EDUCATIONAL MEASUREMENT

EDITORIAL ADVISORY COMMITTEE

Sponsored by National Council on Measurement in Education and American Council on Education

Michael A. Baer, formerly of ACE

Lloyd Bond, Carnegie Foundation

Wendy Bresler, ACE

Linda Crocker, University of Florida

Fritz Drasgow, University of Illinois

Michael T. Kane, National Conference of Bar Examiners

Robert L. Linn, University of Colorado

William A. Mehrens, Michigan State University

Cynthia B. Schmeiser, ACT, Inc.

Wendy M. Yen, Educational Testing Service

EDUCATIONAL MEASUREMENT

Fourth Edition

Sponsored Jointly by
National Council on Measurement in Education and
American Council on Education

Edited by
Robert L. Brennan

Library of Congress Cataloging-in-Publication Data

Educational measurement / sponsored jointly by National Council on Measurement in Education and American Council on Education ; edited by Robert L. Brennan. — 4th ed.
  p. cm. — (ACE/Praeger series on higher education)
 Includes index.
 ISBN 0–275–98125–8
 1. Educational tests and measurements. I. Brennan, Robert L. II. National Council on Measurement in Education. III. American Council on Education. IV. Series: American Council on Education/Praeger series on higher education.
  LB3051.E266 2006
  371.26—dc22   2006015706

British Library Cataloguing in Publication Data is available.

Copyright © 2006 by American Council on Education and Praeger Publishers

All rights reserved. No portion of this book may be reproduced, by any process or technique, without the express written consent of the publisher.

Library of Congress Catalog Card Number: 2006015706
ISBN: 0–275–98125–8

First published in 2006

Praeger Publishers, 88 Post Road West, Westport, CT 06881
An imprint of Greenwood Publishing Group, Inc.
www.praeger.com

Printed in the United States of America

The paper used in this book complies with the
Permanent Paper Standard issued by the National
Information Standards Organization (Z39.48–1984).

10 9 8 7 6 5 4 3 2 1

Contents

Illustrations		vii
Foreword		xiii
Editor's Preface		xv
1.	Perspectives on the Evolution and Future of Educational Measurement *Robert L. Brennan*	1

Part I: Theory and General Principles

2.	Validation *Michael T. Kane*	17
3.	Reliability *Edward H. Haertel*	65
4.	Item Response Theory *Wendy M. Yen and Anne R. Fitzpatrick*	111
5.	Scaling and Norming *Michael J. Kolen*	155
6.	Linking and Equating *Paul W. Holland and Neil J. Dorans*	187
7.	Test Fairness *Gregory Camilli*	221
8.	Cognitive Psychology and Educational Assessment *Robert J. Mislevy*	257

Part II: Construction, Administration, and Scoring

9.	Test Development *Cynthia B. Schmeiser and Catherine J. Welch*	307
10.	Test Administration, Security, Scoring, and Reporting *Allan S. Cohen and James A. Wollack*	355
11.	Performance Assessment *Suzanne Lane and Clement A. Stone*	387
12.	Setting Performance Standards *Ronald K. Hambleton and Mary J. Pitoniak*	433

| 13. | Technology and Testing
Fritz Drasgow, Richard M. Luecht, and Randy E. Bennett | 471 |

Part III: Applications

14.	Old, Borrowed, and New Thoughts in Second Language Testing *Micheline Chalhoub-Deville and Craig Deville*	517
15.	Testing for Accountability in K–12 *Daniel M. Koretz and Laura S. Hamilton*	531
16.	Standardized Assessment of Individual Achievement in K–12 *Steve Ferrara and Gerald E. DeMauro*	579
17.	Classroom Assessment *Lorrie A. Shepard*	623
18.	Higher Education Admissions Testing *Rebecca Zwick*	647
19.	Monitoring Educational Progress with Group-Score Assessments *John Mazzeo, Stephen Lazer, and Michael J. Zieky*	681
20.	Testing for Licensure and Certification in the Professions *Brian E. Clauser, Melissa J. Margolis, and Susan M. Case*	701
21.	Legal and Ethical Issues *S. E. Phillips and Wayne J. Camara*	733

Index 757

Illustrations

Figures

2.1	Toulmin's Model of Inference	28
2.2	Measurement Procedure and Interpretive Argument for Trait Interpretations	33
4.1	Item Characteristic Curves for Two 1PL Items	114
4.2	Item Characteristic Curves for Three 2PL Items	114
4.3	Item Characteristic Curves for Four 3PL Items	115
4.4	The Probability of Incorrect and Correct Responses to a 1PL Item	115
4.5	Item Response Curves and the Item Characteristic Curve for a Three-Level Item	116
4.6	Item Response Curves and the Item Characteristic Curve for a Four-Level Item	116
4.7	Item Response Curves and the Item Characteristic Curve for a 2PPC/GPC Item	117
4.8	Item Response Surface of Item A	119
4.9	Item Response Surface of Item B	119
4.10	Test Characteristic Curve Based on the Four 3PL Items in Figure 4.3 and the PC Item in Figure 4.6	125
4.11	Item Information Functions for Items 2 and 4 in Figure 4.3 and Item 1 in Figure 4.6	128
4.12	Test Information Function and the Test Standard Error Function Based on the Items in Figure 4.11	128
4.13	The Test Standard Error Function Expressed in the Number-Correct Score Metric ($\xi(\theta)$) for the Test in Figure 4.12	129
4.14	Three 3PL Items with Different Item Parameters that Produce Very Similar ICCs	135
4.15	A Log Likelihood Function for the 3PL Model That Has Multiple (Two) Maxima	137
4.16	Ability Estimates for Item Response Vectors Scored with the 3PL Model Using Item-Pattern (Optimal Item Weight) Scoring and Number-Correct Scoring	138
5.1	Schematic Diagram for Different Types of Scores	160
5.2	Relationships between Nominal Weights, Effective Weights, and Composite Reliability	161
5.3	Raw Score Distribution for Normalization	165
5.4	Normalized Score Distribution	165
5.5	Conditional Standard Errors of Measurement for Scales Constructed Using Linear and Nonlinear Transformations	167

5.6	Selected Portions of an Item Map for the 1996 NAEP Fourth-Grade Science Assessment	168
5.7	Illustrative Structure of a Grade-Level Test	172
5.8	Illustration of a Common-Item Design	173
5.9	Illustration of an Equivalent Groups Design	173
5.10	Illustration of a Scaling Test Design	174
6.1	The Three Overall Categories of Test Linking Methods and Their Goals	188
6.2	The Types of Linking Methods within the Overall Linking Category of *Predicting*	190
6.3	The Types of Linking Methods within the Overall Linking Category of *Scale Aligning*	190
6.4	The Types of Linking Methods within the Overall Linking Category of *Test Equating*	194
7.1	A Structural Model Illustration with Five Items for Depicting Item and Test Bias	230
7.2	Depiction of Unbiased Prediction for Two Groups R and F	230
7.3	Depiction of Biased Prediction for Two Groups R and F	231
7.4	Unbiased Regression Showing Probabilities of Success at X_L and Failure at X_h	232
7.5	Uniform DIF Expressed as the Difference in b Parameters for the Item Response Functions (IRFs) for a Reference and Focal Group	236
7.6	Nonuniform DIF Expressed as the Difference in Item Response Functions (IRF) for a Reference and Focal Group	237
7.7	General Notation for the $2 \times 2 \times S$ Data Matrix	238
8.1	Do You See a White Square?	258
8.2	Toulmin's (1958) Structure for Arguments	259
8.3	Elaborated Structure for Assessment Arguments	260
8.4	Two Progressive Matrices	262
8.5	The Wason (1966) Task	264
8.6	Directed Graph Representation of Classical Test Theory	265
8.7	Directed Graph Representation of a Binary-Skills Model	268
8.8	Which Line Is Longer, A or B?	270
8.9	The Structure of Neurode k	274
8.10	A Neural Network with Two Hidden Layers	275
8.11	Two Tasks Concerning Newton's Third Law	278
8.12	A Generic Knowledge Representation	279
8.13	A Set of Responses Consistent with the "Smaller-from-Larger" Bug	281
8.14	Natural Language Problem Statement for a NetPASS Design Task	283
8.15	Network Topology Representation for a NetPASS Design Task	284
8.16	Device Properties Representation in a NetPASS Design Task	285
8.17	Fragment of a Probability Model for Assessing Troubleshooting in NetPASS	297
9.1	Continuum of Content-Related Evidence of Validity	314
9.2	Item-Writing and Review Process	329

9.3	Example of Item Analysis	341
9.4	Sample Fairness Review Quality Control Checklist	350
10.1	Steps in Review of Test Scores on ACT	371
10.2a	Opscan 5001 High Speed Image Scanning System	373
10.2b	Opscan iNSIGHT Desktop Image Scanning System	373
10.3	Work Flow for Writing Assessment	376
10.4	NAEP Reading Achievement Levels for Grade 4	381
12.1	Illustration of the Determination of the Cut Score in the Bookmark Method Given a Response Probability of .67 and a Panelist Bookmark Placement on Item 37	443
12.2	Contrasting Groups Method with Two Performance Categories	445
12.3	Contrasting Groups Method with Four Performance Categories	445
12.4	Illustration of the Hofstee Method	449
13.1	IRT Test Information Function Target for 20-Item Test	481
13.2	Proficiency Scores and Standard Errors for a 50-Item CAT for Two Hypothetical Examinees	489
13.3	Average Standard Errors for a 50-Item CAT vs. 50 Randomly Selected Items	490
13.4	ca-MST from an Examinee's Perspective	491
13.5	A Sample 1-3-3 Compute-Adaptive Multistage Test Panel Configuration (with Multiple Replications)	492
13.6	Reader Interface for OSN Showing a Handwritten Essay Response	495
13.7	Reader Interface for OSN Showing the Same Examinee Essay Response as Annotated by a Reader	496
13.8	A Reading Comprehension Item Presented in High Resolution (1024 by 768)	504
13.9	A Reading Comprehension Item Presented in Low Resolution (640 by 480)	505
13.10	A Reading Comprehension Item Presented with Font Size Set to "Small" in the Microsoft Windows Control Panel and "Smallest" in the Browser (640 by 480 Resolution)	506
13.11	A Reading Comprehension Item Presented with Font Size Set to "Large" in the Microsoft Windows Control Panel and "Medium" in the Browser (640 by 480 Resolution)	507
15.1	Standardized Mean Change on KIRIS and ACT, Mathematics	543
15.2	Schematic Representation of Gains on NAEP and a State Test	544
15.3	Schematic of Elements of Performance and Elements of a Test	546
15.4	Trends in Percentile Ranks of State Means	554
15.5	Performance on a Moderate-Stakes and Audit Test in 3rd-Grade Mathematics	554
15.6	Scores in Two Groups with Two Cut Scores, Simulated Data	560
15.7	Scores after Uniform Gains in Two Groups at Initial Mean, Simulated Data	561
16.1	Description for Proficient Performance in Grade 8 NAEP Mathematics	583
16.2	Sample Item from the Grade 8 NAEP Mathematics Assessment, Mapped to the Proficient Achievement Level, That Illustrates Knowledge and Skills Displayed by Examinees Performing at That Level	584
16.3	Framework of Assessment Approaches and Methods: Types of Items, Tasks, and Prompts That Elicit Responses from Examinees	597
16.4	Multiple Choice Item, *Plumber*	598
16.5	Multiple Choice Item, *Numerical Patterns*	599

16.6	Short Constructed-Response Item, *Keeping Warm*	600
16.7	Short Constructed-Response Item, *Hearth as the Center of the Colonial Home*	601
16.8	Extended Constructed-Response Item, *Native American Beliefs about Land Ownership*	602
16.9	Essay Prompt, A *Book to Save for Future Generations*	603
17.1	An Empirically-Based Progress Map in Writing	630
17.2	An Initial, Instructional-Assessment Task and Illustrative, Near-Transfer Application Tasks	633
17.3	Conceptual (Top) and Conventional Question (Bottom) on the Subject of DC Circuits	635
20.1	Variation of Conditional False-Positive and False-Negative Rates as a Function of Cut Score: 25% Non-Proficient Examinees	710
20.2a	Variation of Conditional False-Positive and False-Negative Rates as a Function of Cut Score: 10% Non-Proficient Examinees	710
20.2b	Variation of Conditional False-Positive and False-Negative Rates as a Function of Cut Score: 40% Non-Proficient Examinees	710
20.3	Variation of Conditional False-Positive Rates as a Function of Test Reliability	711
20.4	Variation of Total Cost Associated with Misclassification Errors as a Function of Cut-Score Placement and the Ratio of the Costs of False-Positive and False-Negative Errors	711
20.5	Comparison of Conditional False-Positive and False-Negative Rates for a Single Administration and a Series of Three Administrations of the Same Test	711
20.6	Conditional False-Positive and False-Negative Rates Associated with a Sequence of Two Separate Tests	712
20.7	Example of Information Classification Errors Provided to Decision Makers	723

Tables

2.1	Interpretive Argument for a Placement Testing System	24
2.2	Interpretive Argument for a Trait Interpretation	34
2.3	Synthetic Multitrait-Multimethod Matrix for Three Traits and Two Methods	39
5.1	ACT Assessment Variances, Covariances, and Effective Weights for Forming the Scale Score Composite	170
6.1	The Design Table for the SG Design	197
6.2	The Design Table for the EG Design	198
6.3	The Design Table for the CB Design	198
6.4	The Design Table for the NEAT Design	199
7.1	OMB Guidelines for Federal Reporting on Race and Ethnicity	224
7.2	Fairness Standards from the 1999 *Standards for Educational and Psychological Testing*	227
7.3	Classification of Fairness Standards	227
7.4	Selection Terminology. The Numbers Falling Into Each Quadrant Are Given by A, B, C, and D as Shown in Figure 7.7, Where N = A + B + C + D	231
8.1	Embretson's (1998) Linear Logistic Test Model for Progressive Matrices	267
8.2	Aspects of Model-Based Reasoning in Science	271
8.3	Excerpt from Polti's (1868/1977) *Thirty-six Dramatic Situations*	277
8.4	A Design Pattern for Assessing "Design under Constraints"	286

8.5	Types of Balance Beam Tasks for Assessing Proportional Reasoning	288
8.6	Stages of Proportional Reasoning	288
8.7	Theoretical Conditional Probabilities of Correct Response	290
8.8	Estimated Conditional Probabilities of Correct Response	291
9.1	Test Purposes, Context of Use, and Inferences	310
9.2	Excerpted Test Content and Cognitive Skill Specifications	317
9.3	Essential Elements in Test and Item Pool Design	325
9.4	Considerations for Selecting Item Types	327
9.5	Considerations in Item Field Testing	331
9.6	Comparison of Classical and IRT-Based Item Statistics	338
9.7	Summary of Item Attributes Typically Stored in Computerized Item Banks	347
10.1	Estimated Power of Copying Indices under Different Copying Conditions	369
10.2	NAEP Reading Achievement Levels for Grade 4	381
11.1	Lifelong Learning Standards	391
11.2	Examples of Different Types of Science Assessments	393
11.3	MSPAP Scoring Rubric: Writing to Express Personal Ideas	396
11.4	Holistic General Scoring Rubric for Mathematics Constructed-Response Items	397
11.5	MSPAP Reading for Literacy Experience Scoring Rubric	398
11.6	Generic and Specific Rubric for Declarative Knowledge Domain	398
12.1	Methods Reviewed in This Chapter, Organized by Type of Rating Provided	438
12.2	Summary of Criteria for Evaluating Standard-Setting Methods	458
13.1	Design of Test Forms for Pretesting Items	478
13.2	Non-overlapping Item Sets	500
13.3	Item Sets with Common Linking Items	501
15.1	Two Standards-Referenced Measures of the Performance of Whites and Blacks in the Simulated Data	561
16.1	Decades of K–12 Achievement Testing	586
16.2	Types of K–12 Achievement Tests and Intended Interpretations, Uses, Content Area Targets, and Decisions for Individual Students	588
16.3	States, Assessments, Content Areas, and Grades Covered in 12 Technical Reports Used To Describe and Evaluate K–12 Achievement Testing	608
16.4	Selected Standards for Reliability of Interpretations and Decisions Based on Test Scores, Organized into Conceptually Similar Groups of Requirements	609
16.5	Selected Standards for Evidence to Support Validity of Intended Interpretations and Uses of Test Scores	611
20.1	Two-by-Two Table for Pass/Fail Outcomes	709

Foreword

Over 55 years ago the American Council on Education saw the need for and had the foresight to ask E. F. Lindquist to assemble a comprehensive, edited book related to educational measurement. The first edition of *Educational Measurement*, published in 1951, became a frequently used and highly regarded reference and classroom text on important and state-of-the-art topics in measurement. After a 20-year span, the second edition was published that was edited by Robert L. Thorndike. It contained chapters written by some of the most prominent names in the measurement community. The second edition both updated topics in the original and introduced new topics, and it became one of the most widely used and referenced books in the measurement field. In 1989, a third edition of this widely known and useful resource was published. The third edition was edited by Robert L. Linn, and in keeping with the previous editions, contained chapters written and reviewed by some of the leading measurement researchers. Now, 17 years later, yet another editor, Robert L. Brennan, has assembled widely known and respected researchers to write and review chapters that bring forth the most current thinking on traditional measurement topics and also to introduce new topics of importance in the educational measurement milieu.

This edition is the second time that the American Council on Education (ACE) and the National Council on Measurement in Education (NCME) have collaborated on the production of this book. These organizations also worked together to produce the third edition. Because these organizations are both concerned about measurement issues and the quality of measurement in educational settings, these collaborations are highly appropriate and fitting.

It is important to note that the editor, the authors, and the chapter reviewers receive no compensation for their hard work. Robert L. Brennan and the various chapter authors and reviewers have worked diligently to assemble an up to date reference book on some of the most critical issues in educational measurement. Many of the topics covered generalize far beyond the confines of education and apply to aspects of measurement in virtually any context. Thus, this work continues the long tradition of *Educational Measurement* in expanding the knowledge base of the entire field. NCME and ACE thank the editor, the authors, and the chapter reviewers for their unselfish contribution.

David Ward, *President*
American Council on Education

James C. Impara, *President*
National Council on Measurement in Education

Editor's Preface

All four editions of *Educational Measurement* have been developed under the aegis of the American Council on Education (ACE), with the last two being collaborative efforts between ACE and the National Council on Measurement in Education (NCME). In the spring of 2002, ACE and NCME began to discuss a revision of *Educational Measurement* under the joint sponsorship of the two organizations. In June 2002, ACE and NCME asked me to assume the role of editor for the fourth edition. Although the contract that formalized the project was not finalized until December 2002, my work on the fourth edition began almost immediately. In particular, I undertook a review of the first three editions of *Educational Measurement,* as well as a review of a substantial body of the literature since the third edition was published, as a basis for constructing a preliminary list of chapters for the fourth edition and potential authors and reviewers.

Also, I identified an Editorial Advisory Committee that was subsequently approved by NCME and ACE. The Editorial Advisory Committee consisted of: Michael A. Baer, who was employed by ACE at that time, Lloyd Bond, Carnegie Foundation, Wendy Bresler, ACE, Linda Crocker, University of Florida, Fritz Drasgow, University of Illinois, Michael T. Kane, National Conference of Bar Examiners, Robert L. Linn, University of Colorado and editor of the third edition, William A. Mehrens, Michigan State University, Cynthia B. Schmeiser, ACT, Inc., and Wendy M. Yen, Educational Testing Service.

The first meeting (and the only formal meeting) of the Editorial Advisory Committee was held in Washington, DC, at the ACE offices on October 29–30, 2002. In addition to the Committee and the editor, other ACE personnel and representatives from the NCME Central Office were in attendance for at least part of the meeting. The Washington meeting was crucial to the project and very productive. The Committee reviewed, discussed, and made suggested revisions to my preliminary list of chapters and chapter lengths. This discussion was followed by an in-depth consideration of potential senior authors for each chapter. Then, potential reviewers for each chapter were identified. I am very grateful for the wise advice and clear support offered to me by the Editorial Advisory Committee.

Shortly after the Washington meeting, I contacted all selected senior authors to ascertain their willingness to write a chapter for the fourth edition. All agreed. Each senior author was given a specified length and told that the writing steps would involve an outline, a draft, and a final submission, with clearly specified deadlines. All authors were given the option of identifying one or more co-authors with my approval. Work progressed steadily but unevenly for the next three years until the final versions of all manuscripts were delivered to me in the fall of 2005.

A comparison of the fourth edition of *Educational Measurement* with the previous three editions illustrates both the enduring nature of many measurement topics and the evolving nature of the field. All editions have chapters devoted to validity, reliability, equating and/or scaling, test development, technology in testing, and measurement in the context of instruction. Also, most editions have chapters dealing with test administration and performance assessment. The titles of some chapters may suggest that a topic is unique to a particular edition, but very often (not always) the issues covered in such chapters are incorporated, at least in part, in other chapters in other editions.

The similarity in chapter titles and/or topics across editions can be quite misleading, however. In particular, although there is overlap in the content coverage of similarly-named chapters, it is almost never the case that a newer chapter is properly viewed as a complete replacement for a previous one. That is as true for the fourth edition as for any other. Many chapters from earlier editions are still relevant in both historical and substantive senses.

The chapters in the fourth edition reflect the authors' perspectives on the considerable changes in the field of educational measurement that have occurred since the third edition was published. Some of these changes occurred as a direct result of developments within the field of educational measurement itself; other changes were substantially influenced by the political and social climate within which the field exists.

This does not mean, however, that there is complete consensus among the authors (or reviewers) of the chapters in the fourth edition, or any previous edition, for that matter. The editor of the fourth edition echoes the warning by Lindquist (1951) in his preface to the first edition that "the reader of this volume ... should not assume that authorities are fully agreed on all ideas expressed therein" (p. x). As part of my review of the drafts of all chapters, I advised fourth-edition authors about certain inconsistencies across chapters; any differences of opinion that remain reflect professional disagreements that characterize any field of scientific endeavor.

Two typical characteristics of edited books of the size and complexity of the fourth edition are the long time it takes to complete and the large number of persons involved. That has been true of all editions of *Educational Measurement*. The fourth edition took approximately four years to complete, involving direct contributions of one kind or another by over 100 persons.

The Editorial Advisory Committee was particularly helpful to me, as were various NCME and ACE personnel. I particularly thank Linda Crocker, who was President of NCME when the project started, and Susan Slesinger, Executive Editor at Praeger, who advised me throughout the four-year developmental cycle.

Principal credit, of course, is reserved for the authors. In addition, the authors and editor gratefully acknowledge the substantial contributions of numerous reviewers and others who offered comments and otherwise supported the development of the chapters in this volume, as outlined below. Of course, the perspectives and opinions expressed do not necessarily reflect the positions or policies of the authors' employers or funding agencies.

Chapter 1, *Perspectives on the Evolution and Future of Educational Measurement*, was written by the editor and reviewed by Michael T. Kane, National Board of Medical Examiners, and Robert L. Linn, University of Colorado. Additional helpful comments were provided by Michael J. Kolen and Won-Chan Lee, both from the University of Iowa.

Chapter 2, *Validation*, by Michael T. Kane, National Conference of Bar Examiners, was reviewed by Robert L. Linn, University of Colorado, and Pamela A. Moss, University of Michigan. Substantial input was also provided by Janet Kane, independent consultant, and Terence Crooks, University of Otago, Dunedin, NZ.

Chapter 3, *Reliability*, by Edward H. Haertel, Stanford University, was reviewed by Leonard S. Feldt and Won-Chan Lee, both from The University of Iowa.

Chapter 4, *Item Response Theory*, by Wendy M. Yen and Anne R. Fitzpatrick, Educational Testing Service, was reviewed by Mark D. Reckase, Michigan State University, and Peter J. Pashley, Law School Admission Council. Additional helpful comments were provided by Daniel Eignor, Dianne Henderson-Montero, Joanne Lenke, Kevin Meara, Robert Smith, and Matthias von Davier, all from Educational Testing Service, as well as Marc Julian, University of Georgia.

Chapter 5, *Scaling and Norming*, by Michael J. Kolen, The University of Iowa, was reviewed by Eugene Johnson, independent consultant. Additional comments were provided by Ming Mei Wang, Educational Testing Service. Comments on portions of an earlier draft were provided by Zhongmin Cui, NooRee Huh, Seonghoon Kim, Dongmei Li, Kyndra Middleton, Yuki Nozawa, and Ye Tong, all from The University of Iowa.

Chapter 6, *Linking and Equating*, by Paul W. Holland and Neil J. Dorans, Educational Testing Service, was reviewed by Nancy S. Petersen, ACT, Inc., and Mary Pommerich, Defense Manpower Data Center. In addition, helpful comments were provided by Tim Davey, Alina von Davier, Daniel Eignor, Kim Fryer, and Samuel Livingston, all from Educational Testing Service.

Chapter 7, *Test Fairness*, by Gregory Camilli, Rutgers, The State University of New Jersey, was reviewed by Lloyd Bond, Carnegie Foundation, and Bert F. Green, Johns Hopkins University. Additional comments were provided by Susan M. Brookhart, Duquesne University, Wayne J. Camara, College Board, Thomas Van Essen, Educational Testing Service, Leonard S. Feldt, University of Iowa, Cynthia B. Schmeiser, ACT, Inc., Amy E. Schmidt, College Board, Lorrie A. Shepard, University of Colorado, and Kevin G. Welner, University of Colorado.

Chapter 8, *Cognitive Psychology and Educational Assessment*, by Robert J. Mislevy, University of Maryland, was reviewed by David F. Lohman, The University of Iowa, and James W. Pellegrino, University of Illinois at Chicago. Additional comments were provided by John Behrens, Cisco Systems, Inc., Jennifer Cromley, Temple University, Geneva Haertel, SRI International, and Michelle Riconscente, University of Maryland. The chapter builds on work with Russell Almond, Educational Testing Service, and Linda Steinberg on evidence-centered assessment design. The chapter benefited from conversations and projects over the years with colleagues at ETS, CRESST, Cisco Systems, SRI International, the Office of Naval Research, the University of Chicago, the University of Maryland, the Spencer Foundation's Idea of Testing project, and the National Research Council's Committee on the Foundations of Assessment. The work reported here was supported in part by the Educational Research and Development Centers Program, PR/Award Number R305B960002, as administered by the Institute of Education Sciences, U.S. Department of Education.

Chapter 9, *Test Development*, by Cynthia B. Schmeiser and Catherine J. Welch, ACT, Inc., was reviewed by Mari Pearlman, Educational Testing Service, and Paul D. Sandifer, independent consultant. Additional helpful comments were provided by Dan Vitale, ACT, Inc.

Chapter 10, *Test Administration, Security, Scoring, and Reporting*, by Allan S. Cohen, University of Georgia, and James A. Wollack, University of Wisconsin, was reviewed by David A. Frisbie, The University of Iowa, and Jeffrey Nellhaus, Massachusetts Department of Education.

Chapter 11, *Performance Assessment*, by Suzanne Lane and Clement A. Stone, University of Pittsburgh, was reviewed by Richard J. Shavelson, Stanford University, Joan Herman, University of California at Los Angeles, and Xiaohong Gao, ACT, Inc. Additional helpful comments were provided by Michael T. Kane, National Conference of Bar Examiners.

Chapter 12, *Setting Performance Standards*, by Ronald K. Hambleton, University of Massachusetts Amherst, and Mary J. Pitoniak, Educational Testing Service, was reviewed by Susan C. Loomis, National Assessment Governing Board, and Barbara S. Plake, University of Nebraska at Lincoln.

Chapter 13, *Technology and Testing,* by Fritz Drasgow, University of Illinois at Urbana-Champaign, Richard M. Luecht, University of North Carolina at Greensboro, and Randy E. Bennett, Educational Testing Service, was reviewed by Cynthia Parshall, independent consultant, and Stephen G. Sireci, University of Massachusetts Amherst. Additional comments were provided by Judy Spray, ACT, Inc., and James Drasgow, independent consultant.

Chapter 14, *Old, Borrowed and New Thoughts in Second Language Testing,* by Micheline Chalhoub-Deville and Craig Deville, University of North Carolina at Greensboro, was reviewed by Lyle F. Bachman, University of California at Los Angeles, and Richard P. Duran, University of California at Santa Barbara. Additional thanks goes to Caroline Clapham and Nick Saville, University of Cambridge, ESOL Examinations, especially for their input on the history of language testing in the UK.

Chapter 15, *Testing for Accountability in K–12,* by Daniel M. Koretz, Harvard Graduate School of Education, and Laura S. Hamilton, RAND Corporation, was reviewed by Linda Crocker, University of Florida.

Chapter 16, *Standardized Assessment of Individual Achievement in K–12,* by Steve Ferrara and Gerald E. DeMauro, American Institutes for Research, was reviewed by Anthony J. Nitko, University of Arizona, Duncan MacQuarrie, Harcourt Assessment, and Andrew C. Porter, Vanderbilt. Additional support of many types was provided by colleagues at American Institutes for Research.

Chapter 17, *Classroom Assessment,* by Lorrie A. Shepard, University of Colorado, was reviewed by Richard Stiggins, Assessment Training Institute, and Mark R. Wilson, University of California at Berkeley.

Chapter 18, *Higher Education Admissions Testing,* by Rebecca Zwick, University of California, Santa Barbara, was reviewed by Daniel R. Eignor, Educational Testing Service, and E. James Maxey, ACT, Inc. The authors also thank Kathleen O'Neill, Ellen Julian, and Jill Burstein for assistance with sections on the GRE, the MCAT, and the e-Rater program, respectively.

Chapter 19, *Monitoring Educational Progress with Group-Score Assessments,* by John Mazzeo, Stephen Lazer, and Michael J. Zieky, Educational Testing Service, was reviewed by Albert Beaton, Boston College, and Terence Crooks, University of Otago, Dunedin, NZ.

Chapter 20, *Testing for Licensure and Certification in the Professions,* by Brian E. Clauser and Melissa J. Margolis, National Board of Medical Examiners, and Susan M. Case, National Conference of Bar Examiners, was reviewed by Steven M. Downing, University of Illinois at Chicago, and James C. Impara, University of Nebraska at Lincoln. In addition, Polina Harik carefully checked calculations used in the figures and Ronald Nungester, Richard Hawkins, Dave Swanson, and Howard Wainer offered comments on earlier drafts; all are from the National Board of Medical Examiners.

Chapter 21, *Legal and Ethical Issues,* by S. E. Phillips, Consultant, and Wayne J. Camara, College Board, was reviewed by Stan von Mayrhauser, Educational Testing Service, and William A. Mehrens, Michigan State University.

Reference

Lindquist, E. F. (1951). Editor's preface. In E. F. Lindquist (Ed.), *Educational measurement* (pp. vii–xi). Washington, DC: American Council on Education.

Robert L. Brennan

1

Perspectives on the Evolution and Future of Educational Measurement

Robert L. Brennan
The University of Iowa

In any scientific field, theorists and practitioners occasionally need to summarize the status of the field, not only to facilitate access to current thinking, but also to enable a reflective consideration of where the field might be headed. That is the principal purpose of this volume. In that spirit, this chapter provides the author's perspectives on various aspects of the evolution and future of educational measurement. These comments are informed by other chapters in this volume, but no claim is made that these comments are always consonant with the perspectives of other authors.

In his introductory chapter to the third edition of *Educational Measurement* Linn (1989a) states:

> A comparison of the current status of educational measurement with that in 1971, when the second edition of this book was published (Thorndike, 1971a), or even with that in 1951, when the first edition appeared (Lindquist, 1951), yields a mixed picture. There are senses in which there has been tremendous change and others in which there has been relatively little. (p. 1)

A similar statement can be made today. While the chapters in this volume reflect the current state-of-the-art in educational measurement, parts of many chapters in the three previous editions are still relevant.

The comments here are organized into two primary sections—measurement theory and measurement practice. The first section traces some of the history of the more technical topics in measurement and concludes with a discussion of the need for more integration of measurement theories. The second section discusses some current issues in measurement practice that are contentious or challenge the field at its boundaries.

1. MEASUREMENT THEORY

To appreciate how measurement theory has evolved since 1950, it is especially instructive to consider how various measurement topics were treated in the three previous editions of *Educational Measurement* (Lindquist, 1951; Linn, 1989b; Thorndike, 1971a) and the five editions of the *Standards for Educational and Psychological Testing* published in 1954, 1966, 1974, 1985, and 1999 by the American Educational Research Association (AERA), the American Psychological Association (APA), and the National Council on Measurement in Education (NCME).[1] The *Educational Measurement* and *Standards* citations in the following sections are ordered chronologically—or, nearly so, and followed by comments about how chapters in the current volume represent an evolution of measurement theory.

1.1. Validity

In the first edition of *Educational Measurement* Cureton (1951) states that, "The essential question of test validity is how well a test does the job it is employed to do" (p. 621). He goes on to say:

> Validity has two aspects, which may be termed relevance and reliability. "Relevance" concerns the closeness of agreement between what the test measures and the function that it is used to measure ... Validity is therefore defined in terms of the correlation between the actual test scores and the "true" criterion scores. (pp. 622–623)

Cureton is faithfully reflecting the fact that, "The theory of prediction was very nearly the whole of validity until about 1950" (Cronbach, 1971, p. 443). Afterward, however, everything changed.

1.1.1. The Trinitarian Model

There is no succinct definition of validity in the first edition of the *Standards* (APA, 1954). The document simply states that, "Validity information indicates to the test user the degree to which the test is capable of achieving certain aims" (p. 13). Rather than giving a definition of validity per se, the 1954 *Standards* provides one of the first published discussions of four types of validity: content, predictive, concurrent, and construct.[2] The committee that developed the first edition of the *Standards* in 1954 included both Meehl and Cronbach, with the latter serving as chair. Clearly, they influenced the dramatic shift from prediction as "the whole of validity" to a more nuanced and deeper appreciation of the topic.

In the second edition of the *Standards* (AERA, APA, & NCME, 1966), the perspective on validity is almost identical to that of the 1954 edition, with two exceptions. First, the validity categories are collapsed from four to three—content, criterion, and construct—which were called "aspects" (p. 12) or "concepts" (p. 14) of validity. (Subsequently, Guion, 1980, called this the trinitarian model of validity.) Second, and much more importantly, the 1966 *Standards* provides an initial discussion of validity of suggested *interpretations*—a notion that resonates to this day.

1.1.2. Inferences and the Centrality of Construct Validity

In the second edition of *Educational Measurement*, Cronbach (1971) states that, "Narrowly considered, *validation* is the process of examining the accuracy of a specific prediction or inference made from a test score ... To explain a test score, one must bring to bear some sort of theory about the causes of the test performance and about its implications" (p. 443). Then, after acknowledging the content/criterion/construct trinitarian model, Cronbach goes on to say, "For purposes of exposition, it is necessary to subdivide *what in the end must be a comprehensive, integrated evaluation of a test*" (p. 445). This statement sounds very much like (nearly) all of validity is construct validity, which Messick (1989, p. 17) later stated, and which is sometimes construed as the "unitary" notion of validity. Subsequently, in the same chapter, Cronbach emphasizes that, "One validates, not a test, but *an interpretation of data arising from a specified procedure*" (p. 447).

The focus on inferences did not escape the committee that authored the third edition of the *Standards* (AERA, APA, & NCME, 1974), which states that, "Questions of validity are questions of what may properly be inferred from a test score; validity refers to the appropriateness of inferences from test scores or other forms of assessment" (p. 25). Still, the 1974 *Standards* retained discussions of content, criterion, and construct validity—what were called "types" of validity.

Over a decade later, the discussion of validity in the fourth edition of the *Standards* (AERA, APA, & NCME, 1985) is, in its essential features, much like that in the 1974 edition. The fourth edition states, "Validity refers to the appropriateness, meaningfulness, and usefulness of the specific inferences made from test scores. Test validation is the process of accumulating evidence to support such inferences" (p. 9). There is a slight change in the trinitarian-model terminology; the three categories are called "types of evidence," rather than "types of validity." Perhaps more importantly, however, content-related and criterion-related evidence are viewed as playing a subordinate (or contributing) role to construct-related evidence.

1.1.3. Validity as an Integrated Evaluation

In the third edition of *Educational Measurement* Messick (1989) begins his extensive treatise on validity as follows:

> Validity is an integrated evaluative judgment of the degree to which empirical evidence and theoretical rationales support the *adequacy* and *appropriateness* of *inferences* and *actions* based on test scores or other modes of assessment ... Broadly speaking, then, validity is an inductive summary of both the existing evidence for and the potential consequences of score interpretation and use ... Thus the key issues of test validity are the interpretability, relevance, and utility of scores, the import or value implications of scores as a basis for action, and the functional worth of scores in terms of social consequences of their use. (p. 13)

In the context of evolving notions of validity, Messick's treatment of the subject is notable on many levels. Perhaps most importantly, he repeatedly emphasizes that validity is an *integrated evaluative judgment* concerning *inferences* and *social consequences* of test use. He supports this perspective with lengthy discussions that cover numerous fields of inquiry including philosophy of science, in particular. Messick's (1989) chapter, however, is not a treatment of validity that provides much specific guidance to those who would undertake validation studies.

The fifth and most recent edition of the *Standards* (AERA, APA, & NCME, 1999) follows Messick (1989) very closely. It states:

> Validity refers to the degree to which evidence and theory support the interpretations of test scores entailed by proposed uses of tests ... The process of validation involves accumulating evidence to provide a sound scientific basis for the proposed score interpretations. It is the interpretations of test scores required by proposed uses that are evaluated, not the test itself. (p. 9)

Subsequent discussion gives considerable attention to notions of construct under-representation and construct irrelevant variance (concepts originally introduced by Cook & Campbell, 1979, and discussed extensively by Messick, 1989), while the content/criterion/construct trinitarian model is essentially replaced by a discussion of sources of validity evidence, including evidence based on consequences of test use.

1.1.4. Validity as Argument

In his treatment of validity in chapter 2 of this volume, Kane provides a perspective on validity that is largely consonant with that of Messick, but there are differences, at least in emphasis. In particular, Kane extends suggestions of Cronbach (1988) and emphasizes a general methodology for validation based on conceptualizing validity as argument. In Kane's formulation, the *validity argument* provides an overall evaluation of the intended interpretations and uses of test scores. The goal is to provide a coherent analysis of all of the evidence for and against proposed interpretations/uses, and to the extent possible, the evidence relevant to plausible competing interpretations. An *interpretative argument* provides a framework for developing a validity argument. In particular, Kane suggests that a convenient basis for discussing the structure of interpretive arguments is to focus on the types of inferences commonly found in test-score interpretations. For example, for a placement testing system, the inferences he discusses are scoring, generalization, extrapolation, and decision making. Many aspects of Kane's perspective on validity are reminiscent of concepts in program evaluation (see, for example, Cronbach, 1982).

Kane's approach to validation can be formulated in terms of the following steps (see Kane, 2001, p. 330):

1. state the proposed interpretation in terms of an interpretative argument, which includes inferences and assumptions involved in the interpretation;
2. create a preliminary version of the validity argument by assembling all available evidence relevant to the plausibility of the interpretive argument;
3. evaluate the most problematic assumptions in detail; and
4. reformulate the interpretive and validity arguments, if necessary, and repeat step three until all inferences in the interpretive argument are considered plausible, or the interpretive argument is rejected.

This is much like the process of theory development in the physical sciences, but Kane's treatment of validity is not influenced solely by philosophy of science. Kane's exposition of validity as argument uses as tools most of the measurement methodologies currently available (particularly generalizability theory) and aims at making validation a more accessible enterprise for educational measurement practitioners. This latter goal is very much consonant with the directive in the 1999 *Standards* that, "the ultimate responsibility for appropriate test use and interpretation lies predominantly with the test user" (p. 112).

1.2. Reliability

Definitions and concepts of validity have evolved considerably since the first edition of *Educational Measurement* was published in 1951. By contrast, the generic definition of reliability has remained largely intact—namely, reliability refers to consistency of scores across replications of a measurement procedure (see Brennan, 2001a). In their treatments of reliability, the various editions of both the *Standards* and *Educational Measurement* differ somewhat in their treatments of types of reliability coefficients (e.g., coefficients of equivalence, stability, and internal consistency), but the primary developments are an increasing attention over time to standard errors of measurement (SEMs) and to generalizability theory (Brennan, 2001b; Cronbach, Gleser, Nanda, & Rajaratnam, 1972; Shavelson & Webb, 1991).

1.2.1. Early 1950s

In the first edition of *Educational Measurement* Thorndike (1951) states: "This tendency toward consistency from one set of measurements to another ... will be designated 'reliability'" (p. 560). Then, almost immediately, Thorndike discussed reliability and analysis of variance (ANOVA). This discussion is too introductory to be characterized as a precursor to generalizability theory, but it might have influenced the editor, who later published an experimental design text (Lindquist, 1953) in which the last chapter foreshadowed the subsequent development of generalizability theory by Cronbach and his colleagues. Interestingly, Cronbach was one of the "collaborators" for Thorndike's chapter, but there is no evidence that the chapter substantially influenced Cronbach's thinking about generalizability theory.

One noteworthy aspect of Thorndike's chapter is what is *not* referenced or even mentioned. For example, there is no reference to Gulliksen's (1950) book, which provided an excellent systematic development of reliability theory up to that time. Also, there is no mention of Cronbach's (1951) paper on coefficient alpha. It seems virtually certain that these publications were overlooked simply because the Thorndike (1951) chapter was largely completed before they were published. (Work on the first edition of *Educational Measurement* began in 1945.)

One undeniable fact about the history of educational measurement is the central role of Cronbach's (1951) paper on coefficient alpha. This paper is widely cited in the social science literature, and probably no statistic related to measurement is reported more frequently. In that sense, the alpha paper has been, and continues to be, extraordinarily influential not only in the field of educational measurement per se but also in many other social science fields. Yet, the emphasis given to Cronbach's alpha is somewhat unfortunate for two reasons. First, as noted by Cronbach (2004) just before his death, coefficient alpha was not particularly novel.[3] Indeed, Cronbach (2004) expressed some embarrassment that his name is uniquely tied to the coefficient.

Second, alpha was never intended by Cronbach to be a universal reliability coefficient. Cronbach had an entirely different goal in mind, as he clearly states in the 1951 paper:

> A ... reason for the symbol is that α is one of six analogous coefficients (to be designated β, γ, δ, etc.) which deal with such other concepts as like-mindedness of persons, stability of scores, etc. (pp. 299–300)

Cronbach abandoned work on "analogous coefficients" when he and his colleagues invented generalizability theory and realized that it was a much richer and more useful approach to conceptualizing and quantifying the influence of different sources of errors on different objects of measurement.

1.2.2. Mid 1950s to Mid 1970s

This two-decade period witnessed the development of the foundations for generalizability theory. In discussing the genesis of the theory, Cronbach (1991) states:

> In 1957 I obtained funds from the National Institute of Mental Health to produce, with Gleser's collaboration, a kind of handbook of measurement theory ... "Since reliability has been studied thoroughly and is now understood," I suggested to the team, "let us devote our first few weeks to outlining that section of the handbook, to get a feel for the undertaking." We learned humility the hard way—the enterprise never got past that topic. Not until 1972 did the book appear ... that exhausted our findings on reliability reinterpreted as generalizability. Even then, we did not exhaust the topic.
> When we tried initially to summarize prominent, seemingly transparent, convincingly argued papers on test reliability, the messages conflicted. (pp. 391–392)

To resolve these conflicts, Cronbach and his colleagues devised a rich conceptual framework and married it to analysis of random effects variance components. The net effect is "a tapestry that interweaves ideas from at least two dozen authors" (Cronbach, 1991, p. 394). The essential features of univariate generalizability theory were largely completed with technical reports in 1960–1961. These were revised into three journal articles, each with a different first author (Cronbach, Rajaratnam, & Gleser, 1963; Gleser, Cronbach, & Rajaratnam, 1965; and Rajaratnam, Cronbach, & Gleser, 1965). The development of multivariate generalizability theory took another decade.

Both the 1966 and 1974 *Standards* were influenced by concepts from generalizability theory, although they do not reference generalizability theory per se. For example, the 1966 *Standards* states: "it is clear that *different methods of determining the reliability coefficient take account of different sources of error* [italics in original]" (p. 25). Also, the 1966 *Standards* states:

> *The estimation of clearly labeled components of error variance is the most informative outcome of a reliability study* [italics in original] both for the test developer wishing to improve the reliability of his instrument and for the user desiring to interpret test scores with maximum understanding. (p. 26)

An identical statement, save for the italics, is in the 1974 *Standards* (p. 49). A very similar statement appears on p. 19 of the 1985 *Standards*.

Stanley's (1971) *Reliability* chapter in the second edition of *Educational Measurement* discusses ANOVA approaches to estimating reliability (pp. 420–431), but the chapter provides only a very limited treatment of generalizability theory for multifaceted universes. Also, Stanley characterizes generalizability theory and classical theory as "competing" (p. 430), whereas Cronbach, Rajaratnam, and Gleser (1963) view generalizability theory as liberalizing classical theory. Stanley (1971) ends his chapter with one of the earliest discussions of estimating reliability for criterion-referenced interpretations.

1.2.3. Mid 1970s to Present

The 1985 *Standards* are noticeably different from earlier editions in their treatment of reliability in at least four respects. First, different types of coefficients receive proportionately less emphasis. Second, SEMs receive more emphasis, and conditional SEMs for particular score regions are mentioned. Third, generalizability theory receives more explicit recognition. Fourth, there is acknowledgement that reliability issues need to be reconceptualized when cut scores are employed.

The Feldt and Brennan (1989) *Reliability* chapter in the third edition of *Educational Measurement* provides a treatment of reliability in classical test theory that is novel in several respects, including its discussion of internal consistency coefficients for different degrees of part-test similarity (influenced in part by Lord & Novick, 1968), and its use of reliability for composites as an organizing theme for a number of issues. In addition, Feldt and Brennan provide a rather lengthy discussion of generalizability theory, and a treatment of reliability for criterion-referenced interpretations.

The treatment of reliability in the 1999 *Standards* continued the evolution seen in the 1985 *Standards*. Categories of coefficients receive little emphasis because, "With the development of generalizability theory, the ... categories may now be seen as special cases of a more general classification: generalizability coefficients" (p. 27). Also, the 1999 *Standards* explicitly attends to relative and absolute comparisons in norm-referenced and criterion-referenced situations, respectively. In addition, the 1999 *Standards* discusses SEMs for different score scales, reliability of group means, and reliability in the context of item response theory.

In this volume, Haertel's treatment of reliability from the perspectives of classical test theory, generalizability theory, and classification consistency parallels the treatment by Feldt and Brennan (1989), but Haertel gives deeper attention to the last two topics than did Feldt and Brennan, and Haertel provides more up-to-date treatments of some reliability issues in classical theory. In addition, Haertel considers the reliability of behavioral observations. The content of Haertel's chapter is partly influenced by the accountability movement of the past decade.

1.3. Item Response Theory

The first well-known treatments of item response theory (IRT) were provided by Lord (1952), Rasch (1960) and Lord and Novick (1968), although precursors were published many years earlier. Lord (1980) provided a mathematically elegant but still very accessible overview of IRT. At that time, however, applications of IRT were relatively rare, primarily because most of the computer programs for IRT that existed were not widely available and/or they demanded computing resources not present in most environments. That all changed in the 1980s with the advent of relatively fast microcomputers and the wide distribution of specialized IRT programs. Still, from a practical point of view IRT has been readily accessible for barely a quarter of a century. In that very short time, it has had a tremendous influence on the field of measurement, but because IRT is relatively new, it has not had a long-standing presence in the various editions of *Educational Measurement* and the *Standards*.

Given the relative youth of IRT, it is not surprising that the first references to IRT in the *Standards* occurred in 1985, mainly in the area of test development (p. 27). Given the meteoric rise in the visibility of IRT after 1985, however, it is noteworthy that in the 1999 *Standards* only two standards refer explicitly to IRT. (Some of the chapter introductions acknowledge IRT in more detail.)

Not surprisingly, the first two editions of *Educational Measurement* are silent with respect to IRT. The third, however, provides an extensive treatment of IRT by Hambleton (1989), and some other chapters reference uses of IRT. The chapter by Yen and Fitzpatrick in the current volume builds upon Hambleton's chapter, and IRT is referenced in many other chapters, as well. The Yen and Fitzpatrick chapter provides substantial discussions of polytomous models, item parameter and ability estimation, and model fit—topics that have evolved considerably since Hambleton (1989).

1.4. Equating, Linking, and Scaling

The topics of equating, linking, and scaling have been part of measurement since at least the early part of the twentieth century (see, for example, Holland & Dorans, this volume). Many of the basic ideas are still intact, but terminology has changed substantially, and there have been numerous methodological developments especially in the last few decades.

In the chapter on *Units, Scores, and Norms* in the first edition of *Educational Measurement* Flanagan (1951) provides the most extensive discussion to that time of various types of scores and score scales. He also provides a prescient discussion of comparability (pp. 747–749), although his use of terminology is unusual by today's standards. For example, Flanagan's notion of *general* comparability is essentially equivalent to today's strictest interpretation of equating. In addition, Flanagan (1951, pp. 750–760) provides perhaps the first integrated discussion of equating and linking methodology.

The 1954 *Standards* seems uninfluenced by Flanagan (1951). It is silent about equating and linking, and its discussion of scaling is restricted to statements of preference for normalized standard scores (p. 35). The 1966 *Standards* again emphasizes standard scores, but does not state a preference for normalization. A section on *Comparability of Forms* (p. 29) is wedged within the *Reliability* section. A rudimentary statement about equipercentile equating is provided, but only for raw scores. Linking, as we understand that term today, is referenced in an "essential" requirement that tables of equivalence between new and old forms be provided when forms have different score scales or content (p. 34).

In the chapter on *Units, Scores, and Norms* in the second edition of *Educational Measurement* Angoff (1971) provides an extensive treatment of score scales, a seminal and masterful treatment of equating, and a treatment of some aspects of linking (what Angoff called "calibration"). To this day, it would be difficult to overstate the influence of Angoff's discussion of equating, although relatively little new research on the topic occurred during the 1970s.

There is little evidence that Angoff's (1971) chapter had much influence on the committee that developed the 1974 *Standards*, perhaps because many of the topics he addressed (particularly equating) were viewed at that time as arcane matters that were best handled behind the scenes at major testing companies. There was relatively little understanding in the measurement community that equating and linking are fallible enterprises that can materially affect score interpretation. The 1974 *Standards* is notable, however, for distinguishing between criterion-referenced and norm-referenced interpretations of scores—a distinction that impacted scaling considerations later.

By the 1980s, scaling, equating, and linking became much more public matters for several reasons (see, for example, Brennan, 1987). First, the number of testing programs that conducted equating had increased substantially, particularly in licensure and certification areas. Second, addressing issues raised by testing critics (e.g., test disclosure and the SAT score decline) required a discussion of equating, at least at some level. Third, institutional and public comparisons of ACT and SAT scores (i.e., concordances) forced discussions of linking. Fourth, high stakes uses of testing (e.g., minimum competency) and the Lake Wobegon effect (most children above average) precipitated score scale discussions. This increased attention to scaling, equating, and linking is reflected in the 1985 *Standards*, which, in a dramatic break from past editions, devoted an entire chapter to the subject. The 1999 *Standards* provided an even longer and deeper discussion.

In their chapter on *Scales, Norms, and Score Comparability*, Petersen, Kolen, and Hoover (1989) view Angoff's chapter as a "supplement" (p. 221) to theirs. In the context of equating, Petersen et al. give considerable attention to data collection designs, a succinct description of the mathematics of equating procedures (including those that use IRT), and brief discussions of smoothing and standard errors of equating. They also provide an extensive treatment of scaling, including the construction of developmental scales for measuring growth.

Since the publication of the third edition, there has been a tremendous amount of research conducted on equating, linking, and scaling, much of which has been discussed by Kolen and Brennan (2004). Given the expanding scope of these topics, in the current volume there are separate chapters on scales and norms by Kolen, and on linking and equating by Holland and Dorans. The chapter by Kolen is particularly noteworthy for the depth and breadth of its treatment of score scales, including developmental score scales that are the focus of much attention in K–12 these days. The chapter by Holland and Dorans is particularly noteworthy for its highly structured treatment of linking and equating methodologies.

1.5. Need for Integration of Models

Our psychometric models are quite well developed, but there are occasional misconceptions and paradoxes (see Brennan, 1998a, 2001c, 2004b) and, in some respects, the models are not well integrated.[4] For example, it is not at all unusual for an assumption used in equating test forms to be blind to an assumption used to document the reliability of scores for those forms. Some equating procedures do not even formally recognize the existence of true scores. Other equating procedures provide transformations in terms of true scores, which are unusable in practice unless one substitutes observed scores for true scores. That is precisely what is usually done, but there is no theoretical justification for doing so.

As another example, consider the truism that "reliability is a necessary condition for validity." This statement is typically explained via corrections for attenuation, which are based on a correlational view of validity. Clearly, current connotations of validity are much broader. Kane's (1982) discussion of the reliability-validity paradox (see, also, Brennan, 2001b, pp. 132–135), which is closely related to his notions of generalization and extrapolation (see Kane, this volume), provides a much richer view of the sense in which reliability is a necessary condition for validity. Still, however, I would argue that validity and reliability are usually too separated in our measurement models.

In considering relationships among models, it is important to pay attention to both mathematical and conceptual issues. Mathematics can address syntactical similarities, but semantics and inference require attention to conceptual issues. Both conceptually and mathematically, it can be argued that classical test theory is largely a special case of generalizability theory.

It can be argued also that classical test theory is a special case of IRT (see, for example, Holland & Hoskens, 2003), but such arguments are sometimes more mathematical than conceptual, even though some of the words used in both theories are the same. From a conceptual perspective, in my view IRT is essentially a scaling model, whereas classical test theory and generalizability theory are measurement models. The essential difference, as I see it, is that a measurement model has a built-in, explicit consideration of error (see section 1.5.3).

Perhaps the most obvious inconsistency among these three models is that IRT pays particular attention to items, whereas classical test theory and generalizability theory are largely test-score based. In this sense, IRT is a micro model, and the other two are macro models that are not yet well integrated with IRT. There are also differences among these models in what constitutes a replication, definitions of true scores, and conceptualization and estimation of error, as discussed next.

1.5.1. What Constitutes a Replication?

Reliability (either a coefficient or an SEM) involves quantifying the consistencies and/or inconsistencies in examinee scores over replications. It follows that grasping the concept of reliability and its estimates involves grappling with the question: "What constitutes a replication of a measurement procedure?" (See Brennan, 2001a.)

Generalizability theory is especially well-suited for dealing with this question. However, we do not need to invoke the full conceptual framework of generalizability theory to capture one very important distinction—namely, the notion of replications is operationalized in part by specifying which sets of conditions of measurement (items, occasions, tasks, raters, etc.) are *fixed* for all replications and which are *random* (i.e., variable) over replications.

Careful thought about replications requires that an investigator have clear answers to two questions: (1) what are the intended (possibly idealized) replications of the measurement procedure, and (2) what are the characteristics of the data actually available, or to be collected, to estimate reliability? It is particularly important to note that if a facet is intended to be random (Question 1), but it is effectively fixed (e.g., only one instance) in a particular set of data (Question 2), then any reliability coefficient computed using the data will likely overestimate reliability and underestimate error variance.

Many apparent conflicts in reliability results can be explained by careful consideration of these matters. For example, conventional wisdom holds that group means are more reliable than scores for individuals. Brennan (1995) shows that this conclusion is not necessarily true, and he has explained why it can be false in terms of which facets are fixed and which are random for various group-mean reliability coefficients. Also, Brennan (2001b, pp. 127–129) shows how differences in the magnitudes of traditional coefficients of reliability are explainable in terms of which facets are fixed and which are random.

Historically, in IRT, the terms "fixed" and "random" have not been used widely. However, these notions play a role in the theory. Specifically, in typical treatments of IRT, the n items are *fixed*, or, more correctly, the parameters of the items are fixed. That is, a replication would involve a set of n items with *identically* the same item parameters. This notion of a replication is much more restrictive than that of classically parallel forms, and dramatically more restrictive than that of randomly parallel forms in generalizability theory. In effect, there is no assumed sampling of content in the usual IRT models, whereas other models permit content sampling. One clear implication is that, all other things being equal, standard errors of ability estimates in IRT will tend to be smaller than SEMs in classical test theory or generalizability theory solely because of model assumptions (see Lee, Brennan, & Kolen, 2000, pp. 14–16).

In theory, one possible route to relaxing the assumption of fixed item parameters in IRT models is to employ Bayesian procedures with prior distributions for the item parameters. Doing so might lead to greater integration of IRT and generalizability theory, but much research remains to be done. (See Kolen & Harris, 1987, for a different ad hoc approach to integrating generalizability theory and item response theory.)

1.5.2. What Are True Scores?

Theories of measurement make repeated reference to true scores (or scores on some latent proficiency). As noted above, the most obvious example is the classical test theory model, but generalizability theory and IRT have their own versions of these concepts. Since true scores are unobservable, they must be defined for these theories to have any utility. The manner in which these entities are defined can make a very big difference. Importantly, "true score" does not mean the same thing in all of these models.

Classical test theory and generalizability theory employ an expected-value notion of true score. By contrast, when IRT is used with dichotomously-scored items, some of the arguments among proponents of the one-parameter logistic (1PL) and two-parameter logistic (2PL) models vis-à-vis the three-parameter logistic (3PL) model are essentially arguments about what shall be considered true score. The 3PL model with its non-zero lower asymptote is reasonably consistent with defining true score as an expected value, because it acknowledges that a low-ability examinee has a positive probability of a correct response. By contrast, the 1PL and 2PL models require that low ability examinees have a probability-of-correct response approaching zero. In this sense, it appears that these latter models are based on defining true score in the more platonic sense of "knowing" the answer to an item, as opposed to getting it correct.[5]

Recall, as well, that in traditional treatments of IRT, the n items in an analysis are fixed, which means that true scores given by the test characteristic curve are for the fixed set of items. By contrast in classical test theory, true score is defined as the expected value of observed scores over forms that are "similar" in some sense, and in generalizability theory, true score (called "universe score") is the expected value over randomly parallel forms. These differences, which are often unacknowledged, have important theoretical and practical implications.

1.5.3. What Is Error?

Differences in notions about true score are a primary contributing factor to different conceptions and estimates of error. In classical theory and generalizability theory, error does not mean mistake, and it does not mean "model misfit" in the usual sense of that term. Rather, important aspects of error are defined directly or indirectly by the investigator. This is eminently obvious in generalizability theory, which requires that the investigator specify a universe of generalization, a data collection design, and the type of error under consideration.

In classical theory, often the investigator indirectly defines error through the choice of a data collection design. For example, different data collection designs are used to estimate traditional coefficients of internal consistency, stability, and stability and equivalence, and these different coefficients typically lead to different estimates of error variance. These different error variances are *not* different estimates of the same quantity; rather, they are estimates of *different* quantities. Investigators often do not appreciate that various design and analysis choices they make are effectively choices about how error is defined.

There is no error term per se in IRT, but there are different notions of error that are often discussed in conjunction with the model. For example, the extent to which the model does not fit the data is a type of error. Rarely, however, is model misfit reported as a quantified amount; rather, various methodologies are employed to assess model (mis)fit. Also, conditional standard errors of ability estimates in IRT are usually used in much the same way that conditional SEMs are used in classical test theory or generalizability theory. Sometimes, however, this can be misleading.

For example, it is often stated that, under IRT assumptions, conditional standard errors of estimates are *larger* at the extremes of the score scale than in the middle. By contrast, in classical test theory and generalizability theory, almost always conditional SEMs are *smaller* at the extremes than in the middle. This difference is almost always an artifact arising from the choice of the θ scale (see Brennan, 1998b, pp. 326–328), and there is no a priori theoretical virtue for any particular choice of scale (Lord, 1980, pp. 84–85).

Also, in traditional IRT, standard errors cannot distinguish among multiple sources of error. In fact, given the unidimensionality assumption of IRT, there is no obvious role for multiple sources of error. Recognizing this last problem, Bock, Brennan, and Muraki (2002) have suggested an ad hoc approach for incorporating multiple sources of error in an IRT analysis for a test consisting of items scored by multiple raters. This is a simple matter in generalizability theory, but as Bock et al. (2002) note:

> Regrettably, a similar straightforward approach to estimation of proficiency from multiple ratings does not exist in present IRT. An essential assumption of IRT is that the scores in the examinee's response ... are conditionally independent, given the examinee's level of proficiency. This is not true of multiple ratings of a response to a given item: They provide additional information ... only to the extent that they attenuate rater error.
>
> Although treating multiple ratings as if they were separate items in an IRT analysis would not in general bias estimation of examinee proficiency, the standard error of estimate would be biased downward. (p. 365)

The ad hoc solution proposed by Bock et al. (2002) involves a modification of information functions based on results from a generalizability analysis. The net effect is an adjustment of the IRT standard errors so that they incorporate error attributable to both items and raters; that is, in a sense, the procedure induces more random error into the model.

On balance, then, different measurement theories are quite different with respect to their conceptions of error, how to quantify it, and how to explain it. Since error is so fundamental in measurement, such inconsistencies among the theories cast considerable doubt on their interchangeability at the current time. For the most part, the different theories do not provide alternative answers to the same questions about error; rather, they more frequently provide answers to *different* questions about error.

1.5.4. No "Right" Model

Given the inconsistencies across models, it is natural to ask which model provides the correct or right answer to the questions posed. For the most part, there is no right answer, and investigators searching for that "Holy Grail" will be forever disappointed. The models are just that—models, not reality; each of them has its own set of definitions and assumptions, and the definitions and assumptions do not mesh perfectly across models. Practitioners sometimes do not realize that model assumptions are not always chosen because they are thought to reflect reality. Assumptions are sometimes chosen because they seem to be natural or efficient ways, in the context of a particular model, to solve or at least simplify otherwise intractable estimation problems.

The 20th century (particularly the second half) witnessed the development of superb measurement and scaling models, but they are not particularly well integrated. Inconsistencies across models are largely attributable to inconsistencies in definitions and assumptions. It follows that integrating these models may require abandoning some definitions or assumptions in favor of others. Such integration, I submit, is a principal psychometric challenge at the beginning of the 21st century.

2. MEASUREMENT PRACTICE

I often view the practice of educational measurement in three different contexts: K–12 (see Ferrara & DeMauro, this volume; Koretz & Hamilton, this volume), admissions to higher education (see Zwick, this volume), and licensure and certification (see Clauser, Margolis, & Case, this volume). Most important theoretical issues pervade all contexts, but practical issues tend to vary by context, at least in emphasis.

In this section, I focus on trends, or what might be called "boundary" issues, that appear to me to have considerable implications for the field of educational measurement in the 21st century. There is a factual and research component to most of the topics covered here, but there are also historical and philosophical perspectives presented here that are surely subject to debate among members of multiple communities including testing professional, users of test scores, the public, etc. Testing is not, and never has been, the sole prerogative or responsibility of measurement experts. Indeed, testing is never an end unto itself—it serves some other purpose(s). Many if not most debates about testing are essentially debates about the value of testing, or a particular kind of testing, for a particular purpose in a particular context.

2.1. Validity and Consequences

Perhaps the most contentious topic in validity is the role of consequences. Since it is now almost universally agreed that validity has to do with the proposed interpretations and uses of test scores, it necessarily follows that consequences are part of validity. One might argue that interpretations do not imply any necessary role for consequences, but the *use* of a test score definitely implies consequences; otherwise, *use* is nothing more than an abstraction. Still, it seems reasonable to ask if *all* consequences of test use should be included under the umbrella of validity.

Consider the four-way classification of intended and unintended, positive and negative consequences. Intended consequences are seldom problematic. Few would argue against the inclusion of intended positive consequences in any notion of validity; indeed, such consequences would seem to be central to most defenses of a proposed test use. With equal force, it is difficult to envision anyone attempting to justify intended negative consequences.

The relevance of unintended consequences, however, is not so easily ascertained. One might think that unintended positive consequences of some particular test use are simply an added, albeit unanticipated, benefit. It may be wise to look such a "gift horse in the mouth," however. The implication is that a test can have a positive benefit for a purpose for which it was not designed. While this may be a possibility, it might be an indication of test design problems.

By far, the most contentious consequences are those that are unintended and negative. Test developers are understandably incensed when others use scores on their test for a purpose unintended by them (the developers) that has negative consequences for some examinees or stakeholders. Tension rises considerably when users are unwilling to accept responsibility for their role in such misuse.

In considering unintended consequences there can be considerable confusion about whose intent is under consideration, as well as heated debate about whether a consequence is positive or negative. Such ambiguity considerably complicates validity judgments. Consider, for example, the use of ACT and SAT scores to rank order states. The developers of these tests have declared that this is an unintended (by them) use of the test scores, and in that sense the developers have typically viewed such use as not valid. Yet, for a former U.S. administration and for the media even now, this use of ACT and SAT scores has wide appeal with positive consequences; for others, it has negative consequences.

Measurement professionals typically attempt to circumvent such ambiguities and conundrums by declaring that the user of test scores has the responsibility to validate that use (see the 1999 *Standards*, p. 112). This may not be an entirely satisfactory answer, however, for at least two reasons. First, it is extraordinarily rare for individuals or entities (e.g., the government or the media) other than test developers to mount even a modest program of research to validate a test use. Second, the ultimate user is often an individual person who has neither the training nor the resources to validate a test use in any substantial sense.

Consider, for example, the reader of a newspaper in which the reported SAT score for the reader's state is lower than that for a neighboring state. Suppose the reader concludes (inappropriately) that the educational system in her state is inferior to that in the neighboring state and, accordingly, the reader moves to the neighboring state. In this case, the reader is the ultimate user of the data, but it does not seem likely that the reader will or could validate the interpretation or use she made of the data. Further, it would seem that the newspaper bears no particular responsibility except to report the data accurately. One might conclude that the responsibility reverts back to the test developer. Clearly, test developers should warn against reasonably anticipated misuses, as they have in the case of using ACT and SAT scores to rank order states. However, often test developers have no ready route for informing the reader of a newspaper about such misuse.

To put it bluntly, "Who is responsible for the negative consequences of a test score use that is not endorsed by a test developer?" When all is said and done, identifying the responsible agent is a matter of central concern not only for the test developer, but also for the body politic. Although it can be argued persuasively that the responsibility for validation of a test use should be borne by the user of the data, that is an empty argument if it is unreasonable to expect that such validation will or could occur.

I have argued elsewhere that validity theory is rich, but the practice of validation is often impoverished (Brennan, 1998a). If validation is to be an attainable goal, it must be clear who is responsible for pursuing a validity argument, and it must be reasonable to expect that the person or entity has the motivation, training, and resources to do so. Otherwise, validation—particularly as it relates to unintended negative consequence—will be an unattainable and perhaps empty goal.

One can surely postulate scenarios in which unintended negative consequences are so egregious that they demand special attention. It is quite another matter to specify who should bear the burden for preventing or remedying such consequences. Although there is a logic for including unintended negative consequences under the umbrella of validity, I would maintain that there is often very little that the measurement profession can do on its own to successfully prevent or remedy such misuse. In this regard, it is worth recalling that the educational testing profession has no mechanism for disciplining those individuals or entities who use test scores inappropriately.

Clearly, test developers have a responsibility to warn users about reasonably anticipated misuses of test scores. However, I would contend that the consequences intended by test developers should have first call on their resources, and test developers should be held to high standards for intended consequences. In particular, documentation relating to validity arguments for intended consequences should be readily available in a timely manner. Unfortunately, publicly available, timely documentation related to validity arguments is often the exception rather than the rule. The uncomfortable reality is that if such documentation is clear, complete, and forthright, it will not always fully support validity arguments. That is intrinsic to the very nature of a validity argument, and it is the price the profession must pay if serious validation is to become routine.

2.2. Reliability and Standardization

In my view, reliability is largely tied to the notion of replications. Specifically, reliability relates to the consistency of scores over replications of the measurement procedure (see Brennan, 2001a). I use the term "reliability" here in a very general sense. It could refer to a coefficient, an error variance, a decision-consistency index, or any other statistic that quantified replicability in some way. In specifying replications, it is almost always the case that a number of conditions are intended to be the same (i.e., fixed) over replications. These fixed conditions are what is meant by "standardization." For example, the same types of essay prompts and/or the same raters might be used over replications.

In general, when conditions of measurement are fixed, reliability tends to increase but validity may decrease (see Kane, 1982). It is particularly important to understand that psychometrics is silent with respect to which conditions of measurement, if any, should be fixed. Such decisions are the responsibility of the body politic or the investigator who seeks an answer to a substantive question of interest to him or her. It is certainly not the case that fixing particular facets is a requirement of valid measurement.

Sometimes, the notion of replicability gets misunderstood as a requirement that there be an actual full replication of every measurement procedure. That is not the case. It is true, however, that one must be able to conceptualize a replication and, when only a single replication is available, one must be willing to make some set of assumptions in order to estimate reliability.

One trend in testing litigation seems to center around arguments that involve tailoring the testing experience, or the decision about a tested examinee, to personal characteristics of the examinee. This trend is understandable in the context of various laws and legal precedents, but it is often at variance with the measurement practice of standardization, which has a two-pronged goal: (a) keep the conditions of measurement the same for all examinees; and (b) use the same standards for making decisions about all examinees. Standardization has been a hallmark of large-scale (often high stakes) testing for decades, largely because it creates a "level playing field," and in this sense contributes to fairness in test scores. This fact, however, should not be construed as a statement that standardization is always required for valid measurement.

The usual argument against standardization (sometimes made in legal and other forums) is that treating everyone the same is not always equivalent to treating everyone fairly. Or, stated in more technical terms, strict adherence to standardization procedures may reduce score validity for some examinees. Consider, for example, administering a paper-and-pencil test to a blind person. Such strict adherence to a standardization condition would be silly, of course. Less extreme examples of accommodating individual needs often present much more difficult challenges that cause considerable tension. This issue is revisited in section 2.5.

2.3. Accountability in K–12

Most educational historians would agree, I think, that Sputnik was the impetus for an evolutionary, and perhaps revolutionary, change in American education. That occurred five decades ago. Years from now, I suspect historians will look back on the current decade and declare that it too was a time of historic change in American education. What distinguishes the current revolution from previous ones, however, is the tremendous emphasis given to testing. Testing can be, and usually is, a positive force throughout our educational system, but many measurement professionals have expressed serious reservations about the current approaches to the use of testing by governmental agencies to advance accountability goals in K–12 (see, for example Brennan, 2004a, and Linn, 2003). It certainly appears that a testing revolution is underway in this country that is based on the nearly unchallenged belief, with very little supporting evidence, that high-stakes testing can and will lead to improved education.

The single most defining event of this revolution was the passage of the revised Elementary and Secondary Education Act of 2001, with the rhetorically brilliant name "No Child Left Behind" (NCLB, 2002). Very few politicians or bureaucrats could or would argue against an act with a name that seemed to promise a quality education for every child. The current conventional wisdom seems to be that NCLB may need "tweaking" and more funding, but otherwise the Act is on target. Others contend that NCLB in anything like its current form is not likely to advance reasonable use of tests in advancing sound educational policy.

Although the appropriateness of NCLB's use of high stakes testing for accountability purposes is subject to debate, the substantial influence of NCLB on K–12 testing at the current time is unarguable. Most persons expect this influence to continue into the foreseeable future. It is not surprising, therefore, that directly or indirectly, NCLB has influenced the content of many chapters in this volume (see, for example, Ferrara & DeMauro, this volume; Koretz & Hamilton, this volume; Chalhoub-Deville & Deville, this volume). For that reason alone NCLB merits further consideration here, although it is acknowledged that some aspects of the following discussion will likely become outdated sooner or later.

2.3.1. Some History

In 1965 congress passed the Elementary and Secondary Education Act (ESEA), which became the cornerstone of the federal government's efforts to help the educationally disadvantaged.[6] During the same decade, the National Assessment of Educational Progress (NAEP) began as a largely invisible (at least to the public) federal testing program that reported how the nation's students were performing at three age/grade levels (roughly fourth, eighth, and twelfth grade) on selected items, not tests.[7] The ESEA and NAEP were not "linked" in any serious measurement or policy sense. Also, from the very beginning of NAEP, scores have never been reported for individual students.

As time went by, both the ESEA and NAEP evolved and became much more prominent and influential.[8] In particular, although the provisions of ESEA under consideration here seemed to focus only on educationally disadvantaged students in the various states, in fact ESEA had tremendous influence on other students and many aspects of K–12 education for two reasons. First, there were strings attached to the receipt of ESEA funds. Second, the amounts of money distributed to the states under ESEA were large enough that they leveraged a great deal of educational policy and practice.

By the late 1980s and early 1990s NAEP had evolved dramatically. For example, item scores were replaced by test scores, many new tests were introduced, reports were beginning to be provided to states on a "trial" basis, and the primary reporting mechanism was beginning to change from scale scores to achievement levels (below basic, basic, proficient, and advanced). Also, there were tentative efforts made during the first Bush administration that could have led to NAEP reporting scores at the student level. Subsequently, President Clinton considered much the same matter when he proposed the so-called "Voluntary National Tests" (VNTs) in his 1997 State of the Union address.[9]

Although NAEP and NCLB are legislatively distinct, there are at least two ways that they are related. First, for both NAEP and NCLB, achievement levels (particularly "proficient") loom large as reporting categories. Second, NAEP will be playing some kind of confirmatory or monitoring role with respect to states' reports of their NCLB status.

Since the 1980s, there has been a series of reports, including "A Nation at Risk" (National Commission on Excellence in Education, 1983) and the "Goals 2000: Educate America Act" of 1994, suggesting that the United States' educational system is in serious trouble. In addition, various international studies (see Mazzeo, Lazer, & Zieky, this volume) have suggested that the United States' educational system is at best "average" compared to other developed countries. It is not my intent to challenge these points, although it can be argued that many of them are at least debatable (see, for example, Berliner, 2004). Rather, I mention these matters as contributing factors in the history that led to NCLB.

In short, in my view, the ever increasing influence of the ESEA, the evolving nature of NAEP, and the high visibility of negative reports about schools in the US have all contributed to a national movement toward the use of tests for high-stakes accountability decisions in K–12 education—a movement that culminated in NCLB.

2.3.2. Testing Stakes

Prior to NCLB, K–12 testing was a low-stakes or medium-stakes activity in most cases. By contrast, the testing required by NCLB is definitely high stakes because the consequences are so serious. Apparently, most policymakers assume that accountability in education can be accomplished only through the imposition of high-stakes testing, although there is no compelling body of evidence to support that assumption.

When testing becomes high stakes, it is almost inevitable that it will drive instructional decisions, usually by narrowing the curriculum in the direction of emphasizing the content and skills tested (i.e., teaching to the test). This may be an unintended outcome, but it has real consequences that may not be desirable. To the extent that tests drive instruction, teachers who are closest to students tend to have less influence over what is taught, how it is taught, and how it is assessed. Classroom assessment represents a kind of counter-revolution that seeks to provide a more seamless integration of testing and assessment that permits formative evaluation of student progress (see Shepard, this volume)—what is sometimes called "assessment for learning" as opposed to "assessment of learning" (see Stiggins, 2005).

There are at least two other potential negative consequences of increasing the testing stakes. First, high stakes testing can have a corrupting influence. Under high stakes conditions, the motivation to misuse tests and test scores can be compelling. Protective mechanisms to preclude such misuse are very expensive (e.g., newly developed forms each year) and/or can create an unpleasant educational environment (e.g., intrusive monitoring of school administrators, teachers, and students). Second, the same test used under high and low stakes conditions can have widely different measurement characteristics, which means that at least some technical documentation for test scores obtained under low stakes conditions may be virtually irrelevant if the test is used under high stakes conditions.

2.3.3. Standards and Standard Setting

Standard setting has been an issue in measurement for decades, especially in licensure and certification testing. However, this is the first edition of *Educational Measurement* that has an entire chapter devoted to the subject (Hambleton & Pitoniak, this volume). The increased emphasis on standard setting is due in large part to NCLB and NAEP.

As noted above, one area of overlap between NCLB and NAEP is the use of achievement-level categories of performance (i.e., below basic, basic, proficient, and advanced) rather than more traditional scale scores. Importantly, under NCLB each state is required to develop its own definitions of these achievement levels, and these definitions do not correspond with those used by NAEP. The net effect is that words such as "proficient" do not mean the same thing in different states. This, in turn raises tension-generating questions such as, "Does it make sense that proficiency in reading for third graders should mean something different in Massachusetts than in Iowa?" Clearly, the body politic has the right to answer this question, "Yes." However, the measurement profession has the ethical responsibility to guard against misuse of scores (see Phillips & Camara, this volume).

2.4. Technology and Computerization

The role of technology in testing has a remarkably enduring quality, which can be traced through all four editions of *Educational Measurement*. Beginning with the second edition, the role of computers has been emphasized repeatedly (see, for example, Baker, 1971, and Thorndike, 1971b). Nearly since the advent of computers, it has been predicted that they would revolutionize education and testing. Some of these predictions have come true, others are beginning to be implemented, and still others have yet to be realized. Some knowledgeable persons might argue that computers have not yet revolutionized testing, but even those persons would agree, I think, that eventually computers will have a major impact on measurement. My own belief is that the role of technology and computers in testing is partly evolutionary and partly revolutionary (see Bunderson, Inouye, & Olsen, 1989; Cohen & Wollack, this volume; Drasgow, Luecht, & Bennett, this volume).

In the 20th century perhaps the single most important technological development in testing was E. F. Lindquist's invention of the optical scanner (see Baker, 1971, and Peterson, 1983). Without Lindquist's invention, it likely would have been impossible for testing to advance at the rate that it did in the second half of the twentieth century. The optical scanner, however, primarily impacts only one aspect of testing—namely, the conversion of bubbled responses on an answer sheet to item and examinee raw scores.[10] Furthermore, the positive impact is largely with respect to speed and cost.

Indirectly, it can be argued that the invention of the optical scanner had consequences that the inventor perhaps did not fully anticipate. It made scoring multiple-choice items so easy, fast, and inexpensive that in most contexts no other testing modality could compete. In this sense, it might be argued that the optical scanner effectively impeded the growth of what are called these days "alternative" assessments. It is interesting to speculate about how Lindquist (the editor of the first edition of *Educational Measurement*) would perceive the influence of his invention. My own guess is that he would strongly encourage innovative use of computers, even if doing so resulted in reduced use of his invention.

Whereas the optical scanner primarily impacts only one aspect of testing, computers have the potential to impact virtually all aspects. Consider the following tasks that are part of just about every testing program: registration, item development, test assembly, test administration, item/test scoring, and score reporting. Computers can facilitate all of these tasks, but not necessarily solve them.

For example, in some testing programs, the development of items is partially automated through the use of algorithmically-generated items (e.g., item forms, item clones, etc), and there are serious efforts underway to use computerized algorithms to implement principles from cognitive psychology in test development (see Mislevy, this volume). However, in most instances item and test development is still an art practiced by highly experienced professionals (see Schmeiser & Welch, this volume). A particularly intractable problem has been the generation of other-than-trivial items to test passage-related reading comprehension. Test assembly is still largely an art, too, but there are testing programs that use sophisticated linear programming software to assign items to tests (or testlets).

2.4.1. Test Administration

It seems likely that most of the public and many educators think that the primary role of computers in testing is for test administration, which is now generally referred to as computer-based testing (CBT). As far back as the 1960s many researchers predicted that computerized test administration would become common practice in the "near" future. Such predictions were largely premature, although they probably will be correct eventually. The principal barriers to widespread use of CBT have not been in the areas of measurement theory or practice; rather they have been cost and/or test volume. To the best of my knowledge, nearly every testing program that has adopted CBT has experienced a dramatic increase in costs, and, except for business environments and the military, almost always these costs are passed on to examinees. Examinees seeking licensure, certification, and occasionally admission to graduate programs have been willing to pay such costs, but examinees in lower-stakes contexts have been less willing or unable to do so. In college admissions testing, CBT is not a "major player," in part because the per-year testing volume is so large. There simply are not enough test centers with enough computers to accommodate the volume, at least not yet.

In the K–12 market, every-student CBT is not likely to be viable in many, if not most, states for years to come. Costs, the number of functioning computers needed, the space to accommodate them, and the technical expertise required to maintain them are not going to be available in the near future without a massive increase in school funding, which does not seem likely. Rather, it seems much more likely that in most of the K–12 arena CBT will be used for "niche" testing for selected purposes.

It is noteworthy that evidence of improved measurement under CBT is relatively rare. Most studies involving CBT focus mainly on the extent to which scores are comparable for paper-and-pencil tests and computerized tests. Often it seems that there is more hype than reality in much of the enthusiasm surrounding CBT, but there are definitely reasons to believe that CBT will become much more prevalent in the future, as discussed next.

First, some of the costs associated with the delivery of major paper-and-pencil testing programs may seem mundane, such as shipping, creation and delivery of score reports, etc. However, these and other costs have been growing and likely will continue to do so. By contrast, computers are becoming cheaper and more ubiquitous. At some point, it seems likely that many paper-and-pencil tests will become "economically-challenged" alternatives, at least in some contexts.

Second, it is undeniable that CBT offers the promise of substantial, positive changes in what is tested and how it is tested. How fast this potential will be realized is subject to considerable debate, but even now there are testing programs that are exploring alternative assessment formats for use in CBT. At a bare minimum, scoring is quicker with CBT, as discussed in the next section.

Third, students who now take tests are intimately familiar with computers in many areas of their lives. For them, a computer is a rather natural modality for testing. In the future, not only students but also those responsible for evaluating student performance will view CBT as a natural way to test, I think. Furthermore, they will likely view paper-and-pencil testing as outdated and perhaps "second-rate" no matter what the measurement arguments may be. This rather superficial reason for adopting CBT may be more compelling than some measurement experts would like to believe.

2.4.2. Item and Test Scoring

For multiple-choice tests delivered via computer, there is no need for an optical scanner to be a "middle man" between the examinee's responses and scoring—the computer can do that, too. In this sense, the future of the optical scanner is to some degree tied to paper-and-pencil multiple-choice testing, and one might speculate that as CBT becomes more pervasive, the use of optical scanners in testing will decline. Perhaps so, but I doubt that will happen soon for two reasons. First, in the near term, economic factors virtually guarantee that optically-scanned multiple-choice tests will survive. Second, even if paper-and-pencil testing were to disappear completely (a very unlikely scenario), scanners likely would still be needed to scan essays and other forms of constructed responses prior to scoring.

Since the third edition of *Educational Measurement* there has been an increasing use of various types of performance assessments instead of, or in addition to, traditional objectively-scored tests (see Lane & Stone, this volume). Essay testing is probably the most prevalent example, but there is a vast range of different types of performance assessments that have been studied and even used operationally. For the most part, these assessments have been delivered in some non-computerized manner, and a persistent and costly problem has been the scoring of such assessments by human raters. Recently, computerized scoring of essays (and other performance assessments) has become a topic of considerable research interest, and there are even testing programs that use computerized scoring operationally at least to some extent. Furthermore, some testing programs are already delivering simulations via computer. There are a number of reasons for believing that many future testing programs may be characterized, at least in part, by sophisticated simulations that are scored in real time. Doing so is likely to be costly, however.

2.4.3. Score Reporting

It might be argued that computers have the greatest potential for immediately advancing testing through improvements in score reports, which have not changed that much in the past several decades. For example, it is still common practice for scores on major testing programs to be reported many weeks (or even months) after test administration. This is particularly problematic for K–12 testing programs for which test performance is intended to guide instruction. When scores are reported so late, the opportunity for instructional improvement is at best delayed substantially. A substantive reason that score reporting is so frequently delayed is that it is driven by a paper-laden process that involves scanning, creating and printing of score reports, and delivery of these reports in traditional ways. By contrast, score reports could be delivered much faster over the internet, with appropriate security precautions, of course. This is being done for some programs, but it is still relatively rare.

Principal changes in score reports in the past several decades are the inclusion of more scores, more details about them, some diagnostic score reporting, and occasionally some rather crude graphical profiles. However, score reports are generally static in the sense that, for the most part, they are dominated by a "one size fits all" approach. There are exceptions. For example, some testing programs provide both narrative and traditional score reports. However, it is relatively rare for a testing company to tailor the information in its reports to the needs of particular types of examinees and users of scores.

Also, computer-delivered score reports could be interactive to some extent, allowing the user to "drill down" to obtain a much deeper level of detail about test scores. Such interactive reports could be provided not only at the student level but also at group levels (e.g., classrooms, schools, districts, etc.). I suggest that computer-delivered, tailored score reports with interactive features would give much more "bang for the buck" than just about any other use of computers in testing, at the present time. After all, the best test in the world is worthless if scores are not understood and used properly, and improved score interpretation enhances the validity and utility of score use.

Another limiting feature of score reports in the K–12 market is the lack of longitudinal information provided to users. Most norm-referenced K–12 testing programs scale the various levels of the tests so that student-level change can be measured from grade to grade. Indeed, the capability of doing so is a highly touted claim of those who market such tests. Yet, score reports are often merely a snapshot of a student's performance in a particular grade without reference to that student's prior performance. The same type of statement applies to group-level reports. In past decades, when data had to be stored on "flat files," it was difficult to incorporate longitudinal data into score reports, but those days are long past. The use of relational databases makes the provision of longitudinal data an attainable goal, although additional costs will be incurred.

2.4.4. Unintended Consequences

The inexorable advancement of computers into testing is not without its perils. First, there is always the danger that this technology will overly influence the nature of what is measured.[11] For example, computerized item generation is extraordinarily attractive largely because it substantially reduces test development costs. However, not all knowledge and constructs are amenable to being tested using item clones, at least not yet. There is a danger, therefore, that tested knowledge and constructs could be twisted to accommodate the capabilities of item generation. It is reasonable to reflect on Marshall McLuhan's dictum that "the medium is the message." If that happens to measurement, it could be a step backward.

Second, it is probably inevitable that the public will believe that tests developed and/or delivered by computer will be "state-of-the-art" and, therefore, less fallible in both a lay sense and a more technical measurement sense. That is by no means certain. "Garbage in, garbage out" is still an applicable aphorism.

2.5. Legislation, Litigation, and Notions of Fairness

Legislation, litigation, and threats of litigation have been playing an ever increasing role in testing, especially for high stakes uses of tests that involve issues of fairness. Here, I focus on a few aspects of these matters that relate to evolutions in testing.

2.5.1. A Sampling of Issues

Phillips and Camara (this volume) provide considerable detail about legislation and litigation in testing. Among the issues that have been addressed in cases that have been decided by the courts are: the use of content validity evidence in defending teacher licensure tests; allegations of reverse discrimination based in part on test scores; the use of IQ tests as a basis for placing students in classes for the educable mentally retarded; the use of a basic skills test to award/deny high school diplomas to African-American students who had attended segregated schools; and allegations of racial discrimination in a high school graduation test.

In addition, there are many matters that began as legal challenges (or the threat of such) but were ultimately resolved out of court. The following are two examples.

In the 1970s and 1980s there were efforts by various states and organizations to force companies involved in admissions testing to release test items used to determine an examinee's score. If these efforts had succeeded to their fullest extent, it would have been virtually impossible to equate test forms, which would have meant that testing companies could not have given assurances that scores earned on different forms were comparable. To protect the integrity of their testing programs, while still bowing to the spirit of their critics' demands, most admissions testing companies decided to release many (but not all) test forms shortly after they were used. This strategy was not optimal from a measurement viewpoint, and it necessitated a substantial and costly increase in test development, but this largely self-imposed settlement seemed to satisfy most of the critics.

In *Breimhorst v. Educational Testing Service (ETS)* (2001) the plaintiff challenged the use of a "flag" on his score report for an ETS test taken with extended-time. (A "flag" is simply some designator, such as an asterisk, indicating that an examinee took a test under one or more unspecified, non-standard conditions.) Before the matter went to court, ETS decided to stop flagging extended-time scores for any of its testing programs. This did not entirely resolve the matter, however, because the best-known test administered by ETS (namely the SAT) is owned by the College Board, which was not immediately willing to endorse the ETS shift in flagging policy. Therefore, as part of the settlement the College Board (in conjunction with the Disabilities Rights Advocate group) convened a blue-ribbon panel to advise them on the matter. The majority of the committee recommended dropping the flag. Subsequently, the College Board decided to drop flagging scores obtained under extended time, and almost immediately ACT (the College Board's competitor in college admissions testing) followed suit.

This last example is particularly illustrative of the extent to which merely raising a legal challenge relative to a seemingly narrow issue can have far-reaching consequences. Even without a court order, three of the largest and most visible testing organizations in the world adopted a dramatic change in policy that each of them had vigorously defended in the past.

2.5.2. Role of the Standards in Legislation and Litigation

In legal contexts and in settlements involving educational tests, considerable weight is generally given to the *Standards*.[12] Still, the legal arena is not bound by the *Standards*, does not accord the *Standards* the same consideration as case law, and does not always concur with the emphases that are explicit or implicit in the *Standards*. This is particularly evident with respect to validity. The courts have not been terribly impressed with complex perspectives on validity; rather, a recurrent theme seems to be the primacy of content validity and predictive validity in the 50-year-old senses of those terms. This is one example of occasional disconnects between the courts and the *Standards*. Such disconnects may be influenced, at least in part, by the lack of a professional mechanism for enforcing the *Standards*, although the *Standards* do have a kind of ethical imperative (see, for example, the NCME, 1995, *Code of Professional Responsibilities in Education*).

As discussed in section 1, often there are close relationships between the treatment of topics in editions of *Educational Measurement* and the *Standards*, but the two play very different roles. The *Standards* usually represent something close to a consensus in the field at a particular point in time, while the various chapters of the editions of *Educational Measurement* provide the authors' perspectives on the topics treated. It often happens that a particular treatment of a topic in *Educational Measurement* influences the next edition of the *Standards*, but there is no professional requirement that this occur. In this sense, it seems appropriate that the courts focus more attention on the *Standards* than on *Educational Measurement*.

The measurement community sometimes forgets that the laws typically used in legal challenges to tests and testing practices are typically not laws that were created primarily to address testing issues. Rather, they tend to be laws deeply embedded in the American legal system that address what are viewed to be fundamental rights of citizens—rights that were often achieved only after intense political debate. For this reason, we should not be too surprised when legislatures and courts do not accord the degree of primacy to measurement standards and principles that measurement experts might prefer. It seems to me that the tension between legislatures and courts vis-à-vis the measurement community has increased in recent decades and is likely to become even more pronounced in the future. One example of this tension centers on matters of standardization, as discussed previously in section 2.2.

2.5.3. Some Potential Consequences of Increased Litigation

Even a cursory review of testing in the legal arena in the last several decades quickly reveals that as the testing stakes increase so does the likelihood of litigation. In our country, this is perhaps inevitable, but it also has a number of possibly unintended, and usually negative, consequences. For example, litigation almost always has the effect of increasing the cost of testing, although the public may not realize it.

Also, contrary to what might be expected, fear of litigation can be a motivation for *avoiding* good validity studies, because such studies inevitably come to conclusions that have a shade of grey, with a healthy amount of reference to the impact of errors of measurement and alternative explanations. As Cronbach (1980) has stated:

> The job of validation is not to support an interpretation, but to find out what might be wrong with it. A proposition deserves some degree of trust only when it has survived serious attempts to falsify it. (p. 103)

Appropriately qualified conclusions often give ammunition to testing critics. This, I think, is one potential explanation for what I perceive to be a dearth of good, thoughtful, published validity studies in high-stakes testing programs.

The involvement of the courts in testing matters is a trend that seems likely to increase. For example, the extraordinarily high stakes associated with NCLB might well lead to legal challenges, and perhaps unprecedented ones. Although I am not a legal scholar, it seems to me that NCLB provides a potential basis for legal challenges that focus on "opportunity to learn." Under NCLB, the stakes are very high for states, districts, schools, and students. Yet, it seems almost self-evident that the resources necessary to attain these extraordinarily high goals are often lacking. If so, does each student truly have an "opportunity to learn" the knowledge and skills that constitute the definition of proficient in the student's state?

Also, I suggest that the steady progression to computer administration of tests may well lead to legal challenges unlike any seen before. For example, one variety of CBT is computerized adaptive testing (CAT). It may be difficult to convince some segments of the public and the courts that CAT gives scores that are equitable for all examinees, even if the measurement arguments are well-crafted and sophisticated. In addition, computerized grading of essays in high-stakes tests may not be accepted routinely by the public and the courts, even if the measurement and cost-savings arguments are compelling.

In our society issues of fairness (see Camilli, this volume) are bound to involve the joint consideration of various measurement standards and legal arguments in the context of historical perspectives. It does not appear to me that there is a "gold standard" that will be accepted universally. I suspect our perspectives on fairness in testing will evolve continually, and arguments about the merits and fairness of particular testing practices will continue as well.

3. CONCLUDING COMMENTS

As reflected in part by the two major sections of this chapter, there are at least two clear trends in testing that show little likelihood of changing in the near future. First, our theoretical models are getting more and more sophisticated. Second, from a practical perspective, social issues are so influential in testing that the boundaries between the two are often blurred.

These two trends have parallels in other areas of science, and they represent substantial progress in many respects. Still, these trends present some challenging problems for the measurement profession. For example, the sophistication of our models has led to a degree of complexity that makes many of them nearly a "black box" even for many measurement professionals. Furthermore, many models are operationalized in proprietary computer programs that too-frequently hide important algorithms and assumptions.

The blurring of social issues and testing makes it imperative that professionals in the field of educational measurement serve as "honest brokers" in supporting the aggressive pursuit of validation efforts. This volume speaks primarily to measurement professionals, but the methods and messages discussed here have important applications and consequences for the broader society served by the field.

NOTES

1. Technically, the first edition was published by APA, only. Also, the titles of the various editions are not all identical; here, the *Standards* refers to any one of them.

2. A preliminary version of the 1954 *Standards* was published in the American Psychologist (1952, vol. 7, 461–475).

3. Some of Cronbach's perspectives on alpha were novel (e.g., the average of all the possible Flannagan split-halves coefficients), but the coefficient itself was not.

4. This section is largely a summary of Brennan (2004a).

5. Of course, these models might be adopted merely as approximations to the 3PL model or some other model.

6. ESEA has numerous provisions. Those of concern here fall mainly within Title I or Chapter I, depending on which version/reauthorization of the Act is under consideration.

7. See Pellegrino, Jones, and Mitchell (1999, pp. 12–20) for a brief history of NAEP; see Jones and Olkin (2004) for an extensive treatment.

8. During the Clinton administration, the reauthorization of the ESEA was called the Improving America's School ACT (IASA). As noted by Linn (2003), it "charted a new direction for testing and reporting for purposes of Title I by the states" (p. 7). According to Cohen (2002), IASA "placed considerable trust in states to work

out the details for themselves" (p. 43). That trust largely evaporated with the next reauthorization of ESEA, namely NCLB.

9. Both Presidents' initiatives failed.

10. Scanners are now being used to scan essays and other types of constructed responses prior to scoring, but that is not my focus at this point.

11. A case can be made that in past decades (and perhaps even now) the optical scanner's capabilities reinforced the use of objectively-scored multiple-choice items.

12. The Uniform Guidelines on Employee Selection Procedures (1985) are also sometimes considered, although they are used primarily in the employment arena. Teacher testing is one highly visible area in which the Uniform Guidelines might be considered relevant.

REFERENCES

American Educational Research Association, American Psychological Association, & National Council on Measurement in Education. (1966). *Standards for educational and psychological tests and manuals*. Washington, DC: American Psychological Association.

American Educational Research Association, American Psychological Association, & National Council on Measurement in Education. (1974). *Standards for educational and psychological tests*. Washington, DC: American Psychological Association.

American Educational Research Association, American Psychological Association, & National Council on Measurement in Education. (1985). *Standards for educational and psychological testing*. Washington, DC: American Psychological Association.

American Educational Research Association, American Psychological Association, & National Council on Measurement in Education. (1999). *Standards for educational and psychological testing*. Washington, DC: American Educational Research Association.

American Psychological Association (APA). (1954). *Technical recommendations for psychological tests and diagnostic techniques*. Washington, DC: Author.

Angoff, W. H. (1971). Scales, norms, and equivalent scores. In R. L. Thorndike (Ed.), *Educational measurement* (2nd ed., pp. 508–600). Washington, DC: American Council on Education.

Baker, F. B. (1971). Automation of test scoring, reporting, and analysis. In *Educational measurement* (2nd ed., pp. 202–234). Washington, DC: American Council on Education.

Berliner, D. C. (2004, March/April). *If the underlying premise for No Child Left Behind is false, how can that act solve our problems?* (The Iowa Academy of Education Occasional Paper #6). Des Moines, IA: FINE Foundation.

Bock, R. D., Brennan, R. L., & Muraki, E. (2002). The information in multiple ratings. *Applied Psychological Measurement, 26*, 364–375.

Breimhorst v. Educational Testing Service (ETS), *Settlement Agreement*, Case No. 99–3387 (N.D. Cal. 2001).

Brennan, R. L. (1987). Introduction to problems, perspectives, and practical issues in equating. *Applied Psychological Measurement, 11*, 221–224.

Brennan, R. L. (1995). The conventional wisdom about group mean scores. *Journal of Educational Measurement, 14*, 385–396.

Brennan, R. L. (1998a). Misconceptions at the intersection of measurement theory and practice. *Educational Measurement: Issues and Practice, 17*(1), 5–9, 30.

Brennan, R. L. (1998b). Raw-score conditional standard errors of measurement in generalizability theory. *Applied Psychological Measurement, 22*, 307–331.

Brennan, R. L. (2001a). An essay on the history and future of reliability from the perspective of replications. *Journal of Educational Measurement, 38*, 295–317.

Brennan, R. L. (2001b). *Generalizability theory*. New York: Springer-Verlag.

Brennan, R. L. (2001c). Some problems, pitfalls, and paradoxes in educational measurement. *Educational Measurement: Issues and Practice, 20*(4), 6–18.

Brennan, R. L. (2004a). *Revolutions and evolutions in current educational testing* (CASMA Research Report No. 6). Iowa City: The University of Iowa, Center for Advanced Studies in Measurement and Assessment. (Available on http://www.education.uiowa.edu/casma)

Brennan, R. L. (2004b). *Some perspectives on inconsistencies among measurement models* (CASMA Research Report No. 8). Iowa City: The University of Iowa, Center for Advanced Studies in Measurement and Assessment. (Available on http://www.education.uiowa.edu/casma)

Bunderson, C. V., Inouye, D. K., & Olsen, J. B. (1989). The four generations of computerized educational measurement. In R. L. Linn (Ed.), *Educational measurement* (3rd ed., pp. 367–407). New York: American Council on Education and Macmillan.

Cohen, M. (2002). Unruly crew: Accountability lessons from the Clinton administration. *Education Next, 2*(3), 42–47.

Cook, T. D., & Campbell, D. T. (1979). *Quasi-experimentation: Design and analysis issues for field settings*. Chicago: Rand McNally.

Cronbach, L. J. (1951). Coefficient alpha and the internal structure of tests. *Psychometrika, 16*, 292–334.

Cronbach, L. J. (1971). Test validation. In R. L. Thorndike (Ed.), *Educational measurement* (2nd ed., pp. 443–507). Washington, DC: American Council on Education.

Cronbach, L. J. (1980). Validity on parole: How can we get it straight? *New Directions for Testing and Measurement: Measuring Achievement Over a Decade, 5*, 99–108.

Cronbach, L. J. (1982). *Designing evaluations of educational and social programs*. San Francisco: Jossey-Bass.

Cronbach, L. J. (1988). Five perspectives on validity argument. In H. Wainer & H. I. Braun (Eds.), *Test validity* (pp. 3–17). Hillsdale, NJ: Erlbaum.

Cronbach, L. J. (1991). Methodological studies—A personal retrospective. In R. E. Snow & D. E. Wiley (Eds.), *Improving inquiry in social science: A volume in honor of Lee J. Cronbach* (pp. 385–400). Hillsdale, NJ: Erlbaum.

Cronbach, L. J. (2004). My current thoughts on coefficient alpha and successor procedures. *Educational and Psychological Measurement, 64*, 391–418.

Cronbach, L. J., Gleser, G. C., Nanda, H., & Rajaratnam, N. (1972). *The dependability of behavioral measurements: Theory of generalizability for scores and profiles*. New York: Wiley.

Cronbach, L. J., Rajaratnam, N., & Gleser, G. C. (1963). Theory of generalizability: A liberalization of reliability theory. *British Journal of Statistical Psychology, 16*, 137–163.

Cureton, E. E. (1951). Validity. In E. F. Lindquist (Ed.), *Educational measurement* (pp. 621–694). Washington, DC: American Council on Education.

Feldt, L. S., & Brennan, R. L. (1989). Reliability. In R. L. Linn (Ed.), *Educational measurement* (3rd ed., pp. 105–146). New York: American Council on Education and Macmillan.

Flanagan, J. C. (1951). Units, scores, and norms. In E. F. Lindquist (Ed.), *Educational measurement* (pp. 695–763). Washington, DC: American Council on Education.

Gleser, G. C., Cronbach, L. J., & Rajaratnam, N. (1965). Generalizability of scores influenced by multiple sources of variance. *Psychometrika, 30*, 395–418.

Goals 2000: Educate America ACT of 1994, 20, U.S.C. 5801 *et seq.*

Guion, R. M. (1980). On trinitarian conceptions of validity. *Professional Psychology, 11,* 385–398.

Gulliksen, H. (1950). *Theory of mental tests.* New York: Wiley. [Reprinted by Lawrence Erlbaum Associates, Hillsdale, NJ, 1987]

Hambleton, R. K. (1989). Principles and selected applications of item response theory. In R. L. Linn (Ed.), *Educational measurement* (3rd ed., pp. 147–200). New York: American Council on Education and Macmillan.

Holland, P. W., & Hoskens, M. (2003). Classical test theory as a first-order item response theory: Application to true-score prediction from a possibly nonparallel test. *Psychometrika, 68,* 123–149.

Jones, L. V., & Olkin, I. (2004). *The nation's report card.* Washington, DC: American Educational Research Association.

Kane, M. T. (1982). A sampling model for validity. *Applied Psychological Measurement, 6,* 125–160.

Kane, M. T. (2001). Current concerns in validity theory. *Journal of Educational Measurement, 38,* 319–342.

Kolen, M. J., & Brennan, R. L. (2004). *Test equating, scaling, and linking: Methods and practices* (2nd ed.). New York: Springer-Verlag.

Kolen, M. J., & Harris, D. J. (1987, April). *A multivariate test theory model based on item response theory and generalizability theory.* Paper presented at the annual meeting of the American Educational Research Association, Washington, DC.

Lee, W., Brennan, R. L., & Kolen, M. J. (2000). Estimators of conditional scale-score standard errors of measurement: A simulation study. *Journal of Educational Measurement, 37,* 1–20.

Lindquist, E. F. (Ed.). (1951). *Educational measurement.* Washington, DC: American Council on Education.

Lindquist, E. F. (1953). *Design and analysis of experiments in psychology and education.* Boston: Houghton Mifflin.

Linn, R. L. (1989a). Current perspectives and future directions. In R. L. Linn (Ed.), *Educational measurement* (3rd ed., pp. 1–10). New York: American Council on Education and Macmillan.

Linn, R. L. (Ed.). (1989b). *Educational measurement* (3rd ed.). New York: American Council on Education and Macmillan.

Linn, R. L. (2003). Accountability: Responsibility and reasonable expectations. *Educational Researcher, 32*(7), 3–13.

Lord, F. M. (1952). A theory of test scores. *Psychometric Monograph No. 7.* Psychometric Society, Center for Educational Research and Evaluation, University of North Carolina at Greenboro.

Lord, F. M. (1980). *Applications of item response theory to practical testing problems.* Hillsdale, NJ: Erlbaum.

Lord, F. M., & Novick, M. R. (1968). *Statistical theories of mental test scores.* Reading, MA: Addison-Wesley.

Messick, S. (1989). Validity. In R. L. Linn (Ed.), *Educational measurement* (3rd ed., pp. 13–103). New York: American Council on Education and Macmillan.

National Commission on Excellence in Education. (1983). *A nation at risk: The imperative for educational reform.* Washington, DC: U.S. Government Printing Office.

National Council on Measurement in Education. (1995). *Code of professional responsibilities in educational measurement.* Middleton, WI: Author.

No Child Left Behind Act of 2001, Pub. L. No. 107-110, 115 Stat. 1425 (2002).

Pellegrino, J. W., Jones, L. R., & Mitchell, K. J. (Eds.). (1999). *Grading the nation's report card: Evaluating NAEP and transforming the assessment of educational progress.* Committee on the Evaluation of National and State Assessments of Educational Progress, Board of Testing and Assessment, National Academy of Sciences. Washington, DC: National Academy Press.

Petersen, N. S., Kolen, M. J., & Hoover, H. D. (1989). Scaling, norming, and equating. In R. L. Linn (Ed.), *Educational measurement* (3rd ed., pp. 221–262). New York: American Council on Education and Macmillan.

Peterson, J. J. (1983). *The Iowa Testing Programs: The first fifty years.* Iowa City: University of Iowa Press.

Rajaratnam, N., Cronbach, L. J., & Gleser, G. C. (1965). Generalizability of stratified-parallel tests. *Psychometrika, 30,* 39–56.

Rasch, G. (1960). *Probabilistic models for some intelligence and attainment tests.* Copenhagen, Denmark: Nielson and Lydiche (for Danmarks Paedagogiske Institut).

Shavelson, R. J., & Webb, N. M. (1991). *Generalizability theory: A primer.* Newbury Park, CA: Sage.

Stiggins, R. J. (2005). *Student involved assessment for learning* (4th ed.). Upper Saddle River, NJ: Pearson/Merrill Prentice Hall.

Stanley, J. C. (1971). Reliability. In R. L. Thorndike (Ed.), *Educational measurement* (2nd ed., pp. 356–442). Washington, DC: American Council on Education.

Thorndike, R. L. (1951). Reliability. In E. F. Lindquist (Ed.), *Educational measurement* (pp. 560–620). Washington, DC: American Council on Education.

Thorndike, R. L. (Ed.). (1971a). *Educational measurement* (2nd ed.). Washington, DC: American Council on Education.

Thorndike, R. L. (1971b). Educational measurement for the seventies. In R. L. Thorndike (Ed.), *Educational measurement* (2nd ed., pp. 3–14). Washington, DC: American Council on Education.

Uniform Guidelines on Employee Selection Procedures [Uniform Guidelines], 29 C.F.R. § 1607 et seq. (1985).

Part I
Theory and General Principles

2
Validation

Michael T. Kane
National Conference of Bar Examiners

Measurement uses limited samples of observations to draw general and abstract conclusions about persons or other units (e.g., classes, schools). To validate an interpretation or use of measurements is to evaluate the rationale, or argument, for the claims being made, and this in turn requires a clear statement of the proposed interpretations and uses and a critical evaluation of these interpretations and uses. Ultimately, the need for validation derives from the scientific and social requirement that public claims and decisions be justified.

Measurement procedures tend to control irrelevant sources of variability by standardizing the tasks to be performed, the conditions under which they are performed, and the criteria used to interpret the results. Such standardization can be effective in controlling irrelevant variability, but it also restricts the range of observations included in the measurements relative to those that are potentially relevant to the proposed interpretations and uses. The use of test scores to make decisions brings in assumptions about consequences, and these assumptions also merit scrutiny. The challenge is to make the connection between limited samples of observations and the proposed interpretations and uses.

The term "validation" and to a lesser extent the term "validity" tend to have two distinct but closely related usages in discussions of measurement. In the first usage, "validation" involves the development of evidence to support the proposed interpretations and uses; in this usage, "to validate an interpretation or use" is to show that it is justified. In the second usage, "validation" is associated with an evaluation of the extent to which the proposed interpretations and uses are plausible and appropriate. In this sense, "to validate an interpretation or use" is to evaluate its overall plausibility. The first usage implies an advocacy role, in the building of a case for the validity of a proposed interpretation. The second usage implies a more-or-less objective appraisal of the evidence, pro and con.

In this chapter, I will focus on validation as the process of evaluating the plausibility of proposed interpretations and uses, and on validity as the extent to which the evidence supports or refutes the proposed interpretations and uses. However, in the early stages of any validation effort, as the measurement procedure is developed, the more confirmationist usage reflects reality. The test developer is expected to make a case for the validity of the proposed interpretations and uses, and it is appropriate to talk about their efforts "to validate" the claims being made. A mature testing program is expected to stand up to criticism, and the accumulated evidence is to be evaluated in an evenhanded way.

The bulk of this chapter can be divided into three parts. The first part, with two sections, will provide a general conceptual analysis of validation. Section 1 examines the historical development of our conceptions of validity. Section 2 develops an argument-based validation framework, which assumes that the proposed interpretations and uses will be explicitly stated as an argument, or network of inferences and supporting assumptions, leading from observations to the conclusions and decisions. Validation involves an appraisal of the coherence of this argument and of the plausibility of its inferences and assumptions.

The second part, Sections 3 to 6, examines a range of common interpretations and uses and focuses on the kinds of evidence needed to evaluate the inferences and assumptions entailed by these interpretations and uses. These sections cover observable attributes and traits (Section 3), theory-based interpretations (Section 4), qualitative interpretations (Section 5), and decision procedures (Section 6).

The last part, Sections 7 and 8, draws some general conclusions about validation. Section 7, on fallacies, examines some ways in which interpretations and decisions based on test results can go awry, and Section 8 presents some concluding remarks.

Writing a chapter like this involves a number of choices about what to include and what to leave out. Validity now has a long history and a very broad scope. Interest in some issues that seemed to be of central concern in the past (e.g., nomological networks) has faded a bit. Other issues that were given little attention (e.g., social consequences) or taken for granted (standard setting) are receiving more attention. Some aspects of validity are quite technical (e.g., analyses of model fit); some are more philosophical (elucidating the meaning of a score); and some raise broad social issues (fairness, unintended consequences).

I will focus mainly on general strategies for validating the interpretations and uses of measurements. I will not give much attention to technical issues, most of which are discussed in detail in other parts of this volume, but will attend to the roles of such issues in validation, particularly where the issues come up and how they get resolved.

Validity theory addresses fundamental questions about the meaning and uses of measurements, and therefore, tends to be quite abstract. It seems to have been more successful in developing general frameworks for analysis than in providing clear guidance on how to validate specific interpretations and uses of measurements. This chapter tries to provide a pragmatic approach to validation, involving the specification of proposed interpretations and uses, the development of a measurement procedure that is consistent with this proposal, and a critical evaluation of the coherence of the proposal and the plausibility of its inferences and assumptions.

1. EVOLVING CONCEPTIONS OF VALIDATION

Validation focuses on interpretations, or meanings, and on decisions, which reflect values and consequences. Neither meanings nor values are easily reduced to formulas, literally or figuratively, and some familiarity with how various models of validity developed may be helpful in understanding the models and how they are used (and sometimes abused). An historical approach is particularly useful in understanding the central concept of construct validity, which has undergone several transformations since its introduction about fifty years ago. As a result of these shifts in interpretation, construct validity has accumulated several layers of meaning that are easily blurred.

1.1. Development of the Criterion Model

Between 1920 and 1950, criterion validity came to be seen as the gold standard for validity (Angoff, 1988; Cronbach, 1971; Moss, 1992; Shepard, 1993). In the first edition of *Educational Measurement*, Cureton (1951) defined validity in terms of "the correlation between the actual test scores and the 'true' criterion score" (p. 623), the test-criterion correlation corrected for unreliability in the criterion. Validation was to address the question of how well a test estimates the criterion, which could be defined in terms of "performances of the actual task" (p. 623). A test was considered valid for any criterion for which it provided accurate estimates (Gulliksen, 1950a). Under the criterion model, the variable of interest was assumed to have a definite value for each person, and the goal was to estimate this value as accurately as possible (Ebel, 1961). Given this goal, it was natural to conceive of validity as the correspondence between test scores and criterion scores.

The criterion model came in two versions, concurrent and predictive. *Concurrent validity* studies employed criterion scores obtained at about the same time as the test scores and could be used to validate a proxy measure that would be cheaper, easier, or safer than the criterion. *Predictive validity* studies employed a criterion of future performance (e.g., on the job, in college), which was not available at the time of testing.

The criterion model worked particularly well in those cases where a plausible criterion was readily available. For example, if the test were used to predict some future performance (e.g., in flight training, in a college course, or on the job), evaluations of actual performance could be used as the criterion. Where a good criterion was available, the criterion model provided a simple, elegant, and effective approach to validation, one that could take advantage of sophisticated quantitative methods (Cronbach & Gleser, 1965; Cureton, 1951). For admissions, placement, and employment testing, the criterion model is still the preferred approach (Guion, 1998).

The data from some early criterion-related studies of employment tests seemed to indicate that criterion-related validity coefficients varied substantially, across similar jobs in similar settings. This variability was attributed to differences in the requirements associated with specific jobs in different settings and to differences in the settings (Ghiselli, 1966). The apparent situational specificity of criterion-related data for employment tests led to suggestions that employment tests be validated separately in every situation in which they were to be used. Schmidt and Hunter (1977) examined the variability in criterion-related validity coefficients for employment tests and found that much of the observed variability could be attributed to such statistical artifacts as sampling error, differences in criterion and test reliabilities, and differences in range restrictions; they concluded that validity coefficients could be generalized across settings.

The criterion model can be implemented more-or-less mechanically once the criterion has been defined, but the specification of the criterion typically involves value judgments and a consideration of consequences (Cronbach & Gleser, 1965). Decision procedures based on the criterion model are generally intended "to optimize some later 'criterion' performance" (Cronbach, 1971, p. 445) and therefore involve judgments about the value of the proposed criterion.

The criterion model has two major advantages. First, in many applications, criterion-related evidence is clearly relevant to the plausibility of the proposed interpretations and uses. If the proposed interpretation claims that applicants with higher scores on the test can be expected to exhibit better performance in some activity (e.g., on the job), it would certainly be reasonable to check on this prediction.

Second, criterion-related validity appears to be (and to some extent actually is) objective. Once the criterion is specified, and data on some sample of individuals is collected, a validity coefficient can be computed in a straightforward way. Of course, the choice of a criterion and the selection of individuals to be included in the study involve a number of value judgments, but once these choices are made and the data are collected, the analyses can be straightforward.

1.1.1. Limitations of the Criterion Model

The main limitation in the criterion model was and is the difficulty in obtaining an adequate criterion. In some cases (e.g., achievement tests), it may be difficult to implement a criterion that is clearly better than the test itself, and in other cases (e.g., intelligence, creativity), it may be difficult to even conceptualize a satisfactory criterion (Cronbach, 1971, 1980a, b; Guion, 1998; Lord & Novick, 1968). As Ebel suggested:

The ease with which test developers can be induced to accept as criterion measures quantitative data having the slightest appearance of relevance to the trait being measured is one of the scandals of psychometry. (1961, p. 642)

Once one begins to question some criteria, it becomes clear that all criteria are questionable.

In addition to the many practical problems that plague criterion-related validity studies, the criterion model faces a fundamental problem. How can the criterion be validated? Even if a second criterion can be identified as a basis for validating the initial criterion, this simply pushes the problem back one step (Ebel, 1961). Without some other way to validate some criterion measures, we clearly face either infinite regress or circularity. The criterion model is quite useful in validating secondary measures of an attribute, assuming that some primary measure is available to be used as a criterion, but, ultimately, it cannot be used to validate the criterion. At some point, the criterion has to be validated in another way.

1.2. Content Model

How can a criterion be validated without appealing to another criterion? One option would be to validate the criterion by establishing a rational link between the procedures used to generate the criterion scores and the proposed interpretation or use of the scores (Cureton, 1951; Ebel, 1961; Gulliksen, 1950b; Rulon, 1946). Where a sample of some type of performance (e.g., typing, flying an airplane, playing the piano) is used to draw conclusions about level of skill in that kind of performance, a good case for the validity of the proposed interpretation can be made on rational grounds (Cronbach, 1971; Cureton, 1951; Ebel, 1961; Kane, Crooks, & Cohen, 1999).

The content model interprets test scores based on a sample of performances in some area of activity as an estimate of overall level of skill in that activity. Assuming that a person's performance is evaluated on a sample of tasks from a domain, it is legitimate to take the observed performance as an estimate of overall performance in the domain, if (a) the observed performances can be considered a representative sample from the domain, (b) the performances are evaluated appropriately and fairly, and (c) the sample is large enough to control sampling error (Guion, 1977).

Validity claims for assessments based on samples of the performance of interest can be challenged on various grounds (e.g., by suggesting that the samples are biased), but such sampling models do provide a basis for validation without resorting to external criteria (Cronbach, 1971; Kane, 1982). This is especially true if the relevant content domain has been defined with care, the tasks have been sampled (or developed) in a way that makes them representative of the domain, the observations were made using procedures that would tend to control random and systematic errors, and the performances were evaluated appropriately. We can find out how well somebody can perform a task by evaluating samples of their performance on the task. This approach tends to work especially well for tests of specific skills, but it can also be applied to more broadly defined measures of achievement (e.g., Flockton & Crooks, 2002).

The content model has most frequently been applied to measures of academic achievement. A content domain is outlined in the form of a test plan or blueprint, which may involve several dimensions (e.g., content per se, cognitive level, item type), with different numbers of items assigned to each cell in the plan. The items are not sampled from the domain; they are created to match the test specifications (Loevinger, 1957), and to the extent that they do, they may be considered to be representative of the content domain described by the test plan.

1.2.1. Limitations of the Content Model

The content model has been subject to a number of criticisms. In particular, content-related validity evidence tends to be subjective and to have a confirmatory bias. Content-based analyses tend to rely on judgments about the relevance and representativeness of test tasks. When these judgments are produced by test developers, they have a natural tendency to confirm the proposed interpretation.

The content model is especially problematic when it is used to argue for the validity of claims about cognitive processes or other theoretical constructs:

Judgments about content validity should be restricted to the operational, externally observable side of testing. Judgments about the subject's internal processes state hypotheses, and these require empirical *construct* validation. (Cronbach, 1971, p. 452; italics in original)

Messick (1989) argued that content-based validity evidence does not involve test scores or the performances on which the scores are based and therefore cannot be used to justify conclusions about the interpretation of test scores. Messick (1989) described content-validity evidence as providing support for "the domain relevance and representativeness of the test instrument" (p. 17) but saw it as playing a limited role in validation because it doesn't provide direct evidence for the "inferences to be made from test scores" (p. 17).

Content-related evidence has an important role to play in validation, but in most cases, it is a limited role. Evidence for the representativeness of the test tasks and the generalizability of scores can make a basic positive case for the validity of an interpretation in terms of expected performance over some universe of possible performances, but to go beyond that basic interpretation, other kinds of evidence are needed.

1.3. The Construct Model

By the early 1950's, the criterion model was well developed, and the content model was used to establish the plausibility of criterion measures. The content model also provided the main framework for validating measures of achievement and measures of various dispositions. However, models for the validation of measures of theoretical attributes were lacking.

In the early 1950s, the APA Committee on Psychological Tests sought to identify the kinds of evidence needed to justify the psychological interpretations that were "the stock-in-trade of counselors and clinicians" (Cronbach,

1989, p. 148). The resulting proposals for construct validation were incorporated in the *Technical Recommendations* (American Psychological Association, 1954), and were further developed by Cronbach and Meehl (1955). In 1971, Cronbach reviewed the events leading up to the 1955 paper:

> The rationale for construct validation (Cronbach & Meehl, 1955) developed out of personality testing. For a measure of, for example, ego strength, there is no uniquely pertinent criterion to predict, nor is there a domain of content to sample. Rather, there is a theory that sketches out the presumed nature of the trait. If the test score is a valid manifestation of ego strength, so conceived, its relations to other variables conform to the theoretical expectations. (Cronbach, 1971, pp. 462–463)

Cronbach and Meehl (1955) framed their discussion of construct validity in terms of the hypothetico-deductive (HD) model of scientific theories, in which a theory consists of a network of relationships linking theoretical constructs to each other and to observable attributes. Each theoretical construct is implicitly defined by its role in the theory.

Under the HD model of theories (Suppe, 1977), if the predictions derived from the theory do not agree with observations, then either the theory is wrong, the measurements are not appropriate indicators of the constructs in the theory, or some ancillary assumption was violated. If diverse predictions based on the theory are confirmed, the theory and the interpretation of scores in terms of the theory are supported.

This model assumes the existence of a well-defined theory from which empirical predictions can be derived. Cronbach and Meehl (1955) recognized the limitation inherent in this requirement:

> The idealized picture is one of a tidy set of postulates which jointly entail the desired theorems ... In practice, of course, even the most advanced physical sciences only approximate this ideal ... Psychology works with crude, half-explicit formulations. (pp. 293–294)

Nevertheless, they suggested that "the network still gives the constructs whatever meaning they do have" (p. 294). The construct is defined by its role in the theory.

Soon after Cronbach and Meehl's (1955) exposition of construct validity, Loevinger (1957) published a seminal analysis of the relationship between tests and psychological theory. Where Cronbach and Meehl basically started with the construct and its theory and posed the question of whether the test was an adequate measure of the construct, Loevinger started from the test and then asked about the plausibility of the proposed interpretation:

> to what extent does the test measure a trait that "really" exists. And how well does the proposed interpretation correspond to what is measured by the test? (Loevinger, 1957, p. 643)

Taking test construction as the starting point, Loevinger (1957) partitioned construct validity into a substantive component (which focused on a theory-based analysis of test content), a structural component (which focused on the internal structure of the test in relation to that of the target construct), and an external component (which focused on relationships to other test and non-test variables and on potential sources of systematic error). Loevinger (1957) considered the criterion and content models to be *ad hoc* because they depended on specific contingencies, proposing that "construct validity is the whole of the subject from a systematic, scientific point of view" (p. 461).

1.4. Evolution of the Construct Model 1955–1989

Cronbach and Meehl (1955) presented construct validity as an alternative to the criterion and content models; it was to be used "whenever a test is to be interpreted as a measure of some attribute or quality which is not operationally defined" (1955, p. 282), and "for which there is no adequate criterion" (1955, p. 299). Shepard (1993, p. 416) has suggested that Cronbach and Meehl introduced construct validity as "the weak sister" to be used when a real criterion is not available.

However, Cronbach and Meehl (1955, p. 282) went on to say that "determining what psychological constructs account for test performance is desirable for almost any test." That is, even if the test is initially validated using criterion or content evidence, the development of a deeper understanding of the constructs or processes accounting for test performance requires a consideration of construct-related evidence. So, Cronbach and Meehl (1955) suggested that construct validity was a fundamental concern, but they did not present it as a general organizing framework for validity.

The 1966 Standards distinguished construct validity from other approaches to validity, particularly criterion-related validity, by suggesting that "construct validity is relevant when the tester accepts no existing measure as a definitive criterion" (American Psychological Association, American Educational Research Association, & National Council on Measurement in Education [APA, AERA, & NCME], 1966, p. 13). The 1974 *Standards* (APA et al., 1974) continued along this track, listing four kinds of validity associated with four kinds of interpretation (predictive and concurrent validities, content validity, and construct validity).

Cronbach (1971) distinguished several approaches to validation and associated construct validation with theoretical variables for which "there is no uniquely pertinent criterion to predict, nor is there a domain of content to sample" (p. 462) and said that any description "that refers to the person's internal processes (anxiety, insight) invariably requires construct validation" (p. 451). He also emphasized the need for an overall evaluation of validity involving multiple kinds of evidence:

> Validation of an instrument calls for an integration of many types of evidence. The varieties of investigation are not alternatives any one of which would be adequate. The investigations supplement one another ... For purposes of exposition, it is necessary to subdivide *what in the end must be a comprehensive, integrated evaluation of the test.* (Cronbach, 1971, p. 445; italics in original)

The construct model continued to serve as one of several possible approaches to validation, but Cronbach also emphasized the need to integrate different kinds of validity evidence in evaluating the proposed interpretations and uses of test scores.

The need to specify and then evaluate the proposed interpretation was also apparent in the development of generalizability theory (Cronbach, Gleser, Nanda, & Rajaratnam, 1972), which deals with the precision (or reliability) of measurements. Generalizability theory, which provides analyses of error variance, required the test developer to specify the conditions of observation (e.g., content areas, test items, raters, occasions) over which generalization is to occur and then to evaluate the impact of the sampling of different kinds of conditions of observation on observed scores.

By the late 1970s, two opposing trends were evident in the development of validity theory. On the one hand, there had been a longstanding interest in a clear specification of the kinds of evidence needed to validate particular interpretations and uses of test scores. On the other hand, there was a perceived need to develop a unified conception of validity. The 1985 Standards (American Educational Research Association, American Psychological Association, & National Council on Measurement in Education [AERA, APA, & NCME], 1985) sought to resolve this tension by treating validity as a unified concept while recognizing that different kinds of evidence were relevant to different kinds of interpretations.

The need for specific rules for validation was particularly acute in employment testing, where employers wanted to know what they had to do to satisfy legal requirements for fairness in testing. For practical reasons, employers tended to prefer content-based strategies. Predictive evidence clearly made sense in employment testing but was expensive and often not feasible. The Uniform Guidelines (Equal Employment Opportunity Commission, Civil Service Commission, Department of Labor, & Department of Justice [EEOC, CSC, DoL, & DoJ], 1978) developed by federal agencies for the implementation of civil rights legislation required that evidence for validity be provided if a test had adverse impact on any protected group. The Uniform Guidelines accepted content or construct evidence but expressed a clear preference for criterion-related, predictive evidence (EEOC et al., 1978; Landy, 1986).

Nevertheless, validity theorists (Cronbach, 1980b; Guion, 1977, 1980; Messick, 1975, 1981; Tenopyr, 1977) preferred a more unified approach and expressed concern about the growing tendency to treat validation methodology as a toolkit, with different models to be employed for different assessments. The criterion model would be used to validate selection and placement decisions, the content model would be used to validate achievement tests, and the construct model would be used for theory-based explanations.

1.4.1. Construct Validation as the Basis for a Unified Model of Validity

Loevinger's (1957, p. 636) suggestion that "since predictive, concurrent, and content validities are all essentially ad hoc, construct validity is the whole of validity from a scientific point of view" took a while to catch on, but by the early 1980s, the construct model was widely accepted as a general approach to validity (Anastasi, 1986; Embretson, 1983; Guion, 1977; Messick, 1980, 1988, 1989). This broad conception of construct validity was taken to encompass all evidence for validity, including content and criterion evidence, reliability, and the wide range of methods associated with theory testing. Messick (1988, 1989) adopted a broadly defined version of the construct model as a unifying framework for validity. He relegated the content model to a subsidiary role in supporting the relevance of test tasks to the constructs of interest, and he treated the criterion model as an ancillary methodology for validating secondary measures of a construct against its primary measures.

The adoption of the construct model as the unified framework for validity had three major positive effects. First, the construct model tended to focus attention on a broad array of issues inherent in the interpretations and uses of test scores, and not simply on the correlation of test scores with specific criteria in particular settings and populations. Second, it emphasized the pervasive role of assumptions in score interpretations and the need to check these assumptions. Finally, the construct model allowed for the possibility of alternative interpretations and uses of test scores.

In the third edition of *Educational Measurement*, Messick (1989, p. 13) defined validity as:

> an integrated evaluative judgment of the degree to which empirical evidence and theoretical rationales support the *adequacy* and *appropriateness* of *inferences* and *actions* based on test scores or other modes of assessment. [italics in original]

He summarized his framework for validity evidence in terms of two interconnected "facets" of validity: the justification for testing (an evidential basis or a consequential basis) and the function or outcome of testing (interpretation or use), yielding a two-by-two matrix. Messick (1989) associated the evidential basis for score interpretation with construct validity and the evidential basis for test use with construct validity and relevance or utility. That is, all interpretations of test scores are to be supported by construct validation, and the appropriateness of the scores for a particular purpose is to be evaluated in terms of the relevance of the construct to the purpose at hand. Under this model, the evaluation of test use is a two-step process, from score to construct and from construct to use.

Messick gave the consequential basis for validity equal billing with the evidential basis. According to Messick (1989), the consequential basis of test interpretation depends on the value implications of the construct label and on the assumptions (theoretical and ideological) supporting the interpretation. Messick associated the consequential basis of test use with "the appraisal of both potential and actual social consequences of the applied testing" (Messick, 1989, p. 20).

1.4.2. Criteria for the Adequacy of Validation Efforts

The broad, unified version of construct validity was quite appealing as a conceptual framework for validity but it did not provide clear guidance for the validation of a test-score interpretation or use. In the absence of strong theories, construct validity tends to be very open ended, and it is not clear where to begin or how to gauge progress. Cronbach suggested that construct validation be viewed "as an ever-extending inquiry into the processes that produce a high or low test score and into the other effects of those processes" (Cronbach, 1971, p. 452), and subsequently characterized validation as "a lengthy, even endless process" (Cronbach, 1989, p. 151). According to Anastasi (1986), "almost any information gathered in the process of developing or using a test is relevant to its validity" (p. 3). If all data are relevant to validity, where should one start, and how much evidence is needed to adequately support a validity claim?

The call for serious consideration of alternative interpretations within the construct model offered one basis for choosing studies to conduct. Those studies that address the strongest competing interpretations would be given the highest priority. However, in practice, most validation research is conducted by test developers and tends to have a confirmationist bias. As Cronbach (1989) observed, "Falsification, obviously, is something we prefer to do unto the constructions of others" (p. 153). In itself, the unified model of construct validity does not necessarily provide clear guidelines for evaluating the adequacy of validation efforts.

1.5. General Principles Emerging from the Construct-Validation Model

Over the period from 1955 to 1989, at least three aspects of the construct-based model gradually emerged as general principles of validation that transcended the theory-dependent context in which construct validity was introduced.

First, by focusing on the role of potentially complex theories in specifying what attributes mean, Cronbach and Meehl (1955) increased awareness of the need to specify the proposed interpretation before evaluating its validity. Within the criterion model, it is relatively easy to develop validity evidence based on a test-criterion correlation without examining the rationale for the criterion too carefully. In marked contrast, the development of construct-related validity evidence requires that the proposed construct interpretation be elaborated in some detail. As a result, between 1955 and 1989, the emphasis gradually shifted from the validation of the test (as a measure of an existing criterion) to the development and validation of a proposed interpretation of test scores (Cronbach, 1971, 1982; Loevinger, 1957).

Second, Cronbach and Meehl (1955) recognized that construct validation would involve an extended research program. The validation of a measure of a theoretical construct involves the specification of a theory and of measures of the constructs in the theory and the empirical evaluation of predictions derived from the theory. The construct-validity model requires a research program, rather than a single empirical study (Cronbach, 1971).

Third, construct validity's focus on theory testing led to a growing awareness of the need to challenge proposed interpretations and to consider competing interpretations. Cronbach and Meehl (1955) did not give much direct attention to the evaluation of alternate interpretations, but this notion is implicit in their focus on theory and theory testing, and it was made fully explicit in subsequent work on construct validity (Cronbach, 1971, 1980a, b, 1982; Embretson, 1983; Messick, 1989).

By the mid-1980's, the model introduced by Cronbach and Meehl (1955) had developed into a general methodology for validation, as these three methodological principles (the need for an explicit statement of the proposed interpretation, the need for extended analysis in validation, and the need to consider alternate interpretations) were accepted as basic principles of validation.

1.6. Argument-Based Approach to Validity

Cronbach (1988) proposed that the validation of score interpretations and uses be based on the logic of evaluation argument (Cronbach, 1982; House, 1980). In program evaluation, it is clearly necessary to specify the program to be evaluated and the contexts in which it will be implemented, and any satisfactory evaluation involves a program of research, rather than a single empirical study. In program evaluation, alternative explanations for any observed changes need to be ruled out through experimental controls and/or through an explicit evaluation of alternative explanations. That is, validation and program evaluation face many of the same issues.

Cronbach suggested that the *validity argument* is to provide an overall evaluation of the intended interpretations and uses of test scores by generating a coherent analysis of all of the evidence for and against the proposed interpretation/use, and to the extent possible, the evidence relevant to plausible alternate interpretations and decision procedures (Cronbach, 1988). Similarly, Messick's (1989) definition of validity required an evaluative judgment of "the *adequacy* and *appropriateness* of *inferences* and *actions* based on test scores" (p. 12).

In order to evaluate a proposed interpretation of test scores, it is necessary to have a clear and fairly complete statement of the claims included in the interpretation and the goals of any proposed test uses. The proposed interpretations and uses can be specified in detail by laying out the network of inferences and assumptions leading from the test performances to the conclusions to be drawn and to any decisions based on these conclusions (Crooks, Kane, & Cohen, 1996; Kane, 1992; Shepard, 1993). The most recent edition of the *Standards* (AERA et al., 1999) has adopted a similar approach, suggesting that, "Validity logically begins with an explicit statement of the proposed interpretation of test scores along with a rationale for the relevance of the interpretation to the proposed use" (p. 9).

The general approach is consistent across applications. The inferences included in the interpretations and uses are to be specified, these inferences and their supporting assumptions are to be evaluated using appropriate evidence, and plausible alternative interpretations are to be considered. However, the model is responsive to differences in proposed interpretations and uses and to the context in which the scores are to be used. The specific inferences and assumptions tend to change from one application to another, and therefore the evidence required to support these claims tends to change, but validation always involves the specification (the interpretive argument) and evaluation (the validity argument) of the proposed interpretations and uses of the scores.

The argument-based approach to validity reflects the general principles inherent in construct validity without an emphasis on formal theories. The interpretive argument is to provide a clear statement of the inferences and assumptions inherent in the proposed interpretations and uses of test results, and these inferences and assumptions are to be evaluated in a series of analyses and empirical studies. Individual studies in a validity argument may focus on statistical analyses, content analyses, or relationships to criteria, but the validity argument as a whole requires the integration of different kinds of evidence from different sources. Plausible rival interpretations can provide particularly effective challenges to a proposed interpretation.

The main advantage of the argument-based approach to validation is the guidance it provides in allocating research effort and in gauging progress in the validation effort. The kinds of validity evidence that are most relevant are those that support the main inferences and assumptions in the interpretive argument, particularly those that are most problematic. In this vein, the 1999 *Standards* suggested that: "validation can be viewed as developing a scientifically sound validity argument to support the intended interpretation of test scores and their relevance to the proposed use" (AERA et al., 1999, p. 9). If some inferences in the argument are found to be implausible given the evidence, the interpretive argument needs to be either revised or abandoned. The proposed interpretations and uses of the test scores determine the kinds of evidence that are needed for validation.

2. VALIDITY AS ARGUMENT

To validate a proposed interpretation or use of test scores is to evaluate the rationale for this interpretation or use. The evidence needed for validation necessarily depends on the claims being made. Therefore, validation requires a clear statement of the proposed interpretations and uses.

2.1. Interpretive Arguments and Validity Arguments

Validation employs two kinds of argument. An *interpretive argument* specifies the proposed interpretations and uses of test results by laying out the network of inferences and assumptions leading from the observed performances to the conclusions and decisions based on the performances.

The *validity argument* provides an evaluation of the interpretive argument (Cronbach, 1988). To claim that a proposed interpretation or use is valid is to claim that the interpretive argument is coherent, that its inferences are reasonable, and that its assumptions are plausible. The analysis "should make clear, and to the extent possible, persuasive the construction of reality and the value weightings implicit in a test and its application" (Cronbach, 1988, p. 5).

The interpretive argument involves inferences leading from observed performances to the claims based on these performances. Each inference involves an extension of the interpretation or a decision. The inferences take the form of "if-then" rules (e.g., if the observed performance has certain characteristics, then the observed score should have a certain value, if an applicant's score is above some cutscore, the applicant is admitted). The assumptions supporting each inference are those that would provide adequate backing for the inference if they were accepted as true; for example, the assumption that a sample of performance is representative of some universe of possible performances supports an inference from the mean score for the sample to the mean over the universe.

There are, potentially, a large number of assumptions in any interpretive argument. We take many of these assumptions for granted, at least until evidence to the contrary develops. On written tests, we typically assume that students can read the questions and understand the instructions, unless special circumstances suggest otherwise. But some of the assumptions cannot be taken for granted, even in ordinary cases, and therefore need to be evaluated. For example, the adequacy with which an achievement test covers a content domain is almost always questionable, because the development of such tests involves a very large number of choices about what to include and what to leave out, and any or all of these choices may be questioned.

The interpretive argument makes the reasoning inherent in the proposed interpretations and uses explicit so that it can be better understood and evaluated. By outlining the claims to be evaluated, it provides a framework for validation. For example, if the interpretive argument includes a statistical generalization from observed performance on a sample of occasions to expected performance over a universe of possible occasions, the validity argument should evaluate the dependability of this generalization over occasions. If the interpretation does not assume generalization over occasions, empirical evidence for consistency over occasions would be irrelevant to the validity of the proposed interpretation and might even cast doubt on its validity. If the attribute being measured is expected to change rapidly over some period of time (e.g., level of achievement during a period of intensive instruction), invariance of the scores over time may indicate a lack of sensitivity in the measurement procedure. Evidence for generalizability over a facet (e.g., items, rater, conditions of measurement) is to be included in the validity argument if and only if the interpretive argument involves generalization over that facet.

Similarly, if the scores are used to predict future performance, the relationship between scores and measures of future performance needs to be examined; on the other hand, if the scores are used to certify current competence, predictive accuracy is not necessarily a concern, but the appropriateness of the passing score becomes a salient issue. If the interpretation depends on a scaling model (e.g., for scoring responses) the fit of the model to the data needs to be examined. If the interpretation does not depend on a scaling model, there is no need to evaluate how well the data fit that model. It is the plausibility of the proposed interpretations and uses that is to be evaluated.

2.2. An Example—Placement Testing

Placement tests are widely used in higher education to assign students within a sequence of related courses. It is assumed that the competencies developed in earlier courses serve as prerequisites for later courses (van der Linden,

1998). The goal is to assign students to courses that will be optimal for them in some sense (i.e., to a course that will be demanding but not overwhelming for the student). The ideal course would be one focusing on competencies that the student has not mastered, but for which the student has mastered all prerequisites.

The development of placement tests usually begins with the identification of the competencies developed in the courses. Once the relevant competencies have been identified, a test covering these competencies can be developed. The intent is not to develop a good, general measure of achievement in the area, but rather to focus on the specific competencies that are needed for courses in the sequence. The intended uses of the placement system drive the test-development process.

The rationale for placement testing is essentially a special case of what Cronbach and Snow (1977) called an aptitude-treatment interaction, with current level of skill in the competencies defining the aptitude, and the different courses constituting different treatments. A student with a very low score on the placement test, indicating a low level of skill in the competencies, would be expected to do poorly in any course beyond the first, which has few if any prerequisites. Students with higher scores would be expected to profit most from higher level courses.

The decision procedures for test-based placement systems are usually defined by specifying a set of cutscores on the test-score scale. Students with scores below the lowest cutscore are placed in the lowest level course; students with scores between the first and second cutscores are placed in the second course, and so on.

For placement tests, the cutscores are generally set empirically using the data from studies in which students who are currently completing the courses take the placement test, and their scores are matched with their grades in the course. Assuming that it is desirable to place each student in the highest level course in which he or she has a good chance of success, and that a student with a grade of B or better in one course is likely to be successful in the next course in the sequence, the lower cutscore for assignment to a course can be set to correspond to an expected score of B in the next lower course. Note that the data used to set the cutscore also provide empirical support for the cutscore and for the relationship between test scores and performance in the different courses.

2.2.1. Interpretive Argument for Placement Testing

An interpretive argument for placement systems, which is outlined in Table 2.1, includes four major inferences: scoring, generalization, extrapolation, and a decision. Each of these inferences depends on several assumptions. The interpretive argument may also involve various technical inferences and assumptions (e.g., equating, scaling) that are not discussed here.

The scoring inference employs a scoring rule to assign a score to each student's performance on the test tasks. For multiple-choice tests, the scoring rule consists of an answer key for the test. For performance assessments, the scoring rule, or rubric, provides guidelines for grading student performances. The scoring inference relies on two basic

TABLE 2.1 Interpretive Argument for a Placement Testing System

I1: *Scoring*: from observed performance to an observed score
    A1: The scoring rule is appropriate.
    A2: The scoring rule is applied accurately and consistently.

I2: *Generalization*: from observed score to universe score
    A1: The observations made in testing are representative of the universe of observations defining the testing procedure.
    A2: The sample of observations is large enough to control sampling error.

I3: *Extrapolation*: from universe score to the level of skill
    A1: The test tasks require the competencies developed in the courses and required in subsequent courses.
    A2: There are no skill irrelevant sources of variability that would seriously bias the interpretation of scores as measures of level of skill in the competencies.

I4: *Decision*: from conclusion about level of skill to placement in a specific course.
    A1: Performance in courses, beyond the initial course, depends on level of skill in the competencies developed in earlier courses in the sequence.
    A2: Students with a low level of skill in the prerequisites for a course are not likely to succeed in the course.
    A3: Students with a high level of skill in the competencies taught in a particular course would not benefit much from taking the course.

assumptions: that the scoring criteria are reasonable and that they are applied appropriately.

The generalization inference extends the interpretation from the observed score to a claim about expected performance over a larger universe of observations allowed by the testing procedure. Generalization depends on two assumptions: that the sample of observations is representative of the universe and that the sample is large enough to control sampling error. If both of these assumptions are met, sampling theory provides support for generalization from the observed score to the expected score over the universe.

The extrapolation inference extends the interpretation from test performance to a claim about competencies required in the courses, and therefore, to expectations about how well the student is likely to do in various courses. The extrapolation inference assumes that the test tasks provide adequate measures of the competencies of interest (those developed in the courses) and are not overly influenced by extraneous factors (e.g., test format).

The decision inference assigns students to courses based on their test scores. This inference depends on a number of value assumptions. It assumes that it is desirable that students be placed in the highest level courses in which they are likely to do fairly well, and that it is important that students not do badly in the courses in which they are placed. These two assumptions are value judgments about possible outcomes of instruction; they represent widely held values, but they are value judgments. As Cronbach (1971) pointed out, any evaluation of a placement decision rests on the assumption that, "the outcome will be more satisfactory under one course of action than another" (p. 448).

2.2.2. Validity Argument for Placement Tests

The validity argument provides an evaluation of the interpretive argument and would begin with a review of the argument as a whole to determine if it makes sense. Assuming that the interpretive argument (e.g., that in Table 2.1) is considered reasonable, its inferences and assumptions would be evaluated using appropriate evidence.

Scoring, generalization, and extrapolation are examined in some detail in Section 3 of this chapter, and decision inferences are analyzed in Section 6. Therefore, the validity argument for placement tests will only be sketched here. Support for scoring inferences relies mainly on expert judgment about the appropriateness of the scoring rule and the thoroughness of quality control procedures. Statistical analyses of the agreement among raters are called for if the scoring involves ratings. If scaling or equating models are employed in generating the final scores, the fit of these models to the data would also be checked empirically.

The analysis of generalizability involves reliability studies or generalizability studies, as well as judgments about the representativeness of the samples of observations included in the test.

Evaluations of the extrapolation inference may be based on judgments about the overlap between the skills measured by the test and those needed in the courses and/or by empirical analyses of the relationship between test scores and measures of performance in courses (e.g., course grades).

Finally, the evaluation of the placement decisions would involve an analysis of the positive and negative consequence resulting from the decisions, relative to those for alternative decision procedures.

In general, several different kinds of evidence would be relevant to each inference and its supporting assumptions, including expert judgment, empirical studies, the results of previous research, and value judgments.

2.3. The Interpretive Argument as Mini-Theory

The interpretive argument is analogous to a scientific theory (Suppe, 1977). Just as a scientific theory provides a general framework for interpreting certain observed phenomena and achieving certain goals, the interpretive argument provides a framework for the interpretation and use of the scores on a test. Both scientific theories and interpretive arguments are evaluated in terms of their clarity, their internal consistency, and the plausibility of their inferences and assumptions, some of which are evaluated by checking their implications against empirical data (Popper, 1962). And just as the applicability of a theory may be questioned in a particular case, the applicability of an interpretive argument to a test performance may be questioned in a particular case.

The generic form of the interpretive argument represents the proposed interpretations and uses of test scores. It is applied every time test results are used to draw conclusions or make decisions. It specifies the reasoning involved in getting from the test results to the conclusions and decisions based on these results. A validity argument that yields a positive evaluation of the reasoning in the interpretive argument provides support for the appropriateness of the proposed interpretations and uses of test results. Neither the interpretive argument nor the validity argument has to be developed anew for each person's test performance.

However, even if the interpretive argument works well in most cases, it may fail in situations in which one or more of its assumptions fails to hold. For example, even if the validity of a test as a measure of achievement in a course is well documented, this interpretation may fail in a special case.

2.4. The Development and Appraisal Stages of Validation

The validation of a proposed interpretive argument can be separated into two stages. In the *development stage*, the focus is on the development of the measurement procedure and the corresponding interpretive argument. In the *appraisal stage*, the focus is on the critical evaluation of the interpretive argument.

In practice, these two stages are likely to overlap considerably, but it is useful to emphasize the shift that needs to occur at some point in the process. Initially the goal is to develop an assessment program that supports the proposed interpretations and uses of scores. It is appropriate (and probably inevitable) that the test developers have a confirmationist bias; they are trying to make the testing program as good as it can be. However, at some point, especially for high-stakes testing programs, a shift to a more arms-length and critical stance is necessary in order to provide a convincing evaluation of the proposed interpretations and uses.

2.4.1. The Development Stage: Creating the Test and the Interpretive Argument

The test developers have some interpretations and/or uses in mind when they begin developing a test. This initial statement of the proposed interpretations and/or uses may be quite general (e.g., to place each student into an appropriate course) but some goal is needed to get started.

The developers decide on a general approach to achieving the goal at hand and then develop the measurement procedure and the accompanying interpretive argument. Efforts to make the measurement procedure consistent with the proposed interpretations and uses provide support for the plausibility of the interpretive argument.

In addition, efforts to identify and control possible sources of extraneous variance may help to rule out certain alternative interpretations. For example, if the test is not intended to be speeded, pilot testing can be used to set appropriate time limits and therefore to make an alternative interpretation in terms of speed less likely. The development stage has a legitimate confirmationist bias; its purpose is to develop the test and a plausible interpretive argument that reflects the proposed interpretations and uses of test scores.

A basic iterative strategy for developing the test and the corresponding interpretive argument can be described in terms of three steps. First, an interpretive argument is outlined (e.g., the interpretive argument for placement tests outlined in the last section) and a test plan is developed.

Difficulty in specifying an interpretive argument for a proposed interpretation or use may indicate a fundamental problem. If it is not possible to come up with a test plan and a plausible rationale for a proposed interpretation or use, it is not likely that this interpretation or use will be considered valid.

Second, the test would be developed. Efforts to develop a test that is consistent with the interpretive argument (e.g., by identifying the relevant competencies and by constructing test tasks that measure these competencies) can make a preliminary case for the interpretive argument.

Third, the inferences and assumptions in the interpretive argument would be evaluated to the extent possible during test development. Any weaknesses unveiled by these analyses may indicate the need to modify the interpretive argument or the test. If the needed changes are substantial, the first two steps would be repeated. This process continues until the test developers are satisfied with the fit between the test and the interpretive argument.

This iterative process is much like the process of initial theory development and refinement in science, with the interpretive argument playing the role of a theory. The initial form of the theory is proposed. Any weaknesses identified in the theory are corrected, if possible, by changing some assumptions in the theory or by changing the scope of the theory (i.e., the range of cases to which it applies). If the evidence reveals inconsistencies that can't be resolved, the theory (or the interpretive argument) is rejected, but this is a last resort. The evidence produced during the development stage tends to be confirmationist; if a problem is identified, it is fixed, if it can be fixed.

2.4.2. Appraisal Stage: Challenging the Interpretive Argument

At some point, the development process is considered complete, and it is appropriate for the validation effort to adopt a more neutral or even critical stance:

> a proposition deserves some degree of trust only when it has survived serious attempts to falsify it. (Cronbach, 1980b, p. 103)

During the appraisal stage, the test is taken as a finished product and the overall plausibility of the interpretive argument is examined.

Some of the evidence for this critical evaluation will come from the development stage. It may seem like a low hurdle, but one product that the development stage is expected to deliver is an explicit, coherent interpretive argument linking test performances to the proposed interpretations and uses. If this minimal expectation has not been met, a critical evaluation of the proposed interpretive argument is premature.

For low-stakes applications involving relatively plausible inferences and assumptions, the evidence derived from the development phase may be sufficient for the appraisal of the interpretive argument. For example, the teacher who uses a performance assessment to provide feedback to students is likely to be on safe ground.

For high-stakes applications, a more extensive appraisal is called for, especially if the interpretive argument makes ambitious claims (e.g., about how well test takers will do in a specific course or institution) that are not fully evaluated during test development. Furthermore, the validity argument for high-stakes testing programs has to be persuasive to a number of audiences (Cronbach, 1988). To meet these varied criteria, a critical evaluation of the proposed interpretations and uses is needed.

During the appraisal stage, studies of the most questionable assumptions in the interpretive argument are likely to be most informative, but it is also prudent to check any inferences and assumptions that are easy to check (Cronbach, 1982, 1988). If the proposed interpretive argument can withstand these challenges, confidence in the claims increases. If they do not withstand these challenges, then either the assessment procedure or the interpretive argument has to be revised or abandoned.

Cronbach (1989) proposed four criteria for identifying the empirical studies to be pursued by the test evaluator:

1. Prior uncertainty: Is the issue genuinely in doubt?
2. Information yield: How much uncertainty will remain at the end of a feasible study?
3. Cost: How expensive is the investigation in time and dollars?
4. Leverage: How critical is the information for achieving consensus in the relevant audience? (Cronbach, 1989, p. 165)

Resources are always limited, and choices have to be made.

The appraisal stage also involves a search for hidden assumptions and investigations of alternative possible interpretations of the test scores. The interpretive argument specified during the development phase may be incomplete in various ways. For example, the criteria used for scoring performances may make a number of value judgments that are not spelled out in any detail. A critical appraisal of that part of the interpretive argument would seek to make any such assumptions explicit and to subject them to scrutiny, perhaps by individuals who espouse different values. Similarly, the interpretive argument may include various assumptions about the outcomes that are likely to result from the proposed uses of the test scores and about the relative values of different outcomes; presumably, these assumptions should be made explicit and critically reviewed.

An emphasis on specific types of evidence to evaluate specific assumptions provides some protection against inappropriate interpretations and uses of test scores. To the extent that the interpretive argument is specified in some detail, gaps and inconsistencies are harder to ignore, and a lack of evidence for one or more steps in the argument may be more apparent. An interpretive argument that has survived all reasonable challenges to its coherence and plausibility can be provisionally accepted, with the understanding that new evidence may undermine its credibility in the future.

Without the discipline imposed by an explicitly stated interpretive argument, it is easy to make claims based on implicit assumptions. For example, a high-school graduation test might be touted as a predictor of future performance in school and life, but be validated as a measure of a limited domain of content knowledge. As Shepard (1993) pointed out, a test label like "developmental maturity" can "smuggle in whole theories without test users being aware of the choices they have made" (Shepard, 1993, p. 425).

2.5. Informal, Presumptive Arguments

In discussing validity arguments, Cronbach (1988) focused on the role of "reasonable argument based on incomplete information" (p. 5). Mathematical models can carry us part of the way and provide a comfortable aura of objectivity and certainty, but many of the core issues in the interpretations and uses of test results take us beyond the safe harbor of strictly deductive inference. As noted earlier, the evaluation of the interpretive argument for a placement test typically involves judgments about the appropriateness of the test tasks to be used, about the appropriateness of scoring criteria, about the relevance of the test tasks to the competencies emphasized in the courses, and about the value placed on completing a higher-level course relative to the risk of failure in a course that may be at too high a level. As a result, interpretive arguments tend to rely on *presumptive or informal reasoning* (Blair, 1995; Pinto, 2001; Toulmin, 1958, 2001; Walton, 1989) as well as mathematical or logical reasoning. Appraisals of presumptive, informal reasoning focus on coherence and on the plausibility of inferences and assumptions.

Formal reasoning is considered *valid* (in the logical sense) if the conclusions can be generated automatically from the premises using rules of inference. For example, the implications of a mathematical model can be derived more or less automatically once the model is accepted and values are assigned to parameters and initial conditions. Such formal reasoning plays an essential but limited role in interpretive arguments. Given that we accept their assumptions, various statistical, psychometric, and cognitive models can be used to draw conclusions from test performances. However, the application of a model to test scores always involves assumptions that are subject to doubt. Real-world arguments (including those based on scientific theories) have to attend to the question of whether the model fits the data and is appropriate given the proposed use. For example, any evaluation of the use of a test score to predict performance in a course involves the choice (implicit or explicit) of a criterion of course performance.

Interpretive arguments are informal and presumptive. They include inferences that do not follow formal rules of inference, and as a result, they exhibit three important characteristics of informal, presumptive arguments. First, their substantive assumptions and conclusions are subject to empirical challenge, and they are, to a large extent, evaluated in terms of how well they stand up to such challenges. If a presumptive argument has survived serious challenges, it is reasonable to have some confidence in its conclusions. The extent to which proposed interpretations and uses of test scores can stand up to serious criticism is a central issue in validation (Cronbach, 1971; Messick, 1989; Moss, 1998a, 1998b).

Second, the claims made by interpretive arguments and other presumptive arguments are always somewhat tentative and often include explicit indications of their uncertainty. Claims based on even highly confirmed scientific theories are subject to some uncertainty because of ambiguity in initial conditions and because all theories are approximations on some level. Many of the inferences in interpretive arguments (e.g., extrapolations from placement test scores to expected performance in a course) are subject to potentially large errors, and the uncertainties in their conclusions are often indicated by correlations, standard errors, confidence intervals, information functions, or Bayesian posterior distributions.

Third, like all presumptive arguments, interpretive arguments are *defeasible* in the sense that even when they are accepted in general, they can be overturned in a particular case (Pinto, 2001; Toulmin, 1958). That is to say, "there are possible facts ... that would cancel the presumptive support if they should come to light" (Pinto, 2001, p. 105). Even if the generic form of an interpretive argument is strongly supported, the conclusions may be overturned if they are contradicted by reliable evidence (e.g., if a student placed in an advanced course cannot keep up with the pace of the course).

Informal, presumptive arguments can establish *presumptions* in favor of conclusions or decisions, but the inferences are not mechanical or certain. Like scientific theories, even well established informal arguments can be challenged in particular cases. However, by establishing a presumption in favor of certain claims, presumptive arguments shift the "burden of proof" onto those who would challenge its claims.

2.5.1. Toulmin's Model of Inference

Toulmin (1958) suggested a general framework and terminology for analyzing arguments, which has been widely used in a variety of contexts including program evaluation (Fournier, 1995) and measurement theory (Mislevy, 1996; Mislevy, Steinberg, & Almond, 2003). According to Toulmin (1958), the assertion of a claim (e.g., a conclusion or decision in an interpretive argument) carries with it a duty to support the claim and defend it if challenged, that is, to "make it good and show that it was justifiable" (Toulmin, 1958, p. 97). For an interpretive argument applied to test scores, this general principle of argumentation is reinforced by the *Standards for Educational and Psychological Testing* (AERA et al., 1999), which require that the claims based on test scores be supported by appropriate evidence.

Toulmin's model, which is represented in Figure 2.1, applies to the individual inferences within an argument. Each inference starts from a *datum* (D) and makes a *claim* (C). The initial inference in a quantitative interpretive argument is likely to be from a record of performance on some tasks (the datum) to a score (the claim). Subsequent inferences may involve generalizations or extrapolations of these scores, explanations of the scores, and decisions. Each interpretive argument is likely to involve a number of inferences, with the conclusions or claims (C) of earlier inferences serving as starting points, or data (D) for later inferences. The interpretive argument for placement tests outlined in Table 2.1 contains four inferences, with the

FIGURE 2.1 Toulmin's Model of Inference

Datum ➡ [warrant] ➡ so {Qualifier} Claim

⇑ ⇑
Backing **Exceptions**

Note: Backing provides the evidence for a warrant. Exceptions indicate conditions under which an otherwise sound inference may fail.

conclusions of each of the first three inferences serving as the datum for the following inference.

Each inference is made using a *warrant* (W), which is a rule for going from D to C. Toulmin suggests that this datum-warrant-claim structure is quite general, but that the warrants are specific to different kinds of inferences. The warrants used in interpreting test results are quite varied. The warrant for the scoring inference is the scoring rule. The warrant for generalization from the observed score to the universe score is a statistical generalization from a sample mean to the expected value over the universe from which the sample is drawn. The warrant for extrapolating to expected performance in a course may be a regression equation. The decision rule for the placement system provides a warrant for assignments to particular courses.

Warrants are not generally self-evident, and therefore, they have to be justified. The evidence supporting the warrant is the *backing* (B) for the warrant. The backing for scoring rules generally consists of expert judgment. The backing for generalization would include evidence that the sample is large enough and representative of the universe. Empirical studies of the relationship between test scores and criterion scores provide the backing for a regression equation. The justification for a decision rule typically relies on an analysis of the likely consequences (positive and negative) of using the rule.

Toulmin (1958) includes two additional components in his analysis of inferences, both of which are relevant to interpretive arguments and their validation. First, he allows for the inclusion of a *qualifier* that indicates the strength of the claim. Many of the inferences employed in the interpretations of test scores have explicit qualifiers. Standard errors and their associated confidence intervals indicate the uncertainty in generalizing from an observed score to a universe score. Inferences from a test score to a criterion score are usually accompanied by standard errors of estimation and/or correlation coefficients. Score-based decisions also tend to have qualifiers indicating their strength. They can have various levels of force ranging from a suggestion (e.g., in a career guidance system), to a strong suggestion (e.g., in a course-placement system), to a firm decision (e.g., in a college admission or licensure decision).

Second, Toulmin's model of argument allows for the specification of exceptions, or *conditions of rebuttal*, indicating conditions under which the warrant (which is defeasible) would not apply. In the context of validity, the exceptions would involve certain cases or categories of cases in which the interpretive argument is not justified.

Some possible exceptions may be explicitly included in the description of the testing program and its associated interpretive argument. The testing procedures and the proposed interpretations may be developed for specific populations, defined by age, educational background, language proficiency, etc. The use of the test with individuals who are not in the specified population might not be consistent with the assumptions built into the interpretive argument. In addition, certain possible contingencies that could interfere with the proposed interpretation may be explicitly identified. For example, a testing program that employs an IRT model as an integral part of its interpretive argument might routinely apply tests of person fit to all examinee's responses (Yen and Fitzpatrick, this volume). An inference from an observed score to a latent variable defined by the IRT model would be suspect for any examinee whose responses do not fit the IRT model.

An important class of exceptions to the applicability of standardized testing procedures and therefore standard interpretive arguments involves examinees with disabilities (Hansen, Mislevy, & Steinberg, 2003; Kane, 1992). Most high-stakes testing programs routinely provide accommodations for individuals with certain disabilities, thus replacing the standard interpretive argument with a modified interpretive argument that takes the accommodations into account. The goal is to reach the same kind of conclusions for all students, and the testing accommodations are designed to achieve this goal (Sireci, Scarpati, & Li, 2005).

In addition to any explicitly stated exceptions, every interpretive argument includes a general assumption to the effect that nothing has interfered with the proposed interpretation. Within the philosophy of science, this kind of general caution is referred to as the *ceteris paribus* (or "all else being equal") assumption. There are many unusual circumstances that could make the "else" unequal enough to interfere with the proposed interpretation and thus to generate an exception. For example, an inference from scores on a reading test to conclusions about a student's reading level may hold ordinarily (i.e., the relevant warrant may have strong empirical and theoretical backing), but not apply to a very farsighted student with broken glasses. Unusual circumstances like this would not ordinarily be anticipated in the interpretive argument, but they would be covered by the ceteris paribus assumption.

Toulmin (1958) treated his model as a dialogue between an advocate for a claim and a challenger. The advocate makes a claim based on an inference. The challenger can question the warrant for the inference or the appropriateness of applying the warrant in a particular case. If the warrant itself is challenged, its backing can be brought forward. The nature of this backing will depend on the nature of the warrant and the nature of the objection to it. For example, if the warrant is a regression equation linking test scores to expected performance in a course, its backing could consist of an empirical study relating test scores to course grades. The challenger can question the quality of the study, and the proponent can respond by defending the study or by questioning specific claims made by the challenger (and thereby shifting the burden of proof to the challenger). A challenger who accepts the warrant can still claim an exception in a particular case (based on special circumstances), and the proponent can agree or argue the point.

The validity argument is to provide an overall evaluation of the evidence for and against the proposed interpretation. Assuming that an interpretive argument lays out the inferences involved in getting from the test scores to the conclusions to be drawn and the decisions to be made, the validity argument would provide a critical appraisal of the warrants and backing for these inferences.

When an inference is drawn (e.g., from an observed performance to a score), the warrant (e.g., the scoring rule) and its backing (judgments by panels of content experts who developed the scoring rule) may not be explicitly mentioned, especially if the inference is fairly routine in a particular context and the audience is friendly. Although they are generally not included in routine score reports, the warrants are an integral part of the interpretive argument and could presumably be supplied if needed. Similarly, the possible exceptions to the interpretive argument would not ordinarily be included in a score report, unless the exception applies to the report and makes a substantive difference in the interpretation or in the confidence with which the interpretation can be stated. The backing for various warrants, qualifiers, and possible exceptions would be included in a technical report or other supporting documentation.

2.6. Criteria for Evaluating Interpretive Arguments

Although they cannot be proven, interpretive arguments can be rigorously evaluated against general criteria for sound presumptive arguments.

Clarity of the argument. The interpretive argument should be clearly stated as a framework for validation. The inferences to be used in getting from the observed performance to the proposed conclusions and decisions, as well as the warrants and backing supporting these inferences, should be specified in enough detail to make the rationale for the proposed claims apparent. Implicit assumptions can be particularly harmful because they may be left unexamined.

Coherence of the argument. The argument is expected to be coherent in the sense that the network of inferences leading from the observed performances to conclusions and decisions makes sense assuming that the individual inferences are plausible. It is also expected to be complete in the sense that no essential inferences or assumptions are left out (AERA et al., 1999; Crooks, Kane, & Cohen, 1996).

Plausibility of inferences and assumptions. The assumptions included in the interpretive argument should be plausible. Some assumptions may be taken for granted, some can be supported by careful documentation and analysis of procedures (e.g., sampling assumptions), and some require empirical evidence to be considered plausible. For highly questionable inferences or assumptions, it is appropriate to consider several parallel lines of evidence. The plausibility of an assumption is judged in terms of all of the evidence for and against it.

Note that procedural evidence cannot go very far in establishing the validity of most interpretations, but it can be decisive in refuting an interpretive argument. If the procedures have not been followed correctly or if the procedures themselves are clearly inadequate, the interpretive argument would be effectively overturned.

If it were necessary to support every inference and assumption with empirical studies conducted after the assessment procedures are developed, validation would be essentially interminable, because most interpretations involve a number of inferences each of which relies on multiple assumptions, and the evaluation of these assumptions will rely on other assumptions. Fortunately, many inferences and assumptions are sufficiently plausible a priori to be accepted without evidence unless there is some reason to doubt them in a particular case.

Like scientific theories, interpretive arguments can be challenged in various ways, but one of the most effective ways to challenge a scientific theory or an interpretive argument is to propose an alternative theory or argument that is more plausible. The evaluation of plausible competing interpretations is therefore an important component in the evaluation of any proposed interpretive argument. The validity argument can make a positive case for the proposed interpretations and uses of scores by providing adequate backing for the interpretive argument and by ruling out plausible alternative interpretations.

2.7. Specifying the Proposed Interpretation

Score interpretations are constructs in the sense that they are constructed by some person or persons, and a test score may have several legitimate interpretations and may be used to make different kinds of decisions, each with its own interpretive argument. The evidence required for validation depends on the proposed interpretation, and it is entirely possible for one or more of these interpretations to be valid, while other interpretations are considered invalid. For example, it is possible that the test scores provide good indications of skill in performing some task but do not support any broader interpretation. The test may provide a good indication of achievement in an area but not be useful for placement testing. The test, the population of examinees, and the context may all remain the same, and yet, validity will vary from one interpretation to another:

> The proper goals in reporting construct validation are to make clear (a) what interpretation is proposed, (b) how adequately the writer believes this interpretation is substantiated, and (c) what evidence and reasoning lead him to this belief. (Cronbach & Meehl, 1955, p. 297)

If the interpretations and uses are not clearly specified, they cannot be adequately evaluated (Cronbach, 1989; Linn, 1998; Ryan, 2002).

In a sense, each interpretive argument is unique, and therefore, the associated validity argument is also unique. A validity argument evaluates a particular interpretive argument in a particular context. Although placement systems have many features in common, each placement program is unique in the instructional options available, the students to be placed, and the consequences of different placements. The appropriateness of a placement program depends on how well it works in a particular context and its appropriateness for any particular student is contingent on that student's satisfying the assumptions built into the system.

The next four sections of this chapter present analyses of four broad categories of interpretive arguments: trait interpretations, theory-based interpretations, qualitative interpretations, and decision procedures. The discussion of specific validation methods is embedded within the analyses of these four categories of interpretive arguments in order to emphasize that the issues to be addressed in a validity argument are determined by the interpretive argument being evaluated.

3. TRAITS

A *trait* is a disposition to behave or perform in some way in response to some kinds of stimuli or tasks, under some range of circumstances. Much of the meaning of the trait is given by the domain of observations over which the disposition is defined, but trait interpretations also assume, at least implicitly, that some underlying or latent attribute accounts for the observed regularities in performance (Loevinger, 1957). For example, some individuals tend to get angry fairly easily, while others can put up with a lot of frustration without losing their tempers. Based on such consistent differences, we postulate an aggressiveness trait. Some students know a lot about chemistry, can answer various questions about this discipline, and can conduct experiments competently, while others cannot generally perform these tasks. We describe these differences in terms of level of proficiency in chemistry.

Messick defined a trait as: "a relatively stable characteristic of a person … which is consistently manifested to some degree when relevant, despite considerable variation in the range of settings and circumstances" (Messick, 1989, p. 15). Trait language tends to be implicitly causal, but no specific mechanisms describe how the trait influences performance or behavior.

Some authors have focused on the domain of observations and see the underlying attribute as shorthand for patterns in the data:

> Much of psychological theory is based on trait orientation, but nowhere is there any necessary implication that traits exist in any physical or physiological sense. It is sufficient that a person behave as if he were in possession of a certain amount of each of a number of relevant traits and that he behave as if these amounts substantially determined his behavior. (Lord & Novick, 1968, p. 358)

Others focus on the underlying attribute and use the domain of observations as a vehicle for clarifying the meaning of the latent attribute:

> The evidence is very strong that there is a "general" factor of intelligence that is involved in a great variety of cognitive tasks…. Whenever a task requires noticing similarities and differences among elements, inferring correspondences, rules and generalities, following a line of reasoning, and predicting consequences, that task is likely to involve the general factor of intelligence—particularly as the elements of the task become more numerous and complex. (Carroll, 1986, p. 53)

Lord and Novick emphasize the observations and their relationships. Carroll emphasizes the underlying attribute. In both cases, the interpretation involves both a domain of observations and an underlying attribute.

3.1. Potential Circularity of Trait Interpretations

Explanations in terms of traits can be circular (Meehl, 1950). The trait is defined as a tendency to behave in particular ways under some circumstances and then the observed regularity is explained by the existence of the trait. Some people tend to get angry easily because they are aggressive and we know that they are aggressive because they tend to get angry easily. Some students can answer questions about chemistry because they are proficient in chemistry, and we know that they are proficient because they can answer the questions. As Cureton put it:

> We must not say that his high score is due to his high ability, but if anything the reverse. We say he has high ability because his performance has yielded a high criterion score. His "ability" is simply a summary statement concerning his actions. (Cureton, 1951, p. 641)

The use of trait language does not necessarily buy us much, and it can be misleading. It can suggest that we have found an explanation for an observed regularity, when we have merely labeled it.

In one sense, there is nothing objectionable about this kind of circularity. The observed regularities in performance are potentially important. We can use this regularity to make predictions about future performance, and it would be reasonable to cite the observed regularity as the basis for the predictions. If talk about traits is nothing more than shorthand for this kind of inference from past experience to expectations about the future, it is a legitimate form of shorthand (Meehl, 1950).

In most cases, however, we do have some sense of component processes involved in the trait, and therefore, the interpretation of the trait does not depend entirely on the performance domain. If nothing else, we know how we feel when we get angry, and we know how we would attempt to answer questions about chemistry. Trait interpretations involve general assumptions about the nature of the trait, and trait language reflects at least a rudimentary effort at theorizing. As a hypothesis about the person, a trait interpretation can be quite useful in interpreting experience.

3.2. Interpretive Arguments for Traits

The conception of a trait, as it is used here, encompasses a wide range of attributes, all of which involve a disposition to behave or perform in some way.

3.2.1. Target Domains

A trait is associated with a *target domain* of possible observations, and a person's expected score over the target domain is the person's *target score*. Some target domains are defined very broadly (e.g., Carroll's definition of intelligence); others are more circumscribed but still broad (e.g., proficiency in algebra), and some are quite narrow (e.g., skill on a specific task). Target domains also vary in the extent to which they allow for varied conditions of observations. Some traits purport to describe how individuals will react in certain situations (e.g., test anxiety); others place few if any restrictions on context (e.g., literacy).

The decision to include certain observations in the target domain, and not other observations, generally relies on experience or prior assumptions about the processes involved in the observations. Certain tasks (e.g., arithmetic items) are included in a target domain because they are thought to require the same or at least overlapping skills or component performances. For traits as defined here, no explicit explanatory model is put forward, but general assumptions about the underlying attribute associated with the trait play a significant role in interpreting the trait scores and in defining the boundary of the target domain.

The target domains of most interest in education are not restricted to test items or test-like tasks, although they may include this kind of formal performance as a subset. A person's level of literacy in a language depends on his or her ability to perform a variety of tasks in a variety of contexts, ranging from the casual reading of a magazine to the careful study of a textbook or technical manual. These performances can occur in a variety of locations and social situations. The fact that it might be difficult to include some of these tasks in an assessment does not indicate that they are not part of the target domain for the trait. The match between the target domain and the measure of a trait is a central issue in developing a trait measure and in validating a trait interpretation.

The target domain may be somewhat fuzzy, in the sense that there are marginal cases in which it is not clear whether an observation should be included in the target domain. Whether a particular piece of technical prose should be included in the definition of literacy may be debatable, but in most cases it is not difficult to decide what's in and what's out. The point is not to define a tidy domain or one that is easy to assess, but to identify the range of observations associated with the attribute of interest.

3.2.2. Measurement Procedures

In some cases, it may be feasible to draw a random or representative sample of observations from the target domain and generalize a person's observed score on this sample to the person's expected score over the target domain. In most cases, however, the measurement procedure is standardized by restricting some conditions of observation. As a result, the range of observations included in the assessment is often much narrower than the range in the target domain. Restrictions may be imposed to promote fairness and replicability (i.e., reliability), for practical reasons (e.g., time limits), or for safety reasons. Consequently, the observations included in measures of traits are typically drawn from a subset of the target domain, often a very small subset (Fitzpatrick & Morrison, 1971; Kane, 1982).

The domain from which the observations are actually sampled by a measurement procedure is referred to as the *universe of generalization* for the measurement procedure, and a person's expected score over the universe of generalization is the person's *universe score* (Brennan, 2001a, 2001b; Cronbach et al., 1972; Shavelson & Webb, 1991).[1]

For standardized tests, the universe of generalization is a restricted subset of the target domain. Some aspects of the measurements may be uniquely specified. The format of the test and the instructions given to test-takers may be specified in detail. Some conditions of observation are specified by general guidelines; different forms of a test may include different sets of items, all following the same test plan. Some conditions of observations may become relevant only if they are extreme; for example, the environment in which observations are made may not be specified in any detail but can become an issue if conditions are extreme (very hot or cold, crowded, noisy, etc.).

While the target domain for adult literacy would include a very wide range of written material (e.g., novels, instructional manuals, magazines, memos, signs), responses (answering specific questions, giving an oral or written summary, taking some action based on the manual or sign), and contexts (e.g., at home, in a library, at work, or on the road), the universe of generalization for a measure of literacy may be limited to responses to objective questions following short passages while sitting at a desk or computer terminal. In most contexts, the reader can start and stop at will; in the testing context, the reader is told when to begin and when to stop. The performances involved in answering questions based on short passages under rigid time limits are legitimate examples of literacy but they constitute a very narrow slice of the target domain for literacy.

Standardization tends to be most extreme in objective tests, but it also occurs in performance testing (Fitzpatrick & Morrison, 1971; Messick, 1994). Students who are asked to conduct experiments for a science assessment are likely to be presented with a set of instructions, a setup including the necessary equipment and supplies, and a list of questions to be answered. The equipment presumably works or is quickly replaced. The work is to be completed under some time limits and without any unauthorized assistance. Actual scientific experiments are messier and longer term than most assessments can afford to be.

As a result of standardization, the samples of tasks included in measurements are not random or representative samples from the target domain, and it is not legitimate to simply generalize from the observed score to the target score. It is certainly not obvious, a priori, that performance on a passage-based objective test of literacy can be extended to the target domain for literacy, even if the observed scores are consistent over replications of the measurement procedure (and therefore generalizable over the universe of generalization).

The universe of generalization is usually a subset of the target domain. The interpretation of observed performance in terms of the target score requires a chain of reasoning from the test results to an observed score, from the observed score to the universe score, and from the universe score to the target score.

3.2.3. Trait Implications

Most trait interpretations carry implications that go beyond the target domain and that need to be addressed in validation. A description "pulls behind it a whole train of implications" (Cronbach, 1971, p. 448), which may include expected relationships to other variables, the expected impact of interventions on the trait, and the extent to which differences are expected between groups.

The target domains for traits can provide a clearer and more definite meaning for existing concepts, like literacy, achievement in some academic subject, proficiency in some activity, or a disposition to behave in some way (e.g., personality traits). However, many trait labels were in use long before anyone decided to measure them, and they have implications that go beyond the specification of a target domain of observations (Bruner, 1990).

Assumptions about trait processes often imply relationships among traits. Two traits that involve similar or overlapping sets of processes are expected to be positively correlated. Traits that seem to involve very different processes would not ordinarily be expected to be highly correlated.

It may be assumed that the trait is or is not likely to change substantially over time. Some traits (e.g., general mental ability) are expected to remain quite stable at least for adults. State variables (e.g., moods) can change abruptly under certain circumstances. Proficiencies in specific areas (e.g., speaking French) can be expected to improve gradually as a result of effective instruction or practice on the activity.

For some traits, certain groups of people may be expected to get similar scores. For other traits, some groups may be expected to score higher than other groups. Experienced workers are expected to have a higher level of job proficiency than trainees. Individuals with certain diagnoses may be expected to have higher values of certain personality traits than individuals with no diagnosis or with a different diagnosis.

Trait measures are often developed for a particular application (e.g., to make placement decisions) and the label may suggest that the trait measure is appropriate for the application (Shepard, 1993). As Cook and Campbell (1979) pointed out, test developers "like to give generalized abstract names to variables" (p. 38), and as a result, trait labels may make implicit claims that the trait can be interpreted more broadly than would be suggested by the test development process.

Trait labels and descriptions typically involve values, as well as assumptions about the traits. Suppose, for example, that a target domain consisting of simple arithmetic tasks was used as the basis for a testing program. The label "test of arithmetic operations" has essentially no excess meaning. The label "test of basic skills in arithmetic" implies that essentially all students should be able to do well on the test. The different implications in the two labels deserve attention in evaluating the proposed interpretations and uses of the test.

A recurring theme in this chapter is the importance of stating the proposed interpretations and uses of test scores explicitly and evaluating all of the inferences and assumptions included in the interpretations and uses. Trait interpretations generally involve both expectations about performance over a target domain and general assumptions about an underlying attribute that accounts for observed regularities in the observations.

3.2.4. Traits as Unidimensional Attributes

Traits have their origins in attempts to account for differences among individuals in their performance in certain kinds of situations or on certain kinds of tasks. Individuals who are high on the trait are expected to do well on the tasks or to perform in a certain way in the situations. Those who are low on the trait are not expected to do well on the tasks or to perform in a different way in the situations. The observed score may vary from one observation to another and from one context to another, but the rank-ordering of individuals is expected to be similar across subsets of observations. In this sense, the trait is conceived of as a unidimensional attribute.

In practice, the unidimensionality assumption is mainly a statistical assumption rather than a substantive assumption about process (Lord & Novick, 1968). In many cases where trait terminology is used, it is known that the attribute being measured involves a combination of more basic components, but the attribute functions, at least approximately, as if it were a single, unidimensional trait in that "it operates in the same way as a determiner of success on all the items of the test" (Henrysson, 1971, p. 146).

3.2.5. Observable Attributes and Operational Definitions

As noted above, most traits have a dual interpretation, with part of their meaning given by the target domain and part of their meaning associated with an underlying attribute of the person. In some cases (e.g., in evaluating scientific theories), it is desirable to employ attributes that are largely devoid of excess meaning. Attributes that are explicitly defined in terms of a target domain of possible observations with few if any implications that go beyond the target domain are referred to as *observable attributes*. Observable attributes simply describe how well people perform some kind of task or how they respond to some kind of stimulus.

Operational definitions were developed to eliminate excess meaning altogether (Bridgeman, 1927). For operationally defined attributes, there are to be no implications that go beyond the universe of generalization defining the measurement procedure. Operational definitions are useful in some contexts, especially in empirical checks on theories. However, they have the potential to be misleading, particularly if the operational definition specifies a relatively narrow, highly standardized domain, but the label assigned to the score suggests a much broader domain or trait. For example, to define intelligence operationally as the score on a specific test but interpret it as a measure of overall cognitive functioning is to invite misinterpretation.

3.2.6. Quantitative Reasoning—An Example

Dwyer, Gallagher, Levin, and Morley (2003) define quantitative reasoning broadly, "as the ability to analyze quantitative information" (Dwyer, et al., 2003, p. 13), and specify that it involves the solving of quantitative problems that are new to the student. If the questions focus on reasoning that has been explicitly taught to some students, they are not included in the target domain for quantitative reasoning.

Dwyer et al. (2003) suggest that quantitative reasoning includes six capabilities: understanding quantitative information in various formats; interpreting quantitative information and drawing inferences from it; solving quantitative problems; estimating answers and checking them for reasonableness; communicating quantitative information; and recognizing the limitations of quantitative methods. Quantitative reasoning is defined in terms of performance on tasks that require these capabilities. The capabilities defining the domain are specified in more detail than is usually the case, but no explicit theory of performance is offered.

For Dwyer et al. (2003), content knowledge is considered an ancillary attribute, which is not part of the definition of quantitative reasoning and therefore should not have much impact on scores:

> the mathematical content in an assessment of quantitative reasoning should include only that which all test takers can be assumed to possess. (Dwyer et al., 2003, p. 17)

The interpretation assumes that the test tasks do not require specific mathematical or substantive knowledge that is unfamiliar to the students, and a finding that some students lack such knowledge could generate an exception to the proposed interpretation in terms of quantitative reasoning.

3.2.7. Overview of Interpretive Arguments for Traits

The interpretive argument implicit in trait interpretations is outlined in Figure 2.2. The interpretation of the trait and its relationship to its measurement procedure are represented in the middle and left side of the figure, and the interpretive argument is represented on the right side of the figure. The interpretive argument is stated in more detail in Table 2.2.

The target domain, representing the full range of possible observations associated with the trait, is in the center of the figure. The underlying attribute or trait is represented by the oval at the top of the figure. It is recognized that the observations in the target domain are also influenced by other traits, by the context in which the observations occur, and by the conditions of observation in potentially complex ways. These factors are represented by the ovals to the left

FIGURE 2.2 Measurement Procedure and Interpretive Argument for Trait Interpretations

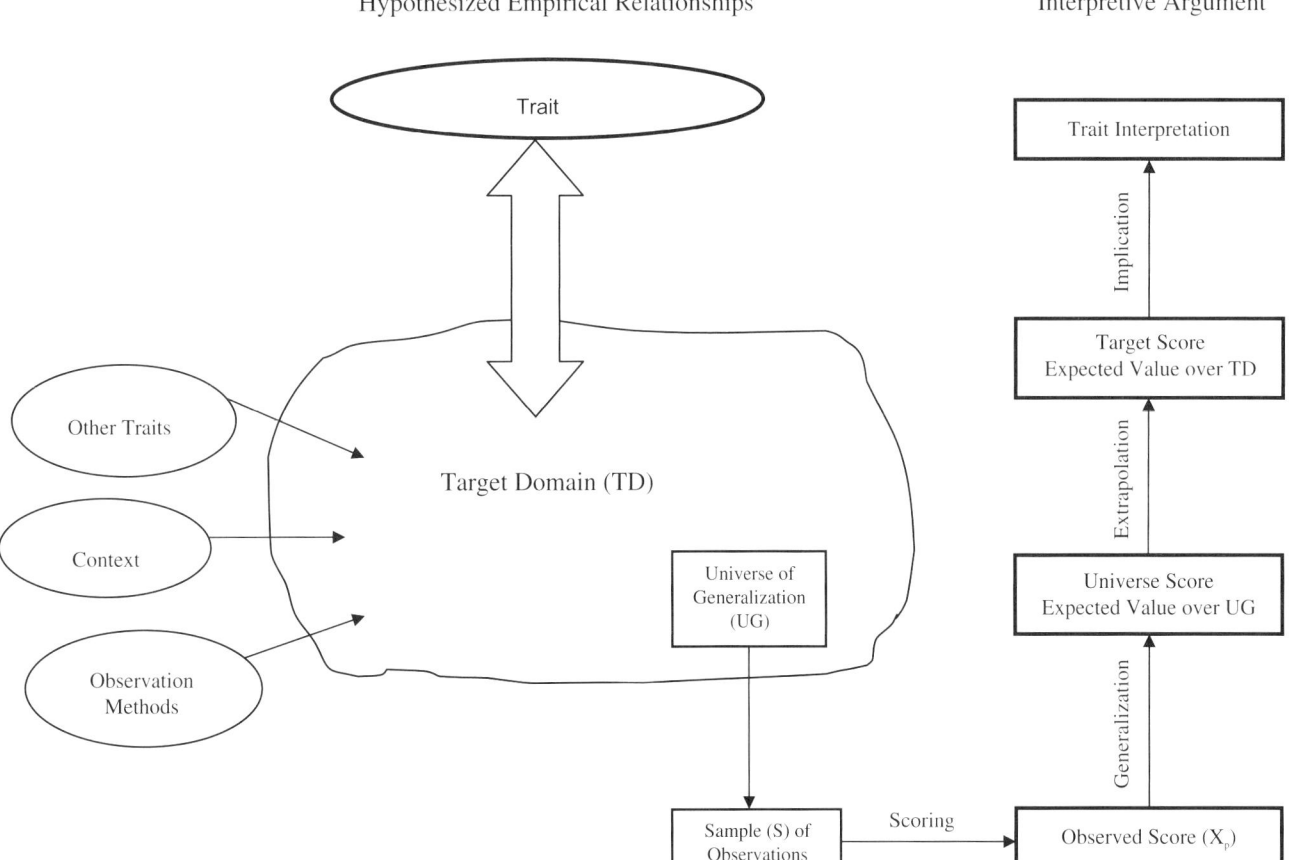

TABLE 2.2 Interpretive Argument for a Trait Interpretation

I1: *Scoring*: from observed performance to the observed score
    A1.1 The scoring rule is appropriate.
    A1.2 The scoring rule is applied as specified.
    A1.3 The scoring is free of bias.
    A1.4 The data fit any scaling model employed in scoring.

I2: *Generalization*: from observed score to universe score
    A2.1 The sample of observations is representative of the universe of generalization.
    A2.2 The sample of observations is large enough to control random error.

I3: *Extrapolation*: from universe score to target score
    A3.1 The universe score is related to the target score
    A3.2 There are no systematic errors that are likely to undermine the extrapolation.

I4: *Implication*: from target score to verbal description
    A4.1 The implications associated with the trait are appropriate.
    A4.2 The properties of the observed scores support the implications associated with the trait label.

of the target domain. The boundary of the target domain is typically not specified with great precision. As indicated in Figure 2.2, the universe of generalization for the measure of the trait is often a small subset of the target domain and tends to be defined more precisely than the target domain.

The interpretive argument on the right side of Figure 2.2 employs four major inferences in interpreting test results in terms of a trait. The observed performance is scored yielding an observed score (a raw score or scaled score of some kind), the observed score is generalized to the universe score, and the universe score is extrapolated to the target score. Finally, the implications associated with the trait are attached to the target score.

The scoring inference assigns a score to each person's performance using a scoring rule, which provides the warrant for the scoring inference. The specific criteria included in the scoring rule will depend on many factors, including the kinds of tasks included in the assessment and its purposes. The scoring inference relies on assumptions that the scoring criteria are appropriate and are applied as intended, that the process is free of bias, and that any statistical models (scaling, equating) employed in scoring are appropriate.

Generalization extends the interpretation of the observed score from an evaluation of a sample of observations to the expected value over the universe of generalization. The value of the score is the same, but its interpretation is expanded from a claim about a specific set of observations to a claim about expected performance over the universe of generalization. The warrant for this inference is derived from statistical sampling theory and depends on assumptions about the representativeness of the sample of observations and about the adequacy of the sample size for controlling sampling error.

Extrapolation from the universe of generalization to the target domain extends the interpretation from the universe score to the target score. The extrapolation inference assumes that the universe score is related (rationally and/or empirically) to the target score and that the extrapolation is relatively free of systematic and random error. Again, the score does not change, but the interpretation of the score is extended from the universe of generalization to the target domain.

The implications involve extensions of the interpretation to include any claims or suggestions associated with the trait. The warrants for trait implications provide authorization for any inferences stated or implied in the trait description, the trait label, and the uses made of scores. Many trait labels have rich associations and are highly value laden, especially those that have been part of the language for centuries. In adopting a preexisting trait label, a test developer is implicitly adopting this excess meaning as part of the proposed interpretation or is taking on an obligation to counteract any unwarranted inferences based on the trait label.

In order for the interpretive argument outlined in Table 2.2 to be convincing, each of the separate inferences must be convincing. A failure of any one of the inferences undermines the interpretive argument as a whole, even if the evidence for the other inferences is compelling (Crooks et al., 1996).

3.3. Validity Arguments for Trait Interpretations

The validation of a proposed interpretation begins with an overall evaluation of its coherence and completeness. For a trait interpretation, this initial review would include an evaluation of the appropriateness of the target domain, given the trait label and description (or conversely, the appropriateness of the label and description given the domain) and an evaluation of the coherence and completeness of the interpretive argument.

The interpretive argument outlined in Figure 2.2 and in more detail in Table 2.2 is intended to provide an outline of how trait measures are actually interpreted. The initial review would examine how well the proposed interpretive argument represents the case at hand. If the interpretive argument does not provide a reasonable explication of the proposed interpretations or uses of the test results, it should be replaced by a more appropriate interpretive argument.

3.3.1. Scoring

Much of the evidence for the scoring inference is based on the judgment of panels of experts who develop and review the scoring criteria, on the care with which the scoring procedures are implemented, and on the procedures used to select and train scorers (Clauser, 2000). These issues are typically addressed during test development.

Several kinds of empirical evidence may also be relevant to the scoring inference. Empirical data can be used to check on the consistency (e.g., interrater reliability) and accuracy (e.g., quality control data) of scoring. A demanding check on the scoring criteria would have two or more panels develop scoring rules independently and would then evaluate the agreement between the scores generated by the two rules (Clauser, Harik, & Clyman, 2000). For many standardized testing programs, statistical models are used to scale or equate scores, and the fit of these models to the data can be evaluated empirically.

The factors that can undermine the warrant for scoring of the observed performance are as numerous as the things that can go wrong in administering and scoring an assessment. The scoring rubrics may reflect inappropriate criteria or fail to include some important, relevant criteria. The selection or training of the scorers may be flawed. Quality control procedures (e.g., checks on the scorers' consistency and accuracy in applying the scoring rubrics) may be inadequate. In addition, exceptions to the scoring inference can arise from violations of the specified procedures.

Procedural evidence cannot establish the plausibility of an interpretive argument, but it can be decisive in refuting it. If the procedures have not been followed correctly (e.g., the wrong scoring key was used) or if the procedures themselves are clearly inadequate (e.g., inadequate training of raters), the interpretive argument would be effectively refuted.

3.3.2. Generalization

The measurement procedure is designed to yield representative samples from the universe of generalization, and if the sample of observations is representative of the universe and is large enough to control sampling error, sampling theory provides a warrant for generalization to the universe score (Loevinger, 1957). If a serious effort has been made to draw a representative sample from the universe of generalization, and there is no indication that this effort has failed, it would be reasonable to assume that the sample is representative (Kane, 1996). As Eisner (1991) pointed out, sampling assumptions are rarely satisfied, and therefore, "inferences are made to larger populations, not because of impeccable statistical logic, but because it makes good sense to do so" (Eisner, 1991, p. 203).

Even if we could draw perfectly representative samples from the universe of generalization, estimates of the universe score would still be subject to sampling errors, and generalization of an observed score to the universe of generalization assume that these sampling errors are not too large. The empirical evidence needed to support generalization over replications of a measurement procedure is collected in reliability studies (Feldt & Brennan, 1989; Haertel, this volume) or generalizability studies (Brennan, 2001b; Cronbach et al., 1972). Any facet that is allowed to vary in the universe of generalization (e.g., tasks, occasions, raters) and is sampled by the measurement procedure contributes to random error. To the extent that reliability or generalizability studies indicate that the sampling errors associated with replications of the measurement procedure are large, inferences from the observed score to the universe score are uncertain.

We have at least two options if the random errors associated with a facet are large. First, during the development phase, we can modify the measurement procedure (e.g., by increasing sample sizes for the facet) so that sampling variability is reduced. Second, we can modify the definition of the attribute so that it does not involve generalization over the facet in question. For example, if the scores are not generalizable over certain kinds of tasks, those tasks could be excluded from both the target domain and the universe of generalization. This has the effect of narrowing the definition of the attribute and thereby may limit its usefulness (Kane, 1982).

Generalizability or reliability studies provide estimates of standard errors of measurement and therefore put limits on the precision of estimates of the universe score (Brennan, 2001a, 2001b). Large standard errors and broad confidence intervals imply weak conclusions about the universe score.

The ceteris paribus assumption plays an important role in claims for generalizability (Kane, 2002a). In particular, if the observations did not occur under conditions consistent with the measurement procedure, they would not constitute a sample from the universe of generalization. For example, if the conditions of observation involve impediments to performance (e.g., faulty equipment) or inappropriate aids to performance, the observations would not be representative of the universe of generalization.

3.3.3. Extrapolation

The extrapolation inference can be evaluated using two kinds of evidence, analytic and empirical. The analytic evidence relies on conceptual analyses and on judgments about the relationship between the universe of generalization and target domain. Much of the analytic evidence tends to be generated during the development stage, as the interpretive argument and measurement procedure are developed. The empirical evidence examines relationships between observed scores and other scores associated with the target domain (e.g., other measures drawn from the target domain).

3.3.3.1. Analytic Evaluation of Extrapolation Inference

Extrapolation depends, at least in part, on the relationship between the universe of generalization and the target domain. It is most plausible if the universe of generalization covers a large part of the target domain or employs high-fidelity simulations covering much of the domain (Flockton & Crooks, 2002). If the universe of generalization constitutes a highly restricted subset of the target domain, the inference from the universe score to the target score is generally more questionable.

The argument for extrapolation may also be based on general notions about overlap in the processes employed in responding to the test tasks and other tasks in the target domain (Snow & Lohman, 1989). For example, if the goal is to make claims about students' skill in using mathematics in a variety of real-world situations, and the test consists of a sample of problems involving the mathematical skills required in the real-world situations, it could be reasonable to assume that students who are successful on the test would also be successful in the real situations and that students who are not successful on the test would not be successful in the real situations.

The processes involved in the test tasks and in other tasks in the target domain can be identified using "think-aloud" protocols. These data could be collected in one-on-one sessions with researchers recording the candidate's self-description of how they approach each task (Bonner, 2005; Cronbach, 1971). If the processes used in responding to test tasks are similar to those used in responding to other tasks in the target domain, confidence in extrapolation is enhanced. To the extent that the performances on the test tasks are substantially different from those for other tasks in the target domain, extrapolation is suspect.

In practice, analytic evidence for extrapolation helps to rule out threats to the credibility of this inference. If a serious effort is made to identify factors that could produce substantial differences between the universe score and the target score, and no such factors are found, the extrapolation is likely to be accepted. If the impact of some factors on the plausibility of extrapolation is unclear, it may be necessary to check on their importance empirically.

The notion of "face validity" refers to the apparent relevance of test tasks to the proposed interpretation or use of scores, and efforts to build face validity into tests are intended to enhance acceptance of the test by those taking it and by various stakeholders (e.g., parents, employers). The appearance of relevance does not go far in supporting the appropriateness of a trait interpretation, but a serious lack of such relevance can lend credibility to certain challenges to the extrapolation inference (Messick, 1989). In particular, to the extent that students put less effort into their performance on a test than they would on the corresponding tasks in other settings, because the test seems irrelevant, the extrapolation inference would be weakened.

Exceptions to the extrapolation inference would generally involve cases in which performance on the test is likely to be different from performance in other parts of the target domain. Any disability that interferes with test performance but not with performance in other parts of the target domain would generate exceptions to the extrapolation inference. Similarly, a lack of some ancillary skill (e.g., a high level of reading comprehension) that is required on the test but is not generally required in the target domain could introduce bias into the estimate of the trait, and could therefore generate an exception. Note however, that a disability or skill deficit that interfered to the same degree with performance on the test and in the target domain would not count against the extrapolation inference.

3.3.3.2. Empirical Evaluation of the Extrapolation Inference

The warrant for extrapolating to the target score could be evaluated empirically by comparing observed scores to criterion scores based on an especially thorough (and representative) sample of performances from the target domain. Criterion-related validity evidence seeks to establish such a direct link between test scores and a demonstrably valid criterion measure (Cronbach, 1971; Messick, 1989).

It is often possible to obtain estimates of the target score that are better than those provided by a standardized test by sampling more broadly from the target domain. Assume, for example, that a test of proficiency in a foreign language consists of sets of objective items asking questions about short printed passages in the foreign language and taped conversations in the foreign language. The question of how well the test represents the target domain for language proficiency can be addressed, at least in part, by developing a criterion measure that samples the target domain more thoroughly than the test. The criterion assessment might include one-on-one interviews, group discussions, or tasks involving the use of printed material, all in the foreign language. Assuming that the criterion measure is only going to be given to a relatively small number of subjects in a validity study, it can be time consuming and expensive.

3.3.3.3. Validity Generalization

Validity generalization involves the application of results from existing criterion-related validity studies to new situations, new populations of examinees, and possibly, to a new test that is similar to those in the existing studies (Murphy, 2003). For example, if several studies of criterion-related validity using a test to predict some criterion in some type of setting have been found to yield consistent results, it can reasonably be concluded that similar results will be found for the test in a new situation, which is similar to those in the earlier studies. The assumption that the new situation is similar in program characteristics, setting, and population to those in the previous studies is based on judgments about the characteristics that could make a substantial difference in the results.

The inference to a new situation or test is strengthened to the extent that it is based on a number studies rather than one or two studies. If all of the studies in a certain kind of setting have yielded consistent results, it would be reasonable to extend the conclusions to a new setting of that kind.

3.3.3.4. Convergent Validity Evidence

Given the difficulties inherent in drawing representative samples from broadly defined target domains, it is often not feasible to develop a clearly valid measure of the target score for use as a criterion measure. An alternate approach is to develop measures of the target score involving different kinds of standardization and therefore different universes of generalization.

Convergent validity evidence (Campbell & Fiske, 1959) is evaluated in terms of the correlations between different measures of a trait. If these correlations are low, at least some of the measures are not adequately representing the target domain. If the correlations of a given measure with other measures drawn from different parts of the target domain are high, extrapolation to the target domain is supported. Convergent evidence may be based on correlations between different tests developed for this purpose or between existing tests with the same label.

It is also possible to use convergent evidence to evaluate specific threats to extrapolation. For example, two teams of qualified test developers could be assigned to develop tests for the same test specifications. A high correlation between the independently developed tests suggests that the systematic errors introduced by assessment teams are small. A low correlation suggests that the test-development team introduces substantial systematic error (Cronbach, 1971).

There are many potential sources of systematic error in most measurement procedures (e.g., testing instructions, time limits, locations, equipment and materials, order of the questions). Standardization of any aspect of the measurement procedure that is not also fixed in the target domain introduces a source of systematic error (Kane, 1982). The goal in designing measurement procedures is to standardize in ways that control random error effectively while introducing as little systematic error as possible.

In practice, it makes sense to check on those aspects of standardization that are most likely to introduce appreciable error. The choice of assessment method (e.g., objective, essay questions, hands-on performance), of scoring rule (Clauser et al., 2000), and of the conditions of observation (Brennan, 2001b) may introduce irrelevant variance and therefore generate systematic error. Decisions about whether to investigate a particular aspect of standardization depend on a number of factors, including the nature of the measurement procedure, the proposed interpretation, previous research on invariance over conditions of the facet, and the stakes associated with the test.

3.3.3.5. Challenges to Extrapolation

Challenges to extrapolation claim that the universe of generalization is sufficiently different from the target domain that extrapolation from the universe score to the target score is not legitimate (Haertel & Greeno, 2003). To the extent that the assessment involves task presentations and/or response formats that are different from most of the tasks in the target domain (e.g., written responses in an area where most responses are oral or involve performances), irrelevant method variance may be introduced (Messick, 1989, 1994). Inferences from highly standardized measures to a broadly defined target domain are more prone to systematic errors than inferences from broadly defined measures (e.g., involving multiple formats, broad content sampling) to the full target domain.

Therefore, it is desirable that the universe of generalization cover as much of the target domain as possible. But there is a downside to this strategy. Performance tasks tend to be time consuming, and therefore, performance assessments tend to include a relatively small number of performances. As a result, generalization from the small sample of high-fidelity performances to a broadly defined universe of generalization may be quite undependable. There is a clear tradeoff here. We can strengthen extrapolation at the expense of generalization by making the assessment tasks as representative of the target domain as possible, or we can strengthen generalization at the expense of extrapolation by employing larger numbers of highly standardized tasks (Kane, Crooks, & Cohen, 1999). The goal is to strike a compromise that supports both generalizability and extrapolation.

Greeno, Pearson, and Schoenfeld (1997) argue that testing is a very specialized activity, and that

> Success in that situation depends on abilities to participate in the practices of test taking, which differ fundamentally from other practices that students need to be learning ....

> We create circumstances in which we can make reliable observations, but in the larger framework, those observations tell us about something that is relatively trivial. (Greeno, Pearson, & Schoenfeld, 1997, p. 170)

Taken literally, this perspective seems to say that extrapolation from standardized test contexts to other contexts is impossible in principle. As a general methodological assumption, this seems overly restrictive. As a warning about the risks inherent in casually extrapolating from standardized testing contexts to work, school, and life, it is a useful caveat (Haertel & Greeno, 2003).

3.3.3.6. Overall Evaluation of the Extrapolation Inference

Generally, a thorough evaluation of the extrapolation inference will require both analytic evidence and empirical evidence. Analytic evidence can be developed during test development by making the test as representative of the target domain as possible. To the extent that standardization is needed to control random error, and therefore the universe of generalization is not representative of the target domain, it may still be possible to design it to tap the core component skills involved in the target domain. For example, in measuring quantitative reasoning as defined by Dwyer et al. (2003), the test tasks could be designed to elicit the six capabilities specified in their framework and to require relatively little specific mathematical or substantive knowledge. In addition, an effort could be made to identify and control the most serious sources of systematic error.

During the appraisal stage, various kinds of empirical evidence that might challenge the proposed interpretive argument would be examined. For example, it might be possible to conduct a criterion-related study by administering a more thorough assessment of the attribute of interest to some sample of students and comparing scores on the test to scores on this more thorough criterion measure.

Convergent evidence might be obtained by comparing the test scores to scores on other measures of the trait. These other measures are not necessarily any better than the test, but they are different from the test and provide an empirical check on extrapolations from test performances to other performances in the target domain.

If the development stage yields a good preliminary case for extrapolation, and this case survives serious empirical challenges, it would be reasonable to accept the extrapolation inference. Under these circumstances, the interpretation of observed scores in terms of expected performance over the target domain would constitute a reasonable presumption.

3.3.4. Trait Implications

The trait label and description and any proposed uses of the test scores generally carry implications that go beyond the definition of the target domain. These implications extend the interpretation beyond a simple inductive summary.

Initial confidence in these implications is likely to depend at least in part on the fit between the target domain and the assumptions implicit in the trait (Cook & Campbell, 1979). If the target domain involves observations that are closely associated with the conception of the trait, and the most likely sources of systematic error have been ruled out, it would be reasonable to draw conclusions based on the conception of the trait. Most analytic evidence for trait implications is generated during the development phase, as the trait interpretation is specified and the test is designed to reflect the trait in terms of content, task types, procedures, context, and scoring (Dwyer et al., 2003; Loevinger, 1957).

Specific implications of the trait interpretation can also be checked empirically. If the conception of the trait suggests that it should be related to some other variable in some way, confirmation of this implication would support the proposed interpretation and disconfirmation would be evidence against the interpretation.

If the trait is expected to remain stable over time, empirical results suggesting that this is so would support the interpretation, and contrary results would undermine it. On the other hand, if the trait is expected to vary as a result of some intervention, change in the expected direction would support the proposed interpretation and stability would count against the interpretation.

For some traits, different groups might be expected to have substantially different score distributions. Individuals with an existing clinical diagnosis might be expected to exhibit extreme scores on some personality traits. Students who read well in class would be expected to perform better on a literacy test than students who are not reading well. These analyses based on categorizations are essentially natural experiments. They take advantage of the fact that the conception of the trait, general as it is, suggests certain patterns in the data.

Score differences between samples of students with similar interests, instructional backgrounds, and overall levels of achievement, but from different ethnic groups, would raise serious questions about the interpretation of the scores. More generally, indications that trait measures depend on any factor that is inconsistent with the conception of the trait would count against the validity of the measure.

To the extent that the implications associated with the trait are supported by data, the plausibility of the trait interpretation is enhanced. To the extent that these implications are disconfirmed, the plausibility of the trait interpretation decreases.

3.4. Trait Underrepresentation and Irrelevant Variance

As discussed in Section 2, challenges to the plausibility of presumptive arguments play a major role in the evaluation of such arguments. The two main threats to the plausibility of trait interpretations fall under the headings of underrepresentation and irrelevant variance (Cook & Campbell, 1979; Messick, 1989).

3.4.1. Trait Underrepresentation

A trait measure is said to under-represent the trait if it fails to adequately represent the range of observations or processes associated with the trait. From the point of view of sampling theory, standardized measurement procedures always underrepresent the target domain, because they treat some conditions of observation that vary in the target domain as fixed (e.g., fixed response formats). The extrapolation inference is supposed to bridge the gap between the universe of generalization and the target domain by indicating that this underrepresentation does not have any substantial impact on scores. For validation, serious underrepresentation occurs when restrictions in the universe of generalization relative to the target domain interfere with the estimation of the target score.

The extent to which extrapolation remains plausible over time can depend, in part, on the stakes associated with the test. In a low-stakes context, performance in various subsets of the target domain may represent performance in the target domain as a whole fairly well. In a high-stakes context, standardization to a subset of the target domain may lead to instruction and test preparation activities aimed specifically at the test, thus making test performance less representative of performance in the target domain as a whole.

The risks posed by different kinds of underrepresentation can often be prioritized based on experience and general assumptions about the processes involved in the trait. The more serious threats can then be evaluated empirically by conducting studies in which the conditions standardized in the measurement procedure are allowed to vary. For example, the impact of response formats could be examined by varying the format across different tasks.

In general, it is desirable for trait measures to include broad sampling of observations, both in terms of the processes involved and in terms of the tasks, situations, and contexts included (Cook & Campbell, 1979; Loevinger, 1957; Messick, 1989). By including a broad sampling of the observations associated with the trait, confidence in extrapolations from scores to trait values is enhanced. The use of multiple measurement methods helps to control irrelevant variance by averaging out method effects. Cook and Campbell (1979) and Messick (1989) raise strong concerns about "monooperational bias" (Messick, 1989, p. 35) resulting from the use of a single observing method to estimate a trait.

Underrepresentation of the trait can constitute a general threat to validity or it can represent a possible exception for some individuals or groups. For example, a test involving novel problems (e.g., maximizing the area enclosed by a certain length of fencing under some constraints) might provide a good measure of problem solving among eighth graders. However, for students who have been taught how to solve such problems, the test would provide a measure of skill in applying these algorithms rather than a measure of problem solving.

3.4.2. Irrelevant Variance and Systematic Error

Trait measures are said to include irrelevant variance to the extent that they are influenced by factors that are not associated with the trait. Concerns about irrelevant variance have a long history under the label of systematic error. There are a number of general sources of irrelevant variance, including traits other than the trait of interest, characteristics of the measurement procedures (e.g., rater bias, item parameter drift, misspecification of a psychometric model), and conditions of observation that affect scores (Downing & Haladyna, 2004; Haladyna & Downing, 2004).

Messick (1989, p. 34) defines construct-irrelevant variance in terms of "excess reliable variance that is irrelevant to the interpreted construct." Therefore, random error is not considered part of construct-irrelevant variance, even though random error variance is construct irrelevant. It is useful to maintain a distinction between random and systematic error, because the steps taken in controlling these two kinds of error are quite different. Random error is generally controlled by standardizing the measurement procedure and by collecting larger samples of performance in the assessment. The systematic errors that produce irrelevant variance have to be addressed in a way that is tailored to particular sources of error.

Standardization tends to promote fairness and to control random error, but it also transforms some sources of random error into sources of systematic error (Kane, 1982). For example, setting time limits on tests eliminates one potential source of random error and promotes fairness across testing sites; however, if speed is not included in the trait definition and individuals vary in the speed with which they work, the imposition of tight time limits can introduce systematic error into the trait measures.

Limiting the test to one method of assessment for a broadly defined trait can lead to both underrepresentation of the trait and irrelevant method variance. These problems can be alleviated by including multiple task formats (Messick, 1989, p. 35). If the observations are sufficiently diverse, "the errors are uncorrelated and more or less cancel each other out" (Loevinger, 1957, p. 648).

Note that an effect might be considered a source of irrelevant variance in measuring a trait but not be considered irrelevant with respect to criterion prediction, "because the criterion *measure* might be contaminated in the same way" (Messick, 1989, p. 34) [emphasis in original]. In this vein, Loevinger (1957) suggested that the empirical keying of items to optimize correlation with some external criterion (psychiatric diagnoses, job success) can produce a test with good predictive efficiency but with no clear trait interpretation. In this case, as in all cases, it is important to be clear about the intended interpretations and uses of test results.

Besides constituting a general threat to validity, irrelevant variance can create an exception for some individuals or groups. For example, a test may take some ancillary competencies (e.g., reading ability, computational skill) for granted. If these skills are variable enough in the population being tested to substantially influence scores, they can be considered sources of irrelevant variance. If the level of proficiency in an ancillary skill (reading English) required by the test is low compared to the levels of skill in the population, this would not constitute a source of irrelevant variance for most students but could be a serious source of systematic error for some students (e.g., those with limited English proficiency).

3.5. Profiles of Traits

In many cases, the focus of the interpretation is not a single trait but a profile of related traits, each with its own target domain and interpretive argument.

3.5.1. Discriminant Evidence for Divergent Traits

The traits included in the profile are expected to be clearly distinct from one another, and therefore the scores on different traits are not expected to be strongly related to each other. A strong relationship between measures of two distinct traits suggests that the two measures may be influenced by some common source of variance.

Empirical evidence on the relationship between distinct traits has been termed *discriminant validity evidence* (Cronbach, 1971). As is generally the case in validation, the role of discriminant evidence is shaped by proposed interpretations. If two measures are expected to be strongly related (e.g., because they are measures of the same trait), a strong empirical relationship between them provides evidence for the proposed interpretation. If two traits are expected to be unrelated, a strong empirical relationship counts against the proposed interpretation. The role of particular kinds of evidence in a validity argument depends on the proposed interpretive argument.

3.5.2. Multitrait-Multimethod Matrices

Campbell and Fiske (1959) proposed that the various kinds of correlational evidence relevant to the validation of a set of trait measures be considered within the context of a multitrait-multimethod matrix, like that presented in Table 2.3. By combining several issues into one analysis, these multitrait-multimethod matrices provide a richer set of conclusions than could be derived from several separate analyses investigating specific concerns.

The multitrait-multimethod matrix in Table 2.3 is based on hypothetical results. It assumes that a sample of individuals have been assessed on three traits, A, B, and C, using each of two methods, 1 and 2. This hypothetical matrix is about as simple as such matrices can be, but it presents evidence relevant to a number of important questions about the validity of the trait measures.

TABLE 2.3 Synthetic Multitrait-Multimethod Matrix for Three Traits and Two Methods

	Method 1			Method 2		
	A1	B1	C1	A2	B2	C2
A1	(.90)					
B1	.40	(.90)				
C1	.60	.40	(.90)			
A2	**.60**	.40	.55	(.70)		
B2	.40	**.65**	.40	.30	(.70)	
C2	.55	.40	**.60**	.65	.30	(.70)

First, the six entries in parentheses along the diagonal represent the correlations across independent measures of a single trait using the same method. Each of these entries can be considered an estimate of the reliability of the scores for that trait-method combination. Since the interpretive arguments for trait measures involve generalization from the observed score to the universe score for the measurement procedure, such generalizability is necessary for the interpretation to be viable. In addition, because limitations in the reliabilities of variables put limits on the correlations among these variables, some understanding of the reliabilities is needed for a clear interpretation of the multitrait-multimethod matrix.

The reliabilities for the three traits are all quite high for method 1 and substantially lower for method 2. One might expect to find the pattern of reliabilities in Table 2.3, for example, if method 1 were an objective test, and method 2 were a performance assessment.

Second, convergence of scores across methods for each of the three traits can be evaluated by examining the monotrait-heteromethod correlations, which are in boldface in the lower left of the matrix. Each of these three entries is the correlation between measures of a single trait using the two different methods. Ideally, these correlations would be large and positive. As a practical matter they are expected to be, "significantly different from zero and sufficiently large to encourage further examination of validity" (Campbell & Fiske, 1959, p. 81). The monotrait-heteromethod correlations in Table 2.3 are all quite high (.60 to .65). The maximum possible value for these correlations given the reliabilities is roughly .80.

Third, the requirement that different traits be distinct or discriminable suggests that the correlations between measures of different traits should not be very high. However, there is no reason to expect a priori that different traits will be independent of each other, and therefore, it is not possible to set any absolute requirement for how low the heterotrait correlations should be. Honesty and diligence are arguably distinct traits, but they are likely to be correlated in many populations. Therefore a fairly high correlation between measures of these two traits employing either the same method or different methods would not necessarily be surprising or distressing.

As Messick (1989) has suggested, investigations of the overlap among traits can be most useful for closely related traits:

> Empirically distinguishing the construct of assertiveness from sociability provides discriminant evidence, to be sure, but it is not as pertinent as distinguishing assertiveness from aggressiveness. (Messick, 1989, p. 48)

As a result, discriminant evidence tends to be most problematic when it is potentially most helpful.

The multitrait-multimethod matrix is particularly effective in providing reasonable relative standards for the discriminability of different trait measures. A modest requirement suggests that the correlations between measures of the same trait using different methods should be higher than the correlations between measures of different traits using different methods. This seems like a fairly minimal requirement, but as Campbell and Fiske (1959) point out, it is not always met. This requirement is met in Table 2.3. All of the heterotrait-heteromethod correlations (the off-diagonal correlations in the lower-left rectangle) are lower than the monotrait-heteromethod coefficients along the diagonal of this rectangle.

A more stringent standard would require that correlations between measures of the same trait using different methods be higher than the correlations between measures of different traits using a common method. This requirement is violated in Table 2.3. In particular, the correlation between Traits A and C for method 1 (.60) is as high as the monotrait-heteromethod coefficients for these variables, suggesting that they are not discriminated very well. The situation is even worse for method 2, where the correlation between traits A and C on method 2 (.65) is higher than the monotrait-heteromethod coefficients for these two traits (.60). This pattern could result from the "halo effect" or some other source of method variance, or it could result from a failure to clearly distinguish between the two traits.

Finally, Campbell and Fiske (1959) also suggest that the general pattern of correlations among the traits be similar across the different methods. Assuming that the different measures of each trait reflect mainly the trait and to a smaller extent the impact of method effects or random error, it would be expected that the pattern of relationships among the traits would be independent of the method. In practice, all measurements contain random errors, and some methods of measurement tend to involve larger random errors than other methods. The pattern of relationships among the three traits is fairly consistent in Table 2.3. All three traits are positively correlated. Traits A and C appear to be closely related, and trait B is relatively distinct from the other two. Overall, it appears that traits A and C are not being clearly distinguished, especially by method 2.

In those cases where they can be deployed, multitrait-multimethod matrices provide a systematic framework for looking at a range of validity issues. The emphasis on multiple methods and multiple traits provides effective criteria for evaluating the discriminability of traits and for evaluating the impact of systematic method effects by comparing correlations involving different methods to correlations involving the same method.

Note, however, that convergence across methods supports validity only if the proposed interpretation is independent of method. In discussing Campbell and Fiske's (1959) willingness to take the correlation of self report and peer ratings as evidence of convergence, Cronbach (1989) made the point that

> their justification could only be that *their* construction viewed self and others as interchangeable perceivers, equally willing to report what they see. For me, self-concept and reputation are distinct constructs, so I would find a high correlation troublesome rather than assuring. (Cronbach, 1989, p. 156)

The relevance of any kind of evidence to the validity of a proposed interpretation depends on the interpretation being proposed.

3.6. Factor Analysis

Traditional factor analysis seeks to model (and thereby to account for) the correlations among a set of variables using a relatively small number of underlying factors (McDonald, 1985; Spearman, 1927). Rather than associate test scores with a single underlying trait, factor analyses assume that these scores depend on a number of factors. They can therefore provide indications of the processes (i.e., factors) involved in the observed performances.

A factor analysis assumes that the test scores depend on a set of factors some of which are common to more than one test, and it uses the observed pattern of correlations among the tests to reason backward to estimates of how much the scores on each test depend on each of the hypothetical factors (i.e., the factor loadings for each factor). If no a priori assumptions are made about the factor loadings, the analysis is referred to as an *exploratory factor analysis*.

Using this kind of reverse inference, exploratory factor analysis seeks to identify a set of hypothetical factors, which can account for the observed pattern of correlations among test scores. The factors and factor loadings derived from the analysis are initially mathematical abstractions. The substantive meaning of the factors is developed by examining the content, format, and measurement procedures for the tests that load on each factor. For example, if all of the tests that load on a factor involve a fair amount of computation, and tests with little or no computation have consistently low or zero loadings on the factor, the factor could be identified with computational skill. The interpretation depends on a combination of formal mathematical modeling and subjective judgments that tie the model to observable phenomena.

The factors can be considered inductive traits, although the induction is not as straightforward as it is when a single trait is associated with a set of positively correlated task performances. The interpretation of the factors is developed inductively by observing the tests that load heavily on the factor, those with modest loadings, and those with no loading or negative loadings. As is true of other inductive traits, interpretations of test scores in terms of factors do not involve any detailed process model describing how the factor operates in producing the observed performances.

In *confirmatory factor analysis*, the general form of the factor structures for different attributes is specified in advance, and the data are used to evaluate the proposed model and to estimate the unconstrained loadings. For example, confirmatory factor analysis can be used to address the issues covered by multitrait-multimethod matrices. If the mix of tests in the analysis includes tests measuring different kinds of performance employing different methods, confirmatory models can be used to identify separate trait and method factors. Large loadings on trait factors and small loadings on method factors provide evidence for the convergence of the indicators for the traits. Large loadings on method factors would indicate a lack of convergence. Similarly, the trait measures are expected to load on the appropriate trait factor and not on factors associated with other traits; such results support the discriminability of the trait (McDonald, 1999; Messick, 1989).

3.7. Item Response Theory (IRT) Scaling

A large number of IRT models are available (see Yen and Fitzpatrick, this volume), each employing a particular mathematical expression to represent the probability that a person will get an item right as a function of the person's ability and the characteristics of the item, as represented by various item parameters. To the extent that the model holds, and the item parameters are known, we can predict how a person with a particular ability level will respond to any item or any set of items that fit the model.

The underlying ability scale (or theta scale) in an IRT model functions as a trait. It provides a summary of how well the person performs on the items used to define the ability scale.

> Fitting an IRT model is an empirical exercise, capturing and quantifying the patterns that some people tend to answer more items correctly than others, and some items tend to be answered correctly less often than others. The conception of ... competence embodied by the IRT model is simply the tendency to perform well in the domain of tasks. (Mislevy, 1996, p. 393)

Because IRT analyses are typically applied to the items included in a test or to all items used in a testing program, the resulting theta scale is tied to this pool of items.

The inference from a person's observed item performances to the person's ability level is analogous to an inference from an observed score to a universe score. Simple generalization relies on sampling models to warrant generalization to a universe score; IRT models warrant inferences from item performance to an ability level on the theta scale. Both models involve inferences from observed performances on some items to claims about overall performance on a universe of possible test items.

The observed performance is "explained or predicted by examinee characteristics referred to as traits or abilities" (Hambleton, 1989, p. 149), but no particular causal mechanism is specified. Nevertheless, the label assigned to the theta scale (e.g., inductive reasoning) may suggest the general nature of the processes involved in successful performance. In addition, the labels may imply that the ability is relevant to expected performance in certain contexts or situations (e.g., in an educational program or work environment). As is the case for any attribute, all of these implications are part of the interpretation.

In general then, IRT ability measures involve essentially the same four steps as the traditional trait interpretations. Item performances have to be scored. The results are extended to a claim about an underlying latent trait that is determined by the items used to define the ability scale, and by extension, is associated with a universe of possible test items that could have been used to define the scale. That is, the latent ability estimates serve a function similar to that of universe scores for traditional traits. The interpretation is then extrapolated to the target domain, and any implications associated with the attribute label are added. The main difference between the two approaches is in the second inference. In the classical approach, sampling models provide warrants for generalization. In IRT scaling, the IRT model provides a warrant for inferences from item responses to the estimated latent ability.

3.8. Trait Measures as Signs and Samples

Traits serve as inductive summaries over their target domains, which carry much of their meaning, but a trait interpretation also assumes that some underlying, latent attribute accounts for the observed regularities in the target domain. As Loevinger (1957) suggested, item responses are always both signs and samples of behavior; they are samples from the universe of generalization and from the target domain, and they are signs of the underlying attribute.

The interpretive argument for trait interpretations depends on substantive assumptions, statistical assumptions, and values. The scoring and extrapolation inferences depend mainly on the substantive and value assumptions implicit in the scoring rules and in the definition of the target domain. Substantive assumptions also play a large role in generating analytic evidence relevant to extrapolation and implication inferences. The statistical assumptions are embedded in sampling models (e.g., in generalizability analyses), scaling and equating models, and in the regression and other statistical models that can be used to examine extrapolation and various implications.

The interpretations and uses of test results are complex, and validation efforts should recognize this complexity. It is more important to state proposed interpretations and uses clearly and to evaluate them fully and critically than it is to have a tidy statistical analysis.

4. THEORY-BASED INTERPRETATIONS

The previous section examined attributes that derive most of their meaning from target domains. This section addresses attributes that are implicitly defined by their role in some theory. The validation of measures of these theoretical constructs necessarily involves an evaluation of the theory.

4.1. Theories, Constructs, Indicators, and Descriptive Attributes

Theory development begins with some phenomena to be explained by the theory. The phenomena are described in terms of existing observable attributes (or traits), which do not depend on the theory for their interpretation. These *descriptive attributes* are, in this sense, theory-neutral. For example, literacy can be defined in terms of a target domain of performances, without specifying any theory of performance, and therefore can function as a descriptive attribute in developing and testing theories of literacy.

The theory postulates some underlying mechanisms or relationships to account for the observed phenomena. In a quantitative theory, the postulates would be stated as equations relating the descriptive attributes to each other and to *theoretical constructs*, which represent aspects or components of the postulated mechanisms or relationships. The theoretical constructs are introduced to specify the theoretical mechanisms or relationships postulated by the theory and are implicitly defined by their roles in their defining theory.

As observable attributes, the descriptive attributes can be measured by drawing samples from their target domains (or more commonly, from standardized subsets of their target domains), and by using the results of these samples to estimate their target scores.

The theoretical constructs are not defined in terms of any domain of observations and therefore cannot be estimated so directly. The estimates of theoretical constructs generally rely on assumptions built into the theory. To take a very simple example, a theory of learning of some skill might assume that skill level (S) is directly proportional to instructional time (T) and to each person's aptitude (a_p):

$$S = a_p T$$

Skill level can be defined and measured as an observable attribute, and instructional time (T) is also observable. The aptitude, a_p, which is simply the slope in the hypothesized linear relationship, is not directly observable, but it can be estimated for a person by taking the ratio of the change in a person's skill level over some period of instruction to the length of instruction. The measurement of the aptitude depends on the theory.

An *indicator* of a theoretical construct is an observable attribute or a combination of observable attributes that is used to estimate the theoretical construct. The indicator does not define the construct, and a construct can have several distinct indicators. The indicator is necessarily based on observable attributes, but as an indicator, it is interpreted as an estimate of the construct defined by the theory. For this interpretation to be plausible, the theory must be plausible, and for the theory to be plausible, its predictions about observed relationships must hold. The simple theory sketched above predicts that skill level will be a linear function of the length of instruction and that the slope will be stable for each person but may vary from one person to another. The theory is evaluated by checking its predictions against data.

Descriptive attributes serve two important functions in the development and testing of theory. First, they specify the phenomena of interest. The phenomena have to be described and understood on some level before theories can be developed to explain them. Second, the descriptive attributes play a key role in evaluating the theory. They provide the "stubborn, dependable, replicable puzzles" (Cook & Campbell, 1979, p. 24) that theories are supposed to solve. If the theory's predictions about the descriptive attributes are accurate, the theory is supported, and if the predictions are inaccurate, at least some part of the theory is questionable.

If a theory is rejected, the interpretations of indicators in terms of the theory would also be rejected, but the interpretation of the descriptive attributes would not change much if at all. The failure of a theory to account for certain phenomena generally leads to a rejection of the theory and not a rejection of the phenomena.

4.1.1. Nomological Theories

Cronbach and Meehl (1955) framed their analysis of construct validity in terms of nomological theories, which specify networks of nomological (or "law-like") relationships among attributes. Structural equation models (SEMs) provide a modern statistical framework for analyzing such nomological theories (Benson, 1998; Benson & Hagtvet, 1996; Jöreskog, 1973; McDonald, 1999). SEMs postulate causal relationships among latent variables and observable or manifest variables. The latent variables function as implicitly defined theoretical constructs that are linked to each other and to the manifest variables that function as descriptive attributes.

An explicit model is developed to explain the relationships among these latent variables and descriptive attributes, and the latent variables are estimated by fitting the model to the data. Empirical evaluations of how well the model fits the data serve as checks on the proposed model and as a basis for comparing alternative models of the same phenomena. These fit analyses also provide an empirical check on the validity of the indicators of the latent variables, which depend on the SEM for their meaning (Benson, 1998).

Cronbach and Meehl (1955) did not limit their discussion of nomological networks to well articulated statistical models. Rather, they suggested that

> the logic of construct validity is invoked whether the construct is highly systematized or loose, used in ramified theory or a few simple propositions ... We seek to specify how one is to defend a proposed interpretation of a test; *we are not recommending any one type of interpretation.* (p. 284) [emphasis in original]

They defined a construct broadly, as "some postulated attribute of people assumed to be reflected in test performance" (Cronbach & Meehl, 1955, p. 283), as in statements like, "Persons who possess this attribute will in situation X act in manner Y (with stated probability)" (p. 284). Given this loose conception of theories, some of the traits discussed in Section 3 can be considered constructs. As indicated in Section 1, Cronbach and Meehl's (1955) emphasis on stating the proposed interpretation clearly and evaluating it critically is generally applicable.

4.1.2. Process Models

Process models postulate specific cognitive processes to account for certain observed performances (Embretson, 1983; Ippel, 1986; Mislevy, Steinberg, & Almond, 2003; Pellegrino, Baxter, & Glaser, 1999; Sternberg, 1979; Tatsuoka, 1990). In addition to descriptive attributes specifying the performances of interest, a process model generally involves parameters (i.e., theoretical constructs) that characterize the latent abilities used to explain the observed performances (Embretson, 1983).

For example, a process model might assume that a number of component processes are called upon (sequentially or concurrently) to perform complex tasks. An IRT model can then provide estimates of latent ability parameters representing each student's level of skill in each of the component processes, as well as item parameters representing the level of processing difficulty of each task on each component (Embretson, 1984; Embretson & McCollam, 2000). The probability of success on a task is assumed to be the product of the probabilities of successfully completing the component processes involved in the task. The parameters serve as theoretical constructs, which are estimated by model-based indicators defined in terms of item responses.

In the context within which a process model is developed and empirically tested, the descriptive attributes describing performance on the tasks are taken as givens, and their definitions do not depend on the process model being proposed. In fact, alternative models could be developed to account for the task performances. A failure of any of these models would not generally have much impact on the measures of the descriptive attributes.

In contrast, the indicators of the model parameters depend on the model for almost all of their meaning. If the model were rejected, the indicators of the model parameters would go with it.

4.2. Interpretive Arguments for Indicators of Theoretical Constructs

A typical interpretive argument for indicators of theoretical constructs has five major inferences:

1. *Scoring*: from observed performance to the indicator score
2. *Generalization*: from indicator score to the universe score for the indicator
3. *Extrapolation*: from the expected indicator score to the target score for the indicator
4. *Theory-based Interpretation*: from the target score for the indicator to the construct as defined by the theory
5. *Implications*: from the construct value to any implications suggested by the construct label or description

The first three inferences support an interpretation as a measure of the observable attribute (or combination of observable attributes) serving as an indicator of the construct. The fourth inference extends the interpretation to the theoretical construct, thereby expanding the interpretation to include all of the claims implicit in the theory. The fifth inference involves any additional implications associated with the construct label or description.

4.3. Validity Arguments for Indicators of Theoretical Constructs

The first step in validating any proposed interpretation is to evaluate the coherence and completeness of the proposed interpretive argument. If the structure of the interpretive argument is considered satisfactory, the specific inferences and assumptions in the argument are evaluated.

The first three inferences in the interpretive argument (scoring, generalization, and extrapolation) serve to define the indicator as an observable attribute, but the scoring inference may be quite complex for indicators of theoretical constructs. In particular, the scoring inference may require that various performances be scored and that the resulting scores be combined to yield the indicator. If the constructs are parameters in IRT models, the scoring inference tends to be relatively straightforward, but the generalization inference is replaced by parameter estimation (see Yen and Fitzpatrick, this volume), and the extrapolation inference is subsumed under the theory-based interpretation.

The interpretation of indicator scores as estimates of a theoretical construct extends the interpretation to a claim about a construct as defined by the theory. Theory-based interpretations of indicator scores assume that the theory provides a sound explanation for the relevant phenomena and that the indicators provide appropriate estimates of the constructs in the theory. The warrant for this inference is the theory. The backing for the warrant would involve analytic and empirical evidence supporting the theory and the appropriateness of the indicator. The analytic evidence relies on analyses of the relevance of each indicator to its construct and is produced during the development stage, as the indicators are designed to fit the theory. The empirical evidence examines how well the theory's predictions agree with observable phenomena.

4.3.1. Analytic Evidence for Theory-Based Inferences

Initial confidence in the theory-based inferences depends in part on judgments about how well the indicator represents the construct as defined by the theory. A theory provides guidance on how to develop indicators for its constructs. If the theory predicts that individuals with high values on a construct are likely to perform well on some tasks and that individuals with low values of the construct are likely to perform poorly on the tasks, performance on the tasks can be used to estimate the value of the construct.

The theory may also indicate various conditions of observation that could have a substantial impact on the observations. In developing an indicator, efforts would be made to control any potential source of irrelevant variation. Basically, indicators are designed to provide plausible estimates of the construct and to be relatively free of systematic and random error.

In general, it is desirable that the indicator involve a broad sampling of relevant observations (Cook & Campbell, 1979; Messick, 1989). By including a broad range of observations associated with the construct, the possibility of construct under-representation is minimized, and by including multiple modes of observation, construct-irrelevant variance can be controlled. If serious efforts are made to identify potential sources of irrelevant variance, and no likely candidates are identified, the interpretation is supported. If any potentially serious sources of systematic error are identified, the accuracy of the indicator as an estimate of the construct is questionable.

4.3.2. Critical Appraisal of Theory-Based Inferences

Most of the evidence needed to evaluate a theory-based inference is that needed to evaluate the theory. The theory is evaluated in terms of its general plausibility and by subjecting it to empirical challenges. A theory that survives serious challenges is accepted as a working assumption (Cronbach, 1980b; Lakatos, 1970; Popper, 1962).

Any prediction about observable attributes that can be made from the theory provides a potential empirical check on the theory. These empirical checks include predictions about performance or behavior in various contexts or by various groups, correlational evidence, and the results of experimental studies. To the extent that the predictions are verified, the plausibility of the theory is enhanced, and therefore, the plausibility of the proposed theory-based interpretation is enhanced.

If the results do not agree with the predictions, some part of the theory is called into question. One option is to reject the theory as a whole. A second option is to reject one or more of the indicators. A third option is to assume that some external factor distorted the results. For any particular study, it is generally not obvious which of these three options would be appropriate, and therefore, no single study will be decisive. The plausibility of the theory and of interpretations based on the theory will depend on the results of a number of studies.

4.3.3. Correlational Analyses

As noted in Section 2.3, correlation coefficients provide much of the empirical evidence produced during test development. In particular, evidence for the homogeneity, or internal consistency, of the observations in the universe of generalization supports generalizability over tasks, and correlations between test performance and non-test performance can support extrapolation from the universe score to the target score for the indicator. When developing indicators of several distinct constructs at the same time or when introducing a new construct indicator, the consistency among different indicators of each construct, and the ability of the indicators to distinguish among different constructs, can be evaluated using multitrait-multimethod matrices or confirmatory factor analysis.

At the appraisal stage, correlational evidence is particularly relevant to the evaluation of nomological theories. Nomological theories predict certain kinds of relationships (e.g., strong or weak, direct or inverse) among observable attributes (descriptive attributes and indicators). If the number of relationships is small or the expected pattern is relatively simple, it may be possible to evaluate the fit between the predicted relationships and the observed relationships directly. More complicated structural, causal, and hierarchical hypotheses can be investigated using relatively general models like structural equation models, confirmatory factor analysis, and hierarchical linear models.

The role of these analyses in the appraisal stage of validation is to subject the proposed theoretical interpretation to empirical challenge. If one theory predicts a positive correlation between two variables and a second theory predicts a negative correlation under the same circumstances, empirical results may support one theory over the other.

4.3.4. Experimental Manipulation

If the theory hypothesizes certain causal relationships, such that a change in one variable is expected to produce some change in a second variable, then it may be possible to check the theory by manipulating the first variable and monitoring the second variable. If the expected changes occur, the theory is supported; if not, the theory tends to be refuted.

For example, some theories of anxiety indicate that motivation to avoid failure would tend to promote test anxiety that would in turn have a negative effect on achievement (Benson, 1998). So, by reducing the need to avoid failure in some way (e.g., by reducing the stakes inherent in testing) it should be possible to reduce test anxiety and thereby to improve achievement. If this pattern were observed, the theory would be more credible; if not, the theory would be less credible.

For process models, it may be possible to improve skill on certain component processes by focusing instruction on the processes. Such focused instruction, if effective, should increase level of skill on that process, and as a result, improve performance on tasks that require that component. Note that the conclusion contains the caveat that the instruction must be effective, and therefore, a finding that instruction has not produced the expected change may not produce a decisive refutation of the theory.

Some attributes are not expected to be affected much by short periods of intense instruction. General abilities (e.g., general verbal or quantitative reasoning) are expected to be less susceptible to targeted instruction than specific skills (e.g., solving algebraic equations). Therefore, if scores on a test of general ability improved substantially after a brief coaching program, the validity of the test scores as indicators of the general ability would be questionable (Messick, 1989).

4.3.5. Evaluating the Backing for Theory-Based Inferences

The overall plausibility of the theory and of theory-based inferences depends on all of the evidence, for and against the theory. The strength of the backing for a theory-based warrant depends on a number of factors, including the number and range of predictions that are examined, the uniqueness or novelty of the predictions, and the quality of each empirical study. Surviving one kind of empirical challenge, even if this challenge has been examined in a number of studies, is not as convincing as surviving a range of different challenges in different contexts (Loevinger, 1957).

Disagreements between the predictions and observations always count against a theory. Agreement between predictions and observations provides strong support only if the predictions cannot be taken for granted in advance. For example, a prediction that performance on some task will generally improve with practice does not provide strong support for a theory of task performance, because this relationship holds for most tasks in most contexts. Agreement between theory and observation does not provide support for one theory relative to another, if both theories make the same prediction.

The impact of any particular study also depends on the quality of the study. A large, well designed study that has eliminated the most serious threats to its conclusions provides more powerful evidence than a smaller study that is subject to various sources of systematic error. For example, finding a predicted positive relationship between two variables that are assessed with the same method (e.g., a rating scale) or the same raters provides weaker confirmation than would be the case if the same correlation resulted from observations involving different raters, using different methods, on different occasions. The latter findings provide stronger evidence because they are less likely to be due to method artifacts.

4.3.6. Challenges to Indicators of Theoretical Constructs

On a fundamental level, theory-based construct interpretations can be challenged by claiming that the theory is not plausible. If the theory cannot stand up to criticism, interpretations based on the theory are not defensible.

Even if the theory as a whole is considered credible, the appropriateness of a particular indicator for a theoretical construct can still be challenged in terms of either construct under-representation or construct-irrelevant variance (Cook & Campbell, 1979; Messick, 1989). For indicators of theoretical constructs, questions about representativeness focus on the extent to which the observations defining the indicator elicit the full range of processes associated with the construct (Bachman, 2002; Borsboom, Mellenbergh, & van Heerden, 2004; Embretson, 1983; Loevinger, 1957). Any factor other than the construct that has an impact on the indicator (e.g., the method or context of observation) is a source of construct-irrelevant variance, or systematic error.

Some systematic errors apply generally in the population and constitute general threats to validity. Some systematic errors may have a particular impact on certain individuals or groups. Toulmin (1953) has argued that scientific laws or theories are not true or false, but that "statements about their range of application can be" (p. 79). If an otherwise successful theory fails to account for certain observations, it may be decided that the theory simply does not apply under certain circumstances. Under this view, the issue in empirically testing a theory is not to find out if it is true or not, but to find out how widely it applies. Exceptions to model-based inferences are triggered by indications that the model does not apply in a particular case.

More general exceptions occur if there is evidence suggesting that the theory does not apply to particular groups, or if almost all or all of the evidence supporting the model or supporting the connection between assessment scores and model parameters was developed for some groups, and there is reason to believe that the model might not apply to other groups. For example, a performance model might have been developed and shown to apply for students in instructional programs based on the model (e.g., with topics covered in a particular sequence), but the performance model might not apply so well to students in other instructional programs. Evidence indicating that the performance of students at one grade level conforms to a particular model does not ensure that the performance of students at a different grade level will conform to the same model. This is not to say that a theory cannot be extended beyond the contexts in which it has been empirically checked, but rather, to suggest that such extensions involve risk.

4.3.7. Evidence for Construct Implications

In addition to the basic interpretation of a construct as defined by its theory, the label or uses of the indicator scores may suggest additional claims. The adoption of a theory of intelligence would define the meaning of intelligence as a theoretical construct within the theory, but claims about the relevance of this construct to success in non-test contexts would typically go beyond the theory.

Embretson (1983, 1998) distinguishes two aspects of validity; construct representation and nomothetic span. *Construct representation* is concerned with "the processes, strategies, and knowledge that persons use to solve items" (Embretson, 1998, p. 382). It is supported by evidence that supports the proposed cognitive models. Embretson (1983, 1998) contrasts the meaning of the construct embodied in the explanatory model from its *nomothetic span*, which describes the relationships of test scores with other measures. Nomothetic span emphasizes significance or utility rather than meaning. Within the framework adopted here, construct representation can be associated with the meaning of the construct, while nomothetic span describes additional implications associated with the construct label.

The validation of a proposed interpretation or use of test scores requires an evaluation of all of the claims inherent in that interpretation or use. For example, the use of aptitude test scores for placement into alternative treatments depends on the assumption that the regressions of achievement on aptitude for the different treatments will cross each other (Cronbach & Snow, 1977). Whether this requirement is satisfied by a particular aptitude test in a particular setting is an empirical question that may transcend the theoretical basis for the aptitude measures.

4.4. The Role of Theories in Interpreting Descriptive Attributes

While theory-based explanations are not necessary for the validation of measures of descriptive attributes, such explanations can provide strong support for some of the inferences in the interpretive arguments for these attributes. The theory may provide explicit guidance for test development and justification for test content, format, and scoring rules by indicating the skills that are most strongly associated with performance on the descriptive attribute.

The theory can also provide support for generalization by indicating the task characteristics or conditions of observation that are likely to have large impacts on performance. For example, the representativeness of a sample of subtraction problems is more plausible if it can be shown that it includes problems requiring all component skills involved in subtraction. To the extent that a model can accurately predict the difficulty of different tasks, the model can be used to control test difficulty by making sure that all persons get tests of the same difficulty or by adjusting the scoring rule for each test to reflect differences in difficulty (e.g., using equating).

To the extent that the model is known or expected to apply in varied contexts (e.g., in the classroom, at work, in the community), it can also provide a solid basis for extrapolating from test performance to performance on other kinds of tasks in other settings (e.g., the workplace). The model thereby provides additional support for extrapolation by providing a rational basis for this inference.

The descriptive attribute does not rely on the theory for its meaning. However, descriptive attributes that are attached to well-confirmed theories can be used to draw conclusions and make predictions based on the theory. The theory thereby adds to the implications or nomothetic span of the descriptive attribute.

4.5. Construct Validity and Theory Testing

In the traditional view of science, the theory's predictions are compared to observations, which "serve as the universal, neutral arbiter among alternative hypotheses" (Galison, 1987, p. 7). The observations are taken as given, and the theory is evaluated by how well it predicts (or explains) the observations (Lakatos, 1970; Popper, 1962). If the theoretical predictions agree with the observations, confidence in the theory increases, and if not, confidence in the theory decreases.

However, in Cronbach and Meehl's (1955) formulation of construct validity, the theory is effectively taken as given, and the appropriateness of the indicators is evaluated by how well the theory fits the data. The evaluation of theories becomes quite complicated if the interpretations of measurements depend on the theory and, therefore, are as much in doubt as the theory (Quine, 1953). A system in which theories are evaluated by comparing their predictions to measurements, and the measurements are validated in terms of the theory, clearly has the potential for circularity. Loevinger (1957) expressed concern that Cronbach and Meehl's use of theories to define constructs could be taken to imply that "validation studies are communicable only among such coteries as are agreed on theoretical issues" (p. 643).

In practice, the distinction between descriptive attributes and indicators of theoretical constructs can be used to cut the circle and make both theory testing and test validation manageable. Theories are developed within a scientific community to explain some phenomena, and the phenomena to be explained can be specified in terms of descriptive attributes without relying on the theory (Galison, 1987; Guion, 1977). The predictions made by the theory about these descriptive attributes provide empirical checks on the theory as a whole, including the choice of indicators for theoretical constructs (Cronbach & Meehl, 1955). That is, the descriptive attributes are taken as given, and the theory is evaluated as a whole by comparing its predictions about the descriptive attributes to the measures of these attributes.

Empirical evaluations of competing theories are possible, because a community can agree on the definition of relevant descriptive attributes and on acceptable measures of these attributes. For example, it is possible to define and measure achievement in arithmetic in terms of a target domain of performances, without developing a theory that explains how schools teach arithmetic or a model that explains how people solve arithmetic problems. The interpretation of the descriptive attribute does depend on various ancillary assumptions, (e.g., about what constitutes an adequate performance on a task) but, once these specifications are agreed on, the measure can be taken as an observable attribute and can serve as a neutral arbiter in evaluating competing theories (Grandy, 1992).

5. QUALITATIVE INTERPRETATIONS

Most decisions in classrooms, clinics, and other real-world settings are based on qualitative assessments, which focus on the interpretation of performance in context and give little or no attention to scores. Qualitative assessments are reported as narrative interpretations, or "thick descriptions" (Geertz, 1973), rather than as interpreted scores. The teacher/clinician collects information and acts on it at the same time, seeking to develop a coherent interpretation that is consistent with all available evidence (Moss, 1994; Shepard, 2001). Classroom assessment of student performance will serve as the primary focus of this section (Frederiksen, 2003; Gipps, 1999; Moss, 1994; Moss & Shutz, 2001; Shepard, 2001, this volume; Stiggins, 2005; Tittle, 1989).

For classroom and other clinical assessments, the goal is not to subsume observations under empirical laws, but, "to place them within an intelligible frame" (Geertz, 1973, p. 26). Different kinds of information from different sources are combined for an interpretation of performance in context (e.g., that of a student in a class). Instead of the observation-scoring-interpretation paradigm prevalent in standardized testing, qualitative assessment involves an active search for meaning from the beginning, with the interpretation being elaborated and extended as data are collected. The goal is to construct a coherent interpretation of performance, "continually revising initial interpretations until they account for all of the available evidence" (Moss, 1994, p. 8). The qualitative approach focuses on evolving interpretations of observations rather than on scores.

Unlike quantitative interpretations, which suppress many interactions among variables by standardizing the measurement procedure and by averaging over any variables that are considered irrelevant, qualitative assessments attend to interactions among the factors that influence performance. As a result, they can provide a richer interpretation of events in environments where interactions among causal factors are the norm (Cronbach, 1975).

5.1. Qualitative Interpretations of Student Performance

Teachers have access to a rich array of data that can be helpful in developing their understanding of each student (Brookhart, 2003; Moss, 2003, Stiggins, 2005; Tittle, 1989). They observe their students' performance on a variety of educational tasks (e.g., participating in classroom activities and discussions, taking tests, completing projects) over an extended period. They talk to the students, to their parents, and to other staff. Teachers may also have scores on standardized tests and information on student's interests, health (including any disabilities), and backgrounds.

Teachers have to make sense of all of this data, and in doing so, they employ an array of conceptual resources and frameworks to organize their observations (Shepard, 2001). They understand the structure of what is being taught and have goals for what students are to achieve. In addition to content-specific skills, most instruction seeks to foster the development of various general skills (reasoning, problem solving, creative expression, reading, writing, mathematical skills), and teachers track each student's progress in developing these skills.

For example, if a second-grade teacher observes a student reading a story aloud but stumbling over some more difficult words, the teacher may conclude that the student can read, but that his or her vocabulary is being stretched by the story. The performance is interpreted in terms of the teacher's conceptual frameworks (e.g., their understanding of the processes involved in reading). To the extent that the teacher is familiar with the student and with the difficulty level of the text, a richer explanation is possible.

Teachers typically have a sense of the kinds of student misconceptions and use this understanding to explain student errors. They also have some sense of the social and organizational context and the expectations and limitations inherent in these contexts and are familiar with various resources (e.g., texts at different levels of difficulty, reference materials) that they and students can make use of in teaching and learning.

Teachers bring a potentially rich set of tools to their observations of student performances. Experienced teachers meeting their new class for the first time have a good sense of the range of skill levels to expect. They know some of the gaps in understanding and skill to expect, and common impediments to learning, and are familiar with "the relevant experience and discourse patterns" (Shepard, 2001, p. 1075) of their students. Their conceptual frameworks provide templates for organizing observations of student performance and for differentiating critical issues from more routine observations. Using these frameworks, teachers interpret student performances as they occur and do not simply keep a record of their observations for later interpretation.

5.1.2. Refinement of Teachers' Views of Their Students

A teacher's understanding of what students know and can do, of their aptitudes, limitations, and interests evolves as the teacher interacts with the students. Initially, the teacher's understanding of each student may be quite general, but over time, it is developed and refined as the teacher interacts with the student. For example, if a student who has shown little interest in reading now exhibits a strong interest in Sherlock Holmes stories, the teacher's view would be modified to reflect this development, and instructional choices could reflect this more nuanced description. The teacher's evolving view of the student is neither complete nor completely accurate, but it is likely to get better over time.

Teachers use their evolving views of the students to guide their interactions with students in various contexts. These views generate expectations about student performances on various tasks in various contexts. The teacher does not generally predict future events but does anticipate them (Geertz, 1973) in the sense that, for a particular student and situation, some kinds of events are seen as more likely than others. If these expectations are confirmed, the teacher's confidence in his or her current views increases. To the extent that the expectations are not confirmed, the teacher may modify assumptions about the student, the tasks, or the context. The teacher's view of each student develops over an extended period and can be self-correcting (Black & William, 1998; Delandshere, 2002; Lane, 2004; Moss, 2003; Stiggins, 2005).

If a teacher's expectations fail for many students in many situations, the teacher may need to rethink some of their basic assumptions. On the other hand, if the teacher's conceptual frameworks are working reasonably well for most students but are failing for a particular student, the teacher is more likely to rethink the assumptions being made about that student. For example, a teacher would use his or her current view of a student in interpreting the performance of the student in reading a passage aloud and answering questions about the passage. Given the difficulty levels of the passages that the student has read with good comprehension and those that seem to be beyond the student, the teacher has expectations about the student's performance on a new book. If a student has trouble with a book that the teacher expected the student to be able to read, the teacher may conclude that the student is a weaker reader than the teacher had thought, that the book is more difficult than the teacher thought, or that the context or some extraneous effect interfered with the student's performance.

Note the lack of symmetry here. If the student reads the book, it is reasonable to conclude that the student has the skills needed to read the book. If the student does not read the book, there are multiple possible explanations for the event, involving the student, the book, or the context. If the student had previously read more difficult books, the teacher may be inclined to attribute the poor performance to something other than a lack of skill in reading (e.g., lack of interest in the book's content, some aspect of the context). If the book is more challenging than those the student had been reading, the student's poor performance could reasonably be attributed to the student's reading level relative to the difficulty of the book. The teacher may adopt (perhaps tentatively) one of these explanations or may defer the choice until more information is available.

The teacher's view of a student may involve some definite expectations (e.g., that a student will be able to perform certain tasks) or some range of possibilities (e.g., that the student may be interested in certain activities). For observations that share many features with those on which the evolving view is based, the expectations may be expressed with some confidence. For new observations that involve many new elements (a substantially different task or setting), the expectations would generally be more tentative.

5.1.3. Interpretive Arguments for Classroom Assessments

The interpretations of teacher assessments of their students can be represented by an iterative interpretive argument:

1. *Development of Initial Views of Students*: Teachers use their conceptual frameworks to develop a view of the student. They use these frameworks to make sense of their initial interactions with students and to develop their initial views of students. The conceptual frameworks provide a basis for evaluating student performance and for anticipating various factors that might influence student learning and performance.
2. *Refinement of the Teacher's View*: Teachers modify their views of students, based on their ongoing interactions with the students. The teachers' evolving views generate expectations (e.g., that a student will or will not be able to read certain books or to solve certain kinds of problems). These expectations provide working assumptions for subsequent instruction and assessment, and comparisons of the expectations to subsequent observations provides feedback on the accuracy of the teacher's views.
3. *Extension of the Teacher's Evolving View to New Contexts*: Teachers may also use their overall assessments of students to draw conclusions about expected performance in new contexts (e.g., beyond the classroom). At various times and for various reasons, the teacher may need to draw general conclusions about student progress (e.g., in making end-of-year promotion decisions).

5.1.4. Teachers' Conceptual Frameworks as Theories

This kind of reasoning represents an informal version of theory testing in science (Cronbach, 1975; Toulmin, 2001), with the teachers' conceptual frameworks and their evolving views of students functioning as theories that generate expectations about what is more or less likely to happen in various situations. If these expectations are confirmed, confidence in the frameworks and evolving views is enhanced. If the expectations are contradicted, changes may be called for in some part of the teacher's views.

Qualitative interpretations are also analogous to the more formal construct interpretations discussed in the last section. In both cases, a general model, or "working hypothesis," provides explanations of performance (Cronbach, 1975), but there are some clear differences between the two approaches. In particular, cognitive-process models assume that the same model applies to all test takers, and second, the assessment procedures based on these models tend to be highly standardized. In such model-based assessment, the goal is to estimate the parameters in the model for each individual. In classroom assessment, the teacher integrates data from a variety of sources, most of which are not standardized, to develop a holistic view, or model, of each student.

5.2. Validity Argument for Classroom Assessments

The validity argument begins with an evaluation of the completeness and coherence of the interpretive argument and an evaluation of whether the interpretive argument provides a reasonable explication of the proposed interpretation. If the general form of the interpretive argument is satisfactory, its inferences and assumptions would then be evaluated. Taking the interpretive argument developed above as a working model, the validity argument would focus on the plausibility of the teacher's conceptual frameworks and of their evolving views of students.

5.2.1. Development of the Teacher's Views

The teacher's conceptual framework cannot generally predict what is going to happen, but it does allow the teacher to anticipate various possibilities, and it can explain observations after they have occurred. The teachers' conceptual frameworks provide the warrants for these interpretive evaluations. The backing for these warrants includes the backing for the teachers' conceptual frameworks (e.g., conceptions and organization of subject matter, pedagogical theories and techniques) and the evidence supporting the ability of the teacher to use these tools effectively, including the training, credentials, and experience of the teacher, the extent to which the teachers have access to relevant data, and any quality-control safeguards that are in place.

Teaching involves an ongoing stream of interactions and decisions, and most of the backing for a teacher's conclusions about students is not publicly available. Teachers do not record all of the reasoning involved in their conclusions, nor do they specify the inferences leading to most of their decisions. However, if asked to do so, a teacher could presumably provide a rationale for his or her choices.

Additional support for the teacher's inferences can be provided by peer or external review. Moss (1994) emphasizes the role of dialogue within a "critical community" of individuals with expertise on the issues involved, as well as those with a stake in the outcome (e.g., parents, community members, students). Dialogue-based warrants are likely to work well in cohesive, autonomous communities with a base of shared assumptions. Within this context, disparate opinions serve several important functions; in particular, they can identify weaknesses in the proposed interpretation and can illuminate implicit assumptions and potential biases (Moss, 1994; Ryan, 2002).

5.2.2. Refinement of the Teacher's Views

Teachers' evolving views of students, supported by their conceptual frameworks, provide the warrants for their ongoing interpretations of their interactions with students. The backing for these warrants is provided mainly by evidence supporting the adequacy of the teacher's evolving views, as a basis for making sense of their interactions with students.

Teachers do not generally rely on statistical inferences in interpreting student performances, but rather on less formal presumptive reasoning. An evaluation of a single performance by a single teacher can justify part of an evolving view. If a qualified teacher evaluates a student's performance on some complex activity (e.g., solving a quadratic equation, making a bowl on a potter's wheel) and uses these observations to draw conclusions about how well a student has mastered the skills needed to perform the activity (e.g., solve equations, make bowls), it is reasonable to accept the teacher's judgment at face value, unless there is some specific reason to question it. As Frederiksen (2003) has suggested, a qualitative analysis of performance

> may reveal that a student has used problem-solving approaches and forms of knowledge that are highly generalizable to other task situations, thus backing a student-model claim about generality of skill. (p. 71)

With the help of their general assumptions about student performance (based on their understanding of task requirements and experience with students) teachers can derive general conclusions about student competencies from samples of performance.

This kind of inference is widely used in evaluating scientific theories and can support strong conclusions. The underlying rationale is analogous to that for Bayes' Theorem; if the probability of an event is high given some hypothesis and is low under all alternative assumptions, then the occurrence of the event provides strong evidence for the hypothesis. For example, given that there is a high probability of getting the correct solution to a quadratic equation if one knows how to solve such equations, and a very low probability of success if one does not know how to solve such equations, students who generate correct solutions to a quadratic equation that they have not seen before can be assumed to know how to solve quadratic equations. In addition, if the teacher asks the student to explain the performance and the student provides an accurate, coherent explanation, it is reasonable for the teacher to conclude that the student can solve quadratic equations.

By examining a body of student work (e.g., in class or in a portfolio), the teacher can form hypotheses about the student's competencies and about gaps in the student's understanding of a topic. If a particular set of conjectures about a student does account for the student's pattern of performance (including the mistakes), and no plausible alternative hypothesis does as well, the proposed conjectures can be accepted as a reasonable conclusion about the student.

Since the qualitative interpretations do not necessarily involve statistical generalization (i.e., from a sample of observations to the expected value over a universe of generalization), it is not necessary to make a case for this kind of generalization (Moss, 1994), but it is necessary to provide support for the inferences from specific observations to a general description of the student. These presumptive inferences are based on content and context-specific warrants. The conclusion about a student's ability to solve quadratic equations rests on our understanding of how such equations can be solved and on experience with students trying to solve them. For content that is less well structured, this kind of model-based inference from performance to competence tends to be less precise. The fact that a student can name the capitol of one state provides little assurance that he or she knows any other state capitols.

If a qualified teacher applies appropriate criteria to a student's performance, the results would have a strong presumptive claim on our confidence. This is the kind of evaluation that might well serve as a criterion in validating some standardized test.

Like all measurements, teacher assessments of their students can be challenged. Even if a qualified, experienced teacher evaluates a student's performance over a long period, a challenge could claim that there was some mistake or omission in the teacher's assessments.

In practice, requests for backing for any particular aspect of a teacher's views of their students may come from the student, a parent, a fellow teacher, or a principal, and the teacher would be expected to respond with an explanation. This kind of dialogue encourages the teacher to articulate and evaluate their own views in a critical way.

5.2.3. Extension of the Teacher's Views to New Contexts

Once a teacher's evolving views of their students have been developed and refined, conclusions based on these views may be extended beyond the particular classroom (e.g., in evaluating a student's readiness for the next grade). The teacher may reasonably draw conclusions about expected performance in settings and on tasks to which student skills would be expected to transfer (based on the teacher's experience, and their understanding of the tasks and situations). As Frederiksen (2003) pointed out, some problem-solving approaches and skills are highly generalizable.

Although formal empirical studies are generally not feasible in evaluating classroom assessments, some kinds of teacher expectations can be compared to subsequent outcomes. For example, it may be possible to examine the subsequent performance of students whom the teacher recommends for promotion or retention.

These extensions of the teacher's conclusions about students to contexts beyond the classroom may be higher stakes than classroom assessments, because they may not be easily correctable (e.g., promotion decisions). The rationale for these extensions is likely to be stated explicitly and in some detail with supporting evidence.

Like all presumptive inferences, teacher assessments are defeasible and can be challenged on various grounds. Information about the student or the environment or the interaction between the two can suggest the need to revise an interpretation. For example, if a teacher had not taken certain information about a student (e.g., limited English language proficiency or a disability) into account in a context in which it was relevant, the interpretation could be questioned. And just as teacher judgments can support challenges to test scores for individual students, test scores can support challenges to teacher judgments.

5.3. Qualitative Approaches to High-Stakes Assessments

As the stakes associated with an assessment go up, the form of the assessment and the shape of the interpretive argument do not necessarily change, but the need to document the procedures being used and to provide backing for the warrants being applied increases. In cases where the proposed interpretation is extended beyond the local classroom setting, it is generally necessary to document the evolving description of each student more thoroughly than would be necessary within a single classroom with a single teacher. In these higher-stakes contexts, the teacher's evolving views may need to explicitly incorporate examples of student work so that readers "may judge its adequacy for themselves in supporting the desired generalization" (Moss, 1994, p. 8).

As the stakes go up, there is also pressure to increase standardization (e.g., by specifying the format and general content of student portfolios) in order to promote comparability of conclusions across settings and occasions, and thereby, to promote a kind of objectivity (i.e., a lack of subjective judgment) that enhances credibility for many audiences (Porter, 2003). As Shepard (2001) has noted, standardization "involves a basic matter of fairness" (p. 1081). Standardization also facilitates aggregation of results to the school, district, and state level.

In high-stakes contexts, where a range of stakeholders have a strong interest in the outcomes, it is generally expected that the analysis of student performance will be documented in a written report, which provides examples of student work and the rationale for the conclusions being drawn. The report would include warrants for major inferences and backing for any warrants that might be questioned by the intended audience. Employing multiple sources of evidence and input from independent observers strengthens the case. Tone and substance that suggest the absence of bias is especially important:

> The vigorous attempt to discover problems with the proposed interpretation—the search for disconfirmatory evidence and for alternative interpretations that account for the same evidence—is central to the development of well warranted interpretations. (Moss, 2003, p. 18)

Contradictory evidence does not necessarily disconfirm the proposed interpretation, but it does introduce notes of caution and can help the reader of the report to form a more complete view of the student.

For assessments that are used within a classroom, consistency in standards across classrooms is largely irrelevant. In fact, it is clearly appropriate that the teacher's assessments be tailored to the needs of his or her students. However, if interpretations and decisions are extended beyond individual classrooms (e.g., in statewide assessment programs) inconsistencies across classes and schools can cause problems.

Empirical research indicates that assessment standards vary across teachers and schools. Essay questions are more standardized than teacher observations, but essay graders generally find it difficult to maintain consistent standards over time. Studies of the consistency in the scores assigned to portfolios are not encouraging (Klein, McCaffrey, Stecher, & Koretz, 1995; Nystrand, Cohen, & Dowling, 1993). In a comparison of standards across states, Linn, Kiplinger, Chapman, and LeMahieu (1992) found that although there was a high consensus about the characteristics of good writing, as indicated by high correlations among graders from different states, there was "substantial diversity in the implicit standards of raters from different states" (p. 104). It is not easy to maintain consistent standards in evaluating complex performances.

Quality-control procedures seem to be the best option for dealing with concerns about the consistency of standards. For example, *social moderation* (or verification) procedures in which teachers' grades on samples of student work are compared to independent ratings by other teachers from the same or different schools and by external expert raters can build confidence in the consistency of standards across classrooms, schools, districts, and states (Linn, 1993). Social moderation aims to build consensus across schools:

> The process of verification of a sample of student papers or other products at successively higher levels in the system

(e.g., school, district, state, or nation) provides a means of broadening the consensus across the boundaries of individual classrooms or schools. It also serves an audit function that is likely to be an essential element in gaining public acceptance. (Linn, 1993, p. 99)

For large-scale, high-stakes assessments (e.g., those used for accountability), the audit function is essential.

5.3.1. The Role of Interactions in Qualitative Interpretations

In general, teachers use their conceptual frameworks and experience to make sense of their encounters with their students and of the students' work. The teacher does not start with an operationally defined scoring inference and then seek to interpret this score. The interpretation is built in from the beginning.

Rather than generalizing from a sample of performances to the expected level of performance over some universe of exchangeable performances, the teacher seeks to integrate all available evidence on each student into a coherent view of the student. The goal is to develop a narrative that makes sense of the full body of available evidence, and the proposed interpretation is refined through an iterative process of developing an interpretation and then checking it against further observations (Tittle, 1989).

In contrast, quantitative models seek to minimize the impact of conditions of observation, of the social and physical context, and of extraneous student characteristics (e.g., motivation, anxiety) by averaging over conditions of observation or by standardizing some conditions of observation (Cronbach, 1975). For many purposes, the use of statistical generalization and extrapolation to average over most interactions is an effective strategy. In most classroom and clinical contexts, the interactions merit attention.

6. DECISIONS

The use of tests to make decisions introduces some new wrinkles into validation, but the same basic approach still applies. The intended interpretations and uses are specified and are evaluated by examining their coherence and the plausibility of their inferences and assumptions.

Test-based decision procedures typically incorporate an interpretation in terms of attributes (traits, constructs, or qualitative descriptions) followed by a decision based on the interpretation. Both the substantive interpretation and the decision rule indicating what to do under various circumstances are included in the rationale for test use.

The addition of a decision rule to an interpretation introduces (or at least brings to the foreground) the issue of consequences. While the interpretations discussed in Sections 3 to 5 are evaluated in terms of their coherence and plausibility, decisions are evaluated in terms of their outcomes, or consequences.

This section has three parts. Section 6.1 discusses general characteristics of test-based decision procedures and their validation, defines some terminology, and raises some salient questions. Section 6.2 analyzes the validation of school accountability programs as an example of a test-based decision program. Section 6.3 addresses the role of consequences in validation (particularly social consequences) a topic that has been somewhat contentious (Guion, 1995; Messick, 1989; Popham, 1997; Sackett, 1998; Shepard, 1997).

6.1. Semantic Interpretations and Decisions

For purposes of this discussion, it will be useful to distinguish between semantic interpretations and decisions. A *semantic interpretation* draws conclusions based on assessment results (e.g., about a trait or construct), and thereby, assigns meaning to these results. The inferences and assumptions involved in the semantic interpretation will be referred to as *semantic inferences* and *semantic assumptions* respectively. A semantic interpretation is evaluated in terms of its plausibility.

A decision procedure implements a policy and involves choices about what to do; it is evaluated in terms of its outcomes, or consequences. The assumptions supporting a decision procedure make claims about the outcomes likely to result from the policy and about the values associated with these outcomes. In particular, they claim that the decisions will generally have positive consequences (e.g., placement of students in appropriate classes) and that any negative consequences will not be too serious. Overall, it is assumed that the positive consequences will outweigh the negative consequences.

Evaluation of a decision procedure necessarily involves an evaluation of values and consequences. Policies are not true or untrue, accurate or inaccurate. They are effective or ineffective, successful or unsuccessful. A policy that achieves its intended goals (positive consequences) at modest cost, and with few undesirable side effects (negative consequences) is considered a success. A policy that does not achieve its goals (lack of positive consequences), and/or that involves relatively high cost or produces significant undesirable side effects (negative consequences) is considered a failure.

For many test-based decisions, the semantic interpretation and the decision are distinct and sequential. For example, a course-placement test typically has a semantic interpretation in terms of level of achievement, and the placement decision is based on this semantic interpretation. The semantic interpretation and the decision may be made by different individuals at different times and in different places (e.g., college admission test scores reported by a testing agency later used by colleges to make admissions decisions). In other cases (e.g., classroom testing), semantic interpretations and decisions are intertwined.

The role of validation in evaluating the plausibility of the semantic interpretation and its role in evaluating the legitimacy of the decision procedure are both recognized in the *Standards*:

> Validation logically begins with an explicit statement of the proposed interpretation of test scores, along with a rationale for the relevance of the interpretation to the proposed use. (AERA et al., 1999, p. 9)

The *Standards* go on to say that validation involves the development of evidence, "to support the intended interpretation of test scores and their relevance to the proposed use" (AERA et al., 1999, p. 9). Although they have differed somewhat in emphasis, both Cronbach (1971, 1980a) and Messick (1975, 1980, 1989), have associated both interpretive accuracy and consequences with validity (Moss, 1992).

In principle, the evaluation of the effectiveness of a decision rule involves an application of utility theory (Cronbach & Gleser, 1965). In practice, the analysis is usually qualitative, because it is generally not feasible to specify the required utility functions. The focus in evaluating decision procedures is on value judgments (what is "desirable") and on empirical claims (about the likelihoods of various outcomes).

6.1.1. Standard Setting

Many test-based decision procedures involve one or more cutscores that define the decision rule (Cizek, 2001). For example, states use licensure tests to decide whether candidates for professional licensure should be allowed to engage in practice. In most cases, it is not feasible to evaluate performance in practice directly, and the standard approach is to assess professional competency over a target domain of cognitive skills that are considered critical for effective performance in practice (AERA et al., 1999). A single cutscore, or passing score, is defined on the score scale for the licensure test. Candidates who pass the licensure test and meet all other requirements get licensed; candidates who do not pass the test do not get licensed (Clauser, Margolis, & Case, this volume).

The interpretive argument for a licensure test typically involves a semantic interpretation of professional competence as a broadly defined trait variable and then a decision procedure that implements a policy about the level of competence required for admission to practice. The validation of such trait interpretations is discussed in Section 3. The target domain of competencies considered critical for effective performance in practice is based on analyses of patterns of practice (LaDuca, 1994; Raymond, 2001).

The choice of cutscore is the main issue in defining the decision rule, and the evaluation of the cutscore is the key issue in validating the decision rule. Standard-setting studies are designed to identify a reasonable cutscore and to provide backing for the choice of cutscore (Hambleton & Pitoniak, this volume). In applying any standard-setting method it is necessary for the participants (e.g., state officials, professional practitioners, members of the public) to develop a conception of the level of competence needed for the intended use (e.g., safe and effective performance in practice). This conception of minimal competence, the *performance standard*, can be based on standards of performance in the practice of the profession (Kane, 2002b). Judgmental standard setting methods (e.g., the Angoff method) are designed to translate the performance standard into a specific score on the score scale for the test. Candidates with scores above this cutscore have presumably met the performance standard, and candidates with scores below this cutscore have presumably not met the standard.

The performance standard provides a description of a minimal level of competence needed in practice. The corresponding cutscore provides an operational definition of the decision rule. An evaluation of the decision rule would address the appropriateness of the proposed performance standard (e.g., as the basis for withholding a license to practice a profession) and of the relationship between the cutscore and the performance standard.

Once the performance standard is defined, various kinds of empirical evidence can be used to evaluate how well the cutscore represents the performance standard (Hambleton & Pitoniak, this volume; Kane, 1994), but the performance standard itself is evaluated in terms of its anticipated consequences. The standard for licensure decisions is supposed to be high enough to provide adequate protection to the public, but not so high as to unduly restrict access to practice. Although licensure programs have social consequences (e.g., the availability of professional services in various areas, the representation of minorities and other subgroups in the professions), the standard setting activities for licensure tests tend to focus on the level of individual competence needed for effective performance in practice.

6.2. Test-Based Accountability Programs

The traditional view of testing programs as essentially non-interactive monitoring devices has been replaced by a recognition that testing programs often have a major impact on those assessed (Crooks, 1988; Frederiksen, 1984; Madaus, 1988; Moss, 1998b), and more recently, by a conception of some standardized tests as the engines of reform and accountability in education. Current test-based school accountability programs use standardized tests to hold schools accountable for student progress. The state develops content standards and develops tests based on these standards. Many of the content standards (particularly those involving more ambitious, extended performances) may be excluded from the test specifications, because they are not amenable to paper-and-pencil testing. The subset of the state standards eligible for inclusion in the tests along with the standardized conditions of observation define the universe of generalization for the state testing program.

The advocates of accountability programs see them as a way to raise academic standards by focusing attention on demanding content. It is assumed that the test-based accountability program will focus attention on the areas tested, and more generally, on the State Standards, and that this will be accomplished without serious loss of attention to other areas.

Under the "No Child Left Behind" (NCLB) Act (NCLB, 2002), student scores are transformed to general achievement levels, intended to reflect different levels of performance (e.g., below basic, basic, proficient, advanced). The achievement levels are defined by cutscores on the score scale for the test. All scores below the basic cutscore are considered below basic, scores between the basic cutscore and the proficient cutscore are considered basic, etc. The goal is to define statewide standards of performance and to encourage all students to reach some predefined level of achievement (e.g., the proficient level). The reduction of the test scores to three or four achievement levels involves a substantial loss of information, but as discussed below, the system is not designed to produce precise information.

The achievement-level scores for each grade are aggregated over students in each school to yield the percentage of students at each achievement level in each grade within the school (and within various subgroups). In general, accountability programs apply rewards or sanctions to the schools based on their students' performances on the tests. The NCLB program focuses on sanctions for failure, particularly failure to achieve certain increases in the percentages of students at or above the proficient level. If a school fails to meet the targets for improvement, it is subject to sanctions.

In adopting high-stakes tests as a way of enhancing educational quality in certain content areas, the focus is not on monitoring achievement, but on improving it. The test is being used to implement a policy, which will have consequences, some of which are likely to be positive and some negative. To evaluate a testing program as an instrument of policy, it is necessary to evaluate its consequences (Cronbach, 1982).

6.2.1. An Interpretive Argument for NCLB Accountability Programs

Interpretive arguments for NCLB accountability programs would involve an initial semantic interpretation of student performance in terms of individual achievement on the state standards (a trait attribute), a conversion of these scores to achievement levels (basic, proficient, advanced), and the computation of the percentages at each level in each grade for a school (and for subgroups), followed by a decision about the school.

The interpretation of individual student performance in terms of achievement of the state standards involves the scoring of student responses, generalization over the universe of generalization, and extrapolation to the trait associated with overall achievement on the state standards.

The first two inferences, scoring and generalization, can be evaluated using the methods described in Section 3. The third inference, extrapolation, is potentially more problematic for accountability tests than for lower-stakes applications. Because the sanctions or rewards associated with the program are based on test scores, they will focus attention on the universe of generalization. As a result, the schools may give less attention to other areas of the curriculum. In particular, they may give less attention to those parts of the state standards not included in the test. There is nothing in the logic of these programs to suggest that achievement in any area not covered by the tests will improve as a result of the testing program. At best, performance on the topics not included in the tests should remain about the same.

Evidence for the extrapolation inference could be generated by examining the relationship between scores on the accountability tests and measures of achievement in areas not covered by the test. The extrapolation inference can also be evaluated by examining the impact of the testing program on the courses taken by the students and on the functioning of these courses. Does the attention given to areas not covered by the tests (e.g., art, music) change? In subjects covered by the accountability tests, does the focus shift away from content areas not covered on the test in favor of test-preparation activities?

Defining performance standards and cutscores for achievement levels introduces an array of value judgments (how good must a performance be in order to be considered proficient), which are made state to state (Linn, 2005). Unlike the cutscores for licensure examinations, which can be based on existing standards of practice, the educational accountability programs are not tied to any particular performance arena and therefore have no established basis for the standards. For example, should the definition of the proficient level in twelfth grade mathematics reflect the level needed in everyday life, in a trade school, or in a college engineering program?

The introduction of value judgments is not necessarily a problem. Decision procedures always rest on value judgments. However, for validation, it is appropriate that the values be made explicit, and that the consequences of the decision rule be evaluated.

The shift from individual student scores to school-based percentages at or above the proficient level shifts the focus from individual students to schools. The school-level results will be skewed if some schools fail to test many low-scoring students. To address this issue, NCLB includes participation rules.

Finally, the NCLB accountability program imposes various sanctions on schools that fail to meet specified requirements for increases in the percentage of students at or above the proficient level. A distinguishing feature of test-based accountability programs is their focus on achieving certain goals, in addition to or instead of focusing on the measurement of any particular attributes. This is particularly true of the NCLB legislation. The provisions of this Act include mandates on when testing is to occur (grades 3 through 8), which students are tested (requirements on participation rates for various groups), and consequences for schools, but the act defers to state standards on the content and format of the tests and on the definition of the achievement levels (Linn, 2005). NCLB says that schools have to test their students and it specifies how the scores are used for accountability, but it leaves the semantic interpretation of the test results to the states.

Test-based accountability programs have a range of potential benefits and costs (Kane, 2002c; Lane, Parke, & Stone, 1998; Linn, 1993; Mehrens, 1997). The potential benefits include increases in student achievement on the content areas covered by the tests (Linn, 2005), increases in achievement on the State Standards, and, possibly, improvements in public confidence in the schools. The potential costs include the time and resources spent on testing, possible narrowing of the curriculum and of student options (e.g., fewer AP courses), and increased dropout rates. These positive and negative consequences are likely to have different impacts on different groups and in different schools (Lane & Stone, 2002).

It is possible to estimate the extent to which the intended outcomes of the testing program actually occur (e.g., higher levels of achievement on the State Standards). It is also possible to estimate the extent to which specific unintended outcomes (e.g., increased dropout rates, decreases in elective course offerings and enrollment, declines in participation rates in extracurricular activities) occur after the introduction of the testing program (McNeil, 2005). Evidence relevant to these questions could also be derived from studies of changes in the schools after the tests are introduced.

The central question is the extent to which the accountability program has an impact (positive or negative) on achievement and other outcomes. To answer this question would require a program evaluation. The accountability program is functioning as an educational intervention and would be evaluated as such.

6.3. The Role of Consequences in Validity

Consequences have always been a part of our conception of validity (Guion, 1974; Messick, 1975, 1998; Shepard, 1997). Traditional definitions of validity in terms of how well a testing program achieves its goals (Cureton, 1951) necessarily raise questions about consequences, positive and negative (Cronbach & Gleser, 1965, Linn, 1997; Moss, 1992). Test-based decision procedures are necessarily evaluated in terms of their outcomes, or consequences, but until the 1970s, the consequences being evaluated tended to be mainly local, direct benefits and costs (e.g., increased efficiency vs. dollar costs).

The civil rights movement of the 1960s brought issues of fairness and equity to center stage (Cole & Moss, 1989; Ebel, 1966), and legislation and judicial decisions changed concerns about social equity into legal issues. Cronbach (1980a) described an environment in which every established testing practice was being criticized by someone who "disliked its consequences" (p. 37).

In 1978, the federal agencies responsible for enforcing civil rights legislation published the *Uniform Guidelines on Employee Selection Procedures* (EEOC et al., 1978). The Uniform Guidelines stated that if a selection procedure or a component of a selection procedure produced adverse impact against a protected group (e.g., racial minorities), the procedure could not be used for employment decisions unless the test scores were shown to be related to performance on the job. Adverse impact was said to exist if the selection rate for the protected group was less than four-fifths of that for the majority group.

Under the Uniform Guidelines, a finding of adverse impact triggers a requirement that the test user "validate" the test for the proposed use (e.g., by showing that test scores are empirically related to job performance). Essentially, adverse impact raises the stakes and creates a presumption of possible bias, which can be answered by supplying evidence that test scores are job related. The Uniform Guidelines struck a balance between the employer's interest in hiring the best candidates for each job and society's interest in group equity.

At about the same time, the courts decided that the state cannot deprive a student of a diploma on the basis of test scores without demonstrating that the student had an opportunity to master the competencies being measured (*Debra P. v. Turlington*, 1983; Linn, 1989). This decision can be viewed as a compromise between the state's interest in promoting high educational standards and students' rights under the Fourteenth Amendment (Jaeger, 1989). In these judicial decisions, the focus was on the balancing of positive and negative consequences.

Messick (1975, 1989, 1995) made social consequences a major issue in his analyses of validity (Moss, 1992). Cronbach (1971, 1980a, 1988) also gave a lot of attention to consequences in his discussions of validity but did not make them an organizing dimension in his analyses. In reaction to Messick's emphasis on the consequential aspect of validity, some authors (Borsboom, Mellenbergh, & van Heerden, 2004; Mehrens, 1997; Popham, 1997; Sackett, 1998) have argued for a more limited definition of validity, involving primarily the semantic interpretation of scores. For example, Popham (1997) acknowledged that consequences were important but preferred not to consider them part of validity. Linn (1997) and Shepard (1997) favored a broader conception of validity, which would include an evaluation of both the meaning of test scores and the consequences of their use.

6.3.1. The Role of Consequences in Evaluating Decision Procedures

Consequences, or outcomes, are the bottom line in evaluating decision procedures, which are always designed to achieve some desired outcomes or to avoid some undesirable outcomes (Cronbach, 1971; Shepard, 1993, 1997). A decision procedure that does not achieve its goals, or does so at too high a cost, is likely to be abandoned, even if it is based on perfectly accurate information. In medicine, a highly accurate diagnostic procedure for an untreatable illness would not be very useful as a screening tool, especially if the diagnostic procedure were costly, painful, or at all risky. In applied settings the bottom line involves a weighing of positive and negative consequences (Cronbach & Gleser, 1965; Debra P. v. Turlington, 1983; EEOC et al., 1978; Jaeger, 1989).

Evidence for the accuracy of the information is certainly relevant to the evaluation of a decision procedure but mainly because more accurate information is expected to lead to better decisions. If the information is shown to be erroneous, confidence in the decisions is likely to collapse. However, even indisputable evidence for accuracy does not justify a decision procedure (Cronbach, 1971, 1988).

As noted earlier, the evaluation of how well a decision procedure achieves its goals and of the immediate negative consequences or costs of testing have always been an integral part of the validation of decision procedures, but social consequences (particularly adverse impact) did not get much attention until the 1970s. Although there is general acceptance within the measurement community of the use of social consequences by the courts and other government agencies in evaluating test-based decision procedures, there has been some debate about whether the evaluation of social consequences should be included under the heading of validity.

Test-based accountability programs (e.g., "No Child Left Behind") blur the distinction between intended consequences and social consequences by adopting as their major purpose the improvement of educational outcomes for all students (Haertel, 1999). These testing programs have moved beyond the traditional monitoring role, to the use of testing as the engine of reform and accountability in education. Since these testing programs are intended to improve (or "reform") educational institutions, it seems reasonable to evaluate them as educational programs. Program evaluations include the evaluation of intended and unintended outcomes of the program being evaluated.

6.3.2. Impact of Consequences on Attribute Definition

Conclusions about the consequences associated with a decision procedure can impact the evaluation of a measurement procedure in two ways. First, information about specific consequences can pinpoint weaknesses or problems in the measurement procedure (Messick, 1989). For example, a finding that many students are being placed into courses that are at too high a level because the placement test does not give enough attention to some critical skill would suggest that the test be modified to give more weight to that skill. Research on differential item functioning (DIF) essentially uses information on group differences in performance to identify items that may be flawed.

Second, information about consequences provides evidence about the appropriateness of the measurement procedure for the purpose at hand. If the decision procedure is not working as intended (e.g., many students are being placed into the wrong course), but no specific problems in the measurement procedure can be identified, it may be reasonable to conclude that the attribute that is being measured is inappropriate (Cronbach, 1971). For example, using a general academic aptitude test to place students into a sequence of engineering courses might not work very well, because the different courses require specific mathematical skills that are not being measured. There is nothing wrong with the test of academic aptitude, but the test does not provide the information that is most critical to effective placement decisions. It is the wrong test for this purpose.

6.3.3. Responsibility for Evaluation of the Consequences

Having drawn a distinction between the semantic interpretation and the decision rule, it is often possible to evaluate the two parts of the interpretive argument separately (Reckase, 1988). Test developers are the obvious candidates to validate the claims they make (explicitly or implicitly in labels and suggested uses) in the proposed semantic interpretation of test scores. Many of the semantic inferences are routinely evaluated in test development (e.g., evaluation of scoring rules, estimation of generalizability).

Test users (i.e., those who make the policy decision to use a test for some purpose) should play a large role in analyzing the consequences of a test use. Test users identify the kinds of decisions to be made and the procedures to be used to make these decisions (Cronbach, 1980b; Taleporos, 1998). They presumably know the intended outcomes, the procedures being employed, and the population being tested, and therefore, they are in the best position to identify the intended and unintended consequences that occur. The test users may choose to rely on evidence and analyses provided by a test developer as one source of information, and it would be reasonable to expect that test developers would provide support for any test uses that they recommended, explicitly or implicitly. (Shepard, 1997).

In spite of the conceptual distinction between the semantic interpretation and the decision and the possibility of having different groups be responsible for the two parts, it is the interpretive argument as a whole that is to be evaluated. Assuming that a test has been found to assess some trait and that a measure of that trait is to be used to make certain decisions, it is not necessarily the case that the procedure will be effective. Aspects of the procedure, the context, or the population being tested may interfere with the effectiveness of the procedure in a particular context. For example, in a high-stakes testing environment, instruction that focuses on the content and format of test tasks (i.e., "coaching") may lead to changes in the meaning of test scores. In particular, the scores may become less indicative of a broad content area to the extent that practice on test questions replaces more general instruction (Heubert & Hauser, 1999). Tests that are susceptible to such subversion may work very well in low-stakes contexts but fail in high-stakes contexts.

Each application of a measurement procedure has to be evaluated on its own merits. Many different kinds of evidence may be relevant to the evaluation of the consequences of a testing system (Lane, Parke, & Stone, 1998), and many individuals, groups, and organizations may be involved in generating the evidence (Linn, 1998).

6.3.4. Social Consequences

Cronbach and Messick have suggested very different approaches to the inclusion of social consequences within their models of validity (Moss, 1992). Messick described the appraisal of social consequences as an aspect of construct validity, because the outcomes of test use "both derive from and contribute to the meaning of test scores" (Messick, 1995, p. 7), and suggested that adverse social consequences invalidate test use mainly if they are due to flaws in the test:

> If the adverse social consequences are empirically traceable to sources of test invalidity, then the validity of the test use is jeopardized. If the social consequences cannot be so traced … then the validity of the test use is not overturned. (Messick, 1989, p. 88)

It is generally agreed that adverse social consequences count against validity when they "can be traced to a source of invalidity such as construct underrepresentation or construct-irrelevant components" (AERA et al., 1999, p. 16).

In a sense, to say that social consequences count against validity only when they are due to sources of invalidity is to give them a secondary role in validation. Under this model, adverse consequences serve mainly to suggest that some cases of invalidity are more serious than others. A threat to validity that might otherwise be ignored (e.g., one that has a small impact on individual test scores) becomes a serious concern if it is shown to have a systematic negative impact on some group. Legal analyses of test consequences and validity have followed this pattern since the 1970s (EEOC et al., 1978). If a test has adverse impact on the hiring of minority workers, the validity of the test has to be demonstrated. If a satisfactory validation is produced, the adverse impact does not count against the legitimacy of the testing program.

For Cronbach (1971, 1988), consequences had a more direct role in validation. He suggested that negative consequences could invalidate test use even if the consequences cannot be traced to any flaw in the test, because "tests that impinge on the rights and life chances of individuals are inherently disputable" (Cronbach, 1988, p. 6). Cronbach (1988) argued that:

> Validators have an obligation to review whether a practice has appropriate consequences for individuals and institutions, and especially to argue against adverse consequences. (p. 6)

He concluded that we

> may prefer to exclude reflection on consequences from meanings of the word *validation*, but ... cannot deny the obligation. (p. 6)

Messick (1989) took exception to Cronbach's flexibility on this matter of definition. After quoting Cronbach's (1988) views, Messick (1989) argued that:

> the meaning of validation should not be considered a preference. On what can the legitimacy of the obligation to appraise social consequences be based if not on the only genuine imperative in testing, namely, validity? (p. 20)

Cronbach (1988) was less insistent than Messick (1989, 1995) about including the evaluation of consequences under validation but was inclined to consider all consequences in evaluating the legitimacy of test use.

Validation has a contingent character in that the evidence required for validation depends on the proposed interpretations and uses. The test user has an obligation to make a case for the appropriateness of the decision procedure in the context in which it is being used. As is the case for all interpretive arguments, there is a ceteris paribus assumption inherent in test uses. In education, as in medicine, there is an obligation to avoid doing harm if it can be avoided. Therefore, the test user has an obligation to consider any negative consequences that can reasonably be anticipated and to weigh them against the potential benefits before adopting the test.

The critic has a right to challenge any assumption or inference in the interpretive argument, including those supporting semantic inferences and those supporting claims about the benefits to be expected from a proposed test use, and the test users should be prepared to defend their choices. All test users have to operate within the bounds of the law, and most test users are also constrained by public opinion. They cannot ignore consequences, even if they would prefer to do so. On the other hand, it is not possible to anticipate all possible consequences of any decision, so it would be counterproductive to demand that all consequences be considered before a decision procedure can be implemented.

Toulmin (1958) has provided a reasonable resolution to this dilemma. He suggested that the general rules of argumentation apply over a wide range of contexts, but that the criteria for evaluating real arguments tend to depend on the context in which they occur. The kinds of consequences to be considered in evaluating a decision procedure vary as a function of the purposes of the procedure and the context in which it operates. So for example, in making selection decisions, businesses tend to be concerned about gains in productivity (a positive consequence) and about costs (a negative consequence). In making placement decisions, schools are concerned about optimizing learning vs. the negative consequences of failure. Licensure organizations seek to protect the public, while not excluding qualified candidates.

Any consequences that are considered significant by stakeholders are potentially relevant to the evaluation of how well a decision procedure is working. The range of consequences that can be considered fair game has evolved over time. Before 1960, adverse impact was not given much attention; by 1980, adverse impact and racial, ethnic, and gender bias were clearly on the agenda. More recently the impact of standardized testing procedures on individuals with disabilities has become a major concern. The measurement community does not control the agenda; the larger community decides on the questions to be asked (Cronbach, 1988).

Cronbach (1988) has pointed out that, for validity arguments to be convincing to diverse audiences, the assumptions in these arguments must be credible to those audiences. This concern is especially salient for the policy assumptions implicit in high-stakes testing programs, because the credibility of these policy assumptions may be highly variable across stakeholders.

The evaluation of the policy assumptions inherent in high-stakes testing programs raises some difficult issues (Sackett, 1998), but they are not any more difficult than the issues routinely faced by program evaluators. To the extent that the purpose of a testing program is to promote certain outcomes, the testing program is functioning as an educational intervention and therefore merits an evaluation of the kind routinely mandated for new educational programs. For stakeholders to make informed decisions about the effectiveness of high-stakes tests, it is necessary that they have information about how well these tests achieve various goals and at what cost. Assuming that there are both positive and negative consequences, the stakeholders and policymakers face the task of weighing these consequences against each other.

7. FALLACIES IN VALIDITY ARGUMENTS

Validity arguments can go wrong in many ways. Any empirical study included in the validity argument can be designed or carried out poorly, and any empirical results can be misinterpreted or misapplied. On a larger scale, the interpretive argument can be misspecified in the sense that it does not correspond to the patterns of actual score interpretations and uses. These misspecifications of the interpretive argument tend to be more serious than technical problems in a particular study, because they are more pervasive and harder to detect.

A fallacy occurs when an unsound argument appears to be sound. Faulty reasoning may appear sound on casual inspection, and if it is subtle enough, it can mislead both proponent and audience (Hansen & Pinto, 1995). It is one of the tasks of validation research to expose any gaps in the formulation of interpretive arguments.

There are at least three ways in which interpretive arguments can be misspecified, each of which is a special case of a classic fallacy: begging-the-question, the straw-man fallacy, and gilding the lily.

7.1. Begging the Question

A common problem in validating interpretive arguments is the tendency to take one or more questionable inferences for granted or to take part of the interpretive argument to be the whole of the interpretive argument. This fallacy has traditionally been referred to as "begging the question," because the question at issue, or a large part of the question at issue, is simply taken for granted (Walton, 1989).

Many real-world applications of testing assume fairly ambitious interpretations of test scores, involving many inferences and assumptions. That some of these inferences and assumptions have not been systematically evaluated at a given point in time is not necessarily a problem, especially if they are reasonably plausible. However, it is a problem if the unexamined assumptions and inferences are not plausible, and it is especially dangerous if the implausible inferences are implicit and rest on hidden assumptions.

As noted in Section 1.2.1, traditional analyses of "content validity" tended to beg questions about implicit trait or construct interpretations. Claims for content validity were often based on studies that evaluated only one assumption, the relevance of items to the attribute being measured, while a sound interpretive argument for an observable attribute generally requires at least three inferences: scoring, generalization, and extrapolation. The traditional content-validity analysis could provide support for the scoring inference. In addition, expert opinion indicating that the sample of performance is representative of the universe of generalization combined with empirical evidence for generalizability over this universe can provide adequate support for generalization to the universe score. However, expert evaluations of test items do not generally provide strong support for extrapolation to the target domain, while the interpretations and uses of the scores typically assume such extrapolation.

The begging-the-question fallacy fits with the confirmationist tendency in many validation studies. For example, the proponents of authentic assessments have tended to emphasize the extent to which the performances observed in testing match the target performance while taking the generalization of observed scores over tasks, occasions, and conditions of observation for granted, even though empirical research consistently indicates that generalizability over performance tasks cannot be taken for granted. Similarly, developers of objective tests have tended to give a lot of attention to content representativeness and generalizability over items, while taking extrapolation to the target performance for granted. In both cases, the more questionable part of the argument is accepted without much critical scrutiny. The fact that some major inferences are being glossed over may not be noticed, especially if other parts of the argument are developed in some detail.

7.1.1. Begging the Question of Consequences

This fallacy is a special case of the begging-the-question fallacy, but it occurs frequently enough that it deserves separate discussion. It is generally inappropriate to assume that evidence supporting a particular interpretation of test scores automatically justifies a proposed use of the scores. That test scores provide accurate estimates of a relevant student attribute does not generally imply that they will be useful to the student's teacher in planning instruction (Tittle, 1989).

A classical example of this fallacy was provided by Cronbach and Snow (1977) in their analysis of aptitude-treatment interactions. Assume, for example, that a test is an excellent predictor of performance in two treatment options, A and B, but that the regression lines for outcomes based on scores are parallel, so that everyone does uniformly better in treatment A than in treatment B. In this case, the test scores are not in themselves at all useful for placement decisions; the optimal policy is to assign everyone to treatment A. The validity of the interpretation as a predictor of performance in the two treatment options does not support the validity of the proposed placement decisions.

Shepard (1993) provides another good example. Suppose that a "readiness" test is an excellent predictor of performance in kindergarten. Does this justify its use in deciding whether to admit children to kindergarten this year or hold them back till next year? If a low "readiness" score indicates a developmental lag that will be resolved by waiting a year, this strategy would make sense. If the low score indicates a home environment that does not promote learning of the skills, keeping the child out of school for another year would be counterproductive. In any case, the validity of the proposed interpretation in terms of mastery of certain skills does not justify the use of the test scores for what is essentially a placement decision (kindergarten or home).

Current accountability programs provide many examples of begging the question. The arguments for these testing programs tend to claim that the program will lead to improvements in school effectiveness and student achievement by focusing the attention of school administrators, teachers, and students on demanding content. Yet, the validity arguments developed to support these ambitious claims typically attend only to the descriptive part of the interpretive argument (and often to only a part of that). The validity evidence that is provided tends to focus on scoring and generalization to the content domain for the test. The claim that the imposition of the accountability requirements will improve the overall performance of schools and students is taken for granted.

The evaluation of the policy assumptions inherent in accountability programs and other high-stakes testing programs requires an evaluation of intended and unintended outcomes. If the primary purpose of a testing program is to promote certain outcomes (e.g., achievement of the demanding content outlined in the state standards) rather than to measure certain variables, the assumption that the testing program will yield these outcomes deserves some attention.

Scriven (1995) has made a similar point in the context of program evaluation. He suggested that a well designed and implemented evaluation effort can lead to well-founded conclusions about a product or program, but that in general, it is not appropriate for the evaluator to make recommendations based on these conclusions. Even if the evaluative conclusions are rock solid given the data, the actions to be taken by decision makers generally depend on many considerations not addressed in the evaluation. In particular, unless the evaluators have examined the potential consequences of different actions that might be taken and the values of the relevant stakeholders, they are not in a position to identify the best course of action.

7.1.2. Overgeneralization or Spurious Precision

The social sciences have, at times, been led astray by trying to mimic the physical sciences too closely, but there is at least one area in which it might be beneficial to follow the example of the physical sciences. Physical scientists are expected to investigate all sources of error that might have a substantial impact on their measurements. As Cronbach et al. (1972) pointed out, reliability studies often implicitly define the universe of generalization too narrowly given their measurement procedures, and in doing so, "they underestimate the 'error' of measurement, that is, the error of generalization" (p. 352).

Generalizability analyses can be used to examine the magnitudes of different sources or random sampling error in any measurement procedure, including the errors due to the sampling from the task, occasion, context, administrator, or rater facets (Brennan, 2001b; Cronbach et al., 1972; Haertel, this volume). Questions about precision are begged if the random errors associated with generalization over some facets are taken to represent unbiased estimates of the total error in generalizing to the expected value over the universe of generalization. In such cases, the estimated random errors underestimate the sampling errors for the full set of facets in the universe of generalization. For example, the use of data from a single administration of an objective test to estimate a standard error based on coefficient alpha includes information on the sampling error for items but does not provide any indication of the impact of other potential sources of error. This limited estimate of sampling error is likely to be an underestimate of the total error in generalizing over occasions, raters, contexts, and other facets.

It may be reasonable to simply assume invariance over some facets that are not expected to have much influence on performance (e.g., the room used for a multiple choice test), and these facets do not necessarily have to be investigated. In addition many facets can be included in the residual error by allowing them to vary randomly in the G study. However, those facets that are expected to introduce substantial error into the generalization inference deserve detailed analysis, and to the extent that some potentially serious sources of error (random or systematic) have not been examined, these limitations should be acknowledged.

7.1.3. Surrogation

Just as correlation does not imply causality, even a very high correlation between two measures does not imply that they have the same meaning. Scriven (1987) has labeled the "use of a correlate ... as if it were an explanation of, or a substitute for, or a valid evaluative criterion of, another variable" as the *fallacy of statistical surrogation* (p. 11). The fallacy involves a "substitution of a statistical notion for a concept of a more sophisticated kind such as causation or identity" (Scriven, 1987, p. 11). Among students who have graduated from American high schools, the correlation between scores on a mathematics test and an English usage test would generally be positive and fairly high; but level of achievement in English is not the same thing as level of achievement in mathematics. The high correlation between English and math scores reflects the fact that successful students typically do well on both tests, and failing students do less well on both tests. However, if math were dropped from the standard high-school curriculum or students from all over the world were included in the analyses, these correlations would probably drop sharply.

Scriven introduces the surrogation fallacy in the context of employee evaluation and distinguishes "primary indicators," which involve samples of the performance of interest from "secondary indicators," which are "only statistically connected with good (or bad) job performance" (Scriven, 1987, p. 17). He points out that it would be inappropriate to dismiss someone from a job because of rumors that they are an alcoholic, even if a statistical relationship can be shown between rumors of this kind and alcoholism, and between alcoholism and poor performance.

The surrogation fallacy is particularly dangerous in high-stakes contexts, because in such contexts, it is predictable that, if the indicators can be manipulated, they will be manipulated. If certain indicators are used for selection decisions because they have been found to be good indicators of future performance, they may not be good indicators for long. If scores on a vocabulary test are used as indicators of language skills in college admissions, applicants will practice this skill, and its value as an indicator of overall verbal competence (e.g., reading, writing, speaking, listening) is likely to decline. Large-scale testing programs tend to be highly standardized to promote fairness and tend to rely on objective formats for practical reasons. Under these circumstances, specific preparation for test tasks is likely to increase and preparation for other tasks is likely to decrease. Test preparation will focus on the formats included in the test in preference to activities not included in the test. The higher the stakes, the more likely it is that the surrogate measures will displace the performances of interest.

7.1.4. Reification

Reification involves a leap from an observed regularity in scores to the existence of some "thing" that is the source of the regularity. For example, it is natural to assume that observed consistencies in performance over some domain of tasks correspond to (and even are caused by) some trait that exists in persons. This tends to be especially true in cases where the performances in the domain all share some structural characteristics (e.g., series completion tasks), and we have some general ideas about how people perform such tasks (e.g., by identifying the pattern in the series and completing it). In such cases, it is natural to talk about "analytic ability," and there is no great harm in doing so as long as we refrain from imbuing the term with a lot of excess meaning (e.g., that it is hereditary, or that it is a prerequisite for success in science). As discussed in Section 3, the scores derived from standardized assessments are interpreted in terms of expected performance over the universe of generalization, and by extrapolation, in terms of the target score. Similarly, IRT models yield estimates of latent abilities derived from performance in some domain of items. Assuming that the data fit the model, the model justifies an interpretation of scores in terms of level of performance in the domain. However, causal inferences about an underlying trait that accounts for the observed regularities requires additional evidence.

Factor analysis provides a framework for analyzing relationships among different domains in terms of factor loadings. The factor loadings summarize the observed pattern of correlations among scores but do not necessarily correspond to any fundamental set of traits. The patterns of factor loadings may in fact be due to common patterns in the sequencing of instruction or other characteristics of the instructional or testing environment.

The point here is not to argue against the use of trait language. Thinking about traits or constructs as underlying causal variables can be a fertile source of insight about behavior and can yield hypotheses for further analysis, and various kinds of statistical analyses can provide useful guidance in defining traits and in defining their target domains. However, if excess meaning is to be brought into an analysis in the form of hypothesized traits or constructs, the claims being made, explicitly or implicitly, should be examined.

7.2. The Straw-Man

The begging-the-question fallacy takes some inferences and assumptions for granted. The second fallacy, the "straw-man fallacy," goes in the opposite direction and adopts an interpretive argument that is more ambitious than that required for the proposed interpretations and uses.

Given the potential for unnecessary difficulties in overstating the interpretation and thereby making it more ambitious than it needs to be, why do interpretations get overstated? I suggest three possible reasons.

First, the details of the interpretive argument implicit in a proposed test interpretation or use are not necessarily obvious in most cases. For example, licensure examinations can be interpreted as measures of current competence or as predictors of future performance. If one does not consider the various options carefully, it is easy to run them together and employ the stronger, predictive model when the competency model is sufficient. The proposed interpretations and uses can easily be overstated through carelessness.

Second, there is some tendency for test developers and vendors to propose ambitious interpretations. Test development projects often start with lofty goals, and correspondingly ambitious interpretive arguments. As development proceeds, compromises may become necessary and some parts of the plan may not get completed, but footnotes and caveats tend to get lost in general statements of the proposed interpretations and uses. In the case of legally mandated testing (federal or state sponsored), there is a tendency for political rhetoric to greatly inflate the claimed benefits of testing programs; if these claims were taken seriously, they would imply the need for a very ambitious validation effort.

Third, individuals who are inclined to challenge a proposed interpretation or use have a natural tendency to state the underlying interpretation of scores in a way that is easy to refute, and overly ambitious assumptions are easy to knock down. So it is tempting for hostile critics to treat the proposed interpretation or use as a "straw man" by overstating its assumptions.

7.3. Gilding the Lily

Any argument can be made to appear more convincing without being substantially strengthened by adding additional evidence for inferences and assumptions that are already quite plausible. This fallacy, referred to as "gilding the lily," is not particularly harmful in itself but can be pernicious when it occurs in connection with other fallacies. It is easier to ignore the fact that support for some key inference is weak, if an extensive array of evidence is provided for other, more plausible inferences or assumptions.

For example, in validity analyses for multiple-choice test scores, it is not unusual to find multiple analyses of generalizability over items, but little or no evidence for more questionable inferences (e.g., extrapolations to performance domains or traits). For objective testing programs, it is generally quite easy to generate internal-homogeneity reliability coefficients (e.g., coefficient alpha), and it is tempting to accumulate lots of this easily available and reassuring evidence. And there is nothing wrong with this in itself.

The problem arises if the accumulation of evidence in support of a relatively safe assumption distracts test developers and users from critically examining other less plausible inferences. For a well developed multiple-choice test with a substantial number of items, it would be surprising if coefficient alpha were not fairly high. Conducting a study to confirm generalizability over items is certainly in order, and monitoring it over time is also appropriate, but it should be recognized that multiple studies of this kind do not add much to our confidence in the interpretive argument as a whole.

8. CONCLUDING REMARKS

Validation involves the evaluation of the proposed interpretations and uses of measurements. The interpretive argument provides an explicit statement of the inferences and assumptions inherent in the proposed interpretations and uses. The validity argument provides an evaluation of the coherence of the interpretive argument and of the plausibility of its inferences and assumptions. It is not the test that is validated and it is not the test scores that are validated. It is the claims and decisions based on the test results that are validated. Therefore, for validation to go forward, it is necessary that the proposed interpretations and uses be clearly stated.

Over the last fifty years, three general principles of validation have developed out of construct validity. The proposed interpretation is to be stated clearly enough to indicate what it implies. The evaluation of the interpretive argument is to involve an extended analysis of the proposed interpretations and uses. Plausible alternative interpretations are to be identified and investigated. The mix of evidence to be used in evaluating a particular interpretive argument depends on the claims being made by that interpretive argument.

For high-stakes testing programs, agreement on the interpretations and uses may require negotiations among stakeholders about the conclusions to be drawn and the decisions to be made (Ryan, 2002). The interpretation of a measure of competence in some area (e.g., writing), may seem simple enough, but in defining the competence and in developing the test, a number of specific issues typically arise, including the kinds of tasks to be included (the writing of short essays on demand or the production of longer works over an extended period), the scoring rules (relative emphasis on the mechanics, organization, style, and creativity), and the conditions under which the performance will occur (e.g., with or without tight time constraints).

The argument-based model provides a relatively pragmatic approach to validation. The goal is to develop a measurement procedure that supports the proposed interpretations and uses and an interpretive argument that is plausible, given the measurement procedure. The initial development effort is legitimately confirmationist. During the appraisal stage, the proposed interpretations and uses are taken as hypotheses or conjectures that are to be subjected to critical evaluation.

An explicitly stated interpretive argument serves three critical functions. First, it provides a framework for test development by indicating the assumptions that need to be met. The development of a measure of current competence in a content area would be different in many ways from the development of an indicator of a theoretical construct.

Second, the interpretive argument provides a framework for the validity argument. The evidence called for in the validity argument is that needed to support the specific inferences and assumptions in the interpretive argument.

Third, the interpretive argument provides a basis for evaluating the adequacy of the validity argument. If the validity argument provides adequate support for the interpretive argument, the proposed interpretations and uses are warranted. If the interpretive argument is incomplete or some of its inferences or assumptions are shaky, some interpretations or uses are not fully justified.

Validation has a contingent character; the evidence required to justify a proposed interpretation or use depends on the proposed interpretation or use. A modest interpretation (e.g., in terms of an observable attribute) makes fewer claims and is therefore easier to justify than a more ambitious interpretation (e.g., in terms of a broadly defined trait or construct).

The fact that we develop the interpretation, rather than discover it, has two major implications. First, we have some flexibility in what we choose to put into the interpretation. Second, the fact that the interpretation is not a given implies that it needs to be specified clearly if it is to be evaluated effectively. The specification of an interpretive argument puts a definite proposal on the table. The proponent has a claim to defend, and the critic has one to challenge. The kinds of evidence required for the validation of a proposed interpretation or use depends on the structure of the corresponding interpretive argument.

In developing a validity argument, the proponent can make a positive case for a proposed interpretation by stating the interpretive argument clearly, thereby demonstrating its coherence, and by providing support for its inferences and assumptions. The critic can challenge the appropriateness of the proposed interpretations and uses of the test results, the adequacy of the interpretive argument given the goals of the testing program, or the plausibility of specific inferences or assumptions. The critic can propose an alternative assessment procedure or interpretation. A critic might also claim that a test-based decision procedure fails to produce the intended outcomes or has serious unintended negative consequences.

A failure to state the proposed interpretations and uses clearly and in some detail makes a fully adequate validation essentially impossible, because implicit inferences and assumptions cannot be critically evaluated. Most fallacies in presumptive reasoning involve the tacit acceptance of doubtful assumptions, and an important function of external critics and alternative interpretations is to make these assumptions explicit.

NOTE

1. The model being proposed here is essentially the same as that in Kane (1982), but the terminology has been changed to make it more natural and more consistent with standard usage in generalizability theory. In the terminology used here, the broader set of observations about which conclusions are to be drawn is called the "target domain," and the narrower set defining the standardized measurement procedure (the set from which observations are drawn and to which statistical generalization is legitimate) is called the "universe of generalization." These two sets approximate what I called the "universe of generalization" and the "universe of allowable observations" respectively in Kane (1982).

REFERENCES

American Educational Research Association, American Psychological Association, & National Council on Measurement in Education. (1985). *Standards for educational and psychological testing*. Washington, DC: American Psychological Association.

American Educational Research Association, American Psychological Association, & National Council on Measurement in Education. (1999). *Standards for educational and psychological testing*. Washington, DC: American Psychological Association.

American Psychological Association. (1954). Technical recommendations for psychological tests and diagnostic techniques. *Psychological Bulletin Supplement, 51*(2) 1–38.

American Psychological Association, American Educational Research Association, & National Council on Measurement in Education. (1966). *Standards for educational and psychological tests and manuals*. Washington, DC: American Psychological Association.

American Psychological Association, American Educational Research Association, & National Council on Measurement in Education. (1974). *Standards for educational and psychological tests and manuals*. Washington, DC: American Psychological Association.

Anastasi, A. (1986). Evolving concepts of test validation. *Annual Review of Psychology, 37,* 1–15.

Angoff, W. H. (1988). Validity: An evolving concept. In H. Wainer & H. Braun (Eds.), *Test validity* (pp. 9–13). Hillsdale, NJ: Lawrence Erlbaum.

Bachman, L. (2002). Alternative interpretations of alternative assessments: Some validity issues in educational performance assessments. *Educational Measurement: Issues and Practice, 21*(3), 5–18.

Benson, J. (1998). Developing a strong program of construct validation: A test anxiety example. *Educational Measurement: Issues and Practice, 17*(1), 10–22.

Benson, J., & Hagtvet, K. (1996). The interplay between design, data analysis and theory in the measurement of coping. In M. Zeidner & N. Endler (Eds.), *Handbook of coping: Theory, research, applications* (pp. 83–106). New York: Wiley.

Black, P., & Wiliam, D. (1998). Assessment and classroom learning. *Assessment in Education, 5*(1), 7–73.

Blair, J. (1995). Informal logic and reasoning in evaluation. *New Directions for Evaluation: Reasoning in evaluation: Inferential links and leaps, 68,* 71–80.

Bonner, S. (2005, April). *Investigating the cognitive processes in responding to MBE questions*. Paper presented at the annual meeting of the National Council on Measurement in Education, Montreal, Canada.

Borsboom, D., Mellenbergh, G., & van Heerden, J. (2004). The concept of validity. *Psychological Review, 111,* 1061–1071.

Brennan, R. (2001a). An essay on the history and future of reliability from the perspective of replications. *Journal of Educational Measurement, 38*(4), 285–317.

Brennan, R. (2001b). *Generalizability theory*. New York: Springer-Verlag.

Bridgeman, P. (1927). *The logic of modern physics*. New York: Macmillan.

Brookhart, S. (2003). Developing measurement theory for classroom assessment purposes and uses. *Educational Measurement: Issues and Practice, 22*(4), 5–12.

Bruner, J. (1990). *Acts of meaning*. Cambridge, MA: Harvard University Press.

Campbell, D. T., & Fiske, D. W. (1959). Convergent and discriminant validation by the multitrait-multimethod matrix. *Psychological Bulletin, 56,* 81–105.

Carroll, J. (1986). What is intelligence? In R. Sternberg & D. Detterman (Eds.), *What is intelligence? Contemporary viewpoints on its nature and definition* (pp. 51–54). Norwood, NJ: Ablex Publishing.

Cizek, G. (2001). *Standard setting: Concepts, methods, and perspectives*. Mahwah, NJ: Lawrence Erlbaum.

Clauser, B. (2000). Recurrent issues and recent advances in scoring performance assessments. *Applied Psychological Measurement, 24,* 310–324.

Clauser, B. E., Harik, P., & Clyman, S. G. (2000). The generalizability of scores for a performance assessment scored with a computer-automated scoring system. *Journal of Educational Measurement, 37,* 245–262.

Cole, N. S., & Moss, P. A. (1989). Bias in test use. In R. L. Linn (Ed.), *Educational measurement* (3rd ed., pp. 201–219). New York: American Council on Education and Macmillan.

Cook, T., & Campbell, D. (1979). *Quasi-experimentation: Design and analysis issues for field settings*. Boston: Houghton Mifflin.

Cronbach, L. J. (1971). Test validation. In R. L. Thorndike (Ed.), *Educational measurement* (2nd ed., pp. 443–507). Washington, DC: American Council on Education.

Cronbach, L. J. (1975). Beyond the two disciplines of scientific psychology. *American Psychologist, 30,* 116–127.

Cronbach, L. J. (1980a). Selection theory for a political world. *Public Personnel Management, 9*(1), 37–50.

Cronbach, L. J. (1980b). Validity on parole: How can we go straight? *New Directions for Testing and Measurement: Measuring Achievement Over a Decade, 5,* 99–108.

Cronbach, L. J. (1982). *Designing evaluations of educational and social programs*. San Francisco: Jossey-Bass.

Cronbach, L. J. (1988). Five perspectives on validity argument. In H. Wainer & H. Braun (Eds.), *Test validity* (pp. 3–17). Hillsdale, NJ: Lawrence Erlbaum.

Cronbach, L. J. (1989). Construct validation after thirty years. In R. E. Linn (Ed.), *Intelligence: Measurement, theory, and public policy* (pp. 147–171). Urbana: University of Illinois Press.

Cronbach, L. J., & Gleser, G. C. (1965). *Psychological tests and personnel decisions*. Urbana: University of Illinois Press.

Cronbach, L. J., Gleser, G. C., Nanda, H., & Rajaratnam, N. (1972). *The dependability of behavioral measurements: Theory of generalizability for scores and profiles*. New York: Wiley.

Cronbach, L. J., & Meehl, P. E. (1955). Construct validity in psychological tests. *Psychological Bulletin, 52,* 281–302.

Cronbach, L. J., & Snow, R. E. (1977). *Aptitudes and instructional methods; A handbook for research on interactions*. New York: Irvington Publishers.

Crooks, T. J. (1988). The impact of classroom evaluation practices on students. *Review of Educational Research, 58,* 438–481.

Crooks, T., Kane, M., & Cohen, A. (1996). Threats to the valid use of assessments. *Assessment in Education, 3,* 265–285.

Cureton, E. E. (1951). Validity. In E. F. Lindquist (Ed.), *Educational measurement* (pp. 621–694). Washington, DC: American Council on Education.

Debra P. v. Turlington, 644 F. 2d 397, 5th Cir. 1981: 564 F. Supp. 177 (M.D. Fla. 1983).

Delandshere, G. (2002). Assessment as inquiry. *Teacher's College Record, 104,* 1461–1484.

Downing, S., & Haladyna, T. (2004). Validity threats: Overcoming interference with proposed interpretations of assessment data. *Medical Education, 38,* 327–333.

Dwyer, C. A., Gallagher, A., Levin, J., & Morley, M. E. (2003). *What is quantitative reasoning? Defining the construct for assessment purposes* (Research Report 03–30). Princeton, NJ: Educational Testing Service.

Ebel, R. (1961). Must all tests be valid? *American Psychologist, 16,* 640–647.

Ebel, R. (1966). The social consequences of educational testing. In A. Anastasi (Ed.), *Testing problems in perspective: Twenty-fifth anniversary volume of topical readings from the Invitational Conference in Testing Problems* (pp. 18–29). Washington, DC: American Council on Education.

Eisner, E. (1991). *The enlightened eye: Qualitative inquiry and the enhancement of educational practice*. New York: Macmillan.

Embretson, S. (1983). Construct validity: Construct representation versus nomothetic span. *Psychological Bulletin, 93,* 179–197.

Embretson, S. (1984). A general multicomponent latent trait model for measuring learning and change. *Psychometrika, 49,* 175–186.

Embretson, S. (1998). A cognitive design system approach to generating valid tests: Application to abstract reasoning. *Psychological Methods, 3,* 380–396.

Embretson, S., & McCollam, K. (2000). Psychometric approaches to understanding and measuring intelligence. In R. Sternberg (Ed.), *Handbook of Intelligence* (pp. 423–444). Cambridge: Cambridge University Press.

Equal Employment Opportunity Commission (EEOC), Civil Service Commission, Department of Labor, & Department of Justice. (1978). Adoption by four agencies of Uniform Guidelines on Employee Selection Procedures. *Federal Register, 43,* 38290–38315.

Feldt, L. S., & Brennan, R. L. (1989). Reliability. In R. L. Linn (Ed.), *Educational measurement* (3rd ed., pp. 105–146). New York: American Council on Education and Macmillan.

Fitzpatrick, R., & Morrison, E. J. (1971). Performance and product evaluation. In R. L. Thorndike (Ed.), *Educational measurement* (2nd ed., pp. 237–270). Washington, DC: American Council on Education.

Flockton, L., & Crooks, T. (2002). *Social studies assessment results 2001.* Educational Assessment Research Unit. Dunedin, New Zealand: University of Otago.

Fournier, D. (1995). Establishing evaluative conclusions: A distinction between general and working logic. *New Directions in Evaluation: Reasoning in Evaluation: Inferential Links and Leaps, 68,* 15–32.

Frederiksen, J. (2003). Issues for the design of educational assessment systems. *Measurement: Interdisciplinary Research and Perspectives, 1,* 69–73.

Frederiksen, N. (1984). The real test bias: Influences of testing on teaching and learning. *American Psychologist, 39,* 193–202.

Galison, P. (1987). *How do experiments end?* Chicago: University of Chicago Press.

Geertz, C. (1973). *The interpretation of cultures.* New York: Basic Books.

Ghiselli, E. E. (1966). *The validity of occupational aptitude tests.* New York: Wiley.

Gipps, C. (1999). Socio-cultural aspects of assessment. *Review of Research in Education, 24,* 355–392.

Grandy, R. E. (1992). Theory of theories; a view from cognitive science. In J. Earman (Ed.), *Inference, explanation, and other frustrations: Essay in the philosophy of science* (pp. 216–233). Berkeley: University of California Press.

Greeno, J., Pearson, P., & Schoenfeld, A. (1997). Implications for the National Assessment of Educational Progress of research on learning and cognition. In R. Glaser, R. Linn, & G. Bohrnstedt (Eds.), *Assessment in transition: Monitoring the nation's educational progress. Background studies* (pp. 151–314). Stanford, CA: National Academy of Education.

Guion, R. (1974). Open a new window: Validities and values in psychological measurement. *American Psychologist, 29,* 287–296.

Guion, R. (1977). Content validity: The source of my discontent. *Applied Psychological Measurement, 1,* 1–10.

Guion, R. M. (1980). On trinitarian conceptions of validity. *Professional Psychology, 11,* 385–398.

Guion, R. M. (1995). Comments on values and standards in performance assessment. *Educational Measurement: Issues and Practice, 14*(4), 25–27.

Guion, R. (1998). *Assessment, measurement, and prediction for personnel decisions.* Mahwah, NJ: Lawrence Erlbaum.

Gulliksen, H. (1950a). *Theory of mental tests.* New York: Wiley.

Gulliksen, H. (1950b). Intrinsic validity. *American Psychologist, 5,* 511–517.

Haertel, E. H. (1999). Validity arguments for high-stakes testing: In search of the evidence. *Educational Measurement: Issues and Practice, 18*(4), 5–9.

Haertel, E., & Greeno, J. (2003). A situative perspective: Broadening the foundations of assessment. *Measurement: Interdisciplinary Research and Perspectives, 1,* 154–162.

Haladyna, T. M., & Downing, S. M. (2004). Construct-irrelevant variance in high-stakes testing. *Educational Measurement: Issues and Practice, 23*(1), 17–27.

Hambleton, R. K. (1989). Principles and selected applications of item response theory. In R. L. Linn (Ed.), *Educational measurement* (3rd ed., pp. 147–200). New York: American Council on Education and Macmillan.

Hansen, E., Mislevy, R., & Steinberg, L. (2003, April). *Evidence-centered assessment design and individuals with disabilities.* Paper presented at NCME Meeting, Chicago.

Hansen, H., & Pinto, R. (1995). *Fallacies, classical and contemporary readings.* University Park: Pennsylvania State University Press.

Henrysson, S. (1971). Gathering, analyzing, and using data on test items. In R. L. Thorndike (Ed.), *Educational measurement* (2nd ed., pp. 130–159). Washington, DC: American Council on Education.

Heubert, J. P., & Hauser, M. H. (1999). *High stakes: Testing for tracking, promotion, and graduation.* Washington, DC: Nation Academy Press.

House, E. R. (1980). *Evaluating with validity.* Beverly Hills, CA: Sage Publications.

Ippel, M. J. (1986). *Component-testing: A theory of cognitive aptitude measurement.* Amsterdam: Free University Press.

Jaeger, R. (1989). Certification of student competence. In R. L. Linn (Ed.), *Educational measurement* (3rd ed., pp. 485–534). New York: American Council on Education and Macmillan.

Jöreskog, K. (1973). A general method for investigating a linear structural equation system. In A. Goldberger & D. Duncan (Eds.), *Structural equation models in the social sciences* (pp. 85–112). New York: Academic Press.

Kane, M. T. (1982). A sampling model for validity. *Applied Psychological Measurement, 6,* 125–160.

Kane, M. (1992). An argument-based approach to validation. *Psychological Bulletin, 112,* 527–535.

Kane, M. T. (1994). Validating interpretive arguments for licensure and certification examinations. *Evaluation and the Health Professions, 17,* 133–159.

Kane, M. T. (1996). The precision of measurements. *Applied Measurement in Education, 9*(4), 355–379.

Kane, M. T. (2002a). Inferences about G-study variance components in the absence of random sampling. *Journal of Educational Measurement, 39*(2), 165–181.

Kane, M. T. (2002b). Practice-based standard setting. *The Bar Examiner, 71*(3), 14–24.

Kane, M. T. (2002c). Validating high-stakes testing programs. *Educational Measurement: Issues and Practice, 21*(1), 31–41.

Kane, M. T., Crooks, T. J., & Cohen, A. S. (1999). Validating measures of performance. *Educational Measurement: Issues and Practice, 18*(2), 5–17.

Klein, S., McCaffrey, D., Stecher, B., & Koretz, D. (1995). The reliability of mathematics portfolio scores: Lessons from the Vermont experience. *Applied Measurement in Education, 6*(1), 83–102.

LaDuca, A. (1994). Validation of professional licensure examinations. *Evaluation and the Health Professions, 17*(2), 178–197.

Lakatos, I. (1970). Falsification and the methodology of scientific research programs. In I. Lakatos & A. Musgrave (Eds.), *Criticism and the growth of knowledge* (pp 91–196). London: Cambridge University Press.

Landy, F. J. (1986). Stamp collecting versus science: Validation as hypothesis testing. *American Psychologist, 41,* 1183–1192.

Lane, S. (2004). Validity of high-stakes assessment: Are students engaged in complex thinking? *Educational Measurement: Issues and Practice, 23*(3), 6–14.

Lane, S., Parke, C., & Stone, C. (1998). A framework for evaluating the consequences of assessment programs. *Educational Measurement: Issues and Practice, 17*(2), 24–28.

Lane, S., & Stone, C. (2002). Strategies for examining the consequences of assessment and accountability programs. *Educational Measurement: Issues and Practice, 21*(1), 23–30.

Linn, R. L. (1989). Current perspectives and future directions. In R. L. Linn (Ed.), *Educational measurement* (3rd ed., pp. 1–10). New York: American Council on Education and Macmillan.

Linn, R. L. (1993). Linking results in distinct assessments. *Applied Measurement in Education, 6*(1), 83–102.

Linn, R. L. (1997). Evaluating the validity of assessments: The consequences of use. *Educational Measurement: Issues and Practice, 16*(2), 14–16.

Linn, R. L. (1998). Partitioning responsibility for the evaluation of the consequences of assessment programs. *Educational Measurement: Issues and Practice, 17*(2), 28–30.

Linn, R. L. (2005, June 28). Conflicting demands of No Child Left Behind and state systems: Mixed messages about school performance. *Education Policy Analysis Archives, 13*(33). Retrieved June 28, 2005, from http://epaa.asu.edu/epaa/v13n33/

Linn, R., Kiplinger, V., Chapman, C., & LeMahieu, P. (1992). Cross-state comparability of judgments of student writing: Results from the New Standards Project. *Applied Measurement in Education, 5*(2), 89–110.

Loevinger, J. (1957). Objective tests as instruments of psychological theory. *Psychological Reports, Monograph Supplement, 3,* 635–694.

Lord, F. M., & Novick, M. R. (1968). *Statistical theories of mental test scores.* Reading, MA: Addison-Wesley.

Madaus, G. F. (1988). The influences of testing on the curriculum. In L. N. Tarner (Ed.), *Critical issues in curriculum* (pp. 83–121). *Eighty-seventh yearbook of the National Society for the Study of Education, Part I.* Chicago: University of Chicago Press.

McDonald, R. (1985). *Factor analysis and related methods.* Hillsdale, NJ: Lawrence Erlbaum.

McDonald, R. (1999). *Test theory.* Mahwah, NJ: Lawrence Erlbaum.

McNeil, L. (2005). Faking equity: High-stakes testing and the education of Latino youth. In A. Valenzuela (Ed.), *Leaving children behind: How "Texas-style" accountability fails Latino youth* (pp. 57–111). New York: State University of New York Press.

Meehl, P. (1950). On the circularity of the law of effect. *Psychological Bulletin, 47,* 52–75.

Mehrens, W. A. (1997). The consequences of consequential validity. *Educational Measurement: Issues and Practice, 16*(2), 16–18.

Messick, S. (1975). The standard problem: Meaning and values in measurement and evaluation. *American Psychologist, 30,* 955–966.

Messick, S. (1980). Test validity and the ethics of assessment. *American Psychologist, 35,* 1012–1027.

Messick, S. (1981). Evidence and ethics in the evaluation of tests. *Educational Researcher, 10,* 9–20.

Messick, S. (1988). The once and future issues of validity. Assessing the meaning and consequences of measurement. In H. Wainer & H. Braun (Eds.), *Test validity* (pp. 33–45). Hillsdale, NJ: Lawrence Erlbaum.

Messick, S. (1989). Validity. In R. L. Linn (Ed.), *Educational measurement* (3rd ed., pp. 13–103.). New York: American Council on Education and Macmillan.

Messick, S. (1994). The interplay of evidence and consequences in the validation of performance assessments. *Educational Researcher, 23,* 13–23.

Messick, S. (1995). Standards of validity and the validity of and standards in performance assessment. *Educational Measurement: Issues and Practice, 14*(4), 5–8.

Messick, S. (1998). Test validity: A matter of consequences. *Social Indicators Research, 45,* 35–44.

Mislevy, R. (1996). Test theory reconceived. *Journal of Educational Measurement, 33,* 379–416.

Mislevy, R., Steinberg, L., & Almond, R. (2003). On the structure of educational assessments. *Measurement: Interdisciplinary Research and Perspectives, 1,* 3–62.

Moss, P. (1992). Shifting conceptions of validity in educational measurement: Implications for performance assessment. *Review of Educational Research, 62,* 229–258.

Moss, P. A. (1994). Can there be validity without reliability? *Educational Researcher, 23,* 5–12.

Moss, P. A. (1998a). Recovering a dialectic view of rationality. *Social Indicators Research, 45,* 55–67.

Moss, P. A. (1998b). The role of consequences in validity theory. *Educational Measurement: Issues and Practice, 17*(2), 6–12.

Moss, P. (2003). Reconceptualizing validity for classroom assessment. *Educational Measurement: Issues and Practice, 22*(4), 13–25.

Moss, P. A., & Schutz, A. (2001). Educational standards, assessment, and the search for consensus. *American Educational Research Journal, 38*(1), 37–70.

Murphy, K. (2003). *Validity generalization: A critical review.* Mahwah, NJ: Lawrence Erlbaum.

No Child Left Behind Act of 2001, Pub. L. No. 107-110, 115 Stat. 1435 (2002).

Nystrand, M., Cohen, A., & Dowling, N. (1993). Addressing reliability problems in the portfolio assessment of college writing. *Educational Assessment, 1*(1), 53–70.

Pellegrino, J. W., Baxter, G. P., & Glaser, R. (1999). Addressing the "Two Disciplines" problem: Linking theories of cognition and learning with assessment and instructional practice. *Review of Research on Education, 24,* 307–353.

Pinto, R. (2001). *Argument, inference and dialectic.* Dordrecht, the Netherlands: Kluwer Academic.

Popham, W. J. (1997). Consequential validity: Right concern—wrong concept. *Educational Measurement: Issues and Practice, 16*(2), 9–13.

Popper, K. R. (1962). *Conjecture and refutation: The growth of scientific knowledge.* New York: Basic Books.

Porter, T. (2003). Measurement, objectivity, and trust. *Measurement: Interdisciplinary Research and Perspectives, 1,* 241–255.

Quine, W. (1953). Two dogmas of empiricism. In W. V. O. Quine (Ed.), *From a logical point of view* (pp. 20–46). New York: Harper and Row.

Raymond, M. (2001). Job analysis and the specification of content for licensure and certification examinations. *Applied Measurement in Education, 14,* 369–415.

Reckase, M. (1998). Consequential validity from the test developer's perspective. *Educational Measurement: Issues and Practice, 17*(2), 13–16.

Rulon, P. (1946). On the validity of educational tests. *Harvard Educational Review, 16*(4), 290–296.

Ryan, K. (2002). Assessment validation in the context of high-stakes testing assessment. *Educational Measurement: Issues and Practice, 21*(1), 7–15.

Sackett, P. R. (1998). Performance assessment in education and professional certification: Lessons for personnel selection? In M. D. Hakel (Ed.), *Beyond multiple choice: Evaluating alternatives for traditional testing for selection* (pp. 113–129). Mahwah, NJ: Lawrence Erlbaum.

Schmidt, F. L., & Hunter, J. E. (1977). Development of a general solution to the problem of validity generalization. *Journal of Applied Psychology, 62,* 529–540.

Scriven, M. (1987). Validity in personnel evaluation. *Journal of Personnel Evaluation in Education, 1,* 9–23.

Scriven, M. (1995). The logic of evaluation and evaluation practice. *New Directions in Evaluation: Reasoning in Evaluation: Inferential Links and Leaps, 68,* 49–70.

Shavelson, R. J., & Webb, N. M. (1991). *Generalizability theory: A primer.* Newbury Park, CA: Sage.

Shepard, L. A. (1993). Evaluating test validity. In L. Darling-Hammond (Ed.), *Review of research in education* (Vol. 19, pp. 405–450). Washington, DC: American Educational Research Association.

Shepard, L. A. (1997). The centrality of test use and consequences for test validity. *Educational Measurement: Issues and Practice, 16*(2), 5–8, 13, 24.

Shepard, L. (2001). The role of classroom assessment in teaching and learning. In V. Richardson (Ed.), *Handbook of research on teaching* (pp. 1066–1101). Washington, DC: American Educational Research Association.

Sireci, S., Scarpati, S., & Li, S. (2005). Test accommodations for students with disabilities: An analysis of the interaction hypothesis. *Review of Educational Research, 75,* 457–490.

Snow, R. E., & Lohman, D. E. (1989). Implications of cognitive psychology for educational measurement. In R. L. Linn (Ed.), *Educational measurement* (3rd ed., pp. 263–332). New York: American Council on Education and Macmillan.

Spearman, C. (1927). *The abilities of man: Their nature and measurement.* New York: Macmillan.

Sternberg, R. J. (1979). The nature of mental abilities. *American Psychologist, 43*(3), 214–230.

Stiggins, R. J. (2005). *Student-involved assessment for learning* (4th ed.). Upper Saddle River, NJ: Pearson/Merrill Prentice Hall.

Suppe, P. (1977). *The structure of scientific theories.* Urbana: University of Illinois Press.

Taleporos, E. (1998). Consequential validity: A practitioner's perspective. *Educational Measurement: Issues and Practice, 17*(2), 20–23, 34.

Tatsuoka, K. K. (1990). Toward an integration of item-response theory and cognitive error diagnosis. In N. Frederiksen, R. L. Glaser, A. M. Lesgold, & M. G. Shafto (Eds.), *Diagnostic monitoring of skill and knowledge acquisition* (pp. 453–488). Hillsdale, NJ: Lawrence Erlbaum.

Tenopyr, M. L. (1977). Content-construct confusion. *Personnel Psychology, 30,* 47–54.

Tittle, C. (1989). Validity: Whose construction is it in the teaching and learning context? *Educational Measurement: Issues and Practice, 8*(1), 5–19, 34.

Toulmin, S. (1953). *The philosophy of science.* London: Hutchinson's Universal Library.

Toulmin, S. (1958). *The uses of argument.* Cambridge: Cambridge University Press.

Toulmin, S. (2001). *Return to reason.* Cambridge, MA: Harvard University Press.

van der Linden, W. (1998). A decision theory model for course placement. *Journal of Educational and Behavioral Statistics, 23*(1), 18–34.

Walton, D. (1989). *Informal logic: A handbook for critical argumentation.* Cambridge: Cambridge University Press.

3
Reliability

Edward H. Haertel
Stanford University

1. INTRODUCTION

The concern of reliability is to quantify the precision of test scores and other measurements. This chapter discusses definitions of error in test scores, the design of data collections to quantify error and precision, and appropriate statistics to characterize score accuracy. Like test validity, test score reliability must be conceived relative to particular testing purposes and contexts. The definition, quantification, and reporting of reliability must each begin with considerations of intended test uses and interpretations. However, whereas validity is centrally concerned with the nature of the attributes tests measure, reliability is concerned solely with how the scores resulting from a measurement procedure would be expected to vary across replications of that procedure. Thus, reliability is conceived in more narrowly statistical terms than is validity. Several important statistical frameworks have been developed for analyzing the reliability of test scores, notably classical test theory and generalizability theory. It is also possible to develop ideas of reliability in the context of item response theory, but accuracy and precision in item response theory are left largely to the chapter devoted to that topic, by Yen and Fitzpatrick (this volume). Throughout, this chapter draws upon the reliability chapters in earlier editions by Thorndike (1951), Stanley (1971), and especially the excellent exposition by Feldt and Brennan (1989).

Reliability theory begins with the idea that an examinee's observed score on a test is the realization of a random variable—A draw from some distribution of possible scores that might have been obtained for that examinee using parallel forms of the test, giving the test on different occasions, perhaps having the test paper scored by different raters, and so forth. Any of these possible scores would have served the purpose of the measurement equally well, but they would not all be identical. Taken together, this hypothetical collection of scores represents the general, enduring attribute of interest. Thus, it is important to determine the extent to which any single result of the measurement procedure is likely to depart from the average score over many replications. Other things being equal, the greater the uncertainty associated with the results of a measurement, the less confidence should be placed in that measurement. Physical measurements, of weight for example, may be regarded in the same way. If a block of wood is weighed repeatedly, the weights obtained will vary slightly from one weighing to another. If that variation is small, then one can be highly confident of the result. Likewise, if an examinee were tested repeatedly, the resulting scores would vary. In testing, however, it is generally not possible to carry out the measurement operation again and again with the same individuals, because their performance would change in response to the testing itself. Thus, the distribution of potential scores may be hypothetical, and its properties (e.g., its standard deviation) must often be estimated indirectly.

Both classical test theory and generalizability theory offer data collection designs and statistical models to estimate the standard deviation of that hypothetical distribution, referred to as the *standard error of measurement*. The standard error of measurement is a number expressed in the same units as the corresponding test score and indicates the accuracy with which a single score approximates the expected value of possible scores for the same examinee. The models treated throughout most of this chapter provide a single numerical estimate of the standard error of measurement, which is taken to be applicable to all examinees' scores in a given population. More complex models yielding *conditional* standard errors of measurement are treated in sections 2.6.2 and 3.9. If derived score scales (e.g., percentile ranks) are constructed, standard errors for those derived scores may be estimated as well but will not be the same as for the original scores. Additional questions about score accuracy arise when scores are transformed to improve comparability across different tests or test forms. The accuracy of test linking or equating is addressed in the chapter on linking and equating by Holland and Dorans (this volume). The reliability of ratings is taken up both in this chapter and in the chapter on performance assessment by Lane and Stone (this volume).

In addition to a standard error of measurement, test score precision is traditionally expressed using a *reliability coefficient*. A reliability coefficient is defined not for a single score, but test scores obtained for a sample from some examinee population. It is a statistic ranging from zero to one, which may be interpreted as the expected correlation between two (actual or hypothetical) replications of a measurement procedure, as the proportion of variance in a set of observed test scores that is replicable or "true-score" variance, or as the expected value of the squared correlation between true and observed scores. Additional statistics expressing score accuracy are introduced later in this chapter.

The set of potential replications may be defined in many ways, and the definition generally determines which of many possible reliability coefficients, standard errors, or other statistics should be employed (Brennan, 2001a). In all cases, however, the consideration of reliability begins with (actual or hypothetical) replications of measurements of the same quality, measured in the same way.[1] Test users are also concerned with the degree to which test scores are predictive of performance on other tests or in nontest settings, but the relation of test scores to measurements of other qualities, or even to alternative measurements of the same quality, is in the domain of test validity, not reliability, addressed in the chapter on validity by Kane (this volume). The correlation between scores on two alternative forms of the same reading test provides an estimate of the test's reliability, because the two forms may be regarded as replications of the same measurement procedure. The correlation between scores obtained using the same form of the reading test, administered twice to the same examinees, would provide an estimate of a different reliability coefficient, referenced to a different set of possible replications. However, the correlation between scores on two different reading tests, say tests produced by different publishers, would generally not be interpreted as a reliability coefficient, even though such a correlation would be influenced by the separate reliabilities of each of the two tests. Two different tests of the same construct are not generally regarded as replications of the same measurement procedure.

As with a standard error of measurement, a coefficient of reliability depends on the definition of some set of possible replications. Different definitions will give rise to different reliabilities as well as different standard errors. Reliability coefficients and standard errors of measurement also depend upon the population of examinees sampled. If a test is administered to a group more homogeneous with respect to the ability the test measures, a reliability coefficient will likely become smaller. Regarding a reliability coefficient as the correlation between measurement replications or as the squared correlation between true score and observed score, the coefficient obtained with a more homogeneous group is reduced due to restriction of range. Regarding that coefficient as the proportion of score variance attributable to stable examinee characteristics, when that stable variation is reduced, the proportion of stable variation relative to stable plus error variation is smaller. Standard errors of measurement also vary as a function of the group tested because, as discussed in sections 2.6.2 and 3.9, most tests provide more accurate measurements in some regions of the score scale than in other regions.

The terms "reliability" and even "accuracy" or "precision" are used here in ways that differ somewhat from everyday usage. One might expect these terms to connote the correspondence between a test score and the true value of some quality the test is intended to measure. Thus, if a certain examinee typically rushed through tests and made many careless errors, the obtained scores might be regarded as inaccurate because they gave too low an indication of that examinee's ability. Such carelessness might be a threat to the validity of inferences from the scores for that examinee but would receive no explicit consideration in an analysis of score reliability. In general, reliability is concerned only with the replicability of measurements, not with the constellation of attributes those measurements reflect. If habitual patterns of carelessness, motivation, speed of work, or test wiseness systematically influence an examinee's scores across replications of a measurement procedure, that is largely an issue of test score validity, not reliability.

The theories of reliability reviewed in this chapter are applicable to a broad range of measurement problems, throughout the social sciences and beyond. The accuracy of ratings of student presentations and annual test score averages for schools are amenable to much the same statistical analysis as number-correct scores on objective examinations. The same models pertain to measurements of the hardness of drinking water, the speed of a car, or the attendance at a parade. Other objects of measurement could be substituted for "examinees" and other kinds of measurements for "test scores." At the same time, there are important distinctions among these different cases, and the routine application of familiar formulas and procedures to different problems may lead to serious mistakes and misunderstandings. As discussed in section 3.6, for example, the accuracy of an average score for a school depends not only on the precision of the separate test scores entering into that average, but also on the variance of those separate test scores.

In addition to cases where the object of measurement is defined at some level of aggregation beyond the individual (e.g., score averages for schools), several other special cases are treated in this chapter. Section 4 addresses the reliability of ratings of examinee performance, as well as the accuracy of classifications created by comparing scores to cutpoints defining categories like pass and fail, or standards-based classifications like "proficient." In these cases, the probabilities of misclassification (of placing examinees in the wrong category) may be more informative than standard errors or reliability coefficients. Standards-based characterizations of schools or districts, like "percent proficient," also call for the use of different models and statistics than do summaries of continuous scores. Another special case, treated in section 5, pertains to the accuracy of behavioral observations. If the measurement procedure is to count instances of some classroom event, for example, somewhat different models are required, and the duration of the observation becomes a critical concern (Rogosa & Ghandour, 1991).

1.1. Criterion-Referenced and Norm-Referenced Interpretations and Decisions

Test score interpretations may be roughly divided into *norm-referenced* (or *relative*) versus *criterion-referenced* (or *absolute*). Norm-referenced interpretations locate an individual examinee's score relative to the distribution of scores for some relevant comparison group. Criterion-referenced interpretations characterize an examinee on the basis of a test performance without reference to the performance of other individuals. In theory, the interpretation is determined by the absolute level of the examinee's score, without reference to the performance of anyone else. The standard error of measurement is relevant to any interpretation of continuous scores for individuals, whether norm-referenced or criterion-referenced. If percentile ranks are reported, for example, it is of interest to know how much an individual's percentile rank might be expected to change upon retesting. If reading speed (words per minute) is estimated, it is again of interest to know how much the estimate might vary upon retesting. One currently popular form of criterion-referenced score interpretation is standards-based. If an examinee is classified into one of a series of performance levels, it may be useful to derive probabilities of misclassification from standard errors.

As noted, the standard error is expressed in the same metric as the corresponding score. That facilitates interpretation of individual scores but complicates the comparison of standard errors for different tests. The reliability coefficient is a dimensionless number, which may be compared across tests for a given population of examinees. For that reason, it provides useful information when choosing among alternative tests for a given purpose, and in test design. Also, because it indicates the consistency with which a test would be expected to rank-order examinees, the reliability coefficient is relevant when tests are used for selection; it shows to what extent individuals' rankings would be expected to change upon retesting. Reliability coefficients are also useful when interpreting correlations involving test scores and other variables, because they indicate the degree to which such correlations are affected by random error inherent in the measurement procedure (see section 2.6.4). Finally, reliability coefficients are often calculated as an intermediate step in the estimation of the standard error of measurement. It should be emphasized, however, that reliability coefficients are much less useful for describing the accuracy of an individual examinee's score. As noted in the *Standards for Educational and Psychological Testing* (American Educational Research Association, American Psychological Association, & National Council on Measurement in Education [AERA, APA, & NCME], 1999, p. 29) "the standard error of measurement is generally more relevant than the reliability coefficient once a measurement procedure has been adopted and interpretation of scores has become the user's primary concern." Measurement textbooks over the years have presented various rules of thumb for the interpretation of reliability coefficients, specifying minimum acceptable levels of reliability for different kinds of test use. It might be stated, for example, that tests with a reliability of less than .70 should not be used for individual student evaluations. All such rules are arbitrary. Despite their wide use and apparent interpretability, reliability coefficients are less informative than commonly believed. Many test users would be surprised to learn, for example, that for an idealized test with a reliability of .90, an examinee whose true score was at the 50th percentile would have only a 58% chance of obtaining an observed score between the 40th and 60th percentiles, inclusive (Rogosa, 1999).

It bears repeating that in describing score accuracy, the statistics used and the ways they are interpreted must be suitable to the context and purpose of the measurement. Kane (1996) notes that tolerance for error, a specification of how large errors must be before they interfere with the intended use of the measurement, varies from one testing application to another. Kane considers "error tolerance ratios" and "signal-to-noise ratios" and illustrates how these statistics may be defined in particular applications. These and other alternatives to the standard error of measurement and the coefficient of reliability are discussed at points throughout this chapter, but especially in section 4, concerning the reliability of classifications.

The remainder of this chapter is divided into four broad sections, concerned with Classical Test Theory (section 2), Generalizability Theory (section 3), the reliability of classifications (section 4), and the reliability of behavioral observations (section 5). A brief concluding section follows.

2. CLASSICAL TEST THEORY

Classical test theory refers to a body of statistical models for test data developed over the past century. It has its roots in the study of individual differences, and patterns of correlation among different measures in biological populations. Thus, classical test theory has traditionally been associated more closely with norm-referenced than with criterion-referenced measurement. The first comprehensive work in the field was *The Essentials of Mental Measurement*, by William Brown and Godfrey H. Thomson (1921), based on an earlier edition by W. Brown (1911). In the United States, a small book produced by L. L. Thurstone (1932), *The Reliability and Validity of Tests*, was highly influential. One of Thurstone's students, Harold Gulliksen, systematized and extended Thurstone's book and added some more specialized material. His *Theory of Mental Tests* (Gulliksen, 1950) was a standard work in the field. Today, the most comprehensive treatment of classical test theory remains *Statistical Theories of Mental Test Scores*, by Lord and Novick (1968). Lord and Novick produced a more rigorously statistical treatment than had been available up to that time and considered a variety of more specialized models and topics, including higher-order moments of score distributions.

Beginning in the 1970s, classical test theory was recast as an important special case of generalizability theory, but the terminology and the statistical results of classical test theory are still widely used. More recent refinements have extended but rarely contradicted the results of the earlier theory. Thus, classical test theory remains an important area of study, both in its own right and as the source of important concepts and methods that have been further developed in more contemporary models.

The most basic formulation of classical test theory derives surprisingly powerful results from very few assumptions. With additional assumptions, stronger results are obtained. Classical theory begins with the assumption that an observed score on a test may be modeled as the sum of two components: the examinee's "true score" and some residual error specific to the particular test score. The true score is often defined as the expected value of the observed score, the expectation being taken over hypothetical repeated testings of the same person. That does not mean, however, that the definition of the true score depends upon some impossible operational procedure. The true score is just a mathematical abstraction. As will be seen, the concept of the true score as a parameter characterizing each examinee is highly useful, even though no examinee's true score can ever be known precisely.

Roughly speaking, the true score reflects systematic influences on test performance—individual examinee characteristics that are stable across repeated testings—and error reflects random, temporary, unstable characteristics. However, there is substantial ambiguity in how the true score is defined. For some purposes, the true score might be the long-run average performance expected on a single form of a test. For other purposes, the true score might be taken as the long-run average performance expected over all possible forms. It must be assumed that an examinee's true score does not vary over some given set of possible measurements—by definition, such variation would be classified as error—but human performance changes over time in response to a multitude of random and systematic influences. For some purposes, the true score might be the expected value of test scores obtained over a period of months or even longer. At the other extreme, the true score might be assumed to change in a matter of hours or even less time. Classical theory does not provide any notational system with which to formalize these alternatives. For that reason, it is important in applying the theory to attend carefully to often implicit choices that in effect define true score versus error, so as to assure that the treatment of different sources of variation as true score versus error is appropriate to the testing situation at hand.

Error, the residual defined by the difference between a person's true score and an observed score for that person, is likewise an abstraction. If it were possible to determine the exact amount of error in any observed score, then the true score could be determined, as well. Even though classical test theory does not provide any formal notation to define or distinguish different sources of error, attention to sources of error is essential if the theory is to be used intelligently. In earlier editions, Thorndike (1951, p. 568) provided a table distinguishing categories of lasting or temporary, general or specific characteristics of the individual; factors affecting test administration; and chance factors not otherwise accounted for. Stanley (1971, p. 364) offered a slight elaboration of the same categories. Feldt and Brennan (1989, p. 107) emphasized that the definition of error is to some extent relative to the context and intended interpretation of a measurement, and briefly discussed the four categories of (1) inherent variability in human performance, (2) variations in the environment within which measurements are obtained, (3) variation introduced by the processes of evaluating responses, and (4) error arising from the selection of test questions asked or the behavioral sample observed. If empirical estimates of reliability or error variance are to reflect the influence of any given source of error, the data collection must be designed to sample across levels of that source. For example, day-to-day variation in performance cannot be estimated from the results of testing completed in a single afternoon.

2.1. Notation

Some common notational conventions will be followed throughout this section. Greek letters will be used for population parameters, including μ, σ^2, and ρ for the mean, variance, and product-moment correlation, respectively. Subscripts will be added as necessary to indicate the variables referred to. The Greek letter σ with two subscripts will be used to denote a covariance, as with σ_{XY} for the covariance of test scores X and Y. Estimates of these quantities will be denoted with a hat (^). Frequency distributions are denoted by a capital F, as in $F(X)$. Typically, n will denote the number of items on a test or the number of parts into which a test is divided. N will be used for the number of examinees tested. The symbol E denotes the expectation operator. For example, $E_p X_p$ denotes the expected value over p of X_p.

The observed score for examinee or person p on form f of test X will be denoted X_{pf}. Uppercase letters with a single subscript may refer to a score for a particular person (e.g., X_p) or the set of scores obtained using a particular test form (e.g., X_f). Uppercase letters will be used for both the variable and for a particular realization of the variable, with the exception that an individual examinee's true score will be denoted τ_p. Where X is decomposed into true-score and error components, these will be designated T and E, respectively. Where it is necessary to refer to the value of some statistic for a subgroup or subpopulation, a designation of the intended subgroup will be appended to the subscript, following a period. For example, the conditional mean of the observed score X given some particular true score τ_p would be denoted $\mu_{X.\tau_p}$. A coefficient of reliability for test X (to be defined subsequently) will be denoted $\rho_{XX'}$. This may be thought of as a correlation between X and a strictly parallel form X'. When it is necessary to distinguish among alternative reliability coefficients, an additional subscript will be appended at the left, as with $_a\rho_{XX'}$ for the coefficient alpha reliability (Cronbach, 1951).

2.2. Definition of Classical Test Theory

Classical test theory begins with little more than the idea that an obtained test score represents a sample from some larger set of scores that might have been obtained instead. Following Feldt and Brennan (1989), the theory may be defined by the following assumptions.[2]

The observed score X_{pf}, obtained when person p is administered form f of test X, is the sum of a true-score component and an error component. Each person p has a true score, τ_p, that is assumed to remain constant over test forms. (Note that in Equation 1, τ does not carry a subscript for test form.) Variation in observed scores across forms is due to form-specific error. In symbols,

$$X_{pf} = \tau_p + E_{pf}. \qquad (1)$$

Form f is one of a set of (actual or hypothetical) *strictly parallel forms*. Strictly parallel forms $f, g, h, \ldots$ are defined by four properties. They have identical test specifications, yield identical observed-score distributions when administered to any (indefinitely large) population of examinees,[3] covary equally with one another, and covary equally with any other measure Z, whether Z is a measure of the same or a different construct. In symbols,

$$F(X_f) = F(X_g) = F(X_h) = \ldots$$
$$\sigma_{X_f X_g} = \sigma_{X_f X_h} = \sigma_{X_g X_h} = \ldots \quad (2)$$
$$\sigma_{X_f Z} = \sigma_{X_g Z} = \sigma_{X_h Z} = \ldots$$

If an examinee could be tested repeatedly, using a different test form each time and assuming that each test administration was unaffected by previous administrations (i.e., with "perfect forgetting" following each test administration), then the average of the resulting errors of measurement would approach zero as the number of test administrations approached infinity. In symbols,

$$E_f E_{pf} = 0, \quad (3)$$

where E_f denotes the expectation taken over forms.

If a group of examinees were tested using any given form f of the test, the average of the resulting errors would approach zero as the size of the group tested approached infinity, unless the group were chosen on the basis of their scores on form f. In symbols,

$$E_p E_{pf} = 0, \quad (4)$$

where E_p denotes the expectation taken over persons.

From these assumptions, it follows that the covariance of true scores and errors is zero for any test form, and that the covariance of errors on any two different forms is also zero. In symbols,

$$\sigma_{TE_f} = 0$$
$$\sigma_{E_f E_g} = 0. \quad (5)$$

It should be emphasized that this linear independence of true score and error, and between errors on different test forms, is not itself an assumption of the theory, but rather a mathematical consequence of the definitions and assumptions preceding. It should also be noted that $\sigma_{E_f X_f} > 0$. Both true score and error are components of the observed score; both are correlated with the observed score. Some implications of this fact are discussed in section 2.6.1.

The fact that true score and error are uncorrelated is sufficient to establish the key result that the variance of observed scores on any form is equal to the sum of the true-score variance and the error variance,

$$\sigma_{X_f}^2 = \sigma_T^2 + \sigma_{E_f}^2. \quad (6)$$

From Equations 1, 2, 5, and 6, it follows that the covariance between parallel forms is equal to the true-score variance. In symbols, $\sigma_{X_f X_g} = \sigma_T^2$. Thus, the correlation between hypothetical strictly-parallel forms is equal to the ratio of the true-score variance to the observed-score variance on either form:

$$\rho_{X_f X_g} = \frac{\sigma_{X_f X_g}}{\sigma_{X_f} \sigma_{X_g}} = \frac{\sigma_T^2}{\sigma_X^2} = \frac{\sigma_T^2}{\sigma_T^2 + \sigma_E^2}. \quad (7)$$

Equation 7 defines the reliability coefficient, denoted $\rho_{XX'}$. (The notation represents the correlation of X with a hypothetical parallel form, X'.) Note that $\rho_{XX'}/(1-\rho_{XX'}) = \sigma_T^2/\sigma_E^2$. This ratio is defined as the *signal-to-noise ratio*, mentioned in section 2.5.4.

The reliability coefficient is also the square of the correlation between the true score and observed score. From Equations 1, 5, and 6, $\sigma_{XT} = \sigma_{(T+E)T} = \sigma_T^2 + \sigma_{TE} = \sigma_T^2$. Thus,

$$\rho_{XT}^2 = \frac{(\sigma_{XT})^2}{\sigma_X^2 \sigma_T^2} = \frac{(\sigma_T^2)^2}{\sigma_X^2 \sigma_T^2} = \frac{\sigma_T^2}{\sigma_X^2} = \rho_{XX'} \quad (8)$$

The definition of strictly parallel forms in Equation 2 avoids the assertion that the expected value of the error is zero when a particular individual responds to a particular test form. Thus, it allows for the (realistic) possibility that an individual will find one or another test form easier or more difficult, perhaps due to specific knowledge relevant to some items on a given form. Note that the true score is defined as an expected value across infinitely many forms, leaving unaddressed the matter of repeated testing of the same individual with the same form. Lord and Novick (1968, p. 48) develop a slightly stronger definition of strictly parallel tests, adding the requirement that the conditions set forth in Equation 2 hold for every subpopulation of the population for which the test is to be used. This requirement implies that for any given examinee, both error variances and expected values of observed scores are constant across strictly parallel measurements.

The assumptions presented thus far also avoid any assertion that if two individuals were each tested repeatedly using parallel forms, the variability across forms of the first individual's scores would be equal to that for the second individual. Both theory and empirical evidence suggest that form-to-form variation in number-correct scores is less for individuals with very high or very low true scores than for those nearer the center of the distribution. In symbols, $\sigma_{E.\tau_p}^2$ varies.[4] The square root of $\sigma_{E.\tau_p}^2$ is the *conditional standard error of measurement* for persons with true score τ_p. It is also useful to define an (unconditional) standard error of measurement for the entire group tested. To obtain this value, the *error variance for the test* is defined as the expected value of the individual error variances, and the standard error of measurement is defined as the square root of the error variance for the test. In symbols, $\sigma_E^2 = E_p \sigma_{E.\tau_p}^2$ and $\sigma_E = \sqrt{\sigma_E^2}$.

It is implicit in this definition that the standard error of measurement can only be defined relative to some true-score distribution. If the expectation of $\sigma_{E.\tau}^2$ were taken over a different population of persons, the result would not, in general, be the same.[5] Thus, "unconditional" standard error is somewhat of a misnomer but is adopted here following general usage. The unconditional standard error of measurement, the reliability, and the observed-score variance are related such that each of these quantities can be expressed in terms of the other two:

$$\sigma_E = \sqrt{\sigma_X^2(1-\rho_{XX'})}$$
$$\rho_{XX'} = 1 - \sigma_E^2/\sigma_X^2 \qquad (9)$$
$$\sigma_X^2 = \sigma_E^2/(1-\rho_{XX'}).$$

2.3. Parallel Forms and Test-Retest Estimates of the Reliability Coefficient

Consider two testing scenarios. In the first, two parallel test forms are administered to a large group of examinees in close succession, on the same day. In the second scenario, the same two parallel forms are administered, several days apart, to another large group of examinees, equivalent to the first. Assuming that under each scenario the second test administration is not influenced by the first, the observed-score variances for the two forms under the two scenarios should all be the same. However, it would typically be found that the correlation between the two forms given on the same day was higher than the correlation between the same two forms given several days apart. Which correlation would better serve as an estimate of the forms' reliability?

The lower correlation between test forms administered several days apart reflects day-to-day variation in examinee performance. If test scores are interpreted as indicators of some enduring examinee characteristic, then such day-to-day variation is appropriately regarded as a source of error. Reliability estimates should reflect the influences of all relevant sources of error; thus, the second, lower correlation would generally be preferred. Note that the choice of testing scenario implies a definition of true score as well as of error. Under the first scenario, the error variance is smaller, and so the true-score variance must be larger. On any given day, an examinee's performance will deviate above or below his or her long-run expected performance. If the true score is defined as the expected value of hypothetical repeated measurements on a single day, then those deviations become part of the definition of the true score.

The first scenario just described might well be impractical, as it would require a double-length test administration on a single day. The second, preferred scenario may be practicable. When two interchangeable test forms are available and are given to the same group of examinees with a suitable time interval between administrations, the observed correlation between scores on those two occasions is a *parallel forms* estimate of reliability, sometimes referred to as a coefficient of *stability and equivalence*. It is generally regarded as the ideal reliability estimate because it reflects the uncertainty in scores arising from examinees' idiosyncratic reactions to different test forms (lack of equivalence between forms), lack of stability over time, and random error (Schmidt, Le, & Ilies, 2003). Note that, with different time intervals, different parallel-forms reliabilities may be obtained. Thus, when reporting a parallel-forms reliability, the interval between test administrations should also be reported (AERA, APA, & NCME, 1999, p. 32). The interval chosen should be long enough to allow for the influence of transient fluctuations in test performance, but not so long as to allow for significant influences from learning or maturation. It would not be appropriate, for example, to interpret the correlation between pretest and posttest scores with intervening instruction as a parallel-forms reliability estimate.

In some cases, it may be appropriate to estimate reliability by repeated administration of the same test form. (If only one form of the test exists, there may be no alternative.) The correlation between repeated testings is then referred to as a *test-retest* estimate of reliability, or sometimes as a coefficient of *stability*. There are two reasons why the test-retest reliability estimate may be less satisfactory than a parallel-forms reliability. First, performance on the second testing is more likely to be influenced by examinees' memories of the first test administration if they are given the identical items. If examinees recognize test items, they may infer that their consistency is being assessed and attempt to respond as they did before, inducing a false consistency. Second, as noted earlier, individual examinees may find particular test forms easier or harder due to their familiarity with the content of specific test questions, for example. With the test-retest reliability, any stable person-by-form interactions are effectively defined as part of the true score instead of as part of the error.

Even if only one form of a test is available, it may be possible to realize the advantages of the parallel-forms reliability estimate using the *staggered equivalent split-half procedure* (Becker, 2000). Under this procedure, a single test form is divided into two half-length tests constructed to be as nearly parallel as possible, and the two half tests are administered a few days or weeks apart, to the same group of examinees. The correlation obtained between the two half tests is not itself a parallel-forms reliability estimate for the original test, but instead for a half-length test. However, it can readily be used to construct a reliability estimate for the original test, as explained by Becker (2000) and as discussed in section 2.4.2 below. Note, however, that the staggered equivalent split-half procedure implicitly assumes that examinee performance on each half-test is unaffected by its administration separately from the remaining half. If the full-length test is fatiguing, for example, or if time limits for the half-tests versus the full-length test are not adjusted properly, this assumption would not be expected to hold. Alternatively, the same intact test form may be administered on two occasions, as for the test-retest reliability estimate, but a reliability estimate may instead be derived from the covariances between different items administered on different occasions (Green, 2003). This procedure correctly treats any stable person-by-form interaction as part of the error but may not be appropriate if test items are particularly memorable. Covariances among different items administered on the same occasion and covariances between administrations of the same item on different occasions can also be examined to estimate different sources of error (Vautier & Jmel, 2003).

In practice, even if alternate forms of a test are carefully designed to the same test specifications, they may have different means and variances. Differences in means are generally unimportant in reliability estimation, but Equation 6 implies that if $\sigma_{X_f}^2 \neq \sigma_{X_g}^2$, then either $\sigma_{T_f}^2 \neq \sigma_{T_g}^2$ or $\sigma_{E_f}^2 \neq \sigma_{E_g}^2$ or both. Under the assumption that $\sigma_{T_f}^2 = \sigma_{T_g}^2$, it follows from Equation 7 that

$$\rho_{X_f X_f'} = \frac{\sigma_{X_f X_g}}{\sigma_{X_f}^2} \text{ and } \rho_{X_g X_g'} = \frac{\sigma_{X_f X_g}}{\sigma_{X_g}^2}. \quad (10)$$

2.4. Internal Consistency Estimates of the Reliability Coefficient

Parallel-forms reliability estimates may be ideal but are often difficult to obtain. Even if parallel forms are available, there may be resistance to the burden of repeated testing, especially in school settings. Thus, there has been an abiding interest in methods for estimating reliability from a single administration of a single test form. Clearly, all such estimates must treat occasion-specific deviations from examinees' long-run performance as part of their true scores. Although there are some practical situations where this is intended, it is rarely ideal. As Feldt and Brennan (1989, p. 110) observe, "When behavioral observations are gathered in an hour or less, certain sources of error 'stand still' for each examinee … [and] are not reflected in the estimate of test error variance. Artful manipulation of the data from a single testing occasion cannot alter this basic fact." The wide use of internal-consistency reliability estimates and the extensive literature on the topic should not obscure the fact that these coefficients may substantially overestimate reliability, especially where day-to-day variation in performance is substantial, as with some affective traits (Schmidt et al., 2003). Because internal consistency reliability coefficients are estimates of variation in performance across randomly parallel forms on a single occasion but cannot indicate variability over time, they are sometimes referred to as coefficients of *equivalence*.

Estimates of reliability obtained using data from a single form on a single occasion all involve dividing the test into two or more constituent parts and in some way estimating reliability from the consistency of performance across these part-tests. For example, the even-numbered versus odd-numbered items on a test might be scored as two separate subtests for purposes of reliability estimation. In other applications, the separate parts might be individual test items, sets of items pertaining to a single reading passage, or different subject area subtests contributing to a composite score for an achievement test battery. All such reliability estimates are referred to as *internal-consistency* estimates of reliability.

The problem of estimating test score reliability from a single administration of a single test form was taken up early in the last century by Spearman (1910) and by W. Brown (1910), who independently arrived at the solution bearing both of their names. The Spearman-Brown procedure requires that a test be divided into two or more parts that largely satisfy the classical test theory assumptions defining strictly parallel tests. Alternative internal-consistency estimation procedures developed more recently require less stringent assumptions. These alternative procedures may be categorized according to the assumptions they require concerning the parallelism of part tests.

2.4.1. Degrees of Part-Test Similarity

Even though the definitions of degrees of parallelism are sometimes applied to the constituent parts of a single test, they are defined in terms of specifications for alternate test forms. As presented earlier, the four assumptions defining strictly parallel tests are identical test specifications, identical observed-score distributions, equal covariances among all such forms, and equal covariances with any other measure. In practice these requirements may never hold exactly, but they are sometimes well approximated by actual test forms and so serve as a realistic and useful model. In many other cases, weaker forms of parallelism may provide better models, again to be approximated by actual test data.

The first such model is referred to as *tau (or τ) equivalence* (Lord & Novick, 1968, p. 50). Under the model of τ-equivalence, each person p is still assumed to have a true score, τ_p, that remains constant over test forms. However, two τ-equivalent test forms f and g do not necessarily measure with equal accuracy. True-score variances are necessarily the same for the two forms, but the error variance may be larger for one form than the other. To illustrate one way that τ-equivalent measures might arise in practice, consider two forms of a test differing only in length, for which scores are expressed in the metric of proportion-correct. For a set of such test forms, only the last two of the four assumptions defining strictly parallel forms, namely equal covariance among all such forms and equal covariances with any other measure, would hold. Observed-score distributions for τ-equivalent forms have the same expected means, but possibly unequal expected variances.

Closely related to τ-equivalence is *essential τ-equivalence* (Lord & Novick, 1968, p. 50). For any two essentially τ-equivalent forms f and g, there is an additive constant C_{fg} such that for every person p, $\tau_{pf} = \tau_{pg} + C_{fg}$.[6] Because covariances are unaffected by the addition of a constant to a variable, essentially τ-equivalent forms have equal covariances with one another and have equal covariances with any other measure. Observed-score distributions for essentially τ-equivalent forms have possibly unequal expected means as well as possibly unequal expected variances.

Congeneric forms (a term introduced by Jöreskog, 1971) are defined by a still weaker form of parallelism, dropping the requirement of equal true-score variances. For any two congeneric forms f and g, there is an additive constant C_{fg} and a positive constant b_{fg} such that for every person p, $\tau_{pf} = b_{fg}\tau_{pg} + C_{fg}$.[7] In other words, true scores on congeneric forms are linearly related, but with possibly unequal means and variances. It follows from this definition that $\rho_{T_f T_g}=1$. Neither true-score variances nor error variances on congeneric test forms need be equal.

Note that τ-equivalent forms also satisfy the assumptions of essential τ-equivalence, and that τ-equivalent and essentially τ-equivalent forms are also congeneric. These differing degrees of parallelism do not exhaust the set of different assumptions under which various internal-consistency reliability estimates are derived. Several of the coefficients described below are derived under the assumption that test parts are congeneric but subject to some additional constraint. Other internal consistency estimation methods may relax the definition of parallelism still further, not even requiring that $\rho_{\tau_f \tau_g} = 1$.

2.4.2. Reliability Estimates Based on Division of a Test Into Two Parts

The first internal consistency reliability estimate, derived by Spearman (1910) and by W. Brown (1910) is based on what has come to be known as the Spearman-Brown formula. If a test is divided into two strictly parallel subparts X_1 and X_2 with $X_1 + X_2 = X$,

$$_{SB}\rho_{XX'} = \frac{2\rho_{X_1 X_2}}{1 + \rho_{X_1 X_2}}. \tag{11}$$

Derivation of the Spearman-Brown formula requires the assumptions that true-score variances for X_1 and X_2 are equal, and that error variances for X_1 and X_2 are equal. It does not require the assumption of equal true-score means for the two test forms. In general, if these assumptions are violated, Equation 11 still gives a good approximation to the true reliability. If X_1 and X_2 are essentially τ-equivalent with different error variances, the reliability will be overestimated. If X_1 and X_2 are congeneric, Equation 11 may give either an overestimate or an underestimate of the true reliability.

Several equivalent formulas have appeared for the *split-half* reliability estimate, which may be derived from the weaker assumptions of essential τ-equivalence. If true-score variances for X_1 and X_2 are equal, then $\sigma_{X_1 X_2} = \sigma_{T_1}^2 = \sigma_{T_2}^2$ and, because the true score for $X = X_1 + X_2$ is twice the true score for either part, $\sigma_T^2 = 4\sigma_{T_1}^2 = 4\sigma_{X_1 X_2}$. This relation is exploited in a formula attributed to John C. Flanagan by Rulon (1939),

$$_F\rho_{XX'} = \frac{4\sigma_{X_1 X_2}}{\sigma_X^2}. \tag{12}$$

Equivalent versions are provided by Rulon (1939) and Guttman (1945, p. 275, Equation 53):

$$_{SH}\rho_{XX'} = 2\left(1 - \frac{\sigma_{X_1}^2 + \sigma_{X_2}^2}{\sigma_X^2}\right) = 1 - \frac{\sigma_{X_1 - X_2}^2}{\sigma_X^2}. \tag{13}$$

The Flanagan and Guttman-Rulon split-half coefficients are algebraically equivalent. For strictly parallel tests, they yield the same population value as Equation 11, although sample values may differ. If $\hat{\sigma}_{X_1}^2 = \hat{\sigma}_{X_2}^2$, Equations 11 and 13 will yield the same numerical value. Otherwise, Equation 11 will yield a higher numerical value than Equations 12 and 13, although the difference is generally small. If the variances of X_1 and X_2 were 6 and 8 and their correlation was .7, the split-half reliability estimate would be .819, and the Spearman-Brown estimate would be .824. The assumption of essential τ-equivalence is generally more defensible than that of strict parallelism, but there appears to be little harm in using the Spearman-Brown formula.

If the two part tests cannot be assumed to be essentially τ-equivalent, there is no unique solution for the reliability estimate. With congeneric tests, both true-score variances and error-variances may differ for the two part tests. Thus, there are four unknown quantities, $\sigma_{T_1}^2$, $\sigma_{T_2}^2$, $\sigma_{E_1}^2$, and $\sigma_{E_2}^2$, which must be estimated from just three independent pieces of information, $\sigma_{X_1}^2$, $\sigma_{X_2}^2$, and σ_X^2 (or, equivalently, $\sigma_{X_1}^2$, $\sigma_{X_2}^2$, and $\sigma_{X_1 X_2}$). Raju (1970) proposed a solution that is applicable when the relative lengths of the two part tests may be assumed known, as when they differ in number of items. Assuming that the relative lengths of X_1 and X_2 are λ_1 and $\lambda_2 = 1 - \lambda_1$, the Raju approach imposes the constraint that $\sigma_{T_1}^2 / \sigma_{T_2}^2 = (\lambda_1 / \lambda_2)^2$. This constraint follows from the assumption that person p's true scores on subtests X_1 and X_2 are $\lambda_1 \tau_p$ and $\lambda_2 \tau_p$, respectively. The covariance between X_1 and X_2 is then $\lambda_1 \lambda_2 \sigma_T^2$, and the reliability is equal to

$$_R\rho_{XX'} = \frac{\sigma_{X_1 X_2}}{\lambda_1 \lambda_2 \sigma_X^2}. \tag{14}$$

Note that no assumption need be made concerning the relative magnitudes of the error variances for the two part tests. Note also that if $\lambda_1 = \lambda_2 = .5$, Equation 14 reduces to the Flanagan estimate given in Equation 12.

Angoff (1953), Kristof (1971), and Feldt (1975) impose a different constraint, which requires estimation of *effective test lengths* for the two parts, for use when these respective test lengths cannot plausibly be assumed known. Their solutions assume that X_1 and X_2 are congeneric, with true-score and error variances related as would be predicted from a simple shortening or lengthening of one part relative to the other. If k is the factor by which the test length is changed, the effect of such shortening or lengthening would be to multiply the true score by k, to multiply the true-score variance by k^2, and to multiply the error variance by k. Horst (1951) generalized the Spearman-Brown split-half formula, deriving a reliability estimate based on the correlation between two part tests of unequal but known lengths, which requires these same assumptions. Note that the error variance changes linearly with test length under the assumption that errors on separate items are independent. Thus, the error variance for the entire test is the sum of the error variances for the separate items. From these assumptions, Angoff (1953) and Feldt (1975) derive the following estimates of effective test lengths:

$$\lambda_1 = (\sigma_{X_1}^2 + \sigma_{X_1 X_2}) / \sigma_X^2 \text{ and} \tag{15}$$
$$\lambda_2 = 1 - \lambda_1 = (\sigma_{X_2}^2 + \sigma_{X_1 X_2}) / \sigma_X^2.$$

As with the Raju (1970) formula, $\sigma_T^2 = \sigma_{X_1 X_2} / \lambda_1 \lambda_2$. This derivation leads to the Angoff-Feldt coefficient,

$$_{AF}\rho_{XX'} = \frac{4\sigma_{X_1 X_2}}{\sigma_X^2 - \frac{(\sigma_{X_1}^2 - \sigma_{X_2}^2)^2}{\sigma_X^2}}. \tag{16}$$

Equivalently, the Angoff-Feldt coefficient may be obtained by calculating λ_1 and λ_2 according to Equation 15 and substituting these values into Equation 14. Feldt (2002b) reviews alternative approaches to reliability estimation when the two part-test lengths are unknown, illustrating the range of coefficients obtained as a function of λ_1 and λ_2, and concludes by recommending the Angoff-Feldt estimate in most cases.

Kristof (1971) treats the general problem of two or more tests differing only in length, formulating test length as a parameter in a model for the population covariance matrix.

Assuming that the covariance matrix of the part-tests follows a Wishart distribution, Kristof treats the problems of testing model fit if test lengths are known, as well as finding confidence intervals for relative test lengths if these parameters must be estimated.

Even though the Spearman-Brown, split-half, Raju, and Angoff-Feldt coefficients were derived under somewhat different sets of assumptions, they are closely related mathematically. All four may be obtained as special cases of Equation 14, with different choices of λ_1 and λ_2. The minimum possible value is obtained when $\lambda_1 = \lambda_2 = .5$, yielding $_{SH}\rho_{XX'}$ or $_F\rho_{XX'}$, which will later be seen to be a special case of coefficient alpha (Cronbach, 1951). Setting $\lambda_1 = .5 \pm \sqrt{((\sigma_{X_1}^2 + \sigma_{X_2}^2)/2 - \sqrt{\sigma_{X_1}^2 \sigma_{X_2}^2})/2\sigma_X^2}$ yields $_{SB}\rho_{XX'}$. When this value is used for λ_1, the term $\lambda_1\lambda_2$ in the denominator of Equation 14 adjusts for the use of the geometric mean, $\sqrt{\sigma_{X_1}^2 \sigma_{X_2}^2}$, in the denominator of the product-moment correlation coefficient, used in the Spearman-Brown formula, versus the arithmetic mean, $(\sigma_{X_1}^2 + \sigma_{X_2}^2)/2$, which appears if the Guttman-Rulon split-half formula is re-expressed as $_{SH}\rho_{XX'} = 2(1-2[(\sigma_{X_1}^2 + \sigma_{X_2}^2)/2]/\sigma_X^2)$. As already noted, if λ_1 and λ_2 are defined as in Equation 15, $_{AF}\rho_{XX'}$ is obtained. Finally, if the effective test lengths of X_1 and X_2 can be determined from other information, λ_1 and λ_2 may be set equal to their respective proportions of X to obtain $_R\rho_{XX'}$.

It is readily shown that for any set of data, $_{SH}\rho_{XX'} \leq {_{SB}\rho_{XX'}} \leq {_{AF}\rho_{XX'}}$, with equality holding only when $\sigma_{X_1}^2 = \sigma_{X_2}^2$. The value of Raju's $_R\rho_{XX'}$ is always greater than or equal to $_{SH}\rho_{XX'}$, with equality holding only if $\lambda_1 = \lambda_2 = .5$. If the true score is conceived in such a way that the difference between X_1 and X_2 reflects all intended sources of error, then the population value of the Flanagan or Guttman-Rulon (or alpha) reliability coefficient is a lower bound to the actual reliability, even under violation of the assumption that the two part tests are congeneric. In the typical case, however, where the true score is conceived as a personal constant that transcends the particular occasion of measurement, any of these coefficients may overstate reliability, because, as has been emphasized, variation between scores on parts of a test administered at one point in time cannot reflect day-to-day variation in examinee performance. Formally, the population value of $_{SH}\rho_{XX'}$ may be either greater than or less than the intended reliability. As a practical matter, these and other internal-consistency reliability estimates are best regarded, in general, as upper bounds to a test's reliability.

For the example introduced earlier, with $\sigma_{X_1}^2 = 6$, $\sigma_{X_2}^2 = 8$, and $\rho_{X_1 X_2} = .7$, the Flanagan or Guttman-Rulon split-half estimate is .8185, the Spearman-Brown estimate is .8235, and the Angoff-Feldt estimate is .8244. These values can be obtained from Equation 14 setting $\lambda_1 = .5$, $\lambda_1 = .4611$, and $\lambda_1 = .4578$, respectively. If $\lambda_1 = .45$, the Raju estimate is .8268. Feldt and Charter (2003) recommend that if the ratio of the standard deviations of X_1 and X_2 (the larger divided by the smaller) is less than 1.15, differences among the three formulas will be trivial. In that case, the simplest, Spearman-Brown calculation may be used, although the Flanagan or Guttman-Rulon split-half formula is preferred. These coefficients, defined by Equations 12 and 13, will be seen to be equivalent to coefficient alpha (Cronbach, 1951). If the ratio of the standard deviations is between 1.15 and 1.30, they recommend the Guttman-Rulon split-half coefficient or the Angoff-Feldt coefficient, and if the ratio is greater than 1.30, they recommend that the Angoff-Feldt coefficient be used. For this numerical example, with $\sigma_{X_1}^2 = 6$, $\sigma_{X_2}^2 = 8$, the ratio of the standard deviations is 1.155.

2.4.3. Methods for Dividing a Test Into Two Parts

For a test consisting of several separately scorable units, there may be many different ways to partition the total test into two separately scored parts in order to estimate reliability. Two principles should be followed in deciding how the test should be divided. First, the two halves should be as nearly parallel as possible, in content, difficulty, and other respects. The reason for this first principle should be clear—One requirement for parallel forms was that they share the same test specifications. The ideals of equal true scores for each examinee (up to an additive constant) and of equal error variances will be best approximated if the two half-tests are as similar as possible in content and difficulty. Even if one of the reliability estimates appropriate for congeneric part-tests is chosen, it is still assumed that $\rho_{T_1 T_2} = 1$. Differences in content or format between the items included in X_1 versus X_2 may result in part-tests measuring slightly different underlying variables, that is, with $\rho_{T_1 T_2} < 1$, biasing the reliability estimate downward. One common default is to place the even-numbered items in one portion and the odd-numbered items in the other, for example. If the items are arranged in order of increasing difficulty, or into a series of distinct subsections, the even-odd split may be a sound choice. Gulliksen (1950, chap. 15) describes a method for dividing test items into two or more equivalent parts by first locating the items on a two-dimensional plot according to their percent correct and the item-test correlation (biserial or point biserial correlation). Items close together are then grouped visually into pairs or larger clusters of the intended size. Finally, within each cluster, items are assigned at random, one to each of the two or more parts. This procedure could be carried out separately for each of several item content or format categories to help assure parallelism with respect to content as well as statistical properties.

The second principle holds that groups of items referring to some common stimulus within the test should generally be kept together (Feldt, 2002a; Feldt & Brennan, 1989; G. Lee, Brennan, & Frisbie, 2000; G. Lee & Frisbie, 1999; Qualls, 1995; Sireci, Thissen, & Wainer, 1991; Wainer & Thissen, 1996, 2001). This is to minimize violation of the assumption that $\rho_{E_1 E_2} = 0$. Consider a reading comprehension test, for example, consisting of a series of passages, each of which is followed by several items. The passages presumably sample some larger domain of reading materials that could have been chosen instead, and scores on the test are intended to reflect reading proficiency with respect to that larger domain. Thus, if an examinee finds a particular passage easier or harder, perhaps due to prior knowledge or to some special interest in or aversion to the passage topic, that passage-level deviation from that examinee's overall reading proficiency level should be regarded as contributing to error. If the items pertaining to that passage are divided between the two part-tests, the examinee's scores on both X_1 and X_2 will be influenced in the same direction, inflating $\sigma_{X_1 X_2}$. If instead, all questions pertaining to a single passage are assigned to the same part-test, either X_1 or X_2, then such passage-specific effects contribute to the variances of the part-tests, but not to their covariance, appropriately treating them as a source of measurement error.

In practice, these two principles may be at odds with one another. Consider a social studies test with a map followed by several questions testing map reading and related reasoning skills. If these items are divided between the two part tests, the content of the two parts may be more nearly parallel than otherwise, but to the extent that particular examinees find the entire set of map items systematically easier or harder due to particular features of the map chosen, dividing the items may lead to some spurious inflation of the reliability estimate. If a fictional map were used, such stimulus-specific effects might be regarded as unlikely, and the items might be divided between the two parts.

2.4.4. Reliability Estimates Based on Division of a Test into More Than Two Parts

Internal consistency reliability estimates are often required for divisions of a test into more than two separate parts. If a test divides naturally into three or more portions, there may be a wish to avoid the arbitrariness of collapsing these portions into just two test parts for purposes of reliability estimation. The objective of creating parallel part tests may be better served by division into three or more parts than just two parts. In addition, the sampling variance of the estimated reliability coefficient is related to the number of units into which the test is divided, and greater precision is obtained if the test can be divided into a larger number of τ-equivalent parts (Kristof, 1963).

It is common practice to base internal-consistency estimates on divisions of tests into the smallest possible units, individual items. This may sometimes be the best choice, but it should not be an automatic default. Division into more parts is only better if model assumptions are satisfied (Brennan, 2001a). As with division into two parts, clusters of items pertaining to a common stimulus should generally be kept together. If items may be classified into categories defined by the test specifications, part tests should be formed so as to maintain the same distribution over categories as the test as a whole.

By far the best known and most widely used internal-consistency reliability estimate is Cronbach's (1951) coefficient alpha (Hogan, Benjamin, & Brezinski, 2000).[8] The formula is usually given in either of two forms,

$$_a\rho_{XX'} = \frac{n}{n-1}\left(\frac{\sigma_X^2 - \sum \sigma_{X_i}^2}{\sigma_X^2}\right) = \frac{n}{n-1}\left(1 - \frac{\sum \sigma_{X_i}^2}{\sigma_X^2}\right), \quad (17)$$

where n is the number of parts into which the test is divided, σ_X^2 is the variance of the total test score, and $\sigma_{X_i}^2$, $i = 1, \ldots, n$ is the variance of the ith part. As already noted, when $n = 2$, $_a\rho_{XX'}$ is equivalent to the Flanagan and the split-half reliability coefficients (Equations 12 and 13). In addition, coefficient alpha is equal to the mean of all possible split-half reliability estimates as defined by Equations 12 and 13 (Cronbach, 1951). Thus, its use eliminates a source of error associated with arbitrary choice of a split (Lord, 1956b). Coefficient alpha is also mathematically equivalent to the coefficient derived by C. Hoyt (1941) from an analysis of variance (ANOVA) framework and is mathematically identical to λ_3, one of the six lower bounds to the reliability coefficient derived by Guttman (1945). From a decision-theoretic perspective, coefficient alpha can also be interpreted as the proportional reduction in expected squared error loss when an observed score is used as an estimator of the corresponding true score (Cooil & Rust, 1994).

If the part-tests are not essentially τ-equivalent, then coefficient alpha is a lower bound to the internal consistency reliability (Novick & Lewis, 1967). As already noted, however, like all internal-consistency estimates, $_a\rho_{XX'}$ may overestimate reliability due to exclusion of fluctuations in performance over time. Thus, in practice, $_a\rho_{XX'}$ may either overestimate or underestimate reliability (Zimmerman, Zumbo, & Lalonde, 1993).

The formula for $_a\rho_{XX'}$ may be understood by noting that $\sigma_X^2 = \sum\sum \sigma_{X_i X_j}$, the sum of all the variances and covariances among test parts. Thus, $\sigma_X^2 - \sum \sigma_{X_i}^2$ is the sum of all the covariances among distinct parts. There are $n(n-1)$ such terms. Under essential τ-equivalence, these terms are all equal (in the population). Furthermore, $\sigma_{X_i X_j} = \sigma_{T_i T_j}$ and $\sigma_{T_i T_j} = \sigma_{T_i}^2 = \sigma_{T_j}^2$ for all $i \neq j$. Thus, $\sigma_T^2 = \sum_i \sigma_{T_i}^2 + \sum\sum_{i \neq j} \sigma_{T_i T_j} = (n/(n-1))(\sigma_X^2 - \sum \sigma_{X_i}^2)$.

If the n parts are all dichotomously scored 0 or 1, an algebraic simplification of Equation 17 is possible. Using φ_i for the proportion of ones, $\sigma_{X_i}^2 = \varphi_i(1-\varphi_i)$. Substituting this expression into Equation 17 gives the Kuder-Richardson formula 20 (Kuder & Richardson, 1937):

$$_{20}\rho_{XX'} = \left(\frac{n}{n-1}\right)\left(1 - \frac{\sum \varphi_i(1-\varphi_i)}{\sigma_X^2}\right). \quad (18)$$

For a test consisting of dichotomously scored items, with each separate item treated as a part-test, $_{20}\rho_{XX'}$ can be estimated from just the test length, the item difficulties (p-values), and the variance of number-correct scores. Violation of essential τ-equivalence is almost inevitable if φ_i varies over items, but in practice Kuder-Richardson formula 20 yields estimates close to split-half reliability estimates. Denoting the sample item difficulties (p-values) by $\hat{\varphi}_i$, $i = 1, \ldots, n$ and the sample variance of total scores by $\hat{\sigma}_X^2$, $_{20}\hat{\rho}_{XX'}$ can be calculated by substituting $\hat{\varphi}_i$, $i = 1, \ldots, n$ and $\hat{\sigma}_X^2$ into Equation 18. However, $\hat{\sigma}_X^2$ should be calculated using the number of examinees, N, instead of $N-1$ in the denominator of the usual formula for the sample variance. Alternatively (and equivalently), if $N-1$ is used in calculating $\hat{\sigma}_X^2$ then $((N/(N-1))\sum \hat{\varphi}_i(1-\hat{\varphi}_i))$ should be used as the estimator of $\sum \hat{\varphi}_i(1-\varphi_i)$.

A further simplification is possible if each φ_i is replaced by the mean across items, $\bar{\varphi}$, so that $\sum \varphi_i(1-\varphi_i)$ becomes $n\bar{\varphi}(1-\bar{\varphi})$. This leads to the Kuder-Richardson formula 21 reliability estimate,

$$_{21}\rho_{XX'} = \left(\frac{n}{n-1}\right)\left(1 - \frac{\mu_X(n-\mu_X)}{n\sigma_X^2}\right). \quad (19)$$

With this formula, reliability for a test consisting entirely of dichotomously scored items can be estimated using just the test length, mean, and standard deviation. As with $_{20}\hat{\rho}_{XX'}$, when substituting sample values to obtain $_{21}\hat{\rho}_{XX'}$, N rather than $N-1$ should be used in calculating $\hat{\sigma}_X^2$, or else $(N/(N-1))\bar{X}(n-\bar{X})$ should be used as the estimator of $\mu_X(n-\mu_X)$. The Kuder-Richardson formula 21 estimate is always less than or equal to the formula 20 estimate, as first shown by Tucker (1949):

$$_{20}\rho_{XX'} = {}_{21}\rho_{XX'} + \frac{n\sum(\varphi_i - \bar{\varphi})^2}{(n-1)\sigma_X^2} = {}_{21}\rho_{XX'} + \frac{n^2\sigma_{\varphi_i}^2}{(n-1)\sigma_X^2}$$

Results of the two formulas are generally close in practice (Lord, 1959).

The close relationships among coefficient alpha and the KR 20 and KR 21 formulas has led to some confusion in referring to these coefficients (Hogan et al., 2000). Although Kuder (1991) called for restricting the term "coefficient alpha" to cases not equivalent to the KR 20 formula, it would seem that "coefficient alpha" properly applies to all such cases. A more common error is the use of "KR 20" to refer to reliability estimates for tests where the items are not dichotomously scored. The KR 21 estimate is mathematically distinct from the other two and should be called by its own name.

If the parts into which a test is divided are assumed not just essentially τ-equivalent but strictly parallel, another simplification is possible. For strictly parallel part tests, $\sigma_{T_i}^2 = \sigma_{X_iX_j}$ for all $i \neq j$. Noting that $\sigma_X^2 = \Sigma\sigma_{X_i}^2 + \sum\sum_{i\neq j}\sigma_{X_iX_j}$, Equation 17 under this more restrictive assumption reduces to

$$\rho_{XX'} = \left(\frac{n}{n-1}\right)\left(\frac{n(n-1)\sigma_{X_iX_j}}{n\sigma_{X_i}^2 + n(n-1)\sigma_{X_iX_j}}\right)$$

Canceling terms and dividing the numerator and denominator by $\sigma_{X_i}^2$ yields

$$_{SB}\rho_{XX'} = \frac{n\rho_{X_iX_j}}{1+(n-1)\rho_{X_iX_j}} \quad (20)$$

This may be seen to be a generalization of the Spearman-Brown split-half reliability estimate, reducing to Equation 11 when $n = 2$. If the mean of the part-test intercorrelations is substituted into Equation 20, a coefficient is obtained that is referred to in some computer programs as a *standardized alpha* (Osburn, 2000). It is equal to the coefficient alpha reliability for a total score created by first standardizing all the part-test scores to equal variances in the sample, then summing those standardized scores to obtain a total score (Li & Wainer, 1997). Unless such a standardized composite score is actually used, however, Equation 20 would seem less useful than the usual coefficient alpha defined by Equation 17.

In some testing applications, examinees may be tested repeatedly and their lowest scores may be discarded. In athletic trials, for example, the mean of a runner's best three times out of five trials might be calculated. Huynh (1986) derives the reliability of the mean of the highest m scores out of a set of n trials, as well as quantifying the expected bias in that mean. (The expected value of the mean discarding lowest scores is greater than the true score.) The formula for the reliability is

$$_H\rho_{XX'} = \frac{m\rho_{X_iX_j}}{\lambda_{nm} + (m - \lambda_{nm})\rho_{X_iX_j}},$$

where λ_{nm} is a coefficient depending only on n and m, derived from order statistics for the normal distribution (Teichroew, 1956). Tables of λ_{nm} are provided by Huynh.

Guttman (1945) offered several lower bounds for the reliability of a test score, of which his λ_2 is still used. By incorporating the sum of squares of covariances as well as the sum of covariances, Guttman obtained a coefficient that is always greater than or equal to coefficient alpha, and less than or equal to the reliability. The form of the equation presented here is chosen to emphasize the relation of Guttman's coefficient to coefficient alpha:

$$_G\rho_{XX'} = \frac{\sigma_X^2 - \sum\sigma_{X_i}^2 + \sqrt{\frac{n}{n-1}\sum\sum_{i\neq j}(\sigma_{X_iX_j})^2}}{\sigma_X^2} \quad (21)$$

If $\sigma_{X_iX_j}$ is the same for all $i \neq j$, Equation 21 reduces to Equation 17. Guttman's coefficient is one of an infinite series of successively closer lower bounds, incorporating higher powers of covariance terms (ten Berge & Zegers, 1978). Additional terms have little effect, however.

The coefficients presented in Equations 17–21 all assume essential τ-equivalence or, for the generalized Spearman-Brown reliability, strict parallelism among part tests. As with split-half estimation procedures, it may sometimes be more realistic to assume that part tests are congeneric. Where the relative lengths of part tests can be specified (as with sections comprising different numbers of similar items), a generalization of Raju's (1970) coefficient may be used (Raju, 1977):

$$_R\rho_{XX'} = \frac{\sigma_X^2 - \sum\sigma_{X_i}^2}{\left(1 - \sum\lambda_i^2\right)\sigma_X^2}. \quad (22)$$

As before, λ_i is the proportion of total test length for part-test i, and $\Sigma\lambda_i = 1$. If all λ_i are equal to $1/n$, Equation 22 reduces to Equation 17, the formula for coefficient alpha.

As noted earlier, for a test composed of two parts of unknown length, there is no unique solution unless an additional constraint is imposed (Feldt, 2002b). For $n = 3$ congeneric parts of unknown length, the problem is just identified, with exactly as many variances and covariances as there are parameters to be estimated. Kristof (1974) offers an elegant solution and shows it to be at least as accurate as coefficient alpha:

$$_K\rho_{XX'} = \frac{(\sigma_{X_1X_2}\sigma_{X_1X_3} + \sigma_{X_1X_2}\sigma_{X_2X_3} + \sigma_{X_1X_3}\sigma_{X_2X_3})^2}{\sigma_{X_1X_2}\sigma_{X_1X_3}\sigma_{X_2X_3}\sigma_X^2} \quad (23)$$

A mathematically identical result may be obtained by using Kristof's (1974) solution for the relative lengths of the part tests, λ_1, λ_2 and λ_3 ($\Sigma\lambda_i = 1$), and substituting these values into Equation 22:

$$\lambda_1 = 1/(1 + \sigma_{X_2X_3}/\sigma_{X_1X_2} + \sigma_{X_2X_3}/\sigma_{X_1X_3})$$
$$\lambda_2 = 1/(1 + \sigma_{X_1X_3}/\sigma_{X_1X_2} + \sigma_{X_1X_3}/\sigma_{X_2X_3})$$
$$\lambda_3 = 1/(1 + \sigma_{X_1X_2}/\sigma_{X_1X_3} + \sigma_{X_1X_2}/\sigma_{X_2X_3})$$

Kristof (1974) reports that his three-part procedure appears to give quite stable results across alternative partitions of a test into three parts. Thus, it may be recommended as a general method for estimating reliability when a division into three congeneric parts is preferable to a division into two parts. Precision will be best if the three parts are of approximately equal length (Sedere & Feldt, 1977).

For tests divided into more than three parts of unknown effective test length, estimation is more complicated because the solution is over-determined. One could, of course, impose a model specifying only that the $n > 3$ parts were congeneric and find a solution via maximum likelihood. Kristof (1971, p. 222, Equation 74) provides such a solution, which requires numerical methods. A maximum-likelihood solution can also be obtained as described by Jöreskog (1971). A least-squares solution is provided by Mayekawa and Haebara (1980). Two approximations suitable for hand calculation are provided by Gilmer and Feldt (1983; Feldt, 2002a; Qualls, 1995) and similar approximations are presented by Liou (1989). All of these approximations are numerically equivalent when $n = 3$.

An elegant solution is provided by Feldt and Brennan (1989, pp. 114–115) for the case they refer to as *classical congeneric*. Test parts are classical congeneric if the true score and error variances of test part i, $i = 1,..., n$ can be expressed as functions of (unknown) parameters λ_i such that the true-score variance of part i equals $\lambda_i^2 \sigma_T^2$ and the error variance of part i equals $\lambda_i \sigma_E^2$, with $\sum_{i=1}^{n} \lambda_i = 1$. These relations can be derived from classical test theory for tests differing only in length—true-score variance changes as the square of test length and error variance changes linearly with test length. From the facts that $\sigma_{X_i X_j} = \lambda_i \lambda_j \sigma_T^2$ for $i \neq j$, $\sigma_{X_i}^2 = \lambda_i^2 \sigma_T^2 + \lambda_i \sigma_E^2$ and $\Sigma \lambda_i = 1$ it follows that $\lambda_i = \sum_{j=1}^{n} \sigma_{X_i X_j} / \sigma_X^2 = \sigma_{X_i X} / \sigma_X^2$. Substituting this expression for λ_i into Equation 22 and simplifying leads to Feldt's coefficient for classical congeneric test parts (unknown lengths):

$$_{CC}\rho_{XX'} = \frac{\sigma_X^2 (\sigma_X^2 - \sum \sigma_{X_i}^2)}{\sigma_X^4 - \sum (\sigma_{X_i X})^2}. \quad (24)$$

Problems in which a test is naturally divided into more than three parts of unknown effective test lengths are most likely to arise in practice in tests with several distinct item formats (Qualls, 1995). If anything more complex than a hand calculation is to be used with such tests, rather than imposing the constraint that test parts are congeneric, it may be preferable to explore the dimensionality of the test parts at the same time as their effective lengths. Such approaches are taken up in section 2.5, on the reliability of composites.

2.5. Reliability of Composite Scores

A composite score, as defined here, is any linear combination of two or more component scores, with fixed weights. All of the internal-consistency reliability estimates discussed to this point are examples of composite scores subject to the constraint (or assumption) that all score components are at least congeneric. The general case includes composites formed from tests of distinct traits or constructs, such as composite scores for achievement test batteries. It also includes cases where the distinct traits or constructs measured by different component scores are more closely related, as with a score on a test including items of several distinct types (Qualls, 1995). Composite scores also include measures of growth or change over time, for example the simple difference between measurements taken prior to and following instruction. Note that in this case, the weight for the posttest is one and the weight for the pretest is negative one. In other cases, other values might be used. Composites with both positive and negative weights also arise in the interpretation of score profiles, as with a contrast between "verbal" and "performance" intelligence score estimates, for example. Such contrasts may be tested for statistical significance or may be evaluated relative to the population standard deviation of the difference scores (Cahan, 1989). In some cases, the weights defining composite scores may be specified a priori or derived from theory. In other cases, they may be derived empirically, as with composites defining predicted values obtained via multiple linear regression (Rozeboom, 1989). The same questions concerning reliability may arise in the interpretation and use of any of these score composites as with scores from single tests. As will be seen, many of the same conceptual and statistical tools can be used to address these questions.

In the discussion to follow, the composite score for person p, formed from k component scores $X_{p_1}, \ldots, X_{p_k}$ with weights $w_1, \ldots, w_k$, will be denoted Z_p. An additive constant may also appear. Thus,

$$Z_p = w_0 + \sum_{i=1}^{k} w_i X_{pi}. \quad (25)$$

As with scores on individual tests, composite scores will be assumed to consist of a true-score component and an error component. Errors will be assumed uncorrelated and with zero expectations, as set forth in Equations 3, 4, and 5. Where it is useful to conceive of a parallel form of a composite measure, it will be assumed that the parallel form is created by applying the same fixed weights to a set of component scores $X'_{p_1}, \ldots, X'_{p_k}$ that are parallel to $X_{p_1}, \ldots, X_{p_k}$, respectively. From these assumptions, it follows that the error variance for a composite score is just the weighted sum of the error variances for its components. The true-score variance for a composite, however, is in general more difficult to obtain directly, because it is a weighted sum of all the covariances among component scores as well as the true-score variances of the component scores. Thus, an especially useful relation in working with composites is

$$\rho_{ZZ'} = 1 - \frac{\sigma_{E_Z}^2}{\sigma_Z^2} = 1 - \frac{\sum w_i^2 \sigma_{E_i}^2}{\sigma_Z^2} = 1 - \frac{\sum w_i^2 \sigma_{X_i}^2 (1 - \rho_{X_i X_i'})}{\sigma_Z^2}. \quad (26)$$

Equation 26 is derived using the facts that $\sigma_{wX}^2 = w^2 \sigma_X^2$ and that $\sigma_E^2 = \sigma_X^2 (1 - \rho_{XX'})$. Note that it expresses the reliability of any composite Z solely in terms of σ_Z^2, $w_1, \ldots, w_k$, and the variances and reliabilities of the component scores (Mosier, 1943).

2.5.1. The Spearman-Brown "Prophecy" Formula

If $X_1, ..., X_k$ are strictly parallel, the reliability of $Z = \Sigma X_i$ is a function of the reliability of the X_i. This relation is presented above in Equation 20, where it was derived as a special case of the coefficient alpha reliability. A slightly different derivation is as follows. Note that if tests X_i and X_j are strictly parallel, then $\sigma_{X_i}^2 = \sigma_{X_j}^2 = \sigma_X^2$ and $\rho_{X_i X_j} = \rho_{XX'}$, the reliability of each test. Because $\sigma_{E_Z}^2 = k\sigma_{E_i}^2 = k\sigma_X^2(1 - \rho_{XX'})$ and $\sigma_Z^2 = k^2\rho_{X_i X_j}\sigma_{X_i}^2 + \sigma_{E_Z}^2 = k^2\rho_{XX'}\sigma_X^2 + \sigma_{E_Z}^2$,

$$\rho_{ZZ'} = 1 - \frac{\sigma_{E_Z}^2}{\sigma_Z^2} = \frac{\sigma_Z^2 - \sigma_{E_Z}^2}{\sigma_Z^2} = \frac{k\rho_{XX'}}{1 + (k-1)\rho_{XX'}}. \quad (27)$$

Equation 27 is widely known as the *Spearman-Brown "Prophecy" Formula* because it can be used to predict the reliability of a lengthened or shortened test. In that application, k (which need not be an integer value) represents the factor by which the test X is lengthened or shortened; $\rho_{XX'}$ represents the reliability of the original test; and $\rho_{ZZ'}$ is the predicted reliability of a test k times as long. Note that solving Equation 27 for $\rho_{XX'}$ yields

$$\rho_{XX'} = \frac{(1/k)\rho_{ZZ'}}{1 + (1/k - 1)\rho_{ZZ'}}.$$

Thus, the Spearman-Brown formula may be used to predict the reliability of a shortened test as well as a lengthened one.

Another useful form of the equation is

$$k = \frac{\rho_{ZZ'}(1 - \rho_{XX'})}{\rho_{XX'}(1 - \rho_{ZZ'})}. \quad (28)$$

Equation 28 can be used to predict the factor by which a test length should be changed to attain a specific target reliability. These formulas may be especially useful in test development. If tests employing different item types are piloted, their reliabilities will not be directly comparable unless they are of the same length. The Spearman-Brown formula can be used to adjust reliability estimates for test length, increasing comparability. Typically, the adjustment of interest would be to tests administered in equal amounts of time, not necessarily tests with equal numbers of items. Obviously, the accuracy of projections using Equations 27 and 28 depend on the assumptions that rate and quality of work will be unaffected by changes in test length, as well as the assumption that true-score variance and error variance change as a function of test length in the manner described.

2.5.2. Stratified Coefficient Alpha

Tests often contain items drawn from two or more distinct categories or types. Specifications for educational achievement tests, for example, often distinguish several content categories as well as distinct processes items are to elicit (factual recall, problem solving, etc.). For tests constructed in this fashion, the assumption that part tests are congeneric is unlikely to be met, let alone the assumption that part tests are essentially τ-equivalent. If items in different categories measured exactly the same dimension (i.e., if their true scores were perfectly correlated), there would be little reason to maintain distinctions among the categories in test construction.[9] Thus, instead of $_a\rho_{ZZ'}$, a more appropriate reliability estimate may be obtained via Equation 26, treating the sets of items in different content categories as separate part tests for purposes of reliability estimation (Rajaratnam, Cronbach, & Gleser, 1965):

$$_{\text{strat }a}\rho_{XX'} = 1 - \frac{\sum \sigma_{X_i}^2(1 - _a\rho_{XX'})}{\sigma_X^2} \quad (29)$$

Other things being equal, $_{\text{strat }a}\rho_{XX'}$ will be greater than $_a\rho_{XX'}$, if, on average, item intercorrelations within content categories are higher than item intercorrelations across different categories. The alpha reliability coefficient as defined by Equation 17 will underestimate reliability if true-score variances differ among part tests or if the part tests are not congeneric. The stratified coefficient alpha could be used to overcome either of these limitations. Coefficient alpha (Equation 17) appears to be robust to violations of essential τ-equivalence (Cronbach, Schöenemann, & McKie, 1965; Enders & Bandalos, 1999; Feldt & Qualls, 1996a). When subsets of items measure distinct content categories, however, stratified alpha may be substantially more accurate than a variety of internal-consistency reliability coefficients derived under the assumption that test parts are congeneric or essentially τ-equivalent (Cronbach et al., 1965; Osburn, 2000).

2.5.3. Reliability of a Battery Composite Score

A general formula for the reliability of a weighted composite score was presented in Equation 26. The reliability of an unweighted mean of k subtest scores from an achievement test battery can be obtained from Equation 26 by setting $w_i = 1/k$, $i = 1, ..., k$:

$$\rho_{ZZ'} = 1 - \frac{\sum \sigma_{X_i}^2(1 - \rho_{X_i X_i'})}{k^2 \sigma_Z^2}.$$

This reliability coefficient for the battery score will reflect whatever sources of error are represented in the reliability coefficients used for the separate component scores. Feldt and Brennan (1989) suggest a practical data collection design for the case where two alternate forms of a test battery have been constructed, say forms A and B. The available examinees are divided into equivalent samples. The first k samples each take Form A of the complete battery, and then, on a separate occasion, each group takes Form B of a different one of the k subtests. The remaining k groups take all of Form B and then one of the Form A subtests. This design permits the calculation of reliability estimates for each subtest according to Equation 10, as well as the reliabilities of the battery composite scores for each form.

2.5.4. Maximal Reliability of a Composite Score

The weights defining a composite score may be dictated by test specifications or adopted as a matter of policy. If some or all component scores are strictly parallel, it is highly unlikely that anything other than equal weighting of those components would be appropriate. In some cases, however, there may be flexibility in choosing weights for score components. The problem of weighting components is not the same as the choice of the numbers of items of different kinds to be included in a test. Here, the composition of each component score (including the length of the component) is assumed fixed. The question addressed is how scores obtained for those fixed components are to be combined. If score components are congeneric, then from a psychometric perspective, the optimum weighting is the one that maximizes the reliability of the composite. By definition, any linear composite of congeneric components is measuring the same underlying dimension, and so the maximally reliable composite will have the highest possible correlation with any other variable (Li, Rosenthal, & Rubin, 1996). Even in cases where score components are not congeneric, the maximum possible reliability may be of theoretical interest, providing a limit against which to evaluate the efficiency of any given weighting.

In practice, reliability may be just one of several considerations in determining test weights. As Rudner (2001) illustrates, when score components are *not* congeneric, cases often arise where the weighting that maximizes composite score reliability is different from the weighting that maximizes the correlation of the composite score with some other criterion variable. Wainer and Thissen (1993) discuss the problem of weighting multiple-choice versus constructed-response component scores in the context of Advanced Placement Examinations and describe arguments for giving constructed-response components relatively higher weights than a consideration of reliability alone would dictate. These include the kinds of skills constructed-response items are assumed to measure and the effects test item formats are assumed to have on classroom instruction and the ways students study. They note that evidence for these possible benefits of constructed-response items is limited.

If component reliabilities are known, the maximal reliability and the required weights to obtain that reliability can be determined from the solution to the eigenvalue problem $\mathbf{u}'(\mathbf{R}^* - \lambda \mathbf{R}) = \mathbf{0}'$ where $\mathbf{R}$ is the correlation matrix of the components and $\mathbf{R}^*$ is the same correlation matrix with component reliabilities instead of unit values on the diagonal. If $\mathbf{u}$ is the eigenvector corresponding to the largest eigenvalue λ, then the maximal reliability $_{max}\rho_{XX'} = (\mathbf{u}'\mathbf{R}^*\mathbf{u}/\mathbf{u}'\mathbf{R}\mathbf{u})$ (Lord & Novick, 1968, pp. 123–124). Expressions for the required weights and a reparameterization in terms of component signal-to-noise ratios $\rho_{X_iX_i'}/(1-\rho_{X_iX_i'})$ are provided by Li (1997; Li et al., 1996). If test components are congeneric but with unknown reliabilities, weights that maximize reliability may be approximated as discussed by Wang (1998). If test components are not congeneric, the maximal reliability may be substantially greater than the coefficient alpha reliability (Osburn, 2000). Beyond the maximally reliable composite, additional orthogonal composites with maximal reliability may also be examined to determine the number of distinct dimensions that can be reliably measured using a given test battery (Cliff & Caruso, 1998; Conger & Lipshitz, 1973; ten Berge, 2000).

An alternative, multivariate conception of reliability for a score battery is developed by Conger and Lipshitz (1973; Rae, 1991). Just as $\rho_{XX'} = \rho_{XT}^2$, a battery reliability index may be defined as the squared canonical correlation between the vectors $\mathbf{x}$ and $\mathbf{t}$. For a battery of k components, this is equal to $\text{Tr}(\mathbf{R}^*\mathbf{R}^{-1})/k$, where $\mathbf{R}^*$ and $\mathbf{R}$ are as defined above (Conger & Lipshitz, 1973, p. 417).

2.5.5. Lower Bound to Reliability of a Composite Score

If the covariances among component scores and the reliabilities of those scores are known (or can be estimated), the reliability of any weighted composite can be determined (or estimated) using Equation 26, and the weights yielding maximal reliability can be determined (or estimated) following the methods of the previous section. Alternatively, if component scores are congeneric, the methods of section 2.4.4 may be used. It may happen, however, that component score reliabilities are not known, the component scores may not be assumed congeneric, but an estimate of reliability is still desired. For example, a set of exercises might be developed for a teacher certification test, requiring the candidate to teach a sample lesson, critique a textbook, plan a lesson using specified materials, and complete several other tasks, each of which is then scored according to some complex rubric. Exercise scores might then be summed to obtain a composite score. Such a mix of tasks cannot be assumed congeneric, and there may not be any straightforward way to estimate the reliability of the separate components. A lower bound to the reliability can nonetheless be obtained, assuming only that covariances among tasks are equal to the covariances among their true scores and that errors are uncorrelated (Bentler, 1972; Bentler & Woodward, 1980).

Given that covariances of observed scores are equal to the covariances of the corresponding true scores, if true-score variances were inserted on the diagonal of the observed-score covariance matrix, the covariance matrix of the true scores would be obtained. Moreover, the trace of the observed-score covariance matrix minus the trace of the true-score covariance matrix would be equal to the sum of the error variances for all components, from which the composite reliability could be obtained using Equation 26. Any covariance matrix must be positive semi-definite. Thus, a lower bound to reliability can be obtained by minimizing the sum of the true-score variances subject to the constraint that the resulting true-score covariance matrix is Gramian. Efficient algorithms exist for this problem (Bentler & Woodward, 1980, 1983; ten Berge, Snijders, & Zegers, 1981) and the sampling distribution of the resulting lower bound has also been investigated (Bentler & Woodward, 1983, 1985; Shapiro, 1982, 1985; Shapiro & ten Berge, 2000, 2002). In applications of the minimum-trace procedure, it is probably best to divide the test into as many separate score components as possible (Cronbach, 1988).

2.5.6. Reliability Estimation Using Structural Equation Models

It is often unclear whether a test or test battery measures one dimension or several, whether part tests or component scores may be assumed essentially τ-equivalent, and how reliable each part test or score component is. Structural equation modeling permits the comparison of alternative models for test data, informing the selection of an appropriate reliability estimate and, often, providing such an estimate directly. Using such modeling approaches, it may also be possible to specify and test a broader range of models than has been considered here, including models with correlated errors (Raykov, 1997, 1998b, 2001; Komaroff, 1997). There is no space here for a systematic review of the large and growing literature on the topic, but illustrative applications are presented by Reuterberg and Gustafsson (1992) and by Hancock (1997). As software programs for such analysis become more widely available and easier to use, there is a risk of misapplication of these models. If part tests or score components are dichotomous or ordered-categorical, for example, appropriate measurement models must be employed (R. Brown, 1989; Muthén, 1984; Muthén & Satorra, 1995), and nonobvious choices may be required in the specification of models for score reliabilities (Bacon, Sauer, & Young, 1995). In particular, it may be necessary to explicitly model multiple sources of error (e.g., error due to sampling of items and of raters) when such models are applied to faceted observations (DeShon, 1998).

2.5.7. Reliability of Differences Among Scores

Score composites in which some weights are positive and some negative may be of interest when examining growth or change over time or when interpreting score profiles. There is little difference in the formal mathematical treatment of reliability for composites in which all the weights w_i are positive versus those with some positive and some negative weights, but such composites do merit some special discussion.

The simple difference score is defined as $X_2 - X_1$. For example, X_1 might be a pretest score and X_2 a posttest score, with "pre" and "post" defined relative to some instructional or therapeutic intervention. In other applications, X_1 and X_2 might be two scores in a profile from an achievement test battery. The true-score and error components of the pretest, posttest, and difference scores may be represented as

$$X_1 = T_1 + E_1$$
$$X_2 = T_2 + E_2$$
$$X_D = (T_2 - T_1) + (E_2 - E_1).$$

Because $\sigma_{E_1 E_2} = 0$,

$$\sigma_{T_D}^2 = \sigma_{T_1}^2 + \sigma_{T_2}^2 - 2\sigma_{T_1 T_2}$$
$$\sigma_{E_D}^2 = \sigma_{E_1}^2 + \sigma_{E_2}^2.$$

Typically, $\sigma_{X_1 X_2} = \sigma_{T_1 T_2} > 0$, which implies that the true-score variance of the difference score will be less than $\sigma_{T_1}^2 + \sigma_{T_2}^2$, whereas the error variance of the difference score is equal to $\sigma_{E_1}^2 + \sigma_{E_2}^2$. Thus, it is not uncommon to find that difference scores have low reliability. Making the substitutions

$$\sigma_{T_D}^2 = \rho_{X_1 X_1'}\sigma_{X_1}^2 + \rho_{X_2 X_2'}\sigma_{X_2}^2 - 2\sigma_{X_1 X_2}$$
$$\sigma_{E_D}^2 = (1 - \rho_{X_1 X_1'})\sigma_{X_1}^2 + (1 - \rho_{X_2 X_2'})\sigma_{X_2}^2,$$

it is straightforward to derive any of several equivalent expressions for the reliability of the difference score. Perhaps the simplest computational formula is

$$\rho_{DD'} = 1 - \frac{(1 - \rho_{X_1 X_1'})\sigma_{X_1}^2 + (1 - \rho_{X_2 X_2'})\sigma_{X_2}^2}{\sigma_{(X_2 - X_1)}^2}. \quad (30)$$

If $\sigma_{X_1}^2 = \sigma_{X_2}^2$, Equation 30 simplifies to

$$\rho_{DD'} = \frac{\bar{\rho}_{XX'} - \rho_{X_1 X_2}}{1 - \rho_{X_1 X_2}}, \quad (31)$$

where $\bar{\rho}_{XX'} = (\rho_{X_1 X_1'} + \rho_{X_2 X_2'})/2$. This simpler formula may aid intuition as to influences on the reliability of difference scores, but may also be conducive to misinterpretation. Except in the case of differences between score components in profiles, which are likely to be standardized to a common mean and standard deviation, equal variance for X_1 and X_2 is probably more the exception than the rule (Feldt & Brennan, 1989; Sharma & Gupta, 1986; Williams & Zimmerman, 1996). Other things being equal, $\rho_{DD'}$ will be higher if $\sigma_{X_1}^2 \neq \sigma_{X_2}^2$. Also, although Equation 31 is a mathematical identity, it cannot be used in any straightforward way to determine the effect on $\rho_{DD'}$ of a change in $\rho_{X_1 X_1'}$ or $\rho_{X_2 X_2'}$, because changes in these reliabilities would also affect $\rho_{X_1 X_2}$ (Feldt, 1995; Zimmerman, 1994).

Simple difference scores have often been criticized as measures of gain from pretest to posttest because they are believed to be unreliable, because the difference score often is negatively correlated with the pretest score,[10] and because an alternative statistic yields a smaller expected mean squared error of estimation (e.g., Cronbach & Furby, 1970; Harris, 1963; Linn & Slinde, 1977). More recent writers, however, have been more favorably disposed to the use of simple difference scores, with due attention to their statistical properties and to their relevance to the use or interpretation at hand. For a randomly chosen individual, the simple difference score is an unbiased estimator of the true difference (e.g., true-score change over time), and if that is in fact the parameter of interest, then the difference score has much to recommend it[11] (Rogosa, Brandt, & Zimowski, 1982; Rogosa & Willett, 1983; Willett, 1988; Williams & Zimmerman, 1996; Zimmerman & Williams, 1982). Moreover, low within-group reliability of difference scores does not imply low statistical power for comparisons among groups (Feldt & Brennan, 1989; Humphreys, 1993; Humphreys & Drasgow, 1989a, 1989b; Nicewander & Price, 1983; Overall, 1989a, 1989b; Zimmerman, Williams, & Zumbo, 1993).

2.5.7.1. Precision of Absolute Versus Relative Interpretations

As discussed in section 1.1, a reliability coefficient alone provides incomplete information about score precision. Because difference scores imply attention to intra-individual comparisons (e.g., the same examinee's performance at two points in time), the standard error of the difference is often more relevant to its intended interpretation than is the reliability coefficient for the difference. If all examinees improve by the same number of points from pretest to posttest, then the reliability of the gain score is zero. Stated differently, the consistency with which examinees may be rank-ordered according to the magnitude of their difference scores is often far less important than the accuracy with which each individual's difference score is estimated (Collins, 1996).

When differences are taken between pairs of scores with the same metric (e.g., profile score components standardized to a common mean and standard deviation, or pretest and posttest scores on the same or parallel test forms), the reliability coefficient may be an unsuitable indicator of score precision for yet another reason. Raw scores on a single test rarely have a meaningful zero point. In most cases, adding a constant to everyone's score would not affect score interpretations. When differences are taken between scores in the same metric, however, the mean difference for the population and the magnitude of the difference for individual examinees become meaningful. Positive versus negative values may indicate growth versus decline. Also, the standard error of measurement may be more meaningfully considered in relation to the magnitude of the difference scores than to the standard deviation of the difference scores (Kane, 1996; Miller & Kane, 2001). Consider two scenarios, one in which pre-post differences for five students were −2, −1, 0, 1, and 2, and the other in which pre-post differences were 98, 99, 100, 101, and 102. Assume in each case that the standard error of measurement for the difference scores is 1.5. In each case, the reliability of the difference scores is 0.1. In the second case, however, the standard error seems trivial relative to the large gains by all students, whereas in the first case, error variance substantially clouds score interpretation.[12]

There are, of course, applications where the reliability coefficient for a difference score does convey important information. Much of the work on difference scores has been motivated by the problem of studying change over time, from pretest to posttest. If a researcher were interested in predicting rate of change, difference scores might be used as a dependent variable in a regression equation. The reliability coefficient for the difference scores would convey important information about statistical power for such an analysis. Reliability of estimates of individual change may be substantially improved by obtaining more than two waves of data (Willett, 1989). Models for reliability of composites involving more than two waves of data are beyond the scope of this chapter, but various models have been proposed (e.g., Mellenbergh & van den Brink, 1998; Rogosa, Brandt, & Zimowski, 1982; Rogosa & Willett, 1985; Willett, 1989; Willett & Sayer, 1994).

2.5.7.2. Alternative Definitions of Difference Scores

As noted, the simple difference score, $X_2 - X_1$, is an unbiased estimator of the true difference but lacks other statistical properties sometimes deemed desirable. Various modifications use weights other than −1 and +1 for X_1 and X_2. One commonly used score is the residual from the regression of X_2 on X_1,

$$Z_{\text{Resid}} = X_2 - a_{2.1} - b_{2.1} X_1,$$

where

$$b_{2.1} = \rho_{X_1 X_2} \sigma_{X_2} / \sigma_{X_1} \text{ and}$$
$$a_{2.1} = \bar{X}_2 - b_{2.1} \bar{X}_1.$$

Z_{Resid} represents the deviation of X_2 from the value predicted by X_1 and is uncorrelated with X_1. A commonly used estimator of the true-score difference simply regresses the observed gain toward the mean gain for the population:

$$Z_{\text{Kelley}} = \rho_{DD'}(X_2 - X_1) + (1 - \rho_{DD'})(\mu_2 - \mu_1). \quad (32)$$

This formula is an application of Kelley's (1947) formula for predicting the true score from the linear regression of true score on observed score, applied to the difference score as proposed by McNemar (1958). It is referred to by Willett (1988) as the *reliability-weighted measure of individual change*. The standard error of Z_{Kelley}, taking into account the substitution of some sample values for population parameters, is derived by Maassen (2000), who points out that it is inappropriate to interpret sample values of Z_{Kelley} relative to the standard error of the simple difference score.

More complicated (and more accurate) formulas incorporate the reliabilities of X_1 and X_2 to estimate the difference in true scores from the two observed scores (Lord, 1956a, 1958; McNemar, 1958). The Lord-McNemar estimate of $T_2 - T_1$ is given by $Z_{L-M} = w_0 + w_1 X_1 + w_2 X_2$, where

$$w_1 = \frac{1}{1 - \rho_{X_1 X_2}^2} \left[\frac{\rho_{X_1 X_2} \sigma_{X_2}}{\sigma_{X_1}} (1 - \rho_{X_2 X_2'}) - \rho_{X_1 X_1'} + \rho_{X_1 X_2}^2 \right] \quad (33)$$

$$w_2 = \frac{1}{1 - \rho_{X_1 X_2}^2} \left[\frac{\rho_{X_1 X_2} \sigma_{X_1}}{\sigma_{X_2}} (\rho_{X_1 X_1'} - 1) + \rho_{X_2 X_2'} - \rho_{X_1 X_2}^2 \right]$$

and

$$w_0 = (1 - w_2)\mu_2 - (1 + w_1)\mu_1. \quad (34)$$

Observed means and correlations and estimated reliabilities are substituted into Equations 33 and 34. The reliability of the Lord-McNemar estimate is given by

$$\rho_{ZZ'_{L-M}} = 1 - \frac{w_1^2 \sigma_{X_1}^2 (1 - \rho_{X_1 X_1'}) + w_2^2 \sigma_{X_2}^2 (1 - \rho_{X_2 X_2'})}{\sigma_{Z_{L-M}}^2}.$$

Extensions to difference scores for multivariate observations, including cases with correlated errors, are given by Brennan (2001b, chap. 12).

2.6. Special Topics

This section includes applications and extensions of the theory developed thus far, beginning with the estimation of true scores from observed scores and the estimation of conditional standard errors of measurement given true scores. Next is prediction of a test's reliability when it is used with a different examinee population. The two subsequent topics concern correction for attenuation due to unreliability and the relation of reliability to statistical power. These show some implications of classical test theory for the use and interpretation of other statistics. The final topics in this section concern the statistical properties of coefficient alpha and intraclass reliability coefficients, including significance testing and the construction of confidence intervals.

2.6.1. Point and Interval Estimation of True Scores

For any given person p, an observed score X_{pf}, obtained when person p is administered a randomly chosen form f of test X, is an unbiased estimator of person p's true score, τ_p. This follows from Equations 1 and 3. However, if a group of (one or more) persons is selected *on the basis of their observed score* X_f^* on form f of test X, then X^* is *not* an unbiased estimator of the selected group's average true score. This seeming paradox arises because the first case, conditioning on person p, is functionally the same as conditioning on person p's true score, τ_p, and from Equations 1 and 3, $E_f(X_{pf}|\tau_p) = \tau_p$. The expected value of the average true score for a group of persons selected on the basis of their observed score X^* is a different quantity. Using f to denote the particular form administered and, to avoid confusion, using g to index all possible forms, $E_g E_p(X_{pg}|X_{pf} = X^*) = E_p(\tau_p|X_{pf} = X^*)$. Note that such selection violates the assumption stated in connection with Equation 4, that the group is not chosen on the basis of their observed scores on form f. If persons with observed score X^* are selected from some larger sample, then assuming $0 < \rho_{XX'} < 1$, the expected value of the error components for their scores falls between 0 and $X^* - \mu$, where μ is the mean for the population represented by the tested sample. For a group chosen *without* regard to their observed scores, of course, the expected value of the errors is zero. Conditioning on observed scores changes the expected value of the errors because errors and observed scores from the same test administration are correlated. From Equation 1, $X_{pf} = \tau_p + E_{pf}$, it follows that observed scores are correlated with both of their constituent parts—the stable, replicable true-score component and the random, nonreproducible error component. The squared correlation of observed score with true score is shown in Equation 8 to be $\rho_{XX'}$. A corresponding derivation would show that the squared correlation of observed score with error is $1 - \rho_{XX'}$.

Consider the subgroup of examinees obtaining an observed score X^* on form f, where X^* is greater than $\overline{X}$, the mean for the group tested. This subgroup would be expected to have a mean true score above the average for the group tested. They would also be expected to have a mean error score component that was greater than zero. If that subgroup were tested again using a strictly parallel form g, their true scores would be the same, but the error components of their scores on form g would have an expected value of zero. Selection based on form f observed scores would not affect the expected error components from the form g administration. Thus, the expected value of (true score plus error) on form g for this subgroup would be somewhere between $\overline{X}$ and X^*. This is the explanation for the familiar phenomenon of "regression toward the mean." If examinees are selected on the basis of their observed scores, they are being selected on the basis of both the true scores and the particular, nonreplicable error components that constitute those observed scores. As will be seen, it follows that using information about the population enables improved estimation of true score conditional on observed score.

The best known formula for point estimation of true scores, attributed to Kelley (1947), is obtained from a model for the linear regression of true scores on observed scores, $\hat{\tau}_p = \mu_T + \beta_{T.X}(X_p - \mu_X)$. From Equations 1 and 4, $\mu_T = E_p(\tau_p) = \mu_X$. From Equation 7 or Equation 8, $\beta_{T.X} = \sigma_{XT}/\sigma_X^2 = \rho_{TX}\sigma_T/\sigma_X = \rho_{XX'}$. Substituting and rearranging terms,

$$\hat{\tau}_p = \mu_{T.X_p} = \rho_{XX'}X_p + (1 - \rho_{XX'})\mu_X. \tag{35}$$

Equation 35 represents the predicted true score as a weighted average of the observed score and the group mean, the weights being $\rho_{XX'}$ and $(1 - \rho_{XX'})$, respectively. It might seem that $\hat{\tau}_p$ would be preferable to X_p when group score information is available, but in most applications, $\hat{\tau}_p$ has little to recommend it. For a single group, there is a linear relation between $\hat{\tau}_p$ as defined by Equation 35 and X_p. Thus, norm-referenced score interpretations and observed correlations with other variables are unchanged when $\hat{\tau}_p$ is substituted for X_p. If examinees were divided into two or more subgroups on the basis of some other characteristic, Equation 35 could be used to regress observed scores toward their respective subgroup means, but this would be unacceptable for nearly any routine testing application, because it would be equivalent to adjusting scores upward or downward as a function of subgroup membership. If subgroups A and B had different mean scores, then persons from subgroups A and B who earned identical observed scores would be assigned different adjusted scores. For the group as a whole, such adjusted scores would be more accurate estimates of true scores, in a least-squares sense, than either unadjusted scores or scores adjusted toward a common population mean. However, any use of such differentially adjusted scores that held consequences for individual examinees would generally be regarded as unfair. Nonetheless, $\hat{\tau}_p$ as defined by Equation 35 may be useful for some forms of criterion-referenced score interpretation, or in research applications if test scores are used to match groups drawn from nonequivalent populations.

It follows from Equations 1, 2, and 3 that the regression of observed scores on true scores must be linear. However, the assumption underlying Equation 35 that the regression of true scores on observed scores is linear holds only under special conditions. If errors of measurement are normally distributed and have the same variance regardless of true score, then the regression of true score on observed score will be linear if and only if true scores are normally distributed (Lord & Novick, 1968, p. 503).

For number-correct or proportion-correct scores, a more realistic model is the beta-binomial strong true-score model (Lord, 1965). This model and the so-called "four-parameter beta" model (Keats & Lord, 1962) are widely used, although other alternatives exist (Hambleton, Swaminathan, Algina, & Coulson, 1978; Hsu, Leonard, & Tsui, 1991; Lin & Hsiung, 1992, 1994; Lord, 1969; Wilcox, 1978). For comparisons among some of these models, see Jarjoura (1985). The beta-binomial model is related to the binomial error model. Suppose that the test score X_{pf} is obtained by randomly sampling n items from some item domain. For examinee p, $\zeta_p = \tau_p/n$ is the probability of a correct response to each such randomly chosen item. Thus, X_{pf} follows a binomial distribution for the sum of n trials with probability ζ_p for each trial. This defines the binomial error model.[13] Algorithms exist for interval estimation of true scores under this model (Lord & Stocking, 1976). The beta-binomial model combines the binomial error model with the assumption that true scores follow a beta distribution. Under this additional assumption, the regression of true scores on observed scores is linear, and the distribution of observed scores is negative hypergeometric. The more general "four-parameter beta-binomial" model is another extension of the binomial error model, modeling the true score distribution as a beta distribution rescaled linearly from the interval (0, 1) to the interval (a, b), $0 \leq a < b \leq 1$. Estimation for the two-parameter and four-parameter beta binomial models can be accomplished by the method of moments (Lord & Novick, 1968, chap. 23; Keats & Lord, 1962; Hanson, 1991).

There are several approaches to interval estimation of true scores. For a chosen individual p, a *confidence interval* may be estimated, which has a specified probability of covering the parameter τ_p. That means that if the measurement procedure were repeated many times and confidence intervals were constructed in the same way, the specified percentage of confidence intervals so constructed would include the parameter. If errors of measurement are assumed to be normally distributed, the traditional confidence interval is $X_p \pm z\sigma_E$, where σ_E is the standard error of measurement and z is determined from the unit normal distribution. For example, to obtain a 95% confidence interval, z would be 1.96.

For a group of persons with a specified observed score X^*, a *tolerance interval* may be constructed. This is an interval that includes a specified percentage of the true scores for that group. It is typically centered at $\mu_{T.X^*}$ as defined by Equation 35. The model for the linear regression of true score on observed score used to derive Equation 35 gives a standard error of estimate of $\sigma_{T.X} = \sqrt{\sigma_T^2(1-\rho_{XT}^2)} = \sqrt{\rho_{XX'} \cdot \sigma_X^2 (\sigma_E^2/\sigma_X^2)} = \sigma_E \sqrt{\rho_{XX'}}$. Thus, under the assumption of normality, a tolerance interval for observed score X^* is

$$(\rho_{XX'}(X^* - \mu_X) + \mu_X) \pm z\sigma_E \sqrt{\rho_{XX'}}, \qquad (36)$$

where z is once again determined from the unit normal distribution. Note that this interval is centered on the point estimate of $\hat{\tau}_p$ given in Equation 35. The tolerance interval in Equation 36 can be calculated for any observed score on any test using sample estimates of the test's mean, reliability, and standard error.

For tests consisting of equally weighted, dichotomously scored items, better results can be obtained by using an estimate of the conditional standard error of measurement (discussed in the following section, 2.6.2) and by using the *score confidence interval* first introduced by Wilson (1927). Let x represent the sum of n binomial trials with a probability π of success on each trial. In the present context, x would be the number correct on a test form constructed by randomly sampling n items from some item domain. Note that if π is person p's probability of success on a randomly chosen item, then $\tau_p = n\pi$. With this notation, $\hat{\pi} = x/n$ and the standard deviation of x is $\sqrt{n\pi(1-\pi)}$, estimated by $\sqrt{n/(n-1)} \sqrt{n\hat{\pi}(1-\hat{\pi})}$. The most familiar estimate of the standard error of x, $\sqrt{x(n-x)/(n-1)}$, is obtained by substituting $\hat{\pi}$ for π, and the most familiar confidence interval for $\tau_p = n\pi$ is $x \pm z \sqrt{x(n-x)/(n-1)}$. This expression is derived from the equation for the test statistic $z = (\hat{\pi} - \pi)/\sqrt{\hat{\pi}(1-\hat{\pi})/(n-1)}$, which is approximately distributed as normal with unit variance. To obtain Wilson's score confidence interval, instead of substituting $\hat{\pi}$ for π, the expression $(\hat{\pi}-\pi)/\sqrt{\pi(1-\pi)/n} = \pm z_{\alpha/2}$ is solved algebraically for π (Agresti & Coull, 1998).[14] Using the notation z for $z_{\alpha/2}$, the score confidence interval for the true score corresponding to observed score x on an n-item test is given by W. Lee, Brennan, and Kolen (in press) as

$$I_S(\tau) = \frac{n(x+z^2/2)}{n+z^2} \pm z \frac{n}{(n+z^2)} \sqrt{x(n-x)/n + z^2/4}. \qquad (37)$$

(W. Lee et al. give a slightly different representation. Notation has been changed for consistency with this presentation.) In simulations based on an actual test form, W. Lee et al. report that the confidence interval given by Equation 37 gave coverages closest to nominal coverage probabilities and recommended it over several alternatives. Agresti and Coull also found that score confidence intervals performed better than alternatives.

Interval estimates of true scores may also be obtained for various derived score scales. For example, a test user might wish to obtain a confidence interval for an examinee's percentile rank or some other scale score. If a derived score scale is obtained as a linear transformation of the raw score, a confidence interval for the true scale score may be obtained by applying the same linear transformation to the endpoints of the confidence interval for the true score on the original, raw score scale. If the scale score is obtained by a nonlinear transformation, the recommended procedure is to obtain a confidence interval on the raw score scale and then transform each endpoint of that confidence interval to the derived score scale (W. Lee, Brennan, & Kolen, in press).

2.6.2. Estimating the Standard Error of Measurement Conditional on True Score

It is sometimes asserted that classical test theory assumes a common standard error of measurement for all examinees. Indeed, the straightforward estimation of the conditional standard error of measurement for a given latent trait value θ_p is often cited as one of the significant advantages of item response theory (IRT) over classical test theory. This perception may arise from the close connection in classical test theory between $\rho_{XX'}$ and the unconditional standard error of measurement, σ_E, as presented in Equation 9. In fact, however, except for a passing reference in section 2.6.1, it has nowhere been assumed to this point that the standard error of measurement is constant for all examinees. To the contrary, it has long been recognized that the standard error of measurement on a fixed-length test with a bounded range of scores varies as a function of the examinee's true score. The standard error of number-correct or proportion-correct scores is larger near the center of the score distribution, and smaller toward the tails of the distribution. The first methods for estimating conditional standard errors of measurement in the context of classical test theory were developed over 50 years ago (Mollenkopf, 1949; Thorndike, 1951, p. 597). Conditional standard errors of measurement are important to test users who wish to construct confidence or tolerance intervals for true scores, and for accurate prediction of the reliability of test scores with a different examinee population. The *Standards* (AERA, APA, & NCME, 1999) calls for reporting of conditional standard errors of measurement in Standards 2.2 and 2.14.

If a test can be divided into two τ-equivalent half-tests, the variance of the difference between the half-test scores is equal to the error variance for the test (cf. the Guttman-Rulon split-half reliability estimate presented in Equation 13). This relation can be exploited to calculate conditional standard errors of measurement by dividing examinees into groups according to their total scores and calculating the variance of half-test differences for each group (Thorndike, 1951). The square root of the resulting error variance estimate, $\sqrt{\sigma^2_{(X_1-X_2)}}$, is an estimate of the conditional standard error of measurement. If two alternate forms can be administered together, examinees may be grouped according to their mean scores, $(X_f + X_g)/2$, and for each group, the conditional standard error of measurement may be estimated by $\sqrt{\sigma^2_{(X_f-X_g)}/2}$. With these methods, small numbers of examinees may lead to erratic estimates, especially for extreme score groups. This problem might be addressed by pooling examinees across a range of scores. An alternative is to smooth the estimates of conditional standard errors of measurement (Mollenkopf, 1949). Note that $\hat{\sigma}^2_{(X_1-X_2)} = \Sigma[(X_{p1}-X_{p2}) - (\overline{X}_1-\overline{X}_2)]^2/(N-1)$, where $\overline{X}_1$ and $\overline{X}_2$ are the half-test means within a given score group. A polynomial regression may be used to predict the mean squared deviations of difference scores for individual examinees, $[(X_{p1}-X_{p2})-(\overline{X}_1-\overline{X}_2)]^2$, as a function of the total score X_p, using a polynomial of whatever degree is required to obtain a satisfactory fit. The regression provides a smooth curve representing the squared conditional standard error of measurement as a function of total score. The same method may be used if scores on two alternate forms X_f and X_g are available.

Several refinements of the Thorndike and Mollenkopf methods have been proposed. Because examinees are necessarily grouped by observed scores, not true scores, slightly different formulas are required to estimate the conditional variance of true scores given observed score versus the conditional variance of errors on a classically parallel test given observed score (Woodruff, 1990, 1991). These quantities may also be related to the standard error of prediction if the score on a parallel test X' is predicted from X. In practice, adjustment for stratification of examinees according to X rather than T has only a small effect on estimates. A generalization of Thorndike's method under which the test is divided into more than two τ-equivalent parts reduces sampling variation and so yields more accurate estimates of conditional standard errors of measurement. These estimates may be again improved by smoothing using a quadratic polynomial regression (Feldt & Qualls, 1996b).

A robust approach to estimating conditional standard errors of measurement for number-correct scores has been derived from the binomial error model. If a test is regarded as a random sample of n dichotomously scored items, then the total score for an examinee with true score τ_p may be modeled as the sum of n draws from a binomial distribution with probability $\varphi_p = \tau_p/n$ of success on each draw. The variance of the number-correct score under this model is $\sigma^2_{X.\tau_p} = \sigma^2_{E.\tau_p} = n\varphi_p(1-\varphi_p)$. Substituting observed scores for true scores and incorporating a correction for the use of the sample estimate of error variance, this model yields

$$\hat{\sigma}^2_{E.\tau_p} = \frac{X_p(n-X_p)}{n-1}. \qquad (38)$$

This is the square of the value widely referred to as Lord's (1955, 1957) conditional standard error of measurement. It is an estimator of the variance expected across hypothetical repeated measurements for a single examinee, where each measurement employs an independent sample of n items from an infinite population of such items. As such, it is appropriate for "absolute" score interpretations, such as constructing confidence intervals for individual examinees' true scores.[15] In many testing applications, however, the intended score interpretations are "relative." If all examinees were given the same form of a test, then score variability due to the sampling of different items for different examinees would not enter into comparisons among their observed scores. The sampling of an unusually easy or difficult set of items would affect all examinees' scores in the same way. For "relative" score interpretations, Equation 38 would overstate the relevant error variance.

There is a close connection between Equation 38 and the formula for the Kuder-Richardson 21 reliability estimate (Equation 19). The estimate of the unconditional error variance obtained by averaging $\hat{\sigma}^2_{E.\tau_p}$ as given by Equation 38 over all examinees is equal to $\sigma^2_X(1-{}_{21}\rho_{XX'})$ (Lord, 1955, 1957). This relation is the basis for a simple correction proposed by Keats (1957), which provides an approximate conditional standard error for relative score interpretations. Keats's formula multiplies the result of Equation 38 by a factor chosen to adjust the average conditional standard error over examinees to equal a more appropriate estimate of the unconditional standard error of measurement. That factor is $(1-\hat{\rho}_{XX'})/(1-{}_{21}\hat{\rho}_{XX'})$, where $\hat{\rho}_{XX'}$ represents any reliability estimate appropriate to the intended use or interpretation. Thus, the recommended formula is

$$\hat{\sigma}^2_{E.\tau_p} = \frac{X_p(n-X_p)(1-\hat{\rho}_{XX'})}{(n-1)(1-{}_{21}\hat{\rho}_{XX'})}. \qquad (39)$$

This approach has the advantage that it does not depend on patterns of part-test scores. It yields a single standard error for each observed score. A disadvantage relative to the earlier approaches is its limitation to tests consisting solely of equally weighted, dichotomously scored items. An extension to the case of polytomously scored items, based on the multinomial error model, is given by W. Lee (2005). A still more general solution would be to use the approach devised by Livingston and Lewis (1995). They show how to approximate the characteristics of tests containing polytomously scored or differentially weighted items using a hypothetical test conforming to the binomial error model assumptions of Equation 38. Their method is further discussed in section 4.1.

As an alternative to the adjustment in Equation 39, items may be stratified according to content categories to capture systematic variation in item difficulty. Equation 38 is then used within strata, and the resulting error variance estimates are summed across strata (Feldt, 1984). This approach provides an estimate of absolute error variance for the case where alternate forms are constructed by random sampling within separate item pools for each stratum. It has the potential disadvantage, however, that different examinees with the same total score may be assigned different conditional error variance estimates according to their patterns of performance across strata.

Six methods for estimating conditional standard errors of measurement were compared empirically by Qualls-Payne (1992). These included the original Thorndike (1951) method, the method incorporating smoothing (Mollenkopf, 1949), Keats's (1957) method given in Equation 39, Feldt's (1984) method incorporating stratification, and two additional methods (Jarjoura, 1986; Lord, 1980). Against a criterion derived from test-retest data, the six methods performed similarly; but against a parallel-forms criterion, Feldt's (1984) stratification approach appeared superior.

Additional methods for estimating conditional standard errors of measurement have been derived within the framework of generalizability theory (e.g., Brennan, 1998). These approaches are discussed in section 3.9. The framework of generalizability theory is helpful in clarifying distinctions between absolute and relative score interpretations and their associated standard errors.

It must be emphasized that all of the foregoing methods yield conditional standard errors of measurement for raw scores. If scale scores are derived by a linear transformation of raw scores, that same transformation may be applied to conditional standard errors of raw scores to obtain standard errors in the scale-score metric. Typically, however, scale scores are derived by some nonlinear transformation, necessitating more complex procedures. Several proposed methods begin with one or another estimate of raw-score conditional standard errors of measurement and then use these estimates to derive conditional standard error estimates for scale scores. For tests comprising equally weighted, dichotomously scored items, strong true-score theory can be used to obtain conditional standard errors of raw scores according to Equation 39 or using an approximation to the more accurate compound binomial model. At the same time, the true-score distribution can be well approximated by a four-parameter beta distribution fitted by the method of moments (Keats & Lord, 1962; Lord, 1965). Under this model, the expected observed score distribution corresponding to any given true score can be generated. If each possible observed score is transformed to its corresponding scale score, the result is the conditional scale score distribution, from which the conditional standard error of measurement for a scale score can be obtained (Kolen, Hanson, & Brennan, 1992; Brennan & Lee, 1999). The same approach may be taken beginning with IRT-based raw-score conditional standard errors of measurement instead of standard errors derived from strong true-score theory, with very similar results (Kolen, Zeng, & Hanson, 1996). A computationally simpler approach approximates the derivative of the scale score with respect to the raw score using a polynomial approximation to the function mapping raw scores to scale scores (Feldt & Qualls, 1998). Each of these methods may be recommended in certain situations, depending on measurement model assumptions and the importance placed on computational simplicity (W. Lee, Brennan, & Kolen, 2000).

2.6.3. Correcting Reliability Coefficients for Restriction in Range

The coefficient of reliability can be expressed as a function of the (unconditional) standard error of measurement and the observed-score variance (Equation 9). Both of these quantities may vary from one population to another. Thus, the reliability coefficient will also vary from one examinee population to another. Consider the problem of using the reliability for population A, $\rho_{XX'_A}$, to estimate the reliability for population B, $\rho_{XX'_B}$. If the (unconditional) error variances are assumed to be the same, i.e., $\sigma^2_{E_A} = \sigma^2_{E_B}$, then $\rho_{XX'_B}$ can be obtained from $\rho_{XX'_A}$ and the observed-score variances $\sigma^2_{X_A}$ and $\sigma^2_{X_B}$ as

$$\rho_{XX'_B} = 1 - \sigma^2_{X_A}(1 - \rho_{XX'_A})/\sigma^2_{X_B}. \quad (40)$$

As discussed in the previous section, the assumption that $\sigma^2_{E_A} = \sigma^2_{E_B}$ is unrealistic. It may, however, provide a satisfactory approximation. For tests consisting of equally weighted, dichotomously scored items, a better estimate can be obtained by modeling the change in the standard error of measurement as well as the change in observed score variance. Using the relation between the KR-21 reliability and the average conditional standard error of measurement as given by Equation 38, the following formula is obtained (Feldt & Brennan, 1989, p. 125):

$$\hat{\rho}_{XX'_B} = 1 - \frac{(1-\hat{\rho}_{XX'_A})(1-_{21}\hat{\rho}_{XX'_B})}{(1-_{21}\hat{\rho}_{XX'_A})}. \quad (41)$$

Applications of Equations 40 and 41 are predicated on the assumption that populations A and B do not differ in other ways that might affect test reliability. In practice, reliability might be influenced by factors extraneous to the statistical models, including characteristics of examinees (e.g., age or membership in some clinical or diagnostic category) or of test administrations (e.g., individual versus group administration, low-stakes versus high-stakes administration). More homogenous populations will almost always have lower reliability coefficients, but there are exceptions (Feldt & Qualls, 1999). Meta-analytic methods have been used to investigate sources of variation across studies in obtained reliability coefficients, following a set of procedures referred to as *reliability generalization* (Henson & Thompson, 2002; Vacha-Haase, 1998). In a special journal issue devoted to this topic, Vacha-Haase, Henson, and Caruso (2002) list over 20 reliability generalization studies that have been conducted. Not surprisingly, different estimates (e.g., test-retest reliability, $_a\rho_{XX'}$, $_{21}\rho_{XX'}$) differ systematically, and alternate forms of the same instrument may vary somewhat in reliability (Lane, White, & Henson, 2002). Work on reliability generalization highlights the importance of investigators estimating and reporting reliability for each study, rather than relying solely on previously published estimates.

2.6.4. Reliability and Corrections for Attenuation

In many measurement applications, intended interpretations pertain more directly to true scores than observed scores. When the interpretation and use of scores for individual examinees is of primary concern, point or interval estimates of true scores can be obtained as discussed in section 2.6.1. In other applications, the relation between true scores on different measures may be of interest. The correlation between true scores on tests X and Y, $\rho_{T_X T_Y}$, can be expressed as a function of the observed-score correlation ρ_{XY} and the reliabilities of the two tests as follows:

$$\rho_{T_X T_Y} = \frac{\sigma_{T_X T_Y}}{\sigma_{T_X} \sigma_{T_Y}} = \frac{\sigma_{XY}}{\sigma_X \sqrt{\rho_{XX'}} \sigma_Y \sqrt{\rho_{YY'}}} = \frac{\rho_{XY}}{\sqrt{\rho_{XX'} \rho_{YY'}}}. \quad (42)$$

Substituting sample statistics into Equation 42 gives the well-known formula used to correct for attenuation due to unreliability in both X and Y. Note that although the population formula is exact, substitution of sample values yields a biased estimate of $\rho_{T_X T_Y}$. In addition, due to sampling error or the selection of an inappropriate reliability estimate, substitution of sample values into Equation 42 may yield values of $\hat{\rho}_{T_X T_Y}$ that are greater than one. It would not be appropriate, for example, to use internal-consistency estimates of $\rho_{XX'}$ and $\rho_{YY'}$ together with an estimate of ρ_{XY} obtained from administrations of tests X and Y on different days.

Cases may arise in which it is useful to correct an observed correlation for attenuation due to unreliability in just one measure. A derivation much like the one in Equation 42 yields an expression with just one term instead of two in the denominator. For example, it might be of interest to compare $\rho_{T_W Y}$ and $\rho_{T_X Y}$ in a situation where W and X have different reliabilities and the reliability of Y is unknown. For that purpose, the correlations $\rho_{T_W Y} = \rho_{WY}/\sqrt{\rho_{WW'}}$ and $\rho_{T_X Y} = \rho_{XY}/\sqrt{\rho_{XX'}}$ could be calculated and compared, perhaps by examining the ratio $\rho_{T_W Y}/\rho_{T_X Y}$. Another special case is the correction of a part-whole correlation for unreliability, for example, estimating the correlation between true scores on a portion of a test and the total test. For this purpose, a formula provided by G. Lee (2000b) may be used.

The usual formulas for ordinary least squares regression are derived under the assumption that predictors (independent variables) are measured without error. In the case of simple linear regression (just one predictor), the regression coefficient in the regression of Y on X is $\beta_{Y \cdot X} = \rho_{XY} \sigma_Y / \sigma_X$. The coefficient for the regression of Y on T_X is

$$\beta_{Y \cdot T_X} = \frac{\rho_{YT_X} \sigma_Y}{\sigma_{T_X}} = \frac{(\rho_{XY}/\sqrt{\rho_{XX'}}) \sigma_Y}{\sqrt{\rho_{XX'}} \sigma_X} = \frac{\beta_{Y \cdot X}}{\rho_{XX'}}.$$

Corresponding formulas in the case of multiple linear regression are complex. Structural equation models can be used to account for the reliabilities of predictor variables (Hancock, 1997).

Statistics other than correlations may also be adjusted for attenuation due to unreliability. In meta-analysis, a commonly used statistic is an *effect size*, equal to a group difference expressed in standard deviation units. In the simplest case of a comparison between two groups, the effect size is just the difference between the two group means divided by the pooled within-group standard deviation. If the reliability of the dependent measure is known, the standard deviation of true scores, $\sqrt{\rho_{XX'}} \sigma_X$, may be used instead of σ_X (Hedges & Olkin, 1985, pp. 131 ff.).

Some uses of these formulas have been controversial, but if accurate and appropriate reliability estimates are available and the statistical procedures are clearly reported, their use can be recommended (Muchinsky, 1996; Schmidt & Hunter, 1996, 1999). It is probably good practice always to report uncorrected statistics together with disattenuated statistics.

2.6.5. Reliability and Statistical Power

Measurement error, together with sampling error, increases the uncertainty of statistical comparisons. The power of statistical tests can be increased by using larger samples. Likewise, statistical power can be increased by using more reliable measures as dependent variables. The simplest case to discuss is a test of equality of means in a one-way analysis of variance with an equal number of observations in each group. The degree to which power can be increased by using a more reliable dependent variable depends on the initial level of reliability and on the degree to which population means actually differ among groups. Trivially, if the null hypothesis holds, then power is unaffected by reliability.

Other things being equal, power is directly related to the noncentrality parameter of the F test for equality of group means,

$$\varphi = \sqrt{\frac{N \sum (\mu_j - \mu)^2}{J \sigma^2}} \quad (43)$$

where μ_j, $j = 1, ..., J$ are group means, N is the sample size in each group, μ is the grand mean, and σ^2 is the within-group variance, assumed homogeneous across groups. Suppose that the original dependent measure X, with reliability $\rho_{XX'}$, is replaced with Y, an essentially τ-equivalent measure with reliability $\rho_{YY'}$. (Essential τ-equivalence of X and Y implies that the numerator under the radical in Equation 43 is unchanged when Y is substituted for X.) By the definition of the reliability coefficient (Equation 8), $\sigma_X^2 = \sigma_T^2/\rho_{XX'}$ and $\sigma_Y^2 = \sigma_T^2/\rho_{YY'}$. Thus, substituting measure Y for X will multiply the denominator under the radical in Equation 43 by $\rho_{XX'}/\rho_{YY'}$. It follows that the effect on statistical power of a change in reliability is given by

$$\varphi_Y = \sqrt{\frac{\rho_{YY'}}{\rho_{XX'}}} \, \varphi_X.$$

It can be seen from Equation 43 that the effect on φ of changing the group size, N, is

$$\varphi_{\text{new}} = \sqrt{\frac{N_{\text{new}}}{N_{\text{old}}}} \, \varphi_{\text{old}}.$$

Thus, the effect of a change in reliability on statistical power is the same as that of increasing the sample size by the ratio of the new to the old test reliabilities. Statistical power has been tabulated as a function of significance level, effect size, sample size, and reliability (Kopriva & Shaw, 1991).

2.6.6. Significance Tests and Confidence Intervals for Estimates of Reliability

In studies of alternative testing procedures, including comparisons of different tests, scoring rubrics, or training procedures for raters or observers, it may be of interest to determine whether observed differences in reliability coefficients are greater than would be expected due to sampling fluctuation. Sampling theory and significance tests are available for various common estimates of reliability.

For parallel forms or test-retest reliability estimates, the reliability estimate is a product-moment correlation coefficient. Standard methods for correlation coefficients can be used to construct confidence intervals or compare coefficients, for example, methods employing Fisher's transformation, $z = \ln((1 + r)/(1 - r))/2$. If split-half reliability estimates were obtained for the same or different tests using two independent groups of examinees, the same methods could be used to compare the product-moment correlations between the two half tests for the respective groups. To construct a confidence interval for a split-half reliability estimate (Equation 13), a confidence interval may first be constructed for $\hat{\rho}_{X_1X_2}$, and the endpoints of that confidence interval then transformed according to Equation 13. It would not be appropriate to apply Fisher's transformation directly to the split-half reliability estimate (Kristof, 1963; Lord, 1974). Parallel forms or test-retest estimates obtained using the same sample of examinees may be compared using methods for correlations involving variables that are not independent (Olkin, 1967; Yu & Dunn, 1982).

Sampling theory for coefficient alpha was developed independently by Kristof (1963) and Feldt (1965). If the coefficient alpha reliability is calculated for a test divided into k strictly parallel parts using a sample of N examinees, then the statistic $(1 - {}_a\rho_{XX'})/(1 - {}_a\hat{\rho}_{XX'})$ is distributed as central F with $(N-1)$ and $(k-1)(N-1)$ degrees of freedom. This result is exact only under the assumption that part-test scores follow a multivariate normal distribution with equal variances and with equal covariances (the compound symmetry assumption). Kristof (1970) presented a method for testing the significance of point estimates and for constructing confidence intervals for alpha calculated from the division of a test into $k = 2$ parts with unequal variances, under the assumption that the two part-test scores are bivariate normally distributed.

The assumption of multivariate normality is quite unrealistic in practice, and so it is important to know the effects of violations of that assumption. For the special case of dichotomously scored items, where alpha is equivalent to the Kuder-Richardson formula 20 coefficient, Feldt (1965) showed that the sampling distribution of alpha is well approximated by the theoretical distribution, even though binary responses obviously are not multivariate normal. More generally, effects of nonnormality are probably negligible if k is large (Bay, 1973). Assuming multivariate normality throughout, van Zyl, Neudecker, and Nel (2000) provide an alternative derivation of the exact sampling distribution under compound symmetry, as well as the asymptotic normal distribution of coefficient alpha for the general case when no assumptions are made about the form of the part-test covariance matrix. (Their general case would include multidimensional tests for which coefficient alpha might not be appropriate.) If multivariate normality is not assumed, the sampling distribution of coefficient alpha may be approximated using bootstrap methods (Raykov, 1998a). Taking a different approach, Wilcox (1992) proposes alternative robust measures of reliability based on variance estimators that are less sensitive to extreme values in the tails of the score distribution and presents a method of constructing confidence intervals for such estimators.

Situations may arise in which it is necessary to establish that the reliability exceeds some minimum threshold using no larger a sample than necessary. Examples include establishing the interrater reliability of a coding procedure or assuring that a test has adequate reliability when used with some small, previously untested population. Sequential probability ratio tests based on the Feldt (1965) and Kristof (1963) sampling distribution have been developed for this purpose by Eiting (1991). Monte Carlo simulations suggest that sample size may be reduced by almost one half using such methods.

A test for the equality of two independent alpha coefficients was introduced by Feldt (1969), who showed that under the null hypothesis $H_0:\alpha_1 = \alpha_2$, the test statistic $W = (1 - \hat{\alpha}_2)/(1 - \hat{\alpha}_1)$ is approximately distributed as a central F with $(N_1 - 1)$ and $(N_2 - 1)$ degrees of freedom, where $\hat{\alpha}_1$ and $\hat{\alpha}_2$ are obtained using samples of size N_1 and N_2, respectively. Hakstian and Whalen (1976) provided an approximate test for equality among three or more independent alpha coefficients, based on a normalizing transformation of the F distribution. The statistical power of Feldt's (1969) test has been investigated in a series of papers (Bonett, 2003; Feldt & Ankenmann, 1998, 1999).

Methods for comparing independent alpha coefficients cannot be used in the common situation where two or more alpha reliability estimates have been obtained using the same sample of examinees. A large-sample likelihood ratio test was developed by Kristof (1964) for the case of two tests each split into two half tests with equal variances. Feldt (1980) developed more general approximate tests for two tests administered to the same sample and split into k_1 and k_2 parts, respectively. Feldt's test statistic for the equality of two dependent coefficients is

$$t = \frac{(W-1)(N-2)^{1/2}}{(4W[1-\hat{\rho}^2_{X_1X_2}])^{1/2}},$$

where once again, $W = (1 - \hat{\alpha}_2)/(1 - \hat{\alpha}_1)$. Feldt and Brennan (1989) give the mathematically equivalent formula,

$$t = \sqrt{\frac{(N-2)(\hat{\alpha}_1 - \hat{\alpha}_2)^2}{4(1-\hat{\alpha}_1)(1-\hat{\alpha}_2)(1-\hat{\rho}^2_{X_1X_2})}}, \qquad (44)$$

which is distributed as t with $N - 2$ degrees of freedom. The critical value is $t_{\alpha/2}$. This test gives good control of Type I error with sample sizes of $N = 50$ or greater and test lengths (or number of part tests for calculation of coefficient alpha) of $k = 20$ or greater, or whenever $Nk > 1000$. A refinement of this test offering greater accuracy at the cost of somewhat greater computational complexity is given by Alsawalmeh and Feldt (1994a). Based on simulations, these authors recommend Equation 44 in cases where $Nk > 1000$ and $k > 10$. With shorter tests or smaller samples, the more complex procedure is recommended.

A test for the equality of K alpha coefficients obtained from the same sample was developed by Woodruff and Feldt (1986), by extending the method of Hakstian and Whalen (1976) to the case of dependent coefficients. That test depends on approximations to the F distribution where the degrees of freedom are high and is recommended for cases in which calculations of $_a\hat{\rho}_{XX'}$ are based on divisions of the tests into at least 20 part tests, or when the product of number of part tests and the number of examinees is at least 1,000.

2.6.7. Sampling Theory and Significance Tests for Intraclass Correlations

An important special case in educational measurement and behavioral measurement more generally concerns the reliability of measurements consisting of single observations. For example, one might be interested in the reliability of a single rater's judgments of examinees' performances, such as scores assigned to student essays by just one rater. Such a reliability coefficient is an *intraclass correlation*, as are test-retest and parallel-forms reliabilities.

Intraclass correlations may be estimated using any of a number of data collection designs, and the distributions of sample estimates will vary depending on the design chosen (McGraw & Wong, 1996). In measurement applications, an intraclass correlation is often estimated using the Spearman-Brown "prophecy" formula (Equation 27) to derive the reliability of a test consisting of a single observation from an estimate of reliability for a sum of two or more observations. Confidence intervals for such intraclass reliability estimates may be obtained by first forming a confidence interval for the original estimate using the methods of the previous section, and then transforming each endpoint of that interval to the corresponding value for a test consisting of a single observation (Feldt, 1990; Kraemer, 1981).

A significance test for comparing two independent intraclass reliability coefficients estimated from a two-way random-effects analysis of variance was derived and illustrated by Alsawalmeh and Feldt (1992), and a similar test for two intraclass coefficients estimated from the same sample was later developed by the same authors (Alsawalmeh & Feldt, 1994b). Their method, which is applicable to estimates derived from coefficient alpha reliability estimates using the Spearman-Brown formula, employs the test statistic $T = (1 - \hat{\rho}_1)/(1 - \hat{\rho}_2)$, which is approximately distributed under $H_0: \rho_1 = \rho_2$ as F with d_1 and d_2 degrees of freedom. Formulas for d_1 and d_2 are complex, and different formulas are required in the independent versus the dependent cases. The methods are more broadly applicable for comparing independent or dependent alpha reliabilities adjusted using the Spearman-Brown formula to any given test length, including cases where different values of k in Equation 27 are used for the two tests (Alsawalmeh & Feldt, 1999, 2000). This latter application might be useful in test development, when two possible test formats or item types are to be compared, and pilot versions of each need to be adjusted to a common test length (or testing time) prior to comparison.

3. GENERALIZABILITY THEORY

Classical test theory models an observed score as the sum of two components, a true score and an error. The true score may be defined as the expected value of the observed score over some set of replications of the measurement procedure, and the error may be defined by subtraction, as the difference between observed score and true score. As noted early in this chapter, there is considerable ambiguity in the definition of the true score, because "some set of replications" might be defined in different ways. The observed score may be conceived instead as a sum of not just two but a number of components in addition to the examinee's attitudes, beliefs, abilities, or character. Among these influences on obtained scores are the occasion of measurement, the test form used, the rater who assigns a score, and possibly interaction terms involving two or more such influences. True score and error may then be formulated in terms of these multiple components, according to the intended use or interpretation of the observed scores. Within classical test theory, there is no common notational system to describe multiple sources of error or alternative definitions of true score and error. A suitable notational system, critical conceptual distinctions, and related computational procedures are provided by generalizability theory.

An application of generalizability theory begins with the specification of a faceted *universe of admissible observations*, defined at the level of the smallest scorable units that might be observed. *Facets* are sources of variance like rater or test form, and each particular rater, test form, and so forth is a *condition* of the corresponding facet. Specifying one condition of each facet defines a potential observation. The ill-defined classical test theory notion of some set of replications is replaced in generalizability theory by a well defined, faceted *universe of generalization*, specifying a set of alternative potential measurements to be regarded as equivalent (i.e., the set of potential replications to which a user intends to generalize, or that the user would accept as equivalent to the measurement obtained). Typically, a measurement in a universe of generalization would be composed of a collection of observations. Instead of a true score, generalizability theory defines a *universe score*, which is the expected value, over a universe of generalization, of observed scores for a single object of measurement. A distinction is drawn between *generalizability studies* (G studies), intended to study the observations comprising potential measurements, and *decision studies* (D studies), in which measurements are obtained in the service of some testing application. The G study characterizes the universe of admissible observations, and the D study is referenced to a universe of generalization. Optimum G-study designs versus D-study designs will often differ. Although generalizability theory employs the statistical machinery of random-effects analysis of variance (ANOVA) models, it is far more than an application of analysis of variance. Rather, it should be viewed as a flexible and powerful family of measurement models, embodying conceptual tools for designing measurement procedures and analyzing their error structures (Brennan, 2000a).

The history of generalizability theory is discussed by Brennan (1997, 2001b). Burt (1936), C. Hoyt (1941), and Ebel (1951) had all proposed analysis of variance approaches to reliability, developing various ideas central to generalizability theory. Lindquist (1953, chap. 16) provided the first extended, formal exposition on the use of ANOVA to analyze components of error and true-score variance. Beginning in the 1960s, Cronbach and others further developed these ideas to create a system of models and statistical methods that was considerably richer than classical test theory (Cronbach, Rajaratnam, & Gleser, 1963; Gleser, Cronbach, & Rajaratnam, 1965). The first full treatment of their theory appeared in a monograph by Cronbach, Gleser, Nanda, and Rajaratnam (1972), titled *The Dependability of Behavioral Measurements: Theory of Generalizability for Scores and Profiles*. Brennan (1983) provided another important exposition of the theory, which was less comprehensive than that of Cronbach et al. (1972), but nonetheless set forth the theory's central concepts and statistical methods. The theory and methods of generalizability theory became more accessible with the appearance that same year of GENOVA (Crick & Brennan, 1983), a specialized computer program for carrying out the analyses required for generalizability studies. Further theoretical developments, including extensions of multivariate generalizability theory, were included in a special journal issue by Fyans (1983). Since then, numerous expositions of the basic theory have appeared, including Feldt and Brennan (1989, pp. 127–140), Shavelson, Webb, and Rowley (1989), Shavelson and Webb (1991), and Brennan (1992a, 1992b, 2000b).

A major recapitulation of the entire theory, with extensions, is Brennan's (2001b) *Generalizability Theory*. That monograph includes a systematic treatment of multivariate generalizability theory (where each object of measurement has multiple universe scores, each associated with conditions of one or more fixed facets). It also addresses recent developments in the estimation of variance components, sampling theory for variance component estimates, conditional standard errors of measurement from a G-theory perspective, and estimation for unbalanced random effects designs. Only a brief introduction to generalizability theory is presented in this chapter.

3.1. Notation and Definitions

This section presents some concepts and notation central to generalizability theory. It begins with a description of the simplest, one-facet designs for G studies and D studies, showing models for the decomposition of observed scores into score components (effects), defining variance components, and introducing the estimation of variance components using expressions for expected mean squares in analysis of variance. Section 3.1.3 turns to the definition of different error terms and corresponding coefficients analogous to, or in some cases identical to, the reliability coefficients of classical test theory. Section 3.1 concludes with an introduction to nested G-study and D-study designs and to multifacet designs.

3.1.1. G-Study p × i Design

Any observation involves a particular condition of each of one or more facets. Consider first the case of a universe consisting of conditions of a single facet, which will be referred to as the *items* facet (i). The observation obtained by administering item i to examinee p is denoted X_{pi}.

To study the precision of X_{pi}, a generalizability study (G study) might be conducted. Assume that each of n_p persons responded to the same set of n_i items. This simplest G-study design would be denoted $p \times i$. It would be described as a one-facet design, because the universe of admissible observations has just one facet, items. The "×" indicates that the items facet is *crossed* with the population of persons. If instead each examinee responded to a different set of items, then items would be said to be *nested* within persons, and the design would be denoted $i:p$, where the ":" is read "nested within." In the simplest case, the n_p persons would be regarded as sampled from an infinite population of persons, and the n_i items for each person ($n_p n_i$ items in all) from an infinite universe of items. Note that the word *population* is used for objects of measurement, and the term *universe* is reserved for conditions of measurement.

The expected value of person p's score over all items is $\mu_p = E_i X_{pi}$. Similarly, the grand mean over both persons and items is $\mu = E_p E_i X_{pi}$. The population mean for item i is $\mu_i = E_p X_{pi}$. Using these definitions and continuing with the case of the $p \times i$ design, score components are defined by Equation 45:

$$\begin{aligned} X_{pi} &= \mu & \text{(grand mean)} \\ &+ \mu_p - \mu & \text{(person effect} = \pi_p) \\ &+ \mu_i - \mu & \text{(item effect} = \alpha_i) \\ &+ X_{pi} - \mu_p - \mu_i + \mu & \text{(person by item effect} = \pi\alpha_{pi}). \end{aligned} \quad (45)$$

The observed score can now be expressed in terms of these components, including the grand mean, score effects, and residual, as

$$X_{pi} = \mu + \pi_p + \alpha_i + \pi\alpha_{pi}. \quad (46)$$

The magnitudes of the score effects and the residual cannot be exactly determined for any particular score, but the fixed effect μ and the variances of the random effects can be estimated.

The definitions of these effects imply that $E_p \pi_p = E_i \alpha_i = E_p \pi\alpha_{pi} = E_i \pi\alpha_{pi} = 0$. The variances of these respective score components are *variance components*. The definitions also imply that $E_p \pi_p \alpha_i = E_i \pi_p \alpha_i = E_p E_i \pi_p \alpha_i = 0$ and that for $p \neq p'$ and $i \neq i'$, $E \pi_p \pi_{p'} = E \alpha_i \alpha_{i'} = E \pi\alpha_{pi} \pi\alpha_{p'i} = E \pi\alpha_{pi} \pi\alpha_{pi'} = E \pi\alpha_{pi} \pi\alpha_{p'i'} = 0$. Standard errors appropriate for different score interpretations and *generalizability coefficients* (which include as special cases some reliability coefficients of classical test theory) are expressed in terms of these variance components. Variance components for this one-facet design are defined as $\sigma^2(p) = E_p \pi_p^2$, $\sigma^2(i) = E_i \alpha_i^2$, and $\sigma^2(pi) = E_p E_i (\pi\alpha_{pi})^2$.

Estimates of these variance components can be obtained from an analysis of variance, using the expected mean square equations for the $p \times i$ design:

$$\begin{aligned} EMS(p) &= \sigma^2(pi) + n_i \sigma^2(p) \\ EMS(i) &= \sigma^2(pi) + n_p \sigma^2(i) \\ EMS(pi) &= \sigma^2(pi). \end{aligned} \quad (47)$$

G-study data are analyzed as for a crossed two-way random-effects analysis of variance design with one observation in each cell. Observed mean squares are set equal to the expressions for the expected mean squares in Equation 47, and the resulting equations are solved for estimators of the variance components in terms of the mean squares, giving $\hat{\sigma}^2(pi) = MS(pi)$, $\hat{\sigma}^2(p) = [MS(p) - MS(pi)]/n_i$, and $\hat{\sigma}^2(i) = [MS(i) - MS(pi)]/n_p$.

Estimates of variance components are the final product of a G study. These estimated variance components could be used to design various decision studies (D studies) in which some measurement procedure would be put to practical use. G-study results would be used to predict the accuracy of D-study score estimates. It is useful to maintain the conceptual distinction between G studies and D studies even though in practice, the same data are often used for both purposes.

3.1.2. D-Study p × I Design

The D-study design begins with the specification of the intended universe of generalization. Potential measurements in the universe of generalization might be derived from the entire universe of admissible observations or a subset of that universe, but facets not defined in the universe of admissible observations cannot be referenced in specifying the universe of generalization. To continue the example, assume the universe of generalization comprises measurements formed by having each examinee respond to a common set of items, sampled from the same universe as the items used in the G study. Note that, whereas the elements of the universe of admissible observations are single (potential) item responses, the elements of the universe of generalization are (potential) scores formed by averaging sets of item responses. In the G study, the number of items employed was denoted n_i. The (possibly different) number of items in the D study is denoted n'_i. It is customary to use the mean of all the observations for an object of measurement as the score from the D study; capital letters are used to indicate averaging across conditions of a facet. Thus, this D-study design is denoted $p \times I$. Person p's score from the D study is defined and modeled as $X_{pI} = \sum_{i=1}^{n'_i} X_{pi}/n'_i = \mu + \pi_p + \sum_{i=1}^{n'_i} \alpha_i/n'_i + \sum_{i=1}^{n'_i} \pi\alpha_{pi}/n'_i = \mu + \pi_p + \alpha_I + \pi\alpha_{pI}$. Using mean scores greatly simplifies notation; conversion to total scores is trivial.

The G-study variance component estimates characterize a single observation. Because D studies typically employ multiple observations for each object of measurement, the magnitudes of G-study variance components versus D-study variance components differ. Notation for D-study variance components again uses capital letters in place of lower-case letters to indicate averaging over two or more conditions of a facet. The *universe score variance* for the D-study is $\sigma^2(p)$. Because effects are uncorrelated, $\sigma^2(I) = E_I \alpha_I^2 = \sigma^2(i)/n'_i$ and $\sigma^2(pI) = E_p E_I (\pi\alpha_{pI})^2 = \sigma^2(pi)/n'_i$.

3.1.3. Coefficients of Generalizability and Dependability

In typical testing applications employing the $p \times I$ D-study design, the test user's primary concern is with the relative scores of different examinees. Under the model shown in Equation 46, if the set of n'_i items actually used is easier or harder than some other set of items that could have been used instead, that will not affect any examinee's relative

standing. Person p's mean score, X_{pI}, is interpreted relative to $\mu_I = E_p X_{pI} = \mu + \alpha_I$, the population mean for the particular test. Substituting into Equation 46, the deviation score $X_{pI} - \mu_I = \pi_p + \pi\alpha_{pI}$. Thus, for purposes of comparing scores of different examinees responding to the same test, the relevant error term, denoted δ_{pI}, is $\pi\alpha_{pI}$. This error term has an expectation of zero and variance of

$$\sigma^2(\delta) = E_p E_I (\pi\alpha_{pI})^2 = \sigma^2(pI). \qquad (48)$$

Cronbach et al. (1972) defined a *generalizability coefficient*, $E\rho^2$, analogous to the reliability coefficient of classical test theory, as the ratio of the universe score variance to the expected value of the observed score variance.[16] For the $p \times I$ design, the expected variance of X_{pI} over persons is $E_p E_I (X_{pI} - \mu_I)^2 = \sigma^2(p) + \sigma^2(pI)$, and so

$$E\rho^2 = \frac{\sigma^2(p)}{\sigma^2(p) + \sigma^2(pI)} = \frac{\sigma^2(p)}{\sigma^2(p) + \sigma^2(\delta)}. \qquad (49)$$

This coefficient may be interpreted and used in much the same way as a reliability coefficient and in fact is equal to the coefficient alpha reliability if $n_i = n'_i$. Moreover, if $n_i \neq n'_i$, Equation 49 gives the same result as would be obtained by adjusting $_a\rho_{XX'}$ for the change in test length using the Spearman-Brown formula (Equation 27). The square root of $\sigma^2(\delta)$ is equal to the standard error of measurement as defined in Equation 9. A consistent, though not unbiased, estimator of $E\rho^2$ is obtained by substituting $\hat{\sigma}^2(p)$ and $\hat{\sigma}^2(pI)$, as defined in connection with Equation 47, for the corresponding quantities in Equations 48 and 49.

For other testing purposes, the user's concern may be not with *relative* scores of different examinees, but instead with the precision of X_{pI} as an estimate of person p's universe score, μ_p. Consider the problem of generalizing X_{pI} to a universe of *randomly parallel* measurements, each conceived as the score from the administration to person p of a sample of n'_i items from an infinite universe of items. The relevant error term for this purpose is $\Delta_p = X_{pI} - \mu_p$. The expected value of the variance of a person's scores across such randomly parallel measurements, $E_p(\sigma^2(\Delta_p)) = \sigma^2(\Delta)$, is equal to $\sigma^2(I) + \sigma^2(pI)$. It is generally the case that *relative* comparisons, and the error δ_{pI}, are most relevant for norm-referenced score interpretations, whereas *absolute* interpretations, and the error Δ_p, are most relevant for various kinds of criterion-referenced (or domain-referenced) interpretations (Brennan & Kane, 1977b). The absolute error variance, $\sigma^2(\Delta) = \sigma^2(I) + \sigma^2(pI)$, is always greater than or equal to the relative error variance, $\sigma^2(\delta) = \sigma^2(pI)$.

Brennan and Kane (1977a, 1977b) define an *index of dependability*, Φ, that is analogous to $E\rho^2$, but using $\sigma^2(\Delta)$ in place of $\sigma^2(\delta)$:

$$\Phi = \frac{\sigma^2(p)}{\sigma^2(p) + \sigma^2(\Delta)}. \qquad (50)$$

Under the $p \times I$ design (all examinees responding to the same set of items), the expected value of the observed score variance will be less than the denominator in Equation 50. If instead each examinee took a different, randomly parallel test form, the denominator in Equation 50 would be equal to the expected value of the variance of their observed scores.

In any case, the denominator is the expected value, over test forms and over persons, of the squared deviation of X_{pI} from μ. Classical test theory does not include any natural analog to the distinction between $\sigma^2(\delta)$ and $\sigma^2(\Delta)$, nor between $E\rho^2$ and Φ. However, there is a surprising connection between Φ and $_{21}\rho_{XX'}$, as discussed in section 4.1.

3.1.4. Single-Facet G-Study and D-Study Designs With Nesting

For the $p \times i$ G-study and $p \times I$ D-study designs just presented, all persons were assumed to respond to the same set of items. If instead each examinee responded to a *different* set of items, items would be said to be *nested* within persons, and the designs would be denoted $i{:}p$ or $I{:}p$. For the $i{:}p$ G-study design, item effects are confounded with the person-by-item interaction. Thus, an individual item response is modeled as $X_{pi} = \mu + (\mu_p - \mu) + (X_{pi} - \mu_p) = \mu + \pi_p + \alpha_{i:p}$. The term $\alpha_{i:p}$ is the sum of the α_i and $\pi\alpha_{pi}$ terms from the $p \times i$ design. Estimators of $\sigma^2(p)$ and $\sigma^2(i{:}p)$ are obtained by setting mean squares obtained from the (nested) one-way analysis of variance equal to their expected mean squares and solving:

$$EMS(p) = \sigma^2(i{:}p) + n_i\sigma^2(i{:}p) \quad (51)$$
$$EMS(i{:}p) = \sigma^2(i{:}p).$$

For the nested D-study design, $\sigma^2(I{:}p) = \sigma^2(i{:}p)/n'_i$.

Note that the $p \times i$ G-study design provides more information than the $i{:}p$ design, in the sense that it affords separate estimates of $\sigma^2(p)$ and $\sigma^2(pi)$. From these separate variance components, it is simple to calculate $\sigma^2(i{:}p) = \sigma^2(i) + \sigma^2(pi)$. Thus, there is no difficulty in using results from a crossed G-study design to plan a D study with a nested design. Because $\sigma^2(i)$ and $\sigma^2(pi)$ are confounded for the $I{:}p$ design, $\sigma^2(\delta) = \sigma^2(\Delta) = \sigma^2(I{:}p) = \sigma^2(i{:}p)/n'_i$. Nesting inevitably results in confounding of some variance components, and for that reason, crossed G-study designs are generally preferred, when feasible. Note, however, that generalizability theory is also applicable to measurement problems where the universe of admissible observations has a nested structure. Examples include samples of individuals' essays or artistic works, or repeated executions of tasks like making a broad jump or hitting a golf ball.

3.1.5. Multifacet G Studies and D Studies

The preceding discussion of the simplest, single-facet designs has served to introduce models and notation for crossed and nested G studies and D studies; the error terms δ and Δ; their corresponding error variances $\sigma^2(\delta)$ and $\sigma^2(\Delta)$; and the coefficients $E\rho^2$ and Φ. The method of estimating variance components using expected mean squares from analysis of variance was also introduced. When the universe of generalization has more than one facet, the number of possible designs increases rapidly, and various trade-offs become possible in D-study designs.

As an example of a two-facet design, consider the measurement of writing proficiency, and assume that the universe of admissible observations contains two crossed facets, prompts or items (i) and raters (r). Assume as well that the population of persons (p) is crossed with the universe of admissible observations. This means that any person might respond to any item, with the response rated by any rater. In order to estimate the variance components for this population and universe of admissible observations, an investigator conducts a G study. Suppose that n_p persons each respond to the same sample of n_i items, and all their responses are then scored by each of the same sample of n_r raters. The resulting G-study design is the fully crossed $p \times i \times r$ design, which mirrors the structure of the universe of admissible observations.

Person p's response to item i as scored by rater r is denoted X_{pir}. The expected value of person p's score over all items and raters is $\mu_p = E_i E_r X_{pir}$. Similarly, the grand mean over all persons, items, and raters is $\mu = E_p E_i E_r X_{pir}$. Population means for item i and rater r are defined as $\mu_i = E_p E_r X_{pir}$ and $\mu_r = E_p E_i X_{pir}$. The mean over persons for the combination of item i and rater r is $\mu_{ir} = E_p X_{pir}$; μ_{pi} and μ_{pr} are defined similarly. Using these definitions, score effects are defined as in Equation 52:

$$\begin{aligned}
X_{pir} = &\mu & \text{(grand mean)} \\
&+\mu_p - \mu & \text{(person effect} = \pi_p) \\
&+\mu_i - \mu & \text{(item effect} = \alpha_i) \quad (52)\\
&+\mu_r - \mu & \text{(rater effect} = \beta_r) \\
&+\mu_{pi} - \mu_p - \mu_i + \mu & \text{(person by item effect} = \pi\alpha_{pi}) \\
&+\mu_{pr} - \mu_p - \mu_r + \mu & \text{(person by rater effect} = \pi\beta_{pr}) \\
&+\mu_{ir} - \mu_i - \mu_r + \mu & \text{(item by rater effect} = \alpha\beta_{ir}) \\
&+X_{pir} - \mu + \mu_p + \mu_i + \mu_r - \mu_{pi} - \mu_{pr} - \mu_{ir} & \text{(residual effect} = \pi\alpha\beta_{pir}).
\end{aligned}$$

As with Equations 45 and 46, the definitions of these effects imply that $E_p\pi_p = E_i\alpha_i = E_r\beta_r = E_p\pi\alpha_{pi} = E_i\pi\alpha_{pi} = 0$. Likewise, expectations of each of the remaining score effects over any of the facets involved in their respective definitions are zero, as are expectations of products of score effects with nonoverlapping sets of subscripts (e.g., α_i and $\pi\beta_{pr}$). Variance components are defined as for the one-facet models. For example, $\sigma^2(pi) = E_p E_i (\pi\alpha_{pi})^2$. For the fully crossed two-facet D-study design, relative and absolute error are defined as $\delta_p = (X_{pIJ} - E_p X_{pIJ}) - (\mu_p - \mu)$ and $\Delta_p = X_{pIJ} - \mu_p$.

Expected mean squares for the $p \times i \times r$ design are as follows:

$$\begin{aligned}
EMS(p) &= \sigma^2(pir) + n_i\sigma^2(pr) + n_r\sigma^2(pi) + n_i n_r\sigma^2(p).\\
EMS(i) &= \sigma^2(pir) + n_p\sigma^2(ir) + n_r\sigma^2(pi) + n_p n_r\sigma^2(i).\\
EMS(r) &= \sigma^2(pir) + n_i\sigma^2(pr) + n_p\sigma^2(ir) + n_p n_i\sigma^2(r).\\
EMS(pi) &= \sigma^2(pir) + n_r\sigma^2(pi) \quad (53)\\
EMS(pr) &= \sigma^2(pir) + n_i\sigma^2(pr)\\
EMS(ir) &= \sigma^2(pir) + n_p\sigma^2(ir)\\
EMS(pir) &= \sigma^2(pir).
\end{aligned}$$

Variance component estimates can be obtained by setting observed mean squares equal to the expected mean squares in Equation 53 and solving the resulting equations, as illustrated for the one-facet design following Equation 47. This is the approach most often used to estimate variance components in G studies. Occasionally, negative estimates may be obtained for some variance components. Although different approaches to the problem of negative variance components have been proposed, the preferred procedure seems to be to carry negative values through intermediate calculations, and then to replace values with zero only after estimates of all variance components have been obtained. Alternatively, negative estimates can be avoided using some of the more complex estimation procedures referred to in section 3.7. Note that the occurrence of negative estimates may indicate model misspecification and should always alert the investigator to interpret results cautiously (Brennan, 2001b, pp. 84–85; Feldt & Brennan, 1989).

The fully crossed 2-facet G-study design permits estimation of seven distinct variance components: $\sigma^2(p)$, $\sigma^2(i)$, $\sigma^2(r)$, $\sigma^2(pi)$, $\sigma^2(pr)$, $\sigma^2(ir)$, and $\sigma^2(pir)$. There are five other possible 2-facet designs in which the p facet is not nested, not counting additional designs that might be obtained by transposing facets i and r. Each of these designs involves some confounding of the seven variance components distinguished in the fully-crossed design. Variance components that can be estimated from the $p \times i \times r$ design as well as these remaining five designs are as follows:

$$\begin{array}{ll}
p \times i \times r & \sigma^2(p), \sigma^2(i), \sigma^2(r), \sigma^2(pi), \sigma^2(pr), \sigma^2(ir), \sigma^2(pir) \\
p \times (i:r) & \sigma^2(p), \sigma^2(r), \sigma^2(i:r), \sigma^2(pr), \sigma^2(pi:r) \\
(i:p) \times r & \sigma^2(p), \sigma^2(i:p), \sigma^2(r), \sigma^2(pr), \sigma^2(ir:p) \quad (54) \\
r:(p \times i) & \sigma^2(p), \sigma^2(i), \sigma^2(pi), \sigma^2(r:pi) \\
(i \times r):p & \sigma^2(p), \sigma^2(i:p), \sigma^2(r:p), \sigma^2(ir:p) \\
r:i:p & \sigma^2(p), \sigma^2(i:p), \sigma^2(i:r:p).
\end{array}$$

Note that the second and third designs shown in Equation 54 distinguish five variance components, the fourth and fifth distinguish four variance components, and the last permits estimation of only three distinct variance components. Any of the variance components in any design can be obtained as the sum of some set of variance components from the fully crossed design. In the $p \times (i:r)$ design, for example, $\sigma^2(i:r) = \sigma^2(i) + \sigma^2(ir)$ and $\sigma^2(pi:r) = \sigma^2(pi) + \sigma^2(pir)$. Thus, provided the two facets in the universe of admissible observations are crossed and that both facets are crossed with the population of objects of measurement, a fully-crossed G-study design enables analysis of any possible D-study design. Two additional designs are possible, in which facets i and r are completely confounded. Continuing the previous example, one of these confounded designs would correspond to a study in which all persons responded to the same set of prompts (items) and all responses to a given prompt were rated once, by a rater who rated responses to that prompt and no others. The other additional design would arise if each person responded to a different set of prompts and each prompt was rated by a different rater.

A facet for which the number of possible conditions is assumed to be infinite is referred to as a *random* facet. Still further variations arise if one or more facets have only a finite number of conditions and all of these are included in the G study. If there is no sampling of conditions of a facet from a larger set of possible conditions, then the facet is referred to as *fixed*. Fixed facets, for which all conditions are sampled, may occur in the definition of the universe of admissible observations or a universe of generalization. The universe of admissible observations for a high school physics test, for example, might have a fixed facet for content area, with conditions like "mechanics," "kinematics," "electricity," "magnetism," and "optics." The test would include specified numbers of items for each level of this (fixed) facet. A facet may be random in the universe of admissible observations, but fixed in the universe of generalization defined for a particular testing application. Rater might be a random facet in the universe of admissible observations, for example, but if only one rater is to be used to score all responses, then a D study might treat rater as fixed. The most common cases are of random facets and of fixed facets where all conditions are sampled. However, intermediate cases may also arise occasionally, in which the proportion sampled out of all possible conditions is significantly greater than zero but less than one. Brennan (1983, 1992a, 2001b; Feldt & Brennan, 1989) gives rules for calculating sums of squares, degrees of freedom, and expected mean squares for any possible design, including designs with fixed facets and with more than two facets. Computer programs are also available to perform these computations for the designs most commonly encountered (e.g., Crick & Brennan, 1983).

3.2. Applications of Generalizability Theory

Generalizability theory enables the precise definition of measurement error appropriate for a specific data collection design and intended inference. One important practical application is in determining optimum designs for test administration and scoring. Continuing with the two-facet universe of admissible observations introduced in section 3.1.5, consider a $p \times I \times R$ D-study design in which each person responds to the same $n'_i = 3$ prompts, and each response is scored by the same $n'_r = 2$ raters. The error variances $\sigma^2(\delta)$ and $\sigma^2(\Delta)$ for this design are as follows:

$$\sigma^2(\delta) = \frac{\sigma^2(pi)}{3} + \frac{\sigma^2(pr)}{2} + \frac{\sigma^2(pir)}{6}$$
$$\sigma^2(\Delta) = \frac{\sigma^2(i)}{3} + \frac{\sigma^2(pi)}{3} + \frac{\sigma^2(r)}{2} + \frac{\sigma^2(pr)}{2} + \frac{\sigma^2(ir)}{6} + \frac{\sigma^2(pir)}{6}. \quad (55)$$

Compare this $p \times I \times R$ design to a $p \times (R:I)$ design in which a *different* pair of raters is trained to score each of the three prompts. Note that the total testing time and the total number of scorings of writing samples are identical for these two designs. For the $p \times (R:I)$ design, however,

$$\sigma^2(\delta) = \frac{\sigma^2(pi)}{3} + \frac{\sigma^2(pr:i)}{6} = \frac{\sigma^2(pi)}{3} + \frac{\sigma^2(pr)}{6} + \frac{\sigma^2(pir)}{6}$$
$$\sigma^2(\Delta) = \frac{\sigma^2(i)}{3} + \frac{\sigma^2(pi)}{3} + \frac{\sigma^2(r:i)}{6} + \frac{\sigma^2(pr:i)}{6} \quad (56)$$
$$= \frac{\sigma^2(i)}{3} + \frac{\sigma^2(pi)}{3} + \frac{\sigma^2(r)}{6} + \frac{\sigma^2(ir)}{6} + \frac{\sigma^2(pr)}{6} + \frac{\sigma^2(pir)}{6}.$$

Comparison of Equations 55 and 56 shows that both relative and absolute error are smaller with the nested D-study design, because the β_r and $\pi\beta_{pr}$ components are each sampled six times instead of two times when separate teams of raters are used. Consequently, $\sigma^2(R:I)=\sigma^2(R)+\sigma^2(IR)$ is only one-third as large for the nested rater design versus the crossed design (cf. Cronbach, Linn, Brennan, & Haertel, 1997).

As noted in section 3.1.3, for one-facet D-study designs, $E\rho^2$ (presented in Equation 49) is the same as $_a\rho_{XX'}$ if $n_i = n'_i$ and the same as $_a\rho_{XX'}$ adjusted for a change in test length using the Spearman-Brown Formula if $n_i \neq n'_i$. With multiple facets, generalizability theory provides a natural extension to the Spearman-Brown Formula. If estimates of variance components from a G study are available, it is straightforward to predict the precision of alternative D-study designs. Thus, one can calculate the effect of changes in the number of conditions of any facet or combination of facets on error variances $\sigma^2(\delta)$ and $\sigma^2(\Delta)$ and on the coefficients $E\rho^2$ and Φ. This enables comparison of possible D-study designs, and the selection of a design with optimum precision subject to a constraint on the total number of observations provided by each examinee (Sanders, Theunissen, & Baas, 1989, 1991). Solutions to D-study optimization problems have also appeared for more complicated situations in which the marginal cost of an additional condition varies from one facet to another (Sanders, 1992; Marcoulides, 1997). For example, the cost of adding another writing prompt might differ from the cost of adding another rater. In the example of the preceding paragraph, the costs of training six versus two raters might weigh against the design offering greater precision. If estimates of costs per observation, of scoring, and so forth are also available, the costs as well as the precision of different D-study designs can be compared.

The theory and application of generalizability theory depend on statistical assumptions that are only rarely satisfied in their entirety. Formally, the estimation of variance components depends on the assumption that the conditions of each facet included in the G study are randomly sampled from among all possible conditions. Likewise, the persons (or other objects of measurement) are assumed to be a random sample from the population. Similar assumptions arise in classical test theory and underlie the use and interpretation of reliability coefficients and standard errors of measurement. In practice, it may be impossible to specify precisely the sets of all possible test items, all possible raters, and so forth. Even if these sets can be specified (e.g., if there is a clear rule for deciding whether a possible test question is or is not included), it may be impossible to determine whether a given subset (e.g., a given set of questions) represents a random sample (Cronbach et al., 1972; Kane, 2002; Loevinger, 1965). Real-world applications may be justified by an appeal to representative (versus random) sampling, under which there is a "claim of absence of selective forces that might introduce bias" (Kane, 2002, p. 172), or by an appeal to the exchangeability of sampled conditions with those not observed (Shavelson & Webb, 1981). The effects of departures from random sampling assumptions can also be minimized by incorporating fixed facets into G-study and D-study designs, so that sampling of facets occurs within relatively more homogeneous strata. For example, items sampled within strata representing content areas may be more similar than items sampled from the full universe. As the universe of conditions becomes more homogeneous, random sampling from among those conditions becomes less important (Kane, 2002). Replications of G-study analyses can also increase confidence that results are not distorted due to violations of sampling assumptions. Although often not ideal for that purpose, D-study data can be used to estimate variance components. Finally, it is important not to lose sight of the degree of precision in variance component estimates that is actually required to support intended test uses and interpretations. In most applications, some uncertainty is tolerable (Kane, 2002).

Another difficulty arises with the assumption of random sampling when occasion of measurement is included in G-study and D-study designs, because points in time are ordered (Cronbach et al., 1972, p. 22). Performances on occasions closer in time are likely to be more similar than performances more widely separated in time. That is why, as noted in section 2.3, the time interval between test administrations should be reported along with test-retest or parallel-forms reliability estimates. In generalizability theory, the fact that covariances between occasions vary as a function of time interval can bias estimates of variance components and coefficients. Although there has been some work quantifying the magnitude of these effects (Bost, 1995; Smith & Luecht, 1992), there is as yet no good solution within the framework of generalizability theory.

The remainder of this section addresses special topics and active research areas within generalizability theory. These include the notion of "hidden facets," the relationship of generalizability theory to varieties of reliability estimates distinguished in classical test theory, multivariate generalizability theory, generalizability theory for group means and multi-level data, special problems in variance component estimation, the precision of variance component estimates, and conditional standard errors of measurement in generalizability theory.

3.3. Hidden Facets in Generalizability Theory

In any G study, no matter how complete the specification of the universe of admissible observations, it is possible to identify additional attributes of observations that have been omitted from consideration. The universe of admissible observations could always be elaborated by introducing one more facet to make another of these implicit attributes explicit. Consideration of such so-called *hidden facets* can highlight interpretational difficulties inherent in the relation between the data collection design and the intended universe of generalization. As a first example, recall that the internal consistency reliability estimates of classical test theory typically employ data from a single occasion of measurement. The resulting limitations in the interpretation of these estimates were referred to in section 2.4 but can be presented more clearly employing the concepts and notation of generalizability theory.

In the most common design for estimating the coefficient of equivalence $_a\rho_{XX'}$, examinees all respond to the same set of n'_i items on just one occasion. This may be viewed as a one-facet $p \times I$ D-study design. As stated in section 3.1.3, $_a\rho_{XX'}$ is mathematically identical to $E\rho^2$ for this design:

$$_a\rho_{XX'} = E\rho^2 = \frac{\sigma^2(p)}{\sigma^2(p) + \sigma^2(pi)/n'_i}. \tag{57}$$

It was noted in section 2.4 that internal consistency estimates cannot reflect variability in examinees' performance from one occasion to another, because only one occasion of measurement is sampled. By introducing occasion as an additional facet, generalizability theory can bring further clarification. In the $p \times I$ design, occasion would be referred to as a *hidden* facet because only one condition of the occasion facet is sampled. This hidden facet can be made explicit by representing the same $p \times I$ data collection design as a two-facet $p \times I \times j$ design, where facet j represents occasion and $n_j = 1$.[17] The seven variance components from this two-facet design cannot all be distinguished, but six of the seven are nonetheless represented in the three sources of variance that can be distinguished with this data collection design, as follows:

$p \times i$ design	$p \times i \times j$ design
$\sigma^2(p)$	$\sigma^2(p) + \sigma^2(pj)$
$\sigma^2(i)$	$\sigma^2(i) + \sigma^2(ij)$
$\sigma^2(pi)$	$\sigma^2(pi) + \sigma^2(pij)$

Using the notation of the $p \times I$ design, $_a\rho_{XX'}$ is given by Equation 57. Using the notation of the $p \times I \times j$ design,

$$_a\rho_{XX'} = E\rho^2 = \frac{\sigma^2(p) + \sigma^2(pj)}{\sigma^2(p) + \sigma^2(pj) + (\sigma^2(pi) + \sigma^2(pij))/n'_i}. \quad (58)$$

Comparing Equations 57 and 58 shows how taking account of the hidden facet of occasion redefines the universe score variance, $\sigma^2(p)$. On any one occasion, the person-by-occasion interaction will cause some individuals to perform a little better and others a little worse than their long-run average performance. These effects, particular to a single occasion, are reflected in the term $\sigma^2(pj)$, which is seen to appear as part of the universe score variance when the notation of the $p \times I \times j$ design is used. The occasion-specific effects become part of the universe score variance when generalization is limited to a single occasion.

Two cases of hidden facets may be distinguished. The hidden occasion facet just described illustrates what Brennan (2001b, pp. 149–153) refers to as a *fixed* hidden facet, because just one condition of the facet is sampled. In other words, the facet of occasion is held constant across all observations. The second case, that of a *random* facet, arises when some additional attribute is completely confounded with persons, with conditions of some other facet, or both. Brennan suggests the case of a piano recital in which each student chooses what piece of music to play. Musical selection may be considered random, but because each student plays just one selection, variance components for student, selection, and the student-by-selection interaction are completely confounded. The same distinction is drawn by Cronbach et al. (1972, pp. 122 ff.).

Commonly used G-study designs for performance assessments illustrate the importance of hidden facets. Consider the two-facet $p \times t \times j$ design, where p represents persons, t tasks, and j judges. Because each task is administered on only one occasion, what appears in this design as $\sigma^2(pt)$ might better be regarded as $\sigma^2(pt) + \sigma^2(pto)$, where o represents the hidden facet of occasion. (Other variance components are similarly confounded. For example, $\sigma^2(t)$ could be viewed as $\sigma^2(t) + \sigma^2(to)$. The occasion of judging could be introduced as an additional hidden facet, o', in recognition that individual judges will not be perfectly consistent over time.) If tasks were more similar to one another, the pt interaction would presumably be diminished. Thus, the precision of a set of performance assessments might be improved by stratifying the domain of performance tasks and specifying that, say, one task be sampled from each narrow stratum. However, improving reliability in this way, by more tightly constraining the construction of randomly parallel forms, will be of limited value if a substantial proportion of $\sigma^2(pt)$ is in fact attributable to $\sigma^2(pto)$. Interactions involving occasion represent sources of error that can only be diminished by administering a larger number of performance assessments (Cronbach et al., 1997). A study involving repeated administration of the same performance assessment found that the magnitude of the person-by-task-by-occasion interaction was greater than that of the person-by-task interaction (Shavelson, Ruiz-Primo, & Wiley, 1999). Although no broad conclusions can be drawn from a single study, it does highlight the fact that occasion is very frequently a hidden facet in psychometric research on performance assessments.

3.4. Traditional Reliability Estimates From the Perspective of Generalizability Theory

As illustrated in the preceding section, study designs for estimating reliability coefficients using classical test theory can also be described using the language and notation of generalizability theory. In addition to clarifying the relation between these two approaches, this view of classical test theory coefficients can clarify their interpretation and their limitations.

Equation 57 states the equivalence between $_a\rho_{XX'}$ and $E\rho^2$ for the $p \times I$ D-study design. As explained in section 3.1.3, generalizability theory offers an additional coefficient for this same design, $\Phi = \sigma^2(p)/(\sigma^2(p) + \sigma^2(i) / n'_i + \sigma^2(pi) / n'_i)$, which has no analog in classical test theory. Φ indicates the degree to which person p's observed score is representative of the expected value of X_{pI} over all randomly parallel test forms.

Turning from internal consistency reliability estimates (coefficients of equivalence) to those obtained from test data on two occasions, the coefficient of stability is obtained by correlating scores from administrations of the identical test form to the same group of examinees on two occasions. In the language of generalizability theory, this is a $p \times i \times j$ design, where once again, p represents persons, i represents items, and j represents occasions, with $n_j = 2$. Item, i, is a fixed facet in this design. The generalizability coefficient for a $p \times I \times J$ D-study with $n'_i = n_i$ and $n'_j = 1$ is

$$E\rho^2 = \frac{\sigma^2(p) + \sigma^2(pi)/n_i}{\sigma^2(p) + \sigma^2(pi)/n_i + (\sigma^2(pj) + \sigma^2(pij)/n_i)}. \quad (59)$$

Note that $n'_j = 1$ because the coefficient describes reliability for a single administration, not the mean of two administrations.

The estimate of $E\rho^2$ obtained by substituting sample estimates of variance components into Equation 59 will differ slightly from the product-moment correlation between scores from the two test administrations, except in the special case where the variances of observed scores on the two occasions turn out to be exactly equal. That is because the theory underlying Equation 59 treats the variance of persons' observed scores on each occasion as an estimate of the same quantity, namely the observed-score variance on a randomly chosen occasion. Thus, the single best estimate of that variance is the average of the observed-score variances on occasions 1 and 2 (in the metric of average scores, not total number correct). That quantity is mathematically identical to the denominator of Equation 55. The theory underlying the product-moment correlation, on the other hand, makes no assumption that the two variables correlated (in this case, persons' scores on occasions 1 and 2) have the same variance. Instead, the covariance between the two variables is standardized by dividing it by the product of their standard deviations, which is the square root of the product of the variances. Thus, the denominator in the correlation coefficient is the geometric mean of the variances and the denominator in Equation 55 is the arithmetic mean of the variances.

As a final example, consider the coefficient of stability and equivalence, equal to the correlation between scores on two test forms administered to the same examinees on separate occasions. Because each item within a form is administered on a single occasion, the data are for a $p \times (i{:}j)$ G-study design. The generalizability coefficient for the corresponding D-study design with $n'_i = n_i$ and $n'_j = 1$ is

$$E\rho^2 = \frac{\sigma^2(p)}{\sigma^2(p) + (\sigma^2(pj) + \sigma^2(pi{:}j)/n_i)}. \quad (60)$$

As with the coefficient of stability, substitution of sample estimates in Equation 60 will generally give a slightly different result from calculation of the product-moment correlation. Comparison of Equations 59 and 60 shows how the definitions of both true-score variance and error variance differ for these two classical test theory coefficients. Comparing the numerators of these equations shows that the universe-score (or true-score) variance is larger for the coefficient of stability (Equation 59) than for the coefficient of stability and equivalence (Equation 60), because the former treats items as fixed. For the same reason, the error variance (in parentheses in the denominator) is larger in Equation 60. From the relation $\sigma^2(pi{:}j) = \sigma^2(pi) + \sigma^2(pij)$ it can be seen that the person-by-item interaction contributes to the error variance instead of the universe score variance when different forms are administered on the two occasions.

3.5. Multivariate Generalizability Theory

The first extensive treatment of multivariate generalizability theory was by Cronbach et al. (1972). Expositions were also provided by Shavelson and Webb (1981), Jarjoura and Brennan (1983), Shavelson, Webb, and Rowley (1989), Webb, Shavelson, and Maddahian (1983), and Brennan (1992a). Brennan (2001b) offers a detailed exposition with some important extensions to the theory, and introduces clearer notation than was used by some earlier authors. The computer program mGENOVA (Brennan, 2001c) can be used to estimate variance and covariance components, as well as many D-study statistics, for a large class of multivariate designs. The calculations for multivariate generalizability theory are somewhat complicated, and no attempt is made here to explain them in detail. Space permits no more than a brief overview; the reader is referred to the references cited.

In multivariate generalizability theory, there is more than one universe score for each object of measurement. Suppose, for example, that responses to writing prompts (i) were scored for both content and mechanics. In a G study, each person might respond to n_i prompts (i), and each response might be scored by n_j judges (j). In this example, suppose that each judge assigned scores both for content and for mechanics. One might analyze such data with a (univariate) mixed-model $p \times i \times j \times s$ design, where s was a fixed facet for score, with two levels, content (c) and mechanics (m), but that analysis would not be entirely satisfactory, for several reasons. First, the three-facet mixed model design would in effect assume that the variance of persons' observed scores for content and for mechanics were equal, and similarly for the variance of judges' ratings for content and mechanics, as well as other variance components. Second, the universe score μ_p defined in that analysis would represent an equally weighted composite of scores on content and mechanics. Information about the properties of the two separate scores or about other (weighted) composites could be derived only with difficulty, if at all.

Alternatively, the content scores and the mechanics scores might be analyzed separately, using (univariate) $p \times i \times j$ G-study designs for each score. Such an analyses would provide separate estimates of variance components for the two scores but would omit important information about covariances. One could not ascertain the covariance between persons' universe scores for the two dimensions, $\sigma_{cm}(p)$. Similarly, there would be no information about the covariance of prompt difficulties with respect to the two dimensions, $\sigma_{cm}(i)$; about the covariance of judge effects, $\sigma_{cm}(j)$; or about $\sigma_{cm}(pi)$, $\sigma_{cm}(pj)$, $\sigma_{cm}(ij)$, and $\sigma_{cm}(pij)$. If there were interest in the properties of (weighted or unweighted) composite scores derived from the content and mechanics scores, a separate $p \times i \times j$ G study would be required for each such composite.

Multivariate generalizability theory provides an elegant conceptual and computational solution and also clarifies the proper analyses for more complex data collection designs. To continue with the same example, a multivariate analysis encompasses the $p \times i \times j$ designs for each score, together with a corresponding design for the covariance between them. The universe score variances for the separate scoring dimensions, $\sigma_c^2(p)$ and $\sigma_m^2(p)$, appear as diagonal elements in a two-by-two variance-covariance matrix, and their covariance appears in the off-diagonal cells. Because a variance-covariance matrix is symmetric, only the lower triangle need be shown:

$$\sum_p = \begin{bmatrix} \sigma_c^2(p) & \\ \sigma_{cm}(p) & \sigma_m^2(p) \end{bmatrix}.$$

Using π_c for the person effect for content scores and π_m for the person effect for mechanics scores, $\sigma_c^2(p) = E\pi_c^2$, $\sigma_m^2(p) = E\pi_m^2$, and $\sigma_{cm}(p) = E\pi_c\pi_m$. Similar matrices are defined for each of the remaining components in the design. In any multivariate G-study design with one fixed facet with k levels, there are k univariate designs for the variances of the separate scores and $k(k-1)/2$ distinct designs for the covariances between scores for pairs of levels.

To illustrate some central concepts in multivariate generalizability theory, it will be helpful to compare the previous illustration to a second example. Suppose now that students are required to respond to writing prompts calling for one of two types of essays. Responses to argumentation (a) prompts are persuasive essays, and responses to expository (e) prompts are informative essays. Assume that each person writes n_a persuasive essays and n_e expository essays, a total of $n_a + n_e = n_i$. Assume once again that all essays are scored by the same n_j judges, each judge this time assigning just a single score to each essay. Note that prompts (i) are now nested within the fixed facet (s) for prompt type. Thus, the univariate mixed-model design would be $p \times (i:s) \times j$. This analysis would be significantly more complicated if n_a and n_e were not equal, but such unequal numbers across levels of the fixed facet would pose no particular difficulties for the multivariate analysis.

In multivariate generalizability theory, these two examples are said to differ in the *linkage* of the facets. Using the notation of Brennan (2001b), the G-study design for the first example (with two scores for each essay) would be $p^\bullet \times i^\bullet \times j^\bullet$. A solid circle indicates that a facet is crossed with the fixed multivariate facet. The design for the second example would be $p^\bullet \times i^\circ \times j^\bullet$. An open circle indicates that a facet is nested within the fixed multivariate facet. For the multivariate $p^\bullet \times i^\bullet \times j^\bullet$ design, the k univariate designs for variances are each $p \times i \times j$ and the $k(k-1)/2$ covariance designs for distinct pairs of levels are also $p \times i \times j$. For the $p^\bullet \times i^\circ \times j^\bullet$ design, the variance designs are again $p \times i \times j$, but the covariance designs are now $p \times j$. Thus, Σ_p, Σ_j, and Σ_{pj} may each have nonzero off-diagonal elements, but Σ_i, Σ_{pi}, Σ_{ij}, and Σ_{pij} are each diagonal matrices. Because different prompts are used for persuasive versus expository essays, covariances across levels are all zero for score components involving the facet i.

Estimates of the (full or diagonal) variance-covariance matrices for all score effects play the same role as estimates of variance components in univariate generalizability theory. As in the univariate case, corresponding D-study components can also be defined. D-study designs may differ from G-study designs. The diagonal elements of the variance-covariance matrices for components provide exactly the same information as univariate generalizability analyses for each separate score. It is also straightforward to calculate variance components for any composite score defined as a linear combination of separate scores, disattenuated correlations between persons' universe scores on separate components, and other useful statistics. The properties of alternative weighted composite scores are readily compared.

One of the earliest multivariate designs analyzed in detail was for a test developed from a table of specifications (Jarjoura & Brennan, 1982, 1983). In the simplest case, the universe of admissible observations has just one random facet, items (i) nested within strata (s). Using Brennan's (2001b) notation, the G-study design is $p^\bullet \times i^\circ$. No particular complexities are introduced in the estimation if the numbers of items, $n_{i:s}$, vary across strata. For a D study with $n'_{i:s} = n_{i:s}$ for all strata, a weighted composite score with stratum weights proportional to $n_{i:s}$ will have a multivariate generalizability coefficient identical to Cronbach et al.'s (1965) stratified alpha, as presented in Equation 29. As with univariate generalizability theory, coefficients from designs with more than one random facet do not, in general, have any direct analogs in classical test theory.

Brennan (2001b) illustrates his discussion with several real-world applications of multivariate generalizability theory. One of these is an analysis presented by Brennan, Gao, and Colton (1995; Brennan, 2001b, pp. 339–343). In this G study to inform the design of a new listening and writing assessment, examinees were asked to take notes while listening to each of 12 tape-recorded stimuli. After listening, they prepared a written summary of each message. These summaries were scored for listening skill (accuracy and completeness) as well as writing skill. Three raters assigned listening scores to all summaries, and a different group of three raters assigned writing scores. Because raters were nested within the fixed facet, this was a $p^\bullet \times t^\bullet \times r^\circ$ G-study design. This entire design was replicated three times, with different groups of 50 examinees, different sets of tapes, and different sets of raters for each replication. Preliminary analysis supported the averaging of variance components across replications of the design. The replications provided a straightforward way to estimate standard errors of the estimates of variance and covariance components. It was anticipated that an operational test would use fewer than 12 tapes and fewer than 3 raters. Major questions addressed by the G study included the tradeoff between number of tapes and number of raters, the (disattenuated) correlation between examinees' universe scores for listening versus writing, and the reliability of difference scores representing the contrast between listening and writing. The G study enabled comparisons among various $p^\bullet \times T^\bullet \times R^\circ$ D-study designs with different numbers of tapes and raters, as well as comparisons with $p^\bullet \times T^\circ \times R^\circ$ designs in which listening versus writing scores are based on different sets of tapes.

3.6. Generalizability Theory for Group Means and Multilevel Data

In applications of generalizability theory considered thus far, the objects of measurement have been individuals. Objects of measurement can also be defined at higher levels of aggregation. In educational accountability systems, for example, school-level scores are often derived from the performance of students within each school. As discussed in this section, for most applications of such school-level scores, it is appropriate to consider the students tested as a random sample from some infinite population of students who might have been enrolled at the time of testing. Thus, in addition to the sources of error that influence individual students' scores, the school mean may also reflect error due to the sampling of students.

Assume for purposes of illustration that testing is conducted in just one subject area, at a single grade level; that all students at that grade level are tested; and that each school's score is defined as the mean of its student's test scores. The resulting data could be analyzed using a one-facet G-study or D-study design, with students or persons (p) nested within schools or groups (g), the objects of measurement. Typically, numbers of students may vary across schools. A $p:g$ generalizability study might be conducted by sampling n_p students from each school to create a balanced design. This design would permit the estimation of variance components for schools, $\sigma^2(g)$, and students within school, $\sigma^2(p:g)$. Typically, the school is conceived as an entity continuing through time, and the school mean is interpreted as a characterization of the school, not just the particular students tested. This interpretation implies that students should be treated as a random facet, even if all students present at a given grade level at the time of testing are included in the assessment. If students were treated as fixed, the resulting standard error would be for "a historical report on the true performance of the student body actually sampled" (Cronbach et al., 1997, p. 393). Note in particular that if school-level test score summaries for different years are compared, then students should be treated as random. Because students are nested within schools, $\sigma^2(\delta) = \sigma^2(\Delta)$ and $E\rho^2 = \Phi = \sigma^2(g)/(\sigma^2(g) + \sigma^2(P:g))$. Substituting sample estimates for $\sigma^2(g)$ and $\sigma^2(P:g) = \sigma^2(p:g)/n_p$ gives an estimate that is algebraically equivalent to a traditional formula for the reliability of group means,

$$\hat{\rho}_{XX'} = \left(\frac{N-1}{N-G}\right)\left(1 - \frac{\hat{\sigma}_X^2}{n\,\hat{\sigma}_{\bar{X}}^2}\right), \quad (61)$$

where N is the total number of individuals summed over all groups, G is the number of groups, $\hat{\sigma}_X^2$ is the variance of individual scores (pooling over groups and ignoring group membership), $\hat{\sigma}_{\bar{X}}^2$ is the variance of the group means, and n is number of individuals in each group. If group sizes are not equal, $\hat{\rho}_{XX'}$ may be calculated by substituting $\tilde{n}$ for n in the denominator of Equation 61, where $\tilde{n}$ is defined as

$$\tilde{n} = \frac{1}{G-1}\left(N - \frac{\sum n_j^2}{N}\right),$$

n_j being the size of group j, $j = 1, \ldots, G$ (Feldt & Brennan, 1989, p. 127).

In the one-facet design just considered, the particular set of items administered to students is ignored. Thus, "test form" may be regarded as a hidden facet; the one-facet design implicitly treats the test administered to all students as fixed. Typically, however, the intended universe of generalization extends to randomly parallel forms of the test (cf. Lord & Novick, 1968, pp. 234–236).[18] Thus, it is useful to consider a two-facet $(p:g) \times f$ G-study design and the corresponding $(P:g) \times F$ D-study design, where the additional facet F represents test forms (Brennan, 2001b). With this design, three different generalizability coefficients may be calculated. Both P and F may be treated as random facets if the intent is to generalize to infinite universes of students and test forms; F may be treated as random and P as fixed if the intent is to generalize across possible test forms administered to the particular groups of students actually tested; or P may be treated as random and F as fixed if the intent is to generalize over persons only. (The second of these three cases, F random and P fixed, is unlikely to arise in practice.) The last case, P random and F fixed, is algebraically equivalent to the value of $E\rho^2 = \Phi$ obtained under the one-facet design described above or from Equation 61. This example again illustrates how the framework of generalizability theory encourages precise formulation of questions about measurement precision and highlights important distinctions that might otherwise be overlooked.

It is sometimes assumed that group-level reliability coefficients must be higher, and group-level standard errors smaller, than at the individual level. Analysis of the two-facet $(p:g) \times f$ design just discussed, and a review of illustrative empirical studies, shows that neither assumption is necessarily true and that in fact, violations of these common assumptions are quite likely to occur in practice (Brennan, 1995).

Accountability systems may employ school-level test score summaries defined in complex ways. Results may be combined across subject areas and/or grade levels. Instead of simple means of student scores, the proportion of students above some cut score (percent above cut, or PAC) may be tabulated (e.g., "percent proficient"). Also, when schools are the objects of measurement and items or test forms are regarded as random, greater precision may be attained by administering different test forms to randomly equivalent subgroups of students in each school, a procedure referred to as "matrix sampling." Although matrix sampling increases precision by employing a larger sample from the universe of possible items, it somewhat complicates the analysis of score accuracy. There has been considerable progress in applying generalizability theory to these more complex cases. When the school summary is in terms of a PAC, students' scores may be recoded to 0 or 1 and then analyzed using standard models to obtain standard errors of the percents of students reaching standards (Brennan, Yin, & Kane, 2003; Cronbach et al., 1997; Yen, 1997). Data from matrix-sampled designs may be analyzed by extracting smaller subsets of data to create data sets with structures more readily analyzed, and results from multiple analyses of data subsets can then be combined to arrive at overall estimates of each source of variation (Chiu & Wolfe, 2002). Where results are combined across multiple tests used for different subject matters or grade levels, multivariate generalizability theory may offer the most appropriate models. It is wise to consider how accuracy will be determined at the time when accountability systems are designed. For example, Cronbach et al. (1997) recommend including classroom as a level in the analysis of school-level score accuracy, modeling students nested within classes nested within schools. They show that treating students as nested within schools, rather than within classes within schools, may be expected to lead to distorted estimates of precision.

Either univariate or multivariate generalizability theory may be useful for examining the reliability of group mean difference scores such as year-to-year changes in school-level performance. As with the treatment of difference scores at the individual level, the standard error of group-level mean difference scores may be more meaningfully compared to the magnitude of a difference score itself than to the standard deviation of the difference scores (cf. section 2.5.7.1). Kane's (1996) "error/tolerance ratio" may be a more suitable index of precision than $E\rho^2$ (Brennan, Yin, & Kane, 2003).

3.7. Variance Component Estimation with Unbalanced or Missing Data

Estimating variance components is straightforward with a balanced design and complete data. Analysis of variance is used to obtain mean squares, which are set equal to their expected mean squares to create a set of equations that can be solved for variance component estimates. When data are not balanced, either due to nesting or because some observations are missing, the estimation of variance components is more complicated. Because estimation for balanced designs with no missing data is so much simpler than available alternatives for other situations, many analysts will randomly sample observations to obtain balanced designs (e.g., Brennan, Yin, & Kane, 2003; Yen, 1997). In some cases, it may be desirable to extract multiple balanced subsets of data from the same dataset, analyze them separately, and then pool the results (Chiu & Wolfe, 2002).

As Brennan (1994) has noted, the term "unbalanced design" may be misleading, as unbalanced situations often arise due to missing data even when the "design" is balanced. He proposes a distinction between unbalanced "designs" and unbalanced "situations," which may be helpful in deciding on an approach to estimation.

If the unbalanced situation arises from nesting with unequal numbers of levels, there are straightforward solutions in many cases. Multivariate generalizability theory can easily accommodate designs that are unbalanced with respect to nesting within levels of a fixed facet. For example, a table of test specifications might involve differing numbers of items within (fixed) content strata. Unambiguous decompositions of sums of squares are also available for certain unbalanced random-effects models (e.g., Jarjoura & Brennan, 1981). For other models, ANOVA-like procedures involving various quadratic forms are available. The most commonly used procedure has probably been Henderson's (1953) Method 1, although this method produces biased estimates in models with fixed effects. The computer program urGENOVA (Brennan, 2001d) can be used to estimate variance components for unbalanced univariate designs.

ANOVA-like procedures, or exact solutions based on ANOVA methods, where available, have the advantage that they do not require any assumptions as to the distributional forms of score effects. When these methods are not applicable, as may happen if there are missing data, for example, maximum likelihood methods can be employed, but these entail distributional assumptions, typically that score effects are normally distributed. An extensive treatment of estimation for unbalanced situations is provided by Brennan (2001b, chaps. 7 & 11).

3.8. Precision of Estimates of Variance Components

Estimates of variance components will vary from one sample to another. To evaluate the accuracy of G-study and D-study results, including estimates of $\sigma^2(\delta)$, $\sigma^2(\Delta)$, $E\rho^2$, Φ, and other statistics based on variance components, it is useful first to determine the accuracy of estimates of variance components themselves.

The soundest method for determining the accuracy of variance component estimates is replication, as illustrated by Brennan et al. (1995), described in section 3.5. In that study, three replications of a $p^\bullet \times i^\bullet \times r^\circ$ G-study design were implemented, with nonoverlapping sets of persons, raters, and stimulus materials for each replication. This yielded three independent and identically distributed estimates of each variance component. For each variance component, the mean of these three estimates was taken as the best point estimate available, and the standard deviation of the three estimates divided by the square root of three was reported as an estimate of the standard error of the variance component estimate. Where it is possible to divide a data set to create independent replications of the full design, this may be the preferred method. Note, however, that if two subsets of the data have levels of any random facet in common, then they will not yield independent estimates of variance components.

In most cases, it will not be possible to divide all of the available data into independent subsets as just described. Under the assumption that score effects have a multivariate normal distribution, standard errors of variance components can be obtained using a formula due to Searle (1971, pp. 415–417; Searle, Casella, & McCulloch, 1992, pp. 137–138), as follows:

$$\hat{\sigma}\left[\hat{\sigma}^2(\alpha \mid M)\right] = \sqrt{\sum_j \frac{2(f_j MS_j)^2}{df_j + 2}}, \qquad (62)$$

where α is a score effect under a given model M, $\hat{\sigma}^2(\alpha \mid M)$ is the estimate of the variance component corresponding to score effect α, and $\hat{\sigma}[\hat{\sigma}^2(\alpha \mid M)]$ is the standard error of that variance component estimate. The estimate $\hat{\sigma}^2(\alpha \mid M)$ is obtained as a linear combination of mean squares, where f_j is the coefficient for MS_j with degrees of freedom df_j. Estimates of standard errors obtained using Equation 62 and estimates obtained from independent replications have shown satisfactory agreement (Gao & Brennan, 2001). These estimates are provided automatically by the GENOVA program (Crick & Brennan, 1983). In addition to standard errors, investigators might wish to obtain confidence intervals for variance component estimates. Although closed-form results for confidence intervals are generally unavailable, approximate confidence intervals may be obtained under appropriate assumptions (Satterthwaite, 1946). Refinements of Satterthwaite's formulas are given by Burdick and Graybill (1992). Confidence intervals can also be obtained using jackknife procedures, as well as the bootstrap methods discussed next.

There are also bootstrap methods that have been developed for estimating the precision of variance component estimates (Brennan, 2001b, chap. 6). These methods avoid the distributional assumptions required with Equation 62 but are computationally intensive. In general, to obtain a bootstrap standard error of a statistic, many data sets are constructed by random sampling *with replacement* from the original data set; the statistic is calculated for each bootstrap replication, and the standard deviation of the resulting estimates is an estimator of the standard error of the original statistic (Efron, 1982). In addition, the percentile points of the distribution of bootstrap estimates can be used to construct confidence intervals, although various refinements to the use of the percentile points themselves are recommended (Efron & Tibshirani, 1986; Shao & Tu, 1995). The bootstrap is closely related to the earlier jackknife procedure due to Tukey (1958), based on work by Quenouille (1949). Jackknife procedures are also discussed by Brennan (2001b, chap. 6).

Application of the bootstrap is complicated when data have a multidimensional structure. In a $p \times i$ design, for example, if items are sampled with replacement, the replication of identical columns will result in inflated covariances between "different" items that are in fact resampled replications of the same item from the original data set. The same difficulties arise with resampling of persons or of both persons and items. In addition, the simple bootstrap variance estimates described above have known biases for estimating the variance of variances. Wiley (2000) reported corrections for the bias found with earlier bootstrap approaches for the $p \times i$ design, and recommended some promising general approaches for more complex designs.

In addition to research on the precision of variance component estimates, some work has addressed the variability of estimates of generalizability coefficients. Schroeder and Hakstian (1990) use a normalizing transformation to develop asymptotic variance expressions for coefficients of generalizability for various one-, two-, and three-facet designs. In addition, Brennan (2001b) shows that various confidence intervals for coefficient alpha derived by Feldt (1965, 1990) are special cases of confidence intervals for ratios of variance components provided by Burdick and Graybill (1992).

3.9. Conditional Standard Errors in Generalizability Theory

The definitions and estimates of the error variances $\sigma^2(\delta)$ and $\sigma^2(\Delta)$ presented thus far may be termed *unconditional* error variances, because they are not conditioned on persons' universe scores. As discussed in section 2.6.2, better characterizations of the error structure of a test can be obtained by conditioning on the true score, and better characterizations of precision for individual examinees can be obtained by conditioning on observed score, or on scores for the parts of the test representing distinct content strata. Conditioning on true score versus observed score corresponds to the distinction between confidence intervals and tolerance intervals.

A parallel development of *conditional* error variances exists for generalizability theory (Brennan, 1998, 2001b). As with other topics in classical test theory, the development in generalizability theory highlights some important distinctions that are less clear in the classical test theory formulation. In particular, the distinction in section 2.6.2 between error variances for "absolute" versus "relative" score interpretations for person p can be framed more precisely as a distinction between $\sigma^2(\Delta_p)$ and $\sigma^2(\delta_p)$.

As defined in section 3.1.3, the absolute error for person p is $\Delta_p = X_{pI} - \mu_p$. An unbiased estimator of the corresponding standard error is

$$\hat{\sigma}(\Delta_p) = \sqrt{\frac{\sum_i (X_{pi} - X_{pI})^2}{n_i'(n_i' - 1)}} \qquad (63)$$

(Brennan, 1998). A special case of Equation 63 for dichotomously scored items is

$$\hat{\sigma}(\Delta_p) = \sqrt{\frac{X_{pI}(1 - X_{pI})}{n_i' - 1}} .$$

Except for the difference in scale between classical test theory results for total scores versus generalizability theory results for mean scores, this formula is identical to Equation 38 in section 2.6.2.

The relative error for person p is defined as $\delta_p = (X_{pI} - \mu_I) - (\mu_I - \mu)$. A complication arises in the derivation of the corresponding standard error, $\hat{\sigma}(\delta_p)$. As stated in section 3.1.1, the expectations of most products of score effects are zero. However, using the notation of section 3.1.1, although $E_p \pi_p \alpha_i = E_i \pi_p \alpha_i = E_p E_i \pi \alpha_{pi} = E_p E_i \alpha_i \pi \alpha_{pi} = 0$, $E_p \pi_p \pi \alpha_{pi}$ and $E_i \alpha_i \pi \alpha_{pi}$ are not necessarily zero (Brennan, 1998). Because these products do not disappear when taking expectations, the expression for $\hat{\sigma}(\delta_p)$ contains a term for $\text{cov}(\alpha_i, \pi \alpha_{pi} \mid p) = E_i \alpha_i \pi \alpha_{pi}$, which is abbreviated $\sigma(i,pi)_p$. Using results from Jarjoura (1986), Brennan derives the following expression:

$$\sigma(\delta_p) = \sqrt{\sigma^2(\Delta_p) + \frac{\sigma^2(i)}{n_i'} - \frac{2\sigma(i,pi)_p}{n_i'}} .$$

The expected value over persons of $\sigma(i,pi)_p$ is zero, but this term can be positive or negative for particular persons. Thus, even though $\sigma(\delta) \leq \sigma(\Delta)$, $\sigma(\delta_p)$ may be greater than $\sigma(\Delta_p)$ for some p. Brennan shows that an estimator of $\sigma(i,pi)_p$ is the observed covariance over items between person p's item scores and the mean item scores for all persons. Using that estimator, he derives an expression for $\hat{\sigma}(\delta_p)$. The value of that estimate may differ among persons with the same number-correct score, and the estimate itself is subject to substantial error. For these reasons, Brennan recommends that an average value be used instead, as follows:

$$\hat{\sigma}(\delta_p) = \sqrt{\hat{\sigma}^2(\Delta_p) - \hat{\sigma}^2(I)} . \qquad (64)$$

For dichotomous data, except for expressing the standard error in terms of a mean score versus a total score, Equation 64 is equivalent to the Keats-Lord conditional standard error shown in Equation 39 (Brennan, 1998).

The foregoing treatment was for the one-facet univariate $p \times I$ D-study design. Similar results can be derived for nested designs and for designs with two or more facets. G. Lee (2000a, 2000c) examines conditional standard errors in tests with testlets, using both simulations (G. Lee, 2000a) and data from large testing programs (G. Lee, 2000c). As expected, standard errors are underestimated with a $p \times I$ design, because that design ignores the higher covariation among items within testlets versus between testlets. Accurate results are obtained with a $p \times (I{:}H)$ design, in which each level of stratum, H, represents a testlet with its own set of items, I_H. Lee also compares conditional standard errors from generalizability theory with results using item response theory (IRT) and finds good agreement between results using the $p \times (I{:}H)$ design and testlet-based IRT models.

4. RELIABILITY OF CLASSIFICATIONS

The theory developed in the previous sections is most directly applicable to continuous scores. When a measurement procedure leads instead to a classification into one of two or more discrete categories, different measurement methods may be appropriate, and reliability (or replicability) may be expressed using different statistics.

Two topics are addressed in this section. First, when continuous scores are interpreted with respect to one or more cut scores, conventional indices of reliability may not be appropriate, and the standard error of measurement may not be directly informative concerning classification accuracy. Such cases arise when examinees above a cut score are classified as passing or proficient, for example. Several coefficients have been developed to index reliability for dichotomous decisions, including Livingston's (1972) coefficient and Brennan and Kane's (1977a) indexes of dependability. Instead of standard errors, users may be concerned with questions such as the following: What is the probability that an examinee with a true score above the cut score will have an observed score below the cut score, or conversely? What is the expected proportion of examinees who would be differently classified upon retesting? The *Standards* (AERA, APA, & NCME, 1999, p. 35) call for estimates of the percentage of examinees who would be classified consistently using the same or alternate forms whenever a test is used to make categorical decisions. Analyses addressing such questions will often begin with an examination of the accuracy of the continuous score on which the classification is based, using the methods of classical test theory or generalizability theory. Additional statistics may then be calculated, such as conditional or unconditional probabilities of misclassification. Such questions may also be addressed using specialized methods. Note that a primary determinant of the probability of misclassification is the difference between an examinee's true score and the cut score. Thus, here more than ever, accuracy inheres not in the measurement procedure per se, but in its use with a specific population. If the cut score is in the tail of the observed-score distribution, misclassifications may be rare even with a test of modest reliability. If the cut score is near the mode of the score distribution, the higher proportion of examinees with true scores close to the cut score will result in a higher proportion of misclassifications.

The second topic addressed is the accuracy of single scores or ratings. In cases where the initial measurement procedure results directly in a classification into one of a small number of discrete categories, as with ratings of essays, portfolios, or other examinee work products, specialized methods may be used to characterize the error structure of the rating process, such as coefficient kappa (Cohen, 1960) and its extensions (e.g., see Agresti, 2002). Work on rater bias and error shades into a broader consideration of score accuracy (e.g., see W. Hoyt, 2000 for an overview). The problem of characterizing agreement between two raters has received considerable attention.

4.1. Reliability Indices for Classification Decisions

As discussed in section 1.1, reliability coefficients are useful for norm-referenced score interpretations, because they indicate the proportion of observed-score variance attributable to examinees' true scores. For criterion-referenced interpretations, reliability coefficients may be misleading. Popham and Husek (1969) observed that if all examinees had the same true score and that value was well above the cut score, then the classical test theory reliability coefficient would be zero even though the test might accurately classify all examinees as masters. Beginning in the 1970s, several coefficients were developed to characterize the accuracy with which criterion-referenced tests classified examinees relative to a cut score.

One of the first of these was Livingston's (1972) coefficient, defined as

$$k^2 \equiv \frac{E_p(T_p-C)^2}{E_p(X_p-C)^2} = \frac{\sigma_T^2 + (\mu_X-C)^2}{\sigma_T^2 + (\mu_X-C)^2 + \sigma_E^2},$$

where C is the cut score (mastery criterion) and μ_X is the mean score for the group tested; σ_T^2 is the variance of persons' true scores τ_p; and σ_E^2 is the error variance. Note that k^2 is of the same form as the reliability coefficient of classical test theory but substitutes squared deviations from the cut score for squared deviations from the mean. If $C = \mu_X$, k^2 reduces to the classical test theory reliability. Livingston also discussed corresponding criterion-referenced notions of the correlation coefficient, the Spearman-Brown formula, and the correction for attenuation due to unreliability.

Brennan and Kane (1977a, 1977b) defined two indexes of dependability, Φ and $\Phi(\lambda)$. The more general index, $\Phi(\lambda)$, is quite similar to Livingston's (1972) k^2 but is derived in the framework of generalizability theory to represent decision consistency over randomly parallel tests, as follows:

$$\Phi(\lambda) \equiv \frac{E_p(\mu_p-\lambda)^2}{E_I E_p (X_{pI}-\lambda)^2} = \frac{\sigma^2(p)+(\mu-\lambda)^2}{\sigma^2(p)+(\mu-\lambda)^2+\sigma^2(\Delta)}. \quad (65)$$

In Equation 65, λ represents the cut score, and the remaining symbols are defined as in section 3, on generalizability theory. Regarding $\Phi(\lambda)$ as a function of λ, it clearly reaches its minimum at $\lambda=\mu$. The value at the minimum is denoted Φ, the index of dependability discussed in section 3.1.3. It was noted in sections 3.1.3 and 3.4 that for the $p \times I$ D-study design with $n_i' = n_i$, $_d\rho_{XX'} = E\rho^2$. Brennan and Kane (1977a, 1977b) show that for this same design, if all items are dichotomously scored and $n_i' = n_i$, then $_{21}\rho_{XX'} = \hat{\Phi}(\lambda = \bar{X})$. Thus, the Kuder-Richardson formula 21 reliability, which was devised as a computational simplification to approximate $_{20}\rho_{XX'}$, turned out to be the appropriate coefficient to use for estimating the correlation between randomly parallel tests composed of dichotomously scored items. It is interesting to note in this connection that Buros (1978, p. 1981) argued that when one is interested in generalization to total raw scores across parallel forms of a test with dichotomously scored items, "Although the contrary is commonly believed to be true, K-R 21 is a better measure than K-R 20."

The k^2 and $\Phi(\lambda)$ coefficients represent the accuracy with which a test indicates examinees' distance from the cut score. Alternative conceptions of precision address the accuracy or consistency of examinee classifications. Consider a two-by-two (or n-by-n) table showing examinees' classifications using two replications of the measurement procedure. The rows (perhaps labeled "0" and "1" or "fail" and "pass") indicate the result of the first replication, and the columns, identically labeled, represent the results of the second. Table entries might represent either frequencies or proportions. A single cut score resulting in a binary classification would correspond to a two-by-two table. Additional cut scores would yield classifications into three or more ordered categories, corresponding to larger tables. In a two-by-two table, let p_{00}, p_{01}, p_{10}, and p_{11} represent the observed proportions of examinees classified nonmaster-nonmaster, nonmaster-master, master-nonmaster, and master-master, respectively, across the two replications. The simplest indicator of decision consistency would be the probability of consistent classification, p_A, estimated by $\hat{p}_A = p_{00} + p_{11}$.

Although p_A could range from 0 to 1, a value greater than zero would be expected by chance, even if the measurements represented by row versus column categories were uncorrelated. To correct for chance agreement, Hambleton et al. (1978) recommended using Cohen's (1960) κ statistic, defined as follows. For the two-by-two table just described, denote the row sums by $p_{0.}$ and $p_{1.}$ and the column sums by $p_{.0}$ and $p_{.1}$. Chance agreement can then be expressed as $p_C = p_0 p_{.0} + p_1 p_{.1}$. The κ statistic is defined as $(p_A - p_C)/(1 - p_C)$. It may be interpreted as the improvement beyond chance, $(p_A - p_C)$, expressed as a proportion of the difference between chance agreement and perfect agreement, $(1 - p_C)$. For n-by-n tables, $n > 2$, with ordered categories, Agresti (2002) describes refinements in which larger discrepancies between ratings (being off by two categories, for example, versus adjacent categories) are treated as indicating more serious lack of agreement.

Several methods have been developed to estimate p_A and κ from a single administration of a criterion-referenced test. Subkoviak's (1976) method estimates each examinee's score on a double-length test, calculates for each examinee the proportion of all possible split halves of the double-length test that result in consistent classifications, and averages that proportion over all examinees. In practice, of course, just one such calculation is required for each number-correct score; all examinees with the same total score have the same predicted proportions. This method is applicable only to tests consisting of equally weighted, dichotomously scored items.

Huynh (1976) estimated the underlying true-score distribution from the single test administration's observed-score distribution, according to the beta-binomial model (Keats & Lord, 1962). He then used the estimated true-score distribution to generate a hypothetical joint distribution of observed scores on two parallel forms of the original test, and estimated p_A from that joint distribution.

From the joint distribution of true scores and observed scores, Huynh (1976) was able to model decision accuracy, the correspondence between true status and observed status with respect to the cut score, as well as decision consistency, the agreement between two observed classifications. Hanson and Brennan (1990) showed that the four-parameter beta-binomial model (Lord, 1965) reproduced the observed-score distribution markedly better than did the two-parameter beta, but that Lord's (1965) compound binomial error model gave nearly the same results as the simple binomial model. W. Lee, Hanson, and Brennan (2002) provide an extension to estimation of decision consistency and accuracy when two or more cut scores are used to classify examinees into three or more score categories. Like Subkoviak's (1976) method, these approaches relying on the two-parameter or four-parameter beta-binomial model are limited to tests composed of equally weighted, dichotomously scored items.

An extension to tests that do not consist of equally weighted, dichotomously scored items was introduced by Livingston and Lewis (1995). Their method replaces the original test with an idealized test consisting of some number of identical dichotomous items. The test length is chosen to produce a test with reliability equal to that of the original test. This "effective test length" is calculated from the mean, variance, and reliability coefficient of the original test. Scores on the original test are linearly transformed to proportion-correct scores on the idealized test, and the four-parameter beta-binomial model is then applied as in Hanson and Brennan (1990). The method appears to give good results for several data sets, including some problems involving multiple cut points, but the authors urge caution until it has been investigated more extensively. The computer program BB-CLASS (Brennan, 2004) can be used for both the Hanson and Brennan method and the Livingston and Lewis method.

A simpler alternative, applicable to any test that can be divided into two parallel half-tests, is provided by Woodruff and Sawyer (1989). They provide two variations of a method based on the Spearman-Brown formula. In the first, a bivariate-normal distribution is assumed for scores on the two half-tests; the Spearman-Brown formula is used to estimate the correlation between scores on two full-length tests from the correlation between the half-tests; and the proportion of consistent classifications on these hypothetical, lengthened half-tests is obtained from a table of the bivariate-normal distribution, assuming the passing rate on each half-test is equal to that on the original test. The Woodruff and Sawyer method not relying on distributional assumptions classifies examinees as passing versus failing each half-test, using cut points chosen so that the half-test passing rates are equal to the original passing rate. The correlation (phi coefficient) between these two binary classifications is then treated as a half-test "pass-fail reliability" and is stepped up directly, using the Spearman-Brown formula. A justification for this procedure is provided, but significant assumptions and approximations are entailed.

Breyer and Lewis (1994) describe a similar split-half method, but one that avoids any assumption about the form of the observed-score distribution. Instead, their method assumes an underlying bivariate normal distribution for unobservable scores underlying the joint distribution of half-test scores. It can be used with tests composed of dichotomously or polytomously scored items, or a mixture of item types. Their index, the estimated probability of consistent classification for a full-length test ($P_{cc,full}$) is derived by dividing the full-length test into half-length tests, then determining a passing score on each half-length test such that the sum of those passing scores is equal to the passing score on the original full-length test. Next, the mean proportion passing the two half-length tests and the proportion passing both half-length tests are used to estimate the tetrachoric correlation between the half-tests, under a model that assumes the true passing rates for the two half-tests are the same. This tetrachoric correlation is then stepped up using the Spearman-Brown formula (Equation 11) to obtain an estimate of the tetrachoric correlation between two full-length tests dichotomized at the passing score. Finally, $P_{cc,full}$ is derived from this correlation and the observed full-length test passing rate by consulting a table of the bivariate normal distribution, as described by Subkoviak (1976). The authors report good agreement with related coefficients. Their $P_{cc,full}$ also performed well in a study in which a test was divided into quarters, so that predicted decision consistency for a half-length test could be compared to observed consistency across two half-length tests. Note that any single-administration estimate of decision consistency shares the same limitation as single-administration estimates of reliability. They cannot reflect error arising from examinees' inconsistency over time and for that reason are likely to overstate decision consistency between test forms administered on separate occasions.

Brennan and Wan (2004) develop a bootstrap procedure (Efron, 1982; Efron & Tibshirani, 1986) for estimating decision consistency for complex assessments, including in principle assessments with polytomously scored items, items scored by multiple raters, unequally weighted item or subtest scores, and nonlinear transformations of raw scores to scale scores. Their method is conceptually related to Subkoviak's (1976) method, in that it estimates decision consistency for one examinee at a time and then averages across examinees. With the Brennan and Wan method, however, unlike the Subkoviak method, examinees with the same total score may have different estimated probabilities of consistent classification. Therefore, multiple bootstrap replications are required for each examinee. For each replication, resampling items, the examinee earns either a passing or a failing score. From the proportion of replications with passing scores, two consistency indices are derived. The first is $\varphi_p = \Pr(pass)^2 + \Pr(fail)^2$. This is the probability of agreement between two randomly chosen bootstrap replications. The second is $\varphi'_p = \Pr(pass)$ if the examinee earned a passing score on the original test and $\varphi'_p = 1 - \Pr(pass)$ if the examinee failed the original test. This is the probability of agreement with the original decision. Thus, φ_p and φ'_p answer different questions about consistency. Brennan and Wan illustrate their method with a small data set from a licensure/certification examination with multiple-choice and constructed-response sections, the latter polytomously scored, and find close agreement with an alternative method requiring stronger distributional assumptions.

4.2. Reliability of Ratings

Many measurement applications involve ratings of examinees' work products. Typically, raters employ some kind of scoring rubric or follow decision rules to assign scores or classify task performances into categories representing varying degrees of success. The component of error associated with the rating process has long been a topic of study in its own right, although in almost all cases, a comprehensive treatment of score accuracy will attend to more than scoring accuracy per se. Generalizability theory provides a unified framework for examining multiple sources of error affecting test scores.

Brennan (2001b) distinguishes between a *standardized* interrater coefficient and a *nonstandardized* interrater coefficient. The standardized coefficient might be obtained by having each of two raters independently score the same task performances by each of a group of examinees and then obtaining the correlation between their ratings. The nonstandardized coefficient might be obtained by obtaining two different task performances for each examinee, having one of these scored by each rater, and then correlating the ratings. As Brennan demonstrates, standardized coefficients would be expected to be markedly higher than nonstandardized. The standardized coefficient ignores the intra-individual variation in task performance; the nonstandardized coefficient appropriately reflects this potentially significant source of measurement error.

In addition to p_A and κ defined in section 4.1, numerous other measures of agreement have been proposed. These are systematized by Blackman and Koval (1993), who show that many of these coefficients may be regarded as chance-corrected intraclass correlation coefficients for different ANOVA models. Based on this formulation, Blackman and Koval provide asymptotic estimates of the variance of different coefficients, including κ and a related coefficient defined by Scott (1955) under the assumption that the true proportion of "pass" ratings is the same for both raters.

As described in section 4.1, the joint distribution of ratings assigned by two raters is conveniently displayed in a two-way table. If n categories are available for ratings, an n-by-n table can represent frequencies or proportions for each possible ordered pair of ratings. The sample n-by-n table of proportions corresponds to a similar table for the population, in which the cell entries are parameters representing probabilities for each ordered pair of ratings. Various models have been developed to represent these population probabilities in terms of a smaller number of underlying parameters (Klauer & Batchelder, 1996; Schuster, 2001; Schuster & Smith, 2002). Different models may be appropriate according to whether categories are ordered and whether marginal probabilities are assumed homogeneous for the two raters.

Throughout this chapter, examinees' true scores (or universe scores) have been defined as the expected value of observed scores. For scores expressed on a scale with a minimum and maximum possible value, this definition implies that no examinee's true score can be equal to the minimum or maximum possible value unless that examinee's observed scores are error-free. This conclusion is the logical extreme of the discussion of conditional standard errors of measurement in sections 2.6.2 and 3.9. If responses to essays are rated on a scale from 1 to 6, then for an examinee to have a true score of 6, that examinee would have to be perfectly consistent in producing "6" essays. Thus, that examinee's observed scores would have zero variance, and so the conditional standard error for that examinee would be zero. In considering interrater reliability, the notion of true score as expected value of observed score is sometimes applied in another way, which may pose conceptual difficulties. The true score for a single essay would customarily be defined as the expected value over raters of the score assigned to that essay. If there is a scoring rubric, however, with clear rules for assigning ratings, typically supported by benchmark essays illustrating "true" scores at each possible level, it may be more sensible to define an essay's true score as the rating dictated by the rubric—a so-called *Platonic* true score (Lord & Novick, 1968, pp. 39–44). Rogosa (1998) begins from this perspective in modeling rater misclassifications. Note that for papers with true scores at the minimum or maximum of the scale, misclassifications can only occur in one direction. Thus, unless all raters assign the identical score, the mean observed score over raters is a biased estimator of the essay's true score. Thus, from this perspective, true score cannot be equal to the expected value of observed score. Useful models for rater accuracy can be derived under this assumption, but paradoxical results are obtained if the variance is decomposed as in classical test theory or generalizability theory. For example, Rogosa presents plausible situations using data from the 1994 California Learning Assessment System (CLAS) in which observed-score variance of ratings is less than true-score variance. This work highlights the importance of clearly specifying what model is used, in particular the definitions of true score and error, and of considering the appropriateness of the model in any particular application.

Special statistical problems arise in large-scale testing programs involving the rating of student responses such as essays. Fitzpatrick, Ercikan, Yen, and Ferrara (1998) analyzed rater performance over successive years with regard to both severity and consistency. They found that raters became more consistent over time, and that rater severity varied from year to year. Different patterns were observed as a function of content area rated.

When essays are rated twice, some rule must be established for assigning a final score in cases where raters disagree. Disagreements involving adjacent versus nonadjacent scoring categories may be treated differently, the latter often triggering adjudication by a third reader. A simple average of the two or three ratings may result in an inadmissible fractional value. Johnson, Penny, and Gordon (2000) compared four common methods of score resolution with respect to their effects on interrater reliability and overall passing rate. Adjudication is also addressed by Brennan (2000b, p. 348). It must be emphasized that when adjudication is used, assumptions for many statistical models are violated. Because the decision rule triggering adjudication depends on previous (observed) ratings, standard errors of measurement and even precise definitions of examinees' universe scores may no longer be entirely clear.

In a systematic treatment motivated by generalizability theory, Longford (1994) provided a unified treatment of the problems of assigning raters to essays and estimating examinees' true scores. His model allowed for variation in both rater severity and rater consistency. Longford began with the additive model $y_{i,j_{ik}} = \alpha_i + \beta_{j_{ik}} + \varepsilon_{i,j_{ik}}$, where α_i is the true score for examinee i; j_{ik} indexes the rater who scored i's response during scoring session k; $\beta_{j_{ik}}$ is the severity of rater j_{ik}; and $\varepsilon_{j_{ik}}$ is a residual representing the examinee by rater interaction. This model is used to develop various score adjustment schemes taking account of the amount of information about severity that is available for raters with large versus small workloads, for example.

5. RELIABILITY AND BEHAVIORAL OBSERVATIONS

In most of test theory, examinees' true scores are in principle unknowable. Thus, it is natural to define the true score as the expected value of the observed score (Lord & Novick, 1968, pp. 39–44.) If one is sampling some continuous stream of observable behavior to infer some property of that behavior stream, it may be appropriate instead to define the target of the measurement as the actual state of the world, akin to what Lord and Novick refer to as a Platonic true score. In their monograph on *Statistical Models for Behavioral Observations*, Rogosa and Ghandour (1991) provide an alternative framework for considerations of score accuracy, with first assumptions quite different from those of classical test theory and generalizability theory. For continuous observation, they consider the statistical and psychometric properties of empirical rates of behavior, empirical proportions or relative frequencies of types of behavior, empirical prevalence (the proportion of time the behavior occurs) and empirical event duration. For time sampling (versus continuous observation), they consider errors due to finite observation time, recorder errors, and variation over occasions of observation in the prevalence of the behaviors observed (Rogosa & Ghandour, 1991, p. 157). The sorts of questions for which they develop error structures are "How many? How often? How long?" Their work highlights the importance of considering the source and nature of the data in choosing an appropriate statistical model. Space does not permit any systematic treatment of the various models Rogosa and Ghandour develop, but it may be useful to list the kinds of models and sources of error they consider, even if omitting their extensive theoretical results.

The authors begin with a simplest case, a two-state behavior stream in which some target behavior is either on or off. An example would be "teacher talking" in research employing classroom observations. The simplest model for such a behavior stream is an alternating renewal process, in which durations of successive on states and of successive off states are mutually independent, identically distributed variables. An observer samples the behavior stream and records its state. In a related model, observers would record the point processes of off-to-on transitions. Sources of error include the finite observation interval (time sampling) and two kinds of recorder errors—thinning (finite probability of failure to observe an event) and superposition (finite probability of over counting events). Reliability is also affected if the actual incidence of the behavior varies over time (heterogeneity over occasions). Observers may be either fixed or random. For fixed observers, individual parameters may be defined for thinning and superposition. For random raters, the distribution of these parameters may be defined. After treating the case of observing a single process, the authors turn to models for populations of individual processes, say for example, observations of teacher talk in many classrooms. In the last part of their monograph, they examine the consequences of applying traditional models from classical test theory and generalizability theory to data arising from the behavioral processes they have developed.

One of Rogosa and Ghandour's (1991) major conclusions is that finite observation time is perhaps the most critical limiting factor on the accuracy of inferences from behavioral observations. Given a choice between more observers versus more occasions or longer durations of observation, increasing the number or duration of observations is likely to produce the greatest benefit. The authors also demonstrate that the Spearman-Brown "prophecy" formula cannot be applied to determine the increase in precision resulting from an increase in the duration of behavioral observations.

In one example, Rogosa and Ghandour (1991) begin with a two-facet $p \times o \times r$ G-study design presented by Medley and Mitzel (1963, p. 316) and reanalyzed by Cronbach et al. (1972, pp. 190–193). For this example, 24 teachers (p) were observed on each of 5 occasions (o) by the same 2 recorders (r). Rogosa and Ghandour point out that the duration of the observations, which is critical for their purposes, is not reported. Within the framework these authors develop, changes in the duration of observations would have complex, but predictable, effects on variance component estimates. They present a model predicting $\sigma^2(o) = \sigma^2(ro) = 0$, in close agreement with the generalizability study findings. Several sets of parameter values for their model are presented, any of which would reproduce the remaining variance component estimates. While there is no claim that these results demonstrate the superiority of either model, the exercise does demonstrate the plausibility of their alternative. The Rogosa and Ghandour monograph was published with two responses, by Brennan (1991) and Floden (1991) and a reply to the discussants by the original authors.

6. FUTURE DIRECTIONS

There have been important changes since Feldt and Brennan (1989) wrote their chapter on "Reliability" for the previous edition of *Educational Measurement*, especially in generalizability theory. New methods have been developed for estimating conditional standard errors of measurement, for quantifying the precision of estimates of variance components and reliability coefficients, for modeling the error structure of group means (e.g., school means in large-scale assessments), and for estimating the reliability of assessments with complex internal structures or complex scoring rules.

There has also been an increasing recognition that alternatives to traditional models may provide better answers to questions of score accuracy in particular situations. For difference scores, accuracy should usually be judged relative to the absolute magnitude of the difference, not the variance of the differences. For behavioral observations, models for time sampling may be more appropriate than conventional models from classical test theory or generalizability theory.

The greater power and lower cost of computers have also brought changes. Some computational shortcuts and approximations are no longer required; estimation methods like the bootstrap are in principle within reach of anyone with a desktop computer.

At the same time, the foundations of classical test theory and generalizability theory were laid long before Feldt and Brennan (1989) wrote their chapter, and most of the new material reviewed in this chapter represents refinements and extensions rather than fundamentally new developments.

Looking to the future, there are at least three areas that may yield such fundamentally new developments. First, the models and methods reviewed in this chapter are concerned primarily with scores obtained as sums of item responses obtained at one point in time. New measurement models (e.g., models using Bayesian inference networks) are now being developed to support more complex patterns of inference from multiple forms of data (Mislevy, 1994). In the future, student models may be maintained over time and updated as new information becomes available. The same basic questions will arise concerning the accuracy of inferences from such models as from more traditional measurements, but methods will change.

Second, fundamental progress is possible in the integration of models from generalizability theory, item response theory, and perhaps other models. As an example, Bock, Brennan, and Muraki (2002) show how results from a generalizability analysis can be used to account for the conditional dependence among multiple ratings and adjust information functions and standard errors obtained in the context of item response theory. As another example, Holland and Hoskens (2003) derive a classical test theory model within the framework of item response theory and use their framework to examine problems in linking or equating possibly nonparallel measures. More generally, it is difficult to predict how such disparate models might be brought together, but practical testing applications, especially large-scale assessments, seem to require both conceptions of items as instances of faceted observations (random effects) and as particular measuring units characterized by their own parameters (fixed effects).

Finally, there is a need for further integration of notions of reliability with evolving conceptions of test validity. Cronbach et al. (1972), Brennan (2001b) and others have observed that there is a sense in which reliability and one aspect of validity fall on a continuum. Classical test theory is primarily concerned with inferences to a universe of generalization in which all sources of error are pooled and treated as a single random variable. Generalizability theory enables consideration of broader universes of generalization but is still limited to measurements comprising elements sampled from well defined, faceted universes of admissible observations. Validity is often concerned, in part, with predictions from test scores to performance in some ill-defined domain of nontest situations. It is conventional wisdom that reliability is prerequisite to validity, and the *Standards* (AERA, APA, & NCME, 1999) clearly state that evaluation of reliability is part of a full consideration of the validity of an intended test use or interpretation. Still, there is room for much progress in integrating notions of score precision more completely with frameworks and methods for test validation.

NOTES

1. Reliability estimates for composite scores, which may combine measurements of different qualities, are usually derived from reliability estimates for the separate score components included, as described in section 2.5.3. However, the composite score from an achievement test battery, for example, could also be regarded as measuring a single, complex "quality," and its reliability could be estimated directly, without regard to its component parts. In some cases, that would be the preferred method.

2. The first assumption here combines Feldt and Brennan's assumptions 1 and 5.

3. Most results require only that the first two moments of the observed-score distributions be identical across test forms.

4. In principle, standard errors of measurement might vary for examinees with the same true score. For example, holding true score constant, the performance of younger children might be more variable than that of older children. The discussion of conditional standard errors of measurement in this chapter, however, is limited to models conditional solely on true score, or on vectors of true scores for test strata. (In practice, estimates of conditional standard errors are based on observed scores for tests or test strata. See sections 2.6.2 and 3.9.)

5. Holland and Hoskens (2003) present the assumptions of classical test theory and derive its fundamental equations using notation chosen to emphasize throughout this dependence of the (unconditional) standard error, as well as the reliability, on some group G of examinees.

6. It may still be useful, for some purposes, to define a single true score $\tau_p = E(X_p)$, the expectation being taken over test forms. One may then define a form-specific constant for each form, such that $\tau_{pf} = \tau_p + C_f$, $\tau_{pg} = \tau_p + C_g$, etc. It follows that over all test forms f, $E(C_f) = 0$.

7. This definition of congeneric tests is unsatisfying in that it does not entail any procedure, even hypothetically, whereby an individual's true score on any particular test form might be inferred. An alternative would be to first define τ_p in terms of an indefinitely large collection of essentially τ-equivalent test forms, then for each congeneric test form f define $\tau_{pf} = a_f \tau_p + C_f$ (Leonard Feldt, personal communication, May 14, 2004.)

8. See also Cronbach's (2004) commentary and reflection on coefficient alpha 50 years later.

9. Even if items in different categories measure the same dimension, distinctions among categories may be maintained for other reasons. For example, if specifications were changed for an achievement test that teachers viewed as consequential, their patterns of content coverage or emphasis might change in response. That in turn might change the correlation between the dimensions measured by the different categories.

10. If the posttest variance is less than the pretest variance, or if the variance of pretest scores is equal to the variance of posttest scores and the correlation of pretest and posttest is less than unity, then difference scores must be negatively correlated with pretest scores. If the posttest variance exceeds the pretest variance, however, the correlation of pretest and difference scores may be positive, negative, or zero (Roberts & Burrill, 1995).

11. If a group of individuals were selected on the basis of either score component forming the difference score (e.g., persons with a given pretest score or a given range of pretest scores), the mean difference score for that group would not, in general, be an unbiased estimator of the mean of their true difference scores. This could be demonstrated by arguments similar to those presented in section 2.6.1 for single test scores. Note that such selection would violate the assumption stated earlier in connection with Equation 4.

12. Thanks to David Rogosa for suggesting a version of this particular example.

13. If the assumption of sampling from an undifferentiated item domain is replaced by sampling fixed numbers of items from each stratum of a stratified item domain (with possibly different mean difficulties for each stratum), then the compound binomial error model is obtained.

14. Note that the bias due to use of n instead of $(n-1)$ in the denominator under the radical tends to zero as n tends to infinity.

15. The true score is defined here as the expected value of the observed score across such hypothetical replications.

16. Note that the observed-score variance is a statistic calculated from sample observations, not a parameter. Thus, the definition of the generalizability coefficient employs the expected value of the observed score variance, which for any given D-study design is a parameter characterizing the population of objects of measurement and the universe of generalization.

17. A lower-case j is used because $n_j = 1$, and so the D-study variance component for facet j is the same as the corresponding G-study variance component. Use of J would be logically consistent, as well.

18. More precisely, the intended universe of generalization probably extends to other forms that might be developed from the same table of specifications. Thus, a better model might be random sampling of items within fixed strata, which is a straightforward application of multivariate generalizability theory.

REFERENCES

Agresti, A. (2002). *Categorical data analysis* (2nd ed.). New York: Wiley-Interscience.

Agresti, A., & Coull, B. A. (1998). Approximate is better than "exact" for interval estimation of binomial proportions. *American Statistician, 52*, 119–126.

Alsawalmeh, Y. M., & Feldt, L. S. (1992). Test of the hypothesis that the intraclass reliability coefficient is the same for two measurement procedures. *Applied Psychological Measurement, 16*, 195–205.

Alsawalmeh, Y. M., & Feldt, L. S. (1994a). A modification of Feldt's test of the equality of two dependent alpha coefficients. *Psychometrika, 59*, 49–57.

Alsawalmeh, Y. M., & Feldt, L. S. (1994b). Testing the equality of two related intraclass reliability coefficients. *Applied Psychological Measurement, 18*, 183–190.

Alsawalmeh, Y. M., & Feldt, L. S. (1999). Testing the equality of two independent α coefficients adjusted by the Spearman-Brown formula. *Applied Psychological Measurement, 23*, 363–370.

Alsawalmeh, Y. M., & Feldt, L. S. (2000). A test of the equality of two related α coefficients adjusted by the Spearman-Brown formula. *Applied Psychological Measurement, 24*, 163–172.

American Educational Research Association, American Psychological Association, & National Council on Measurement in Education. (1999). *Standards for educational and psychological testing*. Washington, DC: American Educational Research Association.

Angoff, W. H. (1953). Test reliability and effective test length. *Psychometrika, 18*, 1–14.

Bacon, D. R., Sauer, P. L., & Young, M. (1995). Composite reliability in structural equation modeling. *Educational and Psychological Measurement, 55*, 394–406.

Bay, K. S. (1973). The effect of non-normality on the sampling distribution and standard error of reliability coefficient estimates under an analysis of variance model. *British Journal of Mathematical and Statistical Psychology, 26*, 45–57.

Becker, G. (2000). How important is transient error in estimating reliability? Going beyond simulation studies. *Psychological Methods, 5*, 370–379.

Bentler, P. M. (1972). A lower-bound method for the dimension-free measurement of internal consistency. *Social Science Research, 1*, 343–357.

Bentler, P. M., & Woodward, J. A. (1980). Inequalities among lower bounds to reliability: With applications to test construction and factor analysis. *Psychometrika, 45*, 249–267.

Bentler, P. M., & Woodward, J. A. (1983). The greatest lower bound to reliability. In H. Wainer & S. Messick (Eds.), *Principals of modern psychological measurement: A festschrift for Frederic M. Lord* (pp. 237–253). Hillsdale, NJ: Erlbaum.

Bentler, P. M., & Woodward, J. A. (1985). On the greatest lower bound to reliability. *Psychometrika, 50*, 245–246.

Blackman, N. J.-M., & Koval, J. J. (1993). Estimating rater agreement in 2 x 2 tables: Corrections for chance and intraclass correlation. *Applied Psychological Measurement, 17*, 211–223.

Bock, R. D., Brennan, R. L., & Muraki, E. (2002). The information in multiple ratings. *Applied Psychological Measurement, 26*, 364–375.

Bonett, D. G. (2003). Sample size requirements for comparing two alpha coefficients. *Applied Psychological Measurement, 27*, 72–74.

Bost, J. L. (1995). The effects of correlated errors on generalizability and dependability coefficients. *Applied Psychological Measurement, 19*, 191–203.

Brennan, R. L. (1983). *Elements of generalizability theory*. Iowa City, IA: American College Testing Program.

Brennan, R. L. (1991). Statistical models for behavioral observations: A review. *Journal of Educational Statistics, 16*, 253–266.

Brennan, R. L. (1992a). *Elements of generalizability theory* (Rev. ed.). Iowa City, IA: American College Testing Program.

Brennan, R. L. (1992b). Generalizability theory. *Educational Measurement: Issues and Practice, 11*(4), 27–34.

Brennan, R. L. (1994). Variance components in generalizability theory. In C. R. Reynolds (Ed.), *Cognitive assessment: A multidisciplinary perspective* (pp. 175–207). New York: Plenum Press.

Brennan, R. L. (1995). The conventional wisdom about group mean scores. *Journal of Educational Measurement, 32*, 385–396.

Brennan, R. L. (1997). A perspective on the history of generalizability theory. *Educational Measurement: Issues and Practice, 16*(4), 14–20.

Brennan, R. L. (1998). Raw-score conditional standard errors of measurement in generalizability theory. *Applied Psychological Measurement, 22*, 307–331.

Brennan, R. L. (2000a). (Mis)conceptions about generalizability theory. *Educational Measurement: Issues and Practice, 19*(1), 5–10.

Brennan, R. L. (2000b). Performance assessments from the perspective of generalizability theory. *Applied Psychological Measurement, 24*, 339–353.

Brennan, R. L. (2001a). An essay on the history and future of reliability from the perspective of replications. *Journal of Educational Measurement, 38*, 295–317.

Brennan, R. L. (2001b). *Generalizability theory*. New York: Springer-Verlag.

Brennan, R. L. (2001c). mGENOVA (Version 2.1) [Computer software and manual]. Iowa City: University of Iowa. (Available from http://www.education.uiowa.edu/casma)

Brennan, R. L. (2001d). urGENOVA (Version 2.1) [Computer software and manual]. Iowa City: University of Iowa. (Available from http://www.education.uiowa.edu/casma)

Brennan, R.L. (2004). BB-CLASS (Version 1.0) [Computer software and manual]. Available from http://www.education.uiowa.edu/casma

Brennan, R. L., Gao, X., & Colton, D. A. (1995). Generalizability analyses of work keys listening and writing tests. *Educational and Psychological Measurement, 55*, 157–176.

Brennan, R. L., & Kane, M. T. (1977a). An index of dependability for mastery tests. *Journal of Educational Measurement, 14*, 277–289.

Brennan, R. L., & Kane, M. T. (1977b). Signal/noise ratios for domain-referenced tests. *Psychometrika, 42*, 609–625.

Brennan, R. L., & Lee, W. (1999). Conditional scale-score standard errors of measurement under binomial and compound binomial assumptions. *Educational and Psychological Measurement, 59*, 5–24.

Brennan, R. L., & Wan, L. (2004). *A Bootstrap procedure for estimating decision consistency for single-administration complex assessments* (CASMA Research Report No. 7). Iowa City: The University of Iowa, Center for Advanced Studies in Measurement and Assessment. (Available from http://www.education.uiowa.edu/casma)

Brennan, R. L., Yin, P., & Kane, M. T. (2003). Methodology for examining the reliability of group mean difference scores. *Journal of Educational Measurement, 40*, 207–230.

Breyer, F. J., & Lewis, C. (1994). *Pass-fail reliability for tests with cut scores: A simplified method* (Report No. ETS-RR-94-39). Princeton, NJ: Educational Testing Service. (ERIC Document Reproduction Service No. ED382655)

Brown, R. L. (1989). Congeneric modeling of reliability using censored variables. *Applied Psychological Measurement, 13*, 151–159.

Brown, W. (1910). Some experimental results in the correlation of mental abilities. *British Journal of Psychology, 3*, 296–322.

Brown, W. (1911). *The essentials of mental measurement* (1st ed.). Cambridge, England: University Press.

Brown, W., & Thomson, G. H. (1921). *The essentials of mental measurement* (2nd ed.). Cambridge, England: University Press.

Burdick, R. K., & Graybill, F. A. (1992). *Confidence intervals on variance components*. New York: Dekker.

Buros, O. K. (1978). Part 2. Some comments on reliability. In O. K. Buros (Ed.), *The eighth mental measurements yearbook* (Vol. 2, pp. 1979–1983). Highland Park, NJ: Gryphon Press. (Reprinted from *Psychological Reports, 42*(3), 1023–1029, 1978)

Burt, C. (1936). The analysis of examination marks. In P. Hartog & E. C. Rhodes (Eds.), *The marks of examiners* (pp. 245–314). London: Macmillan.

Cahan, S. (1989). A critical examination of the "reliability" and "abnormality" approaches to the evaluation of subtest score differences. *Educational and Psychological Measurement, 49*, 807–814.

Chiu, C. W., & Wolfe, E. W. (2002). A method for analyzing sparse data matrices in the generalizability theory framework. *Applied Psychological Measurement, 26*, 321–338.

Cliff, N., & Caruso, J. C. (1998). Reliable component analysis through maximizing composite reliability. *Psychological Methods, 3*, 291–308.

Cohen, J. (1960). A coefficient of agreement for nominal tables. *Educational and Psychological Measurement, 20*, 37–46.

Collins, L. M. (1996). Is reliability obsolete? A commentary on "Are simple gain scores obsolete?" *Applied Psychological Measurement, 20*, 289–292.

Conger, A. J., & Lipshitz, R. (1973). Measures of reliability for profiles and test batteries. *Psychometrika, 38*, 411–427.

Cooil, B., & Rust, R. T. (1994). Reliability and expected loss: A unifying principle. *Psychometrika, 59*, 203–216.

Crick, J. E., & Brennan, R. L. (1983). *Manual for GENOVA: A generalized analysis of variance system* (American College Testing Technical Bulletin No. 43). Iowa City, IA: ACT.

Cronbach, L. J. (1951). Coefficient alpha and the internal structure of tests. *Psychometrika, 16*, 297–334.

Cronbach, L. J. (1988). Internal consistency of tests: Analyses old and new. *Psychometrika, 53*, 63–70.

Cronbach, L. J. (2004). My current thoughts on coefficient alpha and successor procedures. *Educational and Psychological Measurement, 64*, 391–418.

Cronbach, L. J., & Furby, L. (1970). How we should measure change—Or should we? *Psychological Bulletin, 74*, 68–80. (And Errata, *Psychological Bulletin, 74*, 218)

Cronbach, L. J., Gleser, G. C., Nanda, H., & Rajaratnam, N. (1972). *The dependability of behavioral measurements: Theory of generalizability for scores and profiles*. New York: Wiley.

Cronbach, L. J., Linn, R. L., Brennan, R. L., & Haertel, E. H. (1997). Generalizability analysis for performance assessments of student achievement or school effectiveness. *Educational and Psychological Measurement, 57*, 373–399.

Cronbach, L. J., Rajaratnam, N., & Gleser, G. C. (1963). Theory of generalizability: A liberalization of reliability theory. *British Journal of Statistical Psychology, 16*, 137–163.

Cronbach, L. J., Schöenemann, P., & McKie, D. (1965). Alpha coefficients for stratified-parallel tests. *Educational and Psychological Measurement, 25*, 291–312.

DeShon, R. P. (1998). A cautionary note on measurement error corrections in structural equation models. *Psychological Methods, 3*, 412–423.

Ebel, R. L. (1951). Estimation of the reliability of ratings. *Psychometrika, 16*, 407–424.

Efron, B. (1982). *The jackknife, the bootstrap, and other resampling plans*. Philadelphia: SIAM.

Efron, B., & Tibshirani, R. (1986). Bootstrap methods for standard errors, confidence intervals, and other measures of statistical accuracy. *Statistical Science, 1*, 54–77.

Eiting, M. H. (1991). Sequential reliability tests. *Applied Psychological Measurement, 15*, 193–205.

Enders, C. K., & Bandalos, D. L. (1999). The effects of heterogeneous item distributions on reliability. *Applied Measurement in Education, 12*, 133–150.

Feldt, L. S. (1965). The approximate sampling distribution of Kuder-Richardson reliability coefficient twenty. *Psychometrika, 30*, 357–370.

Feldt, L. S. (1969). A test of the hypothesis that Cronbach's alpha or Kuder-Richardson coefficient twenty is the same for two tests. *Psychometrika, 34*, 363–373.

Feldt, L. S. (1975). Estimation of the reliability of a test divided into two parts of unequal length. *Psychometrika, 40*, 557–561.

Feldt, L. S. (1980). A test of the hypothesis that Cronbach's alpha reliability coefficient is the same for two tests administered to the same sample. *Psychometrika, 45*, 99–105.

Feldt, L. S. (1984). Some relationships between the binomial error model and classical test theory. *Educational and Psychological Measurement, 44*, 883–891.

Feldt, L. S. (1990). The sampling theory for the intraclass reliability coefficient. *Applied Measurement in Education, 3*, 361–367.

Feldt, L. S. (1995). Estimation of the reliability of differences under revised reliabilities of component scores. *Journal of Educational Measurement, 32*, 295–301.

Feldt, L. S. (2002a). Estimating the internal consistency reliability of tests composed of testlets varying in length. *Applied Measurement in Education, 15*, 33–48.

Feldt, L. S. (2002b). Reliability estimation when a test is split into two parts of unknown effective length. *Applied Measurement in Education, 15*, 295–308.

Feldt, L. S., & Ankenmann, R. D. (1998). Appropriate sample size for comparing alpha reliabilities. *Applied Psychological Measurement, 22*, 170–178.

Feldt, L. S., & Ankenmann, R. D. (1999). Determining sample size for a test of the equality of alpha coefficients when the number of part-tests is small. *Psychological Methods, 4*, 366–377.

Feldt, L. S., & Brennan, R. L. (1989). Reliability. In R. L. Linn (Ed.), *Educational measurement* (3rd ed., pp. 105–146). New York: American Council on Education and Macmillan.

Feldt, L. S., & Charter, R. A. (2003). Estimating the reliability of a test split into two parts of equal or unequal length. *Psychological Methods, 8*, 102–109.

Feldt, L. S., & Qualls, A. L. (1996a). Bias in coefficient alpha arising from heterogeneity of test content. *Applied Measurement in Education, 9*, 277–286.

Feldt, L. S., & Qualls, A. L. (1996b). Estimation of measurement error variance at specific score levels. *Journal of Educational Measurement, 33*, 141–156.

Feldt, L. S., & Qualls, A. L. (1998). Approximating scale score standard error of measurement from the raw score standard error. *Applied Measurement in Education, 11*, 159–177.

Feldt, L. S., & Qualls, A. L. (1999). Variability in reliability coefficients and the standard error of measurement from school district to district. *Applied Measurement in Education, 12*, 367–381.

Fitzpatrick, A. R., Ercikan, K., Yen, W. M., & Ferrara, S. (1998). The consistency between raters scoring in different test years. *Applied Measurement in Education, 11*, 195–208.

Floden, R. E. (1991). Putting true scores first: A response. *Journal of Educational Statistics, 16*, 267–280.

Fyans, L. J., Jr. (Ed.). (1983). *New Directions for Testing and Measurement: Generalizability theory: Inferences and practical applications, 18*.

Gao, X., & Brennan, R. L. (2001). Variability of estimated variance components and related statistics in a performance assessment. *Applied Measurement in Education, 14*, 191–203.

Gilmer, J. S., & Feldt, L. S. (1983). Reliability estimation for a test with parts of unknown lengths. *Psychometrika, 48*, 99–111.

Gleser, G. C., Cronbach, L. J., & Rajaratnam, N. (1965). Generalizability of scores influenced by multiple sources of variance. *Psychometrika, 30*, 395–418.

Green, S. B. (2003). A coefficient alpha for test-retest data. *Psychological Methods, 8*, 88–101.

Gulliksen, H. (1950). *Theory of mental tests*. New York: Wiley.

Guttman, L. A. (1945). A basis for analyzing test-retest reliability. *Psychometrika, 10*, 255–282.

Hakstian, A. R., & Whalen, T. E. (1976). A k-sample significance test for independent alpha coefficients. *Psychometrika, 41*, 219–231.

Hambleton, R. K., Swaminathan, H., Algina, J., & Coulson, D. B. (1978). Criterion-referenced testing and measurement: A review of technical issues and developments. *Review of Educational Research, 48*, 1–47.

Hancock, G. R. (1997). Correlation/validity coefficients disattenuated for score reliability: A structural equation modeling approach. *Educational and Psychological Measurement, 57*, 598–606.

Hanson, B. A. (1991). *Method of moments estimates for the four-parameter beta compound binomial model and the calculation of classification consistency indexes* (ACT Research Report No. 91-5). Iowa City, IA: American College Testing Program.

Hanson, B. A., & Brennan, R. L. (1990). An investigation of classification consistency indexes estimated under alternative strong true score models. *Journal of Educational Measurement, 27,* 345–359.

Harris, C. W. (Ed.). (1963). *Problems in measuring change.* Madison: University of Wisconsin Press.

Hedges, L. V., & Olkin, I. (1985). *Statistical methods for meta-analysis.* Orlando, FL: Academic Press.

Henderson, C. R. (1953). Estimation of variance and covariance components. *Biometrics, 9,* 226–252.

Henson, R. K., & Thompson, B. (2002). Characterizing measurement error in scores across studies: Some recommendations for conducting "reliability generalization" studies. *Measurement and Evaluation in Counseling and Development, 35,* 113–127.

Hogan, T. P., Benjamin, A., & Brezinski, K. L. (2000). Reliability methods: A note on the frequency of use of various types. *Educational and Psychological Measurement, 60,* 523–531.

Holland, P. W., & Hoskens, M. (2003). Classical test theory as a first-order item response theory: Applications to true-score prediction from a possibly nonparallel test. *Psychometrika, 68,* 123–149.

Horst, P. (1951). Estimating total test reliability from parts of unequal length. *Educational and Psychological Measurement, 11,* 368–371.

Hoyt, C. (1941). Test reliability obtained by analysis of variance. *Psychometrika, 6,* 153–160.

Hoyt, W. T. (2000). Rater bias in psychological research: When is it a problem and what can we do about it? *Psychological Methods, 5,* 64–86.

Hsu, J. S. J., Leonard, T., & Tsui, K. W. (1991). Statistical inference for multiple-choice tests. *Psychometrika, 56,* 327–348.

Humphreys, L. G. (1993). Further comments on reliability and power of significance tests. *Applied Psychological Measurement, 17,* 11–14.

Humphreys, L. G., & Drasgow, F. (1989a). Paradoxes, contradictions, and illusions. *Applied Psychological Measurement, 13,* 429–431.

Humphreys, L. G., & Drasgow, F. (1989b). Some comments on the relation between reliability and statistical power. *Applied Psychological Measurement, 13,* 419–425.

Huynh, H. (1976). Statistical consideration of mastery scores. *Psychometrika, 41,* 65–78.

Huynh, H. (1986). Reliability of composite measurements based on the m highest of n equivalent components. *Journal of Educational Statistics, 11,* 225–238.

Jarjoura, D. (1985). Tolerance intervals for true scores. *Journal of Educational Statistics, 19,* 1–17.

Jarjoura, D. (1986). An estimator of examinee-level measurement error variance that considers test form difficulty adjustments. *Applied Psychological Measurement, 10,* 175–186.

Jarjoura, D., & Brennan, R. L. (1981). *Three variance components models for some measurement procedures in which unequal numbers of items fall into discrete categories* (ACT Technical Bulletin No. 37). Iowa City, IA: American College Testing Program.

Jarjoura, D., & Brennan, R. L. (1982). A variance components model for measurement procedures associated with a table of specifications. *Applied Psychological Measurement, 6,* 161–171.

Jarjoura, D., & Brennan, R. L. (1983). Multivariate generalizability models for tests developed from tables of specifications. *New Directions for Testing and Measurement: Generalizability Theory: Inferences and Practical Applications, 18,* 83–101.

Johnson, R. L., Penny, J., & Gordon, B. (2000). The relation between score resolution methods and interrater reliability: An empirical study of an analytic scoring rubric. *Applied Measurement in Education, 13,* 121–138.

Jöreskog, K. G. (1971). Statistical analysis of sets of congeneric tests. *Psychometrika, 36,* 109–133.

Kane, M. (1996). The precision of measurements. *Applied Measurement in Education, 9,* 355–379.

Kane, M. (2002). Inferences about variance components and reliability-generalizability coefficients in the absence of random sampling. *Journal of Educational Measurement, 39,* 165–181.

Keats, J. A. (1957). Estimation of error variances of test scores. *Psychometrika, 22,* 29–41.

Keats, J. A., & Lord, F. M. (1962). A theoretical distribution for mental test scores. *Psychometrika, 27,* 59–72.

Kelley, T. L. (1947). *Fundamentals of statistics.* Cambridge, MA: Harvard University Press.

Klauer, K. C., & Batchelder, W. H. (1996). Structural analysis of subjective categorical data. *Psychometrika, 61,* 199–240.

Kolen, M. M., Hanson, B. A., & Brennan, R. L. (1992). Conditional standard errors of measurement for scale scores. *Journal of Educational Measurement, 29,* 285–307.

Kolen, M. M., Zeng, L., & Hanson, B. A. (1996). Conditional standard errors of measurement for scale scores using IRT. *Journal of Educational Measurement, 33,* 129–140.

Komaroff, E. (1997). Effect of simultaneous violations of essential τ-equivalence and uncorrelated error on coefficient α. *Applied Psychological Measurement, 21,* 337–348.

Kopriva, R. J., & Shaw, D. G. (1991). Power estimates: The effect of dependent variable reliability on the power of one-factor ANOVAs. *Educational and Psychological Measurement, 51,* 585–595.

Kraemer, H. C. (1981). Extensions of Feldt's approach to testing homogeneity of coefficients of reliability. *Psychometrika, 45,* 41–45.

Kristof, W. (1963). The statistical theory of stepped-up reliability coefficients when a test has been divided into several equivalent parts. *Psychometrika, 28,* 221–238.

Kristof, W. (1964). Testing differences between reliability coefficients. *British Journal of Statistical Psychology, 17,* 105–111.

Kristof, W. (1970). On the sampling theory of reliability estimation. *Journal of Mathematical Psychology, 7,* 371–377.

Kristof, W. (1971). On the theory of a set of tests which differ only in length. *Psychometrika, 36,* 207–225.

Kristof, W. (1974). Estimation of reliability and true score variance from a split of a test into three arbitrary parts. *Psychometrika, 39,* 491–499.

Kuder, F. (1991). Comments concerning the appropriate use of formulas for estimating the internal-consistency reliability of tests. *Educational and Psychological Measurement, 51,* 873–874.

Kuder, G. F., & Richardson, M. W. (1937). The theory of the estimation of test reliability. *Psychometrika, 2,* 151–160.

Lane, G. G., White, A. E., & Henson, R. K. (2002). Expanding reliability generalization methods with KR-21 estimates: An RG study of the Coopersmith Self-Esteem Inventory. *Educational and Psychological Measurement, 62,* 685–711.

Lee, G. (2000a). A comparison of methods of estimating conditional standard errors of measurement for testlet-based test scores using simulation techniques. *Journal of Educational Measurement, 37,* 91–112.

Lee, G. (2000b). A disattenuated part-whole correlation formula. *Journal of Educational Measurement, 37,* 279–280.

Lee, G. (2000c). Estimating conditional standard errors of measurement for tests composed of testlets. *Applied Measurement in Education, 13,* 161–180.

Lee, G., Brennan, R. L., & Frisbie, D. A. (2000). Incorporating the testlet concept in test score analysis. *Educational Measurement: Issues and Practice, 19*(4), 9–15.

Lee, G., & Frisbie, D. A. (1999). Estimating reliability under a generalizability theory model for test scores composed of testlets. *Applied Measurement in Education, 12*, 237–255.

Lee, W. (2005). *A multinomial error model for tests with polytomous items* (CASMA Research Report No. 10). Iowa City: The University of Iowa, Center for Advanced Studies in Measurement and Assessment. (Available from http://www.education.uiowa.edu/casma)

Lee, W., Brennan, R. L., & Kolen, M. J. (2000). Estimators of conditional scale-score standard errors of measurement: A simulation study. *Journal of Educational Measurement, 37*, 1–20.

Lee, W., Brennan, R. L., & Kolen, M. J. (in press). Interval estimation for true raw and scale scores under the binomial error model. *Journal of Educational and Behavioral Statistics*.

Lee, W., Hanson, B. A., & Brennan, R. L. (2002). Estimating consistency and accuracy indices for multiple classifications. *Applied Psychological Measurement, 26*, 412–432.

Li, H. (1997). A unifying expression for the maximal reliability of a linear composite. *Psychometrika, 62*, 245–249.

Li, H., Rosenthal, R., & Rubin, D. B. (1996). Reliability of measurement in psychology: From Spearman-Brown to maximal reliability. *Psychological Methods, 1*, 98–107.

Li, H., & Wainer, H. (1997). Toward a coherent view of reliability in test theory. *Journal of Educational and Behavioral Statistics, 22*, 478–484.

Lin, M.-H., & Hsiung, C. A. (1992). 4 bootstrap confidence-intervals for the binomial-error model. *Psychometrika, 57*, 499–520.

Lin, M.-H., & Hsiung, C. A. (1994). Empirical Bayes estimates of domain scores under binomial and hypergeometric distributions for test scores. *Psychometrika, 59*, 331–359.

Lindquist, E. F. (1953). *Design and analysis of experiments in psychology and education*. Boston: Houghton Mifflin.

Linn, R. L., & Slinde, J. A. (1977). The determination of the significance of change between pre- and posttesting periods. *Review of Educational Research, 47*, 121–150.

Liou, M. (1989). A note on reliability estimation for a test with components of unknown functional lengths. *Psychometrika, 54*, 153–163.

Livingston, S. A. (1972). Criterion-referenced applications of classical test theory. *Journal of Educational Measurement, 9*, 13–26.

Livingston, S. A., & Lewis, C. (1995). Estimating the consistency and accuracy of classifications based on test scores. *Journal of Educational Measurement, 32*, 179–197.

Loevinger, J. (1965). Person and population as psychometric concepts. *Psychological Review, 72*, 143–155.

Longford, N. T. (1994). Reliability of essay rating and score adjustment. *Journal of Educational and Behavioral Statistics, 19*, 171–200.

Lord, F. M. (1955). Estimating test reliability. *Educational and Psychological Measurement, 15*, 325–336.

Lord, F. M. (1956a). The measurement of growth. *Educational and Psychological Measurement, 16*, 421–437.

Lord, F. M. (1956b). Sampling error due to choice of split in split-half reliability coefficients. *Journal of Experimental Education, 24*, 245–249.

Lord, F. M. (1957). Do tests of the same length have the same standard error of measurement? *Educational and Psychological Measurement, 17*, 510–521.

Lord, F. M. (1958). Further problems in the measurement of growth. *Educational and Psychological Measurement, 18*, 437–451.

Lord, F. M. (1959). Tests of the same length do have the same standard error of measurement. *Educational and Psychological Measurement, 19*, 233–239.

Lord, F. M. (1965). A strong true score theory, with applications. *Psychometrika, 30*, 239–270.

Lord, F. M. (1969). Estimating true-score distributions in psychological testing (an empirical Bayes estimation problem). *Psychometrika, 34*, 259–299.

Lord, F. M. (1974). Variance stabilizing transformation of the stepped-up reliability coefficient. *Journal of Educational Measurement, 11*, 55–57.

Lord, F. M. (1980). *Applications of item response theory to practical testing problems*. Hillsdale, NJ: Erlbaum.

Lord, F. M., & Novick, M. R. (1968). *Statistical theories of mental test scores*. Reading, MA: Addison-Wesley.

Lord, F. M., & Stocking, M. (1976). An interval estimate for making statistical inferences about true score. *Psychometrika, 41*, 79–87.

Maassen, G. H. (2000). Kelley's formula as a basis for the assessment of reliable change. *Psychometrika, 65*, 187–197.

Marcoulides, G. A. (1997). Optimizing measurement designs with budget constraints: The variable cost case. *Educational and Psychological Measurement, 57*, 808–812.

Mayekawa, S., & Haebara, T. (1980). *Estimation of the reliability of a test consisting of more than three congeneric parts* (Iowa Testing Programs Occasional Paper No. 28). Iowa City: University of Iowa.

McGraw, K. O., & Wong, S. P. (1996). Forming inferences about some intraclass correlation coefficients. *Psychological Methods, 1*, 30–46.

McNemar, Q. (1958). On growth measurement. *Educational and Psychological Measurement, 18*, 47–55.

Medley, D. M., & Mitzel, H. E. (1963). Measuring classroom behavior by systematic observation. In N. L. Gage (Ed.), *Handbook of research on teaching* (pp. 247–328). Chicago: Rand McNally.

Mellenbergh, G. J., & van den Brink, W. P. (1998). The measurement of individual change. *Psychological Methods, 3*, 470–485.

Miller, T. B., & Kane, M. (2001). The precision of change scores under absolute and relative interpretations. *Applied Measurement in Education, 14*, 307–327.

Mislevy, R. J. (1994). Evidence and inference in educational assessment. *Psychometrika, 59*, 439–483.

Mollenkopf, W. G. (1949). Variation of the standard error of measurement. *Psychometrika, 14*, 189–229.

Mosier, C. I. (1943). On the reliability of a weighted composite. *Psychometrika, 8*, 161–168.

Muchinsky, P. M. (1996). The correction for attenuation. *Educational and Psychological Measurement, 56*, 63–75.

Muthén, B. (1984). A general structural equation model with dichotomous, ordered categorical, and continuous latent variable indicators. *Psychometrika, 49*, 115–132.

Muthén, B., & Satorra, A. (1995). Technical aspects of Muthén's LISCOMP approach to estimation of latent variable relations with a comprehensive measurement model. *Psychometrika, 60*, 489–503.

Nicewander, W. A., & Price, J. M. (1983). Reliability of measurement and the power of statistical tests: Some new results. *Psychological Bulletin, 94*, 524–533.

Novick, M. R., & Lewis, C. (1967). Coefficient alpha and the reliability of composite measurements. *Psychometrika, 32*, 1–13.

Olkin, I. (1967). Correlations revisited. In J. C. Stanley (Ed.), *Improving experimental design and statistical analysis* (pp. 102–128). New York: Rand McNally.

Osburn, H. G. (2000). Coefficient alpha and related internal consistency reliability coefficients. *Psychological Methods, 5*, 343–355.

Overall, J. E. (1989a). Contradictions can never a paradox resolve. *Applied Psychological Measurement, 13*, 426–428.

Overall, J. E. (1989b). Distinguishing between measurements and dependent variables. *Applied Psychological Measurement, 13*, 432–433.

Popham, W. J., & Husek, T. R. (1969). Implications of criterion-referenced measurement. *Journal of Educational Measurement, 6*, 1–9.

Qualls, A. L. (1995). Estimating the reliability of a test containing multiple item formats. *Applied Measurement in Education, 8*, 111–120.

Qualls-Payne, A. L. (1992). A comparison of score level estimates of the standard error of measurement. *Journal of Educational Measurement, 29*, 213–225.

Quenouille, M. (1949). Approximation tests of correlation in time series. *Journal of the Royal Statistical Society B, 11*, 18–24.

Rae, G. (1991). Another look at the reliability of a profile. *Educational and Psychological Measurement, 51*, 89–93.

Rajaratnam, N., Cronbach, L. J., & Gleser, G. C. (1965). Generalizability of stratified-parallel tests. *Psychometrika, 30*, 39–56.

Raju, N. S. (1970). New formula for estimating total test reliability from parts of unequal length. *Proceedings of the 78th annual convention of the American Psychological Association, 5*, 143–144.

Raju, N. S. (1977). A generalization of coefficient alpha. *Psychometrika, 42*, 549–565.

Raykov, T. (1997). Estimation of composite reliability for congeneric measures. *Applied Psychological Measurement, 21*, 173–184.

Raykov, T. (1998a). A method for obtaining standard errors and confidence intervals of composite reliability for congeneric items. *Applied Psychological Measurement, 22*, 369–374.

Raykov, T. (1998b). Coefficient alpha and composite reliability with interrelated nonhomogeneous items. *Applied Psychological Measurement, 22*, 375–385.

Raykov, T. (2001). Bias of coefficient α for fixed congeneric measures with correlated errors. *Applied Psychological Measurement, 25*, 69–76.

Reuterberg, S.-E., & Gustafsson, J.-E. (1992). Confirmatory factor analysis and reliability: Testing measurement model assumptions. *Educational and Psychological Measurement, 52*, 795–811.

Roberts, D. M., & Burrill, D. F. (1995). Gain score grading revisited [Letter]. *Educational Measurement: Issues and Practice, 14*(1), 29–30.

Rogosa, D. R. (1998, May). *Accuracy of individual scores and group summaries.* Presentation at the professional development session for the Council of Chief State School Officers, State Collaborative on Assessment and Student Standards, Technical guidelines for performance assessment, Durham, NC.

Rogosa, D. R. (1999). *Accuracy of individual scores expressed in percentile ranks: Classical test theory calculations* (Report for the National Center for Research on Evaluation, Standards, and Student Testing [CRESST]). Retrieved August 12, 2003, from http://www.cresst.org/products/reports_set.htm

Rogosa, D., Brandt, D., & Zimowski, M. (1982). A growth curve approach to the measurement of change. *Psychological Bulletin, 92*, 726–748.

Rogosa, D., & Ghandour, G. (1991). Statistical models for behavioral observations. *Journal of Educational Statistics, 16*, 157–252.

Rogosa, D. R., & Willett, J. B. (1983). Demonstrating the reliability of the difference score in the measurement of change. *Journal of Educational Measurement, 20*, 335–343.

Rogosa, D. R., & Willett, J. B. (1985). Understanding correlates of change by modeling individual differences in growth. *Psychometrika, 50*, 203–228.

Rozeboom, W. W. (1989). The reliability of a linear composite of nonequivalent subtests. *Applied Psychological Measurement, 13*, 277–283.

Rudner, L. M. (2001). Informed test component weighting. *Educational Measurement: Issues and Practice, 20*(1), 16–19.

Rulon, P. J. (1939). A simplified procedure for determining the reliability of a test by split-halves. *Harvard Educational Review, 9*, 99–103.

Sanders, P. F. (1992). Alternative solutions for optimization problems in generalizability theory. *Psychometrika, 57*, 351–356.

Sanders, P. F., Theunissen, T. J. J. M., & Baas, S. M. (1989). Minimizing the number of observations: A generalization of the Spearman-Brown formula. *Psychometrika, 54*, 587–598.

Sanders, P. F., Theunissen, T. J. J. M., & Baas, S. M. (1991). Maximizing the coefficient of generalizability under the constraint of limited resources. *Psychometrika, 56*, 87–96.

Satterthwaite, F. E. (1946). An approximate distribution of estimates of variance components. *Biometrics Bulletin, 2*, 110–114.

Schmidt, F. L., & Hunter, J. E. (1996). Measurement error in psychological research: Lessons from 26 research scenarios. *Psychological Methods, 1*, 199–223.

Schmidt, F. L., & Hunter, J. E. (1999). Theory testing and measurement error. *Intelligence, 27*, 183–198.

Schmidt, F. L., Le, H., & Ilies, R. (2003). Beyond alpha: An empirical examination of the effects of different sources of measurement error on reliability estimates for measures of individual differences constructs. *Psychological Methods, 8*, 206–224.

Schroeder, M. L., & Hakstian, A. R. (1990). Inferential procedures for multifaceted coefficients of generalizability. *Psychometrika, 55*, 429–447.

Schuster, C. (2001). Kappa as a parameter of a symmetry model for rater agreement. *Journal of Educational and Behavioral Statistics, 26*, 331–342.

Schuster, C., & Smith, D. A. (2002). Indexing symmetric rater agreement with a latent-class model. *Psychological Methods, 7*, 384–395.

Scott, W. A. (1955). Reliability or content analysis: The case of nominal scale coding. *Public Opinion Quarterly, 19*, 321–325.

Searle, S. R. (1971). *Linear models.* New York: Wiley.

Searle, S. R., Casella, G., & McCulloch, C. E. (1992). *Variance components.* New York: Wiley.

Sedere, M. U., & Feldt, L. S. (1977). The sampling distributions of the Kristof reliability coefficient, the Feldt coefficient, and Guttman's lambda-2. *Journal of Educational Measurement, 14*, 53–62.

Shao, J., & Tu, D. (1995). *The jackknife and the bootstrap.* New York: Springer-Verlag.

Shapiro, A. (1982). Rank-reducibility of a symmetric matrix and sampling theory of minimum trace factor analysis. *Psychometrika, 47*, 187–199.

Shapiro, A. (1985). A note on the asymptotic distribution of the greatest lower bound to reliability. *Psychometrika, 50*, 243–244.

Shapiro, A., & ten Berge, J. M. F. (2000). The asymptotic bias of minimum trace factor analysis, with applications to the greatest lower bound to reliability. *Psychometrika, 65*, 413–425.

Shapiro, A., & ten Berge, J. M. F. (2002). Statistical inference of minimum rank factor analysis. *Psychometrika, 67*, 79–94.

Sharma, K. K., & Gupta, J. K. (1986). Optimum reliability of gain scores. *Journal of Experimental Education, 54*, 105–108.

Shavelson, R. J., Ruiz-Primo, M. A., & Wiley, E. W. (1999). Note on sources of sampling variability in science performance assessments. *Journal of Educational Measurement, 36*, 61–71.

Shavelson, R. J., & Webb, N. M. (1981). Generalizability theory: 1973–1980. *British Journal of Mathematical and Statistical Psychology, 34*, 133–166.

Shavelson, R. J., & Webb, N. M. (1991). *Generalizability theory: A primer*. Newbury Park, CA: Sage.

Shavelson, R. J., Webb, N. M., & Rowley, G. L. (1989). Generalizability theory. *American Psychologist, 44*, 922–932.

Sireci, S. G., Thissen, D., & Wainer, H. (1991). On the reliability of testlet-based tests. *Journal of Educational Measurement, 28*, 237–247.

Smith, P. L., & Luecht, R. M. (1992). Correlated effects in generalizability studies. *Applied Psychological Measurement, 16*, 229–235.

Spearman, C. (1910). Correlation calculated from faulty data. *British Journal of Psychology, 3*, 271–295.

Stanley, J. C. (1971). Reliability. In R. L. Thorndike (Ed.), *Educational measurement* (2nd ed., pp. 356–442). Washington, DC: American Council on Education.

Subkoviak, M. J. (1976). Estimating reliability from a single administration of a criterion-referenced test. *Journal of Educational Measurement, 13*, 265–276.

Teichroew, D. (1956). Tables of expected value of order statistics for samples of size twenty or less from the normal distribution. *Annals of Mathematical Statistics, 27*, 410–426.

ten Berge, J. M. F. (2000). Clarification of Cliff and Caruso (1998). *Psychological Methods, 5*, 228–229.

ten Berge, J. M. F., Snijders, T. A. B., & Zegers, F. E. (1981). Computational aspects of the greatest lower bound to reliability and constrained minimum trace factor analysis. *Psychometrika, 47*, 187–199.

ten Berge, J. M. F., & Zegers, F. E. (1978). A series of lower bounds to the reliability of a test. *Psychometrika, 43*, 575–579.

Thorndike, R. L. (1951). Reliability. In E. F. Lindquist (Ed.), *Educational measurement* (pp. 560–620). Washington, DC: American Council on Education.

Thurstone, L. L. (1932). *The reliability and validity of tests: Derivation and interpretation of fundamental formulae concerned with reliability and validity of tests and illustrative problems*. Ann Arbor, MI: Edwards Brothers.

Tucker, L. R. (1949). A note on the estimation of test reliability by the Kuder-Richardson formula (20). *Psychometrika, 14*, 117–119.

Tukey, J. W. (1958). Bias and confidence in not quite large samples. *Annals of Mathematical Statistics, 29*, 614.

Vacha-Haase, T. (1998). Reliability generalization: Exploring variance in measurement error affecting score reliability across studies. *Educational and Psychological Measurement, 58*, 6–20.

Vacha-Haase, T., Henson, R. K., & Caruso, J. C. (2002). Reliability generalization: Moving toward improved understanding and use of score reliability. *Educational and Psychological Measurement, 62*, 562–569.

van Zyl, J. M., Neudecker, H., & Nel, D. G. (2000). On the distribution of the maximum likelihood estimator of Cronbach's alpha. *Psychometrika, 65*, 271–280.

Vautier, S., & Jmel, S. (2003). Transient error or specificity? An alternative to the staggered equivalent split-half procedure. *Psychological Methods, 8*, 225–238.

Wainer, H., & Thissen, D. (1993). Combining multiple-choice and constructed-response test scores: Toward a Marxist theory of test construction. *Applied Measurement in Education, 6*, 103–118.

Wainer, H., & Thissen, D. (1996). How is reliability related to the quality of test scores? What is the effect of local dependence on reliability? *Educational Measurement: Issues and Practice, 15*(1), 22–29.

Wainer, H., & Thissen, D. (Eds.). (2001). *Test scoring*. Mahwah, NJ: Erlbaum.

Wang, T. (1998). Weights that maximize reliability under a congeneric model. *Applied Psychological Measurement, 22*, 179–187.

Webb, N. M., Shavelson, R. J., & Maddahian, E. (1983). Multivariate generalizability theory. *New Directions for Testing and Measurement: Generalizability Theory: Inferences and Practical Applications, 18*, 67–82.

Wilcox, R. R. (1978). Estimating true score in the compound binomial error model. *Psychometrika, 43*, 245–258.

Wilcox, R. R. (1992). Robust generalizations of classical test reliability and Cronbach's alpha. *British Journal of Mathematical and Statistical Psychology, 45*, 239–254.

Wiley, E. W. (2000). *Bootstrap strategies for variance component estimation: Theoretical and empirical results*. Unpublished doctoral dissertation, Stanford University, Stanford, CA.

Willett, J. B. (1988). Questions and answers in the measurement of change. *Review of Research in Education, 15*, 345–422.

Willett, J. B. (1989). Some results on reliability for the longitudinal measure of change: Implications for the design of studies of individual growth. *Educational and Psychological Measurement, 49*, 587–602.

Willett, J. B., & Sayer, A. G. (1994). Using covariance structure analysis to detect correlates and predictors of individual change over time. *Psychological Bulletin, 116*, 363–381.

Williams, R. H., & Zimmerman, D. W. (1996). Are simple gain scores obsolete? *Applied Measurement in Education, 20*, 59–69.

Wilson, E. B. (1927). Probable inference, the law of succession, and statistical inference. *Journal of the American Statistical Association, 22*, 209–212.

Woodruff, D. (1990). Conditional standard error of measurement in prediction. *Journal of Educational Measurement, 27*, 191–208.

Woodruff, D. (1991). Stepping up test score conditional variances. *Journal of Educational Measurement, 28*, 191–196.

Woodruff, D. J., & Feldt, L. S. (1986). Tests for equality of several alpha coefficients when their sample estimates are dependent. *Psychometrika, 51*, 393–413.

Woodruff, D. J., & Sawyer, R. L. (1989). Estimating measures of pass-fail reliability from parallel half-tests. *Applied Psychological Measurement, 13*, 33–43.

Yen, W. M. (1997). The technical quality of performance assessments: Standard errors of percents of pupils reaching standards. *Educational Measurement: Issues and Practice, 16*(3), 5–15.

Yu, M. C., & Dunn, O. J. (1982). Robust tests for the equality of two correlation coefficients: A Monte Carlo study. *Educational and Psychological Measurement, 42*, 987–1004.

Zimmerman, D. W. (1994). A note on interpretation of formulas for the reliability of differences. *Journal of Educational Measurement, 31*, 143–147.

Zimmerman, D. W., & Williams, R. H. (1982). Gain scores in research can be highly reliable. *Journal of Educational Measurement, 19*, 149–154.

Zimmerman, D. W., Williams, R. H., & Zumbo, B. D. (1993). Reliability of measurement and power of significance tests based on differences. *Applied Psychological Measurement, 17*, 1–9.

Zimmerman, D. W., Zumbo, B. D., & Lalonde, C. (1993). Coefficient alpha as an estimate of test reliability under violation of two assumptions. *Educational and Psychological Measurement, 53*, 33–49.

4

Item Response Theory

Wendy M. Yen
Anne R. Fitzpatrick
Educational Testing Service

1. INTRODUCTION

Item response theory (IRT) is a family of statistical models used to analyze test item data. IRT provides a unified statistical process for estimating stable characteristics of items and examinees and defining how these characteristics interact in describing item and test performance. When used appropriately, IRT can increase the efficiency of the testing process, enhance the information provided by that process, and make detailed predictions about unobserved testing situations. IRT is used for many measurement applications including item banking, test construction, adaptive test administration, scaling, equating, standard setting, test scoring, and score reporting.

1.1. Comparisons of IRT and Classical Test Theory

IRT can be distinguished from *classical test theory* (CTT; see the chapter on reliability by Haertel [this volume]) by several characteristics:

- Nature and detail of the assumptions made
- Relative focus on items as unique, independent units rather than on intact tests
- Attention to results for individual examinees versus groups of examinees
- Consideration of a variety of scales or metrics beyond the raw score (number-correct) metric
- Type, range, and depth of predictions
- Importance of testing the accuracy of model assumptions and predictions

CTT uses simple definitions and relatively weak assumptions. Observed raw scores are the sum of true scores and error scores; error scores are uncorrelated with true scores and other error scores. These assumptions produce useful results, related primarily to properties of observed test scores, such as definitions of reliability and the standard error of measurement, corrections for attenuation, and the Spearman-Brown formula. While assumptions about items can enter into CTT (such as the assumptions that all items have the same true score variance and error variance, and that error scores are uncorrelated with true scores within and across items), most of CTT focuses on properties of intact tests. CTT also usually focuses on results for groups of examinees, rather than for individual examinees; that is, CTT usually focuses on unconditional results rather than conditional results. CTT works with item statistics, such as proportion-correct and item-test biserials that are completely dependent on the particular group of examinees tested, and CTT does not provide a ready means for generalizing results from one group of examinees to another. CTT operates in the raw (or number-correct) score metric and is not geared to readily consider the effects of changes in metrics or changes in the items in a test. While CTT is widely applied without examining the accuracy of its assumptions or predictions, it is possible to test some of them (for example, one can compare a Spearman-Brown prediction of increased reliability when doubling a test length with the change in reliability actually observed).

IRT makes stronger assumptions than CTT; these assumptions are related to the probability that an examinee with a particular ability level will produce a particular response to a particular item. IRT models relate item scores to examinee ability levels and item parameters using nonlinear functions. IRT produces a wider range of detailed predictions, both unconditional (for groups of examinees) and conditional (for examinees at one particular ability level). These predictions are more flexible than CTT predictions and are readily expressed in score units other than observed number-correct score units. As its name suggests, a major focus of IRT is on individual items, their unique statistical characteristics, and their independent contributions to tests. Examining the accuracy of IRT assumptions and predictions is an integral part of using IRT models.

1.2. Growth in the Use of IRT Models

While IRT models were rarely used in education in the early 1970s, their use spread rapidly in the late 1970s and 1980s. Research at that time focused on developing procedures and software for implementing models and on examining whether the models described multiple-choice educational test data with sufficient accuracy to make them useful. For example, model-data fit received in-depth attention in the IRT chapter in the third edition of *Educational Measurement* (Hambleton, 1989).

In the 1990s use of the models spread, and they are now used in the majority of large-scale educational testing programs. In the past 15 years, use of IRT models has become commonplace for tests with selected-response (a.k.a. multiple-choice) items, constructed-response items, or combinations of selected-response and constructed-response items, for both paper-and-pencil testing and computerized adaptive testing.

IRT models have become popular because they provide many practical advantages: flexibility, efficiency, and in-depth descriptions of item and test properties, all within one cohesive conceptual framework. IRT models are used in developing banks of items with known statistical properties and in selecting items from those banks to create tests with desirable psychometric characteristics. IRT models provide a conceptual foundation that is helpful when evaluating whether items are measuring the same behaviors for students in different demographic groups. Scaling and equating of tests can be accomplished by IRT, and appropriate use of the models can increase test score accuracy and interpretability.

This chapter begins with a description of commonly used IRT models. Then discussed are the statistical properties of item and test scores that are described by IRT models, including item and test characteristic functions, information functions, and standard error functions. Procedures for estimating the item and examinee characteristics included in the models are described, as are procedures for evaluating the model-data fit of the models. Finally, the chapter considers IRT applications to education in more detail and speculates on future developments. Sources for further information on IRT models are presented at the end of the chapter.

2. MODELS

2.1. General Concepts

The core of every IRT model is a succinct statistical description of the probability that an examinee with particular characteristics will have a particular response to an individual item that has its own particular characteristics. Given that information, it is assumed that responses for different items are conditionally independent (see section 2.7).

The models can be classified by the type of item data that they analyze, the number of dimensions they use to describe examinee and item characteristics, and the number and type of item characteristics they describe relative to each dimension. In addition, models vary with respect to the mathematical function used to describe item responses. Most IRT models make the assumption that item performance is positively (i.e., monotonically increasingly) related to examinee ability, but the models differ in their definition of this relationship.

2.1.1. Types of Item Data

Every test item allows certain types of responses, which are converted into item scores. The item scores can be *dichotomous* (or *binary*, having only two possible outcomes) or *polytomous* (having many possible outcomes). For example, to respond to a typical selected-response item, an examinee selects one answer from among several offered. If an answer key is applied to the answer choice, and the result is scored as correct or incorrect, then the item score is dichotomous. If there are more than two possible answers that receive different item scores, then the item is *polytomous*. Most constructed-response items use scoring rubrics that produce polytomous scores (e.g., 0 = inaccurate answer, 1 = partially correct answer, 2 = completely accurate answer). Rating scales (e.g., 1 = completely disagree, 2 = disagree somewhat, ..., 5 = strongly agree) also produce polytomous item scores.

There are IRT models that describe dichotomous item data, and others that describe polytomous item data. Some assessments have both types of data (e.g., many state-level achievement tests in English/language arts have students respond to selected-response questions related to reading passages as well as to several constructed-response questions). A combination (i.e., joint use) of IRT models is employed for tests with both dichotomous items and polytomous items. The use of combinations of IRT models has become common in educational testing.

2.1.2. Dimensionality

IRT models use *examinee parameter(s)* (also called *person parameter(s)*, *traits*, *proficiencies*, or *abilities*) to describe the dimension(s) on which there are important differences among examinees as measured by the test items being analyzed. These dimensions are commonly referred to as "abilities," but in educational measurement they could be proficiencies, knowledge, skills, attitudes, or other characteristics. In most cases, this chapter will use interchangeably the more accessible terms *ability* or *trait*, rather than the more inclusive but awkward *person parameter*. Models that use one ability to describe quantitative differences among examinees and among items are called *unidimensional*, while models that use more than one ability are called *multidimensional*. For example, an IRT model that analyzes performance on constructed-response math items in terms of mathematics ability and writing ability would be a two-dimensional model. Ways to examine test dimensionality are considered in sections 2.7.2 and 7.2; multidimensional models are discussed in section 2.5. In the vast majority of applications, unidimensional IRT models are used to analyze educational data, and these models will be the primary focus of this chapter.

When IRT models were first used, they were called *latent trait* models (e.g., Birnbaum, 1968). This terminology emphasized the fact that the models postulate "true" abilities for examinees and these abilities cannot be directly observed. Also, these abilities are expressed on a scale that is different from observed number-correct scores. The term "latent" is rarely used today to describe the most commonly used IRT models.

Unidimensional IRT models describe examinee performance on items in terms of a single trait. The numerical value of the trait reflects the examinee's level of ability, achievement, or other major characteristic that is measured by the test. Typically, these trait values are on a scale that ranges from $-\infty$ to $+\infty$ and this scale is nonlinearly related to test raw scores that are bounded by minimum and maximum possible observed raw scores (e.g., 0 to n for an n-item test score). Unidimensional IRT models may be applied to test data containing dichotomous items, polytomous items, and/or combinations of these item types. Unidimensional models applied to dichotomous data are the most commonly used IRT models.

Unidimensional models differ in terms of the number of item parameters that are used to define each item's essential statistical characteristics. Unidimensional models can have one item parameter (almost always a parameter that reflects item difficulty) or several item parameters (which reflect additional statistical properties of the items such as item discrimination) that refer to the single trait reflected in the model. For multidimensional models, items can have one or more parameters referring to each of several traits.

2.1.3. The Item Response Function and Item Characteristic Function

The core of an IRT model is the mathematical expression for the probability of observing a particular item response, given an examinee's trait value(s) and the item parameter(s):

$$P_i(\theta) \equiv P_i(X_i = x_i | \{\theta\}, \{\delta_i\}). \quad (1)$$

Equation 1 is called the *item response function* (IRF). When it is displayed graphically, it is called the *item response curve* (IRC). Equation 1 expresses the probability that an examinee has response x_i to the i-th item, given the examinee has ability level(s) $\{\theta\}$ and the item has parameter(s) $\{\delta_i\}$. The IRC graph displays ability on the x-axis and probability of response x_i on the y-axis. The ability can be measured on one dimension or there can be multiple abilities measured on multiple dimensions; the item can have one or many parameters.

While the item *response* function describes the probability of a given response to an item, the *item characteristic function (ICF)*, and its graphical representation, the *item characteristic curve (ICC)*, define the expected item score as a function of ability. For dichotomous items the expected item score equals 0 times the probability of an incorrect response plus 1 times the probability of a correct response; thus the expected item score for a dichotomous item is simply equal to the probability of a correct response. For dichotomous items, the IRF and the ICF are equal, and the terms are used interchangeably (as are IRC and ICC). In fact, the term ICC is the term more commonly used for dichotomous items. For polytomous items the IRF and ICF are not the same (See section 2.3.1).

The conditional character of the IRF is the key to the special usefulness of IRT models. Because they are conditional on ability, the IRFs convey essential characteristics of the items that are designed to be the same regardless of the sample of students tested. The stability of the IRFs across samples is sometimes called *person-free item measurement*. Similarly, an examinee's trait level is intended to be stable when different items are in the test—this is called *item-free person measurement*. These catchy terms are exaggerations relative to what is found with real tests, but they do convey the ideals that motivate the use of IRT. Studies of model-data fit may include an examination of the stability of ICCs or item parameters across populations of examinees, or the stability of trait estimates when obtained from different sets of items (see section 7).

It is important and useful that IRT models make no assumptions about the shape of the distribution of trait values or abilities.[1] This can be contrasted with scaling models that are dependent on distributional assumptions (e.g., Thurstone models that assume normal distributions; see section 8.4). In educational measurement, a wide variety of educational intervention programs occur that can differentially affect student performance in different parts of the ability distribution (e.g., programs targeted at improving the performance of low-performing students). Thus, in education it is implausible to assume that distributions of abilities always have the same shape, such as a normal distribution. One of the advantages of IRT as a scaling procedure is its lack of constraint on the ability distribution.

2.2. Unidimensional Models for Dichotomous Data

2.2.1. Rasch or One-Parameter Logistic Model

The following equation defines the *Rasch* or *one-parameter logistic (1PL)* model:

$$P_i(\theta) \equiv P_i(X_i = 1|\theta) = \frac{1}{1+\exp[-(\theta-b_i)]}. \quad (2)$$

In Equation (2), X_i is the score for item i, with $X_i = 1$ for a correct response and $X_i = 0$ for an incorrect response. θ is the trait value for an examinee. The function $1/[1 + \exp(-t)] = [1 + \exp(-t)]^{-1}$ is a logistic function, with $\exp(-t)$ denoting e (the natural exponent, 2.718…) raised to the power $-t$. This model is called the Rasch model after its creator (Rasch, 1960), or the one-parameter logistic (1PL) model, because the item response function is a logistic function and it involves only one item parameter, b_i.

Equation (2) depends on the value of θ and the value of the item parameter, b_i. The higher the value of θ, the greater the examinee's ability. The parameter b_i is commonly called the *item difficulty*, and it increases in value as items become more difficult. It is important not to confuse this use of the term "item difficulty" with the item p-value used in CTT. An item p-value, as the proportion-correct score observed for a particular sample of students, decreases in value as the item becomes more difficult and is dependent upon the ability level of the sample of students tested. In contrast, the IRT item difficulty parameter increases in value as the item becomes more difficult and is theoretically not dependent on the ability level of the sample of students tested. The IRT item difficulty parameter, b_i, is expressed on the same scale as the examinee ability θ. Note that for the 1PL model, when $\theta = b_i$ (i.e., when the examinee's ability "matches" the item's difficulty), the slope of the ICC is at its maximum value (0.25), and the probability of a correct response equals 0.50.

Equation 2 is not only the simplest IRT model in use, it may be the most commonly used model. Figure 4.1 is a plot of the ICCs (the solid lines) for two 1PL items. For any given item, the probability of a correct response approaches 0 for very low ability levels and approaches 1 for very high ability levels. The dotted lines in Figure 4.1 show that Item 1 has a b_i value of –0.5, item 2 has a b_i value of 1.5. Item 2 is more difficult than item 1; an examinee needs a higher ability to have a 50% chance of getting item 2 correct. It can also be noted that 1PL ICCs for different items do not intersect. Thus, for the 1PL model, at any given ability level, a more difficult item always has a lower probability of being answered correctly.

Notice how succinct is Equation 2. It needs only one parameter, the item difficulty, to describe a large amount of data (i.e., conditional probabilities of item responses for the entire range of abilities). Other models have more parameters, but they share the power of describing large amounts of information very economically.

2.2.2. Two-Parameter Logistic Model

The slope of an ICC reflects how strongly the item response is related to ability. If the slope is steep, it means that a small change in ability will make a big change in the probability of a correct response; if the slope is flat, it means that the item is not strongly related to ability and a big change in ability level will not have much effect on the probability of a correct response. The IRT item parameter that reflects the strength of the relationship between the item response and ability is the *item discrimination*. The item discrimination is analogous to the item-test biserial correlation used in CTT.[2] The 1PL model assumes that all items have the same item discrimination. However, anyone who reviews empirical item data, either item-test correlations or empirical ICCs (i.e., observed relationships between the proportion of examinees passing an item and their total test scores), is likely to see variation over items in the relationship between item performance and ability. In fact the screening of items for low item-test correlations is a common practice in test construction. In order to reflect differences in item discrimination, the *two-parameter logistic model (2PL)* uses two parameters to describe each item, the item difficulty, b_i, and the item discrimination, a_i:

$$P_i(X_i = 1 | \theta) = \frac{1}{1 + \exp[-Da_i(\theta - b_i)]}. \qquad (3)$$

In Equation 3 a multiplicative constant, D, also has been introduced to the model. As explained in section 2.8, due to scale indeterminacy, the choice of a value for D is a matter of individual preference. D = 1.7 or D = 1.702 is commonly used for the 2PL model to make the logistic model as similar as possible to the normal ogive model (see section 2.2.4). The 1PL model in Equation 2 can be expressed as a special case of the 2PL model defined in Equation 3 by setting $Da_i = 1$ for all items.

For the 2PL model, the slope of the ICC is $P_i'(\theta) = Da_i P_i(\theta)[1 - P_i(\theta)]$ (see Lord 1980, p. 61). When $\theta = b_i$, then $P_i(\theta) = 0.5$ and the slope of the ICC is at its maximum value, $(D/4)a_i$. In other words, when ability matches the item difficulty, there is the strongest relationship between changes in ability and changes in the probability of a correct answer.

Figure 4.2 displays the ICCs for three 2PL items (using D = 1.7). Item 1 has $b_1 = 0$ and $a_1 = 1.0$, and Item 2 has $b_2 = 0$ and $a_2 = 2.0$. Item 2 has a steeper slope than Item 1 for abilities near the item difficulty. Item 3 has $b_3 = 1$ and $a_3 = 1.0$. Item 3 has the same slope as item 1 but its ICC is shifted to right, showing that it is more difficult than Item 1. Notice for models that allow unequal item discriminations, the ICCs can cross; that is, the relative difficulty of the items can vary for examinees in different parts of the ability range.

2.2.3. Three-Parameter Logistic Model

The ICCs for the 1PL and 2PL models show that these models assume that the probability approaches 0 that an examinee with very low ability will correctly answer an item. With multiple-choice items, it is possible for an examinee to guess the correct answer, even if the examinee does not have enough ability to think about the concepts in the item. In order to allow for guessing, the *three-parameter logistic model (3PL)* was created:

$$P_i(\theta) = c_i + \frac{1 - c_i}{1 + \exp[-Da_i(\theta - b_i)]}. \qquad (4)$$

In addition to the item discrimination, a_i, and item difficulty, b_i, the 3PL model uses the item parameter c_i in the

FIGURE 4.1 Item Characteristic Curves for Two 1PL Items

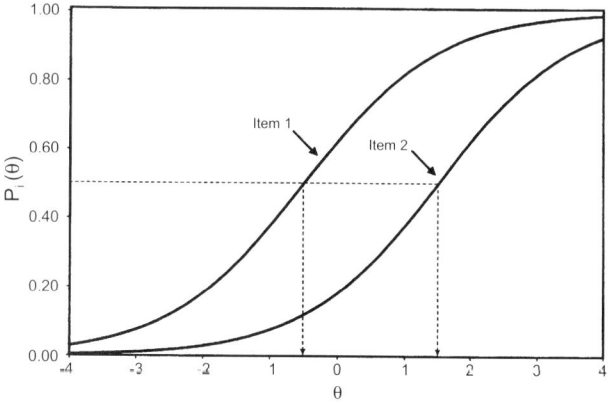

FIGURE 4.2 Item Characteristic Curves for Three 2PL Items

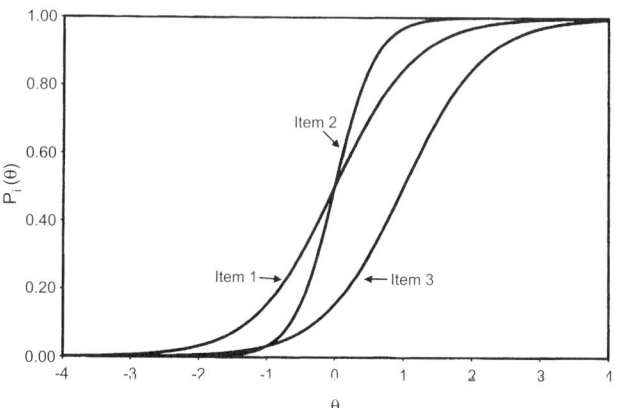

ICF; c_i is the probability that an examinee with infinitely low ability will get the item correct, and it equals the lower asymptote of the ICC. The 2PL model can be expressed as a special case of the 3PL model with $c_i = 0$.

The c_i parameter is commonly called the *guessing* parameter or the *pseudo-guessing* parameter. The latter term is used in order to be clear that guessing, in particular random guessing, may not be the psychological mechanism by which very low ability examinees are getting an item correct. For example, for a 4-choice item, random guessing would produce a probability of getting the item correct of 0.25. However, it is not uncommon for the lower asymptote of well-constructed 4-choice items to be less than 0.25, because examinees with partial knowledge are attracted by well-constructed distractors that reflect their misunderstandings.

For the 3PL model, when $\theta = b_i$, the ICC slope is at its maximum value, $(D/4)a_i(1-c_i)$, and $P_i(\theta) = (1+c_i)/2$; that is, when an examinee's ability matches the item difficulty, the probability of a correct answer is halfway between the value of the guessing parameter and 1.0.

Figure 4.3 contains ICCs for four items with a variety of combinations of a_i, b_i, and c_i values. It can be seen that the 3PL model can describe a wide variety of ICCs that can be found with real test data.

2.2.4. Normal Ogive Models

In the early days of IRT, psychometricians used the cumulative normal distribution (or *normal ogive*) rather than the logistic function to describe S-shaped ICCs (for example, see Lord & Novick, 1968, section 16.5). Later, the logistic function was used because it was mathematically more convenient. It was found that if the scaling constant $D = 1.702$ was used in the logistic function, the absolute difference between the logistic and normal ogive functions was less than 0.01 (e.g., Birnbaum, 1968). While it is not necessary to use this constant in the logistic function, use of $D = 1.7$ or $D = 1.702$ has become standard practice for the 2PL and the 3PL models.

The Rasch model, which has a different historical pedigree, does not use the constant $D = 1.7$. It is technically accurate that say that the Rasch model uses $Da_i \equiv 1.0$ for all items, but researchers using that model understandably omit D entirely from their descriptions of the Rasch model.

The choice to use or not use D is a matter of individual preference; it acts as a linear scaling constant that is irrelevant to the applicability of the model (see section 2.8). It is essential, however, that those who use an IRT model be clear about whether D is being used; if D is not accurately described when it is used, inaccuracies will occur.

2.3. Unidimensional Models for Polytomous Data

2.3.1. General Concepts

The IRT models just described apply to dichotomous item data. When item data are polytomous, more general models are available for use.

Recall that the IRF for dichotomous IRT models describes the probability of a correct response to an item. Normally with dichotomous items, researchers do not consider the IRF for an incorrect response because it is completely known given the IRF for the correct response: The probability of an incorrect response is $P_i(X_i = 0|\theta) = 1 - P_i(X_i = 1|\theta)$. In Figure 4.4 the IRC for the incorrect response for Item 1 in Figure 4.1 is displayed along with the IRC for the correct response. The probability of an incorrect response approaches 1 for examinees with very low ability and approaches 0 as ability increases.

Imagine that a constructed-response item has scores of 0 for a completely incorrect answer, 1 for a partially correct answer, and 2 for a completely correct answer. The IRCs for the three possible scores might appear as in Figure 4.5. For the lowest ability levels, the most likely response would be 0 (completely incorrect). As ability increases to a moderate level, the probability of a completely incorrect answer decreases and that of a partially correct answer increases. However, as ability continues to increase to a high level, the probability of a partially correct answer decreases, and the probability of a completely correct answer increases and approaches 1.0. Note that at any given θ, the sum of the probabilities across all score levels equals 1.0. The IRCs for another polytomous item, this one with four possible scores, is displayed in Figure 4.6.

FIGURE 4.3 Item Characteristic Curves for Four 3PL Items

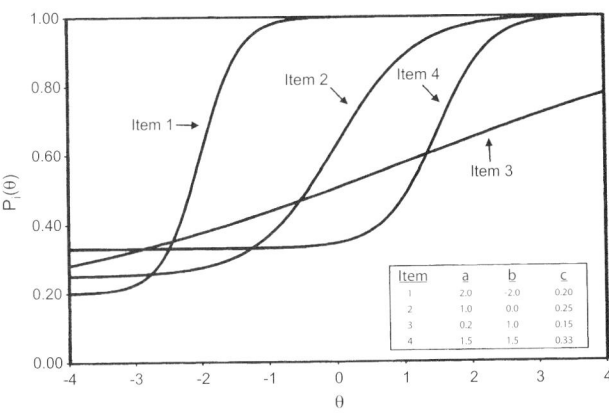

FIGURE 4.4 The Probability of Incorrect and Correct Responses to a 1PL Item

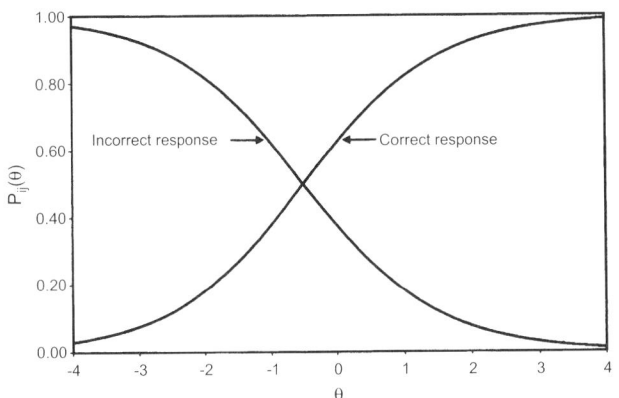

FIGURE 4.5 Item Response Curves and the Item Characteristic Curve for a Three-Level Item

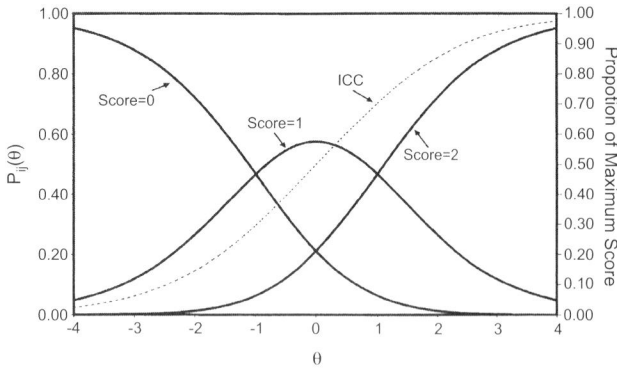

FIGURE 4.6 Item Response Curves and the Item Characteristic Curve for a Four-Level Item

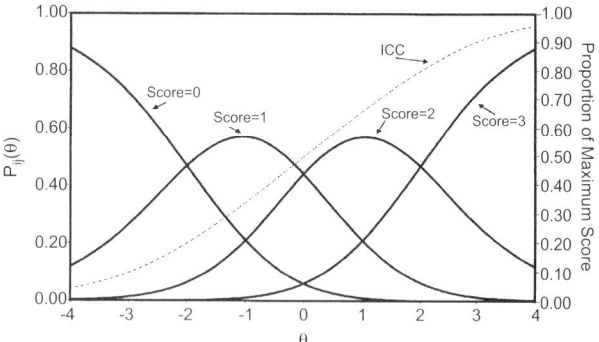

The IRCs for several dichotomous items can be displayed in the same figure without confusion; this is shown in Figure 4.3. However, for polytomous items, it generally would be confusing to display IRCs for several items in the same figure. For polytomous items, the *item characteristic function*, ICF, and the *item characteristic curve*, ICC, provide particularly useful ways to summarize and compare item performance for multiple items. The ICF is the expected item score at a given ability level:

$$E(X_i | \theta) = \sum_{j=1}^{m_i} x_{ij} P(X_i = x_{ij} | \theta). \quad (5)$$

In Equation 5 X_i is the score on the *i*-th item, m_i is the number of possible score levels on the item, and the x_{ij} are the possible scores obtainable on the item. The ICF is simply the sum of the possible scores on an item times the probability of each score. In this chapter, it is generally assumed that item scores range from 0 to $m_i - 1$, that is, the score for the first level is 0, the score for the second level is 1, ... , and the maximum score is $m_i - 1$. ICCs are displayed in Figures 4.5 and 4.6. These ICCs are presented in terms of proportion of maximum scores.

Several models for polytomous items are described in the following sections. These models have been presented in the literature using different terminology; for example, some authors use m_i to stand for the number of score levels, and others use it to stand for the number of nonzero score levels. Thus, readers should use care when comparing model descriptions from different sources.

2.3.2. The Partial Credit Model

The examples given in Figures 4.5 and 4.6 are based on Masters'(1982) *partial credit* (PC) model. In that model Masters expresses the probability that a person with ability θ will obtain a score of x on item i as

$$P_{ix}(\theta) = P(X_i = x | \theta) = \frac{\exp\left[\sum_{s=0}^{x} (\theta - \delta_{is})\right]}{\sum_{k=0}^{M_i} \exp\left[\sum_{s=0}^{k} (\theta - \delta_{is})\right]} \quad x = 0, 1, \ldots, M_i. \quad (6)$$

Item i has M_i "steps," and x can be considered to be the count of the number of successfully completed steps for that item. The $M_i + 1$ item score values range from 0 (no step is successfully completed) to M_i (all steps are successfully completed), and the steps are ordered; that is, for a given item, a higher score (i.e., higher value of X_{ij}) reflects higher ability. The δ_{is} values are called *step difficulties*; δ_{is} is the difficulty of step s of item i. For the sake of notational convenience there is a δ_{i0} value, which is defined to be 0, and the definition is also made that $\sum_{s=0}^{0} (\theta - \delta_{is}) \equiv 0$. The overall scale is anchored using $\sum_{i=1}^{n} \sum_{s=0}^{M_i} \delta_{is} \equiv 0$. See section 2.8 for more information on defining and anchoring scales.

As is true for the 1PL model, Masters' PC model assumes equal item discriminations for all items, and, in fact, the discrimination for all PC items is assumed to equal the discrimination for all 1PL items. Masters (1982) provides further explanation and illuminating examples for the PC model.

With the PC model, the intersections of the IRFs for adjacent score levels correspond to ability values equal to the step difficulties. That is, when $\theta = \delta_{is}$, the examinee has an equal chance of obtaining scores of $s - 1$ and s on item i. In Figure 4.5 Item 1, $\delta_{10} = 0$, $\delta_{11} = -1$, and $\delta_{12} = 1$. In Figure 4.6, Item 2, $\delta_{20} = 0$, $\delta_{21} = -2.0$, $\delta_{22} = 0$, and $\delta_{23} = 2.0$.

It is important to note that the δ_{is} values do not necessarily increase for successive score levels and generally are not interpretable as locations of score levels (e.g., Masters, 1982.). The next section discusses in more detail some concepts of score level locations for polytomous items.

2.3.3. Nominal and Two-Parameter Partial Credit/Generalized Partial Credit Models

For polytomous items there are IRT models that are more general than the partial credit model and that reflect differences among items in characteristics other than difficulty, such as discrimination. Bock's nominal model (1972) is a very general formulation for polytomous items. It expresses the probability that an examinee with ability level θ will respond in the *j*-th category for the *i*-th item:

$$P_{ij}(\theta) = \frac{\exp(z_{ij})}{\sum_{k=1}^{m_i} \exp(z_{ik})} \quad j = 1, \ldots, m_i, \quad (7)$$

where $z_{ij} = a_{ij}\theta + c_{ij}$.

In the nominal model item scores are in m_i unordered categories[3] and a higher item score does not necessarily reflect better performance. The nominal model is suitable in a situation where the user does not know before the data are analyzed how to value item responses. For example, if one wanted to treat the four answer choices for a selected-response reading item as four score categories, it might not be clear *a priori* which answer choices reflect greater ability.

In 1991 Yen used a model that could be expressed as a special case of Bock's nominal model (or as a generalization of Masters' partial credit model) to scale polytomous items in a performance assessment (CTB Macmillan/McGraw-Hill, 1992; Yen, 1993). Given the scoring rubrics for these items, it was known beforehand that higher scores on an item reflected greater ability. This model is called the *two-parameter partial credit* (2PPC) model, and it expresses the probability that an examinee with ability θ would obtain an item score of $j-1$ on the i-th item as

$$P_{ij}(\theta) = P(X_i = j-1 \mid \theta) = \frac{\exp(z_{ij})}{\sum_{k=1}^{m_i} \exp(z_{ik})}, \quad j = 1, \ldots, m_i \quad (8)$$

where

$$z_{ij} = a_{ij}\theta - \sum_{s=0}^{j-1} \delta_{is},$$

and $\delta_{i0} \equiv 0$. Most importantly the following restriction was made:

$$a_{ij} \equiv a_i(j-1). \quad (9)$$

The restriction in Equation 9 assures that higher item scores reflect greater ability, and it allows the polytomous items to vary in their discriminations, a_i. For polytomous items the item discrimination reflects the sharpness of the distinction between the IRFs (i.e., how quickly response probabilities change as a function of ability). Masters' PC model can be expressed as a special case of the 2PPC with all $a_i = 1$.

Independently of Yen, Muraki developed software to estimate parameters for a model he called the *generalized partial credit* (GPC) model (Muraki, 1992). The 2PPC and the GPC models are equivalent models, but they define $P_{ij}(\theta)$ and their item parameters differently. In the GPC model there is an exponential term Z_{ij} (which is used somewhat differently from the z_{ij} in the 2PPC):

$$Z_{ij} = a_{ij}(\theta - b_i + d_{ij}), \quad (10)$$

where b_i is called the *item location* and d_{ij} is called the *category threshold*. Sometimes the D multiplicative constant (e.g., $D = 1.7$) is also incorporated into the GPC model (Muraki & Bock, 1993).[4] Figure 4.7 presents the IRCs and ICC (expressed in terms of a proportion of maximum score) for a 2PPC/GPC item.

As has been noted, the polytomous models use subtly different notation. In order to have some consistency for explanatory supposes, the notation of the 2PPC model is used in other sections of this chapter where information functions, standard

FIGURE 4.7 Item Response Curves and the Item Characteristic Curve for a 2PPC/GPC Item

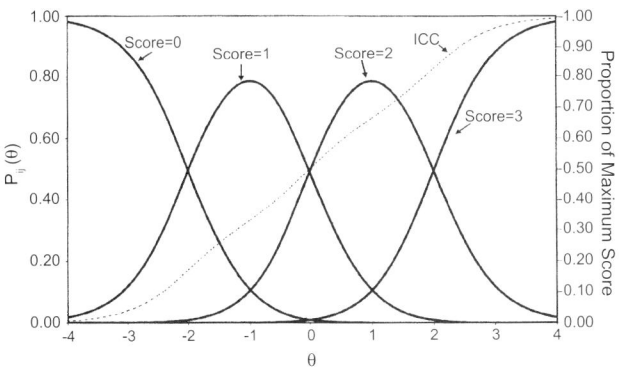

errors, and item locations are discussed, as well as in Table 4.1, where derivatives and information functions are compared.

It is more complex to interpret the parameters for polytomous models than for dichotomous models. For the 2PPC model the score level response curves for adjacent score levels $j-1$ and j intersect at $\theta = \delta_{ij}/a_i$, as noted by Thissen, Steinberg, and Fitzpatrick (1989). As with the PC model, these intersections do not necessarily increase with score level. The IRFs of the intermediate score levels "peak" (have modes) at θ values such that the observed score for that level equals the expected score given θ (i.e., $x_i = E(X_i \mid \theta)$).[5] These θ values can be taken as score level locations. For example, in Figure 4.7 the location of scores of 1 and 2 could be described as $\theta = -1$ and $\theta = +1$, respectively. Other definitions of item locations for polytomous items are also possible (See section 4.5.1).

Either the PC model or the 2PPC/GPC model can be used to analyze a set of polytomous items that differ in their number of score levels. For example, either model could be applied to a test having some items with 3-point rubrics and some with 4-point rubrics; these items can be analyzed together by specifying the appropriate m_i for each item.[6] Both kinds of polytomous models also can be combined with other IRT models for dichotomous items, as described in section 2.4.

2.3.4. Other Models for Analyzing Polytomous Items

While the models described above are far and away those most commonly used with educational tests, Andrich's rating scale model (1978) and Samejima's graded response model (Samejima, 1969) also are notable.

Andrich's model is applicable to items associated with rating scales such as Likert or semantic differential scales that have the same ordered categories. His model is a special case of the PC model where the distances between the score levels are assumed to be constant for all items (i.e., $\delta_{is} = \delta_i + \tau_s$).

Samejima's graded model also is suitable for items with ordered score levels. According to this model, the function of θ associated with each score level reflects the probability of performing at *or above* that score level.

Thissen and Steinberg (1986) presented a useful taxonomy for understanding how a variety of polytomous models relate to each other. For example, they called Samejima's graded model a *difference* model. When this model is used, the probability of an examinee performing at a particular score level j is found by taking the difference between the probability of scoring at or above score level j and the probability of scoring at or above score level $j + 1$. Bock's model and the models that can be expressed as special cases of Bock's model (the 2PPC/GPC model, the PC model, and Andrich's rating scale model), are *divide-by-total* models. For divide-by-total models, an exponential function of θ is associated with each score level; the probability of performing at a particular score level is the ratio of the function for that level to the sum of the functions for all the levels.

2.4. Combinations of Unidimensional Models

A test can contain both dichotomous and polytomous items. Consider a mathematics achievement test with 25 multiple-choice items and 3 open-ended problems whose written answers are scored with 5-point rubrics. Such a test would be analyzed using both dichotomous and polytomous IRT models. The θ that appears in both models is the common scale to which the item responses and examinees' scores refer. It is theoretically possible to combine very disparate item response models, such as a two-parameter normal ogive model for dichotomous items and a one-parameter partial credit model for polytomous items. However, this greatly complicates the interpretation of parameters across item types. It also complicates the calculation of model predictions, such as test information functions, which cut across item types (see section 4).

When two or more IRT models must be used, it is sensible to use compatible item response models. For example, someone approaching the analysis of test data from a Rasch perspective (see section 2.9) typically would use the 1PL model for dichotomous items and the conceptually compatible PC model for polytomous items. In fact, the 1PL model can be expressed as a special case of the PC model. Similarly, a researcher who believes that unequal item discriminations are a necessary part of a model would use a combination of the 2PL or 3PL model and the 2PPC/GPC model. The 2PL model can be expressed as a special case of the 2PPC/GPC model.[7] While the 3PL model cannot be expressed as a special case of the 2PPC/GPC model, these models have compatible logistic parameterizations that make their combined use understandable. In practice, the combination of the 1PL and the PC models and the combination of the 3PL and 2PPC/GPC models are the most common model combinations used today for educational tests.

2.5. Multidimensional Models

Although unidimensional IRT models appear to be adequate for scaling achievement test items in most practical situations, it is reasonable to believe that examinees sometimes need multiple skills to perform well on certain kinds of items. For example, producing high quality responses to writing prompts that refer to a reading passage will require that students have both writing and reading comprehension skills. Certain types of word problems on a mathematics test may assess both reading and mathematics skills.

Some consequences of applying unidimensional models to multidimensional data have been explored by Ackerman (1989, 1992), Ansley and Forsyth (1985), Folk and Green (1989), Luecht and Miller (1992), Reckase (1985), Way, Ansley, and Forsyth (1988), and Walker and Beretvas (2003), among others. For example, Reckase (1985) found that the easy items in a mathematics usage test tended to measure one trait, whereas the hard items measured another trait; thus, low and high scores on the scale did not have the same meaning due to multidimensionality in the test. Ackerman (1992) demonstrated how items calibrated using a unidimensional model may display differential item functioning when used to measure the skills of a group of examinees whose item responses are multidimensional.

In considering these findings, it is important to keep in mind the various ways in which item data can be multidimensional. Multidimensionality can occur when different items in a test assess different skills or when multiple skills are measured to varying degrees by the items in the test. However, when the same skills are assessed to the same degree by all the items, then the item set may appear unidimensional even though more than one skill is required to answer each item correctly (Ackerman, 1992). As Mislevy and Verhelst (1990), Ackerman (1992), and Reckase (1997a), among others, also observed, the number and type of skills measured by the items in a test will depend on what skills examinees bring to bear when they respond to the items, as well as on what skills the items are intended to measure.

Several kinds of multidimensional IRT (MIRT) models have been developed. Most have been developed for use with dichotomous item scores. Some MIRT models are compensatory (i.e., high performance on one ability dimension can compensate for low performance on another dimension), and some are noncompensatory (i.e., high performance on one ability dimension *cannot* compensate for low performance on another dimension). Reckase's multidimensional extensions of the 2PL and 3PL models (Reckase, 1985, 1997a) are the most widely used compensatory models. His 3PL MIRT model for dichotomous items can be expressed as

$$P_i(X_i = 1 | \underline{a}_i, d_i, c_i, \underline{\theta}) = c_i + (1-c_i) \frac{\exp(\underline{a}_i'\underline{\theta} + d_i)}{1 + \exp(\underline{a}_i'\underline{\theta} + d_i)}, \quad (11)$$

where $\underline{a}_i'$ is the vector of item discriminations $\underline{a}_i' = (a_{i1}, a_{i2}, \ldots, a_{ip})$ for item i on each of p dimensions; d_i is a scalar parameter that is affected by the difficulty of item i, where items with positive values are easier than items with negative values; c_i is the probability of a correct response to item i by examinees at the lowest end of the ability scale; and $\underline{\theta}'$ is an examinee's vector of abilities $\underline{\theta}' = (\theta_1, \theta_2, \ldots, \theta_p)$ on the p dimensions.

The additive components in the exponential term of the 3PL MIRT model make it possible for high performance on one ability dimension to compensate for low performance on another dimension. The higher the discrimination parameter, a_{ik}, for a given ability dimension, the more important is the ability in answering the item correctly. When the p discrimination parameters for an item are the same, the relationship between ability dimensions is fully compensatory (Ackerman, 1994).

Whitely's (1980) multicomponent latent trait model (MLTM) is noncompensatory. Superior skills in one ability dimension cannot make up for a lack of skill in another dimension, because the probability of a correct item response is the product of the probabilities of correct responses to the component subtasks. A simple form of the MLTM states that the probability of a correct response to a subtask component for dichotomous item i is

$$P_{ik}(X_{ik}) = P(X_{ik} = 1 \mid \theta_k, b_{ik}) = \frac{\exp(\theta_k - b_{ik})}{1 + \exp(\theta_k - b_{ik})}, \quad (12)$$

where θ_k is the examinee's ability level on component k, and b_{ik} is the difficulty of component k for item i. The probability of success on the item as a whole, X_{iT} is obtained assuming local independence of components:

$$P_i(X_{iT} = 1 \mid \underline{\theta}, \underline{b}_i) = \prod_{k=1}^{K} P_{ik}(X_{ik}). \quad (13)$$

Multidimensional versions of the Rasch 1PL and PC models that are compensatory also have been developed. Kelderman (1996) described a multidimensional partial credit model in which different item responses could be attributed to different latent traits; user-specified weights indicate the relationship between each item response and each trait. Kelderman and Rijkes (1994) discussed application of this model to polytomous items. Adams, Wilson, and Wang (1997) expanded Adams and Wilson's (1996) unidimensional random coefficients multinomial model to accommodate more than one trait.

To make MIRT models easier to understand, Reckase (1985), Reckase and McKinley (1991), Ackerman (1996), and Ackerman, Gierl, and Walker (2003) have developed graphical displays that greatly enhance understanding of the meaning of the item parameters in MIRT models. Examples are given in Figures 4.8 and 4.9, where *item response surfaces* (IRS) for two items, called Items A and B, are displayed. The items are assumed to measure two underlying traits as modeled by Equation 11. For convenience, the two traits are plotted as if they were orthogonal to one another. Item A and Item B differ in the degree to which their discrimination parameters, a_1 and a_2, resemble each other. Item A in Figure 4.8 has two discrimination parameters that are fairly similar, and the plot shows that the slope of the IRS for this item increases at roughly the same rate over levels of θ_1 and θ_2 the two ability dimensions. In contrast, for Item B, shown in Figure 4.9, the slope of the IRS changes much more rapidly over levels of θ_1, because this item's a_1 parameter is much higher than its a_2 parameter. Also, Item B has a $d_i = -2.0$, indicating that it is much harder than Item A, which has a $d_i = 0.4$. This can be seen by comparing the two items in terms of the point on the θ_1 scale where the IRS increases most sharply. Finally, guessing is higher on Item B than on Item A, which is the reason why the lower asymptotes for Item B are higher than they are for Item A.

Other types of graphical displays for multidimensional items are also available. These include equiprobability plots and item vector plots. See Ackerman (1996) for good examples.

FIGURE 4.8 Item Response Surface of Item A

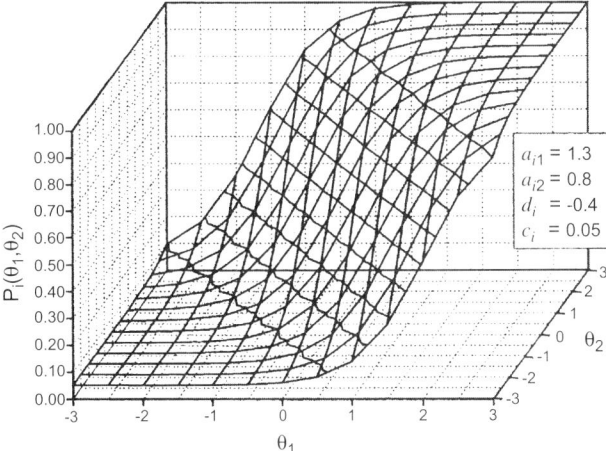

FIGURE 4.9 Item Response Surface of Item B

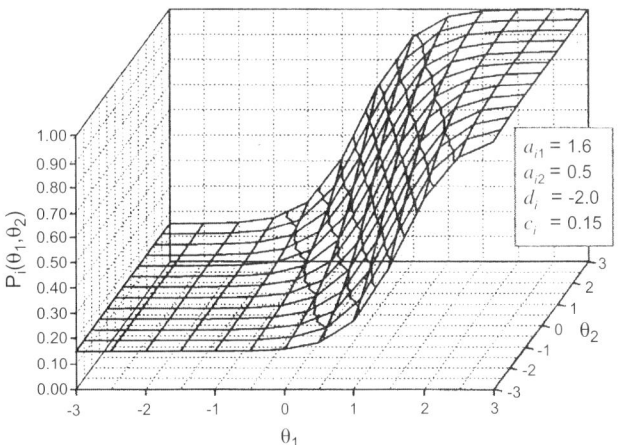

2.6. Other Models

2.6.1. Component Models

The IRT models discussed up to this point are only mathematical in nature, in that they define in mathematical terms what is the relationship between examinees' abilities and their performance on a test item. They do not explain why this relationship occurs. Some researchers have extended these models using psychological theory to identify the cognitive components required for successful performance on test items or tasks; this theory also is used to better understand the constructs that the items measure.

Fischer (1973) carried out some of the earliest work of this kind. His *linear logistic test model* (LLTM), a constrained Rasch model, expresses item difficulty parameters as a linear combination of the cognitive operations required to correctly respond to an item. According to the LLTM,

$$b_i = \sum_{k=1}^{K} \eta_k q_{ik} + c, \quad (14)$$

where b_i is the difficulty of the i-th item, η_k refers to the difficulty of cognitive operation k, q_{ik} is a weight that reflects the importance of cognitive operation k in determining the difficulty of item *i*, and *c* is an arbitrary scaling constant. Fischer applied the LLTM to a calculus problem, where q_{ik} reflected the type of operations that would be needed to differentiate an equation. Note that in the LLTM the difficulty of each cognitive operation (η_k) is the same over items. The LLTM has been applied in a variety of contexts, which include analyses of data generated from matrices tests and spatial ability tests, as well as analyses of cultural differences in cognitive functioning that could be used to explain differential item functioning (DIF) (Fischer, 1997; Fischer & Tanzer, 1994).

To handle polytomous items, Fischer and Parzer (1991) extended Andrich's (1978) rating scale model to include a linear component structure in the item parameters. Fischer and Ponocny (1994) similarly extended Masters's (1982) partial credit model. Noting that statistical tests of fit have tended to reject the LLTM model, Mislevy (1988) concluded that while useful, the LLTM warranted modification, and he proposed a less restrictive model.

Embretson, Schneider, and Roth (1986) used various versions of the MLTM model to assess the construct validity of a verbal reasoning test made up of multiple-choice verbal analogy items. In one model, two cognitive processes were presumed to be needed to correctly answer each analogy item. The first process was discerning the rule underlying the analogy, and the second was evaluating the answer choices in light of this rule. This model and other models that incorporated additional cognitive processes were applied to real data, and their fit was compared to test hypotheses about the cognitive strategies that examinees used.

Embretson (1984) expanded the MLTM to enable the cognitive stimulus features of items to be weighted to reflect their importance in determining the difficulty of item *i* on component *k*. Examples of such stimulus features for reading comprehension might include the number of words, reading grade level, and sentence length. Embretson's expanded model was called the *general latent trait model* (GLTM).

The development of models to assess individual learning and change using IRT component models also has been undertaken by Fischer (1983, 1987, 1989) and Embretson (1991, 1995), among others. An overview of these models has been provided by Verhelst and Glas (1995).

More complex mixture distribution models assume that examinees are not homogenous in the strategies they use to respond to test items. As Rost (1997) explained, in this situation a single IRT model will not fit the item data. This misfit occurs because, although an IRT model may fit the response data for each subpopulation of examinees that use the same problem-solving strategy, the difficulties of the items vary with the strategies examinees use. Mislevy and Verhelst (1990), Rost (1997), von Davier and Yamamoto (2003), and Yamamoto (1989) provide examples from this family of models.

The component models are attractive because of their association of psychometric parameters with the cognitive processes examinees use to answer test questions. As Embretson and Wetzel (1987) noted, the models may help us to understand better what features make an item or task more difficult, which may improve item writing and test development efforts (Sheehan & Mislevy, 1990) and, possibly instruction. In addition, as Embretson and her colleagues (Embretson, 1995; Embretson et al., 1986) have demonstrated, component models may be helpful with construct validation.

All the models considered in this section are complex. Issues of model assumptions, model requirements, sound procedures for estimating parameters, data requirements, and how model-data fit will be evaluated are issues that remain important to address in evaluating the usefulness of the models.

2.6.2. Testlet Response Theory Models

Wainer and Kiely (1987) first proposed using testlets to solve problems created by context and item order effects when test items are administered adaptively.[8] Testlets are groups of items that are administered and scored as a unit, and the items in a testlet often refer to the same stimulus, such as a reading passage. The term *item bundles* has also been used to refer to these kinds of item groups (Rosenbaum, 1988; Wilson & Adams, 1995).

Another problem addressed by forming testlets is that of local item dependence (LID; see section 2.7.1), which can occur among items in paper-and-pencil tests as well as in the computer adaptive testing (CAT) environment. As Wainer, Bradlow, and Du (2000) have noted, locally dependent items often have been calibrated in the usual way as independent items, and their local dependence has been ignored. However, treating locally dependent items as if they were independent can produce overestimates of item discrimination and test precision when there is substantial local dependency among the items in a test (Sireci, Thissen, & Wainer, 1991; Wainer & Thissen, 1996; Yen, 1993).

To calibrate and score testlets, Thissen, Steinberg, and Mooney (1989) suggested summing examinees' scores on the items in a testlet to produce a total score for that testlet, which is then treated as one polytomous item score. Any local item dependence existing among the items contributing to the testlet is absorbed into that testlet score. The nonoverlapping testlet(s) and items then are treated as locally independent scores in the IRT scaling process. Thissen, Steinberg, and Mooney (1989) used a reparameterized version of Bock's (1972) nominal IRT model to calibrate the summed scores from each testlet, in effect treating them as scores from a polytomous item. Wilson and Adams (1995) presented Rasch models for analyses that include testlets, and Yen (1993) gave examples using the 2PPC/GPC model.

Some researchers have proposed integrating LID into the IRT model itself (Bradlow, Wainer, & Wang, 1999; Hoskens & De Boeck, 1997; Jannarone, 1997), thereby possibly permitting use of the models to measure learning when item responses are not locally independent. Bradlow et al. (1999) also suggested that this alternative approach would (1) provide more information from a testlet than the summed scores would give and (2) permit testlets to be composed *ad hoc* during a computerized adaptive test (CAT) administration.

Bradlow et al. (1999) proposed a modification of the 2PL model, adding a random component to represent an examinee-by-testlet interaction. The modified model for dichotomous items can be expressed as

$$P(X_{ij} = 1) = \frac{\exp(a_i(\theta_j - b_i - \gamma_{jd(i)}))}{1 + \exp(a_i(\theta_j - b_i - \gamma_{jd(i)}))}, \quad (15)$$

where $\gamma_{jd(i)}$ refers to the interaction of examinee j with testlet $d(i)$. Bradlow et al. (1999) specified that the value of $\gamma_{jd(i)}$ would be constant for examinee j over all items within a given testlet, although it could vary over testlets, with the constraint that $\sum_j \gamma_{jd(i)} = 0$. An attractive feature of this model is that individual items rather than summed items are modeled, and testlet effects are associated with the individual item rather than a group of items. Wainer et al. (2000) subsequently used these ideas to develop a 3PL testlet model so that guessing behavior could be included.

One potential disadvantage of these models is that the testlet effect is modeled as a random variable; different values can be estimated for different examinees taking the same testlet. These characteristics may not capture important kinds of structural dependency that may be constant across examinees. For example, item dependency can be created when the same rater grades examinees' responses to several items referring to the same stimulus. This kind of dependency would appear to have a far greater effect on item parameters and estimates of test precision than the kind of random examinee-by-item interactions captured by the Bradlow et al. (1999) and Wainer et al. (2000) models. More research is needed to determine what kinds of dependency have the greatest effect on item parameter and information function estimates, and how these dependencies are best treated when IRT models are used.

Some researchers would also argue that because local item independence is the most appropriate means of identifying that a sufficient number of dimensions have been specified in a model (McDonald, 1982), LID should not be incorporated into the model definition. The identifiability and usefulness of models incorporating LID also merit further research.

2.6.3. Group-Level Models

All of the IRT models described up to this point are defined at the level of the individual item (or testlet) and examinee. Specifically, they are concerned with the abilities of individual examinees, and use examinee-level data to estimate item parameters.

For the California Assessment Program (CAP), Bock and Mislevy (1981) defined a group-level IRT model that used school-level data to estimate item parameters. The model specified the probability of a correct response to a multiple-choice item given by a student selected at random from a school with a given proficiency (ability) level (Mislevy, 1983; Mislevy & Bock, 1989).

The purpose of CAP was to provide diagnostic information at the school level on each of a large number of narrowly-defined traits or skills. To that end, the program used a matrix sampling design in which short test forms were randomly assigned to students. Each student responded to multiple items measuring multiple traits, where each item measured just one trait. Results were aggregated at the school level over forms to provide the information needed to determine how a school performed on each narrowly-defined scale (Tate, 1995).

Bock and Mislevy (1988; Mislevy & Bock, 1989) incorporated the approach developed for the CAP program into their *duplex* model. The duplex model provided school-level results for narrowly defined domains, as well as individual student-level results obtained by aggregating item responses over domains.

Tate and his colleagues have used BILOG (Mislevy & Bock, 1990) and PARSCALE (Muraki & Bock, 1993) to apply group-level IRT models to real and simulated data (Tate, 1995; Tate & Heidorn, 1998; Tate & King, 1994). Tate (1995) reported that BILOG's estimates of schools' mean abilities were robust to numerous violations of the stringent distributional assumptions of BILOG's group-level model. Tate and King (1994) examined the precision of school-level and individual student-level scores and factors that affected this precision. They found that the precision of school scores diminished considerably as school size dropped below 50 students per grade, and that the primary sources of imprecision in the school-level and student-level scores are not the same. They noted that test development as well as data collection must proceed differently when precise school level results are of primary interest.

2.6.4. Nonparametric Models

Nonparametric IRT models are less restrictive than the parametric IRT models previously discussed, and they require that the data meet a few relatively weak assumptions in order to be applied. These models do, however, posit that a latent trait underlies the observed responses to test items, and they rest on assumptions that can be used to generate testable hypotheses and predictions. An IRT model is distinctly nonparametric if (1) it restricts item response functions only in terms of order or monotonicity, and (2) the item response functions have no parametric definition (Sijtsma, 1998).

One of the advantages of these nonparametric models is that they are likely to fit data that the parametric models do not. One of their disadvantages is that current nonparametric models do not permit the kind of point estimates of abilities and item parameters usually of interest when educational tests are given. This disadvantage means that nonparametric models do not provide the information needed for test equating, adaptive testing, item banking, and the classification of students relative to a cutscore (Meijer, Sijtsma, Smid, & Eindhoven, 1990; Sijtsma & Molenaar, 2002).

Despite the limitations of the nonparametric models for educational applications, Sijtsma (1998) and Sijtsma and Molenaar (2002) provide abundant examples of other contexts in which the use of nonparametric models has been explored. It should also be noted that the methods developed by Stout and his colleagues (Nandakumar & Stout, 1993; Stout, 1987, 1990; Zhang & Stout, 1999) to assess the dimensionality of educational tests share some concepts and procedures in common with the methodology of nonparametric IRT models (see section 7.2).

Mokken's models and methods have been the most widely investigated of the nonparametric models. Mokken's first model was called the *monotone homogeneity model* (MHM) (Mokken, 1971, 1997; Mokken & Lewis, 1982). It assumes unidimensionality, local item independence, and monotonicity in the IRFs. The monotonicity restriction means that the probability of correctly answering an item is a nondecreasing function of θ. Thus, IRFs can intersect, be horizontal for some values of θ, and/or have asymptotes other than 0 and 1. In addition, examinees can be ordered in terms of their expected item scores, except when an IRF is flat (nondiscriminating) over the interval in which their θ values fall. Items, however, cannot be ordered consistently in terms of difficulty when their IRFs intersect.

Mokken's (1971, 1997; Mokken & Lewis, 1982) *double monotonicity model* (DMM) rests on the same three assumptions made for the MHM and the additional requirement that the IRFs not intersect, which is a second monotonicity assumption (Sijtsma & Molenaar, 2002). This additional requirement means items as well as examinees can be ordered except when there are ties. However, items and examinees are not ordered on the same scale. A DMM for polytomous items was outlined by Molenaar (1997). Scheiblechner (1995) developed models similar to these DMMs.

For the interested researcher who wishes a relatively nontechnical introduction to nonparametric models and methods, Sijtsma and Molenaar's (2002) textbook is recommended. Technical discussions of current issues can be found in Boomsma, van Duijn, and Snijders' (2001) book of essays on IRT. More abbreviated discussions of nonparametric models have been written by Sijtsma (1998) and Sijtsma and Junker (1996). Nonparametric IRT and Rasch models have been compared by de Koning, Sijtsma, and Hamers (2002), Meijer et al. (1990), and de Gruijter (1994).

2.6.5. Models of Rater Effects

When examinees respond to an open-ended test item, raters typically score their responses. Consequently, examinees' scores on the item will be affected by rater characteristics as well by the difficulty of the item and the examinees' abilities.

Saal, Downey, and Lahey (1980) described four ways in which a rater can introduce error into an examinee's item score. The rater can (1) be too severe or lenient, (2) make ratings subject to halo effects, (3) tend to restrict the range of his/her ratings, and (4) tend to be inconsistent with other raters. Raters' evaluations also may drift over time or over items. In addition, some test items could be harder to grade than others, and variation in training will also affect raters' behavior.

Although generalizability theory (see the chapter on reliability by Haertel, this volume) offers a straightforward approach to assessing rater consistency, as Bock, Brennan, and Muraki (2002) observed, there is no straightforward approach to assessing rater consistency when IRT models are used. Most IRT models assume that an examinee's response to a test item is independent of his/her response to any other item when conditioned on the examinee's ability. When multiple raters are used to evaluate the examinee's response to a test item and the multiple ratings are analyzed as if they were separate items, the assumption of local independence is violated. As was noted in the discussion about testlets in section 2.6.2, one consequence of this violation is that the standard error of the examinee's ability estimate will be underestimated. Using generalizability theory, Bock and his colleagues developed a correction for this bias that could be applied to standard error estimates and information functions.

The FACETS program (Linacre, 1991–2003) has been used by Engelhard (1994, 1996) and Lunz, Wright, and Linacre (1991), among others, to demonstrate how an extended Rasch model can be used to assess rater severity. Wilson and Wang (1995) used the random coefficients multinomial logit model for the same purpose. In these applications, items scored by multiple raters are treated as multiple rater-items, and dependency between the ratings is not taken into account.

Patz, Junker, Johnson, and Mariano (2002) explored some of the consequences of failing to model the dependency between ratings, and they have proposed using a hierarchical model to capture the dependency between multiple ratings of the same examinee response. At one level, the model defines an examinee's expected performance on an item as an unobserved latent variable that follows a particular IRT model. At the second level, rater behavior is modeled using a matrix of probabilities that relates examinees' observed and expected performance on an item. Verhelst and Verstralen (2001) discussed a similar approach.

Raters have been found to systematically affect examinees' scores (Engelhard, 1994; Fitzpatrick, Ercikan, Yen, & Ferrara, 1998; Lunz et al., 1991), and assessing rater effects can be useful for (1) calibrating raters, (2) identifying poor raters, and (3) separating item difficulty from a rater effect. As Englehard (1994) noted, developing better understanding of rater behavior would help us to develop a more theory-based approach to assessing rater effects and their most important consequences.

2.7. Local Item Independence and Dimensionality

2.7.1. Local Item Independence

The concept of conditional independence of item scores is used in a variety of forms in classical true score theory, factor analysis, latent class analysis, and IRT (Lord & Novick, 1968). For example, in CTT, errors of measurement are assumed to be uncorrelated given an examinee's true score.[9] When fitting the most commonly used unidimensional IRT models to item data, the assumption is made that the trait value provides all relevant information about the examinee's performance and that once that trait value is taken into account, item responses are independent. This conditional independence is also called *local item independence*, and it is expressed mathematically as

$$P(\{X_i = x_i\} | \theta) = \prod_{i=1}^{n} P(X_i = x_i | \theta), \quad (16)$$

where X_i is the score on item i. Equation 16 defines what is called *strong* local independence. In considering this definition it is important to keep in mind that this independence is conditional on θ. When *un*conditional relationships between items are examined (e.g., by obtaining correlations between the item scores of all examinees who take a particular test), it is expected that item scores will not be independent.

A definition of *weak* local dependence was suggested by McDonald (1979). This definition requires only that the conditional pair-wise covariances among the items in a test be equal to zero for all values of θ. For a pair of items, this concept can be defined as

$$P(X_i = x_i, X_j = x_j | \theta) = P(X_i = x_i | \theta) P(X_j = x_j | \theta). \quad (17)$$

An analogy with factor analysis may be helpful in understanding local item independence. Consider a stepwise factor analysis. The first factor is defined and removed from the data; that step is analogous to conditioning on θ. If the residual item correlations are all zero, then no more than one factor will be defined. However, if there are sets of items with residual correlations, then those items will contribute to the definition of a second factor.

Local item dependence (LID), when it occurs, can be positive or negative. Positive LID between two items means that if examinees perform better than expected (based on their overall test performance as reflected by their $\hat{\theta}$ values) on one item, those examinees also perform better than expected on the other item; similarly, if examinees perform worse than expected on the one item, they perform worse than expected on the other item. Negative LID means that if examinees perform better than expected on one of the items, those examinees perform worse than expected on the other item.

The concept of positive LID is generally easier to understand than negative LID, but both occur if the IRT model does not explain all the important relationships among the item scores. Imagine that a test measures two mathematics skills, addition and subtraction, among first-grade students. Students' total test scores are affected by performance on both types of items: They can have a mediocre total test score by being high on addition and low on subtraction, low on addition and high on subtraction, or mediocre on both. If a unidimensional IRT model is fitted to these two-dimensional test data, it is likely to produce positive LID among the addition items, positive LID among the subtraction items, and negative LID between addition and subtraction items. Habing and Roussos (2003) provide a psychometrically advanced discussion of negative LID.

The concept of local item dependence is relevant regardless of the number of dimensions used in an IRT model. Whether one or several dimensions are incorporated in the model, it is assumed that the model explains all the important relationships among items and is therefore *complete*. In a multi-dimensional modeling situation, LID would be produced by an unmodeled factor that consistently affects the performance of some students on some items. For example, a two-dimensional model for mathematics problem solving items might have dimensions that represent mathematics skill and reading ability. However, if the test were composed of both multiple-choice and constructed-response items, writing skill could produce positive LID among the constructed-response items. Section 7.5 discusses measures of LID, causes of it, and its implications.

2.7.2. Dimensionality

As Hattie (1984, 1985) noted, dimensionality has been defined in a variety of ways. McDonald (1981, 1982) offered a definition that directly linked dimensionality to the concept of local item independence. Specifically he suggested that the dimensionality of a test be defined by the number of traits that must be taken into account in order to achieve weak local independence between the items in the test. McDonald's definition is appealing because it bases dimensionality on the concept of local item dependence, which is central to IRT models and methodology. Also it defines dimensionality in operational terms by specifying that it can be determined by examining the conditional covariance between items.

Drawing upon these ideas, Stout (1987, 1990) proposed a theory of essential item independence and a definition of essential dimensionality based on this theory. The items in a test can be considered *essentially independent* when the average value of the conditional covariances between items approaches zero, as test length increases, for all θ values. Stout defined essential dimensionality as the minimum number of dimensions needed to satisfy the requirement for essential independence.

Stout's definition of essential independence entails slightly weaker requirements than that of either strong or weak local independence, as defined in Equations (16) and (17). The definition of weak local independence states that the conditional covariances between all item pairs will equal zero for all θ when local independence holds; essential independence requires only that the average value of these covariances approach zero as test length increases. Moreover, the definition of weak local independence implies that the traits used by the model of interest completely explain the covariance between all item pairs, whereas essential independence implies that the traits used by the model simply must be dominant traits (Nandakumar, 1991).

2.8. Indeterminacy and Metrics

For the IRT models described in this chapter, the ability and item difficulty parameters are represented on the same scale. For the most commonly used models,[10] this scale (or metric) can be linearly transformed without changing the predictions of the given IRT model, as long as the item discrimination is also transformed appropriately.[11] This circumstance is described as "the scale being indeterminate up to a linear transformation" or as "the results being invariant up to a linear transformation."

For example, imagine that a particular scale is being used for θ, a_i, and b_i, estimated using the 2PL or 3PL model. A new scale can be created: $\theta^* = r\theta + s$, $b_i^* = r b_i + s$, and $a_i^* = a_i/r$, using any constants r and s, as long as $r \neq 0$. The exponent of the IRF is a function of $a_i(\theta - b_i)$. It is clear that $a_i^*(\theta^* - b_i^*) = a_i(\theta - b_i)$, so that all predictions based on the linearly transformed scale will equal predictions based on the original scale.

It is common for the software that estimates item parameters and abilities to use a metric called the theta or logit metric that has θ values that range roughly between –4 and +4. For example, the estimated or theoretical true abilities may be set to have a mean of 0.0 and a standard deviation of 1.0. Another way the metric might be defined is to set the mean item difficulty equal to 0.0 and mean item discrimination equal to 1.0, which will also result in θ values approximately in the +/– 4 range. With these types of metrics, the a_i values will tend to fall between 0.0 and 2.0.

If ability scores are reported to teachers and parents, it would be very unusual to use the theta scores produced by the estimation software, because these scores will include negative ability estimates, which undoubtedly would confuse many users. Instead the scale is transformed by multiplying by a constant and adding a constant, $\theta^* = r\theta + s$. For example, if $r = 40$ and $s = 400$, the reporting scores would fall between approximately 240 and 560. The reporting scores are typically called *scale scores* (or sometimes *scaled scores*) to distinguish them from *theta scores*.

Because only linear transformations are allowed if the form of the IRT model is to be retained, the user has two degrees of freedom in setting the scale score metric. The choice of the reporting scale can be made in many ways, such as choosing a desired mean and standard deviation for a particular sample of examinees or by choosing two cutpoints (such as "basic" and "proficient") and setting the scale scores for those cutpoints equal to some attractive constants (such as 500 and 550). When setting the scale scores, it is essential that the properties of that scale be checked so that, for example, every number-correct score converts to a different scale score[12] (which is accomplished by assuring that the multiplicative constant is sufficiently large). Also it is important that the scale scores stay within reasonable bounds. For example, by convention scale scores in educational measurement usually have three digits, ranging between 100 and 999. The scale score range is determined by the size of the multiplicative constant that is used.

It must be noted that the mathematical function of the model to use in IRT is based on the researcher's choice, not on mathematical necessity. For example, logistic functions are convenient and well researched, so it is logical that the logistic function is commonly accepted as the "default" model. However, other mathematical functions, such as any continuous cumulative density function, are possible and perfectly acceptable to use for an IRT model. The researcher's choice of a particular function is important because it implicitly affects the characteristics of the ability scale produced.

Lord (1975a, 1980) demonstrated that any continuous, strictly increasing function of θ, $\omega(\theta)$ will produce the same predictions as long as the form of the IRT model is changed appropriately. For example,

$$P_i^*(\omega(\theta)) = c_i + \frac{1-c_i}{1+\exp[-Da_i(\omega^{-1}(\omega(\theta))-b_i)]}$$

$$= c_i + \frac{1-c_i}{1+\exp[-Da_i(\theta-b_i)]}$$

$$= P_i(\theta). \qquad (18)$$

P_i^* is an IRT model with a different mathematical function than P_i; that is, if $\omega(\theta)$ is not a linear function of θ, P_i^* is not a logistic function. Nevertheless, $P_i^*(\omega(\theta))$ produces the same predictions as $P_i(\theta)$.

It is not necessary that scores be reported on the θ scale or a linear transformation of that scale. Similarly, the scale that is used for reporting (e.g., number-correct scores, percentiles, grade equivalents, $\omega(\theta)$) is a choice made by the educational researcher. These reporting scales produce scores with different distributional shapes and have advantages and disadvantages (see the chapter by Kolen, this volume, or Allen & Yen, 1979). There is no one scale that is necessarily the "correct" or "natural" one for measuring traits or abilities (Yen, 1986). As described in section 4.6, IRT permits ready calculation of the standard error of any monotonic transformation of the ability score, including such scores as expected number-correct scores, percentiles, and grade equivalents.

2.9. Philosophies of Model Choice

There are different, and sometimes contentious, opinions about which IRT model, if any, should be used. On one end of the continuum are those who "choose a model and then discard data if they do not fit the model." On the other end are those who "choose a data set and then find a model that fits those data."

Those who "choose the model" first identify the measurement properties that are desired and the model that produces those properties (Rasch, 1960). In ideal circumstances, the measurement process (i.e., the test items and scoring rubrics) is designed to be consistent with the model. Items and, less frequently, examinees are discarded if they do not meet the model requirements. Users of the Rasch model(s) typically have a "choose the model" perspective. The Rasch model produces measurement properties that they believe are essential. Specifically, items maintain their difficulty order throughout the ability range (i.e., Rasch ICCs do not cross), and the model is simple, elegant, easily understood, and the estimation of item parameters and abilities are "separable." Moreover, the number-correct score is a sufficient statistic for estimating ability when the Rasch model fits. (See Wright & Stone, 1979, for a presentation on the advantages of the Rasch model.)

Those who "choose the data set and find the model to fit those data" typically believe that it is inappropriate for a scaling model to be the driving force in test construction. For example, in developing a reading test, they would tend to think that content experts should have the primary role in determining the items that belong on the test. The scaling model should be robust so that it places as few restrictions as possible on the items that can be in the test and have the model work. Those who use the 3PL model are likely to be in the "find the model to fit the data" camp, because the 3PL model is very flexible and places only loose restrictions on the items.

More general models are usually developed to be less restrictive with respect to important features. However, more elaborate models are more difficult to understand, more complex to implement, and typically require more data for item parameter estimation. Some models are so general that their parameters may not be estimable or identifiable, even with very large data sets.

In the 1970s and 1980s, when IRT models were first becoming popular in educational measurement, debates between proponents of these different perspectives were often quite heated (e.g., Divgi, 1986). Identifying appropriate measures of fit were part of the debate, as were questions about whether a chosen fit statistic was sufficiently powerful to detect important instances of misfit.

In general, model-data fit is not an all-or-none condition, and a model can be found to be sufficiently accurate for one application but not for another (see section 7.7). Many researchers take a moderate view between "choosing a model" and "choosing a data set," being willing to discard some poor fitting items and willing to relax certain model assumptions provided that there are not serious consequences of doing so.

Generally speaking, the Rasch model typically can work well in equating parallel tests, but it can be inaccurate in linking multiple-choice tests of different difficulty levels (i.e., vertical linking) because it does not take guessing into account (e.g., Kolen, 1981). Also, when using the Rasch 1PL and PC models with mixed format tests, differential item discriminations for the different item types can produce substantial misfit for the Rasch model (Fitzpatrick et al., 1996; Sykes & Yen, 2000). On the other hand, while the 3PL and 2PPC/GPC models can accommodate a wide variety of real items, they are more complex to use and require more substantial sample sizes (see section 5.8). A reasoned choice among models should be based on the particular application being considered.

3. TEST CHARACTERISTIC FUNCTIONS

Equation 5 defines the item characteristic function as the expected item score given θ. The *test characteristic function* (TCF; or graphically the *test characteristic curve*, TCC) is the expected raw score on the total test given θ; the expected raw score is the sum of the item scores assigned to each item response[13] times the probability of obtaining that item response (i.e., the IRF):

$$E(X_. | \theta) = \sum_{i=1}^{n} E(X_i | \theta)$$
$$= \sum_{i=1}^{n} \sum_{j=1}^{m_i} x_{ij} P(X_i = x_{ij} | \theta)$$
$$\equiv \xi(\theta). \quad (19)$$

Equation 19 applies to tests composed solely of dichotomous items, solely of polytomous items, or combinations of the two item types. For a test composed solely of dichotomous items, $E(X_. | \theta)$ looks like the number-correct score, but it is continuous (having fractional expected number-correct scores) and has values higher than $\sum_{i=1}^{n} c_i$.

As described in the chapter on reliability by Haertel (this volume), a true score is a score without measurement error. θ is a true score expressed in one particular metric, the theta metric. $\xi(\theta)$ is a true score expressed in the raw score metric. This raw score can be expressed as the sum of item scores (as in Equation 19), or as a proportion-of-maximum-possible score, also known as a proportion-correct score when all items are dichotomous.

Figure 4.10 displays the TCC for a test composed of the four dichotomous items in Figure 4.3 plus the polytomous item in Figure 4.6. The inverse of the TCC can be used to convert total raw scores to θ estimates (see section 6).

FIGURE 4.10 Test Characteristic Curve Based on the Four 3PL Items in Figure 4.3 and the PC Item in Figure 4.6

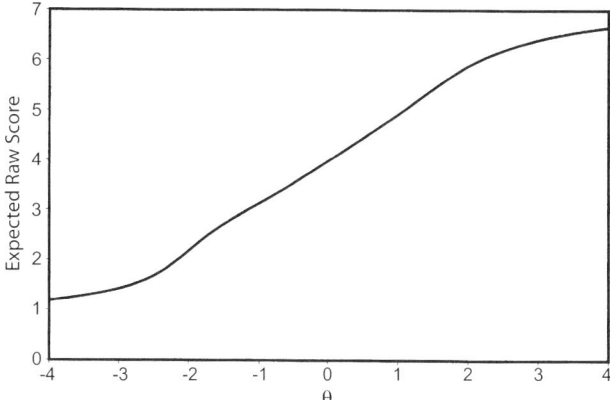

4. INFORMATION FUNCTIONS AND STANDARD ERRORS

In scoring a test there are three important aspects that define the score and determine the standard error of this score: the item data or item scores being used, how these item scores are combined into a single test *raw score* (i.e., a score based on observed performance, which has not been transformed by any scaling procedure), and how this test raw score is transformed into a score that will be reported. Unlike most applications of CTT, in IRT the standard error is expressed as a function of ability level. The IRT standard error is the reciprocal of the square root of a test statistic called *information*. The following discussion describes how information is calculated and related to the standard error, with focus on the effects of the choice of item data, weighting of the item data to produce a raw score, and the transformation of the raw score to a reported score.

4.1. Item Scores

It is most common to use right/wrong (1,0) item scores for multiple-choice items. However, it is also possible to use a score for each multiple-choice item that reflects the particular answer choice the examinee chose for that item (with the assumption that some answer choices reflect greater ability than others; see Thissen, Steinberg, & Fitzpatrick, 1989). For constructed-response items, it is most common to use one rater's score based on a particular scoring rubric (e.g., 0, 1, 2, 3), but an alternative is to base the examinee's item score on some combination of scores provided by two or more raters. With computerized scoring it is possible to imagine more complex algorithms for defining the raw item scores.

4.2. Test Raw Scores

Once item scores are defined, it is necessary to define the procedure for combining them into a single test raw score. Let X be the test raw score that is a particular function of scores for the items in the test. X can take on a wide variety of forms. The vast majority of test raw scores are sums or weighted sums of item raw scores. Such scores are popular presumably because users are familiar with number-correct scores, and weighted sums of scores are just one step removed from number-correct scores. We are all familiar with weighted scores created by teachers, where students get more weight (or credit) for more "important" questions. Weighted raw scores also are highly attractive from a statistical perspective, because their properties are easy to derive. This chapter will be restricted to the standard errors of weighted sums of item scores (which includes as a special case sums of item scores with equal weights, such as number-correct scores), which are far and away the most commonly used scores in educational measurement.[14]

There are many ways to weight item scores. For example, X could be defined as the

- simple sum or "unweighted" sum of the dichotomous scores on the items on a multiple-choice test. In this case, X is the number-correct score and the weight equals 1 for all items;
- unweighted sum of dichotomous and polytomous scores on a test composed of both multiple-choice and constructed-response items;
- weighted sum of dichotomous and polytomous scores, where every multiple-choice item gets a weight of 1 and every score on a constructed-response item gets another weight of, say, 2;
- weighted sum of item scores, where the weights vary item by item but are the same for every examinee;
- weighted sum of item scores, where the weights vary item by item and can vary by examinee; etc.

Thus, while the simple sum of item scores is commonly assumed to be the "default" raw score, there is no inherent reason why that raw score is better than others. In fact, as will be shown, in some circumstances other raw scores are better because they communicate more clearly what the item performance is conveying about examinee ability.

4.3. Transforming Test Raw Scores into Other Scales

For reporting purposes, any raw score (X) on a test can be transformed onto another scale, which can be described with the notation $f(X)$. A linear transformation would be of the form $f(X) = gX + h$, where g and h are constants applied to every raw score. Nonlinear transformations of X are also used. For example, it is common to transform X to be an estimator of the IRT ability. Many other reporting scales can be of interest, ranging from estimated scores on a set of benchmark items to percentiles. As will be seen, IRT offers a simple way of adjusting for such transformations when calculating the standard error of the transformed score.

4.4. Information Functions and Standard Errors of Weighted Sums of Item Scores

We will now examine how the item data, its weighting to produce a test raw score, and the transformation of the raw score into a score that is reported all affect the information and standard error associated with the reported score. In what follows we generally assume that a transformed raw score is going to be used as an estimator of θ.

Let X_i be the score on the i-th item, and $X = \sum_{i=1}^{n} w_i X_i$ be the test scoring function, which is a weighted sum of item scores. Following Birnbaum (1968), the *information* that any test score X provides about θ can be defined as

$$I(X|\theta) \equiv \frac{[\mu'(X|\theta)]^2}{\sigma^2(X|\theta)}, \quad (20)$$

where $\mu' = dE(X|\theta)/d\theta$. The "$X$" in $I(X|\theta)$ stands for the particular scoring function being used; $I(X|\theta)$ varies as a function of θ. The steeper the slope of the regression of the expectation of X given θ (that is, the larger the $\mu'(X|\theta)$) and the smaller the variance of X for any particular value of θ (i.e., $\sigma^2(X|\theta)$), the more strongly X is related to θ and the greater the information X provides about θ.

Let $\tilde{\theta}$ be some estimator of θ. If $\tilde{\theta} = f(X)$ is a consistent estimator of θ, then as the number of items increases, the distribution of $\tilde{\theta}$ approaches a normal distribution with mean θ and variance $1/I(\tilde{\theta}|\theta)$. In other words,

$$SE(\tilde{\theta}|\theta) = 1/\sqrt{I(\tilde{\theta}|\theta)}$$
$$= \frac{\sigma(X|\theta)}{\mu'(X|\theta)}. \quad (21)$$

Thus, the standard error calculated from the test information can be used to construct confidence intervals for θ.

Using Equation (20), an IRT model, and the assumption of local item independence, it is straightforward to derive the information provided by any particular scoring function. For example, for a test composed solely of dichotomous items,

$$I\left(\sum_{i=1}^{n} w_i X_i \middle| \theta\right) = \frac{\left[\sum_{i=1}^{n} w_i P'_i(\theta)\right]^2}{\sum_{i=1}^{n} w_i^2 P_i(\theta)[1 - P_i(\theta)]}, \quad (22)$$

where $P'_i(\theta) \equiv dP_i(\theta)/d\theta$. Table 4.1 contains these derivatives for the major models under discussion here. If $w_i = 1$ for all items, then X is the number-correct score and

$$I\left(\sum_{i=1}^{n} X_i \middle| \theta\right) = \frac{\left[\sum_{i=1}^{n} P'_i(\theta)\right]^2}{\sum_{i=1}^{n} P_i(\theta)[1 - P_i(\theta)]}. \quad (23)$$

For polytomous items or combinations of dichotomous and polytomous items, the appropriate derivatives or conditional score variances are added into the numerator and denominator. For example, for a score based only on polytomous items,

$$I(X|\theta) \equiv \frac{\left[\sum_{i=1}^{n} w_i \sum_{j=1}^{m_i} (j-1) P'_{ij}(\theta)\right]^2}{\sum_{i=1}^{n} w_i^2 \sigma^2(X_i|\theta)}. \quad (24)$$

TABLE 4.1 Derivatives with Respect to θ, Optimal Item Weights, and Item Information Functions

Model	$P'_i(\theta)$	$w'_i(\theta)$	$I(X_i|\theta)$
Rasch/1PL	$Q_i(\theta)P_i(\theta)$	1	$Q_i(\theta)P_i(\theta)$
2PL	$Da_i Q_i(\theta)P_i(\theta)$	Da_i	$D^2 a_i^2 Q_i(\theta)P_i(\theta)$
3PL	$Da_i Q_i(\theta)\left[\dfrac{P_i(\theta)-c_i}{1-c_i}\right]$	$\dfrac{Da_i}{P_i(\theta)}\left[\dfrac{P_i(\theta)-c_i}{1-c_i}\right]$	$D^2 a_i^2 \dfrac{Q_i(\theta)}{P_i(\theta)}\left[\dfrac{P_i(\theta)-c_i}{1-c_i}\right]^2$
PC	$[x_{ti} - E(X_i|\theta)]P_{ij}(\theta)$	1	$\sigma^2(X_i|\theta)$
2PPC/GPC	$\alpha_i [x_{ij} - E(X_i|\theta)]P_{ij}(\theta)$	α_i	$\alpha_i^2 \sigma^2(X_i|\theta)$

Note: For the PC and 2PPC/GPC models, the tabled values for the derivatives are for the item score levels: $P'_{ij}(\theta)$. Notation of the 2PPC model is used for the PC and 2PPC/GPC models.

For a test score based on n_D dichotomous items and n_P polytomous items,

$$I(X|\theta) \equiv \frac{\left[\sum_{i=1}^{n_D} w_i P'_i(\theta) + \sum_{i=1}^{n_P} w_i \sum_{j=1}^{m_i} (j-1)P'_{ij}(\theta)\right]^2}{\sum_{i=1}^{n_D} w_i^2 P_i(\theta)[1-P_i(\theta)] + \sum_{i=1}^{n_P} w_i^2 \sigma^2(X_i|\theta)}. \quad (25)$$

4.5. Optimal Scoring Weights, Item Information, and Maximum Information Functions

Let $\hat{\theta}$ represent a maximum likelihood estimator (MLE) of θ. Because $\hat{\theta}$ is an MLE, it is a consistent estimator, and it has the following information function:

$$I(\hat{\theta}|\theta) = E\left[\frac{d \ln L}{d\theta}\right]^2_{\theta=\hat{\theta}} \quad (26)$$

where L is the likelihood of the observed item data given θ. An MLE provides the maximum information available from a given set of item scores, so that[15]

$$I(\tilde{\theta}|\theta) \leq I(\hat{\theta}|\theta) \quad (27)$$

$$\equiv I(\theta).$$

Using Equation (26) the maximum amount of information available from a test can be obtained. Birnbaum (1968, sections 20.2 and 20.3) and Lord (1980, section 5.3) derived for dichotomous items the *optimal* item weights, which produce maximum test score information, and the *test information function*, which conveys that maximum information. Let the *item information function* for a dichotomous item be defined by

$$I(X_i|\theta) = \frac{|P'_i(\theta)|^2}{\sigma^2(X_i|\theta)}. \quad (28)$$

The optimal weights are

$$w_i^*(\theta) = \frac{P'_i(\theta)}{\sigma^2(X_i|\theta)}. \quad (29)$$

Lord (1980, section 5.6) demonstrated that when the optimal weights are used, the test score information equals the sum of the item information functions, which equals the test information:

$$I\left(\sum_{i=1}^n w_i^* X_i \bigg| \theta\right) = \sum_{i=1}^n \frac{|P'_i(\theta)|^2}{P_i(\theta)[1-P_i(\theta)]} \quad (30)$$

$$= \sum_{i=1}^n I(X_i|\theta) \quad (31)$$

$$= I(\theta). \quad (32)$$

The item scoring weights defined in Equation (29) are optimal weights and produce maximum information and minimum standard error in the θ estimate. A central implication of Equations (30) to (32) is that when optimal weights are used, the information contributed by each item can be considered independently and added into the test score information; this can be done for combinations of models as well. When nonoptimal weights are used, each item influences both the numerator and denominator of Equations (22) to (25), and the effect of any given item is not independent of the other items.

Table 4.1 contains the optimal weights and the item information functions for the major models described in this chapter, including the PC and 2PPC/GPC polytomous models. (To facilitate comparisons across models, 2PPC notation is used in describing the results for the PC and 2PPC/GPC models.) Notice that for some of the models (i.e., the 2PL, 3PL, and the 2PPC/GPC models), the optimal weights vary by item. To employ these optimal weights with these models, it is necessary to take into account the score an examinee obtained on each item; this is called *item-pattern* scoring.

The information functions for Items 2 and 4 in Figure 4.3 and the item in Figure 4.6 are presented in Figure 4.11. All else being equal, items with higher discriminations convey more information at any given θ. The value of c_i also has a predictable effect on item information for 3PL items. As c_i increases, maximum information is provided at higher θ values, and the maximum amount of information that is provided decreases. Birnbaum (1968; Figure 20.4.2) provides a clear example of this effect.

It is important to note that information is a function not only of item discrimination and/or levels of guessing, but also a function of conditional item score variance. Thus, while polytomous items often have lower discriminations than multiple-choice items (Fitzpatrick et al., 1996), they may convey more information than multiple-choice items, because they have more score points and greater variances.

The test information function, $I(\theta)$, based on optimal weighting of the items in Figure 4.11 and its associated test

FIGURE 4.11 Item Information Functions for Items 2 and 4 in Figure 4.3 and the item in Figure 4.6

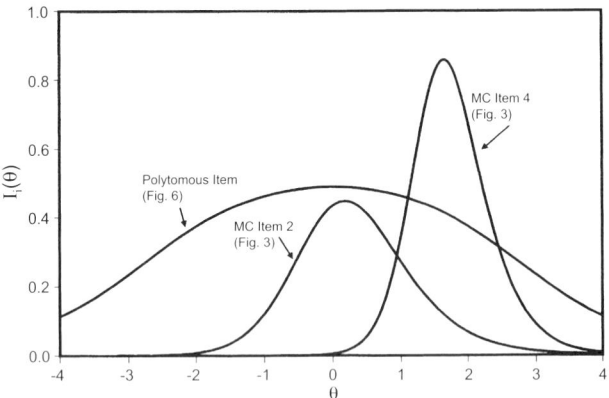

FIGURE 4.12 Test Information Function and the Test Standard Error Function Based on the Items in Figure 4.11

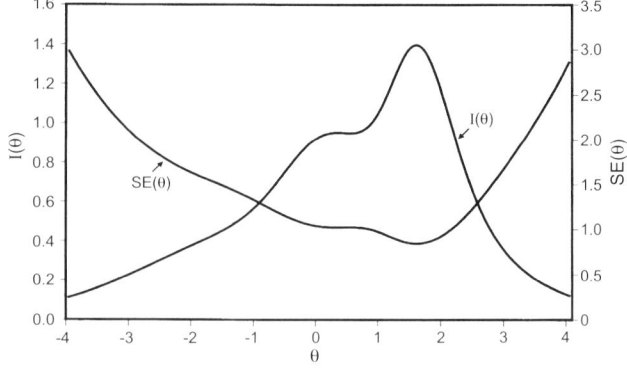

standard error function, $SE(\theta) = 1/\sqrt{I(\theta)}$, are displayed in Figure 4.12. Score accuracy can be evaluated using either information functions or standard error functions. Information functions have the advantage of being roughly proportional to the number of items, and thus easily interpretable in terms of test length. Standard error functions have the advantage of being expressed in units on the same scale as the ability estimate. Also, the concept of a standard error is more familiar to those who have been trained in CTT.

4.5.1. Item Locations

It can be useful to describe the location of an item relative to the IRT ability scale. This is particularly true when attempting to convey concepts of item difficulty to those who are not experts in measurement. For example, in test construction it can be helpful to communicate with test developers (i.e., content experts) by stating that the "passing" score is at a scale score of 500 and that a certain percentage of the items chosen for a test should have locations near that passing score. In another example, in interpreting the meaning of a scale score, it can be helpful to display the location of exemplar items on the scale used to report students' scale scores.

The θ at which the i-th item provides maximum information can be labeled θ_i; θ_i is sometimes called the *item location*. For the 1PL and 2PL models, $\theta_i = b_i$; these items convey their maximum information at abilities that match the item difficulties, and the information they convey at this maximum is $M_i = 1/4$ for the 1PL model and $M_i = D^2 a_i^2 / 4$ for the 2PL model. For the 3PL model where it is assumed that examinees can get items correct by guessing, the item location is (Lord, 1980, section 10.2)

$$\theta_i = b_i + \frac{1}{Da_i} \ln \frac{1 + \sqrt{1+8c_i}}{2}, \quad (33)$$

and the maximum information provided is

$$M_i = \frac{D^2 a_i^2}{8(1-c_i)^2}[1 - 20c_i - 8c_i^2 + (1 + 8c_i)^{3/2}]. \quad (34)$$

For the PC and 2PPC/GPC models θ_i is the θ value at which

$$E\{[X_i - E(X_i | \theta)]^3\} = 0. \quad (35)$$

There are other definitions of item location. For example, sometimes the term *item location* refers to the item b_i value for dichotomous items. Muraki uses the term *item location* for a parameter of the GPC model (Muraki, 1992). When IRT is used to map items for standard setting, the items are ordered in terms of their difficulties or "locations" to help judges find items that reflect content that students should master if they meet a particular standard (see the chapter on standard setting by Hambleton and Pitoniak, this volume). In some cases a particular *response probability* (RP) is chosen as part of the definition of item location. For example, if an RP of 0.50 is chosen for a dichotomous item, then the item location is the θ value at which the examinee has a 50% chance of getting the item correct. Thus, because of the different possible meanings of "item location," it is essential that the meaning of that term be clearly defined when it is used.

4.6. Information Functions of Transformations of Test Raw Scores and Abilities

Lord (1980) presents two very useful results related to information and transformations. The first is that if $f(X)$ is a monotonic transformation of X and certain easily achieved conditions are met,[16]

$$I[f(X) | \theta] = I(X | \theta). \quad (36)$$

In other words, there is a certain amount of information about θ that a test raw score carries. Monotonic transformations of that raw score do not change that information.

The second important result (Lord, 1980, p. 85) is that if $g(\theta)$ is a monotonic transformation of θ,

$$I[X | g(\theta)] = \frac{I(X | \theta)}{[g'(\theta)]^2}, \quad (37)$$

where $g'(\theta) = dg(\theta)/d\theta$. From the definition of the test score information in Equation (20), it is clear that multiplicative transformations of the θ scale will proportionally change the slope of the regression of X on θ. From Equation (37) it follows that

FIGURE 4.13 The Test Standard Error Function Expressed in the Number-Correct Score Metric ($\xi(\theta)$) for the Test in Figure 4.12

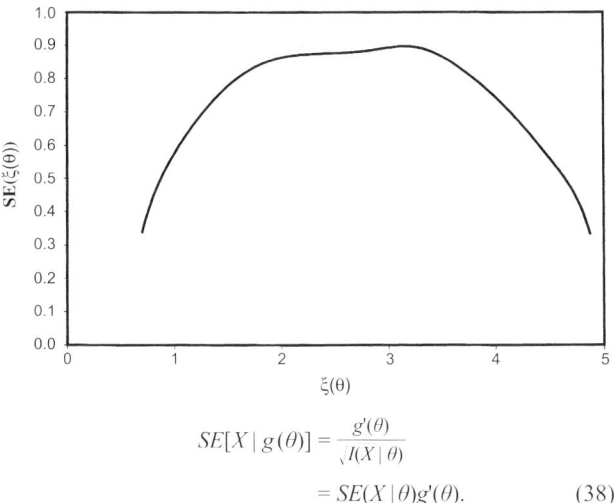

$$SE[X \mid g(\theta)] = \frac{g'(\theta)}{\sqrt{I(X \mid \theta)}}$$
$$= SE(X \mid \theta) g'(\theta). \quad (38)$$

For example, if the θ scale is stretched out (e.g., by multiplying all θ values by 2), the standard errors for estimates of that θ will increase proportionally.

The information functions for nonlinearly transformed θ scales have different shapes (e.g., Lord, 1980, section 6.3), as do standard error functions. For example, Figure 4.12 shows the standard error of a test expressed relative to the θ metric; in Figure 4.13 the standard error is expressed relative to the $\xi(\theta)$ metric (i.e., number-correct metric). In the θ metric, standard errors increase for extreme θ values. In other words, when an examinee is near a perfect or minimal score, the test data can tell us that the examinee has a high θ or low θ, but because θ is unbounded, the test data cannot be precise about how high or low that θ value is. The number-correct metric is bounded by 0 (or Σc_j) and n, so in that metric standard errors become lower for extreme scores (Figure 4.13).

The *relative efficiency* function of two scores is the ratio of their information functions:

$$RE(X,Y) = \frac{I(X \mid \theta)}{I(Y \mid \theta)}. \quad (39)$$

From Equation 37 it is clear that transforming the θ scale will not change the relative efficiency of two scores on a test, because $g'(\theta)$ will cancel out in Equation 39. In general, because information functions are roughly proportional to the number of items in a test, relative efficiencies can be (roughly) interpreted in terms of numbers of items: if $RE(X,Y) = 2$, then the number of items contributing to score Y would have to be doubled for that score to provide roughly the same information as provided by test score X.

Researchers can find it useful to assess the relative efficiency of raw score functions that are based on different item scores or different item weighting schemes. Relative efficiency also can be very helpful in examining the potential effects of making a wide variety of changes in the choice of items to appear in a test (e.g., Lord, 1980). Examining relative efficiencies is particularly helpful if the test designer is concerned about score accuracy at a particular cutpoint, such as that used when examinees are classified on the basis of their test scores.

4.7. Comparing Information Functions Across Models

The results (TCCs, information functions, etc.) of IRT models can be compared in a straightforward manner as in the examples given earlier in this chapter, but only if the θ scales are the same for the different models. Although the models all use the term θ to represent ability, the scales produced by these models when they are applied to the same test data typically are not the same: The θ scales for different models typically have a nonlinear relationship to each other. For example if the 1PL and 3PL models are applied to a multiple-choice test, it is common for the 3PL scale to be more "stretched out" among low ability examinees than the 1PL model (e.g., Yen, 1981). Given that information functions (and standard errors) are affected by the scale, an explicit decision is needed about which scale to use to compare information for the same test across models. In order to determine the relationship between the scales for a particular test, the scales can be related via a metric that they have in common (such as the number-correct metric; for example, see Sykes & Yen, 2000, p. 238).

In order to understand differences that occur between models, it is also necessary to explicitly separate the item data, the scoring function, and the ability metric when comparing models so that these factors are not confounded (e.g., Yen & Candell, 1991). For example, if it is desired to isolate the effect of optimal item weighting on a score's standard error, it is necessary that the standard errors of optimally weighted and nonoptimally weighted scores be compared when both are expressed on the same scale (e.g., the ability metric). In another example, if it is desired to isolate the effect of two metrics on a standard error, such as a 1PL metric versus a 3PL metric, it is essential that the ability scores both be based on the unweighted item scores.

Finally, in comparing information across models, it is important to separate model assumptions from empirical results. For example, because the 1PL model assumes that no guessing occurs, it will predict greater information (and lower standard errors) among low-scoring examinees than that predicted by the 3PL model. However, if the 1PL model's assumption of no guessing is not true, then the model prediction will not be upheld with empirical data. Similarly, if local item independence is inaccurately assumed for a model, and local item dependence inflates the item discriminations for some items, then the greater information predicted by higher item discriminations will not necessarily be seen in empirical evaluations of standard errors (e.g., Yen, 1993).

5. ITEM PARAMETER ESTIMATION

When using IRT models it is necessary to estimate item parameters and abilities from item response data. Estimation of item parameters is also called *item calibration*.[17] This is typically done using software that uses joint maximum likelihood (JML), conditional maximum likelihood (CML), or marginal maximum likelihood (MML) procedures. A description of these procedures as well as some comments about heuristic estimation procedures are provided in this section.

5.1. Heuristic Methods

In the 1960s and 1970s when computers were slower and processing time more expensive than they are now, approximate estimation of item parameters was used. When computer speed improved, these approximate estimates were used as starting values for maximum likelihood estimates of item parameters as well as for screening items for adaptive testing (Schmidt, 1977). These approximate estimates, which relate classical item statistics such a biserials to IRT item parameters, are of continued interest because they provide an additional means of understanding IRT item parameters and relating them to other methods of describing item performance. Hambleton and Swaminathan (1985) and Hambleton (1989) thoroughly discussed these heuristic estimates and the conditions under which they can be reliably calculated. They cautioned that heuristic estimates are likely to be satisfactory only when all assumptions are met, when tests are very long, and sample sizes are very large.

5.2. Joint Maximum Likelihood

JML finds estimates of item parameters and abilities that maximize the likelihood of obtaining the observed item responses. The estimation algorithm typically defines starting item parameter estimates and obtains the MLE of abilities given those item parameter estimates. Then the ability estimates are treated as known, and the MLE of the item parameters are obtained. The algorithm repeats this process iteratively until the program converges on a solution to some preset tolerance level. The joint likelihood function is

$$L = P(\{U = u\} \mid \{\theta\}, \{a, b, c\}) \quad (40)$$

$$= \prod_{k=1}^{N} \prod_{i=1}^{n} \prod_{j=1}^{m} P_{ij}(\theta_k)^{u_{ijk}}, \quad (41)$$

where $u_{ijk} = 1$ if examinee k makes item response j to item i, and $u_{ijk} = 0$ otherwise. The log likelihood function is

$$\ln L = \sum_{k=1}^{N} \sum_{i=1}^{n} \sum_{j=1}^{m_i} u_{ijk} \ln P_{ij}(\theta_k). \quad (42)$$

For dichotomous items the likelihood equations that are solved are

$$\frac{\partial \ln L}{\partial \lambda} = \sum \frac{[u_{ik} - P_i(\theta_k)]}{P_i(\theta_k) Q_i(\theta_k)} \frac{\partial P_i(\theta_k)}{\partial \lambda} = 0, \quad (43)$$

where λ is the parameter or ability being estimated, and the summation is taken over items if an ability is being estimated and over examinees if an item parameter is being estimated.

For the 3PL model, the likelihood equations are the following (Lord, 1980):

For θ_k

$$\sum_{i=1}^{n} a_i \frac{[P_i(\theta_k) - c_i]}{(1 - c_i) P_i(\theta_k)} [u_{ik} - P_i(\theta_k)] = 0. \quad (44)$$

(Note that Equation (44) uses the optimal scoring weights described in section 4.5.)

For a_i

$$\frac{1}{1 - c_i} \sum_{k=1}^{N} \frac{[\theta_k - b_i][P_i(\theta_k) - c_i]}{P_i(\theta_k)} [u_{ik} - P_i(\theta_k)] = 0. \quad (45)$$

For b_i

$$\frac{a_i}{1 - c_i} \sum_{k=1}^{N} \frac{[P_i(\theta_k) - c_i]}{P_i(\theta_k)} [u_{ik} - P_i(\theta_k)] = 0. \quad (46)$$

For c_i

$$\frac{1}{1 - c_i} \sum_{k=1}^{N} \frac{1}{P_i(\theta_k)} [u_{ik} - P_i(\theta_k)] = 0. \quad (47)$$

For the 1PL model, the likelihood equations are very simple:

For θ_k,

$$\sum_{i=1}^{n} [u_{ik} - P_i(\theta_k)] = 0. \quad (48)$$

For b_i

$$\sum_{k=1}^{N} [u_{ik} - P_i(\theta_k)] = 0. \quad (49)$$

In simple terms, for the Rasch 1PL model the MLE of θ_k is the θ value that produces a predicted number-correct score equal to that examinee's observed number-correct score; the MLE estimate of the b_i produces a predicted p-value for each item equal to the observed p-value. Wright and Douglas (1977a, 1977b) provide more information about estimation for the 1PL model.

For the 3PL model a variety of combinations of item parameters can produce very similar ICCs, particularly for easy items. This makes item parameter estimation more complex for that model. In particular, in order to estimate the c_i parameter it is necessary to have examinees whose abilities are far below the item difficulty. In some cases, those data are not available and various procedures are implemented to constrain the c_i value to a reasonable range (e.g., Lord (1975b)). Bayesian priors on parameters are also commonly used to constrain the c_i estimates (e.g., Mislevy & Bock, 1984; Swaminathan & Gifford, 1985, 1986). Standard errors of item parameter estimates are presented by Lord (1980) and Wingersky and Lord (1984).

Research has shown that the JML estimates are not consistent. Specifically, it has been found that the item parameter estimates are biased, and this bias does not disappear when the samples size increases (Andersen, 1972; Lord, 1983, 1986).

5.3. Conditional Maximum Likelihood

Conditional maximum likelihood (CML) estimators, which are consistent, are available for the Rasch 1PL model because number-correct scores are sufficient estimators for ability estimates for this model.[18] The Rasch 1PL model is one of a family of models, which includes Masters' PC model, that have the property of *specific objectivity,* in which it is possible to completely separate the estimation of abilities and item difficulties and eliminate bias in the estimates (Masters & Wright, 1984; Rasch, 1960). In fact, Rasch derived this model in order to have specific objectivity. However, it must be kept in mind that if this model is applied to data that do not fit the model, specific objectivity is not obtained. Andersen (1995), among others, provides a good discussion of the issues related to estimating parameters for polytomous Rasch models.

5.4. Marginal Maximum Likelihood

While software used to estimate IRT parameters in the 1970s and early 1980s was largely based on JML, marginal maximum likelihood (MML; Bock & Aitkin, 1981) became the estimation procedure of choice in the 1980s and 1990s. MML procedures avoid the estimation of abilities[19] and improve the accuracy of the item parameter estimates. The marginal likelihood that is maximized is

$$P(\{U=u\}|\{a,b,c\}) = \int_{-\infty}^{+\infty} \prod_{i=1}^{n} \prod_{j=1}^{m_i} P_{ij}(\theta)^{u_{ij}} g(\theta) d\theta, \quad (50)$$

where $g(\theta)$ is the probability density for θ. Contrasting Equations (41) and (50), we see that because $g(\theta)$ is a hypothesized distribution, there is no estimation of θ values for particular examinees for MML.

The implementation of MML involves further conceptual details. In most cases a continuous $g(\theta)$ is replaced by a finite set of discrete θ values, called *quadrature points*. In addition, an iterative Expectation-Maximization (EM) algorithm is employed. This algorithm iterates to convergence between a) estimating the numbers of theoretical examinees with a particular value of θ that are expected to give response j to item i, and b) finding the item parameters that maximize the likelihood of observing those numbers of examinees with those responses. The EM algorithm for MML parameter estimation is used in software such as BILOG (Zimowski, Muraki, Mislevy, & Bock, 1997), MULTILOG (Thissen, 1991), PARDUX (Burket, 1991), and PARSCALE (Muraki & Bock, 1997).

5.5. Markov Chain Monte Carlo

As unidimensional and multidimensional IRT models become more complex, parameter estimation becomes more difficult to implement using standard estimation methods. *Markov chain Monte Carlo* (MCMC) methods have been proposed as an alternative approach to parameter estimation in these circumstances. One of the advantages of MCMC methodology is that is flexible. The approach easily accommodates complex data sets, which might involve item responses that are multidimensional, have complicated dependencies, or reflect multilevel structures. For example, Patz and Junker (1999a) have considered how MCMC methodology can be used to address missing data issues, polytomous item scores from multiple raters, and guessing behavior.

MCMC methodology involves drawing random samples from a proposed theoretical distribution for a set of parameters and using the sample information to infer characteristics of the theoretical distribution. Gibbs sampling simplifies this complex task (Bradlow et al., 1999) by repeatedly sampling from the complete conditional distribution for each set of parameters assuming that the current values for the other parameters are the true values. MCMC methods are usually carried out using Bayesian models, so that priors are established for the parameters of interest (Patz & Junker, 1999b). Over many iterations, the sampled values are expected to converge on those in the joint distribution. An empirical marginal posterior distribution of each parameter is also obtained; the mean of each distribution can be used as an estimate of the parameter, and the standard deviation of the posterior distribution as the standard error of this estimate.

Albert (1992) first demonstrated the use of Gibbs sampling for a two-parameter normal ogive IRT model. Baker (1998) used Albert's approach in his evaluation of the accuracy of item parameters estimated using BILOG and Gibbs sampling under a variety of test lengths and sample sizes. Bolt, Cohen, & Wollack (2001) applied MCMC methods to explore individual differences in examinees' responses to multiple-choice items, and Kim (2001) compared the accuracy of item and person parameters estimated using MCMC and methods of estimating parameters traditionally used with the Rasch model. Other researchers have used MCMC techniques to estimate the parameters of hierarchical IRT models (e.g., Adams, Wilson, & Wu, 1997; Maier, 2001). Bolt and Lall (2003) explored the use of MCMC procedures to estimate the parameters for both the compensatory 2PL MIRT model and Whitely's noncompensatory MLTM model. In their simulation study comparisons were made between the recovery of parameters based on the 2PL MIRT model when estimated using their MCMC methods and using NOHARM (Fraser, 1988; Fraser & McDonald, 1988).

Results to date for MCMC methods are promising, but very preliminary. Although easily implemented using existing software packages or programming languages, e.g., WINBUGS (Spiegelhalter, Thomas, & Best, 2000), S-Plus (MathSoft, 1995), or FORTRAN (Baker, 1998), MCMC methodology is conceptually complex, and the time required for parameter estimation is very lengthy.

5.6. Unidimensional Estimation Software

To calibrate tests using models from the Rasch family, the Windows™ version of BIGSTEPS (Linacre, 1991–1996), called WINSTEPS (Linacre & Wright, 1991–2000) is available. Users can calibrate dichotomous items using the Rasch model and polytomous items using Andrich's rating scale model (Andrich, 1978), Masters's partial credit model (Masters, 1982), or other models. WINSTEPS implements a two-step process to estimate item and ability parameters. A normal approximation algorithm is used to obtain preliminary estimates, and JML estimation procedures are used to obtain subsequent, more precise estimates (Featherman, 1997). CML estimates for dichotomous and polytomous items calibrated using various Rasch models can be obtained from software programs called RUMM (Andrich, Sheridan, & Luo, 1990–2001) and WINMIRA (von Davier, 2001).

The BILOG™ family of programs offers the option of using the 1PL, 2PL or 3PL model to calibrate dichotomous items, and these programs are widely used. Early versions of BILOG (Mislevy & Bock, 1984) were compared with LOGIST (Wingersky, 1983; Wingersky, Barton, & Lord, 1982), which was at the time the preeminent program for calibrating items using the 3PL model. Both Yen (1987a) and Mislevy & Stocking (1989) found that the two programs generally were similar in their accuracy, although BILOG was slightly more accurate when tests had 15 or fewer items. Mislevy (1986) and Baker (1990) reported that early versions of BILOG™ accurately recovered true parameter values, although Harwell and Janosky (1991) found that this accuracy diminished considerably when sample sizes fell below 500 and tests were very short.

BILOG-MG-3 is a Windows™ version of BILOG-MG (Zimowski et al., 1997), which provides all the functions of BILOG and also offers users a way to calibrate the item responses for multiple groups of examinees. Multi-group analyses can be used to assess differential item functioning when the examinees in all groups take the same items. These multiple group analyses also can be used to assess *item drift,* which is defined as differential changes in item difficulty over time. In theory, multiple group analyses also can be used for equivalent-groups equating, where equivalent groups of examinees take parallel test forms, or for nonequivalent groups equating, where the groups of examinees are not equivalent and they take test forms that include some common anchor items. However, the accuracy of such equating procedures, and the conditions under which they are implemented (i.e., in terms of sample sizes, number of quadrature points, etc.) should be evaluated and understood by the user.

MULTILOG (Thissen, 1991) and PARSCALE (Muraki & Bock, 1997) are designed to calibrate both dichotomous and polytomous items. To calibrate the dichotomous items, these programs give the user the option of applying the 1PL, 2PL or 3PL model. To calibrate the polytomous items the user may choose between several models. MULTILOG 6 offers a range of choices including Bock's (1972) nominal model, Samejima's (1969) graded response model, and Masters's (1982) partial credit model. PARSCALE 3 offers the option of using Andrich's (1978) rating scale model or the generalized partial credit model (Muraki, 1992; Yen, 1993). From their simulation study of the accuracy of MULTILOG, Reise and Yu (1990) concluded that at least 500 examinees were needed to obtain accurate item parameter estimates when Samejima's (1969) graded model was used to calibrate a test with 25 polytomous items. Stone (1992) reported similar findings when the 2PL model was used.

The current versions of MULTILOG and PARSCALE are Windows™ versions published by Scientific Software Inc. (See du Toit, 2003.) Offered with them is a software program called IRT Graphics, which can produce item characteristic curves, item and test information values, and standard error estimates, among other statistics. This kind of output greatly assists the user in understanding item and test behavior.

All of these programs give the user the option to define in detail what calibration process will be implemented and what output should be produced. For example, in addition to choosing the model to use for parameter estimation, the user typically can specify the priors to be used, the number and weighting of quadrature points, the number of estimation cycles, the convergence criterion, and the type of scores to be output. It is essential for the user to understand the effect of each choice on the resulting calibrations.

Reviews of calibration software occasionally appear in journals (e.g., Featherman, 1997; Kim, 1997). Embretson and Reise (2000) provide brief summaries that give more details about the programs discussed in this section as well as other programs that are less commonly used.

5.7. MIRT Estimation Software

Compensatory models have received the most attention from researchers interested in using MIRT models in educational measurement. In part, this focus is due to the availability of procedures and software that can be used to estimate the item parameters defined by these models. Two software programs, NOHARM (Fraser, 1988; Fraser & McDonald, 1988) and TESTFACT (Wood et al., 2003) are available for this purpose. Both programs can be used only for compensatory multidimensional models when data have been dichotomously scored. If a c-parameter (lower asymptote) is desired, both programs require the user to provide values, because this parameter is not estimated. NOHARM fits a multidimensional normal ogive model using nonlinear factor analysis and least squares procedures. Either exploratory or confirmatory analyses can be conducted. Program output includes residual covariances between items after the model is estimated, as well as the root mean square of these residuals as a measure of overall fit. TESTFACT can implement full information factor analyses and provides marginal maximum likelihood estimates of item parameters. TESTFACT can be used to explore the dimensionality of a test, and the user also can perform confirmatory, bifactor analyses. A likelihood ratio test statistic is provided as an overall measure of model fit. See section 7.2 for more discussion of approaches to assessing the dimensionality of a test.

Reckase (1997b) reported that NOHARM and TESTFACT generally produced stable parameters for long tests and sample sizes exceeding 1,000 cases. However, more investigation of the accuracy of parameters estimated by both programs is needed. Included in this work should be studies of the sensitivity of the parameter estimates to sample size, test length, the degree of correlation between dimensions, as well as the shape of underlying ability distributions.

5.8. Recommended Test Lengths and Sample Sizes

Extensive research on the effects of test length and sample size on the parameter estimates for dichotomously-scored items largely was carried out in the 1980s, when the behavior of newly-developed software programs and the effectiveness of alternative parameter estimation methods had yet to be established. Hambleton (1989) provided a succinct summary of those findings. As he noted, there are many factors that affect the accuracy of item and ability parameter estimates. These include choice of IRT model, method of parameter estimation, the shape of the score distributions being analyzed, as well as the software program used to carry out the estimation process and the options exercised within the program.

When making decisions about test length and sample size, it is also very important to consider the stakes associated with the results that are obtained. Longer tests and larger sample sizes are needed in high stakes testing situations when examinees' scores will be used for important decisions and where accurate equating from year to year is required. In contrast, shorter tests and smaller sample sizes may be all that is needed when less accurate estimates are acceptable. This may be the case, for example, when items are being field-tested and only general information about item quality is desired.

With regard to the issue of model choice, Wright and Stone (1979) indicated that 20 items and 200 examinees were needed to obtain adequate parameter estimates using the Rasch model. Hulin, Lissak, and Drasgow (1982) concluded that 30 items and 500 examinees would produce acceptable results when the 2PL model was used, and 60 items and 1,000 examinees were needed to produce acceptable 3PL estimates. Using the same 3PL model, Swaminathan and Gifford (1983) concluded that a 20-item test and 1,000 examinees would produce very good estimates of the b_i and c_i parameters, and fairly good estimates of the a_i parameters and examinee θs. Hulin et al. (1982) noted that tradeoffs between sample size and test length were evident in results they obtained. For example, results based on 60-item tests and 1,000 examinees resembled those based on 30-item tests and 2,000 examinees.

In research focused on sample size and/or test length effects, MML estimates have been found to be more accurate than JML estimates when tests are short and sample size is small (Drasgow, 1989). Bayesian methods also have been found to improve the accuracy of parameter estimates when sample sizes are small (Lim & Drasgow, 1990; Skaggs & Stevenson, 1989; Swaminathan & Gifford, 1986). However, accuracy is adversely affected when a Bayesian prior is misspecified (Harwell & Janosky, 1991; Seong, 1990; Stone, 1992).

True ability distributions that are skewed may produce less accurate item parameter estimates than those obtained from distributions that are normal or uniform (Seong, 1990; Stone, 1992; Swaminathan & Gifford, 1983). As Lord (1980, p.186) noted, when the 3PL model is to be used, examinees performing at the low end of the ability scale are needed if c_i is to be accurately estimated.

Finally, as Baker (1987) observed, the estimation procedures implemented by available software programs are greatly affected by users' choice of options that are offered. Seong (1990) showed that the number of quadrature points, for example, can affect the accuracy of both item parameter and ability estimates. Harwell and Janosky (1991) found that BILOG's default prior variance for discrimination parameters may be inappropriate when tests are short and sample size is small. These examples show that it is important for users to understand thoroughly the implications of any estimation options that they choose.

To date, little research has been done on sample size and test length effects in contexts where polytomous items are used. Reise and Yu (1990) examined the accuracy of MULTILOG's (Thissen, 1991) item and ability parameters estimated using the graded response model (Samejima, 1969) for a 25-item test in which each item had five score categories. They concluded that a sample size of at least 500 examinees was needed to get respectable correlations with true values, and sample sizes between 1000 and 2000 examinees would be needed if accurate estimation of parameter values is required for an important application such as equating.

De Ayala and Sava-Bolesta (1999) evaluated item parameters estimated using Bock's nominal model as implemented by MULTILOG. They found that shape of the true θ distribution substantially affected the accuracy of the nominal model's a_{ij} estimates, but not its c_{ij} estimates. Increases in the sample size also improved accuracy, and they concluded that for a test with three-point items 1,600 cases was adequate, and for a test with four-point items 2,200 cases was adequate provided that the true θ distribution was normal.

In our experience, large sample sizes are needed when tests contain polytomous items that are extremely hard or extremely easy, because the numbers of examinees obtaining extreme scores can be relatively few, indeed at times too few to obtain parameter estimates for these extreme score levels. As an example, sample sizes of about 3,500 cases were expected to be adequate for calibrating a performance assessment developed for a state testing program. Preliminary analyses showed that some items were so difficult for students that none obtained the highest item scores. Doubling the sample size solved the problem, producing sufficient numbers of cases at these extreme score levels to obtain adequate parameter estimates (CTB Macmillan/McGraw-Hill, 1992).

5.9. Aligning Item Parameters from Separate Analyses

As described in section 2.8, IRT scales for commonly used models are determined up to a linear transformation. In many applications it is necessary to align the item parameters obtained from different analyses so that they are on the same scale. For example, two sets of items may have parameters estimated based on two different but equivalent samples of examinees. In other cases, the two analyses have a set of anchor items in common. There are a variety of procedures available to align the parameters from these separate analyses: linear procedures based on ability estimates, holding anchor item parameters fixed, the mean-mean method, the mean-sigma method, and the TCC method. These methods are briefly described below. Hanson and Beguin (1999) described procedures for concurrent calibration, which involves estimating the parameters for items contained in multiple, overlapping test forms in a single calibration run. Hambleton and Swaminathan (1985), Kolen and Brennan (1995), and Peterson, Kolen, and Hoover (1989) provide further discussion of alignment methods.

5.9.1. Linear Methods Based on Ability Estimates

Different test forms can be administered to randomly equivalent groups. This can be effectively done by spiraling test books over students or, in the case of performance assessments where different forms cannot be administered in the same classroom at the same time, students can be randomly assigned to testing groups. The traditional linear procedure (e.g., the chapter on linking and equating by Holland and Dorans [this volume]); Peterson et al., 1989) aligns the means and standard deviations of the ability estimates. The linear transformation used to align the abilities is then applied appropriately to the item parameters.

Because the means and standard deviations of ability estimates are greatly affected by extreme scores, which occur when students perform at the floor or ceiling of a test, equating on the basis of means and standard deviations of ability estimates does not ensure that the score distributions will be aligned. That is, even after the means and standard deviations are made equal, the cumulative frequency distributions for the two test forms may not be aligned through much of the score distribution. This misalignment may cause problems when, for example, the alignment is intended to identify cutscores at various points in the distribution that are to be used to classify examinees in terms of their level of proficiency.

An alternative to aligning means and standard deviations is to use equipercentile methods, which by definition will produce test forms with matching cumulative ability estimate distributions for the samples of students used in the linking. However, the equipercentile method is, except for strictly parallel tests, a nonlinear procedure. For an alignment to be consistent with most IRT models, it must be linear. These considerations lead to the use of the *linear equipercentile* method, in which a linear transformation is identified that aligns the two cumulative ability estimate distributions as closely as possible (e.g., minimizing the sum of squared differences in the cumulative percentage of students at each estimated ability level).

Any alignment procedure based on observed ability estimates or scores can produce inaccurate results if the test forms differ substantially in their standard error functions (e.g., Yen, 1983a). In such situations, procedures that estimate true score distributions can be used (e.g., Mislevy, 1984). In some cases, researchers using MML estimation software rely on a computer program's assumption of a particular prior ability distribution (e.g., normal (0,1)) as a sufficient procedure for aligning true ability estimates. However, such programs do not necessarily produce the needed level of accuracy in the alignment of the results; for example, if the standard deviation of abilities is to be controlled, a sufficient number of quadrature points is needed. Before relying on an assumption that software will align scales, it must be verified, typically through the evaluation of simulated data, that the software is providing the equivalence desired.

Finally, it must always be kept in mind that the quality of an alignment based on matched samples is completely dependent upon the actual equivalence of the samples. If the sampling is not done properly and/or the samples are not sufficiently large, the accuracy of the alignment will be affected; problems caused by nonequivalence between samples are very difficult, if not impossible, to detect during the analyses. The alignment designs described in the following sections involve the use of anchor items and provide a means of examining some aspects of the quality of the alignment during the alignment process.

5.9.2. Holding Anchor Item Parameters Fixed

When parameter estimates already exist for the anchor items that are included in a test being calibrated, these existing parameter estimates can be used for these anchor items during the calibration process. This approach is known as *holding anchor item parameter estimates fixed;* parameters are estimated only for the nonanchor items in the test. This process "pulls" the nonanchor item parameters onto the scale of the fixed parameters. The advantage of this procedure is that it is easy to implement with commonly used software packages. One disadvantage of this procedure is that it does not treat all items equally in terms of estimation error. Holding anchor parameters fixed forces the parameter estimation program to accommodate the anchor item parameter values (i.e., treat them as if they are true values), even if they are not a good fit to the new sample of data, and this can adversely affect the estimation of parameters for nonanchor items.

5.9.3. The Mean-Mean Method

Two sets of parameters are estimated independently, and the means of the anchor item parameters are obtained for the two sets. For example, for the 2PL model the mean anchor item a_i and b_i values are obtained for both samples; call them $\bar{a}_1$, $\bar{b}_1$, $\bar{a}_2$, and $\bar{b}_2$. The values $k_1 = \bar{a}_1 / \bar{a}_2$ and $k_2 = -k_1 \bar{b}_2 + \bar{b}_1$ are calculated. The linear transformation $a_{2i}^* = k_1 a_{2i}$ and $b_{2i}^* = k_1 b_{2i} + k_2$ places all the item parameter estimates from the second set onto the scale for the first set. That is, $\bar{b}_2^* = \bar{b}_1$ and $\bar{a}_2^* = \bar{a}_1$.

Note that for the 1PL model, all $Da_i = 1$, so the only transformation that occurs is $b_{2i}^* = b_{2i} - \bar{b}_2 + \bar{b}_1$. For the 1PL model the multiplicative scaling constant is determined via the implicit assumption of constant a_i values. The degree to which this assumption is correct can be checked by examining plots or relative standard deviations of the anchor item b_i values; the plots should fall along the 45-degree line and the standard deviations should be equal.

The advantage of the mean-mean method is its simplicity. Two disadvantages of this procedure are that item parameters are treated as independent entities and outliers can significantly affect the results. When parameters are estimated, the a_i, b_i, and c_i values are not independent. In essence, the parameter estimation process is finding a set of parameters that accurately describes an ICC. There are different combinations of item parameters, particularly for the 3PL model, that produce very similar ICCs, especially for easy items where the data available to estimate or evaluate the c_i values are sparse (Hulin et al., 1982). For example, see Figure 4.14; these sets of 3PL item parameters all produce very similar ICCs for $-3 < \theta < +3$. By focusing on individual item parameters instead of ICCs for the 2PL and 3PL models, inaccuracies in alignments can occur.

FIGURE 4.14 Three 3PL Items with Different Item Parameters that Produce Very Similar ICCs

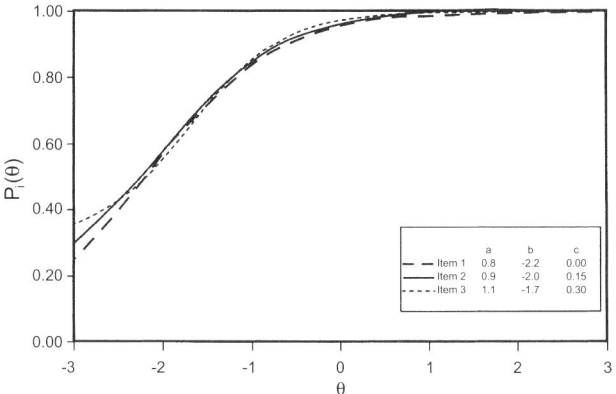

5.9.4. The Mean-Sigma Method

In this method, the standard deviation of the anchor item b_i values replaces the mean a_i values in the role of adjusting for multiplicative changes in scale. (When a scale is stretched out, the a_i values decrease and the standard deviation of the b_i values increases.) The linear transformations described in the previous section are used but with $k_1 = \sigma_{b_1}/\sigma_{b_2}$ and $k_2 = -k_1 \bar{b}_2 + \bar{b}_1$. The result is $\bar{b}_2^* = \bar{b}_1$ and $\sigma_{b_2^*} = \sigma_{b_1}$. The mean-sigma method has essentially the same advantages and disadvantages as the mean-mean method.

To use the mean-mean or mean-sigma methods, robust estimators of means and standard deviations are strongly recommended (e.g., Stocking & Lord, 1983) and bivariate plots of anchor item parameters should be examined for outliers. In some cases standard errors of estimates or other rules of thumb are used to remove outliers. Outliers must be removed with caution, because if they are removed systematically from one part of a bivariate plot, it can significantly affect the outcome of the alignment.

5.9.5. The TCC Method

In order to address the limitations of considering means and standard deviations of item parameters, Stocking and Lord (1983) introduced a method of aligning item parameter estimates based on aligning test characteristic functions. This procedure has the conceptual advantages of (a) considering model predictions in terms of ICCs, which is, in essence, how the estimation programs consider the items, (b) having the effect of minimizing differences between number-correct-to-theta scoring tables based on the anchor items, which often is central to the practical application of an IRT model,[20] (c) using weights for the minimization based on a distribution of abilities, so that more weight is given in parts of the scale where there are more examinees, and (d) minimizing differences in expected scores rather than observed scores or parameters.[21]

This last advantage is particularly important. Observed scores or parameters are the sum of a true score and an error score, and the variance of the observed score or parameter is the sum of true score variance and error variance. It is common for the parameters or thetas that are aligned to be subject to different amounts of error variance. For example, if one set of item parameters estimates is based on a larger sample of examinees than another, all else being equal, it will have less error variance and observed score variance. If the variances of the two sets of estimates are set equal (as in the mean-sigma approach), then a systematic bias in results will occur by "shrinking in" the set of results with greater error variance to match the set with less error variance. That is, the variances of the estimates would be equal but the variances of the true values would not be equal.

There is an application where alignment of results with different error variances is central to the conclusions drawn and where researchers are often misled into an inappropriate procedure that can be avoided by use of the TCC method of alignment. This application is a simulation study, where true parameters and thetas are known and used to generate simulated item responses, which in turn are the basis of estimating item parameters and thetas. In evaluating the accuracy of the estimated values, it is common to want to compare the estimated values to the true values. To do this, given that the estimated scale is undetermined up to a linear transformation, it is necessary to place the estimated values on the same scale as the true values. It is not appropriate to equate means and standard deviations of true and estimated theta values (e.g., by making them both have a mean of 0 and standard deviation of 1.0), because this would result in "shrinking" the observed score scale (which contains both true score variance and error variance) to equal the true score scale. Instead, using the TCC method will provide conceptually appropriate alignment of the estimated and true scales in a simulation.

5.9.6. Removing Outlier Anchor Items from Educational Achievement Tests

It is common for practitioners to review bivariate plots of anchor item parameters from two sets of estimates being aligned, and to remove "outliers" before determining the linking constants. The justification for this practice is that the linking is then based on those items that best fit the IRT model assumption of "sample-free" item calibrations.

However, caution is warranted in removing outliers from linkings for educational achievement tests when the goal is to measure change in achievement from Time 1 to Time 2. To measure change in abilities between Times 1 and 2, one has to have a set of items whose difficulties are held constant at the two testing times. If item difficulties are not known, we cannot tell if change in performance is due to a change in item difficulty or a change in ability.

Testing both times with the same test form using the same item parameters will permit measurement of change in abilities. When the two test forms differ and common anchor items are used, the anchor items in essence are providing the constant part of the test,[22] and they are the only items providing information about change.[23] In other words, all the items at Time 2 contribute to the shape of the Time 2 ability distribution, but it is only the anchor items that are used to linearly shift the mean and standard deviation of that distribution to make it possible to compare it to the Time 1 distribution.

In educational achievement testing, an anchor item can show differential shifts in difficulty (i.e., it can be an outlier) for three main reasons: (1) change in the measurement characteristics of the item due to nonachievement related anomalies, such as an item being edited, context effects, or uncontrolled rater effects, so that the item can no longer be considered the "same" item, (2) poor estimation of an item's parameters due to small N or extreme performance, and (3) variations in relative item parameter estimates due to differential learning or minor sampling variation. To measure change in achievement, in most cases Reasons 1 and 2 justify removing an outlier from an anchor item set, but Reason 3 does not.

When outliers are removed, attention also needs to be paid to systematic effects of the removal. For example, if after examining a bivariate plot of item difficulties, more items are removed from the bottom of the plot than the top, the anchor item removal will have a systematic effect on conclusions about changes in achievement from Time 1 to Time 2.

5.9.7. Aligning the Parameters of Multidimensional Models

Like the scales of unidimensional models, the scales of multidimensional models are indeterminate. That is, they can be transformed linearly without affecting the predictions of the underlying model. To identify a multidimensional scale, the scale location and variance, as well as the covariance between the several ability dimensions, must be defined. Linking a new multidimensional test form to this scale requires finding appropriate transformations for the test form's scale location and variance as well as a rotation of the ability dimensions to maximize their alignment.

Research investigating approaches to multidimensional linking is just beginning. Hirsch (1989), Oshima, Davey, and Lee (2000), and Li and Lissitz (2000) have explored extensions of unidimensional procedures that include a rotational component. At this time, definitive results are not available. In addition to methodological issues related to linking multidimensional scales, ways to identify and maintain the underlying trait structure of test forms administered in different test years are needed, as Min (2003) has noted. Otherwise the linking of these test forms will not produce scores that have the same substantive meaning from year to year.

6. ABILITY ESTIMATION

There are a variety of ways that an examinee's ability can be estimated when using an IRT model. This section discusses the two most commonly used methods, maximum likelihood and Bayesian methods. Throughout this section it is assumed that item parameters are known (i.e., have been previously estimated).

6.1. Maximum Likelihood

Maximum likelihood estimation (MLE) finds the $\hat{\theta}$ that maximizes the likelihood of obtaining the examinee's observed test data, given the item parameters and model. Maximum likelihood estimates have desirable properties: They are consistent (that is, they remain unbiased as the number of items increases) and have minimum standard errors. The test data that are used in the estimation can be item scores, in which case the IRT models define the weights applied to the item scores to produce maximum likelihood estimates (see section 4.5). It is also possible for the test data to be defined as the number-correct score. In that case, the model will describe the transformation that is needed to convert the number-correct score to a θ estimate and will define the information function and standard error of that estimate. Other test data (e.g., arbitrarily weighted sums of item scores) can also be used for ability estimation.

As stated in Equation (48), the MLE of ability obtained from the item responses is based on the number-correct score for the Rasch 1PL; similarly, for the PC model the ability estimate is based on the unweighted raw score. For the 2PL and 2PPC/GPC models (for the 2PL model, see Equation (44), setting $c_i = 0$) the MLE of ability obtained from item responses is based on the weighted sum of item responses, with the weights equal to the item discriminations. In all these cases, the MLE ability estimate is the value for which the expected (weighted or unweighted) raw score equals the examinee's observed (weighted or unweighted) raw score.

For the IRT models discussed in this chapter, the MLE ability estimate for an examinee with a perfect number-correct score is $+\infty$. To anthropomorphize the estimation process, when an examinee achieves a perfect number-correct score, the model knows the examinee is high ability but cannot tell how high that ability is. Similarly, for the models with no guessing, examinees with number-correct scores of 0 have MLE ability estimates of $-\infty$. For the 3PL model, examinees with number-correct scores $\leq \sum_{i=1}^{n} c_i$ (i.e., at or below the "chance level"), also have MLE ability estimates of $-\infty$. Typically it is not appropriate to report scores of $+/-\infty$ in educational applications, and rules of thumb are developed to provide scores for those students. For example, if a "near perfect" student (with only one wrong item) receives an ability estimate equivalent to $+2.8$ (in a logit metric), then a perfect score might receive an ability estimate of $+3.0$. In determining these rules of thumb, it is common to consider conditional standard errors of measurement and TCCs for the "determined" ability estimates. Two other useful options for handling extreme ability estimates are Bayesian methods (see section 6.2) and Warm's (1989) weighted likelihood estimate.

While ability estimation in the absence of guessing is fairly straightforward, for the 3PL model it is worth examining estimation alternatives in more detail.

6.1.1. Maximum Likelihood Ability Estimation for the 3PL Model

When item responses are the test data entering into the estimation and optimal scoring is used, examinees' ability estimates based on the 3PL model depend on the particular items they get right or wrong, not just on the total number-correct score. This is item-pattern scoring, as defined in section 4.5, and it maximizes the likelihood of obtaining the observed pattern of item responses. For IRT models without guessing, the likelihood function will produce one maximum, but when $c_i \neq 0$ it is possible to observe multiple maxima in the likelihood function (Samejima, 1972, 1973; Yen, Burket, & Sykes, 1991). In essence, the possibility of correct guessing introduces ambiguity into a testing process; one cannot be completely sure that a correct response reflects more ability. (If there is guessing, this ambiguity occurs even if the IRT model being used does not acknowledge it.) Thus, when using the 3PL model and MLE based on the pattern of item responses, to find the ability estimate that maximizes the likelihood, it is necessary to use numerical methods that ensure that the global maximum, rather than a local maximum, has been identified.

Figure 4.15 shows an example of a likelihood function with two maxima. This example is based on 10 3PL items, which are ordered by difficulty on the plot. This hypothetical examinee's responses to the items are also indicated. This examinee got wrong the three easiest items, which also have relatively low discriminations; the examinee got right almost all of the harder items. The likelihood function has one maximum at -3 (and the likelihood actually continues to increase for ability values less than -3) and another, local maximum at an ability level near $+0.75$. The likelihood function reveals that there are two alternative "explanations" of this pattern of responses. Either the examinee has very low ability and got the more difficult items correct by "chance," or the examinee has a moderately high ability and got the easier items wrong because they were not very discriminating. The very low ability estimate is the one with the greater likelihood. More examples of likelihood functions with multiple maxima are contained in Yen et al. (1991).

There is a widespread misconception that item-pattern scoring must be used with the 3PL model. That is not true. With the 3PL model one can obtain a MLE ability estimate given the examinee's number-correct score or other weighted raw score. *Number-correct* scoring finds the ability estimate that maximizes the likelihood of obtaining the observed number-correct score:

FIGURE 4.15 A Log Likelihood Function for the 3PL Model That Has Multiple (Two) Maxima

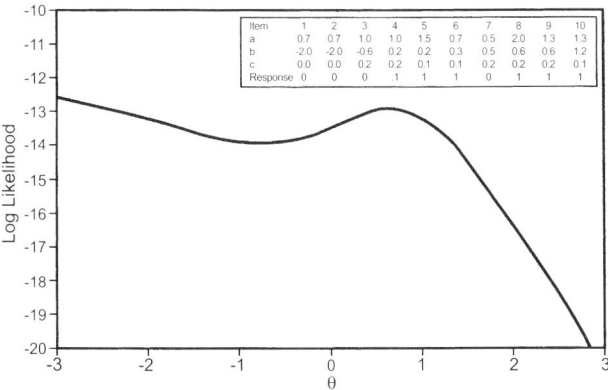

$$L(X_\bullet = x_\bullet | \theta, \{a_i, b_i, c_i\}) = \sum \prod_{i=1}^{n} P_i(\theta)^{x_i}[1 - P_i(\theta)]^{1-x_i}, \quad (51)$$

where the summation is taken over response patterns such that $x_\bullet$ is the sum.

Equation 51 is the compound binomial distribution; if all the items are equivalent (have the same item parameters), Equation 51 is the binomial distribution. Note that it is necessary to evaluate all 2^n possible item response patterns to calculate Equation 51. Lord and Novick (1968, p. 525) provide an alternate statement of the compound binomial that is informative:

$$L(X_\bullet = x_\bullet | \theta, \{a_i, b_i, c_i\}) = \binom{n}{x_\bullet} \varsigma(\theta)^{x_\bullet}[1 - \varsigma(\theta)]^{n - x_\bullet} + e, \quad (52)$$

where the first term on the right-hand side of Equation 52 is the binomial with parameter $\varsigma(\theta)$ (i.e., the test characteristic function expressed in proportion-correct units) and e includes additional terms of decreasing importance that are a function of $x_\bullet$ and the item parameters. It is well-known that a MLE of the parameter of a binomial distribution is the observed proportion-correct score, in this case $x_\bullet/n$. In other words, a first-order approximation to the MLE ability estimate that maximizes the probability of the observed number-correct score can be obtained from the inverse of the easily calculated TCC (Equation 19). It turns out that with tests of, say, 30 or more items, the inverse of the TCC provides a very accurate MLE of ability for the 3PL model (Yen, 1984b). If a precise solution to Equation 51 is needed, Stocking and Lord (1983) provide an easy-to-calculate recursive solution. Thus, with the 3PL model it is possible to provide ability estimates via *item-pattern* or *number-correct* scoring and, in fact, one major standardized test publisher has offered customers a choice between these scoring methods since 1980.

The standard errors of ability estimates obtained using item-pattern and number-correct scoring can be obtained from Equations 30 and 23, respectively. For the 3PL model, standard errors based on item-pattern scoring are not only theoretically lower than standard errors for number-correct scoring, empirical evaluations of the standard errors have verified the model predictions for a wide range of multiple-choice tests (Green & Yen, 1983; Yen, 1984b; Yen & Candell, 1991). These studies and extensive evaluation of operational achievement test data have demonstrated that while item-pattern and number-correct ability estimates differ for individual examinees (i.e., for examinees with the same number-correct score, their item-pattern ability estimate may be higher or lower, depending on which items they got correct), item-pattern and number-correct ability estimates are tau-equivalent for groups of, say, 30 or more examinees. That is, on the average item-pattern and number-correct ability estimates are equal, but they differ in terms of their standard errors.[24] In general, the longer the test and the less the relative influence of guessing (e.g., for multiple-choice tests with many effective distractors, or tests that include constructed-response items that do not allow guessing), the more similar are the results from the two scoring methods.

Figure 4.16 displays an example of how item-pattern and number-correct ability estimates based on the 3PL model

FIGURE 4.16 Ability Estimates for Item Response Vectors Scored with the 3PL Model Using Item-Pattern (Optimal Item Weight) Scoring and Number-Correct Scoring

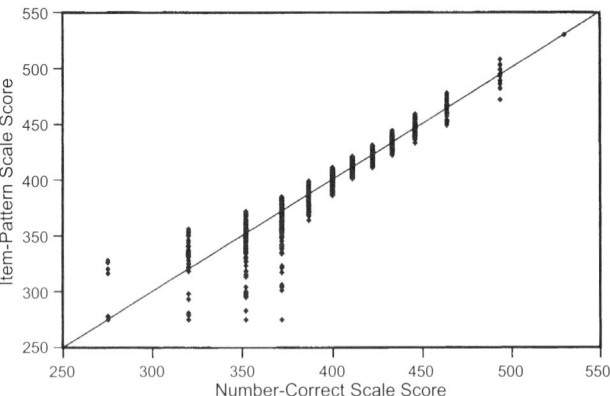

typically relate to each other. It is important to note that multiple examinees can be represented by each point in the plot and, although it cannot be seen, the plot is most dense along the X=Y line. The estimates are tau-equivalent, but the ability estimates can differ for individual examinees, particularly at the low end of the scale where guessing plays the biggest role. It is also important to note that although the correlation of the results of the two scoring methods is high (r = .97), there can be substantial differences in results for individual examinees.

6.2. Bayesian Methods

It is possible to estimate abilities using statistical procedures other than MLE. The most commonly used alternatives involve Bayesian methods, in which a *prior* distribution is assumed for the parameter being estimated. The more confident the user is in the prior information, the smaller is the standard deviation of the prior distribution. The prior information comes from knowledge about examinees that is external to the test, such as concurrent performance on another test (in which case the estimate is an *empirical* Bayes estimate) or the user's belief or knowledge about how a similar population of examinees performed on the test previously.

Bayesian methods are based on Bayes's general theorem:

$$P(Y|X) = \frac{P(X|Y)P(Y)}{P(X)}. \qquad (53)$$

P(Y) is the prior distribution, and this information is combined with information from the current test (X) to produce a *posterior* distribution that reflects the probability, given the test performance, that the examinee has a particular ability value. For example, for a 3PL model the posterior distribution would be

$$P(\theta|\{x_i\}, \{a_i, b_i, c_i\}) = \frac{P[\{x_i\}|\theta, \{a_i, b_i, c_i\}]P(\theta)}{P(\{x_i\})}, \qquad (54)$$

where

$$P(\{x_i\}) = \int P(\{x_i\}|\theta, \{a_i, b_i, c_i\})P(\theta)d\theta. \qquad (55)$$

$P(\{x_i\}|\theta, \{a_i, b_i, c_i\})$ is the likelihood of the observed item scores given the model. $P(\theta)$ is the prior distribution of θ, which is commonly assumed to be a normal distribution. When the mean of the posterior distribution is taken as the ability estimate, it is called an *expected a posteriori* (EAP) estimate. When the ability estimate is the mode of the posterior distribution, it is called the *Bayes modal estimator* or the *maximum a posteriori* (MAP) estimate.[25] The standard deviation of the posterior distribution is used as the standard error of the estimate. This standard error is less than or equal to $1/\sqrt{I(\theta)}$, because of the additional information provided by the prior.

Bayesian estimators are attractive because they avoid infinite and other extreme ability estimates that occur with MLE. Bayesian estimators have lower standard errors than MLE. However, Bayesian estimators are biased: they "pull" the estimate toward the mean of the prior distribution. Also, when estimating a particular examinee's ability, in many practical settings it is seen as inappropriate to use any information external to the test, particularly information about how other examinees have performed.

Warm (1989) describes a weighted likelihood estimate (WLE) for θ that has advantages over MLE and Bayesian methods in some circumstances.

Empirical Bayes estimators have been successfully used in combination with IRT models to provide more accurate subscores on achievement tests. Raw subscore, or objective scores, typically have very high standard errors because the scores are based on small numbers of items. The accuracy of these scores can be improved by using a procedure that (a) considers information about how the examinee did on all the items in the test, (b) examines how consistent that information is with the observed subscore, and, when appropriate, (c) combines the prior estimate based on the entire test with the observed subscore to get a posterior estimate of the subscore. The posterior estimate has a substantially lower standard error than the raw subscore (Wainer et al., 2001; Yen, 1987b; Yen, Sykes, Ito, & Julian, 1997).

7. MODEL-DATA FIT

IRT models are useful because they succinctly describe and predict examinees' performance on items. If an IRT model could be demonstrated to be completely accurate, then all its predictions would be accurate. However, in order to demonstrate that a model is completely accurate, it would be necessary to collect all the empirical data that were the target of the prediction; this would eliminate the efficiency that was motivating the model's use. Also, any IRT model, like all hypotheses that are not tautologies, is surely false when applied to real data and will be proved so with an appropriate statistical test, as long as the sample size is made sufficiently large (McDonald, 1982). Although there are researchers who continue exploration of improved statistical measures of model-fit, many users of these models focus on describing the accuracy of predictions in which they have special interest and generalize their findings to similar situations. For example, if a particular IRT model implemented in a particular way has been shown to provide a necessary level of equating accuracy, practitioners would be likely to generalize that expectation to similar settings and not conduct an exhaustive examination of fit in every application.

7.1. Rational Analysis of Model Features

Before a researcher invests resources into learning about an IRT model and trying it out, it is worthwhile to think through whether the test to be analyzed has special features that may make it more amenable to one model than another. Is the test substantially speeded? If so, the unidimensional IRT models likely will not apply to it, because speededness introduces multidimensionality. Can examinees get items right through guessing, and are items difficult enough so that examinees will be guessing? If so, using the 1PL or 2PL models can have some limitations. Is the number of examinees small? If so, obtaining accurate parameter estimates for the 3PL model may be problematic.

7.2. Assessment of Dimensionality

To assess whether a test is sufficiently unidimensional to apply an IRT model, the methodology developed by Stout and his colleagues (Nandakumar & Stout, 1993; Stout, 1987, 1990) is probably the most widely used. Implementation of the method involves identifying in a test a core set of items believed to measure the dominant trait. A second set of items, used to correct for bias, is selected to match the core set in terms of item counts and the distribution of item difficulties. The remaining items become a third set of items called the partitioning test; examinees are scored on the partitioning test and stratified on the basis of their scores. Subsequently, the covariance between items in the core test is calculated by score group, averaged, and compared to the average item covariance found for the second set of items. To the degree that the test is unidimensional, meaning that the items in the two sets are independent and measure the same thing as the partitioning test, the differences between these average covariances will be small and the test can be deemed essentially unidimensional. Stout's T statistic can be used to test the statistical significance of this difference.

The simple hypothesis that a test is essentially unidimensional can be examined using DIMTEST software (Nandakumar & Stout, 1993; Stout, 1987, 1990). Poly-DIMTEST (Nandakumar, Yu, Li, & Stout, 1998) extends DIMTEST to measures that contain polytomously-scored items. DETECT (Zhang & Stout, 1999) provides more information than DIMTEST by enabling the user to assess the degree of multidimensionality present in a set of dichotomously-scored test data. If the data have simple structure or approximate simple structure, the test can be partitioned into dimensionally distinct, homogeneous clusters of items (Stout et al., 1996). Yu and Nandakumar (2001) have developed Poly-DETECT, which is an extension of DETECT to accommodate tests that contain polytomous items. For more discussion of the conceptual basis for the approach and for details about testing the hypothesis of essential undimensionality, see Junker (1991), Nandakumar and Stout (1993), Stout (1987, 1990), and Stout et al. (1996). For applications of the procedure, see Hattie, Krakowski, Rogers, and Swaminathan (1996), Gessaroli and de Champlain (1996), Nandakumar (1994), and Nandakumar and Yu (1996).

Other approaches to assessing dimensionality are available. Item-level linear factor analysis (LFA) has been commonly used (Hambleton & Rovinelli, 1986; Hattie, 1985). However, LFA is a challenge to implement successfully because of difficulties that often arise when a matrix of phi or tetrachoric item correlations is analyzed (De Ayala & Hertzog, 1991; Hulin, Drasgow, & Parsons, 1983; Mislevy, 1986; Roznowski, Tucker, & Humphreys, 1991). Full information factor analysis (Bock & Aitkin, 1981; Bock, Gibbons, & Muraki, 1988) was developed to avoid the problems posed by analyzing item-level correlation coefficients. Instead, it analyzes vectors of examinee responses. McDonald's (1997) nonlinear factor analysis (NLFA) procedure was developed to account for nonlinear relationships between variables, which traditional LFA cannot do. Structural equation modeling offers a means to investigate in a more complex way the factors underlying a set of test data. The reader is referred to Bollen (1989) and Kaplan (2000) for a thorough discussion of these modeling procedures. Finally, Rosenbaum (1984) and Holland and Rosenbaum (1986) described a general nonparametric test based on theorems they formulated concerning the conditional association between test items.

7.3. Item Fit

The assessment of item fit typically involves comparing examinees' actual performance on an item to the performance predicted by the model used to scale the item. This assessment is what Traub and Lam (1985) called a "first-order" evaluation of model-data fit, because it simply compares examinees' predicted and observed scores at the item level. As discussed by Yen (1984a), these kinds of assessments of item fit are not sensitive to local dependence between items or the presence of multidimensionality among the items in a test.

What can cause poor item fit? Using the wrong IRT model to calibrate an item can produce poor fit. For example, substantial guessing may occur on multiple-choice items calibrated using the 2PL model, which will produce discrepancies between the actual and predicted item scores of examinees who guessed correctly. As another example, a subset of items calibrated using the 1PL model may be identified as poor fitting because they have actual discriminations that differ markedly from those of the other items in the test. Items may also be identified as misfitting when they do not accurately predict the performance of certain subgroups of examinees; this is evidence of differential item functioning. Low sample sizes and item parameters that have been estimated poorly also can produce fit problems. Finally, problems with item stems, item keys, and distractors can also cause a model to do a poor job of describing an item's behavior.

There are a variety of methods used to appraise item fit, but they generally involve a similar approach. Examinees are divided into groups on the basis of their total test score, expressed in either the raw score metric or the IRT ability metric. Actual performance on the item is calculated for each group. The performance for each group is predicted from the model used to calibrate the item. The actual and predicted performances for each group then are compared. To date, most methods of assessing item fit have assumed that the items are dichotomous.

An array of methods have been developed to assess fit to the Rasch model. These procedures are described by Gustafsson (1980) and van den Wollenberg (1982). As Rost and von Davier (1994) observed, many of these procedures involve computing the difference between observed and expected performance at the item level in the interest of obtaining an overall assessment of model-data fit at the test level.

More general methods of assessing fit that are applicable to all IRT models have been suggested by other researchers. Among these methods, analyses of residuals and standardized residuals are the simplest. Hambleton and his colleagues (Hambleton, 1989; Hambleton & Swaminathan, 1985; Hambleton, Swaminathan, & Rogers, 1991) discussed these analyses in detail.

Several indices have been formulated as Pearson chi-squared statistics, in the interest of exploring the use of significance testing to identify the items that are poor fitting (e.g., Bock, 1972; McKinley & Mills, 1985; Mislevy & Bock, 1990; Yen, 1981, 1984a). The Q_1 fit statistic described by Yen (1981) involves dividing the IRT ability scale into 10 score cells, where each cell contains about the same number of examinees. For each cell the observed and expected proportions of examinees getting the item right are calculated and compared:

$$Q_{1i} = \sum_{j=1}^{10} \frac{N_j(O_{ij} - E_{ij})^2}{E_{ij}(1 - E_{ij})}, \tag{56}$$

where O_{ij} and E_{ij} refer, respectively, to the observed and predicted proportions of examinees in cell j that answered item i correctly, and N_j refers to the number of examinees in cell j. For the purposes of significance testing, Yen found that Q_1 was distributed approximately as a χ^2 with 10-m degrees of freedom, where m refers to the number of item parameters estimated for an item. A general form of Q_1 has also been developed for use with polytomous items (Fitzpatrick et al., 1996). It can be noted in Equation 56 that Q_1 will increase proportionally with sample size. Thus, with larger sample sizes, small discrepancies between observed and predicted values may produce higher values of Q_1. Also, Q_1 can lack power for detecting when an inappropriate model is used; noting this, Yen (1981) recommended other procedures for examining model fit.

McKinley and Mills (1985) and Mislevy and Bock (1990) used G^2, a likelihood ratio statistic with J-m degrees of freedom, to measure item fit, where

$$G^2 = 2\sum_{j=1}^{J} N_j \left[O_{ij} \ln \frac{O_{ij}}{E_{ij}} + (1 - O_{ij}) \ln \frac{1 - O_{ij}}{1 - E_{ij}} \right], \tag{57}$$

and J refers to the total number of score cells.

Modifications to the chi-square statistics were proposed by Orlando and Thissen (2000), who noted that the dependency of these statistics on estimates of θ for grouping examinees and in the calculation of the expected proportions were violations of assumptions made with traditional χ^2 statistics. Because of this dependency on a model parameter, these researchers contended that the statistics have sampling distributions that are uncertain because their degrees of freedom are unclear.

Orlando and Thissen suggested assigning examinees to cells using number-correct scores and using a different procedure to find the expected frequencies. Their procedure involves finding two likelihoods for each item and cell. The first is the likelihood of all possible response patterns that produce the number-correct score j. The second is the likelihood of these response patterns when responses to the item in question are excluded. The likelihoods are estimated for all cells, and then they are combined to find the expected proportion of examinees with number-correct score j who correctly answered item i:

$$E_{ij} = \frac{\int T_i S_{k-1}^{*i} \phi(\theta) d\theta}{\int S_k \phi(\theta) d\theta}, \tag{58}$$

where T_i is the ICF for the correct response to item i, S_k and S_{k-1}^{*i} refer to the joint likelihoods for each cell calculated with and without item i, respectively, and $\phi(\theta)$ is the population density for θ.

Finally, Glas and his colleagues (Glas & Falcon, 2003; Glas & Verhelst, 1989) proposed a test using Lagrange multipliers (LM) to assess the fit of ICFs for 1-, 2-, and 3-PL models, as well as for LID. When simulated data were generated to fit the model, the LM test produced Type I error rates that were consistent with the nominal values for tests with sufficient numbers of items and less subject to inflation due to increased sample sizes than other fit measures (such as Yen's Q_1 and Bock's G^2). However, results for detecting misfitting items were mixed.

A few studies have been carried out to compare and evaluate the behavior of item fit statistics (Glas & Falcon, 2003; McKinley & Mills, 1985; Orlando & Thissen, 2000; Reise, 1990). In the typical study, sample size and test length are systematically varied, and the fit statistics are compared in terms of their Type I error rates and their power to detect misfitting items. The studies differed considerably in terms of the test lengths and sample sizes considered. They also differed in terms of the item parameters and θ distributions that were analyzed, the manner in which the score cells were configured, the number of replications, the nature of the misfit to be detected, and the particular fit statistics that were compared. Findings by Orlando and Thissen (2000) suggested that Q_1 and G^2 statistics may have inflated Type I error rates and may be over-identifying misfitting items when tests are very short (fewer than 10 items). Stone (2000) and Stone and Zhang (2003) suggested that imprecision in examinees' ability estimates might cause misclassification errors when estimated θ values are used to form the score groups.

Definitive conclusions about the best way to measure item fit cannot yet be drawn, because few studies have been done to date, and the studies that have been done are not comprehensive. As Henning (1989) noted, to draw solid conclusions about the behavior of the fit statistics, comparative studies over diverse populations, and a range of test lengths, sample sizes, and parameter characteristics are needed. It is also important to investigate the reliability of the fit results over samples and the degree to which the statistics are consistent in their fit classifications.

In large scale testing programs, the most comprehensive evaluation of item quality occurs when items are field-tested; analyses of item fit are one component of this evaluation. Fit results are used to inform decisions about which items are acceptable as they are, which items should be revised, and which items should be excluded from the pool of items later used in an operational test.

When a significance level or other criterion is used to flag items as misfitting, it is important that this designation be followed up with further analyses to determine why the item has been flagged. Sometimes the misfit can be due to a problem with an item's key or content that renders the item unusable. On the other hand, sometimes the causes of apparent misfit are statistical in nature and not at all related to item quality. Small sample sizes can make sampling distributions uncertain (Henning, 1989), and large sample sizes will increase statistical power, so that the number of items identified as misfitting increases. The number of score cells used in an analysis similarly can affect the power to detect misfitting items (Orlando & Thissen, 2003). In addition, score cells with extreme expectations produce high χ^2 values that will cause an item to appear to be misfitting. Interpreting fit results is greatly enhanced when graphics are used, as Gustafsson (1980), Hambleton (1989), Kingston and Dorans (1985), and Ludlow (1986) have shown.

Thus, a compelling case can be made for treating statistical analyses of item fit as informative but not definitive. These statistics can provide a basis for identifying items on which further analyses are needed. The summary statistics should be supplemented by more detailed analyses so that the reasons for the misfit of an item can be better understood.

7.4. Global Measures of Model-Data Fit

A researcher may want to compare the fit of two or more different models to find out which model best fits the data overall. For example, one might want to examine whether the 1PL or 2PL model better fits a data set. As Waller (1981) has suggested, the best way to do this is to compute likelihood ratio statistics based on each model and assess the change in the value of the statistic to evaluate fit of the two models. One way to obtain the overall statistic is to compute a likelihood ratio such as that defined by McKinley and Mills (1985) for each item, and then sum over the items to find a total for the test as a whole. In addition to comparing likelihood ratios to assess overall model fit, these ratios can be subjected to statistical testing. It is known that –2 times the log of a likelihood ratio can be distributed approximately as a χ^2 statistic. However, as Hambleton and Swaminathan (1985) noted, the ratio is distributed as a χ^2 statistic only asymptotically, that is, when sample sizes are very large and there are no sparse or empty cells.

The power of statistical tests increases as the number of observations increases. Thus, the more observations made, the greater the possibility of statistically rejecting a model because of inconsequential deviations from that model. As Lord and Novick (1968) explained,

> it can be taken for granted that every model is false and that we can prove it so, if only we collect a sufficiently large sample of data. The key question, then, is the practical utility of the model, not its ultimate truthfulness. (p. 383)

Thus, it is important to balance the results of statistical tests with descriptive measures of deviations between model predictions and observations.

7.5. Local Item Dependence

7.5.1. Measures of Local Item Dependence

Measures of LID are available for evaluating a particular IRT model for weak local item independence. Yen (1984a, 1993) described a statistic called Q_3, which evaluates the conditional correlation of item scores given model predictions based on ability estimates. For dichotomous items, $d_{ik} = x_{ik} - \hat{P}_i(\hat{\theta}_k)$ is defined as the deviation between the k-th examinee's observed score on the i-th item and the IRT model's prediction using the examinee's estimated θ based on overall test performance. The local dependence between items i and j is estimated using

$$Q_{3ij} = r_{d_i d_j}. \tag{59}$$

where $r_{d_i d_j}$ is the correlation between examinees' deviation scores on the two items.

Huynh, Michaels, and Ferrara (1995) found that a nonparametric procedure proposed by McDonald (1981) and Tucker, Humphreys, and Roznowski (1986) produced essentially the same results as Q_3; this nonparametric procedure involves the calculation of inter-item correlations for examinees at different ranges of total test raw scores. Chen and Thissen (1997) examined Q_3 (including an illuminating bivariate plot of d_{ik} values) and additional LID statistics and found that one statistic based on the likelihood ratio, G^2, and another based on Pearson's chi-square, χ^2, were the most promising. Within the Rasch family of models, Andrich (1985) proposed a likelihood ratio test for examining the hypothesis of item independence versus a model in which items in the same subtest (e.g., associated with the same stimulus) are locally dependent. Wilson (1988) examined local dependence by estimating and comparing item parameters across these same conditions.

As with other measures of model-data fit, it can be useful to practitioners to have available LID measures that do not tend to increase in value as sample size increases. When using such descriptive statistics, users can develop expectations for typical values of the statistic. For example, we have found that Q_3 values greater than 0.20 generally indicate LID worthy of attention.

7.5.2. Causes of LID and Procedures for Managing LID

There are a variety of possible causes of LID, such as those listed in Yen's (1993) compendium. These include: external assistance or interference with some items, speededness, fatigue, practice, special item formats, variation in response format (such as multiple-choice versus constructed-response), a shared stimulus or passage, item chaining, items requiring explanation of a previous answer, cloze items (in which examinees fill in multiple blanks in one passage), scoring rubrics or raters, unique content knowledge or abilities, and differential opportunity to learn. The basic principle involved in producing LID is the existence of an additional factor that consistently affects the performance of some students on some items to a greater extent than on other items.

Best practices for multiple-choice test construction have long emphasized the importance of building items that do not depend on one another. In recent years, greater attention has been paid to LID with the rise in popularity of performance assessments, and the understanding that "authentic" performance assessments intentionally have examinees produce item responses that are interconnected.

LID has been found to occur in a variety of multiple-choice and performance-based tests (Ferrara, Huynh, & Baghi, 1997; Ferrara, Huynh, & Michaels, 1999; Sireci et al., 1991; Thissen, Steinberg, & Mooney, 1989; Yen, 1984a, 1993). However, the magnitude of the LID is not always predictable. Logical analyses of item content tend to identify more item sets as being potentially locally dependent than are actually empirically locally dependent. For example, while LID has been found among items related to a common reading passage, the effect can be minimal (e.g., Yen, 1993). Other types of items (e.g., constructed-response items that require examinees to explain the reasoning behind their answers to a previous item) usually show very strong LID (Ferrara et al., 1999; Yen, 1993). Ferrara et al. (1997) and Ferrara et al. (1999) provide in-depth analyses of various types of contextual effects that produce LID in performance assessments. Further research is needed to establish which factors produce the most significant amounts of LID.

LID and its effects can be minimized by constructing tests with independent items, administering tests under appropriate conditions, modifying scoring rubrics, using statistics to identify LID items, and using testlets or item bundles in analyses (see section 2.6.2).

7.5.3. Practical Implications of LID

When positive LID occurs, it increases the strength of the relationship between some items and strengthens the relationship between the item score and the total test score, thus producing higher discriminations for LID items (Masters, 1988). If item banking is being used, and LID items are separated in subsequent test forms, the predicted item discriminations for those items can be inaccurately high.

LID can affect item response functions (i.e., through the item discrimination), but if a flexible IRT model is used (e.g., one that permits variation in item discriminations), fit measures that examine the match of model predictions to observed item response functions will not identify LID as a problem (Yen, 1984a). If items are locally dependent and their parameters are used to generate a TCC (which is the basis of tables relating raw scores to thetas or scale scores), the accuracy of the TCC is generally not adversely affected (Yen, 1993), nor are maximum likelihood ability estimates based on polytomous items for a particular class of IRT models (Junker, 1991). However, if items are calibrated in an LID context, and later separated and administered in a non-LID context, model predictions can be inaccurate.

In computer adaptive testing, items are chosen adaptively in order to provide the most efficient measurement. Typically, based on the most current estimate of the examinee's ability, the next item is chosen to provide maximum information about the examinee's true ability level. Decisions about item choice are dependent upon the assumption of item independence. For example, it is assumed that an item will have the same measurement characteristics regardless of which item it follows. Locally dependent items will not work in this setting. The possibility of LID in an adaptive testing situation is what motivated the development of testlets (Wainer & Kiely, 1987).

The greatest practical effect of LID appears to be over-predictions of test information and under-predictions of standard errors of test scores (Junker, 1991; Sireci et al., 1991; Thissen, Steinberg, & Mooney, 1989; Wainer & Thissen, 1996; Yen, 1993). For both classical test theory and IRT, predicted standard errors for test scores are based on the assumption of the conditional lack of correlation (or independence) of measurement errors for different items and the independent contribution of each item to the estimation of the true score or true theta. When LID occurs, these assumptions are violated. While the effect of this violation can be very large when estimating the amount of information that comes from particular pairs of LID items, if most item pairs in a test are not LID, the effect of the violation can be relatively minor on the overall test standard error of measurement (Yen, 1993). The prudent practitioner should evaluate the impact of any LID that is discovered on the particular application or model prediction.

7.6. Person Fit and Appropriateness Measures

In recent years, a considerable amount of research has focused on the development of statistical methods of assessing *person-fit,* also called *appropriateness measurement.* This research stems from interest in establishing the validity of examinees' scores. Examinees' item scores may be too high or too low because the examinees lack certain skills or test-taking strategies. Tatsouka (1990, 1996), for example, sought to identify misfitting examinees in order to explore the cognitive processes that underlie aberrant test behavior. Examinees might also misfit because they are guessing, cheating, or mismarking answer documents. Problems with test administration and/or scoring procedures also can produce aberrant patterns of item scores. The assessment of person fit involves identifying examinees whose patterns of item scores differ from the expected patterns. For example, this would occur when examinees are found to correctly answer difficult items but not easy items.

Many person-fit measures have been developed just for use with the Rasch model (e.g., Klauer, 1991; Liou, 1993; Liou & Chang, 1992; Molenaar & Hoijtink, 1990, 1996; Wright & Stone, 1979), although statistics usable with the 2PL and 3PL models are available as well. Most person-fit statistics have been developed for use with dichotomously scored items designed to measure a single trait, except in the case of Drasgow, Levine, and McLaughlin (1991), who developed a multi-test index designed to assess person-fit across tests that measured correlated traits. Nering (1997) as well as van Krimpen-Stoop and Meijer (1999), among others, have evaluated person-fit measures within the context of computer-adaptive testing, but most of the person-fit research has assumed that paper-and-pencil measures were used.

To date, most of the research on person-fit measures has been exploratory, with simulation studies used to ascertain the distributional properties of the statistics and the power of the measures to detect misfitting examinees. Excellent reviews of this research are provided by Meijer (1996), Meijer and Sijtsma (1995, 2001), and Reise and Flannery (1996). From their review, Meijer and Sijtsma (2001) concluded that detection rates for aberrant responses are affected by examinees' θ levels, by test length, as well as by the types of aberrant response pattern present in the data. Further work is needed to demonstrate the usefulness of person-fit in educational testing contexts.

7.7. Evaluation of Other Model Predictions or Features

There are a wide variety of useful predictions that can be made with IRT models, ranging from test equating, to predictions of conditional standard errors, to estimates of raw score statistics for particular samples of examinees. Rather than relying solely on statistical measures of model-data fit, it can be particularly informative to evaluate the use of a model by examining the accuracy of important predictions. For example, rather than debating whether a particular statistical test is sufficiently powerful for a particular model and testing situation, users can examine how close a predicted standard error is to an observed one, and the debate can focus on whether the amount of error in the prediction will affect users.

Equating accuracy (which can also be described as "item-free person measurement") is a model prediction that is often of special interest in educational applications. Following are some general conclusions about equating or linking tests with IRT.

When an item appears in different test forms, the more similar its surrounding context, the more stable the item's parameters will tend to be. Due to fatigue effects, it is common for items to be more difficult when placed at the end of a test than the beginning. The longer the test, the less likely that context effects that influence just a few items will seriously affect the equivalence of the total test score. The more similar the test forms being constructed (in terms of content coverage, range of item difficulty, and standard error functions) the better that IRT (and other equating methods) work, especially when evaluated over different populations of students.

One educational equating issue deserves special mention. IRT has made it easier to customize tests by selecting items for particular applications. However, if customization systematically changes the content emphasis of a test, it is likely that the equivalence of test scores will be negatively affected (Feuer, Holland, Green, Bertenthal, & Hemphill, 1999; Yen, Green, & Burket, 1987).

In terms of person-free item measurement, item parameter estimates are more likely to be stable for different groups of examinees when those examinees have similar test-relevant experiences. However, analyses of differential item functioning indicate that experts cannot necessarily judge via visual inspection which items will be more stable (See the chapter on test fairness by Camilli [this volume].)

This section provides examples of just a few educational applications and how the accuracy of the model predictions can be examined. The many studies that have examined particular IRT applications cannot be covered here, and the reader is referred to the IRT literature (See section 10.). The accuracy of important IRT model predictions should be examined if existing research does not provide a clear conclusion for a particular application of interest.

8. SURVEY OF EDUCATIONAL APPLICATIONS

IRT has been used to enhance the educational measurement process in a wide range of settings, including item generation, test construction, differential item functioning, computerized adaptive testing, scaling, equating, standard setting, and test scoring.

8.1. Item Generation

Researchers are using cognitive science and IRT to explore the possibilities of *automated item generation,* as described by Bejar (1993), Embretson (1999), and Irvine and Kyllonen (2002). In these procedures the salient cognitive factors affecting performance on a particular item are identified and described in an *item model.* Based on previously collected examinee data, a set of IRT parameters is established for items that are consistent with that item model, sometimes using *expected response functions* (Lewis, 1985; Mislevy, Wingersky, & Sheehan, 1994). Systematic application of the model generates new items whose psychometric characteristics are predicted to equal those for that item model. In some cases, this item generation is done "on the fly," during an online testing process (Bejar et al., 2003); in other cases it is done "off line" to generate items that will be used in a paper-and-pencil test or in a pool for computerized testing. The predictions of IRT parameters using these procedures can vary in accuracy. If a model is accurate, it provides excellent validity information, since the test developer can describe with great precision the dimensions being measured by the item.

If necessary, the model predictions can be augmented by student data on the new items. Alternatively this can be thought of as reducing the need for student data for field testing new items by providing priors for the item characteristics based on previous analyses of other items posing the same cognitive demands (Mislevy, Sheehan, & Wingersky, 1993).

Irvine and Kyllonen (2002) provide further discussion of practical applications of these methods. While continued research is needed in the area of item generation, this process has already proved that in some circumstances (where a large number of items of the same well-defined type are needed) it can be cost effective and useful.

8.2. Test Construction

Using IRT, a pool of items that measures a particular domain can be calibrated, producing parameters for all the items on the same scale. All items need not be administered to all examinees, but an appropriate linking design must be used (e.g., section 5.9). These parameters permit prediction and comparison of a wide variety of psychometric properties for items selected for particular tests. Procedures for interactive computer-assisted or automated test selection can be implemented. Early rudimentary procedures (e.g., Yen, 1983b) have been greatly expanded and enhanced over the years (for example, see van der Linden (1998) for a discussion of optimal test assembly).

In test construction, TCCs and standard error functions can be examined to determine if two test forms that are intended to be parallel in fact have matching conditional difficulties and standard errors. Similarly, if two test forms are intended to differ in difficulty, as is true for tests targeted to different grades in school, their TCCs and standard error functions can be compared relative to those intentions. If a test is to be used to help make a decision (such as a promotion, graduation, or admission decision), the standard error at the cut score can be evaluated to determine if it is adequate, and the effect on the standard error of adding or removing individual items can be readily calculated. These IRT capabilities have created the foundation for real-time interactive item selection on a large-scale basis.

In the interests of validity and fairness, it is important that items measure appropriate, comparable dimensions for all students, regardless of their backgrounds. IRT has greatly advanced the theoretical and practical procedures for examining DIF, and use of these procedures has become routine in educational assessment (see the chapter on test fairness by Camilli [this volume]). These procedures compare item performance across selected target groups (e.g., females versus males, English Language Learners (ELL) versus non-ELL students). Items with significant discrepancies are flagged for review of their content. The comparisons can be made in terms of item parameters or in terms of item performance; for the reasons discussed in sections 5.9.3 through 5.9.5, it is preferable to compare conditional item performance rather than item parameters. Problems related to estimating item parameters when a target subgroup is small can be avoided by estimating item parameters in a total sample and comparing predictions based on those parameters to subgroup performance (Linn & Harnisch, 1981).

Using IRT, a wide variety of useful statistics in the item raw score or test number-correct score metric can be estimated for any selected set of calibrated items for any hypothesized group of examinees. This includes: frequency distributions, means, and standard deviations, coefficient alpha, etc. For example, an estimated item p-value can be obtained from

$$\hat{p}_i = \int \hat{P}_i(\theta) g(\theta) d\theta. \tag{60}$$

These estimated statistics are very useful when predicting the test performance of examinees who have not taken a particular test.

8.3. Computerized Adaptive Test Administration

IRT has an important role in computerized adaptive testing (CAT). The flexibility of IRT is particularly valuable when items are chosen to match an examinee's ability level. In such testing an examinee's response to each item is considered in choosing the next item to be administered. Theoretically, adaptive testing is expected to require the administration of fewer items to achieve a particular level of score accuracy than are needed when intact tests are administered. However, practical experience garnered in the last 20 years has found that such testing does pose special challenges (see the chapter on technology and testing by Drasgow, Luecht, and Bennett, this volume).

8.4. Scaling

IRT is commonly used to produce scale scores for educational achievement tests, including vertical scales that run from early elementary grades to high school. Historically, almost all of the vertical scales used in educational measurement have been produced by test publishers, and two major publishers have used IRT procedures for decades to create vertical scales. (The 1PL model is used by Harcourt Educational Measurement, and the 3PL model is used by CTB/McGraw-Hill). Before IRT came to the fore, Thurstonian methods (which usually adopt the convention that ability is normally distributed) were commonly used to build vertical scales. The use of IRT has the advantage that it allows scaling that does not require this kind of assumption of normality.

It was controversial when some early educational achievement tests that were vertically scaled using the 3PL model produced scale scores that showed reduced variance as grade increased; this reduction in scale score variance was accompanied by a parallel reduction in IRT item difficulty variance and an increase in item discrimination. This phenomenon was labeled *scale shrinkage* (Lord, 1975a; Yen, 1985, 1986). Scale shrinkage did not occur for tests scaled using IRT software developed after the mid-1980s, and it has been attributed to JML estimation routines used in early software (Camilli, Yamamoto, & Wang, 1993). However, there have been many changes in achievement test batteries over those years beyond changes in software, and it is not possible to isolate a single factor that produced scale shrinkage (Yen & Burket, 1997). When Thurstonian and modern IRT methods have been applied to the same real or simulated tests, consistent, systematic differences in the scaling results have not been observed (Becker & Forsyth, 1992; Williams, Pommerich, & Thissen, 1998; Yen & Burket, 1997).

The ability scale (θ) that is produced by IRT models is determined up to a linear transformation (see section 2.8). When a model is shown to fit a set of data, it meets traditional criteria for being an equal interval scale (i.e., its predictions are not affected by a linear transformation of the scale and these predictions are falsifiable [i.e., the accuracy of the predictions can be evaluated]). However, IRT models, like other scaling models, are subject to the adoption of conventions, such as the use of the logistic function. The adoption of a different convention (such as the use of the $\omega(\theta)$ scale, described in section 2.8) would produce a different scale (Yen, 1986).

8.5. Test Equating and Linking

Linn (1993) and Mislevy (1993) provide a useful distinction between test equating and linking or calibrating, with the former producing more strict equivalence (see the chapter on linking and equating by Holland and Dorans, this volume). Most traditional equating procedures involve administration of intact tests to collect the needed data. IRT procedures are more flexible, because the item rather than the intact test is the unit of analysis. Once item calibration has been accomplished and items have been selected for a test, the IRT models describe how to score the tests to produce scores that are equivalent to some stated degree. For example, a short test form and a long test form can be designed to produce tau-equivalent scores (i.e., ability estimates that are expected to be equal for every true ability level but that have standard error functions that differ).

8.6. Standard Setting

Because IRT places items and students on the same scale, use of these models has become very popular in the process of setting performance standards (see the chapter on standard setting by Hambleton and Pitoniak, this volume). IRT lends itself to item mapping procedures in which items are presented to standard setting panelists in order of increasing difficulty. Panelists discuss item content as it relates to performance level descriptions for particular performance levels (i.e., descriptions of what students should know and be able to do to be described as Proficient). The panelists make judgments about the location in the ordered item booklet that reflects the least difficult item that a Proficient student should be expected to answer correctly. The IRT item location for that item is then translated into a cut-point on the IRT ability scale. Students who perform at or above that ability level receive Proficient scores.

8.7. Test Scoring and Interpretation

As described earlier, IRT provides a means for scoring and reporting tests in a variety of ways: combining dichotomous and polytomous items, using differential item weights, item-pattern or number-correct scoring, and using the ability scale or some monotonic transformation of that scale to report scores. IRT provides easy-to-calculate conditional standard error functions for any of these procedures and permits the user to determine the most accurate scoring procedure for a given test for the range of ability of interest.

It is not necessary that results from an IRT-scaled test be reported on the ability (θ) scale or a linear transformation of it. For example, the ability score can be transformed to an expected number-correct score for that test or for any set of items that have been calibrated on the same scale. Those benchmark items can help provide concrete meaning to a scale score (Bock, 1996, chapter 20). In another example, the content of test items can be displayed graphically along an IRT ability scale at the items' locations. By locating an examinee's score on that same scale, one can interpret the types of test content that the examinee is likely to know versus the type of content that the examinee is unlikely to know (e.g., Beaton & Allen, 1992; Connolly, Nachtman, & Pritchett, 1976).

IRT is particularly well suited to the scoring of matrix-sampled assessments, in which multiple test forms are created and administered to different students using complex sampling procedures. Matrix-sampled assessments optimize the breadth of the content information that can be obtained for groups of examinees. The National Assessment of Educational Progress (NAEP; see the chapter on monitoring educational progress by Mazzeo, Lazer, and Zieky [this volume]) is the most famous example of a matrix-sampled test, and it has been analyzed using the 3PL model. NAEP is also notable for the use of IRT in combination with advances in missing data technology and hierarchical analyses to estimate population characteristics without estimating individual examinee scores (Mislevy, Johnson, & Muraki, 1992). California used the 2PL model and matrix sampling for the California Assessment Program (Pandey & Carlson, 1983).

Thissen and Wainer (2001) explore an interesting variety of applications of IRT models to test scoring.

9. FUTURE DIRECTIONS

IRT and generalizability theory have developed along paths that have been independent for the most part. Recent work by Brennan (1998) and others has used generalizability theory (see the chapter on reliability by Haertel, this volume) to produce some of the types of predictions found with IRT, such as conditional standard errors of measurement for test raw scores. Bock et al. (2002) present procedures for adjusting IRT information and SE functions based on generalizability theory analyses of constructed-response item scores that are the result of multiple raters scoring student work. A fruitful area for future research is exploration of the connections among the assumptions and results for CTT, generalizability theory, and IRT (see the chapter by Brennan, this volume, and Brennan, 2004).

Future research is likely to expand exploration of existing applications. For example, further delineation of the circumstances that lead to accurate IRT equatings is merited. There are many variations of IRT procedures for equatings: different models, alignment procedures, sampling designs, selection of anchor items, identification of outliers, and procedures for dealing with rater effects. These variations can affect equating results. In many applications the variations in results are too small to be of consequence, but in other applications the variations can affect important decisions. Further research delineating the effects of alternative IRT equating procedures is warranted.

As computing power continues to expand, more complex models and more efficient procedures for estimating their parameters will develop. Interest in unified procedures for analysis is likely to motivate further expansion of models that incorporate a variety of dimensions or effects, such as rater effects, passage dependence, or possibly position effects. IRT procedures that promote computerized testing in general and formative assessment in particular are likely to receive additional attention. Dynamic IRT models in which assessment is integrated with learning and helps direct that learning in real time could be a great benefit to education.

In the interest of minimizing the time and expense associated with testing, practitioners today often want to do more with less, such as estimating item parameters with less data or estimating abilities with fewer items. The use of Bayesian procedures in IRT, as with extending automated item generation or estimation of subscores, is likely to continue and expand. Full advantage has not yet been taken of procedures for squeezing more information out of traditional testing processes. For example, Bock's nominal model (Bock, 1972) has been available for 30 years for scaling answer choices and scoring tests taking an examinee's answer choices into account. Now that computing power has made use of nominal models practicable, perhaps they will be used in operational testing programs.

IRT models have proven their versatility and usefulness. As they have in the past, researchers will turn to those models, and develop new ones, in response to practitioners' needs.

10. SOURCES FOR FURTHER INFORMATION

Embretson and Yang (in press) and Yen (1992) provide basic introductions to IRT with few equations. Hambleton's (1989) chapter on IRT in the third edition of *Educational Measurement* is an excellent survey, with extended attention to fit issues and applications. Hambleton et al. (1991) present a sound introduction to IRT in educational settings, while Hambleton and Swaminathan (1985) is a more advanced presentation requiring greater familiarity with statistical concepts. The book edited by van der Linden and Hambleton (1997) presents a collection of articles on a wide variety of IRT models.

Embretson and Reise (2000) and Hulin et al. (1983) center their attention on IRT applications in psychology, but these books can also be useful to educational researchers. Baker (1992) focuses on IRT estimation techniques, and Wainer (2000) addresses computerized adaptive testing. Wright and Stone (1979) offer a classic treatment of the theoretical advantages of the Rasch model. Fischer and Molenaar (1995) and Wilson (1992) provide interesting collections of articles describing a wide variety of Rasch models and their applications.

Lord (1980) presents an advanced, authoritative treatment of IRT principles and a model of how these principles can be applied to address important practical testing problems.

Professional journals that publish most of the original articles on IRT are *Applied Measurement in Education, Applied Psychological Measurement, Journal of Educational Measurement, Journal of Educational and Behavioral Statistics,* and *Psychometrika.*

NOTES

1. Some parameter estimation software (such as software based on marginal maximum likelihood, section 5.4) does assume a distributional form for abilities, but modern versions of such software are generally structured so that the distributional assumption has little effect on the estimates.

2. For the two-parameter normal ogive model (see section 2.2.4), when θ is distributed N(0,1), the item discrimination $a_i = \rho_i/\sqrt{1-\rho_i^2}$, where ρ_i is the biserial correlation between the item score and θ (Lord & Novick, 1968). See section 5.1 for more connections between classical and IRT statistics.

3. Note that the subscripting and the score level notation of the PC model differ from the nominal and 2PPC/GPC models. There are $M_i + 1$ score levels for the PC model and m_i score categories for the nominal and 2PPC/GPC models.

4. It is possible for one polytomous model to be expressed using different parameterizations. Thissen and Steinberg (1986) provide a conceptual basis for understanding these differences. When comparing results from different models, parameters must be transformed to the same parameterization in order to make legitimate comparisons.

5. These values are obtained by finding the θ that makes $P'_{ij}(\theta) = 0$; see Table 4.1.

6. Since item discrimination may vary with the number of score levels for an item, item fit will be important to evaluate when the PC model is applied to items having different numbers of score levels.

7. A 2PPC model applied to an item with two score levels produces results equivalent to those of the 2PL model, with $a_i = \alpha_i/1.7$ and $b_i = \delta_{i1}/\alpha_i$, or conversely, $\alpha_i = 1.7a_i$ and $\delta_{i1} = 1.7a_ib_i$.

8. In computer adaptive testing (see the chapter on technology and testing by Drasgow, Luecht, and Bennett, this volume), items are selected for administration during the testing process based on the items' statistical characteristics and the examinee's responses to previously administered items. Because an item's statistics can be affected by the context in which it is administered, previous estimates of the items' statistics may not be sufficiently accurate in an adaptive testing situation when there are substantial changes in context.

9. Note that with binary items, the covariance of item scores is $Cov(X_1, X_2) = P(X_1 = 1, X_2 = 1) - P(X_1 = 1)P(X_2 = 1)$, and items have zero covariance if and only if they are pair-wise independent. However, for polytomous items, while independence implies zero covariance, zero covariance does not necessarily guarantee independence.

10. An exception can be some non-parametric IRT models.

11. The lower asymptote c_i is a probability. Because it is not a variable expressed on the theta/item difficulty scale, is not changed or affected by changes in the scale.

12. For models that employ a guessing parameter (e.g., the 3PL model), there is no distinction made among the thetas (or scale scores) related to number-correct scores below the "guessing level" (i.e., $\leq \sum_{i=1}^{n} c_i$). For those models, all number-correct scores below the "guessing level" convert to the same scale score.

13. In most applications the score assigned to an item response equals $j - 1$ but in some cases it does not. For example, a user may decide to assign "half point" credit to some items. In these cases, the score actually assigned to each item response, rather than $j - 1$, is used in calculating the TCC.

14. Rosa, Swygert, Nelson, and Thissen (2001) present an intriguing method of scoring a mixed model test, based on a two-way scoring table with the summed score for the MC items along one axis and the summed score for CR items along the other dimension, and an IRT ability estimate as the table entry.

15. Following Birnbaum, the notation $I(\theta)$ is reserved for the information provided by a maximum likelihood estimate, which is the maximum information possible given a particular set of item scores. (As described in the text, different item scores can be obtained from a test, and they produce different information. Birnbaum did not discuss that distinction.) Birnbaum calls $I(\theta)$ the *test information,* which does not include reference to any particular test score function (i.e., weighted combination of the given item scores). The term *test information* can be contrasted with the term *test score information* (i.e., $I(X|\theta)$), which references a particular scoring function that may or may not be optimal.

16. The conditions are (a) the test raw score is expressed so that its expectation is not affected by n (such as by expressing the raw score in proportion-correct units rather than number-correct units), (b) $f(X)$ is a monotonic transformation of X not involving n, and (c) $\sigma^2(X|\theta)$ is of order $1/n$ and $E[(X - E(X))^3|\theta]$ is of order $n^{-3/2}$ (Lord, 1980, pp. 78-79).

17. Item parameter estimation for computer adaptive testing poses special challenges (see the chapter on technology and testing by Drasgow, Luecht, and Bennett, this volume).

18. Loglinear analysis (Kelderman, 1984) and some forms of latent class analysis (Lindsay, Clogg, & Grego, 1991) also can be used to obtain CML estimators.

19. MML programs such as BILOG offer the option of obtaining θ estimates in a separate step after the MML item parameter estimates are produced.

20. Because number-correct and item-pattern ability estimates for the 3PL model are tau-equivalent, aligning the number-correct-to-theta tables serves to align item-pattern theta estimates.

21. See Haebara (1980) for an approach to equating that involves minimizing the differences between characteristic curves at the item level.

22. In practice, anchor item parameters can be held fixed or a procedure such as one of those described in sections 5.9.2 to 5.9.5 can be used to align the anchor item values. These procedures have the common goal of maintaining constancy in anchor item parameters.

23. For example, if a test has selected-response and constructed-response items, and the anchor contains only selected-response items, only the selected-response items contribute to judgments about changes in abilities from Time 1 to Time 2.

24. In applications of item-pattern scoring in the early 1980s, some users were concerned that because item-pattern scoring "considers guessing" it would necessarily lower student scores. Those concerns were unfounded.

25. Note that if the prior distribution is a uniform distribution (i.e., the prior provides no information), then the Bayes modal estimator is identical to the MLE.

REFERENCES

Ackerman, T. A. (1989). Unidimensional IRT calibration of compensatory and noncompensatory multidimensional items. *Applied Psychological Measurement, 13*(2), 113–127.

Ackerman, T. A. (1992). A didactic explanation of item bias, item impact, and item validity from a multidimensional perspective. *Journal of Educational Measurement, 29*(1), 67–91.

Ackerman, T. A. (1994). Using multidimensional item response theory to understand what items and tests are measuring. *Applied Measurement in Education, 7*(4), 255–278.

Ackerman, T. A. (1996). Graphical representation of multidimensional item response theory analyses. *Applied Psychological Measurement, 20*(4), 311–329.

Ackerman, T. A., Gierl, M. J., & Walker, C. M. (2003). Using multidimensional item response theory to evaluate educational and psychological tests. *Educational Measurement: Issues and Practice, 22*(1), 37–53.

Adams, R. J., & Wilson, M. (1996). Formulating the Rasch model as a mixed coefficients multinomial logit. In G. Englehard & M. Wilson (Eds.), *Objective measurement: Theory into practice* (pp. 143–166). Norwood, NJ: Ablex Publishing.

Adams, R. J., Wilson, M., & Wang, W. C. (1997). The multidimensional random coefficients multinomial logit model. *Applied Psychological Measurement, 21*(1), 1–23.

Adams, R. J., Wilson, M., & Wu, M. L. (1997). Multilevel item response models: An approach to errors in variables regression. *Journal of Educational and Behavioral Statistics, 22*(1), 47–76.

Albert, J. H. (1992). Bayesian estimation of normal ogive item response curves using Gibbs sampling. *Journal of Educational Statistics, 17*(3), 251–269.

Allen, N. L., & Yen, W. M. (1979). *Introduction to measurement theory.* Monterey, CA: Brooks/Cole.

Andersen, E. B. (1972). The numerical solution of a set of conditional estimation equations. *Journal of Royal Statistical Society, Series B-34,* 42–54.

Andersen, E. B. (1995). Polytomous Rasch models and their estimation. In G. H. Fischer & I. W. Molenaar (Eds.), *Rasch models: Foundations, recent developments and applications* (pp. 271–290). New York: Springer-Verlag.

Andrich, D. (1978). A rating formulation for ordered response categories. *Psychometrika, 43*(4), 561–573.

Andrich, D. (1985). *A latent-trait model for items with response dependencies: Implications for test construction and analysis.* Orlando, FL: Academic Press.

Andrich, D., Sheridan, B., & Luo, G. (1990–2001). RUMM: Rasch unidimensional measurement model [Computer software]. Perth, Australia: RUMM Laboratory.

Ansley, T. N., & Forsyth, R. A. (1985). An examination of the characteristics of unidimensional IRT parameter estimates derived from two-dimensional data. *Applied Psychological Measurement, 9*(1), 37–48.

Baker, F. B. (1987). Methodology review: Item parameter estimation under the one-, two-, and three-parameter logistic models. *Applied Psychological Measurement, 11*(2), 111–141.

Baker, F. B. (1990). Some observations on the metric of PC-BILOG results. *Applied Psychological Measurement, 14*(2), 139–150.

Baker, F. B. (1992). *Item response theory: Parameter estimation techniques.* New York: Marcel Dekker.

Baker, F. B. (1998). An investigation of the item parameter recovery characteristics of a Gibbs sampling procedure. *Applied Psychological Measurement, 22*(2), 153–169.

Beaton, A. E., & Allen, N. L. (1992). Interpreting scales through scale anchoring. *Journal of Educational Statistics, 17*(2), 191–204.

Becker, D. F., & Forsyth, R. A. (1992). An empirical investigation of Thurstone and IRT methods of scaling achievement tests. *Journal of Educational Measurement, 29*(4), 341–354.

Bejar, I. (1993). A generative approach to psychological and educational measurement. In N. Frederiksen, R. J. Mislevy, & I. I. Bejar (Eds.), *Test theory for a new generation* (pp. 323–357). Hillsdale, NJ: Erlbaum.

Bejar, I., Lawless, R. R., Morley, M. E., Wagner, M. E., Bennett, R. E., & Revuelta, R. (2003). A feasibility study of on-the-fly item generation in adaptive testing. *The Journal of Technology, Learning, and Assessment, 2*(3), 1–27.

Birnbaum, A. (1968). Some latent trait models and their use in inferring an examinee's ability. In F. M. Lord & M. R. Novick (Eds.), *Statistical theories of mental test scores.* Reading, MA: Addison-Wesley.

Bock, R. D. (1972). Estimating item parameters and latent ability when responses are scored in two or more nominal categories. *Psychometrika, 37*(1), 29–51.

Bock, R. D. (1996). *Domain-referenced reporting in large-scale educational assessments.* Commissioned paper to the National Academy of Education for the Capstone Report of the NAE Technical Review Panel on State/NAEP Assessment.

Bock, R. D., & Aitkin, M. (1981). Marginal maximum likelihood estimation of item parameters: Application of an EM algorithm. *Psychometrika, 46*(4), 443–459.

Bock, R. D., Brennan, R. L., & Muraki, E. (2002). The information in multiple ratings. *Applied Psychological Measurement, 26*(4), 364–375.

Bock, R. D., Gibbons, R., & Muraki, E. (1988). Full-information item factor analysis. *Applied Psychological Measurement, 12*(3), 261–280.

Bock, R. D., & Mislevy, R. J. (1981). An item response curve model for matrix-sampling data: The California grade-three assessment. In D. Carlson (Ed.), *New Directions for Testing and Measurement: Testing in the States* (pp. 65–90). San Francisco: Jossey-Bass.

Bock, R. D., & Mislevy, R. J. (1988). Comprehensive educational assessment for the states: The Duplex design. *Educational Evaluation and Policy Analysis, 10*(2), 89–105.

Bollen, K. A. (1989). *Structural equations with latent variables.* New York: John Wiley & Sons.

Bolt, D. M., Cohen, A. S., & Wollack, J. A. (2001). A mixture item response model for multiple-choice data. *Journal of Educational and Behavioral Statistics, 26*(4), 381–409.

Bolt, D. M., & Lall, V. F. (2003). Estimation of compensatory and noncompensatory multidimensional item response models using Markov Chain Monte Carlo. *Applied Psychological Measurement, 27*(6), 395–414.

Boomsma, A., van Duijn, M. A. J., & Snijders, T. A. B. (Eds.). (2001). *Essays on item response theory.* New York: Springer-Verlag.

Bradlow, E. T., Wainer, H., & Wang, M. M. (1999). A Bayesian random effects model for testlets. *Psychometrika, 64*(2), 153–168.

Brennan, R. L. (1998). Misconceptions at the intersection of measurement theory and practice. *Educational Measurement: Issues and Practice, 17*(1), 5–9, 30.

Brennan, R. L. (2004). *Some perspectives on inconsistencies among measurement models* (CASMA Research Report No. 8). Iowa City, IA: Center for Advanced Studies in Measurement and Assessment, The University of Iowa. (Available from www.uiowa.edu/~casma)

Burket, G. R. (1991). PARDUX [Computer software]. Monterey, CA: CTB/McGraw-Hill.

Camilli, G., Yamamoto, K., & Wang, M. M. (1993). Scale shrinkage in vertical equating. *Applied Psychological Measurement, 17*(4), 379–388.

Chen, W.-H., & Thissen, D. (1997). Local dependence indexes for item pairs using item response theory. *Journal of Educational and Behavioral Statistics, 22*(3), 265–289.

Connolly, A., Nachtman, W., & Pritchett, M. (1976). *KeyMath diagnostic arithmetic test.* Circle Pines, MN: American Guidance Service.

CTB Macmillan/McGraw-Hill. (1992). *Final technical report: Maryland School Performance Assessment Program.* Monterey, CA: Author.

De Ayala, R. J., & Hertzog, M. A. (1991). The assessment of dimensionality for use in item response theory. *Multivariate Behavioral Research, 26*(4), 765–792.

De Ayala, R. J., & Sava-Bolesta, M. (1999). Item parameter recovery for the nominal response model. *Applied Psychological Measurement, 23*(1), 3–19.

de Gruijter, D. N. M. (1994). Comparison of the nonparametric Mokken model and parametric IRT models using latent class analysis. *Applied Psychological Measurement, 18*(1), 27–34.

de Koning, E., Sijtsma, K., & Hamers, J. H. M. (2002). Comparison of four IRT models when analyzing two tests for inductive reasoning. *Applied Psychological Measurement, 26*(3), 302–320.

Divgi, D. R. (1986). Does the Rasch model really work for multiple choice items? Not if you look closely. *Journal of Educational Measurement, 23*(4), 283–298.

Drasgow, F. (1989). An evaluation of marginal maximum likelihood estimation for the two-parameter logistic model. *Applied Psychological Measurement, 13*(1), 77–90.

Drasgow, F., Levine, M. V., & McLaughlin, M. E. (1991). Appropriateness measurement for some multidimensional test batteries. *Applied Psychological Measurement, 15*(2), 171–191.

du Toit, M. (Ed.). (2003). *IRT from SSI.* Lincolnwood, IL: Scientific Software International.

Embretson, S. E. (1984). A general multicomponent latent trait model for response processes. *Psychometrika, 49*(2), 175–186.

Embretson, S. E. (1991). A multidimensional latent trait model for measuring learning and change. *Psychometrika, 56*(3), 495–515.

Embretson, S. E. (1995). A measurement model for linking individual learning to processes and knowledge: Application to mathematical reasoning. *Journal of Educational Measurement, 32*(3), 277–294.

Embretson, S. E. (1999). Generating items during testing: Psychometric issues and models. *Psychometrika, 64*(4), 407–433.

Embretson, S. E., & Reise, S. P. (2000). *Item response theory for psychologists.* Mahwah, NJ: Lawrence Erlbaum.

Embretson, S. E., Schneider, L. M., & Roth, D. (1986). Multiple processing strategies and the construct validity of verbal reasoning tests. *Journal of Educational Measurement, 23*(1), 13–32.

Embretson, S. E., & Wetzel, C. D. (1987). Component latent trait models for paragraph comprehension tests. *Applied Psychological Measurement, 11*(2), 175–193.

Embretson, S. E., & Yang, X. (in press). Item response theory. In G. Camilli, P. Elmore, & J. Green (Eds.), *Complementary research methods in education* (3rd ed.). Washington, DC: American Educational Research Association.

Engelhard, G. J. (1994). Examining rater errors in the assessment of written composition with a many-faceted Rasch model. *Journal of Educational Measurement, 31*(2), 93–112.

Engelhard, G. J. (1996). Evaluating rater accuracy in performance assessments. *Journal of Educational Measurement, 33*(1), 56–70.

Featherman, C. M. (1997). BIGSTEPS Rasch model computer program-Version 2.67. *Applied Psychological Measurement, 21*(3), 279–284.

Ferrara, S., Huynh, H., & Baghi, H. (1997). Contextual characteristics of locally dependent open-ended item clusters in a large-scale performance assessment. *Applied Measurement in Education, 10*(2), 123–144.

Ferrara, S., Huynh, H., & Michaels, H. (1999). Contextual explanations of local dependence in item clusters in a large scale hands-on science performance assessment. *Journal of Educational Measurement, 36*(2), 119–140.

Feuer, M. J., Holland, P. W., Green, B. F., Bertenthal, M. W., & Hemphill, F. C. (Eds.). (1999). *Uncommon measures: Equivalence and linkage among educational tests.* Washington, DC: National Academy Press.

Fischer, G. H. (1973). The linear logistic test model as an instrument in educational research. *Acta Psychologica, 37*(6), 359–374.

Fischer, G. H. (1983). Logistic latent trait models with linear constraints. *Psychometrika, 48*(1), 3–26.

Fischer, G. H. (1987). Applying the principles of specific objectivity and generalizability to the measurement of change. *Psychometrika, 52*(4), 565–587.

Fischer, G. H. (1989). An IRT-based model for dichotomous longitudinal data. *Psychometrika, 54*(4), 599–624.

Fischer, G. H. (1997). Unidimensional linear logistic Rasch models. In W. J. van der Linden & R. K. Hambleton (Eds.), *Handbook of modern item response theory* (pp. 225–243). New York: Springer-Verlag.

Fischer, G. H., & Molenaar, I. W. (Eds.). (1995). *Rasch models: Foundations, recent developments and applications.* New York: Springer-Verlag.

Fischer, G. H., & Parzer, P. (1991). An extension of the rating scale model with an application to the measurement of treatment effects. *Psychometrika, 56*(4), 637–651.

Fischer, G. H., & Ponocny, I. (1994). An extension of the partial credit model with an application to the measurement of change. *Psychometrika, 59*(2), 177–192.

Fischer, G. H., & Tanzer, N. (1994). Some LBTL and LLTM relationships. In G. H. Fischer & D. Laming (Eds.), *Contributions to mathematical psychology, psychometrics, and methodology* (pp. 277–303). New York: Springer-Verlag.

Fitzpatrick, A. R., Ercikan, K., Yen, W. M., & Ferrara, S. (1998). The consistency between raters scoring in different test years. *Applied Measurement in Education, 11*(2), 195–208.

Fitzpatrick, A. R., Link, V. B., Yen, W. M., Burket, G. R., Ito, K., & Sykes, R. C. (1996). Scaling performance assessments: A comparison of one-parameter and two-parameter partial credit models. *Journal of Educational Measurement, 33*(3), 291–314.

Folk, V. G., & Green, B. F. (1989). Adaptive estimation when the unidimensionality assumption of IRT is violated. *Applied Psychological Measurement, 13*(4), 373–389.

Fraser, C. (1988). NOHARM: An IBM PC computer program for fitting both unidimensional and multidimensional normal ogive models of latent trait theory [Computer software]. Armidale, Australia: The University of New England.

Fraser, C., & McDonald, R. P. (1988). NOHARM: Least squares item factor analysis. *Multivariate Behavioral Research, 23,* 267–269.

Gessaroli, M. E., & De Champlain, A. F. (1996). Using an approximate chi-square statistic to test the number of dimensions underlying the responses to a set of items. *Journal of Educational Measurement, 33*(2), 157–179.

Glas, C. A. W., & Falcon, J. C. S. (2003). A comparison of item-fit statistics for the three parameter logistic model. *Applied Psychological Measurement, 27*(2), 87–106.

Glas, C. A. W., & Verhelst, N. D. (1989). Extensions of the partial credit model. *Psychometrika, 54*(4), 635–659.

Green, D. R., & Yen, W. M. (April 1983). *Number-correct versus pattern scoring: Results for ethnic groups.* Paper presented at the annual meeting of the National Council on Measurement in Education, Montreal, Canada.

Gustafsson, J. E. (1980). Testing and obtaining fit of data to the Rasch model. *British Journal of Mathematical and Statistical Psychology, 33*(2), 205–233.

Habing, B., & Roussos, L. (2003). On the need for negative local item dependence. *Psychometrika, 68*(3), 435–451.

Haebara, T. (1980). Equating logistic ability scales by a weighted least squares. *Japanese Psychological Research, 22,* 144–149.

Hambleton, R. K. (1989). Principles and selected applications of item response theory. In R. L. Linn (Ed.), *Educational measurement* (3rd ed., pp. 147–200). Washington, DC: American Council on Education and Macmillan.

Hambleton, R. K., & Rovinelli, R. J. (1986). Assessing the dimensionality of a set of test items. *Applied Psychological Measurement, 10*(3), 287–302.

Hambleton, R. K., & Swaminathan, H. (1985). *Item response theory: Principles and applications.* Boston: Kluwer-Nijhoff Publishing.

Hambleton, R. K., Swaminathan, H., & Rogers, H. J. (1991). *Fundamentals of item response theory.* Newbury Park, CA: Sage.

Hanson, B. A., & Beguin, A. A. (April 1999). *Obtaining a common scale for IRT item parameters using separate versus concurrent estimation in the common item nonequivalent groups equating design.* Paper presented at the annual meeting of the National Council on Measurement in Education, Montreal, Canada.

Harwell, M., & Janosky, J. E. (1991). An empirical study of the effects of small data sets and varying prior variances on item parameter estimation in BILOG. *Applied Psychological Measurement, 15*(3), 279–291.

Hattie, J. (1984). Decision criteria for assessing unidimensionality. *Multivariate Behavioral Research, 19,* 49–78.

Hattie, J. (1985). Methodology review: Assessing unidimensionality of tests and items. *Applied Psychological Measurement, 9*(2), 139–164.

Hattie, J., Krakowski, K., Rogers, J. H., & Swaminathan, H. (1996). An assessment of Stout's index of essential unidimensionality. *Applied Psychological Measurement, 20*(1), 1–14.

Henning, G. (1989). Does the Rasch model really work for multiple-choice items? Take another look: A response to Divgi. *Journal of Educational Measurement, 26*(1), 91–97.

Hirsch, T. M. (1989). Multidimensional equating. *Journal of Educational Measurement, 26*(4), 337–349.

Holland, P. W., & Rosenbaum, P. R. (1986). Conditional association and unidimensionality in monotone latent variable models. *The Annals of Statistics, 14*(4), 1523–1543.

Hoskens, M., & De Boeck, P. (1997). A parametric model for local dependence among test items. *Psychological Methods, 2*(3), 261–277.

Hulin, C. L., Drasgow, F., & Parsons, C. K. (1983). *Item response theory: Application to psychological measurement.* Homewood, IL: Dow Jones-Irwin.

Hulin, C. L., Lissak, R. I., & Drasgow, F. (1982). Recovery of two- and three-parameter logistic item characteristic curves: A Monte Carlo study. *Applied Psychological Measurement, 6*(3), 249–260.

Huynh, H., Michaels, H., & Ferrara, S. (April 1995). *Statistical procedures to identify clusters of items with local dependency.* Paper presented at the National Council on Measurement in Education, San Francisco.

Irvine, S. H., & Kyllonen, P. C. (Eds.). (2002). *Item generation for test development.* Mahwah, NJ: Lawrence Erlbaum.

Jannarone, R. J. (1997). Models for locally dependent responses: Conjuctive item response theory. In W. J. van der Linden & R. K. Hambleton (Eds.), *Handbook of modern item response theory* (pp. 465–479). New York: Springer.

Junker, B. W. (1991). Essential independence and likelihood-based ability estimation for polytomous items. *Psychometrika, 56*(2), 255–278.

Kaplan, D. (2000). *Structural equation modeling: Foundations and extensions.* Thousand Oaks, CA: Sage.

Kelderman, H. (1984). Loglinear Rasch model tests. *Psychometrika, 49*(2), 223–245.

Kelderman, H. (1996). Multidimensional Rasch models for partial-credit scoring. *Applied Psychological Measurement, 20*(2), 155–168.

Kelderman, H., & Rijkes, C. P. M. (1994). Loglinear multidimensional IRT models for polytomously scored items. *Psychometrika, 59*(2), 149–176.

Kim, S. H. (1997). BILOG 3 for Windows: Item analysis and test scoring with binary logistic models. *Applied Psychological Measurement, 21*(4), 371–376.

Kim, S. H. (2001). An evaluation of a Markov Chain Monte Carlo method for the Rasch model. *Applied Psychological Measurement, 25*(2), 163–176.

Kingston, N., & Dorans, N. (1985). The analysis of item-ability regressions: An exploratory IRT model fit tool. *Applied Psychological Measurement, 9*(3), 281–288.

Klauer, K. C. (1991). An exact and optimal standardized person test for assessing consistency with the Rasch model. *Psychometrika, 56*(2), 213–228.

Kolen, M. J. (1981). Comparison of traditional and item response theory methods for equating tests. *Journal of Educational Measurement, 18*(1), 1–11.

Kolen, M. J., & Brennan, R. L. (1995). *Test equating: Methods and practices.* New York: Springer-Verlag.

Lewis, C. (November 1985). *Estimating individual abilities with imperfectly known item response functions.* Paper presented at the annual meeting of the Psychometric Society, Nashville, TN.

Li, Y. H., & Lissitz, R. W. (2000). An evaluation of the accuracy of multidimensional IRT linking. *Applied Psychological Measurement, 24*(2), 115–138.

Lim, R. G., & Drasgow, F. (1990). Evaluation of two methods for estimating item response theory parameters when assessing differential item functioning. *Journal of Applied Psychology, 75,* 164–174.

Linacre, J. M. (1991–1996). BIGSTEPS: Rasch model computer program-Version 2.67 [Computer software]. Chicago: MESA Press.

Linacre, J. M. (1991–2003). *A user's guide to FACETS Rasch-model computer programs.* Chicago: John Linacre.

Linacre, J. M., & Wright, B. D. (1991–2000). *A user's guide to WINSTEPS.* Chicago: MESA Press.

Lindsay, B., Clogg, C. C., & Grego, J. M. (1991). Semiparametric estimation in the Rasch model and related exponential models, including a simple latent class model for item analysis. *Journal of the American Statistical Association, 86,* 96–107.

Linn, R. L. (1993). Linking results of distinct assessments. *Applied Measurement in Education, 6*(1), 83–102.

Linn, R. L., & Harnisch, D. (1981). Interactions between item content and group membership on achievement test items. *Journal of Educational Measurement, 18*(2), 109–118.

Liou, M. (1993). Exact person tests for assessing model-data fit in the Rasch model. *Applied Psychological Measurement, 17*(2), 187–195.

Liou, M., & Chang, C. (1992). Constructing the exact significance level for a person fit statistic. *Psychometrika, 57*(2), 169–181.

Lord, F. M. (1975a). The "ability" scale in item characteristic curve theory. *Psychometrika, 40*(2), 205–217.

Lord, F. M. (1975b). *Evaluation with artificial data of a procedure for estimating ability and item characteristic curve parameters.* Princeton, NJ: Educational Testing Service.

Lord, F. M. (1980). *Applications of item response theory to practical testing problems.* Hillsdale, NJ: Lawrence Erlbaum.

Lord, F. M. (1983). Statistical bias in maximum likelihood estimators of item parameters. *Psychometrika, 48*(3), 425–435.

Lord, F. M. (1986). Maximum likelihood and Bayesian parameter estimation in item response theory. *Journal of Educational Measurement, 23*(2), 157–162.

Lord, F. M., & Novick, M. R. (1968). *Statistical theories of mental test scores.* Reading, MA: Addison-Wesley.

Ludlow, L. H. (1986). Graphical analysis of item response theory residuals. *Applied Psychological Measurement, 10*(3), 217–229.

Luecht, R. M., & Miller, T. R. (1992). Unidimensional calibrations and interpretations of composite traits for multidimensional tests. *Applied Psychological Measurement, 16*(3), 279–293.

Lunz, M. E., Wright, B., & Linacre, J. M. (1991). Measuring the impact of judge severity on examination scores. *Applied Measurement in Education, 3*(4), 331–345.

Maier, K. S. (2001). A Rasch hierarchical measurement model. *Journal of Educational and Behavioral Statistics, 26*(3), 307–330.

Masters, G. N. (1982). A Rasch model for partial credit scoring. *Psychometrika, 47*(2), 149–174.

Masters, G. N. (1988). Item discrimination: When more is worse. *Journal of Educational Measurement, 25*(1), 15–29.

Masters, G. N., & Wright, B. (1984). The essential process in a family of measurement models. *Psychometrika, 49*(4), 529–544.

MathSoft. (1995). S-PLUS-Version 3.3 for Windows [Computer software]. Seattle, WA: Author.

McDonald, R. P. (1979). The structural analysis of multivariate data: A sketch of general theory. *Multivariate Behavioral Research, 14,* 21–38.

McDonald, R. P. (1981). The dimensionality of tests and items. *British Journal of Mathematical and Statistical Psychology, 34,* 100–117.

McDonald, R. P. (1982). Linear versus nonlinear models in item response theory. *Applied Psychological Measurement, 6*(4), 379–396.

McDonald, R. P. (1997). Normal-ogive multidimensional model. In W. J. van der Linden & R. K. Hambleton (Eds.), *Handbook of modern item response theory* (pp. 258–269). New York: Springer Verlag.

McKinley, L. R., & Mills, C. N. (1985). A comparison of several goodness-of-fit statistics. *Applied Psychological Measurement, 9*(1), 49–57.

Meijer, R. R. (1996). Person-fit research: An introduction. *Applied Measurement in Education, 9*(1), 3–8.

Meijer, R. R., & Sijtsma, K. (1995). Detection of aberrant item score patterns: A review of recent developments. *Applied Measurement in Education, 8*(3), 261–272.

Meijer, R. R., & Sijtsma, K. (2001). Methodology review: Evaluating person fit. *Applied Psychological Measurement, 25*(2), 107–135.

Meijer, R. R., Sijtsma, K., Smid, N. G., & Eindhoven, P. (1990). Theoretical and empirical comparison of the Mokken and the Rasch approach to IRT. *Applied Psychological Measurement, 14*(3), 283–298.

Min, K.-S. (2003). *The impact of scale dilation on the quality of the linking of multidimensional item response theory calibrations.* Unpublished doctoral dissertation, Michigan State University, East Lansing.

Mislevy, R. J. (1983). Item response models for grouped data. *Journal of Educational Statistics, 8*(4), 271–288.

Mislevy, R. J. (1984). Estimating latent distributions. *Psychometrika, 49*(3), 359–381.

Mislevy, R. J. (1986). Bayes modal estimation in item response models. *Psychometrika, 51*(2), 177–195.

Mislevy, R. J. (1988). Exploiting auxiliary information about items in the estimation of Rasch item difficulty parameters. *Applied Psychological Measurement, 12*(3), 281–296.

Mislevy, R. J. (1993). *Linking educational assessments: Concepts, issues, methods, and prospects.* Princeton, NJ: Policy Information Center, Educational Testing Service. (ERIC # ED-353–302).

Mislevy, R. J., & Bock, R. D. (1984). BILOG Version 2.2-Item analysis and test scoring with binary logistic models [Computer software]. Mooresville, IN: Scientific software.

Mislevy, R. J., & Bock, R. D. (1989). A hierarchical item-response model for educational testing. In R. D. Bock (Ed.), *Multilevel analysis for educational data* (pp. 57–74). San Diego, CA: Academic.

Mislevy, R. J., & Bock, R. D. (1990). PC-BILOG-Item analysis and test scoring with binary logistic models [Computer software]. Mooresville, IN: Scientific Software.

Mislevy, R. J., Johnson, E. G., & Muraki, E. (1992). Scaling procedures in NAEP. *Journal of Educational Statistics, 17*(2), 131–154.

Mislevy, R. J., Sheehan, K., & Wingersky, M. S. (1993). How to equate tests with little or no data. *Journal of Educational Measurement, 30*(1), 55–78.

Mislevy, R. J., & Stocking, M. L. (1989). A consumer's guide to LOGIST and BILOG. *Applied Psychological Measurement, 13*(1), 57–75.

Mislevy, R. J., & Verhelst, N. D. (1990). Modeling item responses when different subjects employ different solution strategies. *Psychometrika, 55*(2), 195–215.

Mislevy, R. J., Wingersky, M. S., & Sheehan, K. (1994). *Dealing with uncertainty about item parameters: Expected response functions* (Research Report RR-94-28-ONR). Princeton, NJ: Educational Testing Service.

Mokken, R. J. (1971). *A theory and procedure of scale analysis with applications in political research.* Berlin, Germany: de Gruyter.

Mokken, R. J. (1997). Nonparametric models for dichotomous responses. In W. J. van der Linden & R. K. Hambleton (Eds.), *Handbook of modern item response theory* (pp. 351–367). New York: Springer-Verlag.

Mokken, R. J., & Lewis, C. (1982). A nonparametric approach to the analysis of dichotomous item responses. *Applied Psychological Measurement, 6*(4), 417–430.

Molenaar, I. W. (1997). Non-parametric models for polytomous responses. In W. J. van der Linden & R. K. Hambleton (Eds.), *Handbook of modern item response theory* (pp. 369–380). New York: Springer.

Molenaar, I. W., & Hoijtink, H. (1990). The many null distributions of person fit indices. *Psychometrika, 55*(1), 75–106.

Molenaar, I. W., & Hoijtink, H. (1996). Person-fit and the Rasch model, with an application to knowledge of logical quantors. *Applied Measurement in Education, 9*(1), 27–45.

Muraki, E. (1992). A generalized partial credit model: Application of an EM algorithm. *Applied Psychological Measurement, 16*(2), 159–176.

Muraki, E., & Bock, R. D. (1993). PARSCALE: IRT-based test scoring and item analysis for graded open-ended exercises and performance tasks [Computer software]. Chicago: Scientific Software International.

Muraki, E., & Bock, R. D. (1997). PARSCALE 3: IRT-based test scoring and item analysis for graded items and rating scales [Computer software]. Chicago: Scientific Software International.

Nandakumar, R. (1991). Traditional dimensionality versus essential dimensionality. *Journal of Educational Measurement, 28*(2), 99–117.

Nandakumar, R. (1994). Assessing dimensionality of a set of item responses—Comparison of different approaches. *Journal of Educational Measurement, 31*(1), 17–35.

Nandakumar, R., & Stout, W. (1993). Refinements of Stout's procedure for assessing latent trait unidimensionality. *Journal of Educational Statistics, 18*(1), 41–68.

Nandakumar, R., & Yu, F. (1996). Empirical validation of DIMTEST on nonnormal ability distributions. *Journal of Educational Measurement, 33*(3), 355–368.

Nandakumar, R., Yu, F., Li, H. H., & Stout, W. (1998). Validation of Poly-DIMTEST to assess unidimensionality of polytomous data. *Applied Psychological Measurement, 22*(2), 99–115.

Nering, M. L. (1997). The distribution of indexes of person fit within the computerized adaptive testing environment. *Applied Psychological Measurement, 21,* 115–127.

Orlando, M., & Thissen, D. (2000). Likelihood-based item-fit indices for dichotomous item response theory models. *Applied Psychological Measurement, 24*(1), 50–64.

Orlando, M., & Thissen, D. (2003). Further investigation of the performance of s_x^2: An item fit index for use with dichotomous item response theory models. *Applied Psychological Measurement, 27*(4), 289–298.

Oshima, T. C., Davey, T. C., & Lee, K. (2000). Multidimensional linking: Four practical approaches. *Journal of Educational Measurement, 37*(4), 357–373.

Pandey, T., & Carlson, D. (1983). Application of item response models to reporting assessment data. In R. K. Hambleton (Ed.), *Applications of item response theory* (pp. 212–219). Vancouver: Educational Research Institute of British Columbia.

Patz, R. J., & Junker, B. W. (1999a). Applications and extensions of MCMC in IRT: Multiple item types, missing data, and rated responses. *Journal of Educational and Behavioral Statistics, 24*(4), 342–366.

Patz, R. J., & Junker, B. W. (1999b). A straightforward approach to Markov Chain Monte Carlo methods for item response models. *Journal of Educational and Behavioral Statistics, 24*(2), 146–178.

Patz, R. J., Junker, B. W., Johnson, M. S., & Mariano, L. T. (2002). The hierarchical rater model for rated test items and its application to large-scale educational assessment data. *Journal of Educational and Behavioral Statistics, 27*(4), 341–384.

Peterson, N. S., Kolen, M. J., & Hoover, H. D. (1989). Scaling, norming, and equating. In R. L. Linn (Ed.), *Educational measurement* (3rd ed., pp. 221–262). New York: Macmillan.

Rasch, G. (1960). *Probabilistic models for some intelligence and attainment tests.* Chicago: University of Chicago Press.

Reckase, M. D. (1985). The difficulty of test items that measure more than one ability. *Applied Psychological Measurement, 9*(4), 401–412.

Reckase, M. D. (1997a). A linear logistic multidimensional model for dichotomous item response data. In W. J. van der Linden & R. K. Hambleton (Eds.), *Handbook of modern item response theory* (pp. 271–286). New York: Springer-Verlag.

Reckase, M. D. (1997b). The past and future of multidimensional item response theory. *Applied Psychological Measurement, 21*(1), 25–36.

Reckase, M. D., & McKinley, R. L. (1991). The discriminating power of items that measure more than one dimension. *Applied Psychological Measurement, 15*(4), 361–373.

Reise, S. P. (1990). A comparison of item- and person-fit methods of assessing model-data fit in IRT. *Applied Psychological Measurement, 14*(2), 127–137.

Reise, S. P., & Flannery, W. P. (1996). Assessing person-fit on measures of typical performance. *Applied Measurement in Education, 9*(1), 9–26.

Reise, S. P., & Yu, J. (1990). Parameter recovery in the graded response model using MULTILOG. *Journal of Educational Measurement, 27*(2), 133–144.

Rosa, K., Swygert, K. A., Nelson, L., & Thissen, D. (2001). Item response theory applied to combinations of multiple-choice and constructed-response items—Scale scores for patterns of summed scores. In D. Thissen & H. Wainer (Eds.), *Test scoring* (pp. 253–292). Mahwah, NJ: Lawrence Erlbaum.

Rosenbaum, P. R. (1984). Testing the conditional independence and monotonicity assumptions of item response theory. *Psychometrika, 49*(3), 425–435.

Rosenbaum, P. R. (1988). Item bundles. *Psychometrika, 53*(3), 349–359.

Rost, J. (1997). Logistic mixture models. In W. J. van der Linden & R. K. Hambleton (Eds.), *Handbook of modern item response theory* (pp. 449–463). New York: Springer-Verlag.

Rost, J., & von Davier, M. (1994). A conditional item-fit index for Rasch models. *Applied Psychological Measurement, 18*(2), 171–182.

Roznowski, M., Tucker, L. R., & Humphreys, L. G. (1991). Three approaches to determining the dimensionality of binary items. *Applied Psychological Measurement, 15*(2), 109–127.

Saal, F. E., Downey, R. G., & Lahey, M. A. (1980). Rating the ratings: Assessing the psychometric quality of rating data. *Psychological Bulletin, 88*(2), 413–428.

Samejima, F. (1969). Estimation of latent ability using a response pattern of graded scores. *Psychometric Monograph No. 17.*

Samejima, F. (1972). A general model for free-response data. *Psychometric Monongraph No. 18.*

Samejima, F. (1973). Homogenous case of the continuous response model. *Psychometrika, 38*(2), 203–219.

Scheiblechner, H. (1995). Isotonic ordinal probabilistic models (ISOP). *Psychometrika, 60*(2), 281–304.

Schmidt, F. L. (1977). The Urry method of approximating the item parameters of latent trait theory. *Educational and Psychological Measurement, 37*(3), 613–620.

Seong, T. J. (1990). Sensitivity of marginal maximum likelihood estimation of item and ability parameters to the characteristics of the prior ability distributions. *Applied Psychological Measurement, 14*(3), 299–311.

Sheehan, K., & Mislevy, R. J. (1990). Integrating cognitive and psychometric models to measure document literacy. *Journal of Educational Measurement, 27*(3), 255–272.

Sijtsma, K. (1998). Methodology review: Nonparametric IRT approaches to the analysis of dichotomous item scores. *Applied Psychological Measurement, 22*(1), 3–31.

Sijtsma, K., & Junker, B. W. (1996). A survey of theory and methods of invariant item ordering. *British Journal of Mathematical and Statistical Psychology, 49,* 79–105.

Sijtsma, K., & Molenaar, I. W. (2002). Philosophy and assumptions underlying nonparametric IRT models for dichotomous item scores. In K. Sijtsma & I. W. Molenaar (Eds.), *Introduction to nonparametric item response theory* (pp. 9–29). Thousand Oaks, CA: Sage Publications.

Sireci, S. G., Thissen, D., & Wainer, H. (1991). On the reliability of testlet-based tests. *Journal of Educational Measurement, 28*(3), 237–247.

Skaggs, G., & Stevenson, J. (1989). A comparison of Pseudo-Bayesian and joint maximum likelihood procedures for estimating item parameters in the three-parameter IRT model. *Applied Psychological Measurement, 13*(4), 391–402.

Spiegelhalter, D., Thomas, A., & Best, N. (2000). WINBUGS Version 1.3 [Computer software]. Cambridge, UK: MRC Biostatistics Unit, Institute of Public Health.

Stocking, M. L., & Lord, F. M. (1983). Developing a common metric in item response theory. *Applied Psychological Measurement, 7*(2), 201–210.

Stone, C. A. (1992). Recovery of marginal maximum likelihood estimates in the two-parameter logistic response model: An evaluation of MULTILOG. *Applied Psychological Measurement, 16*(1), 1–16.

Stone, C. A. (2000). Monte Carlo based null distribution for an alternative goodness-of-fit test statistic in IRT models. *Journal of Educational Measurement, 37*(1), 58–75.

Stone, C. A., & Zhang, J. (2003). Assessing goodness of fit of item response theory models: A comparison of traditional and alternative procedures. *Journal of Educational Measurement, 40*(4), 331–352.

Stout, W. (1987). A nonparametric approach for assessing latent trait unidimensionality. *Psychometrika, 52*(4), 589–617.

Stout, W. (1990). A new item response theory modeling approach with applications to unidimensionality assessment and ability estimation. *Psychometrika, 55*(2), 293–325.

Stout, W., Habing, B., Douglas, J., Kim, H. R., Roussos, L., & Zhang, J. (1996). Conditional covariance-based nonparametric multidimensionality assessment. *Applied Psychological Measurement, 20*(4), 331–354.

Swaminathan, H., & Gifford, J. A. (1983). Estimation of parameters in the three-parameter latent trait model. In D. J. Weiss (Ed.), *New horizons in testing* (pp. 9–30). New York: Academic Press.

Swaminathan, H., & Gifford, J. A. (1985). Bayesian estimation in the two-parameter logistic model. *Psychometrika, 50*(3), 349–364.

Swaminathan, H., & Gifford, J. A. (1986). Bayesian estimation in the three-parameter logistic model. *Psychometrika, 51*(4), 589–601.

Sykes, R. C., & Yen, W. M. (2000). The scaling of mixed-item-format tests with the one-parameter and two-parameter partial credit models. *Journal of Educational Measurement, 37*(3), 221–244.

Tate, R. L. (1995). Robustness of the school-level IRT model. *Journal of Educational Measurement, 32*(2), 145–162.

Tate, R. L., & Heidorn, M. (1998). School-level IRT scaling of writing assessment data. *Applied Measurement in Education, 11*(4), 371–383.

Tate, R. L., & King, F. J. (1994). Factors which influence precision of school-level IRT ability estimates. *Journal of Educational Measurement, 31*(1), 1–15.

Tatsuoka, K. (1990). Toward an integration of item-response theory and cognitive error diagnosis. In N. Frederiksen, R. Glaser, A. Lesgold, & M. G. Shafto (Eds.), *Diagnostic monitoring of skill and knowledge acquisition* (pp. 453–488). Hillsdale, NJ: Lawrence Erlbaum.

Tatsuoka, K. (1996). Use of generalized person-fit indexes, zetas for statistical pattern classification. *Applied Measurement in Education, 9*(1), 65–75.

Thissen, D. (1991). *MULTILOG user's guide.* Chicago: Scientific Software.

Thissen, D., & Steinberg, L. (1986). A taxonomy of item response models. *Psychometrika, 51*(4), 567–577.

Thissen, D., Steinberg, L., & Fitzpatrick, A. R. (1989). Multiple-choice models: The distractors are also part of the item. *Journal of Educational Measurement, 26*(2), 161–176.

Thissen, D., Steinberg, L., & Mooney, J. (1989). Trace lines for testlets: A use of multiple-categorical-response models. *Journal of Educational Measurement, 26*(3), 247–260.

Thissen, D., & Wainer, H. (2001). *Test scoring.* Hillsdale, NJ: Lawrence Erlbaum.

Traub, R. E., & Lam, Y. R. (1985). Latent structure and item sampling models for testing. *Annual Review of Psychology, 36,* 19–48.

Tucker, L. R., Humphreys, L. G., & Roznowski, M. (1986). *Comparative accuracy of five indices of dimensionality of binary items.* Champaign-Urbana: University of Illinois, Dept. of Psychology.

van den Wollenberg, A. L. (1982). Two new test statistics for the Rasch model. *Psychometrika, 47*(2), 123–140.

van der Linden, W. J. (Ed.). (1998). *Optimal test assembly* [Special issue]. *Applied Psychological Measurement, 22*(3).

van der Linden, W. J., & Hambleton, R. K. (Eds.). (1997). *Handbook of modern item response theory.* New York: Springer-Verlag.

van Krimpen-Stoop, E. M. L. A., & Meijer, R. R. (1999). The null distribution of person-fit statistics for conventional and adaptive tests. *Applied Psychological Measurement, 23*(4), 327–345.

Verhelst, N. D., & Glas, C. A. W. (1995). Dynamic generalizations of the Rasch model. In G. H. Fischer & I. W. Molenaar (Eds.), *Rasch models: Foundations, recent developments and applications* (pp. 181–201). New York: Springer-Verlag.

Verhelst, N., & Verstralen, H. H. F. M. (2001). An IRT model for multiple raters. In A. Boomsma, M. A. J. Van Duijn, & T. A. B. Snijders (Eds.), *Essays on item response theory* (pp. 89–108). New York: Springer-Verlag.

von Davier, M. (2001). WINMIRA: Latent class analysis, dichotomous and polytomous Rasch models [Computer software]. St. Paul, MN: Assessment Systems Corporation.

von Davier, M., & Yamamoto, K. (2003). *Partially observed mixtures of IRT models: An extension of the generalized partial credit model.* Princeton, NJ: Educational Testing Service.

Wainer, H. (2000). *Computerized adaptive testing: A primer.* Hillsdale, NJ: Lawrence Erlbaum.

Wainer, H., Bradlow, E. T., & Du, Z. (2000). Testlet response theory: An analog for the 3-PL model useful in testlet-based adaptive testing. In W. J. van der Linden & C. A. W. Glas (Eds.), *Computerized adaptive testing: Theory and practice* (pp. 245–269). The Hague, Netherlands: Kluwer-Nijhoff.

Wainer, H., Camacho, F., Reeve, B. B., Rosa, K., Nelson, L., Swygert, K. A., et al. (2001). Augmented scores—"Borrowing strength" to compute scores based on small numbers of items. In D. Thissen & H. Wainer (Eds.), *Test scoring* (pp. 343–387). Mahwah, NJ: Lawrence Erlbaum.

Wainer, H., & Kiely, G. L. (1987). Item clusters and computerized adaptive testing: A case for testlets. *Journal of Educational Measurement, 24*(3), 185–201.

Wainer, H., & Thissen, D. (1996). How is reliability related to the quality of test scores? What is the effect of local dependence on reliability? *Educational Measurement: Issues and Practice, 15*(1), 22–29.

Walker, C. M., & Beretvas, N. S. (2003). Comparing multidimensional and unidimensional proficiency classifications: Multidimensional IRT as a diagnostic aid. *Journal of Educational Measurement, 40*(3), 255–275.

Waller, M. I. (1981). A procedure for comparing logistic latent trait models. *Journal of Educational Measurement, 18*(2), 119–125.

Warm, T. A. (1989). Weighted likelihood estimation of ability in item response theory. *Psychometrika, 54*(3), 427–450.

Way, W. D., Ansley, T. N., & Forsyth, R. A. (1988). The comparative effects of compensatory and non-compensatory two-dimensional data on unidimensional IRT estimates. *Applied Psychological Measurement, 12*(3), 239–252.

Whitely, S. E. (1980). Multicomponent latent trait models for ability tests. *Psychometrika, 45*(4), 479–494.

Williams, V. S. L., Pommerich, M., & Thissen, D. (1998). A comparison of developmental scales based on Thurstone methods and item response theory. *Journal of Educational Measurement, 35*(2), 93–107.

Wilson, M. (1988). Detecting and interpreting local item dependence using a family of Rasch models. *Applied Psychological Measurement, 12*(4), 353–364.

Wilson, M. (Ed.). (1992). *Objective measurement: Theory into practice* (Vol. 1). Norwood, NJ: Ablex.

Wilson, M., & Adams, R. J. (1995). Rasch models for item bundles. *Psychometrika, 60*(2), 181–198.

Wilson, M., & Wang, W. C. (1995). Complex composites: Issues that arise in combining different modes of assessment. *Applied Psychological Measurement, 19*(1), 51–71.

Wingersky, M. S. (1983). LOGIST: A program for computing maximum likelihood procedures for logistic test models. In R. K. Hambleton (Ed.), *Applications of item response theory* (pp. 45–56). Vancouver: Educational Research Institute of British Columbia.

Wingersky, M. S., Barton, M. A., & Lord, F. M. (1982). *LOGIST user's guide*. Princeton, NJ: Educational Testing Service.

Wingersky, M. S., & Lord, F. M. (1984). An investigation of methods for reducing sampling error in certain IRT procedures. *Applied Psychological Measurement, 8*(3), 347–364.

Wood, R., Wilson, D. T., Gibbons, R., Schilling, S., Muraki, E., & Bock, R. D. (2003). TESTFACT 4: Classical item and item factor analysis [Computer software]. Chicago: Scientific Software International.

Wright, B. D., & Douglas, G. A. (1977a). Best procedures for sample-free item analysis. *Applied Psychological Measurement, 1*(2), 281–294.

Wright, B. D., & Douglas, G. A. (1977b). Conditional versus unconditional procedures for sample-free analysis. *Educational and Psychological Measurement, 37*(3), 573–586.

Wright, B., & Stone, M. H. (1979). *Best test design*. Chicago: MESA Press.

Yamamoto, K. (1989). *Hybrid model of IRT and latent class models*. Princeton, NJ: Educational Testing Service.

Yen, W. M. (1981). Using simulation results to choose a latent trait model. *Applied Psychological Measurement, 5*(2), 245–262.

Yen, W. M. (1983a). Tau-equivalence and equipercentile equating. *Psychometrika, 48*(3), 353–369.

Yen, W. M. (1983b). Use of the three-parameter logistic model in the development of a standardized achievement test. In R. K. Hambleton (Ed.), *Applications of Item Response Theory*. Vancouver: Educational Research Institute of British Columbia.

Yen, W. M. (1984a). Effects of local item dependence on the fit and equating performance of the three-parameter logistic model. *Applied Psychological Measurement, 8*(2), 125–145.

Yen, W. M. (1984b). Obtaining maximum likelihood trait estimates from number-correct scores for the three-parameter logistic model. *Journal of Educational Measurement, 21*(2), 93–111.

Yen, W. M. (1985). Increasing item complexity: A possible cause of scale shrinkage for unidimensional item response theory. *Psychometrika, 50*(4), 399–410.

Yen, W. M. (1986). The choice of scale for educational measurement: An IRT perspective. *Journal of Educational Measurement, 23*(4), 299–325.

Yen, W. M. (1987a). A comparison of the efficiency and accuracy of BILOG and LOGIST. *Psychometrika, 52*(2), 275–291.

Yen, W. M. (June 1987b). *A Bayesian/IRT index of objective performance*. Paper presented at the annual meeting of the Psychometric Society, Montreal, Canada.

Yen, W. M. (1992). Item response theory. In M. Alkin (Ed.), *Encyclopedia of Educational Research* (6th ed., pp. 657–667). New York: Macmillan.

Yen, W. M. (1993). Scaling performance assessments: Strategies for managing local item dependence. *Journal of Educational Measurement, 30*(3), 187–213.

Yen, W. M., & Burket, G. R. (March 1997). Comparison of item response theory and Thurstone methods of vertical scaling. *Journal of Educational Measurement, 34*(4), 293–313.

Yen, W. M., Burket, G. R., & Sykes, R. C. (1991). Non-unique solutions to the likelihood equation for the three-parameter logistic model. *Psychometrika, 56*(1), 39–54.

Yen, W. M., & Candell, G. L. (1991). Increasing score reliability with item-pattern scoring: An empirical study in five score metrics. *Applied Measurement in Education, 4*(3), 209–228.

Yen, W. M., Green, D. R., & Burket, G. R. (1987). Valid normative information from customized achievement tests. *Educational Measurement: Issues and Practice, 6*(1), 7–13.

Yen, W. M., Sykes, R. C., Ito, K., & Julian, M. (March 1997). *A Bayesian/IRT index of objective performance for tests with mixed item types*. Paper presented at the annual meeting of the National Council on Measurement in Education, Chicago.

Yu, F., & Nandakumar, R. (2001). Poly-Detect for quantifying the degree of multidimensionality of item response data. *Journal of Educational Measurement, 38*(2), 99–120.

Zhang, J., & Stout, W. (1999). The theoretical DETECT index of dimensionality and its application to approximate simple structure. *Psychometrika, 64*(2), 213–249.

Zimowski, M. F., Muraki, E., Mislevy, R. J., & Bock, R. D. (1997). BILOG-MG 3: Multiple-group IRT analysis and test maintenance for binary items [Computer software]. Chicago: Scientific Software International.

5
Scaling and Norming

Michael J. Kolen
The University of Iowa

1. INTRODUCTION

Scores reported to test users are one of the most visible components of educational testing programs. Some reported scores might reflect an examinee's standing relative to different reference groups, other scores might reflect performance relative to standards set by subject matter experts, and still others might reflect performance on subparts of a test. The reason that multiple scores are often reported for an educational test is that such tests often have many purposes.

Scaling is the process of associating numbers or other ordered indicators with the performance of examinees on an educational test. These numbers and ordered indicators are intended to reflect increasing levels of achievement or proficiency. The process of scaling produces a *score scale*, and the scores that are used to reflect examinee performance are referred to as *scale scores*. The term *primary score scale* is used here to refer to the scale that is used to underlie psychometric operations for a test. Scores on the primary score scale often are reported to examinees as an indicator of their performance on an educational test.

Many testing programs also use what Petersen, Kolen, and Hoover (1989) referred to as *auxiliary score scales* to enhance the meaning of the primary score scales. Auxiliary score scales provide information to test users about examinee performance that goes beyond information incorporated in the primary score scale. Percentile ranks for various groups of examinees are widely used auxiliary score scales. Other types of auxiliary score scales include performance levels (e.g., basic, proficiency, and advanced), normal curve equivalents, and percentage correct scores.

Test developers incorporate meaning into score scales to facilitate the interpretation of scores by test users. Normative information is incorporated into a score scale so that the performance of an examinee can be readily compared to examinees nationwide. For example, by setting the nationwide mean scale score equal to 60, the scale score reported to an examinee indicates whether that examinee is above or below the nationwide mean. Score precision information can be incorporated into score scales by choosing a small enough number of distinct score points so that test users will not over-interpret small differences among scores.

Content information is incorporated into score scales so that the performance of an examinee can be compared to a performance standard. For example, the score reported might directly indicate that the examinee is above the level of *proficient*, as defined by subject matter experts.

Score scales, when properly developed, hold their meaning over time. Thus, a score of 60 indicates the same level of proficiency, whether earned last year, this year, or five years from now. When alternate forms of tests exist, *test equating* procedures described by Holland and Dorans (this volume) are used to ensure that scores from all test forms are on the same score scale and have the same meaning. Thus, the use of score scales, often along with test equating procedures, allows for charting trends in scores over time.

Tests are often part of a *test battery*—a set of tests developed together. With test batteries, score scales can be developed that allow for statements about an individual's strengths and weaknesses across tests. For example, the mean score in a nationally representative group of examinees might be set to 60 on each test in a battery. Relative to the nationally representative group, an examinee who scores substantially above 60 in mathematics and substantially below 60 in English could be said to be stronger in mathematics than in English as measured by the tests in the battery. In addition, using common scaling conventions for all tests in a battery can facilitate computation of *composite scores* across tests.

In some testing programs, such as *elementary achievement test batteries*, test developers and users are interested in tracking the growth of individuals, say, from one grade to another. In these situations, a *developmental score scale* can be constructed to allow for comparisons among scores on test levels that differ in difficulty. *Vertical scaling* procedures are used to construct these score scales.

In developing score scales, examinee performance on the test is associated with the scale scores reported to examinees. *Raw scores*, such as number-correct scores on a multiple-choice test, are calculated. The raw scores are transformed to scale scores by either linear or nonlinear transformations. Test developers and psychometricians decide on the particular numbers to use and the form of the transformation of raw scores to scale scores.

In this chapter, score scales for a single test and for a test battery are discussed. The chapter begins by considering perspectives on constructing score scales. Different types of raw scores are considered, followed by a discussion of transformations of raw scores to scale scores. Procedures for incorporating normative, score precision, and content information into score scales are described. Issues associated with maintaining score scales over time, scales for batteries and composites, and constructing developmental score scales are considered. The chapter concludes with a discussion of procedures for developing test norms, followed by a section on future directions.

2. SCALING PERSPECTIVES

The perspective on scaling taken in this chapter is consistent with that of Petersen et al. (1989) who stated that "the main purpose of scaling is to aid users in interpreting test results. In this vein, we stress the importance of incorporating useful meaning into score scales as a primary means of enhancing score interpretation" (p. 222). This perspective derives from the general approach of Lindquist (1953), who stated

> A good educational achievement test must itself define the objective measured. This means that the method of scaling an educational achievement test should not be permitted to determine the content of the test or to alter the definition of objectives implied in the test. From the point of view of the tester, the definition of the objective is sacrosanct; he has no business monkeying with that definition. The objective is handed down to him by those agents of society who are responsible for decisions concerning educational objectives, and what the test constructor must do is to attempt to incorporate that definition as clearly and as exactly as possible into the examination that he builds. (p. 35)

In following this approach with educational achievement tests, test content and test content specifications drive test development. Scaling procedures are applied after the tests are developed.

Other scaling approaches are sometimes used in the development of measures, and many of these are summarized by Kolen and Brennan (2004). In one alternative approach, psychometric models drive the development and scaling of measurement instruments. This approach can be traced to Thurstone (1925, 1928b) who developed one of the first psychometric scaling models. In discussing scaling from the perspective of Rasch's (1960) model, which derives from this approach, Wright (1977) stated,

> When a person tries to answer a test item the situation is potentially complicated. Many forces might influence the outcome—too many to be named in a workable theory of the person's response. To arrive at a workable position, we must invent a simple conception of what we are willing to suppose happens, do our best to write items and test persons so that their interaction is governed by this conception, and then impose its statistical consequences upon the data to see if the invention can be made useful. (p. 97)

As suggested by this statement, the focus of instrument development and scaling in this approach is on fitting psychometric models. When data suggest that examinee responses to test questions do not fit the model, then those test questions might be eliminated from the test. This approach to test development is inconsistent with the perspective in this chapter and is not considered further.

Stevens's (1946, 1951) well-known theory of scaling classified scales as being nominal, ordinal, interval, or ratio. Suppes and Zinnes (1963) further developed this scaling theory, and a summary of their theory is provided by Coombs, Dawes, and Tversky (1970, pp. 7–19). This theory requires that proficiency be clearly and unambiguously defined, and the scaling process is used to associate numbers to reflect levels of proficiency. Coombs et al. (1970, p. 17) stated, however, that because "no measurement theory [of this type] for intelligence is available ... no meaning [from the perspective of this measurement theory] can be given" to the scores from intelligence tests. From this perspective, until the educational and psychological constructs measured by tests are better defined, the scales that are used with these constructs cannot be classified according to this scaling theory. Thus, the use of psychometric models like those of Thurstone (1925, 1928b) or Rasch (1960) is not sufficient to make claims about scale properties (e.g., ordinal or interval) of educational tests based on this scaling theory. A similar point was made by Angoff (1971, pp. 510–511) and Yen (1986, p. 314).

In summary, the approach taken in this chapter is that scaling procedures are intended to facilitate the interpretation of test scores by incorporating normative, score precision, or content information into the score scales. In this approach, scaling procedures are judged by how well they encourage accurate interpretations of test scores and discourage improper score interpretations.

3. SCALES FOR A SINGLE TEST

This section begins with a discussion of various types of raw scores for educational tests. Then different types of raw to scale score transformations are described, followed by a discussion of methods for incorporating normative, score precision, and content information into score scales for a single test.

Traditionally the raw score on a test has been defined as "the number, proportion, or percentage" of test items that an examinee answers correctly (Petersen et al., 1989, p. 222). Implicit in this definition is that items are scored right/wrong and the raw score is based on the number of items correctly answered. Performance assessments (see Lane & Stone, this volume) and computer-based tests (see Drasgow, Luecht, & Bennett, this volume) are now in widespread use with educational tests. Performance assessments typically are scored by judges. Automated scoring of essays and other performance assessments is becoming more prevalent. The use of computers has led to the use of innovative item formats, including complex item types. Many of these innovative items use scoring that is more complex than right/wrong. In addition, the use of item response theory (IRT) models (see Yen & Fitzpatrick, this volume) has led to widespread use of scores that are more complicated than a simple sum of scores on items. For these reasons, an expanded set of terms, beyond that used by Petersen et al. (1989), is needed to handle this variety of test items and scoring procedures.

3.1. Some Test Score Terminology

Consider a situation in which a performance assessment consisting of 4 stimuli is administered, and the examinees provide a written response to each of the 4 stimuli. Two judges rate each written response on a holistic rating scale that ranges from 1 to 5. If the two judges who rate a response differ by more than 1 point, then a third "expert" judge rates the written response. An examinee's score associated with one of the stimuli is the sum of the ratings by the first two judges if the two judges differ by one point or less. Otherwise, the examinee's score is twice the rating of the third judge. The score for an examinee over the 4 stimuli is a function of the scores associated with each of the stimuli.

In this chapter, the term *unit score* refers to the score on the smallest *unit* on which a score is found. This smallest unit is referred to as the *scoreable unit*. In the performance assessment situation just described, for each stimulus there is a unit score for the first judge, a unit score for the second judge, and, possibly, a unit score for the third judge.

The term *item score* refers to the score on a test item. In the performance assessment situation, an item score is a score associated with each stimulus. In this example, each item score ranges from 2 to 10. The item score is the sum of the ratings of the first two judges if their ratings differ by no more than one point, in which case odd item scores (3, 5, 7, 9) are possible. Otherwise, the item score is twice the rating of the third judge, in which case only even item scores are possible. For a multiple-choice item, the item score typically is either 1 for a correct response or 0 for an incorrect response.

The term *raw score* refers to a function of the item scores. In a traditional multiple-choice testing situation, the raw score is the sum of the item scores, which represents the number of items answered correctly. In the performance assessment example, the raw score is a function of the item scores, possibly the sum of the item scores. If it is the sum of item scores, then the raw score ranges from 8 to 40.

3.2. Unit and Item Scores

For traditionally scored multiple-choice tests, the unit scores and item scores often are identical. In other situations, like the performance assessment situation just described, unit and item scores are clearly distinct.

When item response theory (IRT) is used to score tests, the distinction between the unit score and item score might depend on decisions made by the test developer. Consider a test of reading comprehension that consists of 10 passages with 5 dichotomously scored multiple-choice items per passage. This test has 50 scoreable units. Traditionally, each of these scoreable units is treated as an item, so there are 50 item scores. However, a local independence assumption is made in IRT scoring. To handle local independence concerns, the test might be treated as a 10 item (sometimes referred to as testlet) test, with each item score being the number correct over the 5 items associated with a particular passage. In this case, there are 50 unit scores and 10 item scores, with each item score ranging from 0 to 5. Thus, what is considered an item score depends, not only on the number of scoreable units on a test, but on how the test developer decides to define an item on the test. Similar issues occur with computer-based tests.

The relationship between unit and item scores can be complicated for computer-based tests. For example, suppose that both correctness and response time are considered as part of a score for a complex computer-based test. A predetermined procedure might be used to combine correctness and response time into a score on the test. Using the terminology of this section, the unit scores are each piece of information that was collected and used to score the test. The item score is the overall score for the test.

The characteristic that most clearly distinguishes unit scores from item scores is as follows: Whereas there may be operational dependencies among unit scores, item scores are considered operationally independent. That is, it is expected that score on one item does not depend on answers given to previous items. Various types of item scores have been used in practice. Some of the most popular item scores are described next.

3.2.1. Dichotomous Item Scores

Dichotomous item scores, where items are either correct or incorrect, are used with many multiple-choice and other objective test item formats. Let i refer to an item and let V_i be a random variable indicating the score on item i. For an item with a dichotomous item score, the item score is $V_i = 1$ if item i is answered correctly and $V_i = 0$ if the item is answered incorrectly.

3.2.2. "Corrected for Guessing" Item Scores

"Corrected for guessing" item scores are sometimes used with multiple-choice test items. For these item scores, a distinction is made among correct responses, incorrect responses, and omitted responses (where no answer is given to the item). Let A_i be the number of alternatives for a multiple-choice item. One such scoring scheme is $V_i = 1$ if item i is answered correctly, $V_i = -1/(A_i-1)$ if item i is answered incorrectly, and $V_i = 0$ if the item is omitted. In this scoring scheme, examinees who guess at random or omit an item are expected to earn a score of 0 on the item. Other scores can be used to penalize guessing to a greater (or lesser) extent.

3.2.3. Ordered Response Item Scores

Ordered response item scores are used for items that are scored in a set of ordered categories. Categories associated with better performance on the item receive higher scores. For example, for a 3-choice multiple-choice item, a test developer might order the alternatives from best to worst and assign a score of 2 for the correct answer, 1 for the best incorrect alternative, and 0 for the worst alternative. In the performance assessment example considered earlier, the item scores, $V_i = 2, 3, \ldots, 10$, are ordered response item scores.

Ordered response item scoring is used with many complex computer-based assessments. Although item scores often are consecutive integers, the use of consecutive integers is not necessary. Note that "corrected for guessing" item scores actually is one type of ordered response item score.

3.2.4. Other Types of Item Scores

Nominal response item scoring is used for items that are scored in a set of unordered or partially ordered categories. *Continuous response item scoring* is used in situations where there are a very large number of ordered responses. Nominal and continuous response scoring procedures are used infrequently with educational tests. For the purposes of this chapter, it is assumed that items are scored as either dichotomous or ordered responses.

3.3. Raw Scores

Raw scores are defined as a function of item scores on a test. For a test containing n items, the raw score X, is a function of item scores. Many types of raw scores that are used in practice are described in this section.

3.3.1. Summed Scores

The *summed score* is the sum of the item scores over the items on a test. The summed score is

$$X = \sum_{i=1}^{n} V_i. \tag{1}$$

For a test consisting of dichotomously scored items, the summed score is the number of items answered correctly. For the performance assessment example presented earlier, the summed score is the sum of the 4 item scores. Because each item score ranges from 2 to 10 in this example, the summed score ranges from 8 to 40. The summed score is often attractive because it is relatively easy to explain to examinees and to the public. In addition, it equally weights the item scores to form the raw score.

3.3.2. Weighted Summed Scores

Sometimes *weighted summed scores* are used, where the raw score is a weighted sum of the item scores. This score is calculated as

$$X = \sum_{i=1}^{n} w_i V_i, \tag{2}$$

where w_i is a weight that is applied to item i. Various procedures are used to choose the weights. For example, the weights can be chosen to maximize reliability of the raw score. Alternatively, proportional weights can be chosen subjectively so that each item reflects the desired relative contribution of the item to the raw score.

3.3.3. Kelley Regressed Scores

Regressed score estimates of true score are sometimes used as the raw score on a test. A Kelley regressed score (see Haertel, this volume) is of the form

$$X^* = E(\tau \mid X) = \rho_{xx'} X + (1 - \rho_{xx'})\mu, \tag{3}$$

where E is the expected score for an examinee over repeated testings, τ is the true score for an examinee, $\rho_{xx'}$ is test reliability in a particular population of examinees, and μ is the mean score in a particular population of examinees. The use of Kelley regressed score estimates requires an assumption that the regression of true scores on observed scores is linear as well as assumptions for specifying the particular reliability coefficient used, as described in Haertel (this volume). As an estimate of true score, there is less overall error with X^* than with X, unless test reliability is 1. If the test reliability is 1, then X^* equals X. If the test reliability is 0, then X^* equals the population mean. Whereas X is an unbiased estimate of true score, X^* is a biased estimate. For examinees with true scores above the mean, on average, X^* is lower than their true score. For examinees with true scores below the mean, on average, X^* is greater than their true score. A consequence of this bias is that the variability of the Kelley regressed scores is less than or equal to the variability of true scores.

Kelley regressed scores depend on the mean and reliability in the population, as can be seen in Equation 3. As a consequence, two examinees from different populations with the same X might have different values of X^*. Suppose that the mean score for females on a test is 50, the mean score for males is 54, and test reliability in both groups is .7. From Equation 3, a male with a score of 60 would have a Kelley regressed score estimate of 58.2, and a female with a score of 60 would have a Kelley regressed score estimate of 57.

3.3.4. Complicated Scoring Functions

There are situations where the raw score is found using a function that is considerably more complicated than a weighted summation. Such a raw score can be symbolized as follows:

$$X = f(V_1, V_2, ..., V_n), \tag{4}$$

where f is the function used to convert the item scores to a raw score.

3.3.5. IRT Maximum Likelihood Scoring

IRT maximum likelihood scoring is one type of complicated scoring function that is used with IRT models. In these models, IRT proficiency is represented by the variable θ, the response variable for item i is V_i, and a particular response to the item by an examinee is v_i. The application of IRT models requires strong statistical assumptions as described by Yen and Fitzpatrick (this volume). For a unidimensional IRT model, the probability that $V_i = v_i$ is symbolized as $P(V_i = v_i \mid \theta)$. In maximum likelihood scoring, under the assumption of local independence, the value of θ is found that maximizes the likelihood equation

$$L = \prod_{i=1}^{n} P(V_i = v_i \mid \theta). \tag{5}$$

This estimate is symbolized as $\hat{\theta}_{MLE}$. Because this estimate is a function of the item scores, it can be thought of as a raw score and also could be symbolized by X. Note that the maximum likelihood estimate can be found for IRT models used in practice, including the models for items with dichotomous and ordered response scoring. In some cases, such as with the Rasch model, the maximum likelihood estimate can be found from a summed score. In other cases, the scoring function (see Equation 4) is much more complicated. One important property of maximum likelihood estimates is that they are unbiased estimates of θ for long tests. Also, the variance of maximum likelihood estimates ($\hat{\theta}_{MLE}$) in a given population is greater than the variance of the true proficiencies (θ) due to error in estimating proficiency. Maximum likelihood estimates do not exist for some response patterns, such as summed scores of zero correct on a multiple-choice test.

3.3.6. IRT Bayesian Scoring

IRT proficiency can also be estimated using Bayesian methods. The Bayesian *expected a posteriori* (EAP) estimate is calculated as

$$\hat{\theta}_{EAP} = E(\theta \mid V_1 = v_1, V_2 = v_2, ..., V_n = v_n)$$

$$= \frac{\int \theta \prod_{i=1}^{n} P(V_i = v_i \mid \theta) g(\theta) \, d\theta}{\int \prod_{i=1}^{n} P(V_i = v_i \mid \theta) g(\theta) \, d\theta} \quad (6)$$

where $g(\theta)$ is the distribution of θ in the population, E is expected value, and the integrals are over θ. In practice, numerical methods are used and the integrals are replaced by summations. Note that the EAP estimate in Equation 6 contains the likelihood equation from Equation 5 in both the numerator and denominator. Unlike Equation 5, Equation 6 also contains the distribution of θ. Thissen and Orlando (2001) presented a modification of Bayesian EAP estimates that can be used with summed scores.

Similar to the Kelley regressed scores, the EAP is a biased estimate. Examinees whose θ is above the mean in the population, on average, have estimates that are lower than their θ. Examinees whose θ is below the mean in the population, on average, have estimates that are greater than their θ. A consequence of this bias is that in a given population the variability of the EAP estimates of proficiency typically is less than the variability of θ because of shrinkage toward the mean for the EAP estimates. In addition, as with the Kelley regressed scores, the EAP estimate depends on the distribution in the population. If a male and female had the same set of item scores, then their EAP estimates could differ if the score for the male was calculated with respect to the population of males and the score for the females was calculated with respect to the population of females. Unlike maximum likelihood estimates, Bayesian EAP estimates exist for all response patterns, including those for examinees with a zero correct summed score on a multiple-choice test.

3.3.7. Raw Scores and Test Specifications

For educational achievement tests, test specifications typically are developed to reflect the intended importance of content areas. More test questions are chosen from content areas that are considered to be more important for the construct being measured. By using summed scores, the raw score reflects the intended importance in terms of the proportion of score points associated with each of the content areas.

The use of weighted summed scores might not reflect the intended importance when the weights are chosen using criteria other than judged importance, such as maximizing reliability or as is used with IRT models other than the Rasch model. In these situations the weights are based mainly on statistical criteria. In the three parameter logistic IRT model, for example, items that are more highly discriminating near the examinee's proficiency will tend to have greater weight than items that are low in discrimination in this region (see, for example, Lord, 1980, pp. 74–75). For IRT models, it is possible that the weighting used in the weighted summed scores will lead to raw scores that do not reflect the importance of various content areas as intended by test developers. Thus, care should be taken when using weighted summed scores.

3.3.8. Summary: Types of Scores

Figure 5.1 provides a schematic diagram illustrating the different types of scores considered in this chapter. At the bottom of the figure are the unit scores. These scores are the smallest unit on which a score is found. Moving up the diagram, the unit scores for an item are combined to produce the score for that item. The raw score is then calculated as a function of the item scores. As is discussed later in this chapter, scale scores are calculated as a function of the raw scores for the purpose of facilitating meaningful score interpretation.

3.4. Mixed Format Tests

An increasing number of tests are composed of items with different types of formats. For example, some items on a test might be multiple-choice items and other items might be constructed-response items. The items from one format often have different numbers of score points than the items from another format. Developers of mixed format tests need to address the question of how to combine scores from different formats when calculating a total raw score for the test.

Consider, for example, the Advanced Placement Computer Science A Examination (College Board, 2004). This examination contains 40 multiple-choice test items (scored 0/1) and 4 constructed-response sections, each of which has a maximum possible score of 9. The College Board had to decide how to combine the item scores on the multiple-choice and constructed-response sections to arrive at a total raw score over both item types. In this section, issues in deciding how to combine scores are presented.

FIGURE 5.1 Schematic Diagram for Different Types of Scores

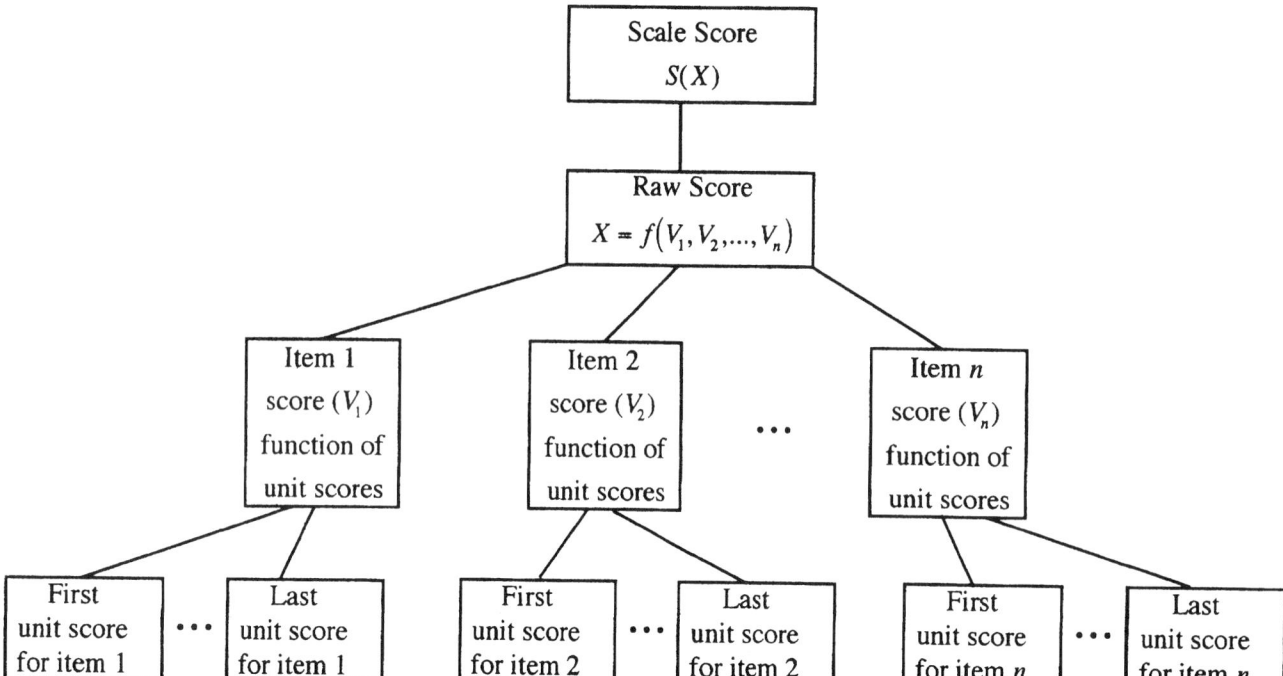

3.4.1. Weights Based on Numbers of Score Points

One way to assign weights is for test developers to decide on the desired proportional contribution of each type of item to the total number of raw score points. This proportion could be chosen based on the viewed importance of each item type to the total test. Numbers of test items, testing time, and the extent to which items from each format cover the domain of content of the test are often considered when assigning weights.

For the Advanced Placement Computer Science A Examination, for example, the College Board decided that the maximum number of score points for each item type should be equal when calculating the total raw score. The total raw score is calculated using Equation 2. A weight of 1 was used for each of the 40 multiple-choice test items, leading to a maximum of 40 points attributable to the multiple-choice test items. Each of the 4 constructed-response items has a maximum score of 9, so the maximum total number of points over the constructed response items is 36. By multiplying the constructed response item scores by $1.\overline{1}$, the maximum score over the constructed response items also is 40 (note that $40 / 36 = 1.\overline{1}$). Thus, using a weight of $1.\overline{1}$ for the constructed response item scores and a weight of 1 for the multiple-choice item scores leads to equal maximum scores for the two item types. Note that in practice College Board uses weights of 1.1 for the constructed response items and then rounds the total score to an integer.

This type of weighting, which is used with many mixed format tests, is straightforward and relatively easy to explain to test users. In addition, weights based on the numbers of score points can be developed prior to administering the test to examinees, so the weighting results are independent of the examinee group taking the test. However, this weighting scheme ignores statistical relationships among the item types and test reliability considerations.

3.4.2. Observed Score Effective Weights

Effective weights are indices of the statistical contribution of each component to the composite. A proportional effective weight is interpreted as the proportion of composite variance that is attributable to a component of the composite.

Assume that a mixed format test is composed of t different item types and that a raw score over all items of type j ($j=1, 2, \ldots, t$), is denoted as X_j. Also assume that weights (u_j) are to be applied to the raw score on each item type so that the raw score over all item types is

$$X = \sum_{j=1}^{t} u_j X_j \qquad (7)$$

Wang and Stanley (1970) referred to the weights u_j as *nominal weights*.

Assume a test is administered to a group of examinees that is representative of the population of test takers. Define the variance of total test raw scores as σ_X^2, of X_j as σ_j^2, and the covariance between X_j and X_k as σ_{jk}. The *proportional observed score effective weight* of item type j is defined as

$$ew_j = \frac{u_j^2 \sigma_j^2 + u_j \sum_{k \neq j} u_k \sigma_{jk}}{\sum_j \left[u_j^2 \sigma_j^2 + u_j \sum_{k \neq j} u_k \sigma_{jk} \right]}. \qquad (8)$$

The summation in the numerator is over raw scores on all of the item types, except item type j. The numerator is a weighted sum of all of the elements in one row (or column) of the variance-covariance matrix among the raw scores on item types. The denominator sums up the numerator values for all of the item types, and it is used to standardize the numerator so that the proportional observed score effective weights sum to 1. The effective weight is an index of the contribution of weighted X_j to the total raw score defined in Equation 7. Note that these weights depend on the nominal weights, the variance of X_j, and the covariance between X_j and the scores on the other item types.

One useful special case occurs when there are two item types, scores on each type are scaled to have a standard deviation of 1, and the weights sum to 1. In this special case, the effective weight for item type 1 is

$$ew_1 = \frac{u_1^2 + u_1 u_2 \rho_{12}}{u_1^2 + u_2^2 + 2u_1 u_2 \rho_{12}}, \quad (9)$$

and the effective weight for item type 2 is $ew_2 = 1 - ew_1$. If the nominal weights are both .5, the effective weights are also .5. Otherwise, the effective weights depend on both the nominal weights and the correlation. If the correlation is 1, then the nominal and effective weights are the same. If the correlation is zero or greater and the nominal weight is below .5, then the corresponding effective weight is smaller than the nominal weight. For example, if the nominal weight for item type 1 is .1 and the correlation is .5, then the effective weight for item type 1 is .06 calculated using Equation 9. Conversely, if the nominal weight is above .5, then the effective weight is larger than the nominal weight. Continuing the example, the nominal weight for item type 2 is .9 and the effective weight is .94.

When using effective weights in practice, test developers state the desired effective weights for each of the item types. Nonlinear estimation procedures can be used to find the nominal weights that lead to the desired effective weights. Wilks (1938) presented such estimation procedures.

3.4.3. True Score Effective Weights

Brennan (2001, pp. 306–307) described effective weights for true scores. Use of a psychometric model such as classical test theory or generalizability theory is required when calculating these weights. Defining $\rho_{jj'}$ as the reliability of X_j, true score effective weights are calculated by substituting true score variance, $\sigma_j^2 \rho_{jj'}$, for each σ_j^2 in Equation 8. These proportional true score effective weights can be used in a manner similar to the proportional observed score effective weights. In general, the two types of effective weights differ, with the proportional true score effective weights affected by the reliabilities as well as the nominal weights and the correlations.

3.4.4. Weights Chosen to Maximize Reliability

Weights can be chosen to maximize the reliability of the total raw score. Based on Feldt and Brennan (1989, p. 116), the reliability of weighted composite scores is

$$\rho_C = 1 - \frac{\sum_j u_j^2 \sigma_j^2 (1 - \rho_{jj})}{\sum_j \left[u_j^2 \sigma_j^2 + u_j \sum_{k \neq j} u_k \sigma_{jk} \right]}. \quad (10)$$

Procedures for finding weights that maximize composite reliability were given by Gulliksen (1950, p. 346), and matrix-based estimation procedures were summarized by Wainer and Thissen (2001).

A special case of Equation 10 given by Wainer and Thissen (2001) is useful when there are two item types, X_1 and X_2, that have been scaled to have a standard deviation of 1, and $u_1 + u_2 = 1$. In this case,

$$\rho_C = 1 - \frac{u_1^2(1 - \rho_{11'}) + u_2^2(1 - \rho_{22'})}{u_1^2 + u_2^2 + 2u_1 u_2 \rho_{12}}. \quad (11)$$

Wainer and Thissen (2001) discussed how to find the weights to maximize reliability in this case.

3.4.5. Weighting Example

Wainer and Thissen (2001) provided an example that is intended to be similar to data for the SAT II Writing Test. In this example, reliability of scores on the multiple-choice portion of the test is .85, reliability of scores on the constructed-response portion of the test is .60, and the correlation between scores on the multiple-choice and constructed-response portion is .43. The scores on each portion are standardized to have a mean of 0 and a standard deviation of 1. The testing time is 40 minutes for the multiple-choice portion and 20 minutes for the constructed-response portion. To be consistent with testing times, the weight for the multiple-choice section is intended to be 2/3.

For this example, reliability of the total raw score for different nominal weights is given in Figure 5.2. Consistent with Wainer and Thissen (2001), for a nominal weight of 2/3 for the multiple-choice section ($v_1 = 2/3$ and $v_2 = 1/3$) reliability of the composite is .851, as calculated using Equation 11. Consistent with Figure 5.2, Wainer and Thissen (2001) also showed that reliability is maximized at .863 when the nominal weight for the multiple-choice section is .82. As can be seen, for low nominal weights, the reliability of the total score can be much less than the reliability of the score over the multiple-choice items (.85).

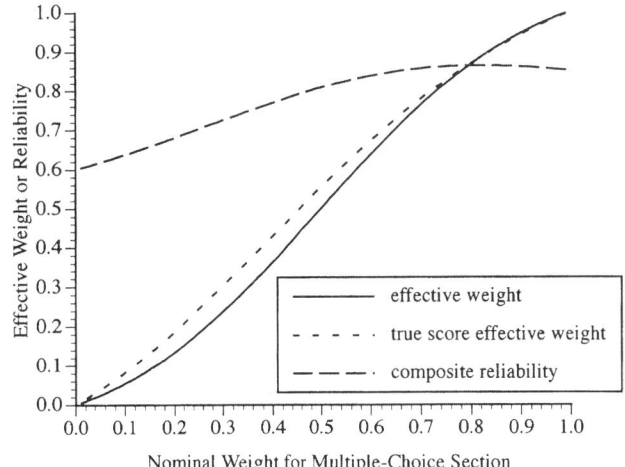

FIGURE 5.2 Relationships between Nominal Weights, Effective Weights, and Composite Reliability

Effective weights also can be calculated for this example using Equation 9. The proportional observed score effective weights for the multiple-choice portion and proportional true score effective weights for the multiple-choice portion also are graphed in Figure 5.2. From this graph, the proportional observed score effective weight equals the nominal weight at a nominal weight of .5. Proportional observed score effective weights are greater than nominal weights for nominal weights above .5 and are less than the nominal weights for nominal weights below .5. Over most of the range of nominal weights, the proportional true score effective weight for the multiple-choice portion is greater than the proportional observed score effective weight for the constructed-response portion, presumably because the multiple-choice portion is more reliable than the constructed-response portion.

The bisection method (Press, Flannery, Teukolsky, & Vetterling, 1989) was used to solve for the nominal weight in Equation 9 given proportional observed score effective weight. In this example, a nominal weight of .621 is associated with a proportional observed score effective weight of 2/3 for the multiple-choice portion. Thus, if the proportional observed score effective weight is intended to be 2/3 for the multiple-choice portion, the nominal weight should be chosen to be .621. Using the bisection method to solve for the nominal weight in Equation 9 given proportional true score effective weight, a nominal weight of .595 is associated with a proportional true score effective weight of 2/3 for the multiple-choice portion.

3.4.6. Some Other Weighting Criteria and Issues

Wang and Stanley (1970) summarized research on using weights that maximize the multiple correlation with external criteria. For example, a composite might be found for a college entrance test battery that maximizes the correlation between college grades and scores on the tests in the battery. Feldt (1997) and Kane and Case (2004) demonstrated that under certain conditions, more reliable composites can be less valid in terms of correlation with a criterion. Brennan (2001, pp. 312–314) discussed issues in optimizing reliability and validity. Rudner (2001) demonstrated that under certain conditions, maximizing validity leads to lower reliability. Noting that constructed-response items are often much more expensive to administer and score than multiple-choice items, Wainer and Thissen (1993) discussed how to incorporate cost into the process of deciding on test length and choosing weights.

3.4.7. Weights in IRT

When applying IRT methodology a crucial first decision is whether or not a single dimension can be used to describe performance over the mixed item types. Recently, Rodriguez (2003) reviewed the construct equivalence of multiple-choice and constructed-response items. Based on the definition of construct equivalence used by Traub (1993) that construct equivalence implies true score correlations of 1, Rodriguez concluded that these item types are measuring different constructs. However, he also found that in certain circumstances the constructs are very similar. Wainer and Thissen (1993) argued that in many cases, the constructs measured with multiple-choice and constructed-response items are similar enough that they can be analyzed together using unidimensional IRT models.

When different item types are considered by the test developer to measure different dimensions, it is possible to fit a unidimensional IRT model separately for each item type. IRT proficiency (θ) can be calculated separately for each item type and a composite formed.

Suppose that the test developer decides that the different item types are similar enough to be analyzed together using unidimensional IRT models. Multiple-choice items then might be fit with a three-parameter logistic model and constructed-response items with a generalized partial credit model. Using suitable software, the item parameters for the different item types could be analyzed together. After item parameters are estimated, proficiency can be estimated using the maximum likelihood or Bayesian methods of Equations 5 and 6. This sort of approach was suggested by Thissen, Wainer, and Wang (1994) and implemented by Ercikan et al. (1998), Rosa, Swygert, Nelson, and Thissen (2001), and Sykes and Yen (2000).

Rosa et al. (2001) developed an alternative unidimensional IRT method for test scoring. In this method, summed scores are calculated for each item type. IRT proficiency is estimated from these summed scores using Bayesian methods. Rosa et al. (2001) suggested that this procedure is preferable to typical pattern scoring, "both to implement and to explain to consumers" (p. 255). Because this method is a Bayesian method, it produces estimates of proficiency that typically are less variable than maximum likelihood estimates when used with Rasch models. In general, however, the weighting of each item type still depends on the extent that the item type discriminates near an examinee's proficiency. Sykes and Hou (2003) used various weighting schemes and then evaluated the psychometric properties using unidimensional IRT methods.

3.4.8. Summary of Issues in Weights for Mixed Format Tests

For many mixed format tests, test developers have clear ideas about the intended weight that should be associated with each item format. As is the case with the Advanced Placement Computer Science A Examination, such weighting is often implemented by considering only the maximum score on each item type. However, this approach does not take into account the statistical characteristics of the test scores. Effective weights are a useful way to take into account these statistical characteristics when deciding on how to weight scores on the different item types.

The reliability of scores associated with constructed-response items often is much lower than the reliability of scores associated with multiple-choice items. In this situation, it is possible that the use of a desired set of effective weights will lead to a composite score that is less reliable than the multiple-choice score. The test developer needs to carefully consider whether the resulting composite reliability is acceptable.

When weights for different item types are chosen based on maximizing reliability or based on an IRT model other than the Rasch model, the resulting weights might be different from the relative contribution of the item types desired by test developers. In these situations, test developers should check the contributions of each item type to the total score to ensure that the actual relative contributions are consistent with the intended relative contributions.

3.5. Transformations of Raw Scores to Scale Scores

Raw scores have serious limitations as primary scale scores for tests. Certain types of raw scores, including number-correct scores, other summed scores, and percent-correct scores depend on the items that are in a particular form of a test. When multiple forms of a test exist, raw scores typically do not have a consistent meaning across forms. For example, on a 50 item multiple-choice test, a number-correct score 35 will be indicative of lower proficiency on an easy test form than on a more difficult test form. One way that number-correct scores might be used as primary scale scores would be to use the number-correct scores for an initial form as the primary scale, and then equate number-correct scores on subsequent forms to the number-correct score of the initial form using procedures described by Holland and Dorans (this volume). For example, if an equating process indicated that the second form of a test is 5 points easier than the initial form, then a number-correct score of 40 on the second form would be judged to indicate the same proficiency as a number-correct score of 35 on the initial form. If scores on the initial form were used as primary scale scores, then the primary scale score would be 35 for an examinee with a number-correct score of 40 on the second form. Such an equating and scaling process could cause much confusion, with this examinee likely questioning why 5 points were being subtracted from his or her score. To eliminate this sort of confusion, scores other than raw scores should be used as primary scale scores whenever multiple forms of a test exist.

When IRT assumptions hold and test items are properly calibrated and placed on the same IRT scale, the IRT proficiency scale does not depend on the particular items taken. So, using IRT-based raw scores avoids many of the problems associated with test scores on a test form depending on the particular items included. However, the scaling conventions used with IRT (often scores with mean of 0, standard deviation of 1, and unrounded) typically do not produce scores that lead to meaningful interpretations without further transformation.

Linear or nonlinear transformations of raw scores are used to produce scale scores that can be meaningfully interpreted. Normative, score precision, and content meaning can be incorporated. Different types of transformations that can be used to incorporate each of these types of meaning are considered in the following sections of this chapter.

3.6. Incorporating Normative Information Into Score Scales

The process of incorporating normative information into a score scale begins with administering the test to a group of examinees, referred to as the *norm group*. Suppose the norm group for an elementary achievement test intended for third graders is a representative group of third grade students nationwide. Statistical characteristics of the scale score distribution (mean, standard deviation, etc.) are set for this norm group. The resulting scale scores are meaningful to the extent that educators judge that it is important to compare the performance by individual third graders to third graders nationwide. Such scale scores would likely be more meaningful than scale scores that were based on the norm group that did not adequately represent the nation.

Sometimes scale scores are set using a norm group based on test users. For example, the SAT I tests were rescaled using a 1990 reference group (Dorans, 2002) of SAT test-takers. In this case, the College Board judged that SAT test-takers were a meaningful group of examinees on which to base the SAT score scale.

Other times, the norm group used to set a score scale is chosen for convenience, such as when a scale is based on the group of individuals who happen to take a test at a particular time. However, in this case, the normative information incorporated into the score scale does little to help users meaningfully interpret test scores.

The particular norm group that is chosen for constructing a scale strongly influences the meaning of the resulting scale scores. Issues associated with the development of norms are considered more fully near the end of this chapter. In the present section, it is assumed that a norm group has been identified and that the norms for this group are collected. It is also assumed that raw scores are calculated using one of the procedures described earlier in this chapter. These raw scores are transformed to scale scores using either linear or nonlinear transformations.

3.6.1. Linear Transformations

Linear transformations can be used if the mean and standard deviation of the scale scores are specified by the test developer and the mean and standard deviation of the raw scores are calculated for the norm group. Define X as the raw score random variable as calculated using any one of the procedures described earlier, x as a particular value (realization) of X, and S as the scale score random variable, where S is calculated as a function of X. The transformation for raw to scale scores is

$$S(x) = \frac{\sigma_S}{\sigma_X} x + \left[\mu_S - \frac{\sigma_S}{\sigma_X} \mu_X\right], \quad (12)$$

where μ_X and σ_X are the mean and standard deviations of raw scores in the norm group and μ_S and σ_S are the desired mean and standard deviation of the scale scores.

Kolen and Brennan (2004) provided an example in which the mean and standard deviation of raw scores are 70 and 10, respectively; the desired mean and standard deviation of the scale scores are 20 and 5, respectively. For this example, using Equation 12,

$$S(x) = \tfrac{5}{10} x + \left[20 - \tfrac{5}{10} 70\right] = .5x - 15.$$

An examinee with a raw score of 50 would receive a scale score of 10 using this equation. Also, any examinee with a scale score above 20 would be above the mean for the norm group.

Another way to linearly transform raw scores to scale scores is to specify scale score equivalents of two raw score points. Defining x_1 and x_2 as these two raw score points $S(x_1)$ and and $S(x_2)$ as the desired scale score equivalents,

$$S(x) = \left[\frac{S(x_2) - S(x_1)}{x_2 - x_1}\right]x + \left\{S(x_1) - \left[\frac{S(x_2) - S(x_1)}{x_2 - x_1}\right]x_1\right\}, \quad (13)$$

defines a linear raw-to-scale score equivalent. Kolen and Brennan (2004) provide another example using a test with a raw score mean of 70. In this example, the mean scale score is intended to be 20 and a raw score of 0 is intended to be equivalent to a scale score of 1. In this case,

$$S(x) = \left[\frac{20-1}{70-0}\right]x + \left\{1 - \left[\frac{20-1}{70-0}\right]0\right\} = .2714x + 1.$$

For example, an examinee with a raw score of 50 would receive a scale score of 14.57.

It might be desirable to specify one scale score equivalent and the standard deviation of the scale scores. In this case, let x_1 be the raw score and $S(x_1)$ be its desired scale score equivalent. Taking σ_S as the desired scale score standard deviation,

$$S(x) = \frac{\sigma_S}{\sigma_X}x + S(x_1) - \frac{\sigma_S}{\sigma_X}x_1. \quad (14)$$

For example, suppose for the norm group used in the other examples, a raw score of 50 is intended to convert to a scale score of 20 and the scale score standard deviation is intended to be 5 points. In this case,

$$S(x) = \frac{5}{10}x + \left[20 - \frac{5}{10}50\right] = .5x - 5.$$

3.6.2. Nonlinear Transformations

Nonlinear transformations can take on almost any monotonically nondecreasing form, such that the scale score corresponding to a particular raw score is greater than or equal to the scale score corresponding to a lower raw score. One of the least complicated nonlinear transformations used in practice is to round to integers the scale scores created by a linear transformation. The use of integer scores as scale scores generally is considered to be easier for test users to interpret than are scale scores reported with decimal places. In the example following Equation 13, $S(x) = .2714x+1$. For this example, a raw score of 50 converts to a scale score of 14.57, which is symbolized by $S(50) = 14.57$. Rounding to integers, a scale score equivalent of 50 is 15 and is symbolized by $S_{int}(50) = 15$, where S_{int} indicates scale scores rounded to integers.

Another nonlinear transformation is truncation, which is used to ensure that all scale scores are within a desired range. In the example following Equation 12, $S(x) = .5x - 15$. Using this transformation, a raw score of 0 converts to a scale score of -15. Suppose that the test developer intends for scale scores to be 1 or higher. In this case, the transformation could be modified so that scale scores below 1 are truncated to a scale score of 1.

Rounding and truncation processes are used in many testing programs when the raw to scale score transformation begins with a linear transformation. Testing programs that use IRT-based proficiencies as raw scores sometimes linearly transform the IRT proficiency estimates, round these estimates to integers, and truncate the scale at minimum and maximum scores.

Sometimes complex nonlinear transformations are used. One of these is to transform raw scores to scale scores that have a particular distributional shape, at least approximately, in a norm group. One shape that is commonly used is a normal distribution, and the process of constructing such scores is referred to as the process of normalizing scores. The following steps can be used to normalize scores:

1. Find the relative frequency distribution of raw scores in the norm group.
2. As an optional step, smooth the relative frequency distribution using a smoothing method such as the log-linear method described by Kolen and Brennan (2004).
3. Find the percentile ranks (see Kolen & Brennan, 2004, for a description of how to compute percentile ranks) for the relative frequency distribution, and refer to these as $Q(x)$.
4. Find the inverse normal transformation of the proportion $Q(x)/100$. That is, find z such that

$$\Phi(z) = Q(x)/100 = \frac{1}{\sqrt{2\pi}}\int_{-\infty}^{z} e^{-w^2/2}\,dw, \quad (15)$$

where Φ is the normal (cumulative) distribution function. The score z can be found from a normal curve table, a statistical package, or a spreadsheet program.

5. Transform z to have a particular scale score mean and standard deviation using the linear transformation $S(x) = \sigma_S z + \mu_S$, where μ_S is the desired scale score mean and σ_S are the desired scale score standard deviation.
6. Round the resulting scale scores to integers, and possibly truncate the transformation at predefined minimum and maximum scores, producing $S_{int}(x)$.

Following these steps produces scores that are approximately normal with approximately the desired mean and standard deviation.

McCall (1939) suggested using T-scores, which are scale scores that are normalized with an approximate mean of 50 and standard deviation of 10. Intelligence test scores typically are normalized with an approximate mean of 100 and a standard deviation of 15 or 16 in a national norm group (Angoff, 1971, pp. 525–526). Stanines (Flanagan, 1951, p. 747) are normalized scores that range from 1 to 9 with an approximate mean of 5 and a standard deviation of 2 for the norm group. Normal curve equivalents (NCE scores), are normalized scores with an approximate mean of 50 and a standard deviation of 21.06 in a national norm group.

Kolen and Brennan (2004) illustrated the 6-step process for normalizing scores using an example. The smoothed raw score distribution for the 24-item multiple-choice test used in their example is given in Figure 5.3. This distribution is negatively skewed and is flatter than a normal distribution. The kurtosis index for the distribution in Figure 5.3 is 2.23, whereas the kurtosis index for a normal distribution is 3.0. This distribution was normalized, with the

Scaling and Norming

FIGURE 5.3 Raw Score Distribution for Normalization

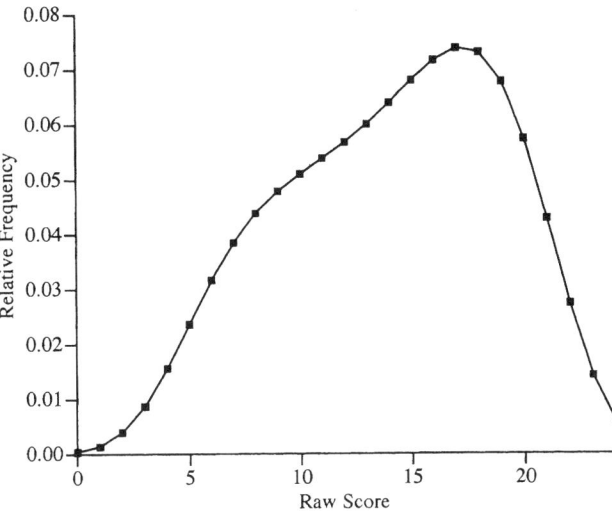

Source: From *Test equating, scaling, and linking: Methods and practices* (Second edition) by M. J. Kolen and R. L. Brennan, Figure 9.1, p. 342. Copyright 2004 by Springer Science and Business Media, Inc. Reprinted with kind permission of Springer Science and Business Media.

resulting distribution being shown in Figure 5.4. Because the resulting distribution is not truly bell-shaped, it is clear that the normalization process does not create a distribution that is perfectly normal. However, the normalized distribution appears to be more peaked and closer to being symmetric as compared to the raw score distribution. The skewness index for this distribution is near 0 and the kurtosis index is near 3. Thus, the normalized distribution is much closer to a normal distribution than is the raw score distribution.

Petersen et al. (1989) pointed out that "the advantage of normalized scores is that they can be interpreted by using facts about the normal distribution. For example, a scale score that is one standard deviation above the mean has a percentile rank of approximately 84 in the reference group" (p. 227). However, they also indicated that "usually there is no good theoretical reason for normalizing scores. Observed scores are not usually normally distributed ..., and there is often reason to expect test score distributions to be nonsymmetric" (pp. 226–227).

Percentile ranks for various examinee groups are nonlinear score transformations that are often used as auxiliary score scales. In addition to using percentile ranks for a national norm group, separate percentile ranks might be reported for national gender groups, racial/ethnic groups, and groups representing different geographical regions. Each of these sets of percentile ranks are auxiliary score scales that can be used to enhance the meaning of the reported score information.

3.7. Incorporating Score Precision Information into Score Scales

Flanagan (1951) pointed out that scale score units should "be of an order of magnitude most appropriate to express their accuracy of measurement" (p. 746). The use of too few score points leads to a loss of precision. For example, referring to stanines, Flanagan (1951) stated that although simple, they "in general are too coarse to preserve all of the information contained in raw scores" (p. 747). On the other hand, the use of very many scale score points might lead test users to inappropriately attach significance to small score differences. The choice of the number of scale score units involves using a sufficient number of scale score units to preserve score precision in the raw scores, but not so many that test users attach significance to score differences that are small relative to measurement error.

3.7.1. Rules of Thumb for Number of Distinct Score Points

Over the years, various rules of thumb have been developed for choosing the number of scale score units. One of these rules was originally used in developing the scale for the Iowa Tests of Educational Development (ITED, 1958). The scale for the ITED was constructed in 1942 using integer scores with the property that an approximate 50% confidence interval for true scores could be found by adding 1 scale score point to and subtracting 1 scale score point from an examinee's scale score. Similarly, Truman L. Kelley (W. H. Angoff, personal communication, February 17, 1987) suggested constructing scale scores so that an approximate 68% confidence interval could be constructed by adding 3 scale score points to and subtracting 3 scale score points from each examinee's scale score. These confidence interval statements

FIGURE 5.4 Normalized Score Distribution

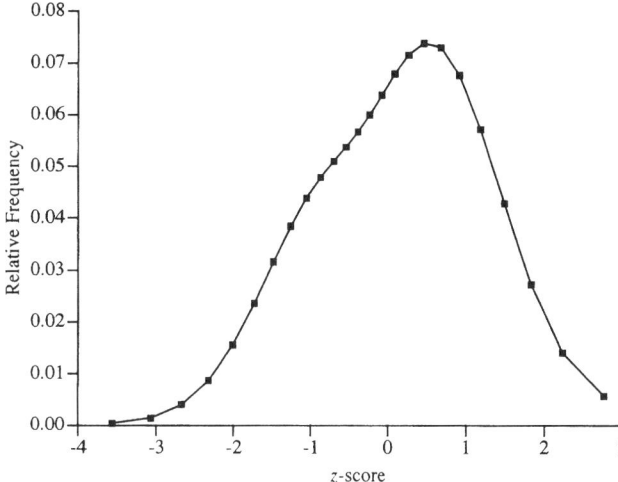

Source: From *Test equating, scaling, and linking: Methods and practices* (Second edition) by M. J. Kolen and R. L. Brennan, Figure 9.2, p. 344. Copyright 2004 by Springer Science and Business Media, Inc. Reprinted with kind permission of Springer Science and Business Media.

were translated into the desired number of discrete scale score points by finding a range of integer scores that are consistent with the confidence interval properties stated. These rules are based on the following assumptions:

1. Linear transformations of raw-to-scale scores are being considered.
2. Measurement error, conditional on true score, is normally distributed.
3. The conditional standard error of measurement is constant along the score scale.
4. The reliability of raw scores, $\rho_{XX'}$, is known or a reasonable estimate exists.
5. The range of scale scores of interest is 6 scale score standard deviations ($6\sigma_s$).
6. The width of the desired confidence interval, symbolized by h, is given. For example, $h = 1$ for the ITED and $h = 3$ for Kelley's rule mentioned earlier.
7. The confidence coefficient, γ, is given, and z_γ is the unit-normal score used to form a $100\gamma\%$ confidence interval. For example, $\gamma = 50\%$ and $z_\gamma \approx .6745$ for the ITED rule; $\gamma = 68\%$ and $z_\gamma \approx 1$ for Kelley's rule.

Based on these assumptions, the standard deviation of scale scores can be found as follows:

$$\sigma_S = \frac{h}{z_\gamma \sqrt{1-\rho_{XX'}}} \qquad (16)$$

as shown by Kolen and Brennan (2004, pp. 346–347). Multiplying σ_s by 6 and rounding to an integer gives the number of distinct score points.

For example, assume that $\rho_{XX'} = .91$ and that the ITED rule is being used, where $h = 1$ and $z_\gamma \approx .6745$. Substituting these values into Equation 16 gives $\sigma_s = 4.94$. Multiplying by 6 and rounding to an integer suggests that 30 scale score points should be used given this rule. Applying Kelley's rule to the same test, $h = 3$, $z_\gamma \approx 1$; in this case Equation 16 indicates that $\sigma_s = 10$, suggesting that 60 score points should be used to cover the range $6\sigma_s$.

From an examination of Equation 16, it can be seen that as reliability decreases, the number of scale score points decreases. Also, Kelley's rule, in general, leads to around twice as many scale score points as the ITED rule.

In practice, to use these rules of thumb, the desired confidence interval properties are stated, an estimate of reliability is used, and the associated number of distinct score points is found. A raw-to-scale score transformation is found that leads to scale scores with an integer score range that is consistent with this number of score points. Using this rule with the ITED, and assuming that $\rho_{XX'} = .91$, the ITED score scale was constructed to have 30 distinct integer scores ranging from 1 to 30. Consistent with Kelley's rule, the SAT score scale (Donlon, 1984) ranges from 200 to 800, with the last digit always being a zero. Thus, there are 61 distinct score points, which is very close to the 60 distinct score points suggested by Kelley's rule for a test with $\rho_{XX'} = .91$.

Although developed making assumptions such as constant and normally distributed measurement errors and linear raw to scale score transformations, these rules of thumb have been used under a much wider set of conditions. Keeping in mind that the confidence interval properties are only approximately achieved when the assumptions are not met, these rules can be used as approximations when errors are not normally distributed or constant, and when the transformations of raw to scale scores are not linear. They can be used for all types of raw scores, including IRT estimates of θ, as long as a reasonable estimate of the reliability of the raw scores is available.

3.7.2. Score Scales with Approximately Equal Conditional Standard Errors of Measurement

In general, conditional standard errors of measurement for raw scores are not constant along the score scale (Feldt & Brennan, 1989; Haertel, this volume). For summed scores, the conditional standard errors of measurement tend to be relatively larger for the middle scores and smaller for very high and low scores. For IRT-based raw scores, such as maximum likelihood and Bayesian EAP estimates of proficiency, the conditional standard errors of measurement typically have a pattern opposite that for summed scores. In this case, the conditional standard errors of measurement are smaller for the middle scores and larger at the extremes. Kolen, Hanson, and Brennan (1992) demonstrated, using a variety of examples, that nonlinear transformations of raw scores can lead to a pattern of conditional standard errors of measurement that is markedly different from that of raw scores.

Standard 2.14 in the *Test Standards* (American Educational Research Association, American Psychological Association, & National Council on Measurement in Education, 1999) states that "conditional standard errors of measurement should be reported at several score levels if constancy cannot be assumed" (p. 35). To follow this standard, test developers should, in general, report standard errors of measurement at various score levels when the standard errors of measurement vary.

In an attempt to simplify score interpretation, Kolen (1988) suggested using a nonlinear transformation that stabilizes the magnitude of the conditional standard error of measurement. The result of applying this transformation is to make the conditional standard errors of measurement approximately equal along the score scale. With equal conditional standard errors of measurement, test developers need only to report a single standard error of measurement, and test users need only use a single standard error of measurement when interpreting test scores.

Kolen (1988) considered a situation in which the raw score was number-correct. He used the following arcsine transformation suggested by Freeman and Tukey (1950) to stabilize the conditional standard errors of measurement:

$$g(x) = .5 \left\{ \sin^{-1}\left[\left(\frac{x}{K+1}\right)^{\frac{1}{2}}\right] + \sin^{-1}\left[\left(\frac{x+1}{K+1}\right)^{\frac{1}{2}}\right] \right\}. \qquad (17)$$

In this equation, K is the number of items on the test, x is the number correct score, and $\sin^{-1}$ is the arcsine function with arguments expressed in radians. The arcsine transformation was used by Freeman and Tukey (1950) to stabilize the variance of random variables that have a binomial distribution.

The arcsine transformation has been used to stabilize error variance of number correct scores using binomial and compound binomial error test theory models (Jarjoura, 1985; Kolen, 1988; Kolen et al., 1992; Wilcox, 1981) and in IRT models (Kolen, Zeng, & Hanson, 1996). Using these test theory models, it has been shown that variance of measurement errors is approximately constant along the score scale when the number-correct scores are transformed using Equation 17. Although no published studies exist, it seems that an equation similar to Equation 17 could be used to stabilize error variance for summed scores other than those that are number-correct.

To stabilize error variance using the arcsine transformation so that the standard error of measurement is a particular value, the number-correct scores are transformed using Equation 17. The standard error of measurement of these arcsine transformed scores is then found. Jarjoura (1985) provided expressions for the standard errors of measurement under strong true score models, which are also given in Kolen and Brennan (2004, p. 350). Under IRT models, the average standard error of measurement for number-correct scores transformed using Equation 17 can be calculated using procedures described by Kolen et al. (1996) and summarized in Kolen and Brennan (2004, p. 302). If a particular standard error of measurement is desired, based on Equation 14, the scale scores can be found by transforming the arcsine transformed scores as

$$S[g(x)] = \frac{sem_s}{sem_g} g(x) + \left\{ S[g(x_1)] - \frac{sem_s}{sem_g} g(x_1) \right\}, \quad (18)$$

where g is the arcsine transformed score from Equation 17, sem_g is the standard error of measurement of the arcsine transformed scores, $S[g(x_1)]$ is the scale score equivalent associated with a prespecified number-correct score on the test, and sem_s is the desired scale score standard error of measurement. Alternatively, scale scores with stabilized conditional standard errors of measurement can be calculated to have a particular mean and standard deviation using Equation 12. The arcsine transformation can be used to stabilize error variance for summed scores. Procedures for stabilizing error variance for IRT proficiency estimates, such as EAP and maximum likelihood estimates, have yet to be developed.

Figure 5.5 illustrates the effect of transformations of raw scores to scale scores on the pattern of the conditional standard error of measurement. Data from the 24-item test used in Figures 5.3 and 5.4 were also used to construct Figure 5.5. Based on an application of Kelley's rule, scale scores were constructed to have a standard error of measurement of approximately 3, and with a raw score of 12 corresponding to a scale score of 50. A scale that is a linear transformation was constructed. In addition, a scale that used the arcsine transformation to stabilize the conditional standard error of measurement was also constructed. This example is provided in much detail in Kolen and Brennan (2004). As can be seen from Figure 5.5 for the linear transformation, the conditional standard errors of measurement are larger for the middle scores and smaller for the extreme scores. Following an arcsine transformation, the conditional standard errors for the nonlinear scale shown in Figure 5.5 are nearly constant along the score scale.

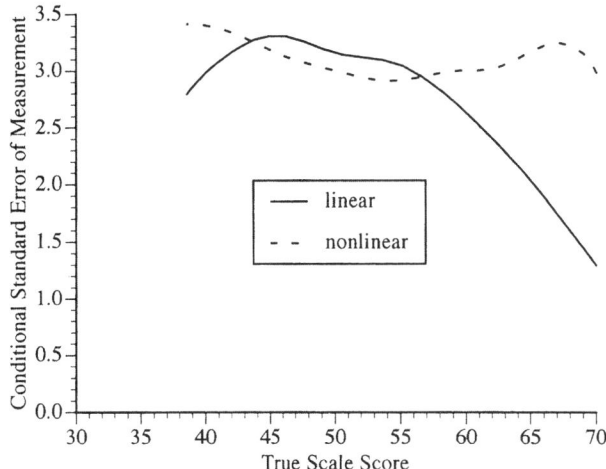

FIGURE 5.5 Conditional Standard Errors of Measurement for Scales Constructed Using Linear and Nonlinear Transformations

Source: From *Test equating, scaling, and linking: Methods and practices* (Second edition) by M. J. Kolen and R. L. Brennan, Figure 9.3, p. 356. Copyright 2004 by Springer Science and Business Media, Inc. Reprinted with kind permission of Springer Science and Business Media.

3.8. Incorporating Content Information Into Score Scales

According to Ebel (1962), "to be meaningful any test scores must be related to test content as well as to the scores of other examinees" (p. 18). Ebel (1962) suggested that content information be provided along with scale scores to aid in score interpretation. He suggested constructing content standard scores, which relate the content of the test to scale scores. Three types of procedures for providing content meaningful scale scores are considered here and referred to as *item mapping, scale anchoring*, and *standard setting*.

3.8.1. Item Mapping

After constructing a primary score scale using one of the methods already discussed, items are found that represent various scale score points. The set of items representing the various scale score points are referred to as item maps. Zwick, Senturk, Wang, and Loomis (2001) reviewed and studied item mapping procedures.

To implement item maps, test items are associated with various scale score points. For dichotomously scored items, the probability of correct response on each item is regressed on scale scores using procedures such as logistic regression or an IRT model. The *response probability* (RP) *level*, which is the probability (expressed as a percentage) of correct response given scale score that is associated with mastery on a test item, is stated by the test developer. The same RP level is used for all dichotomously scored items on the test. Using the regressions of item score on scale score, an item is said to map at the scale score that is associated with an

RP% probability of correctly answering the item. According to Zwick et al. (2001), values of RP ranging from .50 to .80 have been used for item mapping with the National Assessment of Educational Progress (NAEP). Huynh (1998) provided psychometric justifications for choosing RP values.

The choice of RP value has a strong effect on where an item is mapped on the score scale. For example, items are mapped at a much lower scale score if an RP level of .5 is used than if an RP level of .8 is used. Thus, the choice of RP level can affect how test users interpret scale scores.

Additional criteria are often used when choosing the items to report on item maps. For example, items might be chosen only if they discriminate well between examinees who score above and below the score. Also, items might be used only if subject matter experts indicate that an item provides adequate representation of test content. Modifications of item mapping procedures are used for polytomously scored items.

FIGURE 5.6 Selected Portions of an Item Map for the 1996 NAEP Fourth-Grade Science Assessment

NAEP Scale

- 200 — (201) Identify location of Atlantic and Pacific Oceans
- 180 — (185) Identify pattern of ripples
- (177) Understand impact on life cycle of larvae if eaten
- 160 — (164) Identify organism that produces its own food
- (153) Recognize energy source needed for evaporation
- 140 — (140) Understand how fish obtain oxygen
- (132) Understand information needed to identify rock
- 120 — (117) Recognize graph that corresponds to data
- 100 — (94) Identify instrument used to observe stars

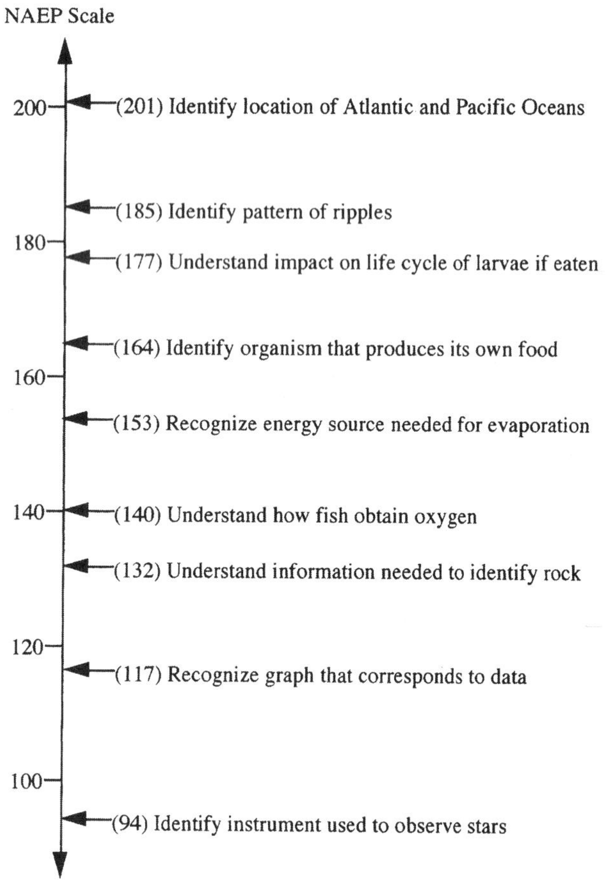

Source: From *Test equating, scaling, and linking: Methods and practices* (Second edition) by M. J. Kolen and R. L. Brennan, Figure 9.4, p. 360. Copyright 2004 by Springer Science and Business Media, Inc. Reprinted with kind permission of Springer Science and Business Media.

The outcome of an item mapping procedure is the specification of test questions that represent various scale score points. Item maps were constructed, for example, using an RP level of 74% for multiple choice test questions on the 1996 NAEP 4th grade Science Assessment (O'Sullivan, Reese, & Mazzeo, 1997). Figure 5.6 shows selected portions of a NAEP item map for this assessment, with scale scores ranging from 0 to 300. A phrase describing what an examinee can do who correctly answers an item, rather than the item itself, is presented. For example, an examinee earning a NAEP scale score of 185 can "identify patterns of ripples."

3.8.2. Scale Anchoring

The goal of scale anchoring is to provide general statements of what students who score at each of a selected set of scale score points know and are able to do. The first step in scale anchoring is to create item maps for the items on a test. Then a set of scale score points is chosen. Typically these points are either equally spaced along the score scale or are selected to be a set of percentiles, such as the 10th, 25th, 50th, 75th, and 90th. Items that map at or near these points are chosen to represent these points. Subject matter experts review the items that map near each point and develop general statements that represent the skills of examinees scoring at these points. In scale anchoring, it is assumed that examinees know and are able to do all of the skills in the statements that are at or below a given score level.

The scale anchoring process used with NAEP is described by Allen, Carlson, and Zelenak (1999). A scale anchoring process was used to develop the ACT Standards for Transition for Explore, PLAN, and the ACT Assessment (ACT, 2001). A process much like scale anchoring was also suggested by Ebel (1962), although he used scores on a subset of items rather than statements to display performance at each of the levels.

3.8.3. Standard Setting

Standard setting procedures (see Hambleton & Pitoniak, this volume) begin with a statement of what competent examinees know and are able to do. Standard setting methods seek to find the score point that divides the examinees who know and are able to do what is stated from other examinees. In professional licensure and certification testing, a statement of what it means for an examinee to be minimally competent to practice in a field is constructed by the test developers. A judgmental process then is used to find the scale score point that differentiates those examinees who are minimally competent from those who are less than minimally competent. In achievement testing situations, various achievement levels are stated, such as basic, proficient, and advanced. Statements are created indicating what students who score at each of these levels know and are able to do. Judgmental techniques are used to find the scale score points that differentiate between adjacent levels.

In a typical standard setting technique, judges are given, or develop, statements about what examinees know and are able to do who score at a particular level (e.g., proficient). The judges are also provided with a set of test questions.

A systematic procedure is used to collect information from judges. They are asked to consider examinees who score just at the score point that divides one level from the next.

In one method used with multiple-choice items, often referred to as the modified Angoff method (Angoff, 1971, p. 514), judges are asked to indicate the proportion of examinees scoring at this point who would be expected to correctly answer each item. The judgments are aggregated over items and judges. In the bookmark procedure (Mitzel, Lewis, Patz, & Green, 2001), which can be used with polytomously-scored test questions, item maps are used in a structured judgmental procedure. Judges are asked to indicate the position of the point on the item map that best divides one level from the next. Note that the results of this procedure depend heavily on the RP-value used to construct the item map. The outcome of these procedures typically is a score that represents the cut-point. Various methods have been used to collect data, to provide feedback to judges, to provide normative information to judges, and to aggregate data.

3.8.4. Usefulness

Forsyth (1991) has questioned whether the outcome of methods for incorporating content information facilitates score interpretation. In considering whether the content information provided on NAEP meets the goal of accurately describing what examinees know and are able to do, he argued that "NAEP, despite its claims, has not achieved this goal to any reasonable extent" (p. 9). He further argued that unless the content domains are very well defined, providing useful content-based information in terms of item mapping or scale anchoring may be unattainable. His argument was based on a detailed analysis of NAEP scale anchoring and item mapping results. Pellegrino, Jones, and Mitchell (1999) argued that the current process for setting NAEP achievement levels is overly subjective and that the judges are given a difficult and confusing task. Hambleton et al. (2000) disputed the argument of Pellegrino et al. (1999). In any case, Ebel's (1962) goal of attaching content meaning to scale scores remains an important one. As Forsyth (1991) stated, "teachers have pleaded for such measures for decades" (p. 9).

3.9. Maintaining Scales

Equating methods described by Holland and Dorans (this volume) are used to maintain score scales as new forms are developed. Over time, however, the information that was originally incorporated into the score scale can become less relevant. For example, the norm group that was central to score interpretation might, over time, become of less interest. The content of a test might slowly evolve, with the cumulative effect that forms used in one year are different in content than forms used a few years later.

Petersen et al. (1989) suggested that professional certification and licensure tests are especially affected by changes in test content. With these tests, a passing score is often set using standard setting methods on an initial test form. Over time, the profession might change in its emphases, knowledge base, and legal context, leading to some items and content becoming less relevant. Even though an equating process can maintain the score scale for some time, the cumulative effects of changes might result in scores at one time being not comparable with scores at a later time. When the test developer judges that these changes have caused the standards to lose their meaning, a study can be conducted to set new standards.

Changes in norm groups can contribute to score misinterpretation. As an example, when the SAT scale was established in 1941, the mean Verbal and Mathematics scores were set to be 500 for the group of examinees who took the test that year. This scale was maintained through the mid-1990s. In the early 1990s, the mean Mathematics score was lower than 500, due, in part, to the changes in the composition of the group of examinees who take the SAT (Dorans, 2002). As indicated by Cook (1994), due to changes in test content, "it is difficult to think of scores on the current SAT as comparable to scores on the version of the SAT that was administered in 1941, even with the effective equating plan that has been used over the years to maintain comparability" (p. 3). These concerns led to a rescaling of the SAT, which was referred to as "recentering." The new scale, which was first used in 1995, was set to have a mean of 500 for students who graduated high school in 1990 and who took the SAT in either their junior or senior year in high school (Dorans, 2002). For similar reasons, the ACT Assessment was rescaled in 1989 (Brennan, 1989).

Some test developers periodically adjust the scaling of their tests. For example, new editions of the Iowa Tests of Basic Skills (ITBS) (Hoover, Dunbar, & Frisbie, 2003) are released approximately every seven years. For each new edition, the developmental scale scores are based on scores for examinees in a national norming study. By periodically adjusting the scale scores, the ITBS scale scores are always referenced to a recent norm group.

Rescaling a test, or setting new standards, makes it difficult to compare scores from before and after the rescaling. Often a study is conducted to link the two scales to help test users make the transition. Because the development of a new score scale causes complexities in score interpretation, the decision about whether to rescale can be difficult. As the examples considered suggest, the decision on when to rescale depends on the context in which the testing program operates.

4. SCALES FOR TEST BATTERIES AND COMPOSITES

Test batteries consist of tests in various areas, with separate scores provided for each area. With test batteries, the processes of test construction and scaling are handled similarly for each test in the battery, making possible the assessment of examinee strengths and weaknesses across test areas. Sometimes composite scores are calculated, which are combinations of scores from some or all of the tests in the battery. Using the same scaling procedures for each of the tests in a battery facilitates the formation of such composites.

4.1. Scale Comparability across Tests in a Battery

When normative information is incorporated into the scale for a test, the same norm group often is used for all of the tests. Using this normative information, the scale can be constructed so that the scale score distributions for the tests in the battery are approximately the same for the norm group. For example, when the SAT was rescaled, the Verbal and Mathematics scores were developed as normalized scores with means of 500 and standard deviations of 110 for the norm group described previously (Dorans, 2002). The use of the same scaling conventions for the two tests allows for straightforward assessment of an examinee's strengths and weaknesses on the test. Consider an examinee scoring 500 on the Verbal test and 610 on the Mathematics test. Because of the normalized scale score property built into the scale, this examinee's score is near the 50th percentile on the Verbal test and near the 84th percentile on the Mathematics test. Relative to the norm group, the examinee is stronger in the Mathematics area than in the Verbal test area.

Primary score scales can be constructed by emphasizing characteristics other than identical score distributions across tests. For example, in the ACT Assessment rescaling (Brennan, 1989), the scale for each test was set to have a mean of 18, with approximately constant conditional standard errors of measurement across the score scale. This process led to unequal scale-score standard deviations from one test to the next, resulting in scores on different tests not being directly comparable to one another. Consider an examinee with scores of 22 on the English Usage test and 25 on the Mathematics test. Although this student readily can be seen to be above the mean on both tests, it is not possible to be sure on which test the examinee ranks higher by looking only at the scale scores. For the ACT Assessment, comparisons of strengths and weaknesses need to be made using percentile ranks in a particular norm group, which can be viewed as an auxiliary score scale in the terminology of this chapter.

The use of common procedures for scale construction across tests in a battery can encourage meaningful score interpretation that goes beyond normative comparisons. For instance, with the ACT Assessment, the standard error of measurement was set to be approximately 2 points for each of the tests in the battery and to be constant along the score scale. Test users can use this information when interpreting test scores. As another example, consider a student who scores 18 on the Mathematics test and is interested in being placed into a particular mathematics course that requires a minimum score of 24. Given that 24 is 3 standard errors of measurement above this examinee's score, this examinee likely would not exceed 24 on a second testing without instructional intervention. This constant standard error of measurement of 2 points can be used by test users to readily make these sorts of interpretations.

Using common procedures for incorporating content information into score scales can also aid test users in interpreting examinee performance across tests in a battery. For example, in NAEP the following policy definition of "proficient" was used: This "level represents solid academic performance.... Students reaching this level have demon-strated competency over challenging subject matter and are well prepared for the next level of schooling" (Bourque, 1999a, p. 739). This policy definition can be used for a variety of subject matter areas, leading to a degree of comparability of the meaning of "proficient" across subject matter areas. Of course, more specific definitions would be needed for each subject matter area to actually set standards. With the NAEP Science test, the following summary achievement level description was used at grade 4:

> Students performing at the Proficient level demonstrate the knowledge and reasoning required for understanding of the earth, physical, and life sciences at a level appropriate to Grade 4. For example, they understand concepts relating to the Earth's features, physical properties, and structure and function. In addition, students can formulate solutions to familiar problems as well as show a beginning awareness of issues associated with technology. (Bourque, 1999b, p. 763)

Still, even though more specific definitions of proficient are needed for each test to set standards, the use of the more general policy definitions creates a degree of comparability among standards across NAEP tests.

4.2. Composites

Composite scores that reflect performance on two or more tests often are used. Composite scores typically are a linear combination of scale scores on different tests. On the ACT Assessment, the Composite score is the average, rounded to an integer, of the English Usage, Mathematics, Reading, and Science Reasoning scale scores. This Composite score is intended to reflect the general educational development over the four tests.

Nominal and effective weights were discussed earlier in this chapter in the context of developing raw scores for mixed format tests. These concepts are also useful when considering composite scores that are linear combinations of scale scores. For composite scores, nominal weights are the weights applied directly to the scale scores for each test used in the composite. For example, for the ACT Assessment Composite scores, the nominal weights are each .25. Equation 8 can be used to find the effective weights of the

TABLE 5.1 ACT Assessment Variances, Covariances, and Effective Weights for Forming the Scale Score Composite

ACT Assessment Test	English	Mathematics	Reading	Science Reasoning
English	27.7	17.0	25.6	15.8
Mathematics	17.0	20.8	18.2	13.1
Reading	25.6	18.2	41.8	21.0
Science Reasoning	15.8	13.1	21.0	19.5
Effective Weight	.26	.21	.32	.21

composite scores by redefining some of the terms in this equation. In this case, ew_j is the effective weight for test j, u_j is the nominal weight for test j, σ_j^2 is the variance of scale scores for test j, σ_{jk} is the covariance between scale scores on test j and test k.

An illustration of the computation of effective weights is given in Table 5.1.

This table is based on data from the 1988 ACT norming study reported by Kolen and Hanson (1989, p. 53). The variance-covariance matrix for the four ACT Assessment scale scores is given in this table. The proportional effective weights shown at the bottom of the table were found from Equation 8. As can be seen, the proportional effective weight for reading is the highest (.32). The main reason that reading has the largest effective weight is that it has a variance of 41.8, which is greater than the variance for the other tests. This finding suggests that even though the nominal weights for the 4 tests are the same (.25), the proportional effective weights are unequal, and the Reading test contributes more to the composite variance than do any of the other tests.

Referring to Equation 8, it can be shown that when tests are scaled to have the same variances, and equal nominal weights are used, the nominal and effective weights differ only due to the covariances. In these cases, as long as the correlations among the tests are similar to one another, the nominal and effective weights will be similar.

When the individual tests are scaled to have similar score distributions, the distribution of the composite score likely will be different from that of the tests. In such cases, the composite score might be rescaled to have a similar distribution to that of the scale scores on the tests.

4.3. Scale Maintenance for Batteries and Composites

The scale scores for the tests in a battery often become less comparable over time. One reason that the SAT was rescaled is because, over time, the mean Verbal and Mathematics scores became considerably different for groups who took the tests (Dorans, 2002). The rescaling was conducted so that the score distributions were the same for a recent group of test users. In the future, as the user groups change over time, the score distributions for Verbal and Mathematics likely will diverge. At some point, the score distributions will differ enough that scores on the two tests will not be comparable. At that point, either test users will need to be cautioned against comparing scores, or another rescaling will be needed. However, even if the Verbal and Mathematics scores cannot be directly compared, percentile ranks in a relevant group could be used to make these comparisons.

When new forms are introduced, test scores are equated using procedures described by Holland and Dorans (this volume) to maintain the score scale. Typically, the composite scores are not separately equated. Equating the test scores does not ensure that the composite scores are equated. If the correlations between scores on one form differ from those on another form, then composites likely will not have identical distributions on the old and new form, regardless of the adequacy of the equating for the scores on the individual tests.

Kolen and Brennan (2004, pp. 371–372) provided an example using ASVAB data reported by Thomasson, Bloxom, and Wise (1994). In this example, alternate forms of three ASVAB tests were equated using equipercentile methods. A composite score was then formed from the three tests. Even though the distribution of scale scores from one form to the next was nearly the same for each of the three tests, the distributions for the composite differed. In particular, the standard deviation of the composite for one of the forms was substantially higher than the standard deviation for the other form. This difference occurred because the correlations among scores on one of the forms were all higher than the correlations among scores on the other form. This example illustrates that when composites are created for tests in a battery, it is important to check whether the composites also are comparable. Although composite scores could be equated, it is rarely done.

5. VERTICAL SCALING AND DEVELOPMENTAL SCORE SCALES

Assessing the extent to which the achievement or aptitude of students grows from one year to the next and over the course of their schooling is important for many educational applications. Growth might be assessed by administering alternate forms of the same test each year, and charting growth as measured by changes in test scores from year-to-year and over multi-year periods. However, students learn so much during their grade school years that using a single set of questions for all grade levels is beset with problems. Most students would be measured imprecisely because the test would not be targeted at their current level of achievement. Students in early grades would be overwhelmed when questioned about material over which they had not been exposed. Students in later grades might be careless or inattentive when taking many test questions that were too easy.

To address these issues, educational achievement and aptitude batteries typically are constructed using multiple test levels, where each level is constructed to be appropriate for students at a particular grade or age. Vertical scaling procedures are used to relate scores on these multiple test levels to a *developmental score scale* that can be used to assess student growth over a range of educational levels.

This section discusses the types of domains that are measured with vertical scales and different definitions of growth. Designs for collecting data for vertical scaling and statistical procedures used to conduct vertical scaling are discussed.

5.1. Structure of Batteries

Vertical scaling procedures are used with achievement test batteries (e.g., Iowa Tests of Basic Skills, Hoover et al., 2003) and aptitude test batteries (e.g., Cognitive Abilities Test, Lohman & Hagen, 2002). These types of batteries typically contain tests in a number of areas and are used with students in a range of grades. For achievement batteries, students are administered test questions that assess achievement relevant to that grade level. Going

FIGURE 5.7 Illustrative Structure of a Grade-Level Test

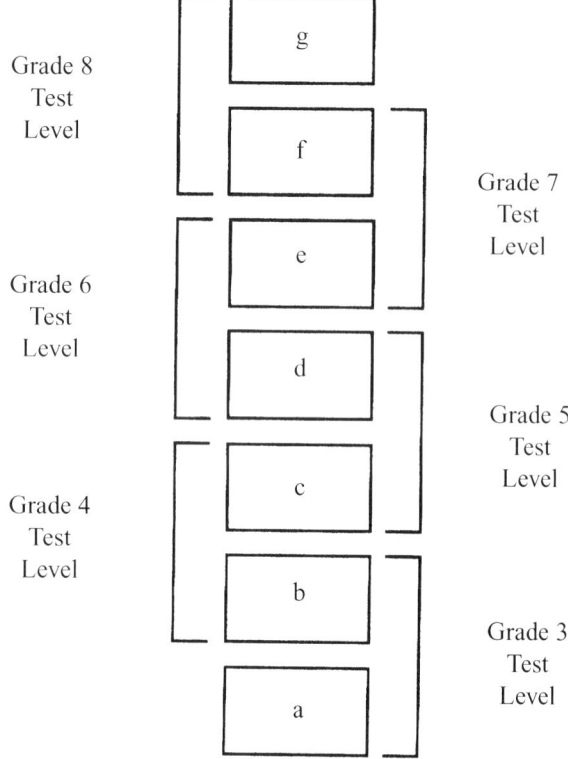

Source: From *Test equating, scaling, and linking: Methods and practices* (Second edition) by M. J. Kolen and R. L. Brennan, Figure 9.6, p. 374. Copyright 2004 by Springer Science and Business Media, Inc. Reprinted with kind permission of Springer Science and Business Media.

from early to later grades, the test questions become more difficult and the content becomes more advanced. In some cases, content covered in later grades is quite different from content covered in earlier grades.

For many such batteries, there is overlap of test questions from one test level to the next. Such overlap is possible because some content is taught in multiple grades. Overlap reduces the development burden, because the same items are used in adjacent test levels.

Figure 5.7 illustrates the overlap. The test illustrated contains 7 blocks of items, labeled *a–g*. Blocks *a* and *b* are administered as part of the grade 3 test level, blocks *b* and *c* as part of the grade 4 test level, blocks *c* and *d* as part of the grade 5 test level, and so on. Beginning with the grade 4 test level, each test level has a block of items in common with the previous level. At least two alternate forms of these tests typically are constructed, so that individuals do not receive the same items in consecutive years.

5.2. Relationship between Content and Growth

The tests that are scaled using vertical scaling procedures differ in the extent to which the subject matter covered is tied to the school curriculum. Most content areas on aptitude tests, and some content areas on educational achievement tests, are not closely tied to the educational curriculum. For example, vocabulary, which is often assessed on aptitude and achievement tests, tends not to be taught systematically by grade level. Other achievement test areas, such as mathematics computation, are closely tied to the curriculum. For such tests, students tend to score higher on the new subject matter areas near the end of the year in which the subject matter is emphasized than they do at the end of the previous year.

Consider a mathematics computation example described by Kolen and Brennan (2004, p. 375). In mathematics computation, "division with whole numbers" is typically covered in grades 3 and 4. "Addition with decimals" is typically covered in grades 5 and 6. Based on what students study in school, students in grades 3 and 4 are expected to grow substantially on items that cover "division with whole numbers." Less growth is expected in this area for students in grades 5 and 6. Students in grades 3 and 4 are expected to do poorly on items covering "addition with decimals" and show little growth. More growth is expected on items covering "addition with decimals" in grades 5 and 6. This example illustrates that for subject matter areas that are closely tied to the curriculum, students will tend to show different amounts of growth, depending on the content areas over which they are tested. When content included on a test is closely tied to the curriculum, the amount of growth exhibited during a year will depend on the content that is assessed. A fifth grade student would be expected to show less growth on some portions of the content that is assessed (e.g., "division with whole numbers") than on other portions of the content (e.g., "addition with decimals").

How should growth be defined in this situation? Should growth be defined over the content that is taught during a particular year? Or should growth be defined over content that is taught over a number of school years? The mathematics computational example just described makes it clear that the amount of growth can depend on which of these definitions is chosen.

To formalize these definitions, Kolen and Brennan (2004) considered a domain as content covered by an achievement test over all grade levels. The *domain definition of growth* refers to growth over all of the content in the domain. Thus, under this definition, growth by a student from one year to the next is defined over the whole domain. One way to think about operationalizing the domain definition would be to administer all of the test levels (e.g. blocks *a* through *g* in Figure 5.7) to students each year. Growth from one year to the next is then defined as changes in scores from one grade to the next over the domain of content. Of course, this process would be difficult to implement in practice, because the test is too long, many of the questions are too difficult for some students and too easy for others, and students would be tested with the same test questions multiple times. More practical procedures for operationalizing the domain definition are described in the next section.

Kolen and Brennan (2004) also described the *grade-to-grade definition of growth*, in which growth is defined over the content that is on a test level appropriate for students in a particular grade. For example, growth from the beginning of grade 3 to the end of grade 3 might be assessed using only the content on the third-grade level, which is item blocks a and *b* in Figure 5.7. One way to operationalize the grade-to-grade definition is to administer the level of the test designed for each grade at the beginning of that grade and at the beginning of the next grade. Thus, under the grade-to-grade definition, growth is defined over the content that is part of the curriculum in a particular grade. For subject matter areas that are closely related to the school curriculum, growth observed between adjacent grades will tend to be different under the grade-to-grade definition than under the domain definition.

5.3. Designs for Data Collection for Vertical Scaling

Data are collected to conduct vertical scaling. Three of the designs used for data collection are considered. The designs are then compared.

5.3.1. Common-Item Design

Taking advantage of the overlapping structure illustrated in Figure 5.7, a *common-item design* can be used to conduct the scaling. Following this design, each test level is administered to students at the appropriate grade, as is shown in Figure 5.8. Performance on the items that are common to adjacent test levels is used to indicate the average amount of growth that occurs from one grade to the next. The data from this design are used to place scores from all test levels on a common scale.

To implement this design, one level is designated as the base level. The item blocks that are common are used to link scores from adjacent levels. A chaining process is used to link

FIGURE 5.8 Illustration of a Common-Item Design

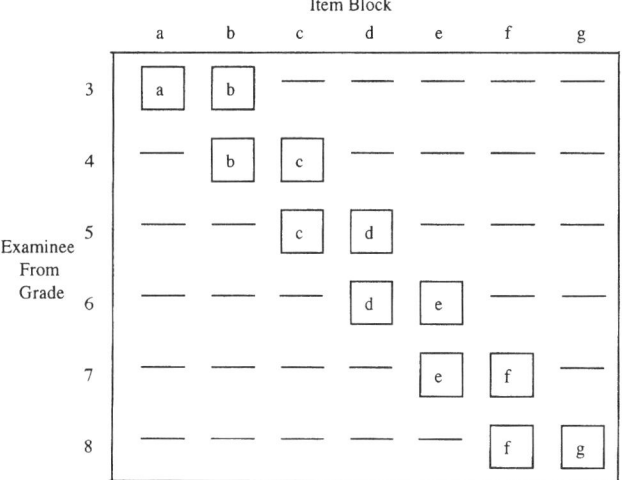

Source: From *Test equating, scaling, and linking: Methods and practices* (Second edition) by M. J. Kolen and R. L. Brennan, Figure 9.8, p. 378. Copyright 2004 by Springer Science and Business Media, Inc. Reprinted with kind permission of Springer Science and Business Media.

FIGURE 5.9 Illustration of an Equivalent Groups Design

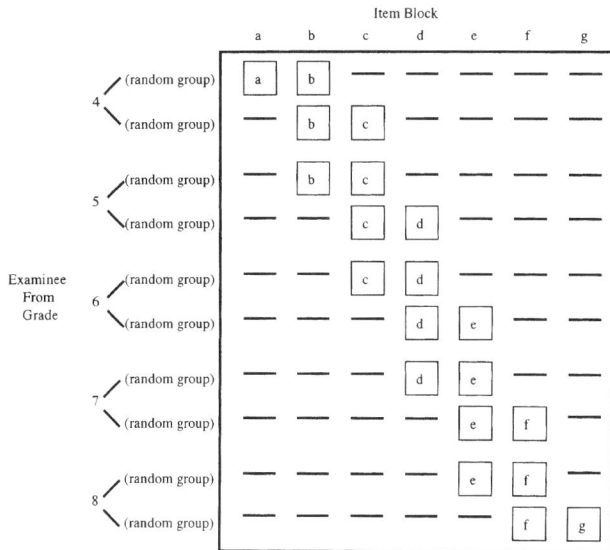

Source: From *Test equating, scaling, and linking: Methods and practices* (Second edition) by M. J. Kolen and R. L. Brennan, Figure 9.9, p. 379. Copyright 2004 by Springer Science and Business Media, Inc. Reprinted with kind permission of Springer Science and Business Media.

scores from all levels to scores on the base level. For example, choosing grade 3 as the base level, scores on the grade 4 level are linked to scores on the grade 3 level using item block b. Scores on the grade 5 level are linked to scores on the grade 4 level using item block c. Scores on the grade 5 level are linked to scores on the grade 3 level through scores on the grade 4 level using a linking chain. A similar process is used to link scores on the grades 6, 7, and 8 levels to scores on the base level. In the end, scores on all levels are linked to scores on the base level. The particular statistical procedures that are used and other scaling issues are described later in this chapter.

5.3.2. Equivalent Groups Design

In the *equivalent groups design*, examinees in each grade are randomly assigned to take either the test level designed for their grade or the test level designed for one or both adjacent grades. One variant of this design is illustrated in Figure 5.9. Randomly equivalent groups of examinees are administered the level appropriate for their grade and the level below their grade. By chaining across grades, the data from this administration are used to place scores from all test levels on a base level. Note that this design does not necessarily make use of the items that are common from one level to the next.

5.3.3. Scaling Test Design

In the *scaling test design*, a special test is constructed that spans the content across all of the grade levels of interest. This *scaling test* is constructed to be of a length

FIGURE 5.10 Illustration of a Scaling Test Design

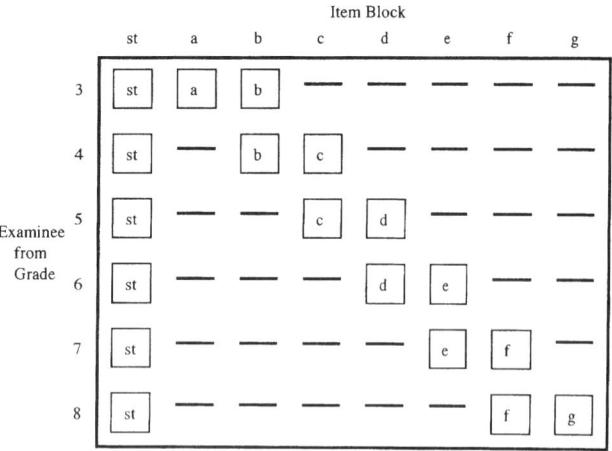

Source: From *Test equating, scaling, and linking: Methods and practices* (Second edition) by M. J. Kolen and R. L. Brennan, Figure 9.10, p. 380. Copyright 2004 by Springer Science and Business Media, Inc. Reprinted with kind permission of Springer Science and Business Media.

that can be administered in a single setting. Students in all grades are administered the same scaling test. Because many items are too difficult for students in the early grades, they are told that there are many difficult items, they should do their best, and they should not guess.

The scaling test design is illustrated in Figure 5.10. All students take the scaling test (*st*) and the item blocks appropriate for their level. The score scale is defined using scores on the scaling test. Scores on each test level are linked to the scaling test.

5.3.4. Contrasting Vertical Scaling Designs

The common-item design is the easiest of the designs to administer when the test battery contains items that are common to adjacent levels. In this case, standard administration conditions are used with the standard test battery when conducting vertical scaling. The equivalent groups design also uses the standard test battery, but requires a special administration. Of the three designs considered, the scaling test design is the most difficult to implement. It requires that a scaling test be constructed, and it requires a special test administration.

A significant potential problem with the common-item design is that it is subject to context effects. In standard administrations, the items common between two levels typically are placed near the end of the lower level test and near the beginning of the upper level test. If items behave differently when administered at the beginning than at the end of a testing session, the vertical scaling might be affected. The equivalent groups design need not be affected, because the linking of adjacent test levels can be based on random groups rather than on common items. Similarly, the scaling test design need not be affected by the context effects associated with the common items, because the linking of each test level to the scaling test can be based on the same students taking the test level and the scaling test.

Although it is the most difficult to implement of the three designs, the scaling test design has the advantage of explicitly considering the domain definition of growth. The scaling test explicitly orders students from all grades on a single set of test questions. The other two designs do not allow for an explicit ordering, because examinees in different grades take different test questions. With these other two designs, the content over which growth is defined can change from grade to grade. Especially for content areas that are closely tied to the curriculum, the scaling test design can be expected to produce scaling results that are different from those produced by the other two designs.

5.4. Scaling Methods

After the test is constructed and data collected, statistical methods are used to construct the score scale. In any approach for constructing the score scale, the performance on the test or tests to be scaled is related to a single *interim score scale*. The interim score scale is transformed to a scale with specified properties. In this section, three general statistical approaches to constructing developmental score scales are considered. Within each of these general statistical approaches, the specific procedures that are used depend on the design used for data collection.

5.4.1. Hieronymus Scaling

Summed scores are used with Hieronymus scaling (Petersen et al., 1989). Although it can be used with any data collection design, this method was developed specifically to be used with data collected under the scaling test design. The data used are score distributions on the scaling test for students in each of the grade levels intended to be covered by the scaling test. Typically, the data are collected from a nationally representative sample so that the score distributions have meaning for a national group.

To conduct the scaling, the median summed score on the scaling test for each grade level is assigned a prespecified score scale value. These prespecified values are based on the test developer's model of patterns of year-to-year median growth that is part of the test developer's specification of the constructs being measured. For example, with the current forms of the ITBS (Hoover et al., 2003), the test developer's model for growth is that the average amount of growth from year-to-year decreases over grades. Consistent with this model, a developmental score scale was constructed so that within-grade raw score medians on the scaling test convert to scale scores as follows: grade 3—185, grade 4—200, grade 5—214, grade 6—227, grade 7—239, grade 8—250. Note that the grade-to-grade change in the median score decreases from 15 points (200–185) between grade 3 and grade 4 to 11 points (250–239) between grade 7 and grade 8.

Other distributional properties of the scale scores are also built into the scale. One property that can be built in is changes in within-grade variability over grades. For the ITBS, the test developer's model for the achievement constructs being measured is that students at lower percentiles tend to grow from grade-to-grade at a slower rate than students at higher percentiles. Consistent with this model, the within-grade variability of scores should increase from grade-to-grade. Scale score conversions are chosen for scaling test score points so the within-grade variability increases in a regular pattern over grades. Another property that can be built into the scale is for the amount of growth exhibited from year-to-year to have a regular pattern at each of a number of selected percentiles. Each of these properties was built into the scaling test score to scale score conversions for the current ITBS developmental score scales.

Note that other properties can be built into the raw score to scale score conversions. For example, earlier versions of the ITBS used grade equivalents as the primary developmental score scale. Grade equivalents were constructed so that at the beginning of third grade, the median scale score was 3.0, at the beginning of fourth grade the median scale score was 4.0, and so forth. As with the current developmental score scale for the ITBS, the scale was constructed so within-grade variability increased over grades.

After the scaling-test-score to scale score conversions are found, scores on each of the test levels are related to the score scale through the scaling test. Recall that in the scaling test design, each student takes both the scaling test and the level appropriate to their grade level. For example, each grade 3 student takes both the grade 3 level and the scaling test. Equivalent groups equipercentile procedures (Kolen & Brennan, 2004; Holland & Dorans, this volume) can be used to relate scores on the test level to the scaling test scores and then to the score scale. Following this linking process, raw to scale score conversions can be found for each of the test levels.

As described by Petersen et al. (1989), Hieronymus scaling uses distributions of Kelley regressed score estimates of true scores (Equation 3) on both the scaling test and the level tests in this linking process rather than raw score distributions. Note that using estimated true scores might better handle differences in reliability between scaling test and level test scores than if raw scores were used.

Hieronymus scaling can be used with data collection designs other than the scaling test design. In Hieronymus scaling with the other designs, raw scores on one test level are set as an interim scale. In the common-item design, common-item equipercentile linking procedures are used to transform scores on each of the levels to the interim score scale. In the equivalent groups design, random groups equipercentile linking procedures are used to transform raw scores on all of the levels to the interim score scale. To construct the developmental score scale using the common-item and equivalent groups designs, scores on the interim score scale are used in place of the scores on the scaling test. The same procedures described for the scaling test design then are used.

Some research questions on using the Hieronymus method include the following: What are the effects of using estimated true score distributions as compared to observed score distributions in the vertical scaling process? What types of analytic methods for smoothing score distributions (Kolen & Brennan, 2004) might best be used in the scaling process? Can analytic techniques be developed for constructing the transformation of scaling test to scale scores to achieve the properties desired by the test developer? How can Hieronymus scaling methods be used with IRT proficiency estimates to produce score scales that have scale score properties desired by the test developers?

5.4.2. Thurstone Scaling

Thurstone (1938) described a scaling method that involves normalizing summed scores within each grade. Gulliksen (1950, p. 284) referred to this method as Thurstone's absolute scaling method. This method has been used to scale achievement test batteries and is referred to here as Thurstone scaling. Using data collected from any of the data collection designs in this chapter, this method is based on the assumption that scale scores are normally distributed within grade group and are linearly related across grade groups. Thurstone scaling is described next for scaling with two grade groups, and is followed by a brief discussion of how to apply this method to more than two grade groups.

Assume, for now, that the same test is administered in two grade groups and raw scores are calculated using summed scores. The scores are then normalized within each group using the first 4 steps in the process for normalizing scores described earlier in conjunction with Equation 15.

Define $z_1^*(y)$ as the summed score y, normalized within grade group 1. Assume that the scale is to be set so that the scores are normally distributed in grade group 1 with mean μ_{S_1} and standard deviation σ_{S_1}. Using notation similar to that previously the raw-to-scale score transformation within group 1 is

$$S(y) = \sigma_{S_1} z_1^*(y) + \mu_{S_1}. \quad (19)$$

Define $z_2^*(y)$ as the summed score y normalized in grade group 2. Note that, in general, $z_1^*(y)$ will not be equal to $z_2^*(y)$, because the two grade groups are expected to differ in their proficiency level. A major step in Thurstone scaling is to relate $z_2^*(y)$ to the score scale, under the assumption that the relationship between $z_1^*(y)$ and $z_2^*(y)$ is linear.

To conduct Thurstone scaling, a subset of the $z_1^*(y)$ and $z_2^*(y)$ are used in the scaling process. Although the choice of $z_1^*(y)$ and $z_2^*(y)$ to use is arbitrary, Williams, Pommerich, and Thissen (1998) found that the points chosen can affect the results. Gulliksen (1950, p. 284) recommended choosing 10 or 20 raw score points when implementing this procedure and constructing a scatterplot for the 10 or 20 $z_1^*(y)$ and $z_2^*(y)$ pairs. Gulliksen (1950, p. 285) stated that if the scatterplot is close to a straight line, then $z_1^*(y)$ and $z_2^*(y)$ can be normalized on the same scale. Otherwise, he suggested abandoning the procedure. Define the following terms:

$\mu_{z_1^*(y)}$ is the mean of the 10 or 20 $z_1^*(y)$ values for group 1,

$\sigma_{z_1^*(y)}$ is the standard deviation of the 10 or 20 $z_1^*(y)$ values for group 1,

$\mu_{z_2^*(y)}$ is the mean of the 10 or 20 $z_2^*(y)$ values for group 2, and

$\sigma_{z_2^*(y)}$ is the standard deviation of the 10 or 20 $z_2^*(y)$ values for group 2.

It can be shown (Kolen and Brennan, 2004, p. 386) that the $z_2^*(y)$ scores can be transformed to the score scale using the following transformation:

$$S(y) = z_2^*(y) \frac{\sigma_{z_2'(y)}}{\sigma_{z_2'(y)}} \sigma_{S_2} + \sigma_{S_2} \left[\mu_{z_2'(y)} - \frac{\sigma_{z_2'(y)}}{\sigma_{z_2'(y)}} \mu_{z_2'(y)} \right] + \mu_{S_2} \qquad (20)$$

Equations 19 and 20 are the basic equations that are used in Thurstone scaling.

Suppose that a scaling test design is used to collect data in which there were two grade groups. Scores on the scaling test are normalized within each grade group. All terms in Equations 19 and 20 are estimated using data on the scaling test. Scores on the level tests are also normalized. The normalized scores on the level test administered to group 1 is substituted for $z_2^*(y)$ in Equation 19 to find the raw to scale score conversion for the level test administered to group 1. The normalized scores on the level test administered to group 2 are substituted for $z_2^*(y)$ in Equation 20 to find the raw to scale score conversion for the level test administered to group 2.

Using the common-item design, scores on the common items are used to find the transformation defined in Equation 20. The transformations in Equations 19 and 20 are applied to normalized scores on each of the complete level tests. Using the equivalent groups design, the level test administered to both grade groups is used to find the transformation in Equation 20. The transformations in Equations 19 and 20 are applied to normalized scores on each of the complete level tests.

The procedures for Thurstone scaling can be readily generalized to three or more grade groups. For any of the three designs, the mean and standard deviation of scale scores for one group are specified. Adjacent group raw scores are transformed to scale scores using the procedures described for two groups. A chaining process is used to convert raw scores on the other levels to the score scale.

5.4.3. IRT Scaling

IRT scaling can be conducted using data from any of the three data collection designs. IRT scaling makes use of the entire set of item-level responses from examinees to the test items. For any of the designs, there are various ways in which item parameter estimation might proceed, which are explicitly considered next for each of the data collection designs.

In the common-item design, each examinee responds to all items appropriate for their grade level. In *separate estimation*, item parameters are estimated separately for each grade level test using responses of examinees at that grade level. For example, an estimation run is conducted using the responses of third graders to the items that are on the test level appropriate for third graders. A computer program such as BILOG 3 (Mislevy & Bock, 1990) or MULTILOG (Thissen, 1991) is used. A separate estimation run is made using responses of fourth graders that are on the test level appropriate for fourth graders. Similar runs are made for fifth, sixth, seventh, and eighth graders.

Because of the indeterminacy of scale location and spread in IRT models, the item parameters from these separate runs are on IRT proficiency scales that are linearly related to one another. Linear transformations are found so that the item parameters all can be placed on the same proficiency scale. Various methods can be used to find these linking transformations, including the mean/mean, mean/sigma, Stocking and Lord, and Haebara methods (Kolen & Brennan, 2004; Yen & Fitzpatrick, this volume). These methods each estimate a linear function that can be used to transform item parameters and proficiencies onto the same IRT proficiency scale. The linear functions are calculated based on the parameter estimates for items that appear on adjacent levels.

The approach taken is to arbitrarily define the proficiency scale for one level as the base scale. Item parameter estimates from the other levels are then transformed to the base level. For example, assume that the proficiency scale for the third grade level is chosen as the base proficiency scale. One computer run is conducted for the third grade level using data for the third grade examinees. This proficiency scale is considered as the base scale. Another computer run is conducted for the fourth grade level using data for the fourth grade examinees. The item parameter estimates for those items that are common to the third and fourth grade levels are used to find the linear function that transforms the parameter estimates from the fourth grade level to the base proficiency scale defined for third graders. Separate runs are also conducted for fifth, sixth, seventh, and eighth graders. The linear transformation is found that transforms parameter estimates from one level to an adjacent level, and a chaining process is used to transform all item parameter estimates to the base proficiency scale. The outcome of this chaining process is that all item parameter estimates are on the same proficiency scale.

Concurrent calibration is an alternative calibration approach using the common item design. In concurrent calibration, data for examinees from all grade levels are calibrated in one computer run. An IRT calibration program that allows for multiple groups of examinees, such as BILOG-MG (du Toit, 2003), is used. (Programs that do not allow for multiple groups, such as BILOG 3, Mislevy and Bock, 1990, should not be used for concurrent calibration because they do not allow for the prior mean and standard deviation of proficiency to vary across grades, and consequently they lead to biased results.) Grade groups are identified so that the program allows for separate proficiency distributions for each grade. In setting up the computer run for concurrent calibration, a response is coded for all items on the test (for levels for grade 3 through grade 8) for each examinee. A "not reached" code is used for all of those items that an examinee does not take. The "not reached" code effectively removes the item from the likelihood calculated for an examinee or item. The result of a single concurrent calibration run is that all item parameters are on the same IRT scale without further transformation.

The data used for IRT scaling under the equivalent groups design are item scores for students on the test levels taken in grades included in the scaling study. Test levels are in common from one grade group to the next, which allows for test levels to be linked to a common scale. Either separate or concurrent calibration can be used with this design.

For separate calibration, assume that the grade 4 group of examinees is chosen as the base group. As can be seen in Figure 5.9, the third grade level (item blocks a and b) and the fourth grade level (item blocks b and c) are administered to random groups of fourth graders. Separate computer runs are conducted for each of the random groups. Because the groups are considered to be randomly equivalent, the item parameter estimates are on the same proficiency scale.

For the fifth grade examinees, separate computer runs are conducted for the fourth grade level (item blocks b and c) and for the fifth grade level (item blocks c and d). The item parameter estimates are linearly transformed to the proficiency scale for the base group. The mean/mean, mean/sigma, Stocking and Lord, or Haebara methods are applied to the item parameter estimates calculated for the fourth grade level (item blocks b and c) for both the fourth and fifth grade examinees. Similar procedures are followed for students at the other grade levels, and a chaining process is used so that all item parameter estimates are placed on the base scale developed using the fourth grade group.

Concurrent calibration procedures can also be used with this design. As with the common-item design, an IRT calibration program that allows for multiple groups of examinees, such as BILOG-MG (du Toit, 2003), is used. A "not reached" code is used for all items an examinee does not take. The result of a single concurrent calibration run is that all item parameters are on the same IRT scale without further transformation.

For the scaling test design with separate estimation, a single estimation run is conducted on the scaling test for all grade groups. An IRT calibration program that allows for multiple groups of examinees, such as BILOG-MG (du Toit, 2003) is used and the grade level of each examinee is identified. The output from the computer run includes an estimate of the mean and standard deviation of the proficiency of each grade group. Separate runs are conducted for each grade level test. The parameter estimates from each separate run are linearly transformed such that the mean and standard of the proficiency distribution from the separate run for a grade level is the same as the mean and standard for the scaling test run for that grade level. Separate linear transformations are developed for each grade level test.

If concurrent estimation is used, the parameters for the scaling test items and the items from each grade level test are estimated in a single computer run. In this run, the grade level of each examinee is identified and each item not taken by an examinee is coded as "not reached."

5.4.4. Separate vs. Concurrent Calibration in IRT Vertical Scaling

Kolen and Brennan (2004, p. 391) pointed out that concurrent calibration is often easier to implement than separate calibration because it requires only one computer run. Concurrent calibration has been shown to produce more stable linking results when the IRT model holds (Hanson & Béguin 2002; Kim & Cohen, 1998). However, when the IRT model does not hold, Béguin, Hanson, and Glas (2000) and Béguin and Hanson (2001) found separate calibration to be more accurate than concurrent calibration. Kolen and Brennan (2004, p. 391) suggested that separate estimation might be preferable because it mitigates the effects of violations of the unidimensionality assumption in IRT on the scaling results. They also pointed out that separate estimation allows for comparison of different item parameter estimates for the same items, which can be used to identify items that are behaving differently in adjacent grades. In addition, because so many items are coded "not reached" in concurrent calibration and so many item scores are included in calibration runs, such runs often have convergence problems.

5.4.5. Test Scoring in IRT Vertical Scaling

The IRT procedures that have been discussed result in item parameter estimates from different test levels being on the same scale. A decision must be made about how to estimate examinee proficiency. One decision that is made when applying many of the IRT methods is whether to use a function of summed scores or a function of the whole response pattern as raw scores. Also, a decision is made about whether to use maximum likelihood, Bayesian, or some other type of estimate of proficiency. The decision of how to estimate examinee proficiency can have a significant effect on the properties of the resulting scale scores.

First, consider raw scores that are a function of the entire response pattern. Maximum likelihood estimates are given in Equation 5 and Bayesian EAP estimates in Equation 6. Within a particular grade g consider the variance of maximum likelihood estimate, $\text{var}_g(\hat{\theta}_{MLE})$, the variance of the Bayesian EAP estimates, $\text{var}_g(\hat{\theta}_{EAP})$, and the variance of the actual (true) proficiencies, $\text{var}_g(\theta)$. Based on the earlier discussion, if the test scores are less than perfectly reliable, the following relationship is expected to hold:

$$\text{var}_g(\hat{\theta}_{EAP}) < \text{var}_g(\theta) < \text{var}_g(\hat{\theta}_{MLE}). \qquad (21)$$

Assuming that the EAP estimates are calculated using as a prior distribution the proficiency distribution for grade group g, and assuming that the maximum likelihood estimates are unbiased, it is also the case that the means of each of these estimates, $mean_g(\hat{\theta}_{EAP})$, $mean_g(\theta)$, and $mean_g(\hat{\theta}_{MLE})$ are all equal, so,

$$mean_g(\hat{\theta}_{EAP}) = mean_g(\theta) = mean_g(\hat{\theta}_{MLE}). \qquad (22)$$

These relationships can have a significant effect on how much separation there appears to be between examinees in different grades. The effect size is one measure of grade-to-grade separation that is often used. Effect size can be calculated as follows:

$$\text{effect size}_{g,g'}(\ ) = \frac{mean_g(\ ) - mean_{g'}(\ )}{\sqrt{[\text{var}_g(\ ) + \text{var}_{g'}(\ )]/2}}, \qquad (23)$$

where subscript g refers to grade g, subscript $g-$ refers to a grade lower than grade g, and the parentheses indicate that one of the estimates of proficiency is placed inside the parentheses. For example, if $\hat{\theta}_{EAP}$ is placed inside the parentheses, then the effect size for the Bayesian EAP estimates is calculated and symbolized by $\textit{effect size}_{g,g-}(\hat{\theta}_{EAP})$. Based on Equations 21, 22, and 23, it can readily be shown that

$$\textit{effect size}_{g,g-}(\hat{\theta}_{EAP}) > \textit{effect size}_{g,g-}(\theta) > \textit{effect size}_{g,g-}(\hat{\theta}_{MLE}). \quad (24)$$

This relationship implies that when examining the extent to which grade groups differ in proficiency, there is more grade-to-grade separation as measured by effect size with EAP estimates than with maximum likelihood estimates. Also, using effect size as a measure, the EAP estimates indicate more grade-to-grade separation than do the true proficiencies; the maximum likelihood estimates indicate less grade-to-grade separation than do the true proficiencies. Note that because summed scores typically are less reliable than scores based on the complete response pattern, the effect size for EAP estimates based on summed scores is even larger than the effect size for scores based on the complete response pattern.

The purpose of the preceding discussion is not to suggest that one estimate of proficiency is preferable to another. Instead the purpose is to demonstrate that the choice of proficiency estimate can have an important effect on the properties of the scores that are reported to examinees.

5.4.6. Scale Transformation in IRT Vertical Scaling

The IRT proficiency scale that results from the scaling procedures just described typically has a mean of 0 and standard deviation of 1 for the base group. This proficiency scale is often linearly transformed to have meaningful units. For example, it might be desired to set the third grade mean to 300 and the eighth grade mean to 800. The IRT proficiency scale also can be nonlinearly transformed to provide growth patterns that are consistent with expected growth patterns. Lord (1980, p. 84) showed that there is no obvious theoretical reason to prefer IRT proficiency estimates to nonlinear transformations of IRT proficiency estimates. Suppose a test developer believes that the variability of scale scores should increase over grades. If the variability of the IRT proficiency estimates does not increase over grades, a nonlinear transformation of the proficiency scale could be used that leads to increasing variability.

5.5. Limitations of Vertically Scaled Tests

As indicated earlier in this section, the levels of vertically scaled tests purposefully differ in content and difficulty. These differences limit interpretations about comparable scores across levels. For example, Kolen (2001) used the scaling of the PLAN (old name is PACT+) Mathematics tests to the ACT Assessment Mathematics test score scale to illustrate some of these limitations. PLAN is intended to be administered to tenth grade students, whereas the ACT Assessment is designed to be administered to eleventh and twelfth grade students. PLAN is shorter, easier, and covers somewhat different content than the ACT Assessment. The ACT Assessment score scale ranges from 1 to 36.

Kolen (2001) reported that the expected scale scores on PLAN and the ACT Assessment were similar for examinees with true scale scores below 27. For true scale scores above 27, however, the expected scale scores on PLAN were too low. This finding was attributed to PLAN's being unable to measure well at the higher score levels, because it did not contain a sufficient number of difficult test questions. Thus, the comparability of scores on these two tests is limited to the range of scores at or below 27. Kolen (2001) also indicated that intermediate algebra and trigonometry items are included on the ACT Assessment but not on PLAN, which also leads to limitations in the comparability of scores. Kolen (2001) suggested that "if a school were to initiate a program where intermediate algebra or trigonometry were taught in ninth or tenth grade, any resulting gains in achievement in these areas likely would not be reflected in PLAN scores" (p. 6). Kolen and Brennan (2004) concluded that "whenever tests are vertically scaled there are serious limitations to interpretability of scores due both to psychometric properties and to content differences among the tests that are scaled" (p. 413).

Because vertical scaling procedures rely on data from samples of examinees, the resulting scale scores contain error due to sampling examinees included in the scaling study. Very little work has been done to study the effect of sampling error in vertical scaling. Procedures for estimating standard errors of equating reviewed by Kolen and Brennan (2004, pp. 231–265) might be adapted to estimate the sampling error in vertical scaling. Based on findings by Johnson (1998) that examined standard errors in linking, such sampling error is likely to be substantial. Estimation and documentation of error variability in vertical scaling is clearly an area for further research.

5.6. Research on Vertical Scaling

Research on vertical scaling has examined differences in results from different scaling methods. Much of this research examined three characteristics of distributions of the resulting scale scores. Kolen and Brennan (2004, pp. 414–418) reviewed much of the research. A summary of their review is given here.

Grade-to-grade growth has been assessed by examining the change in differences in means from one grade to the next. Much of the research on grade level achievement tests shows that growth decelerates over grade for grade-level tests. That is, the grade-to-grade change in mean score tends to be smaller between later grades than between earlier grades. The one major exception to this finding is that developmental score scales can be constructed to force the overall grade-to-grade growth to be constant over grades, as is the case with grade equivalents.

Changes in within-grade variability from one grade to another have been found to differ for different scaling methods. Thurstone scaling has been found, from one grade to the next, to have increasing within-grade (or age) variability in many studies (Andrews, 1995; Thurstone, 1925,

1927, 1928a; Thurstone & Ackerman, 1929; Williams et al., 1998; Yen 1986; Yen & Burket, 1997). Andrews (1995) also found increasing within grade variability for Hieronymus scaling.

IRT methods sometimes have been found to have decreasing within-grade variability across grades (Andrews, 1995; Hoover, 1984a; Yen 1986). Hoover (1984a) criticized scales that showed such decreases, arguing that such decreases occur when low-achieving students increase in scale scores at a *faster* rate than high-achieving students. He argued that such a finding was counter to years of experience with elementary achievement test batteries. (See Burket, 1984; Clemans, 1993, 1996; Hoover, 1984b, 1988; Phillips & Clarizio, 1988a, 1988b; Yen, 1988; Yen, Burket, & Fitzpatrick, 1996 for further discussion).

Simulation studies suggested that decreasing variability with IRT methods could result from multidimensionality (Yen, 1985) and measurement error differences at different grades (Camilli, 1988). Camilli, Yamamoto, and Wang (1993) speculated that problems in estimating IRT proficiency for very high and very low scoring individuals might also be the cause of the decreasing within-grade variability.

Other research using IRT methods has not found decreases in within-grade variability (Becker & Forsyth, 1992; Bock, 1983; Camilli et al., 1993; Seltzer, Frank, & Bryk, 1994; Williams et al., 1998; Yen & Burket, 1997). Camilli (1999) and Williams et al. (1998) speculated that the decreases in within-grade variability found in earlier studies might have been due to the use of the joint maximum likelihood estimation that was used in the LOGIST computer program, because later applications based on BILOG 3 (Mislevy & Bock, 1990) did not show this effect.

Separation of grade distributions is another aspect of vertical scaling that has been studied and is often indexed using effect size. Although closely related to grade-to-grade growth, separation of grade distributions can give a very different picture of changes from year to year. Yen (1986, p. 304) illustrated how the use of effect sizes can lead to different conclusions about how much, on average, students grow from one grade to the next than the use of means. Refer to Equation 23. The numerator of this equation is differences in means. The denominator is a function of variances. In Yen's (1986, p. 304) example, the IRT method showed decreasing within-grade variability and the Thurstone method showed increasing within-grade variability. When examining mean differences, the pattern of year-to-year growth exhibited by Thurstone and IRT methods appeared to be very different. However, when such differences were standardized using effect sizes, the Thurstone and IRT methods appeared to be very similar in terms of separation of grade distributions. Holland (2002) discussed indices that can be used to evaluate separation of score distributions that take into account aspects of score distributions other than the means and variances.

Zwick (1992, pp. 211–214) demonstrated that nonlinear monotonic increasing transformations of score scales can change the pattern of grade-to-grade growth from increasing to decreasing and visa versa. Schulz and Nicewander (1997) illustrated that when scores that show decreasing grade-to-grade growth and equal within-grade variability are transformed to grade equivalents, the resulting scores show constant grade-to-grade growth and increasing within-grade variability.

5.7. Vertically Moderated Standards

Recent federal legislation (referred to as "No Child Left Behind") requires states to test all students every year in grades 3 through 8 in reading and mathematics (and other subject matter areas in the future). The states need to report the percentage of students at each grade and in various subgroups who meet the level "proficient" as defined by the state. States typically use standard-setting methods to define proficient at each grade level. "Annual yearly progress" is based on the percentage of students at a grade level (and for various subgroups at that grade level) who are at or above the "proficient" from one year to the next. Note, as defined, this legislation does not require that developmental score scales be used. Nevertheless, such scales can be used in this process, which has led to a renewed emphasis on developmental score scales by researchers and practitioners.

As pointed out by Lissitz and Huynh (2003), vertical scales can cause interpretational complexities when used to assess annual yearly progress that is based on proficiency levels. Lissitz and Huynh (2003) recommended using what they referred to as "vertically moderated standards" that are developed using a judgmental process. In this process, they "recommend that cut scores for each test be set for all grades such that … each achievement level has the same (generic) meaning across all grades" (p. 7). Judgmental procedures are used to set the proficiency levels. Vertically moderated standards were considered in depth in a special issue of *Applied Measurement in Education* edited by Cizek (2005). Regardless of whether the procedures outlined by Lissitz and Huynh (2003) or others are used, the proficiency levels need to have some constancy of meaning across grades.

5.8. Vertical Scales and Value-Added Models

Value-added models use estimates of student growth in achievement to estimate the effects of schools and teachers on student growth for accountability purposes. Many states are already using, or are considering using, value-added models in their accountability programs. In these programs, the effects of teacher and school on student growth are estimated. These estimates of growth are treated as comparable from school-to-school and from grade-to-grade. Much of the literature on value-added modeling has been involved with describing, developing, and comparing statistical models used for estimating teacher and school effects. A review of these models was completed by McCaffrey, Lockwood, Koretz, and Hamilton (2003), and a special issue of the *Journal of Educational and Behavioral Statistics* edited by Wainer (2004) considered statistical issues in detail. The results from value-added analyses likely are heavily influenced by the particular statistical model chosen and by sampling error in estimating the parameters of the model.

The implementation of value-added models requires the use of a vertically scaled test. McCaffrey et al. (2003) pointed out, however, that

Changes to the scaling of tests, the weight given to alternative topics, or the methods for vertical linking could change our conclusions about the relative achievement or growth in achievement across classes of students. These changes would influence inferences about teacher effects .... We expect that estimated teacher effects could be very sensitive to changes in scaling or other alterations to test construction and vertical linking of different test forms. There is currently no empirical evidence about the sensitivity of gain scores or teacher effects to such alternatives. (p. 89)

In addition, the results may be heavily affected by sampling error in developing the vertical scale and in estimating the parameters of the value-added model. Reckase (2004) added, "before putting a lot of confidence in the results of these analyses, the functioning of the assessments needs to be investigated in great detail" (p. 120). As these comments suggest, much research needs to be done on the influence of measurement aspects of the tests, such as test construction and vertical scaling procedures, before users can be confident that the results are meaningful. Based on the discussion in the present chapter about vertical scaling, it seems likely that procedures used to create the vertical scale could have a serious impact on the results from value-added modeling.

5.9. Conclusions about Vertical Scaling

Kolen and Brennan (2004) concluded, "research suggests that vertical scaling is a very complex process that is affected by many factors. These factors likely interact with one another to produce characteristics of a particular scale. The research record provides little guidance as to what methods and procedures work best" (p. 418). The choice of scale must be based, at least in part, on educational theory about the constructs measured by the test. As Yen (1986) pointed out, "choosing the right scale is not an option. It is important that any choice of scale be made consciously and that the reasons for that choice be carefully considered. In making such choices, appealing to common sense is no guarantee of unanimity of opinion or of reaching a sensible conclusion" (p. 314).

6. NORMS

Norms provide a statistical description of test performance conveyed using summary statistics such as means, standard deviations, and percentile ranks for a group of examinees. The group of examinees used to construct the norms is typically considered to be a sample from a larger population. An individual's performance can be compared to the performance of a relevant group using norms. Norms for test batteries allow for the assessment of individual students' strengths and weaknesses across the tests that make up the battery. The usefulness of norms also depends on the following considerations: (1) the relevance of the examinee population on which the norms are based to the score interpretation test users make, (2) the extent to which the sample of examinees used in the construction of the norms represents the examinee population of interest, and (3) the extent to which the sample size is large enough so that the norms are precise enough estimates for the population of interest. In addition to student-level norms, norms are also developed for aggregates, such as schools, school districts, and states.

In this section, the collection and interpretation of normative data as well as different types of norms and norm groups are considered. Technical issues in norms development are also presented, including some of the basic sampling concepts used to construct nationally representative norms.

6.1. Norms and Norm Groups

Consider a student who scores at the 90th percentile among students who take a particular college entrance examination. Clearly, this student is among the top students taking this examination. Suppose this student is interested in attending a highly selective university, and discovers that this same score is at the 20th percentile among students admitted to this university. This later percentile suggests that the student might have some trouble being accepted into this university. This example illustrates that the norm group to which a student is compared can give a very different impression of the student's proficiency. If the student is compared to students who take the college entrance examination, s/he appears to be doing very well. If the student is compared to students who are admitted to the highly selective university, s/he appears to be doing not so well. Thus, the norm group can have a significant effect on the percentiles reported and on the interpretation of the scores.

Consider another situation in which a third grade student scores at the 45th percentile on mathematics and at the 20th percentile on reading on an achievement test battery whose norms were based on a nationally representative group of third graders. In this norm group, the scores suggest that this student is stronger in mathematics than in reading. Assessment of strengths and weaknesses, such as these, are made possible through the use of a relevant norm group.

With the National Assessment of Educational Progress (NAEP) states are ranked according to their mean scores. Various testing programs also provide group norms at the level of schools and school districts. As this discussion suggests, there are many types of norms that are constructed for standardized tests. Some of these types are described as follows.

National norms are based on nationally representative samples of individuals at the age or educational level for which a test is designed. As described in the following sections of this chapter, national norms typically are developed using a sampling plan that helps ensure the sample accurately represents the population. *National subgroup norms* are national norms provided for members of a particular subgroup. For example, norms might be provided separately for males and females or for students from different geographical regions. *National norms by age or grade* are often provided for educational achievement and aptitude tests. Norms associated with the developmental score scale described earlier in this chapter are examples of grade norms.

Local norms are based on examinees from a particular educational or geographic unit. For example, norms on an elementary achievement test battery might be found for students from a particular state. The state norms might be quite different from national norms for a state that is higher performing than the nation.

User norms are based on examinees who happen to take a test during a given time period. For many testing programs, these are the only norms available. For example, college entrance testing programs in the U.S. provide norms for all students who are administered the test during a particular time period. These user norms cannot be viewed as nationally representative, because they depend on who happens to take a particular test. As stated by Petersen et al. (1989), "the lack of a nationally representative and well-defined norm groups creates some problems in comparing group performance.... Changes in the makeup of the candidate pool are confounded with test performance of groups of examinees" (p. 238). Despite these concerns, user norms can facilitate score interpretation. The user groups for college entrance tests tend to be fairly stable over short periods of time. As suggested by Petersen et al. (1989), "this stability is sufficient to allow the norms to be used for meaningful profile comparisons and to allow an examinee to assess, reasonably accurately, where she or he stands in relation to a group of college-bound students" (p. 238). User norms can also be provided for colleges, allowing examinees to compare their performance to the performance of students enrolled in these colleges.

Convenience norms are based on a group of examinees that happen to be available at the time a test is constructed. Convenience norms typically have very limited usefulness.

Group-level norms are calculated when average performance of groups of examinees is compared to one another. The situation where states are ranked based on their average NAEP scores is one example of group-level norms. Norms for school-level averages is another example of group-level norms. Norms for school averages are constructed by tabulating the average score for each school in a group of schools and forming percentile ranks for school averages. Norms for school averages are typically very different from norms for individuals. As Petersen et al. (1989) discussed, "consider that the mean score of the highest scoring school will be lower than the score of the highest scoring student in that school. Also, the mean of the lowest scoring school will be higher than the score of the lowest scoring student in that school. Therefore, school averages are less variable than student scores, and the percentile rank of a particular score will be more extreme in the norms for school averages than in the norms for student averages" (p. 238).

Item-level norms are sometimes provided for individual items, often as the proportion of students in the norm group who earn each possible score on an item. *Skill-level norms* are sometimes provided based on performance of students in the norm group over sets of items that measure a particular skill. Item- and skill-level norms are used to assess specific strengths and weaknesses of individual students. Although item- and skill-level norms can provide useful information, inferences based on scores on one item or on a small subset of items are often unreliable, so that important decisions for individuals should not be made based on these norms. Item- and skill-level norms can be useful for comparing subgroup performance to that of a national group in specific content areas. For example, the performance of a classroom or a school on specific items and skills can be compared with the performance of a national sample.

6.2. Technical Issues in the Development of National Norms

National norming studies estimate test score characteristics, such as means, standard deviations, and percentile ranks, for a national population of examinees. The development of national norms involves drawing a representative sample of examinees from the national population. Sample survey methodology (Cochran, 1977; Thompson, 2002) is used to design norming studies. In this section, some basic sampling concepts are considered.

The *population of interest* is the population of examinees that the norms are intended to represent. The *population characteristics* or *population parameters*, such as means and percentile ranks for scores on a test, are the estimated quantities. A *sampling design* is the process that is used for sampling examinees from the population of interest. *Statistics* are the estimates of the population characteristics found from the sample.

Refer to π as the population characteristic and $\hat{\pi}$ as the statistic that estimates the population characteristic. The quantities π and $\hat{\pi}$ for a particular sample likely differ because data are available only for the sample from the population rather than for the whole population. Conceive of sampling and calculating the statistic a large number of times. Define E as the expected value over these replications. Thus, $E(\hat{\pi})$ is the expected value of $\hat{\pi}$ over replications of the sampling process. *Bias* is defined as the difference between the expected value of the statistic and the population characteristic, and can be calculated as $E(\hat{\pi}) - \pi$. *Sampling error* on a single replication of a study is defined as $\hat{\pi} - \pi$, and *sampling error variance* is defined as $E(\hat{\pi} - \pi)^2$. Mean squared error is the sum of the bias-squared and sampling error variance.

One goal in norming studies is to minimize bias in estimating the population characteristic(s) of interest. In norming studies, bias typically results from practical problems that cause the sample to be nonrepresentative. For example, schools asked to participate in a norming study often decline to participate, which can lead to bias. A second goal in norming studies is to control sampling error at an acceptable level. The sampling design, and its associated sample size, are used as the primary means for controlling sampling error variance.

Norming studies typically use a combination of sampling plans. In *simple random sampling*, each examinee in the population has an equal and independent probability of being included in the sample. In *stratified random sampling*, the population is divided into strata based on examinee characteristics, such as geographic region or public versus private schools. A sample is drawn from each stratum. Statistics from each strata are often weighted differentially to estimate the population characteristic. Stratification reduces sampling error variance to the extent that the strata differ on the measured variable.

In *systematic random sampling*, every nth examinee is chosen from the population, after the first examinee is randomly chosen from among the first n examinees. If examinees are ordered randomly, then systematic random sampling is the same as simple random sampling. If the examinees are ordered on a variable related to the measured variable, then systematic random sampling can result in substantially lower sampling error than simple random sampling.

Cluster sampling involves sampling at the level of examinee group. For example, schools might be sampled, and then all students within a selected school tested. To the extent that the clusters differ, on average, on the test score of interest, cluster sampling requires testing more students than would be required with simple random sampling to achieve the same sampling error variance.

Most norming studies use a combination of sampling strategies. Simple random sampling usually is not practical for developing test norms, so typically schools are sampled and then students are sampled within the chosen schools. Specialists in sample survey design methodology provide specifics, including the number of schools chosen per stratum and the number of students per school. Such specialists also develop sampling weights, as needed, so that the statistics that are calculated accurately estimate the population characteristics. In addition, indices of the precision of the estimates of the population characteristics are provided.

One significant question encountered in conducting norming studies is the definition of whom to include in the testing. For example, should English language learners be excluded? If so, how is English language learner defined? Should students who need to be tested using special administration procedures be included in the norming study? Also, what sorts of provisions exist for make-up testing? Depending on the use of a test, there may be various federal rules that dictate who should and should not be included in the testing for the development of norms. In addition, nonparticipation of schools and students within schools must be dealt with in these studies. Such nonparticipation can lead to bias in the norms. One procedure for dealing with school nonparticipation is to select substitute schools that are as similar as possible to the nonparticipating schools and then sample students within those schools.

6.3. Illustrative Examples of National Norming Studies

Norming studies use a combination of sampling strategies. In this section, procedures used in two national norming studies are described to illustrate the types and range of sampling procedures used in practice.

National norming studies are conducted for NAEP, which is a national survey of educational achievement that provides information used by policy makers to inform decisions about education in the nation. NAEP is intended to broadly survey educational achievement in areas that include reading and mathematics. The breadth of these subject areas, and the desire to have adequate breadth of content surveyed, requires that each examinee take only a subset of the assessment. Scores are not reported to individual examinees. NAEP results are reported only at the group level, including the nation and various subgroups.

NAEP provides normative data on educational achievement at grades 4, 8, and 12 in various subject matter areas. In the development of norms, NAEP makes extensive use of sampling procedures described in technical manuals that accompany each assessment (e.g., Allen, Carlson, & Zelenak, 1999). Rust and Johnson (1992) described NAEP sampling that was used in 1986 through 1992. The present discussion relies upon their description.

A multistage sampling design was used with NAEP. The first stage involved sampling primary sampling units (PSUs), which are geographical regions that contain either a single metropolitan area, a single county that is not a metropolitan area, or a group of geographically contiguous counties. The nation was divided into approximately 1,000 PSUs. Because of their large size, some of the PSUs that contained a single metropolitan area were included in all NAEP samples (there were 34 of these PSUs in 1986 through 1992). The remaining PSUs were sorted into 60 strata by geographic region, whether or not they were a metropolitan area, the extent of the minority population, and socioeconomic characteristics. One PSU was drawn randomly from each of these strata.

In the second stage, schools with students in the grade to be assessed were selected within the selected PSUs. The schools were chosen with probabilities proportional to size of the schools, with the following exception. So that norms for important subgroups, such as African-Americans and Hispanic-Americans, were sufficiently precise, schools with high proportions of students from these subgroups were sampled at a higher probability. In the third stage, schools provided a list of students eligible for testing. Students were systematically sampled from these lists and assigned to test sessions.

Each student was administered only a subset of items from the entire pool of items. Within a test session, different students were administered different test questions. This procedure is generally referred to as matrix sampling. Different subsets of items were randomly assigned to students in each test session using a procedure referred to as balanced incomplete block spiraling (Beaton & Zwick, 1992).

The records for students included in the sample were weighted to reflect the national population and to adjust for nonparticipation of students and schools. Weights were initially assigned as the reciprocal of the probability of selection of individual students for the assigned session. The weights were adjusted for the effects of nonparticipation of schools and students, and those weights that were extremely large were trimmed, so that they did not overly influence the resulting norms. Poststratification was used to adjust the weights so that over the whole sample they accurately reflected totals for population subgroups, as provided by the U.S. Census Bureau, defined by geographical region, race and ethnicity, and the relationship between student age and grade.

The weights were used to develop the norms on NAEP for the U.S. population as a whole and for various subgroups.

Associated estimates of precision were used to estimate the amount of sampling error present in the norms.

Recently, NAEP sampling was redesigned. A sampling plan now is used within each state to produce state-level norms at a desired level of precision overall and for various subgroups within each state. The state samples are aggregated to produce the national sample.

Another well-documented norming study provides a contrast to the procedures used with NAEP. In 1988 national norms for the ACT Assessment were constructed (Sawyer, 1989). ACT began with a list of all schools in the U.S. that had grades 10, 11, or 12. The schools were stratified by school size, public or private affiliation, geographical region, and the extent to which students at the school took the ACT Assessment. Schools were ordered within stratum by socioeconomic status and systematically sampled within stratum. For most schools, attempts were made to test all eligible students within a school. Weights were assigned as the reciprocal of the probability of selection of the individual student. In addition, a weighting procedure was used to handle the extent of make-up testing.

One difference between the NAEP and ACT sampling procedures was that for NAEP, the first stage sample was at the PSU level whereas for ACT, the first stage sample was at the school level. The NAEP procedures likely provided more control over the sampling process, with the potential drawback that they were more complex than the procedures used with the ACT. A second difference is that NAEP sampled students within school, whereas ACT intended to test all eligible students within school in most schools. By sampling students within school, NAEP was able to greatly reduce the number of students tested. However, by testing all students in a school, ACT may have created fewer practical problems for the schools included in the sample because they did not need to separate those who were included in the testing from those who were not included. These sorts of practical issues are always a concern when conducting national norm studies.

7. FUTURE DIRECTIONS IN SCALING AND NORMING

What does the future hold for scaling and norming? Clearly, there have been substantial changes in how tests are scaled and normed since the Petersen et al. (1989) chapter was written. Some of the likely directions for change are described in this section.

The types of test questions that are used with standardized educational tests have diversified considerably in recent years. Questions are more often scored polytomously, and judges are more often used in the scoring process. The ability to administer tests by computer has led to new types of questions, including simulations. This trend likely will continue, requiring new ways to conceptualize test scoring, to compute raw scores, and to transform raw scores to scale scores.

The consequences on test use of the choice of scoring methods in IRT should receive more attention. Should summed scores be used or should scores that are based on weighted sums be used? Under many IRT models, weighted sum scores are often slightly more reliable, but they are often difficult to explain to test users. In this case, it can be very difficult to explain why two students with the same summed score obtain different scale scores. Should Bayesian estimates or unbiased estimates of proficiency, such as maximum likelihood estimates, be used? Bayesian estimates depend on the population with which the examinee is associated. For example, a female examinee would earn different proficiency estimates if referenced to the overall population as opposed to the population of females. With Bayesian estimates two examinees with exactly the same response pattern could receive different proficiency estimates if they are from different examinee groups. However, Bayesian estimates have less error in estimating proficiency than unbiased estimates, such as maximum likelihood estimates. More research-based guidance is needed to help test developers decide how to score tests under IRT models.

The incorporation of content information into score scales has proliferated in recent years. Many achievement testing programs now use proficiency levels as a major component of their score reports. Such achievement levels typically are constructed using judgmental methods. Likely, there will continue to be a focus on developing procedures for articulating standards over grades in grade-level testing programs.

Recent federal legislation has placed a renewed emphasis on examining student growth in achievement. For example, students will be required to be administered tests each year in grades 3 through 8 in mathematics and reading. Although this legislation does not require that a vertical scale be used, it has led many states to consider vertical scales for measuring growth. The "value-added" movement has also encouraged the use of vertical scales. As concluded earlier in this chapter, research is clearly needed on vertical scaling if such efforts are to be successful.

Mainly due to NAEP, procedures for constructing national norms for tests have become more sophisticated in recent years. As NAEP continues to evolve, with the most recent evolution to providing accurate state-level results for all states, the level of sophistication and complexity used in planning and conducting national norming studies likely will increase.

ACKNOWLEDGMENTS

I thank Eugene Johnson and Robert L. Brennan for their thorough and insightful comments on an earlier draft of this chapter. I also thank Zhongmin Cui, NooRee Huh Seonghoon Kim, Dongmei Li, Kyndra Middleton, Yuki Nozawa, and Ye Tong for their comments on an earlier draft of portions of this chapter.

REFERENCES

ACT. (2001). *EXPLORE technical manual*. Iowa City, IA: Author.

Allen, N. L., Carlson, J. E., & Zelenak, C. A. (1999). *The NAEP 1996 technical report*. Washington, DC: National Center for Education Statistics.

American Educational Research Association, American Psychological Association, & National Council on Measurement in Education. (1999). *Standards for educational and psychological testing*. Washington, DC: American Educational Research Association.

Andrews, K. M. (1995). *The effects of scaling design and scaling method on the primary score scale associated with a multilevel achievement test*. Unpublished Ph. D. dissertation, University of Iowa, Iowa City, Iowa.

Angoff, W. H. (1971). Scales, norms, and equivalent scores. In R. L. Thorndike (Ed.), *Educational measurement* (2nd ed., pp. 508–600). Washington, DC: American Council on Education.

Beaton, A. E., & Zwick, R. (1992). Overview of the National Assessment of Educational Progress. *Journal of Educational Statistics, 19*(2), 95–109.

Becker, D. F., & Forsyth, R. A. (1992). An empirical investigation of Thurstone and IRT methods of scaling achievement tests. *Journal of Educational Measurement, 29*(4), 341–354.

Béguin, A. A., & Hanson, B. A. (2001, April). *Effect of noncompensatory multidimensionality on separate and concurrent estimation in IRT observed score equating*. Paper presented at the annual meeting of the National Council on Measurement in Education, Seattle, WA.

Béguin, A. A., Hanson, B. A., & Glas, C. A. W. (2000, April). *Effect of noncompensatory multidimensionality on separate and concurrent estimation in IRT observed score equating*. Paper presented at the annual meeting of the American Educational Research Association, New Orleans, LA.

Bock, R. D. (1983). The mental growth curve reexamined. In D. J. Weiss (Ed.), *New horizons in testing* (pp. 205–209). New York: Academic Press.

Bourque, M. L. (1999a). Appendix F. Setting the NAEP achievement levels for the 1996 Mathematics assessment. In N. L. Allen, J. E. Carlson, & C. A. Zelenak (Eds.), *The NAEP 1996 technical report* (pp. 739–758). Washington, DC: National Center for Education Statistics.

Bourque, M. L. (1999b). Appendix G. Report on developing achievement level descriptions for the 1996 NAEP Science assessment. In N. L. Allen, J. E. Carlson, & C. A. Zelenak (Eds.), *The NAEP 1996 technical report* (pp. 759–767). Washington, DC: National Center for Education Statistics.

Brennan, R. L. (Ed.). (1989). *Methodology used in scaling the ACT Assessment and P-ACT+*. Iowa City, Iowa: ACT Publications.

Brennan, R. L. (2001). *Generalizability theory*. New York: Springer.

Burket, G. R. (1984). Response to Hoover. *Educational Measurement: Issues and Practice, 3*(4), 15–16.

Camilli, G. (1988). Scale shrinkage and the estimation of latent distribution parameters. *Journal of Educational Statistics, 13*(3), 227–241.

Camilli, G. (1999). Measurement error, multidimensionality, and scale shrinkage: A reply to Yen and Burket. *Journal of Educational Measurement, 36*(1), 73–78.

Camilli, G., Yamamoto, K., & Wang, M.-m. (1993). Scale shrinkage in vertical equating. *Applied Psychological Measurement, 17*(4), 379–388.

Cizek, G. J. (2005). Adapting testing technology to serve accountability aims: The case of vertically moderated standard setting. *Applied Measurement in Education, 18*(1), 1–9.

Clemans, W. V. (1993). Item response theory, vertical scaling, and something's awry in the state of test mark. *Educational Assessment, 1*(4), 329–347.

Clemans, W. V. (1996). Reply to Yen, Burket, and Fitzpatrick. *Educational Assessment, 3*(2), 192–206.

Cochran, W. G. (1977). *Sampling techniques*. New York: Wiley.

College Board. (2004). *Composite-score formula for the 2002 AP Computer Science A examination*. Retrieved February 11, 2004, from http://www.collegeboard.com/ap/teachers/table_3_3.html

Cook, L. L. (1994, April). *Recentering the SAT score scale: An overview and some policy considerations*. Paper presented at the annual meeting of the National Council on Measurement in Education, New Orleans, LA.

Coombs, C. H., Dawes, R. M., & Tversky, A. (1970). *Mathematical psychology: An elementary introduction*. Englewood Cliffs, NJ: Prentice-Hall.

Donlon, T. (Ed.). (1984). *The College Board technical handbook for the Scholastic Aptitude Test and Achievement Tests*. New York: College Entrance Examination Board.

Dorans, N. J. (2002). Recentering and realigning the SAT score distributions: How and why. *Journal of Educational Measurement, 39*(1), 59–84.

du Toit, M. (2003). *IRT from SSI*. Lincolnwood, IL: Scientific Software International.

Ebel, R. L. (1962). Content standard test scores. *Educational & Psychological Measurement, 22*(1), 15–25.

Ercikan, K., Schwarz, R. D., Julian, M. W., Burket, G. R., Weber, M. M., & Link, V. (1998). Calibration and scoring of tests with multiple-choice and constructed-response item types. *Journal of Educational Measurement, 35*(2), 137–154.

Feldt, L. S. (1997). Can validity rise when reliability declines? *Applied Measurement in Education, 10*(4), 377–387.

Feldt, L. S., & Brennan, R. L. (1989). Reliability. In R. L. Linn (Ed.), *Educational measurement* (3rd ed., pp. 105–146). New York: Macmillan.

Flanagan, J. C. (1951). Units, scores, and norms. In E. F. Lindquist (Ed.), *Educational measurement* (pp. 695–763). Washington, DC: American Council on Education.

Forsyth, R. A. (1991). Do NAEP scales yield valid criterion-referenced interpretations? *Educational Measurement: Issues & Practice, 10*(3), 3–9, 16.

Freeman, M. F., & Tukey, J. W. (1950). Transformations related to the angular and square root. *Annals of Mathematical Statistics, 21*, 607–611.

Gulliksen, H. (1950). *Theory of mental tests*. New York: Wiley.

Hambleton, R. K., Brennan, R. L., Brown, W., Dodd, B., Forsyth, R. A., Mehrens, W. A., et al. (2000). A response to "Setting reasonable and useful performance standards" in the National Academy of Sciences' *Grading the Nation's Report Card*. *Educational Measurement: Issues and Practice, 19*(2), 5–13.

Hanson, B. A., & Béguin, A. A. (2002). Obtaining a common scale for item response theory item parameters using separate versus concurrent estimation in the common-item equating design. *Applied Psychological Measurement, 26*(1), 3–24.

Holland, P. W. (2002). Two measures of change in the gaps between CDFs of test-score distributions. *Journal of Educational & Behavioral Statistics, 27*(1), 3–18.

Hoover, H. D. (1984a). The most appropriate scores for measuring educational development in the elementary schools: GE's. *Educational Measurement: Issues & Practice, 3*(4), 8–14.

Hoover, H. D. (1984b). Rejoinder to Burket. *Educational Measurement: Issues and Practice, 3*(4), 16–18.

Hoover, H. D. (1988). Growth expectations for low-achieving students: A reply to Yen. *Educational Measurement: Issues and Practice, 7*(4), 21–23.

Hoover, H. D., Dunbar, S. B., & Frisbie, D. A. (2003). *The Iowa tests: Guide to research and development*. Chicago: Riverside Publishing.

Huynh, H. (1998). On score locations of binary and partial credit items and their applications to item mapping and criterion-referenced interpretation. *Journal of Educational & Behavioral Statistics, 23*(1), 35–56.

Iowa Tests of Educational Development. (1958). *Manual for school administrators. 1958 revision*. Iowa City: State University of Iowa.

Jarjoura, D. (1985). Tolerance intervals for true scores. *Journal of Educational Statistics, 10*(1), 1–17.

Johnson, E. G. (1998). *Linking the National Assessment of Educational Progress (NAEP) and the Third International Mathematics and Science Study (TIMSS): A technical report* (NCES 98–499). Washington, DC: U.S. Department of Education, Office of Educational Research and Improvement, National Center for Educational Statistics.

Kane, M., & Case, S. M. (2004). The reliability and validity of weighted composite scores. *Applied Measurement in Education, 17*(3), 221–240.

Kim, S.-H., & Cohen, A. S. (1998). A comparison of linking and concurrent calibration under item response theory. *Applied Psychological Measurement, 22*(2), 131–143.

Kolen, M. J. (1988). Defining score scales in relation to measurement error. *Journal of Educational Measurement, 25*(2), 97–110.

Kolen, M. J. (2001). Linking assessments effectively: Purpose and design. *Educational Measurement: Issues and Practice, 20*(1), 5–19.

Kolen, M. J., & Brennan, R. L. (2004). *Test equating, scaling, and linking: Methods and practices* (2nd ed.). New York: Springer-Verlag.

Kolen, M. J., & Hanson, B. A. (1989). Scaling the ACT Assessment. In R. L. Brennan (Ed.), *Methodology used in scaling the ACT Assessment and P-ACT+* (pp. 35–55). Iowa City, IA: ACT Publications.

Kolen, M. J., Hanson, B. A., & Brennan, R. L. (1992). Conditional standard errors of measurement for scale scores. *Journal of Educational Measurement, 29*(4), 285–307.

Kolen, M. J., Zeng, L., & Hanson, B. A. (1996). Conditional standard errors of measurement for scale scores using IRT. *Journal of Educational Measurement, 33*(2), 129–140.

Lindquist, E. F. (1953). Selecting appropriate score scales for tests. *Proceedings of the 1952 Invitational Conference on Testing Problems* (pp. 34–40). Princeton, NJ: Educational Testing Service.

Lissitz, R. W., & Huynh, H. (2003). Vertical equating for state assessments: Issues and solutions in determination of adequate yearly progress and school accountability. *Practical Assessment, Research & Evaluation, 8*(10), 1–10.

Lohman, D. F., & Hagen, E. P. (2002). *Cognitive abilities test. Form 6. Research handbook*. Itasca, IL: Riverside Publishing.

Lord, F. M. (1980). *Applications of item response theory to practical testing problems*. Hillsdale, NJ: Erlbaum.

McCaffrey, D. F., Lockwood, J. R., Koretz, D. M., & Hamilton, L. S. (2003). *Evaluating value-added models for teacher accountability*. Santa Monica, CA: RAND Corporation.

McCall, W. A. (1939). *Measurement*. New York: Macmillan.

Mislevy, R. J., & Bock, R. D. (1990). *BILOG 3. Item analysis and test scoring with binary logistic models* (2nd ed.). Mooresville, IN: Scientific Software.

Mitzel, H. C., Lewis, D. M., Patz, R. J., & Green, D. R. (2001). The bookmark procedure: Psychological perspectives. In G. J. Cizek (Ed.), *Setting performance standards: Concepts, methods, and perspectives* (pp. 249–281). Mahwah, NJ: Erlbaum.

O'Sullivan, C. Y., Reese, C. M., & Mazzeo, J. (1997). *NAEP 1996 science report card for the nation and the states*. Washington, DC: National Center for Education Statistics.

Pellegrino, J. W., Jones, L. R., & Mitchell, K. J. (1999). *Grading the nation's report card: Evaluating NAEP and transforming the assessment of educational progress*. Washington, DC: National Academy Press.

Petersen, N. S., Kolen, M. J., & Hoover, H. D. (1989). Scaling, norming, and equating. In R. L. Linn (Ed.), *Educational measurement* (3rd ed., pp. 221–262). New York: Macmillan.

Phillips, S. E., & Clarizio, H. F. (1988a). Conflicting growth expectations cannot both be real: A rejoinder to Yen. *Educational Measurement: Issues and Practice, 7*(4), 18–19.

Phillips, S. E., & Clarizio, H. F. (1988b). Limitations of standard scores in individual achievement testing. *Educational Measurement: Issues and Practice, 7*(1), 8–15.

Press, W. H., Flannery, B. P., Teukolsky, S. A., & Vetterling, W. T. (1989). *Numerical recipes: The art of scientific computing* (Fortran version). Cambridge: Cambridge University Press.

Rasch, G. (1960). *Probabilistic models for some intelligence and attainment tests*. Copenhagen, Denmark: Danish Institute for Educational Research.

Reckase, M. D. (2004). The real world is more complicated than we would like. *Journal of Educational and Behavioral Statistics, 29*(1), 117–120.

Rodriguez, M. C. (2003). Construct equivalence of multiple-choice and constructed-response items: A random effects synthesis of correlations. *Journal of Educational Measurement, 40*(2), 163–184.

Rosa, K., Swygert, K. A., Nelson, L., & Thissen, D. (2001). Item response theory applied to combinations of multiple-choice and constructed-response items—scale scores for patterns of summed scores. In D. Thissen & H. Wainer (Eds.), *Test scoring* (pp. 253–292). Mahwah, NJ: Erlbaum.

Rudner, L. M. (2001). Informed test component weighting. *Educational Measurement: Issues and Practice, 20*(1), 16–19.

Rust, K. F., & Johnson, E. G. (1992). Sampling and weighting in the National Assessment. *Journal of Educational Statistics, 17*(2), 111–129.

Sawyer, R. (1989). Research design and sampling for the Academic Skills Study. In R. L. Brennan (Ed.), *Methodology used in scaling the ACT Assessment and P-ACT+* (pp. 19–33). Iowa City, IA: ACT.

Schulz, E. M., & Nicewander, W. A. (1997). Grade equivalent and IRT representations of growth. *Journal of Educational Measurement, 34*(4), 315–331.

Seltzer, M. H., Frank, K. A., & Bryk, A. S. (1994). The metric matters: The sensitivity of conclusions about growth in student achievement to choice of metric. *Educational Evaluation & Policy Analysis, 16*(1), 41–49.

Stevens, S. S. (1946). On the theory of scales of measurement. *Science, 103*, 677–680.

Stevens, S. S. (1951). Mathematics, measurement and psychophysics. In *Handbook of experimental psychology* (pp. 1–49). New York: Wiley.

Suppes, P., & Zinnes, J. L. (1963). Basic measurement theory. In R. D. Luce, R. R. Bush, & E. Galanter (Eds.), *Handbook of mathematical psychology: Volume* I (pp. 1–76). New York: John Wiley.

Sykes, R. C., & Hou, L. (2003). Weighting constructed-response items in IRT-based exams. *Applied Measurement in Education, 16*(4), 257–275.

Sykes, R. C., & Yen, W. M. (2000). The scaling of mixed-item-format tests with the one-parameter and two-parameter partial credit models. *Journal of Educational Measurement, 37*(3), 221–244.

Thissen, D. (1991). *MULTILOG user's guide* (Version 6) [Computer software]. Chicago: Scientific Software International.

Thissen, D., & Orlando, M. (2001). Item response theory for items scored in two categories. In D. Thissen & H. Wainer (Eds.), *Test scoring* (pp. 73–140). Mahwah, NJ: Erlbaum.

Thissen, D., Wainer, H., & Wang, X.-B. (1994). Are tests comprising both multiple-choice and free-response items necessarily less unidimensional than multiple-choice tests? An analysis of two tests. *Journal of Educational Measurement, 31*(2), 113–123.

Thomasson, G. L., Bloxom, B., & Wise, L. (1994). *Initial operational test and evaluation of forms 20, 21, and 22 of the Armed Services Vocational Aptitude Battery (ASVAB)*. (DMDC Technical Report 94–001). Monterey, CA: Defense Manpower Data Center.

Thompson, S. K. (2002). *Sampling*. New York: Wiley.

Thurstone, L. L. (1925). A method of scaling psychological and educational tests. *Journal of Educational Psychology, 16*(7), 433–451.

Thurstone, L. L. (1927). The unit of measurement in educational scales. *Journal of Educational Psychology, 18*, 505–524.

Thurstone, L. L. (1928a). The absolute zero in intelligence measurement. *Psychological Review, 35*, 175–197.

Thurstone, L. L. (1928b). Attitudes can be measured. *American Journal of Sociology, 33*, 529–554.

Thurstone, L. L. (1938). Primary mental abilities. *Psychometric Monographs. No. 1*.

Thurstone, L. L., & Ackerman, L. (1929). The mental growth curve for the Binet tests. *Journal of Educational Psychology, 20*, 569–583.

Traub, R. E. (1993). On the equivalence of the traits assessed by multiple-choice and constructed-response tests. In R. E. Bennett & W. C. Ward (Eds.), *Construction versus choice in cognitive measurement* (pp. 29–44). Hillsdale, NJ: Erlbaum.

Wainer, H. (2004). Introduction to a special issue of the *Journal of Educational and Behavioral Statistics* on value-added assessment. *Journal of Educational and Behavioral Statistics, 29*(1), 1–3.

Wainer, H., & Thissen, D. (1993). Combining multiple-choice and constructed-response test scores: Toward a Marxist theory of test construction. *Applied Measurement in Education, 6*(2), 103–118.

Wainer, H., & Thissen, D. (2001). True score theory: The traditional method. In D. Thissen & H. Wainer (Eds.), *Test scoring*. Mahwah, NJ: Erlbaum.

Wang, M. W., & Stanley, J. C. (1970). Differential weighting: A review of methods and empirical studies. *Review of Educational Research, 40*(5), 663–704.

Wilcox, R. R. (1981). A review of the beta-binomial model and its extensions. *Journal of Educational Statistics, 6*(1), 3–32.

Wilks, S. S. (1938). Weighting systems for linear functions of correlated variables when there is no dependent variable. *Psychometrika, 3*, 23–40.

Williams, V. S. L., Pommerich, M., & Thissen, D. (1998). A comparison of developmental scales based on Thurstone methods and item response theory. *Journal of Educational Measurement, 35*(2), 93–107.

Wright, B. D. (1977). Solving measurement problems with the Rasch model. *Journal of Educational Measurement, 14*(2), 97–116.

Yen, W. M. (1985). Increasing item complexity: A possible cause of scale shrinkage for unidimensional item response theory. *Psychometrika, 50*(4), 399–410.

Yen, W. M. (1986). The choice of scale for educational measurement: An IRT perspective. *Journal of Educational Measurement, 23*(4), 299–325.

Yen, W. M. (1988). Normative growth expectations must be realistic: A response to Phillips and Clarizio. *Educational Measurement: Issues and Practice, 7*(4), 16–17.

Yen, W. M., & Burket, G. R. (1997). Comparison of item response theory and Thurstone methods of vertical scaling. *Journal of Educational Measurement, 34*(4), 293–313.

Yen, W. M., Burket, G. R., & Fitzpatrick, A. R. (1996). Response to Clemans. *Educational Assessment, 3*(2), 181–190.

Zwick, R. (1992). Statistical and psychometric issues in the measurement of educational achievement trends: Examples from the National Assessment of Educational Progress. *Journal of Educational Statistics, 17*(2), 205–218.

Zwick, R., Senturk, D., Wang, J., & Loomis, S. C. (2001). An investigation of alternative methods for item mapping in the National Assessment of Educational Progress. *Educational Measurement: Issues and Practice, 20*(2), 15–25.

6
Linking and Equating

Paul W. Holland
Neil J. Dorans
Educational Testing Service

1. INTRODUCTION, DEFINITIONS, AND BACKGROUND

This chapter consists of five overall main sections or *parts*. Part 1 provides an introduction to test score linking and gives some important definitions and other background material for the rest of the chapter. Part 2 is concerned with the most common data collection designs that are used to link test scores. In part 3, we discuss the various methods and procedures for forming scaling and equating functions between complete tests. Part 4 discusses various issues involved in the evaluation of scaling and equating functions. In part 5, we give some advice regarding the practice of scaling and equating.

1.1. Relationship to Previous Editions of *Educational Measurement*

A chapter on equating test scores has appeared in each of the three previous editions of *Educational Measurement*. The earlier chapters also included discussions of scales and norms, but these subjects are given separate treatment in this edition—see the chapter by Kolen (this volume). In addition to test equating, this chapter discusses other ways that scores on different tests are connected or linked together.

Readers who are new to test linking will do well to discover the wealth of material that has appeared in the earlier editions of *Educational Measurement*, i.e., Flanagan (1951), Angoff (1971, 1984), and (Petersen, Kolen, & Hoover, 1989). We will exploit the existence of these earlier chapters and refer to them for expansions on, or alternative discussions of, the material we cover.

In addition, at least six books directly address various issues in test linking. Holland and Rubin (1982), an edited volume of conference papers, covers a variety of test equating topics. Kolen and Brennan (2004), in its second edition, is an encyclopedic treatment of the entire field of test equating, scaling, and linking. von Davier, Holland, and Thayer (2004b) focus on a single method of test equating (i.e., kernel equating) in a unifying way that introduces several new ideas of general use in test equating. The two book-length reports from the National Research Council, *Uncommon Measures* by Feuer, Holland, Green, Bertenthal, and Hemphill (1999) and *Embedding Questions* by Koretz, Bertenthal, and Green (1999), provide accessible summaries of informed, professional judgment about the issues involved in linking scores on different educational tests. Finally, Livingston (2004), a training manual for those who will actually do equating and scaling, is a lively and straightforward account of many of the major issues and techniques.

In this chapter we will not attempt to cover all aspects of test linking, but we do attempt to make it a self-contained introduction that describes the important issues and ideas as we see them. In general, our discussion may seem more abstract and theoretical than those in the previous editions of *Educational Measurement*. We intend this level of generality because we want to build upon and not repeat these earlier discussions. Instead, our emphasis is on the unifying ideas and concepts of score linking that have not, in our opinion, had sufficiently wide attention. Whenever appropriate, we will guide readers to other sources for information that we have omitted.

1.2. The Categories of Score-Linking Methods

For two tests, a *link* between their scores is a transformation from a score on one to a score on the other. Several frameworks have been suggested for organizing the different types of links that are used in practice. These are found in Flanagan (1951), Angoff (1971), Mislevy (1992), Linn (1993), Feuer et al. (1999), and Dorans (2000, 2004b). Kolen (2004a) and Kolen and Brennan (2004) gave reviews and syntheses of several frameworks. We will use our own framework that builds on, and we hope, clarifies this prior work. Figures 6.1 through 6.4 illustrate our framework.

We use the term *linking* to refer the general idea of a transformation between the scores from one test and those of another. We will divide linking methods into three basic categories called *predicting*, *scale aligning*, and *equating*. We often shorten scale aligning to *scaling*. Figure 6.1 illustrates the three basic categories of linking.

FIGURE 6.1 The Three Overall Categories of Test Linking Methods and Their Goals

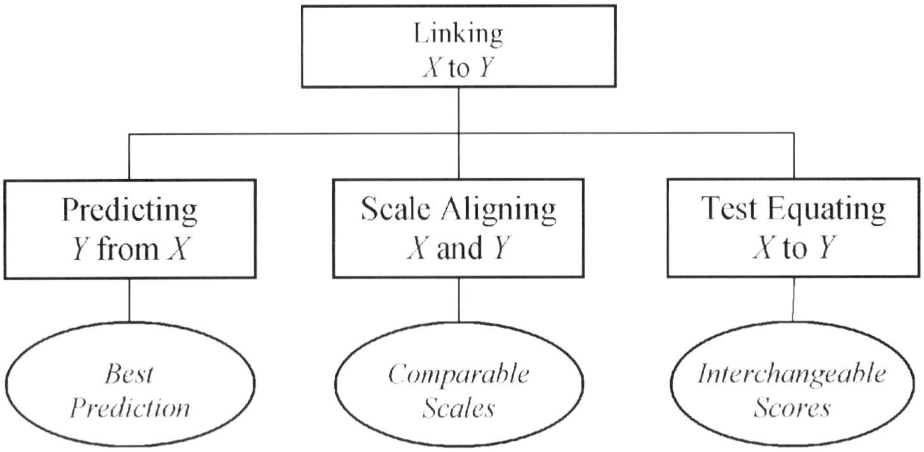

```
                    Linking
                    X to Y
         ┌─────────────┼─────────────┐
    Predicting    Scale Aligning   Test Equating
     Y from X       X and Y          X to Y
         │             │                │
       Best        Comparable      Interchangeable
     Prediction     Scales            Scores
```

Each of these categories contains subcategories of methods for score linking that share common objectives and that are distinct from the objectives of the methods in the other categories. Figures 6.2, 6.3, and 6.4 illustrate the several subcategories within the overall categories of predicting, scale aligning, and equating.

We take the position that the terms used for the various methods of score linking should have restricted meanings so that they may be used with precision. Thus, we have redefined one term that has been used in several ways in the past and created a few new terms for useful, general ideas that had no previous identifiers. We will point out these cases as we come to them.

It is sometimes useful to distinguish between score linkings that are *direct* and those that are *indirect*. A direct link is one that functionally connects the scores on one test directly to those of another. An indirect link is one that connects the scores on two tests through their common connection to a third test or scale. The categories of predicting and equating produce direct links, while the various subcategories of scale aligning typically produce indirect links. This distinction is not always clear-cut, but in many cases it is. We will identify direct and indirect links as they arise.

1.2.1. Predicting

While we include predicting in our three categories of linking, it is not the focus of this chapter. Nonetheless, for completeness and to add some clarity to the rest of the chapter, we give an abbreviated discussion of predicting here because it is both the oldest form of score linking and because predicting has been confused with the other methods of score linking since the earliest days of psychometrics. We will return to this issue in section 3.1.2.3 where we show how Hanson's theorem can shed light on some of the differences between predicting, scale aligning, and equating. In addition, when appropriate, we will point out one version of predicting called *projection* (see Equation 5, below) that is closely related to certain forms of scaling and equating.

The goal of predicting is to predict an examinee's score on one test from some other information about that examinee. This other information might be a score on another test or the scores from several other tests, and it might include demographic or other information. For this reason, there is always an asymmetry between what is predicted and what is being used to make the prediction. The predictors and the predicted quantity may be different both in number and character. This asymmetry is evident even in the case of predicting one test score, Y, from another, X. In this simplest case, it has been known since the 19th century that the usual linear regression function for predicting Y from X is not the inverse of the linear regression function for predicting X from Y (Galton, 1888). This is one aspect of the asymmetry between the predictor(s) and the predicted score.

If X and Y denote the scores on the two tests for examinees who are from a population, P, then the conditional expectation (or conditional mean) of Y given X over P, which we denote by

$$E(Y \mid X = x, P), \qquad (1)$$

is a standard method for predicting Y from X. If X has the value x, then $E(Y \mid X = x, P)$ predicts y, the value of Y. The prediction of Y from X is an example of a direct link between the scores on the two tests.

The error in this prediction is how far $E(Y \mid X = x, P)$ is from y, that is, the difference

$$y - E(Y \mid X = x, P). \qquad (2)$$

The conditional expectation, $E(Y \mid X = x, P)$, is the best predictor of Y in the sense that any other predictor of Y from X, say $y = \text{Pred}(x)$, will have a larger expected squared error in expression 2, that is,

$$\begin{aligned} E[(Y - \text{Pred}(x))^2 \mid X &= x, P] \\ \geq E[(Y - E(Y \mid X = x, P))^2 \mid X &= x, P] \\ = \text{Var}(Y \mid X &= x, P), \end{aligned} \qquad (3)$$

as shown in Cramér (1946), Parzen (1960), and others. Unless Y is functionally dependent on the predictor(s), there is always some amount of error in any prediction.

The conditional variance in Equation 3 is also called the conditional *prediction error variance* in the context of predicting Y-scores from X-scores.

Other types of predictors minimize other measures of prediction error, a subject too large for us to do much more than merely mention. For example, see Blackwell and Girshick (1954), Parzen (1960), or the discussion of best linear predictors in Holland and Hoskens (2003).

Both the conditional expectation, $E(Y \mid X = x, P)$, and the conditional prediction error variance may be estimated (using regression methods) from data in which examinees are sampled from P and tested with both X and Y. Discussions of regression methods are so widely available that we will not give more details here about the variety of possibilities—for example, see Moore and McCabe (1999) or Birkes and Dodge (1993).

An example of an appropriate application of prediction is the use of PSAT scores to forecast how an examinee will perform on the SAT a year or so later. Periodically a year's worth of SAT data from students who have taken both tests is used to estimate the conditional distribution of SAT scores given the corresponding (verbal or mathematical) PSAT score (Educational Testing Service, 1999). This conditional distribution gives a prediction of the range of likely performance on the SAT given an examinee's PSAT score that is accurate for other examinees similar to those in the population from which the prediction equations are derived.

A problem that is related to predicting individual scores on a test is *projecting distributions of scores* on one test from those on another test. In this case, just as we described for predicting a score on Y from a score on X, data obtained from a sample of examinees who take both X and Y is used to estimate the conditional distribution of Y given X on a particular population, say P. We denote the conditional *cumulative distribution function* (cdf) of Y given $X = x$ in P as

$$\Pr\{Y \le y \mid X = x, P\}. \qquad (4)$$

The data may be used to estimate the conditional distributions in Equation 4. Now suppose that in another population, say Q, we have data for the distribution of X, but not for Y. If the distribution of X in Q is somewhat different from that of X in P, we may wish to *project* the distribution of X in Q to obtain an estimate of the cdf of Y in Q, $F_{YQ}(y)$, using methods that are based on the following formula:

$$F_{YQ}(y) = \Pr\{Y \le y \mid Q\} = E[\Pr\{Y \le y \mid X, P\} \mid Q]. \qquad (5)$$

In Equation 5, the expectation or averaging is over the distribution of X in Q. Strictly speaking, Equation 5 is valid only if the conditional distribution of Y given X is the same in both P and Q, that is, if

$$\Pr\{Y \le y \mid X = x, P\} = \Pr\{Y \le y \mid X = x, Q\}. \qquad (6)$$

Equation 6 is a type of p*opulation invariance* assumption because it requires the conditional distribution that holds for one population to also hold for another population. We shall see that identical assumptions also arise in certain cases of scaling and equating. In fact, it is accurate to say that assumptions like Equation 6 or, at least, that are analogous to it, pervade all aspects of scaling and equating

where there are missing data in the sense that in the above example the data for Y in Q are *missing*.

An important example of projecting a score distribution arises when X and Y are both given to a sample of examinees in Year 1, and then in Year 2, only one of them, say X, is given. If we would like to predict what the distribution of Y would have been had it also been given in Year 2, then projection methods provide a way of doing this. They are based on Equation 5, with P representing the data from Year 1 and Q representing the data in Year 2. In this example, the need for the population invariance assumption in Equation 6 to hold is evident.

Pashley and Phillips (1993) provided an example of projecting scores from the International Assessment of Educational Progress to the scale of the National Assessment of Educational Progress (NAEP). Williams, Rosa, McLeod, Thissen, and Sanford (1998) gave a detailed discussion of an example of projecting scores from a state assessment to the NAEP scale.

So far, we have only mentioned prediction methods that directly link *observed scores* on the tests to each other. There is another form of prediction that we will briefly mention here. In this case, an observed score on X is used to predict the *true score* on X. For this section we assume the reader is familiar with the idea of the true scores that lie behind observed scores. For those who are not, we define true scores more carefully in section 3.1.2.1 where they play an important role.

The oldest version of predicting true scores from observed scores is Kelley's formula that predicts true score on Y from an observed score on Y (Kelley, 1927). This idea was generalized in Wainer et al. (2001) to the prediction of true scores on one test from the observed scores on it and some other tests. Holland and Hoskens (2003) considered the problem of predicting true scores from observed scores where the true scores come from one test, Y, and the observed scores come from another test, X.

Figure 6.2 illustrates the subcategories within the overall linking category of predicting.

1.2.2. Scale Aligning

The methods of aligning scales are older than those of test equating, and we feel it is easier to understand test equating when we can compare it to similar scale aligning problems. For this reason, our discussion of scaling is restricted to the brief outlines in the next few subsections and some comments in the rest of the chapter where we discuss data collection designs and equating methods. We refer to the chapter by Kolen (this volume) for more on this large topic.

The goal of scale aligning is to transform the scores from two different tests onto a common scale. Procedures for doing this are about 100 years old and were initially called methods for creating *comparable scores*. These transformations take scores from two different tests, X and Y, and put them onto a common scale. Such aligned scales imply an indirect linking of the scores on X and Y by, for example, transforming an X-score to the common scale and then inverting the Y-to-scale transformation to find the corresponding value for Y.

FIGURE 6.2 The Types of Linking Methods within the Overall Linking Category of *Predicting*

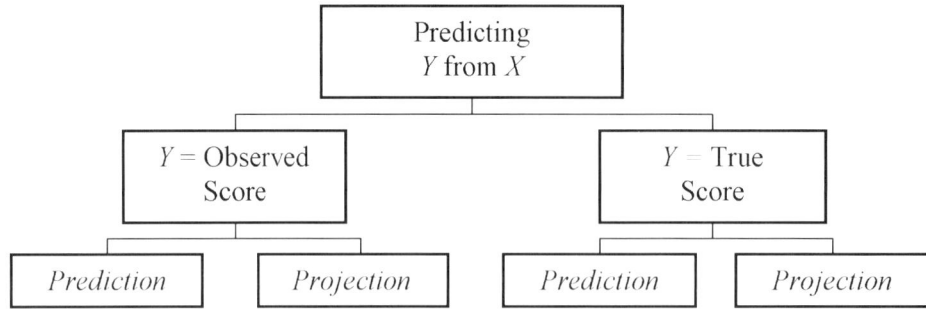

It should be emphasized that while the implied indirect links always exists, their meaningfulness depends on many factors. The indirect link is rarely the main purpose for putting **X** and **Y** onto a common scale.

We divide scale aligning into two basic cases, each of which includes additional subcategories. The two basic cases arise when the tests being linked measure (a) different constructs or (b) similar constructs but with different test specifications. We shall briefly describe six types of scaling within these two cases in the next five subsections. See the chapter by Kolen (this volume) for more discussion of many of these ideas. Figure 6.3 illustrates the subcategories within the overall linking category of scale aligning.

1.2.2.1. Battery Scaling—Different Constructs and a Common Population of Examinees

When two or more tests that measure different constructs are administered to a common population, the scores for each test may be transformed to have a common distribution for this population of examinees (i.e., the *reference population*). Kolen (2004a) referred to this as *battery scal-*

ing. Battery scaling has been used for many years. Flanagan (1951) described it in an educational testing context, but its roots can be traced back at least to Kelley (1914), where the scores on the different tests were given the same mean and variance in the reference population. Kelley (1923) and Angoff (1971) referred to scores from tests that measure different constructs but are scaled so that they have the same distributions on a common population as *comparable measures* (Kelley, 1923) or *comparable scores* (Angoff, 1971). We will use *comparable scales* rather than either of these older terms.

The data collected for battery scaling is usually either (a) a sample of examinees all of whom take all of the tests or (b) several equivalent (i.e., random) samples of examinees from a common population who take some of the tests. In this way, all of the tests are taken by equivalent groups of examinees from the reference population. Thus, for each test being scaled, **Y**, the data can be used to estimate the cumulative distribution function (cdf) of **Y** over the reference population, **P**, that is,

$$F_{\mathbf{YP}}(y) = \Pr\{\mathbf{Y} \leq y \mid \mathbf{P}\}. \tag{7}$$

FIGURE 6.3 The Types of Linking Methods within the Overall Linking Category of *Scale Aligning*

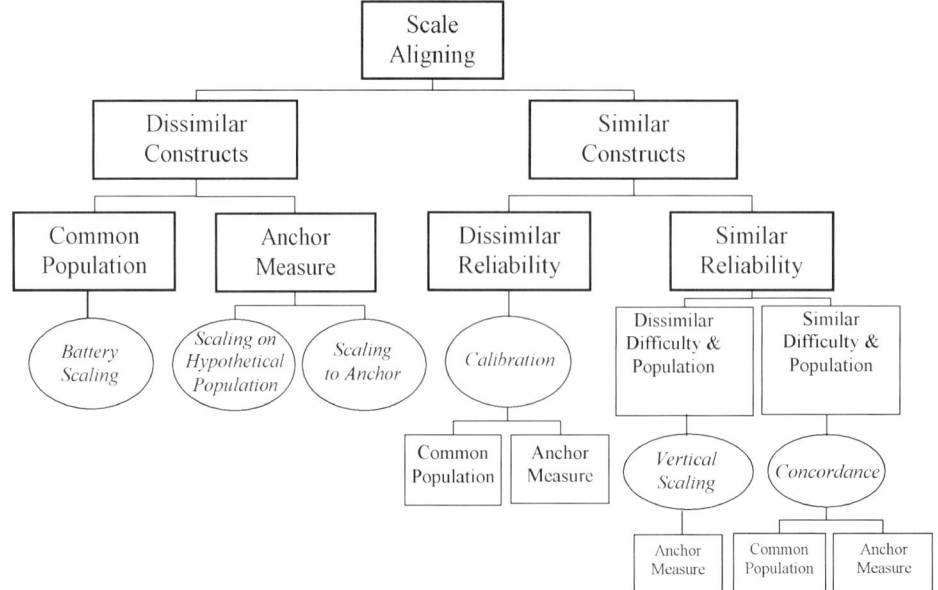

A **Y**-score, y, is then put on the common scale by a transformation of the form

$$s = S(F_{YP}(y)), \quad (8)$$

where $S(u)$ is an arbitrary *scaling function* selected to give the scaled version of **Y** a particular distributional form (see the chapter by Kolen, this volume, for more details).

The value of making the scales of different tests comparable in this sense is that examinees will correctly interpret differences in the scores across the battery of tests. A higher score on one test will indicate better performance (in **P**) on that test when compared to a lower score on another test. Comparing scaled scores becomes similar to comparing percentiles in the reference population when the scales have been aligned this way.

Even though the scales on the different tests are made comparable in this narrow sense, the tests do measure different constructs. The implied indirect link between the scores on the different tests, described above, can be used to indicate comparable performance on the different tests (relative to the reference population), but it has no meaning as a way of transforming a score on a test of one construct into an equivalent score for another construct.

The recentering of the SAT I scale is an example of battery scaling (Dorans, 2002). The scales for the SAT-verbal (SAT-V) and SAT-mathematical (SAT-M) scores were redefined so as to give the scaled scores on the SAT-V and SAT-M the same distribution in a reference population of students tested in 1990. The redefined score scales replaced the original score scales, which had been defined for a reference population tested in 1941. The new score scales enable a student whose SAT-M score is higher than his SAT-V score to conclude that he/she did in fact performed better on the mathematical portion than on the verbal portion, at least in relation to the students tested in 1990. Finally, it should be obvious that the indirect link between the SAT-M and SAT-V has no meaning as a way of turning a score on one of these tests into a score on the other.

1.2.2.2. Anchor Scaling—Different Constructs and Different Populations of Examinees

An important *approximation* to battery scaling arises when two or more tests that measure different constructs are administered to samples of examinees from *different* populations and a common measure (the *anchor measure*) is available for all of the examinees in these different samples. We shall use the term *anchor scaling* to refer to this general class of scaling problems. Mislevy (1992) and Linn (1993) used the term *statistical moderation* to refer to situations that include what we call anchor scaling.

In some applications of anchor scaling it is possible for one or more of the tests being scaled to be completely inappropriate for the examinees taking some of the other tests. Language examinations provide good examples of this—a test of French is inappropriate for examinees that are unfamiliar with French. Another example can occur when examinees choose which test to take based on the courses they have taken in school. Because of these selective factors, the samples of examinees taking the different tests are usually not equivalent, and the anchor measure is the information that is used to adjust for this. Anchor scaling necessarily involves incomplete test data because some tests are given to certain subgroups of examinees, but not to all of them. We say that anchor scaling is an *approximation* to battery scaling because of the potential inequivalence of the samples of examinees taking each of the tests. In contrast, for battery scaling, when different samples of examinees take different tests, they are designed to be equivalent samples of examinees. This is not true for cases of anchor scaling.

The potential inequivalence of the samples used in anchor scaling requires the use of assumptions about the anchor measure that are not easily evaluated. The more strongly the anchor measure is related to the different tests being put on a common scale, the more satisfactory the resulting scale alignment will be, but other than that, little more can be said.

There are two different ways anchor measures are used in practice. The first is similar to projecting score distributions, discussed in section 1.2.1, using the conditional distribution of each test given the anchor measure and Equation 5. This approach has no commonly accepted name so we call it *scaling on a hypothetical population* (SHP) because of the way the anchor measure is used. To briefly outline this approach and to relate it to projecting score distributions, suppose that **Y** denotes a test to be scaled and **A** is the anchor measure. The data for the examinees taking **Y** and **A** are used to estimate the conditional distribution of **Y** given **A** in the population of examinees (which we will denote by $\mathbf{P_Y}$) taking test **Y**. We denote the cdf of this conditional distribution by

$$\Pr\{\mathbf{Y} \le y \mid \mathbf{A} = a, \mathbf{P_Y}\}. \quad (9)$$

Next, this estimated conditional distribution is averaged over a hypothetical distribution for **A**. We call this the distribution of **A** in the *hypothetical* population, **P**. An estimate of the cdf of **Y** in **P** is then given by

$$\Pr\{\mathbf{Y} \le y \mid \mathbf{P}\} = E[\Pr\{\mathbf{Y} \le y \mid \mathbf{A}, \mathbf{P_Y}\} \mid \mathbf{P}]. \quad (10)$$

Equation 10 is the same as the method of projection in Equation 5. The estimated cdf for **Y**, defined in Equation 10, is treated as if it is the cdf of **Y** on a common population. Once this is done for each of the tests to be scaled, the problem is regarded as the simpler case of battery scaling and the same scaling techniques are used from that point on.

Strictly speaking, in order for Equation 10 to hold, a population invariance assumption, similar to Equation 6, must hold. The weaker the correlation between the anchor measure and the test, the less likely it is for this population invariance assumption to hold, even approximately. Checks on the invariance of the scaling across relevant subpopulations may be performed using methods similar to those discussed in section 4.2.

It should be pointed out here that there is nothing in the above analysis that requires the anchor measure to be a single score or number; it could involve more than one score as the example mentioned next illustrates.

An example of SHP is given by the scaling of the various subject area tests of the SAT II. Typically, some of the students who take the SAT I also take one or more tests from the SAT II battery. All of these scores are presented as part of their college admissions materials. The results of the SAT II tests for different examinees are treated as if they are on comparable scales. In this application, the SAT-V and SAT-M scores are used as the anchor measures. The hypothetical population is taken to be similar to the observed joint distribution of the SAT-V and SAT-M scores. This example is discussed in Angoff (1971) under the topic of comparable scores.

In section 3.2.1.1, we will relate *poststratification equating* to the SHP approach to anchor scaling.

The second approach to anchor scaling also has no commonly used name so we call it *scaling to the anchor* (STA). In this approach, the data for the examinees taking both **Y** and **A** are used to estimate a linking function, such as the *equipercentile function* or the *linear linking function*, to link **Y** to **A** (see section 3.1.1.1 for a detailed discussion of both the linear linking and the equipercentile functions). This puts all of the tests to be scaled onto the scale of the anchor measure.

Strictly speaking, in order for STA to be valid, the estimated linking functions should satisfy a type of population invariance assumption that we will discuss in more detail when we consider chain equating in section 3.2.1.2. In that section, we will relate chain equating to the STA approach to anchor scaling.

One difference between STA and SHP is that for STA the measure needs to be a single score or number, whereas, as we indicated earlier, this is not true of SHP. See McGaw (1977) and Keeves (1988) for more discussion of STA, where it was referred to as an example of *moderation*.

Linn (1993) indicated that the STA approach is used to bring comparability to scores on tests that are specific to particular schools in a school district. The anchor measure is a common district-wide examination score, and the scores from the locally developed tests in each school are put on a common scale using the STA approach to anchor scaling.

1.2.2.3. Vertical Scaling—Similar Constructs and Similar Reliability, but Different Difficulty and Populations of Examinees

Tests of academic subjects that are targeted for different school grades may be viewed as tests of similar constructs that are intended to differ in difficulty—those for the lower grades being (at least intuitively) easier than those for the higher grades. It is often desired to put scores from such tests onto a common overall scale so that progress in a given subject, such as mathematics or reading, can be tracked over time. This type of scaling is called *vertical scaling* (Kolen & Brennan, 2004). Alternatively, Angoff (1971) called this process *calibrating tests at different levels of ability*. For a discussion of an example of vertical scaling, see Hoover, Dunbar, and Frisbie (2003).

A topic, such as mathematics or reading, when considered over a range of school grades, has several subtopics or dimensions. At different grades, different dimensions of these subjects are relevant and tested. For this reason, the constructs being measured by the tests for different grade levels may differ somewhat, but the tests are often similar in reliability.

Vertical scaling shares some features with anchor scaling (see section 1.2.2.2). In particular, the tests to be scaled are, to some degree, inappropriate for all but one or a few grades so the samples of examinees that take each test are not equivalent in the sense that they are for battery scaling (see section 1.2.2.1). Moreover, there is no appropriate anchor measure that is available for every examinee (see section 1.2.2.2). Instead, the tests given to neighboring grades may share some common material that can serve as a type of anchor test that connects that pair but not all of the tests being scaled. This common material will be different for the different pairs of tests given to neighboring grades. Methods such as SHP and STA, described briefly in section 1.2.2.2, may be used to put the tests given to neighboring grades onto a common scale, and these can then be connected up to form an overall scale for the entire vertical system of tests. Item response theory (IRT) is also used to link these scales. See Kolen and Brennan (2004), Petersen et al. (1989), Harris, Hendrickson, Tong, Shin, and Shyu (2004), Hoover, Dunbar, and Frisbie (2001), Kolen (2003), and the chapter by Kolen (this volume) for more discussion of vertical scaling.

Vertical scaling produces indirect links between the scores on the different levels of the tests, but these links are rarely of interest to users.

1.2.2.4. Calibration—Same Construct, Different Reliability, and the Same Population of Examinees

We decided to limit the meaning of calibration in this chapter to situations where the tests measure the same construct, have similar levels of difficulty, but differ in reliability (e.g., length). We realize this is a departure from past usage, and it may cause some confusion. Kolen and Brennan (2004) observe that the term *calibration* is used in a variety of senses. In Angoff (1971), *calibration* was used to refer to vertical scaling (see section 1.2.2.3). In Petersen et al. (1989), *calibration* referred to the estimation of item parameters using IRT methods. This usage is reasonably standard in the IRT literature (Lord, 1980; Thissen & Wainer, 2001; and the chapter by Yen & Fitzpatrick, this volume). In Linn (1993), *calibration* referred to methods of score linking for tests that measure the same constructs but that have different statistical characteristics, in particular different reliability *or* difficulty.

To add to the confusion, Angoff (1971) seemed to imply that what we are calling calibration was an example of equating tests of differing reliability. Fortunately, calibration does not play a very important role in this chapter, but we will come back to it again in section 3.1.2.3, where we discuss the application of Hanson's theorem, and in section 3.2.1.2 where we discuss chain equating. The classic case of calibration in our sense is scaling the scores of a short form of a test onto the scale of its full or long form.

For calibration there may be some ambiguity as to whether the linking is direct or indirect. The short form is often derived from the long form so that it usually makes more sense to scale from the less reliable test to the more reliable one than vice versa. It is intuitively obvious as well that simply putting the scores of the short form onto the scale of a more reliable long form cannot increase the actual reliability of the short form.

1.2.2.5. Concordances—Similar Constructs, Difficulty and Reliability, and the Same Population of Examinees

In this case, the tests to be linked all measure similar constructs, but they are constructed according to different specifications. In most cases, they are similar in test length and reliability. In addition, they often have similar uses and may be taken by the same examinees for the same purpose. The use of the linking is to add value to the scores on both tests by expressing them as if they were scores on the other test. Concordances represent scalings of tests that are very similar but are not created with the idea that their scores would be linked. See Pommerich and Dorans (2004) for a thorough discussion of many aspects of concordances.

Many colleges and universities accept scores on either the ACT or SAT I for the purpose of admissions decisions, and they often have more experience interpreting the results from one of these tests than the other. Dorans, Lyu, Pommerich, and Houston (1997) reported a concordance table or function that linked the scores on each of these two tests to each other. This concordance was based on data from more than 100,000 examinees who had taken both tests within a restricted time frame. If their applicants were not widely different from those in this large sample, this concordance enabled university admissions officers to align cutscores on these two similar but somewhat different tests better than they could have using the limited data typically available to them.

Concordances are examples of scalings that produce direct links between the scores on the two tests.

1.2.3. Equating—Same Construct and the Same Levels of Difficulty and Reliability

Equating is the third category of linking methods in our framework. In test equating a direct link is made between a score on one test and a score on another test. The purpose of equating tests is to allow the scores from each test to be used interchangeably, as if they had come from the same test. This purpose puts strong requirements on the tests and on the method of linking. Among other things, the tests must measure the same construct at the same level of difficulty and with the same accuracy.

All linking frameworks define equating as the strongest form of linking between the scores on two tests. In our framework, it represents the endpoint of a continuum that begins with methods that make no assumptions about the relationships between the tests being linked (prediction and battery scaling) and proceeds to methods that are appropriate for linking tests that are very similar (concordances and equating). Because test equating is such an important form of score linking, we will discuss it more extensively in section 1.3. Furthermore, we will base the rest of the chapter on test equating and refer to other linking methods in terms of how similar they are to test equating.

Test equating is a necessary part of any testing program that continually produces new test forms and for which the uses of these tests require the meaning of the score scale be maintained over time. Although they measure the same constructs and are usually built to the same test specifications or test blueprint, different editions or forms of a test almost always differ somewhat in their statistical properties. For example, one form may be harder than another, so without adjustments, examinees would be expected to receive lower scores on this harder form. A primary goal of test equating for testing programs is to eliminate the effects on scores of these unintended differences in test form difficulty. For many testing programs, test equating is necessary to be fair to examinees taking different test forms and to provide score users with scores that mean the same thing, regardless of the tests taken by examinees (Angoff, 1971; Kolen & Brennan, 2004; Petersen et al., 1989).

In high-stakes testing programs, it cannot be overemphasized how important it is that test equating be done carefully and accurately. The released scores are usually the most visible part of a testing program, even though they represent only the endpoint of a long test production, administration, and scoring enterprise. An error in the equating function or score conversion function may change the scores for many examinees. The credibility of testing organizations has been called into question over test equating problems, in ways that rarely occur when, for example, flawed test questions are discovered in operational tests.

Figure 6.4 illustrates the subcategories within the overall linking category of equating.

1.2.4. A Crucial Consideration for Both Scale Aligning and Equating

Suppose that two different tests are given to two different groups of examinees. In examining the distributions of the resulting scores, there are two, ever-present, factors that can influence the results, no matter how similar the score scales of the two tests appear. One is the relative *difficulty* of the two tests (which is what test scaling and equating is concerned about), and the other is the relative *ability* of the two groups of examinees on these tests (which is a confounding factor that should be eliminated in the linking process). In test linking, we are only interested in adjusting for differences in test characteristics, and we wish to control for possible examinee differences in ability when making these adjustments. This basic fact influences both the data that are collected and the methods that are used for test linking. Kelley (1923) includes passages that suggest he was aware of the dual influence of examinee ability and test difficulty on test scores and that this needed to be accounted for in scaling test scores (von Davier et al., 2004b).

1.3. What Makes a Linking an Equating?

All forms of test-score linking involve some of the same ingredients. These include (a) two or more tests and rules

FIGURE 6.4 The Types of Linking Methods within the Overall Linking Category of *Test Equating*

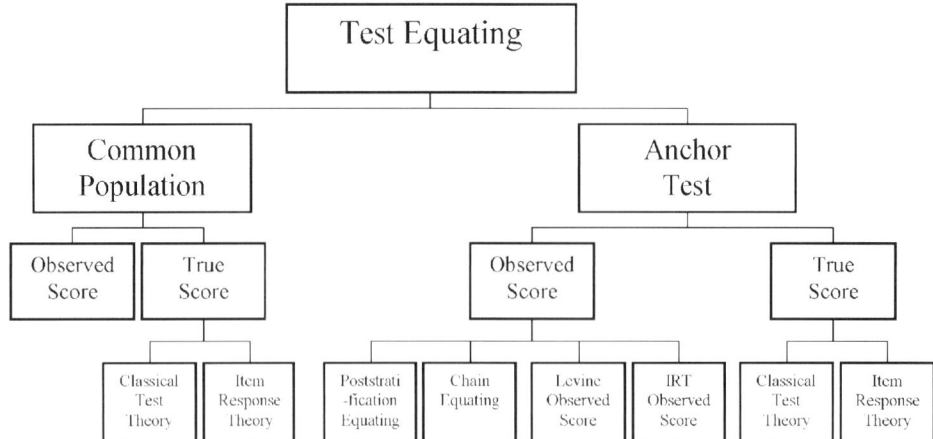

for scoring them, (b) scores on these tests from one or more samples of examinees, (c) an implicit or explicit population of examinees to which the test linking is to be applied, and (d) one or more methods of estimating or calculating the linking function. What distinguishes test equating from other forms of linking is its goal. The goal of equating two tests is to allow the scores from both to be used interchangeably for any purpose. As mentioned earlier, this is a very demanding goal, and experience has shown that, to achieve it, the two tests and the methods used to link them must satisfy very strong requirements.

An *equating function* is a transformation of raw scores on test **X** to the scale of the raw scores on test **Y**. A special property of tests that have been successfully equated is that although the equating function is estimated from data sampled from a given population of examinees, the equating function estimated from any other population is highly similar to it.

It is important to be clear that test equating is usually the first part of a two-step process by which scores on new tests are put onto an existing scale. The first step is the computation of the equating function that links the raw scores on a new test, **X**, to those of an old test, **Y**—the so-called *raw-to-raw equating*. The second step is the conversion of these equated **X**-raw scores to the reporting scale. In practice, there is a scaling function that maps the raw scores of **Y** to the scale, call it $S = s(y)$, and then the **X**-raw-score to **Y**-raw-score equating function, $y = e(x)$, is composed with $s(y)$ to put the raw scores of **X** onto the reporting scale. Braun and Holland (1982) give an illustrative diagram of this two-step process for a testing program that continually produces and equates new test forms. The composition function, $S = s(e(x))$, is called the *score conversion function* for **X**. In this chapter, we will not discuss how scaling functions are obtained, but refer the reader to the chapter by Kolen (this volume) for further information. For most of this chapter, we will ignore the score conversion function and concentrate on linking raw scores, but the score conversion function is one way that different equating functions are compared in practice and they will come up later in parts 4 and 5.

In this section, we paraphrase Dorans and Holland (2000) and outline five requirements that are widely viewed as necessary for test equating to be successful. The order in which they are listed corresponds roughly to the historical order of their appearance in the literature.

a. **The equal construct requirement**: The tests should measure the same constructs.
b. **The equal reliability requirement**: The tests should have the same reliability.
c. **The symmetry requirement**: The equating function for equating the scores of **Y** to those of **X** should be the *inverse* of the equating function for equating the scores of **X** to those of **Y**.
d. **The equity requirement**: It should be a matter of indifference to an examinee to be tested by either one of two tests that have been equated.
e. **The population invariance requirement**: The choice of (sub)population used to estimate the equating function between the scores of tests **X** and **Y** should not matter—that is, the equating function used to link the scores of **X** and **Y** should be *population invariant*.

Both formal and informal statements of these five requirements have appeared in a variety of earlier sources including Lord (1950), Angoff (1971), Lord (1980), Petersen et al. (1989), and Kolen and Brennan (2004). Dorans and Holland (2000) discussed these five requirements and indicate various ways in which the five "...can be criticized as being vague, irrelevant, impractical, trivial or hopelessly stringent" (p. 283). Livingston (2004) argued that requirements (d) and (e) were unattainable in practice, while Lord (1980) regarded (d) as the most fundamental. Regardless of these differences of opinions, we regard these five requirements as having heuristic value for addressing the question of whether or not two tests can be, or have been, successfully equated. Moreover, they provide an intuitive theory of test equating to which we will return in section 3.1.2.2.

In practice, requirements (a) and (b) mean that the tests need to be built to the same specifications, while (c) precludes regression methods from being a form of test equating. Lord (1980) argued that requirement (d) implied both (a) and (b) as follows. If the two tests measure different constructs, examinees will prefer the one on which they believe they will score higher. If the tests measure the same thing but differ in reliability, then more able examinees will prefer the more reliable test, while less able examinees will prefer the less reliable test (but see Appendix B of Dorans and Holland [2000] for a careful analysis of this intuitive claim about the effect of reliability). Requirement (d) is, however, hard to evaluate empirically and its use is primarily theoretical (Lord, 1980; Hanson, 1991).

Furthermore, requirement (e), which is easy to use in practice, also can be used to explain why requirements (a) and (b) are needed. If two tests measure different things or are not equally reliable, then the standard linking methods will not produce results that are invariant across certain subpopulations of examinees. Dorans and Holland (2000) used requirement (e), rather than requirement (d) to develop quantitative measures of equatability; see section 4.2.

If we examine the five requirements, we can see why the other linking methods mentioned earlier will fail as test equatings. Concordances are used with tests that measure similar but different constructs and do not share common test specifications. While they may have similar difficulty and reliability, they will satisfy requirement (a) only approximately and this may be detected by the failure of requirement (e), and possibly requirement (d). Tests that are vertically scaled may be on such different aspects of a school subject that requirement (a) is not satisfied, at least when the gap between the grades is large, and the differences in difficulty may be so great that, regardless of attempts to scale them appropriately, examinees will definitely prefer one test over the other, thus violating requirement (d), and probably requirement (e) as well. Calibrating a short form to a long form violates requirement (b) and is likely to violate requirements (d) and (e).

For either battery scaling or anchor scaling, the tests are usually measures of different constructs so that requirement (a) is not satisfied. Furthermore, scaling tests of different constructs will also tend to fail to satisfy requirements (d) and (e) for important subgroups of examinees. The direct and indirect linkings that arise in scaling are invertible so that requirement (c) is usually satisfied.

Furthermore, prediction methods need not satisfy any of the five requirements. The asymmetry between predictors and outcomes violates requirement (c). In addition, the requirements (a) and (b) play no role in prediction (but they do have consequences for the accuracy of the prediction—that is, less related tests and less reliable tests make for poorer predictors of the scores on another test). Requirement (d) plays no role in prediction. Finally, it often makes sense to include subgroup membership as predictors to improve prediction. This incorporates population sensitivity directly into the prediction, whereas equating functions should not depend on subpopulations according to requirement (e).

As we discuss further in section 1.4, the difference between prediction and equating has been pointed out repeatedly over the last century. To give an example that shows how test equating and predicting can work together but do different things, consider the common way that predictive validity studies are often carried out (Kane, this volume). In these studies, test scores are used to predict future grades. It is common practice in validity studies to use the equated scores that come from different test forms as interchangeable values of the predictor. The prediction benefits from prior test equatings because this eliminates the need to distinguish between the scores on the various forms of the test that are used as predictors. However, the predicted values from the test score would never be construed as an *equating* of test scores and, for example, first-year college grades.

1.4. A Brief History of Test Linking

By the dawn of the 19th century, Legendre, Gauss, Laplace, and their scientific contemporaries understood how to use least squares methods to estimate curves to solve problems in astronomy. By the end of that century, regression methods had been applied to a variety of social and psychological phenomena as well. Notable among these pioneers was Galton, who first observed the effects of regression to the mean (Stigler, 1986). Thus, the use of linear regression methods to predict the scores on one test or measurement from those of another is probably the oldest approach taken for linking scores. However, it was recognized very early that prediction methods were not satisfactory ways of creating *comparable scores*, as the early forms of scale aligning were called. Thorndike (1922) gave intuitive arguments as to why linear regression was not a satisfactory method of finding comparable scores, and Otis (1922) gave a more theoretical discussion of this same topic. Flanagan (1951) emphasized the lack of symmetry of regression functions, thereby connecting regression methods to the failure to satisfy requirement (c) of section 1.3. The distinction between prediction and equating has been repeatedly reaffirmed over the years—Hull (1922), Flanagan (1939, 1951), Lord (1950, 1955, 1982), Angoff (1971), Mislevy (1992), and Linn (1993)—and, following such distinguished scholars, we shall add some additional views in section 3.1.2.3.

The need to make scores on different tests comparable (i.e., scaling) and the invention of methods to do it, has a history almost as old as the field of psychometrics itself. Kelley (1914) discussed problems with the methods proposed in Starch (1913) and modified in Weiss (1914) and Pinter (1914) for putting into comparable units the Ayers and the Thorndike methods of scoring of handwriting. Pinter had a sample of handwriting from examinees that had been judged using both methods. Weiss advocated setting the means of the scores on both tests equal to 50 by a multiplicative factor. Kelley showed that Weiss's method could give absurd results in various circumstances and proposed, instead, to use standard scores as comparable measures, that is, to subtract the mean and divide by the standard deviation of each measure. Using standard scores to scale tests has been used widely since that time. Treating standard scores as equivalent leads to the well-known method of linear equating (see section 3.1.1.1). Kelley explicitly titled his article "Comparable Measures" and used the terms *equate* and *equating* to refer to the results of setting comparable scores equal.

Nine years later, the influential text book by Kelley (1923) had a chapter entitled "Comparable Measures" in which Kelley (a) preferred standard scores to Weiss's method; (b) indicated that Galton had, decades earlier, used a version of standard scores to compare quantities that are measured on different scales; and (c) discussed the "equal successive percentiles method" to define comparable scores—this is an early form of equipercentile equating (see section 3.1.1.1). Kelley referred to even earlier uses of the equal successive percentile method in Otis (1916, 1918).

These references suggest that by the time of the U.S. entry into World War I, those who worked with test data had some familiarity with both the linear and the equipercentile methods of scaling the scores from different tests.

We do not know the earliest example of equating alternative forms of the same tests, but we do know of early examples of alternative forms that *were not equated*—the Alpha test used by the American Army during World War I. This test was devised by the Committee on the Classification of Personnel in the Army, established in 1917. Its membership included the psychologists and early psychometricians E. L. Thorndike, L. M. Terman, R. M. Yerkes, L. L. Thurstone and T. L. Kelley. By the end of 1918 the Army had tested over 1.7 million men using the "Alpha" and "Beta" Army tests. The Alpha was targeted for examinees who could read and write English while the Beta was for those who could not. Yoakum and Yerkes (1920) gave a detailed description of both instruments. They indicated that the Alpha had five different test forms: "To avoid … the risk of coaching, several duplicate forms of this examination have been made available" (p. 18). Thus, by this early date, test security issues had already led to the use of alternate forms, at least for the Army Alpha. Yoakum and Yerkes said little about how the alternate forms of the Alpha were constructed, but the following passage suggests that they used random assignment of test items to forms to help insure the similarity of the alternate forms. "All five forms of the group examination were used in the pre official trial of the tests. The differences in forms were so slight as to indicate the success of the random method of selecting items" (p. 8).

We were not able to find any better description of the test construction process, but under appropriate conditions, assigning test items to forms at random will produce nearly parallel test forms that are similar but not identical in difficulty. In the next sentence, Yoakum and Yerkes (1920, p. 8) indicated that the five forms were not exactly equivalent. "Form B proved more difficult than the other forms."

Nothing more is said about the issue of Form B's difficulty, and we conclude that in all probability, scores on the different forms of the Alpha were treated as sufficiently similar so that they were not equated, even though the linear and equipercentile methods for doing so were known and available by that time.

Of greater concern to the Army psychologists was the comparability of scores achieved on the Alpha and Beta versions of the test. A special sample of military personnel was tested with both, and these data were used to put the Alpha and Beta on a common 7-point scale (A, B, C+, C, C−, D, D −). Because these two tests were quite different in terms of format and questions asked, nowadays we would probably call this a case of battery scaling as defined in section 1.2.2.1 rather than of test equating. Indeed, by 1922 there were three distinct scalings of the Alpha and Beta (Thorndike, 1922).

The example that Kelley criticized in 1914 was also a form of battery scaling rather than equating. The two handwriting scales were arrived at by very different methods and would not, in current terms, be construed to be alternative forms of the same test. The problem that interested Pinter and Starch was to measure the accuracy/stability of these different handwriting measures. Kelley referred to an earlier work, Woodworth (1912), which used standard scores to combine the results of several tests. Otis (1918) was also interested in the problem of combining test results when the tests were on quite different subjects—spelling, arithmetic, synonyms, proverbs, etc. Thus, these early uses of comparable scores were not to equate scores in the sense that we will use this term, but rather as intermediate battery scalings needed to solve other problems.

Terman and Merrill (1937) discussed their revised edition of the Stanford-Binet test. Two alternative forms of the new edition were produced, but they were not equated directly. Rather, both were treated separately and the scores of each one put on the IQ scale using battery-scaling methods (see the chapter by Kolen, this volume). While putting two tests onto a common scale implicitly and indirectly links the scores on the two tests, this was not a significant aspect of the scaling of these two forms. In the next edition of the Stanford-Binet test, the second form was eliminated because it was rarely used.

Thus, the need, or at least the desire, to equate scores on alternate forms of the same test probably arose decades after the invention of scaling methods and of the two standard methods for equating—the linear and equipercentile methods. In 1938 two forms of the College Board's SAT tests were given in the same year, and the need to equate them became evident by 1940. Early versions of anchor test equating were used for the SATs in 1941. In 1942 the SAT scales were equated back to the scales established in 1941 (Donlon & Angoff, 1971; Dorans, 2002). Lord (1950, 1955) credited Ledyard R Tucker with devising the anchor test methods used to equate the SATs during the 1940s; these methods, in various versions, continue to be used to this day (see section 3.2.1).

The theory underlying test equating has evolved slowly over the years. The methods called observed-score test equating (see section 3.1.1) can be viewed as simple adaptations of scale-aligning methods to the problem of equating tests. This includes the linear and equipercentile methods discussed in section 3.1.1.1, as well as the methods adapted to the anchor-test designs discussed in section 3.2.1. Levine (1955) was the first application of classical test theory to the problem of equating tests, and Lord (1980) first applied IRT to test equating. Other attempts to give a theoretical foundation to test equating include Morris (1982), Hanson (1991), and van der Linden (2000). Hanson's theorem (see section 3.1.2.2) is the earliest result we know of that derives an equating function from formalizations of conditions that are related to the requirements of section 1.3. As of this writing, we are unaware of a more general theory of test equating than this initial result, and we believe that work along these lines would be a useful program for future research.

We end this brief account of the early history of test linking with some differing views of the importance of the population invariance requirement (e) given in section 1.3.

Flanagan (1951) was careful to indicate the potential sensitivity of linking functions to the groups and samples used to form them. He even went so far as to state, "Comparability which would hold for all types of groups—that is general comparability between different tests, or even between various forms of a particular test—is strictly and logically impossible" (p. 758). This negative position is rather different from that taken later by Angoff (1971), who stated that "...the resulting conversion should be independent of the individuals from whom the data were drawn to develop the conversion and should be freely applicable to all situations" (p. 563). Thus, both the requirement of population invariance for equating and its denial have roots that are at least 50 years old. See Kolen (2004b) for more on of the history of population invariance and test equating.

2. DATA COLLECTION DESIGNS USED IN TEST SCORE LINKING

There are numerous data collection designs that have been used for scale aligning and equating. Only one of these is useful for predicting. Our emphasis here is on data collection designs used for scale aligning and equating. We restrict our attention to those data collection designs that involve complete tests in the sense that the examinees are given the opportunity to answer all of the questions on one or both of the tests. We make this restriction so that both classical methods and methods that are based on IRT can be applied. IRT methods may also be used for data collection designs that involve substantial amounts of incomplete data (see the chapter by Yen & Fitzpatrick, this volume). Throughout this chapter we will assume that the issues of omitted or not reached items are covered by the rules for scoring the test rather than treating them as a type of missing data.

Data collection designs are crucial to successful test equating and scaling. The need to control for differential examinee ability in score linking was mentioned earlier in section 1.2.4. This control is accomplished through the use of special data collection designs. In this section, we give brief summaries of the important data collection designs that have been used over the years with an attempt to show their similarities and differences. Other good discussions of these designs were given in Lord (1950), Angoff (1971), Petersen et al. (1989), von Davier et al. (2004b), and Kolen and Brennan (2004).

2.1. The Single Group (SG) Design

In the single group (SG) design, all examinees in a single sample from population **P** take both tests. The SG design is used for predicting, scaling, and equating. It is probably the earliest data collection design for test linking. It was used in 1914 to scale the two handwriting scales as well as the scaling of the Army Alpha and Beta tests later in that decade, described in section 1.4. In all likelihood, it was used even earlier than this for predicting test scores on one test from those on another test.

When discussing data collection designs for test linking, it is helpful to introduce the *design table* defined in von Davier et al. (2004b), but used earlier in Petersen et al. (1989) as well as Braun and Holland (1982). The design table is a schematic representation of the examinee-by-test data matrix, with rows representing populations and samples of examinees and the columns representing the different tests, test sections, or test items involved. For the SG design, the design table in Table 6.1 is the simplest possible.

The ✓ mark in the design table indicates that the examinees in the sample for a given row take the tests indicated in the column. In the other data collection designs described in this chapter, a *blank* in a given row and column will indicate that the examinees in the sample for that row are not given the opportunity to take the test items indicated in that column.

The SG design controls for differential examinee proficiency by having the same examinees take both tests. It has several major uses in the practice of scaling and equating. One common case arises for both scaling and equating when it is feasible to (a) have examinees take both tests or to (b) find examinees who already have taken both tests. In addition, it must be plausible that practice or other types of order effects can be ignored. In this case, the common population from which the sample is drawn may be clearly identified as, for example, in the concordance reported in Dorans et al. (1997).

A second use of the SG design in equating arises when a few test questions are deleted from a test after it has been given to a sample of examinees. The link from the slightly shorter test to the full test can be viewed as an example of equating (or calibrating) using the SG design.

A third use of the SG design arises when the scoring procedures for a constructed-response test or performance assessment are changed in a way that changes the scores but the tasks themselves are not altered. The new scores can be linked to the old scores by applying the old and new scoring methods independently to the same sample of examinee responses. This is much the same as the use of the SG design by Pinter (1914) to scale the two different ways of assessing handwriting samples, described in section 1.4.

Predicting requires the use of SG designs in order to estimate the conditional distribution of one test score given the other, as indicated in Equations 1 and 4.

2.2. The Equivalent Groups (EG) Design

In the equivalent groups (EG) design, two equivalent samples are taken from a common population **P**; one is tested with **X** and the other with **Y**. The EG design is often used for battery scaling and equating and could be used for concordances and calibrations, as well.

We have not found an early example of the EG design, but it was probably invented as a solution to the problem that the SG design requires each examinee to take both tests, and the second test taken might be subject to order effects of various sorts. The design table, Table 6.2, for the EG design shows the pattern of missing data in the blank cells.

TABLE 6.1 The Design Table for the SG Design

POPULATION	SAMPLE	X	Y
P	1	✓	✓

TABLE 6.2 The Design Table for the EG Design

Population	Sample	X	Y
P	1	✓	
P	2		✓

TABLE 6.3 The Design Table for the CB Design

Population	Sample	X_1	Y_1	X_2	Y_2
P	1	✓			✓
P	2			✓	✓

Because examinees take only one test, the issue of order effects does not arise for the EG design. The problem is to select samples that are equivalent in whatever the tests are supposed to measure. In practice, this is done in two ways. First, it is sometimes possible to take two random samples from **P** and test each with a single test. To reflect this possibility, this design is sometimes called the *random groups design* (Kolen & Brennan, 2004). The two samples are then as equivalent as two random samples from the same population can be. Second, the more common situation is to construct the two samples by spiraling the two tests together. Spiraling refers to the way that test booklets are packed for distribution. The two tests are alternated in the packaging process so that when the tests are distributed to examinees, they are alternated, first **X**, then **Y**, and then **X** again, and so on. Certain assumptions must hold in order for spiraling to be feasible. For example, if the two tests have separately timed sections, then they must have the same sequence of time limits in the two tests. When well executed, spiraled samples are often somewhat *more* equivalent (i.e., less different) than random samples—however, this effect is usually small. They can be more equivalent because they are approximately *stratified* random samples where the strata are the administrative units of the tested population, i.e., classrooms (Angoff, 1971; von Davier et al., 2004b).

The EG design is a possible option for test equating if relatively large samples are available, and the tests can be reused at least once. When these conditions are met, the EG design is usually regarded as a good choice because it avoids the issue of order effects that can arise in the SG design where each examinee takes *both* tests. For battery scaling, the EG design can be used to reduce the respondent burden by requiring the examinees to take fewer tests.

2.3. The Counterbalanced (CB) Design

In order to allow for the possibility of order effects in the SG design, the sample is sometimes randomly divided in half, and in each subsample the two tests are taken in different orders—**X** first and then **Y** or **Y** first and then **X**. The result is the counterbalanced (CB) design. An early reference to the practice of counterbalancing is Pinter (1914). The CB design may be used for battery scaling, concordances, and equating and it could be used for predicting and calibration, as well.

If we denote a score from **X**, when it is taken first as X_1, and, when it is taken second, as X_2, and similarly for Y_1 and Y_2, then the design table in Table 6.3 describes the CB design.

A comparison of the design table for the CB design with those of the SG and the EG designs reveals that the CB design contains both of the other two designs within it. There is an EG design for X_1 and Y_1 and for X_2 and Y_2. There are SG designs for both X_1 and Y_2 and for X_2 and Y_1. Finally, if the order is ignored and the counterbalancing is regarded as having eliminated the effect of order, the two samples can be pooled and treated as a simple SG design. This variety of interpretations implies that there are several ways to use the data for the CB design to scale or equate **X** and **Y**. von Davier et al. (2004b) describe several approaches and indicate how the naïve pooling of the two samples may not be accurate. Also see Angoff (1971). When the SG design is feasible and the possibility of order effects is substantial, then the CB design may be the preferred option.

2.4. Anchor Test or NEAT Designs

In anchor test designs, there are two populations, **P** and **Q**, with examinees from **P** taking test **X** and those from **Q** taking test **Y**. In addition, both samples take an anchor test, **A**. For this reason, von Davier et al. (2004b) called this the "Non-Equivalent groups with Anchor Test" (or NEAT) design and we follow their terminology. Kolen and Brennan (2004) and others referred to this as the common-item non-equivalent groups design or simply the common item or the anchor test design. In scale aligning, **A** is the *anchor measure* or *anchor test* referred to in section 1.2.2.2.

The use of common items or anchor tests arose later than the other data collection designs for test equating and linking. The earliest methods using anchor tests were probably versions of STA, described in section 1.2.2.2. As a way of equating, the earliest versions that we located are in the early 1940s, when both STA and SHP, described in section 1.2.2.2, were used to equate and scale the SAT (Donlon & Angoff, 1971).

The NEAT design is used for equating, vertical scaling, and both forms of anchor scaling (see section 1.2.2.2). The NEAT design has little use in predicting, but the method of projecting the distribution of scores described briefly in section 1.2.1 is related to both SHP (scaling on a hypothetical population, see section 1.2.2.2) and the poststratification method of equating (section 3.2). Table 6.4 is the design table for the NEAT design.

The role of the anchor test is to quantify the differences between **P** and **Q** in a way that is relevant to the two tests. In addition, the anchor test, **A**, is usually a shorter and less reliable measure of the same constructs that **X** and **Y** measure. It is important that the anchor test quantify the differences between the two groups that affect their performance on the two tests to be equated. See section 2.6 for more discussion of this important issue.

Formally, the NEAT design contains two SG designs within it. This structure underlies both the STA approach

TABLE 6.4 The Design Table for the NEAT Design

Population	Sample	X	A	Y
P	1	✓	✓	
Q	2		✓	✓

to anchor scaling (section 1.2.2.2) and the chain equating methods (section 3.2.1.2).

The relationship of **A** to **X** and **Y** can be of two different types. If **A** is a part of both **X** and **Y**, then it is called an *internal* anchor test, and if it is a separate test from **X** and **Y**, then it is called an *external* anchor test.

The anchor test design improves upon the flexibility of the EG design by allowing the two samples taking **X** and **Y** to be nonequivalent. In addition, it improves upon the SG design by not requiring examinees to take both **X** and **Y**. On the surface, the use of anchor tests may appear to be a minor variation of the previous data collection designs, but, in fact, the use of common items rather than common examinees involves new assumptions that are not necessary in the use of the designs discussed in sections 2.1–2.3. Because **X** is never observed for examinees in **Q** and **Y** is never observed for examinees in **P**, some type of assumption is required to make up for these missing data. For this reason, there are several distinct methods of scaling and equating tests using the NEAT design. All of these methods correspond to making different untestable assumptions about the missing data. We will discuss these methods and assumptions in more detail in section 3.2.

When **P** = **Q**, the NEAT design is called an EG design with anchor test. The two samples are drawn from a common population and the role of the anchor test changes. The anchor test becomes a covariate as in a randomized experimental design. It is used to gain precision in the estimation of the relevant parameters, rather than to adjust for group differences. For this special case, it is not necessary for **A** to measure the same construct that **X** and **Y** do, or even to be a test score. All that matters is for **A** to be correlated with both **X** and **Y**. When this is the case, **A** is useful as a precision-increasing covariate. The poststratification procedures described in section 3.2.1.1 may be viewed as using the anchor test as a covariate. Lord (1955) indicated that Ledyard R Tucker first proposed the EQ design with an anchor test as a way of reaping the benefits of both the EG and the SG designs. The example of an anchor test design given in Liou, Cheng, and Li (2001) is an EG design with both an anchor test and other anchor information as well. These authors pointed out that in this case the missing data are *missing at random* in the technical sense discussed in Little and Rubin (2002).

Lord (1950) showed that the way the anchor test is used in the EG design with anchor test can have dramatic effects on the resulting accuracy of the results. For example, he showed that regardless of the correlation between the anchor measure and the tests, methods like SHP or poststratification produced more stable estimates than did STA or chain equating (see section 1.2.2.2 for more on SHP and STA and section 3.2.1 for poststratification and chain equating).

When **P** and **Q** are different or nonequivalent, the statistical role of **A** is to remove bias as well as to increase precision. When **A** is a miniature version of **X** and **Y** (i.e., a mini test that is a less reliable but otherwise measures the same construct as the two tests to be linked) then it can be expected to do a good job of removing the bias to which the nonequivalence of **P** and **Q** can lead. When **A** is not really a measure of the same construct underlying **X** and **Y**, or if it is not highly correlated with them, **A** is less useful for bias removal or for increasing precision. In situations where (for test security reasons) test material can never be used more than once, the only information that may be available from examinees in both **P** and **Q** is noncognitive demographic information. For test equating purposes, this is an unsatisfactory state of affairs, but it is formally similar to an anchor test design and treating it as such may be the only available approach. Little is known about the properties of such uses of nontest anchor measures other than the fact that if the anchor measure is not highly correlated with the test scores on **X** and **Y**, then it may be almost useless as an anchor test.

One way to think about the difference between the NEAT design and the other three designs discussed so far is as the difference between experimental designs versus observational studies (Rosenbaum, 1995). The EG design is like a randomized experiment with two treatment groups, the SG design is like a repeated measures design with a single group and two treatments, and the CB design is like a repeated measures design with a single group and counterbalanced order of treatment exposure. In contrast, the NEAT design is like an observational study where there are two nonrandomized study groups that are possibly subject to varying amounts of self-selection.

2.5. Practical Differences among the Data Collection Designs

Each of the data collection designs described earlier has advantages and disadvantages that make it more or less useful in particular situations. In general terms, for equating and scaling purposes, the SG design requires the smallest sample sizes and the EG design requires the largest sample sizes to achieve the same level of accuracy as measured by the standard error of equating (see Lord, 1950, and section 4.1.1). The anchor test (i.e., NEAT) designs are somewhere in between depending on how strongly correlated the anchor test is with the two tests and how different the two populations are.

It may be argued that the ideal design, in theory, is a large EG design with an external anchor test. If the anchor test is administered after the others, possible order effects can only affect the anchor test. A comparison of the distributions of the anchor test in the two (equivalent) samples then allows differential order effects to be discovered and if they are substantial, the anchor test can be ignored, resulting in a simple EG design, where no order effects are possible. If the anchor test is internal to the two tests, then issues of context or order effects arise and need to be examined.

The primary drawback of the SG, EG, and CB designs for test equating is that the equated test has to be given at least twice—once to be equated and again for at least one operational use. In some testing programs, this reuse of operational forms may be problematic. If special non-operational test administrations are arranged and one of these three designs is used for equating, then the issue of examinee motivation arises (see sections 5.1.2 and 5.1.3).

The SG design, while requiring a smaller sample size to achieve the same statistical accuracy as the EG design, brings with it issues of order effects, in addition to requiring each examinee to take two tests. In the SG design there is no way to assess whether there are order effects. The CB design allows order effects to be estimated, but if they are large and different for the two tests, then there may be little recourse but to ignore the data from the tests given second and treat the result as an EG design with no anchor test. von Davier et al. (2004b) proposed a formal statistical procedure that used a form of the standard error of equating difference (the SEED, see section 4.1.2), to assess how much the data from the tests administered second in the CB design can affect the resulting equating function. This approach is worth more research to investigate its value in practice.

2.6. The Special Problems of the NEAT Design

When we leave the relative simplicity of the single population designs (EG, SG, and CB) and consider those that use common items and anchor tests, new issues arise. The NEAT design is more flexible than the other three. For test equating, it allows a new operational test to be used at each successive test administration without being previously used or equated. This is desirable in high-stakes situations where test reuse may cause problems of test security. For both scaling and equating, the NEAT design allows flexibility in selecting samples of examinees.

As we will discuss in more detail in section 3.2.1, the use of the NEAT design requires users to make one of several possible sets of untestable, missing-data assumptions to allow the procedures used to be interpreted as bona fide equating methods. However, in addition to requiring these sorts of assumptions, the data in the NEAT design must be collected and analyzed with great care. For example, for both internal and external anchor tests, care needs to be exercised to insure that the statistical properties of the common items have not changed in between the two test administrations. Differential item functioning (DIF) methods may be used to compare the performance of the common items. The two test administrations form the reference and focal groups and the total score on the common items is the matching criterion (see Holland & Wainer, 1993, especially chapter 3). Internal anchor tests are susceptible to context effects because they are embedded in different sets of items in the two administrations. DIF analyses can detect these changes. Items in either type of anchor tests may change because of changes in widely held general knowledge. For example, a hard item on an obscure 19th-century ruling in constitutional law may become easier because of a high-profile Supreme Court decision that brings widespread attention to it. There are many examples of this type of rapid aging of test questions.

2.6.1. External Anchor Tests

External anchor tests are often administered in a separately timed section and do not count as part of the total score. It is often advised that the anchor test should be a "mini version" of the two tests being equated (Angoff, 1971). This advice is sometimes in conflict with the need to disguise an external anchor test to make it look like one of the scored sections on the test. For example, the mini test might require the inclusion of a variety of item types, while the disguise might require that it contain only a limited number of item types.

In addition to disguising an external anchor test, statistical outlier analysis (Barnett & Lewis, 1994) can be used to identify those examinees whose anchor test performance is substantially different from their performance on the operational test. Removing such examinees from the sample used to estimate the equating function prevents their improbable performance from improperly affecting the results.

One advantage of external anchor tests is that the section they are in may also serve other purposes, such as pretesting. This is accomplished by spiraling forms with different content in this variable section that may contain a variety of different section types across the whole test administration. This process can allow the exposure of the anchor test to a relatively small proportion of the group tested, and this in turn may have benefits for test security. Internal anchor tests do not allow this to be done as easily.

2.6.2. Internal Anchor Tests

Items in internal anchor tests are part of the assessment and count toward each examinee's score. Internal anchor items are usually spread throughout the test. For the observed score equating methods described in this chapter, where the score on the anchor test plays an important role, it is often recommended that the anchor test be a mini version of two tests. This may be more feasible for internal anchor tests than for external anchor tests. For the IRT-based methods of equating, the anchor test is used to create a common theta-scale for the tests. This raises other issues that are discussed in Yen and Fitzpatrick (this volume).

Because the items in an internal anchor test count toward the score and are harder to identify than are external anchor tests, examinees are unlikely to skip internal anchor items. For anchor items to be effective, they must maintain their statistical properties across the old and new forms. The primary problems with internal anchor tests are (a) context effects and (b) security breaches. Context effects can occur when common items are administered in different locations, or under different testing conditions (i.e., paper and pencil versus computer delivered), or when adjacent to different kinds of items in the two tests. These effects are well documented (Brennan, 1992; Harris & Gao, 2003; Leary & Dorans, 1985). Security breaches are an unfortunate reality in many circumstances, and great care is required to prevent them or to recognize them when they occur.

2.6.3. Strengthening the Anchor Test

When there are only small differences between the two samples of examinees used in the NEAT design, all linear scaling and equating methods tend to give similar results, as do all nonlinear scaling and equating methods. To the extent that a NEAT design is almost an EG design with anchor test, the need for the anchor test is minimized.

However, when the two samples are very different, as indicated by the anchor test, the use of the anchor test information becomes critical, because it is the only means for separating the *differences between the abilities* of the two groups of examinees from the *differences between the two tests* that are being equated (see section 1.2.4). The most important properties of the anchor test are its integrity and stability over time and its correlation with the scores on the two tests being equated. It is important for the correlation to be as high as possible. Internal anchor tests have an advantage over external anchors because their part-whole relationship with the other tests usually insures that their correlations with the tests being equated are high. Long anchor tests are generally better for equating than short ones because of their higher reliability.

The importance of the test-anchor-test correlation is addressed in several ways. First, the advice that the anchor test be a mini version of the whole tests is offered as one way to do this. Having the anchor test measure the same constructs as the two tests to be equated should increase the correlation with both of them. It is less clear that the anchor test should have the same distribution of statistical characteristics as the two tests. If the difficulties of the items in the full tests are spread over a range of values does that mean that the difficulties of the anchor test items should be spread over the same range? This is a topic where more research would be useful.

Second, will it help to supplement the anchor test with additional information in order to increase the correlation? Wright and Dorans (1993) suggested replacing the anchor test with a propensity score (Rosenbaum & Rubin, 1983) that includes both the anchor test and other examinee data that distinguishes the two groups of examinees. Liou et al. (2001) used a missing data model to include other variables along with the anchor test score to adjust for sample differences before equating. Mislevy, Sheehan, and Wingersky (1993) advocated using collateral information in the absence of common item anchor test data. While collateral, nontest information may be used to make adjustments for examinee differences, such adjustments are likely to under correct for examinee differences when the groups are very different, and result in biased estimates of the equating functions. This is another area that needs more research.

3. PROCEDURES FOR SCALING AND EQUATING SCORES

There are numerous methods that have been developed over the years for scaling and equating tests. For example, the equipercentile function (see section 3.1.1.1) is used for equating; for forming concordances; and for vertical scaling, battery scaling, and calibration. Prediction is primarily based on regression methods, and, because these are better known than the other linking methods, we will only briefly mention prediction to contrast it with the other approaches. The bulk of our discussion of linking procedures concerns methods of equating and concordances.

We have tried to use a systematic classification of equating methods, but it is moderately unwieldy because we must consider these three factors:

1. The designs involve a common population versus common items,
2. Observed-score versus true-score procedures, and
3. Nonlinear versus linear methods.

The first factor is a property of the data collection designs, discussed above. The other two factors are properties of the linking methods and can have several variants. Observed-score procedures are those that directly transform (or link) the scores on **X** to those on **Y**. True-score methods are designed to transform the *true scores* on **X** to the true scores of **Y**. The idea of a true score requires a statistical model that provides a definition of the expected observed test score for an examinee (i.e., his or her true score). The two types of statistical models used to date are those of classical test theory and IRT. Holland and Hoskens (2003) showed how these two statistical models may be viewed as aspects of the same model. In section 3.1.2.2, we will indicate how Hanson's theorem relates the approach based on true scores to the approach based on observed scores.

Linear methods result in a linear function for mapping the scores from **X** to **Y**, while nonlinear methods allow the linking function to be curved. In order to make the discussion manageable, we give detailed discussions for only some of the procedures, pointing to references for the others.

3.1. Procedures for Linking Scores on a Common Population

There are three data collection designs in section 2 that make use of a common population of examinees: the SG, the EG, and the CB designs. They all involve a single population, **P**. Most of what we say in this section applies easily to both the EG and SG designs. To apply them to the CB designs is more complicated and we omit this step. For a careful discussion of the CB design, we refer the reader to von Davier et al. (2004b), as well as to the discussions in Angoff (1971) and Kolen and Brennan (2004).

Several procedures have been developed over the years for linking test scores using a common population. In order to structure our discussion, we separately consider observed-score versus true-score procedures and within these, the nonlinear versus linear methods. In addition, we will be explicit about the population of examinees on which scores are linked or equated. Underlying any linking method is a population of examinees that we will call the *target population* following the usage in von Davier et al. (2004b). In this reference, the target population refers to the source of the samples used to compute the linking function. For the three designs that use a common population, **P** is also the target population, **T**.

3.1.1. Observed-Score Equating and Linking Methods

These are the oldest and most well studied of the linking methods used for scale aligning and equating. We use a single definition of observed-score linking that applies to either linear or nonlinear procedures depending on whether additional assumptions are satisfied. This allows us to consider both linear and nonlinear observed-score linking methods from a single point of view.

We now need to introduce some notation that will be used throughout the rest of this chapter. Let **T** denote the target population of examinees. Our use of the term *target population* is solely to identify that population of examinees from which the *data* that result in the linking function *are assumed to come*. Other authors, specifically Livingston (2004), use the term to mean the population of examinees *to which the linking function is intended to apply*. We do not use *target population* in that sense because intentions and the available data may not have much to connect them other than professional judgment. In our conceptualization of test linking, the data may always be thought of as sampled from and representative of the target population, **T**.

The *cumulative distribution function* (cdf) of the scores of examinees in the target population, **T**, on test **X** is denoted by $F_T(x)$, and it is defined as the proportion of examinees in **T** who score at or below x on test **X**. More formally, $F_T(x) = \Pr\{X \le x \mid T\}$, where $\Pr\{ \cdot \mid T\}$ denotes the population proportion or probability in **T**. Similarly, $G_T(y) = \Pr\{Y \le y \mid T\}$ is the cdf of **Y** over **T**. Cumulative distribution functions increase from 0 up to 1 as x (or y) moves from left to right along the horizontal axis. In this notation, x and y may be any real numbers, not necessarily just the possible scores on the two tests. For the distributions of discrete scores such as number right or rounded formula scores, the cdfs are step functions that have points of increase at each possible score (Kolen & Brennan, 2004). In section 3.1.1.2 we address the issue of the discreteness of score distributions in more detail, but will ignore it until then.

3.1.1.1. The Linear Linking and Equipercentile Functions

The equipercentile definition of *comparable* scores is that x (an **X**-score) and y (a **Y**-score) are *comparable* in **T** if $F_T(x) = G_T(y)$. This means that x and y have the same percentile in the target population, **T**. When the two cdfs are continuous and strictly increasing, the equality of $F_T(x)$ and $G_T(y)$ can always be satisfied and can be solved for y in terms of x. Solving for y leads to the *equipercentile function*, $Equi_{YT}(x)$, that links x to y on **T**, defined by

$$y = Equi_{YT}(x) = G_T^{-1}(F_T(x)). \qquad (11)$$

In Equation 11, $y = G_T^{-1}(p)$ denotes the inverse function of $p = G_T(y)$. We have followed Dorans and Holland (2000) and von Davier et al. (2004b) in explicitly including the target population **T** in the definition of $Equi_{YT}(x)$. The notation is chosen to emphasize that **T** (as well as **X** and **Y**) could influence the form of the equipercentile function.

In general, there is nothing to prevent **T** from having a substantial influence on $Equi_{YT}(x)$, thereby violating requirement (e) of section 1.3. The equipercentile function is used for equating, for forming concordances, and for vertical scaling, battery scaling, and calibration. For equating, we expect the influence of **T** to be small or negligible, and, in that case, we will call the scores *equivalent* or *interchangeable*. In the other cases, **T** can have a substantial effect in which case we will call the scores *comparable in* **T**.

If Equation 11 is satisfied, then $Equi_{YT}(x)$ will transform the distribution of **X**-scores on **T** so that it is the same as the distribution of **Y**-scores on **T**. We will return to this issue in section 4.3.

It is sometimes appropriate to assume that the two cdfs, $F_T(x)$ and $G_T(y)$, have the same shape and only differ in their means and standard deviations. To formalize the idea of a common shape we suppose that $F_T(x)$ and $G_T(y)$ both have the form

$$F_T(x) = K((x - \mu_{XT})/\sigma_{XT}) \text{ and } G_T(y) = K((y - \mu_{YT})/\sigma_{YT}), \qquad (12)$$

where K is a cdf with mean 0 and standard deviation 1. When Equation 12 holds, $F_T(x)$ and $G_T(y)$ both have the shape determined by K. In this case, the reader may show that the equipercentile function is the *linear linking function*, $Lin_{YT}(x)$, defined as

$$Lin_{YT}(x) = \mu_{YT} + (\sigma_{YT}/\sigma_{XT})(x - \mu_{XT}). \qquad (13)$$

The linear linking function may also be derived as the transformation of **X**-scores that gives them the same mean and standard deviation on **T** as the **Y**-scores have. Both of the functions in Equations 11 and 13 satisfy the symmetry requirement (c) of section 1.3. This means that linking **Y** to **X** is the inverse function for linking **X** to **Y**.

There are two special cases of $Lin_{YT}(x)$ that should be mentioned here. The first is the *mean linking function* and the second is the *identity function*. When the two standard deviations in Equation 13 are equal, then $Lin_{YT}(x)$ takes on the form $Mean_{YT}(x) = x + (\mu_{YT} - \mu_{XT})$. The mean linking function adjusts the scores of **X** so that they have the same mean as **Y** does on **T**. When both the means and the variances in Equation 13 are equal, $Lin_{YT}(x)$ takes on the form $Iden(x) = x$. The identity function makes no adjustment at all to the **X**-scores. It corresponds to assuming that the raw scores on **X** and **Y** are already equated and do not need any further adjustments to make them interchangeable. Both $Mean_{YT}(x)$ and $Iden(x)$ are useful when there are very small samples that cannot support accurate estimates of the moments of **X** and **Y** on **T** (Skaggs, 2004). They are discussed in more detail in Kolen and Brennan (2004).

When the equipercentile function is properly defined, the linear linking function can be viewed as the linear part of the equipercentile function (von Davier et al., 2004b). The remainder, $Equi_{YT}(x) - Lin_{YT}(x)$, is the nonlinear part of the equipercentile function. In general, the function, $Equi_{YT}(x)$, fluctuates around the function, $Lin_{YT}(x)$. In the *kernel equating* method of equating (von Davier et al., 2004b), the equipercentile function and the linear linking function are shown to be two members of a family of equipercentile functions that interpolate smoothly between these two special cases.

The linear linking function requires estimates of the means and standard deviations of **X**- and **Y**-scores over the target population, **T**. The ease with which these estimates can be obtained depends on the data collection design. For the EG and SG designs described in section 2, these estimates are straightforward. For more details, see Angoff (1971) or Kolen and Brennan (2004). For the CB design, the situation is more complex. Angoff (1971) gave the details of Lord's (1950) linear procedure for the CB design. von Davier et al. (2004b) described their method that allowed users to control how much the data from the tests that are given second can influence the resulting linear *or* nonlinear kernel equating function.

3.1.1.2. The Need to Continuize the Discrete Distributions of Scores

While there is really only one linear linking function for the SG or EG designs, that is, the one given by Equation 13, the equipercentile function can depend on how $F_T(x)$ and $G_T(y)$ are made continuous or *continuized*. Test scores are typically integers, such as number-right scores or rounded formula scores. Because of this, the inverse function, required in Equation 11, is not well defined—that is, for many values of p, there is no score, y, for which $p = G_T(y)$. This is due to the *discreteness of test scores*. To get around this, there are two methods of continuization of $G_T(y)$ that are in current use.

The first is very old and has been used at least since Otis (1916) and Kelley (1923). The cdf of test scores is a step function but linear interpolation can make it piecewise linear and continuous. This method was described in Angoff (1971), Petersen et al. (1989), and in great detail in Kolen and Brennan (2004). This form of continuization results in a continuous cdf for which the equation, $p = G_T(y)$, can always be solved for y, using linear methods, to produce $G_T^{-1}(F_T(x))$.

The second approach is to use Gaussian kernel smoothing to continuize the discrete distributions. This alternative method of continuization was introduced by Holland and Thayer (1989) and was described in detail in von Davier et al. (2004b). The use of Gaussian kernel smoothing results in a continuously differentiable cdfs for which the equation, $p = G_T(y)$, can also be solved for y but which requires the use of numerical methods. The older, linear-interpolation method of continuization may also be viewed as kernel smoothing using a uniform kernel on $(-\frac{1}{2}, \frac{1}{2})$ rather than a Gaussian kernel (Holland & Thayer, 1989).

There are two primary differences between these two approaches to continuization. First, the use of linear interpolation results in an equipercentile function that is also piecewise linear and continuous. Such functions may have "kinks" that need to be removed by a further process, often called postsmoothing (Fairbank, 1987; Kolen & Brennan, 2004). In contrast, kernel smoothing results in equipercentile functions that are very smooth (i.e., differentiable everywhere) and that do not need further postsmoothing. Second, due to the way that linear interpolation treats the highest and lowest score frequencies, the equipercentile functions obtained by linear interpolation always map the highest score on **X** into the highest score on **Y** and the same for the lowest scores. The use of kernel smoothing to continuize the cdfs does not necessarily have this property, nor does the linear linking function. While it is sometimes desirable, there are cases where the highest score on an easier test should not be mapped onto the highest score of a harder test. For more discussion of this property, see Petersen et al. (1989), Kolen and Brennan (2004), and von Davier et al. (2004b).

3.1.1.3. Presmoothing Score Distributions

Prior to continuizing discrete score distributions, either by linear interpolation or by Gaussian kernel smoothing, consideration should be given to *presmoothing* the raw-score frequencies in some way. The purpose of this step is to smooth out some of the sampling variability that raw-score frequencies exhibit, to produce more stable cdf estimates.

In computing the equipercentile function, it is now generally understood that adequate presmoothing is usually advisable. Kolen and Jarjoura (1987) and Kolen and Brennan (2004) discussed several methods for presmoothing. von Davier et al. (2004b) concentrated exclusively on the use of loglinear models for presmoothing. Their work was based on Holland and Thayer (1987, 2000), and they gave examples of presmoothing for the EG, SG, CB, and NEAT designs. Livingston (1993) showed that for small samples there could be large reductions in equating error when the score frequencies are presmoothed prior to continuization. When the samples are very large, the sampling variability may be small enough that presmoothing does not provide a big improvement, but presmoothing may still be a useful way to remove undesired roughness in the sample frequencies. We refer to the above references for more details about presmoothing. Moses, von Davier, and Casabianca (2004) showed how to use the SAS program to do presmoothing using loglinear models.

The type of data that is available for presmoothing depends on the data collection design (section 2). The EG design is the simplest and results in two independent univariate score distributions, one for **X** and one for **Y**. These may be independently presmoothed. The SG design results in a single bivariate score distribution, the joint frequencies for the (**X**,**Y**)-pairs in the sample. For this case, presmoothing should be done on the joint distribution. Presmoothing is sometimes done on the **X** and **Y** frequencies as if they were from different samples. This ignores the correlation between **X** and **Y** in the SG design and can lead to incorrect standard errors. The CB design, as well as the NEAT design both result in two independent bivariate score distributions. For the CB design, using the notation of section 2.3, the two bivariate score distributions are the joint frequencies for the (X_1, Y_2)-pairs and for the (X_2, Y_1)-pairs. For the NEAT design, using the notation of section 2.4, the two bivariate score distributions are the joint frequencies for the (**X**, **A**)-pairs and for the (**Y**, **A**)-pairs.

In presmoothing a score distribution, it is important to achieve a balance between a good representation of the original data and smoothness. Smoothness reduces sampling variability while a good representation of the data reduces the possibility of bias. For example, if a loglinear model is used, it needs to preserve the most important features of the data, such as means, variances, and skewness and any other special features. The more parameters that are estimated for the model, the better the model will represent the original data, and the *less* smooth the fitted model becomes. Using an inadequate (overly smooth) presmoothing model can introduce bias into the estimated equating functions. In presmoothing for score linking, it is probably better to fit a few extra parameters than to use a model that does not capture the important regularities in the original data. That is, a little overfitting is usually less harmful than underfitting, though this topic needs more research. Holland and Thayer (2000) discussed fitting loglinear models to a variety of data sets that exhibit varying degrees of complexity. von Davier et al. (2004b) gave several additional examples, including a very complicated model for data from a NEAT design.

3.1.1.4. Presmoothing Using IRT Models

We end our discussion of presmoothing with a consideration of the relationship between presmoothing and IRT observed score equating (Lord, 1980).

Suppose $\mathbf{X}$ and $\mathbf{Y}$ denote number-right scores for two tests with dichotomous test items. Using IRT methods, the conditional distributions of $\mathbf{X}$ and $\mathbf{Y}$ given the common latent ability, θ, may be estimated. This produces estimates of $\Pr\{\mathbf{X}=x \mid \theta\}$ and $\Pr\{\mathbf{Y}=y \mid \theta\}$ (Kolen & Brennan, 2004; Lord & Wingersky, 1984). The estimated density function for the ability distribution over $\mathbf{T}$, $f_\mathbf{T}(\theta)$, may be approximated in various ways, and these results combined via numerical integration to obtain

$$\Pr\{\mathbf{X}=x \mid \mathbf{T}\} = \int \Pr\{\mathbf{X}=x \mid \theta\} f_\mathbf{T}(\theta) d\theta,$$

and

$$\Pr\{\mathbf{Y}=y \mid \mathbf{T}\} = \int \Pr\{\mathbf{Y}=y \mid \theta\} f_\mathbf{T}(\theta) d\theta.$$

The resulting estimated probabilities, $\Pr\{\mathbf{X}=x \mid \mathbf{T}\}$ and $\Pr\{\mathbf{Y}=y \mid \mathbf{T}\}$, are IRT model-based estimates of the proportion in the population getting a score of x on $\mathbf{X}$, and the corresponding proportion in the population of a score of y on $\mathbf{Y}$. The estimates, $\Pr\{\mathbf{X}=x \mid \mathbf{T}\}$ and $\Pr\{\mathbf{Y}=y \mid \mathbf{T}\}$, may be regarded as a form of presmoothing of the two, sample score distributions. This is a use of an IRT model to presmooth the data, prior to continuization. Once the presmoothed estimated score probabilities are in hand, they may be continuized by either linear interpolation or Gaussian kernel smoothing and used to produce a version of the equipercentile function, $Equi_{\mathbf{YT}}(x)$.

3.1.2. Linear True-Score Procedures from Classical Test Theory

The use of classical test theory to derive true-score equating procedures is limited to linear methods. While this restricts their usefulness in practice, the ideas of classical test theory give insight into test equating and linking. We shall limit our discussion of linear true-score methods for complete tests linked on a common target population to (a) defining the linear true-score equating function, $TSLin_{\mathbf{YT}}(\tau_\mathbf{X})$, and (b) a discussion of Hanson's theorem. This theorem shows the relationship between linear true-score equating and the linear linking function defined in Equation 13. In addition, this theorem shows the connection between the informally stated requirements of test equating given in section 1.3 and linear equating functions. For a more detailed discussion of true-score equating, see Kolen and Brennan (2004).

3.1.2.1. The Linear True-Score Equating Function

We use the formulation of classical test theory described in Holland and Hoskens (2003). The true scores, $\tau_\mathbf{X}$ and $\tau_\mathbf{Y}$, are latent variables underlying each test and that have these properties: $\tau_\mathbf{X} = E(\mathbf{X} \mid \tau_\mathbf{X}, \mathbf{T})$, and $\tau_\mathbf{Y} = E(\mathbf{Y} \mid \tau_\mathbf{Y}, \mathbf{T})$, for any target population, $\mathbf{T}$. From these properties it follows that $\mu_{\mathbf{XT}} = E(\mathbf{X} \mid \mathbf{T}) = E(\tau_\mathbf{X} \mid \mathbf{T})$, and $\mu_{\mathbf{YT}} = E(\mathbf{Y} \mid \mathbf{T}) = E(\tau_\mathbf{Y} \mid \mathbf{T})$. Lord (1980) takes the position that only true scores can ever really be equated, but it may be argued that this is a consequence of his very stringent interpretation of the equity condition (d) of section 1.3.

To formalize the intuition that $\mathbf{X}$ and $\mathbf{Y}$ measure the same construct, we assume the true scores are *congeneric*, that is, that they are linearly related by

$$\tau_\mathbf{Y} = \alpha \tau_\mathbf{X} + \beta, \quad (14)$$

where α and β may depend on the target population, $\mathbf{T}$. The idea behind true-score equating is to estimate α and β and to use Equation 14 to find the link between the two sets of true scores.

The reliabilities of $\mathbf{X}$ and $\mathbf{Y}$ (over $\mathbf{T}$), which we denote by $\rho^2_{\mathbf{XT}}$ and $\rho^2_{\mathbf{YT}}$, are given by the well-known formulas

$$\rho^2_{\mathbf{XT}} = \sigma^2_{\tau_\mathbf{X}\mathbf{T}}/\sigma^2_{\mathbf{XT}} \quad \text{and} \quad \rho^2_{\mathbf{YT}} = \sigma^2_{\tau_\mathbf{Y}\mathbf{T}}/\sigma^2_{\mathbf{YT}}. \quad (15)$$

Means and variances over $\mathbf{T}$ of both sides of Equation 14 lead to these formulas for α and β:

$$\alpha = (\sigma_{\mathbf{YT}}/\sigma_{\mathbf{XT}})(\rho_{\mathbf{YT}}/\rho_{\mathbf{XT}}) \quad \text{and} \quad \beta = \mu_{\mathbf{YT}} - \alpha \mu_{\mathbf{XT}}. \quad (16)$$

Substituted into Equation 14, these values result in

$$\tau_\mathbf{Y} = TSLin_{\mathbf{YT}}(\tau_\mathbf{X}) = \mu_{\mathbf{YT}} + (\sigma_{\mathbf{YT}}/\sigma_{\mathbf{XT}})(\rho_{\mathbf{YT}}/\rho_{\mathbf{XT}})(\tau_\mathbf{X} - \mu_{\mathbf{XT}}). \quad (17)$$

$TSLin_{\mathbf{YT}}(\tau_\mathbf{X})$ is the *linear true-score equating function* and is very similar to the linear linking function, $Lin_{\mathbf{YT}}(x)$, but its slope also involves the ratio of the square roots of the reliabilities, that is, $(\rho_{\mathbf{YT}}/\rho_{\mathbf{XT}})$.

3.1.2.2. Hanson's Theorem

Hanson's theorem gives a principled justification for the linear linking function, $Lin_{\mathbf{YT}}(x)$, defined in Equation 13. By *principled* we mean that it uses mathematical formalizations of four of the five informally stated equating requirements given in section 1.3 and derives the linear linking function from them. To discuss Hanson's theorem, we first need to define first- and second-order equity in this setting. This type of formalization of the equity condition (d) in section 1.3 was introduced in Lord (1980).

Let $e_Y(x)$ denote a linking function from **X** to **Y**. The function, $e_Y(x)$, satisfies *first-order equity* if

$$E(e_Y(X) | \tau_X, T) = E(Y | \tau_Y, T) = \tau_Y \quad \text{for all } \tau_X \text{ and } \tau_Y, \quad (18)$$

and it satisfies *second-order equity* if, in addition to Equation 18, it also satisfies

$$\text{Var}(e_Y(X) | \tau_X, T) = \text{Var}(Y | \tau_Y, T) \quad \text{for all } \tau_X \text{ and } \tau_Y. \quad (19)$$

These two equity conditions are inspired by requirement (d) of section 1.3. They are (somewhat loosely) interpreted as requiring that a person (characterized by a true-score expressed as either τ_X or τ_Y) have the same expected value and variance for **Y** and $e_Y(X)$. They are weaker than Lord's original requirement, which required that the full conditional distributions of **Y** and $e_Y(X)$ be the same. For additional discussions of these ideas, see Morris (1982) and Kolen and Brennan (2004).

We call the following result Hanson's theorem in honor of the late Brad Hanson, who first published the connection between these ideas (Hanson, 1991). We formulate his results in a setting that is simpler than his.

Hanson's theorem: If $e_Y(x)$ is a linear function, $e_Y(x) = cx + d$, and if the true scores on **X** and **Y** are related by $\tau_Y = \alpha\tau_X + \beta$, with α and β given by Equation 16, then $e_Y(x)$ satisfies first-order equity if and only if $c = \alpha$ and $d = \beta$, so that $e_Y(x) = TSLin_{YT}(x)$. In addition, if $e_Y(x)$ satisfies second-order equity, then $\rho_{YT} = \rho_{XT}$, in which case $e_Y(x)$ is the linear linking function given by Equation 13.

Hanson's theorem is a formal statement of the following ideas that draw on the requirements of section 1.3. If **X** and **Y** measure the same construct (requirement (a)), then first-order equity (requirement (d)) can hold for a linear linking function, $e_Y(x)$, if and only if $e_Y(x) = TSLin_{YT}(x)$. (This treats the linear true-score equating function as an observed score equating function—note that x replaces τ_X.) Furthermore, if second-order equity (requirement (d)) also holds for $e_Y(x)$, then **X** and **Y** must be equally reliable (requirement (b)), and then $e_Y(x)$ must be the linear linking function, because the ratio of reliabilities is unity. Both functions, $TSLin_{YT}(x)$ and $Lin_{YT}(x)$, automatically satisfy the symmetry requirement (c) of section 1.3.

Hence, classical test theory via Hanson's theorem ties up the linear linking function and requirements (a) through (d) of section 1.3, into a neat bundle. Because the target population, **T**, is fixed in this discussion, requirement (e) of section 1.3 is not addressed by this analysis.

If we drop the requirement of equal reliability, then $TSLin_{YT}(x)$, the linear true-score equating function in Equation 17, provides a linking function that satisfies first-order equity, but not second-order equity. In order to apply Equation 17 in practice, the ratio of the square roots of the reliabilities, ρ_{YT}/ρ_{XT}, must be available in addition to the means and variances of **X** and **Y** over **T** (see Kolen and Brennan, 2004).

3.1.2.3. Prediction, Calibration, and Hanson's Theorem

Linear regression methods may be used for predicting the scores on one test from those on another. The linear regression function for predicting **Y** from **X** on **T** is given by

$$RLin_{YT}(x) = \mu_{YT} + (\sigma_{YT}/\sigma_{XT}) \rho_{YXT}(x - \mu_{XT}). \quad (20)$$

It is useful to compare $RLin_{YT}(x)$ to the linear functions, $TSLin_{YT}(x)$ and $Lin_{YT}(x)$. All three linking functions have the same value, μ_{YT}, when $x = \mu_{XT}$, but their slopes can be very different. The slope of $RLin_{YT}(x)$ is always smaller than that of $Lin_{YT}(x)$, and the slope of $TSLin_{YT}(x)$ depends on the square root of the reliability ratio, that is, on ρ_{YT}/ρ_{XT}. Only when $\rho_{YXT} = 1$ are $RLin_{YT}(x)$ and $Lin_{YT}(x)$ identical.

To give an interesting example where Hanson's theorem can shed light on the issues, consider the calibration of the scores on a short form of a test to those of a longer form (see section 1.2.2.4). In this case we would expect the two tests to measure the same construct, be similar in difficulty, but to differ in reliability, so that $TSLin_{YT}(x)$ and $Lin_{YT}(x)$ will be different. In order to obtain a linear linking function that satisfies requirements (a), (c), and the first-order equity version of (d), Hanson's theorem says to use $TSLin_{YT}(x)$ (see section 3.1.2.2). If the linking goes from the less reliable short form to the more reliable long form, we would expect the reliability ratio to exceed 1.0. Thus, $TSLin_{YT}(x)$ will have a higher slope than will $Lin_{YT}(x)$ (see Equations 13 and 17). This is exactly the opposite of the effect of using $RLin_{YT}(x)$ rather than $Lin_{YT}(x)$, where the slope of $RLin_{YT}(x)$ is smaller than that of $Lin_{YT}(x)$. This analysis is yet another way of showing the oft-repeated difference between scaling, equating, and predicting scores on one test from scores on another test.

3.1.3. Nonlinear True-Score Procedures from Item Response Theory

Lord (1980) used item response theory (IRT) to generalize the linear true-score linking methods of classical test theory to nonlinear procedures. Again, we adopt the general version of IRT described in Holland and Hoskens (2003). Assuming a common one-dimensional IRT model with latent variable θ, the true scores of **X** and **Y** may be expressed as

$$\tau_X = v_X(\theta) = E(X | \theta, T) = E(X | \theta), \quad (21)$$

$$\tau_Y = v_Y(\theta) = E(Y | \theta, T) = E(Y | \theta).$$

The functions, $v_X(\theta)$ and $v_Y(\theta)$, are the test characteristic curves for **X** and **Y**, respectively. They may be estimated using the techniques of IRT. The relationship between the two true scores, τ_X and τ_Y, in Equation 21 may be nonlinear, and it is found by solving $\tau_X = v_X(\theta)$ for θ and then substituting for θ in $\tau_Y = v_Y(\theta)$. The result is

$$\tau_Y = v_Y(v_X^{-1}(\tau_X)), \quad (22)$$

where $v_X^{-1}(\tau_X) = \theta$ is the inverse function of $\tau_X = v_X(\theta)$. Equation 22 generalizes the linear true-score equating function in Equation 14.

Hanson's theorem, section 3.1.2.2, suggests using the function in Equation 22 as a transformation of observed scores, that is, as the observed score equating function,

$$y = e_Y(x) = v_Y((v_X^{-1}(x))). \quad (23)$$

As of this writing we know of no justification for the use of Equation 23 that is in the spirit of Hanson's theorem, but this seems like an interesting question for future research in the theory of test linking. It is clear that the use of $e_Y(x) = v_Y(v_X^{-1}(x))$ does produce a symmetric linking relationship as long as the inverse functions of $v_X(\theta)$ and $v_Y(\theta)$ are well defined. When the item response functions have nonzero lower asymptotes (see the chapter by Yen & Fitzpatrick, this volume) and the resulting lower asymptotes of $v_X(\theta)$ and $v_Y(\theta)$ are not the same, the inverse function, $v_X^{-1}(x)$, may not be well defined for the lowest scores on **X**. In these cases, the value of $v_Y(v_X^{-1}(x))$ is often defined by an arbitrary linear extrapolation (Hambleton & Swaminathan, 1985; Kolen & Brennan, 2004; Lord, 1980).

3.1.4. Direct IRT Scaling Procedures

An alternative to using IRT methods to form nonlinear true-score equating functions is to use the same models to scale the raw scores on theta scale. This approach bypasses the equating step and directly puts the scores from **X** onto the common theta scale to which **Y** is already scaled. The chapter by Yen and Fitzpatrick (this volume) discusses this approach more extensively than we can, but for completeness we briefly outline the ideas behind this method.

Once the conditional probability function $\Pr\{\mathbf{X} = x \mid \theta\}$ is estimated as in section 3.1.1.4, the maximum likelihood estimate of θ is obtained by maximizing $\Pr\{\mathbf{X} = x \mid \theta\}$ for each fixed raw score, x. The result, $\theta(x)$, is a transformation of x to the θ-scale. In the special case where the item characteristic curves are all the same, it may be shown that $\theta(x) = v_X^{-1}(x)$, defined in section 3.1.3.

3.2. Procedures for Linking Scores Using Common Items

The use of common items to control for differential examinee ability in linking gives the NEAT design greater operational flexibility than the approaches using common examinees. This flexibility comes with a price. First of all, the target population is less clear-cut for the NEAT design. From the design table for the NEAT design in section 2.4 we see that there are two populations, **P** and **Q**, and either one could serve as the target population. We will return to this issue in a moment. More importantly, the use of the NEAT design always involves making additional assumptions to allow for the missing data in the NEAT design—**X** is never observed in **Q** and **Y** is never observed in **P**. As indicated at the beginning of section 2, our use of the term *missing data* is restricted to data that are missing by design (i.e., the missing data is caused by examinees not being given the opportunity to respond to the test questions). We assume that omitted or not reached items are dealt with by the rules for scoring the tests rather than by being treated as missing data in the sense used here.

The assumptions needed to make allowances for the missing data are not easily tested with the available data, and they are often unstated. We will discuss three distinct sets of assumptions that may be used to justify the *observed score* procedures that are commonly used with the NEAT design. We consider both the definition of the target population and these missing data assumptions next.

Braun and Holland (1982) proposed that for the NEAT design the target population be what they called the *synthetic population* created by weighting **P** and **Q**. They denoted the synthetic population by $\mathbf{T} = w\mathbf{P} + (1 - w)\mathbf{Q}$, by which they meant that distributions (or moments) of **X** or **Y** over **T** are obtained by first computing them over **P** and **Q**, separately, and then averaging them with w and $(1 - w)$ to get the distribution over **T**. The synthetic population forces the user to confront the need to create distributions (or moments) for **X** on **Q** and **Y** in **P**, where there are no data.

When $w = 1$, $\mathbf{T} = \mathbf{P}$ and when $w = 0$, $\mathbf{T} = \mathbf{Q}$. In practice, w is often taken to be proportional to the two sample sizes from **P** and **Q**. This choice of w is implicit when the data for the anchor test is pooled into a total group, as was done in Angoff (1971) and Petersen et al. (1989). Of course, other choices of w are possible, such as $w = ½$, which gives equal weight to **P** and **Q**. There is considerable evidence that in applications to test equating the choice of w has a relatively minor influence on equating results (for example, see von Davier et al., 2004b).

We next discuss two distinct types of missing data assumptions that are commonly employed—the *poststratification equating* (PSE) type and the *chain equating* (CE) type, using the terminology of von Davier et al. (2004b), which we will define in a moment. Each of these types of assumptions asserts that an important distributional property that connects **X** or **Y** to **A** is population invariant and is the same for any $\mathbf{T} = w\mathbf{P} + (1 - w)\mathbf{Q}$. Our emphasis here is on the role of such assumptions for observed-score linking because that is where they are currently most completely understood, but they are likely to have parallels for true-score linking as well, a topic worthy of future research.

The PSE types of assumptions all have the form that the conditional distribution of **X** given **A** is the same for any synthetic population, $\mathbf{T} = w\mathbf{P} + (1 - w)\mathbf{Q}$, and similarly for the conditional distribution of **Y** given **A**. In terms of the missing data in the NEAT design, this means that conditional on the anchor test score, **A**, the distribution of **X** when it is missing (i.e., in **Q**) is the same as when it is not missing (i.e., in **P**).

For an EG design with anchor test, **P** = **Q**. In this case the PSE assumptions hold exactly. When **P** and **Q** are different, the PSE assumptions are not necessarily valid, but there are no data to contradict them.

The CE assumptions all have the form that a linking function from **X** to **A** is the same for any synthetic population, $\mathbf{T} = w\mathbf{P} + (1 - w)\mathbf{Q}$, and similarly for linking **A** to **Y**.

As present, it is not clear what the CE assumptions imply about the missing data in the NEAT design.

For an EG design with anchor test, the CE assumptions also hold exactly as they do for PSE. In this special situation, the corresponding methods based on either the PSE or the CE assumptions will produce identical results. When **P** and **Q** are different, the PSE assumptions and CE assumptions can result in equating functions that are different (von Davier et al., 2004b, gives an empirical example.) However, in this case there are no data to allow us to contradict or choose between either set of assumptions.

An interesting area of theoretical equating research is to clarify the nature of the differences between the CE and PSE assumptions following the general approach to missing data in Little and Rubin (2002). The work of Liou et al. (2001) may provide a useful starting point.

We now discuss the consequences of different missing data assumptions for linking complete tests using common items. To manage our discussion, in parallel to section 3.1, we further divide the procedures into observed-score versus true-score procedures and within these into linear versus nonlinear methods.

3.2.1. Observed-Score Linking Procedures for the NEAT Design

These procedures divide into those of the PSE and those of the CE types, mentioned above. We outline these briefly in turn.

3.2.1.1. The PSE Types of Linking Procedures

There are both nonlinear and linear PSE procedures. They may be viewed as based on these two assumptions, which we adopt from von Davier et al. (2004b).

PSE1: The conditional distribution of **X** given **A** over **T**, $\Pr\{X = x \mid A = a, T\}$, is the same for any **T** of the form $T = w\,P + (1-w)\,Q$.

PSE2: The conditional distribution of **Y** given **A** over **T**, $\Pr\{Y = y \mid A = a, T\}$, is the same for any **T** of the form $T = w\,P + (1-w)\,Q$.

PSE1 and PSE2 are population invariance assumptions because they require that the conditional distributions are the same for any target population.

The clearest examples of procedures of the PSE type are frequency estimation (Angoff, 1971; Kolen & Brennan, 2004; Petersen et al., 1989), and the PSE version of kernel equating (von Davier et al., 2004b). All PSE procedures estimate the score distribution of **X** over **T** via the equation

$$\Pr\{X = x \mid T\} = \sum_a \Pr\{X = x \mid A = a, P\}\,\Pr\{A = a \mid T\}. \quad (24)$$

In Equation 24, assumption PSE1 is used to replace $\Pr\{X = x \mid A = a, T\}$ by $\Pr\{X = x \mid A = a, P\}$. The former should be in the right side of Equation 24 to make it a correct statement, but the latter is all that is available from the data on **X** and **A** in **P**. The other ingredient of the right side of Equation 24, $\Pr\{A = a \mid T\}$, is obtained by

$$\Pr\{A = a \mid T\} = w\,\Pr\{A = a \mid P\} + (1-w)\,\Pr\{A = a \mid Q\}. \quad (25)$$

The combination of Equations 24 and 25 is another example of projecting distributions discussed in section 1.2.1 using Equation 5 with probability functions replacing the cdfs.

PSE2 is used to justify a similar equation for **Y**. These assumptions were discussed extensively in von Davier et al. (2004b).

Once values for the score probabilities, $\Pr\{X = x \mid T\}$ and $\Pr\{Y = y \mid T\}$, are available, they may be continuized via either linear interpolation or Gaussian kernel smoothing (see section 3.1.1.2) to obtain estimates of $F_T(x)$ and $G_T(y)$. From $F_T(x)$ and $G_T(y)$ the equipercentile function, $Equi_{YT}(x)$, is computed via Equation 11.

Frequency estimation and the PSE versions of kernel equating correspond to different ways of continuizing the score probabilities to obtain $F_T(x)$ and $G_T(y)$. Both methods may *presmooth* the joint distributions of **X** and **A** over **P** and **Y** and **A** over **Q**, described in section 3.1.1.3 (see von Davier et al., 2004b, and Kolen and Brennan, 2004, for more details).

Linear observed-score PSE equating procedures include (a) Tucker equating (Angoff, 1971; Kolen & Brennan, 2004; Petersen et al., 1989), (b) the Braun-Holland method (Braun & Holland, 1982; Kolen & Brennan, 2004), and (c) the linear PSE version of kernel equating (von Davier et al., 2004b). The linear PSE version of kernel equating is a way to implement the Braun-Holland procedure and both are directly based on PSE1 and PSE2.

Ledyard R Tucker was originally motivated by selection theory in the development of the linear method that bears his name (Angoff, 1971). However, altering PSE1 and PSE2 to the following two assumptions may also be used to derive Tucker equating with no reference to selection theory.

TUCK1: (a) The conditional mean of **X** given **A** over **T** is linear in **A** and is the same for any $T = w\,P + (1-w)\,Q$, and (b) the conditional variance of **X** given **A** over **T** is constant in **A** and is the same for any **T**.

TUCK2: (a) The conditional mean of **Y** given **A** over **T** is linear in **A** and is the same for any $T = w\,P + (1-w)\,Q$, and (b) the conditional variance of **Y** given **A** over **T** is constant in **A** and is the same for any **T**.

TUCK1 and TUCK2 are population invariance assumptions in the same sense that PSE1 and PSE2 are.

The Braun-Holland and linear PSE version of kernel equating do not make the more restrictive assumptions of linear conditional means and constant conditional variances that appear in TUCK1 and TUCK2. For this reason, they may give somewhat different results from the Tucker method when the conditional means are nonlinear and/or the conditional variances are not constant.

3.2.1.2. The CE Types of Linking Procedures

The idea behind the CE procedures is to first link **X** to **A** using the data from **P**, then link **A** to **Y** using the data from **Q**, and finally combine these two links to link **X** to **Y** through **A**. Braun and Holland (1982) and Kolen and Brennan (2004) expressed concern that this chaining together of two links did not necessarily result in a bona fide equating function, even when **X** and **Y** are alternative forms of the same test. These authors viewed CE as an *ad hoc* chaining together of calibrations of unequally reliable tests (the anchor test is usually less reliable that the other two). However, Livingston (2004) and von Davier et al. (2004b) argued that the CE approach resulted in a bona fide observed-score equating function if certain assumptions held.

The following two assumptions are sufficient to interpret chain equating as an observed-score equating function for any target population of the synthetic population form.

CE1: The equipercentile function linking **X** to **A** on **T** is the same for any **T** of the form $\mathbf{T} = w\,\mathbf{P} + (1-w)\,\mathbf{Q}$.

CE2: The equipercentile function linking **A** to **Y** on **T** is the same for any **T** of the form $\mathbf{T} = w\,\mathbf{P} + (1-w)\,\mathbf{Q}$.

CE1 and CE2 are population invariance assumptions because they require that the same linking function be valid for any target population of the form $\mathbf{T} = w\,\mathbf{P} + (1-w)\,\mathbf{Q}$. These two assumptions share with PSE1 and PSE2 the property of not being directly testable with the data that is available in the NEAT design.

Due to its use of the two SG designs within the NEAT design (see section 2.4) it is likely that CE was the first equating procedure developed for the NEAT design. However, the earliest references to CE procedures that we found was chained equipercentile equating in Angoff (1971). In addition, it was discussed in Marco, Petersen, and Stewart (1983) and Livingston, Dorans, and Wright (1990). The chain version of kernel equating is a CE procedure, described in von Davier et al. (2004b). It differs from the earlier CE methods only in the way that the score distributions are continuized—Gaussian kernel smoothing rather than linear interpolation.

To see that CE procedures based on CE1 and CE2 can be put into the form of Equation 11 so that they are, in fact, bona fide observed-score equating procedures we reproduce the argument of von Davier et al. (2004b).

First, apply CE1 to **P** and to some other **T** of the form $\mathbf{T} = w\,\mathbf{P} + (1-w)\,\mathbf{Q}$. This allows us to conclude that

$$H_\mathbf{P}^{-1}(F_\mathbf{P}(x)) = H_\mathbf{T}^{-1}(F_\mathbf{T}(x)), \qquad (26)$$

where $H_\mathbf{P}(a)$ is the cdf of the anchor test **A** on **P** and $H_\mathbf{T}(a)$ is the cdf for **A** on **T**. Then solve for $F_\mathbf{T}(x)$ in Equation 26, so that

$$F_\mathbf{T}(x) = H_\mathbf{T}(H_\mathbf{P}^{-1}(F_\mathbf{P}(x))). \qquad (27)$$

Similarly, applying CE2 with the target population choices of **Q** and the same **T** as above leads to the equation

$$G_\mathbf{T}^{-1}(u) = (G_\mathbf{Q}^{-1}(H_\mathbf{Q}(H_\mathbf{T}^{-1}(u))). \qquad (28)$$

Then, if we form the equipercentile function from **X** to **Y** on **T** we get

$$G_\mathbf{T}^{-1}(F_\mathbf{T}(x)) = (G_\mathbf{Q}^{-1}(H_\mathbf{Q}(H_\mathbf{P}^{-1}(F_\mathbf{P}(x)))). \qquad (29)$$

The right-hand side of Equation 29 is the chain of links made from the two equipercentile functions (**X** to **A** and **A** to **Y**) that use the data as two SG designs. The left-hand side is the equipercentile function on **T**. Note that the specific **T** does not matter; any $\mathbf{T} = w\,\mathbf{P} + (1-w)\,\mathbf{Q}$ will give the same result. Thus, assuming CE1 and CE2, the CE function given in the right-hand side of Equation 29 is a bona fide equipercentile equating functions on **T**.

There are both linear and nonlinear versions of CE. Linear observed-score CE equating procedures include (a) the chained *linear equating function* (Angoff, 1971) and (b) the linear CE version of kernel equating (von Davier et al., 2004b). Because it is derived as a type of equipercentile function, the linear CE version of kernel equating is based on assumptions CE1 and CE2. However, the fact that the chained *linear equating function* is also a linear linking function on a target population **T**, as defined in Equation 13, also holds when these linear versions of CE1 and CE2 hold.

CL1: The linear linking function linking **X** to **A** on **T** is the same for any **T** of the form $\mathbf{T} = w\,\mathbf{P} + (1-w)\,\mathbf{Q}$.

CL2: The linear linking function linking **A** to **Y** on **T** is the same for any **T** of the form $\mathbf{T} = w\,\mathbf{P} + (1-w)\,\mathbf{Q}$.

Again, CL1 and CL2 are examples of population invariance assumptions.

From CL1 it follows that the mean and standard deviation of **X** in any target population, **T**, is

$$\sigma_{XT} = \sigma_{XP}(\sigma_{AT}/\sigma_{AP}) \quad \text{and} \quad \mu_{XT} = \mu_{XP} + (\sigma_{XP}/\sigma_{AP})(\mu_{AT} - \mu_{AP}). \quad (30)$$

Similarly, from CL2 it follows the mean and standard deviation of **Y** in any target population, **T**, is

$$\sigma_{YT} = \sigma_{YQ}(\sigma_{AT}/\sigma_{AQ}) \quad \text{and} \quad \mu_{YT} = \mu_{YQ} + (\sigma_{YQ}/\sigma_{AQ})(\mu_{AT} - \mu_{AQ}). \quad (31)$$

The reader may show that the linear linking function, $Lin_{YT}(x)$, defined in Equation 13, but using the formulas in Equations 30 and 31 results in exactly the same linear function as does the chain of the two linear linking functions $Lin_{YQ}(Lin_{AP}(x))$. These derivations also may be found in von Davier, Holland, and Thayer (2004a).

3.2.1.3. A Linear Observed-Score Equating Procedure From Classical Test Theory

In addition to the PSE and CE types of procedures, classical test theory may be used to derive an additional *linear observed-score* procedure for the NEAT design—the Levine observed-score equating function, $Lev_{YT}(x)$ (Kolen & Brennan, 2004). This procedure is distinct from the linear true-score equating function, $TSLin_{YT}(\tau_X)$, discussed in section 3.1.2.1 and later, for the NEAT design, in section 3.2.2.1. It is a linear observed-score equating procedure that is not the linear linking function, $Lin_{YT}(\mathbf{x})$. $Lev_{YT}(\mathbf{x})$ may be derived from two population invariance assumptions that are different from those that we have considered so far and that are based on classical test theory. We again use the form of classical test theory discussed in Holland and Hoskens (2003), and the notation of section 3.1.2.

As in section 3.1.2, the true scores are latent variables, τ_X, τ_Y, and τ_A, that underlie the test scores and that satisfy $\tau_X = E(X \mid \tau_X, \mathbf{T})$, $\tau_Y = E(Y \mid \tau_Y, \mathbf{T})$, and $\tau_A = E(A \mid \tau_A, \mathbf{T})$ for any target population, $\mathbf{T}$. From these three assumptions these three equations follow: $\mu_{XT} = E(X \mid \mathbf{T}) = E(\tau_X \mid \mathbf{T})$, $\mu_{YT} = E(\tau_Y \mid \mathbf{T})$, and $\mu_{AT} = E(\tau_A \mid \mathbf{T})$. To formalize the intuition that $\mathbf{X}$, $\mathbf{Y}$, and $\mathbf{A}$ all measure the same construct, assume that their true scores are linearly related in a way that holds for all $\mathbf{T}$, that is, the three measures are *congeneric*. These assumptions are given below to emphasize their similarity to the population invariance assumptions made in sections 3.2.1.1 and 3.2.1.2.

LL1: $\tau_X = \alpha \tau_A + \beta$, where α and β do not depend on the target population, $\mathbf{T}$.

LL2: $\tau_Y = \gamma \tau_A + \delta$, where γ and δ do not depend on the target population, $\mathbf{T}$.

These two congeneric assumptions do not necessarily hold for IRT models. IRT models usually imply that the relationships between the true scores are nonlinear (see section 3.1.3). In this case the equalities in LL1 and LL2 would only be approximate and their approximate validity could very well depend on the choice of $\mathbf{T}$.

From the assumptions, LL1 and LL2, and using reasoning similar to that in section 3.1.2.1 it follows that the means of $\mathbf{X}$ and $\mathbf{Y}$ over any $\mathbf{T}$ are given by

$$\mu_{XT} = \mu_{XP} + (\rho_{XP}/\rho_{AP})(\sigma_{XP}/\sigma_{AP})(\mu_{AT} - \mu_{AP}), \quad (32)$$

$$\mu_{YT} = \mu_{YQ} + (\rho_{YQ}/\rho_{AQ})(\sigma_{YQ}/\sigma_{AP})(\mu_{AT} - \mu_{AP}). \quad (33)$$

Except for the ratios of the square roots of the reliabilities in Equations 32 and 33, these formulas for the means of $\mathbf{X}$ and $\mathbf{Y}$ on $\mathbf{T}$ are similar to those given in Equations 30 and 31 for chain linear equating. In a similar way, the variances of $\mathbf{X}$ and $\mathbf{Y}$ over $\mathbf{T}$ are given by

$$\sigma_{XT} = (\rho_{XP}/\rho_{XT})(\rho_{AT}/\rho_{AP})(\sigma_{AT}/\sigma_{AP})\sigma_{XP}, \quad (34)$$

$$\sigma_{YT} = (\rho_{YQ}/\rho_{YT})(\rho_{AT}/\rho_{AQ})(\sigma_{AT}/\sigma_{AQ})\sigma_{YQ}. \quad (35)$$

Inspection of Equations 34 and 35 reveals that when the reliabilities for $\mathbf{X}$, $\mathbf{Y}$, and $\mathbf{A}$ are insensitive to the population over which they are computed, then the formulas for σ_{XT} and σ_{YT} in Equations 34 and 35 are the same as those derived for the chain linear method in Equations 30 and 31. This suggests a close connection between chain linear equating and Levine observed score equating.

In order to use Equations 32 through 35 to form a linear linking function of the form given in Equation 13, we need estimates of the ratios of the various reliabilities that appear in them. Kolen and Brennan (2004) give a discussion of how these are estimated in practice.

3.2.2. True-Score Procedures for the NEAT Design

In this section we briefly indicate how the discussion of true-score equating methods of sections 3.1.2 and 3.1.3 can be applied to the NEAT design. First we consider the linear procedures of classical test theory and then the nonlinear procedures of IRT.

3.2.2.1. Linear True-Score Procedures From Classical Test Theory

Linear true-score equating for the NEAT design was introduced in Levine (1955). It was extensively discussed in Kolen and Brennan (2004). We continue the notation of classical test theory used in sections 3.1.2.1 and 3.2.1.3 and make the two congeneric Levine assumptions, LL1 and LL2 in section 3.2.1.3. The linear true score equating functions linking $\mathbf{X}$ to $\mathbf{A}$ and $\mathbf{Y}$ to $\mathbf{A}$ on $\mathbf{P}$ and $\mathbf{Q}$, respectively, are denoted by

$$\tau_X = TSLin_{AXP}(\tau_A) \text{ and } \tau_Y = TSLin_{AYQ}(\tau_A). \quad (36)$$

Each of these is a linear true-score equating function that is similar to the one given in Equation 17. Note that in this case, to avoid ambiguity, we indicate the link from τ_A to τ_X on $\mathbf{T}$ by $TSLin_{AXT}(\tau_A)$, etc. The two population invariance assumptions, LL1 and LL2, then imply that it does not matter which population is used to compute these linear true score equating functions so that $TSLin_{AXP}(\tau_A) = TSLin_{AXT}(\tau_A)$ and $TSLin_{AYQ}(\tau_A) = TSLin_{AYT}(\tau_A)$ for any $\mathbf{T}$. Thus, we can use these two linear true-score equating functions to equate the true scores of $\mathbf{X}$ to $\mathbf{Y}$ on any $\mathbf{T}$ in exactly the same way as chain equating works for the NEAT design (see section 3.2.1.2). This requires the inverse function, $\tau_X = TSLin^{-1}_{AXT}(\tau_X)$, that links the true score of $\mathbf{X}$ to the true score of $\mathbf{A}$ on $\mathbf{T}$. Thus, the linear true-score equating function linking τ_X to τ_Y on $\mathbf{T}$ is given by

$$\tau_Y = TSLin_{AYT}(TSLin^{-1}_{AXT}(\tau_X)),$$

and hence, the linear true score equating function linking τ_X to τ_Y is given by

$$\tau_Y = TSLin_{XYT}(\tau_X) = TSLin_{AYQ}(TSLin^{-1}_{AXP}(\tau_X)). \quad (37)$$

In order to compute $TSLin_{XYT}(\tau_X)$ for the NEAT design, estimates of the reliability ratios discussed in section 3.2.1.3 are needed. Kolen and Brennan (2004) gave an extensive discussion of this issue. There is a version of Hanson's theorem (see section 3.1.2.2) for the NEAT design. Results related to it were given in Hanson (1991) and Kolen and Brennan (2004).

3.2.2.2. Nonlinear True-Score Procedures From IRT

In a manner similar to that used in section 3.1.3, IRT can be used to generalize the linear true-score linking methods of classical test theory to nonlinear procedures. As in that discussion, we adopt the version of IRT described in more detail in Holland and Hoskens (2003). We assume a one-dimensional IRT model with latent variable θ. There are three IRT assumptions needed to generalize the two conditions LL1 and LL2 of sections 3.2.1.3 and 3.2.2.1. These three assumptions are again population invariance assumptions and insure that the test characteristic curves (see the chapter by Yen & Fitzpatrick, this volume) for **X**, **Y**, and **A** are the same for any population of examinees, **T**.

IRT1: $\tau_X = E(X \mid \theta, T) = v_{XT}(\theta) = v_X(\theta)$, for any **T**.
IRT2: $\tau_Y = E(Y \mid \theta, T) = v_{YT}(\theta) = v_Y(\theta)$, for any **T**.
IRT3: $\tau_A = E(A \mid \theta, T) = v_{AT}(\theta) = v_A(\theta)$, for any **T**.

If these tests exhibited differential item functioning when the two populations **P** and **Q** are compared, then we would not expect IRT1–IRT3 to hold.

There are various ways to estimate the test characteristic curves in the NEAT design. We shall outline two of them. If the item parameters of **X** and **A** are estimated on **P** and those of **Y** and **A** are estimated on **Q**, we may then obtain estimates of the true-score functions, $v_{XP}(\theta^*)$, $v_{AP}(\theta^*)$, $v_{AQ}(\theta)$, and $v_{YQ}(\theta)$. We have used θ and θ^* to indicate that because they were estimated on different populations the two theta scales may be different. There are several procedures for finding a linear transformation, say $\theta^* = a\theta + b$, to put both tests on the same theta scale. Some methods minimize the difference between $v_{AP}(\alpha\theta + \beta)$ and $v_{AQ}(\theta)$ over the theta scale (see the chapter by Yen & Fitzpatrick, this volume). These approaches force assumption IRT3 to hold as well as possible. Then, $v_{XP}(\theta^*)$ is replaced by $v_{XP}(\alpha\theta + \beta)$, which is then interpreted as $v_{XQ}(\theta) = \tau_X$ from assumption IRT1, above. We then have estimates of the true-score functions for **X** and **Y** on **Q**, and they can be combined to obtain the true-score equating function on **Q** via

$$\tau_Y = v_{YQ}(v_{XQ}^{-1}(\tau_X)). \tag{38}$$

Under the two assumptions IRT1 and IRT2, above, Equation 38 will hold for any population **T**.

Another approach is to simultaneously estimate the parameters of all three tests in a concurrent parameter estimation run (see the chapter by Yen & Fitzpatrick, this volume). This puts all three tests on a common theta scale without the need to adjust one of the scales to the other. However, the population on which this holds is the total population that weights **P** and **Q** proportionately to their respective sample sizes, that is, $T = wP + (1-w)Q$, where w is proportional to the sample size from **P**. If we then assume both IRT1 and IRT2, we may compute $\tau_Y = v_{YT}(v_{XT}^{-1}(\tau_X))$ directly from the estimated true-score functions. See the chapter by Yen and Fitzpatrick (this volume) for more on IRT and additional references.

In addition to this form of true-score equating, the raw scores of **X** may be put directly onto the θ-scale using the maximum likelihood approach mentioned in section 3.1.4.

4. EVALUATING SCALINGS AND EQUATINGS

In this part, we address several topics in the evaluation of links formed by scalings or equatings. Section 4.1 discusses various issues in the measurement of the statistical accuracy of estimated linking functions. In section 4.2, we consider measures of the invariance of equating and scale aligning functions over subpopulations of a larger population. Section 4.3 is concerned with how well observed-score equating functions match the score distributions of the two tests on the target population. In section 4.4, we discuss the value of equating a test back to several old forms and combining the results. Also in that section, we discuss the possible agreement or disagreement of the several methods of equating in the NEAT design.

4.1. Measures of the Statistical Accuracy of Linking Functions

All linking functions are statistical estimates, and they are therefore subject to sampling variability. If a different sample had been taken from the target population, the estimated linking function would have been different. A measure of statistical accuracy gives an indication of the uncertainty in an estimate that is due to the sample selected. In the next subsection, we discuss the SEE, the standard error of equating. Because the same methods are also used for concordances, battery scaling, vertical scaling, calibration, and some forms of anchor scaling, the SEE is a relevant measure of statistical accuracy for these cases of test score linking as well as for equating. Because prediction methods are usually based on linear regression methods, measures of the statistical accuracy of the prediction are available for these procedures. We will not discuss measures of statistical accuracy for prediction in this chapter.

In sections 4.1.1 and 4.1.2, we concentrate on the basic ideas and large-sample methods for approximating the standard errors. These estimates of the SEE and related measures are based on the delta method (Kolen & Brennan, 2004; von Davier et al., 2004b). This means that they are justified as standard error estimates only for large samples and may be only approximately valid in small samples. In section 4.1.3, we briefly discuss bootstrap methods for approximating these measures of statistical accuracy. In section 4.1.4, we discuss the *difference that matters* (DTM) that can be used to evaluate the practical significance of differences among estimated equating functions.

4.1.1. The Standard Error of Equating (the SEE)

The standard error of equating, the SEE, is the oldest measure of the statistical accuracy of estimated linking functions. The first systematic discussion of the SEE for various data collection designs was Lord (1950); a chapter on the SEE is available in Kolen and Brennan (2004). Liou and Cheng (1995) gave a good discussion of the SEE and von Davier et al. (2004b) gave a unified treatment of the SEE for kernel equating for all the data collection designs mentioned in section 2.

The SEE is defined as the standard deviation (SD) of the distribution of the estimated linking function at a particular score. For example, if we are linking from **X** to **Y** on **T**, using the estimated linking function, $\hat{e}_{YT}(x)$, then the SEE for $\hat{e}_{YT}(x)$ is

$$\text{SEE}_{YT}(x) = \text{SD}(\hat{e}_{YT}(x)). \qquad (39)$$

We may use the SEE for several purposes. It gives a direct measure of how accurately the equating or linking function is estimated. Using the approximate normality of the estimate, $\hat{e}_{YT}(x)$, the SEE can be used to form confidence intervals for $e_{YT}(x)$. In addition, comparing the SEE for various data collection designs can indicate the relative advantage some designs have over others for particular sample sizes and other design factors. This can aid in the choice of data collection design for a specific purpose. Lord (1950), Angoff (1971), Holland, King, and Thayer (1989), and von Davier et al. (2004b) discussed some of the ways in which SEEs are sensitive to the choice of data collection design.

The SEE can provide us with statistical caveats about the instability of linkings based on small samples. As the size of the sample(s) increases, the SEE will decrease. As we mentioned in section 3.1.1.3, presmoothing can help increase the effective sample size, relative to not presmoothing, but there is a limit to this increase in precision. Standard errors can only indicate how precise an estimate is, but they cannot make it more precise than the limits imposed by the data. With small samples, there is always the possibility that the estimated linking function is a poor representation of the population linking function.

In principle, every linking method that we have mentioned has a SEE. The adequacy of the SEEs in the published literature is often not satisfactory in the sense of accounting for all of the important factors that influence them. The statistical accuracy of an observed-score linking function depends on four factors: (a) the sample sizes, (b) the effect of presmoothing, (c) the data collection design, and (d) the form of the final equating function including the method of continuization.

The earliest work on the SEE is found in Lord (1950) and reproduced in Angoff (1971). These results are concerned with linear linking methods and assume normal distributions of scores. In addition, Lord (1982) (for the EG and SG designs) and Jarjoura and Kolen (1985) (for the NEAT design) derived the SEE for the equipercentile function using linear interpolation for continuization. However, these SEE calculations for the equipercentile function do not take into account the effect of presmoothing, which can produce reductions in the SEE in many cases (Livingston, 1993). Liou and Cheng (1995) gave an extensive discussion of the SEE for various versions of the equipercentile function that included the effect of presmoothing. Holland et al. (1989) and Liou, Cheng, and Johnson (1997) discussed the SEE for kernel equating for the NEAT design. von Davier et al. (2004b) gave a complete system of statistical accuracy measures for kernel equating for all of the data collection designs described in section 2. Their results account for all four factors that affect the SEE. von Davier and Kong (2003) gave a similar analysis for linear equating in the NEAT design.

4.1.2. The Standard Error of Equating Difference (the SEED) Between Two Linking Functions

Rather than the SEE for a given linking function, we are often more interested in the accuracy of *differences* between linking functions. For example, if we estimate the equipercentile function and the linear linking function, it is often rather obvious that the linear linking function reproduces the essential features of the equipercentile function. Is there a statistically significant difference between the linear linking and the equipercentile functions? If not, then the nonlinearity of the equipercentile function may be an unnecessary embellishment that is added to the linear linking function by the method rather than by some essential features of the data. von Davier et al. (2004b) were the first to explicitly consider the standard error of the distribution of the difference between two estimated linking functions, which they called the standard error of equating difference or the SEED. To parallel Equation 39, the SEED has the form

$$\text{SEED}_{YT,1\,2}(x) = \text{SD}(\hat{e}_{Y1T}(x) - \hat{e}_{Y2T}(x)), \qquad (40)$$

where $\hat{e}_{Y1T}(x)$ and $\hat{e}_{Y2T}(x)$ denote the two estimated linking functions being compared. In principle, there is a SEED for any two linking functions, but, at present, the only available calculations for SEEDs are for kernel equating (von Davier et al., 2004b). For kernel equating methods, using loglinear models to presmooth the data, the same tools used for computing the SEE can be used for the SEED for many interesting comparisons of kernel equating functions.

An important use of the SEED in von Davier et al. (2004b) was to compare the linear and nonlinear versions of kernel equating. They showed how it could be combined with a graphical display of the plot of the difference between the two equating functions. In addition to the plot of the difference, they added a band of ±2SEED to put a rough bound on how far the two equating functions can differ simply due to sampling variability. When the difference curve is outside of this band for a substantial number of values of the X-scores, this is evidence that the two equating functions are reliably different. When the difference curve lies well inside this band, this indicates that the differences are at the level of statistical noise. The ±2SEED band is narrower for larger sample sizes and wider for smaller sample sizes.

In the special situation where we wish to compare an estimated equating function to another nonrandom function, for example, the identity function, then the SEE plays the role of the SEED, that is,

$$\text{SD}(\hat{e}_{YT}(x) - x) = \text{SD}(\hat{e}_{YT}(x)) = \text{SEE}_{YT}(x). \qquad (41)$$

4.1.3. Other Estimates of the SEE and SEED

In addition to the large sample or *asymptotic* standard error calculations used by the writers mentioned in sections 4.1.1 and 4.1.2, both the SEE and the SEED can be estimated using bootstrap methods (Efron & Tibshirani, 1993). Bootstrap methods are more computationally intensive than those using the delta method, but when the asymptotic methods fail for small samples, the bootstrap may be a useful substitute, and in small samples it can be an efficiently computed procedure. Kolen and Brennan (2004) gave a detailed discussion of the bootstrap applied to estimating the SEE and this is a potentially useful topic for additional research on the SEED.

It should be emphasized that neither the SEE nor the SEED give any information about how different the estimated linking function would be if the data were sampled from other populations of examinees. This issue is addressed in section 4.2.

4.1.4. The Difference That Matters (the DTM)

In addition to the statistical significance of the difference between the two linking functions (the SEED), it is also useful to examine whether or not this difference has any important consequences for reported scores. This issue was addressed by Dorans and Feigenbaum (1994) in their notion of a *difference that matters*, or DTM. They called a difference in reported score points a DTM if the testing program considered it to be a difference worth worrying about. This, of course, depends on the test and its uses. As an example of the thinking behind one choice of DTM, consider the SAT. In that case, the DTM is ±5 reported-score points because, in the 200 to 800 point scale of the SAT, scores are rounded and reported in steps of 10 points. Thus, differences of less than ±5 points are not distinguished in the reporting scale and can be ignored.

The SAT equatings involve very large samples so the SEE and the SEEDs are typically very small. Hence, the DTM is usually larger than the ±2SEED band, when this band is transformed to the scale of the reported scores. Typically, if the difference between the score conversions for the linear and equipercentile equating functions is less than 5 scale-score points, the linear linking function is used for the SAT, otherwise the equipercentile function is selected. Of course, the final choice of equating function depends on a variety of factors in addition to this comparison (see section 5).

Establishing a DTM for a testing program is a useful way to formalize an important aspect of equating accuracy. It can be used with the SEE and the SEED to help determine the sample sizes that are necessary for the important uses of the scores. If the DTM that is selected is smaller than two times an appropriate SEE or SEED, then the sample size may not be sufficient for the purposes that the equating is intended to support.

4.2. Measures of the Population Sensitivity of Score-Linking Functions

Methods for checking the sensitivity of linking functions to the population on which they are computed (i.e., population invariance checks) are relatively new diagnostics for evaluating links between tests (especially those that are intended to be test equatings). In practice, it is rare that linkings are repeated on new sets of data, so that the most common way that population invariance checks are made is on subpopulations of examinees within the larger population from which the samples are drawn. Subgroups such as males and females are often easily identifiable in the data. Other subgroups are those based on ethnicity, region of the country, etc. In general, it is a good idea to select subgroups that are known to differ in their performance on the tests in question.

Kolen (2004b) traced the concept of population invariance in equating and linking from the 1950s to the present. Much of that research has occurred since 1980. Central to this body of work is the expectation that requirement (e) of section 1.3, that is, population invariance, ought to hold for good test equatings, while cases of scale aligning are not expected to satisfy this requirement.

Dorans and Holland (2000) developed general indices of the population invariance/sensitivity of linking functions for the EG or SG designs of section 2. In order to study population invariance they assumed that the target population is partitioned into mutually exclusive and exhaustive subpopulations. von Davier et al. (2004b) extended that work to the NEAT design that involves two populations both of which are partitioned into similar subpopulations.

Yin, Brennan, and Kolen (2004) extended the Dorans-Holland indices in a study of concordances between the ACT and the Iowa Tests of Educational Development (ITED). Yang (2004) examined whether the multiple-choice to composite linking functions of the Advanced Placement Program exams remain invariant over regional subpopulations. Related articles on the sensitivity of equating functions to populations of examinees are in Dorans (2004a). von Davier and Liu (2006) and the papers therein gave a variety of applications of the Dorans-Holland indices and include careful and critical discussions of these ideas.

The Dorans-Holland indices all assume that the target population $\mathbf{T}$ is partitioned into several subpopulations, $\mathbf{T}_1$, $\mathbf{T}_2$, … There are two tests to be linked, $\mathbf{X}$ and $\mathbf{Y}$, and this is done on the target population as well as on each of the subpopulations, $\mathbf{T}_j$. Denote the linking function on $\mathbf{T}_j$ by $e_{T_j}(x)$ and the one on $\mathbf{T}$ by $e_T(x)$. Each subpopulation is given a weight, w_j, which could be its relative frequency in the target population or some other proportions such that $\Sigma w_j = 1$. The difference curves, $e_{T_j}(x) - e_T(x)$, are computed for each subpopulation and they are the basis of the Dorans-Holland indices. Their first index is the root-mean-square-difference measure, RMSD(x), defined as

$$\text{RMSD}(x) = \frac{\sqrt{\sum_j w_j [e_{T_j}(x) - e_T(x)]^2}}{\sigma_{YT}}. \quad (42)$$

RMSD(x) is the root-mean-square-difference between the linking functions for each subpopulation and the one for the overall target population. It has a value for each $\mathbf{X}$-score, x.

Each term of the sum in Equation 42 can be averaged over the distribution of $\mathbf{X}$ in $\mathbf{T}$ and the result is a measure of the overall difference of the linking function for $\mathbf{T}_j$ from the one for $\mathbf{T}$. The root expected squared difference, RESD(j), is defined by

$$\text{RESD}(j) = \frac{\sqrt{E_T[e_{T_j}(\mathbf{X}) - e_T(\mathbf{X})]^2}}{\sigma_{YT}}. \quad (43)$$

In Equation 43, E_T denotes expectation or average over the score distribution of $\mathbf{X}$ in $\mathbf{T}$. RESD(j) is a summary index for each subpopulation.

Finally, the REMSD index is an overall summary measure across both score levels and subpopulations. It is the root mean square of the RESD(j) values over the subpopulations, that is,

$$\text{REMSD} = \sqrt{\sum_j w_j \text{RESD}(j)^2}. \quad (44)$$

Each of these indices is in units of proportions of the standard deviation of **Y** over **T**, so they are dimensionless and may be interpreted as effect sizes.

The three measures have different uses. The value of REMSD can be used to summarize the overall differences between the linking functions, whereas RMSD(x) can give detailed information as to which **X**-scores are the most affected by the totality of subpopulation differences. The value of RESD(j) measures the overall difference for subpopulation T_j and is not influenced by its weight, w_j, whereas this weight plays a role in both RMSE(x) and RESD(j).

Dorans and Holland (2000) also considered another way to look at population invariance/sensitivity. If two tests can be equated, then it is plausible that their means should order various subpopulations of examinees similarly. In particular, the standardized mean difference scores for the subpopulations on the two tests should be identical or close. By this we mean that for each subpopulation, Equation 45 below ought to hold, at least approximately,

$$\frac{\mu_{YT_j} - \mu_{YT}}{\sigma_{YT}} = \frac{\mu_{XT_j} - \mu_{XT}}{\sigma_{XT}}. \quad (45)$$

Dorans and Holland (2000) showed that their measures, RMSD(x) and REMSD, were equal when a special system of equating functions was used—those they called the *parallel-linear system of linking functions*. In addition, they showed that for the system of parallel-linear linking functions, RMSD(x) = REMSD = 0 if and only if Equation 45 held. Thus, similar standardized mean differences and similar equating functions are closely related conditions for population invariance/sensitivity.

For situations where tests that are built to the same set of specifications are equated to each other, assessing the population sensitivity of equating functions can be viewed as a form of fairness assessment (Dorans, 2004c).

Feuer et al. (1999) and Koretz et al. (1999) both reported evaluations of the feasibility of linking a variety of tests to the NAEP scale or to any other common scale. Both considered a variety of problems of linkage instability (over subpopulations and over time) that these links would be expected to exhibit and concluded that they would be large enough to invalidate many of the uses of these proposed linkages.

Linking functions between two tests can be computed and the scores on the tests can be linked using them, even when population invariance fails to hold to a sufficient degree. In this situation, however, it is appropriate to claim less for the linking between the two tests—the link may be appropriate for the target population as a whole but inappropriate for some identifiable subgroups. In particular, in order to be fair to different groups of examinees, it may be necessary to consider using *different* links between the tests for different subpopulations of examinees. To support this position we now give a very general result that shows a serious problem that may arise when there is substantial subpopulation sensitivity of linking functions and yet an overall pooled linking function is used instead of two separate linking functions.

Suppose $F(x)$ and $G(y)$, respectively, denote the cdfs for tests **X** and **Y** on a common population. Suppose further that the population is partitioned into two subpopulations of examinees, denoted by 1 and 2. Finally, the form of population sensitivity of the equating functions that we will examine occurs when there is a *reversal* between tests, **X** and **Y**. By a reversal we mean that on **X**, group 1 has lower scores than group 2, but on **Y** the reverse holds. Let F_j and G_j denote the cdfs for **X** and **Y** on group j. A condition that insures a reversal is that

$$F_1(x) > F(x) > F_2(x) \quad \text{and} \quad G_2(y) > G(y) > G_1(y). \quad (46)$$

Next we denote the equipercentile equating functions on group j and on the overall population by $e_j(x) = G_j^{-1}(F_j(x))$ and $e(x) = G^{-1}(F(x))$. From Inequality 46 and the definition of $e_j(x)$ and $e(x)$, it is easy to show that the following inequalities also hold:

$$e_1(x) > e(x) > e_2(x). \quad (47)$$

Inequality 47 shows that when a reversal holds and $e(x)$ is used, rather than $e_1(x)$ and $e_2(x)$, examinees in the lower scoring group, group 1 in this case, will get *lower* converted scores than they would have if separate conversions were used. Thus, when a reversal holds, the group scoring lowest on **X** is always disadvantaged (and the group scoring highest on **X** is always advantaged) by the use of the pooled linking function, $e(x)$. The larger the reversal, the larger this disadvantage will be. We believe that this aspect of unfairness should be considered in addition to the concerns often expressed as to the unfairness of using different linking function for different subpopulations of examinees.

When tests that are built to the same specifications are being equated, reversals like that in Inequality 46 will be small and not a serious concern. For the forming of concordances, however, the possibility of reversals is more likely and should be monitored for major subgroups. Dorans and Holland (2000) give an example of a reversal for male and female examinees for a concordance between two well-known admissions tests.

Dorans and Holland (2000) and Holland (2005) initiated a compilation of REMSD values across different types of test pairs. They included a wide range of linking situations, from linking parallel test forms to linking tests of very different content. As such compilations of results are expanded, we will be better able to answer questions about the consequences of complying with the reoccurring call to link tests that were not constructed to be linked. Feuer et al. (1999) and Koretz et al. (1999) were negative responses to federal requests to link such pairs of tests. The conclusions of these reports would have been strengthened immensely had there been data like that compiled by Dorans and Holland available. We regard this as a very productive line of work because it is likely that requests to link tests that are not equatable will continually arise in the future, as argued by Feuer (2005).

4.3. Measuring How Well Linking Functions Preserve Score Distributions

One of the claims made for the equipercentile function given in Equation 11 is that it will transform the distribution of **X** so that it is nearly identical to that of **Y** on the target population **T**. In fact, due to the discreteness of real score distributions this claim cannot be realized exactly. To measure the degree to which this claim can be achieved, Jaeger (1981) used the Kolmogorov-Smirnov (K-S) 2-sample test to evaluate the similarity of the distributions of **Y** and the transformed scores $e_Y(\mathbf{X})$. This approach has the problem of being a test statistic rather than a measure of difference. In addition, the distribution of the K-S test statistic is affected by the estimation of parameters; in the case of linear equating these are the means and variances. These issues reduce the usefulness of the K-S test statistic so that it becomes just another index of distributional difference.

As an alternative, von Davier et al. (2004b) introduced the *percent relative error in the pth moment* of these distributions, the PRE(p). They used the formula

$$\text{PRE}(p) = 100\{\mu_p(e_Y(\mathbf{X})) - \mu_p(\mathbf{Y})\}/\mu_p(\mathbf{Y}), \quad (48)$$

where $\mu_p(\mathbf{Y})$ is the pth moment of **Y** over **T** and $\mu_p(e_Y(\mathbf{X}))$ is the pth moment of the equated scores, $e_Y(\mathbf{X})$ over **T**. For example, the PRE(p) for $p = 1$ is a measure of the difference in the means of **Y** and $e_Y(\mathbf{X})$, while for $p = 2$ it is a measure of the difference in the second moments of **Y** and $e_Y(\mathbf{X})$. The multiplication by 100 expresses PRE(p) as a percent rather than as a proportion.

PRE(p) is an index of distributional discrepancies that emphasizes the similarities of the moments of the distribution, while the K-S measures the largest difference between the two cdfs. For the linear linking function, both PRE(1) and PRE(2) are zero since the linear linking function matches the mean and variance of the distributions of **Y** and $e_Y(\mathbf{X})$ over **T**.

For the examples in von Davier et al. (2004b), PRE(1) is always less than a hundredth of a percent for the kernel equating method. In general, as p increases PRE(p) tends to increase as well. von Davier et al. (2004b) gave several examples of the values of PRE(p) for values of p from 1 to 10. When the equating function is chosen to match these distributions well, the values of PRE(p) are at most one or two percent even up to the tenth moment. While the linear linking function matches the first two moments perfectly, it need not do well for higher moments using the PRE(p) criterion.

While the K-S statistic and the PRE(p) measure are not the only quantities that are relevant to the assessment of the quality of an linking function, they are directly connected to properties that observed-score linking functions are assumed to have. For this reason, they are useful ways to diagnose the adequacy of any linking function. In particular, neither the linear linking function nor the traditional equipercentile method that uses linear interpolation as the method of continuization explicitly try to match the score distributions of $e_Y(\mathbf{X})$ and **Y** over **T** beyond the first and second moments. A useful research topic is the comparison of various equating methods in terms of how well they match the score distributions using these measures. This may provide a basis for choosing among them.

4.4. The Use of Links to Multiple Tests for Observed-Score Test Equating

In section 1.3, we mentioned that in practice observed-score test equating is the first step in a two-step process—first, equate the raw scores of **X** to those of **Y**, and second, apply the **Y**-conversion function to the equated **X**-scores to map them to the reporting scale (see section 1.3 for definitions). It may happen that the raw-score equating is satisfactory, but the second step has problems because the **Y**-conversion function is unsatisfactory. Experienced test statisticians have faced this frustrating situation at one time or another. The importance of the **Y**-conversion function cannot be overestimated in a testing program that continually produces new tests that need to be equated and put on the reporting scale. It is a critical ingredient to the new **X**-conversion function.

What are some of the causes of poor **Y**-conversions? The primary causes we will discuss are poor past equating. In the EG and SG designs (see sections 2.1 and 2.2), the primary choice of observed score equating functions is between $Equi_{YT}(x)$ and $Lin_{YT}(x)$ (see section 3.1.1.1). With large representative samples, $Equi_{YT}(x)$ is often a reasonable choice. In small samples, especially those that are not representative of the target population, other methods might be better. For example, in smaller samples, $Equi_{YT}(x)$ may be tracking unstable differences from $Lin_{YT}(x)$. The more parsimonious linear model may be preferable. It is wise to check the difference between $Equi_{YT}(x)$ and $Lin_{YT}(x)$ using the methods described in section 4.1. Skaggs (2004) shows that in very small samples it may be preferable, in terms of misclassification, to use either the mean equating function or the identity equating function (see section 3.1.1.1) than either $Equi_{YT}(x)$ or $Lin_{YT}(x)$. In small samples the necessary parameter estimates for the more complicated equating functions may be too inaccurate to be useful.

A different type of problem can lead to poor equatings in the NEAT design, even with large samples. When there are large differences on the anchor test between the samples from **P** and **Q** (see section 2.6), the chances of problems with the equating function are increased. This brings with it the potential for biased equating results that can accumulate over a chain of prior equatings.

To deal with the possibility of linking back to poor equating, testing programs often link to more than one old form **Y**, rather than using a single equating. Kolen and Brennan (2004) and others advocated the use of links to *two or more* past forms. For example, for decades, new editions of the SAT were equated back to two past forms using the NEAT design. Successive new test forms were linked back to different pairs of old forms. In 1994, the SAT equatings began to link new forms back to four old forms. The rationale for this new scheme was that with more links to past forms it is easier to detect a poor past conversion function, and it makes the final new conversion function less reliant on any particular older equating function.

In practice, the true equating function is not known so it is wise to look at several procedures that make different assumptions or that use different data. Given the potential impact of the final score conversion on all participants in an assessment process, it is important to check as many factors that can cause problems as possible. Considering multiple conversions is one way to do this.

In the case of the NEAT design, there are several different linear and nonlinear methods that reflect different assumptions about the missing data in the NEAT design (see section 3.2.1). For this reason, it is possible to estimate several, potentially different, score conversions in order to evaluate the effect of these different assumptions. When the two groups in the NEAT design are similar on the anchor test, the different linear methods are often in close agreement and the nonlinear methods are often similar as well. However, when the two groups differ by substantial amounts on the anchor test there will be noticeable differences between the methods. von Davier et al. (2004b) gave an example where there were statistically reliable differences between the PSE and CE methods of kernel equating. In that case, these differences were larger than the DTM for the testing program (see section 4.1.4). This is, of course, a reason why the NEAT design is best used when the sample differences on the anchor test are smaller and the particular missing-data assumptions made by the different methods are less consequential.

In addition to the comparison of equating functions and score conversions mentioned earlier, we may also ask if a given equating function produces conversions that are consistent with past results. Before scores are released, the new score conversion function should be compared to historical data. The score conversion function can be compared to the historically highest and lowest conversions at each raw-score point on the new form. Unless some special consideration is relevant, once a testing program has put several test forms onto its reporting scale we expect the new score conversions function to lie within the band between the historically highest and lowest conversions. If it falls outside of this band, it might be wise to consider another conversion, especially in testing programs with stable historical data.

It is also wise to examine the *distribution* of the reported scores for the proposed score conversion function to see if it is similar to the distributions of scores on previous test forms administered to comparable samples of examinees. Testing programs build up this type of information as new test forms come into the system, and they provide important quality control checks for the introduction of new versions of the tests.

The use of multiple equating methods to evaluate a given equating function is an area where future research can yield practical results. What tools are useful for evaluating the results of multiple equating methods both across methods on a given set of equating data and across different equatings from the same testing program? Furthermore, we believe that an important area for practical and theoretical research is to devise ways for choosing among the various equating methods for the NEAT design when they give different results.

5. SOUND PRACTICES FOR TEST EQUATING AND LINKING

In this final part, we examine topics in the practice of test equating. Section 5.1 is concerned with doing test equating well, while section 5.2 considers the problem of equating when test specifications change. In section 5.3 we examine a concordance to see if it could be interpreted as an equating. Section 5.4 ends with some final thoughts about the future of test linking.

5.1. Test Equating Practices

The goal of test equating is to allow scores on different tests to be used interchangeably. To achieve this goal, experience has shown that certain practices need to be followed. While we will not emphasize the five requirements of equating from section 1.3, they are explicitly and implicitly used throughout our discussion. Kolen and Brennan (2004) provided another discussion of good equating practices.

5.1.1. The Tests Should Be Measures of the Same Construct

If the tests are built to the same detailed set of specifications, then they are likely to measure the same construct. Expert judgment about the similarity of test content can also be useful, when the specifications are not detailed. In addition, statistical data can sometimes inform this evaluation. Are the scores on the two tests highly correlated? Are their distributions on a common population similarly shaped and close to each other?

However, it is important to point out that there is often more to the same-construct requirement than simply the type of questions that are in the two tests. For example, Feuer et al. (1999) identified both the format of the questions asked (e.g., multiple-choice or constructed-response) and the uses and consequences of the test as factors that can indirectly affect the constructs the tests are measuring. In addition, Koretz et al. (1999) listed the degree of standardization of the test administration, the use of accommodations for certain classes of examinees, the timing of the test in the school year, and test security issues as additional factors that can change the meaning of what the tests are measuring. We consider some of these in more detail below.

5.1.2. The Tests Should Be Administered under Standardized and Secure Conditions

Standardized testing conditions are essential to test equating. The tests should be administered under the same conditions under which they will be used operationally. Special equating administrations need careful consideration in order to be satisfactory. Is the timing the same? Are the examinees motivated to perform on the test in a way that is similar to the motivation of examinees in the operational setting?

Preknowledge of test material, answer copying, and other test security issues compromise standardized administrations and can introduce differences into the equating experiment that undermine its integrity. Special care needs to be taken to prevent these compromises from occurring and to detect them if they do occur.

5.1.3. The Samples of Examinees Should Be Large and Representative of the Target Population

The statistical accuracy of the resulting linking function depends on the number of test takers in the equating sample. The SEE, SEED, and the DTM are described in section 4.1, and they can be used to evaluate how big a sample is needed. Special equating administrations may be smallish due to practical considerations, and this is another of their limitations. However, the usefulness of an equating or linking also depends on the relationship of the equating sample(s) to the population of test takers to which it will be applied. As in all sampling from populations, how well the sample represents the population of intended test takers is a matter of statistical bias rather than of statistical accuracy.

5.1.4. The Test Scores Should Be Equally and Highly Reliable

There are two issues that involve reliability in test equating. The first follows from requirement (b), the tests being equated should be equally reliable or at least nearly so. Hanson's theorem shows that when tests are not equally reliable, linking functions are not expected to satisfy the second-order equity condition. However, there is another, often unappreciated equating issue that involves reliability and that is the need for *enough* reliability. Dorans and Holland (2000) showed there is a relationship between their measures of population sensitivity and the reliability of the two tests. Putting their results into the notation of this chapter, they show that if $\mathbf{X}$ and $\mathbf{Y}$ are alternative test forms with a common reliability, ρ_{XT}^2, over the total target population, $\mathbf{T}$, then their measure of population sensitivity, REMSD (see section 4.2), can be no larger than a quantity that is small when the reliability is large, that is,

$$\text{REMSD} \leq \sqrt{2(1 - \rho_{XT}^2)}. \tag{49}$$

Inequality 49 says that, for alternative forms, the REMSD measure of the subpopulation sensitivity of equating functions cannot be large for very reliable tests. This relationship suggests that to achieve population invariance it is important for the two tests to be reliable enough rather than merely equally reliable.

In fairness to readers, we should report that not all testing professionals agree with our interpretation of the consequences of Inequality 49. For example, see Brennan (2006). This is an area where further research may illuminate the role of test reliability in equating and scaling.

5.2. As Tests Change, Is It an Equating or Just a Concordance?

The process of equating successive forms of a testing program is sometimes at odds with the need to improve, update, and otherwise cause these tests to change and evolve. There can be no doubt that the tests of a testing program will and, often, must change as time goes on. But as test forms go through a process of evolution the first requirement of test equating, that the two test measure the same construct, can be called into question. Sometimes tests change in ways that are more revolutionary than evolutionary, but there is often an overpowering desire on the part of score users to maintain the same reporting scale in spite of the change. Scales for testing programs take on a life of their own as users become familiar with them and develop what they regard as reliable interpretations of different score ranges.

In the face of evolving and changing tests, we regard test equating as a goal that may be achieved only approximately. Concordances, using the data collection designs and computations of test equating, are often the best that we can expect to obtain. Procedurally, concordance and equating are the same, but the characteristics of the tests and what can be inferred from the data are not. When concordances are essentially the same across the important subpopulations, a single concordance may suffice, and then we may be willing to call it an equating function. It is, in our opinion, best to be more circumspect regarding the achievability of population invariance in test linking.

There are two standards (American Educational Research Association, American Psychological Association, & National Council on Measurement in Education, 1999) that directly address the tension between the need for changes in tests and the need for stability of score scales. They are *Standards* 4.16 and 4.17, quoted below.

> *Standard* 4.16: If test specifications are changed from one version of a test to a subsequent version, such changes should be identified in the test manual, and an indication should be given that converted scores for the two versions may not be strictly equivalent. When substantial changes in test specification occur, either scores should be reported on a new scale or a clear statement should be provided to alert users that the scores are not directly comparable with those on earlier versions of the test.
>
> *Standard* 4.17: Testing programs that attempt to maintain a common scale over time should conduct periodic checks of the stability of the scale on which scores are reported.

How can test statisticians balance the need to maintain the constant meaning of a particular scale through test equating with the need to allow the test versions or forms to evolve over time? How can they implement these standards in practice?

When revolutionary change takes place, large alterations in the test are introduced at a new administration. In that case, *Standard* 4.16 recommends the creation of a new score scale, so that there will be no confusion between the scores on the old and new versions of the test. Testing programs sometimes opt for this approach. For example, the reporting scale of the Law School Admissions Test (LSAT) has changed three times over the period 1948 to 1991. The first scale change occurred because the LSAT test specifications were substantially changed and because there was dissatisfaction with the original three-digit, 200–800, scale. The later changes were in response to further changes in the test specifications (Law School Admission Services, Inc., 1991).

The problem with a clean break in the reporting scale is that it may confuse test users who have become familiar with the old scale and do not easily adjust to a new one.

Because of this reality, *Standard* 4.16 also recommends that, if the scale is not changed, the users should be warned that there might be differences between the scores on the old and new versions of the test. For example, the 200–800 scale of the SAT has remained in use despite the significant evolutionary change in this testing program that has occurred over the 60-odd years of its use (Lawrence, Rigol, Van Essen, & Jackson, 2004). Perhaps the most revolutionary shift in the SAT scale occurred in 1995, when the reference group from 1941 was replaced by a more relevant 1990 reference group (Dorans, 2002). Despite the fact that the shift in meaning was well publicized in advance, substantial confusion occurred because scores were reported on the same 200–800 numerical scale.

When evolutionary change takes place, as it almost always will, the differences between subsequent forms are often so slight that a new scale does not seem necessary. However, over a period of time the totality of changes from the older forms to the newer ones can approach revolutionary change and *Standard* 4.17 indicates the need to evaluate the ways in which the scale may or may not have been altered over this longer period.

5.3. Is It a Concordance or an Equating?

We end this discussion with an example that indicates some of the issues that concordances versus equatings involve. In section 1.2.2.5, we mentioned the concordance between the ACT and the SAT I reported in Dorans et al. (1997). That concordance linked the total score on the ACT to the sum of the two SAT I scores, V + M. Dorans (2004b) examined those data in light of other possible linkages between ACT and SAT I scores. In particular, he considered the concordance between the mathematics portions of these two tests denoted here as M-A (from the ACT) and M-S (from the SAT I). The content frameworks for M-A and M-S were similar; the numbers of items were the same, and scores correlated 0.89 in the sample used to form the original concordance. In addition, the Dorans-Holland RMSD value is 1.5% for the gender subpopulations. This value is similar to the value (1.7%) computed for alternate SAT-M forms (Dorans & Holland, 2000). Thus, we have a case of two tests that were constructed to similar but not identical specifications, were both highly reliable (over 0.90), were highly correlated with each other in a substantial sample of real examinees and exhibited a degree of insensitivity to gender differences that was no larger than mathematics test forms that are built to exactly the same specifications. This suggests that we may be more willing to treat the mathematics scores on these two tests as interchangeable than we would be for the concordance of the total scores. Of course, gender differences are only the most easily examined subpopulations, and the case would be substantially clarified if a wider array of subpopulation differences were examined.

The importance of analyses such as those just given will continue to grow with the desire to link scores from tests that were not designed with that intention. The requests that led to the two National Research Council reports, Feuer et al. (1999) and Koretz et al. (1999), should be expected to continue as the importance of testing increases in the face of limited resources.

5.4. A Final Word

Interest in linking scores on different tests has existed for nearly a century, dating back to the 1910s. Equating alternate forms appears to date back to the late 1930s. Much has been learned since then, but some lessons, such as the pitfalls of using regression to produce comparable scores, require relearning in each new generation of psychometricians.

Technological advances have moved practice away from simpler models to more sophisticated ones and away from straightforward complete test data collection designs to complex incomplete test designs. Distinctions among classes of linkages have become prevalent, as educational policy issues have led the drive to link different tests across different populations of examinees. The role of equating within a test fairness framework has begun to be articulated.

In future years, some of the recent advances will be viewed from a broader perspective, just as we view early linking work as a mixture of primitive notions and insightful understandings of the issues surrounding the practice of making scores comparable. We expect that linking practices will become more principled and linking principles more practical over the coming decades. Comparable scores are, and will continue to be, essential to many questions of interest in education and society.

REFERENCES

American Educational Research Association, American Psychological Association, & National Council on Measurement in Education. (1999). *Standards for educational and psychological testing*. Washington, DC: American Educational Research Association.

Angoff, W. H. (1971). Scales, norms and equivalent scores. In R. L. Thorndike (Ed.), *Educational measurement* (2nd ed., pp. 508–600). Washington, DC: American Council on Education.

Angoff, W. H. (1984). *Scales, norms and equivalent scores*. Princeton, NJ: Educational Testing Service.

Barnett, V., & Lewis, T. (1994). *Outliers in statistical data* (3rd ed.). New York: Wiley.

Birkes, D., & Dodge, Y. (1993). *Alternative methods of regression*. New York: Wiley.

Blackwell, D., & Girshick, M. A. (1954). *The theory of games and statistical decisions*. New York: Wiley.

Braun, H. I., & Holland, P. W. (1982). Observed-score test equating: A mathematical analysis of some ETS equating procedures. In P. W. Holland & D. B. Rubin (Eds.), *Test equating* (pp. 9–49). New York: Academic Press.

Brennan, R. L. (1992). The context of context effects. *Applied Measurement in Education, 5*, 225–264.

Brennan, R. L. (2006). A discussion of population invariance. In A. A. von Davier & M. Liu (Eds.), *Population invariance of test equating and linking: Theory extension and applications across exams*. Princeton, NJ: Educational Testing Service, 169–187.

Cramér, H. (1946). *Mathematical methods of statistics*. Princeton, NJ: Princeton University Press.

von Davier, A. A., Holland, P. W., & Thayer, D. T. (2004a). The chain and post-stratification methods of observed-score equating: Their relationship to population invariance. *Journal of Educational Measurement, 41*, 15–32.

von Davier, A. A., Holland, P. W., & Thayer, D. T. (2004b). *The kernel method of test equating.* New York: Springer.

von Davier, A. A., & Kong, N. (2003). *A unified approach to linear equating for the non-equivalent groups design* (Research Report RR-03-31). Princeton, NJ: Educational Testing Service.

von Davier, A. A., & Liu, M. (Eds.). (2006). *Population invariance of test equating and linking: Theory extension and applications across exams.* Princeton, NJ: Educational Testing Service.

Donlon, T. F., & Angoff, W. A. (1971). The Scholastic Aptitude Test. In W. A. Angoff (Ed.), *The College Board Admissions Testing Program: A technical report on research and development activities relating to the Scholastic Aptitude Test and Achievement Tests* (pp. 15–45). New York: The College Entrance Examination Board.

Dorans, N. J. (2000). *Distinctions among classes of linkages* (College Board Research Note No. RN-11). New York: The College Board. Retrieved February 7, 2005, from http://www.collegeboard.com/repository/distinctions_among_cl_10503.pdf

Dorans, N. J. (2002). Recentering the SAT score distributions: How and why. *Journal of Educational Measurement, 39,* 59–84.

Dorans, N. J. (Ed.). (2004a). Assessing the population sensitivity of equating functions [Special issue]. *Journal of Educational Measurement, 41*(1).

Dorans, N. J. (2004b). Equating, concordance and expectation. *Applied Psychological Measurement, 28,* 227–246.

Dorans, N. J. (2004c). Using population invariance to assess test score equity. *Journal of Educational Measurement, 41,* 43–68.

Dorans, N. J., & Feigenbaum, M. D. (1994). Equating issues engendered by changes to the SAT and PSAT/NMSQT. In I. M. Lawrence, N. J. Dorans, M. D. Feigenbaum, N. J. Feryok, A. P. Schmitt, & N. K. Wright (Eds.), *Technical issues related to the introduction of the new SAT and PSAT/NMSQT* (RM-94-10). Princeton, NJ: Educational Testing Service, 91–122.

Dorans, N. J., & Holland, P. W. (2000). Population invariance and the equatability of tests: Basic theory and the linear case. *Journal of Educational Measurement, 37,* 281–306.

Dorans, N. J., Lyu, C. F., Pommerich, M., & Houston, W. M. (1997). Concordance between ACT Assessment and recentered SAT I sum scores. *College and University, 73*(2), 24–34.

Educational Testing Service. (1999). *Score change for PSAT/NMSQT test takers* (ETS SR-99-68). Princeton, NJ: Author.

Efron, B., & Tibshirani, R. J. (1993). *An introduction to the bootstrap.* New York: Chapman & Hall.

Fairbank, B. A. (1987). The use of presmoothing and postsmoothing to increase the precision of equipercentile equating. *Applied Psychological Measurement, 11,* 245–262.

Feuer, M. J. (2005). E Pluribus Unum: Linking tests and democratic education. In C. A. Dwyer (Ed.), *Measurement and research issues in a new accountability era* (pp. 165–183). Mahwah, NJ: Lawrence Erlbaum.

Feuer, M. J., Holland, P. W., Green, B. F., Bertenthal, M. W., & Hemphill, F. C. (Eds.). (1999). *Uncommon measures: Equivalence and linkage among educational tests* (Report of the Committee on Equivalency and Linkage of Educational Tests, National Research Council). Washington, DC: National Academy Press.

Flanagan, J. C. (1939). *The cooperative achievement tests: A bulletin reporting the basic principles and procedures used in the development of their system of scaled scores.* New York: American Council on Education Cooperative Test Service.

Flanagan, J. C. (1951). Units, scores, and norms. In E. F. Lindquist (Ed.), *Educational measurement* (pp. 695–763). Washington, DC: American Council on Education.

Galton, F. (1888). Co-relations and their measurements, chiefly from anthropological data. *Proceedings of the Royal Society of London, 45,* 135–145.

Hambleton, R. K., & Swaminathan, H. (1985). *Item response theory: Principles and applications.* Boston: Kluwer Nijhoff.

Hanson, B. A. (1991). A note on Levine's formula for equating unequally reliable tests using data from the common item nonequivalent groups design. *Journal of Educational Statistics, 16,* 93–100.

Harris, D. J., & Gao, X. (2003, April). A conceptual synthesis of context effect. In *Context effects: Implications for pretesting and CBT.* Symposium conducted at the 2003 annual meeting of the American Educational Research Association, Chicago.

Harris, D. J., Hendrickson, A. B., Tong, Y., Shin, S.-H., & Shyu, C.-Y. (2004, April). Vertical scales and the measurement of growth. In *Methods of establishing vertical scales and their impact on measuring growth.* Symposium conducted at the 2004 annual meeting of the National Council on Measurement in Education, San Diego, CA.

Holland, P. W. (2005). Assessing the validity of test linking: What has happened since *Uncommon measures*? In C. A. Dwyer (Ed.), *Measurement and research issues in a new accountability era* (pp. 185–195). Mahwah, NJ: Lawrence Erlbaum.

Holland, P. W., & Hoskens, M. (2003). Classical test theory as a first-order item response theory: Application to true-score prediction from a possibly nonparallel test. *Psychometrika, 68,* 123–149.

Holland, P. W., King, B. F., & Thayer, D. T. (1989). *The standard error of equating for the kernel method of equating score distributions* (ETS RR-89-06). Princeton, NJ: Educational Testing Service.

Holland, P. W., & Rubin, D. B. (1982). *Test equating.* New York: Academic Press.

Holland, P. W., & Thayer, D. T. (1987). *Notes on the use of loglinear model for fitting discrete probability distribution* (ETS RR 87-31). Princeton, NJ: Educational Testing Service.

Holland, P. W., & Thayer, D. T. (1989). *The kernel method of equating score distributions* (ETS RR 89-7). Princeton, NJ: Educational Testing Service.

Holland, P. W., & Thayer, D. T. (2000). Univariate and bivariate loglinear models for discrete test score distributions. *Journal of Educational and Behavioral Statistics, 25,* 133–183.

Holland, P. W., & Wainer, H. (1993). *Differential item functioning.* Hillsdale, NJ: Erlbaum.

Hoover, H. D., Dunbar, S. D., & Frisbie, D. A. (2001). *Iowa Tests of Basic Skills interpretative guide for teachers and counselors. Forms A and B, Levels 9–14.* Itasca, IL: Riverside.

Hoover, H. D., Dunbar, S. D., & Frisbie, D. A. (2003). *The Iowa Tests: Guide to development and research.* Itasca, IL: Riverside.

Hull, C. L. (1922). The conversion of test scores into series which shall have any assigned mean and dispersion. *Journal of Applied Psychology, 6,* 298–300.

Jaeger, R. M. (1981). Some exploratory indices for selection of a test equating method. *Journal of Educational Measurement, 18,* 23–38.

Jarjoura, D., & Kolen, M. J. (1985). Standard errors of equipercentile equating for the common item nonequivalent populations design. *Journal of Educational Statistics, 10,* 143–160.

Keeves, J. (1988). Scaling achievement test scores. In T. Husen & T. N. Postlethwaite (Eds.), *International encyclopedia of education*. Oxford: Pergamon.

Kelley, T. L. (1914). Comparable measures. *Journal of Educational Psychology, 5*, 589–595.

Kelley, T. L. (1923). *Statistical methods*. New York: Macmillan.

Kelley, T. L. (1927). *Interpretation of educational measurements*. New York: World Book.

Kolen, M. J. (2003, April). *Equating and vertical scaling: Research questions*. Paper presented at the 2003 annual meeting of the National Council on Measurement in Education, Chicago.

Kolen, M. J. (2004a). Linking assessments: Concept and history. *Applied Psychological Measurement, 28*, 219–226.

Kolen, M. J. (2004b). Population invariance in equating and linking: Concept and history. *Journal of Educational Measurement, 41*, 3–14.

Kolen, M. J., & Brennan, R. L. (2004). *Test equating, linking, and scaling: Methods and practices* (2nd ed.). New York: Springer-Verlag.

Kolen, M. J., & Jarjoura, D. (1987). Analytic smoothing for equipercentile equating under the common item nonequivalent populations design. *Psychometrika, 52*, 43–59.

Koretz, D. M., Bertenthal, M. W., & Green, B. F. (Eds.). (1999). *Embedding questions: The pursuit of a common measure in uncommon tests* (Report of the Committee on Embedding Common Test Items in State and District Assessments, National Research Council). Washington, DC: National Academy Press.

Law School Admission Services, Inc. (1991). *The Law School Admission Test: Sources, contents, uses*. Newtown, PA: Law School Admissions Services.

Lawrence, I. M., Rigol, G. W., Van Essen, T., & Jackson, C. A. (2004). A historical perspective on the content of the SAT. In R. Zwick (Ed.), *Rethinking the SAT: The future of standard testing in university admissions*. New York: Routledge Falmer, 57–74.

Leary, L. F., & Dorans, N. J. (1985). Implications for altering the context in which test items appear: An historical perspective on an immediate concern. *Review of Educational Research, 55*, 387–413.

Levine, R. S. (1955). *Equating the score scales of alternate forms administered to samples of different ability* (ETS RB-55-23). Princeton, NJ: ETS.

van der Linden, W. J. (2000). A test-theoretic approach to observed-score equating. *Psychometrika, 65*, 437–456.

Linn, R. L. (1993). Linking results of distinct assessments. *Applied Measurement in Education, 6*, 83–102.

Liou, M., & Cheng, P. E. (1995). Asymptotic standard error of equipercentile equating. *Journal of Educational and Behavioral Statistics, 20*, 259–286.

Liou, M., Cheng, P. E., & Johnson, E. G. (1997). Standard errors of the kernel equating methods under the common-item design. *Applied Psychological Measurement, 21*, 349–369.

Liou, M., Cheng, P. E., & Li, M. Y. (2001). Estimating comparable scores using surrogate variables. *Applied Psychological Measurement, 25*, 197–207.

Little, R. J. A., & Rubin, D. B. (2002). *Statistical analysis with missing data* (2nd ed.). Hoboken, NJ: Wiley.

Livingston, S. A. (1993). Small-sample equating with log-linear smoothing. *Journal of Educational Measurement, 30*, 23–39.

Livingston, S. A. (2004). *Equating test scores (without IRT)*. Princeton, NJ: Educational Testing Service.

Livingston, S. A., Dorans, N. J., & Wright, N. K. (1990). What combination of sampling and equating methods works best? *Applied Measurement in Education, 3*, 73–95.

Lord, F. M. (1950). *Notes on comparable scales for test scores* (ETS RB-50-48). Princeton, NJ: Educational Testing Service.

Lord, F. M. (1955). Equating test scores: A maximum likelihood solution. *Psychometrika, 20*, 193–200.

Lord, F. M. (1980). *Applications of item response theory to practical testing problems*. Hillsdale, NJ: Erlbaum.

Lord, F. M. (1982). The standard error of equipercentile equating. *Journal of Educational Statistics, 7*, 165–174.

Lord, F. M., & Wingersky, M. S. (1984). Comparison of IRT true-score and equipercentile observed-score equatings. *Applied Psychological Measurement, 8*, 453–461.

Marco, G. L., Petersen, N. S., & Stewart, E. E. (1983). *A large-scale evaluation of linear and curvilinear score equating models, Volumes I and II* (ETS RM-83-02). Princeton, NJ: Educational Testing Service.

McGaw, B. (1977). The use of rescaled teacher assessments in the admission of student to tertiary study. *Australian Journal of Education, 21*, 209–225.

Mislevy, R. J. (1992). *Linking educational assessments: Concepts, issues, methods, and prospects*. Princeton, NJ: Educational Testing Service, Policy Information Center.

Mislevy, R. J., Sheehan, K. M., & Wingersky, M. (1993). How to equate tests with little or no data. *Journal of Educational Measurement, 30*, 55–78.

Moore, D. S., & McCabe, G. P. (1999). *Introduction to the practice of statistics* (3rd ed.). New York: W. H. Freeman.

Morris, C. N. (1982). On the foundations of test equating. In P. W. Holland & D. B. Rubin (Eds.), *Test equating* (pp. 169–191). New York: Academic Press.

Moses, T., von Davier, A. A., & Casabianca, J. (2004). *Loglinear smoothing: An alternative numerical approach using SAS* (ETS RR-04-27). Princeton, NJ: Educational Testing Service.

Otis, A. S. (1916). The reliability of spelling scales, including a 'deviation formula' for correlation. *School and Society, 4*, 96–99.

Otis, A. S. (1918). An absolute point scale for the group measurements of intelligence. Part I. *Journal of Educational Psychology, 9*, 239–260.

Otis, A. S. (1922). The method for finding the correspondence between scores in two tests. *Journal of Educational Psychology, 13*, 529–545.

Parzen, E. (1960). *Modern probability theory and its applications*. New York: Wiley.

Pashley, P. J., & Phillips, G. W. (1993). *Toward world-class standards: A research study linking international and national assessments*. Princeton, NJ: Educational Testing Service.

Petersen, N. S., Kolen, M. J., & Hoover, H. D. (1989). Scaling, norming and equating. In R. L. Linn (Ed.), *Educational measurement* (3rd ed., pp. 221–262). New York: Macmillan.

Pinter, R. (1914). A comparison of the Ayres and Thorndike handwriting scales. *Journal of Educational Psychology, 5*, 525–536.

Pommerich, M., & Dorans, N. J. (Eds.). (2004). Concordance [Special issue]. *Applied Psychological Measurement 28*(4).

Rosenbaum, P. R. (1995). *Observational studies*. New York: Springer-Verlag.

Rosenbaum, P. R., & Rubin, D. B. (1983). The central role of the propensity score in observational studies for causal effects. *Biometrika, 70*, 41–55.

Skaggs, G. (2004, April). *Passing score stability when equating with very small samples*. Paper presented at the 2004 annual meeting of the National Council on Measurement in Education, San Diego, CA.

Starch, D. (1913). The measurement of handwriting. *Journal of Educational Psychology, 4,* 445–464.

Stigler, S. M. (1986). *The history of statistics: The measurement of uncertainty before 1900.* Cambridge, MA: Harvard University Press.

Terman, L. M., & Merrill, M. A. (1937). *Measuring intelligence.* Boston: Houghton Mifflin.

Thissen, D., & Wainer, H. (Eds.). (2001). *Test scoring.* Mahwah, NJ: Erlbaum.

Thorndike, E. L. (1922). On finding equivalent scores in tests of intelligence. *Journal of Applied Psychology, 6,* 29–33.

Wainer, H., Vevea, J. L., Camacho, F., Reeve, B. B., Rosa, K., Nelson, L., et al. (2001). Augmented scores—"Borrowing strength" to compute scores based on small numbers of item. In D. Thissen & H. Wainer (Eds.), *Test scoring* (pp. 343–383). Mahwah, NJ: Erlbaum.

Weiss, A. P. (1914). A modified slide rule and the index method of individual measurements. *Journal of Educational Psychology, 5,* 511–524.

Williams, V. S. L., Rosa, K. R., McLeod, L. D., Thissen, D., & Sanford, E. E. (1998). Projecting to the NAEP scale: Results from the North Carolina End-of-Grade Testing Program. *Journal of Educational Measurement, 35,* 277–296.

Woodworth, R. S. (1912). Combining the results of several tests: A study in statistical method. *Psychological Review, 19,* 97–123.

Wright, N. K., & Dorans, N. J. (1993). *Using the selection variable for matching or equating* (ETS RR-93-4). Princeton, NJ: Educational Testing Service.

Yang, W.-L. (2004). Sensitivity of linkings between AP multiple-choice scores and composite scores to geographical region: An illustration of checking for population invariance. *Journal of Educational Measurement, 41,* 33–41.

Yin, P., Brennan, R. L., & Kolen, M. J. (2004). Concordance between ACT and ITED scores from different populations. *Applied Psychological Measurement, 28,* 274–289.

Yoakum, C. S., & Yerkes, R. M. (1920). *Army mental tests.* New York: Henry Holt.

7
Test Fairness

Gregory Camilli
Rutgers, The State University of New Jersey

1. INTRODUCTION

This chapter is about the social context of test fairness, and methods of logical and quantitative analysis for examining test fairness. While there are many aspects of fair assessment, it is generally agreed that tests should be thoughtfully developed and that the conditions of testing should be reasonable and equitable for all students. Many of the chapters in this volume address substantive issues related to this concern; and in particular, the chapters by Kane on validity, and by Haertel on reliability, describe concepts and tools that can be understood as prerequisites for test fairness. Beyond this foundational material, issues of fairness involve specific techniques of analysis, and the more common approaches are reviewed in this chapter.

Some important concepts of social and legal and social justice are summarized initially to provide both context for modern concepts of fairness, and insight into the logic of analyzing fairness. This is important because many unfair test conditions may not have a clear statistical signature, for example, a test may include items that are offensive or culturally insensitive to some examinees. Quantitative analyses infrequently detect such items; rather, such analyses tend to focus on the narrower issues of whether a measurement or prediction model is the same for two or more groups of examinees. Indeed, these statistical models can be the same even when a test or assessment has substantial negative consequences for the members of some groups of test takers. This ostensible contradiction might result from a technically sound test that is developed with a carefully delimited set of purposes, yet used in a manner that is inconsistent with those purposes.

An exhaustive treatment of issues related to fairness is beyond the scope of this, or any single chapter. Rather, I have provided a conceptual framework for understanding both test fairness and the assumptions and modes of inferences that underlie corresponding statistical analyses. Recent methodological developments are examined as well as item sensitivity review, fairness in classroom assessment, and historical themes regarding fairness in college admissions. The current chapter greatly benefited from a number of sources including the *Standards for Educational and Psychological Testing* (American Educational Research Association, American Psychological Association, & National Council on Measurement in Education, 1999); the *Code of Fair Testing Practices in Education* (Joint Committee on Testing Practices, 1988); the *Code of Professional Responsibilities in Educational Measurement* (NCME Ad Hoc Committee on the Development of a Code of Ethics, 1995); *Educational Measurement, Third Edition* (Linn, 1989); and the work of Hartigan and Wigdor (1989), Holland and Wainer (1993), Hubin (1988), and Camilli and Shepard (1994).

Most of the above sources deal largely with test fairness in the United States, though test fairness is obviously not just an American concern. Fairness issues are inevitably shaped by the particular social context in which they are embedded. Thus, while the psychometric methodologies reviewed herein generalize broadly, the substantive generalizations may vary with respect to other cultures and countries. One special emphasis herein is on issues of fairness with respect to race and ethnicity. Many other topics are not considered due to space limitations but are clearly as important including: gender; special populations; licensing and certification; test accommodations; and linguistic diversity. While some of these are treated indirectly, many of the principles in this chapter are directly applicable. Finally, the issue of fairness in high-stakes testing in public K–12 education is not examined. This is a topic unto itself, requiring more space than that of a single section within a broad chapter.

2. SOCIAL AND LEGAL CONTEXT OF FAIRNESS ISSUES

Two fundamental premises of a liberal society are that a republic is a voluntary association between free individuals, and that a free-market economy is based upon fair competition. *Liberal*, in the original sense of the word, referred to the antithesis of social systems based on hierarchy and subordination. In a liberal society, free individuals are members, not subjects, of the state, and government is constituted by the members of society for their mutual benefit. This precept is embodied in the foundational text of the United States, the Declaration of Independence, which holds that "that all men are created equal, that they are endowed by their Creator with certain unalienable Rights, that among these are Life, Liberty and the pursuit of Happiness." And, importantly, "That to secure these rights, Governments are instituted among Men, deriving their just Powers from the consent of the governed...."

In a liberal society, the power of the federal government in regulating social transactions is distributed by design. This idea is embodied in U.S. Congressional representation, which defines "equal representation," in terms of both individual citizens (through the House) and states (through the Senate). However, individual rights were first addressed in the Bill of Rights (the first 10 amendments to the Constitution), which restricted contravention by federal government of individual liberties, including those of freedom of speech, press, assembly, religion, and due process for those accused of committing a crime. Modern interpretations of equality are more directly traceable to the 13th and 14th Amendments, which were designed to dismantle the institution of slavery.

Equality, in the senses of *fair play* and fair competition, was defined with the *individual* as the fundamental unit of both government and society. Ideally, this would have resulted in a *meritocracy* (originally a pejorative term coined in 1958 by Michael Young in the book *The Rise of Meritocracy*), but the scope of individual liberty was limited in early America. For example, women could not vote until 1920, and though all African Americans were legally freed in 1866, another 100 years passed before the Supreme Court decision *Brown v. Board of Education* (1954) began to unravel the apartheid system of racial segregation as established by laws of the Jim Crow era. As opposed to monarchical societies, however, early American political philosophy espoused the principle of accrual of the benefits of society based on merit. Fair competition allows individuals to seek happiness as they prefer *and* allows for the actual accrual of benefits to be unequal. It is only rules and standards for competition that should be impartial to all individuals.

Though some form of merit is frequently appropriate in attaining the benefits of a society (though not all, consider healthcare), there are pitfalls. Young (2001) argued that whereas historically ability was more-or-less randomly distributed among social classes, such ability might become highly concentrated within particular social "castes" if merit is narrowly defined. This may result in potential leaders, artists, scientists, scholars, or technicians being distanced from their various cultural and regional affiliations. Hartigan and Wigdor (1989) recognized alternate conceptions of fair play that characterize equality as more than fair competition, or alternatively, the absence of irrelevant barriers. Instead, they argued that equality may be fostered when individuals with "similar talents have similar life chances" and

> A much more radical interpretation of equal opportunity might call for equalizing the conditions of the development of talent throughout society so that all children enjoy the same material and cultural advantages. (p. 33)

To some, but not others, fairness requires a vision beyond that of competition as embodied by legal statutes of due process. The idea of unqualified individualism (Jensen, 1980), from this perspective, lacks the moral impetus for promoting social change.

2.1. The Fourteenth Amendment

Just after the Civil War, in 1868 the "Radical Republican" members of the 39th Congress intent on protecting newly emancipated African Americans, championed establishment of the 14th Amendment for insuring equal justice under the law. The relevant first section reads,

> All persons born or naturalized in the United States, and subject to the jurisdiction thereof, are citizens of the United States and of the State wherein they reside. No State shall make or enforce any law which shall abridge the privileges or immunities of citizens of the United States; nor shall any State deprive any person of life, liberty, or property, without due process of law; nor deny to any person within its jurisdiction the equal protection of the laws.

Congress, aware of potential resistance in ratifying the 14th Amendment, provided that both state congressional representation and tax allocations would be proportionally decreased according to the number of citizens (excluding Native Americans and, implicitly, women) denied the right to vote. Resistant state governments were eventually compelled to ratify the 14th Amendment, though tangible acceptance of the legal requirements was difficult and slow. This notion of *equal protection* (a close relative of *fair play*) became critical again in the 1950s, 1960s and 1970s for challenging segregation practices ranging from voting rights to school attendance to public accommodations to employment practices. According to Hartigan and Wigdor (1989), this amendment has been the major vehicle for developing substantive meaning for the concept of equality in our society.

Constitutional amendments, as noted above, were limited to infringements by state governments (and their subordinate entities, such as cities, counties, and school boards) and did not pertain to actions by nonstate and private sector entities. The next milestone in legal deliberations on the concept of fairness was the Civil Rights Act of 1964, which was intended

> To enforce the constitutional right to vote, to confer jurisdiction upon the district courts of the United States to provide injunctive relief against discrimination in public accommodations, to authorize the Attorney General to institute suits to protect constitutional rights in public facilities and public education, to extend the Commission on Civil Rights, to prevent discrimination in federally assisted programs, to establish a Commission on Equal Employment Opportunity, and for other purposes.

This law, which was the most significant civil rights legislation since reconstruction, went beyond Congressional enforcement of the 14th Amendment against discriminatory employment actions by state governments. Congress, using its power to regulate interstate commerce, prohibited discrimination based on "race, color, religion, sex or national origin" in public establishments. In the employment context, the Civil Rights Act (Title VI) is enforced by the

Equal Employment Opportunity Commission (EEOC). In the public schools context, the law (Title VI) is enforced by the Office of Civil Rights (OCR). Similarly, Title IX of the Education Amendments of 1972 (20 USC §§ 1681–1688), prohibits discrimination on the basis of sex in education programs and is enforced by the OCR. Most of these laws apply to programs and activities that receive federal financial assistance, while the 14th Amendment applies notwithstanding receipt of federal funding.

2.2. Adverse or Disparate Impact

Title VII of the Civil Rights Act of 1964 concerns discrimination in employment practices, and the Equal Employment Opportunity Commission (EEOC) was created to provide leadership and enforcement regarding Title VII. Section 703(a)(2) declares it unlawful

> to limit, segregate, or classify his employees or applicants for employment in any way which would deprive or tend to deprive any individual of employment opportunities or otherwise adversely affect his status as an employee, because of such individual's race, color, religion, sex, or national origin.

According to Hartigan and Wigdor (1989), the nascent EEOC in 1966 interpreted Title VII discrimination to consist of employment practices *intended* to discriminate or to treat people of protected status differently from others, but includes as well practices having a harmful affect on members of protected groups.

Title VII legitimates challenges to employment practices that adversely affect such groups—whether the outcome was intentional or not (*Griggs v. Duke Power Company*, 1971). *Adverse impact*, which is a measurable outcome related to the Title VII term "adversely affect," has come to denote the selected proportions of people from groups with protected status relative to the largest selection proportion. Yet Congress did not require employers to correct imbalances in their workforce that could not be demonstrated to result from discriminatory practices. In fact, Section 703(j) states specifically that no requirement exists for granting preferential treatment to any individual or group based on extant imbalance with regard to race, color, religion, sex, or national origin.

Adverse impact in employment decisions has been defined as a substantially different rate of selection that creates an imbalanced workforce with respect to a group with protected status. (Note that the phrase "disparate impact" is used in the Civil Rights Act of 1991, PL 102-166). In particular, the usual threshold for adverse impact is established if the selection rate for one group is less than 80% (known as the 4/5s rule) of that for the group with the highest selection rate (EEOC's Uniform Guidelines on Employee Selection Criteria). However, courts have not rigidly interpreted statistical criteria for demonstrating adverse impact, and adverse impact by itself is not a sufficient basis for establishing violation of equal protection. Practices that result in adverse impact are deemed unlawful only (a) if the practice cannot be demonstrated to be job-related and "consistent with business necessity" or (b) if an alternative employment practice with less disparate impact exists and the "respondent refuses to adopt such alternative employment practice." The demonstration of disparate impact establishes the grounds for legal challenge, that is, a *prima facie* argument, and the effect of Title VII was to place the burden of proof on employers in the context of adverse impact given a prima facie case (e.g., one demonstrating the 4/5s rule).

It is important to recognize that the applicability of this law was reduced in 2001 when the Supreme Court ruled in *Alexander v. Sandoval* (2001) that disparate impact arguments could not be brought to federal courts by individual citizens, as had been the case for the previous 35 years. This has effectively rendered disparate impact viable only in the context of OCR administrative enforcement actions (Welner, 2001), and this opinion may reduce the number of venues in which psychometric evidence of disparate impact is salient. It has, nonetheless, no bearing on professional standards for fairness (reviewed in section 3.2). Rather, this course of events serves to illustrate that legal standards and professional responsibilities for ensuring fairness are not necessarily commensurate.

2.3. Individuals Versus Groups

Titles VI and VII represented a dramatic and controversial move beyond the 14th Amendment. As recognized by Hartigan and Wigdor (1989),

> A persistent anomaly in federal civil rights policy has been the adherence, on one hand, to the principle that the Constitution and Title VII protect the rights of *individuals*, and the adoption, on the other, of a definition of discrimination that looks to the effects of employment procedures on *groups*. (pp. 39–40)

Title VII was intended to protect individuals rather than groups, but requires evidence based on the classification of individuals into protected groups. One resulting irony is that discrimination might be demonstrable statistically at the group level, but not in the case of any particular individual. Under Title VII, which is a statutory law, "group" evidence is admissible even though the very same evidence would not be admissible under constitutional law. Thus, statutory law modified the original notion of individual due process in the 14th Amendment: for some purposes, a person on the playing field could now be classified, rather than evaluated individually.

As of 1997, the federal government recognized a number of official group classifications for federal reporting purposes:

2.3.1. Designation of Race

In October 1997, the Office of Management and Budget (OMB) released new categories for collecting data on race and ethnicity (OMB, 1997). The new racial categories (see Table 7.1) established were White; Black or African American; Asian; Native Hawaiian or Other Pacific Islander; and American Indian or Alaska Native. In contrast to *racial* categories, several *ethnic* categories were designated. For designating ethnicity, the OMB categories are Hispanic or Latino and Not Hispanic or Latino. While OMB did not

TABLE 7.1 OMB Guidelines for Federal Reporting on Race and Ethnicity

RACE OR ETHNICITY	DESCRIPTION
American Indian or Alaska Native	A person having origins in any of the original peoples of North and South America (including Central America), and who maintains tribal affiliation or community attachment.
Asian	A person having origins in any of the original peoples of the Far East, Southeast Asia, or the Indian subcontinent including, for example, Cambodia, China, India, Japan, Korea, Malaysia, Pakistan, the Philippine Islands, Thailand, and Vietnam.
Black or African American	A person having origins in any of the black racial groups of Africa. Terms such as "Haitian" or "Negro" can be used in addition to "Black or African American."
Hispanic or Latino	A person of Cuban, Mexican, Puerto Rican, Cuban, South or Central American, or other Spanish culture or origin, regardless of race. The term, "Spanish origin," can be used in addition to "Hispanic or Latino."
Native Hawaiian or Other Pacific Islander	A person having origins in any of the original peoples of Hawaii, Guam, Samoa, or other Pacific Islands.
White	A person having origins in any of the original peoples of Europe, the Middle East, or North Africa.

Source: See OMB, 1997.

offer a "multiracial" category, it allowed that individuals could select one or more races—recognizing that designations of race are becoming more complex and nuanced.

2.3.2. Designation of Ethnicity

One general definition is that an ethnicity is a group of people who see themselves as sharing one or more of the following: language, race, place of origin, values, and history. Members of such a grouping might also differentiate themselves from other groups based on these characteristics. A shorter definition of an ethnicity is a group that shares or is perceived to share a culture. In this sense, "culture" broadly defined is a common heritage or set of beliefs, norms, meanings, and values. A variety of ways exists to define a cultural grouping (e.g., by ethnicity, religion, geographic region, age group, sexual orientation, or profession), and many people consider themselves as having multiple cultural identities. Increasingly, self-identification appears to be driven by factors other than the traditional concept of race.

According to the U.S. Census, there are many distinct ethnicities, and examples may be more useful than definitions in conveying the meaning. Hispanic American (Latino) is an ethnicity according to OMB and may apply to a person of any race, and many people from Caribbean nations identify their ethnicity as Hispanic or Latino and their race as African American. Within the broad category of "Asian Americans and Pacific Islanders," there are 43 ethnic groups speaking over 100 languages and dialects. For "American Indians and Alaska Natives," the Bureau of Indian Affairs currently recognizes 561 tribes.

2.3.3. Other Federal Categories

According to Evinger (1995), the OMB categories were developed largely for collecting data from groups in the United States that have historically suffered discrimination and adverse treatment. Rather than implying a static racial classification, categories are assumed to exist relative to disparate experience.

Under Federal OMB reporting requirements (OMB, 1997), neither gender nor limited English proficiency (LEP) is an official designation. Other laws and regulations (e.g., No Child Left Behind, PL 107-110) require desegregation of data by categories such as grade or gender. The term "protected group" can apply to all of the official designations, and may incorporate other groups established on the bases of equity concerns. For example, an analysis of fairness could designate a protected group as children from highly mobile families, children with special education needs, or even students who are frequently absent.

3. THE STANDARDS FOR TEST FAIRNESS

The 1999 *Standards for Educational and Psychological Testing* (*Standards* for short) followed two previous editions in 1974 and 1985. Revision of the 1985 *Standards* was undertaken by a joint committee of the American Educational Research Association, American Psychological, and National Council for Measurement in Education, and was the first edition to contain explicitly a chapter on test fairness. Comments on draft versions of the 1999 S*tandards* were received from 72 organizations including professional societies, credentialing boards, government agencies, test developers, and academic institutions. As noted in the *Standards*, its purpose is to provide criteria for the evaluation of tests, testing practices, and the effects of test use, where the term *test* here is used to specify a broad range of standardized assessments including particular tests, scales, inventories, and instruments. The term *standardized* here refers not to multiple-choice items, as many misunderstand, but to conditions of test administration that are equivalent for all examinees.

The 1999 *Standards* is a document that reflects a commitment by measurement professionals to address social as well as technical concerns of fairness. This document reflects a broad, rather than a narrow vision:

A full consideration of fairness would explore the many functions of testing in relation to its many goals, including the broad goal of achieving equality of opportunity in our society. It would consider the technical properties of tests, the ways test results are reported, and the factors that are validly or erroneously thought to account for patterns of test performance for *groups and individuals.* [emphasis added] (p. 73)

Tests designed properly and used fairly can facilitate positive educational, social, and economic goals. However, tests are only one source of evidence for informing decisions. For example, in merit-based selections, tests scores are known to correlate modestly with criterion measures of success (e.g., first-year college GPA), and the measurement community has cautioned that test scores are inadequate as a surrogate for merit (Wightman, 2003).

3.1. Relevant Definitions

Prior to considering fairness issues, a number of terms are introduced below including: fairness, statistical bias, disparate impact, fairness, differential item functioning, and test bias. Whereas most of these terms have relatively specific meanings, the term fairness has a much broader usage:

> *Fairness* in testing refers to perspectives on the ways that scores from tests or items are interpreted in the process of evaluating test takers for a selection or classification decision. Fairness in testing is closely related to test validity, and the evaluation of fairness requires a broad range of evidence that includes empirical data, but may also involve legal, ethical, political, philosophical, and economic reasoning.

As noted in the 1999 *Standards*, fairness "is subject to different definitions and interpretations in different social and political circumstances" (p. 80). There are different ways to describe fairness in the context of predictive models for selection (section 5.2), but there are also different ways to conceptualize fairness *per se*.

Given the ubiquity of "groups" in establishing fairness, several definitions are required for the situation in which two groups are compared. Following Holland and Thayer (1988, p. 130),

> The performance of two groups may be compared in terms of a test item, a total test score, or a prediction regarding success on a criterion. The *focal* group (or group F), which is sometimes called the *protected* group, is of primary interest. This group is to be compared to a second group, labeled the *reference* or *base* group (or group R). The previous terminology of minority and majority groups is no longer used.

In typical fairness analysis, the first step is to define groups and then to compute differences between groups R and F in terms of percent selected (say for a job or college position), or average scores on an item or on a test. The obtained difference is described with the label disparate impact:

> In legal analysis, *disparate impact* describes group differences in test performance that result in different group proportions of candidates identified for selection or placement. In studies of test fairness, the term *impact* has been borrowed, and is used to describe the observed difference between the average scores for two groups on a particular test or test item.

Once group differences are estimated, the important task is to distinguish a genuine group difference in proficiency from one that arises from a distorted measurement process. An observed difference (i.e., impact) does not necessarily imply measurement bias.

Disparate impact, to give a simple example, can be thought of as the difference in average running speeds over a fixed distance for two groups using an accurate stopwatch. This difference signals that one group on average is faster than the other. In contrast, statistical bias arises when two groups (R and F) are in reality highly similar in average running time, but stopwatch A for group R is accurate, while the stopwatch B for group F is inaccurate. In the latter case, the running speeds for individuals in group F will be "biased." If it is further established that stopwatch B runs too fast for group F, then the timing information provided by the stopwatch B is *unfair* in the sense that group F is disadvantaged. If stopwatch B runs too slowly, the timing information is *unfair* in the sense that group F is advantaged. In any event, the rankings of runners *within* two groups may be accurate, but comparisons between the best runners from each group and comparisons between group averages would be confounded with the inaccuracy of stopwatch B.

In this chapter, two terms are distinguished that are often used interchangeably elsewhere: fair and unbiased. I use the term *bias* synonymously with the phrase *statistical bias*, except as noted. Specifically,

> *Statistical bias* refers to the under- or over-estimation of one or more parameters in two kinds of statistical models—
>
> 1. In the field of measurement, parameters generally describe properties of examinees or items. Examinee parameters are referred to as person parameters or proficiencies. Item parameters come in three varieties: difficulty, discrimination, and pseudo-guessing.
> 2. In predictive models, parameters describe the intercepts and slopes of regression equations as well as the error variance.

The word bias in this context is reserved for a purely formal concept. This may seem overly technical, but it is better to consider bias as a measurement anomaly, and then to consider fairness in terms of who is advantaged or disadvantaged by the anomaly. Broadly speaking, statistical bias can be thought of as a systematic difference between two parameters that should be equal. Though all estimates embody some level of *random error*, bias is a kind of *systematic error*.

Disparate impact implies neither statistical bias nor unfairness. Differential group performance may be attributable to *bona fide* differences between groups in terms of the test construct. Test fairness does not imply equal outcomes. The purpose of a fairness investigation is to sort out whether the reasons for group differences are due to factors beyond the scope of the test (such as opportunity to learn) or artifactual. For example, immigrant children often score lower than indigenous students do on math items requiring more proficiency in the dominant language. The conclusion that the gap in performance on such an item signified bias would be warranted only if it could be demonstrated that immigrant children and indigenous children of *comparable mathematics proficiency* performed differentially on the item). This leads directly to the definition of statistical bias with respect to item performance:

> *Differential item functioning* or DIF, for short, is said to occur when examinees from groups R and F have the same degree of proficiency in a certain domain, but difference rates of success on an item. The DIF may be related to group differences in knowledge of or experience with some other topic beside the one of interest.

An item that does not show DIF has equivalent measurement properties for groups R and F, or, alternatively, the item is *measurement invariant*. In contrast, DIF occurs when an item's difficulty parameter is different for groups of comparable proficiency. Note that the definition above is also an attempt to shed light on why DIF occurs, a topic is given more attention in section 4, and sections 6 through 9.

The last definition is for the situation in which examinees are selected with a qualifying examination, and the qualifying score is used to make a prediction regarding the candidates' likelihood of success on a criterion. For example, LSAT (Law School Admission Test) is used to predict first year grade point average (GPA) in law school. Then, as Cleary (1968, p. 115) suggested,

> *Test bias* occurs for members of a subgroup of the population if, in the prediction of a criterion for which the test was designed, consistent nonzero errors of prediction are made for members of the subgroup. In other words, the test is biased if the criterion score predicted from the common regression line is consistently too high or too low for members of the subgroup. With this definition of bias, there may be a connotation of "unfair," particularly if the test produces a prediction that is too low. If the test is used for selection, members of a subgroup may be rejected when they were capable of adequate performance.

Parallel to DIF, test bias is also referred to as *differential prediction of a criterion*, or simply differential prediction. Though this definition is widely accepted among psychologists, the term "test bias" is often less descriptive of fairness concerns than the term "selection bias," a point addressed in more detail below. Differential prediction results from bias in measurement or regression parameters; for example, a regression prediction might be two high or too low if the intercepts or slopes of two groups differ and a common regression equation is used. This topic is more fully explored in sections 4 and 5.

3.2. Test Fairness Standards

In this section, an overview is provided of the twelve criteria pertaining to fairness given in the 1999 *Standards for Educational and Psychological Testing*. These appear in Table 7.2.

We note that of the twelve criteria, nine refer to groups or subgroups and three to individuals or aspects of individuals. Along a second dimension, six standards refer to interpretation, reporting, or use of test scores; three to *differential measurement or prediction*; and three to equity or sensitivity. Recall that differential measurement and differential prediction are consistent with the statistician's use of the term *bias*.

The standards regarding test fairness are classified in Table 7.3 according to this heuristic scheme. Standard 7.1 appears in two cells because it is concerned with interpretation and use if differential measurement is detected. Hard-to-classify standards include 7.10 because it is concerned with responsibility for collecting evidence of construct representation in the presence of group differences, and 7.7 because it concerns language, but not different language groups. Standard 7.3 covers *differential item functioning*, and Standard 7.6 covers *differential prediction*. These two aspects of statistical bias are considered in separate sections below. The upper middle cell in Table 7.3 contains standards regarding score interpretation and used, and appropriate limitations on test score use when statistical bias is observed.

Individual fairness requires standardized conditions of testing in which students are treated comparably. This type of fairness is denoted as *equity* (as in Standard 7.12). Standards 7.5 and 7.7 are variations on this theme with respect to language (or reading) and score interpretation. Denotation of group membership is neither required nor implied. The other standards explicitly appeal to group membership—but are not limited to OMB categories (see section 2.3). Evidence can be collected for alternative group definitions, depending on logical assessments of potential adverse or disparate impact. In addition to race and ethnicity, groups (depending on one's purpose) may be identified by social class, age, regions, urbanicity, and so forth.

If a test item is equitable, it is presented to individuals under impartial conditions, meaning that no student is favored over another in answering the item. If a test item is fair, it is (a) invariant across groups with respect to measurement and prediction *and* (b) equivalent across groups with respect to presentation, interpretation, reporting at the item level, and summative or formative use. For both test scores and test item responses, an additional concern regards racial, cultural, and ethnic sensitivity. Testing conditions and test content should avoid stereotyping, culturally offensive material, and other negative implications. Sensitivity problems may lead to statistical bias and thus faulty interpretation of test scores, but they can also be damaging or hurtful to individuals taking tests. The process of screening items in this regard is called *sensitivity review* (see section 10).

3.3. Test Validity and Social Constructions

The 1999 *Standards* stress that validity is addressed by collecting a variety of evidence. Likewise, claims that a test is fair must be supported with evidence. In addition to the general principles of validity and reliability, this requires evidence that the conditions of testing are equitable, and that scores on a test have the same meaning for different groups of examinees. An additional category of evidence concerns the consequences of testing, yet in this regard,

TABLE 7.2 Fairness Standards from the 1999 *Standards for Educational and Psychological Testing*

7.1	When credible research reports that test scores differ in meaning across examinees subgroups for the type of test in question, then to the extent feasible, the same forms of validity evidence collected for the examinee population as a whole should also be collected for each relevant subgroup. Subgroups may be found to differ with respect to appropriateness of test content, internal structure of test responses, the relation of test scores to other variables, or the response processes employed by individual examinees. Any such findings should receive due consideration in the interpretation and use of scores as well as in subsequent test revisions.
7.2	When credible research reports differences in the effects of construct-irrelevant variance across subgroups of test takers on performance on some part of the test, the test should be used if at all only for those subgroups for which evidence indicates that valid inferences can be drawn from the test scores.
7.3	When credible research reports differential item functioning exists across age, gender, racial/ethnic, cultural, disability, and/or linguistic groups in the population of test takers in the content domain measured by the test, the test developers should conduct appropriate studies when feasible. Such research should seek to direct and eliminate aspects of test design, content, and format that might bias test scores for particular groups.
7.4	Test developers should strive to identify and eliminate language, symbols, words, phrases, and content that are generally regarded as offensive by members of racial, ethnic, gender, or other groups, except when judged to be necessary for adequate representation of the construct.
7.5	In testing situations involving individualized interpretations of test scores other than selection, a test taker's score should not be accepted as a reflection of standing on the characteristic being assessed without consideration of alternative explanations for the test takers performance on that test at that time.
7.6	When empirical studies of differential prediction of a criterion for members of different subgroups are conducted, they should include regression equations (or an appropriate equivalent) computed separately for each group or treatment under consideration or an analysis in which the group or treatment variables are entered as moderator variables.
7.7	In testing applications where the level of linguistic or reading ability is not part of the construct of interest, the linguistic or reading demands of the test should be kept to the minimum necessary for the valid assessment of the intended construct.
7.8	When score are disaggregated and publicly reported for groups identified by characteristics such as gender, ethnicity, age, language proficiency, or disability, cautionary statements should be included whenever credible research reports that test scores may not have comparable meaning across these different groups.
7.9	When tests or assessments are proposed for use as instruments of social, educational, or public policy, test developers or uses should proposing the test should fully and accurately inform policymakers of the characteristics of the tests as well as any relevant and credible information that may be available concerning the likely consequences of test use.
7.10	When the use of a test results in outcomes that affect the life chances or educational opportunities of examinees, evidence of mean test scores difference between relevant subgroups of examinees should, where feasible, be examined for subgroups for which credible research reports mean difference for similar tests. Where mean differences are found, an investigation should be undertaken to determine that such differences are not attributable to a source of construct misrepresentation of construct-irrelevant variance. While initially the responsibility of the test developer, the test users bears the responsibility for uses with groups other than those specified by the test developer.
7.11	When a construct can be measured in different ways that are approximately equal, in their degree of construct representation and freedom for construct-irrelevant variance, evidence of mean score difference across relevant subgroups of examinees should be considered in deciding which test to use.
7.12	The testing or assessment process should be carried out so that test takers receive comparable and equitable treatment during all phases of the testing or assessment process.

there is currently no consensus on evidentiary requirements among measurement professionals. Both validity and reliability are considered in more detail in Chapters 2 and 3. Below, a brief treatment of construct definition and testing consequences serves as a backdrop for understanding how the choice of test construct and interpretation of test scores interact with fairness issues.

3.3.1. Construct Definition and Terminology

Test development begins with specifying a *construct*, which can be defined as "the concept or characteristic that a test is designed to measure" (American Educational Research Association, American Psychological Association,

TABLE 7.3 Classification of Fairness Standards

CATEGORY	GROUPS	INDIVIDUALS
Interpretation/use	7.1, 7.2, 7.8, 7.9 (system) 7.10 (evidence), 7.11	7.5
Statistical bias	7.1, 7.3, 7.6	7.7 (language)
Sensitivity	7.4	7.12

& National Council on Measurement in Education, 1999). The notion of construct validity is then derived as the degree to which interpretations of scores on a given test are consistent with the construct. How does one frame the question about what a test measures? This is more complicated than it might seem because typically two different kinds of interpretations are involved. First, extrapolations might be made beyond the particular test items occurring on (say) a mathematics test. Test users seek to know something about a person's competence relative to the domain of all relevant test questions, and the definition of this domain partly identifies the test construct. Second, inferences may be made beyond the item domain to a broader set of desirable mathematical *behaviors*; for example, students who score high on the test should be able to solve job-related problems using statistics and probability, to solve novel problems, to use math to model real-world phenomena, and so forth. The preponderance of the latter behaviors is external to any test, and consequently there is no failsafe method for identifying the most pertinent of these for anchoring inferences. Interpretive preferences are intuitively linked to expectations about what would be the case with students who receive various levels of scores on such a test.

The terminology for denoting constructs in educational testing has fluctuated over the last century. With the advent of intelligence testing, the belief that IQ was a stable characteristic of an individual that was independent of the environment led to the use of synonyms such as ability, aptitude, cognitive ability, mental ability, learning ability, and the ubiquitous "trait." Typically, schools and organization concerned with learning distinguish intelligence and aptitude from achievement. Synonyms for achievement as defined by a construct can include skill, proficiency, attainment, competence or competency, and knowledge. The more nuanced term "developed ability" has been used to acknowledge that abilities are developed by instructional and social practices in the same way that language proficiency is developed. In this sense, the meaning of "ability" is similar to that of "problem-solving proficiency." Not all synonyms work equally well in a given context. Conversely, the distinction between "traits" and "proficiencies" is important from both semantic and social perspectives because the term "proficiency" is often more appropriate for describing learning outcomes. If achievement is being measured, then a score is less aptly described as an ability or aptitude. Since a test can only demonstrate a person's concurrent state, using labels that imply immutability, or even long-term stability, can be dangerous.

3.3.2. Consequences of Testing

Supportable interpretations of tests depend on, but are not limited to, construct definition. One can think of the construct as a nexus of propositions: a student with a higher score on the test will on average do better on homework assignments; lower scores imply disruptions in the learning process that can be identified; higher scores indicate higher levels of initial preparation; reading problems portend problems in mathematics; and so on. These propositions can be used to generate testable hypotheses for the purpose of supporting or disconfirming the validity of test score interpretation.

Yet it is important to distinguish construct-relevant from construct irrelevant variance. If, for example, a great deal of baseball questions on a test of mathematical operations would discourage baseball nonenthusiasts from their best effort, then the consequences of such item content would distort the interpretation of test scores because they would partly reflect enthusiasm (construct-irrelevant variance) for baseball as well as mathematical operations. Similarly, scores from a very long test would partly reflect endurance or test-taking speed. Such extraneous influences may adversely affect the interpretations of test performance. Messick (1994) summarized,

> it is not that adverse social consequences of test use render the use invalid but, rather, that adverse social consequences should not be attributable to any source of test invalidity such as construct under-representation or construct irrelevant variance. (p. 8)

Still other types of hypotheses fall farther outside the original bundle of construct-related propositions. For example, if a student receives inadequate instruction, and as a result, does not pass a test, an accurate conclusion would be that the student does not know the material. Without additional evidence, other interpretations are unsupportable: the student failed to learn; the student was unmotivated; or the student lacked the requisite aptitude. All of the latter are characterized by at least one causal attribution external to and independent of the test construct.

Suppose a testing program is claimed to be successful in promoting achievement. The problem here is that attributing causality to the test itself ("The test increases student achievement") enlarges the construct. Such claims may require serious consideration because there may not be a single perspective for defining a test construct. The previous paragraph implicitly assumed the existence of an indisputable or privileged position for delimiting the appropriate bundle of construct-relevant propositions. Yet authority for determining what is within and outside the realm of the construct is often a shared responsibility, one that requires debate if not consensus. A one-dimensional perspective of "construct-irrelevant" variance falsely suggests a sharp dichotomy between the responsibilities of those who develop or understand assessment theory, and those who use or make practical interpretations of test scores.

4. STRUCTURAL ANALYSIS OF BIAS

Statistical bias and test fairness are usually assessed by comparing item or test performance in different identifiable groups. The use of "groups" is a statistical device, used because potential bias is uncovered by aggregating evidence across test takers within such groups. The mathematical models below acknowledge that there may be individual differences within each group, but also that there may be a component of item or test variance due to group membership *per se*.

In this section, heuristic models are presented for describing statistical bias. For thrift, it is the convention herein to refer to statistical bias simply as bias, which can be assessed logically in two distinct ways. First, there may be a question *internal* to the test "Is this item measuring the same thing for two groups relative to the other items?" Secondly, a question might involve a relationship *external* to the test "Is this item (or test) measuring the same thing for two groups relative to an independent criterion?" This independent or external criterion is often a test of criterion performance in the context of use, or another test thought to be fair—at least fairer than the test being studied. These topics are given a theoretical treatment in this section, and a more general treatment in sections 5 (external analysis) and 6 (internal analysis).

Measurement models are mathematical equations that describe components of test scores. The most common measurement model can be expressed as

$$u_{pi} = t_p + \varepsilon_{pi}. \qquad (1)$$

This equation expresses the idea that an observed measurement u for person p on item i is composed of a *true score* t_{pi} (see the reliability chapter), and an error component ε_{pi} that describes an effect due to a particular combination of person and item. Equation (1) is a theoretical notion of measurement because in actuality only the variable u_{pi} is known, where u in this case represents a scored item response.

4.1. Differential Item Functioning (DIF)

While Equation 1 provides a conceptual basis for measurement, an elaboration is necessary for modeling differential group measurement:

$$z_{gpi} = \alpha_{gi}\theta_{gp} - \delta_{gi} + \varepsilon_{gpi}. \qquad (2)$$

Here, z_{gpi} signifies the propensity of a person p from group g to answer item i correctly, and θ_{gp} is a latent proficiency as defined in item response theory. This expression includes an intercept δ_{gi} representing item difficulty (higher values indicate higher difficulty), a discrimination coefficient α_{gi}, and measurement error ε_{gpi}, where the subscript g indicates that a coefficient can differ for two groups (R and F). Bias in item difficulty is then expressed as $\delta_{ri} \neq \delta_{fi}$, while bias in item discrimination is obtained as $\alpha_{ri} \neq \alpha_{fi}$.

Assumptions of linearity and additivity above are made to facilitate conceptual understanding. In practice, the non-linear expression

$$P(u_{gpi}=1) = \frac{\exp(\alpha_{gi}\theta_{gp} - \delta_{gi})}{1 + \exp(\alpha_{gi}\theta_{gp} - \delta_{gi})} \qquad (3)$$

based on item response theory (IRT) is more common. Here, $P(u_{gpi} = 1)$ is the probability of a correct response on a dichotomous item, and the expected value of z_{gpi} in Equation 2 is defined by the logit link function

$$E[z_{gpi}] = \ln\left(\frac{P(u_{gpi}=1)}{1 - P(u_{gpi}=1)}\right). \qquad (4)$$

When $\delta_{ri} \neq \delta_{fi}$ or $\alpha_{ri} \neq \alpha_{fi}$ is the case, the item is said to function differently for two groups, or, alternatively, to show DIF. Because DIF is based solely on the item scores and group indicators, this is an internal (to the test) analysis of bias.

4.2. Differential Prediction

In some applications, the goal is to use a test score to predict a criterion of interest, such as using an evaluation of student teaching experience to predict supervisory ratings of first-year teaching performance. The measurement model in Equation 1 omits reference to such an *external* variable (i.e., actual teaching performance), and this situation can be addressed by designating a target variable or *criterion* (say y). This choice may depend on a number of reasons, and more than one plausible criterion might exist. Given an explicit choice, predictive bias can be defined, parallel to Equation 2, in terms of

$$y_{gp} = a_g x_{gp} + d_g + e_{gp}, \qquad (5)$$

where x_{gp} is a total score on the predictors test (commonly the sum of scored item responses).

The term a_g in this equation denotes the slope of the regression model, and d_g is the model intercept. Parallel to bias in item parameters, two types of bias also exist in this situation. If the term a_g (or d_g) is not equal for two groups, the bias is present in the model in terms of slopes (or intercepts). Because this approach requires a criterion measurement y independent of the test in question, it is an external analysis of bias.

4.3. Integrated Structural Diagram

In Figure 7.1, a diagram for statistical bias is given for a scenario consisting of a hypothetical five-item test in which three variables can affect item performance. Two of these are proficiency scores, θ and η, where θ is the intended or target construct and η is a secondary factor. The third, G, is a dichotomous group indicator (R or F), which is correlated with θ and η (depicted by bidirectional arrows). The arrow directly from G to item 2 (u_2) represents DIF in an item that is affected by group membership beyond the two proficiencies that contribute to item performance. Item u_5 also may exhibit DIF because is it affected by G indirectly through the secondary factor η (G $\leftrightarrow$ η $\to$ u_5). Simply put, DIF can occur when factors other than target proficiency affect item performance, either directly or indirectly.

Figure 7.1 also contains a scenario containing a criterion y and a predictor variable x, where x is obtained as the simple sum of the scored item responses—indicated by the fixed "1s" on the paths from each u_i to x. Assuming the latent proficiencies, θ and η, would be the ideal predictors of y, but that only x is available, the central question concerns the behavior of the common regression prediction

$$\hat{y} = b_0 + b_1 G + b_2 x. \qquad (6)$$

Because G does not contribute to the prediction of y_1 or y_2, unbiased regression coefficients are obtained with θ and η. It can be shown in this case mathematically that using the observed score x as a proxy for latent proficiency results in

FIGURE 7.1 A Structural Model Illustration with Five Items for Depicting Item and Test Bias

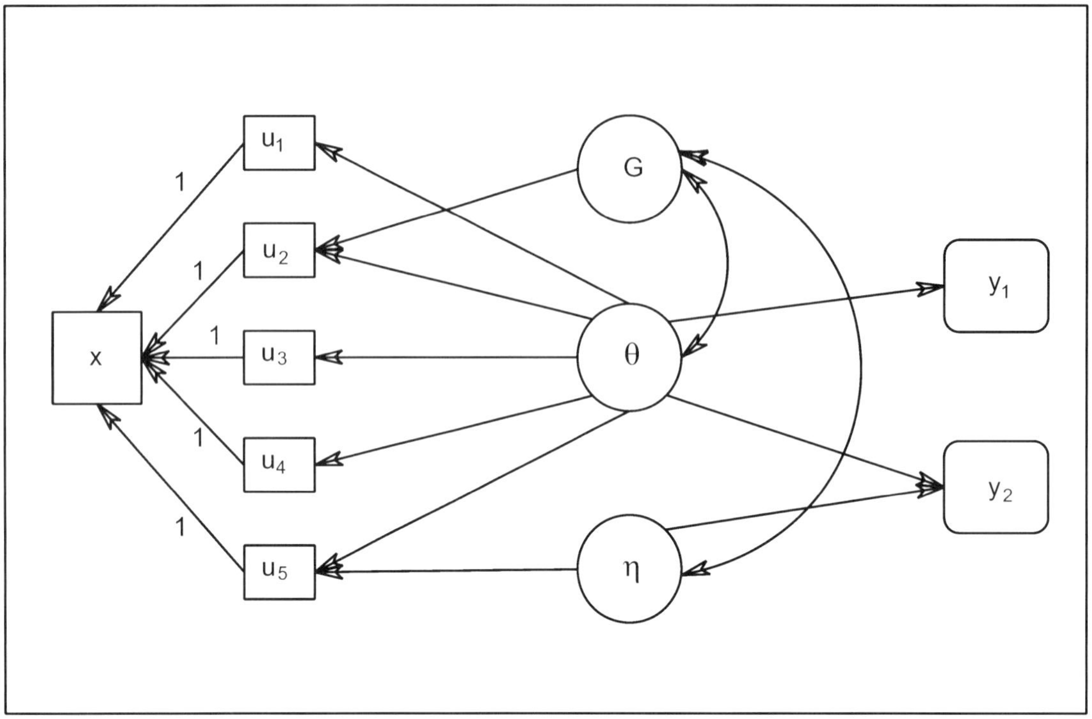

Note: Error terms are not shown. Directional arrows represent causal effects; bidirectional arrows represent co-variances.

$b_1 \neq 0$, due to DIF in u_2 and u_5. Thus, the presence of DIF in this heuristic diagram results in differential prediction, but there are two important qualifications to this statement. First, the structural model could be modified to add a direct path from G to y_1 or y_2, and this would create a scenario in which both measurement bias and predictive bias simultaneously exist. This signifies that predictive bias is not necessarily caused by DIF. Second, the secondary factor η may be relevant to the predicted outcome as in y_2. If this is the case, predictive bias due to DIF is diminished because η validly contributes to both u_5 and the criterion measurement.

In this conceptual approach, statistical bias occurs as a function of G. Bias in the sense of either differential measurement or prediction is not a property of the test *per se*, but rather a property of test use with the particular examinee populations constituting G.

5. EXTERNAL EVIDENCE OF BIAS

External bias detection requires a construct by which a person or student can be deemed successful in a given activity, and is often motivated by the need to make distinctions among examinees *before* they engage in the activity in question. The idea is to *select* examinees using their scores on the *predictor* variable. In Figure 7.2, an example of an unbiased test/criterion regression is illustrated. Following the conventions above, the two groups are labeled R and F. Despite the difference in group distributions on the predictor, the test has equal predictive validity for two groups—they share the same regression line. For any given

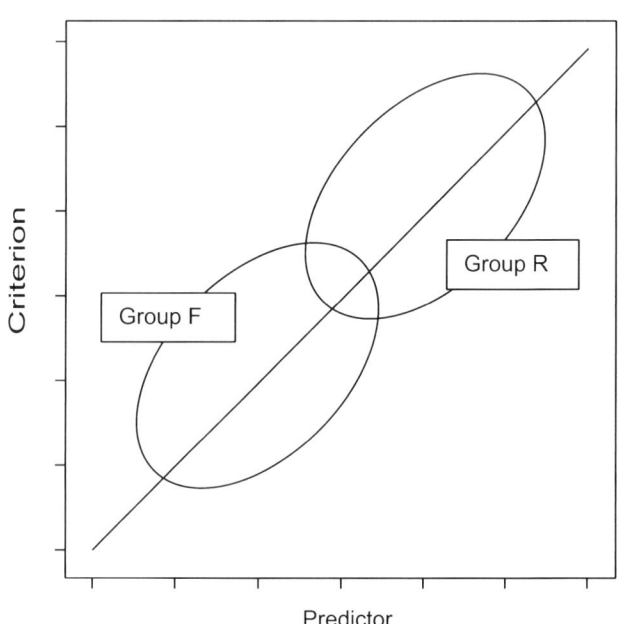

FIGURE 7.2 Depiction of Unbiased Prediction for Two Groups R and F

test score, individuals have the same expected criterion performance, regardless of group membership. Figure 7.3 provides an example of a criterion-predictor relationship that differs for two groups are equal on the criterion but vastly different on the predictor.

FIGURE 7.3 Depiction of Biased Prediction for Two Groups R and F

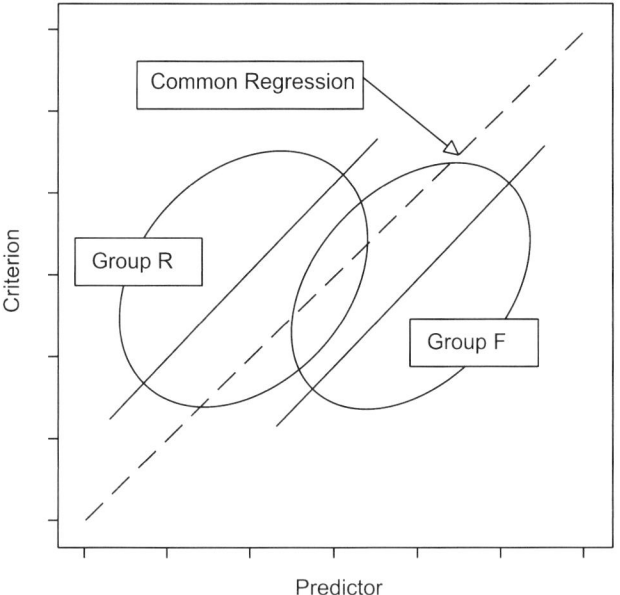

Note: Solid lines are individual group regressions. The dotted line represents the common regression line.

In the latter case, the test differentially predicts the chosen criterion *performance* because there are two different regression lines. Although the regression slopes are the same for both groups, the regression line for the group R has a higher intercept. If a common regression line (dotted line) were used to select candidates for college or a job, the test would lead to overprediction of performance for candidates from group F leading to biased selection. Though the phrase *test bias* is often used to describe this situation, the phrase *differential prediction* more accurately conveys the meaning, and the term *fairness* is bound to a particular use of a test in selecting candidates. It is the selection procedure that is described as fair or unfair, not the test itself.

5.1. Selection Definitions

A number of technical definitions and conventions are commonly used in the analysis of selection procedures, and these are provided in Table 7.4. These terms are used extensively in the following section, and are presented here for easy reference.

A number of potential selection models exist, each having different definitions for and implications about the fairness of the selection process. The conceptual issue these models address differently is that even with unbiased prediction, two candidates from different groups *who could perform equally well on the criterion* may not have the same probability of being selected (Thorndike, 1971). In Figure 7.4, an illustration of selection is given for an unbiased test. One set of candidates has a higher value of the predictor (X_H), and one has a lower value (X_L). If there are many candidates at each score level, a normal distribution can be used to describe the range of scores (on the vertical dimension of the graph) *within* the classes obtaining scores of X_H and X_L. These conditional distributions arise because the criterion is predicted with error.

Now suppose a score X_S is chosen on the X-axis as a cut point for selection, and only examinees with scores equal to or greater than X_S are chosen. The score Y_S denotes the criterion score of an individual that fell precisely at the predictor cut score. Upon examining the distribution of Y for X_H and X_L, an irony of the selection model is evident: some candidates at X_L score higher than Y_S and some candidates at X_H score lower than Y_S. In Figure 7.4, the shaded area above Y_S for candidates at X_L represents the probability of success (false negatives), while the shaded area for candidates at X_H represents the probability of failure (false positives). Given a less-than-perfect correlation between predictor and criterion, any reasonable cut point would result in some selected candidates being less successful than some rejected candidates would have been. As the correlation between predictor and criterion decreases, the problem is that false negative errors occur at a higher rate for the lower-scoring group. Though the test treats *individuals*

TABLE 7.4 Selection Terminology. The Numbers Falling Into Each Quadrant Are Given by A, B, C, and D as Shown in Figure 7.7, Where N = A + B + C + D

Term	Definition	Statistic
Predictor cut score	Select if $X > X_S$	X_S
Criterion cut score	Success if $Y > Y_S$	Y_S
	Number of cases selected	A + B
	Number of cases rejected	C + D
	Number of successful cases	A + C
	Number of unsuccessful cases	B + D
Base rate	proportion of cases deemed "successful" on criterion	(A + D) / N
Selection ratio	proportion of cases selected	(A + B) / N
Success ratio	proportion of selected cases that "succeed" on criterion	A / (A + B)
False positive error	a case predicted to succeed on criterion, but does not	(any case in quadrant B)
False negative error	a case predicted not to succeed on criterion, but does	(any case in quadrant D)

FIGURE 7.4 Unbiased Regression Showing Probabilities of Success at X_L and Failure at X_H

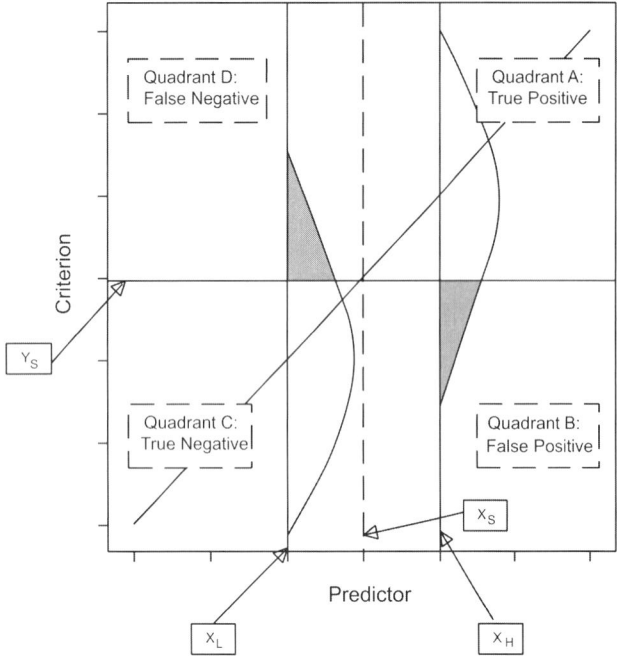

equivalently, regardless of group membership, lower-scoring *groups* bear the burden of the test's fallibility.

Being successful (as in college) is not a lucky happenstance, but depends on effort and achievement. Thus, it is a matter of concern that some rejected candidates would have been successful if they had the opportunity, and this concern leads to two central issues in the analysis of test fairness. First, the choice of criterion construct is of paramount importance. In situations with low or modest correlations of predictor to criterion, the construct of the selection test and errors of measurement drive the selection process more than the construct defining the criterion. The predictor may fail to take into account the genuine factors that lead to success such as motivation, study habits, academic support, and so forth. Second, an elite group would be selected in the case of low predictor correlation, but such elite status would be weakly related to success as defined by the criterion.

Wightman (2003) illustrated the first point with respect to the LSAT:

> The most compelling aspect of the bar admission data is that between 88 and 72 percent of minority law school students who would have been denied opportunity to enter law school under a numbers-only admission model were able to successfully pass the bar and enter the profession. Similar studies in other educational settings should be undertaken to help put the impact of selection based disproportionately on test score results into perspective. (p. 20)

Similarly, Chung-Yan and Cronshaw (2002) found that cognitive ability tests used in employment decisions typically showed a one standard deviation (SD) difference for whites and African Americans. The difference on actual job performance measures shrank to 1/3 SD; and when objective tests were used, rather than subjective rating criteria, the difference shrank to 1/10 SD. Therefore, even if the test measures a competence equally well for two groups in a particular selection process, it cannot be said *unambiguously* that the test use system is fair: two individuals from different groups, with equally likely probabilities of success, may have unequal probabilities of selection. The selection process is fair relative to the predictor, but not (retrospectively) in terms of performance. On the other hand, being fair to a group creates a mechanism in which some individuals with lower scores on the predictor will be chosen over others with higher scores.

5.2. Selection Models

The most widely recognized selection models are briefly reviewed below. These models can be conceptualized in terms of the selection model shown in Figure 7.4 and definitions given in Table 7.4. Additional references for this material can be found in the special spring 1976 issue of the *Journal of Educational Measurement*, Jensen (1980), and Schmidt and Hunter (1998).

5.2.1. Regression Model

In this model, cases having highest predicted criterion scores are selected, regardless of group membership. If groups have different regressions, then these separate regressions are used to make the predictions. This model maximizes the mean criterion score of selected cases relative to other selection models. A probabilistic model called the *equal risk model* (Einhorn & Bass, 1971) bears a strong conceptual similarity to the regression model.

5.2.2. Equal Risk Model (Petersen & Novick, 1976)

In this procedure, a threshold, say Z, for the probability of success (or, conversely, risk) in terms of the criterion score is chosen. The predictor cut score for any of K groups is then chosen so that

$$\text{Prop}(Y \geq y_s \mid X = x_{sg}, Group = g) = Z \qquad (7)$$

for $g = 1, 2, 3, \ldots, K$. This model provides the same cut scores regardless of whether Z is defined in terms of risk or in terms of probability of success. For some selection models, it is problematic that this apparently trivial choice in defining Z results in different cut scores.

5.2.3. Constant Ratio Model (Thorndike, 1971)

Cut scores are set so that the number of selected members of a group $(A + B)$ is proportional to the number who succeed $(A + D)$. For this to occur, the fraction $(A + B)/(A + D)$ must be the same for all groups.

5.2.4. Conditional Probability Model (Cole, 1973; Darlington, 1971)

This has also been described as the equal opportunity model (Wigdor & Sackett, 1993). Cut scores are set so that for candidates who would be successful (A + D), the proportion selected is the same for all groups. For this to occur, the ratio A/(A + D) must be the same for all groups.

5.2.5. Equal Probability Model (Linn, 1973)

Cut scores are set so that for candidates who would be selected (A + B), the proportion who would be successful is the same for all groups. For this to occur, the ratio A/(A + B) must be the same for all groups.

5.2.6. Decision-Theoretic Model (Petersen & Novick, 1976)

In this model, a utility (a quantitative defined benefit to individuals or society) must be assigned to each outcome: true positives, true negative, false positives, and false negatives. Higher utilities are operationalized as a higher weight assigned to any outcome "that has the effect of equalizing opportunity or reducing disadvantage" (Novick & Petersen, 1976, p. 83). A cut score for two or more groups is determined as the value providing the greatest benefit across individuals.

5.3. Summary of Models

The National Research Council Committee on the General Aptitude Test Battery (Hartigan & Wigdor, 1989) categorized selection models into two sets. Methods (5.2.3–5.3.5) that take into account the number of successful candidates are described as "performance fair" in contrast to the rule of the regression and equal risk models (5.2.1–5.2.2), which can be described as "test fair." The former take into account group membership, whereas the latter only recognize individual performance on the predictor test (unqualified individualism). The decision-theoretic model (5.2.6) recognizes that selection takes place in a context of values, and an attempt is made to make these values explicit in the decision rule. This is clearly a desirable approach, yet it is difficult to implement because there may be no consensus for determining the required utilities. Models 5.2.3–5.2.5 attempt to take performance into account in a simpler manner, but these models are internally inconsistent. Depending on whether one seeks to minimize risk or maximize utility, different cut scores are obtained with the identical decision logic (Petersen & Novick, 1976).

Group fairness is not the same as individual fairness, and debate arises regarding quota systems and preferential treatment whenever methods are suggested to correct for the disproportionate effect of fallible tests on protected groups. Jensen (1980) argued that any model other than unqualified individualism is a *quota* method, and the common criticisms of quotas in selection processes are three-fold. First, a quota method runs counter to the American ideal of individual fairness. Under a quota system the rules of play are modified to favor one or more groups of individuals by arbitrarily increasing their likelihood of selection. Second, such methods are criticized as racist because they perpetuate the stereotype that protected group status is correlated with potential for success. The third criticism is that only the individual model "maximizes" utility (Jensen, 1980). In this case, unqualified individualism is the preferred selection procedure; accordingly, scarce resources are allocated to the most talented applicants, who return the highest level of benefit to society.

As a whole, these criticisms constitute less than a complete argument. Because protected groups often have less "access to privilege, power, and position" (Smedley, 2002, p. 174), tests are often used in social contexts of decidedly unbalanced playing fields. Race in this context is a proxy for access, that is, the tools for effectively competing. With respect to the selection procedure itself, fairness is not unambiguously established with a test having low to moderate correlation with a criterion measure of performance. As shown by Wightman (2000) in her analysis of the LSAT, protected status can have a large impact on selection, but has a much smaller degree of association with realized success. The criticism of maximizing utility hinges on the definition of utility. It assumes a single, or at least preferable, criterion that provides a greater benefit to society than all others and that selected applicants do indeed use their talents to benefits society, either directly or indirectly.

For these reasons, a test that can be demonstrated as statistically unbiased still may not meet the criterion of educational or economic necessity if it disparately impacts applicants. The attempt to clarify this issue can be seen in the Supreme Court decision *Grutter v. Bollinger et al.* (2003), where the majority held that the University of Michigan Law School can employ diversity as one component in formulating an admission policy:

> Enrolling a "critical mass" of minority students simply to assure some specified percentage of a particular group merely because of its race or ethnic origin would be patently unconstitutional.... But the Law School defines its critical mass concept by reference to the substantial, important, and laudable educational benefits that diversity is designed to produce, including cross-racial understanding and the breaking down of racial stereotypes. The Law School's claim is further bolstered by numerous expert studies and reports showing that such diversity promotes learning outcomes and better prepares students for an increasingly diverse workforce, for society, and for the legal profession. (pp. 3–4)

Empirical investigations of equal prediction can answer whether a test is performance or individual "fair" for two groups, but cannot address larger questions about the social value of selection procedures (Linn, 1989). The dissenting opinion of Justice Clarence Thomas in *Grutter v. Bollinger* illustrates the difficulty in arriving at a consensus regarding social utility:

> the Law School seeks to improve marginally the education it offers without sacrificing too much of its exclusivity and elite status. The proffered interest that the majority vindicates today, then, is not simply "diversity." Instead the

Court upholds the use of racial discrimination as a tool to advance the Law School's interest in offering a marginally superior education while maintaining an elite institution. Unless each constituent part of this state interest is of pressing public necessity, the Law School's use of race is unconstitutional. I find each of them to fall far short of this standard. (p. 8)

Whereas the majority recognized multiple social values in admissions policies, Thomas argued that the architecture of the selection process is flawed, and consequently students are denied equal protection under the 14th Amendment. The use of developed ability as a predictor of success in combination with a stringent cutoff creates an elite law school, but one without a compelling state interest, Thomas maintained, because few Michigan students attend the law school and of these, most eventually leave the state.

5.4. Empirical Results

Empirical studies have demonstrated a tendency toward overprediction in favor of the focal group performance when a common regression approach is used. Two areas of research are summarized below to illustrate this general conclusion.

In a review of 49 separate studies completed since 1974 on college admission testing, Young (2001) found that for most African Americans and Hispanics, first-year grade point average (FGPA) was slightly *overpredicted* by college admissions test, or about .11 units on a four-point grade scale, meaning that students in these groups perform slightly worse than the test predicts. For women, FGPA was *underpredicted* by about .05 to .06 units. Thus, there is convincing empirical support that the degree of differential prediction is not large for various gender, racial, and ethnic groups on college admissions tests. Young found the average validity coefficient (multiple correlation) to be about .5. Other studies have reached similar conclusions (Linn, 1982; Ramist, Lewis, & McCamley-Jenkins, 1994; Wightman, 2003).

In a review of validity studies concerning the General Aptitude Test Battery (GATB), the GATB Committee identified 70 studies using this test to predict criterion outcomes. Hartigan and Wigdor (1989) reported,

In 26 of the 70 studies the intercepts were significantly different at the .05 level ... in only 1 of the 26 studies in which the intercepts were significantly different was the intercept-greater for black than for nonminority employees. (p. 181)

In this case as in the case of the SAT, the common-groups regression equation is more likely to overpredict than underpredict the performance of black applicants. However, for 72 validity studies "that had at least 50 black and 50 nonminority employees" (p. 188), the average correlation of the GATB with the criterion for the former group was $\bar{r} = .12$, and for the latter group $\bar{r} = .19$. For one quarter of the studies, Hartigan and Wigdor (1989) reported a correlation of $\bar{r} = .03$ or less.

6. INTERNAL EVIDENCE OF BIAS

Procedures using internal evidence to detect bias received considerable attention beginning in the mid-1970s. Methodologically, the intent of DIF analyses was to distinguish *bona fide* group differences from bias in the measurement process. Group differences in test performance cannot be interpreted automatically as evidence of either bias or unfairness because these differences might validly reflect construct-relevant knowledge and opportunity. Therefore, the concept of *relative* difficulty was devised (probably by William Angoff at Educational Testing Service). Absent an external criterion, a variety of internal bias procedures were developed using the other items on the test: an item of interest had a group performance difference relatively larger than the group differences for other items. The modern methods of DIF represent a refinement of this notion.

A major limitation of item bias statistics or indices is that measures of relative difficulty do not provide proof of unfairness. Only if an item is relatively more difficult for one group (statistically biased) *and* the source of this difficulty is irrelevant to the test construct is an item said to be unfair. Holland and Thayer (1988) introduced the term *differential item functioning* to convey this concept more clearly:

The study of items that function differently for two groups has a long history. Originally called "item bias" research, modern approaches focus on the fact that different groups of examinees may react differently to the same test question. These differences are worth exploring since they may shed light both on the test question and on the experiences and backgrounds of the different groups of examinees. We prefer the more neutral terms, differential item performance or *differential item functioning*, (i.e., *dif*), to item bias since in many examples of items that exhibit *dif* the term "bias" does not accurately define the situation. (p. 129)

In other words, DIF is synonymous with statistical bias, whereas unfairness can only be established if these measurement differences are factors irrelevant to the test construct; there is no direct route from statistical bias to unfairness. To maintain the distinction between statistical bias and unfairness, DIF is used as one kind of screening mechanism for quality control. The process of using such an index jointly with a logical analysis of potential attributions is a procedure for *detecting item unfairness*. The term DIF is now widely used in the literature, but, unfortunately, some writers still suggest DIF is sufficient for detecting *unfair* items. Ideally, DIF statistics are used to identify all items that function differently for different groups; then, after logical analysis as to *why* the items seem to be relatively more difficult, the subset of DIF items identified as "unfair" would be eliminated from the test.

Findings from item bias analyses may also help to clarify what a test is measuring and highlight the influence of irrelevant factors. Most major achievement tests have a single dominant or "essential" factor or dimension (Reckase, Ackerman, & Carlson, 1988; Shealy & Stout, 1993b). Because DIF statistics work by signaling systematic group differences, they are highly sensitive to multidimensionality when a secondary dimension is relevant to answering an item correctly *and* when groups differ on one or more secondary dimensions. Therefore, DIF analyses provide insights much like an item-level factor analysis. If a secondary factor is identified in what was believed to be a homogeneous measure of a single proficiency, then the test developer is forced to consider explicitly whether the secondary proficiency is an admissible part of the intended construct. For example, Shepard, Camilli, and Williams (1984) found that verbal math problems were systematically more difficult for African American examinees; differences between this group and Caucasians were larger on this type of problem than on straight computational problems. In this case, findings from the DIF screening might prompt a more conscious appraisal of what proportion of test items should be word problems.

6.1. An Historical Caution

Before describing current methods of DIF analysis, it is useful to reconsider an earlier rationale for defining and operationalizing these procedures. Eells, Davis, Havighurst, Herrick, and Tyler (1951) were not the first researchers to address the question of socioeconomic differences on intelligence test items; however, they drew together much of the literature—nine studies from 1911 to 1947 were reviewed—and performed a primary analysis of more than 650 items from eight IQ tests. Moreover, they defined *cultural bias in test items* as

> differences in the extent to which the child being tested has the opportunity to know and become familiar with the specific subject matter or specific process required by the test item. If a test item requires, for example, familiarity with symphony instruments, those children who have opportunity to attend symphony concerts will presumably be able to answer the question more readily than children who have never seen a symphony orchestra. (p. 58)

Eells et al. were interested in establishing the extent to which observed group differences in IQ scores were dependent on the specific content of the test items rather than an important underlying thinking ability in pupils (p. 4). A test was considered fair if it was composed of items that were equally familiar or unfamiliar to all persons.

The two major purposes of the Eells et al. (1951) study were to detect differential measurement, and then to discover "a) those kinds of test problems on which children from high socioeconomic backgrounds show the greatest superiority and b) those kinds of test problems on which children from low socioeconomic backgrounds do relatively well" (p. 6). This knowledge then would be used to eliminate *cultural bias,* favoring any particular socioeconomic group, from the test (p. 24). When items showing large group differences in performance were detected and analyzed for commonalities, Eells et al. (1951, p. 68) concluded that "variations in opportunity for familiarity with specific cultural words, objects, or processes required for answering the test items seem to the writer to appear..., as the most adequate general explanation for most of the findings."

By eliminating items that relied on opportunity to learn, Eells et al. (1951) believed that group differences then would reflect more accurately an important underlying ability. In 1951 things did not work out so neatly. Eells et al. (1951) concluded their study with the following caution:

> Another important finding in the analysis reported in this chapter is the rather substantial number of items showing large status difference for which no reasonable explanation can be seen. (p. 357)

Thus, about a half century ago analysts had noted that what would later be known as differential item functioning often had no satisfactory explanation. While it is true that the early methods for DIF were unsophisticated statistically, it is also true that findings with no apparent explanation are the same general complaint of analysts today. For example, in studies in which expert judges try to identify DIF-prone items based on substantive or qualitative criteria, little correlation has been found between expert ratings and empirical DIF indices (Englehard, 1989; Reynolds, 1982). Group membership itself, especially with regard to race, is an inference loaded with implicit and usually untestable assumptions, it is not surprising that the observed statistical relationships with this variable have been inconsistent, if not bewildering. As Bond (1994) stated,

> Theories about why items behave differently across groups can be described only as primitive. Part of the problem, as I see it, is that the very notion of differential item functioning by groups implies a homogenous set of life experiences on the part of focal groups that are qualitatively different from the reference group that affect verbal and mathematical reasoning. As I have indicated elsewhere (Bond, 1980, 1981) we are still far from a coherent theory of how knowledge is organized in long-term memory, how it is retrieved, and how it is used in problem solving. (p. 279)

However, some narrow regularities have been noted in DIF research. For an example of substantive findings regarding language, see Schmitt, Holland, and Dorans (1993).

6.2. Other Early DIF Studies

The first well-known studies of test item functioning began in 1910 with Alfred Binet, who was concerned that some items may disadvantage students from lower socioeconomic strata. Binet eliminated certain kinds of items that were considered too dependent on home training or language. William Stern in 1912 also observed such item differences and recommended that procedures be developed for detecting such items. Thurstone (1925, 1931) conducted related studies in which items were examined for group changes in relative scale positions.

Until the 1960s, investigations like that of Eells et al. (1951) tended to focus on items from intelligence tests. More modern investigations began with Coffman (1961), and Cardall and Coffman (1964), who wrote that

> a comparison of the responses of different groups of subjects to a set of test items generates two statistics of interest. First, one may ask whether or not there are mean difference across groups, that is whether the groups differ in average

test score. Second, one may ask whether there is a significant interaction between the items and the groups, that is, whether or not some particular items are relatively easier for one group than for another. (p. 2)

Continuing this work, Angoff and Ford (1973) studied race by item interaction on the Preliminary Scholastic Aptitude Test (PSAT) by matching candidates on total mathematics or verbal subscores. They recommended multivariate matching strategies for DIF investigation, and demonstrated the use of "delta plots," a currently popular graphical procedure (see Camilli & Shepard, 1994, for a fuller description of this method). In the late 1970s and early 1980s, DIF research began to flourish (e.g., Berk, 1982; Ironson & Subkoviak, 1979; Lord, 1977; Scheuneman, 1979; Shepard, Camilli, & Averill, 1981).

7. METHODS OF DIF ANALYSIS

There are two major approaches to DIF analysis. One approach is the use of item response (IRT) theory models, while the other approach relies on methods of observed-score analysis. Both approaches share a core concept: DIF is defined as item performance differences between examinees of comparable proficiency. While IRT methods provide useful results when the item models fit the data *and* a sufficient sample size exists for obtaining accurate estimates of IRT parameters, observed-score methods are frequently used with smaller sample sizes. However, the latter methods contain implicit measurement models, so it is imprecise to refer to them as *nonparametric*. The accuracy of their results depends on how well this implicit model fits the data (Camilli & Shepard, 1994). For example, the Mantel-Haenszel technique (described below) provides an unbiased measure of DIF for a multiple-choice item only when several strong assumptions are satisfied, one of which is that a Rasch model fits the item responses.

7.1. Difference in IRT Parameters

One general approach to assessing the difference in item response functions (IRFs) is a comparison of item parameters. There are various procedures, but the essential feature is the comparison of one of more item parameters across two groups (Lord, 1980). For example, under the 1-paramater logistic model, a test of the of *b*-parameter difference, $H_0:b = 0$, uses an normal approximation test statistic

$$Z = \frac{\Delta \hat{b}}{s(\hat{b})}, \qquad (8)$$

where $\Delta \hat{b} = \hat{b}_F - \hat{b}_R$ and $s(\hat{b})$ is the standard error of the difference. This situation is illustrated in Figure 7.5. Since the item response functions are parallel, this is an instance of *uniform* DIF. For polytomous items, it is convenient to express the item difficulty in terms of an average difficulty parameter and category deviations from this average. Then DIF can be expressed as a shift of the average difficulty parameter for two groups (Muraki, 1999) using Equation 8.

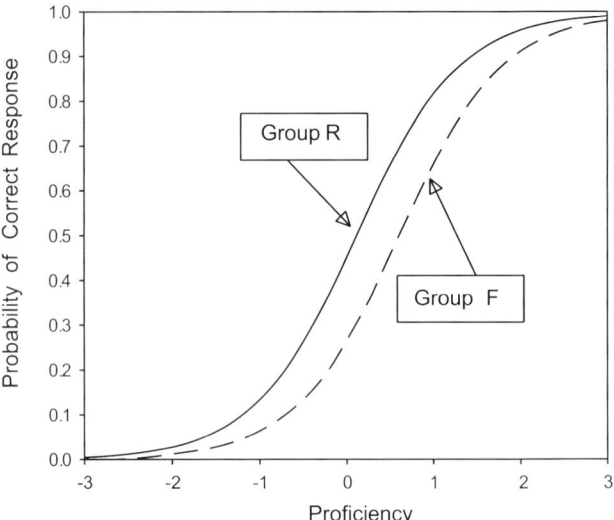

FIGURE 7.5 Uniform DIF Expressed as the Difference in *b* Parameters for the Item Response Functions (IRFs) for a Reference and Focal Group

7.2. Difference in Item Response Functions

When a 2- or 3-PL model is used, a multivariate test of item parameter differences may be more appropriate (Camilli & Shepard, 1994; Hambleton & Swaminathan, 1984). In this case, the test is between IRFs rather than individual IRT parameter estimates. Three general approaches have been taken.

7.2.1. Multivariate Difference in Parameters

Let the vector of item parameter differences be expressed as

$$V = (\hat{a}_F - \hat{a}_R, \hat{b}_F - \hat{b}_R, \hat{c}_F - \hat{c}_R). \qquad (9)$$

The statistic for testing item bias, referred to as Lord's chi-square, is given by

$$Q = V S^{-1} V', \qquad (10)$$

where S is the sample variance-covariance matrix of the differences between the item parameters (Lord, 1980). The statistic Q is distributed as chi-square random variable with degrees of freedom equal to the number of parameters estimated. This case is illustrated in Figure 7.6. As can be seen, the amount of DIF varies by level of proficiency; this phenomenon is known as *nonuniform* DIF.

7.2.2. Area Between IRFs

In simple area measures, DIF is indicated by the area between the IRFs and may be signed or unsigned (Camilli & Shepard, 1994; Raju, 1988). In both cases, the smaller the area, the less DIF. Mathematically these area measures are defined as closed-form solutions to the integrals:

FIGURE 7.6 Nonuniform DIF Expressed as the Difference in Item Response Functions (IRF) for a Reference and Focal Group

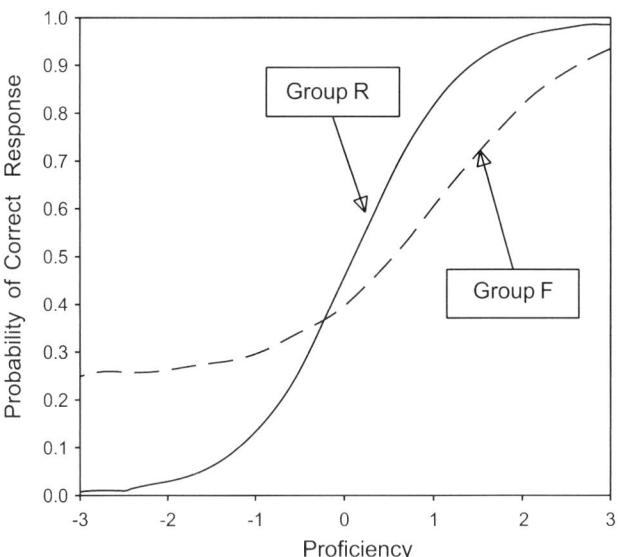

$$\text{Signed-Area} = \int_{-\infty}^{\infty} [P_R(\theta) - P_F(\theta)]\, d\theta, \quad (11)$$

and

$$\text{Unsigned-Area} = \int_{-\infty}^{\infty} |P_R(\theta) - P_F(\theta)|\, d\theta, \quad (12)$$

where $P_G(\theta)$ is the IRF for group G. Both of these measures are effect sizes. If the Signed-Area is positive, then the Reference group is favored. In the case of nonuniform DIF, the Signed-Area would tend to cancel, thus reducing the measure of DIF. In this case, the Unsigned-Area is preferable. A large discrepancy between the two area measures indicates crossing IRFs. Raju (1990) provided asymptotic formulas for the standard errors of Equations 11 and 12, which can be used for obtaining statistical tests. The major weakness of this approach is that these measures may be distorted by IRF differences in sparse regions of the θ continuum. In addition, when the c parameters differ, the integrals do not yield finite values (Camilli & Shepard, 1994).

7.2.3. Likelihood Ratio Test

In this procedure, the fit of an augmented model (A) in which IRT parameters of a studied item are allowed to vary across comparison groups is compared to the fit of a compact model (C) in which item parameters are constrained to be equal across groups (Thissen, Steinberg, & Wainer, 1988, 1993). The likelihood L of the compact model is calculated during a single calibration run. Subsequent runs calculate the likelihood of an augmented model (A) that relaxes some combination of a, b, and c parameters, for a single item for the focal group. This is equivalent to treating the studied item as a different item in each group. The null hypothesis, H_o: Model C (no DIF) is rejected in favor of the alternative, H_a: Model A, using the likelihood ratio test that the simpler model holds. The likelihood ratio test, given by

$$G^2(df) = -2 \ln\left[\frac{L(A)}{L(C)}\right], \quad (13)$$

has a large-sample chi-square distribution with degrees of freedom equal to the difference in number of parameters in the two models (Thissen et al., 1993).

Item response theory DIF methods using 2- and 3-PL models require larger sample sizes, and thus may not be appropriate when one of the comparison groups is relatively small (Clauser & Mazor, 1998). With all three parameters relaxed, the difference between IRFs is tested, and this may be preferable to testing parameters individually because very different combinations of parameters can result in similar IRFs. The likelihood ratio procedure is easily extended to polytomous items, whereas no such extensions of the procedures in 7.2.1 and 7.2.2 have been reported in the literature.

7.3. Observed-Score Methods: Mantel-Haenszel Statistics

Observed score techniques provide an alternative to IRT-based procedures when sample sizes are small or when strong assumptions can be made about underlying models. The most widely used, the Mantel-Haenszel (MH) procedure (Mantel & Haenszel, 1959) was introduced to psychometrics by Holland and Thayer (1988) to study group differences on dichotomously scored items. Applied to test data, the MH procedure pools information across levels (say j) of the matching variable, based on the assumption of a common odds ratio. The resulting estimate is interpreted as the relative likelihood of success on a particular item for comparable members of two different groups of examinees. This odds ratio provides an estimated effect size, and a value of 1.0 (equal odds) indicates no DIF (Dorans & Holland, 1993).

The typical setup for this analysis is a $2 \times 2 \times S$ matrix of items from a K-item test that are dichotomously scored (say 0, 1). The matching variable describing the third dimension of this matrix is typically taken as the total test or number right score ($j = 1$ to $S - 1$). For each level j, the studied item responses are tallied by item score (0, 1) and group (reference, focal) giving the matrix in Figure 7.7. An effect size measure of DIF is then obtained as the Mantel-Haenszel odds ratio:

$$\hat{\alpha}_{MH} = \frac{\sum_j A_j D_j / T_j}{\sum_j B_j C_j / T_j}. \quad (14)$$

This is typically converted to the log-odds scale by the transformation $\hat{\delta}_{MH} = \ln(\hat{\alpha}_{MH})$ with approximate variance (Holland & Thayer, 1988; Phillips & Holland, 1987) given as

$$SE\{\hat{\delta}_{MH}\} = \left(\frac{1}{2U^2} \sum_j T_j^{-2} \left\{A_j D_j + \hat{\alpha}_{MH} B_j C_j\right\} \times \right.$$
$$\left. |A_j + D_j + \hat{\alpha}_{MH}(B_j + C_j)|\right)^{\frac{1}{2}}, \; U = \sum_j A_j D_j / T_j. \quad (15)$$

The log-odds ratio and its associated standard error can be converted to the delta scale (used at Educational Testing Service) with the transformations

$$\text{MH D-DIF} = \Delta_{MH} = -2.35 \cdot \hat{\delta}_{MH},$$

$$SE(\Delta_{MH}) = 2.35 \cdot SE(\hat{\delta}_{MH}). \quad (16)$$

The log-odds and its MH D-DIF cousin take on values from negative to positive infinity. Negative values indicate a higher likelihood of success in the reference group; and positive values indicate a higher likelihood of success in the focal group. The associated null hypothesis is $H_0: \delta_{MH} = 0$, where $\hat{\delta}_{MH}$ is an estimate of the common log-odds across levels of the matching variable. An associated test statistic can be obtained as the MH χ^2, a chi-square random variable with 1 degree of freedom. Alternatively, a z statistic can be obtained by dividing the log-odds estimate by its standard error:

$$z = \frac{\Delta_{MH}}{SE(\Delta_{MH})}. \quad (17)$$

Zieky (1993) described three categories of DIF magnitude, labeled A, B, and C. Both χ^2_{MH} (with $p = .05$) and the absolute value of MH D-DIF are used for this classification:

- A items have Δ_{MH} not significantly different from zero, or $|\Delta_{MH}| < 1$
- B items have Δ_{MH} significantly different from zero and either (a) $|\Delta_{MH}| < 1.5$, or (b) Δ_{MH} not significantly different from 1
- C items have Δ_{MH} significantly greater than 1, and $|\Delta_{MH}| \geq 1.5$

This classification has a significant impact on which item are identified for possible deletion (see section 8.2). In some testing programs type C items are always deleted. A similar classification system for polytomous items is discussed by Zwick, Thayer, and Mazzeo (1997).

A number of simulation studies have shown that Mantel-Haenszel statistics are somewhat over- or underestimated due to several factors including: matching variable (Holland & Thayer, 1988; Swaminathan & Rogers, 1993; Zwick, 1990); multiple DIF items (Zwick et al., 1997); nonuniform odds ratio (Clauser, Nungester, & Swaminathan, 1996); guessing (Camilli & Penfield, 1997); lack of a sufficient statistic for matching (Zwick, 1990); and sample size (Spray, 1989). A polytomous item extension of the Mantel-Haenszel procedure (Mantel, 1963) was adapted for DIF analysis by Zwick, Donoghue, and Grima (1993). Penfield (2001) showed that the generalized Mantel-Haenszel statistic (Mantel & Haenszel, 1959) provided a better assessment than multiple tests conducted on pairs of groups.

7.4. Observed-Score Methods: Logistic Regression

Swaminathan & Rogers (1990) introduced methods of DIF analysis based on logistic regression. In their approach, the matching variable is as the total or number-correct score X, but is treated as a continuous variable. Logistic regression belongs to a broad class of models known as generalized

FIGURE 7.7 General Notation for the $2 \times 2 \times S$ Data Matrix

Group	Score on Studied Item 1	0	Total
Reference (R)	A_j	B_j	n_{Rj}
Focal (F)	C_j	D_j	n_{Fj}
Total	m_{1j}	m_{0j}	T_j

linear models or GLM (Agresti, 1996). In logistic regression, the item response is taken as a random Bernoulli variable Y_i (scored dichotomously) for individuals i with mean and variance

$$E(Y_i | X_i, G_i) = P_i.$$
$$Q_i = 1 - P_i, \quad (18)$$

and

$$Z_i = \ln(P_i/Q_i) = \beta_0 + \beta_1 X_i + \beta_2 G_i + \beta_3 X_i G_i, \quad (19)$$

where P_i is the conditional proportion of individuals that endorse an item in the direction of the latent variable. A dichotomous group membership variable G is often used signifying reference and focal groups (scored 0–1).

The studied item can be evaluated using a likelihood ratio procedure. First, likelihood estimation is performed for the equation $Z_i = \beta_0 + \beta_1 X_i + \beta_2 G_i$. Next, group membership and group-by-total score interaction are added, such that $Z_i = \beta_0 + \beta_1 X_i + \beta_2 G_i + \beta_3 X_i G_i$. The presence of nonuniform DIF is determined with likelihood ratio test (1 df) for improvement in model fit. Similarly, $Z_i = \beta_0 + \beta_1 X_i + \beta_2 G_i$ can be tested against $Z_i = \beta_0 + \beta_1 X_i$. The coefficient $\hat{\beta}_2$ provides an estimate of effect size that is often very similar in value to $\hat{\delta}_{MH}$. This procedure can be extended to multiple groups with the addition of dummy codes.

Logistic regression for DIF analysis is a flexible tool (Clauser & Mazor, 1998; Clauser, Nungester, & Mazor, 1996; Rogers & Swaminathan, 1993; Zumbo, 1999). This procedure typically yields DIF effect sizes highly similar to those obtained by Equation 14. One advantage is that group difference on an item can be modeled with multiple variables, and this may be more efficient than multiple matching required by MH analysis (Mazor, Kanjee, & Clauser, 1995). Moreover, Miller and Spray (1993) and Camilli and Congdon (1999) showed that logistic regression can be adapted to item responses with polytomous outcomes by switching the item response and group membership variable in Equation 19.

7.5. Observed Scores: Standardized Difference

The standardization approach was introduced to DIF analysis by Dorans and Kulick (1983, 1986), who analyzed data form the $2 \times 2 \times S$ matrix by first calculating

$$\Delta p_j = p_{rj} - p_{fj} = \frac{A_j}{n_{rj}} - \frac{C_j}{n_{fj}}, \quad (20)$$

where $p_{r,j} = A_j/n_{r,j}$ and $p_{f,i} = C_j/n_{f,j}$ (see Figure 7.7). This is a measure of the difference in proportions correct at level j, and a weighted average can be obtained across the levels of j by

$$D = \frac{\sum_j w_j \Delta P_j}{\sum_j w_j}, \quad (21)$$

where the weighting factor can be defined in several ways. Using, $w_j = n_{f,j}$, D can be targeted to values of the matching variable most frequently obtained by focal group members. The variance of D (Dorans & Holland, 1993) is given by

$$Var(D) = P_f(1-P_f)/N_f + \sum_j n_{f,j}^2 p_{r,j}(1-p_{r,j})/(n_{r,j}N_f) \quad (22)$$

where P_f is the proportion correct observed in the focal group, and N_f is the number of examinees in the focal group. The measure in (21) is a familiar and useful measure of effect size since it can be interpreted as the average difference (reference minus focal) in proportion correct for examinees of comparable ability.

7.6. Observed Scores: SIBTEST

The methods described thus far analyze one item at a time. The Simultaneous Item Bias procedure or SIBTEST (Shealy & Stout, 1993a, 1993b), a DIF detection method motivated by multidimensional IRT, can be used to detect DIF either in single items or in bundles of items. Bundles or subsets can be constructed to some organizing principle such as test content or item format; and pooling information across items may result in more sensitive tests of group differences. Similar to other DIF techniques, a matching or conditioning variable must be constructed or chosen to create comparable subsets of examinees.

SIBTEST incorporates secondary dimensions, η (a scalar or vector), into the mathematical model for the probability of answering an item or set of items correctly, and conditions on a subtest of items presumed to measure only the target proficiency θ. The basic index for SIBTEST, B_s, represents the average value of the group difference in subtest scores across the focal group ability distribution controlling for the target proficiency factors and is given by

$$B_s = \sum_j w_j \left(\overline{Y}_{rj}^* - \overline{Y}_{fj}^* \right). \quad (23)$$

For dichotomously-scored items, B_s can be interpreted as the average difference in proportion correct. In Equation 23, w_j is the proportion of pooled reference and focal groups on the matching test, $\overline{Y}_{gj}^*$ is the average item score for group g ($g = r$ or $g = f$) at the jth level of the matching variable, and

$$\overline{Y}_{gj}^* = \overline{Y}_{gj} - M_{gj} \left[V_g(j) - V(j) \right],$$

$$M_{gj} = \frac{\overline{Y}_{g,j+1} - \overline{Y}_{g,j-1}}{V_g(j+1) - V_g(j-1)}, \quad (24)$$

where

$$V(j) = \frac{1}{2}\left[V_r(j) + V_f(j) \right]. \quad (25)$$

Finally, the estimated matching true score is given by

$$V_g(j) = \overline{X}_g + \hat{\rho}\left(X_j - \overline{X}_g \right), \quad (26)$$

where $X_i = j$ ($j = 0, 1, 2, 3 \ldots J$) is the value of the matching variable (for creating comparability), $\overline{X}_g$ is the mean of group g on the matching test, and ρ is the reliability coefficient. An important feature of the SIBTEST procedure is the Kelley-type regression adjustment (see Braun, 2006) for measurement error applied to the matching variable given in (26). This controls for score distributions that are affected by measurement error, which also tends to inflate group mean differences based on observed scores. Based on this correction, covariance adjusted estimates are obtained for the average item scores on the studied item for each group according to Equation 24. In SIBTEST, the reliability is estimated by

$$\hat{\rho} = \frac{n}{n-1}\left[1 - \frac{\sum_{i=1}^{n} p_i^*(1-p_i^*)}{Var(X)}\right] \quad (27)$$

where p_i^* is the item p-value adjusted for a chance response

$$p_i^* = (p_i - c)/(1 - c). \quad (28)$$

This differs from Cronbach's Alpha only by the guessing correction applied to item p values in the numerator (Zwick et al., 1997). The standard error of the estimate given in (23) is

$$s(B_s) = \left\{ \sum_{j=0}^{J} w_j^2 \left(\frac{s^2(Y|r,j)}{n_{r,j}} + \frac{s^2(Y|f,j)}{n_{f,j}} \right) \right\}^{\frac{1}{2}}, \quad (29)$$

where $s^2(Y|g,j)$ is the sample variance of the studies subtest scores for examinees of group g with matching test score j. An asymptotically normal test, for the no-DIF hypothesis, $H_o: \beta = 0$ is then provided by

$$z = \frac{B_s}{s(B_s)}. \quad (30)$$

In general, the type 1 and 2 error levels of this procedure have been found to be at least as accurate as those of other procedures (Bolt & Stout, 1996; Zwick et al., 1997).

SIBTEST has been primarily used to study groups of items simultaneously so that $\overline{Y}_{g,j}$ could be the average of the sum of several items. Studying several items may provide a more powerful test of DIF (i.e., DIF amplification) if each item is sensitive to the same secondary dimensions. Single items can also be examined, and the procedure has been extended to accommodate polytomously scored items, and to allow for item bundles that may exhibit either uniform or nonuniform DIF.

8. CURRENT TOPICS IN DIF ANALYSIS

Recent developments in DIF methods have yielded substantial improvements in statistical accuracy. The preponderance of studies has been methodological, rather than addressing issues of fairness directly. Examples of recent studies that apply DIF techniques to substantive problems are exemplified by Takala and Kaftandieva (2000), who studied gender differences on a Level 2 foreign language vocabulary test, and Le (1999), who studied gender DIF on a history achievement examination. O'Neill and McPeek (1993) summarized much of the substantive research on item characteristics associated with DIF. In contrast to substantive findings, this section focuses on methodological developments.

A brief summary of the recent methodological research is useful to consider for numerous reasons, including the fact that DIF has become a major tool in state assessments. In particular, topics are considered regarding testing versus estimation, type 1 errors, item discrimination, multidimensionality, DIF as parameters versus secondary proficiencies, and item difficulty variation (see Camilli & Monfils, 2003; Camilli & Penfield, 1997; Zwick & Lewis, 1999). These topics only scratch the surface of innovation. Other research areas that are not reviewed below include DIF techniques for open-ended items (Hidalgo-Montesinos & Lopez-Pina, 2002; Zwick et al., 1997), computer-assisted testing (Walker, Beretvas, & Ackerman, 2001; Zwick, Thayer, & Wingersky, 1994, 1995), scale purification (Clauser, Mazor, & Hambleton, 1993; Zenisky, Hambleton, & Robin, 2003), latent class analysis (Cohen & Bolt, 2002; Westers & Kelderman, 1991), and cognitive studies (Gierl, Bisanz, Bisanz, & Boughton, 2003). Still others have shown that DIF has very little effect on total score distributions (Burton & Burton, 1993; Hu & Dorans, 1989; Roznowski & Reith, 1999). Several literature reviews cover these issues and estimation methods in more depth (e.g., Camilli & Shepard, 1994; Clauser & Mazor, 1998; Dorans & Holland, 1993; Millsap & Everson, 1993; Penfield, 2001; Penfield & Camilli, in press; Penfield & Lam, 2000; Roussos & Stout, 2004a).

8.1. Inferential Testing Versus Estimation of Effect Size

A number of authors have written about statistical testing versus estimation (Camilli & Shepard, 1994; Holland & Thayer, 1988; Kim & Cohen, 1995). Inferential test statistics are not appropriate as measures of the practical size of DIF, and they should not be used as effect sizes. Rather, parameter estimates such as the log-odds ratio or *p*-value difference should be used to express the degree of differential measurement. For example, effect sizes should be computed for comparing DIF indices across time or test administrations (Longford, Holland, & Thayer, 1993). The parallel idea exists in meta-analysis where effects sizes are used to portray the magnitude of treatment interventions. Descriptive statistics summarizing DIF across a set of items, such as central tendency or variability, should also be expressed with effect size measures. The principle here is that measures of statistical significance are not the same as indicators of *practical significance*.

8.2. Type 1 and 2 Errors

Most testing programs examine test items for group difference in measurement properties. An item is flagged when a statistically significant difference between two groups is found. However, because a statistical test is not perfect, sometimes a flagged item is a false positive and is actually measurement invariant. New testing techniques have resulted in a vast improvement in the reduction of false positive or type 1 errors (e.g., Penfield, 2001). Most problems of this kind (i.e., the actual type 1 error rate is greater than the nominal level) occur when the reference and focal groups have a large mean difference (e.g., Penny & Johnson, 1999).

An interesting trade-off in statistical analysis is the tension between type 1 and 2 errors. Type 2 errors occur when an item functions differentially, yet a statistical test fails to flag the item. A type 1 error rate (alpha level) can be set either to make fewer type 1 or fewer type 2 errors, but not both simultaneously: more type 1 errors imply fewer type 2 errors and vice versa. In most scientific work, type 1 errors are anathema, and much basic research is devoted to developing tests with accurate type 1 error levels. However, the situation in fairness work, where the "cost" of a type 2 error may be high for an examinee, is different from that of quality control in ongoing programs. In contrast, the "cost" of a type 1 error would be high to the test developer because of item development costs and rescoring procedures that may be necessitated by a deleted item. Favoring the examinee would lead to a strategy of reducing type 2 errors at the cost of more type 1 errors. Yet the trade-off should be considered in the context that flagged items are not automatically rejected; they must be reviewed for substantive interpretations of unfairness.

In a hybrid approach to signaling DIF items, Educational Testing Service uses three categories for the degree of DIF in test items (see section 7.3). Each of these categories combines a statistical test with an evaluation of effect size. This approach seems very prudent as a strategy for combining practical considerations with those of statistical hypothesis testing. It is not clear whether the utility of decision making (relative to type 1 and 2 errors) based on this approach has been compared with purely inferential testing strategies.

8.3. Item Statistical Discrimination

Wright, Mead, and Drada (1976) argued that high discrimination indices (e.g., point-biserial coefficients) for some test items could be signs of a problem with a test item. They wrote that

> high SES pupils of a given ability are more likely to be familiar with "sonata" than are low SES pupils of the same ability because of differences in exposure to this culturally biased word.... Typically, high SES students perform better on achievement tests... The greater the difference in the levels of group achievement, the more effective such culturally biased items will appear. If items are selected based on high discrimination, culturally biased items will be selected, producing tests with greater and greater bias. (p. 4)

(Note that in this context, the word *discrimination* is a technical term describing the effectiveness of an item in distinguishing those who demonstrate higher from those who demonstrate lower levels of proficiency. It has no social or legal connotations.) Masters (1993) gave a similar example involving native and nonnative speakers of a language. He argued that an item unclear to native speakers could be thought of as ideal for assessing second-language listening comprehension. One highly discriminating item was identified in which native German speakers did much better than Dutch speakers, probably because the item was based on a conversation about German politics. The contaminating influence of a second dimension can manifest itself in unusually high item discrimination (Masters, 1988), though unusually low discriminations also merit investigation. This claim is given some mathematical justification in section 8.5.2.

8.4. The Multidimensionality Hypothesis

The multidimensionality hypothesis for DIF is attributable to Hunter (1975), who illustrated, using IRT methods, that there is no conceivable way that a unidimensional test can adequately deal with group differences in the distributions of secondary abilities. He also demonstrated that, when two groups differ in average achievement level, point biserial correlations will give a false impression of bias when an item functions identically for two groups; biserial correlations had been proposed earlier as a method of DIF detection by Green and Draper (1972). Using modern measurement theory, Hunter also effectively undermined methods proposed by Angoff and Ford (1973) and Jensen (1974, 1975). Significantly, Hunter proposed multidimensional IRT models for analyzing dimensionally complex test items.

Based on the work in multidimensionality by Stout (1990), Shealy and Stout (1993b) identified three components required to produce statistical test bias: (a) the potential for bias, (b) dependence of correct item responses on secondary test factors, and (c) the test-scoring method. In this case, if two groups differ on the secondary test factors, this difference still must be transferred into a test score by a procedure for scoring. Along these lines, Gelin and Zumbo (2003) showed that an item can show DIF for some methods of scoring but not others using the same detection procedure. They concluded that DIF is a property of the item, scoring method, and purpose of the instrument because the scoring method is dependent upon the purpose of the instrument (p. 65). This underlines the interesting point that a test's purpose creates the conditions in which DIF arises.

Roussos and Stout (1996) proposed a schema for understanding how multidimensionality creates differential measurement on tests. They exhaustively considered the technical requirements for differential measurement to occur. Most importantly, they showed how test items can be combined in DIF analyses to obtain better estimates of DIF as well as more powerful tests (see also Bolt & Stout, 1996; Gierl, Bisanz, Bisanz, Boughton, & Khaliq, 2001; Nandakumar, 1993). Roussos and Stout (1996) also examined the nature of the matching (for comparability) criterion. If a test contains a number of knowledge areas or skills, examinees matched on the total score are not necessarily matched on separate dimensions that items assess (O'Neill & McPeek, 1993). Roussos and Stout (1996, p. 367) concluded that

if the matching criterion is multidimensional, then a statistical test for DIF may reject [the null hypothesis for] a perfectly fair item simply because the examinees differ on one of the auxiliary dimensions (secondary dimensions intended to be measured by the test). Thus, with regard to Type 1 error, perhaps the most insidious cause has been the assumption of a unidimensional matching criterion when in fact the test is measuring either more than one primary dimension or a single primary dimension with several auxiliary secondary dimensions.

That is, the matching criterion, though multidimensional, may not parallel the dimensional content of a particular item. In this case, if examinees are matched on separate measures of the subskill areas, DIF may be diminished or disappear altogether.

This may be true, but it raises several issues. First, if a single score is to be used to make decisions about an examinee, then the criterion of interest is the conditioning or matching score that is most faithful to the intended construct with all of its potential multidimensional complexity (Bolt & Stout, 1996; Camilli & Shepard, 1994, Camilli, 1992). Subdividing the criterion begs the question of the proper dimensional mix of the test; in fact, this is what DIF analysis is most effective at uncovering. Second, a moderate upward bias in the type 1 error rate, as suggested above, may not be such a bad thing in detecting item unfairness.

8.5. DIF Signals: Parameters or Secondary Proficiencies?

Differential item functioning can be conceptualized either as differences in item parameters, or as differences in secondary distributions of ability (a topic similar to that of the previous section). Though the two approaches are related, there are two primary considerations for choosing between them. First, in practical applications the most simple and direct question is often "For examinees of equal proficiency, is this item more difficult for one identifiable subgroup?" The drawback of this approach is that if the answer to this question is "Yes," there is little information for assisting an explanation for *why* the item is more difficult. In the second approach, the reason for the observed difference in item difficulty is postulated to have its origin in multiple proficiencies. While a test typically measures a single dominant dimension (Reckase, 1979; Shealy & Stout, 1993b; Stout, 1987), several other secondary proficiencies may also contribute to item performance. Accordingly, observed differences in item performance for groups of equal ability may be due to group differences in the distributions of one or more secondary proficiencies; once these are identified, a means exists for understanding the nature of the DIF. The basic assumption here is that DIF originates in the knowledge and skills of examines, not the measuring properties of items.

Below several conceptual models are presented for illustrating these issues by using the parameters of IRT model. These models incorporate both item discrimination parameters (labeled a), item difficulty parameters (labeled β), person *proficiency* (labeled θ), and a random measurement error (labeled ε). Finally, the concept of propensity (labeled z) is used to *indicate* the overall likelihood that a person receives a higher score on a test item.

8.5.1. Difference in Parameters

Differences in one or more item parameters can be expressed as

$$z_G = \alpha_G \theta - \beta_G + \varepsilon_G. \quad (31)$$

For two groups G = (r and f), if $\alpha_r = \alpha_f = \alpha$, then DIF is said to be *uniform* across θ. In this case, the expected or average DIF is

$$E[z_r - z_f | \theta] = -(\beta_r - \beta_f). \quad (32)$$

Here, DIF is expressed as the simple conditional difference between the difficulty parameters of two groups. This is because the term $\alpha\theta$ subtracts out when taking the difference, and the error terms average to zero across examinees. If the condition of equal αs is not met, then the expected difference in performance is a more complex function:

$$E[z_r - z_f | \theta] = (\alpha_r - \alpha_f)\theta - (\beta_r - \beta_f). \quad (33)$$

In this case, the expected conditional difference depends on where along the θ dimension the group difference is examined—this DIF is nonuniform (see Figure 7.6). Holland and Thayer (1988) showed that if items on a test followed the Rasch model, then the expected value of Mantel-Haenszel log-odds ratio for a single item having DIF is identical to the right-hand side of Equation 32.

There are two general methods of estimating DIF in the nonuniform case. First, both the discrimination and difficulty parameters can be estimated using IRT techniques and then tested for group differences. The second method is to aggregate the *absolute values* of across the group distributions of θ. This can be done with either IRT techniques (e.g., Raju, 1988, 1990), observed-score techniques (e.g., Zumbo, 1999), or nonparametric techniques (e.g., Shealy & Stout, 1993a, 1993b). In all cases, construction of the conditioning variable is of paramount importance. Absent a sufficient statistic for conditioning, Zwick (1990) showed that all DIF estimates contain some degree of statistical bias.

8.5.2. Difference in Distributions

As explained above, DIF may arise due to group differences in secondary distributions of proficiency. A heuristic model for one primary and one secondary factor can be expressed for a single group as

$$\begin{aligned} z &= \alpha_1 \theta + \alpha_2 \eta - \beta + \varepsilon \\ \eta &= \kappa + \gamma \theta + \nu \end{aligned}. \quad (34)$$

Here z is a propensity score, two proficiencies (θ and η), two items discriminations (α_1 and α_2), a single difficulty parameter β, and a random measurement error ε. Another important aspect of this model is the relationship between the two proficiencies, which is expressed as the linear regression in the second line of (34). The reduced form equation shows that for group equation G,

$$\begin{aligned} z_G &= \alpha_{G1}\theta + \alpha_{G2}(\kappa_G + \gamma_G \theta + \nu_G) - \beta_G + \varepsilon_G \\ &= (\alpha_{G1} + \alpha_{G2}\gamma_G)\theta - (\beta_G - \alpha_{G2}\kappa_G) + (\alpha_{G2}\nu_G + \varepsilon_G). \end{aligned} \quad (35)$$

If it is assumed in this case, that $\alpha_{1r} = \alpha_{1f} = \alpha_1$ and $\alpha_{2r} = \alpha_{2f} = \alpha_2$, and $\gamma_r = \gamma_f$, and it is possible to condition on the primary proficiency θ, then

$$E[z_r - z_f | \theta] = -(\beta_r - \beta_f) + \alpha_2(\kappa_r - \kappa_f). \quad (36)$$

With a strict interpretation of the multidimensionality hypothesis, *all* of the conditional expectation is due to the secondary trait, and so Equation 36 can be rewritten as

$$E[z_r - z_f | \theta] = \alpha_2(\kappa_r - \kappa_f). \quad (37)$$

As above, the conditional group difference does not involve (either) proficiency, but the form of the difference indicates that the item's loading on the secondary dimension η biases its estimate of difficulty. The conditional difference (i.e., DIF) in Equation 37 is a function of the common loading on the secondary dimension and group distributional differences in θ as expressed by different group regressions of η on θ. If the multidimensional model in Equations 34 and 35 is correct, application of a unidimensional model in this case will thus confound the difference in item difficulty with the item and person parameters of the secondary distribution.

If the equality conditions required for Equation 36 are not met, then the expression for the expected difference becomes unwieldy. In most scenarios where the equality assumptions are not met, the conditional difference will be a function of θ, but little else of a simple nature can be concluded. In this case, one can estimate all the parameters of the latent distributions with multidimensional IRT models with the advantage that estimation of the α_2 coefficients leads to identification of the secondary dimension (or dimensions). Once this is done, a mechanism exists for potentially connecting DIF to the educational histories and opportunities of the examinees. Through programmatic research, this may speed the development of more appropriate tests, or provide guidance for instruction. In operational applications, it is more practical for a number of reasons to estimate the average difference between the item response functions using observed score or nonparametric approaches assuming uniform DIF.

8.6. Item Difficulty Variation

Most single analyses of differential item functioning compare the item performance of one focal to one reference group, and the "group" identifier is nearly always a proxy for opportunity variables. In this manner, the notion of "group" can be recast as many levels along one or more measures of opportunity. In other words, there may exist many groups to be compared, and focal versus reference is a reduction of an opportunity continuum. For example, in many states there is tremendous variation among schools (or school districts) in resource variables such as per pupil expenditures, teacher qualifications, instructional materials, building safety, and the like. "School" provides not only an "address," but also access to many process variables collected on a regular basis.

Multilevel mixed models can be used to address the multiplicity or continuum of "groups." Accordingly, data may be analyzed in which item responses are nested within students who are in turn nested within schools. In this design, items receive a multivariate coding and are formally represented by a Rasch model embedded within the random effects (e.g., schools) model (Raudenbush & Sampson, 1999). In the embedded Rasch model, each item is represented by a difficulty parameter. Formally, this is the "fixed" part of the model, which is to say the common part of the model shared by all schools. A number of random effects are also defined within the model, and these describe between-school variation. In one approach (Camilli & Monfils, 2003; Prowker & Camilli, 2004), item difficulties can be conceptualized to have both a fixed (shared) component and a random (school specific) component. Formally, the random component describes variation in item performance across levels of an opportunity variable. For short, this variance component is labeled IDV for Item Difficulty Variation. This index describes the degree to which success on a particular item that is independent of overall proficiency varies by school. If a school does better than expected, this may reflect value added by school factors, including instruction.

Mathematically, this model for a particular item, say j, is represented by

$$f(n_{+sj}/n_{sj}) = \mu_s - \delta_{sj}, \quad (38)$$

where n_{+sj} is the number of correct responses in state s and n_{sj} is the total number of responses, and $f(\bullet)$ represents the logistic link function used to linearize the relationship. In Equation 38, μ_s represents the overall math proficiency of state s, and δ_{sj} represents the difficulty of item j for schools s. Two terms of the above equation can be resolved into fixed and random components:

$$\mu_s = \mu + \theta_s, \quad (39)$$

and

$$\delta_{sj} = \delta_j + \upsilon_{sj}. \quad (40)$$

In this formulation, θ and υ are random variables, and are defined as

$$\theta_s \sim N(0, \sigma_\theta^2), \quad (41)$$

and

$$\upsilon_{sj} \sim N(0, \tau_j^2). \quad (42)$$

Here, the interest is in the parameters

$$\tau_j^2 = Var(\upsilon_{sj}), \quad (43)$$

for each of the $j = 1, 2, 3, \ldots, J$ items on the test or assessment instrument. Each parameter represents how much an item's difficulty varies across schools (or other level of aggregation) independently of school θ_s and fixed item difficulty δ_j. The IDV may indicate items that are more or less instructionally sensitive, and opportunity to learn provides the motivation for examining DIF rather than unfairness.

9. RACE, ETHNICITY, OPPORTUNITY, AND EXPLANATION OF BIAS

Racial and ethnic groups are often referred to as protected groups. Analyses for detecting statistical bias are fundamentally dependent on the existence of groups, yet the definition of "group" can be elusive. If a group is defined in terms of the qualities of its individual members, yet all members within this group are not alike, then how can the meaning of differential prediction or DIF be understood? This seems to have something to do with both similarities and differences among groups, but, in turn, these qualities might depend on the purpose of defining the group. If it is assumed that examinees are alike for some purposes but not others, then what is the underlying reality to the group distinction? These questions are examined in this section.

The focus below is on the status of distinctions based on race and ethnicity, though parallel arguments could be made about other kinds of groups. In particular, the issue is the difference between individual and group interpretations of fairness. For example, one could ask whether a test using English language sentences could disadvantage an *individual* nonnative speaker of English, but on the other hand, one could ask whether *groups* of nonnative speakers are disadvantaged relative to *groups* of native speakers. Although this may seem like the same question, there is an important difference. In addition to the assumption that native and nonnative speakers are different in terms of linguistic processing, the latter question makes the additional assumption that *both* native and nonnative speakers are similar enough to be categorized separately. In other words, individuals *within* each group are assumed similar for the purpose of comparison.

9.1. RACE AND FAIRNESS

Material on race is included in this chapter because of the large differences commonly encountered in test scores among groups of different races and ethnicities, and it is important to understand the extent to which these differences are artifacts of a test rather than true proficiency. Regardless of the origin of racial differences on tests, test professionals are obliged to do everything in their power to remove sources of invalidity in the test or testing situation that contribute to these differences. Although not as frequently as in the past, many people have interpreted such differences as fixed consequences of genetic endowment. Because such interpretations are especially prone to racial stereotyping, we should seek to understand issues of human capital (e.g., access to education or medical care) as well as strive to eliminate group differences from tests that are irrelevant to the test construct. Selection bias and differential item functioning can be assessed by comparing test or item performance in different identifiable groups. Yet as suggested above, the existence of the "groups" in question is a central assumption that cannot be taken at face value. A classification of individuals exists relative to a particular purpose, and it is only this purpose that leads to identification of groups. The assumption that the classification exists with some independent reality runs the risk of stereotyping and is fraught with numerous difficulties including: the complexities of racial identity, multiracial heritage, confusion of race and ethnicity, and the potential difference between self-selected and observer classification. Below, it is argued that to understand—rather than to detect—differential test or item performance, one needs to dig deeper than commonly used group labels.

9.2. Group Membership and Social Address

Bronfenbrenner and Crouter (1983) argued that research that relates a macrosystem such as group identity to an outcome of interest employs a *social address model*. While such a model might correctly reveal a statistical connection between group (the "address") and individual outcomes, it would not clarify the processes that might explain the connection. In other words, the address tells you where you are, not how you got there.

"Social address" measurements make global assumptions about students "at the same address." Examples of social address labels are race, ethnicity, religion, political inclination, and so forth. The different routes to this address, contain the desirable or even necessary information for explaining variance in an outcome of interest. According to de Graaf (1999),

> One must look for mediating processes which link different developmental outcomes with the address label, instead of comparing people from different categories with each other, as is the case in the so called "social address research" (Bronfenbrenner, 1986). For example, stating that socioeconomic-status (SES) or parental IQ affects children's cognitive achievements, does not increase in the slightest our insight into how it does this, into what kind of explanatory model is appropriate to account for those correlations. That is, correlation is not causation. (p. 72)

Reese, Balzano, Gallimore, and Goldenberg (1995) wrote that one criticism of social research has been that individuals with a common race or ethnicity have the same experience when within-group variability may be greater than between-group differences. Using the "social address" approach to group comparisons, classification into groups might be confused with a fixed biological or ethnic classification. As John Stuart Mill (1848) wrote,

> Of all the vulgar modes of escaping the consideration of the effect of social and moral influences on the mind, the most vulgar is attributing the diversities of conduct and character to inherent natural differences. (p. 319)

Lan, Brandley, Tallent-Runnels and Hsu (2002) noted that findings based on social address variables are also easily misconstrued because they sometimes may imply that there are fixed intellectual advantages or disadvantages associated with factors such as SES, ethnicity, or family composition.

There are two additional drawbacks of using labeling variables for fairness analysis. First, even the inference (statistical or otherwise) of no bias could potentially reinforce the apparent reality of the classification, as opposed to refuting its existence. Second, because many individual-level influences are submerged in a "social address," it is likely that the use of such variables will not provide a very powerful means of detecting statistical bias. Thus, the failure to reject hypotheses of differential measurement may not provide convincing support that tests or test items are, in fact, fair.

Whereas the causal examination of ecological influences on performance clearly requires more than social address variables for understanding cause and effect, it is also clear that the "addresses" are laden with social and cultural meanings that affect the lives of examinees. Thus, micro- and macro-processes can be understood in two different ways. The first is that of the analyst or scientist who seeks an understanding of social and educational processes. The second purpose is that of the institutional admissions officer who must balance the two perspectives described by Levin (2003):

> For some, fairness requires treating people as individuals, and for others, fairness requires taking into account the collective representations that matter in society. Ferdman (1997) frames this fairness debate in terms of a distinction between the "individualistic perspective" and the "group perspective." Proponents of the individualistic perspective argue that it is unfair to pay attention to ethnicity because ethnic group memberships should not influence the opportunities and outcomes of individuals in society. Proponents of the group perspective, on the other hand, argue that it is unfair not to take ethnicity into account because of the power differentials that exist between ethnic groups in society. According to this latter perspective, ignoring ethnic group membership obscures the significant ways in which these power differentials influence the opportunities and outcomes of members of different ethnic groups. (p. 8)

Both aspects of fairness must be considered in an evaluation of test bias. The scientist's approach to explaining fairness at the individual and group level should not be taken to imply that the "social labels" have no inherent meaning; indeed, stereotyping and historical discrimination are directed precisely toward the "label" rather than the individual.

10. SENSITIVITY REVIEW

The Office for Minority Education at ETS (Office for Minority Education, 1980) concluded that quantitative studies of item fairness were not likely to result in a set of practical guidelines to prevent cultural influences from interfering with test performance, and an approach coined *sensitivity review* was recommended for developing tests that are socially balanced and evenhanded. According to Bond, Moss, and Carr (1996),

> "Sensitivity review" is a generic term for a set procedures for ensuring (1) that stimulus materials used in assessment reflect the diversity in our society and the diversity of contributions to our culture, and (2) that the assessment stimuli are free of wording and/or situations that are sexist, ethnically insensitive, stereotypic, or otherwise offensive to subgroups of the population. (p. 121)

A panel of trained reviewers is required for examining each item on a test or assessment. Panelists operate with the principle that all students should be treated equitably, and should have a common understanding of the questions and tasks. All items on a test should be reviewed at least once for this purpose, and this process has become especially important for performance items (Bond et al., 1996).

Procedures for creating culturally sensitive tests may seem like unnecessary "add-ons," thus spurring the complaint of political correctness. However, the motive here is to follow the normal professional standards of avoiding irrelevant difficulty, which includes distracting or offensive language, because it is important for test developers to create the least stressful environment possible for test takers. Sensitivity review is a method of procedural due process in establishing test validity; as such, it should be documented in rich detail. Public scrutiny is especially important in preventing both overzealous and lax evaluations.

Below, I draw heavily from documents produced at the Educational Testing Service (ETS) and ACT, Inc. In particular, ETS (2003) provides much valuable detail on constructions to avoid in test item development. These formal documents have an established historical use, are easily available, and are free of charge.

10.1. Panel Formation

A panel of sufficient size (a minimum of 5–10) is usually required for large-scale assessments, and it should be clear *how* panelists were selected. The specific procedures for selecting panelists can vary according to circumstances and may involve both nomination and self-selection. In any event, it is incumbent on the test developer or program personnel to provide public access to descriptions of panel membership (e.g., gender, race, position). Members should also have professional or instructional experience in the subject matter of the test. For example, teachers at the secondary and postsecondary level are prime candidates for sensitivity review of college entrance examinations. Panelists must be able to understand and represent a culturally and ethnically diverse range of perspectives. This is facilitated by a panel that is itself diverse in terms of factors such as race, ethnicity, gender, and geography. As a rule, test authors and item writers cannot provide a sensitivity review of their own work: sensitivity review is an *independent* review to detect unintentional language and biases in the test material.

10.2. Sensitivity Training Procedures

Training should be based on a written policy expressing commitment to the objectives of fair testing, and a set of guidelines compiled in a formal document (Office of Minority Education, 1980). Panelists should be familiar with both the test specifications and sensitivity guidelines. As noted by Ramsey (1993) training is initiated by presenting to panelists a sample of test items and then asking for a set of judgments. These questions include whether there is a problem with an item, to which guideline the problem relates, potential item revisions, and whether modification or deletion of an item should be mandatory. The goal of training is for reviewers to arrive at a consensus on these judgments as they proceed through the set of sample items. Thus, sensitivity training corresponds to procedures used in training raters to score open response items (Bond et al., 1996; Ramsey, 1993) or in setting standards (Camilli, Cizek, & Lugg, 2001; Raymond & Reid, 2001). A typical training session might range from a half to a full day.

10.3. Training Criteria

Ramsey (1993) listed six criteria used at Educational Testing Service: stereotypes, underlying assumptions, controversial material, elitism and ethnocentricity, balance, and examinee perspective. In a more recent document (ETS, 2002), the first four areas above are listed (with "controversial" changed to "inflammatory"); balance and examinee perspective have been dropped or combined into other areas; and the categories "tone" and "inappropriate terminology" have been added. A number of helpful examples are given in ETS (2002) and Office of Minority Education (1980). Other publications (ACT, 2003, 2004) list five general considerations: offensiveness, fair portrayal, diversity and balance, fairness in language, and curriculum-based content and skills. The last consideration specifies that vocabulary, concepts, and experiences (required for understanding test items) should be appropriate for all examinee groups.

There are several general themes within these and other guideline documents. Among these is the principle that racial and ethnic categories have preferred terms. For example, the labels Black American or African American are preferred to earlier terminology, and specific descriptions of ethnicity, such as tribal names of Native Americans, should be used when applicable. Some ethnic descriptions may be preferred to others; for example, the terms *Latina* and *Latino* are more consensual than *Chicana* and *Chicano* as terms for Puerto Rican or Mexican Americans.

The possibility of unintentional stereotyping is a concern in the item writing stage of test development. This concern can include, but is not limited to a number of stereotype categories including, cultural, regional, occupational, religious, and Eurocentric. Implications implying superiority with respect to group status may be difficult to identify; and especially items using the word "minority" may have a subtle implication that minority status is akin to a fixed trait. Similarly, ethnocentrism may be subtle as illustrated in following passage from a test item (Ramsey, 1993, p. 383):

> The Inuvialuit, what the Eskimos of Canada's Arctic prefer to be called, live in the treeless tundra around the Bering Sea.

The problem here is the implication that the real name of the people is Eskimos, that is, the *real* name is determined from the perspective of a different culture.

Condescending material and inflammatory material is less subtle. Reference to a woman as the "lady lawyer" (Office of Minority Affairs, 1980, p. 49), or gratuitous reference to controversial material such as prayer in school, is not likely to be included during item development. However, controversial material may be both appropriate and necessary given the content specifications of a test. An assessment developed for a social studies chapter on *Roe v. Wade* (1973) will necessarily involve contentious or disturbing topics as will the study of euthanasia in Nazi Germany; yet such material would be dubious on a typical test of reading comprehension because it may introduce distractions influencing student performance. Preparing tests for international populations requires additional safeguards.

According to ETS (2003) guidelines, when issues of gender orientation are construct relevant:

> The words *bisexual*, *gay*, *lesbian*, and *transgendered* are all acceptable. Because some people assume that gay refers only to men, use *gay* or *gay people* only when prior reference has specified the gender composition of this term. (p. 21)

References to gender orientation are not consensual (e.g., queer versus gay) and the specific assessment contexts must be carefully considered. Other criteria for sensitivity review include religious beliefs, English as a second language, disability, socio-economic status, and violence. Guidelines should also pertain to gender references in language, and require revision of references to the generic "he" to more gender-neutral constructions (American Psychological Association, 1977).

One last area in this brief sketch of sensitivity review is representational balance. Test items, passages, tasks and so forth should represent population diversity including cultural references, gender roles, disability, and ethnicity. Of course, this does not mean that every test should be perfectly balanced. Rather, the goal is to achieve a reasonable representation of the appropriate populations (American Psychological Association, 1977), to respect the beliefs and experiences of all test takers, and to provide a minimum of distracting content.

10.4. Panel Operation

Formal review can begin with the design of test specifications prior to first drafts of test items, but informal review may occur at any stage of item development. Parallel issues exist in the scoring of examinations, directions to teachers and students, and score reporting. Sensitivity review can be broadened to include scoring procedures (e.g., instructions to scorers) and materials (e.g., scoring rubrics) as well as materials and procedures for reporting test scores. A more detailed description of the logistics of this process is given by Ramsey (1993).

The description in ACT (2003) suggests three stages for a typical fairness review: (1) before materials are pretested, (2) concurrently with pretest item statistics, and (3) before operational forms are administered. Different reviewers at each stage may provide an additional safeguard. In the first stage, reviewers receive packets of items, including directions and prompts. Based on the reviewers' feedback, testing staff may change, modify, or delete material. In the second stage, items are reviewed with quantitative pretest information including DIF statistics. The latter are used to aid identification of items in which irrelevant factors associated with group (e.g., gender or race) contribute to item difficulty. In the third stage, intact test forms are examined. Given that items have already been reviewed once and possibly twice, there is less flexibility in making modifications on the basis of review information in this latter stage.

Fairness reviews can be conducted by mail out for document examination, and by conference or teleconference for deliberation and exchanging views (ACT, 2003). Reviewers typically examine and annotate materials prior to participating in conferences of 1–2 hours at the first and third stages. The second stage review is more likely to be conducted by testing staff (though not item development staff) rather than independently chosen reviewers or consultants. If testing materials are reviewed off-site, it is common that confidentiality agreements are necessary.

11. FAIRNESS IN CLASSROOM ASSESSMENT

In general, the equity concerns addressed by sensitivity review extend beyond the purview of formal assessment. While the technical standards and concepts of validity and fairness are most often applied to standardized tests administered annually, a parallel set of concerns exists for classroom testing, including paper and pencil tests, performance assessments, authentic assessments, and even observational measures of learning. This section concerns fairness issues with *formative* and *summative* classroom evaluation. Shepard (in the chapter on classroom assessment) defines formative assessment as "assessment carried out during the instructional process for the purpose of improving teaching or learning," while summative assessment "refers to the assessments carried out at the end of an instructional unit or course of study for the purpose of giving grades or otherwise certifying student proficiency." Any assessment that eventually affects a grade can be viewed as summative, and therefore many assessments, including standardized tests, can share both summative and formative purposes (Brookhart, 2003, 2004).

A classroom performance assessment by its very nature is more closely connected to instruction than a standardized test, and is typically given to small numbers of students. As a rule, such tests have a short life cycle, and though it would be theoretically possible to examine differential measurement, such an effort would be impractical. Other types of statistical analysis are also of limited application. In the short run, then, different criteria must be brought to bear for insuring fairness in assessment.

Beyond traditional reliability, a number of practices can enhance the fairness of classroom assessments, both in terms of obtaining an accurate evaluation, and the perception of fairness on the part of students. *The kinds of practices and activities that insure testing is fair are also those that provide a solid foundation for attaining learning goals.* Thus, fairness is inherent in, rather than external to, effective classroom instruction. Brookhart (2004) noted the central role of construct validity:

> Particularly important for evaluating the validity of a classroom assessment is defining the construct in its instructional and contextual sense. Is writing part of the skill or irrelevant? Did we discuss this in class? Is this problem the same one as the students have already worked (in which case it measures recall)? Is this problem similar to the ones the students have already worked (in which case it measures transfer)? A close transfer or a stretch? How far did you want them to go? (p. 10)

Given that a clear purpose for the assessment is defined, additional practices are generally recognized (e.g., Brookhart, 2004; Shepard, 2000; Stiggins, 2002). A number of these are briefly examined below. A theme that runs through each of these areas is that all children are not the same. Equity and fairness are insured not by treating all children identically, but by differentiating among children to provide them the most effective opportunities to learn. The chapter by Shepard gives a broader overview of classroom assessment; here the focus is only on fairness issues.

11.1. Clear and Reasonable Assessment Criteria

Students should have an understanding of the content coverage of a test, and all the material on the test is relevant to the course's learning objectives. Students should also understand the process for scoring a test, and for open-response items, this requires a working knowledge of scoring rubrics. Shepard (2001) noted the dual purpose of communicating to students the standards by which their work is judged:

> Although access to evaluation criteria satisfies a basic fairness criterion (we should know the rules for how our work will be judged), the more important reasons for helping students develop an understanding of standards in each of the disciplines are to directly improve learning and to develop metacognitive knowledge for monitoring one's own efforts. These cognitive and metacognitive purposes for teaching students explicitly about criteria then speak to a different sense of fairness than merely being even-handed in evaluating students, that is, they provide students with the opportunity to get good at what it is that the standards require. (p. 1093)

The use of rubrics that define the general characteristics of good work should make assessments fairer in the long run because they help students to visualize their target (Brookhart, personal communication, September 6, 2004). Students should also be exposed to task-specific rubrics, though obviously not prior to a summative assessment activity.

Students should have equivalent understandings of the grading criteria, and according to these criteria, teachers should grade consistently. For example, criteria should remain consistent from the first to the last test or product scored on a particular occasion, and a rubric should be used long enough for students to acquire familiarity. A rational marking system might provide numerical standards for arriving at a grade, or combine a numerical system with judgment in a logical manner. The latter could be implemented, for example, by first establishing a numerical system for marking, and then adjusting grades based on judgment. This might benefit all students if adjustments are based on corroborating evidence from other instances of the same academic work, but absent a systematic and empirical procedure, an "intuitive" adjustment may cause more harm than good. Test scores should be weighted to reflect content area emphases or importance of a particular mark. For example, if a student's grades consist of numerous grades of A and one B+, and the final grade is B+, this provides an inconsistent message about a teacher's standards. Finally, explicit policies are required regarding makeup performances, for transfer students, for students working on group projects, and so on.

11.2. Equity in Assessment and Instruction

Effective classroom assessment supports student learning, and effective assessments, in turn, encourage students to focus on the task rather than their own level of competence *per se* (Black & Wiliam, 1998). Gipps (1999) elaborated:

> Children's evaluations of their ability and feelings toward themselves are more negative when the classroom climate is focused on winning, outperforming one another, or surpassing some normative standard than when children focus on trying hard, improving their performance, or just participating. (p. 383)

Equity is well served by maintaining focus on the learning culture (Shepard, 2000). As Moss (2003, p. 19) wrote, "validity in classroom assessment—where the focus is on enhancing students' learning—is primarily about consequences." It follows that the validity of assessments can be judged in part by their consistency with task-oriented learning activities presented at the appropriate level of difficulty. At its best, assessment in the classroom is more like instruction than testing.

11.3. Opportunity to Learn

The issue of equity raises a number of questions about opportunity to learn. Students should have an opportunity to learn all of the material on a test. In addition, they should understand what opportunity to learn means, and how it can be recognized. Testing for skills and knowledge not taught and practiced in class is problematic unless explicit directions are given regarding learning outside the classroom. Teachers should also consider whether students have equal access to knowledge and instruction. For example, with take-home assignments that are graded, what role should parents have in assisting their children, and how should teachers compensate for such differential access to knowledge?

Research in educational psychology has demonstrated that children and adults learn by incorporating new information and concepts into extant schema. One goal of classroom assessment is to "locate" the presenting proficiencies of students in order to guide instruction along the contours of their strengths and weaknesses. Students who enter at a more advanced level have more places to attach new meaning to old, and it is unreasonable to define fairness as the elimination of individual differences. Teachers can, however, unpack their lesson objectives to see if there is anything that, if not addressed, sets certain students up to fail or otherwise miss significant opportunities to learn. In this regard, it is important for teachers to experience (through initial training or professional development) what students are able to accomplish with help designed on the basis of formative assessment.

11.4. Sensitivity and Construction of Assessments

Test content should be free of cultural, ethnic, racial, religious, and gender stereotypes. It is important, especially with young test takers, to avoid stereotypical material since these children are, to a large extent, learning about themselves through the process of testing. This may require teachers to become familiar with the backgrounds and beliefs of students and their parents. Pellegrino, Chudowsky, & Glaser (2001) warned that

> Apart from the danger of a teacher's personal bias, possibly unconscious, against any particular individual or group, there is also the danger of a teacher's subscribing to the belief that learning ability or intelligence is fixed. Teachers holding such a belief may make self-confirming assumptions that certain children will never be able to learn, and may misinterpret or ignore assessment evidence to the contrary. (p. 240)

Also, familiarity with the prior knowledge of students can help to insure that test items and tasks are developed at an appropriate level of difficulty. Distributions of scores or marks with notable floor and ceiling effects might indicate inappropriate difficulty, lack of clarity, or insufficient instruction.

11.5. Multiple Measures

Assessment tasks should be designed to reflect accurately what students know and can do. Yet it is unlikely that all learners can demonstrate what they know in the same way. According to Shepard (2001), students should be given an accessible opportunity to show their knowledge and this could be provided, for example, by an oral presentation rather a written exam, writing about a familiar topic, or providing translations. These examples illustrate that multiple opportunities should be provided for a student to demonstrate competence; and these opportunities should include alternative assessment formats.

Especially for classroom assessment, the phrase "multiple measures" does not mean multiple opportunities to pass the same test, or even equivalent tests. As in most aspects of fairness in classroom assessment, genuinely alternative measures have a dual role. Not only do multiple measures provide an equitable assessment, they also aid the process of learning. They can facilitate knowledge transfer as well as the diagnosis and remediation of language deficits.

11.6. Modeling Fairness

Because the instructor (or teacher or professor) is the grading authority in the classroom, grading can be a type of modeling of both learning and self-assessment of students. This imparts a serious responsibility to the instructor. In an overt approach to grading, the criteria are explicitly communicated, and students are oriented toward learning rather than social evaluation of themselves or other students. Students in this environment will likely discover that learning depends on effort. When internalized, this becomes a model process for the students' participation in their communities and a larger democratic culture.

12. A BRIEF HISTORY OF COLLEGE ENTRANCE EXAMINATIONS

The measurement topics covered above have all evolved historically, spanning, for the most part, the latter half of the 20th century. In this section, a broader perspective is provided by considering testing issues of the 19th to mid 20th century. Trevelyan and Northcote (as cited in Gipps, 1999, p. 357) wrote with respect to the civil services,

> We are of the opinion that this examination should be in all cases a competing literary examination. This ought not to exclude previous inquiry into the age, health, and moral fitness of candidates. Where character and bodily activity are chiefly required, more, comparatively, will depend upon the testimony of those to whom the candidate is well known; but the selection from among the candidates who have satisfied these preliminary inquiries should still be made by a competing examination. This may be conducted as to test the intelligence, as well as the mere attainments of the candidates. We see no other mode by which (in the case of the inferior no less than superior offices) the double object can be obtained of selecting the fittest person, and of avoiding the evils of patronage.

In this remarkable quotation from 1853, a number of common 20th and 21st century ideas are present. Testing is recognized as a tool for social change, and the distinction is made between intelligence and achievement. The authors presumed that candidates could be ordered along a dimension of "fitness," and also recognized that different types of evidence may be required.

By 1869, Sir Francis Galton had published several articles and a book, *Hereditary Genius*, in which he began to augment informal notions of intelligence. In particular, he suggested that the human traits of "great ability" were inherited, a conclusion that was inspired by the work of his cousin Charles Darwin (Porter, 1986). Based on this idea, Galton proposed the *eugenics* thesis: selective breeding could improve the human species as much as any other (Zenderland, 1998). A number of Americans were deeply influenced by this work including Henry H. Goddard, who translated Alfred Binet's original IQ scales into English; Lewis M. Terman of Stanford University, who adopted Stern's ratio conception of intelligence and coined the shorthand term IQ; and E. L. Thorndike, a pioneer in psychometrics. Intelligence testing in America began in earnest during World War I, when Robert M. Yerkes led a team of social scientists, including Terman and Goddard, Walter V. Bingham, and Carl C. Brigham in adapting Terman's Stanford-Binet intelligence test for group administration to army recruits. This test, the Army Alpha, was used to collect large amounts of data, but the project generated controversy and had little, if any effect on selection and placement during World War I (Gould, 1996; Hartigan & Wigdor, 1989). A number of these and other intelligence theorists and psychometricians were involved in the eugenics movements of the early 20th century (Zenderland, 1998; Lombardo, 2002, 2003); however, an examination of this thread is related beyond the scope of the present chapter.

American and English universities and institutions began using selection and placement examinations as early as the 1850s, and intelligence tests were also thought to hold great promise in the upper reaches of society as tools for selection and placement in higher education. For example, Lazerson (2001, p. 386) noted "by the end of the 1920 academic year, over 200 colleges and universities had given intelligence tests." In the following two sections (12.1 and 12.2), a brief sketch is presented concerning how intelligence testing and the new psychometrics developed relative to two major college entrance examinations. In section 12.3, these developments are linked to current issues in test fairness.

12.1. The SAT

After World War I, Brigham (whose mentor was Yerkes) became a professor at Princeton University and began administering his own version of the Army Alpha—the Princeton Psychological Examination—to Princeton freshmen. Shortly thereafter, he chaired a committee of experts for the College Entrance Examination Board (initially with Yerkes and Henry T. Moore, chair of Dartmouth's psychology department), which was empanelled for recommending a new college admissions test (Hubin, 1988). This test, the Scholastic Aptitude Test (SAT) was completed in 1925, and was given to high school students for the first time the following year. Four of the nine item types on the new tests came from existing psychological tests at Dartmouth, Smith, and Yale; the other five came from Brigham's Princeton test (Hubin, 1988).

The SAT was created to test more integrated and cross-subject thinking as well as to standardize the admission process. Lazerson (2001) noted that the College Board's 1914 Annual Report called for an examination

> so framed as to give the candidate the opportunity to exhibit his power to think independently and to compare or correlate different parts of the field. The ability to reproduce with more or less fidelity the material presented on the pages of a text book would be considered as of secondary importance. (College Board, 1914, pp. 12–13)

At the time, college entrance tests varied widely among institutions of higher education, and individual tests tended to concentrate on factual content. To some degree, this 1914 statement from the Board reflects the mounting pressure to respond to new psychometric developments. Yet the Board was constrained by its "traditional nemesis," the charge that it was attempting to control the college preparatory curriculum (Lazerson, 2001, p. 391). The new SAT was thus crafted to navigate both demands. Testing scholastic "aptitude" tapped critical thinking, yet it did so with test items that for the most part avoided specific curricular knowledge.

In the early 20th century, "merit" in the college admission process, especially at Ivy League schools, was operationally assessed primarily in terms of family privilege, attendance at a small group of eastern preparatory schools, and a brief assessment of moral character (Wechsler, 2001). Shortly after James Bryant Conant was appointed president of Harvard University in 1933, he charged two associate deans, Wilbur Bender and Henry Chauncey, to establish an ambitious new academic scholarship program for students with limited financial resources. To select students for this program, Bender and Chauncey proposed the SAT to Conant as an accurate measure of *intelligence*—a condition upon which Conant had insisted (Lemann, 1999). By 1941, the SAT was required for all Harvard applicants. In the 1950s, the College Board had 300 member institutions administering the SAT as well as a number of nonmembers (Lemann, 1999). Conant's proximal goal was to recruit talented students from a wider geographic area; his broader and enduring social goal was to break up a system of influence, money, and privilege by a fair selection process. Intelligence testing for access to education, as opposed to traditional notions of merit, seemed to provide an objective tool for this purpose.

From the very beginning of the SAT, both Brigham (Hubin, 1988) and the Board (Lazerson, 2001) sought to downplay the connection between intelligence and aptitude: the term *scholastic aptitude* according to this argument makes no assumptions other than a positive correlation with subsequent academic performance:

> The term "scholastic aptitude" makes no stronger claim for such tests than that there is a tendency for individual differences in scores in these tests to be associated positively with individual differences in subsequent academic attainment. (Brigham, n.d., p. 1)

Conant later elaborated:

> as originally developed and used by many educators in the 1920s and 1930s, intelligence tests were thought of as measuring the inherent or genetic qualities of the individual. The evidence at first available seemed to indicate that the chances of a single individual's I.Q. changing over the years were slight. Today, however, when we tend to think of paper-and-pencil intelligence tests, at least in the higher grades, as measuring a type of scholastic aptitude, we are

well aware that we are measuring an aptitude which in part has been developed in the school. The difference between an I.Q. test and a good achievement test is one of degree not kind. Understood in this sense and with evidence accumulating that an individual's aptitude score may change during his school years, there is nothing deterministic about the use of the various forms of intelligence or aptitude tests which are on the market. If they are understood only as giving a prediction of probability of academic success in subsequent schoolwork, they are no more and no less influenced by home or other environmental factors than are the marks for schoolwork given by a conscientious teacher. (Conant, 1961, pp. 13–14)

These views are consistent with other early views of aptitude (e.g., Chauncey & Frederiksen, 1951, p. 89). Zwick (2002, p. 33) provided additional details of this development.

Despite this agnostic position on the meaning of scholastic aptitude, the SAT from its inception began to evolve. While retaining some core elements from its IQ ancestry (analogies, but not antonyms), the reasoning test (now the SAT I) was redesigned for 1994, according to Lawrence, Rigol, Van Essen, and Jackson (2003), "to reflect contemporary secondary school curriculum and reinforce sound educational standards and practices" (pp. 10-11). In 2005, the SAT I was further revised: the verbal section was retooled to assess critical reading, analogies were eliminated, and a new mathematics section added items from third-year college-preparatory mathematics.

12.2. The ACT

E. F. Lindquist, as a new assistant professor of education at the University of Iowa, founded a program in 1928 called the Iowa Academic Meet, dubbed the Brain Derby by the local press (Lindquist, 1970), which was a statewide scholastic contest designed to identify academically talented teens. Lindquist soon discerned "too much emphasis on the competitive features" of this process (Lindquist, 1970, p. 9), and became more interested in a test that would provide guidance in educating a broader population of students. In the 1930s, Lindquist developed the Iowa Every Pupil Achievement Tests (IEPT), the Iowa Tests of Basic Skills (ITBS), and the Iowa Tests of Educational Development (ITED). By the 1940s, Lindquist directed a state assessment program that

> had several remarkable features: every school in the State could participate on a voluntary basis; every pupil in participating schools was tested in key subjects; new editions of the achievement tests were published annually; and procedures for administering and scoring tests were highly structured. (Office of Technology Assessment, 1992, p. 122)

With Phillip Rulon of Harvard, Lindquist in the 1950s designed an electronic scoring machine. The first "Iowa machine" went into production in 1955, and by 1957, it is now clear that the electronic scoring machine reshaped the landscape of educational testing (Office of Technology Assessment, 1992).

Lindquist was also deeply involved with the admissions practices of colleges as a member of the SAT standing committee of College Board (Lindquist, 1970). He advocated expanding college admissions, and sought to develop a test of broad competencies for facilitating selection, and for assisting placement and guidance after selection. Lindquist (1951) had expressed skepticism regarding the use of aptitude tests for this purpose, though an intelligence test (supplied by Thorndike) was used experimentally in the Iowa Testing Program in 1934. While such a test might predict a criterion outcome, Lindquist argued that they were of little use for other educational purposes. What was needed was a test of competencies representing the same kinds of reasoning and problem-solving tasks required in high school and in college:

> the most important consideration is that the test questions require the examinee to do the same things, *however complex*, that he is required to do in the criterion situations. (Lindquist, p. 154, original emphasis)

Lindquist (1951) more ambitiously intended to create an admission test that would stimulate curricular reform; he was highly critical of the traditional high school curricula of his era as well as the extant subject-specific tests used for college admission. Though Lindquist apparently had proposed a new admissions test in which critical thinking was combined with subject matter content to the College Board in 1958 (Coulehan, 2004), he and Theodore McCarrel cofounded the American College Testing (now the initialism ACT) Program to develop a new admission test that soon became the main competitor to the SAT. The ACT test was designed to serve the needs of large state universities as well as state, municipal, and junior colleges rather than elite east-coast institutions.

As Coulehan (2004) observed, "Lindquist's greatest concern was," according to Ralph Tyler, "devising tests to gauge the educational development of each student for purposes of guidance and counseling as well as for college admission and placement." He wanted to design an achievement-oriented admissions test that would provide diagnostic information in the form of four subtest scores of the ITED (Peterson, 1983). After World War II, the Test of General Educational Development (GED) was developed to help youths and adults, especially those who were returning from the war, to demonstrate knowledge for which they would receive academic credit or a high school equivalency diploma. It is not surprising that the GED was also adapted from the ITED with substantial input from Lindquist (Peterson, 1983).

Recent ACT assessments are based on periodic surveys (e.g., in 1998–1999, and most recently in 2002–2003) of state education practices including examination of standards documents, survey of educators, and consultation with content area experts. Based on this information, the four curriculum-based tests are revised and updated (English, Mathematics, Reading, and Science Reasoning). According to current documentation (ACT, 2002), the ACT can be used for a number of purposes including advising and counseling at the high-school level; admissions, recruitment, and course planning and placement at the collegiate level; and scholarship and recognition programs. The stated philosophy of the test remains consistent with Lindquist's view "that the best way to measure students' readiness for postsecondary education is to measure as directly as possible the knowledge and skills students will need to perform college-level work" (ACT, 2002, p. 1). An optional writing test was added to the ACT Assessment in 2005.

12.3. Fairness Issues

Intelligence testing and its aptitude incarnation were conceived as indicators of merit for access to education in the early 1900s. The rationale for aptitude as a democratizing criterion, however, was greatly obscured by the subsequent claims that aptitude was nothing other than a label for a test score that correlates with educational attainment. Indeed, the developmental histories of the SAT and ACT reveal an enduring ambivalence regarding how merit should be defined and measured. According to Lazerson (2001), this ambivalence is expressed as a

> debate that became one of the most intense, fundamental, and divisive of the twentieth century: whether to measure what students knew based on what they were taught or to measure what students were capable of learning. (p. 385)

What examinees know in any given situation is a mixture of educational and informal learning experiences that is strongly affected by access and opportunity to learn. Rather than a simple "individual fair" proposition, the argument for measuring aptitude reflects a concern for recognizing talented students who are highly capable of learning (individual merit) *and* an historical efficiency preference (social or institutional benefit). Yet merit based on potential rather that actual criterion performance is deeply problematic from a philosophic point of view (Rawls, 1971). The SAT and ACT embody these different perspectives to some degree, though they are becoming more similar.

In many institutions of higher education, this dilemma is currently and sensibly resolved by allowing candidates to submit either SAT or ACT scores, to consider subject matter assessments such as the SAT II tests, and to allow for additional student background information (as originally recommended by Brigham) including interviews and high school grade point average. As suggested by Zwick (2002), however, it is not likely that more achievement-oriented selection strategies will substantially alter access to more elite institutions of higher education. Both aptitude and achievement tests reflect the lengthy educational histories of examinees, and equity issues must be addressed either by long-term infrastructure changes, or by affirmative action (as in *Grutter v. Bollinger*).

Other institutional consequences of the intelligence-testing legacy should be considered. Popham (2001, p. 46) warned that IQ-like test items, "are not suitable for evaluating schools." Tests composed of such items are consistent "with assumptions about knowing and learning that existed within the behaviorist perspective" in which knowledge is attained as a set of component skills, without regard to deeper underlying structures or representations (Pellegrino et al., 2001, p. 61). To the degree that a test is constructed with a similar logic, its items are independent samples of these knowledge "bits." Mastery is then defined in a way that is insensitive to effective instruction, on the one hand, and highly susceptible to influences on learning that are weakly related to formal instruction, on the other. As recognized by Lemann (2004, p. 14) "tests don't exist in a social vacuum. The way they are used embodies ideas about how a society should work." Tests have symbolic value regarding the importance of their content, and who can learn the content. Aptitude-dominant tests send weak signals regarding content, and potentially misleading signals regarding who can achieve standards, while achievement-dominant tests may provide clearer messages about the responsibilities of schools in preparing students for college selection and college experience.

13. CONCLUSIONS

Concerns about fairness arise from the intended and unintended consequences of testing. Fairness is thus not a property of a test *per se*, and for this reason, investigations of fairness are framed by test use. The clarity of both questions and answers in these investigations is promoted by involving key stakeholders including test users, test takers, developers and contractors, and measurement scholars. Cole and Moss (1989) recognized that

> Reponses to questions of whether a test *should* be used for a particular purpose and whether that purpose should be served ... are the right and responsibility of all persons affected by test use. This includes test takers and others to whom the consequences of testing are of concern, as well as the measurement profession. (p. 207)

As Linn (1989) suggested, other influential groups have also increasingly begun to appear on the scene including judges, legislators, and administrative agencies.

Constructs are created in (though not by) a social context. In my opinion, there is no single "objective" point of view either for delimiting the construct, or for sorting out intended and unintended consequences. Measurement professionals certainly have a central role to play in any discussion of fairness, but must recognize other important actors. Gardener (1999) asked "Who owns intelligence?" Similarly, one could ask "Who owns developed ability?" or "Who owns achievement?" For this reason, Gipps (1999) argued that rather than analysis by specialists,

> The best defense against inequitable assessment is openness. Openness about design, constructs, and scoring will bring out into the open the values and biases of the test design process, offer an opportunity for debate about cultural and social influences, and open up the relationship between the assessor and learner. (p. 385)

But even the above questions do not go far enough because the central theme of test fairness concerns the match between a test's measurement properties and the purposes and goals for which the test is used. Indeed, an aptitude test may well suit an institution's mission, but a rationale should be provided and defended, rather than presumed. Given a sensible and clear institutional mission, the goal is to understand how decisions can be informed by the full range of evidence regarding an individual's qualifications. (With some modification, this goal is relevant to classroom practices as well.) An adequate analysis of test fairness may involve examining assumptions underlying the test construct as well as the purpose of the test, the consequences of its use, and the responsibilities of test developers and examinees. The latter are further elaborated in the *Code of Fair Testing Practices in Education* (Joint Committee on Testing Practices, 1988) and the *Code of Professional Responsibilities in Educational Measurement* (NCME Ad Hoc Committee on the Development of a Code of Ethics, 1995). In terms of contemporary issues, resolving fairness problems also involves closing the achievement gap, providing opportunity to perform, deterring the misuse of tests, and accommodating individual differences (Cole & Zieky, 2001).

There are now sophisticated methodologies for examining test fairness issues, and these have already helped to distinguish bias in measurement and predictive processes from fairness in test use. With this set of analytic tools, psychologists and measurement experts will continue to play key roles in developing and validating tests. Yet selection, placement, promotion, and certification are mechanisms of social and educational management (and control) that reflect societal tensions—as is the case with recent court decisions—and will continue to do so in the 21st century struggle to reconcile efficient selection with a modern vision of inclusion. Linn (1989, p. 6) recognized that "clarity in definitions and evidence regarding the comparability of prediction systems cannot be expected to resolve the underlying value conflicts."

Test developers do not operate independently of the social context in providing tools for teachers and education managers, just as teachers do not operate independently of prevailing attitudes and beliefs when giving a classroom assessment. Consequently, test developers have the challenging responsibility to construct sound tests, but also to inform clients fairly regarding the purposes, interpretations, and uses of ensuing test scores. In turn, tests users have the significant responsibility to reconcile the choice of test, as well as the potential consequences of its use, with institutional and social goals.

REFERENCES

ACT, Inc. (2002). *Your guide to the ACT assessment*. Iowa City, IA: ACT.

ACT, Inc. (2003). *Consultant's guide for the fairness review of the ACT EPAS tests*. Iowa City, IA: ACT.

ACT, Inc. (2004). *Fairness report for the ACT assessment tests*. Iowa City, IA: ACT.

Agresti, A. (1996). *An introduction to categorical data analysis*. New York: Wiley.

Alexander v. Sandoval, 121 S. Ct. 1511 (2001).

American Educational Research Association, American Psychological Association, & National Council on Measurement in Education. (1999). *Standards for educational and psychological testing*. Washington, DC: American Educational Research Association.

American Psychological Association. (1977). *Guidelines for nonsexist language in APA journals*. Washington, DC: Author.

Angoff, W. H., & Ford, S. F. (1973). Item-race interaction on a test of scholastic aptitude. *Journal of Educational Measurement, 10*, 107–116.

Berk, R. A. (Ed.). (1982). *Handbook for detecting biased test items*. Baltimore: Johns Hopkins University Press.

Black, P., & Wiliam, D. (1998). Assessment and classroom learning. *Assessment in Education: Principles, Policy, and Practice, 5*, 7–74.

Bolt, D., & Stout, W. (1996). Differential item functioning: Its multidimensional model and resulting SIBTEST detection procedure. *Behaviormetrika, 23*, 67–95.

Bond, L. (1980). [Book review of *Bias in mental testing*]. *Applied Psychological Measurement, 3*, 406–410.

Bond, L. (1981). Bias in mental tests. *New Directions for Testing and Measurement: Issues in Testing—Coaching, Disclosure and Ethnic Bias, 11*, 55–77.

Bond, L. (1994). Comments on the O'Neill and McPeek paper. In P. W. Holland & H. Wainer (Eds.), *Differential item functioning* (pp. 277–279). Hillsdale, NJ: Lawrence Erlbaum.

Bond, L., Moss, P., & Carr, P. (1996.) Fairness in large-scale performance assessment. In G. W. Phillips & A. Goldstein (Eds.), *Technical issues in large-scale performance assessment* (pp. 117–140). Washington, DC: National Center for Education Statistics.

Braun, H. (2006). Empirical Bayes. In J. L. Green, G. Camilli, & P. B. Elmore (Eds.), *Complementary methods in education research* (pp. 243–258). Washington, DC: American Educational Research Association.

Brigham, C. C. (n.d.). *Scholastic aptitude tests: A manual for the use of schools*. Prepared by the College Entrance Examination Board. Document is housed in Educational Testing Services Archives, Princeton, NJ.

Bronfenbrenner, U., & Crouter, A. C. (1983). The evolution of environmental models in developmental research. In P. H. Mussen (Series Ed.) & W. Kessen (Vol. Ed.), *Handbook of child psychology: Vol. 1. History, theories, and methods* (4th ed., pp. 357–413). New York: Wiley.

Brookhart, S. M. (2003). Developing measurement theory for classroom assessment purposes and uses. *Educational Measurement: Issues and Practice, 22*, 5–12.

Brookhart, S. M. (2004). *Grading*. Upper Saddle River, NJ: Pearson Education.

Brown v. Board of Education, 347 U.S. 483 (1954).

Burton, E., & Burton, N. W. (1993). The effect of item screening on test scores and test characteristics. In P. W. Holland & H. Wainer H. (Eds.), *Differential item functioning* (pp. 331–335). Hillsdale, NJ: Erlbaum.

Camilli, G. (1992). A conceptual analysis of differential item functioning in terms of a multidimensional item response model. *Applied Psychological Measurement, 16*, 129–147.

Camilli, G., Cizek, G. J., & Lugg, C. A. (2001). Psychometric theory and the validation of performance standards: History and future perspectives. In G. J. Cizek (Ed.), *Setting performance standards* (pp. 445–476). Mahwah, NJ: Lawrence Erlbaum.

Camilli, G., & Congdon, P. (1999). Application of a method of estimating DIF for polytomous items. *Journal of Behavioral and Educational Statistics, 4*, 323–341.

Camilli, G., & Monfils, L. (2003, April). *Item difficulty variation (IDV) approach to school assessment*. Paper presented at the annual meeting of the American Educational Research Association, Chicago.

Camilli, G., & Penfield, D. A. (1997). Variance estimation for differential test functioning based on Mantel-Haenszel statistics. *Journal of Educational Measurement, 34*, 123–139.

Camilli, G., & Shepard, L. A. (1994). *Methods for identifying biased test items*. Thousand Oaks, CA: Sage.

Cardall, C., & Coffman, W. E. (1964). *A method for comparing the performance of different groups on the items in a test*

(Research and Development Reports RDR-64-5 No. 9, College Entrance Examination Board; also Research Bulletin RB-64-61. Princeton, NJ: Educational Testing Service.

Chauncey, H., & Frederiksen, N. (1951). The functions of measurement in educational placement. In E. F. Lindquist (Ed.), *Educational measurement* (pp. 85–116). Washington, DC: American Council on Education.

Chung-Yan, G. A., & Cronshaw, S. F. (2002). A critical re-examination and analysis of cognitive ability tests using the Thorndike model of fairness. *Journal of Occupational and Organizational Psychology, 75*, 489–509.

Clauser, B. E., & Mazor, K. M. (1998). Using statistical procedures to identify differential item functioning test items. *Educational Measurement: Issues and Practice, 17*, 31–44.

Clauser, B., Mazor, K., & Hambleton, R. (1993). The effects of purification for the matching criterion on the identification of DIF using the MH procedure. *Applied Measurement in Education, 6*, 269–279.

Clauser, B. E., Nungester, R. J., & Swaminathan, H. (1996). Improving the matching for DIF analysis by conditioning on both test score and an educational background variable. *Journal of Educational Measurement, 33*, 453–464.

Cleary, T. A. (1968). Test bias: Prediction of grades of Negro and White students in integrated colleges. *Journal of Educational Measurement, 5*, 115–124.

Coffman, W. E. (1961). Sex differences in regard to items in an achievement test. In *Eighteenth yearbook: National Council on Measurement in Education* (pp. 117–124). Washington, DC: National Council on Measurement in Education.

Cohen, A. S., & Bolt, D. M. (2002). *A mixture model analysis of differential item functioning.* Paper presented at the annual meeting of the American Educational Research Association, New Orleans, LA, April.

Cole, N. S. (1973). Bias in selection. *Journal of Educational Measurement, 10*, 237–255.

Cole, N. S., & Moss, P. A. (1989). Bias in test use. In R. L. Linn (Ed.), *Educational measurement* (3rd ed., pp. 201–220). New York: American Council on Education & Macmillan.

Cole, N. S., & Zieky, M. J. (2001). The new faces of fairness. *Journal of Educational Measurement, 38*, 369–382.

College Board. (1914). *Annual report.* New York: College Board.

Conant, James B. (1961). *Slums and Suburbs: A Commentary on Schools in Metropolitan Areas.* New York: McGraw Hill.

Coulehan, M. (2004). ACT now and then. *iJournal, 8.* Retrieved June 24, 2004, from http://www.ijournal.us/issue_08/ij_issue08_MichaelCoulehan_01.htm

Darlington, R. B. (1971). Another look at "culture fairness." *Journal of Educational Measurement, 8*, 71–82.

de Graaf, J. W. (1999). *Relating new to old: a classic controversy in developmental psychology.* University of Groningen (RUG, Ontwikkelingspsychologie en Experimentele Klinische Psychologie, BCN): Regenboog Drukkerij. (Doctoal dissertation thesis, Netherlands).

Dorans, N. J., & Holland, P. W. (1993). DIF detection and description. In P. W. Holland & H. Wainer (Eds.), *Differential item functioning* (pp. 35–66). Hillsdale, NJ: Lawrence Erlbaum.

Dorans, N., & Kulick, E. (1983). *Assessing unexpected differential item performance of female candidates on SAT and TSWE forms administered in December 1977: An application of the standardization approach* (RR-83-9). Princeton, NJ: Educational Testing Service.

Dorans, N. J., & Kulick, E. (1986). Demonstrating the utility of the standardization approach to assessing unexpected differential item performance on the Scholastic Aptitude Test. *Journal of Educational Measurement, 23*, 355–68.

Educational Testing Service. (2002). *ETS standards for quality and fairness.* Princeton, NJ: Author.

Educational Testing Service. (2003). *Fairness review guidelines.* Princeton, NJ: Author.

Eells, K., Davis, A., Havighurst, R., Herrick, V., & Tyler, R. (1951). *Intelligence and cultural differences.* Chicago: University of Chicago Press.

Einhorn, H. J., & Bass, A. R. (1971). Methodological considerations relevant to discrimination in employment testing. *Psychological Bulletin, 75*, 261–269.

Englehard, G. (1989). Accuracy of bias review judges in identifying teacher certification tests. *Applied Measurement in Education, 3*, 347–360.

Evinger, S. (1995). How shall we measure our nation's diversity? *Chance, 8*, 7–14.

Gardener, H. (1999). Who owns intelligence? *Atlantic Monthly, 283*, 67–76.

Gelin, M. N., & Zumbo, B. D. (2003). Differential item functioning results may change depending on how an item is scored: An illustration with the Center for Epidemiologic Studies Depression Scale. *Educational and Psychological Measurement, 63*, 65–74.

Gierl, M. J., Bisanz, J., Bisanz, G., & Boughton, K. (2003). Identifying and content and cognitive skills that produce gender differences in mathematics: A demonstration of the DIF analysis framework. *Journal of Educational Measurement, 40*, 281–306.

Gierl, M. J., Bisanz, J., Bisanz, G., Boughton, K., & Khaliq, S. (2001). Illustrating the utility of differential bundle functioning analyses to identify and interpret group differences on achievement tests. *Educational Measurement: Issues and Practice, 20*, 26–36.

Gipps, C. (1999). Socio-cultural aspects of assessment. In A. Iran-Nejad & P. D. Pearson (Eds.), *Review of research in education* (pp. 355–392). Washington, DC: AERA.

Gould, Stephen Jay (1996). *The mismeasure of man: Revised and expanded.* New York: W. W. Norton. (Original work published 1981)

Green, D. R., & Draper, J. F. (1972). *Exploratory studies of bias in achievement tests.* Paper presented to the American Psychological Association, Honolulu, HI.

Griggs v. Duke Power Company, 401 U.S. 424 (1971).

Grutter v. Bollinger (02–241) 539 U.S. 306 (2003).

Hambleton, R. K., & Swaminathan, H. (1984). *Item response theory: Principles and applications.* Hingham, MA: Kluwer, Nijhoff.

Hartigan, J. A. & Wigdor, A. K. (1989). *Fairness in employment testing: Validity generalization, minority issues and the General Aptitude Test Battery.* Washington, DC: National Academy Press.

Hidalgo-Montesinos, M. D., & Lopez-Pina, J. A. (2002). Two-stage equating in differential item functioning detection under the graded response model with the Raju area measures and the Lord statistic. *Educational and Psychological Measurement, 62*, 32–44.

Holland, P. W., & Thayer, D. T. (1988). Differential item performance and the Mantel-Haenszel procedure. In H. Wainer & H. I. Braun (Eds.), *Test validity* (pp. 129–145). Hillsdale, NJ: Lawrence Erlbaum.

Holland, P. W., & Wainer, H. (Eds.). (1993). *Differential item functioning.* Hillsdale, NJ: Lawrence Erlbaum.

Hu, P. G., & Dorans, N. L. (1989, March). *The effect of deleting items with extreme differential item functioning on equating functions and reported score distributions.* Paper presented at the annual meeting of the American Educational Research Association, San Francisco.

Hubin, D. R. (1988). *The Scholastic Aptitude Test: Its development and introduction, 1900–1948.* Ph.D. dissertation, University of Oregon at Eugene.

Hunter, J. F. (1975, December). A critical analysis of the use of item means and item-test correlations to determine the presence or absence of content bias in achievement test items. A paper presented at the National Institute of Education Conference on Test Bias. Annapolis, MD.

Ironson, G. H., & Subkoviak, M. J. (1979). A comparison of several methods of assessing item bias. *Journal of Educational Measurement, 16,* 209–225.

Jensen, A. R. (1974). How biased are culture-loaded tests? *Genetic Psychology Monographs, 40,* 185–244.

Jensen, A. R. (1975). *Test bias and construct validity.* Invited address at the American Psychological Association, Chicago, September.

Jensen, A. R. (1980). *Test bias.* New York: Free Press.

Joint Committee on Testing Practices. (1988). *Code of fair testing practices in education.* Washington, DC: Author.

Kim, S., & Cohen, A. S. (1995). A comparison of Lord's chi-square, Raju's areas measures, and the likelihood ration test on the detection of differential item functioning. *Applied Measurement in Education, 8,* 291–312.

Lan, W., Bradley, L., Tallent-Runnels, M., & Hsu, P.-Y. (2001, April). *Changes in student academic performance and perceptions of school and self before dropping out from schools.* Paper presented at the annual meeting of the American Educational Research Association, Seattle, WA.

Lawrence, I. M., Rigol, G. W., Van Essen, T., & Jackson, C. A. (2003). *A historical perspective on the content of the SAT.* New York: College Entrance Examination Board.

Lazerson, M. (2001). The College Board and American educational history. In M. C. Johanek (Ed.), *A faithful mirror: Reflections on the College Board and education in America* (pp. 379–400). New York: College Board.

Le, V.-N. (1999). *Identifying differential item functioning on the NELS:88 history achievement test.* Center for the Study of Evaluation, Los Angeles, CA: CRESST/UCLA.

Lemann, N. (2004). A history of admissions testing, In R. Zwick (Ed.), *Rethinking the SAT: The Future of Standardized Testing in University Admissions* (pp. 5–14). New York: RoutledgeFalmer.

Lemann, N. (1995). The structure of success in America. *Atlantic Monthly, 276,* 41–60.

Lemann, N. (1999). *The big test.* New York: Farrar, Straus & Giroux.

Levin, S. (2003). Social psychological evidence on race and racism. In M. Chang, D. Witt, K. Haikuta, & J. Jones (Eds.), *Compelling interest: Examining the evidence on racial dynamics in higher education in colleges and universities* (pp. 97–125). Stanford University Press.

Lindquist, E. F. (1951). Preliminary considerations in objective test construction. In E. F. Lindquist (Ed.), *Educational measurement* (pp. 119–158). Washington, DC: American Council on Education.

Lindquist, E. F. (1970). Iowa Testing Programs—A retrospective view. *Education, 91,* 7–23.

Linn, R. L. (1989). Current directions and future perspectives. In R. L. Linn (Ed.), *Educational measurement* (3rd ed., pp. 1–10). New York: American Council on Education & Macmillan.

Linn, R. L. (1973). Fair test use in selection. *Review of Educational Research, 43,* 139–161.

Linn, R. L. (1982). Ability testing: Individual differences, prediction and differential prediction. In A. K. Wigdor, & W. R. Garner (Eds.), *Ability Testing: Uses, consequences and controversies, Part II* (pp. 335–388). Washington, DC: National Academy Press.

Lombardo, P. A. (2002). "The American Breed": Nazi Eugenics and the origins of the Pioneer Fund. *Albany Law Review, 65*(3), 743–830.

Lombardo, P. A. (2003). Facing Carrie Buck. *Hastings Center Report, 33,* 14–16.

Longford, N. T., Holland, P. W., & Thayer, D. T. (1993). Stability of the MH DIF across populations. In P. W. Holland & H. Wainer (Eds.), *Differential item functioning* (pp. 171–196). Hillsdale, NJ: Erlbaum.

Lord, F. M. (1977). A study of item bias using item characteristic curve theory. In Y. H. Poortinga (Ed.), *Basic problems in cross-cultural psychology* (pp. 19–29). Amsterdam: Swets & Zeitlinger.

Lord, F. M. (1980). *Applications of item response theory to practical testing problems.* Hillsdale, NJ: Lawrence Erlbaum.

Mantel, N. (1963). Chi-square tests with one degree of freedom: Extension of the Mantel-Haenszel procedure. *Journal of the American Statistical Association, 58,* 690–700.

Mantel, N., & Haenszel, W. M. (1959). Statistical aspects of the analysis of data from retrospective studies of disease. *Journal of the National Cancer Institute, 22,* 719–748.

Masters, G. N. (1988). Item discrimination: When more is worse. *Journal of Educational Measurement, 25,* 15.

Masters, G. N. (1993). Undesirable item discrimination. Rasch Measurement Transactions, 7, 289.

Mazor, K. M., Kanjee, A., & Clauser, B. E. (1995). Using logistic regression and the Mantel-Haenszel with multiple ability estimates to detect differential item functioning. *Journal of Educational Measurement, 32,* 131–144.

Messick, S. (1994). Foundations of validity: Meaning and consequence in psychological assessment. *European Journal of Psychological Assessment 10,* 1–9.

Mill, J. S. (1848). *Principles of political economy.* (Reprinted in *Collected works of John Stuart Mill* [Vol. 2], Toronto: University of Toronto Press, 1965)

Miller, T. R., & Spray, J. A. (1993). Logistic discriminant function analysis for DIF identification of polytomously scores items. *Journal of Educational Measurement, 30,* 107–122.

Millsap, R. E., & Everson, H. T. (1993). Methodology review: Statistical procedures for assessing measurement bias. *Applied Psychological Measurement, 17,* 297–334.

Moss, S. M. (2003). Conceptualizing validity for classroom assessment. *Educational Measurement: Issues and Practice, 22*(4), 13–25.

Muraki, E. (1999). Stepwise analysis of differential item functioning based on multiple group partial credit model. *Journal of Educational Measurement, 36,* 217–232.

Nandakumar, R. (1993). Simultaneous DIF amplification and cancellation: Shealy-Stout's test for DIF. *Journal of Educational Measurement, 30,* 293–311.

NCME Ad Hoc Committee on the Development of a Code of Ethics. (1995). *Code of professional responsibilities in educational measurement.* Washington, DC: National Council on Measurement in Education.

Novick, M. R., & Petersen, N. S. (1976). Toward equalizing educational and employment opportunity. *Journal of Educational Measurement, 13,* 77–88.

Office for Minority Education. (1980). *An approach for identifying and minimizing bias in standardized tests* (Educational Testing Service Monograph No. 4). Princeton, NJ: ETS.

Office of Technology Assessment, U.S. Congress. (1992). *Testing in American schools: Asking the right questions* (OTA-SET-519). Washington, DC: U.S. Government Printing Office.

OMB. (1997, October 30). Revisions to the Standards for the Classification of Federal Data on Race and Ethnicity, Federal Register Notice (62FR58782-89). Washington, DC: Author.

O'Neill, K. A., & McPeek, W. M. (1993). Item and test characteristics that are associated with differential item functioning. In

P. W. Holland & H. Wainer (Eds.), *Differential item functioning* (pp. 255–276). Hillsdale, NJ: Erlbaum.

Pellegrino, J. W., Chudowsky, N., & Glaser, R. (Eds.). (2001). *Knowing what students know: The science and design of educational assessment.* Washington, DC: National Academy Press.

Penfield, R. D. (2001). Assessing differential item functioning across multiple groups: A comparison of three Mantel-Haenszel procedures. *Applied Measurement in Education, 14,* 235–259.

Penfield, R. D., & Camilli, G. (in press). Differential item functioning and item bias. In C. R. Rao & S. Sinharay (Eds.), *Handbook of Statistics: Psychometrics,* 25. North Holland: Elsevier.

Penfield, R. D., & Lam, T. C. (2000). Assessing differential item functioning in performance assessment: Review and recommendations. *Educational Measurement: Issues and Practice, 19,* 5–15.

Penny, J., & Johnson, R. L. (1999). How group differences in matching criterion distribution and IRT item difficulty can influence the magnitude of the Mantel-Haenszel chi-square DIF index. *Journal of Experimental Education, 67,* 343–366.

Petersen, N. S., & Novick, M. R. (1976). An evaluation of some models for culture fair selection. *Journal of Educational Measurement, 13,* 3–29.

Peterson, J. J. (1983). *The Iowa Testing Programs: The first fifty years.* Iowa City, IA: University of Iowa Press.

Phillips, A. & Holland, P.W. (1987). Estimators of the variance of the Mantel-Haenszel log-odds-ratio estimate. *Biometrics,* 425-431.

Popham, W. J. (2001). Standardized achievement tests: Misnamed and misleading. *Education Week, 21*(03), 46. (www.edweek.org/ew/newstory.cfm?slug=03popham.h21)

Porter, T. M. (1986). *The rise of statistical thinking 1820–1900.* Princeton, NJ: Princeton University Press.

Prowker, A., & Camilli, G. (2004. *Beyond the composite: An item level methodological study of NAEP mathematics results.* Paper presented at the annual meeting of the American Educational Research Association, San Diego, CA, April.

Raju, N. S. (1988). The area between two item characteristic curves. *Psychometrika, 53,* 492–502.

Raju, N. S. (1990). Determining the significance of estimated signed and unsigned areas between two item response functions. *Applied Psychological Measurement, 14,* 197–207.

Ramist, L., Lewis, C., & McCamley-Jenkins, L. (1994). *Student group differences in predicting college grades: Sex, language, and ethnic groups* (College Board Report No. 93-1). New York: College Board.

Ramsey, P. A. (1993). Sensitivity review: The ETS experience as a case study. In P. W. Holland & H. Wainer (Eds.), *Differential item functioning* (pp. 367–388). Hillsdale, NJ: Erlbaum.

Raudenbush, S. W., & Sampson, R. J. (1999). Ecometrics: Toward a science of assessing ecological settings, with application to the systematic social observation of neighborhoods. *Sociological Methodology, 29,* 1–41.

Rawls, J. (1971). *A theory of justice.* Cambridge, MA: Harvard University Press.

Raymond, M. R. & Reid, J. B. (2001). Who made thee a judge? Selecting and training participants for standard setting. In G. Cizek (Ed.), *Setting performance standards: concepts, methods, and perspectives* (pp. 119–158). Mahwah, N.J.: Erlbaum.

Reckase, M. D. (1979). Unifactor latent trait models applied to multi-factor tests: Results and implications. *Journal of Educational Statistics, 4,* 207–230.

Reckase, M. D., Ackerman, T. A., & Carlson, J. E. (1988). Building a unidimensional test using multidimensional items. *Journal of Educational Measurement, 25,* 193–203.

Reese, L., Balzano, S., Gallimore, R., & Goldenberg, C. (1995). The concept of educación: Latino family values and American schooling. *International Journal of Educational Research, 23,* 57–81.

Reynolds, C. R. (1982). The problem of bias in psychological assessment. In C. R. Reynolds & B. Gutkin (Eds.), *The handbook of school psychology* (pp. 178–201). New York: Wiley.

Roe v. Wade, 410 U.S. 113 (1973).

Rogers, H. J., & Swaminathan, H. (1993). A comparison of the logistic regression and Mantel-Haenszel procedures for detecting differential item functioning. *Applied Psychological Measurement, 17,* 105–116.

Roussos, L., & Stout, W. (1996). A multidimensionality-based DIF analysis paradigm. *Applied Psychological Measurement, 20,* 355–371.

Roussos, L. A., & Stout, W. F. (2004). Differential item functioning analysis: Detecting DIF items and testing DIF hypotheses. In D. Kaplan (Ed.), *The SAGE handbook of quantitative methodology for the social sciences* (pp. 107–115). Thousand Oaks, CA: Sage.

Roznowski, M., & Reith, J. (1999). Examining the measurement quality of tests containing differentially functioning items: Do biased items result in poor measurement? *Educational and Psychological Measurement, 59,* 248–270.

Scheuneman, J. D. (1979). A method of assessing bias in test items. *Journal of Educational Measurement, 16,* 143–152.

Schmidt, F. L., & Hunter, J. E. (1998). The validity and utility of selection methods in personnel psychology: Practical and theoretical implications of 85 years of research findings. *Psychological Bulletin, 124,* 262–274.

Schmitt, A. P., Holland, P. W., & Dorans, N. J. (1993). Evaluating hypotheses about differential item functioning. In P. W. Holland & H. Wainer (Eds.), *Differential item functioning* (pp. 281–315). Hillsdale, NJ: Lawrence Erlbaum.

Shealy, R., & Stout, W. (1993a). A model-based standardization approach that separates true bias/DIF from group ability differences and detects test bias/DTF as well as item bias/DIF. *Psychometrika, 58,* 159–194.

Shealy, R., & Stout, W. (1993b). An item response theory model for test bias and differential test functioning. In P. Holland & H. Wainer (Eds.), *Differential item functioning* (pp. 197–240). Hillsdale, NJ: Erlbaum.

Shepard, L. A. (2000). The role of assessment in a learning culture. *Educational Researcher, 29,* 1–14.

Shepard, L. A. (2001). The role of classroom assessment in teaching and learning. In V. Richardson (Ed.), *Handbook of research on teaching* (pp. 1066–1101) (4th ed.). Washington, DC: American Educational Research Association.

Shepard, L. A., Camilli, G., & Averill, M. (1981). Comparison of procedures for detecting test item bias with both internal and external criteria. *Journal of Educational Statistics, 6,* 317–375.

Shepard, L. A., Camilli, G., & Williams, D. M. (1984). Accounting for statistical artifacts in item bias research. *Journal of Educational Statistics, 9,* 93–128.

Smedley, A. (2002). Science and the idea of *race*. In J. M. Fish (Ed.), *Race and intelligence* (pp. 145–176). Mahwah, NJ: Erlbaum.

Spray, J. A. (1989). *Performance of three conditional DIF statistics in detecting differential item functioning on simulated tests* (ACT Research Report Series 89-7). Iowa City, IA: ACT.

Stiggins, R. J. (2002). Where is our assessment future and how can we get there from here? In R. W. Lissitz & W. D. Schafer (Eds.), *Assessment in educational reform* (pp. 18–48). Boston: Allyn and Bacon.

Stout, W. (1987). A nonparametric approach for assessing latent trait unidimensionality. *Psychometrika, 52,* 589–617.

Stout, W. (1990). A new item response theory modeling approach with applications to unidimensionality assessment and ability estimation. *Psychometrika, 55*, 293–325.

Swaminathan, H., & Rogers, H. J. (1990). Detecting differential item functioning using logistic regression procedures. *Journal of Educational Measurement, 27*, 361–370.

Takala, S., & Kaftandieva, F. (2000). Test fairness: A DIF analysis of an L2 vocabulary test. *Language Testing, 17*(3), 323–340.

Thissen, D., Steinberg, L., & Wainer, H. (1988). Detection of differential item functioning using the parameters of item response theory models. In H. Wainer & H. I. Braun (Eds.), *Test validity* (pp. 67–113). Hillsdale, NJ: Erlbaum.

Thissen, D., Steinberg, L., & Wainer, H. (1993). Use of item response theory in the study of group differences in trace lines. In P. W. Holland & H. Wainer (Eds.), *Differential item functioning* (pp. 147–169). Hillsdale, NJ: Erlbaum.

Thorndike, R. L. (1971). Concepts of culture-fairness. *Journal of Educational Measurement, 8*, 63–70.

Thurstone, L. L. (1925). A method of scaling educational and psychological tests. *Journal of Educational Psychology, 8*, 63–70.

Thurstone, L. L. (1931). Influence of motion pictures on children's attitudes. *Journal of Social Psychology, 2*, 291–305.

Walker, C. M., Beretvas, S. N., & Ackerman, T. A. (2001). An examination of conditioning variables used in computer adaptive testing for DIF analyses. *Applied Measurement in Education, 14*, 3–16.

Wechsler, H. S. (2001). Eastern standard time: High-school college collaboration and admission to college 1880–1930. In M. C. Johanek (Ed.), *A faithful mirror: Reflections on the College Board and education in America* (pp. 41–79). New York: College Board.

Welner, K. (2001). Alexander v. Sandoval: A setback for civil rights. *Educational Policy Analysis Archives, 24*. Retrieved September 12, 2004, from http://epaa.asu.edu/epaa/v9n24.html

Westers, P., & Kelderman, H. (1991). Examining differential item functioning due to item difficulty and alternative attractiveness. *Psychometrika, 57*, 107–118.

Wigdor, A. K. & Sackett, P. R. (1993). Employment testing and public policy: The case of the General Aptitude Test Battery. In H. Schuler, J. L. Farr, & M. Smith (Eds.), *Personnel selection and assessment: Individual and organizational perspectives* (pp. 183–204). Hillsdale, NJ: Lawrence Erlbaum Associates.

Wightman, L. F. (2000). The role of standardized tests in the debate about merit, academic standards, and affirmative action. *Psychology, Public Policy, and Law, 6*, 90–100.

Wightman, L. (2003). Standardized testing and equal access: A tutorial. In M. Chang, D. Witt, K. Haikuta, & J. Jones (Eds.), *Compelling interest: Examining the evidence on racial dynamics in higher education in colleges and universities* (chap. 4). Stanford, CA: Stanford University Press.

Wright, B. D., Mead, R., & Drada, D. (1976). *Detecting and correcting item bias with a logistic response model* (Mesa Research Memorandum 22). Chicago: University of Chicago, MESA Psychometric Laboratory.

Young, J. W. (2001). *Differential validity, differential prediction, and college admissions testing: A comprehensive review and analysis* (Research Report No. 2001-6). New York: The College Board.

Young, M. D. (1958). *Rise of the meritocracy*. Baltimore: Penguin Books.

Young, M.D. (2001, June 29). Down with Meritoocracy. *Guardian Unlimited*. Retrieved August 1, 2005 from http://www.guardian.co.uk/comment/story/0,3604,514207,00.html.

Zenderland, L. (1998). *Measuring minds: Henry Herbert Goddard and the origins of American intelligence testing*. Cambridge: Cambridge University Press.

Zenisky, A., Hambleton, R. K., & Robin, F. (2003). Detection of differential item functioning in large scale assessments: A study evaluating a two-stage approach. *Educational and Psychological Measurement, 63*, 541–564.

Zieky, M. (1993). Practical questions in the use of DIF statistics in test development. In P. W. Holland & H. Wainer (Eds.), *Differential item functioning* (pp. 337–347). Hillsdale, NJ: Erlbaum.

Zumbo, B. D. (1999). *A handbook on the theory and methods of differential item functioning (DIF): Logistic regression modeling as a unitary framework for binary and likert-type (ordinal) item scores* [On-line]. Ottawa, Ontario, Canada: Department of National Defense, Directorate of Human Resources Research and Evaluation. Available: http://www.educ.ubc.ca/faculty/zumbo/DIF/index.html

Zwick, R. (1990). When do item response function and Mantel-Haenszel definitions of differential item functioning coincide? *Journal of Educational Statistics, 15*, 185–198.

Zwick, R. (2002). *Fair game?* New York: Routledge Falmer.

Zwick, R., Donoghue, J. R., & Grima, A. (1993). Assessment of differential item functioning for performance tasks. *Journal of Educational Measurement, 30*, 233–251.

Zwick, R. Thayer, D. T., & Lewis, C. (1999). An empirical Bayes approach to Mantel-Haenszel DIF analysis. *Journal of Educational Measurement, 36*, 1–28.

Zwick, R., Thayer, D. T., & Mazzeo, J. (1997). Descriptive and inferential procedures for assessing differential item functioning in polytomous items. *Applied Measurement in Education, 10*, 321–334.

Zwick, R., Thayer, D. T., & Wingersky, M. (1995). Effect of Rasch calibration on ability and DIF estimation in computer-adaptive tests. *Journal of Educational Measurement, 32*(4), 341–363.

Zwick, R., Thayer, D. T., & Wingersky, M. (1994). A simulation study of methods for assessing differential item functioning in computerized adaptive tests. *Applied Psychological Measurement, 18*, 121–140.

8

Cognitive Psychology and Educational Assessment

Robert J. Mislevy
University of Maryland

1. INTRODUCTION

Cognitive psychology is a young science, but key ideas trace back millennia. Plato puzzled over how we come to know things we had not known before, and Aristotle contemplated visual perception. Kant proposed that a mental representation requires both sensation, which comes to us from the world, and concepts, which we bring to the experience. Important foundations were laid in the first half of the Twentieth Century, as in Gestalt psychologists such as Wertheimer's and Kohler's studies of meaning and perception (Figure 8.1), Piaget's analyses of how rational thinking develops in children, and Vygotsky's and Luria's insights into the situated and social character of learning.

There is no simple answer to "when was cognitive psychology born?" but 1956 was clearly a watershed. That year marked the publication of George Miller's (1956) "The magical number seven, plus or minus two," Chomsky's (1956) *Three Models of Language*, Bruner, Goodnow, and Austin's (1956) *A Study of Thinking*, and Newell and Simon's (1956) "Logic Theorist," the first theorem-proving program. The MIT Symposium on Information Theory began on September 11, 1956. Newell and Simon, Bruner, Miller, and Chomsky presented papers, as well as Nat Rochester on learning in what have come to be called neural networks, and Swets and Birdsall on the relevance of signal detection theory to perception. As Bruner (1990) recounts,

> let me tell you first what I and my friends thought the revolution was about back there in the late 1950s. It was, we thought, an all-out effort to establish meaning as the central concept of psychology—not stimuli and responses, not overtly observable behavior, not biological drives and their transformation, but meaning. The cognitive revolution as originally conceived virtually required that psychology join forces with anthropology and linguistics, philosophy and history, even with the discipline of law. (pp. 2–3)

More focused research areas within cognitive psychology today differ as to their foci, methods, and levels of explanation. They include perception and attention, language and communication, development of expertise, situated and sociocultural psychology, and neurological bases of cognition. All share two complementary premises. The first is that people are essentially alike in terms of cognitive machinery and processes. This human endowment entails both remarkable capabilities and surprising limitations. Examples of our capabilities include learning to use language as toddlers; apparently unlimited long-term memory capacity; and rapid and effortless recognition, judgment, language use, and coordinated bodily action. We are equally subject to sensory limitations, biases in reasoning, working memories of only about seven chunks of information, and unawareness of most of our own cognitive activity. While individuals do vary in these respects, the patterns of development, learning, and thinking are common across people and across cultures. They appear in language and symbol systems, interactions with things in the environment, and interactions with other people as individuals and in social groups.

The second premise is that within broad ranges set by our cognitive machinery and the nature of the world, the contents of learning and thinking are shaped by culture. Every human society uses language, and all languages appear to be built around the same fundamental set of rules for creating sounds, arranging them into larger meanings, and associating them with things, events, and relationships. But particular sounds and syntactic arrangements differ from one language to another. All groups work with symbol systems and classification schemes, but just what the symbols are, how they are used, and what they refer to varies with circumstances and purposes. Everyone uses narratives, stories that "make sense," to interpret their own actions, those of others, and events in their world. But the themes and elements of narratives are shaped by the many communities within which we participate. Everyone interacts with objects in the environments in terms of physical laws that they (and we) must obey, and the affordances (Gibson's [1966] term for ways we can use them to accomplish things) they offer. But the particular things we make and use, and the ends to which we put them, are embedded in culture.

Some aspects of learning, such as acquiring first languages and patterns of social interaction, are natural and seemingly effortless. Other aspects demand intentional effort and focused attention, often over extended periods of

FIGURE 8.1 Do You See a White Square?

time. This learning may require one to acquire a great deal of information, work with symbol systems and knowledge representations, or become proficient at complex activities. Simon (Bhaskar & Simon, 1977) refers to "semantically rich domains," highlighting the concepts, tools, and representational forms that are involved in this kind of learning. Complementary terms such as "community of practice" (Lave & Wenger, 1991) or "affinity group" (Gee, 2003) highlight the groups of people and the patterns of interaction in which these artifacts are employed, in jobs, hobbies, families, and communities. Familiar examples are reading and repairing automobiles. Less familiar examples are gathering food in the forest, and navigating across the open Pacific by means of ocean swells, star movements, and positions of islands—including some that don't even exist, but as constructs help navigators organize and act on what they do observe (D. Lewis, 1973).

Much learning for school and work concerns semantically rich domains. This chapter concerns implications of a cognitive perspective for assessment, with an emphasis on semantically rich domains. What does research into how people think, learn, and act tell us about building and using assessments? How do insights from cognitive psychology help us understand what we are doing when we design and use them?

Our attempt to address these questions sees assessment as a special kind of narrative, an evidentiary argument. It is reasoning from a handful of particular things students say, do, or make in a handful of particular circumstances, to more broadly construed inferences about what they have learned, have accomplished, or might do under various other circumstances (Kane, 1992). Any particular assessment is shaped by its purposes, its constraints, and the context of its use, but also fundamentally by the psychological perspective that gives the argument meaning. This grounding entails the kinds of claims the assessment is meant to support, the kinds of data that are sought and how they are interpreted, and the rationale for each link in a chain of reasoning from observation to inference. An argument is instantiated in the activities and the machinery of operational assessments—tasks, rubrics, measurement models, score reports, and so on. These visible elements of an assessment make sense only in terms of their roles in the underlying argument.

Section 2 provides terminology and representational forms for analyzing assessments as evidentiary arguments. It also offers sketches of psychological perspectives, namely trait or differential, behavioral, developmental, information processing, and sociocultural (Greeno, Collins, & Resnick, 1997). We consider the last three "cognitive," adopting Bruner's inclusive use of the term. While these caricatures necessarily obscure debates and multiple perspectives within and between somewhat arbitrary categories, they help draw out the implications of a psychological stance for assessment.

Section 3 presents an overview of themes from cognitive psychology that are particularly relevant to assessment. Topics include the pattern-driven nature of perception, learning, and action, the development of expertise, and the role of knowledge representations. The discussion focuses on substantive aspects of assessment arguments: What is the nature of claims one might want to make about students, and what does one need to see under what circumstances to back them?

Section 4 brings probability-based reasoning fully into the discussion. A probabilistic framework is an overlay on an assessment argument. It provides machinery for expressing and working with what one knows and does not know, within a simplified representation of the argument's narrative structure. Since Snow and Lohman's (1989) chapter on cognitive psychology in the third edition of *Educational Measurement*, many models have been developed for cognitively based assessment, especially under the developmental and information-processing perspectives. Several are described and illustrated.

Section 5 concludes with thoughts about challenges cognitive psychology raises for educational assessment, and speculations about the role of measurement in meeting them.

2. ASSESSMENT ARGUMENTS

Chi, Feltovich, and Glaser (1981) asked novices and experts in physics to sort cards depicting mechanics problems into stacks of similar tasks. Novices grouped problems in terms of surface features such as pulleys and springs. Experts organized their stacks in terms of more fundamental principles such as equilibrium and Newton's Third Law, each stack containing a mixture of spring, pulley, and inclined plane tasks. Of course experts also differ from novices by being able to solve problems like these, by decomposing forces, chaining equations, solving for unknown variables, and so on. But Larkin (1983) found that before they lay a problem out formally, physicists first construct a "story" for the real-world situations in terms of physics principles. While they ultimately used symbol manipulation to work out the details of a solution, the narratives built around underlying principles linked the symbolic representations to the particulars of real-world situations, and guided the course of the procedure. *Meaning* intertwines with *perception* on the one hand and effective *action* on the other (c.f. Bernstein, 1983).

Tasks and scores are the pulleys and springs of assessments. They are the tangible features of tests; the terms in which most people experience tests, the terms in which most people think about tests. Measurement models and conditional probability distributions correspond to physicists' normal equations and force decompositions. Measurement specialists use them to describe and solve technical problems in assessment design and analysis through principles that are anything but obvious.

What in assessment corresponds to the thinking physicists use to connect configurations of pulleys and springs with variables and equations? Where do we look for the meaning that underlies, unifies, and guides the construction and the operation of items and scores, of parameters and likelihoods? It is the assessment argument. This section concerns the structure of assessment arguments. Upon this structure we can build narratives around the cognitive-psychology themes of section 3, which guide the assembly and use of the machinery of section 4. We begin with argument structures and psychological perspectives in terms of which assessment arguments might be constructed. We then look more closely at how these ideas play out with tests using progressive matrices, a task type conceived under the aegis of trait psychology and later studied by cognitive psychologists.

2.1. The Structure of Evidentiary Arguments

Philosopher Stephen Toulmin (1958) proposed the schema shown as Figure 8.2 for how we reason from particular data to particular claims. A claim is a proposition we wish to support with data. A warrant is a generalization that justifies the inference from the particular data to the particular claim. Theory and experience, formal and informal, provide backing for the warrant. In a particular argument we reason inductively, back up through the warrant. In some cases a claim follows conclusively from data, but usually we must qualify an inference in light of alternative explanations, which further data might support or undercut.

FIGURE 8.2 Toulmin's (1958) Structure for Arguments

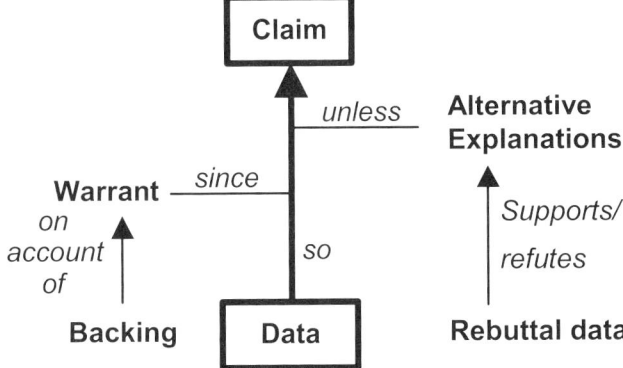

Note: Reasoning flows from *data* to *claim* by justification of a *warrant*, which is supported by *backing*. The inference may be qualified by *alternative explanations*, which *rebuttal evidence* tend to support or refute.

In practice, an argument and its constituent claims, data, warrants, backing, and alternative explanations are more complicated. Arguments generally consist of many propositions and data elements, involve multiple steps of reasoning, and contain dependencies among claims and various pieces of data. In *Science of Judicial Proof*, John Henry Wigmore (1937) introduced a system for charting evidentiary arguments in terms of recurring patterns and principles, to guide thinking across the widely varied and often voluminous particulars in legal contests. His methods accommodate multiple strands of argument, cascaded and conjoined relationships, and multiple points of view, and can be applied with even very large problems. Kadane and Schum's (1996) Wigmore charts for the 395 pieces of evidence from the Sacco and Vanzetti trial span 52 pages. The process of constructing a Wigmore chart forces and organizes thought about how evidence leads to inferences and how inferences interrelate. The product, the diagram itself, serves to communicate this thinking to others, so that they may be persuaded, or moved to propose missing themes, counterexplanations, or new lines of evidence to explore.

To a similar end, we may use Toulmin's and Wigmore's ideas to sketch a general form of an assessment argument (Mislevy, Steinberg, & Almond, 2003). Figure 8.3 applies Toulmin's and Wigmore's ideas to assessment arguments. It is not difficult to relate to formal and familiar assessments, because their visible parts and processes are set up explicitly before the assessment occasion and they map directly to elements of the argument. But at the other extreme, the same structure can be used to analyze a conversation between a student and a teacher as they work through, say, making sense of a poem—in this case with the arguments implicit, constructed iteratively moment by moment as new actions are observed and new meanings are constructed on the fly. Nothing in the argument structure specifies whether the data, nor for that matter the claims, should be among predetermined possibilities or adduced from performances themselves. Typical assessments do, however, rely on determining beforehand the claims of interest and at least some aspects of task conditions and procedures for evaluating performances.

Figure 8.3 actually depicts two arguments, the assessment argument per se in the lower dashed rectangle and an assessment use argument in the upper rectangle (Bachman, 2003). Our attention focuses on the assessment argument, but including the use argument emphasizes that assessment cannot be understood apart from context and use. We begin the discussion with a single "task" and extend later to multiple tasks. We use the term *task* to refer to a goal-directed human activity to be pursued in a specified manner, context, or circumstance (Haertel & Wiley, 1993). A *task* could be an open-ended problem in a computerized simulation, a long-term project such as a dissertation, a language-proficiency interview, or a familiar multiple-choice or essay question.

Assessment claims are shown in the center of the figure, as both the outcome of the assessment argument and data for the use argument. The terms in which they are cast connect our thinking about what is observed in assessment settings and about educational ends such as guiding and evaluating learning. The meaning of the claim is thus integral to

FIGURE 8.3 Elaborated Structure for Assessment Arguments

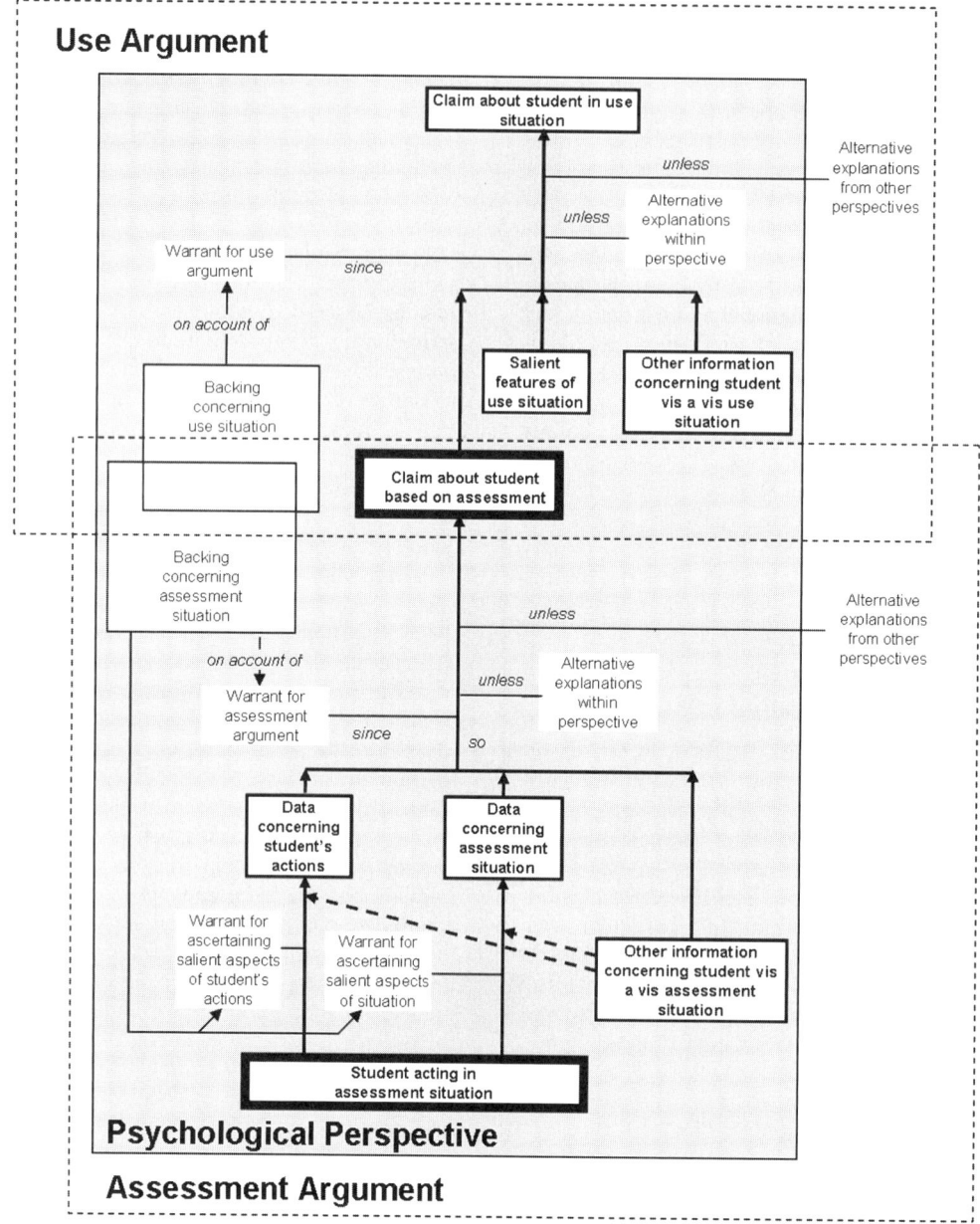

Note: Lower rectangle shows assessment argument proper; upper rectangle shows assessment use argument. They share psychological perspective, backing, and claim about student based on assessment.

both perception of students' performances in assessment situations and as grounds for action in use situations. Highlighted at the bottom of Figure 8.3, toward the left, is a student's action in a situation: The students says, does, or makes something, possibly extending over time, possibly interacting with others. Interpretations of the actions rather than the actions themselves constitute data in an assessment argument. An assessment argument generally encompasses three kinds of data:

- Aspects of the situation in which the person is acting,
- Aspects of the person's actions in the situation, and
- Additional information about the person's history or relationship to the observational situation.

The first two are characterizations of a person acting within a context in terms that might hold value beyond this unique event; that is, in terms that might be used to talk about other actions, other people, and other situations, including in particular the use situations the assessment is meant to support. Assessment designers have influence over the data about situations to varying degrees: considerable control over aspects such as initial conditions and resources, less when the performance will evolve over time in response to the student's own actions or to other events or people that are part of the task (e.g., when assessing language use in live conversations). Students have influence over the data about their performances, through their actions but in some assessments also with their case for how their actions should be interpreted. Both kinds of data can require one or many steps of reasoning, more or less inference to evaluate, more or less synthesis across disparate aspects of the performance and situation (Moss, 1992, 1994). Ascertaining their values in both cases may require human judgment, automated algorithms, or some combination of the two.

"Additional information" data are often tacit, embedded in forms and practices. What we know about a particular student acting in a particular situation may condition how we interpret the interaction. For example, the American Council on the Training of Foreign Languages' reading guidelines (ACTFL, 1989) contrast Intermediate readers' competence with texts "about which the reader has personal interest or knowledge" with Advanced readers' comprehension of "texts which treat unfamiliar topics and situation"—a distinction fundamental to ACTFL's conception of the development of language proficiency. If we know that the context of a given situation is familiar to one student but unfamiliar to a second, the same action from the two students conveys different information about their ACTFL levels.

2.2. Psychological Perspectives

Toulmin's and Wigmore's ideas enable us to say a great deal about the structure of an assessment argument, but nothing about its substance. Here psychological perspectives enter the picture. Perspectives or stances within or across disciplines are marked by characteristic but evolving sets of concepts that focus on some range of phenomena. They take a stand on what is important; how and why to see situations and how and why to act in them; more narrowly, what to see as problems, how to think about them, and how to solve them. A psychological perspective determines the nature of every element in an assessment argument, and the rationale that orchestrates them: the kinds of things one might say concerning students (claims), what kinds of things one wants to see in what kinds of situations (data), and the relationships that justify reasoning from one to the other (warrants).

Of use for our purposes are five psychological perspectives for thinking about knowledge and learning (adapted from Greeno, Pearson, & Schoenfeld, 1996, and Greeno, Collins, & Resnick, 1997): the trait or differential, behavioral, developmental, information-processing, and sociocultural perspectives. They differ as to which of myriad aspects of human learning, thinking, and acting they bring to the foreground.

A trait or differential perspective. Messick (1989, p. 15) defines a trait as "a relatively stable characteristic of a person—an attribute, enduring process, or disposition—which is consistently manifested to some degree when relevant, despite considerable variation in the range of settings and circumstances." Variables are proposed to characterize consistencies across situations *within* individuals, evidenced as systematic differences *between* individuals. Trait psychology's standard-bearers recognize the importance of the uniquenesses of domains of learning and behaving, as witness Cattell's (1963) notion of "crystallized intelligence" to describe particular things people learn in particular domains and situations. But it is commonalities across situations that trait psychology brings to the foreground, such as Cattell's contrasting "fluid intelligence" as a propensity to learn new things quickly.

These patterns are discerned in contexts that range from the unique exigencies of everyday life to replicable settings such as standardized tests. Carroll's (1993) encyclopedic re-analysis of a century of factor analytic research lays out the evidence for individual differences of this type, such as working memory for verbal information, spatial visualization, and the abstract reasoning addressed in the next section. Test scores hold value for prediction and selection to the extent that behaviors observed in the assessment context are manifest in the criterion context, despite differences among the settings' demands for particular knowledge, tools, and ways of interacting with others.

A behaviorist perspective. The behaviorist psychological perspective focuses on targeted behavior in a domain of situations. Details of both the behavior and the situation, as construed by the observer, are brought to the foreground, while internal mechanisms and representations are in the background. Knowledge is viewed as the organized accumulation of stimulus-response associations, developed and strengthened through reinforcement from the environment, to serve as the components of more broadly defined skills. A behaviorist instructional approach requires analysis and decomposition of complex learning goals into well-defined skill hierarchies (Gagné, 1962). Krathwohl and Payne (1971, pp. 17–18) capture the behavioral perspective on assessment by saying "The evaluation of the success of instruction and of the student's learning becomes a matter of placing the student in a sample of situations in which the different learned behaviors may appropriately occur and noting the frequency and accuracy with which they do occur."

A developmental perspective. A developmental perspective brings to the foreground a framework for the patterns in which people develop proficiencies over time. In some areas and at some ages, such as first language acquisition and the phonological awareness that precedes learning to read, interest encompasses physiological aspects of maturation. Learning in conceptual domains and affinity groups can be viewed in similar terms. Two relevant lines of research that illustrate this perspective concern the development of expertise (Ericsson, 1996) and children's understanding of concepts in science and mathematics (Lehrer & Schauble, 2000).

Piaget (1929) proposed paradigmatic stages of development in reasoning: from unstructured, through increasingly refined rules, up to abstract representations and formal operations. The patterns of change in this theory are invariant over people and across domains, but are precipitated by interactions with situations through which a child extends her capabilities to each next level—accommodation, in Piaget's terms. Research has shifted from fixed and broadly applicable stages, to patterns that emerge in experiences in more particular situations (Case, 1987) and through interactions with other, usually more proficient, people (Fischer & Kenny, 1986). Assessment from a developmental perspective seeks observations that evince students' capabilities at various stages or configurations of developing competence, and marks conditions that promote their advance.

An information-processing perspective. Epitomized in Newell and Simon's (1972) *Human Problem Solving*, the information-processing perspective examines the procedures by which people acquire, store, and use knowledge to solve problems. The focus is on "what's happening within people's heads," in terms of patterns through which a person perceives, construes, and interacts with a situation. Parallels with computation as symbol manipulation play an important role in the information-processing perspective, in the use of rules, elementary processes, production systems, task decompositions, and means-ends analyses (VanLehn, 1989). Viewing assessment from this perspective, Snow and Lohman (1989) pointed out in the Third Edition of *Educational Measurement* that "[t]he evidence from cognitive psychology suggests that test performances are comprised of complex assemblies of component information-processing actions that are adapted to task requirements during performance" (p. 317). Carpenter, Just, and Shell's (1990) research on progressive matrices, discussed below, exemplifies research along these lines.

Bringing information-processing ideas to the foreground, an assessor can design tasks explicitly to call upon targeted aspects of perception, interpretation, and action. We will see measurement models that are coarse-grained, looking for students' broadly defined capabilities to carry out targeted reasoning, and others that are fine-grained, detailing their procedures and strategies. Social settings and affinity groups remained in the background in early information-processing research. More recent work suggests a synthesis that recognizes the interplay between phenomena highlighted under information-processing and sociocultural perspectives (Anderson, Greeno, Reder, & Simon, 2000).

A sociocultural perspective. Social structures such as friendships, families, classrooms, professions, cultures, and peer groups influence the processes of acquiring, representing, using, and creating knowledge. These influences are channeled by particular ways of communicating, such as genres, conventions, and knowledge representations. A sociocultural perspective foregrounds the activities through which knowledge is created, conditioned, constrained, and brought to bear, in the contexts of the technologies, information resources, representational forms, and social systems that constitute the situations in which people act. This perspective incorporates explanatory concepts from fields such as ethnography and sociocultural psychology to study "collaborative work ... and other characteristics of interaction that are relevant to the functional success of the participants' activities" (Greeno, Collins, & Resnick, 1997, p. 37). Note the fine grainsize of interactions that may be addressed, and the role played by particulars of interactions among students, situations, and the interrelationships among them.

2.3. An Example

2.3.1. Raven's Progressive Matrices

John Carlyle Raven invented progressive matrices in 1938 to measure abstract reasoning, a component of intelligence as conceived by Spearman, in a way that depended less on language and culture than other then-current tasks (Raven, 1992). Figure 8.4 shows two examples. The relationships among figures across rows and within columns are governed by rules such as identity, addition, rotation, or "the distribution of three"—i.e., the same three tokens must appear in each row. The examinee chooses the alternative that completes the pattern. The publisher's summary of the Raven's Progressive Matrices test clearly takes a trait perspective, saying "Colloquially, the test is best described as a measure of a person's capacity for coherent perception and orderly judgment."[1]

Few people solve progressive matrices in their everyday activities. Their use in, say, employment testing is justified with a warrant framed in terms of a trait labeled abstract reasoning: People who are higher in abstract reasoning ability usually perform better at progressive matrices than people who are lower, and people who are higher tend to do better in the jobs in question because they require abstract

FIGURE 8.4 Two Progressive Matrices

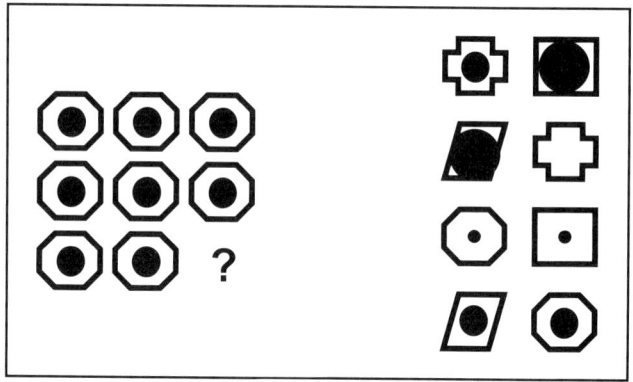

a) Two identity relationships and overlay.

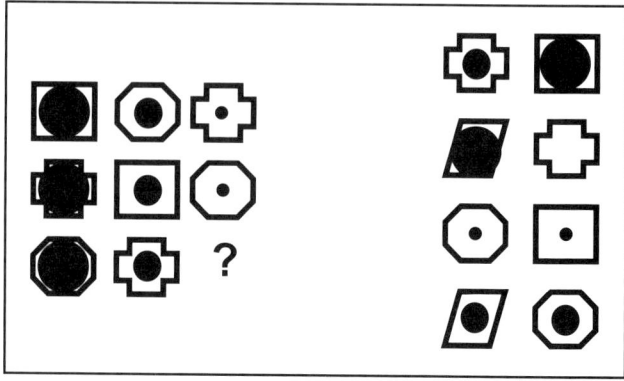

b) One pairwise progression, one rule of three, and overlay.

reasoning with some content, in some contexts. The assessment argument reasons from Sue's correct answer to a matrix item back through the first part of this warrant, to a claim that Sue is high in abstract reasoning. We'll start with the argument from one item, even though a test such as Raven's Standard Progressive Matrices (RSPM; Raven, 1992) contains many.

One kind of data rising from Sue's situated action identifies and characterizes the features of the setting which, from the assessor's point of view, satisfy the situational conditions of the warrant. Historically, the backing includes the correlations of progressive matrix scores with other performances, and the assertion that the tasks' characteristics and resulting demands fall into the broad class that psychologists have viewed as indicators of abstract reasoning based on factor analytic research. Respectively these are "nomothetic span" and "construct representation" validity arguments (Embretson, 1983). Information-processing tools and ideas add depth to the latter, as seen below.

Sue's encounter with the task is a unique sequence of situated activities: emotion, motivation, physical movement, cognition both conscious and unconscious, both relevant and irrelevant. From all this, the assessment protocol isolates as the performance datum her selection from the preconstructed alternatives, which to a predetermined categorization is correct or incorrect. The determination of what to attend to in the performance and how to encode it reflects the broad purposes for which abstract reasoning tests are typically used. The design and procedures of RSPM are tuned to providing evidence for a trait-based argument, to minimize dependence on context, resources, and ancillary information.

2.3.2. Cognitive Analysis of Progressive Matrices Performances

Information-processing analyses of assessment tasks began in the 1970s with work by researchers such as Carroll (1976), Hogaboam and Pellegrino (1978), Hunt, Frost, and Lunneborg (1973), and Sternberg (1977). Features of tasks, one part of the data in the assessment argument, are parsed in light of features suggested by the theory of the domain and studies of peoples' problem-solving in the situations. Student performances are evaluated in terms of behaviors suggested by the same theory and studies. A connection is established among warrants, claims, situation data, and observation data at a finer grainsize than was customary for standard trait-based applications.

Carpenter, Just, and Shell (1990) studied performance on progressive matrices from this perspective. In order to formulate and evaluate their claims about processes by which people solve such tasks, they needed richer data than dichotomous responses, some of it in the form of extracting additional information from the same performance, such as eye-tracking sequences, and some in the form of features of new performances, such as talk-aloud solutions. They needed to dig deeper into the details of interaction between particular people and particular tasks, to look for recurring patterns that would in turn back new, more detailed, warrants about how people solve matrix items.

They found that good matrix solvers scanned across rows, repeatedly proposing, then confirming or discarding in pairwise comparisons, progressions of features according to rules. Back and forth across entries, features become meaningful in light of the whole, the whole becoming meaningful in light of patterns of features. Each task is a new and unique situation, but one comprised in ways to be discovered of tokens and rules, some already familiar, others learned during the process, to complete an emerging pattern.

The tasks in the study differed as to the rules and tokens they presented. Examining subjects' solutions in much the same way as their subjects solved the tasks, the researchers found that subjects differed as to rule knowledge and goal management, or capacity to maintain increasingly many hypotheses as tasks became more complex. Rules based on perceptual features proved easier to propose and test than rules based on abstract features, in line with Piaget. Tasks with more rules and tokens were generally more difficult than tasks with fewer, a goal management load in line with an information-processing perspective. Rules or tokens subjects could assign names to were easier because they reduced the overhead in goal management, in line with a sociocultural perspective because names for patterns and icons are cultural artifacts.

Carpenter et al. wrote computer programs FAIRAVEN and BETTERAVEN based on their observations, to solve matrix problems with designated subsets of rules and varying degrees of working memory capacity. The programs echoed the performance of subjects at different levels of proficiency, in terms of their success on tasks with different predicted demands. They proposed that Ravens tasks reflect higher-level processes such as executive assembly and control processes that are called upon in many and varied real-world activities. Their study constitutes backing from an information-processing perspective for using progressive matrices in trait-based assessment arguments. Moreover, we shall see that studies such as these provide a foundation for creating new tasks and modeling students' performance on them.

Two remarks can be offered from a sociocultural perspective. First, an assessment with a test like RSPM is itself a social situation, and in some ways a peculiar one: The examinee works in isolation, under time limits, without recourse to the interactions and supports that characterize most human activity, to answer not-particularly-meaningful puzzles to which those in charge already know the answers. Alternative explanations abound for poor performance other than deficient goal management and rule knowledge. Because familiarity with and reactions to the usual Raven tasks and testing situation have been found to vary somewhat across cultures, scores are sometimes evaluated with respect to group norms (e.g., de Lemos, 1989). Additional data about students are here used in a trait-based argument to deal with a qualifier from the sociocultural perspective: Information about a student's linguistic and cultural background conditions the interpretation of data about the task and the performance, as evidence for a claim about abstract reasoning.

A second remark is that isolating reasoning processes strips away the contextualized meanings of real-world situations, patterns through which much of our real-world reasoning flows (Rumelhart, 1980). People who struggle with Wason's (1966) analytical reasoning puzzle in Figure 8.5 have no difficulty with a formally identical problem:

> The legal drinking age is 21. A seventeen year old and a thirty-year old are drinking unknown beverages, and two people of unknown ages are drinking water and wine respectively. Who must we check to make sure the law is not being broken? (A: The seventeen year old and the wine-drinker.)

A fuller picture of what a student can and cannot do, in what substantive domains and with what kinds of support and in what social situations, is gained with closer examination of actions in those situations, in light of knowledge about the student's relationship to the situations (Delandshire, 2002). These circumstances are approximated in the informal assessments that characterize contextualized learning situations, where information is available about the relationship of students to assessments in the learning context. Tasks can be selected in light of students' backgrounds and learning experiences, and targeted educational goals and instructional options. This contextualization, through the role of the additional information in the argument, distinguishes local assessments from large-scale assessments in a more fundamental way than task features or modes of performance.

2.4. A First Look at Probability-Based Reasoning

The foregoing Toulmin/Wigmore analysis provides much insight into assessment, but we must go further. How strongly do data support a claim, as to the scope and strength of a warrant, its fit to the situation at hand, and the number and plausibility of alternatives? How do we synthesize the import of the multiple observations, sometimes overlapping, often conflicting, that constitute most assessments? Probability-based reasoning provides a framework to address these issues. This section introduces and illustrates key ideas of probability-based reasoning as they apply to educational measurement, to complete the background needed to see how cognitive psychology can be incorporated in assessment. First, however, a brief digression into nonprobabilistic synthesis of evidence.

A nonprobabilistic approach to synthesizing assessment data seeks to construct a coherent explanation, a story, from all allowable sources of information, such as all the disparate elements of a portfolio and the examinee's explanation of her goals and context. Moss (1994, 1996) calls this a hermeneutic approach, after Gadamer (1960). An evaluator maps a constructed interpretation of performance into one or more scores. The evidentiary value of the data (its reliability, with the term broadly interpreted) depends on the amount of information, its coherence with the proffered explanation, and the presence and plausibility of alternative explanations. This interpretive approach to synthesizing the import of a mass of data is contrasted with adding up scores on discrete tasks.

Rather than viewing the two approaches as opposing poles, it is more useful to see them as different points in a design space of evaluation techniques, not so different as it seems at first blush. In assessments like Advanced Placement Studio Art, interpretive analyses of complex performance are averaged at a later stage (section 4.2.8). Measurement models for developmental stages use probability-based models, but address patterns of responses rather than total scores because that is where the evidence is to be found (section 4.1). A wide variety of options for identifying, evaluating, and synthesizing evidence can all be viewed in terms of their role in an assessment argument. Each is each characterized by its costs, requirements for resources and expertise, strengths and weaknesses as to the kinds of evidence they work well with and implications they hold for the social systems in which they are embedded. A design mind-set helps us think about what kinds of evaluation procedures suit different performances, purposes, and psychological perspectives.

The remainder of this section introduces out the key ideas of probability-based reasoning in assessment arguments. Points are illustrated by applying to progressive matrices a true-score error model, a Rasch item response theory (IRT) model, a linear logistic test model (LLTM), and a cognitive diagnosis model. Section 4 will survey further extensions of measurement models as they apply to cognitively based assessment.

2.4.1. Basic Ideas

The elements of a probability model are variables and a joint probability distribution. What is important technically is that within a probability model, one can calculate how information about any subset of variables changes probabilities for the remaining variables. What is important practically is that one can use probabilities to express strength of belief, and this machinery can be applied to carry out reasoning coherently even in large and complex networks of variables (Gelman, Carlin, Stern, & Rubin, 2003; Lauritzen & Speigelhalter, 1988). A good statistical model embodies the important qualitative patterns in a real-world situation, in terms of entities and their interrelationships. It overlays a substantive model for the situation with a model for our knowledge of the situation, so that we may characterize and communicate what we come

FIGURE 8.5 The Wason (1966) Task

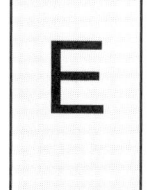  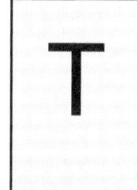 

Note: Each card has a letter on one side and a number on the other. Consider the rule "If there is a vowel on one side, there is an even number on the other." Which cards do you need to turn over to make sure the rule is not violated?

ANSWER: E AND 7.

to believe—as to both content and conviction—and why we believe it—as to our assumptions, our conjectures, our evidence, and the structure of our reasoning (Pearl, 1988; Schum, 1994).

Shafer (1976) coined the term "frame of discernment" for the set of all possible combinations of values of variables in a probability model. This phrase is apt, since "to discern" means "to become aware of" and "to make distinctions among." A frame of discernment circumscribes a universe of all the distinctions one can make within the aegis of a particular model. In assessment, the variables relate to the claims we would like to make about students and the observations we need to make, and probability distributions characterize the relationships among them. All are framed and understood in terms appropriate to the purpose, the context, and psychological perspective that ground the application. This done, tools become available to combine explicitly the evidence that various observations and evaluations convey about claims.

The two most important building blocks for constructing and working with probability models in assessment are conditional independence and Bayes' theorem. We'll use a series of illustrations based on progressive matrix examples to illustrate these ideas, starting with the simplest model, namely the measurement error model of classical test theory (CTT). Although Spearman (1904) developed this model under the trait perspective, the same machinery can be applied for some purposes in assessments cast in cognitive perspectives. Subsequent illustrations use an IRT model, a LLTM (Fischer, 1973), and a cognitive diagnosis model to increasingly incorporate concepts from cognitive psychology.

2.4.2. Classical Test Theory

In probability modeling one builds a model that approximates particular situations and supports reasoning about them, in terms of the kinds of stories through which one means to reason. Spearman's (1904) story line was that a set of observable variables, say number-correct scores on three parallel forms of progressive matrix tasks, X_1, X_2, and X_3, could all be related with one another simply because for each student they were all conveying the same unobserved number (the "true score" θ) plus an unrelated number (noise, or an error term). The corresponding probability model consists of the four variables X_1, X_2, X_3, and θ and a joint probability distribution with the following form:

$$p(x_1, x_2, x_3, \theta) = p(x_1, x_2, x_3 | \theta) p(\theta)$$

$$= \prod_j p(x_j | \theta) p(\theta). \quad (1)$$

Equation 1 formalizes the story that each X_j is related to the others only through their common dependence on θ, by modeling their joint probability given θ as the product of their individual probabilities given θ, i.e., the $p(x_j|\theta)$s. This is conditional independence. The directed graph of Figure 8.6 depicts this relationship with directed edges from θ to each X_j, and no additional edges among the Xs.

This model says it is possible to obtain similar pieces of information X_j in some circumstances that the model itself cannot specify, with their likely values indexed by values of θ via Equation 1. The probability model says nothing about the nature or the meaning of θ or the X_js, or about mechanisms through which the real-world phenomena they refer to may be related. In a behaviorist assessment seeking evidence for a behavioral tendency θ, the X_js could be repeated trials under practically identical circumstances, evaluated mechanically with the utmost reliability. In a socioculturally based assessment, the X_js could be raters' evaluations of the qualities of students' participation in ongoing instruction.

The conditional probabilities $p(x_j|\theta)$ are in the deductive direction of a warrant: from θ, in terms of which claims about a student's unobserved value would be framed, to the potentially observable X_js. Inductive reasoning from a student's observed test scores proceeds in the reverse direction via Bayes' theorem: From initial beliefs about a particular student's value of θ, the probability distribution $p(\theta)$ over all possible values (possibly vague, possibly informed by knowledge about that student), to updated beliefs that incorporate evidence in the form of values of some or all of the X_js. If x_1 and x_2 are observed,

$$P(\theta|x_1, x_2) \propto P(x_1, x_2|\theta) p(\theta). \quad (2)$$

The probability of any particular pattern of test scores can also be calculated. An unlikely set of scores warns us not to trust the common story to understand the performances.

That CTT says so little about situations to which it might be applied is both a strength and a weakness. CTT can play a role under any psychological perspective. One can devise observational settings and evaluation methods under any of the perspectives, and use classical test theory to characterize summary scores. Same model, but different substantive warrants, supporting different kinds of claims, evidenced by different kinds of data. However CTT does not model the patterns within performances. A CTT model cannot establish that data arise in ways that substantive theory would predict; the internal structure needed to validate claims about the nature of scores so obtained is lacking

FIGURE 8.6 Directed Graph Representation of Classical Test Theory

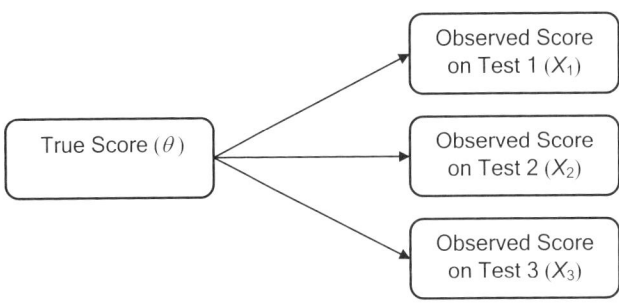

Note: Observed scores are conditionally independent given true score.

(Michell, 1997). It cannot express claims at finer level of detail than overall propensity to perform in such and such a way (as globally indicated by a test score) in such and such situations (as indirectly indicated by definitions of tasks and evaluation procedures).

2.4.3. Item Response Theory

Item response theory (IRT; Yen & Fitzgerald, this volume) takes an important step toward probabilistic models that do build on finer-grained patterns that a substantive psychological perspective would posit. IRT is not a theory about how people respond to items (Goldstein & Wood, 1989), but it opens the door to building models that do. As in classical test theory, claims and data in the substantive argument are the starting point for variables in the probability model. Again qualitative warrants are the starting point for quantitative expressions of relationships among the resulting variables. The difference is that in IRT, modeling is at the level of individual tasks. Although information across several tasks is synthesized for claims about a single overall proficiency, the finer grained modeling grounds a more careful consideration of the meaning of scores, and provides for detecting patterns of response that conflict with the single proficiency conceit.

A trait-based application would again use an unobservable real-valued variable θ to characterize a student's proficiency in the domain of progressive matrix tasks, with higher values simply representing greater chances at giving correct answers to each one of these kinds of tasks. Relationships with other proficiencies and other contexts, to strategies, rules, or processes of solution, and delineation of the scope of applicability all lie outside the model proper. Again what we know about Sue's proficiency before observing her responses is expressed as $p(\theta)$. Correctness of responses are the observable variables, right or wrong (1 or 0) responses x_j, which are modeled as depending on the student variables through conditional probability functions $p(x_j|\theta,\beta_j)$ for each task j. Along with the functional form of $p(x_j|\theta,\beta_j)$, the (possibly vector-valued) variable β_j gives the probability of a correct response to Item j from a person with a given value of θ. The β or Matrix Task 1 would indicate higher probabilities than for Task 2 for any level of θ.

Under the Rasch (1960/1980) model for dichotomous responses, the item parameter β_j indicates the difficulty of Item j and

$$P(X_j = 1|\theta,\beta_j) = \psi(\theta - \beta_j), \quad (3)$$

where the logistic function $\Psi(z)$ maps real numbers into probabilities as $exp(z)/[1+exp(z)]$. The presumption that what a student is likely to do on Task j depends on θ but not otherwise on other tasks is expressed as conditional independence among responses:

$$P(x_1,...,x_n|\theta,\beta_1,...,\beta_n) = \prod_j p(x_j|\theta,\beta_j). \quad (4)$$

Equations 3 and 4 are a quantitative rendition of a warrant in the deductive direction, that is, what a response might be if a student's θ and an items' βs were known. Inductive reasoning from estimated βs and a student's xs moves in the other direction, to inference about the unknown θ, via Bayes' theorem.

This model supports stories of the following form: Some students are more likely to give correct responses than other students by certain odds, some items are more difficult than others, by the same odds for all students, and the more a student's θ exceeds an item's β the more likely she is to get it right. Real data never look exactly like this, and real students will tackle different tasks in different ways, and get them right or wrong for different reasons. This detail lies below the level the probability model speaks to; it is silent about how responses are produced, what θ "really" means, or what information about how a θ instantiated in one context would relate to another context. The role of the model is to enable probability-based reasoning through overall-proficiency stories, motivated in this instance by a trait perspective.

This model goes beyond CTT by making specific predictions about each item-by-student combination, in particular asserting that each item poses the same difficulty to all students. If this is approximately so, then students with the same score have made similar patterns of response, though not necessarily attained in the same ways or from the same knowledge. It is possible to examine which items are harder and which are easier in light of item writers' expectations, reflecting on the validity of substantive warrants. It is possible to discover students with unusual response patterns, missing items that are easy for most students while getting ones right that are generally hard. These validity checks call attention to students whose knowledge or thinking may be different enough from typical patterns to reject the common story line. It is also possible to discover, from patterns of residuals (Smith, 1986) that some items are relatively harder for students with different demographic backgrounds (differential item functioning, or DIF; Holland & Wainer, 1993) or who have studied the content in different ways (Miller & Linn, 1988; Tatsuoka, 1987). Such patterns are unwelcome in assessments aimed at overall proficiency. For studying students' knowledge and strategies at a finer grain size, such patterns can become the object of interest. Assessments are then designed and models are built expressly to support inference in terms of these patterns (section 4.2).

2.4.4. A Linear Logistic Test Model

It was suggested above that an information-processing perspective can be used to improve assessments with purposes cast in trait and behavioral terms. Warrants and backing are framed in an information-processing perspective. Tasks, one part of the data in the assessment argument, are built around features that finer-grained research has found are central to the processes of problem-solving. Student performances, another part of the data, are evaluated in terms of behaviors suggested by the same research.

Fischer's (1973) LLTM extends the Rasch model by expressing each task parameter as the sum of effects related to its salient features:

$$\beta_j = \sum_{k=1}^{m} q_{jk}\eta_k, \qquad (5)$$

where η_k is the contribution to item difficulty from Feature k, and q_{jk} is the extent to which Feature k is represented in Item j. Features of tasks hypothesized to affect performance, always part of the data but hitherto outside the probability model, can be designed into tasks and incorporated in the probability model.

Hornke and Habon (1986) and Embretson (1998) built progressive matrix tasks around the rules required to solve them, then modeled difficulties using the LLTM in terms of these features. Table 8.1 summarizes Embretson's model. The salient task features include the number and kinds of rules employed, with additional features hypothesized to increase demands on memory load and executive processes. To the degree that the LLTM accounts for item difficulties, it provides backing for the nature of the overall proficiency; examinees with higher θs are more capable of carrying out the processes that studies like Carpenter's have disclosed.

When the purpose of assessment is supporting instruction, claims can be connected with instructional options at a finer grain size than overall proficiency. Tasks can be constructed, observations made, and inferences cast in terms of concepts, procedures, strategies, and representations in the domain. Under the LLTM, cognitive analyses of progressive matrices provide backing for inferences cast in a trait perspective. This section illustrates an approach called "cognitive diagnosis" (Junker & Sijtsma, 2001; Nichols, Chipman, & Brennan, 1995). The same research base, the same task types, and the same observable variables are used in an assessment argument and probability model for inference cast in information-processing perspective.

A binary skills model is a particular style of cognitive diagnosis model (Falmagne, 1989; Haertel, 1989; Maris, 1999). The model supports probability-based inference in stories like this: Tasks in a domain are characterized by which components of knowledge or skill they require (data about the situations). Students are characterized by which components they can apply when they are appropriate (the space of claims). If a student can apply all the components a particular task calls for, he is likely to succeed; otherwise, he is likely fail (the warrant). Differences among tasks as to features other than those calling for components in the specified set are not modeled. Differences between students other than vectors of can-apply/cannot-apply components are not modeled. The components that are modeled are selected to reveal key aspects of knowledge or skill, and perhaps guide decisions about further instruction. We construct tasks that demand various combinations of components. When we observe a student's response pattern (data about the student), we reason back up through the warrant to claims about the components he can apply.

In a binary skills model for progressive matrices, the components can be the transformation rules. Define the vector-valued student variable $\emptyset_i = (\emptyset_{i1}, \ldots, \emptyset_{iK})$ by $\emptyset_{ik} = 1$ if Student i can apply Rule k and 0 if not, and the vector-valued task variable $q_j = (q_{j1}, \ldots, q_{jK})$ by $q_{jk} = 1$ if Task j uses Rule k and 0 if not. The q_js are known because the tasks have been constructed around the rules. The following equation posits a "true positive" probability of π_{j1} for a correct response for a student i who can apply all the rules used in Task j (i.e., a conjunction relationship of the student variables for the required rules) and a "false positive" probability of π_{j0} for a correct response for a student i who cannot apply one or more of them:

$$\Pr(X_{ij} = 1 | \theta_i, q_j, \pi_{j1}, \pi_{j0}) = \pi_{j0} + (\pi_{j1} - \pi_{j0}) \prod_k \theta_{ik}^{q_{jk}} \qquad (6)$$

The directed graph of Figure 8.7 depicts this relationship for a simplified set of rules and tasks. The middle row of variables represents the conjunctions of clusters of rules needed by one or more tasks. Some tasks require the same set of rules. They may differ in their details, but they are interchangeable in the eyes of this model.

Let $p(\theta)$ be a (possibly diffuse) probability distribution that expresses belief about a student's knowledge of the rules—a probability distribution over the vector of K rule-knowledge student variables. After we observe Student i's responses Bayes theorem provides posterior probabilities

$$p(\theta_i | x_i, q_1, \ldots, q_n, \pi_1, \ldots, \pi_n) \propto \prod_j p(x_i | \theta_i, q_j, \pi_j) p(\theta_i)$$

Rules for which Student i has low posterior probabilities are candidates for further instruction. This model vastly oversimplifies how people solve matrix tasks. For example, Embretson's research suggests the model might be improved by adding a student variable for working memory capacity, so that even if two students know the same sets of rules, one might be consistently more likely to solve problems because of better goal management. Faithful representation is not the point. The point is whether a model strikes a useful balance between fidelity and simplification to guide action effectively. In a given educational setting, is it a useful model to guide task construction and response evaluation, interpret performances, and plan effective instruction—that is, to guide perception, meaning, and action?

TABLE 8.1 Embretson's (1998) Linear Logistic Test Model for Progressive Matrices

Task Variable	Description	η
Memory load	Weighted sum of rules used, with Identity = 1, Pairwise progression = 2, Figure addition or subtraction = 3, Distribution of three = 4, distribution of two = 5. (integer scale ranging from 3 to 18)	.25
Overlay	Tokens are overlayed, as opposed to adjacent. (0/1 scale)	.62
Distortion	Tokens vary physically. (0/1 scale)	.55
Fusion	Overlay, addition, or subtraction yields a perceptual object. (0/1 scale)	–.42

FIGURE 8.7 Directed Graph Representation of a Binary-Skills Model

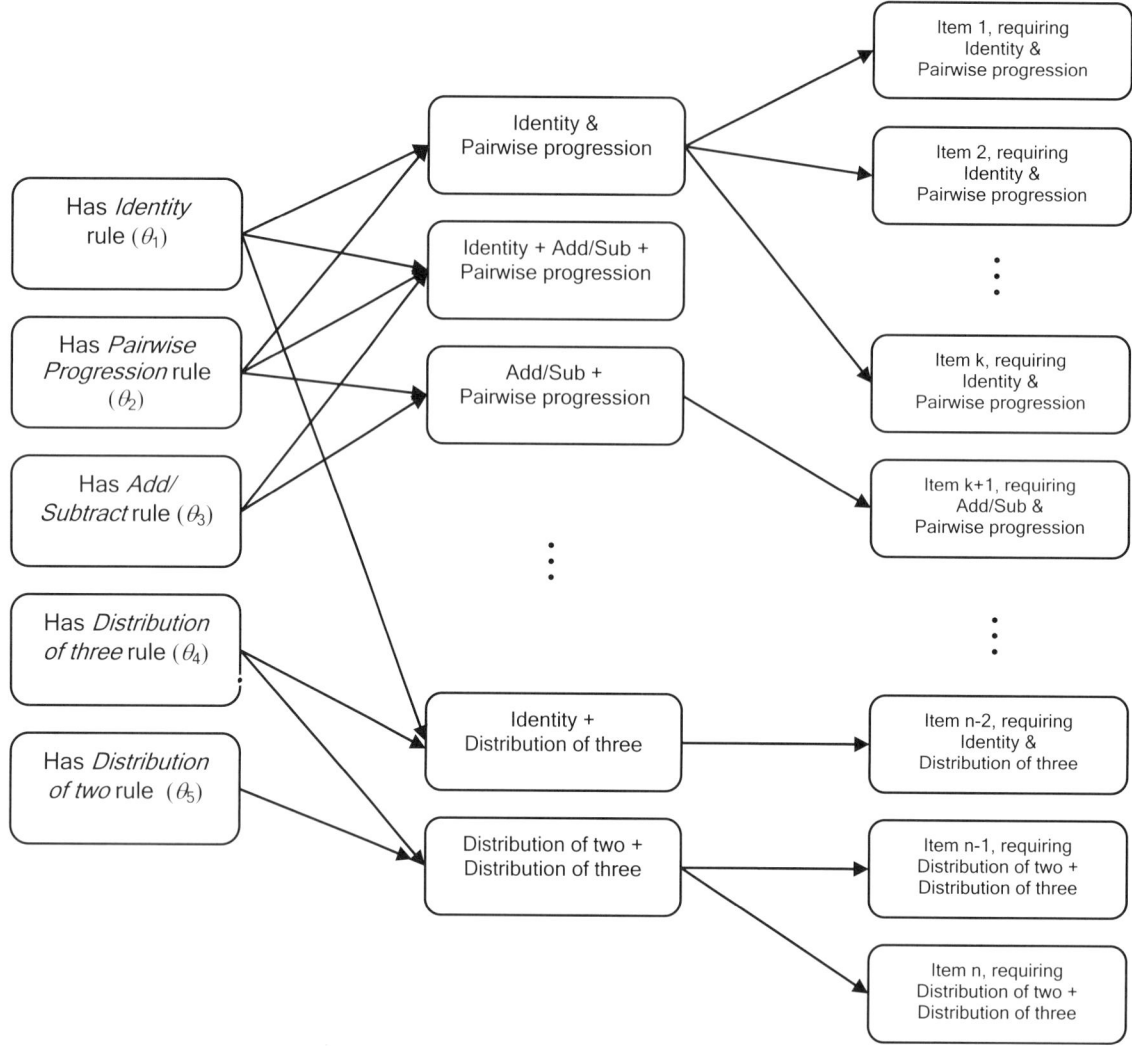

Note: Observed scores are conditionally independent given conjunctions of knowledge of rules.

3. THEMES AND IMPLICATIONS

Anything resembling a thorough review of cognitive psychology lies beyond the scope of this chapter.[2] Rather than attempting to be detailed or comprehensive, it lays out a number of themes that have been emerging over the past thirty years. These themes can be used to ground assessment arguments, as they specialize to learning domains, contexts, and purposes. Some motivate targets of assessment cast in information-processing terms:

> At various stages of learning, there exist different integrations of knowledge, different degrees of procedural skill, differences in rapid access to memory and in representations of the tasks one is to perform. The fundamental character, then, of achievement measurement is based upon the assessment of growing knowledge structures, and related cognitive processes and procedural skills that develop as a domain of proficiency is acquired. (Glaser, Lesgold, & Lajoie, 1987, p. 77)

Others are more comfortably cast in situative/sociocultural terms:

> The situative view of assessment emphasizes questions about the quality of students' participation in activities of inquiry and sense-making, and considers assessment practices as integral components of the general systems of activity in which they occur. (Greeno, Collins, & Resnick, 1997, p. 37)

In any case, the section outlines key themes and relates them to the construction of assessment arguments: Just what sort of things do we want to make inferences about, in order to understand students' learning? What kinds of things we need to see them do, in what kinds of situations?

3.1. Domains, Perspectives, and Levels

The world is a complicated place, and human brains and societies are particularly complicated bits of it. Too complicated, anyway, for people to grasp in their entirety. Hence the need to find ways to think about neighborhoods of it. We acquire much of what we know informally, through patterns that accumulate as we interact with the world and with others. As noted in the introduction, this chapter is aimed at assessment of the kinds of explicit knowledge that we use to think about the world, and to think about our thinking about the world: semantically rich *domains* of school and work, including traditional disciplines such as mathematics and history, professional fields such as medicine and computer networking, and social and recreational spheres such as sports and video games.

Perspectives within or across domains use characteristic sets of concepts to focus on some range of phenomena, and to shape perception, understanding, and action in situations through which they are viewed. The perspectives on knowledge and learning discussed in the previous section are an example. Knowledge domains also typically exhibit *levels* of phenomena and explanatory principles, such as the molecular, cellular, individual, and species levels in biology. Much can be learned by focusing on the entities and processes within such levels, although understanding is deepened by explanations and constraints that cross levels. Snow and Lohman's view of psychological traits as patterns emerging from information processing is an example of such a connection. Psychologists also distinguish among the descriptions of cognitive activities (Markman, 1999, pp. 21, 24):

- The *social or interpersonal* level refers to the social interactions that define and give meaning to information, the focus of the sociocultural perspective.
- The *computational* level refers to the nature and content of information that is involved. It cuts across the sociocultural and information-processing perspectives, and is particularly important in semantically rich domains.
- The *algorithmic* level refers to procedures that people carry out, working with information described at the computational level. Algorithmic analyses are a particular focus of the information-processing perspective.
- The *implementation* level refers to the physical structures and mechanisms that embody cognitive processes.

All hold implications for learning and assessment, and being clear about which level a processing model or an assessment argument addresses helps sort out issues of design and inference in practical applications.

Domains, perspectives, and levels are all marked by what is attended to and how it is thought about; by the entities, relationships, and processes they use; by the kinds of problems they address, the solutions they can conceive, and the methods by which they proceed; by the "generative principles" (Greeno, 1989) through which experts come to reason in a domain. They are also marked by what is not emphasized, indeed what is ignored. The patterns one works with thus at once enable and constrain thinking. This aspect of interpersonal cognition is echoed in intrapersonal cognition, both when explicit and conscious as in scientific investigation, and when tacit and automatic as in visual perception.

3.2. Reflective and Experiential Cognition

The long history and hitherto modest accomplishments of pondering the nature of human cognition is due in large part to our unawareness of so much of our cognitive activity. A useful oversimplification (of many) is distinguishing between *experiential* and *reflective* cognition: "The experiential mode leads to a state in which we perceive and react to the events around us, efficiently and effortlessly.... The reflective mode is that of comparison and contrast, of thought, of decision making. Both modes are essential to human performance" (Norman, 1993, pp. 15, 20).

Experiential cognition is the essence of real-time interaction with the world around us: Comprehending language and assessing motives in a spirited conversation, or making continual minor adjustments to our direction and speed as we drive along curves and hills, in ongoing response to what we see through the windshield and what we feel through our hands on the wheel and the fluids in our inner ear. Our moment to moment actions reveal rapid perception of cues, especially changes, that seem to be important, with or without conscious awareness; interpretation of cues in terms of meaningful patterns; then action in response to the situation as we understand it, updating our understanding or changing the situation as we interact with the affordances we recognize. We enjoy special capabilities for communicating, for classifying and comparing, for recognizing patterns, and for relating physically to the external world. These are neither distinct nor sequential processes. The cues we perceive are linked with the affordances to which we are attuned, and this interrelationship is all of a piece with the meaning we attach to a situation.

Experiential cognition is efficient and effortless, and adaptive, to be sure. But it is not perfect. Cognitive psychologists are beginning to understand the assumptions and the inferences, the interplay between memory and sensation, that underlie experiential cognition. Our impression of complete and continuous awareness of our surroundings turns out to be a clever construction, stitched from a surprisingly incomplete and disconnected patchwork of sights and sounds. Their fragmentary nature was first recognized in individuals who, through disease or injury to particular areas of their brains, lost the capacity to synthesize immediate bits of information with patterns from long-term memory into a coherent whole. Damage to the V5 cortical area of the brain, for example, can cause a condition called akinestopia: experience seems more like discrete snapshots from different angles and different foci than a continuous event. Moving objects are particularly disconcerting, and crossing a street is a perilous undertaking. Processing based on wired-in assumptions about the continuity of objects and the nature of motion is needed to create the perception of continuous motion. Assumptions about constancy of objects across light and space, built in from the very start of visual processing at the retina, enable us to recognize faces and judge distances. We are oblivious to the extensive inferencing and construction that takes place beneath our conscious awareness.

We become aware of some of these assumptions and inferences based on them when we fall prey to an optical illusion. Line **B** in Figure 8.8 seems longer than Line **A** even after a ruler tells us they are the same. Reasoning heuristics using the salience or the representativeness of cues as proxies for their evidentiary value can be similarly misleading (Kahneman, Slovic, & Tversky, 1982). A radiologist excels at detecting subtle cues in cloudy films (Lesgold, Lajoie, Bunzo, & Eggan, 1992), for example, but combines multiple cues for prediction less effectively than a linear regression model (Meehl, 1954). The logical fallacy *post hoc ergo propter hoc* is deep in our bones, or, more literally, in the connections among our neurons. Our natural cognitive capabilities enabled our ancestors to evaluate information rapidly, usually gainfully, and they enable us to do the same in the more complex environments in which we function today. But magicians and con artists understood long before cognitive psychologists how predictably we are fooled by cognitive illusions as compelling as any optical illusion.

Reflective cognition, on the other hand, is conscious and deliberate. It is sequential and reasoned—the kind of thinking we are aware of, if not the processing that underlies it. Its speed and scope are limited in comparison with experiential cognition, but reflective cognition enables us to transcend immediate situations and personal experience, and provides a capability to evaluate our own thinking. We are limited as to both the focus of conscious attention and the capacity of the working memory[3] upon which reflective cognition depends. Miller's (1956) "seven chunks of information, plus or minus two" remains a tolerable approximation. The nature, the size, and the pertinence of the choice of the chunks that we activate from long-term memory determine the effectiveness of reflective cognition. Recalling seven random digits is a challenge, but to many American adults recalling the sixteen digits "1492177618601945" is easy; it can be parsed as only four chunks, each a significant date in the country's history. We leverage our limited resources for reflective cognition by becoming attuned to meanings and affordances of classes of situations, and automatizing recurring sequences of action in them.

Reflection benefits from systematic procedures and methods, which are learned primarily by being taught (Norman, 1993, p. 21). The symbol systems of logic, probability, mathematics, and written language are familiar cross-domain examples, and every domain has its own more specialized tools and methods. These are explicit structures and relationships for thinking about situations we encounter in our jobs and our lives—for thinking about them in our own minds, but also for thinking about them with others, whether or not others happen to be involved in given event. Adding the price of two items in my head is at once a private mental activity and an episode in a nexus of symbols, meanings, and algorithms that embraces millions of people over thousands of years. For this reason Cobb (1994) argues that "mathematical learning should be viewed as both a process of active individual construction and a process of enculturation into the mathematical practices of wider society" (p. 13). Much assessment thus revolves around structures for representing and working with information, by one's self and with others.

The mechanisms of experiential and reflective cognition are common to all humans. All people in all cultures enjoy their capabilities and contend with their limitations. Particular contents and supporting methodologies for reasoning vary across and within cultures, as do the social patterns within which they are used. Some knowledge and practices prove more useful than others. Many embody hard-won insights that reach beyond everyday experience and built-in heuristics. Others involve tools and patterns of interaction among people that enable accomplishments that lie beyond the reach of individuals in isolation. Curriculum design centers on identifying broadly useful structures and patterns of interaction among people, as targets for deliberate learning and reflective cognition. Instructional design centers on figuring out how to help students learn to incorporate these structures and patterns into their perception, understanding, and action. Getting information about these processes and the capabilities they entail is the focus of assessment design.

3.3. Cognition Is Situated and Embodied

Information processing takes as its focus the rules, procedures, principles, and techniques for working with structured information—in particular, what can be accomplished through structure and technique, abstracting above the particular content and context of information. Analogues between information-processing in computers and information-processing in people have been productive for understanding cognition (Newell & Simon, 1972). They have proven their value in practical applications as well, from making can openers easier to use (Norman, 1988), to building intelligent tutoring systems (ITSs; Shute & Psotka, 1996), to helping students learn in domains such as geometry (Anderson, Boyle, & Corbett, 1990), physics (Gertner & VanLehn, 2000), and aircraft electronics (Lesgold et al., 1988). We glimpsed in section 2 how information-processing ideas can help us design tasks and to draw inferences about what students can do from their actions in settings with particular features and affordances.

But information processing is only part of the story. Human cognition is inevitably situated in an environment

FIGURE 8.8 Which line Is longer, A or B?

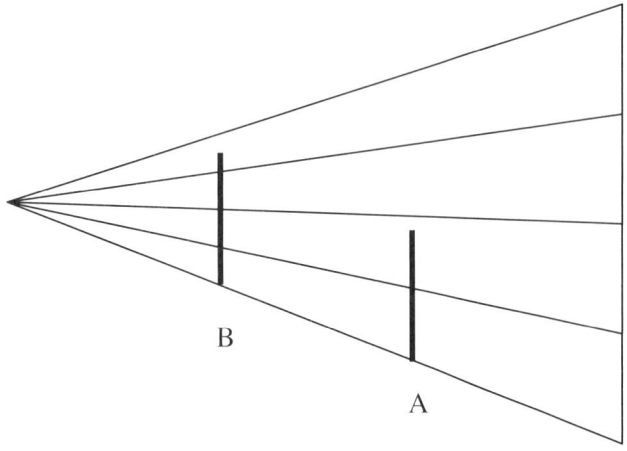

that is internal and material, social and cultural. Internal, in that cognition is inseparable from intentions and emotions, the conative and affective counterparts of the cognitive (Corno et al., 2002). Material, in that the brain is part of a physical body that has evolved to coordinate the actions of that body in a physical world; that is, cognition is embodied, integral with perceiving and acting, quite aside from the fact that patterns that shape perception and guide action can be abstracted, represented, analyzed, and manipulated externally. Social, in that the most important part of environment with which people interact is other people. Cultural, in that particular forms of social interaction, knowledge representation, and informational content are contingent on the communities within which the cognition takes place. We are constantly building, comparing, and integrating patterns with all of these aspects of cognition at once:

> what constitutes the context, how you categorize the world, *arises together* with processes that are coordinating physical activity. To be perceiving the world is to be acting in it—not in a linear input-output relation (act-observe-change)—but dialectically, so that what I am perceiving and how I am moving codetermine each other.... Every activation reinforces physical connections, biasing active hardware to be reincorporated in future compositions, bearing the same temporal relations to perceptual and conceptual maps. Regularities of behavior, including an observer's construction of analogies, develop because every perceptual motor coordination—in both agent and observer—generalizes, includes, and correlates previous perceptions and coordinations. (Clancey, 1993, p. 95)

Recognizing the embodied nature of cognition highlights its intimate connection with acting in the world. In turn, recognizing the central role of cognition as mediating interaction with the environment leads to an interesting and counterintuitive insight: It is not necessary for all the details of the complex activities that people carry out to be somehow fully and explicitly modeled in our heads. Rather, the full complexity of activity is more usefully conceived as residing to a large extent in the environment. Simon (2001) tells of an ant making its way across a sandy beach. Its path is quite complex, as it tries one direction then another, backs up to avoid a chasm, crosses to different grain that is stable—continually winding, reversing, crossing over, moving forward. The ant did not plan this path. At each moment, the ant was interacting with features of its immediate surrounding, in accordance with a relatively small repertoire of behaviors tuned to ant local environments.

Human behavior is more complicated than ant behavior, of course, not to mention affect, reflection, motivation. But it too is characterized by the interplay between a person and a situation, and mediated by the patterns through which the person interprets the situation, both experientially and reflectively. It is the capability to recognize in situations the patterns we have acquired, and to act through such interpretations to modify the situations or ourselves accordingly, that enables complex human behavior despite limited attention and working memory. Static definitions, concepts, and relationships are necessary but not sufficient for expertise; knowledge must be in a form that is primed for percep-

tion in and interaction with particular situations, as seen in Larkin's (1983) study.

It is the exception for the construction of meaning to *not* be interactive, an interplay between the particulars of a situation and patterns from long-term memory. Just as Simon's ant interacts with the details of the beach to construct a path, a video-game player cycles through probes, hypotheses, tests, and reformulations, in order to act, see results, and build patterns that increase her competence in a simulated world (Gee, 2003). A reader evaluating a student's portfolio similarly tries to fit details in broader patterns and newly sees details in relation to emerging patterns, cycling toward a coherent understanding in what Gadamer (1960) calls a hermeneutic circle. A scientist models a particular situation using principles from the domain, mapping a trial version of a model, elaborating its consequences, apprehending both anomalies and points of correspondence, revising the model accordingly in cycles of inquiry (Clement, 1989). Table 8.2 is based on Stewart and Hafner's (1994) and Gobert and Buckley's (2000) parsing of aspects of model-based reasoning in science. They highlight the importance of interactivity and iteration—continually constructing and reconstructing correspondences between unique real-world situations and general structures, using the structures to make sense of the situations provisionally for further perception and action.

TABLE 8.2 Aspects of Model-Based Reasoning in Science

Model formation	Establishing a correspondence between some real-world phenomenon and a model, or abstracted structure, in terms of entities, relationships, processes, behaviors, etc. Includes scope and grain-size to model, and determining which aspects of the situation(s) to address and which to leave out.
Model elaboration	Combining, extending, adding detail to a model, establishing correspondences across overlapping models. Often done by assembling smaller models into larger assemblages, or fleshing out more general models with more detailed models.
Model use	Reasoning through the structure of a model to make explanations, predictions, conjectures, etc.
Model evaluation	Assessing the correspondence between the model components and their real-world counterparts, with emphasis on anomalies and important features not accounted for in the model.
Model revision	Modifying or elaborating a model for a phenomenon in order to establish a better correspondence. Often initiated by model evaluation procedures.
Model-based inquiry	Working interactively between phenomena and models, using all of the aspects above. Emphasis on monitoring and taking actions with regard to model-based inferences vis-à-vis real-world feedback.

Primed-for-action knowledge is an important target for assessment because it is crucial for effective thinking in semantically rich domains. Assessing capabilities to recognize patterns and react accordingly calls to our attention the situations in which a student perceives and acts, the situation changes, and the student acts in response. The focus is on what happened before, what is missing, what to do next, and why, all of which are addressed by reasoning through the patterns that are targets of learning.

Some evidence about interactive capabilities can be obtained with static tasks. Multiple-choice items, for example, serve this purpose when stimulus materials present situations and offer options that require reasoning through patterns to explore precursors, explanations, predictions, or plans for next steps. Aspiring chess players solve "white to win in two moves" puzzles, and study and self-assess by working through games between masters, trying to select the best move for each position (Ericsson, 2004). But recent developments in technology have spurred the use of interactive simulations for learning, and, increasingly, assessment.

In 1997, for example, the National Council of Architectural Registration Boards' Architectural Registration Examination (ARE) became the first fully computerized licensure test to incorporate automated scoring of complex constructed responses in operational testing (Bejar & Braun, 1999). The ARE's paper and pencil predecessor required a candidate to design a building according to a list of requirements and constraints, and execute four architectural drawings to detail the solution. Twelve hours were allotted to the problem, and the resulting solutions were evaluated by expert raters. Both the costs of the exam and the increasing use of computer-aided design (CAD) technology in the profession led NCARB to consider computer-based assessment. Katz's (1994) comparisons of expert and novice architects' solutions helped ground a new family of CAD design problems. The process was invariably iterative: experts and novices alike started from an initial solution that met some constraints, and modified it repeatedly to accommodate more, always working from the representation generated thus far. But while both experts and novices continually revised aspects of provisional designs as they progressed, the novices' rework was more often substantial and discarded much previous work. The novices had encountered conflicting and hard-to-meet constraints when they were further along, whereas the experts identified and addressed these challenges early on. Varying the number of constraints, the challenge of meeting them, and the degree of conflict among them are systematic and cognitively relevant ways to vary task difficulty.

The local environment ARE examinees react to and modify is an evolving design solution, expressed in a representation that encapsulates their previous work and against which they can evaluate remaining constraints. In computer-based troubleshooting tasks such as those of the Hydrive intelligent tutoring system for aircraft hydraulics systems (Steinberg & Gitomer, 1996) and the NetPASS assessment of computer networking skills (Williamson et al., 2004), the environment is a simulation of a physical system that responds to the examinee's queries and changes in response to the examinee's actions (replacing a pump, pinging a router). In Stevens' IMMEX problem-solving scenarios, successive choices of diagnostic tests produce changes in an internal environment, namely the examinee's state of knowledge about, say, a disease in an epidemiology task, as each test rules some possibilities in and others out (Hurst, Casillas, & Stevens, 1997). In the National Board of Medical Examiner's computer-based case simulations (CCS; Clyman, Melnick, & Clauser, 1999), the environment is extended to a patient whose condition changes over (simulated) time in response to an underlying etiology as well as to treatment, and in which many of the human and institutional interactions of medical practice play roles in consultation and treatment. In a networked assessment of negotiation skills, multiple players jointly construct an environment of understanding and action plans as they attempt to solve a problem involving conflicting goals and constrained options (O'Neil, Allred, & Dennis, 1997).

Recognizing the importance of acting in dynamic environments thus sparks a desire to make assessment claims about required capabilities, such as recognizing and understanding patterns, and knowing how to react to them or modify them. What are some implications for other parts of the assessment argument? The environments must be able to provide feedback, offer affordances, and respond accordingly in ways both overt (a patient's results from a diagnostic test) and hidden (an allergenic response to a treatment that only becomes apparent after a day of simulated time). The data concerning the situation in which an examinee acts is evolving, so at some grainsize, salient aspects of the state of the environment and perhaps its history must be tracked in order to evaluate an examinee's actions. Testing the output pressure of a pump half way along the active path in Hydrive suggests expert-level space-splitting if it is the first action, but poor system knowledge if the test follows an earlier action that eliminated it from the problem space. Depending on the aspect of proficiency that is of interest, the evaluation of an action can be evaluated unconditionally (in patient management problems, some actions are dangerous in any circumstances), conditional on the current state of the system, conditional on the current state of the system and previous examinee actions (in Hydrive, what the examinee *could* know from actions taken thus far), or conditional on the examinee's current belief about the system (he is mistaken about the system state, but his choice of diagnostic test would be spot on if his hypothesized model were right: positive evidence about troubleshooting procedure for a class of situations).

3.4. Humans Seek Patterns and Make Meanings

Cognition revolves around patterns: recognizing patterns, assembling and modifying patterns, reasoning through, acting in accordance with, and evaluating outcomes in terms of patterns. This is true of experiential and reflective thinking. Some patterns involved in experiential cognition are innate, such as acoustical features upon which human languages are based, the regularities of interacting with objects in the physical world, and the detection of edges and motion that are the starting point of visual perception. Others are acquired without conscious effort (although not without attention) through the particulars of experience, such as patterns that might be described externally as a "script" for ordering food at a restaurant or a "schema" for a birthday party (Bartlett, 1932; Minsky, 1975; Rumelhart, 1980), or for designing a site plan as in the ARE example, or troubleshooting an aircraft hydraulics system as in Hydrive. Still others, such as the grapheme-phoneme relationships we draw upon when we read, are initially conscious and effortful, but become automatized with practice and use (Rayner, Foorman, Perfetti, Pesetsky, & Seidenberg, 2001).

Useful patterns can concern physical, social, and formal relationships, with interconnections and overlapping among them. They range from grand patterns such as what we think about the nature of the universe to small ones such as the feel of a wallet in a pocket. Some are conscious and available for reflection—in particular many of those we address in assessment—while many more detailed ones are not. Labeling patterns as schemas or scripts provides a useful metaphor for important computational aspects of human cognition, although we should not presume such discreteness and stability at the level of implementation. According to an implementation-level view of situated action, "*the neural structures and processes that coordinate perception and action are created during activity*, not retrieved and rotely applied, merely reconstructed, or calculated via stored rules and pattern descriptions" (Clancey, 1993, p. 94).

Engaging in a conversation, for example, requires integrating patterns of sounds, word meanings, syntactic structures, social situations, and interlocutors' shared and individual purposes, all in a matter of milliseconds, then constructing on the fly equally multilayered patterns to respond. Everyday conversations proceed at a rate of 2 or 3 words a second. How can so much happen so quickly? Only by assembling patterns across the many levels, in accordance with cues from the external environment and our internal intentions. The more patterns we have access to and the more automatized they have become, the more numerous and multileveled chunks we can work with, and the more fluid the interaction and the more successful the communication is apt to be. Attention can then be focused on the most novel or important aspects of the conversation. For example, three distinguishable levels in a conversation concern processing the sounds our interlocutor shapes into words, modeling the intentions that underlie her utterances, and constructing a mental representation of the content. As to the first, parsing a familiar voice is largely automatic, but an unusual accent requires more attentional resources. By default we assume our conversational partner intends to be informative and truthful (Grice, 1975). But suspecting we are being deceived requires us to construct multiple meanings for an utterance: the usual surface meanings, but now also contrary meanings that are consistent with an intention to mislead us. Section 4.2.4 discusses issues of task design and multivariate measurement models for assessment when patterns of different kinds and at different levels are in play simultaneously, as in task-based language assessment.

Discussing the roles of patterns in a series of contexts enables us to highlight some key ideas from cognitive psychology. Visual perception offers opportunities to introduce connectionist models (Rumelhart & McClelland, 1986a) and to discuss the interplay of bottom-up and top-down processing. This leads to a connectionist perspective on knowing and acting. The role of narratives, studied by (Bruner, 1990) in the context of folk psychology—the "natural" way we think about ourselves, others, and the world around us—can be extended to how we make meaning from situations more broadly. It provides one entrée into the development of expertise. A discussion of knowledge structures such as schemas and production rule systems brings up a debate about internal representation of knowledge, and highlights a useful perspective on this issue for those of us who design assessments.

3.4.1. Perception

Perception is a negotiation among patterns we detect in the environment and patterns of accumulated experience, the latter of which we will call knowledge from long-term memory (again at the risk of suggesting discreteness and stability). Visual perception begins with the detection of light by photoreceptor cells, rods and cones, on the retina. Studies of neural structures responsible for the next stages of visual perception illustrate wired-in feature detection, and set the stage for connectionist models of computation and cognition.

A neuron receives information in the form of sensory stimulation, as rods and cones do, or from other neurons at locations called dendrites. When a neuron fires, it passes an electrical charge up along its axon, and sends signals to other neurons across small spaces, synapses, in the form of chemicals called neurotransmitters. A typical neuron receives messages from a thousand other neurons, and sends messages to a thousand others. Transmission at a given synapse can make the receiving neuron more or less likely to fire; that is, it is excitatory or inhibitory. The rate at which a receiving neuron fires depends on all the sending neurons, some excitatory and others inhibitory, each with its own degree of influence.

Neurons called ganglion cells combine information in a cluster of photoreceptor cells, to determine whether there is light in a particular region of the visual field (Kuffler, 1953). An on-off cell is excited by input from a cluster of photoreceptors, inhibited by input from ones a little further from the center of the cluster, and unaffected by input at other parts of the retina. An off-on cell reverses the pattern to detect an area of darkness. Each photoreceptor is connected to many such ganglions, so a first pass of processing combines sensory input into a pattern of light and dark areas. Similarly, neurons in the visual cortex combine messages across ganglions to detect edges (Hubel & Wiesel, 1962). Other neurons detect lines and others, integrating information over time, detect movement. Lettvin, Maturana, McCulloch, and Pitts (1959) found cells in frogs' brains that fired in response to small dark objects moving across their visual fields: bug detectors!

Up to this point, visual processing is driven from the bottom up, detecting light patterns that are wired into the structure of the nervous system. Some of the further processing also involves wired-in procedures, such as heuristics that help us detect the contours of objects and gauge their distance. But perception now also begins to integrate patterns from long-term memory, patterns that have been acquired through previous experience. This is why we "see" a square in Figure 8.1. As in the progressive matrices tasks, expectations based on patterns from accumulated experience influence the search for and the perception of subsequent cues. A comment from a rater of Advanced Placement Studio Art portfolios (College Entrance Examination Board, 1994) makes a similar point in the context evaluating a student's water colors:

> The more I think about it, it's the hundreds and thousands of these that I've seen in the past in my own class ... that helps clarify everything so much more. I hadn't thought about it really until we started this, but I'm sure they all shoot through my head—just instantly whoosh on through, you know. Then, again, that's based on every day for twenty-three years looking at some art work. (Myford & Mislevy, 1995, p. 16)

Higher-level knowledge from long-term memory provides patterns for perception. A familiar sequence occurs as children learn to read. Prereaders detect edges and curves of marks on paper, and learn to recognize certain patterns among them as meaningful clusters called letters (they must be meaningful because they have names, by which our parents and teachers call them to our attention). They often confuse "b" and "d" because they are similar physically. But letter recognition becomes automatic with practice, and more experienced readers can recognize letters in different fonts, even though two versions of a letter in different fonts can differ more than two different letters in the same font. Later still, perception occurs at the level of words, even phrases, as we integrate constructing a meaning of text with perceiving the bits of code by which it is transmitted. The likely occurrence of a word supports the recognition of the letters in the word, just as at a higher level knowing the subject of the text anticipates and helps us recognize the words it is likely to contain—of considerable advantage for reading, albeit a disadvantage for proofreading. Rapid access to patterns through which to perceive and understand input is integral to learning to read, and in much the same way to becoming an expert in semantically rich domains such as chess, physics, and educational measurement (Ericsson, 1996).

Perceptual experience is shaped by and in turn shapes the ever-accumulating patterns that constitute long-term memory. As with other types of experiential learning, aspects of spatial/visual patterns are more apt to modify long-term memory for subsequent perception to the extent that they are meaningful, frequent, and accorded attention. These characteristics of perceptual patterns hold for patterns involving concepts, representational forms, and social interactions.

3.4.2. Connectionist Models

Computational models, known variously as neural networks, connectionist models, and parallel distributed processors (PDP; Rumelhart & McClelland, 1986a), mimic the physical arrangements of multiple layers of neurons, with messages combined stochastically across multiple sources of input. Each neurode in a PDP model receives 0/1 values with certain weights and directions from sending neurodes, and in turn fires with a probability determined by, for example, a logistic function of the weighted sum of inputs (Figure 8.9).

The weights associated with connections can be learned from data, that is, from experience. The path to PDP models was the study of actual neurons. McCulloch and Pitts (1943) first suggested a structure in which the output of a neuron depended on the accumulated impact of contributing signals from other neurons. Hebb (1949) proposed that input signals could have different amounts of influence, and that this influence could strengthen through use, thus a neurological basis of learning. Rosenblatt (1962) combined the McCulloch-Pitts structure and Hebb's learning rule to create "perceptrons," a two-layer model that could learn to recognize patterns. The input layer of perceptrons received 0/1 signals for the presence or absence of features of a target object (e.g., lines, curves, or angles in certain locations), from a defined universe of possibilities (e.g., the digits from 0 to 9). The nodes in the second layer corresponded to possible identities of targets, and weighted sums of signals from the perceptrons determined the activation of each. A network is "trained" with a collection of cases in which both features and target outcomes are known. After each trial, weights are adjusted to strengthen those that contributed to correct identifications and weaken those that led to incorrect identifications. (From a statistician's point of view, a neural network is an underidentified nonlinear regression model.) The resulting weights embody relationships between the lower-level features that characterize the environment and the higher-level features or classifications that are of interest. Two-layered networks stumbled on exclusive-OR patterns (Minsky & Papert, 1969), but "hidden" layers between input and output as in Figure 8.10 extend PDP capabilities to interactions and nonlinear relationships. Further extensions include recursive relationships, weight-learning without known training examples (Kohonen, 1982),

FIGURE 8.9 The Structure of Neurode k

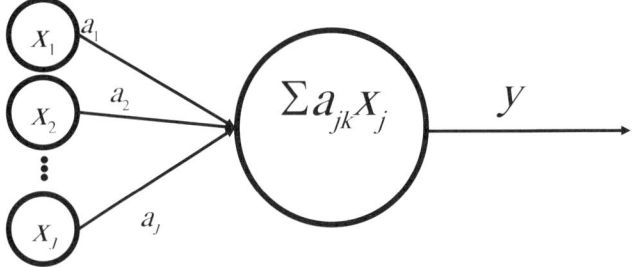

x_j 0/1 signal from input unit j

y_k 0/1 signal as output from neurode k

a_{jk} Weight (influence) of input unit j on neurode k

τ_k Threshold parameter for neurode k

$P_k(\alpha)$ Probability that $y_k = 1$ for given vector of input values;

e.g., $ln(P_k(\alpha)/(1-P_k(\alpha))) \sim N(\Sigma a_{jk} - \tau_k, 1)$.

FIGURE 8.10 A Neural Network with Two Hidden Layers

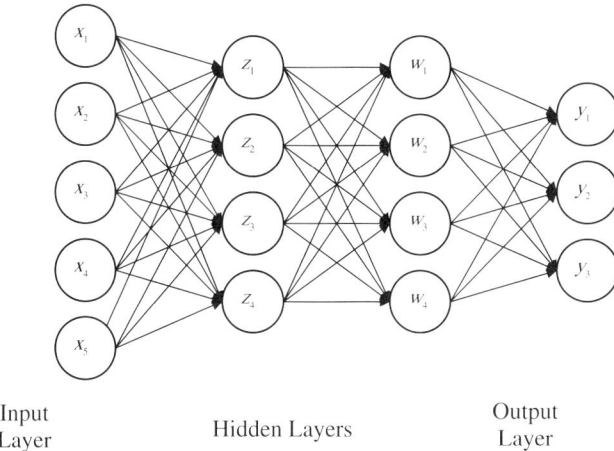

and using outputs from one time point as inputs to subsequent processing in order to recognize temporal patterns.

In addition to perception, neural networks have been used to simulate other aspects of cognition such as learning regular and irregular verb forms as in a well-known and controversial study by Rumelhart and McClelland (1986b). The patterns of their networks' learning over a long series of trials show remarkable similarities to human learning, such as the power law of increasing accuracy and the stage when children overgeneralizing regular tense forms to irregular verbs ("I goed to the store"), and the activation of relevant information in response to perceived cues. Another variation of networks emphasizes the associative nature of memory, as illustrated by McClelland's (1981) Jets and Sharks example. Each of five persons has an age, occupation, education, marital status, and gang membership. Excitatory connections create positive, but less than perfect, associations among the variables. Inhibitory connections among nodes in the same cluster, such as ages and gangs, effects exclusivity: you can't be both a Jet and a Shark. The network can be queried from a node in any cluster. Activating the Shark node, for example, activates nodes for people who are Sharks, and ages and occupations to the degree that they co-occur with Shark membership.

Two features of connectionist models that suggest their relevance for mental representations are these. Knowledge in a network at a given point in time depends on both the initial structure of the network and the connections tuned by the particular examples that have been experienced. Knowledge is not a set of discrete propositions or localized relationships, but a distributed pattern of activation across many nodes. The pattern of associations in McClelland's network that "mean" being a Shark are very different from a propositional definition of a Shark. Human cognition is unquestionably PDP at the level of implementation, for this is how brains work.

Even as we accept cognition as connectionist at the level of implementation, interesting questions remain at the algorithmic and computational level. It is possible, after all, to represent logical propositions and production rule systems in PDP networks. Our physical neural networks too can emulate the actions of formal rules and symbolic processing. We routinely reason in formally structured ways in reflective cognition, and it proves advantageous to organize aspects of instruction and assessment in terms of external representations of these types, quite aside from the way they may be represented internally. Indeed, the reflective and explicit use of symbolic processing, schemas, and other formal structures gain purchase in part because this is not the way human cognition is implemented. They supplement, rather than duplicate, intuitive reasoning.

The situated and social nature of human knowledge lie more to the background in the information-processing perspective. Research from the sociocultural perspective shows that people can become proficient at carrying out inherently mathematical tasks, as in carpentry (Millroy, 1992) or buying groceries (Lave, 1988), that correspond neatly to abstract structures, but without using, indeed without being aware of, the symbolic representation. In work environments and everyday life, underlying relationships are implicit in the tools and procedures that have evolved to do the job at hand. Situated knowledge can be more effective than the abstracted knowledge, but transfer to other contexts proves more difficult. We can use abstract formal structures such as schemas, equations, and representational forms, to circumvent processing limitations because they encapsulate an accumulated wisdom of experience. They provide meaning; but, they must be linked to both perception and action: to perception, so that we may recognize in particular situations the abstracted patterns they embed; to action, so that we may transform those situations in desired ways, reasoning through the structures. Learning how to apply information acquired in abstract terms or in one particular context to other contexts is the problem of transfer.

The possibility of transfer depends on shared elements, or corresponding entities, relationships, and processes, as proposed by Thorndike (1906) from a behaviorist perspective and Singley and Anderson (1989) from an information-processing perspective. From a situative perspective, we come to recognize and acquire facility with particular elements, relationships, and processes in particular contexts. For the young Brazilian candy sellers Saxe (1988) studied, this meant patterns of activities among buyers, sellers, wares, and transactions. The fact that some of these activities could be expressed in the mathematics of proportion was not relevant to their work. For learning in school, the activities involved classrooms, equations, and problems at the end of the chapter. Children who only sold candy were proficient with a higher level of situated mathematical activity than they could express formally. Children with only school learning struggled with candy-selling problems that could be solved with formal representations they had mastered. Connections emerged between situated activity and abstract representations as students of both types gained experience across contexts.

Transfer is uncommon without explicit experiences to forge the connection (Bransford & Schwartz, 1999). To make the broad and generative power of formal structures available to students, learning experiences should illustrate them in multiple settings and make explicit the correspondence between formal structures and particular situations. One should not think of "assessing students' proportional reasoning proficiency" solely by means of facility with formal structures. A richer space of claims addresses proficiency with formal structures, proficiencies in activities that correspond to proportional reasoning in relevant contexts, and facility with correspondences among contexts and between contexts and formal representations.

PDP computer programs play an important role in understanding human cognition, because they add insight into the nature of human knowing and learning. We may note in passing that PDP computer programs can also play a role in assessment operations, to identify and summarize evidence from complex performances. A first stage of analysis is extracting lower-level salient features from a performance, a bottom-up procedure akin to that of visual perception. The second stage is using a PDP program that has been trained on a large number of examples for which higher-level qualities have been established by human judgment. In automated essay scoring, for example, first-stage features concern lexical aspects of a response such as word counts and co-occurrences and syntactic aspects such as sentence structures and cohesive devices (Deane, 2006; Shermis & Burstein, 2003). In one of Stevens's IMMEX problem-solving tasks, a student must identify a disorder. The student can elicit some seventy pieces of diagnostic information in any order, each of which rules some possibilities in and others out. Different combinations can isolate the disorder. Neural nets were better able to distinguish experts' diagnostic solutions from novices' solutions when Stevens used as first-stage features sequenced pairs of the tests they ordered. For the experts were better able than novices to understand the implications of the results of one test to optimally select the next one. This choice of first-stage features reflects the tuned reactions to evolving local situations discussed earlier as a hallmark of developing proficiency.

3.4.3. Narratives

People understand the world by constructing stories, narratives as Bruner (1990) calls them. Stories about why people, including ourselves, do what they do, in terms of beliefs, motives, and plans. Stories about how our cars and our computers work, or don't work. Stories in terms of causes and mechanisms. Stories that are plausible to us, based on personal experiences and what we've picked up, however formally or loosely, from the cultural milieu. We understand situations in terms of stories regardless of the depth of knowledge or expertise we may have. Five-year-olds are driven in the same way as domain experts to understand through narratives what is happening in the world around them, although the elements from which their narratives are constructed differ considerably. Aristotle's narrative for a thrown ball was that it sought its natural place on the ground, whereas Richard Feymann's story for the same event follows a "path of least action" plot line—a story that admits to a rigorous rendering in Newton's laws.

Several properties of reasoning with narratives are relevant to this chapter. Narratives appear to be an innate way of understanding, and figure in experiential as well as reflective cognition. Some of the elements and themes of narratives, such as those dealing with human motives, may be innate. George Polti (1868/1977) claimed to have identified *the* thirty-six essential structures that underlie the whole of literature, such as "Falling Prey to Cruelty or Misfortune" and "Supplication" (see Table 8.3 for an excerpt)—interwoven, juxtaposed, fleshed out in unique personalities and situations. Much content, however, is culturally contingent and learned, both in everyday life such as with games and conversations as well as in semantically rich learning domains. Either way, when we reason with a narrative built from themes in long-term memory, we don't need to fill in or activate all the details. We assemble narrative chunks, with attention drawn to anomalies (Bruner, 1990). Narratives enable understanding but at the same time constrain it, as they provide an interpretive frame into which particulars of a situation are slotted—or stretched, or modified, or ignored. Each instance of use enriches a narrative, through the meanings and connections established in that instantiation.

Reasoning through a narrative is intuitively compelling, whether it is wrong or right. The intuitive feeling of appropriateness of reasoning through narratives leads to cognitive illusions such as mistaking representativeness as strength of evidence, and failing to consider alternative explanations (Kahneman, Slovic, & Tversky, 1982). On the other hand, narrative settings such as permission and obligation relationships can embed abstract rules such as conditional implication, a form that allows people to use them more effectively than the formal expressions alone (Lehman, Lempert, & Nisbett, 1988). This is the rationale for case-based reasoning in domains such as medicine and finance (Watson, 1997). We do well to recall that scientific models and explanations, including educational measurement models, are themselves narrative structures—but ones that can be checked, indeed falsified, by public and explicit methods.

Students do not arrive at school with blank slates, but rather with very powerful and personally satisfactory "theories" for constructing meaning: basic premises about how the world works, story elements or subplots that diSessa (1983) calls phenomenological primitives (p-prims). Examples are found intuitive biology ("things that move are alive"; Carey, 1985) and intuitive physics ("a body can be in motion only if a force is acting on it"; (McCloskey, 1983)). A person's p-prims may not be explicit, organized, or consistent, but they guide reasoning nevertheless. School and the disciplines are supposed to reformulate those theories; to provide concepts and relationships that may be highly nonintuitive at first blush, but with experience come to feel equally natural.

P-prims and the narratives assembled from them are serviceable for most situations in everyday life. But they can lead to trouble in situations outside their range, and they are notoriously resistant to change. College graduates in Schneps and Sadler's (1987) film *A Private Universe* "explain" the seasons in terms of the distance between the earth and the sun. Exposure to scientifically correct explanations of this familiar phenomenon was not sufficient to form associations that would override their intuitive narratives.

Abstract representations cannot be simply loaded into a brain and accessed whenever they are appropriate from an external point of view. A reorganization of our thinking can be precipitated by an experience in which our narrative obviously fails (Vosniadou & Brewer, 1987), or in which an impasse at the limits of our knowledge requires a repair in order to solve a problem (VanLehn, 1990). Planning optimal instruction, therefore, depends on how a student is thinking, to arrange experiences that are most likely to move thinking to the next level—to set the stage for accommodation, in Piaget's developmental terms. An optimal assessment would reveal key facets of a student's understanding, to identify the student's zone of proximal development, in Vygotsky's sociocultural terms.

Much research has been carried out in physics in particular on assessments that reveal students' conceptions and misconceptions. After common misconceptions have be identified through in-depth discussions with students, one can then craft situations such that students with particular ways of thinking are likely provide characteristically different explanations or predictions. Hestenes, Wells, and Swackhamer's (1992) Force Concept Inventory (FCI) contains multiple choice tasks of this type, built around key concepts in introductory mechanics. Figure 8.11 shows two FCI-like tasks concerning Newton's Third Law. No equations or symbol manipulation are involved; claims concern qualitative, narrative structures that students use to reason about physical situations. Each option reflects particular conceptions, and patterns of response across such tasks evidence a student's propensity to reason through different narrative structures. Experts reliably provide explanations across situations that are consistent with Newtonian thinking, but novices' patterns are less consistent—sometimes Newtonian, but sometimes one misconception and sometimes another, depending in part on the surface features a task (Bao & Redish, 2006). The first task in Figure 8.11 is apt to evoke a Newton response, since it is easy to think of equal and opposite forces when the colliding objects are equal in mass and opposite in velocity. The second task is less straightforward. Associating greater force with faster-moving objects leads selecting the car, and associating greater force with heavier objects leads to selecting the truck.

Misconception research provides backing for assessment warrants. It does not, in itself, determine how assessments so grounded ought to be constructed. Contexts, constraints, and purposes also enter into the design problem. Frederiksen and White (1988) carried out a fine-grained implicit assessment inside an intelligent tutoring system designed to bring students through a sequence of increasingly sophisticated models for electricity. No formal statistical model was employed, nor were there detailed comparisons among students. Rather, at any point in time the claim space concerned the model currently in focus, either to give feedback for improved reasoning with it or to decide to move on to the next model. The targeted inference is "What can this student be thinking so that what she just said makes sense to him?" (Thompson, 1982). Minstrell (2000; also see National Research Council, 2001) used a pretest for a unit on separating effects of gravity from the effects of the ambient medium, to plan classroom instruction. Open-ended tasks such as the following revealed students' thinking:

TABLE 8.3 Excerpt from Polti's (1868/1977) *Thirty-six Dramatic Situations*

ATTRIBUTE	VALUE(S)
Name	Supplication
Necessary elements	A Persecutor; a Suppliant; and a Power in authority, whose decision is doubtful.
Summary	Among the examples here offered will be found those of three slightly differing classes. In the first, the power whose decision is awaited is a distinct personage, who is deliberating; shall he yield, from motives of prudence or from apprehension for those he loves, to the menaces of the persecutor, or rather, from generosity, to the appeal of the persecuted? In the second, by means of a contraction analogous to that which abbreviates a syllogism to an enthymeme, this undecided power is but an attribute of the persecutor himself, a weapon suspended in his hand; shall anger or pity determine his course? In the third group, on the contrary, the suppliant element is divided between two persons, the Persecuted and the Intercessor, thus increasing the number of principal characters to four.
Variations	(A1) Fugitives Imploring the Powerful for Help Against Their Enemies
	(A2) Assistance Implored for the Performance of a Pious Duty Which Has Been Forbidden
	…(C2) Supplication to a Relative in Behalf of Another Relative
	(C3) Supplication to a Mother's Lover, in Her Behalf
Examples	Act II of Shakespeare's *King John* (A1); *Oedipus at Colonus* (A3);
Comments	Of what variety … is this trinity capable! The Persecutor, one or many, voluntary or unconscious, greedy or revengeful, spreading the subtle network of diplomacy, or revealing himself beneath the formidable pomp of the greatest contemporary powers; the Suppliant, artless or eloquent, virtuous or guilty, humble or great; and the Power, neutral or partial to one side or the other, perhaps inferior in strength to the Persecutor and surrounded by his own kindred who fear danger, perhaps deceived by a semblance of right and justice, perhaps obliged to sacrifice a high ideal; sometimes severely logical, sometimes emotionally susceptible, or even overcome by a conversion a la Dostoievsky, and, as a final thunderbolt, abandoning the errors which he believed to be truth, if not indeed the truth which he believed to be error!

FIGURE 8.11 Two Tasks Concerning Newton's Third Law

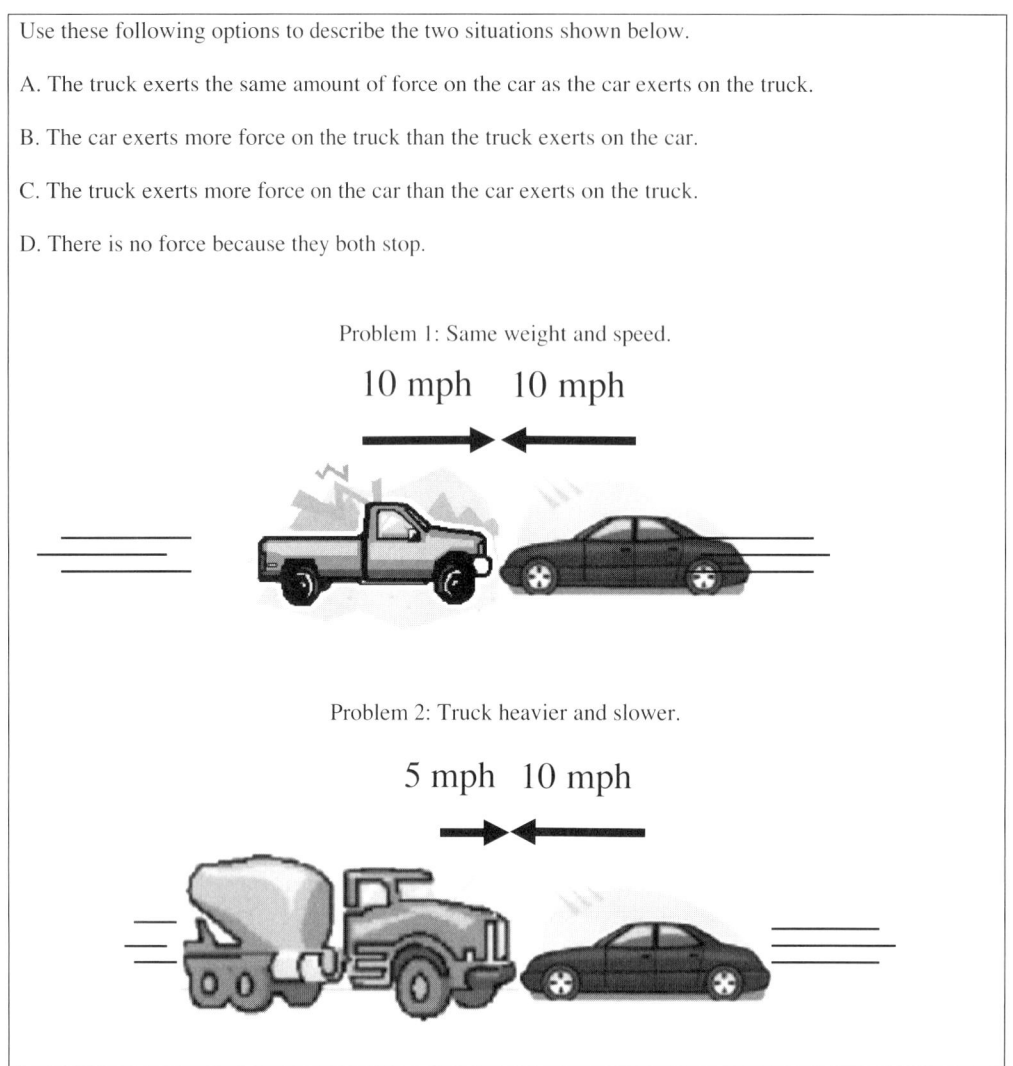

First, suppose we weigh some object on a large spring scale, not unlike the ones we have at the local market. The object apparently weighs 10 pounds, according to the scale. Now we put the same apparatus, scale, object and all, under a very large glass dome, seal the system around the edges, and pump out all the air. That is, we use a vacuum pump to allow all the air to escape out from under the glass dome. What will the scale reading be now? Answer as precisely as you can at this point in time. [pause] And in the space provided, briefly explain how you decided. (Minstrell, 2000, p. 50).

An answer of zero pounds suggests that air pressing down is the only factor at work. Some students say there is no change because gravity is the only factor. Others recognize that buoyancy is involved somehow, but cannot rectify the effects. Working from responses to open-ended tasks such as these and from his experience in the classroom, Minstrill has identified common conceptions and misconceptions, "facets," in a number of domains. As with Frederiksen and White's sequence of models, Minstrill's facets reflect levels of understanding and suggest pathways to more expert understanding (Hunt & Minstrell, 1994).

3.4.4. Knowledge Representations

This section addresses external forms of knowledge representation, or inscriptions (Lehrer & Schauble, 2002). Knowledge representations are physical or conceptual structures that depict entities and relationships, in a way that supports reasoning and can be shared among people or by the same person over time. Good knowledge representations take information and relationships that are otherwise hard to think about (too much, too complicated, too fast, too small), and express it in forms that play to our strengths. An outlier that could hide comfortably in a stream of numbers jumps out from a scattergram (Lewandowsky & Behrens, 1999). Examples of knowledge representations include maps, lists, graphs, wiring diagrams, bus schedules, musical notation, mathematical formulas, and object models for business systems. Markman's (1999) definition of a knowledge representation has four components:

> *A represented world:* The domain that the representations are about. The representation world may be the world outside the cognitive system or some other set of representations inside the system. That is, one set of representations can be about another set of representations.
> *A representing world:* The domain that contains the representations.
> *Representing rules:* The representing world is related to the represented world through a set of rules that map elements of the represented world to elements of the representing world.
> *A process that uses the representation:* It makes no sense to talk about representations in the absence of processes. The combination of the first three components (a represented world, a representing world, and a set of representing rules) create merely the potential for representation. Only when there is also a process that uses the representation does the system actually represent, and the capabilities of a system are defined only when there is both a representation and a process. (pp. 5–8)

The lower left plane in Figure 8.12 shows phenomena in a particular represented-world situation. A mapping is established between this situation and, in the center, patterns that can be expressed in terms of the entities, relationships, and properties of the knowledge representation, that is, its ontology (Greeno, 1983). Reasoning is carried out in these terms in the representing world. This process constitutes an understanding of the situation, which can lead through the machinery of the representation to explanations, predictions, or plans for action. Figure 8.12 is itself a knowledge representation. It brings these points to the foreground: The real-world situation is nebulous, whereas the representation is crisp and well defined. Not all aspects of the real-world situation have correspondents in the representation. The representation conveys ideas and relationships that the real-world situation does not. The reconceived situation shows a less-than-perfect match to the representation, but provides a framework for reasoning the situation itself cannot. On the other hand, Figure 8.12 does not convey the iterative and interactive way we use representations. The reconceived understanding is provisional. The hypothesized missing elements can be used to evaluate the quality of the representation, and spark revisions in the representing world. The hypothesized relationships guide actions that change the represented world, and lead to re-representation.

Under the rubric of knowledge representations, we shall consider rule-based systems for reasoning, including propositional systems (e.g., Buchanan & Shortliffe's [1984] MYCIN) and production systems (e.g., ACT-R, Anderson et al., 2004; SOAR, Newell, 1990; GOMS, Card, Moran, & Newell, 1983; GOMS stands for Goals, Operators, Methods, and Selection rules), and knowledge structures studied variously as mental models (Johnson-Laird, 1983), frames (Minsky, 1975), and schemas (Rumelhart, 1980). This work falls largely under the information processing perspective. It concerns knowledge structures that could in principle be instantiated in and operated upon

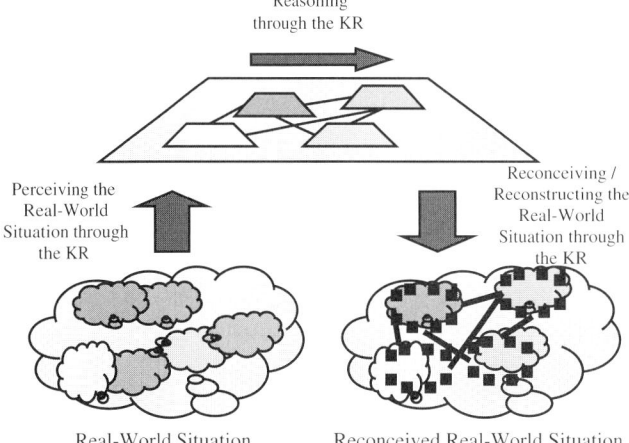

FIGURE 8.12 A Generic Knowledge Representation

by a general computing mechanism—a computer, a Turing machine, or, presumably, a human. These approaches have in fact been implemented in computer programs, often in the form of expert systems, to tackle some of the kinds of problems that humans solve such as diagnosing infections (MYCIN) or learning to solve puzzles (SOAR). Sometimes the motivation for these activities is research on human cognition, as with FAIRRAVEN or for emulating the way children learn to solve word problems (e.g., Dellarosa, 1986). Sometimes the goal is to solve practical applied problems, as when configuring computer systems or predicting weather (Edwards, 1998), quite aside from how computationally equivalent human cognition would be implemented.

Thus one level to discuss these knowledge representations is as computational and algorithmic models that are legitimate targets of learning, to support thinking we somehow do—whether or not we represent and operate on the information the same way computers do. We gain insights about what kinds of processing might be feasible and consonant with the limits of human cognition, such as speed and working memory capacity. Whether propositions, production rules, and schema structures and slots are literally instantiated in the brain, as entities to be operated on in with essentially the same functions that computer programs use is debated by Vera and Simon (1993) from an information-processing perspective and Greeno and Moore (1993) from a situative/sociocultural perspective (also see Clancey, 1993). The question of just how knowledge is represented and used is a current frontier of research, seeking to connect computational and biological perspectives, across informational and neural levels (see Hawkins & Blakeslee, 2004, for a readable discussion of current work).

Quite aside from implementation, these formal structures for reasoning prove useful for designing and conducting assessments. Marshall (1995; also see Derry & the TiPS Research Group, 2001) addresses the implications of schema theory for assessment in the context of arithmetic story problems. She provides students with representational forms for the fundamental relationships Change, Group,

Vary, Compare, and Restate. The Change representation, for example, has slots labeled Original amount, Amount of Change, and Resulting Amount. The slots are associated through a characteristic relationship, expressed in the symbol system of arithmetic as a family of related addition and subtraction equations. In assessment tasks students determine which schemas match various verbal, pictorial, and real-world situations. They map information from the situations into the schema, identifying what is known and what is unknown, and how they are related. They reason through the arithmetic representation and apply the new knowledge to the situation. They combine multiple schemas to tackle more complex problems, filling in a slot in one schema with information obtained through other schemas.

Knowledge representations can also be discussed at the interpersonal level. They are cultural artifacts that people use to express and to transform knowledge, that support the thinking of people individually or collaboratively, that can be taught and learned (Markman, 1999; Stefik, 1995), and therefore around which important learning occurs and assessment is needed. The knowledge structures of disciplines, embodying definitions, principles, and representational forms, are distillations across people and over time of patterns exhibited across countless particular situations—powerful and worth learning because they support understanding and action in new and unique, but appropriately similar, situations.

Collins and Ferguson's (1993) use of the phrase "epistemic *forms*" to describe external knowledge representations underscores their importance in creating knowledge. This is as true of commonplace forms such as lists and tables as it is of blueprints at work and Punnett squares in the lab. Their companion phrase "epistemic *games*" emphasizes that to exploit their potential we must learn the patterns through which people interact with them in particular situations, through time, often collaboratively. Kindfield (1994) contrasted experts' and novices' use of diagrams to reason about crossover in genes during meiosis. Experts' diagrams were often rough and incomplete—but the entities and processes they did include were precisely those that were key to the problem at hand.

Propositional systems are forms of knowledge representation that, as formal structures, date back to Aristotle. If all As are Bs and all Bs are Cs, then all As are Cs, no matter what As, Bs, and Cs happen to be. Historically, the study of meaning in philosophy and branches of linguistics has been logic and its extension to symbol manipulation systems more generally, including mathematics, computer languages, and probability models. Much human knowledge and much human work can be expressed in this form. Computer programs constructed according to these principles can play chess and discover mathematical theorems (Newell & Simon, 1956). Suppose the brain possessed a set of rules such as these, elaborated sufficiently to encompass human language; a dictionary that references As, Bs, and Cs to their real-world counterparts; and operators that can assembly the As, Bs, and Cs into valid strings. Suppose further that visual, acoustical, and other sensory information could be encoded into the same system, running with the same set of operators. We would have, in effect, a universal grammar (Chomsky, 1981), through which actual human languages reflect a common and innate "language of the mind" (Fodor, 1983). But a strictly propositional approach deals poorly with the situated and embodied nature of cognition, as seen by way of contrast with connectionist representations, production rule systems, and schemas.

Thinking about cognition in terms of *production systems* help us bridge the gap between decontextualized operators and symbols on the one hand, and embodied and situated human experience on the other, by characterizing knowledge as propensity to action. A production system is a collection of IF-THEN rules and operators for planning, evaluating, and taking action (Newell & Simon, 1972). The IF clause of a production rule states conditions that can be based on sensory information, goals or subgoals, or results of comparisons. When satisfied, it triggers the THEN clause to revise the external situation, change a goal or subgoal, or gather more information. Production rules are thus about action—some overt actions a behaviorist would study, but others internal, and all subject to the limitations of human processing. One important insight into human cognition is how, with repeated use of sequences, production rules can be chunked into larger more efficient rules. GOMS, SOAR, and ACT-R illustrate a mechanism for this capability. Another insight is how effective and complex activities can be carried out without a comprehensive global plan, but through a series of actions that successively modify the situation in response to contextual cues (Simon, 2001).

As an example, Winograd's (1972) early artificial intelligence computer program SHRDLU encapsulated its knowledge about its world of blocks in terms of production rules for locating and moving them, and planning actions. What "it" means in "Find the red block. Pick it up" was not a fixed dictionary entry, but a set of procedures to be assembled in the particular situation to carry out a particular action. SHRDLU reflects the way words take situated meanings every time people use them better than a propositional system.

Brown and Burton (1978) proposed that children's proficiency in subtraction problems might be characterized in terms of production rules, some correct and others flawed, or "buggy." VanLehn's (1990) list of 121 production rules, garnered through both theory and talk-aloud solutions, includes this bug:

> **Smaller-from-larger.** The student does not borrow, but from each column subtracts the smaller digit from the larger one. (p. 228)

This research provides backing for assessment. Burton and Brown's DEBUGGY computer program and VanLehn's SIERRA instantiate a space of claims about which subset of rules characterizes a student's behavior at some point in time. In a measurement model, the student parameter would be a vector of 0's and 1's corresponding to all the production rules. These are not observable, but a warrant cast in terms of a production rule system would predict patterns of responses that reflected patterns of production rules. For example, Figure 8.13 shows a set of four subtraction responses that is consistent with the "subtract smaller from larger" buggy production rule. For any single problem, a particular correct or incorrect answer can usually have been produced by several different combinations of rules. It is not a response that evidences a pattern of production rules, but triangulation from patterns of responses across tasks with different features. The cognitive diagnosis models introduced in section 2.4.5 and discussed further in section 4.2 support this kind of inference with probability-based reasoning. Anderson's (Anderson & Reiser, 1985) LISP tutor similarly characterizes programming proficiency as a set of 325 production rules. Using production rules as a computational model for cognition, the tutor's instructional sequence reinforces correct rules, and detects and fixes buggy ones.

Schema theory also combines conditional knowledge with recurring patterns, into which we map the particulars of situations. Rumelhart (1980) argued that "Most of the reasoning we do apparently does not involve the application of general purpose reasoning skills. Rather, it seems that most of our reasoning ability is tied to particular bodies of knowledge. ... Once we can 'understand' the situation by encoding it in terms of a relatively rich set of schemata, the conceptual constraints of the schemata can be brought into play and the problem readily solved." A schema is instantiated when one perceives some of its relationships in a situation. This entails filling in missing variables, inferring additional relationships, and checking for specifics that may be at odds with usual expectations. Much of this activity is unconscious and automatic, as when a skilled reader is unaware of details of individual letters as she reads a text. Sometimes aspects of it are conscious and deliberate, as when she ponders the author's intentions.

The schema approach agrees with a connectionist approach that every cognitive act is a construction of meaning, incorporating patterns that have developed up to that point in time. This is a computational level description. The implementation-level issue of just how this would happen is "the binding problem." Binding is a literal problem to be solved when we consider schemas as fixed structures: It is a software design challenge for schemas instantiated in computer programs, and an instructional challenge for schemas used as external forms of knowledge. Assessment tasks can therefore be designed around students' proficiencies to recognize when schemas are applicable and map real-world situations into them.

If perception is an active process (selecting, building, and tailoring representations from currently available schemas), then learning is all the more dynamic: extending, modifying, and replacing elements to create new structures (Rumelhart, 1980). In some cases learning is in fact merely adding bits to existing structures (accretion). Sometimes it involves generalizing or connecting schemas (tuning). Other times it involves wholesale abandonment of important parts of schemas, with replacement by qualitatively different structures (restructuring).

Under what conditions do these changes take place? Piaget's (1968/1970) view of learning combines development and information processing. He tracked how children acquired more powerful concepts and operators as they interact with environments with challenges just beyond their current stage of reasoning. Piaget himself noted unevenness in a given child's development in different circumstances, or décalage; acquiring person permanence before object permanence, for example. Subsequent researchers found it was not at all uncommon that a child would perform at different stages in different domains, depending on task types and prior experience (e.g., Case, 1987) and social context and support (e.g., Fischer & Rose, 2001). One would expect such results from a situative/sociocultural perspective. From this point of view, people acquire concepts and become attuned to affordances largely through their interactions with others in social contexts. Vygotsky (1987) asserts that any higher psychological function appears "twice, or on two planes. First it appears on the social plane and then on the psychological plane. First it appears between people as an interpsychological category and then within the individual child as an intrapsychological category" (p. 57). Then, "the individual's use of this shared understanding is not the same as what was constructed jointly; it is an appropriation of the shared understanding by each individual that reflects the individual's understanding of and involvement in the activity" (Rogoff, 1990, p. 195). Like Piaget, Vygotsky draws attention to the frontiers of a learner's capabilities, but now foregrounding the social aspect, in terms of what can be accomplished with support from others, the zone of proximal development (ZPD). When claims about a learner's ZPD in a given area are of interest, observing levels of performance under fixed conditions is less informative than observing the level of support needed to achieve a given level of performance. The observation in Campione and Brown's (1987) "dynamic testing" is how far into a sequence of hints a child must go to accomplish a task.

FIGURE 8.13 A Set of Responses Consistent with the "Smaller-from-Larger" Bug

```
   821           885
 - 285         - 221
   ───           ───
   664           664

    63            17
  - 15          -  9
   ───           ───
    52            12
```

3.4.5. Knowledge Representations in Assessment

We find knowledge representation throughout the enterprise of educational assessment. An assessment is in itself a knowledge representation, a point of particular importance from the sociocultural perspective (Gipps, 1999). An assessment makes explicit, sharable, and public the knowledge that is valued, the ways it is used, and the qualities of good work. The process of constructing an assessment, done thoughtfully, elicits an understanding of the knowledge that is targeted, the actions of students that provide evidence about it, and the circumstances under which that knowledge should be brought to bear to achieve instructional aims (Wiggins, 1998). An assessment communicates the targets of learning and the standards of performances, and as such serves vital educative purposes before the first student takes it. The Architectural Registration Examination (ARE), NMBE's computer-based case simulations (CCS), and Cisco's NetPASS were all shaped by a desire for assessment that better reflects the profession. As Resnick and Resnick (1989) famously put it, WYTIWYG: What you test is what you get.

The analysis of any domain in which learning is to be assessed must include identifying the knowledge representations that people work with and how they use them. Because developing facility with knowledge representations is central to developing expertise in any domain, claims about students' capabilities will be central to assessment: capabilities to choose representations, express information and obtain information from them, transform information from one representation to another, use representations to coordinate actions in situations and interactions with colleagues.

Assessment tasks can be structured around the knowledge, relationships, and uses of the domain representations. Every assessment task must use forms of knowledge representations to provide information, offer affordances, and capture actions. Explicitly designing tasks around the forms people use and the ways they use them is key to assessing aspects of proficiency with them (Gitomer & Steinberg, 1999). This includes choosing efficacious representations for a given purpose, mapping situations into representations, reasoning through representations, and translating from one representation to another and recognizing when to do so. In a NetPASS design task, for example, students must work from a set of goals and constraints expressed in natural language (Figure 8.14), to topological diagrams (Figure 8.15) and device configurations (Figure 8.16) of a network that meets the client's needs. Natural language specifications are essential for communicating with clients. The topological diagram reflects hardware and connectivity properties of devices. The device setups provide logical information to colleagues who will implement the proposed network. Each representation plays a special role in the design process, and a solution must be coherent across them.

The discipline of assessment employs knowledge representations itself. We use Toulmin diagrams to structure arguments, job analysis questionnaires to determine valued knowledge and skills, scope-and-sequence charts to map curricula, and test specifications to assemble tasks into assessments. Task templates organize the results of domain analyses into schemas that guide task creation, from Hively, Patterson, and Page's (1968) arithmetic item forms to open-ended science inquiry investigations such as SRI's (2002) GLOBE tasks.

Knowledge representations can also structure the creation and conduct of assessments. While the role of technology in assessment is not the focus of this discussion, we note that knowledge representations are the key to its success. They can support every stage of implementing an assessment argument. Expressing targeted knowledge and task settings in appropriate representational forms makes possible model-based dynamic construction and presentation of tasks (Irvine & Kyllonen, 2002). Simulation engines in CCS, NetPASS, and Hydrive use representations not only to render a simulated world, but to characterize the features of the situations and students' actions. Students' work products in ARE and IMMEX take the form of symbol-system representations from which salient features are automatically identified, and interpreted through higher-level rules or neural networks. And for synthesizing evidence across observations, educational measurement has since its inception used the symbol systems of mathematics and probability to combine information, explore complex data, characterize uncertainty, and guide modeling.

3.5. Implications of Expertise Research for Assessment

3.5.1. Research on Expertise

The study of expertise has been a fruitful line of cognitive research (Chi, Glaser, & Farr, 1988; Ericsson, 1996, 2004). Salthouse (1991) describes expertise in terms of circumventing the information-processing limitations that nonexperts face: not knowing what expect or what to do, not knowing what is important or what to focus on, not knowing how variables interact or how to combine information. The expert has acquired, and puts to use, various patterns of the kinds discussed throughout this section, to guide perception, understanding, and action. Capabilities and attunements that are highlighted under both the information-processing and sociocultural perspectives play prominent roles in the development of expertise. In semantically rich domains, high levels of expertise generally take five to ten years to develop—time spent using, extending, practicing with, and reflecting on the concepts, tools, representations, and social interaction patterns of the domain.

Experts in a domain generally command more facts and concepts than do novices, but the key distinction lies in their ways of viewing phenomena, and representing and approaching problems. Chase and Simon (1973) found that Masters' memories for arrangements of pieces on a chessboard was substantially better than that of Novices—but only for positions that arose from games, not random positions. After years of talking and thinking about chess, playing and analyzing games, Masters organize their perceptions in terms of chunks, from such basic patterns as a knight fork to specialized patterns such as the Sveshnikov/Kalashnikov variation of the Sicilian opening defense. And perception is linked to potential for action. Masters do not necessarily search more moves ahead than Novices, but they restrict their search to higher-quality lines of play and more accurately factor in their opponents' responses (de Groot, 1946/1978). The greater degree to which key patterns can

FIGURE 8.14 Natural Language Problem Statement for a NetPASS Design Task

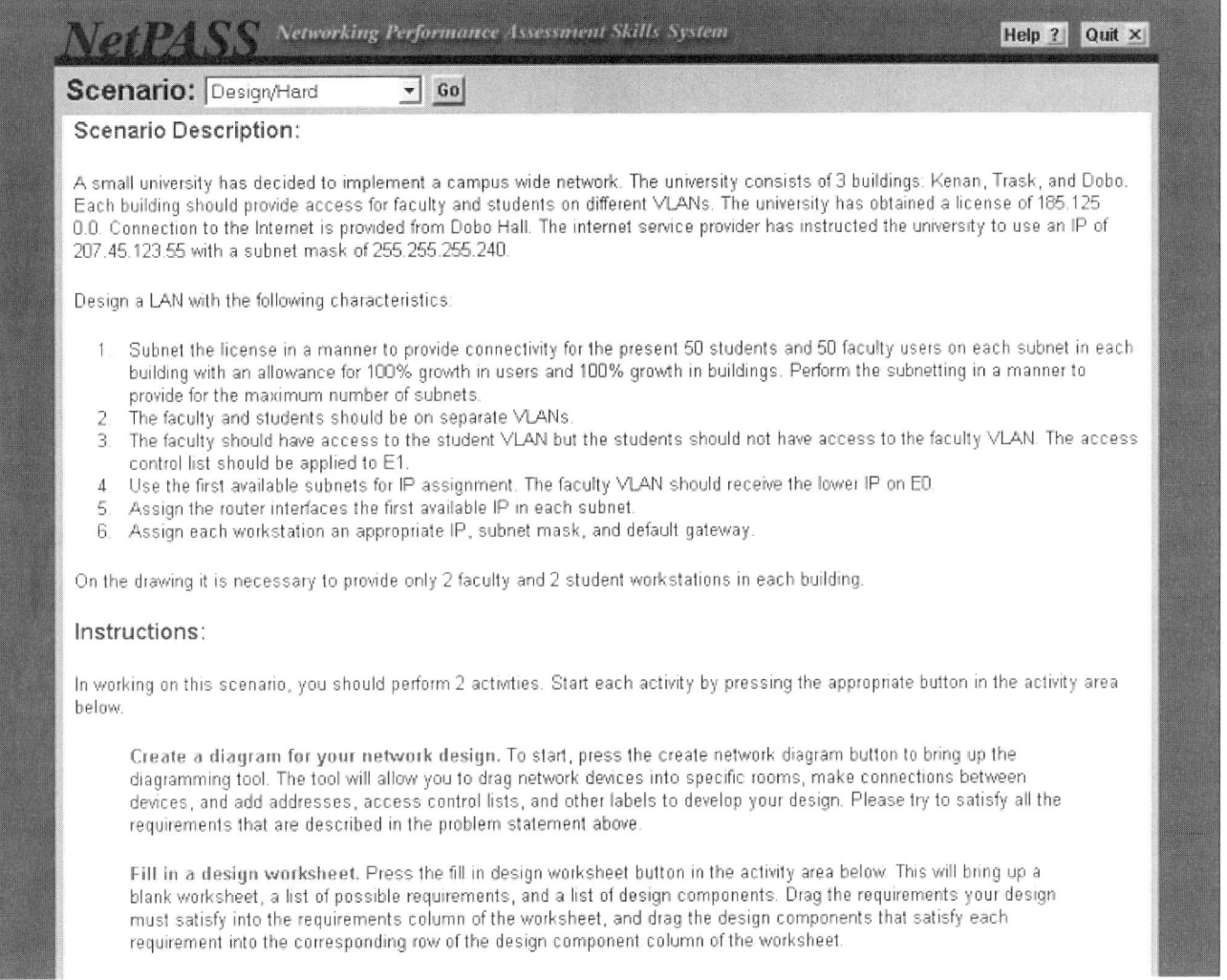

Source: Reproduced with permission from John Behrens.

be perceived and their implications activated experientially enables experts to focus their deliberations on what is novel in the situation at hand. Developing expertise in a domain is marked by the increase of experiential and automatized domain-relevant cognition, and also by increasing of metacognitive capabilities. This means self-awareness at the level of reflective cognition: monitoring one's own use of models and strategies, adapting them to the problem at hand, recognizing when more information is needed or new knowledge must be acquired (Glaser, Lesgold, & Lajoie, 1987).

Cognitive task analysis (CTA; Schraagen, Chipman, & Shalin, 2000) has been a primary tool in expertise research. Early studies took an information-processing stance. Newell and Simon (1972) said that a cognitive task analysis in a domain seeks to shed light on (a) essential features of the situations; (b) internal representations of situations [at a computational level, at least]; (c) the relationship between problem-solving behavior and internal representation; (d) how the problems are solved; and (e) what makes problems hard. Problem-solving is characterized in terms of problem spaces and production rules, with a goal being to identify a subject's Goals, Operators, Methods, and Selection mechanisms (Card et al., 1983). Expertise research from this perspective is marked by observing subjects at different levels of expertise act in the same situations.

The information-processing approach is complemented by an ethnographic approach that studies behavior in more naturally occurring settings, with particular attention to use of tools, knowledge representations, and socially-structured patterns of interaction (e.g., Scribner's 1984 study of dairy workers). Much of the information required by experts resides in an expert's environment and situation as well as in her head; cognition is both supported, in terms of tools and knowledge representations, and distributed, in terms of the interpersonal interactions required in accomplishing a goal. Current CTA work in expertise research integrates both perspectives, therefore, as both are indeed integral to expertise. Examples include studies of nurses in emergency rooms (Patel & Kaufman, 1996) and members of an airline flight crew (Hutchins & Klausen, 2000).

FIGURE 8.15 Network Topology Representation for a NetPASS Design Task

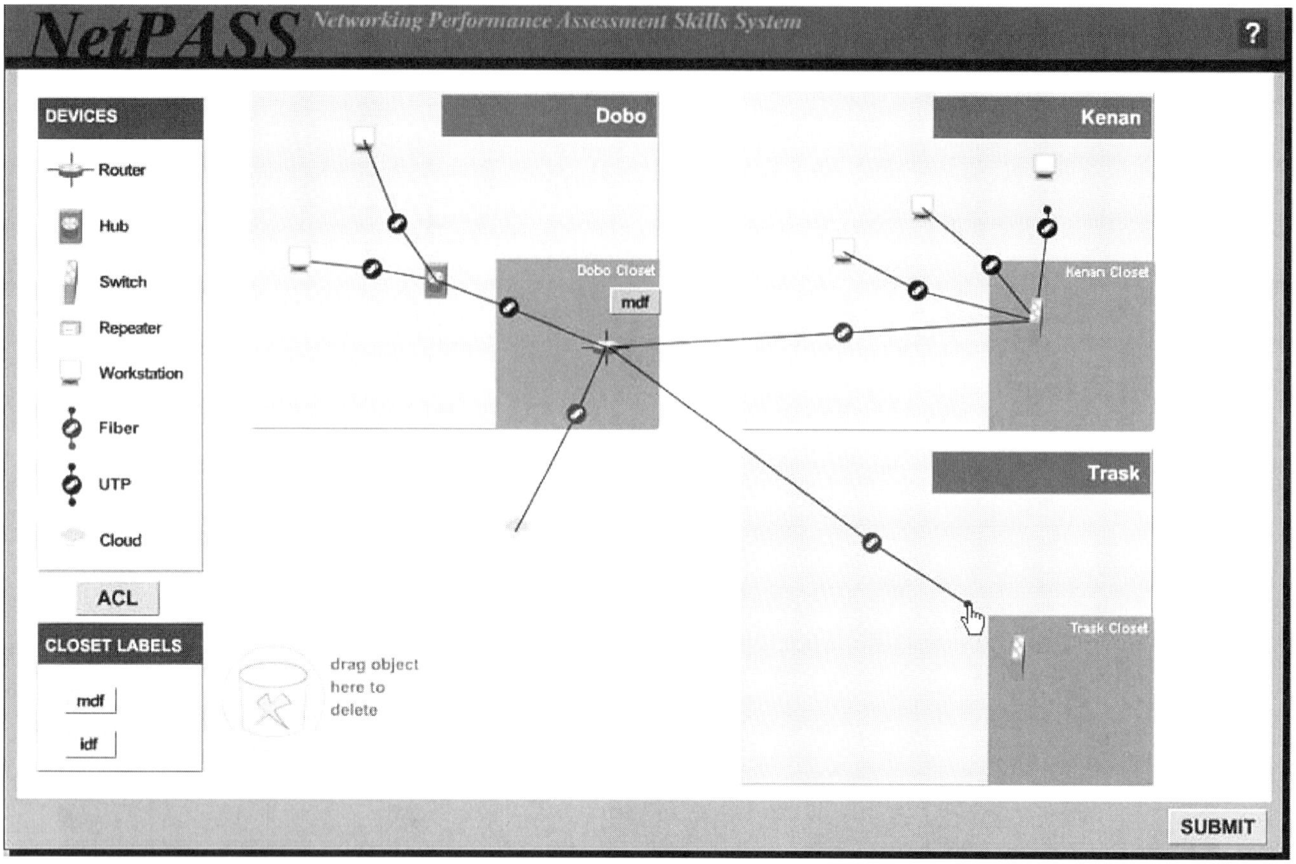

Source: Reproduced with permission from John Behrens.

External knowledge representations are a nexus between the information-processing and sociocultural perspectives on expertise. Representations both constrain and enable expert-like thinking about a domain by an individual, and likewise constrain and enable communication and coordination among individuals. Learning to work with knowledge representations of the domain—to perceive, express, manipulate, transform, explain, and share information—is essential to becoming an expert.

3.5.2. Design Patterns for Assessment

The detailed cognitive task analyses and contextualized observations necessary to discover the nuances of expert performance cannot be carried out in every learning domain, for every learning context, for every assessment occasion. But grounded on the findings of expertise research, coarser models at higher levels explanation can suffice for tracking students' progress and guiding their learning. Emerging from the expertise literature are classes of expertise, each with their own details but with commonalities that can prove helpful in assessment design. We can contrast troubleshooting in finite domains (e.g., repairing avionics test station; Lesgold et al, 1992) with troubleshooting in open-ended domains (e.g., medical diagnosis; Patel & Kaufman, 1996). We can identify domains that demand design under constraints (e.g., programming, architecture, and assessment design itself; Akin, 1986, Katz, 1994), those that require interacting with team members for a common goal (e.g., tank crews and team sports; Helsen, Starkes, & Hodges, 1998), and those that require artistic performances (e.g., music and acting; Sloboda, 1991).

One can develop schemas for designing assessment tasks in different domains that are similar in these broader ways, in terms of patterns suggested by the particulars of detailed cognitive research. Pattern languages are used in architecture (Alexander, Ishikawa, & Silverstein, 1977) and software design (e.g., Gamma, Helm, Johnson, & Vlissides, 1994) to articulate best practices, describe good designs, and capture experience in ways that make it possible for others to capitalize on it. In the same way, design patterns for classes of assessment tasks can be used to organize assessment arguments around the recurring patterns of knowledge and practice, and paradigmatic ways of assessing them (Mislevy, Hamel, et al., 2003). An assessment design pattern sets the stage, in nontechnical terms, for the elements of an evidence-centered assessment argument. Table 8.4 is abstracted from Katz's (1994) ARE research, and offers a starting point for assessment in any domain with problems of design under constraint. The aspects of model-based reasoning in Table 8.2 are seeds for design patterns that could

FIGURE 8.16 Device Properties Representation in a NetPASS Design Task

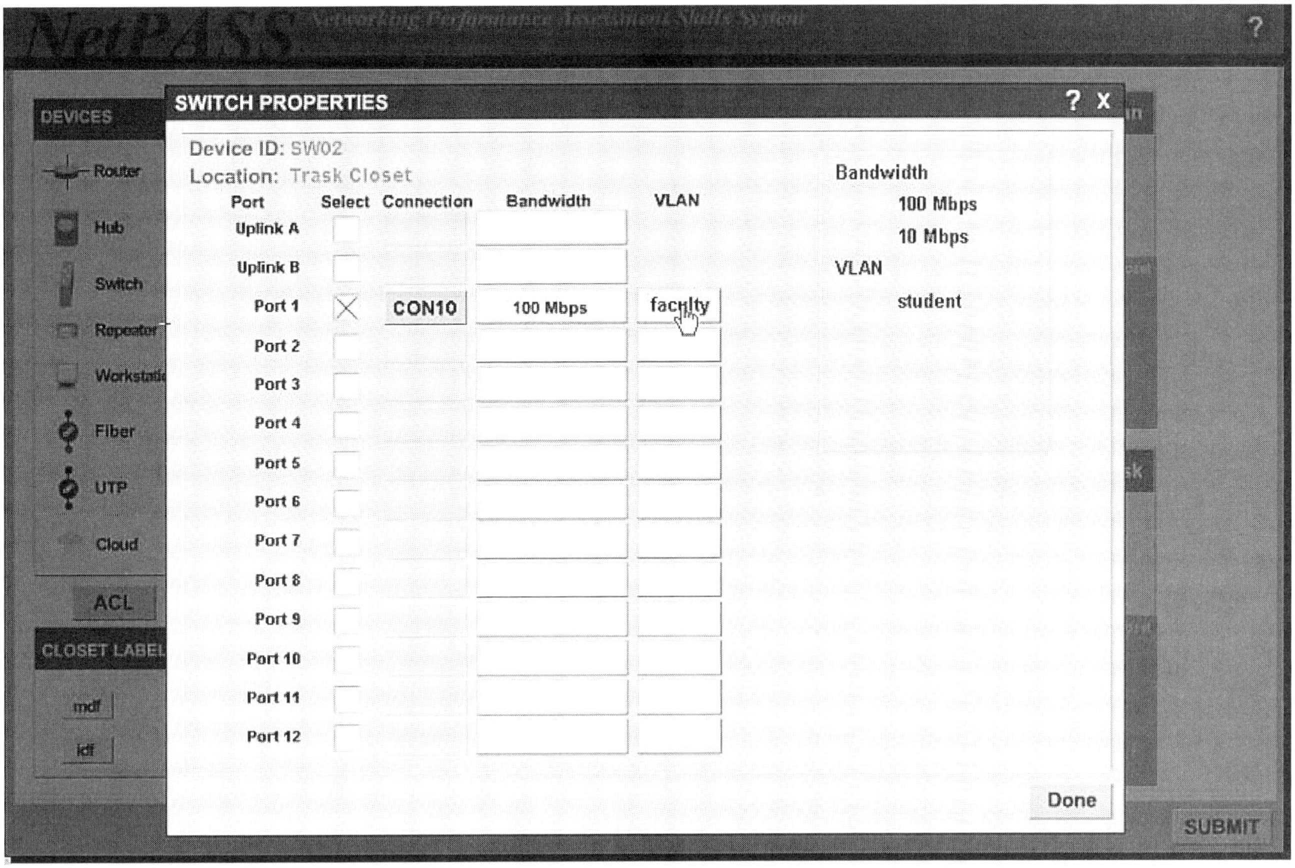

Source: Reproduced with permission from John Behrens.

be developed for use in most scientific domains. Multiple patterns can be called upon for a given design problem; a task might at once arise from patterns for design-under-constraints, peer-collaboration, and self-reflection. Working at the design pattern level can help a designer tailor an assessment argument, preparing to marshal the technical machinery of measurement models to which we now turn.

4. MEASUREMENT MODELS

This section returns to the role of probability-based reasoning in assessment, looking more closely at some specific models and ways of applying them. It highlights the interplay between the technical characteristics of models and the substantive arguments they are meant to support. Section 4.1 views probability models as knowledge representations: They are constructed from recurring themes for particular situations; provisional and revised in light of data; connected to a symbol system that supports reasoning; and fusions of perception, interpretation, and action. Siegler's (1981) balance beam study is used to fix ideas. It has become a paradigmatic example in the psychometric literature (e.g., De Boeck, Wilson, & Acton, 2005; Kempf, 1983; van Maanen, Been, & Sijtsma, 1989). In a simple setting it illustrates inference from a developmental perspective, evidenced by response patterns rather than total scores, and shows children at earlier stages performing better than children at higher stages for some tasks because they give right answers for the wrong reasons. Section 4.2 discusses ways that measurement models have been reconceived in some cases and extended in others to support assessment arguments cast in terms of cognitive psychology. We speak generically of "measurement models," although we see in section 4.1.4 this appellation is not without controversy.

4.1. Measurement Models and Narrative Structures

Probability-based measurement models provide explicit, formal rules for synthesizing evidence from multiple and diverse pieces of information about what a student knows and can do. The statistician Glenn Shafer (quoted in Pearl, 1988) said, "Probability isn't really about numbers; it's about the structure of reasoning." In the context of measurement models, it's reasoning about what we know and what we don't know about students' capabilities, *however we conceive of them*, based on what we see the students say and do.

Measurement models support reasoning about unique events in terms of recurring entities and relationships, within a quantitative framework for managing information and uncertainty. One posits regularities in students' propensities to act in certain ways in certain kinds of situ-

TABLE 8.4 A Design Pattern for Assessing "Design under Constraints"

Attribute	Value(s)
Name	Design under constraint: Creating a design (Other patterns: Implementing a design, Design in cycles, etc.)
Rationale	"Fulfillment of purpose or adaptation to a goal involves a relation among three terms: the purpose or goal, the character of the artifact, and the environment in which the artifact performs" (Simon, 2001, p. 5). This design pattern concerns direct evidence about aspects of these capabilities in a given context
Central claims	Capability to manage/chose/sequence actions & use affordances to achieve design goal in a specified context/domain
Additional knowledge that may be at issue	Substantive knowledge in domain; Familiarity with tools & knowledge representations; Self-regulatory skills in monitoring progress
Characteristic features	Design goal; Multiple conflicting constraints; medium for design
Variable task features	Difficulty/complexity of design problem
	Design goal(s) explicit or implicit?
	Characteristics of constraints:
	Number of constraints; Difficulty of meeting constraints; Degree of interaction among constraints; Presence of implicit constraints, red herrings.
	One possible solution vs many solutions, better or worse with respect to how well they optimize constraints/outcomes
	Kind/degree of support
	Reference materials (e.g., building code, syntax manuals); Advise from colleagues, real or simulated; Feedback on provisional design
	Collaborative work? (If so, draw upon use design pattern for collaboration)
	Familiar vs novel design problem; Limited time
Potential performances and work products	Design rationale; Final design; Sequence of intermediate designs; Trace & time stamps of design actions; Talk-aloud protocol during solution; Video of design activities
Potential features of performance to evaluate	Quality of design rationale; Quality of self monitoring
	Regarding the final product:
	How well final design meets goals; Seriousness of errors
	Regarding performance
	Progression of intermediate products; Severity of rework
Selected references	Akin (1986). On the psychology of architectural design
	Alexander, et al. (1977). Pattern language as design aid
	Gamma, et al. (1994). Design patterns in software engineering

ations—perhaps casting them broadly as under a trait perspective, perhaps narrowly from a situative/sociocultural perspective, perhaps in terms of trajectories of learning through a developmental perspective. These regularities enable us to think at the level of the patterns across relevant situations, whether realized, potential, hypothetical, or even counterfactual (Brennan, 2001).

What is common across all applications of measurement models is the syntax of the symbol system: structures and rules for probability-based reasoning, about variables, by means of conditional distributions. What varies is the connection of these formal entities to people, events, and contexts in the real world, that is, the situated meanings of the symbols and relationships. It is through the processes of model construction, elaboration, and criticism that psychological perspectives and assessment purposes are effected. The key steps in building a measurement model, therefore, are determining variables and specifying their interrelationships.

4.1.1. Determining Variables

A measurement model contains a schematized version of substantive situations and a representation for our knowledge about the entities in those situations. The substantive model concerns students' proficiencies (θs) as relevant to the situations, features of situations (Qs), and features of students' actions (Xs) in the situations. The nature, grain size, and degree of contextualization of the interpretation of the student variables depend on psychological perspective. Psychological and substantive knowledge determine the key relationship, namely conditional distributions of observable variables X given student variables θ, task variables Q, and parameters β that specify the conditional probability distribution; that is,

$$p(x|\theta, \beta, q). \qquad (7)$$

(In many cases, such as IRT, Qs are simply indicators identifying tasks; in more structured models such as the LLTM, formally discerned variables for salient features of task situations.) A joint probability distribution over the student variables and observable variables characterizes an observer's state of knowledge about their values at some point in time, in light of some body of evidence (Mislevy, 1994). All this together is the ontology of measurement models. In the representing world of the model, the machinery of probability-based reasoning indicates how reverse reasoning from Xs to θs is to carried out (through Bayes theorem) and how different kinds and amounts of data should affect our beliefs.

The advantages of probability-based reasoning obtain only for propositions that can be expressed in terms of a model's frame of discernment. There is much flexibility in defining the structure of the relationships in a model and interpreting the variables and relationships, but once it is set, it supports reasoning in a circumscribed narrative space: stories that correspond to configurations of values that the variables can take, which are then interpreted through their situated meanings. Questions concerning features of situations or interactions outside this narrative space cannot be asked or answered.

There is an important difference between the variables in a probability model and the corresponding entities, claims, and data in a Toulmin diagram. In a Toulmin diagram, a claim is a proposition that one seeks to support and a datum is a proposition about an aspect of an observation. A variable addresses not only the particular claim or observation, but other claims or observations that could be entertained. As a datum in an argument, one says that the response to Item j is correct. But as a value of the item response variable X_j, one says that the value of X_j is "correct" *as opposed to* "incorrect." If you know what the value of the variable is, you also know what it is not. This perspective becomes especially important in designing automated scoring procedures for complex performances (Scalise, 2003), since it is not sufficient to simply identify interesting features. One must construct a conceptual frame that allows the results to be compared with what might have been observed but was not.

Similarly, a claim in a Toulmin diagram is a proposition about an aspect of proficiency or propensity for action, whereas a variable θ characterizes ranges or potential values for an aspect of proficiency or propensities for action. The possible values of the possibly vector-valued θ correspond to different states, levels, or configurations of these proficiencies or propensities—each value representing a possible proposition or claim. In the IRT model for progressive matrices, θ was a real-valued scalar that characterizes an examinee's propensity to make correct responses. In the binary skills model, θ was a vector of 1s and 0s that characterized which rules an examinee could and could not apply. The probability distributions $P(\theta)$ and $P(\theta|x)$ represent degree of belief about each of the possibilities, before and after observing x.

The trick is to instantiate a probability model that both captures the salient real-world patterns and suits the purposes of the problem at hand.

Student Variables. With regard to student variables, what distinctions are needed to support the purposes of the assessment, be they selection, evaluation, or feedback for learning? What people know and are able to do in various circumstances differs in myriad ways, but what set of distinctions is minimally sufficient for the job at hand? All other distinctions will not be modeled explicitly, and their influences appear as unmodeled variation in probability distributions, for student variables and for observables given student variables. Persons with the same values of student variables are not considered to be identical, but exchangeable simply with respect to the present modeling effort.

Additional information about the students' relationship to the context, whether acquired or brought about in the system in which the assessment is used, also influences the determination and the interpretation of student variables. The full student models in Anderson's tutoring systems (Anderson et al., 1990) consist of hundreds of production rules, but at any given point in time the measurement model for analyzing performance needs to contain just a few because inference takes place within a carefully constructed instructional sequence. Attainment of production rules from previous lessons can be presumed, because a student demonstrated proficiency on them to reach the current lesson. Attainment of production rules in future lessons can be ignored, because the current lesson avoids them.

Siegler's Balance Beam. To augment the progressive-matrices example, we consider an example from a developmental perspective. Siegler's (1981) balance beam tasks show varying numbers of weights placed at varying locations on a balance beam, and a child predicts whether the beam will tip to the left, tip to the right, or remain in balance (Table 8.5). Following Piaget (Inhelder & Piaget, 1958), Siegler hypothesized that children could be classified into one of five stages shown in Table 8.6. Tables 8.5 and 8.6 summarize the warrant in the assessment argument. It suggests a categorical student-model variable, θ_i, representing Child i's stage—i.e., a latent class model—for interpreting children's responses to a collection of balance beam tasks, and partitioning of tasks into task types denoted by q.

This student model is cast in a developmental perspective, and can support claims about what stage a given child is in at a given point in time, distributions of stage membership with respect to background variables, and differences in stage memberships as a result of experiences. It can support claims about the level of reasoning, through Siegler's developmental progression, about the kinds of reasoning a child can carry out in this domain of tasks. But it cannot address claims about varieties of solution strategies within stages or finer-grained steps in reasoning, issues addressed for example in Noelting (1980). It cannot

TABLE 8.5 Types of Balance Beam Tasks for Assessing Proportional Reasoning

Task Type	Description
Equal (E)	Stacks of weights on each side of the beam have equal number of weights and are equal distance from the fulcrum. Beam will balance.
Dominant (D)	One side has more weight; stacks are equal distance. Side with more weight will tip down.
Subordinate (S)	Sides have equal weight; one is greater distance from the fulcrum. Side with greater distance will tip down.
Conflict Equal (CE)	Sides have unequal weights and unequal distances. Beam will balance.
Conflict Dominant (CD)	Sides have unequal weights and unequal distances. Side with more weight will tip down.
Conflict Subordinate (CS)	Sides have unequal weights and unequal distances. Side with greater distance will tip down.

Source: Based on Siegler (1981).

TABLE 8.6 Stages of Proportional Reasoning

Stage	Description
Stage 0:	**Nonscientific responses.** Responses do not depend systematically on either weights or distances from the fulcrum.
Stage I:	**If the weights on both sides are equal, the beam will balance. If they are not equal, the side with the heavier weight will go down.** Weight is the "dominant dimension" in this domain of tasks. Children are generally aware that weight is important earlier than they realize that distance, the "subordinate dimension," also matters.
Stage II:	**If the weights and distances on both sides are equal, then the beam will balance. If the weights are equal but the distances are not, the side with the longer distance will go down. Otherwise, the side with the heavier weight will go down.** A child at this stage uses the subordinate dimension only when information from the dominant dimension is equivocal.
Stage III:	**Same as Rule II, except that if the values of both weight and distance are unequal on both sides, the child will "muddle through"** (Siegler, 1981, p.6). A child at this stage knows both dimensions matter, but doesn't quite just how they combine.
Stage IV:	**Combine weights and distances by comparing torques** (products of weights and distances).

Source: Based on Siegler (1981).

address issues of internal representations that support children's reasoning, or patterns of change from one stage to the next, as addressed for example by McClelland's (1989) connectionist network for balance beam problems. Modeling correctness of responses with a latent class model does not deny the existence of more detailed processes one could choose to model. There can exist comprehensible reasons for, and procedures by which, children solve certain tasks at certain type correctly and others incorrectly, but they lie below the level of explanation in this model. The response probabilities in the model incorporate uncertainty at this level of analysis.

Not having seen the responses of a particular eight-year-old's responses in a neighborhood school, a probability distribution that expresses our belief about her stage membership might be (.20, 25, .25, .15, .15) for Stages 0 through IV. This is an expression of our belief channeled into the structure of the model, reflecting on what we know and what we don't know about the particular child and the context. A child's experiences with previous instruction, playing with the balance beam, and conversations with others about similar situations influence his propensity to give correct responses. Variation in these factors and many others accounts the spread of stage membership among children of the same age in the same school. Knowing some of these factors for a given child would lead to a different, probably more concentrated, prior distribution over the stages. Because reasoning develops with age, (.05, 10, .15, .30, .40) might be a more plausible prior for a fifteen-year old. Different views of competence in the balance beam context could lead to different models entirely. In probability-based reasoning, mis-

matches between modeled patterns and observed data can spark a change of view. van Maanen, Been, and Sijtsma's (1989) analyses of model fit led them to propose additional rules, including a buggy rule for conflict items: Move the stack that has more weights but is closer to the fulcrum outward, removing one weight for each step out. When the stacks are at the same distance from the fulcrum, say the side with more weight now would have gone down.

The meaning of θ is not anchored until it is related to observable behaviors. If such stages did exist, how would people in different stages tend to act differently in what kinds of situations? Consider the implication for perceiving situations. Among all the ways that balance beam tasks might differ, Siegler's theory suggests partitioning them such that children in different stages tend to respond differently to at least some types of tasks. Stage classes acquire meaning by propensities to act differently on different task types, and task types acquire meaning because they evoke different actions from students in different classes, both through the developmental theory of proficiency.

Observable Variables. Even though every action within an assessment setting is unique, what aspects, and what set of distinctions within those aspects, support the claims that can be framed in the student-model space? Actions with the same evaluations are not considered identical, but exchangeable in light of the modeling effort. In Siegler's study, the observable variable for each child-task interaction was whether the prediction (tip left, tip right, or stay balanced) was correct: X_{ij} = 1 if so, 0 if not. In contrast, van der Maas and Jansen (2003) recorded response time because their study of strategy use revolved around how long the steps in different solution processes took: different warrant, different space of claims, different data required.

Arguments cast in information-processing and sociocultural terms can also require additional information to interpret students' actions and characterize the features of assessment situations. Recall that in Hydrive, it is not the particular actions that constitute data, but the strategy an action accords with in light of actions taken previously. Section B of an AP Studio Art is the student's concentration, "a body of related works based on an individual's interest in a particular idea expressed visually. It focuses on a process of investigation, growth, and discovery.... Students are free to work with any idea in any medium. However, the concentration should grow out of a plan of action or investigation" (College Entrance Examination Board, 1994, pp. 5–6). How can there be comparison when the particulars of every project differ, and the required knowledge to carry out the project is not only idiosyncratic but self-selected? This is dealt with in the step of evaluating students' work: mapping qualities of unique work, in light of information specific to the student, into common variables for the conception and execution.

4.1.2. Specifying Relationships among Variables

The idea that a student's unique actions can be largely understood in more fundamental terms that hold meaning across some circumscribed set of situations is realized in the concept of conditional independence (section 2.4). Conditional independence relationships are central to the knowledge system of probability, and they central to the measurement-model building blocks described later in this section.

In educational measurement models, probability distributions of observable variables X are modeled conditional on values of unobservable variables θ for students and perhaps also known values of additional student variables Z, and on values of variables Q for the salient aspects of tasks. That is, the probability density function for an observable variable X is written as $p(x|\theta, Q, Z)$, where all these variables may be vector-valued. Expressed in narrative terms, knowing the salient aspects of the situation and the person (including things we may know about the person's background with respect to the situation) conditions our belief about the occurrence of the salient aspects of performance. The forms of these distributions and the parameters that are used to characterize them, such as the Rasch model and the LLTM, are building blocks from which a wide range of situations, performances, and conceptions of proficiency can be modeled. Through such models, one uses Bayes' theorem to draw inferences about students' θs in light of the features of their performances x in situations with relevant features q.

Data gathered over time can be used to model occasions and correlates of change, using the same ideas of conditional dependence. Let X_t represent a vector of observable variables and θ_t represent student status at Time t, where both can be vector-valued and θ_t may include elements for discrete class or stage membership as well as continuous aspects of proficiency. Cognitive theory can come into play when a model of change is introduced for current status in light of present and previous information as well—some particularized version of

$$p(\theta_t|\theta_{t-1},...,\theta_1,X_{t-1},...,X_1,Q_{t-1},...,Q_1). \quad (8)$$

That is, status at Time t depends in some way on status θ at earlier time points, previous performances X, and/or situation features Q. The joint probability of responses and states for T time points is thus

$$\prod_{t=1}^{T} p(X_t|\theta_t,Q_t)p(\theta_t|\theta_{t-1},...,\theta_1,X_{t-1}...,X_1,Q_{t-1}...,Q_1)$$

For example, a model for the balance beam could posit zero transition probabilities to stages below or more than two levels above a student's current stage on each task, but a probability of advancing if the task yields to a strategy at the next stage. That is, the features of the next task are optimal for causing an impasse, for provoking accommodation. Latent transition analysis (Collins & Flaherty, 2002) uses similar models to detect changes from one underlying state to another. In a behaviorist tradition, a power function is used to model learning as a function of the number of trials (Anderson, 1995). Anderson uses power functions to approximate students' learning of production rules in his ITSs (Corbett, Anderson, & O'Brien, 1995), illustrating the use of models developed in one perspective (behaviorist) to support applications cast in another (information processing).

4.1.3. Updating Belief

In a latent class model for the balance beam example, $p(x|\theta,Q,Z)$ takes the following form for the probability for Child i will answer Task j correctly, when Child i is at Stage k and Task j is a Task Type c:

$$\text{Prob}(X_{ij}=1|\theta_i=k, q_j=c). \quad (9)$$

There are no Z variables here, concerning other information about the child such as age or instructional background, or known prior experience with balance beam tasks. Any of these factors, or others, could influence performance, but Equation 9 posits that their effect is mediated through θ. That is, item responses are posited to be conditionally independent of background variables given stage membership. This assumption can be tested empirically by comparing the fit of this model with constant conditional probabilities across Zs against a model that allows them to vary across groups. Mixture models (section 4.2.5) allow conditional probabilities to differ across variables we don't know beforehand, such as strategy use.

What are the conditional probabilities in Equation 9? If Siegler's theory were exact, children's stages would tightly control the rates at which they would respond correctly to the various types of tasks, as shown in Table 8.7. Notice in particular the "1" column for CD tasks: Children at Stage I are more likely to get it correct than children in Stage III, but only because their less-expert rule happens to work in this situation.

But any response might be observed from a child in any stage. A probabilistic model expresses expectations for each task type for each stage, allowing for variation in actual performance. Instead of positing that all children in Stage II will respond incorrectly to every "Conflict-Dominant" task, we model the proportion of correct answers in such situations:

$$P(X_{ij} = 1 \mid \theta_i = \text{Stage II}, q_j = \text{CD}).$$

These conditional probabilities play the same role as the item parameters β in the IRT model for progressive matrices: quantifying expectations of potential observations x (here children's predictions) given the unobservable variable of interest θ (here the child's stage of reasoning). Table 8.8 shows probabilities of correct response given reasoning stages estimated under a particular set of assumptions about error rates (Mislevy, 1994).

The *rows* of Table 8.8 give *probabilities* of response to a given task type from students at different stages. This is reasoning in the direction of the warrant: If we knew a student's stage and a task's class, what are probabilities for the outcome? In practice, Child i's stage θ_i is not known and we reason from actions back up through the warrant. Once a particular response to a task is observed, the appropriate *column* of Table 8.8 gives the *likelihoods* that indicate the strength of evidence for each of the possible stages.

For example, suppose a four-year-old answers a CD task correctly. The likelihood function induced over the stages is (.33, .97, .88, .33, .94). By Bayes' theorem, belief is revised from the initial belief of (.20, 25, .25, .15, .15) for an eight-year-old to (.09, .34, .31, .07, .20). Belief increases about the child being in Stages I or II—or in IV. He predicted correctly, probably because he'd say the side with more weight would tip no matter what the distances were (Stages I and II) but possibly because he understands torque (Stage IV). A CS task would sort out the possibilities, shifting belief to (.18, .03, .13, .09, .65) if this prediction too were correct and (.08, .46, .38, .06, .02) if not. And in the latter case, an S item would differentiate Stages I and II. Just as in hermeneutic analysis, the meaning we make of the first prediction contributes to our evolving understanding of the entire set of performances, and the larger understanding shapes our understanding of each.

4.1.4. Do We Really Mean "Measurement" Models?

The term "measurement model" needs comment before we progress further. It is a common practice to sum values of observable variables, 1 for right and 0 for wrong, and treat performances with the same total score as interchangeable. The underlying argument is behavioral, as scores constitute summaries of performance in a defined observational setting. Such scores have proven useful over the past century for purposes of placement, selection, evaluation, and monitoring. While it is also common to refer to these scores as "measures," the term suggests quantitative variables akin to length and force in physics. But are response patterns to a particular collection of tasks from a particular collection of people consistent with an underlying quantitative variable, in terms of which claims about students might then be phrased (Cliff, 1992; Michell, 1999, 2000)?

In physical measurement, extensive quantities such as length are based on an observable comparison with a standard, and derived quantities such as force are inferred from relationships among extensive quantities (Campbell, 1920). Luce and Tukey's (1964) theory of conjoint measurement extends fundamental measurement to simultaneous measures of two quantities inferable from regularities in the interactions between collections of entities such as responses of persons to tasks. The family of Rasch models (Rasch, 1977) provides a compatible basis for quantitative measurement in a probabilistic framework (Fischer, 1995; Perline, Wright, & Wainer, 1979). The hypothesis of quantitative variables for person ability and item difficulty can be tested against observations and rejected (Cressie & Holland, 1983). High-scoring persons responding incorrectly to items that are usually easy and items proving differentially hard for students from different background groups are examples of patterns that tend to disconfirm the model, call into question the hypothesis of a quantitative ability variable, and cast doubt on interpretations of observations through the quantitative measurement narrative.

Debates about measurement properties of test scores lie at a higher level of analysis than the research into the nature, acquisition, and use of knowledge reviewed in section 3. Quantitative measurement, to whatever extent

TABLE 8.7 Theoretical Conditional Probabilities of Correct Response

	\multicolumn{12}{c}{Task Type}											
	E		D		S		CD		CS		CE	
Stage	1	0	1	0	1	0	1	0	1	0	1	0
0	.33	.67	.33	.67	.33	.67	.33	.67	.33	.67	.33	.67
I	1.00	.00	1.00	.00	.00	1.00	1.00	.00	.00	1.00	.00	1.00
II	1.00	.00	1.00	.00	1.00	.00	1.00	.00	.00	1.00	.00	1.00
III	1.00	.00	1.00	.00	1.00	.00	.33	.67	.33	.67	.33	.67
IV	1.00	.00	1.00	.00	1.00	.00	1.00	.00	1.00	.00	1.00	.00

TABLE 8.8 Estimated Conditional Probabilities of Correct Response

	\multicolumn{12}{c}{Task Type}
	E		D		S		CD		CS		CE	
Stage	1	0	1	0	1	0	1	0	1	0	1	0
0	.33*	.67	.33*	.67	.33*	.67	.33*	.67	.33*	.67	.33*	.67
I	.97	.03	.97	.03	.03	.97	.97	.03	.03	.97	.03	.97
II	.88	.12	.88	.12	.88	.12	.88	.12	.12	.88	.12	.88
III	.98	.02	.98	.02	.98	.02	.33*	.67	.33*	.67	.33*	.67
IV	.94	.06	.94	.06	.94	.06	.94	.06	.94	.06	.94	.06

Note: *Denotes fixed value for estimation. True-positive and false-positive probabilities for a given stage are constrained to be equal across task types, to identify the model. Other sets of constraints could be entertained.

and whatever contexts it may be reflected in patterns of test scores, would be an emergent property of cognitive activities and resulting actions in particular contexts. A useful approximation may be found when assessing a certain collection of students with a certain collection of tasks under certain circumstances. But the model should be verified, not presumed, and the interpretation should be through model parameters, not observed scores (Wright & Linacre, 1989).

How does this measurement debate concern cognitively motivated assessment? A first way to bring a cognitive perspective into assessment maintains the traditional behavioral interpretation of student-model variables. One uses insights from cognitive research to design tasks and define evaluation rules, and uses the resulting scores to discuss students' capabilities at the coarse level of overall proficiency. For some researchers, the motivating question will be cast in trait psychology terms, even if emerging from an information-processing or situative foundation: whether a quantitative variable is effected, and if so, across what ranges of situations and populations.

More often, however, the motivation is practical—to use the measurement frame as an approximation simply to help manage test construction and interpretation. Unidimensional IRT offers advantages for model evaluation and model use. Do residuals reveal tasks that are differentially hard for different groups of students in ways related to their instructional or demographic backgrounds (Mead, 1976) or different strategy choices or contextual familiarities (Linn & Harnisch, 1981)? The ARE uses overall scores without asserting they are quantitative. ARE claims concern propensity toward targeted behavior in a domain of tasks grounded on information-processing and sociocultural research. They are connected through task design to targeted knowledge structures and solution processes. The assessment argument can properly be described as cognitively grounded, even though it yields only overall proficiency scores. Within the circumscribed domains of ARE problems and architects with suitable backgrounds, the measurement narrative is a tolerable approximation for interpreting scores for certification decisions.

Further, one can interpret IRT proficiency variables in terms of claims about the kinds of things a student is likely to be able to do in various kinds of task settings. In LLTM analyses of the Document Literacy scale from the Young Adult Literacy Survey (YALS; Kirsch & Jungeblut, 1986, Sheehan & Mislevy, 1990), for example, one can generate a whole family of claims based on tasks' locations on a unidimensional IRT scale, such as "Eighty-percent of the time, the student can do **feature matching** in documents that are **structured according those features**, when **three** features need to be matched and there are **no close distractors** in the text." These claims are stated behaviorally and couched stochastically, but because they acquire their interpretation through a cognitive perspective they can be guide subsequent actions framed in the same perspective. More detailed claims about individuals' knowledge structures, solution processes, and contexts lie below the level the overall-proficiency IRT model can address.

Constraining inference to total scores breaks down if the claims of interest are more complex than overall proficiency in a domain, or if total scores do not capture the evidentiary value of observations for the claims. We may want to make claims about multiple aspects of competence from performances in tasks that vary in their demands for them, as in performance tasks in language testing (Long & Norris, 2000). Students may follow different strategies, so that the same tasks and the same item scores betoken different aspects of competence for different people (Kyllonen, Lohman, & Snow, 1984). Multiple steps may be required in a task, or performance may be continuous. Observations may be confounded as each situation a student encounters depends on performance in previous situations, as in interactive simulation tasks (Clyman et al., 1999).

The models discussed below bring these considerations into the narrative space supported by probability-based reasoning. The analysis is at a coarser level than cognitive task analysis or ethnographic analysis, but the models extend the inferential tools of traditional test theory in directions motivated by cognitive psychology. Sometimes resulting model is a fundamental measurement model, sometimes it isn't. But probability-based reasoning enables us to build and coherently reason through more complex inferences from more complex bodies of evidence, regardless of whether the attributes of interest, the entities in the narrative space, are quantitative variables (Borsboom & Mellenbergh, 2004).

4.2. Measurement Themes and Measurement Models

This section concerns measurement models that can be used address assessment inferences shaped by a cognitive perspective. It begins by noting a general movement to modular construction of statistical models, and its emergence in educational and psychological measurement (e.g., Almond & Mislevy, 1999; de Boeck & Wilson, 2004; Rupp, 2002; von Davier, 2005). More specific model features and narrative elements are then discussed.

4.2.1. Modular Model Construction

The development of expert systems in the 1970s and 1980s rekindled interest in Wigmore's work, particularly as to the question of how the approach might be extended to handle issues of strength and import of evidence in quantitative terms (Schum, 1994). The key insight was to associate with elementary argument fragments with corresponding fragments of probability models, building blocks for assembling probability models to reason about large and complex real-world situations (Pearl, 1988). The development of Markov chain Monte Carlo (MCMC) estimation in statistical computing is similarly tuned to inference in models built up from relatively simple distributions and functions (Gelman, et al. 2003).

In any domain in which these ideas are applied, the probability/narrative building blocks build on the generative principles of the domain. In reliability analysis, basic objects such as pumps and values and their component-level failure rates are combined into larger systems, with emerging implications for overall performance (Almond, 1991). In medical diagnosis, probability fragments are used to model syndromes conditional on disease states and test results conditional on syndromes (Andreassen, Woldbye, Falck, & Andersen, 1987).

In educational measurement, the first building blocks were the conditional independence relationships in classical test theory (observed scores given students' true scores) and factor analysis (test scores given factor values and factor loadings). From these building blocks, one can model students' observed scores on arbitrary sets of appropriate tests. Item response theory and latent class models apply the idea to individual items, modeling response probabilities conditional on student parameters θ and item parameters β. Arbitrary, targeted, and adaptive construction of tests from items in the domain becomes feasible (Wainer et al., 2000). Probability fragments representing these relationships are fundamental to the extensions discussed in the following sections. As important as the technical contributions is the realization that they can be connected to real-world situations through cognitive as well as trait and behavioral themes.

4.2.2. Considerations Regarding Observable Variables

Equation 7 stated that measurement models give conditional probability distributions for observable variables x given student variables θ, and implicitly or explicitly, situation features q (which we recall may be defined to depend on additional knowledge about the student). This section addresses matters both technical and substantive concerning the observable variables and the conditional distributions.

Normal distributions are useful functions to link observed scores to true scores in classical test theory, and Bernoulli distributions suit dichotomous items in IRT and latent class models. Research has extended the kinds of observable variables that can be modeled, supporting wider ranges of performance situations and work products as may be required in cognitively based assessment. For example, building blocks starting from the dichotomous Rasch model provide link functions for counts, multiple categories both ordered and unordered, and response times (Masters & Wright, 1984). Link models for event occurrences (Rogosa & Ghandour, 1991; Singer & Willet, 2003) and continuous performance (Ramsay & Silverman, 1997) are available. All of the structures discussed below for modeling aspects of proficiency can be employed with a wide range of observable variable types by using appropriate link functions.

Types of observable variables do not determine how "cognitively based" an assessment is. It is whether the observable variables characterize aspects of performance that are used to support claims framed in cognitive terms. All the Force Concept Inventory tasks (Hestenes et al., 1992) use a multiple choice format to probe physics misconceptions, and Tatsuoka's (1983, 1990) inferences about the production rules for mixed number subtraction were based on patterns of right/wrong responses from open-ended items. Biggs and Collis's (1982) cross-domain scoring scheme SOLO offers ordered categories for evaluating explanations that reflect a Piaget-like developmental progression: From prestructural responses, to unistructural, multistructural, relational, and finally extended-abstract responses. Ordered rating categories also characterize Bachman and Palmer's (1996) rubrics for integrative essays in language testing: Syntax, Vocabulary, Rhetorical Organization, Cohesion, Register, and Topical Knowledge.

More complex performances are required to obtain direct evidence of interactive and productive capabilities. Evaluations of such performances can themselves be complex, as multiple phases of automated processes glean salient patterns of actions or as human judgments for qualities of work to map to values of observable variables. In the NBME's CCS patient simulations and Cisco's NetPASS tasks, the observable variables are counts, presence, absence, degrees, and sequencing of actions extracted from a first past over the full trace of actions (Clauser, et al., 1997) To rate AP Studio Art Concentration sections, readers assign ratings for ideation and execution in a highly situated context, consistent with a sociocultural model of development as an artist. In Hydrive, the evaluation model traces information revealed by previous actions, then classifies an action as space-splitting, serial elimination, remove-and-replace, redundant, or irrelevant.

4.2.3. Considerations Regarding Task Features

Among the goals of cognitive task analysis is identifying aspects of tasks that make them difficult (Newell & Simon,

1972), that is, which generate demands for knowledge or processing. The LLTM (Fischer, 1973) formally incorporated task features q into IRT by modeling task difficulty in their terms (a random effects version of the LLTM allows items with the same features to vary but share tendencies in difficulty; Rijmen & De Boeck, 2002). Task features enter the probability framework through substantive theory about how students with given values of student variables are likely to act in situations with given task features. Values of task variables are known to the analyst, through determinations of key features either as the task was constructed, as it evolves, or, if required in the argument, when salient aspects of a student's relationship to the task situation is established.

It was noted that language use involves patterns at many levels jointly, a challenge to assessing proficiency in realistic situations. Skehan (1998) said that "if a [task-based assessment] approach is favored, it can only be feasible if we know more about the way tasks themselves influence (and constrain) performance" (pp. 168–169). Psycholinguistc and sociolinguistic research reveals features of language-use situations that tend to make them easier or harder, or shift the focus from one aspect of competence to another (Robinson, 2001a). Linguistic variables, such as syntactic complexity and use of anaphora, were addressed earliest (e.g., Selinker, Tarone, & Hanzeli, 1981). Sociolinguistic features concern settings, participants, and purposes (e.g., Bachman & Palmer, 1996; Skehan, 1998). Features that affect difficulty through cognitive demand include stimulus structure variables and task directives (Mosenthal, 1985; Robinson, 2001b). We see in the next section how knowing which aspects of language use are targets of inference helps the assessment determine which task features to set, which to avoid, and which to vary systematically, in order to focus the evidentiary value of a task on the claims of interest.

4.2.4. Considerations Regarding Student Variables

Student variables provide a space in which to make distinctions. Their meaning arises in interplay among a substantive framework, the construction of tasks, and the aspects of performance to be evaluated. A conception of proficiency and the claims entailed by the assessment's purpose guide their construction for a given application (and the discipline of model checking can force a revision of the model, the tasks, or conception itself). Continuous student variables let us talk about qualities in which people may differ as to degree, such as the IRT θ for proficiency with progressive matrices. Categorical variables as in the balance beam example let us talk about differences in type or character.

The overall proficiency models discussed in section 4.1.4 constitute one approach to cognitively based assessment. But complex performances such as language use and troubleshooting involve many aspects of knowledge and strategy, combining in different ways in different tasks, or at different steps in the same task. The data from any single observation admits to several explanations, and in such situations simply adding scores does not support the meanings we need to make. Probability-based reasoning with finer-grained modeling of knowledge and capabilities can help us sort out the confounding evidence and address multifaceted claims about students' capabilities.

Cognitive diagnosis models provide theoretically derived multidimensional characterizations of persons' knowledge and skills (Nichols, Chipman, & Brennan, 1995). The tasks used to provide observations can tap one or more of several modeled aspects of proficiency, and different tasks may impose different profiles of demand on them. As with task design under the LLTM, substantive theory guides the construction of both the tasks and the probability model for the ensuing performances. The modeling effort builds on a conception of how persons with different configurations of proficiency are likely to act in different ways, in settings with different cognitively relevant features.

In the Hydrive project, Steinberg and Gitomer's (1996) expert-novice studies showed that knowledge of troubleshooting strategies, the subsystem in question, and diagnostic tests were all needed for a mechanic to space split consistently. This finding suggests conjunctive relationship among three θ variables in a task situation, their values defined at the grain size of Hydrive's instructional models. Seeing a trainee carry out space-splitting in, say, the flaps subsystem shifts belief toward higher values for all three of θs that are involved. Failing to space-split produces competing explanations that can be sorted out only with observations that depend on different combinations of knowledge variables: Subsequent space-splitting in the canopy subsystem shifts belief toward lower flaps system knowledge, but failure there too increases belief about low knowledge across systems, low strategic proficiency, or both—again to be disambiguated through further testing in different situations.

The probabilistic conjunctions in Hydrive are one of a number of recurring combinations of knowledge or proficiencies required for performance, along with compensatory, disjunctive, enabler, and selection functions, can be used to build measurement models (von Davier, 2005). Enabler functions say a baseline level of some θs must be met, but after that performance depends on other θs. Familiarity with the conventions of the ARE interface is required before a student can bring design capabilities to bear on a block diagram task. As in the LLTM cognitive diagnosis example, the analyst uses information about the situation, as encoded in task variables, to determine which proficiencies, that is, which subsets of θs, are relevant to performance in a given situation.

Multivariate θs, conjunctions, and link functions to item responses characterize much work in cognitive diagnosis (Junker & Sijtsma, 2001). A widely studied situation is a one-to-one correspondence between salient features q in tasks and elements of θ; for example, each element of θ_k represents a production rule and a corresponding q_{jk} represents a demand for Rule k in Task j (Falmagne, 1989; Haertel & Wiley, 1993; Maris, 1999; Tatsuoka, 1983, 1990). Each Student i is characterized by a vector θ_i of 0/1 variables that indicate which of K designated aspects of knowledge or processing she possesses and each Task j is characterized by a vector q_j of 0/1 task variables that indicate which it requires. This model was illustrated in section 2.4.5, as Equation 6.

Under the modular approach to building measurement models, these ideas are readily adapted to multiple-category and continuous θs and qs, additional θs to handle proficiencies that are not explicitly modeled (Hartz, 2002), alternative functions for combining required θs (Junker & Sijtsma, 2001), and multiple-category and continuous observables (Haertel & Wiley, 1993). Applications include mixed-number subtraction (Tatsuoka, 1983), logic gates (Yamamoto & Gitomer, 1993), and simplifying fractions (Maris, 1999).

Adams, Wilson, and Wang's (1997; also see Kelderman & Rijkes, 1994, and Rijmen, 2002) multivariate random coefficients multinomial logit model (MRCMLM) is another generalization of the LLTM. The tasks can be complex in that each can depend on one or more θs, and different tasks can impose different profiles of demands on them. The probability of a correct response for a dichotomous item is modeled as

$$\Pr(X_j = 1 \mid \theta, \eta, a_j, q_j) = \psi(a_j' \theta + q_j' \eta) \quad (10)$$

Proficiencies combine linearly so that $a_j' = a_{j1}\theta_1 + \ldots + a_{jD}\theta_D$, where θ is a D-dimensional vector representing aspects of proficiency. The a_{jd}s indicate the extent to which proficiency θ_d is required to succeed on item j. As in the LLTM, substantive theory guides the construction of both the tasks and the probability model for ensuing performances. Again the motivating substance narrative says how persons with different configurations of proficiency are likely to act in different ways, in settings with different relevant features. Kelderman (1997) describes an application of a similar model to laboratory investigation tasks, where medium-grain-sized θs represented domain knowledge, calculation through models, and correlating data with substantive information. De Boeck and his colleagues have carried out an active program of research using this approach to investigate processes underlying psychological test performances (e.g., Hoskens & De Boeck, 1995; Janssen & De Boeck, 1997).

Multivariate structured models can be used to sort out what Robinson (2001b) calls the "complexity factors" features in language assessment that increase the load for everybody, such as syntactic complexity and time pressure, and "difficulty factors" that make a task harder or easier for particular persons, such as familiarity with content or experience in a social situation. Complexity factors tend to have information-processing grounding. The kinds of distinctions the assessor needs to make among students in both respects must be reflected in θs. A task's q vector encodes both features that reflect complexity (e.g., memory load) and those that make the task easier or harder as they interact with students' backgrounds (e.g., genre). Its a vector indicates which θs are invoked. The difficulty of a task or step for a given student is the impact of this vector of demands as it matches up with her θ profile through Equation 10. The basic MRCMLM model addresses only a single observable, such as successful use of language to accomplish a goal. It does not address how multiple aspects of communicative performance might be evaluated in a complex task, as with Bachman and Palmer's (op cit.) rubrics. Section 4.2.8 describes probability fragments for modeling the conditional dependence among clustered Xs, on top of modeling each with its own classical test theory, IRT, MRCMLM, or other structure as appropriate.

4.2.5. Mixture Models

A standard IRT model such as the Rasch model posits a single proficiency variable and parameters for task difficulties that are presumed common across students. Factors that make tasks easier for one student but harder for the next constitute measurement error for assessing overall proficiency (Robinson's "difficulty factors"). The previous section described multivariate extensions of IRT to deal with this phenomenon. This section describes an alternative approach that is suited for theories that predict how difficulties will vary for students using different strategies or responding from different developmental stages.

Different students can bring different problem-solving strategies to an assessment setting (Kyllonen, Lohman, & Snow, 1984). Further, comparisons of and theories concerning experts' and novices' problem solving suggest that the sophistication with which one chooses and monitors strategy use develops as expertise grows (Glaser, Lesgold, & Lajoie, 1987). Strategy use is a potential target of inference in assessment. An extension of a taxonomy proposed by Junker (1999) distinguishes five cases for modeling strategy use:

Case 0: No modeling of strategies
Case 1: Model strategy same for all persons
Case 2: Model strategy changes between persons
Case 3: Model strategy changes between tasks, within persons
Case 4: Model strategy changes within task, within persons

Case 0 corresponds to standard IRT models and Case 1 corresponds to LLTM analyses. Case 4 is more often seen in the intelligent tutoring and user modeling literature. Case 2 has been studied most attention in recent psychometric work, and Case 3 is beginning to receive some attention.

Multiple-strategy IRT models for Case 2 build on Rost's (1990) mixtures of Rasch models. Distinct Q-matrices to relate tasks to the different strategies that are used to solve the test items (Mislevy & Verhelst, 1990; Tatsuoka, 1983; von Davier & Carstenson, 2005). Consider M strategies, where a person applies the same strategy to all items. The item difficulty under strategy m is presumed to depend on features of the task that are relevant under this strategy through an LLTM structure, so the difficulty of item j under strategy m is $b_{jm} = \sum_k q_{jmk} \eta_{mk}$. Denoting the proficiency of person i under strategy m as θ_{im} and φ_{im} as 1 if she uses strategy m and 0 if not, the response probability for a dichotomous task takes the form

$$\Pr(X_{ij} = 1 \mid \theta_i, \varphi_i, q_j, \eta) = \prod_m \varphi_{im} \left[\Psi\left(\theta_{im} - \sum_k q_{jmk} \eta_{mk} \right) \right]$$

Yamamoto and Everson (1997) used this model to study the effect of time limitations on response strategies, and Gitomer and Yamomoto (1991) used a further mixture of IRT and latent class models to analyze patterns on logic-gate problems in terms of understanding of its symbol system. Wilson (1989) addressed strategy use associated with developmental stages, extending the latent class approach by positing a continuous proficiency variable within stages.

His examples included whole number subtraction from the perspective of Gagné's (1962) learning hierarchies and geometric figures based on van Hiele's (1986) theory of levels of understanding.

For Case 3, Huang (2003) used a multivariate Rasch model studied by Andersen (1973). His example concerns three approaches to force and motion problems in the Force-Concept Inventory (Hestenes et al., 1992): Newtonian, impetus theory, and nonscientific response. The response of Examinee i to Item j is coded as 1, 2, or 3, for the approach used. An examinee is characterized by three parameters θ_{ik} indicating propensities to use each approach, and an item is characterized by three parameters β_{jk} indicating propensities to evoke each approach. Strategy choice is modeled as

$$\Pr(X_{ij} = k \mid \theta_i, \beta_j) = \frac{\exp(\theta_{ik} - \beta_{jk})}{\sum_{m=1}^{3} \exp(\theta_{im} - \beta_{jm})}.$$

As a stereotypical illustration of the Third Law, the first task in Figure 8.11, has a low β for the Newtonian solution that indicates the attractiveness, while the second task provokes misconceptions related to mass and velocity and has a higher β for the Newton solution.

Finer-grained analyses of solution paths required in Case 4 overlap with the following section, in which individual steps or processes are addressed. Again, tutoring systems are a more typical setting for this work. Martin and VanLehn (1995) and Conati and VanLehn (1996) illustrate probability-based modeling of this type in the context of physics tutors.

4.2.6. Multiple Steps or Processes

The models discussed in the previous sections do not address the sequences of processes that persons may carry out during the course of solution. Behavior at this level is central to cognitive task analysis, and inferences at this level are required in many intelligent tutoring systems to provide feedback or select instruction. Model tracing, as it is called in the ITS literature (e.g., Corbett et al., 1995) lies below the level that can be addressed in the narrative space supported by the LLTM. Steps in the direction of model tracing are seen for example in Embretson's (1985) models for multistep problems: Each subtask is modeled in terms of Rasch model or LLTM-like structures, the probability of a success in each subtask depends on a component of θ associated with that subtask, and the final product is a stochastic outcome of subtask outcomes. Observable variables may or may not be available for intermediate processes. In a simple example, the probability that an examinee will solve an analogy item is the product of probabilities of succeeding on Rule Construction and Response Evaluation subtasks, each modeled by a dichotomous Rasch model:

$$\Pr(X_{jT} = 1 \mid \theta_1, \theta_2, \beta_{j1}, \beta_{j2}) = \prod_{m=1}^{2} \Psi(\theta_m - \beta_{jm}), \quad (11)$$

where x_{jT} is the overall response, θ_1 and β_{j1} are student proficiency and Item j's difficulty with respect to Rule Construction, and θ_2 and β_{j2} are student proficiency and difficulty with respect to Response Evaluation. Both subtask difficulty parameters β_{j1} and β_{j2} could be further modeled in terms of item features as in the LLTM (Equation 5), and multiple θs could be involved in different processes by replacing the Rasch model fragments in Equation 10 with MRCMLM fragments (Equation 10).

4.2.7. Conditional Dependence

The preceding models addressed one observable at a time. Likelihoods computed across tasks combine multiplicatively if conditional independence can be assumed, as with discrete, self-contained tasks. Conditional independence is less plausible in extended and contextualized performances that evidence productive and interactive aspects of proficiency. Extended performances and complex work products can exhibit conditional dependence due to shared context (e.g., materials, representations, content, participants), sequential dependence (later actions depend on early actions), or evaluation of multiple aspects of the same complex performance. Conditional dependence reduces the amount of information observables provide about student variables, and ignoring it produces overly optimistic measures of precision—"double counting evidence," in Schum's terms (1994, p. 129).

The iterative character of problem solving introduces serial dependency into observations. The evaluation of actions at each time point must take into account not only the immediate action, but the situation as it has evolved thus far and the relationship of this action to previous actions. An explanation task in the BioKIDS biodiversity unit (Songer & Gotwals, 2004) consisted of two phases. The first asked students to develop a claim about what would happen to the algae in a pond ecosystem depicted in a diagram if the small fish died; the second asked them to provide evidence to support their claim. Succeeding on the first phase demonstrates some knowledge about the ecosystem relationships, and only then does the second phase provide information whether a student can produce an explanation conditional on this knowledge.

Formally, modeling sequential dependence means including values of relevant previous observed variable on the right side of the conditioning bar. Techniques for doing so include directly modeling the conditional distributions, creating conditionally independent "virtual items" that are in fact the same physical item after different earlier performances (Verhelst & Glas, 1995), and "bundling" responses across dependent items in order to model at the level of patterns rather than individual responses (Wilson & Adams, 1995). These latter two approaches use and reinterpret familiar Rasch-model fragments to extend probabilistic modeling to more complex observational settings.

A random effects approach to handling conditional dependence suits observable variables that share contexts or are multiple aspects of the same performance. An additional student variable appears on the right side of the conditioning bar for each cluster k of related observables, combined with θs in a compensatory relationship (Bradlow, Wainer, & Wang, 1999; Gibbons & Hedeker, 1992):

$$P(x_{ij(k)} = 1 | \theta_i, \beta_j, \emptyset_{ik}) = \Psi(\theta_i - \beta_j + \emptyset_{ik}), \quad (12)$$

where $\emptyset_{ik}$ is a student variable associated with only that cluster, introduced to account for dependence among related observations. In statistical terms, $\emptyset_{ik}$ is a nuisance variable, the presence of which increases uncertainty about θ. In Robinson's language testing terms, it is a difficulty factor. In sociocultural terms, it acknowledges but brackets a contextual effect that could be studied in its own right, were there resources and reasons. A step in this last direction within the framework of probability-based reasoning would be to model the $\emptyset_{ik}$ with LLTM-like structures, as functions of interactions between background variables for students and task/content features.

Figure 8.17 depicts this approach with a fragment of the NetPASS model, here for two troubleshooting tasks (Levy & Mislevy, 2004; Williamson et al., 2004). Three student variables are defined at a coarse grain size, for declarative knowledge (DK), network modeling (NM), and troubleshooting procedures (TP). DK corresponds to knowledge of terminology and concepts for network devices, properties, protocols, and representations. A standard knowledge test also provides evidence about DK. NM goes beyond this foundation, to constructing and reasoning through configurations of devices as they function. TP encompasses effectiveness and efficiency in the iterative process of diagnosing and repairing a faulty network, which requires DK and NM as well. A troubleshooting task yields five observable variables that summarize aspects of an open-ended solution in the simulation environment: Diagram rates the accuracy of a system diagram required at the beginning of the task, SystemOutcome1 and SystemOutcome2 are qualities of the final solution, ProcedureCorrectness indicates whether sufficient and appropriate actions have been taken, and ProcedureEfficiency rates the solution in terms of systematicity and economy. In addition to having student variables as parents, the observables from a given task j additionally have a task-specific parent, TaskContextj, to account for the dependence introduced by evaluating multiple aspects of the same performance.

4.2.8. Models for Raters

Multiple-category IRT models are used to evaluate performances judgmental scales. The framework could be evaluating aspects of performance from a developmental perspective, as with Biggs and Collis's (1982) SOLO rating scheme, or a sociocultural perspective as in AP Studio Art.

From the perspective of evaluating students, variation among ratings of even knowledgeable and well-meaning raters is a source of uncertainty. Generalizability theory (Cronbach, Gleser, Nanda, & Rajaratnam, 1972) has been long used to incorporate the impact of rater variation on scores. Adding terms for raters into the IRT framework (e.g., Linacre, 1989; Patz & Junker, 1999) goes further, both for the practical end of improving score accuracy and for understanding the social systems in which rating processes are embedded. Building blocks for rater effects models can again be cast as an extension of basic IRT building blocks, much like Equation 11 except with a term $\emptyset_{ijl}$ specific to Rater l's evaluation of Student i's performance on Task j. Hypotheses about the rating process further structure $\emptyset_{ijl}$s and their distributions (e.g., fixed versus random rater effects, individual accuracy effects in terms of within-rater variances, and explanatory modeling in terms of LLTM-like structures for rater, task, and student characteristics).

Although rater models rose from a tradition of trait psychology, they can be reinterpreted from a sociocultural perspective as summaries of certain patterns across many unique and situated episodes of evaluation (Schutz & Moss, 2004). In AP Studio Art, probability-based models are used to analyze and summarize patterns in over more than 100,000 ratings across portfolios, students, sections, and raters. Every rating emerged as an individualized evaluation of a unique body of work with problems, media, and themes selected by the students themselves, evaluated in light of contextual information provided by the students. The rater effect models convey amounts of variation typical among raters, signal anomalous scores that merit further attention, and indicate of the accuracy of scores obtained in a given rating design as compared to the ratings that might have occurred had all raters evaluated all work. Those parties responsible for fairness and validity can identify atypical ratings, works, or ratings, and can become aware of new styles or media that need to be accommodated into the evaluation system (Myford & Mislevy, 1995).

5. CONCLUSION

Cognitive psychology concerns the processes and the patterns ways through which people think and act. An information-processing perspective highlights reasoning through patterns, where reasoning encompasses perception, interpretation, and action in context—all of which are aspects of meaning, as Bruner (1990) sees it. A sociocultural or situative perspective highlights action and interaction in material and social situations, which too are negotiated through the patterns through which we perceive and interpret those situations—again, all aspects of meaning as Bruner sees it.

It is through experience that we construct patterns, with certain ones among them, such as language capabilities and perceptual mechanisms, privileged by the way our brains work. Cognition is always and inevitably an interplay between the particulars of situations and the generalities embraced in patterns. The use of patterns "in our head" is embodied and situated, constructed and always reconstructing. Many patterns are social, as to their construction, acquisition, and use. This include concepts, tools for thinking and acting as individuals and with others (in particular, symbol systems and knowledge representations), and ways of interacting with people and situations to accomplish human purposes. Patterns both enable and constrain possibilities. Some of these patterns, these ways of perceiving, interpreting, and acting, we express explicitly and want students to learn to use, as the students participate in activities in which they are useful.

Assessment is structuring situations that evoke evidence about students' thinking and acting in terms of these patterns. It is an exercise of meaning making too: narratives

FIGURE 8.17 Fragment of a Probability Model for Assessing Troubleshooting in NetPASS

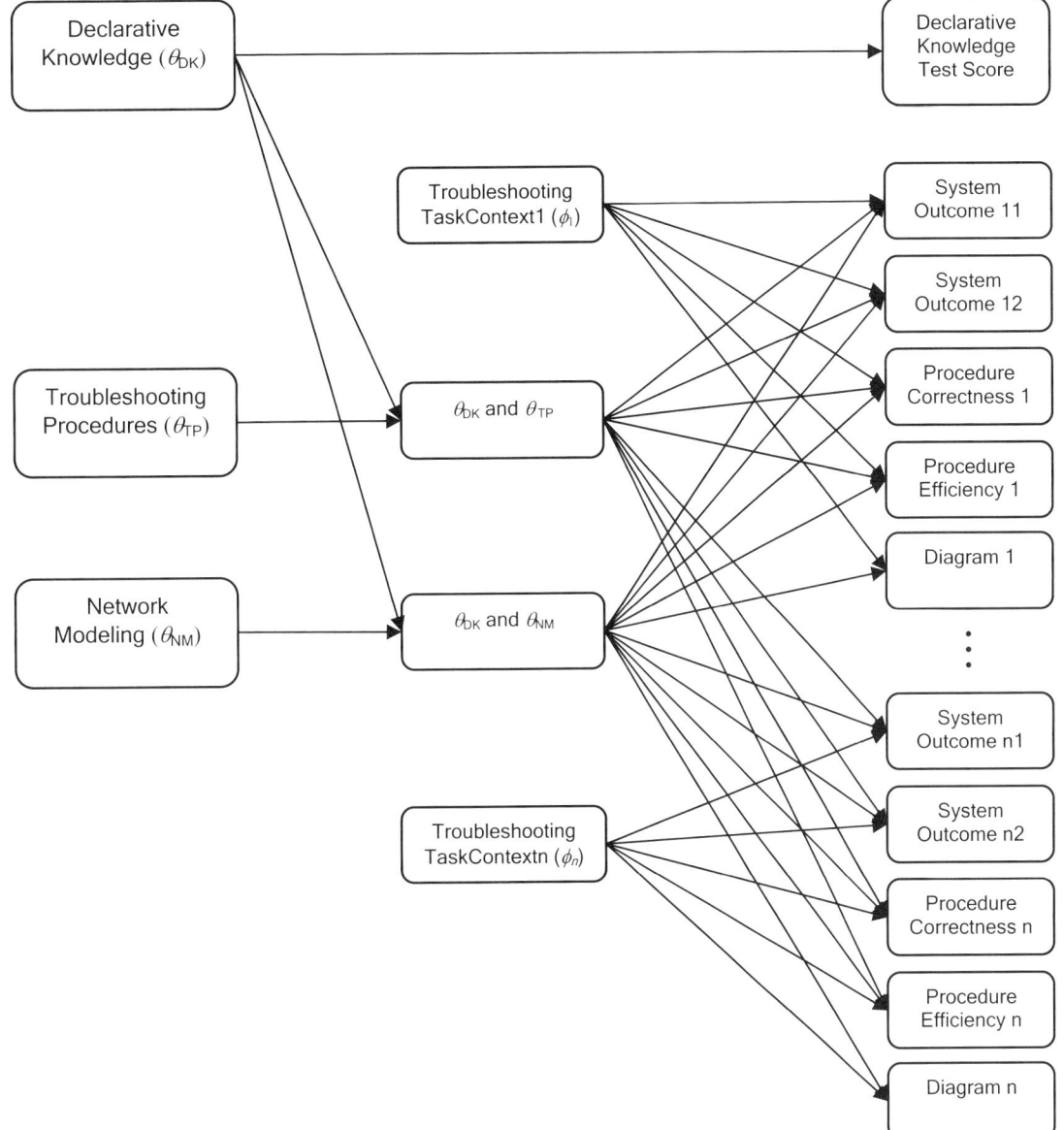

about what students know and can do, in what kinds of situations, narratives cast in some conception of the nature of knowledge, its use, and its acquisition. The perspective suggests the kinds of stories that should be told—the kinds of claims one might make about students; the kinds of things one needs to see them say, do, or make to ground the claims; and the kinds of situations we might find evidence. These patterns, from whatever psychological perspective, both enable and constrain our thinking as designers and users of assessments.

Assessment thus focuses attention and focuses action. It tells us where to look and what to look for as evidence about learning, and draws attention to those situations and behaviors. Designers and users of assessments use their own symbol systems and knowledge representations to manage their activity across time, space, and people. Central among them is the probability based reasoning that underlies educational measurement models. Increasingly with developments in technology, symbol systems and representations support automated ways of producing, evaluating, and managing tasks, and students' interactions with them. Designing and using assessments is always a negotiation between what is unique and what can be understood in terms of more pervasive patterns, such as assessment arguments and measurement models.

As technical machinery of assessment becomes more complex, it becomes more remote from everyday experience of students, parents, teachers, and policymakers. Intuitive test theory fuses ideas about psychology, statistics, and evidence, and the inertia of established practice. Familiar testing practices in fact suffice for many applications of assessment, and insights from cognitive psychology can be applied within familiar frameworks at the level of task design and evaluation. But more complex student models, evaluations of multifaceted performance, and evidentiary dependencies in interactive tasks sometimes require more complex machinery. The details remain the province of experts. But the mediating layer of assessment argumentation both remains accessible to nonexperts and guides the work of technical experts.

The methods that historically grounded educational measurement commingle beliefs about the nature and acquisition of knowledge with ways of gathering and analyzing data. Assessment was cast mainly in the trait and behavioral perspectives. A signal achievement of methodologists was bringing the tools of probability-based reasoning to bear on questions of weight, quality, and coherence of evidence (C. Lewis, 1986). Ironically, the very success of statistical reasoning for assessment cast under the trait and behaviorist paradigms gave rise to a misconception that statistical reasoning applies to assessment framed only within those paradigms.

The same underlying principles of evidentiary reasoning upon which the can be applied to inferences framed in the developmental, information-processing, and sociocultural perspectives. This is an aspect of psychometrics that focuses not on the substance or the purpose of an assessment argument, but on its structure, its assumptions, its chain of reasoning from construction of tasks to interpretations of performance to inferences about students (National Research Council, 2001). The developmental, sociocultural, and information-processing perspectives within cognitive psychology differ from the trait and behavioral perspectives in their conceptions of knowledge and the circumstances in which it is manifest. This entails differences in the nature of claims about students and data required to support them. What remains constant is the need to reason from limited observations of things students say, do, or produce under particular conditions. As Messick (1994) remarked, "validity, reliability, comparability, and fairness are not just measurement issues, but social values that have meaning and force outside of measurement wherever evaluative judgments and decisions are made" (p. 2).

Educators are beginning to integrate insights from cognitive psychology and developments in technology into assessment practices. Applications that demand more technical machinery lie outside traditional and familiar practices. Laboriously at first, we design, from first principles when necessary, methods to gather data and models to make sense of it. Assessment applications that are large scale, high stakes, and dispersed over time, space, and people, benefit especially from a probabilistic framework to examine the qualities of evidence. We may in this way adapt hard-won lessons from the psychometric tradition to assessments based on cognitive foundations, rather than having to rediscover them. What is required to bring cognitively grounded assessment to the fore? Successful examples to emulate, knowledge representations and symbol systems to automatize work, and tools and social processes that embody the principles so users don't need to work them out from scratch. There is much to be done, but we are learning at last to know how to think about it.

NOTES

1. From http://www.jcravenltd.com/info.htm. Retrieved December 19, 2003.
2. See Bechtel, Abrahamsen, and Graham (1998) for a review that is both more historical and technical than the one here, and the National Research Council's (2000) *How people learn* for an overview aimed at education.
3. Actually, working memor*ies*. Among our capabilities are a kind of tape loop for rehearsing a few seconds worth of auditory or verbal information, and a comparable visual sketchpad. This is information we can use for purposes such as determining actions, making plans, comparing current and recent stimuli, and modifying structures in long-term memory.

REFERENCES

Adams, R., Wilson, M. R., & Wang, W.-C. (1997). The multidimensional random coefficients multinomial logit model. *Applied Psychological Measurement, 21,* 1–23.

Akin, O. (1986). *Psychology of architectural design.* London: Pion.

Alexander, C., Ishikawa, S., & Silverstein, M. (1977). *A pattern language: Towns, buildings, construction.* New York: Oxford University Press.

Almond, R. G. (1991). Building blocks for graphical belief models. *Journal of Applied Statistics, 18,* 63–76.

Almond, R. G., & Mislevy, R. J. (1999). Graphical models and computerized adaptive testing. *Applied Psychological Measurement, 23,* 223–237.

American Council on the Training of Foreign Languages. (1989). *ACTFL proficiency guidelines.* Yonkers, NY: Author.

Andersen, E. B. (1973). *Conditional inference and models for measuring.* Copenhagen, Denmark: Danish Institute for Mental Health.

Anderson, J. R. (1995). *Learning and memory: An integrated approach.* New York: Wiley.

Anderson, J. R., Bothell, D., Byrne, M. D., Douglass, S., Lebiere, C., & Qin, Y. (2004). An integrated theory of the mind. *Psychological Review, 111,* 1036–1060.

Anderson, J. R., Boyle, C. F., & Corbett, A. T. (1990). Cognitive modelling and intelligent tutoring. *Artificial Intelligence, 42,* 7–49.

Anderson, J. R., Greeno, J. G., Reder, L. M., & Simon, H. A. (2000). Perspectives on learning, thinking, and activity. *Educational Researcher, 29,* 11–13.

Anderson, J. R., & Reiser, B. J. (1985, April). The lisp tutor. *Byte, 10,* 159–175.

Andreassen, S., Woldbye, M., Falck, B., & Andersen, S. K. (1987). MUNIN: A causal probabilistic network for interpretation of electromyographic findings. In *Proceedings of the 10th International Joint Conference on Artificial Intelligence* (pp. 366–372). Milan: Kaufmann.

Bachman, L. F. (2003). Building and supporting a case for test use. *Language Assessment Quarterly, 2,* 1–34.

Bachman, L. F., & Palmer, A. S. (1996). *Language testing in practice.* Oxford: Oxford University Press.

Bao, L., & Redish, E.F. (2006). Models anaylsis: Assessing the dynamics of student learning. Physical Review Special Topics-Physics Education Research, 2(1). Retrieved June 9, 2006, from http://prst-per.aps.org/abstract/PRSTPER/v2/i1/e010103.

Bartlett, F. C. (1932). *Remembering.* Cambridge: Cambridge University Press.

Bechtel, W., Abrahamsen, A., & Graham, G. (1998). Part I. The life of cognitive science. In W. Bechtel & G. Graham (Eds.), *A companion to cognitive science* (pp. 2–104). Cambridge, MA: Blackwell.

Bejar, I. I., & Braun, H. I. (1999). *Architectural simulations: From research to implementation* (Final Report to the National Council of Architectural Registration Boards, ETS RM-99–02). Princeton, NJ: Educational Testing Service.

Bernstein, R. J. (1983). *Beyond objectivism and relativism: Science, hermeneutics and praxis.* Oxford, England: Blackwell.

Bhaskar, R., & Simon, H. A. (1977). Problem solving in semantically rich domains: An example from engineering thermodynamics. *Cognitive Science, 1,* 193–215.

Biggs, J. B., & Collis, K. F. (1982). *Evaluating the quality of learning: The SOLO taxonomy.* New York: Academic Press.

Borsboom, D., & Mellenbergh, G. J. (2004). Why psychometrics is not pathological: A comment on Michell. *Theory & Psychology, 14,* 105–120.

Bradlow, E. T., Wainer, H., & Wang, X. (1999). A Bayesian random effects model for testlets. *Psychometrika, 64,* 153–168.

Bransford, J. D., & Schwartz, D. (1999). Rethinking transfer: A simple proposal with multiple implications. In A. Iran-Nejad & P. D. Pearson (Eds.), *Review of research in education* (Vol. 24, pp. 61–100). Washington, DC: American Educational Research Association.

Brennan, R. L. (2001). An essay on the history and future of reliability from the perspective of replications. *Journal of Educational Measurement, 38,* 295–317.

Brown, J. S., & Burton, R. (1978). Diagnostic models for procedural bugs in basic mathematical skills. *Cognitive Science, 2,* 155–192.

Bruner, J. (1990). *Acts of meaning.* Cambridge, MA: Harvard University Press.

Bruner, J., Goodnow, J., & Austin, A. (1956). *A study of thinking.* New York: Wiley.

Buchanan, B., & Shortliffe, E. H. (1984). *Rule-based expert systems: The MYCIN experiments of the Stanford heuristic programming project.* Reading, MA: Addison-Wesley.

Campbell, N. R. (1920). *Physics, the elements.* Cambridge: Cambridge University Press.

Campione, J. C., & Brown, A. L. (1987). Linking dynamic assessment with school achievement. In C. S. Lidz (Ed.), *Dynamic assessment: An interactional approach to evaluating learning potential* (pp. 82–115). New York: Guilford.

Card, S., Moran, T., & Newell, A. (1983). *The psychology of human-computer interaction.* Hillsdale, NJ: Erlbaum.

Carey, S. (1985). *Conceptual change in childhood.* Cambridge, MA: Bradford Books, MIT Press.

Carpenter, P. A., Just, M. A., & Shell, P. (1990). What one intelligence test measures: A theoretical account of processing in the Raven Progressive Matrices test. *Psychological Review, 97,* 404–431.

Carroll, J. B. (1976). Psychometric tests as cognitive tasks: A new structure of intellect. In L. B. Resnick (Ed.), *The nature of intelligence* (pp. 27–57). Hillsdale, NJ: Erlbaum.

Carroll, J. B. (1993). *Human cognitive abilities: A survey of factor analytic studies.* New York: Cambridge University Press.

Case, R. (1987). Neo-Piagetian theory: Retrospect and prospect [Special issue: The neo-Piagetian theories of cognitive development: Toward an integration]. *International Journal of Psychology, 22,* 773–791.

Cattell, R. B. (1963). Theory of fluid and crystallized intelligence: A critical experiment. *Journal of Educational Psychology, 54,* 1–22.

Chase, W. G., & Simon, H. A. (1973). The mind's eye in chess. In W. G. Chase (Ed.), *Visual information processing* (pp. 215–281). New York: Academic Press.

Chi, M. T. H., Feltovich, P., & Glaser, R. (1981). Categorization and representation of physics problems by experts and novices. *Cognitive Science, 5,* 121–152.

Chi, M. T. H., Glaser, R., & Farr, M. (Eds.). (1988). *The nature of expertise.* Mahwah, NJ: Erlbaum.

Chomsky, N. (1956). Three models for the description of language. *IRE Transactions on Information Theory, 2,* 113–124.

Chomsky, N. (1981). Principles and parameters in syntactic theory. In N. Hornstein & D. Lightfoot (Eds.), *Explanation in linguistics* (pp. 123–146). London: Longman.

Clancey, W. J. (1993). Situated action: A neuropsychological interpretation response to Vera and Simon. *Cognitive Science, 17,* 87–116.

Clauser, B. E., Ross, L. P., Clyman, S. G., Rose, K. M., Margolis, M. J., Nungester, R. J., et al. (1997). Development of a scoring algorithm to replace expert rating for scoring a complex performance-based assessment. *Applied Measurement in Education, 10,* 345–358.

Clement, J. (1989). Learning via model construction and criticism: Protocol evidence on sources of creativity in science. In J. A. Glover, R. R. Ronning, & C. R. Reynolds (Eds.), *Handbook of creativity: Assessment, theory and research* (pp. 341–381). New York: Plenum Press.

Cliff, N. (1992). Abstract measurement theory and the revolution that never happened. *Psychological Science, 3,* 186–190.

Clyman, S. G., Melnick, D. E., & Clauser, B. E. (1999). Computer-based case simulations from medicine: Assessing skills in patient management. In A. Tekian, C. H. McGuire, & W. C. McGahie (Eds.), *Innovative simulations for assessing professional competence* (pp. 29–41). Chicago: University of Illinois, Department of Medical Education.

Cobb, P. (1994). Where is the mind? Constructivist and sociocultural perspectives on mathematical development. *Educational Researcher, 23*(7), 13–20.

College Entrance Examination Board. (1994). *Advanced placement course description: Art.* New York: Author.

Collins, A., & Ferguson, W. (1993). Epistemic forms and epistemic games: Structures and strategies to guide inquiry. *Educational Psychologist, 28,* 25–42.

Collins, L. M., & Flaherty, B. P. (2002). Latent class models for longitudinal data. In A. L. McCutcheon & J. A. Hagenaars (Eds.), *Applied latent class analysis* (pp. 287–303). Cambridge: Cambridge University Press.

Conati, C., & VanLehn, K. (1996). POLA: A student modeling framework for probabilistic on-line assessment of problem solving performance. In *Proceedings of UM-96, Fifth International Conference on User Modeling.* Kailua-Kona, HI: User Modeling.

Corbett, A. T., Anderson, J. R., & O'Brien, A. T. (1995). Student modeling in the ACT programming tutor. In P. D. Nichols, S. F. Chipman, & R. L. Brennan (Eds.), *Cognitively diagnostic assessment* (pp. 19–41). Hillsdale, NJ: Erlbaum.

Corno, L., Cronbach, L. J., Kupermintz, H., Lohman, D. F., Mandinach, E. B., Porteus, A. W., et al. (2002). *Remaking the concept of aptitude: Extending the legacy of Richard E. Snow.* Mahwah, NJ: Erlbaum.

Cressie, N., & Holland, P. W. (1983). Characterizing the manifest probabilities of latent trait models. *Psychometrika, 48,* 129–141.

Cronbach, L. J., Gleser, G. C., Nanda, H., & Rajaratnam, N. (1972). *The dependability of behavioral measurements: Theory of generalizability for scores and profiles.* New York: Wiley.

De Boeck, P., & Wilson, M. (Eds.). (2004). *Explanatory item response models: A generalized linear and nonlinear approach.* New York: Springer.

De Boeck, P., Wilson, M., & Acton, G. S. (2005). A conceptual and psychometric framework for distinguishing categories and dimensions. *Psychological Review, 112,* 129–158.

De Groot, A. (1978). *Thought and choice in chess.* The Hague, The Netherlands: Mouton. (Original work published 1946)

de Lemos, M. M. (1989). *Standard progressive matrices: Australian manual.* Melbourne, Australia: ACER.

Deane, P. (2006). Strategies for evidence identification through linguistic assessment of textual responses. In D. M. Williamson, R. J. Mislevy, & I. I. Bejar (Eds.), *Automated scoring of complex tasks in computer based testing* (pp. 313–371). Mahwah, NJ: Erlbaum.

Delandshire, G. (2002). Assessment as inquiry. *Teachers College Record, 104,* 1461–1484.

Dellarosa, D. (1986). A computer simulation of children's arithmetic word-problem-solving. *Behavior Research Methods, Instruments, and Computers, 18,* 147–154.

Derry, S. J., & the TiPS Research Group. (2001). *Development and assessment of tutorials in problem solving (TiPS): A remedial mathematics tutor* (Final Report to the Office of Naval Research, N00014-93-1-0310). Madison: University of Wisconsin-Madison, Wisconsin Center for Education Research.

diSessa, A. (1983). Phenomenology and the evolution of intuition. In D. Gentner & A. L. Stevens (Eds.), *Mental models* (pp. 15–33). Hillsdale, NJ: Erlbaum.

Edwards, W. (1998). Hailfinder: Tools for and experiences with Bayesian normative modeling. *American Psychologist, 53,* 416–428.

Embretson, S. (1983). Construct validity: Construct representation versus nomothetic span. *Psychological Bulletin, 93,* 179–197.

Embretson, S. E. (1985). A general latent trait model for response processes. *Psychometrika, 49,* 175–186.

Embretson, S. E. (1998). A cognitive design system approach to generating valid tests: Application to abstract reasoning. *Psychological Methods, 3,* 380–396.

Ericsson, K. A. (1996). The acquisition of expert performance: An introduction to some of the issues. In K. A. Ericsson (Ed.), *The road to excellence: The acquisition of expert performances, sports, and games* (pp. 1–50). Mahwah, NJ: Lawrence Erlbaum.

Ericsson, K. A. (2004). Deliberate practice and the acquisition and maintenance of expert performance in medicine and related domains. *Academic Medicine, 10,* S1–S12.

Falmagne, J.-C. (1989). A latent trait model via a stochastic learning theory for a knowledge space. *Psychometrika, 54,* 283–303.

Fischer, G. H. (1973). The linear logistic test model as an instrument in educational research. *Acta Psychologica, 37,* 359–374.

Fischer, G. H. (1995). Derivations of the Rasch model. In G. Fischer & I. W. Molenaar (Eds.), *Rasch models: Foundations, recent developments, and applications* (pp. 15–38). New York: Springer.

Fischer, K. W., & Kenny, S. L. (1986). The environmental conditions for discontinuities in the development of abstractions. In R. Mines & K. Kitchener (Eds.), *Adult cognitive development: Methods and models* (pp. 57–75). New York: Praeger.

Fischer, K. W., & Rose, L. T. (2001). Webs of skill: How students learn. *Educational Leadership, 59,* 6–12.

Fodor, J. A. (1983). *Modularity of mind: An essay on faculty psychology.* Cambridge, MA: MIT Press.

Frederiksen, J. R., & White, B. Y. (1988). Implicit testing within an intelligent tutoring system. *Machine-Mediated Learning, 2,* 351–372.

Gadamer, G. H. (1960). *Truth and method.* New York: Continuum.

Gagné, R. M. (1962). The acquisition of knowledge. *Psychological Review, 69,* 355–365.

Gamma, E., Helm, R., Johnson, R., & Vlissides, J. (1994). *Design patterns.* Reading, MA: Addison-Wesley.

Gee, J. P. (2003). *What video games have to teach us about learning and literacy.* New York: Palgrave/Macmillan.

Gelman, A., Carlin, J. B., Stern, H. S., & Rubin, D. B. (2003). *Bayesian data analysis* (2nd ed.). London: Chapman & Hall.

Gertner, A., & VanLehn, K. (2000). Andes: A coached problem solving environment for physics. In *Proceedings of Intelligent Tutoring Systems, 5th International Conference, ITS2000, Montreal, Canada, Lecture Notes in Computer Science 1839* (pp. 131–142). New York: Springer-Verlag.

Gibbons, R. D., & Hedeker, D. R. (1992). Full-information item bifactor analysis. *Psychometrika, 57,* 423–436.

Gibson, J. J. (1966). *The senses considered as perceptual systems.* Boston: Houghton Mifflin.

Gipps, C. (1999). Socio-cultural aspects of assessment. *Review of Research in Education, 24,* 355–392.

Gitomer, D. H., & Steinberg, L. S. (1999). Representational issues in assessment design. In I. E. Sigel (Ed.), *Development of mental representation* (pp. 351–370). Mahwah, NJ: Erlbaum.

Gitomer, D. H., & Yamamoto, K. (1991). Performance modeling that integrates latent trait and class theory. *Journal of Educational Measurement, 28,* 173–189.

Glaser, R., Lesgold, A., & Lajoie, S. (1987). Toward a cognitive theory for the measurement of achievement. In R. Ronning, J. Glover, J. C. Conoley, & J. Witt (Eds.), *The influence of cognitive psychology on testing and measurement: The Buros-Nebraska symposium on measurement and testing* (Vol. 3, pp. 41–85). Hillsdale, NJ: Erlbaum.

Gobert, J. D., & Buckley, B. C. (2000). Introduction to model-based teaching and learning in science education. *International Journal of Science Education, 22,* 891–894.

Goldstein, H., & Wood, R. (1989). Five decades of item response modelling. *British Journal of Mathematical and Statistical Psychology, 42,* 139–167.

Greeno, J. G. (1983). Conceptual entities. In D. Gentner & A. L. Stevens (Eds.), *Mental models* (pp. 227–252). Hillsdale, NJ: Lawrence Erlbaum.

Greeno, J. G. (1989). A perspective on thinking. *American Psychologist, 44,* 134–141.

Greeno, J. G., Collins, A. M., & Resnick, L. B. (1997). Cognition and learning. In D. Berliner & R. Calfee (Eds.), *Handbook of educational psychology* (pp. 15–47). New York: Simon & Schuster Macmillan.

Greeno, J. G., & Moore, J. L. (1993). Situativity and symbols: Response to Vera and Simon. *Cognitive Science, 17,* 49–59.

Greeno, J. G., Pearson, P. D., & Schoenfeld, A. H. (1996). *Implications for NAEP of research on learning and cognition* (Report of a study commissioned by the National Academy of Education. Panel on the NAEP Trial State Assessment). Stanford, CA: National Academy of Education.

Grice, H. (1975). Logic and conversation. In P. Cole & J. Morgan (Eds.), *Studies in syntax* (Vol. 3, pp. 83–106). New York: Seminar Press.

Haertel, E. H. (1989). Using restricted latent class models to map the skill structure of achievement test items. *Journal of Educational Measurement, 26,* 301–321.

Haertel, E. H., & Wiley, D. E. (1993). Representations of ability structures: Implications for testing. In N. Frederiksen, R. J. Mislevy, & I. I. Bejar (Eds.), *Test theory for a new generation of tests* (pp. 359–384). Hillsdale, NJ: Lawrence Erlbaum.

Hartz, S. M. (2002). *A Bayesian framework for the unified model for assessing cognitive abilities: Blending theory with practicality*. Doctoral dissertation, University of Illinois, Champaign-Urbana.

Hawkins, J., & Blakeslee, S. (2004). *On intelligence*. New York: Times Books.

Hebb, D. O. (1949). *The organization of behavior*. New York: Wiley.

Helsen, W. F., Starkes, J. L., & Hodges, N. J. (1998). Team sports and the theory of deliberate practice. *Journal of Sport and Exercise Psychology, 20,* 12–34.

Hestenes, D., Wells, M., & Swackhamer, G. (1992). Force concept inventory. *The Physics Teacher, 30,* 141–151.

Hively, W., Patterson, H. L., & Page, S. H. (1968). A "universe-defined" system of arithmetic achievement tests. *Journal of Educational Measurement, 5,* 275–290.

Hogaboam, T. W., & Pellegrino, J. W. (1978). Hunting for individual differences in cognitive processes: Verbal ability and semantic processing of pictures and words. *Memory and Cognition, 6,* 189–193.

Holland, P. W., & Wainer, H. (1993). *Differential item functioning*. Hillsdale, NJ: Erlbaum.

Hornke, L. F., & Habon, M. W. (1986). Rule-based bank construction and evaluation within the linear logistic framework. *Applied Psychological Measurement, 10,* 369–380.

Hoskens, M., & De Boeck, P. (1995). Componential IRT models for polytomous items. *Journal of Educational Measurement, 32,* 364–384.

Huang, C.-W. (2003). *Psychometric analyses based on evidence-centered design and cognitive science of learning to explore students' problem-solving in physics*. Doctoral dissertation, University of Maryland, College Park, Department of Measurement, Statistics, and Evaluation.

Hubel, D., & Wiesel, T. (1962). Receptive fields, binocular interaction and functional architecture in the cat's visual cortex. *Journal of Physiology of London, 160,* 106–154.

Hunt, E., Frost, N., & Lunneborg, C. (1973). Individual differences in cognition: A new approach to intelligence. In G. Bower (Ed.), *Advances in learning and motivation* (Vol. 7, pp. 87–122). New York: Academic Press.

Hunt, E., & Minstrell, J. (1994). A cognitive approach to the teaching of physics. In K. McGilly (Ed.), *Classroom lessons* (pp. 51–74). Cambridge, MA: MIT Press.

Hurst, K., Casillas, A., & Stevens, R. H. (1997). *Exploring the dynamics of complex problem-solving with artificial neural network-based assessment systems* (CSE Technical Report 444). Los Angeles: University of California, National Center for Research on Evaluation, Standards, and Student Testing.

Hutchins, E., & Klausen, T. (2000). Distributed cognition in an airline cockpit. In Y. Engström & D. Middleton (Eds.), *Cognition and communication at work* (pp. 15–34). New York: Cambridge University Press.

Inhelder, B., & Piaget, J. (1958). *The growth of logical thinking from childhood to adolescence*. New York: Basic Books.

Irvine, S. H., & Kyllonen, P. C. (Eds.). (2002). *Item generation for test development*. Hillsdale, NJ: Erlbaum.

Janssen, R., & De Boeck, P. (1997). Psychometric modeling of componentially designed synonym tasks. *Applied Psychological Measurement, 21,* 37–50.

Johnson-Laird, P. N. (1983). *Mental models: Towards a cognitive science of language, inference, and consciousness*. Cambridge: Cambridge University Press; Cambridge, MA: Harvard University Press.

Junker, B. W. (1999). *Some statistical models and computational methods that may be useful for cognitively-relevant assessment*. Paper prepared for the Committee on the Foundations of Assessment, National Research Council Retrieved June 8, 2006, from http://www.stat.cmu.edu/~brian/nrc/cfa/documents/final.pdf

Junker, B. W., & Sijtsma, K. (2001). Cognitive assessment models with few assumptions, and connections with nonparametric item response theory. *Applied Psychological Measurement, 25,* 258–272.

Kadane, J. B., & Schum, D. A. (1996). *A probabilistic analysis of the Sacco and Vanzetti evidence*. New York: Wiley.

Kahneman, D., Slovic, P., & Tversky, A. (1982). *Judgment under uncertainty: Heuristics and biases*. Cambridge: Cambridge University Press.

Kane, M. (1992). An argument-based approach to validation. *Psychological Bulletin, 112,* 527–535.

Katz, I. R. (1994). Coping with the complexity of design: Avoiding conflicts and prioritizing constraints. In A. Ram, N. Nersessian, & M. Recker (Eds.), *Proceedings of the Sixteenth Annual Meeting of the Cognitive Science Society* (pp. 485–489). Mahwah, NJ: Erlbaum.

Kelderman, H. (1997). Loglinear multidimensional item response models for polytomously scored items. In W. J. van der Linden & R. K. Hambleton (Eds.), *Handbook of modern item response theory* (pp. 287–304). New York: Springer.

Kelderman, H., & Rijkes, C. P. M. (1994). Loglinear multidimensional IRT models for polytomously scored items. *Psychometrika, 59,* 149–176.

Kempf, W. (1983). Some theoretical concerns about applying latent trait models in educational testing. In S. B. Anderson & J. S. Helmick (Eds.), *On educational testing* (pp. 252–270). San Francisco: Josey-Bass.

Kindfield, A. C. H. (1994). Understanding a basic biological process: Expert and novice models of meiosis. *Science Education, 78,* 255–283.

Kirsch, I. S., & Jungeblut, A. (1986). *Literacy: Profiles of America's young adults*. Princeton, NJ: National Assessment of Educational Progress/Educational Testing Service.

Kohonen, T. (1982). Self-organized formation of topologically correct feature maps. *Biological Cybernetics, 43,* 59–69.

Krathwohl, D. R., & Payne, D. A. (1971). Defining and assessing educational objectives. In R. L. Thorndike (Ed.), *Educational measurement* (2nd ed., pp. 17–45). Washington, DC: American Council on Education.

Kuffler, S. W. (1953). Discharge patterns and functional organization of mammalian retina. *Journal of Neurophysiology, 16,* 37–68.

Kyllonen, P. C., Lohman, D. F., & Snow, R. E. (1984). Effects of aptitudes, strategy training, and test facets on spatial task performance. *Journal of Educational Psychology, 76,* 130–145.

Larkin, J. (1983). The role of problem representation in physics. In D. Gentner & A. L. Stevens (Eds.), *Mental models* (pp. 75–98). Hillsdale, NJ: Lawrence Erlbaum.

Lauritzen, S. L., & Spiegelhalter, D. J. (1988). Local computations with probabilities on graphical structures and their application to expert systems (with discussion). *Journal of the Royal Statistical Society, Series B, 50,* 157–224.

Lave, J. (1988). *Cognition in practice*. New York: Cambridge University Press.

Lave, J., & Wenger, E. (1991). *Situated learning: Legitimate peripheral participation*. Cambridge: Cambridge University Press.

Lehman, D. R., Lempert, R. O., & Nisbett, R. E. (1988). The effects of graduate training on reasoning. *American Psychologist, 43,* 431–442.

Lehrer, R., & Schauble, L. (2000). Modeling in mathematics and science. In R. Glaser (Ed.), *Advances in instructional psychology. Educational design and cognitive science*, Vol. 5 (pp. 101–159). Mahwah, NJ: Lawrence Erlbaum.

Lehrer, R., & Schauble, L. (2002). Symbolic communication in mathematics and science: Co-constituting inscription and thought. In E. D. Amsel & J. Byrnes (Eds.), *Language, literacy, and cognitive development. The development and consequences of symbolic communication* (pp. 167–192). Mahwah, NJ: Lawrence Erlbaum.

Lesgold, A. M., Lajoie, S. P., Bunzo, M., & Eggan, G. (1992). Sherlock: A coached practice environment for an electronics troubleshooting job. In J. H. Larkin & R. W. Chabay (Eds.), *Computer- assisted instruction and intelligent tutoring systems* (pp. 202–274). Hillsdale, NJ: Erlbaum.

Lesgold, A., Rubinson, H., Feltovich, P., Glaser, R., Klopfer, D., & Wang, Y. (1988). Expertise in a complex skill: Diagnosing X-ray pictures. In M. T. Chi, R. Glaser, & M. J. Farr (Eds.), *The nature of expertise* (pp. 311–342). Mahwah, NJ: Erlbaum.

Lettvin, J. Y., Maturana, H. R., McCulloch, W. S., & Pitts, W. H. (1959). What the frog's eye tells the frog's brain. *Proceedings of the IRE (Institute of Radio Engineers), 47,* 1940–1951.

Levy, R., & Mislevy, R. J. (2004). Specifying and refining a measurement model for a simulation-based assessment. *International Journal of Testing, 4,* 333–369.

Lewandowsky, S., & Behrens, J. T. (1999). Statistical graphs and maps. In F. T. Durso (Ed.), *Handbook of applied cognition* (pp. 513–549). Chichester, England: Wiley.

Lewis, C. (1986). Test theory and *Psychometrika*: The past twenty-five years. *Psychometrika, 51,* 11–22.

Lewis, D. (1973). *We, the navigators.* Honolulu: University of Hawaii Press.

Linacre, J. M. (1989). *Many faceted Rasch measurement.* Doctoral dissertation, University of Chicago.

Linn, R. L., & Harnisch, D. (1981). Interactions between item content and group membership in achievement test items. *Journal of Educational Measurement, 18,* 109–118.

Long, M. H., & Norris, J. M. (2000). Task-based language teaching and assessment. In M. Byram (Ed.), *Encyclopoedia of language teaching* (pp. 597–603). London: Routledge.

Luce, R. D., & Tukey, J. W. (1964). Simultaneous conjoint measurement: A new type of fundamental measurement. *Journal of Mathematical Psychology, 1,* 1–27.

Maris, E. (1999). Estimating multiple classification latent class models. *Psychometrika, 64,* 187–212.

Markman, A. B. (1999). *Knowledge representation.* Mahwah, NJ: Erlbaum.

Marshall, S. P. (1995). *Schemas in problem solving.* Cambridge: Cambridge University Press.

Martin, J. D., & VanLehn, K. (1995). A Bayesian approach to cognitive assessment. In P. Nichols, S. Chipman, & R. Brennan (Eds.), *Cognitively diagnostic assessment* (pp. 141–165). Hillsdale, NJ: Erlbaum.

Masters, G. N., & Wright, B. D. (1984). The essential process in a family of measurement models. *Psychometrika, 50,* 69–82.

McClelland, J. L. (1981). Retrieving general and specific information from stored knowledge of specifics. *Proceedings of the Third Annual Meeting of the Cognitive Science Society,* 170–172.

McClelland, J. (1989). Parallel distributed processing: Implications for cognition and development. In R. G. M. Morris (Ed.), *Parallel distributed processing: Implications for psychology and neurobiology* (pp. 8–45). Oxford: Oxford University Press.

McCloskey, M. (1983). Naive theories of motion. In D. Gentner & A. L. Stevens, (Eds.), *Mental models* (pp. 299–324). Hillsdale, NJ: Erlbaum.

McCulloch, W. S., & Pitts, W. H. (1943). A logical calculus of the ideas immanent in nervous activity. *Bulletin of Mathematical Biophysics, 5,* 115–133.

Mead, R. J. (1976). *Analysis of fit to the Rasch model.* Doctoral dissertation, University of Chicago.

Meehl, P. E. (1954). *Clinical versus statistical prediction: A theoretical analysis and a review of the evidence.* Minneapolis: University of Minnesota Press.

Messick, S. (1989). Validity. In R. L. Linn (Ed.), *Educational measurement* (3rd ed., pp. 13–103). New York: American Council on Education/Macmillan.

Messick, S. (1994). The interplay of evidence and consequences in the validation of performance assessments. *Educational Researcher, 23*(2), 13–23.

Michell, J. (1997). Quantitative science and the definition of measurement in psychology. *British Journal of Psychology, 88,* 355–383.

Michell, J. (1999). *Measurement in psychology: A critical history of a methodological concept.* New York: Cambridge University Press.

Michell, J. (2000). Normal science, pathological science and psychometrics. *Theory & Psychology, 10,* 639–667.

Miller, G. A. (1956). The magical number seven, plus or minus two: Some limits on our capacity for processing information. *Psychological Review, 63,* 81–97.

Miller, M. D., & Linn, R. L. (1988). Invariance of item characteristic functions with variations in instructional coverage. *Journal of Educational Measurement, 25,* 205–219.

Millroy, W. (1992). An ethnographic study of the mathematical ideas of a group of carpenters. *Journal for Research in Mathematics Education, Monograph number 5.*

Minsky, M. (1975). A framework for representing knowledge. In P. H. Winston (Ed.), *The psychology of computer vision* (pp. 177–211). New York: McGraw-Hill.

Minsky, M., & Papert, S. (1969). *Perceptrons: An introduction to computational geometry.* Cambridge, MA: MIT Press.

Minstrell, J. (2000). Student thinking and related assessment: Creating a facet assessment-based learning environment. In J. Pellegrino, L. Jones, & K. Mitchell (Eds.), *Grading the nation's report card: Research from the evaluation of NAEP* (pp. 44–73). Washington, DC: National Academy Press.

Mislevy, R. J. (1994). Evidence and inference in educational assessment. *Psychometrika, 59,* 439–483.

Mislevy, R., Hamel, L., Fried, R. G., Gaffney, T., Haertel, G., Hafter, A., et al. (2003). *Design patterns for assessing science inquiry* (PADI Technical Report 1). Menlo Park, CA: SRI International.

Mislevy, R. J., Steinberg, L.S., & Almond, R.G. (2003). On the structure of educational assessments. *Measurement: Interdisciplinary Research and Perspectives, 1,* 3–67.

Mislevy, R. J., & Verhelst, N. (1990). Modeling item responses when different subjects employ different solution strategies. *Psychometrika, 55,* 195–215.

Mosenthal, P. B. (1985). Defining the expository discourse continuum. *Poetics, 15,* 387–414.

Moss, P. A. (1992). Shifting conceptions of validity in educational measurement: Implications for performance assessment. *Review of Educational Research, 62,* 229–258.

Moss, P. (1994). Can there be validity without reliability? *Educational Researcher, 23*(2), 5–12.

Moss, P. A. (1996). Enlarging the dialogue in educational measurement: Voices from interpretive research traditions. *Educational Researcher, 25*(1), 20–28, 43.

Myford, C. M., & Mislevy, R. J. (1995). *Monitoring and improving a portfolio assessment system* (Center for Performance Assessment Research Report). Princeton, NJ: Center for Performance Assessment, Educational Testing Service.

National Research Council. (2000). *How people learn: Brain, mind, experience, and school.* Committee on Developments in the Science of Learning. J. D. Bransford, A. L. Brown, & R. R. Cocking (Eds.). Washington, DC: National Academy Press.

National Research Council. (2001). *Knowing what students know: The science and design of educational assessment.* Committee on the Foundations of Assessment, J. Pellegrino, R. Glaser, & N. Chudowsky (Eds.). Washington, DC: National Academy Press.

Newell, A. (1990). *Unified theories of cognition.* Cambridge, MA: Harvard University Press.

Newell, A., & Simon, H. A. (1956). The logic theory machine: A complex information processing system. *IRE Transactions on Information Theory, IT 2,* 61–79.

Newell, A., & Simon, H. A. (1972). *Human problem solving.* Englewood Cliffs, NJ: Prentice Hall.

Nichols, P. D., Chipman, S. F., & Brennan, R. L. (Eds.). (1995). *Cognitively diagnostic assessment.* Hillsdale, NJ: Erlbaum.

Noelting, G. (1980). The development of proportional reasoning and the ratio concept. Part 2—Problem structure at the different stages; Problem-solving strategies and the mechanism of adaptive restructuring. *Educational Studies in Mathematics, 11,* 331–363.

Norman, D. A. (1988). *The psychology of everyday things.* New York: Basic Books.

Norman, D. A. (1993). *Things that make us smart.* Boston: Addison-Wesley.

O'Neil, H. F., Jr., Allred, K., & Dennis, R. A. (1997). Use of computer simulation for assessing the interpersonal skill of negotiation. In H. F. O'Neil (Ed.), *Workforce readiness: Competencies and assessment* (pp. 205–228). Mahwah, NJ: Lawrence Erlbaum.

Patel, V. L., & Kaufman, D. R. (1996). The acquisition of medical expertise in complex dynamic environments. In A. Ericsson (Ed.), *The road to excellence: The acquisition of expert performance in the arts and sciences, sports and games* (pp. 127–165). Mahwah, NJ: Erlbaum.

Patz, R. J., & Junker, B. W. (1999). Applications and extensions of MCMC in IRT: Multiple item types, missing data, and rated responses. *Journal of Educational and Behavioral Statistics, 24*(4), 342–366.

Pearl, J. (1988). *Probabilistic reasoning in intelligent systems: Networks of plausible inference.* San Mateo, CA: Kaufmann.

Perline, R., Wright, B. D., & Wainer, H. (1979). The Rasch model as additive conjoint measurement. *Applied Psychological Measurement, 3,* 237–255.

Piaget, J. (1929). *The child's conception of the world.* London: Routledge and Kegan Paul.

Piaget, J. (1970). *Structuralism* (C. Maschler, Trans.). New York: Basic Books. (Original work published 1968)

Polti, G. P. (1977). *The thirty-six dramatic situations* (L. Ray, Trans.). Boston: The Writers. (Original work published 1868)

Ramsay, J. O., & Silverman, B. (1997). *Functional data analysis.* Berlin: Springer.

Rasch, G. (1960/1980). *Probabilistic models for some intelligence and attainment tests.* Copenhagen: Danish Institute for Educational Research/Chicago: University of Chicago Press (reprint).

Rasch, G. (1977). On specific objectivity: An attempt at formalizing the request for generality and validity of scientific statements. *Danish Yearbook of Philosophy, 14,* 58–94.

Raven, J. C. (1992). *Standard progressive matrices: 1992 edition.* Windsor, England: NFER-Nelson.

Rayner, K., Foorman, B. R., Perfetti, C. A., Pesetsky, D., & Seidenberg, M. S. (2001). How psychological science informs the teaching of reading. *Psychological Science in the Public Interest, 2,* 31–74.

Resnick, L. B., & Resnick, D. P. (1989). Assessing the thinking curriculum: New tools for educational reform. In B. R. Gifford & M. C. O'Conner (Eds.), *Future assessments: Changing views of aptitude, achievement, and instruction* (pp. 37–75). Boston: Kluwer.

Rijmen, F. (2002). *A mixed and mixture perspective on item response theory.* Doctoral dissertation, Katholieke Universiteit Leuven, Leuven, Belgium, Department of Psychology.

Rijmen, F., & De Boeck, P. (2002). The random weights linear logistic test model. *Applied Psychological Measurement, 26,* 271–285.

Robinson, P. (Ed.). (2001a). *Cognitive and second learning instruction.* Cambridge: Cambridge University Press.

Robinson, P. (2001b). Task complexity, task difficulty, and task production: Exploring interactions in a componential framework. *Applied Linguistics, 22,* 27–57.

Rogoff, B. (1990). *Apprenticeship in thinking: Cognitive development in social context.* Oxford: Oxford University Press.

Rogosa, D. R., & Ghandour, G. A. (1991). Statistical models for behavioral observations (with discussion). *Journal of Educational Statistics, 16,* 157–252.

Rosenblatt, F. (1962). *Principles of neurodynamics.* New York: Spartan.

Rost, J. (1990). Rasch models in latent classes: An integration of two approaches to item analysis. *Applied Psychological Measurement, 14,* 271–282.

Rumelhart, D. A. (1980). Schemata: The building blocks of cognition. In R. Spiro, B. Bruce, & W. Brewer (Eds.), *Theoretical issues in reading comprehension* (pp. 33–58). Hillsdale, NJ: Erlbaum.

Rumelhart, D. E., & McClelland, J. L. (1986a). *Parallel distributed processing: Explorations in the microstructure of cognition* (Vols. 1–3). Cambridge, MA: MIT Press.

Rumelhart, D. E., & McClelland, J. L. (1986b). On learning the past tenses of English verbs. In D. E. Rumelhart & J. L. McClelland (Eds.), *Parallel distributed processing: Exploration in the microstructure of cognition, Vol. 2: Psychological and biological models* (pp. 216–271). Cambridge, MA: MIT Press.

Rupp, A. A. (2002). Feature selection for choosing and assembling measurement models: A building-block-based organization. *International Journal of Testing, 2,* 311–360.

Salthouse, T. A. (1991). Expertise as the circumvention of human processing limitations. In K. A. Ericcson & J. Smith (Eds.), *Toward a general theory of expertise* (pp. 286–300). Cambridge: Cambridge University Press.

Saxe, G. B. (1988). Candy selling and math learning. *Educational Researcher, 17*(6), 14–21.

Scalise, K. (2003). *Innovative item types and outcome spaces in computer-adaptive assessment: A literature survey.* Berkeley: University of California at Berkeley, Berkeley Evaluation and Assessment Research (BEAR) Center.

Schneps, M. H., & Sadler, P. M. (1987). *A private universe.* New York: Annenberg/Corporation for Public Broadcasting.

Schraagen, J. M., Chipman, S. F., & Shalin, V. J. (Eds.) (2000). *Cognitive task analysis.* Mahwah, NJ: Erlbaum.

Schum, D. A. (1994). *The evidential foundations of probabilistic reasoning.* New York: Wiley.

Schutz, A., & Moss, P. A. (2004). Reasonable decisions in portfolio assessment: Evaluating complex evidence of teaching. *Education Policy Analysis Archives, 12*(33). Retrieved April 15, 2005, from http://epaa.asu.edu/epaa/v12n33/

Scribner, S. (1984). Studying working intelligence. In B. Rogoff & J. Lave (Eds.), *Everyday cognition: Its development in social context* (pp. 9–40). Cambridge, MA: Harvard University Press.

Selinker, L., Tarone, E., & Hanzeli, V. (Eds.). (1981). *English for technical and academic purposes: Studies in honor of Louis Trimble.* Rowley, MA: Newbury House.

Shafer, G. (1976). *A mathematical theory of evidence.* Princeton, NJ: Princeton University Press.

Sheehan, K. M., & Mislevy, R. J. (1990). Integrating cognitive and psychometric models in a measure of document literacy. *Journal of Educational Measurement, 27,* 255–272.

Shermis, M. D., & Burstein, J. (2003). *Automated essay scoring: A cross-disciplinary perspective.* Hillsdale, NJ: Lawrence Erlbaum.

Shute, V., & Psotka, J. (1996). Intelligent tutoring systems: Past, present, and future. In D. Jonassen (Ed.), *Handbook of research for educational communications and technology* (pp. 570–600). New York: Macmillan.

Siegler, R. S. (1981). Developmental sequences within and between concepts. *Monograph of the Society for Research in Child Development, 46* (Serial No. 189).

Simon, H. A. (2001). *The sciences of the artificial* (4th ed.). Cambridge, MA: MIT Press.

Singer, J. D., & Willett, J. B. (2003). *Applied longitudinal data analysis: Modeling change and event occurrence.* New York: Oxford University Press.

Singley, K., & Anderson, J. R. (1989). *The transfer of cognitive skill.* Cambridge, MA: Harvard University Press.

Skehan, P. (1998). *A cognitive approach to language learning.* Oxford: Oxford University Press.

Sloboda, J. (1991). Musical expertise. In K. A. Ericcson & J. Smith (Eds.), *Toward a general theory of expertise* (pp. 153–171). Cambridge: Cambridge University Press.

Smith, R. (1986). Person fit in the Rasch model. *Educational and Psychological Measurement, 46,* 359–372.

Snow, R. E., & Lohman, D. F. (1989). Implications of cognitive psychology for educational measurement. In R. L. Linn (Ed.), *Educational measurement* (3rd ed., pp. 263–331). New York: American Council on Education/Macmillan.

Songer, N. B., & Gotwals, A. (2004). What constitutes evidence of complex reasoning in science? In *Proceedings of the Sixth International Conference of the Learning Sciences* (pp. 497–504). Mahwah, NJ: Erlbaum.

Spearman, C. (1904). "General intelligence" objectively determined and measured. *American Journal of Psychology, 15,* 201–292.

SRI, International. (2002). *GLOBE classroom assessment tools.* Retrieved June 5, 2005, from http://globeassessment.sri.com/index.html

Stefik, M. (1995). *Introduction to knowledge systems.* San Francisco: Morgan Kaufmann.

Steinberg, L. S., & Gitomer, D. G. (1996). Intelligent tutoring and assessment built on an understanding of a technical problem-solving task. *Instructional Science, 24,* 223–258.

Sternberg, R. J. (1977). *Intelligence, information processing and analogical reasoning: The componential analysis of human abilities.* New York: Wiley.

Stewart, J., & Hafner, R. (1994). Research on problem solving: Genetics. In D. Gabel (Ed.), *Handbook of research on science teaching and learning* (pp. 284–300). New York: Macmillan.

Tatsuoka, K. K. (1983). Rule space: An approach for dealing with misconceptions based on item response theory. *Journal of Educational Measurement, 20,* 345–354.

Tatsuoka, K. K. (1987). Validation of cognitive sensitivity for item response curves. *Journal of Educational Measurement, 24,* 233–245.

Tatsuoka, K. K. (1990). Toward an integration of item response theory and cognitive error diagnosis. In N. Frederiksen, R. Glaser, A. Lesgold, & M. G. Shafto (Eds.), *Diagnostic monitoring of skill and knowledge acquisition* (pp. 453–488). Hillsdale, NJ: Erlbaum.

Thompson, P. W. (1982). Were lions to speak, we wouldn't understand. *Journal of Mathematical Behavior, 3,* 147–165.

Thorndike, E. L. (1906). *Principles of teaching.* New York: A. G. Seiler.

Toulmin, S. E. (1958). *The uses of argument.* Cambridge: Cambridge University Press.

van der Maas, H. L. J., & Jansen, B. R. J. (2003). What response times tell of children's behavior on the balance scale task. *Journal of Experimental Child Psychology, 85,* 141–177.

van Hiele, P. M. (1986). *Structure and insight: A theory of mathematics education.* Orlando, FL: Academic Press.

van Maanen, L., Been, P., & Sijtsma, K. (1989). The linear logistic test model and heterogeneity of cognitive strategies. In E. E. Roskam (Ed.), *Mathematical psychology in progress* (pp. 267–287). New York: Springer-Verlag.

VanLehn, K. (1989). Problem-solving and cognitive skill acquisition. In M. Posner (Ed.), *The foundations of cognitive science* (pp. 527–580). Cambridge, MA: MIT Press.

VanLehn, K. (1990). *Mind bugs: The origins of procedural misconceptions.* Cambridge, MA: MIT Press.

Vera, A. H., & Simon, H. A. (1993). Situated action: A symbolic interpretation. *Cognitive Science, 17,* 7–48.

Verhelst, N. D., & Glas, C. A. W. (1995). Dynamic generalizations of the Rasch model. In G. H. Fischer & I. W. Molenaar (Eds.), *Rasch models: Foundations, recent developments, and applications* (pp. 181–201). New York: Springer-Verlag.

Von Davier, M. (2005). *A class of models for cognitive diagnosis* (Research Report RR-05-17). Princeton, NJ: ETS.

Von Davier, M., & Carstensen, C. H. (2005). *Multivariate and mixture distribution Rasch models: Extensions and applications.* New York: Springer.

Vosniadou, S., & Brewer, W. F. (1987). Theories of knowledge restructuring in development. *Review of Educational Research, 57,* 51–67.

Vygotsky, L. S. (1987). *The collected works of L.S. Vygotsky: Vol. 1, Problems of general psychology.* Including the volume *Thinking and speech* (N. Minick, Trans.). New York: Plenum.

Wainer, H., Dorans, N. J., Flaugher, R., Green, B. F., Mislevy, R. J., Steinberg, L., et al. (2000). *Computerized adaptive testing: A primer* (2nd ed.). Hillsdale, NJ: Lawrence Erlbaum.

Wason, P. C. (1966). Reasoning. In B. Foss (Ed.), *New horizons in psychology* (pp. 135–151). Harmondsworth, UK: Penguin Books.

Watson, I. (1997). *Applying case-based reasoning: Techniques for enterprise systems.* San Francisco: Morgan Kaufmann.

Wiggins, G. P. (1998). *Educative assessment: Designing assessments to inform and improve student performance.* San Francisco: Jossey-Bass.

Wigmore, J. H. (1937). *The science of judicial proof* (3rd ed.). Boston: Little, Brown.

Williamson, D. M., Bauer, M., Steinberg, L. S., Mislevy, R. J., Behrens, J. T., & DeMark, S. (2004). Design rationale for a complex performance assessment. *International Journal of Measurement, 4,* 303–332.

Wilson, M. R. (1989). Saltus: A psychometric model of discontinuity in cognitive development. *Psychological Bulletin, 105,* 276–289.

Wilson, M. R., & Adams, R. J. (1995). Rasch models for item bundles. *Psychometrika, 60,* 181–198.

Winograd, T. (1972). *Understanding natural language.* New York: Academic Press.

Wright, B. D., & Linacre, J. M. (1989). Observations are always ordinal; measurements, however, must be interval. *Archives of Physical Medicine and Rehabilitation, 70,* 857–867.

Yamamoto, K., & Everson, H. (1997). Modeling the effect of test length and test time on parameter estimation using the HYBRID model. In J. Rost and R. Langeheine (Eds.), *Applications of latent trait and latent class models in the social sciences* (pp. 89–97). Münster, Germany: Waxmann.

Yamamoto, K., & Gitomer, D. H. (1993). Application of a HYBRID model to a test of cognitive skill representation. In N. Frederiksen, R. J. Mislevy, & I. I. Bejar (Eds.), *Test theory for a new generation of tests* (pp. 275–295). Hillsdale, NJ: Erlbaum.

Part II
Construction, Administration, and Scoring

9

Test Development

Cynthia B. Schmeiser
Catherine J. Welch
ACT, Inc.

1. INTRODUCTION

Test development: art or science?
There is little doubt that some portion of what is known about effective test-development practice has emanated from the opinions of experts who have written seminal test-development textbooks in the last sixty years and from the common sense and experience of test-development practitioners. To a somewhat lesser extent, test-development practice has also been influenced by research that has examined aspects of test design in an experimental context. Certainly there are test developers who believe that the process of developing a clear, unambiguous, challenging test item is an *art*, and they are no doubt correct, at least in part. What is less clear in measurement history is the extent to which the body of test-development practice has been viewed by practitioners as one that should be firmly rooted in a scientific approach from its earliest stages, an approach based on a foundation of validity evidence that drives the entire test-development process, from test design through test administration and evaluation. The *science* of test development is an issue that deserves more professional discussion, and some of the issues that are part of that discussion will be raised in this chapter.

To argue that test development of necessity possesses a scientific component is to argue, in large part, that test development has a role in validation. This seems eminently clear in the sense that test development is undeniably important to the proper interpretation of test scores and the inferences that are drawn from them (see the chapter by Kane, this volume). At a minimum, a user who wants to interpret test scores appropriately must study the specifications for the test and how they were derived, the process by which the test is constructed, and, perhaps, one or more released forms of the test. This is not simply a matter of judging the "content validity" of the test, to use somewhat dated terminology; test development influences many aspects of validity, many types of inferences. It might be argued that, in the past, test development was treated almost entirely as an art, but this has never been entirely true (see, for example, Cronbach, 1971; Haladyna & Downing, 1989a). More efforts are being made to give test development a stronger scientific basis (see, for example, Embretson & Hershberger, 1999; the chapter by Mislevy, this volume).

The purpose of this chapter is to discuss the issues and considerations associated with developing tests, the results of which are used to make educational decisions about students. For simplicity's sake, this chapter refers to these tests as achievement tests and assumes that they are designed to measure educational attainment. This chapter focuses predominantly on the work of the professional test developer rather than the classroom teacher, although many of the principles are applicable to both. The authors of this chapter defer to the authors of other chapters in this volume that address test development in specific contexts, such as the classroom; for specified purposes, such as licensure and certification; for tests administered through specialized delivery platforms, such as computerized testing; and for specified item types, such as performance testing. As expected, many of the practical test-development issues addressed in this chapter have direct connections to the content addressed in nearly every other chapter in this volume.

The recommendations that are provided in this chapter are intended to be consistent with the *Standards for Educational and Psychological Testing* (American Educational Research Association, American Psychological Association, & National Council on Measurement in Education, 1999). The *Standards* constitute a seminal guide for proper test design and development.

This chapter is organized according to seven major components of the test-development process. Following the introduction, Section 2 deals with test and item pool design. Test design begins with identifying test philosophy, test purposes and uses, intended examinee population(s), and other logistical considerations affecting test design and delivery. This section also addresses the need for a more empirical evidentiary process for deriving test specifications.

Section 3 focuses on considerations associated with item development. An item is defined broadly to include "selected-response" and "constructed-response" formats that present a task of some character to an examinee and require a written response. The "how-to's" of item writing are not addressed here, since other test-development professionals have done that well (see Glas & van der Linden, 2003; Haladyna & Downing, 1989b; and Millman & Westman, 1989), but this section does present the considerations associated with designing an item-development process, training item writers, editing and reviewing items, and field testing.

Section 4 presents a discussion of the issues associated with item evaluation, assembly of tests and item pools, and test formatting. Considerations associated with test and item pool assembly by hand and by computer are discussed. These are followed by a review of item and test-formatting issues as they pertain to the test delivery platform.

Section 5 discusses the role of test review: how to select reviewers, train them, and conduct an effective test review process. Section 6 focuses on evaluation of items and tests, and how that information can be used to improve the test-development process. Section 7 examines the considerations associated with item banking, including how to determine what information to store in an item bank and security concerns. Section 8 focuses on the importance of quality control, how to design an effective quality-control process, and the continuous monitoring and improvement of quality-control procedures.

Finally, section 9 concludes the chapter with a reflection on the history of test development and the important role that test development ultimately plays in the educational decisions that are made about students.

2. TEST AND ITEM POOL DESIGN

By far, the most important stage in the development of an educational achievement test is the design stage. In the design stage all of the important overall decisions about the test are made. These decisions include: affirming test philosophy; determining test purposes and uses; defining the intended examinee populations; identifying logistical and administrative constraints on test design (including test length and test timing); identifying relevant legal considerations that affect test design; establishing a validation foundation for the test; designing test specifications; and reviewing, refining, and reaffirming validity evidence for test design.

2.1. Test Philosophy

Before any decisions about test design can be made, it is important that the test developer affirm the philosophy that will serve as the foundation for the test. "Philosophy" in this context is intended to refer to an explicit linkage between test purpose and the criterion that defines the test domain, that is, what will and will not be measured in the test. Test domain in this chapter is used broadly to refer to the various attributes used to define what a test should measure, including content topics, tasks, cognitive skills, and situational context. To be able to develop items that measure the test domain, developers need to define the test domain explicitly.

Perhaps this can be best illustrated by example. Lindquist (1958) stated his philosophy concerning college admissions testing in the following manner:

> While they have not generally done so in the past, wide-scale scholarship and college entrance testing programs can make a significant contribution to these basic educational needs. By providing appropriate types of examinations, the programs can give the students a concrete and immediately effective incentive to work harder at the job of getting ready for college. To serve this purpose, the examinations must measure directly the student's readiness for college, or the extent to which he is prepared to profit by the college experience. That is, they must measure as directly as possible his ability to perform exactly the same kinds of complex tasks that he will have occasion to perform in college and in his later intellectual activities in general. The examination should therefore consist in large part of exercises requiring the students to interpret and to evaluate critically the same kinds of reading materials that he will have occasion to read and study in college, and particularly, that will require him to do the same kinds of complex reasoning and problem solving that he will have to do later both in and out of school. (p. 108)

This statement of test philosophy assumes that the test purposes of scholarship and college admission decisions can be best served by a test that is comprised of tasks that are like those students will be asked to perform in college. Lindquist has defined the test domain criterion to be what students have learned in high school *that is necessary for readiness to perform college-level work*.

Without a philosophy to guide the definition of the test domain, the test developer may define the test domain in unintended, uncontrolled, and/or ambiguous ways. For instance, Lindquist could have defined the test domain criterion as the totality of what students have learned in high school. That domain is substantially different from the domain he described in 1958 and would result in a test that samples from a broad domain of what high schools are teaching, irrespective of whether the knowledge and skills being taught and measured by the test are related to college readiness. The resulting tests would look very different, result in different test-score interpretations, and ultimately likely result in different inferences about students. Thus it is important that a carefully constructed statement of test philosophy be developed at the outset of the test design process.

One of the most frequently debated test philosophy issues in the twentieth century was whether a test used to make educational decisions about students was an achievement test or an aptitude test (Anastasi, 1982; Cooley & Lohnes, 1976; Cronbach, 1984). In an old but still relevant quote, Cronbach (1960) states,

> [A] test is referred to as an achievement test when it is used primarily to examine the person's success in past study, and as an aptitude test when it is used to forecast his success in some future course of assignment. (p. 31)

Cooley and Lohnes (1976) elaborated on this dichotomy by claiming that the distinction is purely a functional one: if a test is used as an indication of past instruction and experience, it is an achievement test; if it is used to predict or forecast future performance, it is an aptitude test. Yet this distinction has been blurred in practice through the years, with so-called achievement tests proving their effectiveness as predictors of future performance and aptitude tests including measures of what students have learned in the past.

Perhaps this achievement/aptitude dichotomy helped to define measurement debates in our history, but in practice this dichotomy has become artificial. It matters less what label a test is given; it matters more that the test philosophy links test purpose with a clear definition of the test domain criterion, delineating how the domain to be measured by the test and the resulting test-score inferences will be defined to fulfill that purpose. If a test is to measure what students have learned in a particular course, for example, its specifications will need to be defined on the basis of the course content that has been taught. Similarly, if a test is to measure what students have learned in high school that is necessary for an entry-level college course, the domain needs to reflect what is taught in high school that is necessary for students to be ready to learn in that first-year college credit-bearing course. And, if a test is to measure whether students have learned the fundamental academic skills that are necessary for upper-division college-level programs, the domain needs to reflect the core knowledge and skills taught in the first two years of college that are necessary for students to be ready for upper-division undergraduate work. In all of these instances, it is the definition of the test philosophy that will drive test design, not a test label. The steps taken to design the test are the same even though the content domains that result from the design process may be substantially different.

2.2. Test Purpose

The measurement literature is full of various categorization schemes for defining the purposes of educational achievement tests. For example, Bloom, Hastings, and Madaus (1971) propose a three-part categorization scheme based in part on when during instruction the assessment is administered: (a) initial evaluation used to diagnose strengths and weaknesses or place students in courses, (b) formative evaluation used to evaluate progress during instruction and prescribe next steps, and (c) summative evaluation used to summarize student attainment after completion of a course or course of study. Mehrens and Lehman (1991) propose four major types of decisions for test data: (a) instructional decisions, including diagnosis, attainment of learning outcomes, and evaluating curriculum; (b) counseling decisions, for occupational, educational, and personal planning; (c) administrative decisions, including selection, classification, placement, and curriculum planning and evaluation; and (d) research and program evaluation decisions. Millman and Greene (1989) offer a two-dimensional scheme: type of inference to be made (i.e., individual attainment, individual mastery, or group attainment), and domain to which inferences will be made (i.e., whether the inference is to be made about the degree to which content knowledge has been attained, cognitive or thinking skills acquired, or likelihood of performance in a future setting).

Because educational tests serve so many different functions in widely different settings, there is no single categorization scheme that is universally accepted. All of these categorization schemes have dimensions in common: all require the test developer to specify the type of decision to be made and the context for that decision. The Millman and Greene scheme adds a third dimension, domain, to which inferences will be made. When considering test purpose, it is important to specify the domain to which inferences will be made on the basis of the test scores. For example, when developers design a test for placing students into one of several courses, they need to define carefully the level of knowledge students need to enter the specific courses ready to learn. If developers do not specify in detail the important prerequisite knowledge and skills needed by students in the particular course, it is possible to end up with a test that does not accurately place students into the right course, ultimately leading to student failure. Similarly, when designing a college admission test, developers need to define the domain of knowledge needed for students to be ready to succeed in college (wherein "college success" is typically defined as first-semester grade-point average, although there are other relevant criteria such as retention in college and graduation). These domains need to reflect the range of subject-matter knowledge and skills that most postsecondary institutions expect their entering students to have in order for them to be ready for credit-bearing college entry courses without remediation.

Selecting the appropriate domains to which test-score inferences are to be made also helps to evaluate the compatibility of multiple purposes for a test. Since most tests are designed to serve more than one purpose, identifying the domains to which test-score inferences will be made helps to identify potentially conflicting purposes. For example, suppose a state requires that students in that state pass an exit test in order to graduate from high school. The exit test needs to define the level of performance in the subject-matter domain defined by the state content standards judged to be sufficient for high school completion. These performance standards are typically established through a standard-setting process. It is not likely, however, that the same test could also be used for college admission, since state standards usually reflect what students need to know to receive a diploma and that level of knowledge is not necessarily the same as the prerequisite knowledge students need to succeed in college. These purposes, if defined for the same test, would be difficult, if not impossible, to reconcile because the domains of knowledge they measure are substantially different.

Table 9.1 presents examples of types of test-score inferences for several different test purposes and uses. Note that the purposes focus on educational decisions about individuals as well as about curriculum and instruction.

2.3. Intended Examinee Population

Another important consideration at the early stages of test design is defining the examinee population(s) for whom the test is intended. It is important to define the characteristics of the students who will constitute the examinee population for the test: by age, geographical location (if relevant), level of education, courses taken, experience taking tests delivered on paper (or computer), and other characteristics that might affect test design, test format, or test delivery. For example, if a test is to be used to diagnose student strengths and weaknesses, it is important to define the age range of the students to be diagnosed and their educational backgrounds (i.e., range of courses these students may have taken) to make sure there is sufficient lower-level content to

TABLE 9.1 Test Purposes, Context of Use, and Inferences

	TEST PURPOSE	CONTEXT OF USE	INFERENCES
INDIVIDUAL			
	Placement	• Course placement • Counseling	• Knowledge needed to enter a specific course "ready to learn"
	Diagnosis	• Remediation • Enrichment • Instructional interventions	• Relative strengths and weaknesses in knowledge across various content domains • Degree of knowledge mastery across various content domains relative to established content standards
	Selection	• College admission	• Knowledge needed to "succeed" in college
	Classification	• Licensure/certification	• Knowledge needed to meet established standards of safe and effective professional practice
	Progress	• Graduation/exit • End-of-course • Grade promotion • Growth over time	• Change in knowledge over time relative to curricular domain or established standard • Level of knowledge upon completion of course, grade, level of education
INSTRUCTIONAL/CURRICULAR			
	Instructional adaptation	• Course pretest	• Distribution of student achievement with regard to course readiness for use in instructional planning
	Instructional effectiveness	• Course posttest • Course/curriculum evaluation and improvement	• Knowledge needed to meet established standard of acceptable course attainment • Comparison of course domain to domains of "like" courses in other schools
	Program effectiveness	• Educational progress across courses in subject-matter area	• Growth in achievement over time across content domains relative to established expectations of progress

diagnose academic weaknesses as well as sufficient higher-level content for those students who may have taken more courses and/or are at higher levels of attainment.

Test format is particularly affected by the age of the examinee population. Many younger students will need larger print and a simple, easy-to-follow layout on paper or an easy-to-follow computer interface. They will also need simple ways to navigate through the test if it is administered on computer. The principles of universal design set forth by Thompson, Johnstone, and Thurlow (2002) are particularly useful to help ensure that the test is accessible and inclusive of as many students as possible in the target population.

Specifying the examinee population must take into account examinee characteristics that fall outside of the requirements of the test, but may constrain or confound the examinee's performance on the test. These characteristics may include disabling conditions, native language where the examinee's first language is other than that used in the test, and reading proficiency. How critical the impact of these factors is on test performance and interpretation depends on the purpose of the test. A minor modification for a visually disabled examinee might involve providing the test in Braille, in large type, or read by a reader. A test that is not dependent on language proficiency that is to be taken by students whose first language is not English should include items that minimize the language load. By contrast, a major confounding factor on examinee performance would be for examinees who are not proficient readers to be confronted with a mathematics computation test that contains items requiring a lot of reading when the test is not intended to measure reading. And, if this test is to be delivered on computer, developers will want to consider how best to instruct students how to navigate through the test without requiring a long, complicated set of navigational instructions. The impact of allowable accommodations needs to be considered early in the test design process. Although many of these considerations are covered in greater detail in subsequent chapters, they are mentioned here because they require early consideration in the test design process.

Another dimension of specifying the intended examinee population(s) is whether individual results, group results, or both will be reported and used. That decision can also affect how the test is designed. For example, if a test is to be used to evaluate the effectiveness of curriculum with no individual results reported or used, then a matrix sampling approach, whereby different items are administered to different students, might be considered in test design, administration, and analysis. If individual results are to be reported, then students need to take the same (or parallel) forms of the paper test or take items on computer from equivalent item pools.

2.4. Administrative Constraints

The administrative constraints consist of the logistical realities of test administration that affect test design. These constraints typically include: amount of available administration time, delivery platform (paper or computer), administrative conditions (location and security), and administration model (individual or group). Considerations associated with each of these are briefly discussed below.

2.4.1. Administrative Time

It is important that examinees have sufficient time to demonstrate adequately those aspects of their achievement measured on a test. Establishing testing time is probably the single most difficult constraint because it is influenced by many factors:

1. Test purpose. Measuring achievement in depth over a broad domain or a large number of standards will require more testing time than a survey measure of the same domain.
2. Technical quality of the test scores. Ensuring that test scores will meet minimum requirements for reliability and support the inferences to be made from them requires that the test be sufficiently long to obtain a precise estimate of student achievement.
3. Age of the students taking the test. Generally, the younger the student, the shorter the testing session should be.
4. Test length. Test length is a function of the accuracy needed in the scores and by the domain coverage required to support the intended test-score interpretations.
5. Practical characteristics of the testing setting. Delivering the test during the school day will require that it be designed around school periods, as compared to administering it in a separate, out-of-school setting.
6. Likelihood of fatigue affecting test scores. The amount of likely fatigue depends on how the test is delivered (computer or paper), the item formats administered (longer, more complicated formats induce fatigue more quickly), and the time of day when testing takes place (end-of-day testing induces fatigue more quickly than testing done at the start of the day).
7. Cost. Generally, the longer the test, the more expensive it will be to produce and deliver (delivering the test on computer may reduce testing time but the unit cost for test delivery is likely to be higher).
8. Item formats. Item formats with shorter stimuli are usually quicker for students to answer because they require less reading than more complicated or stimulus-rich item formats. On the whole, constructed-response items take longer to administer than selected-response items.
9. Domain. Larger, more complex domains will require more test items for adequate coverage and take longer to administer, depending on test purpose and delivery platform.

2.4.2. Delivery Platform

The choice of whether the test should be delivered on paper or on computer is influenced by the following factors:

1. Test purpose. Is the technology consistent with the purpose of the test and can it add value to the information obtained?
2. Availability of computers. Are there sufficient computer workstations and World Wide Web access (if the test is Web-delivered) for the students who will be taking the test?
3. Item formats. Can computer technology be leveraged to improve the item formats?
4. Individual or group administration. Does the test need to be administered to all students at the same time for test security reasons, or can students take the test consecutively if computer workstations are limited?
5. Cost. Who is responsible for paying for the test, and what is the range of realistic costs for the test?
6. Urgency of feedback. Since computers can provide immediate feedback, how important is it that the test results be immediately available after testing?

2.4.3. Location of Administration

The choice of whether to administer the test in a school during or outside the school day or in dedicated test centers outside the school day is affected by the following:

1. Test purpose. Lower-stakes tests (such as diagnostic tests) are more amenable to in-school administration and may not need to be administered under the same level of standardized conditions that are mandated for higher-stakes tests.
2. Cost. In-school test administrations supervised by school personnel tend to cost less than dedicated test centers, but in-school administrations are generally less secure.
3. Availability of test centers. In-school test administrations are usually more convenient than administrations in dedicated test centers, depending on the location, availability, and accessibility of the dedicated test centers.
4. School periods. In-school test administrations need to work around class periods and bell schedules: if the bells aren't synchronized with the test timing, examinees can get confused.
5. Security. Independent test centers span a broad range of security: dedicated centers designed and built for testing typically reflect state-of-the-art security, whereas classrooms or hotel rooms that have been retrofitted as examination rooms tend to be less secure than dedicated centers but more controlled than in-school test administrations.

2.4.4. Administrative Security

The level of security needed for a particular test is directly related to test purpose and use. If the test results are to be used to make high-stakes decisions about students, as in the case of selection tests, then the test centers need to offer highly controlled, standardized testing conditions that enforce security before, during, and after the test. These centers typically require multiple forms of identification when the examinee checks into the center, in-person supervision and/or videotaping of the test session itself, and carefully prescribed sign-out procedures.

If, on the other hand, the purpose of the test is to provide diagnostic feedback about students' strengths and weaknesses so that instructional prescriptions can be provided, then the tests can be administered in a lower-stakes environment such as in the classroom, learning lab, or media center. In this context, one would assume that there would be fewer practical reasons why students might want to cheat, since doing so could result, for example, in placement in inappropriate instructional paths. However, in reality, by late elementary/middle school, there are a number of reasons why students still might cheat on diagnostic tests that seem quite rational to the student themselves, such as avoiding a perceived stigma associated with certain instructional interventions, desire to be grouped with certain peers and/or to avoid certain peers, or pressure from parents. This is an important consideration for teachers in implementing diagnostic testing: the effects of the testing itself on student performance, including cheating.

Another factor affecting administrative security is the frequency of testing opportunities. Most high-stakes standardized tests have explicitly defined test-retake policies that restrict students from retaking the test multiple times without intervening time periods of specified minimum length. Obviously, the frequency with which students are allowed to retest directly affects test item exposure, with more frequent exposure leading to less security. Test item exposure is also related to the size, depth, and number of distinct item pools, topics addressed in the chapter by Drasgow, Luecht, and Bennett (this volume).

With more high-stakes tests being administered on computer, it is important that test developers manage test item exposure through psychometric item selection methodologies that implement exposure control limits through meticulous item pool management. Similarly, it is important that computer-based programs establish limits on the total number of administrations of items defining the point at which the item should be rested from administration or retired from the pool and never reused. Test developers need to manage item pools in ways that assure that no particular item pool becomes overexposed and thereby less secure. Item pool management is a significant concern in preserving the security of computerized tests, as discussed in the chapter by Drasgow et al. (this volume).

2.4.5. Administrative Model

Up to now, most standardized educational achievement tests have been administered to examinees in a group rather than individually. When a test is administered to a group, there are usually few, if any, one-on-one interactions between the test administrator and each examinee, and there are not usually elaborate hands-on equipment or manipulables that require such interaction. Group administrations require simple and clear instructions and item types that do not require special instructions. Using too many different item types can also confuse students, hampering their performance on the test.

Test administrators who are responsible for administering standardized tests need to be carefully trained. They need to understand how to ensure that the conditions are standardized for the examinees and how to prevent extraneous factors that might affect performance. They also need to be trained to handle unexpected issues that might arise before, during, and after the test, while constantly monitoring test security so that no breach of security occurs.

In high-stakes test administrations, test timing is a critical issue not only to ensure that the administration is standardized, but also to make sure a reasonable amount of time is provided for examinees to demonstrate their achievement. Test administrators need to follow the prescribed procedures closely in these types of tests to guarantee that each examinee has the specified amount of time to take the test. Establishing appropriate time limits in tests where speed is not essential to demonstrating achievement is also important.

Individual administrations of paper tests have decreased through the years, but individual administrations of computer-based tests have increased. The use of computer-based testing does not require the same one-to-one administrator-to-examinee ratio, because one test administrator can supervise several examinees taking computer-based tests. Whether the test is administered to a group or by computer, the test developer is responsible for ensuring that the procedures for administration are carefully described and that the training materials for the administrators are effective in guaranteeing standardized testing procedures.

2.5. Legal Considerations

Unfortunately, tests cannot be designed or developed independent of legal considerations. Precedent-setting cases like *Debra P. v. Turlington* (1979/1981/1983/1984) have had an impact on test-development practice and therefore must be considered in the development process. Although these and other legal issues are addressed in far more detail in the chapter by Phillips and Camara (this volume), two legal issues are highlighted here because of their implications for the test design and development process.

2.5.1. Curricular Validity

In 1976, the Florida Functional Literacy Examination was legislated as the state graduation test. Those students who did not pass the test were to receive a certificate of high school completion instead of a diploma. After the first test administration, approximately 2% of Caucasian students failed, compared to 20% of African Americans. A suit was brought in the name of Debra P. alleging that the test was racially biased, given without effective notice, and designed to resegregate African Americans into remedial classes. One of the many issues in the case was whether the test measured what was mandated by the curriculum and what teachers believed should be taught. In effect, the plaintiff asserted that if students have not been taught what the test measures, then these students have been denied a fair opportunity to learn. The judge ruled that the test was shown to have evidence of curricular validity and was aligned with the curriculum.

The ruling in this case highlights the importance of gathering adequate content-related evidence of validity to support the alignment among test philosophy, test purpose, the domain measured by the test, the curriculum on which it is based, the adequacy of the test as a sample from that domain, and the inferences to be made from the test scores. To the extent that a new test designed to induce changes in curriculum and instruction is used for high-stakes purposes, there is a danger that the new test will lack the validation evidence that the law requires. The lesson for the test developer is clear: high-stakes tests, particularly statewide assessments, need to be supported by content-related validity evidence that supports the defined domain as being representative of the important aspects of the curriculum being taught (Phillips, 1993) and the test as a representative sample from that domain.

2.5.2. Adequate Notice

Another legal issue raised in *Debra P. v. Turlington* was whether adequate notice was provided to schools to align their curriculum and instruction to the domain covered by the new high-stakes test. The court ruled that the one-year notice that the state had given the schools was insufficient, and the court enjoined the state from imposing the test requirement for a total of four years. The need for adequate notice is especially important for test developers who are designing new high-stakes tests to be administered in states that have adopted new standards or revised their standards. Adequate notice ensures that there is sufficient time provided to communicate curriculum changes and reflect them in instruction prior to the first test administration.

2.6. Validity Evidence Foundation for Test Design

A reasonable question to ask at the outset of any discussion about test design and development is what should constitute content-related evidence of validity for the knowledge and skills to be measured by an educational achievement test. Mislevy, Steinberg, and Almond (2002) have proposed one such approach, a formal evidentiary framework linking features of the task to the knowledge, skills, and abilities being measured. No matter which approach is used in test design, several important questions must be answered: What evidence is sufficient for solid test design? Should that evidence be based on test developer judgment? Content of popular textbooks? Judgment of teachers and curriculum specialists serving on a test design committee? Or more comprehensive surveys of curriculum? How do we, as developers, evaluate the most effective sources of information to be used in the test design and development process? Figure 9.1 illustrates the continuum of content-related evidence of validity that might be gathered to support the test domain, ranging from subjective opinion to more objective empirical evidence.

Licensure, certification, and employment testing have a rich history of using empirical methods to define the domain to be measured by the test, including job analysis techniques, critical incident techniques, and task analyses. A 1993 document developed by the Council on Licensure, Enforcement, and Regulation (CLEAR) states,

> An examination used in credentialing plays a major role in the protection of the public from incompetent practitioners. It also plays a critical role in protecting the state and the credentialing board itself from the liability associated with failing to license a competent practitioner. The validity of a credentialing examination depends upon two key criteria:
>
> 1. The examination must measure competencies required for safe and effective entry-level job performance.
> 2. The examination must distinguish between candidates who do and do not possess those competencies.
>
> The first of these criteria is met by establishing a link between the questions on the examination and the tasks essential to public safety that are actually performed on the job. This linkage is initially established through a job analysis and maintained by ensuring that all test forms are developed consistently with a test plan that accurately reflects the results of the job analysis. (p. 2)

Guion (1977) identified five conditions that he considered necessary for a measure to be accepted on the basis of its content:

1. the content domain must be rooted in behavior with a generally accepted meaning;
2. the content domain must be defined unambiguously;
3. the content domain must be relevant to the purposes of measurement;
4. qualified judges must agree that the domain has been adequately sampled; and
5. the content of the responses must be reliably observed and evaluated.

In this article, Guion is arguing for a well-defined domain that is relevant to test purpose and to meaningful behaviors. He also emphasizes the importance of adequately sampling the domain in an assessment and the need for systematic scoring approaches that lead to reliable test scores.

Unfortunately, there have been few adaptations of the methodologies frequently used in licensure, certification, and employment testing in K-16 educational testing. In fact, it is not uncommon to find in the technical manuals of widely used standardized grade-level tests that the test domain has been defined by a synthesis of subjective reviews of textbooks, state standards, and curricular frameworks. However, it is not clear how the information synthesized from multiple sources has been translated into test specifications except through judgment and opinion. Should we not seek more objective ways of defining the domains to be measured by these tests?

Perhaps there are lessons developers might learn from the licensure and certification field that can objectify the definition of the domain to be measured by achievement tests. For instance, many licensure tests define the par-

FIGURE 9.1 Continuum of Content-Related Evidence of Validity

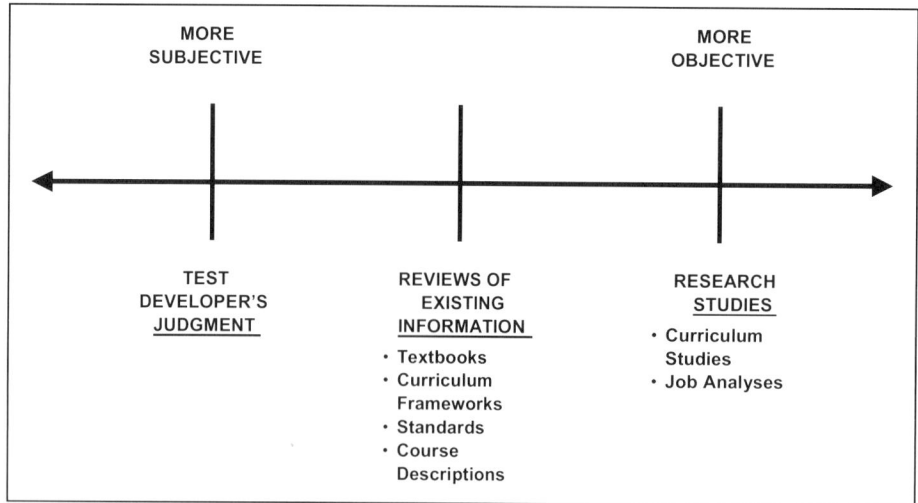

ticular domain by identifying the critical knowledge and skills an entry-level practitioner needs to know to be able to practice safely and competently. Can we define, through more objective means, the important knowledge and skills students need to have in order to be ready to learn at the next educational level? Can we define a college admission test domain by asking professors of entry-level college courses what critical knowledge and skills their entering students need to possess in order to succeed in these entry-level college courses? Can we survey practicing teachers and curriculum specialists in a state to identify those state standards that are the most important priorities for curriculum and instruction—those that are the most important to measure on the statewide high school exit examination?

To do this, developers need to refer to the test-score inferences that were defined at the time the test purposes were established (see Table 9.1). These inferences serve as operational definitions of the populations we might survey to collect more objective content-related evidence of validity. For example, if we were designing a national college algebra placement test that could be used by any college nationwide, we could survey the professors teaching college algebra courses in a representative sample of U.S. postsecondary institutions to define what they think their entering students need to know and be able to do to be ready to learn in their college algebra courses. Recognizing that not all college algebra courses cover the same content or give the same emphasis to course topics, the survey could be sent to a sample of professors at institutions representative of those that would likely use the placement test. By contrast, if we were developing a college algebra placement test for a particular college, we could survey the professors at that particular institution. By collecting information about what students need to know and its relative importance upon entering a course, we have useful evidence upon which to base the definition of the test domain.

It is important that the data sample be sufficiently large and representative of the target audiences so that the evidence gathered is sound. Developers should not be satisfied with test domains defined by one individual as evidence for tests designed to make educational decisions about students; this is neither sufficiently large nor sufficiently representative to be reliable. The way in which the data are collected must be driven by the inferences to be made on the basis of the test scores. If the inference to be made pertains to a specific test use in a defined context, the validity evidence needed will be less demanding than if the inference is to pertain to broader uses of the test in more variable contexts. Once again, test purpose and test-score inferences drive the nature of the empirical validity evidence to be collected. Ultimately, the connection among test philosophy and purpose, test-score inferences to be made, and the evidence gathered constitutes the validation process for the test domain.

One of the major struggles with current state efforts to develop standards-based assessments is the large number of standards that most of the states have adopted and the need to align content standards with curriculum and statewide assessments. There are many issues in alignment, stemming from the wide variation in the specificity and clarity of state standards in defining what students need to know and be able to do, an imbalance between the number of standards and the testing time available, the lack of evidence about how the standards are being interpreted in classroom instruction, and the lack of agreement about the relative importance of the standards and the emphasis each receives in the statewide assessment. Several methods for evaluating alignment have been developed in recent years (Bhola, Impara, & Buckendahl, 2003; Rothman, Slattery, Vranek, & Resnick, 2002; Webb, 1999). Using empirical validation strategies that focus on alignment can help identify, through more objective means, those standards that are the most important priorities for teaching, learning, and testing. When defined in this way, state tests can provide valuable feedback about their students' progress in meeting the most important standards that has instructional utility for classroom teachers.

2.7. Test Specifications

With several of the overall factors affecting test design considered, the next logical step in test design is to specify the important attributes of the items, test forms and item pools, and test delivery. Test specifications are often called blueprints because they specify how the test or pool is to be constructed. Just as an architect's specifications for a building dictate whether the content is wood or steel, the form ranch or skyscraper, and the functional requirements include resistance to hurricanes or imperviousness to earthquake, so also do the specifications for a test form or pool describe its content, form, and functional requirements. Although test developers use different concepts than architects—history may be the content, constructed response may be the form, and a certain targeted statistical distribution may be a functional requirement—the purpose of specifications is the same: to provide direction for construction. Derived directly from test philosophy, test purpose and use, test audience, and empirical validity evidence gathered for the test, test specifications delineate the requirements for the subsequent stages of development, review, field testing, assembly, and evaluation of the end product.

2.7.1. Test Content and Skills

Defining test purposes, uses, and the criteria for test-score inferences provides a broad definition of the test domain: for example, to measure the achievement of students after taking a high school chemistry course or to diagnose strengths and weaknesses in reading. The empirical validity methods described earlier provide the framework through which a more detailed definition of the test domain can be derived. The following five characteristics of the test domain can be used to structure how empirical content-related evidence of validity may be collected and summarized.

2.7.1.1. Sources of Validity Evidence

The domains to which test-score inferences are to be made serve as examples of the sources of validity evidence that can be used to define the test specifications. For example, for a *statewide* end-of-course geometry test, developers would want first to refer to the state curriculum (course) standards describing the intended student outcomes for the course. Since state standards have typically been developed to serve many purposes, they are often not stated in language that can be directly translated into test specifications. More often than not, there are more standards to be measured than there is testing time, without an indication of those that are more important than others.

In this example, we could use an empirical survey to gather information from a representative sample of high school teachers who teach geometry in the state about the standards, topics, and skills taught; the relative importance of the standards, topics, and skills; and those standards and topics that are most important for students to have learned in the course. We could use the results from this survey to identify the important content standards to be measured by the test, and we could establish the relative emphasis each standard should receive in the test through the importance data we collect from the teachers. An additional benefit of this type of approach is that it allows developers to compare the survey results with the state standards and curriculum frameworks, which can lend important insights into how closely the standards are being reflected in instruction.

In addition to the survey data, other instructional materials such as course objectives, syllabi, and assignments can provide useful insights into how the course is being taught, but the synthesis of this information is more subjective and difficult given the variability of instructional approaches taken.

If developers were defining the domain for a *national* end-of-course test in geometry, they would want to survey a nationally representative sample of high school teachers teaching the particular geometry course, asking them to identify what they are teaching in their courses, the relative importance of what they are teaching, and the knowledge and skills they believe are most important for students to have attained when they complete the course.

As is true in any survey research, it is important to make sure that the survey sample is representative of the major attributes of the target population that will take the test and use the results. These attributes would include geographical representation, institutional characteristics (e.g., type of school, size of school), and other relevant socioeconomic factors that should be represented in the sample.

2.7.1.2. Content Domain

The empirical methods described above can be used to define the content topics to be included in the domain measured by a test. The ideal level of specificity of content topics in test specifications is that which ensures adequate control of all crucial elements of the content domain based on the purpose of the test. For instance, a test developed under the single specification "reading" would contain items measuring reading skills in unspecified proportions across unspecified types of reading materials with no assurance that any particular type of reading skill, such as understanding the main idea of a passage, would be tested. The result of this lack of specificity would inevitably be that no two forms of the test would be parallel to each other, and the test scores derived from these forms would not be comparable in meaning. To ensure that particular content topics will be included in the test, they need to be explicitly included in the test specifications.

In defining the content domain, the test developer must understand the structure of the content domain, how topics within the domain relate to each other, and how students build their knowledge over time. For example, mathematics has a hierarchical structure, with students usually developing a sense of whole numbers before they tackle rational numbers. English/language arts is less hierarchical, with students using the same skills but with increasing sophistication. For example, students broaden their vocabulary, use more complex sentence structures, and learn to convey their thoughts in more analytical frameworks over time. Test developers need to understand how these content domains are structured and take these structures into account when specifying the content domain.

The type of test being designed also influences how the content domain is defined. Survey achievement tests, such as end-of-course tests, are designed to cover a broad range of content. These tests may define the domain in more breadth than depth. Diagnostic tests, by contrast, may focus in depth on identifying particular content topics with which students are having difficulty, so the content domain will likely be narrower, focusing on fine distinctions in achievement.

In computer-based tests, how items will be selected for administration to examinees is a factor affecting test blueprint design. Item selection algorithms used in computer-based tests are likely to be predicated on certain assumptions about test content, quantitative attributes of items, and inter-item dependencies (Veldkamp & van der Linden, 1999). For example, if the test is to determine student mastery or nonmastery of specific standards in a particular subject matter area, the item-selection algorithm will need to administer sufficient numbers and types of items associated with each content standard so that sound decisions about mastery can be made. The considerations involved in item pool assembly for computerized tests are addressed in greater depth in the chapter by Drasgow et al. (this volume), but they are mentioned here because of the impact the item-selection algorithm has on defining the content domain, designing the item pool, and assembling the test pool.

2.7.1.3. Cognitive Skills

It is equally important to specify the cognitive requirements of the items in the test. The cognitive requirements are the critical thinking skills students have been taught to use within the context of the content domain. There are many cognitive taxonomies that have been developed, with Bloom's taxonomy (Bloom, Engelhart, Furst, Hill, & Kratwohl, 1956) being one of the best known. Each of these taxonomies defines what it is that students are expected to be able to "do" with what they have learned.

Unfortunately, no current cognitive taxonomy seems to be supported by documented validation evidence. Thus, developers must continue to use logical and empirical methods that allow us to gather data from teachers about the skills that are most important in a particular context. But we also must remember that examinees do not reveal the cognitive skills they used to answer a test item, and we cannot presume to know what skills they used because we don't know their instructional history. Because of this, we must infer the cognitive skill path to a response and classify the item accordingly. In reality, we have no direct knowledge that this is the cognitive path invoked by the item, even by a majority of the test takers. Thus, this type of classification of test items is not merely logical and empirical in nature, it is also inferred by the test developer.

When we design the test specifications, we need to identify the skills pertinent to the content domain and the proportion of items measuring each skill within each major content topic area to be included in the test based on the best empirical data we can gather. The same empirical approach used to define the content domain to be measured by the test can be used to define the cognitive dimensions. The survey can collect information related to the skills students are expected to achieve, the relative importance of these skills overall, and the distribution of these skills across the content domains. This latter information can be used to determine the distribution of items across the cognitive skills and topics. But since we have no way of empirically determining what students are actually doing when they respond to an item, this survey is at best a definition of what students *ought* to be doing.

2.7.1.4. Distribution of Content and Cognitive Skills

Each content topic and cognitive skill needs to have a weight assigned to it in the test specifications that represents the relative emphasis to be placed on the topic or skill in a test form or item pool. Judgments about the emphases to be assigned to content topics and skills can be based on the survey data pertaining to what is actually being taught, or emphasis can be assigned based on a definition of what should be taught as defined by state standards or curriculum frameworks with importance defined through empirical surveys. If the distributions of content and cognitive skills are not specified, test forms will vary widely in their composition and the test scores resulting from multiple test forms will not have comparable meaning. One could conceive of a test with no cognitive specifications that could include only items measuring the rote memorization of information instead of the desired application of that knowledge. Ideally, the weights assigned to both content topics and skills should be based on empirical data collected in a systematic way.

Table 9.2 provides an excerpt from the content and cognitive skill specifications for a national end-of-course test for a college counseling course intended for college sophomores. The purpose of the test is to assess student attainment of the knowledge and skills taught in the course. The data reported in this table were derived from a national survey of college professors who teach this course and reflect the relative importance of the content topics and cognitive skills in the defined domain. Note that, in this example, two cognitive skills were identified as important for students to demonstrate:

1. Comprehension: Students' ability to understand facts, concepts, reasons, relationships, principles, and definitions; to translate words, symbols, formulas and graphs; and to identify procedural errors and inconsistencies in practice.
2. Application: Students' ability to select and apply appropriate principles and rules, analyze situations, interpret situations and draw conclusions, and diagnose needs or problems.

The weights applied to the cognitive categories within content topics cannot exceed the weights assigned to the content topics. Since the skills are applied to the content, the percentages summed across cognitive skill levels must equal the percentage assigned to the respective content topic.

TABLE 9.2 Excerpted Test Content and Cognitive Skill Specifications

		Content Weight	Cognitive Level Weight	
			Comprehension	Application
I.	**Foundations of Counseling**			
	A. Models of counseling	1%	1%	0%
	B. Purpose and objectives of counseling	2%	1%	1%
	C. Ethical and legal considerations	2%	1%	1%
	D. The counseling team	1%	1%	0%
	Category Total	**6%**	**4%**	**2%**
II.	**Individual Counseling**			
	A. Goals of counseling	2%	1%	1%
	B. Theories of counseling	5%	2%	3%
	1. Psychoanalytic	(1%)	(1%)	(0%)
	2. Trait and factor	(1%)	(0%)	(1%)
	3. Client centered	(1%)	(1%)	(0%)
	4. Gestalt	(1%)	(0%)	(1%)
	5. Behavioral	(1%)	(0%)	(1%)
	C. Counseling skills	7%	1%	6%
	D. Process of counseling	6%	1%	5%
	Category Total	**20%**	**5%**	**15%**
III.	**Group Counseling**			
	A. Functions of a group leader	8%	3%	5%
	1. Organizing the group	(2%)	(1%)	(1%)
	2. Facilitating the group	(2%)	(1%)	(1%)
	3. Guidelines for group interaction	(2%)	(1%)	(1%)
	4. Mobilizing group process	(2%)	(0%)	(2%)
	B. Advantages and limitations	2%	2%	0%
	Category Total	**10%**	**5%**	**5%**
IV.	**Career Development**			
	A. Career development theories	6%	3%	3%
	1. Trait and factor	(1%)	(1%)	(0%)
	2. Roe's theory	(1%)	(1%)	(0%)
	3. Holland's theory	(1%)	(1%)	(0%)
	4. Ginzberg's theory	(1%)	(0%)	(1%)
	5. Super's theory	(1%)	(0%)	(1%)
	6. Decision theory	(1%)	(0%)	(1%)
	B. Career counseling information	14%	10%	4%
	1. Delivery systems	(3%)	(3%)	(0%)
	2. Types of information	(3%)	(3%)	(0%)
	3. Sources of information	(4%)	(3%)	(1%)
	4. Evaluating and selecting information	(4%)	(1%)	(3%)
	Category Total	**20%**	**13%**	**7%**
		…	…	…
	Test Total	**100%**	**42%**	**58%**

2.7.1.5. Test Scores

It is important to consider the nature of the test scores that are likely to be reported, in particular whether norm-referenced, domain-referenced, or both types of interpretations will be provided. Domain-referenced interpretations report performance in terms of content and skills domains, and norm-referenced interpretations report interpretation relative to the performance of an identified norm group of students. Some tests are designed to provide both types of interpretations. This requires a careful balancing of testing time, depth or breadth of the domain covered, number of items in the test, and the relative importance of the topics and skills. For instance, there may be items included to support domain-referenced interpretation that would not normally appear on a test from which only norm-referenced interpretations are made and vice versa.

If the test is to report several scores in addition to a total score, it is important that the content and skill dimensions that comprise each of the scores be adequately represented in the test specifications to produce reliable scores that support the intended interpretations. This relates to the dimensionality of the content to be included in the test. Dimensionality refers to the conceptual homogeneity or heterogeneity of the content being measured. If the content is unidimensional, often a single test score derived from a relatively homogeneous set of items is reported. Multidimensional content often results in longer tests from which multiple test scores are reported, each derived from different sets of items. Tests that are more homogeneous are not necessarily easier or simpler in what they are measuring, because they may be measuring the same complexities uniformly across test items. If multidimensional tests report a single composite score to summarize overall achievement, it is important that the composite score reflect the appropriate weightings of the major important dimensions of the test.

Ultimately, the content and skills covered by each score need to be defined in sufficient detail that they can be replicated in parallel forms. This is necessary to ensure that the scores have comparable meaning and characteristics from test form to test form. Jarjoura and Brennan (1983) provide an analysis of issues associated with test scores derived from test specifications.

2.7.2. Item Types

Following the specification of test content and cognitive skills, the next aspect of the test specifications involves identifying the type(s) of items to be developed. At this point, the test developer needs to define the item format features that are required by the content and skills specifications, specify the item types that possess those features, and comparatively evaluate each item type to identify those that might be preferred for reasons of coverage, economy, precision, response time, development and scoring costs, delivery constraints, or feasibility.

The primary concern at this point is to identify the item types that will meet the content and skill specifications and that are administrable through the test delivery platform. More than one item type might be needed if the content and skill specifications are multifaceted. It is also important to determine which item types will generate appropriate samples of student achievement within the time and delivery constraints. The matching of item type to the test domain can conflict with other constraints such as scoring ease, reliability targets, or development time, but above all the test developer needs to promote the item types that are most consistent with and are likely to provide the best measures of content and skill test specifications.

In the 1980s and 1990s, there was much debate in the measurement profession about whether the selected-response or constructed-response item format is inherently better at measuring student achievement. Critics of the selected-response item format argued that only constructed-response items can measure higher-order thinking skills and that the multiple-choice item format is too vulnerable to guessing. Critics of the constructed-response format argued that the format narrows the scope of the test since only a few items can be administered in a particular period of time. They also argued that the scoring of the items is not only subjective, but expensive. Fortunately, as the profession gathered more evidence on the performance of constructed-response items, it was soon recognized that the content and skills to be measured should drive the choice of item type and that, although selected-response items were significantly more efficient in the amount of information they gathered per unit of time, constructed-response items could add a performance dimension to the score and could be scored reliably, although not as inexpensively as selected-response items. With more evidence, researchers showed that both item types could measure higher-order thinking skills (Martinez, 1999), and that while both formats tended to be highly correlated when developed to measure the same domain of knowledge and skills (DeMars, 2000), each format could offer unique insights into student achievement.

In addition to specifying the item type, the test developer also needs to define the characteristics of stimulus materials that will be used to establish the context for the items. For example, a reading test is likely to include a range of textual types and lengths. The item specifications need to define the length, density, complexity, and subject matter of these materials. Similarly, if a test measures students' ability to read and interpret information in charts and graphs, the nature and complexity of the charts and graphs need to be defined.

The nature of an item format has direct implications for the skills that can be measured. For example, a single-sentence format within which students are to identify and correct errors in English grammar cannot measure organizational skills that involve either multiple sentences within a paragraph or multiple paragraphs within a larger passage. Similarly, a short reading passage is limited in its potential to measure higher-order critical reading skills involving analysis of arguments and multiple perspectives. All aspects of the content and skill domains need to be considered in selecting item formats.

Finally, the test developer must consider how the item format, including stimulus materials, will be affected by the delivery platform. If the test is to be delivered on computer, the developer needs to consider how the screen resolution, navigational interface, and screen layout will work with the item formats. Some formats that work well on paper may be more difficult for students to negotiate on computer. For example, an item set in science could present a fairly long description of a number of experiments accompanied by several charts and graphs displaying the results of the experiments. This stimulus could then be followed by a series of items. When displayed in a test booklet, the entire item set can be printed on adjoining pages, but on computer the student needs to scroll through the passage while keeping track of the location of the charts and graphs. The amount of juggling and navigating that students have to do when taking items on computer must be considered when item types are selected.

2.7.3. Test Length

The next substantive consideration under the category of item specifications is test length. The optimum test length is one that is brief enough to be acceptable to those who will use the results and accurate enough to support the inferences that will be made on the basis of the test results. Test length is a function of many concerns, most of which have been described. The strongest determiner of test length is the practical constraint of testing time. The relative emphasis attributed to the content topics and to the cognitive skills across content topics can be derived from the importance ratings of the respondents to the content survey. From the data, emphases can be expressed in terms of percentages of test content (or skills) to be included in the test. Starting with the relative emphases assigned to the major categories, the percentages within categories can be distributed across the important topics or skills in each category based on the survey responses. These percentages can be converted into numbers of items in the test once the total test length has been determined.

Millman and Greene (1989) state: "As a prerequisite to overall test validity, this distribution [of test items across the content domain] should match the relevant domain conceptualization. In practice, this match is accomplished by allocating test items among content components and by weighting schemes applied during test scoring" (p. 342). Both of these approaches are important to ensure that the distribution of test items across the domain will support the inferences to be made from the test scores.

Test length is also affected by the item formats selected for use. If the test developer has no evidence about the average response time for each format to be used, a special research study estimating response time might be necessary. Unless it is relevant to the purpose of the test to measure speed of response, a power test should be planned. That is, there should be sufficient time for most examinees to consider all items. Otherwise the test developer runs the risk of assembling a test that may be highly speeded, resulting in test scores that are related to the speed of test taking rather than to actual achievement. There are several operational definitions of speededness with no single definition universally accepted; most experts would likely agree that the clear majority of examinees should have reached and attempted 90% or more of the items in a test.

Optimum test length finds a balance among competing demands: available administration time, examinee characteristics, scores to be reported, content domain to be covered, cognitive skills to be measured, item formats selected, and target reliability for the reported scores. Constraints on administration time limit the number of items that can be administered (see van der Linden's [2005] approach using linear programming). The age of the examinees can affect how long examinees can reasonably be expected to focus on the test. The number and nature of the scores reported affect test length, particularly in assuring that the test produces scores that meet acceptable standards for reliability. The domain of content topics to be covered and cognitive skills to be measured also affect test length and in many cases the test domain must be prioritized to measure the knowledge and skills judged to be most important by the relevant test audiences. The emphases gathered through empirical survey data can serve as the basis for distributing items across these domains.

2.7.4. Item Scoring

The scoring of many paper-and-pencil multiple-choice tests has historically been fairly straightforward: items have one correct response and are scored dichotomously (1 point for correct answer, 0 points for incorrect answer) with the total raw score equaling the sum of the correct responses. This model becomes slightly more complicated when a correction for guessing is used, which subtracts an additional fractional amount from the total raw score for incorrect responses.

Yet for some types of delivery platforms and types of items, the scoring procedures have necessarily become more complex. For example, in computerized adaptive testing, item response theory is used to derive test scores from item-based calibrated estimates of examinee ability. In constructed-response items, the examinee responses are evaluated according to a rubric wherein each score point is defined. These are only two examples of the many models for item scoring that are in use today, a few of which are briefly described below.

2.7.4.1. Partial Credit Scoring

The use of partial credit scoring can be particularly informative in tests designed to diagnose examinee strengths and weaknesses for the purposes of informing instruction. Partial credit scoring models allocate points to an item response based on the degree of completeness or accuracy of that response. Guttman (1941) proposed a type of partial scoring based on differential weighting of selected-response item options. Partial credit scoring approaches attempt to obtain more information from each item than is obtained by more traditional dichotomous scoring. Haladyna (1985) reviewed the methods and reported the results of a study of option weighting on decision reliability. The test developer needs to consider whether to allow for partial credit in item response scoring early in the test-design process so that items can be written to conform to the format and style needed to compute these scores.

2.7.4.2. Performance Scoring

The scoring of constructed-response items, or performance assessment items, is usually based on detailed scoring rubrics that define the types of scores to be reported and the scales to be used to assign these scores. Although performance assessment is treated in far more detail in the chapter by Lane and Stone (this volume), there are at least two major approaches to scoring constructed-response items with many variations of each. The first is often called analytic scoring, which involves scoring a response on several dimensions each of which has its own scoring rubric. Total scores are often derived as combinations of the analytic scores. Analytic scoring is frequently used when the content and skills are multidimensional and/or when more detailed, diagnostic information might be needed about an examinee's performance. The second type of scoring is often referred to as holistic scoring. This type of scoring is frequently used when the content and skills are more unidimensional. A single rubric is used to score the responses and a single score is assigned. In both types of scoring, it is important that the rubrics be directly tied to the test specifications and focus on the most important dimensions of content and skills defined in the specifications. Again, it is important to consider the implications of the scoring model in the test design phase to ensure that the item-development process takes into account, before the items are written, the subtle yet critical implications of how the items are scored.

2.7.4.3. Test Item Weighting

Since an individual item's contribution to the total score varies according to its item parameters (such as item discrimination), it is important for the test developer to determine whether the actual weighting of any particular component of the test should be controlled through external weighting or left to vary depending on item performance. For example, in a multidimensional test, the content categories containing the more discriminating items will receive more weight in determining unweighted total scores than other content categories. If the test developer believes that this could result in scores that are not representative of the intended specifications, then the developer may well want to consider assigning a nominal item weight to each content category to ensure that the most important content categories receive the intended weight in the total score.

2.7.4.4. Performance Standards

In tests having performance standards, or passing scores, the test developer must consider whether to set standards based on subcomponents of the test specifications or on the test as a whole. Particularly when tests are being used for high-stakes decisions, the test developer must carefully analyze the impact of various approaches to setting standards. For instance, if a statewide assessment has graduated performance standards representing increasing levels of proficiency (e.g., basic, proficient, and advanced), the test developer needs to consider how items will be designed to measure increasingly more sophisticated proficiency within the same test. Or, a test may require examinees to meet or exceed multiple performance standards within the same test, that is, show proficiency in each of several content areas (e.g., adding one- and two-digit numbers, subtracting one- and two-digit numbers). In this case, the test developer needs to determine whether the scores on each part will be compensatory (allow stronger performance in an area to compensate for a weaker performance in another area). This topic is addressed in considerable detail in the chapter by Hambleton and Pitoniak (this volume), but is mentioned here because the developer must consider how the test specifications should address these issues to make sure that the test accommodates the intended scoring scheme.

2.7.4.5. Instructional Sensitivity

In education, one of the critical roles of measurement is to determine what examinees have learned as well as what they are ready to learn next. Developers study the patterns of change from grade to grade, from one age to another, and from before instruction to after instruction. Ideally, one would expect that before instruction all examinees would perform at the lower end of the score scale and after instruction they would perform at the upper end of the score scale. In reality, there is wide variation in the knowledge and skills students bring to the classroom, and there are many intervening factors that affect measurement. So the ideal is rarely seen.

Nevertheless, the concept of instructional sensitivity is important in test development when a test is intended to measure increases in achievement presumed to be tied to instruction. The simplest case of instructional sensitivity is the pre-/posttest model, whereby a teacher measures the level of student proficiency before instruction and again after instruction. One assumes that any increases in achievement are primarily the result of instruction. Haladyna and Roid (1981) examined a set of instructional-sensitivity indices and found a high degree of similarity among them. However, when grade-level tests and other achievement tests are being constructed based on a theory of growth, it is important that the items be constructed, analyzed, and evaluated according to how well they differentiate students who have learned the materials from those who have not. The chapters by Ferrara and DeMauro, Shepard, and Kolen in this volume address the issue of growth in achievement in greater detail.

2.7.5. Test Form Specifications

In addition to item specifications, the test developer must consider the specifications for the test(s) as a whole. This includes consideration of statistical specifications, distribution of content and skills across the test form, test organization, administrative plan, and special accommodations.

2.7.5.1. Statistical Specifications

The test developer must address the statistical characteristics of the items in the test forms (or item pools, if the test is to be administered via computer). Target distributions of item difficulty and discrimination can be identified for the test, as can target test information functions and exposure control functions if the test is to be administered as a computerized adaptive test. In classical theory, item *difficulty* is often computed as the proportion of examinees answering a question correctly, and item *discrimination* is computed as the correlation between the score on an item and some criterion, which may be the total test score, a subscore, or an external test score. There are parallel item difficulty and item discrimination parameters in item response theory. Test information functions identify the point along an ability continuum at which maximum information about examinee ability is achieved, and item exposure rates establish the limits within which items can be exposed through administration.

As with all other aspects of the test specifications, statistical specifications for tests depend on test purpose. Norm-referenced grade-level tests will likely specify statistical distributions that will maximize the discrimination between grade levels and/or age-groups. For many achievement tests, such as mastery tests, end-of-course tests, and diagnostic tests having very well-defined content and skills specifications, the statistical specifications are likely to be subordinated in importance to the content and skills specifications.

Many state assessments currently classify student performance into several different performance levels, such as basic, proficient, and advanced. In these instances, it is important that there are enough items in these ranges to differentiate student performance effectively. This means that the test developer needs to make sure that the test forms and item pools include items measuring content and skills that help to differentiate adjacent performance levels.

In computerized adaptive testing, it is important that the characteristics of the item pool reflect test purposes and uses. If the test is being used for admission decisions, the item pool will need to contain sufficient items across the specified content and skills domain with information functions across a broad range of ability, assuming that the institutions using the test scores also reflect varying admission requirements. The pool also needs to contain enough depth within content and skills categories to facilitate control of item exposure and help ensure item pool security, an issue that is discussed in the chapter by Drasgow et al. (this volume). For high-stakes computerized adaptive tests, current practice suggests creating item pools that are 15 to 20 times the length of the typical adaptive test. For low-stakes computerized adaptive tests, the size of the item pool can be much smaller, between 4 and 6 times the length of the typical test.

Overall, one would also expect particular statistical relationships to exist between and among the tests in a test battery. For instance, one would usually expect higher average intercorrelations among items contained in the same test than between items contained in different tests. Similarly, one would usually expect higher average intercorrelations between the tests having related content and skills domains (such as English usage and reading) than tests having less related content domains (such as reading and mathematics). If the reverse occurs, this can be valuable information to evaluate the test specifications. In this case, developers might want to examine the mathematics test to determine if the reading load is excessive. Further discussion of the role of statistical item characteristics is provided later in this chapter when test evaluation is addressed.

2.7.5.2. Test Form Content and Skills

The earlier stages of test design focused on preparing detailed specifications for each test being developed. Once those specifications have been developed, it is worthwhile to identify any specifications pertaining to content and skills for the test as a whole. If a test battery consists of several tests, it is possible that the test developer could meet the specifications for each test but end up with a total test that has several passages that focus on the same topic. For instance, an English test could measure usage skills within the context of a passage on baseball. In the same test form, a passage in the reading test could also focus on the subject of baseball. Although the subject matter of the passages is not the focus of what is being measured in either test, there may well be an overemphasis on baseball across passages. So the test form specifications should specify how the subject matter of stimulus materials should be distributed across subtests as well as include any specifications for balancing topics of interest by examinee gender, culture, or interests.

It is also possible that more than one test in a test battery might include specifications for the same skills. For instance, understanding and interpreting charts and graphs might be included in a mathematics test, a reading test, and a science test. It is important to examine the test specifications as a whole to ensure that the total emphasis of these skills is appropriate across tests and whether there are different dimensions of these skills to be measured in each test. In this case, the specifications for the battery will need to be very specific about the content and skills to be measured in each test such that each test is fully distinct from the others.

2.7.5.3. Test Organization

Test specifications should include guidelines for how the test is to be organized. The first basic question is whether the test will be presented to examinees as a single unit or in two or more parts, forms, or versions. This decision takes into consideration test content, test length, and test administration time. For example, if a test consists of several separately timed parts, the test may be assembled into one booklet or several booklets. How the test is administered can help determine how the test should be packaged. Separate test administration periods with intervening time periods may make separate booklets easier to manage rather than trying to redistribute the examinees' original test booklets. Other considerations that may affect test organization are the age of the examinees and test security. The younger the student, the shorter the administration periods will likely need to be. If the test developer is concerned about examinee cheating, it may be advantageous to prepare several different test booklets, each containing a version of the test that differs in item sequencing (i.e., scrambled forms, provided that there are no significant differences in performance due to scrambling). Another strategy would feature a common core of items administered to all examinees with each of several variable item sets in a different booklet.

Similar questions about the organization of a computer-based test need to be answered. For instance, the test developer needs to specify the order of testing events as they will be presented on computer to the examinees: login, presentation of demographics, tutorial on navigation, test directions, and test timing. Most, if not all, computer-based tests include a short tutorial describing how examinees are to navigate through the test, how they are to record their answers, and how they can return to items they want to reconsider (if permitted).

Within tests, the essential consideration in item ordering is to minimize factors extraneous to those being measured, such as the number of cognitive shifts the examinees have to make as they move through the test. The goal is to maximize the time examinees spend considering item content and minimize the time necessary to orient themselves to item or test format. For this reason, it is difficult to find a rationale for randomly ordering items in a test. Random ordering requires the examinees to manage the cognitive shifting process on an item-by-item basis when there is likely to be at least one organizing feature of the test (e.g., item format, content, difficulty) that can make test administration for the examinees easier.

The important consideration in test organization is that different item groupings and sequences can influence the psychometric properties of the test. For that reason, once a test-organization approach is selected, it should be consistently applied across parallel test forms and test pools.

Four methods of ordering items within a test are described briefly below.

2.7.5.3.1. CONTENT GROUPING

A logical approach is to group together items with similar content. While this approach helps to reduce the cognitive shifting problem associated with random ordering, it can also provide contextual clues to correct answers, a process known as clueing. For example, grouping together word problems in mathematics may enable students to identify appropriate algorithms for solution when they might not otherwise have been able to do so. This is not necessarily inappropriate depending on the purpose of the test, but decisions to group items by content should be deliberate and possible effects anticipated.

2.7.5.3.2. ITEM TYPE GROUPING

Another possible item grouping approach is by item type or format. This approach works well particularly when item formats may need special directions. If different directions are needed, it may be more efficient to group the items by format.

2.7.5.3.3. ORDER BY DIFFICULTY

This approach is often advocated as a way of decreasing examinees' test anxiety and as the preferred approach in timed paper tests when not all items are likely to be completed. Under this approach, discrete items are sequenced in increasing order of difficulty. When several items are associated with a common stimulus, the items may be ordered within item set by difficulty, unless there is a more logical order based on what the items are measuring. Item sets can be ordered within the test by the average difficulty of the items contained in each item set.

2.7.5.3.4. ADAPTIVE ORDERING

If the test is administered as a computerized adaptive test, then the item selection algorithm needs to take into account not only the target precision needed for ability estimation, but also content domain and item ordering constraints.

2.7.5.4. Administrative Plan

The administrative plan will specify how the test is to be administered, including the ordering of preadministration events (such as examinee check-in, completion of the answer sheet, test directions, questions before administration begins), ordering of tests to be administered, breaks, and postadministration events (such as collection of test booklets, answer sheets, accounting for all materials, dismissal). The more standardized the procedures, the more comparable the test results will be for examinees who take the tests in different administrative settings. The administrative plan should also identify the level of security of the test, whether it is nonsecure (e.g., for diagnostic testing) or highly secure (e.g., for statewide assessment), and the procedures should be designed accordingly.

2.7.5.5. Special Accommodations

The test organization specifications should also identify what type of special testing forms need to be prepared. This may include Braille, large type, audiocassette, reader, and special computer screen and keyboard modifications if the test is delivered on computer. The issue of whether these modifications change the constructs being measured, which was considered much earlier, in the design stage, should be reevaluated at this time.

2.7.6. Test Delivery Specifications

A third category of test specifications focuses on test delivery. Through these specifications, the test developer defines how the test will be delivered, the security requirements for test delivery, item disclosure policies, scoring and reporting requirements, and retesting policies. The considerations associated with each of these are briefly described below.

2.7.6.1. Test Delivery Platform

Although test delivery platform has been considered from the earliest stages of test design, it is important that the test specifications include all assumptions about delivery platform, including whether both paper and computer delivery will be offered and under what conditions. This latter specification has test-score scaling and equating implications as well as platform comparability questions that will need to be researched.

In addition to the delivery platform, the test specifications also need to specify the need for multiple parallel forms and the schedule for administration so that examinee exposure to the same form may be controlled. In computer-delivered tests, the specifications need to define how the item pools will be administered to minimize security risks, the schedule for item pool activation and administration, and how examinee exposure to the same item pools will be controlled.

2.7.6.2. Test Delivery Security Requirements

The security requirements for paper and computer delivery of tests are essential components of the test specifications.

These requirements have implications for the number of test forms that need to be developed annually, the number of item pools that need to be assembled and ready for administration annually, and the plans for replacing test forms and item pools should a security breach occur before administration or during a testing period. Specifications for how suspected security breaches are to be addressed before, during, and after testing should be included.

2.7.6.3. Item Disclosure Requirements

One of the policies that governs the test-development process is whether selected test items or the test form as a whole will be disclosed to examinees after administration. Depending on how many paper test forms or computerized items are disclosed in a given period, the item-development process and schedule must be adjusted accordingly.

2.7.6.4. Scoring and Reporting Requirements

The test specifications need to define the scores to be reported, how they will be computed, and how they will be reported. Decisions need to be made early in the test-design process about the type of inferences to be made on the basis of the scores and the type of information to be reported by the scores because they impact the entire test design process. At this point in the test specifications stage, these decisions need to be formalized in the test specifications and supplemental decisions about scoring need to be made. For example, decisions need to be made about whether partial credit will be awarded to responses, whether a correction for guessing will be used to adjust raw scores, how passing scores will be determined, whether one or more composite scores will be computed and if so how, and the approach used to score constructed-response items. Each of these issues is addressed in other chapters in this volume.

Reporting requirements for the results need to be specified. The specifications need to address turnaround time for the results and, in the case of computer-administered tests, whether a provisional score report will be provided at the end of the test administration, followed by an official report provided after score verification.

2.7.6.5. Retesting Policies

The policies governing how often students can retake a test have implications for test security and administration and ultimately on test development. If a testing program has a fairly liberal retesting policy, then the test developer needs to increase the number of unique test forms and item pools produced so that item, form, and pool security can be preserved.

2.8. Reviewing, Refining, and Reaffirming Validity Evidence for Test Design

This test-design process is one that produces very detailed specifications. Good measurement practice demands detailed specifications, particularly for educational achievement tests, for at least four reasons:

1. To the extent the test specifications are well specified, the test forms produced will be far more parallel than they would be if developed from general specifications.
2. By developing detailed specifications, the test developer considers many specifics of the test-development process before that process is begun, thereby resolving many of the issues that will arise during development. By carefully considering the major aspects of the testing process, the test developer can identify inconsistent or conflicting specifications early in the design process.
3. Well-developed test specifications drive the entire item-development and test-assembly process and serve as helpful directions to item writers, reviewers, and test users. If the specifications for the content and skill domains were less precise, the resulting test would not necessarily measure the intended domain; rather, it would reflect the varying interpretations of the various participants in the test-development process. A consistent set of specifications helps to ensure that the resulting tests fulfill their intended purposes and uses.
4. Detailed test specifications drive an open and fair test-development process and encourage more frequent and more detailed communications with the intended test audiences.

Theoretically, the true measure of test specifications is whether two independent test developers would construct identical test forms from the same item pools. See Cronbach (1971) for a discussion of the duplicate construction experiment.

Once the test specifications are assembled, the test developer may wish to convene a panel of external stakeholders to review them. These stakeholders should include the test audiences defined by considerations of test purpose and use as well as subject-matter experts in the domain being measured. The panel should represent a diversity of experience and viewpoints. The purpose of the panel would be to review the test specifications for appropriateness of content, skills, emphasis attributed to each, and relevance for the purposes of the test. The input received should be considered in view of test purpose and use and the test specifications refined accordingly. This is an important early source of validity evidence intended to affirm or refine preliminary test design.

Once the specifications have been reviewed and refined, the item-development process may begin. The test-design process, however, is never really completed. During the item-development process, it is not uncommon to uncover aspects of the test specifications that need adjustment. Revisions in one aspect of the test specifications often lead to revisions in other aspects. Once the test is administered, the test-evaluation process will provide valuable information that can be used to refine the specifications and the development process.

The content-validation process is also ongoing. Evidence supporting the test design should be reaffirmed on a regular basis. If achievement tests are to reflect the curriculum and the expectations of teachers as to what their students need to be ready to learn or what they should have learned, test developers need to engage in a regular process to collect evidence to adjust or reaffirm the test specifications. Test design is at best an iterative process, one that repeatedly cycles through information gleaned through item development, test administration, and evaluation. This continual cycle of improvement keeps achievement tests current, fresh, and connected to the important audiences they serve: students, educators, administrators, and policymakers.

Table 9.3 provides a summary of the essential elements in test and item pool design.

3. ITEM DEVELOPMENT

Sound test development depends on well-defined, defensible item development. Sound item development is critical for providing the quality and consistency necessary to produce reliable test scores upon which validated test-score inferences can be made. This section discusses various considerations in the item-development process, including design of the item-writing process, training of item writers, implementation of item-development and item-review processes, refinement of items, and field testing.

3.1. Considerations for the Item-Development Process

Prior to 1990, the preeminent view of item writing was as a collection of guidelines (Bormuth, 1970; Cronbach, 1971; Nitko, 1985). However, since that time there have been a number of research studies focusing on the effects of particular item-writing practices (Haladyna, 1997; Linn & Gronlund, 1995; Popham, 1997). This body of work indicates that item writing is still very much an iterative process, but it can be undertaken in a standardized manner. Item-development processes need to establish principles and procedures that take into account the various audiences and purposes of the program. The qualifications of the item writers, the representativeness of item writers, and the security of the process are all essential considerations for the item-development process.

The process adopted for developing items in any testing program is critical and must be considered in relation to issues of validity, reliability, and interpretability. Adams (1992) described the steps involved in item development for the Multistate Bar Examination. These steps included inventory and evaluation of an item pool, assignment of new items to be developed, review, edits, content and key checks, and field testing. This process is similar for many large-scale, highly secure testing programs (Haladyna, 1999) and is the process that serves as the basis for the following sections.

3.1.1. Qualifications of Item Writers

The determination of the source of the item content depends upon test purpose and the inferences that need to be made based upon that content. This chapter assumes that the optimum item-writing resource is the educational expert who is knowledgeable about both the specifics of the content as well as the appropriate difficulty level for the intended assessment. The identification of educational experts to assist in this process can be dependent upon political, fiscal, or logistical considerations. However, the ultimate goal is to identify educational experts who can serve as item writers and produce materials that are defined by the test specifications and are of appropriate levels of difficulty.

In a large-scale assessment program there is a need for a systematic process for identifying, selecting, and contacting item writers to expand and renew the pool of potential item writers on a regular basis. In addition, there is the need to maintain a pool of talented and experienced item writers who can be recontacted on a periodic basis, while ensuring that no individual author exercises an undue influence upon the nature of the test items developed.

The ongoing process of item-writer identification and selection may be accomplished according to a specified set of procedures designed to select item writers who meet the particular qualifications and requirements of the testing program. For example, a particular state may want teachers from state to write the items for their assessment program. Or, another state, concerned about the security of the items, may *not* want teachers from their state participating in item production. In this section some of the criteria used to identify item writers are described; these criteria are followed by a description of resources that may be used to identify those item writers and a description of the mechanism by which these item writers may be selected.

The process for identifying those individuals who are qualified to develop items should reflect a concern for the following demographic characteristics: (a) geographic representation of the examinees, (b) representation of the racial/ethnic backgrounds of the examinee population, and (c) representation of the gender backgrounds of the examinee population. If developing an assessment for undergraduate and graduate educational programs, representation of institutions with student populations similar to the examinee population may also be of interest. The viewpoints of each of these constituencies are important to help the assessment accurately measure the knowledge and skills judged to be necessary.

The above criteria for the identification of item writers are intended to reflect the general and institutional characteristics of the entire pool of item writers; however, criteria reflecting the item writer's individual characteristics may also be considered. Such criteria include knowledge of, and training in, the particular subject matter; accomplishments within the particular area of expertise; current teaching responsibilities; and background and experience in writing test items.

3.1.2. Representativeness of Item Writers

To help ensure that the available pool of item writers is appropriate for the development of the items, item writers may be identified in a variety of ways. One approach is a nomination process where item writers come highly recommended by peers and national organizations, thus ensuring the requisite expertise, teaching experience, and organizational activity. A second approach is the recruitment of individuals with the characteristics of interest. For example, teachers with fourth-grade teaching experi-

TABLE 9.3 Essential Elements in Test and Item Pool Design

I. Test Background Requirements
    A. Test philosophy
    B. Test purpose
    C. Use of test scores
    D. Test score inferences
    E. Intended examinee populations
    F. Special test versions/accommodations

II. Administrative Requirements
    A. Testing time
    B. Administrative model
        1. Delivery platform
        2. Group/individual administration
        3. Retesting policies
    C. Cost/payer
    D. Feedback/reporting requirements
    E. Administrative security
        1. Test disclosure requirements
        2. Number of forms/pools needed
    F. Answer sheet/response requirements

III. Legal Requirements
    A. Curricular validity evidence
    B. Adequate notice

IV. Validity Evidence as Foundation of Test
    A. Domain to be measured
    B. Validity evidence design
    C. Evaluation of validity evidence and test improvement

V. Item Specifications
    A. Content and skills
    B. Test scores computed and reported
    C. Item format
        1. Item set requirements
        2. Stimuli requirements
            a. Word length
            b. Use of tables, graphics
            c. Use of copyrighted material
            d. Number of stimuli
            e. Features
        3. Item requirements
            a. Number by item type
            b. Number of alternatives
            c. Use of graphics
            d. Word limit
            e. Item reuse policies
    D. Total Test Requirements
        1. Number of item sets and research items (test length)
        2. Word requirements
        3. Use of tables, graphics, etc.
        4. Timing requirements
        5. Language requirements
        6. Special accommodations
        7. Diversity requirements (gender, subgroup)
        8. Item/test scoring
            a. Item weighting
            b. Partial credit
            c. Reuse of previously administered items/forms/pools
            d. Other features
        9. Statistical requirements (total test score and subscores)
            a. Joint distribution of item difficulty and discrimination
            b. Range, average, and standard deviation of item difficulty (or IRT parallels)
            c. Range, average, and standard deviation of item discrimination (or IRT parallels)
            d. Estimated target reliability and standard error of measurement
            e. Differential item functioning (DIF) requirements
        10. Test organization
            a. Item grouping
            b. Item sequencing
            c. Booklet organization and layout
        11. Pretest design—item requirements, placement
        12. Equating design—item requirements, placement
        13. Other special features

ence in mathematics may be a requirement for a particular testing program. In this case, the minimum requirements for the item writers serve as a basis for the selection process.

Item writers need to reflect widely diverse focuses. The deliberate search for individuals who will contribute diversity to the item-writer pool results in the ability to reflect diversity in developed test materials. One potential benefit of this diversity is the enhancement of fairness to examinees.

Item writers may be drawn from relevant educational levels. Knowledge of the curriculum and of examinee ability levels is mainly derived from actual teaching experience. Knowledge of examinee capabilities also helps item writers to quickly target appropriate levels of difficulty for test materials, an undeniable benefit when developmental time lines are tight.

3.1.3. Security of the Item-Development Process

Item-writing recruitment procedures should be designed to protect the confidentiality of the development process. Item-writer candidates should be asked to submit credentials so that their qualifications can be checked for security purposes. Each item writer should sign an agreement to indicate adherence to the security and confidentiality procedures, particularly in high-security examinations.

The names of all eligible individuals, together with necessary pertinent information about them—such as institutional affiliation, area of expertise, and demographic information—should be maintained in a database. Individuals can then be selected from the database whose areas of expertise fit the needs of the test specifications. To facilitate the tracking of item-writer performance, information about the active writers may also be maintained.

To protect both the security of test materials in development and the confidentiality of item-writer transactions, no item writer should be engaged in item development who has a direct or indirect connection to any test preparation organization that covers the testing program for which they are writing items, nor should any item writer expect in the near future to take the test for which they are writing items. To ensure this independence, all item writers should sign a contract certifying they do not have a direct or indirect connection to any test preparation organization and that they do not intend to be an examinee for the specific testing program for a predetermined period of time.

3.2. Training of Item Writers

The item-writing process is continuous and varies substantially according to the test program and the availability of resources to support this aspect of item development. However, assuming that the test specifications are developed, the move to item-writer training is the next logical step in the item-development process. Regardless of whether the item writing is completed in a workshop setting, via the World Wide Web, or by mail, the training process is an absolutely critical step. The training methods must be of high quality and consistently applied in programs that require periodic or frequent training. If the training process is of poor quality or poorly applied, the quality of the items will suffer and survival rates for the items will be reduced, leading to increased expenses and possibly lower-quality assessments. This section describes the considerations of the item-writer training process. Critical to the success of this process is an opportunity for feedback and substantial opportunities to review and revise items throughout the training and development process.

After the item writers have agreed to develop items, the item-development process should begin with training in the construction of technically sound test items. Because item writing is not an easy skill to master, there should be a systematic process used to train all item writers who are contributing to a particular testing program. However, this process is not the same for all testing programs and may vary according to the item writers' credentials as well as the logistics of the process.

The test specifications, including a description of the system for classifying items by content area and cognitive skill, should form the foundation for the training materials. In addition, samples of exemplary item sets or stand-alone items from all relevant disciplines and a discussion that highlights the positive features of these samples are an integral part of the training materials. The detailed content specifications should usually form the basis for the item-writing assignments. Item writers must be provided with training materials relevant to the particular test for which they will develop items.

As part of the training process, prospective item writers may be asked to submit a work sample. The item-writing sample helps to evaluate the potential of item writers: ability to follow directions, content knowledge, and writing and test-development skills. This sample may be a section of the actual item-writing assignment for that writer and should be based on the instructions provided in the training materials. Evaluation of the sample serves not only as the basis for determining whether to offer a contract to a writer, but also as the basis for offering potentially acceptable writers both general and specific feedback on their first efforts. This feedback is central to item-writer training. Item writers whose work samples show merit should be given the highest priority and asked to develop items immediately. If the item writer fails the eligibility tests, the work sample should be returned to the item writer as the rightful owner. Care should be taken to ensure that the individual and institutional characteristics of the item-writer pool continue to approximate the targeted item-writer criteria.

Once an item writer's sample has been accepted, an item-writing assignment specifying the number and types of items should be developed. Assignments should be based upon the current specifications and needs of the item pool. This procedure helps to ensure that the pool of newly developed items conforms to the test specifications and, because it guarantees that no item writer has access to the test specifications as a whole, acts as another security safeguard. The size of each writer's assignment should be such that the security of the examination is preserved and that no undue burden is placed on any individual item writer. Moreover, assignments should ensure that no individual has an undue influence on the total pool of new items being developed. Security procedures and ownership regulations must be carefully explained to the item writers. Careful steps should be taken throughout the item-development stage of the project to preserve item security.

As a final step in item-writer training, after an item writer has completed and submitted the items designated in the assignment, the materials should be thoroughly reviewed. If they contain flaws, they should be returned to the item writer with a clear description of the nature of the problems and suggestions for remedying them. This second feedback loop helps to ensure the quality of the test items being produced, but also emphasizes and extends the training process.

3.3. Item-Development Process

An item-development plan must be constructed specifying targets for the number of items to be written and field-tested in each content area, format type, and cognitive skill. This plan should be constructed as part of the item-bank evaluation and according to specific needs in the item bank. The plan should consider the types of items (e.g., selected response, constructed response) and how they interact with the type of assessment that is being designed.

3.3.1. Types of Items

As indicated earlier in this chapter, the identification of the type of item to be developed is typically driven by the content and skills specifications. Lindquist (1951) argued that the item type should match the criterion of interest. He indicated that the test developer should make the item format as similar to the criterion format as possible, recognizing the constraints of efficiency, comparability, and economy. In addition to the specifications, the desired psychometric characteristics of the assessment as well as the logistical aspects of the testing program (e.g., turnaround time, available resources, testing time) need to be considered in the selection of the type of item to be developed.

Haladyna (1999) suggests that the appropriate item format is driven by the inference to be made from the item. He divides item formats into the two general categories of multiple-choice (selected response) and performance assessment (constructed response). Depending upon the types of inferences to be made from the test scores, certain item types may be more successful at capturing the content and cognitive specifications of a testing program than others. Table 9.4 illustrates the types of considerations for the item-development process.

Millman and Greene (1989) divide item types into objective type items, performance assessments, and simulation exercises. Within each of these broad categories are subcategories that include item types such as true/false, matching, or supply item types (i.e., completion, short answer, essay).

Ebel (1972) divides item types into three categories: essay, objective, and problem type. Ebel quickly dispels the myth that some item types test real understanding whereas others only test superficial knowledge. In describing these three item types, however, Ebel distinguishes among them based on ease of development, ease of scoring, and the role objectivity plays in scoring.

More recently, with the growth of accessibility to computer-based testing, there are new item types that capitalize on the capabilities of computer technology. Computers offer a wider array of options for presenting item stimuli to examinees, including video, audio, and complex graphics that can be used to present simulations of real-life contexts or integrated within a multifaceted stimulus. Similarly, computers offer a wide array of options for collecting examinee responses, as characterized more generally by Bennett, Ward, Rock, and LaHart (1990): multiple-choice, selection/identification, reordering/rearrangement, substitution/correction, completion, construction, and presentation. Moreover, with the continued invention of software and other peripheral devices such as light pens, joysticks, trackballs, speech-recognition software, and touch screens, the array of item types in computer-based testing will inevitably increase. Selecting the appropriate item type is not a simple task and must be considered within the larger context of test-design considerations.

3.3.2. Item-Writing Research

Considering that items are the backbone of the assessment industry, research on item writing has been surprisingly sparse. Ebel (1951) stated that there is an insufficiency of relevant research and guidance pertaining to item writing relative to the importance that item writing plays in the field of assessment. Osterlind (1998) states that item writers are routinely left to their own devices because there is no developed theory to undergird item writing, nor is there a comprehensive resource identifying the distinctive features and limitations of test items, the function of test items in measurement, or even basic editorial principles and stylistic guidelines. Haladyna (1994) echoes this concern that item writing has not received the same attention that statistical theories of test scores have received. Moreover, with the relative recency of use of innovative item formats in computer-based tests, little is known about the type of information provided by these items and the relative value of these formats compared to more traditional paper-and-pencil formats.

The research that does exist on item writing suggests that the development of selected-response items is very time consuming and labor intensive. Haladyna (1999) states that it is more difficult to develop technically sound multiple-choice items than to prepare sound performance assessment items. Haladyna and Downing (1989b) took current knowledge about writing selected-response items and created a taxonomy of item-writing rules. Haladyna, Downing, and Rodriguez (2002) updated this taxonomy, reducing it to 30 guidelines for good item writing. However, Haladyna (1999) indicates that the research on item writing is still asystematic and limited only to several rules, but states that encouraging research continues to be done in the hope of advancing the science of item writing.

Research on the design of performance assessment items is also somewhat limited. As Linn and Baker (1996) point out about the development of performance tasks,

> Far too often at this relatively early stage tasks are "created" and then rationalized rather than carefully and systematically designed. More interestingly, design processes can influence external validity criteria, that is, how performance-based assessments perform. (p. 99)

Research relative to the design of performance assessment items has focused on the issues of content representativeness

TABLE 9.4 Considerations for Selecting Item Types

CONSIDERATION	MULTIPLE-CHOICE ITEMS	PERFORMANCE ASSESSMENT ITEMS
Content specifications	Can be matched	Can be matched
Cognitive specifications	Can be matched	Can be matched
Reliability specifications	Will tend to maximize reliability	Will tend to lower reliability
Reporting specifications	Minimal time required	Maximal time required
Item-writing resources	Design of items ranges from very complex to simple	Design of items ranges from very complex to simple; design of scoring rubric is complex
Examinee testing time	Tends to minimize testing time	Tends to maximize testing time
Scoring	Simple and straightforward	Requires training and substantial resources

(Crocker, 1997), content balance and relevance (Linn, Baker, & Dunbar, 1991), and a development process that takes these issues into account (Stiggins, 1995).

3.3.3. Development of Scoring Rubrics

Stiggins (1995) indicates that performance assessments can play a key role in large-scale assessment programs. He indicates that the key to a successful constructed-response item is to make the judgment-based evaluation process as systematic and objective as possible while focusing on the most important attributes of performance.

The development of performance assessment items or constructed-response items requires the development of procedures and criteria to be used during the scoring process. To help guarantee the reliable scoring of performance assessment items, the scoring rubrics are generally developed simultaneously with the items. The item writer is the perfect source for identifying the types of responses to be elicited from a particular item and to identify the necessary components of the response for evaluation. Each performance assessment item tends to require a relatively larger and more complicated combination of skills and knowledge than a single multiple-choice item. The performance assessment item's construct relevance and construct representativeness must be addressed during the design and development of the scoring rubric.

Writers of performance assessment items must adhere to the same rules of item writing used in the development of selected-response items. In addition, the development of successful scoring rubrics is critical to the success of the item. A sound scoring rubric must (a) be consistent with the purpose(s) of the assessment, (b) define the characteristics of the response to be evaluated along a continuum, (c) convey performance criteria in an understandable way, and (d) provide for as full a range of performance as is consistent with the test purpose(s). The language of the scoring rubric is a placeholder until examinee responses to the items are available. The scoring guide is not complete until sample responses that define each level of performance are identified.

3.3.4. Item Rationales

Item rationales provide test developers with the necessary justification to score an item according to the keyed response. Item writers are typically charged with providing the necessary information to verify the correct (keyed) response, or key, to an item and to provide the rationale for why each of the incorrect alternative responses is not correct. The development of the item rationale is a critical part of the item-development process and should not be overlooked.

Item rationales should be included in the content review process. If the content reviewers cannot agree on a rationale for the key, then the item should not be used. Without justifying the key and invalidating the incorrect alternative responses, the test developer risks including a flawed item in a test.

3.4. Item Review

Once new items have been developed, they should be subjected to a multistage, multipurpose review for content accuracy, editorial style, fairness, and psychometric concerns. The various stages of this review are described below and are summarized in Figure 9.2. As with item writers, it is critical that item reviewers be experts in the area for which they are being recruited, that they be representative of the examinee population, and that they receive standardized training on the item attributes they are being recruited to evaluate.

3.4.1. Content Review

Every new item should be reviewed first for content and grammatical accuracy and for sound measurement characteristics according to the established standards of the measurement profession (Osterlind, 1998). The content reviewer should systematically check each item to ensure that it fulfills the general requirements of the item-writing assignment according to the test specifications, including, but not limited to, verifying the accuracy of the content and cognitive classifications. In addition, the content reviewer should review each item and set of stimulus materials to ensure that all are clear, unambiguous, and grammatically consistent. Any problems in the technical quality of the stimulus materials (e.g., passage, tables, graphs) or items should be detected and recorded at this early stage and immediately returned to the item writers for revision.

Detailed explanations for the requested revisions should be provided to the item writers to help them improve their understanding of basic item-writing principles and techniques. Items and stimuli that are judged to be free of any major structural or content flaws after editing should then be prepared for the second stage of the review process.

The content reviewers should then be asked to review the items according to a set of established criteria. These criteria include scrutinizing items for

1. fit within the specified content domain;
2. match to the specified cognitive skill(s);
3. technical correctness;
4. effectiveness of the incorrect alternative responses;
5. clarity (key correct, alternative responses incorrect); and
6. adherence to the specified item format.

Reviewers should also provide guidance on how to rephrase items, propose new incorrect alternative responses, and so on as necessary, in order to clarify the items and/or to render them technically correct.

After the content reviewers have evaluated the items, the items may be reedited to address the content reviewers' concerns. All items judged by the reviewers' to be accurate in terms of content should then be prepared for editorial review. The editorial review helps to ensure consistent editorial standards in the item text.

The editing of artwork and the production of graphics are important tasks in the preparation of test materials for

FIGURE 9.2 Item-Writing and Review Process

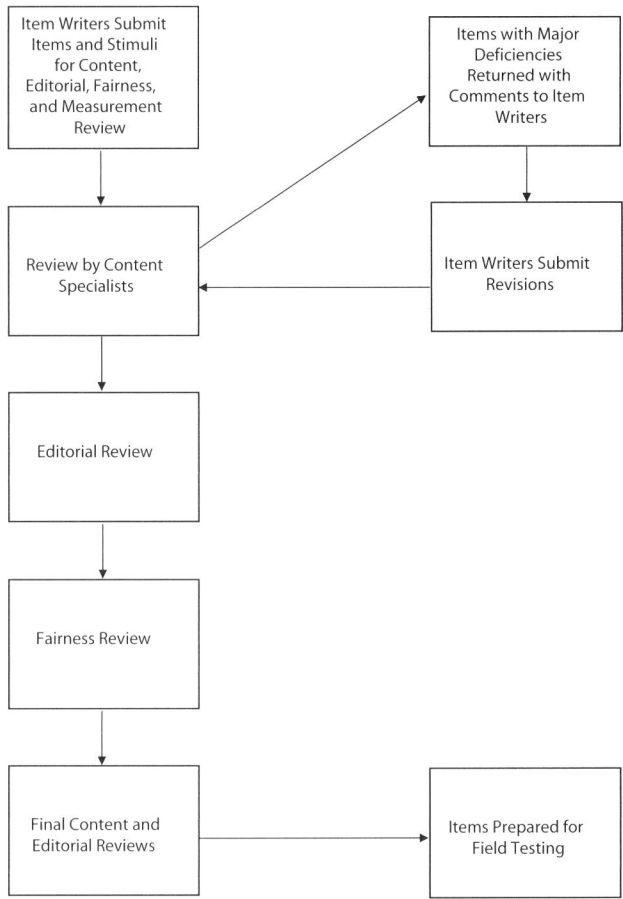

either a paper-and-pencil delivery or a computer-based delivery. Editorial staff contribute to the accuracy of all processing of artwork with numerous checks concerned with: (a) ensuring that each piece of artwork is appropriately identified; (b) matching the relevant piece of artwork to the appropriate test item(s); and, perhaps most critical, (c) proofreading to provide the assurance that no element has been omitted, added, presented in the wrong proportion or relation to other elements, or found to provide an incorrect perspective or angle.

After editorial review, each item is carefully proofread to make sure it is accurate and complete. As will be discussed later, different quality-control steps should be established according to the mode of delivery.

3.4.2. Fairness Review

All item development should be committed to fairness both in principle and in practice. Both the *Code of Fair Testing Practices in Education* (2004) and the *Standards* (1999) include obligations for ensuring fairness to test takers. For example, the *Code* sets forth criteria for fairness in four areas: developing and selecting appropriate tests, administering and scoring tests, reporting and interpreting test results, and informing test takers. The introduction states that the *Code* is "a guide for professionals in fulfilling their obligation to provide and use tests that are fair to all test takers, regardless of age, gender, disability, race, ethnicity, national origin, religion, sexual orientation, linguistic background, or other personal characteristics" (p. 2). Furthermore, test developers should "avoid potentially offensive content or language" (p. 4) and "evaluate the evidence to ensure that differences in performance are related to the skills being assessed" (p. 4).

The *Standards* (American Educational Research Association, American Psychological Association, and National Council on Measurement in Education, 1999) also address obligations to ensure fairness through all stages of test development, test administration, and test use. Fairness plays a critical role in test design as defined by a school of thinking called universal design (Thompson, Johnstone, & Thurlow, 2002), which recommends designing and developing assessments "from the beginning to allow participation of the widest possible range of students, and to result in valid inferences about performance for all students who participate in the assessment" (p. 5).

An essential goal of large-scale assessment programs is ensuring test fairness: that is, providing all test takers a comparable opportunity to demonstrate what they know and can do. Unfairness must be detected and eliminated at all stages of test development, test administration, and test scoring. The work of ensuring test fairness starts with the design of the test and the test specifications. It then continues through every stage of the test-development process, including item writing and review, item field testing, item selection and forms construction, and forms review. The multistage item-development and review process is a highly interactive and complex system, and each of the stages included in the process focuses on a somewhat different aspect or characteristic of the items. This process helps to ensure that items are evaluated from diverse viewpoints, not least of which are multicultural and gender-based perspectives.

It is commonly understood that test material that is inflammatory, insulting, pejorative, or otherwise unfair can seriously impair examinees' efforts to perform to the best of their knowledge and ability. Two types of fairness reviews may be conducted: judgmental reviews by panels of representatives of racial/ethnic groups and other relevant examinee groups, and reviews of statistical analyses conducted to identify any differential item functioning (DIF) based on gender, race, ethnicity, or other characteristic relevant to the test or target examinee population.

The first type of fairness review can occur before field testing, and the second can occur once the items have been administered, for instance in a field test. Judgmental review involves examination of the text of the items by a panel of reviewers who give feedback concerning potential fairness problems. Reviewers may be recruited from a variety of sources. These reviewers must be members of the various groups with an explicit stake in the fairness of the test (e.g., African Americans, Hispanic Americans, Native Americans, women, or those from culturally disadvantaged areas).

Fairness reviewers should be provided guidance and training about what to look for when reviewing items. Generally speaking, four types of concerns should be addressed. The first concern is cultural stereotyping. The second concern involves irrelevant characteristics of an item that might give one examinee group a particular advantage. Examples of such irrelevant characteristics might include regional history or geography that would be unknown to examinees outside the region, references to cultural pursuits that may be less accessible to economically disadvantaged individuals, and topics about which one group is likely to possess more background knowledge than another. The third concern is sensitive topics. In general, religious or sexual topics (e.g., abortion, fetal tissue research) ought to be avoided. The fourth concern is offensive language.

Once the fairness reviewers are trained in how to conduct fairness reviews, they should be provided background information about the test (i.e., purposes, uses, and test specifications) so that they can understand the history of the program. Reviewers should also be provided with the aforementioned guidelines and a document on which they can record their evaluations. If an item violates one of the fairness-review criteria, the reviewer should indicate which guideline was violated and recommend a disposition for the item (revision or replacement). If either revised or replaced, the revised/new item should also undergo a fairness review.

Because these reviews are judgmental, fairness reviewers will disagree with one another. Written, systematic procedures for the review process and for resolution of disagreements are important. No matter how well the fairness-review process is conducted, there is no guarantee that the test is "fair." Statistical analyses of differential item functioning are important to supplement judgmental reviews, as will be described later in this chapter. Other statistical analyses focusing on the fair use of test scores in context are also essential.

3.5. Item Refinement

The evaluations of the item reviewers for content and fairness should then be collated, and a comprehensive evaluation of each item should be conducted after all necessary revisions have been made. The material may need to be resubmitted to an appropriate reviewer for final approval.

Materials that are judged to be acceptable, having successfully passed all the stages of review described above, should be proofread and prepared for field testing.

3.6. Summary of the Item-Development Process

The advantages of the multistage item-development and review process are briefly described below:

1. All items are written by individuals judged to be qualified according to specified criteria. The item writers should represent, as closely as possible, the various institutional and individual requirements considered to be germane to the target examinee population. It is important to the content validity and the credibility of the testing program that the items included in the assessments be developed by members with relevant teaching and/or professional experience.
2. Meticulous and exhaustive item-writer training materials help to produce items that are technically sound, while preserving the security and confidentiality of the test materials themselves. Using carefully prepared item-writing materials, item writers can refine their skills and produce items that are more technically sound and valid than could be achieved without such instruction. The training of item writers can be further enhanced by direct communication with testing specialists who can offer specific suggestions and recommendations for technical improvement of the materials.
3. Providing item writers with specific assignments helps to maintain a proper balance of content coverage in the item pool. Such assignments help guarantee that high-quality items representing the knowledge and skills delineated in the test specifications will be available, providing essential evidence of the content validity of the examination. This procedure also preserves the security of the item pool, since no single item writer will have contributed an undue number of items to the pool in any given developmental cycle.
4. Intensive review of the items by test-development staff helps ensure that the items are consistent with the *Standards* (American Educational Research Association, American Psychological Association, & National Council on Measurement in Education, 1999). Such review serves to detect and correct deficiencies in the technical qualities of the items and item pools early in the development process. In addition, possible problems with race, gender, or other sensitivities can be detected at this stage and corrected.
5. Content evaluation assesses the accuracy, clarity, relevance, and significance of the test materials. This review is also important to the content validity of the test materials.
6. Review of the items by editorial staff ensures that the items are grammatically sound and expressed in a format deemed acceptable. This is desirable because such reviews foster a maximum yield of accurate and useful items.
7. Fairness review helps to detect and eliminate any apparent unfairness in the language, population references and characterizations, and content or format of the test materials. This evaluation should be given careful and deliberate attention.
8. Review of the field-test item pool helps to identify any issues or concerns with the pool at a stage in the development process when adjustments can still be accommodated.

All of these stages are essential to the item-development process. Although each stage takes substantial time in the developmental schedule, each contributes unique perspectives and insights into the item-development process and cannot be ignored. Any item judged to fail any of the criteria during any review stage should be either revised or discarded. Only those items and stimulus materials that satisfactorily pass all review stages can be considered eligible for field testing. Finally, all ratings and comments made during each of these stages should be carefully documented and stored.

3.7. Item Field Testing

Once the items have been reviewed and any problems with the items have been addressed, the items should be prepared for field testing. There are a variety of approaches for field testing items. Two common approaches are embedded field-test administrations and special standalone studies. An embedded field test is typically carried out during an operational administration using items either embedded within or appended to the operational test. Standalone field tests are special administrations usually independent of the administration of the operational test. Standalone field testing not only tends to be more expensive and time consuming, but the technical quality of the resulting item statistics is typically lower than can be obtained through a properly designed embedded field test. Test forms built using field-tested items along with an operational assessment are more stable and predictable in their performance than those built using field-test items from special studies. The characteristics of these two types of field-test strategies are summarized in Table 9.5.

Typically, at least twice the number of items needed in an operational test form should be field tested, but this ratio varies according to complexity of item format, overall test difficulty, and condition of the item pool. Optimally, the ratio of the number of items to be field tested to the number needed operationally should be determined empirically through analysis of actual rates of acceptable items generated from prior field-tests of similar items.

Following the field test, item evaluations should be conducted using the field-test data. Statistical analyses of field-test data typically include item analysis, which is used to identify items that may be problematic. Typical information elicited from an item analysis for selected-response items includes

1. the proportion of examinees selecting each option (the key and the incorrect alternative responses) for each item;
2. the proportions of the upper, middle, and lower percentages of examinees selecting each option based on their total raw score on a given test;
3. the difficulty (p-value and delta) and discriminations (biserial and point biserial) of each item;
4. IRT item difficulty and discrimination indices;
5. discrimination indices for each option for each item;
6. differential item functioning; and
7. internal consistency estimates of reliability for each test.

For constructed-response items, analyses may include (a) descriptive statistics, such as the mean performance, standard deviation of the mean performance, range of responses, and frequency distribution of responses; (b) rater consistency and reliability estimates; and (c) correlations with selected-response items.

Items that appear statistically flawed should be carefully reviewed for possible content-related problems and for structural problems (e.g., inadvertent cues to the key, incorrect alternative responses that are too close to the key).

4. ITEM EVALUATION AND TEST ASSEMBLY

Test assembly includes the process of selecting and organizing a particular set of items that will constitute a given form of a test. Test form assembly requires expert-level knowledge and skills in test construction, including an understanding of the relationships between the characteristics of the items in a test and the test's measurement properties. Although test assembly is guided by test specifications, it also requires the well-reasoned decisions of a test developer who understands the relevant measurement principles and the judgments of content experts.

There are many issues for the test developer to consider prior to the assembly and administration of a test form. This section discusses the various considerations of the test-assembly process. Test formatting is also addressed in this section.

4.1. Test or Pool Assembly

Forms assembly plans provide guidelines for the assembly and review of any assessment. These plans, which are part of the test blueprint, reflect the purpose of the test and specify the content and technical specifications as well as

TABLE 9.5 Considerations in Item Field Testing

CONSIDERATION	EMBEDDED FIELD TEST ADMINISTRATION	STANDALONE FIELD TEST STUDY
Content coverage	Limited to content covered on the operational test (difficult to field test new item types or new content domains)	Forms can be constructed to match the operational content and cognitive specifications
Usefulness of information	Motivation is assumed to be higher, particularly if examinees are unable to distinguish operational test items from embedded items	Motivation of examinees is typically questionable
Costs	Additional editorial time is required to embed multiple field-test forms within an operational form	Recruitment efforts are necessary; payment to examinees may be necessary; separate printing and shipping are required; separate testing sites and administrators are required
Statistics	Student abilities are measured at the same point in time as the operational assessments, thus improving the reliability of the field-test statistics for operational test construction	May be questionable if the motivation level of the participating examinees is questionable
Security	Less of a concern	More of a concern

formatting and logistical considerations. The assembly plan must contain sufficient detail to guide the test developer to assemble parallel test forms or test pools based on the test specifications developed earlier in the process.

The forms assembly plan should require that the forms or pools are balanced with regard to content and cognitive classifications, passage types, numbers of discrete and passage-related items, and number of words. In following such a plan, test developers should strive to develop the necessary number of new forms or pools based on comparable field-test statistics in order to maximize comparability across assembled parallel forms and pools.

The following sections outline the typical information used in the assembly process. In these sections, test form should be interpreted to include both paper-and-pencil forms and test pools assembled for computer-based testing.

4.1.1. Item Characteristics

After field testing, each item should be examined to determine if it is to be eligible for inclusion on a test form. To be included on a form, an item must meet the following criteria:

1. The item's statistics meet the standards established for the specific test.
2. If part of a passage-related set, a specified number of the items of the set must meet the statistical standards set for the specific test.
3. The item has not been flagged as unusable for any other reason.

Once identified as eligible for inclusion on a form, items should be placed into priority categories on the basis of their content and technical characteristics. Those items in the top priority category should be used in the assembly of the next constructed forms if at all possible. Content specialists should examine and prioritize items in terms of content, and measurement staff should examine and prioritize items from a technical standpoint. The final prioritization should be based on a consensus of content and measurement staff.

At the start of any test-development project, the test developer and test users must have decided, consistent with the uses of the assessment, the desirable technical characteristics of the items and stated these in the test specifications. Test developers should review the preliminary item analysis and flag all items that appear not to possess one or more of these characteristics. These flags should vary according to the needs of the testing program. For example, a test whose purpose is to rank-order examinees may eliminate items with difficulty values less than .30 or discrimination values less than .20. The flags should also identify any items in which any incorrect alternative responses drew a larger proportion of the examinee population than the key, or in which an atypical pattern of responses in the upper, middle, or lower groups of the examinee population is observed.

Test developers may also generate a preliminary item analysis from a subsample of the tested population rather than the total group. This preliminary analysis can be used to verify the scoring keys and to identify any items that may be miskeyed.

4.1.2. Form Characteristics

It is also important, prior to the extensive review of a form by content experts, to predict how a test will function. Item-level data (difficulties and discriminations) can be used to project the estimated mean difficulty and estimated reliability of the test scores. In addition to these statistics, the expected distribution of the raw scores can be generated for each new form. These distributions are valuable in examining whether assembled forms would be difficult to equate and whether the distributions' location, spread, and shape are appropriate to their anticipated use. Appropriate analyses are conducted to estimate the distributions, as well as to compute information functions that provide an indication of a test's measurement precision across differing levels of ability.

In addition to the item-level information from the item analysis, the following types of information may be of interest to the test developer after an initial form has been drafted:

1. joint distribution of item difficulty and discrimination;
2. number of items falling in each cell in the joint distribution;
3. mean, range, and standard deviation of item difficulty values;
4. mean, range, and standard deviation of item discrimination values;
5. estimated standard error of measurement;
6. estimates of reliability;
7. summary statistics by content or cognitive classification; and
8. specific examinee-group performance.

This information can be used to refine a preliminary draft of an assessment relative to the requirements of the test specifications. Results can also be used for test analyses after the test is administered.

4.1.2.1. Differential Item Functioning (DIF)

In addition to the items flagged by the preliminary item analysis, a statistical analysis should be conducted to detect any items that appear to be functioning differently for specific sections of the population. Measures of differential item functioning (DIF) help test developers identify items that may be unfair for members of various testing groups. The purpose of DIF analysis is to identify items that may be measuring something extraneous to the intended construct—by determining whether different groups perform more or less well on the items because of the extraneous constructs.

If field-test administrations provide large enough sample sizes to justify the computation of DIF statistics, this information should be used in the identification of eligible items. Depending upon the DIF measure employed, test developers may categorize items into various classifications of eligibility. For example, items for which DIF statistics are statistically significant may be eliminated from the eligible pool, while items for which DIF statistics are more moderate may be classified as usable if they successfully pass all other review stages. In practice, as a result of the considerable efforts made by test developers to incorporate fairness reviews into the item-development process, which has resulted in the elimination of culturally insensitive materials prior to field testing, it has become increasingly difficult to identify the precise characteristics of field-tested items that may be causing DIF. Thus, removing DIF-flagged items has become the more common remedy.

Unfortunately, not all testing programs have access to field-test samples of sufficient size to support DIF analysis. Test developers must decide how large the focal groups must be before analyses can be performed. Obviously, if large sample sizes exist, the statistics will be more stable. However, if the sample sizes are too small, items with no real DIF may be flagged and potentially misclassified, while others with real DIF may be overlooked.

There is a sizable array of methods available for DIF analysis. Historically, multiple measures of DIF have often been used in order to provide as much information to the test developer as possible. For example, the Mantel-Haenszel statistic and the standardized p-difference are two methods routinely used by test developers. The Mantel-Haenszel statistic is the average factor by which the odds that members of one group will answer an item correctly exceed the corresponding odds for comparable members of the other group. The standardized p-difference is the difference in proportion correct on the item between matched members of the group being compared. Zieky (1993) recommends the use of both statistics in order to provide test developers with the particular strengths of each.

While the Mantel-Haenszel statistic and standardized p-difference have been and remain widely accepted and commonly used, other procedures have been developed to address other needs and provide improved power. These include IRT-based procedures (Chang, Mazzeo, & Roussos, 1996; Douglass, Roussos, & Stout, 1996; Shealy & Stout, 1993), regression-based methods (French & Miller, 1996; Swaminathan & Rogers, 1990), and logistic discriminant function analysis (Miller & Spray, 1993). In some cases these procedures were developed to address two limitations of Mantel-Haenszel: insensitivity to DIF where the direction of the DIF reverses itself along the ability scale (sometimes referred to as nonuniform DIF), and incompatibility for nondichotomous items. A generalized version of the Mantel-Haenszel procedure can be applied to nondichotomous items, but the capacity for detailed analysis of categorical response functioning is limited. Poly SIB-Test, logistic regression, and logistic discriminant function analysis (LDFA) are effective for applications to polytomous items. The latter two methods are also powerful for detecting nonuniform DIF. The LDFA procedure is particularly well suited for providing detailed analysis of DIF by score category.

DIF can be an extremely useful tool for test developers both for individual item selection as well as in the refinement of test specifications. The use of DIF statistics has forced test developers to focus more clearly on the knowledge and skills that are being measured. Over time, the continued use of DIF statistics should result in more valid as well as fairer tests (Zieky, 1993).

4.1.3. Other Considerations

4.1.3.1. Field-Testing Needs

There are many different approaches for field-testing items, but at least two approaches affect the construction and assembly of operational forms and must be taken into account in the forms assembly process. When field-test items are embedded within operational forms, the item statistics are very predictable and stable and are therefore reasonably accurate for future forms construction. The examinee is not generally aware of the placement of the field-test items and therefore effects due to motivation and context are minimized. For maximum security, the position of the field-test items should be changed periodically. Field-test item sets embedded in operational forms may vary in length from section to section in order to blend in with the operational items. After the operational forms are assembled, content specialists should carefully review all field-test items in each form. In this way the best blend of content can be achieved and clueing avoided among operational and field-test items.

A second approach to field testing within the operational testing window is to present examinees with an additional testlet or shortened section of the assessment. Examinees are not informed that this section consists of field-test items, and as with embedding, context and motivational factors are minimized. Once again content specialists should carefully review the assignment of testlets to operational forms in order to avoid issues of clueing.

4.1.3.2. Prior Use Restrictions

Another consideration in the assembly of forms is the use of previously administered items. Testing programs may require that a certain percentage of items repeat from previous administrations for purposes of release policies, test security, equating, or limited item availability. Some tests consist only of recently field-tested items. Other test structures require a combination of previously administered items and recently field-tested items. Still other tests comprise previously administered items and items that have not been field tested. Although this latter practice is not recommended, the limitation of the examinee population or the need for highly secure items may warrant this practice. Some tests have a restriction on the proportion of new items that can appear as operational items in a test. The test developer must be aware of the policies for a particular testing program and must adhere to these policies throughout the assembly process.

4.1.3.3. Equating Needs

Equating is often a necessary consideration in the assembly and construction of forms. Equating is only appropriate when the assessments involved are assembled to be similar in content and difficulty. The most successful equatings are accomplished when assessments are constructed to meet well-defined content and statistical specifications. Lord (1980) provides four necessary conditions for equating: (a) assessments must measure the same construct, (b) conditional distributions after equating must be equal, (c) equating transformation should be invariant across populations, and (d) equating transformation should be symmetric.

If equating is deemed necessary, then considerations for the necessary data collection design must be made during the test-assembly process. There are several data collection methods commonly used in equating studies: the single-group design, the random-groups design, and the common-item design. In a common-item data collection design, a new form is equated to an old form by means of a set or sets of items appearing in both the old and the new forms. Common items may or may not contribute to examinee scores, depending upon the testing requirements. If a common-item design is the most appropriate choice in a given application, then the test developer must have clearly in mind the characteristics of the equating section of each content category in the test before the test-assembly process begins. The number of equating items in each link, the content distribution, and the target difficulty and discrimination distribution should all be planned in advance by the test developer. The selection of the common items is often based on the following considerations (Brennan & Kolen, 1987): (a) each set of common items is at least 20% of the total test, (b) each common item set is representative of the total test in terms of content specifications and statistical specifications, (c) each common item occupies approximately the same position in the old and new forms, and (d) the common items (stems, incorrect alternative responses, keys, and stimulus materials) are identical in the old and new forms. See the chapter on equating and linking by Holland and Dorans (this volume) for a more detailed explanation of the test-development requirements for effective equating.

4.2. Performance Assessment Forms Assembly Considerations

Unlike multiple-choice assessments, performance assessments are often complicated by the numerous logistical specifications that must be considered. Test developers must balance financial and practical considerations with desired content and technical considerations. However, no less than with multiple-choice assessments, in the performance assessment forms-assembly process the test specifications must be the first priority of the test developers. During test design, the test developer must work with both content and measurement experts to establish recommendations for distributions of responses, intercorrelations between items, and appropriate levels of difficulty.

To help ensure that constructed-response items are essentially equivalent in difficulty and accessibility, they should be field-tested prior to their operational use. The field-test administration provides information about the expected performance of the items. Similarities in the distributional characteristics of the items should be used to help select those available for operational use. To help ensure that the performance distributions can be accurately compared across performance assessment items, a sufficient number of responses are needed to adequately "fill out" the raw-score distribution of the items. The minimum number of responses per item should be determined by the purpose and use of the test. Field-test responses need to be scored by trained raters. Raters should be trained to score field-test responses using the same procedures used for operational scoring.

Just as they do with multiple-choice assessments, test developers depend on the results of the field-test administration of performance assessments to help select the items that will be available for operational use. However, the appropriate analyses and data explorations are somewhat different from those used with multiple-choice assessments. Test developers should use the observable indices discussed below, as well as input from raters, to help determine which items are eligible for inclusion in operational forms.

Item analysis provides information on score distribution, difficulty, and other information relevant to judging the quality of each item. This information is critical to the selection of items that are equivalent in difficulty. If the assessment is supporting decisions based on rank ordering examinees, seeking items that provide a spread of difficulty should help to maximize the necessary discrimination. Items used for rank ordering should elicit responses at all possible score points on the rubric. Some percentage of respondents should ideally be found in each of the extreme values of the rubric. The results of the field test help test developers revise or eliminate performance assessment items that do not elicit the appropriate distributions. Field-test results also identify the need to modify the scoring rubric.

Rater analysis provides information on the accuracy and reliability of the rating process. High interrater reliability is important when selecting items for operational use. Rater agreement statistics should be examined in addition to interrater correlations to ensure both variability across the scoring rubric and consistency of assigned scores. Test developers should also consider the impact of the interaction between score-point distributions and interrater agreement, because high agreement statistics between raters can indicate the use of a limited number of score points.

The rigor of the training and scoring process is a critical point in the development of technically sound constructed-response items and ultimately in the selection of items for forms. Standardized procedures should guide training and scoring to assure that the reported scores are accurate and reflect the intended specifications. For each item, test developers should construct an extensive scoring guide. Based on the need to deliver consistent and accurate scores in a timely manner, procedures must be developed that address the construction of scoring guides and the assembly of training materials following each administration.

In order to offer the most reliable and efficient approach to scoring, test developers should assume responsibility for overseeing the scoring of constructed-response items once training materials have been assembled and approved.

If an assessment contains both constructed-response and selected-response items, test developers should determine the appropriate method for combining the scores derived from the two item types into a single reported score.

Developers should model various possible combinations of scores in order to determine the most reliable score while still retaining the most appropriate content coverage.

4.3. Computer Assembly of Tests

Test assembly is clearly a time-consuming, labor-intensive process. Content, technical, logistical, and political considerations must be handled simultaneously and balanced. However, research into automated test-assembly procedures over the past twenty years has attempted to make the process more economical and more efficient than the manual process described in the previous sections.

One of the first models for performing these complex tasks was introduced by Theunissen in 1985. Early models such as these were not always able to replicate all the necessary parameters. Enhanced heuristic models (Swanson & Stocking, 1993) and optimization models (van der Linden & Boekkooi-Timminga, 1988, 1989) quickly improved upon the original models.

The more sophisticated computer-based assembly programs use linear programming methodology to optimize the match to specifications for each form and to maximize the statistical parallelism of a set of forms assembled simultaneously from the same item pool. As forms are being assembled and then reviewed by content specialists, scrupulous care needs to be taken to ensure that they meet all relevant technical specifications. In addition, forms need to be assembled so that they are equivalent with respect to total number of words, number of discrete and passage-based items, passage formats, distribution of items across content and cognitive categories, and other requirements of the test specifications. The optimal test models may use either IRT or classical test theory data (Wightman, 1998).

Many of the tools found in the literature today help to streamline certain aspects of the test-assembly process (Armstrong, Jones, & Wang, 1994). These tools help the test developer create initial parallel forms in a relatively short period of time. However, in addition to the interaction that is ultimately required between the test developer and the item bank, automated test-assembly processes are also limited by the following three factors (Luecht, 1998): (a) quality and size of the item bank, (b) reasonableness of the constraints and the targets, and (c) degree to which the content and technical codes can be defined.

Research on automated test assembly seems to support the conclusion that the models are not intended to replace the role of test developers in the test-assembly process. Rather, for those assembly constraints that are quantifiable, automated test assembly helps to eliminate some of the labor involved. As the models expand to include more sophisticated constraints, the utility of the automated test-assembly process will likely become even greater.

4.4. Test Formatting

The format of a test should help examinees perform at their best without interference from factors extraneous to what is being measured. Tests must always be presented as simply as possible if they are to be valid and fair indications of the examinee's ability. Examinees should not be disadvantaged due to the layout or graphics used within an assessment. The challenge in designing test forms is to make the complex as simple as possible. This applies both to paper-and-pencil tests and tests administered on computer (Campion & Miller, 2006).

Good test formatting is inclusive. Universally designed assessments are designed from the beginning to be accessible to the broadest possible group of examinees. To be consistent with universal design principles, assessments should be formatted in a way that will result in validated inferences about the achievement of the widest range of students possible (Thompson, Johnstone, & Thurlow, 2002). Test format should be based on the principles of universal design for all aspects of the test, including the presentation of items, instructions, and test-administration procedures.

Preparing a test for final delivery involves decisions that range from the very general to the very minute. Beginning at the general level, there are decisions about the grouping and ordering of items in a test that should be based upon the test-assembly plan. Items in the test must be grouped into parts, sections, or versions as defined in the test specifications. Embedded equating items should appear in approximately the same position in the form being assembled as they did in the old form. Field-test items should also be in the same positions in each form to the extent possible. Item formatting may also be guided by the need to have items and their associated graphics or stimulus materials presented on the same or facing pages.

In addition to these general guidelines for organizing a test, there are other details to be considered that are specific to delivery method. For paper-and-pencil assessments, decisions about the appearance and placement of all test elements (stems, answer choices, graphics, stimulus materials) on any test page should be a part of the test format specifications. The format specifications must also include information concerning font, margins, line spacing, character spacing, page-number placement, trailers, and headers. Test format will vary from test to test and will depend upon such factors as examinee characteristics, visual appeal, and client preference. For example, single column, large print, and wide margins may be appropriate for examinees at lower levels of reading ability. Defining the optimal specifications requires good communication between the booklet designer and the test developer. Their work should focus on the following three factors (Campion & Miller, 2006), while recognizing that all elements of the test design must work together: (a) legibility (how easily readers can recognize the letters and words and decipher the text), (b) readability (how inviting and understandable the page appears), and (c) reproducibility (how well the materials will look given the selected printing process).

Although computer-delivered assessments require different emphases than do the typical format specifications that are followed for the creation of paper-and-pencil assessments, for the on-screen display of tests the three factors of legibility, readability, and reproducibility remain paramount.

The test developer should work with the test designer to create a graphical user interface. Specifications concerning the text format and the necessary interactive functions must be defined. All hardware and software requirements must also be defined. In addition, acceptable screen resolution must be considered in order to determine desirable font sizes, scrolling needs, and window dimensions.

5. TEST REVIEW

The review of a draft test form, or of operational item pools for a computer-based test, is a critical part of the test-development process. Although each individual item has been selected, approved, and reviewed prior to forms assembly or pool approval, there are additional concerns that can only be addressed when the form or pool is reviewed as a whole.

Test security is a critical aspect of the test-review process and must be tailored to fit the needs of the situation. Up to this point in the development process, only individual items or item sets have been reviewed. The compromise or loss of individual items, item sets, or field-test versions is not as serious as the loss of a complete test form or operational pool. Specific procedures must be developed to monitor all form reviews for security. For example, forms that are being mailed to reviewers must be securely packaged, traceable, and delivery-confirmed. Reviewers must have access to similar procedures for the return of forms. Forms that are being reviewed during panel meetings should never be left unattended by test-development staff.

The various stages of the test-review process are described below.

5.1. Initial Review

After assembly, a technical review of the forms should be completed by the test developer. Each assembled form or operational pool should be scrutinized for technical merit and adherence to technical specifications.

At the same time, a content review should be carried out by the appropriate content expert. This review is for the purpose of detecting content-related problems (e.g., datedness) and ensuring that there are no clueing problems within the form or pool. At this time, content experts should also do a final check of the key for each individual item.

Developers need to be particularly vigilant about ensuring that all items conform to the test-quality requirements.

5.2. Editorial Review

Prior to the release of any assessment, editors must recheck each item to ensure that it is free of grammatical and stylistic errors and (for selected-response items) that it contains one and only one answer choice that is clearly better than the other choices. For constructed-response items, editors must recheck the prompt to make sure that all information needed by the examinees is included and that the rubric is complete.

After reviewing the items, the editors may return the materials to the content experts for further work and the content experts may then forward their changes for an additional round of editorial review. During this collaborative and iterative process, all necessary changes are made to the item in anticipation of its inclusion on the final test or in the operational pool. At this point, if major substantive changes are necessary, an item may be replaced and field-tested in its revised form before it is included.

5.3. Measurement Specialist Review

Measurement specialists should review the test materials, again guided by content and technical standards and item quality requirements. The content distribution and statistical characteristics of each content category and the test as a whole should be compared to the test specifications. Any departures from the specifications should be corrected. A final check of the content and statistical characteristics of the equating links is also important at this stage. It is important that, if an embedded approach to equating is being used, the equating items appear in the new test exactly as they did in the anchor.

5.4. Alignment, Content, and Fairness Reviews

After the review of the items by content and editorial staff, committees may be convened or individual consultants recruited to evaluate test alignment and content quality. These reviews should ensure that the test or pool demonstrates conformity to the test specifications and that all items are content-accurate, clearly phrased, and sound (i.e., the intended key is unambiguously correct, the item contains no defensible alternative responses, and no items function differently for a specific subset of the general population being tested).

As we have seen, each of the individual items selected for inclusion has been previously reviewed for fairness. However, a fairness review of an assembled test form or operational pool is required to identify any imbalances. Examples of the fairness questions that should be asked of a test form or pool as a whole are the following:

1. Is there a balanced representation of relevant groups?
2. Are different groups treated with equal formality?
3. Is there a balanced representation of settings?
4. Are groups balanced with respect to behavior?
5. Are groups balanced with respect to socioeconomic status?
6. Are groups balanced with respect to traditional and nontraditional roles?

5.5. User Reviews

Test users or clients may also be provided the opportunity to review the assembled forms or final pools after they have been approved by test-development staff and prior to release. These reviews help ensure that the coverage is balanced, appropriate, and relevant given the purposes of the test.

5.6. Panel Review

After the forms or operational pools have been assembled, reviewed by test-development content and measurement staff, and approved by the user, they may also be subjected to expert panel review. The panel should be composed of experts in the content areas to be reviewed. Because of the highly secure nature of the forms at this stage, all panelists must adhere to high standards for test security.

For a paper-and-pencil assessment, panel reviews may take place in multiple stages. For example, a first phase may require that the panel members review each form individually, concentrating on the areas of their own expertise, but also examining the form as a whole. As a second phase, panel members may meet as a group, together with content and measurement staff, to review each form item by item. The panel-review process offers several advantages not found in previous item reviews. It puts the items before an informed set of observers with "fresh eyes." In addition, it requires a focus not just on individual items but on the entire set of items as an integrated form. This will result in yet another examination of the forms for possible clueing among items or item sets, and a comparison of the forms to one another in terms of content coverage and general quality. Finally, a panel setting serves to generate discussion of issues that may have been noted but not effectively resolved in earlier stages of review.

5.7. Final Review

All comments or concerns raised by panel members should be addressed by content and measurement staff members in preparing the final forms or operational pools for administration. If item substitutions are required, appropriate panel member(s) may be asked to review the replacement items.

5.8. Proofreading of Forms

For a paper-and-pencil assessment, once the forms are approved, test-development staff proofread all forms to ensure that no errors have been introduced during the typesetting and printing processes.

For a computer-based assessment, a final online proofreading is necessary to ensure that no errors have been introduced during the electronic transfer of items.

5.9. Final Documentation

Test developers should provide supporting documentation for each new assembled form or pool. The following information about the content and technical characteristics of each new form may be appropriate for this documentation:

1. The number of items by format type in each content area and cognitive area should be provided.
2. The characteristics (length, readability, range of topics) of the stimuli included in the test should be provided.
3. Based on pretest statistics, estimated technical characteristics of each test form should be provided. These include the mean and standard deviation of the item difficulties, the range, the distribution of item difficulties, the number of items with acceptable discrimination values, and a comparison with target test specifications.
4. Based on pretest statistics, the projected raw score distributions and the estimated probability and cumulative probability of scoring at each raw score point should be provided.
5. The estimated test statistics, including the mean raw score, standard deviation, standard error of measurement, skewness, kurtosis, and reliability coefficient (KR-20) may be provided and compared to the target test specifications. These statistics may also be compared to the comparable statistics of previous test forms.
6. The answer keys for each test, including counts of how many times each key position is used, should be provided for each new form.

For computer adaptive tests, documentation should include rules for item selection and administration. It may also include exposure rates, item overlap, and pool size.

6. TEST EVALUATION

Evaluating the performance of the individual items in a test and the test as a whole after it has been administered serves a number of purposes. First, the results can be used to evaluate item performance before final scoring, as a quality assurance step to ensure that the items are functioning as expected. Second, the results can be used to evaluate the performance of major subcomponents and the test as a whole. Third, the results can be used to make improvements in the test design and development process. Each of these three purposes is addressed below.

6.1. Evaluating Item Performance

There are two major approaches to evaluating items using item response data, and both can be used, sample size permitting, when items are field-tested as well as when they are administered operationally. The classical approach focuses on traditional item indices such as item difficulty, item discrimination, and the distribution of examinee responses across the alternative responses. The second approach uses IRT to estimate the parameters of an item characteristic curve that provides the probability that an item will be answered correctly based on the examinee's ability level as measured by the test. This section will focus on classical statistics, since the chapter by Yen and Fitzpatrick (this volume) addresses IRT statistics in detail. These two approaches are not exclusive; in fact, most test developers use both models to identify not only mutually reinforcing results but also discrepancies that warrant further evaluation.

Although classical statistics are relatively simple to compute and understand and do not require sample sizes as large as those required by IRT statistics, they are not as likely to be as sensitive to items that discriminate differentially across different levels of ability (or achievement), do not work as well when different examinees take different sets of items, and are not as effective in identifying items that are statistically biased. Table 9.6 compares major characteristics of the two item statistical models.

6.1.1. Item Difficulty Index

The classical item p-value, defined as the proportion of examinees in a particular sample who answered a di-

TABLE 9.6 Comparison of Classical and IRT-Based Item Statistics

Statistic	Classical	IRT
Item difficulty	p-value, proportion of examinees answering the item correctly (sample dependent)	b parameter, location of item on scale of difficulty
Item discrimination	r-biserial or r-point-biserial, correlation between item and total scores (sample dependent)	a discrimination parameter (fit statistic)
Examinee ability (level of achievement)	Raw score on subpart of test or total test form (test dependent)	Θ estimate, location on scale of difficulty or ability
Score accuracy	Reliability and standard error of measurement—usually averaged across test scores (sample dependent)	Standard error of ability estimate

chotomously scored item correctly, is the most common index summarizing item difficulty. The index ranges from zero to one. Note that the p-value pertains to a particular sample of examinees and will vary depending on the nature of the examinee sample responding to the item. This dependency makes it important that the field-test samples be as representative of the target examinee population as possible, so that field-test p-values closely represent actual p-values obtained when the items are administered operationally.

The p-value can serve as the first signal that an item may be keyed incorrectly. Specifically, if an item has a low difficulty index (i.e., few examinees selected the key) and a negative discrimination index (i.e., those who selected the key were among those who scored least well on the test as a whole), the item may be miskeyed. Defining a "low" difficulty index depends on the particular purpose of the test, but as a general rule, test developers should review items for possible miskeys or major ambiguities if one or more of the following exists: (a) difficulty index is less than .30, (b) discrimination (biserial or point-biserial) index is less than .20, and (c) high omit rate in a test that is not intended to be speeded.

The p-value index as a measure of item difficulty has several weaknesses. First, it has an inverse relationship between its value and its interpretation: the higher the p-value, the easier the item. So if an item is described as having a high difficulty, it is important to clarify whether it is a hard item or whether the actual index value is high (i.e., close to one), indicating a very easy item. Second, it is often argued that the p-value is not linearly related to a scale of difficulty with equal intervals, so it cannot be treated like other statistics. Some test developers have transformed p-values into standard scores such as z-scores or a linear transformation of z-scores.

In some multiple-choice assessments, the p-values are corrected for guessing. This correction is predicated on the assumption that students who do not know the answer will select a response randomly. The p-value corrected for guessing is computed as

$$p_g = p - p_w /(a - 1),$$

where p_g is the difficulty index corrected for random guessing, p is the uncorrected p-value, p_w is the proportion of examinees who attempted the item but answered it incorrectly, and a is the number of response alternatives in the item. This type of index is likely to be used in highly speeded tests where the number of omitted items varies widely from examinee to examinee.

When constructed-response items are administered, the items are not dichotomously scored. Rather, the responses are scored according to a scoring rubric defining a number of possible score values. When more than one score category is used to score constructed-response items, item difficulty is typically computed as the item's average score divided by the maximum possible score. The distribution of scores on each item is valuable to evaluate whether the scoring rubric is functioning effectively: that is, whether the scores cover the expected range of scores.

6.1.2. Item Discrimination Index

The discrimination index tells how well the item differentiates among examinees, particularly between those who score highest on the test and those who score the lowest. There are several widely used discrimination indices; these are described briefly below.

6.1.2.1. Biserial and Point-Biserial Correlations

The biserial and point-biserial correlations mediate between the item responses and a criterion, such as the total test score. These indices can suggest whether or not a selected-response item was answered correctly. The biserial correlation provides an estimate of the Pearson product-moment correlation between the criterion score and a hypothesized item continuum, which is dichotomized into right and wrong. The biserial correlation assumes that the distributions of both the criterion and the item scores are continuous and follow the normal distribution curve. The formula for the biserial correlation is shown below:

$$r_{bis} = \frac{M_R - M_T}{S_T}\left(\frac{p}{y}\right),$$

where M_R is the mean criterion score for examinees choosing the key, M_T is the mean of the total sample, S_T is the standard deviation of criterion scores for all students, p is the proportion of examinees choosing the key, and y is the ordinate in the unit normal distribution, which divides the area under the curve in the proportions p and $(1-p)$.

The biserial correlation usually ranges from -1.00 to $+1.00$, with positive values indicating that the item is differentiating the high-scoring examinees from the low-scoring examinees in the same way as the criterion score. A biserial correlation of -1.00 indicates that the item is working opposite the criterion: that is, more low-scoring examinees are answering the item correctly than high-scoring examinees. If the distribution of the criterion scores is bimodal or skewed, the biserial correlation coefficient can yield values higher than 1.00. One way to avoid this is to transform the criterion scores into a scale with a normal distribution.

The point-biserial correlation, r_{pbis}, is also used as an index of item discrimination and is a Pearson product-moment correlation coefficient. The difference between the biserial and point-biserial correlations is that the point-biserial correlation assumes that the distribution of item responses is a true dichotomy: that is, there are only two distinct positions on the item continuum (right and wrong). Also, r_{pbis} does not make any normality assumptions. The formula for the point-biserial correlation is

$$r_{pbis} = \frac{M_R - M_T}{S_T} \sqrt{\frac{p}{1-p}},$$

where the notation is the same as was used for the biserial correlation.

The point-biserial correlation tends to be sensitive to item difficulty and is usually lower in value than the biserial correlation. The relationship between the two indices is shown below:

$$r_{pbis} = r_{bis} \frac{y}{\sqrt{p(1-p)}} \quad \text{and} \quad r_{bis} = r_{pbis} \frac{\sqrt{p(1-p)}}{y}$$

The criterion score for either index should be the best indicator of the aspects of educational development the test developer is trying to measure. Unfortunately, nearly all criteria have contaminating factors, so the test developer is unlikely to find a perfect criterion. Either an internal or an external criterion may be used. An internal criterion is based on some combination of items in the test: the total score or, for example, a subtest score. In either case, it is recommended that the performance on the item being analyzed not be included in the criterion score so as not to artificially inflate the discrimination index for that item. An external criterion can be performance on an independent measure such as a teacher rating or a score from another test designed to measure the same domain. An external criterion, if one exists, may be more independent, since it is separate from the test being analyzed.

The biserial and point-biserial correlations are intended to be used for items scored dichotomously. For constructed-response items that are scored according to a rubric, polyserial correlations can be computed that are simply generalizations of the biserial and point-biserial correlations (see Olsson, Drasgow, & Dorans, 1982). If an examinee is a member of one of two groups, such as those who pass the test and those who fail the test or those who have mastered the content and those who have not, the product-moment correlation can be computed between performance on the item and group membership. The phi coefficient and the tetrachoric coefficient are two such correlations and are analogous to the biserial and point-biserial correlations, respectively.

How the discrimination index is to be interpreted depends on the purposes and uses of the test scores. For example, in a test intended to rank order and differentiate examinees, discrimination indices above .20 are desirable. In tests designed to measure whether examinees have the minimum acceptable level of knowledge and skills in order to be ready for the next level of instruction, maximizing discrimination is far less important than appropriately representing the content and skills domain. In this latter case, there may be several items measuring important content and skills that nearly all examinees answer correctly and other items that nearly all examinees may answer incorrectly, resulting in low or zero discrimination indices. The interpretation and usefulness of the discrimination index depends on how the results will be used.

6.1.3. Omitted and Not-Reached Item Responses

Examinees do not necessarily answer all of the items in a test. When examinees do not respond to an item, it is called an omitted item. When examinees do not answer an item or a string of consecutive items at the end of the test, these items are called not-reached items. Both of these types of nonresponses need to be considered within the context of the test directions: whether students are encouraged to answer every question or whether a correction for guessing is used. If examinees are discouraged from guessing, the rate of omitted items is usually higher than if examinees are encouraged to answer every question.

There are differing perspectives on how omitted and not-reached items should be taken into account when computing item difficulty and discrimination indices. Some believe that the difficulty index should be computed as the number of correct responses divided by the total number of examinees, regardless of whether they attempted the item. Others believe the difficulty should be computed as the number of correct responses divided by the number of examinees who attempted the item, with this number defined as those who responded to the item as well as those who omitted the item but answered subsequent items.

The approach taken to nonresponses also needs to consider whether the test is a speeded or a power test. Most educational achievement tests today are intended as power tests. One prevalent definition of a power test is that at least 90% of the examinees have time to consider all of the items in the test. Under these circumstances, test developers want all examinees to attempt to respond to each item and would use the total number of examinees as the denominator in computing item difficulty. If the test is actually speeded and many examinees do not have time to consider all of the items in the test, item difficulty might be more accurately computed by using the number of examinees who attempted the item as the denominator. The same approach can be used to determine how to treat omitted and not-reached items in computing item discrimination. However, to the extent that the total group of examinees is pared down to include only those who attempted an item, the discrimination index will be lower in value than if it were computed on the basis of the total group.

Most item analysis programs today differentiate between omitted and not-reached items and are flexible in allowing the user to determine how to treat each in the analysis. Items having high omit rates should be examined to determine likely causes, including position in the test, test directions, possible ambiguities or inaccuracies in the item, and complexity. Tests with high not-reached rates should be examined for speededness by examining the criterion score for those examinees who are in the not-reached group compared to the criterion score of those examinees who answered the item correctly. If the criterion score is approximately the same, then it is likely that the test is speeded. If the criterion score for the examinees in the not-reached group is very low compared to those who answered the item correctly, then it is likely that very few of the examinees in the not-reached group would have answered the item correctly even if they had attempted it. If the test is intended to be a power test but is functioning as a speeded test, depending on the consequences for the test specifications the test developer should consider either shortening the test or increasing the administration time.

6.1.4. Analysis of Alternative Responses

Analysis of the pattern of responses to the key and the incorrect alternative responses is one of the most informative aspects of item analysis. Typically, item analyses show the distribution of examinee responses across the alternative responses in an item or across the score categories associated with a scoring rubric for constructed-response items. In selected-response items, it is common for the proportions of high- and low-scoring groups selecting each alternative response to be reported along with the correlation between whether or not the alternative was selected and the criterion score (i.e., biserial or point-biserial correlation computed for each of the alternative responses in an item). Examining the performance of each of the alternative responses can be used to evaluate item effectiveness.

6.1.4.1. Keyed Response

The distribution of examinee responses for the keyed response should reflect, for most test purposes, more higher-scoring examinees selecting it than low-scoring examinees. There are occasions, however, such as in licensure and certification tests and in educational mastery tests, when the proportions in the two groups selecting the keyed response are essentially equivalent, thereby leading to a low overall item discrimination index. This may be expected, particularly when the item focuses on essential knowledge and skills all examinees are expected to (and do) have. Otherwise, the response discrimination index for the keyed response should be positive and above zero.

If the discrimination index for the keyed response is negative, then there may be a fundamental ambiguity in the item that is somehow leading the high-scoring examinees not to select the key, and low-scoring examinees to answer the item correctly. Or, the high-scoring examinees may be interpreting the item at a more complex level than intended—that is, reading more into the item—thereby leading them to select incorrect alternative responses. In these cases, it is important to analyze the item carefully to determine what likely caused the item to function ineffectively.

6.1.4.2. Incorrect Alternative Responses

Item analysis provides information about whether each incorrect alternative response is functioning effectively within selected-response items given the context of the purposes of the test. If an incorrect alternative response is not selected by any examinees, it is nonfunctional and may well have been omitted from the item. If an incorrect alternative response is selected by more high-scoring examinees than low-scoring examinees, it may harbor an ambiguity that may be confusing to the higher-scoring examinees. If an incorrect alternative response has equal numbers of high- and low-scoring examinees, with a high proportion of examinees overall selecting it, the item should be evaluated to determine if it may be ambiguous or confusing. Ideally, one wants each of the incorrect alternative responses to have attracted examinees from the lower-scoring group and have a negative response discrimination value. In reality, many items have one or more incorrect alternative responses that were not selected by many examinees and are essentially nonfunctional.

6.1.4.3. Tabular and Other Methods for Displaying Alternative Response Performance

One of the most commonly used summaries of item performance provided by an item analysis is the distribution of item responses. Figure 9.3 provides a sample item analysis for a selected-response item. Note that the analysis displays the percentage of examinees selecting each response according to criterion groups. In this example, the group was divided into three groups based on total test score. The sample size for each of these three groups is reported. Then, for each response, the percentage of examinees in each criterion score group who selected it is reported along with its discrimination index. The percentage of double grids (number of examinees who gridded in more than one response to the item) and the percentage of examinees who did not reach the item are reported by score group. The analysis also includes identifying information related to the item, such as test date, program name, test name, test-form number, item-bank number (a topic to be discussed later), test-item number, examinee group, item group, discrimination criterion, and grouping criterion. The test developer could have used a different criterion for the score groups, a different number of score groups (another popular option is five score groups, so that 20% of the total group appears in each), or defined different item discrimination indices to be reported using different criteria (such as total test score, subscores, or external test scores).

Another way to portray item analysis results is by using trace lines (Haladyna, 2004). Trace lines graphically dis-

FIGURE 9.3 Example of Item Analysis

```
PROGRAM NAME      ITEM BANK NUMBER
TEST NAME
TEST FORM NUMBER
TEST ITEM NUMBER
TEST DATE
EXAMINEE GROUP
ITEM GROUP
Grouping Criterion                              1      2*      3      4     DG    NR
Disc. Criterion              N=6419    UPP      9     83      6      2     0     0
PBIS R          0.32         N=10937   MID     17     65     12      5     0     0
BIS R           0.42         N=6419    LOW     25     45     20     10     0     0
DIFF            65           N=23775   TOT     17     65     13      6     0     0
                             Response PBIS R  -0.17   0.32  -0.17  -0.15  0.00  0.00
```

- PROGRAM NAME: name of program test represents.
- ITEM BANK NUMBER: unique identifier of the item in the item bank.
- TEST NAME: name of test.
- TEST FORM NUMBER: identifies program and unique test form.
- TEST ITEM NUMBER: sequence number of item in test form.
- TEST DATE: date or testing period when item was administered.
- EXAMINEE GROUP: defines examinee group (total, gender, race/ethnicity, geographical location).
- ITEM GROUP: defines the item group (total, equating, pretest) being analyzed.
- Grouping Criterion: defines how the group being analyzed was divided for analysis (thirds, fourths, fifths).
- Disc. Criterion: defines the criterion used to compute the discrimination indices (total raw test score, subscore).
- 1 2* 3 4 DG NR: Numbers (1-4) refer to the alternative responses in the item: the asterisk denotes the keyed response; DG refers to double gridding; NR refers to no response.
- Numbers in columns and rows: percentages of examinees who selected each response; examinees are sorted into groups based on internal or external criterion; Total row (TOT) refers to percentage of examinees across all groups.
- PBIS R and BIS R: refer to the point-biserial and biserial correlations for the item as a whole.
- RESPONSE PBIS R: refers to the point-biserial correlation for each response.
- DIFF: refers to the item difficulty, expressed as a percentage of the total number of examinees who selected the keyed response.

play the frequency with which each alternative response has been selected by each criterion score group. The trace line for a key typically shows a monotonically increasing line, from the lowest-scoring group to the highest-scoring group. The trace lines for incorrect alternative responses typically show a monotonically decreasing line from the lowest-scoring group to the highest-scoring group, illustrating that an examinee's tendency to choose an incorrect alternative response decreases with his or her achievement level. A flat trace line indicates that the incorrect alternative response did not discriminate across score groups, and a trace line near a frequency of zero shows an incorrect alternative response that was not selected by the examinees in any score group. See Andrich, Lyne, Sheridan, and Luo (2001) for an example of an item analysis and scaling program that provides trace lines for both multiple-choice and rating scales.

Trace lines are particularly helpful in evaluating the effectiveness of rating scales used to score constructed-response items. The trace line shows graphically how well each rating scale point performs. In these graphs, trace lines for each rating scale value are plotted against total score performance with the expectation that high ratings on the rating scale for an item will correspond to high total scores and low ratings on a rating scale for an item will correspond to low total scores. This information provides the test developer with a way to revise, refine, and improve constructed-response items and associated scoring rubrics.

6.1.5. Item Bias

Bias is a threat to the valid interpretation or use of test scores because of a systematic difference in group performance on the item that is attributable to group membership rather than to real differences in the construct being measured. Differential item functioning (DIF), as described earlier, refers to the statistical analysis of item responses that is intended to detect differences in responses associated with one or more subgroups taking the item. Although Camilli addresses this topic in greater detail in the chapter on fairness (this volume), it is mentioned here because it is an important item-level characteristic that needs to be analyzed and evaluated. There are currently a number of statistical approaches to the study of DIF, many of which are supported by the availability of software to analyze DIF. DIF studies are important and essential aspects of test quality, especially when used in conjunction with the fairness reviews described earlier in this chapter. Ultimately, the decision as to whether an item is biased rests on judgment, but both qualitative and quantitative evidence should be used to make the most informed judgment.

6.1.6. Evaluating Item Performance

The information provided by item analysis is helpful not only to evaluate performance, but also to improve item quality. Using the results of the item analysis, the test developer can determine whether the item can be reused as is, whether the item should be revised before reuse, or whether the item should be taken out of the active item bank. What makes an item's performance acceptable should be defined in the test specifications within the context of test purpose and use. An item having a difficulty of .95 might be perfectly acceptable in an end-of-course examination in biology, for example. An item that has a low discrimination index might also be acceptable in the context of a test intended to diagnose student strengths and weaknesses. However, items with negative discrimination indices are not likely to be acceptable in virtually any testing situation; neither are items that have been identified as statistically and logically biased to the disadvantage of one or more examinee subgroups.

6.2. Evaluating Test Performance

Evaluating the performance of the items in a test is not tantamount to evaluating test performance. In addition to evaluating how well individual items perform, it is equally important to evaluate how well the test meets the requirements of the test specifications. And if more than one form of the same test has been administered, it is important to evaluate how consistently the intended parallel forms function. As with item analysis, the test developer needs to determine how the test will be analyzed (as a whole or by subparts), and with which examinee groups (by total group or by subgroups).

6.2.1. Distribution of Raw Scores

The test developer should examine indices of central tendency, such as the mean, mode, and median of the test, along with indices of variability, such as standard deviation, variance, minimum and maximum scores, and range. This information can help to identify whether the test

1. was too difficult for the examinee group, as shown by a larger-than-expected proportion of scores near the lower end of the raw-score scale;
2. was too easy for the examinee group, thereby limiting the amount of information about the upper end of examinee achievement;
3. spread examinee scores across the score scale or clumped them at one or more score levels, making it difficult to differentiate between examinees;
4. may have been insufficient to capture the full range of examinee performance, that is, the lower or upper ends of the score scale may not have been low or high enough;
5. resulted in a test-score distribution that met the test specifications and was not dramatically skewed in one direction, suggesting that the test could have been too difficult or too easy; and
6. resulted in the targeted distribution for decisions, if the test results were used to make decisions relative to performance standards.

6.2.2. Distribution of Item Difficulty and Discrimination Indices

The overall distribution of item difficulty indices and discrimination indices should be examined to determine if they meet the requirements of the test specifications. A joint distribution of item difficulty and discrimination can be used to identify items having out-of-range values. Although test content and skills need to be the primary determiners in educational achievement tests, it is important to evaluate the performance of the items in the test as a whole to determine how closely the statistical specifications were met.

6.2.3. Test-Score Reliability

As addressed in detail in the chapter by Haertel (this volume), the reliability of the resulting test scores should be estimated and evaluated. Estimates should be obtained for both raw scores and scaled scores, since these may differ. Reliability, as test developers also know, is a complicated concept. Although it is often defined as consistency of test scores, defining consistency and selecting an appropriate approach to estimating that consistency is not always straightforward. As Feldt and Brennan (1989) acknowledge,

> In principle, one should gather reliability data in a manner that allows acknowledged error sources to reflect their effects in intra-individual variation and permits true-score components to remain constant. In practice, this is not easy to arrange. (p. 107)

Theoretically, the test developer is confronted with an array of reliability indices from which to choose. For example, Feldt and Brennan (1989) list twelve internal consistency coefficients; Berk (1980) lists thirteen reliability indices for criterion-referenced tests. The task of selecting from among these has been summarized by Stanley (1971):

> Studying the reliability of a measuring instrument for a particular group of examinees involves three types of operations: logical, statistical, and empirical. One must first identify the conditions under which the accuracy of performance needs to be estimated, that is, the type of inference that is to be made from the evidence. Then the procedures for data collection and statistical analysis must be chosen so that they are logically consistent with the inference that is to be made. (p. 358)

In practice, the range of choices confronting the test developer who is doing routine reliability studies on tests measuring educational achievement is considerably narrower. Typically, one may obtain estimates of internal consistency reliability (e.g., KR-20, split-half, alpha), generalizability estimates for performance assessments, agreement or dependability estimates for score interpretations made in reference to one or more performance standards (kappa, phi, phi lambda), and the respective standard errors of measurement associated with each estimate. Depending on the purposes and uses of the test results, one or more of these estimates may be appropriate.

6.2.4. Evaluation of Constructed-Response Rating Process

For constructed-response items that are hand-scored by human raters, it is important that the test developer evaluate both the accuracy and the consistency of the ratings. This would include (a) indices of interrater agreement, to examine agreement of ratings across raters; (b) indices of accuracy, to examine the accuracy of the scores assigned by the raters relative to scores assigned to precalibrated papers; and (c) indices of consistency, to examine the consistency among multiple raters rating the same papers.

Ideally, all raters should complete a training program designed to teach them how to correctly interpret the scoring rubric. All raters should also pass a qualifying test wherein the accuracy of their grading is evaluated. And during training, the ratings assigned by each rater should be checked periodically to ensure that raters are continuing to assign accurate and consistent scores. Those raters whose scores do not meet the requirements of these periodic checks should be either retrained or released from scoring. When scoring is completed, the test developer should review each of the overall indices described above to ensure that the rating process meets the necessary requirements for constructed-response scoring.

6.2.5. Conformity to Test Specifications

Although verification of conformity of the test form or item pool to the specifications is a critical step in the test-assembly process, it is reiterated here at the evaluation stage. Test developers need to evaluate the conformity of a particular test form or item pool to the test specifications to identify any discrepancies and to make any adjustments in the item-development process necessary to ensuring that these discrepancies do not recur.

6.2.6. Multidimensional Analysis of Test Content

Multidimensional scaling uses similarity data to derive dimensions that best summarize qualitative differences among test items. A multidimensional analysis of test content can help to provide the test developer with a visual portrayal of the latent data structure of the test. Each test item is assigned a scale value on each dimension and the dimensions are used to portray the test items as points within the multidimensional space. These data can be used to evaluate whether items that have been developed to measure similar dimensions in fact perform in that way. The results can be used to evaluate the test specifications and to identify content and skill categories that function as expected and those that do not. Ideally, items that have been developed to measure similar content and skills dimensions would clump visually together and they would be situated in proximity to other items with related content and skills dimensions. That information can be used to refine the specifications, clarify the item-development guidelines, and improve the test-construction process. Documentation of the underlying test dimensions is also important to the interpretation and use of IRT-based statistics to evaluate item and test functioning.

6.2.7. Parallelism across Test Forms

When more than one test form is developed and administered, the item and test analyses should be used to evaluate consistency of item and test characteristics across test forms or item pools. The distributions of item characteristics should be similar regardless of test form or test pool, as should the reliability estimates (within reasonable limits). Any multidimensional analyses of test content should show similar dimensions according to the test specifications. Any aberrant indices should be examined and adjustments made in the test specifications to correct these aberrations.

6.3. Test Evaluation and Validity Evidence

The use of item and test analyses has one primary purpose: to improve the test-development process so that the resulting test produces scores that are of the highest quality possible given the test's purposes and uses. Evaluating item performance can help to identify ways in which items can be revised to improve the way they perform. Improving item discrimination has a positive influence on the consistency of the decisions made on the basis of the test scores. Evaluation of the way the test is functioning can help to refine the test specifications, by identifying content and skills that appear to be duplicative or do not appear to be covered by the test, and by maximizing the coverage of the test, given its purposes and uses.

However, while the process of test design begins with a validity foundation that identifies the test purpose and uses and the inferences to be made on the basis of the test scores, the test-evaluation process must evaluate how effectively these inferences can be made by the resulting test scores. The ultimate question must always be: Are the test scores providing the quality and type of information needed to make the intended inferences?

Answering this question requires that the test developer gather the intended evidence of validity as defined by the types of test-score inferences to be made. Suppose we wanted to develop a test to be used to place first-year high school students into the most appropriate English class based on their levels of achievement. At the high school in question, three types of English courses are available: developmental, standard, and advanced. The test must be designed to identify the course each student is ready to enter based upon the level of knowledge and skills the student has already attained. At the outset of the test-design process, we gather empirical evidence that distinguishes the knowledge and skills needed for students to be ready for each of these courses, and we use this information to design the test specifications.

Once the test is administered, we need to gather evidence that the test design and development process resulted in effective educational decisions about students. We therefore gather course grades as evidence of student success in these courses. We also look at retention: whether the students completed the courses into which they were placed. We then analyze the accuracy rate of the placement decisions that were made on the basis of the test scores. If the test scores resulted in a large number of accurate placement decisions, then that evidence would support the test design. If, on the other hand, we found an unacceptable rate of inaccurate course placement based on poor performance in the course or course dropouts, then the validity evidence suggests that we need to go back to the domain specifications, gather additional evidence about the knowledge and skills needed to be ready to enter each of these three courses, and adjust the specifications accordingly.

As stated earlier, the test-design stage is a critical one. If the domain is not well defined through an empirical process, the likelihood of the test being effective in measuring the domain will be dramatically reduced. The results of an ill-defined domain will be evident in the validation process for the test results, a topic treated in depth in the chapter by Kane (this volume). But the inextricable link between the test-development process and validation is one that either provides support that the test is effective in serving the intended test purposes and uses or suggests that the test design needs to be refined and improved through further empirical analysis of the domain(s).

7. ITEM BANKING

An item bank is a collection of test items. The items may be selected response, constructed response, or any other format; they may be used in multiple testing programs; they may be accessed by multiple test developers; and they may be administered on different platforms (e.g., paper, computer, etc.). Item banking is an essential tool for test development, not only to organize items and to keep a history of their development and administration, but also to manage items when multiple test forms and/or item pools are being assembled and interchanged on a regular and frequent basis.

It wasn't all that long ago when item banks comprised sets of index cards, each of which held a copy of an item and its administration history. When tests were assembled, the test developer selected the items to comprise a test form by sorting through the cards and selecting those that best fit the test specifications. This process worked for small item pools and for testing programs with infrequent administrations, but was not particularly efficient or effective for larger item pools or programs that involved multiple test dates and test forms.

Computers have dramatically lessened the burden of item banking. Database management systems allow easy access to item software programs available commercially. There are many associated computer programs that can enhance an item-banking system: item-editing programs, test-assembly programs, and test-publishing programs. The purpose of this section is to provide an overview of the uses of computerized item banks, the information typically stored in item banks, associated functionalities that complement computerized item banking, item-bank maintenance, and item-bank security.

7.1. Uses of Item Banks

Although computerized item banks have many advantages, not all testing programs need to be supported by a computerized item-banking system. If a testing program has a small number of items, administers tests infrequently, and does not have multiple programs or test developers involved, a computerized item bank may not be necessary. There are conditions, however, under which computerized item-banking systems are necessary and important to maintain test quality:

1. large item banks;
2. complicated test specifications;
3. need for multiple test forms or test pools;
4. frequent testing;
5. need for tailored tests;
6. need for multiple test developers to contribute to the item bank or construct test forms or item pools from a single item bank;
7. shared items across testing programs; and
8. multiple item components (multiple stimuli, multiple items associated in a single item set, multiple graphics).

When one or more of these conditions exist, it may make sense for the test developer to use a computerized item-banking system rather than relying on a paper system.

7.2. Information Typically Stored in Item Banks

At a minimum, item banks should store the following information for each item: (a) the item, graphical elements, stimulus, and any other components of the item as it appears for administration; (b) information describing the attributes of the item that are used to sort and select items for test assembly and other test-development purposes; and (c) test-administration history and performance. See Millman and Arter (1984) and Wright and Bell (1984) for discussions of the issues involved in item-bank design. Each of these three categories of information is described below.

7.2.1. Storage of Item Components

It is important to have state-of-the-art word processing capabilities associated with an item bank, particularly if tests are to be published through the banking system. In designing the text storage capabilities of the item bank, the test developer should consider the following:

1. The item-bank text storage capability should be able to store any type of item, regardless of format.
2. The text should be entered into the item bank in a way that is articulated with the test production process. Items should not be reentered for test production. This can lead to errors in the presentation of items to examinees.
3. The text should be formatted in the item bank in a way that facilitates test production. For example, for Web-based computerized tests, the items may be stored in XML format. If items are to be administered in more than one platform, they should be stored in the format that will require the fewest conversions per administration platform.
4. Items that are connected to a single stimulus should be entered into the bank in a way that identifies the stimulus.
5. Items that include graphical elements should be stored in a way that will ensure that all elements of the item will be included when the item is accessed. For instance, if graphics are stored separately, there should be subroutines written to access the appropriate graphics when the item is accessed in the item bank.
6. There should be only one record per item. Parallel or alternative versions of an item, or items that clue each other, should be identified as "enemies" as an attribute in the bank. Items that are identified as enemies are not to be selected for the same test form or item pool.
7. The item-bank text storage capability should have an effective versioning control system that will identify subsequent versions of the item. Older versions of the item should be archived to minimize confusion about which version of the item is the most recent.
8. The item-bank text storage capability should have appropriate levels of security to prevent unauthorized access.
9. The item bank should be backed up regularly to prevent loss of the bank if the computerized storage system fails. If there are daily updates in the bank, the backups should be scheduled accordingly to minimize losses.

7.2.2. Storage of Item Attributes

In addition to item text, it is important that item-banking systems also store descriptive information about the test items for use in sorting and selecting items. These "nontext" attributes of the item are usually stored in a database that allows easy access to the items. In designing the item attributes to be stored in the item bank, the test developer should consider the following:

1. Item banks should be accessible to authorized personnel only for use in authorized testing programs. This is particularly important in high-stakes testing programs where item exposure needs to be carefully controlled and monitored.
2. The item attributes should comprise those features that are likely to be used in various stages of the test-development process, including item writing (to identify the types of items needed in the item bank), test assembly (to identify the candidates for inclusion in future test forms or computerized item pools), and test evaluation (to analyze and evaluate item performance by various attributes).
3. If the item-attribute storage system is to be associated with an item-development software program that maintains the developmental history of an item (e.g., item writer name, status of item, review history, editing history, etc.), then the attributes need to reflect the information required throughout the developmental cycle of the item.
4. The item attributes need to include all of the characteristics defined in the test specifications. For instance, most items in educational development tests will be categorized according to a content and skills classification system, to state standards, and to keywords that can be used to select items.
5. The item attributes should be defined in a way that the test developer can evaluate the coverage of a preliminary assembled test form or item pool. For example, if a particular test has a word limit, the word limits associated with each item in the preliminary form could be summed to a total to make sure that it falls within the targeted word limit. Similarly, the test developer should check the form for similar items (item clones, item enemies) and for items that might clue one another. These relationships can also be coded as item attributes.
6. The item attributes should include test-administration information that identifies the item uniquely within a test form or item pool, information associated with one or more test dates or periods, classical item statistics and the group on which they are based, and IRT item parameters.

7.2.3. Test Administration History and Performance

The administration history of an item is critical to protecting item exposure and security. In designing the test administration history and performance component of the item bank, the test developer should consider the following:

1. Every administration of an item should be documented in the item bank by testing program, test form identifier, test dates or periods, type of administration (e.g., field-test administration, standardization, operational administration), description of examinee group on which classical statistics are based, and item statistics (classical and/or IRT).
2. Any item may have multiple administration records associated with it, depending on item and test reuse policies of the testing program.
3. Any item that has been selected for inclusion in a test form or item pool that has not yet been administered should be designated as such in the item pool to prevent overexposure.
4. Test administration summary statistics can be derived from the bank so that the bank can also store test-form

or item-pool summary statistics such as raw-score mean, standard deviation, reliability, and standard error of measurement.

A summary of these attributes is provided in Table 9.7.

7.3. Associated Functionalities

Item banking has many benefits to offer the test-development process. In the last fifteen years, a number of commercial software programs have become available that have enhanced the capabilities of item banking to span other stages of the test-development process. A few of these associated functionalities are described below.

7.3.1. Item Creation, Editing, and Review

Test developers can use software that combines the capabilities of word processing and database management. Item-creation templates guide item writers through the item-development process, and the database management component records the progress of each item as it proceeds through the various stages of item development, editing, and review. The item attributes that are recorded along the way (such as content and skills classifications) are stored so that they can easily be downloaded to the item-banking system when the item is ready to be formally banked.

There are also a number of computerized item-generation programs available to test developers. The idea of item generation is at least thirty years old (Hively, Patterson, & Page, 1968) and has been extended through intelligent-tutoring models and cognition (Bejar, 1993). These programs use sophisticated techniques to guide the computerized generation of test items. See Millman and Westman (1989) and Bejar (2002) for a discussion of the evolution of current approaches.

7.3.2. Test and Item Pool Assembly

The complexities of test specifications often make it difficult to assemble test forms or item pools that not only conform to the test specifications but also are parallel to other assembled forms and pools. Computerized test-assembly programs are able to consider complex test specifications in ways that are difficult to manage manually and such programs can readily meet the demands of computerized testing for multiple, interchangeable parallel item pools. See van der Linden, Veldkamp, and Reese (2000), Stocking and Swanson (1998), and Armstrong, Jones, and Wang (1994) for discussions of some of these approaches.

7.3.3. Item and Test Analysis

As addressed earlier in this chapter, item and test analysis programs can be interfaced with item-banking programs to download the results of the analyses into the item bank. In testing programs where items are field tested on a continuous basis, once the requisite sample sizes have been attained in field testing the items can be analyzed and the results downloaded into the bank. These programs can also provide a report that identifies items meeting the desired statistical specifications or, conversely, identify those items that fall outside of acceptable statistical performance.

7.4. Item-Bank Maintenance and Security

Just like any other database, the item bank must undergo regular maintenance to make sure that the data are current, that the data pass all integrity checks, and that items that are no longer viable for administration are archived. It is recommended that all item-banking systems conduct routine integrity checks to make sure that the data stored meet internal consistency requirements. For example, all statistical values stored in the item bank should be values that fall within the limits of the particular statistic. Items with statistics that fall outside of the test specifications should be identified for further disposition (either archiving or revision for field testing). Similarly, the parameters for items used in computerized testing programs should be updated routinely, particularly if the item pool is not interchanged on a regular basis. There should also be regular maintenance checks of the items to identify those that meet the limits of exposure or overuse. These should be provided in a report for the test developer.

An equally important aspect of item-bank maintenance is the use of the data stored in the bank to refine and improve the test-development process. Test developers can analyze any group of items based on any attribute stored in the bank. For instance, if a test developer wanted to analyze whether true/false items are more difficult on the whole than selected-response items, the test developer can use administration data to identify the items to be studied. Similarly, test developers may analyze trends that can inform the test-development process. For example, if a test developer suspects that a certain type of reading item is not functioning properly, the test developer can identify the items to be studied to examine the issue. The results of such inquiries can help further refine the test specifications.

Test security is important in all aspects of the test-development process, including item banking. As test developers design their item-banking system, they need to take steps to make sure that the bank is protected from unauthorized access (both internal and external to the testing organization), that the bank is adequately protected by appropriate firewalls and backup facilities, and that off-site access to the item bank is carefully controlled to ensure that only authorized personnel can access features of the bank. The test developer must also consider what type of access (read-only, write, delete) users should have to the bank, and must define explicitly the features of the item-banking system that are made available to others off-site. All of these issues need to be considered in a carefully designed security plan for the item bank.

8. QUALITY CONTROL

Earlier sections of this chapter touched upon quality-control steps as they relate to item review, test formatting, and item evaluation. This section focuses on designing, implementing, monitoring, and refining an overall quality-control process whose goal is the presentation to examinees

TABLE 9.7 Summary of Item Attributes Typically Stored in Computerized Item Banks

Item-identifying information	Item-bank identification number
	Item identification number
	Item security status
Item text	Stimuli (one or more)
	Graphics (one or more)
	Item text (stem and answer choices)
	Correct (or model) answer
Item-writer attributes	Year written
	Item-writer name
	Item-writer identification number
	Item-writer demographics (address, education, etc.)
	Unit number
	Unit type
	Editor identification
	Developmental status
	Reviewer identification
	Status of review
Item attributes	Item type
	Skill categories
	Content classifications
	State-standard classifications
	Keywords
	Item status
	Item enemies or clones
	Item release
	Word count
	Gender reference
	Archive date
	Readability
	Version
	Source supporting key
	Recommended program use (grade or education level)
Item-administration information	Program identification
	Test-form code
	Item-sequence number
	Administration type
	Test date or period
	Examinee group (size, comparison)
	Classical statistics (difficulty, discrimination indices, response distributions)
	IRT parameters
	Evaluation of item performance
	Index of bias

of high-quality items and tests that will result in accurate and reliable assessment of examinee performance.

In a very real sense, each step in the test development process can and should be considered a quality-control step. Aspects such as item content review, measurement staff review, test review and key check, match to specifications, and item analysis all affect the quality of the finished test. Ideally, quality-control steps should begin at the test-design stage and proceed through development, assembly, administration, scoring, and reporting. Each step should be carefully described in writing, recorded as it is implemented, and monitored to make sure it has been implemented properly.

If steps are not taken to ensure that the interaction between test and examinee takes place as cleanly as possible, the worth of other steps in the development process is severely devalued. Large-scale standardized assessment programs, whether paper-and-pencil or computer based, require long-term investments of time, energy, and financial resources, investments that can all too easily be compromised or undermined by lack of attention to detail in the production stages. Conscientious quality-control efforts thus play an essential role in helping to guarantee the proper functioning of items and tests. Campion and Miller (2006) discuss the need for effective quality-control procedures as an adjunct to ensuring test validity.

8.1. Principles for Designing an Effective Quality-Control Process

In general, the design of an effective quality-control process will abide by each of the following principles:

1. Consider characteristics of the final published product throughout the test-development process. In other words, work backward through the test-development process based on what the test will ultimately look like, how it will be administered, and when.
2. Assure that the final test product will be in a form that will help all students do their best and not be distracted by confusing directions, poor layout, distracting typefaces, or errors in form or substance.
3. Follow universal-design principles in test design to assure that the test is accessible and usable by the widest range of students possible.
4. Follow written procedures requiring those engaged in the test-development process to document the steps they take, monitor the process, quantify the errors detected at various stages of the test development process, and evaluate the outcomes of the quality-control process.
5. Capitalize on information stored in the item bank to prepare test answer keys and to quality-control the scoring process to minimize the likelihood of error.
6. Reflect the highest test-security standards, from interactions with item writers through test scoring and reporting.
7. Identify the correct source document to be used to proofread items, test forms, and associated documentation, including answer keys.
8. Customize the quality-control requirements for each step in the test-development process.
9. Standardize procedures so that they are reproducible and can be consistently applied to multiple test forms and pools.
10. Ensure that the quality-control process results in a diminishing error detection curve from editing through test assembly.
11. Take nothing for granted, and check all aspects of a test form/pool to make sure the obvious is not overlooked.
12. Correct errors without introducing new ones.
13. Customize the quality-control process to the task: if checking for format conformity, a read-through by a single person is appropriate, but proofreading to assure accuracy of text requires two proofreaders (one reader, one checker).
14. Check for one type of error at a time, and make multiple passes through the test/pool; it is too difficult to attend to multiple types of error simultaneously.

To minimize redundancy with earlier sections, the remaining subsections discuss those elements of the quality-control process that bear most directly on the production of the physical or electronic object with which examinees must interact. Even these are presented only cursorily, to give the reader an idea of the scope of the topic. Quality-control considerations can be, and sometimes have been, the subject of chapters, monographs, or entire reference works all to themselves. (See, for example, Anderson, 1990; Beach & Kenly, 1999.)

8.2. Quality-Control Considerations for Paper-and-Pencil Tests

The fundamental quality-control consideration in producing paper-and-pencil tests is the avoidance of typographical errors. These can, of course, occur at any stage in the development process and in any element of the test (e.g., item, stimuli, directions). It is crucial that the finished product be free of any such errors because each error can affect how the examinee processes and therefore performs on an item. For example, an error in the directions may compromise the examinee's understanding of the task to be performed, an error in a stimulus may affect the knowledge the examinee brings to an item, and an error in an item may hinder the examinee from understanding what is being asked or from being able to properly distinguish the key from among the answer choices.

Each of these errors in turn can affect the item statistics and therefore the worth of the item for future use. An item that contains such an error needs to be field-tested again with the error removed if the item is to retain its potential value as a true measure of examinee performance, an error in a stimulus necessitates re-field-testing the complete set of items accompanying the corrected stimulus, and an error in the test directions may require an entire section, or even the test itself, to be re–field tested with the error removed. Such additional development steps add time and expense to an already time-consuming and expensive process.

The avoidance of typographical errors also extends to stylistic aspects of item and test presentation, such as item numbering and answer choice numbering or lettering, and accompanying documentation, such as the answer key. A misnumbered or miskeyed item is arguably even more potentially damaging than an item whose text contains an error, because while the latter in many instances may only hypothetically create problems, the former will almost certainly result in the need for a test to be rescored—an error that, if occurring in an operational section of a large-scale assessment program, has the clear potential to affect not just item or test statistics but thousands of examinee records.

8.3. Quality-Control Considerations for Computer-Based Tests

Typographical errors are also a critical quality-control concern in tests presented on computer. All of the potential errors discussed in the previous section are equally a risk with computer-based tests and carry with them the same potential consequences. In addition, there are a number of other potential sources for error that are unique to the computer environment (Campion & Miller, 2006):

1. Errors in Appearance. Because of programming errors or other "glitches," stimulus text, item text, or graphics (including symbols in mathematical equations) may, when viewed on screen, differ in layout or look from how they are intended to appear.
2. Errors in Function. Visual aspects of the computer environment, such as buttons or other navigational devices, may appear as designed but may be inactive or may perform actions other than those they were intended to perform.
3. Psychometric Errors. The "flow" of the test from one item to the next must occur in conformity with the test specifications. This may include aspects such as item-selection rules (for pools and test sessions), item bal-

ance (for fairness and diversity of presentation or variety of topic and tone), and item-exposure rates.

8.4. Implementing a Quality-Control Process

Whether designed for paper-and-pencil tests or computer-based tests, an effective quality-control process must identify all critical points at which text or presentation is subject to alteration, and assign a person or persons to take responsibility for the correctness of the material at each point before it is allowed to pass to the next stage in the development process. For paper-and-pencil tests, critical points may include

1. initial entry of text from a source document into word-processing software;
2. alteration of text in response to content, editorial, or fairness reviewer input;
3. typesetting of text in preparation for printing;
4. photography of typeset text by printer; and
5. printing of test booklets.

At each of the first three critical points, errors usually result from improper keystroking. At the fourth and fifth points, errors may be introduced that can obscure or distort text or otherwise hinder its legibility. The text must be examined closely at each of these points to ensure that material is free of errors. The further an undetected error is permitted to proceed through the development process, the costlier it may be to correct. For example, it is easier and cheaper to fix a typographical error immediately after text has been entered into word-processing software than to fix it in a printed test booklet.

At each critical point, a separate step should be introduced during which an appropriate test-development staff person (usually the content reviewer and/or an editorial reviewer) reviews the text for errors. In the earlier development stages, such as the first three points discussed above, this review may take the form of "single-person" proofreading (i.e., one person reads silently through the document produced in the previous step), or "two-person" proofreading (i.e., one person reads the source document aloud, including punctuation and descriptions of all stylistic features such as boldface or italic type, to a second person who is following along in the document produced in the previous step). In the later stages, such as the fourth and fifth points discussed above, the review may consist of a variation on the single-person proofread, during which the reviewer pays less attention to the actual content of text and more attention to the quality of its appearance on the page. In all cases, quality-control reviewers should possess an eye for detail and will preferably have extensive professional experience with editing and producing text for publication.

8.5. Monitoring and Refining a Quality-Control Process

Each step in a quality-control process should be established and described in writing, and a specific person assigned to complete it. To support the whole of the process, and, where necessary, any individual step in the process, checklists should be created in which each step can be initialed and dated (preferably by the person or persons performing it) as it is completed. The final series of filled-out checklists thus represents a history of the quality-control efforts exerted on each element of test material produced (e.g., item set, field test, test booklet, computer interface). Checklists should be developed to fit the test-development process for each test being developed given test purposes, uses, intended audiences, and administrative requirements. Since each test-development process is unique, its corresponding quality-control process will also be unique.

Figure 9.4 illustrates a checklist that might be used to monitor a fairness-review process.

Errors need to be counted and recorded during each of the major quality-control checks. They can then be plotted so that the error rate can be monitored. If an unexpectedly high rate of errors is detected at a particular stage, then the test developer can reexamine the quality control process at earlier stages to improve the accuracy of error detection. Error detection should be monitored throughout the test-development process and then analyzed more holistically once the test-development process is completed for a series of forms or pools.

Test developers should especially strive to track and understand the history of an error that goes undetected for an unacceptably long period, especially if it is the kind of error that can create problems in the effective functioning of a test item, field test, or test booklet. Developers should identify when the error was introduced and how it was created. If necessary, they should also identify who was responsible for introducing and/or correcting the error; at times, quality control can be a matter of insufficient staff training, and such insufficiencies can thereby be addressed as the need arises. If an error should reasonably have been identified at a much earlier stage in the development process, developers should attempt to determine why it was not.

Most important, test developers should monitor their quality-control process so that any necessary adjustments can be made to the sequencing of steps, or to individual procedures for identifying and correcting errors, for the purpose of ensuring that errors are minimized in the future.

While a completely error-free test may not always be a reality, it should always be the goal of the test developer. Careful attention not only to designing but also to troubleshooting an effective quality-control process is essential to pursuing this goal.

9. SUMMARY

The authors would be remiss if we concluded this chapter without reflecting briefly on the history of test development. Much of the progress that has been made in testing in the last fifty years has been the result of significant landmarks in educational history, and these landmarks have for the most part issued challenges that testing has been asked to meet.

The 1950s and *Sputnik* created an urgency within America's schools. The tensions surrounding the Cold War created a heightened awareness that the United States needed to maintain its competitive position in the world and do what was necessary to identify and develop student aca-

FIGURE 9.4 Sample Fairness Review Quality Control Checklist

Criteria for Ensuring Fairness - Passage

1.	The passage does not contain content that will be offensive to one or more groups of society.	____
2.	The passage does not contain stereotyping of one or more groups.	____
3.	The passage does not contain language that could be offensive to one or more groups.	____
4.	The passage does not contain role, occupational, or personal characterizations that could be offensive to one or more groups.	____
5.	The passage does not contain activities and/or situations that may be unfamiliar to members of one or more groups.	____
6.	The passage does not contain needlessly difficult vocabulary or complex sentence structures.	____

Criteria for Ensuring Fairness - Items

1.	The item format will not be unfamiliar to members of one or more groups of society.	____
2.	The item content is not likely to be unfamiliar to one or more groups.	____
3.	The skill required by the item is not likely to be unfamiliar to one or more groups.	____
4.	The information provided in the item is not presented in such a way that one or more groups will find it needlessly difficult or confusing.	____
5.	The item does not fail to build positive images, mutual understanding, and/or respect for self and others.	____

demic talent. This imposed demands on test developers to create tests that could be used to distinguish those students who were ready for school from those who were not, promote the most talented students, retain those students who were not making sufficient progress, and identify those students who deserved academic honors and who had the potential to go to college.

With the passage of the Elementary and Secondary Education Act (Title I) in 1965, however, standardized tests were now required so that schools could demonstrate that they were improving the academic achievement of all students in order to qualify for federal funds. These new requirements, including an expansion of the National Assessment of Educational Progress (NAEP) in 1969, were often subject to heightened criticisms of cultural bias in testing based on differential performance of students by social class, race/ethnicity, cultural background, gender, and other characteristics. Charges of test bias were rampant, and tests were viewed as being inherently biased against students with disadvantaged backgrounds. Among the responses to these criticisms came the voluntary disclosure of test forms by major national testing programs in an effort to remove the "veil of secrecy" surrounding testing. Over time, the effects of disclosure helped to improve the test-development process while changing the focus of the debate from test bias to awareness of the widespread inequities in the quality of schools across the U.S.

The 1970s brought an escalation in public demands for educational accountability. At least thirty-three states had some form of minimum competency test as part of their student assessments. These tests, which were predominantly criterion referenced, led to much debate in the testing profession about whether norm-referenced or criterion-referenced tests were more effective in certifying that all students could meet a minimum standard of achievement as evidence of school effectiveness. Although this debate was a highly technical one, it was useful in raising awareness of the value that interpretations of student performance relative to content standards could add to interpretations of performance relative to other students. By the 1980s, however, the focus on "minimum competency" was abandoned in favor of high standards of performance as a more ambitious goal.

In 1983, *A Nation at Risk* (National Commission on Excellence in Education, 1983) was released. The focus of education had clearly turned from the need to identify the meritorious few to the setting of rigorous standards and higher expectations for *all* students. Even state progress was publicly audited through Secretary of Education T. H. Bell's wall chart, which was intended to hold states accountable for meeting educational challenges. By 1989, forty-seven states had expanded their statewide assessment programs, but they continued to struggle with defining state standards that applied to all students, communicating these standards to teachers, helping the teachers translate the standards into classroom instruction, and creating tests that were aligned to these standards and to classroom instruction.

With the passage of the No Child Left Behind Act (NCLB) in 2001, all students are required to meet high standards, and schools are being held accountable for their effectiveness. The resulting demands on test development have never been greater. Never before has there been as much interest in, and demand for, the public to understand what examinees need to know and how well they have acquired necessary skills. As this volume is published, the initial results of NCLB are only beginning to be evaluated, but perhaps more importantly, the education debate has been changed to expect high standards for all students and all schools.

Interestingly, and perhaps even ironically, in reflecting on the history of testing, many of the most hotly debated issues were often posited as dichotomies: aptitude tests vs. achievement tests, criterion-referenced testing vs. norm-referenced testing, multiple-choice assessments vs. performance assessments, and item response theory vs. classical test theory.

Yet in reality these issues were not really dichotomies at all: the issues they were intended to address did not demand all-or-nothing answers. Rather, through public debates, research, and development, test developers have found uses for each supposedly antithetical approach, uses that are defined by the contexts and purposes of specific testing occasions. With some relief, developers have been able to focus on the use of tests in context rather than expend energy debating these dichotomous issues.

More important, test developers have witnessed an evolution in testing in the last fifty years, from selecting the meritorious few to educating all students to a standard of readiness for the next level of education and work. This may be the most significant outcome of all, one that is absolutely essential for the United States to compete in a global economy. Educating all students will likely compel us to reexamine our educational system from top to bottom, revisiting such fundamental school-design and organizational principles as size, time, teaching/learning strategies, teacher preparation, content management, and even the meaning of the high school diploma.

Perhaps if test developers have learned anything at all in the last fifty years, it is that the practice of measurement in education is complex and almost wholly dependent on context. From test design through test-score interpretation and application, developers must continuously be cognizant of the context(s) within which test results are used. Each context is unique, and tests must be based on a strong foundation of empirical validity evidence that addresses these varying contexts of use as effectively as possible.

We continue to strive for the right balance between the art and the science of test development. We are making progress.

REFERENCES

Adams, R. (1992). Multiple-choice item writing: Art and science. *The Bar Examiner, 61*(1), 5–14.

American Educational Research Association, American Psychological Association, & National Council on Measurement in Education. (1999). *Standards for educational and psychological testing.* Washington, DC: American Educational Research Association.

Anastasi, A. (1982). *Psychological testing* (5th ed.). New York: Macmillan.

Anderson, L. K. (1990). *Handbook for proofreading.* Chicago: NTC/Contemporary Publishing Group.

Andrich, D., Lyne, A., Sheridan, B., & Luo, G. (2001). RUMM2010: A Windows-based computer program for Rasch unidimensional models for measurement [Computer program]. Perth, Western Australia: Murdoch University, Social Measurement Laboratory.

Armstrong, R. D., Jones, D. H., & Wang, Z. (1994). Automated parallel test construction using classical test theory. *Journal of Educational Statistics, 19*(1), 73–90.

Beach, M., & Kenly, E. (1999). *Getting it printed* (3rd ed.). Cincinnati, OH: North Light Books.

Bejar, I. (1993). A generative approach to psychological and educational measurement. In N. Frederiksen, R. J. Mislevy, & I. Bejar (Eds.), *Test theory for a new generation of tests* (pp. 297–323). Hillsdale, NJ: Lawrence Erlbaum.

Bejar, I. (2002). Generative testing: From comprehension to implementation. In S. H. Irvine & P. C. Kyllonen (Eds.), *Item generation for test development* (pp. 199–217). Mahwah, NJ: Lawrence Erlbaum.

Bennett, R. E., Ward, W. C., Rock, D. A., & LaHart, C. (1990). *Toward a framework for constructed response items* (Research Report 90–7). Princeton, NJ: Educational Testing Service.

Berk, R. A. (1980). A consumer's guide to criterion-referenced test reliability. *Journal of Educational Measurement, 17,* 323–349.

Bhola, D. S., Impara, J. D., & Buckendahl, W. (2003). Aligning tests with states' content standards: Methods and issues. *Educational Measurement: Issues and Practice, 22*(3), 21–29.

Bloom, B. S., Engelhart, M. D., Furst, E. J., Hill, W. H., & Kratwohl, D. R. (1956). *Taxonomy of educational objectives: The classification of educational goals* (Handbook I: Cognitive domain).

Bloom, B. S., Hastings, J. T., & Madaus, G. F. (1971). *Handbook on formative summative evaluation of student learning.* San Francisco: McGraw-Hill.

Bormuth, J. R. (1970). *On the theory of achievement test items.* Chicago: University of Chicago Press.

Brennan, R. L., & Kolen, M. J. (1987). Some practical issues in equating. *Applied Psychological Measurement, 11,* 279–290.

Campion, D., & Miller, S. (2006). Test production effects on validity. In S. M. Downing and T. M. Haladyna (Eds.), *Handbook of test development* (pp. 599–623). Mahwah, NJ: Lawrence Erlbaum.

Chang, H., Mazzeo, J., & Roussos, L. (1996). Detecting DIF for polytomously scored items: An adaptation of the SIBTEST procedure. *Journal of Educational Measurement, 33,* 333–353.

Code of Fair Testing Practices in Education. (2004). Washington, DC: Joint Committee on Testing Practices.

Cooley, W. W., & Lohnes, P. R. (1976). *Evaluation research in education.* New York: Irvington Publishers.

Council on Licensure, Enforcement and Regulation (CLEAR). (1993). *Development, administration, scoring and reporting of credentialing examinations: Recommendations for board members.* Lexington, KY: Council of State Governments.

Crocker, L. (1997). Assessing content representativeness of performance assessment exercises. *Applied Measurement in Education, 10*(1), 83–95.

Cronbach, L. J. (1960). *Essentials of psychological testing* (2nd ed.). New York: Harper & Row.

Cronbach, L. J. (1971). Test validation. In R. L. Thorndike (Ed.), *Educational measurement* (2nd ed., pp. 443–507). Washington, DC: American Council on Education.

Cronbach, L. J. (1984). *Essentials of psychological testing* (4th ed.). New York: Harper & Row.

Debra P. v. Turlington, 474 F. Supp. 244 (M.D. Fla. 1979); *aff'd in part and rev'd in part*, 644 F.2d 397 (5th Cir. 1981); *rem'd*, 564 F. Supp. 177 (M.D. Fla. 1983); *aff'd*, 730 F.2d 1405 (11th Cir. 1984).

DeMars, C. E. (2000). Test stakes and item format interactions. *Applied Measurement in Education, 13*, 55–77.

Douglass, J., Roussos, L., & Stout, W. (1996). Item-bundle DIF hypothesis testing: Identifying suspect bundles and assessing their differential functioning. *Journal of Educational Measurement, 33*, 465–484.

Ebel, R. L. (1951). Writing the test item. In E. F. Lindquist (Ed.), *Educational measurement*. Washington, DC: American Council of Education.

Ebel, R. L. (1972). *Essentials of educational measurement*. Englewood Cliffs, NJ: Prentice-Hall.

Embretson, S. E., & Hershberger, S. L. (Eds.). (1999). *The new rules of measurement: What every psychologist and educator should know*. Mahwah, NJ: Lawrence Erlbaum.

Feldt, L. S., & Brennan, R. L. (1989). Reliability. In R. L. Linn (Ed.), *Educational measurement* (3rd ed., pp. 105–146). New York: American Council on Education and Macmillan.

French, A. W., & Miller, T. R. (1996). Logistic regression and its use in detecting differential item functioning in polytomous items. *Journal of Educational Measurement, 33*, 315–332.

Glas, C. A. W., & van der Linden, W. J. (2003). Computerized adaptive testing with item clones. *Applied Psychological Measurement, 27*, 249–263.

Guion, R. (1977). Content validity: The source of my discontent. *Applied Psychological Measurement, 1*, 1–10.

Guttman, L. (1941). An outline of statistical theory of predictions. In P. Horst (Ed.), *The prediction of personal adjustment* (pp. 253–364). New York: Social Science Research Council.

Haladyna, T. M. (1985, April). *A review of research on multiple-choice item option weighting*. Paper presented at the meeting of the National Council on Measurement in Education, Chicago.

Haladyna, T. M. (1994). *Developing and validating multiple choice questions*. Mahwah, NJ: Lawrence Erlbaum.

Haladyna, T. M. (1997). *Writing test items to evaluate higher order thinking*. Boston: Allyn and Bacon.

Haladyna, T. M. (1999). *Developing and validating multiple choice test items* (2nd ed.). Mahwah, NJ: Lawrence Erlbaum.

Haladyna, T. M. (2004). *Developing and validating multiple-choice test items* (3rd ed.). Mahwah, NJ: Lawrence Erlbaum.

Haladyna, T. M., & Downing, S. M. (1989a). The validity of a taxonomy of multiple-choice item-writing rules. *Applied Measurement in Education, 2*(1), 51–78.

Haladyna, T. M., & Downing, S. M. (1989b). A taxonomy of multiple-choice item-writing rules. *Applied Measurement in Education, 2*(1), 37–50.

Haladyna, T. M., Downing, S. M., & Rodriguez, M. C. (2002). A review of multiple-choice item-writing guidelines for classroom assessment. *Applied Measurement in Education, 15*, 308–313.

Haladyna, T. M., & Roid, G. H. (1981). The role of instructional sensitivity in the empirical review of criterion-referenced test items. *Journal of Educational Measurement, 18*, 39–53.

Hively, W., Patterson, H. L., & Page, S. H. (1968). A "universe-defined" system of arithmetic achievement tests. *Journal of Educational Measurement, 5*, 275–290.

Jarjoura, D., & Brennan, R. L. (1983). Multivariate generalizability models for tests developed according to a table of specifications. In L. J. Fyans (Ed.), *New directions for testing and measurement: Generalizability theory* (No. 18, pp. 83–101). San Francisco: Jossey-Bass.

Lindquist, E. F. (Ed.). (1951). *Educational measurement*. Washington, DC: American Council of Education.

Lindquist, E. F. (1958). The nature of the problem of improving scholarship and college entrance examinations. In *Invitational conference on testing problems* (pp. 104–113). Princeton, NJ: Educational Testing Service.

Linn, R. L., & Baker, E. L. (1996). Can performance-based student assessments be psychometrically sound? In J. B. Baron and D. P. Wolf (Eds.), *Performance-based student assessment: Challenges and possibilities, Ninety-fifth Yearbook of the National Society for the Study of Education* (pp. 84–103). Chicago: University of Chicago Press.

Linn, R. L., Baker, E. L., & Dunbar, S. B. (1991, November). Complex, performance-based assessment: Expectations and validation criteria. *Educational Researcher, 20*(8), 15–21.

Linn, R. L., & Gronlund, N. E. (1995). *Measurement and assessment in teaching* (7th ed.). Englewood Cliffs, NJ: Prentice-Hall.

Lord, F. M. (1980). *Applications of item response theory to practical testing problems*. Hillsdale, NJ: Lawrence Erlbaum.

Luecht, R. M. (1998). Computer-assisted test assembly using optimization heuristics. *Applied Psychological Measurement, 22*, 224–236.

Martinez, M. (1999). Cognition and the question of test item format. *Educational Psychologist, 34*, 207–218.

Mehrens, W. A., & Lehmann, I. J. (1991). *Measurement and evaluation in education and psychology* (4th ed.). Fort Worth, TX: Holt, Rinehart & Winston.

Miller, T. R., & Spray, J. A. (1993). Logistic discriminate function analysis for DIF identification of polytomously scored items. *Journal of Educational Measurement, 30*, 107–122.

Millman, J., & Arter, J. A. (1984). Issues in item banking. *Journal of Educational Measurement, 21*, 315–330.

Millman, J., & Greene, J. (1989). The specification and development of tests of achievement and ability. In R. L. Linn (Ed.), *Educational measurement* (3rd ed., pp. 335–366). New York: American Council on Education and Macmillan.

Millman, J., & Westman, R. S. (1989). Computer-assisted writing of achievement test items: Toward a future technology. *Journal of Educational Measurement, 37*(1), 267–270.

Mislevy, R. J., Steinberg, L. S., & Almond, R. G. (2002). On the roles of task model variables in assessment design. In S. Irvine & P. Kyllonen (Eds.), *Generating items for cognitive tests: Theory and practice* (pp. 97–128). Hillsdale, NJ: Lawrence Erlbaum.

National Commission on Excellence in Education. (1983). *A nation at risk: The imperative for educational reform*. Washington, DC: U.S. Department of Education.

Nitko, A. J. (1985). Review of the book *A technology for test item writing*. *Journal of Educational Measurement, 21*, 201–204.

Olsson, U., Drasgow, F., & Dorans, N. J. (1982). The polyserial correlation coefficient. *Psychometrika, 47*, 337–347.

Osterlind, S. J. (1998). *Constructing test items: Multiple-choice, constructed-response, performance, and other formats*. New York: Kluwer Academic.

Phillips, S. E. (1993). *Legal implications of high-stakes assessment: What states should know.* Oak Brook, IL: North Central Regional Educational Laboratory.

Popham, W. J. (1997). What's wrong—and what's right—with rubrics. *Educational Leadership, 55,* 72–75.

Rothman, R., Slattery, J. B., Vranek, J. L., & Resnick, L. B. (2002). *Benchmarking and alignment of standards and testing* (CSE Technical Report 566). Los Angeles: University of California at Los Angeles, National Center for Evaluation, Standards, & Student Testing.

Shealy, R., & Stout, W. F. (1993). A model-based standardization approach that separates true bias/DIF from group differences and detects test bias/DIF as well as item bias/DIF. *Psychometrika, 58,* 159–194.

Stanley, J. C. (1971). Reliability. In R. L. Thorndike (Ed.), *Educational measurement* (2nd ed.) (pp. 356–442). Washington, DC: American Council on Education.

Stiggins, R. J. (1995). Assessment literacy for the 21st century. *Phi Delta Kappan, 77,* 238–245.

Stocking, M. L., & Swanson, L. (1998). Optimal design of item banks for computerized adaptive tests. *Applied Psychological Measurement, 22,* 271–279.

Swaminathan, J., & Rogers, H. J. (1990). Detecting differential item functioning using logistic regression procedures. *Journal of Educational Measurement, 27,* 361–370.

Swanson, L., & Stocking, M. L. (1993). A model and heuristic for solving very large item selection problems. *Applied Psychological Measurement, 17,* 151–166.

Theunissen, T. J. J. M. (1985). Binary programming and test design. *Psychometrika, 50,* 411–420.

Thompson, S. J., Johnstone, C. J., & Thurlow, M. L. (2002). *Universal design applied to large-scale assessments* (NCEO Synthesis Report 44). Minneapolis: University of Minnesota, National Center on Educational Outcomes.

van der Linden, W. J. (2005). *Linear models for optimal test design.* New York: Springer-Verlag.

van der Linden, W. J., & Boekkooi-Timminga, E. (1988). A zero-one programming approach to Gulliksen's matched random subtests method. *Applied Psychological Measurement, 12,* 201–209.

van der Linden, W. J., & Boekkooi-Timminga, E. (1989). A maximin model for test design with practical constraints. *Psychometrika, 54,* 237–247.

van der Linden, W. J., Veldkamp, B. P., & Reese, L. M. (2000). An integer programming approach to item bank design. *Applied Psychological Measurement, 24,* 139–150.

Veldkamp, B. P., & van der Linden, W. J. (1999). *Designing item pools for computerized adaptive testing* (Research Report 00–03). Twente, Netherlands: University of Twente.

Webb, N. L. (1999). *Alignment of science and mathematics standards and assessments in four states* (Research Monograph No. 18). Madison: University of Wisconsin at Madison, National Institute for Science Education.

Wightman, L. F. (1998). Practical issues in computerized test assembly. *Applied Psychological Measurement, 22,* 292–302.

Wright, B. D., & Bell, S. R. (1984). Item banks: What, why, how. *Journal of Educational Measurement, 21,* 331–345.

Zieky, M. (1993). Practical questions in the use of DIF statistics in test development. In P. Holland & H. Wainer (Eds.), *Differential item functioning* (pp. 337–347). Hillsdale, NJ: Lawrence Erlbaum.

10

Test Administration, Security, Scoring, and Reporting

Allan S. Cohen
University of Georgia

James A. Wollack
University of Wisconsin

1. INTRODUCTION

Administration and scoring are at the heart of maintaining the integrity of an examination. It is the standardization of the administration and scoring that ensure that the test scores can be interpreted: "The usefulness and interpretability of test scores require that a test be administered and scored according to the developer's instructions" (American Educational Research Association, American Psychological Association, & National Council on Measurement in Education [AERA, APA, & NCME], 1999, p. 61). Without careful attention to administration and scoring, it would be difficult, for example, to compare scores among individuals, across administrations or over different forms of a test. Growth in achievement would be potentially inextricably confounded with error. In addition, unless instructions are understandable to all examinees, all examinees are not provided the same opportunity to demonstrate what they know (Willingham et al., 1988). When instructions are vague or misleading, test proctors may direct students in ways that are not standardized. Such practices potentially invalidate certain interpretations and uses of test data (AERA, APA, & NCME, 1999).

Chapters in previous editions of *Educational Measurement* have dealt with the major considerations in administration (Clemans, 1968; Traxler, 1950), scanning (Baker, 1968, 1989), and scoring (Baker, 1968, 1989; Traxler, 1950) of the traditional forms of individual and group-administered paper-and-pencil (P&P) tests. These types of tests have remained essentially unchanged in the last several decades, as have their administration and scoring. However, over the last half century, modern educational measurement has developed rapidly and large-scale educational and psychological testing programs have been at the core of this development. The driving force behind much of this development has been the improvements that arise due to advancements in technology, particularly with respect to computing. Technology has dramatically expanded the ways in which tests are administered, scored, and reported, and has allowed for measuring constructs more completely and in ways not possible using only P&P technology. These developments in computing and psychometric theory have led to major improvements in test administration, scoring, and reporting. Unfortunately, it is these same developments that lie at the root of increasingly serious problems with test security. Because of the tremendous impact of technology on testing since the last printing of *Educational Measurement*, the role of technology in the different phases of testing will be a recurring theme in this chapter.

One topic that has received little attention in previous editions of *Educational Measurement* is test security. Maintaining the security of test items and scores is paramount if tests are to provide useful data. However, due to factors such as technology, widespread testing, and increased stakes associated with tests, the motivation and ability to cheat are alarmingly high. Because test compromise can occur throughout all phases of testing, including administration, scoring, and reporting, the topic of test security will be covered in depth in this chapter.

Our premise for this chapter is that a description and understanding of the areas of test administration, security, scoring, and reporting provides a framework for test developers and test administrators to use to examine the context in which their tests are used. To that end, we will focus on standardized types of tests, mainly because these tests are usually better developed and, in some cases, provide a type of gold standard against which other less well-developed tests might be compared or judged.

We begin this chapter by providing a brief historical perspective on testing, with the particular aim of noting the impact of technology on administration, security, scoring, and reporting. These four domains are covered in more detail, individually, throughout the remainder of the chapter.

1.1. Testing: The Past Is Prelude

The earliest forms of testing reportedly extend back to ancient China, possibly over 2000 years ago (DuBois, 1970). "Examinations" were designed to find the best individuals to serve in the administration of the country (DuBois, 1970), where *best* was defined as both political and *military* and was taken to mean most proficient in the six arts of music, archery, horsemanship, writing, arithmetic, and the rites of public and private life. The methods of testing followed from the purpose and from the available technology. The forms of the tasks were dictated then, as now, by the content and the skills to be measured. Music required the playing of an instrument, archery required demonstrating skill with bow and arrow, and horsemanship required demonstrating riding ability. In general, performance tests were used to measure physical skills for prospective military leaders, and verbal and cognitive skills were tested to assess proficiency in memorization and interpretation of the Confucian classics for political administrators.

By the mid-14th century, these examinations had assumed a clearly structured form with more political than physical objectives (Bowman, 1989; DuBois, 1970). At the latter stages of the examination process, copyists duplicated the compositions so that the identity of each writer would not be known to the two independent readers. Disputes in scoring were resolved by a third reader. Examination security was a concern as the rewards for passing the examinations were large. Some examinees took great risks to have access to reference materials, particularly considering that the punishment for getting caught was sometimes death.

Testing in ancient Greek was likewise used to identify individuals who exhibited the characteristics of the best citizens (Doyle, 1974). These characteristics were primarily physical, so tasks such as running, leaping, and throwing the discus and the javelin were used. Consistency of administrative conditions was enforced to ensure that the conditions under which these skills were measured were the same for all individuals. The concept of standardization was not part of the extant measurement vocabulary, but requiring everyone to "run the same race" was considered necessary to be certain that comparability over administrations was maintained for all examinees and that the best candidates were selected.

Testing in its more modern forms began to emerge in the 19th century as seen in the development of the British civil service examinations as well as in measures of individual differences, exemplified by Galton's studies of individual differences and his development of the questionnaire as a tool for measuring attitudes, although sensory motor measures dominated early testing. Even though paper, which had been invented by the Chinese early in the second century (Hunter, 1947), was available at a relatively low cost in some quantity by the mid-19th century, most schools and pupils could still not afford it. Tests, such as those developed by Binet and his colleagues, were largely individually administered. An important contribution by Binet and his colleagues, however, was the concentration on administering tests under standard conditions, so as to facilitate comparing scores across individuals.

2. ADMINISTRATION

Traxler (1950) noted that test developers had not been overly responsive in providing complete data on administrative conditions and scoring. That has changed somewhat because of the importance that has been attached to the *Standards for Educational and Psychological Tests* (AERA, APA, & NCME, 1974) and the *Standards for Educational and Psychological Testing* (AERA, APA, & NCME, 1985, 1999). These volumes have been instrumental in focusing the attention of both test developers and users on the essential characteristics of educational and psychological tests. More recently, McCallin (in press) discusses the impact of administration on test validity. Consequently, nowadays, the major standardized educational testing programs all provide adequate technical information about the administration and scoring of their tests. A number of programs also provide clear and generally adequate information about the development of the tests and the interpretation of test results. Unfortunately, many licensure and certification testing programs still provide relatively little technical information and many statewide educational testing programs provide relatively little information about the validity of interpretations of test results.

2.1. Types of Administration

Test administration can be defined in terms of (1) mode of presentation, (2) format of the items, (3) the amount of control left in the hands of the examinee for pacing through the examination, and (4) the record left of the copy of the examination that was administered. The simpler modes of administration include oral presentation, slide or overhead presentation, and writing items on a blackboard. For these methods, item format can be either selected response or constructed response, and pacing control is in the hands of the administrator. Too rapid a pace can stress some examinees and too slow a pace can be frustrating to others. Skipping about in a test booklet may be considered by some as good test-taking practice, but it is not possible with these kinds of presentation methods. In addition, when the blackboard is erased or the oral presentation is finished, there may not be an exact record of the examination that was administered, unless an audio or video recording was done.

A second mode of presentation is to create a relatively permanent record of the tasks required such as putting items in individual test booklets or providing a task that the examinee is to perform. Sometimes these can become quite elaborate, such as designing or even constructing an object (Bottge, Heinrichs, Chan, & Watson, 2000). These methods are common in testing of higher-order skills such as in the performance testing methods known as the Objective Structured Clinical Examination (OSCE) format used extensively in medical education (Harden, 1988; Harden & Gleeson, 1979). Pacing is often in the examinee's control even with time limits imposed by the test standardization. Some forms of OSCE offer the option of skipping about in the exam to maximize one's personal probability of a correct response. An exact copy of the test can also usually be retained. Many states have testing programs that require disclosure of operational items after the examination. When this occurs, the individual test booklet may need to be modified to remove pilot items and items included only for equating or linking purposes.

2.1.1. Computer-Based Test (CBT) Administration

Tests administered via computer are becoming increasingly popular. This presentation mode (see Drasgow, Luecht, &

Bennett, Chapter 13, this volume) offers an opportunity to use more varied item formats as well as adaptive presentation with a far greater level of control by the test developer over the conditions of administration. Self-pacing during CBT examinations is usually possible even if the test has time limits. Returning to previously answered questions is also sometimes possible, although some software, notably computer adaptive testing software, may not permit it. CBT may also offer additional potential for development of accommodations-related modifications of tests or testing conditions that measure the same construct as nonaccommodated or nonadapted forms of tests, such as suggested by universal design (e.g., Johnstone, 2003).

Method variance such as that due to differences in mode of administration (e.g., Wang & Kolen, 2001) is a well-known cause of differences in test validity. Therefore, P&P tests and their CBT counterparts may well produce different results. For example, Divgi and Stollof (1986) and Mills and Stocking (1996) suggest that differences in model parameter estimates are likely when modes of administration differ. Recent work (Straetmans & Eggens, 1998), however, suggests that this may not always be the case. Additional research on the impact of differences in modes of administration is needed. Likewise, guidelines for migrating from one mode of administration to another would be useful, especially when performance under the old and new modes may not be comparable.

2.2. Impact of Conditions under Which Test Is Administered

It is reasonable to assume that administration conditions have a nonnegligible effect on examinee performance. If it is too hot or too cold in the testing room, performances of some examinees are likely to be negatively affected. Similarly, if it is too noisy, some examinees may be distracted and perform below their potential. Many such systematic sources of error have been described in previous editions of *Educational Measurement*. Even so, there remains substantial room for further study particularly since, in some cases, new technologies have changed what we need to examine and new methodologies have emerged that can allow us to address these issues. Recent developments in item response theory (IRT), for example, have led to techniques for isolating latent groups of examinees (e.g., Mislevy & Verhelst, 1990; Rost, 1990), which in turn has led to modeling behaviors in groups of examinees that differ with respect to certain characteristics, such as the speededness of the test (e.g., Yamamoto, 1989). Below, we illustrate this approach as it has been used for modeling speededness and then suggest that the method itself can be usefully extended to the study of other aspects of test administration.

Speededness effects arise when examinees change their response strategies as they near the end of the test and have less time to respond. Most educational tests are not intended to measure speed of response so speed is not a desirable influence on test performance (Lord & Novick, 1968). Much of the research on speededness has focused on omissions at the end of the test, but such studies do not directly address the central issue in speededness, namely the ways in which time limits may cause some examinees to change response strategies as time runs out.

Differences in patterns of responses indicate differences in the cognitive strategies that examinees use to answer test questions (Mislevy & Verhelst, 1990). Yamamoto (1989; see also Yamamoto & Everson, 1997) used this rationale to separate examinees into different groups depending on the patterns of their responses in the speeded portions of the test. Examinees who did not change their response strategies were considered to be unaffected by the time limits of the test. Those who did change their strategies to random guessing were considered to be affected by time limits. These different groups of examinees were not manifest groups, but rather were latent and only evident in their patterns of responses in the speeded portions of the test. Boughton, Larkin, and Yamamoto (2004) used this model to identify differential speededness patterns by ethnicity and gender, for both P&P tests and their CBT counterparts. Boughton et al. consistently found little speededness in the computerized tests (which also allowed 33% more time per item), but the P&P tests were often heavily speeded. Tests were found to be most speeded for ethnic minority groups, particularly African Americans and Latinos, and slightly more speeded for males than for females, though the gender effect was small compared to the ethnicity effect. Boughton et al. demonstrated that item parameter estimates from the speededness model were very similar to the parameter estimates under the less speeded CBT administration, whereas uncorrected item parameter estimates typically resulted in underestimating the true probability of a correct response for an item (i.e., item difficulties were spuriously high).

Research on this approach has subsequently been extended to include examinees that do not respond randomly at the end of the test but rather are identified as using a different set of strategies, modeled in the speeded portion of the test by a second IRT model (Bolt, Cohen, & Wollack, 2002). Examinees in the speeded group were found to be qualitatively different from those in the nonspeeded group (Cohen, Wollack, & Mroch, 2002). Although no gender differences were reported in either Bolt et al. (2002) or Cohen et al. (2002), speeded examinees performed less well at the end of the test than they did at the beginning, but were also better students during their first year of college, had higher GPAs, earned more degree credits, and had fewer failing credits. The examinees who were identified as being in the speeded groups in these two studies comprised over 20% of the samples, but less than 5% of the examinees in these studies omitted one or more items at the end of the test. Clearly, there were more examinees whose responses were affected by time limits than could have been detected by simply examining omit rates at the end of the test. The important differences between the speeded and nonspeeded groups were detected by modeling their response strategies. Wollack, Cohen, and Wells (2003) and Wollack, Wells, and Cohen (2003) used the same methodology to examine the impact of speededness on scale stability over relatively long periods. When speeded examinees' responses were removed from the data and item parameters estimates were calibrated only on nonspeeded examinees' responses, the parameter estimates and the score scale were found to be more stable over time.

The research described on speededness demonstrates a new methodology, using discrete mixture IRT models (Mislevy & Verhelst, 1990; Rost, 1990), for differentiating groups of examinees on the basis of their patterns of responses. This new methodology can potentially also be used to study examinee reactions to differences in administration conditions such as time limits, noise, lighting, temperature, and so on, leading to better understanding of how examinees may be affected by administration conditions. Once classified into latent groups, examinees can be further studied to determine what factors are associated with their particular sets of response strategies. These kinds of methodologies may also be useful in understanding the impact of other sources of systematic error, such as modifications in test standardization provided to examinees with disabilities (Cohen, Gregg, & Deng, 2005).

2.3. Standardization

Whenever examinees are to be compared against previous performance, against one another or against some performance criterion, there is a need to be concerned about the testing conditions. Standardization of these conditions is done to help ensure that all examinees are assessed against the same criterion (or criteria) and under the same conditions (e.g., "running the same race"). Standardization requires that tests be administered and scored in the same way for all examinees, under conditions that ensure the results have the same meaning across all forms and administrations, given the purpose for which the test was intended. Developers of tests prescribe the directions, conditions of administration, and scoring as a means of helping to ensure that the results can be used and interpreted in the same way across different samples of examinees, test administrations, and forms of the test. A common misunderstanding is that the use of standard scores or multiple-choice items means a test is standardized. Tests are standardized when the directions, conditions of administration, and scoring are clearly defined and fixed for all examinees, administrations, and forms. A test requiring an examinee to perform a piece of music, paint a picture, or repair an electronic circuit board can be standardized in just the same way as a test with 80 multiple-choice reading comprehension items.

Another common misconception is that standardization is only necessary for norm-referenced tests. In fact, standardization is required whenever results from different test administrations or from different forms are to be aggregated or compared to one another or to some external criterion. If standardized conditions are not maintained, the interpretability of results across the different administrations or forms will be affected. This is the case whether tests are norm referenced, standards based, or criterion referenced, or whether they use performance or selected response item formats.

Standardized directions ensure that all examinees have the same understanding of what is expected on the test. These directions may be detailed or not, but they must indicate exactly what is expected of the examinee. If instructions are overly complex or if they are in a language an examinee cannot understand, examinees are not provided an opportunity to demonstrate that they know the material being tested (Willingham et al., 1988). If an examinee has limited proficiency in the language in which the directions are given, then the administrator needs to provide directions in a language that the examinee does understand. It is likewise necessary to ensure that the examinee has sufficient literacy in the language in which the test is presented so that test results are meaningful. Directions should normally include such things as how to answer the questions on the test, whether or not to write in the test booklet, whether ancillary materials such as a calculator are allowed, applicable time limits, how much help the proctor can be expected to provide, or whether guessing is discouraged (e.g., there is a penalty for guessing), encouraged (e.g., no penalty for guessing), or required (e.g., as is the case on some adaptive tests). Conditions of administration include such things as method of administration of the test, training of administrators, training of examinees to respond appropriately, special instructions for registration, examinee check-in, room lighting and temperature, and seating. Likewise, scoring rules can include machine or hand scoring, training of raters if appropriate, and impact of particular features of the response, such as spelling, handwriting, showing work, length, and so on. Traxler's (1950) concern is still valid today that the information given to test administrators on the reasons for imposing these kinds of conditions and the impact of their violations needs to be spelled out in administrators' manuals.

The impact of instructions on examinee performance has been studied for some time. As an example, Steele and Aronson (1995) presented some evidence on stereotype threat found among African American examinees, as a function of type of instructions given. When African American college-level examinees were asked to take a test that had no direct consequences for them, their performances were equal to or better than those of majority Caucasian college students from the same institution. When similar groups of examinees were told the outcome of the test would affect them academically, performance levels dropped for the African American examinees. Steele and Aronson suggested that this effect was caused by the perceived stereotypes associated with testing instructions.

2.4. Special Accommodations

Anyone with a documented disability, according to the Americans with Disabilities Act of 1990 (ADA), is entitled to receive reasonable accommodations if it is believed that the disability interferes with the ability of the person to demonstrate his/her true skill level. Examinees who are unsighted, for example, will not be able to take a reading test without some form of accommodation such as a Braille version of the test or a reader to read the questions and possibly record the answers. An examinee who has some form of motor impairment may be unable to properly mark a scannable answer sheet or depress a key on a computer keyboard and may need assistance to accomplish these tasks. An examinee with a learning disability may struggle when required to process and respond quickly to test questions, so may need to take the test under modified conditions to allow for additional time. The intent behind the ADA is that disabling conditions may interfere with the measurement of an examinee's ability, so by offering accommodations to examinees with disabilities, the ability of interest will be estimated more accurately. Modifications to testing conditions are typically provided for examinees with visual, auditory, motor, or other physical impairment. In addition, depending on the exact nature of the test, accommodations are common for examinees with learning disabilities, cognitive disabilities, emotional disabilities, and limited English proficiency (Sireci, Li, & Scarpati, 2004), as well as various other forms of mental illness, such as attention deficit disorder (with or without hyperactivity), test anxiety (or generalized anxiety disorder), or depression.

Accommodations are designed to remove or mitigate as much as possible the effects of the disabling condition(s) from the measurement of the ability of interest. Accommodations are not intended to provide an unfair advantage to anyone receiving them (Shepard, Taylor & Betebenner, 1998; Zuriff, 2000), and must not change the nature of the construct being measured (Johnstone, 2003; Sireci et al., 2004). Although reasonable accommodations are generally required under ADA, the exception is that it is not necessary to grant accommodations that will compromise the fundamental interpretations of the test. As an example, for a test to accurately measure reading comprehension, the reading texts, and possibly also the items, must be read by the examinee. If a reader or a taped copy of the test is provided for unsighted examinees, then the construct being measured is no longer reading comprehension.

The use of accommodations is a particular concern for standardized tests because, by definition, such tests are administered under conditions that must remain the same for all examinees. When the standardization is violated, interpretation of the scores on the tests is compromised. The *Standards* (AERA, APA, & NCME, 1999) state that accommodations are to be provided if a disability requires a modification in administration conditions:

> Standard 5.1: "Test administrators should follow carefully the standardized procedures for administration and scoring specified by the test developer, unless the situation or a test taker's disability dictates that an exception should be made." (p. 63)

In the case of accommodated testing, the extent of compromise to the standardization is not always clear. Sireci et al. (2004) noted that a central issue in the debate over what kinds of accommodations to provide is the extent to which standardized testing conditions can be modified without altering the construct being measured. Whenever possible, test developers should provide information about the validity of inferences made and about the effects of modifications for examinees with different types of disabilities (AERA, APA, & NCME, 1999; Standards 10.4, 10.6, 10.7, 10.12).

Changing the task being measured could be a violation of the intent of the test developer and could result in modifying the behavior being measured. Not all accommodations, however, modify the task to the extent that it is no longer the same as that intended by the test developer. The *Standards* (AERA, APA, & NCME, 1999) are clear with regard to the intent of modifications for accommodating individuals with disabilities:

> Standard 10.1: "In testing individuals with disabilities, test developers, test administrators, and test users should take steps to ensure that the test score inferences accurately reflect the intended construct rather than any disabilities and their associated characteristics extraneous to the intent of the measurement." (p. 106)

When necessary, the content or the task may need to be changed to accommodate a particular disability. For example, testing an examinee who has limited proficiency in English may require writing the items in the native language of the examinee, although tests for which English literacy is an important aspect of the construct being measured ought not be accommodated in this way. Oral presentation and extended time are the most common accommodations provided for students with disabilities (Sireci et al., 2004). Oral presentation does not necessarily change the construct being measured unless the ability being measured is something specifically related to the task of visually decoding a page of information, such as reading. Likewise, extended time limits would not necessarily modify the construct unless some function of response speed (e.g., number of words typed in a minute) was part of the construct being measured. As noted earlier, different groups of examinees have been shown to respond differently to test questions, when time limits are imposed (Bolt et al., 2002; Boughton et al., 2004; Yamamoto, 1989; Yamamoto & Everson, 1997). Research along the lines of the speededness studies reported above may be able to determine whether or not there are possibly different groups of examinees who respond differentially to test items when the accommodation is extra time (e.g., Cohen et al, 2005). This type of research would be valuable as it would provide evidence as to the impact of extra time on the cognitive strategies employed by examinees receiving this accommodation.

> Standard 10.4 (AERA, APA, & NCME, 1999) notes that, when modifications are made or recommended for a given test, they should be clearly spelled out in both the test manual and the technical manual. This further requires that the test developer study the impact of these accommodations on the construct being measured as well as on the resulting interpretation of test results. (Standard 10.5)

The impact of testing accommodations is unfortunately not clear. Much of the discussion of accommodations is framed in advocacy studies rather than in cleanly designed studies. Chiu and Pearson (1999) note that, of the few studies that are relatively well designed, there does not appear to be an abundance of clear evidence that accommodations provide an advantage or a disadvantage to accommodated examinees. Instead, in those studies that appear to have useful information, students with disabilities had some improvements in their test performance. The magnitudes of these improvements, however, were relatively small.

Some of the common types of test accommodations and the disabilities for which they are intended to compensate are described below. One difficulty in studying the impact of these accommodations, however, is that most examinees receive multiple accommodations (Sireci et al., 2004), making it unclear what the impact is of any one accommodation (Gregg, Morgan, Hartwig, & Coleman, in press).

2.4.1. Extra Time

One of the most commonly reported types of accommodation is extended time (Sireci et al., 2004; Zuriff, 2000). This kind of accommodation includes increasing the time allowed for testing as well as the length of breaks during the test. Providing extra time, usually time-and-a-half or double time, has been found to improve scores of some disabled examinees but also tends to improve the scores of individuals without disabilities (Zuriff, 2000). Individuals who have a reading disability can often benefit from having extended time for testing. Individuals who have an orthopedic impairment that prevents them from responding quickly, for example, may be more likely to benefit from extended time limits. Extending time limits, however, also may result in unwanted fatigue effects intruding on the estimate of ability (AERA, APA, & NCME, 1999; Standard 10.6, p. 107).

2.4.2. Oral Presentation

Oral presentation of test items is routinely done for individuals who are visually impaired. When the task consists of giving answers to multiple-choice, short answer, or extended response questions (e.g., essay testing), the typical oral accommodation consists of having a test proctor read the question and, if needed, serve as a scribe to write down the examinee's responses. Assistive software has also been available for some time that can read text aloud so that visually impaired examinees can hear the test items without needing to have someone read to them. Some software is also available with voice recognition capabilities so examinees can respond vocally. Oral presentation is sometimes done by audiotaping the test and having a proctor play the audiotape for the examinee.

2.4.3. Assistive Measures

Large print or special equipment for magnifying test copy are also used for individuals who are visually impaired. Not surprisingly, the impact on scores from such accommodations appears to be generally consistent and positive. For unsighted examinees, the use of Braille editions of tests is a common accommodation. Readers are also often provided to read the examination aloud for the examinee. Scribes are often provided for individuals who have a disability that impairs their ability to write or accurately mark answers on an answer sheet. Voice production and recognition equipment removes the need for a second person to serve as a reader or a scribe and enables the examinee to be more independent.

2.4.4. Modifying Test Settings

Individuals who are highly distractible can sometimes be helped by being seated in the testing room so that they cannot see anyone else. In some cases, this can be accomplished by seating the examinee in the front of the testing room. In other instances, it may be necessary to test in a room with minimal decoration or simply in a room by themselves. Some individuals require rooms that have sound-deadening insulation installed to make the room as soundproof as possible, or rooms equipped with white-noise generators to help block out background noises. Likewise, providing a place to lie down may be a helpful accommodation for an examinee with chronic fatigue syndrome.

One needs to be concerned about differences in examinee performance as a function of mode of administration. This is primarily an issue if multiple modes of testing are to be supported. For example, if a P&P test and a CBT are both supported in the same testing program, comparability will usually be important. This would be the case even if both modes are no longer provided but scores from both modes were still available. Such a scenario could easily occur in an admissions testing context, for example, in which the tests are being migrated from a P&P to a CBT platform, since scores from both modes are likely to be available for multiple years. When scores are available from either P&P tests or CBT and the scores aren't comparable (e.g., one format is easier, they measure the intended construct[s] differently, etc.), testing mode becomes a fairness issue.

2.5. Computerized Testing

Computers have been used for over half a century for scoring and analyzing test results. Increasingly, however, they are being used to administer tests as well. The computer offers the capability of presenting item formats that go well beyond those used for P&P tests. Ordering words, phrases, or sequences of statements is possible on a P&P test by having the examinee indicate order by some kind of numbering. On a computer, this same type of item can be converted to a format in which the words, phrases or sentences are dragged by the examinee into the correct answer position. This type of format is particularly useful for asking questions about the order of events in a process. Another example of an item type available with CBT is the hotspot, where examinees are asked to use their mouse to click on the part of a graphic that answers the question. For example, examinees might be shown a picture of the human digestive system, and asked to find the pancreas. It is also possible to use computers to test how examinees perform in simulated scenarios. The United States Medical Licensing Examination (Federation of State Medical Boards of the United States, Inc., & National Board of Medical Examiners, 2005), for example, currently includes nine case simulations. In these simulations, examinees are presented with the clinical setting, a preliminary case history on the simulated patient, and the simulated case time. Examinees provide patient orders to the computer primarily through free-entry text, but some buttons and check boxes may be clicked to select certain features, such as obtaining patient updates, reviewing information, and moving a patient. The use of computers in testing appears to offer the opportunity to test constructs more fully than is possible with P&P tests (Mills & Stocking, 1996).

3. TEST SECURITY

Hand in hand with the earliest use of testing, concern about examination security dates back to the testing done a few thousand years ago in ancient China. Because the passing rate for these tests was in the low single digits and the rewards and responsibilities for those who passed were potentially great (Doyle, 1974), examination security was considered vitally important. Examinees often developed elaborate means to assist them in answering questions, including creating miniature books of notes, writing passages from the Confucian classics on undergarments, copying notes onto the backs of fans, or hiring impersonators to take the exams in their place (Crozier, 2002). Many of these cheating methods are still in use today. The Chinese government often went to extreme measures to prevent and deter cheating. Testing rooms were occasionally sealed to provide a more secure testing environment. Examinees found guilty of cheating were stripped of all previously earned qualifications. In some instances of examiner cheating, guilty examiners were caught and beheaded (Taylor & Taylor, 1995).

Though modern-day methods for addressing the cheating problem are considerably more humane, testing companies continue to spend substantial amounts of money and effort to maintain the integrity of their tests. With tests serving as the gatekeepers to so many professional goals, such as certification, licensure, admission to programs, job retention or promotion, and receiving scholarships or recognition, it could be argued that the motivation to cheat has never been higher. Indeed, it is very easy to find examples of cheating on large-scale, high-stakes testing programs. Some of the more recent examples include the following:

- Two candidates and a test proctor were indicted in January, 2004 on charges that they conspired to allow a person to impersonate six other candidates and take their National Association of Securities Dealers' licensing and qualifying examinations for them. (Associated Press, 2004)
- From 1999–2002, 21 teachers in New York were found to have cheated to improve the scores of their students on state tests. Examples of the types of cheating included reading off answers, photocopying test materials, teaching to the test, encouraging students with wrong answers to re-check their work, and finishing incomplete sentences on essays. Similar stories of teacher cheating have been reported in several other states, as well. (Associated Press, 2003b)
- The November, 2003 administration of the Common Admission Test, used throughout India to enter the top business schools, was cancelled because The Central Bureau of Investigation learned that as many as 150 people throughout the country were involved in selling to candidates question papers that were guaranteed to receive high scores. Candidates paid as much as $11,000 (US currency) for papers. (Times News Network, 2003)

Making the problem more challenging still is that the 21st-century cheaters have at their disposal many new "resources" for compromising tests. Improvements in technology, including availability of better (and smaller) electronic communication devices, has introduced entirely new ways for examinees to cheat. A major concern is that this technology has made it easier than ever for a few individuals to compromise the validity of score interpretations from a given test administration, or even compromise an entire testing program. Recent examples of threats to test security from technology-based cheating include the following:

- Six University of Maryland students, communicating through text messaging on their cell phones, received the exam key for their accounting exam from a friend, after the instructor posted the key to a website during the test. The instructor caught the cheating by posting a bogus key and identifying the examinees who selected those answers. (Associated Press, 2003a)
- National Boards in three health care professions, physical therapy, pharmacy, and podiatric medicine, have all faced cheating problems stemming from electronic sharing of test material. In two of the cases, upward of 200 items were posted on websites or in chatrooms, while the third case involved emailing test questions to friends. (Smydo, 2003)
- In California, a student sitting for the Engineer-in-Training exam was caught using a calculator that had been altered to scan and copy test questions. A subsequent investigation found three years' worth of test items on the candidates' home computer. The California Board for Professional Engineers and Land Surveyors brought charges, and the candidate was sentenced to 90 days in jail. (Boykin, 2004)

3.1. Types of Cheating

Cheating is no longer simply a pragmatic way to improve one's test score. Reasons cited for cheating range from improving scores to showing contempt for an instructor. Some cheat simply because they can. Others cheat because they feel that it has become so commonplace that it is necessary in order to earn the percentile rank they actually deserve. Some teachers and administrators have cheated to help save their jobs. In some cases, cheating is part of an entrepreneurial enterprise where exam information is stolen and sold to interested parties. Davis, Grover, Becker, and McGregor (1992), Haines, Diekhoff, LaBeff, and Clark (1986), and Stevens and Stevens (1987) provide useful discussions of the reasons people cite for cheating.

Methods used for cheating are equally diverse. Although some methods date back to the Chinese civil service examinations thousands of years ago, other methods, particularly those relying on technology, are much more recent. There are many ways to classify types of security breaches. Cizek (1999) categorized cheating into three domains: (a) taking, giving, or receiving information from others; (b) using forbidden materials or information; and (c) circumventing the assessment process. Cizek pointed out that this categorization scheme constitutes a prevalence hierarchy, in that (a) is more common than (b) which is more common than (c). Cheating may also be categorized as hi-tech or low-tech, depending on its level of sophistication. Because of the impact that different types of security breaches can have on a testing program, we choose to categorize cheating as either individual or collaborative. Obviously, testing companies and test consumers, such as licensing boards, are interested in curbing all types of cheating, but it is the organized, collaborative efforts that cause the most concern, because they often result in many individuals receiving inaccurate scores or the exposure of many test items. These two categories of cheating are discussed below.

3.1.1. Individual Security Breaches

Individual security breaches refer to any situation in which one individual, working independently, attempts to cheat. The vast majority of individual security breaches are designed to improve the score of the individual who is cheating. Examples of this include using crib notes or other unauthorized materials, copying answers from an unsuspecting neighboring examinee, and plagiarism. It is also possible that an individual cheats for purposes of collecting information to pass along to other future test takers, possibly for financial gain. A single individual's ability to expose an entire bank of questions is limited, but depending on the individual's resources and the nature of the test, even one person may be able to severely compromise a bank. The use of small electronic devices such as concealed video cameras, cell phones, pagers, voice recorders, personal digital assistants (PDAs), or, in the example given earlier, calculators, make it possible for examinees to capture all of the items to which they are exposed. Illegal access to the internet, particularly for online testing or during unsupervised breaks, presents individuals with the opportunity to look up answers or send detailed information to others.

3.1.2. Collaborative Security Breaches

Collaborative security breaches refer to any situation in which individuals work together to cheat. As with individual security breaches, the objective of the cheating could be to improve the test scores of one or more individuals involved in the cheating. Examples of this include one examinee allowing another to copy answers during a test, examinees agreeing to complete different portions of the test and then to share their answers with each other, or with multiple examinees using a system for communicating answers during a test. However, collaborative security breaches may also include attempts to capture an entire test or test bank. While this is a difficult feat for any one individual, it is much less difficult for a team of people. A few examinees can essentially reproduce an entire test by assigning different parts of the test to each co-conspirator. With computerized adaptive testing (CAT), the item selection algorithms are such that it may be possible for a team of people to reproduce a very large portion of a test bank, by coaching co-conspirators to respond in ways that expose many items at different points along the scale. If a test bank has a limited number of items designed to measure the very high end of the scale, it may be possible to expose nearly all of the items that an examinee would encounter en route to a perfect (or near perfect) score, either by asking high scoring examinees to recall their items or by having experts pose as examinees for purposes of retrieving test information.

3.2. Countermeasures

There are three categories of countermeasures for combating cheating: human observation and prevention, electronic countermeasures, and psychometric countermeasures. These three countermeasures are discussed below.

3.2.1. Human Observation and Prevention

This category refers to anything that humans can do (without the aid of machines) to reduce security breaches. Observation includes using proctors and test administrators who have been educated on the different ways in which examinees cheat during an exam and trained to identify and report behaviors that are suspicious. Examples of things to look for in candidates' behavior include

- presenting fake or improper identification,
- being unusually nervous,
- completing an exam very quickly or spending an unusual amount of time on just a few questions,
- spending lots of time looking around the testing room or at other examinees' papers,
- sitting in unusual positions,
- talking or attempting to communicate with another,
- using prohibited materials, and
- having numerous excuses to leave one's seat (e.g., trips to the bathroom, to sharpen pencils, to ask questions, etc.).

Observation also includes the safekeeping of testing materials by all who have access to them. At the testing company, all test materials should be kept in a secure location, and access to those locations should be reserved for a limited number of people. Test materials, including scraps of paper containing drafts of items, should always be shredded or securely destroyed. Personnel at the printing facilities should be informed of the secure nature of the exams and instructed to take steps to ensure their safekeeping. All exam materials should be boxed promptly after printing, and stored in a secure location until they are ready to be shipped. Misprinted booklets and superfluous pages, such as papers cleared from jammed printers, should be securely destroyed. Tests should be sent to testing sites via secure and traceable means, within a week or two of the scheduled test date. Upon receipt of the testing materials, the facility should take full inventory of everything received. In some cases, it may be helpful to print bar codes onto test booklets for electronic tracking. All materials should be stored at the testing facility in a secure, limited access office. Following the exam, booklets and answer sheets should be collected and counted, and securely shipped back to the testing company. Any discrepancies in the numbers of test booklets and answer sheets before and after testing must be investigated until all materials are accounted for.

Attention to test security at every phase must be ingrained in anyone with access to testing materials and must become a part of the testing organization's culture. Anyone involved in the development, administration, or handling of test materials should be required to sign a confidentiality form, stating that they will not disclose testing materials or internal testing information, and a conflict-of-interest form, stating that they are, and plan to remain, unaffiliated with test preparatory organizations and competing testing companies. Anyone with access to materials from secure testing programs should be subjected to a thorough background check. Although this can be time consuming and costly, and will not identify all people who cannot be trusted with secure exam materials, it can certainly help identify potentially malicious individuals. A surprising number of security breaches stem from disgruntled or dishonest employees. Knowing the backgrounds of potential employees can be an effective step in preventing corruption within the testing organization (Colton, 1998).

Finally, personnel at the testing site must do their part to reduce cheating. Examinees should be required to register for tests in advance. The testing organization should establish the authenticity of all candidates, including whether they have satisfied all prerequisites, and, for certification and licensing exams, verify that no registered candidates have already passed the exam. Seating charts must be developed and the physical layout of the room must be arranged at least a day before the exam to avoid any last-minute complications that can potentially compromise test security (Gundersen, 2002). Testing coordinators must carefully check in examinees, including collecting proper identification, prior to allowing them to test. During the test, proctors must watch for suspicious behavior, use of prohibited materials, and examinees working in unauthorized sections of the test or continuing to work beyond the time limits. Following the test, exams must be collected in an organized manner following the guidelines given in the testing manual, and irregularity reports should be completed documenting any suspicious behavior observed during testing.

3.2.2. Electronic Countermeasures

This category refers to technology that can be installed in a testing room for purposes of preventing or detecting cheating. The most common type of electronic countermeasure is a video surveillance system. Using video cameras to record the test administration can be helpful in identifying and documenting examinees exhibiting suspicious behaviors or using prohibited materials. Specialized equipment can verify each candidate's identity, such as with retinal scans or fingerprinting, and check candidates' information against a database for authenticity.

Another use of electronic equipment is to prevent or detect the use of certain electronic communication devices during testing. A noise generator or nullifier, which scrambles the signal of any device receiving or transmitting information, could be used to prevent an examinee from sending test information to a remote computer. Nullifiers would not help identify the source of the transmission; however, that may be possible using a spectrum analyzer. Also, as many of the prohibited electronic devices include metal, it may be useful to screen entering candidates with a handheld or free-standing metal detector.

Electronic countermeasures can be quite expensive. However, cheating prevention is considerably less expensive than the costs incurred in the aftermath of a significant security breach. Furthermore, cheaters today are relying increasingly on high-tech gadgetry, so it is quite likely that testing companies and test consumers will need to meet this challenge by concentrating more efforts on using sophisticated electronic equipment to combat cheating. A more detailed discussion of electronic devices used for cheating and to combat cheating is presented in Colton (1998).

3.2.3. Psychometric Countermeasures

This category refers to statistical and data analysis approaches to address cheating on tests. Whereas the most common types of observational and electronic countermeasures (e.g., proctors and video cameras) are designed to both prevent and detect cheating, psychometric countermeasures are generally aimed at either prevention or detection. The types of psychometric countermeasures available to a testing program vary depending on the type of testing program. In particular, programs utilizing computer-delivered exams are susceptible to different types of security concerns than are P&P testing programs. Therefore, psychometric approaches to addressing test security will be discussed separately for CBT and P&P testing programs.

3.2.3.1. Maintaining Test Security in CBT

Regardless of how well test administrators are able to maintain test security before or during a test, it is still possible for the security to be compromised after a test. One of the big problems facing any testing program is that of item overexposure. Every time tests are given, there is a chance that examinees will share test content with others who have yet to be tested. The more frequently an item is used, the greater the chance for it to become disclosed. For P&P tests, the impact of item disclosure is typically small because testing windows are very narrow—perhaps only a few days—and the opportunity for leaked information to be useful is limited. Furthermore, within each testing window, an alternate form of the test can be administered that contains only a subset of items that overlap with any other form, so examinees who acquire pretest information are only advantaged proportional to the amount of overlap among forms. Following each testing window, the data can be analyzed and items that are suspected to have been compromised can be retired or temporarily withdrawn from circulation.

The last edition of *Educational Measurement* (Bunderson, Inouye, & Olsen, 1989) argued that CBT provides for increased test security over P&P testing. While it remains true that CBT produces no paper copies of exams or keys to be stolen, enables random administration of items, and allows for various levels of encryption and password protection, it is not at all clear that their claim of improved security is true. CBT is considerably more vulnerable to item disclosure problems than is P&P testing because the testing windows are longer, often two to three months, and tests are administered multiple times per window, perhaps several times per day, every day. Therefore, information that leaks out early in the testing window could potentially affect the scores of many examinees testing later in the window. Furthermore, although it is still possible to analyze data from computerized tests for possible compromise, sufficiently large sets of data needed to detect possible cheating require longer to collect such that compromised items with computer-delivered tests may be allowed to remain in circulation longer than with P&P tests.

CAT programs are particularly susceptible to item compromise. Because CAT exams will predominantly administer items near the examinee's ability level, high-ability examinees performing up to their ability level will be administered items selected from among the most difficult and discriminating in the bank. Obviously, this constitutes a small subset of the entire bank—often a small enough subset that it could be completely reconstructed by just a few individuals whose sole purpose in testing is to try to remember the items they were administered.

As Davey and Fan (2000) point out, given enough time and opportunities, all item pools will eventually be disclosed. Item pools that are disclosed too quickly can render a testing program worthless. Therefore, to sustain a CAT program, it must be possible to monitor item disclosure patterns and replace items or item pools before the test is compromised.

The extent of item overexposure is typically assessed using three criteria: item exposure rates, efficiency of bank utilization, and average item overlap percentage. The exposure rate for an item refers to the percentage of tests administered in which that item was included. In judging the quality of exposure control, it is useful to consider both the average exposure rate across all administered items, as well as the maximum exposure rate for any single item. The efficiency of bank utilization is calculated as the percentage of items in the test bank that were administered to at least one examinee. The fewer the number of items administered over all examinees, the greater the risk of item overexposure. The average item overlap percentage provides a measure of the extent to which two CATs administered to examinees at the same ability level will contain the same items. To monitor item exposure, all three statistics should be computed.

The rates at which items are exposed, the efficiency of the bank utilization, and the percentage of overlapping items are determined to a large degree by the item selection method. It is commonly known that selecting the item that offers the maximum information (max-I) at the examinee's current estimate of θ (i.e., $\hat{\theta}$) results in maximum precision for estimating θ. However, the max-I criterion results in many items never being administered (Chang & Ansley, 2003), and extremely high average item overlaps for all bank sizes and θ levels (Chang & Ansley, 2003; Parshall, Harmes, & Kromrey, 2000; Revuelta & Ponsoda, 1998).

3.2.3.2. Methods to Control Item Over-Exposure

Over the past two decades, substantial work has been done investigating proposed methods to control item exposure rates (e.g., Chang, Quian, & Ying, 2001; Chang & Ying, 1996, 1999; Cheng & Liou, 2003; Davey & Fan, 2000; Davey & Parshall, 1995; Davis, 2003; Hetter & Sympson, 1997; Kingsbury & Zara, 1989; McBride & Martin, 1983; Parshall et al., 2000; Revuelta & Ponsoda, 1998; Stocking & Lewis, 1995, 1998; Sympson & Hetter, 1985). There are essentially two types of item selection methods: those that explicitly model item exposure and those that do not.

Methods that do not explicitly model exposure rely heavily on randomization or stratification techniques. Randomization techniques (e.g., Bergstrom, Lunz, & Gershon, 1992; Cheng & Liou, 2003; Kingsbury & Zara, 1989; McBride & Martin, 1983) work by selecting the next administered item at random from a set of acceptable items. Stratification techniques (e.g., Chang & Ying, 1999; Chang et al., 2001) divide items into strata that are homogeneous with respect to item discrimination parameters. Within each stratum, items are selected for delivery based on the closeness of their b values to the examinee's θ.

Although item selection methods based on either randomization or stratification tend to be relatively easy to implement, some evidence suggests that randomization methods may not be very successful at limiting the amount of overexposure, nor are they effective at utilizing all the items in a test bank. Stratification methods, on the other hand, are much better than randomization methods at utilizing the entire bank and controlling the average exposure rates, but can result in overexposure of individual items (Chang et al., 2001; Leung, Chang, & Hau, 2002; Parshall et al., 2000) and less-than-ideal item-overlap rates (Chang et al., 2001; Leung et al., 2002).

A number of CAT item selection methods have been developed to explicitly model item exposure (Davey & Fan, 2000; Davey & Parshall, 1995; Hetter & Sympson, 1997; Leung et al., 2002; Parshall, Davey, & Nering, 1998; Parshall et al., 2000; Stocking & Lewis, 1995, 1998; Sympson & Hetter, 1985). These methods typically work by assigning each item in an optimal item set a selection probability, based on the frequency with which the item would be selected for a particular subgroup under a max-I criterion.

Comparisons of studies investigating the effectiveness of various methods are difficult to make because most comparison studies include only a few methods, and the study parameters (e.g., length of CAT, distribution of item parameters, bank size, etc.) are often different. Still, in general, the research appears to support the claim that item exposure is controlled better when it is explicitly modeled than when it is not (Chang & Ansley, 2003).

The trade-off in CAT is that implementing methods to control item exposure means that less-than-optimal items are administered and measurement precision is potentially compromised. Although the models including exposure control parameters resulted in higher standard errors, the differences were typically not large. It appears that, in order to strike a balance between item security and measurement precision, CATs using more heavily constrained item selection algorithms need to be slightly longer than originally anticipated.

No matter how good the item-selection algorithm is, given enough time, the items will become overexposed. One way to slow the exposure rate is to use larger test banks. Item banks should include at least enough items to administer 12 nonoverlapping CATs (Stocking, 1994), but bigger banks are better, provided that the item selection method does not rely too heavily on selecting items with high information. Another strategy that may be effective is to rotate item pools so that the set of items available to examinees changes often, perhaps as frequently as every day or two. Rotating item banks around the country or world might be an effective way to limit the exposure of items in any one geographic region. Shortening the testing windows would require more people to be tested in a shorter period of time, making it more difficult for test information to leak and spread quickly enough to compromise the test. Finally, each new testing window can also begin with a refreshed set of banks.

3.2.3.3. Detection Models within CAT

In recent years, researchers have begun to explore the utility of psychometric models to identify item compromise or examinee cheating during the CAT administration. Early detection of compromised items and contaminated response vectors is critical for two reasons. If items are replaced at the first sign of overexposure, it can help minimize the number of examinees with artificially high test scores. Also, if examinees suspected of cheating or using item preknowledge (i.e., specific prior knowledge about some of the items is identified at the time of testing), it may be possible to extend the test length to allow for the administration of more secure items with very low exposure rates, on which to base the estimate of the examinee's ability. If this is not feasible or does not adequately address the problem, it may be necessary to abort the CAT administration and test the individual using an available P&P form in a proctored environment. On-the-fly detection methods are in their infancy, but appear to hold promise for identifying potential security breaches. Some of this work is discussed below.

Segall (2002) developed a model for identifying and describing when items have been compromised or when examinees may have benefitted from item overexposure. Segall's test compromise (TC) model uses Markov chain Monte Carlo methods to estimate the disclosure probability of each item within a set of possibly disclosed items, as well as a measure of the amount of person-specific compromise for each examinee. The TC model provides four pieces of useful information: (1) estimates of the number of examinees who had prior exposure to each item, (2) estimates of the item-level score gains for each item, (3) estimates of the number of items previewed by each examinee, and (4) estimates of the total score gain for each examinee, as a result of item disclosure. The TC model identified very little test compromise in the null case, but was effective at identifying different amounts of simulated disclosure, both at the item and examinee level. This model appears to have potential utility for testing companies, particularly those using CAT, for helping to monitor the extent of item or bank disclosure. One caveat is that for the TC model to work properly, it is necessary to administer a sample of items that are known to be uncompromised. Requiring such a set of items is not an uncommon measurement technique (e.g., SIBTEST for DIF detection, Shealy & Stout, 1993); however, the impact of including items that are to some degree compromised is not known.

Segall (2004) developed a sharing response model (SRM) that explicitly models item sharing in order to improve estimation of item performance for examinees who received test information from informants. Segall's SRM estimates the probability of answering item i correctly as

$$P_i(u_i = 1 \mid \theta, h) = [P_i(u_i = 1 \mid h > 0) \cdot P_i(h > 0)] + [P_i(u_i = 1 \mid h = 0) \cdot P_i(h = 0)],$$

where $P_i(u_i = 1 \mid h)$, the probability of correctly answering item i given h informants, is defined by the IRT model when $h = 0$, and as 1.0 when $h > 0$, and $P_i(h)$ is the probability of the examinee having h informants for item i. The SRM uses information from Trojan items, items that are very difficult and known to be overexposed, to estimate $P_i(h > 0)$ and $P_i(h = 0)$. Scoring well on the Trojan items would result in a high estimate of $P_i(h > 0)$, hence higher expected values of $P_i(u_i = 1 \mid \theta, h)$. Through simulation, Segall showed that by administering 5 to 10 Trojan items, it was possible to improve the estimation precision and accuracy for examinees using informants, without affecting the quality of θ estimates for examinees not using informants.

A separate set of studies have used person-fit methods (Drasgow, Levine, & Williams, 1985; Levine & Rubin, 1979; Meijer & Sijtsma, 1995, 2001; Tatsuoka, 1984) to identify examinees who may have benefitted from preknowledge of some questions. Person-fit measures are designed to detect examinees for whom the IRT model does a poor job predicting the probability of success on an item. There are many reasons that examinees' response patterns might be atypical. Examinees may exhibit a warm-up effect, where performance is worse early in the test than later. Guessing may cause an unusual pattern of responses. Examinees working very slowly and meticulously could produce response patterns that match the model too closely. Examinees with unusual backgrounds could find certain items or test objectives easier or harder than they are for most examinees. As this part of the chapter is on test security, our focus will be on the application of person-fit measures to detect test compromise. Examples of person misfit due to security breaches include item preknowledge and cheating (e.g., copying answers from a neighbor, using prohibited aids, etc.). Because examinees taking CATs are unlikely to see the same sets of questions, most of the person-fit research in CAT has focused on detection of item preknowledge rather than other types of cheating, such as answer copying. Unfortunately, research on person fit to identify item preknowledge has largely yielded discouraging results.

McLeod and Lewis (1999) compared two well-known person fit statistics, l_z (Drasgow et al., 1985) and ECI4$_z$ (Tatsuoka, 1984) with a new index, Z_c, under simulated null and item preknowledge conditions. In the preknowledge condition, 5% of the simulated examinees were assumed to have memorized the 50 most frequently administered items (in a bank of 348). These simulating conditions represented a worst-case scenario, as they maximized both the number of exposed items that would be delivered and the number of previewed items that would be answered correctly. McLeod and Lewis found all three indices had low power to detect item preknowledge, detecting no more than 8.4% of the examinees with preknowledge at $\alpha = .05$.

McLeod, Lewis, and Thissen (2003) examined the utility of a Bayesian posterior log odds ratio computed between one model assuming no preknowledge and one assuming item preknowledge from up to eight independent sources. The indices yielded markedly different results for examinees at different θ levels. Furthermore, hit rates were quite low unless the examinees had preknowledge of over half the items to which they were exposed.

Van Krimpen-Stoop and Meijer (2000, 2001) and Meijer (2002) proposed use of a cumulative sum procedure (CUSUM) for detecting misfit in CAT. CUSUM adds together the residuals associated with strings of correctly or incorrectly answered items. Because of the nature of CAT algorithms, it is expected that examinees will correctly answer approximately half the items, once the algorithms zeroes in on the examinee's θ level. Therefore, if an examinee answers a disproportionately high number of items correctly (or incorrectly) at any point in the test, the cumulative sums of positive (or negative) residuals will become large, and the CUSUM procedure will flag the examinee as misfitting. Van Krimpen-Stoop and Meijer (2001) found that the power (at $\alpha = .01$) of CUSUM to detect small, moderate, and large amounts of preknowledge was approximately .1, .35, and .65. Power of other studied methods was lower.

Another type of aberrance often discussed in the context of person fit is answer copying or cheating. Studies of the utility of person-fit measures for detecting aberrance due to answer copying or cheating have found them to have very low power for this purpose (Chason & Maller, 1996; Drasgow et al., 1985; Iwamoto, Nungester, & Luecht, 1996; Levine & Rubin, 1979), even though most of these have looked at detection rates under a best-case scenario in which all copied items are answered correctly. Such indices are also conceptually unappealing for detection of answer copying because the value of the statistic uses no information from the alleged source examinee, but considers only the item response vector of the examinee in question. Consequently, it may be possible for an examinee to produce a significant person-fit index while producing virtually no answer overlap with neighboring examinees. Fortunately, if the purpose is to detect answer copying, several other better options exist.

3.2.3.4. Maintaining Test Security in P&P Testing

Within the P&P testing environment, the most common threats to the validity of a test are item overexposure, use of prohibited materials such as crib notes, and answer copying (Baird, 1980; Cizek, 1999; Stern & Havlicek, 1986). Controlling item overexposure in P&P testing is much easier than in CAT. By administering the tests during very short testing windows, using multiple test forms, and replacing a large percentage of items between testing windows, it is possible to minimize most advantages to be gained from item preknowledge. Identifying examinees who cheat by using unauthorized aids or copying answers from a neighboring examinee is usually a responsibility of the test proctors. If a proctor observes an examinee using prohibited materials, those materials should be confiscated, as they provide very strong evidence of cheating.

With answer copying, however, aside from a proctor's report of suspicious behavior, the only tangible material that can be used as evidence of cheating is the pattern of answer similarities between the suspected copier and source examinees. Unfortunately, because any two randomly selected examinees will be expected to produce some overlapping answers, it is difficult to know by looking whether the amount of similarity is typical or extreme. Recently, a number of statistical models have been developed for detecting answer copying. These vary in their specific details, but most essentially work by identifying whether the amount of answer similarity can be accounted for by chance alone. If not, barring other counterevidence (such as that the examinees were not sitting within copying distance of one another) and considering the information recorded in the proctor's irregularity report, the most likely scenario is that the unusual amount of similarity in item responses was due to answer copying.

Methods for detection of copying were introduced in the 1920s by Bird (1927), but didn't attain much popularity until the 1970s, when Angoff (1974) developed a set of copying indices for operational use at Educational Testing Service (ETS). Angoff developed a set of eight indices (which he labeled A through H) for detecting answer copying. In developing these indices, Angoff considered five variables he believed would be good indicators of copying: the number of items answered correctly by both the alleged copier (C) and the alleged source (S), the number of items for which identical incorrect answers were provided by C and S, the number of items omitted by both C and S, the number of items jointly omitted or answered identically incorrect, and the highest number of identically marked incorrect answers or omits within a string of consecutively identically marked answers. Angoff's indices involved empirically deriving the sampling distribution of these five dependent variables using examinees known to have not copied. In constructing these distributions, Angoff paired each dependent variable with one of seven different conditioning variables to control for any expected differences due to the performance levels of the particular individuals being studied. The extremity of an examinee pair's score on the dependent variable, given their level on the conditioning variable, was used to measure whether the examinee had copied.

Angoff (1974) eventually determined two of his eight measures, indices B and H, were acceptable, and they were adopted by ETS. Index B examines the number of identically incorrect items, after controlling for the product of the number of items answered incorrectly by the examinees individually. Index H examines the longest stretch of incorrectly answered or omitted items within a block of consecutive identically answered items, after controlling for the number of items not answered correctly (i.e., answered wrong or omitted) by the higher scoring of C or S. Both indices are easy to compute. Angoff found that they resulted in the identification of almost all of the known-copier examinees in a sample containing 50 known copiers. However, B and H are both based on empirical distributions of noncopying examinees and require empirical critical values to maintain Type I error control, making these difficult for some testing programs to implement. In particular, stratification is not well-suited for short tests or tests administered to small groups of examinees (Frary, 1993).

In recommending indices B and H, Angoff (1974) argued that a copying index ought not rely on data from correctly answered items, as an examinee could claim that sharing many right answers in common with another examine is expected when the examinees both know the material. A similar argument has subsequently been made by Holland

(1996). Frary, Tideman, and Watts (1977) and Buss and Novick (1980) proposed using data from all item responses, both correct and incorrect, as matching correct answers do provide some, albeit relatively little, evidence of copying. More importantly, unless information from all items is considered, the indices will fail to consider important evidence against cheating, such as when one examinee selects the correct answer and the other selects an incorrect answer.

Frary et al. (1977) developed an index, g_2, that evaluates the standardized difference between the observed and expected number of answer matches between a pair of examinees:

$$g_2 = \frac{h_{CS} - \sum_{i=1}^{n} P_C(u_{iS})}{\sigma_{h_{CS}}},$$

where h_{CS} is the observed number of answer matches between C and S, $P_C(u_{iS})$ is the probability of C selecting the answer provided by S to item i, and $\sigma_{h_{CS}} = \sqrt{\sum_{i=1}^{n} [P_C(u_{iS})][1 - P_C(u_{iS})]}$. $P_C(u_{iS})$ is estimated by considering the ratio of S's raw score to the test average and the classical test theory p-value of the alternative selected by S. According to Frary et al., g_2 is normally distributed with a mean of 0 and a standard deviation of 1.0.

g_2 has served as a model for several other answer copying indices conceptually quite similar to g_2. These indices differ from g_2 with respect to several variables:

- Replacement of normal distribution with a binomial error similarity analysis (ESA; Bellezza & Bellezza, 1989), P (Cody, 1985), CP (Hanson, Harris, & Brennan, 1987), K-index (Holland, 1996), $\overline{K}_1$ and $\overline{K}_2$ ([Sotaridona & Meijer, 2002), or Poisson [S_1 and S_2 (Sotaridona & Meijer, 2003)] distribution for estimating the likelihood of answer overlaps
- Consideration of only items answered incorrectly by S (ESA; Bellezza & Bellezza, 1989), P (Cody, 1985), CP (Hanson et al., 1987), and K-index (Holland, 1996), S_1 (Sotaridona & Meijer, 2003)
- Estimation of the probability of an answer match (ESA; Bellezza & Bellezza, 1989), P (Cody, 1985), CP (Hanson et al., 1987), K-index (Holland, 1996), $\overline{K}_1$ and $\overline{K}_2$ (Sotaridona & Meijer, 2002), S_1 and S_2 (Sotaridona & Meijer, 2003), and ω (Wollack, 1997)

Much attention in the copying literature has been paid to Frary et al.'s (1977) g_2, Bellezza and Bellezza's (1989) ESA, and the K-index (Holland, 1996), which has been used operationally at ETS for a number of years. However, such studies have consistently shown that these indices suffer from poor statistical characteristics. g_2 has consistently been shown to yield inflated Type I error rates (Hanson et al., 1987; Wollack, 1997, 2003; Wollack, Cohen, & Serlin, 2001), particularly for larger sample sizes and shorter test lengths. Liberal Type I error rates are unacceptable for copying detection indices, as they result in an uncontrolled percentage of examinees being wrongly accused of answer copying. ESA and the K-index, on the other hand, suffer the reverse problem of having very conservative Type I error rates. As a result, ESA and the K-index are underpowered, resulting in the identification of a very low percentage of true copiers (Bay, 1995; Sotaridona & Meijer, 2002; Wollack, 2003).

Although g_2, ESA, and the K-index may be the most widely known indices, better options exist. In particular, S_2 (Sotaridona & Meijer, 2003) and ω (Wollack, 1997) seem to be the most promising. S_2 uses the upper tail of a Poisson distribution to estimate the probability of C having copied from S. The Poisson parameter, μ, is estimated using a log-linear model of the form $\log(\mu_r) = \beta_0 + \beta_1 w_r$, where w_r is the number incorrect score for everyone with r correct answers, evaluated at C's number incorrect score. Therefore, S_2 is given by:

$$S_2 = \sum_{g=m_{CS}}^{n} \frac{e^{-\hat{\mu}} \hat{\mu}^g}{g!}.$$

The variable m_{CS}, which equals the amount of information about answer copying associated with the examinees' pairs of responses, is given by $m_{CS} = \sum_i \delta_i$. Sotaridona and Meijer defined δ_i, the amount of information about copying on item i, as follows:

$$\delta_i = \begin{cases} 0 & \text{if C and S select different answers for item i,} \\ 1 & \text{if C and S select the same incorrect answer for item i, and} \\ \left[\left(\frac{k+1}{k-1}\right)^{-(k+1)P(r)_i}\right]\left[e^{-(k+1)P(r)_i}\right] & \text{if C and S answer item i correctly,} \end{cases}$$

where $P(r)_i$ is the percentage of people in group r who answered item i correctly and k is the number of item alternatives. In choosing to use a Poisson distribution, S_2 is sensitive to the rate of answer matches per incorrect answer by S. Higher rates of matching will result in smaller values of the test statistic and will provide more evidence of copying.

The S_2 index is quite new, so it has been researched little. But the early results suggest that it is one of the most powerful indices available. Sotaridona and Meijer (2003) found that S_2 had substantially more power to detect copiers than did S_1 and $\overline{K}_2$, although its empirical Type I error rate was slightly inflated in some conditions. Wollack (in press) also found that S_2 was the best of these three indices.

The other copying index that consistently performs well compared to others is the ω index (Wollack, 1997). ω compares the amount of observed answer similarity between a pair of examinees with the amount expected due to chance, as shown below:

$$\omega = \frac{h_{CS} - \sum_{i=1}^{n} P_C(u_{iS})}{\sigma_{h_{CS}}}.$$

ω is structurally identical to the g_2 index (Frary et al., 1977), but differs in terms of how $P_C(u_{iS})$ is computed. With ω, $P_C(u_{iS})$ is estimated using the nominal response model (Bock, 1972). The nominal response model, which describes the probability of examinee j with ability θ_j selecting choice k on item i, is given as

$$P_j(u_{ik}) = \frac{\exp(\zeta_{ik} + \lambda_{ik}\theta_j)}{\sum_{q=1}^{K} \exp(\zeta_{iq} + \lambda_{iq}\theta_j)}$$

where ζ_{iq} and λ_{iq} are the intercept and slope parameters for category q, respectively. A more thorough discussion of this model may be found in Yen and Fitzpatrick (Chapter 4, this volume).

For purposes of computing ω, $P_C(u_{is})$ is found by fixing k to the response selected by S to item i, and by using C's ability estimate, $\hat{\theta}_c$, in place of θ_j. The ω index is normally distributed with a mean of 0 and a standard deviation of 1.0; large values of θ indicate unusual amounts of answer similarity.

Studies using both simulated (Sotaridona & Meijer, 2002, 2003; Wollack, 1997; Wollack & Cohen, 1998, Wollack et al., 2001) and real data (Chason, 1997; Wollack, 2003, in press) have found that ω holds good control of the nominal Type I error rate for all test lengths, sample sizes, and α levels studied. In addition, by copying detection standards, ω is a very powerful index. All studies of ω have found it to be the most powerful index in certain conditions, and all studies but two (Sotaridona & Meijer, 2003; Wollack, in press) have found it to be the most powerful in all conditions. Sotaridona and Meijer (2003) found ω to typically be the most powerful index for detecting large amounts of copying (30% or 40% of the items) with small α levels (α < .005). For large amounts of copying with large α levels and small amounts of copying (10% or 20%) for all α levels, S_2 was found to provide the most power. Wollack (in press) found for simulated copying of strings of consecutive items, index H (Angoff, 1974) was the most powerful index at detecting small amounts of copying (10% or 20%) on a 40-item test for all α levels and very small amounts of copying (10%) on an 80-item test for α > .005.

The most comprehensive study of the behavior of copying indices under realistic conditions was conducted by Wollack (in press). In this study, real test data on which copying could not have occurred were manipulated to simulate four different levels of answer copying (ranging from 10% to 40% of the items being copied). Type I error and detection rates were studied for tests of 40 and 80 items, nine sample sizes ranging from 50 to 20,000, and four α levels ranging from .0005 to .01. Wollack considered ω, S_1, S_2, $\overline{K}_2$, B, and H under random copying, strings-based copying, and a combination of random and strings-based copying (i.e., mixed). A summary of the power results are shown in Table 10.1 for the mixed copying condition. For smaller amounts of copying, ω and H were clearly the most powerful; however, to a certain extent, this is a function of the way in which the data were simulated. Index H is particularly sensitive to detection of strings-based copying, so its power numbers will fluctuate based on the type of copying. For comparison, Table 10.1 also includes the power of ω and H under Wollack's random copying condition. While the power of ω remained fairly stable, it is clear that H should be used only when strings-based copying is suspected.

Various indices are differentially sensitive to different types of copying strategies (i.e., strings versus random). Wollack (in press) examined the impact of using multiple copying indices at the same time, but dividing the nominal α among the number of indices used in combination (Dunn, 1961), considered all possible two- and three-way combinations of the indices for each condition. Generally speaking, there was a small improvement in detection rates found by using the ω index and H together. This was particularly evident at small α levels in the 80-item condition, when the data were simulated with either mixed or strings-based copying. When random copying was simulated, the combined ω-H index was less powerful than ω alone. The results of the ω-H combined index in both the mixed and random copying conditions are also provided in Table 10.1 for comparison.

The power of copying indices is influenced by three factors: test length, amount of answer copying, and Type I error rate. As would be expected, detection rates increase as test length or the percentage of items copied increase, and decrease as the Type I error rate decreases. From Table 10.1, it is clear that copying indices generally have very low detection rates when examinees copy no more than 20% of the items on 40- or 80-item tests. Detection rates, however, are much improved when examinees copy 40% of the items, particularly on long tests.

Angoff (1974) proposed that candidates not be charged with answer copying unless either their B or H indexes were larger than 3.72, corresponding to a 1 in 10,000 confidence level that the answer similarity did not arise by chance. Subsequently, false positive rates of .0001 have become the industry standard in answer copying detection. As an example, *Scrutiny!* (Assessment Systems Corporation, 1993), a commercially available software package for copying detection, will not even identify pairs of examinees as being suspicious unless the p-value of their ESA statistic is less than .0001. However, establishing a hard-and-fast rule to this effect is counterproductive. Accusing candidates of answer copying can have extremely serious consequences for the candidate and ought be held to a much higher standard than, say, the criterion necessary to identify an item as exhibiting DIF. However, insisting that all copying analyses be performed using a .0001 criterion is as arbitrary as stipulating that all DIF testing occur with α = .05. As with any type of research, the false positive rate for a copying analysis should be set in advance based on the amount of evidence needed against the null hypothesis to be comfortable concluding that it is false. It stands to reason that the stronger the evidence of copying from other, nonstatistical sources, the less statistical evidence is needed to conclude that copying occurred. As an example, it might be sufficient to use an α = .05 or α = .01 criterion to detect an examinee who was observed copying by two or three proctors, standing in different positions, for extended periods of time. However, if the only other evidence is that a candidate reports after a test that she believes the person seated next to her was copying, a more stringent criterion should be used. Several case studies are described by Wollack (2004) of the different ways in which ω has been used in practice.

It is possible to compute copying indices between all possible pairs of examinees to check the integrity of the testing site, but in practice, indices are usually only computed to corroborate an independent belief that a particular examinee copied from a particular source. The decision to use a statis-

TABLE 10.1 Estimated Power of Copying Indices under Different Copying Conditions

	40-Item Test				80-Item Test			
	20% Copying		40% Copying		20% Copying		40% Copying	
	$\alpha = .001$	$\alpha = .01$	$\alpha = .001$	$\alpha = .01$	$\alpha = .001$	$\alpha = .01$	$\alpha = .001$	$\alpha = .01$
Combined Random and Strings Copying								
$\omega\text{-}H^1$	.08	.25	.49	.74	.18	.44	.85	.95
ω	.07	.22	.52	.75	.16	.39	.77	.90
S_2	.02	.16	.31	.67	.07	.32	.65	.88
$\overline{K}_2$	.01	.11	.30	.64	.05	.25	.69	.88
S_1	.02	.13	.26	.61	.05	.25	.57	.83
B	.00	.04	.02	.25	.00	.05	.02	.32
H^1	.05	.21	.18	.47	.11	.33	.60	.87
Random Copying Only								
$\omega\text{-}H^1$	.06	.20	.49	.74	.11	.30	.69	.85
ω	.08	.25	.55	.77	.15	.36	.73	.88
H^1	.01	.08	.08	.28	.01	.07	.08	.27

Note: Based on data from Wollack (in press); all power data are averaged over nine sample sizes ranging in size from 50–20,000 examinees.

tical index should be the result of a thorough investigation into the matter, including reviewing irregularity reports and seating charts, interviewing key witnesses, and considering any counterevidence that might exist. Copying must be observed by a proctor. Copying indices, for all their value at identifying unusual pairs of item response vectors, cannot be relied on to identify which of the two examinees in question is the copier and which is the source. When one examinee copies from another, both examinees will have an unusual number of answer matches. Although many copying indices provide different values depending upon which examinee is treated as the copier, the indices examining C from S and S from C are highly correlated when one of the examinees is a copier (Wollack et al, 2001). Therefore, even though it is possible to know that answer copying between a pair of examinees was extremely likely, without visual evidence, it is often not possible to distinguish which examinee was the copier and which was the source. In such cases, the best strategy may be to flag both examinees in the database and strongly encourage proctors to monitor them both more closely should they have occasion to test again (Wollack, 1997).

3.3. Teacher Cheating

A special type of cheating, which may be either individual or collaborative, is teacher or administrator cheating. This type of cheating has increased in the past five years— estimates are it occurs in a minimum of 5% of elementary school classrooms (Jacob & Levitt, 2003b)—as standardized test scores and federal and state legislation have led to increased pressure on schools and teachers to increase test scores. Teachers and administrators in many states have been accused or found guilty of artificially increasing students' test scores. Examples of specific types of alleged cheating include changing students' answers after the test, teaching to the test, illegal coaching during a test, using live exams as practice exams, reading off answers during a test, providing extra time, and disallowing low-achieving students from testing.

Numerous studies have focused on teaching to the test and other inappropriate test preparation practices (Anastasi, 1981; Mehrens, 1991; Mehrens & Kaminski, 1989; Mehrens, Popham, & Ryan, 1998; Moore, 1994; Popham, 1991). A good discussion is provided by Schmidt and Shaw (2005), along with a plea to modernize a set of guidelines for appropriate test preparation, in light of current legislation and testing conventions. For all the work that has been done on what constitutes inappropriate teacher intervention on tests, there has been decidedly little research on detecting teacher cheating. Jacob and Levitt (2003a, 2003b) developed an algorithm for identifying teacher cheating based on unusual score gains from successive years and unusual patterns of student answers:

$$SCORE_{cbt} = (PCTILE_{c,b,t})^2 + (1 - PCTILE_{c,b,t+1})^2,$$

where $PCTILE_{c,b,t}$ is the percentile rank of the gain score for class c in subject b for year t. High values of $SCORE_{cbt}$ are expected for classes with large gain scores in the first year and small gain scores in the second year, as might be expected if teachers (at time t) were cheating.

Unusual patterns of students' answers were measured in four different ways. All four indicator variables, designed to be sensitive to different features of a dataset, were hypothesized to be more prevalent in classrooms where the teachers changed answers, supplied students with answers, or taught to the test. The first variable was the most unlikely string of identical answers provided by any set of students in the class, using a multinomial logit model to estimate the probabilities of examinees selecting all item choices. The second variable was a measure of the overall correlation among students' answers within a classroom. The third indicator provided a measure of the variance in inter-item correlations within classrooms. The final variable was essentially a measure of person fit, indicating the extent to which students correctly answered items easy for them and incorrectly answered items hard for them. For each class, these four indicator variables were combined into an overall measure of the unusualness of students' answer patterns by computing

$$ANSWERS_{c,b,t} = (PCTILE_{1,c,b,t})^2 + (PCTILE_{2,c,b,t})^2 + (PCTILE_{3,c,b,t})^2 + (PCTILE_{4,c,b,t})^2,$$

where $PCTILE_{v,c,b,t}$ is the percentile rank of variable v for class c in subject b for year t.

Jacob and Levitt (2003a) used data from Chicago Public Schools to compute SCORE and ANSWERS for all classrooms. Two sets of classrooms were identified as most likely to have cheated. One set included classrooms ranked in the top few percent on both variables; the second set included those whose ANSWERS ranked in the top few percent, but whose SCORE did not. Two groups of classrooms not likely to have cheated were also formed: those with a high SCORE but a low ANSWERS, and a randomly selected group from all remaining schools. A fifth group containing those schools in which allegations of cheating had been made was also formed. Alternate forms of the test were administered to all five groups, under heavily supervised conditions. All three of the groups thought to be cheating showed dramatic decreases in their performances upon retesting, for both reading and math, whereas the two groups not suspected of cheating did not. These data provide some support of this model as a tool for detecting teacher cheating. However, much more work is necessary, including simulation work, to test the appropriateness of the model, determine its error rates, and decide upon appropriate criteria for classifying a classroom as elevated on either SCORE or ANSWERS.

3.4. Test Security in Practice: A Case Study of ACT's Policies

Testing companies must have a fair, well-reasoned policy dictating the means by which misconduct investigations will be instigated, detailing the manner in which these investigations will proceed, and identifying examinees' rights and options at each phase of the investigative process. The following describes ACT's procedures for investigating testing irregularities on the ACT (ACT, 2005). Although specific policies will vary depending on the nature of the testing program, ACT's policy serves as a good example of the type of procedures that testing companies should have in place.

When registering to take the ACT, examinees are informed of ACT's security policy and process for dealing with any irregularities, and must consent to abide by that process. The process for dealing with irregularities consists of two phases: a preliminary internal review of test scores and a formal review of test scores. A flowchart of the steps involved in reviewing test scores on the ACT is provided in Figure 10.1.

All irregularity reviews begin with a trigger; examinees are not randomly reviewed for possible misconduct. The preliminary review phase begins when ACT learns of the possibility of misconduct in one of several ways. For example, ACT's test security procedures provide for an internal audit that systematically compares the test scores of examinees who retest and obtain significantly higher scores on a repeat test. ACT will not formally review a case based on a large score increase alone. There must be additional evidence of a testing irregularity, such as unusual similarity in responses between the answer sheets of two examinees seated near one another or handwriting discrepancies that make it appear that the test was taken by a surrogate examinee. ACT may become aware of testing irregularities through internal sources, such as an irregularity report filed during the test administration (e.g., suspicion of copying or attempting to communicate with another) or through external sources (e.g., a college admission officer requests validation of an ACT score that appears unusually high in light of the examinee's academic record or an examinee reports that another test taker may have looked at his or her answer sheet). As part of the internal review phase, ACT reviews information already on file, including test scores, item responses, seating diagrams, statistical analyses of answer similarity between a suspected copier-source pair, answer sheets, test booklets, and other documentation, for additional evidence of irregularities. ACT uses a variety of statistical methods to detect unusual similarity of responses in an answer sheet pair.

If, after the preliminary internal review, the validity of the scores is still in question, ACT may begin a formal review by sending the examinee a letter and offering a variety of choices for proceeding, including retesting, canceling scores, or providing information to ACT's Test Security Review Panel in support of the score validity. If examinees voluntarily agree to cancellation of their scores, score recipients are notified of the score cancellation.

For examinees who retest and receive an ACT Composite score no more than three points below the questioned Composite score, the investigation closes and the scores remain valid. Examinees scoring more than three points below their questioned Composite, however, have their ACT scores cancelled. Score recipients are notified of the cancellation.

Examinees who choose to present information to the ACT Review Panel must submit a transcript and a statement, along with any other information they would like considered. If the Review Panel decides that the scores are valid, the score review is closed. If the Review Panel finds that the score is not valid, the examinee will again be given the options to privately retest, to cancel the scores or to proceed to arbitration. The arbitrator must ultimately decide whether "ACT acted reasonably and in good faith in deciding to cancel the scores" (ACT, 2006, ¶4). If the arbitrator sides with the examinee, the review closes. If the arbitrator

FIGURE 10.1 Steps in Review of Test Scores on ACT

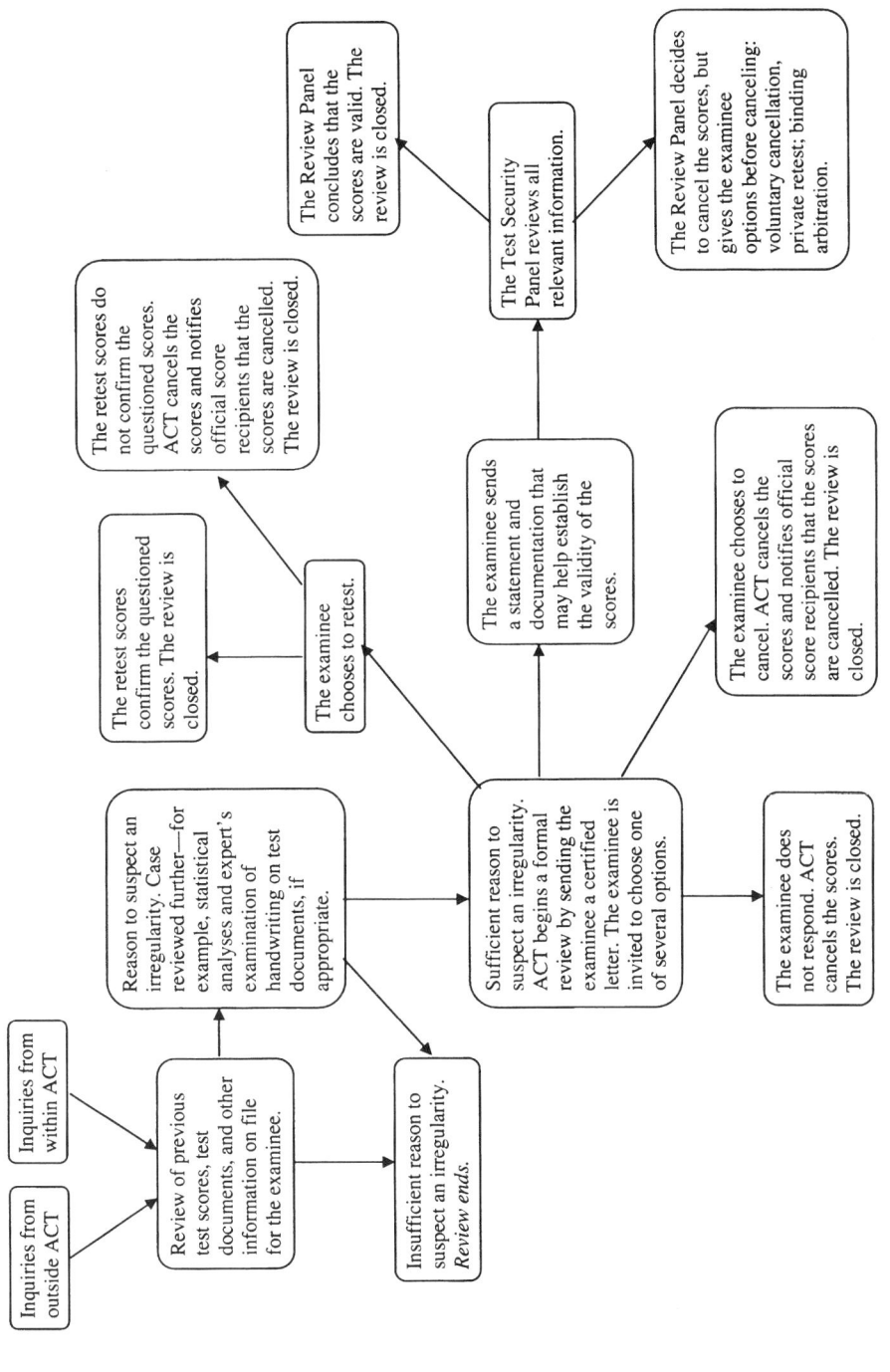

Source: Adapted with permission from ACT (2005). *Procedures for Investigating Testing Irregularities and Questioned Test Scores* [Brochure]. Iowa City, IA: ACT.

sides with ACT, the scores are cancelled. In all cases, the specifics behind score cancellation are confidential and are not divulged to score recipients

3.5. Closing Comments on Test Security

Testing is a multi-billion-dollar a year industry and is used to help make many potentially life-changing decisions about individuals. The capability of tests to yield useful, meaningful scores is predicated on maintaining the security of the test items, test materials, and the exam process. Clearly, the higher the stakes associated with a test, the more some examinees will be tempted to gain an advantage. Unfortunately, with the advances in technology and the increasing reliance on computer-delivered tests, opportunities for examinees to gain that advantage are plentiful. Test developers and administrators must continue to explore and improve current test security measures if we are to ensure that test integrity is maintained.

The importance of test security has led to the formation of companies, such as Caveon, devoted solely to providing security services for testing programs. Test security services are generally aimed at three fundamental levels of security: detection of security breaches, remediation of causes and effects of vulnerability, and prevention of potentially compromising behaviors. Computer software publishers are capitalizing on the increased demand for security by developing user-friendly programs to perform copying analyses (e.g., *Scrutiny!* [Assessment Systems Corporation, 1993] and *Integrity* [Castle Rock Research Corporation, 2005]).

The increase in high-stakes testing for elementary and secondary grades, due largely to the No Child Left Behind (NCLB) legislation signed into law in January 2002, has dramatically raised the threat level to the integrity of the tests developed for these programs. If tests are to be useful for informing decisions about students, schools, candidates for licensure, and so on, then methods for detecting and deterring all forms of cheating need to be developed and continually improved to meet these new threats. Test scores are assumed to reflect the ability levels of the examinees. When examinees have access to test questions prior to or during the test administration, the scores of these examinees do not accurately reflect their ability levels. The *Standards* (AERA, APA, & NCME, 1999) speak directly to this point. Standards 5.7, 11.7, 12.11, and 13.11 each indicate that it is the responsibility of the test users to ensure that testing materials and test preparation activities do not disclose information to examinees that will negatively affect the validity of the inferences made from the test results. Testing conditions that do not ensure the security of the test pose a serious threat to test validity (Crooks, Kane, & Cohen, 1996).

4. SCANNING AND MACHINE-BASED SCORING SYSTEMS

A substantial portion of most large educational testing programs consists of selected response format items (e.g., multiple-choice, true-false) and examinees typically respond by using a pencil to mark their answers on specially prepared answer documents. When examinees can respond in this way, their answers can be scanned and converted to digitized form for subsequent computer processing using some type of automated data capture device. The most common such device is the optical mark reader (OMR). (Baker, 1968, provides a brief history of optical scanning systems.) The OMR scanner captures the examinees' responses from the answer sheet and converts this information into a digital output that can be subsequently scored. OMR document scanners are currently the most common type of scanner used for testing programs of almost any size. These scanners come with capacities that range from very large models designed to process answer sheets for testing programs for an entire country to very small desktop models for processing tests for a classroom.

OMR technology is constrained to read specific locations on special response documents printed on high-quality paper. The response locations on the forms, colloquially referred to as "bubbles," are located in fixed positions on the response document. Small dark marks, called timing tracks, usually along one of the vertical edges of the document are required to identify to the scanner the positions of the rows of bubbles. Special nonoptically sensitive inks are sometimes used to identify the locations that are to be filled in by the examinee. Specialized software is used during scanning to interpret the scanner output for each response location. Most scanning software can differentiate between erasures and light marks intended to be accepted as an answer for an individual sheet. Scanner software can typically determine a mark intensity level for each sheet and then compare each mark to that sheet intensity level to determine whether or not one mark is intended and another is an erasure or a smudge. To ensure that a scanning system is working properly, it must be frequently calibrated to ensure that it can accurately distinguish between multiple marks, erasures, light marks, or omissions. Calibrating at the beginning and during processing of a high-stakes testing program is wise.

OMR cannot recognize hand-printed or machine-printed characters or even the shape of the response bubble, but the technology is mature, relatively inexpensive, fast, and highly accurate. Current OMR scanners are not necessarily faster than they were 30 or 40 years ago, but they are more reliable, run longer without breakdowns, and capture data more accurately than in the past.

One change in optical scanning equipment over the last decade has been the development of reliable and relatively low-cost image scanning systems. These systems come in large-capacity models that can process several thousand documents per hour (such as the OpScan 5000*i*; see Figure 10.2a) and desktop models that can process several hundred documents per hour for smaller applications (such as the OpScan *i*NSIGHT; see Figure 10.2b). The difference in these two systems is both in the throughput capacity as well as in the duty cycle. These systems are capable of capturing both OMR and image data from the same document. Imaging scanners in this class have both intelligent character recognition (*i*CR) and optical character recognition (OCR) capabilities. *i*CR technology enables imaging systems to read and interpret into machine readable form

FIGURE 10.2a Opscan 5001 High Speed Image Scanning System

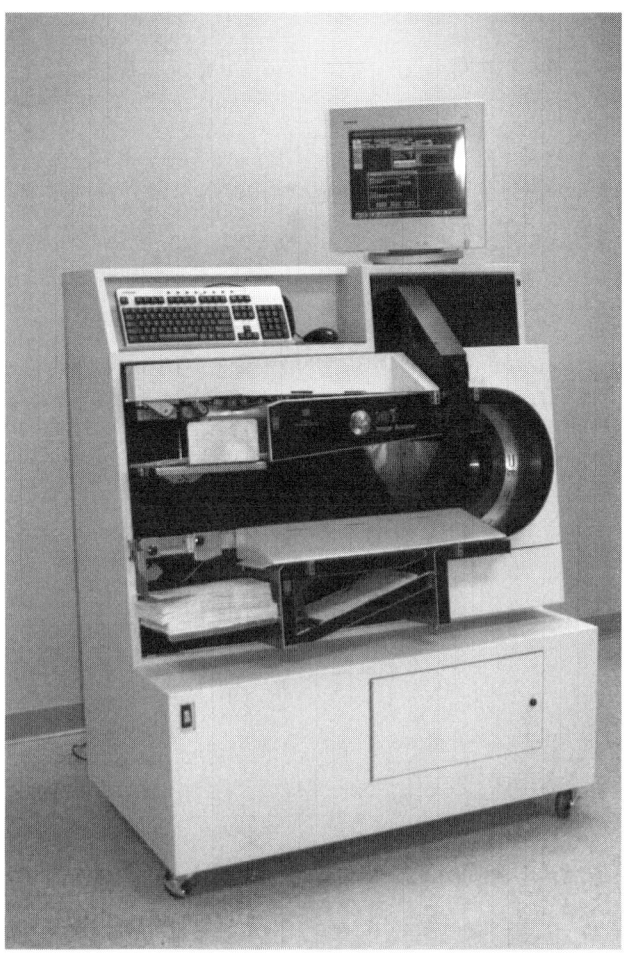

Source: Copyright © 2005 NCS Pearson, Inc. All rights reserved.

FIGURE 10.2b Opscan iNSIGHT Desktop Image Scanning System

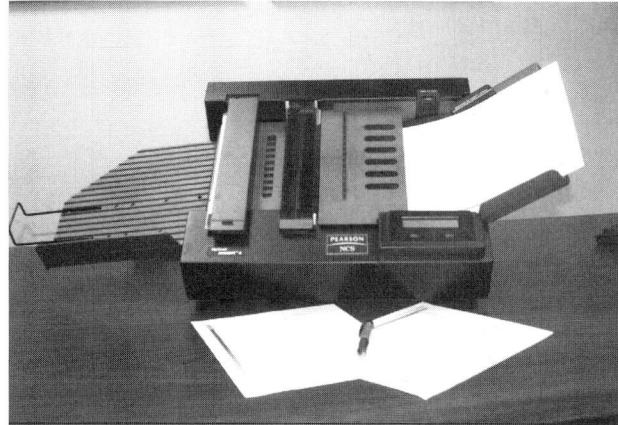

Source: Copyright © 2005 NCS Pearson, Inc. All rights reserved.

machine-printed or numeric hand-printed characters (but not cursive writing). OCR technology can interpret images of machine-printed characters into machine-readable characters. The imaging scanners can generally pick up either pen or pencil, do not require number 2 pencils to be used, and do not require timing tracks on the answer document (although smaller, less obvious registration marks may be needed for some applications). At the current time, imaging scanner technology can eliminate some uses of OMR, although if high levels of accuracy and speed are required, OMR is still the preferred technology.

4.1. Steps in the Processing of Answer Documents

Ensuring data integrity is a process that begins before scanning and continues through the scoring and reporting of results. We consider here the part of the process that starts with processing of answer documents and ends with the checking of results to be certain tests have been scored accurately. For purposes of exposition, we divide this process into three segments—prescanning, scanning, and postscanning—and illustrate using the context of a testing program. Minor modifications in some steps may be required for non-testing-related processing.

The first step, to be completed before scanning and scoring any answer sheets, is verification that (a) the scanning program accurately captures the information on the answer sheet, (b) the answer key is correct, and (c) the scoring program scores correctly. Checking the accuracy of the key and the scoring program normally is done by comparing the output from the scoring program with a small set of hand-scored answer sheets. Actual answer sheets can be used for part of this, but a set of answer sheets should also be constructed that includes different types of possibilities such as all answers correct, all answers incorrect, all answers of the same type (e.g., on a five-choice test, all choices are choice 1 on one sheet, all choices are 2 on one sheet, etc.), multiple marks for each answer, patterns of answers marked, and so on. A sufficient number of sheets, including actual examinees' answer sheets, blank sheets, wrong types of answer sheets (perhaps from previous testing program administrations), and sheets specially prepared to check the scanning and scoring programs, should be scanned and scored. The scanning program should reject the wrong types of answer sheets and not process them. The results from the scanning operation should be compared by hand with each piece of data on the answer sheet to ensure that the scanning program is accurately capturing the information on the answer sheets and recording it properly in a data file. The data file created by the scanning program should then be scored by the scoring program created for the test. Raw scores should be calculated along with any transformations. The results from the machine scoring should be compared with results from hand scoring. Discrepancies between the hand scoring and the machine scoring need to be resolved before proceeding with any further processing. Sometimes simple discrepancies will be found such as when two answers are given for an item, but one is missed in hand scoring because the punched scoring template placed over the answer sheet hides the second mark. If care is not taken to make certain the scanning and scoring programs work correctly at this point, errors in scanning or scoring will be entered into the data set and may be subsequently difficult to locate.

4.1.1. Prescanning

Answer documents received at the scanning facility should be checked first to make certain all documents that should have been received were, in fact, received. The transmittal information from the sending school or teacher should include information such as the number of answer sheets sent, the school and teacher (or class) identification codes, and the type of tests being sent. In many large testing programs, the sheets would then be counted to make sure that the same number was received as indicated on the transmittal form. Checking might also include making sure information such as the name and address of the sender, grade level, and any other information is present that would be required for accurately processing, scoring, and reporting. A general rule is to resolve differences at the stage they are detected. Waiting to a subsequent stage can result in incorporating the error or the differences in counts into the results, thereby increasing the cost and the amount of time needed to find and correct the errors.

The prescanning process is also done to ensure that all documents submitted to the scanner can be mechanically processed by the scanner and that the information on the documents is complete and free of stray marks. If a document has been cut, taped, folded, or modified in some way so that the complete document is no longer available or is substantially compromised, it may not move through the scanner or the information on it may not be properly interpreted by the software. These documents will need to be removed from the feeder and processed by hand.

Answer sheets are typically grouped together in batches for more efficient scanning and scoring. Every different type of answer document requires a tailored computer program written to indicate to the scanner where to find the response locations on that document and how to interpret them. The scanning program contains code that identifies the particular structure of the batch, the individual types of documents included in the batch, and the order of those documents. The first sheet in the batch, usually called a header sheet, identifies important information about the batch to the scanner. Examples of information contained in header sheets include the school, grade, and classroom for the batch. In some scoring systems, this information is copied into each of the answer records so that the batch can be disaggregated in subsequent processing. The prescanning operation also ensures that all documents that need to be in the batch are present and that these documents are in the correct order as expected by the scanning software. Documents that are out of order, reversed, or modified (e.g., mutilated) in some unanticipated way will interrupt and possibly corrupt the data capture process. If the answer document consists of a multiple-page booklet, the booklet will likely have to be disassembled before scanning, because most scanners can only process answer sheets up to 8.5 inches wide by 11 inches in length. Disassembly usually means cutting the spine off the booklet so each page of the booklet can be scanned individually.

4.1.1.1. Editing During Prescanning

The answer sheets need to be edited prior to scanning to make certain that the information on the document is of sufficiently high quality to enable accurate capture by the scanner. The things that need to be edited are determined in large part by the answer sheet being processed. Editing at this point in the process consists of inspecting each answer sheet to make certain a pencil was used (if ink is not recognized by the scanner), that smudges are not so dark that they would interfere with scanning, and that stray marks have not been made on the answer sheet. On some sheets, a check is done to verify that the name or other identifying information is written in, although the bubbles may not necessarily be checked to see if the information was filled in correctly. Editors also need to determine if marks were made in an answer field that was not to be scored. Sometimes examinees will make notes to themselves about an answer or even cross out a section of the answer sheet as not being taken. Since such marks may be interpreted as meaningful information by the scanner, hand editing needs to make certain the sheet is cleaned up before processing through the scanner. Pre-edit is designed to catch as many of these problems as possible before the answer documents are scanned.

4.1.2. Scanning

In addition to calibration of the settings and adjustments on the scanner, most scanners include some checking of the scanner operating system. These checks consist of monitoring internal machine parameters for different aspects of the scanning operation. They also include checking each of the read locations in the scanner for each different type of answer sheet and determining each answer sheet's average light intensity. The average light intensity is used to determine whether or not a particular reading is an actual mark, such as when an erasure occurs. If the mark is too light, relative to this interval, the software can be set to ignore it. On large scanners, documents found to fail a particular check are sometimes shunted into a separate bin. On small scanners, the scanner can be set to stop and the sheet retrieved and checked visually. In large test scoring facilities, tests are not scored during scanning. This is because there is additional checking of the data that may need to be done prior to scoring to ensure that the data have been scanned correctly. Any such checking during scanning will slow down the scanning process.

4.1.2.1. Postscan Editing

Once a document has been scanned, the integrity of the data scanned needs to be checked before scoring is done. Some of this can be done by software specifically designed for this purpose. Scanning software (e.g., ScanTools or Image ScanTools by Pearson NCS) normally contains editing functions that can be applied to each scanned data record to locate errors or potential errors that have been recognized by the software. These edits include checking for multiple marks in fields that should contain only a single mark or making certain that sufficient information is entered in specific fields (e.g., it is possible to check that name fields contain some minimal number of characters or that the identification number has been bubbled in). Rectifying such errors requires locating the answer document and visually checking it to determine what correction needs to be made.

When image scanning is used, even if the scanner is used in OMR mode, software is sometimes available, such as Accra by Pearson NCS, to help in writing editing routines for locating errors on individual answer sheets. Editing software written with a package like Accra can be used to locate errors detected during scanning and display both the error and an on-screen image of the response location on the answer sheet in which the error was detected. The human editor can then view the image of the answer document online, usually without having to physically locate and handle the actual document, and make any necessary corrections. This can result in considerable time savings. Once the documents in a batch have been edited and the data determined to be accurate, the answer records can be scored.

4.1.3. Scoring

Scoring is done only after the integrity of the data have been checked as thoroughly as possible. Large scoring operations have sets of programs designed to check answer records for data integrity prior to scoring. The typical types of checks include checking names and addresses for completeness, checking for long sequences of missing responses, checking the preliminary item analysis information and answer key, and examining score distributions for expected and unexpected kinds of results. Additional checking would include running frequency counts of the numbers of students, the numbers of males and females, the numbers of students receiving special accommodations, the number of different grades, and so on. If there are differences from what would be expected, these need to be resolved before proceeding. For example, if there are too many students listed as receiving a particular type of accommodation, the reason for this needs to be determined. It may be that a field on the answer sheet was scanned incorrectly. In addition, item analyses should be done on each test. This will serve as an added check on the answer key and also on the reasonableness of the response rates for each of the answer choices or omit rates for each of the items. If domain scores are reported, these should be computed and their distributions checked. These distributions should be reasonable when compared with pretest results or with results from administration of previous forms of the test.

4.1.3.1. Steps in the Process of Scoring Constructed Response Items

Performance testing, particularly essay testing, is becoming an increasingly important part of large-scale state-level testing programs (Olson, Bond, & Andrews, 1999). Writing skills, in particular, are often measured by constructed response item formats largely because direct measurement of writing necessitates asking an examinee to provide a sample of writing. A more technical discussion of performance assessment, including development of scoring rubrics and training and monitoring of scorers, is included in Lane and Stone (Chapter 11, this volume). In this section, we examine the general steps to be used in scoring this type of item. To simplify the discussion, we focus on scoring of writing samples. The open-ended nature of this type of item requires a modified version of the steps for processing and scoring answer sheets. The steps in initial processing of response documents, however, should be the same, regardless of the types of items being administered. Figure 10.3 gives a general work flow for the scoring and reporting of writing tests. The steps involved include the basic processing steps plus the development of a scoring rubric, selection of benchmark papers, selection and training of scorers, and monitoring of scorers during scoring to ensure accuracy and consistency.

In large-scale essay testing programs, special answer documents are prepared for examinees to use for writing their essays in order to simplify the handling and subsequent processing needed for scoring. Often, both fixed-response demographic information (e.g., name, birth date, student identification number) and the actual writing sample are captured on the same response document. The demographic information can usually be read in using OMR capability and the actual writing sample read in using an imaging capability. Following pre-edit and resolution of any discrepancies, the documents are moved to the next step in processing.

4.1.3.2. Scanning

Some information on the answer document may need to be scanned in, such as name, identification number, or a bar-coded label to identify the student. If the original answer document is too large to be processed through the scanner, the sheets may need to be disassembled first. If answer booklets for a writing test have to be disassembled for processing, they need to be specially formatted ahead of time so that each of the disassembled portions contains a common linking code that will make it possible to merge the data from the separately scanned sheets into a common record. After data from each of the separated sheets of the answer document are scanned in and interpreted by the scanning programs, this information is recorded in a data file for subsequent editing and processing.

4.1.3.3. Scoring of Essays

In this section, we discuss the general sequence in the typical essay scoring process in which scorers sit at a table and their work is monitored by a table leader. Table leaders are typically trained extensively in the scoring of the prompt(s) used in the essay testing program. The role of the table leader is to maintain control over each scorer's calibration with a performance criterion (usually agreement with the table leader's scoring) within some limit of variability. There are variations on the typical theme of having scorers sit at a table with a table leader. Because of the difficulty of

FIGURE 10.3 Work Flow for Writing Assessment

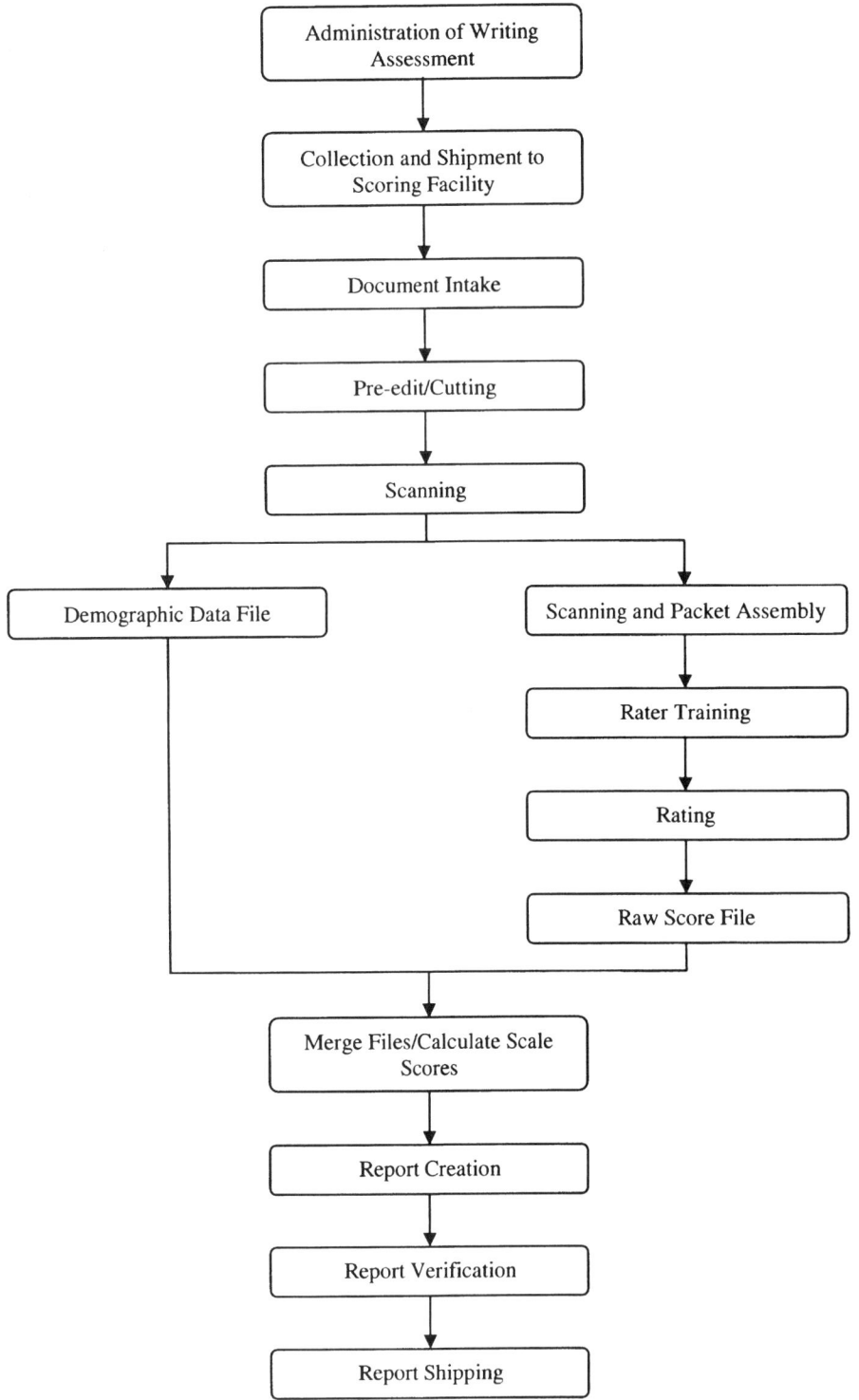

finding individuals who can be trained as table leaders, in some scoring facilities, one scoring center manager and an assistant might be assigned to monitor a larger number of scorers (e.g., 20 or 30 or more). Under this model, scorers would sit at a table in the scoring room and the scoring center manager and the assistant would read and review scores of papers as the raters finished them and turned them in to get their next set.

Technology has played an important role in the scoring of essay tests, as it has allowed essays to be scanned in and sent electronically to scorers not physically located at the same table as the table leader. Online scoring also removes the need for scorers to handle the answer documents. This kind of scoring is currently provided by most large test scoring companies. It is sometimes the case with online scoring that scorers come to a central facility, where "table leaders" are present, to read and score the scanned essays. With online scoring, scorers do not need to congregate in a central location, and "table leaders" can use specialized software to remotely monitor the scoring of each of the raters assigned to their "virtual table."

Selection, training, and monitoring of scorers are discussed in more detail by Lane and Stone (Chapter 11, this volume). Here, we discuss some critical elements. Selection and training of scorers is essential in the scoring process. It is necessary to select raters who are willing to learn to use the test developer's scoring rubric, so that essays may be scored as intended. Applicants should be screened carefully, including being given a sample scoring task similar to those asked of them as scorers. In some cases, it may also be useful to give the applicant a writing sample.

4.1.3.4. Training of Scorers

Training manuals need to be prepared for each essay test to be scored. The training manual typically includes model papers selected from the current administration, selected to represent complete coverage of the range of observed scores. Papers are also selected, where appropriate, to represent particular issues that might arise during scoring, such as atypical approaches to the topic being scored. Model papers are annotated and inserted in the training manual. Table leaders are brought in to help prepare the training manuals, identify model papers, and determine how to score them. Differences in scoring among table leaders are discussed among the table leaders so they are fully understood, and then, if necessary, resolved by the scoring center manager. The training manual needs to be available to table leaders and scorers during the actual scoring.

Table leaders must be trained in the scoring of the essay prior to the rest of the raters coming in. Table leader training should include both taking an extensive training program and passing a qualifying examination. Training is normally done by the scoring center manager; however, as part of their training, table leaders should also be shown how to train new scorers, interpret training materials, monitor accuracy of scorers, and report irregularities to the head scorer or the scoring center manager.

Scorers also need to complete a training program. For lower-stakes essay testing programs, training often includes simply an orientation session to make certain all raters are aware of the intent of the testing program and their role in the program. Training materials would include the rubric for the essay test along with sets of prescored essays selected over the range of scores for the essay. Following the orientation, trainees should discuss the rubric and then begin to score the prescored papers using the rubric. This is still part of the training and usually begins with scoring of one or two papers, followed by a discussion among the raters, during which disagreements are discussed and resolved. The focus of the training is on calibrating raters so that everyone learns to apply the scoring rubric in the same way. The training proceeds by scoring another set of (usually five to ten) prescored papers, followed by discussion. This training process continues through several sets of prescored papers until the scoring center manager is convinced that the scorers at the table are all in agreement with the prescored papers and with each other. Normally, for simple essays of one to three pages, this can be accomplished with less than 20 prescored essays. For longer or more complex essays, or for more complex scoring schemes, scoring of more prescored papers would be necessary.

For high-stakes testing programs, the training needs to be more extensive, including working through the training manual and even passing a qualifying examination. A good training program would have 50 to 100 prescored model papers included in the training manual, which the scorers will have studied, and about 70% of which they will have scored. During training, trainers need to meet with each scorer to go over the agreements or disagreements between their scores and the scores given by the trainers. If necessary, additional practice sets should be provided for scorers who demonstrate they are not yet ready for actual scoring. When the trainer feels the scorer is ready, the scorer is allowed to take the qualifying examination.

A qualifying examination for scorers should look exactly like the task they are to perform in scoring for the testing program. A typical qualifying examination would include scoring 10 or 20 papers. The scores would be compared to the scores agreed to by the table leaders and scoring center manager. Typically, a criterion for agreement with expert scorers would be approximately one-half to two-thirds of the papers scored. Failure on the qualifying test will mean the individual is not eligible to work on the project. All scorers passing the test would need to sign a test security agreement before they are allowed to score actual examination papers.

Papers are then randomly sorted to ensure that papers from one school or one location in a state are not all scored by the same scorers. In high-stakes essay testing programs, each paper may be scored by two scorers but most large-scale testing programs provide a second scoring for only a portion (somewhere between 10% and 20%) of the total papers. Although this is done to keep scoring costs down, it also leaves the scoring process open to potential errors for the remaining papers that are not read more than one time.

4.1.3.5. Monitoring Scorer Accuracy

The accuracy of scorers needs to be monitored continually by the table leader. The table leader often does this by serving as a second reader on a portion of the packets of sheets. When agreement falls below some prespecified level, for example, two-thirds agreement, the scorer needs to go through a modified retraining, a conference with the table leader, or a review of the training manual. If the accuracy of the scorer does not improve after retraining, the scorer should be dismissed Frequent meetings between table leaders and scoring center managers help identify retraining needs.

4.1.4. Computerized Scoring of Essays

One concern with constructed response items is that they are time consuming and costly to score. Because of the appeal of constructed response items to educators and because of the very high cost of scoring this type of item, methods are continually being sought to reduce the cost. An alternative to handscoring that is becoming increasingly feasible is use of computerized scoring algorithms to score essays. Computerized scoring can be done in seconds once the essays are in a computer readable form. The savings in time and cost are obvious. Critics of this approach argue that scoring essays is essentially a subjective process, one that cannot be modeled accurately by a scoring algorithm (Whittington & Hunt, 1999). The subjective nature of scoring essays, however, is not a persuasive rationale for ignoring essay scoring by computer. Furthermore, there is certain appeal for an algorithm that can consistently approximate human scoring, as the savings in cost and time would be enormous (Rudner & Gagne, 2001; Whittington & Hunt, 1999).

What is important to realize is that algorithmic scoring is possible, but once the software is "trained" to score a given prompt, there is usually no feedback mechanism designed to update the kinds of responses that should receive a particular score. Aberrant responses, particularly types not in the initial set of essays used to train the software, will not necessarily be scored the same as by a human grader. Those involved in developing essay scoring software generally agree that the software is ill-suited for scoring very creative responses. Rather than completely replacing humans in the scoring process, the use of computerized scoring can also be combined with a single human scoring, thereby eliminating most of the need for a second human scorer.

Substantial work has been done since the 1980s on operational implementation of computerized scoring algorithms. At the moment, there are four systems that have received the most attention: Project Essay Grade (PEG; Page, 1966), Intelligent Essay Assessor (IEA; Landauer, Laham, & Foltz, 2003), Intellimetric (Elliot, 2003), and e-Rater (Burstein, 2003). Each of these algorithms uses a training or calibration process that first requires humans to score a set of essays. The set of scored essays and the scores comprise the calibration data that are then fed into the software to train the scoring software that is used to score subsequent essays. These systems differ in their selection of the characteristics that are analyzed by the software, the selection of essays for the training set, and the methods used for determining weighting of these characteristics in estimating the essay score.

All four systems are intended to be a surrogate for human scoring so it is not surprising that the primary criterion for determining their effectiveness is often the scores given by human scorers. Proprietary research with these systems indicates that the correlations with scores given by human scorers is generally as good as the correlations between human scorers. To obtain a more stable estimate of the score for an essay, some research has used the average score across multiple human graders. Unfortunately, since each of these systems is proprietary, complete details of their implementation are not generally available. Consequently, descriptions of the algorithms are incomplete from the standpoint of replication. Also, the specific variables included in each of the models are not known, nor are the weights assigned to each (Rudner & Gagne, 2001). This makes these algorithms much less attractive for use either by researchers or test consumers who seek to use the results for subsequent study. Essay scoring software packages have been studied, however, and in some cases extensively, so there is evidence regarding the comparability of these systems with human scoring. Some of this evidence is cited below to give a sense of the kinds of studies that have been done. The increasing sophistication of algorithms in these packages promises to yield results that will become even more accurate approximations of human scorers.

One critical concern for each of these essay scoring algorithms is the method by which papers are fed to the software. Although high-speed scanning systems are already available to provide scanned images of handwritten essays, each of these algorithms requires the essays be in a form that is directly interpretable by the computer so they can be processed. This normally means the essays have to be entered using a keyboard either by the examinee or by scoring center staff. Unfortunately, software for accurately decoding handwriting is not yet available for production-level applications. One current limitation to widespread use of this software, therefore, is the availability of low-cost data entry to the system. Below, we discuss general features of each of these algorithms and present some of the evidence supporting their use in various educational contexts.

4.1.4.1. Project Essay Grade (PEG)

The PEG system is conceptually the simplest of these algorithms. It scores an essay mainly using external features of the essay that are purported to describe the quality of the essay (Page, 1966, 1994). PEG identifies what Page calls trins, which are intrinsic qualities of the essay. Trins are unobservable but can be estimated by means of observable variables called proxes, such as number of words, number of semicolons, number of prepositions, and word frequency, which can be quantified by the software. The PEG software is trained by reading in a set of hand-scored essays (usually from 100 to 400 essays) to estimate values for up to 30 proxes. The proxes are used as predictors and the scores for the hand-graded essays are used as dependent variables in a regression equation. The PEG software uses this information to estimate regression weights for each of the variables in the equation. Once the PEG software is trained (i.e., the regression equation for a particular essay prompt has been estimated), this equation is imposed on all remaining essays (which may or may not have been hand scored), for purposes of calculating the computer-based scores.

4.1.4.2. Intelligent Essay Assessor (IEA)

IEA (Landauer et al., 2003) was initially developed as an algorithm for indexing documents for information retrieval. The approach used is to first define a set of calibration documents and then use these to determine scores on subsequent documents. The documents are compared based on increasingly specific index terms. IEA uses a methodology known as latent semantic analysis (LSA) to measure the quality of writing. LSA is a method that calculates a representation of the meaning relations among words and passages in the document. For essay scoring, LSA determines these relations over a large number of essays written to the same prompt. (Landauer et al. [2003] suggest that 50 is a large number.) The main idea is that the collection of the contexts in which a word does or does not appear defines the set of constraints that are used to indicate similarity of meanings of the words to one another (Landauer et al., 2003). LSA estimates a multidimensional semantic space for the words, phrases, and passages that appear in the essays and then estimates the similarity in meaning among these words, and so on based on their locations in the space (Landauer & Dumais, 1997; Landauer, Laham, & Foltz, 1998). LSA is used in IEA to determine the quality of the semantic content, the components of content and whether they are well covered or not, and sources in texts that can provide needed information to the writer/examinee. (For a more complete description of LSA see Landauer et al., 1998.)

IEA establishes the semantic space for scoring essays by first processing a sufficiently large body of background text in the domain of interest to yield the set of relationships among words, phrases, paragraphs, and so on. (As an example, to establish the semantic space for a given course, IEA would process textbooks and class materials in the subject area to identify words, phrases, etc. that occur in this domain.) Next, IEA processes a training set of hand-scored essays (on a common prompt) to determine the semantic contents of the essay and where each is located in the semantic space. IEA begins by entering each calibration essay in one column of a matrix. The relevant content terms (e.g., words, sentences) appearing in any of the calibration essays are compiled and become the rows in the matrix. The tallies in the cells of the matrix represent the importance of the term to the essay in which it appears or to the content domain being assessed. These tallies can be frequency counts or some other index of the weighting of the row variable. Once the software is trained, the remainder of the essays (i.e., those not used for training) are read into the system. IEA compares the semantic contents of each essay with those in the training set and attempts to predict what score human graders would give to the essay. IEA accomplishes this by identifying the essays in the training set that are most similar (based on their locations in the multidimensional space) to the essay under consideration. The average of the scores for the essays identified as being similar is taken as the score for the essay under consideration (Landauer et al., 1998, 2003).

4.1.4.3. Intellimetric

Intellimetric™ Software is trained on a set of prescored papers identified as "known score" marker papers for each score point in a rubric. Specific information about the Intellimetric™ system is scant. The software is described by its developers as "based on a blend of artificial intelligence, natural language processing and statistical technologies" (Elliot, 2003, p. 71). Intellimetric™ software is reported to analyze over 300 semantic, discourse, and syntactic features classed into five categories: focus and unity, indicating cohesiveness and consistency of purpose and main idea; development and elaboration, representing breadth of content and the support given; organization and structure, describing the logic of discourse; sentence structure; and mechanics and conventions.

4.1.4.4. e-Rater

e-Rater is the automated essay grading system developed by Burstein and her colleagues at ETS (Burstein, 2003). The software was originally designed to provide a single holistic score written to a specific prompt for the analytic writing assessment section of the Graduate Management Record Examination. It is currently used to provide one of the two scores for each of the essays written for this portion of the test (the other score is obtained from a human grader). When the two scores differ by more than a single point (on a 6-point scale), a second human scorer is used. The system has subsequently been enhanced to provide feedback on grammatical and discourse characteristics.

Burstein, Chodorow, and Leacock (2004) describe the e-Rater 2.0 software as identifying 12 linguistically based features from an essay and then using a regression equation developed on a set of 200 to 250 training essays to assign a score to an essay. This equation is unique for each essay prompt and is applied to new essays written to the prompt to produce a predicted value. This predicted value is then converted to the score scale for the essay. Several of the variables used by e-Rater relate to frequency counts of key features, including the number of grammar errors, the number of usage errors, the number of mechanics errors, and the number of style diagnostics each divided by essay length. e-Rater also measures the number of required discourse elements. Eight such elements are expected by e-Rater in a typical essay: a thesis, three main ideas, three supporting ideas, and a conclusion. e-Rater also includes the average length of the discourse elements proportional to the total length of the essay. Topical content is evaluated using content vector analysis in which word frequencies are counted and word weights are determined proportional to the frequency in the essay but inversely related to the number of essays in which the word appears. e-Rater also considers the similarity of the vocabulary to essays in the training set that have the same average length of discourse elements divided by essay length. A ratio is computed of the number of different words in the essay to the total number of word occurrences.

Finally, an index of word frequency is included along with an index of the average word length and the total number of occurrences of each word in the essay.

5. REPORTING OF RESULTS

Tests do not exist in a vacuum. The reasons for which a test was developed become the framework within which results are reported. Test results likewise need to be reported in a form and time frame that matches the purpose of the test. If a test is to have an impact on instruction in the classroom, for example, one requirement is that the teacher needs to receive results in time to implement them in the instructional sequence. If a test matches instruction, the longer it takes to report results, the lower the utility of the test results. In this section, we discuss some derived scores, with an eye toward understanding how different score types can affect reporting and interpretation. In addition, we examine some different reporting formats, again with an eye toward considering how format and time frame need to match the purposes of the test.

Whereas the invariance property of IRT allows for θ estimates from separate administrations or alternate forms to be directly compared, provided the two administrations/forms have been equated (see Yen & Fitzpatrick, Chapter 4, this volume), the same cannot be said of raw scores. Raw scores have little clear meaning beyond the particular set of questions and the specific test administration. To remedy this, a wide variety of types of scores, sometimes called derived scores, are generally used for reporting test results. (The topic of scores is covered in detail by Kolen, Chapter 5, this volume, and by Kolen & Brennan [2004.]) Derived scores represent efforts to provide meaningful information in a useful form and format for the user of the test results. Anastasi (1988) discussed two different types of derived scores: developmental scores and within-group scores.

Developmental scores are useful for showing how far an examinee has advanced, relative to developmental milestones. The two most common developmental scores are grade equivalents and age equivalents. Within-group scores are useful for rank ordering examinees or for determining the trait level of each examinee relative to the normative sample. Examples of within-group scores include percentiles, standard scores (e.g., Z- or T-scores), normalized scores, and stanines.

Although all derived scores contain the same information about an examinee's level on the latent trait, the choice of reporting metric is an important one if the results are to be effectively communicated and interpreted. Developmental scales are conceptually very appealing for communicating educational data, and are still the most common way of reporting standardized test results for students in elementary and middle school (Echternacht, 1977). Developmental scales are useful because students, teachers, and parents are very familiar with the age or grade metric. They can also be valuable in demonstrating the true degree of individual differences within an age or grade (Hopkins, Stanley, & Hopkins, 1990); however, developmental scales are also easily misinterpreted. Because of large within grade variances, a much smaller-than-expected percentage of students at any particular grade will actually test at their own grade level. Many students test above or below grade level, causing many parents to question whether their child is in the appropriate class. Different within-grade or within-age standard deviations mean that students' scores may increase or decrease at apparently different rates. For example, on many educational tests, grade equivalent standard deviations increase with grade. This can cause students to look like they are falling farther and farther behind, even though their position within their grade may not have changed. A student who is one standard deviation below the mean on a test might appear to be one grade level behind at grade 3, but two grade levels behind at grade 6. A similar problem is caused by the standard deviations being different across subject areas. Consequently, a student with the same percentile rank in two different subjects could have different grade or age equivalent scores. Finally, grade and age equivalents are only relevant to the extent that the content on which students are tested is common to all test takers. Curricular differences, as are common across middle schools and high schools, greatly reduce the interpretability of developmental scales. This is particularly true for many students in special education classes.

Though less intuitive than developmental scores, within-group scores are very effective at comparing examinees relative to their peers. Some scores, such as stanines, are appealing for quickly reporting a general pattern or profile of scores. With stanines, examinees are sorted into one of nine categories, based on their test score. Because all students within a particular stanine receive the same score, stanines do not provide the opportunity to make fine discriminations among examinees. However, in simultaneously studying all of a student's scores in the various curricular areas of a statewide achievement test, stanines might be a valuable way to identify the student's relative strengths and weaknesses. For situations where it is necessary to provide finer-grained decisions than can be provided by stanines, scores with a larger number of score points (e.g., percentile ranks, standard scores, normalized scores) are more useful. Within-group scores are generally more difficult to communicate than are developmental scores, but once the logic underlying them is understood, their interpretation is more consistent.

5.1. Uses of Tests

One useful way of categorizing educational tests is as either achievement tests or diagnostic tests. Achievement tests provide information for a wide range of decisions including admissions, course placement, promotion, and program evaluation. Diagnostic tests, such as a reading readiness test, are useful for helping make therapeutic or instructional types of decisions. The types of scores used for these kinds of tests differ somewhat depending on their purpose.

5.2. Reporting Level of Achievement or Performance

One way to report scores is in terms of the achievement standards defined for the test. This kind of score is used mainly for standards-based tests such as those developed by the National Assessment of Educational Progress (NAEP) or tests developed to meet adequate yearly progress (AYP) reporting requirements. NAEP achievement levels for grade 4 reading illustrate this kind of score (see Table 10.2). The achievement levels are Basic, Proficient, and Advanced. Numbers in the table refer to the standard scores on the NAEP Grade 4 Reading Test. Achievement level scores are also reported for norm-referenced tests such as the Iowa Tests of Basic Skills (http://www.uiowa.edu/~itp/downloads/Interp_Guide_(2003_version).pdf).

The achievement level score provides a description of the level of achievement demonstrated by persons receiving a particular score on the test. It is not designed to provide a rubric for grading examination results. Rather, the description provides an indication of what the grade reflects, on average. Achievement levels provide an interpretation of the scores. This interpretation is sometimes also accompanied by an ordinal score indicating relative performance compared to the other achievement levels. The popularity of this type of score is increasing in part because recent legislation (Title I, ESEA reauthorization act, 2002) requires that states report results for their statewide standards-based tests in terms of achievement levels.

5.3. Interpretive Issues in Use of Achievement Levels in Score Reports

Achievement level descriptors for test scores are helpful for describing what test performances mean. The NAEP Reading achievement level descriptors for grade 4, reflect the combined consensus among standard-setting panelists and across different panels as to the meaning of scores on the test. (Mazzeo and Lazer, Chapter 19, this volume, present an extensive discussion of NAEP.) It is important to recognize that results reported on the basis of achievement levels are typically not useful for making instructional decisions. Achievement level descriptors look very much like they were intended to be used for describing the performance of individual students, but such an interpretation is not necessarily appropriate. Achievement level descriptors indicate what would be a typical type (or types) of performance for a given test score or range of test scores. Since individual students do not all achieve in the same way, many students will earn a given score on a test in ways not always well described by the achievement level descriptions. Achievement level descriptions could be misleading, if applied at the individual student level, but may have utility for interpreting group-level performance. For this reason, classroom teachers usually find it difficult to extract much useful information from achievement level scores relative to making instructional decisions. Achievement level scores are generally more often appropriate for making group level decisions such as whether or not students in a school or school system are meeting standards. Instructional decisions for individual students are usually made based on scores that better reflect more finely grained instructional objectives.

5.4. Reporting Growth

Some testing programs are designed to consider achievement over time. In educational contexts, growth in achievement is typically measured over grades. This is, in fact, the intent behind the NCLB legislation, and requires a score scale that retains its meaning over the full scale. Growth scales, usually called vertical scales, have a unique set of problems that make them difficult to develop and maintain. (A thorough discussion of equating issues is given by Kolen, Chapter 5, this volume, and in Kolen & Brennan, 2004.) Grade equivalent scores are typically reported for this type of scale, but as noted earlier, grade equivalents are not without their problems.

5.5. Diagnostic Results

Diagnostic tests are designed to provide information that can be used for making an emotional, instructional, physical, or behavioral diagnosis, or some combination of these, for an individual. Diagnostic tests are used, for example, by almost every school psychologist, reading specialist, and school counselor in the United States. Tests designed to provide diagnostic information generally require

TABLE 10.2 NAEP Reading Achievement Levels for Grade 4

Basic (208)	Fourth-grade students performing at the *Basic* level should demonstrate an understanding of the overall meaning of what they read. When reading text appropriate for fourth-graders, they should be able to make relatively obvious connections between the text and their own experiences and extend the ideas in the text by making simple inferences.
Proficient (238)	Fourth-grade students performing at the *Proficient* level should be able to demonstrate an overall understanding of the text, providing inferential as well as literal information. When reading text appropriate to fourth grade, they should be able to extend the ideas in the text by making inferences, drawing conclusions, and making connections to their own experiences. The connection between the text and what the student infers should be clear.
Advanced (268)	Fourth-grade students performing at the *Advanced* level should be able to generalize about topics in the reading selection and demonstrate an awareness of how authors compose and use literary devices. When reading text appropriate to fourth grade, they should be able to judge text critically and, in general, to give thorough answers that indicate careful thought

Source: http://nces.ed.gov/nationsreportcard/reading/achieveall.asp.

substantial training to administer and to interpret and are often reported in terms of standard scores. One useful reporting method used in many diagnostic tests is the profile chart. The profile chart plots, for each examinee, the scores on all subtests or scales along a common set of axes. Typically, scores for different scales are connected by lines and are sometimes also bounded by error bands. The information is used to indicate to the test administrator the individual subtest scores, the pattern of scores, and, when error bands are present, the error around each of the scores for a particular examinee. Such information is useful for identifying each examinee's relative strengths and weaknesses. Often patterns of scores are as useful as the individual scores themselves in identifying diagnostically useful information.

5.6. Reporting for Different Purposes

There are numerous purposes for which reports are developed. Many of these are covered in this chapter. Reporting for specific types of testing programs are also covered elsewhere in this volume. Shepard covers reporting for instructional tests (Chapter 17, this volume), Zwick covers reporting for placement and selection tests (Chapter 18, this volume), Mazzeo and Lazer cover reporting for program evaluation and accountability (Chapter 19, this volume), and Clauser and Margolis cover reporting for credentialing and certification tests (Chapter 20, this volume).

6. FINAL COMMENTS

We tie the thread of this chapter by noting once again the impact of technology on the past, present, and future of test scoring, security, and reporting. The increased use of technology for scoring constructed response and performance testing is barely in its infancy. This is an area that will see marked expansion as computing power increases and becomes more cheaply and easily available. Managing these new approaches to scoring will require substantial research and effort to ensure that ease of scoring does not contravene accuracy. New forms of technology will also lead to new means for breaching security and, thereby, to new threats to the integrity of tests. As long as tests are used for high-stakes purposes, these threats will remain an important concern for testing programs. This impact is already seen in the development of psychometric models to include detection of forms of cheating, as well as for item selection and exposure. The use of technology by those seeking to gain unfair access to testing materials simply increases the monitoring task. Test reporting is one area that is only just beginning to receive rigorous attention. It is clearly essential to test validity, but most reports are usually developed without much understanding of the impact on the audience. Wainer, Hambleton, and Meara (1999) provide a methodology for development of data displays that focuses on the understanding of the test results by the intended audience. Experimental work such as this will help lead to improvements in the use of technology for reporting and will help ensure that test results are interpreted in ways that are consistent with the design of the test.

REFERENCES

ACT, Inc. (2004) *Cancellation of scores by ACT.* Retrieved June 12, 2006 from http://actstudent.org/scores/cancel.html

ACT, Inc. (2005). *Procedures for investigating testing irregularities and questioned test scores* [Brochure]. Iowa City, IA: ACT.

American Educational Research Association, American Psychological Association, & National Council on Measurement in Education. (1974). *Standards for educational and psychological tests.* Washington, DC: American Educational Research Association.

American Educational Research Association, American Psychological Association, & National Council on Measurement in Education. (1985). *Standards for educational and psychological testing.* Washington, DC: American Educational Research Association.

American Educational Research Association, American Psychological Association, & National Council on Measurement in Education. (1999). *Standards for educational and psychological testing.* Washington, DC: American Educational Research Association.

Americans with Disabilities Act of 1990, Pub. L. No. 101-336, §2, 104 Stat. 328 (1991).

Anastasi, A. (1981). Coaching, test sophistication, and developed abilities. *American Psychologist, 36,* 1086–1093.

Anastasi, A. (1988). *Psychological testing* (6th ed.). New York: Macmillan.

Angoff, W. H. (1974). The development of statistical indices for detecting cheaters. *Journal of the American Statistical Association, 69,* 44–49.

Assessment Systems Corporation. (1993). *Scrutiny!: Software to identify test misconduct.* Advanced Psychometrics, Minneapolis, MN.

Associated Press. (2003a, January 31). 6 confess to cheating on exam with cell phones. *Chicago Tribune.* Retrieved January 13, 2004 from http://www.chicagotribune.com.

Associated Press. (2003b, October 28). Teachers caught cheating. *CBS News* [online]. Retrieved January 12, 2004 from http://www.cbsnews.com.

Associated Press. (2004, January 5). 3 accused of cheating in NASD Broker Test. *Chicago Tribune.* Retrieved January 12, 2004, from http://www.newsday.com

Baird, J. S., Jr. (1980). Current trends in college cheating. *Psychology in the Schools, 17,* 515–522.

Baker, F. B. (1968). Automation of test scoring, reporting, and analysis. In R. L. Thorndike (Ed.), *Educational measurement* (2nd ed., pp. 202–236). Washington, DC: American Council on Education.

Baker, F. B. (1989). Computer technology in test construction and processing. In R. L. Linn (Ed.), *Educational measurement* (3rd ed., pp. 409–428). Washington, DC: American Council on Education.

Bay, L. (1995, April). *Detection of cheating on multiple-choice examinations.* Paper presented at the annual meeting of the American Educational Research Association, San Francisco.

Bellezza, F. S., & Bellezza, S. F. (1989). Detection of cheating on multiple-choice tests by using error-similarity analysis. *Teaching of Psychology, 16*(3), 151–155.

Bergstrom, B. A., Lunz, M. E., & Gershon, R. C. (1992). Altering the level of difficulty in computer adaptive testing. *Applied Measurement in Education, 5,* 137–149.

Bird, C. (1927). The detection of cheating on objective examinations. *School and Society, 25*(635), 261–262.

Bock, R. D. (1972). Estimating item parameters and latent ability when responses are scored in two or more nominal categories. *Psychometrika, 46,* 443–459.

Bolt, D. M., Cohen, A. S., & Wollack, J. A. (2002). Item parameter estimation under conditions of test speededness: Application of a mixture Rasch model with ordinal constraints. *Journal of Educational Measurement, 39*(4), 331–348.

Bottge, B. B., Heinrichs, M., Chan, S. Y., & Watson, E. A. (2000). *Integrating math knowledge of low-achieving students.* Madison: University of Wisconsin, Wisconsin Center for Educational Research.

Boughton, K. A., Larkin, K., & Yamamoto, K. (2004, April). *Modeling differential speededness using a HYBRID psychometric approach.* Paper presented at the annual meeting of the American Educational Research Association, San Diego, CA.

Bowman, M. L. (1989, March). Testing individual differences in ancient China. *American Psychologist, 44,* 576–578.

Boykin, D. (2004, February). New calculators force NCEES to tighten exam security policy. *Engineering Times Online, 26*(2). Retrieved April 19, 2005 from http://www.nspe.org/etweb/1et-0204.asp

Bunderson, C. V., Inouye, D. K., & Olsen, J. B. (1989). The four generations of computerized educational measurement. In R. L. Linn (Ed.), *Educational measurement* (3rd ed., pp. 367–407). Washington, DC: American Council on Education.

Burstein, J. C. (2003). The e-Rater scoring engine: Automated essay scoring with Natural Language Processing. In M. D. Shermis & J. C. Burstein (Eds.), *Automated essay scoring: A cross-disciplinary perspective* (pp. 113–121). Mahwah, NJ: Lawrence Erlbaum.

Burstein, J., Chodorow, M., & Leacock, C. (2004). Automated essay evaluation: The Criterion online writing service. *AI Magazine, 25,* 27–36.

Buss, W. G., & Novick, M. R. (1980). The detection of cheating on standardized tests: Statistical and legal analysis. *Journal of Law and Education, 9,* 1–64.

Castle Rock Research Corporation. (2005). *Integrity* [Computer program]. Edmonton, Alberta, Canada.

Chang, H.-H., Quian, J., & Ying, Z. (2001). a-stratified multistage computerized adaptive testing with b blocking. *Applied Psychological Measurement, 25,* 333–341.

Chang, H.-H., & Ying, Z. (1996). A global information approach to computerized adaptive testing. *Applied Psychological Measurement, 20,* 213–229.

Chang, H.-H., & Ying, Z. (1999). a-stratified multistage computerized adaptive testing. *Applied Psychological Measurement, 23,* 211–222.

Chang, S.-W., & Ansley, T. N. (2003). A comparative study of item exposure control methods in computerized adaptive testing. *Journal of Educational Measurement, 40,* 71–103.

Chason, W. M. (1997, March). *A comparison of several classical and IRT-based methods to detect aberrant response patterns.* Paper presented at the annual meeting of the American Educational Research Association, Chicago.

Chason, W. M., & Maller, S. (1996, April). *Utility of the Rasch person-fit statistic in detecting answer copying: A comparison with traditional cheating indices.* Paper presented at the annual meeting of the American Educational Research Association, New York.

Cheng, P. E., & Liou, M. (2003). Computerized adaptive testing using the nearest-neighbors criterion. *Applied Psychological Measurement, 27,* 204–216.

Chiu, C. W. T., & Pearson, P. D. (1999, June). *Synthesizing the effects of test accommodations for special education and limited English proficient students.* Paper presented at the National Conference on Large Scale Assessment, Snowbird, UT. (ERIC Document Reproduction Service No. ED 433 362)

Cizek, G. J. (1999). *Cheating on tests: How to do it, detect it, and prevent it.* Mahwah, NJ: Erlbaum.

Clauser, B. E., Margolis, M. J., & Case, S. M. (2006). Testing for Licensure and Certification in the Professions. In R. L. Brennan (Ed.), *Educational Measurement* (pp. 703–734). Connecticut: Praeger Publishers.

Clemans, W. V. (1968). Test administration. In R. L. Thorndike (Ed.), *Educational measurement* (2nd ed., pp. 188–201). Washington, DC: American Council on Education.

Cody, R. P. (1985). Statistical analysis of examinations to detect cheating. *Journal of Medical Education, 60,* 136–137.

Cohen, A. S., Gregg, N., & Deng, M. (2005). The role of extended time and item content on a high-stakes mathematics test. *Learning Disabilities: Research and Practice, 20*(4), 225–233.

Cohen, A. S., Wollack, J. A., & Mroch, A. A. (2002, April). *A mixture Rasch model analysis of test speededness.* Paper presented at the annual meeting of the American Educational Research Association, New Orleans, LA.

Colton, G. (1998). Exam security and high-tech cheating. *The Bar Examiner, 67,* 13–35.

Crooks, T. J., Kane, M. T., & Cohen, A. S. (1996). Threats to the valid use of assessments. *Assessment in Education, 3,* 265–285.

Crozier, J. (2002, Summer). A unique experiment. *China in Focus, 12.* Retrieved April 19, 2005 from http://sacu.org/cifc12.html

Davey, T., & Fan, M. (2000, April). *Specific information item selection for adaptive testing.* Paper presented at the annual meeting of the National Council on Measurement in Education, New Orleans, LA.

Davey, T., & Parshall, C. G. (1995, April). *New algorithms for item selection and exposure control with computerized adaptive testing.* Paper presented at the annual meeting of the American Educational Research Association, San Francisco.

Davis, L. L. (2003, April). *Strategies for controlling item exposure in computerized adaptive testing with the generalized partial credit model.* Paper presented at the annual meeting of the National Council on Measurement in Education, Chicago.

Davis, S. F., Grover, C. A., Becker, A. H., & McGregor, L. N. (1992). Academic dishonesty: Prevalence, determinants, techniques, and punishments. *Teaching of Psychology, 19,* 16–20.

Divgi, D. R., & Stollof, P. H. (1986). *Effects of the medium of administration on ASVAB item response curves* (Rep. No. CNA 86–24). Alexandria, VA: Center for Naval Analysis.

Doyle, K. O., Jr. (1974). Theory and practice of ability testing in ancient Greece. *Journal of the History of the Behavioral Sciences, 10,* 202–214.

Drasgow, F., Levine, M. V., & Williams, E. A. (1985). Appropriateness measurement with polychotomous item response models and standardized indices. *British Journal of Mathematical and Statistical Psychology, 38,* 67–86.

Drasgow, F., Luecht, R. M., & Bennett R. E. (this volume). Technology and testing. In R. L. Brennan (Ed.), *Educational measurement* (4th ed., pp. 471–515). Westport, CT: American Council on Education/Praeger.

DuBois, P. H. (1970). *A history of psychological testing.* Boston: Allyn and Bacon.

Dunn, O. J. (1961). Multiple comparisons among means. *Journal of the American Statistical Association, 56,* 52–64.

Echternacht, G. (1977). Grade equivalent scores. *NCME Measurement in Education, 8,* 1–4.

Elliot, S. (2003). Intellimetric™: From here to validity. In M. D. Shermis & J. C. Burstein (Eds.), *Automated essay scoring: A cross-disciplinary perspective* (pp. 71–86). Mawhah, NJ: Lawrence Erlbaum.

Federation of State Medical Boards of the United States, Inc., & National Board of Medical Examiners. (2005). *United States medical licensing examination: Bulletin of information.* Philadelphia: National Board of Medical Examiners.

Frary, R. B. (1993). Statistical detection of multiple-choice answer copying: Review and commentary. *Applied Measurement in Education, 6,* 153–165.

Frary, R. B., Tideman, T. N., & Watts, T. M. (1977). Indices of cheating on multiple-choice tests. *Journal of Educational Statistics, 2,* 235–256.

Gregg, N., Morgan, D., Hartwig, J., & Coleman, C. (in press). Accommodations and the adult population with learning disorders: State of the art research. In L. E. Wolf, H. Scribner, & J. Wasserstein (Eds.), *Adult learning disorders: Contemporary issues, Neuropsychology Handbook Series.* New York: Psychology Press.

Gundersen, J. A. (2002). Testing, testing: Exam security: A constant among the variables in Bar admissions. *The Bar Examiner, 71*(1), 34–37.

Haines, V. J., Diekhoff, G. M., LaBeff, E. E., & Clark, R. E. (1986). College cheating: Immaturity, lack of commitment, and the neutralizing attitude. *Research in Higher Education, 25,* 342–354.

Hanson, B. A., Harris, D. J., & Brennan, R. L. (1987). *A comparison of several statistical methods for examining allegations of copying* (Research Rep. Series No. 87-15). Iowa City, IA: American College Testing.

Harden, R. M. (1988). What is an OSCE? *Medical Teacher, 10,* 19–22.

Harden, R. M., & Gleeson, F. A. (1979). Assessment of clinical competence using an objective structured clinical examination (OSCE). *Medical Education, 12,* 41–54.

Hetter, R. D., & Sympson, J. B. (1997). Item exposure control in CAT-ASVAB. In W. A. Sands, B. K. Waters, & J. R. McBride (Eds.), *Computerized adaptive testing: From inquiry to operation* (pp. 141–144). Washington, DC: American Psychological Association.

Holland, P. W. (1996). *Assessing unusual agreement between the incorrect answers of two examinees using the K-index: Statistical theory and empirical support* (ETS Technical Report No. 96-4). Princeton, NJ: Educational Testing Service.

Hopkins, K. D., Stanley, J. C., & Hopkins, B. R. (1990). *Educational and psychological measurement and evaluation* (7th ed.). Englewood Cliffs, NJ: Prentice Hall.

Hunter, D. (1947). *Papermaking: The history and technique of an ancient craft.* New York: Alfred A Knopf. Reprinted 1974.

Iwamoto, C. K., Nungester, R. J., & Luecht, R. M. (1996, April). *Power of similarity methods and person-fit analysis to detect copying behavior.* Paper presented at the annual meeting of the American Educational Research Association, New York.

Jacob, B. A., & Levitt, S. D. (2003a). Catching cheating teachers: The results of an unusual experiment in implementing theory. In W. G. Gale & J. R. Pack (Eds.), *Brookings-Wharton papers on urban affairs* (pp.185–220). Washington, DC: Brookings Institutional Press.

Jacob, B. A., & Levitt, S. D. (2003b). Rotten apples: An investigation of the prevalence and predictors of teacher cheating. *Quarterly Journal of Economics, 118*(3), 843–877.

Johnstone, C. J. (2003). *Improving validity of large-scale tests: Universal design and student performance* (NCEO Technical Report 37). Minneapolis, MN: University of Minnesota, National Center on Educational Outcomes

Kingsbury, G. G., & Zara, A. R. (1989). Procedures for selecting items for computerized adaptive tests. *Applied Measurement in Education, 2,* 359–375.

Kolen, M. J. (this volume). Scaling and norming. In R. L. Brennan (Ed.), *Educational measurement* (4th ed., pp. 155–186). Westport, CT: American Council on Education/Praeger.

Kolen, M., & Brennan, R. L. (2004). *Test equating, scaling, and linking: Methods and practices.* New York: Springer.

Landauer, T. K., & Dumais, S. T. (1997). A solution to Plato's problem: The Latent Semantic Analysis theory of the acquisition, induction, and representation of knowledge. *Psychological Review, 104,* 211–240.

Landauer, T. K., Laham, D., & Foltz, P. W. (1998). An introduction to latent semantic analysis. *Discourse Processes, 25,* 259–284.

Landauer, T. K., Laham, D., & Foltz, P. W. (2003). Automated scoring and annotation of essays with the Intelligent Essay Assessor®. In M. D. Shermis & J. C. Burstein (Eds.), *Automated essay scoring: A cross-disciplinary perspective* (pp. 87–112). Mahwah, NJ: Lawrence Erlbaum.

Lane, S., & Stone, C. A. (this volume). Performance assessment. R. L. Brennan (Ed.), *Educational measurement* (4th ed., pp. 387–431). Westport, CT: American Council on Education/Praeger.

Leung, C.-K., Chang, H.-H., & Hau, K.-T. (2002). Item selection in computerized adaptive testing: Improving the a-stratified design with the Sympson-Hetter algorithm. *Applied Psychological Measurement, 26,* 376–392.

Levine, M. V., & Rubin, D. B. (1979). Measuring the appropriatness of multiple-choice test scores. *Journal of Educational Statistics, 4,* 269–290.

Lord, F. N., & Novick, M. R. (1968). *Statistical theories of mental test scores.* Boston: Addison-Wesley.

McCallin, R. C. (in press). Test administration. In S. M. Downing & T. M. Haladyna (Eds.), *Handbook of test development.* Mahwah, NJ: Erlbaum.

Mazzeo, J., Lazer, S., & Zieky, M. J. (2006). Monitoring Educational Progress with Group-Score Assessments. In R. L. Brennan (Ed.), *Educational Measurement* (pp. 683–702). Connecticut: Praeger Publishers.

McBride, J. R., & Martin, J. T. (1983). Reliability and validity of adaptive ability tests in a military setting. In D. J. Weiss (Ed.), *New horizons in testing: Latent trait test theory and computerized adaptive testing* (pp. 223–236). New York: Academic Press.

McLeod, L. D., & Lewis, C. (1999). Detecting item memorization in the CAT environment. *Applied Psychological Measurement, 23,* 147–160.

McLeod, L., Lewis, C., & Thissen, D. (2003). A Bayesian method for the detection of item preknowledge in computerized adaptive testing. *Applied Psychological Measurement, 27,* 121–137.

Mehrens, W. A. (1991, April). *Defensible/Indefensible instructional preparation for high stakes achievement tests: An exploratory trialogue.* Paper presented at the annual meeting of the American Educational Research Association, Chicago.

Mehrens, W. A., & Kaminski, J. (1989). Methods for improving standardized test scores: Fruitful, fruitless or fraudulent? *Educational Measurement: Issues and Practice, 8*(1), 14–22.

Mehrens, W. A., Popham, W. J., & Ryan, J. M. (1998). How to prepare students for performance assessments. *Educational Measurement: Issues and Practice, 17*(1), 18–22.

Meijer, R. R. (2002). Outlier detection in high-stakes certification testing. *Journal of Educational Measurement, 39,* 219–233.

Meijer, R. R., & Sijtsma, K. (1995). Detection of aberrant item score patterns: A review and new developments. *Applied Measurement in Education, 8,* 261–272.

Meijer, R. R., & Sijtsma, K. (2001). Methodology review: Evaluating person fit. *Applied Psychological Measurement, 14,* 283–298.

Mills, C. N., & Stocking, M. L. (1996). Practical issues in large-scale computerized adaptive testing. *Applied Measurement in Education, 9*(4), 287–304.

Mislevy, R. J., & Verhelst, N. (1990). Modeling item responses when different subjects employ different solution strategies. *Psychometrika, 55,* 195–215.

Moore, W. P. (1994). Appropriate test preparation: Can we reach a consensus? *Educational Assessment, 2*(1), 51–68.

No Child Left Behind Act of 2001, Pub. L. No. 107-111 (2002). http://www.ed.gov/policy/elsec/leg/esea02/index.html

Olson, J. F., Bond, L., & Andrews, C. (1999). Data from the annual survey: State student assessment programs: Data on 1997–1998 statewide student assessment programs. Washington, DC: Council of Chief State School Officers.

Page, E. B. (1966). Grading essays by computer: Progress report. Notes from the 1966 Invitational Conference on Testing Problems, 87–100.

Page, E. B. (1994). Computer grading of student prose, using modern concepts and software. *Journal of Experimental Education, 62*(2), 127–142.

Parshall, C. G., Davey, T., & Nering, M. L. (1998, April). *Test development exposure control for adaptive testing.* Paper presented at the annual meeting of the National Council on Measurement in Education, San Diego, CA.

Parshall, C., Harmes, J. C., & Kromrey, J. D. (2000). Item exposure control in computer-adaptive testing: The use of freezing to augment stratification. *Florida Journal of Educational Research, 40,* 28–52.

Popham, W. J. (1991). Appropriateness of teachers' test-preparation practices. *Educational Measurement: Issues and Practice, 10*(4), 12–15.

Revuelta, J., & Ponsoda, V. (1998). A comparison of item exposure control methods in computerized adaptive testing. *Journal of Educational Measurement, 35,* 311–327.

Rost, J. (1990). Rasch models in latent classes: An integration of two approaches to item analysis. *Applied Psychological Measurement, 14,* 271–282.

Rudner, L., & Gagne, P. (2001). An overview of three approaches to scoring written essays by computer. *Practical Assessment, Research & Evaluation, 7*(26). Retrieved July 10, 2006 from http://pareonline.net/getvn.asp?v=7&n=26

Schmidt, A. E., & Shaw, E. J. (2005, April). *Test preparation: Where does it cross the line?* Paper presented at the annual meeting of the American Educational Research Association, Montreal, Canada.

Segall, D. O. (2002). An item response model for characterizing test compromise. *Journal of Educational and Behavioral Statistics, 27,* 163–179.

Segall, D. O. (2004). A sharing item response theory model for computer adaptive testing. *Journal of Educational and Behavioral Statistics, 29,* 439–460.

Shealy, R., & Stout, W. F. (1993). A model-based standardization approach that separates true bias/DIF from group differences and detects test bias/DIF as well as item bias/DIF. *Psychometrika, 58,* 159–194.

Shepard, L. A. (this volume). Classroom assessment. In R. L. Brennan (Ed.), *Educational measurement* (4th ed., pp. 623–646). Westport, CT: American Council on Education/Praeger.

Shepard, L., Taylor, G., & Betebenner, G. (1998). *Inclusion of limited-English-proficient students in Rhode Island's grade 4 mathematics performance assessment.* Los Angeles: University of California, Center for the Study of Evaluation/National Center on Research on Evaluation, Standards, and Student Testing.

Sireci, S. G., Li, S., & Scarpati, S. (2004). *The effects of test accommodations on test performance: A review of the literature* (Research Report No. 485). Amherst: University of Massachusetts, School of Education, Center for Educational Assessment.

Smydo, J. (2003, August 3). Health fields fight cheating on tests. *Pittsburgh Post-Gazette.* Retrieved January 1, 2004 from http://www.optometry.org

Sotaridona, L. S., & Meijer, R. R. (2002). Statistical properties of the K-index for detecting answer copying. *Journal of Educational Measurement, 39,* 115–132.

Sotaridona, L. S., & Meijer, R. R. (2003). Two new statistics to detect answer copying. *Journal of Educational Measurement, 40,* 53–69.

Steele, C. M., & Aronson, J. (1995). Stereotype threat and intellectual test performance of African-Americans. *Journal of Personality and Social Psychology, 69,* 797–811.

Stern, E. B., & Havlicek, L. (1986). Academic misconduct: Results of faculty and undergraduate student surveys. *Journal of Allied Health, 15,* 133–136.

Stevens, G. E., & Stevens, F. W. (1987). Ethical inclinations of tomorrow's managers revisited: How and why students cheat. *Journal of Education for Business, 63,* 24–29.

Stocking, M. L. (1994). *Three practical issues for modern adaptive testing item pools* (Research Rep. 94-5). Princeton, NJ: Educational Testing Service.

Stocking, M. L., & Lewis, C. (1995). *A new method of controlling item exposure in computerized adaptive testing* (Research Rep. 95-25). Princeton, NJ: Educational Testing Service.

Stocking, M. L., & Lewis, C. (1998). Controlling item exposure conditional on ability in computerized adaptive testing. *Journal of Educational and Behavioral Statistics, 23,* 57–75.

Straetmans, G. J. J. M., & Eggens, T. J. H. M. (1998). Comparison of test administration procedures for placement decisions in a mathematics course. *Educational Research and Evaluation, 4*(3), 259–275.

Sympson, J. B., & Hetter, R. D. (1985, October). *Controlling item-exposure rates in computerized adaptive testing.* Paper presented at the 17th annual meeting of the Military Testing Association, San Diego, CA.

Tatsuoka, K. K. (1984). Caution indices based on item response theory. *Psychometrika, 49,* 95–110.

Taylor, I., & Taylor, M. M. (1995). *Writing and literacy in Chinese, Korean, and Japanese.* Amsterdam: John Benjamins Publishing.

Times News Network. (2003, November 25). Over 150 doctors involved in exam fiasco. *The Times of India.* Retrieved January 13, 2004 from http://timesofindia.indiatimes.com/articleshow/301967.cms

Traxler, A. E. (1950). Administering and scoring the objective test. In E. F. Lindquist (Ed.), *Educational measurement* (pp. 329–416). Washington, DC: American Council on Education.

van Krimpen-Stoop, E. M. L. A., & Meijer, R. R. (2000). Detecting person-misfit in adaptive testing using statistical process control techniques. In W. J. van der Linden & C. A. W. Glas (Eds.), *Computerized adaptive testing: Theory and practice* (pp. 201–219). Boston: Kluwer Academic Publishers.

van Krimpen-Stoop, E. M. L. A., & Meijer, R. R. (2001). CUSUM-based person-fit statistics for adaptive testing. *Journal of Educational and Behavioral Statistics, 26,* 199–218.

Wainer, H., Hambleton, R. K., & Meara, K. (1999). Alternative displays for communicating NAEP results: A redesign and validity study. *Journal of Educational Measurement, 36,* 301–335.

Wang, T., & Kolen, M. J. (2001). Evaluating comparability in computerized adaptive testing: Issues, criteria, and an example. *Journal of Educational Measurement, 38,* 19–49.

Whittington, D., & Hunt, H. (1999). Approaches to the computerized assessment of free text responses. Loughborough University, *Proceedings of the Third Annual Computer Assisted*

Assessment Conference. (207–219). (Also available at http://cvu.strath.ac.uk/dave/publications/cas99.html)

Willingham, W. W., Ragosta, M., Bennett, R. E., Braun, H., Rock, D. A., & Powers, D. E. (1988). *Testing handicapped people.* Boston: Allyn and Bacon.

Wollack, J. A. (1997). A nominal response model approach to detect answer copying. *Applied Psychological Measurement, 21,* 307–320.

Wollack, J. A. (2003). Comparison of answer copying indices with real data. *Journal of Educational Measurement, 40,* 189–205.

Wollack, J. A. (in press). Simultaneous use of multiple answer copying indices to improve detection rates. *Applied Measurement in Education.*

Wollack, J. A. (2004). Detecting answer copying on high-stakes tests. *The Bar Examiner, 73,* 35–45.

Wollack, J. A., & Cohen, A. S. (1998). Detection of answer copying with unknown item and trait parameters. *Applied Psychological Measurement, 22,* 144–152.

Wollack, J. A., Cohen, A. S., & Serlin, R. C. (2001). Defining error rates and power for detection of answer copying. *Applied Psychological Measurement, 25,* 385–404.

Wollack, J. A., Cohen, A. S., & Wells, C. S. (2003). The effects of test speededness on score scale stability. *Journal of Educational Measurement, 40,* 307–330.

Wollack, J. A., Wells, C. S., & Cohen, A. S. (2003, April). *A comparison of item- and testlet-level scoring on scale stability in the presence of test speededness.* Paper presented at the annual meeting of the American Educational Research Association, Chicago.

Yamamoto, K. (1989). *A hybrid model of IRT and latent class models* (ETS Research Report RR-89-41), Educational Testing Services, Princeton, NJ.

Yamamoto, K., & Everson, H. (1997). Modeling the effects of test length and test time on parameter estimation using the Hybrid model. In J. Rost & R. Langeheine (Eds), *Applications of latent trait and latent class models in the social sciences* (pp. 89–98). Münster: Waxmann, NY.

Yen, W. M. & Fitzpatrick, A. R. (this volume). Item response theory. In R. L. Brennan (Ed.), *Educational measurement* (4th ed., pp. 111–153). Westport, CT: American Council on Education/Praeger.

Zuriff, G. E. (2000). Extra examination time for students with learning disabilities: An examination of the maximum potential thesis. *Applied Measurement in Education, 13*(1), 99–117.

Zwick, R. (this volume). Higher education admissions testing. In R. L. Brennan (Ed.), *Educational measurement* (4th ed., pp. 647–679). Westport, CT: American Council on Education/Praeger.

11

Performance Assessment

Suzanne Lane
Clement A. Stone
University of Pittsburgh

The editions of *Educational Measurement* over the years have provided an indication of the role of performance assessments in educational testing. A chapter on essay examinations by Stalnaker (1951) was in the first edition of *Educational Measurement*. The second edition included a chapter on essay examinations by Coffman (1971) as well as a chapter on performance and product evaluations by Fitzpatrick and Morrison (1971). In the third edition of *Educational Measurement* (Linn, 1989) there were no chapters devoted entirely to essays or performance assessments. The current edition's devotion to an entire chapter on performance assessment suggests the importance of the role of performance assessments in education today.

The purpose of this chapter is to provide an overview on the design, use, and validity of performance assessments for large-scale educational testing. The chapter is divided into four sections. The chapter begins with a description, definition, and rationale for the use of performance assessments. The second section discusses approaches for the design and scoring of performance assessments. Issues and research related to the validity of performance assessments are discussed in the third section. It should be noted, however, that validity issues pertaining to the initial design of performance assessments are also addressed in the second section. The application of generalizability theory and item response theory to performance assessments is the focus of the fourth section. Although portfolios are not directly addressed in this chapter, the reader is referred to the Advanced Placement (AP) Studio Art portfolio assessment, which provides an example of one sustaining large-scale portfolio assessment (Myford & Mislevy, 1995).

As indicated by Fitzpatrick and Morrison (1971), the principles for the design of performance assessments are similar to those for any other form of an assessment. Thus, the other chapters in this volume are applicable to the design of performance assessments. It is important to note that although the focus of this chapter is on performance assessments, the importance of other item formats is acknowledged, including selected-response item formats. Performance assessments, however, can assess important learning outcomes that cannot be assessed by selected-response item formats.

1. INTRODUCTION TO PERFORMANCE ASSESSMENTS

1.1. Description of Performance Assessments

In the early 1980s, performance assessments were considered to be a valuable tool for educational reform (Linn, 1993; Resnick & Resnick, 1992). A prevailing assumption underlying performance assessments was that they serve as motivators in improving student achievement and learning, and that they encourage instructional strategies and techniques that foster reasoning, problem solving, and communication (Frederiksen & Collins, 1989; National Council on Education Standards and Testing, 1992). The way in which they were described was appealing, in that, performance assessments require students to perform an activity (e.g., build a model) or construct an original response (e.g., explain one's solution to a mathematics problem); assess higher-level thinking and problem solving skills; require students to apply their problem solving in relatively novel real-world situations; afford multiple solutions or strategies; access prior knowledge; and require extended periods of time, ranging from several minutes to several days or more (Aschbacher, 1991; Baron, 1991; Herman, Aschbacher, & Winters, 1992; Madaus & O'Dwyer, 1999; Stiggins, 1987). Further, performance assessments may include opportunities for self reflection and collaborative work as well as student choice such as choosing a particular topic for a writing assignment (Baker, O'Neil, & Linn, 1993; Baron, 1991). The evaluation of student performance involves professional judgment that may be amenable to expert-system computer algorithms (Bennett, 1993).

Performance assessments allow for the evaluation of both the process used in solving a task and the product. As Fitzpatrick and Morrison (1971) indicated, sometimes the performance and product are indistinguishable as in the case of dancing and public speaking. The student creates or produces something over a sufficient period of time to allow for the assessment of the process and/or the product (Messick, 1994). Performance assessments may require students to carry out a complex, extended process such as play a musical instrument, conduct a laboratory experiment, or participate in a debate; or produce a meaningful product such as a poem or a report based on conducting an experiment.

This renewed interest in performance assessments in the 1980s was in part due to the call for more direct assessments of students' high level thinking and reasoning skills (Frederiksen, 1984). Performance assessments in education were conceptualized as embodying the features described above. However, the extent to which a performance assessment should require high-level reasoning and problem solving skills is dependent on the performance of interest. For example, if the performance of interest is whether a young child can use a ruler, then directly observing the child measuring an object with a ruler could be considered a performance assessment. The definition of performance assessment adopted for this chapter recognizes that not all performance assessments require complex thinking skills; it is dependent on the construct to be measured. The definition of performance assessment adopted for this chapter is described in the next section.

1.2. Definition of Performance Assessments

The *Standards for Educational and Psychological Measurement* (American Educational Research Association, American Psychological Association, and National Council on Measurement in Education [AERA, APA, & NCME], 1999) stated that performance assessments "attempt to emulate the context or conditions in which the intended knowledge or skills are actually applied" (p. 137). Likewise, Kane, Crooks, and Cohen (1999) defined performance assessment as involving "a sample of performance from some domain of performances, with the resulting scores interpreted in terms of typical, or expected, performance in this domain" (p. 7). They indicated that the "defining characteristic of a performance assessment is the close similarity between the type of performance that is actually observed and the type of performance that is of interest" (Kane et al., 1999, p. 7). This is consistent with the definition of performance assessments provided by Fitzpatrick and Morrison (1971) in the second edition of *Educational Measurement*: "A performance test (performance or product evaluation) has been defined here as a test in which a criterion situation, such as a job, is simulated to a relatively high degree" (p. 268) and "the potential value of the performance test lies in its closer approach to reality—its greater relevance in determining the degree to which the examinee can actually perform the tasks of the criterion job or other situation" (p. 268). It is important to simulate the most critical features of the criterion so as to be able to detect relevant differences and changes in the performance variables of interest (Fitzpatrick & Morrison, 1971).

Kane and his colleagues (1999) linked the definition of a performance assessment with its intended use and score interpretations. In determining whether a test is a performance assessment, one needs to consider how the test is being used and the intended score interpretations (Kane et al., 1999). As an illustration, they suggest that an essay test on the theory of painting in an art theory course would probably be considered a performance assessment; whereas in a studio painting class it would not be considered a performance assessment. This proposed alignment between what constitutes a performance assessment and the intended score interpretations is consistent with the writings of Messick (1989, 1994).

Research has demonstrated that the acquisition of knowledge and skills, and consequently, expertise is domain specific (e.g., Larkin, McDermott, Simon, & Simon, 1980), further suggesting that the nature of performance assessments are linked closely to the construct domain they are intended to assess. As an example, the writing process is considered by writing experts to be an important aspect of writing. Therefore, a performance assessment that best emulates writing would incorporate various facets of the writing process by including a prewriting component, a revision component that may include a critique by a peer, and a proofreading and editing component of the revised draft; whereas, another writing assessment may require only the initial draft. The inclusion of various aspects of the writing process illustrates how performance assessments vary in terms of the extent to which they emulate the conditions of the criterion performance. In deciding on the extent to which performance assessments on large-scale assessments emulate the performance of interest, other measurement (e.g., generalizability and reliability) and practical (e.g., time and cost) issues need to be considered.

Performance assessments in subject areas vary in their format depending on the performance of interest. As an example, scientific inquiry is at the core of science content standards and includes but is not limited to developing questions that can be answered by scientific investigation; designing and conducting scientific investigations; using tools and procedures to collect, analyze, and interpret data; and developing explanations, predictions, and models using evidence (National Research Council, 1996). To fully capture the essence of scientific inquiry requires the use of hands-on performance tasks that may be extended over a number of days. The assessment of particular skills necessary for scientific inquiry however, may be accomplished by smaller hands-on performance tasks and constructed-response items.

As another example, mathematics content standards pertaining to problem solving, reasoning and proof, and communication indicate that students should implement and adapt a variety of strategies to solve problems; develop and evaluate mathematical proofs and arguments; organize, summarize, and communicate their mathematical thinking; and develop and use representations to organize, display, and communicate mathematical phenomena (National Council of Teachers of Mathematics, 2000). Performance tasks that would capture the types of thinking and reasoning reflected in these standards would be extended constructed-response items and to some extent hands-on performance tasks that require the manipulation of tools and materials.

1.3. Rationale for Performance Assessments

As indicated above, one reason for the renewed interest in performance assessments in the 1980s was because of the close similarity between the performance that is observed and the performance of interest. In other words, performance assessments provide a more direct measure of student achievement than traditional multiple-choice tests (Frederiksen, 1984). The skills of interest are directly measured insofar as they are apparent in the performances or products that are elicited (Frederiksen & Collins, 1989). However, regardless of how direct the assessment appears, the skills and knowledge are not measured directly, but are inferred from performances and products (Messick, 1994).

Another reason for the renewed interest in performance assessments is that they have high fidelity (Fitzpatrick & Morrison, 1971). Others refer to this feature of performance assessments as their transparency (Frederiksen & Collins, 1989) or meaningfulness (Linn, Baker, & Dunbar, 1991). Often performance tasks are simulations or representations of criterion activities that are "valued in their own right" (Linn, 1993, p. 9). Performance tasks should be meaningful to students if they are to be a worthwhile educational experience serving to motivate and direct learning. Nevertheless, as Haertel (1999) cautioned, the selection of performance tasks because of their inherent value may jeopardize the generalizability of assessment results. Although the value of a particular task needs to be considered in the design of performance assessments, the overall design of the assessment should be guided by the purpose of the assessment and the construct being assessed.

Performance assessments are considered to be a valuable tool for educational reform by policy makers and advocates for curriculum reform (Haertel, 1999; Linn, 1993; Resnick & Resnick, 1992). They can help shape sound instructional practice (Baron, 1991) by providing an indicator to teachers of what is important to teach and to students of what is important to learn. As summarized by Haertel (1999), in the 1990s inclusion of performance assessments on large-scale assessments was thought of as:

> a vehicle to communicate and popularize new visions of school learning. These new forms of assessment would promote active engagement both in learning and in demonstrating what had been learned. They would serve as models for sound instructional activities. Expectations would rise as teachers saw concrete evidence that students could solve more complex problems than they had thought possible. (p. 664)

Evidence, however, is needed to determine whether these potential benefits have been realized, and such positive benefits should be considered in light of possible limitations of performance assessments. A discussion on the consequential evidence for performance assessments is provided in section 3.4 of this chapter. Performance assessments also serve as a powerful professional development tool when teachers are engaged in the design of performance tasks and in the scoring of student work (Baker et al., 1993).

Further, performance assessments can allow for a particular task to yield multiple scores in different subject areas, which is appealing for practical and pedagogical reasons. As summarized by Goldberg and Roswell (2001), some practical implications for tasks that yield multiple scores are reduced time and cost for item development, test administration, and scoring by raters. Furthermore, tasks that elicit scores in more than one subject area reflect curriculum and instruction that is integrated. Nevertheless, it is important to provide evidence that each score represents the construct it is intended to represent and does not include construct-irrelevant variance (Messick, 1989), and consideration needs to be given to the potential local dependency of scores (Yen, 1993). A discussion on local item dependency is provided in section 4.2 of this chapter.

1.4. Current Uses of Performance Assessments

Large-scale testing programs that are either entirely or partially performance-based involve the annual assessment of students for monitoring students' progress toward meeting national, state, and local standards; promoting educational reform; and holding schools and districts accountable for student learning (Baker et al., 1993; Dunbar, Koretz, & Hoover, 1991; Linn et al. 1991; Mehrens, 1992). Whether the uses involve scores for individual students or groups of students, high-stakes decisions typically accompany them. Further, many of these uses encompass the need to provide scores that are comparable over time, which requires standardization of the content, administration, and scoring of the assessment over time. Extended time periods, collaborative work, choice of task, and the use of ancillary materials, however, pose challenges to the standardization of the administration and scoring of performance assessments. Many state assessment programs incorporate performance assessments, in particular, direct writing assessments. Some states have used performance-based assessments in mathematics as well as writing (e.g., Kentucky, Vermont), while other states had assessment programs that were entirely performance-based (Maryland).

Performance assessments that are used for classroom purposes allow for a direct alignment between assessment and instructional activities. Classroom performance assessment tasks have the potential to simulate better the criterion performance as compared to large-scale assessments given the constraints associated with large-scale assessments. As an example, direct observations of student performances are more amenable to classroom performance assessments than large-scale performance assessments. Purposes of classroom performance assessments may include monitoring student achievement, diagnosing student difficulties, and evaluating the effectiveness of instruction. Regardless of use, the design of classroom performance assessments, including tasks and scoring rubrics, follows the same guidelines as the design of performance assessments for large-scale purposes. However, because of differences in the stakes associated with performance assessments used for classroom purposes, they do not need to meet the same level of standardization and reliability as do large-scale assessments that have high stakes associated with their use.

State assessment programs may adopt a model that includes locally developed classroom assessments (e.g., Nebraska state assessment). These assessments would require a higher level of technical scrutiny than those developed by teachers for classroom use only. Under the Nebraska model, school districts are required to prepare an assessment portfolio that documents the technical quality of their classroom assessments and these portfolios are rated to determine whether they meet the necessary assessment criteria (Nebraska Department of Education, 2002). The success of these types of assessment programs is dependent on the professional development activities provided to teachers to ensure quality assessments.

2. DESIGN AND SCORING OF PERFORMANCE ASSESSMENTS

The design of performance assessments for large-scale assessment programs, like other forms of assessments, is an iterative process that begins with the delineation of the conceptual framework that includes a description of the construct to be assessed, the purpose of the assessment, and the intended inferences to be draw from assessment results. The conceptual framework guides the development of the test specifications that reflect the content, cognitive processes, psychometric characteristics of the tasks, and pertinent information for the administration of the assessment. The tasks and scoring rubrics are then developed iteratively based on a well delineated conceptual framework and test specifications. These aspects of test design are discussed in the next two sections. Issues related to the design of scoring rubrics, the pilot of assessments, and the training procedures for raters are then discussed. It should be noted that validity issues pertaining to the initial design of performance assessments are interwoven in these sections. Many of the same guidelines for designing tests outlined in the chapter on test design by Schmeiser and Welch (this volume) apply to the design of performance assessments.

Throughout the assessment process careful consideration should be given to ensure coherency among the different aspects of the design, from the delineation of the construct to the design of the specific tasks and scoring rubrics. In a large-scale assessment program that assesses students on a variety of subject areas across grades, coordination is needed among the design of the assessments for a particular subject area across grades and among the design of assessments across subject areas within grades. Well-specified standards should reflect this level of coordination across grades and subject areas and the test design process should ensure that it too reflects this coordination. Further, assessments that are used to monitor group performance over time should remain relatively consistent with regard to content, administration procedures, and scoring so as to ensure the comparability of scores over time (Haertel & Linn, 1996).

2.1. Delineation of the Conceptual Framework

The delineation of the conceptual framework begins with a definition of the construct to be assessed. Construct theory as a guide to the development of an assessment provides a rational basis for specifying features of assessment tasks and scoring rubrics as well as for expecting certain empirical evidence, such as the degree of homogeneity of item responses and the relationship between scores with other measures (Messick, 1980; Mislevy, 1996; National Research Council, 2001). Two approaches can be adopted for the design of performance assessments: the construct-centered approach and task-centered approach (Messick, 1994). In the construct-centered approach the construct is defined by identifying the complex set of knowledge, skills or other features that need to be assessed and are valued in instruction. The performances or behaviors that should be elicited by the assessment are then identified. In this way, the construct guides the task development as well as the specification of the scoring criteria and rubrics. As Messick (1994) suggested, focusing on the construct informs one to the possibility of construct-irrelevant variance and construct underrepresentation, which may have an impact on the validity of score interpretations. Further, scores derived from a construct-centered approach may be more generalizable across variations in tasks, settings, and examinee groups than are scores derived from a task-centered approach because of the attention to reducing construct-irrelevant variance (Messick, 1994).

A task-centered approach to performance assessment may be more appropriate when assessing constructs such as listening and artistic creation because the knowledge and skills that contribute to such proficiencies are typically not specified in advance but are specified when designing the scoring rubrics and criteria (Messick, 1994; Wiggins, 1989). In the task-centered approach, however, it is important to ensure that the design of the scoring rubrics and criteria are not driven by features specific to the task, thus limiting the generalizability of the score interpretations (Messick, 1994).

In summary, Messick (1994) suggested that "where possible, a construct-driven rather than a task-driven approach to performance assessment should be adopted" (p. 22). The construct that is defined should not only describe the content to be assessed but also the nature and level of the cognitive thinking and skills that should be elicited, reflecting current theories of cognition and learning when available. In standards-based education, the standards should be derived from the construct. The standards are then used to guide the design of the test specifications, which usually requires further delineation of the standards.

The use of conceptual frameworks for the design of performance assessments results in assessments that are linked to more meaningful educational outcomes and provide more meaningful information that may guide curriculum and instructional reform. As an example, Lane and her colleagues (Lane, 1993; Lane et al., 1995) adopted a construct-centered approach in the design of a mathematics performance assessment consisting of constructed response items requiring students to show their solution processes and explain their reasoning. The conceptual framework they developed guided the development of the assessment tasks and scoring procedures. In defining the construct domain of mathematics, cognitive theories of student mathematics proficiency were considered and as a result four components were specified for the design of the assessment: cognitive processes, mathematical content, mode of representation, and task context. Each component was further delineated; as an example, a wide range of cognitive processes were specified to reflect the complex construct domain of mathematical problem solving, reasoning and communication, including discerning mathematical relations, using and discovering strategies and heuristics, formulating conjectures, and evaluating the reasonableness of answers, to name a few. The detailed specification of the construct domain helped ensure that the assessment results were generalizable to the domain specified.

Other conceptual frameworks also have considered explicitly the content that is specific to an academic discipline as well as cognitive skills and processes that students engage in when solving tasks across academic disciplines. In formulating their conceptual framework for the design of performance assessments, Marzano, Pickering, and McTighe (1993) embedded it within standards-based education. Standards-based education has been one of the driving forces behind the need for performance assessments, requiring a clear identification of what students should know and be able to do specific to the academic discipline. They defined two types of standards that are grounded in cognitive theories of learning: content standards and lifelong learning standards. The knowledge and skills that are specific to an academic discipline are referred to as content standards, and the knowledge and skills that are pertinent to all disciplines and are used outside of classroom are referred to as lifelong learning standards. Content standards are divided into two types of knowledge: declarative and procedural. Within both types of knowledge, a continuum exists that represents different levels of generality. For declarative knowledge, on one end of the continuum there are facts about persons, places, things, and events, while at the other end are concepts and generalizations. For procedural knowledge, on one end of the continuum are algorithms with steps that are executed in a particular order and at the other end are general strategies that apply to a number of problems. Marzano et al. (1993) identified five categories of Lifelong Learning Standards, which are summarized in Table 11.1. Examples of these standards are also provided.

2.2. Test Specifications and Task Design

Performance assessments typically consist of a small number of tasks that may hinder the generalizability of the scores to the broader domain. The use of test specifications will contribute to tasks being developed so as to systematically represent the intended construct. Carefully crafted and detailed specifications are more important for performance assessments than selected-response tests because there are fewer performance tasks and each is designed to measure something unique (Haertel & Linn, 1996). Further, to ensure comparability of scores over time requires that the content assessed remains relatively the same over time (Haertel & Linn, 1996) and clearly delineated test specifications will facilitate the stability of the content of performance assessments. Messick (1994) also called for test specifications that link the assessment of the products or performances to the purposes of the test and to construct theories of relevant skills and knowledge. As Messick (1994) suggested if a task-driven approach to designing performance assessments is adopted, scoring criteria and rubrics may reflect specific properties of the task, which may limit generalizability to the larger construct domain.

2.2.1. Test Specification

A test specification reflects the content and the nature and level of cognitive processes to be assessed. Information about the weighting of the content and cognitive processes as well as the intended psychometric properties of the tasks is included in the test specification. The test specification includes information regarding the administration of the assessment such as administration instructions, time allowed, group versus individual role, whether choice of task is required, and any ancillary or manipulative materials that are needed. The

TABLE 11.1 Lifelong Learning Standards

Complex Thinking	Uses a variety of complex reasoning strategies;
	Translates issues and situations into tasks that have clear purposes (Example processes embedded in these standards include Classifying, Induction, Deduction, Error Analysis, Constructing Support, Analyzing Perspectives, Decision Making, Experimental Inquiry, Problem Solving, Invention)
Information Processing	Uses a variety of information gathering techniques and resources; Interprets and synthesizes information; Evaluates the value of information; Recognizes the benefit of additional information.
Effective Communication	Expresses ideas clearly; Communicates with diverse audiences, in a variety of ways and for a variety of purposes.
Collaboration/Cooperation	Works toward the achievement of group goals; Uses interpersonal skills; Effectively performs a variety of roles.
Habits of Mind	Self-Regulation (e.g., aware of own thinking, makes effective plans, aware of and uses necessary resources, evaluates the effectiveness of own action); Critical Thinking (e.g., accurate and seeks accuracy, clear and seeks clarity, restrains impulsivity, takes a position when needed); Creative Thinking (e.g., engages in tasks even when solutions and answers are not immediately apparent, pushes the limits of own knowledge and abilities, generates, trusts, and maintains own standards of evaluation, generates new ways of viewing a situation outside the boundaries of standard conventions).

Source: Adapted from Marzano, R. J., Pickering, R. J., & McTighe, J. (1993). *Assessing student outcomes: Performance assessment using the dimensions of learning model.* Alexandria, VA: Association for Supervision and Curriculum Dimension.

specification also needs to delineate the nature of the scoring procedures, criteria, and rubrics to ensure the alignment among the defined construct, tasks, and scoring methods.

2.2.2. Task Development

The design of any task or item, including performance tasks, is driven by the test specifications, the purpose of the assessment, the population of examinees, and the intended score interpretations. In designing performance assessment tasks, the degree of structure for the problem posed and the response expected should be considered. Baxter and Glaser's (1998) characterization of performance assessments along two continuums with respect to their task demands provides a framework for designing tasks. The first continuum reflects the task demand for content knowledge from rich to lean, and the second continuum represents the task demand for process skills ranging from open to constrained. A task is content rich if it requires substantial content knowledge for successful performance, and it is process open if it allows for opportunities for students to develop their own strategies and procedures. Crossing these two continuums forms four quadrants. Tasks can be designed along these two continuums and targeted for one or more of these quadrants. This allows for "tasks to be designed with specific cognitive goals in mind, and task quality can be judged in terms of an alignment with the goals and purposes of the developers" (Baxter & Glaser, 1998, p. 40).

In the early 1990s researchers provided general guidelines for the design of performance assessment tasks that are still relevant today (e.g., Baron, 1991; Herman et al., 1992; Linn et al., 1991). Baron (1991) argued that performance tasks need to be content-rich; valued by experts in the domain assessed and the broader educational community; engage teachers and students in meaningful activities; reflect current advances in theories of cognition, learning, instruction, and motivation; communicate effectively the expectations of students allowing students to internalize the criteria for successful performance; and assess processes and skills that cannot be assessed adequately by multiple-choice items. Some of these areas go beyond the design of performance tasks and relate to activities that occur in instruction prior to the administration of the assessment. For example, in preparing students for the assessment, teachers need to engage students in instructional activities that promote deep understandings and are aligned to the assessment, and the scoring criteria can be shared with students throughout the instructional year allowing them the opportunity to self-monitor their own work. In discussing the properties of effective tasks, Baron (1991) suggested that performance tasks embody the following features: require students to formulate their own problems; allow for multiple strategies and/or solutions; allow students to access and use their prior knowledge; and allow for collaboration. Further, some tasks may require sustained work over several weeks or months, allow students a degree of choice and control over how to solve the problems and investigations, require students to design and conduct their own investigations, and require self-assessment and monitoring (Baron, 1991). Clearly some of the areas in this latter category would be difficult to implement in many large-scale assessments; however, the inclusion of portfolios or locally derived assessments in large-scale assessment programs may allow for some of these very open-ended activities. Lastly, the tasks need to be meaningful for students, sufficiently challenging, situated in real-world contexts, and allow for transferring their understanding and skills to other related tasks.

Marzano et al. (1993) provided a specific model for the development of performance assessments. As indicated earlier, they adopted a construct-centered approach to the design of performance assessments by first outlining content and lifelong learning standards. The first step in the model is to identify a content standard. The second step is to structure the task around a complex reasoning process. As an example, they provide a history standard that could be identified under the first step: "Understands that war forces sensitive issues to surface and causes people to confront inherent conflicts of values and beliefs" (p. 27). For this standard several processes could be considered such as error analysis in which the student could "Identify the errors in reasoning by those responsible for interring Japanese Americans during World War I" (p. 27) or decision making in which the student decides "What other alternatives could the United States have used to end the war?" (p. 27). In the second step, the content becomes more explicit as well as the cognitive demands of the task in that the type and level of cognitive activity required by the student is addressed. For this example, the authors point out that the decision-making alternative is more aligned to the content standard than the other alternatives. The third step involves crafting the first draft of the performance task based on the information identified in the first two steps. This process may lead to the following task:

> President Harry S Truman has requested that you serve on a White House task force. The goal is to decide how to force the unconditional surrender of Japan, yet provide for a secure postwar world. You are now a member of a committee of four and have reached the point at which you are trying to decide whether to drop the bomb. Identify the alternatives you are considering and the criteria you are using to make the decision. Explain the values that influence the selection of the criteria and the weights you placed on each. Also explain how your decision has helped you better understand this statement: War forces people to confront inherent conflicts of values. (p. 28)

The fourth step incorporates the information processing category. The direct assessment of standards in this category and the latter categories may not be possible for many large-scale assessments; nevertheless it would be appropriate for classroom assessments. The authors further describe two additional steps, one for incorporating standards from both the habit of mind category and the collaboration/cooperation category. The last step incorporates standards from the communication category. As an example, the task may ask the student to present his or her findings in at least two ways such as a written report, a letter to the President, or an article written for a news magazine. The authors caution not to use more than three or four of the categories of the standards for a particular task so as to keep it manageable.

This approach for designing performance tasks begins with the definition of the construct to be assessed by considering both the content standards and lifelong learning standards. It also allows for the careful specification of what each task will assess and provides a framework to ensure that the assessment represents the defined construct domain. Although they discuss this approach for the design of classroom assessments, it is amenable to the design of large-scale assessments.

Shavelson and Ruiz-Primo (1998) delineated a conceptual framework for science performance assessments, which provides a useful framework for designing performance tasks. In this scheme they cross types of tasks with types of scoring procedures (see also Ayala, Shavelson, Yue, & Schultz, 2002; Ruiz-Primo & Shavelson, 1996). The task types are comparative investigation, component identification, classification investigation, and observation investigation. The types of scoring schemes are analytic and holistic (see Section 2.3 for a discussion on scoring rubrics). The analytic scoring scheme consists of four dimensions: procedure-based, evidence-based, dimension-based and data accuracy-based. Table 11.2 provides examples of different types of assessments, tasks, response formats and their scoring systems for the four dimensions. Ayala, Shavelson, and Ayala (2001) added a fifth dimension to their classification system: Reasoning that consists of three categories: basic knowledge and reasoning, quantitative reasoning, and spatial mechanical reasoning.

Analyses of experts' thinking and reasoning when solving tasks have also been used in designing assessments. As an example, cognitive task analysis using experts' talk alouds (Ericsson & Smith, 1991) has been used to design performance assessments in the medical domain (Mislevy, Steinberg, Breyer, Almond, & Johnson, 1999). Features of the expert's thinking, knowledge, procedures, and problem posing are considered to be indicators of developing expertise in the domain (Glaser, Lesgold, & Lajoie, 1987) and are used systematically to develop assessment tasks. These features can then in turn be used to design the scoring rubrics by embedding them at each score level.

2.2.3. Collaborative Assessment

Some advocates of performance assessments suggest that one benefit of such assessments is that they allow for collaborative work (Resnick & Resnick, 1992). As an example, the Maryland School Performance Assessment Program (MSPAP) required students to work in groups for some of the tasks, but then each student individually submitted written responses to constructed-response items. It should be noted that the purpose of MSPAP was to provide school-level scores and not individual-level scores. In many assessment programs, however, there is a focus on individual student accountability as well as group-level accountability. As Webb (1993) indicated, "it is unclear whether and when the performance of students in collaborative group contexts accurately represents their individual competence" (p. 132).

To determine the extent to which a group score reflected individual competencies and to identify group features that affected individual scores, Webb (1993) compared performance in small-group and individual assessment settings. In this study, 7th grade students worked in small groups to solve arithmetic problems set in a context. Two weeks later they were asked to solve a set of parallel problems individually. Webb (1993) reported that approximately half the

TABLE 11.2 Examples of Different Types of Science Assessments

TYPE OF ASSESSMENT	TASK	RESPONSE FORMAT	SCORING SYSTEM
Comparative Investigation: Saturated Solutions	Given three powders students determine which one saturates water most readily and which least readily.	Asks students to write in detail how they conducted the investigation as well as their finding.	Procedure-based. Focuses on the scientific defensibility of the procedure used and the accuracy of the findings.
Component Identification: Mystery Powders	Given bags of powder mixtures students determine which powders are in each bag.	Asks students to report the tests they used to confirm and/or disconfirm the presence of a substance as well as their observations.	Evidence-based. Focuses on the evidence provided to confirm or disconfirm the presence of a particular powder and the accuracy of the findings.
Classification: Rocks and Charts	Given some rocks, students create a classification scheme by selecting the relevant properties that help classify these and other rocks.	Asks students to show the classification scheme they constructed and to explain why they selected the attributes used in their classification scheme.	Dimension-based. Focuses on the relevance of the attributes selected to construct the scheme and the accuracy of the use of the classification scheme.
Observation: Daytime Astronomy	Given an earth globe students model the path of the sun from sunrise to sunset and use direction, length, and angle of shadows to solve location problems.	Asks students to provide results of their observations and to explain how they collected the information.	Data accuracy-based. Focuses on the adequacy of the mode used to collect the data and the accuracy of the data collected.

Note: From "On the assessment of science achievement: Conceptual underpinnings for the design of performance assessments: Report of year 2 activities," by R. J. Shavelson & M. A. Ruiz-Primo, *CSE Technical Report*, p. 16. Copyright 1998 by the Center for the Study of Evaluation. Reproduced with permission.

students who correctly solved the problems in the collaborative setting were successful in the individual setting, indicating that their group scores were accurate. Slightly less than one-third of the students who had difficulty in solving the problems in the group setting obtained assistance from the group, and half of these students who obtained assistance from the group showed evidence of trying to understand the problem in the group setting and later performed well in the individual assessment setting. The other half of the students did not attempt to gain further insight into the problem in the group setting and performed relatively poorly in the individual setting. Thus, for those students who tried to understand the problem, the collaborative work facilitated the individual work, but their scores for the collaborative setting were most likely inflated. On the other hand, for those students who just copied work in the collaborative setting without attempting to understand the problem also had inflated scores based on the collaborative setting, but subsequently performed poorly in the individual setting (Webb, 1993).

Saner, McCaffrey, Stecher, Klein, and Bell (1994) examined whether an individual score derived after working collaboratively is an independent assessment of a student's achievement and whether working in pairs has an impact on a student's score on subsequent tasks. They used responses to hands-on science tasks developed for grades 5 and 8. Individual scores were obtained for three parts of the assessment. In the first part, students worked individually and then responded. In the second part, students worked in pairs and provided individual written responses, and in the last part, students responded individually to a task. The results indicated that the scores students obtained as they worked in pairs on one part of the assessment correlated more with each other than with the scores two students obtained as they worked independently on the two other parts, but the correlations were slightly higher on these two parts indicating a slight carry-over effect from the collaboration.

2.2.4. Using Computers in Task Design and Administration

Computers are used in a variety of ways in the design and administration of performance assessments. Using computers for simulating tasks, such as computer simulated hands-on science investigations, allows for a more realistic context. As an example, in a computer simulated sow bug science investigation, students investigate how sow bugs respond under different levels of simulated light and moisture (Shavelson, Baxter, & Pine, 1991). Another development is multimedia writing assessments that use CD-ROM technology to embed audio and video features into writing assessment tasks (Breland, Bridgeman, & Fowles, 1999). One such example is the Communication Skills Module from the Core Skills Series in which students perform reading, writing, and listening tasks in a computer simulated work environment (Breland et al., 1999). The assessment requires students to listen to voice mail messages, attend virtual meetings, select documents from computer files, write e-mail messages, and draft position papers on the computer.

Computers provide a more efficient system for not only the administration of the assessment but also for reporting assessment results to the examinee. For example, large-scale writing assessments are administered on the computer (e.g., GMAT, PRAXIS, TOEFL, and GRE), allowing examinees to take the tests at their convenience and providing the opportunity for examinees to preview the pool of essay topics prior to taking the exam (Breland et al., 1999). Some of the assessment programs require examinees to respond using a word processor (e.g., GMAT) while others allow examinees to choose whether to handwrite their responses or use a word processor (e.g., PRAXIS). For these programs, when the assessment is over, the response is sent electronically to a reader who evaluates it on the computer. Drasgow, Luecht, and Bennett (this volume) discuss many innovative developments in using technology for designing and administering assessments.

2.3. Design of Scoring Rubrics

Similar to the design of performance tasks, the design of scoring rubrics is an iterative process and involves coordination across grades as well as across subject areas to ensure a cohesive approach to educating and assessing students. Regardless of whether a construct- or task-centered approach to performance assessment is adopted, Messick (1994) suggested that scoring rubrics should not be "specific to the task nor generic to the construct but are in some middle ground reflective of the classes of tasks that the construct empirically generalizes or transfers to" (p. 17).

The design of scoring rubrics requires the specification of the criteria for judging the quality of performances and the choice of a scoring procedure (e.g., analytic or holistic). Clauser (2000) identified two additional aspects in the design of scoring rubrics: ways for developing criteria and procedures used to apply the criteria. The ways for developing criteria include the process used for developing the criteria and who should be involved in developing the criteria. For large-scale assessments in K–12 education, typically, the scoring criteria are developed by a group of experts as defined by their knowledge of the content domain and experience as educators. These experts have typically been involved in the design of the performance tasks and have knowledge of how students of differing levels of proficiency would perform on the task. Clauser (2000) pointed out that there are alternative approaches to specifying the criteria such as asking experts to think out loud or analyzing expert responses to a task. Two ways in which the scoring criteria can be applied rely on the use of expert raters and computer-automated scoring procedures (Clauser, 2000). This section discusses the specification of the criteria, specification of the scoring procedures, research on scoring procedures, and computer-automated scoring procedures. The review and pilot of assessments, and training procedures for raters are discussed in sections 2.4 and 2.5, respectively.

2.3.1. Specification of the Criteria

The criteria specified at each score level are linked to the construct being assessed, and depend on a number of factors including whether it is an assessment of a product or process, the demands of the tasks in the assessment, the examinee population, and the purpose of the assessment and its intended score interpretations. The number of score levels used depends on the extent to which the criteria across the score levels can distinguish among various levels of performance. The performances reflected at each score level should differ distinctly from those at other score levels. When cognitive theories of learning have been delineated within a domain, the learning progression can be reflected in the criteria. The criteria specified at each score level are then guided by theoretical views on the acquisition of knowledge and processes assessed by the task.

A generic rubric may be designed that reflects the skills and knowledge underlying the defined construct. The development of the generic rubric begins in the early stages of the performance assessment design, and then guides the design of specific rubrics for each task that capture the particular cognitive skills and content assessed by a particular task. An advantage of this approach is that it helps ensure consistency across the specific rubrics and it is aligned with the construct-centered approach to test design. Typically, student responses that cover a wide range of competency are then evaluated to determine the extent to which the criteria reflect the components displayed in the student work. The criteria for the generic and/or specific rubrics may then be modified, and/or the task may be redesigned to ensure it assesses the intended content knowledge and processes. This may require several iterations to ensure the linkage among the construct, tasks, and rubrics.

2.3.2. Scoring Procedures

The design of scoring rubrics has been influenced considerably by efforts in the assessment of writing. There are three major types of scoring procedures for direct writing assessments: holistic, analytic, and primary trait scoring (Huot, 1990; Miller & Crocker, 1990; Mullis, 1984). The choice of a scoring procedure for a particular assessment program depends on the defined construct, purpose of the assessment, and nature of the intended score interpretations. With holistic scoring, the raters make a single, holistic judgment regarding the quality of the writing and assign one score, using a scoring rubric with criteria and usually anchor or (benchmark) papers at each score level. With analytic scoring, the rater evaluates the writing according to a number of features, such as content and organization, mechanics, focus, and ideas, and assigns a score indicating level of quality to each one. Some analytic scoring methods weight the domains, allowing for domains that are assumed to be more pertinent to the construct being measured, such as content and organization, to contribute more to the overall score. As summarized by Mullis (1984), "holistic scoring is designed to describe the overall effect of characteristics working in concert, or the sum of the parts, analytic scoring is designed to describe individual characteristics or parts and total them in a meaningful way to arrive at an overall score" (p. 18). Although the sum of the parts of writing may not be the same as an overall holistic judgment, the analytic method has the potential to provide information regarding potential strengths and weaknesses of the examinee. Evidence, however, is needed to determine the extent to which the domain scores are able to differentiate aspects of students' writing ability (see section 2.3.4).

Primary trait scoring was developed by the National Assessment of Educational Progress (NAEP; Lloyd-Jones, 1977). The primary trait scoring system is based on the premise that most writing is addressed to an audience with a particular purpose, and levels of success in accomplishing that purpose can be defined concretely (Mullis, 1984). As an example, three common purposes of writing are informational, persuasive, and literary or imaginative. The specific task determines the exact scoring criteria, although criteria are similar across similar kinds of writing (Mullis, 1984). The design of a primary trait scoring system involves the identification of one or more traits relevant for a specific writing task. For example, features selected for persuasive writing may include clarity of position and support, whereas characteristics for a literary piece may include plot, sequence, and character development. Thus, the primary trait scoring system reflects aspects of a generic rubric as well as task-specific rubrics. By first using a construct-centered approach the construct, and in this case the type of writing, guides the design of the scoring criteria and rubrics. The development of primary trait rubrics then allows for the general criteria to be tailored to the task allowing for more consistency in raters' application of the criteria to the written response. Thus, in the end there may be one scoring rubric for each writing purpose.

2.3.3. Examples of Holistic and Analytic Scoring Rubrics

Scoring rubrics were developed for assessing the quality of writing on the Maryland School Performance Assessment Program (Maryland State Department of Education, 1996). Table 11.3 provides a holistic rubric for one of the three writing purposes assessed by MSPAP, writing to express personal ideas. Rubrics were also developed for the other two purposes of writing (writing to persuade and writing to be informed). In general, the criteria for each rubric incorporate the same features: development, organization, attention to audience, and language. These features define the construct being assessed and have implications for score interpretation. Further, specific criteria for some of the features varied depending on the purpose of writing; in particular, criteria for the development feature varied across writing purposes. Tailoring the rubric to the particular purpose of writing conveys the unique characteristics that are being assessed, need to be attended to by raters, and need to be considered in interpreting the scores.

Some writing assessment projects have adopted a generic analytic scoring procedure. As an example, Oregon's state writing assessment in 2004 had a scoring rubric for each of six dimensions: ideas and content, organization, voice, word choice, sentence fluency, and conventions. The score levels ranged from one to six for each of the dimensions. The generic analytic scoring rubric was used for tasks across the different purposes of writing and unique characteristics that applied to a particular purpose were embedded in the generic analytic rubric. As an example, below are the scoring criteria at the highest level for the voice dimension:

TABLE 11.3 MSPAP Scoring Rubric: Writing to Express Personal Ideas

Score Level	Score Level Criteria
3	*Development*: The writer consistently develops the ideas into a complete, well-developed whole. *Organization:* The writer purposefully orders ideas. *Attention to Audience:* The writer fully anticipates and answers the audience's needs (audience may include self). *Language:* The writer consistently uses language choices to enhance the text and in a manner appropriate to the literary form.
2	*Development:* The writer partially develops the ideas, but the response is not a complete, well-developed whole. *Organization:* The writer purposefully orders ideas. *Attention to Audience:* The writer somewhat anticipates and answers the audience's needs (audience may include self). *Language:* The writer frequently uses language choices to enhance the text and in a manner appropriate to the literary form.
1	*Development:* The writer tries to develop the ideas, but the response is not well developed and is not complete. *Organization:* The writer orders ideas, but there are some interruptions in the flow of the piece. *Attention to Audience:* The writer attempts to anticipate and answers the audience's needs (audience may include self). *Language:* The writer sometimes uses language choices to enhance the text and in a manner appropriate to the literary form.
0	*Development:* The writer has not developed the ideas into a complete whole. *Organization:* The writer shows little purposeful ordering of ideas. *Attention to Audience:* The writer has not anticipated and answered the audience's needs (audience may include self). *Language:* The writer seldom, if ever, uses language choices to enhance the text and in a manner appropriate to the literary form.

Source: Adapted from Maryland State Department of Education (1996).

The writing is characterized by an effective level of closeness to or distance from the audience (e.g., a narrative should have a strong personal voice, while an expository piece may require extensive use of outside resources and a more academic voice; nevertheless, both should be engaging, lively, or interesting. Technical writing may require greater distance). (Oregon Department of Education, 2004, p. 3)

In subject domains other than writing, holistic and analytic scoring procedures are common. In the adoption of a construct-centered approach in the design of a middle-school mathematics assessment consisting of constructed-response items, Lane and her colleagues (Lane, 1993; Lane et al., 1995) used a construct-driven approach to the design of their holistic scoring rubric. They first developed a generic holistic rubric, as shown in Table 11.4 that reflected the conceptual framework used in the design of the assessment, including mathematical knowledge, strategic knowledge, and communication as overarching features. This generic holistic rubric guided the design of each task-specific rubric, which facilitated the consistency of raters in applying the scoring rubric and the generalizability of the resultant scores to the larger construct domain.

Table 11.5 provides a MSPAP scoring rubric designed for evaluating the learning outcome, Reading for Literary Experience, which was one of three reading purposes specified by Maryland's content standards and performance assessment.

The student had a choice of one of three reading materials, and the rubric was used to evaluate student responses to several items assessing this learning outcome. Below is an example of an item that was scored by this rubric.

> Authors choose the setting of a story for a particular reason. Could the story you read today have taken place in a different setting without affecting the characters and their actions? Elaborate on your answer by referring to the events or characters as well as the setting in the story. (Maryland State Department of Education, 1996, p. 19)

Marzano et al. (1993) provided generic rubrics for each of the categories specified for their content standards and lifelong learning standards. Taking a construct-centered approach to test design, these generic rubrics reflect the overall construct being measured for a particular standard and allow for the generation of specific rubrics to further delineate what is being assessed by a particular task. As an example, Table 11.6 provides the four-point generic rubric for the declarative content standard. The generic rubric was adapted to reflect the generalization assessed by the task discussed previously, "war forces sensitive issues to surface and causes people to confront inherent conflicts of values" (Marzano et al., 1993, p. 30). The specific rubric is also presented in the table. The specific rubric could be expanded to provide examples of student misconceptions

TABLE 11.4 Holistic General Scoring Rubric for Mathematics Constructed-Response Items

Score Level	Score Level Criteria
4	*Mathematical Knowledge:* Shows understanding of the problem's mathematical concepts and principles; uses appropriate mathematical terminology and notations; executes algorithms completely and correctly. *Strategic Knowledge:* May use relevant outside information of a formal or informal nature; identifies all the important elements of the problem and shows understanding of the relationships among them; reflects an appropriate and systematic strategy for solving the problem; gives clear evidence of a solution process, and solution process is complete and systematic. *Communication:* Gives a complete response with a clear, unambiguous explanation and/or description; may include an appropriate and complete diagram; communicates effectively to the identified audience; presents strong supporting arguments which are logically sound and complete; may include examples and counter-examples.
3	*Mathematical Knowledge:* Shows nearly complete understanding of the problem's mathematical concepts and principles; uses nearly correct mathematical terminology and notations; executes algorithms completely; and computations are generally correct but may contain minor errors. *Strategic Knowledge:* May use relevant outside information of a formal or informal nature; identifies the most important elements of the problem and shows general understanding of the relationships among them; and gives clear evidence of a solution process, and solution process is complete or nearly complete, and systematic. *Communication:* Gives a fairly complete response with reasonably clear explanations or descriptions; may include a nearly complete, appropriate diagram; generally communicates effectively to the identified audience; presents strong supporting arguments which are logically sound but may contain some minor gaps.
2	*Mathematical Knowledge:* Shows understanding of some of the problem's mathematical concepts and principles; and may contain serious computational errors. *Strategic Knowledge:* Identifies some important elements of the problem but shows only limited understanding of the relationships among them; and gives some evidence of a solution process, but solution process may be incomplete or somewhat unsystematic. *Communication:* Makes significant progress toward completion of the problem, but the explanation or description may be somewhat ambiguous or unclear; may include a diagram which is flawed or unclear; communication may be somewhat vague or difficult to interpret; and arguments may be incomplete or may be based on a logically unsound premise.
1	*Mathematical Knowledge:* Shows very limited understanding of some of the problem's mathematical concepts and principles; may misuse or fail to use mathematical terms; and may make major computational errors. *Strategic Knowledge:* May attempt to use irrelevant outside information; fails to identify important elements or places too much emphasis on unimportant elements; may reflect an inappropriate strategy for solving the problem; gives incomplete evidence of a solution process; solution process may be missing, difficult to identify, or completely unsystematic. *Communication:* Has some satisfactory elements but may fail to complete or may omit significant parts of the problem; explanation or description may be missing or difficult to follow; may include a diagram, which incorrectly represents the problem situation, or diagram may be unclear and difficult to interpret.
0	*Mathematical Knowledge:* Shows no understanding of the problem's mathematical concepts and principles. *Strategic Knowledge:* May attempt to use irrelevant outside information; fails to indicate which elements of the problem are appropriate, copies part of the problem, but without attempting a solution. *Communication:* Communicates ineffectively; words do not reflect the problem; may include drawings which completely misrepresent the problem situation.

Source: From "The conceptual Framework for the Development of a Mathematics Performance Assessment," by S. Lane, 1993, *Educational Measurement: Issues and Practice,* 12(2), 23. Copyright 1993 by the National Council on Measurement in Education. Reprinted with permission.

TABLE 11.5 MSPAP Reading for Literacy Experience Scoring Rubric

SCORE LEVEL	SCORE LEVEL CRITERIA
3	A completely developed understanding of the text with evidence of connections, extensions and the reader's ideas and text itself are explicit.
2	A generally developed understanding of the text with evidence of constructing meaning. Connections between the reader's ideas and the text itself are implied.
1	Some evidence of constructing meaning, some understanding of the text.
0	Other. No evidence of constructing meaning.

Source: Adapted from the Maryland State Department of Education (1996).

that are specific to the task. To evaluate the other standards embedded in the task, generic rubrics for each standard are provided. This allows for the evaluation of each standard separately. For use in large-scale assessment programs, the examination of local independence of the derived scores would be needed. It would also be possible to combine the criteria across rubrics to obtain one holistic scoring rubric for a task. This approach may be more feasible for many large-scale assessment programs. For additional generic rubrics for each of the content and lifelong learning standards the reader is referred to Marzano et al. (1993).

2.3.4. Research on Analytic and Holistic Scoring Procedures

The validity of score interpretation and use depends on the fidelity between the constructs being measured and the obtained scores (Messick, 1989). Validation of the scoring rubrics includes an evaluation of the match between the rubric and the targeted construct, how well the criteria at each score level captures the defined construct, and for analytic scoring schemes, the extent to which each domain specified measures something unique.

Roid (1994) explored the advantages of analytic scoring in writing assessments. Students in grades 3 and 8 were allowed 45 minutes on each of three days to produce and edit a final piece of writing on Oregon's direct-writing assessment. Students were randomly assigned one of five modes of writing (descriptive, persuasive, expository, narrative, imaginative) and each student chose one of two prompts for the assigned mode. The student responses were scored on six dimensions, including ideas, organization, voice, word choice, sentence fluency, and conventions. Correlations among the six dimensions ranged from .49 to .76 for grade 3 and .54 to .78 for grade 8. The lowest correlation was for voice and conventions, and the highest

TABLE 11.6 Generic and Specific Rubric for Declarative Knowledge Domain

SCORE LEVEL	GENERIC RUBRIC	SPECIFIC RUBRIC
4	Demonstrates a thorough understanding of the generalizations, concepts, and facts specific to the task or situation. Provides new insights to some aspect of that information.	Demonstrates a thorough understanding of the generalization that war forces sensitive issues to surface and causes people to confront inherent conflicts of values. Provides new insights into people's behavior during wartime.
3	Displays a complete and accurate understanding of the generalizations, concepts, and facts specific to the task or situation.	Displays a complete and accurate understanding of the generalization that war forces sensitive issues to surface and causes people to confront inherent conflicts of values.
2	Displays an incomplete understanding of the generalizations, concepts, and facts specific to the task or situation and has some notable misconceptions.	Displays an incomplete understanding of the generalization that war forces sensitive issues to surface and causes people to confront inherent conflicts of values and has some notable misconceptions about this generalization.
1	Demonstrates severe misconceptions about the generalizations, concepts, and facts specific to the task or situation.	Demonstrates severe misconceptions about the generalization that war forces sensitive issues to surface and causes people to confront inherent conflicts of values.

Source: Adapted from Marzano, R. J., Pickering, R. J., & McTighe, J. (1993). *Assessing student outcomes: Performance assessment using the dimensions of learning model.* Alexandria, VA: Association for Supervision and Curriculum Dimension.

correlation was for ideas and organizations for each grade level, suggesting that some of the dimensions were more related than others, but to some extent still measuring unique aspects.

A cluster analysis revealed 11 dimensions, indicating that there were 11 patterns of scores (Roid, 1994). The results showed that 40% of the students at each grade level differed only in the overall level of performance, approximately 20% performed well on all the dimensions and 20% performed poorly on all the dimensions. Approximately 60% of the students had patterns of student-writing ability that had meaningful diagnostic information. The percent of students that were classified into one of these 9 patterns ranged from 5% to 10%. For example, one pattern revealed a relative strength in stylistic aspects of writing such as ideas, organization and voice. Two other patterns indicated either high or low performance on conventions with moderate performance on the other five dimensions. As suggested by Roid (1994), for these 60% of the students, their response patterns provide some useful information for guiding instruction. Although the results suggested that each dimension may not be necessarily unique, relative strengths and weaknesses for some students were identified for combinations of dimensions. Nevertheless, some of the dimensions could be combined in the scoring system without much loss of information.

Other researchers have suggested that analytic and holistic scoring methods for writing assessments may not necessarily provide the same relative standings for examinees. Vacc (1989) reported correlations between the two scoring methods ranging from .56 to .81 for elementary students' essays. Moss, Cole, and Khampalikit (1982) evaluated writing assessments that were scored with an analytic as well as a holistic scoring scheme. In the analytic scheme, student writing was evaluated for errors in spelling, punctuation, capitalization, grammar, and organization of ideas, and holistically student writing was scored for communicative effectiveness and correctness. The correlations between a total score for the analytic method and the holistic score were .21, .24, and .42 for grades 4, 7, and 10, respectively, with interrater reliabilities ranging from .86 to .94. These results suggest that the analytic scores are assessing something different than the holistic scores. However, four of the five analytic dimensions focused on writing conventions in this study, whereas more recent analytic scoring schemes include voice, style and other domains, limiting the number of domains devoted to conventions.

Research that has examined factors that affect rater judgment of writing quality have shown that holistic scores for writing assessments are influenced most by the organization of the text and important ideas or content rather than domains related to mechanics and sentence structure (Breland & Jones, 1982; Huot, 1990; Welch & Harris; 1994). Breland and colleagues (Breland, Danos, Kahn, Kubota, & Bonner, 1994) reported relatively high correlations between holistic scores and scores for overall organization (approximately .73), supporting ideas (approximately .70), and noteworthy ideas (approximately .68).

The validity of three scoring methods for three mathematics performance tasks at the junior and high school level was examined by Taylor (1998). Each of the performance tasks included several steps or items based on the same context or situation. The three scoring methods were task-specific holistic scoring, analytic scoring in which students received one score for understanding mathematical concepts and procedures and one score for mathematical communication, and item-by-item scoring. Correlation and regression analyses revealed that the relationships between the sum of the item scores (i.e., item-by-item scoring) and holistic scores were greater (correlations of .71 to .91) than the relationships between analytic scores and holistic scores (correlations of .55 to .85), suggesting that raters who applied the item-by-item scoring method may have been evaluating similar aspects of student work as those raters who applied the holistic method, whereas raters that used the analytic method, to some extent, evaluated different elements of student work (Taylor, 1998). An exploratory factor analysis indicated that the items within a task explained a relatively large percent of the variance for the holistic score, suggesting that the holistic scoring method and item-by-item scoring method are comparable. Using analytic scores as the criterion variable, smaller and overlapping sets of items explained analytic score variance, suggesting that the two analytic scores (understanding concepts and procedures, and mathematical communication) may represent two unique aspects of students' work.

In the science domain, Klein et al. (1998) compared analytic and holistic scoring of hands-on science performance tasks for grades 5, 8, and 10. The correlations between the total scores obtained for the two scoring methods were relatively high: .71 for grade 5 and .80 for grade 8. The correlations increased to .90 for grade 5 and .96 for grade 8 when disattenuated for the inconsistency among raters within a scoring method. The authors suggested that the scoring method has little unique influence on the raters' assessment of the relative quality of a student's performance. They further suggested that if school performance is of interest, the use of one scoring method over the other probably has little or no effect on a school's relative standing within a state given the relatively high values of the disattenuated correlations. The time and cost for scoring for both of the methods was also addressed. The analytic method took nearly three times as long as the holistic method to score for a grade 5 response and nearly five times as long to score for a grade 8 response, resulting in higher costs for scoring using the analytic method.

Other researchers have examined differences in interrater consistency for analytic and holistic scoring methods. In general, the literature on writing assessments suggests that there is a high degree of interrater consistency with different scoring methods. As an example, Bauer (1981) obtained interrater correlations of .95 with the analytic method and .93 with the holistic method in the scoring of National Assessment of Educational Progress (NAEP) essay responses.

The results in this section suggest that the impact of the choice of scoring method (e.g., analytic versus holistic) may vary depending on the similarity of the criteria reflected in the scoring methods. The more closely the criteria for the analytic method resemble the criteria delineated in the holistic method, the more likely it is that the relative standings for examinees will be similar. The research also suggests that analytic rubrics typically are capable of providing distinct information for only a small number of domains (i.e., two or three).

2.3.5. Computer-Automated Scoring Procedures

Computer-automated scoring of student responses to complex constructed-response items have been developed in an effort to provide more timely assessment results and to reduce the costs associated with scoring. Bennett and Bejar (1998) pointed out that automated scoring procedures have the potential to enhance the quality of assessments because they allow for the construct to be represented systematically in that the response features and feature weights that best illuminate the construct are identified in the scoring procedure, and they allow for the scoring rules to be applied consistently. Bennett (2004) argued for construct-driven, integrated computer-automated assessment systems that include all the aspects involved in the assessment and task design, administration, scoring, and reporting. Sophisticated automated scoring procedures have been designed for computerized performance assessments of architectural problem-solving (Bejar, 1991; Bejar & Braun, 1999), mathematical problem solving (Bennett & Sebrects, 1996), and physician's patient management skills (Clauser, Margolis, Clyman, & Ross, 1997).

In the context of essay scoring, the design of an automated essay scoring system typically involves identifying a large number of responses to a task that have been rated by expert human raters and that represent the full range of the score scale (Breland et al., 1999). A computer program is then designed to analyze the prescored responses by looking for certain features that distinguish the responses at each score level, such as the particular structures, length, and word use. Typically, natural language processing techniques are used in the design of the program. Weights are then assigned to those features considered most important to define a model for scoring the responses to a particular task. Bennett (2004) argued, however, that such scoring procedures should be grounded in a theory of domain proficiency, using experts to help define proficiency in a domain rather than having them as the criterion to be predicted.

A thorough discussion on the design, use, and validity of computer-automated scoring systems can be found in a chapter (this volume) by Drasgow, Luecht, and Bennett. Also see Bennett (2004), Bennett and Bejar (1998), Clauser, Kane, and Swanson (2002), Yang, Buckendahl, Juskiewicz, and Bhola (2002).

2.4. Expert Review and Pilot of Performance Assessments

Performance assessments need to be appraised with regard to the quality and comprehensiveness of the content and processes being assessed and with regard to potential issues of bias in task language and context. The review process is iterative in that when tasks are developed they may be reviewed and modified a number of times prior to and after being piloted. This involves logical analyses of the tasks to help evaluate whether they are assessing the intended content and processes, worded clearly and concisely, and free from anticipated sources of bias. The development process also includes pilot testing the tasks and scoring rubrics to ensure they elicit the processes and skills intended.

Individual pilot analyses may also be conducted. For example, protocol analysis in which students are asked to think aloud while solving a task or to describe retrospectively the way in which they solved the task can be conducted to examine the cognitive processes that the task elicits (Chi, Glaser, & Farr, 1988; Chi, Glaser, & Rees, 1982; Ericsson & Simon, 1984; Newell & Simon, 1972). These individual pilots afford rich information from a relatively small number of students regarding the degree to which the tasks evoke the content knowledge and thinking processes that they were intended to evoke, and allows for additional probing regarding the processes underlying student performance. The individual piloting of tasks also provides an opportunity for the examiner to pose questions to students regarding their understanding of task wording and directions.

A large-scale group pilot administration of the items provides additional information regarding the quality including the psychometric characteristics of the items. Student work from constructed-response items or essays can also be analyzed to ensure that the tasks evoke the content knowledge and cognitive processes that they are intended to evoke, and the directions and wording are as clear as possible. Multiple variants of tasks can also be piloted to further examine the best way to phrase and format tasks to ensure that all students have the same opportunity to display their reasoning and thinking. Any one of these analyses may point to needed modifications to the tasks.

2.5. Training Procedures for Raters

A rating session for a large-scale performance assessment typically involves a large number of raters spending several days together in a training session and then operationally scoring student work. This type of scoring procedure is usually referred to as a centralized scoring procedure. The training for each task begins with a discussion of the task and what it is assessing, the scoring rubric and criteria at each score level, and the features of benchmark papers exemplifying each score level. Raters then practice scoring with prescored papers, followed by a discussion of the scores assigned to each paper to help clarify distinctions between score levels. This process is repeated until raters are scoring sampled papers consistently prior to the operational rating of student responses. For some assessment programs that have high stakes associated with individual scores each student response is rated twice. Typically, if there is a considerable discrepancy between two ratings, an expert rater will rate the response and this third rating can be averaged with the initial ratings or used to replace one or both of the initial ratings. For assessment programs that are not high stakes, typically only a percent of student work is rated twice so as to examine interrater consistency.

In addition to the conventional centralized group scoring procedure, other scoring procedures have been proposed including local group scoring and local computer scoring of performance assessments. Local group scoring occurs when the scoring procedure is decentralized in that there are a number of local scoring sites and each local site has a different set of raters. Decentralized computer scoring typically involves training raters via computer, and then raters evaluate actual student responses on the computer. This procedure involves several trainers training different groups of raters via computer. If scoring is decentralized, issues arise regarding the comparability of scores obtained at different sites and the need for standardized procedures to assure score comparability (Storms, Sheingold, Nunez, & Heller, 1998). As noted by Breland et al. (1999) if an assessment program changes from a group scoring procedure to local or computer scoring, evidence indicating that the scoring procedures produce comparable scores is needed. When referring to computer scoring, Breland et al. (1999) were discussing automated computer programs that score student work, not humans who score student work via computer. Regardless, their comment is applicable to any change in a scoring procedure.

2.5.1. Training Methods for Raters

Two commonly used methods for training raters for scoring performance assessments are the spiral method and the sequential method. As an example, for writing assessment programs that use the spiral method raters are trained to score student essays from a number of writing prompts in a single common training session. In the sequential method, raters are trained sequentially as they score student essays from each new prompt. Moon and Hughes (2002) examined the equivalency of scores under these two scoring methods. They assigned experienced raters to one of the two methods to score 6th grade student essays. Each student was randomly assigned one of ten prompts, and each prompt asked students to compose a personal response. The results indicated that the mean scores for the spiral method were consistently higher across all five analytic domains than the mean scores for the sequential method. The authors suggested that the differences in means for the two methods may be due to raters being exposed to a number of prompts within each set of student responses that they rate under the spiral method as opposed to the same prompt across student performances within each set when using the sequential method. Thus, in the spiral method raters may have to revisit the score scale continually for guidance (Moon & Hughes, 2002).

For assessment programs that monitor changes in performance over time, if each student responds to one prompt each year and the prompts change each year, by default the assessment programs are using a sequential method over time. If these programs change their assessment procedures in later years by administering more than one prompt in a year, the sequential method should continue to be used. If another method is used, it may affect the comparability of scores across years when examining student growth as well as when evaluating instructional changes across years (Moon & Hughes, 2002).

3. VALIDITY OF PERFORMANCE ASSESSMENTS

Validity pertains to the meaningfulness, appropriateness, and usefulness of test score inferences (Messick, 1989) and as stated in the *Standards* (AERA, APA, & NCME, 1999), "Validity refers to the degree to which evidence and theory support the interpretations of test scores entailed by proposed uses of tests" (p. 9). The evaluation of the fairness of an assessment is intimately connected with all sources of validity evidence. As described by Cole and Moss (1989), "bias is differential validity of a given interpretation of a test score for any definable, relevant subgroup of test takers" (p. 205). This conception of bias as differential validity suggests that ensuring a fair assessment requires evidence to support the meaningfulness, appropriateness, and usefulness of the inferences made from test scores for all groups of students. For example, the validity of an assessment is dependent on its capability of evoking the same intended level of cognitive activity for all groups of students regardless of their gender, cultural, or linguistic backgrounds. Therefore, task wording and context should not interfere differentially with student performance. As another example, if an assessment requires students to compose an essay on the computer, equitable opportunity for practice in using the computer for writing is an important consideration. Those students who don't have access to computers would most likely be at a disadvantage. The accumulation of validity evidence for performance assessments, therefore, needs to consider whether "teachers and schools have the capability and do provide all students with the opportunity to learn what is assessed" (Herman & Klein, 1996, p. 246).

A valid assessment of all students requires the development, administration, and validation of the assessment to be interwoven (AERA et al., 1999). Validity evidence for assessments that are intended for students from various cultural, ethnic, and linguistic backgrounds needs to be collected continuously and systematically as the assessment is being developed, administered, and refined. Hambleton and Kanjee (1993) stressed the necessity of considering the diversity of culture and ethnic groups for the entire assessment process from the design to the administration of the assessments. Although they were referring to the use of assessments in cross-cultural studies, this consideration is as important in developing any assessment when the intended population includes a wide range of cultural and ethnic groups.

Six types of validity evidence as defined by Messick (1989) may be evaluated: content, substantive, structural, external, generalizability, and consequential aspects of construct validity. Linn et al. (1991) proposed validity criteria that are specific to performance assessments including content quality, content coverage, cognitive complexity, meaningfulness, cost and efficiency, transfer and generalizability, fairness, and consequences. Others have proposed directness, scope, reliability, and transparency as criteria for examining the validity of performance assessments (Frederiksen & Collins, 1989).

Two sources of potential threats to the validity of score interpretations—construct underrepresentation and construct-irrelevant variance—have been discussed by Messick

(1989). In this chapter, construct underrepresentation was addressed in the section on the design of performance assessments (see section 2) and will also be addressed in the section on the generalizability of performance assessments (see section 4.1). Potential sources of construct-irrelevant variance that are unique to performance assessments will be addressed in the next section. Following this, validity evidence that is particularly germane to performance assessments will be discussed, including construct complexity, directness and meaningfulness, consequences, and group performance differences. The intent of this section is not to cover the range of validity evidence needed for an assessment but instead to focus on validity evidence particularly relevant to performance assessments. For a thorough discussion on validity see Kane's chapter (this volume) and for a comprehensive discussion on fairness in testing see Camilli's chapter (this volume).

3.1. Sources of Construct-Irrelevant Variance

3.1.1. Examinee Choice

A potential threat to the validity of score interpretations is construct-irrelevant variance, which occurs when one or more irrelevant constructs is being assessed in addition to the intended construct (Messick, 1989). Construct-irrelevant variance may occur when examinees are given a choice of prompt or task. Proponents who support student choice of tasks advocate that choice allows examinees to select a task that has context they are more familiar with, which may lead to better performance than if they are assigned a task (Powers, Fowles, Farnum, & Gerritz, 1992). Some have argued, therefore, that allowing for choice may minimize any potential negative impact of irrelevant contextual variables. If the purpose of an essay is to assess students' ability to organize evidence and craft a coherent argument or position on a familiar topic, and not to assess specific content, then choice may be preferable (Bridgeman, Morgan, & Wang, 1997).

Wainer, Wang, and Thissen (1994) argued, however, that choice not only measures the student's proficiency in a given subject area but also measures the student's conception of his or her ability to pick the easiest problem to answer. In this manner, choice introduces a source of construct-irrelevant variance and potentially diminishes the validity of the score interpretations. Nevertheless, not providing choice may disadvantage some students who are unfamiliar with the topic and if the topic is not relevant to the construct being assessed, it will be a source of irrelevant score variance.

Although allowing for choice may address issues regarding perceived fairness of the assessment, equating and test security concerns argue against this practice. Wainer and Thissen (1994) argued that providing choice threatens the comparability of scores. They indicated that the equating of writing forms will be compromised if students are given choice because equating procedures require a random sample from the examinee population to estimate form difficulty and by allowing for choice, task difficulty and the ability of test takers are confounded, leading to biased estimates of difficulty. As researchers have stated, the goal of having the examinee show his or her best work and obtaining a high score is not necessarily in line with the goal of maximum comparability of scores derived from different tasks from different students (Linn, Betebenner, & Wheeler, 1998; Wainer & Thissen, 1994).

Powers and Fowles (1998, 1999) examined the effects of offering a choice of writing topics on the quality of undergraduate students' writing. In one study, students identified their preferences for a set of 20 topics and then chose two topics to write 45-minute essays, one in response to a high-preferred topic and one in response to a low-preferred topic (Powers & Fowles, 1998). There was little or no relationship between preference and essay scores, providing support for the argument that students can write on topics that draw on their personal interests, knowledge, and experiences. Choice of writing prompts on the quality of essays produced by 11th grade students on a statewide assessment was examined by Gabrielson, Gordon, and Engelhard (1995). Fifteen persuasive writing prompts were administered to students where approximately half were assigned a prompt and the other half chose between two presented prompts. Results indicated that providing students with a choice did not have an impact on the quality of their persuasive writing compared to students who were assigned the same writing prompt. Nevertheless, Gabrielson et al. (1995) suggested that the lack of a choice effect may have been due partly to the use of persuasive writing prompts, and if students were given more familiar and less difficult modes of writing, such as narrative and descriptive, an effect might have been observed.

Linn, Betebenner, and Wheeler (1998) examined the effects of providing choice to students on the Grade 10 Mathematics Assessment of the Oregon State Assessment Program. Students were asked to select one of two presented tasks on each of six alternate forms. Results indicated that the choice of problem differed systematically by gender and ethnic group. Further, the scores students obtained differed systematically as a function of choice, jeopardizing the comparability of the passing rates across forms that have different pairs of tasks and within forms when the examinee chooses the task to answer (Linn et al., 1998). The authors concluded that equating adjustments would be needed before making high-stakes decisions based on performance of students when choice is given.

Powers and Bennett (1999) examined the effects of choice on student performance and the psychometric properties of the items for an experimental section of the GRE. The computer-based test items required students to generate 15 explanations or hypotheses for questions posed. Results indicated that there was considerable variation in items in terms of the extent to which they were chosen by examinees. Performance was higher, on average, for every item when examinees were allowed choice rather than when they were assigned the item. On average, the effect was approximately .1 to .2 SD units. Further, internal consistency measures were higher when choice was provided, which may have accounted for the tendency to obtain higher correlations between performance on the items and measures of academic ability, GRE scores and grades (Powers & Bennett, 1999).

Examining the impact of choice of history essay topics on student performance, Bridgeman and colleagues

(1997) showed that for both the U.S. and European History Advanced Placement experimental administration of essay items, scores were approximately .33 SD units higher for a chosen topic than for an assigned topic. They suggested that this effect may be due in part to students working harder on their chosen or preferred essay. As an example, for the European History topic 58% of the students scored higher on their chosen topic and 30% scored higher on the assigned topic. For these history essay tests, it appeared that students tended to make the right choice. Furthermore, essays students wrote on their preferred topics were somewhat better indicators of their ability in history than the written essays on the assigned topics. For example, for the European history exam, the preferred essay correlated .52 with the criterion (i.e., the national administration of the exam consisting of multiple-choice and essay items), compared to .44 for the assigned topic.

Others have examined the effects of choice on younger students. Fitzpatrick and Yen (1995) studied the psychometric characteristics of choice when students in grades 3, 5, and 8 could choose among reading passages on MSPAP. The results suggested that the constructed-response items for non-choice passages and constructed-response items for choice passages did not exhibit differences in difficulty or item-test correlations that could be attributed to student choice, and students' scaled scores were comparable on the choice and assigned passages. They also examined a number of student characteristics in relation to student choice and found that some choices were more attractive to different gender and ethnic groups.

Further research is needed to examine the effects of choice on student performance and on the psychometric quality of tests. In particular, research needs to examine when choice may be appropriate and when it may be a source of irrelevant variance, impacting the fairness of the testing process. Choice may reduce construct-irrelevant variance in the testing process in that students tend to choose tasks that draw on their personal backgrounds and experiences, thus reducing exposure to features of the task that are not familiar to the student and not part of the construct to be measured (Powers & Bennett, 1999). As an example, if the purpose of a history assessment is to assess knowledge of specific historical events, choice would not be appropriate; however, if the purpose is to assess students' ability to organize evidence and present a cohesive argument on a subject, choice may be deemed reasonable to ensure a valid assessment of the construct (Bridgeman et al., 1997). Research also needs to examine the most effective strategies that students should use when making a choice, and students need to be informed about those strategies. In summarizing the results of studies examining the impact of choice on student performance, Powers and Bennett (1999) state that "Test takers do not uniformly make good choices.... The prevalence of poor choices may vary according to the nature of the test and the characteristics of examinees" (p. 265).

3.1.2. Raters' Attention to Irrelevant Features

Construct-irrelevant variance may occur when raters score student responses according to features that do not reflect the scoring criteria and are irrelevant to the construct being assessed (Messick, 1994). In a relatively early study, Stewart and Grobe (1979) reported a relationship between the length of response (i.e., number of words) and the assigned holistic score. To further investigate this relationship between length and the holistic score, Grobe (1981) conducted a study that revealed that length of the response was related to vocabulary diversity, suggesting that vocabulary diversity provides an indication of the quality of the writing.

Breland and colleagues (1994) examined features that affect holistic scores for essays in history. They found that length of response in addition to a historical content score and an English score that reflected both the quality of writing and English mechanics significantly predicted holistic scores for constructed responses on an advanced placement U.S. history examination. Although one may expect length of response to be related to the holistic score because the essay needs to include the required elements, Breland et al. (1995) found that length of response had an impact on the holistic score even after the construct-related features were taken into account. They suggested that the importance of English skills depends on the nature of the performance task. History tests that require students to examine official documents, diaries, and other primary sources, simulating the actual work of a historian, require substantial English skills, whereas more typical straight-forward history essays place less emphasis on English composition skills (Breland et al., 1995).

Using 7th and 10th grade student mathematics and reading responses from the 1996 Kansas Assessment Program, Pomplun, Capps, and Sundbye (1998) examined relevant and irrelevant scoring rubric features that may affect holistic scores. Based on a regression analysis they found that for both reading and mathematics the correctness of the answer was the primary feature reflected in holistic scores. The correct answer across both grade levels and subject areas accounted for over 50% of the holistic score variance. With regard to irrelevant rubric features, the length of response (i.e., number of words) was most influential. Number of words was a significant predictor of holistic score variance when the other rubric features were held constant at both 7th and 10th grade in reading and at 10th grade in math. Additional research needs to determine the construct relevancy of the length of the response as suggested by these authors.

Research indicates that female students tend to score higher on direct writing assessments as compared to male students. Breland, Danos, Kahn, Kubota, and Sudlow (1991) examined the effects of handwriting skills on essay scores obtained on the History Advanced Placement Exams. Under the assumption that males have poorer handwriting than females, they hypothesized that raters may guess the gender of the examinee, impacting the scores they assign. Their results indicated, however, that handwriting did not predict overall essay scores on the History AP exams.

The comparability of scores assigned to handwritten essays and to versions of the same essays typed on a word processor was examined by Powers, Fowles, Farnum and Ramsey (1994). They found that handwritten versions received higher scores. A follow-up interview with the raters revealed that the raters' expectations were higher when essays were written on a word processor, in that raters were more forgiving of mechanical errors (e.g., spelling) when essays were handwritten. Raters were then given special training to help ensure the same criteria were being used for handwritten and word processed essays. Although score differences were reduced, there was still a tendency to score the handwritten essay higher than the word processed essay. A study conducted by Russell and Tao (2004) corroborated the findings of Powers, Fowles, Farnum et al. (1994). Computer versions of essays obtained lower scores than handwritten essays from the Massachusetts Comprehensive Assessment Systems (MCAS) Language Arts Tests for grades 4, 8, and 12. Russell and Tao (2004) reported that raters indicated that they detected more mechanical errors in the computer printed responses. Further, some raters suggested that for the handwritten essays, they identified more with the students and could see the effort students put into their writing. However, a study conducted by Wolfe, Bolton, Feltovich, and Welch (1993) contradicted the findings of these two studies. They found that transcribed computer versions received lower scores than the handwritten original essays. The results of these studies suggest that if assessment programs allow students to either handwrite essays or use a word processor, an irrelevant source of variance may be introduced into the rating of student responses if expert raters are used. Moreover, if assessment programs have raters change from scoring handwritten versions to scoring word processed versions, the comparability of scores over time may be jeopardized.

3.1.3. Computer-Automated Scoring Procedures as a Potential Source of Construct-Irrelevant Variance

The replacement of expert raters with computer-automated scoring procedures may contribute to construct-irrelevant variance. Research on the validity of computer-scoring procedures has focused on comparing ratings by experts with scores produced by automated scoring procedures. The agreement between automated computer-produced scores and expert ratings range from the upper .80s to the upper .90s for percent exact or adjacent agreement (Breland et al., 1999). Keith (2003) compares several automated essay scoring procedures in terms of their validity and in conclusion suggests that these procedures can provide as comparable scores as those based on expert ratings of the same essays.

Clauser, Swanson, and Clyman (1999) compared the generalizability of expert rater scores and computer-produced automated scores for a computer-delivered performance assessment of physicians' patient management skills. Most of the previous research had examined the correspondence between expert rater scores and computer-produced scores at the individual task level; however, they argued for examining the generalizability of computer-produced scores for the entire assessment. One computer scoring procedure used a regression-based algorithm to differentially weight actions identified by the examinee based on the potential benefit or risk to the patient. The other computer scoring procedure attempted to directly operationalize the rules used by experts by identifying the specific combinations of actions, sequence, and timing required for each score level (Clauser, Swanson et al., 1999). The performances of 200 examinees on 16 tasks were analyzed. The results indicated that these two automated scoring systems produced generalizability coefficients that were very similar to each other and the expert raters. A person × task × rater decision study with 16 tasks and 4 expert raters yielded a generalizability coefficient of .81, and person × task decision studies with 16 tasks yielded a generalizability coefficient of .79 for the regression-based system and .75 for the rule-based procedure. As indicated by the authors, typically, only two raters are used in an operational setting, which would result in a generalizability coefficient of .79 for the expert raters, which is equivalent to the coefficient for the regression-based system. They provided additional evidence suggesting that the constructs measured by the expert raters and the automated scoring procedures were comparable.

As previously indicated, however, automated scoring procedures should be grounded in a theory of domain proficiency, using experts to delineate proficiency in a domain rather than having them as a criterion to be predicted (Bennett, 2004). Further, the relationship of automated scores and external criteria should be evaluated and studies that directly assess the extent to which automated scores contribute to construct-irrelevant variance should be conducted (Drasgow, Luecht, & Bennett, this volume). As an example, one study demonstrated that an automated essay scoring program can be tricked into assigning scores that are undeservedly high (Powers, Burstein, Chodorow, Fowles & Kukich [2002]).

3.1.4. Motivation as a Source of Construct-Irrelevant Variance

Researchers have studied whether there are differential effects on performance due to item format and the stakes associated with the assessment. The results suggest that as the stakes increase for the individual student, performance tends to improve on constructed-response items more than on multiple-choice items. For example, DeMars (2000) studied the stakes associated with an assessment for students and the motivation level of students in relation to item format. DeMars reported that increasing the stakes of the science and math sections of the high school proficiency test in Michigan increased student scores on the constructed-response section more so than on the multiple-choice section. O'Neil, Sugrue, and Baker (1995/1996) demonstrated that NAEP math scores on open-ended items were higher than on multiple-choice items when 8th grade students were offered money for correct responses.

3.2. Cognitive Complexity of Performance Tasks

One of the promises of performance assessments is that they can emphasize complex thinking and problem solving skills. As Linn et al. (1991) caution, however, it should not be assumed that a performance assessment measures complex thinking skills; evidence is needed to establish the extent to which it does. Thus, analyses of the cognitive strategies and processes underlying task performance provides relevant information for construct validation. The alignment between the cognitive processes underlying task responses and those underlying the construct domain needs to be made explicit because the goal is to generalize score interpretations to nonassessment construct domain interpretations (Messick, 1989).

The extent to which the design of a performance assessment considers cognitive theories of student proficiency in an academic discipline will therefore affect the validity of the score interpretations. As an example, writing is viewed as a process that entails planning and prewriting, drafting, editing and revising. Researchers have argued that because most tests of direct writing only allow enough time for developing a first draft and not enough time for any meaningful planning or revision, they don't elicit the many processes that writers use, and thus are not representing the writing ability construct fully (Powers & Fowles, 1998). Consequently, this may lead to a less cognitively complex assessment and an underrepresentation of the construct being assessed.

In a study examining the effects of including the planning process on the quality of student writing, Mullis et al. (1994) reported that on the NAEP writing assessment, students who used the provided planning page prior to writing their essays performed significantly higher than those who left it blank. Further, 11th grade students who indicated that they revised and edited their essays frequently performed better than students who indicated that they never or hardly did so (Mullis et al., 1994). Moreover, students of teachers who reportedly encouraged the process of writing, including prewriting, defining purpose and audience, were better writers, on average, than students of teachers who reportedly did not encourage the writing process.

Drafting and revising patterns on writing quality was examined by Zhang (2001) for students in 3rd, 5th, 8th, and 10th grade on the Delaware Student Testing Program. Consistent with previous research, the results showed that engaging in the writing process affected the quality of the written product. Using a holistic scoring rubric, 34% of the essays across grades showed evidence of improvement from the first draft to the second draft, with 9% of the revised essays showing meaningful improvement and 25% of the revised essays showing minimum improvement. Further, those students who reported that their instructional writing activities involved the planning, drafting, and revising process, tended to score higher on the writing assessment than students who reported that their instruction didn't focus on the writing process. This latter finding suggests that having the opportunity to engage in the writing process in the classroom as reported by students is related to student performance on the state writing assessment. In summary evidence suggests that embedding the writing process in a writing assessment improves the quality of students' writing and provides a more accurate measure of student proficiency.

To examine substantive validity evidence, researchers have used Baxter and Glaser's (1998) analytic framework described in section 2 of this chapter. This framework reflects a content-process space depicting the necessary content knowledge and process skills for successful task performance. Using think alouds, Shavelson and Ruiz-Primo (1998) compared expert and novice performance on science performance tasks that were in the content-rich and process-open quadrant of Baxter and Glaser's (1998) content-process space. The results from their think alouds indicated that high school physics students who completed at least two years of high school science were indeed novices, while expert science teachers with 4 to 13 years of experience teaching were indeed experts. Their results also suggested that different performance tasks evoked different reasoning patterns, providing some evidence to support their conjectures regarding the type of reasoning required to solve each task.

In another study designed to obtain substantive evidence for science performance assessments, Ayala, Yin, Schultz, and Shavelson (2002) evaluated whether science performance tasks were eliciting the hypothesized reasoning skills. Each science performance task was intended to measure primarily one of three reasoning skills: basic knowledge and reasoning, spatial-mechanical reasoning, and quantitative reasoning (Ayala et al. 2001). They found that their assignment of the performance assessments to the reasoning categories did not always correspond with their empirical findings. The basic knowledge and reasoning performance task, "Electric Mysteries," behaved as expected, requiring more basic knowledge and reasoning than quantitative science and spatial-mechanical reasoning. However, the spatial-mechanical task, "Daytime Astronomy," was correlated with other measures across the reasoning dimensions but in particular with the quantitative science dimension. The quantitative science task, "Aquacraft," was correlated with measures of basic knowledge and reasoning as well as quantitative science reasoning. In concluding that their assignment of performance tasks to the three reasoning dimensions was problematic, they state that "Student knowledge and experience seems to suggest how a student solves a problem, not the problem alone" (Ayala et al., 2002, p. 23). The results of this study illustrate the need to use think alouds or cognitive labs to ensure that performance tasks are eliciting the intended thinking skills.

Differences in the cognitive complexity of constructed-response items and multiple-choice items have been reported. As an example, the cognitive complexity of computer-based figural constructed-response items and multiple-choice items in architecture was examined by Martinez and Katz (1995/1996). In particular, they examined whether the cognitive demands differed for the two types of items. The computer-based figural response items required examinees to manipulate presented figural material including line illustrations, schematic diagrams, and data graphics (Martinez, 1991, 1993). Using task analysis and verbal protocol analysis for declarative items, learned-procedure items, and discovered-strategy items where examinees were required to discover a correct solution method, their results showed that differences in item difficulties correspond to differences in cognitive processing requirements. Declarative figural response items were more difficult than declarative multiple-choice items, suggesting that there was a greater demand of recall for the figural response items. Differences in format difficulty for learned-procedure items were relatively small. Since both item formats required repeated use of similar procedures, they suggested that the similar difficulties are due to similar cognitive demands. The discovered-strategy figural response items were more difficult than their multiple-choice variants. They attributed the difficulty differences to the differences in processing demand in that the figural response items required design construction whereas the multiple choice items required evaluation of design elements. They indicated that if the types of assessments were limited to multiple-choice items, design construction and the problem solving that it entails would be eliminated or limited.

In an earlier study, Martinez (1993) compared computer-based figural response items and multiple-choice items in predicting architectural problem-solving proficiency as measured by two tasks—one involved a drawing component and the other required only a written verbal response. The results showed that only the figural response scores predicted graphical problem solving, measured by a task that required examinees to design a preschool in three-dimensional space represented by a contour map, whereas both figural response and multiple-choice scores predicted verbal design problem solving. The author suggested that the figural response items more closely resemble actual architectural tasks than do multiple-choice items. This assertion was supported by architects' self-reports indicating that the figural response items as compared to multiple-choice items assess architectural knowledge better and are more comparable to what an architect does.

3.3. Directness and Meaningfulness of Performance Assessments

A validity criterion for performance assessment proposed by Frederiksen and Collins (1989) is directness. They argued that the skills of interest are directly measured insofar as they are apparent in the performances or products that are elicited. To provide validity evidence for the directness of writing essays, Powers, Fowles, and Willard (1994) examined assessment user's satisfaction with the quality of student applicants' writing. Using GRE essays that took students one hour to compose and included three stages of the writing process—draft, write, and revise—college deans and department chairs were asked to indicate their level of satisfaction, from very dissatisfied to very satisfied. The level of satisfaction reported for the essays was compared to the assigned score. They concluded that there was a strong relation between the assigned score and the users' level of satisfaction; however, it was not linear. They suggested that "The extent to which users can readily judge the products of an assessment may provide a reasonable test of whether the criterion of directness has been satisfied" (Powers et al., 1994, p. 98).

Another important validity criteria for performance assessments is their meaningfulness (Linn et al., 1991) or transparency (Frederiksen & Collins, 1989), in that students and teachers need to know what is being assessed, by what methods, the criteria used to evaluate performances, and what constitutes good performance. For large-scale performance assessments that have high-stakes decisions associated with them, it is important to ensure that all students are familiar with the task format and scoring criteria. As an example, throughout the instructional year teachers can use sample or release tasks with their students, and engage them in discussions about what the tasks are assessing and the nature of the criteria used for scoring student performance. Teachers can also engage students in using scoring rubrics to evaluate their own work as well as the work of their peers.

Researchers have examined the effects of instructing students on the nature and format of performance assessment tasks, criteria used for scoring performance, and strategies for scoring well on the tasks in an attempt to reduce construct-irrelevant variance associated with differential format familiarity, and thus allowing for a more valid assessment of student proficiency. As an example, Fuchs et al. (2000) used alternate forms of the mathematics performance assessments for students in grades 2 through 4 and the scoring rubric from the Kansas Quality Performance Assessment (Kansas State Board of Education, 1991) to examine the impact of familiarity with the format of the assessment and the nature of scoring criteria on student performance. Their results showed that performance gains were significantly higher for students whose classes were randomly assigned the brief performance assessment orientation as compared to students whose classes did not receive the orientation. The effect sizes ranged from .54 SD units on the conceptual underpinnings scoring dimension to .75 SD units on the computational applications scoring dimension, suggesting that informing students of the format of the assessment and the scoring criteria helps ensure a valid assessment of the students' competencies. The results further suggested that in the measurement of growth, increases in student performance over time on performance assessments may be partly due to students becoming more familiar with the format and scoring of performance assessments and may not reflect actual increased proficiency on the construct assessed by the performance assessments (Fuchs et al., 2000; Linn, 2000).

3.4. Consequential Evidence for Performance Assessments

Evaluation of both intended and unintended consequences of any assessment is fundamental to the validation of test use and score interpretation (Messick, 1989, 1995). Because performance assessments are intended to improve teaching and learning, "it is important to accrue evidence of such positive consequences as well as evidence that adverse consequences are minimal" (Messick, 1995, p. 7). Likewise, as Linn (1993) suggested, "The need to obtain evidence about consequences is especially compelling for performance-based assessments ... because particular intended consequences are an explicit part of the assessment system's rationale" (p. 6). The primary measurement concern with respect to adverse consequences is that any negative impact on individuals or groups should not derive from any source of test invalidity such as construct-irrelevant variance or construct underrepresentation (Messick, 1989). To identify potential negative effects, one needs to examine whether the purpose of the assessment is being compromised, such as teaching to the assessed version of the content standards rather than to the broader constructs reflected in the standards or teaching specifically to the tasks on the assessment. In the former, the curriculum and instruction can be compromised, and in the latter the validity of score interpretations can be compromised in that the assessment may not be assessing complex thinking skills, but merely the memorization of facts and procedures (Messick, 1994).

Messick (1989) addressed the consequential basis of test use and its role in validity theory in the third edition of *Educational Measurement* as did Cronbach (1971) in the second edition. Others have argued that, although the evaluation of the consequences of the use of a test is important, it should not be subsumed under the umbrella of validity (Mehrens, 1998; Popham, 1997). A prevailing assumption underlying performance assessments is that they serve as motivators in improving student achievement and learning and that they encourage instructional strategies and techniques that foster reasoning, problem solving, and communication (Frederiksen & Collins, 1989). Given these high expectations for performance assessments, the consequences of the uses and interpretations of the assessments need to be addressed, including both negative and positive consequences, and intended and plausible unintended consequences (Cronbach, 1988; Linn et al., 1991; Messick, 1989, 1994; Shepard, 1997). Messick (1994) asserts that adverse consequences bearing on issues of fairness are particularly relevant because "we should not take it for granted that a richly contextualized assessment task is uniformly good for all students... contextual features that engage and motivate one student and facilitate his or her effective task performance may alienate and confuse another student and bias or distort task performance" (p. 19).

3.4.1. Impact on Classroom Instruction

Evidence does exist that large-scale performance assessments are having an impact on instruction and learning. As an example, in a study examining the consequences of Washington's state assessment, Stecher and his colleagues (Stecher, Barron, Chun, & Ross, 2000) indicated that approximately two-thirds of 4th and 7th grade teachers (on-grades) reported that the standards and state assessment short-answer and extended response items were influential in promoting better instruction and student learning. The impact of the Maryland State Performance Assessment Program (MSPAP), which was comprised entirely of performance tasks, was examined by Lane and her colleagues (Lane, Parke, & Stone, 2002; Parke, Lane, & Stone, 2006; Stone & Lane, 2003). They examined the impact of MSPAP on classroom instruction and assessment practices, professional development and student learning. Principals and teachers reported that MSPAP was a useful tool for making positive changes in instruction and teachers were making some positive changes in their mathematics instruction because of MSPAP (Lane et al. 2002). The results further suggested that teachers' positive reaction to MSPAP was due partly to the fact that it was a performance assessment that tapped meaningful aspects of students' proficiency. The majority of principals were also supportive of using MSPAP to hold schools accountable for meeting the state performance standards; however, only 37% of the teachers were supportive of using MSPAP for school accountability.

To examine the impact of MSPAP on students more directly, on-grade students (5th and 8th grade) and off-grade students (4th and 7th grade) were asked to respond to a survey. Three-fourths of the on-grade students whereas only half of the off-grade students said they knew the purpose of MSPAP, and their written descriptions indicated that they knew it was for school accountability reasons regardless of their grade level. Over 90% of the on-grade students as compared to only half of their teachers said it was important to do well on MSPAP and that they tried hard to solve the MSPAP tasks, suggesting that they were motivated to perform their best on MSPAP. Although MSPAP provided only school-level scores, according to the 5th and 8th grade students it appears that they were motivated to perform their best.

3.4.2. Relationship Between Changes in Instruction and Student Performance

Few studies have examined the relationship between changes in instructional practice and improved performance on assessments that are entirely performance-based or include performance tasks. One exception is a study by Stecher and his colleagues in which they compared teachers' reported instructional practices in low and high KIRIS gain schools (Stecher, Barron, Kaganoff, & Goodwin, 1998). Although their study revealed few consistent findings across subject areas and grades, there was a positive relationship between standards-based practices in writing and the KIRIS direct writing assessment at the middle school level. As an example, more 7th grade writing teachers in high- versus low-gain schools in Kentucky reported integrating writing with other subjects and increasing their emphasis on various aspects of the writing process. However, although teachers indicated that they increased coverage on mathematics standards assessed by KIRIS, such as mathematical problem solving and reasoning, there was no evidence of a relationship between instruction practices and increased KIRIS mathematics scores, which reflected performance on both multiple-choice and constructed response items.

Other studies that have examined the relationship between changes in instructional practice and improved performance have been conducted using MSPAP (Lane et al., 2002; Stone & Lane, 2003). The relationship between changes in MSPAP scores for schools and classroom instruction and assessment practices, student motivation, students' and teachers' beliefs about and attitude toward MSPAP, and school characteristics was examined. Their results indicated that teacher-reported instruction-related variables explained differences in performance on MSPSP in four (writing, reading, mathematics, and science) of the five subject areas. Schools in which teachers reported that their instruction over the years reflected more reform-oriented problem types and learning outcomes similar to those assessed on MSPAP had higher levels of school performance on MSPAP than schools in which teachers reported that their instruction reflected less reform-oriented problem types and learning outcomes. More importantly, for the writing and reading domains, teacher-reported reform-oriented instruction-related variables also explained differences in rates of change in MSPAP school performance on writing and reading over time. That is, increased reported use of reform-oriented tasks in writing and reading and focus on the reading and writing learning outcomes in instruction was associated with greater rates of change in MSPAP school performance over a five-year period.

Teacher-perceived impact of MSPAP on instruction and assessment practices was also found to explain differences in MSPAP school performance in writing and reading and in rates of change over a five-year period in mathematics and science. The latter result suggests that the more impact MSPAP had on instruction as reported by teachers, the greater gains in MSPAP mathematics and science school performance over time. The result in the mathematics area was supported by a study conducted by Linn, Baker, and Betebenner (2002). These researchers examined the trends in the percent of 8th grade students meeting the performance standard on MSPAP in mathematics from 1994 through 2001 and the trends in the percentage of 8th grade students scoring at the basic level or higher or at the proficient level or higher for the NAEP mathematics assessments from 1990 through 2000. In their analysis, the slope of the trend line for MSPAP was very similar to the slope of the Maryland NAEP trend line. They concluded that the similarity of these slopes might reflect the fact that both MSPAP and NAEP are challenging assessments. Moreover, their findings provide some additional evidence indicating that the performance gains in Maryland are not specific to the content and format of MSPAP. Thus, the results of the Lane et al. study in conjunction with the findings from the Linn et al. study suggest that teacher-reported changes were not superficial changes on increased performance on MSPAP but were more substantive changes that enhanced students' understanding in mathematics.

Researchers have suggested that using test scores to make inferences regarding the quality of education tends to be problematic and contextual information is needed to inform the inferences and actions taken (Haertel, 1999). Stone and Lane (2003) indicated that a school contextual variable, percent free or reduced lunch that served as a proxy for SES, was significantly related to school-level performance on MSPAP in math, writing, reading, science, and social studies. Schools with a higher percent free or reduced lunch tended to perform poorer on MSPAP. However, there was no significant relationship between percent free or reduced lunch and growth in school-level performance on MSPAP in four of the five subject areas—math, writing, science, and social studies. Thus, improved school performance on performance-based assessments is not necessarily related to contextual factors such as percent free or reduced lunch.

Stein and Lane (1996) examined the relationship between the presence of reform features of middle school mathematics instruction and student mathematics proficiency as measured by a performance assessment consisting of extended constructed-response items. The study was conducted within the QUASAR Project aimed at improving the instructional programs and learning for poor urban students. Extensive observations were conducted in the classroom to examine the quality of mathematics instruction. The analyses of instruction focused on the cognitive demands of the instructional task as represented in the curriculum/instructional material, as set up by the teacher in the classroom, and as implemented by students in the classroom. The mathematics performance assessment consisted of constructed-response items that required students to show their solution processes and explain their reasoning and was developed to monitor school performance over time (Lane et al., 1995). The results indicated that student gains on the performance assessment that required high levels of mathematical thinking and reasoning were related to the extent to which instructional tasks were set up and implemented to allow for multiple solution strategies, multiple representations, and mathematical explanations, and that represented high levels of cognitive demand. The greatest student gains at the classroom level on the mathematics performance assessment were related to the use of classroom instruction tasks that engaged students in high levels of cognitive processing, especially those that encouraged non-algorithmic forms of thinking associated with the doing of mathematics. On the other hand, class-level performance gains on the assessment were relatively small when classroom instruction tasks were procedurally based and able to be solved with a single, easily accessible strategy, single representations, and little or no mathematical communication. Finally, class-level performance gains were found to be moderate for instruction tasks that began as cognitively demanding but were then implemented in such a manner that students often were not engaged in high levels of mathematical reasoning and problem solving. The findings of this study are particularly compelling because the evidence for instructional activities was based on classroom observations by trained observers who were in the mathematics classrooms for three 3-day observations in the fall, winter, and spring for each of three consecutive years. Further, the schools in this study served students who were in economically disadvantaged communities.

3.5. Group Differences on Performance Assessments

As Linn et al. (1991) cautioned, it would be unreasonable to assume that group differences that are exhibited on multiple-choice tests would be smaller or alleviated by using performance assessments. The groups they are referring to are based on the cultural, ethnic, or socioeconomic background of students, and research on ethnic, differences support their assertion. As stated by Linn et al. (1991), differences among groups occur due to differences in learning opportunities, familiarity, and motivation, and not necessarily item format. Researchers have also examined gender differences on performance assessments, and the results examining gender differences indicate that item format may play a role in some subject areas. The analyses of group differences has focused on both the impact of an assessment on two or more groups by examining mean differences and differential group performance on individual items when groups are matched with respect to ability, that is, differential item functioning (DIF). This section discusses both the impact of performance assessments on groups and differential item functioning.

3.5.1. Gender Differences on Essays

Research on gender differences in essay scores has shown that when differences are detected, females tend to outperform males. As an example, a meta-analysis done by Hyde and Linn (1988) indicated that for four of five studies that included a writing assessment, females obtained higher scores than males, and the fifth study showed no significant difference. Eighth grade females also outperformed males on national assessments of direct writing (Applebee, Langer, Jenkins, Mullis, & Foertsch, 1990; Applebee, Langer, & Mullis, 1985).

In examining gender differences in ten areas of academic achievement and across grade levels, Willingham, Cole, Lewis, and Leung (1997) reported that the largest gender difference was in writing—in particular, the production of an essay with a standard mean difference of .57 on the 12th grade NAEP writing assessment. Girls showed substantial gain in writing from 4th grade with a standard mean difference of approximately .3 to 8th grade (D approximately .59), but the gain remained steady at 12th grade (D approximately .57). The ratio of the female to male standard deviation was approximately 1 at 4th grade and decreased slightly (.97) in the 8th and 12th grades, indicating only a very small difference in variability for boys and girls. Overall, there were more males than females among low scorers in writing (bottom 10%), in particular, there was an increase in the number of males among the poor writers from 4th grade to 12th grade. More females were in the top 10% of scorers, with again females showing their relative gain from 4th to 8th grade. As indicated by the authors, this trend is "associated with two factors: changes in overall means for the two genders from grade to grade, and an increase in male variability compared to that of females" (Willingham et al., 1997, pp. 81–82). In comparing female and male students' performance on essays and multiple-choice tests of writing, Willingham and Cole (1997) showed that women tend to perform better than men on both essay and multiple-choice tests of writing. Women average about a tenth of a standard deviation better than men on both essay and multiple-choice parts of the SAT II: Writing Subject Test. Their research also indicates that gender differences do not vary with the required length of the response, and examinee choice does not appear to be associated with gender difference.

3.5.2. Ethnic Differences on Essays

Ethnic differences have also been observed on direct writing assessments. As an example, White 8th grade student essay scores were significantly higher than those of Black 8th grade students on both national and state assessments (Applebee et al., 1990; Engelhard, Gordon, Walker, & Gabrielson, 1994). Ethnic and gender differences in writing quality were also observed by Gabrielson et al. (1995). Fifteen persuasive writing prompts were administered to students where approximately half were assigned a prompt and the other half chose between two presented prompts. The essays were evaluated using an analytic rubric with four domains: content and organization, style, conventions, and sentence formation. Eleventh grade female students wrote higher quality essays than male students, and White students wrote essays of higher quality than Black students. In particular, the domain scores for conventions and sentence formation were more affected by gender and ethnic characteristics than domain scores in content and organization and style. These results are consistent with findings from Engelhard et al. (1994). Research in this area also indicates that student characteristics, such as gender and race, have a much greater effect on writing performance than choice of writing prompt.

3.5.3. Gender Differences in Other Content Areas

Although males typically perform better on multiple-choice sections of some advanced placement examinations, the same degree of difference is not observed on the constructed-response sections. An analysis of several advanced placement examinations (United States History, Biology, Chemistry, and English Language and Composition) by Mazzeo, Schmitt, and Bleistein (1993) revealed that, on average, males performed better than females on both item formats, but on the constructed-response sections, the differences were negligible. The results further showed that differences could not be attributed to differences in score reliabilities for the two item formats nor were such differences due to differential item functioning. As suggested by the authors, specific topics may have influenced the magnitude of gender-related differences, indicating that such differences may be attributed to the construct being measured.

For eleven AP examinations that assessed either language and literature or mathematics, there was little difference in the relative performance of males and females on the multiple-choice and constructed-response sections that consisted of essays, open-ended problems, or short answers (Willingham et al., 1997). However, for sixteen AP exams, females performed relatively better on the constructed response sections. The advantage ranged from a small relative advantage, with a difference of .11 between the two formats, to a larger relative advantage of .39. Because multiple-choice and constructed response differences vary considerably by subject, they suggested that the observed differences may be due to differences in constructs associated with the two item formats. In science and geopolitical subjects, females as compared to males tended to score relatively better on the constructed-response sections than on the multiple-choice sections of the AP exams, whereas in mathematics and language-related subjects, there tended to be no format effect. Willingham et al. (1997) suggested that it may be due to the writing in the science and geopolitical subjects.

For three state assessment programs at the high school level (Georgia, Kansas, and Kentucky), the average gender difference for the multiple choice sections was near zero, but gender differences on the constructed response sections tended to favor females (Willingham & Cole, 1997). This was especially the case for the Kansas and Kentucky mathematics assessment that placed an emphasis on application of math principles in context. For the math and science test on NAEP, where the constructed-response items require a very short answer, item format made no difference in the pattern of female and male performance. In reading, however, where the constructed response items required two or three sentences, the constructed response section was associated with a larger differential in the percent of correct responses favoring females. Whereas for the science constructed-response items that required a figural response, there was a 10% gender differential in the opposite direction, males had relatively more correct responses on the constructed-response items than on the multiple-choice items.

Gender differences were examined by Pollack and Rock (1997) on the 1988 NELS, which included performance assessments in science and mathematics. Each constructed-response section included four questions with multiple parts that were scored analytically. There was no format effect on the mathematics section, whereas the science assessment favored males more on the constructed-response section than on the multiple-choice section. Like NAEP science, NELS constructed-response items involved figural response tasks. Willingham and Cole (1997) pointed out that a common element assessed on the constructed-response section appeared to be spatial and/or mechanical skills, which tend to favor males.

Breland et al. (1994) observed no gender differences in the holistic scores for constructed responses on a 1986 advanced placement U.S. history examination, although males scored considerably higher on the multiple-choice part of the exam, with an effect size of .33. Based on a regression analysis they indicated that there is no support to the hypothesis that females perform better on the constructed-response tasks than expected (based on their performance on the multiple-choice part of the assessment) because raters favor examinees that are neater, have better penmanship, or who have better English composition skills. They suggested that the most reasonable explanation for these format gender differences is that the two types of tests measure somewhat different constructs, both of which are important in history. The multiple-choice test assesses a broad range of historical knowledge, whereas the constructed-response test assesses the ability to work with historical materials that tend to be in written form. Men appear to have greater knowledge of U.S. history as measured by the multiple-choice test. However, when given a performance task in U.S. history women perform as well as men (Breland et al., 1994). Other research has shown that women perform as well as men in college history courses, and that constructed-response tests correlate as well with college history course performance as do multiple-choice tests (Bridgeman & Lewis, 1994).

3.5.4. Differential Item Functioning on Performance Assessments

Fewer studies have examined differential item functioning (DIF) for performance assessments. Differential item functioning is concerned specifically with identifying differences in item performance that are associated with examinee group membership when the groups are matched on ability. The presence of DIF suggests that inferences about test scores may be less valid for a particular group or groups. Although researchers have argued that performance tasks offer the potential for more equitable assessment (Hambleton & Murphy, 1992; Herman, Aschbacher, & Winters, 1992; Supovitz & Brennan, 1997), performance assessments may in fact measure construct-irrelevant factors that contribute to DIF (Penfield & Lamm, 2000). For example, Herman et al. (1992) argued that extended performance-based tasks may favor students with access to higher quality materials. In addition, gender or ethnicity bias could be introduced by the typical contextualized nature of performance tasks, or the use of raters to score responses could introduce another possible source of DIF (Gyagenda & Engelhard, 1999).

In a study of a middle school mathematics performance assessment consisting of constructed-response items requiring students to show their solution processes and explain their reasoning, Lane, Wang, and Magone (1996) found that four of the six constructed-response tasks that exhibited DIF favored female students. Based on an in-depth analysis of differences in male and female students' thinking and reasoning as displayed in their responses, they indicated that females performed better than their matched males because females provided more complete conceptual explanations and were more comprehensive in displaying their solution strategies, whereas males were more likely to provide an answer with little work and an incomplete or procedural explanation. In a study conducted by Garner and Engelhard (1999), they found that the one constructed-response item that exhibited DIF was in favor of females on an 11th grade mathematics assessment. Additional studies examining DIF on performance assessments that include an in-depth analysis of student performance are needed to uncover the features of performance assessment tasks and required responses that have an impact on DIF.

As indicated by Willingham and Cole (1997), content balance on an assessment with respect to gender differences can be done with multiple-choice items because of the large number of items, but is more difficult with performance tasks because of the limited number of tasks on any one assessment. For a more comprehensive discussion on fairness in test design and use the reader is referred to the chapter by Camilli (this volume). In addition, section 4.2.4.2 in this chapter provides a discussion on the methodological issues in examining DIF in performance assessments.

4. APPLICATION OF TEST THEORIES TO PERFORMANCE ASSESSMENTS

Historically, test theories have been applied to assessments to describe how inferences, predictions, or estimates of a particular characteristic, trait, or ability of a person may be made from responses to items (Lord & Novick, 1969). Test theories provide models for explaining test performance in relation to variables that are assumed to influence behavior.

They further provide methods for obtaining scores and for quantifying errors in the measurement process.

In this section, the application of generalizability theory and item response theory (IRT) to performance assessments will be considered. More specifically, the section on generalizability theory focuses on the sources of error or facets more relevant to performance assessments. The IRT section focuses on issues in the application of IRT models to performance assessments. For assessments of student achievement, a sample of item responses is used to infer proficiency to a broader construct domain and generalizability theory can be used to describe the role of errors in generalizing from the sample of behavior. On the other hand, IRT provides models for explaining total test score performance and individual item performance, respectively, as well as methods for determining the precision of model parameter estimates such as the ability being measured by the test. Although methods based on classical test theory have been successfully applied to assessments in the past, the application of IRT addresses shortcomings of CTT and solves many practical issues related to test development (Hambleton & Swaminathan, 1985).

4.1. The Application of Generalizability Theory to Performance Assessments

Generalizability studies are typically conducted to examine the extent to which the scores derived from an assessment can be generalized to the intended construct domain. Generalizability theory allows for the estimation of multiple sources of error in measurement (Brennan, 1983, 2000, 2001; Cronbach, Gleser, Nanda, & Rajaratnam, 1972; Shavelson & Webb, 1991). The generalizability of scores can be examined for both relative decisions as in norm-referenced score interpretations and absolute decisions as in criterion- or domain-referenced score interpretations. Using analysis of variance (ANOVA) procedures, variance components are estimated for the object of measurement (e.g., student, school, district), each facet (i.e., sources of error in measurement such as task, rater, occasion of assessment administration, occasion of rating performance), and each interaction term. Inspection of the estimated variance components provides information about the relative contribution of each facet and interaction term to the measurement error variance. The variance estimates are then used to design efficient measurement procedures. As an example, the researcher can examine the effects of increasing the number of items or number of raters, or both, on the generalizability of the scores. Generalizability coefficients are estimated to examine the extent to which the scores generalize to the larger construct domain for either relative or absolute decisions, or both. The variance components are also combined to estimate a standard error of measurement for relative and absolute decisions. The chapter on reliability by Haertel (this volume) also discusses generalizability theory.

In providing validity evidence for score interpretations, Kane et al. (1999) advised "that the most attention should be given to the weakest part of the interpretative argument because the overall argument is only as strong as its weakest link" (p. 15). For performance assessment, this suggests that careful attention needs to be devoted to investigating the generalizability of the assessment results over a number of facets (Kane, 1982). Facets that need to be considered when examining the generalizability of performance assessment results include task, rater, administration occasion, rater occasion, measurement method, scoring method, and rater committee. As an example, task is a critical facet because only a small number of tasks are typically included in a performance assessment given the amount of time that is needed for each task. This poses a potential threat to the generalizability of performance assessment results.

Generalizability theory often blurs distinctions between reliability and validity (Brennan, 1996; Cronbach et al., 1972; Kane, 1982). As indicated by Shavelson, Baxter, and Gao (1993), traditionally task, rater, and occasion have been considered sources of unreliability in a measurement, whereas the consideration of other facets, such as measurement method or mode and scoring method, moves beyond reliability into a sampling theory of validity (cf. Kane, 1982). For example, examining the comparability of the results over different methods of assessment provides information about convergent validity evidence. Brennan (1996) provides another example of when generalizability theory blurs the distinction between reliability and validity. He points out that the scoring rubric is considered fixed in most analyses, in that only one rubric is used; however, multiple rubrics could be used.

If two or more rubrics are in principal equally acceptable, then the issue is primarily in the realm of reliability. However, if the acceptable rubrics are not equally preferable, then the matter is largely one of validity. For example, the "ideal" rubric may be so costly to implement that a simpler rubric is adopted for operational use ... the issue is the extent to which an investigator can generalize over rubrics, or the extent to which examinee scores are in some sense invariant over rubrics (Brennan, 1996, pp. 47–48).

Haertel and Linn (1996) provided a discussion on the potential threats to the comparability of performance assessment results due to measurements being taken at different times, in different places or using different performance tasks. They point out that comparability is of more concern for performance assessments than multiple-choice tests because administration and scoring procedures are more complicated and more difficult to control, weakening standardization. Comparability is also jeopardized because there are a smaller number of items on a performance assessment than a multiple-choice test. As they explain, students' individual reactions to specific tasks tend to average out on multiple-choice tests because of the relatively large number of items, but such individual reactions to specific items have more of an effect on scores from performance assessments that are composed of relatively few items. When there are a large number of items on a test, unique features of each item have less of an effect on the total score as compared to performance assessments that have a small number of items (Haertel & Linn, 1996).

The section below discusses the generalizability of performance assessment scores when particular facets are considered, and will argue for the need to consider carefully the facets that comprise the universe to ensure that assessment results can be generalized to the larger construct domain.

4.1.1. Error Due to Task and Rater

Research has indicated that performance assessments have relatively low consistency across tasks—that is, students who score relatively high on one task do not necessarily score relatively high on other tasks that measure essentially the same construct and are within the same assessment. Thus, examination of intertask consistency is an essential aspect in the evaluation of performance assessments interpretation (Dunbar et al., 1991; Messick, 1989). Error due to raters can also affect the generalizability of the scores in that raters may differ in their appraisal of the quality of a student's response. As an example, raters may differ in their leniency resulting in rater mean differences, or they may differ in their judgments about whether one response is better than another resulting in an interaction between student and rater facets. The characteristics of the raters who have evaluated their performances can affect student scores, and raters usually differ across years. The consistency among raters who are trained and evaluate student responses during the same rater training session has been documented (Coffman, 1966; Dunbar et al., 1991). Breland (1983) reviewed the results of 15 studies and reported a median correlation of .64 between two sets of ratings across these studies. Dunbar et al. (1991) reviewed nine studies examining the interrater reliability for writing assessments and reported estimates ranging from .33 to .91. These reliability estimates were averages of all the coefficients that were reported in the original studies and were adjusted to reflect an assessment based on one reader and one writing sample. A review of performance assessments used in medical education reported rater reliability estimates ranging from .50 to .93 (van der Vleuten & Swanson, 1990). In general, interrater consistency for science hands-on performance tasks (e.g., Shavelson et al., 1993) and mathematics constructed-response items (Lane, Liu, Ankenmann, & Stone, 1996; Lane, Stone, Ankenmann, & Liu, 1994) tend to be higher than for writing assessments. To help achieve high interrater consistency care is needed in designing precise scoring rubrics, selecting and training raters, and rechecking rater performance (Linn, 1993; Mehrens, 1992).

Researchers have shown that task-sampling variability as compared to rater-sampling variability in students' scores is a greater source of measurement error in performance assessments in science, mathematics, and writing (Baxter, Shavelson, Herman, Brown, & Valdadez, 1993; Gao, Shavelson, & Baxter, 1994; Hieronymus & Hoover, 1987; Lane et al., 1994, 1996; Shavelson et al., 1993). In other words, the number of tasks has a greater effect on the generalizability of the scores than the number of raters (Brennan, 1996).

As an example, Shavelson et al. (1993) reported that task-sampling variability was the major source of measurement error using data from 5th and 6th grade math and science performance assessments. The results of person $\times$ tasks $\times$ rater ($p \times t \times r$) generalizability studies on a math assessment and two science assessments indicated that the pt variance component accounted for the largest percent of total score variation, 49%, 48%, and 82%, respectively. The variance components that included raters were either zero or negligible, indicating that sampling variability due to raters contributed little to no measurement error. They reported that to reach a .80 generalizability coefficient 15 tasks were needed for the math assessment, 8 for the state science assessment, and 23 for the other hands-on science performance assessment.

Another example is based on a mathematics performance assessment, consisting of constructed-response items requiring students to show their solution processes and explain their reasoning (Lane et al., 1996). The results indicated that error due to raters was minimal, whereas there was considerable differential student performance across tasks. Person $\times$ task $\times$ rater ($p \times t \times r$) generalizability studies for each form of the mathematics assessment indicated that between 42% and 62% of the total score variation was accounted for by the pt variance component. The variances due to r, pr, and rt were negligible. When the number of tasks was equal to 9, the generalizability coefficients for the $p \times t \times r$ design ranged from .71 to .84. To examine the generalizability of school-level scores for each form, a (person nested within a school) $\times$ task design was used. The coefficients for absolute decisions ranged from .80 to .97 when the number of tasks was equal to 36 using a matrix sampling design.

4.1.2. Error Due to Administration Occasion

Cronbach, Linn, Brennan, and Haertel (1997) questioned the interpretation of task-sampling variability as the major source of error and suggested that the occasion-sampling variability is an important hidden source of variance given that performance assessments are administered typically on a single occasion. In a typical person $\times$ task $\times$ rater design, the variation of occasions cannot be directly assessed and each of the seven variance components includes the hidden occasion facet. The person component reflects the person $\times$ occasion interaction and "would emphasize the pupil may perform better throughout the week of assessment than usual by virtue of some morale-inducing event or may perform worse because of illness" (Cronbach et al., 1997, p. 384). They further describe the confounding of the person $\times$ task interaction with occasion, indicating that the person $\times$ task interaction:

> consists of two very distinct subcomponents. The pt portion—person-task interaction—describes the reproducible, consistent tendency of the pupil to do especially well on this task and relatively badly on that one. To put it differently, each task taps subskills and motivations on which certain pupils are especially strong and others weak. Second, the e (or pto) portion recognizes fluctuations from occasion to occasion; these arise from mood, distraction, momentary insights and confusions, and, in some tasks, guessing. Whereas, the interaction could be reduced by stratifying tasks in constructing the instrument and recognizing the stratification in the analysis, the e variance could be reduced by lengthening the test. (Cronbach et al., 1997, p. 385)

McBee and Barnes (1998) examined the generalizability of four 8th grade mathematics performance tasks over occasions. Two of the tasks were designed to be very similar so that the effects of task similarity on intertask consistency could be examined in addition to the stability of performance over time. In a person × occasion × task × rater ($p \times o \times t \times r$) generalizability study using only the two similar tasks, the *pt* variance component accounted for less than 1% of the total score variability, whereas the *pto* variance component accounted for 39% of the total score variability. When occasion was excluded from the analysis, the *pt* variance component accounted for 45% of the total variability for the first occasion and 38% for the second occasion. In the person × occasion × task × rater generalizability study using all four tasks, the two very similar tasks and the other two tasks, the results were quite different. The *pt* variance component accounted for 22% of the total score variability and the *pto* variance component accounted for 36% of the total score variability. When occasion was not included in the analysis, the *pt* variance component accounted for 65% of the total score variability on the first occasion and 57% on the second occasion. They further showed that for a design with one occasion, two raters, and using data from only the two similar tasks to obtain a generalizability coefficient of .80, 20 tasks are needed. Under the same scenario but using data from all four tasks, 32 tasks are needed to obtain a generalizability coefficient of .72.

Shavelson and his colleagues (Shavelson et al., 1993; Shavelson, Ruiz-Primo, & Wiley, 1999) provided evidence that large task sampling variability in science performance assessments was due to variability in both the person × task interaction and the person × task × occasion interaction. They conducted a person × rater × task × occasion generalizability study, using data from a science performance assessment administered to 5th and 6th grade students (Shavelson et al., 1993). The *pt* variance component accounted for 32% of the total variability whereas, the *pto* variance component accounted for 59% of the total variability. In a reanalysis of 6th grade science performance assessment data from Ruiz-Primo, Baxter, and Shavelson (1993), Shavelson et al. (1999) provided additional support for the large effects due to occasion. In a person × task × occasion × method generalizability study, the *pt* variance component accounted for 26% of the total variability and the *pto* variance component accounted for 31% of the total variability, indicating that there was a tendency for students to change their approach to each task from occasion to occasion. The variance component for the *po* effect was zero. In summary, "even though students approached the tasks differently each time they were tested, the aggregate level of their performance, averaged over the tasks, did not vary from one occasion to another (Shavelson et al., 1999, pp. 64–65). The results of these studies demonstrate that ignoring occasion in the design leads to an overestimate of the generalizability coefficient as Cronbach et al. (1997) warned.

Webb, Schlackman, and Surgrue (2000) examined the stability of both hands-on and paper-and-pencil science performance tasks administered to 7th and 8th grade students. The hands-on tasks required students to use manipulatives, whereas the paper-and-pencil tasks depicted the equipment in drawings. For the person × task × rater × occasion generalizability study, the *pto* variance component accounted for 24% and 26% of the total score variability, whereas the *pt* variance component accounted for 12% and 0% of the total variability for the hands-on and paper-and-pencil tasks, respectively. When occasion was not included in the analysis, the person variance component accounted again for the largest percent of the total variability, ranging from 58% to 74% for the various combinations of format and occasion. The *pt* variance component accounted for the next largest amount of total score variability, 41% on the first occasion and 33% on the second occasion for the hands-on task, and for the paper-and-pencil task it accounted for 26% of the total score variability on each occasion. All other effects were negligible.

Webb et al. (2000) suggested that the substantial reduction of the *pt* variance component when occasion was introduced in their design, as compared to other two studies (McBee & Barnes, 1998; Shavelson et al., 1999), was due in part to their tasks being much more similar than the tasks used in the other studies. To obtain a generalizability coefficient of .80 for the hands-on method, three tasks were needed for the person × task × rater design, whereas eight tasks were needed for the person × task × rater × occasion design (Webb et al., 2000). For the paper-and-pencil method, a generalizability coefficient of .85 was obtained with two tasks for the person × task × rater design, whereas four tasks were needed to obtain a generalizability coefficient of .80 for the person × task × rater × occasion design. Ignoring occasion in the design led to an inflated generalizability coefficient, regardless of method, hands-on or paper-and-pencil versions of the assessment task. The results from Webb et al. (2000) are consistent with the results of Shavelson et al. (1999) and McBee and Barnes (1998), indicating that when occasion is included in the design, the *pt* variance component reduces substantially and the *pto* variance component contributes the most to the total score variability. In all of these studies, the largest source of error variance is due to a combination of task sampling and occasion sampling.

As suggested by Cronbach et al. (1997) and Shavelson et al. (1999), a potential solution to the relatively high task-sampling variability in performance assessments is to stratify tasks. Using existing science performance assessment data, Shavelson et al. (1999) conducted a person × task nested within stratum × occasion × method ($p \times (t{:}s) \times o \times m$) generalizability study. The *p(t:s)o* variance component was the largest source of error accounting for 40% of the total score variability as compared to 30% for the *pto* in the design without strata. Combining the *p(t:s)* and the *p(t:s)o* variance components to obtain an estimate when occasion is a facet accounted for 45% of the total score variability. The combination of the *pt* and *pto* variance components in the design without strata accounted for 57% of the total variability. Given that the difference in task-sampling variability is reduced only slightly, they suggest that "Stratifying tasks to reduce the person × task variability will only minimally, at best, address the large *pto* component" (Shavelson et al., 1999, p. 68). They further illustrated that to obtain a generalizability coefficient of .80, assuming one occasion, one method, and two tasks per strata, a total of 38 tasks would be needed in the stratified design, whereas only 27 tasks would be needed in a design without strata. Other research has provided additional evidence that stratification does not solve the task-sampling variability in performance assessments (McBee & Barnes, 1998; Solano-Flores, Jovanovic, Shavelson, & Bachman, 1999). As summarized by Shavelson et al. (1999), increasing the number of tasks will reduce measurement error, whereas stratification of tasks due to the occasion confound will not reduce measurement error.

4.1.3. Error Due to Assessment Method

Other research has examined the exchangeability of different methods for assessment. The results from the Shavelson et al. (1993) study suggested that scores on notebook surrogates of 5th and 6th grade science performance assessments were comparable to observation scores on the hands-on tasks (correlations ranged from .71 to .84), but scores obtained from computer simulation, short answer items, and multiple-choice items were not comparable to the observation scores on the hands-on tasks (correlations ranged from .38 to .55). However, in a follow-up study Shavelson et al. (1999) included occasion as a source of measurement error which led to a change in the interpretation of the exchangeability of assessment methods of the study conducted by Shavelson et al. (1993). When occasion was included as a source of error, they concluded that direct observation, notebook, and computer simulations methods are equally exchangeable. Paper-and-pencil methods were not exchangeable with performance assessments. Regardless of method, however, they indicated that student performance across methods was not stable.

The exchangeability of using performance assessments and multiple-choice tests in predicting college performance has also been examined. Bridgeman and Lewis (1994) examined the ability of both essay and multiple-choice scores on the advanced placement exams in American History, European History, English Language and Composition, and Biology in predicting freshman grades. They found that multiple-choice scores from the 1984 American History exam, the 1985 American History Exam, and the Biology Exam had slightly higher correlations with freshman grade point averages—.32, .31, and .36, respectively—than essay scores from the same exams—.23, .25, and .30, respectively. The results were more similar for the European History Exam, in that there was a .25 correlation for the multiple-choice score and a .29 correlation for the essay score. The English Language Exam produced similar correlations with grade point averages for the multiple-choice score, .26, and the essay score, .25. More importantly, the correlations between essay scores with grades from courses most relevant to the exam were essentially equivalent to correlations with multiple-choice scores and the exam. For example, there were no significant differences between the correlations for history GPA and the essay and multiple-choice History AP scores (correlations with essay scores ranged from .22 to .31 and correlations with multiple-choice scores ranged from .20 to .35). After correcting for the unreliability of the multiple-choice scores and the essay scores of the 1984 American History Exam, the correlation between a perfectly reliable essay test and the history grades was .44 while the correlation of a perfectly reliable multiple-choice test with history grades was .31. These results provide external validity evidence for using the AP essay scores to predict freshman grade point average.

4.1.4. Error Due to Rater Occasion

The occasion source of error may be due to the occasion of test administration as well as the occasion of rating student performance. The occasion on which the ratings are obtained reflects the stability of judges' ratings over time. As an example, when a performance assessment is administered on more than one occasion or year, Brennan (1996) points out that the rater occasion facet is complex because "changes in occasion is confounded with change in judges (and perhaps subtle change in rubrics or training procedures)" (p. 46).

For large-scale assessments that are intended to monitor changes in student performance over time, the consistency of scores obtained from raters who evaluated the same student work in different test years needs to be examined (Fitzpatrick, Ercikan, Yen, & Ferrara, 1998). Brennan and Johnson (1995) also cautioned that scores are not stable from occasion to occasion due to differences in raters across occasions. They cite a Johnson and Zwick (1990) technical report illustrating trend data from the 1984 and 1988 NAEP assessment of writing being confounded by variation between the ratings from the 1988 set of raters and the 1984 set of raters. A noticeable difference was observed when 1988 rescores of the 1984 data and original scores assigned to the papers were compared. The results indicated that the 1988 raters tended to be more stringent that the 1984 raters.

Fitzpatrick et al. (1998) examined the consistency of raters over time using scores based on the same student work in different test years for MSPAP. They examined two time periods, each including two consecutive years, 1991–92 and 1992–93. Their results indicated that groups of raters used in different years differed in severity. The absolute mean differences were lower for the 1992–93 analyses than the 1991–92 analyses for all content areas in grades 3, 5, and 8; and the adjusted correlations for the 1992 and 1993 total scores where higher in all content areas assessed in grades 3 and 5. They suggested that this may have been due to the greater continuity of test specifications and scoring of the 1992 and 1993 MSPAP administrations as compared to those of the 1991 and 1992 administrations. Changes in rater severity over years could affect students' proficiency classifications as they suggested, indicating the need to adjust for rater effects during the equating process. They indicated that in their study it was typical for students' second set of total scores to be different from the first set by .1 to .2 SD units on average. As an example, if MSPAP did not adjust for rater effects during the year-to-year equating, about 9% of the grade 5 students would have a different proficiency classification.

They also reported that raters in mathematics produced the most consistent scores, raters in language arts produced the least consistent scores, and the consistency of scores in science and social studies varied over grade levels. They suggested that the nature of the scoring rubrics may have played a role in the differences across content areas in that the mathematics scoring rubrics refer to observable aspects of student performance, whereas the scoring rubrics for language arts refer to abstract qualities that raters need to infer from the student performances. Their results suggest the need for well-trained raters, carefully designed scoring rubrics, and replicable instructions to raters across scoring years (Fitzpatrick et al., 1998).

Most generalizability studies treat raters as being randomly sampled from a universe, and each rater evaluates performance independently on a single occasion. Clauser, Clyman, and Swanson (1999) examined within-rater consistency across rating occasions in the scoring of physicians' patient management skills using computer-based simulations. To examine the effects of rater occasion the raters scored 200 examinees' performances on eight tasks on two separate occasions. Between 6 and 18 months separated the two occasions. The comparison of the variance components from a person × task × rater × occasion generalizability design and a person × task × rater design, treating occasion as a hidden facet in the latter design, revealed that a relatively large percent of the variability was attributable to the hidden occasion facet, which was due to within-rater error reflecting inconsistency across occasions. These results suggest the need to improve not only interrater consistency but also within-rater consistency in training (Clauser et al., 1999).

4.1.5. Error Due to Rater Committee

Many large-scale assessment programs have several groups of committees scoring student performance independently and as a result error may arise due to inconsistency across rater groups. Clauser, Clyman, and Swanson (1999) examined the effects of rater committee in the scoring of physicians' patient management skills using computer-based simulation. To examine the effects of rater committee on performance, they used a person × task × (rater: committee) design. In this study, they calculated the variance components under two scenarios, once after the independent rating within each committee and then again after the raters within each committee discussed their ratings and had an opportunity to adjust their individual ratings if they wanted. For both the initial and final sets of ratings, the variance component due to committee indicated differences in stringency between committees, accounting for approximately 4% to 5% of the total score variation. The *ptc* variance component accounted for 5% of the total variation for the initial ratings and increased to 9% for the final ratings, whereas the *pt(r:c)* variance component accounted for 13% of the variation for the initial ratings and decreased to 3% of the total variation for the final set of ratings.

These results suggest that "committee discussion after initial ratings substantially reduces within-committee differences in ratings ... , but magnifies between-committee differences in these ratings" (Clauser et al., 1999, p. 35). To further illustrate the amount of error due to inconsistency between committees, they compared the generalizability coefficients for two designs, one including the committee facet and one excluding the committee facet, thus treating committee as a hidden facet. The generalizability coefficient for 24 tasks for the design reflecting committee was .70, whereas the coefficient was .87 for the design that treated committee as a hidden facet. These results further demonstrate that generalizability coefficients can be misleading when a relevant facet is not included in the design (Clauser et al., 1999). Typically in many large-scale assessment programs in education, one trainer is used to conduct the overall training session. Factors related to particular aspects of training unique to a trainer may affect the generalizability of scores. Additional studies are needed to examine the stability of scores across rater committees and trainers.

4.1.6. Augmenting Ratings

Other researchers have examined the effect of augmenting ratings on the passing rate and interrater reliability. In a study by Penny, Johnson, and Gordon (2000) using the Georgia 11th grade writing assessment and a four-point analytic rubric including four domains (content and organization, style, conventions of written language, and sentence formation), raters had the opportunity to augment the scores of papers on which the proficiency levels appeared slightly higher or lower than the benchmark papers at the selected level by adding a "+" or "−" to their assigned score. The results indicated that the augmentation did not have an impact on the passing rate, but tended to improve interrater reliability. Penny et al. (2000) suggested that the augmented domain-level scores provided sufficient reliability for providing meaningful feedback to students who did not pass the writing assessment.

4.1.7. Decision Consistency

For large-scale performance assessments that result in high-stakes classification decisions, decision consistency should be evaluated. Linn and Burton (1994) argue that

> although *G* coefficients provide useful information, ... [t]he heavy emphasis on performance standards and on the idea in many recent discussions of assessment that there should be no normative limit to the number of students who meet the standards suggests the need to focus on standard errors and decision consistency rather than on a coefficient that applies to consistency across the distribution of scores. (p. 5)

In a testing scenario where students are classified as proficient or not proficient, inconsistency is due to false negative decisions in which examinees' observed scores are classified as not proficient but their true scores reflect proficiency and false positive decisions in which examinees' observed scores are considered proficient but their true scores lead to a not proficient decision. Using variance components based on Baker's (1992) work on performance assessments in history and a simulated set of data, Linn and Burton (1994) demonstrated that with only two tasks and two raters, there would be a two-point spread of uncertainty between the maximum fail and minimum pass scores on a six-point scale at the 90% confidence level. Further, ten tasks would be required to get a band of uncertainty of about 1.5 points. For a comprehensive discussion on decision consistency, the reader is referred to the chapter on reliability by Haertel (this volume).

4.2. The Application of Item Response Theory to Performance Assessments

IRT models involve a class of mathematical models that may be used to estimate test performance using characteristics of persons that are presumed to underlie performance, and characteristics of items (e.g., item difficulty level). In the context of educational assessment, the models use one or more ability parameters and various item parameters to model or predict item responses (Embretson & Reise, 2000; Hambleton & Swaminathan, 1985). These parameters in conjunction with a mathematical function (normal ogive or logistic functions) may be used to model the probability of a score response as a function of ability. In the models, the item parameters determine the shape of the function. A slope parameter is used to describe how the probability of a response changes as a function of ability (i.e., sensitivity of item to changes in ability), and reflects the degree to which the item is related to the underlying ability or abilities being measured. Parameters related to the score levels are used to describe the probability of responding in one score category as opposed to other score levels.

The remainder of this section summarizes the more commonly applied models to scale performance assessments, as well as other models that have appeared in the literature. Issues that are unique to the context of scaling performance assessments as well as evaluating the applicability of IRT models to performance assessments are also discussed. For detail about the various IRT models, the reader is referred to the chapter on IRT by Yen and Fitzpatrick (this volume).

4.2.1. IRT Models for Performance Assessments

The more commonly applied models assume one underlying ability dimension determines performance or items are homogeneous in their measurement of an ability (Allen & Yen, 1979). These models include: (1) the graded response (GR) model (Samejima, 1969, 1996); (2) the partial credit (PC) model (Masters, 1982); (3) the generalized partial credit (GPC) model (Muraki, 1992); and (4) the general nominal response model proposed by Bock (1972). All of these models accommodate ordinal response scales and therefore can be used with performance assessments. For example, Lane, Stone, Ankenmann, and Liu (1995) discussed the application of the GR model to a mathematics performance assessment, and Allen, Johnson, Mislevy, and Thomas (1994) discussed the application of the generalized partial credit model to NAEP. Although the nominal response model was originally developed for multiple-choice items and capturing information about distractors, Thissen (1993) has described applications of this model to polytomously scored assessments. However, the nominal response IRT model may not be preferred with performance assessments due to the relatively large number of parameters to be estimated.

Derivatives of these models have been discussed where the score category parameters are separated into a location parameter for the item and a set of category threshold parameters that are common to a group of items (modified GR model [Muraki, 1990]; Rating Scale (RS) model described by Andrich [1978] and Masters and Wright [1984]). The location parameter locates the item on the ability continuum being measured and thus reflects the relative difficulty level of the item. A model with a common set of category threshold parameters was argued to be more consistent with responses to rating scales in questionnaires where a set of items share the same response scale. The advantages to these types of models are that fewer parameters require estimation in comparison to standard IRT models, and the model allows for the separate estimation of a location parameter. In the context of performance assessments, if a general rubric is used as the basis for developing specific item rubrics, then the response scales and the differences between score levels may be the same across the set of items. In this case a rating scale or modified graded IRT model could be explored, although use of these models has received little attention with performance assessments.

There are a number of other models that have been successfully applied to dichotomously scored tests. These methods are receiving more attention in the literature, and it is reasonable to expect increased interest in applying these models to performance assessments. One of these methods involves the application of multidimensional IRT (MIRT) models, which assume more than one ability determines item performance. Individuals bring to the testing environment a variety of cognitive skills and some of these skills are separately or in combination relevant to different tasks (Reckase, 1997a). Although unidimensional IRT models can be applied to subsets of tasks that measure one dimension, this approach ignores the potentially valuable information contained in the correlations between dimensions (Segall, 2000). The reader is referred to Ackerman, Gierl, and Walker (2003) for an introduction to MIRT models and to other research for a more technical treatment (Ackerman, 1994, 1996; McDonald, 1999, 2000; Reckase, 1997a, 1997b).

Another class of methods involves nonparametric IRT models, which describe the probability of a response as a function of the ability being measured without specifying a functional form to the relationship. One advantage of nonparametric IRT models is that they are less restrictive than parametric models, and therefore may fit items for which the functional relationship defined by a parametric IRT model may not be appropriate. However, nonparametric IRT models do not provide point estimates and interval scales for the ability being measured. The reader is referred to Sijtsma and Molenaar (2002) for a treatment of nonparametric models to both dichotomous and polytomous item responses as well as to Sijtsma and van der Ark (2000) for a discussion of issues related to the application of nonparametric polytomous IRT models.

Finally, advances in cognitive psychology have led to a deeper understanding of learning and performance assessment provides the opportunity to measure complex cognitive skills, solution strategies, and the structure or representation of knowledge (Bennett, Ward, Rock, & Hart, 1990). Assessment designs based on cognitive characteristics could be particularly useful for explanatory and diagnostic purposes (Baxter & Glaser, 1998; Nichols & Sugrue, 1999). However, standard test theories (CTT and IRT) focus on describing individuals' overall proficiency in a content domain and individuals with the same overall proficiency are indistinguishable (Mislevy, Yamamoto, & Anacker, 1992). Thus, cognitive psychologists have argued that different methods and assessment designs are necessary to capture the information from complex assessments.

Many of these methods are based on a decomposition of tasks into the cognitive processes and attributes necessary for successful performance (e.g., Embretson, 1995, 1997; Hoskens & De Boeck, 2001; Tatsuoka, 1983, 1990, 1995). However, to date, most of these methods have been demonstrated only with dichotomously scored items (e.g., Tatsuoka, 1990; Tatsuoka & Boodoo, 2000; Tatsuoka, Corter, Dean, & Grossman, 2003). In addition, to derive the most benefit from these approaches, test developers should identify the important cognitive characteristics to be measured as part of the conceptual framework and test specifications (Gierl, Leighton, & Hunka, 2000). For more information about different approaches to cognitive measurement the reader is referred to Mislevy and colleagues (1996, 1999, 2002). In this volume Mislevy describes measurement models that reflect the perspective and advances in cognitive psychology.

4.2.2. Using Computer Programs for Scaling Performance Assessments

Yen and Fitzpatrick in their chapter on item response theory (this volume) discussed the more widely used software for applying IRT models to performance assessments. While software is available for estimating MIRT models for dichotomous data (TESTFACT [Wilson et al., 2003]; NOHARM [Fraser, 1988]), software developments for multidimensional polytomous item responses have been limited. Extensions of the methods in TESTFACT to polytomous item responses have been discussed (Muraki & Bejar, 1995; Muraki & Carlson, 1995) and a beta version of such an extension is available (POLYFACT [Muraki, 1993]). Since factor analytic models provide the foundation for some multidimensional IRT models (McDonald, 1999; McDonald & Mok, 1995; Takane & Leeuw, 1987), factor analytic methods for categorical items may prove useful (e.g., MPlus [Muthen & Muthen, 1998]). As noted by Swygert, McLeod, and Thissen (2001), constraints such as those imposed on factor structures in confirmatory factor analysis eliminate the complications associated with indeterminacy and arbitrary rotations in standard factor analytic methods.

With regard to applying unidimensional IRT models to performance assessments, any of the models can be reasonably applied using proven software. For assessments that are administered on a smaller scale, Reise and Yu (1990) recommended a sample of at least 500 examinees for the graded IRT model. Others have suggested ratios of the sample size to the total number of item parameters or to the number of score levels are more important for accurate parameter estimation (Choi, Cook, & Dood, 1997; De Ayala & Sava-Bolesta, 1999; DeMars, 2003). For example, De Ayala and Sava-Bolesta suggested a ratio of 10:1 as a general heuristic for the number of examinees relative to the total number of item parameters (number of parameters per item times number of items) if the sample is normally distributed, and a ratio that is somewhat greater for nonnormal examinee distributions. However, what may be more important is the nature of the response distributions for the score scale. If there are no or few responses for any particular score category even in large samples, no reasonable estimate of a category threshold can be expected. Embretson and Reise (2000) recommended administering the tests to heterogeneous samples so that responses are distributed over the entire score scale for items.

4.2.3. Issues in Scaling Performance Assessments

In this volume, Yen and Fitzpatrick discuss general issues in the application of IRT models. However, there are two issues that are related specifically to performance assessments. First, performance assessment tasks are typically combined with multiple-choice items in assessments and the combination of item formats presents some unique challenges. Second, models being applied to assessments that use human raters to score item responses need to consider the function and effect of raters on the assessment process. Each of these topics is considered below.

4.2.3.1. Combining Performance Assessment Tasks and Multiple-Choice Items

Performance assessment tasks have been combined with multiple-choice items in assessments to capitalize on the advantages of each type of approach. Performance assessment tasks, for example, offer the potential for more direct assessment, more complex items, and more response information. Multiple-choice items, for example, offer the potential for more domain coverage, thus yielding higher reliability and more precise individual-level scores. An assessment that combines these different item formats offers the potential for more direct assessment, more complex items, more response information, and at the same time adequate domain coverage and high reliability for individual-level scores.

Different IRT models may be used to scale simultaneously a combination of different item formats using existing software applications, although as noted by Yen and Fitzpatrick in their chapter (this volume), it is recommended that compatible IRT models be used. For example, if a Rasch model is used with the dichotomous items, a PC model should be used with the performance assessment tasks. The advantage of an IRT approach is that scores on the same scale may be obtained for any combination of item types (Thissen, Nelson, Rosa, & McLeod, 2001).

However, for unidimensional IRT applications, the assumption is that one dimension is being measured "essentially" and it may be that the items associated with the different formats are measuring different dimensions. Any "method factor" associated with the different item formats should also be explicitly examined as part of an evaluation of the dimensionality in the item responses. In addition, although a Rasch or one-parameter model would assume equal slope parameters for items within an item format, the assumption of equal slope parameters across the different formats may be tenuous.

In many of the mixed item type assessments, the use of multiple-choice items dominates the assessment in order to improve the precision of individual scores. One way to increase the contribution of performance assessment tasks to a total score is to increase the number of performance assessment tasks. Although this has practical implications with regard to testing-time requirements, score interpretations from performance assessment tasks may be more valid in regard to the purpose of the assessment. It is also possible to increase the contribution of performance assessment tasks by differentially weighting the different components (Sykes & Hou, 2003). Implicit weighting occurs through a standard application of an IRT model. In this approach, the item discrimination parameter in conjunction with pattern scoring weights items relative to their relationship to the underlying ability being measured. Specific weights can also be utilized with IRT models to explicitly weight items. For example, items can be weighted relative to the amount of testing time required for the different item types, or weighted relative to the total score points contributed by the different items.

When combining item formats in an assessment, however, weighting the different components (performance assessment and multiple-choice items) raises methodological and policy issues. When the weights are selected by committees or based on criteria such as administration time, there is the real chance that the reliability of a composite score will be less than the reliability of one of the components (Wainer & Thissen, 2001). Weighting components based on testing time may also be unjustifiable since different types of items yield different amounts of information for fixed amounts of time. In writing assessments that involve mixed item formats, for example, the essay component is typically less reliable and hence provides less information not because items are scored by judges but because there is a small number of essays that are scored. As for other performance assessment tasks, the person × task interaction is one of the largest sources of error for writing samples—that is, there is a random association between the prompt that is selected and the person that in combination reduces the reliability.

Wainer and Thissen (2001) discussed the reliability of composite scores and further discussed a method for determining a minimum weight for the more reliable component of items when considering weights from unequally reliable subsets of items. They argue that weights should be chosen such that the reliability of the composite scores should be at least as reliable as the component with the highest reliability. As an example, they present the hypothetical case of a writing assessment that consists of two components: a 45-minute multiple-choice component (coefficient $\alpha = .85$) and a 20-minute essay component (scorer reliability = .6) that are correlated .43. If the two components, multiple-choice and essay, are weighted 2:1 to reflect the approximate ratio in testing time, the reliability of the composite score is .85, which is equal to the multiple-choice component by itself. Although the essay component does not enhance overall test score reliability, the validity of score interpretations may be enhanced.

Wainer and Thissen also point out, however, that weights based on mathematical solutions should serve only as a guide for choosing weights. Evaluating different weighting schemes once an assessment is in place is important in determining the effects of different schemes on the reliability and validity of test scores. As an example, Sykes and Hou (2003) found that with a writing assessment explicit weighting of constructed-response items lowered test reliability slightly but improved measurement in the lower range of ability. Kane and Case (2004) argue that simply selecting weights to maximize reliability may not be a useful strategy. They found that weights that maximize reliability are not likely to be the same as those that maximize validity. They also found that the curve representing the relationship between reliability and test component weights was fairly flat. Thus, while choosing less optimal weights may yield slightly lower reliability, there is the potential for gains in validity.

4.2.3.2. Modeling Rater Effects in IRT Models

Engelhard (2002) referred to performance assessments as "rater-mediated" since performance assessments do not provide direct information about the constructs of interest but mediated information through interpretations by raters. He further provided a useful conceptual model for performance assessments in which the observed performance is dependent not only on the measured construct of interest (e.g., math ability) but on rater severity, task difficulty, and the structure of the rating scale (e.g., number of score levels). While task difficulty and the rating scale are under the control of test developers, a major concern with rater-scored assessments is that raters bring a variety of potential sources of construct-irrelevant variance to the rating process. Some examples that Engelhard discusses include differential interpretation of the score scale by raters, halo effects, assignment of different ratings to males versus females, and bias in rater interpretations about the difficulty level of the tasks. These biases contribute to measurement error and can result in less precision in proficiency estimates, lower reliability, and unfair evaluations.

While generalizability studies are important for the design of performance assessments and quantifying sources of error (e.g., error due to item, rater, or occasion samples), it is also important that measurement models applied to performance assessments incorporate rater effects and behaviors into the prediction of performance. Linacre's work (1989) represented the first attempt to model rater effects in IRT models. The model he describes, the many-facet Rasch measurement model (MFRM), is an extended version of the Rating Scale model and implemented in the computer program FACETS (Linacre & Wright, 1992). The MFRM model can be used to detect a number of rater errors. Rater severity or leniency (i.e., the tendency of raters to consistently provide high or low ratings) can be detected using estimates of a rater effect for each rater and estimating the precision of the estimates. Interaction effects can also be modeled to evaluate, for example, whether the application of the scoring scale is invariant over raters or over items and raters. Also, if gender and time facets are included in the model, interaction effects involving these facets and the rater facet could be examined to explore rater bias related to gender or "rater drift" over time. For more detail about the MFRM model as applied to performance assessments and indices to identify various rater errors, the reader is referred to Engelhard (1997, 2002).

One problem with the MFRM model is that it fails to account for the dependency among rater response judgments and research has found that proficiency estimates have lower than expected standard errors (Bock, Brennan, & Muraki, 1999; Donoghue & Hombo, 2000; Junker & Patz, 1998; Patz, 1996; Wilson & Hoskens, 2001). In response to this problem, Patz (1996) and Patz, Junker, and Johnson (2002) discussed the hierarchical structure to performance assessment data (i.e., multiple ratings are nested within item responses that are nested within person parameters) and introduced a hierarchical rating (HR) model to account for the dependencies between rater judgments. This model as well as others (e.g., Verhelst & Verstralen, 2001) introduces an additional parameter into an IRT model that can be considered an "ideal rating" or expected score for an individual. Random errors (e.g., lack of consistency) and systematic errors (e.g., rater tendencies) cause variability in the parameter estimates and reflect rater error or unreliability. These researchers also discuss how covariates introduced to predict rater behaviors can be incorporated into the HR model. For example, parameters could be modeled that examine the effects of rater and examinee background variables or item features. Consideration is also given as to how raters' use of the score scale can be evaluated. For example, differences in the reliability for each of the score levels can be examined. While these types of models extend the HR model in useful ways, research related to these developments is limited. In addition, Bayesian methods that require use of Markov Chain Monte Carlo techniques are required to estimate the models (cf. Patz et al., 2002).

4.2.4. Evaluating the Applicability of IRT Models to Performance Assessments

The appropriateness of using an IRT model to scale item response data affects the validity of inferences based on model parameter estimates. Hambleton and Swaminathan (1985) suggested that model assumptions as well as the degree to which properties of the model are attained (e.g., item and ability parameter invariance) needs to be evaluated. While a description of the procedures for validating IRT models is provided in the chapter by Yen and Fitzpatrick (this volume), there are issues related to validating applications of IRT models that relate specifically to performance assessments. These issues are the focus of this section.

4.2.4.1. Evaluating Dimensionality

While the assessment of dimensionality is relevant to all types of assessments, performance assessments may have unique characteristics that impact the dimensionality of the assessment. Constructed-response items are often designed to capture more complex skills in a more contextual framework (e.g., conducting a science experiment). In addition to the diverse processes being assessed in more complex performance assessment tasks, the development of cognitive skills reflects diverse learning experiences that may impact the number of dimensions measured by a test (Snow & Lohman, 1989). Thus, the empirical analysis of dimensionality should be "guided by substantive hypotheses, analyses, and interpretations" (Ackerman et al., 2003). This can be in the form of a content analysis conducted either by reviewing items and/or the test specifications, or by conducting a cognitive task analysis that examines the skills and processes necessary for performance.

In addition to the stimulus characteristics of performance tasks, the characteristics of scoring schemes may impact the dimensionality of the assessment. With some performance tasks, several different skills may be targeted. For example, mathematics problems may not only require mathematical solutions but also the communication of mathematics through explanations. Analytic rubrics could be developed to assess the communication aspect separate from the procedural component, but holistic rubrics may also be developed to reflect the totality of the response. Thus, holistic scoring rubrics may reflect one or more traits or dimensions on which student responses are scored. In addition, Reckase (1997b) discussed the problem that different points on the score scale may reflect different combinations of skills. The example he provided as an illustration involves a writing assessment in which lower score levels may focus on basic literacy skills and upper score levels may focus on logic, organization, and style.

Because performance assessment tasks typically require more time to respond, these tasks are often combined with multiple-choice tasks in order to obtain more accurate estimates of ability at the individual level. However, performance assessment tasks may assess different aspects of a construct being measured than multiple-choice items. Researchers have attempted to determine whether dimensions measured by multiple-choice tests generalize to performance assessments (e.g., Ayala et al., 2002). Traub (1993) summarized research examining the equivalence of multiple-choice and constructed-response tasks and concluded that the evidence is mixed and beset by methodological problems. When differences exist, they are likely due to the different processes being assessed under the different formats. Thus, when performance assessment tasks are combined with multiple-choice tasks, unidimensional IRT models may not be appropriate.

Traditional linear factor analysis has been used to evaluate the dimensionality of dichotomously scored test items and problems with these methods have been discussed (e.g.,

Ackerman et al., 2003; Bock, Gibbons, & Muraki, 1988; Swygert et al., 2001). While some of these problems may extend directly to performance assessment tasks (e.g., non-normality of response distributions), others may not (e.g., as the number of responses on the ordinal scale increases for performance assessment tasks, a continuous scale is better approximated).

As an alternative, procedures designed specifically for categorical response scales (Christoffersson, 1975; Muthen, 1978) have proved useful. For example, Lane et al. (1995) analyzed several forms of a mathematics performance assessment and found a one-dimensional model "fit" the observed test response data. However, the pattern of factor loadings revealed the possible presence of higher dimensionality. Tasks that required students to provide conceptual explanations exhibited lower factor loadings, whereas tasks with higher factor loadings required students to display their mathematical solutions only. Flora and Curran (2004) recently evaluated these alternative methods and found that the methods were robust to "moderate levels of nonnormality," and that robust weighted least squares (WLS) methods performed well across a variety of simulation conditions.

MIRT models have also been used to assess dimensionality. As discussed by McDonald and Mok (1995), some MIRT models are equivalent to nonlinear factor analysis models. One advantage of MIRT models over linear factor analytic methods is that information from individual response patterns are analyzed as opposed to information from correlation matrices. In addition, nonlinear models may reflect better the relationship between item performance and the underlying ability (Hattie, 1985). These models have been used primarily to assess dimensionality of dichotomously scored tests in which the items reflect different skills, knowledge, or cognitive processes (Embretson & Reise, 2000). As discussed above, programs for polytomous MIRT models are limited.

Stout (1987, 1990) described a nonparametric test for the "essential unidimensionality" that evaluates the presence of a dominant factor and possible nuisance factors in a set of item responses. Stout's procedure has been studied extensively in the context of dichotomously scored items (Hattie, Krakowski, Rogers, & Swaminathan, 1996; Stout, Douglas, Kim, Roussos, & Zhang, 1996). However, there has been less research in the context of polytomously scored items. Nandakumar, Yu, Li, and Stout (1998) evaluated the use of this test with polytomously scored items and found that the procedure was effective in detecting lack of unidimensionality for simulated two-dimensional datasets. They further found that power increased with sample size, test length, and decreased correlations between the ability dimensions. These findings identify possible issues with the application of Stout's method to performance assessments. First, it is likely that ability dimensions will be moderately correlated. Second, unless the performance assessment items are used in conjunction with multiple-choice items, the performance assessment may consist of a small set of items. This has been found to be a limiting factor to the procedure (Stout et al., 1996).

In response to problems in assessing dimensionality in educational testing applications, the application of hierarchical cluster analysis has been explored. Roussos (1995) discussed the use of a different proximity measure for dichotomously scored items, which was later extended to polytomously scored items (Tay-Lim, 1999; Tay-Lim & Stone, 2000). One advantage to cluster analysis methods is that these methods always identify distinct clusters of items irrespective of the dimensionality of the data (Ackerman et al., 2003). A problem with factor analytic approaches to evaluating dimensionality is that these methods focus on assessing simple or approximately simple structure where item responses are determined primarily by one of several dimensions (Ackerman et al., 2003). Due to the more limited focus of these methods, they may not be as useful for exploring structure evidence for more complex performance assessments. For example, Tay-Lim (1999) identified six clusters or dimensions using HCA with constructed response items from the New Standards Mathematics Reference Examination (Resnick, Briars, & Lesgold, 1992). Based on a task analysis, clusters appeared to be classified based on conceptual and procedural complexity.

The presence of multidimensionality in responses to performance assessments may be problematic since the software to estimate models for polytomous responses is more limited and not well studied. However, ignoring the presence of multidimensionality may complicate test development efforts. For example, Luecht and Miller (1992) found decreased item information when unidimensional models were fit to multidimensional polytomous data. The presence of multidimensionality may also impact the comparison of different forms of performance assessments. Muraki, Hombo, and Lee (2000) discussed this issue as well as approaches that could be used to equate or link performance assessments. Finally, Tate (2002) summarized research based on dichotomous responses that indicates ability estimates derived from unidimensional models will typically "reflect the target composite of abilities when the test is multidimensional due to test structure" (p. 188). This finding is conditional on the presence of moderate to strong correlations between the ability dimensions. If this condition does not hold, the ability estimate will represent only one of the component abilities and the validity of any inferences about the composite score will be threatened. This research may generalize to performance assessments, in which case the application of unidimensional models may be reasonably robust. However, even if unidimensional models are found to be robust, analyses examining multidimensionality are useful for establishing validity evidence for score interpretations.

4.2.4.2. Differential Item Functioning and Performance Assessments

Numerous methods have been developed to detect the statistical presence of DIF. However, to uncover the characteristics of items that are responsible for DIF, item content needs to be analyzed in addition to student performance (Lane, Wang, & Magone, 1996). This section focuses on the methods for assessing statistical DIF with performance assessments and the characteristics of performance assessments that may affect methods for assessing DIF.

All DIF methods examine differences in item performance for targeted subpopulations (e.g., males and females; Caucasian and African-American) at comparable levels of the ability being measured by the test. By conditioning on the ability being measured, any differences in performance cannot be attributed to differences in ability. A "matching variable" that is related to the ability being measured is used to determine comparable ability levels. DIF methods for dichotomous items have traditionally used the total score for the test or some function of the total score (e.g., IRT ability parameter estimate) as a basis for the matching variable. Note that for a test that is more multidimensional in nature, Dorans and Holland (1993) discussed that it may be necessary to use different matching criteria for subsets of items.

Differences in item performance are typically measured by comparing the probability of a correct response or odds of a correct response across different values of the matching variable in important subpopulations. Since subpopulation membership reflects an additional person characteristic beyond ability level, DIF assessment involves evaluating the multidimensionality of score responses. Thus, factor analytic methods can also be used to compare the structure or invariance of the responses across groups (Glockner-Rist & Hoijtink, 2003). Penfield and Lam (2000) presented a useful overview of the evaluation of DIF in performance assessments and a summary of the relevant issues. Potenza and Dorans (1995) presented a more technical discussion of these methods as well as issues in their application to polytomously scored tests.

Penfield and Lam (2000) discuss that the total score or a function of the total score is an appropriate matching variable for a dichotomously scored test since the total score typically exhibits high reliability, reflects objective scoring, and is typically unidimensional in nature. However, scores based primarily on performance tasks typically exhibit lower reliability than multiple-choice items since performance assessments generally involve more complex diverse tasks and therefore consist of fewer and more heterogeneous items. In addition, some degree of subjectivity may enter into the scoring of performance assessment tasks (Miller & Welch, 1993). As Zwick (1990) discussed, for DIF analyses, lower reliability in the matching variable increases the chances of falsely identifying items as DIF.

As suggested by Miller and Welch (1993), scores from a multiple-choice test that presumably measures the same trait as the performance assessment could be used as a matching variable. However, these researchers found that scores from a performance assessment may correlate only moderately with scores from a multiple-choice assessment. In addition, studies have found that females perform better on constructed-response items than multiple-choice items (Mazzeo, Schmitt, & Bleistein, 1991; Petersen & Livingston, 1982). Combined with the finding that the construct being measured by constructed responses and multiple-choice items is often different, it may be difficult to use multiple-choice tests as a matching criterion with performance assessments.

For performance tasks, comparing performance across groups is also complicated by the number of score levels for polytomous items. For the dichotomous case, the probability of a correct response or the odds of a correct versus incorrect response can be easily compared for different groups. For example, one can examine whether the advantage of performance (e.g., probability of a correct response) by one group is relatively uniform over the range of values for the matching variable. However, for polytomous items with more than two score levels, there is no simple odds ratio or probability that can be used to reflect item performance. Rather, item category performance information is available. This complicates the identification of DIF in performance assessments since DIF and different types of DIF (uniform and non-uniform) could be observed for some score levels but not others. Finally, the potential for sparseness in the tables used to relate item score response and subpopulation membership at different levels of the matching variable increases as the number of score levels increases.

Penfield and Lam (2000) provided a useful summary of research evaluating the relative advantages and disadvantages of the different methods as applied to performance assessments. These researchers argue that a combination of methods may prove a useful strategy for investigating DIF; however, two methods appear to offer advantages. The method based on regressing item performance onto a CTT true score estimate for the matching variable (Chang, Mazzeo, & Roussos, 1996) offers the advantage of being robust to differences in the mean abilities for the groups being compared. This is a significant advantage since comparing minority and non-minority groups typically reflects overall differences in ability. If the abilities of the groups being compared are approximately equal (e.g., groups based on gender), then a less computationally intensive method based on mean differences may be preferred (e.g., Dorans & Schmitt, 1993). However, neither of these methods can detect non-uniform DIF. To detect non-uniform DIF, IRT-based or logistic regression methods are required and have been found to be effective.

4.2.4.3. Evaluating Model-Data-Fit

A number of tests have been developed to evaluate the Rasch model specifically. These tests are oriented to evaluating a test or evaluating items and focus, for example, on the sufficiency of the sum score, montonicity of item response functions, and the assumption of parallel item response functions (Glas & Verhelst, 1995). However, model-data-fit for the broader class of IRT models has traditionally been assessed for individual items using two-way tables with rows defined by ability (θ) subgroups and columns defined by score levels. The evaluation involves estimating item and θ parameters; constructing an observed score response distribution by cross-classifying examinees using their θ estimate and score response; constructing an expected score response distribution based on the IRT model, item parameter estimates, and a θ level for ability subgroups; and finally, comparing predictions with observed results using a goodness-of-fit (chi-square) statistic (Bock, 1972; Yen, 1981), or examining residuals (Hambleton & Swaminathan, 1985).

Although a number of issues related to using chi-square tests to evaluate model-data-fit have been discussed (e.g., Stone, 2000), evaluating model-data-fit given imprecise ability estimates is a problem most relevant to performance assessments. Stone, Mislevy, and Mazzeo (1994) argued that uncertainty in ability estimation may affect the approximation of the goodness-of-fit statistic to the null distribution. This is particularly likely in tests that are shorter in length, such as performance assessments and assessments incorporating multiple-matrix sampling designs, where ability estimates are likely to be more imprecise. Stone and Hansen (2000) investigated use of Bock's chi-squared statistic for tests comprised of 8, 16, and 32 constructed-response items with a five-point score scale. For tests comprised of 32 constructed-response items, results were consistent with the null chi-squared distribution. For tests with 8 or 16 constructed-response items, serious departures from the null chi-squared distribution were observed, resulting in a marked increase in the false identification of misfitting items.

Alternative approaches to assessing IRT model-data-fit have emerged that could be useful in the context of performance assessment. Orlando and Thissen (2000) described a chi-square fit statistic based on observed and expected frequencies for number correct or total (summed) scores. Observed proportions of individuals responding with a particular response (e.g., correct) for each total score group are compared to expectations based on joint likelihood distributions that consider the likelihood for each total score, t, across all possible response patterns for t. The primary advantage of this approach is that observed frequencies are a function of observed data only (Molenaar & Hoijtink, 1990). In a simulation study involving dichotomous items, Orlando and Thissen found that the procedure was unaffected by test length. This result offers a potential advantage in using the method with performance assessments that are typically shorter in length. However, while the procedure can be extended to polytomously scored items, the number of total score groups increases significantly for polytomously scored items. This increases the computational demands considerably and increases the potential for greater sparseness in observed and expected frequencies.

As another alternative, Stone et al. (1994) proposed a goodness-of-fit statistic based on posterior expectations calculated during MML item parameter estimation. Rather than cross-classifying an individual into a single cell of an item fit table based on point estimates of θ, posterior expectations or probabilities that individuals have θ equal to each ability subgroup are used. Uncertainty in θ estimation is reflected by the degree to which the probabilities for an individual are distributed across a number of different θ subgroups. The probabilities can be summed across all examinees to yield "pseudocounts" of the number of examinees at each ability subgroup and each score level, or a pseudo-observed score distribution for the item. The resulting pseudo-observed score distribution can then be compared with a model-based distribution using a chi-square statistic. However, because posterior probabilities for an individual extend over multiple θ subgroups, the pseudocounts are not independent, and alternative hypothesis testing procedures need to be used (e.g., Donoghue & Hombo, 1999, 2001; Stone, 2000; Stone, Ankenmann, Lane, & Liu, 1993).

A recent study (Stone & Zhang, 2003) compared some of these alternative procedures with regard to their methods, properties (Type I error rates and empirical power), available research, and practical issues (computational demands, treatment of missing data, effects of sample size and sparse data, and available computer programs). Results provided support for the alternative methods but more research is required in the context of performance assessments. For example, performance assessment tasks typically have a number of score levels (4 or 5) and sparseness in cell counts will likely result unless very large samples are available.

4.2.4.4. Local Independence

A number of sources may impact the degree to which local item independence applies in performance assessments, or the degree to which an examinee's true score or ability accounts completely for their performance and responses to items do not influence responses to other items (Yen, 1993). Some sources reflect unintended ability dimensions that are measured, external assistance or interference, fatigue, speededness, practice, item or response format, scoring rubrics or raters, or differential item functioning among subpopulations. Many of these reflect unmodeled person characteristics that result in non-zero covariances between items after conditioning on the modeled ability or abilities. Other sources reflect unmodeled item or rater characteristics (e.g., halo or leniency effects).

Some sources also reflect item interactions and may include dependence that results from use of a common passage or context for a set of items, items that are "chained" or organized into steps, and items that share the same scoring rubric. Performance assessments typically measure more complex skills and as a result may involve more complex stimulus materials and a number of items per task. Tasks that require both an answer and an explanation are common in performance assessments. If the answer and explanation are treated as two distinct items, local dependency may be a result of a number of factors. First, there is a clear item chain between the response and explanation. Second, the explanation reflects verbal ability and if the skills being measured by the item reflect more directly a different domain, then the explanation component may be measuring more than one ability domain. Finally, Yen (1993) noted that items that share the same rubric may exhibit dependence because common skills are measured or because common demands are imposed on raters.

Yen and Fitzpatrick in this edited volume discuss the effect of ignoring local item dependence on the measurement properties of an assessment as well statistical tests to detect the presence of local item dependence. Yen (1993) also discussed several approaches to managing local item dependence in performance assessments. Several of these relate to the development of performance assessments: (1) construct independent items; (2) administer the test under appropriate conditions; and (3) combine the grading of locally dependent items in scoring rubrics. Yen indicates that the philosophy underlying performance assessments is often inconsistent with the requirement of independent items. Performance assessments often reflect complex, more direct assessments, and while item interactions result from having multiple items per task, it would be inefficient to include only one item per stimulus. Administering the assessment under appropriate conditions can help avoid effects due to speededness, fatigue, or undesired interference or assistance. Some items that are "chained" (e.g., response and explanation) can be scored using a rubric that combines the responses to the chained items. Yen notes that identifying a priori these types of items may be difficult and could increase the complexity in scoring rubrics. Also, combining the scoring of items that may involve potentially different skills—for example, a numerical answer and an explanation—introduces the possibility of multidimensionality into the combined score.

Other approaches to managing local item dependence can be implemented with performance assessments. If sets of chained items involve the same relationships between items, then it may be possible to construct separate scales. For example, mathematics performance assessments often consist of item pairs in which students provide a numerical answer and then an explanation. If a number of items of this type exist in the assessment, the numerical answer type items can be scaled separately from the explanation type items instead of combining the grading of the items in each scoring rubric.

A commonly used approach with dichotomously scored tests is to construct "testlets" that combine the scores from each set of the dependent items into a single item that is then scaled using polytomous IRT models (Wainer & Kiely, 1987). One problem with this approach is that information contained in the pattern of item responses is discarded (Bradlow, Wainer, & Wang, 1999; Wainer & Wang, 2000). Also, while the creation of testlets with dichotomous items may not yield an excessive number of score levels to analyze with polytomous IRT models, the creation of testlets from sets of performance assessment tasks scored in more than two levels could result in an excessive number of levels. Finally, Wainer and Thissen (2001) also discuss that testlet reliability is typically lower than item-level reliability. Sireci, Thissen, and Wainer (1991) reported a loss of 10% in reliability based on testlet scores when compared to item-level responses for a reading comprehension test with four passages and 5–12 items per passage. This has implications for test development. If the number of items is based on item-level reliability information when in fact testlet scores will be used, the over-estimated reliability will result in the assembly of a shorter test than if the lower testlet reliability was considered.

Another approach to managing locally dependent item responses is to model the dependency of items. While a number of researchers have proposed methods for modeling item dependency (Ackerman & Spray, 1987; Tuerlinckx & Boeck, 2001), the most promising approach is to model the dependency within a modified IRT model (e.g., Bradlow et al., 1999; Wainer, Bradlow, & Du, 2000; Wainer & Wang, 2000). To model the dependency within the IRT model, a random effect reflecting an interaction between each person and a testlet is modeled. Wainer, Bradlow, and Du (2000) showed that "an increasing testlet effect makes an item appear more difficult" (p. 251). Although much of the focus on testlet models has been in the context of dichotomous item responses (e.g., Wainer et al., 2000), more recent studies have evaluated testlet models in the context of polytomous item responses (Dresher, 2003; Wang, Bradlow, & Wainer, 2002). Although these studies suggest modeling the testlet effect directly within the IRT model holds promise, the complexity of the procedures combined with a lack of available software may limit their use until more research has been conducted.

5. CONCLUDING REMARKS

Performance assessments have always been a part of educational assessment. However, in the 1980s there was a renewed interest in performance assessments. Performance assessments were considered to be an integral aspect of educational reform because of their capability of measuring important educational outcomes that cannot be measured by other forms of assessment. Further, they were considered to be a valuable tool for curricular and instructional changes. This led to an increase in the use of performance assessments in large-scale assessment and accountability programs. As an example, in 1992, 70% of the tests administered in statewide assessment programs included multiple-choice items only (Barton & Coley, 1994). Whereas in 2004, approximately 35% of the states had mathematics assessments that included multiple-choice items only, 22% of the states had mathematics assessments that included multiple-choice and short constructed-response items, and 41% of the sates had mathematics assessments that consisted of multiple-choice and extended constructed-response items. In addition, most states use direct assessments of writing as part of their writing assessment programs. However, the extent to which these assessments emulate the criterion of interest varies. As Shepard (2004) has argued, the "token" constructed-response items in large-scale assessment and accountability programs are not enough.

To fully realize the potential of performance assessments, additional research and development is needed. Designing performance assessments that inform instruction in a meaningful way is particularly important. Additional research on how students acquire and develop knowledge and skills within a content domain is needed so that performance assessments can better reflect domain-based theories of achievement and learning and better emulate the performance of interest. In turn, additional work is needed in identifying techniques for designing performance assessments and scoring procedures that capture these domain-based theories of achievement and learning. Developments in computer-based assessment systems that capture cognitive models of achievement and learning are beginning to emerge and hold promise for the future design of performance assessments. Continued work is needed on measurement models and methods that embody the progression of student thinking and reasoning within domains and provide multiple scores that can inform instruction in a meaningful way. Additional work is also needed to ensure that these models and methods are more accessible to the measurement community so that they can be readily implemented in large-scale testing programs.

Finally, in addition to concerns of generalizability and comparability of performance assessments, there are practical issues that need to be addressed such as the time and cost in administering and scoring performance assessments. Automated scoring procedures of essays and complex constructed-responses address some of these practical issues. However, to ensure that these assessments best reflect the performances of interest and inform instruction, a construct-driven approach is needed for the design of the assessments as well as their automated scoring approaches.

REFERENCES

Ackerman, T. A. (1994). Using multidimensional item response theory to understand what items and tests are measuring. *Applied Measurement in Education, 7*(4), 255–278.

Ackerman, T. A. (1996). Graphical representation of mulitidimensional item response theory analyses. *Applied Psychological Measurement, 20,* 311–330.

Ackerman, T. A., Gierl, M. J., & Walker, C. M. (2003). An NCME instructional module on using multidimensional item response theory to evaluate educational and psychological tests. *Educational Measurement: Issues and Practice, 22,* 37–53.

Ackerman, T. A., & Spray, J. A. (1987). *A general model for item dependency* (No. 87–10). Iowa City, IA: American College Testing Program.

Allen, M. J., & Yen, W. M. (1979). *Introduction to measurement theory.* Prospect Heights, IL: Waveland Press.

Allen, N. L., Johnson, E. G., Mislevy, R. J., & Thomas, N. (1994). Scaling procedures. In N. J. Allen, D. L. Kline, & C. A. Zelenak (Eds.), *The NAEP 1994 technical report* (pp. 247–266). Washington, DC: U.S. Department of Education.

American Educational Research Association, American Psychological Association, & National Council on Measurement in Education. (1999). *Standards for educational and psychological testing.* Washington, DC: American Educational Research Association.

Andrich, D. (1978). A rating formulation for ordered response categories. *Psychometrika, 43,* 561–573.

Applebee, A. N., Langer, J. A., Jenkins, L. B., Mullis, I., & Foertsch, M. A. (1990). *Learning to write in our nation's schools: Instruction and achievement in 1988 at grade 4, 8, and 12.* Princeton, NJ: Educational Testing Service.

Applebee, A. N., Langer, J. A., & Mullis, I. (1985). *Writing: Trends across the decade, 1974–84.* Princeton, NJ: Educational Testing Service.

Aschbacher, P. R. (1991). Performance assessment: State activity, interest and concerns. *Applied Measurement in Education, 4*(4), 275–288.

Ayala, C. C., Shavelson, R., & Ayala, M. A. (2001). *On the cognitive interpretation of performance assessment scores* (CSE Technical Report 546). Los Angeles: UCLA, Center for Research on Evaluation, Standards, and Student Testing.

Ayala, C. C., Shavelson, R. J., Yue, Y., & Schultz, S. E. (2002). Reasoning dimensions underlying science achievement: The case of performance assessment. *Educational Assessment, 8,* 101–121.

Ayala, C. C., Yin, Y., Schultz, S., & Shavelson, R. (2002). *On science achievement from the perspective of different types of tests: A multidimensional approach to achievement validation* (CSE Technical Report 572). Los Angeles: UCLA, Center for Research on Evaluation, Standards, and Student Testing.

Baker, E. L. (1992). *The role of domain specifications in improving the technical quality of performance assessment* (Technical Report). Los Angeles: UCLA, Center for Research on Evaluation, Standards, and Student Testing.

Baker, E. L., O'Neil, H. F., & Linn, R. L. (1993). Policy and validity prospects for performance-based assessment. *American Psychologist, 48*(12), 1210–1218.

Baron, J. B. (1991). Strategies for the development of effective performance exercises. *Applied Measurement in Education, 4*(4), 305–318.

Barton, P. E., & Coley, R. J. (1994). *Testing in America's schools.* Princeton, NJ: Educational Testing Service, Policy Information Center.

Bauer, B. A. (1981). *A study of the reliability and cost-efficiencies of three methods of assessment for writing ability.* Champaign, IL: University of Illinois (ERIC Document Reproduction Service No. ED 216357)

Baxter, G. P., & Glaser, R. (1998). Investigating the cognitive complexity of science assessments. *Educational Measurement: Issues and Practice, 17*(3), 37–45.

Baxter, G. P., Shavelson, R. J., Herman, S. J., Brown, K. A., & Valdadez, J.R. (1993). Mathematics performance assessment: Technical quality and diverse student impact. *Journal for Research in Mathematics Education, 24,* 190–216.

Bejar, I. I. (1991). A methodology for scoring open-ended architectural design problems. *Journal of Applied Psychology, 76,* 522–532.

Bejar, I. I., & Braun, H. I. (1999). *Architectural simulations: From research to implementation* (RM-99–2). Princeton, NJ: Educational Testing Service.

Bennett, R. E. (1993). On the meanings of constructed response. In R. E. Bennett & W. C. Ward (Eds.), *Construction versus choice in cognitive measurement* (pp. 1–27). Hillsdale, NJ: Erlbaum.

Bennett, R. E. (2004). *Moving the field forward: Some thoughts on validity and automated scoring* (ETS RM-04–01). Princeton, NJ: ETS.

Bennett, R. E., & Bejar, I. I. (1998). Validity and automated scoring: It's not only the scoring. *Educational Measurement: Issues and Practice, 17*(4), 9–17.

Bennett, R. E., & Sebrechts, M.M. (1996). The accuracy of expert-system diagnoses of mathematical problem solutions. *Applied Measurement in Education, 9,* 133–150.

Bennett, R. E., Ward, W. C., Rock, D. A., & Hart, C. L. (1990). *Toward a framework for constructed-response items* (RR-90–7). Princeton, NJ: Educational Testing Service.

Bock, R. D. (1972). Estimating item parameters and latent ability when responses are scored in two or more nominal categories. *Psychometrika, 37,* 29–51.

Bock, R. D., Brennan, R. L., & Muraki, E. (1999, April). *The introduction of essay questions into the GRE: Toward a synthesis of item response theory and generalizability theory.* Paper presented at the annual meeting of the American Educational Research Association, Montreal, Canada.

Bock, R. D., Gibbons, R., & Muraki, E. J. (1988). Full information item factor analysis. *Applied Psychological Measurement, 12,* 261–280.

Bradlow, E. T., Wainer, H., & Wang, X. (1999). A Bayesian random effects model for testlets. *Psychometrika, 64,* 153–168.

Breland, H. (1983). *The direct assessment of writing skill: A measurement review* (College Board Report No. 83–6). New York: College Entrance Examination Board.

Breland, H. M., Bridgeman, B., & Fowles, M. E. (1999). *Writing assessment in admission to higher education: Review and framework* (College Board Report No. 99–3). New York: College Entrance Examination Board.

Breland, H., Danos, D., Kahn, H., Kubota, M., & Bonner, M. (1994). Performance versus objective testing and gender: An exploratory study of an Advanced Placement History Examination. *Journal of Educational Measurement, 31*(4), 275–293.

Breland, H., Danos, D., Kahn, H., Kubota, M., & Sudlow, M. W. (1991). *A study of gender and performance on advanced placement history examinations* (College Board Report No. 91–04). New York: College Entrance Examination Board.

Breland, H. M., & Jones, R. J. (1982). *Perceptions of writing skills* (College Board Report No. 82–4 and ETS Research Report No. 82–47). New York: College Entrance Examination Board.

Brennan, R. L. (1983). *Elements of generalizability theory.* Iowa City, IA: American College Testing Program.

Brennan, R. L. (1996). Generalizability of performance assessments. In G. W. Phillips (Ed.), *Technical issues in large-scale performance assessment* (NCES 96–802) (pp. 198–258). Washington, DC: National Center for Education Statistics.

Brennan, R. L. (2000). Performance assessments from the perspective of generalizability theory. *Applied Psychological Measurement, 24,* 339–353.

Brennan, R. L. (2001). *Generalizability theory.* New York: Springer-Verlag.

Brennan, R. L., & Johnson, E. G. (1995). Generalizability of performance assessments. *Educational Measurement: Issues and Practice, 14*(4), 9–12, 27.

Bridgeman, B., & Lewis, C. (1994). The relationship of essay and multiple-choice scores with grades in college courses. *Journal of Educational Measurement, 31*(1), 37–50.

Bridgeman, B., Morgan, R., & Wang, M. (1997). Choice among essay topics: Impact on performance and validity. *Journal of Educational Measurement, 34*(3), 273–286.

Chang, H., Mazzeo, J., & Roussos, L. (1996). Detecting DIF for polytomously scored items: An adaptation of SIBTEST procedure. *Journal of Educational Measurement, 33,* 333–353.

Chi, M. T. H., Glaser, R., & Farr, M. (Eds.). (1988). *The nature of expertise.* Hillsdale, NJ: Erlbaum.

Chi, M. T. H., Glaser, R., & Rees, E. (1982). Expertise in problem solving. In R. Sternberg (Ed.), *Advances in the psychology of human intelligence* (pp. 7–70). Hillsdale, NJ: Erlbaum.

Choi, S. W., Cook, K. F., & Dood, B. G. (1997). Parameter recovery for the partial credit model using MULTILOG. *Journal of Outcome Measurement, 1,* 114–142.

Christoffersson, A. (1975). Factor analysis of dichotomized variables. *Psychometrika, 40,* 5–32.

Clauser, B. E. (2000). Recurrent issues and recent advances in scoring performance assessments. *Applied Psychological Measurement, 24*(4), 310–324.

Clauser, B. E., Clyman, S. G., & Swanson, D. B. (1999). Components of rater error in a complex performance assessment. *Journal of Educational Measurement, 36*(1), 29–46.

Clauser, B. E., Kane, M. T., & Swanson, D. B. (2002). Validity issues for performance-based tests scored with computer-automated scoring systems. *Applied Measurement in Education, 15*(4), 413–432.

Clauser, B. E., Margolis, M. J., Clyman, S. G., & Ross, L. P. (1997). Development of automated scoring algorithms for complex performance assessments: A comparison of two approaches. *Journal of Educational Measurement, 34,* 141–161.

Clauser, B. E., Swanson, D. B., & Clyman, S. G. (1999). A comparison of the generalizability of scores produced by expert raters and automated scoring systems. *Applied Measurement in Education, 12*(3), 281–300.

Coffman, W. E. (1966). On the validity of essay tests of achievement. *Journal of Educational Measurement, 3*(2), 151–156.

Coffman, W. E. (1971). Essay examinations. In R. L. Thorndike (Ed.), *Educational measurement* (2nd ed., pp. 271–302). Washington, DC: American Council on Education.

Cole, N. S., & Moss, P. A. (1989). Bias in test use. In R. L. Linn (Ed.), *Educational measurement* (3rd ed., pp. 201–220). New York: American Council on Education and Macmillan.

Cronbach, L. J. (1971). Test validation. In R. L. Thorndike (Ed.), *Educational Measurement* (2nd ed., pp. 443–507). Washington, DC: American Council on Education.

Cronbach, L. J. (1988). Five perspectives on validity argument. In H. Wainer & H. I. Braun (Eds.), *Test validity* (pp. 3–17). Hillsdale, NJ: Erlbaum.

Cronbach, L. J., Gleser, G. C., Nanda, H., & Rajaratnam, N. (1972). *The dependability of behavioral measurements: Theory of generalizability of scores and profiles.* New York: John Wiley.

Cronbach, L. J., Linn, R. L., Brennan, R. L., & Haertel, E. H. (1997). Generalizability analysis for performance assessments of student achievement or school effectiveness. *Educational and Psychological Measurement, 57*(3), 373–399.

De Ayala, R. J., & Sava-Bolesta, M. (1999). Item parameter recovery for the nominal response model. *Applied Psychological Measurement, 23,* 3–19.

DeMars, C. E. (2000). Test stakes and item format interactions. *Applied Measurement in Education, 13*(1), 55–77.

DeMars, C. E. (2003). Sample size and the recovery of nominal response model item parameters. *Applied Psychological Measurement, 27,* 275–288.

Donoghue, J. R., & Hombo, C. M. (1999, June). *Some asymptotic results on the distribution of an IRT measure of item fit.* Paper presented at the Psychometric Society, Lawrence, KS.

Donoghue, J. R., & Hombo, C. M. (2000, April). *A comparison of different model assumptions about rater effects.* Paper presented at the annual meeting of the National Council on Measurement in Education, New Orleans, LA.

Donoghue, J. R., & Hombo, C. M. (2001). *The distribution of an item-fit measure for polytomous items.* Paper presented at the annual meeting of the National Council on Measurement in Education, Seattle, WA.

Dorans, N. J., & Holland, P. W. (1993). DIF detection and description: Mathel-Haenszel and standardization. In P. W. Holland & H. Wainer (Eds.), *Differential item functioning* (pp. 35–66). Hillsdale, NJ: Erlbaum.

Dorans, N. J., & Schmitt, A. P. (1993). Constructed response and differential item functioning: A pragmatic perspective. In R. E. Bennett & W. C. Ward (Eds.), *Construction versus choice in cognitive measurement* (pp. 135–165). Hillsdale, NJ: Erlbaum.

Dresher, A. R. (2003, April). *An empirical investigation of local item dependency in NAEP data.* Paper presented at the annual meeting of the American Educational Research Association, Chicago.

Dunbar, S. B., Koretz, D. M., & Hoover, H. D. (1991). Quality control in the development and use of performance assessments. *Applied Measurement in Education, 4*(4), 289–304.

Embretson, S. E. (1995). A measurement model for linking individual learning to processes and knowledge: Application to mathematical reasoning. *Journal of Educational Measurement, 32,* 277–294.

Embretson, S. E. (1997). Multicomponent response models. In W. J. V. d. Linden & R. K. Hambleton (Eds.), *Handbook of modern item response theory* (pp. 305–321). New York: Springer Verlag.

Embretson, S. E., & Reise, S. P. (2000). *Item response theory for psychologists.* Mahwah, NJ: Lawrence Erlbaum.

Engelhard, G. (1997). Constructing rater and task banks for performance assessments. *Journal of Outcome Measurement, 1,* 19–33.

Engelhard, G. (2002). Monitoring raters in performance assessments. In G. Tindal & T. M. Haladyna (Eds.), *Large-scale assessment programs for all students: Validity, technical adequacy, and implementation* (pp. 261–287). Mahwah, NJ: Erlbaum.

Engelhard, Jr., G., Gordon, B., Walker, E.V., & Gabrielson, S. (1994). Writing tasks and gender: Influences on writing quality of black and white students. *Journal of Educational Research, 87,* 197–209.

Ericsson, K. A., & Simon, H. A. (1984). *Protocal analysis. Verbal reports as data.* Cambridge, MA: MIT Press.

Ericsson, K. A., & Smith, J. (1991). Prospects and limits of the empirical study of expertise: An introduction. In K. A. Ericsson & J. Smith (Eds.), *Toward a general theory of expertise: Prospects and limits* (pp. 1–38). Cambridge: Cambridge University Press.

Fitzpatrick, A. R., Ercikan, K., Yen, W. M., & Ferrara, S. (1998). The consistency between raters scoring in different test years. *Applied Measurement in Education, 11*(2), 195–208.

Fitzpatrick, R., & Morrison, E. J. (1971). Performance and product evaluation. In R. L. Thorndike (Ed.), *Educational measurement* (2nd ed., pp. 237–270). Washington, DC: American Council on Education.

Fitzpatrick, A. R., & Yen, W. M. (1995). The psychometric characteristics of choice items. *Journal of Educational Measurement, 32*(3), 243–260.

Flora, D. B., & Curran, P. J. (2004). An empirical evaluation of alternative methods of estimation for confirmatory factor analysis with ordinal data. *Psychological Methods, 9,* 466–491.

Fraser, C. (1988). NOHARM: A computer program for fitting both unidimensional and multidimensional normal ogive models of latent trait theory (Version II) [Computer program]. Armidale, Australia: University of New England: Center for Behavioral Studies.

Frederiksen, N. (1984). The real test bias: Influences of testing on teaching and learning. *American Psychologist, 39,* 193–202.

Frederiksen, J. R., & Collins, A. (1989). A systems approach to educational testing. *Educational Researcher, 18*(9), 27–32.

Fuchs, L. S., Fuchs, D., Karns, K., Hamlett, C. L., Dutka, S., & Katzaroff, M. (2000). The importance of providing background information on the structure and scoring of performance assessments. *Applied Measurement in Education, 13*(1), 1–34.

Gabrielson, S., Gordon, B., & Engelhard, G. (1995). The effects of task choice on the quality of writing obtained in a statewide assessment. *Applied Measurement in Education, 8*(4), 273–290.

Gao, X., Shavelson, R. J., & Baxter, G. P. (1994). Generalizability of large-scale performance assessments in science. Promises and problems. *Applied Measurement in Education, 7,* 323–334.

Garner, M., & Engelhard, Jr., G. (1999). Gender differences in performance on multiple-choice and constructed response mathematics items. *Applied Measurement in Education, 12*(1), 29–51.

Gierl, M., Leighton, J. P., & Hunka, S. M. (2000). Exploring the logic of Tatsuoka's rule-space model for test development and analysis. *Educational Measurement: Issues and Practice, 19,* 34–44.

Glas, C. A. W., & Verhelst, N. D. (1995). Tests of fit for polytomous Rasch models. In G. H. Fischer (Ed.), *I.W. Molenar* (pp. 325–352). New York: Springer-Verlag.

Glaser, R., Lesgold, A., & Lajoie, S. (1987). Toward a cognitive theory for the measurement of achievement. In R. Ronning, J. Glover, J. C. Conoley, & J. Witt (Eds.), *The influence of cognitive psychology on testing and measurement: The Buros-Nebraska Symposium on measurement and testing* (Vol. 3, pp. 41–85). Hillsdale, NJ: Lawrence Erlbaum.

Glockner-Rist, A., & Hoijtink, H. (2003). The best of both worlds: Factor analysis of dichotomous data using item response theory and structural equation modeling. *Structural Equation Modeling, 10,* 544–565.

Goldberg, G. L., & Roswell, B. S. (2001). Are multiple measures meaningful?: Lessons from a statewide performance assessment. *Applied Measurement in Education, 14*(2), 125–150.

Grobe, C. (1981). Syntactical maturity, mechanics, and vocabulary as predictors of quality ratings. *Research in the Teaching of English, 15,* 75–85.

Gyagenda, I. S., & Engelhard, G. (1999, April). *Using classical and modern measurement theories to explore rater, domain, and gender influences on student writing ability.* Paper presented at the annual meeting of the American Educational Research Association, Montreal, Canada.

Haertel, E. H. (1999). Performance assessment and education reform. *Phi Delta Kappan, 80*(9), 662–667.

Haertel, E. H., & Linn, R. L. (1996). Comparability. In G. W. Phillips (Ed.), *Technical issues in large-scale performance assessment* (NCES 96–802). Washington, DC: U.S. Department of Education.

Hambleton, R. K., & Kanjee, A. (1993, April). Enhancing the validity of cross-cultural studies: Improvements in instrument translation methods. Paper presented at the annual meeting of the National Council on Measurement in Education, Atlanta, GA.

Hambleton, R. K., & Murphy, E. (1992). A psychometric perspective on authentic measurement. *Applied Measurement in Education, 5,* 1–16.

Hambleton, R. K., & Swaminathan, H. (1985). *Item response theory.* Boston: Kluwer-Nijhoff.

Hattie, J. (1985). Methodology review: Assessing dimensionality of tests and items. *Applied Psychological Measurement, 9,* 139–164.

Hattie, J., Krakowski, K., Rogers, H. J., & Swaminathan, H. (1996). An assessment of Stout's index of essential unidimensionality. *Applied Psychological Measurement, 20,* 1–14.

Herman, J. L., Aschbacher, P. R., & Winters, L. (1992). *A practical guide to alternative assessment.* Alexandria, VA: Association for Supervision and Curriculum Development.

Herman, J. L., & Klein, D. C. D. (1996). Evaluating equity in alternative assessment: An illustration of opportunity-to-learn issues. *The Journal of Educational Research, 89*(4), 246–256.

Hieronymus, A. N., & Hoover, H. D. (1987). *Iowa tests of basic skills: Writing Supplement teacher's guide.* Chicago: Riverside.

Hoskens, M., & De Boeck, P. (2001). Multidimensional componential item response theory models for polytomous items. *Applied Psychological Measurement, 25,* 19–37.

Huot, B. (1990). The literature of direct writing assessment: Major concerns and prevailing trends. *Review of Educational Research, 60*(2), 237–263.

Hyde, J. S., & Linn, M. C. (1988). Gender differences in verbal ability: A meta-analysis. *Psychological Bulletin, 104,* 53–69.

Johnson, E. G., & Zwick, R. (1990). *Focusing the new design: The NAEP 1988 technical report* (No. 19–TR-20). Princeton, NJ: Educational Testing Service.

Junker, B. W., & Patz, R. J. (1998, June). *The hierarchical rater model for rated test items.* Paper presented at the North American Meeting of the Psychometric Society, Champaign, Urbana, IL.

Kane, M. (1982). A sampling model for validity. *Applied Psychological Measurement, 6*(2), 125–160.

Kane, M., & Case, S. M. (2004). The reliability and validity of weighted composite scores. *Applied Measurement in Education, 17*(3), 221–240.

Kane, M., Crooks, T., & Cohen, A. (1999). Validating measures of performance. *Educational Measurement: Issues and Practice, 18*(2), 5–17.

Kansas State Board of Education. (1991). *Kansas quality performance accreditation.* Topeka, KS: Author.

Keith, T. Z. (2003). Validity and automated essay scoring systems. In M. D. Shermis & J. C. Burstein (Eds.), *Automated essay scoring* (pp. 147–168). Mahwah, NJ: Lawrence Erlbaum.

Klein, S. P., Stecher, B. M., Shavelson, R. J., McCaffrey, D., Ormseth, T., Bell, R. M. et al. (1998). Analytic versus holistic scoring of science performance tasks. *Applied Measurement in Education, 11*(2), 121–137.

Lane, S. (1993). The conceptual framework for the development of a mathematics performance assessment instrument. *Educational Measurement: Issues and Practice, 12*(3), 16–23.

Lane, S., Liu, M., Ankenmann, R. D., & Stone, C. A. (1996). Generalizability and validity of a mathematics performance assessment. *Journal of Educational Measurement, 33*(1), 71–92.

Lane, S., Parke, C. S., & Stone, C. A. (2002). The impact of a state performance-based assessment and accountability program on mathematics instruction and student learning: Evidence from survey data and school performance. *Educational Assessment, 8*(4), 279–315.

Lane, S., Silver, E. A., Ankenmann, R. D., Cai, J., Finseth, C., Liu, M. et al. (1995). *QUASAR Cognitive Assessment Instrument (QCAI).* Pittsburgh, PA: University of Pittsburgh, Learning Research and Development Center.

Lane, S., Stone, C. A., Ankenmann, R. D., & Liu, M. (1994). Reliability and validity of a mathematics performance assessment. In R. J. Shavelson (Ed.), *International Journal of Educational Research* [Special issue on performance assessment], *21*(3), 247–266.

Lane, S., Stone, C. A., Ankenmann, R. D., & Liu, M. (1995). Examination of the assumptions and properties of the graded item response model: An example using a mathematics performance assessment. *Applied Measurement in Education, 8,* 313–340.

Lane, S., Wang, N., & Magone, M. (1996). Gender related DIF on a middle school mathematics performance assessment. *Educational Measurement: Issues and Practice, 15,* 21–27, 31.

Larkin, J. H., McDermott, J., Simon, D. P., & Simon, H. A. (1980). Models of competence in solving physics problems. *Cognitive Science, 4,* 317–345.

Linacre, J. D. (1989). *Many-facet Rasch measurement.* Chicago: MESA Press.

Linacre, J. D., & Wright, B. D. (1992). *A user's guide to FACETS: Rasch measurement computer program.* Chicago: MESA Press.

Linn, R. L. (Ed.). (1989). *Educational measurement* (3rd ed.). New York: American Council on Education and Macmillan.

Linn, R. L. (1993). Educational assessment: Expanded expectations and challenges. *Educational Evaluation and Policy Analysis, 15,* 1–16.

Linn, R. L.(2000). Assessments and accountability. *Educational Researcher, 29*(3), 4–16.

Linn, R. L., Baker, E. L., & Betebenner, D. W. (2002). Accountability systems: Implications of requirements of the No Child Left Behind Act of 2001. *Educational Researcher, 31*(6), 3–16.

Linn, R. L., Baker, E. L., & Dunbar, S. B. (1991). Complex performance assessment: Expectations and validation criteria. *Educational Researcher, 20*(8), 15–21.

Linn, R. L., Betebenner, D. W., & Wheeler, K. S. (1998). *Problem choice by test takers: Implications for comparability and construct validity* (CSE Tech. Rep. No. 482). Los Angeles: University of California, National Center for Research on Evaluation, Standards, and Student Testing.

Linn, R. L., & Burton, E. (1994). Performance-based assessment: Implications of task specificity. *Educational Measurement: Issues and Practice, 13*(1), 5–8, 15.

Lloyd-Jones, R. (1977). Primary trait scoring. In C. R. Cooper & L. Odell (Eds.), *Evaluating writing: Describing, measuring and judging* (pp. 33–60). Urbana, IN: National Council for Teachers in Education.

Lord, F. N., & Novick, M. R. (1969). *Statistical theories of mental test scores.* Reading, MA: Addison Wesley.

Luecht, R. M., & Miller, R. R. (1992). Unidimensional calibrations and interpretations of composite abilities for multidimensional tests. *Applied Psychological Measurement, 16,* 279–294.

Madaus, G. F., & O'Dwyer, L. M. (1999). A short history of performance assessments. *Phi Delta Kappan, 80*(9), 688–696.

Martinez, M. E. (1991). A comparison of multiple-choice and constructed figural response items. *Journal of Educational Measurement, 28*(2), 131–145.

Martinez, M. E. (1993). Problem-solving correlates of new assessment forms in architecture. *Applied Measurement in Education, 6*(3), 167–180.

Martinez, M. E., & Katz, I. R. (1995/1996). Cognitive processing requirements of constructed figural response and multiple-choice items in architecture assessment. *Educational Assessment, 3*(1), 83–98.

Maryland State Department of Education. (1996, March). *1996 MSPAP public release task: Choice in reading and writing scoring guide* [On-line]. Available: http://mdk12.org/mspp/mspap/look/prt_mspap.html.

Marzano, R. J., Pickering, R. J., & McTighe, J. (1993). *Assessing student outcomes: Performance assessment using the dimensions of learning model.* Alexandria, VA: Association for Supervision and Curriculum Dimension.

Masters, G. N. (1982). A Rasch model for partial credit scoring. *Psychometrika, 47,* 149–174.

Masters, G. N., & Wright, B. D. (1984). The essential process in a family of measurement models. *Psychometrika, 49,* 529–544.

Mazzeo, J., Schmitt, A. P., & Bleistein, C. G. (1991, April). *Do women perform better, relative to men, on constructed-response tests or multiple-choice tests? Evidence from the advanced placement examinations.* Paper presented at the annual meeting of the National Council of Measurement in Education, Chicago.

Mazzeo, J., Schmitt, A., & Bleistein, C. (1993). *Sex-related performance differences on constructed-response and multiple-choice sections of the Advanced Placement Examinations* (RR-93-5). Princeton, NJ: Educational Testing Service.

McBee, M. M., & Barnes, L. L. B. (1998). The generalizability of a performance assessment measuring achievement in eighth-grade mathematics. *Applied Measurement in Education, 11*(2), 179–194.

McDonald, R. P. (1999). *Test theory: A unified treatment.* Mahwah, NJ: Lawrence Erlbaum.

McDonald, R. P. (2000). A basis for multidimensional item response theory. *Applied Psychological Measurement, 24,* 99–114.

McDonald, R. P., & Mok, M. M. C. (1995). Goodness of fit in item response models. *Multivariate Behavioral Research, 30,* 23–40.

Mehrens, W. A. (1992). Using performance assessment for accountability purposes. *Educational Measurement: Issues and Practice, 11,* 3–9, 20.

Mehrens, W. A. (1998). Consequences of assessment: What is evidence? *Education Policy Analysis Archives 6(13).* Retrieved December 3, 2004 from http://epaa.asu.edu/eppa.

Messick, S. (1980). Test validity and the ethics of assessment. *American Psychologist, 35*(11), 1012–1027.

Messick, S. (1989). Validity. In R. L. Linn (Ed.), *Educational measurement* (3rd ed., pp. 13–104). New York: American Council on Education and Macmillan.

Messick, S. (1994). The interplay of evidence and consequences in the validation of performance assessments. *Educational Researcher, 23*(2), 13–23.

Messick, S. (1995). Standards of validity and the validity of standards in performance assessment. *Educational Measurement: Issues and Practice, 14*(4), 5–8.

Miller, M. D., & Crocker, L. (1990). Validation methods for direct writing assessment. *Applied Measurement in Education, 3*(3), 285–296.

Miller, T. R., & Welch, C. J. (1993, April). *Issues and problems in assessing differential item functioning in performance assessments*. Paper presented at the annual meeting of the National Council on Measurement in Education, Atlanta, GA.

Mislevy, R. J. (1996). Test theory reconceived. *Journal of Educational Measurement, 33*, 379–416.

Mislevy, R. J., Steinberg, L. S., Breyer, F. J., Almond, R. G., & Johnson, L. A. (1999). A cognitive task analysis, with implications for designing a simulation-based assessment system. *Computers and Human Behavior, 15*, 335–374.

Mislevy, R. J., Steinberg, L. S., Breyer, F. J., Almond, R. G., & Johnson, L. (2002). Making sense of data from complex assessments. *Applied Measurement in Education, 15*(4), 363–390.

Mislevy, R. J., Yamamoto, K., & Anacker, S. (1992). Toward a test theory for assessing student understanding. In R. A. L. S. Lamon (Ed.), *Assessments of authentic performance in school mathematics* (pp. 293–318). Washington, DC: American Association for the Advancement of Science.

Molenaar, I. W., & Hoijtink, H. (1990). The many null distributions of person fit indices. *Psychometrika, 55*(1), 75–106.

Moon, T. R., & Hughes, K. R. (2002). Training and scoring issues involved in large-scale writing assessments. *Educational Measurement: Issues and Practice, 21*(2), 15–19.

Moss, P. A., Cole, N. S., & Khampalikit, C. (1982). A comparison of procedures to assess written language skills at grades 4, 7, and 10. *Journal of Educational Measurement, 19*(1), 37–47.

Mullis, I. V. S. (1984). Scoring direct writing assessments: What are the alternatives? *Educational Measurement: Issues and Practice, 3*(1), 16–18.

Mullis, I. V. S., Dossey, J. A., Campbell, J. R., Gentile, C. A., O'Sullivan, C., & Latham, A. S. (1994). *NAEP 1992 trends in academic progress*. Washington, DC: National Center for Education Statistics.

Muraki, E. (1990). Fitting a polytomous item response model to Likert-type data. *Applied Psychological Measurement, 14*, 59–71.

Muraki, E. (1992). A generalized partial credit model: Application of an EM algorithm. *Applied Psychological Measurement, 16*, 159–176.

Muraki, E. (1993). *POLYFACT*. Princeton, NJ: Educational Testing Service.

Muraki, E., & Bejar, I. I. (1995, June). *Full information factor analysis of polytomous item responses of NCARB exams*. Paper presented at the annual meeting of the Psychometric Society, Princeton, NJ.

Muraki, E., & Carlson, J. E. (1995). Full-information factor analysis for polytomous item responses. *Applied Psychological Measurement, 19*, 73–90.

Muraki, E., Hombo, C. M., & Lee, Y.-W. (2000). Equating and linking performance assessments. *Applied Psychological Measurement, 24*, 325–337.

Muthen, B. O. (1978). Contributions to factor analysis of dichotomous variables. *Psychometrika, 43*, 551–560.

Muthen, L. K., & Muthen, B. O. (1998). *Mplus user's guide*. Los Angeles: Muthen and Muthen.

Myford, C. M., & Mislevy, R. J. (1995). *Monitoring and improving a portfolio assessment system* (Center for Performance Assessment Research Report). Princeton, NJ: Educational Testing Service.

Nandakumar, R., Yu, F., Li, H.-H., & Stout, W. F. (1998). Assessing unidimensionality of polytomous data. *Applied Psychological Measurement, 22*, 99–115.

National Council of Teachers of Mathematics. (2000). *Principles and standards for school mathematics*. Reston, VA: Author.

National Council on Education Standards and Testing. (1992). *Raising standards for American education*. Washington, DC: Author.

National Research Council. (1996). *National science education standards*. National Committee on Science Education Standards and Assessment. Coordinating Council for Education. Washington, DC: National Academy Press.

National Research Council. (2001). *Knowing what students know: The science and design of educational assessment*. J. Pellegrino, N. Chudowsky, & R. Glaser, editors. Board on Testing and Assessment, Center for Education. Division of Behavioral and Social Sciences and Education. Washington, DC: National Academy Press.

Nebraska Department of Education. (2002). *Stars: School-based teacher-led assessment and reporting system*. Lincoln: Nebraska: Author.

Newell, A., & Simon, H. (1972). *Human problem solving*. Englewood Cliffs, NJ: Prentice Hall.

Nichols, P., & Sugrue, B. (1999). The lack of fidelity between cognitively complex constructs and conventional test development practice. *Educational Measurement: Issues and Practice, 18*, 18–29.

O'Neil, H. F., Sugrue, B., & Baker, E. L. (1995/1996). Effects of motivational interventions on the National Assessment of Educational Progress Mathematics Performance. *Educational Assessment, 3*, 135–157.

Oregon Department of Education. (2004). *Official scoring guide, writing 2003–2004*. Available from http://www.ode.state.or.us/tls/english/writing

Orlando, M., & Thissen, D. (2000). Likelihood-based item-fit indices for dichotomous item response theory models. *Applied Psychological Measurement, 24*, 50–64.

Parke, C. S., Lane, S., & Stone, C. A. (2006). Impact of a state performance assessment program in reading and writing. *Educational Research and Evaluation, 12*(3), 239–269.

Patz, R. J. (1996). *Markov Chain Monte Carlo methods for item response theory models with applications for the National Assessment of Educational Progress*. Unpublished manuscript, Carnegie Mello University, Pittsburgh, PA.

Patz, R. J., Junker, B. W., & Johnson, M. S. (2002). The hierarchical rater model for rated test items and its application to large-scale educational assessment data. *Journal of Educational and Behavioral Statistics, 27*, 341–384.

Penfield, R. D., & Lam, T. C. M. (2000). Assessing differential item functioning in performance assessment: Review and recommendations. *Educational Measurement: Issues and Practice, 19*, 5–15.

Penny, J., Johnson, R. L., & Gordon, B. (2000). Using rating augmentation to expand the scale of an analytic rubric. *Journal of Experimental Education, 68*(3), 269–288.

Petersen, N. S., & Livingston, S. A. (1982). *English composition test with essay: A descriptive study of the relationship between essay and objective scores by ethnic group and sex* (No. SR-82-96). Princeton, NJ: Educational Testing Service.

Pollack, J. M., & Rock, D. A. (1997). *Constructed response tests in the NELS:88 school effects study*. Washington, DC: National Center for Education Statistics.

Pomplun, M., Capps, L., & Sundbye, N. (1998). Criteria teachers use to score performance items. *Educational Assessment 5*(2), 95–110.

Popham, W. J. (1997). Consequential validity: Right Concern—Wrong Concept. *Educational Measurement: Issues and Practice, 16*(2), 9–13.

Potenza, M. T., & Dorans, N. J. (1995). DIF assessment for polytomously scored items: A framework for classification and evaluation. *Applied Psychological Measurement, 19*, 23–37.

Powers, D. E., & Bennett, R. E. (1999). Effects of allowing examinees to select questions on a test of divergent thinking. *Applied Measurement in Education, 12*(3), 257–279.

Powers, D. E., & Burstein, J. C., Chodorow, M., Fowles, M. F., & Kukich, K. (2002). Stumping e-rater: Challenging the validity of automated scoring of essays. *Journal of Educational Computing Research, 26*, 407–425.

Powers, D. E., & Fowles, M. E. (1998). Test takers judgments about GRE writing test prompts (GRE No. 94–13). Princeton, NJ: Educational Testing Service.

Powers, D. E., & Fowles, M. E. (1999). Test-takers' judgments of essay prompts: Perceptions and performance. *Educational Assessment, 6*(1), 3–22.

Powers, D. E., Fowles, M. E., Farnum, M., & Gerritz, K. (1992). *Giving a choice of topics on a test of basic writing skills: Does it make any difference?* (ETS Research Report No. 92–19). Princeton, NJ: Educational Testing Service.

Powers, D. E., Fowles, M. E., Farnum, M., & Ramsey, P. (1994). Will they think less of my handwritten essay if others word process theirs? Effects on essay scores of intermingling handwritten and word-processed essays. *Journal of Educational Measurement, 31*(3), 220–233.

Powers, D. E., Fowles, M. E., & Willard, A. E. (1994). Direct assessment, direct validation? An example from the assessment of writing. *Educational Assessment, 2*(1), 89–100.

Reckase, M. D. (1997a). A linear logistic multidimensional model for dichotomous item response data. In W. J. v. d. Linden & R. K. Hambleton (Eds.), *Handbook of modern item response theory* (pp. 271–286). New York: Springer-Verlag.

Reckase, M. D. (1997b). The past and future of multidimensional item response theory. *Applied Psychological Measurement, 21*, 25–36.

Reise, S. P., & Yu, J. (1990). Parameter recovery in the graded response model using MULTILOG. *Journal of Educational Measurement, 27*, 133–144.

Resnick, L. B., Briars, D., & Lesgold, S. (1992, April). *Certifying accomplishments in mathematics: The New Standards examination system.* Paper presented at the International Conference on Mathematics Education, University of Chicago.

Resnick, L. B., & Resnick, D. P. (1992). Assessing the thinking curriculum: New tools for educational reform. In B. G. Gifford & M. C. O'Conner (Eds.), *Changing assessment; Alternative views of aptitude, achievement and instruction* (pp. 37–55). Boston: Kluwer Academic.

Roid, G. H. (1994). Patterns of writing skills derived from cluster analysis of direct-writing assessments. *Applied Measurement in Education, 7*(2), 159–170.

Roussos, L. A. (1995). *A new dimensionality estimation tool for multiple-item tests and a new DIF analysis paradigm based on multidimensionality and construct validity. Dissertation Abstracts International, 57*(04). (UMI No. 9624474).

Ruiz-Primo, M. A., Baxter, G. P., & Shavelson, R. J. (1993). On the stability of performance assessments. *Journal of Educational Measurement, 30*(1), 41–53.

Ruiz-Primo, M. A., & Shavelson, R. J. (1996). Rhetoric and reality in science performance assessments: An update. *Journal of Research in Science Teaching, 33*,1045–1063.

Russell, M., & Tao, W. (2004). Effects of handwriting and computer-print on composition scores: A follow-up to Powers, Folwes, Farnum & Ramsey. *Practical Assessment, Research and Evaluation, 9*(1). Retrieved January 15, 2005 from http://PAREonline.net/getvn.asp

Samejima, F. (1969). Estimation of latent ability using a response pattern of graded scores. *Psychometrika Monograph* (No. 17).

Samejima, F. (Ed.). (1996). *The graded response model.* New York: Springer.

Saner, H., McCaffrey, D., Stecher, B., Klein, S., & Bell, R. The effects of working in pairs in science performance assessments. *Educational Assessment, 2*(4), 325–338.

Segall, D. O. (2000). Principles of multidimensional adaptive testing. In W. J. v. d. Linden & C. A. W. Glas (Eds.), *Computerized adaptive testing: Theory and practice* (pp. 53–73). Boston: Kluwer Academic.

Shavelson, R. J., Baxter, G. P., & Pine, J. (1991). Performance assessment in science. *Applied Measurement in Education, 4*(4), 347–362.

Shavelson, R. J., Baxter, G. P., & Gao, X. (1993). Sampling variability of performance assessments. *Journal of Educational Measurement, 30*(3), 215–232.

Shavelson, R. J., & Ruiz-Primo, M. A. (1998). *On the assessment of science achievement conceptual underpinnings for the design of performance assessments: Report of year 2 activities* (CSE Technical Report 481). Los Angeles: UCLA, Center for Research on Evaluation, Standards, and Student Testing.

Shavelson, R. J., Ruiz-Primo, M. A., & Wiley, E. W. (1999). Note on sources of sampling variability. *Journal of Educational Measurement, 36*(1), 61–71.

Shavelson, R. J., & Webb, N. M. (1991). *Generalizability theory.* Newbury Park, CA: Sage.

Shepard, L. A. (1997). The centrality of test use and consequences for test validity. *Educational Measurement: Issues and Practice, 16*(2), 5–8, 13.

Shepard, L. A. (2004, September). *Conceptual coherence between large-scale and classroom assessment.* Presentation at the CRESST Conference, Los Angeles.

Sijtsma, K., & Molenaar, I. W. (2002). *Introduction to nonparametric item response theory.* Thousand Oaks, CA: Sage.

Sijtsma, K., & van der Ark, L. A. (2000). Progress in NIRT analysis of polytomous item scores: Dilemmas and practical solutions. In A. Boomsma, M. A. J. v. Duijn, & T. A. B. Snijders (Eds.), *Essays on item response theory* (pp. 297–318). New York: Springer.

Sireci, S. G., Thissen, D., & Wainer, H. (1991). On the reliability of testlet-based tests. *Journal of Educational Measurement, 28*, 237–247.

Snow, R. W., & Lohman, D. F. (1989). *Implications of cognitive psychology for educational measurement.* Unpublished manuscript.

Solano-Flores, G., Jovanovic, J., Shavelson, R. J., & Bachman, M. (1999). On the development and evaluation of a shell for generating science performance assessments. *International Journal of Science Education, 21*(3), 293–315.

Stalnaker, J. M. (1951). The essay type of examination. In E. F. Lindquist (Ed.), *Educational measurement* (pp. 495–530). Washington, DC: American Council on Education.

Stecher, B., Barron, S., Chun, T., & Ross, K. (2000). *The effects of the Washington state education reform in schools and classrooms* (CSE Tech. Rep. NO. 525). Los Angeles: University of California, National Center for Research on Evaluation, Standards and Student Testing.

Stecher, B., Barron, S., Kaganoff, T., & Goodwin, J. (1998). *The effects of standards-based assessment on classroom practices: Results of the 1996–97 RAND survey of Kentucky teachers of mathematics and writing* (CSE Tech. Rep. No. 482). Los Angeles: University of California, National Center for Research on Evaluation, Standards, and Student Testing.

Stein, M. K., & Lane, S. (1996). Instructional tasks and the development of student capacity to think and reason: An analysis of the relationship between teaching and learning in a reform mathematics project. *Educational Research and Evaluation, 2*(1), 50–80.

Stewart, M. R., & Grobe, C. H. (1979). Syntactic maturity, mechanics and vocabulary and teachers' quality ratings. *Research in the Teaching of English, 13,* 207–215.

Stiggins, R. J. (1987). Design and development of performance assessments. *Educational Measurement: Issues and Practice, 6*(1), 33–42.

Stone, C. A. (2000). Monte-Carlo based null distribution for an alternative fit statistic. *Journal of Educational Measurement, 37,* 58–75.

Stone, C. A., Ankenmann, R. D., Lane, S., & Liu, M. (1993, April). *Scaling QUASAR's performance assessment.* Paper presented at the annual meeting of the American Educational Research Association, Atlanta, GA.

Stone, C. A., & Hansen, M. (2000). The effect of errors in estimating ability on goodness-of-fit for IRT models. *Educational and Psychological Measurement, 60,* 974–991.

Stone, C. A., & Lane, S. (2003). Consequences of a state accountability program: Examining relationships between school performance gains and teacher, student, and school variables. *Applied Measurement in Education, 16*(1), 1–26.

Stone, C. A., Mislevy, R. J., & Mazzeo, J. (1994, April). *Classification error and goodness-of-fit in IRT models.* Paper presented at the annual meeting of the American Educational Research Association, New Orleans, LA.

Stone, C. A., & Zhang, B. (2003). Comparing three new approaches for assessing goodness-of-fit in IRT models. *Journal of Educational Measurement, 40*(4), 331–352.

Storms, B. A., Sheingold, K., Nunez, A. M., & Heller, J. I. (1998). *The feasibility, comparability, and value of local scorings of performance assessments.* Princeton, NJ: Center for Performance Assessment, ETS.

Stout, W. F. (1987). A nonparametric approach for assessing latent trait dimensionality. *Psychometrika, 52,* 589–617.

Stout, W. F. (1990). A new item response theory modeling approach with applications to unidimensional assessment and ability estimates. *Psychometrika, 55,* 293–326.

Stout, W. F., Douglas, J., Kim, H. R., Roussos, L., & Zhang, J. (1996). Conditional covariance-based nonparametric multidimensionality assessment. *Applied Psychological Measurement, 10,* 331–354.

Supovitz, J. A., & Brennan, R. T. (1997). Mirror, mirror on the wall, which is the fairest test of all? An examination of the equitability of portfolio assessment relative to standardized tests. *Harvard Educational Review, 67,* 472–506.

Swygert, K. A., McLeod, L. D., & Thissen, D. (2001). Factor analysis for items or testlets scored in more than two categories. In D. Thissen & H. Wainer (Eds.), *Test scoring* (pp. 217–250). Hillsdale, NJ: Erlbaum.

Sykes, R. C., & Hou, L. (2003). Weighting constructed-response items in IRT-based exams. *Applied Measurement in Education, 16,* 257–275.

Takane, Y., & Leeuw, J. D. (1987). On the relationship between item response theory and factor analysis of discretized variables. *Psychometrika, 52,* 393–408.

Tate, R. (2002). *Test dimensionality*. Mahwah, NJ: Lawrence Erlbaum.

Tatsuoka, K. K. (1983). Rule-space: An approach for dealing with misconceptions based on item response theory. *Journal of Educational Measurement, 20,* 34–38.

Tatsuoka, K. K. (1990). Toward an integration of item response theory and cognitive diagnosis. In N. Frederiksen, R. Glaser, A. Lesgold, & M. C. Shafto (Eds.), *Diagnostic monitoring of skill and knowledge acquisition* (pp. 543–588). Hillsdale, NJ: Erlbaum.

Tatsuoka, K. K. (1995). Architecture of knowledge structures and cognitive diagnosis: A statistical pattern recognition and classification approach. In P. D. Nichols, S. F. Chipmann, & R. L. Brennan (Eds.), *Cognitively diagnostic assessment* (pp. 327–359). Hillsdale, NJ: Erlbaum.

Tatsuoka, K. K., & Boodoo, G. M. (2000). Subgroup differences on GRE Quantitative test based on the underlying cognitive processes and knowledge. In A. E. Kelly & R. A. Lesh (Eds.), *Handbook of research design in mathematics and science education* (pp. 821–857). Mahwah, NJ: Erlbaum.

Tatsuoka, K. K., Corter, J., Dean, M., & Grossman, J. (2003, April). *Exploring mathematical thinking skills in TIMMSS.* Paper presented at the National Council of Measurement in Education, Chicago.

Tay-Lim, S. H. (1999). *Assessing the dimensionality of constructed-response tests using hierarchical cluster analysis: A Monte Carlo study with application.* Dissertation Abstracts International, 61(01). (UMI No. 9957759).

Tay-Lim, S. H., & Stone, C. A. (2000, April). *Assessing the dimensionality of constructed-response tests using hierarchical cluster analysis: A Monte Carlo study with application.* Paper presented at the annual meeting of the American educational Research Association, New Orleans, LA.

Taylor, C. S. (1998). An investigation of scoring methods for mathematics performance-based assessments. *Educational Assessment, 5*(3), 195–224.

Thissen, D. (1993). Repealing rules that no longer apply to psychological measurement. In N. Frederiksen, R. J. Mislevy, & I. I. Bejar (Eds.), *Test theory for a new generation of tests* (pp. 79–97). Hillsdale, NJ: Lawrence Erlbaum.

Thissen, D., Nelson, L., Rosa, K., & McLeod, L. D. (2001). *Item response theory for items scored in more than two categories.* Mahwah, NJ: Lawrence Erlbaum.

Traub, R. E. (1993). On the equivalence of traits assessed. In R. E. Bennett & W. C. Ward (Eds.), *Construction versus choice in cognitive measurement: Issues in constructed response, performance testing, and portfolio assessment* (pp. 29–44). Hillsdale, NJ: Erlbaum.

Tuerlinckx, F., & Boeck, P. D. (2001). The effect of ignoring item interactions on the estimated discrimination parameters in item response theory. *Psychological Methods, 6*(2), 181–195.

Vacc, N. N. (1989). Writing evaluation: Examining four teachers' holistic and analytic scores. *The Elementary School Journal, 90,* 87–95.

van der Vleuten, C. P. M., & Swanson, D. B. (1990). Assessment of clinical skills with standardized patients: The state of the art. *Teaching and Learning in Medicine, 2,* 58–76.

Verhelst, N. D., & Verstralen, H. H. F. M. (2001). An IRT model for multiple raters. In A. Boomsma, M. A. J. V. Duijn, & T. A. B. Snijders (Eds.), *Essays on item response theory* (pp. 89–108). New York: Springer-Verlag.

Wainer, H., Bradlow, E. T., & Du, Z. (2000). Testlet response theory: An analog for the 3PL model useful in testlet-based adaptive testing. In C. A. W. Glas (Ed.), *Computerized adaptive testing: Theory and practice* (pp. 245–269). Boston: Kluwer Academic.

Wainer, H., & Kiely, G. L. (1987). Item clusters and computerized adaptive testing: A case for testlets. *Journal of Educational Measurement, 27,* 1–14.

Wainer, H., & Thissen, D. (1994). On examinee choice in educational testing. *Review of Educational Research, 64,* 159–195.

Wainer, H., & Thissen, D. (2001). True score theory: The traditional method. In D. Thissen & H. Wainer (Eds.), *Test scoring* (pp. 23–72). Hillsdale, NJ: Erlbaum.

Wainer, H., & Wang, X. (2000). Using a new statistical model for testlets to score TOEFL. *Journal of Educational Measurement, 37*(3), 203–220.

Wang, X., Bradlow, E. T., & Wainer, H. (2002). A general Bayesian model for testlets: Theory and applications. *Applied Psychological Measurement, 26*(1), 109–128.

Webb, N. M. (1993). *Collaborative group versus individual assessment in mathematics: Group processes and outcomes* (CSE Tech. Rep. No. 352). Los Angeles: University of California, Center for the Study of Evaluation.

Webb, N. M., Schlackman, J., & Surgrue, B. (2000). The dependability and interchangeability of assessment methods in science. *Applied Measurement in Education, 13*(3), 277–301.

Welch, C. J., & Harris, D. J. (1994, April). *A technical comparison of analytic and holistic scoring methods.* Paper presented at the annual meeting of the National Council on Measurement in Education, New Orleans, LA.

Wiggins, G. (1989). A true test: Toward more authentic and equitable assessment. *Phi Delta Kappan, 79,* 703–713.

Willingham, W. W., & Cole, N. S. (1997). Research on gender differences. In W. W. Willingham & N. S. Cole (Eds.), *Gender and fair assessment* (pp.17–54). Mahwah, NJ: Lawrence Erlbaum.

Willingham, W. W., Cole, N. S., Lewis, C., & Leung, S. W. (1997). Test performance. In W. W. Willingham & N. S. Cole (Eds.), *Gender and fair assessment* (pp. 55–126). Mahwah, NJ: Lawrence Erlbaum.

Wilson, D., Wood, R., Gibbons, R., Schilling, S., Muraki, E., & Bock, R. D. (2003). TESTFACT: Test scoring and full information item factor analysis (Version 4.0) [Computer Software]. Lincolnwood, IL: Scientific Software International.

Wilson, M., & Hoskens, M. (2001). The rater bundle model. *Journal of Educational and Behavioral Statistics, 26,* 283–306.

Wolfe, E., Bolton, S., Feltovich, B., & Welch, C. (1993). *A comparison of word-processed and handwritten essays from a standardized writing assessment* (RR. 93–8). Iowa City, Iowa: American College Testing.

Yang, Y., Buckendahl, C. W., Juskiewicz, P. J., & Bhola, D. S. (2002). A review of strategies for validating computer-automated scoring. *Applied Measurement in Education, 15*(4), 391–412.

Yen, W. M. (1981). Using simulation results to choose a latent trait model. *Applied Psychological Measurement, 5,* 245–262.

Yen, W. M. (1993). Scaling performance assessments: Strategies for managing local item dependence. *Journal of Educational Measurement, 30*(3), 187–213.

Zhang, L. (2001, April). *Examining the effects of drafting and revising patterns on students' writing performance and the implications in writing instruction.* Paper presented at the annual meeting of the American Educational Research Association, Seattle, WA.

12

Setting Performance Standards

Ronald K. Hambleton
University of Massachusetts Amherst

Mary J. Pitoniak
Educational Testing Service

1. INTRODUCTION

Whenever educational assessments are used to categorize individuals, performance standards must be established along the score range. Examinees may be classified as "pass" or "fail," or may be placed into a greater number of ordered performance categories with labels such as "below basic," "basic," "proficient," and "advanced." The importance of setting of performance standards on assessments has been highlighted in recent years as the use of assessments for accountability purposes in education has increased; for example, a student may be required to reach one of the aforementioned performance levels in order to receive a high school graduation diploma. The prominence of performance standards is reflected in the fact that for many state testing programs and credentialing agencies, examinees may not even see their actual scores, instead receiving information only about their performance category or classification.

Numerous methods are available for setting performance standards. The types reviewed in this chapter are judgmental methods used to set standards on criterion-referenced tests. These methods thus lie in contrast to norm-referenced approaches, with which many members of the public are more familiar (Goodman & Hambleton, 2005; Plake, 2005). Norm-referenced methods are designed to pass or fail prespecified percentages of examinees, in contrast to criterion-referenced methods in which the content standards outlining the knowledge, skills, and abilities are used as the basis of judgments about performance standards (Meskauskas, 1976). As Sireci (2005) noted, a "norm-referenced passing score is not defensible for high school graduation, licensure, or certification tests because scores are interpreted with respect to being better or worse than others, rather than with respect to the level of competence of a specific test taker" (p. 118). Within this chapter, we therefore focus on methods in which experts bring their informed judgments to bear on different aspects of the testing process.

The practice of setting performance standards has been and continues to be controversial for high-stakes assessments and credentialing examinations. Among the reasons for such intense debate is the critical role that judgment plays in setting performance standards, as just mentioned. Performance standards depend to some extent on informed judgments about several critical factors—the composition of the panel that is used in the process, the amount of training panelists receive, the specifics of the method that is implemented, whether panelists receive impact data—as well as other factors. There are likely hundreds of variables that can potentially impact the results. The extent to which the standard-setting process is a judgmental one will be reviewed in more detail below.

In the educational context, not only examinees, but also schools, districts, and states, are being judged; for this and other reasons, performance standards are carefully scrutinized and often hotly debated (see, for example, Hambleton, Brennan et al., 2000; Pellegrino, Jones, & Mitchell, 1999; Shepard, Glaser, Linn, & Bohrnstedt, 1993). Because the standard setting process does have subjective elements, it has at times been criticized as "arbitrary" (Glass, 1978). However, many theorists and practitioners have countered such criticisms. For example, Popham (1978) pointed out that the very word that Glass used to criticize standard setting arbitrary can not only be defined as "capricious," but as "involving judgment." Popham noted that it is erroneous to insist that the latter implies the former, stating that "it is patently incorrect to equate human judgment with arbitrariness in this negative sense" (p. 298).

Due in part to criticisms regarding the judgmental nature of standard setting, many attempts have been made to introduce procedural and evaluative rigor into the process. Substantial effort has been devoted to documenting how a process can be established that will produce defensible and valid performance standards. Examples of guidelines for standard setting range from early efforts by Livingston and Zieky (1982), Hambleton and Powell (1983), and Berk (1986), through more recent work by Cizek (1996a, 1996b, 2001), Cizek, Bunch, and Koons (2004), and Kane (1994, 2001). Some authors have developed categorization schemas for different types of methods (Cizek, 1996a; Hambleton, Jaeger, Plake, & Mills, 2000; Jaeger,

1989), while others have focused on steps that generally characterize all standard setting methods (Hambleton, 1998, 2001). The need to evaluate the results of a standard setting study within a validity framework has also been stressed by standard-setting experts (Cizek, 1996b; Kane, 1994).

The purposes of the chapter are to present the steps that are typically involved in setting performance standards on educational assessments and credentialing examinations, and to review the critical topics that are involved with carrying out those steps, including those mentioned in the preceding paragraph. Those critical topics include: (1) selecting a method; (2) preparing performance category descriptions; (3) forming a standard-setting panel; (4) training panelists; (5) providing feedback to panelists during the standard-setting process, and (6) evaluating and documenting the validity of the process. Some additional topics will also be addressed, and future topics for research discussed.

1.1. Professional Guidelines for Setting Performance Standards

A framework for designing and evaluating the process for setting performance standards is provided by the *Standards for Educational and Psychological Testing* (hereafter referred to as "the *Standards*"; American Educational Research Association, American Psychological Association, and National Council on Measurement in Education [AERA, APA, & NCME], 1999). Six of the standards are especially relevant to the establishment of performance standards, or cut scores (as they are referred to in the *Standards*):

Standard 1.7

When a validation rests in part on the opinions or decisions of expert judges, observers, or raters, procedures for selecting such experts and for eliciting judgments or ratings should be fully described. The qualifications, and experience, of the judges should be presented. The description of procedures should include any training and instructions provided, should indicate whether participants reached their decisions independently, and should report the level of agreement reached. If participants interacted with one another or exchanged information, the procedures through which they may have influenced one another should be set forth.

Standard 2.14

Conditional standard errors of measurement should be reported at several score levels if constancy cannot be assumed. Where cut scores are specified for selection or classification, the standard errors of measurement should be reported in the vicinity of each cut score.

Standard 4.19

When proposed interpretations involve one or more cut scores, the rationale and procedures used for establishing cut scores should be clearly documented.

Standard 4.20

When feasible, cut scores defining categories with distinct substantive interpretations should be established on the basis of sound empirical data concerning the relation of test performance to relevant criteria.

Standard 4.21

When cut scores defining pass-fail or proficiency categories are based on direct judgments about the adequacy of item or test performances or performance levels, the judgmental process should be designed so that judges can bring their knowledge and experience to bear in a reasonable way.

Standard 14.17

The level of performance required for passing a credentialing test should depend on the knowledge and skills necessary for acceptable performance in the occupation or profession and should not be adjusted to regulate the number or proportion of persons passing the test.

These six standards clearly address many issues relevant to the setting of performance standards. *Standard* 1.7 calls for a detailed description of the qualifications and experience of the panelists involved in the setting of performance standards as well as how the panelists went about their tasks. *Standard* 2.14 requires the testing agency to report the conditional standard error of measurement at each of the performance standards and, preferably, for other scores near the performance standards (see also *Standard* 2.15 regarding decision consistency). *Standard* 4.19 focuses on the need for documentation of the rationale for setting performance standards, and the basis for setting them (*Standards* 6.5 and 6.12 also reference the importance of documentation relative to performance standards when they are relevant for test interpretation). *Standard* 4.20 addresses the desirability of obtaining external evidence to support the validity of test score interpretations associated with the performance category descriptions. *Standard* 4.21 stresses the importance of designing a process where panelists can optimally use the knowledge that they have to influence the process. Finally, *Standard* 14.17 addresses the need to embed performance standards for credentialing tests in the context of content and what test candidates need to know and to be able to do, rather than adopting a straight normative approach to obtain a prespecified pass rate. Relevant standards will be addressed as appropriate in subsequent sections of the chapter.

1.2. General Issues in Setting Performance Standards

Three points about the issues and methods for setting performance standards will be addressed before specific issues regarding methods and their implementation are reviewed. Issues to be discussed are: (1) terminology regarding standards, (2) the role of judgment in setting performance standards, and (3) differences in standard-setting methods across item types.

1.2.1. Terminology Regarding Standards

The word "standards" can be used both in conjunction with (1) the content and skills candidates are viewed as needing to attain, and (2) the scores they need to obtain in order to demonstrate the relevant knowledge and skills. Within the context of assessments used in educational settings, a distinction must be made between the former *(content standards)* and the latter *(performance standards)* since confusion on the difference between these concepts often arises among policymakers, educators, and the public. The establishment of content standards, while a critical activity, is usually the domain of policymakers and educators (Kane, 2001). Content standards are reflected in the curricula, and specify what examinees are expected to know and to be able to do. Content standards provide direction to instructors on what they need to teach. Performance standards, in contrast, define the levels of test performance examinees are expected to attain in relation to the content standards (Linn & Herman, 1997). Performance standards may thus be viewed as an operationalization of the content standards to the test or assessment that has been constructed to measure the content standards. With many credentialing examinations it is common to set a single performance standard to distinguish certifiable and non-certifiable candidates. In educational testing, the number of performance standards often varies from one (to distinguish "passing" and "failing" candidates) to as many as four or five.

Many different terms are used in the measurement and assessment literature to refer to performance standards. They may also be referred to as "passing scores," "cut scores," "cutoff scores," "performance levels," "achievement levels," "mastery levels," "proficiency levels," "thresholds," and "standards." Within this chapter the term performance standard will generally be used, though abbreviated phrases such as "setting standards" may also be used at times. Performance categories, on the other hand, are the intervals between the performance standards on the score reporting scale. In practice, detailed descriptions of the knowledge and skills of candidates located in these performance categories are developed and used to communicate test results (Hambleton, 2001). It should also be noted that terms such as tests and assessments, and examinees and candidates, will be used interchangeably throughout the chapter.

1.2.2. The Role of Judgment

The setting of performance standards is a blend of judgment, psychometrics, and practicality. In the words of the *Standards*, "cut scores embody value judgments as well as technical and empirical considerations" (AERA, APA, & NCME, 1999, p. 54).

It is thus impossible to avoid using judgment in setting performance standards. The nature of the judgments often differ from method to method, but judgment always plays a critical role. Judgment is used when a method for setting standards is chosen, as well as in the determination of the demographic composition of the panel(s). Panelists' judgments are also the cornerstone on which the resulting performance standards are based. The goal of serious standard-setting work is to make these judgments as informed as possible. Performance standards should not be found lacking because judgments are involved, since judgments must be involved in every aspect of education including the specifications of curriculum frameworks (i.e., content standards), the choices of textbooks and other instructional materials, and the selection of teaching methods to match students' learning styles and capabilities. The focus must instead be on providing adequate training so that panelists can provide their judgments in an informed manner, and establishing a proper context within which to interpret those judgments (Hambleton, 1978).

In order to provide a context for the role of judgment, and to assist in the discussion of steps employed in standard setting before methods are reviewed, at this point it is useful to give a brief description of two methods. In one version of the often-used Angoff (1971) method that is applied to multiple-choice items, for example, panelists are asked to estimate independently the probability that the borderline examinee (an examinee believed to be located at a performance standard of interest) will answer each item correctly; those probabilities are summed over items for each panelist to arrive at a panelist performance standard, and then these panelist performance standards are averaged to obtain a performance standard for the panel on the test. The process can be repeated for all performance standards of interest. Basically, the panelists are estimating the expected score of the borderline candidate on each item and then these expected item scores are summed to obtain an estimated true score for the borderline candidate on the collection of test items. The panelist's estimated true score on the test for the borderline examinee is taken as the panelist's estimate of the performance standard.

In other, more examinee-centered methods, panelists are asked to directly categorize the performance of given examinees (e.g., "qualified," "borderline," or "unqualified"). A performance standard can be determined by taking the median test score of examinees judged as just-qualified (borderline group method), or by contrasting two different groups of examinees, one containing examinees above the standard and the other below (contrasting groups method). Often the performance standard on the test is then chosen to maximize the accuracy of panelist classifications.

A key concept in the methods briefly described above, as well as in other approaches, is that of the borderline examinee. It is critical that the reference group(s) be clearly established so that panelists develop an operational definition of what they expect in terms of examinee performance. While the formulation of this concept may vary depending on method, panelists are generally asked to imagine how examinees who are "just good enough" to meet a given performance standard would perform. Many different terms may be used to describe these examinees, such as just-qualified candidate, borderline candidate, and minimally competent practitioner, among others. Within this chapter, the term borderline examinee will generally be used.

1.2.3. Item Types

Methods for setting performance standards on educational assessments that use the multiple-choice item type are well developed and steps for implementation are generally clear (see Cizek, 2001; Cizek et al., 2004; Livingston & Zieky, 1982). However, standard-setting methods for educational assessments that include constructed-response items such as writing samples and performance tasks are not nearly as well developed, and none of them have been fully researched and validated (see Hambleton, Jaeger, et al., 2000). The relative lack of research makes the use of these new methods more problematic. Well-designed and implemented field testing may be advised before these methods are used operationally so that their use with the test under consideration can be evaluated. The extensive amount of field testing of standard-setting methods carried out by the National Assessment Governing Board (NAGB) for use with the National Assessment of Educational Progress (NAEP; National Center for Educational Statistics, 2005; see also Loomis & Bourque, 2001; Reckase, 2000a, 2000b) is an excellent example of the pursuit of a research agenda prior to the implementation of new standard-setting methods.

2. TYPICAL STEPS IN SETTING PERFORMANCE STANDARDS

Regardless of method, performance standards must ultimately be defensible and valid; therefore, the process used in setting the standards needs to be reasonable, systematic, and thoughtful as well (Cizek, 1996b; Hambleton & Powell, 1983; Plake, 1997). The defensibility of the resulting performance standards is considerably increased if the process reflects careful attention to: (1) the selection of the method; (2) the selection and training of panelists; (3) the sequence of activities in the process; (4) validation; and (5) careful documentation of the process.

Within this section, nine steps for setting performance standards are described briefly. The purpose of this overview is to provide a framework for the more in-depth discussion of issues in the remainder of the chapter. In practice these steps are often combined in different ways and in different orders; also, depending on method, all steps may not be essential.

It should also be kept in mind that there are numerous other steps, both administrative and more substantive, that need to be undertaken in order to implement the overall process. For example, a timeline should be set that takes into account the date by which performance standards need to be established; this date may be determined by a legislative body or a testing agency. Plans need to be developed that can be reasonably implemented given this time frame. For example, the choice of a method must reflect the realities of available resources, including development of materials such as booklets containing test questions, rating forms, spreadsheets, etc. One or more facilitators must be located who are familiar with the method and can implement it effectively, given appropriate training. Many otherwise excellent studies have failed because of untrained facilitators. If the method is a newly developed one, a pilot study may need to be conducted to assess whether it can be used with the test for which the performance standards are being set. Similarly, randomly-equivalent panels could be established to investigate the generalizability of the performance standards. All of the features of a given method and resources required for its implementation should be carefully considered before steps described below are undertaken.

2.1. Step 1: Select a Standard-Setting Method

Many methods for setting performance standards appear in the measurement literature (see, for example, Cizek, 2001). As is described later in this chapter, methods can be classified in terms of the task that is asked of panelists—specifically, on the types of materials on which the panelists will focus their judgments. For example, some methods require panelists to review items, while others require them to look at candidate work. The choice of a particular standard-setting method will depend on: (1) the types of items in the assessment; (2) the time and resources required by the method; (3) an agency's prior experience with the method; and (4) the availability of validity evidence for the method. In general, the method chosen should also align with the approach used to compute scores on the assessment. Sometimes it is suggested that two or even three methods be implemented so that the results can be compared, but this is usually an expensive and time-consuming process, and would be rarely done except in pilot or research studies. Detailed information about available methods is presented in section 3.

2.2. Step 2: Choose a Panel and Design

One of the first questions to be asked is who the stakeholders are in the decisions that will be made with the assessments. These stakeholders represent the constituencies who should be involved in the standard-setting process. The types of constituencies that are relevant to a given standard-setting effort will differ depending on the type of assessment involved. The types of panelists needed will also depend on the choice of method, since some methods (for example, the Angoff method) require panelists to have substantial knowledge of the test content, whereas others (for example, borderline or contrasting groups approaches) require considerably less content knowledge on the part of panelists. The number of panelists must also be considered carefully, as well as their diversity in terms of geography, ethnic background, gender, age, work experience, and often other factors (Jaeger, 1991; Jaeger & Mills, 2001). The defensibility of the performance standards will ultimately depend on many factors including the acceptability of the composition of the standard-setting panel.

It is important for the agency setting performance standards to be able to demonstrate that the issue of panel composition was considered, that a target range of panelist characteristics was established (e.g., 70% teachers, 30% curriculum specialists; 80% of the teachers with over five years of experience, 20% of the teachers with less than five years of experience, etc.), and that there was a rationale for the composition of the panel that was ultimately used. Additional discussion of the composition of panels, including qualifications of panelists and how many panelists are needed, is presented in section 4.

A second consideration at this early stage in the planning process is the desirability of conducting parallel standard-setting studies so that the generalizability of the resulting performance standards over panels can be studied. Sometimes separate panels are drawn, thus doubling the number of panelists needed, and totally independent standard-setting studies are carried out. Other times, double the number of panelists is drawn, but all panelists may participate together in the orientation and training aspects of the study, after which they are separated into carefully matched panels and kept independent for the remainder of the process. Standards from independent panels provide an excellent basis for calculating standard errors associated with the performance standards (see Brennan, 2001).

2.3. Step 3: Prepare Descriptions of Performance Categories

Performance category descriptions consist of statements of the knowledge, skills, and abilities that characterize examinees in these categories. The focus on clear descriptions of borderline examinees and performance categories is one of the most important advances in recent years in standard-setting, and follows in large part from NAGB's experiences with setting performance standards on NAEP. The development of these descriptions may be undertaken by a separate panel meeting earlier in the process, or by the standard-setting panelists. Section 5 provides further detail on preparing performance category descriptions.

2.4. Step 4: Train Panelists to Use the Method

Effective training and the use of practice exercises are needed in order to thoroughly familiarize panelists with the tasks ahead of them. Effective training includes: (1) providing an orientation to the standard-setting process and clarifying the goals of the session and the purpose of the test; (2) explaining and demonstrating the steps to follow in setting standards; (3) showing the scoring keys and/or scoring rubrics and ensuring they are understood; (4) giving instructions in how to complete the rating forms; (5) allowing time for practice in providing ratings on tasks similar to those on the actual test; (6) explaining any normative data that will be used in the process; (7) familiarizing panelists with the content of the test; (8) facilitating the panelists' gaining confidence in working with the performance category descriptions; (9) developing descriptions of just-qualified candidates (if used); and (10) taking the test under standard or near-standard conditions. The amount of time allotted to training will vary based on the method chosen, as well as other factors. Retraining on some concepts may also be warranted if panelists' responses to daily evaluation questionnaires indicate that they are not comfortable with one or more parts of the process. Information on training of panelists is included in section 6.

2.5. Step 5: Collect Item Ratings

This step involves panelists' conduct of one of the most critical tasks in standard setting—that of providing judgments. The form that this step takes will, of course, vary based on the standard-setting method chosen. In most cases, panelists enter their ratings onto a form, and those data are then entered into a spreadsheet or program, either manually or electronically via a scannable form. A summary of the panelists' ratings is usually prepared, with that information being provided to the panelists in order to provide feedback on their ratings and to initiate discussion about the performance standard(s). A general description of the panelist task for each of the popular methods is given in Table 12.1, with more detailed information being provided in section 3.

2.6. Step 6: Provide Feedback and Facilitate Discussion

Panelists are often asked to work through the method and set preliminary standards and then to participate in a discussion of these initial standards and actual examinee performance data on the assessment. The purposes of the discussion and feedback are to provide the opportunity for panelists to reconsider their initial ratings and to identify errors or any misconceptions or misunderstandings that may be present. The precise form of the feedback depends on the method, but with several methods the feedback might include average performance and examinee score distributions on the items or tasks of the assessment, and descriptive statistics of the ratings of the panelists.

An iterative process incorporating further ratings, discussion, and feedback is common but not essential. A two- or three-stage rating process is typically used, whereby panelists provide their first ratings (independent of other panelists or performance data of any kind), discussion follows, and then panelists complete a second set of ratings. It is not required that panelists change their initial ratings, but they are given the opportunity to do so. This iterative process may often be continued for one or two more rounds.

An optional step in the standard-setting process involves the presentation of consequence data to panelists. A panel may, for example, be informed about the percentage of examinees who would pass the test with the recommended performance standard, or may be given the percentage of examinees falling into each performance category. Panelists may be given an additional opportunity to revise their ratings in order to increase or decrease one or more of their performance standards.

It is important to stress that the implementation and timing of panelist discussion and different types of feedback should be carefully considered on a case-by-case basis given the type of method employed and the knowledge sets of the panelists. Section 7 contains additional information relevant to these topics.

2.7. Step 7: Compile Panelist Ratings and Obtain Performance Standards

At this stage, panelists' ratings are compiled to determine performance standards, if this has not been done already in step 6. An average of the performance standards set by each panelist is generally used. Depending on method, the

TABLE 12.1 Methods Reviewed in This Chapter, Organized by Type of Rating Provided

Method	Overview of Panelists' Task
Methods Involving Ratings of Test Items and Scoring Rubrics	
Angoff	Panelists estimate the probability that the borderline examinee will answer each multiple-choice item correctly. (The yes/no and item score string estimation methods are similar to Angoff, but call for panelists to make a yes[1]/no[0] rating for each item instead of estimating probability.)
Extended Angoff and related methods	This method is similar to Angoff for multiple-choice items, except that the panelists rate polytomous items (or with the analytic method, items within a simulation specifically) and indicate the number of score points (or average score of 100 borderline examinees) that the borderline examinee will obtain.
Ebel	Panelists classify each item along two dimensions—difficulty and relevance—and for each combination of the dimensions estimate the percentage of items that the borderline examinee will answer correctly.
Nedelsky	Panelists estimate for each item the number of distractors that they think the borderline examinee would be able to rule out as incorrect; the reciprocal of the number of distractors not ruled out, plus one (for the correct answer), is taken as the probability that the borderline examinee will answer the item correctly by resorting to random selection among the remaining answer choices.
Jaeger	Panelists make a yes/no rating for each item in terms of whether *every* examinee (not just the borderline examinee) should be able to answer the item correctly.
Bookmark and other item mapping methods	In the bookmark method, panelists review test items that are ordered according to their difficulty parameter and place a bookmark where the items preceding it represent content that the borderline examinee should, with a specified probability, be able to answer correctly. See the text for other item mapping methods.
Direct consensus	Panelists review clusters of items and provide an estimate for each cluster of the number of items that the borderline examinee will be able to answer correctly (or an estimate of the average score over 100 borderline examinees), and are encouraged to come to a consensus on this number for each cluster of items in the test.
Methods Involving Rating of Candidates	
Contrasting groups	Raters review lists of candidates and identify one group whose members are clearly above a particular performance standard and another group whose members are clearly below that standard.
Borderline group	Raters review lists of candidates and identify those that they view as borderline.
Methods Involving Ratings of Candidate Work	
Item by item (paper selection)	Panelists review, item by item, samples of candidate responses to items in the test representing each test score and select the papers they view as representing the borderline examinee.
Holistic (body of work, booklet classification, generalized examinee-centered)	Panelists review, holistically, a sample of entire candidate test booklets and place them into different performance categories.
Hybrid (analytic judgment, integrated judgment, work classification)	Panelists review samples of candidate responses, proceeding section by section through the test booklet, and place them into different performance categories, perhaps followed by an adjustment of the ratings at the overall test level.
Methods Involving Ratings of Score Profiles	
Judgmental policy capturing	Panelists review score profiles across exercises making up a performance assessment and assign each score profile to a proficiency category; these data are then analyzed to determine each panelist's latent standard-setting policy.
Dominant profile	Panelists review score profiles across different exercises in the assessment and attempt to come directly to a consensus on the policy to be used in setting a standard (compensatory, conjunctive, or a combination of both).
Item cluster	Panelists review patterns of candidates' responses to multiple-choice items and rate them on a four-point scale.

(continued)

TABLE 12.1 (*continued*)

METHOD	OVERVIEW OF PANELISTS' TASK
	Compromise Methods
Beuk	Panelists provide estimates of the expected percent correct for the borderline examinees and the expected passing rate for the examinee population.
de Gruijter	Panelists provide estimates of the expected percent correct for the borderline examinees and the expected failing rate for the examinee population, plus an estimate of uncertainty for both values.
Hofstee	Panelists provide estimates of the highest and lowest acceptable passing scores for the test and the highest and lowest failure rates that would be acceptable.

mean or median may be calculated. For example, the mean is generally used with the Angoff method, while the median is typically used for the borderline group method. Median ratings may be preferable with a small number of panelists or when non-symmetric distributions of panelist ratings are observed. However, sometimes the mean is preferred because when the panelists' ratings are independent (as they often are after the first round of ratings), the standard error of the mean (based on the assumption of independent ratings) can be used as a measure of the performance standard stability for the panel (across replications or parallel panels). In contrast, a formula for the stability of the performance standard based on the median rating of panelists is not readily available.

It is also common to report the variability of the performance standards across any subpanels that may have been formed to set standards. This variability may be used in deciding on the viability of the resulting performance standards; a large amount of variability may lead to concern about the standards, while a small amount of variability may build confidence in the standards. This variability may also be used in adjusting a performance standard to reflect uncertainty among the panelists (see Beuk, 1984).

2.8. Step 8: Conduct Panelist Evaluation

A panelist evaluation of the process should also be conducted. Information about the panelists' level of satisfaction with or understanding of the performance descriptors, training, amount of time allotted for each activity, the rating task used in the standard-setting process, the use of feedback data and discussion, and final recommended performance standards is an important piece of the evidence for establishing the validity of the performance standards. Further information about panelist evaluations is included in section 8.

2.9. Step 9: Compile Validity Evidence and Prepare Technical Documentation

Standard 4.19 stipulates that "when proposed score interpretations involve one or more cut scores, the rationale and procedures used for establishing cut scores should be clearly documented" (AERA, APA, & NCME, 1999, p. 59). Thus it is necessary to leave a "paper trail" documenting the work that was done and by whom it was conducted.

Summarizing this information soon after the completion of the standard-setting session is important so that it is available to policymakers or others setting the final performance standard.

It is critical to compile validity evidence derived from several sources. As is described in section 9, such evidence may be one of three major types—procedural, internal, and external. Collecting information related to each source should be viewed as an integral component of the standard-setting process. Such documentation will also prove invaluable should legal challenges arise; an overview of legal issues is also provided in section 9.

Nearly every factor or feature of a standard-setting process can impact on the performance standards, at least in a small way, and some of these factors are potentially very influential (e.g., the role of the facilitator). In the following sections, six of the most critical topics will be considered. All of these topics relate back to the steps outlined in this section (however, not every step in section 2 will have a specific critical topic connected with it).

3. SELECTING A STANDARD-SETTING METHOD

As noted earlier, choice of a standard-setting method will depend on several factors. First, the mix of items in the assessment plays a role; for example, with multiple-choice tests, the Angoff method or the bookmark method has been popular; with performance assessments, paper selection or body of work methods may be more suitable choices. Second, the time and resources available to set performance standards will vary and impact the choice of method and how it is implemented. For example, in state testing programs three days are often allocated for the process, while in credentialing, one or two days may be all that is available; in the information technology (IT) industry, an agency once requested that the task of standard-setting be completed within three or four hours. Limited resources may eliminate the possibility of using methods that are very labor intensive, such as any of the methods that require extensive amounts of material to be prepared. Amount of time available may also influence the amount of training that is possible, the number of rounds of ratings that are possible, etc. Third, an agency's prior experience with the method may be an issue; methods less familiar to the testing agency would require materials development and field testing, thus driving up the cost of the process and taking more time. Fourth, beliefs about the validity evidence for particular methods may play a role; for example, some testing agencies may avoid particular methods because of a lack of validity evidence for them.

Increased attention has been given to establishing the credibility of existing standard-setting methods and investigating new methods in recent years. Many of the new approaches have been developed in an attempt to present panelists with meaningful activities (e.g., reviewing the test booklets of candidates), and to better accommodate the changing nature of assessments, including the common use of more than one performance standard and the frequent inclusion of polytomously scored items.

As methods have evolved, ways of categorizing them have advanced from the simple to the more complex. In the next section of this chapter, different ways of classifying methods will be outlined. In later sections, existing methods will be classified along different dimensions, and their features and characteristics described.

3.1. Ways of Classifying Methods

A dichotomy long used to classify standard-setting methods is that of test-centered methods versus examinee-centered methods (Cizek, 1996a; Jaeger, 1989; Kane, 1994, 1998). Test-centered standard-setting methods require panelists to make judgments about assessment tasks. During their review of test items, panelists provide judgments regarding expected levels of performance on each item by examinees on the border between two levels of performance. In contrast, examinee-centered methods focus more directly on the candidates by asking persons who know the candidates to place them into ordered performance categories, usually without knowledge of their test performance.

However, as newer standard-setting methods have been developed, this classification schema has become limited in its ability to characterize different approaches. In response, Hambleton, Jaeger, et al. (2000) developed a more comprehensive classification approach. One of the dimensions along which they classified methods is the focus of panelists' judgments, which can be viewed as expanding the previous test-centered vs. examinee-centered dichotomy into four categories:

1. methods that involve review of test items and scoring rubrics;
2. methods that involve review of candidates;
3. methods that involve looking at candidate work; and
4. methods that involve panelist review of score profiles.

Within the following section, available standard-setting methods are classified along these four dimensions. In addition, compromise methods that take into account both absolute (i.e., levels of examinee test performance necessary for assignments to ordered performance categories) and relative (i.e., with a focus on acceptable percentages of examinees in the performance categories) standards are described. Table 12.1 provides a listing of the methods and a brief description of the panelist rating task required by each of them.

Several caveats are warranted before the review of methods is provided. First, the methods listed do not exhaust the full complement of approaches available to the practitioner. They represent instead the most well-known traditional methods as well as a selection of those developed more recently. Omission from this review does not mean that a method cannot be used effectively. Second, the description for each method is necessarily concise and should be viewed only as a summary of key points, not as a full set of steps for implementation. Any given implementation of a method may also vary in its details (e.g., how many rounds of ratings were conducted, whether empirical data were provided). For example, the Angoff method is characterized by the way panelists judge items, but there may be 100 or more "modified-Angoff methods" that have been used in the field that vary the amount and nature of training, the number of rounds of ratings, the use or non-use of consequence data, and so on. Even the basic judgmental task with the Angoff method comes in at least two versions: In some studies panelists are asked to estimate the probability of a correct response from a borderline examinee, and in other studies they are asked to imagine 100 borderline examinees and estimate the number who will answer the item correctly. Third, where applicable, critiques of the method that have been noted in the literature are included; this information is given only to give the reader a general sense of other viewpoints and not to indicate whether a method should or should not be used. All of the methods described next, and several others not included, seem worthy of use in practice and deserve to be researched further.

3.2. Methods Involving Review of Test Items and Scoring Rubrics

3.2.1. Angoff Method

The Angoff method was first introduced in the "Scales, Norms, and Equivalent Scores" chapter of the second edition of Educational Measurement (Angoff, 1971). There are in fact, however, two variations on the Angoff method outlined therein. Paradoxically, the method described in a footnote in the chapter is the one most frequently employed, and most commonly known as the Angoff method. In that method, panelists review multiple-choice items and provide, for each item, an estimate of the probability of minimally competent candidates answering an item correctly. The probability ratings for each panelist are typically summed over items in the test, and these sums are averaged across panelists, to determine the panel performance standard. The process can, of course, be repeated to set multiple performance standards.

In contrast, the method described in the main text of Angoff (1971) is a simpler version of the method (and one that Angoff attributed to Ledyard Tucker), in which the standard-setting panelist provides an estimate of whether the just-qualified candidate would answer the item correctly or not. Although this method clearly stems from the suggestion of Angoff, it does not always carry that name; it has been referred to in the literature as either the yes/no method (Impara & Plake, 1997) or the item score string estimation method (Loomis & Bourque, 2001). Research has suggested, however, that estimates of borderline performance tend to be biased lower for the lower performance standards and higher for the higher performance standards (Reckase & Bay, 1999). For that reason, the method was not recommended for use with NAEP (Loomis & Bourque, 2001).

Most implementations of the method use the term "modified Angoff" to reflect the addition of one or more features not present in the original formulation. These added elements include the provision of empirical item data to participants, encouragement of discussions among panelists, and the conduct of several rounds of ratings to enable panelists to revise their estimates (Cizek & Fitzgerald, 1996; Mills, 1995). Reviews of research related to many of the features of the Angoff method can be found in Brandon (2004) and Hurtz and Auerbach (2003).

The Angoff method, while widely used (Kane, 1994; Meara, Hambleton, & Sireci, 2001; Mehrens, 1995, Plake, 1998; Sireci & Biskin, 1992), has been subject to criticism from those who claim that the very task inherent in this method—evaluating the difficulty of test items for borderline candidates—is too difficult for panelists to accomplish in an accurate manner (Shepard et al., 1993). One of the most vocal attacks on the Angoff method took place within the context of NAEP. Shepard (1995) noted, for example, that panelists systematically overestimated performance on difficult items and underestimated performance on easy items. Accurately estimating performance probabilities was viewed by researchers reviewing 1990 NAEP standard setting as an "unreasonable cognitive task" (Shepard et al., 1993, p. 72). The procedures that were followed with NAEP Angoff-based standard setting have, however, been strongly defended by both policymakers and psychometricians. For example, NAGB, which coordinated these standard-setting efforts, responded by stating that the alternative methods suggested in the United States General Accounting Office (USGAO) report "appear naïve and unsupported by research evidence" (USGAO, 1993, p. 88). This position was articulated further by Kane (1995). Further support for the procedures was provided by Hambleton, Brennan, et al. (2000), who presented a rebuttal to a critical summary of NAEP standard setting compiled by Pellegrino et al. (1999). Hambleton and colleagues concluded that the Pellegrino et al. report "presents a very one-sided and incomplete evaluation that is based largely on dated and second-hand evidence" (p. 6); they also presented a review of evidence that they felt refuted the report and supported the credibility of the Angoff standard-setting method as implemented for NAEP.

Angoff himself acknowledged that more attention should be paid to factors affecting the reliability of item judgments, and noted that lack of agreement in performance standards may stem from two factors (Angoff, 1988). First, the panelists may not have a clear picture of the competency of the borderline examinee. Second, even if panelists did have a clear picture, they may not be able to accurately determine probabilities of correct responses to these items. Research has been conducted to directly investigate the ability of panelists to provide accurate ratings. For example, evidence for the accuracy of panelists' item ratings is reviewed by Brandon (2004; see also Plake & Impara, 2001). Overall, it appears that the degree to which panelists can accurately estimate the probability of an examinee getting an item correct depends on the training of the panelists, the type of empirical data they receive, and the difficulty levels of the items being rated. In general, Brandon concluded that research has shown that item ratings are moderately correlated with those items' actual difficulties.

3.2.2. Extended Angoff and Related Methods

The Angoff procedure described above can be expanded to tests that include polytomously scored items. In a study by Hambleton and Plake (1995), the method was applied to a multidimensional performance assessment and termed the extended Angoff method. Instead of providing an estimate of the proportion of borderline candidates who would get a multiple-choice item correct, panelists in the extended version gave an estimate of the expected score a just-qualified candidate would obtain on a polytomously scored item.

In Hambleton and Plake (1995), panelists estimated the scores the borderline examinee would get on each of the three dimensions used to score, on a four-point scale, each performance task for the National Board of Professional Teaching Standards (NBPTS) certification exam. Then, these estimates were summed to derive the expected score for the borderline examinee on each exercise. Panelists were also allowed to suggest weights to use in combining scores across items. There were multiple rounds in which panelists set standards, indicated their confidence level in those standards, received feedback about their standards and those of the group, engaged in discussion, and provided relative weights.

Plake (1995) noted in a critique of the method that it appears to be the easiest to administer (of the ones studied for use with the NBPTS exam; the other two methods—judgmental policy capturing and dominant profile—are described below), and speculated that it would yield more replicable results. The extended Angoff method did not, however, take into account the underlying decision rule of the panelists, as observed by Hambleton and Plake (1995). Although the Angoff method is a fully compensatory model, in which a high score on one exercise can balance a low score on another exercise, panelists appeared to want a conjunctive model in which candidates must pass certain exercises in order to be certified. A discrepancy was thus revealed between two sets of questionnaire data: first, the high degree of confidence the panelists felt in the standard (which was set using a compensatory model); and second, the fact that the panelists theoretically viewed the conjunctive model as most appropriate. The authors were troubled by this disparity, and they concluded that in this study, the standard that was ultimately set was not solidly in line with the panelists' preferences.

Several other methods have been used that bear similarity to the extended Angoff approach. These include the analytic method, which was implemented by Pitoniak, Hambleton, and Biskin (2003) in a performance assessment comprised of simulations. Panelists reviewed the items contained within each simulation and estimated the number of score points that they expected the just-qualified candidate to obtain. The method was implemented in an iterative manner, with discussion and feedback taking place between rounds.

3.2.3. Ebel Method

The Ebel (1972) method is characterized by the following panelist tasks. First, panelists make item-by-item judgments and classify those items along two dimensions—difficulty and relevance. The three difficulty levels suggested by Ebel were easy, medium, hard, and the four relevance levels were essential, important, acceptable, and questionable, yielding a matrix of 12 cells. (He developed the method for setting a single performance standard, but the method is easily extended to handle multiple standards.) Next, for each cell, or combination of difficulty level and relevance level, panelists provide a judgment, in terms of expected percent correct, as to how the borderline examinee will perform on the items contained within that cell. Each panelist's performance standard is obtained by multiplying the number of test items in each cell by the percentage assigned by the panelist, summing those products, and dividing by the total number of test items. These scores are then averaged across panelists to produce the panel's performance standard. (Berk, 1986, noted that the cell values may also be calculated based on the panel's cell values, which would yield a different performance standard.) The Ebel method may be used for both dichotomous and polytomous items.

It has been questioned whether keeping the highly correlated dimensions of difficulty and relevance distinct is too difficult a task for panelists (Shepard, 1984). In addition, Cizek (1996a) has pointed out that the Ebel method may prompt questions about the test construction process, since the method identifies items that are of questionable relevance. He also noted that requiring panelists to come up with item difficulty levels may not seem a necessary task to them since empirical item data are often available and may be provided.

3.2.4. Nedelsky Method

In the Nedelsky (1954) method, which can only be used with multiple-choice items, the panelists' task is to estimate for each item the number of answer choices that they think the borderline examinee would be able to rule out as incorrect. The reciprocal of the number of choices not ruled out represents the probability that the borderline examinee will answer the item correctly by random guessing after eliminating the choices he/she knows to be incorrect. The probability estimates are then summed across items to obtain each panelist's performance standard, and then averaged across panelists to yield a final performance standard. Nedelsky suggested that the value then be adjusted using a procedure designed to take measurement error into account. The adjustment uses both a constant determined by considerations of the types of items on the test, and an estimate of the standard deviation of the performance standard based on the likely values of the reciprocals. The adjustment has, however, rarely been used in practice, though the method itself has been popular for some time, especially with credentialing exams.

The assumption underlying the Nedelsky method is that the borderline examinee eliminates the answer choices he or she thinks are incorrect, and then chooses at random among the remaining choices (Livingston & Zieky, 1982).

The accurateness of this assumption has been questioned (Jaeger, 1989; Plake & Melican, 1989; Shepard, 1984). It also limits panelists to a discrete set of probabilities dependent on the number of answer choices (Brennan & Lockwood, 1980; van der Linden, 1982), and a probability of .50 is frequently assigned (Shepard, 1984). The low performance standards that the method would tend to produce as a result of these factors have also been viewed as problematic (Shepard, 1980), a concern that has been borne out in some studies (e.g., Chang, 1999; Melican, Mills, & Plake, 1989; Subkoviak, Kane, & Duncan, 2002).

3.2.5. Jaeger Method

The Jaeger method (Jaeger, 1982, 1989), though a test-centered method, differs from those just described in that it deliberately takes into account the various constituents who may have a stake in the performance standard being set and was proposed for use with high school graduation tests. The focus in this method is on whether panelists, via the use of a yes/no method, think that *every* examinee *should* be able to answer the item. As Kane (1994) pointed out, the focus is shifted from estimating a probability for a hypothetical group of examinees to a more overtly value-laden judgment. In addition, the task does not require panelists to conceptualize a borderline examinee (Jaeger & Keller-McNulty, 1991). The Jaeger method was originally formulated as an iterative process, which is now a common feature of other standard-setting methods (such as Angoff) as well. Jaeger himself noted that the method may, however, yield standards that are impractically high, particularly if separate standards are set for each task and satisfactory performance is necessary on all the tasks sampled for the test (Jaeger & Keller-McNulty, 1991).

3.2.6. Bookmark and Other Item Mapping Methods

Item mapping refers to the use of spatially representative displays—item maps—to illustrate the relationship between item difficulty and examinee performance on a given test; item difficulty is generally estimated in conjunction with item response theory models (see Hambleton, Swaminathan, & Rogers, 1991). Item mapping may be used as a part of standard-setting and/or to illustrate what examinees at a given performance standard or in a performance category can do. Confusion sometimes arises, however, because there are several different types of item mapping standard-setting approaches, including one specifically named the item mapping method; others include bookmark and mapmark. Since bookmark is the most commonly used of the item mapping approaches, it will be described first.

The bookmark method requires panelists to review specially constructed booklets, termed "ordered item booklets," in which the test items are ordered according to their difficulty parameter as estimated with an IRT model (Lewis, Green, Mitzel, Baum, & Patz, 1998; Lewis, Mitzel, & Green, 1996; Mitzel, Lewis, Patz, & Green, 2001). For constructed-response items, each score point has a unique location in the ordered item booklet (corresponding also to its difficulty level), and the rubric and a sample examinee response at that score point is presented along with the item itself. Panelists are also given an item map, in which each row contains an item, sequenced in terms of its location in the ordered booklet. Other information also included for each item is its scale location (i.e., its difficulty level on the reporting scale), an indication of the item's position in the original test booklet, and its content categorization.

The task for the panelist is to place a bookmark between the two items in the ordered item booklet such that from his or her perspective, those items before the bookmark represent content that borderline examinees at a given performance standard should be likely to know and be able to do. It should be noted that although Lewis and colleagues (Lewis et al., 1996, 1998; Mitzel et al., 2001) described the placement as being between two items, others have operationalized the task for panelists as putting the bookmark on the last item the borderline examinees would be likely to answer correctly. As Cizek, Bunch, and Koons (2005) pointed out, however, both approaches lead to the same result. Each panelist's performance standard is obtained by taking the IRT item location value of the item immediately preceding the bookmark (or on which the bookmark is placed, depending on the implementation method). Figure 12.1 shows the relationship between the bookmark's placement and the score scale. The panel's performance standard is then obtained by calculating the mean or median of the panelists' scale score performance standards (see Cizek et al., 2004, for a detailed review of the method).

A key concept in the bookmark method is that of the value that is given to panelists for their use in estimating the likelihood of a borderline examinee's answering a given multiple-choice item correctly, or, for constructed-response items, obtaining at least the score point indicated. This likelihood is termed the response probability (RP). Lewis et al. (1996, 1998) have used an RP of .67. While acknowledging that other RP values are, of course, possible, Mitzel et al. (2001) pointed out that the concept of mastery used in

FIGURE 12.1 Illustration of the Determination of the Cut Score in the Bookmark Method Given a Response Probability of .67 and a Panelist Bookmark Placement on Item 37

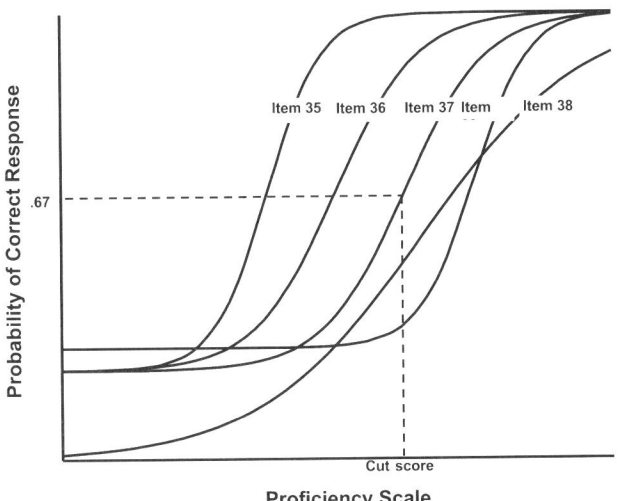

bookmark training implies an RP value greater than .50, and that a value of .50 is more in line with the idea of uncertainty, "which is both unfamiliar to most panelists and not aligned with the criterion task of specifying the skills and academic content that students should know and be able to do" (p. 262). Mitzel et al. acknowledged, however, that attention needs to be given to the effect of the chosen RP value and its impact on both the ordering of items due to different measurement models and the ability of panelists to provide judgments using that value. Others have echoed this suggestion (see, for example, Hambleton, 1998; Hambleton, Jaeger, et al., 2000; and Reckase, 2000a).

Some researchers have addressed the topic of the choice of RP value. Huynh (1998) provided a psychometric framework for the discussion of item score locations, and reported that an RP of .67 has the property of maximizing the information function of the test when a two-parameter IRT model is used. Wang (2003) concluded that an RP of .50 is more appropriate when the Rasch model is used since in that model the likelihood of an examinee's getting a correct response is .50 when his or her ability is equal to the item difficulty. Research by Beretvas (2004) confirmed that different measurement models and RP values do affect the placement of items in the booklet; however, the impact of these differently ordered booklets on performance standards would require actual panelist ratings, not available in this simulation study. Kolstad (1996) also addressed the issue of RP values, though not in the context of judgmental standard setting.

Empirical research that has explored the use of different RP values in standard-setting studies is perhaps most informative. Several studies investigated the comparability of performance standards set using different RP values with the same set of items by randomly equivalent panels. In theory, panelists using a lower RP value such as .50 would place the bookmark later in the ordered item booklet than panelists using a higher RP value such as .80. However, the performance standard connected with the bookmarked items would theoretically be equivalent, leading to identical standards. However, research has not borne out this speculation. In a study conducted in relation to the National Adult Assessment of Literacy, the National Research Council (2005) compared RP values of .50, .67, and .80. They found that while for two of the three literacy dimensions there was a general tendency for bookmark placement to vary in the predicted manner in relation to RP value, this was not the case for the third dimension or for some performance standards within the other dimensions. And perhaps more importantly, when the ultimate target of inference—scale scores—were analyzed, the researchers found that the differences in placement across the panels using different RP values were not enough to yield comparable performance standards. In general, higher RP values led to higher performance standards.

Williams and Schulz (2005) also reported on a study where different RP values were used. Two field trials, one using an RP value of .50 and one using a value of .67, were conducted for the mapmark method developed in conjunction with NAEP standard setting, which begins with a bookmark-like task. As in the National Research Council (2005) study, panelists set higher performance standards with the higher RP value. The higher performance standards resulting from the use of the .67 RP value were more in line with the current standards (set previously with an item rating method) for that NAEP assessment. It should be noted, however, that there were differences other than RP value between the field trials, and therefore results should be interpreted with caution. Panelist feedback indicated a preference for the .67 RP value; panelists who used the .67 value thought they would have had difficulty with the .50 value, and those who used the .50 value said they would have felt more comfortable with the .67 RP. The concept of a mastery task (.67 RP) appeared to have been easier to comprehend and implement than that of an even chance task (.50 RP).

Thus, as some psychometricians have suspected, the use of different RP values does appear to produce systematically different performance standards. The results of Williams and Schulz (2005) suggested that an RP value of .67 is easier for panelists to use and yields more reasonable standards. However, as pointed out by the National Research Council (2005), the selection of RP value, as with any other feature of a standard-setting method, call for consideration of the specific test and its uses:

> Like many decisions made in connection with developing a test, the choice of a response probability value requires both technical and nontechnical considerations. The decision should be based on the level of confidence one wants to have that examinees have truly mastered the content and skills assessed, but it should also reflect the objectives for the test, the ways the test results are used, and the consequences associated with these uses. Choice of a response probability value requires making a judgment, and reasonable people may disagree about which of several options is most appropriate. (p. ES-3)

However, the bookmark method, which is used for setting performance standards on many statewide student assessments (Council of Chief State School Officers, 2001), does have some positive features. Advantages include its being viewed favorably by panelists, who find the task of placing bookmarks to be meaningful and feel confident about the standards that are set (Lewis et al., 1996; State of Wisconsin, 1997).

As noted previously, there are methods other than bookmark that use item maps. These include one termed "item map" (Shen, 2001) and another called "item mapping" (Wang, 2003). Both utilize the Rasch model for item ordering (the bookmark method usually uses a three-parameter-logistic/two-parameter-partial-credit model; Mitzel et al., 2001). In terms of RP criterion, Wang noted that item mapping uses an RP criterion of .50; Shen did not mention an RP criterion, though he indicated that panelists were given instructions that used the term "mastery." Wang also noted that item mapping has an additional graphic element, a histogram, and that only a representative sample of items needs to be rated.

An additional method mentioned previously is mapmark, recently investigated for use with NAEP standard setting (Schulz & Mitzel, 2005). Mapmark builds on the bookmark method but adds in domain feedback (a domain being a group of items with similar content), which appears to facilitate panelists' understanding of student achievement in different subareas (Schulz, Lee, & Mullen, 2005).

3.2.7. Direct Consensus Method

The direct consensus method was conceptualized as a way to streamline the standard-setting process, reducing the complexity of the rating task and, as a result, the amount of time needed to arrive at performance standards. In this method, panelists review multiple-choice test items that are grouped into clusters of approximately eight items each according to their content specifications. For each item cluster, panelists are asked to individually indicate on a rating form the number of items that they think the borderline examinee would answer correctly. After ratings for the first item cluster are completed, the ratings for each panelist are placed into spreadsheet form and projected onto a screen visible to all panelists. Panelists then discussed their ratings for the cluster, consider the item statistics (p values), and then modify, as appropriate, their ratings. Any changes are incorporated into the spreadsheet immediately. This process is repeated for each of the item clusters.

Following a review of all of the ratings for the item clusters, the relative ranks of clusters by difficulty in terms of (1) actual operational performance data and (2) panelist ratings are shown to panelists. Both panelist ratings and the projected performance standard are also displayed to panelists after ratings for all item clusters are completed. Upon viewing this information, panelists are given an additional chance to change their performance standard if they feel that the sum of their cluster scores does not reflect their overall sense of how well candidates should be expected to perform, in what is termed the *global modification step*. Next, the panel discusses how viable they see the panel mean of the performance standard on the total test to be, and adjust it as they see fit. If the panel does not arrive at a consensus regarding a performance standard, the mean score across panelists is used as the final group performance standard.

The direct consensus method has been implemented in three studies (Sireci, Hambleton, Huff, & Jodoin, 2000; Pitoniak, Hambleton, & Sireci, 2002; Pitoniak et al., 2003; see also Sireci, Hambleton, & Pitoniak, 2004). In each study, it was compared to another method—the Angoff method in the first study, and an approach termed the item cluster method (described later in the chapter) in the remaining studies. In all three studies, two panels used both methods, which enabled data on replicability to be collected as well. In each study, the direct consensus method did, as anticipated, take less time than the other method used. With five of the six panels used across the studies, consensus was reached; for the remaining panel (Sireci et al., 2004), the average of panelists' ratings was taken for the final standard. In all of the studies, the direct consensus method yielded higher performance standards than the other method considered. In one of the studies (Pitoniak et al., 2002), the panels had a large difference in performance standards, but in the other studies the across-panel differences within method were fairly similar across methods.

3.3. Methods Involving Review of Candidates

Methods falling in this category require direct ratings of a sample of candidates. For credentialing exams, candidates would be judged in terms of their qualifications to practice or not practice in a profession, or to be "just barely qualified" to practice. For educational assessments, candidates would be placed into performance categories, or on the borderlines of performance categories. These ratings might be made by the candidates' teachers or others capable of making valid judgments about candidates' proficiency levels, but the raters generally do not have knowledge of the candidates' test scores. The role of a standard-setting panel or possibly a technical advisory committee might be to design a rating form and directions, choose raters, draw samples of candidates, oversee the collection of data, and ultimately to determine the best approach for deriving performance standards from the ratings.

3.3.1. Borderline Group Method

As its name suggests, in the borderline group method a group of borderline examinees is identified for each performance standard based on the ratings of teachers and/or other qualified persons to judge them. Then, the test scores for these borderline examinees are gathered, and their median test score is typically used as the performance standard (though a different performance standard may be chosen depending on the perceived relative importance of false positive and false negative errors in classification; Schoon & Smith, 1996).

Although the method is simple conceptually, it may have some disadvantages operationally. Mills (1995) noted that the borderline group may consist of a small number of examinees, resulting in performance standards being set on limited and possibly unstable test score distributions. Livingston and Zieky (1982) and Jaeger (1989) also observed that raters may have difficulty restricting their judgment to how the examinees would perform on the content that is covered by the test to the exclusion of other factors, both cognitive and non-cognitive, or may tend to classify examinees into the borderline group if they are unsure of their knowledge and skills. It is also noted that if the borderline group were to contain examinees who are "just qualified," choosing the performance standard to be placed at the median of the actual test scores would result in half the examinees being placed in the lower performance category, when all of them would deserve to be placed in the higher performance category. The temptation might be to lower the performance standard, but then the number of false positive errors would increase.

A recent development related to both the borderline group method and the contrasting group method is the use of the cluster analysis technique, which has been suggested as a way to empirically determine the composition of the groups through inspection of item score data (Sireci, 2001; Sireci, Robin, & Patelis, 1999).

3.3.2. Contrasting Groups Method

In the contrasting groups method, raters are asked to identify one group of examinees whose members are clearly above a particular performance standard and another group whose members are clearly below that performance standard. Then, the test score distributions of these two groups are contrasted to select the performance standard (see Figure 12.2). The method is easily extended to more than two categories by asking raters to sort known

FIGURE 12.2 Contrasting Groups Method with Two Performance Categories

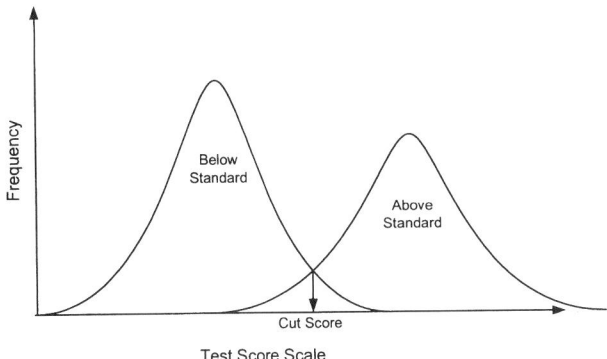

candidates into more than two performance categories, with the approach to data analysis being basically the same as for two categories. Adjacent categories are used to derive each performance standard (see Figure 12.3).

Several approaches exist for determining the performance standards. Livingston and Zieky (1982) described dividing the score scale into intervals and calculating the percentage of examinees at each level who are judged to be qualified; this distribution can then be smoothed, and the point at which 50% of the candidates were judged qualified used as the performance standard. An alternative approach is to select the test score that results in the fewest "false positive" errors (i.e., classifying a below-standard candidate as meeting the standard) and "false negative" errors (i.e., classifying an above-standard candidate as not meeting the standard) or some weighted combination of the two types of errors. Also, logistic regression can be used to find the test score that minimizes these two types of errors (Livingston & Zieky, 1989). This approach was also used by Sireci, Rizavi, Dillingham, and Rodriguez (1999) and Sireci, Robin, and Patelis (1999). A review of the contrasting groups literature can be found in Brandon (2002). However, it should be noted that some of the research he described as "response-focused contrasting groups" would be classified within this chapter as being methods involving

FIGURE 12.3 Contrasting Groups Method with Four Performance Categories

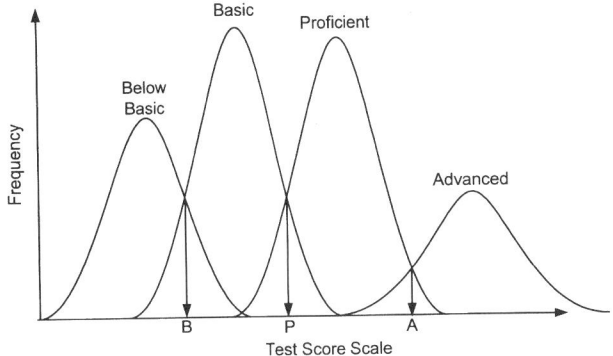

candidate work, as opposed to traditional contrasting group methods.

A likely challenge with both the contrasting groups and borderline group methods is finding raters who are familiar with the examinees. The achievement of this goal is most probable in the context of an educational assessment, where teachers are familiar with the capabilities of their students. Even in that setting, however, there is the danger of the performance standards not being generalizable beyond the examinee sample used for analysis (Hambleton, Jaeger, et al., 2000). An additional difficulty may arise in the contrasting groups approach when score distributions overlap and a clear demarcation to be used as the performance standard is not apparent.

3.4. Methods Involving Review of Candidate Work

Contained within this section are several methods that are very similar but have been given different names by the authors who implemented them, perhaps because they were being developed concurrently in the same general time period when methods were being explored that could deal with tests containing constructed-response items. The main differences among the methods include: (1) the types of items on the assessment, whether just constructed-response or a combination of multiple-choice and constructed-response; (2) whether the rating task is done holistically or item by item; (3) the nature of the rating task, which may be identifying either the work of just-qualified candidates or that of candidates at the top of one performance category and the bottom of another; and (4) for the item-by-item type of task, the method of calculating the performance standard.

An attempt has been made in the following subsections to group the methods by the type of ratings provided by panelist: item-by-item, holistic, or hybrid. Since the following descriptions of methods are necessarily brief, the reader is encouraged to consult the source articles cited in order to obtain specific details about the features of the method and its implementation (a caveat that applies to all methods described in this chapter).

3.4.1. Item-by-Item Approaches

The paper selection method is the only item-by-item method to be reviewed within this section. As its name implies, the paper selection method is used for constructed-response items that yield "papers" or other samples of candidate performance; multiple-choice items have not been included in its use to date. In this method (Loomis & Bourque, 2001), ratings are done item by item, as opposed to viewing the candidate's work holistically. After examples of candidate work from every score point are given to panelists, they are asked to select the papers they view as representing the borderline examinee for the performance standard of interest. Performance standards are obtained by averaging the scores of those papers selected as borderline for each item.

Scores for the papers are not revealed to the panelists, which is desirable from the point of view of making sure selections were based on the performance category descriptions and not the score points. However, this may make it difficult for the panelists to adjust their performance standards from round to round since they do not know which direction in which to adjust ratings for individual papers; this difficulty is exacerbated, noted Loomis and Bourque (2001), when there is less of a correspondence between the knowledge and skills related to a score point versus the performance standard. It may also be difficult to educate panelists that, for example, a score of 3 out of 5 on one task may represent borderline performance at a given performance standard (for example, basic), while for another task it may represent borderline performance at another level (for example, proficient).

With this approach it is critical that the scoring of responses be done carefully so that scores assigned to papers very clearly match the scoring rubric. Alternately, papers are selected from those where scoring had been replicated by a second set of raters. However, there may not be papers viewed by panelists as representing the borderline examinee, or there may be a lack of papers at a given score point (Loomis & Bourque, 2001). The time needed to prepare a large set of papers in order to prevent such an occurrence as much as possible should not be underestimated. As noted by Loomis and Bourque, the paper selection method was used as an actual rating method for NAEP standard setting in 1992, but since then has been used only as an adjunct to the process as a means of familiarizing panelists with borderline student performance, the scoring rubrics, and the range of responses actually given by NAEP examinees.

3.4.2. Holistic Approaches

Discussed within this subsection are the body of work, booklet classification, and generalized examinee-centered methods. In each, panelists view the samples of examinee performance, comprised of both multiple-choice and constructed-response items, holistically.

In the body of work method (Kingston, Kahl, Sweeney, & Bay, 2001), panelists review entire sets of examinee test responses that are sorted from lowest to highest total scores, including both a display of answers to multiple-choice items and responses to the constructed-response items. The panelist rating task consists of assigning each set of examinee work into one of the performance categories. A multi-step process involves training, initial evaluations of examinee work to determine approximate ranges of the performance standards, and then a more intensive look at the entire set of test responses for an increased number of examinees with total scores in the vicinity of likely performance standards. The increased number of examinee papers to rate increases the stability of the determination of performance standards. Performance standards may be calculated using logistic regression (Kingston et al., 2001) or an averaging technique (Olson, Mead, & Payne, 2002).

The body of work method has been used in several statewide student assessment programs. In a review of these implementations, Kingston et al. (2001) concluded that although this method—which utilizes a task similar to that which educators are accustomed to doing (reviewing a rich body of candidate work)—is promising, more work is needed to explore why it often produces higher performance standards than other methods. Kingston et al. described a study in which performance standards obtained using the body of work method were compared to those obtained with an approach using classroom teacher judgments, and the former produced higher performance standards than the latter. They suggested that this could perhaps be addressed by giving panelists in the body of work method information about how classroom teachers rated the examinees whose test booklets were examined (though this obviously adds a level of complexity to the implementation of the method).

One advantage of the body of work method noted by Hambleton (1998) is that it allows panelists to provide judgments about the overall performance of an examinee rather than focusing on the performance of individual items or sections of an assessment. However, further research would help define the method's strengths and limitations. For example, one possible area for further study is whether there is a maximum booklet length beyond which panelists cannot make valid and reliable judgments about the material contained therein (Hambleton, Jaeger, et al., 2000).

The booklet classification method, pilot tested on NAEP assessments, is very similar to the body of work method. Panelists are given assessment booklets representing a range of performance, and are asked to place each booklet into a performance category. Booklets may be ordered by score level to facilitate the rating task, though the panelists are then told that their classifications do not need to reflect this ordering (Loomis & Bourque, 2001). Hanson, Bay, and Loomis (1998) tried several approaches to transforming proficiency estimates into performance standards, but concluded further work was needed in this area; this issue was one factor that resulted in the rejection of the method for NAEP (Loomis & Bourque, 2001). Hanson et al. also noted that performance standards obtained with this method may appear too high, and were in fact higher than those obtained with an item rating method. In addition, panelists may not take the holistic approach reflected in the design of the method, instead estimating item or task performance levels and then adding them together (Loomis & Bourque, 2001); the time allowed for ratings may need to be restricted to prevent this activity.

The generalized examinee-centered method was developed by Cohen, Kane, and Crooks (1999). It is very similar to both methods just described, with a slight difference being that the rating scale is broken down into greater numbers of categories (i.e., borderline categories were added). With this method, several approaches were explored for transforming panelist ratings of examinee work into performance standards. The authors concluded that an "equating" approach, in which the ratings were rescaled to have the same mean and standard deviations as the scores, was most appropriate.

3.4.3. Hybrid Approaches

For the remaining methods, panelists review sections of tests as either an interim or final step in the process. Relevant methods include the analytic judgment, integrated judgment, and work classification methods.

In the analytic judgment method, samples of examinee performance may be reviewed either item by item or by sections of the test (Plake & Hambleton, 2001). The method first requires that a subset of test booklets from examinees be carefully chosen for analysis; all booklets must be previously scored, but these scores are not revealed to the panelists. The selection of examinee work is structured so as to obtain work across the total score scale. The method is termed "analytic" because panelists' ratings are based on components of the test, rather than on the entire test. Breaking up the test booklet into smaller collections of test items was done to reduce the cognitive complexity of the rating task by reducing it to judging more modest sets of items. The researchers had observed in preliminary studies that when panelists were presented with the complete work of examinees, they tended to skip over some of that work and key in on selected questions or the first part of the students' work.

Panelists place examinees' responses into one of 12 achievement categories (each of the four performance categories was subdivided into three categories—low, medium, and high). Panelists may accomplish these ratings by either sorting the examinee work into four performance categories and then dividing them again into low, medium, and high, or by directly classifying the examinee papers into the rating scale categories. The process is then repeated for each set of student work. Panelists who are teachers like the sorting procedure because they are more comfortable sorting candidate papers into ordered performance categories than they are providing Angoff-type estimates; the former task is most likely a common one for teachers. The ratings can be transformed into performance standards by using either a boundary method (i.e., averaging the scores of papers assigned to the high end of one performance category and the low end of the next higher performance category) or a regression approach for each set; the performance standards established for each set of test items are then summed in order to obtain performance standards for the total test.

In the integrated judgment method (Jaeger & Mills, 2001), panelists review entire test booklets for candidates and place them into one of 12 achievement categories (for each of the four performance categories, there are three subgroupings—barely within the category, clearly within the category, and almost in the next higher category). Operationally, however, the ratings are made first for each of three sections, and these judgments are taken into account by the panelists when making a final rating for the whole booklet. The performance standards can be calculated by using either a boundary or regression approach with the ratings in the almost-in-the-next-higher and the barely-within categories for adjacent categories.

In the work classification method (Pitoniak et al., 2003), panelists review samples of candidate responses to the items within a performance assessment comprised of several simulations. Approximately 20 candidate responses are provided for each simulation; while each simulation contains a set of items, panelists rate the simulations holistically. For each simulation, panelists are presented with a variety of candidate responses ranging across the score continuum from poor to excellent. The task of the panelists is to assign each of the sets of candidate simulation responses to one of the performance categories. Panelist ratings can be transformed into performance standards in several ways: (1) boundary, which takes the mean score of candidate response patterns assigned by panelists to the borderline categories; (2) regression, in which a non-linear regression line is fit to the mean scores of candidate response patterns assigned to each of the four performance categories, or (3) "equating," through use of an equipercentile relationship between response pattern scores and assigned performance categories. The first approach is simple enough for panelists to do themselves; the second and third require more time and are more likely to be conducted after the session has concluded. For another application of this basic method in the field of medicine using videotapes of candidate work, see McKinley, Boulet, and Hambleton, 2005.

3.5. Methods Involving Review of Score Profiles

3.5.1. Judgmental Policy Capturing Method

The judgmental policy capturing (JPC) method was developed for use with performance-based credentialing exams containing complex multidimensional exercises. As the method's name suggests, its goal is to capture the standard-setting policy used by panelists through a statistical analysis of their ratings. The assumption is that panelists cannot articulate their policies about the vector of candidate scores needed to pass; they instead rate a large number of vectors of scores (called "score profiles"), after which their policies are inferred from a statistical analysis of their ratings. Later these can be averaged to provide a passing score that can be applied to all candidates.

The panelists' task in the JPC method is to review hypothetical score profiles for the exercises comprising the assessment and assign each score profile to one of four performance categories. These data are then analyzed to determine each panelist's latent standard-setting policy, including the weights that the panelist assigns to each exercise and the type of policy used: compensatory, where the total score is a weighted total of scores on individual exercises, or conjunctive, where some of the exercises would have a minimum required level. A weighted average of the panelists' policies is then calculated in order to obtain the latent standard-setting policy for the entire group of panelists.

Jaeger (1995a, 1995b) described two slightly different implementations of the method, both with multidimensional performance assessments developed by the National Board of Professional Teaching Standards. The use of the method varied across the studies; the differences stemmed from both the different characteristics of the assessments and the degree to which the overall process was an iterative one. In Jaeger (1995a), the method was implemented in two stages since each exercise, as well as the entire assessment, was scored multidimensionally. However, the process was not iterative, as it was in Jaeger (1995b), where panelists were provided with information about their own ratings of profiles and the ratings of the entire panel.

Jaeger (1995b) viewed the method as feasible, concluding that panelists are up to the task of providing ratings on numerous complex assessment components in a reasonable amount of time, and that there is a high level of intrapanelist consistency in responses to the score profiles. In Jaeger (1995a), the standards resulting from the JPC method were higher than those obtained using the extended Angoff method, and appeared to be too high; the iterative process implemented in Jaeger (1995b) might ameliorate this problem, though since that study did not compare methods that conclusion is speculative. Hambleton (1998) noted that the task of finding statistical models that fit the panelists' ratings and then explaining the overall process to panelists for deriving a performance standard is a challenging one.

3.5.2. Dominant Profile Method

The dominant profile method (DPM) was also developed and implemented with multidimensional NBPTS assessments. As with the JPC method, in the DPM panelists review score profiles across different exercises in the assessment. However, with the DPM panelists attempt to come *directly* to a consensus on the policy to be used in setting a standard (Plake, Hambleton, & Jaeger, 1997).

Two investigations of the DPM have been conducted, the first by Putnam, Pence, and Jaeger (1995), and the second by Plake, Hambleton, and Jaeger (1997). In both implementations, the first stage required panelists to review score profiles, state their decision policies, and create profiles of borderline examinees that represent their "bottom line," or the lowest levels of performance that would justify certification. In the Putnam et al. study, subsequent steps, including receiving feedback and reviewing additional profiles, took place by mail. In the Plake et al. study, the second round took place in person, with panelists discussing their policies in small groups and then rewriting their policies individually. In theory, consensus in policy could have been achieved at the end of the second round, but since this was not the case, a follow-up mailing was sent to panelists listing three policies synthesized from round two data. Panelists provided endorsement, confidence, and preference ratings for these policies; while one policy was rated most highly by a majority of panelists, differences still remained. The challenge of reconciling panelists' views into one group policy was noted as a troubling outstanding issue of the method (Plake et al., 1997). The confounding of the method with that of the JPC method, which preceded it in both studies, is also an issue requiring further study.

3.5.3. Item Cluster Method

In the item cluster method, the score profile information that panelists review consists of responses from approximately 20 examinees to a group of item clusters, each comprised of approximately six or seven items. The examinee profiles are selected to be representative of those of the overall pool of examinees. The first-round data presented to panelists include not only an indication of whether the candidate got the item correct, but if he or she got it incorrect, the identity of the distractor that was chosen. In addition, panelists are provided with detailed information about the nature of the error reflected in each distractor. Candidate profiles are presented in order from lowest to highest score on that cluster. The task of the panelists is to review the candidate profiles on the cluster of items and rate each candidate's performance on a four-point scale; the possible ratings are failing, just below borderline, just above borderline, and solid/exceptional. The process includes, as do many methods, panelist feedback, discussion, and the provision of a second round of ratings. Panelist ratings can be transformed into performance standards in the same manner as for the work classification method—boundary, equating, and regression.

Three studies have looked at the item cluster method: Mills et al. (2000); Pitoniak et al. (2002), and Pitoniak et al. (2003). Parallel panels were used in each study, and the method was in general shown to be consistent across panels. In the studies comparing it to the direct consensus method, the item cluster method yielded lower performance standards, and ones that appeared to be more plausible. Panelists viewed the method favorably, though they stressed that adequate time needs to be allotted for the provision of ratings; these time requirements may be a drawback to the method.

3.6. Compromise Methods

The standard-setting methods described above can be termed "absolute" methods in that they attempt to establish a performance standard that is not influenced by normative information. Performance standards that do reflect norm-referenced procedures, such as setting a performance standard so that a certain percentage of the examinees pass, are termed "relative" or "normative" standards (Nedelsky, 1954). As Cizek (1996a) noted, in the 1970s absolute performance standards became more popular, and in most cases replaced normative ones. However, several methods were developed in an attempt to effect a compromise between relative and absolute standards. These methods, to be described next, are intended for high-stakes assessments with a single pass-fail performance standard, and can be used in several ways. They can be used as freestanding procedures to set performance standards, or can be used as an adjunct process to adjust scores obtained by other standard-setting methods. As such, Cizek observed that these methods can be seen as balancing two competing perspectives—a cognitive one linked to the judgmental task panelists are asked to make, and a political one tied to the realities resulting from setting a given performance standard. Within this section, three compromise methods will be reviewed: the Hofstee, Beuk, and de Gruijter methods. For space reasons, only the Hofstee method will be explained fully and accompanied by a figure illustrating its calculation. For the Beuk and de Gruijter methods, the reader is encouraged to consult the references given for further detail and graphical representations.

3.6.1. Hofstee Method

In the Hofstee (1983) method, panelists are asked to provide four judgments: (1) the maximum acceptable required passing score (as defined on the total test score scale) for the test; (2) the minimum acceptable required passing score for the test; (3) the maximum failure rate that would be acceptable; and (4) the minimum failure rate that would be acceptable. Figure 12.4 displays a graph that uses the candidate test score distribution (the S-shaped curve) to link failure rates to possible passing scores. For each of the four judgments, the average of the panelists' ratings are compiled, two points—(4,1) and (3,2)—are placed in the graph, and the points are then joined by a straight line. It is along this line that an optimal solution balancing the panelists' acceptable passing scores and failure rates can be found. Where the line cuts the curve is the optimal placement for the passing score. The final passing score (P) and the associated percentage of failures can be read from the graph. Additional detail regarding this method may be found in Hofstee (1983), Mills (1995), and Norcini (2003). The Hofstee compromise method was used by Mills et al. (2000). However, a possible outcome noted by Cizek (1996a) and Mills and Melican (1988) did occur, in that the line drawn from the panelists' preferences did not intersect with the curve reflecting the candidate test score data. When this situation occurs, panelists need to reconsider one or more of their four judgments.

FIGURE 12.4 Illustration of the Hofstee Method

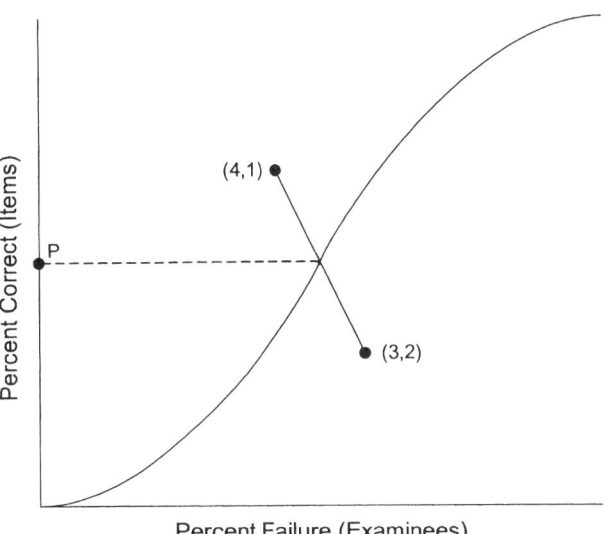

The S-shaped curve is based on the candidate test score distribution and highlights the passing score (from 0 to 100%) corresponding to each possible failure rate (from 0 to 100%). As the desired failure rate is increased, so is the corresponding passing score (and vice versa). The values of the points are as follows: (1) the maximum acceptable passing score; (2) the minimum acceptable passing score; (3) the maximum failure rate that would be acceptable; and (4) the minimum failure rate that would be acceptable. P is chosen as the performance standard on the test because it is the optimal placement that is consistent with the four preferences of the panelists.

3.6.2. Beuk Method

In order to implement the Beuk (1984) method, panelists provide two judgments: (1) based on the total possible test score, the percent correct that a borderline examinee should be able to get, and (2) the expected pass rate for the examinee population. The mean and standard deviation of these judgments are calculated over panelists. An adjusted value for percent correct passing score and passing rate is obtained by graphing a line that takes the panelist values into account and determining its intersection with the curve linking pass rates (vertical axis) to possible passing scores (horizontal axis) using the distribution of candidate total test scores. In practice, as Mills noted the adjustments to percent correct and passing rate will be smaller to the extent to which the panelists agree on their estimates of the two values. Graphical depictions of this method may be found in Beuk (1984), Cizek (1996a), and Mills (1995). One potential difficulty with the method noted by Mills (which could be applied to each of the compromise methods) is that panelists who do not have a great deal of experience with the performance of examinees may find it difficult to estimate a passing rate for them.

3.6.3. de Gruijter Method

In the de Gruijter (1985) approach the panelists provide estimates similar to that given in the Beuk (1984) method: (1) the percent correct that a borderline examinee should ideally be able to obtain, and (2) the expected failing rate for the examinee population (as opposed to the passing rate for the Beuk method). In addition, however, panelists provide an estimate of the uncertainty of values, which is used in the graphical determination of the adjustment to the performance standard. Graphical representations of the method may be found in de Gruijter (1985) and Mills (1995). Mills observed that the method requires complex computations and is difficult to explain, and that panelists may find the provision of uncertainty estimates a challenging task (see, e.g., Mills & Melican, 1988) despite the appeal of including this information in the process.

3.7. Compensatory Versus Conjunctive Standards

Standard-setting policies may be compensatory, conjunctive, or a combination thereof (Hambleton, 1995). In compensatory models, candidate scores from items are combined in such a way that a high score on one item can compensate for a low score on another one. The Angoff method is a good example of a compensatory standard-setting policy, in that what places candidates in the performance categories is their total test score. Candidate performance on particular items or even subsets of items, regardless of panelist perceptions of their criticality, is unimportant to the ultimate candidate classifications as long as a specified total score is obtained. For example, with a test containing 10 exercises, each with a four-point score scale, a compensatory model may allow a candidate to pass if he or she obtained the performance standard of 28 overall, regardless of how these scores were obtained. A candidate could conceivably pass by getting a score of 1 on four exercises and a 4 on the six remaining ones (as improbable as such a scoring pattern might be).

In contrast are conjunctive models, which are known as multiple-cutoff models (Mehrens & Phillips, 1989) in that candidates must attain a stated performance standard on each exercise to pass the test. In the earlier example, a combination policy containing conjunctive and compensatory components would require candidates to obtain a score of at least 2 on all ten exercises (the conjunctive component), and an overall total score of at least 28 points (the compensatory component).

Conjunctive models are often preferred by panelists when standards are being set on a test comprised of performance assessments or different skills (see Hambleton, Jaeger, et al., 2000; Hambleton & Plake, 1995). For example, for a reading literacy test measuring both reading and writing skills, policymakers were concerned that candidates might pass the test with relatively low writing scores, an outcome that appeared unsatisfactory to them. They seriously considered a conjunctive policy where candidates would need to achieve a performance standard set on the reading and writing portions of the assessment. Conjunctive standards are, however, problematic in practice. Because measurement error can be rather large at the level of a portion of the assessment, an inflated false-negative error rate can result at the test level when conjunctive standards are employed. In this example, the writing component of the assessment was relatively short and score reliability was modest. The result would have been many candidates failing the writing portion, and subsequently the test, simply because of large measurement errors on the writing component. With relatively low test score reliability on one or more portions of the assessment, false-negative error rates would be relatively high.

Hambleton and Slater (1997) demonstrated in a simulation study the effects of number of exercises and the intercorrelations between exercises on decision consistency and decision accuracy, using several different standard-setting policies. They found that a policy with conjunctive features such as those described above can lead to high decision consistency (with enough exercises, nearly every candidate would fail at least one of the exercises simply because of measurement error, and would fail every time they took the test, so decision consistency over parallel administrations would be high) and low decision accuracy (just about all candidates who deserve to pass would, however, fail the test), particularly when the intercorrelations between the exercises are low and the test contains many exercises that must be passed. In general, they concluded, "choices about scoring models and standard-setting policies need to be made with full knowledge of their implications for both decision consistency and decision accuracy as well as other types of validity" (p. 36). Those considering a standard-setting policy with conjunctive features need to consider carefully the scoring model and the features of the test before implementing such an approach.

3.8. Comparative Studies

Comparative studies of methods are plentiful in the research literature and will not be reviewed here. Often these studies are inconclusive, and do not produce generalizable results for the assessment field, because of many factors: (1) the test may be unique in some way, (2) the methods were implemented in ways that may be unique to the particular research studies, and so on. Recent empirical studies, current publications, or review of standard-setting studies may, however, be especially helpful to those interested in reviewing relatively recent comparative studies of methods (e.g., Brandon, 2002, 2004; Buckendahl, Smith, Impara, & Plake, 2002; Cizek, 2001; Green, Trimble, & Lewis, 2003; Hurtz & Auerbach, 2003).

4. CHOOSING A STANDARD-SETTING PANEL

As noted previously, standard setting is a judgmental process. Key to this process, therefore, are the panelists (also sometimes called judges in the measurement literature). The selection of an effective standard-setting method will be for naught if an appropriate panel is not assembled to implement it. Within this section, both the qualifications of the panelists and the number of panelists that are needed are reviewed.

4.1. Qualifications of Panelists

One of the important issues faced by those who set performance standards concerns the composition of the standard-setting panel. Who should be included on panels and what skills do they need? Many options are possible. When setting performance standards on a statewide assessment of students, for example, one could assemble a panel composed of classroom teachers, curriculum specialists, school principals, district superintendents, state school board members, local school board members, representatives of the business community, parents, or college admissions officers, either alone or in combination. Clearly, some guidelines are needed. *Standard* 1.7 (AERA, APA, & NCME, 1999) addresses the issue of panelists' qualifications in terms of documentation, but the *Standards* provide no assistance in determining the particular composition of a standard-setting panel.

A popular approach is to support a broadly based selection of standard-setting panelists, perhaps including representatives of all groups that have a legitimate stake in the outcome of an assessment and the decisions that will derive from its use. The panels used to set performance standards for NAEP approximate this perspective, in that about 70% of their members are classroom teachers and other educators, while 30% of the panel is composed of non-educators who are selected from such populations as the business community, the military, and parents' groups. It is also common to select panels that demonstrate balance in terms of gender, ethnicity, geography, age, and experience.

Seeking broad representation of constituency groups when assembling a standard-setting panel provides political advantages. Knowledge about the content is, however, a more important criterion in panel section since standard-setting methods often require complex judgments and insights into factors such as school curricula, the abilities of examinee groups, the characteristics of test items that determine their difficulty, and the demands likely to be placed on examinees later in their schooling (or, in the case of licensure and certification examinations, in their occupational or professional roles). Obtaining reasonable results requires standard-setting panelists who are knowledgeable in these areas.

Not only should standard-setting panelists be knowledgeable about test content and the examinees, they must be capable of accessing relevant knowledge rapidly, and integrating that knowledge during a time-constrained procedure that has them considering various types of assessments and sometimes scoring rubrics. In a qualitative study by Skorupski and Hambleton (2005) of panelists setting standards, the complexities that panelists go through on their way to finalizing their judgments were reviewed. The authors reported that for some panelists the process itself remained mysterious and challenging. It remains to be seen whether improved training or an application of a more stringent criterion for knowledge of the content in panel member selection could improve the process.

Examples of procedures followed to select panelists, illustrating factors that need to be taken into account during this process, can be found in Raymond and Reid (2001). As noted earlier, for NAEP standard setting there are specific distributional requirements that must be met in terms of panel composition. Raymond and Reid described the sampling plan developed by the contractor (ACT, 1997) in order to meet these requirements. A process is used in which persons within each sampling unit are contacted in order to nominate potential panelists that meet certain qualifications (characteristics desired for panelists to be selected from that sampling unit). After individuals are nominated, and their qualifications verified, panelists are selected from the database in a manner that ensures as much as possible that the target distribution of characteristics is met. In NAEP, it is required that the target distribution be compared to the actual distribution of panelist characteristics. It is advisable that the details regarding the recruitment and ultimate composition of every standard-setting panel be reported in this way to ensure that the panel is as representative of the desired population as possible.

4.2. Number of Panelists and Design Considerations

The question "How many panelists should be used in a standard-setting study?" is just another manifestation of the common question in research: "How large a sample do I need?" The simple answer is "Get as many as panelists as can be afforded!" But this answer is sometimes unreasonable, because "getting as many panelists as can be afforded" might well be insufficient or might result in a panel producing performance standards with much more precision than is needed.

In general, as Kane (1994) indicated, the number should be sufficient to ensure that the standard errors of the performance standards are within acceptable ranges. When they are not, the number of false positive and false negative errors will be large. However, obtaining an acceptable panel size is not so easy to do. The very experts who make up an important part of the panel may be very busy, and it can be difficult to gain their commitment for the time required. Also, the sizes of the standard errors depend to a considerable extent on the standard-setting process itself—the facilitators, the panel members, the success of the training, etc; panel size is just one of the factors. In addition, any calculations that might be made at the beginning of a standard-setting process to guide the choice of panel size are going to need to be based on strong assumptions about the sampling (or non-sampling) of panelists and test items (Brennan, 1995, 2001).

Several guidelines for the number of panelists necessary for an effective panel that yields reliable judgments can be found in Raymond and Reid (2001). Using the framework of generalizability theory, they reviewed the results of studies looking at the number of panelists required for a study. Although they noted that there was a great deal of variability in the findings, a range of 10 to 15 panelists appeared to be needed to ensure an acceptable level of dependability in many contexts. In educational assessments, 15 to 30 is generally viewed as acceptable because of the desire (1) to have both broad representation on panels setting standards and (2) to obtain stable results.

Often the question is asked about whether a second sample of panelists chosen to reflect the same characteristics as the first set of panelists would produce a similar set of performance standards applying the same method. Evidence for the generalizability of the performance standards across randomly parallel panels is information often valued by policymakers, and so sometimes double the number of panelists needed for a single panel is chosen so that parallel standard-setting studies can be carried out. In one cost-effective variation of running two totally independent panels, double the number of panelists that would be suitable for a single panel is chosen. All panelists receive common training, after which the panelists are divided into two independent and randomly parallel panels, each with its own facilitator, to produce panel performance standards. The two sets of results can then be compared. When the results are close, the two sets of results are often combined to produce a single set of performance standards (Mills et al., 2000) and the separate results are used to highlight the generalizability of the findings over two more or less equivalent panels for a single test. When the results are not close, normally a review is conducted to determine if one set of results may be preferable to the other (for example, there may have been substantial confusion among the panelists in one panel, or one of the facilitators may have been judged as doing a poor job). If each performance standard is set at the mean of the performance standard set by the panels, the standard error associated with each (mean) performance standard is equal to the absolute value of the difference in the panel estimates, divided by two (Brennan, 2002).

Application of generalizability theory, using a variety of assumptions about the sampling of panelists and items, can be employed to provide estimates of the standard errors of the performance standards that are a function of the number of panelists and test items. For more on this approach, see Brennan (1995, 2001), Brennan and Lockwood (1980), Haertel (this volume), and Kane and Wilson (1984). With the judgmental item level ratings from a group of panelists (data that might come from a pilot administration), standard errors could be preliminarily calculated and used as a basis for studying the number of panelists that might be needed on a panel to obtain a desired level of precision.

5. PREPARING DESCRIPTIONS OF PERFORMANCE CATEGORIES

Time spent defining the performance category and/or borderline candidate descriptions has increased considerably in recognition of the importance of these descriptions for producing valid performance standards (see, e.g., Mills & Jaeger, 1998). This focus on clear descriptions is one of the most important advances in recent years in standard setting and is derived from NAGB's experiences in setting performance standards on NAEP (see Reckase, 2000b).

Detailed descriptions of the performance categories are normally established early in the process by a content panel in advance of the standard setting study, or they are developed as the first step in the standard-setting process. These descriptions are needed to provide the framework for panelists to make meaningful judgments about the performance standards. If performance category descriptions are developed, then panelists are told to consider borderline candidates as those just good enough or just qualified to be in that performance category. Other times, a panel of content experts will try to develop descriptions of those candidates who are at the borderline of performance standards.

Here, for example, are the performance category descriptors used in Massachusetts at the 10th grade level in mathematics:

> *Needs Improvement*—A student at this level demonstrates partial understanding of the numeration system; performs some calculations and estimations; identifies examples of basic math concepts; reads and constructs graphs, tables, and charts; applies learned procedures to solve routine problems; and applies some reasoning methods to solve simple problems.
>
> *Proficient*—A student at this level demonstrates solid understanding of the numeration system; performs most calculations and estimations; defines concepts and generates examples and counter examples of concepts; represents data and mathematical relationships in multiple forms (e.g., equations, graphs); applies learned procedures and mathematical concepts to solve a variety of problems, including multi-step problems; and uses a variety of reasoning methods to solve problems and explains steps and procedures.
>
> *Advanced*—A student at this level connects concepts from various areas of mathematics, and uses concepts to develop generalizations; performs complex calculations and estimations; selects the best representation for a given set of data and purpose; generates unique strategies and procedures to solve non-routine problems; and uses multiple reasoning methods to solve complex problems, and justifies strategies and solutions.

Mills and Jaeger (1998) produced the first published set of steps for producing test-based descriptions of performance categories:

1. Convene and orient a panel. The requirements for the panel are very much like the requirements for a standard-setting panel. But because of the time involved to do this job well, convening separate panels is usually advantageous. Otherwise potentially valuable contributors may be lost because they are not able to make the necessary time commitment. Multiple panels also allow more persons to participate in the process. Panelists need to be informed of the intended use of the performance category descriptions so that they have a clear expectation for how their work will be used.
2. Review the content specifications for the test and the specific content strands that serve as the basis for organizing the specifications. Just as the content specifications for the test drive the test development process and item selection, these same specifications are valuable to the panel developing the descriptions. Panelists need to be familiar with the breadth of the content specifications because this breadth needs to be reflected in their descriptions.
3. Train the panelists in test content and scoring methods. Performance category descriptions need to be broad enough to reflect the proposed test content but not so broad that they go beyond it. Mills and Jaeger (1998) have argued for administering the test to panel members and reviewing in detail with them the scoring rubrics as ways for familiarizing panelists with the test and scoring.
4. Match test content to the content specifications. Mills and Jaeger (1998) recommended that panel members match the test items to the content specifications for the test. This will familiarize the panel members with the relative emphases given to the different strands of content and lead to discussions about just how well the items match the content specifications. These discussions are intended to help prepare the panel for the next steps.
5. Present the policy descriptions of the performance categories. Generally it is a policy decision as to the number of performance categories, and usually these performance category labels (e.g., failing, needs improvement, proficient, and advanced), along with very general descriptions, are given to the panel at this time. For example, the policy description for the NAEP Proficient category is "Solid academic performance for each grade assessed. Students reaching this level have demonstrated competency over challenging subject matter including subject-matter knowledge, application of such knowledge to real-world situations, and analytical skills appropriate to the subject matter" (ACT, 1998a, p. 101). The NAEP descriptions are so general that they can be used across all the content areas, and at grades 4, 8, and 12. The task of the panel will be to develop narrative descriptions of these performance categories in terms of the test content. Preliminary discussions can begin about these more detailed narratives that are needed for setting standards.
6. Familiarize panel members with samples of candidate performance. At this step, panelists begin to look at candidate responses to the test items and link them if they can to the general descriptions of the performance categories. They might look at a piece of work and describe it as Proficient because it has all the elements of very accurate work in solving equations, but falls short of Advanced because no justification for the solution is offered. According to Mills and Jaeger (1998) it is important not to inundate the panelists with too many candidate papers; otherwise they start classifying them without really carefully studying the work and discussing it.
7. Begin to draft the performance category descriptions. At this point, panelists or small groups of panelists are asked to begin writing out descriptions with specific content knowledge and skills that should be expected of candidates who are placed in each performance category. Obviously, this too applies to borderline candidates, who will be the most minimally qualified of candidates assigned to the performance category. Mills and Jaeger (1998) preferred that panelists start by specifying the knowledge and skills of candidates in a content strand at a middle performance category and build on these knowledge and skills to arrive at the Advanced level, or take away or lower the knowledge and skills to get to the descriptions at the lower levels: Choose a content strand (e.g., geometry), and write what candidates at a middle performance category should be able to do, and then extend it to get to the Advanced level, and subtract to get to the lower performance categories. This insures that the progression in each content strand across performance categories can be seen. This process is repeated for each of the content strands or categories covered in the content specifications.
8. Develop consensus. At this final step, all panelists come back together from their independent work or small group work and try to reach consensus about the descriptions. This consensus should be for each performance category and each of the major content strands that is represented in the content specifications. For example, in Massachusetts, the mathematics curriculum at each grade level is currently organized into five content strands. These five content strands and the progression of knowledge and skills are represented in the performance category descriptions.

Mills and Jaeger (1998) were the first to offer a set of steps for developing test-based performance category descriptions. As they noted, the importance of these descriptions is central for both effective standard setting and communicating results, but the topic has not received much attention. More research is clearly needed to validate the steps and to increase the likelihood of presenting standard-setting panels with clearly written and meaningful performance category descriptions.

6. TRAINING PANELISTS

Raymond and Reid (2001) outlined several key steps in the development of the process for training standard-setting panelists: Specifying the tasks that the panelist will be required to complete; determining the knowledge, skills, and abilities necessary for performing those tasks; and formulating the instruction that is needed to ensure that the panelists develop these essential knowledge, skills, and abilities.

The training plan resulting from the employment of those steps should, Raymond and Reid (2001) indicated, reflect four components previously detailed by Mills (1995). First, the process should be reviewed with the panelists so that they have a good idea of what to expect. An agenda should be distributed that lists each activity and how much time is allotted for it. Ideally, this agenda is sent to panelists in advance of the session along with other introductory information.

Second, the context of the standard-setting study should be clarified. Issues to be discussed include the purposes of the assessment, how it was developed, the content covered on it, why performance standards are being set, what the consequences of the performance standards are, and what the role of the panel is; each of these issues will be discussed in turn. Raymond and Reid (2001) pointed out that panelists need to know not only what the purpose of the assessment is, but also what it is not. To better familiarize panelists with the purpose of the test, they suggest having panelists contrast different possible purposes and discussing how each could influence the standards ultimately set, reviewing sample items that are both on and not on the test as a way of refining their understanding, and discussing the content covered by the test.

An overview of the test development process can also provide a useful background for standard-setting participants; as Raymond and Reid (2001) noted, panelists may then better understand the capabilities and limitations of testing programs. Familiarizing panelists with the content specifications is also a key part of establishing the framework of the standard-setting endeavor (Raymond & Reid, 2001). Giving a reason as to why the standard-setting activity is taking place is an additional key step in providing a context to panelists. As noted earlier, many people are more familiar with normative standards than with criterion-referenced ones, and may need to be educated as to why establishing the latter are preferable in the case under consideration. In addition to the idea of judgmental standard setting, panelists should be told why the specific method being used was chosen.

Another consideration when establishing a context for a standard-setting endeavor, Raymond and Reid (2001) indicated, is that of discussing the consequences of setting a standard at a given level and of passing or failing the test. Providing an overview of the concepts of false positives and false negatives can help panelists understand the consequences of passing an unqualified examinee and failing a qualified one. Finally, and most importantly, panelists must understand that their role as a panel is often, though not always, in an advisory capacity to a policy board who must ultimately set the performance standards. Failing to make this clear can frustrate and anger panels when they learn that the performance standards they set are only recommendations to a policy board.

A third component of training is establishing the reference group(s) so that panelists develop an operational definition of what they expect in terms of examinee performance. Examples of reference groups include the borderline examinee, the minimally competent practitioner, or the group of examinees in a particular performance category. As discussed in section 5, descriptions of performance categories that help illustrate the characteristics of the reference groups may be developed before the session by a separate group or by the panelists themselves. In either case, it is important that the facilitator work effectively with the panelists to form a clear conception of the reference groups that may be used when making judgments about what examinees in each group can or cannot do. Useful information to be reviewed includes characteristics of the population of examinees for the test, the level of education and training they will have encountered prior to the test, and data on the performance of the examinees on the test items (Raymond & Reid, 2001).

Fourth, panelists should be given instruction in the specific rating task they will be performing, be allowed some practice in doing it, and receive feedback on their ratings. After the task is described to the panelists, the facilitator should assist them in performing it, step by step. Materials that resemble those that will be used for actual ratings should be available for training the panelists, though it is important that no test items overlap across the two sets since judgments on the former could influence those on the latter. Any dimensions on which operational items may vary—for example, difficulty, format, complexity—should be reflected in the training set. In addition, panelists need to be informed about factors that may influence examinee performance and need to be considered when providing ratings. These might include (1) any time limit for the assessment; (2) the artificiality of educational assessments (examinees do not always perform as well on tests as they might in more natural situations); (3) distractors in multiple-choice items that may be nearly correct and therefore increase the difficulty of the item for examinees; and (4) the role of guessing in the performance of examinees on multiple-choice items. Administering the assessment to panelists early in the process is often an effective way to demonstrate the knowledge and skills required to do well on the assessment and to familiarize panelists with the conditions under which examinees are expected to demonstrate their knowledge and skills. The latter aim is facilitated if panelists take the assessment under timed conditions and are told that their answer sheets will be collected (even if they are not). Of course, panelists need to be debriefed following the test administration as to the reason that they were misled (the reason being that it is the best way for them to experience the test anxiety and pressure that candidates often feel).

Training can often take a full day. When the assessment and scoring are complex, considerably more time may be needed. For example, with NAEP, different facets of training may take two or more days. Additionally, with NAEP and other assessments training often continues throughout the session, particularly when new information is introduced (i.e., feedback data). The use of training materials that have been field tested is important and can be a key factor in ensuring a smoothly run and productive session. For example, a miscalculation of the time required to complete various steps in the process can result in panelists needing to rush their ratings to finish on time (see Hambleton & Bourque, 1991). Raymond and Reid (2001) may be consulted for additional information about training provided to panelists involved in setting performance standards for NAEP and for certification exams. These descriptions illustrate the types of activities that can be undertaken in order to familiarize panelists with the process and the tasks required of them. (See also ACT, 1998b, for more in-depth information about the NAEP training process.)

7. PROVIDING FEEDBACK TO PANELISTS

As noted previously, panelists are often provided with feedback throughout the standard-setting process. Such information may include performance and consequence data, as well as feedback in the form of discussion with other panelists. Kane (1994) viewed the provision of feedback to panelists as a measure of the procedural validity of a standard-setting process, as it contributes to the consistency in the data collected. Reckase (2001) stated that feedback is one of the more underappreciated aspects of the process, but that it is a key element that differentiates one implementation of a given method (i.e., Angoff) from another.

Reckase (2001) referenced two areas of psychological research that may provide a theoretical framework for the importance of feedback. First, research in industrial/organizational psychology has shown that individuals are able to provide more accurate ratings of employees' job performance when feedback is provided because it helps to create a common understanding of performance, that is, a frame of reference. Second, research in cognitive psychology suggests that feedback can assist raters in correcting flaws in their knowledge—that is, misinterpretations of data and procedures.

According to Reckase (2001), types of feedback relevant to the standard-setting process can be placed along a continuum, with feedback related to the two effects described above being at different ends of the spectrum. On one end of the continuum is feedback related to process, which Reckase noted could be used to assist panelists in understanding the task they are asked to do—that is, differentiating items based on their difficulty level and providing consistent ratings, which can be viewed as error-correcting in nature. On the other end is normative feedback, which can help to provide a frame of reference in that it connects panelists' ratings to actual examinee performance. In the middle of the continuum is feedback related to the location of panelists' ratings relative to the ratings of others.

Process-related feedback includes information about item difficulty provided to panelists so that they can better understand how items function. One common example of this feedback are *p* values, which indicate the proportion of examinees answering each item correctly. The group of examinees may be defined as all examinees or a subset—for example, those within a certain distance of each performance standard. Similar feedback is provided by the Reckase Chart, which allows panelists to see how their ratings correspond to the expected difficulty of the items based on their IRT calibrations rather than classical item difficulty statistics (Reckase, 2001). Used for NAEP standard setting, which has utilized an item rating technique based on the Angoff method, these charts graphically illustrate the degree to which the panelist's ratings correspond to the ways in which examinees responded to the item (assuming of course that the IRT model actually fits the item response data). The data provide panelists with information not only about their perceptions of item difficulty relative to actual item performance, but also on the relative difficulty of items to each other. Reckase observed, however, that if item difficulty data were provided more to give feedback on the capabilities of the examinees than to understand the ways in which the items function, this type of information could actually fall toward the normative side of the continuum.

Another form of process-related feedback is information on the extent to which panelists are internally consistent in their ratings (van der Linden, 1982). Panelists who set higher performance standards on difficult tasks than on easier tasks would be identified as being "inconsistent" in their ratings. They would then be given the opportunity to revise their ratings or explain the basis for their ratings. Sometimes the so-called inconsistencies in the ratings can be defended; in any case, however, panelists would rarely be required to revise their ratings if they were comfortable with them. For a full review of factors affecting intrajudge consistency in standard-setting, the reader is referred to Plake, Melican, and Mills (1991).

Normative feedback are generally data related to consequences. Panelists may, for example, be given the estimated percentage of examinees scoring above a performance standard that they set individually and/or as a group. If the consequence data are not consistent with the panelists' experiences and sense of reasonableness, they may want to revise their performance standards. For example, panelists may feel that a performance standard that resulted in a very large percentage of candidates failing is simply not reasonable or consistent with other available data about the examinees, and so they may want to lower the standard.

An additional form of feedback, panelist location feedback, provides information to the panel members about how their performance standards relate to those of other panelists. This feedback can be tabular or graphic in format, though the latter can be most helpful in illustrating for the panelists the distribution of ratings. In particular, these displays can highlight the presence of outliers, who may, if they choose, modify their judgments to be more in line with those of other panelists.

One last type of feedback that is not in the form of data captured for display to panelists, as the previous types are, is that of discussion. When panelists voice their opinions and share viewpoints, they are giving each other feedback that may be either process-oriented or normative. In the former case, panelist discussion would be aimed at facilitating an understanding of the process; in the latter, it would shape a group norm that could influence subsequent rounds of ratings. Of course, discussion can take each of these forms at different points in a standard-setting session. For a review of factors influencing the role that discussion can play in a standard-setting session, the reader is referred to Fitzpatrick (1989).

Reckase (2001) noted that though training efforts often focus heavily on other aspects of the training process, feedback sometimes does not get adequately explained to panelists. It is critical that panelists understand what the feedback means and how to use it. One possible outcome of poor understanding of the data could be an unwelcome tendency to systematically change their ratings to be in line with data such as *p* values, without considering the actual content of the items. Also important is determining when the feedback should be provided. Generally, multiple rounds of ratings are implemented when feedback is used; that is, an iterative process is employed. The first round of ratings is usually done before any feedback is given; after feedback is given, second-round ratings can reflect that data; a third round, if conducted, can allow panelists to further revise their ratings, perhaps after receiving additional information. It is routine in many standard-setting studies to use two or three rounds of ratings. The timing of multiple types of data should also be given consideration, since when information is presented could affect how it is used.

Panelists often report that they appreciate the opportunity to view feedback data and to discuss their ratings with their colleagues, and find these activities valuable. Performance standards do sometimes shift significantly up or down, especially when the feedback information is a surprise to panelists (see Hambleton & Plake, 1995; Plake & Hambleton, 2000). Often, the main impact of feedback and discussion is consensus among the panelists, in that the variability of the panelists' performance standards is decreased. Although the performance standards themselves often remain about the same, this is not always the case, and the iterative process is generally viewed as worthwhile; panelists are often more confident about the performance standards when there have been discussion and feedback (see, e.g., Plake & Hambleton, 2000).

Research specific to the effects of providing item difficulty information (p values) was reviewed by Brandon (2004), in an examination of studies in which variations of the Angoff method were used. He summarized findings in relation to three outcomes: the correlation between p values and item estimates; changes in performance standards; and changes in the reliability and variability of item estimates. While the literature was not entirely consistent, Brandon did draw some conclusions based on the majority of studies within each category. First, he noted that providing this type of empirical information does usually have a positive effect on the correlation between panelist ratings and the p values in the subsequent round. Second, when p values are provided, performance standards tend to change across rounds. Third, providing p values often reduces the variability of ratings across panelists. However, it should be stressed that there were exceptions to these general conclusions for each type of outcome in the standard-setting literature.

It should be noted that there is some debate about the merits of providing different types of feedback, the timing of the presentation of information, and even the format in which it is presented. For example, many policymakers believe that panelists should set performance standards without knowledge of the consequences, and that it is the policymaking board's prerogative to review the consequences and take appropriate actions. As regards timing, one view is that if the normative data are provided too early, this may unduly influence the panelists because they have not had the chance to settle on their own views. However, if the data are provided too late in the process, panelists may be reluctant to consider them because they are often fairly confident in the process they went through and the performance standards that they have set. The standard-setting process should be planned carefully, with attention being given to factors such as the purpose of the test, method being used, and the panelists' backgrounds, and the types of feedback that are available when a decision is being made about whether and when to provide such information during the session.

8. CONDUCTING PANELIST EVALUATIONS

Obtaining information from the panelists about different parts of the process is a key step in standard setting. No matter how well the facilitator and observers view the session as having been conducted, the opinions that matter just as much (or more) are those of the people who performed the requisite tasks. As Cizek et al. (2004) noted, "on-site evaluations of the process of standard setting, by the participants themselves, serve as an important internal check on the validity and success of the process" (p. 44).

Evaluations are conducted at least twice during the session, but often more frequently. Cizek et al. (2004) suggested that input be gathered after panelists undergo orientation, training in the rating task, and administration of the representative test form (if applicable). It is critical to get a sense of how prepared panelists feel about key concepts and the task before them before the process proceeds any further. If only two evaluations are conducted, the second takes place at the end of the session. However, it may be argued that panelists need to be consulted more frequently for their feedback. For example, in NAEP there may be as many as six process evaluation questionnaires administered (see Schulz & Mitzel, 2005). In this way, potential gaps in knowledge or lack of confidence in the process can be addressed before the next set of tasks is undertaken.

Sample evaluation forms are provided by Hambleton (2001) and Cizek et al. (2004). Information obtained from the panelists may include their ratings of the following: (1) how well they understood the performance standards and performance category descriptions and the definition of the reference group (e.g., borderline examinees); (2) the quality of the training, perhaps broken down by its different aspects; (3) the amount of time allowed for different aspects of the study such as training, providing ratings, discussion, etc.; (4) their level of understanding of and comfort with the rating task they were asked to perform, and of the types of feedback they were provided when doing so; (5) an indication of the degree to which they used different factors such as the definition of the reference group, the difficulty of the items, other panelists' opinions, their experience in the field, etc., as they provided their ratings; (6) whether they thought the performance standards were too low, about right, or too high; and (7) their level of confidence in the resulting performance standards.

Panelists may be given statements to which they simply agree or disagree; for example, "the orientation provided me with a clear understanding of the purpose of the meeting" (Cizek et al., 2004). Or they may be given a rating scale on which they can indicate responses at a greater degree of specificity. For example, to the question "what confidence do you have in the classification of students at the Basic level," panelists may be asked to respond "very high," "high," "medium," or "low" (Hambleton, 2001). Open-ended questions may also be asked. Summaries of these evaluation data, both in tabular and descriptive form, are an integral part of any documentation of the process, as discussed in the following section.

9. EVALUATING AND DOCUMENTING THE VALIDITY OF THE PROCESS

Standard setting is not finished after the performance standards have been obtained. After the completion of the study, the important task of evaluating and documenting the process must begin. As there are no absolute criteria against which specific performance standards can be validated, there are no perfect criteria for evaluating different standard-setting studies (Kane, 1994, 2001). That there are no absolute criteria does not, however, allow a testing agency to abdicate the responsibility to provide evidence that the performance standards and associated performance category descriptions are reasonable and appropriate. Nor does it mean that any standard-setting method is as good as any other (Hambleton, 1998; Jaeger, 1991; Linn, 1998).

A review of the literature yields several sets of guidelines for carrying out a standard-setting study (Cizek, 1993, 1996a, 1996b; Hambleton, 1998; Hambleton & Powell, 1983; Jaeger, 1991; Livingston & Zieky, 1982; Norcini & Shea, 1997; Plake, 1997). The *Standards* (AERA, APA, & NCME, 1999) also provide recommendations for conducting and evaluating standard-setting studies (see, e.g., *Standards* 1.7, 2.14, 4.19, 4.20, 4.21, and 14.17, as noted in section 1.1). A common feature of the guidelines is the need for the careful design, conduct, evaluation, and documentation of the standard-setting study. Important constituencies, including the courts and psychometricians, use the degree to which such guidelines have been followed as critical criteria for evaluating the validity of examinee classifications based on performance standards (Sireci & Green, 2000).

A useful grouping of categories of evidence that can be used to support the validity of standards is provided by Kane (1994, 2001). Three sources of evidence that are useful to examine are those termed procedural, internal, and external. In Table 12.2, different sources of standard-setting validity evidence are placed within these three broad categories. Different authors have grouped their evaluation criteria in different ways, but in general their concepts can be contained within this three-part framework. (For an overview of evaluation guidelines grouped by author, see Plake, 1997.)

9.1. Procedural Evidence of Validity

Kane (2001) noted that "procedural evidence is especially important in evaluating the appropriateness of performance standards... We can have some confidence in standards if they have been set in a reasonable way (e.g. by vote or consensus) by persons who are knowledgeable about the purpose for which the standards are being set, who understand the process they are using, and who are considered unbiased" (pp. 63–64). Kane (1994) observed that the reasonableness of procedures is often, in fact, the primary source of evidence, particularly when policy decisions are being evaluated. Carson (2001) indicated that providing evidence of procedural validity is often one of the most successful ways of establishing the rationality of performance standards used for licensure and certification (see also Plake, 1998). This is the case even though the reasonableness of such evidence is best suited to rule out a performance standard rather than establishing it as appropriate, as is the case with other aspects of validity (Kane, 1994). Among the sources of procedural evidence, the following five areas may be considered: explicitness, practicability, implementation of procedures, panelist evaluations, and documentation.

9.1.1. Explicitness

According to van der Linden (1995), the explicitness criterion "stipulates that all steps should be based on explicit definitions and procedures" (p. 107). He offered two reasons in support of this criterion. First, he asserted that meeting this criterion would allow for the communication of the results of the study in a clear and meaningful manner. Second, he noted that it would be very difficult to apply the other validity criteria if the groundwork for the standard-setting process was not applied in a thorough fashion. As an example, he offers the observation that it would be impossible to repeat the implementation of a method to assess variability across replications if the details of its first execution were not made explicit.

9.1.2. Practicability

Although a standard-setting procedure should, of course, be technically defensible, attention must also be paid to "real-world" logistics. Berk (1986) argued that this criterion could be addressed by evaluating the degree to which a standard-setting method could be implemented without great difficulty, data analysis could be addressed without laborious computations, and the procedures would be seen as credible and interpretable by laypeople.

Berk (1986) noted that a standard-setting method may be technically defensible in a psychometric sense, but if it cannot be implemented adequately because the panelists are confused about the rating task, the method is not practicable. *Standard* 4.21 is relevant to this point, in that it stipulates that when performance standards are based on panelists' judgments, "the judgmental process should be designed so that judges can bring their knowledge and experience to bear in a reasonable way" (AERA, APA, & NCME, 1999, p. 60).

A method may also not be practicable if the time required to prepare materials and/or to carry out the study is excessive and unreasonable. One component of the time required is that needed for data analysis; methods that require laborious hand computations either at the session or afterward could be impracticable; software may help in this regard, but only if it is fully understood and usable by those implementing the study.

The "understandability" of each of the methods used is also of interest. Berk (1986) noted that educators and members of the public who are interested and involved in

TABLE 12.2 Summary of Criteria for Evaluating Standard-Setting Methods

Evaluation Criterion	Description	Sources
Procedural		
Explicitness	The degree to which the standard-setting process was clearly and explicitly defined *before* implementation	van der Linden (1995)
Practicability	The ease of implementation of the procedures and data analysis, and the degree to which procedures are credible and interpretable to laypeople	Berk (1986)
Implementation of procedures	The degree to which the following procedures were systematic and thorough: selection and training of panelists, definitions of the performance categories and/or borderline candidates, and data collection	Kane (1994, 2001)
Panelist feedback	The extent to which panelists feel comfortable with the process and with the performance standards and performance category descriptions	Kane (1994, 2001)
Documentation	The extent to which features of the study are reviewed and documented for evaluation purposes	Cizek (1996b); Hambleton (1998); Mehrens (1995)
Internal		
Consistency within method	The precision of the estimates of the performance standards, or the extent to which same performance standards would be obtained if the method were replicated; also termed across-panel consistency	Cizek (1996b); Kane (1994, 2001); van der Linden (1995)
Intrapanelist consistency	The degree to which a panelist is able to provide ratings that are consistent with the empirical item difficulties, and the degree to which ratings change across rounds	Berk (1996); Chang, van der Linden, & Vos (2004); Cizek (1996b); van der Linden (1982)
Interpanelist consistency	The consistency of item ratings and performance standards across panelists; includes "caution indices," whereby panelists are flagged whose ratings are inconsistent with the majority	Berk (1996); Cizek (1996b); Jaeger (1988, 1991)
Other measures	The consistency of performance standards across item types, content areas, and cognitive processes	Kane (1995); Shepard et al. (1993)
External		
Comparisons to other standard-setting methods	The consistency of performance standards across replications with other standard-setting methods	Jaeger (1991); Kane (1994, 2001)
Comparisons to other sources of information	The relationship between decisions made using the test to other criteria (e.g., grades, performance on a similar test, etc.)	Berk (1996); Giraud et al. (2000); Kane (1994, 2001); Shepard et al. (1993)
Reasonableness of performance levels	The extent to which the resulting performance standards are feasible or realistic, including impact on pass rates	Kane (1998, 2001); van der Linden (1995)

the use of the scores from the test need to be able to comprehend descriptions of the method and interpret the results appropriately. To facilitate this understanding and a sense that the results are reasonable, the method also needs to be credible, or intuitively sound, to laypeople.

9.1.3. Implementation of Procedures

For Kane (1994), an important source of procedural validity evidence is whether goals of the decision procedure are made explicit, and the degree to which the selection and training of panelists, definition of the performance standards, and data collection were implemented in a systematic and thorough fashion. First, Kane noted that establishing the purpose of the standard-setting activity—for example, readiness for entry-level practice in a profession, or identifying students with sufficient knowledge and skills to obtain a high school graduation diploma—is important, and the description of the purpose needs to be specific enough to guide the work of the standard-setting panel. This is an important first step before planning and implementation of the study are begun.

Second, the selection of panelists is a critical area for review. As Kane (1994) observed, since the standard setting process requires the involvement of panelists, it is essential to ensure that they are qualified. The number of panelists required is also an important factor. Both of these issues are discussed in more detail in section 4.

A third factor critical to the sound implementation of a standard-setting method is the training provided to the panelists. As Camilli, Cizek, and Lugg (2001) observed: "It cannot be overstated: participants involved in standard-setting procedures need to understand and perform their tasks within a common framework . . . Training, or practice within this framework, is an essential component of the due process argument; indeed, demonstrating that training was effective strengthens a validity argument" (p. 453). Information about training that should be provided to panelists is contained in section 6.

Returning to Kane's (1994) criteria for the implementation of procedures, the fourth is the provision of definitions of the performance standards or associated performance categories. Kane's (1995) guideline about establishing a reference group is relevant here, but also important is the development and/or dissemination of a thorough description of performance in each performance category. The descriptions of the performance categories may have been developed before the study by an entity such as a licensing agency, governmental body, group of educators, or may be drawn up by the panel itself. In any case, it is essential that the performance standards and performance categories are clear, understandable, and can be linked to the decision being made on the basis of the test results. Further detail about this important issue is provided in section 5.

Fifth and finally for the implementation-of-procedures criterion, Kane (1994) noted that the procedures used for data collection need to be systematic and accurate, and the degree to which strategies were used that can improve the quality of the data collected should be evaluated. These strategies include (1) iterative procedures in which the panelists provide ratings more than once; (2) efforts to promote consistency in the data, such as panel discussions and providing empirical performance data; and (3) use of external checks on the ratings and projected results, such as consequence data (see section 7).

9.1.4. Panelist Evaluations

Kane (1994) identified feedback from panelists as an important source of validity information on the procedural criterion. It is important to gather this input to establish whether the panelists felt the process and outcome were appropriate. The types of questions that may be asked of panelists are reviewed in section 8, and include topics such as the efficacy of the orientation, provision of performance category descriptors, and training in the rating task; the helpfulness of discussion and feedback; and the level of confidence in the resulting standards. This evidence cannot establish the validity of the performance standards, but as Kane observed, "if the judges who developed the standard do not have confidence in it, it is not clear why anyone else should" (p. 443).

9.1.5. Documentation

The final criterion for the procedural component of validity evidence is the extent to which the standard-setting process has been documented. Hambleton (1998) noted that technical documentation is of great value when defense of the resulting performance standards is required. Such documentation will also be helpful to the ultimate agency or governing body that is responsible for approving and communicating the performance standards.

Ideally, the documentation should include all of the types of information mentioned within this section, as all types of validity evidence are relevant. The *Standards* state the following:

> If a judgmental standard-setting process is followed, the method employed should be clearly described, and the precise nature of the judgments called for should be presented, whether those are judgments of persons, of item or test performances, or of other criterion performances predicted by test scores. Documentation should also include the selection and qualification of judges, training provided, any feedback to judges concerning the implications of their provisional judgments, and any opportunities for judges to confer with one another. (AERA, APA, & NCME, 1999, pp. 59–60)

Examples of technical documentation include, for NAEP, Chen, Loomis, and Fisher (2000), Hambleton and Bourque (1991), and Reckase (2000b); and for the Uniform CPA Examination, Mills et al., (2000). Other excellent examples of technical documentation can be found in technical manuals prepared by state departments of education (see, e.g., Massachusetts Department of Education, 2003, New Jersey Department of Education, 2005) and by credentialing agencies (see, e.g., Boulet, Sprafka, & Gimpel, 2005).

9.2. Internal Evidence of Validity

Evidence to be discussed within this section includes consistency within method, and intrapanelist and interpanelist consistency, as outlined in Table 12.2.

9.2.1. Consistency within Method

The *Standards* (AERA, APA, & NCME, 1999) indicate that "whenever feasible, an estimate should be provided of the amount of variation in cut scores that might be expected if the standard-setting procedure were replicated" (p. 60). Kane (2001) noted that there are two ways in which to estimate the variation across implementations (in addition, a third was described earlier in the chapter).

The first, and most direct, way to estimate the standard error of the performance standard is to convene different groups of panelists on the same or different occasions. One could then estimate the standard error of the mean using a simplified formula provided by Brennan (2002): $\sigma_{\bar{x}} = |\bar{X}_1 - \bar{X}_2|/2$ where $\bar{X}_1$ is the performance standard for the first implementation and $\bar{X}_2$ the performance standard for the second.

However, as Cizek (1996b) observed, convening two panels on the same or different occasions may not always be feasible, which leads to the second, less direct, method—using generalizability theory to estimate the variance components associated with panelists, tasks, and, when applicable, occasion. Both approaches to estimating the standard error of each performance standard involve first defining the universe of generalization, or specifying which aspects of the method's implementation are viewed as being allowed to vary across replications (Brennan, 1995; Kane, 1994, 2001; van der Linden, 1995). However, other issues that Kane (1995) recommended be taken into account when conducting a generalizability study are item/subscale weighting, unit of analysis, dimensionality, and the transformation of ratings to the scale score metric.

An example of generalizability theory applied to standard setting can be found in Brennan and Lockwood (1980), where the Nedelsky and Angoff methods were subjected to analysis. Kane and Wilson (1984) later extended those analyses to allow different types of error to covary. Lee and Lewis (2001) applied generalizability theory to the bookmark approach, and concluded that even within method, different patterns of variability applied to performance standards for different tests (e.g., grades). In addition, they noted the degree to which the conceptualization of universe of generalization can affect the estimation of standard errors. A discussion of generalizability theory as applied to standard setting can also be found in Camilli et al. (2001).

9.2.2. Intrapanelist Consistency

Berk (1996) distinguished between two types of intrapanelist consistency (or reliability, as he termed it): (1) between steps, and (2) within steps. In the first type, the degree to which panelists' ratings vary across steps, or rounds, is examined. If panelists are taking in and synthesizing the information they are provided after each round, including empirical data and discussions with the rest of the panel, their ratings should show some variability. If, in contrast, panelists are staying with their initial ratings from round to round, the reliability coefficient will be very high, calling into question the effectiveness of efforts to provide information that could help them refine their judgments. High reliability is not necessarily a sign of a poor standard-setting process, but certainly it ought to be used as a sign for additional investigation. Panelists' evaluations may provide additional data for interpreting the across steps reliability.

In the second type of intrapanelist consistency—within rounds—the degree to which a panelist's ratings is consistent with other sources of information is examined. Empirical data may include performance data such as percent correct, difficulty parameters from IRT modeling, etc. The correlation between a panelist's ratings and the *p* values of items may then be calculated. Berk (1996) noted that this type of consistency check should be done at several points in the process, as the level may decrease over the course of the study.

9.2.3. Interpanelist Consistency

The *Standards* state that "where applicable, variability over judges should be reported" (AERA, APA, & NCME, 1999, p. 60). Evidence for this criterion is provided by the degree to which ratings are consistent across panelists, and an important source of information is interrater reliability estimates. The extent to which interpanelist agreement increases across rounds can be viewed as an index of convergence (Berk, 1996).

The standard deviation of individual panelists' performance standards is often used as an index of interpanelist agreement as well. The standard deviation of performance standards across panelists is computed for each performance standard, and the lower the standard deviation, the more agreement there is among panelists. Monitoring these standard deviations over rounds is often of assistance to facilitators. The standard deviations associated with panelists' final recommended performance standards are often of considerable interest to policy boards and evaluators because they provide information about the extent to which the panelists agree among themselves about the recommended performance standards. Acceptance of standards is obviously easier to defend when the panelists are in agreement about their recommendations.

Berk (1996) noted that many factors can contribute to a low level of interpanelist consistency, including a lack of clarity in the definition of the performance standards, the types of items being reviewed, and differences in the backgrounds, competencies, and even political agendas of the panelists. Cizek (1996b) pointed out, however, that such differences (as reflected by higher standard deviations) may actually lend credibility to the process, since a lack of consensus may indicate that a desired diversity of perspectives has been achieved.

Jaeger (1988) described an alternative approach to comparing panelists' judgments. He reviewed the use of the modified caution index with the Jaeger standard-setting method to investigate how it performed in identifying panelists who had patterns of item-level judgments that were aberrant when compared to that of the overall group (e.g., the panelist gave the items a "yes" rating that other panelists gave a "no" rating, and vice versa). Jaeger concluded that the reasons underlying panelists' aberrant behavior are difficult to deduce, and that the implementation of such indices should be undertaken cautiously, particularly if they are used to screen out panelists and discount their ratings.

9.2.4. Other Measures

Evaluation of the consistency of performance standards across item types, content areas, and cognitive processes may provide useful information. Shepard et al. (1993) described a series of studies in which the consistency and coherence of item judgments across these dimensions were investigated in the context of setting performance standards for the 1992 NAEP Trial State Assessment. They concluded that there were differences across item type and item difficulty, but not across content area and cognitive processes. Specifically, they noted that ratings based on polytomously scored extended constructed-response items yielded higher performance standards than those based on dichotomously scored items, and that the same pattern held for short answer versus multiple-choice items. They also found that different performance standards were generated by ratings made on items of different difficulty levels. Panelists underestimated borderline students' performance on easy items and overestimated performance on difficult items. Though Shepard et al. (1993) used these results to question the viability of the standard-setting method implemented—the Angoff method—Brennan (1995) countered that some of the results have plausible explanations, and that modification of the method could counter other issues raised. The reference to the research by Shepard and colleagues is included here because it highlights the variety of investigations that might be carried out to address the validity of a set of performance standards.

9.3. External Evidence of Validity

Kane (2001) observed that comparing standard-setting results to external sources of information is a way of checking whether the performance standards are at approximately the right level. However, he also noted that the criteria to which the study's results are being compared are often open to question themselves and that, as a result, such comparisons are usually not definitive. Nonetheless, a convergence of data supporting the performance standards would be a valuable source of evidence. Types of information external to the process include the results of other standard setting methods, information from other sources, and evidence of the reasonableness of the outcomes.

9.3.1. Comparisons of Results among Methods

Jaeger (1989) acknowledged that the question of whether different procedures applied to the same test produce similar standards is most often answered negatively. He presented a summary of 12 studies in which 32 contrasts across methods were made, and concluded that the results were sobering: "there is little consistency in the results of applying different standard-setting methods under seemingly identical conditions, and there is even less consistency in the comparability of methods across settings" (p. 500). He echoed others' suggestions that, when possible, several methods should be used in a given study and their results considered in conjunction with other factors when determining final performance standards.

Despite the evidence that different methods usually produce different performance standards—Zieky (2001) termed it perhaps one of the most widely replicated research findings in the area of standard-setting—comparisons across methods are useful. As Kane (2001) noted, such comparisons would be most informative if we have confidence in each of the methods and its implementation, although the evaluation of the quality of a study and the resulting performance standards are often a difficult task.

If the results of two standard-setting methods used with the same test do not yield the same or very similar performance standards, Kane (2001) observed, that should not be viewed with great surprise since methods require different types of ratings by panelists, using different sources of data. If the discrepancy between the two performance standards is too large, however, it may call into question the validity of the results from both standard-setting processes. In contrast, if different standard-setting methods produce identical or very close performance standards, our level of confidence in both sets of results is increased.

Relevant to this criterion is research conducted by Green et al. (2003), in which they compared the results of three standard-setting methods used with different tests within a statewide assessment system. In addition to comparing the features of the methods and how they might have affected the resulting performance standards, the study called for a final step in which the results of the three methods were synthesized. They concluded that although the methods did not yield the same results, "the view that getting different results from different procedures invalidates them all does not stand up; although they are different, the bases of the judgments are each relevant" (p. 28).

Other studies in which the results of different methods were compared include Giraud, Impara, and Buckendahl (2000); Kaufman, Mann, Muijtjens, and van der Vleuten (2000); Norcini and Shea (1992); Pitoniak et al. (2003); and Subkoviak, Kane, and Duncan (2002). Such studies provide valuable information about the features of the methods and allow consideration of their strengths and weaknesses.

9.3.2. Comparisons to Other Sources of Information

In the *Standards* (AERA, APA, & NCME, 1999), *Standard* 4.20 states that "when feasible, cut scores defining categories with distinct substantive interpretation should be established on the basis of sound empirical data concerning the relation of test performance to relevant criteria" (p. 60).

As Kane (2001) described, perhaps the most simple and direct approach to evaluating performance standards through the use of an external criterion would be to administer the assessment for which the performance standard is being determined to a sample of examinees, and then have them perform the activity and be evaluated on it. If the pass rates are comparable, that serves as evidence that the performance standard is reasonable. Other performance standards could be evaluated in much the same way. As he noted, however, this paradigm is usually difficult to implement. It would require a performance standard to be set on the performance activity, which would raise the same issues as the establishing of the original performance standard had. But even more importantly, it is usually problematic to evaluate how examinees who failed an assessment would perform at a given activity, particularly if that activity could endanger the public (for example, allowing an unlicensed physician to practice medicine or an unqualified teacher to teach). For these reasons, the use of this type of external criterion is usually not feasible. And as the *Standards* acknowledge, "a carefully designed and implemented procedure based solely on judgments of content relevance and item difficulty may be preferable to an empirical study with an inadequate criterion measure or other deficiencies" (AERA, APA, & NCME, 1999, p. 60).

However, other sources of external validity evidence such as tests measuring similar constructs, and other types of assessments such as portfolios or interviews, may provide useful information. If a test measures a similar construct, its results may be compared to that of the test under consideration for the same group of examinees. However, as Kane (2001) noted, the choice of criterion test must be made carefully, not out of convenience, and care should be taken to be sure that the content is comparable. Even so, it may be difficult to reconcile the results if they are different, since it may not be clear whether it is due to the characteristics of the tests, the standard-setting methods, or a difference in stringency of performance standards. If there is fidelity between the results of the two tests, this can provide support for the performance standards; however, if there is divergence, it may be difficult to determine the weight to give to this evidence.

Giraud et al. (2000) conducted a study in which information from schools, in the form of teacher ratings and course information, was triangulated with the results of several standard-setting methods (Angoff, borderline group, and contrasting groups). Although one of their conclusions was that the collection of the criterion information could take the place of conducting standard setting studies, they also acknowledged that it could be used to support (or question) the findings if such studies were conducted.

9.3.3. Reasonableness of Performance Standards

This criterion focuses directly on the reasonableness of the distribution of achievement that results from the application of the performance standards. The percentages of licensure candidates that are classified as masters or nonmasters, or students who are sorted into performance categories such as below basic, basic, proficient, and advanced (ACT, 1998a), are direct illustrations of the stringency of the performance standards, and the reasonableness of the number of examinees placed in each category can be evaluated by looking at the distribution of the population in other circumstances. For example, a state might compare its performance on a recent NAEP administration with its own state assessment results. If the two sets of results are more or less in agreement, the state might assume that its performance standards are reasonable. If results were very different, many explanations can be hypothesized including problems associated with the setting of its own performance standards.

As Kane (2001) observed, if for example a licensure test has had a pass rate of 90%, practitioners' performance has been seen to be acceptable, and no changes have taken place to impact candidate competence or skills required in the profession, then the performance standard should be expected to yield approximately the same percentage of passing examinees. Evidence from different groups on the same test may also provide useful information. For example, experienced practitioners may be expected to have a higher pass rate than students just completing training, depending on the test content. In general, Kane concluded that such reasonableness evidence is most relevant if the results are extreme—that is, if the pass rates are very different from what is expected. They thus can serve as a reality check more than as a way to distinguish between performance standards that are relatively close to each other.

"Feasibility" is a criterion described by van der Linden (1995) as relating to another aspect of the reasonableness of the performance standards. Feasibility in this case refers to the degree to which resources are available to enable the target to be met. He pointed out that given a fixed pool of resources, trade-offs must usually be made as to which goals will be met. He offered as an example the idea that students at a school may be able to meet high achievement standards for a given subject, such as geography, if all of its resources were devoted to that subject. However, such a scenario is unrealistic, and ignores the trade-offs that are made. Similar arguments could be made, for example, about a state's administration of an assessment when the curriculum has not been fully implemented or the teachers oriented to it. He acknowledged that feasibility is a more practical criterion, and that many standard-setting approaches would not encompass it. It could be argued that this criterion belongs more in the domain of the policymaker; however, van der Linden pointed out that panelists may set unrealistically high standards if they do not take competing priorities into account.

9.4. Legal Issues

Relevant to the evaluation process are legal ramifications that may arise when performance standards are set. Setting a standard that grants or denies access to practice of a profession, or that allows or prevents a student from graduating, is obviously an endeavor that can lead to legal challenges due to the high stakes nature of these decisions. Carson (2001) and Phillips (2001) described the legal issues relevant to setting performance standards in each of these areas. While some of the issues are relevant more to the general use of the test to make classification decisions than to the standards in particular, a brief review of the general legal considerations is informative.

Carson (2001) reviewed challenges to licensure and certification tests that were undertaken on the basis of several different legal grounds. For example, a test may be challenged on the basis of constitutional law, either through the provision of due process (the principle that individuals are treated fairly from both substantive and procedural perspectives) or through that of equal protection (which requires that similarly situated individuals be treated equally). Likewise, an examinee could seek redress under Title VII of the Civil Rights Act (1964), in which employers are prohibited from discriminating on the basis of color, sex, religion, or national origin. Carson also described cases in which antitrust laws were used to challenge a test on the basis that it suppresses competition. And lastly, the Americans with Disabilities Act (1990) has been invoked when testing accommodations were not allowed or test scores were flagged when accommodations were used. The extent to which the challenges were successful across these legal bases varied, though in general courts have upheld the rights of states to institute reasonable standards for licensure (see also Sireci & Green, 2000, for examples specific to teacher certification testing). Though the details of all of these cases are beyond the scope of this chapter, Carson noted that precepts of good standard setting go far to protect the test agency from a successful challenge:

> Although licensing and certifying examinations have generally withstood judicial scrutiny, it is in the best interest of a licensing authority or certifying entity and the public it serves to have as much as evidence as possible available to support its standard-setting judgment.... The guiding principles under the law are the three Rs: rationality, relatedness, and reasonableness. These would all seem to be desirable and attainable goals for those involved in standard setting even in the absence of any legal imperative. (p. 442)

The validity evidence referred to by Carson (2001) includes those types described earlier in this section. In particular, Carson stressed that procedural evidence is critical. More important than the exact procedures used is the degree to which those procedures existed, that they were reasonable and defined clearly ahead of time, and that they were implemented as designed.

In the area of educational assessments, Phillips (2001) reviewed legal aspects of both content standards and performance standards (especially the performance standard distinguishing examinees who pass from those who fail). Relevant to content standards are the provision of sufficient notice to students, parents, and other stakeholders before a change in content is implemented, opportunity to learn that content, availability of remediation, opportunity for success, the difficulty of defining observable behaviors, and the effects of cheating. Phillips, like Carson, also described legal issues related to the provision of testing accommodations and modifications, and the importance of carefully considering whether the accommodations altered the construct being measured. If states implement tests in a manner that takes each of these factors into effect, legal challenges are less likely to be successful.

For performance standards, Phillips (2001) described the importance of evaluating the balance of false positives versus false negatives (i.e., passing a student who should fail, and failing a student who should pass). She noted that when students are given multiple attempts to pass, adjusting the performance standard downward might not be warranted since false negatives would already be greatly minimized (see Geisinger, 1991; Millman, 1989). Doing so would also increase the number of false positives, resulting in students who needed remediation not being offered it.

In general, Phillips (2001) echoed the view of Carson (2001) that most critical to the successful defense against legal challenge is the use of a sound and carefully executed standard-setting methodology. This is particularly important when a given test is being used for a different purpose than originally designed. Phillips concluded that "it appears that courts will uphold a state's passing standards if all the facts and circumstances indicate that the resulting standard is not arbitrary or capricious and has been adopted by the requisite authorities based on legitimate goals and relevant information" (p. 420).

9.5. Conclusions about Validity Evidence

The process of setting performance standards is clearly not over once the session has been completed. In order to evaluate the validity of interpretations made on the basis of performance standards and to safeguard the legal basis for such decisions, it is critical that many sources of evidence be considered.

Validity evidence is able to most effectively play a role in ruling out a standard-setting method, since a performance standard can never technically be ruled in, or established as unassailable (Kane, 1994). However, the lack of an absolute criterion by which a performance standard can be judged as acceptable does not excuse one from gathering as much evidence as possible. Kane also noted in regard to external validity evidence that, "although any particular empirical check is likely to be inconclusive, a pattern of agreement between the results of the proposed decision process and other sources of information supports the reasonableness of this process, and a pattern of disagreement with the results of other decision processes may suggest that the passing score is inappropriate" (p. 457). The idea of a pattern of evidence is a helpful concept that may be applied to all three sources of validity information. The gathering of many types of evidence allows for the evaluation of an even richer tapestry. It is very important to assemble information related to all three criteria and to document these findings. Only then can the standard-setting process be considered complete.

10. ADDITIONAL TOPICS

In the following sections, two additional topics related to the setting of performance standards are addressed.

10.1. Setting Performance Standards for Alternate Assessments

Increasing numbers of examinees who have disabilities and/or are English language learners are administered assessments under accommodated conditions or are given alternative assessments. Both legislation and educational initiatives have reinforced the need to give individuals with disabilities and English language learners the same testing opportunities, and thus access to the same life experiences in education and employments, as other individuals. Relevant legislation includes the Americans with Disabilities Act (1990) and the Individuals with Disabilities Educational Act (1991, 1997). The No Child Left Behind Act (2001) also heightened the focus on the importance of not only including students with disabilities and English language learners in standardized test administrations, but also including their scores in the reporting of student progress and achievement for accountability purposes.

While testing students with disabilities and English language learners with accommodations does raise serious validity considerations (see Pitoniak & Royer, 2001), those students are generally held to the same performance standards as are students not tested with accommodations. However, some students, most often those with significant cognitive disabilities, cannot be assessed with general state-and-district wide assessments programs, and are instead given alternative assessments. These assessments may take different forms, including checklists, observation in structured and unstructured settings, performance assessments, samples of student work, and portfolios (Roeber, 2002; see also Kleinert & Kearns, 2001; Quenemoen, Rigney, & Thurlow, 2002; Thompson, Quenemoen, Thurlow, & Ysseldyke, 2001).

Theoretically, any standard-setting method may be used to set performance standards on alternative assessments. For example, Roeber (2002) reviewed many methods described in this chapter, including contrasting groups, modified Angoff, bookmark, body of work, and judgmental policy capturing. Roeber noted that the choice of standard-setting method is closely tied to the type of alternative assessment used. Among the factors to be considered are the amount of time that a given method will take with a given type of alternative assessment. As an example, Roeber pointed out that using a body of work method with extensive student portfolios may not be practical.

However, Olson et al. (2002) did implement the body of work approach with a state's alternative assessment, but chose to have panelists review only a subset of portfolio entries for each student so as to allow a greater number of students' work to be examined. They used two different approaches to calculating performance standards. In the first approach, the mean score was calculated for the portfolios placed into each classification category, and the average of the two adjacent categories was used as the performance standard. In the second approach, the mean of the classification categories assigned to each portfolio was calculated. The cut score dividing two adjacent categories was then calculated by interpolating between the portfolio scores that best defined the border between the categories, with best being defined as the performance standard that minimized classification errors. They concluded that the second method was preferable since it was more robust to outliers.

Olson et al. (2002) noted several limitations and qualifications to their study. They observed that some panelists felt uncomfortable with the incomplete portfolios and were concerned that student work was not displayed in multiple settings. In addition, due to limitations of time and availability of portfolios, only the first step of the body of work method was implemented (i.e., the step to obtain an approximate idea of the location of the performance standards). The more detailed second step, during which additional portfolios in the vicinity of the performance standards are reviewed, was not conducted. This caused some confusion for the panelists and impacted the reliability of the performance standard. The authors noted that including this second step in subsequent implementations of the body of work method with alternative assessments is advisable. It is likely that research in this area of standard setting will grow as state assessment systems continue to administer alternative assessments and are required to categorize students with severe disabilities for accountability purposes.

10.2. Adjusting Performance Standards

As noted previously, the role of the standard-setting panel is to provide information, in the form of recommended performance standards, to the decision-making body. That group may then choose to make adjustments to the performance standards before implementing them. Geisinger (1991) outlined various sources of information that may be considered when adjusting standards. Several of these require consideration of the nature of the test and the effect of varying pass rates over time with the change in performance standards; this information includes organizational or societal needs, acceptable passing and failing rates, adverse or disparate impact data, opportunities for re-testing, and relative costs of misclassification errors. Other adjustment approaches relate more closely to data obtained in the standard-setting process, and are considered here.

One option for adjusting a performance standard is to lower it by a standard error of measurement. This step may be undertaken in the beginning of a testing program in order to allow for a phased-in process. However, it may be argued that making such an adjustment with the goal of preventing false negatives is misguided when examinees are given multiple attempts to pass a test, since false negatives in that case are extremely rare (see Mehrens, 1986; Millman, 1989; Phillips, 2000). A second type of approach involves the use of an estimate that takes into account error related to interjudge variability. Jaeger (1991) developed an index that Geisinger (1991) termed the standard error of the test standard, which reflects both the unreliability of the test and error due to sampling of panelists.

Geisinger (1991) also described adjustments that may be made when there are anomalies in the rating process; for example, if some or all of the panelists were not qualified, did not understand the rating task, had a personal stake in the outcome of the session, or did not make ratings independently, ratings from these panelists may be removed when the standards are calculated. Geisinger also pointed out that evidence from different standard-setting methods implemented on the same test, perhaps within the same study, could inform the ultimate decision on the value of the performance standards. He cautioned, however, that consideration of all of the information described above should be made systematically and explicitly, with the rationale and procedures clearly documented, as required by the *Standards*

(AERA, APA, & NCME, 1999) for all elements of the standard-setting process.

11. SUMMARY

Performance standards are being set by just about every state department of education, many school districts, and every credentialing exam agency in the country. The steps described in the second section of this chapter should be helpful to agencies planning standard-setting studies. The steps are based on the best standard-setting practices found in the educational measurement field (Cizek, 2001). The section on methods includes detailed descriptions and some evaluative results on many of the available methods. Following the steps described in this chapter, consulting studies that are cited, implementing the steps well, and compiling validity evidence along the lines recommended earlier in the chapter should go a long way toward establishing the defensibility and validity of the process used to set performance standards for educational tests and credentialing exams.

Many researchers, policymakers, and educators today are still not comfortable with several of the current performance standard-setting methods (see, e.g., Pellegrino et al., 1999). Criticisms center on the logic of the methods, the ways in which several of the methods are being implemented, and the lack of validity evidence to support their use. What is needed is more commitment on the part of agencies setting standards to follow best practices and ensure that their process is documented, and that substantial validity evidence is compiled and used in the ultimate determination of the suitability of a set of performance standards for their intended use. Improved standard-setting practices would address many of the criticisms that are being heard.

Clearly, too, there is need for new ideas and more research. Probably the most important topic for research today is the vertical alignment of performance standards across grades within a subject, and across subjects at a grade level (see Ferrara, Johnson, & Chen, 2005; Huynh & Schneider, 2005). Consider a state setting three performance standards in three subjects from grades 3 to 8. The state would be setting 54 performance standards. Unless some integrated approach to setting these standards is adopted, 18 standard-setting panels would be needed, and with the systematic and random errors associated with the formation of these panels, with the idiosyncrasies of facilitators, and recognizing the inevitable errors associated with performance standards, it is impossible to believe that the result would be a coherent set of performance standards. The percent of proficient students over grades would go up or down in a subject due not only to any achievement growth taking place but due to the errors in the performance standards themselves. Research is now underway to build coherence into the standard-setting process by developing performance category descriptors that are meaningful and show progression across grades using curriculum specialists and teachers representing multiple grades and subjects. With empirical data available that address impact, performance standards are being adjusted to smooth out the results so that, for example, a high passing rate at one grade is not followed by substantially lower pass rates at higher grades (unless strong justification can be offered). Of course, when performance standards are moved, then the associated performance category descriptions need to be modified as well. Many of the states now are grappling with this complex standard-setting problem, and research findings to identify best practices are needed.

Another important topic, because it is the final step prior to performance standards becoming policy, concerns the best ways to present the results of a standard-setting study to a policy board (see, e.g., Boulet et al., 2005; New Jersey Department of Education, 2005). How can the material be packaged to maximize understandability and ultimately serve the purpose of informing board members without overwhelming them? Provide too much information and the board members' task may become overwhelming in the time available to make the decisions. Provide too little and it is likely that only the impact data will drive any final modifications of the performance standards, and these modifications will be made without the full benefit of knowing the demographics of the panelists, the process they went through, the time that was spent, the validity evidence available, and so on.

Cognitive laboratories have been valuable in helping test developers better understand the way candidates approach solving test items. Much more could be learned too about the way panelists work through a standard-setting study (Skorupski & Hambleton, 2005). What preconceptions do they have? Do they understand the need for performance standards and the important role they play in monitoring educational achievement? Skorupski and Hambleton found that panelists benefited from several common standard-setting practices—effective orientation, extensive training, and time to deliberate with their ratings. At the same time, their finding came from a single study with an item mapping method using a questionnaire approach to data collection. Much more needs to be learned about panelists and their thoughts during a standard-setting study. The findings would likely impact on (1) the ways performance category descriptions are prepared and presented, (2) training practices, (3) rating tasks and feedback, (4) the role of normative data, and more.

In conclusion, the importance of credible standard-setting procedures for any test cannot be overstated. As the *Standards* note, "the validity of the inference drawn from the test depends on whether the standard for passing makes a valid distinction between adequate and inadequate performance. . . . Verifying the appropriateness of the cut score . . . is a critical element of the validity of test results" (AERA, APA, & NCME, 1999, p. 157). The background, guidelines, and criteria for evaluation contained here and in other cited resources should be carefully used by all practitioners implementing or using the results of a standard-setting study in order to enhance the validity of such inferences.

Cizek (2001) observed that "never before has the technology or epistemology of standard setting been so controversial or its methods and results so scrutinized" (p. 8), and that as a result "it is a dynamic time to be involved in the art and science of standard setting" (p. 14). It is hoped that the material presented in this chapter promotes investigation of current methods and exploration of alternative approaches, since the need for such continued work is clear.

REFERENCES

ACT, Inc. (1997). *Developing achievement levels on the 1998 NAEP in civics and writing: The design document.* Iowa City, IA: Author.

ACT, Inc. (1998a). 1998 civics and writing level-setting methodologies. In M. L. Bouque (Ed.), *Proceedings of achievement levels workshop* (pp. 99–106). Washington, DC: National Assessment Governing Board.

ACT, Inc. (1998b). *Briefing booklet: 1998 writing NAEP achievement levels setting.* Iowa City, IA: Author.

American Educational Research Association, American Psychological Association, & National Council on Measurement in Education. (1999). *Standards for educational and psychological testing.* Washington, DC: American Educational Research Association.

Americans with Disabilities Act of 1990, 42 U.S. C. § 12101 et seq.

Angoff, W. H. (1971). Scales, norms, and equivalent scores. In R. L. Thorndike (Ed.), *Educational measurement* (2nd ed., pp. 508–597). Washington, DC: American Council on Education.

Angoff, W. H. (1988). Proposals for theoretical and applied development in measurement. *Applied Measurement in Education, 1,* 215–222.

Beretvas, S. N. (2004). Comparison of bookmark difficulty locations under different item response models. *Applied Psychological Measurement, 28,* 25–47.

Berk, R. A. (1986). A consumer's guide to setting performance standards on criterion-referenced tests. *Review of Educational Research, 56,* 137–172.

Berk, R. A. (1996). Standard setting: The next generation (where few psychometricians have gone before!). *Applied Measurement in Education, 9,* 215–235.

Beuk, C. H. (1984). A method for reaching a compromise between absolute and relative standards in examinations. *Journal of Educational Measurement, 21,* 147–152.

Boulet, J., Sprafka, S., & Gimpel, J. (2005). *Standard setting for COMLEX-USA Level 2 performance evaluation.* Conshohocken, PA: NBOME.

Brandon, P. R. (2002). Two versions of the contrasting-groups standard-setting method: A review. *Measurement and Evaluation in Counseling and Development, 35,* 167–181.

Brandon, P. R. (2004). Conclusions about frequently studied modified Angoff standard-setting topics. *Applied Measurement in Education, 17,* 59–88.

Brennan, R. L. (1995). Standard setting from the perspective of generalizability theory. In *Proceedings of the joint conference on standard setting for large scale assessments of the National Assessment Governing Board (NAGB) and the National Center for Educational Statistics (NCES), Volume II* (pp. 269–287). Washington, DC: U.S. Government Printing Office.

Brennan, R. L. (2001). *Generalizability theory.* New York: Springer-Verlag.

Brennan, R. L. (2002). *Estimated standard error of a mean when there are only two observations* (CASMA Technical Note No. 1). Iowa City, IA: University of Iowa, Center for Advanced Studies in Measurement and Assessments.

Brennan, R. L., & Lockwood, R. E. (1980). A comparison of the Nedelsky and Angoff cutting score procedures using generalizability theory. *Applied Psychological Measurement, 4,* 219–240.

Buckendahl, C. W., Smith, R. W., Impara, J. C., & Plake, B. S. (2002). A comparison of Angoff and Bookmark standard-setting methods. *Journal of Educational Measurement, 39*(3), 253–263.

Camilli, G., Cizek, G. J., & Lugg, C. A. (2001). Psychometric theory and the validation of performance standards: History and future perspectives. In G. J. Cizek (Ed.), *Setting performance standards: Concepts, methods, and perspectives* (pp. 445–475). Mahwah, NJ: Erlbaum.

Carson, J. D. (2001). Legal issues in standard setting for licensure and certification. In G. J. Cizek (Ed.), *Standard setting: Concepts, methods, and perspectives* (pp. 427–444). Mahwah, NJ: Erlbaum.

Chang, L. (1999). Judgmental item analysis of the Nedelsky and Angoff standard-setting methods. *Applied Measurement in Education, 12,* 151–165.

Chen, W.-H., Loomis, S. C., & Fisher, T. (2000). *Developing achievement levels on the 1998 NAEP in civics and writing: Technical report.* Iowa City, IA: ACT.

Civil Rights Act of 1964, 42 U.S.C. §2000e-2, Supp. V (1993).

Cizek, G. J. (1993). Reconsidering standards and criteria. *Journal of Educational Measurement, 30,* 93–106.

Cizek, G. J. (1996a). Setting passing scores. *Educational Measurement: Issues and Practice, 15*(2), 20–31.

Cizek, G. J. (1996b). Standard-setting guidelines. *Educational Measurement: Issues and Practice, 15*(1), 12–21.

Cizek, G. J. (2001). Conjectures on the rise and call of standard setting: An introduction to context and practice. In G. J. Cizek (Ed.), *Setting performance standards: Concepts, methods, and perspectives* (pp. 3–17). Mahwah, NJ: Erlbaum.

Cizek, G. J., Bunch, M. B., & Koons, H. (2004). Setting performance standards: Contemporary methods. *Educational Measurement: Issues and Practice, 23*(4), 31–50.

Cizek, G. J., Bunch, M. B., & Koons, H. (2005). Clarification for the ITEMS module, Setting performance standards: Contemporary methods. *Educational Measurement: Issues and Practice, 24*(2), 43.

Cizek, G. J., & Fitzgerald, S. M. (1996, April). *A comparison of group and independent standard setting.* Paper presented at the meeting of the American Educational Research Association, New York.

Cohen, A. S., Kane, M. R., & Crooks, T. J. (1999). A generalized examinee-centered method for setting standards on achievement tests. *Applied Measurement in Education, 12,* 327–366.

Council of Chief State School Officers. (2001). *State student assessment programs annual survey* (Data Vol. 2). Washington, DC: Author.

Ebel, R. L. (1972). *Essentials of educational measurement* (2nd ed.). Englewood Cliffs, NJ: Prentice-Hall.

Ferrara, S., Johnson, E., & Chen, W.-H. (2005). Vertically articulated performance standards: Logic, procedures, and likely classification accuracy. *Applied Measurement in Education, 18*(1), 35–59.

Fitzpatrick, A. R. (1989). Social influences in standard setting: The effects of social interaction on group judgments. *Review of Educational Research, 59,* 315–328.

Geisinger, K. F. (1991). Using standard-setting data to establish cutoff scores. *Educational Measurement: Issues and Practice, 10*(2), 17–22.

Giraud, G. T., Impara, J. C., & Buckendahl, C. W. (2000). Making the cut in school districts: Alternative methods for setting cut-scores. *Educational Assessment, 6,* 291–304.

Glass, G. V. (1978). Standards and criteria. *Journal of Educational Measurement, 15,* 237–261.

Goodman, D., & Hambleton, R. K. (2005). Some misconceptions about large-scale educational assessments. In R. Phelps (Ed.), *Defending standardized testing* (pp. 91–110). Mahwah, NJ: Erlbaum.

Green, D. R., Trimble, C. S., & Lewis, D. M. (2003). Interpreting the results of three different standard setting procedures. *Educational Measurement: Issues and Practice, 22*(1), 22–32.

de Gruijter, D. (1985). Compromise models for establishing examination standards. *Journal of Educational Measurement, 22,* 263–269.

Hambleton, R. K. (1978). On the use of cutoff scores with criterion-referenced tests in instructional settings. *Journal of Educational Measurement, 15,* 277–290.

Hambleton, R. K. (1995, August). *Setting standards on performance assessments: Promising new methods and technical issues.* Paper presented at the meeting of the American Psychological Association, New York.

Hambleton, R. K. (1998). Setting performance standards on achievement tests: Meeting the requirements of Title I. In L. Hansche (Ed.), *Handbook for the development of performance standards: Meeting the requirements of Title I* (pp. 87–114). Washington, DC: Council of Chief State School Officers.

Hambleton, R. K. (2001). Setting performance standards on educational assessments and criteria for evaluating the process. In G. J. Cizek (Ed.), *Setting performance standards: Concepts, methods, and perspectives* (pp. 89–116). Mahwah, NJ: Erlbaum.

Hambleton, R. K., & Bourque, M. L. (1991). *The levels of mathematics achievement: Initial performance standards for the 1990 NAEP Mathematics assessment* (Technical Report, Vol. 3). Washington, DC: National Assessment Governing Board.

Hambleton, R. K., Brennan, R. L., Brown, W., Dodd, B., Forsyth, R. A., Mehrens, W. A., et al. (2000). A response to "Setting reasonable and useful performance standards" in the National Academy of Sciences' *Grading the nation's report card. Educational Measurement: Issues and Practice, 19*(2), 5–14.

Hambleton, R. K., Jaeger, R. M., Plake, B. S., & Mills, C. N. (2000). Setting performance standards on complex educational assessments *Applied Psychological Measurement, 24,* 355–366.

Hambleton, R. K., & Plake, B. S. (1995). Using an extended Angoff procedure to set standards on complex performance assessments. *Applied Measurement in Education, 8,* 41–55.

Hambleton, R. K., & Powell, S. (1983). A framework for viewing the process of standard-setting. *Evaluation & the Health Profession, 6,* 3–24.

Hambleton, R. K., & Slater, S. C. (1997). Reliability of credentialing examinations and the impact of scoring models and standard-setting policies. *Applied Measurement in Education, 10*(1), 19–38.

Hambleton, R. K., Swaminathan, H. R., & Rogers, J. (1991). *Fundamentals of item response theory.* Thousand Oaks, CA: Sage.

Hanson, B. A., Bay, L., & Loomis, S. C. (1998, April). *Booklet classification study.* Paper presented at the meeting of the National Council on Measurement in Education, San Diego, CA.

Hofstee, W. K. B. (1983). The case for compromise in educational selection and grading. In S. B. Anderson & J. S. Helmick (Eds.), *On educational testing* (pp. 109–127). San Francisco: Jossey-Bass.

Hurtz, G. M., & Auerbach, M. A. (2003). A meta-analysis of the effects of modifications to the Angoff method on cutoff scores and judgment consensus. *Educational and Psychological Measurement, 63,* 584–601.

Huynh, H. (1998). On score locations of binary and partial credit items and their application to item mapping and criterion-referenced interpretation. *Journal of Educational and Behavioral Statistics, 23,* 35–56.

Huynh, H., & Schneider, C. (2005). Vertically moderated standards: Background, assumptions, and practices. *Applied Measurement in Education, 18*(1), 99–113.

Impara, J. C., & Plake, B. S. (1997). Standard setting: An alternative approach. *Journal of Educational Measurement, 34*(4), 353–366.

Individuals with Disabilities Educational Act of 1991, 20 U.S.C. § 1400 *et seq.*

Individuals with Disabilities Educational Act of 1997, 20 U.S.C. § 1412(a) (17)(A).

Jaeger, R. M. (1982). An iterative structured judgment process for establishing standards on competency tests: Theory and application. *Educational Evaluation and Policy Analysis, 4,* 461–475.

Jaeger, R. M. (1988). Use and effect of caution indices in detecting aberrant patterns of standard-setting judgments. *Applied Measurement in Education, 1,* 17–31.

Jaeger, R. M. (1989). Certification of student competence. In R. Linn (Ed.), *Educational measurement* (3rd ed., pp. 485–514). Englewood Cliffs, NJ: Prentice-Hall.

Jaeger, R. M. (1991). Selection of judges for standard-setting. *Educational Measurement: Issues and Practices, 10*(2), 3–6, 10, 14.

Jaeger, R. M. (1995a). Setting performance standards through two-stage judgmental policy capturing. *Applied Measurement in Education, 8,* 15–40.

Jaeger, R. M. (1995b). Setting standards for complex performances: An iterative, judgmental policy-capturing strategy. *Educational Measurement: Issues and Practice, 14*(4), 16–20.

Jaeger, R. M., & Keller-McNulty, S. (1991). Procedures for eliciting and using judgments of the value of observed behaviors on military job performance tests. In A. K. Wigdor & B. F. Green (Eds.), *Performance assessment in the workplace: Volume I* (pp. 258–304). Washington, DC: National Academy Press.

Jaeger, R. M., & Mills, C. N. (2001). An integrated judgment procedure for setting standards on complex, large-scale assessments. In G. J. Cizek (Ed.), *Standard setting: Concepts, methods, and perspectives* (pp. 313–338). Mahwah, NJ: Erlbaum.

Kane, M. (1994). Validating the performance standards associated with passing scores. *Review of Educational Research, 64,* 425–461.

Kane, M. (1995). Examinee-centered vs. task-centered standard setting. In *Proceedings of the joint conference on standard setting for large scale assessments of the National Assessment Governing Board (NAGB) and the National Center for Educational Statistics (NCES), Volume II* (pp. 119–141). Washington, DC: U. S. Government Printing Office.

Kane, M. (1998). Choosing between examinee-centered and test-centered standard-setting methods. *Educational Assessment, 5,* 129–145.

Kane, M. (2001). So much remains the same: Conception and status of validation in setting standards. In G. Cizek (Ed.), *Standard setting: Concepts, methods, and perspectives* (pp. 53–88). Mahwah, NJ: Erlbaum.

Kane, M., & Wilson, J. (1984). Errors of measurement and standard setting in mastery testing. *Applied Psychological Measurement, 8,* 107–115.

Kaufman, D. M., Mann, K. V., Muijtjens, A. M. M., & van der Vleuten, C. P. M. (2000). A comparison of standard-setting procedures for an OSCE in undergraduate medical education. *Academic Medicine, 75,* 267–271.

Kingston, N. M., Kahl, S. R., Sweeney, K., & Bay, L. (2001). Setting performance standards using the body of work method. In G. J. Cizek (Ed.), *Standard setting: Concepts, methods, and perspectives* (pp. 219–248). Mahwah, NJ: Erlbaum.

Kleinert, H., & Kearns, J. (2001). *Alternate assessment: Measuring outcomes and supports for students with disabilities.* Baltimore: Brookes Publishing.

Kolstad, A. (1996, April). *The response probability convention embedded in reporting prose literacy levels from the 1992 National Literacy Survey.* Paper presented at the meeting of the American Educational Research Association, New York.

Lee, G., & Lewis, D. M. (2001, April). *A generalizability theory approach toward estimating standard errors of cutscores set using the bookmark standard setting procedure.* Paper presented at the meeting of the National Council on Measurement in Education, Seattle, WA.

Lewis, D. M., Green, D. R., Mitzel, H. C., Baum, K., & Patz, R. J. (1998, April). *The bookmark standard setting procedure: Methodology and recent implementations.* Paper presented at the meeting of the 1998 National Council on Measurement in Education, San Diego, CA.

Lewis, D. M., Mitzel, H. C., & Green, D. R. (1996, June). Standard setting: A bookmark approach. In D. R. Green (Chair), *IRT-based standard setting procedures utilizing behavioral anchoring.* Symposium presented at the Council of Chief State School Officers National Conference on Large-Scale Assessment, Phoenix, AZ.

Linn, R. L. (1998). Validating inferences from National Assessment of Educational Progress achievement-level reporting. *Applied Measurement in Education, 11,* 23–47.

Linn, R. L., & Herman, J. (1997). *A policymaker's guide to standards-led assessment.* Denver, CO: The Education Commission of the States.

Livingston, S. A., & Zieky, M. J. (1982). *Passing scores: A manual for setting standards of performance on educational and occupational tests.* Princeton, NJ: Educational Testing Service.

Livingston, S. A., & Zieky, M. J. (1989). A comparative study of standard-setting methods. *Applied Measurement in Education, 2,* 121–141.

Loomis, S. C., & Bourque, M. L. (2001). From tradition to innovation: Standard setting on the National Assessment of Educational Progress. In G. J. Cizek (Ed.), *Standard setting: Concepts, methods, and perspectives* (pp. 175–217). Mahwah, NJ: Erlbaum.

Massachusetts Department of Education. (2003). *2003 MCAS technical report.* Malden, MA: Author.

McKinley, D. W., Boulet, J. R., & Hambleton, R. K. (2005). A work-centered approach for setting passing scores on performance-based assessments. *Evaluation & The Health Professions, 28*(3), 349–369.

Meara, K. C., Hambleton, R. K., & Sireci, S. G. (2001). Setting and validating standards on professional licensure and certification exams: A survey of current practices. *CLEAR Exam Review, 7*(2), 17–23.

Mehrens, W. A. (1986). Measurement specialists: Motive to achieve or motive to avoid failure? *Educational Measurement: Issues and Practice, 5*(4), 5–10.

Mehrens, W. A. (1995). Methodological issues in standard setting for educational exams. In *Proceedings of the joint conference on standard setting for large scale assessments of the National Assessment Governing Board (NAGB) and the National Center for Educational Statistics (NCES), Volume II* (pp. 221–263). Washington, DC: U.S. Government Printing Office.

Mehrens, W. A., & Phillips, S. E. (1989). Using college GPA and test scores in teacher licensure decisions: Conjunctive versus compensatory models. *Applied Measurement in Education, 2,* 277–288.

Melican, G. J., Mills, C. N., & Plake, B. S. (1989). Accuracy of item performance predictions based on the Nedelsky standard setting method. *Educational and Psychological Measurement, 49,* 467–478.

Meskauskas, J. A. (1976). Evaluation models for criterion-referenced testing: Views regarding mastery and standard setting. *Review of Educational Research, 46,* 133–158.

Millman, J. (1989). If first you don't succeed: Setting pass-rates when more than one attempt is permitted. *Educational Researcher, 18*(6), 5–9.

Mills, C. N. (1995). Establishing passing standards. In J. C. Impara (Ed.), *Licensure testing: Purposes, procedures, and practices* (pp. 219–252). Lincoln, NE: Buros Institute of Mental Measurements.

Mills, C. N., Hambleton, R. K., Biskin, B., Kobrin, J., Evans, J., & Pfeffer, M. (2000). *A comparison of the standard-setting methods for the Uniform CPA Examination.* Jersey City, NJ: American Institute for Certified Public Accountants.

Mills, C. N., & Jaeger, R. M. (1998). Creating descriptions of desired student achievement when setting performance standards. In L. Hansche (Ed.), *Handbook for the development of performance standards: Meeting the requirements of Title I* (pp. 73–85). Washington, DC: Council of Chief State School Officers.

Mills, C. N., & Melican, G. J. (1988). Estimating and adjusting cutoff scores: Features of selected methods. *Applied Measurement in Education, 1,* 261–275.

Mitzel, H. C., Lewis, D. M., Patz, R. J., & Green, D. R. (2001). The bookmark procedure: Psychological perspectives. In G. J. Cizek (Ed.), *Standard setting: Concepts, methods, and perspectives* (pp. 249–281). Mahwah, NJ: Erlbaum.

National Center for Educational Statistics. (2005). *The Nation's Report Card: An introduction to the National Assessment of Educational Progress (NAEP)* (NCES 2005454). Washington, DC: U.S. Department of Education, Institute of Education Sciences, National Center for Education Statistics.

National Research Council. (2005). *Measuring literacy: Performance levels for adults, interim report.* Washington, DC: The National Academies Press.

Nedelsky, L. (1954). Absolute grading standards for objective tests. *Educational and Psychological Measurement, 14,* 3–19.

New Jersey Department of Education. (2005). *Standard setting for the New Jersey Assessment of Skills and Knowledge for Grade 4 (NJ ASK4).* New Brunswick, NJ: Author.

No Child Left Behind Act of 2001, 20 U.S.C. § 6301 *et seq* (2001) (PL 107–110).

Norcini, J. J. (2003). Setting standards on educational tests. *Medical Education, 37,* 464–469.

Norcini, J., & Shea, J. (1992). The reproducibility of standards over groups and occasions. *Applied Measurement in Education, 5*(1), 63–72.

Norcini, J. J., & Shea, J. A. (1997). The credibility and comparability of standards. *Applied Measurement in Education, 10,* 39–59.

Olson, B., Mead, R., & Payne, D. (2002). *A report of a standard setting method for alternate assessments for students with significant disabilities* (Synthesis Report 47). Minneapolis: University of Minnesota, National Center on Educational Outcomes. Retrieved January 19, 2004, from http://education.umn.edu/NCEO/OnlinePubs/Synthesis47.html

Pellegrino, J. W., Jones, L. R., & Mitchell, K. J. (1999). *Grading the nation's report card: Evaluating NAEP and transforming the assessment of educational progress.* Washington, DC: National Academy Press.

Phillips, S. E. (2000). GI Forum vs. Texas Education Agency: Psychometric evidence. *Applied Measurement in Education, 13,* 343–385.

Phillips, S. E. (2001). Legal issues in standard setting for K–12 programs. In G. J. Cizek (Ed.), *Standard setting: Concepts, methods, and perspectives* (pp. 411–426). Mahwah, NJ: Erlbaum.

Pitoniak, M. J., Hambleton, R. K., & Biskin, B. H. (2003). *Setting standards on tests containing computerized performance tasks* (Center for Educational Assessment Research Report No. 488). Amherst: University of Massachusetts, Center for Educational Assessment. This paper was presented at the April, 2003 annual meeting of the National Council on Measurement in Education, Chicago.

Pitoniak, M. J., Hambleton, R. K., & Sireci, S. G. (2002). *Advances in standard setting for professional licensure examinations* (Center for Educational Assessment Research Report No. 423). Amherst: University of Massachusetts, Center for Educational Assessment. This paper was presented at the April, 2002 meeting of the American Educational Research Association, New Orleans, LA.

Pitoniak, M. J., & Royer, J. M. (2001). Testing accommodations for examinees with disabilities: A review of psychometric, legal and social policy issues. *Review of Educational Research, 71,* 53–104.

Plake, B. S. (1995). An integration and reprise: What we think we have learned. *Applied Measurement in Education, 8,* 85–92.

Plake, B. S. (1997). *Criteria for evaluating the quality of a judgmental standard setting procedure: What information should be reported?* Unpublished manuscript.

Plake, B. S. (1998). Setting performance standards for professional licensure and certification. *Applied Measurement in Education, 11,* 65–80.

Plake, B. S. (2005). Doesn't everybody know that 70% is passing? In R. Phelps (Ed.), *Defending standardized testing* (pp. 175–185). Mahwah, NJ: Erlbaum.

Plake, B. S., & Hambleton, R. K. (2000). A standard-setting method designed for complex performance assessments: Categorical assignments of student work. *Educational Assessment, 6,* 197–215.

Plake, B. S., & Hambleton, R. K. (2001). The analytic judgment method for setting standards on complex performance assessments. In G. J. Cizek (Ed.), *Standard setting: Concepts, methods, and perspectives* (pp. 283–312). Mahwah, NJ: Erlbaum.

Plake, B. S., Hambleton, R. K., & Jaeger, R. M. (1997). A new standard setting method for performance assessments: The dominant profile judgment method and some field-test results. *Educational and Psychological Measurement, 57,* 400–411.

Plake, B. S., & Impara, J. C. (2001). Ability of panelists to estimate item performance for a target group of candidates: An issue in judgmental standard setting. *Educational Assessment, 7,* 87–98.

Plake, B. S., & Melican, G. J. (1989). Effects of item context on intrajudge consistency of expert judgments via the Nedelsky standard setting method. *Educational and Psychological Measurement, 49,* 45–51.

Plake, B. S., Melican, G. J., & Mills, C. N. (1991). Factors influencing intrajudge consistency during standard setting. *Educational Measurement: Issues and Practice, 10*(2), 15–16, 22, 25–26.

Popham, W. J. (1978). As always, provocative. *Journal of Educational Measurement, 15,* 297–230.

Putnam, S. E., Pence, P., & Jaeger, R. M. (1995). A multi-stage dominant profile method for setting standards on complex performance assessments. *Applied Measurement in Education, 8,* 57–83.

Quenemoen, R., Rigney, S., & Thurlow, M. (2002). *Use of alternate assessment results in reporting and accountability systems: Conditions for use based on research and practice* (Synthesis Report 43). Minneapolis: University of Minnesota, National Center on Educational Outcomes.

Raymond, M. R., & Reid, J. B. (2001). Who made thee a judge? Selecting and training participants for standard setting. In G. J. Cizek (Ed.), *Standard setting: Concepts, methods, and perspectives* (pp. 119–157). Mahwah, NJ: Erlbaum.

Reckase, M. D. (2000a). A survey and evaluation of recently developed procedures for setting standards on educational tests. In M. L. Bourque & S. Byrd (Eds.), *Student performance standards on the National Assessment of Educational Progress: Affirmations and improvements* (pp. 41–69). Washington, DC: National Assessment Governing Board.

Reckase, M. D. (2000b). *The evolution of the NAEP achievement levels setting process: A summary of the research and development efforts conducted by ACT.* Iowa City, IA: ACT.

Reckase, M. D. (2001). Innovative methods for helping standard-setting participants to perform their task: The role of feedback regarding consistency, accuracy, and impact. In G. J. Cizek (Ed.), *Setting performance standards: Concepts, methods, and perspectives* (pp. 159–173). Mahwah, NJ: Erlbaum.

Reckase, M. D., & Bay, L. (1999, April). *Comparing two methods for collecting test-based judgments.* Paper presented at the meeting of the National Council on Measurement in Education, Montreal, Quebec, Canada.

Roeber, E. (2002). *Setting standards on alternate assessments* (Synthesis Report 42). Minneapolis: University of Minnesota, National Center on Educational Outcomes. Retrieved January 18, 2004, from http://education.umn.edu/NCEO/OnlinePubs/Synthesis42.html

Schoon, C. G., & Smith, I. L. (1996). Standard setting. In A. H. Browning, A. C. Bugbee, Jr., & M. A. Mullins (Eds.), *Certification: A NOCA handbook* (pp. 149–190). Washington D.C: National Organization for Competency Assurance.

Schulz, E. M., Lee, W., & Mullen, K. (2005). A domain-level approach to describing growth in achievement. *Journal of Educational Measurement, 42,* 1–26.

Schulz, E. M., & Mitzel, H. C. (2005, April). *The Mapmark standard setting method.* Paper presented at the meeting of the National Council on Measurement in Education, Montreal, Quebec, Canada.

Shen, L. (2001, April). *Comparison of Angoff and Rasch model based item map methods in standard setting.* Paper presented at the meeting of the American Educational Research Association, Seattle, WA.

Shepard, L. A. (1980). Standard setting issues and methods. *Applied Psychological Measurement, 4,* 447–467.

Shepard, L. A. (1984). Setting performance standards. In R. A. Berk (Ed.), *A guide to criterion-referenced test construction* (pp. 169–198). Baltimore: Johns Hopkins University Press.

Shepard, L. A. (1995). Implications for standard setting of the National Academy of Education evaluation of the National Assessment of Educational Progress achievement levels. In *Proceedings of the joint conference on standard setting for large scale assessments of the National Assessment Governing Board (NAGB) and the National Center for Educational Statistics (NCES), Volume II* (pp. 143–160). Washington, DC: U.S. Government Printing Office.

Shepard, L. A., Glaser, R., Linn, R., & Bohrnstedt, G. (1993). *Setting performance standards for student achievement.* Stanford, CA: National Academy of Education.

Sireci, S. G. (2001). Standard setting using cluster analysis. In G. J. Cizek (Ed.), *Standard setting: Concepts, methods, and perspectives* (pp. 339–354). Mahwah, NJ: Erlbaum.

Sireci, S. (2005). The most frequently unasked questions about testing. In R. Phelps (Ed.), *Defending standardized testing* (pp. 111–121). Mahwah, NJ: Erlbaum.

Sireci, S. G., & Biskin, B. J. (1992). Measurement practices in national licensing examination programs: A survey. *CLEAR Exam Review, 3*(1), 21–25.

Sireci, S. G., & Green, P. C. (2000). Legal and psychometric criteria for evaluating teacher certification tests. *Educational Measurement: Issues and Practice, 19*(1), 22–31, 34.

Sireci, S. G., Hambleton, R. K., Huff, K. L., & Jodoin, M. G. (2000). *Setting and validating standards on Microsoft Certified Professional examinations* (Center for Educational Assessment Research Report No. 395). Amherst: University of Massachusetts, Center for Educational Assessment.

Sireci, S. G., Hambleton, R. K., & Pitoniak, M. J. (2004). Setting passing scores on licensure exams using direct consensus. *CLEAR Exam Review, 15*(1), 21–25.

Sireci, S. G., Rizavi, S., Dillingham, A., & Rodriguez, G. (1999). *Setting performance standards on the ACCUPLACER Elementary Algebra Test* (Center for Educational Assessment Research Report No. 368). Amherst: University of Massachusetts, Center for Educational Assessment.

Sireci, S. G., Robin, F., & Patelis, T. (1999). Using cluster analysis to facilitate standard setting. *Applied Measurement in Education, 12,* 301–325.

Skorupski, W., & Hambleton, R. K. (2005). What are panelists thinking when they participate in standard-setting studies? *Applied Measurement in Education, 18,* 233–255.

State of Wisconsin, Department of Public Instruction. (1997). *Final summary report of the proficiency score standards for the Wisconsin Student Assessment System (WSAS) Knowledge and Concept Examinations for elementary, middle, and high school at grades 4, 8, and 10.* Madison, WI: Office of Educational Accountability.

Subkoviak, M. J., Kane, M. T., & Duncan, P. H. (2002). A comparative study of the Angoff and Nedelsky methods: Implications for validity. *Mid-Western Educational Researcher, 15*(2), 3–7.

Thompson, S. J., Quenemoen, R., Thurlow, M. L., & Ysseldyke, J. E. (2001). *Alternate assessments for students with disabilities.* Thousand Oaks, CA: Corwin Press.

United States General Accounting Office. (1993). *Educational achievement standards: NAGB's approach yields misleading interpretations* (GAO/PEMD Publication No. 93–12). Washington, DC: Author.

van der Linden, W. J. (1982). A latent trait method for determining intrajudge consistency in the Angoff and Nedelsky techniques of standard setting. *Journal of Educational Measurement, 19,* 295–308.

van der Linden, W. J. (1995). A conceptual analysis of standard setting in large-scale assessments. In *Proceedings of the joint conference on standard setting for large scale assessments of the National Assessment Governing Board (NAGB) and the National Center for Educational Statistics (NCES), Volume II* (pp. 97–117). Washington, DC: U. S. Government Printing Office.

Wang, N. (2003). Use of the Rasch IRT model in standard setting: An item mapping method. *Journal of Educational Measurement, 40,* 231–253.

Williams, N. J., & Schulz, E. M. (2005, April). *An investigation of response probability (RP) values used in standard setting.* Paper presented at the meeting of the National Council on Measurement in Education, Montreal, Quebec, Canada.

Zieky, M. J. (2001). So much has changed: How the setting of cutscores has evolved since the 1980s. In G. J. Cizek (Ed.), *Standard setting: Concepts, methods, and perspectives* (pp. 19–51). Mahwah, NJ: Erlbaum.

13

Technology and Testing

Fritz Drasgow
University of Illinois at Urbana-Champaign

Richard M. Luecht
University of North Carolina at Greensboro

Randy E. Bennett
Educational Testing Service

1. INTRODUCTION

This chapter describes our vision of a 21st-century testing program that capitalizes on modern technology and takes advantage of recent innovations in testing. Using an analogy from engineering, we envision a modern testing program as *an integrated system of systems*. Thus, there is an item generation system, an item pretesting system, an examinee registration system, and so forth. This chapter discusses each system and illustrates how technology can enhance and facilitate the core processes of each system.

An engineering perspective is becoming increasingly important because of a profound change in the test administration model used by many testing programs. Traditionally, high stakes tests were administered only a few times a year, with a large number of individuals tested via paper-and-pencil at each administration. However, continuous testing—where examinees schedule their exam at a time that is convenient for them—is increasingly popular. Test takers greatly prefer this approach to scheduling rather than being required to take the test at the time mandated by the testing program.

Continuous testing provides great challenges to testing programs. Perhaps foremost among these challenges is test security: Use of a single test form for an extended time period invites test compromise. Consequently, multiple forms or some type of adaptive testing must be used. This, in turn, means that many more items must be generated for the testing program. Technology—and an engineering approach—is critical for mass production of items.

Another challenge is examinee registration and test administration. Continuous testing programs typically rely on computerization to ensure standardization in the test administration process. Registration is then much more complex than simply "signing up for the test." The registration system must ensure that a computer seat is available at the time requested by the examinee; moreover, the computer must have the capability to properly administer the test (e.g., it must have a sound card and headphones if the test requires audio).

Technology offers solutions to many of the challenges faced by testing programs. From automating item generation and forms assembly to registering and scheduling test takers to scoring and providing results, this chapter describes how computerization can improve the testing process. It is important to note that these innovations have costs. For example, implementing a continuous testing program typically requires many additional items to be written and pretested. Moreover, some of the technology described in this chapter is new and testing programs would be well advised to conduct their own research before implementation.

The testing program we describe in this chapter is certainly a Cadillac system. But any testing program can utilize some of the advantages we describe, even small programs that cannot implement everything. Thus, we present this chapter as an idealized conceptualization of a testing program. We encourage testing practitioners to think of their tests in terms of the systems we describe and consider the use of technology to enhance their work.

2. NEW TECHNOLOGY AND TEST DESIGN

A consequence of moving testing to computers, and also a prime reason for conceptualizing computerized testing programs as a system of systems, is that decisions made in one system affect the functioning of other systems. Bennett and Bejar (1998) noted this fact in the context of designing computer-based tests that included automated scoring. Their conception focused on the following components: construct definition, along with a test and task design that operationalizes the construct; an examinee interface; a tutorial; test development tools; an automated scoring routine; and some method for communicating assessment results. Construct definition and test and task design (including test items) work in tandem to define what test designers *intend* an examination to measure. The implementation of that design in the examinee interface, tutorial, test development tools, automated scoring, and reporting define what the test *actually* measures. Intention and actuality may not be identical, with the latter being more or less than the former. If the intention is to measure some construct domain, the difference between actuality and intention can be phrased in terms of Messick's (1989) twin threats to validity. When actuality does not fully cover intention, the result is construct under-representation. When actuality exceeds intention, it is construct-irrelevant variance.

The interaction between intention and implementation is magnified in computer-based testing because the component systems are so tightly intertwined (Bennett & Bejar, 1998). For example, by allowing the examinee more or less freedom in what can be entered as a response, the interface can affect what is measured, as when, for example, the interface admits only a final answer as opposed to the intermediary work that led to that answer. Additionally, the scoring system must process what the interface admits. Here, too, intention and actuality may fail to converge if the automated—or human—scoring does not effectively capture the relevant features of responses. How the interface functions must, in turn, be explained in the test tutorial. If the tutorial fails to prepare the examinee sufficiently, the test may wind up measuring computer familiarity more than the intended construct. As a final example, the tools test developers use to create items limit what they can create. If those tools do not permit developers to interact with, review, and change item presentation easily, or test and change scoring keys, developers may be forced to create tasks that fall within frequently used structures they know will work effectively but that under-represent the intended construct domain.

Managing the match between intention and actuality, then, makes computer-based testing particularly challenging from a validity perspective. And, the more complex the assessment in terms of the stimulus presentation, the response openness, or the interactivity, the more serious these challenges become. To make matters worse, the same interdependencies that make computer-based testing challenging from a validity perspective can also make it extremely costly. Even for new response types that are structurally simple, costs can be high due to the need to create multimedia stimulus components (e.g., an animation or audio clip), interfaces that allow new ways of responding (e.g., for entering and editing a mathematical expression), and scoring for those responses. For highly interactive tests that interleave item presentation and responding to form extended tasks like simulations, the costs and time required for development and scoring can quickly become untenable, especially when the test is created anew and not from existing infrastructure components.

One approach to managing more effectively the validity and cost challenges posed by computer-based testing, and especially by the more complex tests that computer-based approaches allow, is *evidence-centered design* (ECD; Mislevy, this volume; Mislevy, Almond, & Lukas, 2003). This approach was developed from the realization that traditional design methods did not afford the conceptual, linguistic, or data structures needed for creating complex computer-based assessments efficiently. ECD can be viewed from at least four perspectives: as a way of reasoning about assessment design, a way of reasoning about examinee performance, a data framework for more efficiently creating new assessments, and a model for structuring test delivery around four key processes.

As a way of reasoning about design, ECD proceeds from first identifying the claims that test users wish to make about proficiency, to specifying the evidence needed to support those claims, to finally describing the tasks capable of eliciting that evidence. ECD structures the development process so that validity is built in *by design* because the resulting assessment is more tightly tied to inferences that users wish to make and because each "item" can be linked directly back to the proficiency claim it is intended to support.

As a way of reasoning about examinee performance, the inference process proceeds in the opposite direction, this time from task responses, to evidence (i.e., item scores), to claims about proficiency. ECD structures the scoring process so that rules are established for evaluating each examinee action and for combining those evaluations into proficiency claims.

These two ways of reasoning—from claims to tasks and from task responses back to claims—help focus design on validity issues, as well as on the practical constraints limiting the type and number of tasks that may be included. For computer-based tests, especially ones that incorporate complex tasks, that focus is invaluable in preventing developers from spending unnecessary time creating interesting (yet expensive) assessment exercises that have no clear links to the target construct and, possibly, no hope of implementation in a practical setting.

Whereas these first two ECD elements—reasoning about design and reasoning about performance—are aimed primarily at creating valid, practically deliverable tests, the two remaining key ideas that ECD contributes center on the infrastructure for designing assessments in a repeatable and sustainable manner. Thus, ECD is also a data framework in which assessments are made up of software components drawn, in theory, from large, relationally structured "object" libraries. These libraries contain such things as proficiency claims, evidence types, task templates, evaluation rules (that specify how an examinee's task response is to be judged), and accumulation rules (such as measurement models, that dictate how scored task responses are to be combined to produce estimates of proficiency). These components are objects in the software sense of the word. That is, they are built according to a set of programming conventions, and contain information, that allows them to act in concert with other objects in prescribed ways.

Using a library, a test designer would create a new assessment as follows:

- Choose from among the library's proficiency claims those that match the requirements of test users.
- For each claim, choose from among the type of evidence associated with that claim.
- For each type of evidence, choose from among the task templates associated with that evidence type.
- Write items to correspond to those task templates, using a tool that stores the items as software objects.
- Choose from among the evaluation rules associated with those task templates.
- Choose from among the accumulation rules.

The chosen software objects are then used by the various test systems to assemble, deliver, and score the test. When the library does not have the required objects, those components can be created anew and added so that they may be used in future projects.

The promise of ECD from an efficiency perspective is the reusability of these software objects. This reusability can, at least in principle, dramatically reduce the cost and time required for developing complex, computer-based assessments and related products (e.g., test preparation materials, diagnostic measures, and instructional software). However, this reduction presumes the existence of a library of interoperable design objects that comprehensively cover a given domain. Further, it assumes that a reasonably large amount of new product development is expected in this domain. The creation of this object library is, in itself, an extremely expensive undertaking that can only be cost-justified through extensive reuse.

ECD is, last, a model for structuring test delivery around four modular processes: activity selection, presentation, evidence identification, and evidence accumulation (Mislevy, Almond, & Steinberg, 2003). *Activity selection* is the process that decides what "item" to present next, where the item may be anything from a multiple-choice question to a complex simulation. The CAT algorithm is an example of an activity selection mechanism. *Presentation* is the process that displays an item for an examinee and collects the response(s). *Evidence identification* is the process that scores the response. It may be done by machine or by a human judge. Finally, *evidence accumulation* translates item scores into proficiency estimates. These proficiency estimates may, in turn, be used by the activity selection process to choose the next task.

Why is it important from the ECD perspective that processes be modular? Processes are modular so that software objects can be swapped in and out of one process without having to modify modules associated with the other processes. For example, the same complex tasks can be employed for both generating a single score and for detailed diagnosis simply by changing the relevant objects in the evidence identification and evidence accumulation modules.

In sum, ECD exemplifies an approach that attempts to rationalize the design of computer-based assessments through validity as well as software engineering frameworks. Design within these frameworks may allow such assessments to be built more effectively, efficiently, and synergistically in terms of linkages to related products.

3. AUTOMATIC ITEM GENERATION

With the advent of continuously administered computerized tests, such as in the Graduate Record Examinations (GRE) General Test and the Graduate Management Admission Test (GMAT), has come the need for large numbers of test items. Large numbers of items are needed because test content is exposed almost daily and item pools must be constantly replenished to maintain security. In cases where the tests are administered adaptively, the need extends beyond test items to the calibrations required for item selection and scoring.

This demand for large numbers of items is challenging to satisfy because the traditional approach to test development uses the item as the fundamental unit of currency. That is, each item is individually hand-crafted—written, reviewed, revised, edited, entered onto computer, and calibrated—as if no other like it had ever been created before. A second issue with traditional approaches is that it is notoriously hard to hit difficulty targets, which results in having too many items at some levels and not enough at other levels. Finally, the pretesting needed for calibration in adaptive testing programs entails significant cost and effort.

One potential solution to these problems is automatic item generation (Bejar, 1993; Irvine & Kyllonen, 2002). Ideally, automatic item generation has two requirements. The first requirement is that an item class can be described sufficiently for a computer to create instances of that class automatically or at least semi-automatically. The second requirement is that the determinants of item difficulty be understood well enough so that each of the generated instances need not be calibrated individually.

In the terminology of automatic item generation, the abstract description the computer uses to generate instances of a class is called an item "model" and the instances are called "variants." Item models can be created and large numbers of variants can be inexpensively generated with software tools such as the Mathematics Test Creation Assistant (Singley & Bennett, 2002). To the degree that a testing program can employ large numbers of variants effectively, automatic item generation can increase efficiency considerably.

Automatic item generation has its roots in the criterion-referenced testing movement of the 1960s. A key milestone was Hively's (Hively, Patterson, & Page, 1968) "item forms." In this approach, items were generated from templates that had fixed and variable elements. The class of item was defined by the fixed elements and the variable elements defined how members of the class—the variants—differed from one another. Items created from such a template were intended to function similarly; that is, to measure the same homogeneous skill and be at the same difficulty level. Absent the assumptions of homogeneity and equivalent difficulty, the mastery decision for any given student might vary from one sample of items to the next (Macready & Merwin, 1973). In these early attempts, the questions produced by an item form were often of similar difficulty but not necessarily homogeneous (Hively, Patterson, & Page, 1968; Macready, 1983); that is, they produced a large person-by-task interaction within item forms, such that an individual who answered one item correctly did not necessarily get the next item right, even though the items were variants of one another. One reason for this outcome was that the cognitive-psychological tools to make possible the generation of equivalently difficult and homogeneous items were not available.

Automatic item generation advanced with the emergence of cognitive approaches to instruction and diagnosis, as exemplified by intelligent tutoring systems (e.g., see Wenger, 1987). Intelligent tutoring systems attempt to dynamically characterize student understanding in a domain so that the tutors can adjust instruction in real-time. The advance made by this field was to generate items based on cognitive-domain analysis; that is, on a deep understanding of the cognitive mechanisms—the strategies, processes, knowledge structures—that made for proficiency in a given subject-matter domain (e.g., Burton, 1982). This was a significant advance because, in principle, it allowed for achieving control over—and psychometric characterization of—item functioning that eluded earlier attempts at automatic generation (e.g., Hively, Patterson, & Page, 1968). But, of course, being concerned mainly with instruction and not assessment, this generation was done without exploring its psychometric implications. The integration of the psychometric and cognitive perspectives did not occur until relatively recently, with Bejar's (1993) work on *response generative modeling* and Embretson's (1999) work on *cognitive design systems*. That integration is more or less evident in three approaches to automatic item generation. Those approaches are based on strong theory, weak theory, and art, or personal theory.[1]

3.1. Automatic Item Generation from Strong Theory

The goal of automatic item generation from strong theory is to generate *calibrated* items automatically from design *principles* by using a *theory* of difficulty based on a cognitive model. That theory needs to posit the cognitive mechanisms required to solve items and the features of items that cause difficulty. So, the intent is to model *both* content and responses; only by modeling item content in terms of the difficulty demands it places on the cognitive apparatus is it possible to (1) predict the parameters of some response model and (2) control homogeneity and difficulty in item production (Bejar, 1993). Note that strong theory links test development directly to construct validity, in particular to Embretson's (1983) notion of construct representation, which is centered on specifying and providing evidence for the cognitive mechanisms underlying item performance. These mechanisms determine the construct(s) measured by items. If one builds a test based on knowledge of these mechanisms, every time the test is given, the theory is challenged because comparing the theoretical description with the responses of examinees is a continual test of the validity of scores (Bejar, 1993).

Automatic item generation from strong theory is best suited to narrow domains where cognitive analysis is more feasible and, as a result, well-developed theory is more likely to exist. Among the best examples of automatic item generation from strong theory are Bejar's (1990) work on mental rotation tasks and Embretson's (1998) work on matrix completion items. In the former case, the examinee's task is to determine if a rotated figure is the same as a given figure. There is a large literature from experimental psychology on the cognitive mechanisms underlying performance in this domain and the features that affect item functioning. This literature suggests that, for any given figure, angular disparity drives difficulty (i.e., the difference in the amount of rotation between the given and the comparison figures). In this domain, a single item model can be created that, by virtue of manipulating angular disparity, produces items that range widely, but predictably, in difficulty.

For matrix completion, the work of Carpenter, Just, and Shell (1990) provides a reasonably strong basis for identifying the cognitive processes brought to bear in item solution, as well as the features of items that can be manipulated to generate questions that vary predictably in their operating characteristics. In this domain, Embretson (1998) created a series of item models, or *structures* as she calls them, where each model was written to produce items of a constant difficulty. The models varied in their manipulation of critical features so that the variance in difficulty was across models, rather than across the items coming from any given model.

Although there is uncertainty in parameter estimation even for empirically calibrated items, generation from strong theory introduces another source of error in that parameters are *predicted* rather than estimated from data. According to Embretson (1998), empirically estimated parameters typically correlate in the high .90s with true parameters. Parameters predicted from cognitive models, however, correlate with true parameters only in the .70s–.80s (Embretson, 1998). As a result, greater impact on ability estimates should result when items are calibrated through strong theory as opposed to brute empirical methods. Simulations reported by Embretson (1999) showed that both predicted, as well as empirically estimated, parameters contained some amount of bias and imprecision.

In one of the most extensive empirical analyses of item generation from strong theory, Embretson (1998, 1999) found automatically generated matrix completion tests to function similarly to longer, conventionally created tests of the same construct in terms of percentage correct scores, alpha reliability, correlations with reference tests, and loadings on reference factors. She also found that difficulty was predicted quite strongly by the item models, which were written to vary in difficulty, as well as by the individual item features hypothesized to cause that variation.

3.2. Automatic Item Generation from Weak Theory

In contrast to generation from strong theory, automatic item generation from weak theory is the preferred approach when one can do no better. The idea behind this approach is to generate *calibrated* items automatically from design *guidelines* by using a "theory" of *invariance*. Thus, one starts with a "parent" item whose psychometric characteristics are known. Then the test developer finds, through experience, intuition, theory, or research, some features that do *not* affect item operating characteristics. Finally, these features are varied to create items. Obviously, a lot less knowledge is required for a theory of invariance than to understand the cognitive mechanisms and item features that cause difficulty. Hence the name, "weak theory."

Generation from weak theory is best suited to broad domains—such as the mathematics covered by the quantitative section of the GRE General Test—where cognitive analysis is not as feasible and where well-developed theory is less likely to exist. Perhaps the best illustration of generation from weak theory is Bejar's work with the GRE quantitative section (Bejar et al., 2003). As in the models created by Embretson (1998), the models Bejar et al. designed specified the elements of the item class that remain fixed, the elements that were to be varied, and the constraints that governed variation. Many items can be created from any such model. However, because the determinants of difficulty are not well understood, fewer characteristics can be varied simultaneously and the items generated may consequently be more visibly similar than those generated through strong theory. As a result, examinees may recognize items on the operational exam as variants of ones from a practice test and coaching schools may begin teaching these narrow models. Further, because there is no strong theory from which to predict functioning, new models must be calibrated empirically so that the items produced can inherit those calibrations.

Obviously, item parameters will shift and construct validity will be threatened if irrelevant strategies help examinees solve items. The chances for irrelevant strategies to succeed increase if the items are more similar in appearance *within* than across models, the number of items produced per model is large, and the total number of models is small. But, of course, generating too many models could be less efficient than simply writing items in the traditional way.

One possible solution to this dilemma lies in the cognitive psychology literature, which shows that experts in a domain rapidly perceive problem situations in terms of their underlying principles or solution structure (Glaser, 1991). Experts are able to see beyond surface features to deep structure. This literature suggests that experts represent problems by category based on solution structure. Categories direct problem solving by eliciting schema that may contain potential solution methods. Categorization restricts search to a small range of potential solution paths. Novices get caught up with surface features and, consequently, have trouble detecting the underlying problem structure (Chi, Feltovich, & Glaser, 1981).

In the testing context, these same principles appear to hold. Bennett and Sebrechts (1997) asked GRE examinees to choose from among several mathematical word problems the one that most closely matched a given problem in terms of such features as the principles required for solution, the form of any equations that model the problem, the methods that could lead to solution, the role of variables, and the nature of the steps or operations in the solution. Results showed that those who were able to match problems according to deep structure tended to have higher GRE General Test scores and college grades than examinees who performed less effectively on the matching task. In a subsequent study, Morley, Bridgeman, and Lawless (2003) randomly assigned undergraduates to *deep-structure* and *deep-structure-plus-surface-feature* conditions. Students in both conditions took the same posttest composed of mathematical reasoning problems, including both word problems and pure mathematical problems. In the deep-structure condition, examinees took a pretest in which all items were paired with one and only one posttest item. The pairing was either of pretest and posttest items that shared the same deep-structure (termed, "close variants"), or of pretest and posttest items that had different deep structures but shared difficulty level and mathematical content classification (termed, "matched items"). In the second study condition, examinees took the same posttest but a pretest that included, in addition to the close variants and the matched items, items that shared surface features with posttest items but *not* deep-structure (termed, "surface variants"). In analyzing the posttest results, the investigators found that examinees performed better on the close variants than on the other types of items, suggesting some amount of irrelevant transfer. However, the group taking the posttest that included surface variants performed lower on the close variants than did the comparison group, suggesting that mixing close and surface variants can forestall irrelevant transfer.

Given this research, item pools might be designed to *interleave* deep structure and surface features. That is, for any parent item, it may be possible to create a family of models, some of which produce variants with different surface features but the same deep structure as the parent item, and other models that produce variants having a different deep structure from the parent item but the same surface features as that item (e.g., such items could use the same contextual information but vary the operations the examinee must perform). Items could then be distributed so that no more than one instance from any given family of superficially and structurally related models appears in every nth test form, where n is a changing number. If such interleaving were feasible for a sufficient number of model families, remembering surface features as a cue to item solution should not work. What should work is learning generalized problem schema—that is, learning how to recognize and solve the many and varied categories of mathematical reasoning problems that compose a tested domain.

But, assuming that large numbers of items can be generated and used securely in operational testing programs, how would one calibrate them absent strong theory? Weak theory offers no cognitive model from which to predict calibrations and it is clearly unreasonable to empirically calibrate all variants from an item model. To do that would lose one of the main promises of automatic item generation.

One approach, proposed by Bejar et al. (2003) is to pretest a sample of variants and use that information to calibrate the model. However, the parameters for the variants that have never been empirically calibrated will still be unknown. Further, there will be departures from *isomorphicity* among these variants because every item generated by a model may not be absolutely identical in the demands it places on the cognitive system. And, clearly, such departures are more likely to occur in the context of weak—as opposed to strong—theory.

Bejar suggests a way to account for this uncertainty by calibrating models using the expected response function (Lewis, 1985; Mislevy, Wingersky, & Sheehan, 1994). Operationally, the process might proceed as follows. First, generate some variants from a model. Next, randomly spiral them among examinees. Third, collapse the response vectors for the variants to produce a single vector. Fourth, fit an item response model to that vector. Finally, use that *attenuated* item characteristic curve (ICC) for all existing and new variants produced by that model. Other, more sophisticated approaches to modeling the variation in item parameters both within and across models are possible, including hierarchical approaches described by Glas and van der Linden (2001), and by Sinharay, Johnson, and Williamson (2003). Regardless of the specific method used, the implication is that to the degree that variants differ in their ICCs, ability may need to be estimated with parameters that are less precise than usual, which may mean having to administer a somewhat longer test.

To evaluate these ideas, Bejar et al. (2003) created an experimental, adaptive GRE quantitative section, where each examinee was administered 28 items, with between 14 and 21 of those items generated in real time from models; the remaining items were drawn from previously disclosed GRE test questions. The item parameters were taken from analyses of responses to the previously existing questions and expected response functions were used for the models. The expected response functions assumed spread in parameters among the variants for a model equal to the largest spread observed on operational recalibrations of GRE quantitative items. Bejar et al. (2003) found that the correlation between the experimental test score and operational GRE score was .87, very close to the alternate-forms reliability observed for the operational test. Thus, even using attenuated item parameters for half or more of the test, the test as a whole functioned similarly to the operational measure, at least in the way it rank-ordered examinees.

3.3. Automatic Item Generation from Art

The last approach to automatic item generation is from art. Generation from art means creating item models on the basis of the personal theories, beliefs, or principles of individual test developers, which are likely to be idiosyncratic, implicit, and undocumented. In such generation, the goal is simply to produce as many items as possible, with little attempt to control difficulty.

In this approach, the test developer uses art to create item models that generate variants of different classifications and difficulties. Standard procedures are then used for calibrating the individual variants.

Generation from art is noteworthy because, of the three approaches to automatic item generation, art is the one that most closely resembles standard test development practice. Thus, in measurement organizations where the practice of test development has evolved to take a "guild-like" form, automatic generation from art may be an attractive, but theoretically and practically limiting, option.

4. ITEM PRETESTING

In the absence of methods for generating already-calibrated items, it is important to pretest items prior to using them in operational tests. Even items that have been reviewed many times by content experts and an experienced editorial staff sometimes fail to function as expected. Small test development programs that do not have technical editors may need to pretest twice (Nunnally, 1978) as many items as needed for operational test; larger programs with experienced editors may discard only 10–20% of the new items. In any case, it is crucial to write a sufficient quantity of surplus items so that any with unsatisfactory psychometric properties can be discarded.

The goal of pretesting is to obtain item statistics such as the traditional proportion correct $\hat{p}$, item-total correlation, r_{pb} (which is sometimes called a "point-biserial correlation," but is nonetheless a Pearson product-moment correlation), and item-total biserial correlation, r_b, and item response theory (IRT) parameter estimates such as the difficulty $\hat{b}$, discrimination $\hat{a}$, and lower asymptote $\hat{c}$. Although all of these item statistics can be useful, the IRT statistics are critical for most computerized testing programs because examinees are typically administered adaptive tests or one of many alternate test forms. When examinees are administered different sets of items, the number right test score $X = \sum_{i=1}^{n} u_i$, where $u_i = 1$ if the ith item is answered correctly and $u_i = 0$ if incorrect, is an inappropriate measure of performance because the difficulty of the different sets of items can (and probably will) vary. The IRT ability estimate $\hat{\theta}$, in contrast, is on the same scale regardless of differences in the difficulty of the items administered.

How do testing programs obtain item statistics? There are two general situations to consider when answering this question. First, in the transition from a conventional paper-and-pencil test administered a few times a year to a computerized test with continuous administration, testing programs may need to pretest many thousands of new items. The second situation arises for continuous testing programs that have the need to refresh their item pools by replacing frequently administered items with new and hopefully secure items.

In both of these situations, it is critical to ensure that item parameters are on the same scale. To illustrate this point, suppose that a testing program that administers a professional licensing exam is in the process of converting from a paper-and-pencil format to a computerized format. Suppose it obtains permission to pretest items with seniors at a highly selective college where the mean SAT total score (verbal plus math) exceeds 1,400 and at a city college with open admissions. It would be a serious mistake to exclusively pretest one set of items at the highly selective college and exclusively pretest another set of items at the city college because these two groups are likely to differ in their skill level. More generally, unless test forms are randomly or systematically assigned to examinees, test developers should assume that any pre-existing groups differ in their skill levels. Consequently, it would be vastly preferable to administer both test forms to students at both colleges, either by randomly assigning test forms to students or by spiraling, where the first student from each college is administered form 1, the second student receives form 2, the third completes form 1, and so forth.

4.1. Calibration before Operational Use

The key issue here is: How many items need to be calibrated to start up the program? For high stakes college admissions, licensing or credentialing, and employment tests, it may be necessary to calibrate several thousand items before initiating continuous testing.

Directly related to the question of how many items need to be calibrated is the question of how many people are needed for pretesting. Although the point of pretesting items is to obtain item parameter estimates, the ultimate goal is to estimate accurately the ability level of examinees. To gain insight into the sample sizes needed to obtain adequate ability estimates, Chuah, Drasgow, and

Luecht (2006) simulated a computer adaptive multistage test (ca-MST; Luecht, 2000; Luecht & Nungester, 1998, 2000) licensing exam based on the three-parameter logistic model. When they used the simulation item parameters to estimate ability, they correctly classified 94.1% of the ca-MST simulees as masters or nonmasters (i.e., both θ and $\hat{\theta}$ were above the cut score for passing or both were below the cut score). When item parameters were first estimated using the BILOG (Mislevy & Bock, 1990) computer program with a samples of $N = 300$ simulees, the correct classification rate was 93.6% for the ca-MST simulees. When $N = 1,000$ simulees were used to estimate item parameters, the correct classification rate was 93.7% for the ca-MST. Evidently, relatively small samples can be used to estimate item parameters accurately enough for subsequent use in licensing and certification testing.

Chuah et al. (2006) used the sampling plan shown in Table 13.1 to estimate item parameters for their simulated items. The first set of 50 items (items 1 to 50) were used for linking; one set of simulees answered these items. The second test form consisted of items 1 to 5 and 51 to 95 (Chuah et al. assumed that the number of items that could be completed by examinees was 50; test developers obviously want examinees to complete as many items as possible, but do not want fatigue or boredom to affect examinees' performance and consequently must limit the number of items administered). Items 6 to 10 and 96 to 140 constituted the next test form. It would have been simpler to use items 1 to 5 as the linking items for all test forms, but Chuah et al. did not use this approach because they felt using just one set of items would lead to overexposure. Table 13.1 shows eleven test forms for pretesting 500 items; additional items could be included as illustrated for the last test form.

Obtaining a sample to pretest items can be a significant challenge. For example, estimating item parameters for the 11 test forms shown in Table 13.1 with 300 examinees per form requires a sample of 3,300; where would the test developers obtain such a sample? Obviously, it is desirable to have the pretest sample as similar as possible to the actual examinee population. However, it can be very challenging to satisfy this desideratum. Examples of approaches taken include:

- A private sector employer developing a computerized test to be used when hiring new employees hired individuals registered at a temporary help agency to answer items.
- The United States Department of Defense developing a computerized adaptive version of its enlistment test (Segall & Moreno, 1999; Segall, Moreno, & Hetter, 1997) used newly inducted service members (note that this sample is unlike the applicant population because service members constitute a restricted range of talent—they all passed the enlistment test).
- The American Institute of Certified Public Accountants developing a computerized version of the licensing exam for certified public accountants pretested many newly written items with samples of volunteer accounting majors at colleges and universities across the United States.

In each of these cases, the pretesting sample differs from the examinee population in some nontrivial way. However, the subpopulation invariant nature of IRT item parameters provides some justification for using the pretest sample. Traditional item parameters such as $\hat{p}$ are very sensitive to subpopulation differences, whereas IRT parameters are invariant across subpopulations when the model fits (see Hulin, Drasgow, & Parsons, 1983, pp. 43–46, for details) and empirically often show only small differences across subgroups.

4.2. Calibration for Operational Testing Programs

There are two issues here. First, at what point is it useful to recalibrate items whose parameters were estimated as described in the above paragraphs? Second, how should newly written items be calibrated in an ongoing computerized testing program?

The answer to the first question is not straightforward when a testing program uses branching or fully adaptive testing. In this case, the sample that responds to an item may have a restricted range of ability on the trait that is being assessed. Do, Chuah, and Drasgow (2005), for example, found that the re-estimation sample may need to be several times larger than the original pretest sample when there has been substantial restriction of range.

It is important to recalibrate items whose parameters were originally estimated in pretest samples consisting of examinees answering under nonoperational conditions. Such examinees cannot be assumed to be as highly motivated as examinees being tested under operational conditions. If the pretest sample is less motivated, the examinees' performances will be lower, and item difficulty measures such as $\hat{p}$ and $\hat{b}$ will be affected such that the items will appear more difficult (i.e., $\hat{p}$ will be too small and $\hat{b}$ will be too large). Moreover, some item types may be more affected (e.g., synonyms and antonyms may be relatively unaffected because examinees either know or do not know the answer; paragraph comprehension items that require substantial effort by the examinee to ascertain answers may be more affected). In sum, item parameters originally estimated from samples of examinees answering under nonoperational conditions should be re-estimated from a sample answering under operational conditions to empirically verify the accuracy of item parameter estimates.

As noted in the previous subsection, it is essential to keep item parameter estimates on the same scale. The ability level of examinees can vary over time (e.g., examinees tested in some months may tend to be more able than those tested in other months—as in a licensing exam where those tested in June are recent college graduates and those tested in November and December are mostly individuals who failed in June). Consequently, data from an entire year should be used, or known item parameters from some anchor items should be held constant to fix the scale.

There is a continuous need to estimate parameters of newly written items. Such items can be "seeded" in an operational testing program. The items should be administered to a randomly selected sample but not used to determine examinees' test scores. It is desirable to

TABLE 13.1 Design of Test Forms for Pretesting Items

Items	1–5	6–10	11–15	16–20	21–25	26–30	31–35	36–40	41–45	46–50	51–95	96–140	141–185	186–230	231–275	276–320	321–365	366–410	411–455	456–500	Total Items
n	5	5	5	5	5	5	5	5	5	5	45	45	45	45	45	45	45	45	45	45	
	X	X	X	X	X	X	X	X	X	X											50
	X										X										50
		X										X									50
			X										X								50
				X										X							50
					X										X						50
						X										X					50
							X										X				50
								X										X			50
									X										X		50
	X																			X	50

Source: Table adapted from Chuah, Drasgow, & Luecht (2006).

administer the new items to individuals with a wide range of talent (i.e., do not administer one set of new items only to high ability examinees and another set to low ability examinees). Item parameter estimates for the new items can be placed on the scale of the operational items when estimating item parameters by including data from operational items and holding constant the known values of their item parameters.

4.3. Item Banking

All important information about each item should be contained in a testing program's item bank, which is sometimes called the item database. The item bank is a repository for information about the item: the item's text, images, sound or video clips, content codes, word count and readability measures, item statistics (traditional items statistics and IRT item parameter estimates and their standard errors), item impact and differential item functioning information, exposure, and other relevant information.

In modern approaches to computerized testing, items can have scripts that allow the item to administer itself. That is, the item is administered by executing the script. These scripts should also be contained in the item bank.

It is important for testing programs to code each item for its content and archive this information in the item bank. Generally, the test blueprint specifies the content of the test (and this information should be available electronically). For example, the blueprint may state that each test form should have three items from Category A, four items from Category B, and so forth. In traditional test development, as each form of a test is assembled, subject matter experts ensure that the test blueprint and other specifications are satisfied. That is, test committees function in part as test constructors and in part as quality controllers. During automated test assembly (ATA), software selects items that satisfy the test blueprint and various other optimization criteria and consequently each item's content codes and the test blueprint need to be accessible by the software.

Item banks are typically customized database applications built on powerful commercial database software platforms such as Oracle™ or Microsoft SQL Server™. These products provide the capability to store data in multiple formats and to establish user-definable, complex, relational links among the data (e.g., linking item statistics from multiple IRT calibrations to each item, linking text, graphics, or even sound files to an item or an item set). These types of commercial products have the apparent advantage of being portable across hardware platforms and operating systems and are scalable as a testing program grows. In some cases, the data is even portable across item banking systems. An example is the BUILDER™ content management system (Promissor, Inc., 2003), which is built on Oracle. Builder can also export to a variety of formats, including extensible mark-up language (XML). Sometimes, proprietary item banking software is used for item banking. Examples include FASTTEST™ (Assessment Systems Corporation, 2003) and BENCHMARK™ (Thomson Prometric, 2003). These item packages are typically developed to work with a specific computer-based test (CBT) delivery driver and often use a test definition language (TDL) with complex field structures and data formats understood only by the test delivery driver. Because of that specialization, they may provide limited database functionality and end-user customization capabilities. Unfortunately, little to no research has been done to compare the features, advantages, and disadvantages of these various item banking applications.

5. TEST ASSEMBLY AND PACKAGING

Under CBT, a number of test forms are composed and administered in real-time by a computer program called the *test delivery driver*. The test delivery driver interfaces with two types of data input files: (1) eligibility files and (2) test resource files. The eligibility files contain information about authorized test takers (identification and access information for eligible examinees, filters on any previously seen test forms, special testing accommodations needed, etc.). The test resource files contain both item and test form presentation and administration information. That is, the test resource file contains all of the data needed by the test delivery driver to administer all test forms within a particular period of time. These resource files therefore function as both a temporary item bank and a repository for test administration data for all test forms.

Test assembly and packaging is essentially the process of building a resource file used by the test delivery driver. In practice, test assembly and packaging are distinct test development procedures, each requiring different types of systems support. Test assembly involves procedures for selecting items from an item bank for one or more test forms. At one extreme, all aspects of test assembly are performed before the test administration takes place. At the other extreme, all test assembly is performed in real-time, either immediately before or while the examinee is taking the examination.

Test packaging—which is sometimes called publishing or test composition—follows test assembly. For paper-and-pencil testing, publishing literally means producing the text and graphic pages for each test form. Under CBT, packaging involves extracting from the item bank all relevant information needed for administering the selected test items (e.g., item identifiers, item text, graphics, scripts, answer keys), combining that information with test administration data such as test-taker instructions and timing controls needed by the test delivery driver, and generating one or more formatted files used by the test delivery driver that actually administers the tests to the examinees. Most CBT test delivery drivers use a customized data format for their resource files called a test definition language (TDL). Using a TDL allows the test developers to access reusable software components, functions, and data structures. Recently, some test delivery drivers have started using TDL based on customizable versions of Microsoft's extensible mark-up language.

5.1. Models of Test Assembly and Packaging

There are three basic models for test assembly and packaging. The first model is the *intact forms model*. Under this model, items are selected from the item bank for one or more intact test forms; each form is individually packaged in the test resource file. This test assembly and packaging model is useful for computerized fixed forms (see *Test Delivery Models*). The test resource files tend to be more compact and can be efficiently downloaded over the Internet or over other transmission channels.

The second model is the *item-pool model*. This model creates one or more item pools for use by the test delivery driver and is usually associated with computerized adaptive tests or linear-on-the-fly tests (Folk & Smith, 2002). All relevant item data and test delivery information are prepackaged in the resource file, which acts as a temporary item pool. Under this model, *no* item-to-test form assignments are specified within the file. Instead, the test delivery driver assembles the test (i.e., carries out the item selections by random selection or by using an adaptive heuristic) in real-time, either immediately preceding the start of the test or while the examinee is taking the examination. Way, Steffen, and Anderson (2002) describe a sophisticated application of the item-pool model that is used for the GRE. Their item-pool model employs collections of item pools called "item vats." Automated test assembly algorithms and item exposure simulations are used to construct the vats. Item pools within a vat can be systematically rotated over time to reduce threats to test security for CAT.

The third test assembly and packaging model is the *encapsulated, self-adaptive test form model*. This type of model carries out most of the test assembly beforehand and prepackages unique testlets for administration by the test delivery driver. Testlets are small test delivery modules or item sets containing a relatively small number of items (see Luecht & Nungester, 1998; Wainer & Kiely, 1987; Wainer & Lewis, 1990). The testlets can be adaptively or randomly administered under computerized-mastery testing (Adema, 1990; Lewis & Sheehan, 1990; Sheehan & Lewis, 1992) or preassigned as groups of testlets that are packaged together with self-administering scripts for testlet selection and scoring under a test delivery model heading called "computer-adaptive multistage tests" (Luecht, 2000; Luecht, Brumfield, & Breithaupt, 2002; Luecht & Burgin, 2003; Luecht & Nungester, 1998, 2000; Luecht, Nungester, & Hadadi, 1996).

5.2. Automated Test Assembly

Automated test assembly (ATA) can be essential technology for all three of these models. ATA involves the use of sophisticated mathematical optimization procedures to select items from an item bank for one or more "test forms." These optimization procedures are programmed into a computer. The computer program is then run to select items from the item bank and "packages" them for delivery to the test takers on a computer. Most ATA algorithms and heuristics work in more or less the same way. That is, given some goal—usually a statistical target or criterion to be optimized—the algorithm or heuristic attempts to select items or units that achieve the goal and that meet various other test development requirements called "constraints."

There is a fairly extensive literature concerning ATA heuristics, algorithms, and many examples of test construction applications. Some of the more common methods include linear programming (van der Linden, 1998; van der Linden & Adema, 1989, 1998; van der Linden & Boekkooi-Timminga, 1989), mixed integer programming (MIP) with shadow test technology (van der Linden, 2000; van der Linden & Reese, 1998), network flow algorithms (Armstrong, Jones, & Kunce, 1998; Armstrong, Jones, Li, & Wu, 1996; Armstrong & Little, 2003), and specialized item selection heuristics like the weighted deviations model (Stocking & Swanson, 1993; Swanson & Stocking, 1993) and the normalized weighted absolute deviation heuristic (Luecht, 1998b, 2000; Luecht & Hirsch, 1992). An in-depth explanation of these ATA algorithms and heuristics is beyond the scope of this chapter. Nonetheless, a simple example of an ATA problem is provided below for the purposes of illustration. Van der Linden (1998, 2004) provides more comprehensive reviews of some of the popular ATA heuristics and mathematical programming techniques.

An ATA problem starts with the specification of a quantity to minimize or maximize. This quantity is called the *objective function* and can be formulated as a mathematical function to be optimized by linear programming algorithms or heuristics. *Constraints* are imposed on the solution, usually reflecting the content blueprint or other qualitative features of the items that we wish to control (e.g., word counts). The constraints are expressed as equalities (exact counts of items to select for a testlet) or inequalities (upper or lower bounds on the frequency of items selected within particular content categories).

Suppose that we want to maximize the reliability of a 20-item test and further fix the difficulty of the test so that it provides most of its reliability near the mean of a population of test takers. In ATA, it is very common to deal with this type of problem in terms of IRT test information functions. IRT test information functions allow us to estimate the amount of score precision at particular points of a score scale. The exact mathematical form of the information function varies by IRT model (Lord, 1980) and the amount of information will tend to vary at different levels of proficiency.

In this example, we wish to maximize the test information near the mean (i.e., where $\theta = \mu$). We further need to define a binary decision variable, x_i, $i = 1, \ldots, I$ that indicates that item i is selected ($x_i = 1$) or not ($x_i = 0$) from the item bank for inclusion on a test form. Given this decision variable, the objective function to be minimized is the difference between the IRT test information function $\Sigma I(\theta = \mu, \xi_i)$ for the selected items and the target test information function $I^*(\theta = \mu)$; that is,

$$\text{minimize} \left| \sum_{i=1}^{I} I(\theta=\mu, \xi_i) x_i - I^*(\theta = \mu) \right|, \qquad (1)$$

where ξ_i denotes the vector of item parameters for the ith item from the item bank, $i = 1, \ldots, I$ (e.g., $\xi_i = [a_i, b_i]$ for the two-parameter logistic model where a_i and b_i refer to the discrimination and difficulty parameters). Now, further suppose that we have two content areas, C_1 and C_2, and wish to have at least five items from content area C_1 and no more than 10 items from content area C_2. This ATA problem can be modeled as minimizing Eq. 1 subject to:

$$\sum_{i \in C_1}^{I} x_i \geq 5 \text{ (constraint on } C_1) \quad (2)$$

$$\sum_{i \in C_2}^{I} x_i \leq 10 \text{ (constraint on } C_2) \quad (3)$$

$$\sum_{i=1}^{I} x_i = 20 \text{ (test length)} \quad (4)$$

$$x_i \in \{0,1\}, i = 1, \ldots, I. \text{ (range of variables)} \quad (5)$$

It is relatively straightforward to extend these basic ATA procedures to more complicated test assembly problems. For example, ATA can be used to enhance computerized adaptive tests by adding complex content constraints to ensure that test forms meet various test blueprint requirements (Stocking & Swanson, 1993; van der Linden, 2000; van der Linden & Adema, 1998). For fixed test forms, it is common to employ test information function (TIF) targets that represent the amount of score precision across the entire proficiency scale. For example, Figure 13.1 displays a target TIF that might be used for a 20-item academic achievement test. The goal here would be to build every test form to meet this same TIF curve, subject to also meeting all relevant content constraints and other test development requirements (e.g., test pacing, reading loads, etc.).

ATA is also mandatory for preconstructing computer-adaptive multistage tests implemented under the self-adaptive test form assembly and packaging model (Luecht, 2000; Luecht, Brumfield, & Breithaupt, 2002; Luecht & Nungester, 1998). A typical ATA problem in this context would employ multiple, simultaneous TIF objective functions and multiple constraint sets. The goal would be to simultaneously build from a common item bank various numbers of testlets meeting different target TIFs as well as complex content constraints.

FIGURE 13.1 IRT Test Information Function Target for 20-Item Test

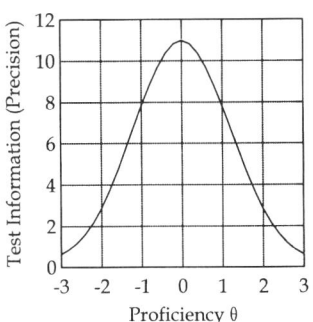

There are two possible ways to implement ATA. One approach is to implement ATA as an *offline* process that is used to preconstruct and package intact test forms or multistage test forms (see descriptions of the intact forms model and the self-administering adaptive test form model, above). The second approach to implementing ATA incorporates the item selection algorithms as part of the *online* test delivery driver-that is, the software that actually administers the test to each examinee. This is the item-pool model described above; whereas the item bank is prepackaged, specific test forms are not. Instead, the test delivery software performs the item selections in *real-time*. There are advantages and disadvantages to each approach. Online ATA can typically generate more test forms and even customize the test forms for each test taker. Computerized adaptive testing (CAT) can be seen as a type of online ATA. In contrast, offline ATA and packaging of test forms offers numerous quality assurance capabilities—principally a review or audit of test forms by human content experts—that are not viable with an online test production system.

6. EXAMINEE REGISTRATION, SCHEDULING, AND ACCOMMODATIONS

The proliferation of commercially operated, computer-based testing facilities has generated a need for innovative ways to register eligible examinees and schedule their examinations. This system must verify an individual's eligibility to sit for an exam, schedule a time and place to administer the test, and provide for any authorized special accommodation.

6.1. Eligibility

Eligibility implies that the applicant has met specified criteria to take a particular test and may include a variety of educational or professional requirements (e.g., having completed a professional curriculum, meeting graduation/degree requirements from an accredited college or university, sponsorship by a licensing authority). Obviously, there are almost no eligibility requirements—beyond paying required testing fees—for low-stakes tests that are open to the general public. In contrast, high-stakes examination programs may go to great lengths to guarantee the eligibility of every examinee. Furthermore, eligibility for high-stakes examinations is typically provided for a specified period of time. For example, a candidate may be authorized to take the test within 12 months from the date on which eligibility was granted. Eligibility may also restrict test retake attempts within prescribed time windows. For example, the eligibility may be limited to three attempts within any 12-month period, with a waiting period of at least one month between retake attempts.

An eligibility system is typically constructed as a dynamic database system that holds a complete listing of everyone authorized to take a particular examination. In addition to listing the examinees who are authorized to test, the eligibility database must also include eligibility rules such as the termination date for the eligibility and the allowable number of attempts remaining within the eligibility window. The eligibility database may also contain information concerning testing accommodations for candidates authorized to have those accommodations (see below). In some cases, the required accommodations may limit which testing facilities can be used.

6.2. Scheduling

Examination scheduling services provide the test taker with seat availabilities by location, date, and time. Most computer-based testing organizations and vendors offer three ways for candidates to schedule their test: (a) by mail application; (b) by telephone (usually a toll-free number with operator-assisted registration and scheduling); and (c) via the Internet.

Commercial scheduling systems are often modeled after airline scheduling systems that attempt to find seats on flights in a dynamically changing environment, subject to passenger preferences for price, times, numbers of connections, and so forth. In a very simplistic way, a test scheduling system can be conceptualized like a huge grid with days and times listed in the columns and testing sites (including special facilities offerings) listed in the rows. Unavailable sites, days, and times are blocked from the grid. The goal is for the candidate to choose a particular cell in the grid (representing an open seat) at a convenient site on the desired date of testing.

The constraints on the selection of seats are four-fold: (1) proximity of the testing site to the candidates' preferred location (i.e., close to home, school, or work); (2) choice of testing days/times (morning, afternoon, evenings, weekends, etc.); (3) special facility or physical accommodations if required; and (4) maximum utilization of seat time for the test. Proximity constraints can be introduced into the scheduling algorithm by searching for zip codes that contain testing centers or by directly computing actual mileage via map search algorithms. Facility and physical accommodations may include "quiet rooms," high-resolution monitors, special software for visually impaired examinees, and so forth for individuals authorized to receive a particular type of testing accommodation. Not all testing centers may provide certain accommodations, resulting in a restricted set of possible testing seats for some examinees.

The maximum time limit for testing is another potential constraint. This is, without a doubt, the most dynamically changing constraint in a test scheduling system. Long tests—requiring several hours or even several contiguous days—are more difficult to schedule than short tests lasting only one to three hours. Therefore, testing programs that have relatively long tests may find it difficult to locate centers with seats available for extended time periods. Although a testing program may advise its candidates to call months in advance, other testing programs competing for seats may use that same strategy. It is tempting to recommend to the commercial CBT vendors that they offer reserved block seating on limited testing dates for particular examinations. However, vendors are usually reluctant to reserve large blocks of seats without prepaid security deposits and stiff restrictions on dates and times. The scheduling problem can be further exacerbated by the policies that some CBT testing firms use to fill seats. For example, many fixed-venue, dedicated testing centers schedule their computer-based testing seats by filling up the time slots from the morning first, and then stacking the test appointments, by seat, until center closing time. Examinees could therefore be told that there are no seats available in the afternoon on a preferred testing date, simply because the morning time slots have not been filled.

Obviously, scheduling is a complicated process. Ideally, examinees should be able to schedule or choose an open slot via the Internet, by telephone, or by mail at any testing center, whether dedicated or temporary. However, each additional access route also potentially adds constraints to the system and creates possible conflicts and overbooking of seats.

6.3. Accommodations

According to the Americans with Disabilities Act of 1990 and Section 504 of the Rehabilitation Act, a person is considered to have a disability if he or she has a physical or mental impairment that substantially limits one or more life activities, has a record of such impairment, or is regarded as having such an impairment. Covered disabilities may include deafness/hearing impairments, blindness/visual impairments, autism, mental retardation, traumatic brain injury, orthopedic impairments, learning disabilities, and speech or language impairments. There are several broad categories of testing accommodations offered for examinees classified as having one or more disabilities (American Educational Research Association, American Psychological Association, & National Council on Measurement in Education [AERA, APA, & NCME], 1999; Goh, 2004).

Modification of the *testing setting* refers to changing the environment, location, or conditions of testing. Examples include preferential seating, individualized testing in a distraction-free, private testing room, or using a bilingual test administrator.

Modification of the *testing format* covers all changes to the medium of the test and/or test administration. Examples might include presenting oral, Braille, or large-print instructions for a blind or visually impaired examinee. The test materials themselves might also be presented orally, in Braille, in a large-print version, or by using a computer-based zoom/magnification software application that the test taker has been extensively trained to use.

Modification of the *response format* refers to changing the way in which the test taker answers the items. Typically, the response format is changed to accommodate the examinee's preferred mode of communication. For example, examinees with orthopedic/motor impairments may prefer to point to a multiple-choice answer response or give their answers orally, either recording their responses or having them transcribed. Responses may also be allowed in sign language for individuals with deafness or speech and hearing impairments. Ideally, the accommodation should not modify the response. This type of accommodation can be especially challenging when using written transcriptions of the scored constructed response or essay-type items where the transcriber may be given the latitude to correct spelling, insert punctuation, or even correct grammar.

Timing and test scheduling modifications are the most common accommodations allowed. Extended testing time limits are usually authorized for examinees with documented learning disabilities, and sometimes examinees classified as English language learners—that is, individuals for whom English is not their first or native language. Extended time may also be required as part of another accommodation. For example, listening to recorded speech or a Braille reader may take more time than reading from print. Two complications that arise from extended time are scheduling and data management across testing days. Scheduling problems are the same as those discussed above regarding long tests. That is, it is more difficult to locate an available time slot for a long test than a short test at most testing centers. Data management is complicated if the extended time crosses days of testing. Many administration systems cannot keep a test session "live" over multiple days. Adaptive tests that use previous information to select future test materials are especially challenged if the previous information cannot be stored and used over several days of testing.

Eliminating or substituting portions or sections of a test may be offered as an accommodation when the required skills or abilities to complete particular items or test sections interferes with, or is not feasible for, an individual's physical, sensory, or linguistic abilities. An example would be requiring a blind or severely visually impaired examinee to read a statistical graph or interpret pictorial material. Although a tactile version of the images might be created, the expense of doing so would likely be prohibitive. In addition, questions of test construct validity would remain if the basic abilities being tested were fundamentally changed.

In sum, issues and concerns related to testing accommodations are complex. Legal requirements, fairness to examinees, and meaningfulness of test scores must all be considered. Goh (2004) provides an excellent overview of the current issues and practices related to providing testing accommodations in educational settings.

6.4. The Internet

The Internet provides a convenient mechanism for determining eligibility and scheduling (with accommodations when necessary). In commercial aviation, passengers can now go online and purchase tickets for the specific flight that they desire. Test takers desire a similar level of convenience: They want to be able to schedule their exam at a time and place that is convenient to them. Eligibility determination can add a layer of complexity to this process because a state licensing board may need to verify the educational credentials of candidates. Consequently, one-step scheduling (i.e., the test taker goes to a Web page and schedules his/her exam) may be difficult in some cases. Nonetheless, test takers desire this feature.

7. TEST DELIVERY

From a test taker's perspective, most CBT software systems may seem like a simple software application. The software logs the examinee into the system, provides one or more screen pages of general instructions, may offer a brief practice test, and then launches into the test, presenting the test items in some prescribed or random sequence. The test taker responds to each item, usually answering one or more items at a time. An online clock automatically manages timing. For many computer-based tests, the examinees can navigate around the test and even mark items for later review. The testing sequence typically ends when all items have been answered and submitted for scoring, when time has expired, or when a particular test stopping rule is reached.

In reality, what happens underneath the test delivery interface depends on the type of testing facility and connectivity used, the CBT delivery models employed by the test delivery software, and the types of items employed. With varying degrees of intervention from test administrators and proctors, the test delivery software performs all of the test administration tasks at a test center, from authenticating the examinees' identification to terminating the test and administering a postexamination survey.

7.1. CBT Facilities

Testing organizations using paper-and-pencil testing have successfully managed to administer tests to very large numbers of test takers for many years. Several "testing events" are scheduled each year and only a small number of scrambled hard-copy test forms are usually sufficient to handle security concerns related to copying, memorizing, and other forms of cheating. In contrast, CBT has required a paradigm shift and, with it, has created some significant cost and connectivity challenges. The reality is that almost every testing program that has transitioned to CBT has experienced major cost increases (e.g., Mills, 2004; Mills & Stocking, 1996). Although some of the costs can be attributed to start-up research and systems development, a majority of the costs appear to be related to two factors: (1) item production costs (i.e., the cost of writing, editing, and pretesting items) and (2) testing seat costs. The type of CBT facility used affects both factors.

There are two basic types of CBT facilities (at least for large-scale testing applications): (1) *dedicated test centers* and (2) *multipurpose distributed testing sites*. Dedicated test centers typically occupy a small suite of offices in major cities, employ a full-time test administration staff, and have 10 to 30 testing stations running on a local network. Data communications with the central test processing facility are usually handled by any of a variety of channels, ranging from telephone modems to high-speed leased communications lines, broadband, or even satellite links. This type of facility has the advantage of standardization and secure control of the testing environment and computer equipment.

Commercial CBT vendors note that their dedicated test centers offer conveniences to test takers ranging from the flexible scheduling (i.e., on-demand testing) to ergonomically designed testing stations. While this may be true, it is clear is that dedicated test centers have fixed operating costs and restricted testing capacity. This capacity limitation can indirectly lead to significant cost increases for large-scale operational testing. Continuous CBT—that is, tests scheduled over a substantial period of time to accommodate large numbers of test takers within limited-capacity computerized test centers—inherently creates an ongoing demand for large numbers of new, high-quality, pretested items. The item banks for high-stakes CBT can quickly become compromised and the integrity of examination scores and decisions will become suspect (Luecht, 1998a; Mills & Stocking, 1996; Stocking & Lewis, 2000). The obvious solution is to increase the number of test items in the bank and to establish an item-inventory management plan for renewing, rotating, and replacing item banks over time. This solution is expensive.

Stepped-up item production typically means periodically commissioning and training large numbers of item writers to compose new items to meet the demands. Each item must also be pilot tested on a sufficiently large sample of motivated test takers to provide the statistical data needed to evaluate the quality of the items. Item statistics are also essential for test assembly (discussed below). The practical costs and challenges of creating a pipeline of high-quality, pilot-tested items cannot be trivialized.

In contrast to dedicated testing centers, multipurpose distributed testing sites are temporary testing sites that are typically set up in computer laboratories on college and university campuses or even at businesses. These types of facilities may offer a single network or clusters of private networks. The only requirement is a local network of computers that meets technical specifications and that has access to the Internet (or a compatible connectivity channel for the test delivery model used). In principle, an enormous number of testing seats could be activated on a single day of testing—similar to the way in which large-scale paper-and-pencil testing is done as a scheduled event. On-site security can be handled in the "old-fashioned" manner—using human proctors hired exclusively for each testing event. The facility serves purposes other than testing most of the time (e.g., its primary function as a computer learning laboratory).

The primary advantage of using multipurpose distributed testing sites is that a testing program can conduct high-volume testing events at multiple, convenient locations on a limited number of days and avoid substantial item production costs associated with continuous testing. In terms of disadvantages, there are clearly nontrivial logistical and engineering challenges associated with establishing a robust, wide area network of multipurpose distributed testing sites. Regardless, this approach appears to be the only way to create the capacity required for large-scale testing events and drive down testing costs.

An alternative to testing at dedicated testing centers and multipurpose testing sites is unproctored Internet testing. Here the physical location of the test taker can be anywhere with a connection to the Web: a dorm room, living room, café, and so forth. The examinee connects to the test's Web page and takes the test. The obvious question is: Who is actually taking the test? Although a number of technologies have been suggested for verifying the test taker's identity (e.g., Web cameras, voice recognition), no foolproof method has yet been devised to ensure that the person providing answers to a test is indeed who he/she claims to be.

Do, Shepherd, and Drasgow (under review) have suggested that the likelihood of cheating on an unproctored Internet test is a function of the stakes. Obviously, there is little motivation to cheat on a low-stakes test, whereas by definition much can be gained in a high-stakes setting. In a laboratory study using students enrolled in Introductory Psychology, Do et al. found no evidence of cheating in the unproctored condition; the stakes in this study were $100 prizes where a student's chances of winning were based on his/her number of correct responses. Do et al. also examined a higher-stakes setting: Individuals applying for supervisory positions in a large retailing organization. Here the Internet was used to administer a battery of tests under either proctored or unproctored conditions. Interestingly, Do et al. found scant evidence of score inflation for unproctored Internet testing despite the fact that desirable jobs were at stake.

Tippins et al. (2006) provide the views of a number of measurement experts on unproctored Internet testing. These views range from total opposition under any circumstances to enthusiasm for unproctored testing in a first stage, which would then be followed by a confirmation test that would be given under secure conditions to individuals who passed the first stage. Clearly, there is a need for research on unproctored Internet testing to determine the conditions under which it can yield meaningful scores.

7.2. Connectivity

Connectivity is a subtle but essential technology that affects many aspects of test delivery, from security and speed of data transmissions to the level of interactivity possible within a test. In a generic sense, connectivity implies that there are computers or networks of computers linked by one or more channels. A channel is a method of transmitting data between computers and networks. A CBT system may use a variety of connection channels, including telephone modems, digital subscriber lines (DSL), digital cable service (DCS) with cable modems, and fiber optic Ethernet. In general, connectivity is rated by the capacity of the channel (which is usually called bandwidth) and the speed of the transmission allowed by using a particular channel.

The capacity and speed of connections employed in CBT directly affect the extent of interactivity possible between workstations and servers, the efficiency and accuracy of the data transmitted, and even the security of the data within certain channels. For example, a high-level data link, such as a 10-gigabyte fiber optic Ethernet channel, is vastly superior to 56K modem technology because it provides a great deal more bandwidth and speed (i.e., more data can be moved more quickly in the former case). However, increasing the speed and bandwidth of a channel can have serious cost implications. For example, a telephone modem connection rarely costs more than two hundred dollars to establish per workstation or server. In contrast, a dedicated "T1 line" can cost tens of thousands of dollars for each installation. As a result, one of the appealing aspects of subscriber services like DSL and DCS is relatively low-cost transmission with moderately high-bandwidth and speed.

A thorough technical discussion of connectivity issues is beyond the scope of this chapter. Nonetheless, a brief discussion of issues germane to test delivery is useful. As described above, two of the fundamental characteristics of any transmission medium are channel capacity (bandwidth) and speed. Both characteristics are important for test delivery because large-scale CBT requires test materials and data to be transmitted over extended distances. In fact, testing organizations must deal with potentially different communication channels between various system layers. For example, local area networks (LANs) that connect the individual testing workstations to a local file server can usually support dedicated channels (i.e., full-duplex) and controlled timing between the sender and receiver (synchronous communications) for transmitting block data between the server and workstations. Bandwidth and speed are usually not serious considerations on a LAN. As a result, the connections on a LAN can be highly interactive, while remaining efficient, accurate, and secure, usually with minimal administrative overhead. The implication is that, within a test center or site running a LAN, connectivity issues do not greatly affect test delivery.

In contrast, the transmission medium used to move data between the remote testing sites and a central processing facility typically lacks the bandwidth or speed required for highly interactive connections. The reason is simple—cost. As noted previously, a T1 line is very expensive. Therefore, many CBT vendors and testing organizations use a less-expensive transmission medium.

Unfortunately, slower communication media may preclude highly interactive test delivery models such as computer-adaptive testing, the use of multipart, interactive item types, like performance simulations and video-based assessments. Also, despite being initially cheaper to implement, a slower and lower bandwidth transmission medium tends to be less efficient and less accurate than faster, higher bandwidth media. Ultimately, the issue of connectivity is related to the real-time performance of the test delivery system and should be evaluated given the needs of a particular testing program. This is especially true as testing programs consider use of the Internet as the primary delivery channel connecting workstations with the central processing test file servers and wish to have highly interactive tests like adaptive tests.

There are two connectivity-related factors that can seriously affect real-time CBT performance: (1) the amount of test data that needs to be transmitted for real-time activities and (2) the extent of interactivity between various communication channels. High-resolution graphics, large sound files, and video can generate extremely high bandwidth demands. Modern data compression and streaming technologies can help, but may still be affected by uncontrollable factors (e.g., Internet traffic). Because of storage and bandwidth limitations, some testing organizations have moved almost exclusively toward distributing CDs or DVDs containing large graphics and sound files to their local test centers. However, physically sending CDs and DVDs around the world is hardly efficient and introduces potential system capability problems, data synchronization problems, and possible security breaches.

A similar problem arises with respect to large item banks. Database design experts usually advocate a "single source" paradigm—that is, data that officially exist in one and only one place. In a CBT context, this paradigm suggests that it is optimal to have a single version of the item bank. Unfortunately, some of the connectivity issues discussed here create difficulties for the single source model. Instead, a version of the item bank is often broadcast to remote test centers in anticipation of testing that will take place in the near future. In addition to the potential security risks associated with having an entire item bank "out there," it is also difficult to ensure that changes and updates to the item bank and/or test driver components are completely synchronized across the entire testing enterprise. For example, consider the possibility that two examinees in two separate locations get the same test question—except one examinee is administered the new version of the item that is correct while the other examinee receives the old version with a critical flaw. This is a very plausible event, if the items presented to each of these two examinees are stored locally at their respective test centers and have not been properly updated. The inability to ensure simultaneous, fully synchronous updating of all test materials everywhere is a special case of propagation delay. Barring the capability to ensure continuous updates (e.g., using high-speed WAN technology), one solution is to move toward distributed systems that move smaller packets of data more often over the Internet with embedded code similar to asynchronous communication.

The extent of interactivity relates to the types of data communications associated with various system-wide connections; that is: central processor-to-local server(s); central processor-to-workstations; and local server(s)-to-workstations. The choice of testing model and the degree to which the software uses "distributed processing technology" or "middleware" may also affect system interactivity. For example, CATs tend to be far more interactive (i.e., demanding in terms of channel resources) than conventional tests, because a rather sophisticated scoring procedure and a possibly even more sophisticated item selection heuristic must be utilized after each item is administered. When these operations are resident on each local workstation, performance is usually excellent. When those scoring and item selection operations are moved to a middleware, distributed processing layer—either the local server or off-loaded to a processor farm, grid, or cluster—performance may not be degraded. However, if a central processor handles every exchange, item by item, the performance decrement can be significant. For example, if 10,000 examinees each take a 50-item CAT, the central processor will receive 1,000,000 multifunction operations (scoring + item selection = $2 \times 50 \times 10,000$). In addition, the likelihood of propagation delays and intermittent transmission failures will increase by an order of magnitude, simply because there are more "events" that can be affected.

Most test delivery drivers are designed to support one or more CBT delivery models. For example, some drivers only support the administration of intact fixed-length test forms. Others support a particular type of CAT. Still others support various multistage testing designs. Adding support for each of these models obviously adds to the complexity of the test delivery driver. The environment in which the test is administered (computer laboratories, dedicated test centers, remote PCs connected over the Internet, etc.) can have dramatic impact on performance of the test delivery driver.

7.3. CBT Delivery Drivers

The software that actually administers the test is called a *CBT delivery driver*, or test driver. The test driver performs nine basic operations: (1) decrypting and restructuring of the resource file (see *Test Assembly and Packaging*); (2) logging in, verifying, and authenticating the test taker; (3) selecting the items to administer (e.g., fixed sequence, random or heuristic-based such as an adaptive test); (4) populating a navigation control and enforcing authorized navigation through the test by the examinee; (5) rendering of the test items and running scripts to add animations, interactivity, and so forth to the items; (6) capturing and storing responses; (7) executing timing controls (e.g., enforcing section time-outs) and providing pacing help to the examinee; (8) scoring responses in real-time—which may be needed for adaptive testing as well as final scoring, if a score report is immediately provided to the examinee; and (9) encrypting results and transmitting them to a central storage repository. Commercial test drivers vary in their capabilities to perform these operations for different types of tests and test units (e.g., item selection and timing controls at the level of multi-item testlets).

A test driver typically supports one or more CBT delivery models. CBT delivery models are distinguished by the degree of adaptation used, the size and type of test units used, and the user interface (e.g., pacing and navigation). In essence, then, one may be able to discriminate among test drivers based on their capabilities to support adaptivity, test units of varied size, and flexibility of the user interface.

A fundamental distinction among many CBT models is the degree to which the test is *adaptive*. The basic mechanism behind an adaptive test is relatively simple. An adaptive test tailors the difficulty of the test items to the apparent ability or proficiency of each examinee. The specific goal in a purely adaptive test is to maximize the test reliability (score precision) for every examinee, regardless of his or her ability level. Items that are too easy or too difficult for particular examinees add little to the reliability of their scores. By tailoring the difficulty of the items to the ability of a particular examinee, it can be shown that the reliability of test scores is maximized.[2] Tailored or adaptive testing therefore leads to measurement efficiencies where a particular level of reliability can be achieved with fewer items or score precision can be improved for a fixed-length test.

Since the 1970s a plethora of adaptive strategies have emerged, including adapting on item sets or modules (Adema, 1990; Luecht & Nungester, 1998; Luecht, Nungester, & Hadadi, 1996; Sheehan & Lewis, 1992; van der Linden & Adema, 1998; Wainer, Kaplan, & Lewis, 1992; Wainer & Kiely, 1987; Wainer & Lewis, 1990); using sophisticated item selection heuristics for balancing content and other test features (Kingsbury & Zara, 1989, 1991; Stocking & Swanson, 1993; van der Linden, 2000; van der Linden & Reese, 1998), using stratification schemes to block on item characteristics—effectively using less discriminating items earlier in an adaptive test (Chang, Qian, & Ying, 2001; Chang & van der Linden, 2000; Chang & Ying, 1997, 1999), selecting items with information proportional to the error variance of provisional proficiency scores (Luecht, 1995); stochastically controlling the exposure of test materials within the population (Davey & Parshall, 1995; Stocking & Lewis, 1995, 1998, 2000; Sympson & Hetter, 1985), and even simultaneously estimating multiple abilities or proficiencies using multidimensional IRT adaptive testing algorithms (Luecht, 1996; Segall, 1996). Despite the increased sophistication of modern adaptive algorithms, the central goal of the algorithm is still to either maximize the test information function or to achieve a targeted amount of information at various points of the proficiency scale. "Maximizing the information function" refers to seeking the most information possible at each ability level whereas seeking a prescribed amount of information at each ability level is termed "targeting." This latter approach is used for some types of multistage adaptive tests and for nonadaptive tests, including computerized fixed tests.

CBT delivery models also differ in the size and nature of their delivery units. For example, a single test item is often thought of as the fundamental unit of test administration (i.e., one item = one test administration object). However, test administration *units* can be small or large. For example, sets of items assigned to a reading passage or to a particular problem scenario can also be packaged to present as a single unit or module. In fact, any cluster of items can be preconstructed and packaged as a unique test administration unit. By extension, modules can be also be grouped into fairly large, discrete test administration units (e.g., subtests or test sections).

The term "testlet" has become a common way to refer to a test module or item set that is larger than a single item. Although the term "testlets" is sometimes explicitly associated with layered-problem item sets that may involve internal branching (Wainer & Keily, 1987) or sometimes with computerized mastery tests using multi-item modules (Sheehan & Lewis, 1992), there is nothing precluding the use of that label in almost any type of CBT model to describe a preconstructed test module that includes everything ranging from a cluster of items to a set of computerized performance exercises (Luecht, 2002; Luecht, Brumfield, & Breithaupt, 2002). As unique test administration units, testlets can be selected and administered to examinees by a variety of mechanisms, including random selection from a pool of testlets, sequentially from a list, or by an adaptive algorithm. Some of the multistage adaptive test models described below specifically combine the modular features of testlets with adaptive selection and scoring mechanisms. Surveys of examinees have consistently reported that examinees prefer being allowed to navigate through an examination section, rather than being forced to answer a single item at a time, with no chance to review and change previously answered items, or to skip ahead (e.g., Hadadi, Luecht, Swanson, & Case, 1998; Parshall, Spray, Kalohn, & Davey, 2002; Wise, 1996, 1997).

From a data management perspective, creating uniquely identified, hierarchically related "structured data objects" (test forms, testlets, or modules) is also very efficient. Modern CBT requires enormous amounts of data to be moved, usually on a near-continuous basis, with the concomitant chance for error. In virtually any database management situation, *structure reduces error*. If more structure can be imposed on the data, fewer errors are likely because preventative measures are easier to implement. And when errors do occur, it is easier to detect them in highly structured data than in less-structured data.

There is no magical size that qualifies as the optimal test administration unit size. Intermediate test administration units such as testlets are indeed easier to handle from a data management perspective and examinees seem to prefer them. However, some amount of flexibility and mobility is always sacrificed through consolidation. The trade-offs largely depend on the choices of costs and benefits, some of which may be indirect and even intangible (e.g., perceptions of fairness, trust, or integrity by the test users). In any case, a test driver that restricts the test administration unit size to a single item or a fixed size testlet or module may be overly restrictive in terms of future flexibility.

Test drivers also differ in terms of various user interface considerations. These include issues that affect how examinees take the test, aspects of the software or test design that have some direct effect on examinee performance, and test or software design factors that directly affect examinee perceptions (but not necessarily their performance). Two important interface considerations that seem to distinguish the various CBT delivery models from one another are timing/pacing issues and navigation.

Pacing and *speededness* are problematic aspects of any time-limited, standardized test. The fact that some examinees either fail to reach certain items on speeded tests, or are induced to engage in "rapid guessing" behaviors, is troubling to most test developers and psychometricians, and is certainly a serious concern for most examinees. Unlike paper-and-pencil tests, where it is impossible to distinguish between intentionally omitted and not-reached items, the speededness problem is easily detectable under CBT (Hadadi & Luecht, 1998). Under CBT, where the tests are often administered at commercial test centers, the speededness problem can be exacerbated by the fact that seat time directly contributes to the cost of the examination. Where time equals money, policies may be made that tend to minimize rather than maximize the time allotted for examinees to take the examination. Empirical (real data) studies of speededness using actual item-by-item response times are rare (e.g., Hadadi & Luecht, 1998; Swanson, Featherman, Case, Luecht, & Nungester, 1997). For tests with highly restrictive time limits, there tends to be a moderate to high degree of correlation between the time spent on test items and the difficulty of the items (van der Linden, Scrams, & Schnipke, 1999). As a result, tests that provide differentially difficult items for low, medium, and high proficiency examinees—which includes most types of adaptive tests—may be speeded for higher ability examinees (van der Linden, 2000). At the same time, empirical studies conducted with medical students have shown that higher-ability examinees may pace themselves better than lower-ability examinees (Hadadi & Luecht, 1998; Swanson et al., 1997).

Pacing aids can range from online clocks to "pacer mechanisms" to designing the test in a way that facilitates pacing for most examinees. For example, Hadadi et al. (1998) empirically showed that using reasonably sized modules as the basic test administration units facilitated all examinees and specifically helped the lower-ability examinees whose pacing skills on a timed, multiple-choice CBT appeared to be underdeveloped. Automated test assembly procedures (see *Test Assembly and Packaging*) can also be used to reduce speededness. That is, average response latencies can be incorporated into the test assembly constraints to ensure that average item response time is equalized across all test forms (see, e.g., van der Linden, 1998; van der Linden et al., 1999).

Navigation relates to how the examinee moves around in a test. There are two aspects to navigation: (1) the design of the navigation control; and (2) blocking review and/or changing answers to previously seen items. The design navigation software controls differ across test delivery drivers (and sometimes across test delivery system platforms). Every test has some navigation mechanisms. Some CBT test delivery drivers merely use "forward/next" and "back" keys or mouse-clickable buttons to move item by item. Other CBT test drivers include a "jump" control that allows the examinee to enter the number of a test item and immediately go to that item. Some CBT test delivery drivers provide a full-page "review screen" to display all of the items, the examinee's item response (if any), and any flags left by the examinee indicating that he or she wants to possibly review the item later. Many of the recent genre of CBT graphical user interfaces provide an "explorer" or "helm" style of navigation control that continuously shows an ordered list of the test items in a narrow scrollable window within some segment of the display screen.

The style of the navigation control can affect performance and/or examinee perceptions in positive or negative ways. *Review*, for example, refers to a navigation control that allows examinees to return to previously seen materials or skip ahead to view upcoming materials. Some of the early CBT review screens completely covered up the test item display when the examinee selected the on-screen "review" button. Inexperienced CBT examinees sometimes panicked because they believed that the computer had lost their test. The "no review/no changing answers" aspect of item-by-item adaptive testing is strongly criticized by most examinees (Pommerich & Burden, 2000; Wise, 1996, 1997). When review and answer changes are precluded, examinees report that they felt overly restricted in their test-taking strategies. Some of the multi-item, modular test designs, discussed below, attempt to avoid that criticism by allowing examinees to freely navigate and change answers within each testlet or module. The examinees are required to electronically *submit* their testlet or module (analogous to physically turning in a paper-and-pencil test booklet and answer sheet at the end of a test section). Once a testlet or module is submitted, the examinee is prohibited from revisiting it. What is not clear from the research is how small the testlets or modules can be before examinees perceive that their choices in test-taking strategies are limited.

8. TEST DELIVERY MODELS

There are (at least) five categories of test delivery models: (1) computerized fixed tests; (2) linear-on-the-fly tests; (3) item-level computer-adaptive tests (including computer-adaptive tests with shadow testing technology and stratified adaptive tests); (4) testlet-based CAT and computerized mastery tests; and (5) structured computer-adaptive multistage tests. Additional reviews and comparisons of these models can be found in Luecht (2005a, 2006).

8.1. Computerized Fixed Tests

Computerized fixed testing (CFT) is a delivery model category that encompasses most varieties of preconstructed, intact test forms that are administered by computer. Different examinees may see different forms of the test; however, all examinees administered a given form see exactly the same items—although the presentation sequence may be scrambled at runtime. In the typical implementation of this model, several test forms (of the same fixed length) are available for administration and one is selected—perhaps randomly—for each examinee. The different forms are parallel with respect to test content and are either formally equated for difficulty (using classical test theory or item response theory; see Kolen & Brennan, 2004) or are assumed to be randomly equivalent. A CFT is directly analogous to having fixed-item paper-and-pencil test forms (PPT).

One advantage of a CFT over a PPT is that the presentation sequence for the items may be scrambled or randomized at runtime. Scrambling the item presentation sequence prevents certain types of cheating (e.g., coming in with an ordered list of illicitly obtained answers for the test). For multiple-choice questions, the answer options may further be scrambled within each item as an added measure of security. Scrambling the item sequence creates a minor data management challenge, because the scrambled test items (or components of test items) must be unscrambled or otherwise dealt with as part of the test scoring process.

8.2. Linear-on-the-Fly Tests

The second category of CBT delivery models is a variation on CFT called *linear-on-the-fly testing* (LOFT). Unlike CFT, however, LOFT incorporates real-time test assembly algorithms as part of the CBT delivery driver to generate a unique (but not adaptive) test for each examinee (Folk & Smith, 2002). Classical test theory or IRT can be used to generate randomly parallel LOFT test forms (Gibson & Weiner, 1998). There are at least two variations of the LOFT model: A large number of unique test forms can be developed far in advance of test administration (which is merely a special case of CFT, where ATA is employed, as noted above) or test forms can be generated immediately prior to testing (i.e., in real-time). An advantage of developing the test forms in advance is that content and measurement experts can review each form.

The primary advantage of the LOFT model is that numerous forms can be developed in real-time from the same item pool. Furthermore, there is typically some overlap of items allowed across the test forms. When test forms are assembled just prior to administration, the current exposure levels of the items can be considered in the test assembly algorithm. Overexposed items can be made unavailable for selection. For real-time LOFT, explicit item exposure controls can be used to limit the exposure of particular items (e.g., Sympson & Hetter, 1985). The benefits of LOFT include all those associated with CFTs with the addition of more efficient item pool usage and reduced item exposure.

8.3. Item-Level Computer-Adaptive Testing

The third category of CBT delivery models is *item-level computerized adaptive testing* (CAT). CAT adapts or tailors the difficulty of the test to each examinee, item by item. The idea of using the computer to match the difficulty of an item to the proficiency of an examinee was initially proposed by Lord (1977). Under the purest form of CAT, this tailoring is done by keeping track of an examinee's performance on each test item and then using this information to select the next item to be administered. A CAT is therefore sequentially developed in real-time by the test delivery software, using a simple item-selection heuristic. The primary item-selection criterion in CAT is to maximize the test information function and thereby minimize the measurement error of the examinee's score.

Figure 13.2 shows what happens to the provisional proficiency scores and associated standard errors for two hypothetical examinees taking a 50-item CAT. The proficiency scale is shown as the vertical axis (−3.0 to +3.0). The sequence of 50 adaptively administered items is shown on the horizontal scale. Although not shown in the picture, initially, both examinees start with proficiency estimates of zero. After the first item is given, the estimated proficiency scores immediately begin to separate. Over the course of 50 items, the individual proficiency scores for these two examinees systematically diverge to their approximate true values of +1.0 for Examinee A and −1.0 for Examinee B. The difficulties of the 50 items selected for each examinee's CAT would track the provisional proficiency scores: Examinee A would be administered more difficult items than Examinee B.

Figure 13.2 also indicates the estimation errors present throughout the CAT. The size of each error band about the proficiency score, denotes the relative amount of error associated with the scores, with larger bands indicating more error than narrower bands. Near the left side of the plot the error bands are quite large, indicating fairly imprecise scores. During the first half of the CAT, the error bands rapidly shrink. After 20 items or so, the error bands have stabilized; they continue to shrink, but more slowly. This figure demonstrates how the CAT quickly reduces error variance and improves the efficiency of a test.

There are several different methods for ending a computerized-adaptive testing session. In many situations,

FIGURE 13.2 Proficiency Scores and Standard Errors for a 50-Item CAT for Two Hypothetical Examinees

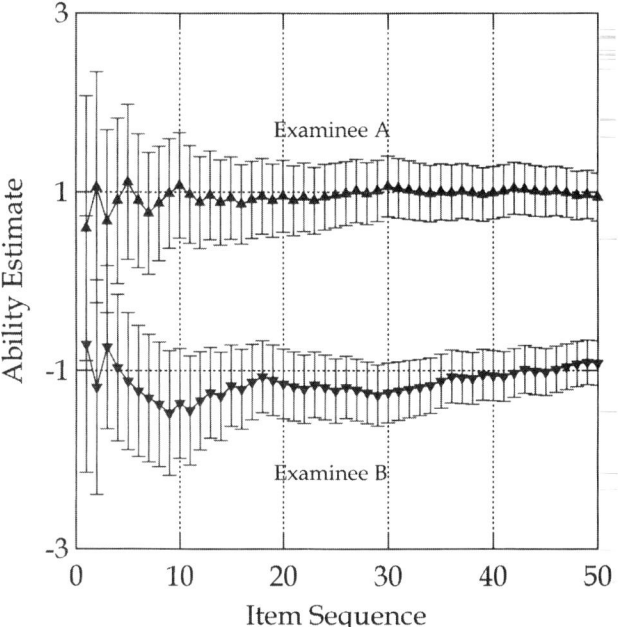

fixed-length CATs are used, where all examinees are administered the same number of items, regardless of the measurement error associated with their score. However, some testing programs use a variable-length CAT procedure in which the test session ends when some prespecified level of measurement precision is reached. Test stopping rules for variable length CATs typically use one of two methods, depending on the testing context. In a norm-referenced context, where no performance standards are set on the test, a minimum standard error criterion is typically used. In this situation, an examinee's test ends when the measurement error associated with her or his score falls below a prespecified level (Lord, 1980). This criterion assures that the scores for all examinees meet a minimum standard of reliability. In mastery or criterion-referenced testing situations, such as in academic placement, licensure, or certification testing, a test session ends when it is clear that an examinee's proficiency is above or below a specific threshold, such as a passing score. Confidence intervals or loss functions are typically used in the latter case.

A CAT offers improved testing efficiency, which means more precise estimates of examinees' ability of skill level can be obtained using fewer items than are typically required on non-adaptive tests. This gain in efficiency stems directly from the CAT item selection algorithm, which avoids administering items that are too easy or too hard for an examinee. Therefore, CATs are often significantly shorter than their paper-and-pencil counterparts. In principle, a CAT needs to be about half as long as a parallel non-adaptive test to achieve the same measurement precision (Wainer, 1993); however, content balancing, limited numbers of items in the item pool, and other practical constraints prevent CATs from achieving optimal efficiency. Figure 13.3 shows the efficiency gains of a hypothetical CAT, compared to a test for which the items were randomly selected. The plot shows the *average* standard errors of the proficiency estimates over 50 items (horizontal axis). The standard errors are averaged for examinees having different proficiency scores.

Figure 13.3 demonstrates how the measurement errors decrease over the course of the two tests. It is important to realize that the errors decrease for a randomly selected set of items, too. However, CAT clearly does a better job of reducing the errors. For example, at 20 items, the CAT achieves nearly the same efficiency as the 50-item random test; at 50 items, the average standard error for the CAT is approximately half as large as for the random test.

8.3.1. Item Selection Algorithms

There are many types of item selection algorithms. Traditional approaches that are cited in the psychometric literature include maximum information item selection (Lord, 1977), maximum information item selection with the Sympson-Hetter (unconditional) item exposure control procedure (Hetter & Sympson, 1997; Sympson & Hetter, 1985), maximum information with Stocking and Lewis (conditional) item exposure control (Stocking & Lewis, 1995, 1998), and maximum information with stochastic (conditional) exposure control (Revuela & Ponsoda, 1998; Robin, 1999, 2001).

Van der Linden and Reese (1998; also see van der Linden, 2000) proposed a special type of CAT that incorporates content balancing capabilities. They call this method *shadow testing*. Shadow testing conceptualizes the goals of the real-time item selection algorithm—which must be programmed into the test driver—as a series of optimization problems that include both dynamically changing objective functions and modified test constraints. This is conceptually similar to the way that ATA heuristics work in a CAT environment (see Luecht, 1998b; Stocking & Swanson, 1993). For shadow testing, a complete test is reassembled following each item administration, using ATA (see *Test Assembly and Packaging*). This test, called the *shadow test*, incorporates maximum information item selection for the as-yet-unadministered items subject to all of the required content constraints, item exposure rules, and other constraints (e.g., cognitive levels, total word counts, test timing requirements, clueing across items, etc.). Research is needed to explore how this technology can be incorporated in an operational test driver and determine how it performs in a highly demanding operational testing environment.

a-stratified computerized adaptive testing (Chang & Ying, 1997, 1999) is another interesting modification on the adaptive theme. a-stratified CAT adapts the test to the examinee's proficiency—like a traditional CAT. However, this variation eliminates the need for formal exposure controls and makes use of a greater proportion of the test bank than traditional CAT by formally partitioning the test bank into ordered layers, based on statistical characteristics of the items (Chang & Ying, 1997, 1999). First, the items are sorted according to their estimated IRT item discrimination parameters. Second, the sorted list is partitioned into layers (the strata) of a fixed size. Finally, one or more items are selected within each stratum by the usual CAT maximum

FIGURE 13.3 Average Standard Errors for a 50-Item CAT vs. 50 Randomly Selected Items

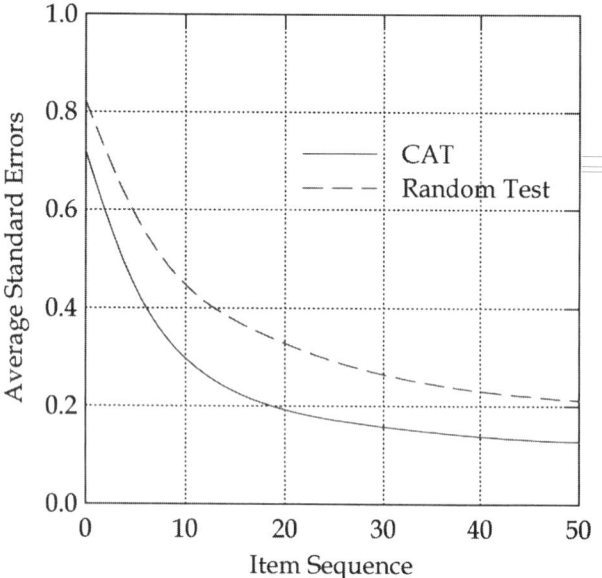

information algorithm. The CBT delivery driver proceeds sequentially through the strata, from the least to the most discriminating strata. The item selections may or may not be constrained by applicable content specifications. Chang and Ying reasoned that, during the initial portion of an adaptive test, less discriminating items could be used since the proficiency estimates have not yet stabilized. This stratification strategy effectively ensures that most discriminating items are saved until later in the test when they can be more accurately targeted to the provisional proficiency scores. In short, the a-stratified CAT approach avoids wasting the "high demand" items early in the test and makes effective use of the low demand items that, ordinarily, are seldom selected in CAT. Chang, Qian, and Ying (2001) went a step further to also block the items based on the IRT difficulty parameters.

There are numerous examples of successful, large-scale CAT testing programs. These include the ACCUPLACER postsecondary placement exams (College Board, 1993), the Graduate Record Exam (Eignor, Stocking, Way, & Steffan, 1993), the Armed Service Vocational Aptitude Battery (Sands, Waters, & McBride, 1997), and several licensure and certification tests such as the Novell certification exams and the licensure exam for registered nurses (Zara, 1994).

8.4. Testlet-Based CAT and Computerized Mastery Tests

Wainer and Kiely (1987) introduced the concept of a *testlet* to describe a subset of items or a "mini-test" that could be used in an adaptive testing environment (see also Lewis & Sheehan, 1990; Sheehan & Lewis, 1992; Wainer & Lewis, 1990). A testlet-based CAT involves the adaptive administration of preassembled *sets* of items to an examinee, rather than single items. This means that the test driver must: (a) be aware of the testlet as the primary adaptive "unit"; (b) provide real-time scoring of the testlets; (c) be capable of adaptively selecting the next testlet to be administered; and (d) be able to terminate the test when the final testlet has been administered or when some other termination criterion has been reached. (Note: testlet-based CAT uses preconstructed pools of testlets with non-overlapping items. Once the testlet pool is generated, any testlet can be selected by the real-time selection algorithm for any examinee. In contrast, structured ca-MST, described in section 8.5, preassigns the items to testlets and then further preassigns the testlets to test units called "panels." The "panel" concept is not used with testlet-based CAT.)

Examples of testlets include sets of items that are associated with a common reading passage or visual stimulus, or carefully constructed subsets of items that mirror the overall content specifications for a test. After completing the testlet, the computer scores the items within it and then chooses the next testlet to be administered. Thus, this type of test is adaptive at the testlet level rather than at the item level. This approach allows for better control over exam content and can be used to allow examinees to skip, review, and change answers within a block of test items. It also allows for content and measurement review of these sets of items prior to operational administration.

It should be clear that testlet-based CATs are only partially adaptive because items within a stage (testlet) are administered in a linear fashion. However, both the multistage adaptive tests described below and testlet-based CAT model offer a compromise between the traditional, non-adaptive format and the purely adaptive model. Advantages of multistage testing include increased testing efficiency relative to non-adaptive tests; the ability of content experts and sensitivity reviewers to review individual, preconstructed testlets to evaluate content quality; and the ability of examinees to skip, review, and change answers to questions within a testlet or stage.

On the surface, *computerized mastery testing* (CMT) is similar to testlet-based CAT. Lewis and Sheehan (1990; also see Sheehan & Lewis, 1992) proposed the CMT model for computerized mastery testing applications, although extensions to the non-mastery situation have also been proposed (Smith & Lewis, 1995). Under the original CMT framework, testlets are randomly selected from a pool of parallel testlets. The test proceeds—usually beyond some minimum number of testlets—until a prescribed minimum amount of error is achieved relative to decisions about the examinee passing or failing.

There are two disadvantages to testlet-based CAT and CMT. First, the testlets cannot contain any item overlap. That is, all active testlets in the testlet pool must be unique because it is not feasible for a test driver to track which testlets have testlet enemies (i.e., pairs of testlets that might share items, provide answer cues, or merely have common themes) and filter them in real-time for each examinee. This unique testlet requirement can severely restrict the number of testlets that can be produced from an item bank and increase risks of overexposing the testlets if a testing program is required to have continuous or near-continuous testing (see *CBT Facilities* for a discussion of capacity issues). The second limitation is that testlet-based CAT and CMT, despite the use of ATA to build the testlets, may yield test forms that do not meet all of the test-level content specifications when various testlets are combined. Provided that all of the test specifications can be stated at the testlet level and incorporated into the ATA constraints, this is not a serious problem. However, various programs attempting to implement these models have encountered quality control problems when test developers review samples of complete tests (e.g., criteria for test assembly used by the test developers but not specified as content constraints for ATA can be violated).

8.5. Structured Computer-Adaptive Multistage Tests

Structured computer-adaptive multistage tests (ca-MST) are self-administering adaptive tests that use testlets. These tests are designed to adhere to object-oriented design (OOD) software engineering principles and provide many quality control and data management advantages over computer-based CAT and CMT. Luecht and Nungester (1998; also see Luecht, Nungester, & Hadadi, 1996; and Luecht, 2000) introduced ca-MST under the heading of computer-adaptive sequential testing (CAST). Recently, the ca-MST acronym has been adopted as a more descriptive title for this delivery model. In any case, the structured ca-MST model has gained increasingly more interest over the past few years as a practical framework for implementing an adaptive testlet model without the quality control and data management complications of testlet-based CAT or CMT (Armstrong & Little, 2003; Hambleton & Xing, 2002; Jodoin, Zenisky, & Hambleton, 2002; Luecht, 2000; Luecht, Brumfield, & Breithaupt, 2002; Luecht & Burgin, 2003; Patsula & Hambleton, 1999).

Functionally, ca-MST is a preconstructed, multistage adaptive testlet model. The model uses a strong manufacturing-engineering paradigm that incorporates multistage adaptive technologies and automated test assembly (ATA) in a way that allows test developers to maintain a greater degree of control over the quality of test forms and data. It can be used for adaptive testing applications related to proficiency scoring or mastery testing applications. ca-MST is adaptive in nature and is therefore more efficient than a CFT or LOFT. Yet, ca-MST provides very explicit control over content validity, test form quality, and the exposure of test materials (Luecht, 2000; Luecht & Burgin, 2003).

ca-MST uses as a fundamental building block a unit termed a "module" or "testlet." These modules or testlets are preconfigured sets of items that may range in size from several items to well over 100 items. Modules may include discrete items or items that share a common stimulus (e.g. sets of 10 to 12 items, each associated with a particular reading passage). These modules or testlets are usually targeted to have specific statistical properties (e.g., a particular average item difficulty or level of precision) and all content balancing is built into the construction of the module. In turn, the test modules are assembled into a "panel" and are assigned to a particular stage of testing within the panel. This approach of assigning items to modules and modules to panels makes adaptive testing viable under ca-MST and further provides a concrete way of controlling exposure of items and/or modules over time, via the reuse or overlap rules associated with panels.

From an examinee's perspective, ca-MST appears to function as a multistage linear test. Figure 13.4 shows a three-stage ca-MST as a series of three modules or testlets. After each stage, a scoring and routing process is initiated. The scoring and routing process may involve test adaptation or mastery decision-making but is largely invisible to the examinee.

From a psychometric perspective, each series of three testlets (the "test form" actually seen by the examinee) needs to meet a specific statistical target, which is operationally defined as a prescribed level of measurement precision within a particular region of the score scale via an IRT test information target. From a test development perspective, each "test form" must also meet a variety of categorical test specifications, including the content and other specifications. Automated test assembly is ordinarily used to preconstruct testlets so that they individually meet all statistical and content specifications.

As part of the ATA process, the preconstructed testlets are packaged into panels. Each panel contains four to seven (or more) testlets, depending on the panel design chosen by the test developer—an issue addressed below. Each testlet is explicitly assigned to a particular stage and to a specific route within the panel (easier, moderate, or harder) based on the average difficulty of the testlet. Multiple panels can be prepared with item overlap precisely controlled across different panels. Figure 13.5 presents what is called a "1-3-3 multistage panel design." One testlet (A) is assigned to Stage 1. Three testlets are assigned to Stage 2 (B, C, D) and three more testlets are assigned to Stage 3 (E, F, G). The difficulty of each testlet is controlled through ATA, using IRT test information functions to target the difficulty of each testlet to a specific region of the relevant score scale. Thus, there are seven explicit target test information functions underlying the 1-3-3 panel design.

There are multiple panels depicted in Figure 13.5. These panels would be simultaneously constructed, using ATA, and incorporated as "test forms" in the test driver resource

FIGURE 13.4 ca-MST from an Examinee's Perspective

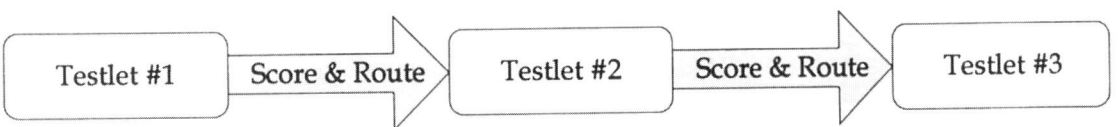

FIGURE 13.5 A Sample 1-3-3 Computer-Adaptive Multistage Test Panel Configuration (with Multiple Replications)

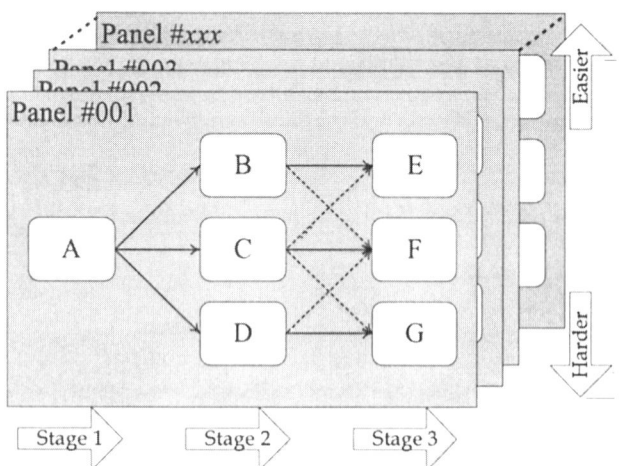

file (see *Test Assembly and Packaging*). When an examinee sits for the examination, a panel is selected at random.

The six solid arrows drawn on each panel in Figure 13.5 denote the primary adaptive routes allowed within the panel. The four dotted arrows denote secondary routes. Certain routes can even be de-activated to prevent examinees from making extreme jumps across routes. Routing from Stage 1 to Stage 2 is based solely on the examinee's performance on Testlet A. Lower performing examinees are routed to Testlet B, moderate performing examinees are routed to Testlet C and top performing examinees are routed to Testlet D. Routing to Stage 3 (Testlets E, F, and G) is based on cumulative performance for all prior testlets.

There are seven viable pathways through each 1-3-3 panel depicted in Figure 13.5: A+B+E, A+B+F, A+C+E, A+C+F, A+C+G, A+D+F, and A+D+G. Each panel is explicitly constructed so that any of those pathways provides a content-balanced test that meets all relevant test-level specifications (item counts, content balance, word counts, etc.). Multiple panels are simultaneously preconstructed for operational use, using ATA. By mixing and matching testlets across panels, hundreds of panels can be constructed if the item pool is large enough.

Once constructed, each panel therefore becomes a formal "data object" for purposes of test administration. That is, a panel "knows" how to adaptively administer itself. Creating panels as formal data objects provides many operational system advantages in terms of security, quality control, and data management. Test committees can review the content and quality of the "test forms" within each panel. Furthermore, trial runs can be made to make sure each panel is working properly, before activation in the live examination pool. From a security perspective, panels can be randomly assigned to examinees, the items can be randomly scrambled within testlets, and item overlap across panels can be explicitly controlled during ATA as a mean of controlling item exposure risks. Finally, the panels concretely deal with retest issues—that is, previously seen panels should be precluded from selection when an examinee is retested.

In real-time, scoring and routing of the examinees can be greatly simplified by including a *score routing table* for each panel. The score routing mechanism uses cumulative number-correct scoring and predetermined cut-offs to mimic the maximum information criterion used in CAT. The number-correct cut-offs can be packaged as part of the panel data. For example, the 1-3-3 design shown in Figure 13.5 requires exactly ten score look-up values (A→B, A→C, A→D, A+B→E, A+B→F, A+C→E, A+C→F, A+C→G, A+D→F, and A+D→G). This feature simplifies the operational scoring and routing functionality needed by the test delivery driver and potentially could improve performance of the test delivery driver (i.e., involve less complex data processing and computational steps—especially in a Web-enabled testing environment).

It is important to realize that the 1-3-3 panel design shown in Figure 13.5 is merely an example of a ca-MST panel. Virtually any panel configuration can be custom-designed to fit a particular assessment scenario by merely implementing a *template* for the desired configuration (number of stages, number of difficulty levels per stage, size of the testlets or modules within each stage, etc.). Some of the ca-MST panel designs proposed to date include the 1-3 (two-stage) design, the 1-2-2, the 1-3-4, the 1-3-4-5, and the 1-3-3-3. Note that more stages consisting of shorter modules add to adaptive flexibility. Luecht (2000) presented a number of practical design strategies and ATA considerations for implementing ca-MST designs.

The structured ca-MST test model is essentially a compromise solution that affords some degree of adaptation, while ensuring adherence to the content specifications for every examinee as well as limiting overexposure of the test items. There are some distinct advantages. First, research has shown that examinees like the ability to review the items within testlets. Second, the adaptive nature of ca-MST capitalizes on many of the same measurement efficiencies as CAT, especially for longer tests or tests having severe content and other constraints (Luecht & Nungester, 1998). Third, ca-MST simplifies some of the needs for developing, testing, and implementing costly new software systems. In fact, many of the largest commercial CBT test delivery software vendors have already incorporated the essential functionality for ca-MST in their systems. Fourth, ca-MST makes strong use of ATA as a front-end process, eliminating the need to implement ATA (i.e., constrained adaptive testing or shadow testing) in a real-time test delivery driver. The simultaneous construction of multistage panels using ATA has already been shown to be feasible (Armstrong & Little, 2003; Luecht, 2000; Luecht, Brumfield, & Breithaupt, 2002). Fifth, because the panels can be preconstructed, they can also be reviewed for quality of every "test form." Where human review is not entirely feasible, quality control software mechanisms can be constructed to flag potentially problematic panels.

The final advantage relates to a somewhat technical data management issue. As noted earlier, the ca-MST panel framework follows a formal object-oriented design schema that greatly facilitates how tests are stored, processed, and checked for quality (Luecht, Brumfield, & Breithaupt, 2002; Luecht & Nungester, 1998). The object-oriented design of the panels and the simultaneous construction of multiple panels, using ATA, further provides some very powerful ways of precisely controlling item exposure and managing related examination security risks, including: (a) precise control within and across panels of item overlap by placing appropriate constraints on the ATA test construction model; (b) specific reuse of testlets on various panels proportional to the risk of exposure for the different panel routes (a "mix-and-match" capability that allows multiple panels to be systematically constructed from an initial "parent" set of panels); (c) precise control over the presentation of pretest materials (i.e., who sees them and when); (d) capability to randomly scramble item presentation order within each testlet; and (e) the capability to randomly assign panels to examinees as "test objects," screening out previously seen panels for test retakers (Luecht & Burgin, 2003).

9. SYSTEMS FOR SCORING RESPONSES

Responses must be scored after the exam is administered. It is a simple matter to score the traditional multiple-choice item—regardless of whether a test is computerized or not—but many measurement specialists believe that this format is inadequate for assessing some important skills and competencies. Wainer, Bradlow, and Du (2000) suggest that multiple-choice items "yield a task that is abstracted too far from the domain of inference for many potential uses" (p. 245) because of the "atomistic nature of single independent small items" (p. 246). A good example is provided by the National Council of Architect Registration Boards' (NCARB) site-design subtest. Multiple-choice items can assess whether a candidate recognizes desirable features of a design, but appear incapable of assessing a candidate's ability to create a structure.

This section describes systems and research focusing on scoring constructed-response items. Two general approaches are presented. First, the use of technology to facilitate human scoring is described. Human scoring is, of course, time consuming and expensive, but can be implemented in a relatively short time frame. Second, we describe computerized scoring of constructed-response items. As exemplified by Bejar's (1991) description of computerized scoring for the NCARB site-design subtest, this approach may require substantial inspiration and perspiration to be developed successfully.

9.1. Technologies for Constructed-Response Scoring

Paper testing programs have traditionally been limited in their use of constructed-response items by the high cost of scoring and by the delay in reporting that manual scoring of these items requires. Reporting delay is especially problematic for K–12 programs that use year-end tests for making promotion or graduation decisions.

These added cost and time requirements are also problematic for continuously administered computer-based testing programs (CBT), like the Graduate Record Examinations (GRE) General Test or the Graduate Management Admission Test (GMAT), which include writing measures containing essay questions. In fact, this type of continuous CBT with constructed response has necessitated the redesign of scoring operations. In paper programs with occasional fixed administrations, human readers can be gathered periodically at central locations to score responses to a small number of questions. For continuous CBT, however, responses must be scored throughout the year. Moreover, readers must grade many different open-ended questions concurrently.

Two technological solutions have been applied to reducing the cost and time associated with constructed-response scoring. One solution has been automated scoring (see below), which involves replacing, or at least supplementing, human scoring with technology. A less radical solution, appropriate when automated scoring does not meet validity, cost, or credibility standards, has been online scoring, which uses technology to make traditional human scoring more efficient. Hybrids that combine these approaches are also possible.

In online scoring, responses generated as part of paper test administrations are sent to a processing facility where the responses are scanned into digital form. These digitized responses are then transmitted to a local or to a remote computer display, where they are presented to a human reader for scoring. For computer-entered responses, the scanning step is unnecessary, because responses are entered into the computer directly by the examinee. Once entered, those responses can be transmitted and displayed for scoring.

Online scoring has been employed for over a decade, first by NCS Pearson, which has been using this approach with a variety of NAEP item types since the early 1990s. More recently, ETS began using the technology for the GRE General Test, the GMAT, Praxis™, TOEFL, and some K–12 state assessment programs. CTB/McGraw-Hill also acquired such a capability with the purchase of Uniscore in 2001 (McGraw-Hill Acquisition, 2001).

Online scoring systems typically store examinee responses, provide readers with access to those responses from scoring centers or from remote locations via the Web, provide support materials required for scoring (including rubrics and essays that benchmark each score point), schedule readers, and tabulate statistical information regarding reader and topic performance. One system for which the functional details are publicly available is the Online Scoring Network (OSN) used by ETS (Odendahl, 1999). OSN houses the prompt or essay question, scoring notes that explain how a general rubric applies to the prompt, benchmarks and explanations for delineating score points, "rangefinders" for practice scoring, certification tests for qualifying readers initially, calibration papers for qualifying readers daily, monitor papers for supervisors to employ in the real-time quality control of readers, and the operational papers to be scored.

As the foregoing implies, OSN incorporates several procedures to ensure the quality of scoring. First, readers take a preoperational training tutorial that may be either delivered at a central scoring center or via the Internet to the reader's office or home. Second, each reader takes a certification test. For the GRE, the test involves 50 essay responses divided among five Issue topics and 50 divided among five

Argument topics, the two question types used on the General Test's Analytical Writing Assessment. Third, there is daily calibration. Every scoring day, each certified reader must score one or more calibration sets consisting of prescored essays. If the reader cannot calibrate, he or she cannot score at that session.

Once daily calibration is completed, the readers self-train on each operational topic to be scored that day. This training involves reviewing the scoring guide, topic notes (which customize the scoring guide to that topic), benchmark responses for each score point and explanations of how each benchmark fits that point, and the rangefinder essays that offer an opportunity to practice scoring the topic.

Several quality assurance procedures are used once operational scoring begins. First, prescored "monitor" essays are interspersed in the operational set. The scoring leader monitors readers' real-time performance by watching how the reader scores these monitor essays and assists as needed. The supervisor may also compare such things as the reader's score distribution and reading rate to the values taken across all readers for that prompt, or may back-read a sample of the reader's essays. Finally, test development staff members evaluate topic and reader performance over the long term and may remove topics or readers that do not perform as required.

Figure 13.6 shows the reader scoring interface from the OSN Web version. In the display window is a digitized version of the student's handwritten essay. (Essays written by students on computer can also be displayed in OSN.) Along the top border of the display window appear tools for manipulating the essay image, including ones that allow zooming in or out, and that allow magnifying specific portions (e.g., a word or phrase). On the left border are tools for annotating the image with text notes, arrows, and other devices. Along the far left is a list of links, including such resources as the scoring guide, benchmark responses for each score point, and prompt notes that customize the general scoring guide to a particular essay task. Just below the display window is a place to record scores. For this particular scoring session, two scales are displayed, one for the essay content and one for a holistic writing score.

Figure 13.7 shows the same essay response after annotation by a reader. The annotation shows a word highlighted in yellow, with an associated comment inserted into the examinee's response. Also shown are the use of a red circle and arrow to indicate a spelling error. At the bottom of the screen is a blank text box into which the reader can type a more extensive comment.

OSN collects a variety of real-time statistics about reader performance that can be useful to scoring managers. For each reader, managers can view such things as the total number of papers read; the number and percentage of exact, adjacent, and discrepant scores; the hourly rate of papers read; the average number of papers in the reader's queue; the mean score awarded over all papers for that prompt, and the percentage of scores awarded at each score point. Similarly, managers can review real-time topic (i.e., prompt) statistics, including the number and percentage of exact, adjacent, and discrepant scores; the average reading rate; the mean score; the percentage of scores awarded at each point; and the number of third and fourth readings required to resolve score disagreements.

Two comparability issues are associated with online scoring. The first issue concerns whether responses—be they essays or answers to open-ended mathematics problems—receive equivalent scores when the grading is conducted in the traditional way on *paper* versus *online*. The second issue, which is not limited to online scoring, is whether responses submitted in *handwritten* and *typed* form are graded equivalently. Note that the question here is not how delivery mode affects the examinee's performance but, rather, how the form of the response affects the *scorer's judgment* of that performance. Also note that these two presentation conditions—scoring mode and format—are independent. Responses may be submitted in either handwritten or typewritten format. Handwritten responses can be presented for scoring as submitted or they can be scanned for computer display. Likewise, key-entered responses can be scored from printed copy or from a computer screen.

Surprisingly, there is very little published research in peer-reviewed journals on this type of comparability. The most comprehensive study is probably that conducted by Zhang, Powers, Wright, and Morgan (2003). These investigators studied scores from more than 11,000 high school students who had taken either the Advanced Placement Program® English Language and Composition test or the AP® Calculus test. All exams had been scored in handwritten, paper form through the operational AP reading by readers gathered in one or more common locations. As part of the reading, 500 of the exams for each subject were independently re-scored to estimate inter-rater reliability. Those 500 exams were subsequently scanned and again scored twice independently, this time by different readers working from individual home or office locations through the Internet. Zhang et al. compared the score level, variability, and inter-rater agreement for the individual questions composing each exam, as well as the overall exam passing rates, across modes. They found little, if any, practical difference on their comparability indicators (e.g., differences of less than .1 standard deviations for the English language and composition test and less than .02 standard deviations for the calculus test). These findings are basically consistent with an older study conducted for NAEP at grades 4, 8, and 12 in each of five subject areas (ETS, 1993), and with smaller studies using college-age students by Powers, Farnum, Grant, and Kubota (1997) for GMAT essays, and by Powers and Farnum (1997) for The Praxis Series: Professional Assessments for Beginning Teachers essays.

Whereas the limited available research has generally supported the comparability of online and traditional paper scoring, the same cannot be said for the scoring of handwritten versus typed responses. While some studies have found mixed or null effects (e.g., Harrington, Shermis, & Rollins, 2000; MacCann, Eastment, & Pickering, 2002), the evidence suggests that readers generally give lower scores to typed responses. For example, Powers, Fowles, Farnum, and Ramsey (1994) used answers from 32 college-age students, who each wrote two essays, one key-entered and one handwritten, in connection with pilot tests for the

FIGURE 13.6 Reader Interface for OSN Showing a Handwritten Essay Response

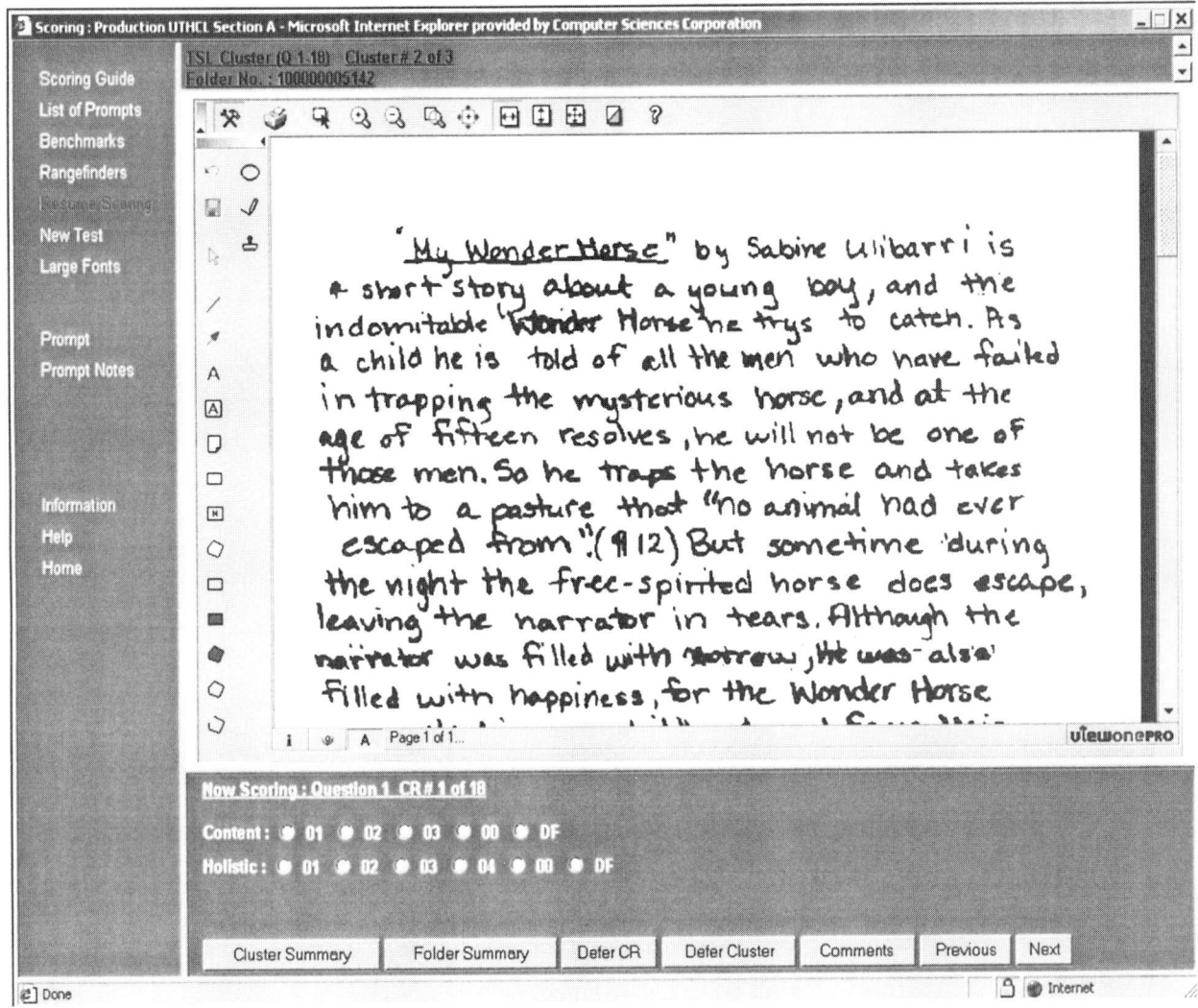

Source: Copyright ETS. Used with permission.

Praxis I Series: Academic Skills Assessments. Each essay was then transcribed to the other format, and the essays were presented on paper to two pairs of readers. The investigators found that the handwritten versions of the essays were graded significantly higher than the typed ones. In a second experiment, the investigators were able to reduce the scoring effect somewhat by training a new set of readers with both types of essays and calling their attention to the different impressions format might make. Powers and his colleagues concluded that the size of the performance difference was of little practical importance, in part because the essay was only one component of the Praxis I writing score (which also included performance on multiple-choice questions).

In a subsequent study, Powers and Farnum (1997), presented 40 Praxis essays on-screen and on paper, and in both typed and handwritten formats, to four pairs of readers. As noted above, the investigators found no differences for scoring on-screen versus on paper. However, they did find that the handwritten versions of essays were graded .2 standard deviations higher than the typed versions of the same text. This effect was virtually the same size as that found in the earlier study described above by Powers et al. (1994).

Russell and Tao (2004a) replicated in the school population the scoring presentation effect that Powers and his colleagues found for college students. These investigators analyzed 52 essays in grade 4, and 60 in each of grades 8 and 10, written in response to questions taken from the Massachusetts Comprehensive Assessment System (MCAS) Language Arts Test. All essays were handwritten by students and subsequently typed on computer by the investigators. Once typed, the essays were presented on paper to six raters at each grade level in one of three formats—handwritten, printed in single-spaced 12-point text, and printed in double-spaced 14-point text. The last condition was intended to correct for any difference in appearance between handwritten and typed essays due to length. Russell and Tao found the handwritten versions to receive significantly higher scores than the typed ones, but detected no difference between typed essays of different apparent lengths.

FIGURE 13.7 Reader Interface for OSN Showing the Same Examinee Essay Response as Annotated by a Reader

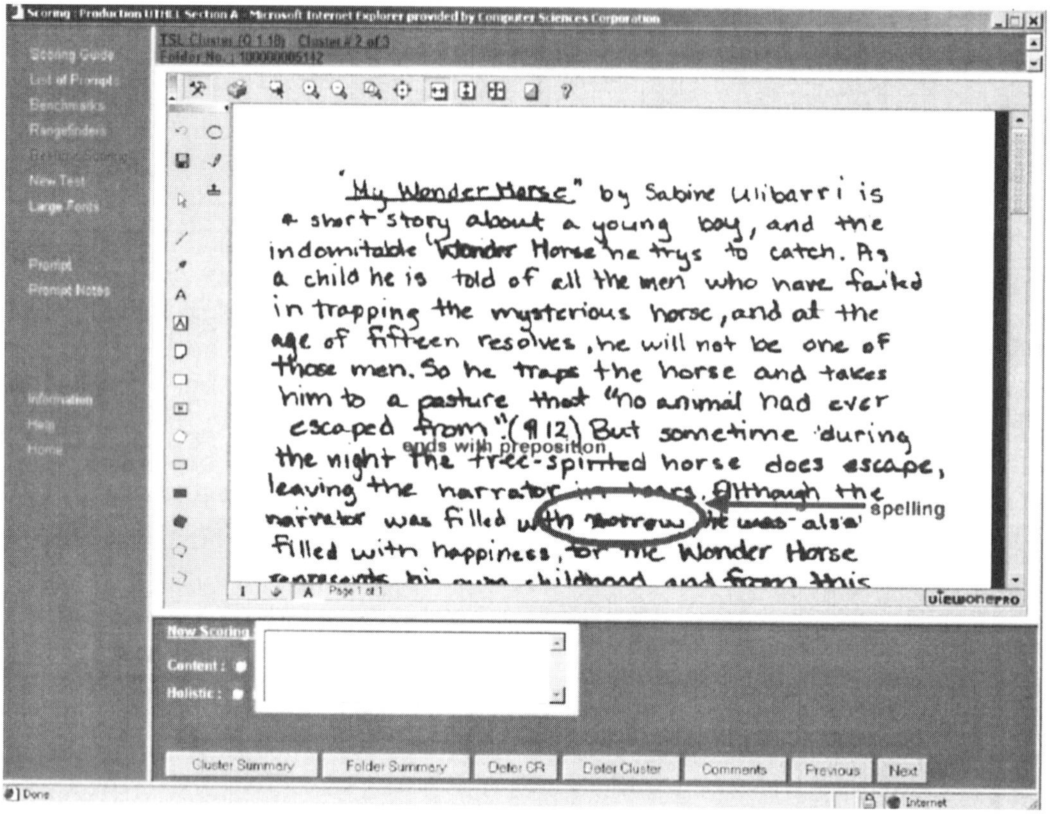

Source: Copyright ETS. Used by permission.

As part of their study, Russell and Tao (2004a) also asked two readers to identify and categorize errors in each of 30 grade 8 essays. Half of the essays appeared in handwritten form and half appeared in print, with the half seen in print by the first reader presented as handwritten to the second reader. The error categories were spelling, punctuation, capitalization, awkward transitions, and confusing phrases or sentences. Results showed that the two raters detected significantly more spelling errors and more confusing phrases or sentences when the essays were presented in print.

In a second study, Russell and Tao (2004b) had handwritten 8th grade MCAS essays entered onto computer. They then presented the responses on paper to eight readers in four formats—handwritten, printed in single-spaced type font, printed in a single-spaced script font to simulate handwritten text, and printed in single-spaced type font with all spelling errors corrected. Results showed that the scores for the handwritten versions and for the script-font versions did not differ from one another, but that both were graded significantly higher than the same essays represented in typed font. The effect on scores of corrected spelling was not significant for any comparison.

Russell and Tao (2004b) next repeated the scoring with a second set of four readers trained to avoid the presentation effect. These readers graded only the original handwritten responses and their verbatim transcriptions in type font (i.e., without spelling corrected). In this scoring, the presentation effect was eliminated. That is, no significant difference was found between the scores awarded to the handwritten and typed versions.

In sum, online scoring can provide several advantages to testing programs. One such advantage is in eliminating the need to package, ship, and handle paper for scoring sessions, which can reduce processing time and cost. A second advantage is in allowing readers to train, qualify, and score remotely, eliminating reader subsistence and transportation costs. Finally, online scoring can permit grading to be ongoing, a requirement for continuous computer-based testing programs.

The available research concerning online scoring suggests little, if any, effect for computer versus paper display but, in general, a consistent difference for typed compared with handwritten presentation. Why typed essays receive lower scores is not completely clear, though the results of one study suggest that substantive and mechanical errors may stand out more since these responses are easier to read. However, other possibilities include that raters' expectations for typed responses are higher because such responses have the look of a final draft, and that typed text may encourage a weaker connection with the reader because the student's attempts at revision are not apparent.

9.2. Automated Scoring

Automated scoring is necessitated by the need to incorporate in tests question types that more faithfully reflect the tasks examinees encounter in academic and work settings but which can be scored in a cost-effective manner. At least three general classes of tasks may come to mind. The first class covers questions that can be graded by a simple match between the key and response. For the verbal domain, an example might be a reading passage that requires the examinee to click on the point at which a given sentence should be inserted. For math, examples would include problems that call for ordering values by dragging and dropping them into slots, extending a bar on a chart to represent a particular amount, clicking the appropriate point on a number line, or entering a numeric response. At this writing, machine-scored tasks like these were being used in several large-scale tests.

A second general class consists of static problems for which the responses are too complex to be graded by a simple match. The problems are static in the sense that the task does not change in response to the actions taken by the examinee. There has been considerable experimental work on such tasks. In mathematics, investigators have developed and evaluated mechanisms for scoring students' step-by-step solutions to algebra word problems (Bennett & Sebrechts, 1996; Bennett, Sebrechts, & Rock, 1991; Sebrechts, Bennett, & Rock, 1991), graphs plotted on Cartesian coordinate systems (Bennett, Morley, Quardt, & Rock, 2000), symbolic expressions (Bennett, Steffen, Singley, Morley, & Jacquemin, 1997), and numerical responses to questions having no predetermined set of quantitatively equivalent correct answers (Bennett et al., 1999). Work has also been conducted in the scoring of students' computer programs (Bennett, Gong, et al., 1990; Bennett, Rock, et al., 1990; Braun, Bennett, Frye, & Soloway, 1990), verbal responses to divergent thinking tasks (Bennett, Rock, et al. 1995; Enright, Rock, & Bennett, 1999), and concept mapping as an indicator of history knowledge (Herl, O'Neil, Chung, & Schacter, 1999).

One operational illustration of this task class can be found in the Architect Registration Examination of the National Council of Architectural Registration Boards. A section of this test asks the examinee to use computer-assisted design tools to produce building plans, which are then automatically graded (Bejar, 1995; Kenney, 1997). A second example is the essay section in the Graduate Management Admission Test, in which the responses to each of two essay questions are scored automatically as well as by a human reader (Burstein, 2003). A final example relates to derivatives of the mathematical tasks described above that call for students to enter symbolic expressions or plot graphs on Cartesian coordinates. These derivatives have been used operationally in the Indiana Core 40 End-of-Course Assessment in Algebra, a state assessment administered to recognize outstanding performance among schools.

The third class covers those problems that change because of actions the examinee takes in the course of problem solution. Interactive simulations exemplify this class. One such operational simulation that is automatically scored is the Primum CCS patient management test developed by the National Board of Medical Examiners for the United States Medical Licensing Examination (Clyman, Melnick, & Clauser, 1995). Experimental approaches for scoring interactive problems in a variety of content domains also have been developed (Stevens, Lopo, & Wang, 1996).

Regardless of task class, at a high level, automated scoring can generally be decomposed into three separable processes: feature extraction, feature evaluation, and feature accumulation. (In terms of the four ECD processes mentioned at the beginning of this chapter, these three processes can be seen as subcomponents of evidence identification.) These three processes will be present in most automated scoring applications, though one or another of them may sometimes be folded together. *Feature extraction* involves isolating scorable components of the response. For essay scoring, one such component might focus on content and include all of the words in the responses except for the function words (i.e., articles, prepositions). *Feature evaluation* involves judging the extracted components. Continuing the example for essay scoring, the extracted words for an individual's essay might be compared to the words used in a sample of essays at different score levels, with the content component of the examinee's response receiving an evaluation based on the closest score level. Finally, *feature accumulation* involves combining the various feature evaluations to produce an overall score for the response. So, the content component score might be combined with other feature scores to create a composite rating for the task.

Note that for any given process, the methods used may vary from one domain to the next or, within a content domain, from one scoring approach to the next. For example, words may be extracted from an essay response through conventional programming techniques that involve taking everything between markers (e.g., spaces, punctuation) that is not an article or preposition. Alternatively, more specialized natural language processing techniques might be used to parse the text so that the function of each word can be identified for subsequent use in feature evaluation. Similarly, for purposes of feature accumulation, logical or empirical methods might be employed to combine features into a task score. Multiple regression is one commonly used method. It is employed in combining feature evaluations in the Primum CCS patient management test (Clauser et al., 1995), as well as in such automated essay scoring programs as *e-rater* (Burstein, 2003), the Intelligent Essay Assessor (Landauer, Laham, & Foltz, 2000), and Project Essay Grade (Page, 2003).

The calibration of automated systems often proceeds as follows, especially among programs for essay scoring. First, two or more human experts manually score a sample of responses to a particular question. Next, the same sample of responses is submitted for automated processing. Third, the human scores are regressed on the feature evaluations generated by the automated processing. Finally, a new sample of responses is evaluated by human judges and is processed automatically. The judges' scores are contrasted with the scores produced by applying the regression weights to the feature scores automatically extracted from this new sample. If the automated scores agree with the human judges to about the same degree as the human judges agree among themselves, the automated system is considered to be interchangeable with the scores of the typical judge.

Whereas this procedure is the one that is typically followed, it has clear limitations, the most important of which is that it gives too much weight to modeling the scores of human judges (Bennett, 2006; Bennett & Bejar, 1998). Although human scores might be one reasonable criterion, they should not be the only one and they might not even be the best one, especially if the scores were generated under operational conditions by only a pair of judges, which is most often the case. Under operational conditions, judges score papers very quickly and not necessarily with optimal validity. Further, the smaller the number of judges, the greater will be the noise in any estimates of examinee true score that are derived. Regression will model whatever variance is systematic in a set of human scores, whether that variance is valid or not. If a regression equation is estimated for each new task, another often-followed procedure, differences in the equations—especially if derived through stepwise regression—may reflect nothing more than differences in the samples of examinees taking the prompt or of judges grading it.

Instead of searching for features that best predict the scores of human judges, a far more theoretically satisfying approach would be to derive a set of features based on an analysis of what makes for proficiency in the domain of interest (Bennett, 2006). Then, a scoring program should be built to extract those features, weighting them according to substantive criteria, and using human judges only to verify that the features are being correctly extracted.

This agreement of automated scores with the judgments of human experts must, however, be only one component of the validation effort. Relations of the automated scores with a *variety* of external criteria (e.g., other measures of the same construct, measures of related constructs, measures of unrelated constructs) should be evaluated. Powers, Burstein, Chodorow, Fowles, and Kukich (2002a), for example, examined the relations of both automated and human essay scores with nine criteria, including writing samples from courses, self-evaluations of writing skill, self-reported grades from courses that required considerable writing, self-reported documentable accomplishments in writing (e.g., published a short story), and self-reported success with various kinds of writing and writing processes. These investigators found reasonably similar relations with the external indicators for human and for automated scores, though the relations for the automated scores were somewhat weaker than for the scores awarded by humans.

In addition to relations with external criteria, the degree to which automated scores are subject to construct-irrelevant sources of variation should be tested. For example, Powers, Burstein, Chodorow, Fowles, and Kukich (2002b) looked at the extent to which an automated essay scoring program could be fooled into giving scores that were either higher than deserved or lower than warranted. Results suggested that the automated scoring could be tricked more easily into assigning scores that were too high than into awarding scores that were too low.

10. POSTADMINISTRATION ANALYSIS SYSTEMS

Continuous testing programs in computerized settings—as with all high-stakes testing programs—have a need for postadministration item analysis. In addition to the usual reasons for postadministration item analysis (e.g., checking for miskeys), continuous testing programs must be particularly vigilant with regard to test compromise. High-stakes exams administered continuously may tempt examinees to conspire in one way or another to obtain high scores. For example, a program that rotates item pools on a monthly basis provides ample opportunity for examinees who took the exam early in the cycle to help examinees taking the exam later. Such examinees can post items they recall on a bulletin board; before long, enough items may be available to inflate scores. The decision by the sponsors of the Graduate Record Exam to abandon continuous testing in several Pacific Rim countries is a testament to the seriousness of this issue.

This section describes analyses that should be conducted on a regular basis by continuous testing programs. The purpose of these analyses include ascertaining whether items function as desired and whether some type of anomaly has occurred that warrants closer investigation.

10.1. Banking Statistics

The data in the master exam should be analyzed on a weekly or monthly basis (depending on examinee flow) to track the psychometric properties of items and to identify any anomalous changes. Traditional difficulty ($\hat{p}$) and discrimination (point biserial r_{pb} and/or biserial r_b) item statistics should be re-computed when sample size permits (responses from several hundred examinees are needed for these statistics to be stable). Graphing these indices as a function of time allows anomalous changes to be readily apparent.

Re-computing IRT item parameters is more difficult. In the past, the software that performs IRT analyses had sharp limits on the number of items and examinees that could be analyzed simultaneously. However, as the cost of computer memory chips has decreased dramatically and operating systems have increased the amount of memory that can be addressed, the capacity of software has increased. The recently released version of BILOG-MG (Zimowski, Muraki, Mislevy, & Bock, 2003), for example, can analyze approximately 1,000 items with data from 250,000 examinees (or 2,000 items and 125,000 examinees, 4,000 items and 62,500 examinees, etc. [Leo Stam, personal communication, 2003]) when run on a Windows XP computer with 2 gigabytes of memory installed.

Although computational limitations have diminished, accurate estimation of IRT item parameters remains a challenge: A thousand or more responses per item are needed to ensure small standard errors of item parameter estimates (paradoxically, accurate ability estimation does not necessarily require small errors in item parameter estimates; see Chuah et al., 2006). In addition to large sample sizes, the pattern of item-examinee interactions is critical. To place all item parameter estimates on the same scale, there must be overlap in item administrations across examinees. Table 13.1, for example, shows how this can be done for a conventional test. Table 13.2, on the other hand, depicts a short adaptive test where examinees 1 to 5 were administered an item pool consisting of items 1 to 10, but examinees 6 to 10 were administered items from a disjoint set of items

(items 11 to 20). Unless examinees are randomly assigned to item pools, item parameter estimates cannot be placed on a common scale for designs with disjoint sets of examinees and items. Moreover, even when examinees are randomly assigned, very large samples are needed because "randomly equal" groups are not "virtually equal" until sample size is quite large. Items 1 to 3 in Table 13.3 are linking items; even though items 4 to 10 and 11 to 17 were administered to disjoint sets of examinees, their IRT item parameter estimates can be placed on a common scale because the linking items provide a connection. Kolen and Brennan (2004) provide details on designs for linking.

10.2. Finding Miskeys

An item is miskeyed when the answer that is scored as correct is not the correct answer or if another answer can be considered as correct in addition to the keyed answer. There are rare but highly publicized cases where an examinee is able to demonstrate that an option deemed incorrect by the test developers is actually correct. Although embarrassing to testing programs, such instances are quite rare. It is far more common to find items on operational forms with near-zero or even negative r_b coefficients. Including such items in test scores unfortunately adds error and consequently they should be removed from the item pool. It is a good idea to return such defective items to the item writers so that they can identify the source of the problem. Luecht (2005b) summarizes some methods for conducting item analysis within the context of CBT.

10.3. Differential Item Functioning

As a part of the development process, testing programs conduct sensitivity reviews of the materials they create because there is consensus that tests should not contain anything that is offensive to test takers. Despite the best efforts of developers and review panels, it is possible that some items are unexpectedly difficult to members of some subpopulation. Differential item functioning (DIF) analyses should be conducted to identify such items.

It is important to note that subgroups are not expected to perform equally well. Groups differ in their experiences, interests, motivation, and so forth. Consequently, only groups formed by random assignment should be expected to perform equally well.

DIF methods examine whether an item is *relatively* more difficult or easier across relevant groups. Non-IRT approaches such as Mantel-Haenszel (Holland & Thayer, 1988) and simultaneous item bias test (SIBTEST; Shealy & Stout, 1993a, 1993b) can be used for this purpose. Alternatively, IRT methods include Lord's chi-square (Lord, 1980) and its extension to multiple groups (Kim, Cohen, & Park, 1995), and the likelihood ratio approach (Thissen, Steinberg, & Wainer, 1988, 1993) can be used. Raju and Ellis (2002) provide a lucid description of these methods and related issues.

Computerized scoring of essays (Shermis & Burstein, 2003), architectural designs (Bejar, 1991; Bejar & Braun, 1999), and other open-ended assessments provides an interesting twist on DIF analysis. Here, the issue is whether each group's computer-determined score agrees with a human grader equally well across subpopulations. It is possible that, in the development of the automated scoring system, processes were created that artificially penalize (or reward) members of some specific group. Therefore, as part of the postadministration analysis system, it is important to examine the relation across groups of computer-assigned scores with scores given by a human grader. Note that a correlation coefficient is an inadequate measure of association in this context because it is insensitive to an additive constant; it would be very important to learn that scores given to members of a minority group by the computer are, on the average, a half-point lower than the scores given by a human grader. Therefore, the equality of regression lines or equating lines of computer-assigned scores and human grader scores should be examined.

10.4. Scaling Drift

With conventional paper-and-pencil tests, testing programs administer a new form at almost every administration. Equating (Kolen & Brennan, 2004) is then used to place scores from the new test onto the scale used in previous administrations. Thus, a score of, say 700, on the SAT-Verbal test indicates the same skill level, regardless of which form was administered to an examinee.

In computerized testing programs, item pools, testlets, or ca-MST panels are changed on a regular basis to maintain test security. IRT item parameters, hopefully on a common scale, are used to obtain the ability estimate $\hat{\theta}$ for each examinee and then a pseudo-number right score is computed as $X = \sum_{i}^{n} P_i(\hat{\theta})$ for a fixed set of n items (actually, just the item parameters for the n items are used), and then X can be equated as with a conventional test.

Scaling drift can occur when item parameters for successive item pools are not on exactly the same scale. This can occur due to estimation error in item parameters, perhaps compounded by changes in the distribution of skill among the examinees used to estimate item parameters. Moreover, any IRT model is only an approximation and there will be some model misfit. This is likely to be an especially thorny issue for testing programs using the one-parameter logistic (a.k.a., Rasch) model, as this model provides only a very rough approximation to the way examinees actually respond to items.

To examine the extent of scaling drift, testing programs can occasionally re-introduce previously used items, re-estimate their IRT item parameters, and then compute the difference between ability estimates obtained using the original and new item parameters. One fly in the ointment is that the psychometric properties of items can change over time. For example, old forms of an electronics information test might include items asking about vacuum tubes; obviously, the properties of outdated items will be different than they were many years ago. Chan, Drasgow, and Sawin (1999) examined a test battery (the U.S. Department of Defense's Armed Services Vocational Aptitude Battery) that included tests of cognitive ability such as verbal and

TABLE 13.2 Non-overlapping Item Sets

Examinee	1	2	3	4	5	6	7	8	9	10	11	12	13	14	15	16	17	18	19	20
1	X		X	X	X		X													
2	X	X		X	X	X														
3	X		X		X	X		X												
4		X		X			X		X											
5			X			X	X	X		X										
6										X	X	X				X	X			X
7												X	X	X	X		X		X	
8											X			X	X	X	X	X	X	
9													X	X	X	X				X
10											X	X	X		X	X		X		

ITEM

TABLE 13.3 Item Sets with Common Linking Items

									ITEM								
EXAMINEE	1	2	3	4	5	6	7	8	9	10	11	12	13	14	15	16	17
1	X		X		X		X		X								
2	X	X		X		X			X								
3	X		X		X	X		X									
4		X	X	X			X			X							
5		X	X			X		X		X							
6	X	X									X					X	X
7		X	X									X	X				X
8	X		X								X			X		X	
9	X	X												X	X		X
10		X	X									X	X		X		

math skills as well as technical tests such as electronics information. They found that the IRT item parameters of a substantial number of items changed over a 16-year period.

11. COMPARABILITY AND TECHNOLOGY

Comparability refers to the commonality of score meaning across testing conditions. In the context of technology and assessment, the testing conditions of interest include delivery mode (i.e., paper vs. computer) and computer platforms. When comparability exists, scores from different testing conditions can be used interchangeably. For example, scores derived from one condition can be referenced to norms collected, or to cut scores set, in another.

The American Psychological Association's *Guidelines for Computer-based Tests and Interpretations* (American Psychological Association [APA], 1986, p. 18) states that scores may be considered equivalent when individuals are rank ordered in approximately the same way and when the score distributions are approximately the same. If the rank-ordering criterion is met but the distributions are not the same, it may be possible to make scores interchangeable by equating. Although the *Guidelines* pose these criteria in the context of comparability across computer and paper delivery, the criteria are generally applicable to any difference in testing conditions.

Comparability is required when scores need to have common meaning with respect to one another, to some reference group, or to a content standard. If scores are not comparable across delivery modes or computer platforms, and the test varies along one or more of these dimensions, the decisions we make from assessment may be wrong. Wrong decisions may be made about students for such things as promotion, graduation, diagnosis, or progress reporting. They may be made about workers for hiring, promotion, or training. Wrong decisions also may be made about institutions. For example, under *No Child Left Behind*, a school's standing with respect to Adequate Yearly Progress, the federal law's performance metric, could be incorrect. Finally, these wrong decisions—or at least, interpretations—may be made about population groups when the lack of comparability is associated more with some types of individuals than others.

11.1. Comparability of Delivery Modes

Comparability across delivery modes is important when assessments need to be delivered on both computer and paper. This need for dual delivery may exist when there are not enough readily available computers to allow all examinees to test electronically or when not all examinees have the skills or comfort levels needed to take computer-based tests.

The scores from paper and computer versions of the same test can diverge for several reasons. For one, differences in such *presentation characteristics* as the number of items on the screen versus the number on the printed page, or the size of text fonts, could impact performance. Differences in *response requirements* also may affect scores. For example, to take a paper test, an examinee need only know how to use a pencil to mark correct answers to multiple-choice problems and how to write in answers for the open-ended questions. In contrast, a computer-based test may require additional skills. The examinee may have to point, click, drag, drop, and scroll with the mouse, as well as use the keyboard to enter and edit text. A third reason scores could diverge across delivery modes is differences in *general administration characteristics*. For instance, the online test might present items adaptively, so that every examinee gets a different test, while the paper test contains the same items in the same order for all individuals. Additionally, the paper administration would typically require test takers to wait until time elapses before moving on to the next section, while the online administration may permit individuals to proceed at their own discretion. Finally, the two versions may be differentially speeded because differences in presentation, response, and other administrative characteristics are not appropriately accounted for in setting test timing.

Many studies have investigated the comparability of paper and computer tests among adults. Mead and Drasgow (1993) reported a meta-analysis of studies that estimated the correlation of scores across testing modes after correcting for unreliability and that compared differences in mean performance across modes. Based on 159 estimates, they found the correlation for timed power tests like those used in educational settings to be .97, suggesting score equivalence, but the correlation for speeded measures, such as clerical tests, to be .72. For the timed power tests, the standardized mean difference between modes was .03 and the standard deviation of the differences was .15. Computerized tests, therefore, were harder than paper versions, but only trivially so, and the spread in the size of this mode difference from one study to the next was minimal.

Gallagher, Bridgeman, and Cahalan (2000) examined comparability for population groups on the Graduate Record Examinations® (GRE®) General Test, Graduate Management Admission Test® (GMAT®), SAT® I: Reasoning Test, Praxis: Professional Assessment for Beginning Teachers®, and Test of English as a Foreign Language™ (TOEFL®). These investigators discovered that delivery mode consistently changed the size of the differences between focal- and reference-group performance for some groups, but only by small amounts. For African American and Hispanic students, for example, the difference in performance relative to White students was smaller on computer-based tests than on paper tests. From one mode to the other, the difference in performance between groups changed by up to .25 standard deviation units, depending upon the test. For White females, the difference relative to White males was smaller on the paper versions than on the online editions. This difference changed as a function of delivery by up to .14 standard deviations, again depending on the particular test.

At the elementary and secondary school level, very few large studies have been published. The most extensive effort has probably been that undertaken through the National Assessment of Educational Progress (NAEP). The NAEP effort is particularly noteworthy for its use of nationally representative samples, hands-on tests of computer skill to estimate the impact of computer familiarity on performance, and both between- and within-groups designs that evaluate comparability from multiple perspectives. In mathematics, NAEP compared the performance of a nationally representative sample of 8th grade students taking a test on paper to a second nationally representative sample taking the same items on computer (Sandene, Bennett, Braswell, & Oranje, 2005). Both multiple-choice and constructed-response questions were included. Results showed that the computer version was significantly harder than the paper version, but only by a trivial amount (about .14 standard deviation units). The effect appeared to be greater for the constructed-response than the multiple-choice items, for students taking the test on NAEP laptop as compared to school computers, and for those students who experienced interruptions due to technical difficulties during the testing session. Within-group analyses were also conducted for the 8th grade students as well as for a nationally representative sample of 4th graders taking an online mathematics test of multiple-choice and constructed-response items. In these analyses student performance on the computer mathematics test was regressed on hands-on computer skill and self-reported computer experience, after controlling for score on a paper mathematics pretest administered as part of the study. For 4th grade level, hands-on computer skill and computer experience significantly added to the incremental prediction of online mathematics performance. Paper math score accounted for approximately 33% of the variance in online math performance. Computer experience and hands-on skill added another 11%, arguably a *non*-trivial amount. At the 8th-grade level, hands-on computer skill added significantly to prediction but self-reported computer experience did not. The increment in prediction over paper math score was from 49% to 57% of the variance.

NAEP conducted a similar study in writing, also using between- and within-groups designs (Horkay, Bennett, Allen, & Kaplan, 2005). This study found no significant difference in score between a nationally representative sample of 8th graders taking two essays on paper and a comparable sample taking the same two essays on computer. However, as in the mathematics study, the within-groups analysis showed that hands-on computer skill was associated with online writing score, after controlling for performance on a paper writing assessment. The variance accounted for in online writing score by the paper test was 36%. This percentage increased to 47% with the addition of the hands-on computer-skills measure. Other, smaller studies have also suggested that scores from productive writing tests may not be the same across delivery mode and that computer experience may interact with mode in determining performance (e.g., Russell, 1999; Russell & Haney, 1997; Russell & Plati, 2001; Wolfe, Bolton, Feltovich, & Niday, 1996).

The NAEP studies illustrate why, as the APA *Guidelines for Computer-based Tests and Interpretations* (APA, 1986) suggest, judgments of comparability should never be based solely on the analysis of mean differences across testing modes. In the NAEP studies, mean differences were trivial in math and non-significant in writing. Yet, the mix of skills measured in each mode was notably different, implying that the rank orders of individuals across modes would not be closely similar. In both studies, the online test appeared to require computer competencies that, logically speaking, the paper version should not invoke. Differences among examinees in their levels of computer skill will, hopefully, become less of a concern with time. As students do more of their academic work on computer, computers become easier to use, and designers learn to create more intuitive online tests, the impact of computer familiarity on performance may become inconsequential. But, at least at the time these studies were conducted (2001–2002), and for the grades, school subjects, and task types involved, computer familiarity did appear to be a significant source of irrelevant variance in online test scores.

11.2. Comparability of Computer Platforms

One of the attractions of Internet testing is that, in principle, any connected computer can run the test. This fact means that tests can be delivered to a wide variety of locations, including school computer labs and classrooms. The hardware and software configurations in these locations, however, will undoubtedly differ. This variation may have measurement consequences because the presentation of items may not be the same from one machine to the next.

One way in which item presentation can be affected is by the Internet connection. This connection is, in reality, not a single electronic link but a chain of connections between the test center and the testing agency (or agency vendor). In test delivery models that fetch questions from a remote server one at a time, the flow of information through this chain dictates how long an examinee will need to wait before seeing the next item. That delay will be determined by several factors. The first factor is the test center link to its Internet service provider (ISP). The quality of this connection is determined by two things: its bandwidth and the number of computers that are actively sharing it. For example, if the test center is in a school district, all of the district's classroom and administrative computers may go to the ISP through the same high-speed line, which may effectively support only a portion of those computers simultaneously. This arrangement means that response time on test center machines may be slowed if many other computers in the district are accessing the Internet during the testing session. The chain between the test center and testing agency also will be affected by conditions at the ISP itself. Individual ISPs do occasionally encounter problems and, when they do, all traffic entering or exiting the Internet through them may come to a halt. Third, the Internet has an impact. If demand is high because of time of day, or an unusual news event, response time everywhere may slow. Quality may be affected too by the testing agency's ISP and, of course, by the testing agency server itself.

Besides the Internet connection, item presentation may be influenced by other factors, including differences in screen size, screen resolution, operating system settings, and browser settings (Bridgeman, Lennon, & Jackenthal, 2001).

How does screen size impact item presentation? All other things equal, differences in screen size do *not* affect the amount of information displayed. Smaller monitors make the same information look smaller because the text displayed on such monitors is, in fact, physically littler. As a result, a question presented on a smaller monitor may be harder to read than the same question presented on a larger one. But the amount of information displayed will be the same on both screens.

What about resolution? Resolution affects the size of text *and* may affect how much information is shown. Given the same screen size and font size, text displayed at high resolution will be smaller than text displayed at a lower resolution. The higher-resolution screen is packing more pixels (picture elements) into the same physical area, so the pixels themselves will be smaller. As a result, a text character containing a fixed number of pixels will be smaller on the higher- than on the lower-resolution monitor. And because the text is smaller, there can be more of it. Higher resolution allows more words per line and lines per screen.

Figure 13.8 shows a reading comprehension item from Bridgeman et al. (2001) displayed in a high resolution (1,024 by 768). Notice that the entire passage fits on the screen and that each option takes only one line. In particular, note that the first line of the passage contains two complete sentences. Figure 13.9 depicts the same item in a much lower resolution (640 by 480). Notice that the text lines break differently—now only the first sentence fits on the opening line. Also note that the examinee must scroll to read the complete passage. Finally, the answer options each take more than one line.

The practical impact of these differences in screen resolution, then, is that lower resolutions may require examinees to spend more time locating information. Why? Because they may need to do more scrolling and make more visual sweeps to process shorter lines of text. Lower resolutions also may increase processing difficulty if critical information is split between screens, perhaps making more prominent than intended the role of short-term memory in item solution.

What about font size? What do differences in font size imply? Font size affects the size of text and the amount of information displayed. That is, smaller letters allow the display of more information. If resolution is held constant, smaller fonts permit more characters per line and lines per screen. Unfortunately, font size can be changed in multiple ways, including through operating system settings, browser settings, and Web-page coding. As a result, font size may not be identical across machines or test centers under some Internet delivery models.

Figure 13.10 shows a reading comprehension item from Bridgeman et al. (2001) displayed in a low resolution (640 by 480). The font size has been set to "small" in the Microsoft Windows control panel and "smallest" in the browser. The passage pane on the left side of the window shows one partial paragraph at the top followed by two complete paragraphs. The item stem and all five options are visible in the right-hand pane.

The same question is shown in Figure 13.11, this time displayed at the identical resolution but with the font size set to "large" in the Microsoft Windows control panel and "medium" in the browser. Now *only* the last paragraph in the passage is visible in the left pane. Also, the lines of text are shorter. Finally, only three of the five question options appear.

The effect of changing font size, then, is similar to the effect of allowing adjustments to resolution. At one extreme, the examinee may need to spend more time locating information or may have to use different cognitive processing. At the other, the text will be smaller and possibly harder to read.

What is the effect of differences in item presentation on test scores? Unfortunately, there appears to be almost no research that addresses this question directly and systematically in an assessment context.[3] Perhaps the most relevant study was conducted by Bridgeman, Lennon, and Jackenthal (2003). They looked at the effect of variations in screen size, resolution, and item-presentation latency on test performance for SAT I: Reasoning Test items. These investigators randomly assigned 357 high school juniors to a variety of item presentation conditions. Two tests were administered, one consisting of SAT I Mathematical quantitative comparisons questions and one of SAT I Verbal multiple-choice comprehension questions with their associated reading passages. Bridgeman and his colleagues found no effect on scores for

FIGURE 13.8 A Reading Comprehension Item Presented in High Resolution (1,024 by 768)

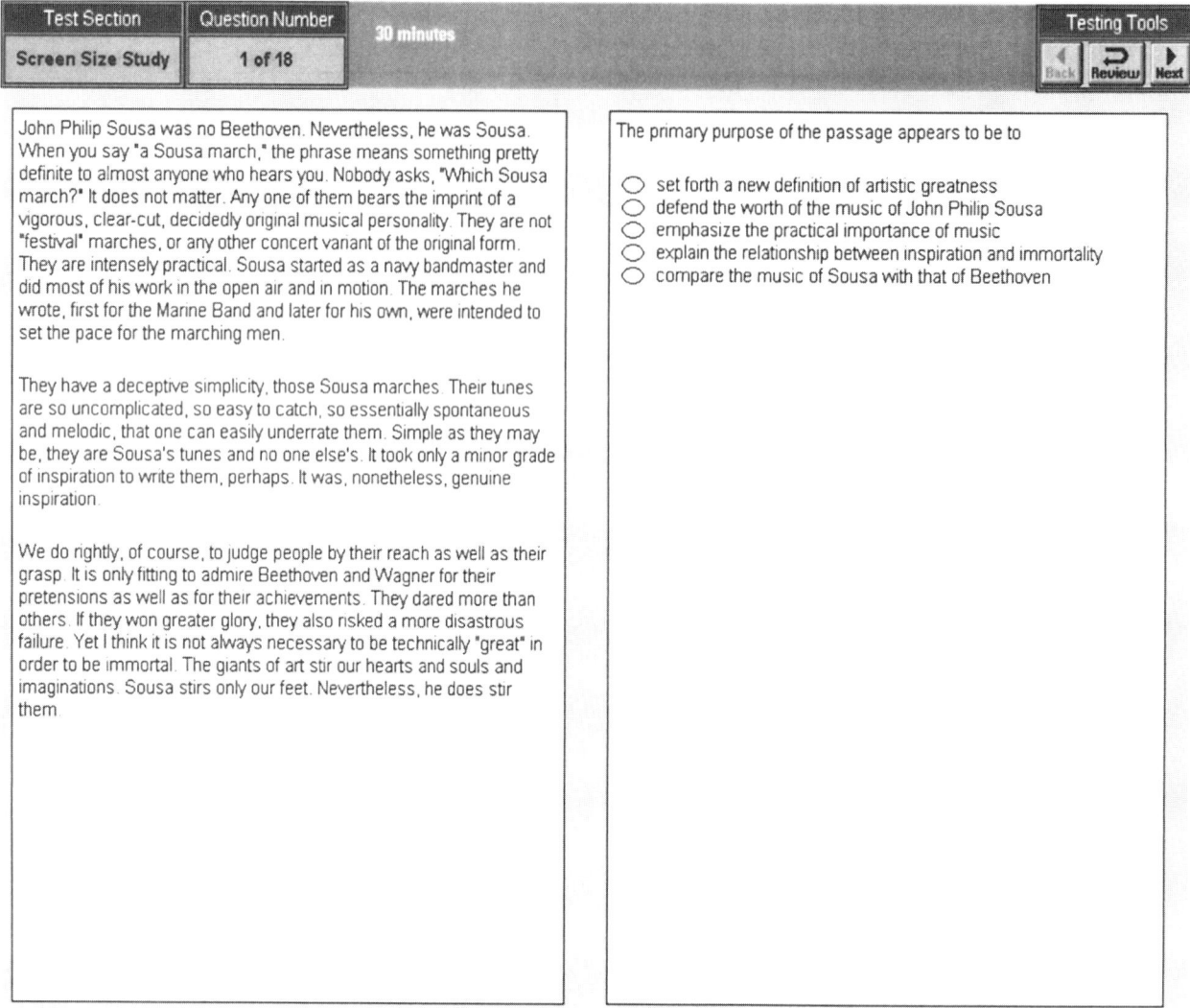

Source: From *Effects of Screen Size, Screen Resolution, and Display Rate on Computer-Based Test Performance* (RR-01-23) (p. 3) by B. Bridgeman, M. L. Lennon, & A. Jackenthal, 2001. Princeton, NJ: ETS.

the Mathematical items. Reading comprehension scores, however, were higher by about .25 standard deviations for students using a larger, higher-resolution display than for students using a smaller, lower-resolution screen. (The effects of screen size and resolution could not be separated in the analysis.) Finally, the only test feature rated as interfering by the majority of students was scrolling. Bridgeman et al. (2001) suggest that a prudent approach in Web delivery of high-stakes tests would be to attempt to have comparable scrolling across computer configurations.

Fortunately, variation in item presentation can be controlled to a substantial degree. One approach is to establish hardware and software standards to limit presentation differences. Delivery to a limited range of configurations is the approach that many high-stakes computer-based testing programs, such as the GRE General Test and GMAT, have typically taken. A second possibility is to manipulate presentation characteristics through choice of the Internet delivery model. That is, testing software can be designed to adjust font size, font type, and resolution by taking control of the examinee machine at the operating system level. This approach may not be the first choice of some test centers, however, because it typically requires installation of special software on center machines. Absent such fine control through software, a third possibility is to have proctors set display characteristics before starting the test and reset them after the examination concludes, so that other software used on those machines runs properly. A fourth possibility is to design items for the lowest common denominator—for example, for the lowest likely resolution to ensure that all answer options fit on a single screen. Finally, test delivery software can attempt to render items intelligently by automatically scaling text to wash out differences in resolution. If a machine's resolution is high, the text can be made a little bigger, so that roughly the same information ends up on the screen as in the low-resolution display.

FIGURE 13.9 A Reading Comprehension Item Presented in Low Resolution (640 by 480)

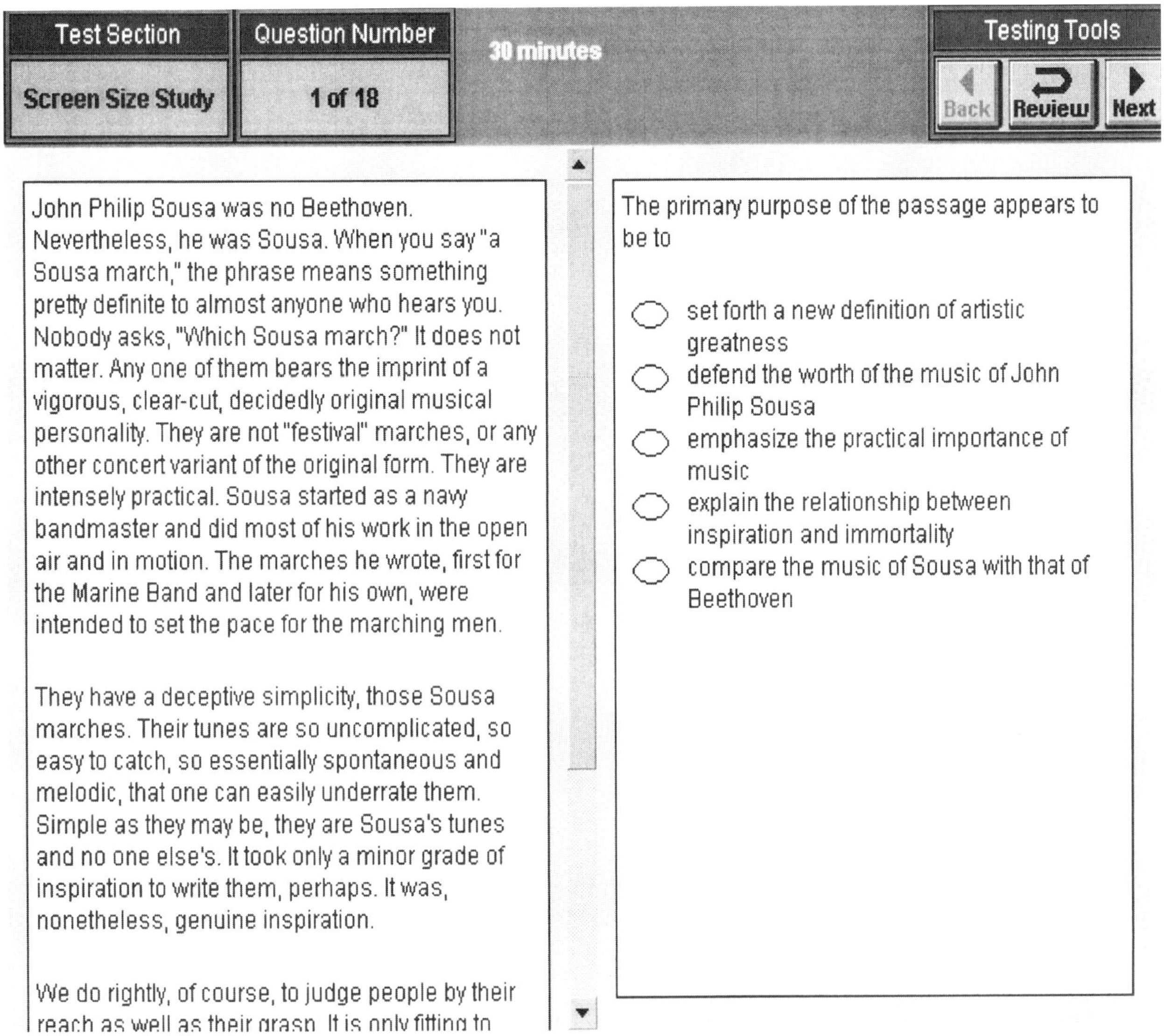

Source: From *Effects of Screen Size, Screen Resolution, and Display Rate on Computer-Based Test Performance* (RR-01-23) (p. 3) by B. Bridgeman, M. L. Lennon, & A. Jackenthal, 2001. Princeton, NJ: ETS.

12. REPORTING SCORES

After scores have been computed and saved to a database, score reports can be generated. Score reports, sometimes called "report forms," can be created with database software. Each form has common text and several fields. Results for a particular examinee are communicated by inserting the examinee's name in a field, his/her test scores and percentiles in other fields, and so forth. Modern database software allows sophisticated reports to be created, including graphical displays, so that as much—or as little—information is communicated as desired by the test developer.

Information about test performance is typically provided to two distinct groups. First, and obviously, the test takers must be informed about their scores. In high-stakes settings, test takers can gain or lose much depending on their test performance. They are understandably anxious about their scores, and it is important to provide results in a timely manner.

Sponsoring boards and various other types of policy-makers constitute a second group requiring test results. Licensing and credentialing boards closely monitor passing rates; any substantial and unexplained change is a source of great concern. State and local boards of education carefully monitor scores on achievement tests, and the National Assessment of Educational Progress (NAEP) tracks academic performance across the entire United States. Again, any change in performance is important to such groups.

12.1. Providing Results to Examinees

In some computerized testing programs, test scores are computed as soon as an examinee finishes the exam and score reports can be printed immediately. Other testing programs perform a postadministration item analysis—and may remove some poorly functioning items—and perform additional analyses to place scores on some pre-existing score

FIGURE 13.10 A Reading Comprehension Item Presented with Font Size Set to "Small" in the Microsoft Windows Control Panel and "Smallest" in the Browser (640 by 480 Resolution)

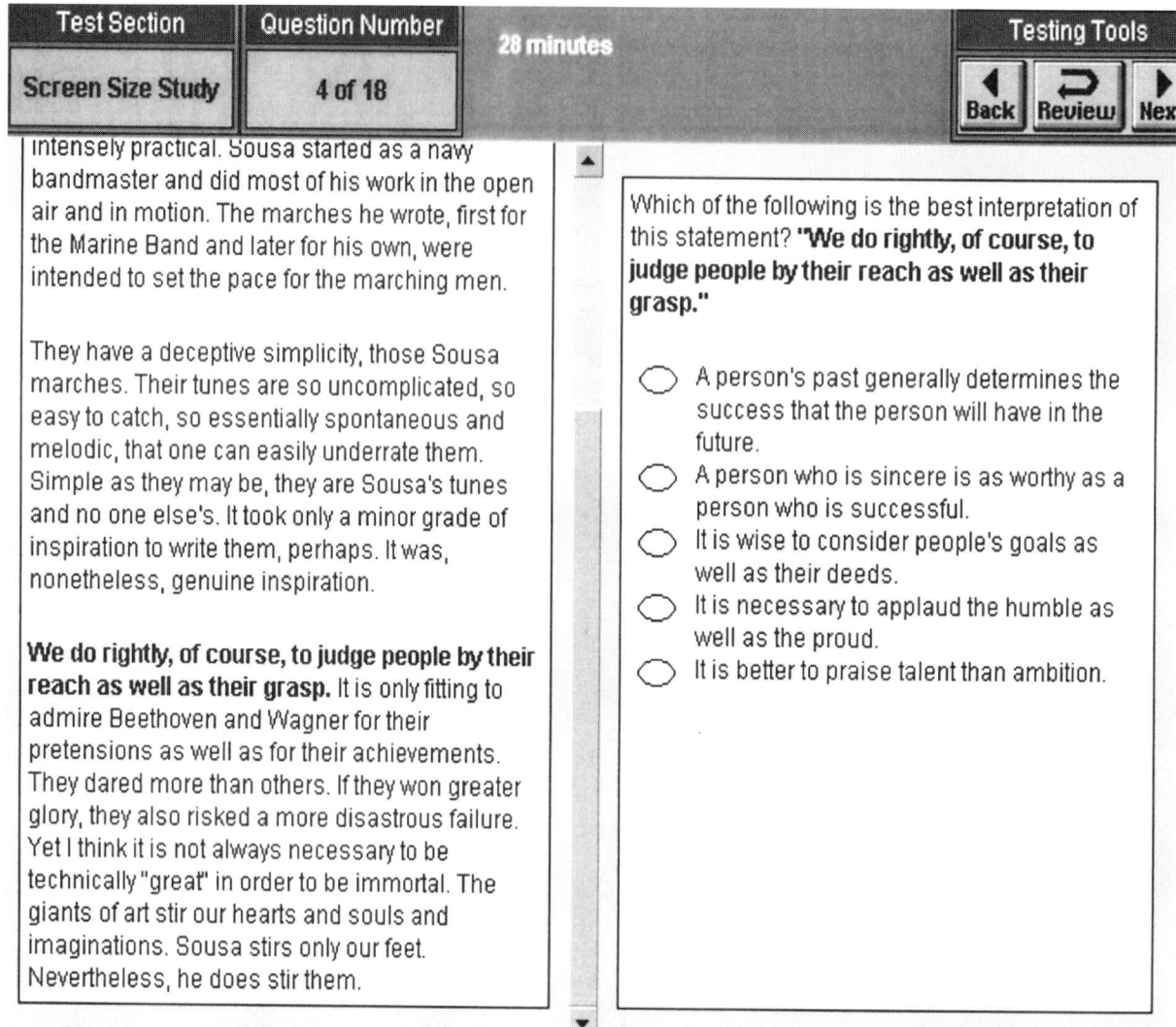

Source: From *Effects of Screen Size, Screen Resolution, and Display Rate on Computer-Based Test Performance* (RR-01-23) (p. 4) by B. Bridgeman, M. L. Lennon, & A. Jackenthal, 2001. Princeton, NJ: ETS.

scale. Thus, these analyses must be complete before final scores are available for score reports. Once the analyses have been completed and final scores entered into the system, the database system can create score reports immediately.

Authoring the score report is simply a matter of choosing what information to provide and then creating a form with text, fields for the examinee's results, and fields for any graphic displays to be generated from normative data and/or the examinee's scores. The score reports can then be printed, automatically stuffed in envelopes, and mailed. Alternatively, if examinees can select a personal identification number, the results can be made available on a Web site.

Online score reporting greatly increases the possibilities for customizing score reports. Consider, for example, a national licensing exam. The examinee might view his/her results in relation to national norms. Or, the examinee could choose an option to see his/her scores in relation to state or local norms. Same sex, opposite sex, and overall results might be requested by the examinee or results might be given for an overall group, university bound, and four-year college bound. Interpretative material could be provided that is relevant for the specific comparison group.

Although the creation of score reports is straightforward, the specific details of the material included in the reports are a matter of concern. The authors of this chapter have seen reports that they cannot understand; these reports were intended for examinees or their parents who presumably do not have graduate degrees in psychometrics. What value is a score report to a parent when it defies comprehension by a trained psychometrician?

Thus, it is very important to pretest score reports. Individuals or groups from the intended audience can be interviewed to determine what they understand, what they do not understand, and what other information they would

FIGURE 13.11 A Reading Comprehension Item Presented with Font Size Set to "Large" in the Microsoft Windows Control Panel and "Medium" in the Browser (640 by 480 Resolution)

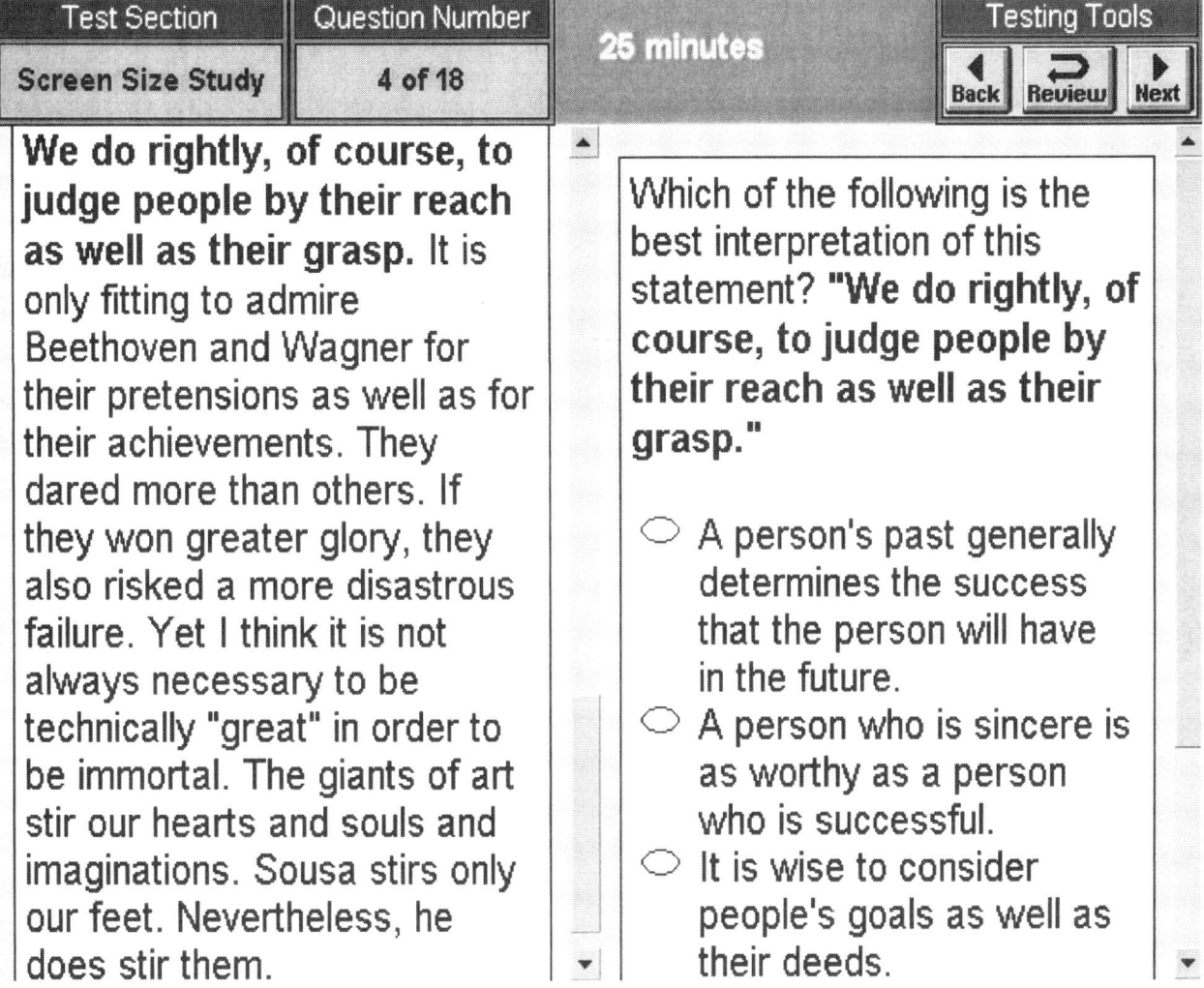

Source: From *Effects of Screen Size, Screen Resolution, and Display Rate on Computer-Based Test Performance* (RR-01-23) (p. 4) by B. Bridgeman, M. L. Lennon, & A. Jackenthal, 2001. Princeton, NJ: ETS.

like to see in the report. In sum, it is important to empirically ascertain what is comprehended rather than simply assume that the score report is meaningful to examinees.

12.2. Providing Results to Boards and Policymakers

Interestingly, Hambleton and Slater (1996; see also Hambleton, 2002) evaluated what policymakers glean from executive summaries. Hambleton and Slater asked a sample of 59 policymakers to read an actual NAEP executive summary and they conducted interviews to ascertain what was understood and how the report was interpreted. The policymakers' responses to the question, "What does statistically significant mean?" are illuminating. The responses included

"more than a couple of percentage points"

"ten percentage points"

"at least a five point increase"

"more than a handful—you have enough numbers"

"the results are important"

"I wish you hadn't asked me that. I used to know"

(Hambleton & Slater, 1996, p. 8).

Of this sample, about half had taken more than one course in statistics or testing and another quarter had taken one course.

Hambleton and Slater (1996) made several recommendations based on their findings. For example, they suggested that tables and figures should be simple and understandable without reference to accompanying text. Perhaps their most important recommendation is to always field test figures and tables on focus groups consisting of the intended audience; as the noted athlete-philosopher Yogi Berra is reputed to have said, "You can see a lot just by looking."

With the understanding that reports will be comprehensible to their audiences, interactive summaries available via the Internet provide exciting possibilities. As with the customizable score reports described above, it is possible to allow policymakers to view findings from different perspectives. Results can be presented for an overall group and by various subgroups of particular interest to the policymaker. In this way, different policymakers could explore the dataset and understand key findings that are important to them. An excellent example is the NAEP Data Tool. This Internet application allows any interested individual to analyze NAEP data within or across years. Among other things, results for groups delineated by one, or by combinations of, demographic or background questionnaire factors can be computed, tables and graphs created, significance tests conducted, and results exported to other software programs (e.g., Excel). See Lazer (2004) for more information on this application.

12.3. Improving Diagnostic Scores

One additional aspect of score reporting merits comment: Many high-stakes testing programs receive considerable pressure to report diagnostic scores so that individuals with low scores are given feedback about the specific areas in which they are weak. However, consider a licensing exam with, say 100 items that assesses seven distinct competencies. If diagnostic feedback is given in each of the seven competencies, these scores would be based on an average of just 14 items. Clearly, issues about reliability and validity are apparent when diagnostic feedback is based on such small numbers of items.

When diagnostic information is important to test takers, technology may provide a solution. Specifically, standard errors of estimate can be computed for IRT-based scores in each competency. If time permits, CAT methods could be used to draw additional items from the item pool to improve the accuracy of diagnostic scores with large standard errors. At a minimum, we urge testing programs to evaluate the precision of any diagnostic scores that they plan to report. If technology is not used to improve scores with substandard precision, care should be taken so that test takers do not misinterpret their results.

13. ADDITIONAL SYSTEMS

13.1. Research System

Testing programs as envisioned in this chapter are quite different from traditional paper-and-pencil programs. Consequently, much research is needed to compare and evaluate alternatives and determine the characteristics of these new approaches. For example, this chapter has described a variety of test delivery models. Further research is needed on how practical testing problems—writing and pretesting items, maintaining test security, minimizing scale drift, and so forth—affect the usefulness of each model.

One of the greatest opportunities for research lies in using the capabilities of personal computers to create innovative assessments. Traditional paper-and-pencil tests are static and presented via a single—and highly limited—medium. Computerized assessments, on the other hand, can be dynamic and incorporate color, sound, and motion. Clearly, there is considerable opportunity to create new types of assessments.

Parshall, Davey, and Pashley (2000) described five dimensions of innovation for computerized tests. First, *item format* refers to the type of response made by the examinee. In contrast to the traditional selected response format (e.g., the multiple-choice item), researchers can use constructed-response formats to provide improved measurement. Bennett, Morley, and Quardt (2000) investigated a new item format—mathematical expressions—where examinees are asked to write an equation to solve a problem. An example item is, "If M is the mean of 4, 13, and X, what is the value of X in terms of M?" The examinee would then enter an equation such as $X = 3M - (4+13)$ or $X = 3M - 17$. Computerized scoring of open-ended responses is, of course, a considerable challenge; Bennett et al. used symbolic computation principles to devise a highly accurate scoring engine.

Response action, the second dimension of innovation described by Parshall et al. (2000), describes what the examinee must do physically to answer an item. Examples include clicking on a button with a mouse, dragging and dropping, and speaking into a microphone. A wide variety of item formats and response actions is described by Zenisky and Sireci (2002).

A third dimension of innovation is *media inclusion*. Multimedia computers allow test developers to utilize sound, animation, high-resolution color images, and video clips. Examples include:

a. Ackerman, Evans, Park, Tamassia, and Turner's (1999) test of dermatological skin disorders that allows examinees to pan in and out to view color photographs of skin disorders;
b. Vispoel's (1999) test of musical aptitude that adaptively presents short melodies; and
c. Olson-Buchanan et al.'s (1998) assessment of conflict resolution skills that presents video clips of workplace situations with various types of interpersonal disputes.

Parshall et al.'s (2000) fourth aspect of innovation is interactivity, which is defined as the extent to which the computer interacts with the examinee. Computerized adaptive tests provide the most widely studied example (e.g., Sands et al., 1997). Another example is provided by the National Board of Medical Examiners' (NBME) case simulation (Clyman, Melnick, & Clauser, 1999). Here a candidate physician is presented with a brief description on a patient's presenting symptoms. The candidate physician can request a medical history, order laboratory tests, conduct a physical exam, or provide a treatment. The simulated patient's medical status progresses as would a real patient, and realistically responds to appropriate and inappropriate treatments.

The final dimension of innovation described by Parshall et al. (2000) is the scoring algorithm. Extensive research has shown that IRT scoring is appropriate for CATs where the test deliberately administers easier items to some examinees and harder items to others. More challenging is computerized scoring of essays. Powers et al. (2002b) described an interesting evaluation of one approach to scoring essays (*e-rater*) where people from a variety of disciplines were invited to submit essays that could deceive *e-rater* and consequently receive spuriously high or low scores. The clear winner was a professor of computational linguistics who wrote a few paragraphs and then repeated them 37 times; *e-rater* gave this essay the highest score possible whereas human graders gave it the lowest possible score. Nonetheless, grades given by *e-rater* were in generally good agreement with human graders even though all essays were designed to trick its scoring algorithm.

In sum, there are many opportunities for research on computerized assessment systems. For example, what are the psychometric properties of innovative items? Interestingly, Jodoin (2003) found innovative items provided more information about ability than multiple-choice items, but multiple-choice items provided more information per unit of time. Do new item types improve the substantive richness of the constructs assessed or assess heretofore unmeasured skills and abilities? Do they provide improved measurement of achievement and competence? Do they enhance prediction of future performance? And do the people being tested believe that the new tests are fair and effective (Tonidandel, Quinones, & Adams, 2002)? These and other questions provide fertile grounds for new research.

13.2. Quality Control System

As described here, a modern testing program is a system of systems. Not only must each system function correctly, but it also must interface appropriately with several other systems. Ensuring the integrity of the system is difficult but critical.

Consider a nationally administered licensing exam working in concert with state boards of licensing. To schedule an exam, a candidate's eligibility must first be ascertained by his or her state board. Following a determination of eligibility, a candidate can schedule a time from among those when the exam is being administered; a computer must be available with the functionality needed for the licensing exam. During the test administration, the computer must deliver the intended set of items and score responses with the correct answer key. All pertinent information about the test administration must be uploaded to the testing agency for postadministration analyses. Finally, score reports must be sent to the state boards and/or the candidates. Note that it is very important for the score report for a particular examinee to be based on his/her responses and not result from some "computer glitch."

It is the responsibility of the quality control system to verify the accuracy of the testing process. This system is actually a metasystem because it envelops all the other systems. Obviously, all of the individual systems described above must work correctly and they must work together. Moreover, system integrity must be maintained in the face of problems with the computer administering the exam, the local area network at the testing site, the system for uploading examinee records to the testing agency, and the server at the testing agency. Consequently, extensive testing of the system is necessary, under both normal operating conditions as well as when some part fails.

14. CONCLUSIONS AND DISCUSSION

As described in this chapter, technology can enhance measurement in many ways. Traditional tests and item types can be made more efficient by tailoring the test to each examinee as in CAT and ca-MST. By individualizing the test, it is possible to offer continuous testing yet maintain test security. Construct-based design principles can facilitate the efficient production of large numbers of items. New types of items and tests can improve the measurement of skills and abilities traditionally assessed via multiple-choice items and allow us to measure other individual differences heretofore poorly assessed.

Many challenges must be confronted by measurement specialists. For the approach advocated here to become widely implemented, costs must be reduced. Licensing boards that charge hundreds of dollars to a hundred-thousand candidates per year have the resources to implement very sophisticated testing programs. However, many boards and private sector organizations test far fewer individuals and consequently have budgets that are much smaller. A valuable contribution to the measurement community would be a scalable software system with the diverse functionality described here sold at a price that small testing programs can afford.

Examinees find new assessments interesting (Richman, Olson-Buchanan, & Drasgow, 2000). But do they truly add to assessment? A subtest consisting entirely of the new format should show divergent validity: The disattenuated correlation of such a new measure with the old test should be substantially less than 1.0. Bennett et al. (1999) provided such an evaluation for a new type of quantitative item and found a disattenuated correlation of .77, which adds considerably to the construct validity of the new item type. Similarly, Clyman et al. (1999) reported moderate disattenuated correlations between the NBME computerized case simulations measure and multiple-choice tests of medical knowledge.

Bennett et al. (1999) and Clyman et al. (1999) present important information about their new measures. However, this type of research needs to become the norm, not the exception, in the development of new item formats and tests.

The decades ahead promise many new and creative advances in testing made possible by technology. Many of the topics discussed here—construction of items, the test driver, postadministration analysis—are the focus of intense research efforts. Certainly, they will evolve to become, simultaneously, less costly but more sophisticated. Thus, we can look forward to improved assessment of a wide range of critical skills and abilities.

What specific technology trends might aid this improved assessment? One emerging trend is inexpensive, wireless devices like personal digital assistants (PDAs), that make possible traditional large-scale delivery to big groups, as well as delivery to individuals on demand. A second trend is toward more sophisticated test delivery technologies that allow the use of performance tasks, like simulation, as well as more efficient ways to build and re-purpose such tasks. Third is the development of more powerful automated scoring technologies that permit the use of open-ended assessments without the same, high backend processing expense such assessments now incur. Finally, is the creation of more informative reporting technologies, like the NAEP Data Tool, that permit test users to ask their own questions of the data.

These technological developments are being accompanied by advances in cognitive and measurement science. Cognitive science is producing a better understanding of what it means to be proficient in a domain and how domain proficiency develops. Similarly, we are seeing from psychometrics the creation of measurement models capable of reflecting this more complex understanding of proficiency (Mislevy, this volume). Finally, and perhaps most important, we are witnessing the emergence of a science of assessment design (Mislevy, this volume), that will allow us to combine advances in technology, cognitive science, and measurement to create assessments that serve the needs of test takers and institutions more effectively and efficiently.

Perhaps, in the future, the science of assessment design will, itself, become a blend of principles derived from technology (software and systems engineering), cognitive science, and modern psychometrics. At least we would hope that such a blend of those fields is considered.

NOTES

1. Kevin Singley should be credited with introducing us to the distinction between strong and weak theory in item generation.

2. In practice, the IRT item information function is maximized at the provisional estimate of proficiency.

3. There is an extensive literature on the design characteristics that affect a computer user's ability to interact with software, including the characteristics that influence reading speed and comprehension. However, connecting this literature to computer-based tests is not straightforward (M. Lennon, personal communication, July 16, 2005). Among other things, the display technology has improved dramatically since many of these studies were conducted and some findings may no longer hold. Second, the reading tasks used in these studies were generally unlike the items employed in achievement and ability tests (Bridgeman, Lennon, & Jackenthal, 2001).

REFERENCES

Ackerman, T. A., Evans, J., Park, K. S., Tamassia, C., & Turner, R. (1999). Computer assessment using visual stimuli: A test of dermatological skin disorders. In F. Drasgow & J. B. Olson-Buchanan (Eds.), *Innovations in computerized assessment* (pp. 137–150). Mahwah, NJ: Erlbaum.

Adema, J. J. (1990). The construction of customized two-stage tests. *Journal of Educational Measurement, 27,* 241–253.

American Educational Research Association, American Psychological Association, & National Council on Measurement in Education. (1999). *Standards for educational and psychological testing.* Washington, DC: Author.

American Psychological Association. (1986). *Guidelines for computer-based tests and interpretations.* Washington, DC: Author.

Armstrong, R. D., Jones, D. H., & Kunce, C. S. (1998). IRT test assembly using network-flow programming. *Applied Psychological Measurement, 22,* 237–247.

Armstrong, R. D., Jones, D. H., Li, X., & Wu, I.-L. (1996). A study of a network-flow algorithm and a non-correcting algorithm for test assembly. *Applied Psychological Measurement, 20,* 89–98.

Armstrong, R. D., & Little, J. (2003, April). *The assembly of multiple form structures.* Paper presented at the annual meeting of the National Council on Measurement in Education.

Assessment Systems Corporation. (1999). *FastTest™ Professional,* Version 1.6 [Computer Program]. St. Paul, MN: Author.

Bejar, I. I. (1990). A generative analysis of a three-dimensional spatial task. *Applied Psychological Measurement, 14,* 237–245.

Bejar, I. I. (1991). A methodology for scoring open-ended architectural design problems. *Journal of Applied Psychology, 76,* 522–532.

Bejar, I. I. (1993). A generative approach to psychological and educational measurement. In N. Frederiksen, R. J. Mislevy, & I. I. Bejar (Eds.), *Test theory for a new generation of tests* (pp. 323–359). Hillsdale, NJ: Lawrence Erlbaum.

Bejar, I. I. (1995). From adaptive testing to automated scoring of architectural simulations. In E. L. Mancall & P. G. Bashook (Ed.), *Assessing clinical reasoning: The oral examination and alternative methods* (pp. 115–130). Evanston, IL: American Board of Medical Specialties.

Bejar, I. I., & Braun, H. I. (1999). *Architectural simulations: From research to implementation* (Research Memorandum 99–2). Princeton, NJ: Educational Testing Service.

Bejar, I. I., Lawless, R. R., Morley, M. E., Wagner, M. E., Bennett, R. E., & Revuelta, J. (2003). A feasibility study of on-the-fly item generation in adaptive testing. *Journal of Technology, Learning and Assessment, 2*(3). Retrieved July 13, 2003, from http://www.bc.edu/research/intasc/jtla/journal/v2n3.shtml

Bennett, R. E. (2006). Moving the field forward: Some thoughts on validity and automated scoring. In D. M. Williamson, R. J. Mislevy, & I. I. Bejar (Eds.), *Automated scoring of complex tasks in computer-based testing* (pp. 403–412). Hillsdale, NJ: Erlbaum.

Bennett, R. E., & Bejar, I. I. (1998). Validity and automated scoring: It's not only the scoring. *Educational Measurement: Issues and Practice, 17,* 9–17.

Bennett, R. E., Gong, B., Kershaw, R. C., Rock, D. A., Soloway, E., & Macalalad, A. (1990). Assessment of an expert system's ability to grade and diagnose automatically student's constructed responses to computer science problems. In R. O. Freedle (Ed.), *Artificial intelligence and the future of testing* (pp. 293–320). Hillsdale, NJ: Erlbaum.

Bennett, R. E., Morley, M., & Quardt, D. (2000). Three response types for broadening the conception of mathematical problem solving in computerized tests. *Applied Psychological Measurement, 24,* 294–309.

Bennett, R. E., Morley, M., Quardt, D., & Rock, D. A. (2000). Graphical modeling: A new response type for measuring the qualitative component of mathematical reasoning. *Applied Measurement in Education, 13,* 301–320.

Bennett, R. E., Morley, M., Quardt, D., Rock, D. A., Singley, M. K., Katz, I. R., et al. (1999). Psychometric and cognitive functioning of an under-determined computer-based response type for quantitative reasoning. *Journal of Educational Measurement, 36,* 233–252.

Bennett, R. E., Rock, D. A., Braun, H. I., Frye, D., Spohrer, J. C., & Soloway, E. (1990). The relationship of expert-system scored constrained free-response items to multiple-choice and open-ended items. *Applied Psychological Measurement, 14,* 151–162.

Bennett, R. E., & Sebrechts, M. M. (1996). The accuracy of expert-system diagnoses of mathematical problem solutions. *Applied Measurement in Education, 9,* 133–150.

Bennett, R. E., & Sebrechts, M. M. (1997). Measuring the representational component of quantitative proficiency. *Journal of Educational Measurement, 34,* 62–75.

Bennett, R. E., Sebrechts, M. M., & Rock, D. A. (1991). Expert-system scores for complex constructed-response quantitative items: A study of convergent validity. *Applied Psychological Measurement, 15,* 227–239.

Bennett, R. E., Steffen, M., Singley, M. K., Morley, M., & Jacquemin, D. (1997). Evaluating an automatically scorable, open-ended response type for measuring mathematical reasoning in computer-adaptive tests. *Journal of Educational Measurement, 34,* 163–177.

Braun, H. I., Bennett, R. E., Frye, D., & Soloway, E. (1990). Scoring constructed responses using expert systems. *Journal of Educational Measurement, 27,* 93–108.

Bridgeman, B., Lennon, M. L., & Jackenthal, A. (2001). *Effects of screen size, screen resolution, and display rate on computer-based test performance* (ETS RR-01–23). Princeton, NJ: ETS.

Bridgeman, B., Lennon, M. L., & Jackenthal, A. (2003). Effects of screen size, screen resolution, and display rate on computer-based test performance. *Applied Measurement in Education, 16,* 191–205.

Burstein, J. (2003). The e-rater® scoring engine: Automated essay scoring with natural language processing. In M. D. Shermis & J. C. Burstein (Eds.), *Automated essay scoring: A cross-disciplinary perspective* (pp. 113–121). Mahwah, NJ: Erlbaum.

Burton, R. R. (1982). Diagnosing bugs in a simple procedural skill. In D. Sleeman & J. Brown (Eds.), *Intelligent tutoring systems* (pp. 157–183). New York: Academic Press.

Carpenter, P. A., Just, M. A., & Shell, P. (1990). What one intelligence test measures: A theoretical account of processing the Raven's Progressive Matrices Test. *Psychological Review, 97,* 404–431.

Chan, K.-Y., Drasgow, F., & Sawin, L. L. (1999). What is the shelf life of a test? The effect of time on the psychometrics of a cognitive ability test battery over 16 years. *Journal of Applied Psychology, 84,* 610–619.

Chang, H. H., Qian, J., & Ying, Z. (2001). *a*-stratified multistage computerized adaptive testing item *b*-blocking. *Applied Psychological Measurement, 25,* 333–342.

Chang, H. H., & van der Linden, W. J. (2000, April). *A zero-one programming model for optimal stratification of item pools in a-stratified computerized adaptive testing.* Paper presented at the annual meeting of the National Council on Measurement in Education, New Orleans, LA.

Chang, H. H., & Ying, Z. (1997, June). *Multistage CAT with stratification designs.* Paper presented at the annual meeting of the Psychometric Society, Gatlinburg, TN.

Chang, H. H., & Ying, Z. (1999). A-stratified multi-stage computerized adaptive testing. *Applied Psychological Measurement, 23,* 211–222.

Chi, M. T., Feltovich, P. J., & Glaser, R. (1981). Categorization and representation of physics problems by experts and novices. *Cognitive Science, 5,* 121–152.

Chuah, S. C., Drasgow, F., & Luecht, R. (2006). How big is big enough? Sample size requirements for CAST item parameter estimation. *Applied Measurement in Education, 19,* 241–255.

Clauser, B. E., Subhiyah, R. G., Nungenster, R. J., Ripkey, D. R., Clyman, D. R., & McKinley, D. (1995). Scoring a performance-based assessment by modelling the judgement process of experts. *Journal of Educational Measurement, 32,* 397–415.

Clyman, S. G., Melnick, D. E., & Clauser, B. E. (1995). Computer-based case simulations. In E. L. Mancall & P. G. Bashook (Ed.), *Assessing clinical reasoning: The oral examination and alternative methods* (pp. 139–149). Evanston, IL: American Board of Medical Specialties.

Clyman, S. G., Melnick, D. E., & Clauser, B. E. (1999). Computer-based case simulations from medicine: Assessing skills in patient management. In A. Tekian, C. H. McGuire, & W. C. McGahie (Eds.), *Innovative simulations for assessing professional competence* (pp. 29–41). Chicago: University of Illinois, Department of Medical Education.

College Board. (1993). *ACCUPLACER: Computerized placement tests: Technical data supplement.* New York: Author.

Davey, T., & Parshall, C. G. (1995, April). *New algorithms for the item selection and exposure control with computerized adaptive testing.* Paper presented at the annual meeting of the American Educational Research Association, San Francisco, CA.

Do, B.-R., Chuah, S. C., & Drasgow, F. (2005). *Effects of range restriction on item parameter recovery with multistage adaptive tests.* Manuscript submitted for publication.

Do, B.-R., Shepherd, W. J., & Drasgow, F. (under review). *Measurement equivalence across proctored and unproctored administration modes of web-based measures.* Manuscript submitted for publication.

Eignor, D. R., Stocking, M. L., Way, W. D., & Steffen, M. (1993). *Case studies in computer adaptive test design through simulation* (RR-93-56). Princeton, NJ: Educational Testing Service.

Embretson, S. E. (1983). Construct validity: Construct representation versus nomothetic span. *Psychological Bulletin, 93,* 179–197.

Embretson, S. E. (1998). A cognitive design system approach to generating valid tests: Application to abstract reasoning. *Psychological Methods, 3,* 380–396.

Embretson, S. E. (1999). Generating items during testing: Psychometric issues and models. *Psychometrika, 64,* 407–433.

Enright, M. K., Rock, D. A., & Bennett, R. E. (1999). Improving measurement for graduate admissions. *Journal of Educational Measurement, 35,* 250–267.

ETS (1993). *The results of the NAEP 1993 field test for the 1994 National Assessment of Educational Progress.* Princeton, NJ: Author.

Folk, V. G., & Smith, R. L. (2002). Models for delivery of CBTs. In C. Mills, M. Potenza, J. Fremer, & W. Ward (Eds.), *Computer-based testing: Building the foundation for future assessments* (pp. 41–66). Mahwah, NJ: Erlbaum.

Gallagher, A., Bridgeman, B., & Cahalan, C. (2000). *The effect of computer-based tests on racial/ethnic, gender, and language groups* (GRE Professional Board Report 96–21P, ETS RR-00–08). Princeton, NJ: ETS. Retrieved August 5, 2003, from ftp://ftp.ets.org/pub/gre/gre_96–21p.pdf

Gibson, W. M., & Weiner, J. A. (1998). Generating random parallel test forms using CTT in a computer-based environment. *Journal of Educational Measurement, 35,* 297–310.

Glas, C. A. W., & van der Linden, W. J. (2001). *Modeling variability in item parameters in educational measurement* (OMD-Report 01–11). Newtown, PA: Law School Admission Council.

Glaser, R. (1991). Expertise and assessment. In M. C. Wittrock & E. L. Baker (Eds.), *Testing and cognition* (pp. 17–30). Englewood Cliffs, NJ: Prentice-Hall.

Goh, D. S. (2004). *Assessment accommodations for diverse learners.* Boston: Pearson.

Hadadi, A., & Luecht, R. M. (1998). Some methods for detecting and understanding test speededness on timed multiple-choice tests. *Academic Medicine, 73,* S47–50.

Hadadi, A., Luecht, R. M., Swanson, D. B., & Case, S. M. (1998, April). *Study 1: Effects of modular subtest structure and item review on examinee performance, perceptions and pacing.* Paper presented at the annual meeting of the National Council on Measurement in Education, San Diego, CA.

Hambleton, R. K. (2002). How can we make NAEP and state test score reporting scales and reports more understandable? In R. W. Lissitz & W. D. Schafer (Eds.), *Assessment in educational reform* (pp. 192–205). Boston: Allyn & Bacon.

Hambleton, R. K., & Slater, S. C. (1996, April). *Are NAEP Executive Summary reports understandable to policy makers and educators?* Paper presented at the annual meeting of the National Council on Measurement in Education, New York.

Hambleton, R. K., & Xing, D. (2002). *Comparative analysis of optimal and non-optimal computer-based test designs for making pass-fail decisions* (Center for Educational Assessment Research Report No. 457). Amherst, MA: University of Massachusetts, School of Education.

Harrington, S., Shermis, M. D., & Rollins, A. L. (2000). The influence of word processing on English placement test results. *Computers and Composition, 17*(2), 197–210.

Herl, H. E., O'Neil, H. F., Chung, G. K. W. K., & Schacter, J. (1999). Reliability and validity of a computer-based knowledge mapping system to measure content understanding. *Computers in Human Behavior, 15*, 315–333.

Hetter, R. D., & Sympson, J. B., (1997). Item exposure control in CAT-ASVAB. In W. A. Sands, B. K. Waters, & J. R. McBride (Eds.), *Computerized adaptive testing: From inquiry to operation* (pp. 141–144). Washington, DC: American Psychological Association.

Hively, W., Patterson, H. L., & Page, S. (1968). A "universe-defined" system of arithmetic achievement tests. *Journal of Educational Measurement, 5*, 275–290.

Holland, P. W., & Thayer, D. T. (1988). Differential item performance and the Mantel-Haenszel procedure. In H. Wainer & H. Braun (Eds.), *Test validity* (pp. 129–145). Hillsdale, NJ: Erlbaum.

Horkay, N., Bennett, R. E., Allen, N., & Kaplan, B. (2005). Online assessment in writing. In B. Sandene, N. Horkay, R. E. Bennett, N. Allen, J. Braswell, B. Kaplan, et al. (Eds.), *Online assessment in mathematics and writing: Reports from the NAEP Technology-Based Assessment Project* (NCES 2005-457) (pp. i–79). Washington, DC: National Center for Education Statistics, U.S. Department of Education.

Hulin, C. L., Drasgow, F., & Parsons, C. K. (1983). *Item response theory: Application to psychological measurement.* Homewood, IL: Dow Jones-Irwin.

Irvine, S., & Kyllonen, P. (Eds.). (2002). *Item generation for test development.* Hillsdale, NJ: Erlbaum.

Jodoin, M. G. (2003). Measurement efficiency of innovative item formats in computer-based testing. *Journal of Educational Measurement, 40*, 1–15.

Jodoin, M., Zenisky, A., & Hambleton, R. K. (2002, April). *Comparison of the psychometric properties of several computer-based test designs for credentialing exams.* Paper presented at the annual meeting of the National Council on Measurement in Education, New Orleans, LA.

Kenney, J. F. (1997). New testing methodologies for the Architect Registration Examination. *CLEAR Exam Review, 8*, 23–28.

Kim, S.-H., Cohen, A. S., & Park, T.-H. (1995). Detection of differential item functioning in multiple groups. *Journal of Educational Measurement, 32*, 261–276.

Kingsbury, G. G., & Zara, A. R. (1989). Procedures for selecting items for computerized adaptive tests. *Applied Measurement in Education, 2*, 359–375.

Kingsbury, G. G., & Zara, A. R. (1991). A comparison of procedures content-sensitive item selection in computerized adaptive tests. *Applied Measurement in Education, 3*, 241–261.

Kolen, M. J., & Brennan, R. L. (2004). *Test equating, scaling, and linking: Methods and practices* (2nd ed.). New York: Springer.

Landauer, T. K., Laham, D., & Foltz, P. W. (2000). The Intelligent Essay Assessor. *IEEE Intelligent Systems, 15*, 27–31.

Lazer, S. L. (2004). Innovations in instrumentation and dissemination. In L. V. Jones & I. Olkin (Eds.), *The nation's report card: Evolution and perspectives* (pp. 469–487). Bloomington, IN: Phi Delta Kappa Educational Foundation.

Lewis, C. (1985, June). *Estimating individual abilities with imperfectly known item response functions.* Paper presented at the annual meeting of the Psychometric Society, Nashville, TN.

Lewis, C., & Sheehan, K. (1990). Using Bayesian decision theory to design a computer mastery test. *Applied Psychological Measurement, 14*, 367–386.

Lord, F. M. (1977). A broad-range tailored test of verbal ability. *Applied Psychological Measurement, 1*, 95–100.

Lord, F. M. (1980). *Applications of item response theory to practical testing problems.* Hillsdale, NJ: Erlbaum.

Luecht, R. M. (1995). *Some alternative CAT item selection heuristics* (NBME Technical Report RES95031). Philadelphia: National Board of Medical Examiners.

Luecht, R. M. (1996). Multidimensional computerized adaptive testing in a certification or licensure context. *Applied Psychological Measurement, 20*, 389–404.

Luecht, R. M. (1998a, April). *A framework for exploring and controlling risks associated with test item exposure over time.* Paper presented at the annual meeting of the National Council on Measurement in Education, San Diego, CA.

Luecht, R. M. (1998b). Computer assisted test assembly using optimization heuristics. *Applied Psychological Measurement, 22*, 224–236.

Luecht, R. M. (2000, April). *Implementing the computer-adaptive sequential testing (CAST) framework to mass produce high quality computer-adaptive and mastery tests.* Paper presented at the annual meeting of the National Council on Measurement in Education, New Orleans, LA.

Luecht, R. M. (2002, February). *An automated test assembly heuristic for multistage adaptive tests with complex computer-based performance tasks.* Invited paper presented at the annual meeting of the Association of Test Publishers, Carlsbad, CA.

Luecht, R. M. (2005a). Computer-based testing. In *Encyclopedia of social measurement* (Vol. 1, pp. 419–427). San Diego, CA: Academic Press.

Luecht, R. M. (2005b). Item analysis. In B. Everitt & D. Howell (Eds.), *Encyclopedia of statistics in behavioral science.* West Sussex, UK: John Wiley & Sons.

Luecht, R. M. (2006). Operational issues in computer-based testing. In D. Bartrum & R. Hambleton (Eds.), *Computer-based testing and the Internet* (pp. 91–114). West Sussex, UK: John Wiley & Sons.

Luecht, R. M., Brumfield, T., & Breithaupt, K. (2002, April). *A testlet assembly design for the uniform CPA examination.* Paper presented at the annual meeting of the National Council on Measurement in Education, New Orleans, LA.

Luecht, R. M., & Burgin, W. (2003, April). *Test information targeting strategies for adaptive multistage testing designs.* Paper presented at the annual meeting of the National Council on Measurement in Education, Chicago.

Luecht, R. M., & Hirsch, T. R. (1992). Item selection using an average growth approximation of target information functions. *Applied Psychological Measurement, 16*, 41–51.

Luecht, R. M., & Nungester, R. J. (1998). Some practical examples of computer-adaptive sequential testing. *Journal of Educational Measurement, 35*, 229–249.

Luecht, R. M., & Nungester, R. J. (2000). Computer-adaptive sequential testing. In W. J. van der Linden & C. A. W. Glas (Eds.), *Computerized adaptive testing: Theory and practice* (pp. 117–128). Dordrecht, Netherlands: Kluwer Academic.

Luecht, R. M., Nungester, R. J., & Hadadi, A. (1996, April). *Heuristic-based CAT: Balancing item information, content and exposure*. Paper presented at the annual meeting of the National Council of Measurement in Education, New York.

MacCann, R., Eastment, B., & Pickering, S. (2002). Responding to free response examination questions: Computer versus pen and paper. *British Journal of Educational Technology, 33*(2), 173–188.

Macready, G. B. (1983). The use of generalizability theory for assessing relations among items within domains in diagnostic testing. *Applied Psychological Measurement, 7,* 149–157.

Macready, G. B., & Merwin, J. C. (1973). Homogeneity within forms in domain referenced testing. *Educational and Psychological Measurement, 33,* 351–360.

McGraw-Hill acquisition to complement Sacramento. (2001, November 30). *Sacramento Business Journal.* Retreived December 17, 2003, from http://sanjose.bizjournals.com/sacramento/stories/2001/11/26/daily39.html

Mead, A. D., & Drasgow, F. (1993). Equivalence of computerized and paper-and-pencil cognitive ability tests: A meta-analysis. *Psychological Bulletin, 114,* 449–458.

Messick, S. (1989). Validity. In R. L. Linn (Ed.), *Educational measurement* (3rd ed., pp. 13–103). New York: Macmillan.

Mills, C. (2004, February). *That costs how much?* Paper presented at the annual meeting of the Association of Test Publishers, Palm Springs, CA.

Mills, C. N., & Stocking, M. L. (1996). Practical issues in large-scale computerized adaptive testing. *Applied Measurement in Education, 9,* 287–304.

Mislevy, R. J., Almond, R. G., & Lukas, J. F. (2003). *A brief introduction to evidence-centered design* (RR-03–16). Princeton, NJ: Educational Testing Service.

Mislevy, R. J., Almond, R. G., & Steinberg, L. (2003). *A four-process architecture for assessment delivery, with connections to assessment design* (CSE Report 616). Retrieved January 13, 2004, from http://cresst.org/products/reports_set.htm

Mislevy, R. J., & Bock, R. D. (1990). *BILOG 3: Item analysis and test scoring with binary logistic models* [Computer software]. Mooresville, IN: Scientific Software.

Mislevy, R. J., Wingersky, M. S., & Sheehan, K. M. (1994). *Dealing with uncertainty about item parameters: Expected response functions* (RR-94–28–ONR). Princeton, NJ: Educational Testing Service.

Morley, M. E., Bridgeman, B., & Lawless, R. R. (2004). *Transfer between variants of quantitative items* (RR-04-36). Princeton, NJ: Educational Testing Service.

Nunnally, J. C. (1978). *Psychometric theory* (2nd ed.). New York: McGraw-Hill.

Odendahl, N. (1999, April). *Online delivery and scoring of constructed-response assessments*. Paper presented at the annual meeting of the American Educational Research Association, Montreal, Quebec, Canada.

Olson-Buchanan, J. B., Drasgow, F., Moberg, P. J., Mead, A. D., Keenan, P. A., & Donovan, M. A. (1998). Interactive video assessment of conflict resolution skills. *Personnel Psychology, 51,* 1–24.

Page, E. B. (2003). Project Essay Grade (PEG). In M. D. Shermis & J. C. Burstein (Eds.), *Automated essay scoring: A cross-disciplinary perspective* (pp. 43–54). Mahwah, NJ: Erlbaum.

Parshall, C. G., Davey, T., & Pashley, P. J. (2000). Innovative item type for computerized testing. In W. J. van der Linden & C. A. W. Glas (Eds.), *Computerized adaptive testing: Theory and practice* (pp. 129–148). Norwell, MA: Kluwer.

Parshall, C. G., Spray, J. A., Kalohn, J. C., & Davey, T. (2002). *Practical considerations in computerized-based testing.* New York: Springer-Verlag.

Patsula, L. N., & Hambleton, R. K. (1999, April). *A comparative study of ability estimates obtained from computer-adaptive and multi-stage testing.* Paper presented at the annual meeting of the National Council on Measurement in Education, Montreal, Quebec, Canada.

Pommerich, M., & Burden, T. (2000, April). *From simulation to application: Examinees react to computerized testing.* Paper presented at the annual meeting of the National Council on Measurement in Education, New Orleans, LA.

Powers, D. E., Burstein, J. C., Chodorow, M., Fowles, M. E., & Kukich, K. (2002a). Comparing the validity of automated and human scoring of essays. *Journal of Educational Computing Research, 26,* 407–425.

Powers, D. E., Burstein, J. C., Chodorow, M., Fowles, M. E., & Kukich, K. (2002b). Stumping e-rater: Challenging the validity of automated essay scoring. *Computers in Human Behavior, 18,* 103–134.

Powers, D., & Farnum, M. (1997). *Effects of mode of presentation on essay scores* (ETS RM-97–08). Princeton, NJ: Educational Testing Service.

Powers, D., Farnum, M., Grant, M., & Kubota, M. (1997). *A pilot test of online essay scoring.* Princeton, NJ: Educational Testing Service.

Powers, D. E., Fowles, M. E., Farnum, M., & Ramsey, P. (1994). Will they think less of my handwritten essay if others word process theirs? Effects on essay scores of intermingling handwritten and word-processed essays. *Journal of Educational Measurement, 31,* 220–233.

Promissor, Inc. (2003). BUILDER™ [Computer program]. Philadelphia: Author.

Raju, N. S., & Ellis, B. B. (2002). Differential item and test functioning. In F. Drasgow & N. Schmitt (Eds.), *Measuring and analyzing behavior in organizations* (pp. 156–188). San Francisco: Jossey-Bass.

Revuela, J., & Ponsoda, V. (1998). A comparison of item exposure control methods in computerized adaptive testing. *Journal of Educational Measurement, 35,* 311–327.

Richman, W. L., Olson-Buchanan, J. B., & Drasgow, F. (2000). Examining the impact of administration medium on examinee perceptions and attitudes. *Journal of Applied Psychology, 85,* 880–887.

Robin, F. (1999, March). *Alternative item selection strategies for improving test security and pool usage in computerized adaptive testing.* Paper presented at the annual meeting of the National Council on Measurement in Education, Montreal, Quebec, Canada.

Robin, F. (2001). *Development and evaluation of test assembly procedures for computerized adaptive testing.* Unpublished doctoral dissertation, University of Massachusetts, Amherst, School of Education.

Russell, M. (1999). Testing on computers: A follow-up study comparing performance on computer and on paper. *Education Policy Analysis Archives, 7.* Retrieved August 5, 2003, from http://epaa.asu.edu/epaa/v7n20/

Russell, M., & Haney, W. (1997). Testing writing on computers: An experiment comparing student performance on tests conducted via computer and via paper-and-pencil. *Education Policy Analysis Archives, 5.* Retrieved August 5, 2003, from http://epaa.asu.edu/epaa/v5n3.html

Russell, M., & Plati, T. (2001). Effects of computer versus paper administration of a state-mandated writing assessment. Retrieved April 19, 2002, from the *TC Record.Org* Web site: http://www.tcrecord.org/Content.asp?ContentID=10709

Russell, M., & Tao, W. (2004a). Effects of handwriting and computer-print on composition scores: A follow-up to Powers, Fowles, Farnum, & Ramsey. *Practical Assessment, Research and Evaluation, 9*(1). Retrieved July 10, 2005, from http://PAREonline.net/getvn.asp?v=9&n=1

Russell, M., & Tao, W. (2004b). The influence of computer-print on rater scores. *Practical Assessment, Research and Evaluation, 9*(10). Retrieved July 10, 2005, from http://PAREonline.net/getvn.asp?v=9&n=10

Sandene, B., Bennett, R. E., Braswell, J., & Oranje, A. (2005). Online assessment in mathematics. In B. Sandene, N. Horkay, R. E. Bennett, N. Allen, J. Braswell, B. Kaplan, et al. (Eds.), *Online assessment in mathematics and writing: Reports from the NAEP Technology-Based Assessment Project* (NCES 2005-457) (pp. v–67). Washington, DC: U.S. Department of Education, National Center for Education Statistics.

Sands, W. A., Waters, B. K., & McBride, J. R. (Eds.). (1997). *Computerized adaptive testing: From inquiry to operation*. Washington, DC: American Psychological Association.

Sebrechts, M. M., Bennett, R. E., & Rock, D. A. (1991). Agreement between expert system and human raters' scores on complex constructed-response quantitative items. *Journal of Applied Psychology, 76*, 856–862.

Segall, D. O. (1996). Multidimensional adaptive testing. *Psychometrika, 61*, 331–354.

Segall, D. O., & Moreno, K. E. (1999). Development of the computerized adaptive testing version of the Armed Services Vocational Aptitude Battery. In F. Drasgow & J. B. Olsen-Buchanan (Eds.), *Innovations in computerized assessment* (pp. 35–65). Mahwah, NJ: Erlbaum.

Segall, D. O., Moreno, K. E., & Hetter, R. D. (1997). Item pool development and evaluation. In W. A. Sands, B. K. Waters, & J. R. McBride (Eds.), *Computerized adaptive testing: From inquiry to operation* (pp. 117–130). Washington, DC: American Psychological Association.

Shealy, R., & Stout, W. (1993a). A model-based standardization approach that separates true bias/DIF from group ability differences and detects test bias/DTF as well as item bias/DIF. *Psychometrika, 58*, 159–194.

Shealy, R., & Stout, W. (1993b). An item response theory model for test bias and differential item functioning. In P. W. Holland & H. Wainer (Eds.), *Differential item functioning* (pp. 197–239). Hillsdale, NJ: Erlbaum.

Sheehan, K., & Lewis, C. (1992). Computerized mastery testing with nonequivalent testlets. *Applied Psychological Measurement, 16*, 65–76.

Shermis, M. D., & Burstein, J. (Eds.). (2003). *Automated essay scoring: A cross-disciplinary perspective*. Mahwah, NJ: Erlbaum.

Singley, M. K., & Bennett, R. E. (2002). Item generation and beyond: Applications of schema theory to mathematics assessment. In S. Irvine & P. Kyllonen (Eds.), *Item generation for test development* (pp. 361–394). Hillsdale, NJ: Erlbaum.

Sinharay, S., Johnson, M. S., & Williamson, D. (2003). Calibrating item families and summarizing the results using family expected response functions. *Journal of Educational and Behavioral Statistics, 28*, 295–313.

Smith, R., & Lewis, C. (1995, April). *A Bayesian computerized mastery model with multiple cutscores*. Paper presented at the annual meeting of the National Council on Measurement in Education, San Francisco.

Stevens, R. H., Lopo, A. C., & Wang, P. (1996). Artificial neural networks can distinguish novice and expert strategies during complex problem solving. *Journal of the American Medical Informatics Association, 3*, 131–138.

Stocking, M. L., & Lewis, C. (1995). *A new method for controlling item exposure in computerized adaptive testing* (Research Rep. No. 95-25). Princeton, NJ: Educational Testing Service.

Stocking, M. L., & Lewis, C. (1998). Controlling item exposure conditional on ability in computerized adaptive testing. *Journal of Educational and Behavioral Statistics, 23*, 57–75.

Stocking, M. L., & Lewis, C. (2000). Methods of controlling the exposure of items in CAT. In W. J. van der Linden & C. A. W. Glas (Eds.), *Computerized adaptive testing: Theory and practice* (pp. 163–182). Boston: Kluwer.

Stocking, M. L., & Swanson, L. (1993). A method for severely constrained item selection in adaptive testing. *Applied Psychological Measurement, 17*, 277–292.

Swanson, D. B., Featherman, C., Case, S. M., Luecht, R. M., & Nungester, R. J. (1997, April). *Relationship of response latency to test design, examinee proficiency, and item difficulty in computer-based test administration*. Paper presented at the annual meeting of the National Council on Measurement in Education, Chicago.

Swanson, L., & Stocking, M. L. (1993). A model and heuristic for solving very large item selection problems. *Applied Psychological Measurement, 17*, 151–166.

Sympson, J. B., & Hetter, R. D. (1985, October). *Controlling item exposure rates in computerized adaptive tests*. Paper presented at the annual meeting of the Military Testing Association, San Diego, CA.

Thissen, D., Steinberg, L., & Wainer, H. (1988). Use of item response theory in the study of group differences in trace lines. In H. Wainer & H. I. Braun (Eds.), *Test validity* (pp. 147–169). Hillsdale, NJ: Erlbaum.

Thissen, D., Steinberg, L., & Wainer, H. (1993). Detection of differential item functioning using the parameters of item response models. In P. W. Holland & H. Wainer (Eds.), *Differential item functioning* (pp. 67–113). Hillsdale, NJ: Erlbaum.

Thompson Prometric, Inc. (2003). BENCHMARK™ [Computer program]. Stamford, CT: Author.

Tippins, N. T., Beaty, J., Drasgow, F., Gibson, W., Pearlman, K., Segall, D., & Shepherd, W. (2006). Unproctored Internet testing in employment settings. *Personnel Psychology, 59*, 189–225.

Tonidandel, S., Quinones, M. A., & Adams, A. A. (2002). Computer-adaptive testing: The impact of test characteristics on perceived performance and test takers' reactions. *Journal of Applied Psychology, 87*, 320–332.

van der Linden, W. J. (1998). Optimal assembly of psychological and educational tests. *Applied Psychological Measurement, 22*, 195–211.

van der Linden, W. J. (2000). Constrained adaptive testing with shadow tests. In W. J. van der Linden & C. A. W. Glas (Eds.), *Computer-adaptive testing: Theory and practice* (pp. 27–52). Boston: Kluwer.

van der Linden, W. J. (2004). *Linear models for optimal test design*. New York: Springer-Verlag.

van der Linden, W. J., & Adema, J. (1989). Algorithms for computerized test construction using classical item parameters. *Journal of Educational Statistics, 14*, 279–290.

van der Linden, W. J., & Adema, J. J. (1998). Simultaneous assembly of multiple test forms. *Journal of Educational Measurement, 35*, 185–198. [Erratum in Vol. 36, 90–91]

van der Linden, W. J., & Boekkooi-Timminga, E. (1989). A maximin model for test design with practical constraints. *Psychometrika, 54*, 237–248.

van der Linden, W. J., & Reese, L. M. (1998). A model for optimal constrained adaptive testing. *Applied Psychological Measurement, 22*, 259–270.

van der Linden, W. J., Scrams, D. J., & Schnipke, D. L. (1999). Using response-time constraints to control for differential speededness in computerized adaptive testing. *Applied Psychological Measurement, 23*, 195–210.

Vispoel, W. P. (1999). Creating computerized adaptive tests of musical aptitude: Problems, solutions, and future directions. In F. Drasgow & J. B. Olson-Buchanan (Eds.), *Innovations in computerized assessment* (pp. 151–176). Mahwah, NJ: Erlbaum.

Wainer, H. (1993). Some practical considerations when converting a linearly administered test to an adaptive format. *Educational Measurement: Issues and Practice, 12*, 15–20.

Wainer, H., Bradlow, E. T., & Du, Z. Testlet response theory: An analog for the 3PL model useful in testlet-based adaptive testing. In W. J. van der Linden & C. A. W. Glas (Eds.), *Computerized adaptive testing: Theory and practice* (pp. 245–269). Boston: Kluwer.

Wainer, H., Kaplan, B., & Lewis, C. (1992). A comparison of the performance of simulated hierarchical and linear testlets. *Journal of Educational Measurement, 29*, 243–251.

Wainer, H., & Kiely, G. L. (1987). Item clusters and computerized adaptive testing: A case for testlets. *Journal of Educational Measurement, 24,* 185–201.

Wainer, H., & Lewis, C. (1990). Toward a psychometrics for testlets. *Journal of Educational Measurement, 27,* 1–14.

Way, W. D., Steffen, M., & Anderson, G. S. (2002). Developing, maintaining, and renewing item inventory to support CBT. In C. N. Mills, M. T. Potenza, J. J. Fremer, & W. C. Ward (Eds.), *Computer-based testing: Building the foundation for future assessments* (pp. 143–164). Mahwah, NJ: Erlbaum.

Wenger, E. (1987). *Artificial intelligence and tutoring systems: Computational and cognitive approaches to the communication of knowledge.* Los Altos, CA: Kaufmann

Wise, S. L. (1996, April). *A critical analysis of the arguments for and against item review in computerized adaptive testing.* Paper presented at the annual meeting of the National Council on Measurement in Education, New York.

Wise, S. L. (1997, April). *Examinee issues in CAT*. Paper presented at the annual meeting of the National Council on Measurement in Education, Chicago.

Wolfe, E. W., Bolton, S., Feltovich, B., & Niday, D. M. (1996). The influence of student experience with word processors on the quality of essays written for a direct writing assessment. *Assessing Writing, 3,* 123–147.

Zara, A. R. (1994, March). *An overview of the NCLEX/CAT beta test.* Paper presented at the annual meeting of the American Educational Research Association, New Orleans, LA.

Zenisky, A. L., & Sireci, S. G. (2002). Technological innovations in large-scale assessment. *Applied Measurement in Education, 15,* 337–362.

Zhang, Y. L., Powers, D. E., Wright, W., & Morgan, R. (2003). *Applying the online scoring network (OSN) to Advanced Placement Program® (AP®) tests* (ETS RR-03–12). Princeton, NJ: ETS.

Zimowski, M., Muraki, E., Mislevy, R., & Bock, R. D. (2003). BILOG-MG. In M. Du Toit (Ed.), *IRT from SSI* (pp. 29–256). Lincolnwood, IL: Scientific Software International.

Part III
Applications

14

Old, Borrowed, and New Thoughts in Second Language Testing

Micheline Chalhoub-Deville
Craig Deville
University of North Carolina at Greensboro

1. INTRODUCTION

In this chapter we discuss something "old" in that we provide a brief history of language testing, something "borrowed" as we take from our own work and experience in the field, and something "new" as we present fresh ideas concerning how we define the constructs of language ability and context. Instead of surveying the literature of language testing, which has been accomplished recently and ably by Alderson and Banerjee (2001, 2002), or focusing on a pressing issue, such as the assessment of English language learners (see Duran, 1989, in the previous edition of this publication), we have identified and addressed issues that would be of interest to both measurement professionals and language testers alike.

Our primary intention in this chapter is to introduce language testing to measurement specialists unfamiliar with this somewhat unique field. We will explain what language testing is; spend some space discussing the history of the field; provide a brief account of the various professional enterprises concerned with language testing; talk in some detail about the industry of language assessment—especially with regard to the testing of English across the globe and the tradition of foreign language testing in the United States and elsewhere—and provide a review of the kinds of issues language testing researchers have investigated over the years with an eye toward where the field is headed. Many educators and psychometricians may not be aware that a huge, worldwide industry exists for the assessment of languages; that various local, national, and international organizations and agencies are devoted specifically to language testing; that national and local language policies are often couched in terms of language assessment; and that there are numerous university programs in the world where one can specialize in this discipline.

To begin, however, an explanation is in order as to what is meant by language testing. Historically, this field is concerned with the assessment of *foreign* and *second* language learners, whereby the distinction as to whether a person is learning a foreign or second language is not always clear-cut. (In the field we use the shorthand L2 to refer to both foreign and second language.) That being said, *foreign* language learners typically live, study, and learn the language in their home country, that is, in an environment where the language of interest, referred to as the *target* language, is not spoken by the populace. *Second* language learners, on the other hand, reside in the country where the target language is spoken, meaning that they have ready access to communicative interactions in the target language in everyday life, and not only (or perhaps not at all) in a formal, classroom setting. Immigrants are generally second language learners as they often learn the local language after having settled in their adopted country.

The next point of clarification is to explain who language testers are. Put simply, a language tester has research training in both foreign/second language acquisition and measurement. This simplification, however, fails to give expression to the diversity of professional fields, experiences, and training from which language testers emerge—for example, from linguistics, literature, psychology, education, among many other fields. Language testers work at schools and universities, within government, testing organizations, publishers, policy institutes, language institutes, and private companies. They can communicate via various listservs devoted to the topic. Language testers often belong to several local, national, and international organizations and can publish their research in journals and book series that deal specifically with language testing. Before turning our attention to language testing research and thought, we will briefly outline some historical tidbits that may help explain how this discipline has evolved.

2. SOME HISTORY

Language testers never tire of depicting the first language test on record—from the Bible—whereby the required test task was employed to uncover potential enemy infiltrators:

> The Book of Judges (12: 4-6) in the Bible records an early language test. Guarding the fords on the River Jordan, Gileadite patrols asked anyone approaching to say the word *shibboleth*.... The Shibboleth test was, technologically, a single-item, objective, oral, phonological test, individually administered: the 42,000 who failed it were slaughtered on the spot. There was nothing educational about the test, which served an immediate political purpose. (Spolsky, 1995, p. 15)

While such an extreme example might redefine our connotative measurement notions of high stakes, error, false positives, rater consistency, etc., the language tester, while certainly not ignoring these measurement principles, would likely focus on such questions as: is the native speaker criterion the most appropriate? What was the context in which the speech task was performed? What model of language proficiency underlies the test task? Was the performance rated on a hierarchical scale of language development? Is the testing of this particular phoneme indicative of pronunciation mistakes made by enemy language learners?

As can readily be seen, the language tester will want to examine not only issues of measurement per se, but also investigate what constitutes language ability and language performance—that is, how is language proficiency defined and, given the definition, how is this construct then measured? Language testers have long called for an agreement between how language proficiency is understood and how it is measured, and this insistence on conformity of construct definition and test method is a pervasive element in the history of language testing and will be a topical strand followed throughout this chapter.

3. LARGE-SCALE LANGUAGE TESTING

The following sections focus on the enterprises of large-scale English and foreign language testing throughout the world. With regard to the English language tests, we will highlight how different approaches to testing have evolved in the United Kingdom and the United States. As for foreign language testing, discussion will address the role the U.S. government language schools have played in shaping the practices used in academia in the United States and around the world. The most prominent English as a Second Language (ESL) and foreign language (FL) testing programs have essentially existed in parallel worlds. The traditions, orientations, practices, and research of ESL and FL testers have evolved to accommodate their respective learner populations and users' needs. While these two worlds have crossed paths at times, they still remain somewhat separate.

3.1. English as a Foreign Language Testing

3.1.1. Large-Scale Language Testing in the United Kingdom

The start of large-scale, modern language testing of English as a foreign language is usually dated 1913 (Spolsky, 1995; Weir, 2003). At that time the University of Cambridge Local Examinations Syndicate, often referred to as UCLES, began testing the English proficiency of people overseas who intended to become teachers of English (see http://www.cambridgeesol.org/index.htm). It is worth noting that UCLES had been testing other subjects in English-medium schools within British possessions overseas since about 1860, where "[e]xaminations proved eminently suitable for export" (Roach, 1971, p. 145). At the turn of the century, these school-leaving exams were administered to colonial candidates in 36 countries.

By 1930 UCLES was administering its English language test, called the Certificate of Proficiency in English (CPE), to prospective language teachers in some 30 countries around the world. The earliest versions of the examination were quite long and very demanding; in structure they were "academic in orientation and initially modeled on the traditional, essay-based, native-speaker language syllabus" (Weir, 2003, p. 2). The examination consisted of: an English literature paper, an essay, a phonetics paper, a grammar test, a translation from and into French/German, a dictation, and a read aloud/conversation task. The exam required approximately 12 hours of the test taker's time, probably a similar amount of time for a test administrator, and one can only guess at the time needed by the headmaster to mark a single exam. Not unexpectedly, the literature and essay topics were anglocentric, for example, English pre-Raphaelitism (Weir, 2003), but the expectations of the students were in line with the syllabus and teaching practices that had been established in the network of UCLES'S colonial teaching centers. Moreover, the format of the exams corresponded to the kinds of examinations administered at British universities at the time.

Today UCLES has, in addition to the CPE, the Certificate in Advanced English (CAE) and the First Certificate in English (FCE), among others. These Cambridge Certificate Exams are employed to evaluate test takers' English language proficiency for academic use as well as for functioning in commerce and industry. The UCLES tradition with respect to testing, exemplified by the Cambridge Certificate Exams, has been one that views examinations as a reflection of the teaching and learning process, including the eclectic practices encountered in the classroom. Early on UCLES concerned itself with issues of consequential validity, or washback, by considering how the content and format of its examinations were likely to influence teachers and what was taught. This close alignment between what students see in the classroom and what they see in their exams is understandable given that UCLES was (and is) engaged in both the teaching and testing of foreign students. The examinations were (are) a natural outgrowth of the teaching and learning practices of the classroom.

It is worth pointing out that UCLES/University of Cambridge ESOL Examinations has partnered with the British Council, and IDP Education/IELTS Australia to administer another major battery of tests that has been gaining in popularity. The battery is the International English Language Testing System (IELTS), which in some ways departs from the traditional UK approach to assessment (Clapham, 1996). (See http://www.ielts.org/.) IELTS is more of a proficiency-based measure, that is, independent in its orientation from any specific instructional program. The academic language component of the battery is primarily used for admissions purposes and is administered around the world, including the United States.

3.1.2. Large-Scale English Language Testing in the United States

One could argue that the watershed year 1961 marks the beginning of large-scale language testing in the United

States. That year saw the publication of Lado's (1961) seminal book on language testing as well as a conference that launched the Test of English as a Foreign Language (TOEFL) program at Educational Testing Service (ETS). (See http://www.toefl.org/.) Before proceeding with a historical account of TOEFL, however, it should be pointed out that several other institutions in the United States had already embarked on language testing. In the 1950s the University of Michigan's English Language Institute, under the direction of Lado, developed a battery of English language exams for use overseas.[1] In addition, the Foreign Service Institute (FSI) at about this time instituted a hierarchical language proficiency scale linking various proficiency levels to descriptions of tasks that a prototypical learner at the different levels could be expected to perform. This FSI language scale is discussed in more detail below, but for our purpose here it is important to note that the scale was used widely by other governmental agencies and had an enormous impact on language testing in the United States and abroad.

The keynote speaker for the 1961 conference that spawned TOEFL was John Carroll. Carroll had been involved with language testing for some time and had served as a consultant in the development of the FSI scale mentioned above. At the time of the conference, university and college administrators were lamenting the lack of a standardized measure that could be used to determine if foreign student applicants possessed a suitable level of English proficiency that would allow them to pursue university-level academic work. Carroll recommended that a needs analysis be undertaken to identify and describe typical communication tasks that foreign students face. He saw the need for an assessment battery that would cover more than just grammar and other discrete elements, but would also include performance measures, for example, speaking tasks. Validation evidence should indicate the predictive power of the test. Finally, perhaps due to his work with the FSI scale, Carroll wanted to see score reporting that included not only normative information but also descriptions of language skills and behaviors that examinees at various score levels would likely exhibit.

The first TOEFL was 2 1/2 hours long and consisted entirely of multiple-choice items. The areas tested were reading, listening, writing, grammar, and vocabulary. As is true with any test construction process, practical and political constraints contributed to what material found its way onto the assessment and what was rejected. Not all of Carroll's recommendations could be followed at the outset, but it should be noted that ETS has since developed several performance measures to supplement the multiple-choice TOEFL.

3.1.3. The U.K. Versus the U.S. Approach to Language Testing

Even from this very brief survey of English language admissions tests in the United Kingdom and the United States it will be clear to the reader that quite different considerations led to the development of quite different kinds of examinations in the two countries. Spolsky (1995), in his history of large-scale English language testing, characterizes the two countries' ideologies as follows:

> there are two major ideologies underlying the testing and assessment of human characteristics, which I might characterize as the humanistic-scepticist descriptive approach on the one hand, and the rationalist-empiricist measurement approach on the other. The former ... the *traditional* ... is the one that is associated with examinations of the British university style.... Characterized in the 1920s as old-type questions, it used open-ended interviews, or more typically, essays, marked intuitively by selected judges.... The latter approach is that typified by the true-false or multiple-choice test ... whose internal consistency and other technical kinds of reliability can be demonstrated ... it is popularly known as the American test, and not altogether incorrectly associated with such other modern technological innovations as television, computers, and mass-market hamburgers.... [W]ith the traditional examination we think we know what we are assessing, but remain ... uncertain about the accuracy or replicability of our assessment; with the modern examination, we are sure enough of our measurement, but are ... uncertain as to what exactly we have measured. (p. 5)

To be sure, Spolsky's dichotomy clearly separates the British and U.S. American schools of thought regarding English language assessment, and this distinction is especially clear when one looks back on the historical development of language needs and testing in the two countries. The British/UCLES exam system grew out of a concerted effort by the government to spread the British culture, language, and policy—including education—to the many peoples across the globe under its sphere of influence. The teaching of English (British) language, literature, among other things, was an integral part of this effort. As already mentioned, the examinations were tied very closely to the instructional practices of the classroom, and the achievement of a certificate—that is, passing the CPE meant one was proficient not only in the use of the language, but also the use of it to learn and appreciate aspects of British life and culture of the time.

The TOEFL, on the other hand, was designed to be program-free. In other words, the scores from the tests were meant to be interpreted as an indication of the test taker's level of English proficiency with respect to his/her readiness for university academic work—generally without regard for where the student had studied, what his/her course of study had been, or what the student's planned course of study might be. The multiple-choice format of the test with its various language components allowed it to exhibit healthy reliability estimates, be administered and scored in an efficient manner, and keep costs down (see Davidson & Bachman, 1990).

Alderson and Buck (1993) caution against an uncritical acceptance of the stereotype that depicts U.S. American measurement specialists as concerned mainly with a test's psychometric qualities while their British counterparts ignore such technicalities and concentrate solely on test content. While Spolsky's characterization of the two ideologies leads us to think that the two programs still represent distinct assessment philosophies and approaches, this perception changes upon closer examination of the expanding purposes and uses of the tests in recent times, as well as the changing orientations of the two organizations.

In terms of purpose, both UCLES and ETS promote the use of their instruments beyond academic purposes. In terms of expanding to non-academic environments, IELTS includes, in addition to its academic language test, a general language assessment intended to measure English language proficiency for work-related or for immigration application purposes. IELTS has been marketed primarily in the United Kingdom, Australia, and New Zealand, and is now making significant inroads in the United States and Canada as well. As for TOEFL, the test has traditionally been thought of as a measure of academic English language proficiency for international students who plan to study in the United States or Canada. TOEFL publications increasingly indicate, however, that TOEFL scores are employed by institutions/agencies in other countries and for other purposes such as professional licensing and certification. ETS's promotional material thus implies that such uses are appropriate.

In terms of content, IELTS has consistently been described as more communicative in its orientation. It includes all four modalities (i.e., reading, writing, listening, and speaking). TOEFL, in its more recent computer-delivered format, measures the original skills mentioned above plus writing. Speaking is not part of the battery and is assessed separately through a test called the Test of Spoken English. Nevertheless, ETS has recently released a new version of TOEFL, referred to as 'TOEFLiBT,' which is an internet-based test and measures all four modalities. The NGT is said to be grounded in communicative language theory and research (see *TOEFL Monograph Series,* http://www.toefl.org/research/rmonogph.html) and uses integrated modalities—for example, test takers read a lengthy text and then write about it.

Other indicators reveal that UCLES and ETS learn lessons from each other. Alderson (1990) notes, for example, that IELTS is unlike other EFL exams developed in the United Kingdom, and "is a secure test that has been trial-tested, extensively validated, and is in widespread international use" (p. 44). In addition, research documentation similar to that found with standardized tests in the United States is available and accessible (e.g., Clapham, 1996). As for TOEFL, a noted change in the orientation of that program is its venture into the creation of an "array of sophisticated teaching and learning tools that support English language learning" (Pearlman, 2003). TOEFL, as such, is departing from its traditional position as removed from the learning environment to now designing and developing teaching and learning tools.

In conclusion, the intensifying competition between UCLES and ETS to capture more and more of the constantly expanding market for English language tests has fostered some healthy criticism and change in the ways the two organizations conceptualize and practice language testing. Language testers trained according to the American ideology have been very vocal in their criticism of UCLES's lack of attention to reliability (e.g., Bachman, Davidson, Ryan, & Choi, 1995; Chalhoub-Deville & Turner, 2000; Spolsky, 1995). UCLES has not been deaf to such criticism and has taken major steps to address issues of psychometric quality (see Weir & Milanovic, 2003). For their part, ETS's TOEFL program has invested considerable resources into moving beyond multiple-choice tests of discrete language points by developing a new generation of tests that are more communicative and authentic. So in many ways, the two organizations are retaining their respective strengths while addressing critical psychometric and construct issues within their bailiwicks.

3.1.4. Predictive Evidence

A discussion of large-scale ESL tests such as TOEFL and IELTS entails a consideration of the salient role these tests play in the admission process. Two issues are especially of note here. The first issue is a commonly held belief that the primary function of TOEFL and IELTS scores is to serve as predictors of academic success. A second and related issue is the perception that the higher the score on these tests the more likely it is the test takers will succeed in their academic studies. In terms of prediction, available research indicates that the predictive power of ESL admissions tests such as TOEFL and IELTS is relatively small (Des Brisay, 1994; Hale, Stansfield, & Duran, 1984; Henning, 1990; Loyd, 1985).

In a discussion of the topic on LTEST-L, the professional listserv for language testers, Stansfield (2002) speaks to the predictive validity of TOEFL:

> The median correlation [of TOEFL] with first semester GPA was about .25. Not very impressive! There are many reasons for this. Apart from the small N in these single institution studies, there is a restriction of range, in that people who score low on the English proficiency test don't get admitted. As one approaches the native speaker level, or if one is a native speaker, we see no relationship between being a native speaker and GPA. Such a relationship would not be logical in a university setting where the vast majority of students are native speakers.
>
> There are other more subtle factors too, such as the course load of a student, the language load of the courses (math or engineering vs. philosophy), the student's knowledge of the discipline, study habits, financial situation, remedial support provided by the institution, etc. When you consider how all these other factors impact GPA, .25 becomes more impressive.

The principal function of these ESL admissions tests is "to provide information regarding the student's academic language ability, not information about the student's qualifications in his/her course of study or the student's personal qualities, both of which contribute to successful academic work" (Chalhoub-Deville, 2003b). In other words, it is more accurate to conceive of these tests as measures of whether test takers have achieved a linguistic threshold that enables them to approach academic work in English in a meaningful manner. If the test takers have indeed achieved that requisite level, then their language proficiency should not be a factor in terms of their potential for academic success.

Given this focus on linguistic threshold, then it follows that setting higher English language admissions score standards does not ensure success in academic work. Haas (1990), an admissions officer at Indiana University, writes that ESL admissions test scores "are not guarantees of academic success, no matter how high the scores" (p. 11). Lumley (2002), as part of the above cited exchange on the LTEST-L listserv, echoes Haas' statement. Lumley criticizes the high standard on IELTS—a score of 7.5—mandated by Australian universities for admission of non-native speakers of English. He makes reference to a study by Elder (1993) that suggests that an IELTS score of 4.5 best predicted academic success in coursework for a diploma in Australia. Lumley goes on to mention another study, by Hamilton, Lopes, McNamara, and Sheridan (1993), relating how these authors discovered that English native speakers:

> do not necessarily score more highly than "non-native speakers," nor highly enough on IELTS (the test chosen for the studies reported here, but the findings might equally apply to other tests) to reach the levels required nowadays by many institutions. This raises the possibility of claims of discrimination against all these "non-native speakers."

Setting high English language admissions scores then seems to run against the conceptualization of the purpose of these tests and contrary to the modest research evidence available. Moreover, setting high scores is likely to result in rejecting applicants who have the requisite threshold of language ability to handle academic work and so have the potential to succeed in their academic pursuits. Measurement professionals involved in advising on or setting admissions standards are, therefore, encouraged to consider setting more reasonable levels of required language performance. Moreover, institutions/academic programs need to determine within their local contexts the nature and threshold levels of English needed by incoming students whose native language is not English.

3.2. Foreign Language Testing

The most significant development in foreign language testing in the United States is the Oral Proficiency Interview (OPI) from the American Council on the Teaching of Foreign Languages (ACTFL). (See http://www.actfl.org/.) The OPI is typically 10 to 25 minutes of structured, live face-to-face spoken interaction between a trained interlocutor/rater and test taker on a series of topics of varied language difficulty (Omaggio Hadley, 1993). The interviewer initiates the interactions and attempts to build on the interviewee's responses, guided throughout by the ACTFL description of language use at different levels. The ACTFL Guidelines is a widely recognized hierarchy of language use, that is, descriptions of tasks that learners of various proficiency levels can accomplish. The Guidelines are essentially a language behavioral scale used to determine an examinee's proficiency in a given foreign language (most modern languages except English). The ACTFL Guidelines include nine successive levels that extend from novice to superior. As mentioned, each level includes a description of functions, structures, contexts, and degrees of accuracy expected of interviewees as they perform language tasks. (For detailed information about the OPI see ACTFL, 1999b).

The OPI and the ACTFL Guidelines have their genesis in the interview procedure and rating scale developed by government language agencies. In the 1950s the FSI was involved in the standardization of an oral interview and a rating scale to be used with its personnel. The oral testing procedure then, like now, was a face-to-face interview on a variety of topics that vary in difficulty with a trained interviewer. The FSI scale is holistic but emphasizes five traits: accent, comprehension, fluency, grammar, and vocabulary (Adams, 1980; Wilds, 1979). The scale, which ranges from 0 to 5, was first published in 1958. Not long thereafter other government agencies involved in the teaching and testing of foreign language proficiency (e.g., Defense Language Institute, Central Intelligence Agency, National Security Agency, and Peace Corps) took interest in the interview procedure and scale and adopted it for their uses. In an effort to create a unified testing system in the government, these agencies pooled their expertise to create a joint standardized oral assessment system that is commonly referred to as the Interagency Language Roundtable (ILR) (Jones, 1975; Lowe, 1987). The ILR scale (see http://www.dlielc.org/testing/round_table.pdf), which is regarded as the grandfather of all language rating procedures, is still in existence and use today (Fulcher, 1998).

In 1981, ACTFL and Educational Testing Service received funding to adopt and modify the oral ILR interview and scale for academic purposes. Prior to this and influential for the modification of the original ILR scale, Carroll (1967) had administered the oral interview to college majors of French, German, Russian, and Spanish, and showed that very few language majors were able to achieve a level above 2/2+ (Level 3 is the minimum proficiency rating required of government professionals). So the rating scale was modified. New categories were created to provide greater differentiation of ability below the ILR 2+ level, and categories above 2+, where few students scored, were collapsed (Clark, 1988; Liskin-Gasparro, 1984a, 1984b; Lowe, 1983, 1987). The ACTFL Provisional Proficiency Guidelines appeared in 1982 (ACTFL, 1982) and the complete ones in 1986 (ACTFL, 1986). The Guidelines were revised in 1999 (ACTFL, 1999a).[2]

Criticism in the L2 field is widespread in terms of the lack of research evidence to support many of the claims made by the ACTFL Guidelines and its OPI (Bachman & Savignon, 1986; Brindley, 1991; Chalhoub-Deville, 1997; Chalhoub-Deville & Fulcher, 2003; Fulcher, 1996; Lantolf & Frawley, 1985; van Lier, 1989; Young & He, 1998). Critics of the Guidelines have questioned the legitimacy of a committee-produced description of language use without any research to support the claims made; the generic use of the "educated native speaker" as a criterion for performance; the asymmetrical interaction and skewed performance due to the power of the interviewer; the narrow contexts of communication depicted in testing and the sweeping generalizations that ensue; and the circular logic in rating language use in the interview based on the Guidelines, which are said to be based on OPI performances; among other criticisms.

Despite pervasive and sustained criticisms, the ACTFL Guidelines have thrived. As Liskin-Gasparro (2001) argues, they have been incorporated into the development of language textbooks, curriculum frameworks, teacher preparation programs, and national foreign language learning standards (National Standards in Foreign Language Education Project, 1996). Moreover, the ACTFL Guidelines, originally created for speaking, have since been developed for the other modalities as well. The Guidelines have also influenced the development of a national foreign language test, which is to be released under the auspices of the National Assessment of Educational Progress (NAEP). OPI ratings are increasingly being used for making major decisions in terms of licensure and certification, employment, promotion, admission, graduation, etc. (see ACTFL, 1999b). ACTFL's prosperity and power is also seen in the founding of a professional testing arm, Language Testing International, to administer and process OPIs. Finally, and perhaps most significant, is the fact that the ACTFL Guidelines have been promulgated in various forms worldwide. The International Second Language Proficiency Ratings (ISLPR), and the Common European Framework (CEF) are patterned after the FSI/ACTFL hierarchy (Fulcher, 1998, 2003). See North (2000) and Fulcher (2003) for an extensive discussion of these hierarchies and their scales. A fundamental question here is, why have the Guidelines thrived despite pervasive and sustained criticisms?

McNamara (2003) attributes the success of scales such as ACTFL to the political machinery that propels them. In considering the forces that impact testing considerations, McNamara questions the assumption "that test-developers [are] responsible for the central work of defining the construct in the test, and subjecting it to evaluation as part of the validation process" (p. 471). McNamara argues that "test constructs are typically determined by pragmatic considerations, and are often in fact politically mandated entirely" (p. 471). McNamara goes on to make reference to the dubious but nonetheless influential role that various hierarchical scales play in shaping assessment practices, saying that:

> a particularly potent example is the growing role of the Common European Framework for languages (Council of Europe, 2001) as dictating the construct in assessment projects throughout Europe, a fact which is mandated politically. The success of the ILR (Interagency Language Roundtable) and ACTFL (American Council on the Teaching of Foreign Languages) scales in the USA—in the face of the sort of powerful critique articulated in Bachman (1990) and elsewhere—is testimony to the imperviousness of the test constructs to academic criticism. (p. 471)

While hierarchical scales have some basis in functional linguistics and communicative language teaching and testing, these scales are powerful primarily because of their political/governmental support. As an example, we reference the policy that underpins the promotion of the CEF. The CEF has been declared an important component in helping the Council of Europe accomplish its overall language policy "to promote plurilingualism and pluriculturalism among citizens in order to combat intolerance and xenophobia" (http://www.coe.int/T/E/Cultural_Co-operation/education/Languages/Language_Policy/downloaded 11/4/2003). CEF is the first item listed on the Web page as a practice devised and used to help implement the stated policy. With regard to assessment, one implication of this policy of plurilingualism has been the formulation and dissemination of the CEF in the testing community. Saville (2002) states that, "Examination providers are one of the key target groups for which the CEF was developed: one of the main examples of the way in which the CEF has been used effectively is … the use of the CEF by The Associate of Language Testers in Europe."[3] In sum, to promote the Council of Europe's laudable language policies, most language instructional programs and assessment products are being linked to the CEF.[4]

As with the ACTFL Guidelines, the CEF has been subject to criticism (Fulcher, 2003). Nevertheless, such criticisms do not mean much in the face of the solid political base that the CEF enjoys. It can be of little consequence what the knowledge base in the field reveals about the CEF and the other hierarchies, in the end it seems that "politics trumps psychometrics."[5]

In conclusion, Deville and Chalhoub-Deville (2006) acknowledge that different pragmatic purposes drive our assessment practices. What is distinctive, however, about politically driven assessments is their widespread and potent impact, their imperviousness and/or tardy reaction to compelling professional criticisms, and the lack of a focused research agenda to support or evaluate their use and the interpretations and decisions that ensue. Concerted discussions of the assessment problems begotten by these politically mandated language frameworks is needed worldwide and across professional disciplines to help curb the tide of their impact.

3.3. Concluding Remarks about Large-Scale L2 Testing

Large-scale ESL tests such as the CPE, IELTS, and TOEFL and FL assessments such as ACTFL's OPI and its offshoots like the CEF have influenced practices in the field considerably and will continue to do so. As to be expected, the ESL and FL tests have been motivated by different concerns, have served diverse populations, and have engendered divergent assessment practices and research interests. Despite these differences, the tests in general come from a traditional orientation to defining the L2 construct that is essentially cognitive, psycholinguistic in nature. This depiction represents—for the most part—current trends and practices in the field.

The following section of the chapter recounts representations of the L2 construct and concomitant practices that have been embraced in the language testing field. The section also discusses new ideas that have been emerging in the field with regard to defining language ability as a social endeavor, one that is difficult—if not impossible—to interpret without acknowledging context as well. We argue that these fresh ideas are worth serious consideration as the profession moves forward.

4. CONSTRUCT DEFINITIONS OF LANGUAGE PROFICIENCY

4.1. More History and Perspective

Theories and practices of second/foreign language learning, teaching, and testing have been influenced by dominant and popular paradigms from psychology, education, and linguistics. One prominent example is the audio-lingual method (ALM), with its roots in behaviorism and structuralist linguistics (i.e., extensive description of the grammatical features of a language). A behaviorist hallmark of ALM was its use of language labs where learners sat for hours, headphones on, repeating drill after drill. It was immaterial that students were sometimes unable to attach meaning to their utterances. Instead, language teachers and theorists expected learners to master the various linguistic structures through memorization and drill. Emphasis was placed on the learner's ability to conjugate verbs, master verb tenses, recite noun declensions, construct adjective-noun agreements, and so on.

Knowing the linguistic bits and pieces of a language, however, is not at all the same thing as knowing how to use the language. This important distinction was embraced and promoted by the linguist Noam Chomsky (1965), who distinguished between a person's competence, that is, knowledge of the language, and a person's performance, that is, actual linguistic behavior. Chomsky and his followers have focused on the study of competence, which they postulated to be internal, intrinsic, cognitive mechanisms that explain how language is generated. Competence is what an ideal native speaker would utter when unfettered by confounding, messy variables such as memory, interest, emotion, dialogue partner, and so on. These variables come into play when examining performance, but again, this aspect of language production was of no interest to Chomskyans. An emphasis on language as competence would dictate assessments that tap a predominantly cognitive language construct that resides within the test taker.

The anthropologist Dell Hymes (1972) found Chomsky's view of language to be much too narrow. Hymes saw language as the rich, dynamic interaction of participants in a social setting. He argued that the study of language should not be restricted to postulations about intrinsic, idealized mechanisms, but should also concern itself with language behavior exhibited by people in real environments. This view of language would necessitate assessments that are performance- and context-driven.

In essence, the various construct definitions of proficiency and attendant practices of language testing can be schematized along several dimensions: assessing a test taker's knowledge of language versus the person's ability to use language; viewing language proficiency as essentially something internal to the test taker versus something generated in a dynamic interaction among participants; developing language tests to tap hypothesized cognitive abilities versus tests, which are based on specific tasks of interest and are meant to illustrate what a test taker can do. We encourage the reader to keep these dimensions in mind as we outline the dominant construct definitions of language proficiency that have guided testers over the decades.

4.2. Cognitive, Psycholinguistic Perspective

4.2.1. Definitions

Researchers have defined L2 ability in different ways at different times. We begin our discussion of how language testers have represented the construct with Lado's (1961) seminal publication. Lado defines the ability or knowledge that underlies a test taker's performance within a structuralist linguistic approach. In other words, language knowledge is essentially examined in terms of skills (reading, writing, listening, and speaking) and elements (e.g., grammatical structure, vocabulary, pronunciation, cultural understanding). Lado's perspective of what should be measured focuses on what Chomsky (1965) later calls competence, and not on performance or ability to use the language (Hymes, 1972).

Carroll (1961) maintains that while it is important to assess what a learner knows about the L2, for example, discrete grammar and/or vocabulary elements, it is equally important to measure more integrated skills using what are now called performance assessments. Looking back on 25 years of language testing and restating his position once again, Carroll (1986) wrote, "language tests should measure those aspects of language performance that call upon skills in putting together utterances or written statements in more or less real-life situations, or in understanding or reading connected speech or text" (pp. 123–124). Carroll promotes two characteristics of language testing that have driven the field from early on, that is, performance-based measurement and real-life or authentic testing.

Oller (1979) advocates integrative methods of testing based on a psychological theory of language processing and use. He calls his theory, which presents language as a unidimensional construct, the unitary competence hypothesis (UCH).[6] The underpinning of the UCH is pragmatic expectancy grammar, which means that language users process sequences of language elements that are constrained by their immediate linguistic context. Oller's theory of expectancy grammar seems quite reasonable when one considers the type of assessments he researched and analyzed, namely dictation and cloze tests. These tasks tap the so-called receptive language skills, listening and reading, and require the test taker to process sequential chunks of language and anticipate what is to come based on his/her comprehension of what has been heard/read and what the context—lexical and grammatical—permits. Oller's work reflects another attempt to explicate the psychological and linguistic processes that underlie language use by linking construct theory and test operationalization.

Canale and Swain (1980) introduce sociolinguistic and strategic competence as prominent features in their model of language teaching and testing, along with grammatical competence. These features represent a person's knowledge of appropriate language in different social contexts and a person's ability to employ various strategies of communication. In 1983 Canale adds discourse competence to the model, that is, one's knowledge of the language in terms of constructing cohesive text. These researchers emphasize issues pertaining to the knowledge of language in terms of components but do not deliberate on how these components come together to result in performance.

While Canale and Swain do present a more comprehensive view of the L2 construct, they still essentially adhere to a Chomsky-like (1965) abstract representation of language knowledge, and not to the broader view as put forth by Hymes (1972), that is, ability to use language knowledge in specific contexts. As Ellis (1994) puts it, "although Canale and Swain prefer to exclude 'ability to use' from their definition of 'competence', they argue in favour of including sociolinguistic, discourse, and strategic knowledge within its compass" (p. 158). In other words, the Canale and Swain model with its emphasis on knowledge—and not performance—remains cognitive and psycholinguistic in its depiction of the L2 construct. Yet, while it may be possible to view grammatical competence simply in terms of knowledge, it is more difficult to conceptualize the other competences, especially sociolinguistic and discourse competence, as divorced from a particular performance context.

Many language testers would cite the Bachman (1990) and Bachman and Palmer's (1996) communicative language ability (CLA) model as the current state of the art. The CLA model is an extension and amplification of Canale and Swain's work, and it advances Carroll's (1986) call for both discrete-point and authentic measurement as it attempts to model both language knowledge and language use. The authors postulate an interaction among language knowledge, topical knowledge, affective schemata, and individual characteristics together with the test task. The model sees this interaction between internal cognitive variables and external task factors being mediated through strategic competence. Bachman and Palmer (1996) state that strategic competence represents "higher order executive processes that provide a cognitive management function in language use, as well as in other activities" (p. 70). In addition, the discussion of affect in the model is also cognitive in nature. According to Bachman and Palmer (1996), affect, like background knowledge and experience are stored information that can hinder or help a learner's performance.

The CLA model, like its predecessors, is essentially a psycholinguistic representation of language ability and performance. Bachman and Palmer (1996) do address the social and contextual nature of language in their discussion of task demands, but a social, interactional perspective goes well beyond registering task characteristics (see next section). Bachman and Palmer would, therefore, agree with Sharwood Smith (1994) that "[performance] has, of course, sociolinguistic relevance, but social factors are not the immediate concerns" (p. 111).

In summary, the review of the prominent models in language testing shows that the cognitive, psycholinguistic perspective has been the dominant approach in the field to representing language. Even CLA, the most influential model and one that embraces language use in context, portrays the interaction of the language user with the features of the task as cognitive in nature, whereby knowledge and skills are stable entities stored *within* a language user.

Increasingly researchers are considering views advanced by those within the social camp who provide more elaborate accounts of how language components and other variables interact in a given language use situation. The idea that performance can be attributed almost solely to an individual test taker's array of internal, cognitive competences or abilities is abandoned in favor of a model that views the interaction between the dynamic language exchange of participants and the external social context as the primary determinant of performance (see Halliday and Hasan, 1985). Criticisms of the cognitive orientation to representing language ability as well as the main ideas deliberated in the social camp are discussed next.

4.2.2. Limitations of the CLA Model

Recently, several authors (see Chalhoub-Deville, 2003a; Chalhoub-Deville & Deville, 2005; Johnson, 2001, 2004; McNamara, 2003) have questioned the cognitive, generic, and a priori nature of L2 use depicted in the most notable model in the language testing field, that is, CLA. McNamara (2003), for example, recognizes that the "function of the general model of communicative ability in Bachman's approach is to outline a repertoire of aspects of knowledge and skill which are in turn drawn upon in modeling the criterion, the domain of generalization of the test" (p. 467). McNamara, however, argues against such a generic, psycholinguistic representation. He writes:

> The *a priori* nature of abilities in the Bachman model is ... increasingly problematic. The problem lies ... in the question of context and the context-dependent nature of inferences. As Bachman (1990: 311) himself puts it: "instances of language use are by definition context dependent and hence unique". And there is a further fundamental problem here: the model is essentially psychological, seeing communicative language ability as a mental ability, while the context of use is increasingly understood theoretically as a social arena, as in virtually all current work in discourse analysis. (p. 468)

Similar arguments are advanced by Johnson (2004). Johnson maintains that context in Bachman and Palmer's (1996) model is "viewed as being autonomous and separated from other components. The possibility that language can create social context and vice versa during actual interaction is not addressed in their model" (p. 95). She goes on to state that Bachman seems to be more concerned with enumerating the stable characteristics of context than with attempting to:

> understand what that social context means to different individuals engaged in real-life communication. This understanding of how the individual views social context is essential for our ability to understand the individual's behavior, or performance, in a particular social context. Perhaps Bachman's background in language testing has something to do with this static view of social context. (p. 95)

Johnson is probably referring to the dominance of the cognitive perspective in language testing and the very pragmatic concern for generalizability of scores that prompts testers to characterize language knowledge and skills as stable and thus transferable entities. In fairness to Bachman (and Palmer, 1996), however, they do define language use as "the creation or interpretation of intended meanings in discourses by an individual, or as the dynamic and interactive negotiation of intended meanings between two or more individuals in a particular situation" (p. 63). Yet while elements of interaction and social context are clearly acknowledged, the authors maintain a division of construct and context (see also Chapelle, 1998).

Chalhoub-Deville (2003a) acknowledges that in recent publications, Bachman (2002a, 2002b) advocates more attention to context. She writes that he supports "both a construct-based and a task-based approach to test design, which gives tasks (or contexts) equal prominence in test design and interpretation. Nonetheless, Bachman still posits a distinction between the abilities targeted and the context in which they are observed" (p. 372). Chalhoub-Deville makes the case, based on emerging arguments in the field with regard to interactional competence (Johnson, 2001; Kramsch, 1986; Swain, 2001; Young, 2000), that L2 ability, language user, and context are inextricably interconnected. Chalhoub-Deville advocates moving away from a generic and cognitive representation of the construct to examining the interaction of L2 features and related variables of a given context. She proposes, following Snow's (in Cronbach, 2002) notation, a representation that emphasizes an *ability-in-language user-in-context* as a way to represent this latter approach.

Researchers in language testing are increasingly calling for a move away from all-inclusive, generic models of ability to instead a delineation of *local* theories of L2 abilities (Chalhoub-Deville, 2003a; McNamara, 2003). This call finds support in the larger educational research field (e.g., Schoenfeld, 1999; Sfard, 1998). Educational psychologists, such as Snow (in Cronbach, 2002), also endorse *local* theories. In taking stock of Snow's work, Cronbach points out that:

> Snow abandoned at an early date all visions of a synoptic theory or of theory that merely links up variables from refined but separate taxonomies of person characteristics and situation characteristics. Adequate theories would give thorough treatment to behavior in situations of one or another type. (p. 234)

In developing local theories that document features of *ability-in-language user-in-context* we essentially elaborate the characteristics unique to those contexts. However, these theories are also likely to afford a picture of the manner in which some characteristics overlap.

4.3. Social, Interactional Competence Perspective

In recent years, the social orientation to characterizing language ability has been gaining influence in the general educational as well as the L2 learning and testing fields. Influenced by the work of the Russian developmental psychologist Lev Vygotsky (1978) and his followers (e.g., Cole, 1996; Wertsch, 1985), a number of L2 researchers have been calling for the consideration of the social viewpoint in language testing research and development (see McNamara, 1997; Swain, 2001; Young, 2000). In language testing, the work that is most often referred to when discussing this perspective is probably that by Kramsch (1986, 1998), an applied linguist.[7] Kramsch employs the term interactional competence to characterize the social orientation of language use. She defines interactional competence as follows:

> Whether it is face-to-face interaction between two or several speakers or the interaction between the reader and the written text, successful interaction presupposes not only a shared knowledge of the world, the reference to a common external context of communication, but also the construction of a shared internal context or "sphere of inter-subjectivity" that is built through the collaborative effort of the interactional partners. (1986, p. 367)

In this definition, Kramsch emphasizes notions of interaction and the co-construction of communication among participants. It is also critical to note that in this definition Kramsch advances two interrelated notions of context, external and internal, both of which are social in their orientation.

This social perspective is new to the field of language testing and, as one might expect, there are no useful models to guide testers. What researchers have been discussing are the research tools needed to start deriving such models. For example, Young (2000) defines the L2 construct in terms of discursive practices that refer to recurring, stable episodes of language interaction in context among participants. In his research, Young advocates the investigation of six interactional resources that interactants utilize in a given context to co-construct their communication. These resources comprise: sequences of speech acts; the register of semantic relations expected with its syntactic and lexical structures; patterns of turn taking; topic management; participation configuration; and transitions across discursive practices. Young underscores that these resources are not set in advance but are contingent on the specifics of the social context. As such, researchers like Young provide the profession with investigative mechanisms to garner the evidence that can support theory formulation.

Models inspired by the interactional competence approach view L2 knowledge and skills as *local* and *jointly constructed* by the interactants. Developing assessments following this framework offers serious challenges to our traditional practices. As Chalhoub-Deville (2003a) explains, this perspective compels us to consider two basic challenges:

- amending the construct of **individual** ability to accommodate the notion that language use in a communicative event reflects dynamic discourse, which is co-constructed among participants; and
- the notion that language ability is **local** and the conundrum of reconciling that with the need for assessments to yield scores that generalize across contextual boundaries. (p. 373)

In other words, fundamental to a testing operation are the need to award scores to individual test takers and the aim to generalize the scores beyond the testing situation to similar but non-testing and authentic contexts of use. These are complex notions and responses to these challenges are not readily forthcoming.

In conclusion, a social perspective of language use and interaction could be represented as *ability-in-language user-in-context*. Some may argue that this perspective is too narrow, not permitting generalization of scores beyond a given context, while others will see this construct definition as too murky, offering little guidance as to what constitutes context. Regardless of how we characterize the relationship between ability and context, we need to attend more closely to the challenging task of defining and explicating context. The next section will be devoted to the slippery issue of context.

5. CONTEXT

Anastasi (1986) asserts the central role of context in all aspects of testing. She writes: "when selecting or developing tests and when interpreting scores, consider context. I shall stop right there, because those are the words, more than any others, that I want to leave with you: *consider context*" (p. 484). Anastasi urges testers to take into account context features when designing tests and when validating test scores. Yet, while many testing professionals would concur with Anastasi's position, it is not clear what exactly the plea to consider context entails.

It is significant to note that the two leading authorities of validity theory, Cronbach (1971, 1989) and Messick (1989, 1996), differ in their views with regard to context (Moss, 1992). Messick makes the case that context is more relevant when generalizing performance to like contexts and discounts the importance of context for score interpretation, stating that: "the intrusion of context raises issues more of generalizability than of interpretive validity. It gives testimony more to the ubiquity of interactions than to the fragility of score meaning" (1989, p. 15). Cronbach (1989), on the other hand, upholds the position that the generalizability of context is indeed tied to score interpretation and validation. He asserts that "[a]ny interpretation invokes constructs if it reaches beyond the specific, local, concrete situation that was observed" (Cronbach, 1989, p. 151). As such, Cronbach clearly ties generalizations across contexts to issues of construct validation.

In language testing, Chalhoub-Deville (2003a) has made a similar argument, that is, context and construct are intertwined. She advocates an approach that proposes *ability-in-language user-in-context* as the unit of analysis for both theoretical and practical validation work. This assertion of the significant weight of context requires consideration of the role it plays in the measurement of constructs. Before delving into a discussion of the interaction of ability and context, however, it is important to understand what is being referred to when talking about context.

An earlier version of this chapter included a longer section devoted to context. (Because of the space allotted here, we needed to shorten the present section.) We surveyed the use of the term in diverse areas of language and educational research and our review uncovered the reality that context is not a particularly well-explicated term. Context is a vague and imprecise term, used generically with different meanings (see Erickson and Shultz, 1981; Frederiksen, 1981; Gilbert, 1992; Rex, Green, Dixon, & the Santa Barbara Discourse Group, 1998). Conceptualizations of context seem to range from relatively narrow definitions (for example, context as an aspect of task), to broader definitions (for example, context as community, culture, and world view). Context has been used to refer to physical, psychological, and cultural characteristics of a situation, and can denote micro- as well as macro-conditional features that set the scene for performance. Language researchers have also conceptualized context in terms of temporal elements and processes that regulate the communicative event. In short, such vague and disparate representations of the term prompted Culler (1983) to observe that: "context is boundless" (p. 124). In the present treatment of context we grudgingly limit the discussion to the task aspect of context as this is, in our minds, the prevalent approach to context among testers. We do urge readers to consider and explore the larger, slipperier facets of context.

Snow (1994), the renowned educational psychologist whose work revolutionized aptitude theory and research, delineates four research approaches to dealing with interaction. The first approach, *independent* interaction, posits that person and task variables are independent from one another. Person and task variables are viewed as separate entities and can be examined independently. In language testing, the ILR/ACTFL proficiency scales advocate such a position. The ILR/ACTFL proficiency scales, for example, follow a system whereby reading passages are analyzed linguistically and assigned a difficulty level. The passages are then administered to test takers and proficiency scores are awarded based on the examinee's performance reading the specified difficulty texts.

The second approach Snow (1994) discusses is *interdependent* interaction where the person and task variables are viewed in relation to one another, for example, task difficulty must be interpreted with respect to person ability. Bachman's (2002b) work could be classified within this approach, as he contends that "difficulty does not reside in the task alone, but is relative to any given test-taker" (p. 462). As described earlier, while Bachman argues against examining task difficulty factors independent from test takers, he opposes viewing person-task as the unit of analysis.

Snow's remaining two representations of interaction differ from the first two, as now person and task are considered inseparable. The third perspective of interaction is *reciprocal*, that is, person and task variables are continuously acting to change one another. Work by interactionalists and co-constructionists (Johnson, 2001; Kramsch, 1986; Swain, 2001; Young, 2000) could be viewed as advocating a reciprocal interactional perspective. For example, consider a testing task where two test takers are given a newspaper with ads for different apartments and each is assigned specific likes/dislikes or preferences. Then these test takers are asked to communicate to find an apartment agreeable to both of them. The test developer may have constructed the task to target specific aspects of the construct. However, the test takers may negotiate, digress, and discuss the pros and cons of city versus rural living, and even disagree in the end. The question, proponents of the reciprocal perspective posit, then is how to evaluate these performances in terms of the intended construct and the unintended, yet authentic and appropriate, test behavior. Additionally, they point out that examinees' performances are intertwined and evaluation criteria should reflect this co-constructed performance.

The fourth approach to interaction is the *transactional*. In a transactional system, person and task exist only in the relations and actions between them. The focus of any inquiry then is to examine the relations or actions of person-in-task systems. Again, viewpoints by some interactionalists and co-constructionists might fit within this perspective. Also, those who uphold the assessment of language for specific purposes—for example, language tests for aircraft pilots—as being firmly context-bound would support a transactional viewpoint.

While Snow (1994) views his work in aptitude theory as representing both reciprocal and transactional interaction, he cautions against an extreme variety of transaction, which he refers to as "new situationism." A new situationism perspective contends that nothing could be learned from studying person or situation/context independently. In arguing against new situationism, Snow cites Allport, who in 1955 wrote:

> there are *some* things about both organism and environment that can be studied and known about in advance of ... [as well as after] their interrelationship, even though the fact that in their relationship they contribute something *to each other* is undeniable. What then, *is* this residual nature or property of the parties to a transaction? (p. 287, emphasis in original)

If we were to explore *ability-in-language user-in-context* in language testing, we need to consider how to incorporate the reciprocal and transactional approaches into our research. This implies, among other things, the need to focus research less on the effects of variables across persons and more on the understanding of dynamic systems and processes within person × context interactions. As Chalhoub-Deville and Tarone (1996) argue:

> the nature of the language proficiency construct is not constant; different linguistic, functional, and creative proficiency components emerge when we investigate the proficiency construct in different contexts. (p. 5)

In summary, we maintain that in our research we need to explore constructs not simply to document whether they are susceptible to features of the context, but also to investigate how their make-up changes dynamically as a communicative event unfolds.

6. CONCLUSION

In conceptualizing and writing this chapter we have attempted to address both measurement experts and language testers. At the beginning of the chapter we acknowledged that measurement experts are our primary audience. Nevertheless, we believe that some of the topics we have addressed, especially those dealing with future research trends, would appeal to language testers and measurement experts alike.

The chapter begins with an abbreviated history of foreign and second language testing—with an emphasis on large-scale testing of English. The discussion reveals that language testers have a long history, that there are different traditions or approaches to assessing language (each of which has its strengths and weaknesses), and that this intellectual and pragmatic enterprise, together with the commercial- and policy-driven industry, are widespread and still growing.

Another topic dealt with in this chapter is how L2 ability has been defined over time. Our discussion of the prominent representations of L2 ability shows that the construct has generally been conceptualized as a stable construct that resides within an individual and sits still as we measure it. We make the case that context plays a critical role in shaping the L2 abilities measure. We call on researchers to investigate the relationship between context and the construct of interest—in our case, language ability. Our position is buttressed by evidence of performance variability across tasks from the language testing and general measurement literature (e.g., Brennan, 2001; Lee, Kantor, & Mollaun, 2002; Shavelson, Baxter, & Goa, 1993). The consistent finding of the instability of test takers' performances across measures leads us to reconceptualize our construct research as examining *ability-in-language user-in-context*.

We conclude the chapter by asserting that *ability-in-language user-in context* representations will result in local theories, which attend more closely to and detail the L2 features and connections most salient in particular contexts, and which may be more useful for test development and construct research. As a final comment, it is our hope that the present chapter provides constructive information as researchers begin to work toward the development of such local theories.

NOTES

1. The Michigan tests are still widely used today. For details on these tests see http://www.lsa.umich.edu/eli/testing.htm.

2. The ACTFL Guidelines have four principal categories (novice, intermediate, advance, and superior). Here is a description of the ACTFL Guidelines (1999a) at the intermediate level: "[Speakers] produce relatively short, discrete sentences, ask simple questions, and handle straightforward survival situations in language which is basically in present time. In contrast, Advanced speakers can speak in paragraphs, describe and narrate in the major time-frames, and can handle situations with a complication, while Novice speakers operate primarily with memorized material using mostly isolated words and phrases" (p. 15).

3. The Associate of Language Testers in Europe (ALTE) consists of major, influential language testing organizations/centers in Europe.

4. Both IELTS and TOEFL are required to be linked to CEF as well. IELTS has already made such links to CEF. TOEFL is currently conducting a standard-setting study to link scores to certain CEF levels.

5. An oft-repeated saying in the measurement field, attributed to Larry Snowhite.

6. Several models such as those described in the present section as well as research evidence and theoretical arguments (e.g., Bernhardt, 1999; Buck 1994; Grabe, 1999) assert that the L2 construct is multidimensional. Oller (1983) retracted his assertions about the unidimensionality of language ability and acknowledged that the construct comprises several interacting components and processes.

7. Bachman (1990) makes reference to this definition by Kramsch (1986) when discussing interactional communicative ability. Bachman writes that the "'interactional' aspect of the [CLA] approach is rooted in the same views of language and language use that have informed communicative language teaching, an aspect that Kramsch (1986) has referred to as 'interactional competence'" (p. 302). However, as the discussion shows, CLA is not really in line with Kramsch's social orientation.

REFERENCES

Adams, M. L. (1980). Five cooccurring factors in speaking proficiency. In J. R. Firth (Ed.), *Measuring spoken language proficiency* (pp. 1–6). Washington, DC: Georgetown University Press.

Alderson, J. C. (1990). British tests of English as a foreign language. In D. Douglas (Ed.), *English language testing in U.S. colleges and universities* (pp. 41–50). Washington, DC: National Association for Foreign Student Affairs.

Alderson, J. C., & Banerjee, J. (2001). Language testing and assessment (Part 1). *Language Teaching, 34,* 213–236.

Alderson, J. C., & Banerjee, J. (2002). Language testing and assessment (Part 2). *Language Teaching, 35,* 79–113.

Alderson, J. C., & Buck, G. (1993). Standards in testing: A study of the practice of UK examination boards in EFL/ESL testing. *Language Testing, 10,* 1–26.

Allport, F. H. (1955). *Theories of perception and the concept of structure.* New York: Wiley.

American Council on the Teaching of Foreign Languages. (1982). *ACTFL provisional proficiency guidelines.* Hastings-on-Hudson, NY: Author.

American Council on the Teaching of Foreign Languages. (1986). *ACTFL proficiency guidelines.* Hastings-on-Hudson, NY: Author.

American Council on the Teaching of Foreign Languages. (1999a). *Revised ACTFL proficiency guidelines—speaking.* Yonkers, NY: Author.

American Council on the Teaching of Foreign Languages. (1999b). *ACTFL oral proficiency interview tester training manual.* Yonkers, NY: Author.

Anastasi, A. (1986). Evolving concepts of test validation. *Annual Review of Psychology, 37,* 1–15.

Bachman, L. F. (1990). *Fundamental considerations in language testing.* Oxford: Oxford University Press.

Bachman, L. F. (2002a). Alternative interpretations of alternative assessments: Some validity issues in educational performance assessments. *Educational Measurement: Issues and Practice, 21,* 5–18.

Bachman, L. F. (2002b). Some reflections on task-based language performance assessment. *Language Testing, 19,* 453–476.

Bachman, L. F., Davidson, F., Ryan, K., & Choi, I.-C. (1995). *An investigation into the comparability of two tests of EFL: The Cambridge-TOEFL comparability study.* Cambridge: Cambridge University Press.

Bachman, L. F., & Palmer, A. S. (1996). *Language testing in practice.* Oxford: Oxford University Press.

Bachman, L. F., & Savignon, S. J. (1986). The evaluation of communicative language proficiency: A critique of the ACTFL oral interview. *The Modern Language Journal, 70,* 380–390.

Bernhardt, E. (1999). If reading is reader-based, can there be a computer-adaptive test of reading? In M. Chalhoub-Deville (Ed.), *Issues in computer-adaptive testing of reading proficiency* (pp. 1–10). Cambridge: Cambridge University Press.

Brennan, R. L. (2001). *Generalizability theory.* New York: Springer-Verlag.

Brindley, G. (1991). Defining language ability: The criteria for criteria. In S. Anivan (Ed.), *Current developments in language testing* (pp. 139–164). Singapore: Regional Language Center.

Buck, G. (1994). The appropriacy of psychometric measurement models for testing second language listening comprehension. *Language Testing, 11,* 145–170.

Canale, M. (1983). One some dimensions of language proficiency. In J. W. Oller, Jr. (Ed.), *Issues in language testing research* (pp. 333–342). Rowley, MA: Newbury House Publishers.

Canale, M., & Swain, M. (1980). Theoretical bases of communicative approaches to second language teaching and testing. *Applied Linguistics, 1*(1), 1–47.

Carroll, J. B. (1961). Fundamental considerations in testing for English proficiency of foreign students. In *Testing the English proficiency of foreign students* (pp. 31–40). Washington, DC: Center for Applied Linguistics.

Carroll, J. B. (1967). The foreign language attainments of language majors in the senior year: A survey conducted in U.S. colleges and universities. *Foreign Language Annals, 1,* 131–151.

Carroll, J. B. (1986). LT + 25, and beyond? Comments. *Language Testing, 3,* 123–129.

Chalhoub-Deville, M. (1997). Theoretical models, assessment frameworks and test construction. *Language Testing, 14,* 3–22.

Chalhoub-Deville, M. (2003a). Second language interaction: Current perspectives and future trends. *Language Testing, 20,* 369–383.

Chalhoub-Deville, M. (2003b). Fundamentals of ESL admissions tests: MELAB, IELTS, and TOEFL. In D. Douglas (Ed.), *Revised English language testing in U.S. colleges and universities* (2nd ed., pp. 11–36). Washington, DC: National Association of Foreign Student Affairs.

Chalhoub-Deville, M., & Deville, C. (2005). A look back at and forward to what language testers measure. In E. Hinkel (Ed.), *Handbook of research in second language teaching and learning* (pp. 815–832). Mahwah, NJ: Lawrence Erlbaum.

Chalhoub-Deville, M., & Fulcher, G. (2003). The oral proficiency interview: A research agenda. *Foreign Language Annals, 36,* 498–506.

Chalhoub-Deville, M., & Tarone, E. (1996, March). *What is the role of specific contexts in second-language acquisition, teaching, and testing?* Paper presented at the annual meeting of the American Association for Applied Linguistics, Chicago.

Chalhoub-Deville, M., & Turner, C. (2000). What to look for in ESL admissions tests: Cambridge Certificate Exams, IELTS, and TOEFL. *System, 28,* 523–539.

Chapelle, C. A. (1998). Construct definition and validity inquiry in SLA research. In L. F. Bachman & A. D. Cohen (Eds.), *Second language acquisition and language testing interfaces* (pp. 32–70). Cambridge: Cambridge University Press.

Chomsky, N. (1965). *Aspects of the theory of syntax.* Cambridge, MA: MIT Press.

Clapham, C. (1996). *The development of IELTS: A study of the effect of background on reading comprehension.* Cambridge: Cambridge University Press.

Clark, J. L. D. (1988). *The proficiency-oriented testing movement in the United States and its implications for instructional program design and evaluation.* Mimeo: Defense Language Institute, California.

Cole, M. (1996). *Cultural psychology.* Cambridge, MA: Belknap Press of Harvard University Press.

Cronbach, L. J. (1971). Test validation. In R. L. Thorndike (Ed.), *Educational measurement* (2nd ed., pp. 443–507). Washington, DC: American Council on Education.

Cronbach, L. J. (1989). Construct validation after thirty years. In R. E. Linn (Ed.), *Intelligence: Measurement theory and public policy* (pp. 147–171). Urbana: University of Illinois Press.

Cronbach, L. J. (Ed.). (2002). *Remaking the concept of aptitude: Extending the legacy of Richard E. Snow.* Mahwah, NJ: Lawrence Erlbaum.

Culler, J. (1983). *On deconstruction: Theory and criticism after structuralism.* London: Routledge.

Davidson, F., & Bachman, L. F. (1990). The Cambridge-TOEFL comparability study: An example of the cross-national comparison of language tests. *AILA Review, 7,* 24–45.

Deville, C., & Chalhoub-Deville, M. (2006). Old and new thoughts on test score variability: Implications for reliability and validity. In M. Chalhoub-Deville, C. Chapelle, & P. Duff (Eds.), *Inference and generalizability in applied linguistics:*

Multiple perspectives (pp. 9–25). Amsterdam: John Benjamins Publishing Company.

Des Brisay, M. (1994). Problems in developing an alternative to the TOEFL. *TESL Canada Journal, 12,* 47–57.

Duran, R. P. (1989). Testing of linguistic minorities. In R. L. Linn (Ed.), *Educational measurement* (3rd ed., pp. 573–587). New York: American Council on Education & Macmillan.

Elder, C. (1993). Language proficiency as predictor of performance in teacher education. *Melbourne Papers in Language Testing, 2,* 1–17.

Ellis, R. (1994). *The study of second language acquisition.* Oxford: Oxford University Press.

Erickson, F., & Schultz, J. (1981). When is context? Some issues and methods in the analysis of social competence. In J. Green & C. Wallat (Eds.), *Ethnography and language in educational settings* (pp. 147–160). Norwood, NJ: Ablex.

Frederiksen, C. H. (1981). Inference in preschool children's conversations—a cognitive perspective. In J. Green & C. Wallat (Eds.), *Ethnography and language in educational settings* (pp. 303–350). Norwood, NJ: Ablex.

Fulcher, G. (1996). Invalidating validity claims for the ACTFL oral rating scale. *System, 24,* 163–172.

Fulcher, G. (1998). Testing speaking. In C. Clapham & D. Corson (Eds.), *Language testing and assessment (Encyclopaedia of language and education, Vol. 7)* (pp. 75–86). Amsterdam: Kluwer.

Fulcher, G. (2003). *Testing second language speaking.* London: Pearson Education Limited.

Gilbert, R. (1992). Text and context in qualitative educational research: Discourse analysis and the problem of contextual explanation. *Linguistics and Education, 4,* 37–57.

Grabe, W. (1999). Developments in reading research and their implications for computer-adaptive reading assessment. In M. Chalhoub-Deville (Ed.), *Issues in computer-adaptive testing of reading proficiency* (pp. 11–48). Cambridge: Cambridge University Press.

Haas, G. J. (1990). English language testing: The view from the admission office. In D. Douglas (Ed.), *English language testing in U.S. colleges and universities* (pp. 9–18). Washington, DC: National Association for Foreign Student Affairs.

Hale, G. A., Stansfield, C. W., & Duran, R. P. (1984). *Summaries of studies involving the Test of English as a Foreign Language, 1963–1982.* Princeton, NJ: Educational Testing Service.

Halliday, M. A. K., & Hasan, R. (1985). *Language, context, and text: Aspects of language in a social-semiotic perspective.* Victoria, Australia: Deakin University.

Hamilton, J., Lopes, M., McNamara, T., & Sheridan, E. (1993). Rating scales and native speaker performance on a communicatively oriented EAP test. *Language Testing, 10,* 337–354.

Henning, G. (1990). Interpreting test scores. In D. Douglas (Ed.), *English language testing in U.S. colleges and universities* (pp. 82–90). Washington, DC: National Association for Foreign Student Affairs.

Hymes, D. H. (1972). On communicative competence. In J. B. Pride & J. Holmes (Eds.), *Sociolinguistics: Selected readings* (pp. 269–293). Harmondsworth, Middlesex, England: Penguin.

Johnson, M. (2001). *The art of nonconversation: A re-examination of the validity of the oral proficiency interview.* New Haven, CT: Yale University Press.

Johnson, M. (2004). *A dialogic philosophy of second language acquisition.* New Haven and London: Yale University Press.

Jones, R. L. (1975). Testing language proficiency in the United States government. In R. L. Jones & B. Spolsky (Eds.), *Testing language proficiency* (pp. 1–9). Arlington, VA: Center for Applied Linguistics.

Kramsch, C. (1986). From language proficiency to interactional competence. *The Modern Language Journal, 70,* 366–372.

Kramsch, C. (1998). *Language and culture.* Oxford: Oxford University Press.

Lado, R. L. (1961). *Language testing: The construction and use of foreign language tests: A teacher's book.* New York: McGraw-Hill.

Lantolf, J. P., & Frawley, W. (1985). Oral proficiency testing: A critical analysis. *The Modern Language Journal, 69,* 337–345.

Lee, Y.-W., Kantor, R., & Mollaun, P. (2002, April). *Score dependability of the writing and speaking sections of New TOEFL.* Paper presented at the annual meeting of the National Council on Measurement in Education (NCME), New Orleans, LA.

Liskin-Gasparro, J. E. (1984a). The ACTFL proficiency guidelines: Gateway to testing and curriculum. *Foreign Language Annals, 17,* 475–489.

Liskin-Gasparro, J. E. (1984b). The ACTFL proficiency guidelines: A historical perspective. In T. V. Higgs (Ed.), *Teaching for proficiency: The organizing principle* (pp. 11–42). Lincolnwood, IL: National Textbook Company.

Liskin-Gasparro, J. E. (2001, February). *L2 speaking as proficiency.* Paper presented at the annual meeting of AAAL—LTRC/AAAL Joint Colloquium, St. Louis, MO.

Lowe, P. (1983). The ILR oral interview: Origins, applications, pitfalls, and implications. *Die Unterrichtspraxis, 16,* 230–244.

Lowe, P. (1987). Interagency language roundtable proficiency interview. In J. C. Alderson, K. J. Krahnke, & C. W. Stansfield (Eds.), *Reviews of English language proficiency tests* (pp. 43–47). New York: TESOL.

Loyd, B. H. (1985). Review of the Test of English as a Foreign Language. In J. V. Mitchell, Jr. (Ed.), *The ninth mental measurement yearbook* (pp. 1568–1569). Lincoln, NE: Buros Institute of Mental Measurements.

Lumley, T. (2002, March 26). Email communication on the listserv LTEST-L.

McNamara, T. (1997). 'Interaction' in second language performance assessment: Whose performance? *Applied Linguistics, 18,* 446–466.

McNamara, T. (2003). Looking back, looking forward: Rethinking Bachman. *Language Testing, 20,* 466–473.

Messick, S. (1989). Validity. In R. L. Linn (Ed.), *Educational measurement* (3rd ed., pp. 13–103). New York: American Council on Education and Macmillan.

Messick, S. (1996). Validity and washback in language testing. *Language Testing, 13,* 241–256.

Moss, P. (1992). Shifting conceptions of validity in educational measurement: Implications for performance assessment. *Review of Educational Research, 62,* 229–258.

National Standards in Foreign Language Education Project. (1996). *Standards for foreign language learning: Preparing for the 21st century.* Yonkers, NY: American Council on the Teaching of Foreign Languages, Inc.

North, B. (2000). *The development of a common framework scale of language proficiency.* New York: Peter Lang.

Omaggio Hadley, A. C. (1993). *Teaching language in context* (2nd ed.). Boston, MA: Heinle & Heinle Publishers.

Oller, J. W., Jr. (1979). *Language tests at school: A pragmatic approach.* London: Longman.

Oller, J. W., Jr. (1983). Evidence for a general language proficiency factor: An expectancy grammar. In J. W. Oller, Jr. (Ed.), *Issues in language testing research* (pp. 3–10). Rowley, MA: Newbury House.

Pearlman, M. (2003, February). *Next generation TOEFL: Focus on communication.* Presentation at the University of Texas, Austin.

Rex, L., Green, J., Dixon, C., & the Santa Barbara Discourse Group. (1998). What counts when context counts?: The uncommon "common" language of literacy research. *Journal of Literacy Research, 30,* 405–433.

Roach, J. (1971). *Public examinations in England 1850–1900.* Cambridge: Cambridge University Press.

Saville, N. (2002, December). *Plurilingualism and partial competence: Implications for language assessment.* Presentation at the annual Language Testing Research Colloquium, Hong Kong, China.

Schoenfeld, A. (1999). Looking toward the 21st century: Challenges of educational theory and practice. *Educational Researcher, 28*(7), 4–14.

Sfard, A. (1998). On two metaphors for learning and the dangers of choosing just one. *Educational Researcher, 27*(2), 4–13.

Sharwood Smith, M. (1994). *Second language learning: Theoretical foundations.* London: Longman.

Shavelson, R. J., Baxter, G. P., & Goa, X. (1993). Sampling variability of performance assessments. *Journal of Educational Measurement, 30,* 215–232.

Snow, R. E. (1994). Abilities in academic tasks. In R. J. Sternberg & R. K. Wagner (Eds.), *Mind in context* (pp. 3–37). Cambridge: Cambridge University Press.

Spolsky, B. (1995). *Measured words.* Oxford: Oxford University Press.

Stansfield, C. (2002, March 24). Email communication on the listserv LTEST-L.

Swain, M. (2001). Examining dialogue: Another approach to content specification and to validating inferences drawn from test scores. *Language Testing, 18,* 275–302.

van Lier, L. (1989). Reeling, writhing, drawling, stretching, and fainting in coils: Oral proficiency interviews as conversation. *TESOL Quarterly, 23,* 489–508.

Vygotsky, L. S. (1978). *Mind in society: The development of higher psychological processes.* Cambridge, MA: Harvard University Press.

Weir, C. (2003). A survey of the history of the Certificate of Proficiency in English (CPE) in the twentieth century. In C. Weir & M. Milanovic (Eds.), *Continuity and innovation: Revising the Cambridge Proficiency English Examination 1913–2002* (pp. 1–56). Cambridge: Cambridge University Press.

Weir, C., & Milanovic, M. (Eds.). (2003). *Continuity and innovation: Revising the Cambridge Proficiency in English Examination 1913–2002.* Cambridge: Cambridge University Press.

Wertsch. J. V. (1985). *Vygotsky and the social formation of mind.* Cambridge, MA: Harvard University Press.

Wilds, C. (1979). The measurement of speaking and reading proficiency in a foreign language. In M. L. Adams & J. R. Frith (Eds.), *Testing kit: French and Spanish* (pp. 1–12). Washington DC: Department of State, Foreign Services Institute.

Young, R. F. (2000, March). *Interactional competence: Challenges for validity.* Paper presented at the annual meeting of the Language Testing Research Colloquium, Vancouver, Canada.

Young, R., & He, A. (Eds.). (1998). *Talking and testing.* Amsterdam: John Benjamins Publishing Company.

15

Testing for Accountability in K–12

Daniel M. Koretz
Harvard Graduate School of Education

Laura S. Hamilton
RAND Corporation

The past several decades have witnessed sweeping and fundamental changes in the uses of large-scale group achievement tests in the elementary and secondary grades. Some of the uses of tests that are now nearly ubiquitous, such as the imposition of concrete sanctions and rewards for schools based on changes in students' scores, were seen as revolutionary only a few years ago.

These many changes in the uses of tests have numerous important implications for measurement. The mix of inferences users base on scores has changed substantially. For example, normative inferences have become less salient, and standards-based inferences have become correspondingly prominent. Conclusions about aggregates and about changes in performance have become increasingly important. As a consequence of both these changes and the shifting uses of tests—in particular, the growth of high-stakes uses—the mix of threats to the validity of inferences has changed, which has implications for the methods used in validation. For example, because of the pressures of test-based accountability, the potential for corruption or inflation of test scores must now be a central concern in the evaluation of validity.

The first section of this chapter provides a brief history of large-scale K–12 achievement testing in the United States, focusing primarily on trends in the uses of tests over the past several decades. The following section provides a framework for evaluating the validity of inferences about performance under high-stakes conditions, links this to educators' responses to testing, and suggests new directions for evaluating validity under high-stakes conditions. The remainder of the chapter draws frequently on this framework and makes use of terminology defined in section 2. The remaining sections explore the implications of changes in testing described in the first section. Throughout these sections, our primary focus is on implications for the validity of inferences.

1. TRENDS IN K–12 GROUP TESTING

Recent years have been a period of intense ferment in K–12 group achievement testing. The amount of testing increased sharply during the 1990s and early 2000s, and the characteristics and uses of tests underwent many changes, some fundamental. Yet at the same time, many of these changes can be seen as continuations of trends that stretch back decades and that have taken different forms over the years.

At the time of this writing, a primary focus of debate about large-scale testing is the No Child Left Behind Act of 2001 (NCLB, federal legislation that mandates that states accepting federal Title I funds implement a specific form of accountability based on group achievement tests).[1] NCLB requires states to implement annual testing in at least seven grade levels; link their assessments to standards; report results in terms of specific performance standards, including a Proficient standard that indicates the level of performance expected of all students in a grade level; hold all but a very small percentage of students to this standard; maintain specified rates of inclusion in testing programs; and report results separately for a number of subgroups of the student population, such as students with disabilities. It holds schools accountable for meeting a series of increasingly stringent targets, ending at 100% of students meeting the Proficient standard at the end of 12 years. It specifies that each reporting subgroup, not just the entire student population, is expected to meet these targets, and it requires the use of a complex measure, called Adequate Yearly Progress (AYP), for determining whether schools are meeting their targets during the 12-year period.

These provisions of NCLB have required sweeping changes of practice in many states, but even this statute can be seen to have its roots in earlier developments in large-scale testing. When NCLB was passed, many of its provisions had already been implemented in various states, although the specific details of some provisions were new, and no state had put in place the entire package of testing provisions mandated by the statute.

In this section, we present a brief discussion of trends in K–12 group testing. Our goal is not to be comprehensive but rather to provide sufficient context to clarify the implications of these changes for measurement, which we discuss in the following sections. This section is divided into two parts. The first part provides a brief sketch of the origins of large-scale achievement testing and its evolution through the mid-1980s. The second section, which is organized thematically rather than historically, provides an overview of the most important changes in testing since the late 1980s. Among the changes discussed in this section are the following:

1. Increased stakes for both educators and students, accompanied by an increased emphasis on measurement-driven instruction
2. Changes in the mix of item formats used
3. Reliance on criterion-referenced or standards-based, as opposed to norm-referenced, reporting, coupled with pressure to align tests with state standards
4. Increased use of custom or state-specific tests
5. Mandates for inclusion of students with disabilities, students with limited proficiency in English, and other students who have previously been exempt from testing, accompanied by restrictions on the use of alternative tests or alternative performance standards for all but the most severely disabled students[2]
6. Reporting strategies that focus on increasingly small aggregates (such as the subgroup reporting requirements of NCLB), with high stakes attached to the performance of these groups
7. Reporting focused more on changes in scores, and on cohort-to-cohort changes in particular, than on levels of performance at a single point in time, including a growing interest in value-added modeling of test scores to measure school and teacher effects.

1.1. Origins and Development of Large-Scale Testing in the United States through the 1980s

Large-scale, group-administered tests have influenced public education in the United States since at least the 1840s, when an examination to monitor schools' effectiveness was implemented in Boston (Resnick, 1982). This test had many of the features associated with today's large-scale state and district tests and was intended to provide efficient measurement for large numbers of students and to facilitate comparisons across classrooms and schools. The use of this type of standardized test increased over the ensuing decades, frequently taking the form of a high school entrance examination (Resnick, 1982). Although these entrance examinations were originally intended for selection of individuals and were not administered to representative groups of students, they were often used as measures of school effectiveness. School administrators and state and district supervisors found the use of these tests for monitoring educators' performance appealing despite arguments from teachers and their representatives that these tests should not be used to compare teachers or schools (Tyack, 1974).

World War I marked the beginning of a new use for standardized, group-administered tests. Schools and institutions such as the armed services demanded more efficient ways to measure individuals' abilities and their potential for educational or occupational success. Group intelligence tests became a primary mechanism for selecting individuals into programs, positions, and institutions (Goslin, 1963). The first large-scale group intelligence test, the Army Alpha, was published in 1917 and was used to determine placements for large numbers of army recruits. The use of the Army Alpha led to an expansion of group intelligence testing into workplaces and schools and fostered the development of the test publishing industry. Schools, in particular, found the new tests useful for placing students into homogeneous ability groups, which many educators believed would result in more efficient and effective instruction (Resnick, 1982).

The development of standardized achievement test batteries designed to provide information on student learning and school effectiveness across multiple grade levels began at about the same time. The first such battery, the Stanford Achievement Tests, was published in 1923, and was followed by the development of a number of measures designed to assess student learning rather than simply intelligence. An example is the Iowa Tests of Basic Skills (ITBS), developed in the late 1930s, which assessed a broad range of abilities and was intended to help teachers diagnose student needs and adapt their instruction to these needs (Resnick, 1982).

1.1.1. Development of Assessments to Monitor Aggregate Achievement Trends

During the years following World War I, the use of testing in schools expanded significantly (Haney, 1981), but the primary purposes of testing continued to be individual selection and diagnosis and, to a lesser extent, evaluation of programs (Goslin, 1963; Goslin, Epstein, & Hallock, 1965). Beginning in the 1960s, however, large-scale testing took on a new role, that of monitoring the performance of educational systems. In earlier decades, the use of tests for monitoring was limited to local jurisdictions. This changed with the development of the National Assessment of Educational Progress (NAEP), which was established in the 1960s to measure the achievement of the nation's students and, in particular, to provide the public with information about trends in performance. NAEP was designed to measure student achievement in core subjects on a recurring basis and to provide descriptive information on student performance (Koretz, 1992). As we discuss later, the uses of NAEP eventually expanded beyond these original intentions.

The increased use of tests for monitoring was also influenced by the Elementary and Secondary Education Act (ESEA) of 1965, which established the Title I compensatory education program. The law included provisions for the evaluation of the program's effects, marking the first time that major social-program legislation required program evaluation (David, 1982). The ESEA evaluation requirement resulted in the Title I Reporting and Evaluation System (TIERS), which used standardized norm-referenced achievement tests for this purpose—that is, tests that report performance in terms of students' positions on a distribution of performance. This system led to an increase in the use of these tests. This was also the origin of the Normal Curve Equivalent (NCE) scale, which is a normalized scale with mean 50 and standard deviation 21.06 (e.g., Linn, 2000), parameters chosen to align the scale with percentile ranks at values 1, 50, and 99.

The creation of NAEP and the evaluation requirements of the 1965 Title I legislation represent the first formal uses of tests as instruments for monitoring the performance of the nation's students (Koretz, 1992). Although neither of these testing programs imposed specific consequences for individual educators or students, some consider them to have been precursors of today's emphasis on using tests as tools for holding educators accountable for student performance (Roeber, 1988). Moreover, some argue that the growing use of tests for monitoring led policymakers and the public to view test scores as the primary measure of the success of the public education system and to accept an increasing level of centralized control of schools, thereby creating a context that would facilitate later test-based reforms (Airasian, 1987).

1.1.2. Minimum-Competency Testing and Measurement-Driven Instruction

For the most part, these new applications of testing to monitoring and evaluation emphasized the performance of groups of students rather than individuals. Beginning in the 1970s, however, testing began to carry consequences for individuals beyond those imposed by the earlier use of tests as selection mechanisms. This occurred primarily as a result of the growth of state-mandated, minimum-competency testing (MCT) programs that were designed to ensure that students reached an acceptable minimal level of proficiency, generally in basic skills. These programs used scores on tests to make decisions about individual students' access to educational programs or credentials; most imposed an exit test as a requirement for high school graduation, while a smaller number instituted "promotional gates" tests used as a requirement for promotion between grades (Jaeger, 1982).

The first statewide minimum-competency testing programs were enacted in 1971, and by the end of the decade at least 35 states had such programs (Jaeger, 1982). The rationales put forth by proponents of this form of testing indicate that the movement was largely a political one, intended to improve the level of public confidence in the education system and to serve as a mechanism to ensure that schools were serving their student populations adequately (Airasian, 1987; Gorth & Perkins, 1979). Minimum-competency testing was the first recent, large-scale, formal use of K–12 achievement tests as tools to hold students and, by extension, their teachers accountable for performance. In addition, minimum-competency tests were intended to signal to students and teachers what should be taught and learned. Although the movement withered during the 1980s, it had at least three major influences on large-scale testing.

The minimum-competency movement contributed to a dramatic increase in the number of states with uniform, statewide testing programs. Although some state programs, such as the New York Regents examinations, were in place long before minimum-competency testing, most states did not develop such programs until the 1970s and after. By the end of that decade, roughly 60% of states had systems of uniform, statewide assessments, and by 1990, most of them did. The states' role in testing has continued to expand since then.

The spread of MCTs also gave impetus to the use of criterion-referenced testing, which foreshadowed the standards-referenced testing that began spreading nationwide about two decades later. The term "criterion-referenced" test was coined by Robert Glaser to refer to assessments designed to assess "the degree to which the student has attained criterion performance" (1963/1994, p. 6). He noted that he was not using the term to refer only to end-of course (or other terminal) behaviors, but rather for information about students' placement on a "continuum of attainment" that "provides explicit information about what the individual can or cannot do" (p. 6). Glaser's use of the term criterion-referenced test thus was similar in many respects to Lindquist's (1951) notion of a direct measure of educational achievement. This approach stood in contrast to the norm-referenced approach to reporting typical of large-scale testing programs up to that time. Glaser's seminal paper was written not in reference to large-scale achievement testing used for monitoring or accountability, but rather in response to a number of problems in psychology, including the assessment of performance in "man-machine systems" such as flying airplanes (Glaser, 1994). Nonetheless, criterion-referenced reporting gained favor in some large-scale testing programs because advocates claimed that it was more useful than norm-referenced testing for helping students and teachers focus their efforts to improve (Popham & Husek, 1969) and because it fit with many educators' dislike of ranking students (Hambleton, 1994). The shift toward this form of reporting also reflected a practical constraint: many of the new assessments of the MCT era were developed at the local or state levels, and national norms were generally not available for them.

Within a short time, however, Glaser's concept of criterion-referenced testing accrued what Linn (1994) called "surplus meaning[s]," one of which is the notion of a cut score to determine mastery. MCT programs primarily employed tests designed to be criterion-referenced, and they all imposed cut scores to determine which students had attained sufficient mastery to deserve graduation or promotion. By the end of the MCT era, the term "criterion referenced" carried both meanings—that is, reporting in terms of what students know and the employment of a cut score. Although Glass (1976) and Linn (1994) have argued that cut scores are a "nonessential meaning" (Linn, 1994, p. 13) of the term criterion-referenced, this meaning has been central to the evolution of large-scale testing, and the two meanings are rarely distinguished in public discussion. By the end of the 1990s, reporting in both senses of the term had become the expected method for describing schools' and students' performance on large-scale, state-mandated tests, although as noted below, the term "criterion referenced" was in some instances replaced by the terminology of standards-based reporting.

Finally, the use of MCTs to influence instruction marked a shift toward what Popham and others (Popham, 1987; Popham, Cruse, Rankin, Sandifer, & Williams, 1985) called *measurement-driven instruction*, reflecting a belief that instruction can and should be shaped directly by tests.[3] Although evidence indicates that testing influenced instruction even as early as the beginning of the 20th century (Perrone, 1979), many tests used before the minimum-competency movement, such as standardized achievement test batteries, were designed with the primary goal of providing information about performance. These tests were expected to have an indirect effect on instruction by informing educators and parents about the relative strengths and weaknesses of students' performance. In contrast, advocates of measurement-driven instruction argued that tests should be designed explicitly to influence decisions about what was taught and learned. This foreshadowed future waves of test-based education reform discussed below: the enthusiasm for performance assessments and the ascendancy of standards-based testing.

1.1.3. The Education Reform Movement

This emphasis on using tests to influence instruction continued into the 1980s, a decade characterized by deep concern over what was perceived to be poor performance on the part of American students. Although student performance had begun improving by the early 1980s (College Board, 1985; Koretz, 1986), the public debate focused little on this and instead emphasized the bad news: NAEP scores that showed that many students did not demonstrate even a basic level of skills and knowledge, international comparisons that showed the achievement of U.S. students trailing that of their peers in many other countries, and the sizable decline in mean scores on the SAT during the 1960s and 1970s.

These concerns were expressed vividly in *A Nation at Risk* (National Commission on Excellence in Education, 1983), which led to a nationwide reform effort (known as the "education reform movement") that included an increased reliance on testing (Pipho, 1985) as well as an expansion of the kinds of stakes attached to scores. These stakes were intended to motivate improved performance on the part of teachers and administrators. By 1989, for example, nine states had enacted policies that allowed state agencies to take over school or district management as a consequence of poor performance on tests (National Governors' Association, 1989). States began experimenting with other sanctions as well. For example, The ISTEP program implemented by Indiana in the late 1980s established cut scores as the primary criterion for promotion between most grades, beginning with first grade. Several states, including Indiana and California, experimented with financial incentives to schools or districts for high scores on state-mandated tests (Koretz, 1992)—efforts that seemed to most observers to be revolutionary at the time but became commonplace not many years later.

Statewide tests also became more challenging during this period, beginning a shift in emphasis from minimum competency to high expectations for all students. This shift resulted from a widespread concern that too few American students were attaining the high levels of achievement thought necessary to compete economically with other countries, especially in the areas of science and mathematics. Some tests were also redesigned to measure a broader range of skills and content knowledge than in the past, though most states relied on off-the-shelf, multiple-choice tests that used norm-referenced reporting.

This period also saw the first widely publicized report of problems with the validity of information from high-stakes tests. John Cannell, a physician in private practice in West Virginia, discovered that most districts and states were reporting average test scores that were above the national average as defined by test-publisher norms and published a report documenting these findings (Cannell, 1988). This phenomenon was labeled the "Lake Wobegon effect" (Koretz, 1988; Phillips, 1990). Subsequent research suggested that Cannell's findings were essentially accurate, if not correct in all details, and that state and district scores on standardized tests were overstating students' actual achievement. In particular, Linn, Graue, and Sanders (1990) showed that performance as measured against test-publisher norms increased throughout the 1980s for most published tests, but these gains were not replicated on NAEP. This discrepancy between NAEP and high-stakes tests suggested that a large portion of the gains on the latter did not generalize beyond those specific tests.

The general phenomenon of increased test scores without a corresponding increase in the construct the test was designed to measure is often called "score inflation" (Koretz, 2003). Research from the late 1980s until the present day indicates that score inflation continues to compromise the validity of information from high-stakes tests (Jacob, 2002; Klein et al., 2000; Koretz & Barron, 1998; Koretz, Linn, Dunbar, & Shepard, 1991). Although the general causes of score inflation are understood (see section 2), the specific causes in most instances are not known. The type of inflation documented by Cannell may have resulted in part from outdated test publisher norms. Most tests are re-normed every 6 or 7 years. Because student achievement was increasing before Cannell's report, referencing performance to older norms overstated performance relative to the current distribution of achievement nationwide (Linn, Graue, & Sanders, 1990). However, this explanation probably accounts for only part of the inflation (Shepard, 1990). Moreover, old norms are not relevant to several studies that found inflation by comparing trends on high-stakes and other tests using metrics other than normative scales. A significant portion of the score inflation probably stems from inappropriate test-preparation activities, which we discuss in section 2. Many educators attributed the problems of score inflation and excessive test preparation to the multiple-choice format that was then used in nearly all standardized tests, though as we discuss later, score inflation turned out not to be limited to the multiple-choice format.

1.2. Changes in Testing Beginning in the Late 1980s

A confluence of trends during the 1980s, including the shift from focusing on minimum competency to expecting high levels of performance from all students, the continuing faith placed in the power of measurement-driven instruction to improve education, and growing concerns about the validity of information from large-scale, multiple-choice tests, led to additional changes in the nature of testing beginning in the late 1980s and continuing through the following decade.

1.2.1. Experimentation with Performance Assessment

Throughout the 20th century, the item format most commonly used in large-scale tests was multiple choice.

The multiple-choice format became popular because of its low cost and reliability of scoring, and the feasibility of testing large numbers of students using this format contributed to the expansion of large-scale testing early in the century.

Despite its advantages, however, the multiple-choice format fell out of favor with many education reformers in the late 1980s. By the late 1980s and early 1990s, many reformers and educators were calling for a shift to alternative formats often called "performance assessments," which require examinees to construct rather than select a response and which typically rely on human raters for scoring.[4] The terminology was not used consistently. Some used "performance assessment" to subsume almost any constructed response format, including short-answer items, items calling for more extended written responses, standardized hands-on performance tasks (e.g., those requiring manipulation of scientific apparatus), tasks that included both group activities and individually written products, portfolios of tasks generated during ongoing instruction, and other unstandardized tasks, such as oral presentation and defense of projects. Others, however, reserved the term for the more complex of these tasks and would not apply it to formats such as short answer.

The interest in performance assessment had at least three roots. One was the call for higher levels of achievement for all students, which included a shift in emphasis from knowledge of basic facts to more sophisticated reasoning and higher-order thinking skills. Some expressed concern that multiple-choice items might be poorly suited to assessing these more complex skills (see, e.g., National Research Council, 2001). A second motivation, seemingly in response to the Cannell (1988) report and related studies suggesting widespread score inflation on state and district tests, was the apparent susceptibility of multiple-choice tests to inappropriate test-preparation practices.

A third motivation followed the logic of the push for measurement-driven instruction: a desire to use assessment to shape instruction. Some reformers argued that assessment formats should mirror and therefore encourage the kinds of instructional activities that require higher-level skills (Madaus, 1993; Resnick & Resnick, 1992; Wiggins, 1992). Some assessment reformers used the phrase "tests worth teaching to," an ambiguous phrase that was used to imply both that preparation for these tests would be instructionally valuable and that it would not inflate scores. As explained in section 2, however, the second does not logically follow from the first.

Numerous states experimented with the inclusion of performance tasks in their large-scale testing programs during the late 1980s and early 1990s. Vermont was one of the first and most ambitious. In 1988 Vermont began developing a statewide testing program based largely on portfolios of student work collected over the course of the school year rather than on standardized, on-demand items or tasks. The motivations for this program, as expressed by the Commissioner of Education and State Education Department staff, were similar to those expressed by many performance assessment advocates—to reduce score inflation and promote good instruction (Koretz, Stecher, Klein, & McCaffrey, 1994). The program was designed to provide local educators with a great deal of autonomy in the selection of tasks and to involve them in scoring. Although evaluations of the program eventually revealed that the quality of information it produced was generally poor (Koretz, Stecher, Klein, and McCaffrey, 1994), the program received widespread national attention. Kentucky also included portfolios in its assessment system, but no state relied as heavily on unstandardized tasks as did Vermont. Maryland and Kentucky both used tasks that involved group activities followed by individual writing of responses: Kentucky abandoned these after several years for technical reasons, while Maryland used them from 1992 through 2002. Other states included varying mixes of constructed-response formats.

Perhaps the most far-reaching effort to develop a large-scale performance assessment program was the New Standards Project. A joint effort of the University of Pittsburgh Learning Research and Development Center and the National Center on Education and the Economy, the project initially involved a national coalition of approximately 17 states and seven districts that worked to develop a performance assessment system that was intended for eventual use in large-scale state or district testing programs (Spalding, 2000). Performance assessment was one part of a broader system of tests linked to standards (see section 1.2.2). The system was eventually to have consisted of a combination of short, performance-based tasks, projects, exhibitions, and portfolios that would replace existing large-scale multiple-choice tests (O'Neil, 1993) and that its advocates hoped would result in improved quality of curriculum and instruction offered to all students (Simmons & Resnick, 1993).

1.2.2. The Shift Back to Multiple-Choice Format

The influence of the performance assessment movement can still be seen in many large-scale assessments. Both Rhode Island and Vermont used New Standards assessment tasks as of 2003 (Arenz & Bohlin, 2003). Many large-scale assessments continue to include short-answer and more extended pencil-and-paper constructed-response items. For example, constructed-response items constituted a modest share of the total number of items on the Massachusetts MCAS assessments in 2002 (Massachusetts Department of Education, 2003a) and roughly half of the items on the NAEP mathematics assessments in 1996, 2000, and 2003 (National Center for Education Statistics [NCES], 2004). Because of the time required to write responses as well as the large size of some tasks for which constructed responses are required, constructed-response items sometimes require the bulk of examinees' testing time. For example, approximately 80% of testing time was allocated to short and extended constructed-response items on the 1996 NAEP science assessment (NCES, 2001).

Nonetheless, the enthusiasm for complex formats waned rather quickly, and the 1990s saw a substantial shift back to a reliance on the multiple-choice format, often coupled with short constructed-response items. In part, the reduced reliance on such complex performance tasks stemmed from concerns about what those tasks measure. Several studies have demonstrated that performance tests frequently fail to tap the processes and skills their developers intended (Baxter & Glaser, 1998; Hamilton, Nussbaum, & Snow, 1997; Linn, Baker, & Dunbar, 1991) and that they are not immune to score inflation (Koretz & Barron, 1998). In addition, performance typically generalizes poorly across complex tasks, even writing samples (e.g., Dunbar, Koretz, & Hoover, 1991), because of often unintended idiosyncratic aspects of the tasks. As a result, studies have typically shown that a substantial number of complex tasks is needed to obtain reliable scores for individual students (e.g., Koretz, Stecher, Klein, McCaffrey, & Deibert, 1993; Shavelson, Baxter, & Gao, 1993; Wainer & Thissen, 1993). Given the cost and time required by complex tasks, however, administering a sufficiently large number is burdensome and often impractical. Therefore tests comprising complex performance tasks often include only a small number of items, the consequence of which is both limited content sampling and poor generalizability. Concerns about technical quality and costs are also likely to dissuade most states from relying heavily on performance assessments in their accountability systems (Linn, 1993; Mehrens, 1998; NCES, 1996), particularly when states are facing heavy testing demands and severe budget constraints.

The problem of high costs may be the most important factor contributing to states' reliance on multiple-choice testing. The magnitude of the problem is evident in a study by the U.S. General Accounting Office (2003), which estimated states' costs for implementing large-scale testing. The total estimated cost for states using only multiple-choice tests was approximately $1.9 billion, whereas the cost if states also included a small number of hand-scored open-response items such as essays was estimated to be about $5.3 billion. The magnitude of this difference suggests that many states may remain reluctant to abandon extensive reliance on the multiple-choice format, at least until the alternative testing technologies become less expensive. The increase in the volume of testing required of many states by the recent No Child Left Behind legislation (2001) may strengthen this reluctance.

1.2.3. Standards-Referenced Testing

As performance assessment began to gain in popularity, a related and longer-lived movement was taking hold: a drive for rigorous standards and for assessments aligned to them. The tests spawned by this movement go by several terms, but we refer to them as standards-referenced tests (SRTs) to distinguish them from norm-referenced and earlier criterion-referenced tests. SRTs dominated state-level testing during the early 21st century and were required for jurisdictions accepting Title I funds under the terms of the No Child Left Behind Act (e.g., 2 0 U.S.C. 6311 § 6311(b)(3)(C)(ii)).

In the late 1980s, educators, policymakers, and other reformers began calling for the publication of high, rigorous standards that would apply to all students and that would clearly communicate to students, teachers, and others the high level of achievement expected (Resnick & Resnick, 1992; Smith & O'Day, 1990). One impetus for this movement was the 1989 Charlottesville, Virginia Education Summit in which the president and governors developed a set of national goals (Linn, 2003). The federal legislation that eventually emerged from this effort, the Goals 2000: Educate America Act of 1994, encouraged the use of two types of standards: content standards that would convey what students should learn, and performance standards that would indicate how well students would be expected to perform with respect to these content standards. Although performance standards (also sometimes called achievement standards) were generally communicated via written descriptions of expectations, in practice they were implemented in the form of cut scores on tests. The rationale and vision for national standards were described by the National Council on Education Standards and Testing, a group that was formed to explore the feasibility of a national system of standards and tests and that played a role in shaping Goals 2000 (NCEST, 1992). The group called for an overarching vision statement for each subject; content and performance standards describing knowledge, skills, and understandings as well as the levels of competence expected; and school delivery standards that were intended to ensure opportunity to learn.

The standards movement rapidly gained momentum, and numerous national groups and individual states began working on the development of standards. The first of the national efforts was that of the National Council of Teachers of Mathematics, which published its *Curriculum and Evaluation Standards for School Mathematics* in 1989. The New Standards Project, described above, was a major contributor to the development of standards during this period. During the same time, several states, including California, Vermont, and Connecticut, developed statewide curriculum standards that encompassed many of the features espoused by national organizations advocating the use of standards.

An emphasis on higher-order thinking skills was central to standards-based reform. One reason was a widespread belief that minimum-competency testing had led to an excessive emphasis on low-level skills and had therefore hindered the academic progress of some students, particularly those who were not assigned to college-bound tracks (Smith & O'Day, 1990). Of the characteristics that NCEST asserted were essential for a national system of standards, the first was that "Standards must reflect high expectations, not expectations of minimum competency" (NCEST, 1992, p.3). The NCTM standards emphasized higher-order skills such as problem solving and communication in mathematics. In science, the National Research Council's National Science Education Standards (1996) and the American Association for the Advancement of Science's Benchmarks for Science Literacy (1993) emphasized the importance of promoting inquiry skills and an understanding of science processes in addition to knowledge of facts and vocabulary. The importance of higher-order skills was similarly a central tenet of The New Standards Project.

Two attributes characterized the testing spawned by the standards movement: an emphasis on alignment between tests and content standards, and reporting test scores in terms of performance standards. Alignment was a central part of the argument put forward by NCEST and was a focus of much of the assessment-development work that took place during this period. The New Standards Project, for example, developed assessments linked to its curriculum standards and disseminated both the standards and the assessments to states and localities.

The standards movement created a rapid shift toward reporting of performance in terms of performance standards rather than in terms of norm-referenced or other conventional scales. The primary motivation for this shift appears to have been a desire to compare performance to expectations—how much students should know—rather than to the distribution of current performance, which many reformers considered unacceptably low. The levels of the performance standards varied substantially from state to state (Linn, 2000), but most states established only a small number of them, thus creating a coarse and clearly ordinal scale on which to report performance. In the 2001–2002 school year, 29 states (including the District of Columbia) reported on scales comprising four or fewer levels based on three or fewer standards, and an additional 9 states reported using scales of five levels (Council of Chief State School Officers, 2003). Both reporting in terms of standards and the use of standards in accountability were mandated by NCLB (2001). Despite the pervasiveness of standards-based reporting and the explicit disparagement of normative reporting often heard in the policy debate, the demand for norm-referenced information remained, as evidenced by the continuing popularity of school rankings, the attention granted to state rankings on NAEP (see section 1.2.9), and the incorporation of normative data into the reports of some standards-referenced tests, such as the comparisons of school-level to district-level and statewide performance provided for the Massachusetts MCAS assessment (e.g., Massachusetts Department of Education, 2003b).

The SRT movement shows both similarities to and differences from both the MCT and performance assessment movements that preceded it. The standards movement retained the emphasis on higher-order thinking skills that characterized the performance-assessment movement, even though most SRTs avoided highly complex performance assessments and places considerable reliance on the multiple-choice format (see section 1.2.2). Standards-based reform continued the use of cut-scores and the goal of measurement-driven instruction first manifested in the MCT movement of the 1970s, but with two important differences. First, many advocates of standards-based reform argued that the published standards, rather than just the test, should determine what is taught in the classroom. The extent to which this expectation has been met remains an empirical question (see section 3). Second, in contrast to the MCTs, the standards movement emphasized high rather than minimal standards, although in practice the standards set by states have been highly variable (see, e.g., Linn, 2000).

1.2.4. Increase in States' Use of Custom-Developed Tests and Standards

Content and performance standards have been developed primarily by individual states. The development process typically involves the convening of educators and other subject-matter experts to identify the skills and knowledge expected at each grade level, sometimes with supplementary input from members of the business community, parents, or other stakeholders (La Marca, Redfield, & Winter, 2000). Several national organizations have developed content standards in core academic subjects (e.g., National Council of Teachers of Mathematics, 1989; American Association for the Advancement of Science, 1993; National Research Council, 1996), but these have served largely to influence states' own development of standards.

One result of states' involvement in the development of standards has been pressure for states to adopt either tests designed specifically for their own use or more broadly used tests that have been customized for them. The logic of standards-based reform requires that the tests used to measure student progress must be aligned with standards—that is, the content, skill requirements, and difficulty levels of the tests must match those of the standards. Clear links among testing, standards, and curriculum were believed not only to drive curriculum in a desirable direction but also to enhance the motivation of educators and students by giving them an unambiguous message about how to focus their efforts (Smith, O'Day, & Cohen, 1990). With the enactment of No Child Left Behind, this logic is now clearly incorporated into federal statute (see, for example, 20 U.S.C. § 6311(b)(3)(C)).

Nonetheless, as states began to establish their standards-based systems, some simply purchased existing tests from commercial publishers, often with little effort to ensure alignment with state standards beyond a fairly cursory inspection of the items (Rothman, Slattery, Vranek, & Resnick, 2002). More recently, however, as stakes have increased and the emphasis on standards-based or criterion-referenced reporting has grown, states have put more effort into creating systems designed to be aligned, which has resulted in a proliferation of custom-built tests either developed by states themselves or purchased from publishers. The emphasis on alignment has therefore substantially increased the diversity of tests that must be constructed for state systems.

1.2.5. Incorporation of Tests into Accountability Systems

The statewide testing programs enacted or expanded during this period increasingly emphasized the use of tests for accountability purposes. The minimum-competency movement imposed stakes on students and thereby held their teachers accountable to some extent, but formal stakes for educators were rare. Over the ensuing decades, however, states began incorporating both rewards and sanctions such as threats of reconstitution into their testing systems. By the end of the 1990s, many states had implemented explicit systems of rewards and sanctions for schools. For example, an *Education Week* survey reported that as of 1998, 18 states had systems for rewarding schools based on test scores, and a smaller number had implemented formal sanctions based on scores (Jerald & Boser, 1999). Moreover, while some early efforts focused on the threat of sanctions for the lowest performing schools, these systems were increasingly designed to affect all schools. The Kentucky KIRIS system, implemented in 1992, was in many ways a model for this change; it imposed both sanctions and rewards for schools based on the size of test-score changes from one two-year period to the next. The presumed positive effects of testing on both student and teacher motivation was a primary rationale for expanding the stakes attached to scores (NCEST, 1992).

This period also saw a resurgence of high stakes for students. Although some exit examination systems had persisted as the wave of enthusiasm for minimum-competency testing abated, in many states, attention had moved to school-level accountability. However, during the 1990s, many states again began imposing high stakes for students, primarily in the form of exit examinations. As of 2003, 19 states had high school exit examinations in place, and 4 more had implementation planned between 2004 and 2008 (Gayler, Chudowsky, Kober, & Hamilton, 2003). In many cases, these new exit exams required a much higher level of performance than did minimum-competency tests, and some states (e.g., Texas) that had maintained exit exam systems increased the difficulty of their tests, making them a serious consideration for a larger percentage of students and schools. In addition to exit examinations, a number of states (e.g., Texas) and districts (e.g., New York and Chicago) implemented promotional-gates testing, making promotion between specified grades contingent on exceeding a cut score on a test.

1.2.6. Mandates for Full Inclusion and Greater Uniformity in Testing

In recent years, there have been repeated efforts to increase the inclusiveness of large-scale assessments. Accompanying this change have been policies requiring uniformity in the tests administered to most students and in the performance standards used to evaluate them.

One particular focus has been the participation of students with disabilities or limited proficiency in English in the assessments used with the general student population. In this chapter, we use the term "students with special needs" to refer to both of these groups. This trend is evident in a series of federal statutes that have imposed increasingly specific requirements for the inclusion of students with special needs, especially students with disabilities. However, the impetus for this change was broadly based, and several states undertook ambitious efforts to increase inclusion before federal mandates required that they do so. For example, in the early 1990s, Kentucky adopted a system for assessing students with disabilities that is very similar to that mandated by a federal statute enacted several years later, the Individuals with Disabilities Education Act Amendments of 1997 (IDEA). Kentucky's policy required that most students with disabilities be assessed with the regular state assessment, that these students be provided special accommodations as needed, and that a small number of students with severe disabilities be assessed with special assessments labeled alternate assessments (e.g., see Koretz, 1997)—all policies that were later included in IDEA. Nonetheless, it is simplest to chart this evolution by considering policy changes at the federal level, which affect large-scale assessment nationwide.

Although most statewide testing programs were intended to provide information about the performance of all students in the state, it had been common practice in the 1980s and 1990s to exclude substantial numbers of students with disabilities from testing. Guidelines for the inclusion of these students varied across states, and the implementation of those guidelines varied across schools within a state, resulting in widely discrepant and generally low inclusion rates (e.g., Erickson & Thurlow, 1996). Advocates for students with disabilities worried that until the inclusion of these students was mandated, schools faced incentives to exclude students who would be expected to score poorly and therefore would not be held accountable for the performance of these students (see, for example, National Research Council, 1997).

Beginning in the early 1990s, a series of policy federal statutes and policy initiatives undertaken by some states pushed for greater inclusion of students with disabilities in large-scale assessments. Title I of the Improving America's Schools Act of 1994, which reauthorized the Elementary and Secondary Education Act of 1965 (ESEA), implied that states receiving Title I funds should include students with disabilities in their assessments. It required states to develop or adopt "a set of high-quality, yearly student assessments, including assessments in at least mathematics and reading or language arts" and that these "be the same assessments used to measure the performance of all children" (20 U.S.C. §6301(3)). It further mandated that these assessments provide for "the reasonable adaptations and accommodations for students with diverse learning needs, necessary to measure the achievement of such students relative to State content standards" (20 U.S.C. §6301(3)(F)(ii)). In the 1997 reauthorization of the Individuals with Disabilities Education Act, Congress moved further in this direction. As Karger observed, the 1997 reauthorization was "the first time that IDEA explicitly mandated that States and districts include students with disabilities in their assessment systems, with appropriate accommodations or by means of alternate assessments, and that States report on the results of these assessments" (Karger, 2003, p. 13). The statute requires that children with disabilities be included in general state and district programs; that appropriate accommodations be provided when necessary; and that the state develop alternate assessments for students who are unable to participate in state and district programs (20 U.S.C. §1412(a)(17)(A)). In addition, the law requires that state education agencies report the performance of students with disabilities on both the general and alternate assessments "with the same frequency and in the same detail as it reports on the performance of nondisabled children" (20 U.S.C. §1412(a)(17)(B)).

The No Child Left Behind Act of 2001, the most recent reauthorization of ESEA, moved farther in this direction, reestablishing certain requirements and adding others. It mandates that the same assessments be used for all students, with a few exceptions noted below, and that these assessments provide for "the reasonable adaptations and accommodations for students with disabilities ... [and] the inclusion of limited English proficient students, who shall be assessed in a valid and reliable manner and provided reasonable accommodations ... including, to the extent practicable, assessments in the language and form most likely to yield accurate data on what such students know and can do in academic content areas" (20 U.S.C. §6311(b)(3)(C). NCLB also requires disaggregated reporting "within each State, local educational agency, and school by gender, by each major racial and ethnic group, by English proficiency status, by migrant status, by students with disabilities as compared to nondisabled students, and by economically disadvantaged students ..., except that, in the case of a local educational agency or a school, such disaggregation shall not be required in a case in which the number of students in a category is insufficient to yield statistically reliable information or the results would reveal personally identifiable information about an individual student" (20 U.S.C. §6311(b)(3)(C)(xiii)). This disaggregated reporting for four groups—the economically disadvantaged, major racial/ethnic groups, students with disabilities, and students with limited proficiency in English, is used to measure Adequate Yearly Progress for accountability purposes (20 U.S.C. § 6311(b)(2)(C)(v)(II)), as described in section 1.2.8.2.

It is clearly impossible to assess "all students," and this series of statutes and the accompanying implementing regulations have gradually clarified who must be included. As noted, IDEA allows the use of alternate assessments for the small percentage of students whose disabilities are sufficiently severe as to preclude their participation in general-education assessments. In recent regulations implementing NCLB, the Education Department accepted these provisions of IDEA and clarified that while the expectation is that few students will be administered the alternate assessments, NCLB does not further limit the percentage of students so assessed (34 CFR Part 200, pp. 68698 ff.). NCLB requires that for an entity to make AYP, at least 95% of each of the subgroups noted above, including students with disabilities and with limited proficiency in English, must be tested with assessments meeting the requirements of the statute, either the general assessments or the alternate assessments (20 U.S.C. §6311(2)(I)(ii)).

While not limiting the percentage of students assessed with alternate assessments, the implementing regulations for NCLB do severely limit the percentage of students who can be assessed using "alternate achievement standards," a term that includes anything other than grade-level standards and includes out-of-level testing (Department of Education, Title 1 Implementing Regulations, 2003). The regulations specify that this is permitted only for students "with the most significant cognitive disabilities" (Department of Education, Title 1 Implementing Regulations, 2003, p. 69702). For states, but not necessarily for individual schools, these students are not permitted to exceed 1% of the total, and any students in excess of 1% are automatically counted as not being proficient for accountability purposes, as explained further below (Department of Education, Title 1 Implementing Regulations, 2003, p. 68703). Draft regulations published seven months earlier explained that the provision was intended to permit the use of alternate standards with students with moderate or more severe mental retardation, explicitly noting that mildly retarded students were to be assessed with grade-level standards. The draft further explained that this meant that only students more than three standard deviations below the mean should be assessed using alternate standards; the cap was set at 1% to allow for variations in prevalence (Department of Education, Title 1 Notice of Proposed Rulemaking, 2003, pp. 13796 ff.). The final regulations removed the references to both categories of retardation and standard deviations—the latter because of a view that it would have "placed unwarranted reliance on an IQ test" (Department of Education, Title 1 Implementing Regulations, 2003, p. 68704)—but retained the 1% cap.

1.2.7. School- and Group-Level Reporting Requirements

The test-based accountability systems that states enacted through the late 1980s and 1990s emphasized school-level rewards and sanctions. As a consequence of these systems, nearly all states developed reporting systems that provided the public with school-level scores, and many of these reported on smaller units within schools, such as grade levels or racial/ethnic subgroups. Many of these reports were made available over the Internet and therefore were more broadly disseminated than in the past. The increasing availability of school-level measures of performance led members of the news media, politicians, and others to increase their use of these results to rank and compare schools and districts.

1.2.8. Emphasis on Score Changes

Trends in test scores, such as declines in performance on college-entrance examinations, have long captured the attention of the public as well as educators and policymakers. However, until the emergence of state test-based accountability systems, evaluations of schools, classrooms, or individual students focused primarily on cross-sectional data, and psychometric methods, such as those used for validation, accordingly focused on cross-sectional relationships (see section 2). In recent years, however, attention has increasingly shifted to changes in performance over time, and in current large-scale K–12 testing, many of the most important inferences—in particular, those used in accountability—evaluate change. The increasing availability of school-level measures of performance, combined with a growing level of sophistication of national, state, and district databases, has facilitated this shift in emphasis.

Until the passage of NCLB, the most commonly used measure of change was the cohort-to-cohort difference in student performance. For example, in numerous test-based accountability systems of the 1990s, scores for one year's 4th graders would be compared with those of the previous year's 4th graders to obtain a measure of school improvement. This approach to measuring change may be the only feasible one for states that test students at non-consecutive grade levels or that administer different tests at different grade levels. Some systems also aggregate across specified grades, comparing performance of that aggregate in one year to the performance of the similar aggregate the previous year. Although this latter approach combines individual grade cohorts, it is logically a cohort-to-cohort model, with most of the same advantages and disadvantages as approaches that compare single-grade cohorts.

Change may also be measured with longitudinal and quasi-longitudinal approaches. A true longitudinal approach requires tracking individual students and measuring their growth across grades. We discuss this method, which is often called the value-added approach, later in this section. Measures of change may also be constructed using a quasi-longitudinal approach (Linn, 2001), in which a school's average score for this year's 4th graders (for example) is compared with that of last year's 3rd graders. This type of change measure should be less strongly influenced by changes in the mix of students from year to year than the cohort-to-cohort approach because in many instances, the two groups compared would largely comprise the same students.

Although quasi-longitudinal and value-added methods have garnered some interest, most state accountability systems have relied primarily on cohort-to-cohort approaches. The approach specified by NCLB is not a true cohort-to-cohort model, but it appears to have evolved from this approach.

1.2.9. Performance Targets

Accountability systems that measure score levels or changes typically specify a target that schools or other units are expected to meet to receive rewards or avoid sanctions and interventions. Two common approaches for setting performance targets are discussed below.

1.2.9.1. Straight-Line Improvement Models

During the 1990s, numerous test-based accountability systems implemented straight-line improvement models. This approach specifies for each school (or other group) a required rate of improvement that begins with the school's initial score and terminates at a specified date at a target that was generally uniform across all schools. As the name implies, the required improvements are typically a straight line (albeit sometimes with room for deviations) from the starting point to the ending point, using whatever metric the accountability system employs.

Kentucky was one of the first states to adopt this approach, in the KIRIS testing and accountability system implemented at the beginning of the 1990s (see Koretz & Barron, 1998). The KIRIS system entailed an index for each school that was based largely but not entirely on changes in scores on the KIRIS test. The test-based portion of the index was created by crediting the school with a specified number of points for each child in each of the four performance bands created by three performance standards (0, 40, 100, and 140 points, respectively) and taking an average. Each school's performance targets were established by drawing a straight line from its starting point to a value of 100 20 years later. The ending value of 100 corresponded to having all students at the proficient level, although the additional points that accrued for students in the top level meant that schools could reach this target while some students failed to reach the proficient standard. Schools were expected to achieve an improvement in the performance index of at least 1/10 of the distance between the starting value of the index and 100 every two years. Note that this system required a straight line of improvement only relative to the particular way in which the index was scaled. By the end of the decade, a number of additional states had established systems that included some variant of this approach (see Goertz, Duffy, & Carlson-LeFloch, 2001). In some cases, the straight lines were modified over time, resetting the lines after each round of accountability in response to the amount of progress made by schools in the preceding interval.

These systems result in more ambitious targets for initially low-performing schools than for higher-performing schools, and the targets have rarely been based on empirical information or other evidence regarding what expectations would be realistic (see, e.g., Linn, 2003). As a result, targets for low-performing schools in particular may be virtually impossible to meet by legitimate means (Koretz & Barron, 1998). The problem of unrealistic targets is relevant to the discussion of score inflation discussed in section 3.

1.2.9.2. The NCLB Model

The NCLB accountability requirements appear to have evolved from a straight-line cohort-to-cohort improvement model, but the law incorporated a number of differences, one of which makes it not an actual cohort-to-cohort change model for most schools. Cohort-to-cohort change models, including straight-line models, compare each cohort's performance to that of one or more previous cohorts in the same school. In contrast, the NCLB model establishes a series of targets for each entire state; the ending point is 100% proficient, and the starting point is either the 20th percentile school (ranked in terms of percent proficient) or the percent proficient in the lowest-scoring reporting group, as described above (20 U.S.C., § 6311(b)(2)(E)). The performance of each cohort in each school in any given year is compared to the statewide target. For most schools, the performance of previous cohorts in the school is irrelevant. NCLB retains a true cohort-change model in the form of a "safe harbor provision" that applies only to schools in which the total school population does make adequate progress but the school fails to make AYP because one or more of the specified subgroups does not meet the state's target. These schools may be designated as making AYP if the percentage of students in the subgroup(s) who failed to reach proficient level declined by at least 10% from the preceding year and if the school met its targets for other academic indicators as well as percent of students tested. For these schools, AYP is a hybrid measure, one part of which is a true cohort-to-cohort change indicator.

NCLB also substitutes for a straight-line improvement model a complex measure called Adequate Yearly Progress (AYP). The state can employ a straight-line model but can also institute various alternatives, such as changing rates of progress over the 12-year period and short-term averaging. Unlike the straight-line improvement model described above, the NCLB targets are not based on change scores but on performance at a single point in time. In addition, if the numbers of students in each group permit reliable reporting (which is not defined by the statute or its implementing regulations), the reporting groups must also meet these targets (No Child Left Behind, 2001: 20 U.S.C. § 6311(b)(2)(C)(v)(II)). Finally, each state's definition of AYP must include at least one other indicator, which for secondary schools must be the graduation rate, and may include other indicators at the state's discretion (20 U.S.C. § 6311(b)(2)(C)(vi)).

1.2.10. Value-Added Modeling

The growing use of straight-line improvement and other cohort-to-cohort change models for schools contrasts with another trend that emerged during this period: a heightened interest in evaluating teachers or schools on the basis of the achievement growth of their students. Several trends—the growing interest in measures of change, technological advances in database construction and statistical computing, and a continuing belief that test-score information could inform instruction—facilitated this change. The various approaches to monitoring growth in this way are often labeled "value-added modeling" or "value-added assessment" because they attempt to show how much schools or teachers contribute to student achievement growth, net of other factors such as student background characteristics. The most commonly known application of value-added modeling is the Tennessee Value Added Assessment System, or TVAAS (Sanders & Horn, 1998), though there are several other examples of value-added approaches in the literature (e.g., Rivkin, Hanushek, & Kain, 2005; Webster, Mendro, Orsak, & Weerasinghe, 1998), and a number of states are exploring ways to incorporate value-added methods into their assessment and accountability systems. Although most applications of value-added modeling appear incompatible with the NCLB accountability requirements described in the previous section, this approach to measuring achievement growth and evaluating teachers and schools may gain in popularity as data systems and computing resources improve.

Value-added modeling has attracted interest in large part because measures of student growth are generally believed to be less influenced by non-school factors than cross-sectional measures. In addition, several studies (Rivkin et al., 2005; Sanders & Rivers, 1996; Wright, Horn, & Sanders, 1997) claim to demonstrate that teachers' effects on achievement growth are quite large. A review of these studies was more cautious, concluding that the studies do show an effect of teachers but are not sufficient to clearly estimate its magnitude (McCaffrey, Lockwood, Koretz, & Hamilton, 2003). If additional research substantiates large teacher effects on growth, this could have profound effects on efforts to improve education through teacher selection or training and could greatly affect the ways test-score data are used to evaluate teachers' performance. The use of value-added modeling places certain demands on how tests are constructed and how scores are reported; for example, some approaches require vertically equated scale scores, a type of score that is becoming less common in large-scale testing applications as a result of the growing emphasis on standards-referenced reporting. Value-added modeling raises a number of additional issues of measurement and statistical modeling that are noted in section 7.

1.2.11. Changes to NAEP

Throughout the 1980s and 1990s, large-scale testing was frequently used as a mechanism to document publicly the performance of American students and thereby provide political justification for the need for reforms (Linn, 1993; U.S. Congress, Office of Technology Assessment, 1992). One element of this trend was a growing importance of NAEP to debate about K–12 education. Accompanying this increased prominence was a series of changes in the design of NAEP that reflected its changing roles. Some of these changes closely paralleled developments in local and state-level testing.

As noted earlier, NAEP was first established in the 1960s to monitor the achievement of the nation's youth. Because NAEP was not intended to evaluate the effectiveness of schools, it initially sampled children regardless of whether they were enrolled in school, it sampled by age rather than grade, and the samples were not designed to provide representative data below the level of regions and large population subgroups. No summary scale scores were provided; performance was reported with simple descriptive statistics, such as the percentage of items of a given type answered correctly. These statistics were accompanied in NAEP reports with numerous illustrative items. No formal linking was carried out across years.

The first major change in the design of NAEP occurred in 1984, when the Educational Testing Service (ETS) took over management of the assessment from the Education Commission of the States. The new ETS design, which persists with modifications until the present, instituted grade-level as well as age-based sampling and uses IRT scaling both to produce summary scores and to link across years (Messick, Beaton, & Lord, 1983).

A second change, with no parallels in state and local testing, was the bifurcation of NAEP into two separate assessments: a main assessment that is periodically revised, and a trend assessment, administered to a smaller sample and used to track long-term trends, that is kept constant over time. This change stemmed from an abrupt and implausibly large change in scaled scores in reading in 1986, an occurrence rapidly dubbed "the reading anomaly." Two reports (Beaton & Zwick, 1990; Haertel et al., 1989) suggested that this change in scores was an artifact of seemingly minor changes in the assessment, and as a result, a decision was made to keep one form of the assessment invariant over time. The long-term trend assessment was modified in several ways before the 2004 assessment—for example, to allow accommodations for students with disabilities—and some items will be replaced after 2004, but efforts will be made to keep the assessment as consistent over time as is practical (see National Assessment Governing Board, 2002a).

A third change was an expansion of NAEP to permit state-level reporting. Even after the original ETS redesign, the NAEP sample was designed to provide estimates only for regions and the nation as a whole. State samples were neither large enough nor sufficiently representative to permit meaningful state-level reporting. Because of interest in the policy community in information comparing states, other performance indicators, such as state-level SAT scores, were being used to rank and compare states (see, e.g., U.S. Department of Education, 1985), but these were recognized by many users as being inappropriate for this purpose. A National Academy of Education study group recommended that NAEP be expanded to provide a valid method for comparing states' education systems (Alexander & James, 1987), and the first administration of "state NAEP" occurred in 1990. State NAEP results quickly captured the attention of policymakers and researchers who were interested in ranking states and identifying factors associated with those ranks (see, e.g., Grissmer, Flanagan, Kawata, & Williamson, 2000), marking the most dramatic expansion in the use of NAEP scores since the program's inception.

At about the same time, NAEP began reporting results in terms of performance standards, called Achievement Levels and labeled Basic, Proficient, and Advanced. The 1988 reauthorization of NAEP established the National Assessment Governing Board (NAGB) to manage NAEP, focused attention on establishing standards for what students should know, and gave NAGB responsibility for setting appropriate goals for performance. Achievement Levels were first used in reporting the results of the 1990 assessment in mathematics. The initial performance standards were the subject of intense controversy (see General Accounting Office, 1993; Linn, Koretz, Baker, & Burstein, 1991; National Assessment Governing Board, 1991; Stufflebeam, Jaeger, & Scriven, 1991). Several revisions ensued, but the controversies continued. Debate focused on inconsistencies in standard-setting across methods, item difficulties, and item types; the difficulty levels of the standards; the adequacy of the descriptions of the cut scores; and the adequacy of validity evidence for the cut scores. (For a brief summary of some of these arguments and sources on both sides, see Pellegrino, Jones, & Mitchell, 1999.) Although the performance standards established in state programs have typically been far less controversial, many of the arguments raised in both criticism and support of the NAEP Achievement Levels would apply also to them.

Changes in the NAEP tracked broader trends in state assessments in one other respect as well: the greater inclusion of students with disabilities and with limited proficiency in English. Responding to the same policy concerns that motivated greater inclusion in many state assessments, NAEP conducted an experiment in the 1996 assessments of mathematics and science in which one sample was selected as in earlier assessments and administered the test with no accommodations; a second sample was selected with new rules designed to increase inclusion but was administered the test with no accommodations; and a third sample was selected using the new rules and allowed accommodations with students with special needs. (For a description of the results, see Reese, Miller, Mazzeo, & Dossey, 1997; for an analysis of the effects of these alternatives, see Mazzeo, Carlson, Voelkl, & Lutkus, 2000.) The split-sample experiment was continued in the 2000 assessment (Braswell et al., 2001), after which the assessment was switched to the new, more inclusive procedures.

NAEP took on an even more prominent role under NCLB, which mandates administration of the test in mathematics and reading every two years and requires all states to participate in the state NAEP assessment. Although the legislation attaches no formal stakes to NAEP performance, it refers to the use of NAEP as a way to "help the U.S. Department of Education verify the results of statewide assessments" (U.S. Department of Education, 2002), a use that is likely to lead to increased public scrutiny of the results. How NAEP should be used to confirm or disconfirm the results of state assessments remains controversial. The essential issues are not specific to NAEP but rather are relevant to the interpretation of disparities in trends between scores on high-stakes tests and lower-stakes tests. If both tests show positive trends but the increase is far smaller on NAEP or another lower-stakes test, what does this imply about inferences about improved achievement? NAGB has issued a policy statement about this that does not address the size of a disparity in trends and instead asserts that "any amount of growth on the National Assessment should be sufficient to 'confirm' growth on state tests" (National Assessment Governing Board, 2002b, p. 9). In contrast, several studies have presented large disparities in trends between high-stakes tests and audit tests (usually but not always NAEP) as an indication of score inflation (e.g., Jacob, 2002; Klein et al., 2000; Koretz et al., 1991; Koretz & Barron, 1998). This issue is discussed further by Koretz (2003) and in the following section on validating inferences under high-stakes conditions.

2. Validating Inferences under High-Stakes Conditions[5]

An overarching psychometric issue raised by some of the trends in test use described in section 1 is the validity of scores obtained under high-stakes conditions. Test scores can become inflated—that is, can be higher than proficiency in the measured domain warrants—when teachers or examinees respond to testing in certain ways, and these responses are likely to be particularly severe when the consequences for scores are substantial. (For a summary of evidence about these behavioral responses and the inflation of scores, see section 3.)

Therefore, an essential aspect of validating score-based inferences under high-stakes conditions is evaluating the possibility of score inflation. Traditional approaches to validation, while necessary, are insufficient for this purpose. This section explains the reasons for this inadequacy, provides a conceptual framework for validating gains under high-stakes conditions, describes categories of teacher behavior that influence the validity of scores, and sketches several possible approaches for evaluating score inflation.

Much of the previous research on score inflation has examined between-cohort gains and has reflected an assumption that scores become progressively more corrupted by behavioral response over time (see, e.g., Jacob, 2002; Klein et al., 2000; Koretz et al., 1991; Koretz & Barron, 1998; Koretz, McCaffrey, & Hamilton, 2001; Linn, 2000). Although it is often a convenient shorthand to describe this issue in terms of the validity of score gains, the underlying issue is not gains as such, but rather the possibility of inflation in one or more cross-sections (i.e., inflation that occurs in a single testing administration). As Koretz et al. (2001) point out, inflation of gains need not indicate inflation of scores in any given cross-section. If a new assessment is sufficiently novel, initial scores may be biased downward, and a decrease in negative cross-sectional bias over time as teachers and students gain familiarity will create a positive bias in score trends.

Accordingly, we focus here on the validity of inferences under high-stakes conditions (VIHS). In discussing both extant research and hypothetical examples, we will often refer to the validity of gains, but even in those cases, the underlying issue is always threats to the validity of one or more cross-sections.

2.1. The Inadequacy of Traditional Validation

Traditional approaches to validation are insufficient for evaluating VIHS for several related reasons:

- With the exception of predictive criterion-related evidence, traditional empirical validity evidence is generally cross-sectional and correlational.
- Traditional approaches implicitly assume stability in the relationships among elements of the domain relevant to the inferences based on scores.
- These approaches largely ignore behavioral responses to testing.

Cross-sectional correlations, such as convergent/discriminant validity evidence, are insensitive to differences in mean levels of performance. This is of no consequence when scales are arbitrary and one has no reason to expect the overall location of the distribution of scores on the scale to be biased. However, it is critically important when evaluating VIHS because of the possibility of an artifactual elevation of the distribution of scores. Correlational measures may capture inflation of scores if it is sufficiently non-uniform across schools or other units, but otherwise, these methods may miss it entirely. This problem was illustrated in a study of Kentucky's high-stakes KIRIS (Kentucky Instructional Results Information System) assessment in which trends in KIRIS scores were compared to trends on the ACT Assessment for students who took both tests. Among these students, the mean score in mathematics on KIRIS rose about .7 *SD* over three years, while the mean on the ACT mathematics test dropped trivially (Koretz & Barron, 1998; see Figure 15.1). During that time, however, the correlations between the tests were reasonably stable. Koretz and Barron (1998) interpreted these marked disparities in trends as evidence of score inflation, but whether they were correct in this specific case is immaterial. The essential point is that these disparities in trends could be a sign of inflation and that the correlations are insensitive to them. Nonetheless, some analysts cite high cross-sectional correlations between scores on high-stakes tests and other measures as evidence of the validity of the former without recognizing their insufficiency for this purpose (e.g., Greene, Winters, & Forster, 2003; Hannaway & McKay, 2001).

FIGURE 15.1 Standardized Mean Change on KIRIS and ACT, Mathematics

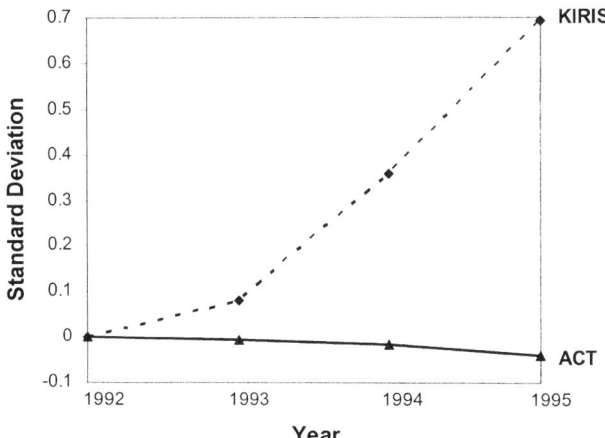

Source: Koretz & Barron (1998).

Traditional approaches to validation, as well as many other methods in psychometrics, assume a stability in the relationships among elements of the domain about which inferences are drawn. One assumption is that the relationships among tested elements remain reasonably stable. This assumption is essential, for example, for some methods of equating. Perhaps logically more important for VIHS, however, is the assumption of stability in the relationships between tested and untested elements of the domain about which inferences are drawn. This assumption, which is not warranted under high-stakes conditions, is examined in detail in subsection 2.4.

Finally, traditional approaches to validation do not examine teachers' or students' behavioral responses to testing, although they do implicitly make some assumptions about behavior—for example, that examinees and teachers do not cheat and that proctors adhere to standard procedures for administration. Under high-stakes conditions, however, examinees, teachers, proctors, and scorers can behave in ways that undermine the validity of scores. This issue is inextricably tied up with the previous one because some of the behaviors that undermine the validity of scores do so by altering the relationships between tested and untested elements of the domain. This too is discussed in detail in section 2.4.

2.2. Early Methods for Validating Scores under High-Stakes Conditions

Most of the relatively few studies of VIHS have examined concordance in trends rather than just cross-sectional concordance—specifically, the degree to which gains on high-stakes tests generalize to lower stakes tests such as NAEP (e.g., Klein et al., 2000; Koretz & Barron, 1998; Koretz et al., 1991; Linn, 2000; and Linn & Dunbar, 1990). We refer to the high-stakes test on which scores are to be validated as the *focal test* and to the lower-stakes test as the *audit test*.

In some cases, the disparity in trends has been so great as to lead the researchers to conclude that scores on the focal test were clearly inflated (e.g., Klein et al., 2000; Koretz & Barron, 1998; Koretz et al., 1991; see section 3). Research of this type, however, suffers from two important limitations: difficulties in obtaining an appropriate audit measure, and ambiguities in the interpretation of the divergence in score trends.

2.2.1. Limitations of Audit Tests

Studies of VIHS are limited by the scarcity of suitable audit measures. These studies require measures that are administered over the same period of time in the same grades, that support similar inferences, that are not themselves corrupted, and that meet the methodological demands of particular designs, such as comparability of samples and the ability to link over time and between tests. In practice, it is difficult to find jurisdictions that have audit measures that meet these criteria, and researchers do not always have access to the needed data when they do exist.

Audit tests may themselves be affected by score inflation. This inflation may be a direct result of the test's use if it is part of a jurisdiction's routine testing program. For example, Schemo and Fessenden (2003) concluded on the basis of a large disparity in trends in Houston between the Texas Assessment of Academic Skills (TAAS, the Texas statewide high-stakes test at the time) and the Stanford-9 (SAT9) that score gains on the former were inflated. However, the SAT9 was part of the Houston Independent School District's accountability system and was used, along with TAAS scores, to provide school performance ratings (Houston Independent School District, 2002). Thus, while the stakes attached to SAT9 were lower than those on TAAS, they may have been sufficient to inflate scores on the SAT9 and thus to understate the inflation of TAAS scores.

Scores on an audit measure may also become corrupted indirectly if the focal test is designed to mirror it closely enough. That is, by focusing unduly on the specific content of the focal test, teachers and students would by the same token be doing the same for the audit test. This has not been true of the studies reported in section 3, but it could prove important in the future. In particular, recent changes in policy and the prominence of several recent studies might lead administrators to anticipate that NAEP may be used as an audit test and to design their high-stakes tests accordingly.

A final limitation of audit tests is that they require a compromise between two conflicting goals. The audit test must be similar enough to the focal test in terms of intended or actual inferences to justify the comparison of scores. However, if the two tests are too similar, generalization from one to the other will overstate the generalizability of performance on the focal test to mastery of the domain about which inferences are made.

2.2.2. Ambiguity in the Interpretation of Disparities in Trends

The interpretation of disparities in score trends is clouded by differences in the intended inferences and design of high-stakes and audit tests. Because of differences between the tests, it is not always clear how much generalizability to expect in the absence of score inflation and therefore what share of a divergence should be interpreted as an indication of inflation (Koretz, 2002; Koretz & Barron, 1998). As explained in section 2.3.3, differences in design reflecting dissimilarities in inferences excuse disparities in trends, whereas incidental differences in design do not. Even when the disparity in trends is great enough to warrant an inference that scores have been appreciably inflated, differences between the focal and audit test generally preclude estimating the degree of inflation with any precision.

This ambiguity is illustrated by the Venn diagram in Figure 15.2. The rectangle represents all gains on a state focal test. The partially overlapping ellipse represents gains on the audit test, in this case, state NAEP. Gains stemming from score inflation—for example, teaching the specific items on the test—are represented by area A. Meaningful gains on the focal test that do not generalize to the audit test because of differences in intended inferences and resulting differences in test construction are represented by area B. Meaningful gains that do generalize to the audit test are represented by area C. NAEP gains have only two subdivisions—meaningful gains that do and do not generalize to the state's focal test—because until recently, educators have had little incentive to teach in ways that would inflate gains on NAEP.

In most instances, the relative size of the five regions is unknown, and for that reason, the degree of validity or inflation cannot be well estimated. The delineation of area B from area C and of area C from area D—in each case, the distinction between meaningful gains that are and are not generalizable because of differences in the inferences intended for the two tests—is obscured by the incomplete and often vague specification of the intended inferences. The distinction between areas A and B—between non-generalizable score gains that do and do not represent meaningful increases in student learning—is obscured both by this incompleteness of specification and, in most cases, by a lack of information on the roots of performance gains (e.g., the extent to which they are dependent on particular formats, rubrics, inessential details of content, and so on).

FIGURE 15.2 Schematic Representation of Gains on NAEP and a State Test

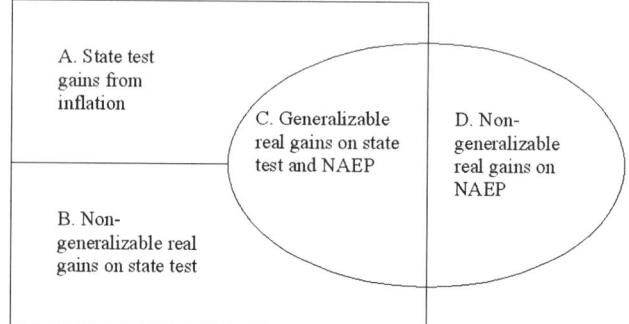

Source: Adapted from Koretz (2002).

2.3. A Framework for Evaluating VIHS

In response to the difficulties in validating scores under high-stakes conditions, Koretz et al. (2001) suggested a conceptual framework for VIHS and suggested possible methodological approaches consistent with it. This framework applies to tests that support inferences about student mastery of domains. It does not apply to predictive inferences unless those are directly tied to inferences about current proficiency. Thus, for example, it does not apply to the validity of predictive inferences about college performance based on SAT-I scores.

The traditional view of test construction focuses on the whittling down of the possible focus of measurement through the specification of the domain, definition of a framework, choice of test specifications, and selection of items or tasks (e.g., Koretz, Bertenthal, & Green, 1999). It focuses on the material included in a test and does not clarify the nature of excluded material or its relevance to particular inferences. This traditional view also focuses on intentional decisions about inclusion or emphasis and does not address inadvertent emphasis. VIHS, however, hinges on the relevance to inferences of both excluded and unintentionally emphasized material, and it also depends on the degree to which the emphasis assigned to material on the test comports with the emphasis inherent in the inference. The framework that follows takes these factors into account.

2.3.1. Elements of Performance

The framework begins with the deliberately general term, *elements of performance*, which subsumes all the aspects of performance that underlie both performance on tests and inferences about it. *Substantive* performance elements contribute either explicitly or tacitly to the definition of the domain about which inferences are drawn. In elementary mathematics, examples include knowledge of arithmetic algorithms and the skills needed to apply them to meaningful problems. *Non-substantive* elements are not the focus of inference and do not differentiate one domain from another. An example would be facility with a particular format that is of no particular importance for the intended inference.

These elements of performance are conceptually distinct, but they are not necessarily empirically independent, either in cross-section or over time. They must be treated as distinct, however, if differences among them are pertinent to inferences about performance and *if they have the potential to vary independently over time*. For example, algebra and geometry skills will normally be highly collinear in cross-section, but if a test of high school mathematics proficiency tested only algebra, teachers might respond to the test by increasing their emphasis on algebra while reducing time spent on geometry, and performance in algebra could increase independently of performance in geometry.

Test construction requires selecting a subset from the range of potentially relevant performance elements. This is illustrated in Figure 15.3. The first stages resemble traditional models of test construction. The set of substantive elements is divided into domains, some tested and others not. Within a tested domain, the set of substantive elements is subdivided into those included in a given test and those not tested. Inclusion here refers solely to representation in the test, not to importance for intended inferences or presence in a test-development framework. Elements excluded from the test may be central to the inferences based on scores.

2.3.1.1. Effective Test Weights

Scores on a test will be more sensitive to changes in performance on some elements than on others. One obvious source of these differences in sensitivity is simply the number of items that tap each element, but numerous other factors can contribute as well, depending on the nature of the items and the manner of test construction. For example, sensitivity can be affected by scoring rubrics, scaling procedures, differences in item discrimination, and relative difficulty. We call the aggregate impact of those factors the *effective test weight,* indicated by w_i in Figure 15.3.[6]

The term *test weight* does not imply that test scores need be a weighted linear composite of performance on individual elements. Rather, the model is general. Let θ_i represent performance on any element i. Then test score Y is a function of the vector of θ values:

$$Y = f(\boldsymbol{\theta}). \qquad (1)$$

The effective test weight of a given element is the sensitivity of Y to changes in performance on that element, that is, the partial derivative of Y with respect to θ_i:

$$w_i = \frac{\partial Y}{\partial \theta_i}. \qquad (2)$$

This representation is important because some sources of score inflation stem from biased estimates of performance on individual items—that is, biased estimates of one or more θ_i—while others result from distortions in the aggregation of these θ_i estimates into scores. This is discussed further in section 2.4.

2.3.1.2. Unintentional Emphasis and Overweighting

Critical to the framework is the distinction between intentional and unintentional weighting of performance elements, which refers both to the inclusion or exclusion of an element and to its effective test weight if included. Unintentional weighting can arise because of unforeseen effects of the factors contributing to effective test weights (such as unintended differences in item discrimination). More important sources may be an incorrect anticipation of the skills and knowledge students will bring to bear in answering items and inattention to the distribution of ancillary skills required by items.

An example of unintentional weighting was provided by the pilot form of a state high school mathematics assessment reviewed by one of the authors several years ago. The state's standards made several references to geometry, but most simply noted the subject area in general. They included only one brief reference to coordinate geometry, in the context of using geometry as a tool for understanding functions and patterns. The pilot test, however, placed a substantial emphasis on coordinate geometry, not because

FIGURE 15.3 Schematic of Elements of Performance and Elements of a Test

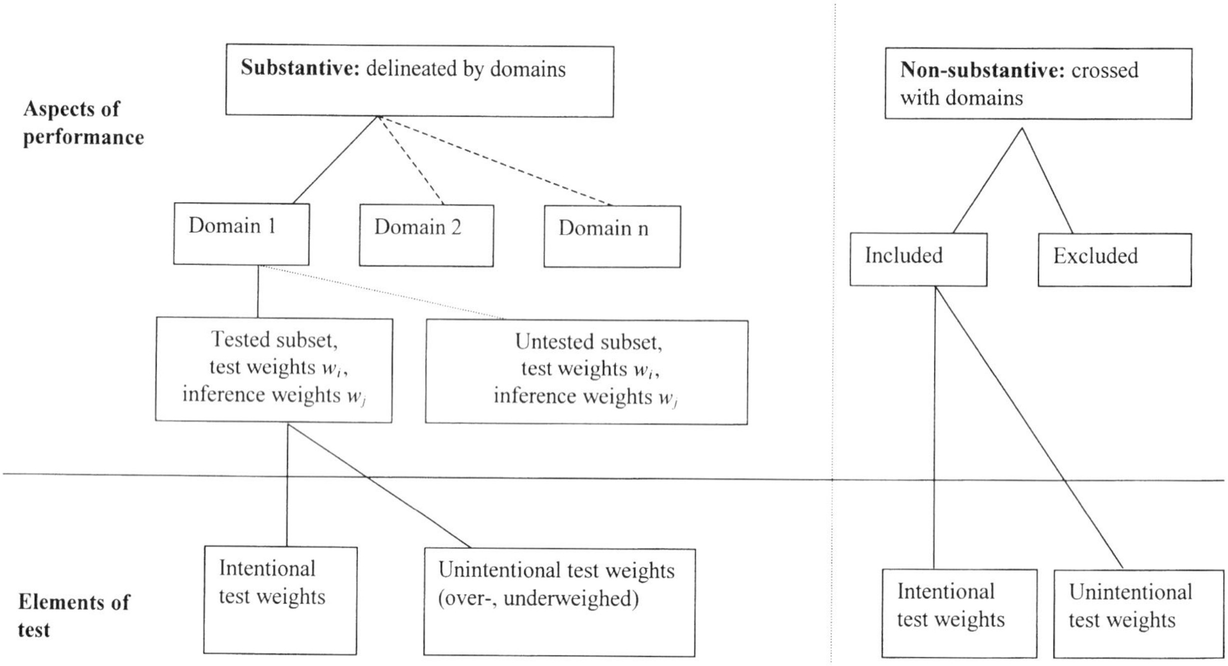

```
Aspects of          Substantive: delineated by domains              Non-substantive: crossed
performance                                                         with domains

              Domain 1    Domain 2    Domain n                      Included      Excluded

        Tested subset,          Untested subset,
        test weights w_i,       test weights w_i,
        inference weights w_j   inference weights w_j

Elements of   Intentional    Unintentional test weights    Intentional      Unintentional
test          test weights   (over-, underweighed)         test weights     test weights
```

it was a deliberate substantive focus of the developers, but rather because it provides a handy vehicle for assessing numerous aspects of proficiency in algebra. In this manner, performance elements may be unintentionally *overweighted*—that is, given more emphasis in a test than the intended inferences warrant. Similar issues arise with non-substantive elements as well.

Seen this way, the elements included in a test are of the four types arrayed at the bottom of Figure 15.3. Both substantive and non-substantive performance elements may have either intentional or unintended effective weights. Generalizability of performance or of gains could be threatened by differences among tests in the inclusion or weighting of elements in any of these categories of performance elements. The meaning of a failure of generalizability will hinge on the types of elements involved and their relevance to the inferences supported by scores.

2.3.2. Targets of Inference

Scores on a test are used as the basis for inferences about a *target of inference*—in the case of achievement tests, students' proficiency on a bundle of skills and knowledge. Validity depends on the consistency between performance on the tested elements and the target of inference, but evaluating that consistency is difficult, particularly when inferences pertain to change.

The inferences users base on scores are often simple and vague. For example, newspaper articles typically reference broad constructs such as proficiency in mathematics with little attention to the specific elements of performance underlying the inference (e.g., Koretz & Deibert, 1996). This simplification is not merely a convenience and is not limited to the lay press. Many users of scores lack a clear notion of the array of proficiencies implied by them, and even more sophisticated consumers of scores who agree on a simple interpretation of a score increase may have widely varying opinions about the elements of performance that should be implied by it. Even performance standards and test guidelines leave considerable room for uncertainty and disagreement about intended or appropriate inferences.

Nonetheless, it is useful to conceptualize targets of inference as paralleling the construction of tests. Targets of inference can be seen as comprising elements comparable to the elements of a test shown in Figure 15.3, although the distinction between intentional and unintentional representation is not pertinent to the description of the target. The target of inference also includes non-substantive elements of performance. For example, users of test scores may have in mind contexts or ways in which examinees should be able to manifest substantive proficiencies, and these may correspond to non-substantive elements of tests.

2.3.2.1. Implicit Performance Elements

Some performance elements may appear in the target but not the test, or vice versa. Those that are irrelevant to the inference but have substantial test weights go by the traditional term of *construct-irrelevant* elements. To evaluate the validity of gains, however, we need also to consider elements that are important to an inference but that are not included in the test, which we call *implicit elements* because they are included in the inference but are not directly measured.

2.3.2.2. Inference Weights

The relative importance of performance elements to users' inferences about performance can be conceptualized as *inference weights*, indicated by w_j in Figure 15.3.

Inference weights are a logical counterpart to test weights but are more elusive. Test weights are an empirical attribute of a test, reflecting its content, the method used to scale performance, and so on. In contrast, inference weights are often tacit and are generally too vague to quantify easily even when explicit. For example, debate among users about the relative importance of communication and computation in mathematics proficiency or of usage and voice in composition reflects differences in inference weights, but even those participating in the debates would often find it difficult to quantify their own weights. Moreover, a user's inference weights may not be uniform. They may depend, for example, on students' level of performance. For example, proponents of phonics and the whole-language approach may differ in terms of the relative importance of decoding and comprehension in evaluating the proficiency of beginning readers, but this disagreement is likely to be far less important—that is, their inference weights would be more similar—when evaluating more advanced readers.

2.3.3. VIHS in Terms of Test and Inference Weights

Validity of inferences about current proficiency under any conditions can be expressed in terms of the inference and test weights assigned to elements of performance. Any difference in scores (often, in current uses of high-stakes tests, a cohort-to-cohort gain in scores) represents variations in performance on the particular elements that have substantial effective test weights. Validity then depends on the extent to which variation in performance on these particular elements justifies an inference of comparable variation on the elements with substantial inference weights. In the case of VIHS, we are concerned about positive differences, usually gains—that is, the extent to which an increase in scores reflecting an increase in performance on elements with substantial test weights justifies an inference about a comparable increase in proficiency in the set of elements with substantial inference weights.

If tests included all important substantive elements, the strength of the inference would depend on the vector of actual changes in performance on the tested elements and the consistency of test and inference weights on those elements. This would include the degree to which changes in scores result from changes in performance on elements (substantive or not) with appreciable test weights but little or no relevance to the inference—for example, from practice with specific formats or rubrics. The greater the influence of these elements, the lower the validity of the inference.

Because of the incompleteness of tests, however, validity also depends on the degree to which change on *implicit* elements with substantial inference weights can be inferred from changes on measured elements. In traditional validation, one needs to assume or demonstrate only that the cross-sectional relationship between measured and unmeasured elements is consistent with the construct. That cross-sectional consistency, however, does not necessarily imply that under high-stakes conditions, changes in performance on implicit elements are consistent either with change on measured elements or with the inference.

2.3.3.1. Evaluating the Similarity of Focal and Audit Tests

The degree to which dissimilarities in trends between focal and audit tests indicate inflation of scores has been a source of disagreement. For example, Koretz and Barron (1998) maintained that markedly smaller growth on NAEP than on Kentucky's KIRIS test indicated inflation of gains on the latter. In contrast, the Ad Hoc Committee on Confirming Test Results of the National Assessment Governing Board argued that "Any amount of growth on the National Assessment should be sufficient to 'confirm' growth on state tests" (Ad Hoc Committee, 2002, p. 9).

The framework described here provides a way of reconciling these disparate views. The key is the relevance of the audit test to the inferences supported by the focal test.

A complete lack of confirmatory gains on an audit test, as has been found in some studies (see section 3), is a threat to the validity of gains on the focal test unless the audit test is inappropriate. Specifically, unless the sum of the inference weights on the focal test is near zero for the almost all of the performance items included in the audit test, valid gains on the focal test should show an echo in scores on the audit test. This condition of near-zero inference weights is unlikely to arise with tests focusing on similar domains.

More problematic is the situation, also found in several studies (e.g., Klein et al., 2000; Koretz & Barron, 1998) in which the audit measure shows gains, but these are far smaller than those shown by the focal test. Seemingly with such situations in mind, the Ad Hoc Committee on Confirming Test Results reasoned:

> Potential differences between NAEP and state testing programs include: content coverage in the subjects, definitions of subgroups, changes in the demography within a state over time, sampling procedures, standard-setting approaches, reporting metrics, student motivation in taking the state test versus taking NAEP, mix of item formats, test difficulty, etc. Such differences may be minimal or great in number and in size and cannot reasonably be expected to operate in all states in equal fashion. The greater the differences between the respective state tests and NAEP, the greater the complexity in using NAEP as confirmatory evidence for state test results and the greater the cautions in interpretation that should accompany the weighing of the confirmatory evidence. (2002, p. 9)

However, the importance of differences in trends stemming from factors such as standard-setting procedures, format mix, and content depend on the inference weights for both tests of the performance elements responsible for the divergence. Consider three instances, all cases in which an audit test shows appreciable but much smaller gains than does a focal test. In one instance, the performance elements responsible for the disparity in trends have high inference weights for both tests. In this case, the divergence clearly threatens the validity of inferences about gains on the focal test. In the second instance, the divergence in performance arises from performance elements with low or zero inference weights for the focal test. For example, suppose that performance gains are lower on an audit test because of a lack of improvement in trigonometry, when trigonometry is not considered important for the inferences the focal test is designed to support. In this case, the divergence would be unthreatening to the validity of inferences about gains on the focal test.

The third case is more complex. Consider a classic example presented by Shepard (1988):

> When students were asked to add decimals in vertical format, the state percent passing was 86 percent. In horizontal format for identically difficult decimals, the percent passing was 46 percent. For subtraction of decimals in the two formats the passing rates were 78 percent and 30 percent, respectively (drawing on data from New Jersey Department of Education, 1976).

In this case, one can assume that the choice of vertical or horizontal format had zero inference weights for many users. Subtraction, on the other hand, would have had a substantial inference weight. Teachers seeking diagnostic information would find the difference in performance across formats useful information, but users drawing inferences about the level of proficiency of the state's students in addition or subtraction would not be likely to make inferences specific to one or the other format. As Shepard (1988) argued, the failure to generalize across formats was a clear threat to the validity of inference. Thus, in this case, the failure of generalizability affects a performance element with a substantial inference weight but is attributable to one with a zero or near zero weight. In such cases, validity is undermined.

Thus, although differences between focal and audit tests on attributes such as format and content make the task of validation more difficult, they do not make the divergence of trends between focal and audit tests irrelevant to VIHS. The degree of acceptable disparity between the two tests depends on inference weights. The extent to which differences in test design and test weights make a disparity acceptable hinges on the relationship between those design elements and both intended and actual inferences.

This point is particularly important when there are broad secular trends in achievement. For example, NAEP has shown increases in mathematics proficiency nationwide since the mid-1970s in elementary and middle school and since the mid-1980s in high school (Braswell et al., 2001; Campbell, Hombo, & Mazzeo, 2000). These increases rival and in some cases exceed the magnitude and rate of the nationwide decline in test scores in the 1960s and 1970s (Koretz, 1986). In the presence of such trends, the position of the Ad Hoc Committee would in effect treat all increases in scores on any state mathematics test to be "confirmed."

2.4. Methods of Test Preparation and VIHS

As used here, the term *test preparation* refers all steps educators take, both desirable and undesirable, to prepare students for tests and has no negative connotations. We distinguish among seven types of test preparation:

- teaching more
- working harder
- working more effectively
- reallocation
- alignment
- coaching
- cheating.

The first three of these types of test preparation can produce unambiguously meaningful increases in scores. One is *teaching more*—for example, providing more instructional time by adding days to the school year, instituting remedial classes outside of normal school hours, or devoting more of the school year to actual instruction. Assuming that these changes are focused on tested knowledge and skills and are not accompanied by a deterioration of gains per unit of time, they will produce meaningful gains in achievement. An example of *working harder* would be covering more material per hour of instructional time. Assuming that this is done effectively and does not exceed the ability of students to keep pace, this too will produce meaningful gains. An example of *working more effectively* would be adopting a better curriculum or more effective teaching methods. All of these methods are consistent with Mehrens and Kaminski's (1989) description of ethical test-preparation practices.

The other four types of test preparation, however, can produce inflated scores. All but cheating can also produce meaningful increases in scores, depending on how they are conducted.

2.4.1. Reallocation

Reallocation refers to shifts in resources among substantive elements of performance. For example, numerous studies have found that teachers report shifting instructional time to focus more on the material emphasized by an important test, both within and across domains (see section 3 for a review of these studies). The resources relevant to reallocation are not limited to instructional time; they include all of the resources that parents and students as well as teachers must allocate among performance elements. Assuming that resources are applied effectively, a shift of resources will result in a reallocation of achievement as well.

Reallocation within domains can have various effects on both test scores and validity, depending on the test and inference weights of the elements given both increased and decreased emphasis. For example, if the elements receiving increased emphasis have both higher effective test weights and higher inference weights than the elements receiving lowered emphasis, increases in scores will support valid inferences about increases in achievement. This case is discussed further under *alignment.*

Reallocation can also inflate scores, however, if it decreases emphasis on elements with substantial inference weights but relatively low or zero test weights. If teachers begin focusing disproportionately on elements with large test weights (including those that were inadvertently overweighted) while deemphasizing important elements excluded from the test, then performance on included elements will become less representative of the broader set relevant to the inference. Reallocation can inflate scores even if the emphasized material is important to the inference and the deemphasized material is not specified in standards or other test-construction guidelines, as long as the deemphasized material has substantial inference weights.

In terms of the model above, reallocation inflates scores by distorting the aggregation of estimates for individual elements into scores so that the aggregate misrepresents meaningful gains in achievement. This distortion may involve misaligned weights for tested elements, but perhaps more important, it may also undermine the ability of performance on measured elements to represent performance on implicit elements.

Reallocation also occurs among domains; for example, a school may shift instruction from science to mathematics in response to a testing program that assesses the latter but not the former. Whether the gains caused by reallocation among domains is inflation again depends on the inferences based on scores. In this example, if performance on a test were used strictly to support the inference that students were learning more mathematics, the between-subjects reallocation would not make the increase in scores misleading. If, on the other hand, users inferred that the increase in mathematics scores represented a net increase in learning and that there was no compensating decrease in performance in other important areas, the increase in scores would be misleading.

2.4.2. Alignment

At the time of this writing, "alignment" between tests and the standards they are intended to reflect is a cornerstone of education policy and is often presented as being unambiguously desirable. In the terminology used here, standards identify elements of performance that warrant high inference weights in the eyes of those drafting the standards (which may or may not be given high inference weights by users), and alignment gives these elements high test weights as well. Some observers argue that alignment provides protection against score inflation because it focuses instruction on elements deemed valuable by those who drafted the standards.

However, the argument that alignment protects against score inflation is simplistic. Increased alignment is a form of reallocation, and its impact on the validity of gains depends on the same considerations that arise in other types of reallocation. The extent to which alignment may inflate gains depends not only on which elements receive greater emphasis, but also on which elements receive less. When tests are not exhaustive and some performance elements with large inference weights have small or zero test weights, alignment is not sufficient to protect against inflation from reallocation. Efforts to align tests and standards may not address all dimensions of performance and tend to focus primarily on content (see section 4). Finally, alignment is also not sufficient to protect against inflation from coaching, as discussed in the following section.

2.4.3. Coaching

The term "coaching" has been used to refer to many types of test preparation. Here we restrict its use to two types of preparation, one focusing on substantive elements, the other on non-substantive elements.

Substantive coaching refers to an instructional emphasis on narrow aspects of substantive performance elements to comport with the style or emphasis of test items. The object of this focus may not be an intentional emphasis of test developers. For example, a teacher may notice that a test's items about the area of polygons focuses entirely on certain classes of polygons—say, only regular polygons, or only polygons with five sides or fewer—and may focus instruction unduly on those classes of figures at the expense of other types of polygons. As a result, students might exhibit facility in calculating areas that does not generalize well to other types of polygons.

The distinction between substantive coaching and reallocation may sometimes appear hazy in practice, but they are fundamentally different in terms of the framework presented here. Reallocation moves resources and achievement among substantively important performance elements, thus changing the meaning of composite scores. When it inflates gains, it does so by undermining the ability of change in the composite scores to represent change in achievement consistent with the user's target of inference. In contrast, coaching, whether substantive or non-substantive, distorts the estimates of performance on the elements themselves; that is, it biases estimates of one or more θ_j.

The distinction between substantive coaching and cheating (discussed further below) can also be indistinct. Consider the following newspaper report of test preparation in Montgomery County, Maryland:

> The question on the review sheet for Montgomery County's algebra exam [provided by district officials] reads in part: "The average amount that each band member must raise is a function of the number of band members, b, with the rule f(b)=12000/b." The question on the actual test reads in part: "The average amount each cheerleader must pay is a function of the number of cheerleaders, n, with the rule f(n)=420/n." (Strauss, 2001, p. A09)

The author asked, "Is this good test preparation or—as some parents claim—institutional cheating?" and noted that it was defended as appropriate by some district officials (Strauss, 2001, p. A09). One might argue about whether this test preparation should be classified as cheating, but if not, it would be an example of substantive coaching.

Non-substantive coaching refers to forms of test preparation that focus instruction on elements that are largely or entirely unrelated to the definition of the domain the test is intended to represent—that is, elements that are largely or entirely non-substantive.

Limited non-substantive coaching can be appropriate and can increase the validity of scores by removing construct-irrelevant impediments to performance. For example, if a format is sufficiently novel for students, it may cause them to perform more poorly than their mastery of substantive elements of the test would warrant. Some amount of coaching to increase familiarity would lessen this barrier and improve validity of scores.

However, once familiarity with format and other non-substantive elements is no longer a barrier to performance, additional coaching is usually inappropriate, either inflating scores or simply wasting instructional time. When non-substantive coaching inflates scores, it does so in the same manner as substantive coaching, that is, by biasing estimates of individual θ_i values.

2.4.4. Cheating

Cheating comprises a wide variety of forms of inappropriate test preparation, including, for example, providing answers, correcting students' responses, alerting students to incorrectly answered items so that they can review them, providing access during testing to inappropriate material, violating test administration procedures, and allowing students to practice secure test items in advance. Cheating is not always clearly differentiated from extreme forms of other types of test preparation, especially coaching. Cheating is often motivated by an intent to bias scores, but for present purposes, intent is not a useful way of differentiating between cheating and coaching. Cheating, unlike coaching, can never produce a valid increase in scores. It distorts scores by inflating estimates of performance on individual performance elements.

2.5. New Directions for Evaluating VIHS

The preceding discussion clarifies that traditional approaches to validation, although necessary, are insufficient to evaluate many score-based inferences under high-stakes conditions. Several additional approaches may prove fruitful.

2.5.1. Clarifying Inference Weights

Evaluating VIHS may require considerably more clarification of inference weights than is traditional, in order to interpret disparities in trends between focal and audit tests when the tests are notably different or when the audit test also shows gains. Similarly, when behavioral responses to testing erode the relationships between elements with large and small test weights, for example, by reallocation away from the latter, the inference weights of elements that do not show comparable gains are central to the evaluation of validity.

Two sets of inference weights are important: those of test developers and sponsors and those of other users. Developers and sponsors—the policymakers and agencies that design and implement testing programs—have *intended inference weights*, which are the weights corresponding to the inferences they intend test scores to support. Different inference weights may be applied by other users, such as parents, the press, and (in most settings) teachers, who generally play little or no role in determining the intended inferences. Sponsors are also users, and their inference weights may shift over time.

Intended inference weights may be easier to discern than actual weights because the former are reflected in published test specifications or frameworks and are sometimes even specified at the level of individual items (e.g., Hoover et al., 1994, pp. 36–37). States' content standards often provide more general information about weights intended for statewide testing, and in some cases, maps of items to standards are provided for them (e.g., Massachusetts Department of Education, 2003c, p. 216). Statements of intent may also be found in state laws that pertain to the state's testing program or in statements that are made by the test's sponsors (e.g., press releases that discuss changes in test scores and what they mean). Even combined, these sources will often be incomplete, but they may provide sufficient information about intended inference weights to help evaluate failures of generalization.

The actual inference weights applied by users are also important for validation but are more problematic because they are generally less well thought out, highly variable, and undocumented. Rudimentary information about the inference weights of writers for the media can be gleaned by studies of published articles about test results (e.g., Koretz & Deibert, 1996). Information about the inference weights of other key stakeholder groups would require primary data collection, for example, surveys of parents. These efforts would be burdensome, and the most effective methods of gathering this information is not clear. For example, surveys of stakeholders could base questions on elements of test frameworks, test items (e.g., Koretz & Hamilton, 2003), or specific inferences about performance.

2.5.2. Ascertaining Effective Test Weights

Ascertaining effective tests weights can serve two functions in evaluating VIHS: clarifying the nature of changes in performance, so that these can be compared to the target of inference; and identifying potential avenues for score inflation by means of reallocation and coaching.

Methods for clarifying test weights are not well established and face several difficulties. One hurdle is the need to determine an appropriate level of detail, one that is specific enough to capture important differences in change over time but general enough to provide a meaningful and useful basis for comparison. A second difficulty is that information about weights can be obtained from numerous sources, but these sources may yield discrepant information.

Classification of items based on test content (see, e.g., Bond & Jaeger, 1993) may help clarify how various constructs are weighted on a test and may help users evaluate whether these weights are consistent with those suggested by standards documents or other published materials. However, content standards and intended inference weights are often not sufficiently well defined to facilitate clear classification. Moreover, even when these are clear, the classification of items is typically not straightforward. Many items are inherently ambiguous and difficult to classify under a single category, and simple inspections of item content are generally insufficient for understanding the specific skills and sources of knowledge upon which examinees draw.

Approaches that elicit information about how examinees respond to items may be especially powerful for clarifying the actual test weights assigned to performance elements. Messick (1989) includes these approaches in his discussion of methods for gathering validity evidence. For example, gathering evidence of the cognitive processes in which examinees engage while responding to test items may help to illuminate the constructs that are measured (see, e.g., Hamilton et al., 1997). In some cases these methods may identify performance elements that differ from those noted in the formal test specifications. While this evidence may be particularly helpful for validating inferences about skills, it is likely to be less useful for identifying possible inflation because the skills illuminated by these investigations will often not be readily apparent to teachers and students searching for ways to improve scores.

Teachers may be a valuable source of information about effective test weights—particularly recurrent patterns—because under high-stakes conditions, they have a strong incentive to identify them. Stecher, Barron, Chun, and Ross (2000), for example, found that teachers in a high-stakes testing context generally paid more attention to what is on the test than to the state's published standards. If one's goal is simply to raise scores, it is not important whether a test weight is intended, and surveys noted in section 3.2 suggest that many teachers attend both to unintended weights and to aspects of item style—that is, non-substantive performance elements—such as format and types of presentation. Information about teachers' perceptions of effective test weights could be obtained by various methods, including structured surveys somewhat like those suggested above for parents. Commercial test preparation materials might provide another source of information, though it is generally not possible for researchers to evaluate the approaches used in creating these materials, so any conclusions based on them should be confirmed using another source of information.

2.5.3. Examining Changes in Dimensionality

Evaluation of VIHS might be furthered by a variety of approaches to examining the dimensionality of score data. Conventional approaches applied to tests of a single academic subject most often indicate a structure that can be treated as unidimensional for purposes of scaling even when a test comprises a range of content. As noted by Muthén, Khoo, and Goff (1997), however, there will often nonetheless be potentially useful distinctions that can be made from an analysis that is designed to detect deviations from unidimensionality. Even the finding that a test is unidimensional in cross-section does not mean that dimensional differences are unimportant for validating gains. Performance on elements that are dimensionally indistinct (i.e., very highly correlated) in cross-section may nonetheless change independently over time.

Test preparation efforts could cause a change in the dimensionality of scores. Such changes could arise, for example, if the variability of performance on one dimension were reduced through test preparation efforts; in this case, a dimension that was observed at the first administration may not be observed at a later administration. Similarly, coaching focused on certain performance elements could result in the emergence of new dimensions of performance.

One way to explore changes in dimensionality is to classify items in terms of the direction and magnitude of change in performance over time. The characteristics of high- and low-gain items could then be examined for patterns relevant to VIHS and possible inflation. For example, this could be done with a DIF analysis, with low-gain schools as the reference group and high-gain schools as the focal group. At the initiation of a testing program, one will find a baseline distribution of DIF across all schools as a result of variations in the alignment of the test with instruction. Over time, if some schools generate large gains by focusing unduly on certain performance elements, that resulting change in dimensionality should result in a change in the distribution of DIF relative to that in lower-gain schools. (For explanation and an initial exploration of this approach, see Koretz & McCaffrey, 2005.)

2.5.4. Examining Between-Level Differences in Correlational Structure

Typically, correlations between scores on various tests and between scores and student background characteristics will be higher at the classroom and school levels because of the effects of aggregation. School-level interventions could alter this relationship in several ways. If introduced disproportionately into low-scoring schools, school-level interventions that create meaningful improvements in instruction could reduce school-level correlations between scores and background variables while leaving high correlations between alternate achievement measures. School-level interventions that inflate scores in initially low-scoring schools could reduce aggregate correlations between a high-stakes measure and both background variables and scores on other tests, again without necessarily reducing student-level correlations. The latter pattern, suggesting inappropriate test preparation, was found in a small sample of schools in one Texas district by Klein et al. (2000).

3. EFFECTS OF LARGE-SCALE, HIGH-STAKES TESTING

The sweeping changes in the uses of large-scale tests described in section 1 have sparked research into the effects of high-stakes testing. Studies have explored a variety of outcomes, including the validity of score gains and the effects of testing programs on educational practice, teacher and student morale, classroom climate, and organizational cohesiveness. Because our primary purpose is to explore implications for measurement, and in particular implications for validity of inferences, we describe here illustrative findings from studies of educational practice and the validity of scores. These two outcomes are linked: The framework described in section 2 explains ways in which the instructional responses of teachers and other educators may affect validity. A review by Hamilton (2003) addresses these and other outcomes.

3.1. Effects on Instructional Practice

The research indicates that testing can exert a strong influence on instruction and that some of the resulting changes are likely to affect the validity of scores. However, it is important to note that testing policies are typically enacted in the context of other reforms, and the effects of testing will almost certainly interact with the effects of these other reforms and with factors such as teachers' beliefs about pedagogy, the curriculum in place in their schools, and their professional development experiences (Cimbricz, 2003; Cohen, 1995; Haertel, 1999; O'Day, Goertz, & Floden, 1995). Moreover, the effects of testing on instruction are likely to vary as a function of the severity of stakes attached to them (Mehrens, 1998; Pedulla et al., 2003). Most of the studies of effects on practice report average responses that mask some of these important variations and interactions.

Some studies suggest that in certain instances, large-scale testing has led to some of the behavioral responses that are described in section 2 as likely to produce meaningful gains in scores. In particular, some teachers have reported that they work harder and focus more on achievement than they had before the implementation of high-stakes testing (Bishop & Mane, 1999; Wolf, Borko, McIver, & Elliott, 1999). In addition, there is evidence that some testing programs may lead teachers to make other changes consistent with the goals of the assessment programs, particularly in contexts where performance assessment was adopted as a means of promoting certain kinds of instructional changes. For example, teachers in Vermont reported increasing their emphasis on mathematics applications and problem solving in response to that state's portfolio assessment program (Koretz et al., 1994), and teachers in Kentucky reported that they increased time spent on writing about mathematics and using "meaningful tasks" as a result of the state's performance-based KIRIS assessment (Koretz, Barron, Mitchell, & Stecher, 1996). In Colorado, the use of high-stakes mathematics tests that required students to explain their answers was associated with teacher reports of increased emphasis on explanation in their classes (Taylor, Shepard, Kinner, & Rosenthal, 2003), and several other studies describe increases in teachers' use of innovative instructional approaches (Borko & Elliott, 1999; Lane, Parke, & Stone, 2002; Wolf & McIver, 1999). These changes were all consistent with the goals of the assessment programs.

At the same time, a growing body of literature suggests that teachers often respond to high-stakes testing in ways that can undermine the validity of inferences about improved student performance. Numerous studies have found that teachers report reallocating time among topics and skills within a subject area. One form of reallocation involves changing the order in which topics are presented to ensure that tested material is covered before the testing date; evidence of this type of response has been described by Corbett and Wilson (1988) and by Darling-Hammond and Wise (1985). More problematic is the form of reallocation that involves devoting more emphasis overall to tested material and neglecting material that is not tested. Shepard and Dougherty (1991) studied high-stakes testing in two districts and found that substantial majorities of teachers reported increasing the amount of time allocated to skills such as vocabulary and computation while decreasing time spent on activities that did not mirror the content and format of the tests. Another study found that a majority of 8th grade mathematics teachers reported increasing emphasis on basic skills and computation while decreasing emphasis on extended projects and other activities not emphasized by most tests (Romberg, Zarinia, & Williams, 1989). A study of Arizona teachers by Smith, Edelsky, Draper, Rottenberg, & Cherland (1991) found that language arts teachers reduced their emphasis on non-tested parts of the curriculum, including certain types of writing. Numerous studies report reallocation among subject areas (e.g., Jones et al., 1999; Koretz, Barron, et al., 1996; Shepard & Dougherty, 1991; Smith et al., 1991; Stecher & Barron, 1999; Stecher et al., 2000; Taylor et al., 2003), but as noted in section 2, this form of reallocation does not threaten the validity of subject-specific inferences.

Several studies have identified responses that focus heavily on the specific format in which test questions are presented, which is a form of coaching as that term is defined in section 2. Examples include the use of word problems that mirror those on the state test in mathematics (Smith & Rottenberg, 1991) and an emphasis on having students look for mistakes in their written work rather than produce their own writing, in response to the format of a state writing test (Shepard & Dougherty, 1991). Pedulla et al. (2003) found the practice of adopting instructional materials that are designed to mirror the format of the state test to be more commonly reported among teachers in states with high-stakes testing programs than in other states, although this finding is weakened by the survey's low response rate.

There is no comprehensive source of information on how much time schools devote to coaching activities such as practicing on released test forms, but some studies suggest these activities are widespread. Teachers in Arizona, for example, reported up to 100 hours per course (M. L. Smith, 1994), and in North Carolina teachers said they devoted more than 20% of instructional time to test practice (Jones et al., 1999). Use of practice tests and emphasis on test-taking strategies have been found to be more common among teachers at low-performing schools than they are in more-successful schools (Taylor et al., 2003). The introduction of high stakes can be a catalyst for a focus on test preparation, as Tepper (2002) found among teachers in Chicago. Teachers in states with high-stakes testing programs, as compared with those in states without such programs, report spending more time on test preparation, beginning it earlier in the year, and making more extensive use of commercial or state-developed test-preparation materials (Pedulla et al., 2003).

In addition to the test items themselves, the methods for scoring the items have been found to affect instruction. Stecher and Mitchell (1995) reported that teachers used the scoring rubrics from Kentucky's performance-based assessment as indicators of what should be taught and how it should be presented. More recent evidence of teachers' shifting instruction and evaluation strategies to match scoring rubrics was reported by Mabry (1999). As with other forms of reallocation, adapting instruction in response to scoring rubrics is not necessarily problematic if done in moderation. However, excessive emphasis on specific rubrics may limit teachers' attention to skills or knowledge that are difficult to measure using a particular form of scoring but that are nonetheless important for the inferences based on scores.

Reallocation was discussed in section 2 in terms of the shifting of instructional resources among performance elements, but teachers also sometimes respond to high-stakes testing by shifting attention among students in a classroom. When scores are reported in a standards-based form (see section 3.5), changes in aggregate scores are solely dependent upon the numbers of students who move from one side of the cut score to the other. As a result, teachers may focus their efforts on students at the cusp of passing state tests, who are often called "bubble kids" (Taylor et al., 2003). Pedulla et al. (2003) found this practice to be more common in states with high-stakes tests than in those without, although again, the survey's low response rate weakens the finding. As noted in section 5, when performance is reported in terms of a coarse, standards-based scale, this form of reallocation can bias estimates of aggregate changes in performance.

While some of these effects on practice pose clear threats to the validity of important inferences, reallocation and coaching in general may have either beneficial or detrimental effects on the validity of inferences. The only unvaryingly negative response described in section 2.4 is cheating, which may involve a number of clearly unethical actions such as deliberately failing to follow test administration instructions, inappropriately providing advance copies of a test, and modifying student responses. As with coaching, there are no comprehensive studies of the frequency of cheating across schools in the United States. In studies of teachers in two states, however, sizable minorities of teachers reported that inappropriate test-administration practices such as rephrasing questions during testing occurred in their schools (Koretz, Mitchell, Barron, & Keith, 1996; Koretz, Barron, et al., 1996). As would be expected, the introduction of high stakes has been found to increase the frequency of cheating (Jacob & Levitt, 2003).

3.2. Other Effects on Schooling

Research has also explored the apparent effects of high-stakes testing programs on non-instructional changes in practice, some of which also could affect VIHS. In surveys, many principals have reported that they responded to high-stakes testing by increasing teacher professional development opportunities, adding summer or after-school sessions to provide additional instruction to low-performing students, and revising curriculum programs (Stecher et al., 2000; Stecher & Chun, 2001). Most of these actions correspond to the set of responses we classified as "working harder" in section 2.4, though the revisions of curriculum programs are likely to involve reallocation. Principals also report engaging in actions that appear to be designed to improve test scores without necessarily improving the overall quality of education in their schools. For example, Koretz, Mitchell et al. (1996) reported that approximately one third of principals in Maryland said they reassigned teachers between tested and untested grades to improve performance.

Another set of responses involves efforts to improve scores by changing the composition of the cohort that takes the test. Figlio and Getzler (2002), in a study of six counties in Florida, reported that school administrators frequently reclassified students as disabled to exempt them from testing, and a study by Deere and Strayer (2003) came to a similar conclusion about school administrators in Texas. The introduction of high stakes in Chicago was accompanied by a substantial increase in the proportions of students placed in special education classes or excluded from testing (Jacob, 2002), though it is not entirely clear whether the high stakes alone caused this change. Efforts to manipulate the cohort of test-taking students threaten the validity of inferences about score changes when school-level averages are reported. In response to these problems, many state accountability systems, as well as NCLB, have included strict rules regarding inclusion and test participation rates.

3.3. Effects of High Stakes on the Validity of Scores

The net effect of test-based accountability on student achievement remains controversial, and many of the studies of this question suffer substantial methodological weaknesses. (For a review of relevant studies, see Hamilton, 2003.) The question of net effects, however, is distinct from the issue of score inflation; severe inflation of scores could accompany no change in achievement, a smaller increase, or a decrease.

The possibility of score inflation is suggested by the long-recognized sawtooth pattern shown by trends in scores on many large-scale achievement tests. It has been noted for many years that it is common for scores to drop when a jurisdiction implements a new testing program, to rise (often at a decreasing rate) for some years thereafter, and to drop abruptly again when another new test is put into place. Linn (2000) showed that this pattern was apparent in the aggregate in trends in the national percentile ranks of state means on norm-referenced tests in the 1980s and 1990s (see Figure 15.4). The most obvious explanation of this pattern is that scores are increased by growing familiarity with the specifics of a particular test and that the effects of this familiarization do not generalize. However, in the absence of audit testing, this hypothesis cannot be tested.

The first systematic study of score inflation included several tests of the generalizability of gains, one of which explored the common sawtooth pattern by readministering tests that had previously been used in the jurisdictions in which the study was conducted. Koretz et al. (1991) evaluated the validity of gains in a district that used commercially available multiple-choice tests and that imposed stakes primarily through the publication of scores rather than through concrete rewards or sanctions. This system was considered moderately high-stakes by the standards of the times but would be judged quite low-stakes by current standards. The district had switched from one commercial achievement test (called Test C in the study) to another (Test B) four years before the study. Classrooms in two elementary grades were randomly assigned to administer one of several tests a few weeks after the district's own tests were administered. The motivational conditions for the two test administrations were nominally similar, since neither involved any stakes for students or educators, but as a check against motivational biases, some classrooms administered parallel forms of the district's own tests. Other classrooms

FIGURE 15.4 Trends in Percentile Ranks of State Means

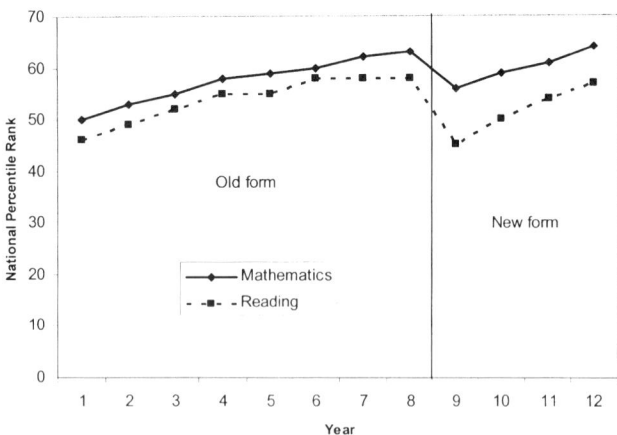

Source: From Linn (2000).

FIGURE 15.5 Performance on a Moderate-Stakes and Audit Test in 3rd-Grade Mathematics

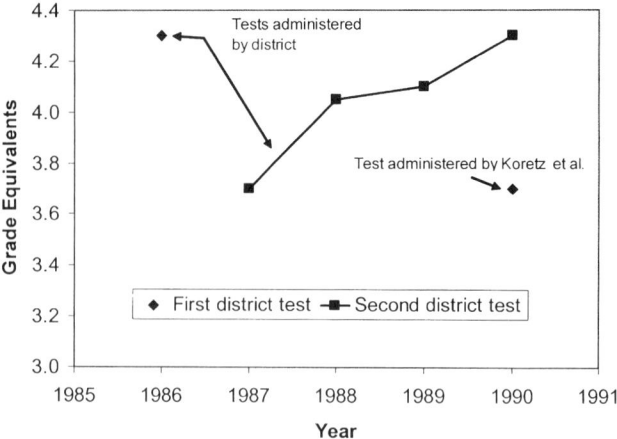

Source: Adapted from Koretz, Linn, Dunbar, & Shepard (1991).

administered the test that the district had used until four years previously.

The study revealed substantial score inflation. The usual sawtooth pattern was present (see Figure 15.5). Although it is not apparent from Figure 15.5, scores on Test C had risen substantially before the district stopped using it. A switch to Test B produced the usual drop in scores: In mathematics in the spring of 3rd grade, the median grade-equivalent score for the district dropped from 4.3 to 3.7. This was followed by the usual rebound: Scores rose on Test B during the subsequent three years of administration, and by the final year had reached 4.3, equivalent to the score on Test C during the year preceding the change of tests. Readministration of Test C showed that over the four years during which it had not been administered, performance on it had dropped to a GE of approximately 3.7, similar to the score obtained on Test B in its first year. Thus, both the comparison across the two tests within one cohort and the comparison between two cohorts within one test (Test C) showed a substantial lack of generalizability, with scores on the test with moderate stakes approximately half an academic year higher than scores on the audit measure.

Two studies of the generalizability of scores under high-stakes conditions examined the assumption, widespread in the early 1990s, that performance-based tests are less subject to score inflation than are multiple-choice tests. Kentucky's state assessment program, called the Kentucky Instructional Results Information System (KIRIS), included multiple-choice items as well as open-response on-demand tasks, writing portfolios, and "performance events." However, apart from writing, the only portion of the assessment that continued uninterrupted during the full period of the program was the portion using on-demand open-response tasks. Schools received financial rewards for exceeding their KIRIS targets, which were ambitious, requiring gains of roughly 2 standard deviations over a 20-year period for the typical school, and even larger improvements for schools with low achievement initially. Schools that failed to meet targets were sanctioned.

Comparisons of KIRIS gains with gains on NAEP showed that the former were much larger than the latter. For example, between 1992 (when KIRIS was first administered) and 1994, 4th grade reading scores on KIRIS increased by roughly three-fourths of a standard deviation, while NAEP scores remained fairly constant (Hambleton et al., 1995). In mathematics, KIRIS showed a gain of approximately 0.6 standard deviation from 1992 to 1996, while the NAEP gain was only 0.17 standard deviation (Koretz & Barron, 1998). These studies cast doubt on the claim that performance-based tests are not susceptible to score inflation. The findings are similar to those of Klein et al. (2000), who found that gains on the multiple-choice high-stakes test in Texas were several times as large as gains on NAEP.

The use of NAEP as an audit mechanism has been criticized because of the possibility that the lack of stakes on NAEP may result in low motivation and artificially depress scores. The topic of the effects of student motivation on NAEP has been the subject of considerable discussion in the field (e.g., Reckase, 2001), but there is as yet little empirical evidence to inform this debate. (Two studies that explored the impact of motivational conditions on performance on NAEP are Kiplinger & Linn, 1995, and O'Neil, Sugrue, Abedi, Baker, & Golan, 1997.) However, for studies that examine changes in NAEP performance, the impact of low motivation on NAEP scores presents a problem only if this impact increases rapidly over time, which seems unlikely.

A second analysis in the Koretz and Barron study examined trends on the ACT, which would not be affected by low motivation but which was less similar to KIRIS in terms of intended inferences. The study included only students who took both tests so that changes in selectivity would affect both trends. The results were consistent with those obtained using NAEP: In mathematics, KIRIS scores rose approximately two-thirds of a standard deviation in three years but declined slightly on ACT. Similar but less severe disparities were found for reading and science (Koretz & Barron, 1998).

The research described so far focused on aggregate achievement trends. A study by Jacob (2002) examined generalizability of gains by following individual students over time using data from the Chicago Public Schools. Scores on the Iowa Test of Basic Skills (ITBS), which had been improving over time, showed a greater degree of improvement after the district introduced an accountability system that imposed stakes on schools (e.g., reassignment of staff) and on students (retention in grade). Scores on the lower-stakes state test also improved, but the slope of the trend did not change when the accountability system was implemented. This study also revealed that scores on tests of science and social studies, which were not part of the accountability system, increased much less than scores on reading and mathematics, which were the focus of the accountability system.

The empirical evidence on score inflation is consistent with the views of teachers obtained in two studies. In surveys administered by Koretz, Barron, et al. (1996) to representative samples of teachers in Kentucky, more than half of respondents said that "increased familiarity with KIRIS" and "work with practice tests and preparation materials" had contributed to score gains a great deal, whereas only 16% attributed score gains to "broad improvements in knowledge and skills." Similar responses were obtained in a study of teachers in Maryland (Koretz, Mitchell, Barron, & Keith, 1996), where the testing program had fewer formal stakes than Kentucky's but was perceived as high-stakes.

4. ALIGNMENT BETWEEN TESTS AND STANDARDS

The test-based accountability systems developed in the 1990s and early 2000s included content standards, performance standards, and tests that were intended to operate together to communicate learning goals, document the extent to which these goals were achieved, and reward or sanction educators or students accordingly. An essential assumption underlying these systems is that the tests and standards will be *aligned*—that is, the knowledge, skills, and other constructs measured by the tests will be consistent with those specified in the standards. Alignment was one of the core ideas put forth by proponents of systemic reform in the early 1990s (Smith & O'Day, 1990) and is critical for accountability systems to work as intended (Stecher, Hamilton, & Gonzalez, 2003). By the end of the century, the notion of alignment had become one of the core principles of education reform. Rothman et al. (2002) noted that the term "alignment" appears more than 100 times in the NCLB legislation. Moreover, there is evidence that the degree of alignment between what teachers say they teach and the content of assessments is a strong predictor of test-score gains (Porter, 1998), so measurement of alignment may be helpful in evaluating the meaning and validity of these gains.

While the terminology of alignment was new, the idea was not. Guidelines for test validation have long included the representativeness of content (formerly called "content validity," but more recently conceptualized as content-related evidence of a unitary validity; see American Educational Research Association, American Psychological Association, & National Council on Measurement in Education, 1999). Testing programs have traditionally provided written description of the tests' content, such as the content-by-process specification tables provided by publishers of large-scale achievement tests (e.g., Hoover et al., 1994). Although the degree of alignment between tests and specifications provided by publishers is important for conveying accurate information about what the tests measure, the issue of alignment is especially critical today because of the demands placed on test-based accountability to improve instruction through communication of goals and through the motivational effects of rewards and sanctions.

4.1. Measuring Alignment

The requirement for aligned standards and tests has prompted the development of a number of approaches to evaluating alignment. The nature of each method tends to reflect the developer's definition of "alignment." Webb (1997) provided a basic definition: "the degree to which expectations and assessments are in agreement and serve in conjunction with one another to guide the system toward students learning what they are expected to know and do" (p. 3). It is not clear from this definition, however, what aspects of agreement should be considered or how strong the agreement must be. Bhola, Impara, and Buckendahl (2003) distinguished among low, moderate, and high complexity models of alignment. Low complexity models focus on content standards or test specifications and rely on content experts such as teachers or curriculum coordinators to rate the degree of agreement between the content measured by an item and the content specified by a standard. Moderate complexity models extend beyond content to consider the cognitive complexity of the items and standards. High complexity models address additional dimensions; for example, they may examine the relative weights given to particular skills or knowledge in the tests and in the standards and may consider conditions of administration, such as whether students are permitted to use calculators on mathematics items (La Marca et al., 2000). Because higher complexity models involve more dimensions, the measured degree of alignment will tend to be inversely correlated with the complexity of the model applied to any given set of tests and standards.

The use of expert raters is the typical method for evaluating content representativeness or alignment (Sireci, 1998). Porter (2002), for example, described a method that produces a quantitative index of alignment. He illustrated this with a topic-by-process matrix in mathematics. The topic dimension included "multiple-step equations," "inequalities," and several others, and the cognitive demand dimension included skills and processes such as "memorize," "perform procedures," and "solve nonroutine problems." Test items and standards can be assigned on the basis of expert judgment to the cells of this matrix, and a quantitative index can be calculated to indicate the degree to which the proportions assigned to each cell in the assessment matrix match those in the standards matrix.

Rothman et al. (2002) described another approach, which has been used by Achieve, Inc. in its work with states.

This method considers four dimensions: content centrality (i.e., degree of match between the content of the standards and test); performance centrality (i.e., cognitive demand); challenge; and balance and range. The challenge dimension addresses both the level of the challenge and its source—whether it stems from the knowledge and skills required or from some ancillary factor. The balance and range dimension represents relative emphasis and coverage of material across the set of items or standards. This method provides richer information than most because it considers a number of dimensions of match and provides evidence of the ways in which a test may fail to cover the entire range of material specified in the standards. Achieve's alignment analyses for several states showed that while states' tests generally included only material that appeared in the standards, the set of items on the test typically failed to assess the full range of the standards, and the more challenging standards were less well represented than the easier ones (Rothman et al., 2002).

Webb (1997) proposed an even more complex model, with five broad categories and several subcategories. His method addresses the factors considered by Achieve's model, along with additional criteria such as pedagogical implications. The Third International Mathematics and Science Study (TIMSS) applied his method but only used the Content category and its six subcategories. The broader set of categories was used in alignment studies of four states, described by Webb (1999).

All of the methods discussed here are designed to consider alignment in both directions—from standards to tests, and from tests to standards. This is typically done by filling in cells in matrices for both standards and tests, and evaluating the degree of match between the two resulting matrices. Rothman et al.'s (2002) finding, however, suggests that in the development of many state tests, alignment was evaluated primarily in one direction. That is, each test item was evaluated for alignment with standards, whereas apparently no effort was made to ensure that each standard was addressed in the test. This may stem from the sequential nature of many standards and assessment development efforts, in which the publication of standards often precedes the development or selection of a test, and the latter activity is often contracted to an external organization.

The nature of state content standards complicates analysis of alignment. Standards vary in clarity and specificity (American Federation of Teachers, 2001), and many states have multiple levels of standards—for example, general guidelines followed by more detailed descriptions of specific skills and knowledge (Bhola, Impara, & Buckendahl, 2003). States sometimes use different names for these documents; for example, the more general guidelines might be called standards, whereas the detailed descriptions may be labeled a curriculum framework. The degree of specificity in a standard or framework element affects the meaning of "alignment" and may have implications for the methods used to evaluate it.

In addition, there are currently no criteria for determining what level of alignment is acceptable. Perfect correspondence between tests and standards is infeasible because tests typically require sampling from the domain of interest. Moreover, a higher value on a given alignment index need not correspond to a better-aligned system. Factors such as the number of dimensions considered (i.e., the degree of complexity of the alignment model), the number of topics included, and the type of rating scale used will affect the magnitude of the alignment index. Even when the same method is applied across contexts, features of the standards and assessment systems, such as the complexity of the test items and the degree of specificity of the standards, may lead to differences in the measured degree of alignment that do not necessarily reflect meaningful differences in the test-standards match. It is also not clear how items or standards that address more than one cell should be handled or whether an item that addresses part of a standard but not the entire standard should be considered "aligned." These may be some of the reasons that discrepancies have been found between alignment results reported by test publishers and those produced by teachers (Buckendahl, Plake, Impara, & Irwin, 2000).

To illustrate the problem of differences in breadth between standards and test items, Webb (1997) provided an example of a 1995 Virginia standard specifying that students should be able to read four types of maps: bathymetric, geologic, topographic, and weather. A single test item that required students to read a topographic map would probably be classified as being aligned with this standard, even though the item does not address the entire standard. The method of alignment described by Webb addresses this potential mismatch through a "range of knowledge correspondence" criterion, which shares features of Rothman et al.'s "balance and range" dimension, described earlier. Judgments about range may be relatively easy to make in cases such as this example, in which the standard is clearly described, but are likely to be much more difficult when standards are vague or focus on more generic skills such as problem solving. Even in this case, however, it is not clear what is meant by "able to read," and it is possible that a test item that requires some map reading will fail to capture the full range of skills intended by the standards developers.

The accuracy and consistency of the raters who conduct the alignment ratings is critical. Using generalizability theory, Porter (2002) has estimated the reliability of his system of rating standards to be approximately 0.7 when two raters were used and approximately 0.8 when four were used. He obtained similar results for ratings of assessment items. However, high rates of consistency, while necessary, are insufficient to imply accuracy. It is possible that raters tend to share biases or response tendencies that lead to high levels of agreement but low levels of accuracy. For example, teachers tend to be generous when deciding whether a test item matches a standard and often try to make sure that each item has at least one match (Buckendahl, Impara, Plake, & Haack, 2001). Bhola et al. (2003) note the critical importance of providing adequate training to raters.

Studies have shown that the cognitive complexity dimension is particularly difficult to rate (Le, 2002; Sanford & Fabrizio, 1999). This difficulty stems in part from the fact that items can often be solved in multiple ways, sometimes as a function of the examinee's proficiency or the curriculum to which he or she was exposed. A simple multiplication item, for example, could be solved quickly and automatically by a student who had memorized the multiplication facts, but might call on problem solving ability among students who did not have the relevant facts memorized. Even the most well-trained rater will generally be unable to determine unambiguously what cognitive processes are required by most items. Ratings could be supplemented by talk-along studies of students solving items on the assessments (e.g., Hamilton et al., 1997), but this has not generally been done with studies of alignment.

4.2. Alignment and Validity

For present purposes, a central question is the utility of alignment studies for validating inferences, given the current uses of tests. This is a particularly demanding use of alignment studies, and studies of alignment that are useful for other purposes may be insufficient for validation.

When used in validation, alignment studies are merely a new variant of content-related validity evidence. Both the importance and the insufficiency of content-related evidence has long been a matter of agreement. Other forms of evidence—in particular, empirical evidence based on relationships between scores and other variables—are essential. The shift in emphasis toward standards and aligned assessments in no way alters this, and the growing consequences for test scores makes empirical evidence even more important.

The necessary incompleteness of alignment studies (and of content-related evidence more generally) is an important limitation for their use in validation, particularly given the current uses of large-scale tests. This incompleteness has three aspects. First, even when alignment studies use high-complexity models and evaluate alignment in both directions (from standards to tests and from tests to standards), the nature of large-scale state testing programs makes it nearly impossible to assess the full range of what is specified in the standards. Second, the standards themselves will generally be incomplete representations of the set of performance elements with substantial inference weights (see section 2). Third, the focus of alignment studies on substantive elements—that is, content and process—while appropriate for many purposes, is insufficient for validation under high-stakes conditions.

These considerations suggest how alignment studies might best be used for validation under high-stakes conditions such as those in many large-scale K–12 testing programs. Alignment studies should evaluate alignment in both directions in order to identify omissions and underweighting that could provide an opportunity for inappropriate test preparation. For the same reason, alignment studies will also need to examine overweighting. High-complexity models are likely to be more useful for these purposes than low-complexity models. When testing programs replace forms over time, alignment studies should examine alignment over time. Ideally, this would show that representation of the standards is more comprehensive over the moderate term than in any one year, but conversely, it would also reveal recurrent patterns of content and style that afford opportunities for inappropriate coaching and reallocation.

For purposes of investigating VIHS, it may be necessary to extend current test-based alignment studies in two ways. First, to the extent that alignment studies ignore non-substantive elements that may be pertinent to the generalizability of performance, they should be complemented by examination of these elements. Second, validity depends on the consistency of test weights with inference weights (see section 2), and standards are only a proxy for the latter. The adequacy of standards as a proxy will vary depending on the nature of the standards and the particular inferences users base on scores. Therefore, it may be essential to generate information about inference weights and to include in alignment studies performance elements with large inference weights but little or no representation in the standards.

Alignment studies, as any content-related evidence, must be considered jointly with empirical validity evidence, and the nature of that empirical evidence also depends on the uses of tests. Under high-stakes conditions, content-based evidence must be paired not only with traditional forms of empirical evidence, such as convergent/discriminant evidence, but also with evidence pertaining to the generalizability of performance from focal to audit measures. In many cases, it would be particularly useful to link alignment studies to examination of clusters of items showing particularly large or small increases in performance, as suggested in section 2.5.3.

5. REPORTING IN TERMS OF PERFORMANCE STANDARDS

Reporting performance on large-scale K–12 assessments in terms of a small number of performance standards had become increasingly common by the end of the 1990s, and the enactment of NCLB in 2001 made standards-based reporting of results on certain tests a statutory requirement for states accepting federal funding under the Elementary and Secondary Education Act. In some instances, for example, in NAEP and some state assessments, standards-based reporting is coupled with reporting on one or more additional scales. For present purposes, however, we consider issues raised by standards-based reporting in isolation, without regard to the use of additional reporting scales.

In this section, we consider the effects of three aspects of standards-based reporting: the coarseness of the scale, the robustness of the standards, and the reliance on measures of non-central tendency. All three pose problems of validity that have yet to be adequately addressed and that should be weighed along with other advantages and disadvantages of standards-based reporting. Other issues raised by the use of standards-based reporting are discussed in other chapters of this volume. The chapter by Hambleton and Pitoniak (this volume) provides an extensive discussion of the recent use of performance standards, including numerous psychometric issues. The chapter by Haertel (this volume) discusses the reliability of standards-based measures.

5.1. The Coarseness of Standards-Based Scales

In much of the psychometric literature, "precision" is used synonymously with "reliability." For example, Linn (2001) wrote that "Reliability refers to the precision of assessment scores and is usually gauged in terms of the consistency of scores obtained using alternate sets of assessment tasks, or different occasions, or when different raters score open-ended responses." In the case of standards-based reporting, reliability in this sense of consistency or dependability often takes the form of the consistency of classification (see the chapter by Haertel, this volume).

However, "precision" also has another meaning, closer to "accuracy": the closeness of a point estimate to its target or "true" value. As Rogosa and others have shown (e.g., Rogosa, 1999), this aspect of precision is distinct from reliability in the sense of consistency of estimates. For example, as the variance of true scores decreases, the reliability corresponding to any fixed level of precision will decrease because error will constitute a growing proportion of the variance of observed scores.

Precision in the sense of accuracy is a particularly important issue with standards-based reporting because the coarse scales generally used (see section 1.2.3) can provide only very approximate information about student performance or change. The performance intervals established by common standard-setting methods can be of any width, but at least one must necessarily encompass a broad range of performance, and typically most of the intervals do. This coarseness is exacerbated when the highest or lowest standard is in an extreme location, as is the case in some states presently (see Linn, 2003; McLaughlin & Bandeira de Mello, 2002) because most students are then distributed among yet fewer categories.

Thus, standards-based reporting as commonly implemented is imprecise in the sense of being inexact. This imprecision does not necessarily imply a high rate of misclassification. The probability that an individual will be inconsistently classified across repeated instances of measurement will depend on the individual's distance from the cut score (Kane, 1996), the precision of the test itself (that is, its conditional standard error at the relevant point in the distribution), and the level of the cut score relative to the distribution. Moreover, Brennan, Yin, and Kane (2003) demonstrated that criterion-related inferences about aggregate change can be more dependable than normative inferences.

Nonetheless, the coarseness of the reporting scale poses substantial threats to some inferences about performance. Even large differences in performance that do not cross a performance standard are not reflected on this scale, while very small differences that cross a cut score do register, so cross-sectional comparisons among students or groups may be distorted. The same issues can arise in drawing inferences about individual and aggregate change over time.

Behavioral responses to test-based accountability may exacerbate these distortions. As noted in section 3.1, in response to pressure to increase the percentage of students reaching a particular performance standard, some teachers may place disproportionate emphasis on the achievement of students near the cut score. If this response is sufficiently prevalent (and effective), the result would be to bias some inferences about aggregate change based on standards-based statistics. In contrast, changes in means on conventional scales would accurately reflect change across the full range of performance.

5.2. The Robustness of Performance Standards

Much of the argument surrounding the use of judgmentally set performance standards has focused on the arbitrariness of the standards. Popham (1978) and Hambleton (1998) noted that the word "arbitrary" has two meanings: a positive meaning connoting appropriate use of judgment and a negative meaning connoting capriciousness. Both argued that the careful setting of performance standards is arbitrary in the first sense but not capricious.

For purposes of validating inferences, argument about capriciousness obscures a more fundamental issue: the robustness or generalizability of the standards. That is, if one assumes that standards are set by reasonable and not capricious methods, how consistent are the results across equally reasonable alternatives?

Research to date indicates that the generalizability of performance standards is often poor. Hoover (2003) showed that the percentages of students in national samples rated as "proficient" or "advanced" varied greatly across three competing achievement test batteries and, in the three available grades, the National Assessment of Educational Progress. For example, in the third grade, one of the three batteries labeled 14% of students proficient or advanced, while another rated 56% as proficient or advanced. One source of inconsistency is the method chosen to set standards. Although some studies have found consistency of results across methods (e.g., Buckendahl, Smith, Impara, & Plake, 2002), many have not (see Jaeger, 1989; Linn, 2003). Linn (2003) noted that the composition of panels of judges also can introduce inconsistency, although he noted the limitations of current data pertaining to this. Shepard (1994) found substantial differences between the results obtained by holistic and item-based standard-setting. She also presented evidence that using the modified Angoff method, the levels of standards were not robust to variations in item difficulty and format.

The implications of this lack of robustness for the validity of inferences remains a matter of disagreement. From the perspective of the sampling theory of validity (Kane, 1982; see also the chapter on validity by Kane in this volume), such inconsistencies are a clear threat to the validity of inferences. The threat appears particularly severe when the factors causing the inconsistency are irrelevant to the intended inference. For example, one could imagine an inference that assumes a specific format of tasks, and in such a case, inconsistencies in the levels of standards stemming from differences in format might not be problematic. It is more difficult to imagine, however, intended inferences that are specific to a particular standard-setting method or even a particular mix of item difficulties, and for inferences that make no such assumption, inconsistencies stemming from these factors would pose a serious threat to validity.

Haertel and Wiley (1995) offered a fundamentally different view of standards-based inference, one in which arbitrariness of the standards, and by implication inconsistency, becomes unimportant over time. In a defense of the standards used with Kentucky's KIRIS assessment program in the 1990s, they argued that the initial arbitrariness of standards would become less problematic as the standards accrued meaning with continued use:

> What was done [in the KIRIS system]...was to set the three cut points rather arbitrarily. Since then, however, substantial meaning has accrued to those cut points and the categories they define. Their definitions inhere not in the original standard setting process, but in the creation and dissemination of scoring rubrics for much larger numbers of tasks; in the training of teachers to use those rubrics; and in the acceptance of the NAPD [Novice, Apprentice, Proficient, Distinguished] categories into public discourse. In short, their meanings are found in their present use. With the possible exception of a few measurement specialists, historians, and perhaps philosophers, people who understand and use the NAPD categories today have no more need of an exegesis on their origins than a typical user of the Fahrenheit temperature scale has for the original definitions of zero and one hundred degrees. (Haertel & Wiley, 1995, p. 6)

A reconciliation of Haertel and Wiley's view and the sampling notion of validity may lie in greater specificity about inferences. Haertel and Wiley's logic presupposes an inference that reflects only patterns of performance on the assessment itself, does not entail external comparisons (for example, across grades, over time, or to standards on different tests), and does not reflect any inherent meaning in the label it is given. Such conditions apply to some common test-based inferences. For example, most applicants to highly competitive colleges know that a score 750 on the mathematics scale of the SAT-I is very good and would be considered competitive at even the most selective schools. The label of 750 has no inherent meaning and is not given any verbal label, such as "proficient," that carries any. Comparisons over time are mooted by the linking of the scale, and with the exception of some users who need to compare this score to a score on the ACT, comparisons to other standards are not essential to the inference. However, the SAT scale has been in use long enough that it has accrued meaning, albeit a normative one: without knowing the actual norms, students know that this score is very high both relative to the distribution of scores and to the expectations of colleges. Much the same phenomenon could occur over time with standards-based scales, as Haertel and Wiley (1995) suggested, although there is at present no empirical evidence documenting this.

Many inferences based on standards, however, entail some manner of external comparison or carry with them a prior meaning because of the label used for the standard. In these cases, the lack of robustness of the standards would pose a serious threat to validity. Koretz and Deibert (1996), for example, found that writers for the lay press relied heavily on the verbal labels attached to performance standards in interpreting performance on the NAEP. Some users may be encouraged to draw incorrect inferences when jurisdictions use similarly named but differently set standards. For example, before the enactment of NCLB, many states gave the same names to some or all of their performance standards, and NCLB now mandates the establishment of "proficient," "advanced," and "basic" standards (20 U.S.C. 6311 §1111(a)(1)(D)). No studies have clarified the extent to which users interpret these identically labeled standards to have comparable meaning. However, the large differences among states in the levels of standards (in particular, the proficient standard) have been the source of considerable controversy (e.g., Kingsbury, Olson, Cronin, Hauser, & Houser, 2003; Linn, 2003; Olson, 2002). These variations would be uncontroversial if the similarly named standards were used only to support inferences specific to the standards in each state.

Developmental inferences are an instance in which the lack of robustness of performance standards may be particularly problematic. Examples would include inferring that students who are proficient in one grade are on track to be proficient in a later grade or that performance in a middle school is not as good as performance in the elementary schools feeding it. Because standards-setting processes traditionally were not linked across grades, the percentages of students reaching a given standard have often been erratic (e.g., Hoover, 2003). Moreover, there is no evidence that the between-grades relationships among performance standards are robust to differences in standard-setting method, item type, and so on. These cross-grade inconsistencies have been problematic to policymakers, and in recent years, a number of efforts have been undertaken to link standards across grades (see, e.g., Buckendahl, Huynh, Siskind, & Saunders, 2005; Ferrara, Johnson, & Chen, 2005; Huynh, Barton, Meyer, Porchea, & Gallant, 2005; Huynh & Schneider, 2005; Lewis & Haug, 2005). However, these efforts are in their infancy, and their reasonableness and utility have yet to be evaluated.

5.3. The Reliance on Measures of Non-Central Tendency

Because performance standards will only by chance be located near a measure of central tendency, the shift to standards-based measures entails a reliance on measures of non-central tendency. The implications of this for estimation of reliability has been the focus of considerable investigation (e.g., the chapter by Haertel, this volume). However, this approach to reporting has ramifications for the interpretation of differences among groups independent of the issue of reliability. These issues are not specific to performance standards; measures of non-central tendency are used in a variety of contexts. They affect the validity of many of the most important inferences based on scores, including cross-sectional differences among groups (or jurisdictions) that differ substantially in performance and estimates of trends over time.

The importance of this issue is illustrated by a concrete example. Figure 15.6 shows 2,000 simulated observations representing an unexceptional difference between Whites and African Americans. For simplicity, the database includes only two groups, Whites and African Americans, constituting 85% and 15%, respectively. The African American and White distributions are both random draws from normal distributions, with a mean difference of 0.8 standard deviation and a variance ratio of approximately 0.8.

None of these details is essential; the contrasts among measures described here will arise whenever the distributions of scores in two groups are concentrated near substantially different means. Two performance standards have been superimposed: one at the overall mean and a second one standard deviation below the overall mean.

One of the simplest questions one might ask of these data is the size of the difference between the groups. In the absence of performance levels, this difference would normally be expressed either in scaled scores or as an effect size. When performance standards are used, this difference would typically be expressed using one of two sets of percentages: the percentages of African Americans and Whites scoring below (or above) a standard, or the percentages of the failing (or passing) group who are African American and White. Passing and failing rates appear to be more common in the reporting of K–12 assessments, but statistics of the latter type arise in discussion of equity and access in postsecondary education, which often focuses on measures such as the percentage of minority students among the applicants accepted for admission to a college.

When these common standards-based measures are used, the apparent severity of the cross-sectional difference between African Americans and Whites varies depending on the level of the standard. When the lower standard is applied, the failure rate is roughly three times as high for African Americans, whereas using the higher standard, the differential is roughly a factor of two (Table 15.1). Focusing on the passing rate reverses the pattern: a higher standard makes the group difference appear larger. The same problem arises with the latter statistic: the percentage of failing students who are African American appears more negative when the standard is lower (38%) than when the standard is higher (24%). This same phenomenon arises in college admissions, although there the focus is on those above the cut (selected students) rather than those below. The more selective a college becomes, the more severe the underrepresentation of low-scoring groups among students selected, all else being equal (e.g., Koretz, 2000).

Whether these standards-based measures are misleading depends on the particular inference supported by the scores. If the inference is about the overall difference between Whites and African Americans in this example, the mean difference and standard deviations (being sufficient statistics by construction in this artificial example) fully describe it. Therefore, for this inference, the two seemingly different answers provided by the standards-based measures are misleading. On the other hand, the standards-based measures are appropriate if the inference is specifically about differential success with respect to a particular performance standard.

This difficulty with standards-based reporting arises also when comparing trends among groups that differ in initial levels of achievement. In the case of current K–12 programs, these trends, such as the relative trends of African American and White students, are often reported in terms of changes in the percentages of students scoring proficient or above.

Just as the apparent size of group differences varies with the level of performance standards, so does the apparent difference in trends over time. Figure 15.7 shows the same data as in Figure 15.6 but with an identical increment (one standard deviation) added to the score of every individual. The higher of the two cut scores, at the initial grand mean, is retained. (In most large-scale K–12 testing programs, trends would compare one cohort with the next rather than one group at two points in time, but recasting the problem in terms of a change in a single cohort simplifies the discussion.) Although the increase in performance is identical by construction in the two groups in this example, common standards-based metrics show apparent differences in gains. This occurs regardless of whether one uses the percent of each group failing to reach (or succeeding in reaching) the standard or the percent of those failing (or passing) who belong to each group. This can be seen from Table 15.1, in which the "low standard" columns now reflect the rates with the higher standard but after a uniform improvement of one standard deviation. Here again, the standards-based measures are appropriate for inferences that are specific to those standards but are misleading as indicators of overall trends in the two distributions.

6. INCREASED INCLUSION AND UNIFORMITY OF ASSESSMENT

The increased inclusion of students with special needs and the emphasis on uniformity in group assessment raise issues of the appropriateness of the difficulty and content of assessments. The broader the proficiency range of a tested population, the more difficult it becomes to provide a reasonable level of reliability. Moreover, when the range of proficiency is sufficiently broad, the content of students' instruction is varied enough that the approximation to unidimensionality required for most scaling is increasingly untenable.

The inclusion of students with special needs in general-education assessments, however, raises important issues

FIGURE 15.6 Scores in Two Groups with Two Cut Scores, Simulated Data

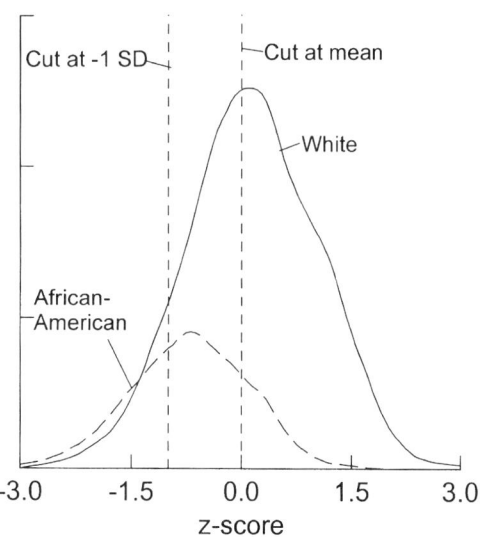

FIGURE 15.7 Scores after Uniform Gains in Two Groups at Initial Mean, Simulated Data

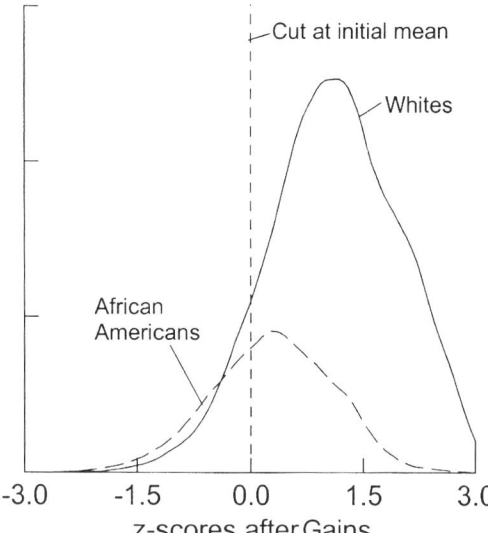

TABLE 15.1 Two Standards-Referenced Measures of the Performance of Whites and Blacks in the Simulated Data

	PERCENT FAILING		PERCENT OF FAILURES	
	Low Standard	High Standard	Low Standard	High Standard
Whites	10	44	62	76
Blacks	33	79	38	24

beyond these. The specific attributes that lead to students being identified as having a disability or limited proficiency in English may impede their performance on achievement tests. The relationships between their special needs and their performance on tests pose particularly difficult issues pertaining to test design, administration, and validation.

6.1. The Heterogeneity of Students with Special Needs

One fundamental difficulty for designing assessments for students with special needs and evaluating the validity of their scores is the heterogeneity of these populations. The U.S. Education Department estimates, based on state administrative data, that 11.3% of students ages 6–17 are served under IDEA Part B, the major state grant program under IDEA (U.S. Department of Education, 2001). For administering IDEA, the U.S. Department of Education recognizes 13 categories of disability, including some that are cognitive (e.g., mental retardation), some that are unambiguously non-cognitive (e.g., visual disabilities), and yet others the cognitive aspects of which are more ambiguous for purposes of assessment (in particular, specific learning disabilities) (U.S. Department of Education, 2001). Moreover, each of these 13 disabilities can take a variety of different forms, and because of comorbidity, they can occur in many combinations.

There is also substantial heterogeneity among students classified as having limited English proficiency (LEP). By one estimate, LEP students constituted 9.6% of total public school enrollments in pre-K through grade 12 in 2000–2001, and states reported more than 460 languages spoken by students nationwide. Spanish is spoken by almost 80% of LEP students, but no other single language was reported for more than 2% of LEP students (Kindler, 2002).

One corollary of this heterogeneity is that some groups with specific special needs are extremely small. For example, students identified as visually disabled for purposes of IDEA section B constitute only about five one-hundredths of one percent of all children ages 6–17, and numerous other disability groups are also very small (U.S. Department of Education, 2001). Similarly, while the language-minority populations of individual jurisdictions are often very different from the national statistics cited above, it is common for states and districts to have many very small language groups. For example, Maine, one of the most homogeneous states in the nation, has identified 80 native languages in the state's public schools (not counting American Sign Language), of which only four are spoken by more than 300 students (Maine Department of Education, n.d.).

This heterogeneity and small group size hinder research and design. For example, even with census testing data from Kentucky, Koretz and Hamilton (2000) were able to evaluate the assessment of only a few disability groups. The small size of groups also constrains practical responses to the difficulties confronting students with special needs. For example, the heterogeneity of the LEP population in most jurisdictions makes it impractical to offer many LEP students assessments in any relevant language other than English. As a result, this heterogeneity results in a *de facto* system in which students in one or a few second language groups can be assessed in their native languages (or with language-specific aids, such as glossaries), while the others cannot.

6.2. Construct-Relevant and Construct-Irrelevant Impediments to Performance

A key to assessing the proficiency of students with special needs is whether the impediments caused by their special needs are relevant to the inferences based on scores—that is, whether these impediments are construct-relevant or construct-irrelevant. If the impediment is unrelated to the construct about which inferences are drawn, the result is a bias in scores. An example would be the effects of visual disabilities on performance on a test measuring comprehension of mathematical concepts. Visual acuity would in this case be construct-irrelevant, and a severely visually disabled student's difficulty reading a printed test form would result in a downward bias in the estimate of that student's proficiency. At the other extreme, mental retardation, by definition a generalized cognitive deficit, is relevant to most of the inferences based on achievement test scores, and therefore the effect of the disability on test scores will generally not be bias.

In the case of most K–12 group assessments of achievement, the construct-relevance of special needs is unambiguous for only a minority of identified students. For example, as noted, only 0.05% of all students ages 6–17 were identified in 1999 as having a visual disability as their primary disability. Only 0.14% of students were identified as having hearing impairments. Conversely, mental retardation, which clearly is construct-relevant, was somewhat more common but still relatively rare: approximately 1.1% of all students ages 6–17 were identified as having retardation (U.S. Department of Education, 2001, Table AA10).

Most identified students have disabilities the consequences of which are more difficult to categorize as relevant or irrelevant to the constructs about which inferences are drawn. These include specific learning disabilities, which is the largest category under IDEA, emotional disturbance, and speech and language impairments (U.S. Department of Education, 2001, Table AA10). Whether these disabilities are construct-relevant may depend on the assessment and the specific inference intended. For example, consider an assessment of basic mathematics. If the intended inferences focus on knowledge of and the ability to apply arithmetic algorithms, a dyslexic student's difficulty reading text in which problems are embedded or writing answers in verbal form would arguably be a construct-irrelevant source of bias in the student's score. In contrast, if the inferences pertain to a broader definition of mathematical competence that includes communication skills or the ability to solve mathematical problems in the contexts in which they naturally occur, then an inability to read text and write verbal answers would not be entirely construct-irrelevant (National Research Council, 1997).

6.3. The Use of Accommodations and Modifications

The terms "accommodations," "modifications," and "adaptations" are all variously used to describe departures from standardization for students made in response to special needs. The use of these terms is inconsistent. The most recent edition of the *Standards for Educational and Psychological Testing* (American Educational Research Association, American Psychological Association, & National Council on Measurement in Education, 1999) suggests using the term "accommodations" to refer to all departures from standardization:

> Here accommodation is used as the general term for any action taken in response to a determination that an individual's disability requires a departure from established testing protocol. Depending on circumstances, such accommodation may include modification of test administration processes or modification of test content. (*Standards,* p. 101)

More common usage reserves the term "accommodation" for changes in administration that do not directly change test content: changes in setting, in time allowed, in mode of presentation, or in allowed mode of response. The term "modification" is then used to refer to changes in content, such as eliminating or altering test items. "Adaptation" appears to have no consistent use. We use "accommodations" here to refer to alterations that are not intended to change the construct measured by the test.

The psychometric function of accommodations is to increase the validity of inferences about students with special needs by offsetting specific disability-related, construct-irrelevant impediments to performance. A National Research Council study suggested the metaphor of a corrective lens: "Accommodations are intended to function as a corrective lens that will deflect the distorted array of observed scores back to where they ought to be—that is, back to where they provide a more valid image of the performance of individuals with disabilities" (National Research Council, 1997, p. 176).

Both federal statute, as explained above, and the policies of most states require that appropriate accommodations be offered to students with special needs. If one could identify reliably the construct-irrelevant impediments caused by a student's special needs, if those impediments could be reliably distinguished from construct-relevant ones, and if research showed clearly which accommodations offset these impediments without having other effects on performance, this requirement would be practicable, but in fact, these conditions rarely apply. As a consequence, neither researchers nor educators have reached agreement on which accommodations are appropriate under various conditions. State policies about the use of accommodations are inconsistent and have changed rapidly (e.g., National Center on Educational Outcomes, 1993; Thurlow, House, Boys, Scott, & Ysseldyke, 2000; Thurlow, Seyfarth, Scott, & Ysseldyke, 1997). Moreover, studies have shown that teachers often assign accommodations either inconsistently with state guidelines or without accurately predicting their benefits (e.g., Fuchs, Fuchs, Eaton, Hamlett, & Karns, 2000; Koretz & Hamilton, 2000). Research on the effects of accommodations in K–12 testing programs has been sparse and is insufficient to provide adequate guidance for practice (National Research Council, 1997). While recent years have seen a marked increase in this work, it remains limited (Koretz & Barton, 2004).

Because of the intended incentive effects of testing, the use of tests for accountability, and the increased focus on aggregate scores, a second function of accommodations has recently become salient: enabling students with special needs to participate in large-scale assessments. Although it is logical to expect that the provision of accommodations will increase participation, empirical evidence is sparse, in part because there have been few instances in which a policy prohibiting accommodations was changed to allow them. One clear source of evidence is the NAEP, which did change from a policy of prohibiting accommodations to allowing them, at the same time changing rules for exclusion. In the 1996 assessment of mathematics, when NAEP first allowed accommodations and changed exclusion rules, an increase in the participation of both students with disabilities and students with limited proficiency in English was found in both grades 4 and 8 but not in grade 12 (Reese et al., 1997). Increased participation was again found four years later (Braswell et al., 2001). However, these findings from NAEP may not generalize to state or local testing programs. In such programs, incentives to exclude students (see section 3.2 and Hamilton, 2003) or statutory or regulatory requirements for inclusion rates may be sufficiently powerful to offset the effects of accommodations on participation.

The goal of increasing participation is related to the traditional aim of increasing validity because of the potential effects of increased participation on the validity of inferences about aggregates. If the effect of providing accommodations is to increase participation without altering the assessment of students who would have been assessed without the change, and if the information about the newly included students is of reasonably high quality, the validity of inferences about aggregates should improve. However, it is not necessarily true that the conditions of assessment would remain the same for students who would be assessed under either set of rules. The experience of NAEP is inconsistent in this respect: the 1996 assessment suggested that some students who otherwise would have been assessed without accommodations were instead assessed with them because of the change of rule (Reese et al., 1997), while the 2000 assessment did not reveal the same pattern (Braswell et al., 2001). Changes in the conditions of assessment for students who would participate under either set of rules could have either positive or negative effects on the validity of inferences both about them and about aggregates, depending on the appropriateness of the accommodations.

The importance of such changes in inclusion and the provision of accommodations will depend on the specific inferences based on scores. When the inferences pertain to the entire tested population, the effects of these changes may be modest unless the proportion of students affected is large. However, under current policy, some of the most important inferences, for example, some that determine whether schools make Adequate Yearly Progress, pertain to students with disabilities and with limited proficiency in English. Because of the much smaller size of these two groups, changes in inclusion and the provision of accommodations could have a substantial impact on inferences about their performance.

6.4. Inconsistencies of Identification and Classification

The identification and classification of students with disabilities are strikingly inconsistent across states, schools, and classrooms. Consistent with common usage in special education, we use "identification" to refer to the determination that the student has a recognized disability under IDEA or Section 504 of the Rehabilitation Act of 1973 and "classification" to refer to the labeling of the student's primary disability.

Identification is highly inconsistent at all levels of the educational system. IDEA requires that states provide annual reports to the Congress on the implementation of IDEA, including prevalence data. In 1999, the percentage of students ages 6–17 identified as disabled for purposes of IDEA Part B (the principal state grant program under IDEA) ranged from a low of 9% in Colorado to a high of almost 16% in Rhode Island (U.S. Department of Education, 2001). It is likely that a substantial part of this variation represents inconsistent identification rather than real differences in prevalence. Moreover, studies have shown that there are substantial inconsistencies in identification rates at lower levels of aggregation, including teachers and schools (e.g., Clarizio & Phillips, 1992; National Research Council, 1997; Shepard, 1993; Ysseldyke & Algozzine, 1982).

Classification is even more inconsistent. The reported prevalence rates for many of the federally recognized disability categories vary dramatically from state to state. Among students ages 6–17, a particularly extreme case is mental retardation, the reported prevalence of which varied tenfold in 1999, from 0.3% in New Jersey to 3.0% in West Virginia. Several other categories had maximum rates two to four times the reported minimum rates (U.S. Department of Education, 2001, Table AA 10). Inconsistent classification is particularly important in the case of specific learning disabilities because of the size of this group. The diagnostic criteria for this disability are ambiguous. Research is inconsistent with respect to whether students with learning disabilities are functionally or psychometrically distinct from other low-achieving students and whether they respond differently to specific educational treatments (National Research Council, 1997). In 1999, the prevalence rates for specific learning disabilities among students ages 6–17 ranged from a low of 3.0% (in Kentucky) to a high of 9.1% (in Rhode Island; see U.S. Department of Education, 2001, Table AA10).

Although classification is widely considered in the special education community to be unimportant for assigning services, both identification and classification are critically important for assessment. Inconsistencies in identification are problematic because they indicate that the benefits of statutes such as IDEA—for present purposes, particularly the testing accommodations—are misallocated. This could undermine the validity of inferences about students inappropriately granted or denied the accommodations to which identification entitles them, and it could result in other harm to students not appropriately identified. Classification is important for numerous reasons. Research exploring the best way to assess students with special needs requires the establishment of groups that vary in known ways in terms of disability characteristics. The appropriate assignment of accommodations requires that one identify the functional implications of disabilities and their relevance to test-based inferences, and that requires reliable information on students' disabilities (National Research Council, 1997). Finally, evaluation of the impact of accommodations and of the validity of inferences about students with special needs requires accurate information about relevant aspects of disabilities.

6.5. Approaches to Validation

Several of the factors noted here—the heterogeneity of students with special needs, the small size of many subgroups, the strikingly inconsistent classification of students with disabilities, the construct-relevance of some of the impediments caused by special needs, and the inability in many cases to clearly delineate construct-relevant from construct-irrelevant impediments—pose formidable barriers to the validation of inferences about the performance of students with special needs. These difficulties are compounded by the lack of a criterion measure for the validation of many K–12 assessments. In the case of college-admissions testing, the predictive criterion of later performance has been used to help evaluate the validity of standard and nonstandard administrations for students with disabilities (see Willingham et al., 1988). In the case of most K–12 tests, however, no suitable criterion measure exists. Because the appropriate accommodations remain largely undetermined, alternative standardized measures are no more trustworthy than the measure requiring validation, and teachers' grades may be biased or simply highly unreliable in the case of some students with special needs.

Faced with these difficulties, researchers have taken a variety of approaches to validation. Several studies have explored the internal psychometric properties of the performance of students with special needs under both standard and non-standard conditions, for example, item discrimination, item difficulty, the monotonicity of empirical item characteristic curves, and DIF (e.g., Anderson, Jenkins, & Miller, n.d.; Koretz, 1997; Willingham et al., 1988). Koretz (1997) and Koretz and Hamilton (1999) examined the plausibility of total scores for specific combinations of disability classification and accommodations but warned that this approach is useful only in the relatively rare cases in which one has a reasonable prior expectation. Phillips (1994) suggested using the criterion of differential gain (that is, an interaction between accommodation and disability) to examine the validity of scores obtained with accommodations, an approach that was used by Fuchs et al. (2000). She argued that an appropriate accommodation would produce improvements in scores for the target group but not for other students. However, Elliott and McKevitt (2000) argued against this approach, maintaining that appropriate accommodations that would improve the validity of inferences about students with disabilities might fail this test. While work on this problem has grown markedly in recent years, it remains one of the most difficult issues confronting K–12 assessment.

7. INFERENCES ABOUT CHANGE

Scores from K–12 group tests are now often used to support inferences about change. Although many of the topics we have addressed in earlier sections of this chapter are relevant to both status and change measures, reporting performance in terms of change introduces additional issues. In this section we focus on aggregate change measures, such as those used to report progress at the school level. Linn (2001) described three broad approaches to measuring aggregate change: cohort-to-cohort, quasi-longitudinal, and true longitudinal or value-added (see also Carlson, 2000). We discuss each of these below.

7.1. Cohort-to-Cohort Change Measures

One common method for measuring change noted in section 1 involves comparing average scores (or some other summary score, such as percent passing) for a unit (e.g., a school) from one year to the next. These comparisons may involve only a single grade or may incorporate information from multiple grade levels—for example, the difference between a summary score for grades 3, 4, and 5 from one year to the next. In the first case, almost none of the students whose scores were included in year 1 would be included in year 2 (with the exception of students who were retained in grade). In the second type of comparison, some students will have scores included at both time points (e.g., students who were in grade 3 in year 1 and grade 4 in year 2). In either case, a substantial number of students whose scores are included in year 2 will not have been included in year 1, and vice versa. Although this approach is widely used in test-based accountability systems, it can only support certain kinds of inferences about improvement, and cannot support inferences about the effectiveness of schools or teachers.

Perhaps the most serious threat to inferences based in cohort-to-cohort change models is instability in aggregate scores. Recent studies have investigated the magnitude of this instability, its relationship to the size and composition of schools, and its sources. Nonetheless, several key questions about this instability have yet to be answered, and therefore the implications for validity remain incompletely explored.

Instability in cohort-to-cohort change measures stems from several sources, including measurement error, sampling error, and one-time events that affect scores one year but not the next (e.g., a disruption during testing or a particularly unfavorable match between students and teacher; see Kane & Staiger, 2002). The effects of measurement error are likely to be small in the context of most large-scale testing programs, but sampling variability and the effects of one-time events may be substantial. Sampling error arises even with census testing because each year's cohort of tested students is a sample of possible students over time, and these cohorts differ from each other independently of school effects. As simple statistical theory indicates, sampling error is a problem particularly for small schools and for schools at which test scores for only one or two grade levels are included in the performance index. Moreover, inferences made from cohort-to-cohort measures rest on the assumption that student characteristics do not show substantial systematic change from one year to the next. Linn (2001) notes that this assumption may be reasonable in most instances but may not hold for certain types of schools that are characterized by rapid turnover in student population.

Kane and Staiger (2002) analyzed state test-score data in an effort to disentangle the effects of sampling error, non-persistent factors, and persistent factors related to the actual performance of the school. As expected, their analysis revealed that instability due to sampling error was quite large, especially for smaller schools, and that instability due to one-time events was also substantial. Using data from North Carolina's state testing program, Kane and Staiger estimated that nearly 80% of the between-school variability in change scores for a combined measure of math and reading achievement in elementary schools was due to sampling variability and non-persistent factors. Moreover, they noted that the typical elementary school includes 68 students per grade, making sampling variability a significant problem for those schools in particular. They concluded that simple annual change scores are too volatile to be of use to policymakers or educators. Linn and Haug (2002), using data from Colorado's state testing program, reached a similar conclusion.

Although these studies clearly indicate that aggregate, cohort-to-cohort change scores should be interpreted with caution, the current literature does not allow us to determine to what extent score gains provide information about real school effects. One problem is that percent-of-variance calculations are dependent upon the amount of variance in true change. If schools are approximately equally effective at promoting growth, or if change is heavily dependent upon factors such as maturation, which are relatively consistent across schools, then sources of error may constitute a fairly large proportion of variance in change scores even when aggregate achievement is measured with high precision (see Rogosa, 2002).

Perhaps more important, the studies conducted to date fail to indicate what proportion of variance in score gains is attributable to real behavioral responses that are relevant to the construct of interest, and what proportion is attributable to the various sources of error. Kane and Staiger (2002) estimated the proportion of variability due to nonpersistent factors but did not address the fact that those factors are of two types. Their description focuses on one type—the one-time events that affect scores in a way that detracts from their validity. Specific examples given by Kane and Staiger include dogs barking in the playground and a wave of flu that occurs one year but not the next. The other type of one-time events involves the behavioral responses made by teachers, students, or others that affect the underlying achievement construct as well as the scores themselves. In fact, these responses may be influenced by prior performance in a way that contributes to inconsistency in gains over time. For example, in accountability systems that impose sanctions or offer assistance to particularly low-performing schools, educators in schools at which performance drops may be especially motivated to improve performance the subsequent year. In this case, a large drop followed by a large increase in scores would reflect real responses rather than simple error, and a low correlation between two sets of year-to-year change scores may not necessarily indicate measurement problems. Accurate inferences about change scores depend on an understanding of how these various factors contribute to those scores, and to date the literature does not provide such an understanding.

7.2. Quasi-Longitudinal Change Measures

A second type of change measure involves using aggregate scores to track changes in achievement from one grade to the next. For example, the mean score for 5th graders in year 2 would be compared with the mean score for 4th graders in year 1. This quasi-longitudinal approach (Carlson, 2000; Linn, 2001) represents an effort to address one of the shortcomings of cohort-to-cohort change measures by focusing on the same group of students over time.

Quasi-longitudinal change scores are less heavily influenced by sampling variability and between-cohort differences in student background characteristics than are cohort-to-cohort measures, though they are not immune to these problems. In addition, they require a testing program that uses a vertical scale, which may be especially problematic in testing systems that use standards-based reporting, and they are affected by the scaling issues we discuss in the next section. However, because they are relatively simple to construct and to explain to the public, quasi-longitudinal change scores may be attractive for some reporting purposes and may represent an effective compromise between the simplicity of cohort-to-cohort measures and the emphasis on growth provided by the value-added approach, discussed below.

7.3. True Longitudinal or Value-Added Measures

The final type of change measure we discuss is the true longitudinal or value-added measure, which relies on longitudinally linked student-level data to obtain estimates of growth for aggregates, generally either teachers or schools (see section 1.2.10). We refer here to estimates for teachers, but the issues noted here apply to other aggregates as well. Applications of this approach range from the reporting of simple averages of student-level change scores to the implementation of complex multivariate models, such as the Tennessee Value-added Assessment System or TVAAS (Sanders & Horn, 1998). As we discussed in section 1.2.8, value-added modeling (VAM) methods such as TVAAS have gained attention from the research and policy communities in large part because proponents of these methods have asserted that they can be used to isolate the effects of schools or teachers and therefore measure effectiveness.

Despite its popularity, the use of VAM raises a variety of statistical, measurement, and practical issues. Here we briefly note some of the major issues; for a comprehensive discussion, see McCaffrey, Lockwood, Koretz, and Hamilton (2003).

7.3.1. Statistical Issues

VAM may be implemented using a variety of modeling approaches, and analysts must make decisions about the specific form that VAM models take. First, a decision needs to be made about whether to treat teacher effects as fixed or random. Most recent VAM studies use mixed models that treat the teacher effects as random (e.g., Ballou, Sanders, & Wright, 2003; Rowan, Correnti, & Miller, 2002; Sanders, Saxton, & Horn, 1997), but earlier applications of VAM approaches have used fixed effects (e.g., Hanushek, 1972; Murnane, 1975). Fixed effects estimates can be highly sensitive to sampling error because teachers tend to teach only small numbers of students. The random effects models used in VAM are empirical Bayes methods that shrink the estimate for each teacher back toward the overall mean based on the amount of sampling error in each teacher's estimate. This shrinkage has optimal statistical properties on average across teachers but will tend to underestimate effects for teachers who are far from the mean, and is likely to be difficult to explain to users of the data and those who are affected by the system (such as teachers whose job performance is evaluated using this method).

A second statistical consideration involves the decision about how to use the longitudinal data—whether to model change scores, estimate a series of models using single-year outcomes, or conduct a single multivariate analysis of the full set of data. The full multivariate approach tends to be more flexible and efficient than the other approaches, but is computationally demanding.

A third issue stems from the possible effects of omitted variables. There is debate in the research community on the effects of omitting student background variables from the models used in recent VAM analyses. Ballou et al. (2003) found that this omission did not affect VAM estimates, whereas McCaffrey, Lockwood, Koretz, and Hamilton (2003) found that the omission of background variables may bias estimates, depending on the interplay of a number of factors. In general, the potential for bias exists when classrooms or schools differ in terms of student background characteristics that are related to outcomes (McCaffrey, Lockwood, Koretz, & Hamilton 2003, p. 69). Related problems involve possible confounding of school and teacher effects and biases resulting from incomplete student records.

An additional statistical consideration is the uncertainty resulting from sampling error, which may lead to imprecise estimates of school and teacher effects. A simulation by McCaffrey et al. (2003) showed that many VAM estimates are likely to be sufficiently precise for some types of inferences, such as determining which teachers are far from the mean, but are inadequate for other purposes, such as ranking all teachers.

7.3.2. Measurement Issues

The other broad category of issues related to VAM stems from the use of large-scale achievement tests as outcome measures. We discuss three of these: the timing of test administration, the scaling of the test, and test dimensionality. Again, these discussions are relatively brief; additional details are provided in McCaffrey, Lockwood, Koretz, and Hamilton (2003).

7.3.2.1. Timing of Test Administration

Most large-scale assessment programs involve annual testing, typically in the spring. The interval between two administrations in such cases generally includes portions of two academic years and a summer break. Although research suggests that achievement trends over summer break may be related to student characteristics such as socioeconomic status (Alexander, Entwisle, & Olson, 2001), a simulation conducted by McCaffrey, Lockwood, Koretz, and Hamilton (2003) indicates that differential summer achievement changes do not represent a significant threat to the validity of VAM-based inferences. Moreover, the logical alternative of using fall-to-spring gains, in addition to being costly, may introduce biases stemming from student selection, scale conversion errors, mismatch between administration dates and norming dates, practice effects, and score inflation (Linn, 2000). Still, additional work needs to be done to explore the validity of inferences about teacher or school effects in the context of testing programs that do not correspond to the timeline about which users make inferences.

7.3.2.2. Scaling

Most inferences based on VAM require an interval scale of teacher or school effectiveness. Because achievement tests are used in VAM as proxies for teacher or school effectiveness, these inferences require two assumptions to be met: (1) that the achievement measures themselves are on an interval scale; and (2) that the mapping of the achievement scale onto the latent scale of teacher or school effectiveness is reasonably linear. With respect to the first of these assumptions, concerns about interval scaling arise from two sources: the general indeterminacy of cross-sectional scales, and additional complications that arise from the use of vertical scales.

The general indeterminacy of cross-sectional scales is an issue in value-added modeling because some VAM-based inferences are sensitive to nonlinear transformations of the scale. Applications of VAM typically rely on a small number of commonly used scaling approaches, and most of these approaches yield scores that are highly correlated with one another. Even highly correlated scales, however, may show clearly non-linear relationships in part of their ranges. McCaffrey, Lockwood, Koretz, and Hamilton (2003) illustrated this by scaling scores on an algebra test with a 2-PL IRT model and comparing the theta scale to a simple number-correct score. The correlation between the two scales was .97, even though the relationship between them was clearly nonlinear in the tails, as one would expect. Therefore, even when nonlinearly related scales show very high correlations, some VAM-based inferences, such as those stemming from the estimation of effects for teachers whose students' scores are mostly in the tails, would be affected by choice of scaling.

The construction of vertical scales, which are often used in VAM, exacerbates the indeterminacy problem in a number of ways that are relevant to VAM-based inferences (see the chapter by Kolen in this volume for detailed discussion of vertical scaling). One example is the fact that scales often show different trends in variability over time, with some indicating that achievement becomes more variable as students mature, and others suggesting that it does not (e.g., Yen, 1986). A number of studies of this phenomenon have generated conflicting findings (compare, for example, Becker & Forsyth, 1992; Williams, Pommerich, & Thissen, 1998; Yen, 1986; and Yen & Burket, 1997). The accumulated research therefore does not clarify how the construction of a vertical battery, the method chosen for linking across grades, and the method chosen for scaling interact to influence trends in variance across grades, but it does make clear that variations in these trends are common. A simulation study showed that VAM-based inferences about teacher or school effectiveness are affected by these differences in variance trends, particularly when the estimated effectiveness of teachers of high- and low-scoring students is compared (McCaffrey, Lockwood, Koretz, & Hamilton 2003).

An inference about the effectiveness of teachers (or schools) based on a value-added analysis of scores also requires an assumption that the mapping from the score scale to the latent scale of teacher effectiveness is linear. That is, even if the achievement measure is truly interval (which is unlikely to be known), these inferences require the additional assumption that a teacher who raises scores a given amount at one point along the distribution is equally effective as a teacher who raises scores that same amount at another point along the distribution. To illustrate, a teacher who achieves a given score increase among average readers and a teacher who achieves the same increase among remedial readers would be considered equally effective by typical VAM models, even though the second teacher's task may in fact have been much more difficult (see McCaffrey, Lockwood, Koretz, & Hamilton 2003, for a more extended discussion of this example). Although issues related to the achievement scale and to the mapping between achievement and effectiveness could pose threats to VAM-based inferences, there is currently little empirical evidence that would clarify the degree of sensitivity of various VAM-based inferences to different choices among scaling approaches.

7.3.2.3. Dimensionality and Test-Curriculum Match

Related to the problems associated with scaling are issues of test dimensionality and of the match between test and curriculum. Although most methods that are used to scale achievement tests treat the construct of interest as unidimensional, in fact virtually all such tests incorporate a mix of content and measure achievement across multiple dimensions. Thus, a summary score necessarily represents a weighting of dimensions, although not always the intended ones (see section 2.3.1.3).

Rankings of schools, states, or other units may be affected by the specific mix and weighting of dimensions included in the test and by the match between the test and the curriculum (e.g., Koretz, 1986; Wolfe, 1997), and some VAM-based inferences are likely to be affected by these factors as well. For example, an 8th-grade mathematics test that focuses on basic skills may be more sensitive to the instruction provided in general mathematics classes than that provided in algebra classes. A teacher who is effective at improving her students' algebra skills may not appear effective if the test does not adequately sample algebra content. Thus, rankings of observed or modeled gain confound latent gain with the alignment between the curriculum of the teacher or school and the dimensional mix and weighting of the test.

This problem is exacerbated by the reliance of many VAM approaches on tests that use a vertical scale, because between-grade differences in curricula are often substantial. Problems of mismatch are likely to be greater for wide grade spans than for narrow ones. Mismatch is also likely to be more prevalent in secondary schools, which are typically characterized by extensive curricular differentiation, than in elementary schools. The existing VAM research literature provides limited guidance on the severity of the problem or its effects on estimates of teacher or school effects (Martineau, in press).

7.3.2.4. Other Measurement Issues Affecting Value-Added Modeling

Two other measurement issues discussed above are pertinent to change measures, including value-added modeling of test scores. Score inflation, which can be very large relative to meaningful gains in scores, has the potential to badly bias estimates of change. There is no reason to expect score inflation to be uniform, and indeed there is limited evidence suggesting that it is not (see Klein et al., 2000). Non-uniform score inflation could render rankings meaningless, and correlation between the degree of inflation and other variables could distort inferences about the characteristics of effective teachers or schools. The use of standards-based reporting also presents a problem for VAM-based inferences about growth, for reasons discussed in section 5. Although VAM and other approaches to measuring change provide promising alternatives to a reliance on status measures, there is a need for research that clarifies the effects of these measurement issues.

8. TEST DESIGN AND CONSTRUCTION

The changes in test use noted in section 1 and the problem of inappropriate test preparation noted in sections 2 and 3 have important implications for test design. Here we focus on the implication of three of these changes: the sheer volume of testing, the increased inclusion and uniformity of testing, and the imposition of high stakes.

8.1. Volume of Test Development

The changes outlined in section 1 will substantially increase the number of large-scale K–12 achievement tests produced. The overall amount of mandated testing has increased, and both the evolution of state policy and the enactment of NCLB increased pressure on states to tailor tests to their own particular standards rather than use tests aimed at national markets. In many instances, these state tests are customized versions of national tests rather than tests developed from scratch, but even these require additional resources for development. Perhaps in response to the pressures of high stakes, many states administer new forms of their tests every year, and because of high stakes imposed on students, many offer forms for retesting as well.

This sharp increase in volume raises issues of capacity and quality. The pool of individuals with doctoral training in psychometrics and test development is small, and the production of new graduates is currently very limited. Whether the field will be able to absorb this large increase in the volume of test development while maintaining quality is uncertain.

8.2. Inclusion and Uniformity of Assessment

As noted in section 6, the increase in the inclusion of students in large-scale testing, in conjunction with pressures for uniformity of testing, raise numerous issues of reliability and validity. These in turn raise several issues of test design.

The first issue is designing tests to be appropriate across a very wide range of proficiency. Adaptive testing, computer-assisted or otherwise, has been a common approach for addressing this issue, and one might anticipate greater use of adaptive testing in statewide achievement testing programs in response to the recent changes in testing, unless costs or NCLB and its implementing regulations are seen as prohibiting it. Adaptive testing as conventionally implemented, however, is not likely to be fully adequate for addressing the issues raised by current testing. Adaptive testing is typically premised on the assumption of a unidimensional domain within which items vary only in difficulty. However, when the tested range of proficiency is sufficiently broad, curricular and other differences may make this assumption untenable, particularly in the secondary grades, where curricular differentiation is greater. Research exploring the practical importance of these limitations and ways of addressing them is needed.

The second issue is designing testing systems to better assess students with special needs. There are two basic approaches for addressing this issue: accommodations and "universal design." The potential of both approaches is unclear. Although there has been a growing amount of research on the use and effects of accommodations (Koretz & Barton, 2004), several of the factors noted in section 6, such as the inconsistency of classification of students and the prevalence of disabilities related to measured constructs, pose both practical and logical obstacles to the progress of this work. Universal design has recently been proposed as an alternative. The term originally referred to design of facilities that made them accessible to people both with and without disabilities, such as wide doorways to accommodate wheelchairs and sidewalks with curb cuts. Recently, some have begun exploring the possibility of applying this concept to assessment design:

> The term "universally designed assessments" refers to assessments that are designed and developed from the beginning to be accessible.... Universal design in assessments may not be as obvious as curb cuts or ramps. It involves thinking about designing assessments that are appropriate for the widest range of students. For example, it involves very precise and explicit descriptions of what the assessment intends to measure, so that it is possible to avoid measuring unintended factors. It involves eliminating items that preclude the use of appropriate accommodations. It involves field testing assessments with a diverse group of students, including those who use accommodations during testing. It also involves ensuring that floor or ceiling effects do not prevent good measurement of all students. (National Center on Educational Outcomes, 2003)

At the time of this writing, however, it remains unclear how well this concept can be applied to testing and how successfully it will overcome the difficulties of obtaining valid information about students with special needs from large-scale K–12 tests.

8.3. High Stakes

High-stakes uses of tests raise numerous issues of design because of their function in creating incentives for teachers and students and their potential for inducing undesirable responses, including those that lead to score inflation.

High stakes create a tension between the goals of comparability and novelty in assessment. Many high-stakes uses create pressure for comparability across forms for the sake of fairness. This is most important when high stakes are imposed on students. One wants to minimize the percentage of students who would fail to get a diploma, for example, solely because they were administered a form used in one year rather than one used in another year. Some such inconsistency is inevitable, but generally one would strive to minimize it by increasing the reliability of the test at the cut score and by maintaining comparability of forms over time. Comparability is also important, however, when high stakes are imposed on educators. For example, inconsistency in forms over time could unfairly disadvantage some educators and advantage others in an accountability system that considers change in performance over time. At the same time, the more similar and hence predictable test forms are over time, the easier it becomes to prepare students for tests inappropriately and thus to inflate scores.

Striking the best balance between these competing goals may require departures from conventional approaches to test development. First, it may require more precise specification of intended inferences in order to facilitate distinguishing desirable from unnecessary comparability. Second, it may require careful scrutiny of test forms to identify aspects of item style and unintended test weights that might encourage inappropriate test preparation, and it may similarly necessitate efforts to avoid repetition of these over time.

Because even careful attention to unneeded similarities across forms is not likely to eliminate fully the potential for inappropriate test preparation, high-stakes uses suggest the importance of audit mechanisms to confirm gains in scores and to identify areas in which scores are particularly inflated. These audit mechanisms could take several forms. For example, an ongoing test could incorporate small, matrix-sampled sections that match intended inferences but are deliberately different in terms of item style and other attributes with low substantive inference weights. Alternatively, a testing program could be designed to include periodic administration of an alternative test, perhaps on a sample basis.

Many high-stakes systems present an additional tension because of the use of high-stakes tests to create incentives. The test designs best suited to producing desired incentives may not be the best for other purposes. For example, consider a state that wants to encourage teachers to focus on both writing across the disciplines and the solving of complex and realistic problems. To encourage these styles of teaching, the state might want to administer a test that includes a variety of constructed-response formats, including some involving substantial writing, as well as some fairly large and complex tasks. These design choices, however, are likely to reduce reliability relative to a test that utilizes primarily the multiple-choice format because of both a reduced number of tasks and the introduction of additional task-specific and potentially construct-irrelevant variance. Yet high reliability may be essential for some high-stakes uses. Here again, the test designer would need to strike a balance between two competing goals.

Finally, high-stakes testing raises numerous issues about the characteristics of formative tests and other materials aligned with the high-stakes test. Surveys of school and classroom responses to test-based accountability in three states suggest that the use of these materials is booming in many systems (Barney & Robyn, 2005; Hamilton, Berends, & Stecher, 2005), and many practitioners are clamoring for more highly "aligned" materials. Adequate alignment is certainly essential for standards-based accountability systems to work as intended, and resources that help teachers understand the links among assessments, standards, and curriculum might reduce the tendency for teachers to focus excessively on a specific test (Stecher, Hamilton, & Gonzalez, 2003). Yet as noted earlier, alignment is not an unmitigated good (see sections 2 and 4). Insufficient alignment between these materials and the high-stakes test may waste time and attenuate improvement, but excessively tight alignment may lead to inappropriate reallocation and coaching and hence produce inflated gains. The balance needed in the design of these materials mirrors the issue above concerning the degree of novelty in successive test forms.

9. DESIGN OF ACCOUNTABILITY SYSTEMS

The validity of inferences from large-scale achievement tests is inextricably linked to the design of the accountability systems in which these tests are often embedded. Earlier sections address some implications of accountability system design, such as those arising from including students with special needs and the use of cut scores. In this section we discuss several additional implications of accountability system design for the validity of inferences.

9.1. Alignment with Curriculum

Although many of today's test-based accountability systems are predicated on the assumption that tests and standards are aligned, the extent to which districts and schools have implemented curricula consistent with either their states' tests or the standards is often unknown. The potential mismatch between the content of a state's test and the material to which students are exposed in the classroom would weaken the utility of the test as a measurement instrument and as a tool for holding educators accountable—for example, creating an underestimate of student learning or a misestimation of cohort-to-cohort gains. The most severe mismatch is likely to occur at the higher grade levels, which are typically characterized by extensive curricular differentiation that makes alignment of a single test with implemented curricula more difficult.

It is equally important, however, to consider the potential for excessive or inappropriate alignment. Efforts to align instruction with the test, if carried to extremes, can inflate scores by diverting instructional resources away from aspects of the curriculum weakly represented in the test or by focusing attention on unimportant specifics of the particular test employed. High-quality curriculum materials, professional development, and other resources designed to help teachers understand how to present the desired content without relying too heavily on the test might help mitigate some of the undesirable effects of high-stakes testing.

9.2. Use of Multiple Measures

There is a widespread consensus among measurement professionals that important decisions should be based on more than a single measure. This principle is stated explicitly in the *Standards*, and NCLB specifies that multiple measures should be incorporated into accountability systems. An obvious reason to avoid reliance on a single measure is that simple measurement error will lead to some incorrect or inappropriate decisions. Measurement error, however, is not the only or even necessarily the most important reason to avoid using a single measure in isolation, particularly in systems that are intended to evaluate schools or educators (Koretz, 2003). The necessary incompleteness of standardized tests as measures of important educational objectives has long been recognized even by the developers of these measures. For example, Lindquist (1951) characterized standardized testing as only a proxy for the ideal but impractical direct measurement of desired outcomes. He noted that direct measurement is often impossible because many of the important outcomes of education occur long after schooling ends, occur infrequently, are inaccessible to examiners, and are manifested in various forms by different individuals (Lindquist, 1951, p. 143). Other measures may capture additional important outcomes, albeit often without the advantages conferred by standardization. More recent uses of tests in accountability systems also raise additional concerns about the incentive effects of undue focus on a single measure, beyond the more traditional issues of measurement quality. These incentive effects can result in score inflation as well as other unwelcome outcomes.

Although many developers of accountability systems acknowledge the importance of using multiple measures to evaluate school and student performance, most of today's systems rely almost exclusively on a single test score for each student in each subject. When alternative measures are used, they are often given relatively little weight, either deliberately, because of limited variance, or both (e.g., Koretz & Barron, 1998). Incorporating other sources of information could both improve the quality of information about performance and reduce the likelihood of undesirable behavioral responses, such as those described in sections 2 and 3. Additional measures might include both achievement measures and other measures, such as student work samples, classroom artifacts such as lesson plans or teacher-developed assessments, survey- or observation-based measures of classroom practices, and surveys or interviews of students and families (Hamilton & Stecher, 2002; Koretz,

2003; Lane, Parke, & Stone, 1998). Well-designed measures of instructional practice might reduce the likelihood of excessive emphasis on test preparation, help policymakers and administrators monitor the effects of accountability systems and deal with undesirable consequences when they arise, and address the issue of potentially inadequate alignment described above.

While the desirability of basing accountability on multiple measures is apparent, the practicality of doing so remains unproven. Many of the additional measures noted here are costly, and there are as yet no well-evaluated and accepted approaches for implementing some of them. To take one example, accurate measurement of instructional practice requires overcoming a number of challenges, including a diversity of curricula across classrooms, the possibility of response bias, the probability of political backlash, and high costs (Koretz, 2003). Moreover, we lack evaluations of the functioning and effects of multiple-indicator systems of this sort. At the time of this writing, systems of multiple measures remain an area in pressing need of research and evaluation, and designers of accountability systems will need to make decisions in the absence of good research evidence.

9.3. Locus of Incentives

Most state accountability systems that existed during the decade before NCLB imposed sanctions, rewards, or both at the school level, and under NCLB, all states are required to adopt accountability systems that include school-level sanctions and interventions. In systems that impose consequences on individual students, these most often take the form of high school exit exams, although some states and districts have also implemented promotional-gates testing. Such student-level incentives are likely to be felt most acutely by those students at risk of not passing the test; students whose performance is well above the cut score may experience little pressure.

At the time of this writing, it is widely held that optimal accountability systems would hold both educators and students accountable for performance. In systems that impose stronger incentives on schools and educators than on students, there is a risk that students will not put forth their best effort on the tests, and sanctions for educators therefore may be imposed inappropriately. The CRESST *Standards for Educational Accountability Systems* (Baker, Linn, Herman, & Koretz, 2002) recommend the use of incentives that are balanced between educators and students and that support the goals of the accountability system. Of course, some of the measures useful for school- or teacher-level accountability, such as direct measures of practices, cannot be applied to students, which limits the degree to which systems may be truly "balanced."

However, the research investigating the effects of different types of accountability systems is meager. There is as yet no clear empirical evidence about the mix of incentives that would be most balanced, and there is not yet sufficient empirical evidence comparing the outcomes produced by balanced and unbalanced accountability systems.

9.4. Conjunctive and Compensatory Models

All accountability systems require a method for combining information across measures and groups of students. For example, a school's score on an accountability index might be constructed by synthesizing test scores in several subjects and across several grade levels. The method for combining such information involves either a compensatory or conjunctive approach, or some combination of both. In a compensatory model, good performance on one measure may offset poor performance on another, as is the case if a simple mean across subjects and grade levels is used. A conjunctive model, by contrast, requires a minimum level of performance on each of several measures, so that poor performance on one measure may result in a school's failure to meet its accountability targets regardless of how well the school performed on all other measures. Some systems combine elements of both approaches. Under NCLB, for example, states can opt for a system in which poor performance in 3rd grade reading may be offset by high scores in 4th and 5th grade reading, but poor performance in reading overall cannot be offset by good performance in mathematics.

There are three ways in which information is commonly combined in today's accountability systems: across outcomes (including test subjects as well as non-test information such as graduation rates) within students; across outcomes within schools or other aggregates; and across groups within aggregates. Conjunctive or compensatory models can be applied to all three of these. Systems that are conjunctive across groups are new but are now ubiquitous because of the requirement in NCLB that each student subgroup—major racial/ethnic groups, economically disadvantaged students, students with disabilities, and students with limited proficiency in English—achieve a minimum level of proficiency in each tested subject in order for a school to avoid sanctions. Conjunctive models increase the likelihood of missing a target because of random chance; for example, in a system that is conjunctive across groups, each additional subgroup into which a group is broken increases the likelihood that a school will fail to meet its targets solely as a result of error in the estimates of performance (Kane & Staiger, 2001). A compensatory approach to combining scores would address this problem but has offsetting disadvantages. For example, a model that is compensatory across groups does not provide as clear an incentive for schools to focus on all groups, and a model that is compensatory across subjects does not permit a state or other entity to set a minimum level of performance in any subject. Research is needed to evaluate the practical effects of using various combinations of compensatory and conjunctive models.

10. CONCLUSION

Recent decades have seen major changes in large-scale K–12 achievement testing: changes in the nature of the tests, the delineation of the tested populations, the reporting of scores, and the uses of test scores. These have been accompanied by important shifts in the primary inferences users base on test scores and have markedly altered the behavioral responses of educators and students to testing.

The implications of these changes are numerous and significant. They have important implications for the design of testing programs and of the accountability systems in which they are often embedded. These changes have a major bearing on reliability and validity, and they have implications for the methods needed for the evaluation of both reliability and validity. Indeed, in some instances—in particular, in the case of evaluating validity under high-stakes conditions—these changes push the field beyond the range of currently available analytical methods, indicating the importance of methodological development tailored to the currently dominant forms of test use.

NOTES

1. All discussion of this and other statutes and implementing regulations refer to those in effect as of March 2005 unless otherwise noted.

2. It has become conventional to refer to students who are not native speakers of English and have not yet attained a high degree of proficiency in the language as "English language learners" rather than "limited English proficient" students. However, for purposes of the validity of test-based inferences, the relevant issue is not whether students are learning English but rather whether they are less than proficient at the time of assessment. Accordingly, we do not use the term "English language learner."

3. In his more recent work, Popham has expressed concerns about the negative effects of using tests in this manner, particularly when tests are not designed to support high-quality instruction. See, for example, Popham (2004).

4. The need for human raters has since in principle diminished as new technologies have been developed to facilitate automated scoring of open-ended responses, but conventional scoring has been the norm in large-scale achievement testing programs.

5. Substantial portions of this section are reprinted or adapted with permission from Koretz et al. (2001).

6. The term "effective weight" is often used to denote the contribution of a variable to a weighted linear composite, which is a function of any nominal weight assigned to the variable, its variance, and its covariance with other variables in the composite (Wang & Stanley, 1970, p. 665; see also Feldt & Brennan, 1989). Our use of the term is loosely analogous, although it refers to change rather than cross-sectional variance and is otherwise entirely general, that is, it does not depend on any particular mathematical algorithm for forming the composite scores from item performance.

REFERENCES

Ad Hoc Committee on Confirming Test Results. (2002). *Using the National Assessment of Educational Progress to confirm state test results*. Washington, DC: National Assessment Governing Board.

Airasian, P. W. (1987). State mandated testing and educational reform: Context and consequences. *American Journal of Education, 95*, 393–412.

Alexander, K. L., Entwisle, D. R., & Olson, L. S. (2001). Schools, achievement, and inequality: A seasonal perspective. *Educational Evaluation and Policy Analysis, 23*(2), 171–191.

Alexander, L., & James, H. T. (1987). *The nation's report card: Improving the assessment of student achievement* (Report of the study group). Washington, DC: National Academy of Education.

American Association for the Advancement of Science. (1993). *Benchmarks for science literacy*. New York: Oxford University Press.

American Educational Research Association, American Psychological Association, & National Council on Measurement in Education. (1999). *Standards foreducational and psychological testing*. Washington, DC: American Educational Research Association.

American Federation of Teachers. (2001). *Making standards matter*. Washington, DC: Author.

Anderson, N. E., Jenkins, F. F., & Miller, K. E. (n.d.). *NAEP inclusion criteria and testing accommodations: Findings from the NAEP 1995 Field Test in Mathematics*. Princeton, NJ: Educational Testing Service.

Arenz, B., & Bohlin, C. F. (2003). *National Council of Teachers of Mathematics News Bulletin*. Reston, VA: National Council of Teachers of Mathematics. Last accessed February 6, 2004, from http://www.nctm.org/news/assessment/2003_11nb.htm

Baker, E. L., Linn, R. L., Herman, J. L., & Koretz, D. M. (2002, Winter). Standards for educational accountability systems. CRESST Line, pp. 1–4.

Ballou, D., Sanders, W., & Wright, P. (2004). Controlling for student background in value-added assessment of teachers. *Journal of Educational and Behavioral Statistics, 29*(1), 37–65.

Barney, H., & Robyn, A. (2005). *School improvement, interventions, and technical assistance* (Working Paper WR-257-EDU). Santa Monica, CA: RAND Corporation.

Baxter, G. P., & Glaser, R. (1998). Investigating the cognitive complexity of science assessments. *Educational Measurement: Issues and Practice, 17*(3), 37–45.

Beaton, A. E., & Zwick, R. (1990). *The effect of changes in the national assessment: Disentangling the NAEP 1985–86 reading anomaly* (Report No. 17-TR-21). Princeton, NJ: Educational Testing Service, National Assessment of Educational Progress.

Becker, D. F., & Forsyth, R. A. (1992). An empirical investigation of Thurstone and IRT methods of scaling achievement tests. *Journal of Educational Measurement, 29*(4), 341–354.

Bhola, D. S., Impara, J. C., & Buckendahl, C. W. (2003). Aligning tests with states' content standards: Methods and issues. *Educational Measurement: Issues and Practice, 22*(3), 21–29.

Bishop, J. H., & Mane, F. (1999). *The New York state reform strategy: The incentive effects of minimum competency exams*. Philadelphia: National Center on Education in Inner Cities.

Bond, L., & Jaeger, R. M. (1993). *Judged congruence between various state assessment tests in mathematics and the 1990 National Assessment of Educational Progress item pool for grade 8 mathematics* (Report prepared for the National Academy of Education Panel on the NAEP Trial State Assessment). Stanford, CA: National Academy of Education.

Borko, H., & Elliott, R. (1999). Hands-on pedagogy versus hands-off accountability. *Phi Delta Kappan, 80*(5), 394–400.

Braswell, J. S., Lutkus, A. D., Grigg, W. S., Santapau, S. L., Taylim, B. S.-H., & Johnson, M. S. (2001). *The nation's report card: Mathematics 2000*. Washington, DC: National Center for Education Statistics.

Brennan, R. L., Yin, P., & Kane, M. T. (2003). Methodology for examining the reliability of group mean difference scores. *Journal of Educational Measurement, 40*(3), 207–230.

Buckendahl, C. W., Huynh, H., Siskind, T., & Saunders, J. (2005). A case study of vertically moderated standard setting for a state science assessment program. *Applied Measurement in Education, 18*(1), 83–98.

Buckendahl, C. W., Impara, J. C., Plake, B. S., & Haack, K. (2001). *Evaluating the alignment of selected nationally norm referenced achievement tests to Nebraska's 4th, 8th, and high school reading/writing and mathematics content standards.* Lincoln: Nebraska Department of Education.

Buckendahl, C. W., Plake, B. S., Impara, J. C., & Irwin, P. M. (2000, April). *Alignment of standardized achievement tests to state content standards: A comparison of publishers' and teachers' perspectives.* Paper presented at the annual meeting of the National Council on Measurement in Education, New Orleans, LA.

Buckendahl, C. W., Smith, R., Impara, J. C., & Plake, B. S. (2002). A comparison of Angoff and bookmark standard setting methods. *Journal of Educational Measurement, 39*(3), 253–263.

Campbell, J. R., Hombo, C. M., & Mazzeo, J. (2000). *NAEP 1999 trends in academic progress: Three decades of academic progress.* Washington, DC: National Center for Education Statistics.

Cannell, J. J. (1988). Nationally normed elementary achievement testing in America's public schools: How all 50 states are above the national average. *Educational Measurement: Issues and Practice, 7*(2), 5–9.

Carlson, D. (2000, June). *All students or the ones we taught?* Annual Conference on Large-Scale Assessment, Council of Chief State School Officers, Snowbird, UT.

Cimbricz, S. (2003). State-mandated testing and teachers' beliefs and practice. *Education Policy Analysis Archives, 10*(2). Retrieved June 1, 2005 from http://epaa.asu.edu/epaa/v10n2.html

Cohen, D. K. (1995). What is the system in systemic reform? *Educational Researcher, 24*(9), 11–17.

Clarizio, H. F., & Phillips, S. E. (1992). A comparison of severe discrepancy formulae: Implications for policy consultation. *Journal of Educational and Psychological Consultation, 3,* 55–68.

College Board. (1985). *National college-bound seniors, 1985.* New York: Author.

Corbett, H. D., & Wilson, B. L. (1988). Raising the stakes in state-wide mandatory minimum competency testing. In W. L. Boyd & C. T. Kerchner (Eds.), *The politics of excellence and choice in education: The 1987 Politics of Education Association yearbook* (pp. 27–39). New York: Falmer Press.

Council of Chief State School Officers. (2003). *State education accountability reports and indicator reports: Status of reports across the states—2003.* Washington, DC: Author.

Darling-Hammond, L., & Wise, A. E. (1985). Beyond standardization: State standards and school improvement. *Elementary School Journal, 85,* 315–336.

David, J. L. (1982). Local uses of Title 1 evaluations. In E. R. House, S. Mathison, J. A. Pearsol, & H. Preskill (Eds.), *Evaluation studies review annual* (Vol. 7, pp. 412–425). Beverly Hills, CA: Sage.

Deere, D., & Strayer, W. (2003). *Competitive incentives: School accountability and student outcomes in Texas.* Unpublished working paper.

Department of Education, Title 1 Implementing Regulations (2003, December 9)—Improving the Academic Achievement of the Disadvantaged, 68 Fed. Reg. 68698, 34 C.F.R. Part 200.

Department of Education, Title 1 Notice of Proposed Rulemaking (2003, March 20)—Improving the Academic Achievement of the Disadvantaged, 68 Fed. Reg. 13796 (to be codified at 34 C.F.R. Part 200).

Dunbar, S., Koretz, D., & Hoover, H. D. (1991). Quality control in the development and use of performance assessment. *Applied Measurement in Education, 4*(4), 289–303.

Elliott, S. N., & McKevitt, B. C. (2000, April). *Testing accommodations decisions: Legal and technical issues challenging educators or "good" test scores are hard to come by.* Paper presented at the annual meeting of the American Educational Research Association, New Orleans, LA.

Erickson, R. N., & Thurlow, M. L. (1996). *State special education outcomes 1995.* Minneapolis: University of Minnesota, National Center on Educational Outcomes.

Feldt, L. S., & Brennan, R. L. (1989). Reliability. In R. L. Linn (Ed.), *Educational measurement* (3rd ed., pp. 105–146). New York: American Council on Education/Macmillan.

Ferrara, S., Johnson, E., & Chen, W.-H. (2005). Vertically articulated performance standards: Logic, procedures, and likely classification accuracy. *Applied Measurement in Education, 18*(1), 35–59.

Figlio, D. N., & Getzler, L. S. (2002). *Accountability, ability and disability: Gaming the system* (NBER Working Paper W9307). Cambridge, MA: National Bureau of Economic Research.

Fuchs, L. S., Fuchs, D., Eaton, S. B., Hamlett, C., & Karns, K. (2000). Supplementing teacher judgments of test accommodations with objective data sources. *School Psychology Review, 29,* 65–85.

Gayler, K., Chudowsky, N., Kober, N., & Hamilton, M. (2003). *State high school exit exams put to the test.* Washington, DC: Center on Education Policy.

General Accounting Office. (1993). *Educational achievement standards: NAGB's approach yields misleading interpretations.* Washington, DC: Author.

Glaser, R. (1963). Instructional technology and the measurement of learning outcomes: Some questions. *American Psychologist, 18,* 519–521. (Reprinted in *Educational Measurement: Issues and Practice, 13*(4), 6–8 [1994]).

Glaser, R. (1994). Criterion-referenced tests: Part I. Origins. *Educational Measurement: Issues and Practice, 13*(4), 9–11.

Glass, G. V. (1976). Standards and criteria. *Journal of Educational Measurement, 15,* 237–261.

Goals 2000: Educate America Act of 1994, 20 U.S.C. 5801 et seq.

Goertz, M., Duffy, M., & Carlson-LeFloch, K. (2001). *Assessment and accountability systems in the 50 states: 1999–2000.* Philadelphia, PA: The Consortium for Policy Research in Education [CPRE] No. RR-046.

Gorth, W. P., & Perkins, M. R. (1979). *A study of minimum competency testing programs* (Final program development resource document). Amherst, MA: National Evaluation Systems.

Goslin, D. A. (1963). *Teachers and testing.* New York: Russell Sage Foundation.

Goslin, D. A., Epstein, R. R., & Hallock, B. A. (1965). *The use of standardized tests in elementary schools.* New York: Russell Sage.

Greene, J. P., Winters, M. A., & Forster, G. (2003). *Testing high-stakes tests: Can we believe the results of accountability tests?* (Civic Report 33). New York: Manhattan Institute for Policy Research.

Greenwald, R., Hedges, L. V., & Laine, R. D. 1996). The effect of school resources on student achievement. *Review of Educational Research, 66,* 361–396.

Grissmer, D. W., Flanagan, A., Kawata, J., & Williamson, S. (2000). *Improving student achievement: What state NAEP scores tell us* (Publication MR-924–EDU). Santa Monica, CA: RAND.

Haertel, E. H. (1999). Performance assessment and education reform. *Phi Delta Kappan, 80,* 662–666.

Haertel, E., Forgione, P. D., Walberg, H. J., Baldwin, J., Bock, R.D., Burstein, L., et al. (1989). *Report of the NAEP technical review panel on the 1986 reading anomaly, the accuracy of NAEP trends, and issues raised by state-level NAEP comparisons* (CS 89–499). Washington, DC: National Center for Education Statistics.

Haertel, E. H., & Wiley, D. E. (1995). *Response to the OEA panel report, "Review of the measurement quality of the Kentucky Instructional Results Information System, 1991–1994."* Unpublished paper prepared for the Kentucky Department of Education and Advanced Systems in Measurement and Evaluation.

Hambleton, R. K. (1994). The rise and fall of criterion-referenced measurement? *Educational Measurement: Issues and Practice, 13*(4), 21–26.

Hambleton, R. K. (1998). Setting performance standards on achievement tests: Meeting the requirements of Title I. In L. N. Hansche (Ed.), *Handbook for the development of performance standards: Meeting the requirements of Title I* (pp. 87–115). Washington, DC: Council of Chief State School Officers.

Hambleton, R. K., Jaeger, R. M., Koretz, D., Linn, R. L., Millman, J., & Phillips, S. E. (1995). *Review of the measurement quality of the Kentucky Instructional Results Information System, 1991–1994.* Frankfort: Office of Education Accountability, Kentucky General Assembly, June.

Hamilton, L. S. (2003). Assessment as a policy tool. *Review of Research in Education, 27,* 25–68.

Hamilton, L. S., Berends, M., & Stecher, B. M. (2005). *Teachers' responses to standards-based accountability* (Working Paper WR-259–EDU). Santa Monica, CA: RAND.

Hamilton, L. S., Nussbaum, E. M., & Snow, R. E. (1997). Interview procedures for validating science assessments. *Applied Measurement in Education, 10,* 181–200.

Hamilton, L. S., & Stecher, B. M. (2002). Improving test-based accountability. In L. S. Hamilton, B. M. Stecher, & S. P. Klein (Eds.), *Making sense of test-based accountability in education* (pp. 121–144). Santa Monica, CA: RAND.

Haney, W. (1981). Validity, vaudeville, and values: A short history of social concerns over standardized testing. *American Psychologist, 36,* 1021–1034.

Hannaway, J., & McKay, S. (2001, Fall). Taking measure. *Education Next, 1*(3). Available at http://www.educationnext.org/20013/6hannaway.html

Hanushek, E. (1972). *Education and race.* Lexington, MA: D.C. Heath and Company.

Holland, P. W. (1986). Statistics and causal inference. *Journal of the American Statistical Association, 81,* 945–960.

Hoover, H. D. (2003). Some common misconceptions about tests and testing. *Educational Measurement: Issues and Practice, 22*(1), 5–14.

Hoover, H. D., Hieronymus, A. N., Frisbie, D. A., Dunbar, S. B., Oberly, K. R., Cantor, N. K., et al. (1994). *Iowa Tests of Basic Skills interpretive guide for school administrators.* Chicago: Riverside.

Houston Independent School District. (2002). *HISD school accountability system 2002.* Houston, TX: Author. Retrieved January 16, 2004, from http://dept.houstonisd.org/research/Presentations/presentations_splash.htm

Huynh, H., Barton, K. E., Meyer, J. P., Porchea, S., & Gallant, J. (2005). Consistency and predictive nature of vertically moderated standards for South Carolina's 1999 Palmetto Achievement Challenge Tests of Language Arts and Mathematics. *Applied Measurement in Education, 18*(1), 115–128.

Huynh, H., & Schneider, C. (2005). Vertically moderated standards: Background, assumptions, and practices. *Applied Measurement in Education, 18*(1), 99–113.

Improving America's Schools Act of 1994. Public Law 103-382. Individuals with Disabilities Education Act, 20 U.S.C. § 1400 et seq.

Jacob, B. (2002, May). *Accountability, incentives and behavior: The impact of high-stakes testing in the Chicago public schools* (Working paper W8968). Cambridge, MA: National Bureau of Economic Research.

Jacob, B. A., & Levitt, S. D. (2002). Rotten apples: An investigation of the prevalence and predictors of teacher cheating. *Quarterly Journal of Economics, 2003, 168*(3), 843–878.

Jaeger, R. M. (1982). The final hurdle: Minimum competency achievement testing. In G. R. Austin & H. Garber (Eds.), *The rise and fall of national test scores* (pp. 223–246) New York: Academic Press.

Jaeger, R. M. (1989). Certification of student competence. In R. L. Linn (Ed.), *Educational measurement* (3rd ed., pp. 485–514). New York: American Council on Education/Macmillan.

Jerald, C. D., & Boser, U. (1999). Taking stock. In *Quality counts.* Bethesda, MD: Education Week (January 11). Retrieved March 12, 2004, from http://www.edweek.org/sreports/qc99/ac/tables/ac-intro.htm

Jones, G., Jones, B. D., Hardin, B., Chapman, L., Yarbrough, T., & Davis, M. (1999). The impact of high-stakes testing on teachers and students in North Carolina. *Phi Delta Kappan, 81,* 199–203.

Kane, M. T. (1982). A sampling model for validity. *Applied Psychological Measurement, 6,* 125–160.

Kane, M. T. (1996). The precision of measurements. *Applied Measurement in Education, 9*(4), 355–379.

Kane, T. J., & Staiger, D. O. (2001). *Improving school accountability measures.* Cambridge, MA: National Bureau of Economic Research.

Kane, T. J., & Staiger, D. O. (2002). Volatility in school test scores: Implications for test-based accountability systems. In D. Ravitch (Ed.), *Brookings papers on education policy* (pp. 235–269). Washington, DC: Brookings Institution Press.

Karger, J. S. (2003). *Ensuring access to the general curriculum for students with disabilities: An analysis of the legal and educational obligations of states and school districts.* Unpublished qualifying paper, Harvard Graduate School of Education.

Kindler, A. L. (2002). *Survey of the states' limited English proficient students and available educational programs and services 2000–2001 summary report.* Washington, DC: National Clearinghouse for English Language Acquisition & Language Instruction Educational Programs.

Kingsbury, G. G., Olson, A., Cronin, J., Hauser, C., & Houser, R. (2003). *The state of state standards.* Portland, OR: Northwest Evaluation Association.

Kiplinger, V. L., & Linn, R. L., (1995). Raising the stakes of test administration: The impact on student performance on the National Assessment of Educational Progress. *Educational Assessment, 3*(2), 111–134.

Klein, S. P., Hamilton, L. S., McCaffrey, D. F., & Stecher, B. M. (2000). *What do test scores in Texas tell us?* (Issue Paper IP-202). Santa Monica, CA: RAND. Retrieved January 12, 2004, from http://www.rand.org/publications/IP/IP202/

Koretz, D. (1986). *Trends in educational achievement.* Washington, DC: Congressional Budget Office, April.

Koretz, D. (1988). Arriving at Lake Wobegon: Are standardized tests exaggerating achievement and distorting instruction? *American Educator, 12*(2), 8–15, 46–52.

Koretz, D. (1992). State and national assessment. In M. C. Alkin (Ed.), *Encyclopedia of educational research* (6th ed., pp. 1262–1267). Washington, DC: American Educational Research Association.

Koretz, D. (1997). *The assessment of students with disabilities in Kentucky* (CSE Technical Report 431). Los Angeles: University of California, Center for the Study of Evaluation.

Koretz, D. (2000). *The impact of score differences on the admission of minority students: An illustration.* Chestnut Hill, MA: National Board on Educational Testing and Public Policy.

Koretz, D. (2002). Limitations in the use of achievement tests as measures of educators' productivity. In E. Hanushek, J. Heckman, & D. Neal (Eds.), *Designing Incentives to Promote Human Capital* [Special issue]. *Journal of Human Resources, 37*(4), 752–777.

Koretz, D. (2003). Using multiple measures to address perverse incentives and score inflation. *Educational Measurement: Issues and Practice, 22*(2), 18–26.

Koretz, D., & Barron, S. I. (1998). *The validity of gains on the Kentucky Instructional Results Information System (KIRIS)* (MR-1014–EDU). Santa Monica, CA: RAND.

Koretz, D., Barron, S., Mitchell, K., & Stecher, B. (1996). *The perceived effects of the Kentucky Instructional Results Information System (KIRIS)* (MR-792–PCT/FF). Santa Monica, CA: RAND.

Koretz, D., & Barton, K. (2004). Assessing students with disabilities: Issues and evidence. *Educational Assessment, 9*(1).

Koretz, D. M., Bertenthal, M. W., and Green, B., Eds. (1999). *Embedding Common Test Items in State and District Assessments.* (National Research Council, Committee on Embedding Common Test Items in State and District Assessments.) Washington: National Academy Press.

Koretz, D., and Deibert, F. (1996). Setting standards and interpreting achievement: A cautionary tale from the National Assessment of Educational Progress. *Educational Assessment, 3*(6), 53–81.

Koretz, D. & Hamilton, L. (1999). *Assessing students with disabilities in Kentucky: The effects of accommodations, format, and subject* (CSE Technical Report 498). Los Angeles: University of California, Center for the Study of Evaluation.

Koretz, D., & Hamilton, L. (2000). Assessment of students with disabilities in Kentucky: Inclusion, student performance, and validity. *Educational Evaluation and Policy Analysis, 22*(3), 255–272.

Koretz, D., & Hamilton, L. S. (2003). *Teachers' responses to high-stakes testing and the validity of gains: A pilot study* (CSE Technical Report 610). Los Angeles: University of California, Center for the Study of Evaluation.

Koretz, D., Linn, R. L., Dunbar, S. B., & Shepard, L. A. (1991, April). The effects of high-stakes testing: Preliminary evidence about generalization across tests. In R. L. Linn (Chair), *The effects of high stakes testing.* Symposium presented at the annual meetings of the American Educational Research Association and the National Council on Measurement in Education, Chicago.

Koretz, D., & McCaffrey, D. (2005). *Using IRT DIF methods to evaluate the validity of score gains* (CSE Technical Report 660). Los Angeles: University of California, Center for the Study of Evaluation.

Koretz, D., McCaffrey, D., & Hamilton, L. (2001). *Toward a framework for validating gains under high-stakes conditions* (CSE Technical Report 551). Los Angeles: University of California, Center for the Study of Evaluation.

Koretz, D., Mitchell, K., Barron, S., & Keith, S. (1996). *The perceived effects of the Maryland School Performance Assessment Program* (CSE Technical Report 409). Los Angeles: University of California, Center for the Study of Evaluation.

Koretz, D., Stecher, B., Klein, S., & McCaffrey, D. (1994). The Vermont portfolio assessment program: Findings and implications. *Educational Measurement: Issues and Practice, 13*(3), 5–16.

Koretz, D., Stecher, B., Klein, S., McCaffrey, D., & Deibert, E. (1993). *Can portfolios assess student performance and influence instruction? The 1991–92 Vermont experience* (CSE Technical Report 371). Los Angeles: University of California at Los Angeles Center for Research on Evaluation, Standards, and Student Testing.

LaMarca, P. M., Redfield, D., & Winter, P. C. (with Bailey, A., & Despriet, L. H.). (2000). *State standards and state assessment systems: A guide to alignment.* Washington, DC: Council of Chief State School Officers.

Lane, S., Parke, C. S., & Stone, C. A. (1998). A framework for evaluating the consequences of assessment programs. *Educational Measurement: Issues and Practice, 17*(2), 24–28.

Lane, S., Parke, C. S., & Stone, C. A. (2002). The impact of a state performance-based assessment and accountability program on mathematics instruction and student learning: Evidence from survey data and school performance. *Educational Assessment, 8*(4), 279–315.

Lindquist, E. F. (1951). Preliminary considerations in objective test construction. In E. F. Lindquist (Ed.), *Educational measurement.* Washington: American Council on Education (pp. 119–158).

Linn, R. L. (1993). Educational assessment: Expanded expectations and challenges. *Educational Evaluation and Policy Analysis, 15,* 1–16.

Linn, R. L. (1994). Criterion-referenced measurement: A valuable perspective clouded by surplus meaning. *Educational Measurement: Issues and Practice, 13*(4), 12–14.

Linn, R. L. (2000). Assessments and accountability. *Educational Researcher, 29*(2), 4–16.

Linn, R. L. (2001). *The design and evaluation of educational assessment and accountability systems* (Technical Report 539). Los Angeles: University of California, Center for the Study of Evaluation.

Linn, R. L. (2003). Performance standards: Utility for different uses of assessments. *Education Policy Analysis Archives, 11*(31). Retrieved October 20, 2003, from http://epaa.asu.edu/epaa/v11n31/

Linn, R. L., Baker, E. L., & Dunbar, S. B. (1991). Complex performance-based assessment: Expectations and validation criteria. *Educational Researcher, 20*(8), 15–21.

Linn, R. L, and Dunbar, S. B. (1990). The Nation's report card goes home: Good news and bad about trends in achievement. *Phi Delta Kappan, 72*(2), October, 127–133.

Linn, R. L., Graue, M. E., & Sanders, N. M. (1990). Comparing state and district test results to national norms: The validity of claims that "everyone is above average." *Educational Measurement: Issues and Practice, 9*(3), 5–14.

Linn, R. L., & Haug, C. (2002). Stability of school-building accountability scores and gains. *Educational Evaluation and Policy Analysis, 24,* 29–36.

Linn, R. L., Koretz, D. M., Baker, E. L., & Burstein, L.(1991). *The validity and credibility of the achievement levels for the 1990 National Assessment of Educational Progress in mathematics* (CSE Technical Report No. 330). Los Angeles: UCLA, Center for Research on Evaluation, Standards, and Student Testing.

Lord, F. M. (1969). Statistical adjustments when comparing pre-existing groups. *Psychological Bulletin, 72*(5), 336–337.

Mabry, L. (1999). Writing to the rubric: Lingering effects of traditional standardized testing on direct writing assessment. *Phi Delta Kappan, 80,* 673–679.

Madaus, G. (1993). A national testing system: Manna from above? A historical/technological perspective. *Educational Assessment, 1,* 9–26.

Maine Department of Education. (n.d.). *1997–98 language minority student demographics in Maine schools.* Retrieved January 12, 2004, from http://www.state.me.us/education/esl/esl/lmsd.htm

Martineau, J. A. (in press). Distorting value added: The use of longitudinal, vertically scaled student achievement data for growth-based value-added accountability. *Journal of Educational and Behavioral Statistics.*

Massachusetts Department of Education. (2003a). *2002 MCAS technical report.* Malden, MA: Author. Retrieved December 23, 2004, from http://www.doe.mass.edu/mcas/2003/news/02techrpt.pdf

Massachusetts Department of Education. (2003b). *Guide to interpreting the spring 2003 reports for schools and districts.* Malden, MA: Author. Retrieved October 24, 2003, from http://www.doe.mass.edu/mcas/interpretive_guides.html

Massachusetts Department of Education. (2003c). *Massachusetts Comprehensive Assessment System: Release of spring 2003 test items.* Malden, MA: Author. Retrieved January 30, 2004, from http://www.doe.mass.edu/mcas/2003/release/testitems.pdf

Mazzeo, J., Carlson, J. E., Voelkl, K. E., & Lutkus, A. D. (2000). *Increasing the participation of special needs students in NAEP: A report on 1996 NAEP research activities.* Washington DC: National Center for Education Statistics, U.S. Department of Education, Office of Educational Research and Improvement.

McCaffrey, D. F., Lockwood, J. R., Koretz, D. M., & Hamilton, L. S. (2003). *Evaluating value-added models for teacher accountability* (MG-158–EDU). Santa Monica, CA: RAND.

McLaughlin, D. & Bandeira de Mello, V. (2002). Comparison of state elementary school mathematics achievement standards using NAEP 2000. Paper presented at the Annual Meeting of the American Educational Research Association, New Orleans, LA, April.

Mehrens, W. A. (1998). Consequences of assessment: What is the evidence? *Educational Policy Analysis Archives, 6*(13). Retrieved May 15, 2005 from http://epaa.asu.edu/epaa/v6n13.html

Mehrens, W. A., & Kaminski, J. (1989). Methods for improving standardized test scores: Fruitful, fruitless, or fraudulent? *Educational Measurement: Issues and Practice, 8*(1), 14–22.

Messick, S. (1989). Validity. In R. L. Linn (Ed.), *Educational measurement* (3rd ed., pp. 13–103). New York: American Council on Education/MacMillan.

Messick, S., Beaton, A., & Lord, F. (1983). *National Assessment of Educational Progress reconsidered: A new design for a new era.* Princeton, NJ: Educational Testing Service.

Murnane, R. J. (1975). *The impact of school resources on the learning of inner city children.* Cambridge, MA: Ballinger Publishing.

Muthén, B., Khoo, S., & Goff, G. (1997). *Multidimensional description of subgroup differences in mathematics achievement data from the 1992 National Assessment of Educational Progress* (CSE Tech. Rep. No. 432). Los Angeles: University of California, National Center for Research on Evaluation, Standards, and Student Testing.

National Assessment Governing Board. (1991). *Response to the draft summative evaluation report on the National Governing Board's inaugural effort to set achievement levels on the National Assessment of Educational Progress.* Washington, DC: Author.

National Assessment Governing Board. (2002a). *Long-term trend policy statement.* Washington, DC: Author.

National Assessment Governing Board. (2002b). *Using the National Assessment of Educational Progress to confirm state test results.* Washington, DC: Author.

National Center for Education Statistics. (2001). *NAEP 1996 science state reports, revised December 1997* (Updated March 21, 2001). Retrieved December 23, 2004, from http://nces.ed.gov/nationsreportcard//pubs/stt1996/97499.asp

National Center for Education Statistics. (2004). *More about NAEP mathematics* (Updated May 21, 2004). Retrieved December 23, 2004, from http://nces.ed.gov/nationsreportcard/mathematics/moreabout.asp

National Center on Educational Outcomes. (1993, March). *Testing accommodations for students with disabilities: A review of the literature* (Synthesis Report 4). St. Cloud State University & National Association of State Directors of Special Education. (ERIC Document Reproduction Service No. ED 358 656)

National Center on Educational Outcomes. (2003). *Special topic area: Universally designed assessments.* Minneapolis: University of Minnesota. Retrieved March 25, 2003, from http://education.umn.edu/nceo/TopicAreas/UnivDesign/UnivDesign_topic.htm

National Commission on Excellence in Education. (1983). *A nation at risk.* Washington, DC: U.S. Department of Education.

National Council of Teachers of Mathematics. (1989). *Curriculum and evaluation standards for school mathematics.* Reston, VA: Author.

National Council on Education Standards and Testing. (1992). *Raising standards for American education.* Washington, DC: Author.

National Governors Association. (1989). *Results in education: 1989.* Washington, DC: Author.

National Research Council. (1996). *National science education standards.* Washington, DC. National Academy Press.

National Research Council. (1997). *Educating one and all: Students with disabilities and standards-based reform.* Washington, DC: National Academy Press.

National Research Council. (2001). *Knowing what students know: The science and design of educational assessment.* Washington, DC: National Academy Press.

New Jersey Department of Education. (1976). *Educational assessment program: State report 1975–76.* Trenton, NJ: Author.

No Child Left Behind Act of 2001, 20 U.S.C. 6311 *et seq.*

O'Day, J., Goertz, M. E., & Floden, R. E. (1995). *Building capacity for education reform* (CPRE Policy Brief RB-18). Philadelphia: Consortium for Policy Research in Education.

Olson, L. (2002, February 20). A 'Proficient' score depends on geography. *Education Week.* Retrieved December 12, 2003, from http://www.edweek.org/ew/newstory.cfm?slug=23proficient.h21

O'Neil, H. F., Sugrue, B., Abedi, J., Baker, E. L., & Golan, S. (1997). *Final report of experimental studies on motivation and NAEP test performance* (CSE Tech. Rep. 427). Los Angeles: University of Califormia at Los Angeles Center for Research on Evaluation, Standards, and Student Testing.

O'Neil, J. (1993). On the New Standards Project: A conversation with Lauren Resnick and Warren Simmons. *Educational Leadership, 50*(5), 17–21.

Pedulla, J. J., Abrams, L. M., Madaus, G. F., Russell, M. K., Ramos, M. A., & Miao, J. (2003). *Perceived effects of state-mandated testing programs on teaching and learning: Findings from a national survey of teachers.* Boston: National Board on Educational Testing and Public Policy.

Pellegrino, J. W., Jones, L. R., & Mitchell, K. M. (1999). *Grading the nation's report card: Evaluating NAEP and transforming the Assessment of Educational Progress.* Washington, DC: National Academy Press.

Perrone, V. (1979). Competency testing: A social and historical perspective. *Educational Horizons, 58,* 3–8.

Phillips, G. W. (1990). The Lake Wobegon effect. *Educational Measurement: Issues and Practice, 9*(3), 3, 14.

Phillips, S. E. (1994). High-stakes testing accommodations: Validity versus disabled rights. *Applied Measurement in Education, 7*(2), 93–120.

Pipho, C. (1985). Tracking the reforms, Part 5: Testing—Can it measure the success of the reform movement? *Education Week, 4*(35), 19.

Popham, W. J. (1978). *Criterion-referenced measurement.* Englewood Cliffs, NJ: Prentice-Hall.

Popham, W. J. (1987). The merits of measurement-driven instruction. *Phi Delta Kappan, 68,* 679–682.

Popham, W. J. (2004). All about accountability: Tawdry tests and AYP. *Educational Leadership, 62*(2), 85–86.

Popham, W. J., Cruse, K. L., Rankin, S. C., Sandifer, P. D., & Williams, P. L. (1985). Measurement-driven instruction: It's on the road. *Phi Delta Kappan, 66,* 628–634.

Popham, W. J., & Husek, T. R. (1969). Implications of criterion-referenced measurement. *Journal of Educational Measurement, 6,* 1–9.

Porter, A. C. (1998). The effects of upgrading policies on high school mathematics and science. In D. Ravitch (Ed.), *Brookings papers on education policy 1998* (pp. 123–172). Washington, DC: Brookings.

Porter, A. C. (2002). Measuring the content of instruction: Uses in research and practice. *Educational Researcher, 31*(7), 3–14.

Raudenbush, S., & Bryk, A. (2002). *Hierarchical linear models: Applications and data analysis methods* (2nd ed.). Newbury Park, CA: Sage.

Reckase, M. D. (2001). The controversy over the National Assessment Governing Board Standards. In *Brookings Papers on Educational Policy* (pp. 231–253). Washington, DC: The Brookings Institution.

Reese, C. M., Miller, K. E., Mazzeo, J., & Dossey, J. A. (1997). *NAEP 1996 mathematics report card for the nation and the states: Findings from the National Assessment of Educational Progress.* Washington, DC: National Center for Education Statistics.

Rehabilitation Act of 1973, 29 U.S.C. §701 *et seq.*

Resnick, D. P. (1982). History of educational testing. In A. K. Wigdor & W. R. Garner (Eds.), *Ability testing: Uses, consequences, and controversies, Part II* (pp. 173–194). Washington, DC: National Academy Press.

Resnick, L. B., & Resnick, D. P. (1992). Assessing the thinking curriculum: New tools for educational reform. In B. R. Gifford & M. C. O'Connor (Eds.), *Changing assessment: Alternative views of aptitude, achievement, and instruction* (pp. 37–75). Boston: Kluwer.

Rivkin, S. G., Hanushek, E. A., & Kain, J. F. (2005). Teachers, schools, and academic achievement. *Econometrica, 73*(2), 417–458.

Roeber, E. (1988, February). *A history of large-scale testing activities at the state level.* Paper presented at the Indiana Governor's Symposium on ISTEP, Madison, IN.

Rogosa, D. (1999). *Accuracy of individual scores expressed in percentile ranks: Classical test theory calculations.* Los Angeles: University of California, Center for the Study of Evaluation.

Rogosa, D. (2002, October). *Irrelevance of reliability coefficients to accountability systems: Statistical disconnect in Kane-Staiger "Volatility in school test scores."* Unpublished working paper. Retrieved May 15, 2005 from http://www-stat.stanford.edu/~rag/api/kscresst.pdf

Romberg, T. A., Zarinia, E. A., & Williams, S. R. (1989). *The influence of mandated testing on mathematics instruction: Grade 8 teachers' perceptions.* Madison: University of Wisconsin, National Center for Research in Mathematical Science Education.

Rothman, R., Slattery, J. B., Vranek, J. L., & Resnick, L. B. (2002). *Benchmarking and alignment of standards and testing* (CSE Technical Report 566). Los Angeles: University of California, Los Angeles, Center for Research on Evaluation, Standards, and Student Testing.

Rowan, B., Correnti, R., & Miller, R. J. (2002). What large-scale survey research tells us about teacher effects on student achievement: Insights from the *Prospects* study of elementary schools. *Teachers College Record, 104,* 1525–1567.

Sanders, W., & Horn, S. (1998). Research findings from the Tennessee Value-Added Assessment System (TVAAS) database: Implications for educational evaluation and research. *Journal of Personnel Evaluation in Education, 12,* 247–256.

Sanders, W. L., & Rivers, J. C. (1996). *Cumulative and residual effects of teachers on future student academic achievement.* Knoxville: University of Tennessee Value-Added Research Center.

Sanders, W., Saxton, A., & Horn, B. (1997). The Tennessee Value-Added Assessment System: A quantitative outcomes-based approach to educational assessment. In J. Millman (Ed.), *Grading teachers, grading schools: Is student achievement a valid evaluational measure?* (pp. 137–162). Thousand Oaks, CA: Corwin Press.

Sanford, E. E., & Fabrizio, L. M. (1999, April). *Results from the North Carolina—NAEP comparison and what they mean to the End-of-Grade Testing Program.* Paper presented at the annual meeting of the American Educational Research Association, Montreal, Canada.

Schemo, D. J., & Fessenden, F. (2003, December 3). Gains in Houston schools: How real are they? *New York Times.* Retrieved December 3, 2003, from http://www.nytimes.com.

Shavelson, R. J., Baxter, G. P., & Gao, X. (1993). Sampling variability of performance assessments. *Journal of Educational Measurement, 30*(3), 215–232.

Shepard, L. A. (1988, April). *Should instruction be measurement-driven? A debate.* Paper presented at the annual meeting of the American Educational Research Association, New Orleans, LA.

Shepard, L. A. (1990). Inflated test score gains: Is the problem old norms or teaching the test? *Educational Measurement: Issues and Practice, 9*(3), 15–22.

Shepard, L. A. (1993). Identification of mild handicaps. In R. L. Linn (Ed.), *Educational measurement* (3rd ed., pp. 545–572). New York: American Council on Education/Macmillan.

Shepard, L. A. (1994). Implications for standard setting of the National Academy of Education evaluation of the National Assessment of Educational Progress Achievement Levels. In *Proceedings of the joint conference on standard setting for large-scale assessments, Vol. II.* (pp. 143–160). Washington, DC: National Assessment Governing Board and National Center for Education Statistics.

Shepard, L. A., & Dougherty, K. C. (1991, April). *Effects of high-stakes testing on instruction.* Paper presented at the annual meeting of the American Educational Research Association and National Council on Measurement in Education, Chicago.

Simmons, W., & Resnick, L. (1993). Assessment as the catalyst of school reform. *Educational Leadership, 50*(5), 11–15.

Sireci, S. G. (1998). Gathering and analyzing content validity data. *Educational Assessment, 5,* 299–321.

Smith, M. L. (1994). *Old and new beliefs about measurement-driven instruction: "The more things change, the more they stay the same"* (CSE Tech. Rep. 373). Los Angeles: University of California, Los Angeles, Center for Research on Evaluation, Standards, and Student Testing.

Smith, M. L., Edelsky, C., Draper, K., Rottenberg, C., & Cherland, M. (1991). *The role of testing in elementary schools* (CSE Tech. Rep. 321). Los Angeles: University of California, Los Angeles, Center for Research on Evaluation, Standards, and Student Testing.

Smith, M. L., & Rottenberg, C. (1991). Unintended consequences of external testing in elementary schools. *Educational Measurement: Issues and Practice, 10*(4), 7–11.

Smith, M. S., & O'Day, J. Systemic School Reform. In S. Fuhrman & B. Malen (Eds.), *The politics of curriculum and testing: The 1990 yearbook of the politics of education and association* (pp. 233–267). Philadelphia: Falmer Press.

Smith, M. S., O'Day, J., & Cohen, D. K. (1990). National curriculum American style: Can it be done? What might it look like? *American Educator, 14*(4), 10–17, 40–47.

Spalding, E. (2000). Performance assessment and the New Standards Project: A story of serendipitous success. *Phi Delta Kappan, 81*(10), 758–764.

Stecher, B. M., & Barron, S. I. (1999). *Quadrennial milepost accountability testing in Kentucky* (CSE Tech. Rep. No. 505). Los Angeles: University of California, Los Angeles, Center for Research on Evaluation, Standards, and Student Testing.

Stecher, B. M., Barron, S. L., Chun, T., & Ross, K. (2000). *The effects of the Washington state education reform on schools and classrooms* (CSE Tech. Rep. No. 525). Los Angeles: University of California, Los Angeles, Center for Research on Evaluation, Standards and Student Testing.

Stecher, B. M., & Chun, T. (2001). *School and classroom practices during two years of education reform in Washington state* (CSE Tech. Rep. No. 550). Los Angeles: University of California, Los Angeles, Center for Research on Evaluation, Standards, and Student Testing.

Stecher, B. M., Hamilton, L. S., & Gonzalez, G. (2003). *Working smarter to leave no child behind*. Santa Monica, CA: RAND.

Stecher, B. M., & Mitchell, K. J. (1995). *Portfolio driven reform: Vermont teachers' understanding of mathematical problem solving* (CSE Tech. Rep. No. 400). University of California, Los Angeles: Center for Research on Evaluation, Standards, and Student Testing.

Strauss, V. (2001, July 10). Review tests go too far, critics say. *The Washington Post*, p. A09.

Stufflebeam, D. L., Jaeger, R. M., & Scriven, M. (1991). *Summative evaluation of the National Governing Board's inaugural effort to set achievement levels on the National Assessment of Educational Progress*. Kalamazoo, MI: Western Michigan University.

Taylor, G., Shepard, L., Kinner, F., & Rosenthal, J. (2003). *A survey of teachers' perspectives on high-stakes testing in Colorado: What gets taught, what gets lost* (CSE Technical Report 588). Los Angeles: University of California, Los Angeles, University of California, Loss Angeles, Center for Research on Evaluation, Standards, and Student Testing.

Tepper, R. L. (2002). *The influence of high-stakes testing on instructional practice in Chicago*. Unpublished doctoral dissertation, Harris Graduate School of Public Policy, University of Chicago.

Thurlow, M., House, A., Boys, C., Scott, D., & Ysseldyke, J. (2000). *State participation and accommodation policies for students with disabilities: 1999 update* (Synthesis Report 33). Minneapolis: University of Minnesota, National Center on Educational Outcomes.

Thurlow, M., Seyfarth, A. L., Scott, D., & Ysseldyke, J. (1997). *State assessment policies on participation and accommodations for students with disabilities: 1997 Update* (Synthesis Report 29). Minneapolis: University of Minnesota, National Center on Educational Outcomes.

Tyack, D. (1974). *The one best system: A history of American urban education*. Cambridge, MA: Harvard University Press.

U. S. Congress, Office of Technology Assessment. (1992). *Testing in America's schools: Asking the right questions* (Publication OTA-SET-519). Washington, DC: U.S. Government Printing Office.

U. S. Department of Education. (1985). *State education statistics: State performance outcomes, resource inputs, and population characteristics, 1982 and 1984*. Washington, DC: Author.

U.S. Department of Education. (2001). *To assure the free appropriate public education of all children with disabilities: 23rd annual report to Congress on the implementation of the Individuals with Disabilities Education Act*. Washington, DC: Author. (Table AA 10 online at http://www.ed.gov/about/reports/annual/osep/2001/appendix-a-pt1.pdf. Last accessed May 19, 2005.)

U.S. Department of Education. (2002). *Fact sheet on No Child Left Behind*. Washington, DC: Author. Last accessed January 27, 2004, from http://www.ed.gov/nclb/overview/intro/factsheet.html?exp=0

U.S. General Accounting Office. (2003). *Title I: Characteristics of tests will influence expenses; information sharing may help states realize efficiencies* (Publication GAO-03-389). Washington, DC: Author.

Wainer, H., & Thissen, D. (1993). Combining multiple choice and constructed response test scores: Toward a Marxist theory of test construction. *Applied Measurement in Education, 6*, 103–118.

Wang, M. C., & Stanley, J. C. (1970). Differential weighting: A review of methods and empirical studies. *Review of Educational Research, 40*(5), 663–705.

Webb, N. L. (1997). *Criteria for alignment of expectations and assessments in mathematics and science education* (Research Monograph No. 8). Washington, DC: Council of Chief State School Officers.

Webster, W., & Mendro, R. (1997). The Dallas value-added accountability system. In J. Millman (Ed.), *Grading teachers, grading schools: Is student achievement a valid evaluation measure?* (pp. 81–99). Thousand Oaks, CA: Corwin Press.

Webster, W., Mendro, R., Orsak, T., & Weerasinghe, D. (1998, April). *An application of hierarchical linear modeling to the estimation of school and teacher effects*. Paper presented at the annual meeting of the American Educational Research Association, San Diego, CA.

Wiggins, G. (1992). Creating tests worth taking. *Educational Leadership, 49*, 26–33.

Williams, V. S. L., Pommerich, M., & Thissen, D. (1998). A comparison of developmental scales based on Thurstone methods and Item Response Theory. *Journal of Educational Measurement, 35*(2), 93–107.

Willingham, W. W., Rogosta, M., Bennett, R. E., Braun, H., Rock, D. A., & Powers, D. E. (1988). *Testing handicapped people*. Boston: Allyn & Bacon.

Wolf, S. A., Borko, H., McIver, M. C., & Elliott, R. (1999). *"No excuses": School reform efforts in exemplary schools of Kentucky* (CSE Tech. Rep. 514). Los Angeles: University of California, Los Angeles, Center for Research on Evaluation, Standards, and Student Testing.

Wolf, S. A., & McIver, M. C. (1999). When process becomes policy. *Phi Delta Kappan, 80*(5), 401–406.

Wolfe, R. (1997, April). Country-by-item interactions: Problems with content validity in scaling. In *Validity in cross-national assessments: Problems and pitfalls*. Symposium presented at the annual meeting of the American Educational Research Association, Chicago.

Wright, S. P., Horn, S. P., & Sanders, W. L. (1997). Teacher and classroom context effects on student achievement: Implications for teacher evaluation. *Journal of Personnel Evaluation in Education, 11*, 57–67.

Yen, W. M. (1988). Normative growth expectations must be realistic: A reply to Phillips and Clarizio. *Educational Measurement: Issues and Practice, 7*(4), 16–17.

Yen, W. M., & Burket, G. R. (1997). Comparison of Item Response Theory and Thurstone methods of vertical scaling. *Journal of Educational Measurement, 34*(4), 293–313.

Ysseldyke, J. E., & Algozzine, B. (1982). Bias among professionals who erroneously declare students eligible for special services. *Journal of Experimental Education, 50*(4), 223–228.

16

Standardized Assessment of Individual Achievement in K–12

Steve Ferrara
Gerald E. DeMauro
American Institutes for Research

1. INTRODUCTION AND OVERVIEW

In this chapter we describe and evaluate the state of the art in standardized assessment of individual achievement in kindergarten through grade 12. The last two editions of *Educational Measurement* provide superb documentation of the best thinking and practice in the state of the art up to 1971 and 1989, respectively. In this chapter we endeavor to uphold that tradition.

We begin the chapter by discussing the two broad purposes for achievement testing: providing information for public accountability and instructional decisions. We then describe current practice in score reporting. We address score reporting early because the information in score reports is the penultimate product of the assessment process. (Users' interpretations and uses of test scores are the ultimate product.) Following that discussion, we survey the K–12 achievement testing landscape. We describe the types of achievement tests used in grades K–12 and selected salient features of state assessment programs. We also examine in some detail the item formats most widely used in achievement assessments: multiple-choice and short and extended constructed-response items. We complete our survey of the state of the art by examining evidence provided in technical reports from 12 assessment programs. We focus on evidence of test score reliability and the validity of test score interpretations and uses. We also describe traditional and emergent approaches to achievement test design and development. We complete our description and evaluation of the state of the art with a brief discussion of some issues and concerns for the future.

Much of the discussion in this chapter focuses on state assessment programs. That is by design. Much of the activity in K–12 achievement assessment has been managed and directed from state departments of education since the rise of minimum competency testing in the late 1970s (e.g., Jaeger & Tittle, 1980). Further, state assessments play a significant role in education reform policy and programs. Our focus on state assessment programs also reflects our long years of experience working on state assessment programs, including as state directors of student assessment in Maryland, New Jersey, and New York.

In discussing K–12 achievement testing, it is necessary to acknowledge assessment and reporting requirements in the *No Child Left Behind* legislation. We describe K–12 achievement testing during the early years of implementation of those requirements. We do not make *No Child Left Behind* the central focus of the chapter, however. The long term viability of *No Child Left Behind* requirements will not be clear until after the 2008 presidential elections or later, if large numbers of schools fail to meet annual progress goals on the way to 2013–14.

1.1. *No Child Left Behind* Testing and Reporting Requirements

President George W. Bush signed the *No Child Left Behind Act of 2002* (No Child Left Behind) at the end of his first year in office. *No Child Left Behind* obliges states, school systems, and schools to take steps necessary to ensure that 100% of students in grades 3–8 and high school achieve proficient performance on state assessments no later than the 2013–2014 school year. In announcing *No Child Left Behind*, President Bush expressed concern that "too many of our neediest children are being left behind, despite the nearly $200 billion in Federal spending since the passage of the Elementary and Secondary Education Act of 1965 (ESEA)" (retrieved September 21, 2005 from http://www.ed.gov/No Child Left Behind/overview/intro/execsumm.html).

No Child Left Behind prescribes a range of requirements relevant to K–12 achievement testing programs, but passes down responsibility for the specifics. *No Child Left Behind* requires states to:[1]

- Implement content standards for reading/language arts and mathematics for grades 3–8 and high school and corresponding annual assessments by 2005–06.
- Implement content standards for science in one grade at each of three schooling levels (i.e., grades 3–5, 6–9, and 10–12) by 2005–06 and corresponding assessments by 2007–08.
- Include all enrolled students in administrations of all state content area assessments, including all students with disabilities and English language learners.
- Provide alternate assessments that are linked to grade level academic content standards for students with significant cognitive disabilities who cannot participate meaningfully in the state reading/language arts, mathematics, and science assessments.

- Ensure that local school systems administer annual assessments of English language proficiency for English language learners by the beginning of the 2002–03 school year.
- Establish Adequate Yearly Progress (AYP) goals that follow a trajectory to 100% of students achieving the proficient level in reading/language arts, mathematics, and science assessments by the 2013–14 school year.
- Report assessment results at the state, school system, and school levels for all students and separately for key student subgroups: males and females, racial/ethnic subgroups, economically disadvantaged students, students with disabilities, and English language learners.

No Child Left Behind also prescribes corrective actions for schools that fail to meet Adequate Yearly Progress goals.

The impacts and implications of *No Child Left Behind* requirements for K–12 achievement testing are profound. State assessment programs have expanded from assessing achievement in selected grades to grades 3–8 and high school. In 2001–2002, 41 states and jurisdictions assessed science achievement; under *No Child Left Behind* all states do so. Prior to *No Child Left Behind*, English language proficiency assessment was conducted at the local school system level with little coordination across school systems. In addition, alternate assessments for students with significant cognitive disabilities focused primarily on life skills (e.g., sorting tasks, using vending machines) rather than academic content as they do now. State assessment programs now play an even more significant role in education reform: the consequences for schools that do not meet Adequate Yearly Progress goals are severe.

2. PURPOSES FOR USING K–12 ACHIEVEMENT ASSESSMENTS

In this section we discuss the two broad intended purposes for using K–12 standardized achievement assessments: providing information for (a) public accountability, and (b) instructional decisions. Assessment information used for accountability purposes illuminates what goes on in schools (i.e., the inputs paid for by public funds) by publicizing how well students are achieving educational goals (i.e., the output). Accountability testing typically is mandated externally (e.g., as in statewide assessment programs). Assessment information intended to guide instruction should support teachers as they make ongoing, day-to-day instructional decisions to guide student learning (Stiggins, 2002). In this section we discuss these two purposes and then examine current practice in score reporting.

2.1. Intended Purposes for Achievement Assessment Information

The success of large-scale individual achievement testing in grades K–12 is remarkable. You may take the perspective that K–12 achievement testing functions as an information gathering tool for professional educators and school systems, a policy lever for legislators and educational reformers, or as a detail in the larger scheme of public education as social policy. Or you may view it as a blunt instrument that narrows curriculum, restricts teacher autonomy and creativity, damages children's self-esteem, and undermines their natural inclination to learn. Whatever your perspective, the history of K–12 achievement testing dates at least to the New York Regents examinations in 1865 (see Nitko, 1983, inside front cover). That history includes a mixture of positive, neutral, and negative impacts on society, schools, teachers, and students. We do not trace that history here (though we provide some details in section 3).

Of course, externally mandated testing in schools has endured considerable criticism, especially in the last 25 years. Some parents and educational professionals contend that most of K–12 achievement testing has not been effective (e.g., state assessment program results are punitive and not useful for instructional decision making, and even rather harmful; for example, Kohn, 2000). Even with these criticisms, support is strong for student achievement testing in schools.

- For example, 62% of teachers and 61% of superintendents and principals agree with the statement that "standardized tests are a necessary evil" (from a Public Agenda survey completed in September 2003; retrieved from http://www.publicagenda.org/issues/red_flags_detail.cfm?issue_type=education&list=5&area=2)
- In addition, 53% of Americans say that "class work and homework" are the best measures of academic achievement (from a Gallup/Phi Delta Kappa poll conducted in June 2002; retrieved from http://www.publicagenda.org/issues/red_flags_detail.cfm?issue_type=education&list=4&area=2)
- However, 70% of Americans agree with the statement that standardized tests "should be used...to ensure that all students meet national academic standards" (from a Pew/Kaiser poll completed in October 2003; retrieved from http://www.publicagenda.org/issues/red_flags_detail2.cfm?issue_type=education&red_flag_graphic=rfedutestsevaluate.jpg).

According to these poll results, fully two-thirds of the American public supports the use of standardized achievement testing to account for what goes on in schools and the achievement of students. Similarly, more than 60% of teachers agree that standardized achievement testing serves an important purpose.

The American public supports accountability testing. Many teachers do not (e.g., 18% of teachers in the Public Agenda poll felt that "standardized tests do more harm than good"), at least as a guide for making ongoing classroom instructional decisions. This disagreement reflects competing needs and goals. No single assessment or assessment system can serve both accountability and classroom instructional guidance goals simultaneously, and do it well (e.g., Stiggins, 2003). Annual large-scale content area assessments cannot serve the daily informational needs of teachers. Likewise, teacher classroom assessments cannot achieve the technical rigor requirements of accountability reporting.[2] A National Research Council committee acknowledged the need to bridge the gap between large-scale and classroom assessment and described efforts to align classroom and large-scale efforts (National Research Council, 2003). Other writers have observed that K–12 achievement testing is out of balance—that state testing requirements emphasize public accountability goals even though the ultimate goal is to improve student achievement. These writers propose balanced assessment systems that support accountability information needs and that provide information that is instructionally supportive (Commission on Instructionally Supportive Assessment, 2001; National Research Council, 2003; Popham, 2003; Stiggins, 2003). They echo earlier calls for linking both external and internal assessments to instruction (e.g., Nitko, 1989). Integrating large-scale and classroom assessments into balanced systems is necessary because each serves different purposes, provides information for different intended users, and focuses on different achievement targets (Stiggins, 2003, pp. 5–10).

The rhetoric in support of instructionally supportive assessment is enthusiastic. For example, the five school administrator and teacher professional organizations that created the Commission on Instructionally Supportive Assessment wrote, "teachers, principals, and district superintendents will readily embrace accountability measures if they are tied to effective assessment systems designed and implemented to improve classroom instruction" (2001, from the Preface). The commission's nine requirements to achieve a system of instructionally supportive assessments emphasize both large-scale and classroom assessments. Their vision seems clear. The steps for implementing such a system and the impetus for pursuing those steps are not clear at this time. However, several countries around the world are training teachers and promoting the role of classroom assessment in improving student achievement (Olson, 2005). Several of these efforts may lead the way to balancing the emphasis on assessment for learning with assessment for accountability.

Some school systems develop and require use of curriculum embedded assessments as a supplement to both state assessments and teachers' classroom assessment activities. Typically, these assessments are administered and scored in the classroom by teachers. The information generated is intended to inform teachers about student mastery of, specifically, the school system curriculum. This information can be useful to teachers, who need information to adjust instruction so that students achieve classroom instructional goals; to principals, who must ensure that their schools meet school system and state performance goals; and to school system administrators, who must ensure that the school system meets state performance goals. Classroom teachers object to the amount of time they must spend to prepare students for administrations of externally mandated achievement assessments and that they wait for weeks to receive score reports that contain only summary test score information that does not guide daily instructional decisions. Many would prefer to see tests items and student responses as a supplement to summary test score information. Student responses to test items—that is, student work—is information that teachers use every day to assess student learning and make instructional decisions. Curriculum embedded assessments often offer this information, in part because items and tasks from these assessments may not be held secure as are items from external tests. We discuss curriculum embedded assessments in section 3. We observe there that little systematic information is available about curriculum embedded assessments.

A goal in score reporting in K–12 achievement testing is to provide information that is useful for instructional decisions as well as for description of achievement. Achievement test score reports typically include subscale scores (e.g., computation and problem solving in mathematics) as well as total content area scores. Over time, limitations in reporting student achievement in relation to other students' achievement (i.e., norm referenced score interpretations) became apparent. In response, in the 1970s psychometricians developed the concept of criterion referencing to enable interpretations of student achievement in relation to a domain of content or prescribed level of achievement (e.g., Berk, 1980, p. 3). A recent development in criterion referencing—standards-based reporting in state assessment programs—integrates state content standards that are explicitly targeted by state assessments, multiple performance levels, and performance level descriptions that define knowledge and skills that examinees in each performance level are expected to display. Even with these developments, teachers do not find achievement test score reports useful in day-to-day decision making, as we discussed above. It is also clear that score reports are misunderstood and misinterpreted, as we discuss below.

2.2. Test Score Reporting

Score reports are the user interface, so to speak, between test developers and test users. They are one of the most visible products of the achievement testing enterprise. Yet of all the conceptual and technical phases in achievement testing—definition of test content, test development, and psychometrics—score reports and score reporting probably have received the least amount of attention from researchers (e.g., Goodman & Hambleton, 2004). Score reports must be technically accurate to support reasonable and warranted interpretations and must contain supportive explanations to minimize unwarranted inferences and decisions. Score reports must be understandable to the range of audiences that interpret them to guide a range of decisions and actions. Score reports designed for students and their families should pass the "kitchen table test." If students and their families can understand the information in a score report and interpret it appropriately, then the report is effective for that audience.[3] These design requirements are significant.

2.2.1. Types of Scores and Score Scales and General Features of Score Reports Available for Educational Achievement Assessments

Score reports from educational achievement assessments are developed for specific audiences (e.g., individual students and their parents, teachers, principals, and school system leaders) so that they can make intended interpretations and decisions. Student scores also are reported in other contexts for other audiences, such as school, school system, and state report cards. Score reporting includes three elements: types of scores provided on score reports, other information provided on or with the score reports, and other supporting information that may be available.

2.2.2. Types of Test Scores

Other writers have defined and discussed the advantages and drawbacks of the various types of scores that typically are available from educational achievement assessments (see Cohen & Wollack, this volume). Perhaps the most widely known test score types used in score reports of individual student achievement are number correct and percentage correct scores (i.e., raw scores); holistic scores for writing assessments; norm referenced scores such as percentiles, normal curve equivalents, grade equivalents, and stanines; and test-specific scale scores. Performance levels with labels such as basic, proficient, and advanced also are widely used. Here we discuss score types, grouped according to the ways in which they communicate to users about student academic achievement.

Virtually all educational achievement tests produce raw scores in the form of the number of items answered correctly or the number of points earned on items that are scored correct/incorrect and items scored in multiple levels (e.g., 0, 1, and 2). Raw scores usually have no intrinsic meaning. Scoring rubrics and performance scales that indicate levels of quality directly are an exception. Examples of such rubrics and performance scales are common in performance assessments, especially in content areas beyond the traditional academic areas (e.g., rating scales in physical education), scoring rubrics for essay tests, and performance scales in language proficiency assessments (e.g., the speaking proficiency guidelines provided by the American Council on the Teaching of Foreign Languages, or ACTFL; see http://www.languagetesting.com/scale.htm). Raw scores most typically are a first step toward deriving scores that are intended to aid interpretation of test performances. Scale scores may be derived normatively (e.g., percentiles) or by transformation of IRT ability estimates (e.g., as in many commercial norm referenced tests and state content area achievement tests). Scale scores can acquire meaning over time. For example, college admissions staff and much of the general public know what it means when a high school student achieves a mathematics score of 500 versus a 770 on the Scholastic Assessment Test or a 20 versus a 33 on the ACT Assessment. Such meaning accretes over time, as a result of comparing student scores and levels of achievement in school over time.

Scores that support norm referenced interpretations of test performance and student achievement include percentiles, grade equivalents, and normal curve equivalents. Percentile scores are widely available with commercial achievement assessments and probably are interpreted reasonably accurately by a wide range of educators and the general public. Parents of school age children usually are interested to know how well their children have achieved in relation to other students. Other scores support criterion referenced interpretations or, more recently, standards-based interpretations (e.g., National Research Council, 1999, pp. 36 ff.). Standards-based interpretations of test performance incorporate content standards and performance standards, typically by reporting student and group performance in relation to multiple performance levels and performance level descriptions. Standard setting committees set cut scores (see Hambleton & Pitoniak, this volume) to delineate performance levels (e.g., basic, proficient, and advanced) on a test score scale. Performance level descriptions are developed to guide understanding and interpretation of the performance levels.

2.2.3. Performance Level Descriptions

Rapid expansion in the use of performance levels and performance level descriptions in the 1990s is a significant advance in score reporting. The ideas of multiple performance levels and performance level descriptions (i.e., distillations of what students who perform at a level know and can do, based on the knowledge and skills demands of items mapped to each level) are a logical extension of the pass/fail cut scores on minimum competency tests in the 1970s and 1980s. Providing performance level descriptions with test scale scores clarifies what it means to say that a student has passed a high school exit examination or is performing at the proficient level of performance.

Figure 16.1 contains the performance level description for grade 8 mathematics for the National Assessment of Educational Progress (NAEP) from 1992 through 1998. We have selected NAEP descriptions because they are developed following rigorous procedures and illustrate important features that aid interpretation of student test performance. In fact, NAEP has led the way in developing and using performance level descriptions. NAEP Achievement Level Descriptions and development procedures serve as models for a large number of state and other assessment programs. From the point of view of interpreting and understanding student test performance, there are three important components of NAEP descriptions: (a) a single set of policy definitions of advanced, proficient, and basic performance for all grades and content areas; (b) performance level descriptions that are specific to a content area and grade level assessment; and (c) items that illustrate performance at each level. The NAEP policy definition of proficient performance is "solid academic performance exhibiting competency over challenging subject matter" (National Assessment Governing Board, 2001, p. 2). The basic and advanced levels are defined and described in relation to the definition for proficient. A benefit of policy definitions like these is their potential for lending coherence to performance levels and descriptions for an entire achievement assessment program, across grade levels and content areas. Articulating performance standards—that is, ensuring that performance standards and performance level descriptions are consistent across content areas and grades—has become central to setting performance standards for state assessment programs in recent years (see, for example, Ferrara, Johnson, & Chen, 2005). Also, policy definitions provide an easy-to-remember way of thinking about the performance levels for an assessment program.

The shaded section of the description in Figure 16.1 defines proficient grade 8 mathematics performance succinctly. As

FIGURE 16.1 Description for Proficient Performance in Grade 8 NAEP Mathematics

> Eighth-grade students performing at the proficient level should apply mathematical concepts and procedures consistently to complex problems in the five NAEP content strands.
>
> 8th graders performing at the proficient level should be able to conjecture, defend their ideas, and give supporting examples. They should understand the connections among fractions, percents, decimals, and other mathematical topics such as algebra and functions. Students at this level are expected to have a thorough understanding of basic level arithmetic operations—an understanding sufficient for problem solving in practical situations.
>
> Quantity and spatial relationships in problem solving and reasoning should be familiar to them, and they should be able to convey underlying reasoning skills beyond the level of arithmetic. They should be able to compare and contrast mathematical ideas and generate their own examples. These students should make inferences from data and graphs; apply properties of informal geometry; and accurately use the tools of technology. Students at this level should understand the process of gathering and organizing data and be able to calculate, evaluate, and communicate results within the domain of statistics and probability.

Source: Adapted from National Assesment Governing Board (2001), p. 8.

with the policy definition for proficient performance, it provides a brief, easy-to-remember definition. It links to the policy definition of Proficient (provided above) with references to consistent application of knowledge and "competency over challenging subject matter." It also introduces the notion that students who perform at this level "should" be able do the things described. This word choice makes the description consistent with the probabilistic nature of estimating student performance on a test's score scale and with mapping items onto a score scale (see, e.g., Zwick, Senturk, Wang, & Loomis, 2001). The second section provides details about performance at the proficient level in two paragraphs. These details are based on the content knowledge and mathematical ability demands identified in items mapped to the range of scores in the proficient level on the NAEP grade 8 mathematics score scale. The content knowledge demands are defined as content strands in NAEP mathematics assessments (e.g., number sense, properties, and operations; algebra and functions). Mathematical abilities (i.e., conceptual understanding, procedural knowledge, and problem solving) also are defined for NAEP mathematics assessments. The description is meticulous in referring explicitly to the content strands and mathematical abilities in the NAEP assessment framework, and only those that are evident in the items mapped to this level. The precision and defensibility of performance level descriptions is crucial to supporting warranted inferences about what students who achieve a particular level know and are able to do. In fact, such rigorously detailed descriptions may challenge the understanding of students, their families, and their teachers because they require strong familiarity with the content standards that underlie test content.

Sample items can provide concreteness to performance level descriptions. Figure 16.2 displays an item mapped to the NAEP grade 8 mathematics proficient level.

This item is mapped to the proficient level based on its IRT difficulty parameter and other criteria. It was selected, based on rigorous content and statistical criteria, as an appropriate item to illustrate the mathematical knowledge and skill that students whose achievement is at or above the proficient level are likely to possess (see Ryan, 2003; Zwick et al., 2001). A small collection of items mapped to the proficient and other achievement levels provides concrete illustrations of the likely knowledge and skills that students at and above those levels demonstrate through test performance. Sample items can enhance the concreteness of performance level descriptions and illustrate the relationship between the demands in test items and the content standards targeted by the test.

Performance level descriptions are unique to the achievement test for which they define levels of performance. Little guidance exists for developing clearly interpretable performance level descriptions (e.g., see Hambleton, 2001, p. 97). This is somewhat ironic since the research and methodological literature on setting performance levels is expansive. As a result, standard setting methods have proliferated but principles for conceptualizing and developing performance level descriptions—which have become fundamental to setting performance standards judgmentally—are limited.

2.2.4. Subdomain Scores

Typically, users of test score information are interested in receiving information about examinee performance on subsections of an achievement test as well as on the total test. For example, teachers and parents typically are interested in knowing whether a student's achievement is as strong in understanding algebra and functions as it is in arithmetic computation subsections in a mathematics assessment. Scores on these subsections typically are referred to as "subscale scores," "subtest scores," or more generically, "subscores." Because no standard use of these terms exists, users must be clear about the psychometric basis and interpretation of these scores. For example, "subscale scores" could refer to raw scores on subsets of items in a mathematics assessment (as in the example above) or scores derived from IRT item parameters that have been estimated at the total test level.

Psychometricians, test developers, and others seem to take competing views on subdomain scores, even if the debate is not conducted face to face. (Here we mean scores that

FIGURE 16.2 Sample Item from the Grade 8 NAEP Mathematics Assessment, Mapped to the Proficient Achievement Level, That Illustrates Knowledge and Skills Displayed by Examinees Performing at That Level

From a shipment of 500 batteries, a sample of 25 was selected at random and tested. If 2 batteries in the sample were found to be dead, how many dead batteries would be expected in the entire shipment?

Ⓐ 10
Ⓑ 20
Ⓒ 30
● 40
Ⓔ 50

Probability of correct response	
Basic	34%
Proficient	74%
Advanced	96%

Source: From National Assesment Governing Board (2001), p. 18.

represent performance on a subset of items in an achievement test.) Some argue that subdomain scores should not be provided unless they are highly reliable (e.g., with internal consistency reliability estimates of .85 or higher) and should not be highly correlated, even if the intended uses of the scores do not necessarily require such technical rigor and discriminability. Others argue that subdomain scores can be useful to examinees, families, and teachers if the scores are used as indicators of relative strengths and weaknesses, along with other corroborating indicators of course, to guide instructional targeting. Wainer and colleagues (2001; chap. 9) make a persuasive argument for augmenting scores—that is, "'borrowing strength' [from other items on the test] to compute scores based on a small number of items" (p. 343)—to improve the reliability of scores from test subsections. Of course, augmented scoring obscures the relationship between the examinee's raw score and the augmented subdomain score.

In a study of score reports and interpretive guides for 11 U.S. states, two Canadian provinces, and three U.S. commercial testing companies, Goodman and Hambleton (2004) reported that all entities provide some information at the subdomain level. The appeal and usefulness of such information seems self-evident. The reliability of differences between subdomain scores is the crucial issue. Typically, subdomain scores in educational achievement tests, which may contain as few as 40 items at the elementary school level, may be based on 10 or even as few as 5 items. A quick perusal of achievement assessment technical reports demonstrates that reliabilities for such scores can be quite low (e.g., .65), and the reliability of differences between two subdomain scores would be considerably lower. Further, correlations between subdomain scores may be as high as the correlation between each subdomain score and the total test score, suggesting that all subdomains are facets of a unidimensional achievement construct. (This is not surprising, of course, because achievement assessments typically are constructed to be as unidimensional as possible.) In essence, subdomain scores are highly desired for instructional reasons and may not provide precise and sensitive information to detect differences in subdomain achievement where differences exist.

2.2.5. Typical Features of Score Reports

The variety in content and formats of score reports is substantial. Virtually every achievement testing program, whether commercial, national, state, or local, produces customized score reports. Typically, they provide individual student score reports on a single page or on several pages. In addition, classroom reports may be available to teachers and principals, and school, school district, and state level reports typically are produced for state assessment programs. Examinee subgroup reports often are available so that relative performance of racial/ethnic subgroups, boys and girls, and some instructional subgroups (e.g., students in special instructional programs) can be compared and monitored. In addition, score interpretation guides that explain the content of score reports, appropriate interpretations of the information, and even unwarranted interpretations are widely available (Goodman & Hambleton, 2004).

Goodman and Hambleton (2004) and Ryan (2003) provide the most comprehensive reviews of score reporting for individual students on large-scale assessments. Goodman and Hambleton (2004) provide 32 examples of score reports, report approaches, and features of score reports and supporting score interpretation guides. They summarize the types of information that appear in score reports based on a content analysis of score reports and interpretation guides from the U.S. and Canadian sources noted above. The information types include overall test scores (e.g., raw scores, scale scores, percentile rank scores), reporting in relation to performance levels, and diagnostic information (i.e., subdomain scores). In an analysis of score reporting strategies, Ryan (2003) developed a framework of eight characteristics that can be considered in designing a score reporting system: (a) audience for the report (e.g., student, teacher), (b) reporting metric (e.g., raw score, scale score), (c) reference for interpretation (i.e., norms or standards), (d) assessment unit (i.e., item, subdomain, total test), (e) reporting unit (e.g., student, school, state), (f) error of measurement (i.e., explicitly for each unit, metric, and test level combination for which score reports are provided), (g) mode of presentation (i.e., numeric, graphical, narrative), and (h) reporting medium (i.e., print, static, and interactive Web based). Goodman and Hambleton (2004) report promising and problematic features of score reports and score interpretation guides.

2.2.6. Score Reporting Research, Conceptualization, and Practice

Several venerable and recent conceptual developments and efforts illustrate the state of the art in score reporting. For example:

- Concepts of norm referenced and criterion referenced test interpretations are well understood and have informed test design and supported score reporting for decades.
- The introduction of performance level descriptions and related practices (e.g., item mapping; see Zwick et al., 2001) to support test score interpretation have enhanced criterion referenced score reporting.
- Standards-based assessment practices have expanded the notion of interpreting test performance in relation to performance levels and descriptions to incorporate consideration of the content standards to which test items are aligned (e.g., Porter, 2002).
- Haertel & Lorié (2004) have proposed a conceptual framework for validity arguments that support standards-based score interpretations. The framework explicitly unifies all elements of achievement testing—the content standards that are targeted by a test, test content and item formats, standard setting, test score validation, and test score interpretation.
- Commercial test developers and niche companies (e.g., the Grow Network; see http://info.grow.net/grow.html) emphasize score reporting in a number of ways. They now offer color reports with high-quality graphics, Web-based score reporting, and customized reports that link curriculum recommendations and materials to student performance on state and other achievement assessments.
- Kane's work (this volume) and other work on validity evidence and argumentation for intended test score interpretations reinforce the preeminence of test score interpretation in validity theory and validation practice. (See also the *Standards for Educational and Psychological Testing*,[4] chap. 1.)

The *Standards* require testing program managers to provide score reports that are "understandable to the test taker and others" (standard 11.6) and "appropriate interpretations" of test score information (standard 5.10) but place most of the responsibility with test users, not necessarily test developers.

These developments and efforts represent significant refinements in the quality of score reports and reporting, especially in terms of aligning test score interpretation to content and performance standards. The National Council on Measurement in Education has used external funding to develop and validate materials to train teachers in interpreting and communicating test results (Plake, Impara, & Wise, 1997). However, the (limited) research on score reporting "shows confusion among policymakers, educators, and the public over the meaning and interpretation of large scale assessment results" (Goodman & Hambleton, 2004, p. 146). It is not clear that recent developments and efforts will alleviate this confusion.

Score reporting is conducted as one-way communication in which score reports and score interpretation guides transmit information about test performance, and teachers, parents, and students receive the information. Other models of human communication explicitly include the receiver's role in making meaning of the information that is transmitted (e.g., Berko, Wolvin, & Wolvin, 1998, pp. 17–21). School staff can provide two-way communication with students and their families. But it seems unlikely that interpretation of achievement assessment information would get significant attention in parent-teacher and student conferences. Other fields, such as public health, use social marketing techniques (e.g., Lefebvre & Rochlin, 1997) to convey information and change behavior. Continuing emphasis on score reporting as both an information communication function and a change agent for individual students and schools may provide additional dividends.

3. THE LANDSCAPE: K–12 ASSESSMENTS AND ASSESSMENT PROGRAMS

3.1. Introduction

Having discussed purposes for K–12 achievement assessments and score reporting, we now turn to K–12 assessment programs and the types of tests that appear in those programs. In this section we describe 10 types of achievement tests used to assess students in kindergarten through high school and summarize the interpretations and uses intended for each type. Following that, we describe general features of state assessment programs. Our goal is to illustrate and comment on the current state of the art in assessing individual achievement in grades K–12.

3.1.1. A Brief and Selective History of Externally Mandated Achievement Testing

Table 16.1 provides a highly selective portrayal of the evolutionary history of K–12 achievement testing since its modern beginnings (arguably) in the 1920s. Our goal is to give a sense of that evolution and to provide a broad context for ensuing descriptions, discussions, and evaluations. Modern K–12 achievement testing has its beginnings in two developments in the 1920s (see Nitko, 1983, inside back cover): (a) Commercial achievement test publishers and developers opened for business (i.e., Psychological Corporation, California Test Bureau), and (b) the first of the major achievement tests became available (i.e., Stanford Achievement Test, Iowa Every Pupil Examination). Two phases are evident in the evolution of purposes and uses for K–12 educational achievement assessments:

- Use of commercially developed standardized norm referenced achievement tests, selected primarily by local school systems

TABLE 16.1 Decades of K–12 Achievement Testing

Main Features of Achievement Testing	Coincidental and Precipitating Activities
1920s through 1970s: Use of commercial norm referenced achievement tests	
Achievement tests provide information on student, classroom, school, and school system achievement	1954: In *Brown vs. Board of Education*, the U.S. Supreme Court determines that "separate educational facilities are inherently unequal"
Developed by commercial publishers; adopted primarily by school systems, later by states for statewide use	1955: The National Education Association releases *Technical Recommendations for Achievement Tests*
Some specialized applications (e.g., special education diagnostic tests)	1957: The Soviet Union launches *Sputnik*; the United States has fallen behind in science, mathematics, and technology
	1965: The Elementary and Secondary Education Act (ESEA) triples federal education spending to supplement the education of economically disadvantaged children and improve their achievement
	1969: The first administration of the National Assessment of Educational Progress (NAEP)
	1974: In *Lau vs. Nichols*, the U.S. Supreme court establishes education rights of English language learners
	1975: Public Law 94-142 requires a Free Appropriate Public Education for school age children with disabilities
1980s: Rise of minimum competency tests and statewide assessment programs	
Minimum competency tests administered in state assessment programs are intended to ensure that high school graduates have mastered basic skills; passing becomes a high school graduation requirement in some states	Test scores are reported publicly; schools and school systems are publicly accountable for student achievement
	Racial/ethnic subgroup performance differences are reported publicly
Essay tests come into wide use	Ensuring that students master basic skills in language arts and mathematics prior to high school graduation comes to the forefront as a public issue
Use of commercial norm referenced tests continues	1981: President Ronald Reagan reduces federal education categorical funding by providing block grants to states, enabling state departments of education to expand their role in monitoring student achievement
	1983: The National Commission on Excellence in Education produces its report, *A Nation At Risk*, citing a "rising tide of mediocrity" in American education
	1989: The National Council of Teachers of Mathematics releases *Curriculum and Evaluation Standards for School Mathematics*, which emphasizes conceptual understanding and problem solving
1990s: Proliferation of assessment approaches and purposes in statewide assessment programs	
Performance-based assessments (i.e., use of constructed-response items) expand into state content area assessments	Incorporating higher-order thinking skills (i.e., "HOTS") into curriculum and assessments comes to the forefront in debates about education
High school exit examinations begin to supplant minimum competency tests	Educational reform, school improvement, and raising expectations for achievement of all students come to the forefront as a public issue
States and school systems require end-of-course examinations for selected high school courses	1991: President George H. W. Bush calls for *American Achievement Tests* in grades 4, 8, and 12 in five content areas
	1997: President Bill Clinton initiates *Voluntary National Tests* in grade 4 reading and grade 8 mathematics
	1997: Reauthorization of the *Individuals with Disabilities Education Act* (IDEA) strengthens academic expectations and accountability for disabled students; test administration accommodations and alternate assessments become a requirement to enable participation of students with disabilities in state assessment programs

(continued)

TABLE 16.1 (*continued*)

MAIN FEATURES OF ACHIEVEMENT TESTING

2000s: Era of *No Child Left Behind* testing and reporting requirements

President George W. Bush signs the *No Child Left Behind (NCLB) Act of 2002*

States and schools must:
- Implement annual student assessments in reading and mathematics in grades 3–8 and high school and in science
- Demonstrate annual progress in raising the percentage of students who are proficient in reading and mathematics and narrow the test score gap between advantaged and disadvantaged students

All students must be included in state content area assessments
- Test administration accommodations continue to be important; attention to the needs of English language learners, as well as students with disabilities, is emphasized
- States must provide alternate assessments for students with significant cognitive disabilities

English proficiency of English language learners must be assessed and reported annually

- Development of state-specific assessments, supplemented in some cases by local school system curriculum embedded assessments

3.1.2. Types of K–12 Educational Achievement Tests

Table 16.2 summarizes the most prevalent types of K–12 educational achievement assessments. We provide the table to document the current landscape of K–12 achievement assessment. It is convenient to refer to *types* of assessments (e.g., content area achievement surveys), even if it is more meaningful to discuss intended interpretations of test scores for specified decisions and actions. The test types included here are not exhaustive. This classification of test types is not exclusive, as is true for many typologies. Table 16.2 organizes test types into three groups of primary intended uses: (a) Draw summative conclusions about the level and pace of student achievement, (b) draw formative or diagnostic conclusions about student achievement in an academic content area or other school related areas, and (c) make decisions about selection, placement, and continuation in special programs and services. These groupings are based on ideas from Millman and Greene (1989, p. 336).

Some general observations are warranted about the test types listed. First, many of these test types are designed for group administration (e.g., content area achievement surveys). Others are designed for individual administration (e.g., some academic area achievement and diagnostic assessments, school readiness assessments). Educators, families, the general public, and policymakers are the audience for test scores intended for informing summative conclusions. In addition, educators most often use test scores intended to guide formative conclusions and to make selection, placement, and continuation decisions. Finally, some of the assessment types in Table 16.2 are not, strictly speaking, assessments of achievement in academic content areas. Specifically, school readiness, special education diagnostic, and gifted and talented screening assessments serve purposes beyond describing a student's current level of achievement. We include them here because they provide information related to past and future achievement and because they are used in conjunction with achievement information for making decisions about instruction.

What conclusions can be drawn about K–12 individual achievement testing on the basis of Table 16.2? First, test types exist to provide information on most academic program functions of K–12 education and on virtually all students. In addition, test types have been devised to serve major social and educational policy concerns that have arisen over the years. For example:

- Are students learning the academic content that schools deliver? Is that level of achievement satisfactory? Are all students (e.g., students from economically disadvantaged backgrounds) achieving at satisfactory levels?
- Are students leaving K–12 education well prepared for post secondary education and training and the world of work?
- Are students with special instructional needs receiving the instructional services that they need? Are they afforded opportunities to learn rigorous academic content?

3.2. Types of Educational Achievement Assessments

In this section we describe details on the test types summarized in Table 16.2. The descriptions address purposes and intended uses, test design, and content. The descriptions also include examples of each test type and some details on who develops the tests, the grade levels they target, item formats, psychometrics, score interpretation, and other relevant features. We do not evaluate each type of test individually. In subsequent sections we evaluate K–12 educational achievement testing in general, in terms of assessment items and design and reliability and validity of achievement test score interpretations and uses.

3.2.1. Content Area Achievement Surveys

Content area achievement surveys are perhaps the best known, most widely and longest used of large-scale achievement assessments in grades K–12. They include custom developed state assessments and commercial, off-the-shelf, norm referenced tests. Virtually everyone who has attended

TABLE 16.2 Types of K–12 Achievement Tests and Intended Interpretations, Uses, Content Area Targets, and Decisions for Individual Students

Test Type	Intended Interpretations and Content Area Targets	Intended Decisions
Primary intended use: Draw summative conclusions about level and pace of student achievement		
1. Content area achievement surveys	Is this student achieving at a satisfactory level and pace? Typically, state content area standards (available from state departments of education and their Web sites)	Decisions related to the student's curriculum and instruction
Examples (a) Statewide assessments in reading, writing, mathematics, science, and social studies (b) Commercial norm referenced tests such as the Iowa Tests of Basic Skills and Iowa Tests of Educational Development (Riverside Publishing), the Stanford Achievement Tests (Harcourt Assessment), and TerraNova (CTB McGraw-Hill). Schools and school systems may use these tests as published or states may work with the publisher to augment them with additional items to improve alignment with state content standards		
2. End-of-course examinations	Has this student learned enough of the course content standards to receive course credit or a specific course grade? Typically, state content standards for a high school course or a course syllabus or objectives	Student receives or does not receive credit for a course (if other requirements are met), receives a specific grade in a course, or a course grade is weighted by the test score
Examples (a) End-of-course exams in four states in, for example, English I, algebra I, biology, and U.S. history (b) Commercially produced tests that correspond to typical high school courses (c) Advanced Placement and International Baccalaureate examinations		
3. High school exit examinations, minimum competency tests, and grade promotion tests	Has this student achieved at a level high enough to receive a high school diploma or to be promoted to the next grade? State content standards	Student is eligible or not eligible to receive a high school diploma or for grade promotion (if other requirements are met)
Example Standards-based high school exit exams in reading, writing, and mathematics		
4. Alternate assessments for students with significant cognitive disabilities	Is this significantly cognitively disabled student achieving at a satisfactory level and pace? State alternate content and achievement standards	Decisions related to the student's curriculum and instruction
Example Alternate assessment portfolios developed by states		
Primary intended use: Draw formative or diagnostic conclusions about student achievement in an academic content area or other school related areas		
5. Curriculum embedded assessments	Has this student achieved curriculum goals addressed during instruction? Learning goals for a unit of instruction	Decisions about remedial instruction for individual students or an entire group or class
Examples (a) Chapter and unit tests provided with curriculum materials (b) Curriculum-based measurement procedures used in special education		
6. Academic area achievement and diagnostic assessments	Is this student achieving adequately in the targeted academic area?	Decisions related to the student's curriculum and instruction

(continued)

TABLE 16.2 (continued)

TEST TYPE	INTENDED INTERPRETATIONS AND CONTENT AREA TARGETS	INTENDED DECISIONS
	Content objectives specified for the particular test	
Examples		
Content area assessments available in commercial test publisher catalogues and listed in the *Mental Measurements Yearbooks*		
7. School readiness assessments	Has this student developed adequate levels of academic, behavioral, social, and other skills to succeed in kindergarten? What supports and services will this child need to succeed in school?	Student may receive special services (e.g., all-day kindergarten) or may be screened for special education or other services
	Academic (typically literacy and mathematics concepts and skills), behavioral, and social skills considered necessary to benefit from and succeed in kindergarten	
Examples		
(a) Norm referenced readiness assessments available from commercial publishers		
(b) Standardized observational assessments such as the Work Sampling System		

Primary intended use: Make decisions about selection, placement, and continuation in special programs and services

8. Special education diagnostic assessments	Does this student exhibit evidence of a specific learning disability or other cognitive disability that may impede learning and, thus, meet the diagnostic criteria to qualify for special education services?	Student will or will not receive or continue to receive special education or 504 services
	Instructional activities and interactions in mainstream classrooms (with or without special education support services)	
Example		
Woodcock-Johnson Psycho-Educational Battery-Revised		
9. English language proficiency and screening assessments	Is this student's English proficiency in reading, listening, writing, and speaking sufficient to enable him or her to benefit from instruction delivered in English?	Student will receive content area instruction in English-only classrooms (with or without native language supports)
	Content area instructional activities and interactions in English-only classrooms (with or without native language supports)	Student may or may not continue to receive additional instruction to develop English language proficiency
Examples		
(a) The English Language Development Assessment (ELDA)		
(b) English proficiency assessments available from commercial test publishers		
10. Gifted and talented screening instruments and procedures	Which students may be eligible for gifted and talented services and programs? Is this student eligible for the specific gifted and talented services and programs available?	Student is eligible for specific services and programs
	Instructional and developmental outcomes targeted by specific instructional services and programs	
Example		
Intelligence and aptitude tests, achievement tests, teacher recommendations and structured observations, parent recommendations and structured observations, self-assessments by older students, and student products and performances relevant to specific programs and services (e.g., in the arts)		

school in the United States during grades K–12 has taken one of these tests, such as the "Iowas" (i.e., Iowa Tests of Basic Skills) and the "CAT" (California Achievement Tests). The primary purpose and intended use of content area surveys is to determine and describe a student's achievement of a fairly broad range of content. Additional purposes and intended uses may include determining eligibility for grade promotion and high school graduation (see section 3.2.2 below) and indicating areas of relative strength and weakness within a content area (see section 3.2.6 below).

Custom state assessments are developed by state departments of education, most often in conjunction with test development and services companies. In 2001–02, 34 states administered custom developed content area assessments (see Council of Chief State School Officers, 2003, chart 2–9). Some states implemented custom developed achievement surveys as early as the late 1970s. State-specific achievement surveys are developed in alignment with state-specific content standards. They are likely to include multiple-choice items, short constructed-response items, extended constructed-response items (e.g., essay prompts to assess writing skill), and sometimes grid-in items in mathematics (i.e., constructed-response items for which examinees "bubble in" a numerical or other response rather than select from response options). The goal of including a variety of item formats is to represent the range of knowledge and skills in a content area, encourage teachers to teach a range of content area knowledge and skills, and to avoid "multiple-choice teaching." States also use "augmented NRTs"; that is, commercial norm referenced tests with additional state-specific items that provide more complete alignment with state content standards. Student achievement typically is reported on test-specific score scales and in relation to performance levels with accompanying performance level descriptions. (See section 2 for details.)

Commercial norm referenced tests (NRTs) are developed and marketed to state and public school systems primarily by three commercial test companies: CTB McGraw-Hill, Harcourt Assessment, and Riverside Publishing (in conjunction with the Iowa Testing Program at the University of Iowa). Commercial NRTs provide broad coverage of content and skills in reading, language arts, mathematics, science, social studies, and other areas (e.g., writing and study skills) that appear in virtually all state curriculum frameworks and content standards—hence the label content area "surveys." Usually, they include a primary multiple-choice component with optional add-on sections of short and longer constructed-response items. (See examples of multiple-choice and constructed-response items in section 4 of this chapter.) Typically, commercial norm referenced tests are available for grades kindergarten through 12 and are vertically scaled so that growth in individual student achievement can be tracked on a score scale that is intended to represent achievement across all grades. Individual examinee achievement typically is reported as percentile scores based on nationally representative samples, grade equivalent scores, and test-specific scale scores. Many provide subscale scores referenced to groups of objectives within content areas (e.g., a score for mathematics computation within the mathematics assessment). (See section 2.2 for a discussion of score scales and score types.)

3.2.2. High School Exit Examinations, Minimum Competency Tests, and Grade Promotion Tests

Students in 20 states are required to pass high school exit examinations (i.e., standards-based, high school exit, and minimum competency examinations; Center on Education Policy, 2004, Figure 1) in order to be eligible for a high school diploma. High school exit examinations are intended to ensure that students who receive a high school diploma have acquired basic concepts and skills in key academic areas by the time they leave high school. High school exit examinations cover a range of content standards in an academic area rather than the contents of a specific high school course (e.g., 20 states in English language arts and mathematics, 10 in science, 9 in social studies in 2004; Center on Education Policy, 2004, Figure 3). High school exit examinations implemented in recent years cover more challenging content than their predecessors, minimum competency tests used for high school graduation, which were first implemented in the late 1970s and early 1980s (e.g., Jaeger & Tittle, 1980). They include multiple-choice items, short and extended constructed-response items, and essay prompts (Center on Education Policy, 2004, Figure 4). States typically develop state-specific exit examinations. They typically are administered initially in grades 10 or 11. Students who fail on the first attempt are provided multiple opportunities to retake tests. Student performance is reported in terms of passing or failing the test. Additional performance levels and subscale information may be provided to guide review work for students who have failed an administration and are preparing to retake a test.

States and some school systems began implementing minimum competency tests in the late 1970s and early 1980s to assess students' acquisition of basic skills and to ensure that student achievement of those skills reached a minimally acceptable level prior to receiving a high school diploma. (See Michaels & Ferrara, 1999, for a more detailed discussion.) Most often, minimum competency tests have been used as high school exit examinations, but they also have been used to determine student eligibility—thought of as readiness—for promotion to the next grade level. Essay tests, which typically require students to write one or two essays that may require 20–60 minutes each, set the stage for the introduction of performance assessments into state assessment programs in the 1990s. During the 1990s, and partly in response to pressures to help students acquire and demonstrate their acquisition of "higher order thinking skills," many minimum competency tests were supplanted by more challenging high school exit examinations and end-of-course examinations (e.g., Center for Education Policy, 2004, p. 7).

3.2.3. High School End-of-Course Examinations

Responsibility for high school course final examinations and course grades in the United States traditionally has rested with individual teachers or departments within high schools. State assessment programs began to introduce high school end-of-course examinations beginning in 2000 as a means of encouraging high schools and teachers to incorporate rigorous state content standards into specified courses. As of 2004, end-of-course examination programs in four states were required for grade 9 or 10 English, algebra, biology, government, U.S. history, global history, and geography (Center for Education Policy, 2004, Table 7). State end-of-course examination scores are incorporated into course final grades, to help standardize course grading. They also have been planned as high school graduation requirements.

In addition to end-of-course examinations administered to all students, schools offer assessments that cap special programs of instruction, such as Advanced Placement courses and the International Baccalaureate program. These programs expand typical high school curriculum by providing advanced and demanding high school coursework. The College Board develops more than 30 Advanced Placement (AP) examinations in 20 content areas (see http://www.collegeboard.com/student/testing/ap/about.html). They assess the contents of course syllabi delivered over a school year to high school students. AP examinations contain multiple-choice questions and a free-response section (i.e., an essay or an extended problem to solve); the Studio Art examination is a portfolio. Students who score high enough (3 or 4 out of a possible 5) on AP examinations can receive course credit from the colleges they attend after high school graduation. Over 1,200 secondary education programs worldwide offer an International Baccalaureate (IB) diploma, granted by the International Baccalaureate Organization (see http://www.ibo.org/ibo/index.cfm?page=/ibo&language=EN) when students complete a two-year curriculum and meet performance standards in a rigorous assessment system. Students select courses in each of six areas (i.e., literature, foreign language, social science, experimental science, mathematics and computer science, and the arts) each year. Assessment components required of IB diploma candidates worldwide include standardized assessments with a wide range of item types (i.e., small numbers of multiple-choice items, short response questions, structured problem solving questions, open-ended problem solving questions, essay questions, data analysis questions, case studies, and commentaries on supplied texts) and extended projects (e.g., music investigations, theory of knowledge essays). Teachers score the classroom assessments they develop; scores are moderated by the International Baccalaureate Organization.

3.2.4. Alternate Assessments

Alternate assessments are designed to assess academic and other skills (e.g., life skills such as using vending machines) acquired by students with the most significant and limiting cognitive disabilities (which often are accompanied by physical disabilities as well). Most students with significant cognitive disabilities (estimated at approximately 1% of all enrolled students) cannot participate meaningfully in statewide content area assessments required for all other students. Alternate assessments provide the opportunity for them to participate in statewide standards-based assessments that are appropriate and meaningful. Alternate assessments have proliferated since they became a requirement in the reauthorization of the Individuals with Disabilities Education Act (IDEA) in 1997 (e.g., Hitchcock, Meyer, Rose, & Jackson, 2002). Early versions of alternate assessments generally focused on life skills, with some attention to skills in reading and mathematics. *No Child Left Behind* requires all states to provide alternate assessments in reading, mathematics, and science knowledge and skills that are linked meaningfully to grade level content standards (i.e., in grades 3–8 and high school) in reading, mathematics, and science. The predominant approaches to alternate assessment have involved teacher judgments of student achievement using rating scales and checklists, assessing progress on goals from student individual educational plans (IEPs), and assessment portfolios. In recent years, and because of evidence indicating that the psychometric rigor of these approaches has been inadequate, other approaches have been implemented. These approaches include larger performance tasks referred to as "performance events" (e.g., a theme-based task in mathematics with 15–20 activities) and smaller performance tasks with summative rating scales.

3.2.5. Curriculum Embedded Assessments

We use the term "curriculum embedded" assessments to refer to a range of assessment activities that focus on student learning in K–12 classrooms. They are intended to provide information on learning in the classroom on an ongoing basis to guide teachers in adjusting instruction. Web-based searches (using the terms curriculum embedded and curriculum based in conjunction with assessment and measurement) return large numbers of documents and journal articles. The results address assessment of young children (i.e., preschool through grade 2), students in special education, and students at risk of failing in school. We also consider here (a) chapter tests, project ideas, and other assessment activities that accompany commercial curriculum materials and textbooks, (b) assessment ideas included in school system curriculum guides, (c) assessments implemented by local school systems to monitor student progress in relation to school system curricula, and (d) teachers' own classroom assessment activities. Curriculum embedded assessments are activities that are conducted as part of the teaching-learning process and that are intended to be closely aligned with school system curriculum guides and classroom instructional activities. It seems reasonable to conclude that curriculum embedded assessments comprise a considerably large percentage of the time devoted to assessing achievement in grades K–12.

Often, curriculum embedded assessments include a wider range of item types and assessment approaches than do other large-scale K–12 assessments. Administration, scoring, and use of curriculum embedded assessments in instructional decision making may be closely managed by a school system or teachers may be afforded significant latitude. Some school systems develop and require use of curriculum embedded assessments as a supplement to both state assessments and teachers' classroom assessment activities. Typically, school system curriculum embedded assessments are administered and scored by teachers in the classroom. The psychometric quality of curriculum embedded assessments—and validity of inferences about student achievement as the result of instruction—are determined in large measure by general design features of the assessment, the fidelity of alignment of the assessment activities to curriculum and instruction goals, and the rigor with which teachers administer, score, and use the assessments. Nitko (2004) observes that questions in textbook-based tests tend to focus on low-level cognitive skills (p. 372). Teacher classroom assessment is addressed in detail by Shepard (this volume). The measurement literature on curriculum embedded assessment practices and quality is nearly nonexistent, despite the large number of references available via the Web and literature searches.

3.2.6. Academic Area Achievement and Diagnostic Assessments

Academic area achievement and diagnostic assessments are available for a wide range of subjects and grade levels. These assessments focus on specific academic content areas such as reading, writing, mathematics, science, social studies, fine arts, and foreign languages. They are distinct from content area achievement surveys (see section 3.2.1.) in at least three ways: (a) Typically, they are not closely aligned with state content standards or school system curricula but, instead, assess achievement in a general or specific academic subject (e.g., written expression, numeration and computation) and provide information on relative strengths and weaknesses; (b) some are individually administered and scored by the administrator rather than group administered; and (c) they may be selected for use by a school system, school, or individual teacher rather than required by a state or school system. In general, they are available commercially rather than custom designed and developed.

The term "diagnostic" may call to mind a medical model of diagnosis and prescription leading to alleviating symptoms or curing an illness. Nitko (1989) points out that commercial diagnostic assessments provide information on learning goals that are not achieved, but not on the causes of the failure to achieve them. Web and literature searches on academic area diagnostic assessments provide little evidence of advancements in identifying such causes. Nitko (1989) also provides a detailed review of five approaches to diagnostic assessment and proposes them for instructional use (pp. 455–465).

3.2.7. School Readiness Assessments

School readiness assessments—that is, assessments of a child's preparedness to function successfully and benefit from kindergarten—have received much attention over the years from educators of young children and relatively little from the educational measurement community at large. Conceptions of school readiness and domains for readiness assessment are broad. Readiness domains include health and physical, social and emotional, language and literacy, and cognitive development (Niemeyer & Scott-Little, 2001, p. 4) and the preparedness of schools to educate all children who are eligible by age for kindergarten. A National Education Goals Panel report (Shepard, Kagan, & Wurtz, 1998) identifies five purposes for assessing young children, including to help teachers adapt teaching and improve learning and to identify children for subsequent evaluation for special services. The report recommends against high-stakes assessment of children until they reach the end of 3rd grade (p. 54). In 2002, at least 17 states required assessment of school readiness of kindergarten students; six states required assessments to gauge school readiness statewide (see Quality Counts, 2002, p. 66).

School readiness assessments fall generally into two approaches: naturalistic approaches and standardized, norm referenced assessments (Maxwell & Clifford, 2004). Typically, data collection involves observation in settings or individual assessment, either just before or soon after children enter kindergarten. A review of state pre-kindergarten evaluation reports identified 42 different readiness assessments in use in 13 state evaluations of preschool programs during 1997–1998 (Gilliam & Zigler, 2000). Niemeyer and Scott-Little (2001) provide a review of commercially available school readiness instruments. Information about the psychometric quality of these instruments is limited primarily to reliability estimates and concurrent validity correlation coefficients; predictive and classification accuracy information is not widely provided. The news on readiness assessment practices in most local school systems is not good (Shepard, 1997). According to Mashburn and Henry (2004):

> Current practices of assessing young children have evolved from a legacy of questionable practices and objectionable uses to a search for ways to assess young children appropriately that contribute to accountability for external audiences and improving programs and instruction. (p. 17)

3.2.8. Special Education Diagnostic Assessments

Schools have been required to provide special education services for students with a range of school-related cognitive and other disabilities since the passage of *Education for All Handicapped Children Act* (Public Law 94–142), in 1975. *The Individuals with Disabilities Education Improvement Act of 2004* (IDEA) identifies 10 categories of disabilities that may make students eligible for special education services in kindergarten through grade 12 (see http://www.ed.gov/policy/speced/guid/idea/idea2004.html). Cognitive disability categories include mild to moderate learning disabilities and mild to significant cognitive disabilities (mental retardation). Diagnostic assessments of achievement in school curriculum areas (see section 3.2.6 above) play a significant role in identifying disabilities and determining eligibility for a range of services under IDEA and Section 504 of the *Rehabilitation, Comprehensive Services, and Developmental Disabilities Act of 1978* (see http://www.firstgov.gov/).

Special education diagnostic assessments are used to refer students to formal special education evaluation processes; determine existence of a disability that interferes with learning; determine eligibility for services; plan services, including specification of goals for an Individualized Educational Plan (IEP); and reevaluate students. Special education teachers also use informal assessment procedures to monitor student progress in relation to IEP goals. Curriculum-based assessment approaches (or curriculum-based measurement; see Fuchs, Fuchs, Hosp, & Hamlett, 2003) play a significant role in monitoring progress and targeting instruction for students in special education. Special education diagnosticians have used a range of formal assessments to identify the presence and absence of a range of cognitive disabilities. In assessing students for special education, diagnosticians typically integrate results from achievement, behavioral, developmental, intelligence and aptitude, neuropsychological and sensory-motor, and speech and hearing assessments. Identification of the existence of specific learning disabilities usually is based on a discrepancy between achievement test scores and school aptitude or intelligence scores. The existence and degree of cognitive disabilities (e.g., mental retardation) is determined primarily based on intelligence test scores. Inappropriate selection, use, and interpretation of measures used to diagnose learning disabilities documented more than 20 years ago (e.g., Shepard, 1983) appear enduring (e.g., Keogh & MacMillan, 1996).

3.2.9. English Language Proficiency Assessments

English language screening and proficiency assessments have been implemented in states with large English language learner populations to identify students whose English is limited, to monitor their progress toward full English proficiency, and to determine when students are ready to benefit from content area instruction in English. Under *No Child Left Behind*, states must ensure that local school systems administer annual assessments of English language proficiency that are aligned with state English language development standards. Chalhoub-Deville and Deville (this volume) address second language testing extensively.

3.2.10. Gifted and Talented Screening Instruments and Procedures

The responsibility in K–12 public education to provide appropriate services for gifted and talented students came to the forefront in the late 1960s. The purposes for identifying and providing special educational services for school age children with high potential are to (a) provide such students with opportunities to develop their cognitive potential and seek fulfillment, and (b) increase the U.S. reservoir of talent to produce solutions to society's problems as well as apply existing solutions (Renzulli, 1999). These purposes are rooted in philosophies of universal education and early goals of intelligence testing. Renzulli (1999) identifies two types of giftedness: "school house" giftedness and "creative-productive" giftedness. School house giftedness refers to learning in school and is most easily assessed using standardized tests. Creative-productive talent is not as easily assessed, in part because constructs and evaluative criteria are difficult to define for assessment purposes and because an individual's creativity and productivity vary across time and situations. The National Association for Gifted Children (NAGC) defines a gifted person as "someone who shows, or has the potential for showing, an exceptional level of performance in one or more areas of expression" (National Association for Gifted Children, 2005a). NAGC also quotes the federal definition of gifted students, which indicates giftedness in intellectual, creative, artistic, leadership, and specific academic areas.

Not surprisingly, no single type of instrument or procedure exists to identify gifted and talented students or to monitor development of their identified gifts and talents. Identification and monitoring require broad approaches to assessment, both standardized and informal. School systems may require or consider information from intelligence and aptitude tests, achievement tests, teacher recommendations and structured observations, parent recommendations and structured observations, self-assessments by older students, and student products and performances relevant to specific programs and services (e.g., in the arts). Assessment purposes in gifted education include broad searches to identify potentially gifted and talented students; screening to identify eligible students, specify their strengths and weaknesses, and match them to appropriate programs and services; and monitoring the appropriateness of program placements and progress. Students may be identified for enrichment programs in specific areas (e.g., writing, mathematics, leadership, visual and performing arts) or readiness for acceleration (e.g., skipping a grade, starting college early; see Colangelo, Assouline, & Gross, 2004). The field acknowledges that no single measure can serve all or any one of these purposes. Leaders in the field call for gathering information for identifying gifted and talented students from multiple sources (e.g., families, teachers, students themselves, and others), different ways of assessing (e.g., observation, nomination, performances, products, portfolios, and interviews), and from settings in and outside of school (National Association of Gifted Children, 2005b). Problems in identification (Coleman, 2003) include disproportionate representation (i.e., under-representation of students from linguistically, culturally, and economically disadvantaged backgrounds), disregard of theories of intelligence (i.e., using only IQ scores and narrow views of gifts and talents), inappropriate use of statistical formulas (e.g., creation of composite scores that increase rather than reduce disproportionality), and mismatching students with services (e.g., use of visual-spatial measures to identify students for highly verbal programs). Lewis (2001) cites evidence of the promise of nonverbal standardized measures that assess problem solving using graphical figures to identify students from linguistically, culturally, and economically disadvantaged backgrounds for gifted and talented services. NAGC acknowledges the need for expertise in using standardized tests for identification and placement and to seek "comprehensive assessment alternatives" (National Association for Gifted Children, 2005b).

3.3. Features of K–12 Statewide Assessment Programs

Descriptions of K–12 assessments have been fairly general to this point. To bring some concreteness to our characterization of the state of the art, we now provide some detail on statewide assessment programs. It is relatively straightforward to summarize the most salient features of state assessment programs using the State Student Assessment Programs (SSAP) Annual Survey Summary Report. The most recent version is the 2001–2002 survey, which provides a database and descriptive report of the use of content area and other assessments in each state. The Council of Chief State School officers surveyed assessment programs in all 50 states and seven U.S. jurisdictions. (See Council of Chief State School Officers, 2003, chap. 2 for details.) We summarize some of the most salient features of state assessment programs as of 2002. We note that these results reflect state and jurisdiction assessment programs in transition, as they began to implement components of *No Child Left Behind* testing requirements.

1. Statewide census assessments (i.e., administrations including all eligible students) were administered in 46 of 57 states and jurisdictions in grade 4, 51 states and jurisdictions in grade 8, and 44 states and jurisdictions in grade 10.[5] Between 32 and 40 states and jurisdictions administered assessments in grades 3–11 (excluding grades 4, 8, and 10). Three states administered statewide assessments at kindergarten, 7 at grade 1, and 12 at grades 2. The emphasis on testing in grades 4, 8, and 10 and limited testing in grades K–3 are consistent with the organization of schooling. Grade 4 is commonly considered a transition grade in which young children, who require extensive teacher support to develop basic academic skills and productive school behaviors, are required to be more independent learners who acquire much of their learning through reading. Grade 8 is the point at which students complete elementary and middle school education and prepare for the transition to secondary education. Grade 10 is a winnowing grade at which students select higher-level college preparatory courses or courses that may prepare them for other postsecondary activities. Grade 10 also often is selected as the first time to administer high school exit examinations. The small numbers of states and jurisdictions that required student assessments in grades K–3 is consistent with popular and official views (see Shepard, Kagan, & Wurtz, 1998).

2. In 2002, 54 of the 57 states and jurisdictions reported using state assessments for instructional purposes, 51 reported school accountability purposes, and 39 reported individual student accountability purposes. The large numbers of states and jurisdictions using assessments to account for outcomes of educational inputs reflect the educational accountability and reform movements of the 1980s and 1990s.

3. Language arts/reading and mathematics were assessed by the most states (54 states and jurisdictions in each area), followed by writing (47), science (41), and social studies (33). These numbers reflect relative curricular emphases around the United States and probably the influence of imminent *No Child Left Behind* testing requirements.

4. Fifty of the states and jurisdictions reported involvement of commercial test publishers and other testing companies to deliver or support development and implementation of state assessment programs. States and jurisdictions relied heavily on commercial test publishers' off-the-shelf norm referenced tests; 39 states and jurisdictions used off-the-shelf or customized off-the-shelf tests.

5. Forty reported using direct writing assessments, 19 using performance assessments (in which students produce a response rather than select one), and 3 using portfolios assessments (not including alternate assessments for students with significant cognitive disabilities). Multiple-choice items were the most widely used item format (in 54 states and jurisdictions), followed by extended constructed-response items (46) and short constructed-response or fill-in-the-blank items (39). Smaller numbers of states and jurisdictions reported using examples of student work (10) and hands-on performance tasks (10).

Statewide K–12 achievement assessment programs vary widely, even if they do influence one another and were influenced by similar external pressures. Although state assessment programs arose in part because of Reagan era block grant funding, and although *No Child Left Behind* requires testing in specified grades and content areas, both federal policies provide considerable latitude to states regarding achievement testing. States are likely to continue to vary widely on the content and performance standards in reading, mathematics, and science they assess; the ongoing use of writing assessments; and the role of the state in assessing social studies achievement. In addition, many large urban and affluent suburban school systems have implemented their own curriculum embedded K–12 assessment programs to fulfill local school system information needs. Many of these programs are likely to continue into the future.

3.4. Selected Issues in K–12 Achievement Testing

To this point, we have described the K–12 achievement testing landscape. We did comment on some features of the landscape along the way. In other sections of this chapter we have been more analytic about K–12 achievement testing and have provided evaluative observations. Here we comment on the state of the art in K–12 achievement testing by acknowledging selected current and ongoing issues in the field. Our selection and treatment of the issues is representative rather than exhaustive.

3.4.1. Issues Surrounding Test Administration Conditions and Interpretation of Test Performance

One of the most salient issues in K–12 achievement testing in recent years has been the debate about use of tests for high-stakes decisions (e.g., National Research Council, 1999). High-stakes decisions make a difference in the schooling and lives of students in grade K–12. They include decisions about grade promotion and high school graduation, inclusion in special instructional programs (e.g., special education), and access to rigorous academic content and high expectations (e.g., counseling students about course selection in high school). High-stakes testing is considered potentially harmful and may induce anxiety that inhibits optimal test performance. It may also produce negative effects on the curriculum that teachers deliver to students. On the other hand, some students may not be motivated to give their best effort on tests that do not matter to them (i.e., low-stakes tests).

Test administration accommodations and testing modifications also have been salient issues since the 1990s. Test administration accommodations are provided in state and other achievement assessments for students with disabilities and students whose English proficiency is limited. Accommodations are intended to reduce impediments to optimal test performance posed by disabilities and language limitations without changing the knowledge and skill requirements targeted by the items on a test—that is, without changing the targeted achievement construct. Reducing these impediments without altering the achievement construct enables valid inferences from test scores about what examinees know and can do that are comparable to inferences about examinees that do not need such accommodations. Accommodations such as reading mathematics test items aloud to students with reading disabilities and permitting English language learners to use English-first language glossaries are believed not to alter testing conditions enough to alter the achievement construct that is assessed. Modifications to test content and test administration conditions—for example, reading passages aloud to examinees on a reading comprehension test—are believed to alter the achievement construct that is assessed. The veracity of these beliefs is crucially important, of course. Accommodations and modifications that alter the targeted achievement construct introduce construct irrelevance and undermine the comparability of score interpretations compared to those of other examinees. A synthesis of 46 studies of a range of test administration accommodations indicates that accommodations related to timing of test administrations (e.g., time extensions) do not alter the comparability of items; however, accommodations involving computer administrations of tests, oral presentation of items, and administration of items using sign language did alter the comparability of items in some studies (Thompson, Blount, & Thurlow, 2002).

The rapidly expanding availability of affordable digital devices (e.g., laptops and personal digital assistants, or PDAs), psychometric and automated scoring software (see Shermis & Burstein, 2003), and accessibility to the Internet have amplified the importance of comparability of paper-pencil and computer-based testing. Some studies suggest that interpretations of results from the same achievement test given in paper-pencil and computer-based formats may not be fully comparable. This issue is addressed in detail by Drasgow, Luecht, and Bennett (this volume).

3.4.2. Issues Surrounding Validity, Broadly Conceived: Fairness and Appropriateness

Disputes about the fairness and appropriateness of standardized testing and the focus of those disputes have evolved over the years. Early debates about cultural, language, and other sources of bias in standardized tests (e.g., Jensen, 1980) evolved into explications of misuses of tests (e.g., Cole & Moss, 1989; Gould, 1996) and development of procedures for reducing sources of unfairness and invalidity. Psychometricians and test developers implement procedures to avoid inappropriately sensitive topics (cf. Ravitch, 2003, chap. 4 regarding censorship and achievement testing) and stereotypical portrayals (e.g., women shown only in the kitchen); identify and reduce differential item functioning (DIF; see Camilli, this volume) for racial/ethnic, sex, and first language subgroups; and reduce unnecessarily complex vocabulary and language usage that may impede understanding for some students (e.g., Abedi, Lord, Hofstetter, & Baker, 2001). These advances seem to have had some role in quieting concerns about unfairness in tests and test items (even though average minority-majority subgroup performance differences persist).

The accuracy with which achievement tests categorize students and schools into performance levels is treated primarily as a psychometric issue. It soon could become a controversial policy issue as schools strive to meet increasingly more demanding Adequate Yearly Progress (AY) goals under *No Child Left Behind* (see Porter, Linn, & Trimble, 2005, for an explication of school growth trajectories). As schools fall just short of meeting annual goals for the percentages of students reaching or exceeding proficient performance, educators are likely to request evidence of the classification consistency and accuracy of achievement tests that are used to categorize students. As we discuss later, few technical reports contain classification consistency and accuracy evidence (see section 5).

Beginning in the late 1970s, concerns about curriculum narrowing (e.g., Broudy, 1980, p. 110; Kohn, 2000), teaching to the test, and test score inflation (see Koretz & Hamilton, this volume) arose as using test scores for public accountability reporting and for high-stakes decisions for students increased. Over the years, discussion of the issues has evolved. The potential desirability of teaching to the test has been acknowledged—when instruction appropriately focuses on content standards or is appropriately remedial (e.g., National Research Council, 1999, p. 280) or if assessment activities elicit authentic "intellectual performance" (Wiggins, 1993, p. 229). These concerns are likely to persist and evolve as tests are used for important decisions about students and for schools under *No Child Left Behind*.

3.4.3. The Role of K–12 Achievement Testing and Test Information in Educational Policy and Practice

The powerful influence of educational achievement tests on classroom instruction—that is, what is taught and how it is taught—has been well known in the educational measurement community (e.g., Popham, 1985) and to policymakers (e.g., McDonnell, 2004, p. 5). The power of its influence explains the controversy over the expansion of achievement testing over the last 25 years. Numerous studies suggest that achievement testing can effect changes in school and classroom practices (McDonnell, 2004, p. 9) and educators' expectations for student learning (e.g., Koretz, Mitchell, Barron, & Keith, 1996). But this influence is most powerful when it is supported by teacher training and adequate instructional materials (McDonnell, 2004, p. 175).

No Child Left Behind capitalizes on this influence by specifying some testing and reporting requirements and leaving others for individual states to decide. For example, *No Child Left Behind* requires states to establish content and performance standards in reading, mathematics, and science and to align assessments with those requirements. However, it requires each state to specify its own content and performance standards and implement its own assessments. *No Child Left Behind* exerts federal influence on schools by requiring states to assess three content areas (reading, mathematics, and science) and remaining silent on others (e.g., social studies, the arts); test students every year (i.e., in grades 3–8 and high school); and establish annual growth goals and growth trajectories leading to 2014. These requirements aspire to achieve equitable outcomes (e.g., by requiring all schools to help all students reach proficient standards) and provide focus (e.g., on only three academic content areas), goals that state assessment programs and local school systems did not reach prior to *No Child Left Behind*. We do not suggest that *No Child Left Behind* will succeed; skepticism about its requirements and goals abounds. Further, *No Child Left Behind's* requirements may consume state and local attention and resources to the detriment of other goals and academic subjects (e.g., Burroughs, Groce, & Webeck, 2005).

4. K–12 ASSESSMENT ITEMS, TASKS, AND PROMPTS AND ASSESSMENT DESIGN APPROACHES

Our goal in this section is to illustrate and evaluate the state of the art in K–12 assessment in terms of types of assessment items, tasks, and prompts and approaches to designing K–12 assessments of achievement.

4.1. K–12 Assessment Items, Tasks, and Prompts

A wide range of formal and informal approaches is available for assessing student achievement in grades K–12. To aid discussion of the approaches used most widely, we have adapted in Figure 16.3 the Framework of Assessment Approaches and Methods (McTighe & Ferrara, 1998, Fig. 2). This framework has been used previously to portray approaches to classroom assessment (McTighe & Ferrara, 1998), to assessing student thinking (Ferrara & McTighe, 1992), and for large-scale assessments. Other writers provide alternative typologies (e.g., Nitko, 2004, p. 239, Table 11.1; Stiggins, 2001, p. 87, Fig. 4.2).

The framework organizes assessment approaches in three broad categories: when examinees select responses, when examinees construct responses, and when examiners observe examinee behaviors. The framework distinguishes constructed-response items, tasks, and prompts in terms of the length and complexity of student responses: short constructed-response items (e.g., short written answers, creating a graph or data table) and performance-based assessment tasks and prompts. In the framework, performance-based tasks and prompts include (a) student products (e.g., essays, research papers, portfolios), and (b) student performances (e.g., oral presentations, athletic and dance performances). Process-focused assessment is a hybrid category that includes approaches that are intended to illuminate student understanding and thinking (e.g., processes students follow to complete a task or reach a conclusion) using a variety of methods (e.g., oral questioning by teachers, reviewing student learning logs, and asking students to think aloud as they complete a task). The role of the evaluator—the person who scores or rates student responses, products, or performances—becomes prominent in performance-based and process-focused assessments.

At least 6 of the 27 approaches and methods in the framework are used widely in large-scale K–12 achievement assessments. For example, multiple-choice and short constructed-response items are pervasive in large-scale achievement assessments (e.g., 54 and 39 of the 54 responding states and jurisdictions, respectively, in 2001–2002; Council of Chief State School Officers, 2003). Essay prompts and other extended constructed-response tasks also are widely used (e.g., 46 of 54 respondents; Council of Chief State School Officers, 2003). Assessment portfolios have been used widely as alternate assessments for students with significant cognitive disabilities who cannot participate meaningfully in mandatory statewide content area assessments (see section 3.2.4). The Kentucky and Vermont content area portfolio assessments (e.g., Fontana, 1995; Koretz, Stecher, Klein, & McCaffrey, 1994) are other well-known examples. Several other approaches and methods are used in K–12 assessments in non-academic areas such as the performing arts, physical education, and vocational-technical education.

4.2. Examples of K–12 Assessment Items, Tasks, and Prompts

In this section we illustrate and examine multiple-choice and short and extended constructed-response items that are typical of those currently in use on K–12 achievement assessments.[6] We also hypothesize about the response requirements of each item type. Selecting items to represent the range of design features and response requirements of items that appear on operational achievement assessments in grades K–12 is no simple matter. First, that range is quite diverse. Second, items from operational assessments usually are kept secure from public view. We could have selected items from state assessment programs that release items publicly. We have chosen to use items released on the World Wide Web from the National Assessment of Education Progress (NAEP; also referred to as "The Nation's Report Card") to exemplify items that appear on a range of K–12 achievement assessments. These items are appropriate illustrations because (a) they assess well-known content frameworks that serve as models for other K–12 assessments, (b) they are representative of items from many K–12 achievement assessments, and (c) their difficulty for students in the United States is known.

4.2.1. Item Response Requirements

In presenting achievement test items to examinees of any age or grade level, the goal is to determine whether examinees possess and can use appropriately the knowledge, skills, and cognitive processes required to respond successfully. Item response requirements are the declarative, procedural, and strategic knowledge that examinees must bring to bear in order to respond successfully to an item. Test blueprints

FIGURE 16.3 Framework of Assessment Approaches and Methods: Types of Items, Tasks, and Prompts That Elicit Responses from Examiness

Examinees Select a Response	Examinees Construct a Response			Examiner Observes Examinee Behavior
	Short Constructed Response Items	Performance Based Tasks and Prompts		Process Focused Assessments
		Products	Performances	
Multiple choice items	Fill-ins (words, phrases, diagram labels)	Essays or other extended written responses	Oral presentations	Oral questioning
True-false items	Short answers (sentences, paragraphs)	Stories, poems, plays	Debates	Interview, conference
Matching items	"Show your work"	Science lab reports	Science lab demonstrations	Observation
	Visual representations (drawings, tables, graphs, flow charts, concept maps)	Science and other projects	Musical performances	Process description
		Research papers	Athletic, dance, and other physical performances	Think-aloud
		Spreadsheets, PowerPoint presentations		Student learning log
		Artwork for exhibit		
		Video or audiotapes		
		Portfolios		

Source: Adapted from McTighe and Ferrara, 1998. Fig. 2.

typically delineate content area knowledge and skills to be targeted in a K–12 achievement assessment, sometimes in a content-by-process matrix (e.g., Crocker & Algina, 1986, p. 74, Fig. 4.2). Cognitive processes and skills often are defined only broadly (e.g., problem solving). Several frameworks are available to guide item writers in targeting types and levels of cognitive processes. Probably the most widely used framework in educational assessment is Bloom's taxonomy of educational objectives (Bloom, Engelhart, Furst, Hill, & Krathwohl, 1956). Marzano (2001) reviewed the conceptual and practical criticisms of Bloom's taxonomy and updated it. Recent studies of item response requirements have identified knowledge, skills, and processes that examinees appear to use when they respond to test items (e.g., Ferrara et al., 2004). Other studies address English language proficiency requirements (e.g., Abedi et al., 2001; Solano-Flores & Trumbull, 2003). Snow and colleagues (Snow, Corno, & Jackson, 1996) proposed a *Provisional Taxonomy of Individual Difference Constructs* to distinguish among the cognitive, affective, and conative functions that influence examinee responses to assessment items.

As we examine examples of K–12 achievement assessment items, we hypothesize about their response requirements.[7] In discussing the response requirements of these example items, we refer to construct relevance and irrelevance and "item construct validity" (see Ferrara et al., 2004). The *Standards* (American Educational Research Association, American Psychological Association, & National Council on Measurement in Education, 1999) defines construct irrelevance as "the degree to which test scores are affected by processes that are extraneous to its intended construct" (p. 10). Haladyna and Downing (2004) give examples of sources of construct irrelevant processes such as the influence of verbal abilities on test performance and test anxiety, motivation, and fatigue (see Haladyna & Downing, 2004, Table 1). Ferrara et al. (2003) define item response requirements as the "content area knowledge and skills and broader cognitive processes that are required to respond to test items" (p. 2).

4.2.2. Multiple-Choice Items

Multiple-choice items can be administered in a relatively short amount of time, which enables coverage of considerable numbers of content area standards. In most circumstances, multiple-choice items are relatively inexpensive to develop, very inexpensive to score, and efficient to evaluate for psychometric quality. Opponents of large-scale assessment or high-stakes testing assert that multiple-choice items engender "multiple-choice teaching." They claim that such items narrow the curriculum objectives that teachers cover and limit approaches to learning and opportunities to develop skills and thinking that other items encourage. These criticisms seem misdirected at multiple-choice items when they should, perhaps, be directed at instructional decisions to "teach to the test" (e.g., National Research Council, 1999). Other criticisms are over-generalized to all multiple-choice items; for example, that they can elicit only recall of low-level knowledge (i.e., facts) or relatively unreflective applications of concepts and algorithms. Of course, examples of poorly developed multiple-choice test items are not rare. Research and guidelines to support the technical quality of multiple-choice items is extensive (e.g., Haladyna, 2004, chaps. 8–10).

Below we provide two examples of multiple-choice items from the NAEP grade 8 mathematics assessment. The first is an example of a moderately difficult item (i.e., 58% of U.S. students responded correctly). It requires examinees to (a) process and understand the item stem, (b) connect to prior knowledge about appropriate operations and setting up algebraic expressions with one unknown, and (c) select the correct response option (see Figure 16.4).

Examinees must recognize that the three elements in the stem correspond to the elements in the equations in the response choices and must determine the correct relations among the elements. Examinees may use different strategies to respond to items like this. For example, some examinees may write out what they think is the correct equation and then find the matching or similar response option. Other examinees may scan the response options, eliminate implausible options, and select the most likely correct response. Both strategies require examinees to use some knowledge of algebraic equations. Others may simply guess. The incorrect response options represent logical errors that would indicate in many cases a failure to understand the relationships among the elements in the item (i.e., the hourly rate, the fixed travel cost, and the unknown, the number of hours worked). Following the correct order of arithmetic operations, which is important to arriving at the correct response, also plays a role in the distracters for this item. Examinees who choose an incorrect option may have committed a logical error because they do not understand the relationship among these elements, may have misread the problem, or may simply have guessed at a response. The first possibility contributes construct relevant information to estimates of examinee proficiency in mathematics; the latter two possibilities may or may not contribute construct relevant information to the overall test score.

The second example is a difficult multiple-choice item (i.e., only 25% of U.S. students responded correctly), intended to elicit higher-order thinking from students (i.e., problem solving, as defined in the NAEP mathematics framework). It requires examinees to (a) process and understand the item stem, (b) discern the relationship between the ordered pairs in the accompanying table, (c) connect to prior knowledge about numerical sequences and functional relationships, and (d) select the correct response option (see Figure 16.5).

This item is intended to require more complex thinking than the first example. The NAEP definition of mathematical problem solving includes recognizing problems, using strategies, using reasoning in new settings, and judging the reasonableness and correctness of solutions. Examinees must discern the functional relationship in the first four rows (i.e., 2X+1), relate it to the last row, and recognize the role of the break in the series, using the series of numbers in column A and/or the portrayal of ripped paper in the original graphic. Some examinees may recognize that they can write a simple equation to solve the problem (i.e., B = 2A + 1) and arrive at the response choice keyed as correct, 29. However recognizing patterns, formulating equations, and other algebra fundamentals are not taught to all U.S. students prior to grade 8. The remaining 75% of exam-

FIGURE 16.4 Multiple-Choice Item, *Plumber*

Example 1. NAEP grade 8 mathematics, 1996

A plumber charges customers $48 for each hour worked plus an additional $9 for travel. If h represents the number of hours worked, which of the following expressions could be used to calculate the plumber's total charge in dollars?

A) 48 + 9 + h
B) 48 x 9 x h
C) 48 + (9 x h)
D) (48 x 9) + h
E) (48 x h) + 9

(Correct response is E)

Description provided by the National Center for Education Statistics
Find (x, y); solution of a linear equation
Content strand: Algebra and functions
Target mathematical ability: Conceptual understanding

National performance results provided by the National Center for Education Statistics
P value=58
Omitted=0%

Source: Retrieved from http://nces.ed.gov/nationsreportcard/itmris/qtab.asp.

inees (including the 1% who omitted the item) may not have been exposed to or mastered the skills and developed the insights necessary to respond correctly. For example, 45% chose option B (i.e., 21), may have overlooked the gap in Column A from 8 to 14, and focused on the "add 4" pattern in Column B (i.e., 5 + 4 = 9, 9 + 4 = 13, 13+ 4 = 17, 17 + 4 = 21). In contrast, 18% chose option D (i.e., 25) and may simply have added 8 + 17 in the last row, failing to recognize the relationship between Columns A and B. Determining the sources of difficulty and errors in this item would require studies of opportunity to learn the specific knowledge and skills it requires and analyses of examinee processing of the item (e.g., "think-alouds" in "cognitive lab" studies; see Ferrara et al., 2004; Leighton, 2004; Sudman, Bradburn, & Schwarz, 1996, p.17).

4.2.3. Short Constructed-Response Items

Short constructed-response items represent an attempt to capture the efficiency and breadth of coverage that multiple-choice items provide and facets of examinee skill, knowledge, and depth of conceptual understanding that multiple-choice items may not capture. They may be somewhat less difficult to develop, especially if generic scoring rubrics and scoring benchmarks (i.e., examples of responses at each score level on a scoring rubric) are used in place of item specific scoring rubrics. Hand-scored short constructed-response items are more costly to score than are multiple choice items. Item analysis statistics and criteria for judging psychometric quality for multiple-choice items are applicable to short constructed-response items (American Educational Research Association, American Psychological Association, & National Council on Measurement in Education, 1999, p. 42). Constructed-response items are not widely criticized for narrowing curriculum and teaching, even though some short constructed-response items may elicit low-level knowledge and skills.

We provide two examples of short constructed-response items from a NAEP grade 4 reading assessment. These items are intended to assess comprehension of accompanying reading passages. The passage describes ways in which North American colonists kept warm during cold weather months and is written in a light, whimsical style to engage the interest of 4th graders. The first item is relatively easy (i.e., 76% of examinees achieved partial or full credit). It requires examinees to describe two differences between how 18th-century colonists kept warm and how people keep warm today. The item provides scaffolds for responding to the item in three ways: (a) It directs examinees to "tell about" the differences, which suggests indirectly, but

FIGURE 16.5 Multiple-Choice Item, *Numerical Patterns*

Example 2. NAEP grade 8 mathematics, 1992	
A	B
2	5
4	9
6	13
8	17
14	?

If the pattern shown in the table were continued, what number would appear in the box at the bottom of column B next to 14?

A) 19
B) 21
C) 23
D) 25
E) 29

(Correct response is E)

Description provided by the National Center for Education Statistics
Complete patterns in a table
Content strand: Algebra and functions
Target mathematical ability: Problem solving

National performance results provided by the National Center for Education Statistics
P value=25%
Omitted=1%

Source: Retrieved from http://nces.ed.gov/nationsreportcard/itmris/qtab.asp.

does not require, that examinees should describe, discuss, and perhaps refer to examples in the passage and a modern day example; (b) It directs examinees to address two differences; and (c) It provides five lines (perhaps too closely spaced for eight- and-nine-year-old 4th graders) for the response (see Figure 16.6).

Examinees must recognize that this is a compare/contrast item and that they must adhere to the response instructions in order to write a response that will receive full credit. Some constructed-response items provide a scaffold for thinking about how to respond; for example, "First, pick two ways that people today keep warm. Then think about the ways described in the article that colonists kept warm. Then think about two ways that keeping warm today is different." This item does not provide a scaffold for thinking about how to select differences between ways of keeping warm. The benchmark responses for score level 0 (available at http://nces.ed.gov/nationsreportcard/itmrls/qtab.asp) indicate that examinees do refer to ways of keeping warm today but do not refer to differences in ways of keeping warm. Benchmark responses at score level 1 provide only one difference or do not connect descriptions from the passage to contemporary ways of keeping warm. Responses like these may reflect only partial understanding of the information in the reading passage, misunderstanding of the item response requirements, limitations in writing proficiency, or reticence to write. A "strict constructionist" view of reading achievement would not include oral and written expression in assessing comprehension of a reading passage. Under this view, examinee responses that are limited by misunderstandings of the item response requirements, writing skills deficiency, or reticence to write would be construct irrelevant and would undermine item construct validity (i.e., inferences about reading achievement from performance on this item).

The second example of a short constructed-response item is relatively easy (i.e., 66% of examinees achieved partial or full credit) but 11% of examinees omitted this item. This item provides some response scaffolding: Examinees are (a) directed to give two reasons, (b) directed to give reasons that are stated in the article, and (c) are provided five lines to write the response (see Figure 16.7).

In order to respond successfully to this item, examinees must recognize among other requirements that their responses must refer explicitly to information implied in the reading selection. Benchmark responses for score level 0 (available at http://nces.ed.gov/nationsreportcard/itmrls/qtab.asp) indicate that examinees understand key vocabulary (i.e., "hearth") but do not explain it as the center of colonial homes. Responses at score level 1 provide only one reason from the passage. As discussed above, responses like these may reflect incomplete understanding of the reading passage or other limitations such as misunderstanding of the response requirements or reticence to write. The omit rate of 11% (i.e., examinees who left the response lines blank) suggests that the item was difficult for some examinees. Omit rates typically are higher for constructed-response items than for multiple-choice items (typically, as low as 1%), especially those that require lengthier responses,

FIGURE 16.6 Short Constructed-Response Item, *Keeping Warm*

Example 3. NAEP grade 4 reading, 2000

Reading passage: A Brick to Cuddle Up To
This 11-paragraph passage describes clever ways in which colonists in the New World kept warm, including slipping heated stones or bricks into their beds, using bed warmers, covering themselves with animal skins and blankets, and a range of other methods while traveling, at home, and while bathing. The first and last paragraphs of the passage refer to current times; the remainder of the text describes keeping warm in colonial times.

Item
Some of the ways colonists kept warm during the winter were different from the ways that people keep warm today. Tell about two of these differences.

(5 lines for response)

Description provided by the National Center for Education Statistics
Brick: Compare keeping warm—colonial to today
Context for reading: Reading for information
Target aspect of reading: Making reader/text connections

National performance results provided by the National Center for Education Statistics
Score level (in parentheses) and label:
(2) Evidence of full comprehension=17%
(1) Evidence of partial or surface comprehension=59%
(0) Evidence of little or no comprehension=21%
(0) Omitted=2%
(0) Omitted=1%

Note: NCES provides only score labels and descriptions; score levels are added.
Source: Retrieved from http://nces.ed.gov/nationsreportcard/itmris/qtab.asp.

more complex responses, or unusual effort to complete. Black and Hispanic students tend to omit items at higher rates than White and Asian students, even after controlling for achievement level (e.g., Jakwerth, Stancavage, & Reed, 1999). Omit rates for this item were 10% (White), 4% (Asian), 18% (Black), and 16% (Hispanic). Omitting items, especially constructed-response items, may indicate that examinees do not understand the problem posed by the item, that they do not possess the knowledge and skills required to respond, or motivation-related explanations (Jakwerth et al., 1999).

4.2.4. Extended Constructed-Response Items

Extended constructed-response items, tasks, and prompts often are included in educational achievement tests as much for their expected influence on instruction and learning (e.g., Wolf, Bixby, Glenn, & Gardner, 1991) as for their contributions to content validity and other psychometric properties of tests. Essay tests have a long history as a staple of student assessment in English, history, and other subjects. Essay testing remained in wide use in educational and selection testing (Coffman, 1971, p. 271) despite decades of criticism regarding fairness of scoring (i.e., standardization and accuracy) and sampling of topics (Coffman, 1971, pp. 276–283), availability of optical scoring machines beginning in the 1930s (see http://www-03.ibm.com/ibm/history/exhibits/specialprod1/specialprod1_9.html), and the popularity of multiple-choice items (e.g., Baker, 1971, p. 227). Essay tests, or more precisely, direct assessments of writing proficiency, came into new prominence in large-scale testing in the 1980s. Writing assessments typically contain one or more writing prompts. In the 1990s, extended constructed-response items began to appear in reading/language arts, mathematics, science, and social studies assessments to elicit written and other forms of responses that were longer, more complex, and took more time and effort to produce. Extended constructed-response items are intended to elicit higher-order thinking and skills, knowledge, and depth of conceptual understanding that may not be accessed by multiple-choice and briefer constructed-response items. Scoring rubrics for extended constructed-response items typically contain more score points (e.g., 4, 6, or more in some assessments), require more detailed specification of rhetorical features and content elements required in examinee responses, and are more difficult for scorers to score reliably and validly.

We provide two examples of extended constructed-response items, with an eye toward suggesting their variety. Both are from NAEP: an extended constructed-response item from a grade 12 history assessment and an essay prompt from a grade 12 writing assessment. This history item scaffolds examinee responses into three briefer responses. Other extended constructed-response items might scaffold response requirements to produce a single, integrated response. This history item requires examinees to know about likely 19th-century White Americans' beliefs about landownership. The three-part response, table title (i.e., Ways in Which Beliefs ...), and direction to refer to the Black Hawk quote and prior knowledge of history are intended to scaffold comparisons and contrasts about beliefs of the two groups. Comparison and contrast in the first part of the response should facilitate responding to the second part of the item, in which examinees are directed to explain the effects of differences in those beliefs (see Figure 16.8).

FIGURE 16.7 Short Constructed-Response Item, *Hearth as the Center of the Colonial Home*

Example 4. NAEP grade 4 reading, 2000

Reading passage: A Brick to Cuddle Up To
One paragraph near the end of the passage refers to hearth-side family activities and states, "So you can see why the fireplace was the center of a colonial home." (See Example 3 above for additional details about the passage.)

Item
Give two reasons stated in the article why the hearth was the center of the home in colonial times.

(5 lines for response)

Description provided by the National Center for Education Statistics
Brick: Hearth center of home - reasons why
Context for reading: Reading for information
Target aspect of reading: Developing interpretation

National performance results provided by the National Center for Education Statistics
Score level (in parentheses) and score label:
(2) Evidence of full comprehension=20%
(1) Evidence of partial or surface comprehension=46%
(0) Evidence of little or no comprehension=20%
(0) Omitted=11%
(0) Off task=3%

Note: NCES provides only score labels and descriptions; score levels are added.
Source: Retrieved from http://nces.ed.gov/nationsreportcard/itmris/qtab.asp.

This item is scored as a testlet (Wainer & Keily, 1987): the three short responses are interdependent and scored as a single response. The item is fairly easy for U.S. 12th graders: 72% wrote full or partial credit responses. However, only 4% of 12th graders achieved a maximum score of 3 by writing an appropriate response (i.e., a response that identifies two differences in views and explains with some specificity how differences affected relationships between Native and White Americans). Twenty-eight percent of the responses received a score of 0 because the responses were inappropriate, off task, or omitted. Seven percent of 12th graders did not respond to this item. It is not uncommon to see relatively high omit rates for extended constructed-response items, even in high-stakes assessments such as end-of-course examinations and high school exit examinations. Since the history of treatment of Native Americans in the 19th century permeates U.S. culture, most 12th graders are likely to possess prior knowledge required to respond to part two of this item. Response requirements that also are explicit in the scoring rubric explain the national performance results in this example. The requirements for essential and partial responses focus on identifying both the differences in beliefs and the effects on relationships between White and Native Americans; benchmark responses at these score levels indicate that examinees tended to provide weak, non-specific explanations or provided and explained only one difference in beliefs.

The second example of an extended constructed-response item is an essay prompt from the NAEP grade 12 writing assessment. The essay prompt, that appears to be inspired by Ray Bradbury's 1953 novel and the 1967 movie *Fahrenheit 451*, illustrates the distinctiveness of essay prompts from other extended constructed-response items. For example, it scaffolds the structure of the essay by posing a question (i.e., "Which book would you save?"), providing "be sure to" reminders about the two critical issues to address (i.e., "Why the book is important to you" and "Why it would be important to future generations"), and by signaling examinees to "discuss in detail." General directions for the NAEP writing assessment provide additional response scaffolding about rhetorical requirements that are explicit in the scoring rubric

FIGURE 16.8 Extended Constructed-Response Item, *Native American Beliefs about Land Ownership*

Example 5. NAEP grade 12 history, 2001

Both parts of Question 3 are about the statement below.

"My logic teaches me that land cannot be sold. The Great Spirit gave the land to his children to live upon...Nothing can be sold but such things as can be carried away."

-Black Hawk, Chief of the Sac and Fox

On the table below, list two ways in which the beliefs about landownership held by many Native Americans (such as Black Hawk) differed from the beliefs about landownership probably held by many White Americans. In your answer, use both the quote above and your knowledge of history.

WAYS IN WHICH BELIEFS ABOUT
LANDOWNERSHIP DIFFERED

1. (2 lines for response)
2. (2 lines for response)

In the space below, explain how the differences in beliefs about landownership you identified affected the relationship between White Americans and Native Americans.

(5 lines for response)

Description provided by the National Center for Education Statistics
Land ownership—American Indian v. White
Historical theme: Gathering of people, culture, ideas
Target cognitive level: Historical analysis and interpretation

National performance results provided by the National Center for Education Statistics
Score level (in parentheses) and score label:
(3) Appropriate=4%
(2) Essential=33%
(1) Partial=35%
(0) Inappropriate=19%
(0) Omitted=7%
(0) Off task=2%

Note: NCES provides only score labels and descriptions; score levels are added.
Source: Retrieved from http://nces.ed.gov/nationsreportcard/itmris/qtab.asp.

(e.g., relevance and organization of details, writing style elements such as varying sentences, and grammatical correctness). Unlike many items in other content areas, this essay prompt requires examinees to imagine a hypothetical situation. Essay prompts that do not require prior content area knowledge often include this requirement (see Figure 16.9).

This was a moderately difficult prompt for U.S. 12th graders in 2002: 52% achieved the sufficient level or higher. However, only 17% wrote essays of skillful or excellent quality. As few as 3% of examinees wrote off-task responses or did not respond to this prompt. Essay prompts like this one feature a unique item response requirement: examinees must make conscious choices about the position or point of view they take, the topic they choose to write about, and rhetorical strategies. These choices can influence the score assigned to the written product in a number of ways. For example, examinees may choose to write about a topic that (a) is more complex than other topics, (b) does not facilitate producing an adequately detailed response, or (c) may become uninteresting and de-motivating. Of less concern is the influence of examinee decisions in biasing scorer decisions. Research suggests that when examinees can choose items and topics to respond to, they may make choices that result in performance that is lower than expected. Research on scorer performance while scoring responses to writing prompts and other constructed-response items indicates that typical human responses toward non-objectivity (e.g., affective response to topics selected by examinees or word choices) or inaccuracy in judgment (e.g., Plous, 1993) can be addressed and minimized by effective training and recalibration.

This prompt requires examinees to write an essay to inform the reader (in this case, scorers) by explaining their choice of a book. It also implicitly requires persuasion in the form of support; that is, it directs examinees to explain "what it is about the book that makes it important to save" and "why it would be important to future generations." The target cognitive response requirements for this prompt are quite broad. Some examinees may be required to recall a similar classroom discussion or writing assignment, perhaps even about this book. For other examinees, this prompt may pose significant cognitive demands, including "a range of thinking skills," as the prompt explicitly targets (see Figure 16.9).

Assessment items, tasks, and prompts like those described here and the content area knowledge, skills, and processes that they target are the basic components of K–12 educational achievement assessments. The design for an achievement assessment provides an explicit framework and systematic process for combining these components into a test. The conceptual, theoretical, and procedural characteristics of an assessment design significantly influence the alignment between the assessment and the achievement construct that the assessment targets. We

FIGURE 16.9 Essay Prompt, *A Book to Save for Future Generations*

Example 6. NAEP grade 12 writing, 2002

A novel written in the 1950s describes a world where people are not allowed to read books. A small group of people who want to save books memorize them, so that the books won't be forgotten. For example, an old man who has memorized the novel *The Call of the Wild* helps a young boy memorize it by reciting the story to him. In this way, the book is saved for the future.

If you were told that you could save just one book for future generations, which book would you choose?

Write an essay in which you discuss which book you would choose to save for future generations and what it is about the book that makes it important to save. Be sure to discuss in detail why the book is important to you and why it would be important to future generations.

(Three-quarters of a page of blank space is provided for the response)

Description provided by the National Center for Education Statistics
Which book would you save?
Purpose for writing: Informative writing
Target cognitive level: Informative writing may span the range of thinking skills from recall to analysis to evaluation

National performance results provided by the National Center for Education Statistics
Score level (in parentheses) and score label:
(4) Excellent=4%
(3) Skillful=13%
(2) Sufficient=35%
(1) Uneven=30%
(0) Insufficient=12%
(0) Unsatisfactory=7%
(0) Off task or omitted=3%

Note: NCES provides only score labels and descriptions; score levels are added.
Source: Retrieved from http://nces.ed.gov/nationsreportcard/itmris/qtab.asp.

next describe approaches to designing K–12 achievement assessments.

4.3. Traditional and Emergent Approaches to K–12 Assessment Design and Development

It is standard practice in large-scale operational educational assessment programs to use psychometric theory, conception, and models for analysis and quality control, scaling and equating, and score reporting. Cognitive psychological theory, conception, and models for how examinees respond to test items are less evident.

Educational achievement assessment item and test development is guided by over a half century of standard practices, conventional wisdom, and insightful technique, most of it well documented (e.g., Haladyna, 2004; Millman & Greene, 1989; Popham, 1984; Schmeiser & Welch, this volume). In addition, several groups and individual researchers have expanded current technology for generating psychometrically and conceptually sound items by, for example, expanding earlier ideas about item templates for generating parallel items (e.g., Irvine & Kyllonen, 2002; Roid & Haladyna, 1980) and investigating item features associated with examinee cognitive processing (e.g., Baxter & Glaser, 1998; Ferrara et al., 2004; Hamilton, Nussbaum, & Snow, 1997; Kupermintz, Le, & Snow, 1999; Solano-Flores & Shavelson, 1997) and item difficulty (e.g., Embretson, 2002; Embretson & Gorin, 2001). Other researchers and theorists argue that assessment development models and theories also should account explicitly for linguistic demands on examinees, especially English language learners (e.g., Abedi et al., 2001) and the needs of students with cognitive disabilities who participate in K–12 assessments (e.g., Tindal & Haladyna, 2002). This empirical work and emerging theories, conceptions, and models for item development and assessment design—in contrast to theories of true scores and item response probabilities—have set the stage for a psychology of K–12 achievement testing that may catch up with the advanced development of psychometric theory. Advances in the technology of assessment design and development tend to transpire independent of one another. No practical theory or system brings together psychometrics, cognitive psychology, linguistics, and operational test development into a unified approach for designing and developing K–12 achievement assessments and for validating interpretations and uses of achievement test scores. Theory and conception tend to be implicit in or even absent from current practice. However, recent advanced work may be setting the stage for explicit approaches to achievement assessment design, development, and validation that may become practically feasible. These explicit approaches attempt to integrate cognitive and psychometric principles into the design of achievement assessments, development of assessment items and tasks, and validation of interpretation of examinee performance in relation to cognitive models of examinee achievement. We describe briefly several of these models and then discuss implications for current and future practice in educational achievement assessment.

4.3.1. Traditional "Task Driven" Approaches to Assessment Design and Development

Traditional task driven approaches to assessment design and development (Messick, 1994; Mislevy, Steinberg, & Almond, 2002) address links in an inferential chain from assessment purposes, to construct definition, and through to supportable interpretations and warranted decisions, but do so implicitly. For-example, targets of inference typically are defined as well-organized lists of content standards and test objectives rather than as well-defined achievement constructs; that is, as a coherent set of knowledge, skills, and processes organized to show relationships among components that enable predictions about performance in learning and assessment situations (see, for example, Ferrara et al., 2005). Also, traditional approaches typically do not capitalize on findings from cognitive research to inform assessment task design. Current practice, in general, includes explicit guidelines for selecting items and scoring rubric development to enable the use of psychometric models. However, evidence of the alignment of items with achievement targets is highly inferential and indirect, based on judgments of content experts, rather than built explicitly into item design. Likewise, analyses to generate evidence of construct validity, construct representativeness, and construct relevance are conducted after an achievement assessment has been assembled and administered rather than built explicitly into the design and development process. This characterization is not meant to suggest that current practice in test design and development is somehow faulty. On the contrary, K–12 educational achievement testing functions extremely well in a range of school settings and provides technically rigorous and useful information about student achievement for a range of important purposes and uses. But the characterization does illustrate the implicitness of connections among steps in the assessment process and links in the inferential chain from learning targets to score interpretations and actions. This lack of explicitness points to opportunities to make refinements in conceptualizing assessment design, conducting assessment task development, and gathering validity evidence for K–12 achievement assessments.

4.3.2. Emergent Conceptions and Models: Explicit Assessment Design

Messick (1994) and Snow and Lohman (1989) have been in the forefront of advocating for the role that cognitive psychology could play in educational achievement test design. Their thinking is reflected in literatures relevant to aptitude and intelligence testing (e.g., see Embretson, 2002, p. 221). Messick, Snow and Lohman, and a National Research Council report (2001) have exhorted the educational assessment community to modernize approaches to assessment design and development and have provided some illustrations to guide modernization efforts. Measurement researchers have made significant strides in applying theory and empirical findings from cognitive psychology to the design of educational assessments. There is little evidence so far that these advances have influenced operational K–12 achievement assessments (cf. Lane, 1993).

4.3.2.1. Construct Driven Assessment Design

In extending his conception of consequential validity to suddenly pervasive educational performance-based assessments of the 1990s, Messick introduced the notion of construct driven assessment design (1994). Construct driven design of assessments and assessment tasks, applied to K–12 educational testing in general, requires specification of three things:

1. The complex of knowledge, skills, and other attributes to be assessed; that is, the definition of the achievement construct.
2. Examinee knowledge and performances that are expected to illuminate this construct; that is, procedures to draw inferences about what students know and can do in relation to the targeted achievement construct and evidence to support those inferences.
3. Tasks or situations that are expected to elicit these behaviors and performances; that is, test items, tasks, and prompts that are closely aligned to the achievement construct.

The concept of construct driven assessment design is intended to minimize construct under-representation and avoid eliciting construct irrelevant behavior from examinees. It links assessment design and item development directly to achievement constructs, with the goal of supporting valid interpretation and use of achievement test scores.

4.3.2.2. Scientifically Principled Assessment Design

Messick's conception is evident in the work of a committee of the Board on Testing and Assessment of the National Research Council (2001). In their comprehensive review of research and design work in cognitive and educational psychology, the committee proposed that "a cognitive model of learning should serve as the cornerstone of the assessment design process" (p. 54). They did not stop there. They described in detail three "pillars" of assessment design:

1. A *cognitive model* of how students represent knowledge in memory and develop competence in academic content areas.
2. Tasks or situations that enable *observation* of student performance in an academic content area.
3. An *interpretation method* to draw inferences about what students know and can do in an academic content area, based on the observed performances.

As in construct driven design, the report calls for designing assessments so that achievement constructs and assessment items, tasks, and prompts are closely aligned and intended interpretations of test performance and decisions are warranted by the evidence elicited from examinee responses. The report proposes additional details for assessment design. For example, cognitive models and corresponding assessments would target content area knowledge, but more specifically, what examinees know, how they know it, and how they can use it. Further, such models would specify thinking processes and proficiencies such as problem solving strategies, metacognition, and use of knowledge and skills in other contexts. Finally, cognitive models and such assessments would distinguish novices and experts in the content domain.

4.3.2.3. Cognitive Design System Approach

Embretson (2002) argues for the importance of cognitive theory in item generation; that is, in model-based rather than solely expert-based test item writing. Her cognitive design system for generating test items contains a conceptual framework and a procedural framework. The conceptual framework provides a representation of the target construct via "the processes, strategies, and knowledge structures that are involved in item solving" (p. 222). Describing these features using cognitive psychology principles enables manipulation of item cognitive demands and prediction of item difficulty and discrimination. The procedural framework guides test designers in managing the relationship of the features that item writers write into items (e.g., content knowledge and skill demands) to item difficulty and psychometric quality (e.g., fit to an item response model). This framework includes the following stages:

1. Specify the goals of measurement including, specifically, the target construct.
2. Identify, using cognitive psychology principles, item design features that are relevant to the target construct.
3. Develop a cognitive model, based on existing and new research and theory that explicates the influences of item design features on examinee cognitive processing and on item difficulty and discrimination.
4. Generate items based on the cognitive model and assemble a test.
5. Evaluate the item generation model by predicting item performance and fit of items to a psychometric model.
6. Evaluate the test's fidelity with the representation of the target construct using correlations with external measures.

Embretson (2002) demonstrates the cognitive design system approach for generating abstract reasoning items and acknowledges that few applications to operational tests have emerged (p. 221).

4.3.2.4. Evidence Centered Assessment Design

Mislevy, Steinberg, and Almond (2002) provide a model for designing and developing assessments, which they call a conceptual assessment framework.[8] Their goal is to provide a "formal evidentiary framework for linking ... [assessment tasks] ... to those knowledge, skills, and abilities (KSAs) which are the targets of inference" (p. 97). The evidence centered assessment design framework contains three primary models (see pp. 100–102 for an overview):

1. A *student model*, which specifies the target achievement construct and describes what students know and can do in relation to that construct.
2. An *evidence model*, which contains rules of evidence for relating student test performances to the achievement construct.
3. A *task model*, which describes the features of the assessment activities that produce evidence of what students

know and can do in relation to the target achievement construct.

These models coincide with the Messick and National Research Council conceptions. (The authors acknowledge the conceptual similarities.) The design framework is comprehensive in that it also includes an *assembly model* to specify how assessment tasks should be combined to form an assessment, a *delivery model* to describe the environment and other requirements of the assessment situation, and an *environment model* to describe the overall assessment situation.

4.3.2.5. Commonalities

These four explicit design models share a common goal: To enable interpretations of performance on achievement assessments as a process of reasoning from evidence (Mislevy, Steinberg, & Almond, 2002, p. 98; National Research Council, 2001, p. 42) about examinee status in relation to a well-specified achievement construct. Reasoning from evidence makes explicit the inferential connections from intended score interpretations (a) to achievement construct definition, assessment and task design and development, administration, scoring, and analysis; and (b) warranted decisions and actions based on those interpretations. Further, these approaches provide a framework for developing assessments that should enable (a) reliable predictions of overall task difficulty or conditional task difficulty for examinees at different levels of proficiency in relation to the target construct (Embretson, 2002), and (b) inferences about what students know and can do in terms of declarative, procedural, and strategic knowledge. These explicit predictions and inferences stand in contrast to those possible under current traditional, less explicit approaches. Under traditional approaches to test design and development, the primary goal is to create assessment items, tasks, and prompts that are aligned with a set of content standards.

4.4. Implications of Explicit Approaches: The State of the Art in K–12 Assessment Design and Development

What do these emergent design approaches mean—in practical terms—for designing, developing, operating, and validating inferences from K–12 assessments? Simply stated, and setting aside the complexity of these approaches, they require a fundamental shift in test design and item development:

> Characteristics of tasks are determined by the nature of the behaviors they must produce to constitute evidence for the targeted aspects of proficiency. This perspective stands contrary to a task centered approach, under which the primary emphasis is on creating tasks, with the target of inference defined only implicitly as the tendency to do well on those tasks. (Mislevy, Steinberg, & Almond, 2002, p. 116)

A fundamental shift would entail the following changes in conception and practice:

- Definition of achievement constructs based on content standards as models of cognition that are the target for achievement assessments (i.e., in the case of state assessments).
- Specification of assessment items, tasks, and prompts that elicit the knowledge, skills, and processes specified by the achievement construct.
- Empirical verification that inferences from test performances to the achievement construct about what students know and can do are warranted and that planned instructional actions in relation to content standards are likely to be effective.
- Score reporting that is understandable to families and educators and faithful to the assessment design.

And what might be gained from undertaking more explicit approaches to design and development of K–12 achievement assessments? Using them should (a) support accuracy in achieving difficulty and cognitive demand targets during test development, and (b) produce explicit evidence that assessment tasks elicit from examinees the intended knowledge, skills, and processes, and with a minimum of construct irrelevant cognitive activity. Clarity and coherence can be gained by defining what is to be tested as an achievement construct derived from content standards. When achievement targets are defined clearly as achievement constructs, assessment tasks can be aligned with targeted procedural knowledge and cognitive processes in fact as well as in intent. Further, when achievement constructs are defined rigorously, interpretations of test scores can be clearer, more strongly supportable, and more likely to provide more directly useful information to guide instructional decisions and planning (Ferrara et al., 2005).

Closing the gap between this vision and current practice in the near future may be unrealistic. Suggesting a unifying theory for educational achievement assessment practice may seem far fetched. However, advances in the state of the art since 1980 have been quite remarkable. Demonstrations of explicit design models, continuing work on IRT models, advances in aligning tests with intended content and cognitive targets, and other ongoing work suggest that we can expect to see the gap closed by some amount by the publication of the fifth edition of *Educational Measurement*.

Development and validation of survey and interview questions is based on a simple model of respondent cognitive processes (see Sudman, Bradburn, & Schwarz, 1996, Table 2.1). An adaptation of that model for educational achievement assessment items would be as follows: (a) Comprehend or interpret the item response requirements (e.g., content area knowledge and skills, response elements specified or implied by the item); (b) retrieve required knowledge, activate and apply required skills and processes; (c) formulate or locate a response; and (d) decide on a response (e.g., consider plausibility of response options) and record the response. Implementing an explicit examinee responding model and findings from studies of examinee response strategies into assessment design and item development would be a good start to closing the gap.

5. THE STATE OF THE FIELD OF K–12 ACHIEVEMENT TESTING: A DESCRIPTION AND EVALUATION

In previous sections we described the K–12 achievement assessment landscape. In this section we review the state of the field of K–12 achievement assessment. We summarize and draw conclusions about the technical quality of K–12 assessments, including the evidence of reliability of scores from K–12 achievement assessments and evidence of validity to support interpretations and uses of these assessments. We have gathered information on reliability and validity from readily available technical reports. We use technical reports because they (a) are prepared by testing program and contractor staff who are responsible for all aspects of development, validation, and use of a test; and (b) contain relevant information generated by a range of groups involved in developing, delivering, and analyzing tests, including content area experts, psychometricians, outside contractors, and school staff who administer tests. Technical reports currently are the one best place for documenting all types of information about the validity of K–12 assessments. Chapter 16 of the *Standards for Educational and Psychological Testing* (American Educational Research Association, American Psychological Association, & National Council on Measurement in Education, 1999), "Supporting Documentation for Tests," includes 15 standards relevant to the contents of technical reports and other related documents.

This is an illustrative review of the state of the field of K–12 achievement assessment prior to reauthorization of the federal Elementary and Secondary Education Act (ESEA) under *No Child Left Behind* (NCLB; see No Child Left Behind Act of 2002). This review is not intended to be definitive, comprehensive, or exhaustive, nor strictly representative (in the sampling sense) of the technical quality of all K–12 achievement assessments represented in Table 16.2. It is reasonable to say that these technical reports typify in a general way the state of the field of K–12 achievement testing. In fact, creating a definitive review of the field of K–12 assessment would be a challenge. State assessment programs have evolved rapidly since the late 1970s. That evolution has accelerated considerably with the passage of NCLB. The review is based on the technical reports available on state department of education Web sites during December 2003 to January 2004. It includes technical reports from 11 state assessment programs and one commercial norm referenced K–12 achievement survey. Table 16.3 indicates the assessments and assessment programs, content areas, grades, and administration periods covered by the 12 technical reports.

The assessment programs include some of the test types represented earlier in Table 16.2. The technical reports cover assessments and programs administered during 1998 through 2003. Nine or 10 of the reports cover reading/English language arts assessments, 6–7 cover writing assessments, 9–10 cover mathematics assessments, 6–7 cover science assessments, and 5–6 cover social studies assessments. (The numbers of reports vary across grade clusters 3–5, 6–8, and 9–12.) Many of the technical reports contain information for assessments in several content areas and grades. One report includes information on a listening assessment; another includes an assessment of computers and technology. Two reports cover high school exit examinations (i.e., Alaska and Minnesota) in reading, writing, and mathematics. Technical reports from two states provide information on end-of-course examinations in English (which may specify reading and writing separately), mathematics, science, and social studies. The technical reports come from state assessment programs in the East, Southeast, Midwest, Southwest, and West Coast sections of the United States and large, small, populous, and sparsely populated states (i.e., Alaska, Colorado, Delaware, Florida, Illinois, Michigan, Minnesota, New Hampshire, Texas, Virginia, and Washington state) and one commercial norm referenced K–12 achievement survey, TerraNova (2nd ed.).

5.1. Evaluation Criteria

Similarly, we have not tried to provide exhaustive coverage of all considerations in evaluating the state of the field. We have selected two fundamental evaluation categories: reliability and validity evidence. In the following tables we summarize these evaluation categories and specific types of evidence in each category. We have organized the evidence using selected standards from the *Standards for Educational and Psychological Testing* (American Educational Research Association, American Psychological Association, & National Council on Measurement in Education, 1999; referred to here as the *Standards*). A more comprehensive review would include standards from all three parts of the *Standards* (i.e., Test Construction, Evaluation, and Documentation; Fairness in Testing; and Testing Applications) and standards from all four sections of the *Code of Fair Testing Practices* (i.e., Developing and Selecting Appropriate Tests, Administering and Scoring Tests, Reporting and Interpreting Test Results, and Informing Test Takers; see Joint Committee on Testing Practices, 2004).

In the summary tables below we use the term "test developers" in its most inclusive sense, following the definition in the *Standards*: "The person(s) or agency responsible for the construction of a test and for the documentation regarding its technical quality for an intended purpose" (p. 183). Some standards refer to test users, defined in the *Standards* as "The person(s) or agency responsible for the choice and administration of a test, for the interpretation of test scores produced in a given context, and for any decisions or actions that are based, in part, on test scores" (p. 183). The validity of interpretations and decisions based on test scores are dependent on the professional judgment and actions of these two distinct groups of professionals.

5.2. Documentation of Evidence of Test Score Reliability

The *Standards* specify types of reliability evidence required for a range of assessment situations (e.g., for examinee subgroups, when cut scores and performance levels are used in score reporting). Selected requirements appear in Table 16.4, organized into conceptually similar groups. We have summarized and evaluated the explanation and interpretation of evidence of reliability of score interpretations

TABLE 16.3 States, Assessments, Content Areas, and Grades Covered in 12 Technical Reports Used to Describe and Evaluate K–12 Achievement Testing

STATE	ASSESSMENT(S)/ PROGRAM(S)	CONTENT AREAS	GRADE LEVELS	TESTING PERIOD
Alaska	Alaska Comprehensive System of Student Assessment: Benchmark Assessments; High School Graduation Qualifying Examination	Reading, writing, mathematics	3, 6, 8, high school	Spring 2003
Colorado	Colorado Student Assessment Program (CSAP)	Reading, writing, mathematics	3–10	Spring 2002
Delaware	Delaware Student Testing Program (DSTP)	Reading, writing, mathematics, science, social studies	3, 4, 5, 6, 8, 10, 11	Spring 2001
Florida	Florida Comprehensive Assessment Test (FCAT)	Reading, mathematics	4, 5, 8, 10	Spring 2000
Illinois	Illinois Standards Achievement Tests (ISAT)	Reading, writing, mathematics, science, social studies	3, 4, 5, 7, 8	April 2003
Michigan	Michigan Educational Assessment Program (MEAP)	Reading, writing, mathematics, science, social studies	4, 5, 7, 8, 11	1998–99 school year
Minnesota	Minnesota Basic Standards Test (BST)	Reading, writing, mathematics	8, high school	January–July 2001
New Hampshire	New Hampshire Educational Improvement and Assessment Program (NHEIAP)	English language arts, mathematics, science, social studies	3, 6, 10	May 2002
Texas	Texas Assessment of Academic Skills (TAAS); Texas Assessment of Knowledge and Skills (TAKS) field tests	Reading, writing, mathematics; English II, algebra I, biology, U.S. history	3–8, high school	2001–02 school year
Virginia	Virginia Standards of Learning (SOL) Assessments	Reading, writing, mathematics, science, history and social science, computer/technology; 11 end-of-course exams in the areas of English, mathematics, science, and social studies	3, 5, 8, high school	Spring 1998
Washington	Washington Assessment of Student Learning (WASL)	Reading, writing, listening, mathematics	4	April–May 2001
--	TerraNova (2nd ed.)	Reading/language arts, mathematics, science, social studies, word analysis, vocabulary, language mechanics, spelling, mathematics computation	K–12	Fall, winter, spring 2001 and on

Note: This summary table illustrates generally the grades and content areas covered by these 12 technical reports. Some content areas and grade levels do not coincide with one another. The table does not define all assessments, content areas, and grades included in each assessment or program.

and decisions provided in the 12 technical reports. We gathered information on (a) internal consistency reliability estimates (e.g., coefficient alpha), (b) standard errors and score confidence intervals, (c) rater consistency and accuracy, (d) test-retest and alternate forms reliability, (e) generalizability analyses and decision studies, and (f) classification consistency, accuracy, and standard errors.

The selected standards for reliability evidence emphasize the importance of using score reliability indicators appropriately, interpreting specific estimates of reliability accurately, estimating reliability for examinee subgroups, reporting standard errors of measurement as well as reliability coefficients, reporting reliability information for test score levels and ranges, and estimating the consistency and accuracy with which test scores categorize students into performance levels. This latter requirement has grown in importance since minimum competency tests became widely used (e.g., Berk, 1984), performance levels grew in popularity for reporting performance on NAEP and state assessment programs, and recently with NCLB reporting requirements (see No Child Left Behind Act of 2002: section 1111, State Plans, (D) Challenging Academic Standards). To what degree do K–12 achievement assessment developers provide evidence consistent with these standards? And how reliable are scores from K–12 achievement assessments?

TABLE 16.4 Selected Standards for Reliability of Interpretations and Decisions Based on Test Scores, Organized into Conceptually Similar Groups of Requirements

STANDARDS	REQUIREMENTS IN THE STANDARDS
Fundamentals	
2.1, 2.2	Test developers should report for all scores:
	— Estimates of reliability and the SEM
	— Conditional SEMs for raw scores and all derived scores
Examinee subgroups	
2.11, 2.12, 2.18	Test developers should report:
	— Separate estimates of reliability and the SEM when examinee subgroup differences are expected
	— Reliability data for each reported age and grade group
	— Reliability analyses for examinees for whom significant variation in test procedures is allowed
Explanation and interpretation	
2.4, 2.5	Test developers should:
	— Provide clear explanations of reliability estimates and the sample of examinees on which estimates are based
	— Avoid misinterpreting reliability estimates as interchangeable in terms of their conceptions of measurement error
Reliability for scoring of constructed-response items	
2.10, 2.13	When judgmental scoring of examinee responses is required, test developers should:
	— Report rater consistency and within-examinee consistency
	— Provide reliability information when local scoring is conducted
Classification consistency and accuracy for categorizations using cut scores and performance levels	
2.14, 2.15	Test developers should:
	— Report conditional standard errors if reliability is expected to differ with score level
	— Report SEMs in the vicinity of cut scores
	— Report estimates of the reproducibility of percentages of examinees in performance levels

Note: SEM=standard error of measurement.
Source: Adapted from the *Standards* (1999); details and some qualifying statements are excluded for the sake of brevity.

All 12 technical reports provide internal consistency reliability estimates for content area total scores (e.g., reading) primarily using coefficient alpha. One report (i.e., New Hampshire) includes the stratified alpha coefficient for its English language arts, mathematics, science, and social studies assessments in grades 3, 6, and 10, which include multiple-choice and constructed-response items, as recommended elsewhere (e.g., Feldt & Brennan, 1989, pp. 117–118). Most of the internal consistency estimates (including stratified alphas) are greater than .85 and range into the low to mid .90s. Estimates lower than .85 are reported for short tests (e.g., alpha =.60 for the Washington state grade 4 listening test, which includes six multiple-choice and two short-answer items). Only the Minnesota and Texas reports provide reliability estimates for six and racial/ethnic subgroups. Six reports include score reliability information for content area subscores (e.g., number concepts in mathematics). Most reports include standard errors for scale scores or raw scores. The Michigan report, which is brief and provided as a Web page rather than a full-length technical report, does not provide standard errors; the Illinois report provides item information functions but not standard errors. Standard errors tend to be relatively small in relation to the number of score points available on these tests, as expected for these highly reliable (i.e., internally consistent), homogenous tests. In a random sample of three of the reports, standard errors typically are 5% of the raw score points available in reading and mathematics assessments; 2% to 4% of the scale score range on reading and mathematics assessments; and 6% of the available raw score points in writing, science, and social studies. Most reports contain information on the consistency with which trained scorers assign scores to constructed-response items, typically as percentages of agreement between two blind and randomly paired scorers, either when all examinee responses are scored twice (e.g., typically in direct writing assessments) or when a random sample of responses (e.g., 10%) is scored a second time to produce rater agreement information. Exact agreement is reported as low as 48% and up to 94% and higher (e.g., Alaska). Three reports do not contain rater agreement information for constructed-response items even though they provide extensive analyses of other psychometric considerations (e.g., one state does report local item dependence statistics). The lowest exact rater agreement rates appear in a range of content areas and grades, typically depending on the degree of open endedness of items and rubrics, number of score points in rubrics, and the rigor of rater training. For example, exact rater agreement rates for extended responses to mathematics items range from 51% to 72% (i.e., Illinois grade 3 and 5 mathematics Explanation scores; the range of rubric score points is not given) and tend to be lower than exact agreement rates in other content areas (e.g., reading exact agreement rates range 63–71%). Exact agreement rates for writing assessments tend to be in the 60–70% range (e.g., Illinois and other states), as expected according to other sources (e.g., Ferrara, 1993). Other reports provide rater accuracy results; that is, percentages of agreement of scorer decisions with "validity papers" (i.e., responses with scores assigned by consensus within a committee of scoring experts). For example, the Illinois report includes exact agreement with validity papers between 62% and 96%. In place of rater agreement and accuracy rates, the TerraNova report provides intraclass correlations and weighted *kappa* coefficients (to account for chance rater agreement) that are greater than .90 in the vast majority of cases and rarely below .80.

None of the technical reports includes test-retest or alternate forms of reliability estimates. Several of these assessments include multiple parallel forms, and technical information on these parallel test forms does appear in other technical reports. Typical explanations for not providing this information (when explanations are provided) include concerns about deleterious fatigue and motivation effects. Reports for five state assessment programs (Florida, Illinois, Minnesota, New Hampshire, and Virginia) provide evidence of classification consistency and accuracy using a variety of statistics. Several of the reports provide decision consistency and accuracy internal estimates plus *kappa* coefficients and cite Livingston and Lewis (1995) on these statistics. The Minnesota and Texas reports include only the probabilities of passing a specific test (grade 8 reading and the high school reading exit exam, respectively) on subsequent administrations (with the assumption of no growth in achievement). The Florida report provides the most extensive information: classification accuracy and consistency internal estimates of .56 to .79 for reading and mathematics in grades 4, 5, 8, and 10; the highest classification accuracy estimates (.80 to .89) for performance level 1, the lowest for level 4 (.57 to .84; grade 10 reading is .35); decision accuracy for percentages of students at or above each performance level ranging from .83 to .99; and discussion of false positive and false negative classification rates of approximately 4% (and 8% for grade 10 reading).

5.3. Development and Documentation of Evidence of the Validity of Score Interpretations and Uses

Validity in educational achievement assessment is about inferences and actions. The process of validating interpretations of test scores—that is, supporting interpretations and actions based on interpretations—requires integrating validity evidence (*Standards*, p. 17) and constructing a line of argument (see, for example, Kane, this volume). More specifically, standards 1.1–1.4 require test developers to provide evidentiary support for making intended interpretations about examinee achievement and performance. Logically, validation of interpretations of test scores should begin with statements of proposed interpretations and uses of test scores. The discussion of validation in the *Standards* suggests a logic chain that should be followed in the validation process:

> Validation logically begins with an explicit statement of the *proposed interpretation* of test scores, along with a rationale for the *relevance of the interpretation to the proposed use*. The proposed interpretation refers to the *construct or concepts* the test is intended to measure. Examples of constructs are mathematics achievement... (p. 9; emphases added)

The logic chain suggests that test developers must (a) define the achievement construct or concepts that a test is intended to assess, then (b) propose interpretations of test performance in relation to the targeted achievement construct or concepts, and finally (c) demonstrate that the proposed interpretations are relevant to intended decisions (i.e., uses) of those interpretations. Some readers may prefer metaphors other than a chain linking these three concepts. What is important is that test developers address the three concepts as part of the validation process. How explicitly do developers of K–12 achievement assessments address intended interpretations, intended uses, and targeted achievement constructs?

In this section we examine types of evidence reported in the 12 technical reports to support the validity of interpretations of K–12 achievement test scores and decisions based on those interpretations. We also examine what that evidence suggests about the validity of interpretations typically made about student knowledge and skills based on performance on K–12 assessments. We do not address broader interpretations such as using test scores to evaluate school quality or assessing potential positive and negative side effects of high-stakes assessment programs. (See Koretz & Hamilton, this volume, on these topics.) We have sampled from the index of the *Standards* some of the most salient standards on test score interpretation (see "Score interpretation," p. 190) and use (see "Test use," p. 193). We have organized selected validity requirements into conceptually similar groups in Table 16.5. The first group of standards focuses on providing support for interpreting test scores. The other three groups provide guidance on developing validity evidence.

5.3.1. Statements of Intended Score Interpretations and Uses

While interpretations and uses are separate links in the logic chain, they are inseparably connected as a practical matter. Test users cannot use results from a test administration without first interpreting results, and it is a challenge to interpret test results without having at least a vague purpose for making interpretations. All 12 of the technical reports contain a simple declaration of the interpretations that the assessments are intended to enable. It should come as no surprise that all of the state assessment program technical reports refer to state content standards as the academic content targeted by the tests and as the basis for interpreting test performance. After all, we have been working in an era of standards-based assessment at least since the early 1990s. And the current era was preceded by its evolutionary predecessors, the basic skills and minimum competency testing movements of the 1970s (see Michaels & Ferrara, 1999).

Only the Michigan report contains the popularly used phrase "what students know and can do" regarding intended interpretations, along with a reference to the state content standards. According to the report for TerraNova, this nationally normed commercial test, is intended to "measure concepts, processes, and skills taught throughout the nation"

TABLE 16.5 Selected Standards for Evidence to Support Validity of Intended Interpretations and Uses of Test Scores

STANDARDS	REQUIREMENTS IN THE STANDARDS
Test score interpretations	
1.1–1.4, 1.10–1.12	Test developers should:
	—Present rationales, evidence, and theory to support all recommended interpretations and uses of test scores
	—Describe the construct being assessed
	—Describe evidence to support interpretations of subsets of items, individual items, score differences and profiles, and composite scores
	—Identify interpretations for which no evidence exists or for which evidence is contradictory
Development of validity evidence	
1.5–1.8, 1.13, 1.14, 13.3	In developing and providing validity evidence, test developers should:
	—Describe test content in relation to the target content objectives or achievement construct
	—Describe theoretical and empirical support for premises about cognitive processes used by examinees
	—Describe and provide rationales for data collection, analysis, and interpretation procedures
	—Provide rationales for external measures used in analyses of convergent and discriminant validity
Development of evidence of construct under-representation and construct irrelevant score variance	
7.3, 7.10	Test developers should conduct studies to:
	—Detect and eliminate sources of differential item functioning
	—Determine that examinee subgroup mean test score differences are not attributable to construct under-representation or construct irrelevant sources
Development of evidence of impacts of tests and interpretations of test scores	
1.23, 1.24	Test developers should:
	—Provide rationales and evidence to support claims for positive impacts of tests and testing programs
	—Attempt to investigate sources of construct irrelevance and construct under-representation that may be related to unintended consequences

Source: Adapted from the *Standards* (1999); details and some qualifying statements are excluded for the sake of brevity.

(p. 1). The most frequently used interpretive verb in these reports is "measure," as in measure student achievement in relation to content standards. More modest verbs like "document" and "test" appear once each in a report. Another interpretive verb, "determine," appears in conjunction with other terms like "meeting," "achieving," and "making progress toward" (performance standards and proficiency levels). Three state reports describe broader intended interpretations and make more explicit references to intended uses. The Minnesota and New Hampshire reports state that test results are intended to enable decision making to improve curriculum, instruction, and student achievement. (Actually, the New Hampshire legislation mandates this intention.) The Texas report states that results are intended to measure student progress toward achieving academic excellence and that test results "are used as a gauge for institutional accountability" (p. 1). Rhetoric aside, this is one of the only explicit references in the context of test score interpretation and use from the 11 state assessment program reports to the role of the assessments in state accountability systems and educational improvement efforts. None of the reports identifies intended interpretations that may not be supported by evidence or evidence to contradict intended interpretations. Two reports include cautions about misinterpreting test scores. The Minnesota report recommends using multiple indicators (including test scores) for decisions about student promotion and grade retention. The Texas report contains a section on cautions for score use that focuses primarily on interpreting scores at the extremes of the score scale.

5.3.2. Definitions of Achievement Constructs

It continues to be true that validity theory runs far ahead of validation practice in K–12 achievement testing. One of the biggest distances between theory and practice is in construct definition. The discussion in section 5.3.1 above suggests that, in K–12 assessment practice, specifying "targets of inference" (National Research Council, 2001, p. 45) or targeted achievement constructs (Haertel, 1985) is a matter of declaring that an assessment is intended to assess a set of content standards that should be taught in schools and learned by students. State content standards are designed to guide local curriculum development and instructional planning, not test development. They are written to communicate to teachers and local school system instructional supervisors and to capture public acceptance (or at least minimize public outcry). Content standards typically do not describe achievement in a content area in a way that is readily translatable to clear test specifications. Clarity and coherence can be gained by defining what is to be tested as an achievement construct that is derived from content standards. When achievement targets are defined clearly as achievement constructs, assessment tasks can be aligned with targeted procedural knowledge and cognitive processes in fact as well as in intent. Further, when achievement constructs are defined rigorously, interpretations of test scores can be clearer, more strongly supportable, and more likely to provide more directly useful information to guide instructional decisions and planning (Ferrara, Duncan, et al., 2005).

Achievement constructs depict (a) educational outcomes in school content areas (e.g., reading, writing, mathematics) that encompass instructional objectives defined by curriculum specialists (Haertel, 1985), and (b) models of cognition and learning (Haertel, 1985; National Research Council, 2001, p. 178) that might be described by educational and cognitive psychologists. Some explications exist on defining constructs to support assessment development and valid interpretation. The *Standards* suggest that definitions of constructs like mathematics achievement delineate "the knowledge, skills, abilities, processes, or characteristics to be assessed" (p. 9). Fiske (1971) provides a chapter on specifying personality constructs that is so practical it seems readily adaptable to educational assessment. He calls for "a comprehensive delineation of it [the target construct], one that indicates with some clarity how one should go about measuring it" (p. 91). He describes 10 steps for arriving at a working conceptualization of a construct (summarized on p. 117), including (a) the setting for the construct (e.g., supporting theory, variables that comprise the construct), (b) delineation of the construct (e.g., its essence and differentiation from overlapping constructs), and (c) planning for measurement of the construct (e.g., assessment approaches). Haertel (1985) provides a well developed illustration of defining and validating an achievement construct that is an intended outcome of schooling, functional literacy. He describes studies to support generalizations from test performance to broader outcome domains and to investigate facets of the tested construct that do not generalize beyond test performance.

Wiley (2002) describes three partially formulated construct definitions in terms of assessment tasks. For example:

> *Conceptual understanding* tasks are broadly described as those that usually create the opportunity for students to analyze an idea, to reformulate it, and to express it in their own terms. Tasks designed to assess conceptual understanding are usually non-routine, short, and cast in a context. Conceptual understanding tasks can be thought of as "idea probes." Usually the accomplishment of a conceptual understanding task draws heavily on reconstruction rather than on recall; solutions are characterized by representation or explanation rather than by manipulation. Often a short written explanation is sufficient to accomplish the task. These are the kinds of tasks that students can do easily if they understand the mathematics involved. (p. 218; emphasis in original)

As clear and explicit as this achievement construct definition is, it is only partially formulated. Ferrara, Duncan, et al. (2005) suggest four features for defining complex educational achievement constructs. (They refer to others, as well, from National Research Council, 2001.) They are: (a) specification of content knowledge, including what is known, how the knowledge is organized, how well it can be accessed and used; (b) specification of procedural knowledge, including content area specific strategies, thinking processes, and communication skills; (c) a measurement plan, including examples of assessment tasks and guidance on supportable inferences about what examinees know and can do based on test performance; and (d) hypotheses and evidence of the relation of the construct to other constructs, including similar and different achievement constructs.

The definition of the conceptual understanding achievement construct specifies only procedural knowledge and a measurement plan.

Much of the work on specification of educational assessments provides guidance relevant to defining achievement constructs. Nitko's (2004, chap. 2) update of the large literature on developing instructional objectives distinguishes general learning targets typically portrayed in state content standards from specific learning targets for teachers. The distinction appears related to Fiske's notion of construct delineation (1971, pp. 98–101). Crocker and Algina (1986) list suggested activities to produce information relevant to defining constructs (e.g., content analysis, identification of critical incidents; see p. 68). And Popham's prescriptions for domain, test, and item specifications (Popham, 1984) have served as a model for much of the test conceptualization, design, and development work in state assessment programs for several decades. Millman and Greene (1989) classify test purposes that emphasize differences in kinds of decisions made using test scores (see p. 336). They distinguish three sources of test content (i.e., construct) for defining the domain to be tested and the domain of inference[9] from a test performance: inferences to a curricular domain, inferences to a cognitive domain, and inferences to future performances. In doing so, they anticipate the National Research Council's call (2001) for using in the assessment design and validation process a model of cognition and learning that informs assessment design (pp . 178 ff.), components of cognition (pp. 65 ff.), and the nature and development of subject matter expertise (p. 72). The National Research Council report provides brief descriptions of models of thinking, reasoning, and conceptual understanding (2001, pp. 92–96). It also acknowledges that the work of specifying declarative and procedural knowledge in academic content areas requires significant effort (see Recommendation 2, p. 299).

None of the 12 technical reports we reviewed attempts to define achievement constructs. Rather, the common approach is to list the content standards that each test targets. For state assessments the targets are state content standards for which all school systems, schools, teachers, and students are responsible. For commercial norm referenced tests the targets are the instructional objectives that appear most frequently in the content standards of as many states as possible (e.g., p. 1 of the TerraNova report). The 12 technical reports list and sometimes elaborate on the content standards that are targeted by each test, almost always describe the process for matching test items with state content standards, typically provide tables with the number of item types assigned to each content standard (i.e., test blueprints), and describe other test design information. The reports do not suggest that test designs are intended to support inferences about student achievement in relation to models of cognition and learning. Rather, the reports reflect the pervasive concept in K–12 assessment design: standards-based assessment. In this conception, content standards are described and items that are purported to be aligned with those standards are included in the test. Three reports (Minnesota, Texas, and Washington) begin with a brief discussion of intended and appropriate uses for test scores and reports. Many of the reports describe types of scores provided with the tests and leave discussions of interpretation and use of test scores to separate score interpretation guides for test users.

5.3.3. Evidence Based on Test Content

It is no surprise that all 12 technical reports document the relationship between test content and the content standards targeted by the tests. Typically, technical reports provide descriptions of the process of developing and refining test items and test blueprints that summarize information such as numbers or proportions of items that are intended to assess each content standard or test objective included in the test design. The reports provide these accounts as evidence that assessments cover the content area material intended. The surprise is that three of these reports provide only brief and general descriptions of the test development process and the role of the descriptions as validity evidence. Even more surprising, two states do not present test blueprints. In these cases, the evidence presented actually is declarations by content expert committees or testing program staff and their contractors that these tests cover the content area knowledge and skills intended in the corresponding content standards.

For several decades, evidence that an achievement test covers intended curricular objectives, usually summarized in test blueprints or tables of specifications, was adequate. In the 1980s, the Debra P. case raised the standards for test content based evidence by introducing notions of curricular and instructional validity (see Madaus, 1983). Systematic alignment studies published in recent years (e.g., Porter, 2002; Rothman, Slattery, Vranek, & Resnick, 2002; Webb, 2002) have produced more explicit examination of the content knowledge and cognitive processes that test items require of examinees and of the degree to which these demands are consistent with the content knowledge and procedural requirements intended in content standards and corresponding item and test specifications. None of these 12 reports refers explicitly to alignment studies since, of course, these reports document tests and test administrations prior to publication of influential alignment studies. Recent development and application of rigorous methods for examining the alignment between test and content standards suggest that the quality of validity evidence based on test content soon will improve significantly.

5.3.4. Evidence Based on Internal Structure and Response Processes

Prior to the publication of the *Standards* (1999), this concept was referred to as "construct validity." Evidence of the relationship of K–12 assessments with the achievement constructs they target varies widely in these reports. Two of the reports mention construct validity but do not provide relevant evidence. Six additional reports do not even mention construct validity. Three reports refer to various types of evidence about the tests they document (e.g., factor analysis results as evidence of unidimensionality in the Michigan and Virginia reports, item point biserial correlations and Rasch fit statistics in the Minnesota report) and state simply that the evidence supports the validity of the tests. Two other reports construct arguments relevant to supporting the validity of test score interpretations, as required by the *Standards*, but with little reference to score interpretations. Part 3 of the Washington report, "Evidence for the Validity of Inferences from Test Scores," provides (a) internal subscale correlations of roughly .40–.60 (a small number are lower than .40); (b) factor analysis results with 12 reading and mathematics subscales with high loadings on separate reading and mathematics factors (i.e., 10 communalities greater than .60, two approximately equal to .50) and with 60% of the variance explained by a two-factor solution; and (c) factor analysis results indicating that Washington assessment reading and writing subscores load on an English language arts factor with Iowa Tests of Basic Skills (ITBS) reading items, and Washington and ITBS mathematics items load on a second factor (18 of 20 communalities greater than .60, two greater than .45, $R^2 = .36$). Discussion of these results does not often refer explicitly to implications for interpreting corresponding test scores. Rather, it mentions the need to reconceptualize test subscales with low factor loadings. The TerraNova report provides arguments about the relationship between presented evidence and the validity of test score interpretations. The evidence includes correlations between TerraNova scores and scores from InView, an academic abilities test developed and co-normed with TerraNova. The correlations range between .35 (grade 2 spelling and analogies) and .76 (mathematics composite and InView total score). The report asserts that the correlations are "in agreement with expectations of convergent and discriminant validity" (p. 254) without referring to implications for score interpretation. The report does include a set of "construct validity statements" (pp. 267–275). The statements are discussions of the content knowledge and cognitive skills targeted in each content area subtest with references to content area conceptualization, theory, and research that support these targets. In fact, these validity statements actually approximate construct definitions (see section 5.3.2 above).

Finally, only five reports refer explicitly to the cognitive processes that are likely to be required to respond to the items on the tests they document. It may seem unfair to evaluate tests using this criterion since only recently have measurement researchers begun investigating examinee cognitive processing during test taking (e.g., Ferrara et al., 2003, 2004; National Research Council, 2001). However, in the third edition of *Educational Measurement* Snow and Lohman observed that methodology existed and such investigations had already begun (1989, p. 314). In addition, the *Standards* discuss such evidence (1999, pp. 12–13). Typically, content standards and test objectives refer to cognitive skills and processes as well as content knowledge requirements. These five technical reports refer specifically to cognitive processes required by items in discussions of content standards and other topics (e.g., standard setting). They do not provide evidence of examinee cognitive processing. The Michigan technical report contains a section titled "Validity of Test Items." The report argues that item p values, DIF statistics, item discrimination statistics, the range of item difficulty on each test, and other factors (e.g., rater agreement for constructed-response items) provide assurance that items measure what they are intended to measure.

5.3.5. Evidence of Relations to Other Measures

Criterion related evidence does not play as prominent a role in validation in educational assessment as it does in other contexts. We do not need to catalogue the limited information provided in six of these 12 technical reports to support this point. It would seem obvious to provide correlations of achievement test scores with external measures such as scores from other achievement tests, course grades, and other teacher ratings. And the predictive validity of high school graduation tests with measures of postsecondary attainment (i.e., in higher education achievement, training, employment, and the military) seems crucial. The evidence in these technical reports on relations with external measures is generated most often when it is convenient and affordable to do so. For example, the Virginia report contains correlations with a commercial norm referenced test (correlations of approximately .6 to .8) for students in grades 3, 5, and 8. According to the technical report, these data are intended to answer a question directly relevant to score interpretation: Do schools and students that score well on the external criterion also score well on the state assessments? One report argues that external measures that are available are not appropriate because they are based on different subject matter. Other reports do provide evidence of relations to other measures that required special data collection. The New Hampshire report displays line plots to show the positive relationship between state assessment average scores and, for example, amount of homework; the Texas report refers to correlations with course grades published in previous technical reports; and the Washington report provides correlations with a commercial norm referenced test (ranging between .44 and .77). These reports provide little discussion of the relevance of these correlations to supporting interpretations of test scores. Another report suggests that local school systems and university researchers will collect data to produce evidence of the state assessment's relations to other measures.

5.3.6. Evidence Regarding Construct Under-Representation and Construct Irrelevance

Only two of the 12 reports mentions construct under-representation or construct irrelevant variance explicitly. (Both reports are written by the same contractor, but not all reports in this sample from that contractor make similar mention.) The Alaska report provides test blueprints as evidence to refute construct under-representation. The TerraNova report offers as evidence of minimizing construct irrelevant variance the steps in the test development and refinement process, item selection process (i.e., by selecting items based on their point biserial correlations, IRT model fit statistics, and DIF statistics), and rater accuracy rates in scoring responses to the writing assessment.

One way to minimize sources of construct irrelevant variance is to exclude items that are flagged for differential item functioning (DIF; Haladyna & Downing, 2004). This topic—especially development of analytic procedures, statistics, and decision criteria—has received abundant attention recently in professional conferences and journals. DIF receives similar attention in these technical reports. Only two of the reports do not mention DIF. All 12 reports refer to committees that review items for fairness and that DIF results or fairness criteria are used in item selection. Seven reports indicate that DIF analyses are conducted for male-female differences. DIF for racial/ethnic subgroups depends on the diversity of the student population in a state (or the United States, in the case of TerraNova). For example, Alaska provides DIF analysis results for community type and Alaskan natives. The Alaska, New Hampshire, and TerraNova reports tabulate numbers of items that are and are not flagged for levels of DIF; two additional states observe that only small numbers of items are flagged.

5.3.7. Evidence Based on Consequences and Impacts of Tests

Debate has subsided about whether evidence of the consequences of interpreting test scores and making decisions about students and impacts of testing programs (e.g., curriculum narrowing) is relevant to test score validity. The *Standards* distinguish evidence about consequences that is relevant to social policy (e.g., valid differences in group performance on a validated job skills test) from evidence that "can be traced to a source of invalidity" (e.g., a sophisticated literacy test for a job that requires minimal literacy skills; see p. 16). Standards 1.23 and 1.24 in Table 16.5 above reflect this distinction. Standard 1.23 requires test developers to support claims that an educational assessment produces intended positive impacts. Standard 1.24 requires test developers to attempt to investigate sources of invalidity. Recent work demonstrates the kinds of evidence that *are* relevant to positive impacts of assessment programs (e.g., Firestone, Mayrowetz, & Fairman, 1998; Lane, Parke, & Stone, 1998). Haladyna and Downing (2004) catalogue potential sources of construct irrelevant score variance that could be investigated for educational assessments.

How do these 12 technical reports address evidence of consequences and impacts? The Washington report mentions consequences among many validity considerations. Other reports refer to uses of test scores that are relevant to consequences and impacts. For example, the Michigan report states that test results can be used for school improvement but does not support the claim, and the Minnesota report suggests using test scores as evidence for school program evaluations.

5.4. Quality of the Evidence and the State of the Field of K–12 Achievement Testing

We began this section by describing 12 state assessment program technical reports that cover a generally representative sample of the grade levels, content areas, and test purposes that comprise K–12 achievement testing in the United States. This sample of reports enables a number of evaluative conclusions about the state of the art of the field

early in the 21st century. The *Standards* require that assessment documents, including technical reports, should be made available at the time when a test is published and used (see standard 6.1). It is probably reasonable to assume that technical documentation is available for virtually all state-level and commercially Published K–12 assessments, and even for some curriculum-based assessments developed by local school systems. General availability—specifically via state assessment program Web sites—is not good. Many of the 51 state assessment programs (including Washington, DC) and U.S. territories would be expected to produce at least one technical report each year during the period prior to *No Child Left Behind* (i.e., before 2002). We were able to find only 11 technical reports on 50 state Web sites, covering the years 1998–2003. Although we assume that documentation of technical adequacy in K–12 achievement testing is comprehensive, it certainly is not widely disseminated. It should be. K–12 testing serves governmental and societal functions; information on the quality and appropriateness and technical soundness of K–12 assessments should be accessible publicly. Further, documentation of evidence of some critical validity questions is inadequate, as we discuss below.

5.4.1. Evidence of Score Reliability

The evidence in the sampled technical reports suggests that test score reliability is quite good, especially for tests with more than 40 items. Standard errors of measurement (both average and conditional) are relatively low in relation to the numbers of score points available on raw score and scale score scales. Reliability tends to be a bit higher in reading and mathematics. All of this is expected, given that these tests tend to be long enough, are scored rigorously, and are homogenous in terms of content. Rater agreement and accuracy tend to be high, as well. The industry knows how to develop achievement assessments for school age children that produce internally consistent scores.

These technical reports provide almost no information on the stability of scores over occasions and parallel forms and other evidence of score reliability. Only two of the reports provide score reliability information for examinee sex and racial/ethnic subgroups, six on content area subscores. Three reports provide information on the consistency and accuracy with which test scores classify examinees into performance levels (e.g., proficient). These types of information are required by the *Standards*. The critical importance of the reliability of examinee classifications is increasingly important with the widespread popularity of reporting test performance in performance categories and reporting requirements in *No Child Left Behind*.

5.4.2. Evidence of the Validity of Intended Score Interpretations and Uses

The limited evidence in these reports to support interpretations about student achievement is, perhaps, marginally adequate. We know from the reports that K–12 achievement assessments cover intended content standards. That has been the standard for evidence for test score validity at least since the 1980s. Additional, more rigorous evidence that is required in the *Standards* to support score interpretations is not widely available. For example, explicit statements of intended interpretations and uses tend to be general and formulaic (e.g., intended interpretations refer to content standards in a general way). Other validity evidence typically is not explicitly linked in these reports to intended score interpretations and uses. Similarly, when evidence is provided relevant to the internal structure of tests (e.g., subscale correlation analyses) and external relations with other measures of achievement, the evidence is not linked explicitly to intended interpretations and uses. Other validity evidence appears not to be part of current thinking about supporting intended interpretations and uses of scores from K–12 assessments. None of these reports referred to evidence from studies of test alignment or cognitive processes elicited from examinees by test items. A handful of reports refer to the importance of addressing construct under-representation, construct irrelevant variance, and consequences and impacts of the assessment programs they document but provide little relevant evidence.

5.4.3. The State of the Art

We have evaluated the availability and quality of evidence relevant to validity. Our conclusions are rather disappointing. The types of evidence provided fall far short of current thinking and recent methodological developments relevant to developing validity evidence. Technical reports tend to describe evidence without integrating it into statements about the validity of various interpretations and uses (see the *Standards*, p. 17). In contrast, the robustness and influence of K–12 achievement testing is unmistakable. The general public supports testing in schools (e.g., 70% of Americans, according to a 2003 Pew/Kaiser poll) and legislators and boards of education recognize the power of tests as levers for focusing teaching and other resources on improving student achievement. Further, the evidence about technical adequacy that is provided (e.g., reliability of scores, coverage of test objectives) is positive, if far from comprehensive.

6. SELECTED ONGOING CONCERNS AND ISSUES FOR THE FUTURE

Throughout this chapter we have commented on the state of the art in K–12 achievement testing. To those observations we add discussion of ongoing concerns and issues for the future of K–12 achievement testing. We have selected a small number of what we consider the most interesting and potentially influential issues.

We begin by suggesting what may seem obvious. We anticipate that K–12 achievement testing will continue indefinitely in its prominent role in K–12 education. Achievement assessment information will be used for public accountability purposes and will be provided to support curriculum and instruction decisions. Achievement assessments will be used for high-stakes decisions for schools and for students. It is difficult to imagine that K–12 achievement testing will continue to expand in terms of numbers of test administrations and amount of time spent on preparation and administration. Likewise, it is difficult to imagine continuing expansion in test types and assessment purposes, especially after recent expansions in assessing students with disabilities and English language learners. It is not difficult to imagine that the dollars spent on achievement assessments will continue to grow.

We have organized our concerns and issues into five themes. We recognize that some issues may be our hopes for the future as much as they are our predictions.

6.1. Coordination of State, Local School System, and Classroom Assessment Activities

Earlier, we discussed points of view about the value of large-scale K–12 achievement testing for accountability purposes and guiding instructional decisions. K–12 achievement testing operates on several parallel and loosely coupled levels. States require external, large-scale assessments to serve accountability requirements and spur school improvement. They strive to make test information relevant at least for broad curriculum and instruction decisions at the state, local, and school levels. Some school systems with financial and technical resources operate curriculum embedded assessments to monitor school and student achievement of curriculum area goals. Some states implement high school end-of-course examinations for similar reasons. And teachers assess their students in the classroom as part of the teaching-learning process. We also discussed calls for improving the balance between large-scale and classroom assessment and for instructionally supportive assessments (see section 2.1). Additional emphasis at any level on providing assessment information that supports instruction and student achievement is, obviously, desirable.

Coordination or improved balance across these levels seems unlikely in the near future. State departments of education, local school systems, and classroom teachers each have different information needs and different purposes for assessing students. Coordination and balance are likely to increase only as information produced from local school system curriculum embedded assessments, for example, is perceived as valuable for state accountability and education reform efforts. There are reasons for modest optimism. We have observed that teachers who follow curriculum guides prescribed by their school systems do use information from curriculum embedded assessments to focus instruction for students. And we have observed that the practice and quality of classroom assessment have received enormous attention in the last 20 years in pre-service and in-service training. In addition, countries around the world are recognizing the effects that effective formative assessment has on learning (e.g., Olson, 2005). (See also section 2.1 above on instructionally supportive assessment.)

6.2. A Psychology of Assessing Achievement and Practical Applications to Operational Testing Programs

Earlier, we described research that attempts to clarify the knowledge and skill demands that assessment items and tasks place on examinees (see section 4.2.1 above) and assessment models that link test performance interpretations explicitly to evidence of student knowledge, skills, and cognitive processing (see section 4.3 above). We suggested that this work would improve accuracy in achieving item cognitive demand and difficulty targets during test development and enhance the clarity of interpretations from test scores about what students know and can do. We expect that work in this area will continue to be productive. We observed that using findings from this research would require a shift in current conception and practice in assessment design and development. We also expect that principles from explicit assessment design approaches eventually will be adapted for operational K–12 achievement assessments.

6.3. Achievement Test Design

Methods for systematic study of the alignment between test items and targeted content standards are widely used (see section 5.3.3 above). These methods address demands on content area knowledge and skill and on cognitive processing. Other proposals would unify all elements of achievement assessment—from defining content standards to score reporting. Alternate assessments for students with significant cognitive disabilities assess academic content that is reduced in complexity while remaining linked to grade level content standards. We expect this close attention to linking achievement assessment items and tasks tightly to content standards to reinforce the development and practical application of a psychology of assessing achievement.

6.4. Digital Technology Applications

In the 1980s, the most significant applications of technology in large-scale achievement testing were evident at the back end of the assessment process. Optical scanners captured answer sheet bubbles highly accurately, at a rate of thousands of sheets per hour. Sorting machines sliced test booklet bindings and shunted booklet sections to different piles for distribution to hand-scoring teams. In subsequent years, high-speed optical image processing machines created digital images of test booklet pages, which enabled integration of multiple-choice and constructed-response items in a single test booklet/answer document. More recently, a range of powerful digital electronic devices, sophisticated analysis programs, and use of the Internet have become evident in virtually all phases of achievement testing: Automated item generation, assessment task formats that are not feasible in printed test booklets, delivery and administration of tests to examinees (e.g., computer adaptive testing, Internet delivery of tests), voice recognition software in language testing, automated scoring of constructed responses, psychometric analysis, easy and meaningful tabulation of test scores by educators who are not formally trained in data analysis, and delivery of test scores and customized remedial advice and support. These applications are addressed in detail by Drasgow, Luecht, and Bennett (this volume).

Delivery and administration of assessments using technology will continue to expand. Many school age children, their families, and their schools have limited or no access to the Internet, personal computers, and hand-held digital devices. These limits will constrain how quickly and widely digital applications can pervade K–12 achievement testing. Concerns about the comparability of assessment results from paper-pencil and technology-based administrations will continue to be worrisome, as will concerns about generalizing achievement results from technology-based administrations to classrooms without access to technology.

6.5. National Content Standards, National Performance Standards, and National Tests

Are we on a path toward national content standards, national individual achievement assessments, and corresponding performance standards? Developments since the 1980s would suggest that we may be. President George H. W. Bush proposed American Achievement Tests in 1991; President Bill Clinton proposed Voluntary National Tests in 1997 (see Table 16.1). The National Assessment of Educational Progress (NAEP) now includes state assessments and Trial Urban District Assessments. And NAEP assessment frameworks, psychometric innovations, and achievement levels are influential models for state assessment programs. In addition, national content area organizations publish national standards for their content areas (e.g., the National Science Education Standards), with the endorsement of the National Governors Association (National Research Council, 1996, p. 13). States collaborate on a number of assessment-related activities, including development of assessments. For example, a collaborative of 18 states managed by the Council of Chief State School Officers developed the English Language Development Assessments (ELDA). Five states administered ELDA operationally in spring 2006 to assess the English proficiency of English language learners in order to meet *No Child Left Behind* requirements.

The idea of mandatory achievement tests controlled by the federal government seems a bit far fetched. National curricula and student assessments have been predicted in the past and their potential benefits described (Ferrara & Thornton, 1988). Potential drawbacks of a national curriculum also have been described (American Educational Research Association, 1995). A third proposal to implement a system of national content and performance standards and individual student achievement tests cannot be ruled out.

NOTES

1. For the sake of simplicity, we exclude some details and provide a general outline of the most significant requirements. References to states also include U.S. jurisdictions such as the District of Columbia and Puerto Rico.

2. There are notable exceptions, including perhaps local assessments in Nebraska's School-Based Teacher-Led Assessment and Reporting System (STARS); see Brookhart (2005).

3. Consider applying the kitchen table test for 3rd graders, whose numeracy and literacy are limited. Also consider, for example, the limited English proficiency of parents who recently emigrated to the United States. We acknowledge that applying the kitchen table test could rule out score reporting scales other than number correct scales.

4. Throughout this chapter we refer to "the *Standards*." See American Educational Research Association, American Psychological Association, and National Council on Measurement in Education (1999).

5. Throughout this section, a single affirmative response to a survey question could refer to one grade or several grades.

6. We use the term "item" generically here. Some K–12 assessments include assessment "prompts" (e.g., essay prompts) or assessment "tasks," which may include a coherent collection of items and prompts (e.g., see Yen & Ferrara, 1997).

7. We order the example items in a conventional way; we do not intend the order to suggest importance or any other comparative value of item types.

8. See Mislevy (this volume) for a comprehensive and up-to-date perspective.

9. This terminology is no longer widely used, and it is somewhat inconsistent with current conceptions of validation as described, for example, by Kane (this volume).

REFERENCES

Abedi, J., Lord, C., Hofstetter, C., & Baker, E. (2001). Impact of accommodation strategies on English language learners' test performance. *Educational Measurement: Issues and Practice, 19*(3), 16–26.

American Educational Research Association. (1995). *The hidden consequences of a national curriculum*. Washington, DC: Author.

American Educational Research Association, American Psychological Association, & National Council on Measurement in Education. (1999). *Standards for educational and psychological testing*. Washington, DC: American Educational Research Association.

Baker, F. B. (1971). Automation of test scoring, reporting, and analysis. In R. L. Thorndike (Ed.), *Educational measurement* (2nd ed.) (pp. 202–234). Washington, DC: American Council on Education.

Baxter, G. P., & Glaser, R. (1998). Investigating the cognitive complexity of science assessments. *Educational Measurement: Issues and Practice, 17*(3), 37–45.

Berk, R. A. (Ed.). (1980). *Criterion-referenced measurement: The state of the art*. Baltimore: Johns Hopkins University Press.

Berk, R. A. (Ed.). (1984). *A guide to criterion-referenced test construction*. Baltimore: Johns Hopkins University Press.

Berko, R. M., Wolvin, A. D., & Wolvin, D. R. (1998). *Communicating: A social and career focus*. Boston: Houghton Mifflin.

Bloom, B. S., Engelhart, M. D., Furst, E. J., Hill, W. H., & Krathwohl, D. R. (Eds.). (1956). *Taxonomy of educational objectives: The classification of educational goals. Handbook I: Cognitive domain*. New York: David McKay.

Brookhart, S. M. (2005). The quality of local district assessments used in Nebraska's School-Based Teacher-Led Assessment and Reporting System (STARS). *Educational Measurement: Issues and Practice, 24*(2), 14–21.

Broudy, H. S. (1980). Impact of minimum competency testing on curriculum. In R. M. Jaeger & C. K. Tittle (Eds.), *Minimum competency achievement testing: Motives, models, and consequences* (pp. 108–121). Berkeley, CA: McCutchan.

Burroughs, S., Groce, E., & Webeck, M. L. (2005). Social studies education in the age of accountability testing. *Educational Measurement: Issues and Practice, 24*(3), 13–20.

Center on Education Policy. (2004). *State high school exit exams: A maturing reform*. Washington, DC: Author.

Coffman, W. E. (1971). Essay examinations. In R. L. Thorndike (Ed.), *Educational measurement* (2nd ed.) (pp. 271–302). Washington, DC: American Council on Education.

Colangelo, N., Assouline, S. G., & Gross, M. U. M. (2004). *A nation deceived: How schools hold back America's brightest students (Vol. I)*. Iowa City: University of Iowa.

Cole, N. S., & Moss, P. A. (1989). Bias in test use. In R. L. Linn (Ed.), *Educational measurement* (3rd ed.) (pp. 201–219). New York: Macmillan.

Coleman, M. R. (2003). *The identification of students who are gifted*. (ERIC Document Reproduction Service No. EDi480431) ERIC Clearinghouse on Disabilities and Gifted Education, Arlington, VA.

Commission on Instructionally Supportive Assessment. (2001, October). *Building tests to support instruction and accountability: A guide for policymakers*. Retrieved September 19, 2003 from http://www.nea.org/accountability/buildingtests.html

Council of Chief State School Officers. (2003). *Annual survey of state student assessment programs: Summary report (2001–02)*. Washington, DC: Author.

Crocker, L., & Algina, J. (1986). *Introduction to classical and modern test theory*. New York: Holt, Rhinehart and Winston.

Embretson, S. E. (2002). Generating abstract reasoning items with cognitive theory. In S. H. Irvine & P. C. Kyllonen (Eds.), *Item generation for test development* (pp. 219–250). Mahwah, NJ: Lawrence Erlbaum.

Embretson, S. E., & Gorin, J. (2001). Improving construct validity with cognitive psychology principles. *Journal of Educational Measurement, 38*, 343–368.

Feldt, L. S., & Brennan, R. L. (1989). Reliability. In R. L. Linn (Ed.), *Educational measurement* (3rd ed.) (pp. 105–146). New York: Macmillan.

Ferrara, S. (1993). Generalizability and scaling: Their roles in writing assessment and implications for performance assessments in other content areas. In G. Phillips (Moderator), *After a decade of authentic writing assessment, what advice do frontier states have to offer authentic assessment developers in other subject areas?* Symposium conducted at the annual meeting of the National Council on Measurement in Education, Atlanta, GA.

Ferrara, S., Duncan, T., Freed, R., Velez-Paschke, A., Burke, A., McGivern, J., et al. (2005, April). *Comparing the achievement constructs targeted and achieved in a statewide middle school science assessment*. Paper presented at the annual meeting of the National Council on Measurement in Education, Montreal, Canada.

Ferrara, S., Duncan, T. G., Freed, R., Velez-Paschke, A., McGivern, J., Mushlin, S., et al. (2004, April). *Examining test score validity by examining item construct validity: Preliminary analysis of evidence of the alignment of targeted and observed content, skills, and cognitive processes in a middle school science assessment*. Paper presented at the annual meeting of the American Educational Research Association, San Diego, CA.

Ferrara, S., Duncan, T., Perie, M., Freed, R., McGivern, J., & Chilukuri, R. (2003, April). *Item construct validity: Early results from a study of the relationship between intended and actual cognitive demands in a middle school science assessment*. In S. Ferrara (Chair), *Cognitive and other influences on responding to science test items: What is and what can be*. Symposium conducted at the annual meeting of the American Educational Research Association, Chicago.

Ferrara, S., Johnson, E., & Chen, W.-H. (2005). Vertically articulated performance standards: Logic, procedures, and likely classification accuracy. *Applied Measurement in Education, 18*(1), 35–59.

Ferrara, S., & McTighe, J. (1992). Assessment: A thoughtful process. In A. Costa, J. Bellanca, & R. Fogarty (Eds.), *If minds matter: A foreword to the future* (Vol. 2) (pp. 337–348). Palatine, IL: Skylight Publishing.

Ferrara, S., & Thornton, S. (1988). Using NAEP for interstate comparisons: The beginnings of a "national achievement test" and "national curriculum." *Educational Evaluation and Policy Analysis, 10*(3), 200–211.

Firestone, W. A., Mayrowetz, D., & Fairman, J. (1998). Performance-based assessment and instructional change: The effects of testing in Maine and Maryland. *Educational Evaluation and Policy Analysis, 20* 2), 95–113.

Fiske, D. W. (1971). *Measuring the concepts of personality*. Chicago: Aldine Publishing.

Fontana, J. (1995). Portfolio assessment: Its beginnings in Vermont and Kentucky. *National Association of Secondary School Principals (NASSP) Bulletin, 79*(573), 25–30.

Fuchs, L. S., Fuchs, D., Hosp, M. K., & Hamlett, C. L. (2003). The potential for diagnostic analysis with curriculum-based measurement. *Assessment for Effective Intervention, 28*(3–4), 13–22.

Gilliam, W. S., & Zigler, W. F. (2000). A critical meta-analysis of all evaluations of state-funded preschool from 1977 to 1998: Implications for policy, service delivery, and program evaluation. *Early Childhood Research Quarterly, 15*(4), 441–473.

Goodman, D. P., & Hambleton, R. K. (2004). Students test score reports and interpretive guides: Review of current practices and suggestions for future research. *Applied Measurement in Education, 17*(2), 145–220.

Gould, S. J. (1996). *The mismeasure of man* (Rev. ed.). New York: Norton.

Haertel, E. (1985). Construct validity and criterion-referenced testing. *Review of Educational Research, 55*(1), 23–46.

Haertel, E. H., & Lorié, W. A. (2004). Validating standards-based test score interpretations. *Measurement: Interdisciplinary Research and Perspectives, 2*(2), 61–103.

Haladyna, T. M. (2004). *Developing and validating multiple-choice test items* (3rd ed.). Mahwah, NJ: Lawrence Erlbaum.

Haladyna, T. M., & Downing, S. M. (2004). Construct-irrelevant variance in high-stakes testing. *Educational Measurement: Issues and Practice, 23*(1), 17–27.

Hambleton, R. K. (2001). Setting performance standards on educational assessments and criteria for evaluating the process. In G. J. Cizek (Ed.), *Setting performance standards: Concepts, methods, and perspectives* (pp. 89–116). Mahwah, NJ: Erlbaum.

Hamilton, L. S., Nussbaum, E. M., & Snow, R. E. (1997). Interview procedures for validating science assessments. *Applied Measurement in Education, 10*(2), 181–200.

Hitchcock, C., Meyer, A., Rose, D., & Jackson, R. (2002, March 27). *Access, participation, and progress in the general curriculum* (Technical Brief). Wakefield, MA: National Center on Accessing the General Curriculum/Center for Applied Special Technology.

Individuals with Disabilities Education Act Amendments of 1997, 20 U. S. C. §1400 *et seq.* (ERIC Document Reproduction Service No. ED412721) IDEA amendment published June 4, 1997.

Irvine, S. H., & Kyllonen, P. C. (Eds.). (2002). *Item generation for test development*. Mahwah, NJ: Lawrence Erlbaum.

Jaeger, R. M., & Tittle, C. K. (Eds.). (1980). *Minimum competency achievement testing: Motives, models, measures, and consequences*. Berkeley, CA: McCutchan.

Jakwerth, P. M., Stancavage, F. B., & Reed, E. D. (1999). *An investigation of why students do not respond to questions* (Paper commissioned by NAEP Validity Studies Panel). Palo Alto, CA: American Institutes for Research.

Jensen, A. R. (1980). *Bias in mental testing*. New York: The Free Press.

Joint Committee on Testing Practices. (2004). *Code of fair testing practices in education*. Retrieved August 31, 2005 from http://www.apa.org/science/fairtestcode.html

Keogh, B. K., & MacMillan, D. L. (1996). Exceptionality. In D. C. Berliner & R. C. Calfee (Eds.), *Handbook of educational psychology* (pp. 311–330). New York: Macmillan.

Kohn, A. (2000). *The case against standardized testing: Raising the scores, ruining the schools*. Portsmouth, NH: Heinemann.

Koretz, D., Mitchell, K., Barron, S., & Keith, S. (1996). *Perceived effects of the Maryland School Performance Assessment Program* (CSE Technical Report No. 409). Los Angeles: University of California, CRESST.

Koretz, D., Stecher, B., Klein, S., & McCaffrey, D. (1994). The Vermont portfolio assessment program: Findings and implications. *Educational Measurement: Issues and Practice, 13*(3), 5–16.

Kupermintz, H., Le, V., & Snow, R. E. (1999). *Construct validation of mathematics achievement: Evidence from interview procedures* (CSE Technical Report 493). Los Angeles: UCLA, Center for the Study of Evaluation. (ERIC Document Reproduction Service No. ED428125)

Lane, S. (1993). The conceptual framework for the development of a mathematics performance assessment instrument. *Educational Measurement: Issues and Practice, 12*(2), 16–23.

Lane, S., Parke, C. S., & Stone, C. A. (1998). A framework for evaluating the consequences of assessment programs. *Educational Measurement: Issues and Practice, 17*(2), 24–28.

Lefebvre, R. C., & Rochlin, L. (1997). Social marketing. In K. Glanz, F. M. Lewis, & B. Rimer (Eds.), *Health behavior and health education: Theory, research, and practice* (2nd ed.) (pp. 384–402). San Francisco: Jossey-Bass.

Leighton, J. P. (2004). Avoiding misconception, misuse, and missed opportunities: The collection of verbal reports in educational achievement testing. *Educational Measurement: Issues and Practice, 23*(4), 6–15.

Lewis, J. D. (2001). *Language isn't needed: Nonverbal assessments and gifted learners*. (ERIC Document Reproduction Service No. ED453026). Paper in the American Council on Rural Special Education 2001 Conference Proceedings.

Livingston, S. A., & Lewis, C. (1995). Estimating the consistency and accuracy of classifications based on test scores. *Journal of Educational Measurement, 32*(2), 179–197.

Madaus, G. F. (Ed.). (1983). *The courts, validity, and minimum competency testing*. Boston: Kluwer-Nijhoff.

Marzano, R. J. (2001). *Designing a new taxonomy of educational objectives*. Thousand Oaks, CA: Corwin Press.

Mashburn, A. J., & Henry, G. T. (2004). Assessing school readiness: Validity and bias in preschool and kindergarten teachers' ratings. *Educational Measurement: Issues and Practice, 23*(4), 16–30.

Maxwell, K. L., & Clifford, R. M. (2004, January). Research in review: School readiness assessment. *Journal of the National Association for the Education of Young Children* National Association for the Education of Young Children, Washington DC. Retrieved September 13, 2005 from http://www.journal.naeyc.org/btj/200401/maxwell.asp.

McDonnell, L. M. (2004). *Politics, persuasion, and educational testing*. Cambridge, MA: Harvard University Press.

McTighe, J., & Ferrara, S. (1998). *Assessing learning in the classroom* (Rev. ed.). Washington, DC: National Education Association.

Messick, S. (1994). The interplay of evidence and consequences in the validation of performance assessments. *Educational Researcher, 23*(2), 13–23.

Michaels, H., & Ferrara, S. (1999). Evolution of educational reform in Maryland: Using data to drive state policy and local reform. In G. J. Cizek (Ed.), *Handbook of educational policy* (pp. 101–127). San Diego: Academic Press.

Millman, J., & Greene, J. (1989). The specification and development of tests of achievement and ability. In R. L. Linn (Ed.), *Educational measurement* (3rd ed.)(pp. 335–366). New York: Macmillan.

Mislevy, R. J., Steinberg, L. S., & Almond, R. G. (2002). On the role of task model variables in assessment design. In S. H. Irvine & P. C. Kyllonen (Eds.), *Item generation for test development* (pp. 97–128). Mahwah, NJ: Lawrence Erlbaum.

National Assessment Governing Board. (2001). *National assessment of educational progress: Achievement levels (1992–1998) for mathematics*. S. C. Loomis & M. L. Bourque (Eds.). Washington, DC: Author.

National Association for Gifted Children. (2005a). *Frequently asked questions*. Retrieved October 9, 2005, from http://www.nagc.org

National Association for Gifted Children. (2005b). *Position paper: Using tests to identify gifted students*. Retrieved October 9, 2005, from http://www.nagc.org/index.aspx?id=404

National Research Council. (1996). *National science education standards*. Washington, DC: National Academy Press.

National Research Council. (1999). *High stakes: Testing for tracking, promotion, and graduation*. Committee on Appropriate Test Use. J. P. Heubert & R. M. Hauser (Eds.). Washington, DC: National Academy Press.

National Research Council. (2001). *Knowing what students know: The science and design of educational assessment*. Committee on the Foundations of Assessment. J. Pellegrino, N. Chudowsky, & R. Glaser (Eds.). Washington, DC: National Academy Press.

National Research Council. (2003). *Assessment in support of instruction and learning: Bridging the gap between large-scale and classroom assessment* (Workshop report, Committee on Assessment in Support of Learning). Washington, DC: National Academies Press.

Niemeyer, J. A., & Scott-Little, C. (2001). *Assessing kindergarten children: A compendium of assessment instruments*. Retrieved September 14, 2005 from http://www.serve.org/_downloads/REL/Assessment/rdakcc.pdf

Nitko, A. J. (1983). *Educational tests and measurement: An introduction*. New York: Harcourt Brace Jovanovich.

Nitko, A. J. (1989). Designing tests that are integrated with instruction. In R. L. Linn (Ed.), *Educational measurement* (3rd ed.) (pp. 447–474). New York: Macmillan.

Nitko, A. J. (2004). *Educational assessment of students* (4th ed.). Upper Saddle River, NJ: Pearson Education.

No Child Left Behind Act of 2002, Pub Law No. 107–110 (2002, January). Retrieved August 21, 2005 from http://www.ed.gov/policy/elsec/leg/esea02/107-110.pdf

Olson, L. (2005). Classroom assessments stir growing global interest. *Education Week, 25*(6), 8.

Plake, B. B., Impara, J. C., & Wise, V. L. (1997). Development and validation of professional development resource materials for teachers covering communicating and interpreting assessment results. *Educational Measurement: Issues and Practice, 16*(2), 19–24.

Plous, S. (1993). *The psychology of judgment and decision making*. New York: McGraw-Hill.

Popham, W. J. (1984). Specifying the domain of content or behaviors. In R. A. Berk (Ed.), *A guide to criterion-referenced test construction*. Baltimore: Johns Hopkins University Press.

Popham, W. J. (1985). Measurement-driven instruction: It's on the road. *Phi Delta Kappan, 66,* 628–634.

Popham, W. J. (2003). *Test better, teach better: The instructional role of assessment*. Alexandria, VA: Association for Supervision and Curriculum Development.

Porter, A. C. (2002). Measuring the content of instruction: Uses in research and practice. *Educational Researcher, 31*(7), 3–14.

Porter, A. C., Linn, R. L., & Trimble, S. (2005). The effects of state decisions about NCLB adequate yearly progress targets. *Educational Measurement: Issues and Practice, 24*(4). 32–39.

Quality Counts. (2002). *Building blocks for success: State efforts in early-childhood education*. Bethesda, MD: Education Week.

Ravitch, D. (2003). *The language police: How pressure groups restrict what students learn*. New York: Knopf.

Renzulli, J. S. (1999). What is this thing called giftedness, and how do we develop it? A twenty-five year perspective. *Journal for the Education of the Gifted, 23*(1), 3–54.

Roid, G. H., & Haladyna, T. M. (1980). The emergence of an item-writing technology. *Review of Educational Research, 50,* 293–314.

Rothman, R., Slattery, J. B., Vranek, J. L., & Resnick, L. B. (2002). *Benchmarking and alignment of standards and testing* (CSE technical report 566). Los Angeles: UCLA Center for the Study of Evaluation. Retrieved February 7, 2004, from http://www.cse.ucla.edu/products/reports_set.htm

Ryan, J. M. (2003, October). *An analysis of item mapping and test reporting strategies*. Available from SERVE, P.O. Box 5367, Greensboro, NC 27435; http://www.serve.org

Shepard, L. (1983). The role of measurement in educational policy: Lessons learned from the identification of learning disabilities. *Educational Measurement: Issues and Practice, 2*(3), 4–8.

Shepard, L. (1997). Children not ready to learn? The invalidity of school readiness testing. *Psychology in the Schools, 34*(2), 85–97.

Shepard, L. A., Kagan, S. L., & Wurtz, E. (1998). Public policy report. Goal 1 early childhood assessments resource group recommendations. *Young Children, 53*(3), 52–54.

Shermis, M. D., & Burstein, J. C. (Eds.). (2003). *Automated essay scoring: A cross-disciplinary perspective*. Mahwah, NJ: Lawrence Erlbaum.

Snow, R. E., Corno, L., & Jackson, D. (1996). Individual differences in affective and conative functions. In D. C. Berliner & R. C. Calfee (Eds.), *Handbook of educational psychology* (pp. 243–310). New York: Macmillan.

Snow, R. E., & Lohman, D. F. (1989). Implications of cognitive psychology for educational measurement. In R. Linn (Ed.), *Educational measurement* (3rd ed.) (pp. 263–331). New York: Macmillan.

Solano-Flores, G., & Shavelson, R. J. (1997). Development of performance assessments in science: Conceptual, practical, and logistical issues. *Educational Measurement: Issues and Practice, 16*(3), 16–24.

Solano-Flores, G., & Trumbull, E. (2003). Examining language in context: The need for new research and practice paradigms in the testing of English language learners. *Educational Researcher, 32*(2), 3–13.

Stiggins, R. J. (2001). *Student-involved classroom assessment* (3rd ed.). Upper Saddle River, NJ: Prentice-Hall.

Stiggins, R. J. (2002). Assessment crisis: The absence of assessment FOR learning. *Phi Delta Kappan, 83*(10), 758–765.

Stiggins, R. J. (2003). *Balanced assessment: The key to accountability and improved student learning*. Washington, DC: National Education Association.

Sudman, S., Bradburn, N. M., & Schwarz, N. (1996). *Thinking about answers: The applications of cognitive processes to survey methodology*. San Francisco: Jossey-Bass.

Thompson, S., Blount, A., & Thurlow, M. (2002). *A summary of research on the effects of test accommodations: 1999 through 2001* (NCEO Technical Report 34). Minneapolis: University of Minnesota, National Center on Educational Outcomes. Retrieved September 15, 2005 from http://education.umn.edu/NCEO/OnlinePubs/Technical34.htm

Tindal, G., & Haladyna, T. M. (Eds.). (2002). *Large-scale assessment programs for all students: Validity, technical adequacy, and implementation*. Mahwah, NJ: Erlbaum.

Wainer, H., & Keily, G. L. (1987). Item clusters and computerized adaptive testing: A case for testlets. *Journal of Educational Measurement, 24*, 185–201.

Wainer, H., Vevea, J. L., Camacho, F., Reeve, B. B., Swygert, K., Rosa, K., et al. (2001). Augmented scores—"borrowing strength" to compute scores based on small numbers of items. In D. Thissen & H. Wainer (Eds.), *Test scoring*. Mahwah, NJ: Erlbaum.

Webb, N. L. (2002). *Alignment study in language arts, mathematics, science, and social studies of state standards and assessments in four states*. Washington, DC: Council of Chief State School Officers.

Wiggins, G. P. (1993). *Assessing student performance: Exploring the purpose and limits of testing*. San Francisco: Jossey-Bass.

Wiley, D. E. (2002). Validity of constructs versus construct validity. In H. I. Braun, D. N. Jackson, & D. E. Wiley (Eds.), *The role of constructs in psychological and educational measurement*. (pp. 263–331). Mahwah, NJ: Lawrence Erlbaum.

Wolf, D., Bixby, J., Glenn, J., & Gardner, H. (1991). New forms of student assessment. *Review of Research in Education*, 31–74.

Yen, W. M., & Ferrara, S. (1997). The Maryland School Performance Assessment Program: Performance assessments with psychometric quality suitable for high-stakes usage. *Educational and Psychological Measurement, 57*(1), 60–84.

Zwick, R., Senturk, D., Wang, J., & Loomis, S. C. (2001). An investigation of alternative methods for item mapping in the National Assessment of Educational Progress. *Educational Measurement: Issues and Practice, 20*(2), 15–25.

Technical Reports

Alaska Department of Education and Early Development. (n.d.). *Alaska Comprehensive System of Student Assessment 2003 spring technical report: Benchmark Assessments and High School Graduation Qualifying Exam*. Retrieved December 26, 2003, from http://www.eed.state.ak.us/tls/assessment/HSGQE/TechnicalReports/Spring03TechReport.pdf

Colorado Department of Education. (2003). *Colorado Student Assessment Program technical report, 2002*. Retrieved December 26, 2003, from http://www.cde.state.co.us/cdeassess/reports/2002/as_tech02.htm

CTB McGraw-Hill. (2002). *TerraNova* (2nd ed., CAT technical bulletin 1). Monterey, CA: Author.

Delaware Department of Education. (2002, July). *Delaware Student Testing Program technical report—2001*. Retrieved December 26, 2003, from http://www.doe.state.de.us/aab/tech_report_21.pdf

Florida Department of Education. (2002, March 27). *Technical report for operational test administrations of the Florida Comprehensive Assessment Test*. Retrieved December 26, 2003, from http://www.firn.edu/doe/sas/fcat/pdf/fc00tech.pdf

Illinois State Board of Education. (n.d.). *The Illinois State Assessment 2003 technical manual*. Retrieved December 26, 2003, from http://www.isbe.net/assessment/PDF/2003ISATTech.pdf

Michigan Department of Education. (n.d.). *Design and validity of the MEAP test*. Retrieved December 27, 2003, from http://treas-secure.state.mi.us/meritaward/mma/design.htm

Minnesota Department of Children, Families, and Learning. (2001, June 12). *Minnesota Basic Standards Test technical manual for the academic year 2000–2001*. Retrieved December 26, 2003, from http://education.state.mn.us/content/004211.html

New Hampshire Department of Education. (n.d.). *New Hampshire Educational Improvement and Assessment Program 2001–2002 technical manual*. Retrieved December 26, 2003, from http://www.ed.state.nh.us/Assessment/assessme(NHEIAP).htm

Texas Education Agency. (n.d.). *Texas student assessment program technical digest for the academic year 2001–2002*. Retrieved December 27, 2003, from http://www.tea.state.tx.us/student.assessment/resources/techdig/contents.pdf#xml=http://www.tea.state.tx.uswww.tea.state.tx.us/cgi/texis/webinator/search/xml.txt?query=technical+digest&db=db&id=08f8b88240b44e02

Virginia Department of Education. (2000, October). *Virginia standards of learning assessments: Virginia technical report*. Retrieved December 26, 2003, from http://www.pen.k12.va.us/VDOE/Assessment/VA01–Techrpt.pdf

Washington Office of the Superintendent of Public Instruction. (2002, May 15). *Washington Assessment of Student Learning grade 4 2001 technical report*. Retrieved December 1, 2003, from http://www.k12.wa.us/assessment/techrpts/techreport2001/2001TechRptGr4.doc

17

Classroom Assessment

Lorrie A. Shepard
University of Colorado at Boulder

The model of classroom assessment elaborated in this chapter is quite different from the model of testing and measurement that predominated in classrooms and schools in the last century. In the early 1900s, measurement experts believed that new, objective tests could be used to study and improve schooling outcomes and to provide for the diagnosis and placement of individual students according to their learning needs (Symonds, 1927; Thorndike, 1913). The prevailing view was that experts should construct standardized tests to be used by teachers to increase the accuracy of their decision making. In addition, measurement experts began to teach teachers how to make their own tests according to scientific measurement principles. In those early years, a familiar framework was developed for measurement textbooks to teach teachers about validity and reliability (using largely quantitative representations), test construction, item formats, item analysis, and statistical analysis of test results. This framework—focused almost exclusively on formal tests, quizzes, and grading—has continued as the template for textbooks to the present day.

In contrast to this technical and quantitative model, a transformed view of classroom assessment, developed at the end of the 20th century, is focused much more on eliciting students' understandings and the formative use of assessment as part of the learning process (Black & Wiliam, 1998; Gipps, 1999; Shepard, 2000). Interest in reforming assessment practice was spurred by the increased use of standardized tests for accountability purposes beginning in the 1980s and by mounting evidence that narrow test formats had a deleterious effect on the quality of instruction and student learning (Resnick & Resnick, 1992; U.S. Congress, Office of Technology Assessment, 1992). Ahead of measurement experts, subject-matter specialists began to develop assessment strategies that were more closely tied to curricular goals (Kulm, 1990; Mathematical Sciences Education Board, 1993; Morrow & Smith, 1990; Valencia & Calfee, 1991). In addition, research in cognitive and motivational psychology provided both theory and evidence pointing the way for needed changes (Black & Wiliam, 1998; Crooks, 1988; Pellegrino, Chudowsky, & Glaser, 2001). Ultimately, this new model of classroom assessment has been manifest in a new kind of assessment textbook grounded in instructional practice (Stiggins, 2001; Taylor & Nolen, 2005). Also, signaling the fundamental nature of this shift, a few measurement experts have begun to ask how traditional notions of validity and reliability should change in classroom contexts (Brookhart, 2003; McMillan, 2003; Moss, 2003; Smith, 2003).

In this chapter, I present both the vision and the research base for classroom assessment strategies designed to be a integral part of teaching and learning. I begin with a historical preamble to describe the view of testing in classrooms held by measurement theorists of the past. I focus specifically on the viewpoints presented in earlier editions of *Educational Measurement*, edited by Lindquist (1951), Thorndike (1971), and Linn (1989), respectively. My intention is to identify enduring ideas as well as those that are currently contested. The main body of the chapter is organized in three sections: (1) formative assessment, (2) summative assessment and grading, and (3) external, large-scale assessments. In a concluding section, I consider the implications of these transformative ideas for the field of educational measurement. I propose a program of research and suggest needed changes in the conceptualization of validity and reliability for classroom purposes.

1. A HISTORIC VIEW OF EDUCATIONAL MEASUREMENT AND CLASSROOMS

The achievement testing movement—which began in 1908 with the publication of arithmetic and handwriting tests by Thorndike and his students—was closely tied to the scientific management or social efficiency movement. Its leaders, who believed that schools were failing (U.S. Congress, Office of Technology Assessment, 1992), developed instruments to document the need and set the direction for improvement. Standard tests were required to allow for comparison and summary across schools; and the "new-type," objective examination was seen as a remedy to the "scandalous" unreliability of teachers' examinations demonstrated in a number of early studies (Thorndike, 1922). From the beginning there were also critics who complained that objective tests measured "mere facts or bits of information" instead of "reasoning capacity, organizing ability" etc. (Wood, 1923). However, speaking for the dominant view,

Wood (1923) laid down the basic arguments for the benefits of objective measurement,[1] which were repeated throughout the century:

> The information test is highly reliable not only because of its objective scoring but because of the adequacy samplings which it affords of the performances of the examinee and of the material on which he is tested. Moreover, it is flexible enough that it can be made to test not only "information" but also judgment, and the appreciation of relations, causes, and consequences. (p. 162)
>
> There is not as much opposition between "information" and "reasoning" as some teachers would have us believe ... (F)acts are not only a legitimate and undoubted aspect of thinking, ... they can be acquired, retained, and reproduced only by thinking, only by organizing material in a logical and systematic manner. (p. 162)
>
> Every experimental study thus far made and reported has shown a very high relationship between measurement of information in a field and the intelligence or ability to think in the material of that field. (p. 163)

Additionally, as achievement tests were developed in the same time period and by the same authors as IQ tests, the two types of tests came to share the same item formats and the same statistical models with their roots in individual differences psychology.

After World War I, the use of standardized achievement tests grew dramatically because of the practical, large-scale success of the Army Alpha test, the establishment of large city school research offices and bureaus of cooperative research, and Ralph Tyler's conceptualization of the field of educational evaluation intended to assess how well instructional programs had achieved their objectives (Cook, 1941; Madaus & Stufflebeam, 2000; U.S. Congress, Office of Technology Assessment, 1992).

The first edition of *Educational Measurement*, published in 1951 and edited by E. F. Lindquist, reflected and extended this view that standardized tests were central to the process of evaluating and improving education. Although 1951 chapter authors wrote that the "functions of educational measurement are concerned...with the facilitation of learning" (Cook, 1951 p. 4), they had in mind that this would be accomplished by tests developed outside the classroom. Their vision was of testing *programs* at the school district level, which today might be called data management or data-driven systems. The distinction made in our contemporary *Knowing What Students Know* report (Pellegrino et al., 2001)—between the kinds of assessment data needed for large-scale policy purposes versus everyday decisions in the classroom—was not a distinction apparent in 1951.

Walter Cook (1951), in his chapter entitled, "The Functions of Measurement in the Facilitation of Learning" advocated the use of objective measurement to adapt instruction to individual learning needs. While he acknowledged that, "Superior teachers constantly carry on the process of checking learning through direct observation of behavior and informal testing," he argued for the value of "expertly prepared tests" because:

1. They are more thoroughly analytical than most teachers are able to prepare.
2. They make the teachers aware of the important elements, necessary sequences, and difficulties of the process.
3. They save the teacher's time and energy in diagnosis and leave more for individual remedial work.
4. They help the pupil recognize his learning needs by systematically emphasizing his errors.
5. Remedial procedures are usually suggested or provided that save the teacher's time and also aid in systematizing the process. (p. 37)

In the related chapter on "The Functions of Measurement in Improving Instruction," Tyler (1951) noted that "educational measurement is conceived, not as a process quite apart from instruction, but rather as an integral part of it" (p. 47). Despite the resonance between these words and current conceptions of classroom assessment, the processes Tyler had in mind would occur almost wholly *outside* the classroom. While some of Tyler's examples allowed for the possibility that an individual course instructor could go through the instructional planning process—specifying objectives, designing learning experiences, and appraising effects—Tyler was for the most part concerned that a district's achievement testing program be "planned and developed as an integral part of the program of curriculum and instruction" (p. 64). Teachers would learn by participating in the development of objectives and the development of tests and from the resulting data.

For the second edition in 1971, Robert Glaser, a cognitive psychologist, and Anthony Nitko, a measurement theorist, wrote the chapter on "Measurement in Learning and Instruction." Their formal instructional design perspective was influenced by behaviorist and computer-adaptive instructional assumptions popular at the time. Like Tyler and Cook, their vision called for instructionally-relevant tests to be developed outside of the classroom and provided to teachers. "(A)s instruction proceeds, information for instructional decisions must be provided to the teacher, the student, and possibly to a machine" (pp. 626–627). Given the complexity of designing appropriate tests, including validation of quantitative instructional adaptation models, "it would seem further that the burden of designing and constructing such tests, of processing response data, and of providing preliminary analysis of test data must be handled by someone other than the classroom teacher." Again like Tyler, Glaser and Nitko saw that test data could serve a program evaluation function, by providing formative feedback to system developers. Unlike Tyler, however, they were more interested in test data that could be used on an ongoing basis to tailor instruction for individual students, and they believed that their externally devised testing system could be embedded seamlessly in instruction. "If appropriately and subtly done, teaching, instruction, and testing would fade into one another" (p. 646).

Writing alone for the third edition, Nitko (1989) again offered an instructional design approach that would tap an increasingly sophisticated cognitive research base to provide instructionally relevant tests for classroom use. He reviewed the literature on diagnostic tests based on prerequisite knowledge and skills and mastery of behavioral objectives—approaches that reflected a very lock-step notion of how learning proceeds and a relatively impoverished representation of content mastery. In contrast, Nitko (1989) also reviewed emergent diagnostic literatures focused on analysis of errors and students' knowledge structures. These latter categories provided a glimpse at research themes that would be foundational for today's conception of learning and assessment. For example, "(a) test designer's understanding of the meaning and structure of the knowledge a student brings to the instructional system" might be used to identify "everyday understandings of terms and phenomena ... at odds with the experts' canonical understandings" (p. 461). Importantly, Nitko (1989) also noted that, "(R)ecent research in instructional psychology indicates that the ways in which students mentally represent knowledge are as important for the development of students' problem-solving skills and for advanced learning as the ways in which they manifest their knowledge behaviorally" (p. 466). Although Nitko (1989) still imagined a formal instruction and assessment system developed outside the classroom and delivered to teachers, his standpoint reflected an important, substantive shift—away from pass-fail posttests of student mastery to richer assessments of students' understandings and proficiency in a domain.

Although earlier volumes of *Educational Measurement* had little to say about teacher-made tests or classroom assessment practices, the standardized testing movement and program evaluation paradigm nonetheless determined what teachers were taught about assessment. Measurement theorists, responsible for "Tests and Measurements" courses for teachers, believed that teachers should be taught how to emulate the construction of standardized achievement tests as well as how to use a variety of standardized measures. Typical textbooks from the 1940s through the 1990s included the following chapters:

  I. The purpose of measurement and evaluation
  II. The statistical analysis of test results
  III. Validity
  IV. Reliability
  V. General principles of test construction (includes specifying instructional objectives)
  VI. Principles of objective test construction
  VII. Principles of essay test construction
  VIII. Item analysis for classroom tests
  IX. Grading and reporting
  X. I. Q. testing and scholastic aptitude
  XI. Standardized achievement tests
  XII. Measures of interest and personality
  XIII. Interpreting test norms

Measurement textbooks focused on constructing formal tests primarily for the purpose of grading. Although a number of authors mentioned the importance of using test information to revise instruction, textbooks provided little explication about how teachers were to make sense of assessment data so as to redesign instruction. Some authors assumed that it would be straightforward to "reteach certain items" (Torgerson & Adams, 1954). Statistics and quantitative presentations of reliability and validity were highly salient in what teachers needed to know. In the preface to his *Educational Measurement* text, Travers (1955) pointed out that many of his colleagues preferred textbooks on psychological measurement because they provided "more substantial intellectual fare than books on educational measurement" (p. vi). Accordingly he increased the technical level of his book "to help strengthen a point of weakness in the preparation of teachers" (p. vi). In a sample of 30 textbooks reviewed for this historical analysis, I found only two that had a section or subsection devoted to the use of classroom observation. I found one text that mentioned the use of assessment for feedback.[2] Most texts had a chapter on specifying instructional objectives; and, if grasped, an understanding of the main message from these books would help teachers become more systematic in their use of various item formats to represent important content. Nonetheless, it would be fair to say that the technical aspects of test construction received far more attention than the connections between assessment and instructional activities.

The measurement community's emphasis on formal and technical topics can also be found in the research literature on measurement training for teachers. This literature spanning several decades sounds a constant lament that teachers have been poorly prepared to carry out their measurement and evaluation responsibilities. Historically, many studies assumed that teachers needed to know what was taught in Tests and Measurement courses and reported the adequacy of preparation according to how many colleges offered such courses, how many states required them, and how many teachers took them (Goslin, 1967; Noll, 1955; Roeder, 1972; Ward, 1980). When researchers attempted to identify directly the specific skills deemed essential for teachers, their survey instruments unfortunately confined the potential knowledge base to the contents of measurement books. In Mayo's 1964 study, for example, teachers and principals as well as college professors and testing experts were asked to rank the importance of 70 competencies. Thirty-two of these competencies were statistical items having to do with computing and interpreting the mean, median, and mode, standard deviations, standard scores, correlations, and so forth. The remaining competencies, receiving relatively higher ratings, corresponded closely to the chapter titles of measurement textbooks cited previously. Similarly, in 1973, Goehring used tests and measurement textbooks to generate a list of 116 competencies and then asked teachers and principals to analyze their relative importance.

Only rarely, and relatively recently, have measurement specialists begun to look at the classroom context to try to understand teachers' needs for competence in assessment. In 1973, Farr and Griffin challenged the measurement literature, which seemed to make measurement an end in itself, arguing instead that skills should be tied directly to instructional decisions that teachers needed to make. Several studies, focused initially on how standardized tests were used in classrooms, revealed the much greater importance for teachers' day-to-day decision making of teacher-made tests, curriculum-embedded tests, and informal interactions and observations (Dorr-Bremme, 1983; Salmon-Cox, 1981; Yeh, Herman, & Rudner, 1981). From interview data, Dorr-Bremme (1983) concluded that teachers act as practical reasoners and as clinicians, orienting their assessment activities to the practical tasks they have to accomplish in everyday routines, such as "deciding what to teach and how to teach it to students of different achievement levels; keeping track of how students are progressing and how they (the teachers) can appropriately adjust their teaching; and evaluating and grading students on their performance" (p. 3). For these purposes, teachers rely most heavily on teacher-made tests and interactions with and observations of students. Stiggins and Conklin (1992) published results from a series of field-based studies documenting what teachers do in assessing their students, and they analyzed what teachers would need to know to do these tasks well. Stiggins (1991) concluded that traditional measurement training has been "chronically misfocused," so much so that we have only ourselves to blame for the neglect of formal measurement training in teacher education programs.

Quite separate from the measurement literature, subject-matter experts also began to develop alternatives to standardized tests for classroom purposes, impelled by an aversion to the effects of accountability testing but also because of profound shifts in conceptions of learning and subject-matter proficiency (Shepard, 2000). In reading, for example, researchers working from an emergent literacy perspective (Clay, 1985; Teale & Sulzby, 1986), focused much more on observing and supporting children's developing skills in social contexts, rather than on isolated and decontextualized skills. Clay (1985) invented assessment strategies embedded in the acts of reading, pointing out that research had failed to demonstrate improved learning from diagnostic placements based on either reading readiness tests or tests of prerequisite skills such as language abilities or visual discrimination. Goodman (1985) reintroduced the concept of "kidwatching," a carryover from the much earlier child-study movement. Unlike single-moment-in-time standardized tests, kidwatching is ongoing. It legitimizes the importance of professional observation in the classroom and allows for richer learning experiences than those that can be "safely entombed in the test" (Goodman, 1985, p. 14). Collecting samples of student work (Teale, Hiebert, & Chittenden, 1987) became a rich resource both to gain insight into children's thinking and to document progress over time. Story retelling was found to be more effective, for both instructional and assessment purposes, than traditional reading comprehension questions (Morrow, 1985), and so forth. Ironically, these researchers were doing exactly as Tyler had admonished decades before by clarifying their instructional goals and seeking as faithful a representation of those goals as possible in their assessment devices. What Tyler did not anticipate, however, were the limitations of objective test formats, which by the end of the 20th century were no longer adequate to match new conceptions of subject matter learning (Shepard, 2000).

In the mathematics community, the impetus and direction for changes in assessment paralleled those in reading. In the mathematics chapter for the third *Handbook of Research on Teaching*, Romberg and Carpenter (1986) noted that a major shift had occurred in research on teaching and learning. Because of the cognitive science revolution, research no longer focused only on observable behaviors but also considered internal cognitive processes. Instead of a model of learning where teachers transmit and students absorb knowledge, the new model of learning holds that students actively construct new knowledge. In the National Council of Teachers of Mathematics (NCTM) *Curriculum and Evaluation Standards for School Mathematics* (1989) and *Everybody Counts*, a report of the National Research Council (1989), learning mathematics was redefined as a process of inquiry and sense making rather than "mindless mimicry." For assessment this meant that more extended, non-routine problems were needed to engage students and to assess "mathematical power"—defined as the ability to use one's mathematical knowledge "to reason and think creatively and to formulate, solve, and reflect critically on problems" (NCTM, 1989, p. 205). In addition, classroom discourse became a focus of the math reforms in order to provide students with the opportunity to conjecture and explain their reasoning. These new instructional routines at the same time increased the importance of embedded, informal assessments—observations, teacher questioning, and journal writing—as means for gaining insights into students' thinking (Silver & Kenney, 1995). Rather than prevailing practice wherein teachers oriented their own tests to emulate both the form and content of external, multiple-choice tests, Silver and Kilpatrick (1989) argued that a serious effort should be made to *reskill* teachers to conduct problem-solving lessons and to assess their students' problem-solving abilities and dispositions in the context of those lessons.

Similar stories can be told for other subject areas such as science and social studies. In each case, late 20th-century reformers were motivated by constructivist learning theory and the need for more authentic instruction and assessment tasks (Resnick & Resnick, 1992; Wiggins, 1993). For the measurement community in the United States the impact of these changes was focused primarily on reforming large-scale assessment programs as a number of states launched innovative, performance-based assessments (Baron & Wolf, 1996). Perhaps because of the salience of external accountability tests, the measurement community was slow to consider implications of these theoretical changes for classroom assessment. A small Special Interest Group was formed within the American Educational Research Association; but during the 1990s, for example, classroom assessment or related topics, such as grading, accounted for only 4% of the sessions at the annual meetings of the National Council on Measurement in Education. In Great Britain, however, the organized response to the negative effects of standardized testing took a quite different direction. The Assessment Reform Group (1999), which began in 1989 as a Task Group of the British Educational Research Association, focused on the critical link between classroom assessment and teaching and learning. The Assessment Reform Group coined the term "*assessment for learning*" to refer to assessment that supports the learning process in contrast to assessment that measures the outcomes of learning. Following Sadler (1989), Black and Wiliam (1998) made this learning focus the defining characteristic of formative assessment, saying that assessment is formative "only when comparison of actual and reference levels yields information which is then used to alter the gap" (p. 53).

In the next section on formative assessment I elaborate on this idea of assessment used as part of the learning process. *Formative assessment* is defined as assessment carried out during the instructional process for the purpose of improving teaching or learning. Formative assessment may involve informal methods such as observation and oral questioning or the formative use of more formal measures such as traditional quizzes, portfolios, or performance assessments. I also address issues of coherence and how formative and summative assessment strategies could be made mutually supportive. The distinction between formative and summative assessment parallels Michael Scriven's (1967) original use of these terms, in the context of program and curriculum evaluation, to distinguish between evaluation conducted during the process of development to inform the process versus evaluation of the final product. *Summative assessment*, considered in a subsequent section, refers to the assessments carried out at the end of an instructional unit or course of study for the purpose of giving grades or otherwise certifying student proficiency. As we will see, the new, formative assessment model aspires to make assessment an integral part of instruction, just as early measurement theorists proposed. The important difference is that the strategies described here are built upon a very different model of teaching and learning and do not rely on standardized instruments developed outside the classroom.

2. FORMATIVE ASSESSMENT

For teachers to be effective in supporting student learning, they must constantly be checking for student understanding. Moreover, they must convey to students the importance of students themselves taking responsibility for reflecting on and monitoring their own learning progress. A landmark review by Black and Wiliam (1998) found that focused efforts to improve formative assessment produced learning gains greater than one-half of a standard deviation. In other words, formative assessment, effectively implemented, can do as much or more to improve student achievement than any of the most powerful instructional interventions, intensive reading instruction, one-on-one tutoring, and the like.

In this section, I begin with a summary of contemporary learning theories and then present a model of formative assessment showing its compatibility with both cognitive and sociocultural learning theory. I then consider several specific strategies and tools comprising the general model that teachers use as part of everyday instructional routines. These recursive assessment processes are essential for ongoing revision and improvement of teaching as well as for improving student learning.

Before proceeding, however, a caveat is needed. The ideal assessment practices described here, based on research, are consistent with the practices of particularly adept, expert teachers, but they do not necessarily reflect typical assessment practices. In fact, the majority of practicing teachers has limited knowledge of formative assessment strategies and continues to think about assessment as being primarily for the purpose of grading. Therefore, the concluding section on future research must address teacher learning and professional development as well as the efficacy of specific assessment tools.

2.1. Learning Theory and Coherence in Assessment Design

Knowing What Students Know (Pellegrino et al., 2001) was the product of a National Research Council committee charged with bringing together theoretical and empirical advances in both cognitive science and measurement. A central premise underlying *Knowing What Students Know*'s recommendations is that assessment observations and interpretations must be connected to a well-conceived cognitive model of student learning in a domain. This underlying model must reflect up-to-date understandings of how learning develops in a field rather than the "highly restrictive beliefs" (Pellegrino et al., 2001, p. 54) upon which the most widely used assessments of academic achievement are based. A model of learning serves "as a unifying element—a nucleus that brings cohesion to curriculum, instruction, and assessment" (Pellegrino et al., 2001, p. 54). Moreover, the *Knowing What Students Know* authors go on to argue for this same substantive *coherence* between external and classroom level assessments. To work together to support student learning, assessments at both levels of an assessment system must rest on compatible models of student learning—although the classroom-level models might be much more fine-grained. In this chapter, I use the concept of coherence to talk about how formative and summative assessments within classrooms can be made mutually supportive.

In the historical overview, changes in learning theory were mentioned several times as the impetus for changes in how subject matter experts conceptualized instruction and assessment. Contemporary views of learning have shifted our understandings of how learning occurs, but more fundamentally, they have altered our conceptions of what learning is, what it means to be proficient in a field, and therefore how we would look for evidence of proficiency. The cognitive revolution was a revolt against individual differences psychology and behaviorism, which as a central tenant had focused on the acquisition of competence through reinforcement of observed behaviors rather than trying to explain underlying mental processes. In contrast, according to cognitive theory, learners construct knowledge by connecting new information to prior knowledge structures. Mental schema, in the brain or mind, serve to organize knowledge for subsequent retrieval and use in problem situations; and executive processes, called *metacognition*, allow learners to monitor and manage their own understanding and learning. Cognitivists emphasize conceptual understanding and have demonstrated that transfer, the use of knowledge in new situations, is enabled by the apprehension of generalized principles and the use of schema, whereby similarities in problem types are recognized. The cognitive perspective predominates in the theoretical and empirical work presented in two significant National Research Council publications, *How People Learn* (Bransford, Brown, & Cocking, 1999) and *Knowing What Students Know*, although both acknowledge the influence of social context and the relevance of sociocultural or situative perspectives.

A sociocultural model of learning arises from a resurgent interest in the work of Vygotsky (1978) and other Russian psychologists. It focuses on the social nature of learning and the idea that competence and one's identity as a learner are developed through socially mediated participation in meaningful, practical activity. An individual learns to think and reason through a variety of supports provided by more knowledgeable adults and peers. This model of learning is best characterized as a process of induction or an apprenticeship model of learning whereby novices are allowed to participate and contribute within the context of actual work but are still given tasks tailored to their particular level of competence. The paradigmatic example, of course, is the way that language is acquired through a process of socially mediated practice (Bruner, 1985). A key understanding in sociocultural theory is that the products of activity (learning outcomes) are embedded in the cultural practices of the activity setting. Thus, learning to know means becoming adept at participating in the ways of speaking, representations of knowledge, and use of tools associated with a particular community of practice.

Elsewhere, I have argued for a "social-constructivist"[3] view of learning that brings together cognitive and sociocultural theories (Shepard, 2000). Although there are many unsettled points of contention between and within these two perspectives, I view them as compatible. Vygotsky (1978, p. 57) argued that "Every function in the child's cultural development appears twice: first, on the social level, and later on the individual level; first *between* people (*interpsychological*), and then *inside* the child (*intrapsychological*)." Following Vygotsky's lead then, we can use sociocultural research to understand the social processes that support and define learning and cognitive theory to understand the subsequent and recursive mental processes of the individual. Note, however, that even seemingly private reasoning and reflections by an individual are socially embedded because an individual carries with her the ways of reasoning, expectations, criteria, and so forth from the social world. More recently I have centered my work in sociocultural theory because I believe it is the more encompassing theory.

2.2. A Model of Formative Assessment

Sadler (1989) provided the most widely accepted model of formative assessment. He pointed out that it is insufficient for teachers merely to give feedback about whether answers are right or wrong. Instead, to facilitate learning, it is equally important that feedback be linked explicitly to clear performance standards and that students be provided with strategies for improvement. This model of formative assessment is further explicated in a recent report on classroom assessment in science by Atkin, Black, and Coffey (2001). They frame the learning-assessment process with these key questions:

- Where are you trying to go?
- Where are you now?
- How can you get there?

By answering the assessment question (#2, Where are you now?) in relation to the instructional goal (question #1) and specifically addressing what is needed to reach the goal (question #3), the formative assessment process directly supports improvement.

Setting clear targets for student learning involves more than posting an instructional goal for students to see. It also requires elaboration of the criteria by which student work will be judged. How will the teacher and student know that a concept is understood? How will the student's ability to defend an argument be evaluated? Then, the assessment step must occur during the learning process, while the student is working on tasks that directly embody the intended learning goal. This assessment, in the midst of learning, could happen by means of student questioning during group work, at the overhead projector when a student explains to the class how he or she solved a problem, or by examining written work. Finally, in the third step, for formative assessment to actually aid learning, feedback must be given that provides insight about how to close the gap. For example, when a student is still confused about a fundamental concept, is there a different approach to the problem that might be taken or prerequisite knowledge that should be revisited? If the reasoning in a paper is poorly developed, how might the student revise it after first considering what is lacking in relation to assessment criteria?

This formative assessment model is more than its data-gathering step. It is a model for learning that directly corresponds to the zone of proximal development (ZPD) and sociocultural learning theory. As envisioned by Vygotsky (1978), the zone of proximal development is the region, on an imaginary learning continuum, between what a child can do independently and what the same child can do with assistance. Wood, Bruner, and Ross (1976) further developed the idea of *scaffolding* to characterize the support, in the form of guidance, coaching, hints, and encouragement, that adults provide in the ZPD to enable (and indeed challenge) the learner to perform at a level of accomplishment that she would otherwise not have been able to reach. The assessment step in the formative assessment model (Where are you now?) provides the insight needed to enable effective support. And the complete formative model, which includes clarification of the goal and identification of the means to get there, can be seen as essentially synonymous with instructional scaffolding. Indeed, Sadler's fully elaborated version of formative assessment requires that teachers and students have a shared understanding and ownership of the learning goal and, ultimately, that students be able to self-monitor their own improvement. This corresponds to the goal of scaffolding, which is to foster internalization and the taking over of responsibility by the learner.

In the real world, teachers rarely have time for one-on-one tutoring sessions or dynamic assessments that would allow them to pursue scaffolded instruction with one student through an entire learning cycle. And, to be sure, planning instruction for an entire classroom filled with students whose ZPDs are highly varied, is challenging. Nevertheless, classroom routines can be established to ensure that the basic elements of formative assessment and scaffolding are in place and functioning in the guise of ordinary instructional interactions. For example, conferencing with individual students is a normal part of writing instruction along with peer editing and author's chair, where one student shares a piece of writing with the whole class. Another strategy is to develop students' abilities to provide feedback to each other. One of the reasons that classroom discourse has received such attention in research on instructional reform is that patterns of group interaction, especially students questioning and explaining their reasoning, can scaffold student learning without requiring one-on-one teacher time. Cobb, Wood, and Yackel (1993) describe scaffolded whole-class discussions in which students are able not only to clarify their understandings of mathematical concepts but also to practice the social norms and ways of speaking in that discipline. Similarly, in science inquiry classrooms (Hogan & Pressley, 1997), students learn to provide evidence to support a position and also to critique their classmates' unsupported conclusions—a valuable form of feedback. Such public displays of developing thinking also create the perfect opportunity for formative assessment.

Ideally, then, formative assessment should be seamlessly integrated with instruction. In the paragraphs that follow I elaborate on the specific elements of the formative assessment process that have an extensive research base. I begin with a focus on content, because assessment is meaningless if it does not engage those things that we most want students to learn. Then I consider learning progressions because, within subject matter domains, teachers must also have a working idea of typical learning progressions so that they know what they are helping students toward, and also how to back up when comprehension fails. Then I consider specific aspects of assessment-instruction interactions, accessing prior knowledge, making criteria explicit, providing feedback, and so forth. None of these processes, however, need to interrupt instruction, but rather should continuously feed back into ongoing learning. Even if time is taken for a formal quiz, the results can be used for instructional diagnosis to decide what concepts still need further discussion and work. And students can come to understand that such assessments have a learning purpose.

2.3. The Importance of Content: Selecting Instructional and Assessment Tasks That Embody Learning Goals

Assessment cannot promote learning if it is based on tasks or questions that divert attention from the real goals of instruction. Historically, traditional tests often misdirected instruction if they focused on what was easiest to measure instead of what was important to learn. Classroom instruction should engage students in learning activities that are as directly as possible instantiations of the real goals for learning. For example, if we want students to be able to read books, newspapers, and poems, they should, in fact, do these things and not be given shortened, simulated materials except to make them age appropriate. Similarly, in science, if we want students to be able to use and reason with scientific knowledge, then students should have the opportunity to figure out how things work by conducting investigations and developing explanations in their own words that connect their experiences with textbook theories. Assessment, then, must be conducted as part of such meaningful learning activities. If students are doing a research project in history or showing the class how they solved a math problem, then the instructional task is the assessment task.

A defining feature of standards-based reform has been the development of curriculum standards that served to reinvigorate and elevate what it means to know and demonstrate proficiency in each of the disciplines. For example, the NCTM (1989) *Curriculum and Evaluation Standards for School Mathematics* set out expectations, emphasizing problem solving, communication, mathematical reasoning, and drawing connections, that went well beyond the mastery of basic skills and concepts. Not surprisingly, assessment reform was an equally important part of the standards movement because of the need to capture these more ambitious goals. The term *alignment* has been used to specify the desired correspondence between assessments and curriculum standards. Unfortunately, the meaning of alignment has been cheapened somewhat when test publishers show that all of their multiple-choice items can be matched to the categories of a state's content standards, even if altogether they tap only a narrow subset of the intended standards. Previously, I have suggested the term *embodiment* as a way to better characterize the more complete and substantive alignment that occurs when the tasks, problems, and projects in which students are engaged represent the full range and depth of what we say we want students to understand and be able to do (Shepard, 2003).

As illustrated by Wiggins and McTighe (1998), devising assessments that manifest learning goals is central to good teaching, not just a matter of measuring outcomes. Instead of instructional planning that focuses on interesting activities, Wiggins and McTighe use a process of "backward design" that begins with instructional goals, then asks what would be compelling evidence or demonstrations of learning, and last plans activities that would enable students to develop those understandings. With understanding as the goal of instruction, an emphasis on assessment forces teachers to spell out what evidence of understanding would look like—and these descriptions of performance propel them to provide students with opportunities to develop and practice these skills that might otherwise have been missed if "understanding" had been left only as the globally-stated goal of the unit. For example, evidence of understanding would be found if students could explain their reasoning or apply their knowledge in a new context. And each of these facets can be further elaborated to make it clear what it is that students would be able to do. For example, Wiggins and McTighe's (1998) criterion for an explanation that demonstrates understanding includes giving credible reasons, providing a systematic account, or using helpful mental models. While it is true that being able to explain a concept is more demanding than knowing it, knowing and explaining are closely related, and the additional reasoning and thinking required to produce a credible explanation is exactly the kind of mental effort needed to develop more flexible and deeper understandings.

2.4. Learning Progressions

Learning progressions or learning continua are important for monitoring and supporting learning and development over time. Unlike content standards, which have received intensive attention over the past decade, much less research and development has been devoted to explicating learning progressions. Of course, most teachers have some intuitive sense of what comes next, or they would not be able to help students do better. However, even master teachers could benefit from more formally developed models of how learning typically unfolds within a curricular domain as well as knowing the natural variations and departures from the typical pattern. While empirically validated progressions can enable more insightful instructional scaffolding, progressions should never be interpreted as lock-step or an absolute sequence of prerequisites.

The writing *progress map* in Figure 17.1 is an example of a learning progression from Australia's National School English Literacy Survey, which was designed to collect baseline data on the literacy achievement of Year 3 and Year 5 students in reading, viewing, speaking, listening, and writing (Masters & Forster, 1997). A student's progress in gaining control of language structures and conventions can be mapped or reported on this continuum, which provides a picture of individual growth against a backdrop of normatively established expectations. In contrast to assessment reports that look more like a checklist of grade-level objectives, progress maps have more direct implications for instruction because they provide simultaneously a picture of strengths and weaknesses and a way to look ahead at what comes next for each facet of the domain. For example, a second-grade student might be quite advanced in use of punctuation (capitals and periods) and spelling common words correctly (Level 3), but may need help to experiment and move beyond repetitive sentence structures (Level 2).

In Australia, coherent assessment systems with classroom and large-scale assessments linked to the same underlying progress map are relatively well developed (Forster & Masters, 2004). Similarly, in the Netherlands, "learning-teaching trajectories" are being developed to provide pedagogical insights needed to support the development of students' thinking over time (Van den Heuvel-Panhuizen, 2001). By contrast, in the United States the development of instructionally useful learning progressions has been limited by the cross-sectional, patchwork-way that large-scale assessment systems have been developed over time. State and national assessments, originally intended to monitor cross-sectional trends, focused on grade level expectations for milestone grades (e.g., 4, 8, 12). More recently, with increased requirements for individual testing, states have filled in the intervening grades and interpolated curricular expectations. However, these expectations, especially when "world class standards" were set on never-before-implemented curricula, do not necessarily reflect the developmental trajectory of real students. At the same time, there is the danger that relying on normative means

FIGURE 17.1 An Empirically-Based Progress Map in Writing

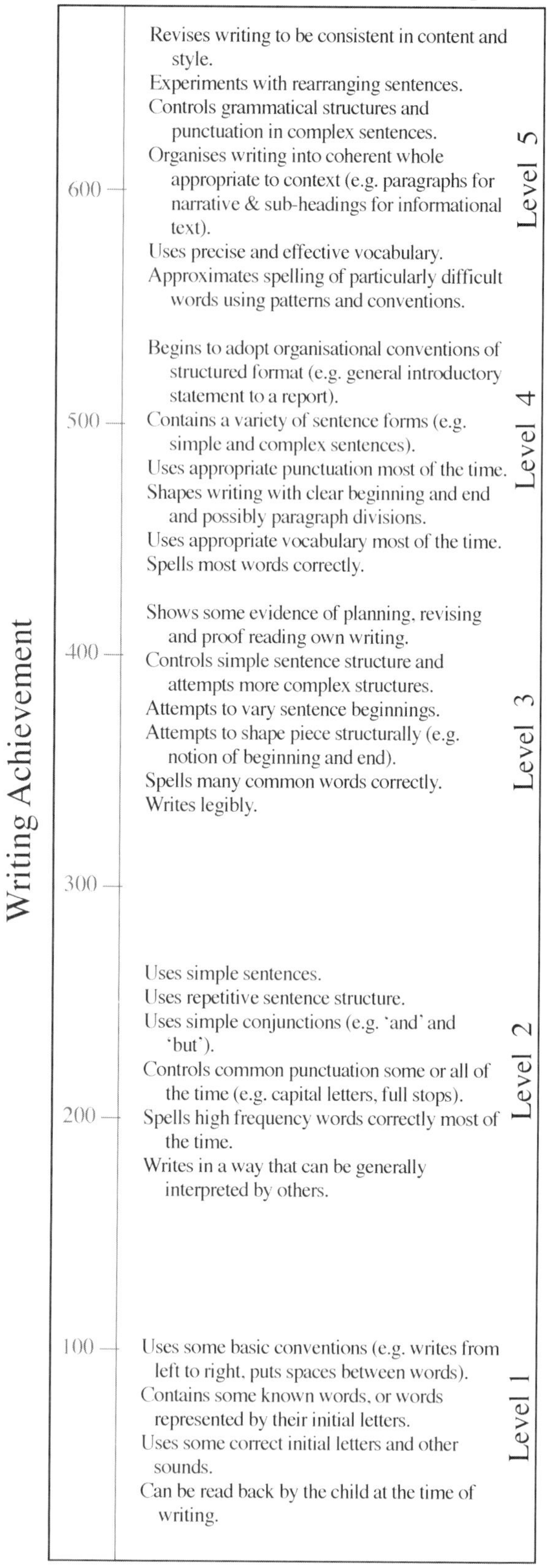

Writing Achievement

600 —
- Revises writing to be consistent in content and style.
- Experiments with rearranging sentences.
- Controls grammatical structures and punctuation in complex sentences.
- Organises writing into coherent whole appropriate to context (e.g. paragraphs for narrative & sub-headings for informational text).
- Uses precise and effective vocabulary.
- Approximates spelling of particularly difficult words using patterns and conventions.

Level 5

500 —
- Begins to adopt organisational conventions of structured format (e.g. general introductory statement to a report).
- Contains a variety of sentence forms (e.g. simple and complex sentences).
- Uses appropriate punctuation most of the time.
- Shapes writing with clear beginning and end and possibly paragraph divisions.
- Uses appropriate vocabulary most of the time.
- Spells most words correctly.

Level 4

400 —
- Shows some evidence of planning, revising and proof reading own writing.
- Controls simple sentence structure and attempts more complex structures.
- Attempts to vary sentence beginnings.
- Attempts to shape piece structurally (e.g. notion of beginning and end).
- Spells many common words correctly.
- Writes legibly.

Level 3

300 —

200 —
- Uses simple sentences.
- Uses repetitive sentence structure.
- Uses simple conjunctions (e.g. 'and' and 'but').
- Controls common punctuation some or all of the time (e.g. capital letters, full stops).
- Spells high frequency words correctly most of the time.
- Writes in a way that can be generally interpreted by others.

Level 2

100 —
- Uses some basic conventions (e.g. writes from left to right, puts spaces between words).
- Contains some known words, or words represented by their initial letters.
- Uses some correct initial letters and other sounds.
- Can be read back by the child at the time of writing.

Level 1

Source: From Masters, G. & Forster, M. (1997). *Mapping Literacy Achievement: Results of the 1996 National School English Literacy Survey.* Canberra, Australia: Department of Employment, Education, Training and Youth Affairs (DEETYA). Reproduced by permission.

for establishing progressions will reify outmoded curricular expectations or set expectations that are too low—because they "average in" the results of failed instruction. For example, based on empirical data, the *Keymath Diagnostic Arithmetic Test* (Connolly, Nachtman, & Pritchett, 1972) uses items in the form of 4 1/2 × 5 as an example of the arithmetic that students would be expected to master during the ninth grade year.

What is needed is a process for creating learning continua based on both research and expert judgment that includes validation of proposed continua in the context of well-implemented curriculum. To date some of the most grounded and instructionally relevant research has been done in the area of emergent literacy and numeracy, which might serve as a model. For example, in early, prephonemic spelling, children first write letters that stand for words without relating letters sounds to the intended word. Then, an important developmental step occurs as they begin to write letters that match the most salient phonemes in a word, and so forth (Hiebert &Raphael, 1998). Similarly, children's natural addition strategies develop over time, from counting-on to use of number facts (Carpenter & Moser, 1984), and research on teaching has shown that teachers become more effective when they are made aware of these typical problem-solving strategies (Fennema & Franke, 1992).

2.5. Prior Knowledge Assessment

Prior knowledge is essential to learning. In fact, the process of learning can be thought of as what one does to connect and reintegrate new understandings with existing knowledge. Prior knowledge includes formal learning, such as a preschooler learning the rule about not crossing the street without looking both ways, but it also includes a multitude of implicit, self-taught explanations about how the world works. These intuitions or self-taught theories can sometimes facilitate new learning, as when scientific explanations are easily mastered because they "make sense" and jibe with our previous experience. Intuitive theories can also be the source of serious misconceptions that hinder new learning and are relatively impervious to instructional change unless students are given a structured way to work through the inconsistencies between their intuitions and other evidence.

Effective instructional strategies draw on students' prior knowledge as a resource. Moreover, by using knowledge-activation routines at the beginning of new lessons and units of study, teachers help students develop the habit of asking, when faced with a new learning or problem-solving task, "what do I already know to help me figure this out?" Many prior-knowledge activities—such as instructional conversations (Tharp & Gallimore, 1988) and K-W-L techniques (Ogle, 1986)—are not seen as assessments per se by either students or teachers. Nevertheless, they do yield valuable data for revising instruction, as when teachers find gaps in assumed knowledge or discover that students know far more about a topic than anticipated. Given the research evidence on the need to engage misconceptions when they occur, explicitly acknowledging assessed misconceptions as the reason for subsequent instructional activities could be a way to heighten students' awareness that assessment serves learning purposes.

Prior knowledge is more than a set of facts that a student has amassed at home and in previous grades. Prior knowledge also includes language patterns and ways of thinking that students develop through their social roles and cultural experiences. Differences in cultural practices can sometimes be misinterpreted by teachers as evidence of "deficits." For example, white middle-class children are more accustomed to being asked decontextualized questions, like "what color is this?" than children from other social groups (Heath, 1983). Implicit rules of interaction can make it difficult for teachers to see the strengths of students outside their own social group unless they have a means for drawing out those strengths in a way that is culturally responsive. For example, Moll, Amanti, Neff, and Gonzalez (1992) use "funds of knowledge" as a way to describe the household knowledge of children from poor families based on farming, carpentry, medicine, religion, childcare, and budget management activities, that can be used to support school knowledge.

2.6. Explicit Criteria and the Use of Rubrics

The formative assessment model requires that teacher and student have a shared understanding of the goals for learning. In cognitive theory, goals must be explicitly defined and visible to students. In sociocultural theory, an understanding of the goal is jointly constructed as the learner is supported toward improved performance. When teachers help students understand and internalize the standards of excellence in a discipline—that is, what makes a good history paper or a good mathematical explanation—they are helping them develop the metacognitive awareness about what they need to attend to as they are writing or problem solving. Indeed, learning the rules and forms of a discipline is part of learning the discipline, not just a means to systematize or justify grading. Moreover, this coming to understanding what standards of excellence mean is not likely to occur simply because scoring rubrics are posted on the wall (though these can be a helpful reference point). Rather, students develop understandings of expectations through feedback and self-assessments whereby criteria are tied directly to their own learning efforts.

2.7. Feedback

One of the oldest findings in psychological research (Thorndike, 1931) is that feedback facilitates learning. Without feedback, about conceptual errors or an inefficient backstroke, the learner is likely to persist in making the same mistakes. In an extensive meta-analysis of 131 controlled studies, Kluger & DeNisi (1996) reported an average effect size or gain due to feedback of .4. They also acknowledged significant study variation with roughly one-third of studies showing negative effects. In attempting to identify characteristics of feedback most associated with positive effects, Kluger and DeNisi found that learning is more likely to be fostered when feedback focuses on features of the task and emphasizes learning goals. This important finding from the feedback literature is consistent with my previous argument for rubrics that allow performance to be judged in relation to well-defined criteria (rather than in comparison to other students), and it jibes with findings from the motivational literature discussed later in the context of grading practices.

According to research evidence, it is a mistake to give false praise in an effort to motivate students and boost self-esteem. At the same time, straightforward, let-the-chips-fall-where-they-may, negative feedback can undermine learning and students' willingness to make subsequent effort. Therefore, an understanding of the motivational consequences of feedback is as important as knowing its cognitive purposes. The formative assessment model, consistent with the cognitive literature, shows that feedback is most effective when it focuses on particular qualities of a student's work in relation to established criteria and provides guidance about what to do to improve. In addition, teachers must establish a climate of trust and develop classroom norms that enable constructive criticism. This means strategically that feedback must occur during the learning process (not at the end when learning on that topic is finished); teacher and students must have a shared understanding that the purpose of feedback is to facilitate learning; and it may mean that grading should be suspended during the formative stage.

For effective feedback to occur, teachers need to be able to analyze student work and identify patterns of errors and gaps that most need to be addressed (not every possible error). In an intervention study, Elawar and Corno (1985) found that teachers dramatically improved the effectiveness of feedback by focusing on these questions: "What is the key error? What is the probable reason the student made this error? How can I guide the student to avoid the error in the future?" (p. 166). Teachers must also understand the theory of how feedback enhances learning so that they can develop classroom routines that check for student understanding and ensure that students are not left alone to persist in bad habits or misconceptions.

2.8. Teaching and Assessing for Transfer

Transfer refers to the ability to use one's knowledge in new contexts. Transfer is obviously a goal of learning. What good is knowledge if it can't be accessed or applied? Yet, studies of students' abilities to use relevant information even from a recently successful lesson are notoriously disappointing. Transfer is inhibited when students learn by rote and go through mechanical routines to solve problems without thinking. Examples are numerous, ranging from regrouping (or borrowing) by rote in second grade arithmetic to "plug and chug" problem solutions in college physics. In contrast, expert-novice research and transfer studies show us that transfer is more likely to be supported when initial learning focuses on understanding of underlying principles, when cause and effect relationships and reasons why are explicitly considered, and when principles of application are directly engaged.

Teaching for transfer requires that initial instruction focus on understanding. It also means visibly working to extend students' understandings. For example, it should be commonplace—as soon as students appear to have mastered a new problem type or one way of solving a problem— for teachers to ask a new question that connects with but extends that knowledge. The initial problem and follow-up applications in Figure 17.2 are from *Connected Mathematics* (Lappan, Fey, Fitzgerald, Friel, & Phillips, 1998). These are exemplary tasks in a number of respects. First, they illustrate that good assessment tasks can be interchangeable with good instructional tasks. Second, the complete investigation from which these problems are drawn clearly helps develop understanding of the underlying principle of equivalency by asking students to make connections between tabular, graphical, and algebraic representations. Third, the application problems can be thought of as near-transfer tasks that can be used to make sure students can generalize what they learned in the investigation. But, students will have to think a bit about the unique features of the new task. They can't just apply the rule from Problem 1 by rote to Applications 1 and 2.

One reason that experts have better transfer skills than novices is that they are able to recognize the features of problems that are the same and different from problems previously solved. Therefore, it is important for students to learn to think specifically about how they can use what they already know. In this sense, teaching for transfer strategies, especially far-transfer, also dovetail with prior knowledge techniques.

2.9. Student Self-Assessment

Engaging students in critiquing their own work serves both cognitive and motivational purposes. Ultimately the habit of self-assessment leads to the self-monitoring of performance that is the goal of instructional scaffolding as well as the goal of Sadler's (1989) formative assessment model. The process of self-assessment builds on the metacognitive benefits of explicit criteria by requiring students to think about and apply criteria in the context of their own work. In so doing, students make sense of and come to understand what the criteria mean in a deeper way than if they merely read a list. More broadly, this kind of supported, metacognition practice—that is, where students learn strategies to monitor their own learning—helps develop students' metacognitive abilities. At the same time, self-critique can increase student responsibility for their own learning and make the relationship between teacher and student more collaborative. This does not mean that teachers relinquish responsibility, but by sharing it, they gain greater student ownership, less distrust, and more appreciation that expectations are not capricious or out of reach.

In case studies of two Australian and English sites, Klenowski (1995) found that students who participated in self-evaluation became more interested in the criteria and substantive feedback than in their grade per se. Students also reported that they had to be more honest about their own work as well as being fair with other students, and they had to be prepared to defend their opinions in terms of the evidence. Klenowski's (1995) data support Wiggins's (1992) earlier assertion that involving students in analyzing their own work builds ownership of the evaluation process and "makes it possible to hold students to higher standards because the criteria are clear and reasonable" (p. 30). In an experimental study by White and Frederiksen (2000), students learned to

FIGURE 17.2 An Initial, Instructional-Assessment Task and Illustrative, Near-Transfer Application Tasks

Problem 1

In this problem, you will explore this question: If a square pool has sides of length s feet, how many tiles are needed to form the border?

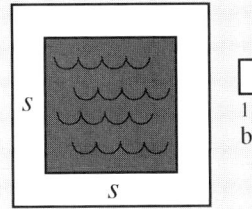

A. Make sketches on grid paper to help you figure out how many tiles are needed for the borders of square pools with sides of length 1, 2, 3, 4, 6, and 10 feet. Record your results in a table.
B. Write an equation for the number of tiles, N, needed to form a border for a square pool with sides of length s feet.
C. Try to write at least one more equation for the number of tiles needed for the border of the pool. How could you convince someone that your expressions for the number of tiles are equivalent?

Applications

1. a. How many 1-foot-square tiles are needed to form a border for a pool that is 10 feet long and 5 feet wide?
   b. Write an expression for the number of border tiles needed for a pool that is L feet long and W feet wide.

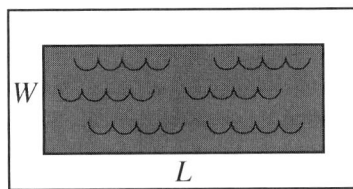

   c. Write a different expression for the number of tiles needed. Explain why your expressions are equivalent.

2. A square hot tub has sides of length s feet. A border is created by placing square tiles measuring 1 foot on each side along the edges of the tub and triangular tiles in the corners. The triangular tiles were made by cutting square tiles in half.

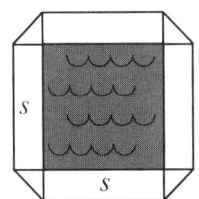

   a. If the hot tub has sides of length 7 feet, how many square tiles are needed to make the border?
   b. Write two equations for the number of square tiles, N, needed to build this type of border for a square tub with sides of length s feet.

Source: From *Connected Mathematics, Say It with Symbols: Algebraic Reasoning* © 1998 Michigan State University, Glenda Lappan, James T. Fey, William M. Fitzgerald, Susan N. Friel, & Elizabeth Difanis Phillips. Published by Pearson Education, Inc. publishing as Pearson Prentice Hall. Used by permission.

use science inquiry criteria to evaluate their own work. As part of the protocol, students in the experimental group had to write a rationale each time they self-evaluated pointing to the features of their work that supported their ratings. In addition, students used the criteria to give feedback to classmates when projects were presented orally in class. Compared to controls, students who had participated in self-assessment produced projects that were much more highly rated by their teachers (on the shared criteria). In addition, initially low-achieving students showed dramatic gains on a measure of conceptual understanding.

As part of curricular reforms, content experts in various subject areas have developed assessment reforms to better integrate assessment and instruction. Some of these strategies, in particular, serve to make self-assessment and peer-assessment a normal part of classroom instruction. For example, "author's chair" is a literacy practice where students learn explicitly the norms for listening and giving feedback to classmates about a piece of writing (Routman, 2000). Conferencing with students can also be a means to see if they are developing the ability to self-evaluate. Both the Klenowski and White and Frederiksen studies above involved a self-assessment step that became a part of normal instruction. Importantly, the purpose of engaging students in self-assessment is not to give a grade but for students to gain insight that can be used to further learning.

2.10. Evaluation of Teaching

The formative assessment model focuses on student learning. An equally important use of classroom assessment is the evaluation and improvement of teaching. At the same time that teachers are gathering evidence about student understanding, they are also considering which teaching practices are working and which are not, and what new strategies are needed. The NCTM (1995) *Assessment Standards for School Mathematics* identified three types of instructional decisions that are informed by assessment data: moment-to-moment decisions, short-term planning, and long-term planning. When assessment and instruction are effectively intertwined, then assessment insights can be used in real time to adjust instruction. For example, if several students are making the same type of error, it may be useful to stop and spend some time on the underlying misconception. Whereas formative assessment focuses on what the student can do to improve, the parallel evaluation of teaching asks whether students have had adequate opportunity to learn.

Teachers who are reflective about their practice use data systematically to make judgments about the specific aspects of instructional strategies that may be hindering learning. They are looking for explanations of learning success or failure, and especially for teaching decisions that may be the cause. For example, are there certain tasks that seem to elicit a great deal of student thinking, because they are high-interest and allow multiple solutions? Are there some activities that engage most of the boys but leave the girls slumped in their seats? Do two second-language learners struggle with assignments when there is not adequate time to talk about relevant background knowledge or to clarify expectations? In a now classic reexamination of his own teaching, Mazur (1997) discovered that students could do problems like number 2 in Figure 17.3, but not problems like number 1. His extended analysis of why students could do algorithmic problems but not conceptual ones and what he was doing to foster their search for recipes (including the form of his exams), led Mazur to completely revise his teaching to focus on more active learning strategies.

When teachers use assessment data to modify their instruction they are also setting an important example for students. As I argued previously, "if we want to develop a community of learners—where students naturally seek feedback and critique their own work—then it is reasonable that teachers would model this same commitment to using data systematically as it applies to their own role in the teaching and learning process" (Shepard, 2000, p. 12).

3. SUMMATIVE ASSESSMENT AND GRADING

Summative assessment and grading pose a serious threat to the learning purposes avowed for formative assessment. According to findings from the motivational literature and from surveys of teachers and students, grading practices can undermine the learning process in several ways: First, tests and graded assignments convey what is important to learn. If these measurements diverge from valued learning goals, then students focus their attention and effort only on the graded portion of the curriculum. Second, the use of grades as rewards and punishments can undermine intrinsic motivation to learn. Third, for those students for whom grading standards seem out of reach, grades can reduce effort and subsequent learning. Fourth, the comparative nature of traditional grading practices can reduce the willingness of students to help or to learn from each other.

In this section, I consider the purposes for grading and summarize the research on current practices. Then, after reviewing relevant empirical findings from the measurement, cognitive psychology, and motivational psychology literatures, I outline the grading practices that are expected to be both valid in reporting achievement and conducive to student learning. If they are built on the same underlying model of developing competence in a knowledge domain, then formative and summative assessment practices can be made coherent and mutually supportive.

3.1. Age Appropriate Purposes for Grading

Textbooks in educational measurement and educational psychology assume that grading is something that teachers must do. Little rationale is provided except that school district policies require teachers to give grades, often with detailed specifications as to the information required on report cards. I likewise assume that teachers will have to give grades primarily because parents want them. However, I note that there have been virtually no systematic studies of the effects of grading practices on student achievement. I assume further that there are three important audiences for grades: parents, external users such as employers and college admissions officers, and students themselves. Students

FIGURE 17.3 Conceptual (Top) and Conventional Question (Bottom) on the Subject of DC Circuits

1. A series circuit consists of three identical light bulbs connected to a battery as shown here. When the switch *S* is closed, do the following increase, decrease, or stay the same?

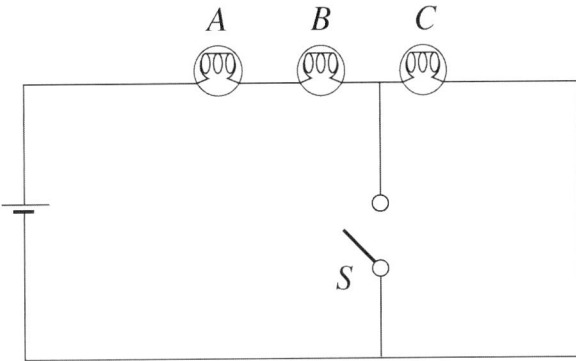

(a) The intensities of the bulbs *A* and *B*
(b) The intensity of bulb *C*
(c) The current drawn from the battery
(d) The voltage drop across each bulb
(e) The power dissipated in the circuit

5. For the circuit shown, calculate (a) the current in the 2-Ω resistor and (b) the potential difference between points *P* and *Q*.

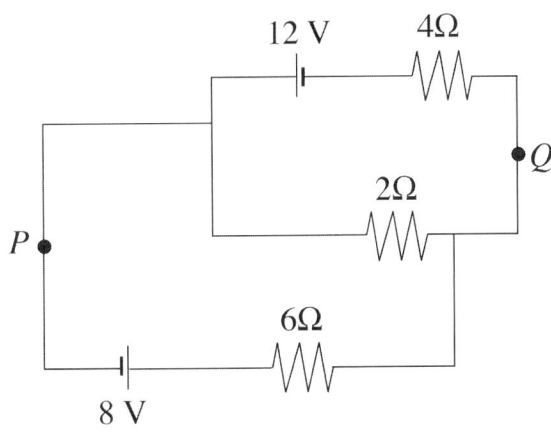

Source: From Mazur, Eric. *Peer instruction: A user's manual*, 1st Edition, © 1997. Reprinted by permission of Pearson Education, Inc., Upper Saddle River, NJ.

become the primary audience for grades because what others will be told about their achievement comes to play a powerful roll in learning interactions. However, if students were the only audience, it is not clear that grades per se would add useful information. Rather, what teachers and students need most are summative assessments used to verify attainment of important milestones in students' developing competence that are tied to the same performance continua used in formative assessment.

Age appropriate grading principles suggest that grades should be much less salient in elementary classroom life than they are for high school students. By the time students reach high school, there is a greater expectation that grades have meaning for external audiences. For example, a grade of A or B in English should mean that the student can write a well-organized essay; and a g.p.a. of 3.0 should mean that a senior is well prepared for college work. A basic purpose of the standards movement, in fact, has been to assure these kinds of shared understandings about the meaning of grades. In contrast, it is much more difficult to conduct formal assessments of young children and much less necessary. Principles articulated by the National Association for the Education of Young Children (NAEYC) (1990) emphasize that assessments of young children should be based on observation conducted during the ordinary activities of classroom life and should be used for formative purposes and to report to parents. The NAEYC concluded that for children in the early grades, "The method of reporting to parents (should) not rely on letter or numerical grades but rather (should) provide more meaningful, descriptive information in narrative form" (p. 15).

Evidence is limited about what kind of information parents find useful. In one study, strikingly, parents of third graders placed the highest value on talking with the teacher about their child's progress; 77% said they found this very useful (Shepard & Bliem, 1995). The next most useful was "seeing graded samples of my child's work." Sixty percent of parents reported this was very useful in contrast to report cards and standardized tests, which were said to be very useful by only 43% and 14% of parents, respectively. In interview data, parents explained that talking with the teacher was valued most because of the first-hand knowledge it gave them of their child's specific strengths and weaknesses in the context of the classroom curriculum. One additional generalization from this research has significant implications for grading practices. Parents want normative comparisons. However, they appear to be willing to have teachers tell them how their child is doing in relation to grade-level expectations rather then requiring a norm-referenced test. This substitution, of grade-level standards for norm-referenced comparisons, is important in the context of standards-based reporting and, as we will see, because of the de-motivating consequences of normative grading practices.

3.2. Research on Current Practice

Brookhart (1994) identified 19 studies published within 10 years of her review that examined teachers' grading practices. Study methods varied from teacher surveys to case studies. Supported by highly consistent results across studies, Brookhart (1994) identified the following generalizations:

- Teachers try hard to be fair to students, including informing them up front what the components of a grade will be.
- Achievement measures, especially tests, are the major components in grades, but effort and ability are also commonly considered.
- There is a grade-level effect on grading practices. Elementary teachers use more informal evidence and observation. At the secondary level, paper-and-pencil achievement measures and other written activities comprise a much larger portion of the grade.
- There is individual variation among teachers' grading practices. Different teachers perceive the meaning and purpose of grades differently, and consider achievement and non-achievement factors differently.

The practices identified in findings 1 and 3—that teachers try to be fair and communicate grading standards and that they use more informal evidence at younger grade levels—are consistent with research-based professional standards. However, the use of effort and ability factors to adjust achievement grades is contrary to recommendations from measurement experts and from standards-based reformers. In a study of 143 midwestern elementary and secondary teachers, Cizek, Fitzgerald, and Rachor (1995/1996) similarly found that 52% said they took individual student ability into account and 42% said they considered student effort in assigning grades. Cizek et al. noted that teachers use a diverse array of non-achievement factors in ways that create a "success bias," helping them to raise student grades. Experts argue against considering effort, ability, and attitude in grading because they undermine the validity of grades as indicators of achievement. Moreover, these factors cannot be measured accurately, they create inequities, they invite students to dissemble, and they confuse most or all audiences about the meaning of grades.

In trying to explain the large gap between practice and theory, Brookhart (1994) advances several arguments on teachers' behalf: effort is seen as part of "earning" a grade; work habits are closely related to the feedback that students need about how to do better; and participation is essential to the student's relationship with the teacher as coach. While it is critical to understand teachers' viewpoints and the practical realities of classrooms, teachers' intuitive beliefs about what is fair and motivating to students may not be supported by research. We must also consider whether teachers are using effort grades to *manage* student behavior, which is not the same thing as creating a learning environment that is *motivating* to students. In a case study of teachers' assessment methods (Lorsbach, Tobin, Briscoe, & LaMaster, 1992), a major finding was that "Tasks and systems of aggregating scores often reward completion of tasks and motivation to learn rather than what is known" (p. 310). Teachers appeared to be operating within a "school is work" metaphor (Marshall, 1988), creating an elaborate system to keep track of student work, but without evaluating the quality or content of that work.

3.3. Importance of Content and Format: What Gets Valued

The content of tests—what gets tested and how it is tested—and the content of assignments that are evaluated for a grade communicate the goals of instruction to students and focus their attention and effort. (Note, however, that merely giving points for assignments does not ensure that attention is paid, if the quality of work is never examined; see Lorsbach et al., 1992). I addressed the issue of assessment content previously in the context of formative assessment and visit it again when considering the effect of external tests on teaching and learning in classrooms.

Historically, classroom teachers, especially at the secondary level, have relied on formal tests for grading purposes and used predominantly low-level test questions. Fleming and Chambers (1983) analyzed 8,800 test questions from elementary through high school tests and found that nearly 80% were at the *knowledge* level in Bloom's (1956) taxonomy. Similar results were found a decade later. In a nationally representative survey, Madaus, West, Harmon, Lomax, and Viator (1992) found that 53% of high school and 73% of elementary math teachers reported using textbook tests at least once a month. When analyzed by Madaus et al. (1992), only 3% of items on text-embedded final tests sampled high-level conceptual knowledge and about 5% sampled higher level thinking skills. The remaining 95% of items sampled recall of information, computation, and use of algorithms and formulas in routine problems similar to those students had worked in the text. A higher percentage of teachers reported making their own tests, but when these were examined in field studies, Madaus et al. (1992) found them to be close adaptations of textbook tests. More recently, Cizek et al. (1995/1996) reported a surprising finding that novice teachers were more likely to develop their own assessments than were experienced teachers who tended to rely on commercially prepared tests. This finding could be the result of beginning teachers having more knowledge of and access to reform-based materials and problem types.

As I have stressed previously, the nature of accomplishment in each of the disciplines cannot be adequately represented by low-level recall-type questions. Assessment reform has been an integral part of educational reform because of the need to engage students in authentic tasks so as to develop, use, and extend their knowledge. More meaningful work aimed at conceptual understanding not only provides better evaluation data about how well students are doing, it also has both cognitive and motivational benefits. For example, Crooks (1988) reviewed studies that examined the link between evaluation format and the study strategies of college students. Numerous studies corroborated the earlier findings of Marton and Saljo (1976) that students' approaches to learning tasks could be categorized as *deep* or *surface* approaches. Deep approaches involved active search for meaning, underlying principles, and structures that linked different concepts. Surface approaches focused primarily on memorization of isolated facts without looking for connections among those facts. While other factors affect students' tendency to use deep or surface approaches, especially interest and motivation, their perceptions of the demands of anticipated evaluations were clearly influential across studies in their choice of strategy.

Subject-matter experts value conceptually rich instructional tasks because they capture what is most important for students to learn. Cognitivists prefer challenging tasks because they engage students in reasoning and they support generalization, if transfer tasks are used as a normal part of instruction. Authentic tasks that require higher-order thinking and active problem solving also increase student motivation because they are intrinsically more interesting than memorizing or applying simple procedures (Stipek, 1998). For example, Mitchell (1993) found that students' beliefs about the real-world significance of what they are learning was a strong predictor of their interest and enjoyment in math class. In addition, challenging tasks increase intrinsic motivation by enhancing students' feeling of competence. Newmann (1992), for example, found that students give the highest interest ratings to classes that make them think hard and required them to participate actively in thinking and learning.

3.4. Research Base in Measurement, Cognitive Psychology, and Motivational Psychology

Most teachers dislike evaluating their students and giving grades (Brookhart, 1993; Nava & Loyd, 1992). Given the distorting effects of grading practices reviewed above and negative motivational effects of grades considered here, it would be easy to regard grades as only a misguided and oppressive mandate. However, there is some evidence of positive cognitive benefits from summative assessments that should be considered along with findings from the motivational literature. Most importantly, students appear to study more and learn more if they expect to be tested. As summarized by Crooks (1988), the benefits from testing can be explained by three factors. First, follow-up testing engages students in review and relearning, which works like a limited form of distributed practice. Second, the testing experience itself engages students in mental processing of the content, although this depends very much on the quality of the test questions. Third, as I have noted previously for good or ill, the test directs attention to the topics and skills tested, which has implications for students' study efforts.

Cognitive theory also suggests that students benefit from the opportunity to demonstrate competence and to work toward increasing proficiency as defined by criteria that are mutually understood by teacher, student, and the community (Pellegrino, Baxter, & Glaser, 1999). As I described earlier, providing students with a clear understanding of goals makes goals more attainable. And, helping students learn the meaning of criteria in the context of their own work helps them develop the metacognitive awareness of what they need to do to improve. Cognitive theory would not predict that withholding summative evaluations would improve learning. In fact, from a cognitive perspective, the best system would be one where formative and summative assessments were mutually aligned with conceptually-oriented learning goals, and where summative assessments were used as milestones of accomplishment (perhaps acknowledged by family and friends) following successful learning periods supported by formative assessment.

The most devastating evidence showing the negative effects of grading and schooling practices come from the motivational literature. Strikingly, in a comprehensive review of research on children's motivation, Wigfield, Eccles, and Rodriguez (1998) report that many aspects of classroom organization have such pervasive negative effects that children's competence beliefs, achievement goals, interest in school subjects, and intrinsic motivation to learn all decline as students move through the elementary and middle school years. With respect to grading practices, the most important issues have to do with the role of grades as rewards (or punishments), students' orientations toward performance or learning goals, and the use of normative versus mastery evaluation standards. These factors along with other factors such as students' locus of causality and feelings of competence all interact in complex ways. Here I summarize only the most significant and consistent patterns.

The use of grades as rewards contributes to what Lave and Wenger (1991) termed the "commoditization of learning" (p. 112). When there is no cultural value for increasing one's skill and participation in an endeavor, the only reason to participate is to obtain surface knowledge that can be displayed for evaluation. In reviews of experimental studies, researchers found that the use of external rewards can actually undermine students' intrinsic interest in a task (Deci & Ryan, 1985; Lepper, 1983). As summarized by Stipek (1996), rewards work to decrease intrinsic motivation when they are perceived as controlling and are not directly related to successful performance. Consistent with the positive findings from research on feedback, rewards or praise that convey positive information about competence are more likely to increase intrinsic motivation.

Findings about the effects of rewards are closely related to research on students' goal orientations. Dweck (1986) distinguishes between children with mastery goals and those with performance goals. These dispositions are independent of students' academic abilities. Students with mastery goals are intrinsically motivated. They seek challenging tasks and enjoy opportunities to develop new competencies. They are less likely to be fearful of evaluation because they see the teacher as a resource. When students with a mastery orientation are faced with a difficult task, they are likely to persist, maintain a positive attitude, and look for solution strategies. A mastery orientation has also been termed a task orientation by related theories. In contrast, students with a performance orientation are extrinsically motivated. They are more concerned about looking competent rather than being competent and will tend to avoid situations where they might appear to be incompetent. Related theories suggest that performance orientation are induced by ego-involving environments. When faced with a difficult task, performance-oriented students will often comment on their lack of ability, act bored or anxious, and exhibit a marked deterioration in performance. Dweck came to call these behaviors "learned helplessness." Because of their fear of evaluation, students in this category may try to hide their lack of understanding from the teacher.

Importantly, mastery versus goal orientations are not fixed student attributes; they can be created or elicited to different degrees by the learning environment and have been experimentally induced (Elliot & Dweck, 1988). For example, in a study of college students, two groups developed very different levels of conceptual understanding depending on whether they were told they would be tested at the end of the study or that they would need to teach the material to others (Benware & Deci, 1984). Students are more likely to develop a learning orientation when teachers emphasize effort, learning, and working hard rather than performing or getting the right answer, when mistakes are treated as a normal part of learning, and when evaluation of progress is accompanied by opportunities to improve (Ames, 1992; Stipek, 1996).

Perhaps the most serious negative consequences of traditional grading practices have come from the use of normative comparisons. As Ames (1984) suggested, competitive class structures make social comparisons and judgments about ability more salient. In a series of studies, Butler (1987, 1988) and Butler and Nisan (1986) found that normatively distributed grades resulted in lower interest, less willingness to persist, and lower performance compared to students who received substantive feedback. In a classic study, Harackiewicz, Abrahams, and Wageman (1987) found that evaluation based on social norms reduced interest in a task while evaluation based on achieving a predetermined standard increased interest. Stipek's (1996) general conclusion from this literature was that evaluation, especially of difficult tasks, tends to undermine intrinsic interest. However, the exception she identified is noteworthy and foreshadows my recommendations for grading practices in this chapter.

> Substantive evaluation that provides information about competencies and guidance for future efforts, and evaluation that is based on mastery rather than social norms, however, appear not to have these negative effects and can even enhance intrinsic interest in academic tasks. (Stipek, 1996, p. 99)

3.5. Benchmarks of Developing Competence

To be mutually supportive, formative and summative assessments must be conceptually aligned. They must do a good job of representing important learning goals and should use the same broad range of tasks and problem types to tap students' understandings. However, summative assessments should not be mere repeats of earlier formative tasks. Rather, they should be culminating performances that invite students to exhibit mastery and to use their knowledge in ways that generalize and extend what has come before. Summative assessments can be thought of as important milestones on the same learning continua that undergird formative assessment.

Formative and summative assessments have different purposes. One enables learning and the other documents achievement. Given the known negative effects of grading, a critical question is how often to engage in summative assessment? Measurement specialists argue for frequent grading of assignments to gather sufficient data to ensure reliability. Cognitivists want students to have practice with the criteria that will be used to evaluate culminating performances. However, the formative assessment model and motivation research argue that grading could undermine students' learning orientation. Therefore, to make formative assessment truly for learning, teachers may need to postpone giving grades or use them only student self-assessment and "as if" grades to help students stay focused on substantive feedback. Most certainly, teachers should avoid interrupting and judging as-if-finished the quality of learning that is still in progress. Of course the issue of reliability is important. And students should not be graded on the basis of only one or two isolated formal tests. However, if summative assessments are embedded in learning progressions, then the reliability of graded events is supported by other evidence of each student's developing competence along that underlying continuum.

Summative assessments and the grades based on them should represent achievement. Consistent with Stipek's (1996) summary of motivation research above, evaluation of achievement should be based on mastery standards, rather than social norms. Achievement-based grades will be more transparently aligned with feedback on the same standards used for formative assessment and will communicate better to external audiences. When teachers adjust grades to take account of effort and improvement, they are often responding to issues of fairness. Is it fair to hold students of very different abilities to the same standards? And, isn't it the case that low-ability students are likely to stop trying if the standards are out of reach? In heterogeneous classrooms, grading in terms of mastery standards will require other support systems for students of different abilities including strategies such as: differential pace for learning and timing of benchmark assessments, identification of intermediate, attainable goals, and differential scaffolding. If taken seriously, the commitment for grades to represent achievement would mean doing away with the various elements of compliance grading such as extra credit points, points for turning in note cards and preliminary drafts, points for turning in homework that is never graded, and so forth. The effects of assignments that help students learn should be evaluated ultimately in culminating assessments, where that learning will be manifest. At the same time, other ways of helping students soften worries about grades would be allowed if in each case they provide opportunities for students to demonstrate mastery. These would include replacement assignments and replacement tests or throwing out test scores when learning is verified by subsequent assessments.

4. EXTERNAL, LARGE-SCALE ASSESSMENTS

National, state, and district-level assessments are used to collect data to answer the questions of policymakers at some distance from the classroom. In an era of high-stakes accountability, however, external tests can also have profound effects on classroom practices. Ideally, an external assessment that was well aligned with conceptually rich learning goals would have positive impacts on instruction by exemplifying significant learning targets, providing useful feedback to teachers about curricular strengths and weaknesses, and verifying individual students' attainments. The authors of *Knowing What Students Know* (Pellegrino et al., 2001) envisioned for the future a more *balanced* and *coherent* assessment system, where formative classroom assessment would receive attention equal to that of external, high-stakes tests and where classroom and external assessments would be coherently linked to the same underlying model of learning.

At present, the *Knowing What Students Know* idealization has not been realized. Indeed, an extensive body of literature has documented the negative effects on teaching and learning (Heubert & Hauser, 1999; Pedulla et al., 2003; Pellegrino et al., 2001; U.S. Congress, Office of Technology Assessment, 1992), caused primarily by the distorting effects of teaching to tests with limited formats and less-than-adequate representation of significant learning goals.

In a more extensive treatment of both the positive and negative effects of high-stakes testing (Shepard, Hammerness, Darling-Hammond, & Rust, 2005), my coauthors and I concluded that two factors appear to mediate the way that external tests reshape the curriculum. The first is the adequacy of test content for capturing learning goals, and the second is the classroom teacher's ability to keep classroom instruction focused on real learning. Based on these lessons from the teaching-the-test research literature, we identified strategies for test preparation that help to maintain a focus on student learning consistent with the formative assessment vision of classroom culture. Thus, in addition to content coherence between internal and external tests, we sought to preserve a philosophical coherence between the attitudes toward learning and assessment conveyed during ordinary lessons and the stance toward learning taken when preparing for external tests.

To protect against the narrowing effects of a test-driven curriculum, individual teachers, or preferably teams of teachers, should develop an explicit rationale for situating test-related knowledge and skills within the larger boundaries of real curricula. We call this technique "domain mapping." Starting with the state's curriculum frameworks or national content standards, teachers might draw a Venn diagram or construct a table to illustrate what subpart of the desired curriculum is covered by the test and what is not. Many commercially developed tests cover the easiest-to-measure part of each content strand in a domain, but this does not mean that the domain has been adequately represented. Saying what has been left out helps to make clear the limitations of the test as a curriculum guide. Based on this explicit analysis, teachers can then consciously plan units of study and allocation of instructional time in ways that keep attention to tested content in its proportional place. Accordingly, low-level, basic-skills tests that represent only a subpart of intended content standards would not be allowed to have as much influence on classroom instruction as more challenging, conceptually based assessments.

In keeping with the idea that students should be self-aware about their own learning progress, it also makes sense to help students understand the relationship between the knowing that is required on tests and how this compares to the ways that they use their knowledge in other settings. For example, Calkins, Montgomery, and Santman (1998) suggest that we teach children how to "read" tests just as we teach them to master the peculiarities of any other genre. "If our youngsters are accustomed to gathering on the carpet to read a shared, and perhaps enlarged, text together and then talking about strategies for approaching this text or for handling difficulty in the text, why wouldn't they do the same to read an excerpt from a standardized reading test?" (p. 71). Similarly, in McNeil's 1988 study, experienced teachers at magnet schools resisted the "fragments and facts" required on the test by helping students keep parallel sets of notes, one set for the real knowledge and one for the knowledge they would need for the test. Although students, especially in elementary school, deserve to have some practice with test formats such as open-ended math tasks or writing to a prompt so as not to be flummoxed by unfamiliar demands, such practice should be provided in the context of the instructional goals to which these tasks connect. And given what we know about the lack of transfer when only one problem type is used, teachers can work to ensure the development of more robust understandings by focusing on underlying principles and continuing to ask for extensions and applications.

Much of this advice about how to maintain one's professional integrity in the face of high-stakes testing pressures has to do with attitude and stance. The basic idea is to pay attention to the test only in so far as it connects with the curriculum, rather than giving over to the test and letting it become the center of instructional planning. Such a stance enables teachers to use test results to make only appropriate and needed improvements in curriculum and instruction. As Wiggins (1998) pointed out, good teachers have the ability to self-assess, but still there are blind spots and a lack of external referents. For the most part, teachers with a good working knowledge of content standards, as they are represented by the test, and a good grasp of what their students know, can generally predict how their students will do. Therefore, the greatest insights from external tests results can often come from the surprises, as teachers attempt to disentangle answers to these questions: Why were my students unable to solve this problem (or perform this task)? How would my teaching have to change to help them solve problems of this type? Why didn't I know what they didn't know? In addition, even when results jibe with predictions, teachers can evaluate the adequacy of their own efforts by examining relative strengths and weaknesses across curricular strands. For example, are students doing as well on higher order thinking skills as on basic skills? When teachers have well-developed professional knowledge about how test-based information fits within a larger framework of rich curricular goals, it becomes possible to attend to insights gained from test results without fearing curriculum narrowing and distortion, so well documented in the literature.

5. CONCLUSIONS: IMPLICATIONS FOR RESEARCH AND MEASUREMENT THEORY

Ralph Tyler is an iconic figure in the history of educational measurement. I began this chapter with a historical analysis because I wanted to address explicitly the tension between my continued belief in Tyler's vision—that educational measurement should be an integral part of instruction—and my need to challenge his inadvertent legacy—the long-standing tests-and-measurement model for classroom assessment founded primarily on externally developed objective tests. The transformed vision of classroom assessment presented in this chapter is dramatically different from the image of classroom testing put forth in previous volumes of *Educational Measurement* and in measurement textbooks. The transformed vision focuses on much richer conceptualizations of student learning in the context of meaningful activities and emphasizes the formative use of assessment to improve learning.

This idealized, new model is well grounded in contemporary, cognitive and sociocultural learning theories and motivation theory, but in some sense it is still untried, given that it has not yet been implemented on a wide scale. Much remains to be learned about what additional insights and adaptations will be needed to make such a vision work in practice. I conclude by considering four major categories for future research: (1) studies of assessment tools and processes, (2) development of learning progressions, (3) studies of teacher development, and (4) new conceptualizations of reliability and validity.

5.1. Studies of Assessment Tools and Processes

In *Knowing What Students Know*, Pellegrino et al. (2001) argued that assessment practices and interpretations must be built on a well-conceived model of student learning. The same can be said for the importance of the theoretical model underlying research studies. When Black and Wiliam (1998) undertook their massive review of research on classroom formative assessment, they cited primary studies, meta-analyses, and reviews representing well over 1000 studies. Yet, many of the studies cited are inadequate for our purposes because they were derived from learning models incommensurate with contemporary theory. For example, a great majority of the studies on feedback were conceptualized from a behaviorist perspective and relied on pre-and posttests that closely resembled instructional materials. In the motivational literature, the admonition to avoid challenging tasks may not hold in a standards-based rather than norm-referenced environment or when the classroom culture supports students in developing a learning orientation. New studies are needed that reflect constructivist and sociocultural models of supported learning.

A few studies cited in the chapter illustrate how a specific assessment practice, consistent with social-constructivist theory, can be introduced and studied. For example, Elawar and Corno (1985) created an intervention to help teachers focus on making feedback useful for student improvement. White and Frederiksen (2000) and Klenowski (1995) examined the effect of self-assessment on student learning and on attitudes about grades, knowledge of the criteria, and so forth. More studies like these are needed. They should be designed to answer research questions such as the following: How well do instructionally embedded assessments capture important learning goals? What insights do such assessments provide to teachers and students, and how do these insights promote further steps to move learning forward? How can assessment occasions and strategies be made to fit with instructional routines? (Portfolios, student conferencing, and explaining problem solutions to the class at the overhead are examples of such strategies.) Can the processes derived from learning theory—prior knowledge assessment, feedback, metacognitive awareness, self-assessment, etc.—be introduced self-consciously as a means to increase student learning and motivation? Under what conditions and for whom are these strategies effective? Can formative and summative assessment be made coherent and mutually supportive? When they are coherent, are student learning and motivation enhanced? Speculative extrapolations from existing research and theory should also be explicitly tested. For example, would postponing grading increase the effectiveness of formative assessment, that is, foster a learning orientation and increase achievement?

5.2. Studies of Teacher Development

One-variable-at-a-time or one-assessment-feature-at-a-time studies like those cited above are helpful for research purposes because they help focus on the effects of a specific strategy and the ways by which that particular assessment practices support student learning. In addition, I find these studies to be useful examples of how change might occur—that is, how teachers who like the theory of formative assessment might take the initial steps to change their practice. Ultimately the goal is to make a complete paradigm and cultural shift (Shepard, 2000). Indeed, adopting a formative assessment "technique" without a corresponding philosophical shift is likely to undermine efforts by leaving in place traditional attitudes, about performing for the sake of grades, for example. However, we know from the research on educational reform and teacher change that it is impossible to install a reform whole. Therefore, it is quite pragmatic to consider theoretical arguments and then adopt a specific assessment strategy, as the focal point for self-conscious change in practice, along with ongoing mentoring and reflection to address the inevitable practical as well as theoretical repercussions. The single assessment intervention strategy might be: special training to give feedback focused on improvement, documenting students' funds of knowledge, examining student work in grade-level teams and brainstorming instructional interventions, introducing self-assessment, and so forth. In an impressive study in England where median classroom gains were on the order of one-third of a standard deviation, Black and Wiliam (2004) acquainted teachers with the theory of formative assessment and then invited them to develop their own plans by selecting strategies from the literature such as rich questioning, comment-only marking, sharing criteria with learners, and student peer- and self-assessment.

Research on teacher learning and professional development provides us with several general principles for supporting change. In essence, we (who are promoting change) need to treat teachers, as learners, in the same way we would have them treat their students. We need to have a well-conceived model of ideal professional practice toward which we are inducting them and at the same time must realize that teachers will contribute to and modify the tools and practices of the community in which they participate (Lave & Wenger, 1991). For teachers to make meaningful changes in pedagogical beliefs and accompanying practices, they themselves will need to try out and reflect on new approaches in the context of their own classrooms (Putnam & Borko, 2000). Research studies conducted in the context of practice should focus on questions such as the following. What conditions, prior beliefs, or supports enable or frustrate the use of assessment as theoretically intended? How does subject matter knowledge mediate beliefs and the enactment of effective formative assessment practices? How can formative assessment practices be integrated with other curricular reforms or with other cultural shifts aimed at developing a community of learners, which are also grounded in a sociocultural model of learning? How must issues surrounding grading and external assessments be addressed so as to help rather than hinder formative assessment efforts? How do school context and the implied social contract (Perrenoud, 1991) students bring with them about grading affect renegotiating formative assessment purposes?

5.3. New Conceptualizations of Reliability and Validity

My historical preamble portrayed the measurement field as slow to move away from a traditional view of testing in classrooms focused on summative assessment. The turn of the 21st century, however, has seen dramatic changes. The publication of *Knowing What Students Know* (Pellegrino et al., 2001) was one watershed event. A second was the publication of a special issue of *Educational Measurement: Issues and Practice* on "Changing the Way Measurement Theorists Think about Classroom Assessment" (Brookhart, 2003). Leading the charge, Brookhart (2003) argued that developments in reliability and validity theory have been forged in the context of large-scale assessment programs. Given the need to integrated classroom assessment and instruction, as I have described in this chapter, Brookhart (2003) makes the case that "doing" reliability and validity work in classrooms must also be fundamentally different.

A cardinal principle of measurement theory has always been that reliability and validity depend on test use. In the classroom context, the reliability of any one assessment need not meet the same standard for stability as a measure used to determine high school graduation or college entrance. Because formative assessment in classrooms is ongoing, a misperception of a student's skills or knowledge one day can be corrected by new information and demonstration of proficiency the next (Shepard, 2000). More importantly, notions of scaffolding and dynamic assessment (Lidz, 1987), based on Vygotsky's zone of proximal development, are intended to change a student's level of proficiency in the very midst of assessing. As Moss (2003) argues in the *EM:IP* special issue, as a teacher, "I have no need to draw and warrant fixed interpretations of students' capabilities, rather it is my job to help them make those interpretations obsolete" (p. 16). Smith (2003), also in the special issue, suggested that perhaps "sufficiency of information" would be the most appropriate standard for reliability in classroom contexts. "Do I have enough information here to make a reasonable decision about this student with regard to this domain of information?" (p. 30). As Moss noted, the standard would be quite different depending upon whether the decision was summative, as for a letter of recommendation, or formative as when a teacher tailors feedback to help a student improve a paper.

Just as formative assessment may not require that a fixed "score" be reported, it is also the case that correlation coefficients may seldom be the appropriate indicators of reliability. In classrooms, making sense of observational and work sample data means looking for patterns, checking for contradictory evidence, and comparing the emerging description against models of developing competence. Like a number of other authors, I argue for an interpretivist approach to analysis and synthesis of data (Gipps, 1999; Graue, 1993; Moss, 1996, 2003; Shepard, 2001). In my own case, I see a strong connection between the use of qualitative research methods, formative assessment practices, and my training as a clinician when I used observations to form a tentative hypothesis, gathered additional information to confirm or revise, and planned an intervention (itself a working hypothesis). Indeed, some time ago, Geertz (1973) drew an analogy between clinical inference as used in medicine and the way in which cultural theorists "diagnose" the underlying meaning of social discourse, meaning that they use grounded theory to generate cogent interpretations, or generalizations, that have explanatory power beyond thick descriptions. Note that checking for patterns and justifying the warrant for particular interpretations blurs the boundaries between reliability and validity, as Smith (2003) had to acknowledge in his argument for sufficiency of information as the way to define reliability for classroom purposes. In fact, the line of questioning that Smith (2003) proposed to evaluate reliability corresponds closely to the interpretive process of reasoning from evidence that Moss (2003) offers as the standard for validity. Given that validity is the more encompassing concept, I prefer to use the term validity to refer to the process of warranting interpretations and to limit use of the term reliability to narrower consistency requirements such as inter-judge agreements for scoring rubrics.

Brookhart (2003), Moss (2003), and Smith (2003) have made a start in speculating about how reliability and validity theory will have to be reformulated to make sense for classroom purposes, but theirs is only the beginning of a major reconceptualization effort. Many old adages may need to be modified or even turned on their heads. For example, we know that computed quantitatively the difference between two scores is usually much less reliable than either score alone. However, if we were to take seriously the recommendation from *Knowing What Students Know* to represent student progress along well-developed learning continua, "difference scores" or progress measures would be highly reliable, because the classroom-based measure of growth would have the warrant of all the data collected in between, and would not depend on just the two end-points. A program of research to study reliability for classroom purposes should begin by examining the kind and degree of consistency required to support classroom decisions.

Validity is the appropriate place to begin or end any essay on educational measurement. In classrooms, formative assessment is valid if it contributes to the furtherance of student learning. As Moss (2003) suggests, validity in classroom contexts is primarily about consequences, about how well interpretations from assessments inform instructional decisions and help to move students along a trajectory of increasing competence. To outline a research agenda for developing validity theory appropriate to classroom assessment one need only reprise the important themes of the chapter. To be mutually supportive, formative and summative assessments must be conceptually aligned. They should embody important learning goals using a broad range of tasks and problem types to tap student understandings. Validity investigations should examine how well various assessment tools represent students' knowledge, skills, attitudes, and developing identities for summative purpose and how well they support deep, mastery approaches to learning when used formatively. Validity studies should also explicitly address whether assessment processes work as intended. For example, do students use substantive feedback to improve their work? The program of research outlined above to examine the effects of assessment tools and processes is, in fact, a program of validity research. A greater understanding gained from research that tests the model of formative assessment, its relation to learning theory, and so forth will also help to illuminate new understandings of validity theory needed for classroom assessment.

NOTES

I am grateful to Rick Stiggins and Mark Wilson for their encouraging and prodding reviews of earlier drafts of this chapter.

1. To be fair, Wood (1923) was arguing for the use of information tests with their greater reliability *to supplement* direct measurement using traditional essay examinations. However, this same reasoning was later used by others *to substitute* more reliable objective tests for essay tests.

2. Prophetically, Brown (1981) commented, "(T)he effective aspect of the feedback is knowing whether a question was answered correctly or, if it was answered incorrectly, knowing where the error occurred and what needs to be done to correct the error. This information is provided by the teacher's indication of the correctness of the response and/or by his comments, not by the grade. Thus, a test that is scored but not graded can provide as much useful feedback to students as one which is graded" (p. 171).

3. In this chapter, I do not define and use the term social-constructivism as the conjoining of cognitive and sociocultural theories because some authors use social-constructivism more narrowly to refer only to a variant of cognitive theory.

REFERENCES

Ames, C. (1984). Competitive, cooperative, and individualistic goal structures: A cognitive-motivational analysis. In R. E. Ames & C. Ames (Eds.), *Research on motivation in education* (Vol. 1, pp. 177–207). New York: Academic Press.

Ames, C. (1992). Classrooms: Goals, structures, and student motivation. *Journal of Educational Psychology, 84,* 261–271.

Assessment Reform Group. (1999). *Assessment for learning: Beyond the black box*. Cambridge: University of Cambridge School of Education.

Atkin, J. M., Black, P., & Coffey, J. (2001). *Classroom assessment and the National Science Education Standards*. Washington, DC: National Academy Press.

Baron, J. B., & Wolf, D. P. (Eds.). (1996). *Performance-based student assessment: Challenges and Possibilities, Ninety-fifth Yearbook of the National Society for the Study of Education* (Part 1). Chicago: University of Chicago Press.

Benware, C., & Deci, E. (1984). Quality of learning with an active versus passive motivational set. *American Educational Research Journal, 21*, 755–765.

Black, P., & Wiliam, D. (1998). Assessment and classroom learning. *Assessment in Education: Principles, Policy, and Practice, 5*(1), 7–74.

Black, P., & Wiliam, D. (2004). The formative purpose: Assessment must first promote learning. In M. Wilson (Ed.), *Towards coherence between classroom assessment and accountability: 103rd Yearbook of the National Society for the Study of Education* (Part 2, pp. 20–50). Chicago: University of Chicago Press.

Bloom, B. S. (Ed.). (1956). *Taxonomy of educational objectives: The classification of educational goals*. New York: David McKay Company.

Bransford, J. D., Brown, A. L., & Cocking, R. R. (1999). *How people learn: Brain, mind, experience, and school*. Washington, DC: National Academies Press.

Brookhart, S. M. (1993). Teachers' grading practices: Meaning and values. *Journal of Educational Measurement, 30*, 123–142.

Brookhart, S. M. (1994). Teachers' grading: Practice and theory. *Applied Measurement in Education, 7*(4), 279–301.

Brookhart, S. M. (2003). Developing measurement theory for classroom assessment purposes and uses. *Educational Measurement: Issues and Practice, 22*(4), 5–12.

Brown, F. G. (1981). *Measuring classroom achievement*. New York: Holt, Rinehart, & Winston.

Bruner, J. S. (1985). Vygotsky: A historical and conceptual perspective. In J. V. Wersch & Center for Psychosocial Studies (Eds.), *Culture, communication, and cognition: Vygotskian perspectives* (pp. 21–34). New York: Cambridge University.

Butler, R. (1987). Task-involving and ego-involving properties of evaluation: Effects of different feedback conditions on motivational perceptions, interest, and performance. *Journal of Educational Psychology, 79*, 474–482.

Butler, R. (1988). Enhancing and undermining intrinsic motivation: The effects of task-involving and ego-involving evaluation on interest and performance. *British Journal of Educational Psychology, 58*, 1–14.

Butler, R., & Nisan, M. (1986). Effects of no feedback, task related comments, and grades on intrinsic motivation and performance. *Journal of Educational Psychology, 78*, 210–216.

Calkins, L., Montgomery, K., & Santman, D. (1998). *A teacher's guide to standardized reading tests: Knowledge is power*, Portsmouth, NH: Heinemann.

Carpenter, T. P., & Moser, J. M. (1984). The acquisition of addition and subtraction concepts in grades one through three. *Journal for Research in Mathematics Education, 15*(3), 179–202.

Cizek, G. J., Fitzgerald, S. M., & Rachor, R. E. (1995/1996). Teachers' assessment practices: Preparation, isolation, and the kitchen sink. *Educational Assessment, 3*(2), 159–179.

Clay, M. M. (1985). *The early detection of reading difficulties*. Auckland, New Zealand: Heinemann.

Cobb, P., Wood, T., & Yackel, E. (1993). Discourse, mathematical thinking, and classroom practice. In E. A. Forman, N. Minick, & C. A. Stone (Eds.), *Contexts for learning: Sociocultural dynamics in children's development* (pp. 91–119). New York: Oxford University Press.

Connolly, A., Nachtman, W., & Pritchett, M. (1972). *Keymath diagnostic arithmetic test*. Circle Pines, MN: American Guidance Service.

Cook, W. W. (1941). Achievement tests. In W. S. Monroe (Ed.), *Encyclopedia of educational research* (pp. 1283–1301). New York: Macmillan.

Cook, W. W. (1951). The functions of measurement in the facilitation of learning. In E. F. Lindquist (Ed.), *Educational Measurement* (pp. 3–46). Washington, DC: American Council on Education.

Crooks, T. J. (1988). The impact of classroom evaluation practices on students. *Review of Educational Research, 58*(4), 438–481.

Deci, E., & Ryan, R. (1985). *Intrinsic motivation and self-determination in human behavior*. New York: Plenum.

Dorr-Bremme, D. W. (1983). Assessing students: Teachers' routine practices and reasoning. *Evaluation Comment, 6*(4), 1–12.

Dweck, C. (1986). Motivational processes affecting learning. *American Psychologist, 41*, 1040–1048.

Elawar, M. C., & Corno, L. (1985). A factorial experiment in teachers' written feedback on student homework: Changing teacher behavior a little rather than a lot. *Journal of Educational Psychology, 77*, 162–173.

Elliott, E., & Dweck, C. (1988). Goals: An approach to motivation and achievement. *Journal of Personality and Social Psychology, 54*, 5–12.

Farr, R., & Griffin, M. (1973). Measurement gaps in teacher education. *Journal of Research and Development in Education, 7*(1), 19–28.

Fennema, E., & Franke, M. L. (1992). Teachers' knowledge and its impact. In D. A. Grouws (Ed.), *Handbook of research on mathematics teaching and learning* (pp. 147–164). New York: Macmillan.

Fleming, M., & Chambers, B. (1983). Teacher-made tests: Windows on the classroom. *New Directions for Testing and Measurement: Testing in the Schools, 19*, 29–38.

Forster, M., & Masters, G. (2004). Bridging the conceptual gap between classroom assessment and system accountability. In M. Wilson (Ed.), *Towards coherence between classroom assessment and accountability: 103rd Yearbook of the National Society for the Study of Education* (Part 2, pp. 51–73). Chicago: University of Chicago Press.

Geertz, C. (1973). *The interpretation of cultures*. New York: Basic Books.

Gipps, C. V. (1999). Socio-cultural aspects of assessment. In P. D. Pearson & A. Iran-Nejad (Eds.), *Review of research in education* (Vol. 24, pp. 355–392). Washington, DC: American Educational Rescrach Association.

Glaser, R., & Nitko, A. J. (1971). Measurement in learning and instruction. In R. L. Thorndike (Ed.), *Educational measurement* (2nd ed., pp. 625–670). Washington, DC: American Council on Education.

Goehring, H. J., Jr. (1973). Course competencies for undergraduate courses in educational tests and measurement. *The Teacher Educator, 9*, 11–20.

Goodman, Y. M. (1985). Kidwatching: Observing children in the classroom. In A. Jaggar & M. T. Smith-Burke (Eds.), *Observing the language learner* (pp. 9–18). Newark, DE: International Reading Association and National Council of Teachers of English.

Goslin, D. A. (1967). *Teachers and testing*. New York: Russell Sage.

Graue, M. E. (1993). Integrating theory and practice through instructional assessment. *Educational Assessment, 1,* 293–309.

Harackiewicz, J., Abrahams, S., & Wageman, R. (1987). Performance evaluation and intrinsic motivation: The effects of evaluative focus, rewards, and achievement orientation. *Journal of Personality and Social Psychology, 53,* 1015–1023.

Heath, S. B. (1983). *Ways with words: Language, life, and work in communities and classrooms.* Cambridge: Cambridge University Press.

Heubert, J., & Hauser, R. (Eds.). (1999). *High-stakes: Testing for tracking, promotion, and graduation.* Washington, DC: National Academy Press.

Hiebert, E. H., & Raphael, T. E. (1998). *Early literacy instruction.* Fort Worth, TX: Harcourt Brace College Publishers.

Hogan, K., & Pressley, M. (1997). Scaffolding scientific competencies within classroom communities of inquiry. In K. Hogan & M. Pressley (Eds.), *Scaffolding student learning: Instructional approaches and issues* (pp. 74–107). Cambridge, MA: Brookline Books.

Klenowski, V. (1995). Student self-evaluation process in student-centered teaching and learning contexts of Australia and England. *Assessment in Education, 2,* 145–163.

Kluger, A. N., & DeNisi, A. (1996). The effect of feedback interventions on performance: A historical review, a meta-analysis, and a preliminary feedback intervention theory. *Psychological Bulletin, 119,* 254–284.

Kulm, G. (Ed.). (1990). *Assessing higher order thinking in mathematics.* Washington, DC: American Association for the Advancement of Science.

Lappan, G., Fey, J. T., Fitzgerald, W. M., Friel, S. N., & Phillips, E. D. (1998). *Connected mathematics, say it with symbols: Algebraic reasoning* (Student ed.). Menlo Park, CA: Dale Seymour Publications.

Lave, J., & Wenger, E. (1991). *Situated learning: Legitimate peripheral participation.* Cambridge: Cambridge University Press.

Lepper, M. (1983). Extrinsic reward and intrinsic motivation: Implications for the classroom. In J. Levine & M. Wang (Eds.), *Teacher and student perceptions: Implications for learning* (pp. 281–317). Hillsdale, NJ: Lawrence Erlbaum.

Lidz, C. S. (1987). *Dynamic assessment: An interactional approach to evaluating learning potential.* New York: Guilford Press.

Lindquist, E. F. (Ed.). (1951). *Educational measurement.* Washington, DC: American Council on Education.

Linn, R. L. (Ed.). (1989). *Educational measurement* (3rd ed.). New York: American Council on Education & Macmillan.

Lorsbach, A. W., Tobin, K., Briscoe, C., & LaMaster, S. U. (1992). An interpretation of assessment methods in middle school science. *International Journal of Science Education, 14*(3), 305–317.

Madaus, G. F., & Stufflebeam, D. L. (2000). Program evaluation: A historical overview. In D. L. Stufflebeam, G. F. Madaus, & T. Kellaghan (Eds.), *Evaluation models: Viewpoints on educational and human services evaluation* (2nd ed., pp. 3–18). Boston: Kluwer Academic.

Madaus, G. F., West, M. M., Harmon, M. C., Lomax, R. G., & Viator, K. A. (1992, October). *The influence of testing on teaching math and science in grades 4–12: Executive summary.* Chestnut Hill, MA: Boston College, Center for the Study of Testing, Evaluation, and Educational Policy.

Marshall, H. H. (1988). Work or learning: Implications of classroom metaphors. *Educational Researcher, 17*(9), 9–16.

Marton, F., & Saljo, R. (1976). On qualitative differences in learning: 1. Outcome and process. *British Journal of Educational Psychology, 46,* 4–11.

Masters, G., & Forster, M. (1997). *Mapping literacy achievement: Results of the 1996 National School English Literacy Survey.* Canberra, Australia: Department of Employment, Education, Training and Youth Affairs (DEETYA).

Mathematical Sciences Education Board. (1993). *Measuring what counts: A conceptual guide for mathematics assessment.* Washington, DC: National Academy Press.

Mayo, S. T. (1964, February). *What experts think teachers ought to know about educational measurement.* Paper presented at the annual meeting of the National Council on Measurement in Education, Chicago.

Mazur, E. (1997). *Peer instruction: A user's manual.* Upper Saddle River, NJ: Prentice Hall.

McMillan, J. H. (2003). Understanding and improving teachers' classroom assessment decision making: Implications for theory and practice. *Educational Measurement: Issues and Practice, 22*(4), 34–43.

McNeil, L. M. (1988). *Contradictions of control: School structure and school knowledge.* New York: Routledge.

Mitchell, M. (1993). Situational interest: Its multifaceted structure in the secondary school mathematics classroom. *Journal of Educational Psychology, 85,* 424–436.

Moll, L. C., Amanti, C., Neff, D., & Gonzalez, N. (1992). Funds of knowledge for teaching: Using a qualitative approach to connect homes and classrooms. *Theory Into Practice, 31*(2), 132–141.

Morrow, L. M. (1985). Retelling stories: Strategies for improving children's comprehension, concept of story structure, and oral language complexity. *Elementary School Journal, 85,* 647–661.

Morrow, L. M., & Smith, J. K. (1990). *Assessment for instruction in early literacy.* Englewood Cliffs, NJ: Prentice Hall.

Moss, P. A. (1996). Enlarging the dialogue in educational measurement: Voices from interpretive research traditions. *Educational Researcher, 25,* 20–28, 43.

Moss, P. A. (2003). Reconceptualizing validity for classroom assessment. *Educational Measurement: Issues and Practice, 22*(4), 13–25.

National Association for the Education of Young Children. (1990). *Guidelines for appropriate curriculum content and assessment in programs serving children ages 3 through 8.* Washington, DC: National Association for the Education of Young Children.

National Council of Teachers of Mathematics. (1989). *Curriculum and evaluation standards for school mathematics.* Reston, VA: Author.

National Council of Teachers of Mathematics. (1995). *Assessment Standards for School Mathematics.* Reston, VA: Author.

National Research Council. (1989). *Everybody counts: A report to the nation on the future of mathematics education.* Washington, DC: National Academy Press.

Nava, F. J. G., & Loyd, B. H. (1992, April). *An investigation of achievement and non-achievement criteria in elementary and secondary school grading.* Paper presented at the annual meeting of the American Educational Research Association, San Francisco.

Newmann, F. (1992). Higher order thinking and prospects for classroom thoughtfulness. In F. Newmann (Ed.), *Student engagement and achievement in American secondary schools* (pp. 62–91). New York: Teachers College Press.

Nitko, A. J. (1989). Designing tests that are integrated with instruction. In R. L. Linn (Ed.), *Educational measurement* (3rd ed., pp. 447–474). New York: American Council on Education & Macmillan.

Noll, V. H. (1955). Requirements in educational measurement for prospective teachers. *School and Society, 80,* 88–90.

Ogle, D. M. (1986). K-W-L: A teaching model that develops active reading of expository text. *The Reading Teacher, 39*(6), 564–570.

Pedulla, J. J., Abrams, L. M., Madaus, G. F., Russell, M. K., Ramos, M. A., & Miao, J. (2003). *Perceived effects of state-mandated testing programs on teaching and learning: Findings from a national survey of teachers.* Boston: Boston College, National Board on Educational Testing and Public Policy.

Pellegrino, J. W., Baxter, G. P., & Glaser, R. (1999). Addressing the "Two Disciplines" problem: Linking theories of cognition and learning with assessment and instructional practice. In P. D. Pearson & A. Iran-Nejad (Eds.), *Review of research in education* (Vol. 24, pp. 307–353). Washington, DC: American Educational Research Association.

Pellegrino, J. W., Chudowsky, N., & Glaser, R. (2001). *Knowing what students know: The science and design of educational assessment.* Washington, DC: National Academy Press.

Perrenoud, P. (1991). Towards a pragmatic approach to formative evaluation. In P. Weston (Ed.), *Assessment of pupils' achievement: Motivation and school success* (pp. 77–101). Amsterdam: Swets and Zeitlinger.

Putnam, R. T., & Borko, H. (2000). What do new views of knowledge and thinking have to say about research on teacher learning? *Educational Researcher, 29*(1), 4–15.

Resnick, L. B., & Resnick, D. P. (1992). Assessing the thinking curriculum: New tools for education reform. In B. R. Gifford & M. C. O'Connor (Eds.), *Changing assessments: Alternative views of aptitude, achievement, and instruction* (pp. 37–75). Boston: Kluwer Academic.

Roeder, H. H. (1972). Are today's teachers prepared to use tests? *Peabody Journal of Education, 59,* 239–40.

Romberg, T., & Carpenter, T. (1986). Research on teaching and learning mathematics: Two disciplines of scientific inquiry. In M. Wittrock (Ed.), *Handbook of research on teaching* (3rd ed., pp. 850–873). New York: Macmillan.

Routman, R. (2000). *Conversations: Strategies for teaching, learning, and evaluating.* Portsmouth, NH: Heinemann.

Sadler, R. (1989). Formative assessment and the design of instructional assessments. *Instructional Science, 18,* 119–144.

Salmon-Cox, L. (1981). Teachers and standardized achievement tests: What's really happening? *Phi Delta Kappan, 69*(9), 631–634.

Scriven, M. (1967). The methodology of evaluation. In R. A. Tyler, R. M. Gagne, & M. Scriven (Eds.), *Perspectives of curriculum evaluation* (pp. 39–83). Chicago: Rand McNally.

Shepard, L. A. (2000). The role of assessment in a learning culture. *Educational Researcher, 29*(7), 4–14.

Shepard, L. A. (2001). The role of classroom assessment in teaching and learning. In V. Richardson (Ed.), *Handbook of research on teaching* (4th ed., pp. 1066–1101). Washington, DC: American Educational Research Association.

Shepard, L. A. (2003). Reconsidering large-scale assessment to heighten its relevance to learning. In J. M. Atkin & J. E. Coffey (Eds.), *Everyday assessment in the science classroom* (pp. 121–146). Arlington, VA: NSTA Press.

Shepard, L. A., & Bliem, C. L. (1995). Parents' thinking about standardized tests and performance assessments. *Educational Researcher, 24*(8), 25–32.

Shepard, L., Hammerness, K., Darling-Hammond, L., & Rust, F. (2005). Assessment. In L. Darling-Hammond & J. Bransford (Eds.), *Preparing teachers for a changing world: What teachers should learn and be able to do* (pp. 275–326). San Francisco: Jossey-Bass.

Silver, E. A., & Kenney, P. A. (1995). Sources of assessment information for instructional guidance in mathematics. In T. A. Romberg (Ed.), *Reform in school mathematics and authentic assessment* (pp. 38–86). Albany, NY: State University of New York Press.

Silver, E. A., & Kilpatrick, J. (1989). Testing mathematical problem solving. In R. Charles & E. Silver (Eds.), *Teaching and assessing mathematical problem solving* (pp. 178–186). Hillsdale, NJ: Lawrence Erlbaum.

Smith, J. K. (2003). Reconsidering reliability in classroom assessment and grading. *Educational Measurement: Issues and Practice, 22*(4), 26–33.

Stiggins, R. J. (1991). Relevant classroom assessment training for teachers. *Educational Measurement: Issues and Practice, 10*(1), 7–12.

Stiggins, R. J. (2001). *Student-involved classroom assessment* (3rd ed.). Upper Saddle River, NJ: Prentice-Hall.

Stiggins, R. J., & Conklin, N. F. (1992). *In teachers' hands: Investigating the practices of classroom assessment.* Albany: State University of New York Press.

Stipek, D. J. (1996). Motivation and instruction. In D. C. Berliner & R. C. Calfee (Eds.), *Handbook of educational psychology* (pp. 85–113). New York: Simon & Schuster Macmillan.

Stipek, D. (1998). *Motivation to learn: From theory to practice* (3rd ed.). Boston: Allyn & Bacon.

Symonds, P. M. (1927). *Measurement in secondary education.* New York: Macmillan.

Taylor, C. S., & Nolen, S. B. (2005). *Classroom assessment: Supporting teaching and learning in real classrooms.* Upper Saddle River, NJ: Pearson Education.

Teale, W. H., Hiebert, E., & Chittenden, E. (1987). Assessing young children's literacy development. *The Reading Teacher, 40,* 772–777.

Teale, W. H., & Sulzby, E. (Eds.). (1986). *Emergent literacy: Writing and reading.* Norwood, NJ: Ablex.

Tharp, R. G., & Gallimore, R. (1988). *Rousing minds to life: Teaching, learning, and schooling in social context.* New York: Cambridge University Press.

Thorndike, E. L. (1913). *Introduction to the theory of mental and social measurements.* New York: Teachers College, Columbia University.

Thorndike, E. L. (1922). Measurement in education. In *Twenty-first yearbook of the National Society for the Study of Education, Part I,* pp. 1–9. Bloomington, IL: Public School Publishing.

Thorndike, E. L. (1931). *Human learning.* New York: Century.

Thorndike, R. L. (1971). *Educational measurement* (2nd ed.). Washington, DC: American Council on Education.

Torgerson, T. L., & Adams, G. S. (1954). *Measurement and evaluation for the elementary-school teacher with implications for corrective procedures.* New York: Dryden Press.

Travers, R. M. W. (1955). *Educational measurement.* New York: Macmillan.

Tyler, R. W. (1951). The functions of measurement in improving instruction. In E. F. Lindquist (Ed.), *Educational measurement* (pp. 47–67). Washington, DC: American Council on Education.

U.S. Congress, Office of Technology Assessment. (1992). *Testing in American schools: Asking the right questions* (OTA-SET-519). Washington, DC: U.S. Government Printing Office.

Valencia, S. W., & Calfee, R. C. (1991). The development and use of literacy portfolios for students, classes, and teachers. *Applied Measurement in Education, 4,* 333–346.

Van den Heuvel-Panhuizen, M. (2001). A learning-teaching trajectory description as a hold for mathematics teaching in primary schools in the Netherlands. In M. Tzekaki (Ed.), *Didactics of mathematics and informatics in education. 5th Panhellenic Conference with International Participation* (pp. 21–36).

Thessaloniki: Aristotle University of Thessaloniki, University of Macedonia, Pedagogical Institute.

Vygotsky, L. S. (1978). *Mind in society: The development of higher psychological processes.* Cambridge, MA: Harvard University Press.

Ward, J. G. (1980). Teachers and testing: A survey of knowledge and attitudes. In L. M. Rudner (Ed.), *Testing in our schools* (pp. 15–24). Washington, DC: National Institute of Education.

White, B. Y., & Frederiksen, J. R. (2000). Metacognitive facilitation: An approach to making scientific inquiry accessible to all. In J. Minstrell & E. van Zee (Eds.), *Inquiring into inquiry learning and teaching in science* (pp. 33–370). Washington, DC: American Association for the Advancement of Science.

Wigfield, A., Eccles, J. S., & Rodriguez, D. (1998). The development of children's motivation in school contexts. In P. D. Pearson & A. Iran-Nejad (Eds.), *Review of Research in Education* (Vol. 23, pp. 73–118). Washington, DC: American Educational Research Association.

Wiggins, G. (1992). Creating tests worth taking. *Educational Leadership, 49,* 26–33.

Wiggins, G. (1993). Assessment: Authenticity, context, and validity. *Phi Delta Kappan, 74,* 200–214.

Wiggins, G. (1998). *Educative assessment: Designing assessments to inform and improve student performance.* San Francisco: Jossey-Bass.

Wiggins, G., & McTighe, J. (1998). *Understanding by design.* Alexandria, VA: Association for Supervision and Curriculum Development.

Wood, B. D. (1923). *Measurement in higher education.* Yonkers-on-Hudson, NY: World Book.

Wood, D., Bruner, J. S., & Ross, G. (1976). The role of tutoring in problem-solving. *Journal of Child Psychology and Psychiatry, 17,* 89–100.

Yeh, J. P., Herman, J. L., & Rudner, L. M. (1981). *Teachers and testing: A survey of test use* (CSE Report No. 166). Los Angeles: UCLA, Center for the Study of Evaluation.

18
Higher Education Admissions Testing

Rebecca Zwick
University of California, Santa Barbara

1. HISTORY OF ADMISSIONS TESTING[1]

Although it is often assumed that standardized testing originated in the 20th century, it actually has its roots in the assessments administered by the Chinese Imperial Civil Service, beginning at least as far back as 200 B.C.[2] Test-takers had to undergo an elaborate selection process with several rounds of examinations that could take years. These tests covered not only such areas as history, philosophy, and literature, but calligraphy, poetry, and painting as well. University admissions tests apparently began in Europe, although there is some disagreement about the time and location of the first such test. According to Webber (1989, p. 37), most historians agree that "[t]esting for admissions to universities ... did not begin in Europe until the eighteenth century." Another account of testing history by the Congressional Office of Technology Assessment, however, alludes to a Sorbonne entrance examination that was required in the 13th century (Office of Technology Assessment, 1992), and a College Board publication titled "Why Hispanic Students Need to Take the SAT" claims that "the idea of testing students for college admission has Hispanic roots. It was in Madrid in 1575 that a scholar ... proposed that the king establish an examination board to determine university admission" (Stewart, 1998). Most accounts agree that admissions testing had been instituted in Germany and England by the mid-1800s. In most countries, the use of tests to get *out* of universities preceded the use of tests to get *in*. In the early part of the 19th century, when Oxford and Cambridge established stricter examination procedures for graduation, it was still the case that anyone who could afford a university education could get into these prestigious institutions.

Standardized admissions testing first took root in the United States during the early part of the 20th century. In 1900, only about 2% of 17-year-olds—more than three-quarters of them men—went on to receive a college degree.[3] Those applying to college at the turn of the century were faced with a bewildering array of admissions criteria. Course requirements and entrance examinations differed widely across schools. In an attempt to impose order on this chaos, the leaders of 12 top northeastern universities formed a new organization, the College Entrance Examination Board, in 1900. The College Board created a set of examinations that were administered by the member institutions and then shipped back to the Board for painstaking hand scoring. Initially, the Board developed essay tests in nine subject areas, including English, history, Greek, and Latin; it later developed a new exam that contained mostly multiple-choice questions—the Scholastic Aptitude Test. This precursor to today's SAT was first administered in 1926 to about 8,000 candidates.

The first SAT consisted of questions similar to those included in the Army Alpha tests, which had been developed by a team of psychologists for use in selecting and assigning military recruits in World War I. These Army tests, in turn, were directly descended from IQ tests, which had made their first U.S. appearance in the early 1900s. (It is clear, though, that the Alpha test questions were revised with the military in mind. A sample arithmetic problem: "A certain division contains 5,000 artillery, 15,000 infantry, and 1,000 cavalry. If each branch is expanded proportionately until there are in all 23,100 men, how many will be added to the artillery?" [Brigham, 1923, p. 9].) The relationship between the Army Alpha and the SAT is just one example of the ongoing interplay between the educational testing world and the U.S. military, which today boasts the world's largest testing program (Sellman & Arabian, 1997, p. xv). The needs of the military fueled the growth of standardized testing in the United States in several ways. In World War II, as in World War I, tests played a role in screening individuals for military service and assigning them to jobs. During this period, both the College Board and the Iowa Testing Programs, which would later spawn the testing company ACT, Inc., helped the military develop personnel tests. Although the publicity about wartime testing was not always favorable, it produced a surge of interest by educational institutions.

World War II also fueled an expansion in the use of standardized testing by creating an urgent need for well-trained individuals who could be recruited into the military; this led to an increased emphasis on college study in the United States. The passage of the GI Bill in 1944 sent thousands of returning veterans to college as well, boosting the popularity of the efficient multiple-choice SAT. Between 1940 and 1950, the number of college degrees granted more than doubled to about 400,000 (Snyder, Hoffman, & Geddes, 1997, Table 244).

Between the Wars, another development took place that was to have a major impact on the testing enterprise—the automatic scoring of tests. Beginning in 1939, the monumental task that had once required many hours of training and tedious clerical work—scoring the SAT—was done by a machine. This change effectively transformed testing from an academic venture to a bona fide industry. The stage was now set for the birth of Educational Testing Service (ETS).

ETS, currently the largest U.S. testing organization, was founded in Princeton, New Jersey in 1947 through the merger of the testing activities of three companies: The College Entrance Examination Board, the Carnegie Foundation for the Advancement of Teaching, and the American Council on Education. The parties to the merger had painstakingly negotiated the terms of their union over a period of 10 years. (All three continue to exist as separate organizations.)

The 1949–1950 ETS annual report gives an idea of the astonishing optimism about testing that prevailed at that time. The claims made by ETS president Henry Chauncey sound stunningly naive from today's perspective: "[W]ith respect to knowledge of individuals, the possibilities of constructive use [of tests] are far greater than those of misuse. Educational and vocational guidance, personal and social adjustment most certainly should be greatly benefited. Life may have less mystery, but it will also have less disillusionment and disappointment … [T]he field of testing is exceedingly broad and the opportunities for ETS almost limitless" (ETS, 1950, pp. 9–10, 14).

In 1959, ETS gained a competitor in the college admissions test market. The American College Testing Program was begun in Iowa City "with no equipment and not even one full-time employee," according to the organization's own description.[4] (Today, the company is "ACT, Inc." and the test is simply "the ACT." Like "SAT," "ACT" is no longer considered an acronym.) ACT, Inc. was founded by E. F. Lindquist, a University of Iowa statistician and a man of many talents. Lindquist was the director of the Iowa Testing Programs, which instituted the first major statewide testing effort for high school students. As an acknowledged expert in standardized testing, he served on ETS's first advisory committee on tests and measurements. Remarkably, he was also the inventor, with Phillip Rulon of Harvard, of the "Iowa scoring machine." First described at a conference sponsored by rival ETS in 1953, this device was the first to use electronic scanning techniques (rather than simply a mechanical approach) to score test answer sheets.

The founding of ACT, Inc. was, in fact, closely tied to the development of this test scoring machine, "a marvel of blinking panels backed by a forest of cables that could ingest pulsations and emit a record of achievement from the brief encounter of small black marks on paper and the photocells in a reading head" (Peterson, 1983, pp. 111, 114). In 1953, Professor Lindquist formed the not-for-profit Measurement Research Corporation, which was to continue the development of test processing systems and offer services to other testing programs. ACT, Inc., in turn, was a spinoff of the MRC and the Iowa Testing Programs (Peterson, 1983, p. 164).

1.1. The Early Promoters of Admissions Tests

As test critics point out, the beliefs held by some of the early proponents of standardized testing were nothing short of abhorrent. This is particularly true of Carl Brigham, an early College Board advisor who has been called "the father of the SAT." Although he later famously recanted, Brigham, in his early writings, sounds like an almost absurd caricature of bigotry. Based on his extensive analysis of test results collected solely from (male) Army recruits during World War I, Brigham published a number of conclusions. First, immigrants were less intelligent than native-born Americans, and each succeeding wave of immigrants was less intelligent than the last. (He explicitly rejected the explanation that newer immigrants scored lower because they were less familiar with English.) Second, Americans of Nordic heritage were superior in intelligence to those of Alpine or Mediterranean heritage. (In particular, Brigham noted that his data "would rather tend to disprove the popular belief that the Jew is highly intelligent … The able Jew is popularly recognized not only because of his ability, but because he is able and a Jew" [Brigham, 1923, p. 190].) And finally, American intelligence was expected to deteriorate rapidly if action was not taken to halt a particularly "sinister" form of immigration, "the importation of the negro" (Brigham, 1923, p. xxi). Ironically, Brigham himself remarked that "it is difficult to keep racial hatreds and antipathies out of the most scholarly investigations in this field" (Brigham, 1923, p. xix).

Many opponents of standardized testing believe that today's SAT remains tainted by the views of its early promoters. Yet some early champions of college admissions tests were, in fact, staunch supporters of equal opportunity. The prime example is James Bryant Conant, the Harvard president who in the late 1930s promoted the idea that the leading U.S. testing agencies be merged into a single centralized company, and who eventually served as the first chairman of the ETS Board of Trustees.[5] In a series of *Atlantic Monthly* articles in the early 1940s, Conant cautioned against the development of a caste system in America and argued for a fluid society where people's roles would be determined by their merit (Lemann, 1995). Conant continued to be an advocate of educational reform throughout his career, deploring the continued existence of segregated schools and calling for an educational policy that would "mitigate [the] evil influence" of racial prejudice (Conant, 1964).

Even Brigham, after collecting several years' worth of data on immigrants, revised his opinions, not only on minority groups, but on the entire testing enterprise. Seven years after his 1923 book, *A Study of American Intelligence*, he published an article on intelligence testing in immigrant groups, in which he acknowledged that his earlier analyses had been misleading. In particular, in a passage that is in some ways strikingly modern, Brigham critiqued his earlier failure to understand the impact of test-takers' native language on their scores: "For purposes of comparing individuals or groups, it is apparent that tests in the vernacular [i.e., American English] must be used only with individuals having equal opportunity to acquire the vernacular of the test ... Comparative studies of various national and racial groups may not be made with existing tests ... [O]ne of the most pretentious of these comparative racial studies—the writer's own—was without foundation" (Brigham, 1930, p. 165).

The sharp distinction between the bigotry of Carl Brigham's early writings and the egalitarian stance of James B. Conant is reflected in the dual perceptions of the role of admissions testing that exist today: To some, tests like the SAT are harsh and capricious gatekeepers that bar the road to advancement; to others, they are gateways to opportunity.

2. OVERVIEW OF ADMISSIONS TESTS USED IN HIGHER EDUCATION IN THE UNITED STATES

This section describes the primary admissions tests used in the United Sates today—the SAT, GRE, MCAT, LSAT, GMAT, and ACT (presented in order of development). Sample items for each of these tests appear in Zwick (2002).[6]

2.1. Today's SAT

The SAT testing program is sponsored by the College Board; the tests are administered by ETS under a contract with the Board. The SAT Reasoning Test (previously called the SAT I: Reasoning Test) is claimed to measure "developed" critical thinking and reasoning skills needed for success in college.[7] Until recently, the SAT provided math and verbal scores; as described below, it now provides scores in math, critical reading, and writing. When they register for the SAT, students can choose to complete the Student Descriptive Questionnaire, which asks about demographic background, course preparation, interests, and plans. This information is then passed on to the colleges to which students send their scores.

In addition to the SAT Reasoning Test, the current SAT program also includes the SAT Subject Tests (formerly called the College Board Achievement Tests and later, the SAT II: Subject Tests), which assess the candidates' knowledge in particular areas. Twenty SAT Subject Tests are available, in literature, U.S. and world history, math, biology, chemistry, physics, and foreign languages. (When the new SAT writing test was unveiled in 2005, the SAT Subject Test in writing was eliminated.)

The SAT has changed substantially since it was first administered in 1926 (complete with instructions indicating that the "pencil is preferable to the fountain pen for use in this sort of test"). The 1926 test, for example, included a set of deductive reasoning items, as well as a set of items requiring test-takers to translate sentences to and from an artificial language whose vocabulary and rules were provided. A history of the changes in the content of the SAT is provided by Lawrence, Rigol, Van Essen, and Jackson (2004).

Two key events in the history of the SAT occurred in the mid-1990s: In 1994, major changes in content and procedures were implemented. Math items that required students to compute the answer rather than merely select it from several alternatives were introduced. Also, an earlier prohibition on the use of calculators was lifted. In addition, antonym items were eliminated from the verbal section, reading comprehension items were made more complex, and sentence completion items were added. (An early plan to include an essay section in the SAT was dropped, but a writing test that included an essay component was incorporated in the SAT Subject Tests.) Beginning in 1995, scores for the mathematics and verbal sections were reported on scales that had been "recentered" so that a score of 500 would represent an average score for each section, as in the original SAT. The SAT Subject Tests were also rescaled at this time. Post-recentering scores are not comparable to pre-recentering scores without adjustment; equivalence scales have been created to facilitate such comparisons. (See section 4.3 for more on recentering and section 4.4 on the linkage of the SAT Reasoning Test and SAT Subject Test scales.)

In 2005, the SAT changed once again, reflecting modifications agreed upon following a nationwide controversy about the SAT that came to a head in 2001, with a speech by Richard C. Atkinson, then the president of the University of California. Atkinson recommended the elimination of the SAT Reasoning Test as a criterion for admission to the university and advocated an immediate switch to college admissions tests that were tied closely to the high school curriculum (see section 2.5). In 2002, after months of discussion with UC representatives, the College Board Trustees approved several significant changes to the SAT. The new SAT, which made its debut in March 2005, substitutes short reading items for the verbal analogy items that were formerly part of the verbal section, incorporates more advanced math content, eliminates "quantitative comparison" items, and adds a writing section. All the critical reading questions and most of the math questions are multiple-choice. Each SAT also includes some math questions that require "student-produced" answers—there are no response choices. The newly added writing section includes both multiple-choice questions and an essay. (Essay and multiple-choice subscores for writing are provided, along with an overall writing score.)

Field trials of the new SAT were conducted in 2003, based on more than 45,000 students at 680 high schools. According to the College Board, changes to the verbal and math sections "will not affect the difficulty or reliability of the test" and will not exacerbate score disparities among ethnic or gender groups. Furthermore, the Board stated that math and critical reading score scales on the new SAT can be considered equivalent to the previously existing math and verbal score scales, so that "longitudinal data will be maintained." Based on a smaller study of the new test, the College Board also expected the addition of the new writing section to enhance the predictive validity of the SAT ("The new SAT 2005," 2004).

2.2. The GRE, MCAT, and LSAT

The ETS calendar of testing programs for 1949–1950 listed 22 distinct exams—quite an impressive array for a brand-new company. In addition to some tests that have now faded into obscurity—"Knights of Columbus" and "National College Home Economics Testing Program"—were the Graduate Record Examinations, the Medical College Admission Test, and the Law School Admission Test: Three of today's principal admissions tests for graduate and professional school were already in existence more than 50 years ago.[8]

2.2.1. The GRE

The Graduate Record Examinations program of the Carnegie Foundation for the Advancement of Teaching administered its first exam in 1937. In 1948, the GRE program was transferred to the newly formed ETS. Today, the GRE, which is used to evaluate candidates for admission to graduate school, is developed and administered by ETS under the direction of the Graduate Record Examinations Board, an independent 19-member committee that is affiliated with the Association of Graduate Schools and the Council of Graduate Schools. The exam is available in test centers around the world.

The GRE has undergone several content changes since its inception. In 1937, the "Profile Tests" (as the fledgling GRE was called) consisted of assessments in eight areas, including literature and fine arts as well as math, science, and verbal skills. The test, later renamed the GRE Aptitude Test and then the GRE General Test, was eventually streamlined to provide only verbal reasoning and quantitative reasoning scores, while separate "Advanced Tests" (subsequently renamed the GRE Subject Tests) measured achievement in other areas. In 1985, a new analytical reasoning section became an official part of the General Test. This section was intended to measure the "ability to understand structured sets of relationships, ... analyze and evaluate arguments, ... draw sound inferences, and identify plausible causal explanations" (ETS, 2000, p. 8).

The next major content change to the GRE Testing program occurred in 1999 with the introduction of a writing assessment that was separate from the General and Subject Tests. Beginning in October, 2002, the writing assessment, now called analytical writing, became a component of the GRE General Test, replacing the analytical reasoning section. According to the GRE program, this change was made "in order to (1) respond to the need to help the admissions process by assessing higher level critical thinking and analytical writing skills of applicants, and (2) provide a performance assessment that measures a test-taker's ability to make and critique arguments, which is central to the work done by graduate students in most fields" (ETS, 2003a).

According to the test bulletin, today's GRE General Test "measures analytical writing, verbal, and quantitative reasoning abilities that have been acquired and developed over a long period of time" (ETS, 2003b, p. 4). The verbal and quantitative reasoning items are all multiple-choice; the analytical writing section consists of two essay tasks, one asking the candidate to take a perspective on an issue, and one requiring the candidate to analyze an argument. According to the GRE score guide, the "Issue task states an opinion on an issue of general interest and asks test takers to address the issue from any perspective(s) they wish, so long as they provide relevant reasons and examples to explain and support their views. The Argument task presents a different challenge: it requires test takers to critique an argument by discussing how well reasoned they find it" (ETS, 2003b, p. 4).

The GRE was the first major admissions test to be administered as a computerized adaptive test (CAT; see section 4), beginning in 1993. In 1999, the paper-and-pencil GRE was discontinued, except for limited administrations outside the United States. The GRE analytical writing assessment is not adaptive, but is administered on the computer for test-takers who take the General Test on the computer. Students key in their essays using an elementary word processor. Most students who take the paper-and-pencil GRE write their essays by hand.

The GRE program announced in 2006 that changes would be made in the content and administration of the GRE General Test beginning in fall 2007. According to ETS, the modifications constitute "the most significant overhaul of the GRE General Test in its nearly 60-year history" (ETS, 2006). The verbal reasoning section will have a greater emphasis on high-level cognitive skills and the quantitative reasoning section will contain more data interpretation and real-life scenarios. The verbal and quantitative sections will be longer than they are at present, and the score scales for these sections will change. The writing section will include more focused prompts that are intended to reduce reliance on memorized materials, and test-takers' essays will be made available to designated score recipients. In addition, the GRE will change from an adaptive test to a computer-based "linear" test with fixed administration dates. All test-takers who take the exam at the same time will receive the same questions. The GRE will be administered via an Internet-based testing network, an approach that is already being used for the Test of English as a Foreign Language.

In addition to the General Test, the following eight GRE Subject Tests are available: biochemistry, cell and molecular biology; biology; chemistry; computer science; literature in English; mathematics (rescaled);[9] physics; and psychology. These exams are multiple-choice, and are administered in paper-and-pencil format only.

2.2.2. The MCAT

The Medical College Admission Test began in 1946 as the Professional Aptitude Test. (An earlier medical school admission test, called the Scholastic Aptitude Test for Medical School or the Moss Test, was used between 1930 and 1946.) From the beginning, sponsorship and overall responsibility for the MCAT have resided with the Association of American Medical Colleges, which currently represents about 125 medical schools, 400 teaching hospitals, and various academic societies and medical professionals. Various companies, however, have been involved in item development, test administration, scoring, and psychometric analyses for the test. ETS inherited the contract for the operation of the MCAT program (along with the GRE) from the Carnegie Foundation, and continued to develop and administer the test until 1960. Over the next four decades, The Psychological Corporation, ETS, ACT, Inc., and other contractors had responsibility for various aspects of the MCAT. In late 2004, the AAMC, which had been pilot-testing a computerized version of the MCAT, announced its intention to move exclusively to (nonadaptive) computer-based testing in 2007. Thomson Prometric, a technology-based testing company, will administer the exam, and ACT, Inc. will be in charge of item development and psychometric analysis (E. Julian, personal communication, December 19, 2004). The computer-based MCAT is being administered in a limited number of cities in 2005. The last paper-and-pencil administration of the MCAT is expected to occur in 2006. The AAMC hopes to shorten the test substantially by the time the transition to computer administration is completed.

As described in an MCAT bulletin, the test assesses skills and concepts "identified by physicians and medical educators as prerequisite for the practice of medicine" including "mastery of basic concepts in biology, chemistry, ... and physics; facility with scientific problem solving and critical thinking; and writing skills." The scoring and content of the MCAT were overhauled in 1991. The test now consists of three multiple-choice sections—verbal reasoning, physical sciences, and biological sciences—as well as a writing sample composed of two essay questions. For each essay, the candidate is presented with a "statement that expresses an opinion, discusses a philosophy, or describes a policy," according to MCAT materials. The test-taker is asked to perform three tasks: interpret the statement, describe circumstances under which the statement could be contradicted, and present a resolution of the conflict between the statement and the contrary viewpoint offered in the response to the second task.

In 2003, the MCAT program implemented some minor modifications to the content of the biological sciences section, reduced the length of verbal reasoning, and made some minor changes in scoring and score reporting. A separate score is reported for each section, along with a total score for the three multiple-choice sections.

2.2.3. The LSAT

The LSAT was conceived at a 1947 meeting between College Board staff and representatives of an association of nine law schools. This group of institutions, the precursor of the Law School Admission Council, wanted an SAT-like test that would be appropriate for use by law schools. In 1948, the first LSAT was administered by ETS, which had just assumed responsibility for the testing activities of the College Board. Since 1979, however, the LSAT has been developed by the LSAC itself, which today has about 200 member institutions in the United States and Canada. Portions of the work have been contracted out to other companies; for example, from 1992 through 2004, ACT, Inc. assisted in the development of the LSAT items and sections.

The LSAT is "designed to measure skills that are considered essential for success in law school: the reading and comprehension of complex texts with accuracy and insight; the organization and management of information and the ability to draw reasonable inferences from it; the ability to reason critically; and the analysis and evaluation of the reasoning and argument of others" (Law School Admission Council, 1999). Four sections serve as the basis for a single score: one reading comprehension, one analytical reasoning, and two logical reasoning sections. The current LSAT score scale was adopted in 1991.

All LSAT questions are multiple-choice except a writing sample, added in 1982, which is not graded, but is sent to the law schools to which the candidate applies. (Other writing assessments had been included in earlier versions of the LSAT.) In June, 2005, the LSAC increased the length of time for the writing sample from 30 to 35 minutes, increased the length of the sample, and introduced a new type of prompt. The writing sample remains unscored, but according to the LSAC Web site, a scored sample is under consideration for the future.

2.3. The GMAT

In the late 1940s and early 1950s, the GRE was used to screen business school applicants. In 1953, however, representatives of nine graduate schools of business agreed that they needed an admissions test of their own. They commissioned a feasibility study by ETS, and, just a year later, the first Admission Test for Graduate Study in Business—later renamed the Graduate Management Admission Test—was administered.[10] For five decades, the test was developed and administered by ETS for the Graduate Management Admission Council. In 2003, the Council, which includes about 140 "governing schools" of business and management, announced that its partnership with ETS would soon end. As of 2006, GMAT test development is managed by ACT, Inc., and the test is administered by Pearson VUE, a company specializing in computer-based testing.

The 1954 business school test included four sections, called verbal, quantitative, best arguments, and quantitative reading. Today's GMAT, according to its information bulletin, "measures general verbal, mathematical, and analytical writing skills that are developed over a long period of time ... The GMAT does not presuppose any specific knowledge of business ... [and] does not measure achievement in any particular subject areas" (Graduate Management Admission Council, 2000, p. 5). Since 1997, the GMAT has been a computerized adaptive test.

The test contains verbal and quantitative sections, both of which are multiple-choice, and an analytical writing section, which was added in 1994. The writing section requires the test-taker to produce essay responses to two questions, with half an hour allowed for each. One requires candidates to analyze an issue and explain their points of view; the other asks for an analysis of the reasoning behind a given argument. As in the GRE, candidates use a simple word-processing system to write their essays. The GMAT essay scoring procedures have sparked a great deal of controversy because computers, as well as humans, participate in the grading (see section 4.2.3).

Separate scores are reported for each of the three sections of the GMAT; a total score that reflects performance on the verbal and quantitative sections (but is not the total of the verbal and quantitative scores) is also reported.

2.4. The ACT

In 1959, when the ACT program began, the SAT was already well-established. Why start a new college admissions testing program? In Iowa testing circles, the SAT was considered to be geared toward the elite institutions of the east, and its developers were viewed as sluggish and resistant to change. From the beginning, the ACT was somewhat different from the SAT in terms of underlying philosophy: While the SAT consisted only of verbal and mathematical sections, the ACT was more closely tied to instructional objectives. The original version of the ACT had four sections—English, mathematics, social studies reading, and natural sciences reading. It is no coincidence that these subject areas were also included in the Iowa Tests of Educational Development, which had been used to assess Iowa high schoolers since 1942. In fact, because of scheduling constraints, the first form of the ACT assessment was constructed from the same pool of test items that was being used to assemble new forms of the ITED. In its early years, the ACT was administered primarily in midwestern states, but it is now used much more widely.

The content of the modern-day ACT is based on an analysis of the material that is taught in grades 7 through 12. The test specifications and items are developed from information obtained from regular surveys of secondary school teachers and curriculum experts that ask about the major themes being taught in the ACT subject areas. All questions in these subject areas are multiple-choice. The information bulletin notes that "test passages and questions used in the ACT Assessment are deliberately chosen to reflect the range of cultures in our population" (ACT, Inc., 2000, p. 2).

In 1989, major changes in the test content were implemented and the current four subject areas were introduced: English, mathematics, reading, and science reasoning (now renamed "science"). At the same time, the scoring of the test was changed (see section 4.3). Scores on this "enhanced ACT" cannot be compared to scores on the original ACT without adjustment. Students receive a score in each subject area, as well as a composite score. Seven subscores are also reported—two in English, three in mathematics, and two in reading.

In 2002, after the College Board announced that a writing component would be added to the SAT, ACT, Inc. announced that it would add a writing test to the ACT. Unlike the SAT writing section, however, the ACT writing test, first administered in 2005, is optional. Students who elect to take it along with the ACT receive two additional scores: a writing test score and a combined English/writing score.

As well as being more strongly linked to instructional goals than the SAT, the ACT also places a greater emphasis on facilitating course placement and academic planning (Beatty, Greenwood, & Linn, 1999, p. 5). In keeping with this goal, the ACT registration booklet includes a questionnaire on high school courses and grades, educational and career aspirations, extracurricular activities, and educational needs, as well as a career interest inventory (UNIACT).

2.5. Do Admissions Tests Measure Aptitude or Academic Achievement?

Despite the entrenchment of standardized tests in our systems of undergraduate, graduate, and professional school admissions, questions have persisted about their precise function: Are admissions tests intended to measure specific academic achievements, or to assess intellectual aptitude? Testing experts have not been particularly helpful in clarifying the niche that admissions tests are intended to fill. As an example, consider the GRE. While a 1960 document from the ETS archives says that its purpose is "to offer standardized evaluation of student learning in college," a 1965 archival note says the GRE is intended "to assist in appraising intellectual qualities of individual candidates." From the perspective of most testing professionals, the failure to unambiguously identify admissions test as measures of either aptitude or achievement is not particularly troubling. Instead, achievement tests and aptitude tests are typically viewed as endpoints of a continuum, with exams that focus on specific course material lying closer to the "achievement test" pole, while those that are less reliant on mastery of particular content falling near the "aptitude test" end.

Where do the various admissions tests lie on the aptitude-achievement continuum? Historically, the content of the SAT has not been tied to particular high school courses; instead, it was claimed to measure "developed verbal and mathematical reasoning abilities" that are relevant to success in college. According to the College Board, the new SAT that emerged in 2005 remains "a test of developed reasoning," but is "more closely tied to what students learn in the high school classroom than ever before. The college success skills measured by the exam have been identified through research and discussions with college faculty, high school teachers, and subject area experts across the country" (College Entrance Examination Board, 2004, p. 3). The new SAT, then, is somewhat closer to the achievement end of the continuum than its predecessor and is more similar to the ACT, which is based on an analysis of the material that is taught in grades 7 through 12 in each of 4 areas of "educational development"—English, math, reading, and science. The GRE General Test, GMAT, and LSAT are similar to the (pre-2005) SAT in that they too focus on verbal, math, and reasoning skills rather than course content. The MCAT, which was previously more of a general ability test, now includes an assessment of candidates' knowledge of material taught in undergraduate biology, chemistry, and physics courses. The SAT Subject Tests and GRE Subject Tests are, of course, based on specific curricular content, as described in sections 2.1 and 2.2.1.

Reinforcing the view that aptitude and achievement are not clearly distinguishable is the high correlation between "aptitude" and "achievement" measures. For example, although the SAT Reasoning Test and the ACT were created using different frameworks, the (pre-2005) SAT total score (verbal score plus math score) and the ACT composite score are highly correlated—.92 in a recent large-scale study (Dorans, 1999). Similarities in the functioning of the SAT Reasoning Test and SAT Subject Tests are discussed by Crouse and Trusheim (1988), Kobrin, Camara, and Milewski (2004), Bridgeman, Burton, and Cline (2004), Geiser and Studley (2004), and Zwick (2004a).

Nevertheless, the designation of admissions tests as aptitude or achievement tests does have implications for the perceived fairness of these tests and the educational practices that result from their administration. For these reasons, the controversy is unlikely to die, particularly as it applies to college admissions tests. In a recent reemergence of this debate, Richard C. Atkinson, then president of the University of California, announced in 2001 that he opposed the use of the SAT Reasoning Test as a university admissions criterion, arguing that it is viewed as being "akin to an IQ test" and hence unfair, and that it promotes undesirable instructional practices, such as the implementation of analogies drills in the classroom. He recommended that standardized tests be developed that would be directly tied to the college preparatory courses required of applicants to the University of California, and said that he hoped to eventually move away from quantitative admissions formulas in order to "help all students, especially low-income and minority students, determine their own educational destinies" (Atkinson, 2001; see Zwick, 2004b).

A different view is presented by Lohman (2004), who suggests that "aptitude tests that go beyond prior achievement have an important role to play in admissions decisions, especially for minority students." He presents evidence that scores on "well-constructed measures of developed reasoning abilities" show smaller disparities among ethnic groups than scores on good achievement tests, and argues that tests of reasoning ability can help admissions officers to identify students who do not do well on curriculum tests but can succeed academically if they try hard. According to Lohman, the "problem with the [2001] version of the SAT I may not be that it is an aptitude test, but that it is not enough of an aptitude test" (2004, p. 50).

Despite the fact that these debates are unresolved, the use of admissions tests continues to grow, presumably because of their demonstrated utility as a predictor of subsequent grades.

3. HOW ARE ADMISSIONS TESTS USED BY UNIVERSITIES?

How widespread is the use of standardized admissions tests, and how heavily weighted are test scores in admissions decisions? In what other ways do universities use standardized admissions tests? These are the questions addressed in sections 3.1. and 3.2.

3.1. How Are Admissions Tests Used by Undergraduate Institutions?

The sorting procedure that ultimately leads to admittance to college starts with the applicants themselves, who typically consider a combination of academic and nonacademic factors in deciding where to apply. For candidates who pick one of the "open-door" colleges, tests play no role in the admissions process: All that is required is to complete an application and, in some cases, show proof of high school graduation. Eight percent of the 957 four-year institutions that responded to a survey conducted by ACT, Inc., the Association for Institutional Research, the College Board, Educational Testing Service, and the National Association for College Admission Counseling (referred to hereafter as "the joint survey"),[11] fell into the open-door category; 80% of the 663 two-year institutions were open-door (see Breland, Maxey, Gernand, Cumming, & Trapani, 2002, p. 15). But even for applicants who prefer not to attend open-admissions schools, chances of getting admitted to some institution are still quite good, because about 71% of four-year institutions admit at least 70% of their applicants (see Breland et al., 2002, p. 23).

Of course, the degree to which standardized test scores and other academic criteria are regarded as useful in admissions decisions depends entirely on the goal of the institution's admissions policies. As Harvard public policy professor Robert Klitgaard pointed out in his thought-provoking 1985 book, *Choosing Elites*, the "first question to ask about selective admissions is why it should be selective at all" (p. 51). Klitgaard notes that we as a society have mixed feelings about selectivity. On one hand, we think it "has unpleasant connotations of elitism, unfairness, snobbishness, and uniformity." On the other hand, we "laud excellence, recognize its scarcity and utility, and endorse admissions on the basis of merit" (p. 51). This puts us in a bind, Klitgaard points out: If we truly wanted all applicants to have equal access to an education at the college of their choice, we could institute a "first come, first served" policy, or even a lottery as a means of choosing an entering class. (More recently, lottery admissions have been discussed by Sturm & Guinier, 2000/2001.) But although a lottery does provide equal access, most people find this solution unreasonable precisely *because* it is blind to student characteristics: The lottery seems unfair because it does not reward academic excellence, unusual motivation, or hard work. In fact, according to a recent College Board report, the lottery approach "was experimented with several decades ago [in] at least one institution, but abandoned when highly qualified applicants were not 'selected' over others who had considerably weaker records from the same school" (Rigol, 2003, p. 45).

Another argument for selectivity in college admissions is that it encourages high schools to provide a quality education; the same argument could be extended to the graduate and professional school admissions process. But most institutions are selective for a more immediate reason: They consider it desirable to admit candidates who are likely to be able to do the academic work required of them. Standardized admissions tests, along with other criteria, are considered in an attempt to identify these candidates.

Just how widespread is the use of standardized tests in undergraduate admissions? According to the joint survey, the percentage of four-year colleges requiring either the SAT or ACT held steady at slightly over 90% between 1979 and 2000 (Breland et al., 2002). The number of students taking either of these tests increased from about half of those graduating from high school in 1979 to about two-thirds of the 1998 graduates (Breland, 1998, pp. 3, 7).[12]

Although this has not always been true, the ACT and SAT are now used interchangeably by the majority of institutions. To allow at least rough comparisons to be made between the two tests, both individual colleges and testing companies have created tables of "concordance" between ACT and SAT scores (usually between the ACT composite and the sum of SAT verbal and math scores). The most recent large-scale effort to produce one of these concordance tables was undertaken jointly by researchers from ETS and ACT, Inc., using data from more than 100,0000 students who took the tests between 1994 and 1996 (Dorans, Lyu, Pommerich, & Houston, 1997). The linkage, however, is only approximate. Because the content of the tests is not identical, the association between SAT and ACT scores may not be the same for all types of test-takers. In particular, the relationship between the scores is likely to depend on whether the test-takers have been exposed to the curricular content in the ACT.

How heavily are test scores weighted in undergraduate admissions decisions? Four-year institutions responding to the joint survey rated high school grade-point average (GPA) or class rank as the most important factor in admissions, as was the case in similar surveys conducted in 1979, 1985, and 1992. Admissions test scores had the second-highest average rating, and showed a slight increase in average importance between 1979 and 2000 (Breland et al, 2002, p. 67). The third-most important factor in all four surveys was "pattern of [high school] course work."

About 70% of four-year institutions reported that test scores were "routinely considered in reaching an overall judgment regarding admissibility"; another 6% of these schools said they used scores only when other credentials were weak (Breland et al., 2002, p. 61). Roughly 40% of four-year schools reported that they had minimum test score requirements for admission; 57% had minimum requirements for high school GPA (see Breland et al., 2002, p. 59). Scores on achievement tests such as the SAT Subject Tests "were not viewed as highly important in admissions decisions in any of the four surveys between 1979 and 2000" (Breland et al., 2002, p. xi), a finding that is interesting in light of the renewed focus on achievement-based testing in California (see section 2.5).

What nonacademic aspects of a candidate's background are likely to be considered in undergraduate admissions? Leadership ability, extracurricular activities, community activities, motivation, work experience, and compatibility were all rated as "sometimes important" or "often important" by at least half of the four-year institutions (see Breland et al., 2002, p. 74). The average rating for "minority group membership" was low, falling between "not considered" and "a minor factor" (p. 67). Only 16% of four-year institutions (down from 31% in 1992) reported granting exceptions to formal admissions criteria for racial/ethnic minorities (see p. 65).

Colleges use standardized test scores for a variety of purposes other than making decisions about applicants. Approximately 45% of four-year schools reported using admissions test scores for placement and more than one-third of four-year schools stated that admissions test scores were used "by [the] institution for class profiles and by applicants in [the] self-selection process" (Breland et al., 2002, p. 61). Among two-year institutions, tests were widely used for diagnosis and placement, although the tests employed for this purpose were not specifically identified as admissions tests. In each of four areas—reading, writing, arithmetic, and algebra—roughly 80 to 90% of two-year schools reported that they required diagnosis or placement tests for at least some students (Breland et al., 2002, p. 48).

3.2. How Are Graduate and Professional School Admissions Tests Used?

The graduate and professional school admissions process is quite different from its undergraduate counterpart.[13] Graduate and professional school programs tend to be smaller, and admissions policies less formalized and less public. Decisions are typically in the hands of faculty, rather than admissions officers, and although a great deal of self-selection by applicants takes place, admission rates tend to be much lower than at undergraduate institutions. The use of standardized test scores as a factor in admissions decisions is widespread in Ph.D. programs and nearly universal at professional schools.

Admissions policies and rates vary widely over the hundreds of fields of doctoral study available in the United States Decisions tend to be made by faculty at the department level, and procedures are typically very flexible. As a 1997 College Board report noted, "published statements about [doctoral] admissions provide ample latitude for almost any decision" (Rigol & Kimmel, 1997, p. 13). Attiyeh and Attiyeh (1997) conducted a study of 48 leading graduate schools in which they examined admissions rates in 1990 and 1991 for doctoral programs in biochemistry, economics, English, mathematics, and mechanical engineering. Counter to stereotype, English was the most selective of these five disciplines, accepting only 20% of its applicants in 1991, while math, with a 1991 admission rate of 47%, was the least selective (Attiyeh & Attiyeh, 1997, p. 528). Surveys have shown that standardized admissions tests are widely used in graduate admissions, in combination with undergraduate grades and other factors (Kuncel, Hezlett, & Ones, 2001; Rigol & Kimmel, 1997; Skager, 1982). Many graduate programs require the GRE General Test; some require certain GRE Subject Tests as well. The Miller Analogies Test, developed by The Psychological Corporation is accepted by a small percentage of graduate programs as an alternative to the GRE.

What about the medical school admissions process? According to the Association of American Medical Colleges (AAMC), admission to medical school is extremely selective. AAMC data show that more than 60% of applicants were not accepted anywhere for the 1996–1997 academic year, though most applied to 10 to 12 institutions (Rigol & Kimmel, 1997, p. 12). The MCAT is required by nearly all American medical schools. College grades, the quality of the undergraduate institution, and letters of recommendation are also important factors in admissions decisions. Medical schools are unique in their heavy emphasis on personal interviews: A survey of accredited U.S. medical schools found that 98% of the responding institutions used interviews in the admissions process; in fact, the 92 responding schools conducted an average of about 2 interviews per applicant (Johnson & Edwards, 1991). Overall, the interview was rated as the most crucial factor in selecting among candidates, followed by undergraduate GPA in science courses, letters of recommendation, MCAT scores, and undergraduate non-science GPA, in that order.

Law school admissions, like medical school admissions, can be very competitive. A recent survey showed that the most prestigious law schools received more than 20 applications for each slot; about 40% of schools received at least ten applications for each available place. Overall, though, nearly 60% of the applicants do eventually get admitted somewhere (Nix, 1996; Wightman, 1997). Test scores and undergraduate grades tend to be weighted heavily in law school admissions decisions; schools often use an index score that combines LSAT score and undergraduate GPA. All American and Canadian law schools that belong to the Law School Admission Council (LSAC) require the LSAT, and most other law schools do as well.

According to its Web site, the GMAT is used by "thousands of graduate management programs around the world." Undergraduate grades and math background are also important factors in business school admissions, and according to a GMAC brochure, "[t]he vast majority of schools specifically require applicants to have work or military experience" (Graduate Management Admission Council, 1998). Essays, letters of recommendation, and interviews may also be considered. Business schools do not usually require a specific undergraduate major and tend to attract a student body with diverse academic backgrounds. The more prestigious schools admit only 10 to 15% of applicants, while some part-time Masters of Business Administration programs accept more than 60% of those who apply.

Studies indicate that commitment to affirmative action principles was a substantial factor in graduate and professional school admissions decisions during the 1990s. In doctoral programs (Attiyeh & Attiyeh, 1997), medical schools (Jolly, 1992), law schools (Nix, 1996; Wightman, 1997),[14] and business schools (Dugan, Baydar, Grady, & Johnson, 1996), African-American and Hispanic applicants, and sometimes members of other under-represented groups, were found to have higher admission rates than other students with similar undergraduate grades and test scores.

4. TEST DEVELOPMENT, SCORING, AND EQUATING

How are admissions tests developed, scored, and equated? These processes depend in part on the administration mode of the test. The GRE and GMAT are now computerized adaptive tests (CATs), whereas the SAT, ACT, and LSAT are paper-and-pencil tests. (As noted in section 2.2.1, a new nonadaptive version of the GRE will replace the current test in fall 2007.) The MCAT, primarily given as a paper-and-pencil test at present, is in the process of a transition to computerized (but nonadaptive) administration (see section 2.2.2).

In a CAT, items are selected for administration from a pool in such a way as to target the difficulty of the exam to the test-taker's proficiency level. Therefore, a CAT can measure proficiency much more efficiently than conventional tests; the multiple-choice sections of the GRE and GMAT CATs have fewer items than their paper-and-pencil counterparts. All the major admissions testing programs have investigated the use of CATs: Experimental CAT versions of the SAT and ACT already exist, and the sponsors of the LSAT and MCAT have investigated the possibility of developing a CAT version. CATs are discussed in further detail in the chapter by Cohen and Wollack and the chapter by Drasgow, Luecht, and Bennett (this volume).

In a CAT, test development involves the development of a pool of test items from which the candidates' items will be drawn, rather than the creation of a test form. Scoring and equating procedures must accommodate a situation in which the composition of the test varies from one test-taker to another even if they take the exam simultaneously. The multiple-choice test items are assumed to be consistent with the three-parameter logistic item response model (see the chapter on item response theory by Yen and Fitzpatrick [this volume]). Under that model, the probability that the response to dichotomous item i is equal to 1 (indicating a correct answer), given proficiency θ, can be expressed as follows:

$$P(x_i = 1 \mid \theta) = c_i + (1-c_i)[1 + \exp(-a_i(\theta - b_i))]^{-1} \quad (1)$$

The discrimination (a), difficulty (b), and "guessing" (c) parameters are estimated in advance for all the items in the CAT pool. (The c parameter is better described as the probability of correct response for a test-taker with a very low level of proficiency.) The test-taker's proficiency, θ, is re-estimated after the administration of each item. The item selection and estimation algorithm implemented in the GRE and GMAT CATs involves constrained optimization procedures. The algorithm uses the principles of maximum likelihood estimation to select for administration the item that, according to its estimated item parameters, will maximize the estimated item information function (see the chapter by Yen and Fitzpatrick [this volume]) at the test-taker's estimated proficiency level, provided that certain other constraints involving item content are met.

4.1. Overview of the Test Development Process

The sponsoring organization for each test (for example, the College Board in the case of the SAT, or the Graduate Management Admission Council in the case of the GMAT; see section 2) makes the broad policy decisions about the purpose, content, length, and method of administration of the test. The next step in the process usually involves the development of a framework or blueprint that specifies the content areas—and sometimes the cognitive skills—that are to be included in the test, along with the importance to be accorded to each of these areas and skills. This framework is typically developed by a committee of testing professionals and subject-area experts and then submitted for review to numerous other individuals and panels. The tests have statistical specifications as well, typically including a target range of item difficulties and item discrimination values, which measure the relationship between an item score and a test or section score.

With the exception of the writing assessments and a small number of short-answer items included on the math section of the SAT Reasoning Test, higher education admissions tests consist entirely of multiple-choice questions. The way items are composed varies to some degree across tests and testing organizations. Some companies rely mainly on in-house staff, some contract with other testing companies, and others primarily use hired consultants—usually classroom teachers or university professors—to develop test questions. After the items are created, they are reviewed by expert panels and by test editors who check the grammar, spelling, and format of the items.

Another type of evaluation that typically takes place is a "sensitivity" review of the items to eliminate content that could be disturbing to test-takers. According to the guidelines used at ETS, for example, the test "must not contain language, symbols, words, phrases, or examples that are generally regarded as sexist, racist, or otherwise potentially offensive, inappropriate, or negative toward any group." For example, "[w]omen should not be portrayed as overly concerned with their appearance or as more intuitive than men," and phrases like "the little woman" are unacceptable. In addition, "African Americans should not be characterized as people who live in depressed urban areas or who excel only in sports," and "[o]lder people should not be characterized as feeble, incompetent, or dependent" (ETS, 1999, pp. 3–5). Also prohibited is content that could be upsetting or inflammatory. For example, topics like abortion or euthanasia are usually taboo.

The items that pass muster are then field-tested. This may be done by embedding a special section (which typically does not count toward the test-taker's score) in a test that is given at a regular administration, or by conducting a separate experimental administration. The results of this field test are analyzed to determine whether the new items meet the established statistical specifications. Analyses of differential item functioning (see sections 6.3 and 6.5 and the chapter on test fairness by Camilli [this volume]) are typically conducted at this point too. The surviving items are deemed eligible for inclusion in a CAT pool or in a bank of items from which paper-and-pencil test forms can be constructed.

One fairly recent change in test development methods is that the initial versions of paper-and-pencil test forms are sometimes assembled using automatic item selection, which relies upon a computer program that incorporates both content and statistical specifications, and can monitor the degree to which the test form conforms to the blueprint (Stocking, Swanson, & Pearlman, 1991). If the test designer wants to make sure that "A" is not always the right answer to the multiple-choice items, that a certain number of reading passages include content expected to be of interest to minority test-takers, or that a particular set of items stays together, the procedure can accommodate these constraints too. Test specialists can then select the best of the automatically produced test forms, and can modify them as needed.

4.2. Scoring and Equating

This section addresses the scoring and equating of admissions tests. The main portions of the four paper-and-pencil tests are considered in section 4.2.1 first, followed by the two CATs, in 4.2.2. The scoring procedures for the essay components of the MCAT, GRE, and GMAT are described in section 4.2.3. (The essay that accompanies the LSAT is sent to the law schools unscored.)

4.2.1. Scoring and Equating the Paper-and-Pencil Tests (SAT, ACT, MCAT, and LSAT)

For the paper-and-pencil admissions tests, scoring consists of two basic steps:

Step 1. A raw score is computed, based on the number of correct answers.

Step 2. The process of test equating, described below, is used to translate the raw score to the reporting scale (for example, the 200-to-800 scale for the SAT). The equating process adjusts for differences in difficulty between test forms.

For the ACT, MCAT, and LSAT, the raw score is simply the number of correct answers, but for the multiple-choice questions on the SAT Reasoning Test, the SAT Subject Tests, and the GRE Subject Tests, a formula score is used. The formula score includes a "correction for guessing," which is intended to adjust the score to compensate for random guessing. The idea underlying the correction is that test-takers who guess randomly (in contrast to those who make informed guesses) should not be allowed to increase their scores by doing so. Specifically, the formula score is $R - W/(C - 1)$, where R is the number of right answers, W is the number of wrong answers, and C is the number of response choices. No points are subtracted for omitted items. The formula score is intended to be an estimate of the number of items for which the test-taker actually knew the answer (see Gulliksen, 1987, pp. 246–249 for a rationale). The formula score, which can include a fraction, is rounded to the nearest whole number before proceeding to Step 2.

As an example (based on the 1998–1999 *Admission Staff Handbook for the SAT Program*), consider the scoring and equating process for the verbal section included until recently in the SAT Reasoning Test. Suppose a test-taker answered 71 of the 78 questions correctly, got 4 five-choice items wrong, and omitted 3 items. The test-taker's raw (formula) score would be computed by subtracting 1/4 point for each wrong answer from the number of right answers, yielding a score of 70. A test equating process, described further below, would then be applied to determine the correspondence between raw and scaled scores for the particular SAT version at hand. The 1998–1999 *Handbook* shows that, for SAT forms then in use, a raw score of 70 on the verbal section could correspond to a scaled score of 720 on a relatively easy form, but could translate to a scaled score of 760 on a harder version of the test (The College Board and Educational Testing Service, 1998, p. 27). If the test-taker had received an SAT form of average difficulty, her verbal score would have been about 740.

The purpose of the equating process is to assure that scores on new test forms can be used interchangeably with scores on earlier forms. Even though the intention of test-makers is to create new test forms that are equivalent in difficulty to the old ones, some differences will inevitably exist, requiring that score adjustments be made. Each testing program uses a somewhat different equating method. Consider a particular section of the SAT as an example. Each new form of the SAT includes sets of equating items that serve as "anchor tests" to link the new form to previous (and future) forms. (Responses to these anchor items are not included in the scoring of the test.) One of several technical procedures used to establish the linkages among SAT Reasoning Test forms is IRT true-score equating, which is based on item response theory. (Some details of the SAT procedures are omitted here for simplicity; see Donlon, 1984 for additional information.) Specifically, the three-parameter logistic item response model in Equation 1 is assumed. Test-taker response data for the new and old forms are combined, and the a, b, and c parameters for the new, old, and anchor items are estimated. Including the anchor items (which have been administered as a portion of both the new and old SAT forms) in this item calibration process serves to put the two forms on the same scale. Now, item response theory can be used to derive the expected raw (formula) score at each level of θ for the new and old forms. The two expected raw scores (one for each SAT form) corresponding to a given value of θ are then considered equivalent and assigned the same scaled score (Donlon, 1984, p. 19). For more information on this and other approaches to test equating, see the chapter by Holland and Dorans (this volume).

4.2.2. Scoring and Equating the GRE and GMAT CATs

The scoring procedure for the GRE and GMAT CATs uses the three-parameter logistic item response model in Equation 1 to take into account the fact that candidates receive tests that differ in terms of the difficulty of the items (and in terms of the items' discrimination and guessing parameters). For each main section of the exam, a test taker's proficiency level, θ, is estimated based on his item responses and on the estimated parameters of the items he took. Two candidates who answer the same number of questions correctly will not, in general, get the same score on the test: All other things being equal, the more difficult the item, the more credit the candidate receives for answering it correctly. Each test-taker's estimated skill level, $\hat{\theta}$, is then converted to a raw test score through a statistical process that essentially asks the question, "How many items on a standard paper-and-pencil version (the reference test) would a candidate with this level of skill be expected to answer correctly?" Scores of this type are discussed by Stocking (1996). The raw score for a test-taker with estimated proficiency $\hat{\theta}$ can be expressed as follows for a reference test of n items:

$$Raw\ score = \sum_{i=1}^{n} \hat{P}(x_i = 1 \mid \hat{\theta}), \quad (2)$$

where $\hat{P}(x_i = 1 \mid \hat{\theta}) = \hat{c}_i + (1 - \hat{c}_i)[1 + \exp(-\hat{a}_i(\hat{\theta} - \hat{b}_i))]^{-1}$

As the final step in scoring, an equating process similar to that described in the preceding section is used to translate this raw score to the reporting scale. This last step, in effect, equates the CAT scores to scores from previous test administrations, assuming that the item response model holds.[15] The final score, then, should be comparable to scores on either paper-and-pencil or CAT versions of the test.

4.2.3. Scoring the MCAT, GRE, and GMAT Writing Assessments

The MCAT writing sample consists of two handwritten essays, which are scored by raters using conventional essay-grading procedures (see the chapter on performance assessment by Lane and Stone [this volume]). Two raters score the overall effectiveness of each of the two essays on a 1-to-6 scale. Disagreements of more than one point are adjudicated by a third rater. The resulting four scores (two per essay) are summed and then converted to an alphabetic score that ranges from J to T.

Essay-scoring procedures are very similar for the GRE: Two raters score each essay on overall quality, using a six-point scale; discrepancies of more than one point are adjudicated by a third rater. The scores on the two essays are averaged and rounded up to the nearest half-point to produce the final analytical writing score. According to the GRE score guide, essay responses are "reviewed by ETS essay-similarity-detection software and by experienced essay readers during the scoring process" to detect plagiarism or other forms of cheating (ETS, 2003b, p. 5).

In the GMAT writing assessment, as in the MCAT and GRE, test-takers respond to each of two essay questions. In terms of scoring procedures, however, the GMAT writing assessment is quite different from the MCAT and GRE: Each essay is evaluated by a computerized essay-scoring program called e-rater, and by one human rater. Both human and computer score the essay on a six-point scale. If the human and machine raters disagree by more than a point, another human rater resolves the disagreement. The candidate's writing score is the average of the four essay scores (two ratings for each of two essays), rounded to the nearest half-point.

How does this electronic scoring program work? E-rater counts the occurrence of various linguistic features in each essay, including sentence complexity, rhetorical structure (identified by the presence of certain "cue" words or phrases), and topical similarity to essay responses to the same question that received high grades from humans in the past. The importance e-rater assigns to each feature is determined through stepwise regression analyses that attempt to maximize the correspondence of e-rater scores to human experts' scores. For example, if the degree to which the essay adheres to its intended topic is an effective predictor of the human experts' evaluation, that feature will receive a large weight in e-rater's scoring system.

According to ETS, which created e-rater and has now conducted nearly a decade of research on its performance, e-rater agrees with its human counterpart about as often as two human raters agree: About 87% to 94% of the time, the two scores are within one point of each other (Burstein, Kukich, Wolff, Lu, & Chodorow, 1998).[16] How is it possible that a machine-human pair can agree roughly as well as a pair of trained human beings? One reason is that grading essays is often less than straightforward for *human* raters. Even with training, the task of assigning a number to a piece of writing is still complex and subjective. The success of e-rater relative to humans is less remarkable in light of the inconsistencies, biases, and errors that live raters cannot entirely avoid.

4.3. Score Scale Revisions: The Enhanced ACT and the Recentered SAT

Most testing programs revise their score scales from time to time. The ACT underwent a substantial change in its reporting scale in 1989, and the SAT began reporting scores on a "recentered" scale in 1995. The original ACT score scale was based on the 1959 version of the scale used for the Iowa Tests of Educational Development, originally established in 1942. By the 1980s, the ACT scales had developed some properties that were less than ideal (Brennan & Kolen, 1989, pp. 8–10). For example, the means for the individual tests departed from their original intended values and were quite different from each other. Also, ceiling effects were becoming severe for some candidate groups on some of the tests. In addition, the content of the ACT had changed substantially. In 1989, a new score scale for the "enhanced ACT" was introduced on which the scores for each of the four ACT tests and for the composite ranged from 1 to 36, and the means were set equal to 18 for a nationally representative sample of 1988 college-bound seniors. The new score scales for each of the ACT tests and for the composite were intended to have standard errors of measurement that were constant throughout the score scales, a goal that was approximately met through a process of scale transformation. The purpose of this novel feature was to aid in the interpretation of scores and score differences (Brennan & Kolen, 1989, pp. 10–11). (The additional goal of making the standard errors of measurement equal across the four ACT tests was not met, however; see Kolen & Hanson, 1989, pp. 53–54).

Just as the properties of scores on the ACT changed over time, so did the properties of SAT scores. After a lengthy period of study and debate, the College Board made a decision in the 1990s to change the reporting scales for the SAT, a change that ultimately took effect in 1995. Before this recentering, SAT scores were reported on a scale established in 1941. At that time, each of the SAT sections (verbal and math) was scaled so that scores would range from 200 to 800, with an average score of 500 and a standard deviation of 100. Subsequent versions of the test were then equated to the 1941 version. Under this scaling system, if a student had a verbal score of 600 and a math score of 620, then we could say that her math performance was "better" in the sense that it exceeded the average score by a larger number of standard deviation units. But over the years (particularly between 1963 and 1980), SAT scores "drifted" downward and lost their intended meaning. A score of 500 was no longer the average on either section, and the math and verbal averages were no longer the same. By 1993, the math average was 478, while the verbal average was 424. Now, a student with a verbal score of 600 and a math score of 620 would actually have a more impressive verbal performance (176 points above average) than math performance (142 points above average), but this would not be apparent without consulting the percentile ranks corresponding to the scores.

What explains the downward drift of SAT scores? A federally funded study concluded that much of the early part of the decline resulted from changes in the academic backgrounds of the students taking the SAT: More students from the lower ranks of their high school classes were taking the test. By the early 1970s, this shift in the test-taking population stabilized, but test scores continued to drop. The federal study suggested several other reasons for the score decrease (which was paralleled by a dip in scores on the ACT and other educational tests), including declining school and textbook quality and a reduced emphasis on the teaching of writing, which could explain the greater decrease in verbal scores. William Turnbull, then president of ETS, conjectured that this later phase of the decline was indirectly related to population changes as well: Because of reductions in the high school dropout rate, the average achievement level among high school seniors was decreasing, and high school education was becoming less rigorous (Turnbull, 1985). Turnbull also speculated that a decrease in the verbal complexity and vocabulary level of textbooks had contributed to the larger decline on the verbal SAT.

The recentering was, in essence, an adjustment procedure that assigned a label of 500 on the "new" SAT scale to the average score obtained by a special sample of about one million 1990 high school seniors (Dorans, 2002). This adjustment made it possible, once again, to interpret individual test scores relative to a mean of 500. The recentering did not change the percentile rank of an individual's score. If a student scored at the 65th percentile on the old scale, he would be at the 65th percentile on the recentered scale, but the numerical label attached to his score would change.

Unlike the change in the ACT scale, the SAT recentering, which had the effect of boosting the math average by about 25 points and the verbal average by about 75 points,[17] was assailed from all political quarters. Five years after the fact, the recentering was listed in an *Education Week* opinion piece as one of the 10 worst educational disasters of the 20th century, leading to the destruction of "an accurate and valuable barometer of the nation's educational achievement" (Weinig, 2000). The substantial negative reaction most likely reflects the deeply entrenched beliefs held by admissions counselors and members of the general public about the meaning of particular SAT scores.

4.4. Scaling the SAT Subject Tests and GRE Subject Tests

This section gives a brief description of the procedures for achieving an approximate linkage of the SAT Subject Test scales to the SAT Reasoning Test (prior to the introduction of the new SAT in 2005), as well as the scaling of the GRE Subject Tests. Any effort to link the Subject Tests to the Reasoning Test is complicated by the fact that the population of students who choose to take a particular Subject Test is not equivalent to the population taking the SAT Reasoning Test, nor is the population consistent across the various Subject Tests. Adjustments for these population differences were made by basing the Subject Test score scales on a hypothetical reference group, which was specified in terms of its SAT Reasoning Test score distribution. The original scaling of most of the Subject Tests (then called the Achievement Tests) was conducted by assuming that the reference group had a mean of 500 and a standard deviation of 100 on both the verbal and math scales of the SAT, and a verbal-math correlation of .4. (These assumptions were modified for the language tests, and were revised in subsequent scalings.) The goal was to scale each Subject Test in such a way that it would have a mean of 500 and standard deviation of 100 for the reference group. (See Donlon, 1984, pp. 21–23.)

For the group taking each Subject Test, the linear regression of the Subject Test raw score, S, on the SAT verbal and math scores, V and M, was estimated. The mean and standard deviation of S in the hypothetical reference group were then predicted using the results of this regression analysis; the means, standard deviations, and intercorrelations of V, M, and S among the Subject-Test-takers; and the specified properties of the joint distribution of SAT math and verbal scores in the reference group. A linear transformation of S was then derived to produce a scale score mean of 500 and a scale score standard deviation of 100 on the Subject Test for the reference group. As explained in the 1984 SAT technical handbook, this "system has the effect of raising the scale score values for a test that is typically taken by high-ability students (as measured by the SAT) and lowering the scale for a test that is typically taken by lower-ability students ... It broadens the scales for tests that are taken by heterogeneous groups of students (heterogeneous in terms of SAT scores ...) and produces narrow scales for tests taken by homogenous groups of students" (Donlon, 1984, p. 23).

This entire scaling process was carried out when a given Subject Test was introduced and was sometimes repeated later on. More typically, however, new forms of each Subject Test have been linked to earlier forms using linear or equipercentile equating methods (see the chapter by Holland and Dorans [this volume]).

The GRE Subject Tests were originally linked to the GRE General Test scale using a method similar to that used to link the SAT Subject Test scales to the SAT Reasoning Test scale. The intention was to make the Subject Test scores comparable to one another. But after that linkage was achieved in 1952, changes in the test-taker population and in the curricula in the various subject areas caused the comparability of the scales to erode (Briel, O'Neill, & Scheuneman, 1993, p. 36). A 1968 study verified that across-field comparisons were not warranted. The lack of comparability is not considered to be a serious problem because most graduate school admissions decisions "are made within a field (such as Chemistry), so examinees with different tests are not being evaluated by the same department" (Kathleen O'Neill, personal communication, November 17, 2003). Linear or equipercentile equating procedures are used to link the new and old forms of each Subject Test (Daniel Eignor, personal communication, January 20, 2004).

5. PREDICTIVE VALIDITY OF ADMISSIONS TESTS

Although they differ somewhat in the skills they are alleged to measure, all college, graduate school, and professional school admissions tests share one particular claim—that they are useful for predicting the first-year grades students will receive in the educational programs they enter. Research on the association between test scores and college grades began more than a hundred years ago. In the late 1800s, several studies at Columbia and Yale found that scores on psychological tests were nearly useless for predicting grades in various subjects (Gulliksen, 1987, p. 1), but around 1920, researchers did have some success in predicting college grades using intelligence test scores, obtaining correlations ranging from .35 to .60 (McKown, 1925; see Crouse & Trusheim, 1988, pp. 21–22).

In 1939, T. R. Sarbin conducted a particularly interesting study that compared two methods of predicting first-quarter college grade-point averages of 162 college freshmen. One method used a regression equation that included the students' high school ranks and college aptitude test scores; the other was based on the judgments of counselors, who used the students' high school standings and test scores, plus additional background information and personal interviews to make the predictions. Sarbin found that the regression equation was more accurate—the counselors tended to overestimate the student's future grades (Sarbin, 1942; see Gough, 1962, p. 556). Although the superiority of the statistical approach in the Sarbin analysis was small, 2 studies of the prediction of academic performance conducted 30 years later—Dawes (1971) and Wiggins & Kohen (1971)—showed a substantial advantage for the statistical approach (see Dawes & Corrigan, 1974, p. 98).

While early investigations of the prediction of college grades focused on the psychological implications of the findings, present-day researchers typically study the association between admissions test scores and subsequent grades as a way of evaluating the tests themselves: The validity of admissions tests as a selection tool for higher education institutions is judged largely by the degree to which test scores can predict later grades. Thousands of these prediction studies have been conducted—more than 3,000 for the SAT alone as of 1988, according to one estimate (Crouse & Trusheim, 1988, p. 6).

Predictive accuracy alone is, of course, insufficient evidence of test validity. According to the eminent validity theorist Samuel Messick, validity "is an overall evaluative judgment ... of the *adequacy* and *appropriateness* of *inferences* and *actions* based on test scores" (Messick, 1988, p. 33; italics in original). A comprehensive evaluation of a test's validity, then, must involve a consideration of the test's design, development, content, administration, and use. The validity of admissions tests for people of color, language minorities, people with disabilities, and women are addressed in section 6; misuses of admissions test scores are considered in section 7. General issues of test validity are addressed in the chapter by Kane (this volume).

5.1. Prediction of First-Year Grades

How can the predictive value of a standardized test—say, the SAT—be measured? Conducting a predictive validity study requires that the first-year grade-point averages (FGPAs) for the cohort of interest be available so that the predicted FGPAs (estimated using test scores and high school grades) can be compared to the FGPAs actually earned by the admitted students. Predictive validity studies are usually conducted within a single institution, although results may later be averaged across institutions.

Linear regression analysis is typically applied to estimate an equation for predicting FGPA using high school GPA, SAT math score, and SAT verbal score. The resulting multiple correlation (which is equal to the simple correlation between the observed and predicted FGPAs) provides an index of the effectiveness of the prediction equation. The regression analysis can then be repeated using high school GPA alone as a predictor. Comparing the predictive effectiveness of the two equations gives an estimate of the "value added" by using SAT scores.

For example, analyses of this kind were performed as part of a comprehensive study of the utility of the SAT as a predictor of college grades, conducted by Ramist, Lewis, and McCamley-Jenkins (1994). The research was based on 1985 data from a total of about 45,000 students from 45 colleges. All analyses were performed separately within each school and then averaged. The regression analysis using only high school GPA as a predictor yielded a moderately high correlation of .39; using only the SAT produced a correlation of .36. When high school GPA, SAT math, and SAT verbal scores were used in combination, the correlation rose to .48, yielding an "SAT increment" of .09 (.48 minus .39). (Correlations given in this chapter are not "corrected," except where noted. Corrected correlations are often larger by as much as .2; see section 5.5.) These findings parallel the results of many other test validity analyses in two basic ways. First, prior grades alone were more effective in predicting subsequent grades than were admissions test scores alone. Second, adding test scores to prior grades improved the prediction.

How important is the improvement that is achieved by using the SAT to predict FGPA? In their book, *The Case Against the SAT*, Crouse and Trusheim (1988) argued that the typical SAT increment is so small as to make the SAT useless. Essentially, their claim was that SAT scores are largely redundant with high school grades. By contrast, a recent study by Bridgeman, Pollack, and Burton (2004), based on data from 41 institutions, showed that even for students with similar high school grades and course backgrounds, SAT scores contributed substantially to the prediction of college "success," defined as the attainment of a college GPA above a particular criterion level. (Cutpoints of 2.5 and 3.5 were considered, as were GPAs at the end of freshman and senior years.) From an institutional perspective, even a small improvement in prediction accuracy is often perceived as worthwhile, especially by large schools that do not have the opportunity to interview candidates or review applications in elaborate detail. From the point of view of these institutions, in fact, admissions tests are often considered great bargains: The students themselves pay to take the tests, and the cost to the schools of collecting and processing the scores is minimal.

Also, as described in section 6.1, using only high school grades, without test scores, to predict freshman grades tends to produce predictions that are systematically off target for some ethnic groups, a problem that can occur despite the sizeable correlation between high school and college grades. Including test scores in combination with high school grades to predict college performance often reduces these systematic distortions.

What does current research say about the predictive validity of admissions tests in college, graduate school, and professional school? An examination of large-scale studies (focusing on multi-institution studies and reviews published in 1985 or later), reveals some consistent patterns. The multiple correlation of ACT score (all four section scores considered together) or SAT score (verbal and math scores considered together) with FGPA is about .4, on average (ACT, 1997; Camara & Echternacht, 2000; The College Board & ETS, 1998; Noble, 1991; Ramist et al., 1994; Rigol, 1997; Willingham, 1998). This correlation—the validity coefficient—is usually slightly lower than the correlation between high school GPA and FGPA. Considering ACT or SAT scores as predictors along with high school grades yields correlations with FGPA that average about .5.

Occasionally, test scores are found to do a better job than high school grades in predicting college GPA, as in a 1990 study at Dartmouth ("SAT's better freshman predictor than grades," January 16, 1991). In addition, Ramist et al. (1994) found that SAT scores tended to be more effective than high school GPA in predicting grades in individual college courses and that, among African-American students, SAT scores were slightly more effective than high school grades in predicting FGPA.

In a second large study conducted using data from 1982 and 1985, Ramist, Lewis, and McCamley-Jenkins (2001) studied the validity of the SAT Subject Tests (then called the College Board Achievement Tests). They found that validity coefficients for the individual Subject Tests ranged from .17 for Spanish and German to .58 for Chemistry and Mathematics II (p. 36). (These coefficients were corrected for restriction of range and for the upward bias of the sample multiple correlation.) Ramist et al. also found that the average of a student's SAT Subject Test scores tended to be a slightly better predictor of FGPA than was the SAT Reasoning Test. The correlation between the SAT Subject Test average and FGPA was about the same as the correlation between high school GPA and FGPA. Adding the SAT Subject Test scores to a prediction equation that included SAT Reasoning Test score and high school GPA further boosted the multiple correlation by a small amount (p. 35).

More recently, several studies based on University of California data have found the SAT Subject Tests, particularly the writing test, to be more predictive of FGPA than the SAT Reasoning Test in most instances (Geiser & Studley, 2004; Kobrin, Camara, & Milewski, 2004; Zwick, Brown, & Sklar, 2004). In a study comparing various admissions criteria, Bridgeman, Burton, and Cline (2004) used high school grades in combination with either SAT Reasoning Test or Subject Test scores to select hypothetical entering classes. (The admissions criteria were applied to data from students who had, in fact, already been admitted to college, rather than to data from applicants.) The mean FGPAs were nearly identical for the "entering classes" selected by the two models, a finding that was not surprising given that admissions decisions were the same for 86% of the students.

Most GRE validity research predates the substitution of the writing assessment for the analytical reasoning component in the main part of the test. Results from the GRE Validity Study Service collected between 1986 and 1990, which are based on more than 1,000 departments and more than 12,000 test-takers (ETS, 2003b), show that the predictive validity of the GRE (as formerly constituted) is quite similar to that of the SAT and ACT. GRE scores (verbal, quantitative, and analytical reasoning combined) typically have a validity coefficient of .3 to .4, and this is usually slightly smaller than the correlation between college GPA and first-year graduate school GPA. When college GPA and GRE scores are considered in combination, their correlation with graduate school GPA is typically .4 to .5. Including scores on the GRE Subject Tests as predictors usually boosts the correlation to between .5 and .6. The reported validity coefficients for individual Subject Tests are .27 for Physics, .32 for Literature in English, .37 for Biology and for Psychology, and .51 for Chemistry. Within the smaller samples used to assess the validity of the Subject Tests (ranging from 20 to 110 departments), the Subject Test validity always exceeded the validity for the verbal, quantitative and analytical reasoning sections combined.[18] Kuncel et al. (2001, p. 175), who conducted a meta-analysis of GRE validity that included corrections for range restriction and criterion unreliability, came to a somewhat more favorable conclusion about the validity of the verbal, quantitative, and analytical reasoning sections, and a somewhat less favorable conclusion regarding the Subject Tests.

Separate validity analyses of the GRE writing assessment (before it was added to the main assessment) were conducted based on approximately 2,000 college juniors, college seniors, and first-year graduate students. Analyses showed that the writing assessment (the combined score on two essays) had correlations of about .4 with the combined score on two course-related writing samples that had been scored by specially trained readers. The writing assessment had correlations of about .3 with a GPA based on courses that "required considerable writing." Correlations with overall GPA were about .2, and correlations with GPA in the students' major field were even smaller (Powers, Fowles, & Welsh, 1999, p. 33).

What about the professional school admissions tests? The GMAT (verbal and quantitative scores combined) has been found to have a correlation of .2 to .3 with business school GPA, similar to the correlation between college GPA and business school GPA (Wightman & Leary, 1985; Zwick, 1990, 1993). According to a recent summary, the LSAT typically does a better job of predicting law school GPA than do college grades, yielding correlations averaging about .4, compared to slightly under .3 for college GPA (Anthony, Harris, & Pashley, 1999). A recent summary of MCAT validity studies reported that the typical correlation between MCAT scores and medical school grades was over .4, higher than the correlation between college grades and medical school GPA. Using college grades and MCAT scores together produced a correlation of .5 (Beran, 1997; E. Julian, personal communication, March 13, 2001).

In summary, test scores tend to be slightly less effective than previous grades as predictors of college and graduate school GPA. Including test scores in addition to past grades in the prediction equation tends to increase the validity coefficient by about .1. In predicting professional school grades, however, test scores are frequently found to be more effective than are past grades.

5.2. Prediction of Academic Performance beyond the First Year

The evidence is fairly strong that tests can be useful in predicting grades beyond the first year of college, graduate school, or professional school. A recent College Board report summarized the results of 19 studies (all appearing since 1985) of the association between students' SAT scores and their cumulative grade-point averages upon completing college (Burton & Ramist, 2001). These studies were based on results from 227 institutions and over 64,000 students. SAT verbal score and SAT math score each had correlations averaging about .4 with the final college GPA, as did high school achievement (grades or class rank). These correlations are at least as large as those typically reported for first-year college GPA.

In another research project funded by the College Board, University of Minnesota researchers conducted a meta-analysis of more than 1,700 previous studies of the predictive value of the SAT. In a report of their initial findings (Hezlett et al., 2001), they concluded that the SAT was useful for predicting grades obtained both early and late in college, as well as other factors. The corrected correlations between SAT scores and grade-point averages earned in the second, third, and fourth years of college ranged from roughly .35 to .45.

Recent MCAT research also found test scores useful for predicting grades beyond the first year. In a study of the 1992 and 1993 entering classes at 14 medical schools, MCAT scores were found to have an average correlation of more than .4 with cumulative GPA for the first two years of medical school, and an average correlation of .3 with third-year GPA (E. Julian, personal communication, March 13, 2001). Another study showed that MCAT scores were useful for predicting performance in third-year clerkships, which are typically graded on the basis of both exams and ratings by supervisors (Huff, Koenig, Treptau, & Sireci, 1999). A recent University of Michigan study found that a composite of LSAT scores and undergraduate GPA had a correlation of more than .6 with final law school GPA (Chambers, Lempert, & Adams, 1999). In my own 1993 study of doctoral programs in business, I found a smaller association between test scores and subsequent GPA. Although GMAT scores predicted final grades about as well as they predicted first-year grades, the correlations were quite low in both cases—about .2 (Zwick, 1993).

Outside the realm of grades, several studies have found GRE scores to be moderately useful for predicting performance on departmental examinations and faculty ratings of students (Burton & Turner, 1983; Kuncel et al., 2001; Schneider & Briel, 1990; Willingham, 1974). On the other hand, a well-publicized 1997 study at the psychology department at Yale yielded less favorable results about the predictive value of the GRE. Yale intelligence theorist Robert J. Sternberg and Cornell professor Wendy M. Williams found that, although GRE psychology test scores were correlated about .4 with first-year GPA, GRE scores were not, in most cases, useful for predicting second-year grades or six different types of ratings of students by faculty (Sternberg & Williams, 1997). "Tests like the GRE measure only a fairly narrow aspect of intelligence," Sternberg said about these findings. "They may predict grades, but they won't predict much beyond that." ("Study finds that GRE doesn't predict success in psychology," 1997). In a flurry of responses to Sternberg and Williams (e.g., see Kuncel, Campbell, & Ones, 1998; Thayer & Kalat, 1998), GRE defenders pointed out that some studies have found GRE scores to be useful in predicting criteria other than grades. These critics suggested that the Yale study may have been marred by technical problems or that the faculty rating scales, rather than the GRE, may have been flawed.

5.3. Prediction of Graduation

Isn't it more important to predict who will complete a degree than to foretell first-year grades? This very reasonable question often arises in discussions of the utility of admissions tests. In an article in *Science* 30 years ago, Warren Willingham, then a research director at ETS, neatly summarized the pros and cons of graduation as a measure of academic success. Although his article was about graduate education, his remarks are equally applicable at the college level: "Regardless of what other judgments a faculty may make about a ... student, the acid test is whether he or she is granted the degree. Consequently, this is probably the single most defensible criterion of success. On the negative side, one must wait a long time for this criterion. Another difficulty is the fact that whether or not a student graduates may frequently depend upon extraneous influences. [Also,] this criterion places a premium on academic persistence and probably does not differentiate very well the most promising scholars and professionals" (Willingham, 1974, p. 275).

How well *can* admissions test scores predict who will graduate? As in so many aspects of admissions testing research, the evidence is mixed, with some studies showing that tests are moderately useful for this purpose and others concluding that test scores are of little value in predicting who will attain a degree.

Burton and Ramist (2001) reviewed the research conducted in the last 20 years about the association between SAT scores and college graduation. A 1996 study of more than 75,000 freshmen at 365 institutions showed a rather remarkable link between SAT scores and rates of college graduation within 4 years. Even among the 9,000 students with high school GPAs of A or A+, the SAT was a valuable predictor: The graduation rate was 28% for those with total SAT scores (math plus verbal) of less than 700. The rate rose steadily as SAT score increased, reaching 80% for the A and A+ students with combined scores over 1300 (Astin, Tsui, & Avalos, 1996), and preliminary findings of a recent College-Board-sponsored study showed, based on 11 earlier analyses, that SAT scores were somewhat useful for predicting both persistence through the first year of college and completion of the bachelor's degree (Hezlett et al., 2001).

A 1999 U.S. Department of Education report described a strong relationship between a "mini-SAT" (a one-hour test with items drawn from old SATs) and the likelihood of completing college. Results from a national sample of more than 7,000 college students showed that only 7% of those who scored in the bottom fifth on this test completed a bachelor's degree, compared to 67% of those who scored in the top fifth. High school grades were slightly less useful in predicting college completion; the rigor of the student's course background was a slightly better predictor (Adelman, 1999, p. 15). In their extensive analysis of data from the National Longitudinal Study of the High School Class of 1972, Manski and Wise (1983, p. 15) also found a strong relationship between SAT score and persistence in college, even among students with similar class ranks in high school. On the other hand, several analyses of large national data bases have yielded only moderate correlations between SAT scores and graduation (about .3, slightly greater than the typical correlation between high school grades and college graduation), and some analyses conducted within single institutions found correlations of only .1 or .2 between test scores and graduation (see the summary in Burton & Ramist, 2001, pp. 16–19). In another study, my coauthor Jeffrey C. Sklar and I used survival analyses to study college graduation patterns over seven years for the sophomore cohort of the High School and Beyond Survey conducted by the National Center for Education Statistics. We considered four groups of students: Hispanic students who said their first language was Spanish, and Hispanic, African-American, and White students who said their first language was English. Total SAT score was a statistically significant predictor of college graduation, after taking high school GPA into account, in the Hispanic/English and White/English groups, but not in the remaining two groups (Zwick & Sklar, 2005).

Results for graduate and professional school are quite scarce. In a 1974 review of more than 40 validity studies of the GRE, Willingham concluded that GRE scores tended to be moderately useful—and more useful than college GPA—in predicting Ph.D. attainment (Willingham, 1974; see also Rock, 1974). A recent study of 31 institutions also found GRE verbal and quantitative scores to be useful in predicting completion of the doctorate (Attiyeh, 1999). A meta-analytic study by Kuncel et al. (2001) offered some evidence that GRE Subject Test scores were useful in predicting degree attainment; verbal, quantitative, and analytical reasoning scores were not found to be strong predictors. My own 1991 research, based on an analysis of 11 graduate programs at each of 3 selective universities, showed that degree attainment was not well predicted by either GRE scores or college GPA (Zwick, 1991), and my 1990 analysis of data from 25 doctoral programs in business revealed very little association between degree completion and either GMAT scores or undergraduate grades (Zwick, 1990).

One pattern that becomes evident in the results of this body of research is that single-institution studies tend to find smaller correlations between test scores and degree completion than studies based on large national data bases. In a large study that includes many colleges, there will be a much larger range of test scores and graduation rates than in a single school. Multi-institution analyses of graduation are usually based on the *combined* data from all the schools (unlike multi-institution GPA prediction studies, which usually involve analyses that have been conducted *within* institutions and then averaged). To some extent, then, the apparent association between test scores and graduation will reflect the fact that some *schools* have both higher test scores and higher graduation rates than others. (This phenomenon was noted by Willingham, 1985, p. 105.)

What is the final word on the usefulness of admissions test scores for predicting who graduates from college, graduate school, or professional school? Admissions test scores may be of some use for this purpose, but their predictive value *within a particular school* is likely to be quite small. Most students admitted to higher education are quite competent academically. In deciding whether to remain in school, they are influenced by an array of nonacademic factors, involving finances, mental and physical health, and family responsibilities. For these reasons, it is unlikely that any measure of academic performance can do a very accurate job of predicting who gets a degree.

5.4. Prediction of Career Success

Investigating the role of tests in predicting career accomplishments is a complex venture. Several studies have demonstrated that admissions test scores are correlated with scores on tests of professional knowledge (see Hezlett et al., 2001; Klitgaard, 1985, Appendix 2; Wiley & Koenig, 1996). For example, LSAT scores have been found to be predictive of performance on the bar exam, MCAT scores have been shown useful for predicting scores on medical boards and medical licensing exams, and SAT scores have proved to be correlated with performance on nursing exams. But, of course, the bar exam and medical and nursing tests do not directly assess professional competence, and, as test critics are quick to point out, the fact that one test score predicts another is not terribly impressive.

Before determining whether test scores predict career success, it is necessary to consider a basic question: How should success be defined and measured? Income is, of course, one criterion, but a mediocre businessman may earn far more than an excellent professor. Supervisor ratings may be useful in some occupations, but they are notoriously imprecise and subjective. Prizes and titles are another possibility, but customs for awarding these kinds of recognition differ widely across fields. Another knotty question is *when* people's career accomplishments should be assessed. If it is soon after they have finished school, individuals may not yet have had time to bloom. If it is late in their careers, countless life events that can affect career progress will have intervened. In addition to determining what and when to measure, researchers attempting to investigate career success are also faced with the practical problem of tracking down an appropriate group of individuals for study and attempting to locate their test scores, which may be decades old.

Further complicating this kind of research is the "credential effect"—the fact that employees with high test scores may have certain personal qualifications that are likely to lead to career advances, regardless of actual ability. As Harvard psychologist David McClelland described this phenomenon in a much-quoted 1973 article (based on a presentation at ETS), the same social class advantages that are associated with high test scores also confer certain credentials on the employee that facilitate his success: "the habits, values, accent, interests, etc.—that mean he is acceptable to management and to clients" (McClelland, 1973, p. 3). To explain the concept even more vividly, McClelland sketched out a hypothetical scenario in which a "ghetto resident" from Roxbury wants to be a policeman, but is condemned to being a janitor because he cannot "play analogy games" and define words like quell, pyromaniac, and lexicon. Data from the would-be policeman—his poor test scores and menial job—then contribute to the "celebrated correlation of low intelligence with low occupational status" (McClelland, 1973, p. 4). McClelland contended that any association between aptitude test scores and career accomplishments was probably due only to the credential effect, rather than to any actual predictive value of the tests. Although McClelland's claims are still being debated decades after his article (Barrett, 1994; Barrett & Depinet, 1991; Boyatzis, 1994; Cowen, 1994; McClelland, 1994), it is wise to keep in mind the possibility that a credential effect may influence the apparent association between test scores and later success.

The credential effect may help to explain the results of a 1998 study of the LSAT. The analysis found LSAT scores to be highly predictive of post-law school earnings—each score point was "worth thousands of dollars to the test-taker"—but the effect diminished when the quality of the law school the graduate had attended was taken into account (Berkowitz, 1998, p. 84). Those with higher test scores went to better law schools; the superior education, rather than the test scores themselves, may have been primarily responsible for the greater earnings. On the other hand, a recent University of Michigan study found that a composite of LSAT score and undergraduate GPA was not predictive of later income or career satisfaction. The composite, however, did have a slight negative association with the number of hours of postgraduation pro bono service—the higher the composite, the lower the service contribution. According to the authors, this might have occurred because "Michigan seeks ... students who subscribe to the legal profession's aspirational norms of service and so admits applicants who appear committed to serving others on somewhat weaker numerical records" than would otherwise be required (Chambers, Lempert, & Adams, 1999, p. 19).

In a 1978 study of 215 Ph.D.-level psychologists, ETS researcher William B. Schrader found that the GRE Advanced Test (now "Subject Test") in Psychology and, to some degree, the GRE quantitative test, were moderately useful in predicting the number of professional publications and the number of times the psychologists' work had been cited. On the other hand, SAT scores were of little value for predicting these criteria, and test scores were clearly of no use in predicting which psychologists were subsequently elected to fellow status in the American Psychological Association (Schrader, 1978). Schrader later conducted a similar study of Ph.D.-level historians, in which he examined the association between GRE scores and several indexes of career accomplishment, including citations, books, and awards. Although he concluded that the scores were "correlated with productivity as measured by citations" (Schrader, 1980, p. 13), the reported relationships appear quite weak. In yet another study, Mary Jo Clark and John A. Centra (1982), found little relationship between either grades or GRE scores and the career accomplishments of Ph.D.s in the physical, biological, and social sciences.

A 1985 review of the literature on the prediction of career accomplishments concluded that, "[a]cross a rather large spectrum of the population, both test scores and grades tend to have modest predictive power for many kinds of 'later-life contributions'" (Klitgaard, 1985, p. 130). Based on the information that has accumulated to date, this assessment seems a bit too rosy. For each study that shows a relationship, another does not. How well, then, do admissions test scores predict eventual career success? Overall, the answer appears to be "not very well." An equally accurate answer might be "better than expected." After all, a test is just a small sample of a candidate's skills. It is extremely limited both in duration and in breadth—a point often emphasized by test critics. Career success, on the other hand, depends on many factors that are unrelated to competence, including health, family situation, and national economic conditions, not to mention luck. From that perspective, it is surprising that tests have occasionally proven useful in predicting career accomplishments.

5.5. Effects of Range Restriction and Criterion Unreliability on Validity Coefficients

A factor that complicates the interpretation of validity coefficients is selection, or restriction of range: A very basic limitation of test validity research is that only a portion of the college, graduate school, or professional school applicants is available for analysis. For example, in an SAT validity study conducted by a particular college, students whose SAT scores were too low to allow admission will not, of course, have freshman GPAs. Some high-scoring applicants who were, in fact, admitted may also be unavailable for analysis because they chose another school. Because of this restriction of range (of SAT scores, and, as a result, of other predictors and of FGPAs as well), validity coefficients tend to be smaller for the admitted students than they would be for the entire population of applicants. As a result, the apparent association between test scores and FGPA is smaller than it would be if the entire group of applicants could be considered. A simple correlation or regression approach to the analysis of test validity will, therefore, produce a more pessimistic picture than is warranted, given that the intended goal of a validity study is to estimate the usefulness of tests in selecting students *from the overall applicant pool*. The range restriction problems that affect validity analyses at the college level lead to even greater distortions in the case of graduate and professional school admissions, where the selection process is more stringent. To compensate for the effects of selection, statistical corrections are sometimes applied in an attempt to estimate how big the association would have been if the range had not been restricted (see Gulliksen, 1987, pp. 165–166). These adjustments, which are based on the disparity between the sample covariance matrix of the predictors for the admitted students and the covariance matrix for the applicant pool (or some other reference population) are only approximate because they require the unrealistically simple assumption that selection takes the form of truncation of the predictor distributions. (A multivariate normal distribution of the predictor variables and the criterion is assumed.) In actuality, the determination of which college, graduate school, or professional school applicants are accepted at a particular institution is quite complex, involving a combination of self-selection and institutional selection.

An additional drawback of traditional validity studies is that they ignore the inaccuracies and inconsistencies of GPA as a criterion of academic performance. As in the case of range restriction, statistical corrections can be applied to validity coefficients to adjust for the unreliability of grades. In evaluating the results of a validity analysis, it is important to determine whether validity coefficients have been adjusted for range restriction or criterion unreliability, since the effect of these corrections can be substantial. For example, Ramist et al. (1994) found the uncorrected multiple correlation of verbal and math SAT scores with FGPA to be .36; with adjustments for restriction of range and criterion unreliability, the correlation rose to .57, a sizable increase.

Several researchers, using approaches of varying sophistication, have attempted to improve the precision of grade-point averages by taking into account the fact that some college courses are harder than others and that some fields of study have more stringent grading practices than others (see Johnson, 1997; Stricker, Rock, Burton, Muraki, & Jirele, 1994; and Willingham, Pollack, & Lewis, 2000 for reviews.) Adjusting GPAs for course difficulty—not a trivial task—usually leads to a slight increase (up to .1) in the correlation between test scores and GPAs. Even a relatively simple refinement—achieved by using only specific academic courses as the basis for computing GPA—has been found to make GPAs more comparable across students and more highly correlated with test scores.[19]

Another subtle and complex aspect of validity analysis is the problem of "underprediction" and "overprediction." Suppose a college uses data from all freshmen to obtain a regression equation for use in predicting FGPA for future applicants. Will this equation work equally well for all groups of students, or will it lead to predicted GPAs that are systematically too high or too low for certain groups, such as African-American or Hispanic test-takers, or women? In fact, prediction errors of this kind have consistently been found to occur, whether high school grades or test scores are used as predictors. This phenomenon is discussed further in section 6.

6. FAIRNESS OF ADMISSIONS TESTS TO PEOPLE OF COLOR, WOMEN, AND OTHER SPECIAL POPULATIONS

Standardized admissions test results often reveal substantial average score differences across ethnic, gender, and socioeconomic groups. In the popular press, these differences are often regarded as sufficient evidence that these tests are biased. From a psychometric perspective, a test's fairness is inextricably tied to its validity. According to Cole and Moss (1989), test bias occurs (i.e., fairness is violated) "when a test score has meanings or implications for a relevant, definable subgroup of test-takers that are different from the meanings or implications" for other test-takers. "[B]ias is differential validity of a given interpretation of a test score" (p. 205).

Psychometric assessment of the fairness of admissions tests typically comprises two broad types of investigations. One type consists of analyses of differential prediction of a criterion, usually a grade-point average. Two distinct questions are typically addressed: First, are the test scores equally predictive of later grades for all groups? This question is investigated by obtaining separate prediction equations for each group and then comparing correlation or regression coefficients across groups. Second, if we obtain a single prediction equation for students as a whole, how accurate are the predictions, on average, for particular student groups? In a least squares regression analysis, the sum of the prediction errors across all observations must be zero, but this need not be true within each group of interest. It is useful, therefore, to determine whether the equation produces predicted GPAs that are systematically too high or too low for some groups. (Analyses of this kind often include key predictors in addition to test scores. For example, in the case of college admissions tests, high school GPA would typically be included in the regression equations.) Analyses of differential prediction allow a determination of whether a test is biased according to Cleary's (1968) definition, which says that a test is biased against a particular subgroup of test-takers "if the criterion score [in this case, GPA] predicted from the common regression line is consistently too high or too low for members of the subgroup" (p. 115). (This definition of test bias was proposed earlier by Humphreys [1952]. Most researchers today would use the term "prediction bias" rather than "test bias," to reflect the fact that prediction errors may stem from causes external to the test.)

Another common component of fairness assessment is an examination of item content. Before an item is approved for inclusion in an admissions test, it undergoes a "sensitivity review" to make sure its content is not disturbing to certain student groups or offensive in some other way (see section 4.1). Later, after the test is administered, a differential item functioning (DIF) screening is performed (see the chapter on test fairness by Camilli [this volume]) to determine whether equally skilled members of different groups (e.g., men and women) have statistically different rates of correct response on some items. The ultimate purpose of the DIF analysis is to identify test items with content that may be problematic for some student group. For example, the item may include content that is irrelevant to the construct being assessed, and is more familiar to some student groups than others, such as sports content in a mathematics test. Items found to have DIF are either discarded immediately or "flagged" for further study. Typically, a flagged item is reviewed by panelists from a variety of backgrounds who are expert in the subject-matter of the test. If the question is considered legitimate despite the differential functioning, it remains on the test. If the item is determined to be biased, it is modified or eliminated.

In sections 6.1 through 6.6, findings on differential prediction and differential item functioning on admissions tests are summarized for key student groups. Section 6.7 addresses fairness issues related to test coaching.

6.1. Are Admissions Tests Fair to People of Color? Differential Performance and Differential Prediction Findings

In America, any discussion of limited educational resources, such as space in selective schools, leads inevitably to the issue of race. For African-, Hispanic, and Native Americans, the rate of participation in U.S. higher education is strikingly low. While these groups constituted 27% of the enrollment in elementary and secondary schools in 1986, they collectively earned fewer than 7% of the doctorates granted by U.S. institutions 10 years later.[20] In addition, differences among racial and ethnic groups in standardized test performance have been pervasive. Typically, White and Asian-American test-takers perform better than African-American, Hispanic, and Native American test-takers; some differences show up as early as preschool (Nettles & Nettles, 1999, p. 2). Researchers, social theorists, and politicians have offered an array of reasons for this score gap, including socioeconomic, instructional, cultural, linguistic, and genetic factors, as well as test bias. Given the disturbing patterns of performance differences, it is particularly important to determine how well admissions tests work as a measuring device for people of color.

Two findings that have recurred in SAT validity studies involving ethnic groups are that correlations of test scores with FGPA tend to be somewhat smaller for African-American and Hispanic students than for White students (see Young, 2004, p. 291), and that use of a common regression equation to predict FGPA using SAT scores and high school grades produces overpredictions (predicted grades higher than actual grades) for these groups. Based on 11 studies, Young (2004, pp. 293–294) found the average overprediction for African-American students to be .11 (on a 0-to-4 scale); based on eight studies, the average overprediction for Hispanic students was .08. The lower correlations and the tendency toward overprediction also occur when high school GPA only is used to predict FGPA. In fact, although high school GPA is usually more highly correlated with FGPA than is SAT, overprediction tends to be worse if only high school GPA is included in the prediction equation (e.g., Ramist et al., 1994; Zwick & Schlemer, 2004; Zwick & Sklar, 2005).

The overprediction of subsequent college achievement for African-American students (and often for Hispanic students too) occurs for the ACT (Noble, 2004), GMAT (Braun & Jones, 1981), MCAT (Koenig, Sireci, & Wiley, 1998), and LSAT (Wightman & Muller, 1990), but a 1985 study did not find similar evidence of overprediction on the GRE (Braun & Jones, 1985). Educational researchers have long been aware of the overprediction phenomenon (e.g., Cleary, 1968; Linn, 1983). With the publication of *The Shape of the River* (Bowen & Bok, 1998) and *The Black-White Test Score Gap* (Jencks & Phillips, 1998), overprediction has become more widely recognized.

There are a number of theories about the reasons for the overprediction findings. A brief overview of the most prevalent hypotheses appears here. (See also Zwick, 2002, pp. 117–124.) One conjecture is that minority and White students are likely to differ in ways that are not fully captured by either their test scores or their high school grades. For example, an African-American student and a White student who both have high school GPAs of 3.5, SAT verbal scores of 600, and SAT math scores of 650 may nevertheless differ in terms of factors like the quality of early schooling, the environment in the home, and the aspirations of the family, all of which can influence academic preparation.

A related technical explanation is that overprediction occurs because both SAT scores and high school grades are imprecise measures of academic abilities. The effect is simplest to understand in the case of one predictor. Suppose a test score is being used to predict subsequent GPA. Under typical classical test theory and regression assumptions, the unreliability of the score can be shown to produce a regression line that is less steep than the line that would theoretically be obtained with an error-free predictor. Specifically, if the slope of the regression of GPA on the true test score is β, the slope of the regression of GPA on the observed test score will be $\rho\beta$, where ρ is the test reliability (see Snedecor & Cochran, 1967, pp. 164–166). Therefore, to the degree that the test score is affected by measurement error, groups with lower test scores will tend to be overpredicted while those with higher scores will tend to be underpredicted. But two findings argue against this factor as an all-purpose explanation: On standardized admissions tests, women often score lower than men, yet their later grades tend to be *underpredicted* (see section 6.4). Second, because the reliability of admissions tests typically exceeds .90, the impact of measurement error on prediction accuracy is small (under the model described above).

Another category of hypotheses about overprediction is based on the assumption that in college, minority students do not fulfill their academic potential, which is assumed to be accurately captured by the tests. This "underperformance" could occur because of outright racism or because of a campus environment that is inhospitable to people of color, or it could be related to a greater occurrence among minority students of life difficulties, including financial problems, that interfere with academic performance. It has also been hypothesized that anxieties, low aspirations, or negative attitudes may interfere with the academic success of minority students (e.g., Bowen & Bok, 1998, p. 84).

The "stereotype threat" theory of Steele and Aronson (1998) has been offered as another possible explanation for overprediction (e.g., Bowen & Bok, 1998, p. 81). Stereotype threat—"the threat of being viewed through the lens of a negative stereotype, or the fear of doing something that would inadvertently confirm that stereotype"—produces stress, which causes students to "learn to care less about the situations ... that bring it about" and, ultimately, to perform more poorly (Steele, 1999, pp. 4, 5). In some circumstances, the researchers claim, merely asking test-takers to state their sex or ethnic group can be damaging to their performance. But, although the stereotype threat research is intriguing, it does not provide a straightforward explanation of the overprediction phenomenon. If stereotype threat depressed standardized test performance, but didn't affect subsequent academic work, it would be expected to lead to *underprediction* because the affected students would perform *better* in college than their (depressed) test scores would indicate. To explain the existing pattern of test results and college grades, we would have to hypothesize that stereotype threat had *more* effect on college grades than on admissions test performance, which seems contrary to the researchers' implication that standardized testing situations are particularly evocative of stereotype threat (Steele & Aronson, 1998, pp. 425–426).

It seems evident that unmeasured differences between White students and African-American and Hispanic students with the same test scores and previous grades play a role in the recurrent finding of overprediction. It seems plausible as well that a greater incidence among minority students of life difficulties and financial problems in college contributes to the phenomenon.

6.2. Are Admissions Tests Fair to Students with Limited English Skills? Differential Prediction Findings

SAT validity findings for language minorities are quite mixed. This inconsistency in results is probably due in part to the fact that language minority groups have been defined in varying ways (see Zwick & Sklar, 2005). In a six-institution study of SAT validity for Hispanic and non-Hispanic students, Pennock-Román (1990) found that "in the prediction of college achievement, English proficiency did not have much of an added effect beyond the accuracy obtained from test scores and other predictors. It seems likely that persons with somewhat limited English proficiency are handicapped both on test scores and in college achievement ... their achievement in the first year is commensurate with their lower SAT scores" (1990, pp. 122–126).

Ramist et al. (1994) compared students who said English was their best language to those who said it was not. High school GPA and SAT verbal score were more effective as predictors for those students who said English was their best language. However, when high school GPA, SAT math score, and SAT verbal score were used in combination, prediction was equally strong for both groups. Any combination of predictors that included SAT verbal score led to underprediction of FGPA for students whose best language was not English.

Zwick and Schlemer (2004) studied the prediction of FGPA using SAT scores and high school GPA in two freshman cohorts at the University of California, Santa Barbara. They divided students into 10 groups, based on language background and ethnicity, and compared predictive effectiveness and accuracy across these groups. They found substantial overprediction of FGPA among language minorities (especially Hispanic test-takers) when high school GPA alone was used to predict FGPA; this overprediction was mitigated by inclusion of SAT scores in the prediction equation. In other respects, the results of the study were somewhat inconsistent: For students whose first language was not English, SAT verbal score was in some cases found to be a better predictor of FGPA than were SAT math score or high school GPA, but in other cases, high school GPA was the best of these three predictors. Also, prediction of FGPA tended to be less effective for language minorities than for native English speakers in one of the two freshman cohorts, but the reverse sometimes held true in the other cohort.

Zwick and Sklar (2005) studied SAT validity for four groups of students from the High School and Beyond sophomore cohort of 1980: Hispanic students who said their first language was Spanish, and Hispanic, African-American, and White students who said their first language was English. The Zwick and Sklar study examined the prediction of both FGPA and college graduation using high school GPA and SAT scores. Results on the prediction of FGPA suggested that, when compared to Hispanic/English group members with similar high school GPAs and SAT scores, Hispanic/Spanish group members received higher college grades. This was particularly surprising in light of the fact that a greater proportion of the Hispanic/Spanish group attended selective colleges, which, presumably, would grade more stringently. A second difference between the two Hispanic groups was that both FGPA and graduation were better predicted by high school grades and SAT scores in the Hispanic/English group than in the Hispanic/Spanish group.

6.3. How Does Test Content Contribute to Ethnic and Language Group Differences in Test Performance? Differential Item Functioning Findings

What kinds of items have shown evidence of DIF in ethnic group analyses? Findings about verbal items tend to be somewhat more consistent and interpretable than results for math questions. It has been a recurrent finding that African-American, Hispanic, and Asian-American test-takers do not perform as well as a matched group of Whites on verbal analogy items (Bleistein & Wright, 1987; Rogers & Kulick, 1987; Schmitt, 1987). (As of 2005, verbal analogy items no longer appear in the SAT.) The same is true for test questions containing homographs—words that have two (or more) completely different meanings, such as "light," which can mean "not heavy" or "not dark" (O'Neill & McPeek, 1993; Schmitt & Dorans, 1988). The following item is an example of an SAT verbal analogy question on which Mexican-American and Puerto-Rican test-takers did not perform as well as a matched group of Whites. The item has two homographs—*bark* and *wake* (Schmitt, 1987, p. 22).

BARK : TREE ::

(A) skin : fruit [correct answer]

(B) dew : grass

(C) seed : flower

(D) peak : hill

(E) wake : boat[21]

ETS researcher Alicia Schmitt and her colleagues also found that items containing similar words with common roots in English and Spanish—true cognates—favor Hispanic test-takers if the Spanish version is used more frequently than its English cognate. Consider the following SAT antonym item (an item type no longer included on the SAT), which contains five true cognates:

TURBULENT

(A) aerial

(B) compact

(C) pacific [correct response]

(D) chilled

(E) sanitary[22]

Hispanic test-takers performed better on this item than a matched group of Whites (O'Neill & McPeek, 1993, p. 266). One reason may be that the correct answer—"pacific"—is a more unusual word than its cognate, the Spanish "pacífico" (peaceful). There is some evidence that Hispanic test-takers are disadvantaged by false cognates—similar words that have different meanings in the two languages.

DIF findings on math items are quite mixed. Some studies have found that minorities perform better than a matched group of Whites on "pure math" items—those involving algebraic manipulations in the absence of any context—and do worse on word problems. One speculation about the reason for this is that pure math items tend to resemble textbook problems, which may be the focus of instruction at schools with fewer resources (O'Neill & McPeek, 1993, p. 270). Some research has also found that African-American test-takers do not perform as well as a matched group of Whites on test questions that include graphs, charts and diagrams, although the reasons for this remain unclear.

Other studies have shown that questions on topics of "minority interest" show evidence of DIF in favor of people of color. For example, one study of the SAT found results of this kind on a reading comprehension passage about an African–American mathematician and on passages about civil rights and poverty (Rogers & Kulick, 1987, p. 7; see also O'Neill & McPeek, 1993, pp. 262–263). These findings suggest that DIF can be caused by differences in test-takers' interest in the content of the test items. Differences across groups in training and course background can also result in DIF.

To what degree do problem test items contribute to overall test score differences among ethnic groups? Burton and Burton (1993) examined ethnic group performance differences on the SAT before and after DIF screening began at

ETS in 1989. Essentially, there was no change over time in the score disparities among ethnic groups. For one thing, the number of test questions found to have problems was fairly small. Also, on some items that were eliminated, ethnic minorities had an advantage. Even in the absence of evidence that it affects overall scores, however, DIF screening is important as a precaution against the inclusion of unreasonable test content and as a source of information that can contribute to the construction of better tests in the future.

6.4. Are Admissions Tests Fair to Women? Differential Performance and Differential Prediction Findings

On average, men score better than women on the SAT math and verbal sections, the ACT math test, the ACT science test, and the ACT composite; the MCAT verbal reasoning, physical sciences, and biological sciences tests; the GRE verbal, quantitative, and analytical reasoning tests; the GMAT verbal and quantitative tests, and the LSAT (Wightman, 1994). Women tend to score better then men on the ACT English and reading tests, the GMAT writing assessment (Bridgeman & McHale, 1996), and the GRE writing assessment (Schaeffer, Briel, & Fowles, 2001), and the same as men on the MCAT writing sample.[23] (At one time, women scored better than men on the verbal SAT but this changed beginning in 1972. Ironically, some researchers have speculated that the reversal may have resulted from ETS attempts to make the content of the verbal exam more "gender neutral" in order to improve the scores of men; see Clark & Grandy, 1984.)

What accounts for the fact that men perform better than women on most standardized admissions tests, especially on the math sections? It has been suggested that this test score gap occurs in part because women and men differentially self-select to take these tests, producing sex differences in average economic and academic background. More young women than men take the SAT, for example, and, according to a College Board research summary, a "much higher proportion of females than males taking the SAT come from families with lower levels of income and parental education" (The College Board, 1998, p. 2).[24] More women than men take the ACT, GRE, MCAT, and LSAT as well.

The College Board research summary also noted that "important differences still persist in the proportion of males and females completing advanced courses in math, science, and computer programming" in high school (The College Board, 1998, p. 2). But a recent College Board profile of high school seniors shows that disparities in course background have decreased substantially over the last 10 years. The Board reported that in 2000, male and female SAT-takers were equally likely to have taken at least four years of math, and that 22% of girls and 26% of boys had taken calculus. Girls and boys had each taken an average of 3.4 years of natural science courses; 45% of girls and 53% of boys had taken physics (The College Board, 2000; see also Coley, 2001).

Along with differences in course preparation, countless other reasons have been offered to explain the gender gap in test scores, including test bias, biological differences, diverging interests and aspirations, and societal influences. Over the years, various conjectures about sex differences in test performance have become psychometric legends: Women are often assumed to perform more poorly on standardized tests because the content is oriented toward men, because they are afraid to guess, or because the multiple-choice format is disadvantageous to women. Each of these speculations has gleaned support in some studies, but none have held up consistently. More recently, the "stereotype threat" phenomenon described in section 6.1 has also been invoked as an explanation for the performance discrepancy between men and women on standardized tests. This threat—the fear of inadvertently confirming a cultural stereotype—"dramatically depresses the standardized test performance of women and African Americans" in areas in which society regards them as inferior (Steele, 1997, p. 613). According to Steele, this phenomenon could explain the typically lower math scores earned by women: "[T]he stereotype threat that women experience in math-performance settings derives from a negative stereotype about their math ability that is disseminated throughout society" (Steele, 1997, p. 619).

In SAT research, it is typical to find that validity coefficients are higher for women, although the reasons are not clear. One frequent speculation is that men are more likely to skip classes and homework assignments, making their college grades less predictable. In more selective colleges, where both men and women are presumably more dedicated to their academic work, validities for men and women tend to be more similar to each other (see Young, 2004 for a review; see also Bridgeman, McCamley-Jenkins, & Ervin, 2000, Table 4, page 5; Ramist et al., 1994, Table 18, p. 25). Another recurrent finding is that, when a common regression equation, based on men and women, is used to predict college grades using SAT scores and high school GPA, women's predicted grades tend to be lower than the FGPAs they actually earned, and the reverse is true for men (e.g., Ramist et al, 1994, p. 15). Based on consideration of 17 studies, Young (2004) found an average underprediction of .06 (on a 0-to-4 scale) for women. Although this is smaller than the average *overprediction* found for African-American and Hispanic test-takers (see section 6.1), Young noted that, because women constitute the majority of college students in the United States, "the net impact of the differential prediction by sex has a much greater overall effect than the overprediction problem for minority students" (p. 296).

Research on the underprediction of women's grades dates at least as far back as 1972 (see Young, 2001, p. 7). The SAT, the ACT, and most of the SAT Subject Tests have been found to underpredict women's college grades (see Willingham & Cole, 1997, Leonard & Jiang, 1999, and Young, 2004, for reviews; see also Ramist et al., 2001). In a widely publicized study based on data from the University of California at Berkeley, Leonard and Jiang (1999) argued that even a small degree of underprediction can disadvantage women in the admissions process. They analyzed the records of 10,000 Berkeley freshmen admitted between 1986 and 1988. At every level of Berkeley's academic index score—a composite of high school grades and SAT scores—women received higher cumulative college GPAs than men. For the most part, this finding held up even when results were examined within each major.[25] This makes it unlikely that differences between men and women in their selection of college major had a large influence on the results.

According to the College Board (1998, February, p. 1), both the SAT and high school grade-point average "slightly underpredict FGPA for females. However, when these measures are used together, this underprediction is reduced to a lower level." But this is a somewhat misleading portrayal of the findings. For example, Ramist et al. (1994, p. 15) found that underprediction was *smallest* when high school GPA alone was used as a predictor of FGPA. When the combination of high school GPA and SAT scores was used, the underprediction actually increased. Leonard and Jiang (1999) found similar results.

What accounts for the underprediction phenomenon? Ramist et al. (1994) found that a portion of the underprediction of women's FGPAs could be explained by the fact that women are less likely than men to take college courses that are stringently graded. When a measure of the grading severity of students' courses was included in the prediction equation, the validity coefficients for both men and women increased, and the average underprediction of women's FGPAs shrank from .06 to .03, a small fraction of a grade point. The researchers found that similar reductions in underprediction could be achieved by predicting the grades in individual college courses and then averaging those results, rather than predicting the FGPA. Although this did not occur in the UC Berkeley study, some researchers have found that including college major in the prediction equation served to decrease the underprediction of women's grades (Pennock-Román, 1994). In the same vein, Stricker, Rock, and Burton (1993) found that, at a large university, underprediction could be reduced by including in the regression model various measures of academic preparation, attitudes toward mathematics, and studiousness (see also Dwyer & Johnson, 1997; Willingham, Pollack, & Lewis, 2000).

Another frequent finding is that underprediction of women's grades is reduced when writing test scores play a substantial role in the prediction equation. For example, Ramist et al. (1994) found that if the Test of Standard Written English (a separately scored exam administered with the SAT between 1974 and 1994) was included in the regression equation along with SAT and high school GPA, underprediction of women's FGPAs was slightly reduced, and Leonard and Jiang (1999) reported that giving a heavy weight to the College Board English Achievement Test (predecessor to the SAT Subject Test in writing) eliminated underprediction at Berkeley. These findings suggest that the underprediction of women's college grades may be reduced as a result of the addition of a writing component to the SAT.

A possible clue to the puzzling pattern of grade predictions for men and women is the recurrent finding that underprediction is slight or even absent at very high academic levels (although again, the UC–Berkeley research appears to be an exception). Ramist et al. (1994) found that "[a]t more selective colleges, the typical underprediction for females and overprediction for males was substantially reduced; there was no under- or overprediction using HSGPA, SAT scores, and [Test of Standard Written English] to predict course grade." Also, in recent studies, underprediction has not occurred at the graduate or professional school level (Koenig, Sireci, & Wiley, 1998; Ramist et al., 1994, p. 27; see also Young, 1991, 2001). Some researchers speculate that underprediction is minimized at graduate and professional schools and at elite colleges because nearly all students at these institutions take difficult courses. In this situation, differences between men and women in the grading stringency of their coursework is likely to be reduced. At typical colleges, by contrast, men may be more likely than women to gravitate toward fields of study with stricter grading standards.

Some intriguing results on prediction accuracy emerged from a study of SAT validity by Bridgeman et al. (2000), who grouped students on the basis of both sex and ethnic background and then studied the patterns of over- and underprediction. The analysis was based on about 47,000 students from 23 (mostly selective) colleges. The analyses revealed that it was primarily White women who were affected by the underprediction problem, while the college grades of men from all ethnic groups tended to be overpredicted.[26] Within each of the four ethnic groups, men's FGPAs were found to be overpredicted by amounts ranging from .07 to .15 when high school GPA and SAT verbal and math scores were included in the equation. College grades were underpredicted by small amounts for African-American (.01) and Asian-American (.03) women and overpredicted by .02 for Hispanic women. For White women, however, FGPAs were underpredicted by nearly a tenth of a grade point (.09).[27]

From a statistical perspective, then, the claim that college admissions tests are biased against women could be considered more convincing than the case for ethnic bias: Women tend to receive lower test scores than men *and* (at least in the case of White women) to earn higher college GPAs than predicted by their test scores. The bias conclusion is mitigated, however, by the finding in several analyses that underprediction of women's grades is reduced when the grading stringency of college courses is taken into account. Also, some researchers paint a picture of female "overperformance" in college, suggesting that underprediction occurs because women are more serious than men about their studies, more diligent about attending class and doing assignments, and more likely to be neat and careful in their work. According to this conjecture, women actually do perform better in college than men with equivalent academic preparation, and this is appropriately reflected in their college grades.

6.5. How Does Test Content Contribute to Sex Differences in Test Performance? Differential Item Functioning Findings

Awareness that certain test content may be disadvantageous to women dates back as least as far as 1923, when Carl Brigham, a rather unlikely forefather of today's test critics, noted with regard to the Army Alpha exams, "As a rule women object to the information test more than men because the test samples rather heavily the fields of sport, mechanical interests, etc. The chances are that this test would penalize women rather heavily" (Brigham, 1923, p. 30). The following analogy item, which appeared on a 1977 SAT verbal test, might be considered a latter-day equivalent of the Army Alpha items:

DECOY: DUCK ::

(A) net : butterfly

(B) web : spider

(C) lure : fish [correct answer]

(D) lasso : rope

(E) detour: shortcut[28]

Women were less likely to answer this question correctly than men with equivalent SAT verbal scores, presumably because it required knowledge of hunting and fishing jargon that is more familiar to men in our society (Dorans & Holland, 1993, p. 46). Today, testing companies take great pains to avoid test questions about topics that might be relatively unfamiliar to women or people of color. As described in sections 4.1 and 6, test items go through "sensitivity review" to eliminate content thought to be racist, sexist, or potentially offensive in some other way. An ETS document decrees that among the types of test questions that should generally be avoided are those that involve violence or harm, sports knowledge, or military topics, particularly "specialized military language such as rapier or muzzle" (ETS, 1999). Test items that unnecessarily include these subjects are thought to put men at an unfair advantage.

Certain DIF findings have emerged fairly consistently from comparisons of men and women. Women tend not to do as well as a matched group of men on verbal SAT and GRE items about scientific topics or about stereotypically male interests, like sports or military activities. An example is this item from the SAT (Bridgeman & Schmitt, 1997, p. 194):

CONVOY : SHIPS ::

(A) flock : birds [correct answer]

(B) ferry : passengers

(C) barn : horses

(D) dealership : cars

(E) highway : trucks.[29]

On the other hand, women tend to perform better than their male counterparts on questions about human relationships or questions about the arts, like the following GRE analogies item (O'Neill & McPeek, 1993, p. 262):

TILE : MOSAIC ::

(A) wood : totem

(B) stitch : sampler [correct answer]

(C) ink : scroll

(D) pedestal : column

(E) tapestry : rug.[30]

It seems likely that these particular performance disparities stem from differences in interests and pastimes, and perhaps high school course work (although these course preparation differences are vanishing). But for the vast majority of items that show evidence of DIF, the reasons are murky at best. In general, it is harder to understand the findings about math questions than the results for verbal tests. In their review of DIF findings, O'Neill and McPeek (1993) noted that on several ETS tests and on the ACT, women perform better on algebra questions than men with equivalent quantitative scores; men do better on geometry and mathematical problem-solving. Also, analyses of the GRE, GMAT, SAT, and ACT have shown that women do better on "pure mathematics" problems (23/2 + 23/3 + 23/6 = ?), and men tend to perform better on word problems framed in terms of an actual situation. The authors gave this example of a word problem (O'Neill & McPeek, 1993, p. 269):

> The rectangular bed of a truck is 6 feet wide and 7 feet long and has sides 1 1/2 feet high. A type of gravel weighs about 95 pounds per cubic foot. If the truck bed were filled level to the top of its sides with this gravel, approximately how many tons would the gravel weigh? (1 ton = 2,000 pounds)[31]

(A) 1/2

(B) 2/3

(C) 3 [correct answer]

(D) 8

(E) 36

The reason for the performance difference on this question is not clear, and the finding is hard to reconcile with the conclusion of a later study that women have an advantage on GRE items that require "modeling of a word problem as an algebraic expression" (Gallagher, Morley, & Levin, 1999).

As in the case of ethnic group score differences, Burton and Burton (1993) found that there was essentially no change in the SAT score gap between men and women after DIF screening began at ETS in 1989. A fairly small number of items were found to have problems, and some of those eliminated were items on which women had an advantage.

6.6. Are Admissions Tests Fair to People with Disabilities?

A standardized test is meant to be administered under uniform conditions and time constraints, but fairness dictates that test scores should not be affected by any limitations of the test-taker that are not relevant to the skills being assessed. In this spirit, various types of special accommodations are made available to admissions test candidates with disabilities. Test-takers with visual impairments, for example, are offered Braille, cassette, or large-type versions of the test, or are provided with assistants who read the test aloud. Other special arrangements that are typically available include scribes for individuals with physical impairments that make writing impossible and sign language interpreters who can relay spoken instructions to deaf test-takers. Extended time is also permitted for candidates with disabilities. The rationale for offering these accommodations is that "the standard procedures … impede [these] test takers from performing up to their ability" (Mandinach, Cahalan, & Camara, 2001, p. 5). Ideally, scores on the accommodated admissions tests should be comparable to scores obtained from nondisabled test-takers under standard conditions—they should measure the same cognitive abilities and should be of equivalent difficulty and precision.

The provision of special testing arrangements gives rise to a vast array of questions. What should "count" as a disability in an admissions testing situation? How can we determine whether the difficulty of an accommodated test for a candidate with a disability is equal to the difficulty of the standard test for a nondisabled test-taker? Should scores that are sent to schools be "flagged" if they have been obtained under nonstandard conditions? Do admissions test scores predict grades as well for people with disabilities as for other test-takers?

At the recommendation of a National Academy of Sciences panel, a four-year research program that focused on candidates with disabilities who take the SAT or the (paper-and-pencil) GRE was undertaken during the 1980s, under the sponsorship of Educational Testing Service, the College Board, and the Graduate Record Examinations Board (Willingham et al., 1988). The research showed that blind test-takers found some SAT math items with figures or special symbols (which must be described verbally or rendered in Braille) to be excessively difficult, and that deaf test-takers found the verbal content of the GRE to be particularly hard. In general, though, the researchers concluded that the scores of test-takers who received accommodations were roughly comparable to scores obtained by nondisabled test-takers under standard conditions. (The one major exception, described below, involved test-takers who were granted extended time.)

Prediction of subsequent grades was found to be somewhat less accurate for candidates with disabilities, whether test scores or previous grades were used as predictors. The researchers speculated that one reason may be the exceptionally wide range in the quality of educational programs and grading standards for these students. Individuals with disabilities may also be more likely than other students to experience difficulties in college or graduate school that affect their academic performance, such as inadequate support services or insufficient funds.

In general, students who receive extended time were found to be more likely to finish the test than candidates at standard test administrations. Willingham et al. (1988, p. 156) stated that, for SAT-takers claiming to have learning disabilities, "the data most clearly suggested that providing longer amounts of time may raise scores beyond the level appropriate to compensate for the disability." In particular, these students' subsequent college grades were lower than their test scores predicted, and the greater the extended time, the greater the discrepancy. By contrast, the college performance of these students was consistent with their high school grades, suggesting that their SAT scores were inflated by excessively liberal time limits. Similar conclusions have been obtained in more recent SAT analyses (Cahalan, Mandinach, & Camara, 2002), as well as studies of ACT and LSAT results for candidates with learning disabilities (Wightman, 1993; Ziomek & Andrews, 1996).

Developing fair policies for candidates with learning disabilities has been particularly troublesome for testing companies because even the definition of "learning disability" is murky and subject to manipulation. The College Board reported in 1998 that the "number and proportion of students with learning disabilities requesting accommodations on the SAT I has been increasing annually at a rate substantially faster than for students with any other type of disability, and represents approximately 90 percent of students receiving accommodations on the test" (Camara, Copeland, & Rothchild, 1998, p. 3). Two-thirds of these accommodations involve only extra time. Recent research suggests that some SAT-takers have sought to gain extra time by falsely claiming to have learning disabilities. A *Los Angeles Times* analysis of national data from the College Board showed that students who received extra SAT time in 1999 because of supposed learning disabilities tended to be Whites from high-income families (Weiss, 2000). Auditors in California produced a similar finding and expressed suspicions that some students who were granted extra time did not deserve it and that some students who needed it did not request it (Leatherman, 2000; see also California State Auditor, 2000). In recent years, the SAT program has implemented more rigorous criteria for granting extra testing time to candidates claiming learning disabilities, and the number of requests has decreased.

A longstanding controversy about testing accommodations for people with disabilities is whether score reports should contain a "flag" indicating that the test was given under nonstandard conditions. Proponents of flagging (who include most college admissions officers and high school guidance counselors, according to a recent survey [Mandinach, 2000]) say that information about testing conditions is needed to interpret test scores correctly. Test users, such as universities, are misled when this information is withheld, they contend, possibly to the test-taker's disadvantage. Advocates of flagging say that it can also help to discourage dishonest "game-players" from requesting undeserved extra time, and can thus increase the fairness of the test to those who play by the rules. Those who argue against flagging, however, say that it stigmatizes test-takers with disabilities and constitutes both a privacy violation and a form of discrimination that is prohibited by law.

The *Standards for Educational and Psychological Testing* offer a reasonable guideline for determining when flagging is appropriate. "[I]mportant information about test score meaning should not be withheld from test users who interpret and act on the test scores," the *Standards* say, "and ... irrelevant information should not be provided. When there is sufficient evidence of score comparability across regular and modified administrations, there is no need for any sort of flagging" (American Educational Research Association, American Psychological Association, & National Council on Measurement in Education, 1999, p. 105). The one accommodation for which comparability evidence is clearly lacking is the provision of extended time to candidates claiming learning disabilities. From this perspective, flagging the scores from these administrations seems appropriate.

The flagging debate, however, has been more heavily influenced by legal than by psychometric considerations: ETS announced in 2001 that it would discontinue flagging scores of test-takers who received extra time on some tests—the GRE, GMAT, Test of English as a Foreign Language, and certain teacher tests (Foster, 2001). The action came in response to a federal lawsuit filed against ETS by a GMAT test-taker with a disability. The decision did not affect the SAT because it is owned by the College Board, which was not a defendant in the suit. The parties to the lawsuit and the College Board agreed, however, that an expert panel would be formed to address SAT flagging issues. The deliberations of this panel led to a decision in 2002 to discontinue flagging for the SAT as well, and a corresponding decision regarding the ACT soon followed. The MCAT and LSAT programs, however, continue the practice of flagging ("ACT to stop flagging scores of disabled students who need extra time on test," 2002).

6.7. Does Coaching Undermine the Fairness of Admissions Tests?

The effectiveness and ethics of commercial test preparation for admissions tests, particularly the SAT, have long been the subject of controversy. During the last 15 years, several well-designed research studies have produced consistent results about the magnitude of score improvement that results from SAT coaching. Becker (1990), Powers and Rock (1999), and Briggs (2001, 2004) all concluded that the average gain from SAT coaching is between 6 and 8 points on the verbal section and between 14 and 18 points on the math section. Coaching studies on tests other than the SAT are quite scarce. Research suggests that coaching produces small benefits on the ACT (Briggs, 2001; Scholes & McCoy, 1998), the paper-and-pencil GMAT (Leary & Wightman, 1983), and the quantitative section of the paper-and-pencil GRE (Powers, 1983), and essentially no effect on the MCAT (Koenig & Leger, 1997) or the verbal section of the paper-and-pencil GRE (Powers, 1983). (See Zwick, 2002, Chapter 7, for a more detailed review of coaching research.) Although many testing companies long maintained the position that test preparation programs were largely ineffective, the sponsors of all major admissions tests now produce test preparation materials, seemingly a tacit acknowledgment that preparation can be beneficial.

Currently, the coaching debate tends to focus on the question of whether coaching, because it is likely to be most accessible to those who have already benefited from a lifetime of educational advantages, presents an impediment to test fairness for poor and minority test-takers. Some studies by testing companies have challenged the belief that Whites are much more likely than people of color to receive coaching. According to a survey conducted by the Law School Admission Council during the 1996–1997 academic year, about 38% of Hispanic candidates, 31% of Whites, and 28% of African-Americans had attended a commercial LSAT-preparation course (Mangan, 1998); a 1989 LSAC study revealed a similar pattern (Wightman & Muller, 1990). A 1983 study of the GMAT showed minority test-takers were slightly more likely to have participated in a prep course than White candidates (Leary & Wightman, 1983). On the other hand, Powers and Rock (1999) and Briggs (2001) found that coached SAT-takers came from more affluent families than uncoached candidates; they were also more motivated and were more likely to be Asian-American.

Although average coaching effects are apparently quite small and studies of the demographic makeup of coached and uncoached candidates have been inconclusive, it is legitimate to question the fairness of a system in which some test-takers can afford coaching and others cannot. It is clear that coaching programs are here to stay, and that it is impractical, if not impossible, to create admissions tests that are not susceptible to coaching. Minimizing the impact of coaching on test fairness, then, requires that the availability of free and low-cost test preparation be increased. In the case of the college admissions tests, many efforts of this kind are already underway. A 1996 survey found that slightly over half of secondary schools offered SAT coaching, and that many of these programs were free (College Board, 1998, November). In 1998, the California legislature made a bold move to improve access to college education by passing a bill that set aside $10 million for a five-year program of SAT and ACT coaching aimed at students from low-income households. Students could be charged no more than $5 for a course that was required to offer at least 20 hours of instruction. In recent years, other states and school districts have also adopted test preparation plans. Georgia's legislators, for example, approved a quarter of a million dollars to provide commercial SAT prep software to every public high school, Florida funded a program to train teachers in test preparation, and districts in Maryland, North Carolina, and Texas developed subsidized test preparation programs as well. The National Association for the Advancement of Colored People, which believes that standardized tests should be de-emphasized in the admissions process, has nevertheless urged the adoption of programs like California's state-sponsored test preparation plan (Weissert, 1999).

7. MISUSES AND MONITORING OF ADMISSIONS TESTS

Admissions test scores are sometimes used for purposes unrelated to the screening of university applicants or the placement of students in college courses. Some misuses are particularly flagrant. According to the *Wall Street Journal*, for example, submission of sufficiently high SAT scores is a "common requirement" for entry-level financial services jobs. In a weak job market, "employers see the scores as one more way to differentiate among applicants" (Dunham, 2003). This practice is a clear-cut misuse, because the SAT has not been validated for this purpose.

More frequently, misuses of admissions test scores involve the treatment of average scores as evidence of the educational quality of a school, district, or state. For example, between 1984 and 1991, the U.S. Department of Education issued a "wall chart" that compared states in terms of educational resources and educational performance, including average SAT and ACT scores. A major flaw in this type of comparison is that the test-takers are not random samples of the high school populations in their states; furthermore, the proportions of students who take these two tests vary widely across states.[32] The College Board's annual statistics typically show that in the states with the highest SAT averages, only a small percentage of high school graduates took the test; these are usually states in which the ACT is preferred. Correspondingly, the proportions of graduates taking the SAT tend to be large in the states with the lowest averages. After the existence of this pattern sparked criticism of the original wall chart, the Department of Education began reporting either the ACT or the SAT for each state, depending on which test was taken by more students. Although this was an improvement, it was still misleading because the samples of students who take college admissions tests are self-selected and, therefore, are not representative of the populations of interest. Another problem with the use of average admissions test scores as a basis for ranking education systems is that these tests are not designed as measures of instructional quality. The ACT has stronger links to the high school curriculum than the SAT, but neither test can claim to be based on a comprehensive assessment of the material taught in American high schools.

Such misuses raise the question of who is monitoring college, graduate school, and professional school admissions testing. The testing profession itself has, of course, established codes such as the *Standards for Educational and Psychological Testing* (American Educational Research Association, American Psychological Association, & National Council on Measurement in Education, 1999), and testing companies have their own sets of standards as well. Various government entities are also involved in monitoring standardized tests and their uses in admissions. For example, the federal government commissions studies on testing through the National Academy of Sciences, which published *Myths and Tradeoffs: The Role of Tests in Undergraduate Admissions*, a report that endorsed the use of testing as part of admissions screening, but warned against over-reliance on test scores (Beatty, Greenwood, & Linn, 1999). The Office for Civil Rights of the U.S. Department of Education deals with testing complaints that involve discrimination and has also published guidelines for high-stakes testing. In one of the more unusual instances of federal involvement, the Federal Trade Commission launched an investigation of the test coaching business in the late 1970s. In addition to government agencies, advocacy groups like the National Center for Fair and Open Testing (FairTest) keep a constant critical watch, and university-based centers like the National Center for Research on Evaluation, Standards, and Student Testing (CRESST) at UCLA and the National Board on Educational Testing and Public Policy (NBETPP) at Boston College devote themselves to testing research. Federal and state judicial decisions and legislation play a role as well. For example, bills passed in California and New York in the late 1970s permanently altered testing practice by requiring public disclosure of some admissions test questions.

Although numerous organizations are involved in monitoring admissions testing, it is clear that oversight is extremely decentralized and lacks enforcement mechanisms. Periodically, there are calls for centralized official oversight of standardized testing in general. In an essay titled, "Standardized Testing Needs a Consumer-Protection Agency," Madaus (1990) argued that a regulatory organization, possibly modeled after the Food and Drug Administration, was needed to make sure exams meet professional standards, to monitor the use of tests, and to deal with individual complaints. A subsequent National Academy of Sciences report renewed the call for "new methods, practices and safeguards" for ensuring appropriate test use, possibly involving government regulation or an independent oversight body (Heubert & Hauser, 1999, p. 8).

In particular, a body dedicated specifically to issues of admissions testing could play a valuable societal role by producing balanced, accessible information briefs on key testing issues (such as the effects of coaching and the underprediction of college grades for women); providing a hotline for consumer questions and complaints; offering arbitration for testing disputes; monitoring misuses; and censuring testing companies or test users that administered or utilized tests improperly.[33] In addition to providing a service to consumers, a monitoring agency of this kind could cut down on costly and time-consuming litigation. Finally, it could help to foster a balanced and informed public conversation about admissions testing.

NOTES

1. Information on admissions testing programs appearing in this chapter is accurate as of June, 2006 but may soon be outdated because of rapid changes in the testing industry. Portions of this chapter are adapted from *Fair Game: The Use of Standardized Admissions Tests in Higher Education*, RoutledgeFalmer, 2002. Copyright © 2002 by Rebecca Zwick.

2. This account is based on Webber, 1989 and Miyazaki, 1976. Miyazaki chose to ignore the testing that took place in the Han dynasty (see p. 9) and instead placed the beginning of the Chinese examination system in 589 A.D. Wainer (1990), on the other hand, says that formal testing procedures for candidates for office began in China in 1115 B.C.

3. Computations based on tables 99 and 244 in Snyder, Hoffman, & Geddes, 1997.

4. Historical material on the ACT is based on ACT, Inc. (1999), Brennan, (1999), Haney, Madaus, & Lyons (1993), and Peterson (1983).

5. The first to suggest the merger was evidently Ben D. Wood, the director of an organization called the Educational Records Bureau. Wood was an early proponent of multiple-choice testing and one of the developers of the first test-scoring machine.

6. Tests that are not discussed in this chapter include the Preliminary SAT/National Merit Scholarship Qualifying Test, which serves as a practice SAT for high school sophomores and juniors and is used in awarding National Merit Scholarships, the PLAN assessment (formerly the P-ACT+), which is billed as a "pre-ACT" test and is typically administered to high school sophomores, the Test of English as a Foreign Language, which is required of foreign students by some U.S. colleges or graduate schools (discussed in the chapter by Chalhoub-Deville and Deville [this volume]), and the Miller Analogies Test, which is accepted by a small percent of graduate programs as an alternative to the GRE.

7. Originally, "SAT" stood for "Scholastic Aptitude Test," which was later changed to "Scholastic Assessment Test." Now, "SAT" is no longer considered to be an acronym, but the actual name of the test.

8. Section 2.2 draws on material in Briel, O'Neill, and Scheuneman (1993), ETS (1950), Saretzky (1992), and Winterbottom (1995).

9. The score scale for the Mathematics Subject Test was changed in 2001; the test is now labeled "rescaled" to alert test users that scores are not comparable to those obtained on earlier versions of the test.

10. Historical material in section 2.3 is based on Hecht and Schrader (1986) and Schmotter (1993).

11. Because the respondents to this survey do not constitute random samples of the corresponding populations of institutions, the survey results need to be interpreted with caution.

12. The watchdog organization FairTest claims that this percentage has declined in recent years ("Critics of SAT and ACT," 1997).

13. The general information in this section is based primarily on Skager (1982) and Rigol and Kimmel (1997), as well as materials from the testing programs themselves.

14. Kidder (2000) arrived at an opposite conclusion concerning law schools, asserting that women and minorities are disadvantaged in the admissions process. Many of Kidder's arguments, however, rest on an *a priori* assumption that differences among groups on LSAT scores are "artificial," while differences in undergraduate grades (e.g., the typical edge of women over men) are "real."

15. Model assumptions would be violated, for example, if an item's "behavior" depended on its position within the test.

16. A newer version of e-rater has been developed (Attali & Burstein, 2004), but the older version continues to be used by the GMAT program (Jill Burstein, personal communication, October 8, 2004).

17. The SAT Subject Tests and the PSAT were affected as well, because their score scales are linked to those of the SAT.

18. The GRE validity coefficients reported here are estimated based on the results of empirical Bayes regression analysis, rather than least squares regression.

19. A more troublesome question about the validity of GPAs is whether grades reflect biases against particular groups of students, such as people of color, individuals with disabilities, or foreign students. This issue is rarely investigated. In general, grades are subject to far less scrutiny than tests when it comes to investigating bias.

20. Snyder and Hoffman, 2000, Table 45, p. 60 and Table 275, p. 318. For the doctoral data percentages were recalculated using the total number of doctorates, rather than the number of doctorates granted to U.S. citizens, as a base. A quarter of U.S. doctorates were earned by foreign students.

21. Reprinted by permission of the College Entrance Examination Board, the copyright owner. Permission to reprint SAT materials does not constitute review or endorsement by Educational Testing Service or the College Board of this publication as a whole or of any other questions or testing information it may contain.

22. Reprinted by permission of Lawrence Erlbaum Associates, Inc.

23. Supplementary information on gender differences in test performance was obtained from National Center for Education Statistics (1998); Willingham, Cole, Lewis, and Leung, 1997, pages 84–85; and testing program documents.

24. Also, average test score differences between males and females who have been "selected" on the basis of academic criteria are likely to be larger than the differences that exist before the selection criteria are applied. See Hoover and Han, 1995; Lewis and Willingham, 1995. Similar phenomena may apply in the case of ethnic group differences.

25. The one substantial exception is engineering: Here, men's college grades were slightly better than those of women with the same academic index scores.

26. The main purpose of this study was to determine whether the changes to SAT content in the 1990s and the recentering of the score scale affected validity conclusions. The results included here are for the newer, recentered version of the SAT; these proved to be nearly indistinguishable from those for the old version.

27. To complicate things further, the same degree of underprediction for White women was evident when high school GPA alone was used as a predictor—a departure from the results obtained when all women were considered together.

28. Reprinted by permission of Lawrence Erlbaum Associates, Inc.

29. Reprinted by permission of Lawrence Erlbaum Associates, Inc.

30. Reprinted by permission of Lawrence Erlbaum Associates, Inc.

31. Reprinted by permission of Lawrence Erlbaum Associates, Inc.

32. Because of the complexity of the process of deciding whether and where to apply to college, attempts to statistically adjust average ACT or SAT scores to "correct" for differing participation rates have had limited success. Competing adjustment methods, based on seemingly sensible conclusions, have been found to produce very different rankings of the 50 states (Wainer, 1989).

33. Testing companies already offer arbitration of test-taker complaints, and testing organizations, coaching companies, and anti-testing groups publish information briefs on testing issues. None of these entities, however, can be considered disinterested parties. The NBETPP, according to its Web site, monitors admissions tests (as well as other types of educational tests) "for appropriate use and technical adequacy," but this monitoring primarily takes the form of conducting and publishing research that is relevant to testing policy issues. It does not regulate testing programs or respond to consumer complaints.

REFERENCES

ACT, Inc. (1997). *ACT Assessment technical manual.* Iowa City, IA: Author.

ACT, Inc. (1999). *ACT Assessment user handbook 1999.* Iowa City, IA: Author.

ACT, Inc. (2000). *Preparing for the ACT Assessment 2000–2001.* Iowa City, IA: Author.

ACT to stop flagging scores of disabled students who need extra time on test. (2002, August 9). *The Chronicle of Higher Education,* p. A36.

Adelman, C. (1999). *Answers in the tool box: Academic intensity, attendance patterns, and bachelor's degree attainment.* Washington, DC: U.S. Department of Education.

American Educational Research Association, American Psychological Association, & National Council on Measurement in Education. (1999). *Standards for educational and psychological testing.* Washington, DC: American Educational Research Association.

Anthony, L. C., Harris, V. F., & Pashley, P. J. (1999). *Predictive validity of the LSAT: A national summary of the 1995–1996 correlation studies* (LSAT Technical Report 97–01). Newtown, PA: Law School Admission Council.

Astin, A., Tsui, A., & Avalos, J. (1996). *Degree attainment rates at American colleges and universities: Effects of race, gender, and institutional type.* Los Angeles: University of California, Higher Education Research Institute.

Atkinson, R. (2001, February). *Standardized tests and access to American universities.* The 2001 Robert H. Atwell Distinguished Lecture, delivered at the 83rd annual meeting of the American Council on Education, Washington, D.C.

Attali, Y., & Burstein, J. (2004, June). *Automated essay scoring with e-rater V.2.0*. Retrieved December 22, 2004, from http://www.ets.org/research/erater.html

Attiyeh, G. M. (1999). *Determinants of persistence of graduate students in Ph.D. programs* (ETS Research Report 99–4). Princeton, NJ: Educational Testing Service.

Attiyeh, G., & Attiyeh, P. (1997). Testing for bias in graduate school admissions. *The Journal of Human Resources, 32*, 524–548.

Barrett, G. V. (1994). Empirical data says it all. *American Psychologist, 49*, 69–71.

Barrett, G. V., & Depinet, R. L. (1991). A reconsideration of testing for competence rather than for intelligence. *American Psychologist, 46*, 1012–1024.

Beatty, A., Greenwood, M. R., & Linn, R. (Eds.). (1999). *Myths and tradeoffs: The role of testing in undergraduate admissions*. Washington, DC: National Academy Press.

Becker, B. J. (1990). Coaching for the Scholastic Aptitude Test: Further synthesis and appraisal. *Review of Educational Research, 60*, 373–417.

Beran, R. (1997). *Evolution of the MCAT* (AAMC Internal Document). Washington, DC: American Association of Medical Colleges.

Berkowitz, R. (1998). One point on the LSAT: How much is it worth? Standardized tests as a determinant of earnings. *American Economist, 42*(2), 80–89.

Bleistein, C. A., & Wright, D. J. (1987). Assessment of unexpected differential item difficulty for Asian-American examinees on the Scholastic Aptitude Test. In A. P. Schmitt & N. J. Dorans (Eds.), *Differential item functioning on the Scholastic Aptitude Test* (ETS Research Memorandum No. 87–1). Princeton, NJ: Educational Testing Service.

Bowen, W. G., & Bok, D. (1998). *The shape of the river: Long-term consequences of considering race in college and university admissions*. Princeton, NJ: Princeton University Press.

Boyatzis, R. E. (1994). Rendering unto competence the things that are competent. *American Psychologist, 49*, 64–66.

Braun, H. T., & Jones, D. H. (1981). *The Graduate Management Admission Test prediction bias study* (GMAC Report 81–4). Princeton, NJ: Educational Testing Service.

Braun, H. T., & Jones, D. H. (1985). *Use of empirical Bayes methods in the study of the validity of academic predictors of graduate school performance* (ETS Research Report 84–34). Princeton, NJ: Educational Testing Service.

Breland, H. M. (1998, December). *National trends in the use of test scores in college admissions*. Paper presented at the National Academy of Sciences Workshop on the Role of Tests in Higher Education Admissions, Washington, DC.

Breland, H., Maxey, J., Gernand, R., Cumming, T., & Trapani, C. (2002, March). *Trends in use college admission 2000: A report of a survey of undergraduate admissions policies, practices, and procedures* (Sponsored by ACT, Inc., Association for Institutional Research, The College Board, Educational Testing Service, and the National Association for College Admission Counseling). Retrieved October 6, 2003, from http://www.airweb.org

Brennan, R. L. (1999, July). *A perspective on educational testing: The Iowa testing programs and the legacy of E. F. Lindquist*. Paper presented to the National Institute for Testing and Evaluation, Jerusalem: Israel.

Brennan, R. L., & Kolen, M. J. (1989). Scaling the ACT assessment and P-ACT +: Rationale and goals. In R. L. Brennan (Ed.), *Methodology used in scaling the ACT assessment and P-ACT+* (pp. 1–17). Iowa City: The American College Testing Program.

Bridgeman, B., Burton, N., & Cline, F. (2004). Replacing reasoning tests with achievement tests in university admissions: Does it make a difference? In R. Zwick (ed.), *Rethinking the SAT: The future of standardized testing in university admissions* (pp. 277–288). New York: RoutledgeFalmer.

Bridgeman, B., McCamley-Jenkins, L., & Ervin, N. (2000). *Prediction of freshman grade-point average from the revised and recentered SAT I: Reasoning Test* (College Board Report 2000–1). New York: College Entrance Examination Board.

Bridgeman, B., & McHale, F. (1996). *Gender and ethnic group differences on the GMAT Analytical Writing Assessment* (ETS Research Report 96–2). Princeton, NJ: Educational Testing Service.

Bridgeman, B., Pollack, J., & Burton, N. (2004). *Understanding what SAT Reasoning Test scores add to high school grades: A straightforward approach* (College Board Research Report No. 2004–4). New York: College Entrance Examination Board.

Bridgeman, B., & Schmitt, A. (1997). Fairness issues in test development and administration. In W. W. Willingham & N. Cole (Eds.), *Gender and fair assessment* (pp. 185–226). Mahwah, NJ: Lawrence Erlbaum.

Briel, J. B., O'Neill, K. A., & Scheuneman, J. D. (1993). *GRE technical manual*. Princeton, NJ: Educational Testing Service.

Briggs, D. (2001). The effect of admissions test preparation: Evidence from NELS: 88. *Chance, 14*(1), 10–18.

Briggs, D. C. (2004). Evaluating SAT coaching: Gains, effects and self-selection. In R. Zwick (Ed.), *Rethinking the SAT: The future of standardized testing in university admissions* (pp. 217–233). New York: RoutledgeFalmer.

Brigham, C. C. (1923). *A study of American intelligence*. Princeton, NJ: Princeton University Press.

Brigham, C. C. (1930). Intelligence tests of immigrant groups. *Psychological Review, 37*, 158–165.

Burstein, J., Kukich, K., Wolff, S., Lu, C., & Chodorow, M. (1998, April). *Computer analysis of essays*. NCME Symposium on Automated Scoring. Educational Testing Service. Retrieved July 3, 2000, from http://www.ets.org

Burton, E., & Burton, N. W. (1993). The effect of item screening on test scores and test characteristics. In P. W. Holland & H. Wainer (Eds.), *Differential item functioning* (pp. 321–336). Hillsdale, NJ: Lawrence Erlbaum.

Burton, N. W., & Ramist, L. (2001). *Predicting success in college: SAT studies of classes graduating since 1980* (Research Report 2001–2). New York: College Entrance Examination Board.

Burton, N. W., & Turner, N. (1983). *Effectiveness of Graduate Record Examinations for predicting first year grades: 1981–82 summary report of the Graduate Record Examinations Validity Study Service*. Princeton, NJ: Educational Testing Service.

Cahalan, C., Mandinach, E., & Camara, W. (2002). *Predictive validity of SAT I: Reasoning test for test takers with learning disabilities and extended time accommodations* (College Board Research Report RR 2002–05). New York: College Entrance Examination Board.

California State Auditor. (2000). *Standardized tests: Although some students may receive extra time on standardized tests that is not deserved, others may not be getting the assistance they need* (Summary of Report 2000–108). Sacramento, CA: Bureau of State Audits.

Camara, W. J., Copeland, T., & Rothchild, B. (1998). *Effects of extended time on the SAT I: Reasoning test score growth for students with learning disabilities* (College Board Report 98–7). New York: College Entrance Examination Board.

Camara, W. J., & Echternacht, G. (2000, July). *The SAT and high school grades: Utility in predicting success in college* (College Board Research Note RN-10). New York: College Entrance Examination Board.

Chambers, D. L., Lempert, R. O., & Adams, T. K. (1999, Summer). *Doing well and doing good: The careers of minority and white graduates of the University of Michigan Law School 1970–1996.* Retrieved July 20, 1999, from University of Michigan Law School Web site: http://www.law.umich.edu

Clark, M. J., & Centra, J. A. (1982). *Conditions influencing the career accomplishments of Ph.D.s* (GRE Board Report 76–2R). Princeton, NJ: Graduate Record Examinations Board.

Clark, M. J., & Grandy, J. (1984). *Sex differences in the academic performance of Scholastic Aptitude Test-takers* (College Board Report 84–8). New York: College Entrance Examination Board.

Cleary, T. A. (1968). Test bias: Prediction of Negro and White students in integrated colleges. *Journal of Educational Measurement, 5*(2), 115–124.

Cole, N. S., & Moss, P. A. (1989). Bias in test use. In R. L. Linn (Ed.), *Educational measurement* (3rd ed., pp. 201–219). New York: American Council on Education/Macmillan.

Coley, R. J. (2001). *Differences in the gender gap: Comparisons across racial/ethnic groups in education and work* (ETS Policy Information Report). Princeton, NJ: Educational Testing Service.

The College Board. (1998, February). *SAT and gender differences* (College Board Research Summary RS-04). New York: The College Board, Office of Research and Development.

The College Board. (1998, November 23). *New studies document limited value of coaching on SAT scores: Strong academic preparation key to success.* Retrieved May 8, 1999, from http://www.collegeboard.org

The College Board. (2000). *College-bound seniors 2000.* Retrieved September 1, 2000, from http://www.collegeboard.org

The College Board & Educational Testing Service. (1998). *Admission staff handbook for the SAT program 1998–1999.* Princeton, NJ: Authors.

College Entrance Examination Board. (2004). *The SAT program handbook 2004–2005.* New York: Author.

Conant, J. B. (1964). *Shaping educational policy.* New York: McGraw-Hill.

Cowen, J. J. (1994). Barrett and Depinet versus McClelland. *American Psychologist, 49,* 64.

Critics of SAT and ACT hail decline in colleges that use them. (1997, August 8). *The Chronicle of Higher Education,* p. A41.

Crouse, J., & Trusheim, D. (1988). *The case against the SAT.* Chicago: University of Chicago Press.

Dawes, R. M. (1971). A case study of graduate admissions: Application of three principles of human decision making. *American Psychologist, 26,* 180–188.

Dawes, R. M., & Corrigan, B. (1974). Linear models in decision making. *Psychological Bulletin, 81*(2), 95–106.

Donlon, T. F. (Ed.). (1984). *The College Board technical handbook for the Scholastic Aptitude Test and Achievement Tests.* New York: College Entrance Examination Board.

Dorans, N. J. (1999). *Correspondences between ACT and SAT I scores* (College Board Report 99–1). New York: College Entrance Examination Board.

Dorans, N. J. (2002). Recentering and realigning the SAT score distributions: How and why. *Journal of Educational Measurement, 39,* 59–84.

Dorans, N. J., & Holland, P. W. (1993). DIF detection and description: Mantel-Haenszel and standardization. In P. W. Holland & H. Wainer (Eds.), *Differential item functioning* (pp. 35–66). Hillsdale, NJ: Lawrence Erlbaum Associates.

Dorans, N. J., Lyu, C. F., Pommerich, M., & Houston, W. M. (1997). Concordance between ACT assessment and recentered SAT I sum scores. *College and University, 73*(2), 24–32.

Dugan, M. K., Baydar, N., Grady, W. R., & Johnson, T. R. (1996). Affirmative action: Does it exist in graduate business schools? *Selections,* 11–18.

Dunham, K. J. (2003, October 28). More employers ask job seekers for SAT scores. *Wall Street Journal,* pp. B1, B10.

Dwyer, C. A., & Johnson, L. M. (1997). Grades, accomplishments, and correlates. In W. W. Willingham & N. Cole (Eds.), *Gender and fair assessment* (pp. 127–156). Mahwah, NJ: Lawrence Erlbaum.

Educational Testing Service. (1950). *Educational Testing Service annual report to the Board of Trustees (1949–1950).* Princeton, NJ: Author.

Educational Testing Service. (1999). *Overview: ETS fairness review.* Retrieved August 30, 1999, from http://www.ets.org

Educational Testing Service. (2000). *GRE 2000–2001 information and registration bulletin.* Princeton, NJ: Author.

Educational Testing Service. (2003a). *GRE for educators: The general test.* Retrieved September 24, 2003, from http://www.gre.org

Educational Testing Service. (2003b). *GRE 2003–2004 guide to the use of scores.* Princeton, NJ: Author.

Educational Testing Service. (2006). *How can you tell who's cut out for grad school success?* Princeton, NJ: Author.

Foster, A. L. (2001, February 23). ETS agrees to alter policy on reporting tests taken under modified conditions. *The Chronicle of Higher Education,* p. A49.

Gallagher, A., Morley, M. E., & Levin, J. (1999). *Cognitive patterns of gender differences on mathematics admissions tests* (The GRE, FAME Report Series 3, pp. 4–11). Princeton, NJ: Educational Testing Service.

Geiser, S., & Studley, R. (2004). UC and the SAT: Predictive validity and differential impact of the SAT and SAT II at the University of California. In R. Zwick (Ed.), *Rethinking the SAT: The future of standardized testing in university admissions* (pp. 125–153). New York: RoutledgeFalmer.

Gough, H. G. (1962). Clinical versus statistical prediction in psychology. In L. Postman (Ed.), *Psychology in the making: Histories of selected research problems* (pp. 526–584). New York: Alfred A. Knopf.

Graduate Management Admission Council. (1998). *MBA Q. & A.* McLean, VA: GMAC and Design Partners.

Graduate Management Admission Council. (2000). *GMAT information bulletin.* McLean, VA: Author.

Gulliksen, H. (1987). *Theory of mental tests.* Hillsdale, NJ: Lawrence Erlbaum.

Haney, W. M., Madaus, G. F., & Lyons, R. (1993). *The fractured marketplace for standardized testing.* Boston: Kluwer Academic.

Hecht, L. W., & Schrader, W. B. (1986). *Graduate Management Admission Test: Technical report on test development and score interpretation for GMAT users.* Princeton, NJ: Graduate Management Admission Council.

Heubert, J. P., & Hauser, R. M. (Eds.). (1999). *High stakes: Testing for tracking promotion, and graduation.* Washington, DC: National Research Council.

Hezlett, S. A., Kuncel, N. R., Vey, M., Ahart, A. M., Ones, D. S., Campbell, J. P., et al. (2001, April). *The effectiveness of the SAT in predicting success early and late in college: A meta-analysis.* Paper presented at the annual meeting of the American Educational Research Association and the National Council on Measurement in Education, Seattle, WA.

Hoover, H. D., & Han, L. (1995, April). *The effect of differential selection on gender differences in college admission test scores.* Paper presented at the annual meeting of the American Educational Research Association, San Francisco.

Huff, K. L., Koenig, J., Treptau, M., & Sireci, S. G. (1999). Validity of MCAT scores for predicting clerkship performance of medical students grouped by sex and ethnicity. *Academic Medicine, 74*(10), 41S–44S.

Humphreys, L. G. (1952). Individual differences. *Annual Review of Psychology, 3,* 131–150.

Jencks, C., & Phillips, M. (Eds.). *The black-white test score gap.* Washington, DC: Brookings Institution Press.

Johnson, V. E. (1997). An alternative to traditional GPA for evaluating student performance. *Statistical Science, 12*(4), 251–278.

Johnson, E. K., & Edwards, J. C. (1991). Current practices in admission interviews at U. S. medical schools. *Academic Medicine, 66*(7), 408–412.

Jolly, P. (1992). Academic achievement and acceptance rates of underrepresented-minority applicants to medical school. *Academic Medicine, 67*(11), 765–769.

Kidder, W. G. (2000). The rise of the testocracy: An essay on the LSAT, conventional wisdom, and the dismantling of diversity. *Texas Journal of Women and the Law, 9*, 167–218.

Klitgaard, R. E. (1985). *Choosing elites.* New York: Basic Books.

Kobrin, J. L., Camara, W. J., & Milewski, G. B. (2004). The utility of the SAT I and SAT II for admissions decisions in California and the nation. In R. Zwick (Ed.), *Rethinking the SAT: The future of standardized testing in university admissions* (pp. 251–276). New York: RoutledgeFalmer.

Koenig, J. A., & Leger, K. F. (1997). Test-taking behaviors and their impact on performance: A comparison of retest performance and test-preparation methods for MCAT examinees grouped by gender and race-ethnicity. *Academic Medicine, 72*(10), S100–S102.

Koenig, J. A., Sireci, S. G., & Wiley, A. (1998). Evaluating the predictive validity of MCAT scores across diverse applicant groups. *Academic Medicine, 73*(10), 1095–1106.

Kolen, M. J., & Hanson, B. A. (1989). In R. L. Brennan (Ed.), Scaling the ACT assessment. *In Methodology used in scaling the ACT assessment and P-ACT+* (pp. 35–55). Iowa City, IA: The American College Testing Program.

Kuncel, N. R., Campbell, J. P., & Ones, D. S. (1998). Validity of the Graduate Record Examination: Estimated or tacitly known? [Comment on Sternberg & Williams]. *American Psychologist, 53*(5), 567–568.

Kuncel, N. R., Hezlett, S. A., & Ones, D. S. (2001). A comprehensive meta-analysis of the predictive validity of the Graduate Record Examinations: Implications for graduate student selection and performance. *Psychological Bulletin, 127*, 162–181.

Law School Admission Council. (1999). *LSAT & LSDAS registration information book.* Newton, PA: Author.

Lawrence, I., Rigol, G., Van Essen, T., & Jackson, C. (2004). A historical perspective on the content of the SAT. In R. Zwick (Ed.), *Rethinking the SAT: The future of standardized testing in university admissions* (pp. 57–74). New York: RoutledgeFalmer.

Leary, L. F., & Wightman, L. E. (1983). *Estimating the relationship between use of test-preparation methods and scores on the Graduate Management Admission Test* (ETS Research Report 83–22). Princeton, NJ: Educational Testing Service.

Leatherman, C. (2000, December 4). California study finds racial disparities in granting of extra time on SAT. *The Chronicle of Higher Education.* Retrieved December 5, 2000 from http://www.chronicle.com

Lemann, N. (1995, August). The structure of success in America. *The Atlantic Monthly,* pp. 41–60.

Leonard, D., & Jiang, J. (1999). Gender bias and the college prediction of the SATs: A cry of despair. *Research in Higher Education, 40*(4), 375–408.

Lewis, C., & Willingham, W. W. (1995). *The effects of sample restriction on gender differences* (ETS Research Report 95–13). Princeton, NJ: Educational Testing Service.

Linn, R. L. (1983). Predictive bias as an artifact of selection procedures. In H. Wainer & S. Messick (Eds.), *Principals of modern psychological measurement: A Festschrift for Frederic M. Lord* (pp. 27–40). Hillsdale, NJ: Lawrence Erlbaum.

Lohman, D. F. (2004). Aptitude for college: The importance of reasoning tests for minority admissions. In R. Zwick (Ed.), *Rethinking the SAT: The future of standardized testing in university admissions* (pp. 41–55). New York: RoutledgeFalmer.

Madaus, G. (1990, September 5). Standardized testing needs a consumer-protection agency. *The Chronicle of Higher Education.* Retrieved July 31, 1999, from http://www.chronicle.com

Mandinach, E. B. (2000, April). *Flagging: Policies, perceptions, and practices.* Paper presented at the annual meeting of the American Educational Research Association, New Orleans, LA.

Mandinach, E. B., Cahalan, C., & Camara, W. J. (2001, April). *The impact of flagging on the admissions process: Policies, practices, and implications.* Paper presented at the annual meeting of the American Educational Research Association, Seattle, WA.

Mangan, K. S. (1998, May 11). Law-school council says access to LSAT courses is unrelated to racial disparity in scores. *The Chronicle of Higher Education.* Retrieved May 23, 2000, from http://www.chronicle.com

Manski, C. F., & Wise, S. A. (1983). *College choice in America.* Cambridge, MA: Harvard University Press.

McClelland, D. C. (1973). Testing for competence rather than intelligence. *American Psychologist, 28*, 1–14.

McClelland, D. C. (1994). The knowledge-testing-educational complex strikes back. *American Psychologist, 49*(1), 66–69.

McKown, H. (1925). *The trend in college entrance requirements, 1913–1922* (Department of Interior Bureau of Education Bulletin no. 35). Washington, DC: Government Printing Office.

Messick, S. (1988). The once and future issues of validity: Assessing the meaning and consequence of measurement. In H. Wainer & H. I. Braun (Eds.), *Test validity* (pp. 33–45). Hillsdale, NJ: Lawrence Erlbaum.

Miyazaki, I. (1976). *China's examination hell: The civil service examinations of Imperial China.* New York: Weatherhill.

National Center for Education Statistics. (1998). *Digest of education statistics 1998.* U.S. Department of Education. Retrieved December 15, 1999 from http://nces.ed.gov

Nettles, A. L., & Nettles, M. T. (1999). Introduction: Issuing the challenge. In A. L. Nettles & M. T. Nettles (Eds.), *Measuring up: Challenges minorities face in educational assessment* (pp. 1–11). Boston: Kluwer Academic.

The new SAT 2005. (2004). Retrieved December 22, 2004, from http://www.collegeboard.com

Nix, D. (1996). The LSAT and affirmative action in U.S. law schools. *The Mankind Quarterly, 21*(3,4), 335–361.

Noble, J. P. (1991). *Predicting college grades from ACT assessment scores and high school course work and grade information* (ACT Research Report 91–3). Iowa City, IA: American College Testing Program.

Noble, J. (2004). The effects of using ACT composite scores and high school averages on college admissions decisions for ethnic groups. In R. Zwick (Ed.), *Rethinking the SAT: The future of standardized testing in university admissions* (pp. 303–319). New York: RoutledgeFalmer.

Office of Technology Assessment. (1992). *Testing in American schools: Asking the right questions.* Washington, DC: U.S. Government Printing Office.

O'Neill, K. A., & McPeek, W. M. (1993). Item and test characteristics that are associated with differential item functioning. In P. W. Holland & H. Wainer (Eds.), *Differential item functioning* (pp. 255–276). Hillsdale, NJ: Lawrence Erlbaum.

Pennock-Román, M. (1990). *Test validity and language background: A study of Hispanic American students at six universities.* New York: College Entrance Examination Board.

Pennock-Román, M. (1994). *College major and gender differences in the prediction of college grades* (College Board Report 94–2). New York: College Entrance Examination Board.

Peterson, J. J. (1983). *The Iowa testing programs.* Iowa City, IA: Iowa University Press.

Powers, D. E. (1983). *Effects of coaching on GRE aptitude test scores* (GRE Board Report 83–7). Princeton, NJ: Graduate Record Examinations Board.

Powers, D. E., Fowles, M. E., & Welsh, C. K. (1999). *Further validation of a writing assessment for graduate admissions* (GRE Board Research Report No. 96–13R, ETS Research Report 99–18). Princeton, NJ: Educational Testing Service.

Powers, D. E., & Rock, D. A. (1999). Effects of coaching on SAT I: Reasoning test scores. *Journal of Educational Measurement, 36*(2), 93–118.

Ramist, L., Lewis, C., & McCamley-Jenkins, L. (1994). *Student group differences in predicting college grades: Sex, language, and ethnic groups* (College Board Report 93–1). New York: College Entrance Examination Board.

Ramist, L., Lewis, C., & McCamley-Jenkins, L. (2001). *Using Achievement Tests/SAT ll Subject Tests to demonstrate achievement and predict college grades: Sex, language, ethnic, and parental education groups* (Research Report No. 2001–5). New York: College Entrance Examination Board.

Rigol, G. W. (1997, June). *Common sense about SAT score differences and test validity* (College Board Research Notes RN-01). New York: College Entrance Examination Board.

Rigol, G. W. (2003). *Admissions decision-making models.* New York: College Entrance Examinations Board. Retrieved November 11, 2003, from http://www.collegeboard.com

Rigol, G. W., & Kimmel, E. W. (1997). *A picture of admissions in the United States.* New York: The College Board and Educational Testing Service.

Rock, D. A. (1974). *The prediction of doctorate attainment in psychology, mathematics and chemistry* (GRE Board Report 69–6aR). Princeton, NJ: Educational Testing Service.

Rogers, H. J., & Kulick, E. (1987). An investigation of unexpected differences in item performance between Blacks and Whites taking the SAT. In A. P. Schmitt & N. J. Dorans (Eds.), *Differential item functioning on the Scholastic Aptitude Test* (ETS Research Memorandum No. 87–1). Princeton, NJ: Educational Testing Service.

Sarbin, T. R. (1942). A contribution to the study of actuarial and individual methods of prediction. *American Journal of Sociology, 48,* 593–602.

Saretzky, G. (1992). *Return of the MCAT* (Bulletin No. 57, ETS Archives). Princeton, NJ: Educational Testing Service.

SAT's better freshman predictor than grades. (1991, January 16). *Chronicle of Higher Education,* A35.

Schaeffer, G. A., Briel, J. B., & Fowles, M. E. (2001). *Psychometric evaluation of the new GRE writing assessment* (GRE Board Professional Report No. 96–11P, ETS Research Report 01–08). Princeton, NJ: Educational Testing Service.

Schmitt, A. P. (1987). Unexpected differential item performance of Hispanic examinees. In A. P. Schmitt & N. J. Dorans (Eds.), *Differential item functioning on the Scholastic Aptitude Test* (ETS Research Memorandum No. 87–1). Princeton, NJ: Educational Testing Service.

Schmitt, A. P., & Dorans, N. J. (1988). *Differential item functioning for minority examinees on the SAT* (ETS Research Report 88–32). Princeton, NJ: Educational Testing Service.

Schmotter, J. W. (1993). The Graduate Management Admission Council: A brief history 1953–1992. *Selections, 9*(2), 1–11.

Schneider, L. M., & Briel, J. B. (1990). *Validity of the GRE: 1988–89 summary report.* Princeton, NJ: Educational Testing Service.

Scholes, R. J., & McCoy, T. R. (1998, April). *The effects of type, length, and content of test preparation activities on ACT assessment scores.* Paper presented at the annual meeting of the American Educational Research Association, San Diego, CA.

Schrader, W. B. (1978). *Admissions test scores as predictors of career achievement in psychology* (GRE Board Report 76–1R). Princeton, NJ: Graduate Record Examinations Board.

Schrader, W. B. (1980). *GRE scores as predictors of career achievement in history* (GRE Board Report 76–1bR). Princeton, NJ: Graduate Record Examinations Board.

Sellman, W. S., & Arabian, J. M. (1997). Foreword. In W. A. Sands, B. K. Waters, & J. R. McBride (Eds.), *Computerized adaptive testing: From inquiry to operation* (pp. xv–xvii). Washington, DC: American Psychological Association.

Skager, R. (1982). On the use and importance of tests of ability in admission to postsecondary education. In A. K. Wigdor & W. R. Garner (Eds.), *Ability testing: Uses, consequences, and controversies* (pp. 286–314). Washington, DC: National Academy Press.

Snedecor, G. W., & Cochran, W. G. (1967). *Statistical methods* (6th ed.). Ames, Iowa: Iowa State University Press.

Snyder, T. D., Hoffman, C. M., & Geddes, C. M. (1997). *Digest of education statistics, 1997* (NCES 98–015). Washington, DC: National Center for Education Statistics.

Steele, C. M. (1997). A threat in thin air: How stereotypes shape intellectual identity and performance. *American Psychologist, 52*(6), 613–629.

Steele, C. M. (1999, August). Thin ice: "Stereotype threat" and Black college students. *The Atlantic Monthly.* Retrieved September 19, 1999, from http://www.theatlantic.com

Steele, C. M., & Aronson, J. (1998). Stereotype threat and the test performance of academically successful African Americans. In C. Jencks & M. Phillips (Eds.), *The Black-White test score gap* (pp. 401–427). Washington, DC: Brookings Institution Press.

Sternberg, R. J., & Williams, W. M. (1997). Does the Graduate Record Examination predict meaningful success in the graduate training of psychologists? *American Psychologist, 52*(6), 630–641.

Stewart, D. M. (1998, January 25). *Why Hispanic students need to take the SAT.* Retrieved April 4, 1999, from The College Board Web site: http://www.collegeboard.org

Stocking, M. (1996). An alternative method for scoring adaptive tests. *Journal of Educational and Behavioral Statistics, 21,* 365–389.

Stocking, M. L., Swanson, L., & Pearlman, M. (1991). *Automatic item selection (AIS) methods in the ETS testing environment* (ETS Research Memorandum 91–5). Princeton, NJ: Educational Testing Service.

Stricker, L. J., Rock, D. A., & Burton, N. W. (1993). Sex differences in predictions of college grades from Scholastic Aptitude Test scores. *Journal of Educational Psychology, 85*(4), 710–718.

Stricker, L. J., Rock, D. A., Burton, N. W., Muraki, E., & Jirele, T. J. (1994). Adjusting college grade point average criteria for variations in grading standards: A comparison of methods. *Journal of Applied Psychology, 79*(2), 178–183.

Study finds that GRE doesn't predict success in psychology. (1997, August 15). *The Chronicle of Higher Education,* A33.

Sturm, S., & Guinier, L. (2000, December/2001, January). The future of affirmative action. *The Boston Review.* Retrieved May 21, 2001, from http://www.bostonreview.mit.edu

Thayer, P. W., & Kalat, J. K. (1998). Questionable criteria [Comment on Sternberg and Williams]. *American Psychologist, 53*(5), 566–567.

Turnbull, W. W. (1985). *Student change, program change: Why SAT scores kept falling* (College Board Report 85–2). Princeton, NJ: Educational Testing Service.

Wainer, H. (1989). Eelworms, bullet holes, and Geraldine Ferraro: Some problems with statistical adjustment and some solutions. *Journal of Educational Statistics, 14* (2), 121–140.

Wainer, H. (1990). Introduction and history. In H. Wainer (Ed.), *Computerized adaptive testing: A primer* (pp. 1–21). Hillsdale, NJ: Lawrence Erlbaum.

Webber, C. (1989). The mandarin mentality: University admissions testing in Europe and Asia. In B. R. Gifford (Ed.), *Test policy and the politics of opportunity allocation: The workplace and the law* (pp. 33–57). Boston: Kluwer Academic.

Weinig, K. M. (2000, June 14). The 10 worst educational disasters of the 20th century: A traditionalist's list. *Education Week,* 31, 34.

Weiss, K. R. (2000, January 9). New test-taking skill: Working the system. *The Los Angeles Times.* Retrieved December 20, 2000, from http://www.latimes.com

Weissert, W. (1999, December 17). NAACP urges support for test-prep courses for minority students. *The Chronicle of Higher Education,* p. A34.

Wiggins, N., & Kohen, E. S. (1971). Man vs. model of man revisited: The forecasting of graduate school success. *Journal of Personality and Social Psychology, 19,* 100–106.

Wightman, L. F. (1993). *Test takers with disabilities: A summary of data from special administrations of the LSAT* (LSAC Research Report 93–03). Newtown, PA: Law School Admission Council.

Wightman, L. F. (1994). *Analysis of LSAT performance and patterns of application for male and female law applicants* (LSAC Research Report 94–02). Newtown, PA: Law School Admission Council.

Wightman, L. F. (1997, April). The threat to diversity in legal education: An empirical analysis of the consequences of abandoning race as a factor in law school admission decisions. *New York University Law Review, 72,* 1–53.

Wightman, L. E., & Leary, L. F. (1985). *GMAC validity study service: A three-year summary.* Princeton, NJ: Graduate Management Admission Council.

Wightman, L. F., & Muller, D. G. (1990). *Comparison of LSAT performance among selected subgroups* (Law School Admission Council Statistical Report 90–01). Newton, PA: Law School Admission Council.

Wiley, A., & Koenig, J. A. (1996). Undergraduate performance assessment and prediction: The validity of the medical college admission test for predicting performance in the first two years of medical school. *Academic Medicine, 71*(10), S83–S85.

Willingham, W. W. (1974). Predicting success in graduate education. *Science, 183,* 273–278.

Willingham, W. W. (1985). *Success in college: The role of personal qualities and academic ability.* New York: College Entrance Examination Board.

Willingham, W. W. (1998, December). *Validity in college selection: Context and evidence.* Paper presented at the National Academy of Sciences Workshop on the Role of Tests in Higher Education Admissions, Washington, DC.

Willingham, W., & Cole, N. (1997). *Gender and fair assessment.* Mahwah, NJ: Lawrence Erlbaum Associates.

Willingham, W. W., Cole, N. S., Lewis, C., & Leung, S. W. (1997). Test performance. In W. W. Willingham & N. Cole (Eds.), *Gender and fair assessment* (pp. 55–126). Mahwah, NJ: Lawrence Erlbaum.

Willingham, W. W., Pollack, J. M., & Lewis, C. (2000). *Grades and test scores: Accounting for observed differences* (ETS Research Report 00–15). Princeton, NJ: Educational Testing Service.

Willingham, W. W., Ragosta, M., Bennett, R. E., Braun, H., Rock, D. A., & Powers, D. E. (1988). *Testing handicapped people.* Boston: Allyn & Bacon.

Winterbottom, J. A. (1995). *A historical survey of test development in the Law School Admission Test program 1947–1978* (Report in ETS Archives). Princeton, NJ: Educational Testing Service.

Young, J. W. (1991). Improving the prediction of college performance of ethnic minorities using the IRT-based GPA. *Applied Measurement in Education,* 4(3), 229–239.

Young, J. W. (2001). *Differential validity, differential prediction, and college admissions testing: A comprehensive review and analysis* (Research Report No. 2001–6). New York: The College Board.

Young, J. W. (2004). Differential validity and prediction: Race and sex differences in college admissions testing. In R. Zwick (Ed.), *Rethinking the SAT: The future of standardized testing in university admissions* (pp. 289–301). New York: RoutledgeFalmer.

Ziomek, R. L., & Andrews, K. M. (1996). *Predicting the college grade point averages of special-tested students from their ACT assessment scores and high school grades* (ACT Research Report 96–7). Iowa City, IA: ACT.

Zwick, R. (1990). *The validity of the GMAT for the prediction of success in doctoral study in business and management* (ETS Research Report 90–24). Princeton, NJ: Educational Testing Service.

Zwick, R. (1991). *Differences in graduate school attainment patterns across academic programs and demographic groups* (ETS Research Report 91–17). Princeton, NJ: Educational Testing Service.

Zwick, R. (1993). The validity of the GMAT for the prediction of grades in doctoral study in business and management: An empirical Bayes approach. *Journal of Educational Statistics, 18*(1), 91–107.

Zwick, R. (2002). *Fair game? The use of standardized admissions tests in higher education.* New York: RoutledgeFalmer.

Zwick, R. (Ed.). (2004a). Is the SAT a "wealth test"? The link between educational achievement and socioeconomic status. In R. Zwick (Ed.), *Rethinking the SAT: The future of standardized testing in university admissions* (pp. 203–216). New York: RoutledgeFalmer.

Zwick, R. (2004b). *Rethinking the SAT: The future of standardized testing in university admissions.* New York: Routledge Falmer.

Zwick, R., Brown, T., & Sklar, J. C. (2004, July). *California and the SAT: A reanalysis of University of California admissions data.* Center for Studies in Higher Education, UC Berkeley, Research and Occasional Papers Series. Retrieved July 20, 2004, from http://ishi.lib.berkeley.edu/cshe/publications/papers/papers.html

Zwick, R., & Schlemer, L. (2004). SAT validity for linguistic minorities at the University of California, Santa Barbara. *Educational Measurement: Issues and Practice, 25,* 6–16.

Zwick, R., & Sklar, J. C. (2005). Predicting college grades and degree completion using high school grades and SAT scores: The role of student ethnicity and first language. *American Educational Research Journal, 42,* 439–464.

19

Monitoring Educational Progress with Group-Score Assessments

John Mazzeo
Stephen Lazer
Michael J. Zieky
Educational Testing Service

1. INTRODUCTION

The purpose of this chapter is to discuss the uses and major features of large-scale survey assessments constructed to provide data about the educational progress of groups of people at district, state, national, and international levels. We will refer to such assessments as *group-score assessments*. From their inception in the 1960's, group-score assessments have played an increasingly important and increasingly visible role in educational measurement, a role that cannot be met by individual-score tests. Policymakers, researchers, educators, and the press rely on group-score assessments as highly valued and trusted sources of data.

Group-score assessments are designed to answer questions about what groups of students know and can do, as well as to provide comparisons of student performance across jurisdictions, to provide information concerning educational performance trends, and to indicate the extent to which jurisdictions are meeting their educational goals. Such assessments typically have very broad content coverage, use both content and test-taker sampling (see sections 5 and 6), and contain both cognitive and background instruments. They generally use analytic methods such as *item response theory* (see section 7) and *marginal estimation* (see section 8) to calculate the performance of groups of people on entire assessments when no single person has responded to all of the items in those assessments. Data regarding groups of people are the main outcomes of group-score assessments, and not subsidiary byproducts as is the case with tests used for the evaluation of individuals.

We begin with a brief history of group-score assessment and we describe some of the major group-score assessments currently in use. Then we discuss several aspects of the design and development of group-score assessments that differ in important ways from those used in individual-score tests. Because of the importance of sampling test-takers and items for group-score assessments, we describe those sampling processes in some detail. We then explain the use of item-response theory and marginal estimation procedures in group-score testing and we describe attempts to link scores on different group-score assessments.[1] We explain how scores are reported for group-score assessments, and we discuss some of the current challenges facing such assessments.

2. BRIEF HISTORY OF GROUP-SCORE ASSESSMENT

Since the 19th century, most industrial nations have gathered educational data about basic indicators such as the literacy rates of citizens. Until relatively recently in the United States, however, these data were not based on consistent definitions of knowledge or skills, were not derived from standardized measures, and were not collected in a consistent fashion (Vinovskis, 1998). The situation was the same in many other nations, and there was also no way to make meaningful international comparisons.

Tests used in the United States in the first half of the 20th century were given to non-representative samples of students, and covered limited content. This rendered them inappropriate providers of representative data on the educational achievement and progress of large groups. After the launching of Sputnik in 1957 by the Soviet Union, policymakers in the United States felt an increased need to acquire meaningful and reliable data about national and international educational performance. These concerns led to the development of early group-score assessments such as Project Talent, beginning in 1960; the First International Mathematics Study (1964); the Equal Opportunity Survey (1965); and the National Assessment of Educational Progress (NAEP, 1969).

In the early years of group-score assessments (circa 1960–1980), there was no appropriate way to produce a reporting scale, discuss score distributions, or describe performance at desired proficiency levels. In the 1980s, programs began to use item-response theory (IRT) and marginal estimation approaches to allow for the reporting of performance distributions in terms of a score scale. First used in NAEP, these approaches became common to most group-score assessments through the 1980s and 1990s.

In the United States, the No Child Left Behind Act ([NCLB]; 2002) made testing more prevalent, more prominent, and more controversial. (See http://www.ed.gov/nclb for information about the law.) NCLB did not solve problems of the lack of comparability of data collected on different tests in the different states. Increased emphasis is, therefore, being placed on group-score assessments to provide the desired comparisons across states and to provide both national data and international comparisons. (For more information about the historical background of group-score assessment, see Cohen, 1974; Jones & Olkin, 2004.)

3. DESCRIPTIONS OF SOME MAJOR GROUP-SCORE ASSESSMENTS

3.1. The National Assessment of Educational Progress (NAEP)

First administered in 1969, the National Assessment of Educational Progress (NAEP) has served as the only representative, ongoing measure of what students in the United States know and can do in a variety of subject areas. The modern program, with its use of IRT scaling, marginal estimation approaches, and state-level samples, took form in the 1980s and 1990s. In addition to this program, called *main NAEP*, there are assessments of long-term trends that have continued to use older methods.

The goal of the main NAEP assessments is to measure student performance on content currently taught in schools using state-of-the-art assessment methodologies. Main NAEP assessments have been constructed to measure domains described in frameworks created by the National Assessment Governing Board (NAGB). The current generation of main NAEP assessments was first administered in 1990. Assessments have been given in reading, mathematics, science, writing, U.S. history, geography, civics, economics, and the arts.

Main NAEP assessments are usually administered to national samples of students at grades 4, 8, and 12. At the time this chapter is being written (2005), assessments in reading and mathematics at grades 4 and 8 are conducted every 2 years, science and writing every 4 years. Grade 12 assessments in these 4 "core subjects" occur every 4 years. Assessments in all other subjects are administered less frequently. Certain subjects are assessed only at one grade, such as economics at grade 12 and the arts at grade 8.

In reading, mathematics, science, and writing, national samples at grades 4 and 8 are large enough to allow reporting of results on a state-by-state basis.[2] On a trial basis beginning in 2002, samples were expanded to allow results to be reported for certain large urban school districts. All NAEP national samples include both public and nonpublic schools, although state- and district-level estimates are reported only for public schools. In addition to answering content-area questions, students complete background questionnaires to provide demographic data and information about their educational experiences. The teachers of the tested students and school officials complete questionnaires as well, providing information about teacher training, classroom instructional practices, and school policies.

From 1990 to 2001, the NAEP that was used to collect data for states was separate from the main NAEP assessments. By 2002, however, the instruments and administration procedures used in the main and state NAEP programs had become identical in subjects in which state assessments were conducted, and the national sample had largely become an aggregate of the state samples.

Main NAEP instruments garner most of the attention from policymakers; however, NAEP has another set of instruments that measure trends going back to the earliest days of the program. First created as instruments separate from the main assessments in the mid-1980s, the long-term trend assessments (LTT) use exercises that were developed in the 1970s and 1980s. They measure trends in student performance going back to 1971 in reading and 1973 in mathematics. LTT NAEP included, until 1999 and 1996 respectively, science and writing assessments. Because LTT NAEP was designed to continue a trend line begun long ago, it has been limited to continued use of the assessment techniques of an earlier era.

In addition to studies of trends, NAEP has conducted a number of special studies including those of oral reading fluency (Daane, Campbell, Grigg, Goodman, & Oranje, in press; Pinnell et al., 1995), of the performance of groups of students working together (Goodman, Lazer, Mazzeo, Mead, & Pearlmutter, 1998), of advanced students in mathematics and science (O'Sullivan & Grigg, 2001), of the effects of letting students choose assessment texts (Campbell & Donahue, 1997), and of classroom instructional practices regarding writing (Solomon, Lutkus, Kaplan, & Skolnik, 2004).

3.2. Progress in International Reading Literacy Study (PIRLS)

PIRLS is designed to allow comparisons of the literacy skills acquired by fourth-graders in different countries (Martin, Mullis, & Kennedy, 2003). PIRLS assesses students in the upper of the two grades that include the most nine-year-olds—fourth grade in most countries. PIRLS was given in 2001 for the first time, with 35 countries participating. (See http://isc.bc.edu/pirls2001.html for details.)

Sponsored by the International Association for the Evaluation of Educational Achievement (IEA) and funded by the governments of participating nations, PIRLS shares many features with the NAEP reading assessment, including a similar content framework and sampling approach. PIRLS also examines instructional practices, students' attitudes toward reading, and students' reading habits.

Students, their teachers, and their principals complete background questionnaires. In some participating countries, questionnaires are also administered to parents of sampled students. PIRLS follows rigorous translation and verification approaches designed to help ensure that the assessment measures the same content and skills in different nations. A PIRLS assessment is scheduled for 2006.

3.3. Programme for International Student Assessment (PISA)

Coordinated by the governments of participating countries under the auspices of the Organization for Economic Cooperation and Development (OECD), PISA was first conducted in 2000 with 41 countries participating, was repeated in 2003, and is scheduled to be repeated every 3 years. PISA assesses samples of 15-year-olds in reading, mathematics, and science. The program is designed to measure the ability of students to apply and use knowledge in practical, and not solely academic, settings.

All three subject areas are assessed each time PISA is conducted, but one of them forms the focus during each assessment cycle. As in NAEP and PIRLS, a matrix sampling approach is used, in which samples of students in participating nations are tested on samples of assessment items. Unlike NAEP and PIRLS, however, PISA tests individual students across multiple subject areas. PISA uses student and teacher questionnaires in addition to the cognitive testing.

3.4. Trends in International Mathematics and Science Study (TIMSS)

Sponsored by the IEA and various governmental agencies in participating nations, TIMSS (formerly known as the Third International Mathematics and Science Study) was first administered in 1995 in grades 3 and 4, in grades 7 and 8, and in the last year of secondary school. In 1999, the assessment was administered at grade 8. In 2003, TIMSS was given at grades 4 and 8. Between 32 countries (in 1999) and 50 (in 2003) have participated in TIMSS. In addition to assessing national samples, TIMSS assesses interested jurisdictions (states, provinces, or school districts), at their own expense, providing them with results so that they can determine how they perform against international benchmarks. TIMSS also uses matrix sampling. Unlike NAEP (but like PISA), TIMSS assesses a student in multiple subject areas (both mathematics and science).

3.5. The National Assessment of Adult Literacy

Conducted in 2003, the National Assessment of Adult Literacy (NAAL) is the U.S. Department of Education's successor to the earlier National Adult Literacy Study (NALS), which was conducted in 1992 (Kirsch, Jungeblut, Jenkins, & Kolstad, 1993), and the Young Adult Literacy Study, conducted in 1985 (Kirsch & Jungeblut, 1986). The NAAL is administered to a multistage probability sample (see section 6.2) of people age 16 and older living in households in the United States. The NAAL cognitive assessment covers document, prose, and quantitative literacy (National Assessment of Adult Literacy, n.d.).

NAAL is conducted through in-person household interviews that make use of paper-and-pencil literacy components. NAAL includes a background questionnaire, which is administered through computer-assisted personal interviews. After respondents complete the questionnaire, participants complete seven relatively easy items. A cut score for performance on these items identifies people whose literacy skills would place them in approximately the lowest 5% of the population. Participants who score above this cut score complete the main literacy assessment as well as an oral fluency measure. Participants with low scores on the initial seven items complete the Adult Literacy Supplemental Assessment instead of the main instrument.

3.6. The International Adult Literacy Survey

The International Adult Literacy Survey (IALS) is designed to allow comparisons of the literacy skills of adults in various countries around the world. Funding has been provided by various organizations, including the National Center for Education Statistics (NCES) in the United States. Between 1994 and 1998, IALS data were collected in three rounds. Twenty-three countries (representing 19 language groups) participated. In addition to completing a literacy survey, respondents answered an extensive background questionnaire. Like NAAL, IALS uses a screening instrument. After completing the background questionnaire, respondents complete six simple tasks. Failure to complete at least two tasks correctly leads to the conclusion of the interview. Those who continue are given a more extensive array of literacy tasks, presented in a separate, untimed booklet (Organisation for Economic Co-Operation and Development, 2000). IALS tasks are based on a content framework similar to that used in NALS. Literacy is divided into three distinct areas: prose, document, and quantitative literacy (Kirsch, 2001). Scores are reported for each area, and there is also an overall score that is a composite of performance in the three literacy areas.

4. SOME DIFFERENCES BETWEEN GROUP-SCORE ASSESSMENTS AND INDIVIDUAL-SCORE TESTS

Group-score assessments differ significantly from individual-score tests in a number of features. In this section we discuss several of these: content specifications, constructed-response items, item pools, and background data. We discuss two of the most important differences—the use in group-score assessments of item and population sampling—in sections 5 and 6.

4.1. Content Specifications

Because group-score tests are administered across jurisdictions that lack a common curriculum, there is no single set of content or curricular standards to determine what should be measured. This makes the definition of content and skills to be measured an inherently political process, involving policymakers and stakeholders in the outcomes of the assessment, in addition to educators, measurement experts, and subject-matter experts. In international assessments, participating nations are generally given the power to eliminate content they believe to be inappropriate either from their own assessments or from the assessments used in all countries.

Because group-score assessments are often given to populations that have no common instructional background, the assessments must be broad enough to encompass different curricula. In addition, because the goal of these assessments is to measure the performance of educational systems in broad content domains, the specifications and frameworks for these assessments usually imply more extensive content and skills "coverage" than would be common in an individual-score test.[3] For example, if the United States wants to know how fourth-graders are performing in different areas of mathematics, it is important that the assessment cover all areas in ways that allow the provision of this information. This requirement tends to yield specifications that call for assessments that are quite long, in terms of the amount of time it would take an individual to answer all questions. Combined with the use of constructed-response questions, and the need to reduce respondent burden, these broad specifications necessitate the use of matrix sampling and marginal estimation approaches.

4.2. Constructed-Response Items

The use of samples of items administered to samples of people allows the affordable use of expensive, constructed-response or performance item types on group-score assessments, because only a relatively small proportion of the population of interest is administered any item. Constructed-response items are particularly useful for measuring the broad content and skills commonly covered by group-score assessments; therefore, such assessments tend to have a larger proportion of constructed-response items than do standardized individual-score tests (Glaser & Baxter, 2000; Lazer, Mislevy, Whittington, & Ward, 1997; Mazzeo, Yamamoto, & Kulick, 1993). Because respondents do not receive scores and there are no performance stakes, however, low motivation might possibly lead people to be less likely to respond to items that require more effort than selecting an option (Hawkins, Stancavage, Mitchell, Goodman, & Lazer, 1998). Furthermore, international group-score assessments face special scoring issues related to the evaluation of constructed responses in different languages (Martin et al., 2003).

4.3. Item Pools

Group-score assessments must be designed and reviewed at the level of total item pools rather than at the level of individual test forms, because the entire pool of items is the unit on which reported results are based. Pool design is influenced both by content coverage demands and by subscale reporting goals. If subscores are reported, the item pool must be rich enough in each subscale domain to support such reporting. Even if relatively few skills are measured, the need to represent different types of stimuli, as in the measurement of reading, will increase the number of items required in the pool.

Decisions about the pools are also influenced by the item types required to meet the specifications. Assessments that use high proportions of multiple-choice and short constructed-response items may have modest aggregate testing time. Those that make extensive use of lengthy tasks will, of course, prove longer. The NAEP writing assessment contains twenty 25-minute essay tasks at each grade and would require 500 minutes to administer to an individual.

At times frameworks require special-purpose blocks, and these influence pool design decisions as well. For example, the NAEP science assessment uses blocks devoted to hands-on experiments; the history assessment calls for blocks focused on specific themes. These blocks are not efficient contributors to overall content coverage because they contain relatively few items, all focused in a specific content area, and each item consumes a large amount of time. The remainder of the assessment must bear the weight of content coverage. Therefore, assessments with special-purpose blocks tend to require longer aggregate pools.

Pools that require longer aggregate assessment times may require larger samples of students, assuming that testing time per student is fixed. Stable IRT scaling requires a certain number of students per item. Therefore, the portion of an aggregate pool any student completes is an important factor in determining the overall sample size required. For example, in the NAEP U.S. history assessment, each student takes one-fifth of the pool. If 2,000 students per item are required for analysis, the aggregate sample size required will be 10,000. In the case of the NAEP writing assessment, because each item takes longer to answer, each student takes only one-tenth of the pool. Therefore, the sample required to get the same count per item is 20,000. It is important to note that in cases where samples are large for other reasons (NAEP assessments that do state-level reporting, for example), increases in the size of the item pool need not lead to concomitant increases in samples.

Reviews of group-score assessments differ from reviews of individual-score tests primarily because reviews of group-score assessments must be conducted at the level of the assessment pool (that is, the unit on which results will be reported), in addition to reviews of items and assembled blocks of items. Reviews must ensure that the pool sufficiently covers the specifications, does not contain unwanted overlap, and has the appropriate mix of item types.

4.4. Background Data

Group-score assessments usually obtain data about background and instructional variables, such as the amount of homework students do, the types of training received by teachers, and levels of absence and tardiness in schools. Data from the assessments are used to examine the relationship between these reported variables and achievement. Obtaining accurate estimates for the performance of groups as defined by responses to these background questionnaires has implications for the analysis of results, as discussed below.

The interest in background variables has often placed unrealistic expectations on group-score assessment results. The data rarely support causal inferences, yet the presence of the data appears to encourage such inferences.

5. SAMPLING OF ITEMS IN GROUP-SCORE ASSESSMENTS

5.1. Matrix Sampling

Group-score assessments usually have many more items in total than individual-score tests have. In addition, the broad skills to be measured often require use of time-consuming item types. An extremely important aspect of group-score tests is, therefore, the administration of samples of items to samples of test-takers. We refer to the use of both samples of students and samples of items as *matrix sampling*.

Generally, individuals take between one-third and one-tenth of the entire assessment. However, the assessment design must allow the estimation of how groups *would* have performed had individuals taken the entire assessment. The results must represent a best estimate of what respondents know and can do, and must not be overly influenced by fatigue or item context. To accomplish these goals, virtually all group-score assessments use some form of matrix sampling.

5.2. Block Designs

An important version of matrix sampling is called the Balanced Incomplete Block (BIB). The BIB approach has several key features, some of which are common to other matrix sample designs. Once developers have determined the aggregate pool length required to cover a content area, they determine the amount of time that an individual can spend taking the assessment. The assessment pool is then divided into units or "blocks" that can be administered in the time allowed. It is optimal for IRT scaling that the blocks be short enough for two or more to be administered to participants during an assessment session.

In a full BIB design, each block is paired with all other blocks, allowing IRT analyses to estimate item parameters on a common scale. The blocks are balanced by position—that is, each block occurs in each position an equal number of times so that results are not biased by position effects. Many assessments rely on a partial BIB (pBIB) design or some other form of matrix sampling in which each block is not paired with all other blocks. This compromise is made because meeting the demands of a complete BIB design would involve the printing of massive number of test books, and unrealistically complex plans for spiraling (see next section). However, IRT linkages are stronger where the blocks overlap directly.

BIB and pBIB designs are used in NAEP (for examples of these designs see Allen, Carlson, & Donoghue, 2001, pp. 20–21; Lazer, 1999). Several group-score assessments use forms of matrix sampling other than the BIB design. In TIMSS, for example, blocks are rotated among assessment booklets, with the exception of a core item cluster that is placed in all booklets. The core cluster is used in the IRT analysis to ensure that parameter estimates for all items are expressed on a common scale.

While designers normally try to ensure that blocks show up in all booklet positions an equal number of times, unbalanced designs are sometimes impossible to avoid in the case of special-purpose blocks. Hands-on NAEP science tasks, for example, always occur in the last assessment position, because it would be too disruptive for some students to be conducting science experiments when others were working on traditional items.

In a *focused* sample, students are assessed in a single subject area. Focused samples are used in NAEP, IALS, and PIRLS, and have the advantage of providing optimal measurement in a subject area. In an *unfocused* sample, respondents are tested in more than one area (for example, in both reading and mathematics). Unfocused samples are used in TIMSS and PISA, and have been used in the past in parts of NAEP. Unfocused samples have the advantage of allowing estimates of the correlations among different subject areas. They also make it harder to develop the matrix design optimally for IRT scaling. Unfocused designs work best when individual testing time is longer than would be required for a focused design.

Matrix sampling is acknowledged to be an effective method of administering group-score tests. Matrix sampling, however, necessitates complex and time-consuming analysis procedures, and some reviewers have raised questions about whether simpler designs could yield equally useful results (see, for example, Bay et al., 1997).

5.3. Spiraling

The BIB design will satisfy the requirements of statistical analysis only if the numbers of respondents called for in analysis plans actually complete each book in the design and randomly equivalent populations answer each item. When these conditions are satisfied, performance on different items can be validly compared, and more complex summary analyses such as IRT scaling can be undertaken in a relatively straightforward fashion.

Some assessments, such as adult literacy measures and early childhood studies, involve one-on-one testing and individual interviews. Protocols for administration ensure that roughly the right sample of respondents will answer each item. However, most academic group-score assessments involve testing relatively large numbers of students together. Therefore, administration systems must be developed to ensure that the items are administered to appropriate samples of students.

For large surveys involving thousands of sites, assessment books cannot be packaged on a site-specific basis. To make the system feasible, some prepackaging must be accomplished. Assessment books may be placed in a certain order and packaged for shipping by processes called *spiraling* and *bundling*. Books are distributed and assigned to schools and students in the preset order in which they are packaged, and thus all assessment items and blocks are given to appropriate-size, randomly equivalent samples.

6. SAMPLING OF POPULATIONS IN GROUP-SCORE ASSESSMENTS

6.1. Probability Sampling

Probability sampling techniques are used by all modern group-score assessments to select test-takers. In probability sampling, every element in the target population has a known probability of being chosen (Kish, 1965). Probability sampling techniques provide a set of tools for drawing samples, making valid inferences about population quantities, and quantifying the amount of uncertainty (or sampling error) inherent in those inferences. The goal is to produce samples from which reasonably precise estimates of population achievement can be obtained while satisfying economic and operational constraints.

In most group-score assessments, the primary element or unit of analysis is the student or individual respondent. However, group-score assessments rarely, if ever find it economically or operationally feasible to select a simple random sample of students. Instead, all modern group-score assessments make use of *multistage cluster sampling* techniques.

6.2. Multistage Cluster Sampling

Cluster sampling is typically employed in situations where the *frame* (i.e., a listing of all the possible primary analysis units eligible to be included in the sample) is not available or is inconvenient or inefficient to use. Fortunately, especially when testing students, the population of primary analysis units is naturally grouped into clusters for which an adequate frame exists. For example, there are up-to-date, comprehensive lists of the public school districts and private schools in the United States.

Group-score assessments have, for the most part, used either a three-stage or two-stage cluster sampling design. A good example of the former is the design used by NAEP during the 1980s and 1990s to select its national samples (Rust & Johnson, 1992). In the first stage of sample selection, a frame of primary sampling units (PSUs) was established, in which each PSU was a geographic area in the United States. A nationally representative sample of PSUs was selected. In the second stage, a sample of schools was selected from a list of all of the eligible schools in each sampled PSU. In the final stage of sampling, a sample of students was selected from a listing of all the eligible students in the school.

School-based group-score assessments have taken one of two approaches to student sampling from across the different classrooms within schools. Some, like NAEP, draw random samples of students. TIMSS and certain other studies sample intact classrooms. The student-sampling approach typically yields more statistically efficient samples. However, this approach can be more disruptive to schools, and the resulting data will be less useful for studies in which classrooms are the unit of analysis. Classroom samples tend to be preferred by teachers and schools because students can be tested in their normal classes. The resulting data are, of course, better suited to analyses that examine the associations between classroom-level variables and achievement. Classroom samples, however, tend to have larger sampling errors than do random samples of students.

Frequently, the complex sample designs used in these assessments result in different probabilities of selection for certain subpopulations. This is accounted for in data analysis by using case weights. Each examinee is assigned a weight that is the reciprocal of the probability of selection. The case weights are then used in calculating average achievement or other important outcomes to obtain consistent and approximately unbiased estimates of the corresponding population quantities (Johnson & Rust, 1992).

6.3. Standard Errors

The degree of uncertainty associated with particular results is frequently quantified by including an estimated standard error, or confidence interval, associated with each of those results. The use of multistage cluster designs requires more complex procedures for the estimation of standard errors than are typically required for simple sampling designs. Most group-score assessments use resampling-based estimators, typically variants such as the jackknife or balanced repeated replications, to obtain estimates of sampling variability (Johnson & Rust, 1992).

The standard errors of estimates of the average achievement of states or countries (or of subgroups within those jurisdictions) calculated from cluster samples will be larger than standard errors for simple random samples of comparable size. Data from sampled students who attend the same school cannot be considered independent observations. Thus, a simple random sample of 4,000 students is likely to cover the diversity of the population better than a sample of 100 schools with 40 students observed with each school.

In addition, within a school, samples in which the 40 students are selected from across all classrooms are likely to cover the diversity of the population better than a design in which the 40 students are taken from an intact classroom. In general, therefore, the greater the level of clustering in a multistage sample, the greater the uncertainty induced (Monseur, Rust, & Krawchuck, 2002).

6.4. Other Commonly Used Sampling Techniques

A number of other common sampling techniques have been employed to try to offset the loss in statistical efficiency inherent in the use of cluster sample design. These techniques include stratified sampling, sampling with certainty, sampling with probability proportional to size, and oversampling.

6.4.1. Stratified Sampling

Most of the national and international group-score assessments have made use of some amount of stratification in sample selection. With *stratified sampling*, sampling units are divided into a set of mutually exclusive groups, or strata, and samples are then selected from each stratum. The strata are often formed on the basis of practical considerations (e.g., geographic location, administrative convenience). When the strata are formed such that the units within the strata are homogenous with respect to the main variables of interest (e.g., educational achievement), stratification can lead to gains in precision (see, for example, Rust & Johnson, 1992).

6.4.2. Sampling with Certainty and with Probability Proportional to Size

In some instances, particular PSUs are so large (i.e., contain such a substantial portion of the population of interest), that an optimal cost-efficient sample requires that they be sampled with certainty. For example, in NAEP's three-stage national sampling design, the 22 largest geographic areas are included with certainty in the sample. These include, for example, the New York metropolitan area (Rust, Krenzke, Qian, & Johnson, 2001, pp. 35–36). Among PSUs not sampled with certainty, strata-specific samples are often assigned a selection probability proportional to their size (PPS), that is, larger PSUs are included with higher probability than smaller PSUs. PPS sampling provides a number of practical and statistical advantages over the more familiar simple random sampling. In NAEP, PPS sampling has been used at the first level of sampling to select geographic regions from noncertainty strata. At the second level of sampling, it was used to choose school samples from each of the chosen PSUs.

6.4.3. Oversampling

The practice of increasing the probability of inclusion in the sample for certain target population groups is referred to as *oversampling*. It is done to produce larger sample sizes than would otherwise occur for groups of particular policy interest. For example, schools with high concentrations of African-American and Hispanic students may be over-sampled to ensure better precision of estimation for those groups than could otherwise be obtained.

6.5. Implementing Sampling Plans for Group-Score Assessments

Unless procedures ensure that samples are representative of their intended populations and are comparable across jurisdictions, the validity of results in general, and in particular of comparisons across jurisdictions, will be diminished. Obtaining comparability of samples is particularly difficult in international comparisons. Critical discussions of sampling practices in international studies have raised a number of issues (Chromy, 2002; Medrich & Griffith, 1992; Prais, 2003). For example, in different countries, children start and leave school at different ages, are subject to different grade progression and tracking policies, and may enter specialized training programs at different ages. In response to criticisms of the early international studies, at least two organizations have published documents that address sample-design issues in comparative educational studies (Bradburn & Gilford, 1990; Martin, Rust, & Adams, 1999). The design and conduct of recent international surveys have attempted to address many of these issues.

The general model that has been followed in recent years by international studies is one in which each of the participating countries may do its own sampling or may have its sample drawn by the study managers or by an independent contractor. Most participants have chosen the first option, and their activities were carried out in accordance with a set of approved procedures and standards. Tools, such as a procedures manual and sampling software, as well as technical assistance are provided to those in each country responsible for sample selection. Each country's sampling practices and outcomes are systematically reviewed by an oversight body. Although important sampling design and implementation issues remain (Prais, 2003), the design and selection of samples in recent international studies have improved markedly from earlier attempts (Chromy, 2002).

6.6. School and Student Nonparticipation

Voluntary group-score assessments face challenges in securing school and student participation. Lack of participation has the potential to undermine the validity and comparability of results by introducing nonresponse bias. To the degree that the schools or students declining to participate differ from participants with respect to group-score outcomes, results from the sample may incorrectly estimate achievement. Differences in the nature and degree of nonparticipation across states and countries threaten the validity of comparisons. Differences in participation over time within a country can pose equally serious threats to the interpretation of trends.

6.6.1. Substitution

Many recent group-score assessments have attempted to address nonresponse issues by permitting the use of substitute schools. In addition to the initial list of sampled schools, sampling experts prepare a second list of schools matched to those in the original sample with respect to sampling frame variables. If the original school refuses to participate, attempts are made to recruit an appropriate substitute for it. Although the use of substitution does not eliminate bias due to nonresponse, if the substitutes are carefully matched to the original participants the extent of nonresponse bias can be reduced, with an additional benefit of maintaining target sample sizes.

6.6.2. Weighting-Class Adjustments

Group-score assessments routinely make use of weighting-class adjustments (Kish, 1965) to attempt to offset the biasing impact of school and student nonresponse. To carry out school-level nonresponse adjustments, all sampled schools (those that did and those that did not agree to participate) are formed into groups, usually on the basis of the school-level stratification variables used in the design. Within each group, the weights for students from participating schools are increased to compensate for the students from schools that did not participate. Similar adjustments are applied to offset student absenteeism and refusal.

6.6.3. Nonresponse

Group-score assessments now routinely report both school and student response rates. Such rates are defined to indicate the percentage of the population directly covered by the sample, prior to any nonresponse adjustments (i.e., the percentage of the population to which, strictly speaking, the results can be generalized absent nonresponse adjustments). Most group-score assessments also suppress or flag data that do not meet defined criteria for response rates.

6.7. Exclusion of Students from Samples

The practice of excluding schools and students from the target population raises additional challenges to the validity of group-score assessment results. For purposes of this discussion, *exclusion* should be understood as different from nonresponse. The latter case involves schools that or students who may be presumed to be conditionally missing at random. Exclusion, on the other hand, involves populations of students (such as those with disabilities) who cannot be meaningfully assessed, in the judgment of school staff, and who should thus be thought of as outside of the target sample. For example, NAEP has permitted sampled schools to exclude students who, in the opinion of officials, could not be tested because of mental or physical disability, or because of limited English proficiency.

During the 1990s, NAEP officials became increasingly aware of potential fairness, validity, and comparability problems associated with exclusion policies. Because NAEP results were supposed to describe the performance of *all* students, increases in the numbers of students with disabilities and English language learners excluded from national NAEP assessments weakened the generalizabilty of results and threatened the comparability of trend comparisons to earlier assessments. This was particularly true as states decided that students could be assessed only with accommodations or adaptations that NAEP did not, at the time, allow. Moreover, throughout the 1990s it became obvious that considerable differences existed across states in the percentages of students with disabilities and English language learners excluded from state NAEP, and that the differences threatened the validity of cross-state comparisons. Some of these differences were due to changes in the populations (e.g., changing numbers of English language learners in states like California and Florida); others were due to differences in identifying students with disabilities and in state policies about allowing accommodations in testing programs.

Beginning in 1995, the NAEP program made changes to its inclusion and accommodations policies. Accommodations were phased in between 1996 and 2002 and are now permitted in all subjects. The NAEP program conducted a series of research studies to quantify and control for the effects of these policy changes (Lutkus, 2004; Lutkus & Mazzeo, 2003; Mazzeo, Carlson, Voelkl, & Lutkus, 2000). Experience with NAEP reading and mathematics assessments after the new procedures were adopted suggests that the changes have reduced the amount of exclusion and induced greater consistency in exclusion rates across states.

Exclusion remains a concern for NAEP, which has sponsored a variety of research studies on these issues. McLaughlin (2001), for example, has conducted a number of innovative analyses that attempt to produce full population estimates reflecting the achievement of both included and excluded students.

7. ITEM-RESPONSE THEORY (IRT) SCALING

7.1. The Role of IRT in Group-Score Assessments[4]

Group-level outcomes for individual items have been and continue to be one of the important ways in which results from group-score assessments are presented (see, for example, Grigg, Daane, Jin, & Campbell, 2003; Silver & Kenney, 2000). Despite the utility of item-level reporting for some purposes, the many ways in which the data from group-score assessments are used require some summary measure of achievement (Linn, 2002). Such summaries are used to compare overall performance levels across states or countries (see, for example, Braswell et al., 2001; Grigg et al., 2003). Summary measures are also useful to researchers interested in examining associations between achievement and a wide range of policy-relevant factors such as student and school demographics, school organization, and teacher instructional practices (Messick, Beaton, & Lord, 1983).

Because of the interest in summary measures, many group-score assessments in earlier periods tried alternatives to simple item-level reporting. For example, before 1984 NAEP (as well as several international surveys) sometimes reported results in terms of simple average percent-correct scores for specific collections of items (Bertrand, Dupuis, Johnson, Blais, & Jones, 1992; Phillips et al., 1993). These early approaches to summary reporting were of limited utility (Beaton & Johnson, 1992). Perhaps the most salient limitation of this approach is that, in matrix sample designs, it is not possible to describe the distribution of performance within and across groups (Phillips et al., 1993).

Today, most group-score assessments employ IRT scaling methods to generate summary measures of achievement. IRT is discussed extensively by Yen and Fitzpatrick (this volume). A single properly executed IRT-based analysis allows the results of all participants to be placed on a common scale, regardless of the particular collection of items individuals received, and allows for the reporting of distributional information, such as the percentages of students at or above particular score values. Moreover, IRT can provide a metric for the reporting scale that is independent of the particular test forms and items included in the assessment (Lord, 1980; Lord & Novick, 1968).

All of the modern national and international surveys use unidimensional IRT measurement models. While many produce multiple scales for a given content area, each item in the assessment is treated as measuring only one of these scales. Adams, Wilson, and Wang (1997) refer to these kinds of measurement models as *multidimensional between-item models*.

Many of the recent group-score assessments are based on instruments that make use of a combination of multiple-choice, dichotomously scored, and polytomously scored constructed-response items. The scales on which results are reported summarize over these different item types (i.e., they do not produce separate scales by item type). A large number of these assessments, including NAEP (Allen, Carlson, Johnson, & Mislevy, 2001), TIMSS-1999 (Yamamoto & Kulick, 2000), PIRLS (Gonzalez, 2003), NALS (Kirsch et al., 2001, chapter 9), IALS (Yamamoto, 1998), have used the same item-scaling models: three-parameter logistic (3PL) for multiple-choice items, two-parameter logistic (2PL) for dichotomous constructed-response items, and generalized partial credit (GPC) for polytomous constructed-response items. Some, like the 1991 PIRLS (Atash & Binkley, 1994), TIMSS-1995 (Adams, Wu, & Macaskill, 1997; Macaskill, Adams, & Wu, 1998), and PISA (Adams, 2002) have used the Rasch model for dichotomously scored items and partial credit (PC) for polytomously scored items.[5]

7.2. Critiques of the Use of IRT in Group-Score Assessments

The use of IRT scaling as the principal basis for summarizing group-score assessment results has critics. For example, Goldstein (2004) and Blum, Goldstein, and Guering-Pace

(2001) have raised concerns about how the assumption of IRT unidimensionality affects the meaningfulness of assessment results. In particular, they question the practice in international assessments of deleting from the scales items that show evidence of differential functioning across countries. Similar concerns are also relevant to group comparisons within national assessments.

Most group-score assessments have responded in some degree to these criticisms by attempting to provide separate scales for various subdomains within a general content area. But such an approach only partly addresses the issue. No single summary measure of a content area can adequately capture all the ways in which different groups and countries differ with respect to achievement (Mislevy, Johnson, & Muraki, 1992).

Brennan (2001) pointed out that each scaling methodology brings with it a set of assumptions and values, frequently masked by the complexities of the methods, and that these assumptions and values have a direct impact on the meaning of the resulting scales. He argued that the assumptions of some scaling procedures, particularly IRT, "can lead to weighting types of items and/or areas of content in a manner that is dramatically different from that intended by the developers of the assessment" (Brennan, p.11).

Despite the acknowledged limitations of IRT scaling, it is indisputable that the use of IRT scaling in group score assessments to produce summary measures is extremely common and has contributed to the growth in utility and visibility of such assessments over the last two decades.

7.3. Establishing IRT-Based Scales for Group-Score Assessments

The application of IRT models to group-score assessments requires estimation of two types of parameters: *item parameters* (e.g., item difficulty and discrimination) and *population parameters* (e.g., scale score means, standard deviations, and percentiles for the different groups for which assessment results are reported). Group-score assessments using IRT models have, to date, taken what Patz and Junker (1999a, 1999b) refer to as a "divide and conquer" strategy; that is, IRT analysis is carried out in two distinct phases.

In the first phase, which is described in this section, item parameters and a limited set of provisional population parameters are jointly estimated. The item parameters establish the scale on which the group-score results will be reported.[6] In the second phase, which is described in section 8, the provisional population parameters are ignored and a second comprehensive set of population parameters is estimated and reported. The item-parameter estimates of the phase 1 set are treated as fixed and known during phase 2 of the analyses. Assessments using the 2PL, 3PL, and GPC models for the most part use some variant of the PARSCALE computer program (Muraki & Bock, 1997), while the more recent assessments based on Rasch and PC models have used the ConQuest software (Wu, Adams, & Wilson, 1997) to obtain their phase-1 item parameter estimates.[7]

All of the group-score assessments have made use of what are typically referred to as *concurrent calibration* strategies to establish and maintain their IRT-based scales.

The most straightforward application of the concurrent calibration strategies involves establishing scales that apply to a single target population group (e.g., fourth-graders in public schools) in a single year. Such situations arise typically in one-time-only group-score assessments or in the initial year of a time series. Examples may be seen in PISA (Adams & Wu, 2002), NAEP (Allen, Carlson, & Zelenak, 1999), TIMSS (Martin & Kelly, 1997, 1998), and PIRLS (Martin et al., 2003).

The test booklets for these assessments were constructed so that at least some portion of the item pool appears in more than one test booklet and each item in the assessment is paired, either directly or indirectly, with every other item in the assessment. This linking system permits the calibration of all the items in the pool on a common IRT scale. This is accomplished by constraining the IRT parameters for the items that appear multiple times to be the same for each of the booklets in which they appear. In other words, only a single set of item parameters is estimated for each item, regardless of the number of booklets in which it appears.

Both the PARSCALE and ConQuest programs use a *marginal maximum likelihood* approach to estimate item parameters (Bock & Aitkin, 1981; Muraki & Bock, 1991). This approach requires that some provisional population model be specified and concurrently estimated along with the item parameters. The assessments noted above have typically specified a single population model. In some cases (e.g., PISA) the normal has been used, whereas in NAEP the multinomial discrete approximation has been the model of choice. It should be noted that both PARSCALE and ConQuest permit the analyst to specify more complicated population structures. For example, separate group distributions could be concurrently estimated for males and females, or for different racial/ethnic groups, with the implied estimate of the overall distribution being a mixture of these separate group distributions. However, theoretical work by Mislevy (1987) and Mislevy and Sheehan (1989) shows that there is little to be gained in the accuracy of item-parameter estimation in designs like these, where the items have been assigned to individuals independent of group membership. Adams, Wilson, and Wu (1997) obtained results in simulation research using Rasch-family measurement models that were consistent with the theoretical results.

7.4. Developmental Scales

Some of the group-score assessments, most notably NAEP in reading and mathematics, have chosen to report the results for students in different grades or at different ages on a common set of "developmental scales." Such scales are used when content from multiple levels of an assessment item pool is viewed as defining a developmental continuum across grades or across ages for a particular area of achievement (Barton & Coley, 1998; Coley, 2003; Petersen, Kolen, & Hoover, 1989).

The establishment of developmental scales in NAEP and other group-score assessments has been based on a concurrent calibration approach. The item pools administered to each of the target populations are constructed so that they share a subset of items (see, for example, Yamamoto & Jenkins, 1992). Developmental scaling is achieved by estimating a single set of parameters for each item in the assessment—both the items unique to a single grade and the items that appear in multiple grades. The use of a common set of item parameters across grades or ages during the proficiency estimation phase of the analysis produces results for the age/grade groups on a common developmental scale.

Of course, it is an assumption that common item-characteristic curves exist for items that appear in multiple age groups. The data from any given assessment may or may not be consistent with this assumption. If the assumption does not hold, the validity of at least some of the comparisons of the performance distributions across the different age group would be suspect. Group-score assessment programs routinely check for the appropriateness of these kinds of assumptions and take appropriate corrective action when necessary.

In the context of group-score assessments, developmental scales have had proponents and critics. Proponents have argued that such scales support useful and meaningful analyses and inferences that are not available when separate scales are used for each level of the assessment. Critics of developmental scales have raised a number of concerns about validity, accuracy, and susceptibility to misinterpretation (Haertel, 1991; Zwick, 1992). Controversy will no doubt continue regarding the technical soundness of developmental scales and the defensibility of interpretations based on such scales. Many national and international group-score assessments use only within-grade scales. Even in subject areas with developmental scales, the scales may have limited use. Official NAEP reports, for example, discuss comparisons of results only within each grade or age level, and current NAEP program policy gives preference to within-grade scaling.

7.5. Maintaining IRT Scales over Time

Several of the national and international group-score assessments measure trends in academic performance. In NAEP and TIMSS, trend measurement is accomplished by comparing successive cohorts of students. Comparing performance over time depends on results from the different assessment years being reported on the same scales.

To ensure valid trend measurement, successive assessments in the time series must have at least some portion of the item pool in common. This design constraint was accomplished in the TIMSS-1995/TIMSS-1999 time series, for example, by reusing the same instrument. In main NAEP, each successive pair of item pools has shared a common set of items. From the standpoint of IRT analysis, a number of strategies are possible for placing multiple years on the same scale (see, for example, Donoghue & Mazzeo, 1992; Hedges & Vevea, 1997; Petersen et al., 1989; and Yamamoto & Mazzeo, 1992).

To date, group-score assessments have typically used a variant of the concurrent calibration approach (similar to that used in building developmental scales) to maintain score scales across years. Specifically, scales have been maintained by conducting an ongoing series of concurrent calibrations, using the data from successive pairs of adjacent years in the time series that share common items and constraining item parameters for each item that was administered in more than one assessment to be equal across the assessments (see Jenkins, Chang, & Kulick, 1999, for an example).

Donoghue and Mazzeo (1992) and Hedges and Vevea (1997) compared the concurrent calibration used for NAEP to some of the alternatives. Both studies suggest the NAEP procedure works well in maintaining the comparability of results across assessment years.

8. MARGINAL ESTIMATION OF GROUP SCALE SCORE RESULTS

8.1. The Need for Marginal Estimation Methods in Group-Score Assessments

Analyses of group-score assessments focus on the estimation of group-level results. Specifically, these results are the group means, percentages at/above specific score levels (e.g., the NAEP achievement levels or the TIMSS international benchmarks), or the parameters of the regression of a latent proficiency variable (e.g., NAEP or TIMSS scale scores) on a collection of independent variables (typically, student, teacher, and school background variables). Virtually all IRT-based group-score assessments use complex *marginal estimation procedures* to obtain assessment results. While such procedures are complex and, in general, less familiar than the IRT procedures used in individual student testing, they are essential to obtain results in the group-score assessment context.

Marginal estimation procedures are sometimes called *direct estimation procedures* because results are derived directly from students' responses to the test items (Mislevy & Sheehan, 1987). No estimates of individual student scores are produced. The need for marginal estimation procedures in the group-score assessment context became apparent with early experiences in applying IRT-based analysis methods in NAEP. The use of IRT scaling as the primary basis for the analysis and reporting of group-score assessment results first occurred with the NAEP assessments of 1984. The plan was to apply IRT to group-score assessment results as it was used in individual student testing (Messick et al., 1983). This proposed analysis approach ran into difficulties almost immediately. One such difficulty was that individual IRT scores for about 15% of the NAEP sample could not be estimated. Furthermore, according to Beaton (1987, p. 231), "the inability to compute a reading score was associated with various background and attitude items; for example, different ethnic groups had different rates of inestimable scores."

The absence of finite estimates of proficiency for substantial portions of the sample was one symptom of a more general problem—measurement error in educational assessment and the inherent potential biases it introduces in estimates of group-level quantities. Using the distribution of individual student-level scores to estimate group-level parameters (such as the percentage of students performing at or above a NAEP achievement level) can result in biased estimates of both group-level results and associations between educational achievement and demographic and educational policy variables. These biases are not mitigated by increases in sample size (Mislevy, 1991).

The impact of measurement error on the accuracy of assessment results is particularly pernicious within the context of group-score assessments that use matrix sampling. In such contexts, the psychometric properties of the individual student scores differ across the numerous test booklets used within an assessment year, as well as over time. These differences in the measurement-error properties of individual-level scores introduce distortions when used as the basis of comparisons of group achievement results within years, comparisons of results for a single group over time, or correlations between achievement and instructional factors.

Such distortions are present to some degree in all testing programs, because all tests imperfectly measure the target proficiency underlying performance. However, in individual-score tests there are relatively few different test forms, each form contains relatively many items, and the test forms are usually constructed to be parallel with respect to their measurement properties. None of these conditions is typical in group-score assessments. The distortions in target statistics that result from the aggregation of imprecise scores, such as those that would result from test lengths like those found in most group-score assessments, are particularly problematic. The marginal estimation approaches used in the vast majority of IRT-based group-score assessments mitigate these distortions and allow for more accurate estimation of group-level results within and across assessment years (see Adams, Wilson, & Wu, 1997; Mislevy, Beaton, Kaplan, & Sheehan, 1992; and Wingersky, Kaplan, & Beaton, 1987).

8.2. How Marginal Estimation in Group-Score Assessments Is Carried Out

Phase 2 analysis for IRT-based group-score assessments, the marginal estimation of group-level results, has been performed similarly in all the major group-score assessment programs. Phase 2 analysis proceeds through two general steps. The first involves marginal estimation of the multiple regression function of the latent variable θ (in the NAEP context, scale scores) on a set of predictor variables χ (school, teacher, and student background variables). The second subphase involves the production of estimates of group-score assessment targets of inference (e.g., subgroup means, standard deviations, percentages above cut points, and percentiles) implied by this regression relationship. Both the estimated regression coefficients and the estimates of residual variance are used in the second subphase to produce the group-level means, standard deviations, percentages above cut points, and percentiles.

The marginal estimation approach described above does not, in general, provide accurate results for groups, unless the regression model explicitly includes the classification variables corresponding to the groups for which results are to be reported among the independent variables. As the number of potential groups of interest is quite large, the number of classification variables required is concomitantly large. As in simple multiple regression situations (i.e., regressions where the predictors and dependent variable are both observed), estimation of highly parameterized models like these is often numerically challenging. Low sample-size-to-predictor-variable ratios, high correlations among the predictor variables, and small variances associated with particular predictors can cause the estimation algorithms to fail and can result in numerical instabilities in the estimation of the regression coefficients.

These challenges have been addressed in NAEP, TIMSS, PIRLS, PISA, and the other IRT-based group-score assessments through the use of principal components regression (Jolliffe, 1986, pp. 129–145). Principal components are linear combinations of the original predictor variables that are uncorrelated and retain the variation present in the variables. Specifically the analysis proceeds by taking principal components of the original set of predictor variables and conducting the estimation using these derived components in place of the original set. In practice, NAEP and the other IRT-based group-score assessments do not use the full set of components. In NAEP and TIMSS, for example, the subset of principal components with the largest variances is used, such that the sum of the variances for this subset is equal to at least 90% of the sum of the variances for the full set. Use of a subset of this size is a practical compromise, arrived at in the early 1990s, with the intention of mitigating estimation problems while maintaining as much of the information in the original contrasts as is practical (Mazzeo, Johnson, Bowker, & Fong, 1992).

All the IRT-based group-score assessments carry out the marginal estimation process—specifically, the conversion of the original predictor variables to principal components, and estimation of the regression—separately for each jurisdiction for which results will be reported. Each of the separate runs is carried out with a common set of item parameters, which ensures that the results for each of the states or countries are expressed on a common scale. Variability by state and country in educational outcomes, and the degree to which such variability can be associated with differences in educational organization and instructional practices, is one of the subjects about which proponents of cross-state and international assessments hope to learn. Both the theory of marginal estimation (Mislevy, 1991) and practical work (Mazzeo et al., 1992) have demonstrated the need to conduct marginal analysis separately in each jurisdiction in order to allow the detection of such differences.

In subphase 2, the estimated regression model is used to derive estimates of the group-level statistics typically reported. For practical reasons NAEP and the other IRT-based group-score assessment programs have relied on a multiple-imputation-based approach modeled after the missing-data procedures of Little and Rubin (1987) to carry out subphase 2 and to generate their official reported statistics. Historically, these imputations have been referred to in NAEP as *plausible values* (PVs). Coupled with the weighting procedures used by NAEP's sampling contractor, plausible values can support a unified approach to both point estimation and standard error calculations for a variety of different types of statistics and for the large array of potential reporting groups.

Plausible values (PVs) are random draws from the subphase 1 model-implied distribution of scale scores for each examinee. Following Rubin (1987), NAEP takes five sets of draws (a set consists of one draw for each individual). The PVs are then used to calculate the needed estimates of group means, standard deviations, achievement-level percentages, correlations, and a large number of other potential statistics of interest.

The use of PVs has been questioned on "equity" grounds, because the model-implied distribution for each examinee from which the plausible values are sampled depends on student background characteristics as well as on student responses to the test items. In the context of individual student testing, it would be inappropriate to have a student's test score depend on any influence beyond his or her responses to the test items. It cannot be emphasized enough, however, that plausible values are *not* scores for individual students. They are intermediate calculations that, when properly analyzed, provide marginal estimates of group-level statistics. A number of studies (e.g., Adams, Wilson, & Wu, 1997; Cohen & Jiang, 2002) demonstrate that the PV approximations work well in reproducing the directly calculated marginal estimates of group-level statistics.

9. LINKING RESULTS FROM DIFFERENT ASSESSMENTS

9.1. Linking NAEP, IAEP, and TIMSS

There has been a good deal of interest since the early 1990s in linking the results of various national and international group-score assessments. (For general information about the types of linking that are possible see Kolen & Brennan, 2004; Linn, 1993; Mislevy, 1992; and von Davier, Holland, & Thayer, 2004.) Considerable effort has been expended in attempting to establish links between the NAEP mathematics and science assessments and international assessments in the corresponding subjects, specifically the IAEP and TIMSS assessments. The interest in such links is twofold: examining the performance of foreign students in relation to NAEP achievement levels, and comparing the performance of the various states and jurisdictions that participate in NAEP to that of the countries that have participated in the international assessments.

Two of the earliest of these studies established links between the NAEP grade 8 mathematics assessments and the IAEP mathematics assessments administered to 13-year-olds (Beaton & Gonzalez, 1993; Pashley & Phillips, 1993). Because the instruments being linked were highly similar in content, were low-stakes assessments designed for group-level reporting, and used similar scaling and proficiency estimation methodologies, the results of the linking were useful. However, the authors of both studies urge caution in using linked scores. Beaton and Gonzalez emphasize that different methods of linking produce somewhat different results. Pashley and Phillips caution that there is no guarantee that the relationship established in their study would hold in subsequent years, or that use of their methodologies with less closely related tests would provide satisfactory results. For details of more recent linking studies see Johnson and Owen (1998) and Johnson, Cohen, Chen, Jiang, and Zhang (in press).

9.2. Linking NAEP with State Tests and ASVAB

Researchers have attempted to link results from state tests to NAEP to provide estimates of results at the student, school, and district levels, and to produce state-level results for years in which NAEP was not administered (Williams, Billeaud, Davis, Thissen, & Sanford, 1995). Despite the desire to link state tests and NAEP (Feuer, Holland, Green, Bertenthal, & Hemphill, 1999), few efforts to do so have produced satisfactory results, particularly when the focus was on producing student-level scores. Differences in test content, test format, reliability, and test-taker motivation make such linking difficult to carry out successfully. For details, see Bloxom, Pashley, Nicewander, and Yan (1995); Ercikan (1997); Feuer et al. (1999); Linn and Kiplinger (1995); McLaughlin (1998); McLaughlin and Bandiera de Mello (2002, 2003); Qian and Braun (2004); Waltman (1997); and Williams et al. (1995).

10. REPORTING RESULTS FROM GROUP-SCORE ASSESSMENTS

Addressing the interests and needs of different audiences requires a variety of reports (see http://nces.ed.gov/nations reportcard/ for examples of the types of reports described in this section). Primary reports, available in print and on the Internet, typically contain basic summary results such as overall average scores and percentages reaching achievement levels or international benchmarks. Scores are reported for major subsets of the population, including states and countries and their major demographic groups (see Braswell, Daane, & Grigg, 2003; Donahue, Daane, & Grigg, 2003).

Group-score assessment programs have developed specialized tools and products that provide detailed access to their results. For example, NAEP has developed a "NAEP Questions Tool" (http://nces.ed.gov/nationsreportcard/ itmrls), which provides access to a large collection of sample items. Interested parties can review these sample items, with associated constructed-response scoring guides, and have simultaneous access to detailed item-level performance data for the nation, for states, and for a variety of demographic subgroups. Both NAEP and TIMSS now also provide online data analysis capabilities that allow users to create customized data displays. Finally, most of the group-score assessment programs produce public or restricted-use data files, statistical tools, and software designed to support analyses by independent researchers.

10.1. Encouraging Valid Inferences and Comparisons

The results of group-score assessments are subject to uncertainties because of the use of student and item sampling. Virtually all these surveys include estimates of the standard errors of reported statistics somewhere in their reporting systems.

While standard errors are available, an important reporting challenge is encouraging the users of the data to take error into account when interpreting results. For example, in cross-state and international surveys, there is considerable interest in the "horse race" aspect of the assessment results. (Did eighth-grade students in Texas "beat" eighth-grade students in California in mathematics?) Setting aside questions about the meaningfulness of such comparisons, it is necessary to take error into account when interpreting rankings. The official reports issued by the sponsors of group-score assessments typically use formal statistical tests to determine which differences will be discussed and how they will be described. For example, reports may restrict their discussion of group differences to those that are statistically significant, or use alternative displays that discourage inappropriate inferences by going beyond simple rank-ordered lists of groups, states, or countries.

10.2. Imparting Meaning to Scales

Norm-referenced interpretations of assessment results are useful, but limited. They do not provide information about what students know, nor whether the achievement is at a level that policymakers, educators, and the public consider acceptable. Group-score assessment programs have taken various approaches to impart such meaning to their scales. One common practice is to include *item maps*, displays that show item descriptions at positions along the scale at points where students have a high likelihood of success on the item (see, for example, Grigg et al., 2003; Kirsch et al., 1993.)

The numbers of items that can be displayed on an item map are limited, and the choice of a percent correct required to indicate "high likelihood of success" is necessarily arbitrary and varies in different group-score assessments (Kolstad et al., 2001). Unfortunately, many people interpret the charts as indicating what students at certain score levels can and cannot do, rather than what students at different score levels are more or less likely to be able to do.

A second method of imparting meaning to scales is anchoring. Scale anchoring has both statistical and judgmental components (Beaton & Allen, 1992). Specific score locations, referred to as *anchor levels*, are selected for description. Data from a particular assessment year are analyzed to identify a set of anchor items associated with each level. The items must be correctly answered by most of the assessed students at the associated anchor level, but answered correctly by relatively few students at the anchor level below it. The anchor items are examined by content specialists who develop descriptions of the knowledge and skills demonstrated by students at each of the levels. In addition, the committees select exemplar items for each level. Expressing group-score assessment results in terms of anchor levels typically involves reporting the percentages of students at or above each of the anchor levels, along with the content descriptions. (For examples, see Beaton & Allen, 1992; Campbell, Hombo, & Mazzeo, 2000; and Lapointe, Mead, & Phillips, 1989.)

The use of anchor-level reporting has been criticized for not yielding valid criterion-related inferences when applied to certain domains (Forsyth, 1991). Linn and Dunbar (1992) expressed concern that it is difficult for the press and the public to grasp the distinction between the percentage of students at/above an anchor level and the percentage of students at each anchor level who successfully complete an item. Furthermore, statistical criteria for anchor items are arbitrary, and the anchor-level descriptions may not generalize across different committees used to write the descriptions.

Achievement levels or standards are yet another method used to give meaning to scales. In 1988, NAEP reauthorization legislation assigned to the National Assessment Governing Board (NAGB) the responsibility to identify "appropriate achievement goals" for each grade and assessment. NAGB operationalized this directive by establishing *achievement levels* (performance standards) for each of the main NAEP subject areas, beginning with the mathematics assessments in 1990 (Loomis & Bourque, 2001).

The goal of having achievement levels is to set performance standards for what students should know and should be able to do. NAGB has established three achievement levels: *Basic*, *Proficient*, and *Advanced*. To date, the setting of standards (cut scores) to define achievement levels operationally for NAEP has been carried out primarily using variations of the Angoff method (Angoff, 1971; see Reckase, 2000, for a description of the evolution of the NAEP standard-setting process.)

The use of achievement levels in NAEP has been controversial. Some of the early debate focused on the concern that a federally sponsored program to establish achievement goals and performance standards might lead to a federal curriculum. (See Vinovskis, 1998, for a history of NAGB's early standard-setting activities.) More recently, much of the debate has centered on the technical issues associated with the standard-setting process used, and whether or not the resulting standards represent reasonable expectations for student performance (see, for example, Glaser, Linn, & Bohrnstedt, 1993; Linn, Baker, & Dunbar, 1991; Pellegrino, Jones, & Mitchell, 1999; Stuffelbeam, Jaeger, & Scriven, 1991; U.S. General Accounting Office, 1993; for more favorable views of the standards, see, e.g., Brennan, 1998; Cizek, 1993; Hambleton et al., 2000; Kane, 1993; Mehrens, 1995; National Assessment Governing Board and National Center for Education Statistics, 1995; and Pellegrino, 2000).

Despite the controversies, achievement-level results are featured prominently in NAEP reports. With the passage of NCLB in 2002, virtually all states adopted performance standards for use in reporting their state testing programs. However, despite their widespread use in U.S. testing programs, they have not been applied in international surveys.

These international surveys have often used *benchmarking* approaches to impart meaning to scales. One commonly used approach is to select cases of agreed-upon high achievement (e.g., the average score of the highest performing state or country) and to show where that level of achievement would fall on the scale. Other groups can then compare their results to this established benchmark (see Martin et al., 2001, pp. 55–92, and Mullis et al., 2001, pp. 55–90, for examples).

10.3. Effectiveness of Reports of Group-Score Assessment Results

Much of the work that has been done to date on the effectiveness of group-score assessment score reports has focused on NAEP reporting practices. Hambleton and Slater (1996) investigated the extent to which executive summaries of the NAEP 1992 mathematics report cards (Mullis, Dossey, Owen, & Phillips, 1993) communicated with intended audiences. Considerable confusion was evident about the meaning of statistical terms such as "standard error," "statistically significant," and "confidence interval." The use of cumulants (i.e., percentages at or above a given score point) to report achievement levels also caused confusion, as did the design and layout of specific displays included in the reports. Hambleton and Slater made recommendations for improving reports, including simplification of tables and figures, focus-group testing of graphs, figures, and tables prior to their inclusion, reduction of jargon, and provision of glossaries.

Wainer, Hambleton, and Meara (1999), extending the work of Hambleton and Slater (1996) and earlier work by Wainer (1997a, 1997b), conducted a study using displays from the 1994 NAEP Reading Report Card (Williams et al., 1995). Several displays used in NAEP reports were redesigned as a result of this research. For example, NAEP tables and graphs in recent reports have been simplified (e.g., Grigg et al., 2003), standard errors have been removed from tables (e.g., Braswell et al., 2001), and shorter special-purpose publications for a more general audience have been designed, such as the NAEP highlight reports (Braswell et al., 2003; Donahue et al., 2003).

11. SOME CURRENT CHALLENGES

Group-score assessments in the United States are under increasing scrutiny because of their role in accountability systems. Discrepancies between the results of state assessments and NAEP will add new consequences or "stakes" to state NAEP results. One concern is that the new pressure on educators to raise NAEP scores (as distinct from raising real achievement) may lower NAEP's validity. Another concern is that the increased mandatory testing required for accountability has made schools less likely to participate in voluntary testing. Programs such as PISA and PIRLS and the NAEP subjects not mandated by NCLB have had increasing difficulty recruiting samples of test-takers in the United States. Weak response rates will continue to threaten validity.

The diversity of populations in the United States complicates the study of differences in educational performance. Whether or not to "standardize" populations for demographic differences before comparing scores has become controversial. Finn (2004), for example, called adjustments for demographics and economic status "bizarre." Wainer (1994), and Wainer and Saka (1994), on the other hand, argued for demographic adjustments to compare how groups of students in various jurisdictions would have performed if their demographics had matched those of the United States as a whole. To avoid even the appearance of deceit, NAGB passed a policy forbidding the prime contractor to make adjustments of the type proposed by Wainer and Saka.

Changes in disciplines complicate the study of trends in educational performance. To study trends, it is important to keep the assessment constant (Beaton & Zwick, 1990), but to maintain validity the assessment should be congruent with current educational practices. For example, in 1984 few fourth-grade students used a computer as a writing tool. In 2002, well over half of the students assessed in writing did so. At some point, the validity of a trend line based on a paper-and-pencil assessment of writing will become questionable.

Moving from paper and pencil to computer-based testing is unavoidable. Though the shift may cause some complications (Sandene et al., 2005), computer-based testing will certainly increase the efficiency and flexibility of group-score assessments (Bock & Zimowski, 1998). Computer-based testing will at some point become cheaper than paper-and-pencil testing, and the use of paper and pencil for assessment will become anachronistic.

NOTES

1. Most of the chapter is accessible to readers with no specialized knowledge. The sections on item-response theory and marginal estimation procedures, however, assume that the reader has some familiarity with statistical concepts.
2. Writing will not be included in the 2007 state-level assessment at grade 4. It may be included in later assessments.
3. The distinction between assessment "frameworks" and "specifications" is not entirely clear, and at times the terms are used interchangeably. In the case of NAEP, frameworks are brief documents that are meant to communicate the content domain to the public. Assessment specifications are more fully articulated documents that give specific and detailed meaning to the general content and skills categories described in the framework.
4. Group-score assessments use item analysis for quality control purposes, and conduct DIF analyses. However, these are not different from approaches used in individual-score tests, so are not discussed here.
5. These scaling models can also be described equivalently as specific instances of the more general random coefficients multinomial logit models presented by Adams and Wilson (1996) and Adams, Wilson, and Wang (1997).
6. Of course, the actual reporting scales of most assessments involve some form of linear transformation of the scales implied by the phase-1 item parameter estimates. Because the IRT scales are indeterminant up to a linear transformation, results on the transformed scales are essentially identical to those implied by the original scaling.
7. The NAEP and recent TIMSS assessments make use of a specialized BILOG/PARSCALE program, which combines Mislevy and Bock's (1982) BILOG and Muraki and Bock's (1991) PARSCALE programs, and which has been adapted to make use of student sampling weights. This NAEP/BILOG/PARSCALE program was developed by ETS solely for its own use under a licensing agreement with the publishers of BILOG and PARSCALE, Scientific Software Incorporated.

REFERENCES

Adams, R. (2002). Scaling PISA cognitive data. In R. Adams & M. Wu (Eds.), *PISA 2000 technical report* (pp. 99–108). Paris: OECD.

Adams, R. J., & Wilson, M. R. (1996). Formulating the Rasch model as a mixed coefficients multinomial logit. In G. Engelhard & M. Wilson (Eds.), *Objective measurement: Theory into practice* (Vol. 3, pp. 143–166). Norwood, NJ: Ablex.

Adams, R. J., Wilson, M., & Wang, W. (1997). The multidimensional random coefficients multinomial logit model. *Applied Psychological Measurement, 21,* 1–23.

Adams, R. J., Wilson, M., & Wu, M. (1997). Multilevel item response models: An approach to errors in variables regression. *Journal of Educational and Behavioral Statistics, 22,* 47–76.

Adams, R. J., & Wu, M. (2002). *PISA 2000 technical report.* Paris: OECD.

Adams, R. J., Wu, M. L., & Macaskill, G. (1997). Scaling methodology and procedures for the mathematics and science scales. In M. O. Martin & D. L. Kelly (Eds.), *Third International Mathematics and Science Study technical report, volume II: Implementation and analysis—primary and middle school years* (pp. 111–146). Chestnut Hill, MA: Boston College, Center for the Study of Testing, Evaluation, and Educational Policy.

Allen, N. L., Carlson, J. E., & Donoghue, J. R. (2001). Overview of part I: The design and implementation of the 1998 NAEP. In N. L. Allen, J. R. Donoghue, & T. L. Schoeps (Eds.), *The NAEP 1998 technical report* (NCES 2001–509, pp. 5–23). Washington, DC: U.S. Department of Education, Office of Educational Research and Improvement, National Center for Education Statistics.

Allen, N. L., Carlson, J. E., Johnson, E. G., & Mislevy, R. J. (2001). Scaling procedures. In N. L. Allen, J. R. Donoghue, & T. L. Schoeps (Eds.), *The NAEP 1998 technical report* (NCES 2001–509, pp. 227–254). Washington, DC: U.S. Department of Education, Office of Educational Research and Improvement, National Center for Education Statistics.

Allen, N. L., Carlson, J. E., & Zelenak, C. A. (1999). *The NAEP 1996 technical report* (NCES 1999–452). Washington, DC: U.S. Department of Education, Office of Educational Research and Improvement, National Center for Education Statistics.

Angoff, W. H. (1971). Scales, norms, and equivalent scores. In R. L. Thorndike (Ed.), *Educational measurement* (2nd ed., pp. 508–600). Washington, DC: American Council on Education.

Atash, N., & Binkley, M. (1994). The scaling procedures. In M. Binkley & K. Rust (Eds.), *Reading literacy in the United States: Technical report* (NCES 94–259). Washington, DC: U.S. Department of Education, National Center for Education Statistics.

Barton, P. E., & Coley, R. J. (1998). *Growth in school: Achievement gains from the fourth to eighth grade.* Princeton, NJ: Educational Testing Service, Policy Information Center.

Bay, L., Chen, L., Hanson, B. A., Happel, J., Kolen, M. J., Miller, T., et al. (1997). *ACT's NAEP redesign project: Assessment design is the key to useful and stable assessment results* (Working Paper No. 97-30). Washington, DC: U.S. Department of Education, National Center for Education Statistics.

Beaton, A. E. (1987, March). *Implementing the new design: The NAEP 1983–84 Technical Report* (NAEP Tech. Rep. No. 15-TR-20). Princeton, NJ: Educational Testing Service.

Beaton, A. E., & Allen, N. (1992). Interpreting scales through scale anchoring. *Journal of Educational Statistics, 17,* 191–204.

Beaton, A. E., & Gonzalez, E. J. (1993). Comparing the NAEP trial state assessment results with the IAEP international results. In L. Shepard, R. Glaser, R. Linn, & G. Bohrnstedt (Eds.), *Setting performance standards for student achievement: Background studies* (pp. 171–180). Stanford, CA: National Academy of Education.

Beaton, A. E., & Johnson, E. G. (1992). Overview of scaling methodology used in the national assessment. *Journal of Educational Measurement, 29,* 163–175.

Beaton, A. E., & Zwick, R. (1990, February). *Disentangling the NAEP 1985–86 reading anomaly* (NAEP Rep. No. 17-TR-21). Princeton, NJ: Educational Testing Service.

Bertrand, R., Dupuis, F. A., Johnson, E. G., Blais, J. G., & Jones, R. (1992). *IAEP technical report Part III: Data analysis.* Princeton, NJ: Educational Testing Service.

Bloxom, B., Pashley, P. J., Nicewander, W. A., & Yan, D. (1995). Linking to a large scale assessment: An empirical evaluation. *Journal of Educational and Behavioral Statistics, 20,* 1–26.

Blum, A., Goldstein, H., & Guering-Pace, F. (2001). International adult literacy survey (IALS): An analysis of international comparisons of adult literacy. *Assessment in Education: Principles, Policy & Practice, 8,* 225–246.

Bock, R. D., & Aitkin, M. (1981). Marginal maximum likelihood estimation of item parameters: An application of the EM algorithm. *Psychometrika, 46,* 443–459.

Bock, R. D., & Zimowski, M. F. (1998). *Feasibility of two-stage testing in large-scale educational assessment: Implications for NAEP.* Palo Alto, CA: American Institutes for Research.

Bradburn, N. M., & Gilford, D. M. (Eds.). (1990). *A framework and principles for international comparative studies in education.* Board on International Comparative Studies in Education, Commission on Behavioral and Social Sciences and Education, National Research Council. Washington, DC: National Academy Press.

Braswell, J., Daane, M., & Grigg, W. (2003). *The nation's report card: Mathematics highlights 2003* (NCES 2004-451). Washington, DC: U.S. Department of Education, Institute of Education Sciences, National Center for Education Statistics.

Braswell, J. S., Lutkus, A. D., Grigg, W. S., Santapau, S., Tay-Lim, B., & Johnson, M. (2001). *The nation's report card: Mathematics 2000* (NCES 2001-517). Washington, DC: U.S. Department of Education, Office of Educational Research and Improvement, National Center for Education Statistics.

Brennan, R. L. (1998). Misconceptions at the intersection of measurement, theory and practice. *Educational Measurement: Issues and Practice, 17*(1), 5–9, 30.

Brennan, R. L. (2001). Some problems, pitfalls and paradoxes in educational measurement. *Educational Measurement: Issues and Practice, 20*(4), 6–17.

Campbell, J. R., & Donahue, P. L. (1997). *Students selecting stories: The effects of choice in reading assessment: Results from The NAEP Reader special study of the 1994 National Assessment of Educational Progress* (NCES 97-491). Washington, DC: U.S. Department of Education, Office of Educational Research and Improvement, National Center for Education Statistics.

Campbell, J. R., Hombo, C. M., & Mazzeo, J. (2000, August). *NAEP 1999 trends in academic progress: Three decades of student performance* (NCES 2000-469). Washington, DC: U.S. Department of Education, Office of Educational Research and Improvement, National Center for Education Statistics.

Chromy, J. R. (2002). Sampling issues in design, conduct, and interpretation of international comparative studies of school achievement. In A. C. Porter & A. Gamoran (Eds.), *Methodological advances in cross-national surveys of achievement* (pp. 80–114). Washington, DC: National Research Council, Board on Testing and Assessment, Center for Education, Division of Behavioral and Social Sciences and Education, National Academy Press.

Cizek, G. J. (1993). *Reaction to the National Academy of Education report,* Setting performance standards for student achievement. Washington, DC: National Assessment Governing Board.

Cohen, J., & Jiang, T. (2002). *Direct estimation of statistics for the National Assessment of Educational Progress (NAEP).*

Unpublished paper. Washington, DC: American Institutes for Research.
Cohen, S. (Ed.). (1974). *Education in the United States: A documentary history*. New York: Random House.
Coley, R. J. (2003). *Growth in school revisited: Achievement gains from the fourth to the eighth grade*. Princeton, NJ: Educational Testing Service, Policy Information Center.
Daane, M. C., Campbell, J. R., Grigg, W. S., Goodman, M. J., & Oranje, A. (in press). *Fourth-grade students reading aloud: NAEP 2002 special study of oral reading*. Washington, DC: U.S. Department of Education, Institute of Education Sciences, National Center for Education Statistics.
von Davier, A. A., Holland, P. W., & Thayer, D. T. (2004). *The kernel method of test equating*. New York: Springer-Verlag.
Donahue, P., Daane, M., & Grigg, W. (2003). *The nation's report card: Reading highlights 2003* (NCES 2004-452). Washington, DC: U.S. Department of Education, Institute of Education Sciences, National Center for Education Statistics.
Donoghue, J. R., & Mazzeo, J. (1992, April). *Comparing IRT-based equating procedures for trend measurement in a complex test design*. Paper presented at the annual meeting of the National Council on Measurement in Education, San Francisco.
Ercikan, K. (1997). Linking statewide tests to the National Assessment of Educational Progress: Accuracy of combining test results across states. *Applied Measurement in Education, 10*, 145–159.
Feuer, M. J., Holland, P. W., Green, B. F., Bertenthal, M. W., & Hemphill, F. C. (Eds.). (1999). *Uncommon measures: Equivalence and linkage among educational tests*. Board on Testing and Assessment, Commission on Behavioral and Social Sciences and Education, National Research Council. Washington, DC: National Academy Press.
Finn, C. E., Jr. (2004, February 2). Education in urban America. *Hoover Institution weekly essays*. Retrieved April 23, 2004, from http://www-hoover.stanford.edu/pubaffairs/we/2004/finn02.html
Forsyth, R. A. (1991). Do NAEP scales yield valid criterion-referenced interpretations? *Educational Measurement: Issues and Practice, 10*(3), 3–9, 16.
Glaser, R. G., & Baxter, G. P. (2000). *Assessing active knowledge* (CSE Tech. Rep. No. 516). Los Angeles: University of California, National Center for Research on Evaluation, Standards, and Student Testing.
Glaser, R., Linn, R., & Bohrnstedt, G. (1993). *The trial state assessment: Prospects and realities. The third report of the National Academy of Education panel on the evaluation of the NAEP trial state assessment: 1992 trial state assessment*. New York: The National Academy of Education.
Goldstein, H. (2004). International comparisons of student attainment: Some issues arising from the PISA study. *Assessment in Education: Principles, Policy and Practice, 11*, 319–330.
Gonzalez, E. (2003). Scaling the PIRLS reading assessment data. In M. O. Martin, I. V. S. Mullis, & A. M. Kennedy (Eds.), *PIRLS 2001 technical report* (pp. 151–168). Chestnut Hill, MA: Boston College, Lynch School of Education, International Study Center.
Goodman, M., Lazer, S., Mazzeo, J., Mead, N., & Pearlmutter, A. (1998, September). *1994 NAEP U.S. history group assessment* (NCES 98-533). Washington, DC: U.S. Department of Education, Office of Educational Research and Improvement, National Center for Educational Statistics.
Grigg, W. S., Daane, M. C., Jin, Y., & Campbell, J. R. (2003). *The nation's report card: Reading 2002* (NCES 2003-521). Washington, DC: U.S. Department of Education, Institute of Education Sciences, National Center for Education Statistics.

Haertel, E. H. (1991, October 29). *Report of the TRP analyses of issues concerning within-age versus cross-age scales for the National Assessment of Educational Progress*. Washington, DC: National Center for Education Statistics. (ERIC Document Reproduction Service No. ED404367)
Hambleton, R. K., Brennan, R. L., Brown, W., Dodd, B., Forsyth, R. A., Mehrens, W. A., et al. (2000). A response to "Setting reasonable and useful performance standards" in the National Academy of Sciences' *Grading the nation's report card*. *Educational Measurement: Issues and Practice, 19*(2), 5–14.
Hambleton, R. K., & Slater, S. (1996, April). *Are NAEP executive summary reports understandable to policymakers and educators?* Paper presented at the annual meeting of the National Council on Measurement in Education, New York.
Hawkins, E., Stancavage, F., Mitchell, J., Goodman, M., & Lazer, S. (1998). *Learning about our world and our past: Using the tools and resources of geography and U.S. history* (NCES 98-518). Washington, DC: U.S. Department of Education, Office of Educational Research and Improvement, National Center for Education Statistics.
Hedges, L. V., & Vevea, J. L. (1997). *A study of equating in NAEP*. Palo Alto, CA: American Institutes for Research.
Jenkins, F., Chang, H.-H., & Kulick, E. (1999). Data analysis for the mathematics assessment. In N. L. Allen, J. E. Carlson, & C. A. Zelenak (Eds.), *The NAEP 1996 technical report* (NCES 1999-452, pp. 255–289). Washington, DC: U.S. Department of Education, Office of Educational Research and Improvement, National Center for Education Statistics.
Johnson, E. G., Cohen, J., Chen, W.-H., Jiang, T., & Zhang, Y. (in press). *2000 NAEP–1999 TIMSS linking report*. Washington, DC: National Center for Education Statistics.
Johnson, E. G., & Owen, E. (1998). *Linking the National Assessment of Educational Progress (NAEP) and the Third International Mathematics and Science Study (TIMSS): A technical report* (NCES 98-499). Washington DC: National Center for Education Statistics, Office of Educational Research and Improvement, U.S. Department of Education.
Johnson, E. G., & Rust, K. F. (1992). Population inferences and variance estimation for NAEP data. *Journal of Educational Statistics, 17*, 175–190.
Jolliffe, I. T. (1986). *Principal component analysis*. New York, NY: Springer-Verlag.
Jones, L. V. & Olkin, I. (2004). *The nation's report card: Evolution and perspectives*. Bloomington, IN: Phi Delta Kappa Educational Foundation.
Kane, M. (1993). *Comments on the NAE evaluation of the NAGB achievement levels*. Washington, DC: National Assessment Governing Board.
Kirsch, I. (2001). *The international adult literacy survey (IALS): Understanding what was measured* (RR 01-25). Princeton, NJ: Educational Testing Service.
Kirsch, I. S., & Jungeblut, A. (1986). *Literacy: Profiles of America's young adults* (Report No. 16-PL-02). Princeton, NJ: Educational Testing Service.
Kirsch, I. S., Jungeblut, A., Jenkins, L., & Kolstad, A. (1993). *Adult literacy in America: A first look at the results of the National Adult Literacy Survey* (NCES 93-275). Washington, DC: U.S. Department of Education, Office of Educational Research and Improvement, National Center for Education Statistics.
Kirsch, I., Yamamoto, K., Norris, N., Rock, D., Jungeblut, A., O'Reilly, P., et al. (2001). *Technical report and data file user's manual for the 1992 National Adult Literacy Survey* (NCES 2001-457). Washington, DC: U.S. Department of Education,

Office of Educational Research and Improvement, National Center for Education Statistics.

Kish, L. (1965). *Survey sampling*. New York: John Wiley & Sons.

Kolen, M. J., & Brennan, R. L. (2004). *Test equating, scaling, and linking: Methods and practices* (2nd ed.) New York: Springer-Verlag.

Kolstad, A., Cohen, J., Baldi, S., Chan, T., DeFur, E., & Angeles, J. (2001, October). *The response probability convention used in reporting data from IRT assessment scales: Should NCES adopt a standard?* (Working Paper No. 2001-20). Washington, DC: U.S. Department of Education, Office of Educational Research and Improvement, National Center for Education Statistics.

Lapointe, A. E., Mead, N. A., & Phillips, G. W. (1989). *A world of differences: An international assessment of mathematics and science* (Rep. No. 19-CAEP-01). Princeton, NJ: Educational Testing Service.

Lazer, S. (1999). Assessment instruments. In N. L. Allen, J. E. Carlson, & C. A. Zelenak (Eds.), *The NAEP 1996 technical report* (NCES 1999-452, pp. 75–95). Washington, DC: U.S. Department of Education, Office of Educational Research and Improvement, National Center for Education Statistics.

Lazer, S., Mislevy, R. J., Whittington, K., & Ward, W. C. (1997). Measuring cognitive skills. In E. G. Johnson, S. Lazer, & C. Y. O'Sullivan (Eds.), *NAEP reconfigured: An integrated redesign of the National Assessment of Educational Progress* (pp. 4-2–4-52). Princeton, NJ: Educational Testing Service.

Linn, R. L. (1993). Linking results of distinct assessments. *Applied Measurement in Education, 6*, 83–102.

Linn, R. L. (2002). The measurement of student achievement in international studies. In A. C. Porter & A. Gamoran (Eds.), *Methodological advances in cross-national surveys of educational achievement* (pp. 25–57). Washington, DC: National Academy Press.

Linn, R. L., Baker, E. L., & Dunbar, S. B. (1991). Complex, performance-based assessment: Expectations and validation criteria. *Educational Researcher, 20*(8), 15–21.

Linn, R. L., & Dunbar, S. B. (1992). Issues in the design and reporting of the National Assessment of Educational Progress. *Journal of Educational Measurement, 29*, 177–194.

Linn, R. L., & Kiplinger, V. L. (1995). Linking statewide tests to the National Assessment of Educational Progress: Stability of results. *Applied Measurement in Education, 8*, 135–156.

Little, R., & Rubin, D. (1987). *Statistical analysis with missing data*. New York: Wiley.

Loomis, S. C., & Bourque, M. L. (2001). *National Assessment of Educational Progress achievement levels, 1992–1998 for reading*. Washington, DC: National Assessment Governing Board.

Lord, F. M. (1980). *Applications of item response theory to practical testing problems*. Hillsdale, NJ: Erlbaum.

Lord, F. M., & Novick, M. R. (1968). *Statistical theories of mental test scores*. Reading, MA: Addison-Wesley.

Lutkus, A. D. (2004, March). *Including special-needs students in the NAEP 1998 reading assessment: Part II. Results for students with disabilities and limited-English-proficient students* (ETS NAEP Report No. 04-R01). Princeton, NJ: Educational Testing Service.

Lutkus, A. D., & Mazzeo, J. (2003, February). *Including special-needs students in the NAEP reading assessment: Part I. Comparison of overall results with and without accommodations* (NCES 2003-467). Washington, DC: U.S. Department of Education, Institute of Education Sciences, National Center for Education Statistics.

Macaskill, G., Adams, R. J., & Wu, M. L. (1998). Scaling methodology and procedures for the mathematics and science literacy, advanced mathematics, and physics scales. In M. O. Martin & D. L. Kelly (Eds.), *Third International Mathematics and Science Study technical report, volume III: Implementation and analysis—final year of secondary school* (pp. 91–120). Chestnut Hill, MA: Boston College, Center for the Study of Testing, Evaluation, and Educational Policy.

Martin, M. O., & Kelly, D. L. (1997). *Third International Mathematics and Science Study technical report, volume II: Implementation and analysis—primary and middle school years*. Chestnut Hill, MA: Boston College, Center for the Study of Testing, Evaluation, and Educational Policy.

Martin, M. O., & Kelly, D. L. (1998). *Third International Mathematics and Science Study technical report, volume III: Implementation and analysis—final year of secondary school*. Chestnut Hill, MA: Boston College, Center for the Study of Testing, Evaluation, and Educational Policy.

Martin, M. O., Mullis, I. V. S., Gonzalez, E. J., O'Connor, K. M., Chrostowski, S. J., & Smith, T. A. (2001). *Science Benchmarking Report-TIMSS 1999-Eighth grade*. Chestnut Hill, MA: Boston College, The International Study Center.

Martin, M. O., Mullis, I. V. S., & Kennedy, A. M. (Eds.). (2003). *PIRLS 2001 technical report*. Chestnut Hill, MA: Boston College.

Martin, M. O., Rust, K., & Adams, R. (1999). *Technical standards for IEA studies*. Amsterdam: IEA.

Mazzeo, J., Carlson, J. E., Voelkl, K. E., & Lutkus, A. D. (2000). *Increasing the participation of special needs students in NAEP: A report on 1996 NAEP research activities* (NCES 2000-473). Washington, DC: U.S. Department of Education, Office of Educational Research and Development, National Center for Education Statistics.

Mazzeo, J., Johnson, E., Bowker, D., & Fong, Y. F. (1992, April). *The use of collateral information in proficiency estimation for the trial state assessment*. Paper presented at the annual meeting of the American Educational Research Association, San Francisco.

Mazzeo, J., Yamamoto, K., & Kulick, E. (1993, April). *Extended constructed-response items in the 1992 NAEP: Psychometrically speaking, were they worth the price?* Paper presented at the National Council on Measurement in Education, Atlanta, GA.

McLaughlin, D. (1998). *Study of the linkages of 1996 NAEP and state mathematics assessments in four states: Final report*. Palo Alto, CA: John C. Flanagan Research Center, Education Statistics Services Institute, American Institutes for Research.

McLaughlin, D. H. (2001). *Exclusions and accommodations affect state NAEP gain statistics: Mathematics, 1996 to 2000* (Report to the NAEP Validity Studies Panel). Palo Alto, CA: American Institutes for Research.

McLaughlin, D., & Bandeira de Mello, V. (2002, April). *Comparison of state elementary school mathematics achievement standards, using NAEP 2000*. Paper presented at the annual meeting of the American Educational Research Association, New Orleans, LA.

Medrich, E. A., & Griffith, J. E. (1992). *International mathematics and science assessments: What have we learned?* (NCES 92-011). Washington, DC: U.S. Department of Education, Office of Educational Research and Improvement, National Center for Education Statistics.

Mehrens, W. A. (1995). Methodological issues in standard setting for educational exams. In *Proceedings of the joint conference on standard setting for large scale assessments of the National Assessment Governing Board (NAGB) and the National Center for Educational Statistics (NCES), Volume II* (pp. 221–263). Washington, DC: National Assessment Governing Board.

Messick, S. J., Beaton, A. E., & Lord, F. M. (1983). *National Assessment of Educational Progress reconsidered: A new design for a new era* (NAEP Report 83-1). Princeton, NJ: Educational Testing Service.

Mislevy, R. J. (1987). Exploiting auxiliary information about examinees in the estimation of item parameters. *Applied Psychological Measurement, 11*, 81–91.

Mislevy, R. J. (1991). Randomization-based inference about latent variables from complex samples. *Psychometrika, 56*, 177–196.

Mislevy, R. J. (1992). *Linking educational assessments: Concepts, issues, methods, and prospects*. Princeton, NJ: Educational Testing Service.

Mislevy, R. J., Beaton, A. E., Kaplan, B., & Sheehan, K. M. (1992). Estimating population characteristics from sparse matrix samples of item responses. *Journal of Educational Measurement, 29*, 133–161.

Mislevy, R. J., & Bock, R. D. (1982). BILOG: Item analysis and test scoring with binary logistic models [Computer program]. Mooresville, IN: Scientific Software.

Mislevy, R. J., Johnson, E. G., & Muraki, E. (1992). Scaling procedures in NAEP. *Journal of Educational Statistics, 17*, 131–154.

Mislevy, R. J., & Sheehan, K. J. (1987). Marginal estimation procedures. In A. E. Beaton (Ed.), *Implementing the new design: The NAEP 1983–84 technical report* (Rep. No. 15-TR-20, pp. 293–360). Princeton, NJ: Educational Testing Service.

Mislevy, R. J., & Sheehan, K. J. (1989). The role of collateral information about examinees in item parameter estimation. *Psychometrika, 54*, 661–679.

Monseur, C., Rust, K., & Krawchuk, S. (2002). Sampling outcomes. In *PISA 2000 technical report* (chapter 12). Paris: OECD.

Mullis, I. V. S., Dossey, J. A., Owen, E. H., & Phillips, G. W. (1993). *Executive summary of the NAEP 1992 mathematics report card for the nation and the states* (Rep. No. 23-ST03). Washington, DC: Office of Educational Research and Improvement, U.S. Department of Education.

Mullis, I. V. S., Martin, M. O., Gonzalez, E. J., O'Connor, K. M., Chrostowski, S. J., & Garden, R. A. (2001). *Mathematics Benchmarking Report-TIMSS 1999-Eighth grade*. Chestnut Hill, MA: Boston College, The International Study Center.

Muraki, E., & Bock, R. D. (1991). PARSCALE: Parameter scaling of rating data [Computer program]. Chicago: Scientific Software.

Muraki, E., & Bock, R. D. (1997). PARSCALE: IRT item analysis and test scoring for rating scale-scale data. Chicago: Scientific Software.

National Assessment of Adult Literacy. (n.d.). *Assessment design. The 1992 National Adult Literacy Survey: Instrument design*. The National Center for Education Statistics, U.S. Department of Education. Retrieved April 12, 2004, from http://nces.ed.gov/naal/design/design92.asp

National Assessment Governing Board and National Center for Education Statistics. (1995). *Proceedings of the joint conference on standard setting for large scale assessments of the National Assessment Governing Board (NAGB) and the National Center for Educational Statistics (NCES), Volume II*. Washington, DC: Authors.

No Child Left Behind Act of 2001, Pub. L. No. 107-110, 115 Stat. 1425 (2002).

Organisation for Economic Co-Operation and Development. (2000). *Literacy in the information age: Final report of the International Literacy Study*. Paris and Ottawa: OECD and Minister of Industry.

O'Sullivan, C. Y., & Grigg, W. S. (2001). *Assessing the best: NAEP's 1996 assessment of twelfth-graders taking advanced science courses* (NCES 2001-451). Washington, DC: U.S. Department of Education, Office of Educational Research and Improvement, National Center for Education Statistics.

Pashley, P. J., & Phillips, G. W. (1993). *Toward world class standards: A research study linking international and national assessments*. Princeton, NJ: Educational Testing Service, Center for Educational Progress.

Patz, R. J., & Junker, B. W. (1999a). A straightforward approach to Markov Chain Monte Carlo methods for item response models. *Journal of Educational and Behavioral Statistics, 24*, 146–178.

Patz, R. J., & Junker, B. W. (1999b). Applications and extensions of MCMC in IRT: Multiple item types, missing data, and rated responses. *Journal of Educational and Behavioral Statistics, 24*, 342–366.

Pellegrino, J. W. (2000). A response to ACT's technical advisers on NAEP standard setting. *Educational Measurement: Issues and Practice, 19*(2), 14–15.

Pellegrino, J. W., Jones, L. R., & Mitchell, K. J. (Eds.). (1999). *Grading the nation's report card: Evaluating NAEP and transforming the assessment of educational progress*. Committee on the Evaluation of National Assessments of Educational Progress, Board on Testing and Assessment, Commission on Behavioral and Social Sciences and Education, National Research Council. Washington, DC: National Academy Press.

Petersen, N. S., Kolen, M. J., & Hoover, H. D. (1989). Scaling, norming, and equating. In R. L. Linn (Ed.), *Educational measurement* (3rd ed., pp. 221–262). New York: American Council on Education/Oryx.

Phillips, G. W., Mullis, I. V. S., Bourque, M. L., Williams, P. L., Hambleton, R. K., Owen, E. H., et al. (1993). *Interpreting NAEP scales*. Washington, DC: U.S. Department of Education, Office of Educational Research and Improvement, National Center for Education Statistics.

Pinnell, G. S., Pikulski, J. J., Wixson, K. K., Campbell, J. R., Gough, P. B., & Beatty, A. S. (1995). *Listening to children read aloud: Data from NAEP's integrated reading performance record (IRPR) at grade 4* (NCES 23-FR-04). Washington, DC: U.S. Department of Education, Office of Educational Research and Improvement, National Center for Education Statistics.

Prais, S. J. (2003). Cautions on OECD's recent educational survey (PISA). *Oxford Review of Education, 29*, 139–163.

Qian, J., & Braun, H. (2004). *TOC Study 2.4.1.4: Mapping state performance standards onto the NAEP scale* (Interim Report from ETS to NCES). Unpublished report.

Reckase, M. D. (2000). *The evolution of the NAEP achievement levels setting process: A summary of the research and development efforts completed by ACT*. Iowa City, IA: ACT.

Rubin, D. B. (1987). *Multiple imputation for nonresponse in surveys*. New York: Wiley.

Rust, K. F., & Johnson, E. G. (1992). Sampling and weighting in the national assessment. *Journal of Educational Statistics, 17*, 111–129.

Rust, K. F., Krenzke, T., Qian, J., & Johnson, E. G. (2001). Sample design for the National Assessment. In N. L. Allen, J. R. Donoghue, & T. L. Schoeps (Eds.), *The NAEP 1998 technical report* (NCES 2001-509, pp. 31–59). Washington, DC: National Center for Education Statistics.

Sandene, B., Horkay, N., Bennett, R. E., Allen, N., Braswell, J., Kaplan, B., et al. (2005). *Online assessment in mathematics and writing: Reports from the NAEP technology-based assessment project, research and development series* (NCES 2005-457). Washington, DC: U.S. Department of Education,

National Center for Education Statistics. Washington, DC: Office.

Silver, E. A., & Kenney, P. A. (Eds.). (2000). *Results from the seventh mathematics assessment of the National Assessment of Educational Progress*. Reston, VA: National Council of Teachers of Mathematics.

Solomon, C., Lutkus, A. D., Kaplan, B., & Skolnik, I. (2004). *Writing in the nation's classrooms: Teacher interviews and student work collected from participants in the NAEP 1998 writing assessment* (ETS-NAEP 04-R02). Princeton, NJ: Educational Testing Service.

Stufflebeam, D. L., Jaeger, R. M., & Scriven, M. (1991). *Summative evaluation of the National Assessment Governing Board's inaugural effort to set achievement levels on the National Assessment of Educational Progress*. Kalamazoo: Western Michigan University, The Evaluation Center.

U.S. General Accounting Office. (1993). *Educational achievement standards: NAGB's approach yields misleading interpretations* (Report No. GAO/PEMD-93-12). Washington, DC: U.S. Government Printing Office.

Vinovskis, M. A. (1998). *Overseeing the nation's report card: The creation and evolution of the National Assessment Governing Board*. Washington, DC: National Assessment Governing Board.

Wainer, H. (1994). *On the academic achievement of New Jersey's public school children: I. Fourth and eighth grade mathematics in 1992* (Report No. RR-94-29). Princeton, NJ: Educational Testing Service.

Wainer, H. (1997a). Improving tabular displays, with NAEP tables as examples and inspirations. *Journal of Educational and Behavioral Statistics, 21*, 1–30.

Wainer, H. (1997b). Some multivariate displays for NAEP results. *Psychological Methods, 2*, 34–63.

Wainer, H., Hambleton, R. K., & Meara, K. (1999). Alternative displays for communicating NAEP results: A redesign and validity study. *Journal of Educational Measurement, 36*, 301–335.

Wainer, H., & Saka, T. (1994). *On the academic achievement of Hawaii's public school children: I. Fourth & eighth grade mathematics in 1992* (Report No. RR-94-43). Princeton, NJ: Educational Testing Service.

Waltman, K. K. (1997). Using performance standards to link statewide achievement results to NAEP. *Journal of Educational Measurement, 34*, 101–121.

Williams, V. S. L., Billeaud, K., Davis, L. A., Thissen, D., & Sanford, E. E. (1995). *Projecting to the NAEP scale: Results from the North Carolina end-of-grade testing program* (Tech. Rep. No. 34). Chapel Hill: University of North Carolina, National Institute of Statistical Sciences.

Wingersky, M. S., Kaplan, B. A., & Beaton, A. E. (1987). Joint estimation procedures. In A. E. Beaton (Ed.), *Implementing the new design: The NAEP 1983–1984 technical report* (Rep. No. 15-TR-20, pp. 285–292). Princeton, NJ: Educational Testing Service.

Wu, M. L., Adams, R. J., & Wilson, M. R. (1997). ConQuest: Multi-aspect test software [Computer program]. Camberwell, Victoria, Australia: Australian Council for Education Research.

Yamamoto, K. (1998). Scaling and scale linking. In T. S. Murray, I. S. Kirsch, & L. B. Jenkins (Eds.), *Adult literacy in OECD countries: Technical report on the First International Adult Literacy Survey* (NCES 98-053, pp. 161–178). Washington, DC: U.S. Department of Education, Office of Educational Research and Improvement, National Center for Education Statistics.

Yamamoto, K., & Jenkins, F. (1992). Data analysis for the mathematics assessment. In E. G. Johnson & N. L. Allen (Eds.), *The NAEP 1990 technical report* (Report No. 21-TR-20, pp. 243–274). Washington, DC: U.S. Department of Education, Office of Educational Research and Improvement, National Center for Education Statistics.

Yamamoto, K., & Kulick, E. (2000). Scaling methodology and procedures for the TIMSS mathematics and science scales. In M. O. Martin, K. D. Gregory, & S. E. Stemler (Eds.), *TIMSS 1999 technical report: Description of the methods and procedures used in IEA's repeat of the Third International Mathematics and Science Study at the eighth grade* (pp. 237–263). Chestnut Hill, MA: Boston College, Lynch School of Education, International Study Center.

Yamamoto, K., & Mazzeo, J. (1992). Item response theory scale linking in NAEP. *Journal of Educational Statistics, 17*, 155–173.

Zwick, R. (1992). Statistical and psychometric issues in the measurement of educational achievement trends: Examples from the National Assessment of Educational Progress. *Journal of Educational Statistics, 17*, 205–218.

20

Testing for Licensure and Certification in the Professions

Brian E. Clauser
Melissa J. Margolis
National Board of Medical Examiners

Susan M. Case
National Conference of Bar Examiners

Work on this chapter by Brian Clauser and Melissa Margolis was supported by The National Board of Medical Examiners (NBME), but the views expressed are those of the authors and do not necessarily represent the position or policy of the NBME.

1. INTRODUCTION

Testing for licensure and certification is intended to provide evidence that an individual possesses some part of the overall set of knowledge and skills necessary for professional practice. In the United States, licensure differs from certification in that licensure is a legal requirement for practice. States (or other jurisdictions) typically establish educational, practical, and testing requirements for licensure; these requirements are designed to protect the public from unqualified individuals who are seeking either to enter a profession or to function as an independent practitioner in that profession. By contrast, certification denotes a status that exceeds the minimum legal requirements for practice.

The aforementioned distinctions between licensure and certification exist in principle, but in practice the distinctions are often elusive. For example, if a licensed physician practicing in one jurisdiction wishes to relocate to another, and if more than 10 years have passed since the physician successfully completed the licensing examination sequence, the individual may be required to re-test. If, however, the individual has completed the requirements for specialty certification, the requirement for re-testing may be waived; in effect, certification replaces licensure. Similarly, although licensure bestows the status of legal independent practitioner, for practical reasons certification may become a kind of *de facto* license. For example, hospitals may require a physician to have specialty certification in order to be granted privileges. To the extent that hospital privileges are essential for practice, certification may function as the true minimum standard for independent practice. There are also professions in which licensure is not required for practice, but in which practice without certification is significantly limited. For example, the settings in which primary and secondary school teachers can function are likely to be limited if they lack the appropriate teaching certification. Finally, although professional organizations typically establish requirements for certification, in some cases states impose legal requirements as they do for licensure.

The distinction between licensure and certification also may be influenced by the nature and extent of the licensing bodies' obligations to various constituencies. It is generally assumed that the primary obligation of licensing examinations is to the public (i.e., the consumers of professional services). Laws regulating professional practice are intended to protect the public, and the public reasonably might view the license as evidence that the practitioner possesses the necessary knowledge and skills to provide safe and effective professional services. As such, the licensing body is expected to establish requirements that are sufficiently extensive and demanding to meet the public's expectations with reasonable certainty. This is the view endorsed by the current *Standards* for credentialing examinations, a category that includes both licensing and certifying tests (American Educational Research Association, American Psychological Association, National Council on Measurement in Education [AERA, APA, & NCME], 1999, p 156):

> Tests used in credentialing are intended to provide the public ... with a dependable mechanism for identifying practitioners who have met particular standards.... Credentialing also serves to protect the profession by excluding persons who are deemed to be not qualified to do the work of the occupation. Tests used in credentialing are designed to determine whether the essential knowledge and skills of a specified domain have been mastered by the candidate.

Raising professional standards should increase confidence that licensed practitioners possess the necessary knowledge and skills to provide safe and effective professional services, but doing so also may reduce the number of licensed practitioners and so deny some individuals access to professional services. Insofar as a marginally competent practitioner may be better than none at all, the public actually may suffer from increased protection. The extent to which this is true likely will vary across professions and across time. From this perspective, the licensing body has a responsibility to the public to establish requirements that are neither too high nor too low.

In addition to the public, there generally are three other constituencies in the credentialing process: (1) candidates who are interested in assurances that the requirements are not so burdensome that they may be prevented from practicing in the profession for which they have trained; (2) professionals and the organizations that represent them who are interested in maintaining high professional standards and protecting their economic self interest; and (3) members of the educational/training system who are interested in recruiting and retaining students who will commit to years of training with the expectation that their training will prepare them for credentialing. For a more thorough understanding of factors impacting the licensing process, it is important to consider some historical aspects of licensure and certification.

1.1. Historical View

The extent to which different constituencies influence the licensing process varies from profession to profession and for some professions from jurisdiction to jurisdiction. Because licensure is a legal requirement, it is by definition a political process subject to the influence of political pressures; this has been true throughout the history of licensure. Medical and legal practice have been regulated for more than two millennia. Chinese civil service requirements have included written assessments for close to three millennia, and medical and legal practice were included sometime before 500 B.C.E. (DuBois, 1970). Legal regulation of the professions in Europe followed by several centuries. Garcia-Ballester, McVaugh, and Rubio-Vela (1989) list four motivating factors in describing the forces that led to the institution of legal standards for the practice of medicine in the early part of the last millennium: (1) concern for quality healthcare; (2) a wish to control entry into the profession on the part of those already established ("there is certainly reason to suspect that...monopolistic self-interest rather than concern for public welfare was a principle motive," p. 8); (3) ongoing political confrontation over the power to regulate professional activities; and (4) struggles between Christian, Muslim, and Jewish interests. While this last consideration may not be as important as it was historically, the other three remain relevant. Similar issues have motivated the institution of licensure in other professions.

The requirements for professional practice also have remained relatively unchanged. By the 12th century, the practices of law and medicine were controlled through legislation. Early in the 14th century, practitioners were required to meet minimal educational requirements and to pass an examination. The prescribed form of examination was the *lectio* in which the examinee was required to read a passage from a medical text and then was asked questions about the meaning of the passage. Surgeons additionally were required to demonstrate their skills in the form of surgery that they intended to practice (Garcia-Ballester et al., 1989).

Since these early beginnings, assessment for licensure has evolved in much the same way as other areas of testing. Written and/or oral examinations were used along with what would now be referred to as performance assessments. For example, early in the 20th century, the National Board of Medical Examiners' (NBME) examination required the candidate to suture a severed animal intestine. The intestine then was attached to a source of water at a specified pressure and if the suture held the candidate received credit for that portion of the examination (Hubbard & Levit, 1985).

By the early part of the 20th century, measurement experts voiced concerns about the objectivity of scoring essay examinations. Hartog and Rhodes (1936) presented a series of studies examining the stability of the marks produced by examiners for university-level essay examinations. The results argued strongly against the use of this type of assessment. Influenced by this and other empirical evidence, testing agencies searched for alternative methodologies. The NBME, for example, made a decision in 1954 to replace essay questions with objectively-scored multiple-choice items. This break with tradition was so controversial at the time that some states ceased to recognize the NBME examinations.

A similar trend was evident in performance-based assessment. During the 1960s, the NBME discontinued use of the bedside oral examination because of concerns about standardization and the objectivity of scoring. This trend toward objectivity was not limited to testing for licensure. The first and second editions of this volume (Lindquist, 1951; Thorndike, 1971) included chapters on essay tests and performance examinations. By the third edition (Linn, 1989), these chapters no longer were included (although the topics were considered in other chapters).

1.2. Current Practice

Despite trends toward objectively scorable formats, licensing bodies continued to use essay, oral, and practical examinations. Currently, certification in psychiatry requires successful completion of a multiple-choice examination as well as an examination in which the candidate is observed examining and interviewing a patient. Numerous other medical specialties require similar examinations. Assessment of architects requires a performance-based component in which the candidate is required to produce designs. Similarly, certified public accountants are required to complete both knowledge and performance assessments. The licensing examination for most of those seeking admission to the bar includes multiple-choice, essay, and written performance test components. Certification in some medical specialties such as orthopedic surgery has taken this a step further by requiring applicants to submit records based on actual practice; medical records for a defined group of patients from the applicant's practice are evaluated as part of the certifying process, and an oral examination is based on a subset of these patients.

One trend in licensing assessment during recent decades is the increasing use of computers to administer and score exams. The National Council of Architectural Registration

Boards (NCARB) invested considerable effort in research and development to allow for computerized scoring of architectural design problems and has been successfully administering and scoring a computer-based examination for several years (Bejar & Braun, 1999). Examinees are required to produce designs that meet specifications similar to those that would commonly occur in practice (for example, to design an office suite in the available floor space that provides a meeting room to accommodate 20 people, office space for 5 people and cubicle space for 15 people). The computer program then compares the resulting design to the specifications and applies scoring rules that account for the extent to which the design meets those specifications, complies with relevant building codes, and is of good overall quality.

This same trend is evident in medical licensure. The NBME spent more than two decades developing a computer-administered and computer-scored examination format designed, in part, to replace the bedside-oral examination that had been dropped from testing for licensure in the 1960s (Margolis & Clauser, 2006). These computer-based case simulations, which now are a part of the United States Medical Licensing Examination (USMLE®), require the examinee to manage a patient in a simulated patient-care environment. The examinees are able to order diagnostic tests, treatments, and consultations and they receive realistic feedback on the patient's condition as simulated time is advanced on a clock under their control. The simulations are scored using a regression-based algorithm designed to produce a score that approximates that which would have been received if the performance had been reviewed and rated by trained clinician raters.

The American Institute of Certified Public Accountants and National Association of the State Boards of Accountancy (NASBA) along with Thompson Prometric similarly have launched a computer-administered and scored assessment for certified public accountants. The assessment includes both multiple-choice items and performance tasks designed to reflect routine activities that accountants are called upon to perform in practice.

This continued commitment to the use of performance tasks in licensure and certification is not limited to computer-delivered assessments. In 2004, the USMLE implemented a large-scale performance assessment as part of the sequence of tests required for licensure (Hawkins et al., 2005). The test utilizes laypersons (known as standardized patients) trained to portray the part of patients with specific medical problems. Examinees interact with 12 of these patients in a way that is similar to how they might evaluate patients in a real clinical setting; they have 15 minutes to interview each patient and perform a focused physical examination and 10 minutes following the patient interview to record their findings in a structured note. Each interaction is scored using several instruments designed to capture information about the examinee's ability to gather and record pertinent information and to communicate effectively. The examination is required of all U.S. and internationally trained medical graduates who intend to practice medicine in the United States. A similar test has been part of licensure in Canada since 1992 (Reznick et al., 1993).

Licensure for the bar provides another example of the trend toward standardization, the use of multiple-choice item formats, and more recently toward the use of performance tasks. In 1931, the National Conference of Bar Examiners (NCBE) was founded with the purpose of increasing the efficiency of state boards in admitting qualified applicants to the bar. Following the trend toward the use of performance assessment formats, the NCBE introduced the Multistate Essay Examination in 1988 and the Multistate Performance Test in 1997 (Karge, 1996). The essay format requires the applicant to demonstrate an ability to communicate effectively in writing. The Multistate Performance Test was designed to assess the use of fundamental skills in a realistic situation; each test evaluates an applicant's ability to complete a task that a beginning lawyer should be able to accomplish. A file including the facts of the case is provided; this file might include a memorandum from a supervising attorney, transcripts of interviews, depositions, pleadings, correspondence, client documents, contracts, newspaper articles, medical records, police reports, and lawyer's notes. Because the intent is to mirror practice, the file may include irrelevant facts as well as ambiguous, incomplete, or even conflicting information. Examinees also are provided with a library that includes cases, statutes, regulations, and rules, some of which may not be relevant to the assigned task. Library materials provide sufficient substantive information to complete the task, and the applicant is expected to extract from the library the legal principles necessary to analyze the problem and perform the task.

1.3. Multiple Requirements

In understanding the place of testing in professional licensure, it is important to note that entrance into a profession typically is not based on successful completion of an examination alone. As noted previously, the requirement of university training for medical licensure dates back at least to the 14th century (Garcia-Ballester et al., 1989). Similarly, medical licensure requires completion of a period of supervised practice and specialty certification typically requires additional supervised practice. Specifics, however, vary from profession to profession and across jurisdictions.

Until 1830, almost all lawyers in the United States entered the profession by undergoing a lengthy apprenticeship in a lawyer's office. With the rise of popularism during the Jacksonian era, it became more common to allow free access to the law without any educational or apprenticeship training. Standards began to be raised in the early 1900s and today most, but not all, of the jurisdictions require formal legal educational training (Kargar, 1996).

The variation across professions and jurisdictions aside, licensure and certification typically require completion of a formal educational program, a period of supervised practice, and a standardized assessment. The requirement for formalized training has implications for test construction and score validity. If candidates for licensure only had to pass a standardized test in order to qualify for a license, it would be necessary to develop a test that reliably assessed each of the components of knowledge required for competent practice. The argument that a candidate can be considered competent because of acceptable performance on a test covering a *sample* of that knowledge base becomes more credible when the candidate also has successfully completed a course of study at an accredited school with a curriculum covering the *entire* knowledge base.

In addition to the fact that standardized assessment is only one component of the licensing process, it is important to note that for many professions that one component is not a single step. For example, the medical licensing assessment in the United States currently is a multi-stage process. Examinees must demonstrate proficiency in the basic medical sciences, clinical science, clinical skills, and patient management in four separately administered (and separately scored) tests. Certification in a medical specialty often requires successful completion of an additional written examination as well as an oral or practical examination.

This brief introduction provides an overview of the purpose, history, and current practice of testing for licensure. The remainder of the chapter will provide a more detailed consideration of five important topics within the context of testing for licensure and certification: test development, reliability issues, validity issues, establishing standards, and legal issues. Several of these topics are covered by individual chapters in this volume; the aim of the present chapter is to provide specific focus in terms of how these topics relate to testing for licensure and certification. The intention is that the information provided should be relevant to the broad field of testing for licensure and certification. However, much of the specific discussion focuses on practice in the learned professions. There are several reasons for this focus. One consideration is that the authors' knowledge and experience is in this area. In addition, these professions generally have more resources to invest in assessment procedures and they therefore tend to be leaders in establishing assessment practice. It is understood that many professions will not have similar resources and that in many circumstances the nature of professional practice in these fields and the need to balance the requirements of protection of the public against other competing interests does not justify such expenditure. Moreover, the examples provided are intended as illustrations of conceptual issues and not as prescriptions for practice.

2. TEST DEVELOPMENT

Although there often are additional requirements for licensure, it is almost inevitable that in order to obtain a professional license or certification an applicant will be required to pass an examination. Generally, the examination is developed by an outside agency that retains independence and separation from the educational arm of the licensing process. This separation from the educational component is viewed as critically important in ensuring to the public that the practitioner is safe. In testing for licensure and certification, an examination should provide independent evidence that the applicant is at least minimally competent to practice in the profession. This section focuses on the initial steps in developing a testing program: deciding what to test, deciding how to test, and deciding which formats to use.

2.1. Deciding What to Test

Deciding what to test involves several considerations, among which are the underlying purpose for the examination, the relevant content given the stated purpose, the types of questions to be used, and the relevance of the questions to the purpose of the examination. A discussion of each of these issues follows.

The first step in developing a testing program is to create an explicit statement of the purpose of the test that indicates why the examination is an important component of the licensing process. Because the overall objective of licensure and certification is to protect the public from practitioners who do not have the knowledge and skills necessary to practice in a competent manner, the test should focus on differentiating between those who have sufficient knowledge and skills and those who do not. The focus should be on the knowledge and skills required of the new practitioner, *which are not necessarily the knowledge and skills that were taught in school*. These two knowledge domains often are congruent, but to the extent that there are discrepancies, the focus should be on requirements for successful practice.

The purpose statement for tests used for licensure and certification in the professions often takes the following form:

> This test is designed to measure whether or not an examinee has the requisite knowledge and skills that are required of new practitioners.

If the examination produces scores (as opposed to just pass/fail results), the purpose statement might be altered to read:

> This test is designed to measure *the extent to which* an examinee has the requisite knowledge and skills that are required of a new practitioner.

In the latter case, actual examination scores (rather than pass/fail decisions) might be used as part of the selection criteria for a job or for entry into further training. In medicine, for example, actual scores are considered for entrance into residency training; in law, the emphasis is on the pass/fail result.

The purpose statement should be highlighted in each place that the examination is described. It is difficult to overstate the importance of the wide distribution of a clear purpose statement: it helps to steer the test development and item writing efforts; it provides direction to examinees who are preparing for the test; and it can, as an ancillary benefit, help faculty who teach courses in the field.

An example from medical licensure can be used to illustrate these principles. The purpose statement of the USMLE is included on the examination program Web site and in the USMLE Bulletin of Information. It includes a general statement related to the overall examination: "The three Steps of the USMLE assess a physician's ability to apply knowledge, concepts, and principles, and to demonstrate fundamental patient-centered skills, that are important in health and disease and that constitute the basis of safe and effective patient care" and a specific purpose statement for each individual examination. The focus for the series of examinations is on content that is necessary for practice rather than on content that has been taught; this allows medical schools to define the curriculum based on what they deem to be important, but at the same time it allows for an independent assessment of whether each examinee demonstrates sufficient knowledge and skills in order to practice safely and effectively.

While there likely is a close association between what is taught and what is included on the examination, a result of this separation is that some of the questions on USMLE might assess knowledge not taught uniformly in medical school. Conversely, topics taught in some medical schools might be omitted from the examination. For example, the examination might appropriately include a question that describes a patient and asks the examinee to indicate the next step in patient care. A correct answer to this question for one examinee might require recall and synthesis of information learned in an anatomy or physiology class with information learned in several clinical courses; an examinee from another school, however, might draw on material learned in a course on clinical diagnosis, while a third examinee could have used information gleaned from independent reading because no course covered the particular type of patient being assessed.

2.2. Basic Considerations of Examination Content

After the purpose is specified, the next step is to develop a content outline or test specifications; these provide a more explicit statement of examination content. The content outline specifies what will be covered on the examination, and, at least by omission, what will not be on the examination. It also should specify the relative weights or numbers of questions allocated to each topic.

Several methods can be used to provide information that is helpful in developing the content outline. A job (or practice) analysis commonly involves surveying members of the profession about what new practitioners do, how often they do it, and how important each topic or task is for effective entry-level practice (Raymond, 2001). A group of content experts—typically including both practitioners and teachers in the field—develops a draft list of tasks or topics that are believed to represent required knowledge or skills for entry-level practice. This initial list is circulated to a larger group in order to ensure that it is reasonable and that there are no obvious gaps in the task list. The last data-gathering step involves transforming the final list into a survey that asks respondents to indicate both the frequency with which each task or topic occurs and the importance of each. Following the data-gathering phase, the survey is sent to a sample of individuals—perhaps newly-licensed practitioners and supervisors of new licensees—who indicate how often the topic or task arises and how critical it has been for them to be competent in that area. If the topic or task list is too large, it can be divided and each subset can be sent to a representative sample of respondents.

The topic or task list should include only those elements that are necessary to protect the public; entries that might be necessary for success in the field but are not required for safe practice (e.g., efficient billing practices) should be omitted. The list also should cover variations in practice—including any areas that are covered by the license or certification—even if those areas are not widely practiced. For example, in medicine the survey should include tasks that might pertain to practices ranging from those in large cities to rural areas, with patients ranging from neonates to the elderly, and from general practice to neurosurgery. A job analysis should be undertaken periodically, with the frequency determined by the rapidity of changes in practice.

Another method that can be used to gather data is a critical incident study in which participants or observers are asked to document incidents that together help to describe the critical requirements for practice (Flanagan, 1947). Respondents list incidents that were observed and believed to have had a substantial positive or negative impact on patient or client outcomes (e.g., a nurse notices that a patient's diet is not consistent with medication orders and has the inconsistency corrected). Hundreds to thousands of incidents then are summarized and used to help guide the development of the content outline or test specifications.

Regardless of the specific method, considerable work remains even after a list of topics or tasks is defined and the data are collected; judgment is required to turn the data into something useful. For example, though an analysis of the patterns of practice among pediatricians might show that diagnosing and treating children with ear infections is required much more frequently than diagnosing and treating children with leukemia, the latter may be viewed as more critical. Activity lists also might show that considerable time is spent on office procedures that might not be of any testing interest because they are not related to client outcomes. Although it is inevitable that there will be topics that cannot be tested and topics that are not worth testing, documenting what new practitioners actually do in practice can provide useful information to the decision makers who determine what will be on the test.

It is not uncommon for test designers to convene a group of content experts or policymakers to generate a content outline by consensus. Some programs will require that these groups develop the specifications based on their own knowledge and experience, while others will provide them with some empirical data from a practice analysis, a critical incident study, or another source. Those involved in defining the examination content should include a diverse group of practitioners; among others, factors such as ethnicity, race, gender, urban/rural setting, and geographic region should be considered in selecting members for the group.

In terms of structure, it is common for content outlines to be developed as a matrix with one dimension listing the topics to be covered. The other dimension can vary, but it commonly represents either cognitive level or task (as will be discussed below). One issue that arises in designing and using such test specifications is the extent to which questions should be framed narrowly within a topic area or be interdisciplinary in nature. In general, interdisciplinary questions are appropriate in licensing and certifying examinations (e.g., a set of facts that crosses torts and criminal law). It is common for real-life challenges to span several areas, and this element of real life can be mirrored on the exam. At the same time, care should be taken to avoid unnecessary complexity.

2.3. Classification of Questions by Cognitive Level

Classifying test questions by cognitive level long has been a popular method of test construction. One system that remains in use, Bloom's taxonomy, classifies questions at one of six levels (knowledge, comprehension, application, analysis, synthesis, and evaluation) depending on the cognitive processes that are believed to be required to answer the question (Bloom, Engelhart, Furst, Hill, & Krathwohl, 1956). Using this scheme, a test developer may decide that an examination should include a particular percentage of questions classified as "knowledge," a particular percentage classified as "comprehension," etc. The difficulty with such classifications is that the cognitive processes required to answer a question are as dependent on the knowledge base of the examinee as they are on the question content. Those with expertise on a particular topic may be able to answer the question with little or no conscious thought, whereas others may need to analyze or synthesize information in order to formulate a response. The cognitive processes involved in responding to a question are specific to the examinee, thus making the taxonomic approaches difficult or perhaps even impossible to use. Even when this is not the case, classifications based on cognitive level are likely to be made in the absence of empirical evidence; the classification is likely to be subjective at best.

A simpler approach classifies items either as "recall of an isolated fact" or "application of knowledge." To qualify as an "application of knowledge" question, a question must require the examinee to reach a conclusion, make a prediction, or select a course of action. The advantage of this simpler classification approach is that the questions can be classified without any reference to the thought processes of the examinee.

The sample questions shown below assess knowledge of the same basic topic. Both are shown in a short-answer response format, but options easily could be added to convert them to a multiple-choice format. It is clear that the isolated fact item requires the examinee simply to recall isolated pieces of information. The application of knowledge question, on the other hand, assesses understanding of much the same information, but the task is framed more realistically; the examinee must interpret the clinical findings and arrive at a diagnosis.

Isolated Fact Question: What are the signs and symptoms of gastroesophageal reflux disease?

Application of Knowledge Question: A 55-year-old man comes to the physician because of recurring pain in his chest that has occurred with increased frequency for the past two months. The pain occurs mostly in the evening after dinner, but occasionally occurs while he is eating. He describes it as a burning sensation in the center of his chest at his sternum. Occasionally, he feels as if he can't swallow his food. Physical examination is unremarkable. What is the most likely diagnosis?

Scenario-based questions such as the one shown above provide many advantages. The criticism that many examinations—regardless of format—only assess knowledge of unimportant facts can be reduced greatly by use of questions with clinical (client or patient) vignettes as item stems. Scenario-based items have the potential to enhance the validity of the examination by requiring examinees to solve problems that they would be expected to handle as new practitioners. In addition, questions in the form of realistic problems are more likely to focus on important information than on trivia. Finally, these questions require not only that examinees have an appropriate level of factual knowledge, but also that they are able to analyze factual situations and apply their knowledge of facts to solve problems.

2.4. Classification of Questions by Examinee Task

As discussed above, simple cognitive-level classification may not be appropriate in the context of licensure and certification. Instead, it may be appropriate to classify all items by examinee task and to require that all items assess application of knowledge by framing each question within a context that is relevant for a new practitioner. Items for licensing and certifying examinations should reflect the tasks that examinees will have to perform once they are in practice; generally, these are tasks such as determining the underlying cause of the problem, determining the next step in resolving the problem, identifying what additional information is needed in order to solve the problem, and describing the solution. In the health sciences, these tasks might include gathering data from the patient, determining the diagnosis, and deciding the next step in patient care. These tasks then would be applied to items reflecting a range of logically categorized content groupings such as organ system (respiratory or gastrointestinal) or patient problem (joint or back pain). The challenge is to ensure that the tasks are ones that would be expected of a new practitioner; it is not sufficient to ensure that the questions assess relevant content without taking the second step of asking whether the tasks themselves are relevant.

2.5. Evaluating the Relevance of the Questions

Each test question, regardless of format, should be subject to a review that addresses whether or not the question is relevant to new practitioners. At least periodically, a formal study of the relevance of questions on an exam should be conducted. Ratings of the relevance of questions should be obtained from a cross-section of practitioners who are familiar with what a new practitioner needs to know.

In assessing the relevance of a particular question, reviewers should be asked to consider whether both the contextual information and the examinee task are relevant to the new practitioner; whether or not a topic typically is taught in schools is not a sufficient reason to include or exclude a particular question from the examination. While in most cases what is taught is what should be learned, the focus of the item writer should be on the skills that are required to practice and not on what was taught (Cuddy et al., 2004).

2.6. Deciding Which Formats to Use

Examinations used for licensure and certification initially tended to be essay and oral examinations that involved the discussion of directly observed performance. The examination in medicine consisted of essay questions and an oral examination that was conducted at the bedside of a real patient. In the 1950s, testing agencies began exploring the use of multiple-choice questions (MCQs), and in medical licensure MCQs ultimately replaced essay questions. This trend was supported by research in the 1970s showing that "problem solving" was not a generic skill and that examinees had strengths and weakness that varied substantially from problem to problem or from case to case. This phenomenon, which became known as "problem specificity" or "case specificity," was identified in numerous research studies and highlighted the need for broad content sampling that allowed for assessing knowledge, skills, and performance in many different contexts in order to achieve a reproducible score. Regardless of the assessment format, performance has been found to generalize poorly from item to item, from task to task, and from case to case (Elstein, Shulman, & Sprafka, 1975). This line of research highlighted the importance of using more problems that were shorter and more focused rather than fewer problems that were covered in greater depth.

Research also has shown that, once reproducible scores are obtained, all the various testing methods produce scores that are correlated strongly with scores on multiple-choice tests (Norcini, Swanson, Grosso, Shea, & Webster, 1985; van der Vleuten, van Luijk, & Beckers, 1989). Research comparing scores from items with listed responses and items that require examinees to construct a response has shown that the corrected correlation is near 1.00; scores from the selected-response version are higher than the constructed-response version, but the rank-ordering of examinees is nearly identical (Newble, Baxter, & Elmslie, 1979; Norman et al., 1987). While most of the published research has been in the field of medicine, these phenomena also are likely to be seen in other professions.

Despite the concerns about the reproducibility of scores from performance assessments, searching for measures that go beyond standard MCQs has been an ongoing quest (Case, Holsgrove, et al., 1994). The search has led in three directions. First, there has been an effort to enhance the quality of MCQs by (1) increasing the fidelity of the stimulus through use of scenario-based items and (2) increasing the number of options to reduce the likelihood of guessing the correct answer (Case, Swanson, & Ripkey, 1994; Veloski, Rabinowitz, Robeson, & Young, 1999). Second, there has been an effort to enhance the quality of simulations by: (1) utilizing the increased capabilities provided by computer-administration; (2) shortening the simulations to allow greater sampling of cases; and (3) enhancing the scoring to ensure that scores reflect the quality of performance rather than some artifact. Third, there has been an effort to enhance the quality of performance testing by (1) shortening each case to allow for greater content sampling; and (2) enhancing the scoring to ensure that scores reflect the quality of performance rather than some artifact. For methods that utilize subjective scoring, particularly when the examinee is observed by the grader, additional challenges include the need to ensure that (1) graders are calibrated with each other; (2) graders remain consistent over time; and (3) scores reflect the construct of interest and are not systematically influenced by sources of construct-irrelevant variance. Each of these challenges is described in further detail below.

Examinations for licensure and certification in the professions now include a variety of formats, and undoubtedly the most prevalent format is the MCQ. Each method has its advantages and disadvantages and has both high- and low-quality exemplars; it is therefore important to level the playing field in comparing the formats (Norman, Swanson, & Case, 1996). The following section considers advantages and disadvantages and good and bad illustrations of each format. Oral and essay examinations are discussed, but emphasis is placed on multiple-choice questions because they continue to serve as the linchpin of licensing examinations in the professions.

2.7. Oral Examinations

Oral examinations remain a popular form of assessment, particularly for professional certification. Content experts often believe that spending time questioning an examinee yields a more valid assessment of that examinee's ability than do scores derived from other forms of assessment. The potential advantage of oral examinations is that examiners are able to adapt the questions to the responses of the examinee and to investigate a topic in depth, which can provide insight into the examinee's thought process. The primary disadvantage of oral examinations is poor content sampling and the often poor level of agreement achieved by independent examiners. Some organizations have tried to increase the reliability of the assessment by shortening the amount of time spent on each topic and requiring that each topic be assessed by an independent examiner. Reliability is governed largely by content sampling (number of cases or interactions) and number of independent examiners; research in several areas has shown that a dozen or so examiners and topics are required to achieve a reasonable level of reliability, and the basic strategy should be to sample as many different situations and raters as is feasible (Swanson, 1987).

2.8. Essay and Short Answer Examinations

Essay examinations continue to be used in some professions (such as law). Proponents of essay examinations cite three main advantages over MCQs. First, essays can probe an examinee's knowledge in more depth. Second, they can assess an examinee's ability to write coherently about a topic. Finally, because they don't provide a list of possible responses, they don't provide examinees with the ability to guess the correct answer. Proponents of essay examinations also see advantages over oral examinations and face-to-face simulations. Essay exams maintain the anonymity of examinees. Grades are not affected by personal attributes of the examinee or by the interaction between the examinee and the grader.

There are also disadvantages of essay examinations. The first is the relatively limited content coverage; a typical essay examination includes far fewer questions than a typical multiple-choice examination. Second, while essay questions seem much easier to develop, questions must be very clear in order to ensure that examinees answer the question that is intended. Finally, essay responses are difficult to grade; considerable efforts therefore are required to ensure that grading is fair, impartial, and consistent. Equating scores produced by oral and essay examinations where items are not repeated across administrations is difficult at best. This becomes an issue in the context of licensure and certification due to the criticality of maintaining consistent standards across test administrations.

For licensure in the legal profession, most jurisdictions use essay questions within the bar examination and most use a multiple-choice component as well. The multiple-choice component generates a scaled score that is equated and is sufficiently reliable to stand alone. Most jurisdictions scale their essays to this multiple-choice component, and that process helps to ensure that the essay scores are equated over time.

Research has shown that large numbers of essays are required to generate a reasonably reliable score. One study of essay scores in medicine found that the number of essays necessary to achieve a reliability of .8 was larger with analytic grading (which would require 72 essays) than with holistic grading (which would require 22 essays; Norcini et al., 1990). The large number of oral examinations and essay questions required to achieve a reasonably generalizable or reliable score raises concerns about the appropriateness of these formats for high-stakes testing unless the scores are combined with scores obtained from other assessments before making pass/fail decisions. The research on content specificity should lead test developers to generate a larger number of shorter, more focused questions rather than a smaller number of longer questions. At least a dozen essays likely would be required if the score were to be used for an independent decision (Day et al., 1990). This relatively pessimistic view of the reliability of essay examinations may be surprising to readers familiar with the use of essays to assess K through 12 writing skills, but such results are not uncommon in contexts in which essays are used to assess content-specific professional skills.

2.9. Multiple-Choice Questions

There is little reason to use essays, oral examinations, and simulations to assess knowledge and skills that can be assessed adequately using MCQs. MCQs are the clear winner in terms of efficiency; you can ask more questions and sample more content in a shorter period of testing time with MCQs than with any other format. Another advantage of MCQs is that the examinees are anonymous; scores depend only on the responses that have been selected, and potentially irrelevant confounds such as examinee appearance or penmanship are excluded from consideration. In addition, mechanisms for equating scores across forms of the test and across time are well defined and ensure a measure of fairness that is much more difficult to achieve with other methods.

Despite the advantages of MCQs, there are disadvantages to this format that cannot be ignored. First, responses are selected and not constructed. Even though this is not supported by research, as noted above, many believe that this changes the nature of the challenge to reward a subset of examinees who can "guess well." Second, MCQs assess what an examinee knows, not what an examinee can do. Exposés that identify licensed practitioners who fail to perform properly provide fuel to the debate that licensing those with adequate knowledge fails to ensure adequate performance in practice. Of course, some practitioners who were licensed after demonstrating adequate skills on a simulation (or any other method) also will end up failing to adequately perform some action in practice. Finally, the ubiquitous nature of MCQs and the poor quality of MCQs developed for lower-stakes uses has added to their reputation as a format that rewards those with knowledge of trivial facts and those who are "test-wise." Numerous books provide advice on how to take multiple-choice tests, as if following their advice will substitute for knowing the content. And, in fact, too frequently multiple-choice questions are so poorly developed that knowledge of some test-taking rules will enable examinees to succeed even if they lack the basic proficiency the item is intended to assess.

The universe of multiple-choice questions can be divided into two basic groups: true/false-type questions and one-best-answer questions. The options for true/false questions must be absolutely true or absolutely false, under all conditions, and without exception. If this condition is not met, an option may be viewed as partially true, and the challenge for examinees is to decide if the option is true enough to be keyed as true. This decision may not be as linked to expertise in the subject matter as it is to test-taking skill and skill in deciding where the item writer drew the cut-off point between true and false.

Research has shown that true/false items don't perform as well as one-best answer questions on licensing and certifying examinations, even when substantial effort has been directed at ensuring that the items are clear and the options are unambiguous (Case & Downing, 1989; Grosse & Wright, 1985; Swanson & Case, 1992, 1995). Well-constructed one-best-answer questions that assess application of knowledge are far superior to true/false questions for licensing and certifying examinations, even if the true/false questions are constructed well.

This section has described test development issues relevant for licensing and certifying examinations. The next section considers approaches for assessing the reliability of scores produced by these examinations.

3. RELIABILITY

Tests developed for licensure and certification ultimately are used to make classification decisions. Conceptually, this is true whether or not the testing program reports scores. This does not make measurement error an irrelevant concept; increased measurement error and lower reliability translate into reduced classification accuracy. For licensing tests, however, indices reflecting classification accuracy provide important information that may not be evident from typical indices of reliability. This section includes a discussion of indices that may be appropriate in such applications. Many of these indices were developed during the period in which the psychometric community was devoting considerable attention to criterion-referenced testing and, more specifically, to mastery testing. This discussion also includes consideration of testing conditions that were given relatively little attention in previous examinations of classification accuracy. For example, some assessment systems have multiple (conjunctive) hurdles. Each component yields an independent score or pass/fail decision, and examinees must pass all of the components for successful completion of the assessment system.

3.1. Classification Accuracy

Under classical test theory assumptions, classification accuracy will be a function of the reliability of the test, the score distribution, the proportion of examinees with a level of proficiency that meets the standard, and the placement of the cut score. In the classical test theory framework, an examinee with a level of proficiency that meets the standard is an examinee with a true score at or above the cut score associated with that standard. In this framework, classification errors occur when examinees have a true score above the cut score on the true-score scale and an observed score below the cut score on the observed-score scale or when examinees have a true score below the cut score on the true-score scale and an observed score above the observed-score cut score. (For simplicity, in the discussion that follows the fact that there are conceptually two distinct cut scores, one on the true-score scale and one on the observed-score scale, will be made explicit only when the context otherwise would be confusing; throughout, this distinction should be considered implicit.)

The concepts of false-positive and false-negative errors may appear to be straightforward, but an explicit statement is justified because these terms have been used in different ways in different contexts. Let x and τ be scores on the observed- and true-score scales and let x_0 and τ_0 be cut scores on the observed- and true-score scales, respectively. Typically, x will be discrete and τ will be continuous. Table 20.1 presents the relevant 2 × 2 table. Cells in that table can be defined as

P00 = Pr($x < x_0$ and $\tau < \tau_0$)
P01 = Pr($x < x_0$ and $\tau > \tau_0$)
P10 = Pr($x \geq x_0$ and $\tau < \tau_0$)
P11 = Pr($x \geq x_0$ and $\tau > \tau_0$)

TABLE 20.1 Two-by-Two Table for Pass/Fail Outcomes

		True Scores		
		0	1	Marginal
Observed Scores	0	P00	P01	P0•
	1	P10	P11	P1•
Marginal		P•0	P•1	1

and the marginals can be defined as

P0• = Pr($x < x_0$)
P1• = Pr($x \geq x_0$)
P•0 = Pr($\tau < \tau_0$)
P•1 = Pr($\tau > \tau_0$).

Using this notation, P10 represents the proportion of examinees who have passing status based on the observed scores and failing status based on true scores. In applications such as medical diagnosis and engineering (e.g., McNeil, Keeler, & Adelstein, 1975), the false-positive rate typically is defined as fp=P10/ P•0 and the false-negative rate is defined as fn=P01/ P•1. However, an alternative formulation often is used in the educational measurement literature. For example, Hanson and Brennan (1990) and Brennan (2004) have defined the false-positive rate as fp = P10 and false-negative as fn = P01 (these rates also may be referred to as the joint false-positive and joint false-negative rates); they have used the term *conditional false-positive rate* to describe cfp = P10/ P•0 and the term *conditional false-negative rate* to describe cfn = P01/ P•1.

The difference between these definitions is not trivial and the interpretation of the indices may be significantly different. In the context of medical diagnosis, the two indices are linked by the concept of prevalence. Prevalence represents the proportion of subjects in the population who actually have the diagnosis of interest. The analogue in licensure might be the proportion of examinees who have (or, depending on an arbitrary choice of definition, lack) the proficiency of interest. The conditional false-positive rate does not reflect the prevalence of false-positive errors within the full population. If 10% of examinees who lack the proficiency of interest are classified as passing, the conditional false-positive rate is 10% regardless of the overall proportion of examinees who are misclassified; if half of the examinees in the population lack the proficiency of interest, this 10% represents 5% of the full population. If only 20% of the examinees in the population lack the proficiency of interest, this 10% represents 2% of the entire population. By contrast, fp is sensitive to prevalence but has the limitation that it approaches zero as the proportion of examinees with $\tau < \tau_0$ approaches zero regardless of the accuracy of classification. In the following discussion, the distinction made by Brennan and others will be made explicit when clarification is needed based on the context.

The relationship between classification accuracy and measurement error for credentialing examinations is

FIGURE 20.1 Variation of Conditional False-Positive and False-Negative Rates as a Function of Cut Score: 25% Non-Proficient Examinees

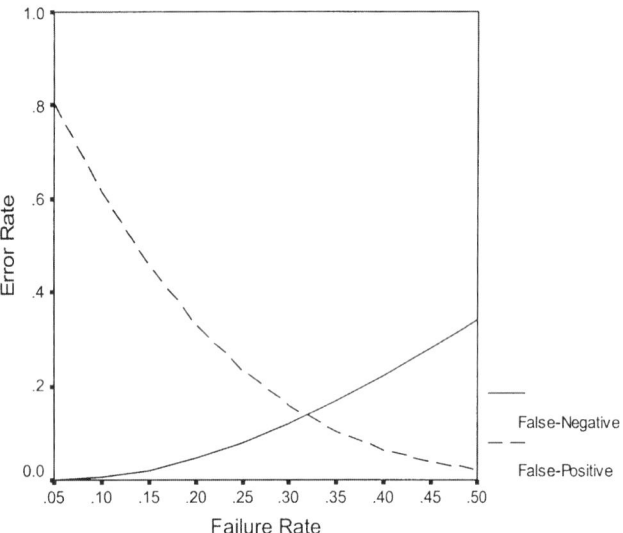

FIGURE 20.2a Variation of Conditional False-Positive and False-Negative Rates as a Function of Cut Score: 10% Non-Proficient Examinees

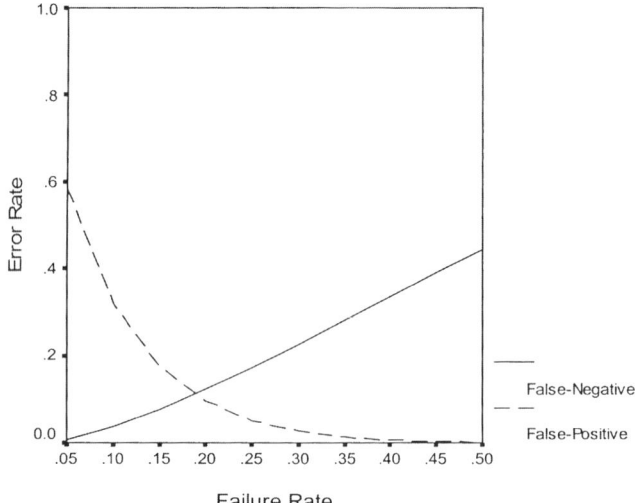

complicated. The simplest scenario is that in which examinees complete a single-stage examination on a single occasion. In this situation, both the joint and conditional false-positive rates will decrease and the false-negative rates will increase as the cut score is raised. As an example, Figure 20.1 illustrates how the conditional false-positive and false-negative rates vary as the cut score is increased from a value that fails 5% of all examinees to a value that fails 50% of all examinees. This figure represents a hypothetical test that produces scores that are normally distributed with a reliability of .8, and it is based on the assumption that 25% of the examinees actually lack the defined level of proficiency. With this level of reliability and a cut score established to fail 25% of examinees, more than 20% of the non-proficient examinees will pass due to measurement error. (The reader should note that the x-axis is defined in terms of the proportion of examinees failing the test. This is a convenience that allows for a demonstration of the relationship of interest; the cut score typically would be defined on a score scale and not in terms of percent passing. It should also be noted that the results assume a bivariate normal distribution in which both the true and observed scores are continuous. In practice, observed scores typically are discrete.)

Figures 20.2a and 20.2b show how the results vary as the proportion of proficient examinees in the population varies. Figure 20.2a provides results for conditions equivalent to those in Figure 20.1 but assumes that 10% of the examinees are actually non-proficient; Figure 20.2b provides results for analogous conditions in which 40% of examinees are non-proficient. Again, for both of these conditions the conditional false-positive rate is close to 20% when the cut score is established so that the proportion of examinees failing is equal to the proportion defined as non-proficient.

Figure 20.3 presents information about how conditional false-positive rates vary under the conditions exemplified in Figure 20.1 (scores are normally distributed and 25%

FIGURE 20.2b Variation of Conditional False-Positive and False-Negative Rates as a Function of Cut Score: 40% Non-Proficient Examinees

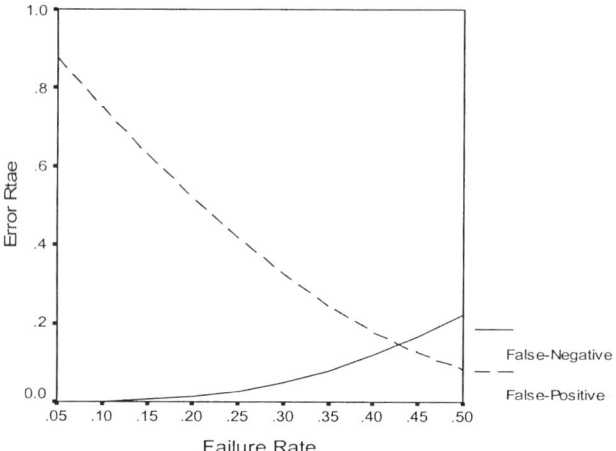

of examinees lack the identified level of proficiency) as the reliability of the test varies from .6 to .9; this range is intended to reflect the difference in reliability that might be expected between oral and other performance-based assessments (.6) and long, standardized MCQ-based assessments (.9). The figure indicates that raising the cut score reduces the conditional false-positive rate, but this occurs at the expense of increasing the conditional false-negative rate. For a given set of testing conditions (reliability, score distribution, and proportion of proficient examinees in the population), the only tradeoff available is to reduce one type of error at the expense of the other. There is no perfect answer, but there will be an optimal answer in the sense that it

FIGURE 20.3 Variation of Conditional False-Positive Rates as a Function of Test Reliability

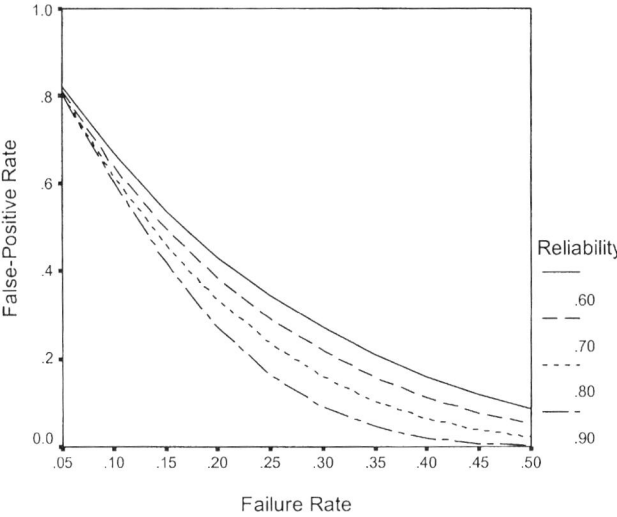

FIGURE 20.4 Variation of Total Cost Associated with Misclassification Errors as a Function of Cut-Score Placement and the Ratio of the Costs of False-Positive and False-Negative Errors

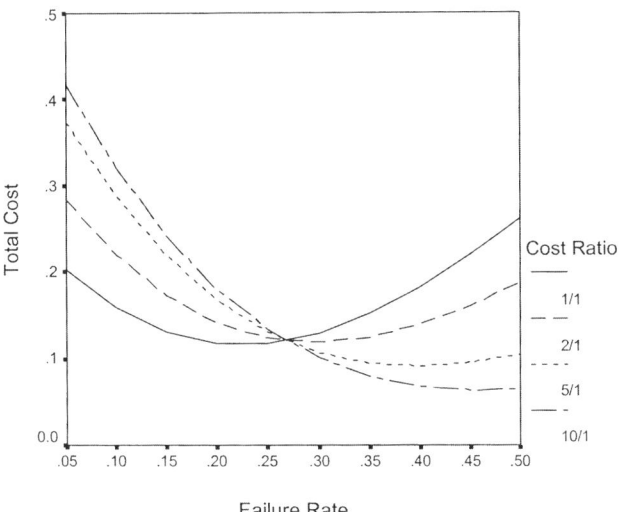

minimizes the costs associated with misclassification errors. Within the type of decision-theoretic framework presented by Cronbach and Gleser (1957), the total cost of misclassification errors will be a function of the number of each type of error and the costs associated with each. Figure 20.4 illustrates the costs associated with misclassification errors for a test with reliability of .8 and the other conditions represented in Figures 20.1 and 20.3. The lines show the total costs as the relative costs associated with false-positive and false-negative errors vary from 1/1 to 2/1, 5/1, and 10/1. The figure makes it clear that the point that minimizes the total cost moves up the score scale as the ratio increases.

FIGURE 20.5 Comparison of Conditional False-Positive and False-Negative Rates for a Single Administration and a Series of Three Administrations of the Same Test

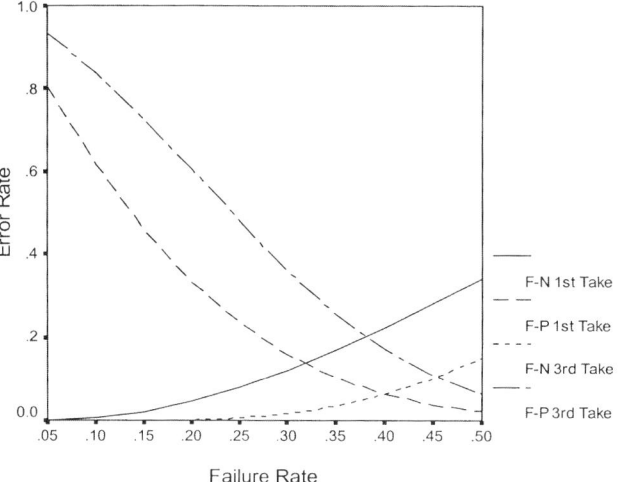

In Figure 20.4, the line labeled 1/1 also identifies the point at which the total number of misclassification errors is at a minimum.

The problem of classification accuracy for credentialing tests is further complicated by the fact that such testing is usually best conceptualized in terms of a sequence of test administrations. Examinees passing an examination typically do not re-test, while failing examinees may re-take the test multiple times (although some credentialing examinations limit the number of re-takes, limiting examinees to a single attempt is unusual). Across multiple re-takes, the misclassification of proficient examinees who fail due to measurement error is systematically reduced. At the same time, there is an increase in the rate of misclassification of examinees who are not proficient. Figure 20.5 illustrates the effects of this cumulative process; the four lines reflect the conditional false-positive and false-negative error rates associated with a single administration and those same rates accumulated across three administrations. The testing conditions for the single administration (and the resulting error rates) are the same as those represented in Figure 20.1. The error rates resulting from three administrations reflect the same testing conditions but assume that only failing examinees re-test. The cut score is unchanged, and the axis labeled "Failure Rate" represents the failure rate for the first administration. Under these conditions, with a cut score established to fail 25% of examinees (a value equal to the proportion of examinees defined as non-proficient) the opportunity to re-test essentially doubles the false-positive rate (increasing it from 24% to 48%) and reduces the false-negative rate from approximately 8% to approximately 1%.

In addition to the opportunity to re-take examinations, the issue of classification accuracy is further complicated by the fact that candidates for licensure may be required to complete and pass multiple, independently scored examinations. For example, medical licensure in the United States requires successful completion of USMLE Step 1, Step

FIGURE 20.6 Conditional False-Positive and False-Negative Rates Associated with a Sequence of Two Separate Tests

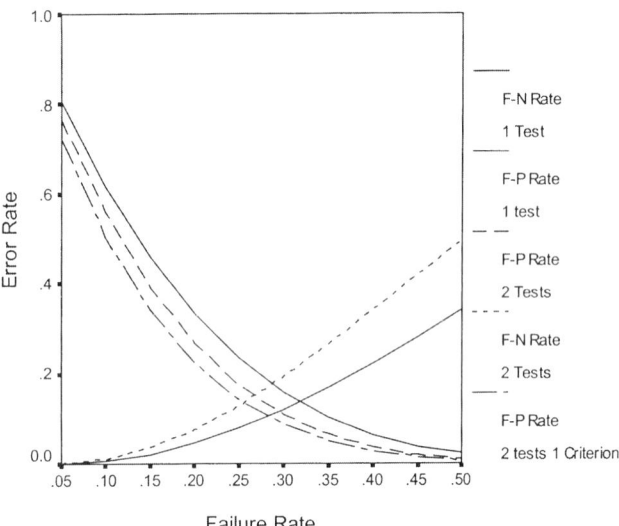

2CS, Step 2CK, and Step 3. Figure 20.6 presents the conditional false-positive and false-negative rates associated with a sequence of two tests. Both tests have a reliability of .8 and the tests have a true-score correlation of .5. For both tests, 25% of examinees are non-proficient. For all examined conditions, the cut scores are the same for both tests. The value represented on the axis labeled "Failure Rate" is the proportion of examinees failing each of the tests. As a frame of reference, with 25% non-proficient examinees on each test, 38% of examinees are non-proficient on at least one of the tests. Similarly, the point on the horizontal axis representing a 25% failure rate on each of the tests is associated with an approximately 38% failure rate for the sequence of two tests.

The conditional false-positive and false-negative rates for the sequence of two tests are graphed with those from either of the tests considered independently. These latter values are the same as those presented in Figure 20.1. This comparison is complicated by the fact that the overall proportion of non-proficient examinees has changed, and for any given value on the horizontal axis the overall failure rate also has changed. As an additional comparison, the conditional false-positive rates are graphed for the condition in which the pass-fail classification is based on the sequence of two tests but the criterion proficiency is for the first test only. That is, a line representing the proportion of examinees who pass both tests but lack the criterion proficiency measured by the first of the two tests (owing to measurement error on at least the first test) is included. Figure 20.6 makes it clear that all else being equal, requiring an examinee to demonstrate proficiency on multiple related but distinct measures decreases the overall false-positive rate and increases the false-negative rate.

The previous figures are intended to give the reader a practical sense for how test reliability relates to classification accuracy. The implications of these results for practice will be discussed in a subsequent section. In the next sections, consideration is given to a range of indices appropriate for tests intended for classification decisions.

3.2. Measures of Classification Consistency and Accuracy

Driven by trends in curriculum development, psychometricians in the 1970s developed procedures for assessing the decisions made using criterion-referenced (or domain-referenced) mastery tests. These procedures can be divided into two types: those based on squared-error loss functions and those based on threshold loss functions. Brennan and Kane (1977) refer to their procedure and that proposed by Livingston (1972) as representing a squared-error loss function. This contrasts with procedures that they refer to as representing a threshold loss function. This latter group of procedures includes a variety of contingency-table-based procedures. In principle, this group of procedures includes measures such as conditional and joint false-positive and false-negative error rates. It also includes indices of classification consistency such as that presented by Subkoviak (1976) and applications of Cohen's κ as recommended by Swaminathan, Hambleton, and Algina (1974). Indices of classification consistency will be discussed next followed by a discussion of classification accuracy.

3.2.1. Indices of Classification Consistency

Indices of classification consistency represent a reliability-like assessment of the performance of tests used to make classification decisions. If a test (or parallel forms of a test) can be administered to a sample of examinees on two occasions, classification consistency can be summarized in terms of the proportion of examinees who are classified the same way on both administrations. Huynh (1976), Subkoviak (1976, 1988), and Livingston and Lewis (1995) have presented procedures for estimating classification consistency based on a single administration. The earlier procedures presented by Huynh and Subkoviak require assumptions that typically will not be appropriate for licensing tests (e.g., equal item difficulty), but they have been shown to provide a good approximation even when these assumptions are not met (Algina & Noe, 1978; Huynh & Saunders, 1980). The basic model presented by Huynh was subsequently extended by Hanson and Brennan (1990), who used a more complex four-parameter beta distribution to model the underlying proficiencies (i.e., true scores).

More recently, Breyer and Lewis (1994) used a split-half approach to estimate the same index of consistency. With this approach, the test is split in half, the half-test cut score is applied to both halves, the decisions are compared, and the results are stepped up to the full test length. Livingston and Lewis (1995) also have presented a procedure based on the four-parameter beta model. This approach differs from previous procedures in several ways, including that it provides a measure of both classification accuracy and classification consistency. Although available evidence suggests that these more recent procedures are effective, they have not been studied thoroughly.

These various procedures differ in their level of computational complexity. In the 1970s, the limited availability of high-powered computers made this a significant issue that led to the development of approximation procedures. Although evaluations of these approximations showed them to be useful (Peng & Subkoviak, 1980; Subkoviak, 1988), computing power is no longer as significant an issue and there is currently little need for such approximations.

One limitation of classification consistency as an index of the usefulness of a test for making classification decisions is that the index can be high even if the test-based classifications are random. For example, if 10% of examinees fail the test on each of two occasions, even if the classifications are completely random 82% of examinees would be expected to be classified consistently across occasions. Swaminathan, Hambleton, and Algina (1974) recommended Cohen's κ as an alternative to the index of classification consistency because it accounts for differences in this level of chance agreement. Cohen's κ takes the form

$$\kappa = \frac{P_o - P_c}{1 - P_c}.$$

P_o represents the observed proportion of examinees classified the same way on both administrations. P_c represents the level of agreement expected to occur by chance. The coefficient reflects the improvement in classification consistency for the test over and above that expected by chance.

This adjustment for chance is important, but the κ coefficient has some potential-conceptual limitations. Because it is based on a threshold loss function, the loss associated with a nearly-proficient examinee being misclassified as proficient is considered to be equal to the loss associated with a far-from-proficient examinee being similarly misclassified. Another potential problem is that there may be instances in which basing the definition of chance on the observed marginals is undesirable (Brennan & Prediger, 1981).

3.2.2. Classification Accuracy and Decision-Theoretic Formulations

Classification accuracy differs from classification consistency in that it requires an explicit criterion. If classification consistency can be seen as providing reliability-like information, classification accuracy provides validity-like information. This change in perspective has several important implications. Perhaps most obviously, consistency is not a virtue in itself; consistent classification may be *wrong* consistently. The presence of a criterion replaces "consistent" classification with "correct" classification. It also allows for a distinction between false-positive and false-negative classification errors. This is important because the costs associated with these two types of error are not likely to be equal; requiring a proficient examinee to re-test may be less problematic than licensing a non-proficient candidate.

Cronbach and Gleser (1957) dealt explicitly with this issue in their discussion of the use of tests to make personnel decisions. The decision-theoretic framework that they developed, in part following the mathematical formulation laid down by Wald (1947), was taken up in the mastery-testing context by Hambleton and Novick (1973) and Swaminathan, Hambleton, and Algina (1975). They apply separate weights for false-positive and false-negative errors.

These latter presentations also apply a Bayesian framework to the problem, which allows for estimates of the probability that an examinee is or is not proficient (the examinee's true score is above and below the cut score, respectively) based on the Bayesian posterior distribution for the examinee. If the product of the probability that an examinee is proficient and the loss associated with failing a proficient examinee is greater than the product of the probability that an examinee is non-proficient and the loss associated with passing a non-proficient examinee, the examinee is classified as proficient. Defining the loss associated with a false-positive error as l_{fp} and the loss associated with a false-negative error as l_{fn}, the examinee is classified as passing if

$$\Pr(\tau < \tau_0) l_{fp} < \Pr(\tau > \tau_0) l_{fn}.$$

If the reverse is true,

$$\Pr(\tau < \tau_0) l_{fp} > \Pr(\tau > \tau_0) l_{fn},$$

the examinee is classified as non-proficient.

Consistent with the decision-theoretic framework, this approach minimizes the expected total cost of classification errors. The decision-theoretic formulation does not result in a simple index of the usefulness of a test for making classification decisions, although the expected total loss could be used for comparison purposes. In a certain sense, the major theoretical strength of this type of decision-theoretic procedure is also its major practical limitation. The procedure explicitly accounts for the relative costs of false-positive and false-negative errors, which requires that these costs can be made explicit. Some of the associated costs will defy quantification. This has led practitioners to avoid using decision theory. Unfortunately, avoiding these difficult questions is not an answer. Ultimately, the practical interpretation of any measure of classification accuracy requires an implicit consideration of these relative costs. For example, the choice to minimize misclassification errors rather than the cost associated with such errors simply reduces to setting these two types of error to be equal. If this is clearly an unfounded assumption, then the resulting interpretation similarly will be inappropriate.

3.2.3. Some Alternative Procedures for Assessing Classification Accuracy

Two procedures have become practical since the period in the 1970s and 1980s when domain-referenced mastery tests had an important place in the curriculum reform movement. The increasing use of these procedures has resulted in part from the wide availability of powerful computers. The first of these relies on bootstrap methodologies. These methods provide an obvious means of estimating classification consistency based on a single test administration. Consider the example in which a group of examinees has completed a 100-item test. For simplicity, further assume that the cut score can be defined in terms of the percent correct. The bootstrap approach treats the 100 item responses (scored 0/1) as a pool that represents the best available estimate of the distribution of an examinee's responses. Scores on randomly equivalent tests are constructed by sampling from the pool with replacement. The score on the re-sampled test can be classified by comparison to the cut score. This process can be completed n times for each of N examinees. For each examinee, a 2 × 2 table can be constructed and the classification consistency can be estimated. The coefficient for the test can be produced by averaging across the N examinees. The dimensions represented in the 2 × 2 table can represent either classification on the original test and bootstrap replications or classifications on two independent bootstrap replications.

This general approach can be adapted for circumstances in which simple random sampling is not appropriate. For example, if the test is built to a table of specifications, simple random sampling can be replaced with proportional stratified random sampling from within the various categories. For reasonably long tests where sampling is from a relatively small number of categories, this will provide a reasonable alternative. However, for a fixed-length test, as the number of content categories increases the number of items within each category will decrease; as the number of categories approaches the number of items, the usefulness of the procedure will decline. This logic holds equally well whether the categories are based on content or response format. For example, if a test contains 100 multiple-choice items and 5 constructed-response items, stratified bootstrap sampling can be applied. If, however, the test design calls for 100 multiple-choice items, 2 short essays, and 1 long essay, the procedure is not applicable. A recent paper by Brennan and Wan (2004) examines this application of the bootstrap in detail. In that paper, Brennan and Wan discuss an important distinction between classification consistency using pairs of bootstrap procedure replications and classification consistency using the actual test and a random bootstrap replication. Brennan and Wan also relate the bootstrap framework to the well-established constructs of generalizability theory.

The simplicity of the bootstrap approach is attractive. In the present application, it also is likely to be adequate. However, limitations of the procedure have led statisticians to recommend parametric bootstrapping as an alternative. With this approach, the available sample (e.g., examinee responses from a single test form) is used to estimate the parameters of a distribution. The characteristics of the data drive the choice of the distribution and its parameterization. Sampling then proceeds from the distribution rather than the observed data. This parametric approach to bootstrap sampling is discussed by Brennan and Wan (2004) as well.

This potential to use parameter estimates based on actual data as the starting point for computer simulations within a specified measurement model opens up the possibility of moving from estimates of classification consistency to estimates of classification accuracy. The procedure presented by Livingston and Lewis (1995) represents a variation on this approach. The results presented in Figures 20.1 through 20.6 were produced using a simulation based on classical test theory assumptions. In the classical test theory framework, a computer-generated variable can be treated as the true score for simulated examinees. Based on an estimate of the reliability of the test of interest, an error term can be generated and added to the true score; this produces the simulated observed score. Estimates of classification accuracy then can be made by comparing classifications based on the true score with those based on the observed score. If an estimate of classification consistency is needed, an independent error term with the same variance as that for the original error term can be generated. This can be added to the original true-score term to produce a second observed score. Classification consistency can be estimated by comparing the classifications made using the two simulated observed scores. Classifications based on both the true and observed scores can be made in conformance with assumptions about the proportion of proficient examinees in the population and the proportion of examinees who failed using the test. As the number of simulated examinees is increased, the precision with which the simulation results will approximate the theoretical values increases.

This approach is limited to the extent that the classical test theory assumptions fail to approximate the conditions in practice. This general approach, however, can be extended by simulating the data to conform to more complex models. For example, simulations could be based on dichotomous or polytomous item response theory models. Similarly, consistent with the generalizability theory framework, multiple independent sources of error could be included in the model representing the person by item interaction as well as terms for item difficulty, rater stringency, and the associated interactions.

3.2.4. Dependability Measures for Mastery Tests

The previous paragraphs discuss indices based on a threshold loss function. This section describes indices based on a squared-error loss function and focuses on a measure of dependability for mastery tests. Conceptually, the measure of dependability for mastery tests differs from the typical classical test theory measure of reliability in two important respects. First, the concept of dependability differs from that of reliability. Reliability can be viewed as an index of the precision of measurement in the context of a specific test; dependability is an analogous metric used when the scores are to be interpreted as measures of mastery of a domain from which the specific test items were sampled. Additionally, these procedures provide indices appropriate for the scores that are intended for classification decisions (that is, conditions in which the observed score was to be interpreted relative to a cut score).

Both Livingston (1972) and Brennan and Kane (1977) presented procedures that extended existing test theory to mastery-testing applications. Livingston presented an index that paralleled the traditional reliability coefficient-with one important difference: rather than defining score deviations in terms of variability around the mean, deviations were defined in terms of distance from the cut score. The Brennan-Kane index was conceptually similar to that proposed by Livingston except that it was constructed within a generalizability framework rather than a classical test theory framework. As such, Livingston attempted to extend classical test theory to the mastery-testing context. By contrast, the Brennan-Kane index moves both from the norm-referenced framework of classical test theory to the domain-referenced interpretation made possible by generalizability theory and then redefines the metric to make it appropriate for mastery testing.

Brennan and Kane describe the index of dependability for mastery tests as

$$M(C) = \frac{\sigma^2(\pi)+(\mu-C)^2}{\sigma^2(\pi)+(\mu-C)^2+\frac{1}{n_i}[\sigma^2(\beta)+\sigma^2(\pi\beta,e)]}.$$

In this formulation, $\sigma^2(\pi)$ is the person variance. In generalizability theory terms, this is referred to as universe-score variance and is conceptually similar to true-score variance in classical test theory. μ represents the population mean and C is the cut score. The number of items on the test is represented by n_i. The variance associated with the item effect is $\sigma^2(\beta)$. This represents the variability in difficulty of the items in the domain. Finally, $\sigma^2(\pi\beta,e)$ represents the residual variance. This includes the examinee by item interaction effect and other sources of error unaccounted for in the model. This index is equivalent to the dependability or phi coefficient commonly used in generalizability theory except that it also includes a term that accounts for the distance between the cut score and the group mean.

The Brennan-Kane index has the advantage that it appropriately reflects the fact that the extent to which a given level of measurement error will impact decision accuracy is in part a function of the placement of the cut score. This index also sensibly reflects the fact that the loss associated with misclassifying an examinee with a true score very close to the cut score is typically not as significant as that of misclassifying an examinee whose true score is well above or well below the cut score.

Harris (1972) criticized Livingston's (1972) proposed index on the grounds that a larger coefficient "does not imply a more dependable determination of whether or not a true score falls below (or exceeds) a given criterion value" (p. 27). This is a necessary consequence of the fact that the index is sensitive to the placement of the cut score relative to the distribution of examinees. As such, it is both an advantage and disadvantage of the index. This criticism applies similarly to the Brennan-Kane index. Brennan and Kane respond to this potential criticism by emphasizing the importance of clearly defining the index as a function of both the placement of the cut score and the length of the test. They recommend that users of the index be presented with additional information including estimates of measurement error. The indices presented by Brennan and Kane (1977) and Livingston (1972) also are limited by the fact that there is no differentiation between measurement error that results in misclassification and measurement error that results in overconfidence in the correct classification. That is, in many cases measurement error will result in (1) an examinee who is in fact proficient receiving a score that exaggerates the extent to which that examinee's proficiency exceeds the standard; or (2) an examinee who is not proficient receiving a score that exaggerates the extent to which the examinee fails to meet the standard. Such errors interfere with the ability to provide accurate feedback regarding the examinee's position relative to the standard, but they do not contribute to misclassification.

3.3. Implications for Practice

The previous section reviewed several indices that are useful for describing the precision of test scores in contexts in which the scores are used to make classification decisions. The array of indices raises an obvious question: "Which of these indices is preferred?" The simple answer is that an appropriate evaluation in the context of a high-stakes assessment will include multiple indices. An estimate of the standard error of measurement will be appropriate regardless of whether or not the test is used to make classification decisions. Measures that more directly reflect classification accuracy also will be needed. The presentation on classification accuracy makes it clear that these measures must be interpreted in the context of a specific examinee distribution and a specified cut score. For any given examinee population and assessment, it will be possible to eliminate either false-positive or false-negative classification errors by adjusting the cut score; reducing (or eliminating) either type of error, however, comes at the cost of increasing the other type. Optimal performance for a given test will result from placing the cut score to minimize the total cost associated with classification errors. Although this is theoretically straightforward, it requires specifying the ratio of costs associated with these two types of error. As a practical matter, this is problematic because it requires measuring the costs associated with credentialing an unqualified practitioner with the same metric used to measure the costs associated with failing to credential a qualified individual. In both cases, this includes costs both to society and to the individual. When a proficient examinee is denied a license, society loses access to a practitioner and the examinee must bear the costs associated with being denied the opportunity to practice and having to re-test. When practitioners are in short supply, the cost to society may mean that some individuals will not be able to access professional services. By contrast, the costs to the individual primarily will be financial and emotional. When a non-proficient examinee is licensed as a result of classification error, society pays the cost of having an unqualified practitioner enter practice. There also may be costs for the individual; for example, an individual's career ultimately may be enhanced by the additional study that is prompted by initial failure on a credentialing examination. Issues related to the costs of classification errors are further complicated by the fact that some of these expected costs are mediated by the extent to which test scores accurately quantify readiness for subsequent practice.

From a practical perspective, the main complication in interpreting indices of classification accuracy or consistency is that ultimate licensing or certifying decisions result from an overall testing process and not from a single administration. Failing examinees will have the opportunity to re-test and examinees may be required to demonstrate proficiency on multiple occasions based on multiple measures. Classification accuracy for the assessment system is the issue of interest. As Figure 20.5 demonstrates, multiple administrations—under the condition that only failing examinees re-test—lead to inflated false-positive error rates; an increased number of examinees with inadequate credentials will pass. Controlling this source of error obviously is a significant issue. Numerous procedures have been recommended for this purpose (Clauser & Nungester, 2001; Millman, 1989). For example, an examinee's score across multiple administrations could be averaged. This averaging could be across all administrations, the best two administrations, or the most recent two administrations. Averaging in this way minimizes the impact of measurement error in any single administration, but it puts the examinee at a significant disadvantage if he or she has performed unexpectedly poorly on an initial administration. An examinee performing at a level well below his or her actual proficiency owing to illness or other extraneous factors that existed on the day of the administration could be disadvantaged significantly. Another strategy for controlling the false-positive error rate across multiple administrations is to increase the cut score for subsequent administrations. Increasing the cut score for each subsequent administration that an examinee attempts would decrease the incremental false-positive rate. As with approaches that involve averaging across administrations, this strategy would put a subset of examinees at what may be perceived to be an unfair disadvantage. It is also true that even if one of these procedures is used, permitting re-takes still will increase the false-positive error rate. One alternative strategy that avoids the limitations of the previously described procedures is to establish the cut score for all administrations at a level such that the false-positive rate associated with a sequence of administrations is acceptable. For example, Figure 20.5 suggests that if an overall false-positive rate of approximately 20% is acceptable for the modeled test, a cut score that fails between 25% and 30% of examinees is appropriate if examinees are permitted only one attempt. If examinees are permitted up to three attempts, the cut score would need to be adjusted to fail approximately 40% of examinees on the first administration to maintain that same false-positive rate across the sequence of up to three administrations. This logic will be considered in greater detail in the subsequent section on standard setting, but it is important to note that the size of the adjustment to the cut score will be a function of the number of re-takes that are allowed. This in itself suggests one of the most important strategies for controlling false-positive errors across a sequence of administrations: limit the number of re-takes permitted. The practical implementation of limits on an examinee's opportunity to re-take an examination could be categorical, or the requirements could be in terms of the allowable number of re-takes either within a given time span or without documentation of having undertaken additional training.

Figure 20.5 highlights the implications of multiple re-takes: increasing the false-positive rate and decreasing the false-negative rate. Figure 20.6 demonstrates how an assessment system that requires the examinee to pass multiple hurdles pushes the false-positive and false-negative error rates in opposite directions: the false-negative rate increases and the false-positive rate decreases. The interplay of multiple re-takes and multiple conjunctive hurdles will be influenced by the specifics of the assessment.

This section has examined issues of score reliability and the reproducibility of decisions for licensing and certifying examinations. The next section turns to the larger question of score validity.

4. VALIDITY ISSUES

Broadly speaking, score interpretations can be thought of as valid to the extent that evidence and theory support those interpretations. The *Standards* (AERA, APA, NCME, 1999) define validity as "the degree to which evidence and theory support the interpretation of test scores entailed by proposed uses" (p. 9). The process of validation is viewed as the collection of evidence providing "a sound scientific basis for the proposed score interpretations" (p. 9). Because the primary interpretation based on scores from licensing and certifying tests is that the examinee is (or is not) suitable for licensed or certified practice, it follows that a central issue of validity theory in this context is the question of whether the test scores properly classify examinees.

4.1. Predictive Validity

The holy grail of validity evidence for licensing examinations is a demonstration that examinees who pass the test perform satisfactorily in practice and those who do not pass do not perform satisfactorily in practice. There are many reasons that such evidence is elusive. Foremost among these is the fact that failing examinees typically are not permitted to practice and their inadequacy therefore cannot be documented. Examining the relationship between practice and test scores within the more restricted group of passing examinees has the potential to provide supportive evidence, but a test that is carefully constructed to distinguish between the unacceptable and the just-acceptable practitioner may not discriminate well between other levels of practice. Conversely, information demonstrating that test scores within the passing range discriminate between more and less competent practitioners is not direct evidence that those test scores around the cut score produce appropriate classifications.

Some researchers have produced evidence relating test scores to performance in practice (e.g., Tamblyn et al., 2002), but the problem of establishing a criterion against which to assess the test scores adds to the elusive nature of this type of validity evidence. There are many reasons that a practitioner's performance may be unacceptable. If a test is developed to assess the extent to which professionals possess the skills required for practice, it is sensible that examinees with lower levels of those skills will be less-fit practitioners. But examinees who possess these skills may fail to use them; knowing how and doing what is required are two different things. In this respect, a passing score on a licensing examination may be seen as a *prerequisite* for acceptable practice but not a *guarantee* of acceptable practice. The potential for aspects of individual behavior that are not measured by the test to impact practice further complicates the problem of defining a criterion by which score validity can be evaluated. A lack of professional integrity, substance abuse, or other personal problems may influence professional performance. To the extent that the scores are intended to be interpreted as evidence that the examinee possesses the required skills and proficiencies for practice, poor performance in practice may be associated with exceptional test scores without reflecting on the validity of the scores. The criterion problem is further complicated by the fact that any identified criterion will itself need to be supported by validity evidence. Criteria, no matter how appealing, are not revealed. This results in a kind of infinite regression.

4.2. The Interpretative Argument

The previous paragraphs are not intended to deny the potential usefulness of collecting validity evidence that includes a comparison of practice-based performance to test outcomes. Instead, these comments are intended to argue that when such evidence can be collected it is likely to be flawed and in itself insufficient to provide compelling support for the intended interpretations of scores from licensing and certifying examinations.

When the first edition of *Educational Measurement* (Lindquist, 1951) was published, criterion-related validity was central. Since that time, the concept of test validity has evolved, first to include the notion of construct validity and more recently to view the validation process as the development of an argument in support of the interpretations and inferences drawn from test scores. The process of developing support for a proposed interpretation involves the production of a coherent argument for that interpretation. The *interpretative argument* provides an overall evaluation of the plausibility of the intended interpretation including evidence for and against the proposed interpretation as well as a balanced evaluation of plausible alternate interpretations (Cronbach, 1988; House, 1980; Kane, 1992).

This interpretative argument can be represented as a chain or network of inferences leading from test scores to conclusions to be drawn to decisions based on those conclusions (Kane, 1992). It provides an explicit statement of the inferences and assumptions inherent in the interpretation and provides a framework for evaluating the proposed interpretation in some detail. All inferences and assumptions must be sound if the interpretative argument is to be accepted; the plausibility of the interpretation therefore is limited by the plausibility of its weakest links (Cronbach, 1971; Messick, 1989). Evidence that provides further support for a highly plausible assumption does not add much to the overall argument. Evidence relevant to the most questionable inferences in the interpretive argument provides the most effective contribution to the validity argument. All of the inferences and assumptions in the interpretative argument must hold for the proposed interpretation to be considered valid.

Several general types of inferences and assumptions appear in interpretive arguments: (1) the acceptance of a number as a test score assumes that the number was assigned using appropriate procedures; (2) generalizations from the observed score to the expected score over some universe of possible observations rest on assumptions about the invariance of observed scores over different conditions of observation; (3) extrapolations beyond the testing context are based on assumptions about the relationship between the performances observed during the assessment and the ("real-world") performances of ultimate interest; (4) any theory-based inferences are only as credible as the theory; and (5) the decisions based on test scores make assumptions about the desirability of various kinds of outcomes (i.e., about values and consequences). These five types of arguments are referred to by Kane, Crooks, and Cohen (1999) as evaluation, generalization, extrapolation, explanation, and decision.

4.2.1. Evaluation and Generalization

For professionally developed licensing and certifying tests, the evidence to support the first two of these inferences is likely to be compelling. Generally, great effort is expended to insure that tests are administered under highly structured and standardized conditions and that violations or variations in the conditions of administration are documented by annotations to the reported score or considered as a basis for invalidating the administration. Similarly, evidence to support the level of generalizability of test scores for professional licensing and certifying tests is typically compelling. To insure generalizability, these tests tend to be lengthy and constructed to meet highly structured content and statistical specifications.

4.2.2. Extrapolation and Interpretation

In contrast to the steps in the argument representing evaluation and generalization, collecting the evidence required to support inferences relating to extrapolation from the conditions of testing to those in practice is likely to be more challenging. It may be that the difficulties in this step in the process are the result of efforts to improve standardization and generalizability. As described previously, assessment for licensure historically was based on observation and interactive oral examination. Though this approach provided a close link between the physical and cognitive conditions of testing and those of practice, it was at the expense of standardization and generalizability. Replacing these methods with multiple-choice items created the opportunity for standardization and substantially increased generalizability at the risk of widening the gap between the conditions of testing and those of professional practice. The relative weakness of this link has been a major motivation for the recent movement toward the use of complex constructed-response formats in testing for licensure and certification.

The primary evidence to support inferences related to extrapolation is to be found in rigorous test construction procedures (described in a previous section). Empirical evidence is collected through job analyses, practice analyses, critical incident reports, and related techniques to establish the range of skills and knowledge required for practice. To the extent that the test is constructed to reflect that range of proficiencies, a credible link may be established. Additional evidence may be produced by asking content experts and practitioners to make judgments about the relevance of test items (c.f. Cuddy et al., 2004). This type of evidence is important, but it may miss limitations associated with the cognitive challenge represented by an item format. Narrowing the gap between the cognitive challenge of responding to test items and the demands of professional practice is a driving force behind the use of complex item formats.

Certified public accountants, architects, lawyers, and physicians all complete such items as part of assessment for licensure. This said, it should be noted that although the complex items appear to provide a closer approximation to practice, there is little empirical evidence to support this contention.

In general, fact-based tests for professionals function on the basis that knowledge of the facts and ability to apply the facts are prerequisites to using information to make nuanced professional decisions. Cognitive theories (or assumptions) of this type are necessary to support inferences based on test scores. Such inferences often have strong support in common sense, but again, empirical evidence to support these inferences is needed.

4.2.3. Decision

The final type of evidence required to support the validity argument is that associated with the decision. In testing for licensure and certification, the associated decisions are important to both the examinee and the public. The decision process is based on establishing a cut score that defines the distinction between adequate and inadequate proficiency in the domains evaluated by the test. Considerations related to establishing cut scores are addressed in more detail in a subsequent section, but ultimately the adequacy of this process limits the extent to which decisions based on the test scores can be supported.

For the interpretive argument to be credible, it must include evidence for and against the proposed interpretation; this includes any evidence for or against plausible alternative interpretations. To make the validity argument credible, particular attention must be given to threats to validity. The following section describes some of the prominent threats to the validity of interpretations made based on the scores from licensing and certifying examinations.

4.3. Threats to Validity

4.3.1. Security Issues

The stakes involved in testing for licensure are extremely high. Given the importance of passing, it is inevitable that some examinees will attempt to subvert the system. When examinees are successful in gaining an advantage through such efforts, the validity of interpretations based on those scores will be threatened. Producing convincing evidence for the evaluation step in the validity argument therefore requires evidence that threats to the security of the test can be discounted. Conceptually, there are three points in the process of secure test delivery: (1) test items must remain secure until the test is administered; (2) it must be verified that examinees had no assistance in completing the examination; and (3) it must be verified that responses were not altered after the examination was completed (and that resulting scores are not altered before they are reported).

These problems are not new; a century ago, Sherlock Holmes was called upon to solve a case in which a student had gained prior access to a test (Doyle, 1904). But although these problems are not new, technological advances have complicated them. With paper-and-pencil testing, it is common practice to administer a test on a small number of occasions per year. If items are reused across administrations, it is often after a lag of several administrations if not several years in order to reduce the usefulness of memorizing test material to share with examinees planning to complete the examination in the future. The most significant threat to security under these conditions is the possibility that individual copies of the test might be stolen during transport to the testing location or from storage prior to administration. (Of course, if items are to be reused, it remains necessary to maintain control over test books after administration as well.)

Moving to computer administration does much to solve the problem of test booklets being lost or stolen (e.g., materials can be encrypted until administration). But when large-scale tests are administered electronically, the limited availability of secure administration facilities typically dictates that the test will be administered more frequently—if not continuously—throughout the year. Even with large item banks, this administration approach will lead to the need to reuse items with relatively little lag time. Under these circumstances, items can and likely will be memorized and shared with other test-takers. The potential impact of such memorization is exacerbated by the fact that these items can be shared across the internet.

There are no easy answers to this problem. Increasing the number of items in the pool is likely to limit the advantage that examinees gain as a result of prior access, but item production is costly. Monitoring the Internet and closing down sites shown to present copyrighted test items also may provide some relief. Automated systems for item generation may provide an answer in the future, but considerable research remains to be completed before these procedures are appropriate for operational use in testing for licensure (Irvine & Kyllonen, 2002).

As computer technology has complicated the problem of ensuring that test material remains secure prior to administration, other forms of technology have added to the difficulty in verifying that examinees do not receive assistance in completing the examination. Computer delivery largely has eliminated one potential problem with paper-and-pencil administered tests: copying answers from another examinee. Even if two examinees are completing the same form of the test, the computer can administer the items in a different order. But cell phones and other means of portable communication have made it more difficult to ensure that examinees are not able to communicate with others. Monitoring in the testing area is a partial answer, but without intrusive searching it is impossible to be sure that examinees do not have such devices. Additionally, unmonitored breaks during testing give examinees who do not bring communication devices to the test area an opportunity to use them outside the room where the test is being administered.

Perhaps the simplest way for an examinee to receive help with a test is to have someone more competent complete the examination. Requiring multiple forms of identification in addition to photographing, fingerprinting, or retinal scanning of examinees for comparison and verification by the licensing authority should provide reasonable security against identity fraud. However, these approaches require that the proctoring staff be both diligent and honest.

Finally, threats to security also exist to the extent that someone is in a position to alter examinee responses after testing is completed. Again, computerization may make this type of alteration more difficult. It also may make it more difficult to identify the fact that an alteration has occurred.

Whether a licensing examination is administered on computer or paper, these types of threats to validity must be taken seriously and thoughtful procedures must be developed and implemented to limit them. Statistical procedures may provide some useful information that allows test developers to monitor performance over time. Many of the procedures developed to examine differential item functioning may be useful to assess changes in item difficulty over time to determine if item exposure is having a substantial impact (Clauser & Mazor, 1998; Davy & Stone, 2004). Logistic regression procedures are particularly useful because they allow time (or number of exposures) to be modeled as a continuous variable. The extent to which these tools will be sensitive is likely to be a function both of the extent of the exposure and the pattern of the exposure. If only the poorest performing examinees take advantage of available materials, the impact on the score validity could be significant while the changes in statistical performance of the items may be minimal. When tests are being delivered by computer at a large number of testing centers, statistical procedures also may be useful for indentifying center-level changes in performance. Such information could indicate that a security problem exists at a given center.

4.3.2. Teaching to the Test and Teaching the Test

It is hoped that the high stakes associated with testing for licensure will drive relatively few examinees to cheat; the importance of these tests, however, gives examinees a strong interest in being as prepared as possible for the examination. This interest is likely to motivate professional schools to make sure that their curriculum is well matched to the demands of the test. It also will motivate examinees to take courses specifically designed to prepare for the examination.

The issue of professional schools teaching to the test is complicated. In principle, if the test provided a full and balanced assessment of all skills and proficiencies needed to practice in the profession, teaching to the test would not be a concern. In fact, teaching to the test would be identical to preparing the student for practice. This is, however, never fully the case. Licensing tests are likely to assess a subset of the material in the curriculum and a subset of the proficiencies needed for practice. Insofar as scores are interpreted as representing an examinee's overall readiness for practice, teaching to the test may undermine the validity of the interpretations because it will mean that examinees are receiving more instruction in the areas that are tested. This issue is a double-edged sword, because curricular focus on the content of the test means that a well-structured test built to a thoughtfully produced and empirically supported blueprint can be a force to improve professional education.

The logic in assessing the validity implications of test prep courses is much the same as that which is relevant to assessing the impact of tests on a curriculum. In some sense, test prep courses are the ultimate example of teaching to the test. A well-designed course focuses only on the skills required for success on the test. Again, to the extent that the test assesses the proficiencies required for success in the profession, improving those proficiencies can and should lead to higher scores. A problem arises, however, when the test also measures secondary proficiencies unrelated to the construct the test is intended to assess. For example, if a prep course teaches examinees how to eliminate incorrect multiple choice options based on weaknesses of item writing rather than knowledge of the content, the scores produced by examinees completing the course may lead to less valid inferences.

4.3.3. Other Sources of Construct-Irrelevant Variance

The fact that performance on test items may be influenced by factors other than the proficiency the test is intended to measure represents a central threat to score interpretation. One common conceptualization of the impact of such effects is manifest in approaches for examining differential item functioning (Clauser & Mazor, 1998; Holland & Wainer, 1993). The basic concept is that if examinees from one subgroup have a differential likelihood of success on an item (after conditioning on the proficiency measured by the test), the item must be sensitive to some secondary proficiency. This general conceptualization covers a range of influences, and the challenge is to determine whether this secondary influence is relevant. In the case of licensing tests, it is not uncommon that a single examination contains items relating to specialized areas; for example, real estate law and criminal law, pediatrics and surgery. In these circumstances, items may perform differentially for subgroups that are more likely to be familiar with specific content areas. For example, in medicine, women may perform differentially better on pediatrics and obstetrics items than do men. This might be a matter of concern were it not for the fact that women are more likely to specialize in these areas; when this difference in training is taken into account, performance differences are reduced or even eliminated (Clauser, Nungester, & Swaminathan, 1996). Because of the complexity of the content of licensing tests, differential performance based on item content is difficult to interpret. When differences exist, it may not be evidence that the item is flawed but it will be evidence that the inclusion of such items in the test should be controlled through the test specifications. It is fine if women do better on obstetrics items, but it is a threat to validity when these items are represented disproportionately on the test.

Differential performance may be manifest as a result of item characteristics other than content. For example, issues of examinee pacing and test speededness may cause items at the end of the test to be more difficult for some examinees. Whether viewed in the context of differential item functioning or in some other analytic framework, time constraints may threaten the validity of score interpretations.

In order to maintain standardized testing conditions, large-scale high-stakes tests are administered with time limits. There are likely to be some instances in which the test developers believe that the proficiency of interest includes answering items both correctly and quickly, but more often time limits are a matter of administrative practicality. When the examination is administered on paper, it may be that examinees are running out of time at the end of the test. However, it is difficult to evaluate the level of speededness because examinees are unlikely to leave items blank; instead, they may answer items rapidly, possibly without even reading the question. With computer administration, it has become possible to record the amount of time that each examinee spends on each item. This makes it possible to assess the relationship between the position of the item in the test sequence, the time spent on the item, and the probability of success on the item. When examinees use less time on a given item when it appears later in the test and have a lower probability of success, this provides evidence that timing constraints may be influencing examinee scores. Two recent papers examining timing on a computer-administered licensing test provide evidence that examinees used less time and performed less well on the final items in each separately timed section of the examination (Swanson, Case, Ripkey, Clauser, & Holtman, 2001; Swygert, Muller, Clauser, Dillon, & Swanson, 2004). Interestingly, results of these papers indicate that the pattern of performance across item position was unchanged when the total time allowed for the sections was increased.

A final source of potential construct-irrelevant variance is item format. With the advent of widespread computer-based testing, test developers have been attracted to the idea of moving beyond the one-best-answer item format to development of more complex response types. The purpose of these new formats is to assess examinee proficiencies that may not be well measured with simpler fixed-format response types. There is often a wish that the form of the response should more closely approximate the real-world behavior of interest. But with current technology, although these new item formats may require responses that more closely approach the real-world behavior of interest, the responses only provide an approximation of that behavior. Artifacts in how the examinee is required to respond or how those responses are interpreted and scored by the computer may introduce construct-irrelevant variance into the scores. Bennett, Steffen, Singley, Morley, & Jacquemin (1997) described a computer-delivered response type that requires examinees to produce a mathematical expression that represents the relationship presented in the item stem. They provide the following example: "During one week in Trenton in January, it snowed for s days and was fair on the other days. What is the probability that a randomly-selected day from that week was fair?" (p. 164). The task for the examinee is to use the interface to produce a mathematical expression that could be used to represent the relationship. Either of the following examples might be considered correct:

$$(1)\ 1-\frac{s}{7}\ \text{or}$$

$$(2)\ \frac{7-s}{7}.$$

The interface and scoring procedure were limited by the fact that if the examinee labeled the response

$$\frac{7-s}{7}\ days,$$

this conceptually correct answer would be scored as incorrect.

A scoring algorithm sensitive to this type of behavior would measure the examinee's understanding of the scoring rules as well as the underlying mathematical relationship; this artifact undermines the validity of the resulting scores. This example from outside of licensure is a reasonably simple one, but it shows by analogy how the response interface and scoring algorithm simultaneously can extend the boundaries of testing and undermine the validity of the resulting interpretations. This issue also is not limited to computerized testing. Similar problems can arise with any complex item format.

The problem of format-specific variance is of particular concern because of the trend toward the use of such alternative formats in testing for licensure and certification. There has been relatively little systematic study to assess the presence of format-specific variance on scores. One exception is a paper by Margolis, Clauser, Harik, and Guernsey (2002) that investigated subgroup performance differences on the computer-based case simulation component of the USMLE Step 3 examination. The hypothesis was that if such effects were present, they may be manifest as performance differences between groups that might differ in familiarity with computers and facility with written English. The results provided little evidence of such an influence. Consistent with Cronbach's admonition that, "A proposition deserves some degree of trust only when it has survived serious attempts to falsify it" (Cronbach, 1980, p. 103), more of this type of research is needed before any of these new and complex item formats can be accepted fully. These innovations that are designed to expand the bounds of assessment for licensure must be supported by critical evaluation.

The significance of cut scores has been raised in this section in the context of the validity argument. In the next section, issues related to establishing cut scores will be addressed more broadly.

5. ESTABLISHING STANDARDS AND CUT SCORES

A variety of procedures have been developed for estimating cut scores (see Hambleton and Pitoniak, this volume; Cizek, 2001). Standard setting for licensing examinations is not conceptually different than standard setting in most other testing contexts, and this section examines some of the conceptual issues that arise in applying existing standard-setting procedures to licensing and certifying tests.

Standards typically do not exist in nature, waiting to be found or estimated by scientific procedures. Establishing a standard is a policy decision and so it is, by definition, a political activity; given this political nature, it is not surprising that standard-setting procedures historically have been a source of controversy (Glass, 1978; Shepard, 1995; Zieky, 2001). In spite of the related challenges, the difficult task of establishing a credible standard must be done in a manner that avoids the charge that it is capricious (Kane, 1994). This is not a simple task and there is no single right answer.

One widely-accepted requirement for standards for licensing tests is that they be absolute, rather than norm-referenced. This view is represented in the *Standards* (AERA, APA, & NCME, 1999) and rests on the strict notion that a standard should reflect the level of proficiency required for practice in the profession. Once a decision establishing that level of performance is made, in theory it should be possible for all candidates to receive passing scores or for all candidates to fail the examination.

The limitation of this view is that for most professional activities it reduces to a circular argument. The level of proficiency required to practice in a profession is in part defined by the standards of practice in that profession, and standards of practice are necessarily norm-referenced. If a profession experiences an influx of highly qualified practitioners, their entry into the work force will lead to changes in expectations for the profession and the standards of practice. With this change in standards for practice would come a change in the level of proficiency required for practice. The reverse is true also; if the best and brightest reject one profession in favor of another, over time the standards of practice may be lowered. It is the nature of the professions that professional judgment is required; these judgments will not be flawless. The incompetent physician is not simply the physician whose patients die. Instead the incompetent physician is the physician whose patients die when they would have been expected to survive in the care of most other physicians. The incompetent teacher similarly is defined not by failure with individual students or classes but by failure under conditions in which success could be expected.

Of course this does not deny the possibility of an absolute standard in the sense that once that standard is established the subsequently demonstrated proficiency of examinees testing under that standard will not come into play. A distinction must be drawn between an absolute standard and a purely content-based standard. An absolute standard may be based on consideration of a range of evidence that includes information about the proportion of examinees within some defined group who have passed under the previous standard (and possibly a projection about the proportion in that group expected to pass under some alternate standard). A purely content-based standard would be absolute, but presumably such a standard would not take the population of examinees into account. Conceptually this is problematic because it ignores the norm-based aspect of standards of practice.

The view that strictly content-referenced standards can be achieved is further limited by empirical evidence. Far and away the most commonly used methods for setting standards on professional licensing tests in the United States are variations on the Angoff procedure. These procedures require the standard setters to make judgments about the proportion of "borderline examinees" that would be expected to select the correct answer for each studied item. Numerous authors have examined the judgments that experts make in this context. The repeated results of these studies show that in the absence of normative data about examinee performance, experts are extremely limited in their ability to make judgments about the performance of "borderline examinees" (e.g., Clauser, Swanson, & Harik, 2002; Impara & Plake, 1998).

In the Impara and Plake study, high school teachers made judgments about the expected performance of borderline students in a science class. Borderline was defined in terms of the grade that those students received in the class. Because of this definition, unlike the situation in most licensing tests, it was possible to identify the "borderline examinees" and to compare their actual performance with the expectations reflected in the judgments. The results provided little support for the use of this type of judgment for establishing standards.

The paper by Clauser and colleagues (2002) examines the performance of content experts who made judgments about the performance of borderline candidates for medical licensure. The results show wide disparities both within and between groups of judges. Additionally, the results suggest that judgments from independent groups of experts converge when empirical performance evidence is provided.

These studies argue against the view that a strictly content-based standard can be established with variations on the Angoff procedure. Some antagonists have argued against the Angoff procedure on these grounds, suggesting that examinee-based procedures are preferable (Shepard, Glaser, Linn, & Bohrnstedt, 1993). There is considerable evidence that this approach can be useful, but the suggestion that this procedure achieves criterion-referenced standards while avoiding the circular argument that supports the Angoff procedure is misguided. Ultimately, there is no way to separate standards for licensure from standards for practice.

In the end, standard setting is a political process that is informed by evidence. The question then becomes one of deciding on the information that should inform this decision. Expert judgments about examinee performance are one important source of information, but whether these judgments focus on the expected performance of examinees on specified items (in the context of the Angoff procedure) or on the adequacy of the skills of individuals (as in the contrasting groups procedure), they represent only a single source of information. To fully inform decision makers, at least four types of evidence should be considered: (1) the results from independent groups completing judgments using the Angoff or other procedures; (2) the proportion of a defined reference group of examinees that would be expected to fail with any given cut score as well as comparative information that shows how performance has changed across cohorts of examinees; (3) survey information representing the opinions of constituency groups regarding the adequacy of current standards and information about expected fail rates for a defined group; and (4) information about the expected impact of measurement error on classification accuracy. (See Nungester, Dillon, Swanson, Orr, & Powell [1991] for a discussion of the first three of these sources of information and Orr & Nungester [1991] for a discussion of constituency surveys.)

Although a procedure using all of these sources of information may be more elaborate than that used in most licensing contexts, these sources of information provide a useful framework for comment. First, establishing the standard typically is not the responsibility of the judges participating in the Angoff exercise. The final decision rests with a policy group that bears overall responsibility for the examination. Integrating this type of information to make a policy decision regarding the standard requires that the decision makers be knowledgeable about the population of interest, the standards of practice in the field, and the content of the examination. These are characteristics that should be common to the judges in the content-based standard-setting exercise as well. In addition, the decision makers must credibly be able to represent and balance the conflicting political pressures and interests (AERA, APA, & NCME, 1999; Raymond & Reid, 2001). A level of independence from the organization that produces the test also may be beneficial. If the decision makers are employees of the testing organization, examinees may believe that a decision to raise the cut score has been motivated by the increase in revenue from failing examinees re-taking the examination.

The first three of the previously-listed sources of information allow the decision makers to identify the standard. Conceptually, this answers the question, "How much is enough?" The simplest approaches to standard setting, and those that likely are the most common, depend on the results of a content-based standard-setting procedure (typically the Angoff procedure) and information about the impact of the resulting decisions. The more elaborate procedure described previously extends this model by adding the results of replications of the Angoff procedure across multiple groups. This allows decision makers to integrate information about variability in the results of this procedure into the overall decision. Information about the variability of the procedure across replications is explicitly recommended in the *Standards* (AERA, APA, & NCME, 1999).

Experts planning such exercises may benefit from a more technical examination of that variability. Generalizability theory provides an ideal framework for examining the sources of this variability (Brennan, 2001; Cronbach, Gleser, Nanda, & Rajaratnam, 1972). As with other estimates based on sampling, the precision will increase as the sample sizes increase; as the number of items judged, the number of judges within groups, and the number of groups increase the precision also will increase (Brennan, 1995). In this context, Clauser and colleagues (2002) present results suggesting that the group effect may be a nontrivial source of variance. That is, a more precise estimate may be produced using two groups of five raters each than with one group of ten raters. Both theory and empirical results also would suggest that nesting items within raters should be advantageous because more items can be judged while holding the total number of judgments fixed. This said, it is important to remember that projections based on generalizability analysis provide estimates of error variance associated with the mean score of interest for various data collection designs. This information provides no insight into the social-psychological effects of increasing the size of the group that is working to produce content-based standard-setting judgments, and there is relatively little empirical evidence about the impact of these effects (Fitzpatrick, 1989). Practical issues also must be considered in designing these exercises.

Another potential source of information that may guide decision makers in establishing a standard comes from surveying groups that are knowledgeable about the population and are invested in the standard. The specifics will vary across professions, but groups including recent examinees, individuals involved in professional training, and individuals representing state licensing boards are obvious choices for inclusion (Raymond & Reid, 2001). Again, results of these procedures may inform the decision makers; the judgment regarding how this information is to be used rests with the decision-making group.

The information described in the previous paragraphs is collected to help the decision makers establish a standard. There is, however, no reason to assume that the standard represents the point on the score scale that will result in optimal classifications. Optimal classification requires a decision-theoretic framework; it requires at least implicit consideration of the relative costs of failing a proficient examinee (one whose true score is above the standard) as opposed to passing a non-proficient examinee (one whose true score is below the standard). In testing for licensure, this represents balancing three considerations: (1) the loss to the public associated with licensing an examinee that lacks the expected proficiency; (2) the loss to the proficient individual who is denied the opportunity to practice; and (3) the loss to the public that is denied access to the misclassified practitioner. Figure 20.7 provides an example of the type of information that might be provided to decision makers. The graph presents the fail rates for proficient examinees assuming a prespecified standard and a range of cut scores at or above that standard. In the common circumstance in which failing examinees re-test, graphics such as Figure 20.7 help decision makers to conceptualize how the false-negative rate changes across administrations. Similar graphics could be provided for the analogous pass rates for non-proficient examinees under the same conditions.

This type of information is most directly applicable when decision makers identify the standard before considering the impact of classification errors, but in principle there is no reason that the varying sources of information might not be combined into a single decision. As discussed in a previous section, the type of information presented in Figure 20.7 must be the result of a theoretical model (e.g., classical test theory). Observed scores in isolation provide no means of identifying examinees with a true score above the cut score.

These four sources of evidence will not insure that the selected cut score is appropriate, but they will insure that decision makers are well informed. Again, standard setting is a policy decision that requires balancing multiple legitimate interests. Each of these sources of information may offer important evidence, but there are no fixed rules that describe how these types of evidences should be weighted or combined to produce a decision.

FIGURE 20.7 Example of Information Classification Errors Provided to Decision Makers

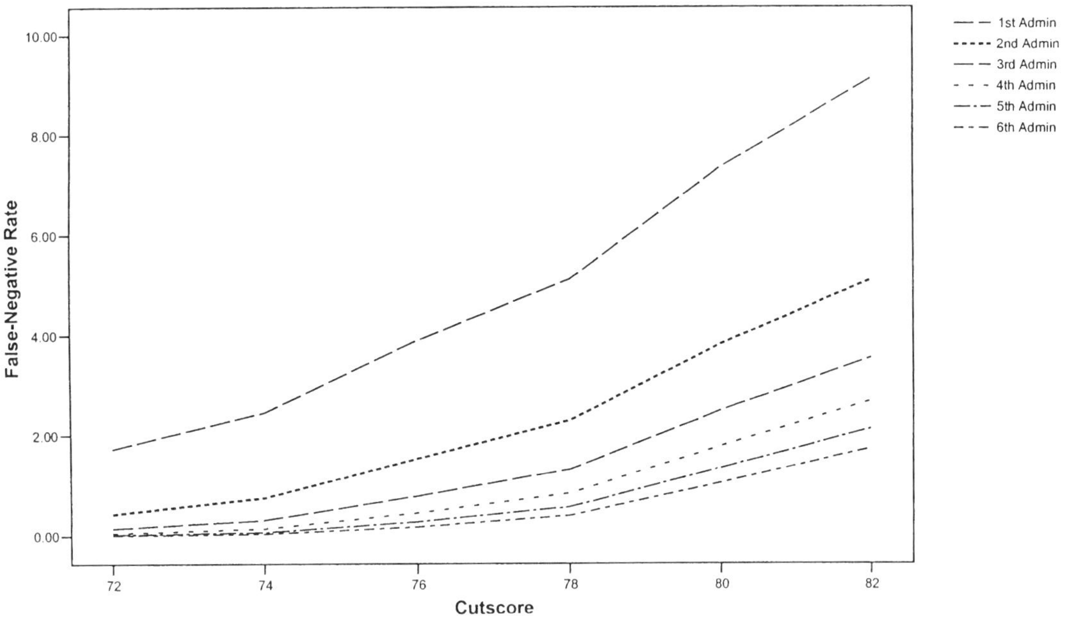

6. LEGAL ISSUES

The stakes involved in professional licensure and certification are sufficiently high that restrictions and decisions made based on these tests, as well as the specifics of test construction and administration, have been subject to legal challenge. The following pages provide an overview of the legal issues relevant to these challenges. Constitutional and statutory protections that impact licensure and certification are discussed first, followed by a review of issues relating to the Americans with Disabilities Act and the need for score annotation that results from test accommodations (also see Phillips & Camara, this volume).

6.1. Constitutional Protections

Carson (2001) describes three legal bases for challenging tests for licensure and certification: (1) the Fourteenth Amendment of the U.S. Constitution; (2) the Civil Rights Act; and (3) antitrust laws. The Fourteenth Amendment guarantees due process and equal protection under the law. Because it is intended to protect individuals from purposeful discrimination, these protections have the potential to limit a state's authority in licensure. Carson (2001) quotes from the 1957 decision of the Supreme Court in *Schware v. Board of Bar Examiners of the State of New Mexico*:

> A State cannot exclude a person from the practice of law or from any other occupation in a manner or for reasons that contravene the Due Process or Equal Protection Clause of the Fourteenth Amendment.... A State can require high standards of qualification ... but any qualification must have a rational connection with the applicant's fitness or capacity to practice. (p. 429)

On the face of it, this decision would seem to offer considerable protection to candidates for licensure. O'Brien (1986), however, interprets other decisions as lowering the proverbial bar on that standard. O'Brien quotes the Supreme Court in the case of *Williamson v. Lee Optical Co.* (1955) saying: "The ... law may exact a needless, wasteful requirement in many cases, but it is for the legislature, not the courts to balance advantages and disadvantages of the new requirement" (p. 174). Subsequently, expert testimony in the case of *Delgado v. McTighe* (1981) called into question the relevance of the Pennsylvania Bar examination by disputing its validity and reliability. O'Brien concludes:

> A review of the cases leads to the conclusion that no examination that asks questions related to the domain of knowledge popularly associated with the profession will fail to pass the constitutional requirement that it be rationally related to the regulatory objective of protecting the public from incompetent practitioners. (p. 175)

Subsequent decisions have been consistent with the view that these constitutional protections are weak at best. Carson (2001) cites several cases in which courts concluded that evidence of individual wrong decisions did not represent a denial of due process, nor would evidence of broader imprudent or unnecessary decisions, provided some rational relationship existed between the testing procedure and some legitimate state goal.

In contrast to the courts setting a low bar for the evidence required to show a relationship between the standards for licensure and the requirements of professional practice, they have set a high bar for evidence showing a denial of equal protection through discrimination. O'Brien (1986) cites Supreme Court decisions that broadly establish the precedent that disparate impact against a minority group is necessary but not sufficient evidence to establish discrimination. In *Personnel Administrator v. Feeney* (1979), the Court concluded that it was necessary not only to demonstrate that the state's action had a disparate impact but that the policy had been established because of its adverse impact on an identifiable group. It seems that an evolution in the Court's thinking will be necessary before the protections of the Fourteenth Amendment will impact assessment for licensure significantly.

6.2. The Civil Rights Act of 1964

The Civil Rights Act of 1964 prohibits employment discrimination on the basis of sex, color, religion, or national origin. Title VII of that act prohibits discrimination in employee selection procedures, including examinations. Within the context of employee selection, if an examination displays adverse impact on a minority group, the test user would be required to demonstrate both the relationship between the test and the job and the absence of an alternative instrument that would have a less discriminatory effect (O'Brien, 1986). Because licensing and certifying tests have the potential to limit employment, the provisions of the Civil Rights Act may impact these activities.

The broadest decisions relating to this Act have excluded credentialing examinations from coverage because the administering boards are not employers. There are, however, two important respects in which the requirements of the Act may remain a concern for licensing and certifying organizations. First, California has by state statute extended these standards to licensing and certifying examinations; other states may follow. Secondly, Carson (2001) cites two cases in which the plaintiff made claims against both the prospective employer and the certifying board because failure to pass a certifying examination resulted in the inability to gain employment (*Morrison v. American Board of Psychiatry and Neurology, Inc.*, 1996; *Veizaga v. National Board of Respiratory Therapy*, 1979). In both cases, the courts denied a motion to dismiss on the part of the certifying board on the grounds that the board was not the employer. Carson notes that these cases have not initiated a trend in court decisions regarding the applicability of the Title VII protections to licensing and certifying testing, but they do make it clear that the potential exists for successful litigation. Certifying organizations should be prepared to defend the validity of decisions made on the basis of their assessments.

6.3. Antitrust Law

The Sherman Antitrust Act (2004) prohibits unreasonable restraint of trade. Although this does not generally include state licensure, certification is more clearly vulnerable to restrictions imposed by this act because certifying organizations typically are groups of practicing professionals. The Supreme Court repeatedly has upheld the view that restraint of trade resulting from actions of the state government and intended to advance the legitimate goals of the state is beyond the restrictions of antitrust laws (Carson, 2001). Under this interpretation, the power of the states to establish standards for practice in a profession is explicitly protected (*Goldfarb v. Virginia*, 1975; *Virginia State Board of Pharmacy v. Virginia Citizens Consumer Council, Inc.*, 1976). O'Brien (1986) points out that although these specific state activities remain exempt from restrictions under antitrust law, the Supreme Court has distinguished between "public service" and "business" aspects of state control over professional activity. State actions imposing minimum fee schedules, prohibitions on advertising, and restrictions on competitive bidding have been struck down. These steps may be viewed as a weakening of the 1943 Supreme Court decision that appeared more broadly to place anticompetitive activities imposed by the state beyond the control of antitrust legislation. It is important to note that in order for a licensing activity to be protected under this interpretation, it must be carried out by the state. That is, it must be imposed by the state or a state agency and implemented by a state agency or under the direct supervision of the state.

This limitation clearly removes most certifying organizations from exemption to antitrust law. In the case of such activities, legitimacy is evaluated in terms of the extent to which trade is restrained and in terms of the reasonableness of the standards for certification. Generally speaking, licensure represents a requirement for practice. A lack of certification does not prevent an individual from practicing, and this may be seen as reducing the extent of the restraint of trade. Courts have ruled that the actions must have an appreciable effect on interstate commerce or unreasonably suppress competition (Carson, 2001). Arguments also have been made that certification actually promotes competition because it places important information in the hands of consumers (O'Brien, 1994). To the extent that the decision to certify can be supported with a credible validity argument, the line of reasoning is sensible. This argument has yet to be considered by the courts.

6.4. The Americans with Disabilities Act

Pitoniak and Royer (2001) reference three pieces of legislation that impact testing practices for individuals with disabilities: the Rehabilitation Act of 1973, the Americans with Disabilities Act (ADA), and the Individuals with Disabilities Educational Act of 1991 and 1997. The first of these required that accommodations be made in any program or activity receiving federal funds. Testing is, of course, an activity that falls within the purview of this legislation. The ADA broadened the requirements of this legislation by extending them to the private sector. The third piece of legislation extends the rights and requirements within educational settings. Of these three acts, the ADA has far and away the greatest impact on licensing assessment. The ADA states that:

> a private entity offering an examination … is responsible for selecting and administering the examination in a place and manner that ensures that the examination accurately reflects the individual's aptitude and achievement level, or other factors that the examination purports to measure, rather than reflecting [an] individual's impaired sensory, manual, or speaking skills, except where those skills are the factors that the examination purports to measure. (quoted in Pitoniak & Royer, 2001, p. 55)

The requirements of the law are clear enough; disabled individuals must be provided accommodations unless: (1) the accommodation would fundamentally alter the skills or knowledge that the test is intended to measure; or (2) the implementation of the accommodation would represent an undue burden. A relevant example is recounted by Carson (2001): An applicant failed the Florida Bar examination with an accommodation that allowed extended time. The applicant then requested a modified scoring process that would combine scores from different parts of the examination that had resulted from separate exam administrations, with the resulting combined score yielding a single decision. The court considered this to be a fundamental alteration (Carson, 2001).

There has been relatively little litigation relating to this aspect of the ADA. The test development community appears to have accepted the notion that a fundamental alteration requires changing the construct assessed rather than simply modifying the test in a manner that impacts the validity of the resulting scores. This is evident in the case of administrations with increased time (an accommodation offered by most testing organizations). There is empirical evidence indicating that providing additional time, in the absence of a technology that perfectly matches the accommodated time to the disability, may provide an advantage to the accommodated examinee (Cahalan, Mandinach, & Camara, 2002; Swygert et al., 2004; Wightman, 1993; Zuriff, 2000). Such an accommodation clearly has the potential to impact the resulting score interpretation. In the case of a licensing examination, where the primary interpretation focuses on whether or not the examinee has demonstrated minimal competence, an accommodation that systematically biases scores to the advantage of the accommodated group has a clear potential to impact the validity of the resulting score interpretations. This type of alteration is common, but the psychometric literature has not supported the practice consistently. For example, Phillips (1994) suggests that in considering a departure from standard administration, test administrators should ask: (1) "Will scores of examinees tested under standard conditions have a different meaning than scores for examinees tested with the requested accommodation?"; and (2) "Would nondisabled examinees benefit if allowed the same accommodation?" (p. 104). Perhaps future litigation will focus on the question of whether the accommodation changes not only the construct that is assessed but the scale on which that construct is measured.

Although some cases have addressed the reasonableness of the identified accommodation, the primary basis of contention has been the question of who qualifies as disabled (Carson, 2001). The courts have been less than consistent on this point. In 1997, a group of medical students was denied requested accommodations. The court ruled against the students and concluded that they were not substantially impaired in their ability to conduct life functions when compared to *most people* (*Price v. National Board of Medical Examiners*, 1997). By contrast, in *Bartlett v. New York State Board of Law Examiners* (2000), a learning-disabled law school graduate sued for relief under the ADA. The court found that, unlike most major life activities for which the appropriate reference group is the general public, for job-related activities the relevant comparison is the average person with comparable skills. Because her inability to successfully complete the bar examination without accommodation prevented her from practicing law, Bartlett was viewed as disabled. It is interesting to note that the court considered the relevant reference group for the major life activity of "test-taking" to be the general public. Bartlett's accommodation on the test was required only because the test barred access to work (Searns, Howard-Martin, & Hopper, 1999).

Subsequently, in *Gonzales v. National Board of Medical Examiners* (2000), the court judged a medical school student's claim of a learning disability against the standard of performance expected of *most people*. This decision, specific to the context of testing for licensure, is consistent with three 1999 Supreme Court decisions related to employment; in each case, the comparison group was "most people." The decision is also consistent with the ninth circuit court's 2004 decision in *Wong v. Regents of the University of California*. In that case, a medical student was denied accommodation for a claimed learning disability when he began to perform unsatisfactorily during his third year of training.

In *Baer v. National Board of Medical Examiners* (2005), the court denied a preliminary injunction to a medical student seeking additional time to complete the USMLE Step 1 examination. Baer had submitted reports form several psychologists indicating that she had a learning disability. Although the court concluded that Baer had shown that she likely suffers from some impairment, she had not shown that the impairment was severe enough to limit a major life activity substantially. In this case the court drew a clear distinction between a diagnosis of "learning disability" and the level of impairment required to justify protection under the ADA. The court went on to question whether timed tests could be considered a major life activity and concluded that Baer was not likely to succeed on the merits of her case because the evidence suggested that her impairment substantially limited her performance on timed tests in math and science only.

6.5. Score Annotation

Providing an accommodation typically represents violating the prescribed conditions of standardization for test administration. The accommodation most commonly results in modifying the timing of the administration, but changes in the presentation of the material, the response modality, or the testing environment also are common. When such modifications are made, the current *Standards* provide guidance regarding the importance of providing the score user with information about the modification (AERA, APA, & NCME, 1999). Because the user (e.g., the licensing or certifying authority) ultimately is responsible for defending the specific uses that are made of test scores, the *Standards* state that "important information about test score meaning should not be withheld from test users who interpret and act on test scores" (AERA, APA, & NCME, 1999, p. 105). This general guidance is defined further in two specific standards. Standard 10.4 states that:

> Unless evidence of validity for a given inference has been established for individuals with the specific disabilities, test developers should use cautionary statements ... regarding confidence of interpretations based on such test scores. (p. 108)

Standard 10.11 states:

> When there is credible evidence of score comparability across regular and modified administrations, no flag should be attached to the score. When such evidence is lacking, specific information about the nature of the modification should be provided, if permitted by law, to assist test users properly to interpret and act on test scores. (p. 108)

The *Standards* are not law, hence the inclusion of "if permitted by law" in Standard 10.11. The extent to which flagging is permitted by law is being addressed in D*oe v. National Board of Medical Examiners* (1999). In this case, the appellate court vacated the preliminary injunction entered by a lower court. The court concluded that "it is not possible to know how scores of exams taken with accommodations compare to scores of exams taken under standard conditions" (Carson, 2001, p. 17). As of this writing, this case is still in litigation.

The outcome of the Doe case aside, the issue raised by the court has been the subject of considerable empirical investigation. The question at hand is whether scores from exams taken with accommodations can be viewed as comparable to those produced under standard conditions. Though most of the studies are outside of the context of licensure and certification, they are reviewed briefly for two reasons. First, the methodology used in these studies has applicability in the context of licensure and certification. Second, to the extent that the results of these studies argue for caution in assuming comparability for scores from accommodated administrations, they provide empirical evidence that commonly used accommodations may impact the interpretability of test scores.

Producing unambiguous empirical evidence is difficult. It is impossible to randomly assign individuals to disabled and non-disabled conditions. It is similarly impossible to identify disabled and non-disabled populations of examinees with identical distributions of the proficiency that the test is intended to measure. Such controlled experimental designs are out of the question, but even observational studies are problematic. Sample sizes for disabled examinees are likely to be small and a simple categorization of "disabled" is likely to be insufficient. Results may differ if the group categorized as "disabled" is made up of learning-disabled individuals as opposed to individuals with a limitation in manual dexterity. Even categorizing all learning-disabled examinees into a single group may be inappropriate because of differing levels of disability.

Working within these limitations, several studies have been implemented to examine the comparability of scores for standard and accommodated test administrations. Zuriff (2000) summarized the results of several studies in which disabled and non-disabled examinees were administered tests with and without time limits. The purpose of the studies was to examine the hypothesis that additional time improves the performance of examinees with disabilities while having no impact on the performance of examinees without disabilities. In general, the examinees with disabilities did show significant improvement when additional time was provided; examinees who did not have disabilities also showed improved performance in many of the comparisons.

The studies summarized by Zuriff varied in specifics. Some included more careful matching of examinees than others, but all five studies were limited by small sample sizes. More importantly, in each of the studies, examinees knew that they were completing the examination as part of a research project. This raises issues about the level of motivation and the extent to which these results generalize to high-stakes test administrations.

Bennett, Rock, Kaplan, and Jirele (1988) examined the extent to which reliability remained unchanged across accommodated and standard versions of the SAT. Substantial changes in reliability across testing conditions would call into question the extent to which scores from accommodated administrations are comparable to those from standard administrations. Their results suggested only modest differences between the administrations.

Rock et al. (1988) used factor analysis to examine scores from the SAT across accommodated and standard administrations. Evidence that the factor structure had changed would support the view that the constructs measured by the assessment were not stable across administration conditions. The investigators found little difference across conditions; as with the examination of reliability, comparability in the factor structure might be viewed as necessary but not sufficient evidence that the scores from accommodated and standard test administrations are comparable.

Another important type of evidence is the extent to which the relationship between the test scores and other external measures remains unchanged when the test is administered with accommodations. Cahalan et al. (2002) examined the extent to which the relationship between scores from the SAT I and freshman grade point average remained stable across accommodated and standard administrations. The results showed a weaker relationship for examinees testing with accommodations. For male examinees completing the examination with extended time, the SAT I scores substantially over-predicted freshman grade point average. These results are consistent with those from Wightman (1993), which showed that examinees completing the LSAT with extended time had scores that overpredicted their first-year grades in law school.

Although none of these studies are directly applicable to testing for licensure or certification, they do provide examples of relevant methodologies. The studies described in the previous paragraphs are based on a comparison of performance across conditions of administration for disabled and non-disabled examinees. Another potential approach to arguing that scores are comparable with and without accommodation is to make the case that providing the accommodation to non-disabled examinees would provide them with no meaningful advantage. If all non-disabled examinees complete the test with time to spare, in most cases offering an accommodation that provides additional time would not be seen as impacting the comparability of the scores. Some advocates have argued that because the tests in question are not intended to be speeded, the same logic applies; scores from extended time and standard administrations should therefore be considered comparable. The problem with this argument is that although these tests are not primarily speeded examinations, under standard conditions some significant portion of non-disabled examinees would benefit from additional time. Bridgeman, Trapani, and Curley (2003) present evidence that the math section of the SAT I is speeded to such a degree that allowing time-and-a-half would be expected to increase performance by 10 to 20 points and that the largest increases would be expected for higher-proficiency examinees. Clearly, the assumption that additional time would not help a non-disabled examinee is faulty in this instance. Data for the studies examining the SAT I were produced by varying the number of items presented in an experimental block within the operational SAT I administration. Swygert et al. (2004) provide similar results for two timing conditions in a medical licensing examination. In this case, the total number of items presented in each separately timed block was changed for operational testing. A comparison based on common items presented before and after the timing change suggests that increasing the time per item improved the mean performance. The analysis assumed equivalence of the cohorts responding before and after the timing change. Evidence based on other assessments supports this assumption. Interestingly, increasing the time allowed per item increased scores most for the least proficient examinees; the most proficient examinees gained relatively little from the timing change. Again, this evidence argues against the assumption that because a test is not intended to be speeded, increasing the available time will have no impact on the performance of non-disabled examinees.

Advocates for the disabled also have argued that annotation may be inappropriate when there is evidence that additional time affords a disproportionate advantage to disabled over non-disabled examinees. Empirical evidence is available to support the view that disabled examinees may gain disproportionately from such accommodations; Camara, Copeland, and Rothschild (1998) showed that the gains for disabled examinees were substantially greater than those for non-disabled examinees. Although this sort of evidence supports the potential usefulness of accommodations, it does nothing to demonstrate that accommodated and standard scores are comparable. Simply speaking, this type of evidence has no bearing on the question of whether scores should be annotated. The issue is not whether disabled individuals may need more time (or other accommodations) to display their proficiency appropriately, but one of whether the resulting scores are comparable to scores from non-disabled examinees testing under standard conditions. In the presence of evidence that non-disabled examinees may gain from additional time and the absence of evidence that the allocated additional time perfectly accounts for the disabled individual's disability, such a contention is questionable.

7. THE FUTURE OF TESTING FOR LICENSURE AND CERTIFICATION

The extent of the evolution of practice in testing for licensure and certification varies across the five areas representing the major sections of this chapter. In terms of test development, oral and practical examinations in which established practitioners evaluate candidates remain common; these approaches were also the standard 500 years ago. At the same time, the range of item formats has expanded and more complex testing modalities have been developed to provide standardized, realistic evaluations of performance. Even with the continued use of oral and practical examinations, multiple-choice items have become a central part of most testing programs. In addition, the use of systematic data collection procedures to establish the content of such tests has become an accepted part of test construction that serves to enhance test quality.

In addition to changes in test modality, the last century similarly has seen the development of complex psychometric theories of reliability and validity. These perspectives have supported the move away from the reliance on oral and practical examinations but at the same time cautioned against overvaluing the efficiency of multiple choice items. More recently, a great deal of interest and attention has been focused on procedures for establishing standards.

Finally, legal and political issues and pressures that shape licensure and certification largely have remained constant over centuries. Current law and specific political contexts are always unique, however, and it is expected that both normal evolution and the introduction of novel testing formats will give rise to new legal and political challenges.

Given this evolutionary process, it is sensible to ask how testing for licensure and certification will change and what trends are currently evident. One conclusion appears unavoidable: There is a clear trend toward the use of technology in the hope that it will improve testing practice. Several professions currently use computer-delivered simulations as part of licensure, and significant advances have been made in automated scoring of these complex item formats (Williamson, Mislevy, & Bejar, 2006). Considerable effort also has gone into efforts to allow computers to generate test items (Irvine & Kyllonen, 2002). Advances in this area would increase the flexibility of test administration and enhance test security (because the items would not exist until the test was administered).

The learned professions generally have well-financed programs for licensure and certification. This allows for significant investment into the types of technological improvements described in the previous paragraph. But it should be remembered that these improvements are incremental. Substituting a computer simulation for a practical examination may broaden the range of content that can be assessed and provide a level of standardization and control; it does not, however, eliminate the problem of content specificity, which limits the generalizability of scores. Similarly, it should be remembered that there is very little research investigating the extent to which scores from these simulations are influenced by construct irrelevant variance (such as effects arising from familiarity with the simulation interface). Nonetheless, these technical innovations are promising. Although they are unlikely to revolutionize testing, they are almost certain to make contributions to the evolution of testing for licensure and certification.

A second important trend in the professions may be less obvious; this trend also is tied to technical, electronic innovation. Advances in Internet technology and the increased availability of high-speed data, voice, and image transfer has reduced the importance of geographic proximity. An x-ray taken in a New York hospital now can be examined and interpreted in San Francisco or Delhi as conveniently as down the hall. Surgery can be performed by robotic hands controlled by a physician hundreds of miles away. Physicians, lawyers, and high school teachers all can perform their professional functions from across state lines. These innovations raise questions about how long state licensure will remain sensible and appropriate. If the requirements of interstate commerce lead to federal licensure, legal issues could be transformed substantially. The complexities of test construction also could be increased as the target list of knowledge and skills is expanded to include the broader range required for practice across state lines.

While our ability to see the implications of current and future technological advances is limited, one final trend is easier to foresee: continuing advances in the psychological and statistical theories of testing. These advances in theory and practice are the primary focus of this chapter, and it is hoped that a focus on guiding changes to and enhancements in testing practice will remain a primary concern of all with a stake in the process of licensure and certification for the professions.

REFERENCES

Algina, J., & Noe, M. J. (1978). A study of the accuracy of Subkoviak's single-administration estimate of the coefficient of agreement using two true-score estimates. *Journal of Educational Measurement, 15,* 101–110.

American Educational Research Association, American Psychological Association, & National Council on Measurement in Education. (1999). *Standards for educational and psychological testing.* Washington, DC: American Educational Research Association.

Baer v. National Board of Medical Examiners, 392 F. Supp. 2d 42 (D. Mass, 2005).

Bartlett v. New York State Board of Law Examiners, 226 F. 3d 69 (2nd Cir. 2000).

Bejar, I. I., & Braun, H. I. (1999). *Architectural simulations: From research to implementation* (ETS Rep. No. RM-99-2). Princeton, NJ: Educational Testing Service.

Bennett, R. E., Rock, D. A., Kaplan, B. A., & Jirele, T. (1988). Psychometric characteristics. In W. W. Willingham, M. Ragosta, R. A. Bennett, H. Braun, D. A. Rock, & D. E. Powers (Eds.), *Testing handicapped people* (pp. 83–97). Boston: Allyn & Bacon.

Bennett, R. E., Steffen, M., Singley, M. K., Morley, M., & Jacquemin, D. (1997). Evaluating an automatically scorable, open-ended response type for measuring mathematical reasoning in computer-adaptive testing. *Journal of Educational Measurement, 34,* 162–176.

Bloom, B. S., Engelhart, M. D., Furst, E. J., Hill, W. H., & Krathwohl, D. R. (1956). *Taxonomy of educational objectives, Book 1: Cognitive domain.* New York: David McKay Company.

Brennan, R. L. (1995). Standard setting from the perspective of generalizability theory. In M. L. Bourque (Ed.), *Joint conference on standard setting for large-scale assessments* (pp. 269–287). Washington, DC: NCSE-NAGB.

Brennan, R. L. (2001). *Generalizability theory.* New York: Springer.

Brennan, R. L. (2004). *A computer program that uses the beta-binomial model for classification consistency and accuracy (Version 1.0)* (CASMA Research Report No. 9). Iowa City: University of Iowa, Center for Advanced Studies in Measurement and Assessment.

Brennan, R. L., & Kane, M. T. (1977). An index of dependability for mastery tests. *Journal of Educational Measurement, 14,* 277–289.

Brennan, R. L., & Prediger, D. J. (1981). Coefficient Kappa: Some uses, misuses, and alternatives. *Educational and Psychological Measurement, 41,* 687–699.

Brennan, R. L., & Wan, L. (2004). *Bootstrap procedures for estimating decision consistency for single-administration complex assessments* (CASMA Research Report No. 7). Iowa City: University of Iowa.

Breyer, F. J., & Lewis, C. (1994). *Pass-fail reliability for tests with cut scores: A simplified method* (ETS Research Report No. 94–39). Princeton, NJ: Educational Testing Service.

Bridgeman, B., Trapani, C., & Curley, E. (2003). *Effect of fewer questions per section on SAT I scores* (College Board Research Report No. 2003–2). New York: College Entrance Examination Board.

Cahalan, C., Mandinach, E. B., & Camara, W. J. (2002). *Predictive validity of SAT I: Reasoning Test for test takers with learning disabilities and extended time accommodations* (College Board Research Report No. 2002–5). New York: College Entrance Examination Board.

Camara, W., Copeland, T., & Rothschild, B. (1998). *Effects of extended time on the SAT I: Reasoning Test score growth for students with disabilities* (College Board Research Report No. 98–7). New York: College Entrance Examination Board.

Carson, J. D. (2001). Legal issues for standard setting for licensure and certification. In G. J. Cizek (Ed.), *Setting performance standards: Concepts, methods, and perspectives* (pp. 427–444). Mahwah, NJ: Lawrence Erlbaum.

Case, S. M., & Downing, S. M. (1989). Performance of various multiple-choice item types on medical specialty examinations: Types A, B, C, K and X. *Proceedings of the Twenty-Eighth Annual Conference of Research in Medical Education* (pp. 167–172). Washington, DC: Association of American Medical Colleges.

Case, S. M., Holsgrove, G., McCann, B., McRae, C., & Saunders, N. (1994). Methods of assessment in certification. In D. I. Newble, B. Jolly, & R. Wakeford (Eds.), *The certification and recertification of doctors: Issues in the assessment of clinical competence* (pp. 105–125). New York: Cambridge University Press.

Case, S. M., Swanson, D. B., & Ripkey, D. R. (1994). Comparison of items in five-option and extended-matching formats for assessment of diagnostic skills. *Academic Medicine, 69*(Suppl. 10), S1–S3.

Cizek, G. (Ed.). (2001). *Standard setting: Concepts, methods, and perspectives.* Mahwah, NJ: Lawrence Erlbaum.

Clauser, B. E., & Mazor, K. M. (1998). Using statistical procedures to identify differentially functioning test items (ITEMS Module). *Educational Measurement: Issues and Practice, 17*(1), 31–44.

Clauser, B. E., & Nungester, R. J. (2001). Classification accuracy for tests that allow re-takes. *Academic Medicine, 76*(Suppl. 10), S108–S110.

Clauser, B. E., Nungester, R. J., & Swaminathan, H. (1996). Improving the matching for DIF analysis by conditioning on both test score and an educational background variable. *Journal of Educational Measurement, 33,* 453–464.

Clauser, B. E., Swanson, D. B., & Harik, P. (2002). A multivariate generalizability analysis of the impact of training and examinee performance information on judgments made in an Angoff-style standard-setting procedure. *Journal of Educational Measurement, 39,* 269–290.

Cronbach, L. J. (1971). Test validation. In R. L. Thorndike (Ed.), *Educational measurement* (2nd ed., pp. 443–507). Washington, DC: American Council on Education.

Cronbach, L. J. (1980). Validity on parole: How can we go straight? New directions for testing and measurement: Measuring achievement over a decade. In *Proceedings of the 1979 ETS Invitational Conference* (pp. 99–108). San Francisco: Jossey-Bass.

Cronbach, L. J. (1988). Five perspectives on validity argument. In H. Wainer & H. Braun (Eds.), *Test validity* (pp. 3–17). Mahwah, NJ: Lawrence Erlbaum.

Cronbach, L. J., & Gleser, G. C. (1957). *Psychological tests and personnel decisions.* Urbana: University of Illinois Press.

Cronbach, L. J., Gleser, G. C., Nanda, H., & Rajaratnam, N. (1972). *The dependability of behavioral measurements: Theory of generalizability for scores and profiles.* New York: Wiley.

Cuddy, M. M., Dillon, G. F., Clauser, B. E., Holtzman, K. Z., Margolis, M. J., McEllhenney, S. M., et al. (2004). Assessing the validity of the USMLE Step 2 Clinical Knowledge Examination through an evaluation of its clinical relevance. *Academic Medicine, 79*(Suppl. 10), S43–S45.

Davy, T., & Stone, E. (2004, June). *A trend model for monitoring item security under continuous testing.* Paper presented at the meeting of the Psychometric Society, Monterey, CA.

Day, S. C., Norcini, J. J., Diserens, D., Cebul, R. D., Schwartz, J. S., Beck, L. H., et al. (1990). The validity of an essay test of clinical judgment. *Academic Medicine, 65*(Suppl. 9), S39–S40.

Delgado v. McTighe 522 F. Supp. 886 (E. D. PA 1981).

Doe v. National Board of Medical Examiners 199 F. 3d 146 (3rd Cir. 1999).

Doyle, A. C. (1904, June). The three students. *Strand Magazine, 27,* 603–613.

DuBois, P. H. (1970). *A history of psychological testing.* Boston: Allyn & Bacon.

Elstein, A. S., Shulman, L. S., & Sprafka, S. A. (1978). *Medical problem solving: An analysis of clinical reasoning.* Cambridge, MA: Harvard University Press.

Fitzpatrick, A. R. (1989). Social influences in standard-setting: The effects of social interaction on group judgments. *Review of Educational Research, 59,* 315–328.

Flanagan, J. C. (1947). The critical incident technique. *Psychological Bulletin, 51,* 327–358.

Garcia-Ballester, L., McVaugh, M. R., & Rubio-Vela, A. (1989). *Medical licensing and learning in fourteenth century Valencia.* Philadelphia: American Philosophical Society.

Glass, G. V. (1978). Standards and criteria. *Journal of Educational Measurement, 15,* 237–261.

Goldfarb v. Virginia, 421 U.S. 773 (1975).

Gonzales v. National Board of Medical Examiners, 225 F. 3d 620 (6th Cir. 2000).

Grosse, M. E., & Wright, B. D. (1985). Validity and reliability of true-false tests. *Educational and Psychological Measurement, 45,* 1–13.

Hambleton, R. K., & Novick, M. R. (1973). Toward an integration of theory and method for criterion-referenced tests. *Journal of Educational Measurement, 10,* 159–170.

Hanson, B. A., & Brennan, R. L. (1990). An investigation of classification consistency indexes estimated under alternative strong true score models. *Journal of Educational Measurement, 27,* 345–359.

Harris, C. W. (1972). An interpretation of Livingston's reliability coefficient for criterion-referenced tests. *Journal of Educational Measurement, 9,* 27–29.

Hartog, P., & Rhodes, E. C. (1936). *The marks of examiners.* London: Macmillan.

Hawkins, R. E., Swanson, D. B., Dillon, G. F., Clauser, B. E., King, A. M., Scoles, P. V., et al. (2005). The introduction of clinical skills assessment into the United States Medical Licensing Examination (USMLE): A description of USMLE Step 2 Clinical Skills (CS). *Journal of Medical Licensure and Discipline, 91*(3), 22–25.

Holland, P. W., & Wainer, H. (1993). *Differential item functioning.* Hillsdale, NJ: Lawrence Erlbaum.

House, E. R. (1980). *Evaluating with validity.* Beverly Hills, CA: Sage.

Hubbard, J. P., & Levit, E. J. (1985). *The National Board of Medical Examiners: The first seventy years.* Philadelphia: National Board of Medical Examiners.

Huynh, H. (1976). On the reliability of decisions in domain-referenced tests. *Journal of Educational Measurement, 13,* 253–264.

Huynh, H., & Saunders, J. C. (1980). Accuracy of two procedures for estimating reliability of mastery tests. *Journal of Educational Measurement, 17,* 351–358.

Impara, J. C., & Plake, B. S. (1998). Teachers' ability to estimate item difficulty: A test of the assumptions of the Angoff standard setting method. *Journal of Educational Measurement, 35,* 69–81.

Irvine, S. H., & Kyllonen, P. C. (2002). *Item generation for test development.* Mahwah, NJ: Lawrence Erlbaum.

Kane, M. (1992). An argument-based approach to validation. *Psychological Bulletin, 112,* 527–535.

Kane, M. (1994). Validating the performance standards associated with passing scores. *Review of Educational Research, 64,* 425–461.

Kane, M., Crooks, T., & Cohen, A. (1999). Validating measures of performance. *Educational Measurement: Issues and Practice, 18* (2), 5–17.

Kargar, A. (1996, May). The continuing role of the NCBE in the bar admission process, *The Bar Examiner,* pp. 14–22.

Lindquist, E. F. (Ed.). (1951). *Educational measurement.* Washington, DC: American Council on Education.

Linn, R. L. (Ed.). (1989). *Educational measurement* (3rd ed.). New York: American Council on Education, Macmillan.

Livingston, S. A. (1972). A criterion-referenced application of classical test theory. *Journal of Educational Measurement, 9,* 13–26.

Livingston, S. A., & Lewis, C. (1995). Estimating the consistency and accuracy of classifications based on test scores. *Journal of Educational Measurement, 32,* 179–197.

Margolis, M. J., & Clauser, B. E. (2006). A regression-based procedure for automated scoring of a complex medical performance assessment. In D. M. Williamson, R. J. Mislevy, & I. I. Bejar (Eds.), *Automated scoring for complex tasks in computer based testing* (pp. 123–167). Hillsdale, NJ: Lawrence Erlbaum.

Margolis, M. J., Clauser, B. E., Harik, P., & Guernsey, M. J. (2002). Examining subgroup differences on the computer-based case simulation component of USMLE Step 3. *Academic Medicine, 77*(Suppl. 10), S83–S85.

McNeil, B. J., Keeler, E., & Adelstein, S. J. (1975). Primer on certain elements of medical decision making. *The New England Journal of Medicine, 293,* 211–215.

Messick, S. (1989). Validity. In R. L. Linn (Ed.), *Educational measurement* (3rd ed., pp. 13–103). New York: American Council on Education, Macmillan.

Millman, J. (1989). If at first you don't succeed: Setting passing scores when more than one attempt is permitted. *Educational Researcher, 18*(6), 5–9.

Morrison v. American Board of Psychiatry and Neurology, Inc., 908 F. Supp. 582 (N. D. Ill. 1996).

Newble, D. I., Baxter, A., & Elmslie, R. G. (1979). A comparison of multiple-choice tests and free-response tests in examinations of clinical competence. *Medical Education, 13*, 263–268.

Norcini, J. J., Diserens, D., Cebul, R. D., Schwartz, J. S., Beck, L. H., Webster, G. D., et al. (1990). The validity of an essay test of clinical judgment. *Academic Medicine, 65*(Suppl. 9), S39–S40.

Norcini, J., Swanson, D., Grosso, L., Shea, J., & Webster, G. (1985). Reliability, validity, and efficiency of multiple choice questions and patient management problem item formats in the assessment of physician competence. *Medical Education, 19*, 238–247.

Norman, G., Smith, E., Powles, A., Rooney, P., Henry, N., & Dodd, P. (1987). Factors underlying performance on written tests of knowledge. *Medical Education, 2*, 297–304.

Norman, G. R., Swanson, D. B., & Case, S. M. (1996). Conceptual and methodological issues in studies comparing assessment formats. *Teaching and Learning in Medicine, 8*(4), 208–216.

Nungester, R. J., Dillon, G. F., Swanson, D. B., Orr, N. A., & Powell, R. D. (1991). Standard-setting plans for the NBME Comprehensive Part I and Part II Examinations. *Academic Medicine, 66*, 429–433.

O'Brien, T. L. (1986). Legal trends affecting the validity of credentialing examinations. *Evaluation and the Health Professions, 9*, 171–185.

O'Brien, T. L. (1994). Legal issues in board certification. In E. L. Mancall, P. G. Bashook, & J. L. Dockery (Eds.), *Establishing standards for board certification* (pp. 91–94). Evanston, IL: American Board of Medical Specialties.

Orr, N. A., & Nungester, R. J. (1991). Assessment of constituency opinion about NBME examination standards. *Academic Medicine, 66*, 465–470.

Peng, C. J., & Subkoviak, M. J. (1980). A note on Huynh's normal approximation procedure for estimating criterion-referenced reliability. *Journal of Educational Measurement, 17*, 359–368.

Personnel Administrator v. Feeney, 422 U.S. 256 (1979).

Phillips, S. E. (1994). High-stakes testing accommodations: Validity versus disabled rights. *Applied Measurement in Education, 7*, 121–140.

Pitoniak, M. J., & Royer, J. M. (2001). Testing accommodations for examinees with disabilities: A review of psychometric, legal, and social policy issues. *Review of Educational Research, 71*, 53–104.

Price v. National Board of Medical Examiners, 966 F. Supp. 419 (S.D. W. Va. 1997).

Raymond, M. R. (2001). Job analysis and the specification of content for licensure and certification examinations. *Applied Measurement in Education, 14*, 369–415.

Raymond, M. R., & Reid, J. B. (2001). Who made thee a judge: Selecting and training participants for standard setting. In G. Cizek (Ed.), *Standard setting: Concepts, methods, and perspectives* (pp. 119–157). Mahwah, NJ: Lawrence Earlbaum.

Reznick, R. K., Blackmore, D., Cohen, R., Baumber, J., Rothman, A., & Smee, S. (1993). An objective structured clinical examination for the licentiate of the Medical Council of Canada: From research to reality. *Academic Medicine, 68*(Suppl. 10), S4–S6.

Rock, D. A., Bennett, R. E., Kaplan, B. A., & Jirele, T. (1988). Construct validity. In W. W. Willingham, M. Ragosta, R. A. Bennett, H. Braun, D. A. Rock, & D. E. Powers (Eds.), *Testing handicapped people* (pp. 99–107). Boston: Allyn & Bacon.

Schware v. Board of Bar Examiners of State of New Mexico, 353 U.S. 232 (1957).

Searns, J. A., Howard-Martin, J., & Hopper, D. B. (1999). *Public accommodations under the Americans with Disabilities Act: Compliance and litigation manual*. St. Paul, MN: West Group.

Shepard, L. A. (1995). Implications for standard setting of the National Academy of Educational Evaluation of the National Assessment of Educational Progress achievement levels. In M. L. Bourque (Ed.), *Joint conference on standard setting for large-scale assessments* (pp. 143–160). Washington, DC: NCSE-NAGB.

Shepard, L. A., Glaser, R., Linn, R. L., & Bohrnstedt, G. (1993). *Setting performance standards for student achievement* (Final Report). Stanford, CA: National Academy of Education.

The Sherman Antitrust Act of 1890, 15 U.S.C. § 1 (2004).

Subkoviak, M. J. (1976). Estimating reliability from a single administration of a criterion-referenced test. *Journal of Educational Measurement, 13*, 265–276.

Subkoviak, M. J. (1988). A practitioner's guide to computation and interpretation of reliability indices for mastery tests. *Journal of Educational Measurement, 25*, 47–55.

Swaminathan, H., Hambleton, R. K., & Algina, J. (1974). Reliability of criterion-referenced tests: A decision theoretic formulation. *Journal of Educational Measurement, 11*, 263–267.

Swaminathan, H., Hambleton, R. K., & Algina, J. (1975). A Bayesian decision-theoretic procedure for use with criterion-referenced tests. *Journal of Educational Measurement, 12*, 87–98.

Swanson, D. B. (1987). Measurement framework for performance-based tests. In I. Hart & R. Harden (Eds.), *Further developments in assessing clinical competence* (pp. 13–42). Montreal, Canada: Can-Heal Publications.

Swanson, D. B., & Case, S. M. (1992). Trends in written assessment: A strangely biased perspective. In R. Harden, I. Hart, & H. Mulholland (Eds.), *Approaches to assessment of clinical competence* (pp. 38–53). Norwich, CT: Page Brothers.

Swanson, D. B., & Case, S. M. (1995). Variation in item difficulty and discrimination by item format on Part I (basic sciences) and Part II (clinical sciences) of U.S. licensing examinations. In A. I. Rothman & R. Cohen (Eds.), *Proceedings of the Sixth Ottawa Conference on Medical Education* (pp. 285–287). Toronto, Canada: University of Toronto Bookstore Custom Publishing.

Swanson, D. B., Case, S. M., Ripkey, D. R., Clauser, B. E., & Holtman, M. (2001). Relationships among item characteristics, examinee characteristics and response times on the USMLE Step 1. *Academic Medicine, 76*(Suppl. 10), S114–S116.

Swygert, K., Muller, E., Clauser, B., Dillon, G., & Swanson, D. (2004). The impact of timing changes on examinee pacing on the USMLE Step 2 exam. *Academic Medicine, 79*(Suppl. 10), S52–S54.

Tamblyn, R., Abrahamowicz, M., Dauphinee, W. D., Hanley, J. A., Norcini, J., Girard, N., et al. (2002). Association between licensure examination scores and practice in primary care. *Journal of the American Medical Association, 288*(23), 3019–3026.

Thorndike, R. L. (Ed.). (1971). *Educational measurement* (2nd ed.). Washington, DC: American Council on Education.

van der Vleuten, C., van Luijk, S., & Beckers, H. (1989). A written test as an alternative to performance testing. *Medical Education, 23*, 97–107.

Veizaga v. National Board of Respiratory Therapy, 1979 WL 1591 (N. D. Ill. 1979).

Veloski, J. J., Rabinowitz, H. K., Robeson, M. R., & Young, P. R. (1999). Patients don't present with five choices: An alternative to multiple-choice tests in assessing physicians' competence. *Academic Medicine, 74*, 539–546.

Virginia State Board of Pharmacy v. Virginia Citizens Consumer Council, Inc., 425 U.S. 748 (1976).

Wald, A. (1947). *Sequential analysis*. New York: John Wiley and Sons.

Wightman, L. (1993). *Test takers with disabilities: A summary of data from special administrations of the LSAT* (LSAC Research Report 93–03). Newtown, PA: Law School Admissions Council.

Williamson, D. M., Mislevy, R. J., & Bejar, I. I. (2006). *Automated scoring for complex tasks in computer based testing*. Hillsdale, NJ: Lawrence Erlbaum.

Williamson v. Lee Optical Co., 348 U.S. 483 (1955).

Wong v. Regents of the University of California, 379 F. 3d 1097 (2004).

Zieky, M. J. (2001). So much has changed: How the setting of cut scores has evolved since the 1980s. In G. Cizek (Ed.), *Standard setting: Concepts, methods, and perspectives* (pp. 19–51). Mahwah, NJ: Lawrence Erlbaum.

Zuriff, G. E. (2000). Extra examination time for students with disabilities: An examination of the maximum potential thesis. *Applied Measurement in Education, 13*, 99–117.

21

Legal and Ethical Issues

S. E. Phillips
Consultant

Wayne J. Camara
College Board

1. INTRODUCTION

In the last decade, the uses of tests have become increasingly high-stakes with a concomitant increase in related legal and ethical issues. When a testing requirement has the potential for depriving individuals or institutions of something of value, a legal challenge of unfairness often results. Resolution of such disputes may result in the passage of new regulatory laws, a court opinion articulating specific psychometric testing requirements, or a settlement agreement used as leverage for seeking changes in other jurisdictions. Determining when and how to apply these resolutions to a specific testing program requires an understanding of the legal process, the specific factual situation at issue, the characteristics of the testing program, and expert opinion based on relevant psychometric standards.

The purpose of this chapter is to discuss major legal and ethical issues related to tests and to explore the implications of current law and professional standards on the legal and ethical defensibility of specific testing practices. The focus of the chapter is primarily K–12, large-scale, high-stakes testing, with reference to licensure and employment testing where relevant to particular topics.

This chapter is not intended to provide specific legal advice. Its purpose is to provide a broad outline of the legal, ethical, psychometric, and policy issues involved in the topics discussed. In applying these principles to a specific set of circumstances, testing programs are advised to seek individual counsel from an appropriate legal source.

2. DISPARATE IMPACT CHALLENGES

In the past, the performance of some minority group examinees on standardized achievement tests has been lower than that of Caucasian (majority group) examinees. This differential test performance has led to allegations that the use of the test in question is *biased against or discriminates against* the lower-performing minority group and may be labeled *disparate impact* when the difference in performance is too large. Disparate impact is one form of legal challenge to a test and is asserted under the federal Civil Rights Act (Title VI & Title VII) or the U.S. Constitution (Fourteenth Amendment, equal protection clause).

2.1. Title VII

Title VII of the Civil Rights Act (1964) prohibits discrimination by employers on the basis of race. Title VII specifically makes it permissible for an employer to use a professionally developed test "provided that such test ... is not designed, intended or used to discriminate because of race, color, religion, sex or national origin." As part of its Title VII enforcement responsibilities, the federal Equal Employment Opportunity Commission (EEOC) issued the *Uniform Guidelines on Employee Selection Procedures* (1985) that further define the permissible boundaries of employer testing. The *Uniform Guidelines* defines presumptive disparate impact, requires its elimination or the use of less discriminatory alternatives, and requires employment tests to be job-related. Disparate impact challenges under Title VII do not require evidence of overt, intentional discrimination because, when Title VII was enacted, Congress supplied past societal discrimination as the violation to be remedied (*Alexander v. Sandoval*, 2001; Phillips, 1990). In practice, this has made it easier for plaintiffs to initiate Title VII lawsuits because they need only demonstrate significant differential test performance between majority and minority groups.

In the *Wards Cove* case (1989), the U.S. Supreme Court articulated the shifting of burdens in a Title VII challenge. Plaintiffs have an initial burden of demonstrating disparate impact. The burden then shifts to the defendants to show that the test is necessary to achieve an important business goal and that the test is job-related. The latter requirement is satisfied if the test has been properly validated for its intended purpose. The burden then shifts back to the plaintiffs to show that a valid and effective alternative selection practice with less adverse impact exists. Court cases disagree as to whether the alternative(s) proposed by the plaintiffs at this stage must be *equally* valid and *equally* effective. An equally valid and equally effective alternative would measure the same knowledge and skills with equivalent reliability, validity, and other psychometric properties at similar cost. If plaintiffs propose no acceptable alternatives, the original test, if found to be job-related and valid, may be upheld despite a finding of disparate impact.

2.2. Equal Protection and Title VI

The equal protection clause of the Fourteenth Amendment to the U.S. Constitution provides that "[n]o State shall make or enforce any law which shall ... deny to any person within its jurisdiction the equal protection of the laws." A successful equal protection challenge requires the plaintiffs to demonstrate that racial or ethnic group members have been denied a property right by the intentional discrimination of a state governmental entity. Discriminatory intent means that the government entity acted (e.g., chose a test instrument) deliberately because of, not merely in spite of, its disparate effects upon an identifiable, minority group (*Personnel Administrator v. Feeney*, 1979). Absent a law or official policy of discrimination, intent is proven by all the surrounding facts and circumstances, including such factors as legislative history, disparate impact, sequence of events, deviation from normal procedures, and historical background (*Village of Arlington Heights*, 1977).

Analogous standards apply to the federal government through Fifth Amendment equal protection guarantees. Private actors are covered by Title VI of the Civil Rights Act (1964), which prohibits racial discrimination by recipients of federal funding. Like equal protection, Title VI requires proof of intentional discrimination, and as with Title VII, Title VI litigation follows the shifting burdens of proof format. At the time the *GI Forum* case (2000; see section 4.2) was litigated, challenges based on the Title VI Regulations required proof of disparate impact but not intent to discriminate. Subsequently, the U.S. Supreme Court has held that consistent with the Title VI statute, Title VI Regulations also require proof of intent to discriminate.

2.3. Defining Disparate Impact

An important issue in Title VI, Title VII, and equal protection challenges is determining when differential performance becomes large enough to qualify as disparate impact. Two types of significant differences are commonly used to assess disparate impact: practical significance and statistical significance. Statistical significance is important when the group differences being used to evaluate potential disparate impact represent samples from their respective populations. In such cases, the relevant question is whether the sample differences are the result of random error or true population differences. Statistical tests can be used to evaluate whether the differential performance among the samples is large enough to justify the conclusion that there is differential performance among the respective minority and majority populations.

Statistical significance tests are appropriately applied in employment cases to calculate the probability of population differences based on the full population when only a sample of the potential applicant pool has been tested. Alternatively, in graduation testing cases, typically data are available for nearly all students in each group across multiple years of testing. In this context, most inferential statistical tests are likely to be inappropriate because (1) the large numbers of students tested annually effectively provide population data, and (2) attempts to use these numbers as if they were sample sizes creates meaninglessly large values that label extremely small differences (e.g., 1%) as statistically significant when such differences have little practical significance.

Another distinction between employment and graduation testing in the calculation of data for evaluating disparate impact involves the appropriate passing rate calculation. Employment cases typically involve hiring or promotion decisions based on a single administration of a test instrument. Initial passing rates are appropriate here because applicants typically are not given additional opportunities to retake the test. However, state graduation testing programs typically provide students with multiple testing opportunities and targeted remediation following each unsuccessful attempt. Diplomas are withheld only for students who have not yet passed the graduation test at the time of their scheduled graduation. In this case, cumulative passing rates more accurately describe the differential performance of majority and minority groups in completing the graduation testing requirement.

Once differential performance has been established for a minority population via statistical inference or through direct population comparisons using initial or cumulative passing rates, one must decide if the difference in group performance is large enough to justify the label of disparate impact. This requires a judgmental evaluation of the practical significance of the observed difference. The *Uniform Guidelines* (1985) for employment testing create a presumption of disparate impact when the passing rate for the minority group is less than 80% of the passing rate for the majority group. Courts have not clearly indicated whether the 80% rule is the standard for state graduation tests but such data are typically contained in expert witness reports and testimony for graduation testing challenges.

3. DUE PROCESS CHALLENGES

Due process challenges arise under the Fourteenth Amendment to the U.S. Constitution and apply only to state and local governments. A property or liberty interest is a threshold requirement for a due process claim against a test. Due process claims may be procedural or substantive in nature.

3.1. Fundamental Fairness

The due process clause guarantees fundamental fairness. The courts have interpreted this requirement to invalidate testing procedures that are arbitrary, capricious, or fundamentally unfair to some examinees. The *curricular validity* requirement for graduation testing (discussed in section 4.1) is one aspect of fundamental fairness. All aspects of testing covered by professional standards may be included in a due process challenge to a testing program.

3.2. Role of Professional Standards

Professional standards assume a central role in testing litigation. The *Standards for Educational and Psychological Measurement* (American Educational Research Association, American Psychological Association, & National Council on Measurement in Education [AERA, APA, & NCME],

1999; *Standards*) is cited by expert witnesses, and the interpretation and applicability of specific standards are debated. Introductory material in the *Standards* supports the appropriateness of professional judgment in interpreting the standards:

> Evaluating the acceptability of a test or test application does not rest on the literal satisfaction of every standard in this document, and acceptability cannot be determined by using a checklist. Specific circumstances affect the importance of individual standards, and individual standards should not be considered in isolation. Therefore, evaluating acceptability involves (a) professional judgment that is based on a knowledge of behavioral science, psychometrics, and the community standards in the professional field to which the tests apply; (b) the degree to which the intent of the standard has been satisfied by the test developer and user; (c) the alternatives that are readily available; and (d) research and experiential evidence regarding feasibility of meeting the standard.
>
> When tests are at issue in legal proceedings and other venues requiring expert witness testimony it is essential that professional judgment be based on the accepted corpus of knowledge in determining the relevance of particular standards in a given situation. The intent of the *Standards* is to offer guidance for such judgments. (p. 4)

4. GRADUATION TESTING

State testing for the award of a high school diploma began in the 1970s. The landmark *Debra P.* case (1979/1981/1983/1984) established new legal requirements for a defensible graduation test. A decade and a half later the *GI Forum* case (2000; see section 4.2) reaffirmed these requirements while also supporting states' rights to mandate graduation tests despite differential performance by minority groups.

4.1. The Florida Debra P. Case

In 1981, a federal appeals court first articulated new requirements for a high school graduation test. The *Debra P.* (1979/1981/1983/1984) case challenged Florida's use of a basic skills test to award diplomas to African-American students who had attended segregated elementary schools. Statewide test data indicated that the proportion of African-American students who passed the graduation test was substantially lower than the proportion of Caucasian students who passed. When asked to find the graduation test constitutionally invalid, the appeals court crafted two new requirements for graduation tests: notice and curricular validity.

Notice requires the state to disseminate information about graduation test requirements to all affected students well in advance of implementation. The courts have not mandated a specific length for the notice period but have found notice periods of 4 or more years acceptable (*Debra P.*, 1979/1981/1983/1984; *GI Forum*, 2000) and notice periods of less than 2 years unacceptable (*Anderson v. Banks*, 1981/1982; *Board of Educ. of Northport*, 1981/1982/1983).

Curricular validity (also referred to as opportunity to learn) means that students must be given the opportunity to learn the skills tested on a graduation test. In practice, curricular validity evidence is often gathered by examining the official curricular materials used in instruction and by surveying teachers to determine whether they are teaching the tested content. The curricular validity requirement was incorporated into the 1985 revision of the *Standards* and appears as Standard 13.5 in the 1999 revision.

The *Debra P.* case was sent back to the district court to determine whether the Florida graduation test met the new requirements. Initially, the *Debra P.* court had determined that Florida students' 1 1/2 years' notice of the graduation test requirement was insufficient, but by the time the court reconsidered its decision, students had been given 4 years notice, which the court found sufficient. The *Debra P.* court upheld the curricular validity of the Florida graduation test based on evidence including formal surveys of districts' curricular materials, teachers, and students, which demonstrated that on average, students had 2.7 opportunities to learn the tested skills. In addition, on remand 4 years after the case was initially filed, the *Debra P.* court found that current minority graduating seniors had never attended segregated schools, and that remediation efforts had increased the passing rate for African Americans from an initial 22% in 1979 to 91% in 1983. These findings were upheld on appeal.

4.2. The Texas GI Forum Case

In 1999, the Texas graduation test was challenged in federal court based on differential passing rates for Hispanic and African-American students. The challenged academic skills test was a revision of an earlier basic skills graduation test. The *GI Forum* (2000) challenge to the Texas high school graduation test alleged racial discrimination in violation of federal Title VI Regulations (34 CFR § 100.3) and constitutional due process. The court dismissed Title VI and equal protection challenges for lack of evidence of intent to discriminate and an Equal Educational Opportunity Act (20 USC § 1703) challenge on the grounds that lack of a Spanish version of the test was not a barrier to participation in instructional programs. In its decision, the court summarized the *GI Forum* case as follows: "The issue before the Court is whether the use of the Texas [graduation test] as a requirement for high school graduation unfairly discriminates against Texas minority students or violates their right to due process."

Although the plaintiffs argued for similarity, the situation in Texas when its graduation test was implemented was distinguishable from that of Florida at the time of the *Debra P.* case. Texas had a state-mandated curriculum; Florida did not. Unlike the Florida students in the *Debra P.* case, African-American and Hispanic minority students subject to the graduation test requirement in Texas had not been required by statute to attend segregated schools. Moreover, graduation testing was not a new concept in Texas as it had been in Florida. At the time the *GI Forum* case was filed in 1997, high school graduation tests had been in existence for nearly two decades nationwide and for a decade in Texas, beginning with the challenged test's predecessor implemented in 1985. However, the *GI Forum* court did reaffirm the *Debra P.* court's holding that a high school diploma is a property interest "created by the requirement of compulsory education, attendance requirements, and the statute detailing graduation requirements."

The factual issue in dispute under the due process claim was the validity of the graduation test; that is, whether the implementation and use of the graduation test was a substantial departure from accepted professional standards, specifically including fairness and opportunity to learn. Under Title VI Regulations, the issues included the appropriate method for calculating and interpreting disparate impact data and whether the parties had met their shifting burdens of proof. At trial, the *GI Forum* plaintiffs presented a variety of psychometric and statistical arguments related to the quality of the Texas graduation test and its impact on African-American and Hispanic students. These arguments focused on historical misuses of tests, validity, reliability, opportunity to learn, setting passing standards, disparate impact, use of a single test score, conjunctive versus compensatory models, differential item performance, item discrimination, factor analyses, and dropout/retention rates.

4.3. Disparate Impact

Relative to the disparate impact issue, the court stated, "Unfortunately, there is not a clear consensus on what type of statistical analysis is to be used in cases in which racial discrimination is asserted." The court concluded that cumulative statistics were more appropriate than initial passing rates for evaluating relative subgroup performance and applied the 80% rule from the employment context to assess disparate impact. However, the court also credited statistical tests applied to subpopulation differences that would have found majority/minority group passing percentage differences of less than 1% significant due to the large numbers of subgroup students tested.

Nonetheless, after finding disparate impact, the court held that the state had met its burden of demonstrating an educational necessity for the test in establishing minimum academic standards for all students and identifying inequalities in minority student achievement and remediating them. The court further determined that the plaintiffs had not met their burden of identifying a valid and effective alternative to the graduation test. In doing so, the court rejected the plaintiffs' arguments for adding teacher grades (a different standard) or substituting a compensatory model (high scores in one subject offset low scores in another) for the existing conjunctive model (passing scores required for each subject).

4.4. Due Process

In finding the Texas graduation test constitutional with respect to due process requirements, the court found that the test met applicable legal standards for notice and curricular validity, and satisfied relevant professional standards for content validity, reliability, and standard setting. The court made extensive findings of fact related to test construction and adherence to professional standards in support of the validity of the graduation test. The court stated:

> [T]he test measures what it purports to measure, and it does so with a sufficient degree of reliability.... [T]he disparities in test scores do not result from flaws in the test or in the way it is administered.

The *GI Forum* court also found that the Texas graduation test provided sufficient notice (3 years prior to initial administration in 10th grade and 5 years prior to graduation) and satisfied curricular validity requirements. The *GI Forum* plaintiffs argued that Texas should have collected exactly the same curricular validity data as Florida presented to the court in the *Debra P.* case. However, the *GI Forum* court found that (1) the widely-disseminated, state-mandated curriculum, (2) surveys of teachers and curricular materials for the prior graduation test based on the same curriculum, (3) adequacy of preparation reviews by Texas educator committees and bias review panels asked to respond "yes or no" to the following question for each test item: "Would you expect students in your class to have received sufficient instruction by the time of the test administration to enable them to answer this item correctly?", (4) eight testing opportunities with mandated remediation, (5) distribution of study guides, and (6) availability of released tests, provided sufficient evidence to satisfy the curricular validity requirement. Further, the *GI Forum* decision indicated:

> The Court has determined that the use and implementation of the [graduation test] does identify educational inequalities and attempts to address them. While lack of effort and creativity at the local level sometime frustrate those attempts, local policy is not an issue before the Court. The results of the [graduation test] are used, in many cases quite effectively, to motivate not only students but schools and teachers to raise and meet educational standards. (pp. 29, 31, citations omitted)

The *GI Forum* court also held that Texas set a constitutionally valid passing standard for the graduation test without having used a specific standard setting methodology. The court stated:

> Texas relied on field test data and input from educators to determine where to set its cut score. It set initial cut scores 10 percentage points lower, and phased in the 70-percent score. While field test results suggested that a large number of students would not pass at the 70-percent cut score, officials had reason to believe that those numbers were inflated. Officials contemplated the possible consequences and determined that the risk should be taken. The Court cannot say, based on the record, that the State's chosen cut score was arbitrary or unjustified. Moreover, the Court finds that the score bears a manifest relationship to the State's legitimate goals. (pp. 24–26)

4.5. Lessons from the GI Forum Case

In sum, the court's decision upholding the Texas graduation test concluded that:

> While the [graduation test] does adversely affect minority students in significant numbers, the [state] has demonstrated an educational necessity for the test, and the Plaintiffs have failed to identify equally effective alternatives.... The

[state] has provided adequate notice of the consequences of the exam and has ensured that the exam is strongly correlated to material actually taught in the classroom. In addition, the test is valid and in keeping with current educational norms. Finally, the test does not perpetuate prior educational discrimination.... Instead, the test seeks to identify inequalities and to address them. (pp. 31–32)

The *GI Forum* decision provided guidance for state graduation testing programs in the following key areas:

- Upheld the *Debra P.* requirements of notice and curricular validity implicated by a property interest in a high school diploma.
- Credited the professional judgment of psychometric experts who had extensive, direct experience with large-scale achievement testing.
- Used reasonable common sense interpretations of professional standards for evaluating test quality.
- Supported the use of cumulative rather than initial passing rates and the 80% rule for disparate impact analyses.
- Recognized that there was no evidence of a causal link between the graduation test and differential minority performance and that a variety of nontest factors may have contributed to the observed differences.
- Found that the graduation test was not the sole criterion for receipt of a high school diploma.
- Indicated that graduation test developers are not required to minimize differential performance among racial/ethnic groups or to validate the test against criteria (e.g., teacher grades) that measure different student attributes from those measured by the test.
- Found evidence of successful remediation of minority students convincing and compelling.
- Upheld passing standards for a graduation test based on all the facts and circumstances, including field test data, multiple retest, and a 2-year phase-in, but absent use of a specific standard setting method.
- Found extensive test construction documentation and KR_{20} reliabilities by subgroup in the upper 80s and low 90s sufficient to satisfy professional standards for validity and reliability for a graduation test.
- Found a graduation test administered only in English to be valid for all students, including those whose native language was not English.
- Found notice of the graduation test 3 years prior to initial testing and 5 years prior to expected graduation adequate.
- Found adequate curricular validity based on all the facts and circumstances, including a state-mandated curriculum, successful remediation, and adequacy of preparation judgments by educator item review committees, but absent formal surveys of teachers and students.
- Noted that high dropout and retention rates among minority students were reason for concern but not shown to have been caused by the graduation test.
- Indicated that decisions of whether and what to test for high school graduation are the province of the legislature, not the courts. (Phillips, 2000, pp. 380–381)

In addition, the *GI Forum* case demonstrated that:
- A technical manual is a valuable document for collecting and memorializing important graduation test procedures, decisions, and psychometric data needed to defend a court challenge.

- A potential finding of disparate impact can trigger comprehensive scrutiny of all facets of a graduation test and of the statewide testing program of which it is a component.
- Absent any evidence that a graduation test caused other educational outcomes, courts may still be receptive to and troubled by evidence of higher dropout and retention rates among members of minority subgroups.
- The time elapsed from the initiation of a lawsuit against a graduation test to a final court decision may be 2 years or more. (Phillips, 2000, pp. 382–383)

4.6. The Massachusetts Challenge

In 2003, students who had not yet passed the required graduation test in English language arts and mathematics sought an injunction in state and federal courts to prohibit the state of Massachusetts from conditioning the award of a high school diploma on passage of the test (*Student 1 v. Mass. Bd. of Educ.,* 2003). Both state constitutional claims and federal due process, equal protection, and Title VI claims were raised. The graduation testing program included a performance appeal initiated by the district for a student with 95% attendance, 3 unsuccessful attempts with at least one within 4 points of the passing standard, and specified alternative evidence of competency. Students with disabilities were permitted to complete an alternate portfolio assessment of the tested skills.

After 4 testing opportunities, cumulative passing rates in the spring of 2003 were 75%, 70%, and 94% for African-American, Hispanic, and Caucasian students, respectively. The federal court abstained pending resolution of the state claims. The state court denied the injunction after determining that it was permissible for the state to phase in the five subject area tests specified in the statute over time beginning with English language arts and mathematics, and that the state was not required to offer portfolio assessment to all students. The court stated:

[I]t bears note that if the current graduation requirement were enjoined, the thousands of public school students who have passed the [graduation test] could be adversely affected. These students' hard work and successful improvement in performance and attainment of knowledge, for which the graduation requirement was at least in part the catalyst, will be devalued. (p. 30)

4.7. Summary

Successful defense of a graduation test requires cooperation among several key players: state education agency staff, the contractor, outside consultants, and the attorneys representing the state. Significant time and resources must be found to deal with discovery requests, depositions, production of documents, and coordination of defense efforts while maintaining the quality of the testing program. Because a challenge to a graduation test allows scrutiny of all facets of the testing program, the ready availability of well-organized and thorough written documentation of program activities is a major advantage. The defense of substantive aspects of a graduation testing program rest primarily on the *Standards*

(AERA, APA, & NCME, 1999) and expert testimony interpreting relevant individual standards.

5. TEACHER LICENSURE TESTING

Most states require prospective teachers to pass a test before being licensed to teach (Mitchell, Robinson, Plake, & Knowles, 2001). Typically, the test consists of a pedagogy subtest and a content subtest in the subject area for which the applicant seeks to be licensed. The state derives its authority to impose teacher licensure requirements from its power to protect the public welfare. The purpose of a teacher licensure test is to protect the public from incompetent teachers. Unlike an employment test, which is designed to distinguish levels of ability so that the most qualified persons can be selected, a licensure test is designed to ensure that all licensees have minimal knowledge and skills. Licensure tests distinguish two levels of performance: competent (passing) and incompetent (failing).

Technically, Title VII and the *Uniform Guidelines* apply only to fairness in employment testing, not licensure testing (Phillips, 1991). The selection of a single candidate from a pool of candidates to fill a specific vacancy is clearly a different task than establishing minimum competence that allows a candidate for licensure to become a part of the pool of eligible candidates. Moreover, there is a difference between a state's determining which candidates have adequate knowledge and skills to be licensed to teach and an individual school district's selecting a prospective teacher from a pool of applicants that the state has determined meet minimum requirements for licensure. Nonetheless, disparate impact under Title VII and validity requirements from the *Uniform Guidelines* have provided the basis for challenges to state teacher licensure programs. Although courts have held that an interest in practicing a profession, including teaching, is not a fundamental right, there may be a protected liberty interest based on the right to pursue a chosen occupation free from "arbitrary or discriminatory interference from the state" (*United States v. Texas*, 1985, pp. 318–319).

An important issue in teacher licensure testing litigation is the appropriate standard for validity. In teacher licensure testing, the inference one wishes to make is prospective; that is, the goal is to weed out those teachers who, if allowed to practice the profession, may cause future harm to students (Mehrens, 1987). In contrast, a diploma test such as that in the *Debra P.* and *GI Forum* cases, is retrospective in that it seeks to measure what students learned in a past education program. Therefore, the match between what is taught in the training program and what is tested (i.e., curricular validity) is important in the diploma testing situation but irrelevant to a teacher licensure test. If one were to tie a licensure test to what happened to be taught in a particular teacher training program, the test would not fulfill its function of ensuring a minimal level of competence for all licensed teachers. While some preparation programs might be right on target in teaching what a teacher must know in order not to harm the public, there is no guarantee that this will be so. Additionally, no person has a "legitimate expectation" of receiving a teaching license by virtue of having spent four years in a teacher preparation program. Thus, teacher competence should not be measured by past performance or knowledge but by the current knowledge and skills deemed important for minimally competent performance.

This latter definition is consistent with content validity evidence described in the *Standards* (AERA, APA, & NCME, 1999) and the job-relatedness requirement of the *Uniform Guidelines* (1985). Job relatedness requires that the test measure bona fide occupational skills that have been demonstrated to be necessary for success as a teacher. The U.S. Supreme Court upheld a lower court's application of a content validity standard to a challenged teacher licensure test (*United States v. South Carolina*, 1977/1978). The lower court found that although the test did not measure "teaching skills," it did "measure the content of the academic preparation [expected] of prospective teachers" (p. 1108).

Much of the debate about teacher licensure testing has centered on the degree to which such tests predict successful teaching but courts have uniformly rejected predictive validity as necessary for teacher licensure testing (*AMAE v. California*, 1996/2000; *United States v. South Carolina*, 1977/1978). However, there are several reasons why predictive validity is usually an inappropriate standard for teacher licensure tests. First, there is the problem of identifying an outcome measure that represents a consensus of what constitutes successful teaching and obtaining valid and reliable measures of it. Second, while it is true that good teachers possess skills that the test does not measure and passing the test does not guarantee that a candidate will become a good teacher, it is not the purpose of teacher licensure tests to measure variables outside the test content or to guarantee the success of all teachers who are licensed. Conversely, despite other skills such as excellent rapport with students, candidates who are not able to demonstrate the tested minimal knowledge and skills, particularly subject matter knowledge and skills that overlap with the state content standards that must be taught to students, do not have the necessary prerequisite competencies for effective teaching.

When making pass/fail decisions as in a teacher licensure testing program, two kinds of errors can be made: false positives and false negatives. A false positive is a candidate who passes the licensure test and is granted a license to teach but, in fact, lacks the prescribed minimal level of knowledge and should not have been licensed. A false negative is a candidate who fails the licensure test and is denied a license to teach, but actually has the required knowledge and skills and should have been licensed. These errors have different social costs and their magnitudes are inversely related. For example, the interest of the state in protecting the public might lead the state to set passing standards that minimize the number of erroneously certified teachers (false positives). In doing so, the state will increase the number of erroneous rejects (false negatives) on the initial testing, but this difference may be more than offset by allowing multiple retests. Alternatively, critics of licensure tests have argued for more lenient standards (e.g., setting the passing standard three standard errors of measurement below the recommended value) to decrease the disproportionate number of unsuccessful minority candidates who are excluded from becoming role models for minority students (Mehrens, 1986). However, if a state sets such a lowered standard, it also significantly increases the number of certified teachers who lack the requisite skills (false positives). Courts must balance these competing interests when judging the legality of a teacher licensure testing requirement.

Despite evidence of disparate impact on African-American and Hispanic candidates, courts have generally upheld teacher licensure tests. In Texas, the courts upheld a basic literacy test for veteran teachers (*State v. Project Principle*, 1987) and a preprofessional basic skills test required of prospective teacher education candidates (*United States v. LULAC*, 1986), with passing rates for Caucasians, African-Americans, and Hispanics of 99%, 81%, 94% (*State v. Project Principle*) and 73%, 23%, 34% (*United States v. LULAC*), respectively (Phillips, 1991, pp. 531, 520). With respect to the test required for entry into a teacher education program, the court held that minority teachers who lacked the requisite reading and mathematics basic skills would not satisfy the state mandate to provide unitary schools and would be both inappropriate role models and ineffective teachers (*United States v. LULAC*, pp. 639, 643). In upholding the testing requirement for veteran teachers, the court held that "competency testing bears a rational relation to the legitimate state objective of maintaining competent teachers in the public schools" (*State v. Project Principle*, p. 391).

However, a teacher licensure test with failure rates of 2% and 31%, respectively, for Caucasians and African-Americans was disallowed by the court on job-relatedness grounds because the test had not been validated to show the minimum academic knowledge an applicant must have to be a competent teacher (*United States v. North Carolina*, 1975/1977). In addition, the settlement of a disparate impact challenge to an Alabama teacher licensure test sought to attenuate differential group performance by using a discredited item selection procedure from another licensure testing case (see section 6).

In a more recent disparate impact challenge, a class of prospective Mexican-American, African-American, and Asian-American educators in California sought elimination of a required basic skills licensure test (CBEST) of reading, mathematics, and writing (*AMAE v. California*, 1996/2000). A compensatory total passing standard of approximately 70% correct allowed a score above passing on one of the 3 subtests to compensate for a score below passing on another. The CBEST had been revised in 1995 to eliminate mathematics items, such as geometry, that tested "higher order skills." The plaintiffs alleged that the CBEST violated Title VII because it had a disparate impact on minority candidates and had not been adequately validated.

According to the *Uniform Guidelines* (1985), validation of an employment exam requires: (1) specifying the skills to be measured, (2) demonstrating the job relevance and importance of those skills, and (3) establishing the connection between the skills intended to be measured and the test items. To address these criteria, the state cited validation studies providing job relevance and importance ratings of the tested skills/items and psychometric expert testimony that the test had been constructed in accord with professional standards.

Affirming the district court, the appeals court held that: (1) Title VII applied to the CBEST because its implementation was not solely an exercise of the state's police power, (2) the plaintiffs had demonstrated a disparate impact of the CBEST on minority candidates, (3) the CBEST had been properly validated according to professional standards of content validity, (4) the passing standard was based on reasoned professional judgment, (5) the plaintiffs had failed to identify any equally effective but less discriminatory tests, (6) it was proper for the court to hire its own psychometric consultant who did not prepare an expert report and was not subject to cross-examination, and (7) it was not an abuse of its discretion for the district court to refuse to award taxable costs to the state as the prevailing party due to the limited financial resources of the challengers and the importance and complexity of the issues. Using initial passing rates because licensure is denied each time a candidate fails the CBEST, the district court cited disparate impact statistics of 38% for African-Americans, 49% for Hispanics, and 73% for Caucasians.

The holding by 6 of 11 judges that Title VII applies to a teacher licensure test is significant due to the lack of a direct employer/employee relationship between licensure candidates and the state. The court held that Congress intended Title VII to apply to any party who "interferes with a candidate's employment opportunities or controls access to the job market." Moreover, in the court's view, the special circumstances of extensive state control over public schools and application of the licensure test requirement to public but not private school educators distinguished this case from state licensure exams in other fields for which courts have held Title VII inapplicable. It is also noteworthy that the appeals court upheld the validity of the CBEST based on traditional surveys of majority and minority educators regarding the job relevance and importance of tested skills and individual test items, and on expert testimony regarding test construction, content validation, and standard setting procedures that were consistent with the *Standards*, the *Uniform Guidelines*, and professional psychometric judgment.

As part of the job-relevance review of skills included on their teacher licensure exams, some states are now including the knowledge and skills from their student content standards because the content knowledge requirements of many basic skills tests used for teacher licensure are below what states expect of their high school graduates. Along with the NCLB requirement for *highly qualified teachers*, the consideration of student content standards during the development of teacher licensure tests may lead states to move beyond basic skills and include more advanced academic content. If so, Title VII disparate impact challenges may increase. Detailed documentation of test development, validation, and standard setting procedures consistent with professional standards will be critical in defending such challenges.

6. SCREENING ITEMS FOR DIFFERENTIAL PERFORMANCE

When minority and majority examinees exhibit differential levels of performance on an achievement test, some observers believe that the test items are "biased" against members of the lower-scoring minority group. However, an alternate explanation for the differential performance is a true difference in average achievement levels for the two groups. To address the issue of differential performance, testing programs typically calculate differential item functioning (DIF) statistics for examinees of equal ability with total test score serving as the ability surrogate. Comparisons are made of correct answer rates among racial, ethnic, and gender subgroups whose representation in the testing population is large enough to permit statistically robust comparisons. Test items flagged by this statistical review are then reviewed by content experts with proportional representation from relevant minority groups. Differential correct answer rates on a test item do not necessarily indicate unfairness; it is up to the trained reviewers to evaluate the DIF flagged items for the purpose of determining the fairness and appropriateness of such items.

Accepted professional practice has established that comparisons designed to quantify differential performance must compare groups of equal ability. To the extent that p-value differences are based on groups of unequal ability, a purported measure of differential performance based on p-value differences is confounded by achievement differences in the two groups. The settlement of an early legal case temporarily established such a practice for choosing items for an insurance licensure test (*Golden Rule Life Insurance Co. v. Washburn*, 1984). The settlement required items with Caucasian/African-American p-value differences of less than 15% and p-values in both groups of at least 40% in a content category to be used first. Supporters of the procedure believed that the settlement achieved its goal of decreasing performance differences between majority and minority groups. At the time, the test contractor (ETS) believed that because the quality of this particular test would not be affected, it would be less costly to agree to implement the p-value difference procedure than to continue the litigation. Subsequently, after condemnation by many psychometricians, including some with a reputation for disfavoring standardized tests, and following numerous attempts by test critics to force other testing programs to adopt the procedure, ETS declared that the *Golden Rule* settlement was a mistake (Phillips, 1990).

A settlement is not a court order; it is an agreement between two parties to a lawsuit. In dismissing a case after settlement, the court merely acknowledges that the parties have settled their differences and that there are no longer any issues requiring judicial intervention. The court does not evaluate the content of the settlement and makes no ruling regarding it. Thus, a settlement is binding only on the parties who agree to it and provides no legal precedent for any other lawsuit in any other court. Nonetheless, a settlement with one entity may be used to pressure another to agree to the same terms.

For example, proposed legislation in California, Massachusetts, New York, Texas, and Wisconsin sought to mandate various cutoff values for *Golden Rule* type item selection procedures. These legislative proposals were ultimately defeated. However, to settle a teacher licensure lawsuit alleging discrimination against African-Americans, Alabama was pressured to accept a more stringent version of the *Golden Rule* item selection procedure that preferred items with less than a 5% p-value difference between Caucasians and African-Americans and disallowed the use of all items with p-value differences between the two groups greater than 15% (*Allen v. Alabama State Bd. of Educ.*, 1985/1986/1987). Due to political maneuvering and procedural defects, the Alabama settlement was never implemented.

The *Golden Rule* case would have been merely a footnote in psychometric history had it not been for its revival in the *GI Forum* litigation by the same plaintiffs' expert that pushed for its adoption in the *Golden Rule* case. In the *GI Forum* case, the plaintiffs argued that the graduation test was *biased* because p-value differences between majority and minority groups correlated highly with total group point-biserials. Thus, the plaintiffs' expert argued that test development procedures for the graduation test were flawed because use of item point-biserial statistics in the selection of items failed to reduce racial/ethnic differences in item performance. Instead, the plaintiffs' expert opined that point-biserial statistics should not be used in the test development process, or in the alternative, minority group point-biserials should be used. Contrary to any legal or professional standard, this argument implied that the state had a duty to minimize majority/minority p-value differences as reflected in correlations with point-biserial statistics, and was a backdoor attempt to reinstitute the *Golden Rule* procedure renounced by ETS and soundly discredited by measurement professionals. The state's expert demonstrated that, all else being equal, the use of minority rather than total point-biserials to select items would result in substantially similar tests. However, in the few cases where there were differences, test validity would be compromised by the substitution of less complex items measuring lower-level skills (Phillips, 2000).

The *GI Forum* court declined to invalidate the graduation test based on evidence that items with higher point-biserials tended to have larger majority/minority p-value differences. The *GI Forum* Court held:

> The Court also finds that the Plaintiffs have not demonstrated that the [graduation test] is a substantial departure from accepted academic norms or is based on a failure to exercise professional judgment....
>
> The Court, in reaching this conclusion, has considered carefully the testimony of Plaintiffs' expert ... demonstrating that the item-selection system chosen by [the state] often results in the favoring of items on which minorities will perform poorly, while disfavoring items where discrepancies are less wide.... However, the Court finds that the Plaintiffs have not been able to demonstrate that the test as validated and equated, does not best serve the State's goals of identifying and remediating educational problems. Because one of the goals of the [graduation test] is to identify and remedy problems in the State's educational system, no matter their source, then it would be reasonable for the State to validate and equate test items on some basis other than their disparate impact on certain groups. (pp. 29–30)

It seems likely that this decision will put to rest any further attempts to pressure testing programs or courts to adopt *Golden Rule* type item selection procedures.

7. TEST SECURITY AND PARENTAL RIGHTS

Test security is an aspect of due process fairness that has created tension between test administrators, educators, parents, and the media. Constant vigilance, decisive action and political negotiation have been necessary to protect the validity of test scores from potential compromise by adults with access to test materials. Educators can also threaten the validity of test scores by engaging in inappropriate test preparation activities.

7.1. Inappropriate Test Preparation

There has been extensive debate about the appropriateness of "teaching to the test." Teaching the domain of knowledge and skills sampled on the test is appropriate instruction. But if the rewards and sanctions associated with high-stakes testing cause some educators to teach specific test items, or drill students excessively using test items from parallel forms, that is inappropriate test preparation (Mehrens & Kaminsky, 1989). Deterring such unethical behavior is an important state responsibility. To prevent disclosure of actual test items prior to testing and minimize inappropriate test preparation and other unethical behaviors, states can adopt a code of ethics with penalties for specific violations, increase staff education efforts, adopt and enforce strict test monitoring and security procedures, investigate reports of suspicious circumstances, conduct random site visits during testing, and sanction proven violators.

7.2. Review of Tests by Parents

However, some parents have objected to test security policies that prohibit the public from viewing and/or disclosing actual test items. In *Maxwell v. Pasadena ISD* (1994), Texas parents alleged that the statewide assessment violated First Amendment guarantees of free exercise of religion and freedom of speech by requiring their children to answer personal questions and to respond to questions contrary to their religious beliefs. The parents demanded the right to review all assessments prior to administration to their children and asserted that the state's nondisclosure policy violated their fundamental constitutional right to direct the upbringing and education of their children.

Although the *Maxwell* court found no violation of the First Amendment right to free exercise of religion, the court held that the parents' fundamental liberty right to direct the education of their children had been violated. The violation of a fundamental right can be upheld only if the state has a compelling interest and the means are narrowly tailored. Even though the *Maxwell* court found that the state had a compelling interest in assuring an adequate education for Texas children, the court ruled that the state's nondisclosure policy was not narrowly tailored to serve that interest. The final judgment of the court enjoined the state from administering tests to Texas students unless parents of such students were provided an opportunity to view the test within 30 days after it had been administered.

While the *Maxwell* decision was on appeal by the state, the Texas legislature passed a law requiring annual release of all assessment items administered by the state to Texas students. Pretest items were exempted from release, and annual release of scored items allowed for reuse of items within the year prior to release. The exemption for pretest items allowed data to be collected from regular test administrations to evaluate the quality of new items without compromising their security prior to use on actual test forms. The pretested items also provided a common item link for placing new forms on the common scale and for establishing equivalent passing standards.

In a similar challenge, the Ohio state supreme court ruled that Ohio's graduation test was a public record and that administered tests must be released to interested persons upon request (*State ex rel Rea v. Ohio Dept. of Educ.*, 1998). Prior to this case, Ohio had allowed post-administration review if the requestor signed a nondisclosure agreement. Nondisclosure agreements prohibit reviewers from revealing the content of the test questions. Subsequent to the court decision, the Ohio legislature enacted specific provisions similar to the Texas legislation. In both states, educators are still prohibited from disclosing test questions to students prior to test administration. Test security violations are investigated and the licenses of violators may be suspended. In Texas, released tests are often used for student practice but in Ohio, due to the inclusion of copyrighted material in test forms, teachers are not permitted to use released forms as practice tests for students.

While the disclosure procedures in Texas and Ohio have defused claims of inappropriate item content, they have also substantially increased testing costs due to the need to field test a much larger number of items each year and the increased complexity of equating designs necessary to ensure a comparable standard across administrations. To reduce costs, the Texas legislature has recently changed the law to allow disclosure every other year.

In situations where review of secure assessment materials is permitted, a written policy may be helpful in ensuring fair and consistent administration across reviews. To protect security, it is also desirable for all persons with access to secure test materials to sign a nondisclosure agreement and be supervised by staff. Review of secure materials at a central location is desirable to ensure an orderly process with maximum protection for secure materials. It is desirable to have at least two staff members supervise each review to provide two witnesses. In addition, if the attention of one of the supervisors is diverted for any reason, the other supervisor can maintain the continued security of the room and materials.

7.3. Adult Malfeasance and Copyright Infringement

There have been a number of cases in multiple states where teachers have been disciplined or lost their licenses due to failure to follow state test administration and security procedures (e.g., AOL News, 2003). Adults have also jeopardized test security in other ways including unauthorized release of test items and tampering with answer documents.

In a newsletter critique, a veteran teacher in Chicago, IL published secure district English and social studies items after a pilot test. An injunction prevented further disclosure of items in other content areas. The district fired the teacher based on security and copyright violations and sought $1.4 million in reimbursement for the cost of developing new test items. The court held that the teacher did not have a First Amendment right to destroy the tests by indiscriminate publication but awarded the district only $500 in damages (*Chicago Public Schools v. Schmidt*, 2003). In other locales, copies of the Stanford-9 used in California and a Georgia school district exam were sent to local media outlets but were not published (Boser, 2000).

The tests in some statewide programs consist of state-developed items and items from a nationally standardized achievement test item bank. The latter items belong to the test publisher, which typically prohibits their disclosure to the public. Based on the state's freedom of information law and a large failure rate, an Arizona newspaper sought the right to publish items from one form of the state graduation test that included some items from the contractor's item bank. Post-administration review was available at multiple sites but required agreement not to discuss or copy the test items. A state judge ruled in favor of the newspaper with the exception of the contractor's anchor items. The state appealed and subsequently settled the case by agreeing to establish a timetable for releasing test forms except for a small number of items reserved for reuse. The state also delayed implementation of the graduation requirement until 2006 (Kossan, 2002).

In addition to compromising test security, adult malfeasance has also compromised the validity of student test scores. For example, in an affluent Connecticut school district, officials became suspicious of an elementary school with extremely high achievement test composite scores (none below the 98th percentile) when they discovered an abnormally high number of erasures on student answer sheets (Lindsay, 1996). A high percentage of the erasures were from wrong answers to right answers and in a few cases from the right answer to the same wrong answer. In an unannounced retest in the target school and two comparison schools, proctored by district personnel, erasures and student scores declined at the target school to levels similar to the demographically comparable control schools. Parents at the affected school denied that any cheating had occurred and a local realtor unsuccessfully sued the test publisher for reporting results of the tampering investigation, which the realtor claimed had depressed property values. Based on all the facts and circumstances, the district concluded that the school principal had tampered with the answer sheets and his employment was terminated.

State and district student testing programs are not the only venues in which adult malfeasance has compromised test security. Recently, the leader of a national group of teacher education colleges circulated copies of pretest questions from a teacher licensure test designed as an alternative for candidates who have not completed a teacher preparation program (Mathews, 2003). The security breach destroyed six months of work and required replacement of all the pretested items.

8. TESTING ACCOMMODATIONS AND MODIFICATIONS

Concern for appropriate treatment of persons with disabilities has become a national testing issue, as test administrators receive increasing numbers of requests for alterations in standard test administration conditions, and new statutory and case law requirements are adopted and interpreted. In 1992, the Americans with Disabilities Act (ADA, 1990) became effective and imposed on private entities the same obligations for accommodating persons with disabilities as Section 504 of the Rehabilitation Act (1973) had earlier imposed on public entities. Although a major focus of the ADA is the removal of physical barriers in building construction, there are also provisions that prohibit discrimination against persons with disabilities in employment and education.

8.1. Federal Statutes

Section 504 of the Rehabilitation Act prohibits discrimination against an otherwise qualified handicapped individual in any federally funded program. Section 504 Regulations (1997) further provide:

> A recipient [of federal funds] shall make *reasonable accommodation* to the known physical or mental limitations of an *otherwise qualified* handicapped applicant or employee unless the recipient can demonstrate that the accommodation would impose an *undue hardship* on the operation of its program. (§ 104.12, emphasis added)

The ADA made minor changes in the wording of Section 504. The major change relevant to testing involved the substitution of *qualified individual with a disability* for *otherwise qualified handicapped individual*. The ADA section on requirements for tests states:

> Any person that offers examinations or courses related to applications, licensing, certification, or credentialing for secondary or post-secondary education, professional, or trade purposes shall offer such examinations or courses in a place and manner accessible to persons with disabilities or offer alternative accessible arrangements for such individuals. (§ 309)

Regulations interpreting this section of the ADA (1992) require:

> The examination is selected and administered so as to best ensure that, when the examination is administered to an individual with a disability that impairs sensory, manual, or speaking skills, the examination results accurately reflect the individual's aptitude or achievement level or whatever other factor the examination purports to measure, rather than reflecting the individual's impaired sensory, manual, or speaking skills [*except where those skills are the factors that the examination purports to measure*]. (emphasis added)

As recognized in the ADA, the conditions under which a test is administered can significantly affect what the test measures, which in turn can affect the validity of the intended score interpretation. Technically, whenever testing conditions deviate from a standard administration, score comparability may be affected. However, test scores are differentially affected by alterations in testing conditions depending on the type of test and the nature of the specific alteration. For example, changing the table height for a reading test would likely have a negligible effect on the comparability of test scores but providing a reader could have a substantial effect.

8.2. Physical Versus Cognitive Disabilities

In the past, it was common practice to alter standard testing conditions for persons with physical disabilities such as sensory deficits and mobility impairments. For example, visually impaired examinees were given large print or Braille test booklets and examinees in wheelchairs were supplied with tables at a comfortable height. Because physical disabilities were obvious even to the untrained, there was no need for verification of the disability. Moreover, there was little question about the appropriateness of these alterations because they primarily involved the removal of physical barriers and did not affect the cognitive skills being tested (Phillips, 1994). There was also little debate about testing condition alterations for persons with physical disabilities because it was obvious when the disability itself disqualified the person for a particular activity. For example, even though a visually impaired person might pass a Braille version of a written driving test for bus drivers, denial of this alteration would not be disputed because sight is a job requirement for employment as a bus driver.

However, cognitive disabilities such as attention deficit disorder, dyslexia, dysgraphia, dyscalculia, and other learning disabilities have different characteristics than physical disabilities. Although physical disabilities are usually distinct from the cognitive skills being assessed, the nexus between cognitive disabilities and the cognitive skills intended to be tested may be extremely close. Providing a testing condition alteration for a cognitive disability may effectively exempt the person with a disability from demonstrating the cognitive skills the test measures (e.g., use of a calculator on math estimation items) or it may substitute a different skill for the one intended to be measured (e.g., listening comprehension for reading comprehension when a reader is provided for a reading test).

8.3. Legal Interpretations

Historically, educators have often used the term *accommodation* to refer to any testing condition alterations provided to persons with disabilities. This is unfortunate because it is not consistent with the legal requirement for the provision of reasonable accommodations. According to its legal definition, an accommodation must be:

- *needed* by a disabled person
- to *access* the test
- while maintaining valid and comparable scores.

An alteration needed to access the test means that the disabled person is unable to respond to the test questions without it. The phrase *needed for access* requires more than simply providing assistance that helps the person with a disability to obtain a higher score; the assistance must be essential for participation in the testing program. The phrase *maintaining valid and comparable scores* means that the change in test administration conditions produces scores that are free from extraneous (content irrelevant) factors while preserving the skills intended to be measured and producing scores that have the same interpretation as scores from standard test administrations.

Language from prior testing accommodation cases under Section 504 supports the definition of *reasonable accommodation* described above. For example, in a Georgia diploma testing case involving developmentally disabled students (*Anderson v. Banks*, 1981/1982), a federal district court stated that:

> [I]f the [disability] is extraneous to the activity sought to be engaged in, the [person with a disability] is "otherwise qualified." ... [But] if the [disability] *itself* prevents the individual from participation in an activity program, the individual is not "otherwise qualified." ... To suggest that ... any standard or requirement which has a disparate effect on [persons with disabilities] is presumed unlawful is far-fetched. The repeated use of the word 'appropriate' in the regulations suggests that different standards for [persons with disabilities] are not envisioned by the regulations. (pp. 510–511)

In another diploma testing case involving disabled students, the Court listed Braille, large print, and testing in a separate room as required accommodations but specifically stated that changing the test questions is not required (*Brookhart v. Illinois State Board of Education*, 1983). Similarly, a federal court found that an applicant for teacher certification was not entitled to an interactive, oral administration of the required teacher licensure test (*Pandazides v. Virginia Bd. of Educ.*, 1990/1991). An earlier U.S. Supreme Court case that held that accommodations do not include "lowering or substantial modification of standards" refused to require a nursing program to exempt a severely hearing impaired applicant from required clinical assignments (*Southeastern Community College v. Davis*, 1979). The *Brookhart* court elaborated this point as follows:

> Altering the content of the [test] to accommodate an individual's inability to learn the tested material because of his [disability] would be a "substantial modification" as well as a "perversion" of the diploma requirement. *A student who is unable to learn because of his [disability] is surely not an individual who is qualified in spite of his [disability].* (p. 184, emphasis added)

In a more recent challenge to a graduation test involving students with disabilities who did not receive all requested accommodations (*Rene v. Reed*, 2001), the court stated:

> The IEP represents "an educational plan developed specifically for the child [that] sets out the child's present educational performance, establishes annual and short-term objectives for improvements in that performance,

and describes the specially designed instruction and services that will enable the child to meet those objectives." The [graduation test] by contrast, is an assessment of the outcome of that educational plan. We therefore decline to hold that an accommodation for cognitive disabilities provided for in a student's IEP must necessarily be observed during the [graduation test], or that the prohibition of such an accommodation during the [graduation test] is necessarily inconsistent with the IEP. (p. 746)

Examinees whose disabilities interfere with the cognitive skills tested by an academic test are not *otherwise qualified* according to the definitions provided in the above cases and are therefore not entitled to earn a diploma or license by altering the tested skills or substituting different skills in their place. Thus, students with disabilities who must take alternate assessments because they are being taught nonacademic skills or simplified academic skills substantially below grade level are not *otherwise qualified* for a high school diploma when passing a graduation test is one of the requirements.

8.4. Psychometric Interpretations

The *Standards* agree that factors extraneous to the intended measurement should be accommodated. The introduction to the chapter on testing individuals with disabilities states:

> While test takers should not be disadvantaged due to a disability *not* relevant to the construct the test is intended to assess, the resulting accommodation should not put those taking a modified test at an undue advantage over those tested under regular conditions. As research on the comparability of scores under regular and modified conditions is sometimes limited, decisions about appropriate accommodations in these contexts involve important and difficult professional judgments. (pp. 101–102, 105)

The testing principles articulated in the text above are summarized in Standard 10.1:

> In testing individuals with disabilities, test developers, test administrators, and test users should take steps to ensure that the test score inferences accurately reflect the intended construct rather than any disabilities and their associated characteristics *extraneous to the intent of the measurement.* (p. 106, emphasis added)

A valid test score on a cognitive test should be affected by the examinee's knowledge of the tested skills (constructs) but should not be affected by extraneous factors such as lack of physical ability (e.g., a paraplegic unable to blacken ovals on an answer sheet) or lack of cognitive skill (e.g., recall of complex math formulas) not intended to be measured. When a cognitive test score is affected by extraneous factors, score differences among examinees represent a combination of real differences in cognitive skills and differences attributable to the effects of the extraneous factors (construct irrelevant variance). *To be fair to all examinees, accommodations should counteract sources of construct irrelevant variance but not sources of construct relevant variance.*

The *Standards* also distinguish between comparable and noncomparable scores in the context of determining when notations (flags) indicating nonstandard test administrations are appropriate. Standard 10.11 states:

> When there is credible evidence of score comparability across regular and modified administrations, no flag should be attached to a score. When such evidence is lacking, specific information about the nature of the modification should be provided, if permitted by law, to assist test users properly to interpret and act on test scores. (p. 108)

In the *Standards*, the terms *accommodation* and *modification* are used interchangeably to refer to alterations in standard testing conditions. For convenience in distinguishing between nonstandard test administrations that produce comparable scores and nonstandard test administrations for which evidence of score comparability is lacking, I have urged testing programs to use the term *accommodation* for the former and *modification* for the latter (Phillips, 2002). Testing programs routinely make decisions about whether scores obtained from nonstandard test administrations should be interpreted as comparable to scores obtained from standard test administrations. Many have found it helpful in communicating with students, parents, educators, professionals, examinees, and the public to have different words to describe alterations in standard testing conditions that they judge do and do not result in comparable scores. This distinction has allowed them to explain more clearly to others why some scores *count* for satisfying requirements such as diploma testing while others do not.

The recommendation that the term *accommodation* be used as a shorthand referent for nonstandard test administrations that produce *comparable* scores and the term *modification* be used as a shorthand referent for nonstandard test administrations that produce *noncomparable* scores is consistent with the plain English meaning of these terms. According to the *American Heritage Dictionary*, *accommodate* means *to adapt or adjust* while *modify* means *to change in form or character.* Making an *adjustment* for a paraplegic individual in a wheelchair who needs a taller table to make room for a wheelchair during the administration of a cognitive test is typically judged by psychometricians to produce a comparable score. On the other hand, psychometricians typically view a *change* in the construct being measured, such as occurs when a reading test is read aloud (reading comprehension becomes listening comprehension) or a math computation test is administered with a calculator (math skill in applying calculation algorithms becomes pushing calculator keys in the correct sequence), as producing noncomparable scores. Thus, the use of the term *accommodation* for the former example and *modification* for the latter examples is consistent with the English meanings of those words as applied to mainstream psychometric opinions about score comparability. This usage will be employed in the remainder of this chapter.

8.5. Essentially Comparable Scores

To maintain the validity of test score interpretations, testing condition alterations must produce scores that are comparable to those obtained under standard testing conditions. Rather than viewing test score comparability as a dichotomous characteristic that is either present or absent, it is more accurate to view it as spanning a continuum from absolutely comparable (standard administration) to clearly noncomparable (administering a different test). In between are testing condition alterations with varying degrees of effects on the validity of test score interpretations including alterations that produce essentially comparable scores and alterations with significant effects that compromise score comparability.

For example, setting changes, such as additional lighting or seating near the door are generally viewed by psychometricians as having a negligible effect on score comparability. Psychometricians typically also view equated alternate forms of a test and test administrations on different days or at different times within a testing window as producing comparable scores. Alternatively, alterations in testing conditions that change the nature of what is being assessed, such as the use of a calculator for math computation items, substantially impact score comparability.

It is appropriate to inform test users when test scores have been obtained with modifications (by a notation or score flag) because the resulting test scores have been judged noncomparable or because evidence of score comparability is lacking, but not to do so for test scores obtained with accommodations for which the effects on score comparability, if any, are negligible.

Test scores obtained with modifications may receive little interpretive feedback. Normative data will not be valid, nor will achievement classifications such as "proficient" or "basic"; therefore, they should not be reported. Thus, valid reporting of scores from modified test administrations may be limited to raw scores only. Further, aggregate statistics that include test scores from standard administrations and test scores obtained with modifications are likely to be misinterpreted. Test scores from modified administrations also may have little meaning when summarized as a group due to the diversity of disabilities and types of modifications provided.

8.6. Classifying Testing Condition Alterations

To decide whether an alteration in standard test administration conditions affects the validity and comparability of score interpretations, psychometricians consider a variety of evidence including the:

- purpose of the test;
- skills intended to be measured;
- reason for the alteration;
- effects of the alteration on the tested skills;
- comparisons of reliability, validity, and other psychometric evidence;
- speededness of the test;
- consequential validity of test use and score flags (e.g., invasion of privacy, score misinterpretation, degree of comparability, stakes for individuals);
- feasibility of more comparable alternatives; and
- relevant professional standards, statutory language, and interpretive guidelines.

Based on these factors, psychometricians agree on the appropriate classification for many testing condition alterations. However, some situations are more difficult to evaluate. The following questions may assist a decision maker in classifying a testing condition alteration as an accommodation or a modification:

1. Are the test questions totally inaccessible to the disabled person without the alteration?
2. Will the test score obtained under altered testing conditions have a different interpretation than scores obtained under standard test administration conditions (i.e., are the scores comparable)?
3. Is the alteration in test format or administration conditions part of the skill or knowledge being tested (i.e., is it construct relevant variance)?
4. Would allowing the alteration for all students help nondisabled students achieve higher scores or change the interpretation of their test scores?
5. Will the classification of the alteration and its provision to examinees be based on a uniform written policy that includes an opportunity to appeal?

8.7. Undue Burden

An accommodation is not required if it imposes an *undue burden*. To qualify as an undue burden, the accommodation must involve extreme expense or disruption. An expensive testing accommodation applicable to a single student may qualify as an undue burden.

For example, in one statewide program, a student requested a 99-point large print version. This size print allowed only one or two words per page and required special large paper versions for diagrams. The cost of producing such a large print version for a single test form was over $5,000. Because it was a graduation test, there was a possibility that additional versions would need to be created if the student was unsuccessful on the initial attempt. In addition, due to fatigue, the student could only work for about 10 minutes at a time and for only a few hours each day, so testing was scheduled over several weeks.

In this situation, the examinee had a visual impairment that could not be further corrected. Thus, it was impossible for the student to take the test without the requested alteration. However, the cost was significant for the state to pay repeatedly for a single student. In such a situation, if the court views the cost as excessive, the requested alteration might be judged an undue burden and the state might not be required to provide it.

8.8. Public Policy Exceptions

Normally, the award of diplomas, licenses, and credentials conditioned on the achievement of a specified test score should only be made for standard and accommodated test administrations. However, there may be extraordinary circumstances for which a special waiver of the testing requirement may be appropriate.

For example, suppose a student who has been taking accelerated college-prep courses and receiving A grades is involved in a tragic automobile accident just prior to the initial administration of the graduation test in tenth grade. Suppose further that there was extensive evidence that the student's academic achievement in reading and math had already exceeded the standards tested by the graduation test and that the student had been expected to pass easily with a high score. However, due to the accident, the student is now blind and has no hands. The student is now unable to read the material on the reading test visually or in Braille. Administering the reading test aloud via a reader would alter the tested skills from reading comprehension to listening comprehension producing noncomparable scores.

However, as a matter of public policy, such a case might be deserving of a waiver of the requirement in recognition of the extraordinary circumstances and compelling evidence of achievement of the tested skills. Based on the student's medical records, transcripts, references, and a passing score on the graduation test obtained with a read aloud modification, an appeals board might determine that this student should receive a waiver of the testing requirement and be eligible to receive a high school diploma if all other graduation requirements are satisfied. Granting an exception to the testing requirement when a student is otherwise qualified, rather than treating a modification as if it were an accommodation, is preferable because it preserves the integrity of the testing program. It is rare for a disabled student to be able to document achievement of high school level competencies but be unable to access the graduation test without a modification. Thus, to avoid lowering standards by granting testing exemptions to students who are not otherwise qualified, public policy exceptions should be reserved for truly extraordinary circumstances expected to occur rarely.

8.9. Extended Time

Extended time used to compensate for slow work speed on the test items is a particularly difficult alteration to classify as an accommodation or modification. The decision depends in part on the degree of speededness of the test and in part on the reason for the slow work speed.

A speeded test is one for which most examinees have difficulty responding to all the test items in the allotted time. Speeded tests are used when rate of work is an important aspect of the skill being measured. However, when academic skills are measured, the main focus is usually on whether the examinees have the knowledge and skills being tested, not on how fast the examinees can complete the test. Such tests are referred to as power tests.

Rather than viewing speededness and power as dichotomous characteristics of a test, it is more accurate to view them as falling on a continuum from a pure power (nonspeeded) test administered with unlimited time (e.g., a state 5th grade math test) to a pure speed test for which the fastest individuals achieve the highest scores (e.g., a 100-yard dash). In between these extremes are tests that are primarily power (norm-referenced achievement test) or primarily speeded (typing test) (Mehrens & Lehmann, 1987).

A typing test is an example of a primarily speeded test. To pass a typing test, an examinee typically must type a minimum number of words per minute with no more than a specified number of errors. A typing test intentionally measures typing speed because a rapid rate of work is an important job qualification for a typist (Cronbach, 1970; Sax, 1989).

Norm-referenced achievement tests are examples of primarily power tests for which reasonable time limits are imposed on a test intended to be a power test. The mere imposition of a time limit does not make a test primarily speeded (Anastasi, 1976). Developers of standardized achievement tests typically try out the test ahead of time to find out how long it takes most examinees to complete it. They then establish realistic time limits so that most examinees have adequate time to attempt all the test items.

Test developers need to establish reasonable time limits for primarily power tests. If given unlimited time, some examinees will continue working on an academic test well beyond the point of productivity. Reasonable time limits are also needed to facilitate orderly test administration and to deter examinees from spending too much time on items for which they are unsure of the correct answer. Further, it is appropriate to allow enough time so that examinees who have a reasonable amount of facility with the tested skills can answer all the items while not providing the excessive amounts of time an unprepared or underprepared examinee might desire.

When a test is designed to be a power test and is administered with reasonable time limits (i.e., the test is primarily a power test), additional testing time will have a negligible effect on most test scores. Nonetheless, if an examinee has poor English skills, reads slowly, has difficulty comprehending complex text, or struggles with the cognitive demands of the tasks presented in the test items, the examinee may not possess all of the skills intended to be measured and may have difficulty finishing in a reasonable amount of time. Allowing extra work time in this case may inappropriately provide the examinee with compensation for lack of skills intended to be measured.

However, when manual dexterity and speed of work are not part of the skills intended to be measured by a cognitive test, examinees with physical disabilities that cause fatigue, decreased motor coordination, or unpredictable needs to leave the testing room may be disadvantaged when tested under standard time limits. Such physically disabled examinees may effectively have less time to answer the test items than nondisabled examinees because they must use some of the testing time to attend to the physical effects of their disabilities. As a result, the scores for such examinees may underestimate their skills and be invalid.

Standard 10.6 of the *Standards* recommends:

> If a test developer recommends specific time limits for people with disabilities, empirical procedures should be used, whenever possible, to establish time limits for modified forms of timed tests rather than simply allowing test takers with disabilities a multiple of the standard time. When possible, fatigue should be investigated as a potentially important factor when time limits are extended.
>
> *Comment:* Such empirical evidence is likely only in the limited settings where a sufficient number of individuals with similar disabilities are tested. Not all individuals with the same disability, however, necessarily require the same accommodation. In most cases, professional judgment based on available evidence regarding the appropriate time limits given the nature of an individual's disability will be

the basis for decisions. Legal requirements may be relevant to any decision on absolute time limits. (p. 107)

The alterations for some physical disabilities, such as Braille versions for blind examinees, are known to require more testing time. However, for most physical disabilities that cause fatigue, decreased manual dexterity, or frequent needs to leave the testing room, it is difficult to estimate the amount of time required to compensate for these effects because of differences in type of disability, number of effects, severity of effects, and presence of concurrent disabilities.

In addition, there may be too few examinees with a specific physical disability to provide reliable research results to address the timing issue (Mehrens, 1997). This has led researchers to conduct studies in which categories of physical disability are combined or a specific alteration, such as extra time, is studied for the group of all examinees with disabilities (physically and learning disabled) who received it. While not specific to any particular disabled examinee, such research has led many test administrators to conclude that in general, time and a half or double time are reasonable amounts of extra time for most examinees with disabilities who need extra time (Ragosta & Wendler, 1992).

8.10. Flagging Test Scores

Flags are notations on score reports that indicate the scores were obtained under nonstandard test administration conditions where the resulting test scores were judged not comparable to scores from standard test administrations or evidence of score comparability is lacking. Typically, test scores have been flagged when the examinee has received a modification of standard test administration conditions because the resulting score does not have the same validity or interpretation as scores obtained under standard conditions or with accommodations. Alternatively, to avoid flagging, some testing programs deny requests for alterations in testing conditions that would otherwise be flagged. Flagging test scores is controversial because: (1) there are differences of opinion about the classification of specific testing condition alterations as accommodations or modifications; and (2) the existence of flags on test scores may identify unwilling examinees as disabled because only persons with disabilities are eligible for nonstandard test administrations.

Neither the ADA nor its guidelines specifically address flagging test scores. When a judgment has been made that test scores obtained under nonstandard conditions are not comparable to test scores obtained under standard conditions or evidence of score comparability is lacking, Standards 10.11 (quoted in section 8.4) and 10.4 support flagging to facilitate proper interpretation of test scores by test users. Score comparability and accurate communication are the central principles articulated in these Standards. Summarizing these recommendations, the *Standards* states:

The fundamental principles relevant here are that important information about test score meaning should not be withheld from test users who interpret and act on the test scores, and that irrelevant information should not be provided. (p. 105)

9. ALTERATIONS IN TESTING CONDITIONS FOR NONNATIVE ENGLISH SPEAKERS

Many states provide accommodations for persons whose native language is not English (commonly referred to as English language learner [ELL] or limited English proficient [LEP]). However, the term *accommodation* is inappropriate because classification as an ELL has not been legally recognized as a disability protected by the ADA. *Disabilities are typically characteristics a person cannot change and are not reversible over time.* But ELL students are not disabled because they can become proficient in English through instruction. Moreover, the testing condition alterations typically provided to ELLs, such as transadapted tests (translated from English versions where feasible and appropriate; adapted where necessary due to constraints of language or culture), dictionaries, and simplified language, may substantially change the content and difficulty of the knowledge and skills being assessed and result in noncomparable scores. As a result, given the legal and definitional distinctions described earlier in this chapter, testing condition alterations provided to ELLs are more appropriately termed *modifications*.

9.1. Policy Considerations

The desirability of transadapting tests into languages other than English or exempting ELLs from testing has been extensively debated. Psychometrically, the decision depends on the articulated purpose(s) of the test. If the purpose of the test is to provide a pure measure of content knowledge such as mathematics apart from English language proficiency, then policymakers may consider transadapting the test into other languages or exempting ELLs from testing. A typical rationale for such actions is that ELLs should not be tested in a language in which they are not proficient (i.e., language proficiency is construct irrelevant variance). However, there are native English speakers who are also unable to demonstrate their true content knowledge (e.g., mathematics ability) due to poor English skills but they are not exempted from testing or given language assistance. Unfortunately, if all students with poor English skills were exempt from testing, the very students (and schools with many such students) who most need additional educational assistance would not be identified.

Alternatively, if the purpose of the test is to provide a measure of achievement of academic skills in English, then translation or exemption would be inappropriate. Tests used to award diplomas or licenses typically fall in this category. Moreover, in a recent settlement, several districts challenging statewide accountability testing of ELLs in English agreed to continue such testing (*San Francisco Unified School District et al. v. State Bd. of Educ. et al.*, 2000).

9.2. Accountability Testing in English for ELLs

In the *San Francisco* case, the San Francisco, Oakland, Hayward, and Berkeley Unified School Districts joined together to oppose a state legislative requirement that an achievement test designated by the State Board of Education be administered annually to all students in grades 2–11. In particular, the districts objected to the requirement that English language learners with less than 30 months of public school instruction (ELLs<30) be required to take the state-designated test. Test scores were used for school accountability with scores for students enrolled for less than 12 months excluded from the computation of a school's accountability index. The designated achievement test was the Stanford Achievement Test Ninth Edition (SAT9) plus an additional set of items selected to measure state standards not measured by the SAT9. There were no state-imposed consequences for individual students.

The plaintiffs argued that administration of the SAT9 to ELLs<30 was unfair because the test measured English language skill in addition to content knowledge. They argued that students with limited English proficiency should either be tested in their native language or be exempt from testing. State law provided that ELLs with less than 12 months of public school instruction (ELLs<12) be administered a second achievement test in their native language when available. ELLs<12 were also eligible for test modifications when tested in English.

Plaintiffs' experts opined that ELLs<30 would suffer psychological harm from taking the SAT9 in English because their low scores would be stigmatizing, would diminish their self esteem, and would cause them to be inappropriately placed in special education programs and portrayed as having inferior employment skills. In addition, plaintiffs' experts argued that ELLs<30 would score at the chance level resulting in unreliable test scores. Plaintiffs also objected to rules prohibiting educators from encouraging ELL parents to invoke statutory provisions allowing them to exclude their children from testing.

In response, the state argued that a reasonable interpretation of state law indicated an intent to measure academic skills in English, that a fair accountability system requires the inclusion of all students, that the districts and their ELL students benefited from the receipt of state funds targeted toward the improvement of academic skills for low-scoring students, that the districts failed to show that any ELLs were harmed by the test administration, and that the data demonstrated that most ELLs scored above chance and their test scores were reliable. In addition, the state argued that 30 months was an arbitrary exclusion criteria and that there was significant overlap in the performance of ELLs<30 and ELLs>30. Further, over the three-year period the SAT9 had been administered statewide, ELLs had made substantial gains in some districts.

The case settled out of court just prior to trial. The districts agreed to administer the state-designated achievement test to all ELL students as provided by state law. The state agreed to clarify the rules regarding educator communications with parents about exemptions, to consider, among other factors, English Language Development scores when considering school waiver requests, and to make other minor modifications to program procedures.

9.3. Majority and Minority ELL Groups

When a test developer chooses to provide transadapted tests, issues of validity, fairness, methodology, and cost need to be considered. Existing resources will typically support at most a handful of valid transadapted tests. In many cases, the only translation available may be Spanish because that language group often represents the majority of ELLs.

The equal protection clause of the U.S. Constitution requires similarly situated persons to be treated equally. Court cases based on this clause have invalidated educational programs that favored a majority ethnic group. In particular, any allocation of benefits based on race or ethnicity has been considered suspect and high standards required by the courts to justify such programs have rarely been met. It therefore seems conceivable that the courts would take a dim view of a program that provides a benefit of native language testing to speakers of language 1, but denies that same benefit to speakers of language 2, who are given the option to test in English or not test at all. In the context of the ELL classification, majority group ELLs (speakers of language 1) would be treated differently than minority group ELLs (speakers of all other non-English languages). It is not clear whether the courts will accept numerical dominance as a compelling reason for providing transadapted tests in some languages and not others, particularly when there is disagreement about whether English language proficiency represents construct relevant variance. However, in other noneducational contexts, some courts have accepted numerical dominance as an appropriate criteria for selecting a limited number of languages for translations.

9.4. Psychometric Issues

Aside from possible legal challenges to transadapted tests, there are psychometric difficulties as well. Creating a transadapted test for which the scores have the same interpretation as the English version is a difficult task. Direct translation will work on only some of the items and the adaptations made for other items may change the skills being measured. Moreover, linking transadapted tests is complicated because ideally it requires a group of students who are equally proficient in both languages—a difficult condition to define and assess. Other alternatives to a single group design, such as a random group, common item design or social moderation, may be equally problematic (Kolen & Brennan, 2004). Even if equivalent tests could be developed, the purported equivalence may be illusory if educators or employers are not indifferent between two examinees who are equally proficient on all relevant variables, the only difference being one is proficient in English and the other in another language. In addition, all ELLs may not be proficient or may not be receiving instruction in their native language. Thus, for some ELLs, administration of transadapted tests may not remove a language barrier but rather may create a new one.

Another suggested option has been to review items for *bias* against ELLs during test development. However, attempts to simplify language, include more pictures, change vocabulary, or avoid idioms may significantly alter the difficulty of the test and the match of the test items to the content intended to be tested. A more valid procedure may be to administer an English language proficiency test to all ELLs and use the results to track progress in learning English and to interpret the results of academic tests administered in English. The No Child Left Behind Act (NCLB, 2000) requires states to develop and administer English language proficiency tests to all ELLs.

10. ALTERNATE ASSESSMENTS

Congress has determined that schools should be held accountable for the achievement of all students they serve. The NCLB Implementing Regulations for Standards & Assessments (NCLB Implementing Regulations, 2002) require states to provide alternate assessments for students with disabilities whose Individualized Educational Program (IEP) teams have determined cannot participate in the state's regular assessments with *appropriate accommodations*. Alternate assessments must initially be provided in the subject areas of language arts and math; science must be added beginning in the 2007–2008 school year. In addition, the Individuals with Disabilities Education Act (IDEA, 1991) requires that students with disabilities be included in regular state assessment programs with accommodations where possible or be administered appropriate alternate assessments.

10.1. Types of Alternate Assessment

Besides modification of a regular assessment, other types of alternate assessment include: (1) a test in the same academic subject designed for a lower grade level where the tested skills match the instruction specified in the student's IEP (also called out-of-level testing); (2) an individually administered standardized achievement test covering the same academic subject; (3) a test constructed to measure the specific academic curriculum prescribed by an individual student's IEP; (4) a portfolio of student academic work in the subject area; (5) a checklist or rating scale of prerequisite behaviors that must be learned prior to beginning instruction on the tested subject matter; and (6) an evaluation of progress in achieving and maintaining nonacademic skills specified in the student's IEP. In providing for such alternate assessments, the intent of the NCLB Act, consistent with the IDEA and the ADA, is to include students with disabilities in regular, on-grade-level instruction and assessment to the maximum extent possible and, when students with disabilities cannot do so, to ensure that schools are held accountable for systematic evaluation of their progress in meeting IEP goals related to state standards in the tested subject.

10.2. Competing Policy Goals

The NCLB Act and its regulations state conflicting goals that have not yet been totally reconciled. On the one hand, all students are to be assessed at grade level based on the same state content standards. On the other hand, alternate assessments are to be provided when students with disabilities are unable to participate in regular state assessments with appropriate accommodations. By definition, students taking alternate assessments are being tested on different content and skills than students taking the regular assessment because the content has been modified, is at a lower grade level, or involves nonacademic behaviors. The provision of alternate assessments meets the policy goal of including all students in the assessment system but does not meet the policy goal of holding all students to the same grade level content standards. However, the IDEA requires that students with disabilities be tested on the content and skills prescribed by their IEPs and covered by their instructional programs.

In response, some states have expanded their content standards to include prerequisite and developmental skills necessary for achieving each grade level content standard. In addition, severely disabled students within the allowable exemption percentage may be administered appropriate nonacademic behavior assessments. However, it is still not clear for the long term how students with disabilities functioning significantly below grade level academically are to be tested and reported in school accountability data.

10.3. Reporting Results

When students with disabilities take different tests, including regular statewide assessments administered with modifications, the resulting test scores are not comparable to scores from the regular statewide assessment. Thus, it is not valid to aggregate the scores from these disparate measures into a single statistic purporting to indicate the percent of students who have met state standards. For example, if some students with disabilities are administered regular math computation tests with and without a calculator, some students with disabilities take math computation tests designed for students two or more grades below the student's grade placement, and some students with disabilities are administered oral tests of counting skills, the resulting math scores are not comparable. Thus, a single standard for grade-level proficiency cannot be applied, and the results of those disparate tests also cannot validly be aggregated to produce a meaningful result. The most that could be said for an aggregate measure of proficiency for those disabled students is that it indicates the percent of students with disabilities who met whatever standard (at or below grade level) on whatever content that had been set for them in their IEPs. Unfortunately, this broad interpretation does not answer the policymakers' question: How many students have achieved state standards in each academic subject at each grade level?

A compromise position may be to separately report: (1) the percent of students taking regular assessments who met state standards (with or without accommodations); (2) the percent of students with disabilities taking alternate *academic* tests who met state standards or those specified for them in their IEPs; (3) the percent of students with disabilities who met the *nonacademic* goals specified for them in their IEPs; and (4) the total percent of students who met on-grade-level state standards (including all students in the denominator and only those students from (1) above in the numerator). Each of these statistics could be included in the state accountability system. It may also be helpful for states to provide incentives for instructing and assessing students with disabilities at the highest academic levels possible.

The alternate assessment requirement is more than the development of a single test. The alternate assessment administered to a student with a disability must be matched to the specific instruction that student is receiving. Different students will require different alternatives depending on what their IEPs prescribe. As a state begins planning for alternate assessments, consideration must be given to the various types of alternate assessments that will be needed. It may be relatively straightforward to modify regular assessments. Assessments may already be available for students who need to test one or two grade levels below their grade placement. Rated portfolios or state-developed observations/checklists may be appropriate for the most severely disabled students who are focusing on enabling skills or nonacademic behaviors. English language proficiency tests (reading, writing, and speaking) are required for ELLs who are not yet proficient in English. In short, alternate assessment is really a system of assessments appropriate for different types and degrees of disability and consistent with IEP requirements.

Once a state has decided which tests or assessment procedures will be administered as alternatives to which types of students, the difficult task remaining will be to determine how to incorporate that information into the state's accountability system. As long as each student with a disability is assessed, and nearly all are assessed on academic skills in reading, math, and later science as required by the NCLB Act, the states should have some flexibility in determining how those results will be reported to provide valid and meaningful information about attainment of standards by students within the state. The state must strive to provide information that is accurate and not misleading while providing all students with disabilities the opportunity to achieve grade level academic standards when the IEP team concurs. The challenges for the state are (1) to raise expectations for students with disabilities while retaining enough flexibility for IEP teams to prescribe appropriate goals for each disabled student, and (2) to ensure that schools are held accountable for the progress of their disabled students.

10.4. Application to Graduation Tests

A reasonable educational and psychometric interpretation of the NCLB and IDEA statutes is that Congress intended to require states to assess the progress of all students with disabilities on the curricula prescribed by their Individualized Education Program (IEP) teams but that it did not intend to modify the academic requirements established by states for the awarding of a high school diploma. Unlike earlier practice in which students with disabilities were routinely exempted from statewide tests administered to regular education students, this requirement ensures that, in judging school effectiveness, states will consider the performance of all students, including those with disabilities. However, this does not mean that all tests will be appropriate for all students or that there must be an alternate assessment for every statewide test.

This interpretation would require the provision of alternate assessments for students with disabilities to be included among the mix of different assessments comprising the state testing program. From the available choices, the IEP team would select the most appropriate assessment for measuring the progress of a disabled student in achieving the educational goals specified in the student's IEP. For example, a learning disabled tenth grader who reads at a fourth grade level might take an elementary level reading test; an emotionally impaired tenth grader in a special day class who is learning how to interact appropriately with other students might be administered a portfolio assessment including a behavior checklist.

Assessing each disabled student with an instrument that measures progress on the educational goals specified in the student's IEP ensures that schools are held accountable for the progress of disabled students as well as regular education students. This process also ensures that the assessment administered to each disabled student measures that student's individualized educational goals. Moreover, under this interpretation, any student with a disability who wanted to earn a high school diploma would be given the opportunity to do so when the IEP team concurs. However, a disabled student would not be guaranteed a passing score on the exit exam or passing grades in required high school level academic courses, nor would the *opportunity* to earn a high school diploma create an *entitlement* to a diploma for all students with disabilities who attend school and complete the instructional programs selected by their IEP teams. Meeting IEP requirements does not automatically entitle a disabled student to a high school diploma because the instructional program selected by the IEP team may not be at the same academic level as the state standards required for graduation.

That is, using the examples given above, the learning disabled student who passes a fourth grade reading test or the emotionally impaired student who receives a favorable rating on a behavior checklist would be counted and included in their schools' accountability results but would not be eligible for a high school diploma because their IEP teams had determined that high school level academic coursework and testing were not appropriate for them. Only those disabled students whose IEP teams determined that high school level academic coursework was appropriate, who completed all required courses at a high school level of proficiency, and who passed the graduation test indicating achievement of the high school level standards would be eligible for the award of a high school diploma. The *Brookhart* (1983) and *Rene* (2001) cases upheld the right of the state to deny high school diplomas to special education students who were not able to demonstrate mastery of the language arts and mathematics skills tested on the state graduation test. However, because the IEP process is time consuming, the *Brookhart* court held that the notice period for special education students must be at least as great as that afforded regular education students.

In California, high school students with disabilities are currently allowed to take the high school graduation test with modifications, including a reader for the language arts test and a calculator for the mathematics test. If a disabled student who tested with modifications achieves the equivalent of a passing score, has a supporting IEP, and has sufficient high school level coursework to have attained the tested skills, the student's school district must grant the student a waiver of the testing requirement. Based on the waiver option and postponement of the graduation test requirement to the class of 2006, federal and state courts dismissed challenges to the graduation testing requirement by students with disabilities in the classes of 2004 and 2005 (*Chapman v. Calif. Dept. of Educ.*, 2003). It remains to be determined how districts will assess the attainment of the tested high school level skills when students with disabilities are administered modified tests. For example, will a student who completes all required high school English language arts classes with all written materials read aloud be judged to have attained the tested skills?

11. ETHICAL ISSUES AND PROFESSIONAL RESPONSIBILITIES

Professional conduct and responsibilities in the use of educational assessment can raise legal issues, ethical issues, issues concerning professional responsibilities, and issues relating to technical/professional practices. Distinctions among these categories are not always clear, and what may be considered inappropriate professional conduct by some, could also constitute an ethical violation and even an unlawful act in certain situations. Legal and regulatory mandates affecting assessment have been described earlier in this chapter. This section discusses the National Council on Measurement in Education *Code for Professional Responsibilities in Educational Measurement* (1995; *NCME Code*). The *Code of Fair Testing Practices in Education* (Joint Committee on Testing Practices, in press) also provides ethical guidance for test users and test developers and encourages dissemination on Web pages and in publications.

11.1. The *NCME Code*

The *NCME Code* was developed to:

> guide the conduct of NCME members who are involved in any type of assessment activity in education ... [and] as a public service for all individuals who engage in educational assessment activities ... such as classroom teachers, principles and superintendents; state and national technical, legislative and policy staff in education; staff in research, evaluation and testing organizations; providers of test preparation services; colleges and university faculty and administrators; and professionals in business and industry who design and implement educational training programs. (p. 1)

Nearly all other ethical and professional codes explicitly state that they are intended to apply only to members, while the *NCME Code* goes further in encouraging others who engage in assessment activities to endorse and abide by these principles. The *NCME Code* identifies the following general expectations of those involved in educational assessment:

- Protect the health and safety of all examinees;
- Be knowledgeable about, and behave in compliance with, state and federal laws relevant to the conduct of professional activities;
- Maintain and improve their professional competence in educational assessment;
- Provide assessment services only in areas of their competence and experience, affording full disclosure of their professional qualifications;
- Promote the understanding of sound assessment practices in education;
- Adhere to the highest standards of conduct and promote professionally responsible conduct within educational institutions and agencies that provide educational services; and
- Perform all professional responsibilities with honesty, integrity, due care, and fairness.

The remainder of this section discusses issues regarding professional responsibilities and practice in major assessment areas identified in the *NCME Code*. These areas include: selecting and modifying, marketing, administering, scoring, and interpreting assessments, educating others, and evaluation and research.

11.2. Selecting and Modifying Assessments

Educators who select among *off-the-shelf* achievement tests have a responsibility to ensure that the content specifications of the tests are aligned to the curriculum and that assessment formats are relevant. Similarly, test users must ensure that testing programs that are in place continue to be relevant and appropriate for their intended use(s) and population(s). In the case of norm-referenced tests, the population tested in the norming sample should be representative of the population to which the test user wishes to generalize. Special attention should be given to the age appropriateness of any assessment with younger children. Those involved in the process of selecting assessment products also have an ethical responsibility to disclose any relevant associations, affiliations, or conflicts of interest (*NCME Code*, 1995).

In addition, test developers who produce *off-the-shelf* tests and do contract work for others may face a number of potential dilemmas. For example, a test contract may require a developer to produce many more items in a short period of time than the organization is capable of developing while meeting acceptable quality standards. The increased assessment demands from local, state, and federal arenas may require test developers to take actions to meet scheduling and economic constraints that can threaten the technical quality of an assessment program. Sometimes the demands of test production may outstrip the resources of a test publisher and result in errors that may have been prevented with a more reasonable schedule.

The development of standardized administrative procedures and appropriately modified forms of tests and administrative procedures is also a responsibility of test developers (*NCME Code*, 1995). Modifications in test forms, response format, and test setting or content for students with disabilities or diverse linguistic backgrounds should be clearly described for test users to aid them in interpreting test scores appropriately. The *NCME Code* also notes that current technical documentation should be provided, including test content descriptions and sample items.

There are no professional standards that require an educational institution or test developer to make secure forms of a test available to the public for review prior to its administration; however, many state and district testing programs have developed limited policies covering test review prior to and immediately after administration. Several state assessment programs have adopted annual disclosure policies for all scored items their tests. In addition, truth in testing legislation passed in New York compels national admissions testing programs to disclose a limited number of forms annually. Initially, disclosure of some test items can assist teachers and examinees to better understand the domain of tested skills but repetitive disclosure of administered forms significantly increases test development costs and may encourage inappropriate test preparation activities.

11.3. Marketing and Sales

Issues relating to professional responsibilities in the marketing and sales of tests are addressed directly in the *NCME Code* (1995). Thirteen separate statements address issues such as claims about tests, reasonable fees, recommended uses, limiting access to qualified users, test preparation, and endorsements. The *NCME Code* states that test developers should provide users with accurate information about the recommended uses and limitations of their assessments, as well as cautions about the most common misinterpretations and misuses.

A second area of concern involves unsubstantiated claims about tests and test preparation services. The *NCME Code* warns against incomplete and inaccurate marketing of assessment products and services. It includes warnings about test preparation products that could cause individuals to receive scores that misrepresent their actual levels of attainment. False, deceptive, or fraudulent statements concerning qualifications, credentials, services, scientific results, or degree of success associated with services and products are also of concern; honesty, full disclosure of qualifications, and avoiding false or misleading data or statements in applied and research settings are very important. In addition, educational researchers should not agree to undue or questionable influence by funding agencies in the reporting of research.

Nearly every profession that produces technical, professional, or ethical standards directly addresses the need to limit the sale of assessments and the release of assessment data to qualified individuals. The term *qualified user* is not explicitly defined in any of these documents, and several professional associations that might have attempted to restrict access to assessments to licensed or credentialed professionals or their own members have avoided this because of fear that such policies would raise legal issues.

11.4. Administering Assessments

Teachers, school administrators, assessment personnel, counselors, and proctors are directly and indirectly involved in the administration of educational assessments. The *NCME Code* and *Code of Fair Testing Practices* (in press) identify a number of related issues and responsibilities including: informing test-takers of the purposes, uses, and consequences of the assessment; ensuring the security of testing materials before, during, and after the administration; administering the standardized assessment according to prescribed procedures and conditions and notifying appropriate persons of exceptions; including all qualifying students in the assessment; and protecting student data and scores. Students and parents, as well as educators and other stakeholders, should be informed of the purpose(s), use(s), and consequences associated with an assessment prior to its administration. In particular, colleges are expected to provide prospective students with accurate and complete information about the uses of test scores in admissions and to refrain from using minimum scores as the sole criterion for admissions.

There are often incentives to exclude lower-performing students from assessments when results are used to evaluate teachers, schools, and districts. Students with disabilities, students who recently transferred to a school, and even students who are expected to perform below state standards on tests may be inappropriately excluded from assessment programs. For example, Advanced Placement teachers may discourage lower-performing students from taking the exam if they fear exam grades might be used as a measure of teacher effectiveness. Eyde et al. (1993) state that "decisions about which students to exclude from group analyses need careful thought and consideration" (p. 196). These authors note that two separate ethical questions emerge in such situations: (1) When is it appropriate to exclude certain students from group assessment? and (2) How should exclusion be noted and aggregate data be reported?

Test professionals need to ensure that any equipment (e.g., computers, calculators, laboratory equipment) is functioning properly prior to testing. In addition, the *NCME Code* states that there should be reasonable opportunities for individuals to ask questions about the assessment or its directions prior to test administration. Standardized administration helps ensure that all test-takers have the same opportunity to demonstrate competency and helps maintain test security so no one has an unfair advantage (*Standards*, AERA, APA, & NCME, 1999). Administrators who allow unapproved deviations from standardized administration procedures (e.g., providing additional time to some test-takers) or permit distractions and disruptions in the testing environment may inappropriately affect the performance of test-takers (Mehrens & Kaminsky, 1989).

There are numerous anecdotes and media reports of test security violations by educators (Cizek, 1999; Gay, 1990). To avoid security breaches, it is important to keep test booklets in a secure location until the day of testing, and it is preferable to avoid having teachers of students who will be taking the test be responsible for receipt, distribution, and administration of tests. A student's teacher may be more inclined to provide a hint to a student who is struggling during a test or to allow a few additional minutes or other changes to standard administration conditions than an educator who has had minimal direct contact with the student (McGinn, 2000). In addition, when consequences are associated with student test performance, teachers may have an added incentive to inappropriately help students perform well. Shepard and Dougherty (1991) reported that teachers in two large districts who felt substantial pressure to improve students' scores also believed that a number of questionable administrative practices occurred often or frequently at their school. They included: providing hints to correct answers (23%), giving students more time on a test than directions permitted (20%), rephrasing test questions during testing (18%), and reading questions to students that they are supposed to read to themselves (14%). To avoid possible pressure on teachers to provide inappropriate assistance or to deviate from standard test administration procedures, the Advanced Placement program, which administers high school subject matter tests nationally, prohibits students' classroom teachers from administering the examinations.

Multiple studies have demonstrated that for a substantial proportion of teachers, their attitudes and beliefs about appropriate testing practices conflict with professional standards that address standardized administration and scoring procedures (Cizek, 1999). Test preparation activities range from highly unethical to acceptable depending on the intended use of the assessment and the perspectives of the test user (Mehrens & Kaminsky, 1989). Providing teachers with explicit instructions and guidance on appropriate and inappropriate test preparation practices for a state or national testing program can reduce unethical practices.

Using old items and test forms is a common method of preparing students for assessments. However, when the same form of a test is reused over multiple years, educators should be informed so they understand the importance of maintaining test security. Mehrens & Kaminsky (1989) reported that the majority of teachers in one large district felt that using an old form of a standardized norm-referenced test for practice prior to administration of a current form of the same test was not cheating. APA issued a comprehensive statement on the disclosure of test data (Committee on Psychological Tests and Assessment, 1996) noting that exposure to tests and test items can invalidate the test for future use with students and advising that simulated items be used for classroom purposes when feasible. Clearly, these sources indicate that secure forms of tests should not be used for instruction (e.g., a current form of a norm-referenced achievement test, an intelligence test that is still used for assessment).

11.5. Scoring Assessments

Score comparability is a component of the scoring process that can raise professional and ethical issues. The *NCME Code* states that measurement professionals should minimize irrelevant factors in ratings and that quality control procedures should be in place to ensure the accuracy of scoring. It also notes that when errors occur, corrected score reports should be issued to all recipients as soon as possible. In addition, test-takers in state programs should be informed of the procedures for requesting rescoring or appealing test scores. The *NCME Code* also states that reporting schedules and fees should be disclosed in advance to test-takers.

Users who rely on computers to score assessments and develop score reports also have responsibilities related to these services. Psychologists should select such services on the basis of evidence of the validity of the program while retaining responsibility for the appropriate application, interpretation, and use of the resulting scores.

Protecting the confidentiality of individual examinees is addressed in virtually every professional and technical code concerned with assessment. Some test publishers have developed detailed guidelines that attempt to protect college, school, district, and student data and have specific requirements before aggregate data can be released to the media, policymakers, state agencies, or researchers (College Board, 2002). In addition, aggregate data is reported to the public only when the group is large enough (typically 10 or more) to ensure that no students will be individually identified.

11.6. Interpreting Assessments and Communicating Results

A number of different standards and guidelines address issues of score interpretation and reporting. These guidelines include: informing test-takers of the use and interpretations that will be made of results; providing information about the limits of any test and score (e.g., error bands), communicating results in an understandable way that reduces the likelihood of misinterpretations; considering student background characteristics, multiple sources of data, and various types of information whenever possible in decision making; ensuring informed consent of test-takers; and disclosing to examines who will receive results and how long they will be retained. In addition, if automated reports are generated, test users must ensure that appropriate factors (e.g., characteristics of test-takers, situations, intended uses) are considered (*Standards*, AERA, APA, & NCME, 1999).

In state assessment reporting, when scores are used to compare or rank schools or districts, the participation rates and other factors that can moderate performance should be considered in any interpretative materials. The *Code of Fair Testing Practices* (in press) states that test reports should warn against assigning greater precision to results than is warranted. The *Standards* (AERA, APA, & NCME, 1999) recommend reporting confidence intervals or the standard error of measurement to prevent users from over-interpreting small differences in test scores. The *NCME Code* stresses the need to provide understandable score reports and to inform test score recipients of how assessment results may be used and could affect them.

11.7. Educating Others

The *NCME Code* addresses teaching and instruction in assessment and the use of assessments in the instructional process in more detail than other ethics codes. It has specific guidelines addressing the need to distinguish expressions of opinion and substantiated knowledge when educating others about any specific assessment method, product, or service;

disclosing any financial interest or potential conflicts that could influence the evaluation of assessment services; avoiding the administration of assessments in a course if that assessment could harm any student; and protecting the security of assessments and materials used in courses. Finally, educational professionals have a responsibility to model responsible practice and to educate test users about professional responsibilities (*NCME Code*, 1995).

11.8. Evaluation and Research

Measurement professionals also have responsibilities in program evaluation, research, and consultative activities. The AERA *Ethical Standards* (American Educational Research Association, 2000) strive to protect populations that educational researchers work with and to maintain the integrity of research activities and colleagues with whom they have professional relations. They address a range of issues concerning reporting results honestly and fully, describing research methods in sufficient detail to allow others to understand them, providing informed consent to research participants, conducting sponsored research, and publishing results.

12. CONCLUSION

The increased stakes associated with educational testing and a rising demand for assessment services that are faster, more authentic, and low-cost have intensified the pressure on students, teachers, principals, school boards, and others in the educational system and have created additional professional and ethical demands on measurement and testing professionals. Legal and ethical challenges to testing programs can come from a variety of groups on an assortment of issues. To be prepared, testing programs must follow legal, ethical, and psychometric standards, comprehensively document program decisions and activities, and work closely with relevant stakeholders. Maintaining a defensible testing program is a challenging but achievable goal.

REFERENCES

ADA Regulations, 28 C.F.R. § 36.309[b][1][I] (1992).
Alexander v. Sandoval, Case # 99-1908 (U.S. Supreme Court, 2001).
Allen v. Alabama State Bd. of Educ., 612 F. Supp. 1046 (M. D. Ala. 1985), *reh'g*, 636 F. Supp. 64 (M.D. Ala. 1986), *rev'd*, 816 F.2d 575 (11th Cir. 1987).
AMAE v. California, 937 F. Supp. 1397 (N.D. Cal. 1996), *aff'd*, 195 F. 3d 465 (9th Cir. 2000).
American Educational Research Association. (2000). *Ethical standards of AERA*. Washington, DC: Author.
American Educational Research Association, American Psychological Association, & National Council on Measurement in Education. (1999). *Standards for educational and psychological testing*. Washington, DC: American Educational Research Association.
Americans with Disabilities Act [ADA], 42 U.S.C. § 12101 *et seq.* (1990).
Anastasi, A. (1976). *Psychological testing* (4th ed.). New York: Macmillan.

Anderson v. Banks, 520 F. Supp. 472, 510–11 (S.D. Ga. 1981), *reh'g*, 540 F. Supp. 761 (S.D. Ga. 1982).
AOL News. (2003, October 28). Teachers caught cheating on standardized tests. *Associated Press.* Retrieved on November 1, 2003 from http://www.aolsvc.news.aol.com/news
Board of Educ. of Northport-E. Northport v. Ambach, 436 N.U.S.2d 564 (1981), *aff'd with mod,* 458 N.Y S.2d 680 (A.D. 1982), *aff'd,* 457 N.E.2d 775 (N.Y. 1983).
Boser, U. (2000, November 30). *Opponents of high-stakes tests seek to breach exam security.* Retrieved on October 2, 2003 from the NCME Web site: www.ncme.org/news
Brookhart v. Illinois State Board of Education, 697 F.2d 179 (7th Cir. 1983).
Chapman v. Calif. Dept. of Educ., Superior Court for the State of Calif., County of Alameda, Case No. 2002049636 (2003); Chapman v. Calif. Dept. of Educ., U.S. District Court, Northern District of Calif., Case No. C01 1780 CRB (2003).
Chicago Public Schools v. Schmidt, Case No. 03–1479 (7th Cir. 2003).
Cizek, G. J. (1999). *Cheating on tests.* Mahwah, NJ: Erlbaum.
College Board. (2002, June). *The release of college board data.* New York: Author.
Committee on Psychological Tests and Assessment. (1996). Statement on the disclosure of test data. *American Psychologist, 51,* 644–648.
Cronbach, L. J. (1970). *Essentials of psychological testing* (3rd ed.). New York: Harper & Row.
Debra P. v. Turlington, 474 F. Supp. 244 (M.D. Fla. 1979), *aff'd in part, rev'd in part,* 644 F.2d 397 (5th Cir. 1981); *on remand,* 564 F. Supp. 177 (M.D. Fla. 1983), *aff'd,* 730 F.2d 1405 (11th Cir. 1984).
Eyde, L. D., Robertson, G. J., Krug, S. E., Moreland, K. L., Robertson, A. G., Shewan, C. M., et al. (1993). *Responsible test use: Case studies for assessing human behavior.* Washington, DC: American Psychological Association.
Gay, G. H. (1990). Standardized tests: Irregularities in administration affect test results. *Journal of Instructional Psychology, 17*(2), 92–103.
GI Forum v. Texas Education Agency, 87 F. Supp.2d 667 (W.D. Tex. 2000).
Golden Rule Life Ins. Co. v. Washburn, Settlement Agreement & General Release, No. 419–76 (Ill. 7th Jud. Cir. Ct. Sangamon County, November 20, 1984).
Individuals with Disabilities Education Act [IDEA], 20 U.S.C. § 1400 et seq. (1991).
Joint Committee on Testing Practices. (in press). *Code of fair testing practices in education* (Rev. ed.). Washington, DC: American Psychological Association.
Kolen, M. J., & Brennan, R. L. (2004). *Test equating, scaling and linking: Methods and practices* (2nd ed.) (B5). New York: Springer-Verlag.
Kossan, P. (2002, March 9). State will release AIMS test questions. *Arizona Republic*
Lindsay, D. (1996, October 2). Whodunit? Someone cheated on standardized tests at a Connecticut school. *Education Week,* p. 25.
Mathews, J. (2003, June 10). Education effort meets resistance. *The Washington Post,* p. A8.
Maxwell v. Pasadena I.S.D., Case No. 92–017184, 295th Dist. Ct. of Harris County Tex. (December 29, 1994).
McGinn, D. (2000, June 13). Learning from the SATs: Tips stopping test cheating. *Newsweek.* Retrieved on October 5, 2003 from http://newsweek.com
Mehrens, W. A. (1986). Measurement specialists: Motive to achieve or motive to avoid failure? *Educational Measurement: Issues and Practice, 5*(4), 5–10.

Mehrens, W. A. (1987). Validity issues in teacher licensure tests. *Journal of Personnel Evaluation in Education, 1,* 195.

Mehrens, W. A. (1997). *Flagging test scores: Policy, practice and research.* Background paper prepared for the National Academy of Sciences.

Mehrens, W., & Kaminsky, J. (1989). Methods for improving standardized test scores: Fruitful, fruitless, or fraudulent? *Educational Measurement: Issues & Practice, 8*(1), 14.

Mehrens, W. A., & Lehmann, I. J. (1987). *Using standardized tests in education* (4th ed.). New York: Longmann.

Mitchell, K., Robinson, D. Z., Plake, B. S., & Knowles, K. P. (Eds.). (2001). *Testing teacher candidates: The role of licensure tests in improving teacher quality.* Washington, DC: National Academy Press.

National Council on Measurement in Education. (1995). *Code of professional responsibilities in educational measurement.* Middleton, WI: Author.

NCLB Implementing Regulations for Standards & Assessments [NCLB Regulations], 34 C.F.R. Part 200, § 200.6 (2002).

No Child Left Behind Act [NCLB], 20 U.S.C. § 6300 *et seq.* (2000).

Pandazides v. Virginia Bd. of Educ., 752 F. Supp. 696 (E.D. Va. 1990), *rev'd* 946 F.2d 345 (4th Cir. 1991).

Personnel Administrator v. Feeney, 442 U.S. 256 (1979).

Phillips, S. E. (1990). The golden rule remedy for disparate impact of standardized testing: Progress or regress? *Education Law Reporter, 63,* 383–428.

Phillips, S. E. (1991). Extending teacher licensure testing: Have the courts applied the wrong validity standard? *T.M. Cooley Law Review, 8*(3), 513–546.

Phillips, S. E. (1994). Testing accommodations: Validity versus disabled rights. *Applied Measurement in Education, 7*(2), 93–120.

Phillips, S. E. (2000). GI Forum v. TEA: Psychometric evidence. *Applied Measurement in Education, 13*(4), 343–385.

Phillips, S. E. (2002). Legal issues affecting special populations. In G. Tindal & T. Haladyna (Eds.) *Large-scale assessment programs for all students: Validity, technical adequacy, and implementation* (pp. 109–148). Mahwah, NJ: Lawrence Erlbaum.

Ragosta, M., & Wendler, C. (1992). *Eligibility issues and comparable time limits for disabled and nondisabled SAT examinees* (College Board Report #92–5). New York: College Entrance Examination Board.

Rene v. Reed, 751 N.E.2d 736, 746 (Ind. App. 2001).

San Francisco Unified School District et al. v. State Bd. of Educ. et al., Case No. 99409 (Sup. Ct. Cal. December 2000).

Sax, G. (1989). *Principles of educational and psychological measurement and evaluation* (3rd ed.). Belmont, CA: Wadsworth.

Section 504 of the Rehabilitation Act, 29 U.S.C. § 701 *et seq.* (1973).

Section 504 Regulations, 7 C.F.R. § 156.13(a) (1997).

Shepard, L. A., & Dougherty, K. C. (1991, April). *Effects of high-stakes testing on instruction.* Paper presented at the annual meeting of the American Educational Research Association, Chicago. (ERIC Document Reproduction Service No. ED 337 468)

Southeastern Community College v. Davis, 442 U.S. 397, 406 (1979).

State ex rel Rea v. Ohio Dept. of Educ., 692 N.E.2d 596 (1998).

State v. Project Principle, Inc., 724 S.W.2d 387 (Tex. 1987).

Student 1 v. Mass. Bd. of Educ., Case No. 03–0071 (Suffolk Superior Court, April 4, 2003).

Title VI of the Civil Rights Act, 42 U.S.C. § 2000d (1964).

Title VII of the Civil Rights Act, 42 U.S.C. § 2000e *et seq.* (1964).

Uniform Guidelines on Employee Selection Procedures, 29 C.F.R. § 1607 *et seq.* (1985).

United States v. North Carolina, 400 F. Supp. 343 (E.D. N.C. 1975), *vacated,* 425 F. Supp. 789 (E.D. N.C. 1977).

United States v. South Carolina, 445 F. Supp. 1094 (D.S.C. 1977), *aff'd mem,* 434 U.S. 1026 (1978).

United States v. Texas, 628 F. Supp. 304 (E.D. Tex. 1985), *rev'd on other grounds.*

United States v. LULAC, 793 F.2d 636 (5th Cir. 1986).

Village of Arlington Heights v. Metropolitan Housing Dev. Corp., 429 U.S. 252 (1977).

Wards Cove Packing Co. v. Antonio, 490 U.S. 642 (1989).

Index

Abedi, J., 554, 595, 597, 604
Ability estimation, 4, 136, 322, 422, 498
Abrahams, S., 638
Absolute interpretations, 89
Accommodations, appropriate, 539, 562, 564, 568, 744, 749
Accountability programs, test-based, 52–55
ACCUPLACER, 490
Achievement constructs, definitions of, 612–13
Ackerman, L., 179
Ackerman, T. A., 119, 234, 240, 416, 419, 420, 423, 508
ACT, Inc., 245, 647, 648, 650, 651, 652, 653, 654, 673
ACT Assessment, 168; admissions testing, higher education, 651–54; composite scores, 170–71; fairness of, 665–73; FGPAs and, 660–61; history of, 250–51; K–12 accountability testing and, 543; Mathematics test score, 178; national norms for, 183; policies, case study of, 370–72; rescaling of, 169, 170, 658; scoring, 656–57
Activity selection, 473
Acton, G. S., 285
ACT-R, 280
Adams, A. A., 509
Adams, G. S., 625
Adams, J. H., 324
Adams, M. L., 521
Adams, R. J., 120, 131, 294, 295, 687, 688, 689, 691, 692, 694
Adams, T. K., 661, 663
ADA Regulations
Adelman, C., 662
Adelstein, S. J., 709
Adema, J. J., 480, 481, 486
Ad Hoc Committee on Confirming Test Results, 221, 547, 548
Adjudication, 102
Administration, 356–59; of computerized testing, 360; conditions for, impact of, 357–58; special accommodations for, 358–59; standardization of, 358; types of, 356–57
Admissions testing, higher education, 647–73; ACT, 651–52, 658; aptitude and achievement, measures of, 652–53; fairness of, 665–72; GMAT, 651; graduate and professional institutions, use of, 654–55; GRE, 650, 658–59; history of, 647–48; LSAT, 651; MCAT, 650–51; misuses, monitoring of, 672–73; promoters of, early, 648–49; SAT, 649, 658–59; score scale revisions, 658; scoring and equating, 656–58; test development, process of, 655–56; undergraduate institutions, use of, 653–54; validity of, predictive (see Validity of higher education admissions testing, predictions)
Advanced Placement Examinations, 78; Computer Science A, 159, 160
Adverse impact, 223
Agresti, A., 82, 99, 100, 238
Airasian, P. W., 533
Aitkin, M., 131, 139, 689
Akin, O., 284, 286
Albert, J. H., 131
Alderson, J. C., 517, 519, 520
Alexander, C., 284, 286
Alexander, K. L., 566
Alexander, L., 542
Alexander v. Sandoval, 223, 733
Algina, J., 81, 597, 613, 712, 713
Algozzine, B., 563
Alignment, 549, 555–57, 569
Allen, M. J., 124, 416
Allen, N. L., 124, 145, 168, 182, 416, 502, 685, 688, 689, 693
Allen v. Alabama State Board of Education, 740
Allport, F. H., 527
Allred, K., 272
Almond, R. G., 27, 43, 259, 292, 313, 393, 472, 473, 604, 605, 606
Alpha Army test, 196
Alsawalmeh, Y. M., 86, 87
AMAE v. California, 738, 739
Amanti, C., 631
American Achievement Tests, 617
American Association for the Advancement of Science, 536, 537
American Association for the Advancement of Science's Benchmarks for Science Literacy, 536

American College Testing Program, 250
American Council on the Teaching of Foreign Languages, 521, 522, 582
American Council on the Training of Foreign Languages (ACTFL), 261, 526
American Educational Research Association, 20, 21, 60, 67, 216, 221, 224, 307, 329, 330, 355, 388, 434, 482, 555, 562, 597, 599, 607, 617, 626, 671, 673, 701, 734
American Educational Research Association (AERA), 1, 754
American Federation of Teachers, 556
American Institute of Certified Public Accountants, 703
American Psychological Association (APA), 1, 2, 14, 19, 20, 21, 60, 67, 70, 82, 99, 166, 216, 221, 227, 246, 307, 329, 355, 356, 359, 360, 372, 388, 401, 434, 435, 439, 451, 457, 459, 460, 461, 462, 465, 482, 501, 502, 555, 562, 599, 607, 664, 671, 673, 701, 716, 721, 722, 725, 734, 738, 752, 753; Committee on Psychological Tests, 19; *Technical Recommendations*, 20
Americans with Disabilities Act of 1990 (ADA), 358, 463, 464, 482, 723, 724–25, 742–43
Analogous coefficients, 3
Analysis of variance (ANOVA), 3, 4, 74, 87–88, 97
Anastasi, A., 21, 22, 308, 369, 380, 526, 746
Anchor item parameters, 134, 135–36
Anchor levels, 693
Anchor scaling, 191–92
Anchor tests, 198–201
Andersen, E. B., 130, 131, 295
Andersen, S. K., 292
Anderson, G. S., 480
Anderson, J. R., 262, 270, 275, 281, 289, 348
Anderson, L. K., 287
Anderson, N. E., 564
Anderson v. Banks, 735, 743
Andreassen, S., 292
Andrews, C., 375
Andrews, K. M., 178, 179, 671
Andrich, D., 117, 118, 120, 131, 132, 141, 341, 416

Angoff, W. H., 201, 203, 206, 207, 208, 211, 217, 234, 236, 241, 366, 368, 435, 436, 438, 439, 440, 441, 442, 444, 447, 448, 450, 455, 456, 460, 461, 462, 464, 558, 693, 721, 722
Angoff-Feldt coefficient, 72–73
Ankenmann, R. D., 412, 416, 422
ANOVA. *See* Analysis of variance (ANOVA)
Ansley, T. N., 118, 364
Answer documents, processing steps of, 373–80; essays, computerized scoring of, 378–80; prescanning, 374; scanning, 374–75; scoring, 375, 377–78; work flow for writing assessment, 375, 376
Anthony, L. C., 624, 661
Antitrust Law, 724
AOL News, 742
Applied Measurement in Education, 146, 179
Applied Psychological Measurement, 146
Appropriateness measures (person-fit), 142–43
Approximations, 76
AP Studio Art, 296
Arabian, J. M., 647
Architectural Registration Examination (ARE), 272, 282
Arenz, B., 535
Armed Service Vocational Aptitude Battery, 490
Armstrong, R. D., 335, 346, 480, 491, 492
Aronson, J., 358, 666
Aschbacher, P. R., 387, 410
Assessment, classroom, 623–42; content, importance of, 629–30; external, large-scale, 639–40; fairness in, 246–48; feedback, 631–32; formative, 627–29; historical view of, 623–27; interpretive arguments for, 48; learning progressions, 630–31; prior knowledge, 631; reliability and validity, new conceptualizations of, 641–42; rubrics, criteria and use of, 631; student self-assessment, 632, 634; summative, and grading, 634–39; teacher development, studies of, 641; teaching, evaluation of, 634; tool and processes for, studies of, 640–41; transfer, teaching and assessing for, 632; validity argument for, 48–50
Assessment arguments, and cognitive psychology, 258–98; design patterns for, 284–85; evidentiary, structure of, 259–61; expertise research for, 282–84; probability-based reasoning, 264–67; psychological perspectives, 261–64; themes and implications, 268–85. *See also* Measurement models, for assessment
"Assessment for learning," 626
Assessment Reform Group, 626
Assessments: alternate, 749–50; explicit designs of, 604–6; high-stakes, 50–51; *for* learning *vs. of* learning, 10; legal and ethical issues in, 751–53; performance, delivery of, 12; psychological perspectives on, 261–62
Assessments, group-score, 681–94; background data, 684; challenges of, current, 694; constructed-response items, 684; content specifications, 683–84; history of, 681–82; IALS, 683; IRT scaling in, 688–90; item pools, 684; linking, 692; marginal estimation procedures in, 690–92; NAAL, 683; NAEP, 682; PIRLS, 682; PISA, 682–83; reporting of results, 692–94; sampling (*see* Sampling, in group-score assessments); TIMSS, 683
Assessment Standards for School Mathematics (NCTM), 634
Assessment Systems Corporation, 368, 372, 479
Associated Press, 361
Association of American Medical Colleges (AAMC), 654
Assouline, S. G., 593
Astin, A., 662
A Study of Thinking, 257
ASVAB, 171, 692
Atash, N., 688
Atkin, J. M., 628
Atkinson, R., 649, 653
Attenuation, reliability and corrections for, 84–85
Attiyeh, G. M., 654, 655, 662
Attiyeh, P., 654, 655
Attribute definition, 55
Audio-lingual method (ALM), 523
Audit tests, 544, 547–48
Auerbach, M. A., 441, 451
Automated item generation, 143, 473–76; from art, 473–76; from strong theory, 474; from weak theory, 474–76
Automated test assembly (ATA), 480–81
Auxiliary: cultural, definition of, 235; external evidence of, 230–34; internal evidence of, 234–36; structural analysis of, 228–30; systematic error and, 225
Avalos, J., 662
Ayala, C. C., 393, 405, 419
Ayala, M. A., 393

Bachman, L. F., 45, 259, 292, 293, 294, 519, 520, 521, 522, 524, 525, 526, 527
Bachman, M., 414
Backing (B), 28
Bacon, D. R., 79
Baer v. National Board of Medical Examiners, 725
Baghi, H., 142
Baird, J. S., Jr., 366
Baker, E. L., 146, 327, 328, 387, 389, 404, 408, 415, 536, 542, 554, 570, 595, 693
Baker, F. B., 11, 131, 132, 133, 355, 372, 601
Balance beam (Siegler's), 287–88
Ballou, D., 566
Balzano, S., 244
Bandalos, D. L., 77
Bandeira de Mello, V., 558
Banerjee, J., 517
Bao, L., 277
Barnes, L.L.B., 413, 414
Barney, H., 569
Baron, J. B., 387, 389, 392, 626
Barrett, G. V., 663
Barron, S. I., 407, 534, 540, 542, 543, 544, 547, 551, 552, 553, 554, 555, 569, 595

Bartlett, F. C., 273
Bartlett v. New York State Board of Law Examiners, 725
Barton, K. E., 559, 562, 568
Barton, M. A., 132
Barton, P. E., 423, 689
Bass, A. R., 232
Batchelder, W. H., 101
Batteries. *See* Test batteries
Bauer, B. A., 399
Baum, K., 442
Baxter, A., 707
Baxter, G. P., 43, 392, 394, 405, 411, 412, 413, 417, 527, 536, 604, 637, 684
Bay, K. S., 86
Bay, L., 367, 441, 446, 447, 685
Baydar, N., 655
Bayesian expected a posteriori (EAP), 138, 159, 177–78
Bayes modal estomator, 138
BB-CLASS, 100
Beach, M., 348
Beaton, A. E., 145, 182, 541, 688, 690, 691, 692, 693, 694
Beatty, A. S., 652, 673
Becker, A. H., 361
Becker, B. J., 672
Becker, D. F., 144, 179, 566
Becker, G., 70
Beckers, H., 707
Been, P., 285, 288
Begging-the-question fallacy, 57–59
Béguin, A. A., 133
Behavioral observations, reliability in, 4, 102–3
Behrens, J. T., 273, 283, 284, 285
Bejar, I. I., 143, 272, 346, 400, 417, 471, 472, 473, 474, 475, 476, 493, 497, 498, 499, 703, 727
Belief, updating, 289–90
Bell, R. M., 394
Bellezza, F. S., 367
Bellezza, S. F., 367
BENCHMARK™, 479
Benchmarking, 693
Benjamin, A., 74
Bennett, R. E., 11, 144, 146, 156, 312, 327, 357, 387, 394, 400, 402, 403, 404, 417, 471, 472, 473, 475, 497, 498, 502, 508, 509, 595, 617, 655, 720, 726
Benson, J., 43, 45
Bentler, P. M., 78
Benware, C., 638
Beran, R., 661
Berends, M., 569
Beretvas, S. N., 118, 240, 443
Bergstrom, B. A., 364
Berk, R. A., 236, 343, 433, 442, 457, 458, 460, 581, 608
Berko, R. M., 585
Berkowitz, R., 663
Berliner, D. C., 10
Bernhardt, E., 527
Bernstein, R. J., 258
Bertenthal, M. W., 143, 187, 545, 692
Bertrand, R., 688

Index

Best, N., 131
Beta Army test, 196
Betebenner, D. W., 402, 408
Betebenner, G., 359
BETTERAVEN, 263
Beuk, C. H., 439, 449, 450
Bhaskar, R., 258
Bhola, D. S., 314, 400, 555, 556
Bias, and test fairness: cultural, definition of, 235; external evidence of, 230–34; internal evidence of, 234–36; structural analysis of, 228–30; systematic error and, 225
Bias, item, 342; definition of, 181
Biggs, J. B., 292, 296
BIGSTEPS, 131
Billeaud, K., 692
BILOG, 121, 131, 132, 133, 477
BILOG-MG, 132, 176, 177
BILOG-MG-3, 132
BILOG 3, 176, 179
Binkley, M., 688
Binomial error model, 81–82
BioKIDS, 295
Bird, C., 366
Birnbaum, A., 126, 127, 146
Bisanz, G., 240, 241
Bisanz, J., 240, 241
Bisection method, 162
Bishop, J. H., 552
Biskin, B., 441
Bixby, J., 601
Black, P., 47, 247, 623, 626, 627, 628, 640, 641
The Black-White Test Score Gap, 666
Blair, J., 27
Blais, J. G., 688
Blakeslee, S., 279
Bleistein, C. A., 667
Bleistein, C. G., 421
Bliem, C. L., 636
Block designs, 685
Bloom, B. S., 309, 316, 597, 637, 706
Bloxom, B., 171, 692
Blum, A., 688
Board of Education of Northport-E. Northport v. Ambach, 735
Bock, R. D., 7, 103, 116, 117, 118, 120, 121, 122, 130, 131, 132, 133, 139, 140, 145, 146, 176, 179, 367, 416, 419, 420, 421, 422, 477, 498, 689, 694
Boeck, P. D., 120, 285, 292, 293, 294, 417, 423
Boekkooi-Timminga, E., 335, 480
Bohlin, C. F., 535
Bohrnstedt, G., 433, 693, 721
Bok, D., 666
Bollen, K. A., 139
Bolt, D. M., 131, 239, 240, 241, 357, 359, 404, 502
Bolton, S., 404, 502
Bond, L., 235, 245, 375, 550
Bonett, D. G., 86
Bonner, M., 399
Bonner, S., 36
Boodoo, G. M., 417
Boomsa, A., 122

Bootstrap procedures, 97–98, 101, 210, 211, 212, 713–14
Borko, H., 552, 641
Bormuth, J. R., 324
Borsboom, D., 45, 54, 291
Boser, U., 537, 742
Bost, J. L., 92
Bottge, B. B., 356
Boughton, K. A., 240, 241, 357, 359
Boulet, J. R., 448, 459, 465
Boundary issues, 8
Bourque, M. L., 170, 436, 440, 441, 446, 447, 454, 459, 693
Bowen, W. G., 666
Bowker, D., 691
Bowman, M. L., 356
Boyatzis, R. E., 663
Boykin, D., 361
Boyle, C. F., 270
Boys, C., 562
Bradburn, N. M., 599, 606, 687
Bradlow, E. T., 120, 121, 131, 295, 423, 493
Brandon, P. R., 441, 445, 451, 456
Brandt, D., 79, 80
Bransford, J. D., 275, 627
Braswell, J. H., 502, 542, 548, 562, 563, 688, 692, 694
Braun, H. I., 194, 197, 206, 207, 208, 217, 239, 272, 400, 497, 499, 692, 703
Braun, H. T., 666
Breimhorst v. Educational Testing Services (ETS), 13
Breithaupt, K., 480, 481, 486, 491, 492
Breland, H. M., 394, 399, 400, 401, 403, 404, 410, 412, 653, 654
Brennan, R. L., 4–9, 14, 31, 35, 37, 58, 65, 66, 68, 71, 73, 74, 76, 77, 79, 80, 82, 84, 86, 87, 88, 89, 91–103, 133, 145, 156, 161–80, 183, 187, 192, 193, 194, 197, 198, 200–210, 212, 214, 215, 216, 217, 267, 286, 293, 318, 334, 342, 343, 367, 380, 381, 410, 411, 412, 414, 419, 433, 437, 441, 442, 452, 460, 461, 488, 499, 527, 558, 609, 658, 673, 689, 692, 693, 703, 712, 713, 714, 715, 722, 748
Brewer, W. F., 277
Breyer, F. J., 100, 393, 712
Brezinski, K. L., 74
Briars, D., 420
Bridgeman, B., 394, 402, 403, 410, 414, 475, 502, 503, 504, 505, 506, 507, 652, 660, 668, 669, 670, 727
Bridgeman, P., 32
Briel, J. B., 659, 662, 668
Briggs, D. C., 672
Brigham, C. C., 249, 251, 647, 648, 649, 670, 699
Brindley, G., 521
Briscoe, C., 636
British Council, 518
British Educational Research Association, 626
Bronfenbrenner, U., 244
Brookhart, S. M., 47, 246, 247, 617, 623, 636, 637, 641, 642
Brookhart case, 743–44, 750
Broudy, H. S., 595

Brown, A. L., 281, 627
Brown, F. G., 642
Brown, J. S., 280
Brown, K. A., 412
Brown, R. L., 79
Brown, T., 660
Brown, W., 67, 71, 72, 73, 75, 77, 87, 89, 92, 99, 100, 101, 103, 111
Brown v. Board of Education, 222
Brumfield, T., 480, 481, 486, 491, 492
Bruner, J. S., 32, 257, 258, 273, 276, 296, 628
Bryk, A. S., 179
"Bubble kids," 553
Buchanan, B., 279, 508, 509
Buckendahl, C. W., 314, 400, 451, 461, 555, 556, 558, 559
Buckley, B. C., 271
BUILDER™, 479
Bunch, M. B., 433, 443
Bunderson, C. V., 11, 363
Bunzo, M., 270
Burden, T., 487
Burdick, R. K., 97, 98
Burgin, W., 480, 491, 493
Burket, G. R., 131, 137, 143, 144, 179, 566
Buros, O. K., 99
Burroughs, S., 593
Burstein, J. C., 276, 378, 379, 404, 497, 498, 499, 595, 657
Burstein, L., 542
Burt, C., 87
Burton, E., 240, 415, 416, 667, 670
Burton, N. W., 240, 652, 660, 661, 662, 664, 667, 669, 670
Burton, R., 280
Burton, R. R., 473
Bush, George H. W., 10, 617
Buss, W. G., 367
Butler, R., 638

Cahalan, C., 502, 671, 725, 726
Cahan, S., 76
Calibration, 192–93
California Assessment Program (CAP), 121, 145
California Learning Assessment System (CLAS), 102
Calkins, L., 640
Camara, W. J., 11, 13, 312, 652, 660, 671, 723, 725, 727, 733
Camilli, G., 14, 143, 144, 179, 221, 235, 236, 238, 240, 241, 243, 245, 342, 402, 410, 459, 460, 595, 656, 665
Campbell, D. T., 2, 32, 36, 38, 39, 40, 42, 44, 45
Campbell, J. P., 662
Campbell, J. R., 548, 682, 688, 693
Campbell, N. R., 290
Campion, D., 335, 347, 348
Campione, J. C., 281
Canale, M., 523, 524
Candell, G. L., 129, 137
Cannell, J. J., 534, 535
Capps, L., 403
Card, S., 279, 283
Cardall, C., 235

Carey, S., 276
Carlin, J. B., 264
Carlson, D., 145
Carlson, J. E., 168, 182, 234, 417, 542, 564, 565, 685, 688, 689
Carlson-LeFloch, K., 540
Carpenter, P. A., 262, 263, 267, 474
Carpenter, T. P., 626, 631
Carr, P., 245
Carroll, J. B., 30, 261, 263, 519, 521, 523, 524
Carson, J. D., 457, 462, 463, 723, 724, 725, 726
Caruso, J. C., 78, 84
Case, R., 281
Case, S. M., 418, 486, 487, 707, 708, 720
The Case Against the SAT, 660
Casella, G., 97
Casillas, A., 272
Castle Rock Research Corporation, 372
Category threshold, 117
Cattell, R. B., 261
CBEST, 739
Center for Research on Evaluation, Standards, and Student Testing (CRESST), 673; *Standards for Educational Accountability Systems,* 570
Center on Education Policy, 590
Centra, J. A., 664
Certificate in Advanced English (CAE), 518
Certificate of Proficiency in English (CPE), 518
Certification exams, 5
Ceteris paribus (all else being equal), 28
Chain equating (CE), 206–7, 208
Chalhoub-Deville, M., 520, 521, 522, 524, 525, 526, 527, 593, 673
Chambers, B., 637
Chambers, D. L., 661, 663
Chan, K.-Y., 499
Chan, S. Y., 356
Chance agreement, 100, 713
Chang, C., 142
Chang, H., 333, 421
Chang, H. H., 364, 486, 489, 490, 690
Chang, L., 442
Chang, S.-W., 364
Change measures, 564–67; cohort-to-cohort, 565–65; measurement issues, 566–67; quasi-longitudinal, 565; statistical issues, 565–67; true longitudinal or value-added, 565–67
Chapelle, C. A., 524
Chapman v. California Department of Education, 751
Charter, R. A., 73
Chase, W. G., 282
Chason, W. M., 366, 368
Chauncey, H., 249, 250, 648
Cheating: by teachers, 369–70; in test preparation, 550; types of, 361–62
Chen, W.-H., 141, 459, 465, 559, 582, 692
Cheng, P. E., 199, 210, 211, 364
Cherland, M., 552
Chi, M.T.H., 258, 282, 475
Chicago Public Schools v. Schmidt, 742
Chipman, S. F., 267, 283, 293

Chi-square tests, 140, 141, 421–22, 724
Chiu, C. W., 96, 97, 359
Chodorow, M., 379, 404, 498, 657
Choi, I.-C., 520
Choi, S. W., 417
Chomsky, Noam, 257, 280, 523
Choosing Elites, 653
Christoffersson, A., 420
Chromy, J. R., 687
Chuah, S. C., 476, 477, 498
Chudowsky, N., 248, 538, 623
Chun, T., 407, 551, 553
Chung, G.K.W.K., 497
Chung-Yan, G. A., 232
Cimbricz, S., 552
Civil Rights Act of 1964, 222–23, 723–24, 733–34; Title VII, 223, 633, 738, 739; Title VI, 222–23, 734
Civil rights movement, 54
Civil Service Commission, 21
Cizek, G. J., 52, 179, 245, 361, 366, 433, 434, 436, 440, 441, 442, 443, 449, 450, 451, 456, 457, 458, 459, 460, 465, 636, 637, 693, 720, 752, 753
Claim (C), 28–29
Clancey, W. J., 271, 273, 279
Clapham, C., 518, 520
Clarizio, H. F., 179, 563
Clark, J.L.D., 521
Clark, M. J., 664, 668
Clark, R. E., 361
Classical congeneric, 76
Classical test theory (CTT), 4, 6, 67–87; battery composite score, reliability of, 77; composite scores in, 76–78; definition of, 68–70; error variance in, 68; internal consistency estimates, 71; IRT comparisons, 111; linear procedures, 208–9; notations used in, 68; parallel forms and test-retest estimates, 70–71; part-test similarities, degrees of, 71–72; probability-based reasoning and, 265–66; score differences, reliability of, 79–80; *Spearman-Brown "Prophecy" Formula,* 72–73, 77; stratified coefficient alpha, 77; structural equation models, reliability estimation using, 78–79; test division and, 72–76
Classifications, 99–102
Clauser, B. E., 394, 400, 404, 415, 497, 508, 701, 703, 716, 719, 720, 721, 722
Clay, M. M., 196, 626
Cleary, T. A., 226, 665, 666
Clemans, W. V., 179, 355
Clement, J., 271, 387
Cliff, N., 78, 290
Clifford, R. M., 592
Cline, F., 652, 660
Clinton, Bill, 10, 617
Cluster sampling, 182
Clyman, S. G., 34, 272, 291, 400, 404, 415, 497, 508, 509
Coaching, 549–50, 672
Cobb, P., 270, 629
Cochran, W. G., 181, 666
Cocking, R. R., 627

Code of Fair Testing Practices in Education (Joint Committee on Testing Practices), 221, 329, 607, 753
Code of Professional Responsibilities in Educational Measurement (NCME), 221, 751–54
Cody, R. P., 367
Coefficients: alpha, 3, 75; correlation, 44; Flanagan's split-half, 72–73, 74; generalizability, 89–90; Guttman-Rulon split-half, 72–73, 83; Guttman's, 75; interrater, standardized/nonstandardized, 101; phi, 100, 339, 715; reliability, 3, 65–67, 84; of stability, 70, 93, 94; stratified, 77
Coffey, J., 628
Coffman, W. E., 235, 387, 412, 601
Cognitive analysis: connectionist models, 274–76; domain perspectives, levels of, 268–69; knowledge representations, 278–82; narratives, 276–78; perception, 273–74; of progressive matrices performances, 263–64; reflective and experential, 269–70; seeking patterns and making meanings, 272–73; situated and embodied cognition, 270–72
Cognitive design systems, 474, 605
Cognitive psychology. *See* Assessment arguments, and cognitive psychology
Cognitive task analysis (CTA), 283–84
Cohen, A. S., 11, 14, 22, 29, 37, 50, 131, 177, 240, 355, 357, 358, 359, 367, 368, 372, 388, 447, 499, 552, 582, 655, 717
Cohen, D. K., 537
Cohen, J., 99, 100, 692
Cohen, S., 682
Colangelo, N., 593
Cole, M., 525
Cole, N. S., 54, 251, 399, 401, 410, 595, 665, 668
Coleman, C., 360
Coleman, M. R., 593
Coley, R. J., 423, 668, 689
The College Board, 13, 159, 160, 163, 249, 250, 490, 534, 591, 642, 648, 649, 651, 652, 653, 654, 655, 656, 658, 660, 661, 662, 668, 669, 671, 672, 673, 753
College Entrance Examination Board, 249, 274, 289, 647, 648, 652
Collins, A. M., 258, 261, 262, 268, 280, 387, 389, 401, 406, 407
Collins, L. M., 79, 289
Collis, K. F., 292, 296
Colton, D. A., 95
Colton, G., 363
Commission on Instructionally Supportive Assessment, 581
Committee on Psychological Tests and Assessment, 753
Committee on the Classification of Personnel in the Army, 196
Common-item design, 173, 174
Communicative language ability (CLA), 524–25
"Comparable Measures" (Kelley), 195
Comparable scores, 189, 195
Compensatory models, 570

Index

Composite scores, in CTT: lower bound to reliability of, 78; maximal reliability of, 77–78; reliability of, 76
Computational models, 274
Computer-aided design (CAD), 272
Computer-based case simulations (CCS), 272, 282
Computer-based testing (CBT), 11–12; connectivity, 484–86; continuous, 484; delivery drivers, 479, 486–88; facilities, 483–84
Computerized adaptive testing (CAT), 14, 120, 144
Computerized mastery testing (CMT), 490–91
Computer technology, 11; consequences of, unintended, 12–13; in score reporting, 12; in test administration, 11–12; in test assembly, 11
Conant, James, B., 249, 250, 648, 649
Conati, C., 295
Concordances, 193, 217
Concurrent calibration, 176–77
Concurrent validity, 1, 18, 20
Conditional dependence, 295–96
Conditional error variances, 98
Conditional false-negative/positive rates, 709–10
Conditional maximum likelihood (CML), 130–31
Conditional probability model, 233
Conditional standard errors of ability, 7, 98–99
Conditional standard errors of measurement, 166–67
Conditions of rebuttal, 28
Confidence intervals, 82, 85–86, 97–98
Confirmatory factor analysis, 41
Congdon, P., 238
Conger, A. J., 78
Congeneric forms, 71
Conjunctive models, 570
Conklin, N. F., 626
Connected Mathematics, 632
Connectionist models, 274–76
Connectivity, 484–86
Connolly, A., 145, 631
Consequences in validity, role of, 8–9, 54; attribute definition, impact of, 55; begging-the-question of, 57–58; evaluating, responsibilities for, 55; in evaluating decision procedures, 54–55; social, 2, 55–56
Constant ratio model, 232
Constraints, 480
Construct driven assessment design, 605
Constructed-response component scores, 78
Constructed-response items, 684
Construct-irrelevant elements, 546
Construct-irrelevant variance, sources of: computer-automated scoring procedures as source of, 404; examinee choice, 402–3; motivation as source of, 404; raters' attention to irrelevant features, 403–4
Construct representation, 46
Construct validity, 19–20; adequacy of, criteria for, 21–22; evidence for, 45–46; evolution of, 20–21; HD model of scientific theories and, 20; interpretive arguments for indicators of, theoretical, 43; irrelevance variance, 2; principles of, 22; theory testing and, 46; under-representation, 2; as unified model of validity, 2, 21; validity arguments for indicators of, theoretical, 43–46
Content validity model, 1, 19, 20
Continuous response item scoring, 158
Convenience norms, 181
Convergent validity evidence, 36–37
Cooil, B., 74
Cook, K. F., 417
Cook, L. L., 169
Cook, T. D., 2, 32, 38, 42, 44, 45
Cook, W. W., 624
Cooley, W. W., 308
Coombs, C. H., 156
Copeland, T., 671, 727
Copyright infringement, 741–42
Corbett, A. T., 270, 289, 295
Corbett, H. D., 552
Corno, L., 271, 597, 632, 640
Corrected for guessing item scores, 157
Correct response: estimated conditional probabilities of, 291; theoretical conditional probabilities of, 290
Correlational structure, between-level differences, 551
Correnti, R., 565
Corrigan, B., 659
Corter, J., 417
Coulehan, M., 250
Coull, B. A., 82
Coulson, D. B., 81
Council of Chief State School Officers, 444, 537, 590, 594, 596, 617
Council on Licensure, Enforcement and Regulation (CLEAR), 313
Counterbalanced design (CB), 198
Cowen, J. J., 663
Cressie, N., 290
Crick, J. E., 88, 91, 97
Criterion-referenced interpretations, 4, 5, 66–67
Criterion validity model, 18–19
Crocker, L., 395, 597, 613
Cronbach, L. J., 1–4, 14, 18–24, 26, 27, 29, 31, 32, 36, 39, 40, 42–44, 46–48, 51–58, 68, 73, 74, 77–79, 88, 89, 92, 96, 103, 239, 296, 307, 308, 323, 324, 407, 411–13, 525, 526, 711, 713, 717, 720, 722, 746
Cronin, J., 559
Cronshaw, S. F., 232
Crooks, T. J., 19, 22, 29, 34, 35, 37, 52, 372, 388, 447, 623, 637, 717
Crouse, J., 652, 659, 660
Crouter, A. C., 244
Crozier, J., 361
Cruse, K. L., 533
CTB Macmillan-Hill, 117, 133, 144, 493, 588, 590
CTB McGraw-Hill, 493
Cuddy, M. M., 707, 717
Culler, J., 526
Cumming, T., 653
Cumulative distribution function (cdf), 189, 202

Cumulative normal distribution, 115
Cureton, E. E., 1, 18, 19, 30, 54
Curley, E., 727
Curran, P. J., 420
Curriculum and Evaluation Standards for School Mathematics, 536, 626, 629

Daane, M. C., 682, 688, 692
Danos, D., 399, 403
Darling-Hammond, L., 552, 639
Darlington, R. B., 233
Darwin, Charles, 249
Data collection designs, in test score linking, 5, 197–201; anchor test or NEAT designs, 198–99, 200–201, 206, 207–10; counterbalanced design (CB), 198; differences among, 199–200; equivalent group design (EG), 197–98, 206, 207; error, estimating, 7; single group design (SG), 197
Datum (D), 27–28
Davey, T. C., 136, 364, 486, 508
David, J. L., 532, 663
Davidson, F., 519, 520
Davis, A., 235
Davis, L. A., 692
Davis, L. L., 364
Davis, S. F., 361
Davy, T., 719
Dawes, R. M., 156, 659
Day, S. C., 708
Dean, M., 417
Deane, P., 276
De Ayala, R. J., 133, 139, 417
De Boeck, P., 120, 285, 292, 293, 294, 417, 423
Debra P. case, 735–36
Debra P. v. Turlington, 54
DEBUGGY, 280
De Champlain, A. F., 139
Deci, E., 638
Decisions, test-based, 51–56; accountability programs, 52–54; consequences in, role of, 54–56; semantic interpretations and, 51–52; standard setting for, 52
Decision study (D-study), 87–99; multifacet, 90–91; p x i design, 89; single facet, with nesting, 90
Decision-theoretic model, 233
Dedicated test centers, 483
Deep-structure, 475
Deere, D., 553
De Graaf, J. W., 244
De Groot, A., 282
De Gruijter, D.N.M., 122, 439, 449, 450
Deibert, E., 536, 546, 550, 559
De Koning, E., 122
Delandshere, G., 47
Delaware Student Testing Program, 405
De Lemos, M. M., 263
Delgado v. McTighe, 723
Dellarosa, D., 279
DeMars, C. E., 318, 404, 417
Deng, M., 358
DeNisi, A., 631
Dennis, R. A., 272

Department of Justice, 21
Department of Labor, 21
The Dependability of Behavioral Measurements: Theory of Generalizability for Scores and Profiles, 88
Depinet, R. L., 663
Derry, S. J., 279
Des Brisay, M., 520
Descriptive attributes, 42
DeShon, R. P., 79
Designs, balanced/unbalanced, 96, 97, 695
Design table, 197
"Design under constraints" design pattern, 286
DETECT, 139
Developmental score scale, 155
Deville, C., 9, 517, 520–27, 593, 673
Dichotomous data, 6, 100, 101, 112, 113–15. *See also* Unidimensional models, for dichotomous data
Dichotomous item scores, 157
Diekhoff, G. M., 361
DIF analysis, 239–43; inferential testing *vs.* estimation of effect size, 240; item difficulty variation, 242–43; item statistical discrimination, 240–41; methods of, 236–39; multidimensionality hypothesis, 241; parameter differences, 242; signals, 241–42; type 1 and 2 errors, 240
Difference model, 118
Difference that matters (DTM), 212
Differential item functioning (DIF), 55, 120, 144, 200, 226, 229, 499; differential performance issues, 740; on performance assessments, 410, 420–21; studies in, early, 235–36. *See also* DIF analysis
Differential performance, screening items for, 739–41
Differential prediction, 229
Digital cable service (DCS), 484
Digital subscriber lines (DSL), 484
Dillingham, A., 445
Dillon, G. F., 720, 721
Dimensionality, in IRT models, 112–13, 123, 419–20; changes in, examining, 551; test-curriculum match and, 567
DIMTEST, 139
Disabilities Rights Advocate group, 13
Disabled individuals: accommodations for, 359, 482–83, 562–63, 595, 688; alterations in testing conditions, classifying, 745; extended time for, 746–47; federal statutes for, 742–43; flagging of test scores and, 747; legal interpretations for, 743–44; mentally retarded, educable, 13; modifications for, 359, 482, 562–63, 595, 751; physical *vs.* cognitive disabilities, 743; psychometric interpretations and, 744; public policy exceptions and, 745–46; score interpretations and, 744–45; special education diagnostic assessments, 592–93; test fairness and, 665, 666, 670–72; undue burden and, 745
Discriminate validity evidence, 39
DiSessa, A., 276
Disparate impact, 733–34, 736
Divgi, D. R., 124, 357

Divide-by-total models, 118
Dixon, C., 526
Do, B.-R., 477
Doe v. National Board of Medical Examiners, 726
Domain definition of growth, 172
Donahue, P. L., 682, 692, 694
Donlon, T. F., 166, 196, 198, 657, 659
Donoghue, J. R., 238, 419, 422, 685, 690
Dood, B. G., 417
Dorans, N. J., 5, 65, 134, 141, 145, 155, 163, 169, 170, 171, 175, 187, 191, 193, 194, 195, 196, 197, 200, 201, 208, 212, 213, 216, 217, 235, 237, 238, 239, 240, 334, 339, 421, 652, 654, 657, 658, 659, 667, 670
Dorans-Holland indices, 212–13
Dorr-Bremme, D. W., 625
Dossey, J. A., 542, 694
Double monotonicity model (DMM), 122
Dougherty, K. C., 552, 753
Douglas, G. A., 130
Douglas, J., 333, 420
Dowling, N., 50
Downey, R. G., 122
Downing, S. M., 39, 307, 327, 597, 615, 708
Doyle, A. C., 718
Doyle, K. O., Jr., 356, 361
Drada, D., 240
Draper, J. F., 241
Draper, K., 552
Drasgow, F., 11, 79, 133, 139, 142, 144, 146, 156, 312, 316, 321, 339, 356, 365, 366, 394, 400, 404, 471, 476, 477, 484, 499, 502, 509, 595, 617, 655
Dresher, A. R., 423
Du, Z., 423
DuBois, P. H., 355, 356, 702
Due process challenges, 735–36
Duffy, M., 540
Dugan, M. K., 655
Dumais, S. T., 379
Dunbar, S. B., 169, 192, 328, 389, 412, 534, 536, 543, 554, 693
Duncan, P. H., 442, 461
Duncan, T., 612
Dunham, K. J., 672
Dunn, O. J., 86, 368
Duplex model, 121
Dupuis, F. A., 688
Duran, R. P., 517, 520
Du Toit, M., 132, 176, 177
Dweck, C., 638
Dwyer, C. A., 32, 33, 37, 38, 669

Eaton, S. B., 562
Ebel, R. L., 18, 19, 54, 87, 167, 168, 169, 327, 438, 442
Eccles, J. S., 638
Echternacht, G., 380, 660
Edelsky, C., 552
Educational measurement: contexts of, 7–8; standards in, and controversy, 10–11
Educational Measurement: Issues and Practice, 641
Educational Measurement, Third Edition (Linn), 221, 262, 407

Educational Testing Service (ETS), 13, 111, 187, 189, 217, 234, 238, 240, 244–46, 245, 246, 366, 367, 433, 493, 494, 496, 504, 505, 506, 507, 519–20, 520, 521, 541, 641, 648, 649, 650, 651, 652, 653, 654, 656, 657, 658, 660, 661, 662, 663, 667, 668, 670, 671, 672, 681, 694, 740
Education Amendments of 1972: Title IX, 223
Education for All Handicapped Children Act, 592
Edwards, J. C., 654
Edwards, W., 279
Eells, K., 235
Effective test lengths, estimation of, 72, 73, 76, 100
Efron, B., 98, 101, 211
Eggan, G., 270
Eggens, T.J.H.M., 357
Eignor, D. R., 490, 659
Eindhoven, P., 121
Einhorn, H. J., 232
Eisner, E., 35
Eiting, M. H., 86
Elawar, M. C., 632, 640
Elder, C., 521
Elementary and Secondary Education Act of 1965 (ESEA), 10, 532
Elementary and Secondary Education Act of 2001. *See* No Child Left Behind (NCLB)
Elliot, S., 378, 379
Elliott, E., 638
Elliott, R., 552
Elliott, S. N., 564
Ellis, B. B., 499
Ellis, R., 523
Elmslie, R. G., 707
Elstein, A. S., 707
Embretson, S. E., 21, 22, 43, 45, 46, 120, 143, 146, 263, 267, 295, 307, 416, 417, 420, 474, 604, 605, 606
Embretson's LLTM for progressive matrices, 267
Encapsulated, self-adaptive test form model, 480
Enders, C. K., 77
Engelhard, G. J., 402, 410, 418, 419
Engelhard, G. J., Jr., 122, 410
Engelhart, M. D., 316, 597, 706
English as a foreign language testing (ESL), 518–21; predictive evidence, 520–21; U.K. *vs.* U.S. approach to, 519–20; in U.K., 518; in U.S., 518–19
English Language Development Assessments (ELDA), 617
English Language Learners (ELLs), 144, 747–49; test condition alterations for, 747–49
Enright, M. K., 497
Entwisle, D. R., 566
Epitemic forms, 280
Epstein, R. R., 532
Equal Employment Opportunity Commission (EEOC), 21, 54, 56, 62, 222, 223, 733
Equal Opportunity Survey, 681
Equal probability model, 233
Equal risk model, 232
Equating. *See* Linking and equating

Index

Equating function, 194
Equipercentile function, 134, 192, 5202–203
Equivalent group design (EG), 173, 197–98, 206, 207
E-rater, 509
Ercikan, K., 102, 122, 162, 414, 692
Erickson, F., 526
Erickson, R. N., 538
Ericsson, K. A., 261, 272, 274, 282, 393, 400
Error, 7; ad hoc solution, 7; conditional standard, in generalizability theory, 7, 98–99; conditional standard errors of ability, 7; defining, by investigator, 7; multiple sources of, 7; in performance assessment, 412–16; recorder, 102–3; sampling, 181; systematic, and irrelevant variance in traits, 38–39; tolerance ratios, 67. *See also* Standard errors of measurement (SEMs)
Error variance, 69–71, 73, 78, 80, 83–84, 90, 98, 135, 166–67, 181–82
Ervin, N., 668
ESOL Examinations, 518
Essays, 409
Essential independence, 123
Essentially independent test items, 123
The Essentials of Mental Measurement (Brown, W. and Thomson, G. H.), 67
Essential *t*-equivalence, 71
Ethical issues: in administering assessments, 752–53; in educating others, 753–54; in evaluation and research, 754; in interpreting assessments and communicating results, 753; in marketing sales, 752; NCME code, 751; in scoring assessments, 753; in selecting and modifying assessments, 751–52
Ethical Standards (AERA)
Evans, J., 508
Everson, H. T., 240, 294, 357, 359
Everybody Counts, 626
Evidence accumulation, 473
Evidence-centered assessment design, 605–6
Evidence-centered design (ECD), 472–73
Evidence identification, 473
Evinger, S., 224
Examinee parameters, 112; accommodations, 482–83; eligibility, 481–82; examination scheduling, 482
Expectation-Maximization (EM), 131
Expected a posteriori (EAP), 138, 159, 177–78
Expected response functions, 143
Expertise, research on, 282–84
Exploratory factor analysis, 41
Explore, 168
Exploratory factor analysis, 41
Extensible markup language (XML), 479
Extrapolation inferences, 5, 24, 25, 34; analytic evaluation of, 35–36; challenges to, 37; convergent validity evidence, 36–37; evaluation of, empirical, 36; evaluation of, overall, 37; interpretation and, 717–18; validity generalization, 36
Eyde, L. D., 752

Fabrizio, L. M., 556
FACETS, 122, 419

Facets: fixed, 93; hidden, 92–93; random, 93
Face validity, 36
Factor analysis, 41
FAIRHAVEN, 263, 279
Fairman, J., 615
Falck, B., 292
Falcon, J.C.S., 140
Fallacy of statistical surrogation, 58
Falmagne, J.-C., 267, 293
Fan, M., 364, 400
Farnum, M., 402, 403, 404, 494, 495
Farr, M., 282, 625
FASTTEST™, 479
Featherman, C. M., 131, 132
Feature accumulation, 497
Feature evaluation, 497
Feature extraction, 497
Federal Trade Commission, 673
Federation of State Medical Boards of the United States, Inc., 360
Feldt, L. S., 4, 35, 65, 68, 71, 72, 73, 75, 76, 77, 79, 83, 84, 86, 87, 88, 91, 96, 98, 103, 161, 162, 166, 342, 343, 609
Feldt-Brennan's classical congeneric, 76
Feldt's method, 84
Feltovich, B., 404, 502
Feltovich, P., 258, 475
Fennema, E., 631
Ferguson, W., 280
Ferrara, S., 7, 9, 102, 141, 142, 320, 414, 465, 559, 579, 582, 590, 596, 597, 599, 604, 606, 610, 611, 612, 614, 617
Fessenden, F., 544
Feuer, M. J., 143, 187, 213, 215, 217, 692
Fey, J. T., 632, 633
Figlio, D. N., 553
Finn, C. E., Jr., 694
Firestone, W. A., 615
First Certificate in English (FCE), 518
First International Mathematics Study, 681
First-year grade point average (FGPA), 234, 660, 666–67
Fischer, G. H., 119, 120, 146, 265, 266, 290, 293
Fischer, K. W., 262, 281
Fisher, T., 86, 459
Fiske, D. W., 36, 39, 40, 612, 613
Fitzgerald, S. M., 266, 441, 636
Fitzgerald, W. M., 632, 633
Fitzpatrick, A. R., 4, 28, 41, 43, 65, 102, 111, 117, 122, 125, 127, 140, 156, 158, 176, 179, 192, 197, 200, 206, 210, 337, 368, 380, 403, 414, 415, 416, 417, 419, 422, 455, 655, 688, 722
Fitzpatrick, R., 31, 387, 388, 389
Fixed item parameters, 6
Flagging policy, 13, 747
Flaherty, B. P., 289
Flanagan, A., 542
Flanagan, J. C., 5, 72, 73, 74, 164, 165, 705
Flanagan's split-half coefficients, 72–73, 74
Flannery, B. P., 162
Flannery, W. P., 143
Fleming, M., 637
Flockton, L., 19, 35

Floden, R. E., 103, 552
Flora, D. B., 420
Focal tests, 547–48
Folk, V. G., 118, 480, 488
Foltz, P. W., 378, 379, 497
Fong, Y. F., 691
Fontana, J., 596
Foorman, B. R., 273
Force Concept Inventory (FCI), 277
Ford, S. F., 236, 241
Foreign Service Institute (FSI), 519
Formative assessment, 627, 628–29
Forster, G., 543
Forster, M., 630
Forsyth, R. A., 118, 144, 169, 179, 566, 693
FORTRAN, 131
Foster, A. L., 672
Fournier, D., 27
Four-parameter beta-binomial error model, 82
Fourteenth Amendment, 222–23
Fowles, M. E., 394, 402, 403, 404, 405, 406, 494, 498, 661, 668
Frank, K. A., 179
Franke, M. L., 631
Frary, R. B., 366, 367
Fraser, C., 131, 132, 417
Frawley, W., 521
Frederiksen, C. H., 526
Frederiksen, J. R., 47, 49, 50, 277, 278, 387, 389, 401, 406, 407, 632, 634, 640
Frederiksen, N., 52, 250, 388, 389
Freeman, M. F., 166
French, A. W., 333
Friel, S. N., 632, 633
Frisbie, D. A., 73, 169, 192
Frost, N., 263
Frye, D., 497
Fuchs, D., 406, 562, 564, 593
Fuchs, L. S., 562, 593
Fulcher, G., 521, 522
Furby, L., 79
Furst, E. J., 316, 597, 706
Fyans, L. J., Jr., 88

Gabrielson, S., 402
Gadamer, G. H., 264, 271
Gagne, P., 378
Gallagher, A., 32, 502, 670
Gallant, J., 559
Gallimore, R., 244, 631
Galton, Sir Francis, 248–49
Gamma, E., 284, 286
Gao, X., 95, 97, 200, 411, 412, 536
Garcia-Ballester, L., 702, 703
Gardener, H., 251
Garner, M., 410
GATB Committee, 234
Gay, G. H., 752
Gayler, K., 538
Geddes, C. M., 648, 673
Gee, P. J., 258, 271
Geertz, C., 47, 642
Geiser, S., 652, 660
Geisinger, K. F., 463, 464
Gelin, M. N., 241
Gelman, A., 264, 292

Gender differences, 409–10, 665, 668–70
General administration characteristics, 501
General Aptitude Test Battery (GATB), 234
General comparability, 5
General Education Development (GED), 250
Generalizability coefficient, 89–90
Generalizability study (G-study), 87–97; multifacet, 90–91; p x i design, 88–89; single facet, with nesting, 90
Generalizability theory, 3, 5, 6, 87–99; analyses of, 58; applications of, 91–92; coefficients of, and dependability, 89–90; conceptual framework of, 3–4; conditional standard errors in, 98–99; D-study p x i design, 89; facets in, hidden, 92–93; for group means and multilevel data, 95–97; G-study pxi design, 88–89; multifacet G-studies and D-studies, 90–91; multivariate, 4, 94–95; reliability estimates, traditional, from the perspective of, 93–94; single-facet G-study and D-study designs with nesting, 90; univariate, 4, 94–95; variance component estimation, 33, 97–98
Generalized partial credit model (GPC), 117
General latent trait model (GLTM), 120
GENOVA, 88, 94, 97
Gernand, R., 653
Gerritz, K., 402
Gershon, R. C., 364
Gertner, A., 270
Gessaroli, M. E., 139
Getzler, L. S., 553
Ghandour, G. A., 66, 102, 103, 292
Ghiselli, E. E., 18
Gibbons, R. D., 139, 295, 420
Gibson, J. J., 257
Gibson, W. M., 488
Gierl, M. J., 119, 240, 241, 416, 417
Gifford, J. A., 130, 133
GI Forum v. Texas Education Agency, 734–38, 740–41
Gilbert, R., 526
Gilding the lily fallacy, 59
Gilford, D. M., 687
Gilliam, W. S., 592
Gilmer, J. S., 76
Gilmer-Feldt's approximations, 76
Gimpel, J., 459
Gipps, C. V., 47, 247, 248, 251, 282, 623, 642
Giraud, G. T., 458, 461, 462
Gitomer, D. G., 293
Gitomer, D. H., 272, 282, 294
Glas, C.A.W., 120, 140, 177, 295, 307, 421, 475
Glaser, R. G., 43, 248, 258, 268, 282, 283, 294, 392, 393, 400, 405, 417, 433, 475, 533, 536, 604, 623, 624, 637, 684, 693, 721
Glass, G. V., 433, 533, 720
Gleeson, F. A., 356
Gleser, G. C., 3, 4, 18, 21, 52, 54, 77, 88, 296, 411, 711, 713, 722
GLOBE tasks, 282
Glockner-Rist, A., 421
GMAT, 493
Goa, X., 527

Goals 2000: Educate America Act, 10
Gobert, J. D., 271
Goehring, H. J., Jr., 625
Goertz, M. E., 540, 552
Goff, G., 551
Goh, D. S., 482, 483
Golan, S., 554
Goldberg, G. L., 389
Goldenberg, C., 244
Golden Rule Life Insurance Co. v. Washburn, 740–41
Goldfarb v. Virginia, 724
Goldstein, H., 266, 688
GOMS, 280
Gong, B., 497
Gonzales v. National Board of Medical Examiners, 725
Gonzalez, E. J., 692
Gonzalez, G., 555, 569, 688
Gonzalez, N., 631
Goodman, D. P., 433, 581, 584, 585
Goodman, M. J., 682, 684
Goodman, Y.M., 626
Goodness-of-fit, 421–22
Goodwin, J., 407
Gordon, B., 102, 402, 415
Gorin, J., 604
Gorth, W. P., 533
Goslin, D. A., 532, 625
Gotwals, A., 295
Gould, Stephen Jay, 595
Grabe, W., 527
Graded response model (difference model), 117, 118
Grade-grade definition of growth, 172–73
Grade-point average (GPA), 654–55, 660–69
Graduate Management Admission Council (GMAC), 379, 473, 493, 497, 502, 651, 655
Graduate Management Admission Test (GMAT), 473, 502, 504, 651, 657, 661, 665–73
Graduate Record Examinations General Test (GRE), 402, 406, 473, 490, 493, 502, 504, 650, 657–62, 664–73
Graduation testing, legal and ethical issues in: *Debra P.* case, 735; disparate impact, 736; due process, 736736; *GI Forum* case, 735–37; Massachusetts challenge, 737; summary of, 737–38
Grady, W. R., 655
Grandy, J., 668
Grandy, R. E., 46
Grant, M., 494
Graue, M. E., 534, 642
Graybill, F. A., 97, 98
Green, B. F., 118, 143, 187, 545, 692
Green, D. R., 169, 241, 442, 451, 461
Green, J., 526
Green, P. C., 457
Greene, J., 309, 319, 327, 543, 587, 604, 613
Greeno, J. G., 37, 258, 261, 262, 268, 269, 279
Greenwood, M. R., 652, 673
Gregg, N., 358, 360
Grice, H., 273

Griffin, M., 625
Griffith, J. E., 687
Grigg, W. S., 682, 688, 692, 693, 694
Grissmer, D. W., 542
Grobe, C. H., 403
Groce, E., 596
Gronlund, N. E., 324
Gross, M.U.M., 593
Grosse, M. E., 708
Grossman, J., 417
Grosso, L., 707
Group-level models, 121
Group-level norms, 181
Group testing, in K–12, 531–42; accountability system, incorporating tests into, 537–38; aggregate achievement trends, monitoring assessments, 532–33; changes in testing, late 1980s, 534–42; custom-developed tests and standards, increased use of, 537; education reform movement, 534; inclusion and uniformity in, mandates for, 538–39; large-scale testing in U.S., origins and development of, 532–34; minimum-competency testing and measurement-driven instruction, 533–34; multiple choice format, shifting back to, 535–36; NAEP changes, 541–42; performance assessment, experimentation with, 534–35; performance targets, 540–41; reporting requirements, 539; score changes, 539–40; standards-referenced testing, 536–37; value-added modeling, 541
Grover, C. A., 361
Grutter v. Bollinger, 233–34, 251
Guering-Pace, F., 688
Guernsey, M. J., 720
Guessing parameter, 115
Guidelines for Computer-based Tests and Interpretations (APA), 501, 502
Guinier, L., 653
Guion, R., 18, 19, 21, 46, 51, 54, 313
Guion, R. M., 2
Gulliksen, H., 3, 18, 19, 67, 73, 161, 175, 656, 659, 664
Gundersen, J. A., 363
Gupta, J. K., 79
Gustafsson, J.-E., 79, 141
Guttman, L. A., 72, 73, 74, 75, 83, 319
Guttman-Rulon split-half coefficient, 72–73, 83
Guttman's coefficient, 75
Gyagenda, I. S., 410

Haack, K., 556
Haas, G. J., 520, 521
Habing, B., 123
Habon, M. W., 267
Hadadi, A., 480, 486, 487, 491
Haebara, T., 76, 176, 177
Haebara method, 177
Haenszel, W. M., 236, 237, 238, 242, 333, 499
Haertel, E. H., 4, 35, 54, 65, 92, 111, 122, 125, 145, 158, 166, 221, 259, 267, 293, 294, 342, 389, 390, 391, 408, 411, 412, 416, 452, 541, 552, 557, 558, 559, 585, 612, 690

Index

Haertel, G., 37
Hafner, R., 271
Hagen, E. P., 171
Hagtvet, K., 43
Haines, V. J., 361
Hakstian, A. R., 86, 98
Haladyna, T. M., 39, 307, 319, 320, 324, 326, 327, 340, 597, 598, 604, 615
Hale, G. A., 520
Halliday, M.A.K., 524
Hallock, B. A., 532
Hambleton, R. K., 4, 10, 41, 52, 81, 100, 130, 133, 140, 141, 146, 168, 206, 236, 240, 320, 401, 410, 411, 416, 419, 421, 433, 434, 435, 436, 440, 441, 442, 443, 444, 446, 447, 448, 450, 451, 454, 456, 457, 458, 459, 465, 491, 507, 533, 554, 557, 558, 581, 582, 583, 584, 585, 693, 694, 712, 713, 720
Hamel, L., 284
Hamilton, J., 521
Hamilton, L. S., 7, 9, 531, 536, 541, 542, 550, 551, 553, 555, 557, 561–67, 569, 595, 604, 610
Hamilton, M., 538
Hamlett, C. L., 562, 593
Hammerness, K., 639
Hancock, G. R., 79, 85
Haney, W. M., 502, 532, 673
Hannaway, J., 543
Hansen, E., 28
Hansen, H., 57
Hansen, M., 422
Hanson, B. A., 82, 84, 100, 133, 166, 167, 171, 177, 188, 192, 195, 196, 201, 204–6, 209, 216, 367, 447, 658, 709, 712
Hanson's theorem, 188, 196, 204–5
Hanushek, E. A., 541, 565
Hanzeli, V., 293
Harackiewicz, J., 638
Harden, R. M., 356
Harik, P., 34, 720, 721
Harmes, J. C., 364
Harmon, M. C., 637
Harnisch, D., 144, 291
Harrington, S., 494
Harris, C. W., 715
Harris, D. J., 6, 367, 399
Harris, V. F., 661
Hart, C. L., 417
Hartigan, J. A., 221, 222, 223, 233, 234, 249
Hartog, P., 702
Hartwig, J., 360
Hartz, S. M., 294
Harwell, M., 133
Hasan, R., 524
Hastings, J. T., 309
Hattie, J., 123, 139, 429
Hau, K.-T., 364
Haug, C., 559, 565
Hauser, C., 559
Hauser, M. H., 55, 639, 673
Havighurst, R., 235
Havlicek, L., 366
Hawkins, E., 684
Hawkins, J., 279

Hawkins, R. E., 703
He, A., 521
Heath, S. B., 631
Hebb, D. O., 274
Hebb's learning rule, 274
Hedeker, D. R., 295
Hedges, L. V., 85, 690
Heidorn, M., 121
Heinrichs, M., 356
Heller, J. I., 401
Helm, R., 284
Helsen, W. F., 284
Hemphill, F. C., 143, 187, 692
Henderson, C. R., 97
Henning, G., 140, 141, 520
Henry, G. T., 592
Henrysson, S., 32
Henson, R. K., 84
Hereditary Genius (Galton), 248
Herl, H. E., 497
Herman, J. L., 387, 392, 401, 410, 435, 570, 625
Herman, S. J., 412
Herrick, V., 235
Hershberger, S. L., 307
Hertzog, M. A., 139
Hestenes, D., 277, 292, 295
Hetter, R. D., 364, 477, 486, 488, 489
Heubert, J. P., 55, 639, 673
Heuristic methods, 130
Hezlett, S. A., 654, 661, 662, 663
Hidalgo-Montesinos, M. D., 240
Hieronymus, M., 175, 179, 412
Hieronymus scaling, 174–75
High-stakes accountability, 10; in K–12 accountability, 551–55, 568–69; qualitative approach to, 50–51
Hill, W. H., 117, 316, 706
Hirsch, T. M., 136
Hirsch, T. R., 480
History Advanced Placement Exams, 403
Hitchcock, C., 591
Hively, W., 282, 346, 473
Hodges, N. J., 284
Hoffman, C. M., 648, 673
Hofstee, W.K.B., 439, 449
Hofstetter, C., 595
Hogaboam, T. W., 263
Hogan, K., 629
Hogan, T. P., 74, 75
Hoijtink, H., 142, 421, 422
Holland, P. W., 5, 6, 65, 103, 134, 139, 143, 145, 155, 163, 169, 171, 175, 179, 181, 189, 194, 195, 197, 200, 201, 203, 204, 205, 206, 207, 208, 209, 210, 211, 212, 213, 216, 217, 221, 225, 234, 235, 237, 238, 239, 240, 242, 266, 290, 317, 334, 366, 367, 421, 499, 657, 659, 670, 692, 719
Holsgrove, G., 707
Holtman, M., 720
Hombo, C. M., 419, 420, 422, 548, 693
Hoover, H. D., 5, 133, 155, 169, 171, 174, 179, 187, 192, 389, 412, 536, 550, 555, 558, 559, 689
Hopkins, B. R., 380

Hopkins, K. D., 380
Hopper, D. B., 725
Horkay, N., 502
Horn, B., 541, 565
Horn, S. P., 541, 565
Hornke, L. F., 267
Horst, P., 72
Hoskens, M., 6, 103, 120, 189, 201, 204, 205, 209, 210, 294, 417, 419
Hosp, M. K., 593
Hou, L., 162, 418
House, A., 562
House, E. R., 22, 717
Houser, R., 559
Houston, W. M., 193, 654
Houston Independent School District, 544
Howard-Martin, J., 725
How People Learn, 627
Hoyt, C., 74, 87
Hoyt, W. T., 99
Hsiung, C. A., 81
Hsu, J.S.J., 81
Hsu, P.-Y., 244
Hu, P. G., 240
Huang, C.-W., 295
Hubbard, J. P., 702
Hubel, D., 273
Hubin, D. R., 221, 249
Huff, K. L., 444, 661
Hughes, K. R., 401
Hulin, C. L., 133, 134, 139, 146, 477
Humphreys, L. G., 79, 139, 141, 665
Hunka, S. M., 417
Hunt, E., 263, 278
Hunt, H., 378
Hunter, D., 356
Hunter, J. E., 18, 85, 232, 241
Huot, B., 395, 399
Hurst, K., 272
Hurtz, G. M., 441, 451
Husek, T. R., 99, 533
Hutchins, E., 283
Huynh, H., 75, 100, 141, 142, 168, 179, 443, 465, 559, 712
Hymes, D. H., 523
Hypothetico-deductive (HD) model of scientific theories, 20

IDP Education/IELTS Australia, 518
IF-THEN rules, 280
Ilies, R., 70
Illinois State Board of Education, 743
IMMEX, 272, 276
Impara, J. C., 440, 441, 451, 461, 556, 558, 585, 721
Impara, J. D., 314, 555, 556
Implicit performance elements, 546
Improving America's Schools Act of 1994, 538
Indeterminacy, metrics and, 123–24
Index of dependability, 89
Individual education plans (IEPs), 591, 749–50
Individual Education Program (IEP), 749–51
Individuals with Disabilities Education Act Amendments (IDEA), 538, 539, 561, 592

Individuals with Disabilities Education Improvement Act of 2004 (IDEA), 592
Inferences, 2; Theory-based inferences; decision, 24–25; generalization, 24, 25, 34; implications, 34; scoring, 24, 25, 34, 43; targets of, 546–48; Toulmin's model of, 27–29; weights, 546–47, 550. *See also* Extrapolation inferences
Information functions, and standard errors, 125–29
Inhelder, B., 287
Inouye, D. K., 11, 363
Intact forms model, 480
Integrated evaluative judgment, 2
Integrated structural diagram, 229–30
Interagency Language Roundtable (ILR), 522, 526
Internal-consistency estimates of reliability, 71
International Adult Literacy Survey (IALS), 683
International Assessment of Education Progress, 189
International English Language Testing System (IELTS), 518, 520, 521
Internet, 483
Internet service provider (ISP), 503
Interpretations: absolute, 89; criterion-referenced, 4; norm-referenced, 4, 5, 66–67, 89; relative *vs.* precision of absolute, 79–80
Interpretative arguments, qualitative: of high-stakes assessments, 50–51; interactions in, role of, 51; of student performance, 47–48
Interpretative arguments, theory based: descriptive attributes, 42, 46; for indicators of theoretical constructs, 43–44; for nomological theories, 42–43; process models for, 43; theoretical constructs of, 42
Interpretive arguments, 2, 23, 717; for classroom assessments, 48; defensible nature of, 27; evaluating, criteria for, 29; informal and presumptive reasoning, 27; as mini-theory, 25; for placement testing, 24–25; specifying for evaluation, 29–30; Toulmin's model of inference and, 27–29
Interpretive arguments, for traits: implications, trait, 31–32; measurement procedures, 31; overview of, 33–34; target domains, 30–31
Intraclass correlation, 87
Iowa Every Pupil Achievement Tests (IEPT), 250
Iowa Tests of Basic Skills (ITBS), 169, 174–75, 250, 532, 555, 614
Iowa Tests of Educational Development (ITED), 165–66, 169, 171, 212, 250, 381, 588, 590, 614, 652, 658
Ippel, M. J., 43
IQ tests, 13
Ironson, G. H., 236
IRT. *See* Item response theory (IRT)
IRT Bayesian scoring, 159
IRT Graphics, 132
IRT maximum likelihood scoring, 158–59
IRT models: choice, philosophies of, 124–25; component, 119–20; concepts of, 112–13; group-level, 121; information functions, comparing, 129; integration of, need for, 5–6; multidimensional, 118–19; non-parametric, 121–22; for performance assessment, 416–23; polytomous, 118–20, 131–33, 146, 416, 420–23; presmoothing, 204; of rater effects, 122; testlet response, 120–21; use of, growth in, 111–12. *See also* Model-data fit, in IRT; Unidimensional IRT models
Irvine, S. H., 143, 282, 473, 604, 718, 727
Irwin, P. M., 556
Ishikawa, S., 284
Isomorphicity, 475
ISTEP program, 534
Item bundles, 120
Item calibration, 129
Item characteristic curve (ICC), 113–15, 116, 475
Item characteristic function (ICF), 113, 116
Item difficulty, 113
Item discrimination, 114
Item drift, 132
Item fit, 139–41
Item format, 508
Item-free person measurement, 113
Item information function, 127
Item-level norms, 181
Item location, 117, 128
Item mapping, 167–68
Item model, 143
Item parameter, and ability estimation, 4, 129–36; aligning, from separate analyses, 133–36 (*see also* Item parameters, aligning); conditional maximum likelihood, 130–31; heuristic models, 130; joint maximum likelihood, 130; marginal maximum likelihood, 131; Markov chain Monte Carlo, 131; MIRT estimation software, 132; test lengths and sample sizes, 132–33; unidimensional estimation software, 131–32
Item parameters, aligning, 133–36; holding anchor item parameters fixed, 134; linear methods based on ability estimates, 134; mean-mean method, 134–35; of multidimensional models, 136; outlier anchor items, removing from educational achievement tests, 135–36; TCC method, 135
Item-pattern scoring, 127, 137
Item pool model, 480
Item pools, 346, 684
Item pretesting, 476–79; calibration before operational use, 476–77; calibration for operational testing programs, 477, 479; item banking, 479
Item response curve (IRC), 113
Item response functions (IRFs), 236–37
Item response surfaces (IRS), 119
Item response theory (IRT), 4; ability estimation, 136–38; CCT comparisons, 111; *vs.* classical test theory, 111; computer programs for, 4; dimensionality, 123; educational applications, survey of, 143–45; evolving notions of, 4; future directions of, 145–46; indeterminacy and metrics, 123–24; information sources, 146; item parameter, and ability estimation, 4, 129–36; local item independence, 122–23; model fit, 4; nonlinear true-score procedures from, 205–6, 209–10; parameters, difference in, 236; performance assessments and, 416–23; IRT models for, 416–17; polytomous models, 4; probability-based reasoning and, 266; proficiency estimates, 164, 167, 175, 178; reliability of, 4; scaling in, 41, 176–78, 206; standard error and information functions, 125–29; test characteristic functions, 125. *See also* IRT models
Item scores, 125, 157–58; corrected for guessing, 157; dichotomous, 157; location of, 128; ordered response, 157–58; weighted sums of, 126–28
Item selection algorithms, 489–90
Item sets with common linking items (graph), 501
Item unfairness, detecting, 234
Iwamoto, C. K., 366

Jackenthal, A., 503, 504, 505, 506, 507
Jackknife procedures, 97, 98, 686
Jackson, C. A., 217, 250, 649
Jackson, D., 597
Jackson, R., 591
Jacob, B. A., 369, 370, 534, 542, 553, 555
Jacquemin, D., 497, 720
Jaeger, R. M., 54, 214, 433, 436, 438, 440, 442, 443, 445, 446, 447, 448, 450, 452, 453, 457, 458, 460, 461, 464, 533, 542, 550, 558, 579, 590, 693
Jakwerth, P. M., 601
James, H. T., 249, 355, 542, 633, 648, 649
Jannarone, R. J., 120
Janosky, J. E., 133
Jansen, B.R.J., 289
Janssen, R., 294
Jarjoura, D., 81, 84, 94, 97, 98, 167, 203, 211, 318
Jencks, C., 666
Jenkins, F. F., 564, 690
Jenkins, L. B., 683
Jensen, A. R., 222, 232, 233, 241, 595
Jerald, C. D., 537
Jiang, J., 668, 669
Jiang, T., 692
Jim Crow era, 222
Jin, Y., 688
Jirele, T. J., 664, 726
Jmel, S., 70
Jodoin, M., 444, 491, 509
Johnson, E. G., 145, 178, 182, 211, 414, 416, 465, 559, 582, 685, 686, 688, 689, 691, 692
Johnson, E. K., 654
Johnson, M. S., 122, 419, 475, 524, 525, 526
Johnson, R. L., 102, 240, 284, 415
Johnson, T. R., 655
Johnson, V. E., 664, 669
Johnson-Laird, P. N., 279
Johnstone, C. J., 310, 329, 335, 357, 359
Joint Committee on Testing Practices, 221, 607, 751
Joint maximum likelihood (JML), 130

Jolliffe, I. T., 691
Jolly, P., 655
Jones, D. H., 335, 346, 480, 666
Jones, L. R., 14, 169, 542, 552, 693
Jones, L. V., 682
Jones, R. J., 399, 433, 688
Jones, R. L., 521
Jöreskog, K., 43, 71, 76
Journal of Educational and Behavioral Statistics, 146, 179
Journal of Educational Measurement, 146
Jovanovic, J., 414
Julian, M., 138, 651, 661
Jungeblut, A., 291, 683
Junker, B. W., 122, 131, 139, 142, 267, 294, 296, 419, 689
Juskiewicz, P. J., 400
Just, M. A., 262, 263

Kadane, J. B., 259
Kaftandjieva, F., 239
Kagan, S. L., 592, 594
Kaganoff, T., 407
Kahl, S. R., 446
Kahn, H., 399, 403
Kahneman, D., 270, 276
Kain, J. F., 541
Kalat, J. K., 662
Kalohn, J. C., 486
Kaminski, J., 369, 548
Kane, M. T., 2, 3, 5, 9, 17, 19, 22, 28, 29, 31, 35, 37, 39, 43, 52, 53, 60, 66, 67, 80, 89, 92, 96, 97, 99, 162, 195, 221, 258, 307, 344, 372, 388, 400, 402, 411, 417, 418, 433, 435, 440, 441, 442, 447, 451, 452, 455, 457–63, 558, 585, 610, 659, 712, 714, 715, 717, 721
Kane, T. J., 564, 565, 570
Kanjee, A., 238
Kansas Assessment Program, 403
Kansas Quality Performance Assessment, 406
Kansas State Board of Education, 406
Kantor, R., 527
Kaplan, B. A., 486, 502, 682, 691, 726
Kaplan, D., 139
Kargar, A., 703
Karger, J. S., 538
Karns, K., 562
Katz, I. R., 272, 284, 405
Kaufman, D. M., 461
Kaufman, D. R., 283, 284
Kawata, J., 542
Kearns, J., 464
Keats, J. A., 81, 82, 83, 84, 98, 100
Keats's method for estimating conditional standard errors of measurement, 83, 84
Keeler, E., 709
Keily, G. L., 486, 602
Keith, S., 553, 555, 595
Keith, T. Z., 404
Kelderman, H., 119, 240, 294
Keller-Mcnulty, S., 442
Kelley, T. L., 80, 81, 158–59, 165, 166, 167, 175, 189, 190, 193, 195, 196, 203, 239
Kelley, Truman L., 165–66
Kelley regressed scores, 158

Kelly, D. L., 689
Kempf, W., 285
Kenly, E., 348
Kennedy, A. M., 682
Kenney, J. F., 497
Kenney, P. A., 626, 688
Kenny, S. L., 262
Keogh, B. K., 593
Keymath Diagnostic Arithmetic Test, 631
Khaliq, S., 241
Khampalikit, C., 399
Khoo, S., 551
Kiely, G. L., 120, 142, 423, 480, 486, 490
Kilpatrick, J., 626
Kim, H. R., 420
Kim, S.-H., 131, 132, 177, 240, 499
Kimmel, E. W., 654
Kindfield, A.C.H., 280
Kindler, A. L., 561
King, F. J., 121
King, G. F., 211
Kingsbury, G. G., 364, 486, 559
Kingston, N. M., 141, 446, 447
Kinner, F., 552
Kiplinger, V. L., 50, 554, 694
KIRIS, 407, 537–38, 543, 554
Kirsch, I. S., 291, 683, 688, 693
Kish, L., 685, 687
Klauer, K. C., 101, 142
Klausen, T., 283
Klein, D.C.D., 401
Klein, S. P., 50, 394, 399, 534, 535, 536, 542, 543, 544, 547, 551, 554, 567, 596
Kleinert, H., 464
Klenowski, V., 632, 634, 640
Klitgaard, R. E., 653, 663, 664
Kluger, A. N., 631
Knowing What Students Know, 624, 627, 639, 640, 641
Knowledge, skills, and abilities (KSAs), 605
Knowledge representations, 278–82
Knowles, K. P., 738
Kober, N., 538
Kobrin, J. L., 652, 660
Koenig, J. A., 661, 663, 666, 669, 672
Kohen, E. S., 659
Kohn, A., 580, 595
Kohonen, T., 274
Kolen, M. J., 5, 6, 124, 125, 133, 155, 156, 163–68, 171–78, 180, 187, 189, 190–94, 196, 197, 198, 201, 203–12, 214, 215, 320, 334, 357, 380, 381, 488, 499, 566, 658, 689, 692, 748
Kolen, M. M., 82, 84, 167
Kolstad, A., 443, 683, 693
Koons, H., 433, 443
Kopriva, R. J., 85
Koretz, D. M., 7, 9, 50, 179, 187, 213, 215, 217, 389, 531–38, 540–55, 559–62, 564–67, 569, 570, 595, 596, 610
Kossan, P., 742
Koval, J. J., 101
Kraemer, H. C., 87
Krakowski, K., 139, 420
Kramsch, C., 525, 526, 527
Krathwohl, D. R., 261, 597, 706

Krenzke, T., 686
Kristof, W., 72, 73, 74, 75, 76, 86
Kristof's three-part procedure formula, 75–76
Kromrey, J. D., 364
K–12 achievement testing, description and evaluation of, 607–16; criteria for, 607; reliability of test scores, evidence of, 607–10, 615; validity of test scores, evidence of (*see* Validity of K–12 achievement test scores)
K–12 assessment items, 596–604; extended constructed-response, 601–4; multiple-choice, 597–99; response requirements, 596–97; short constructed-response, 599–601
K–12 educational achievement assessments: academic area achievement and diagnostic, 592; alternate, 591; content area achievement surveys, 587, 590; curriculum embedded, 591–92; English language proficiency, 593; gifted and talented screening instruments and procedures, 593; high school exit examinations, 590–91; school readiness, 592; special education diagnostic, 592–93; uniformity of, 560–64
K–12 test score reporting, 581–85; features of, 584–85; performance level descriptions, 582–83; research, 585; subdomain scores, 583–84; types of, 581–82
K–12 individual achievement tests, standardized assessment of, 579–618; decades of (chart), 586–87; design and development approaches to, 604–6; externally mandated, 585; features of, 593–94; future issues and concerns, 616–17; information, purposes for, 580–81; issues in, 594–96; items, tasks, prompts, 596–604 (*see also* K–12 assessment items); performance studies, reporting of, 557–60; state of the field of (*see* K–12 achievement testing, description and evaluation of); test score reporting (*see* K–12 test score reporting); types of (*see* K–12 educational achievement assessments)
K–12, testing for accountability in, 9, 531–71; accountability systems, design of, 569–70; alignment, between tests and standards, 555–57; assessment, inclusion and uniformity of, 560–64; change inferences, 564–67; group testing, trends in, 531–42; high-stakes testing on large-scale, effects of, 551–55; reporting, performance standards, 557–60; test design and construction, 567–69. *See also* Group testing, in K–12; Validity of score-based inferences under high-stakes conditions (VIHS)
Kubota, M., 399, 403, 494
Kuder, G. F., 74, 75, 83, 86, 99
Kuder-Richardson formula 20 and 21 estimate of reliability (KR 20 and KR 21 formulas), 74–75
Kuffler, S. W., 273
Kukich, K., 404, 498, 657
Kulick, E., 238, 667, 684, 688, 690
Kulm, G., 623
Kunce, C. S., 480

Kuncel, N. R., 654, 662
Kupermintz, H., 604
Kurtosis index, 164
Kyllonen, P. C., 143, 282, 291, 294, 473, 604, 718, 727

LaBeff, E. E., 361
Lado, R. L., 519, 523
LaDuca, A., 52
Laham, D., 378, 379, 497
LaHart, C., 327
Lahey, M. A., 122
Lajoie, S. P., 268, 270, 283, 294, 393
Lakatos, I., 44, 46
Lake Wobegon effect, 5, 534
Lall, V. F., 131
Lalonde, C., 74
Lam, T. C., 240, 421
Lam, Y. R., 139
Lan, W., 244
Landauer, T. K., 378, 379, 497
Landy, F. J., 21
Lane, G. G., 84
Lane, S., 6 15, 12, 47, 53, 55, 65, 156, 319, 375, 377, 387, 390, 396, 397, 407, 408, 410, 412, 416, 420, 422, 552, 570, 604, 657
Lantolf, J. P., 521
Lapointe, A. E., 693
Lappan, G., 632, 633
Larkin, J. H., 258, 271, 388
Larkin, K., 357
Latent trait models, 112
Lauritzen, S. L., 264
Lave, J., 258, 275, 638, 641
Lawless, R. R., 475
Lawrence, I. M., 6 49, 217, 250
Law School Admission Council, 651, 655, 672
Law School Admissions Test (LSAT), 216, 232, 651, 655, 663
Lazer, S., 10, 145, 381, 508, 681, 682, 684, 685
Lazerson, M., 249, 251
Le, H., 70
Le, V.-N., 239, 604
Leacock, C., 379
Learning progressions, 630–31
Leary, L. F., 200, 661, 672
Least-squares solution, 76
Leatherman, C., 671
Lee, D. M., 460
Lee, G., 73, 85, 98, 99, 460
Lee, K., 136
Lee, W., 6, 82, 83, 84, 100
Lee, Y.-W., 420, 527
Leeuw, J. D., 417
Lefebvre, R. C., 585
Leger, K. F., 672
Legislation and litigation, in testing: consequences in, 14; *Educational Measurement* and *Standards*, influence on, 13; flagging policy and, 13; issues, sampling of, 13; *Standards*, role in, 13–14; Uniform Guidelines, 21
Lehman, D. R., 276, 309

Lehmann, I. J., 746
Lehrer, R., 261, 278
Leighton, J. P., 417, 599
LeMahieu, P., 50
Lemann, N., 249, 251, 648
Lempert, R. O., 276, 661, 663
Lennon, M. L., 503, 504, 505, 506, 507
Leonard, D., 668, 669
Leonard, T., 81
Lepper, M., 638
Lesgold, A. M., 268, 270, 283, 284, 294, 393
Lesgold, S., 420
Lettvin, J. Y., 273
Leung, C.-K., 364
Levin, J., 32, 670
Levin, S., 244
Levine, M. V., 142, 196, 208, 209, 365, 366
Levit, E. J., 143
Levitt, S. D., 44, 117
Levy, R., 296
Lewandowsky, S., 278
Lewis, C., 74, 83, 100, 121, 122, 143, 217, 234, 240, 249, 364, 365, 410, 414, 475, 480, 484, 486, 489, 490, 610, 660, 664, 669, 712, 714
Lewis, D. M., 169, 258, 442, 443, 444, 451, 460, 595
Lewis, J. D., 593
Li, D., 183
Li, H.-H., 139
Li, S., 28, 359
Li, X, 480
Li, Y. H., 136
Liberal, definition of, 221
Licensure and certification testing, 701–28; classification, consistency and accuracy of, 706, 709–15; content considerations, 705–6; current practice of, 702–3; development of, 704–8; essay and short answer examinations, 707–8; formats of, deciding on, 707; future of, 727–28; historical view of, 702; interpretative argument, 717–18; legal issues, 723–27; mastery tests, measures for, 714–15; multiple-choice questions, 708; multiple requirements of, 703–4; performance standard for, 52; practice implications, 715–16; relevance of questions, evaluating, 706–7; reliability of, 709–16; oral examinations, 707; score annotation, 725–27; standards and cut scores, establishing, 720–22; teacher, legal and ethical issues in, 738–39; validity issues, 716–20
Lidz, C. S., 641
Likelihood ratio test, 237, 499
Lim, R. G., 133
Limited English proficiency (LEP), 561
Lin, M.-H., 81
Linacre, J. D., 122, 131, 291, 296
Linacre, J. M., 418, 419
Lindquist, E. F., 1, 3, 11, 87, 156, 250, 308, 326, 533, 569, 623, 624, 648, 702, 717
Lindsay, D., 742
Linear equating function, 208
Linear equipercentile method, 134
Linear factor analysis (LFA), 139

Linear linking function, 192, 202–3
Linear logistic test model (LLTM), 119–20; probability-based reasoning and, 266–67
Linear transformations, 163–64
Linear true-score equating function, 204
Link, V. B., 292
Linking and equating, 5, 144–45; considerations for, crucial, 193; data collection used in, 197–201; difference that matters (DTM), 212; direct and indirect, 188; distinction between, 144–45; errors of, 5; evaluating, 210–15; history of, 195–97; interpretation of, 5; mathematics of, 5; population sensitivity of, 212–13; practices for, 215–17; in previous editions of *Educational Measurement*, 187; procedures for, 201–10; requirements of, 193–95; score-linking and, 193–95; standard error of equating difference (SEED), 211–12; standard error of (SEE), 210–12. *See also* Data collection designs, in test score linking; Score-linking, categories of
Linn, R. L., 1, 9, 14, 29, 50, 51, 53, 54, 55, 79, 92, 144, 187, 191, 192, 195, 196, 199, 221, 233, 234, 251, 266, 291, 324, 327, 328, 387, 389, 390, 391, 392, 401, 404, 406, 407, 408, 411, 412, 415, 416, 433, 435, 457, 532, 533, 534, 536, 537, 540, 541, 542, 543, 553, 554, 557, 558, 559, 564, 565, 566, 570, 595, 623, 652, 666, 673, 688, 692, 693, 702, 721
Liou, M., 76, 142, 199, 201, 207, 210, 211, 364
Lipshitz, R., 78
Lissak, R. I., 133
Lissitz, R. W., 136, 179
Litigation, 9, 13–14; fairness and, 13; increased, consequences of, 14; standardization and, 9, 13–14. *See also* Legislation and litigation, in testing
Little, J., 480
Little, R., 199, 691
Liu, M., 217, 412, 416, 422
Livingston, S. A., 83, 99, 100, 187, 194, 203, 208, 211, 421, 433, 436, 442, 445, 457, 610, 712, 714, 715
Lloyd-Jones, R., 395
Local area networks (LANs), 485
Local item dependence (LID), 120; causes of, and procedures for managing, 141–42; implications of, practical, 142; measures of, 141
Local item independence, 122–23, 422–23
Lockwood, J. R., 179, 541, 565, 566, 567
Lockwood, R. E., 442, 452, 460
Loevinger, J., 19, 20, 21, 22, 30, 35, 38, 39, 42, 45, 92
"Logic Theorist," 257
LOGIST, 132, 179
Logistic regression, 238
Lohman, D. E., 35, 258, 262, 269, 291, 294, 419, 604, 614
Lohman, D. F., 653
Lohnes, P. R., 308
Lomax, R. G., 637
Lombardo, P. A., 249

Long, M. H., 291
Longford, N. T., 102, 240
Long-term trend assessments (LTT), 682
Loomis, S. C., 167, 436, 440, 441, 446, 447, 459, 583, 693
Lopes, M., 521
Lopez-Pina, J. A., 240
Lopo, A. C., 497
Lord, C., 595
Lord, F. M., 4, 7, 74, 75, 80, 81, 82, 83, 84, 86, 100, 114, 124, 127, 128, 129, 130, 133, 135, 137, 144, 146, 159, 176, 177, 178, 192, 194, 195, 196, 197, 199, 203, 204, 205, 206, 210, 211, 236, 334, 480, 488, 489, 499, 541, 688
Lord, F. N., 4, 18, 30, 32, 67, 69, 71, 78, 81, 82, 96, 102, 115, 122, 137, 141, 146, 357, 410, 688
Lorsbach, A. W., 636, 637
Lowe, P., 521
Loyd, B. H., 395, 520, 637
LTEST-L, 520, 521
Lu, C., 657
Luce, R. D., 290
Ludlow, L. H., 141
Luecht, R. M., 4 87, 11, 92, 118, 144, 146, 156, 312, 335, 356, 366, 394, 400, 404, 420, 471, 477, 480, 481, 484, 486, 488, 489, 491, 492, 493, 499, 595, 617, 655
Lugg, C. A., 245, 459, 652
Lukas, J. F., 472
Lumley, T., 521
Lunneborg, C., 263
Lunz, M. E., 122, 364
Luo, G., 131, 341
Lutkus, A. D., 542, 682, 688
Lyne, A., 341
Lyons, R., 673
Lyu, C. F., 193, 654

Maassen, G. H., 80
Mabry, L., 552
Macaskill, G., 688
MacCann, R., 494
MacMillan, D. L., 593
Macready, G. B., 473
Madaus, G. F., 52, 309, 387, 535, 613, 624, 637, 673
Maddahian, E., 94
Magone, M., 410, 420
Maier, K. S., 131
Maine Department of Education, 561
Maller, S., 366
Mandinach, E. B., 671, 725
Mane, F., 552
Mangan, K. S., 672
Mann, K. V., 461
Manski, C. F., 662
Mantel, N., 236–38, 242, 333, 499
Mantel-Haenszel statistics, 237–38, 499
Many-facet Rasch measurement model (MFRM), 418–19
Marcoulides, G. A., 92
Marginal maximum likelihood (MML), 129–30, 131, 133, 134, 422
Margolis, M. J., 7, 52, 400, 701, 703, 720

Mariano, L. T., 122
Maris, E., 267, 293, 294
Markov chain Monte Carlo (MCMC), 131
Marshall, H. H., 636
Marshall, S. P., 279
Martin, I.V.S., 682, 684
Martin, J. D., 295
Martin, J. T., 364
Martin, M. O., 687, 689
Martineau, J. A., 567
Martinez, M. E., 318, 405, 406
Marton, F., 637
Maryland School Performance Assessment Program (MSPAP): classroom instruction, impact on, 407; performance, and teacher-reported instruction-related variables, 407–8; rater inconsistencies, and proficiency classification, 414–15; Reading for Literacy Experience Scoring Rubric, 395; Scoring Rubric: Writing to Express Personal Ideas, 396
Maryland State Department of Education, 395, 396, 398
Marzano, R. J., 391, 392, 396, 398, 597
Mashburn, A. J., 592
Massachusetts Comprehensive Assessment System (MCAS), 404, 495, 496, 535
Massachusetts Department of Education, 459, 535, 537, 550
Masters, G. N., 116, 117, 120, 131, 132, 142, 240, 241, 272, 282, 292, 416, 630
Mathematical Sciences Education Board, 623
Mathematics Test Creation Assistant, 473
Mathews, J., 742
MathSoft, 131
Matrices, multitrait-multimethod, 39–40
Matrix sampling, 96, 145, 182, 684–85
Maturana, H. R., 273
Maxey, J., 653
Maximum a posteriori (MAP), 138
Maximum likelihood estimation (MLE), 127, 136–38; Bayesian methods, 138; for 3PL model, 136–38
Maxwell, K. L., 592
Maxwell v. Pasadena ISD, 741
Mayekawa, S., 76
Mayekawa-Haebara's least squares solution, 76
Mayo, S. T., 625
Mayrowetz, D., 615
Mazur, K. M., 237, 238, 240, 719
Mazur, E., 634, 635
Mazzeo, J., 10, 145, 168, 238, 333, 381, 421, 422, 542, 548, 681, 682, 684, 688, 690, 691, 693
McBee, M. M., 413, 414
McBride, J. R., 364, 490
McCaffrey, D. F., 50, 179, 394, 535, 536, 541, 542, 551, 565, 566, 567, 596
McCall, W. A., 164, 356
McCallin, R. C., 356
McCamley-Jenkins, L., 234, 660, 668
McClelland, D. C., 663
McClelland, J. L., 273, 274, 275, 288
McClelland's Jets and Sharks example, 275
McCloskey, M., 276

McCollam, K., 43
McCoy, T. R., 672
McCulloch, C. E., 97
McCulloch, W. S., 273, 274
McCulloch-Pitts structure, 274
McDermott, J., 388
McDonald, R. P., 41, 43, 121, 122, 123, 131, 132, 138, 139, 141, 416, 417, 420
McDonnell, L. M., 595
McGinn, D., 752
McGraw, K. O., 87
McGraw-Hill, 117, 133, 144, 493, 588, 590
McGregor, L. N., 361
McHale, F., 668
McIver, M. C., 552
McKay, S., 543
McKevitt, B. C., 564
McKie, D., 77
McKinley, L. R., 140, 141
McKinley, R. L., 119
McLaughlin, D. H., 142, 558, 688, 692
McLeod, L. D., 189, 365, 417
McLuhan, Marshall, 13
McMillan, J. H., 623
McNamara, T., 521, 522, 524, 525
McNeil, B. J., 709
McNeil, L. M., 54, 640
McNemar, Q., 80
McPeek, W. M., 240, 241, 667, 670
McTighe, J., 391, 398, 596, 597, 629, 723
McVaugh, M. R., 702
Mead, A. D., 502
Mead, N., 682, 693
Mead, R. J., 240, 291, 446
Mean-mean method, 134, 177
Mean-sigma method, 135, 177
Meara, K. C., 441, 694
Measurement-driven instruction, 533–34
Measurement models, for assessment, 285–96; conditional dependence, 295–96; measurement debate and, 290–91; mixture models, 294–95; modular model construction, 292; narrative structures and, 285–86; observable variables, considerations regarding, 292; for raters, 296; student variables, considerations regarding, 293–94; task features, considerations regarding, 292–93; variables, determining, 286–89; variables, relationships among, specifying, 289
Measurement theory, 1, 6
Media inclusion, 508
Medical College Admission Test (MCAT), 650–51, 657, 661, 665–73
Medley, D. M., 103
Medrich, E. A., 687
Meehl, P. E., 1, 20, 22, 30, 42, 43, 46, 270
Mehrens, W. A., 53, 54, 309, 369, 389, 407, 412, 441, 450, 458, 464, 536, 548, 552, 693, 738, 741, 746, 747, 752, 753
Meijer, R. R., 121, 122, 142, 143, 365, 366, 367, 368
Melican, G., 442, 449, 450, 455
Mellenbergh, G. J., 45, 54, 80, 291
Melnick, D. E., 272, 497, 508
Mendro, R., 541
Mentally retarded, educable, 13

Merwin, J. C., 473
Meskauskas, J. A., 433
Messick, S. J., 2, 19, 21, 22, 27, 30, 31, 36, 37, 38, 39, 40, 41, 44, 45, 51, 52, 54, 55, 56, 228, 261, 387, 388, 389, 390, 391, 394, 398, 401, 402, 403, 405, 406, 407, 412, 471, 526, 541, 550, 604, 605, 606, 659, 688, 690, 717
Metacognition, 627
Meyer, A., 591
Meyer, J. P., 559
MGENOVA, 94
Michaels, H., 141, 142, 590, 611
Michell, J., 266, 290
Microcomputers, 4
Microsoft SQL Server™ 479
Milanovic, M., 520
Milewski, G. B., 652, 660
Mill, J. S., 244
Miller, G. A., 257, 270
Miller, K. E., 542, 564
Miller, M. D., 266, 395
Miller, R. J., 565
Miller, R. R., 420
Miller, S., 335, 347, 348
Miller, T. B., 80
Miller, T. R., 118, 238, 333, 421
Millman, J., 307, 309, 319, 327, 345, 346, 463, 464, 587, 604, 613, 716
Millroy, W., 275
Mills, C. N., 140, 141, 357, 360, 433, 436, 441, 442, 445, 447, 449, 450, 452, 453, 454, 455, 459, 483, 484
Millsap, R. E., 240
Min, K.-S., 136
Minimal competence, 52
Minimum competency testing (MCT), 533
Minimum competency tests, 5, 350
Minstrell, J., 278
Miskeys, 499
Mislevy, R. J., 2 84, 11, 27, 28, 41, 43, 103, 118, 120, 121, 130, 131, 132, 134, 139, 140, 143, 144, 145, 176, 179, 187, 191, 195, 201, 257, 259, 274, 287, 290, 291, 292, 294, 296, 307, 313, 357, 358, 387, 390, 393, 416, 417, 422, 472, 473, 475, 477, 498, 604, 605, 606, 684, 688, 689, 690, 691, 692, 694, 727
Missing data, 206
Mitchell, J., 684
Mitchell, K. J., 14, 169, 433, 542, 693
Mitchell, K. M., 552, 553, 555, 595, 738
Mitchell, M., 637
Mitzel, H. C., 169, 442, 443, 444
Mitzel, H. E, 103
Mitzel, M. C., 444, 456
Mixed format tests, 159–63
Mixed integer programming (MIP), 480
Mixture models, 294–95
Miyazaki, I., 673
Model-based reasoning in science, 271
Model-data fit, in IRT, 138–43; dimensionality, assessment of, 139; evaluating for performance assessments, 421–22; features of model, and rational analysis of, 139; item fit, 139–41; local item dependence, 141–42; measures of, global, 141; person-fit (appropriateness measures), 142–43; predictions or features of other models, evaluation of, 143
Models: choice, philosophies of, 124–25; inconsistencies in, 7; integration of, 5–6; misfit, 7
Moderation, 192
Modular model construction, 292
Mok, M.M.C., 417, 420
Mokken, R. J., 121, 122
Molenaar, I. W., 121, 122, 142, 146, 416, 422
Moll, L. C., 631
Mollaun, P., 527
Mollenkopf, W. G., 82, 83, 84
Monfils, L., 240, 243
Monotone homogeneity model (MHM), 121–22
Monseur, C., 686
Montgomery, K., 640
Moon, T. R., 401
Mooney, J., 120, 142
Moore, J. L., 279
Moore, W. P., 369
Moran, T., 279
Moreno, K. E., 477
Morgan, D., 360
Morgan, R., 402, 494
Morley, M. E., 32, 475, 497, 508, 670, 720
Morrison, E. J., 387, 388, 389
Morrison v. American Board of Psychiatry and Neurology, Inc., 724
Morrow, L. M., 623, 626
Mosenthal, P. B., 293
Moser, J. M., 631
Mosier, C. I., 76
Moss, P. A., 18, 27, 49, 52, 54, 55, 245, 251, 261, 264, 296, 399, 401, 526, 595, 650, 665
Moss, S. M., 47, 50, 247, 623, 641, 642
Mroch, A. A., 357
Muchinsky, P. M., 85
Muijtjens, A.M.M., 461
Mullen, K., 444
Muller, D. G., 666, 672, 720
Mullis, I.V.S., 395, 405, 682, 693, 694
Multicomponent latent trait model (MLTM), 119
Multidimensional between-item models, 688
Multidimensional item response theory (MIRT), 118–19; compensatory 2PL, 131; for dichotomous data, 417; for dimensionality assessment, 420; estimation software, 132
Multidimensionality hypothesis, 241
MULTILOG, 132, 133, 176
MULTILOG-6, 132
Multiple-choice questions (MCQs), 417, 535, 597–99, 707–8
Multipurpose distributed testing sites, 483
Multistage cluster sampling, 685–86
Multistate Essay Examination, 703
Multistate Performance Test, 703
Multitrait-multimethod matrices, 39–40
Multivariate random coefficients multinomial logic model (MRCMLM), 294

Muraki, E. J., 1 39, 7, 103, 117, 121, 122, 131, 132, 145, 236, 416, 417, 419, 420, 498, 664, 689, 694
Murnane, R. J., 565
Murphy, E., 410
Murphy, K., 36
Muthen, B. O., 417, 420
Muthen, L. K., 417
MYCIN, 279
Myford, C. M., 274, 296, 387
Myths and Tradeoffs: The Role of Tests in Undergraduate Admissions, 673

Nachtman, W., 145, 631
Nanda, H., 21, 88, 296, 411, 722
Nandakumar, R., 121, 123, 139, 241, 420
National Academy of Sciences, 673
National Assessment Governing Board (NAGB), 436, 541, 542, 547, 582, 682, 693
National Assessment of Adult Literacy (NAAL), 683
National Assessment of Educational Progress (NAEP), 10, 145, 168, 169, 170, 180, 182–83, 381, 399, 493, 494, 502, 505, 532, 533, 534; as audit mechanism, 554; Data Tool, 508; description of, 682; 4th grade Science Assessment, 168; K–12 accountability testing, changes to, 541–42; mathematical problem solving, definition of, 598; schematic representation of gains, 544; Trial Urban District Assessments, 617
National Association for Gifted Children, 593
National Association for the Education of Young Children (NAEYC), 636
National Association of the State Boards of Accountancy (NASBA), 703
National Board of Medical Examiners (NBME), 272, 360, 497, 508, 701, 702, 725, 726
National Board on Educational Testing and Public Policy (NBETPP), 673
National Center for Education Statistics (NCES), 436, 535
National Center on Educational Outcomes, 562, 568
National Commission on Excellence in Education, 10, 350, 534, 586
National Conference of Bar Examiners (NCBE), 703
National Council of Architectural Registration Board (NCARB), 272, 493, 702–3
National Council of Teachers of Mathematics (NCTM), 388, 536, 537, 586, 626
National Council on Education Standards and Testing (NCEST), 387, 536
National Council on Measurement in Education (NCME), 1, 20, 21, 60, 67, 166, 216, 221, 227, 307, 329, 355, 388, 397, 434, 482, 555, 562, 585, 597, 599, 607, 626, 671, 673, 701, 734, 751–53; *Code of Professional Responsibilities in Education,* 13, 221, 751
National Governors Association, 534, 617
National norms, 180, 182–83

Index

National Research Council, 187, 217, 233, 277, 287, 388, 390, 443, 444, 535, 536, 537, 538, 562, 563, 580, 581, 582, 594, 595, 598, 604, 605, 606, 612, 613, 614, 617, 626, 627; Committee on the General Aptitude Test Battery, 233; National Science Education Standards, 536
National Standards in Foreign Language Education Project, 522
National subgroup norms, 180
A Nation at Risk (NCEA), 10, 350–51, 534
Nava, N.F.G., 637
Navigation, 487
NCME Ad Hoc Committee on the Development of a Code of Ethics, 1, 2, 13, 20, 21, 67, 70, 82, 99, 221, 355, 356, 359, 360, 372, 388, 401, 434, 435, 439, 451, 457, 459, 460, 461, 462, 465, 482, 701, 716, 721, 722, 725, 734, 738, 751, 752, 753
NCS Pearson, 493
NEAT designs, 198–99, 200–201, 206, 207–10
Nebraska Department of Education, 390
Nedelsky, L., 438, 442, 449, 460
Neff, D., 631
Nel, D. G., 86
NELS, 410
Nelson, L., 146, 162, 417
Nering, M. L., 142, 364
NetPASS design task, 272; device properties representation in, 285; fragment of a probability model for assessing troubleshooting in, 296, 297; natural language problem statement for, 282, 283; network topology representation for, 284
Nettles, A. L., 665
Nettles, M. T., 665
Neudecker, H., 86
Neural network, 275
Neurode *k*, structure of, 274
Newble, D. I., 707
Newell, A., 257, 270, 279, 280, 283, 292
New Jersey Department of Education, 459, 465, 548
Newmann, F., 637
The New SAT 2005, 249, 649, 652, 658
New Standards Mathematics Reference Examination, 420
New Standards Project, 536–37
Nicewander, W. A., 79, 179, 692
Nichols, P. D., 267, 293, 417
Niday, D. M., 502
Niemeyer, J. A., 592
Nisan, M., 638
Nisbett, R. E., 276
Nitko, A. J., 324, 580, 581, 585, 592, 596, 613, 624, 625
Nix, D., 655
Noble, J. P., 660, 666
No Child Left Behind Act (NCLB), 9, 10, 14, 52, 53, 372, 381, 531, 532, 537, 539, 540, 541, 542, 553, 555, 557, 559, 567, 568, 569, 570, 587, 607, 608, 681, 693, 694, 739, 749, 750; accountability requirements, 540–41; achievement-levels of, 10–11, 52–53; high-stakes debate associated with, 10, 14, 52–53, 531–32; history of, 9, 10; Implementing Regulations for Standards and Assessments, 749; interpretive argument for, 52–53; legal challenges of, 14; psychometric interpretation of, 750; testing and reporting requirements, 579–80; uniformity in testing mandates, 538–39
Noe, M. J., 712
Noelting, G., 287
NOHARM, 131, 132, 417
Nolen, S. B., 623
Noll, V. H., 625
Nominal model, 116–17, 118
Nominal response item scoring, 158
Nominal weights, 160
Nomological theories, 42–43
Nomothetic span, 46
Nonlinear factor analysis (NLFA), 139
Nonlinear transformations, 164–65
Non-overlapping item sets (graph), 500
Nonparametric models, 121–22
Norcini, J. J., 449, 457, 461, 707, 708
Normal Curve Equivalent (NCE), 164, 532
Normal ogive models, 115
Norman, D. A., 269, 270
Norman, G., 707
Norm-referenced interpretations, 4, 5, 66–67, 89
Norm referenced tests (NRTs), 590
Norms, 180–83; development of, technical issues in, 181–82; future directions in, 183; norm groups and, 180–81; studies, illustrative examples of, 182–83
Norris, J. M., 291
North, B., 522
Notation, 68
Novell certification exams, 490
Novick, M. R., 4, 18, 30, 32, 67, 69, 71, 74, 78, 81, 82, 96, 102, 115, 122, 137, 141, 146, 232, 233, 357, 367, 410, 688, 713
Number-correct scoring, 137
Nunez, A. M., 401
Nungester, R. J., 238, 366, 477, 480, 481, 486, 487, 491, 492, 716, 719, 721
Nunnally, J. C., 476
Nussbaum, E. M., 604
Nystrand, M., 50

Objective function, 480
O'Brien, A. T., 289
O'Brien, T. L., 723, 724
Observable attributes, 32
Observable variables, 288–89, 292
Observed-score methods: linking procedures, 189, 206–9; logistic regression, 238; Mantel-Haenszel statistics, 237–38; SIBTEST, 239; standardized difference, 238–39
Observed-score test equating, 196, 214–15, 217
Observed-score variance, 69, 84, 94, 99, 102
O'Day, J., 536, 537, 552, 555
Odendahl, N., 493
O'Dwyer, L. M., 387
Office for Minority Education at ETS, 244–45
Office of Civil Rights (OCR), 223

Office of Management and Budget (OMB), 223–24
Office of Technology Assessment, U. S. Congress, 250, 541, 623, 624, 639, 647
Off-the-shelf achievement tests, 751
Ogle, D. M., 631
Olkin, I., 14, 85, 86, 682
Oller, J. W., Jr., 523, 527
Olsen, J. B., 11, 363
Olson, A., 559
Olson, B., 446
Olson, J. F., 375
Olson, L. S., 464, 559, 566, 581, 616
Olson-Buchanan, J. B., 508, 509
Olsson, U., 339
Omaggio Hadley, A. C., 521
OMB, 223, 224, 226
O'Neil, H. F., 272, 387, 404, 497, 554
O'Neil, J., 535
O'Neill, K. A., 240, 241, 659, 667, 670
One-parameter logistic model (1PL), 6, 113–14
Ones, D. S., 654, 662
Online Scoring Network (OSN), 493–94
Online scoring systems, 493–94
Operational definitions, 32
Optical scanners, 11, 12
Oracle™, 479
Oral Proficiency Interview (OPI), 521, 522
Oranje, A., 502, 682
Ordered response item scores, 157–58
Oregon Department of Education, 396
Organization for Economic Cooperation and Development (OECD), 682, 694
Orlando, M., 140, 141, 159, 422
Orr, N. A., 721
Orsak, T., 541
Osburn, H. G., 75
Oshima, T. C., 136
Osterlind, S. J., 327, 328
O'Sullivan, C. Y., 168, 682
Other-than-trivial items, 11
Overall, J. E., 79
Overgeneralization, 58
Owen, E. H., 692, 694

Pacing, 487
Page, E. B., 497
Page, S. H., 282, 346, 378, 473
Palmer, A. S., 292, 293, 294, 524
Pandazides v. Virginia Board of Education, 743
Pandey, T., 145
Panelists, performance standards of: evaluations of, 456–57; panelists, choosing, 451–542; providing feedback to, 455–56; training, 453–55
Papert, S., 274
Parallel distributed processors (PDP), 274–76
Parallel-forms: classically, 6; estimate of reliability, 70; estimates of reliability, 70, 71; randomly, 6
Park, K. S., 508
Park, T.-H., 499
Parke, C. S., 53, 55, 407, 552, 570, 615

PARSCALE, 121, 132
PARSCALE 3, 132
Parshall, C. G., 364, 486, 508
Parsons, C. K., 139, 477
Partial credit model (PC), 116
Parzer, P., 120
Pashley, P. J., 189, 508, 661, 692
Pass-fail: classification, 704, 712; performance standard, 449; posttests, 625; reliability, 100
Patel, V. L., 284
Patelis, T., 445
Patsula, L. N., 491
Patterson, H. L., 282, 346, 473
Patz, R. J., 122, 131, 169, 296, 419, 442, 689
Payne, D. A., 261, 446
Pearl, J., 285, 292
Pearlman, M., 520, 656
Pearlmutter, A., 682
Pearson, P. D., 37, 261
Pedulla, J. J., 552, 553, 639
Pellegrino, J. W., 14, 43, 169, 248, 251, 263, 441, 465, 542, 623, 624, 627, 637, 639, 640, 641, 693
Pence, P., 448
Penfield, D. A., 238, 240
Penfield, R. D., 238, 240, 410, 421
Peng, C. J., 713
Pennock-Román, M., 666, 669
Penny, J., 102, 240, 415
Percent above cut (PAC), 96
Perception, 273–74
Perceptrons, 274
Perfetti, C. A., 273
Performance assessment, 387–424; administration occasion, error due to, 412–14; augmenting ratings, and error, 415; comparability of, 411; current uses of, 389–90; decision consistency, and error, 415–16; definition of, 388; description of, 387–88; of DIF, 420–21; dimensionality, evaluating, 419–20; IRT models, 418–19; of K–12, reporting of, 557–60; of local independence, 422–23; method of assessment, error due to, 414; model-data-fit evaluation, 421–22; rater committee, error due to, 415; rater occasion, error due to, 414–15; rationale for, 388–89; scaling, 417–19; task and rater, error due to, 412; tasks and multiple choice items, combining, 417–18; of testing for accountability in K–12, 534–35; of test theories, 410–23. *See also* Performance assessment, design and scoring of; Validity, of performance assessment
Performance assessment, design and scoring of, 390–401; conceptual framework, delineation of, 390–91; expert review and pilot performance, 400; lifelong learning standards, 391; raters, training procedures for, 400–401; rubrics, 394–400. *See also* Test specifications and task design
Performance standards, 52, 433–65; adjusting, 464–65; for alternate assessments, 463–64; comparative studies, 450–51; compensatory *vs.* conjunctive, 450; guidelines for, professional, 434; guidelines for setting, professional, 434; issues in, general, 434–36; non-central tendency, 559–60; performance categories, preparing descriptions of, 452–53; robustness of, 558–59; standards-based scales, coarseness of, 557–58; standard-setting method, selecting, 439–51; steps in, typical, 436–39. *See also* Panelists, performance assessments of; Standard-setting method, selecting; Validity evidence, for setting performance standards
Perkins, M. R., 533
Perline, R., 290
Perrenoud, P., 641
Perrone, V., 533
Person-fit (appropriateness measures), 142–43
Person-free item measurement, 113
Personnel Administrator v. Feeney, 724, 734
Pesetsky, D., 273
Petersen, N. S., 5, 155, 156, 157, 165, 169, 174, 175, 181, 183, 187, 192, 193, 194, 197, 203, 206, 207, 208, 232, 233, 421, 689, 690
Peterson, J. J., 250, 648, 673
Peterson, N. S., 133, 134
Phillips, A., 237
Phillips, E. D., 632
Phillips, G. W., 189, 534, 688, 692, 693, 694, 740
Phillips, J., 13
Phillips, M., 666
Phillips, S. E., 11, 13, 179, 312, 313, 450, 462, 464, 563, 564, 723, 725, 733, 737, 738, 739, 740, 743, 744
Piaget, J., 257, 261, 263, 277, 281, 287, 292
Piaget's view of learning, 281
Pickering, R. J., 391, 398
Pickering, S., 494
Pine, J., 394
Pinnell, G. S., 682
Pinto, R., 27, 57
Pipho, C., 534
Pitoniak, M. J., 10, 52, 128, 145, 168, 320, 433, 441, 444, 447, 449, 461, 464, 557, 582, 720, 724
Pitts, W. H., 273, 274
Placement testing, 23–24
Plake, B. S., 433, 436, 440, 441, 442, 447, 448, 450, 451, 455, 456, 457, 556, 558, 585, 721, 738
PLAN, 168, 178
Plati, T., 502
Platonic true score, 102
Plausible values (PVs), 691–92
Plous, S., 603
Pollack, J. M., 410, 660, 664, 669
Polti, G. P., 276, 277
Poly-DETECT, 139
Poly-DIMTEST, 139
POLYFACT, 417
Polytomous data, 4, 101, 112, 115–18, 420. *See also* Unidimensional models, for polytomous data
Polytomous items, 118–19, 236–37, 238, 421
Polytomous models, 118–20, 131–33, 146, 416, 420–23
Pommerich, M., 175, 193, 654
Pomplun, M., 403
Ponocny, I., 120
Ponsoda, V., 364, 489
Popham, W. J., 51, 54, 251, 324, 369, 407, 433, 533, 558, 581, 595, 604, 613
Popper, K. R., 25, 44, 46
Population characteristics, 181
Population invariance, 189
Population of interest, 18
Population parameters, 181
Porchea, S., 559
Porter, A. C., 555, 556, 585, 595, 613
Porter, T., 50, 249
Posterior distribution, 138
Post hoc ergo propter hoc, 270
Poststratification equating (PSE), 192, 206, 207
Potenza, M. T., 421
Powell, R. D., 721
Powell, S., 433, 436, 457
Powers, D. E., 402, 403, 404, 405, 406, 494, 495, 498, 508, 661, 672
P-prims, 276
Prais, S. J., 687
Praxis™, 493
Praxis I Series: Academic Skills Assessments, 495
The Praxis Series: Professional Assessments for Beginning Teachers, 494
Prediction error variance, 188
Predictive validity, 1, 18, 20
Prediger, D. J., 713
Presentation, 473; characteristics, 501
Presmoothing, 203–4
Press, W. H., 162
Pressley, M., 629
Price v. National Board of Medical Examiners, 725
Primary sampling units (PSUs), 182, 682
Primary score scale, 155
Primum CCS patient management test, 497
Pritchett, M., 145, 631
Probability-based reasoning, 264–67; basic ideas, 264–65; in classical test theory, 265–66; in item response theory, 266; linear logistic test model, 266–67
Probability-of-correct response, 6
Probability sampling, 685
Process models, 43
Production rules, 280–81
Program for International Student Assessment (PISA), 682–83
Progress in International Reading Literacy (PIRLS), 682
Projection, 188–89
Project Talent, 681
Promissor, Inc., 479
Proportional observed score effective weight, 160
Proportional reasoning, stages of, 288
Propositional systems, 280
Provisional Taxonomy of Individual Difference Constructs, 597
Prowker, A., 243
Pseudo-guessing parameter, 115

Index

Psotka, J., 270
Psychological Corporation, 654
Psychometrics, 9, 188, 195, 237, 249
Psychometrika, 146
Putnam, R. T., 641
Putnam, S. E., 448

Qian, J., 486, 490, 686, 692
Quadrature points, 131
Qualifier, 28
Quality control process, in test development, 346–49; computer-based test considerations, 348–49; design principles of, 346–47; fairness review Quality control checklist, 350; implementing, 349; paper-and-pencil test considerations, 348
Quality Counts, 592
Qualls, A. L., 73, 76, 77, 83, 84
Qualls-Payne, A. L., 84
Quantitative reasoning, 32–33; capabilities of, 33; definition of, 32
Quardt, D., 497, 508
Quenemoen, R., 464
Quenouille, M., 98
Quian, J., 364
Quine, W., 46
Quinones, M. A., 509

Rabinowitz, H. K., 707
Race and ethnicity, fairness in testing: for African-American students, 182; bias and, explained, 243; designation of, 223–24; essays, performance assessments on, 409; fairness in testing, 243–44, 665–66, 667–68; OMB reporting requirements, 224; panel formation/operation, 245, 246; racial discrimination, 13; sensitivity review, 244–45; sensitivity training procedures/criteria, 245–46; social address model, 244
Rachor, R. E., 636
Rae, G., 78
Ragosta, M., 747
Rajaratnam, N., 3, 4, 21, 77, 88, 296, 411, 722
Raju, N. S., 72, 73, 75, 236, 237, 242, 499
Raju coefficient, 72, 73, 75
Ramist, L., 234, 660, 661, 662, 664, 665, 666, 668, 669
Ramsay, J. O., 292
Ramsey, P. A., 245, 246, 403, 494
Randomly parallel measurements, 89
Random groups design, 198
Random item parameters, 6
Rankin, S. C., 533
Raphael, T. E., 631
Rasch, G., 4, 113, 115, 118, 119, 120, 122, 124, 125, 130, 131, 133, 136, 139, 141, 142, 146, 156, 159, 162, 163, 236, 242, 243, 264, 266, 289, 290, 292, 294, 295, 417, 418, 421, 443, 444, 499, 613, 688, 689
Rasch model, 6, 113–14, 124, 125
Raters: construct-irrelevant variance and, 402–4; *e-raters,* 509; errors, in performance assessment, 412, 414–15; models, 122, 296; training procedures for, 400–401
Rating scale model, 117, 118

Raudenbush, S. W., 243
Raven, J. C., 262, 263
Raven's Standard Progressive Matrices (RSPM), 262–63
Ravitch, D., 595
Rawls, J., 251
Raw scores, 11, 158–59; definition of, 158; IRT-based, 84, 163, 166; score scales, transforming to, 163; test specifications and, 159
Raw-to-raw equating, 194
Raykov, T., 79, 86
Raymond, M. R., 52, 245, 451, 452, 453, 454, 705, 722
Rayner, K., 273
Reading readiness tests, 380, 626
Reallocation, 548–49
Reckase, M. D., 55, 118, 119, 132, 180, 234, 241, 416, 419, 436, 441, 443, 452, 455, 459, 554, 693
Reder, L. M., 262
Redfield, D., 537
Redish, E. F., 277
Reed, E. D., 601, 743
Rees, E., 400
Reese, C. M., 168, 542, 562, 563
Reese, L., 244
Reese, L. M., 346, 480, 486, 489
Regression model, 232
Rehabilitation, Comprehensive Services, and Developmental Disabilities Act of 1978, 592
Rehabilitation Act, 482, 563, 724, 742
Reid, J. B., 245, 451, 452, 453, 454, 722
Reification, 58–59
Reise, S. P., 132, 133, 140, 146, 416, 417, 420
Reiser, B. J., 281
Reith, J., 240
Relative efficiency function, 129
Reliability: attenuation, and corrections for, 84–85; in behavioral observations, 4, 102–4; in classical test theory, 4, 67–87; of classifications, 99–102; coefficients, 3, 65–67, 84; of composite scores, 76–80; conflicts in, 6; for criterion-referenced interpretations, 4, 5, 66–67; evolving notions of, 3–4; future directions of, 103–5; generalizability theory, 84, 87–99; of group means, 4; internal-consistency estimates of, 71, 74; intraclass correlations, sampling theory and significance tests for, 87; of item response theory, 4; KR 20 and 21 formula estimates of, 74–75; in 1950s, early, 3; in 1950s to 1970s, mid, 3–4; in 1970s to present, 3–4; parallel forms estimates of, 70, 71; significance tests and confidence intervals for estimates of, 85–87; split-half estimate of, 72–75, 86; standardization and, 9; statistical power and, 85; test-retest estimates of, 70; *vs.* validity, 5; variance and, analysis of, 3; weights chosen to maximize, 161
The Reliability and Validity of Tests (Thurstone)
Rene v. Reed, 743, 750
Renzulli, J. S., 593

Replication, 6, 9, 65–66, 100–101; bootstrap, 97–98, 101, 713–14; some set of, 87
Resnick, D. P., 282, 387, 389, 393, 535, 536, 623, 626
Resnick, L. B., 258, 261, 262, 268, 282, 314, 387, 389, 393, 420, 532, 535, 536, 537, 613, 623, 626
Response action, 508
Response format, modifications of, 482
Response generative modeling, 474
Response probability (RP), 128, 167–68
Response requirements, 501
Reuterberg, S.-E., 79
Reverse discrimination, in test scoring, 13
Revuelta, J., 364
Rex, L., 526
Reynolds, C. R., 235
Reznick, R. K., 703
Rhodes, E. C., 702
Richardson, M. W., 74
Richman, W. L., 509
Rigney, S., 464
Rigol, G. W., 217, 250, 649, 653, 654, 660
Rijkes, C.P.M., 119, 294
Rijmen, F., 293, 294
Ripkey, D. R., 707, 720
Rivers, J. C., 541
Rivkin, S. G., 541
Rizavi, S., 445
Roach, J., 518
Robeson, M. R., 707
Robin, F., 240, 445, 489
Robinson, D. Z., 738
Robinson, P., 293, 294, 296
Robyn, A., 569
Rochlin, L., 585
Rock, D. A., 327, 410, 417, 497, 662, 664, 669, 672, 726
Rodriguez, G., 445
Rodriguez, M. C., 162
Rodriquez, D., 638
Roeber, E., 464, 533
Roeder, H. H., 625
Roe v. Wade, 246
Rogers, H. J., 667
Rogers, J. H., 139, 140, 238, 333, 420, 442
Rogoff, B., 281
Rogosa, D. R., 66, 67, 79, 80, 102, 103, 292, 558, 565
Roid, G. H., 320, 398, 399, 604
Rollins, A. L., 494
Romberg, T. A., 552, 626
Root expected square difference (RESD), 212–13
Root-mean-square-difference measure (RMSD), 212–13
Rosa, K., 146, 162, 189, 417
Rose, D., 591
Rose, L. T., 281
Rosenbaum, P. R., 139, 199, 201
Rosenblatt, F., 274
Rosenthal, J., 78, 552
Ross, G., 628
Ross, K., 407, 551
Ross, L. P., 400
Rost, J., 120, 140, 357, 358

Roswell, B. S., 389
Roth, D., 120
Rothchild, B., 671
Rothman, A., 314, 537, 555, 556, 613
Rothschild, B., 727
Rottenberg, C., 552
Roussos, L. A., 123, 240, 241, 333, 420, 421
Routman, R., 634
Rovinelli, R. J., 139
Rowan, B., 565
Royer, J. M., 464, 724
Rozeboom, W. W., 76
Roznowski, M., 139, 141, 240
Rubin, D. B., 78, 187, 199, 201, 207, 217, 264, 365, 366, 691, 692
Rubio-Vela, A., 702
Rubrics: in classroom assessment, 631. *See also* Scoring rubrics, design of
Rudner, L. M., 78, 162, 378, 625
Ruiz-Primo, M. A., 93, 393, 405, 413
Rulon, P., 19, 72, 83, 250, 640
Rumelhart, D. A., 264, 273, 279, 281
Rumelhart, D. E., 273, 274, 275
RUMM, 131
Rupp, A. A., 292
Russell, M. K., 404, 495, 496, 502
Rust, F., 639
Rust, K. F., 182, 686, 687
Rust, R. T., 74
Ryan, J. M., 369, 583
Ryan, K., 29, 520
Ryan, R., 638

Saal, F. E., 122
Sackett, P. R., 51, 54, 56, 233
Sadler, P. M., 276
Sadler, R., 626, 628, 632
Saka, T., 694
Saljo, R., 637
Salmon-Cox, L., 625
Salthouse, T. A., 282
Samejima, F., 117, 118, 416
Sampling, in group-score assessments, 684–88; block designs, 685; exclusion of students from, 687–88; matrix, 684–85; multistage cluster, 685–86; nonparticipation in, 687; nonresponse, 687; oversampling, 687; probability, 685; size, sampling with certainty and with probability proportional to, 686; spiraling, 685; standard errors in, 686; stratified, 686; substitution in, 687; weighting-class adjustments, 687
Sampling design, 181–82
Sampling error variance, 181
Sampson, R. J., 243
Sandene, B., 502, 694
Sanders, N. M., 534
Sanders, P. F., 92
Sanders, W. L., 541, 565
Sandifer, P. D., 533
Sands, W. A., 490, 508
Saner, H., 394
Sanford, E. E., 189, 556, 692
San Francisco case, 748
Santa Barbara Discourse Group, 526
Santman, D., 640

Sarbin, T. R., 659
SAT (Stanford Achievement Tests): admissions testing, higher education, 649–54, 658–59; fairness of, 665–73; FGPAs and, 660–61; history of, 196, 249–50, 532, 649; rescaling of, 169, 170, 658–59; scoring, 656–57
SAT-M, 191, 192
SAT9, 748
SAT I, 191, 726, 727; Reasoning Test, 502
SAT II, 191
SAT-V, 191, 192
Satorra, A., 79
Satterthwaite, F. E., 97
Sauer, P. L., 79
Saunders, J. C., 559
Sava-Bolesta, M., 133, 417
Savignon, S. J., 521
Saville, N., 522
Sawin, L. L., 499
Sawyer, R. L., 100, 183
Sax, G., 746
Saxe, G. B., 275, 565
Saxton, A., 565
Sayer, A. G., 80
Scaffolding, 600, 602, 628–29, 630, 632, 639, 641
Scale anchoring, 168
Scale shrinkage, 144
Scaling: of performance assessments, 417–19. *See also* Score scales
Scaling drift, 499, 501
Scaling on a hypothetical population (SHP), 191–92
Scaling test design, 173–74
Scaling to anchor (STA), 192
Scalise, K., 287
Scarpati, S., 28, 359
Schacter, J., 497
Schaeffer, G. A., 668
Schauble, L., 261, 278
Scheiblechner, H., 122
Schematheory, 281
Schemo, D. J., 544
Scheuneman, J. D., 236, 659
Schlackman, J., 413
Schlemer, L., 665, 667
Schmidt, A. E., 3
Schmidt, F. L., 18, 70, 71, 85, 130, 232
Schmitt, A. P., 235, 421, 667, 670
Schneider, C., 465, 559
Schneider, L. M., 120, 662
Schneps, M. H., 276
Schnipke, D. L., 487
Schöenemann, P., 77
Schoenfeld, A. H., 37, 261, 525
Scholes, R. J., 672
Schoon, C. G., 445
Schraagen, J. M., 283
Schrader, W. B., 663, 664
Schroeder, M. L., 98
Schultz, S. E., 393, 405
Schulz, E. M., 179, 443, 444, 456
Schum, D. A., 259, 265, 292, 295
Schuster, C., 101
Schutz, A., 296

Schware v. Board of Bar Examiners of State of New Mexico, 723
Schwartz, D., 275
Schwarz, N., 599, 606
Science of Jusicail Proof, 259
Scientifically principled assessment design, 605
Scientific Software, Inc., 132
Score-linking, categories of, 187–93; equating, 193; predicting, 188–89; scale aligning, 189–93. *See also* Linking and equating
Score reports, 380–82; of achievement or performance, 380–81; of diagnostic results, 381–82; for different purposes, 382; of growth, 381; of test uses, 380
Scores: comparable, 189, 195; composite, 76–80, 170–71; confidence intervals, 82, 85–87; conversion function, 194; difference, alternative definitions of, 80; essentially comparable, 744–45; interpretation of, 5; interpretations of, absolute *vs.* relative, 98; item, 125, 12, 126-128; K–12 accountability testing, changes in, 539–40; number-correct, 124, 125, 126, 129, 130, 136–40, 163, 166–67; points, rules for number of, 165–66; pseudo-observed, 422; raw, 11, 125–26, 128–29, 159; reliability coefficients and, 65–66; reporting of, computer-delivered, 12; reporting of, longitudinal information, 12; scale, 124; subdomain, 583–84; summed, 158; target, 30; terminology for, 157; theta, 124; true, 6–7; types, summary of, 159; universe, 7, 31
Score scales, 5, 41, 144, 155–80; with approximately equal conditional standard errors of measurement, 166–67; auxiliary, 155; composites, 170–71; content meaningful, 167–69; developmental, 171; developmental, for measuring growth, 5; future directions in, 183; interim, 174; linear transformations, 163–64; maintaining, 169; nonlinear transformations, 164–65; normative information, incorporating, 163; perspectives on, 156; primary, 155; raw scores, transforming to score scales, 163; score precision information, incorporating, 165; single test, 156–69; test batteries, 169–70, 171; VAM requirements, 566–67; vertical, and developmental score scales, 171–80 (*see also* Vertical scaling)
Scoring: adjacent *vs.* nonadjacent, 102; automated, 496–98; computer-automated, 400; functions, complicated, 158; inferences, 24, 25, 34, 43; item and test, future of, 12; optimal scoring weights, 127–28; reports, flagging policy, 13
Scoring rubrics, design of, 394–400; computer-automated scoring procedures, 400; criteria specifications, 394–95; Generic and Specific Rubric for Declarative Knowledge Domain, 398; holistic and analytic, 395–400; Holistic General Scoring Rubric for Mathematics Constructed-Response Items, 397; MSPAP Reading for Literacy Experience Scoring Rubric, 398; MSPAP Scoring Rubric: Writing to

Express Personal Ideas, 396; scoring procedures, 395
Scoring systems, scanning and machine-based, 372–80. *See also* Answer documents, processing steps of
Scott, D., 562
Scott, W. A., 101
Scott-Little, C., 592
Scrams, D. J., 487
Scribner, S., 283
Scriven, M., 58, 542, 627, 693
Searle, S. R., 97
Searns, J. A., 725
Sebrechts, M. M., 475, 497
Second language testing: *ability-in-language user-in-context*, 525, 526, 527; CLA model, limitations of, 524–25; cognitive, psycholinguistic perspective, 523–254; construct definitions of language proficiency, 522–25; context, 526–27; of foreign language, 521–22; history of, 517–18, 522–23; interaction, 526–27; social, interactional competence perspective, 525. *See also* English as a foreign language testing (ESL)
Sedere, M. U., 76
Segall, D. O., 365, 416, 477, 486
Seidenberg, M. S., 273
Selinker, L., 293
Sellman, W. S., 647
Seltzer, M. H., 179
Semantic assumptions, 51
Semantic inferences, 51
Semantic interpretation, 51–52
SEMs. *See* Standard errors of measurement (SEMs)
Sensitivity review, 244–45
Senturk, D., 167, 583
Seong, T. J., 133, 183
Separate estimation, 176
Serlin, R. C., 367
Seyfarth, A. L., 562
Sfard, A., 525
Shafer, G., 265, 285
Shalin, V. J., 283
Shao, J., 98
The Shape of the River, 666
Shapiro, A., 78
Sharwood Smith, M., 524
Shavelson, R. J., 3, 31, 88, 92, 93, 94, 393, 394, 405, 411, 412, 413, 414, 527, 536, 604
Shaw, D. G., 85
Shaw, E. J., 369
Shea, J. A., 457, 461, 707
Shealy, R., 234, 239, 241, 242, 333, 365, 457, 461, 499, 707
Sheehan, K. M., 120, 143, 201, 291, 475, 480, 486, 490, 689, 690, 691
Sheingold, K., 401
Shell, P., 262, 263, 474
Shen, L., 444
Shepard, L. A., 10, 18, 20, 22, 27, 32, 47, 50, 51, 54, 55, 57, 221, 235, 236, 237, 240, 241, 246, 247, 248, 359, 407, 423, 433, 441, 442, 458, 461, 534, 548, 552, 554, 558, 563, 592, 593, 594, 623, 626, 628, 629, 634, 636, 639, 641, 642, 720, 721, 753
Shepherd, W., 484
Sheridan, E., 521
Sheridan, G., 131, 341
Sherman Antitrust Act, 724
The Sherman Antitrust Act of 1890, 724
Shermis, M. D., 276, 494, 499, 595
Shortliffe, E. H., 279
SHRDLU, 280
Shulman, L. S., 707
Shute, V., 270
SIBTEST, 239
Siegler, R. S., 285, 287–89
Siegler's balance beam, 287–88
SIERRA, 280
Signal-to-noise ratios, 67, 69
Significance tests, 80, 85–87, 140, 508, 734
Sijtsma, K., 121, 122, 143, 285, 288, 293, 294, 365, 416
Silver, E. A., 626, 688
Silverman, B., 292
Simmons, W., 535
Simon, D. P., 388
Simon, H. A., 257, 258, 262, 270, 271, 279, 280, 282, 283, 286, 292, 388, 400
Simple random sampling, 181
Simultaneous item bias test (SIBTEST), 499
Singer, J. D., 292
Single group design (SG), 197
Singley, K., 275
Singley, M. K., 473, 497, 720
Sinharay, S., 475
Sireci, S. G., 28, 73, 120, 142, 359, 360, 423, 433, 441, 444, 445, 457, 463, 508, 555, 661, 666, 669
Siskind, T., 559
Siverstein, M., 284
Skager, R., 654
Skaggs, G., 133, 214
Skehan, P., 293
Skill-level norms, 181
Sklar, J. C., 660, 662, 665, 666, 667
Skolnik, I., 682
Skorupski, W., 451, 465
Slater, S. C., 450, 507, 694
Slattery, J. B., 314, 537, 613
Slinde, J. A., 79
Sloboda, J., 284
Slovic, P., 270, 276
Smedley, A., 233
Smid, N. G., 121
Smith, D. A., 101
Smith, I. L., 445
Smith, J. K., 393, 623, 641, 642
Smith, M. L., 552
Smith, M. S., 536, 537, 555
Smith, P. L., 92
Smith, R. L., 480, 488
Smith, R. W., 266, 451, 490, 558
Smith, S., 524
Smoothing, 5, 84
Smydo, J., 361
Snedecor, G. W., 666
Snijders, T.A.B., 78, 122

Snow, R. E., 24, 46, 57, 291, 294, 525, 526, 527, 536, 597, 604
Snow, R. W., 35, 258, 262, 269, 419, 604, 614
Snyder, T. D., 648, 673
SOAR, 279, 280
Social address model, 244
Social consequences, 2, 55–56
Social moderation, 50–51
Solano-Flores, G., 414, 597, 604
Solomon, C., 682
SOLO rating scheme, 296
Soloway, E., 497
Songer, N. B., 295
Sotaridona, L. S., 367–68
Southeastern Community College v. Davis, 743
Spalding, E., 535
Spearman, C., 7 5, 41, 71, 72, 73, 77, 87, 92, 103, 262, 265
Spearman-Brown "Prophecy" formula, 72–73, 77
Special needs students, 561. *See also* Disabled individuals
Specific objectivity, 131
Speededness, 487
Spiegelhalter, D. J., 131
Spiraling, 685
Split-half estimate of reliability, 72
Spolsky, B., 517–20
Sprafka, S. A., 459, 707
Spray, J. A., 238, 333, 423, 486
Staggered equivalent split-half procedure, 70
Staiger, D. O., 564, 565, 570
Stalnaker, J. M., 387
Stancavage, F. B., 601, 684
Standard error of equating difference (SEED), 211–12
Standard error of equating (SEE), 210–12
Standard errors of measurement (SEMs), 3, 4, 65, 67; conditional, 7, 65, 69, 98–99; unconditional, 3, 4, 65, 67; information functions and, 125–29; true scores, estimating, 82–84
Standardization, in measurement procedures: reliability of, 9; validity of, 31, 37, 38, 39, 50
Standardized alpha, 75
Standard setting, 10–11, 145, 168–69
Standard-setting method, selecting, 439–51; Angoff method, 440–41; Beuk method, 450; bookmark, and other item mapping methods, 442–44; borderline group method, 445; candidate reviews, methods involving, 444–45; classifying methods, ways of, 440; compromise methods, 449; contrasting groups method, 445–46; criteria summary for, 458; de Gruiter method, 450; direct consensus method, 444; dominant profile method (DPM), 448; Ebel method, 442; extended Angoff method, and related methods, 441; Hofstee method, 449; holistic approaches, 446–47; hybrid approaches, 447–48; item-by-item approaches, 446; item cluster method, 448–49; Jaeger method, 442; judgmental policy capturing method (JPC), 448; Nedelsky method, 442

Standards for Educational and Psychological Testing (AERA, APA, NCME): 1985, 1, 4, 5, 21, 224; 1954, 1, 5; 1999, 1, 3, 4, 5, 22, 23, 24, 27, 51, 67, 83, 221, 224–25, 226, 227, 307, 359; 1974, 1, 2, 5; 1966, 1, 2, 4, 20
Standards for Transition, 168
Standards-referenced tests (SRTs), 536, 537
Stanford-Binet test, 196
Stanley, J. C., 4, 65, 68, 160, 162, 343, 380
Stansfield, C. W., 520
Starkes, J. L., 284
State Student Assessment Program (SSAP), 594
State v. Project Principle, Inc., 739
Statistical Models for Behavioral Observations, 102
Statistical moderation, 191
Statistical Theories of Mental Test Scores (Lord and Novick), 67
Stecher, B. M., 50, 394, 407, 535, 536, 551, 552, 553, 555, 569, 596
Steele, C. M., 358, 666, 668
Steffen, M., 480, 497, 720
Stefik, M., 280
Stein, M. K., 408
Steinberg, L. S., 27, 28, 43, 117, 120, 125, 142, 146, 237, 259, 272, 282, 293, 313, 393, 473, 499, 604, 605, 606
Step difficulties, 116
Stern, A. H., 264
Stern, E. B., 366
Sternberg, R. J., 43, 263, 662
Stevens, F. W., 361
Stevens, G. E., 361
Stevens, R. H., 497
Stevens, S. S., 156
Stevenson, J., 133
Stewart, D. M., 647
Stewart, J., 271
Stewart, M. R., 403
Stiggins, R. J., 10, 47, 247, 328, 387, 580, 581, 596, 623, 626, 642
Stipek, D. J., 637, 638, 639
Stocking, M. L., 81, 132, 135, 137, 176, 177, 335, 346, 357, 360, 364, 480, 481, 483, 484, 486, 489, 490, 656, 657
Stocking and Lord method, 137, 176, 177
Stollof, P. H., 357
Stone, C. A., 12, 53, 55, 65, 124, 132, 133, 140, 142, 146, 156, 319, 375, 377, 387, 407, 408, 412, 416, 420, 422, 552, 570, 615, 657
Stone, E., 719
Storms, B. A., 401
Stout, W. F., 121, 123, 139, 234, 239, 240, 241, 242, 333, 365, 420, 499
Straetmans, G.J.J.M., 357
Straight-line improvement models, 540
Stratified coefficient alpha, 77
Stratified sampling, 868; random, 181–82
Strauss, V., 549
Straw-man fallacy, 59
Strayer, W., 553
Stricker, L. J., 664, 669
Strictly parallel forms, 69
Structural equation models (SEMs), 42–43

Student 1 v. Massachusetts Board of Education, 737
Student performance, qualitative interpretations of, 47–48
Student variables, 287, 293–94
Studley, R., 652, 660
A Study of American Intelligence, 648
Stufflebeam, D. L., 542, 624
Sturm, S., 653
Subkoviak, M. J., 100, 101, 236, 442, 461, 712, 713
Substantive/non-substantive coaching, 549
Sudlow, M. W., 403
Sudman, S., 599, 606
Sugrue, B., 404, 417, 554
Sulzby, E., 626
Summative assessment, 627
Sundbye, N., 403
Superposition, 103
Supovitz, J. A., 410
Suppe, P., 20, 25
Suppes, P., 156
Surgrue, B., 413
Surrogation fallacy, 58
Swackhamer, G., 277
Swain, M., 523, 524, 525, 526
Swaminathan, H., 81, 130, 133, 139, 140, 141, 206, 236, 238, 333, 411, 416, 419, 420, 421, 442, 712, 713
Swanson, D. B., 400, 404, 412, 415, 486, 487, 656, 707, 708, 720, 721
Swanson, L., 335, 346, 480, 481, 486, 489
Sweeney, K., 446
Swygert, K. A., 19, 99, 126, 144
Sykes, R. C., 125, 129, 137, 138, 162, 418
Symonds, P. M., 623
Sympson, J. B., 364, 486, 488, 489
Synthetic population, 206
Systematic random sampling, 182

Takala, S., 239
Takane, Y., 417
Taleporos, E., 55
Tallent-Runnels, M., 244
Tamassia, C., 508
Tamblyn, R., 716
Tanzer, N., 120
Tao, W., 404, 495, 496
Target domains, 30–31
Target populations, 201
Tarone, E., 293, 527
Task features, considerations regarding, 292–93
Tate, R. L., 121, 420
Tatsuoka, K. K., 43, 266, 293, 294, 365, 417
Tay-Lim, S. H., 420
Taylor, C. S., 399, 623
Taylor, G., 359
Taylor, I., 361
Taylor, M. M., 361
Teachers: classroom assessment, studies on, 641; conceptual framework of, as theories, 48; developmental studies of, 641; development of, views on, 48–49; evaluation of, 634; extending to new contexts, views on, 50; licensure, testing for, 13; student refinement, views of, 47–48, 49

Teacher-talking, 102
Teale, W. H., 626
Technical Recommendations (APA), 20
Technological advancements, 11, 471–510; accommodations, 482–83; for automated scoring, 496–98; automatic item generation, 473–76; banking statistics, 498–99; computer platforms, comparability of, 502–4; for constructed-response scoring, 493–96; delivery modes, comparability of, 501–2; differential item functioning, 499; eligibility, 481–82; Internet, 483; item pretesting, 476–79; miskeys, finding, 499; nonoverlapping item sets, 500; postadministration analysis systems, 498–501; in quality control system, 509; in reporting scores, 505–8; in research system, 508–9; scaling drift, 499, 501; scheduling, 482; test assembly and packaging, 479–81; in test delivery, 483–88; in test design, 471–73. *See also* Test delivery models
Teichroew, D., 75
Ten Berge, J.M.F., 75, 78
Tennessee Value-added Assessment System (TVAAS), 565
Tenopyr, M. L., 21
Tepper, R. L., 552
T-equivalence (or *tau*), 71
TerraNova, 610, 614
Test administration: CBT *vs.* paper-and-pencil, 11–12; critics of, 5; essay, 12; multiple-choice, 11, 12; stakes, levels of, 10
Test assembly and packaging, 11, 479–81; automated, 480–81; models of, 480
Test batteries, 77, 155, 169–70; elementary achievement, 155; maintenance for, 171; scale comparability, 170; scaling of, 190–92; structure of, 171–72
Test characteristic curve (TCC), 125, 129, 135
Test characteristic functions, 125
Test construction, 143–44
Test definition language (TDL), 479
Test delivery models, 488–93; computerized fixed tests (CFT), 488; item-level computerized adaptive testing (CAT), 488–89; item selection algorithms, 489–99; linear-on-the-fly tests (LOFT), 488; structured computer-adaptive multistage tests (ca-MST), 477, 491–93; testlet-based CAT and computerized mastery testing (CMT), 490–91
Test design, 308–24; administrative constraints and, 311–12; delivery specifications and, 322–23; form specifications and, 320–22; intended examinee population and, 309–11; item scoring and, 319–20; item types and, 318; legal considerations and, 312–13; length of test and, 318–19; philosophy of test and, 308–9; purpose of test and, 308–9, 310; specifications of test and, 315–18; validity evidence and, 323–24; validity evidence foundation for, 313–14
Test development, 307–51; assembly, 331–36; banking of items, 344–46; designing, 308–24 (*see also* Test design); of items, 324–31

(*see also* Test item development); quality control, 346–49; review, 336–37. *See also* Test evaluation
Test equating practices, 215–16
Test evaluation, 336–44; of item performance, 337–42; of test performance, 342–43; validity evidence and, 343–44
TESTFACT, 132, 417
Test fairness, 221–52; in classroom assessment, 246–48; college entrance exams, 248–51; consequences of testing and, 228; definitions, relative, 225–26; empirical studies on, results of, 234; legislation and litigation in, 13; selection models, 232–34; sensitivity review, 244–46; social and legal issues, 221–24; standards for, 224–28; validity and social constructions, 226–28. *See also* Bias, and test fairness; Differential item functioning (DIF); Race and ethnicity, testing fairness
Test information function (TIF), 127, 481
Test item banking, 344–46; associated functionalities, 346; banking statistics, 498–99; information stored in, 344–46; item pretesting and, 479; maintenance and security, 346; uses of, 344
Test item development, 324–31; essential items in, 325; field testing, 330–31; format modifications, 482; item writers, training of, 326; process of, 324–28; refinement of items, 330; review of items and, 328–30; setting modifications, 482; summary of, 330. *See also* Test item evaluation and assembly
Test item evaluation and assembly: assembly, 331–32; of characteristics, 332–33; computer assembly, 335; formatting, 335–36; performance assessment, 334–35
Testlet response theory models, 120–21
Test of English as a Foreign Language™ (TOEFL), 493, 502, 519; TOEFLiBT, 520
Test of Spoken English, 520
Test-retest estimates of reliability, 70
Test review, 336–37
Tests: admissions, 13; basic skills, 13; change over time, and maintaining standards, 216–17; eliminating or substituting portions or sections of, 483; full length, 70, 100, 101, 197, 201, 712; half, 70, 83, 86, 100–101, 712; IQ, 13; length and sample sizes of, recommended, 132–33; significance, 80, 85–87, 140, 508, 734
Test scores, distribution of: discreet, 203; preserving, 214; presmoothing, 203–4
Test scores, interpretation of: criterion-referenced, 66–67, 145; inferences found in, 2; in IRT vertical scaling, 177–78; norm-referenced, 66–67; proposed, 610
Test security, 361–72; adult malfeasance and copyright infringement, 741–42; cheating, types of, 361–62; countermeasures, 362–69; inappropriate test preparation and, 741; parental review of tests and, 741741; in practice, case study of ACT's policies, 370–72; teacher cheating, 369–70
Test weights, 545–55
Teukolsky, S. A., 162

Texas Assessment of Academic Skills (TAAS), 544
Tharp, R. G., 631
Thayer, D. T., 187, 203, 204, 208, 211, 217, 225, 234, 237, 238, 240, 242, 499, 692
Thayer, P. W., 662
Theoretical constructs, 42
Theory-based inferences: analytic evidence for, 44; backing for, evaluating, 45; correlational analyses of, 44; critical appraisal of, 44; experimental manipulation of, 44–45
Theunissen, T.J.J.M., 92, 335
Think-aloud protocols, 35, 400, 405, 496, 499
Thinning, 102–3
Third International Mathematics and Science Study (TIMSS), 556
Third Law, Newton's, 277, 278, 295
Thirty-six Dramatic Situations (Polti), 276, 277
Thissen, D., 73, 78, 117, 120, 125, 131, 132, 133, 140, 141, 142, 144, 145, 146, 159, 161, 162, 176, 189, 192, 237, 365, 402, 416, 417, 418, 422, 423, 499, 536, 566, 692
Thomas, A., 131
Thomas, C., 233, 234
Thomas, N., 416
Thomasson, G. L., 171
Thompson, B., 84
Thompson, P. W., 277
Thompson, S. J., 310, 329, 335, 464
Thompson, S. K., 595
Thompson Prometric, Inc., 703
Thomson, G. H., 67, 479, 651
Thorndike, E. L., 195, 196, 275, 623, 631
Thorndike, R. L., 1, 3, 11, 68, 82, 83, 84, 217, 231, 232, 249, 250, 623, 702
Thorndike's method for estimating standard errors of measurement, 83, 84
Thornton, S., 617
Three Models of Language, 257
Three-parameter logistic model (3PL), 6, 114–15
Thurlow, M. L., 310, 329, 335, 464, 538, 562, 595
Thurstone, L. L., 67, 113, 156, 175, 176, 178, 179, 196, 235
Thurston scaling, 175–76
Tibshirani, R., 98, 101, 211
Tideman, T. N., 367
Times News Network, 361
Timing and test scheduling modifications, 483
Tindal, G., 604
Tippins, N. T., 484
Title I Reporting and Evaluation System (TIERS), 532
Tittle, C. K., 47, 51, 57, 579, 590
Tobin, K., 636
Tolerance interval, 82
T1 line, 484, 485
Tonidandel, S., 509
Torgerson, T. L., 625
Toulmin, S. E., 27, 28, 48, 56, 259, 282, 287
Toulmin's model of inference, 27–29
Traits, 30–42; circularity of, 30; definition of, 30; divergent, discriminant evidence for, 39;

factor analysis, 41; implications, 31–32, 37–38; irrelevant variance and systematic error, 38–39; IRT scaling, 41; measurement procedures, 31; measures as signs and samples, 42; multitrait-multimethod matrices, 39–40; observable attributes, 32; operational definitions, 32; quantitative reasoning, 32–33; target domains, 30–31; underrepresentation, 38; unidimensional attributes, 32. *See also* Interpretive arguments, for traits; Validity arguments, for traits
Transfer, definition of, 632
Trapani, C., 653, 727
Traub, R. E., 139, 162, 419
Travers, R.M.W., 625
Traxler, A. E., 355, 356
Trends in International Mathematics and Science Study (TIMSS), 683
Treptau, M., 661
Trial Urban District Assessments, 617
Trimble, C. S., 451
Trimble, S., 595
Trinitarian model of validity, 1, 2
True scores, 6–7; distribution, estimating, 82, 84, 100, 134, 175; effective weights, 161; examinees', 83, 99, 101, 102; expected-value of, 6; linear equating function, 204; nonlinear, procedures from IRT, 205–6; Platonic, 102; point and interval estimation of, 80–82; standard error of measurement conditional on, estimating, 82–84
Trumbull, E., 597
Trusheim, D., 652, 659, 660
Tsui, A., 662
Tsui, K. W., 81
Tu, D., 98, 709
TUCK1 and Tuck2, 207
Tucker, L. R., 75, 139, 141, 196, 199, 207, 440
Tucker, Ledyard R., 207
Tuerlinckx, F., 423
Tukey, J. W., 98, 166
Turnbull, W. W., 658
Turner, C., 520
Turner, N., 662
Tversky, A., 156, 270, 276
Two-parameter logistic model (2PL), 6, 114
Two-parameter partial credit model (2PPC), 117
Tyack, D., 532
Tyler, R. W., 235, 250, 624, 626, 640

U.S. Census Bureau, 182
U.S. Congress, Office of Technology Assessment, 250, 541, 623, 624, 639, 647
U.S. Department of Education, 542, 561, 562, 563, 662, 672, 673
U.S. General Accounting Office, 536
Underprediction, 666
Undue burden, 745
Unidimensional estimation software, 131–32
Unidimensional IRT models: for combinations of, 118; for dichotomous data, 113–15; for performance assessments, 416–17, 419; for polytomous data, 115–18; for weighting, 162
Unidimensional models, for dichotomous data, 113–15; normal ogive, 115; Rasch

or one-parameter logistic, 113–14; three-parameter logistic, 114–15; two-parameter logistic, 114
Unidimensional models, for polytomous data: analyzing, other models for, 117–18; concepts of, 115–16; nominal partial credit/generalized, 116–17; partial credit, 116; two-parameter partial credit/generalized, 116–17
Uniform Guidelines on Employee Selection Procedures, 223, 733
Uniform Guidelines on Employee Selection Procedures, 21, 54, 733, 734, 738, 739
Unitary competence hypothesis (UCH), 523
United States General Accounting Department, 441, 536, 542, 693
United States Medical Licensing Examination (USMLE), 497, 703, 705
United States v. LULAC, 739
United States v. North Carolina, 739
United States v. South Carolina, 738
United States v. Texas, 738
Universe of admissible observations, 87
Universe of generalization, 31
Universe scores, 7, 31
University of Cambridge Local Examinations syndicate (UCLES), 518, 519, 520
UrGENOVA, 97
User norms, 181

Vacc, N. N., 399
Vacha-Haase, T., 84
Valdadez, J. R., 412
Valencia, S. W., 623
Validation, 17–60; argument-based approach to (see Validity arguments); begging-the-question fallacy, 56–59; concepts or aspects of, 2; concurrent, 1, 18, 20; consequences (see Consequences in validity, role of); construct, 19–22; content, 1, 19, 20, 57; decisions, 51–56; definition of, 2; in employment testing, 21; evolving conceptions of, 1–3, 18–23; face validity, 36; gilding the lily fallacy, 59; as integrated evaluation, 2; predictive, 1, 18, 20; qualitative interpretations, 47–51; vs. reliability, 5; straw-man fallacy, 59; theory-based interpretations, 42–47; traits, 30–42; Trinitarian model of, 1, 2. See also Construct validity model
Validity, of performance assessment, 401–10; cognitive complexity of performance tasks, 404–6; consequential evidence for, 406–8; construct-irrelevant variance sources of, 402–4; directness and meaningfulness of, 406; group differences on, 408–10
Validity arguments, 2–3, 23; appraisal stage of, 26–27; for classroom assessments, 48–50; developmental stage of, 25–26; fallacies in, 56–59; for indicators of theoretical constructs, 43–46; for placement testing, 25
Validity arguments, for trait interpretations, 34–38; extrapolation inference, 35–37; generalization inference, 35; scoring inference, 34–35

Validity evidence, for setting performance standards, 457–63; comparisons to other sources of information, 461–62; conclusions, 463; consistency within method, 460; documentation, 459; explicitness, 457; external evidence of, 461; intra/inter panelist consistency, 460–61; intrapanelist consistency, 460; legal issues, 462–63; other measures of, 461; panelist evaluations, 459; practicability, 457, 459; procedures, implementation of, 459; reasonableness of performance standards, 462; result comparisons among methods, 461
Validity generalization, 35, 36
Validity of higher education admissions testing, predictions, 659–65; of academic performance beyond first year, 661–62; of career success, 663–64; coefficients, range restriction and criterion unreliability on, 664–65; of first-year grades, 660–61; of graduation, 662–63
Validity of K–12 achievement test scores, 610–16; achievement constructs, definitions of, 612–13; consequences and impact of tests, evidence based on, 615; construct under-representation and irrelevance, evidence based on, 614–15; intended score interpretations and uses, evidence of, 615–16; relations to other measures, evidence based on, 614; statements of intended score interpretations and uses, 611–12; structure and response processes, evidence based on, 613–14; test content, evidence based on, 613
Validity of score-based inferences under high-stakes conditions (VIHS), 542–51; audit tests, limitations of, 544; early methods of, 543–45; evaluating, framework for (see VIHS, evaluating); test preparations (see VIHS test preparations, methods of); traditional validation, inadequacy of, 543; trends disparity, ambiguous interpretation of, 544
Value-added modeling (VAM), 179–80, 541, 565–67
Value judgments, 53
Van den Brink, W. P., 80
Van den Heuvel-Panhuizen, M., 630
Van den Wollenberg, A. L., 140
Van der Ark, L. A., 416
Van der Linden, W. J., 23, 144, 146, 196, 307, 316, 335, 346, 442, 455, 457, 458, 460, 462, 475, 480, 481, 486, 487, 489
Van der Maas, H.L.J., 289
Van der Vleuten, C.P.M., 412, 461, 707
Van Duijn, M.A.J., 122
Van Essen, T., 217, 250, 649
Van Heerden, J., 45, 54
Van Krimpen-Stoop, E.M.L.A., 142, 366
VanLehn, K., 295
Van Lier, L., 521
Van Luijk, S., 707
Van Maanen, L., 285, 288
Van Zyl, J. M., 86
Variance component estimation, 97–98
Vautier, S., 70

Veizaga v. national Board of Respiratory Therapy, 724
Veldkamp, B. P., 316, 346
Veloski, J. J., 707
Vera, A. H., 279
Verhelst, N. D., 118, 120, 122, 140, 294, 295, 357, 358, 419, 421
Verstralen, H.H.F.M., 122, 419
Vertical scaling, 171–80; battery structures, 171–72; calibrating tests at different levels of ability, 192; common-item design, for data collection, 173; conclusions about, 180; content and growth, relationship between, 172–73; contrasting vertical scaling, for data collection, 174; equivalent groups design, for data collection, 173; Hieronymus methods of, 174–75; IRT methods of, 176–77; limitations of, 178; moderated standards, 179; research on, 178–79; scale transformation in IRT, 178; separate vs. concurrent calibration in IRT, 177; test scoring in IRT, 177–78; Thurstone methods of, 175–76; value-added models and, 179–80
Vetterling, W. T., 162
Vevea, J. L., 690
Viator, K. A., 637
VIHS, evaluating, 545–48, 550–51; between-level differences in correlational structure, examining, 551; coaching, 549–50; dimensionality, examining changes in, 551; inference targets, 546–47; inference weights, clarifying, 550; performance elements, 545–46; in terms of test and inference weights, 547–48; test weights, ascertaining effective, 550–56
VIHS test preparations, methods of, 548–50; alignment, 549; cheating, 550; coaching, 549–50; reallocation, 548–49
Village of Arlington Heights v. Metropolitan Housing Development Corp., 734
Vinovskis, M. A., 693
Virginia State Board of Pharmacy v. Virginia Citizens Consumer Council, Inc., 724
Vispoel, W. P., 508
Vlissides, J., 284
Voelkl, K. E., 542, 688
Voluntary National Tests (VNTs), 10, 617
Von Davier, A. A., 120, 131, 140, 292, 293, 294
Von Davier, M., 187, 193, 197, 198, 200, 201, 203, 204, 206, 207, 208, 210, 211, 212, 214, 215, 217, 692
Vosniadou, S., 277
Vranek, J. L., 314, 537, 613
Vygotsky, L. S., 257, 277, 281, 525, 628, 641

Wagner, M. E., 504, 507
Wainer, H., 73, 75, 78, 120–21, 138, 142, 145, 146, 161–62, 179, 189, 192, 200, 221, 237, 266, 290, 292, 295, 402, 418, 423, 480, 486, 489, 490, 493, 499, 536, 673, 584, 602, 694, 719
Wald, A., 713
Walker, C. M., 118, 119, 240, 416
Waller, M. I., 141
Waltman, K. K., 692

Index

Walton, D., 27, 57
Wan, L., 101, 714
Wang, J. B., 167, 583
Wang, M., 402
Wang, M. C., 160, 162
Wang, M. M., 120, 144, 179, 295
Wang, N., 410, 420, 423, 443, 444
Wang, P., 496
Wang, T., 78, 357
Wang, W. C., 119, 122, 688, 694
Wang, X.-B., 120, 162, 402, 423
Wang, Z., 335, 346
Ward, J. G., 625
Ward, W. C., 327, 417, 684
Wards Cove case, 733
Wards Cove Packing Co. v. Antonio, 733
Warrent, 28–29
Wason, P. C., 264
Waters, B. K., 490
Watson, E. A., 356
Watson, I., 276
Watts, T. M., 367
Way, W. D., 118, 480, 490
Webb, N. L., 314, 555, 556
Webb, N. M., 3, 31, 88, 94, 393, 394, 411, 413
Webber, C., 647, 673
Webeck, M. L., 596
Webster, W., 541, 707
Wechsler, H. S., 249
Weerasinghe, D., 541
Weighted likelihood estimate (WLE), 138
Weighted summed scores, 158
Weighting: criteria and issues in, 162–63; example of, 161–62; in IRT, 162; observed score effective, 160–61; reliability, maximizing, 161; score points, based on numbers of, 160; true score effective, 161
Weiner, J. A., 488
Weinig, K. M., 658
Weir, C., 518, 520
Weiss, K. R., 195, 671
Weissert, W., 672
Welch, C. J., 11, 307, 390, 399, 404, 421, 604
Wells, C. S., 357
Wells, M., 277
Welner, K., 223
Welsh, C. K., 661
Wendler, C., 747
Wenger, E., 258, 473, 638, 641
Wertsch, J. V., 525
West, M. M., 534, 563, 607, 637
Westers, P., 240
Westman, R. S., 307, 346
Wetzel, C. D., 120
Whalen, T. E., 86
Wheeler, K. S., 402
White, A. E., 84
White, B. Y., 277
Whitely, S. E., 119, 131
Whittington, D., 378, 684
Wiesel, T., 273
Wigdor, A. K., 221, 222, 223, 233, 234, 249
Wigfield, A., 638
Wiggins, G. P., 535, 595, 626, 629, 632, 640

Wiggins, N., 659
Wightman, L. E., 661, 672
Wightman, L. F., 225, 232, 233, 234, 335, 655, 666, 668, 671, 672, 725, 726
Wigmore, J. H., 259, 261, 264, 292
Wigmore, R. R., 81, 86, 167
Wilds, C., 521
Wiley, A., 663, 666, 669
Wiley, D. E., 259, 293, 294, 558, 559, 613
Wiley, E. W., 413
Wilks, S. S., 161
Willard, A. E., 406
Willett, J. B., 79, 80
William, D., 47
Williams, D. M., 235
Williams, E. A., 365
Williams, N. J., 443, 444
Williams, P. L., 533
Williams, R. H., 79
Williams, S. R., 552
Williams, V.S.L., 144, 178, 179, 189, 566, 692, 694
Williams, W. M., 662
Williamson, D. M., 272, 296, 475, 727
Williamson, S., 542
Williamson v. Lee Optical Co., 723
Willingham, W. W., 355, 358, 410, 564, 660, 662, 663, 664, 668, 669, 671
Wilson, B. L., 141, 552
Wilson, D. T., 417
Wilson, E. B., 82
Wilson, J., 452, 460
Wilson, M. R., 119, 120, 122, 131, 285, 292, 294, 295, 419, 688, 689, 691, 692, 694
WINBUGS, 131
Wingersky, M. S., 130, 132, 143, 201, 204, 240, 475, 691
WINMIRA, 131
Winograd, T., 280
WINSTEPS, 131
Winter, P. C., 537
Winters, L., 387, 410
Winters, M. A., 543
Wise, A. E., 552
Wise, L., 171
Wise, S. A., 662
Wise, S. L., 486, 487
Wise, V. L., 585
Woldbye, M., 292
Wolf, D. P., 601, 626
Wolf, S. A., 552
Wolfe, E. W., 96, 97, 404, 502, 567
Wolff, S., 657
Wollack, J. A., 11, 131, 355, 357, 367, 368, 369, 582, 655
Wolvin, A. D., 585
Wolvin, D. R., 585
Wong, S. P., 87
Wong v. Regents of the University of California, 725
Wood, B. D., 623, 624, 642
Wood, D., 628
Wood, R., 132, 266
Wood, T., 629
Woodruff, D., 83, 86, 100
Woodward, J. A., 78

Wright, B. D., 1 30, 122, 124, 131, 133, 142, 146, 240, 290, 291, 292, 345, 416, 419, 708
Wright, D. J., 667
Wright, P., 201, 208
Wright, S. P., 541, 565
Wright, W., 494
Writing progress map, 630
Wu, I.-L., 480
Wu, M. L., 131, 688, 689, 691, 692
Wurtz, E., 592, 594

Xing, D., 491

Yackel, E., 629
Yamamoto, K., 179, 294, 357, 359, 417, 684, 688, 690
Yan, D., 692
Yang, X., 146
Yang, Y., 400
Yeh, J. P., 625
Yen, W. M., 4, 28, 41, 43, 65, 96, 97, 102, 111, 117, 120, 122, 124, 125, 129, 132, 134, 137, 138, 139, 140, 141, 142, 143, 144, 146, 156, 158, 162, 176, 179, 180, 192, 197, 200, 206, 210, 266, 337, 368, 380, 389, 403, 414, 416, 417, 419, 421, 422, 423, 566, 655, 688
Yin, P., 96, 97, 212, 405, 558
Ying, Z., 364, 486, 489, 490
Young, J. W., 222, 234, 665, 668, 669
Young, M. D., 79, 222
Young, P. R., 707
Young, R. F., 521, 525, 526
Ysseldyke, J. E., 464, 562, 563
Yu, F., 139, 420
Yu, J., 132, 133, 417
Yu, M. C., 86
Yue, Y., 393

Zara, A. R., 364, 486, 490
Zarinia, E. A., 552
Zegers, F. E., 75, 78
Zelenak, C. A., 168, 182, 183, 689
Zenderland, L., 249
Zeng, L., 84, 167
Zenisky, A., 240, 491, 508
Zhang, B., 121, 139
Zhang, J., 140, 420, 422
Zhang, L., 405
Zhang, Y. L., 494
Zieky, M. J., 10, 145, 238, 333, 433, 436, 442, 445, 457, 461, 681, 720
Zigler, W. F., 592
Zimmerman, D. W., 79
Zimowski, M. F., 79, 80, 131, 498, 694
Zinnes, J. L., 156
Ziomek, R. L., 671
Zone of proximal development (ZPD), 281, 628
Zumbo, B. D., 238, 241, 242
Zuriff, G. E., 359, 360, 725, 726
Zwick, R., 7, 167, 168, 179, 182, 238, 239, 240, 242, 250, 251, 414, 421, 541, 583, 585, 647, 649, 652, 653, 660, 661, 662, 663, 665, 666, 667, 672, 673, 690, 694